by Thomas Rowlandson

Founded in 1744 to auction fine books, Sotheby's is now the leading firm of art auctioneers and appraisers in the world.

Sotheby's, 1334 York Avenue, New York, New York 10021.
Telephone: (212) 606-7385

Sotheby's, 34-35 Bond Street, London W1A 2AA.
Telephone: 44 (71) 493-8080.

THE WORLD'S LEADING AUCTION HOUSE

SOTHEBY'S
FOUNDED 1744

"American book prices current"

A.B.M.R.

ANTIQUARIAN BOOK MONTHLY REVIEW

FEATURES
    NEWS
        REVIEWS
            WORLDWIDE

SUBSCRIBE NOW!

U.S.A.	£26
U.K.	£22
EUROPE	£24
AUSTRALIA & FAR EAST	£29

* We take Amex, Visa and Access – number, expiry date (& signature for postal applications), + subscription address.

AMBR, Suite G, Bullingdon House, 174b Cowley Road, Oxford, OX4 1UE, UK.

ADVERTISING RATES ON REQUEST

Tel: (0865) 794704   Fax: (0865) 794582

AUSTRALIAN BOOK COLLECTOR

The monthly magazine for buyers and sellers of secondhand, out-of-print, and rare books.

Trade news, calendar, auction reports, book reviews, recent catalogues, bibliographies and price guides, books wanted, books for sale, articles of interest to collectors.

Send for a free copy and details of subscription and advertising sales.

Fax (067) 78 4516   Phone (067) 78 4682

PO Box 2, Uralla, NSW 2358, Australia.

Offering & Purchasing Rare Books & Autographs in all Fields.

Catalogues issued regularly.

Philadelphia: Gallery and Offices:
1215 Locust Street Philadelphia, PA 19107
215-546-6466 • Fax: 215-546-9064

New York Gallery:
The Waldorf-Astoria Hotel, Lobby Level
301 Park Avenue • New York, NY 10022
212-759-8300 • Fax: 212-759-8350

THE BIBLIOGRAPHICAL SOCIETY OF AMERICA

The Society was founded in 1904. Membership is open to all who share its aims and interests in the promotion of bibliographical research and publication.

Membership is available at a cost of $30.00 per year, which includes a subscription to the quarterly *Papers* of the Society, as well as substantial discounts for the Society's monographic publications.

The BSA sponsors an annual short-term (one or two months) fellowship program, in support of bibliographical inquiry as well as research in the history of the book trades and publishing history. Details of the program are available from the Executive Secretary.

The *Papers of the Bibliographical Society of America (PBSA)* publishes contributions dealing with books and manuscripts, in any field, which treat them as artifacts of historical evidence, as well as studies of the printing, publishing, and allied trades.

For further information, address the BSA Executive Secretary, P. O. Box 397, Grand Central Station, New York, N. Y. 10163, U. S. A.

Bloomsbury Book Auctions

London's only specialist book auction house is approaching its 200th sale.

We hold about 22 sales a year including two devoted to prints, drawings and photographic material, and two of Hebrew books and manuscripts.

Each of our sales is divided into different categories for the convenience of our clients. We specialise in the dispersal of Libraries, particularly those of an academic nature.

Please write to us for further information and a free sample catalogue.
Bloomsbury Book Auctions
3 & 4 Hardwick Street, London EC1R 4RY
Tel: 011 441 833 2636/7
Fax: 011 441 833 3954

BONHAMS
KNIGHTSBRIDGE & CHELSEA HARBOUR

AUCTIONS OF RARE BOOKS AND MANUSCRIPTS

Including Natural History, Travel, Atlases and Maps, English Literature, Science, Private Press and Modern First Editions, Art Reference, Autograph Letters and Historical Documents.

For further information on buying or selling please contact:

MICHAEL LUDGROVE
on (071) 351 7111

KNIGHTSBRIDGE:
Montpelier Street, London SW7 1HH   Tel: 071 584 9161 Fax: 071-589 4072
CHELSEA:
65-69 Lots Road, Condon SW10 ORN   Tel: 071 351 7111 Fax: 071 351 7754

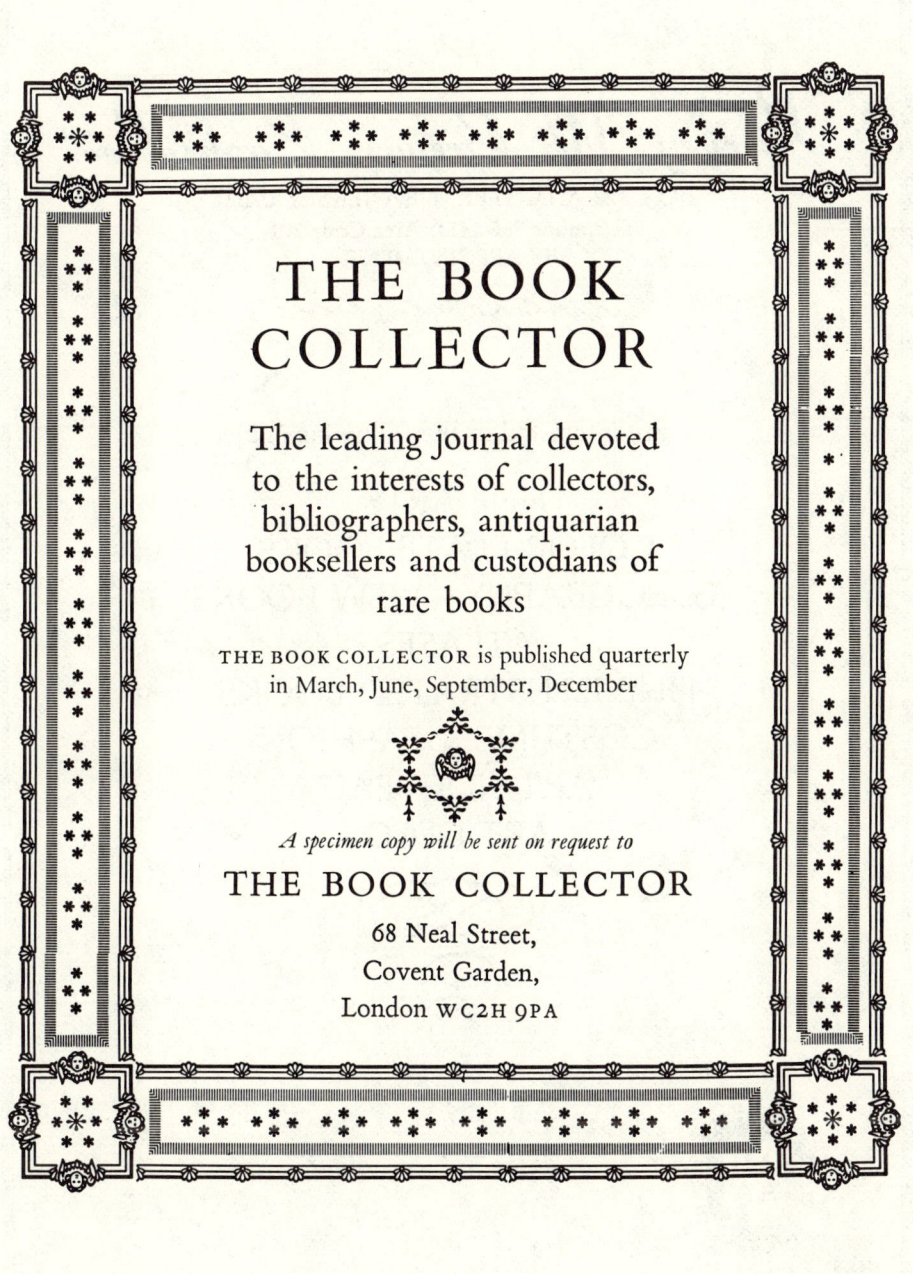

THE BOOK COLLECTOR

The leading journal devoted to the interests of collectors, bibliographers, antiquarian booksellers and custodians of rare books

THE BOOK COLLECTOR is published quarterly in March, June, September, December

A specimen copy will be sent on request to

THE BOOK COLLECTOR

68 Neal Street,
Covent Garden,
London WC2H 9PA

Harvey W. Brewer, Bookseller

BOX 322, CLOSTER, NEW JERSEY 07624
Telephone 768-4414. Area Code 201
BY APPOINTMENT

We are interested in the following subjects

**FINE ARTS
COLOR PLATE BOOKS
TOPOGRAPHY - VIEW BOOKS
ATLASES
FINE ILLUSTRATED BOOKS
COSTUME & FASHION
ART NOUVEAU
ART DECO**

BUTTERFIELD & BUTTERFIELD
Fine Art Auctioneers and Appraisers since 1865

Auctions of Rare Books and Manuscripts

Butterfield and Butterfield holds quarterly auctions of
Rare Books, Bindings, Manuscripts & Sets in many categories
including: Americana, Antiquarian, California & Western History.

Bi-Monthly auctions featuring books as in our quarterly
auctions and great quantities of secondary books.

For information about buying and selling fine books and
manuscripts at Butterfield's or to purchase an auction catalogue:

Jack Evans or Andrew Johnston
Telephone: (415) 861-7500 ext. 325
Facsimile: (415) 861-8951
220 San Bruno Avenue, San Francisco, California 94103

State Lic. No. 578

FINE AND RARE BOOKS & MANUSCRIPTS MAPS AND ATLASES

Buy and sell through the largest and oldest rare book auction house in the West.

Auctions Held Weekly ❧ Catalogues Issued
Appraisals ❧ Consignments Welcome
Newsletters on Request

CALIFORNIA BOOK AUCTION GALLERIES

965 Mission Street, Suite 730, San Francisco, CA 94103
Tel: (415) 243-0650 or Fax: (415) 243-0789

5225 Wilshire Blvd., Suite 324, Los Angeles, CA 90036
Tel: (213) 939-6202 or Fax: (213) 939-6298

859 Lexington Avenue   New York, NY 10021
Telephone (212) 249-690; Fax (212) 988-0539

English & American Literature

Americana

Color Plate

Sporting

Private Press

Fine Bindings

Catalogues issued

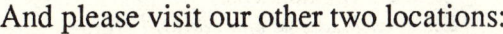

And please visit our other two locations:

The Country Annex	*The Mill*
PO Box 232	Pottersville Road East
Pottersville, NJ 07979	Pottersville, NY 07979
Tel & Fax: (908) 439-3803	Tel: (908) 439-272
General Fine Books	**Sets, Bindings, Fine Prints**
Catalogues issued	*By appointment*

HARTUNG & HARTUNG

Antiquariat-Auktionen

KAROLINENPLATZ 5 A · D-8000 MÜNCHEN 2
Telephone: (089) 284034 · Cables: Buchauktion
GERMANY

*Illuminated Manuscripts · Incunabulas
Books on Medicine and Natural History
Illustrated Books from the 15th to the 20th century
German Literature in First Editions
Autographs · Fine Bindings
Atlases · Decorative Prints · Maps and Views*

 **AUCTIONS**

as usual twice a year, May and November

Richly illustrated catalogues and lists of results

Dr. Ernst Hauswedell & Co.

Jahrbuch der Auktionspreise fur Bucher, Handschriften und Autographen

(Central european auction prices for books, manuscripts and autographs)

Vol. 41 (1990) includes prices of 41,000 books, manuscripts, and autographs sold at 62 public sales in Germany, the Netherlands, Switzerland, and other middle European countries in 1990. Among the appendices of the book is to be found a list of antiquarian booksellers according to their specialities and an English/German index of the keywords used in this list. 1991. Royal octavo. 992 pages. Cloth DM 340,-.

A few copies are still in stock of vols. 11 to 20, 23, and 29 to 40, moreover of the index vols. 1-10 (DM 360,-), 11-20 (DM 360,-), 21-30 (2 vols. DM 560,-), and 31-35 (DM 480,-).

The index volume 36-40 is in preparation for March 1992.

We are publishers since 1927:

Books about Books — Typography

Book Trade — Fine Arts

Illustrated Books

Catalog sent on request
DR. ERNST HAUSWEDELL & CO.
Rosenbergstrasse 113 — D-7 Stuttgart, 1

- POLYGRAPHICUM -

Books • Paintings • Prints • Drawings

PETER A. HELM

Backgasse1   Tel. 06271 • 1387
D-693 Eberbach am Neckar
EURO-BOOK AUCTION SERVICE

We wish to buy Fine Prints & Books i.e. single titles and collections of Old Master & Decorative Prints, European Travel, Art, Natural History, Literature, etc.
(Colour) Plate Books

Fine Topographical Paintings & Works of Art relating Mannheim, Heidelberg, Heilbrown (River Neckar Valley)
— **Fine Paintings by R. EPP (1834-1910)**

We are always interested in acquisition and would be please to discuss outright purchase or other possible arrangements with collectors interested in disposal. Consultations with bankers and attorneys representing estates are welcome.

Heritage Book Shop, Inc. and Bindery

We are one of the largest buyers and sellers in the U.S.A. of:

- Rare Books and Manuscripts
- First Editions
- Fine Bindings
- Illustrated Books
- Fine Printing
- Americana
- Early Voyages and Travels
- Science and Medicine
- Natural History
- African-American Literature

Our Autograph Gallery has a large selection of letters and manuscripts.

**8540 Melrose Avenue
Los Angeles, California 90069**

(310) 659-3674   Fax: (310) 659-4872

Louis, Ben, and Jerry Weinstein

PHILATELIC BOOKS WANTED

Any out of print book pertaining to postage stamps bring substantial money, especially those by Ashbrook, Dietz, Brazer or Chase. (I pay $150.00 for Ridgway's Color Guide.) No Scott catalogs (unless prior to 1880) are wanted, and no "how to" books or any printed for juveniles are wanted. All correspondence promptly answered.

STAMP COLLECTIONS ALSO WANTED

Especially United States before 1940. There is little demand for first day covers, commemorative sheets before 1935, nor modern plate number blocks.

I am a Senior Member of the American Society of Appraisers, and a former director of the American Stamp Dealers' Association and the Philatelic Traders' Society of London. For forty years I was a Licensed Auctioneer in New York City, selling at public auction stmaps, coins, manuscripts, autographs and philatelic books. I have been in business sinece 1933.

Give me a RING AT ANY TIME OF DAY OR NIGHT (Sundays included) on my toll free number and tell me what you have for sale. I will be glad to give you an honest appraisal of its value, and to solicit its purchase if of interest to me.

OLD LETTERS ESPECIALLY WANTED

I am one of the nation's leading buyers of ninetheenth century letters, with or without stamps, especially those from the Civil War, California, or prior to the use of stamps in 1845. Offers made subject to your acceptance. Payment in Sterling may be easily arranged from my Barclay's account in London.

HERMAN HERST, JR.
P.O. Box 1583, Boca Raton, FLA. 33429-0494
Telephone: (407) 391-3223 - (407) 391-8868
1-800-321-6180

Rare Books & Manuscripts
sought for auction

Ephemera
Photographs
Etchings, Lithographs, Engravings
Oil Paintings & Watercolors
Period Furniture & Statuary
Porcelains
Ethnological Artifacts
Militaria

Metropolitan
Arts & Antiques Pavilion
110 West 19th Street
New York, New York 10011

Catalogues and information
212-463-0200 TEL
212-463-7099 FAX

Regular Book Auctions Held
NYS DEPT CONSU AFFRS LIC#867203

New Hampshire Book Auctions
92 Woodbury Road, P.O. Box 86
Weare, NH 03281
(603) 529-1700 or 529-7432

Some 1991 Sales We're Pleased To Report

ASSASSINATION OF JOSEPH SMITH. 1844.	$5,500.
Ruskin. WORKS OF.... 39 vols. 1903-12.	4,070.
Morden. GEOGRAPHY RECTIFIED. 1700.	1,540.
[Jane Austen] EMMA. A Novel. 1816.	1,870.
ORIENTAL NAVIGATOR. Philadelphia. 1801.	1,155.
COURT MARTIAL OF GEN. ST. CLAIR. 1778.	1,760.
Du Verney. L'ORGANE DE L'OUIE. 1683.	1,075.

May we auction your books, maps, prints, photos, ephemera?

RICHARD & MARY SYKES, FRANK SYKES,
ROBINSON MURRAY III

*Small or Large Consignments Are Invited.
Packing and Transportation Can Be Arranged.
Send For Sample Catalogue And Terms.*

NEW ENGLAND'S MARKETPLACE FOR BOOKS

CATALOGUE SUBSCRIPTION W/PRICES REALIZED
$20./DOMESTIC: $30./FOREIGN

RARE BOOKS, AUTOGRAPH LETTERS & HISTORICAL DOCUMENTS, ATLASES & MAPS

For information
about buying or selling at Phillips
Please contact Elizabeth Merry (London).

Direct Line: (071) 629-1824

Phillips London, 101 New Bond Street, London W1A 0AS.
Telephone: (071) 629 6602.
Phillips New York, 406 East 79th Street, New York 10021.
Telephone: (212) 570 4830

LONDON · PARIS · NEW YORK · GENEVA · BRUSSELS · ZURICH
THE HAGUE · DÜSSELDORF
*Twenty nine salerooms throughout the United Kingdom.
Members of the Society of Fine Art Auctioneers.*

AUCTIONS AT SWANN

SWANN GALLERIES is the oldest and largest U.S. auctioneer specializing in

RARE & ANTIQUARIAN BOOKS

AUTOGRAPHS & MANUSCRIPTS

19TH & 20TH CENTURY PHOTOGRAPHS

HEBRAICA & JUDAICA

WORKS OF ART ON PAPER

We conduct some 35 sales a year.
For our Newsletter and Catalogues,
and to discuss consignments to future sales,
please call Swann at (212) 254-4710.

SWANN GALLERIES
104 East 25 Street, New York, N.Y. 10010 ■ (212) 254-4710

Titles, Inc.

FLORENCE SHAY
1931 Sheridan Rd.
Highland Park, ILL. 60035

708-432-3690

DEALERS IN
RARE & FINE BOOKS
IN ALL CATEGORIES

SEARCH SERVICE

Do you have books to sell us?

EIGHT AUCTIONS YEARLY
OF
FINE & RARE BOOKS
DECORATIVE & FINE ART PRINTS
MAPS & ATLASES
AUTOGRAPHS & MANUSCRIPTS

Catalogues And Prices Realized
Available Individually And
By Subscription

Information Regarding Auction Schedule, Consignments
Or Subscriptions, Write or Call Dale A. Sorenson

4931 Cordell Avenue, Suite AA
Bethesda, Maryland 20814
(301) 951-8883

Zubal Auction Company
2969 West 25th Street
Cleveland, Ohio 44113 U.S..A.

Conducts Auctions
Of
Rare, Antiquarian, and
Unusual Books
Manuscripts and Periodicals
in all subjects
but especially in
Americana, the Arts, Science,
and Travel
Ten times each year

Consignments Invited
We buy bookstores and library duplicates

Please Contact

John T. Zubal or Michael T. Zubal
Phone: 216-241-7640 • Fax: 216-241-6966

NATURAL HISTORY
OUR SPECIALITY SINCE 1948

Scholarly books wanted at all times.
We are interested single important volumes,
small collections and complete libraries.

**AMPHIBIANS • ANIMALS • BIRDS • BOTANY
CRYPTOGRAMS • DARWIN • FISHES • INSECTS
INVERTEBRATES • PALEONTOLOGY
REPTILES • SNAKES
VOYAGES AND EXPLORATIONS**

John Johnson

NATURAL HISTORY BOOKS
R.D. #1 - BOX 513, NO. BENNINGTON, VT 06257
(802) 442-6738

PLEASE QUOTE

**MANUSCRIPT and PRINTED MATERIAL BY and ABOUT
GUN INVENTORS and GUN COMPANIES**

**BOOKS ABOUT ANTIQUE and MODERN FIREARMS,
HUNTING, MILITARY, etc.**

RUTGERS BOOK CENTER
**127 RARITAN AVENUE
HIGHLAND PARK, NJ 08904
(908) 545-4344**
Specialists in Gun Literature

G. W. WALFORD (Booksellers)

15 Calabria Road · Highbury Fields · London N5 1JB · England
Tel: 071-226 5682 · Fax: 071-354 4716 · Telex: 8813271 Gecoms G (Walford)

We issue the catalogues in 4 series: Let us know your interests.

A ARTS – *Illustrated Books of all kinds and ages, Books with Coloured Plates, Atlases, Art History and Technique etc.*

T TRAVEL – *Worldwide.*

H HUMANITIES – *Social History, Sports and Education, Literature in Important Editions or Standard Fine Sets, Reference Works.*

S SCIENCES – *Botany and Biology, Physics, Chemistry, Mathematics, Medicine etc.*

We exhibit regularly at major book fairs worldwide and cover the Major International auctions.

BIELEFELD AUCTIONS

Several Auction Sales each year
■ Fine Books ■ Manuskrips ■ Old Paintings and Prints ■ Modern Art

Catalogues may be orderd according to particular fields of interest.

Our antiquarian book firm
ANTIQUARIAT GRANIER GMBH
is ready as it has been for more than 20 years, to accommodate your needs in buying and selling books.

GRANIER
AUKTIONSHAUS
WELLE 9 ■ 4800 BIELEFELD 1 ■ GERMANY
TELEFON 0521/67148 ■ TELEFAX 0521/67146

Walter R. Benjamin
Autographs, Inc.
Established 1887

Specialists in
letters and documents
of literary,
historical, musical
and scientific interest

P.O. Box 255
Scribner Hollow Road
Hunter, N.Y. 12442
Telephone: (518) 263-4133

Publishers of
"THE COLLECTOR"

AMERICAN BOOK PRICES CURRENT INDEX

1987 - 1991

AMERICAN
BOOK PRICES CURRENT
1987 — 1991

Index
The auction seasons September 1987 — August 1991

Autographs & Manuscripts
Books A — B

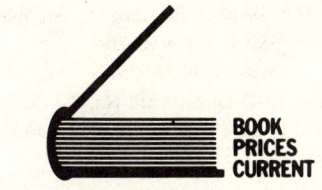

BANCROFT-PARKMAN, INC.
1992

EDITORS

KATHARINE KYES LEAB
DANIEL J. LEAB

Please send all inquiries and suggestions to:

American Book Prices Current
P.O. Box 1236
Washington, CT 06793
TEL: (212) RE 7-2715
     (203) 868-7408

Copyright © 1992 by Bancroft-Parkman, Inc. All rights reserved
ISBN: 0-914022-26-1
ISSN: 0091-9357
Library of Congress Card No. 3-14557
Printed in the United States of America

CONTENTS

	Page
Abbreviations	vi
Foreword	vii
Named Consignors	ix
Part I: Autographs & Manuscripts	1
Part II: Books, Broadsides, Maps & Charts	811

ABBREVIATIONS

ad, ads Advertisement(s)
ACs Autograph Card, signed
ADs Autograph Document, signed
ALs Autograph Letter, signed
A Ls s Autograph Letters, signed
Amst. Amsterdam
anr Another
Anon Anonymous
ANs Autograph Note, signed
armorial bdg Binding with coat of arms on cover
Balt. Baltimore
bdg Binding
bds Boards
Birm. Birmingham
Bost. Boston
c. Circa
Cambr. Cambridge
cat Catalogue
cent Century
contemp Contemporary
def Defective
Ds Document, signed
d/j Dust-jacket
Ed Edition; Edited; Editor
Edin. Edinburgh
extra bdg Elaborate binding
f, ff Folio(s)
frontis Frontispiece
H of R House of Representatives
illus, illusts Illustrate(d); Illustrations
imperf Imperfect
inscr Inscribed; Inscription
intro Introduction

L London
lea Leather
lev Levant
litho Lithograph
L.p. Large paper
Ls Letter, signed
Ls s Letters, signed
Ltd Limited
mor Morocco
Ms, Mss Manuscript; Manuscripts
mtd Mounted
n.d. No date
n.p. No place
n.y. No year
NY New York
no, nos Number; Numbers
orig Original
pbd, pbr Published; Publisher
Phila. Philadelphia
port Portrait
pp Pages
prelim Preliminary
pseud. Pseudonym
ptd, ptg, ptr Printed; Printing; Printer
pvtly Privately
Sen. Senate
sgd Signed
syn Synthetic
tp Title-page
trans Translated; Translation; translator
vol, vols Volume; volumes
w.a.f. With all faults
Wash. Washington
wrap, wraps Wrapper; Wrappers

Book sizes are listed as:
folio   **12 mo**
4to   **16 mo**
8vo   etc.

FOREWORD

This priced Index to *AMERICAN BOOK PRICES CURRENT* follows the pattern of the previous indexes. Note, however, that we have included *all* place names in imprints, that we have included formats, and, in a goodly number of instances, we have provided both edition and uniform titles.

The arrangement of the ABPC 1987-91 Index is that of the annual volumes 94 through 97, covering the four years from September 1987 through August 1991. The Index is divided into two parts; Part I, Autographs & Manuscripts, includes original illustrations for printed books, documents, letters, typescripts, corrected proofs, signed photographs, and signatures, as well as manuscripts. Part II, Books, also includes broadsides, single-sheet printings, printed maps & charts and uncorrected proof copies.

AUTOGRAPHS & MANUSCRIPTS (Part I of the Index) are arranged in a single alphabet by author, by title, or by subject (e.g., Bible Manuscripts, Latin; Chronicles; Horae B.M.V.; New Jersey) Autograph manuscripts and typescripts are arranged alphabetically under the author. Preceding each price is the year of the volume (*not* the volume number) of the ABPC in which the full entry will be found, with the abbreviated form (87) for 1987, (88) for 1988 and so on. Each letter or document now is listed to begin a separate line, with more information being given on specialized or high priced items.

BOOKS (Part II of the Index) are arranged alphabetically by author whenever possible, by title when the author's name is not readily available, or by Private Press, Club, printer or publisher headings, if such are the associations which attract the collector. In general, illustrated books are listed under the author of the text. A few subject headings have also been used, such as England, Maps & Charts, Hebrew Books, and Miniature Books, or those for individual U.S. states or cities. There are cross-references to Club or Press books, to books bound together, and to books by more than one author.

Main entries under each author listing are identified by a one-em dash. Sub-entries (later states or issues, etc.) begin on spearate lines without the dash. A few headings, such as the Bible listings and those for the *Rubaiyat* and *The Compleat Angler,* are arranged chronologically for the user's convenience.

Following the title of each work is the year of publication, when known; then, edition, issue or state information when pertinent; then, the format for books published before 1901; and then in parenthesis, the year of the volume of ABPC in which the entry will be found, followed by price or prices realized, with dollar sales listed first, then British pounds, and then other currencies in alphabetical order, each in ascending order within the year concerned when there were multiple sales. The annual volumes are referred to by year (rather than volume number), with the abbreviated form (87) for 1987, and so on.

Incunabula are listed with place of printing and printer (when known) immediately following the title. The Goff number or other pertinent reference is included. Prices out of the ordinary often have immediately preceding them a clue to the reason for the variation, such a "Inscr" (inscribed by the author) or "Doheny copy," Other information pertaining to condition,, limitation, and extra-illustration is given when necessary to explain price variations. Errors and blunders found in the annual volumes have been corrected in this Index without comment.

Throughout this Index the prices used are hammer prices, that is, no buyer's premium of any kind has been added in. The following buyers' surcharges should be noted: In Holland 16% and 10 cents per item; in France, 16% up to F6,000, 11.5% up to F20,000, 10% above F20,000; in England, 10%; and in the United States, 10% at most houses.

Among the people responsible for the good things in this book are Jane Mallison, Marie-Luise Frings, Williston R. Benedict, various under-age Leabs, and Kathy Thorp. Audrey Smith of Columbia University Press continues to provide us with wisdom about production; Pam Kjellerstedt of Halliday-Arcata guides our book through the printing process. Everybody at Stebco Printers patiently puts up with our front matter coming in to them at the last possible moment. Finally, (and we're repeating it because we mean it) without Bill King at Inforonics, madness would have overtaken us years ago.

NAMED CONSIGNORS

Refer to annual volumes under dates given for auction house and catalogue dates.

Abbey, J.R.	1989
Adler, Mr. & Mrs. Fred P.	1990
Abrams, George	1989
Affron, Lawrence C.	1989
Aitchison, Christopher	1991
Alexander, Thomas J.	1990
Angus, Donald	1990
Arlott, John	1987
Arnot Art Museum	1987
Ash, Lee	1988
Asian Art Museum of San Francisco	1987
Astor Collection, William Waldorf	1987
Auchincloss, Louis	1989
Austin, James Bliss	1990
Baker, Larry E.	1989
Barnes Gallery	1989
Baron, Salo W.	1991
Barrett, Ellen & Mary	1988
Barrett, Roger W.	1987, 1988
Bartholomew, John	1990
Bassine, Charles C. 1988	
Bates, Joseph D., Jr.	1989
Belcher, Nathan, III	1990
Belding Memorial Library	1989
Bastard, Mrs. John	1987
Beebe, Lucius	1989
Bellow, Saul	1988
Bergstrom-Mahler Museum	1990
Bewick, Thomas	1990
Blanchi, H.	1991
Billington, Ralph H.	1988
Binney, Edwin, 3d	1990
Bishop, William P.	1991
Blackmer, Harry	1989
Boehm, Edward Marshall	1991
Boerth, Mrs. E.H.	1990
Bok, Mrs. Cary W.	1988
Boone, James R. Herbert	1988
Borowitz, David	1987
Borthwick-Norton, Mrs. E.S.	1988
Bowen, Henry	1991
Boxted Library	1988
Breitbart Collection	1990
British Rail Pension Fund	1988
Brooklyn Museum	1989
Brooklyn Public Library	1988
Browne, William A.	1988
Brummer, Susie	1990
Brundage, Avery	1987
Bryan Kirke	1988
Bulkley, Martha Lambert	1990
Bullock, Hugh	1987
Bullock, Marie	1987
Bunin, Buzz	1990
Buxton, Mrs. W. Dimmock	1988
Byer, Mr. & Mrs. Stephen	1990
Cann, R.J.	1989
Carmichael, P.O.	1990
Cavalry and Guards Club	1988
Chancellor, John	1990
Christensen, Stanton, C.	1989
Chrysler, Walter P., Jr.	1989
Clegg, Charles	1989
Cockerell, Sydney	1990
Cohen, Albert	1990
Cohn, Leo R.	1989
Coleman, William R.	1990
Conant, Mrs. James B.	1989
Crahan, Marcus & Elizabeth	1989
Crimmins, Cyril	1990, 1991
Crohn, Frank & Helen	1988
Curtis, William	1990
Curwen Studio Archive	1988
Dahlgren, Eva Drexel	1988
Dalton, Charles Grant	1989
d'Amboise, Cardinal	1991
Darien Library	1990, 1991
Davis, Chester	1991
Day, Dennis	1990
Delaware Art Museum	1987
De La Fontaine, Alfred Cart	1990
De Mille, Cecil B.	1988
Dent-Brocklehurst, Mrs. J.H.	1988
de Saumarez, the Lord	1990

Desmarais, R.B.G.	1988
Devine, Douglas & Garnet	1989
Doheny Collection, Estelle	1987, 1988,
Doherty Archive, Edward	1988
Dolger, Henry	1989
Dorset County Library	1988
Downing, Kenneth	1989
Downshihre, the Marquess of	1990
Dring, E.M.	1991
Duarte, Francisco, J.M.	1990
Duke-Elder, the Lord & Lady	1989
Duschnes, Fanny S.	1989
Eastern Baptist Theological Seminary	1990
Edwin Forrest Home for Retired Actors	1989
Ehrenfeld, William K.	1990
Ekstrom, Parmenia M.	1990
Evans, Bruck Llewellyn	1989
Fairfax, James	1987
Faridany, Edward	1987, 1990
Felix, David H.	1990
Fellowship of Friends Library	1991
Fertig, Lawrence	1988
Fiebleman, Peter	1989
First, William	1989
Flagg, Lowrie S.	1989
Fleming, John	1988, 1989
Fletcher-Moulton, Sylvia	1990
Fontaine, Janet des Rosiers	1988
Forster, Thomas	1989
Foster, Gary	1989
Franklin Institute	1988
Fraser, Eric	1988
French Institute	1988
Frick Art Reference Library	1988
Fried, Henry K.	1989
Furness, Simon	1991
The Garden Ltd.	1989
Gardner, Maurice B.	1989
Gaute, J.H.H.	1991
Gavin, George D.	1990
Gerdau, Allan	1990
Ghandi, Arun	1989
Gill, Joseph O.	1988
Gillam, J.P.	1987
Gillet, James McHenry	1991
Girwood, Joy	1989
Girton College, Cambridge	1990
Goetz, William & Edith Mayer	1989
Graef, Alma	1990
Graham, Lloyd	1989
Gratsos, Panos	1990
Gray, Graham, F.	1990
Greenfield Museum	1990
Grendel, E.	1987
Griffin, Jonathan	1990
Grosset, A. Donald, Jr.	1991
Gump, Richard B.	1990
Gunner, Colin	1990
Gustin, Gunnar F., Jr.	1990
Haddington, the Earl of	1988
Halliday, Alice & David	1988
Hammond Family Libraries	1987
Harper, C.G.	1988
Harriman Foundation	1988
Harrington, Phyllis	1987
Harrison, Rex	1990
Haworth, Karl F.	1989
Haxton, Kenneth	1990
Hemingway, Doris	1991
Henry Ford Museum	1990
Herb Society	1990
Hetherington, John R.	1991
Heyer, Geroge S., Jr.	1991
Hill Library, James	1987
Hillwood Museum	1987
Home, Gordon Cochrane	1988
Hornby, Ann	1988
Hotine, William	1990
Houghton, Arthur A., Jr.	1988, 1989
Houghton, Monica	1990
Howell, John C.	1990
Huerlimann, Erwin	1990
Hughes, Gordon	1988
Hunt, Nelson Bunker	1990
Isham, Ralph H.	1989
Jack, Ian	1991
Jeffrey, Sheldon R.	1988
Jeanson, Marcel	1988
Jessup, Rondald R.	1991
Johns Hopkins University	1988
Johnson, James	1988
Kahn, Carolyn	1987
Kauffman, Lazare M.	1988
Kaufman, Kim	1988
Kay, Henry Cassels	1990
Kebabian, Eleanor	1991
Kababian, John S.	1991
Keen, E.A.	1990
Kemper, William T.	1990
Kennerley, Morley	1988
Kenyon, the Lord	1989
Kineon, James C	1991

Kissner, Franklin H.	989, 1990	Newberry Library	1989
Klemperer, Vjictor von	1991	New Hampshire Historical Society	1991
Koch Foundation, Frederick R.	1990	Newman, James	1990
Koelz, Walter N.	1990	New-York Historical Society	1991
Kollek, Teddy	1991	Nordholt, J.W. Schulte	1988
Korner, Eric	1990	Northumberland, Dukes of	1990
Krelle, Lloyd	1991	Novello & Co.	1989
Kump, Peter	1990	O'Connor, Edward J.	1990
Kuser, Lynda	1988	Oresman, Gertrude, JB.	1989
Lambert Collection	1990	Parsons, Fanny	1988
Lancaster, Sir Osbert	1990	Pattle, J.E.	1988
Lanchester, Elsa	1988	Payne, Robert C.	1988
Landau, Horace de	1991	Peabody, George	1989
Lathrop, Dorothy P.	1990	Pease, Lucy, Helen & William	1988
Latymer, the Lord	1988	Pepper, Graham	1991
Lawrence, Harry	1991	Pforzheimer Foundation	1989
Leeds, 10th Duke of	1990	Philip, Francis Higginson	1990
Lewis, Mrs. Robert A.	1990	Plaut, Martin E.	1989
Lloyd, Stacey B., III	1991	Poor, Alfred Easton	1988
Loughborough School of Library Service	1988	Powers, Maurice F.	1990, 1991
Lowe, Samuel, L., Jr.	1991	Pratley, H.W.	1988
Mackenzie, John, Jr.	1988	Pribek, Mrs. Gordon	1991
Macmillan Archive	1990	Prinzmetal, Myron	1988
McKell, Jospeh Scott	1990	Radbill, Samuel X	1988
McPherson, Gertrude Huntington Wright	1990	Reid, Whitelaw & Ogden	1988
		Reilly, Pamela, G.	1989
Malbin, Lydia Winston	1990	Reissman, Milton	1991
Malora, Stanley E.	1988	Robinson, Philip	1988
Manhattan College	1991	Roche-Guyon, Duc de la	1987
Martin, Henry Bradley	1989, 1990	Rochester, University of	1990
Massa, Pamela	1988	Rockefeller, John D., IV	1990
May, Marjorie	1990	Roelker, Naila K.	1990
Medhurst, R.G.	1988	Roosevelt, James	1988
Messore, Carman Harriot	1991	Roosevelt, Theodore	1991
Methley, K.	1991	Rosen, Victor	1989
Meyer-Kehr, Elise	1990	Rosenbloom, Charles J.	1987
Michaelis, Anthony	1988	Royal Institute of British Architects	1988
Middendorf, J. William, II	1989, 1990	Royal Society	1988
Miller, John	1990	Ruddy, James	1988
Miller, Phyllis J.	1990	Rumley, Peter	1988
Minshall, India Early	1988	Rylands Library	1988
Miro, Joan	1989	Salloch, Williams	1991
Montgomery County Community College	1991	Salzer, Felix & Hedwig	1990
Mount Charles, the Earl of	1988	Sang, Mrs. Philip D.	1987, 1989, 1990
Muirhead, Arnold	1987		
Munson, George	1989	Santy, Rosalyn W.	1990
Myers, Gilbert	1990	Sassoon, Siegfried	1991
Myres, Nowell	1990	Sawyer, Roland	1988
Neuman, Mary Stuart	1989	Schapiro, Robert D.	1990

Schatra, August W.	1989	Tropper, Gary	1988
Schiff, Dorothy	1990	Union Club	1988
Schiff, John M.	1990	Van den Brink,	
Schimmel, Stuart B.	1991	J.N. Bakhuizen	1988
Schorscher John	1990	van Fenema, Greta	1990
Schuster, Mrs. Leonard	1989	Vlaste, Philip	1989
Scott, Stanley	1990	Vogelius, Federico M.	1988
See, Neil	1990	Wagner, Henry	1991
Seligson, Ellen	1988	Wagner-Johnson, Livingston	1990
Sementchenkoff, Alexandre	1987	Walcott-Soliday	1990
Semsrott, William H.	1991	Walker, Benson Peter	1990
Senate Library	1991	Wastby, E.P. John	1987
Siegel, Henry A.	1990	Webb, Samuel E.	1991
Skilton, Charles	1990	Weeks, Harvey C.	1988
Skinner, E.W.	1987	Weems, F. Carrington	1990
Sligh, Nigel	1989	Welch, Edmund	1988
Slocum, John Jermain	1988	Wellington, Duke of	1990
Smith, Keywin Lehman	1990	Western Pennsylvania	
Smith, C.R.	1988	Museum	1989
Somerset House	1990	Western Reserve Historical	
Stevenson, Adlai E.	1987	Society	1987
Stirling, William	1990	Wetherell, Cortright	1987
Stokes, Lettice S. Phelps	1989	White, Edward A	1989
Stone, Florence & Philip	1989	Whitman, Enda Jardine	1988
Sullivan, Margaret M.	1987	Whiton, Joan	1988
Tate, Vernon D.	1990	Wills, Patricia	1988
Taylor, Howard H.	1988	Winchell, Walda	1990
Taylor, Lord & Lady	1988	Winter, W.H.	1987
Tennant, Stephen	1987	Wittgenstein, Matthias	1989
Tesone, Fountain Oliva	1990	Witzel, Annie L.	1989
Thimm, Gary G.	1989	Wolf, Edwin, 2d	1989, 1990
Thompson, Lawrence S.	1991	Wolfe, Donald C.	1989
Thornton, J.F.D.	1991	Wojlpe, Berthold	1990
Tomash, Erwin	1990	Wreden, William P.	1990
Tovee, Mrs. E. Bruce	1990	Yablon, Ralph & Phyllis	1988
Traub, Daniel L.	1990	Yeats, W.B.	1990
Tregoning Family	1990	Zeitlin & Ver Brugge	1988
Trinity College	1989	Zerbe, Jerome B.	1989

PART I

Autographs & Manuscripts

A

ABBA
[The signatures of all 4, [n.d.], on 8vo postcard with ABBA design, sold at wa on 21 Oct 1989, lot 430, for $50.]

Abbe, Salomon van
Original drawings, (13), to illus Louisa M. Archives of J. M. Dent & Son. (88) £260

— Original drawings, (15), to illus Louisa M. Archives of J. M. Dent & Son. (88) £520

— Original drawings, (25), to illus Thomas Hughes' Tom Brown's Schooldays, 1948. Archives of J. M. Dent & Son. (88) £850

— Original drawings, (27), to illus Joyce Reason's The Secret Fortress, 1950. Archives of J. M. Dent & Son. (88) £200

— Original drawings, (31), to illus Carola Oman's Robin Hood, 1939. Archives of J. M. Dent & Son. (88) £500

— Original drawings, (33), to illus Nathaniel Hawthorne's A Wonder Book, 1949. Archives of J. M. Dent & Son. (88) £550

— Original drawings, (38), to illus Nathaniel Hawthorne's Tanglewood Tales, 1950. Archives of J. M. Dent & Son. (88) £700

— Original drawings, (45), to illus R. Archives of J. M. Dent & Son. (90) £580

Abendroth, William H., 1895-1970
[The personal files of Gen. Abendroth containing hundreds of letters & photographs of prominent military, political & other notables, 1913 to 1968, sold at R on 24 Feb 1990, lot 50, for $1,500.]

Abt, Franz, 1819-85
ALs, 5/18 Nov 1870. (90) DM270
— 22 June 1877. (88) DM320

Accorimboni, Agostino, 1739-1818
Ms, Sonata for piano & violin in D-major, full score; [n.d.]. Heyer collection. (88) DM900

— Ms, Sonata per Pian-forte, e Violino, in D major, [n.d.]. Heyer collection. (89) DM800

Account Books
Ms, account book kept by the silversmith [Miguel?] Jeronimo, [Spain?], July 1579 to June 1580. (90) £500

— ARCHEDALE, RICHARD. - 2 Mss, ledgers of accounts as merchant in London, 1623 to 1637. About 600 pp in 2 vols, large folio, in contemp vellum bdg. Listing shipments, sales & prices of wine, cloth & other goods, naming agents & clients, etc. Marquess of Downshire collection. (90) £3,000

Achenbach, Oswald, 1827-1905
Series of 7 A Ls s, 26 Sept 1856 to Oct 1869. (91) DM700

1

ACQUAVIVA

Acquaviva, Baldassare, 1464-1528
Ms, De Prestantia Fidei. De Venatione et de Aucupio. [Rome, c.1523-25] 106 leaves only plus 2 flyleaves, vellum, 303mm by 215mm, in 16th-cent mor gilt. With full-page frontis, added half-page miniature & 38 large illuminated initials & borders & headings in gold on colored panels. Dedication copy presented to Pope Clement VII. Schiff Ms (91) $100,000

Adalbert, Prince of Prussia, 1811-73
ALs, 10 Jan 1870. (91) DM420
Series of Ds s, 3 Ds s, 4 May 1863 to 25 July 1869. Schroeder collection. (89) DM220

Adam, Adolphe, 1803-56
A Ls s (2), 19 Oct 1842 & [n.d.]. (90) DM460
ALs, [n.d.]. (91) DM230

Adam Brothers
Ds, 9 July 1774. (88) £380

Adams, Abigail Smith, 1744-1818
ALs, 2 May 1775. 2 pp, 4to. To Mercy Warren. About the military situation in Massachusetts & expressing hope for the American cause. Doheny collection. (89) $17,000

Adams, Andrew, 1736-97
ALs, 27 Oct 1792. (91) $120

Adams, Frank
Original drawings, (19), to illus W. (89) £400
— Original drawings, (20), to illus The Story of the House that Jack Built, [n.d.]. Various sizes. In ink & watercolor; 14 sgd. (89) £1,800
— Original drawings, (25), to illus The History of Sam the Sportsman, 1909. Mostly 372mm by 270mm. In ink & watercolor. Mostly sgd or initialled. (89) £1,700
— Original drawings, (26), to illus Three Jolly Anglers, 1913. 372mm by 270mm. In ink, watercolor & wash. 13 sgd. (89) £1,700
— Original drawings, (27), to illus A Book of Quaint Old Rhymes, 1912. Various sizes. In ink & watercolor. Mostly sgd or initialled. With related material. (89) £2,000

AMERICAN BOOK PRICES CURRENT

— Original drawings, (27), to illus The Frog Who Would A-Wooing Go, [c.1904]. 375mm by 272mm. In ink & watercolor. 12 sgd. (89) £2,600
— Original drawings, (3), to illus Alice's Adventures in Wonderland, 1911. 398mm by 245mm. In ink & watercolor; sgd. 1 def. (89) £1,900
— Original drawings, (32), to illus The Story of Simple Simon, [c.1904]. Mostly 373mm by 270mm. In ink & watercolor. 14 sgd. With related material. (89) £1,700
— Original drawings, (32), to illus The Three Little Pigs, [c.1904]. Various sizes. In ink & watercolor. Mostly sgd or initialled. (89) £3,800
— Original drawings, (32), to illus The Story of Old Dame Trot and her Pig, [c.1904]. Various sizes. In ink & watercolor. Mostly sgd or initialled. With related material. (89) £1,800
— Original drawings, (32), to illus Tom Tom the Piper's Son, 1910. Various sizes. In ink & watercolor; mostly sgd or initialled. (89) £2,000
— Original drawings, (33), to illus The Story of Jack and Jill, [c.1904]. Various sizes. In ink & watercolor. Mostly sgd or initialled. (89) £2,000
— Original drawings, (33), to illus The Story of Mother Goose, [c.1904]. Various sizes. In ink & watercolor. Mostly sgd or monogrammed. With related material. (89) £2,600
— Original drawings, (39), to illus various fairy tales, 1914. Various sizes. In ink & watercolor. Mostly sgd or initialled. (89) £2,600
— Original drawings, (4), to illus The Three Jovial Huntsmen, 1911. (89) £600
— Original drawings, (43), to illus Old Mother Hubbard (19) & other books, [n.d.]. (89) £400
— Original drawings, (7), to illus Little Jack Sprat, 1912. (89) £800

Adams, Henry, 1838-1918
ALs, 13 Sept 1871. Doheny collection. (89) $325

Adams, John, 1735-1826

ALs, 5 Sept 1777. 1 p, folio. To the Deputy Master Gen. Regarding the transmission of a Congressional resolve. Also sgd by Richard Henry Lee & Henry Laurens; free franked by Laurens. (89) $4,200

— 24 Oct 1777. 1 p, 4to. To Gen. James Warren. Requesting intelligence; speaks of legislatie actions. (91) $26,000

— 6 Feb 1778. 2 pp, 4to. To William Ellery, Jr. Discussing the fate of Burgoyne's army, & responding to Ellery's recommendation of a young man. (90) $18,000

— 26 June 1783. 2 pp, 4to. To Charles William Frederic Dumas. Reflecting his impatient mood while waiting for work of American & British ratification of the Treaty of Peace. (91) $3,750

— 20 Nov 1783. 1 p, 4to. To Mr. Cerisier. About "our American Constitutions." (91) $4,000

— 6 July 1785. 2 pp, 4to. To Elbridge Gerry. About his negotiations in London, & commenting on American politics. Was mtd. (89) $6,000

— 2 Oct 1793. 2 pp, 4to. To [Jean] Luzac. Letter of introduction for Tobias Lear. Seal tears repaired. Pratt collection. (89) $8,000

— 15 Oct 1797. 1 p, 4to. To Sec of War James McHenry. Requesting information about things "necessary to be communicated ... to Congress". (90) $7,500

— 27 July 1799. 1 p, 4to. To Sec of War [James McHenry]. Voicing his fear of the European "system of Debt and Taxes". (90) $12,000

— 23 Jan 1800. 1 p, 4to. To the Rev. Samuel Miller. Thanking for a copy of recipient's sermon on the death of George Washington. Encapsulated. (90) $5,500

— 20 Feb 1801. 1 p, 4to. To Thomas Jefferson. Informing him about horses & carriages belonging to the President's household. Repaired; framed. (90) $14,000

— 28 Feb 1803. 1 p, 4to. To Lyman Spalding. Informing him that he has forwarded his "Bills of Mortality" to the Secretary of the American Academy [of Arts and Sciences]. McVitty collection. (90) $6,000

— 10 Oct 1808. 4 pp, 4to. To Benjamin Rush. Reflecting on Jefferson's political errors & the mistakes of his administration. (90) $22,000

— 9 Mar 1809. 4 pp, 4to. To Jedediah Morse. Commenting on the Ms of Benjamin Trumbull's History of the US & reminiscing about events leading to the Revolution. Sang collection. (91) $26,000

— 17 June 1812. 2 pp, 4to. To Samuel Malcolm. About his recommending Malcolm for a judgeship, NY politics, & John Randolph. Some text loss; repaired. Mtd with a port. Rosenbloom collection. (88) $1,800

— 8 Dec 1812. 3 pp, 4to. To Benjamin Rush. Recounting an allegorical dream. (91) $18,000

— 29 Jan 1813. 3 pp, 4to. To Benjamin Rush. About his son-in-law's election to Congress, American naval heroes, & other matters. (90) $6,500

— 2 Feb 1814. 1 p, 4to. To Mercy Warren. Sending & commenting on a letter from Thomas McKean regarding the vote for independence in 1776. Sang collection. (91) $24,000

— 12 Feb 1818. 2 pp, 4to. To I. LeRay de Chaumont. Thanking for a copy of an agricultural address. (89) $5,500

— 6 Oct 1818. 1 p, 4to. To James Donatien Le Ray de Chaumont. About recipient's praise of American women & Madison's address to the Virginia Agricultural Society. (89) $6,000

— 20 Sept 1819. 1 p, 4to. To John Binns. Acknowledging receipt of a facsimile of the Declaration of Independence. With 10-line explanation [in Binn's hand?] at bottom. Tipped to card. Doheny collection. (89) $6,500

— 7 Aug 1821. 1 p, 4to. To "Cousin Boyleston". Acknowledging a letter, & talking about his children's visits. (90) $4,200

— 31 Aug 1821. 1 p, 4to. Recipient unnamed. Responding to a query concerning a Roman dictator. (89) £2,000

Ls, 29 May 1798. 1 p, 4to. To "Citizens of the Lower end of Frederick County".

ADAMS

Acknowledging a message of support. Pratt collection. (89) $6,000
— 16 July 1798. 1 p, 4to. To William North. Circular, requesting him to attend the Senate Chamber on the following day. (89) £2,100
— 18 Jan 1809. 3 pp, 4to. To Joseph B. Varnum. Discussing the effects of the Napoleonic Wars on European possessions in America. Mtd. (89) £7,500
— 20 Feb 1818. 1 p, 4to. To M. LeRaydechaumont. Content not given. (91) $4,600

ADs, 14 Dec 1792. 1 p, 4to. As President of the US Senate, certifying receipt of Connecticut's votes for President. With engraved port. (90) $7,500

Ds, 27 Mar 1797. 1 p, folio. Ship's papers for the ship The Two Sisters. Countersgd by Pickering. Repaired. (89) $1,200
— 13 June 1797. 1 p, folio. Military land grant in the Northwest Territory to descendants of John Quarles. Countersgd by Timothy Pickering. Doheny collection. (89) $2,800
— 14 June 1797. 1 p, folio. Ship's papers in 4 languages for the brig The Edmund of Newburyport. Countersgd by T. Pickering. Framed. (91) $4,250
— 13 Oct 1797. 1 p, folio. Ship's papers in 4 languages for the Industry of Bath. Countersgd by Pickering. Imperf. (90) $1,800
— 17 Oct 1797. 1 p, folio. Ship's papers in 4 languages for the schooner Sally of Baltimore. Countersgd by Pickering. (89) $2,200
— 19 Oct 1797. 1 p, folio. Ship's papers in 4 languages for the schooner Ruby. Countersgd by Timothy Pickering. (90) $1,900
— 13 Nov 1797. 1 p, folio. Ship's papers in 4 languages for the brig Lewis. Countersgd by Timothy Pickering. Repaired. (88) $1,050
— 26 Feb 1798. 1 p, folio. Ship's paper in 4 languages for the schooner Sisters of Baltimore. Countersgd by Timothy Pickering. (89) $1,900
— 16 Mar 1798. 1 p, folio. Land grant to William Nelson. Countersgd by Pickering; endorsed by Sec of War James McHenry on verso. (91) $2,750
— 26 Apr 1798. 1 p, folio. Appointment for Edward Wyer as midshipman. Whiton collection. (88) $1,700
— 30 June 1798. 1 p, folio. Ship's papers in 4 languages for the Betsey of NY. Countersgd by TImothy Pickering. Tape repairs. (89) $1,900
— 30 June 1798. 1 p, folio. Mediterranean Pass for the brigantine Columbia of New York. Countersgd by Timothy Pickering. (89) $1,850
— 17 July 1798. (90) $1,000
— 7 Mar 1799. 1 p, folio. Appointment for Samuel C. Crafts as Commissioner. Countersgd by Timothy Pickering. Partly ptd. (88) $2,400
— 17 Apr 1799. 1 p, folio. Appointment of Hugh Brady as Captain of Infantry. (91) $1,200
— 1799. (90) $750
— 20 Mar 1800. 1 p, folio. Grant of 4,000 acres to Jonathan Dayton in a tract appropriated for military services & for the Society of the United Brethren for propagating the Gospel. Framed. Byer collection. (90) $1,900
— 14 Apr 1800. (88) $450
— 28 June 1800. 1 p, folio. Ship's paper for the Lark. Countersgd by T. Pickering. (91) $3,500
— 13 Nov 1800. 1 p, folio. Ship's paper for the brig Luna. Countersgd by Charles Lee. (88) $1,800
— 16 Jan 1815. 1 p, 12mo. Receipt to Josiah Nightingale "for the Rent of Babel pasture". Text in the hand of Abigail Adams. (91) $1,400
— 17 Oct 1797. 1 p, folio. Ship's papers in 4 languages for the schooner Sally of Baltimore. Countersgd by Timothy Pickering. (90) $3,250

Cut signature, 22 Mar 1798. (90) $1,000
Franking signature, [28 Mar 1791]. Alexander collection. (90) $1,100
— Anr, [20 Sept 1819]. (90) $950

Adams, John, 1735-1826 —&
Adams, John Quincy, 1767-1848
[A group of 3 autographs, including an autograph document by John Adams, July 1763, 1 p, 8vo, statement of plaintiff's costs in the case of Belcher vs. Tirell, & franking signature & ADs of John Quincy Adams, 11 June 1793, 4 pp, 4to & 8vo, writ of attachment on the estate of Samuel Nicholson, sold at

P on Oct 23, lot 1, for $650.]

Adams, John Quincy —& Others
Ls, 13 Dec 1847. Doheny collection. (89) $600

Adams, John Quincy, 1767-1848
[An autograph envelope, front panel only, sgd & addressed to Solomon Lincoln, [15 Nov n.y.], sold at sg on 24 Mar 1988, lot 3, for $100.]
[2 franking signatures, each with autograph address, n.d., sold at wa on 1 Oct 1988, lot 98, for $325.]
Autograph Ms, 4-line poem in Greek, with heading requesting a trans. (91) $600
— Autograph Ms, comments on the controversy between Dr. Waterhouse & the Medical Society over smallpox vaccination; [n.d.]. 4 pp, 4to. (91) $2,600
Collection of ALs, Ds & franking signature, 19 July 1819, 3 Dec 1821 & [n.d.]. (88) $1,000
ALs, 2 Aug 1789. 3 pp, 4to. To Nathaniel Freeman. About his personal life & the new judicial system. Byer collection. (90) $3,200
— 20 Nov 1790. 3 pp, 4to. To his sister, Abigail Adams Smith. About their father's fame as an impediment to their own success. (91) $16,000
— 29 Aug 1792. 1 p, 8vo. To his mother. About domestic matters & the smallpox epidemic. Byer collection. (90) $2,800
— 4 Apr 1802. 2 pp, 4to. To his father John Adams. Forwarding a letter, & discussing financial arrangements & a court case. (89) $2,200
— 27 Oct 1802. (90) $1,000
— 7 Jan 1809. 1 p, 8vo. To his father John Adams. Discussing a financial matter. Docketed by recipient. (90) $1,800
— 10 Apr 1811. 4 pp, 4to. To Thomas B. Adams. Discussing his sons' education, his own prospects & plans, etc. Sang collection. (91) $9,000
— 14 Aug 1811. 2 pp, 4to. To Oliver Wolcott. As Minister to Russia, regarding commercial matters in connection with some vessels. Byer collection. (90) $1,200
— 16 June 1812. 2 pp, 4to. To [Peter] P[aul] F[rancis] Degrand. Commenting about public events in the USA. (89) $3,000
— 23 June 1813. 1 p, 4to. To Robert Fulton. Commenting on modern technology & the war. (88) $8,500
— 16 Feb 1816. (89) £750
— 17 Jan 1817. 4 pp, 4to. To Gov. William Plumer. Praising Plumer's speech & analyzing European attitudes towards America. Pratt collection. (89) $12,000
— 9 Sept 1817. 1 p, 4to. To Richard Rush. Responding to an urgent summons & informing him that he is about to leave for Washington. (91) $2,000
— 9 Sept 1817. 1 p, 4to. To Richard Rush. Informing him of his departure for Washington. Endorsed by Rush on verso. (89) $1,600
— 8 Oct 1817. 1 p, 4to. To Dr. J. Morse. Expressing willingness to support his efforts concerning Indian missions. Mtd. (89) £1,600
— 25 May 1820. 1 p, 4to. To John Howard March. Requesting a bill for wine received from Madeira. With related material. Pforzheimer collection. (90) $3,750
— 1 Mar 1822. Whiton collection. (88) $850
— 3 Dec 1826. 1 p, 4to. To Thomas Boylston Adams. Responding to inquiries on behalf of John Kirkland regarding the Adams genealogy & John Adams's diary. Pratt collection. (89) $3,000
— 31 Aug 1827. 1 p, 4to. To Sec of State Henry Clay. Discussing the charges directed against the US minister to Mexico Joel Poinsett. (90) $6,000
— 1 July 1829. 1 p, 4to. To Joseph Blunt. Thanking for his pamphlet on the Cherokee question & commenting on changing the American flag with every new state. Rosenbloom collection. (88) $4,250
— 30 Sept 1829. Christensen collection. (90) $500
— 2 Nov 1830. 1 p, 4to. To his son Charles. Asking him to send a grate & coal for his wife's bedroom. Inlaid. (90) $1,100
— 15 Jan 1831. 2 pp, 4to. To Samuel L. Southard. Discussing the congressional election & requesting an account of

ADAMS

2 occurrences in Monroe's cabinet. (90) $2,000
— 10 Jan 1832. 1 p, 4to. To Susan Decatur. Acknowledging her letter & documents relating to her efforts to obtain a pension. (90) $2,200
— 1 Mar 1837. 2 pp, 4to. To Benjamin Lundy. Asking for his opinion about an enclosed document relating to the slave trade (not present). (91) $11,000
— 24 June 1838. 1 p, 4to. To Joseph Coleman Fisher & others. Regretting that "public duties" prevent him from attending 4th of July ceremonies in Philadelphia. (90) $2,500
— 21 Sept 1838. 4 pp, 4to. To the Ed of the Quincy Patriot. Reporting about his activities in Congress, the Cilley duel, the Texas question, etc. Stained. (88) $5,500
— 22 Aug 1840. McVitty collection. (90) $600
— 11 Nov 1840. 1 p, 4to. To Roger L. Baldwin. About the Amistad case. (91) $4,800
— 29 Oct 1841. 1 p, 4to. To R. E. Lockwood. Declining an invitation to address the Mercantile Library Association. (91) $1,200
— 27 Nov 1841. 1 p, 4to. To George Roberts. Forbidding the publication of his lecture on the Opium War in the Boston Times and Notion. Sang collection. (91) $1,800
— 28 Sept 1843. 2 pp, 4to. To William B. Read. Content not given. (91) $1,500
— 22 Nov 1844. (90) $600
— 24 Jan 1825. 2 pp, 4to. To Joseph R. Ingersoll. Requesting the return of papers withdrawn from the Department of State by Levett Harris. Pforzheimer Foundation. (90) $3,500

Ls, 15 Nov 1817. (90) $300
— 20 Apr 1818. (90) $450
— 30 July 1821. (88) $400
— 16 May 1822. (88) $350
— 26 July 1823. (90) $400

Ds, 1 Apr 1825. (90) $300
— 6 May 1825. (91) $750
— 25 May 1825. (90) $300
— 31 Mar 1826. (91) $800
— 31 Mar 1826. (88) $170
— 30 June 1826. (88) $350
— 1 Dec 1826. (90) $250

AMERICAN BOOK PRICES CURRENT

— 26 Feb 1827. (91) $225
— 23 Apr 1827. (91) $300
— 23 Apr 1827. (90) $325
— 5 May 1827. 3 pp, folio. Answer in a suit brought against him by James Corcoran. (90) $1,400
— 10 May 1827. (88) $200
— 24 May 18l27. (91) $550
— May 1827. (89) $500
— 20 June 1827. (89) $275
— 20 June 1827. (89) $225
— 26 June 1827. (88) $130
— 20 Sept 1827. (90) $160
— 20 Jan 1828. (91) $200
— 30 Jan 1828. (90) $180
— 21 Feb 1828. (88) $700
— 20 Mar 1828. (91) $250
— 24 Apr 1828. (90) $1,000
— 1 May 1828. (90) $200
— 4 June 1828. 1 p, folio. Appointment of William Clark as Treasurer. Countersgd by Henry Clay. Fold splits. (88) $1,300
— 1 Dec 1828. (88) $310
— 14 Jan 1848. 2 pp, 4to. Contract with William H. Powell for a painting for the rotunda of the Capitol. Sgd twice. Also sgd by Sen. James Alfred Pearce & Powell. (90) $3,250

Check, sgd, 27 Nov 1826. (91) $425
Cut signature, 4 June 1822. (90) $140
— Anr, 19 June 1826. (91) $225
— Anr, [n.d.]. (91) $130
— Anr, [n.d.]. (90) $120

Engraving, profile view of Adams by N. Dearborn, [n.d.]; sgd by Adams in top margin. Also sgd in facsimile. (90) $4,000

Franking signature, [1820]. (89) $180
— Anr, [n.d.]. (90) $180
— Anr, 1825. (89) $170
— Anr, 17 Sept 1831. (90) $220
— Anr, [n.d.]. (88) $120
— Anr, [n.d.]. Alexander collection. (90) $350

Signature, 21 Aug 1823. (91) $375
See also: Adams, John & Adams

Adams, Louisa Catherine Johnson, 1775-1852
ALs, 18 June 1847. Doheny collection. (89) $1,000
— 5 Dec [n.y.]. (91) $120
— [n.d.]. 1 p, 12mo. To an unnamed lady. Postponing a visit. (90) $1,100

Adams, Samuel, Signer from Massachusetts
Ls, 9 Oct 1793. 2 pp, folio. To Joshua Clayton. In his first day as governor, taking up his quarrel with the Supreme Court over "the first principles of a federal government." (91) $7,000
Ds, 16 Aug 1753. (90) $375
— 30 Aug 1776. (88) $350
— 15 Dec 1794. (91) $650
— 26 May 1796. (88) $270
— 1 Oct 1796. Christensen collection. (90) $350

Adcock, Frederick
Original drawings, (55), to illus A. Archives of J.M.Dent & Son. (88) £280

Addams, Jane, 1860-1935
ALs, 17 Mar 1899. (89) $80
— 16 Nov 1922. (90) $65
Ls, 24 Apr 1933. (91) $300

Addams, John, 1737-1823
[A collection of 62 items relating to Major Addams & his family, including deeds for tracts in NY & Vermont, c.1790 to 1826, & c.20 family letters sold at wa on 17 Oct, lot 298, for $140.]

Adenauer, Konrad, 1876-1967
Autograph Ms, notes taken during the Paris Conference discussing the project of a European Community, [10/11 Apr 1951]. 4 pp, 4to. With autograph corrections on 3 related typescripts by Herbert Blankenhorn, 8 pp, mostly 4to. (91) DM7,500
Ls, 10 Nov 1959. (89) DM200
— 4 July 1925. (90) DM380
— 18 Dec 1941. (91) DM420
— 30 Apr 1951. (88) DM220
— 11 Mar 1955. (89) DM280
— 24 Feb 1959. (89) DM320
— 10 Nov 1959. (90) DM380
— 7 Jan 1960. (90) DM400
ANs, Jan 1960. (89) DM220

Photograph, sgd, 1955. (89) DM420
— Anr, 1963. (90) DM280
— BLANKENHORN, HERBERT. - Typescript, draft of a speech dealing with the political situation in Europe, 22 June 1951. 2 pp, 4to. With autograph annotations by Adenauer. (91) DM1,900

Adler, Alfred, 1870-1937
Collection of 3 A Ls s, 10 Ls s & 3 autograph postcards, sgd, [c. 1914] to 14 Mar 1935. Length not stated, 4to & 8vo. To Erwin O. Krausz & his wife Tilde. About his work & his efforts to improve his professional situation in America. With related material. Ernst Gottlieb collection. (88) DM3,000
ALs, 21 May 1914. (88) DM900
— 7 Sept 1916. (91) DM780
Ls, 26 Feb 1931. (89) DM540
— 18 Feb 1932. (90) DM700

Adolf, Grand Duc de Luxembourg, 1817-1905
ALs, 1 Aug 1849. (89) DM550
Ds, 9 July 1866. (90) DM320

Adorno, Theodor Wiesengrund, 1903-69
Autograph Ms, addenda to p 239 of a treatise dealing with methodology & the social sciences, [n.d.]. 1 p, folio, on verso of hotel letterhead. (89) DM1,300
— Autograph Ms, notes taken from Johannes Buehler's Deutsche Kultur des Mittelalters; 1931. (88) DM650
Series of 5 Ls s, 20 May 1963 to 17 Jan 1964. 6 pp, folio. To a record company. About texts for a recording of songs by Schoenberg & Webern, & declining to write a commentary to songs by Winfried Zillig. File holes. (89) DM2,400

Adrian, Gilbert, 1901-59
Ms, measurement book of film stars while costume designer for MGM, in the hand of his chief fitter Hanna Lindfors, [1930s]. Length not stated. (89) $3,200

Adshead, Mary
Original drawings, (27), to illus Mary Norton's Bonfires and Broomsticks, 1947. Archives of J.M.Dent & Son. (88) £200

ADSHEAD

See also: Bone, Stephen & Adshead

Aeneas Sylvius Piccolomini, (Pope Pius II), 1405-64

Ms, Dialogus de somnio quodam, [Germany, Trier?, late 15th cent]. 57 leaves (3 lacking), 280mm by 205mm. Disbound. In a secretary-influenced bookhand presumably by I. W. G. With 2 large initials in red. Dampstained. (88) £1,150

Afghan War, Second

— STOKES, CORPORAL HENRY. - ALs, [1881]. 27 pp, folio. To Miss E. Stokes. Giving an account of his march through Southern Afghanistan to Quetta. (89) £320

Africa

— SPEAR, F. GORDON. - Autograph Ms, travel journal consisting of letters & diaries written as medical missionary to the Belgian Congo, 1922 & 1923. About 700 leaves, 8vo, in a folding box. (90) £720

Agassiz, Louis, 1807-73

ALs, 15 Feb 1856. (91) DM220
— 29 June 1873. (89) DM260
Photograph, sgd, [n.d.]. (91) $180

Agnese, Battista. See: Maps & Charts

Agnew, Spiro T.

Transcript, sgd, of his letter to President Nixon resigning the Vice Presidency, 10 Oct 1973. (91) $425
Signature, [c.Jan 1969]. (89) $60

Agoult, Marie, Comtesse d', 1805-76

ALs, 29 Jan [1875]. (88) DM280
— [n.d.]. (90) DM220
— [n.d.]. (89) DM220

Agricola, Johann Friedrich, 1720-74

ALs, [11 Nov 1771]. 4 pp, 4to. To Friedrich Nicolai. Discussing the merits of contemp composers. (90) DM9,500

Ahier, Herbert C.

Original drawings, (15), mostly to illus works by Robert Louis Stevenson, [n.d.]. Archives of J.M.Dent & Son. (88) £150

AMERICAN BOOK PRICES CURRENT

Ahlefeldt, Charlotte von, 1781-1849

Autograph Ms, collection of poems, Andenken; [n.d.]. (90) DM320

Aichinger, Ilse

Autograph transcript, poem, Gebirgsrand. (88) DM220
Collection of 15 A Ls s, 3 Ls s, ANs, & autograph Ms, 12 Apr 1973 to 13 Feb 1982. 29 pp, various sizes. Recipient unnamed. Letters to a friend, commenting about his poems, mentioning her work, etc. Poem, Bild im Mai; 7 lines, sgd & inscr. (90) DM1,400

Ainsworth, William Harrison, 1805-82

[A collection of autograph drafts, fragments, notes, letters & plates, [c.1840 to 1880], c.230 pp, 4to, & c.450 plates, 8vo, sold at S on 21 July 1988, lot 40, for £3,000 to Johnson.]
Autograph Ms (2), drafts of 2 unpbd plays, Second Sight or The Fireside Traveller, & My Housekeeper, [c.1820]. About 95 pp, 4to & folio, & 75 pp in a 4to notebook. Including 40 pp in anr hand. (88) £3,800
Autograph Ms, drafts of part of [Old Saint Paul's, pbd 1841]. (89) £290
— Autograph Ms, Jack Sheppard, drafts of 2 sections, with revisions, [c.1839]. (88) £900
— Autograph Ms, part of Crichton, [pbd 1837]; draft. 127 pp, 4to. Including c.50 of H. K. Browne's plates. (88) £1,700
— Autograph Ms, part of The Tower of London, draft, [c.1840]. 27 pp, 4to. Including related notes & material by George Cruikshank. With 25 plates & model of the Tower used by Ainsworth as reference. (88) £1,200

Akeley, Carl, 1864-1926

[An archive of correspondence addressed to Akeley & his wife by various correspondents including members of the Roosevelt family, 33 items, sold at P on 31 Oct 1989, lot 147, for $700.]

Alain-Fournier, Henri, 1886-1914
ALs, "Tuesday" [1913/14]. 1 p, 8vo. To [Marie Scheikevitch]. Thanking for an introduction to M. Hebrard. (90) DM8,500

Alaleo, Paolo
Ms, diaries recording Papal ceremonies, 1582 to 1638; c.10,000 pp in 11 vols, 4to; in contemp vellum bdg. Fair copy in several hands. Doheny collection. (89) $11,000

Alaska
Letter, 34 [sic] Feb 1898. (90) $200
— OTLER[?], WILLIAM. - ALs, 18 Dec 1879. 4 pp, size not stated. Recipient unnamed. Apologizing for the slowness in paying a debt, & describing his voyage to Alaska. (90) $100
— SMITH, J. S. - ALs, 20 May 1887. 2 pp, size not stated. To his sister Edith Smith. Referring to the land boom in Alaska, the growth of Juneau, hunting, etc. (90) $160

Alba, Fernando Alvarez de Toledo, Duke of, 1507-82
Ls, 14 May 1547. 1 p, folio. To Anton Fugger. Promising to support Sebastian Schertl[in]'s efforts to effect a reconciliation with the Emperor; with autograph subscription. With engraved port. (90) DM2,800
— 17 Feb 1569. Byer collection. (90) $475
— 1 Sept 1569. 1 p, folio. To the mayor & magistrates of the city of Louvain. Informing them of an investigation to be conducted by [Jacob] Hessels. In French. (90) DM2,200
Ds, 29 Dec 1567. 1 p, vellum, folio. Order regarding the confiscation of the estates of Count Hoorn & their administration by Nikolaus van Outheusden. (90) DM2,800

Albani, Dame Emma, 1852-1930 —& Gye, Ernest
[A collection of c.80 A Ls s addressed to Emma Albani & her husband by various musicians, singers, & literary figures, 1878 to 1915, sold at S on 21 Nov 1990, lot 1, for £900 to Macnutt.]

Albeniz, Isaac, 1860-1909
ALs, 19 June 1897. (89) DM250

Albers, Josef, 1888-1976
ALs, 12 May 1948. (90) DM220

Albert, 1819-61, Prince Consort of Victoria of England
Collection of ALs & ANs, 24 Apr 1861 & [n.d.]. Doheny collection. (89) $300
ALs, 10 Nov 1851. (90) £190
— 9 Nov 1854. (88) £120
Ds, 15 Oct 1852. (88) $225
See also: Victoria & Albert

Albert, King of Saxony, 1828-1902
Ds, 8 Apr 1885. (90) DM200
— 4 Feb 1896. (91) DM200

Albert, Eugen d', 1864-1932
Autograph music, song, Voeglein wohin so schnell, for voice & piano; [n.d.]. (90) £400
Typescript, comments about Johann Strauss, [n.d.]. (88) DM240
Collection of 5 A Ls s & 3 A Ns s, 1903 to 1930. (91) DM800
— Collection of 4 A Ls s & autograph postcard, sgd, [25 July] to 5 Sept 1922. (90) DM370
A Ls s (2), 16 Jan 1891 & 13 Jan 1900. (88) DM230
ALs, 11 Jan 1886. (89) DM320
— 25 Oct 1896. (90) DM340
— 6 Mar 1903. (89) DM200
— 20 Sept 1910. (90) DM220
Autograph quotation, 3 double bars of music, sgd; 27 Oct 1900. (91) $110

Albrecht, Herzog von Sachsen-Coburg, 1648-99
Ds, 7 July 1690. (89) DM650

Albrecht, Herzog von Preussen, 1490-1568
Autograph Ms, prayer, beginning "Zukum dein reich O ewiger vatter..."; [n.d.]. 1 p, 8vo. With authentication by the archivist Faber, 1818. (90) DM7,000
ALs, [9 Sept] 1513. 7 pp, folio. To his brother Markgraf Kasimir von Brandenburg. As Grand Master of the Teutonic Order, asking for advice about his differences with the King of Poland. (90) DM23,000

ALBRECHT

Albrecht, Prince of Prussia, 1837-1906
Ms, "Sieges-Hymnus, 1866", for piano. Schroeder collection. (89) DM270
ALs, 22 June 1888. Schroeder collection. (89) DM200
— 11 Mar 1893. (90) DM320
Photograph, sgd, 15 Oct 1880. (91) DM480

Albrecht Achilles, Kurfuerst von Brandenburg, 1414-86
Letter, [19 Mar] 1441. (90) DM650
Document, [27 Dec] 1472. 1 p, folio; vellum. Confirmation of privileges for Friedrich, Bishop of Lebus. Schroeder collection. (89) DM2,800

Albrecht Alcibiades, Markgraf von Brandenburg-Kulmbach, 1522-57
Ls, [25 Mar] 1551. 1 p, 4to. To Melchior Zobel von Giebelstadt, Bishop of Wuerzburg. Asking that Veit Zigk be invested with property near Uttenreuth. (91) DM1,100
— 13 Feb 1553. 3 pp, 4to. To the chapter at Eichstaedt & the magistrates at Nuernberg, Rothenburg & Windsheim. Demanding that they accept his agreements with the Emperor. Sgd AMzB. (90) DM1,900

Albrecht VII, Archduke, Regent of the Netherlands, 1559-1621
Ls, 10 Mar 1604. (88) DM300

Albrecht von Brandenburg, Kurfuerst von Mainz, 1490-1545
Ds, [29 June] 1538. 1 p, 4to. Receipt for taxes paid by the cloister at Hadmersleben. Schroeder collection. (89) DM1,100
Document, [15 Sept] 1519. (90) DM400

Album
Ms, album of Albert Scholten, 1770 to 1811. (88) £170
— Ms, album of C. B. M. Kiefhaber, 1790 to 1812. 162 leaves, 8vo, in contemp bds. With 109 entries by family members & friends in Nuernberg, Bayreuth, Offenbach (Sophie von La Roche, Gunda von Savigny) etc.; including 4 watercolors. (90) DM1,600
— Ms, album of Christiane Erdmuthe von Beust, 1788 to 1792. (88) DM900
— Ms, album of Christoph Andreas Nilson, 1780 to c.1820. 317 pp, 8vo. Vellum bdg. 130 entries by members of his family, August Ludwig, Dorothea & Caroline Schloezer, C. G. Heyne, J. Claproth, C. W. Gatterer & other professors at Goettingen, & numerous acquaintances at Augsburg. With 15 drawings & 2 engravings. Kuehlmann collection. (88) DM6,600
— Ms, album of Heinrich Herwartt, 1583 & later. 25 leaves, 191mm by 130mm, in quarter vellum bds. With entries by relatives & friends at Augsburg & Wittenberg & 22 pages illuminated with armorials, colored borders, etc. Some leaves lost, many loose. (90) $1,500
— Ms, album of Joh. Ernst Seidlitz, 1763 to c.1802. 330 pp & 7 index leaves, 8vo. Lea bdg. 285 entries, mostly dating from his student days at Helmstaedt. With several illusts, including 9 in watercolors. (88) DM2,200
— Ms, album of Johannes Friedrich Kielman von Kielmannsegg, 1589 to 1600. 116 leaves, 150mm by 105mm. Contemp blindstamped brown lea. With c.100 entries in Latin, German, Italian & French, 26 painted coats-of-arms, & full-page miniature. Decorated with numerous specimens of paper of oriental origin. (90) DM5,100
— Ms, album of Mme F. Friedland, 1846 to 1862. 34 leaves, 170mm by 255mm. Contemp green velvet. With 28 entries by acquaintances in Paris (Adolphe Adam, Theophile Gautier, etc.), Prague, Berlin, London, etc.; including 2 drawings & 12 musical quotations. (90) DM1,400
— Ms, album of the apothecary J. J. Bentzien, 1773 to 1803. 118 leaves, 110mm by 202mm, in contemp lea bdg. With 176 entries by family members & friends in Germany, East Prussia, Kopenhagen, etc. Illus with 15 watercolors, 9 drawings, 4 engravings, & 4 silhouettes. (91) DM1,600
— Ms, [c.1895]; size not stated. (88) $230
— Ms, [Germany, 1595-1616]. 176 leaves, 142mm by 97mm. Contemp blindstamped calf gilt. With 14 brief entries. Including 31 leaves of marbled paper in colors. Bdg chewed by rodents. (90)

DM4,300
— Ms, [Germany], 1806 to 1866. 173 leaves, 127mm by 205mm. Contemp extra red mor bdg; with fore-edge painting. With 22 entries, & including 3 watercolors & colored engraving. (90) DM5,400
See also: Moerike, Eduard

Alby, Henri
Ms, La Vie de S. Schiff Ms (90) $475

Alchemical Manuscripts
Ms, anthology of alchemy containing over 140 recipes, in Latin & Italian. [Northeast Italy, 2d half of 15th cent]. 85 leaves & 2 flyleaves, 214mm by 152mm. Tanned lea over pastebds, c.1500. In black ink in a skillful humanistic cursive bookhand. 5 pp with illusts of scientific or chemical apparatus. Some leaves with 17th-cent alchemical notes. (88) £34,000
— Ms, compilation of alchemical recipes, [c.1742]. 102 leaves, 205mm by 160mm, in contemp vellum bdg. In several hands. (91) DM2,800
— Ms, compilation of alchemical & pharmaceutical receipts derived from 2 late 16th-cent Tuscan manuals; [Tuscany, 17th cent]. (91) £500

Alcock, Sir John William, 1892-1919 —& Brown, Arthur Whitten, Sir, 1886-1948
Menu, for banquet at the Savoy Hotel honoring 1st non-stop transatlantic flight; 23 June 1919. (90) $500

Alcott, Louisa May, 1832-88
Autograph Ms, fragment (p 90) from her work Jack And Jill, [1880]. (90) $750
— Autograph Ms, Jack and Jill: A Village Story, fragment; [1880]. Doheny collection. (89) $700
— Autograph Ms, story, Jerseys, or The Girls' Ghost, [pbd July 1884]. 52 pp, 8vo, on rectos only. In blue mor gilt by Bennett. Ptr's copy. Doheny collection. (89) $14,000
Cut signature, [n.d.]. (88) $65

Alden, John, 1599?-1687
Autograph endorsement, sgd, 8 Jan 1665/66. 1 p, 4to. Witnessing the mark of Quechataset on a deed dated 9 June 1665. Repaired. Sang & Middendorf collections. (89) $11,000

Alderotti, Taddeo, 1215-95
Ms, Libello per conservare sanita. [Italy, mid-13th century] Portions only, bound with fragment on the conversion to Christianity of Theodorus (in Latin). 18 leaves, vellum, 230mm by 156mm, in modern lea. In semi-cursive gothic script in black ink. (90) $3,800

Aldhelm of Malmesbury, Saint, 640?-709
Ms, De Laude Virginitatis. [Worcester?, late 8th or early 9th cent]. 2 leaves (bifolium), 180mm by 134mm. Orange-brown mor. In dark brown ink in a calligraphic very early Anglo-Saxon minuscule with some majuscule forms. With illuminated initial monogram. In Latin, with 17 glosses in Old English added in the 10th cent. Ludwig MS.XI.5. (89) £50,000

Aldobrandinus de Toscanella
Ms, Sermones de Tempore. [Italy, c.1400]. 96 leaves, vellum, 324mm by 230mm. Def 18th-cent Belgian brown calf. In a regular rounded gothic bookhand. With painted initials throughout. (89) £4,200

Aldrin, Edwin E.
Collection of ALs & group photograph, 31 May 1975. (91) $85
Photograph, sgd & inscr, [n.d.]. (91) $300

Alembert, Jean le Rond d', 1717?-83
ALs, 24 Apr 1770. (91) DM650

Alexander, Grand Duke of Russia
A Ls s (2), 11 June & 14 Sept 1919. Doheny collection. (89) $400

Alexander I, Emperor of Russia, 1777-1825
ALs, 1 Oct 1806. 2 pp, 4to. To Queen Luise of Prussia. Thanking for a letter delivered by the Duchess of Kurland. In French. (90) DM2,400
— 27 Sept 1824. (91) DM340
Ls, 5 Aug 1801. (88) DM360
— 31 July 1804. Byer collection. (90) $800
— 15 Jan 1808. (89) £350
— 30 Sept 1812. (90) DM950
— 14/26 July 1819. Byer collection. (90) $550
— 18 Jan 1820. (89) DM400
— 2/14 June 1825. (88) DM420

ALEXANDER I

Ds, 9 Sept 1807. (88) DM460

— 18 Dec 1810. 3 pp, size not stated. Appointment as Court Counsellor & grant of arms to Ivan Varvatsi. Including large Imperial Seal in silver gilt case. (90) £5,000

— 1 June 1825. (89) $250

Alexander II, Emperor of Russia, 1818-81

[A brass-bound lea photograph album, the personal property of Alexander II, containing 30 photographs mostly of Yekaterina Mikhailovna Dolgorukaya (later Princess Iurievskaya), dated in Alexander's hand & inscr on verso by the Princess, sold at S on 5 Apr 1990, lot 4, for £6,500.]

[A writing album, 29cm by 44cm, in extra bdg with crowned silver monogram & dates 1855-1880, with silver ropework borders & Romanov crown, c.1880, sold at CNY on 12 Apr, lot 17, for $1,400.]

Series of over 400 A Ls, 19 Aug 1866 to 7 Jan 1880. To Yekaterina Mikhailovna Dolgorukaya, Princess Iurievskaya. Love letters. With c.130 autograph letters by Yekaterina Dolgorukaya to Alexander. Together about 1,500 pp, 8vo. Mostly in French. (90) £45,000

— Series of 595 A Ls, Jan 1868 to Jan 1870. To Yekaterina Mikhailovna Dolgorukaya, Princess Iurievskaya. Love letters. With 370 A Ls by Yekaterina Dolgorukaya to Alexander, May 1869 to Jan 1872, & 40 telegrams. Together about 5,000 pp, 8vo. Mostly in French. (91) £11,000

Ls, 7 June 1858. (88) DM280

— 19 Aug 1858. (90) DM500

Ds, 4 Nov 1867. 7 pp, 31cm by 46.2cm. Letter of nobility for Peter, son of Alexis Moritz. In cyrillic calligraphy in gold & black, large painting of the arms, illuminated border incorporating imperial eagle & small coats-of-arms on 1st page, & illuminated floral scrollwork borders. In orig green velvet portfolio attached to orig imperial silver seal-box, 1867. With letter of authenticity. (88) $4,000

— 16 Apr 1878. (89) DM650

Autograph telegram, sgd, [c.1870s]. (91) $950

AMERICAN BOOK PRICES CURRENT

Alexander III, Emperor of Russia, 1845-94

Series of 3 A Ls s, 22 Mar 1866 to 22 Dec 1884. Length not stated. To Prince Nikolai Alexeevich Orlov. Commenting on family matters & world events. (90) £3,000

Alexander the Great, 356-323 B.C.

— THE ROMANCE OF ALEXANDER. - Ms, in French; [Southern Netherlands, early 14th cent]. 1 leaf only, vellum, 365mm by 239mm. In a formal gothic hand. With 3 two-line initials & large miniature showing the battle of Alexander & King Porus. Framed. (90) £7,000

Alexander VI, Pope, 1431?-1503

[2 autograph endorsements (4 words) on a Dispensation, 11 July 1494, 1 p, folio, sold at CNY on 17 Oct 1988, lot 1036, for $300 to Heritage Bookshop.]

Document, 25 Sept 1492. 1 p, vellum, 306mm by 430mm. Papal Brief addressed to Ulrich Ammann regarding the appointment of Jakob Haushamer to a church at Ramering, Bavaria. (91) DM1,200

— 6 Oct 1494. 1 p, folio; vellum. Bull addressed to 3 bishops in Dalmatia regarding income from a church at Veglia. Lacking seal. (90) DM1,600

— ANON. - Ms, Vita d'Alessand. VI. [Italy, c.1600]. 72 leaves of laid paper, 270mm by 195mm, in 18th-cent half vellum bdg. In cursive script. Phillipps Ms.7235. (91) $600

Alexander VI, Pope, 1431?-1503 —& Julius II, Pope, 1443-1513

Document, 20 Jan 1491. 1 p, vellum, 715mm by 945mm. Indulgence granted to a congregation of laymen at the Parish of St. Mary's at Glatz in Bohemia by Rodrigo Borgia [Alexander VI], Giuliano della Rovere [Julius II] & 18 other cardinals. Including certification by Paul Stephan Poucek von Talmberg, 19 Jan 1492, below. Illuminated. Stained. (89) DM3,600

Alexander VII, Pope, 1599-1667

Document, 30 July 1661. (90) DM350

Alexander, Sir William, 1567-1640 — & Mason, John, 1586-1635
Ds, 9 Apr 1622. 1 p, c.27 by 24 inches. Contract with Thomas Hopkins, master of the ship Planter, for a voyage to be made to North America. Also sgd by others. Marquess of Downshire collection. (90) £38,000

Alexander, William ("Lord Stirling"), 1726-83
[An important collection of 220 items from Alexander's archives, 14 July 1767 to 14 Dec 1782, mostly letters addressed to him during his service in the Continental Army, including letters by Washington, Hancock, Hamilton, Monroe, & many others, mtd in 2 mor gilt vols, sold at P on 31 Jan 1990, lot 2540, for $290,000.]
ADs, 15 Nov 1765. (91) $200

Alexandra, Queen of Edward VII of England, 1844-1925
Photograph, sgd, [n.d.]. (91) £90

Alexandra Fyodorovna, Empress of Nicholas I of Russia, 1798-1860
ALs, 1 Oct 1825. (90) DM300
— 27 Apr/9 May 1834. (91) DM500

Alexandra Fyodorovna, Empress of Nicholas II of Russia, 1872-1918
ALs, [n.d.]. (91) $700
ANs, [n.d.]. (90) DM900
— [n.d.]. 1 p, 12mo (card). Recipient unnamed. Expressing the wish to see Princess Obolensky. Sgd A. In English. In pencil. (89) DM1,100
See also: Nicholas II & Alexandra Fyodorovna

Alexis, Willibald, 1798-1871
Autograph Ms, essay regarding examinations for the legal professions, sgd & dated 29 Nov [n.y.]. (89) DM320
— Autograph Ms, poem, Liebes Macht, [n.d.]. (91) DM350
ALs, 11 May 1835. (91) DM330
— 29 Oct 1849. 3 pp, 8vo. To Karl von Holtei. Commenting on the revolution in Germany. (91) DM1,050
— 15 Nov 1852. (90) DM320

Alfalfa
Signature, [n.d.]. (89) $100

Alfonso, Infante of Castile, 1453-68
Ls, 20 Sept 1465. 3 pp, folio. To Juan Ponce de Leon, Conde de Arcos. Offering wealth & honors if he will change his allegiance. Sgd Yo el Rey. Contemp endorsements. (88) £1,050

Alfonso V, King of Aragon & Sicily, 1396-1458
Ds s (2)7 Oct 1430 & 20 Apr 1440. 2 pp, vellum, folio. Acknowledging debts to Juan Fernandez de Heredia, & discussing financial matters relating to Barcelona. (90) £1,500

Alfonso XIII, King of Spain, 1886-1941
ALs, 18 Dec 1907. (90) DM220
Ls, 1 June 1906. (90) $300
Signature, 1931. (88) $70

Algrinus, Joannes ab Abbatisvilla, Cardinal
Ms, Expositio in cantica canticorum. [N.p., c.1220] 55 leaves, vellum, 105mm by 75mm, in modern bdg of early Ms vellum. In a small gothic hand in black ink. (90) $3,800

Ali, Muhammad
Signature, on limited Ed serigraph from a painting by Ali, no 127/250; [n.d.]. (91) $200

Alibert, Jean Louis, 1768-1837
A Ls s (2), 25 July 1823 & [n.d.]. (88) $225

Allen, Ethan, 1738-89
ALs, 12 Jan 1787. 2 pp, folio. To Guy [Carleton], Lord Dorchester. Hinting at an alliance between Vermont & Quebec. (91) $38,000

Allen, Fred
Ls, [n.d.]. (91) $225

Allen, Gracie, 1905-64. See: Burns, George & Allen

Allende, Salvador, 1908-73
Ds, 25 May 1955. (88) £50

Allut, Jean
Ms, detailed account of his preaching, etc., [c.1726-1736]. (88) £160
See also: Marion, Elie

Almirantes Family
[A group of 38 documents, 1535 to 1689, pertaining to the Almirantes Family & Spanish colonization in the New World, some sgd by Kings Charles II & Philip IV, & Queen Mariana of Austria, sold at P on 27 June 1989, lot 92, for $8,000.]

Alonso of Aragon, Archbishop of Zaragoza
Ls, 19 Nov 1512. (90) £600

Al-Sabah, Sheikh Jabir al-Ahmad al-Jabir, Emir of Kuwait
Signature, 17 Jan 1991. (91) $100

Altenberg, Peter, 1859-1919
Autograph Ms, Hysterie; [n.d.]. (89) DM420
— Autograph Ms, literary text, Philosophie; [n.d.]. (91) DM350
— Autograph Ms, literary text, Portrait-Malerei; [n.d.]. (91) DM400
— Autograph Ms, literary text, "Sehnsucht"; [n.d.]. (90) DM300
— Autograph Ms, [n.d.]. (90) DM370
— Autograph Ms, [n.d.]. (88) DM250
— Autograph Ms, [n.d.]. (88) DM400
— Autograph Ms, Stammtisch, [n.d.]. (91) DM380
Series of 8 A Ls s, 1918 & [n.d.]. 13 pp, 4to. To Alfred von Schebeck. Desperate letters about his declining health, financial problems, etc. (91) DM2,200
ALs, [n.d.]. (88) DM220
— [1918]. (90) DM440
— [n.d.]. (90) DM700
Autograph sentiment, commenting on Alpine flowers, 1914. (91) DM310

Altieri, Luigi, Cardinal, 1805-67. See:
Haslinger, Tobias

Alverdes, Paul, 1897-1979
Autograph Ms, story, Vergeblicher Fischzug, 10 Oct 1937. (90) DM320

Amalie, Queen of Otto of Greece, 1818-75
ALs, 10 May 1845. (90) DM660

Ambrosiaster
Ms, Tractatus in Epistolas S. Pauli. [Winchcomb Abbey, Gloucestershire, c.1140]. 129 leaves, vellum, 345mm by 255mm. 15th-cent calf over wooden bds by the Oxford "Fishtail" binder. In black & dark brown ink in a compressed English minuscule hand. With numerous large pen initials & 4 large decorated initials. Doheny collection. (88) £90,000

Ambrus, Victor
Original drawings, (5), to illus Francis Dickie's Husky of the Mountains, 1966. Archives of J. M. Dent & Son. (88) £70

American Revolution
[A collection of 33 items relating to figures & events of the American Revolution sold at P on 16 Apr 1988, lot 53, for $1,500.]
[A group of 3 autographs by Generals Philip Schuyler, John Sullivan & von Steuben, 31 Oct 1776 to 3 Mar 1787, 6 pp, various sizes, sold at R on 4 Mar 1989, lot 285, for $900.]
[A group of 4 autographs by different Revolutionary War generals & officers, 10 May 1777 to Dec 1787, sold at R on 4 Mar 1989, lot 298, for $180.]
[A soldier's letter, 30 Apr 1778, 1 p, to Gen. Edward Hand, complaining of lack of provisions & mentioning an Indian attack, sold at rf on 5 Dec, lot 54, for $900.]
[2 items relating to the military discharge of James Shop, a free black soldier of the Connecticut line, 25 Sept & 15 Dec 1780, 2 pp, 4to & 8vo, sold at wa on 17 Oct, lot 299, for $85.]
[A group of 33 letters, 1821 to 1860, requesting certification of service in the Revolution, sold at rf on 22 Apr 1989, lot 4, for $425.]
[A group of 19 autographs, mostly cut signatures, of military figures of the Revolutionary War, each with engraved port, sold at CNY on 8 Dec 1989, lot 70, for $2,800.]
Ms, Brigade Orders Book for a Connecticut Brigade, 27 Oct to 19 Dec

1781. 148 pp, size not stated; disbound. Listing assignments, general orders, courts martial, etc. Lacking some pages. (89) $6,000
— Ms, general court martial of Lieut. (89) $110
— Ms, General Orders Book for the Headquarters of the Continental Army in Rhode Island, kept by Major Gibbes, 8 to 28 Aug 1778. 135 pp, 16mo, in quarter calf bdg. (89) $4,000
— Ms, Naval Order Book, containing transcripts of letters from commanders of various ships of Gen. (88) £300
— Ms, notebook containing descriptions of the outbreak of rebellion at Boston & the British attack on 17 June 1775, copies of letters between Washington & Gen. (88) £680
— Ms, orderly book for a unit commanded by Capt. John Douglass of Pennsylvania, 3 - 29 Aug & 22 - 31 Oct 1776; c.65 pp, 4to. Incomplete; also containing some accounts, lists, etc. With related material. (90) $4,250
— Ms, patriot treatise, dealing with New Jersey's responsibility for the revolutionary cause, [n.d.]. (89) $280
— Ms, petition addressed to Col. (89) $350
Document, Sept 1774. (91) $450
— 4 July 1776. (91) $275
— BATTLE OF PENSACOLA. - Ms, Apuntes de las occurrencias..., contemp copy of the diary kept by the secretary of the Governor of Havana, 3 Aug 1780 to 28 Jan 1781. About 100 pp, folio, in 7 unbound quires. Detailing preparations for the capture of Pensacola by Bernardo de Galvez. (90) £5,800
— BIRCH, SAMUEL. - ADs, 3 Oct 1780. 1 p, folio. As British Commander of NY, authorizing B. Galway & others to sail to Delaware with a flag of truce. With approval, sgd by Admiral G. B. Rodney, on verso. Repaired. (89) $220
— CONTINENTAL CONGRESS, MARINE COMMITTEE. - Ds, 26 June 1777. 2 pp, folio. Instructions to John Hodge, Commander of the frigate Montgomery, regarding defense of the Hudson River & the appointment of officers. Sgd by 9 members of the committee, including 6 signers of the Declaration of Independence. Martin collection.

(90) $18,000
— CRAFTS, THOMAS. - Autograph Ms, A Journal of my March from Bridgewater to N York [From Courtland's Manour, to Bridgewater]. 24 July through 9 Dec 1776. 23 pp, 8vo, in home-made book. With miniature port of Crofts. (91) $10,000
— DARTMOUTH, MASSACHUSETTS. - Document, 1777. 1 p, folio. Ms broadside, fixing prices for a number of articles. (91) $150
— DE HAAS, COL. JOHN PHILIP. - Letter and orderly book of Phillips, who was commander of the 1st Pa Battalion, 26 Nov 1775-5 Sept 1776. 37 leaves remaining, folio, in orig sheep. (89) $1,700
— GIBBES, MAJOR CALEB. - Orderly Book for the Continental Army in Rhode Island. 8 to 28 Aug 1778. 125 pp, oblong 4to, in several hands, in orig half calf. (91) $10,000
— GLEN, HENRY. - ALs, 6 July 1776. 1 p, size not stated. To Col. Dayton. Concerning supplies. (88) $400
— GRAY, REV. ROBERT. - Autograph Ms, Marsden Manor, or Murder Will Out, sgd; [c.1900]. About 38 pp, in 4to vol; on rectos only. With numerous corrections. In pen & ink. "Domestic generational melodrama centering on the Revolution." (88) $120
— HOAKESLEY, ROBERT. - Ds, 16 June 1780. 1 p, folio. British officer's parole after imprisonment in Virginia; also sgd by Aide-de-Camp A. Collyer. (89) $300
— HOUSTON, DR. JAMES. - ALs, 2 June 1777. 2 pp, folio. To Gen. Lachlan McIntosh. Reporting about his efforts to obtain medical supplies at Philadelphia. (89) $450
— HUNTINGTON, EBENEZER. - ALs, 16 Mar [17]82. 1 p, folio. To Col. Joshua Huntington. Regarding supplies. (91) $80
— KIRBY, EPHRAIM. - ALs, 7 May 1777. 1 p, 4to. To his father A. Kirby. Patriotic letter from a soldier joining the Light Dragoons. Def. (89) $280
— LAUGCAY, JEAN. - Ds, 2 July 1779. 2 pp, folio. Petition to the Supreme Executive Council of Pennsylvania for a display of fireworks to celebrate the

AMERICAN REVOLUTION

anniversary of independence. Silked. (89) $450

— MASSACHUSETTS. - Broadside, We the Subscribers, ... [Watertown: Benjamin Edes, 1776]. Folio, in quarter mor slipcase. Declaration of non-cooperation with the British, with 28 ink signatures. Repaired. Evans 14840. John F. Fleming Estate. (89) $850

— MASSACHUSETTS. - Document, 30 June 1781. 3 pp, folio. Ptd act of the Massachusetts House of Representatives to raise soldiers for the Continental Army. With hand-written notation at head, sgd by Sec of the Commonwealth of Massachsetts John Avery. (91) $450

— MASSACHUSETTS. - Ls, 9 Apr 1773. 1 p, folio. To the Town Clerk of Lincoln. Ptd circular from the Boston Committee of Correspondence, reporting about the revolt against the Stamp Act in Virginia. Sgd by William Cooper, Town Clerk of Boston. (91) $1,000

— MASSACHUSETTS. - Document, 17 to 24 July 1775. 1 p, 12 by 6.6 inches. Enlistment broadside; partly ptd with signatures of enlistees. (89) $400

— MASSACHUSETTS. - Document, [c.1775]. 1 p, folio. Ms Oath of Allegiance; signature not stated. (89) $300

— MERRILL, COL. ISAAC. - ALs, 19 Apr 1775. 1 p, 4to. To Capt. John Currier. Informing him about the Battles of Lexington & Concord, & ordering him to mobilize troops. Framed. (91) $12,000

— OLIVE BRANCH PETITION. - A group of 14 A Ls s, A Ds s, & Ds s by different signers of the Olive Branch Petition, 1755 to 1805, sold at CNY on 22 Feb 1989, lot 2191, for $2,500 to Richards. 89

— PENNSYLVANIA. - Document, 25 July 1780. 3 pp, 7 by 12 inches. Orders from the Supreme Executive Council to procure wagons & horses requested by Washington; addressed to John Moore. In the hand of Timothy Matlack; sgd by Joseph Reed. (91) $1,000

— PLYMOUTH & SANDWICH, MASS., COMMITTEES OF CORRESPONDENCE. - An ALs by John Torrey for the Plymouth Committee to the Sandwich Committee, & the draft of a letter from the Sandwich Committee to committees at Truro & Provincetown, 14 & 17 Dec 1773, 6 pp, 4to, discussing measures to prevent the landing of tea. (90) $5,500

— PRESTON, CAPT. THOMAS. - Autograph Ms, The Case of Captain Thomas Preston, 14 Mar 1770. 5 pp, folio, in modern paper bds. Account of the Boston Massacre by the British officer in charge; sgd. With related material. (89) $80,000

— RHODE ISLAND. - Document, ptd copy of the minutes of the General Assembly, 28 June 1775; attested by Sec of the Colony Henry Ward. 7 leaves, folio. (89) $950

— RICHARDSON, WILLIAM. - ALs, 9 Oct 1781. 1 p, 8vo. To Major Gen. Greene. Requesting military supplies. (89) $300

— SHAW, NATHANIEL. - ALs, 29 May 1775. Length not stated. To the Treasurer of Connecticut. Informing him that his vessel is ready to sail, & requesting funds. (89) $260

— SHELDON, COL. ELISHA. - ADs, 1 Oct 1777. 1 p, 8vo. Orders received from Gen. Pulaski & conveyed to Cornet Brown "to collect all the Horse proper for Cavalry that belong to Tories". (90) $250

— SINCLAIR, PATRICK. - ALs, 13 Mar 1775. 3 pp, 4to. Recipient unnamed. Commenting on the crisis in America. (89) $150

— SMITH, PASCHAL. - ALs, 5 Oct 1779. 4 pp, 4to. To Col. Lewis Morris. Commenting on the military situation in Massachusetts. (89) $180

— STAMP ACT. - An ALs, 8 June 1766, 3 pp, size not stated, from William Wallace, mentioning the commotion occasioned by the Stamp Act in Richmond, Virginia, sold at rf on 4 June 1988, lot 32, for $210. 88

— TRAILLE, J. - Ls, 1 Sept 1780. Recipient unnamed. Ordering issue of ordnance items during the British occupation of Charleston. (89) $280

— WENDELL, JOHN. - ALs, 27 May 1776. 4 pp, 4to. Recipient unnamed. About the war in Canada, mentioning Hancock & others. (91) $350

— WHITING, SAMUEL. - Ds, bill for the hire of a horse from Fredericksburg to

Washington's headquarters, 6 June 1779. 1 p, 4to. (89) $140
See also: Strachey, Sir Henry

Amherst, Jeffrey Amherst, Baron, 1717-97
ALs, 24 May 1782. (90) $400
— 26 Sept 1788. (89) £150
— 21 Sept 1790. (90) £120
Ls, 17 Jan 1761. (88) $425

Amherst, Mary Rothes Margaret Cecil, Baroness, 1857-1919
[A large collection of papers relating to her book A Sketch of Egyptian History, including orig Ms, typescript, proofs, & related collections & correspondence, in a metal trunk, sold at S on 21 Sept, lot 90, for £340 to Spake.]

Amici, Giovanni Battista, 1786-1863
ALs, 18 Feb 1841. (91) DM550

Ammon, Friedrich August von, 1799-1861
ALs, 6 June 1846. (91) DM550

Ampere, Andre M., 1775-1836
ALs, [c.1806]. 3 pp, 4to. To M. Chatelain. Expressing his attachment to the friends left in Lyon. (89) DM1,300
— 31 Jan 1808. 2 pp, 4to. Recipient unnamed. Sending a requested report & apologizing for the delay. (91) £1,100
— 28 Oct 1809. (88) $700
— 5 July 1828. (91) $250

Amundsen, Roald, 1872-1928
[A collection of 6 autograph subscriptions, sgd, 1912, on 4to sheets, sold at star on 30 Nov 1988, lot 396, for DM550.]

Anatomy
Ms, 40 anatomical drawings with text, in French, probably for the Etudes de l'anatomie a l'usage des peintres; [c.1770]. 82 pp, folio, in vellum bds. (91) £4,200

Ancillon, Jean Pierre Friedrich, 1767-1837
Series of 4 A Ls s, [1829]. Schroeder collection. (89) DM320

Andersen, Hans Christian, 1805-75
[An engraved port, [c.1850], c.32cm by 24cm, sgd & inscr to J. A. Josephson, laid down on album leaf, sold at S on 5 May 1988, lot 146, for £520 to Baskett.]
Autograph Ms, poem, beginning °Igaar kom en Hilsen fra Britlands Kyst°, [June 1867]. (88) DM900
— Autograph Ms, poem, Des Dichters letztes Lied. 16 lines, sgd, inscr & dated 8 Nov 1843. 1 p, 4to. Margin cut; was mtd. (90) DM2,100
— Autograph Ms, quatrain entitled "Josephson", sgd & dated 3 June 1846. (88) £380
Collection of ALs & Ls, 31 Dec 1868 & 14 May 1870. 6 pp, 8vo. To George Bell. Thanking for an invitation & for royalties, & discussing editions of his fairy tales. In English. (91) £1,100
ALs, 16 May 1850. 3 pp, 8vo. To J. A. Josephson. Enclosing Mss, discussing an opera libretto, & mentioning Jenny Lind & Gade. (88) £2,100
— 10 Sept 1850. (89) £400
— 5 May 1852. (89) £500
— 7 Apr 1854. (91) £600
— 28 July 1859. (89) £420
— 7 Feb 1862. 2 pp, 8vo. To [his German pbr?]. Expressing disappointment that his new collection of fairy tales has not been pbd, & mentioning other stories. In German. (89) £1,100
— 28 Jan 1864. (88) £240
— 20 June 1864. 4 pp, 8vo. To Mrs. Collins. About personal, financial & literary matters, & sending an autograph poem, sgd (present). Worn. With related material. (91) $1,600
Ns, [n.d.]. (91) DM850
Autograph sentiment, poem, beginning "Min Digtning si omkring i Verden saad", Dec 1853. 1 p, 8vo. 4 lines, sgd. On verso of tp of the German Ed of his Gesammelte Werke, vol 1, Leipzig 1853. (89) DM1,400
— Anr, "Impromptu", quatrain addressed to Thorvaldsen recalling a visit made together; [n.d.]. (89) £480
Photograph, sgd & inscr, [n.d.]. (91) £600
— KLETKE, HERMANN. - ALs, 24 Jan 1844. 2 pp, 4to. To Andersen. Sending one of his publications & praising

ANDERSEN

Andersen's works. Seal tear. (88) DM240

Anderson, Judith

[A group of 7 photographs, 2 sgd, n.d., 11 by 14 inches, sold at pnNY on 3 Dec 1988, lot 38, for $50.]

Anderson, Philip Warren

Ls, 2 Apr 1979. (88) DM260

Anderson, Robert, 1805-71

ALs, 14 Apr 1866. (90) $200
— [n.d.]. (90) $120

Anderson, Samuel R.

ALs, 5 Oct 1866. (88) $80

Anderson, Sherwood, 1876-1941

ALs, [4 May 1928]. (89) $220
— 28 Oct [19]38. (89) $160
Ls, 28 July 1938. (91) $130

Anderson, Wayne

Original drawings, (4), dragons in different surroundings, to illus The Enchanted World, 1984. (90) £1,000

Original drawing, 2 children riding toy horses, to illus The Magic Inkstand, 1981. (90) £500

— Original drawing, 2 mice in human clothing with bearded figures at their feet, to illus Mouses Tale, 1983. (90) £750

— Original drawing, 2 tearful mice in human clothing with an evil creature looking out of a rose, to illus Mouses Tale, 1983. (90) £380

— Original drawing, 3 people & 2 birds flying through the air, to illus Magic Circus, 1979. (90) £720

— Original drawing, 3 people with birds & animals, to illus Magic Circus, 1979. (90) £500

— Original drawing, animals & birds amongst miniature trees, to illus Ratsmagic, 1977. (90) £450

— Original drawing, fantastic figures in a spray of leaves; cover design for The Magic Inkstand, 1981. (90) £450

— Original drawing, mouse seated on dragon's back between tall candles, to illus Mouses Tale, 1983. (90) £500

AMERICAN BOOK PRICES CURRENT

Andre, John, 1751-80

Collection of 2 A Ls s & document, 14 May & 19 July 1772, & 7 June 1777. 7 pp, 4to, & 20 by 23.5 inches. To his uncle John Lewis Andre, reporting about a fire in Amsterdam, in French; & discussing the securing of a commission, in English. Contemp probate copy of his testament. With a collection of Andre family papers. (89) £3,800

Andrea di Jacobo de Mangabotti da Barberino, c.1370-c.1432

Ms, romance of Meschino da Durazzo, in Italian. [Northwest Italy, 1472]. 214 leaves, 237mm by 160mm. Def contemp bdg of square wooden bds. In brown ink in a regular small gothic bookhand. With 4-line illuminated initial & small initials in red. Some dampstaining. (88) £4,000

Andreas-Salome, Lou, 1861-1937

Autograph transcript, Rilke's poem Der Panther, copied for Helene Voigt-Diederichs; 26 June 1922. (91) DM1,000

Series of 3 A Ls s, 3 Feb 1919 & [n.d.]. (90) DM600

— Series of 5 A Ls s, 4 Mar 1922 to 18 Apr 1935 & [n.d.]. (90) £600

Andres, Stefan, 1906-70

Autograph Ms, poem, Mass der Zeit. (90) DM400

Photograph, sgd & inscr, 11 Oct 1953. (90) DM250

Andrews Sisters

[Their signatures (3 individually, & 2 items sgd by all 3), on 4 photographs & a small sheet of paper, [n.d.], sold at Dar on 4 Oct 1990, lot 48, for $100.]

Anker, Albert, 1831-1910

ALs, 7 July 1865. (88) DM750

Anna, Consort of Emperor Matthias, 1585-1618

Ls, 31 May 1618. 2 pp, 4to. To Franz Christoph Khevenhueller. Giving instructions concerning a payment. (91) DM2,200

Anna Ivanovna, Empress of Russia, 1693-1740
Ds, 19 Aug 1736. (91) £500

Anne, Princess of England. See: Elizabeth & Anne

Anne, Queen of England, 1665-1714
ALs, 30 June [c.1690]. 1 p, 4to. To [Douwe Bothnia van] Burmania. Requesting him to secretly inform her of the text of A. Heinsius's letter to her brother-in-law William III. In French. (90) DM2,200
Ls, 30 Nov 1704. (89) £500
Ds, 4 Apr 1706. 1 p, folio. Order addressed to the Duke of Montagu to provide accoutrements of the Order of the Garter for the future George II. Byer collection. (90) $1,100
— 2 July 1712. (88) £320
Document, 29 Mar 1706. (89) £550

Anne, Consort of Prince William IV of Orange, 1709-59
ALs, 10 Aug [1738]. (90) DM400

Anouilh, Jean, 1910-87
ALs, [21 Mar 1966]. (89) DM360
— [n.d.]. (91) DM360

Anschuetz-Kaempfe, Hermann, 1872-1931
ALs, 8 Oct [19]08. (89) DM400
See also: Einstein, Albert & Anschuetz-Kaempfe

Anson, George, Baron Anson, 1697-1762
Collection of 2 A Ls s & Ds, 5 Mar 1762 & [n.d.]. (89) £240
Series of 9 A Ls s, 27 Sept to 9 Dec 1743. 14 pp, folio & 4to. To Edward Page of the East India Company at Canton. Mostly regarding negotiations with the Chinese. With retained copies of Page's answers & Page's account of his transactions with Anson & the Chinese, 86 pp, 4to. (88) £3,800
Ds, 26 July 1744. (88) £240

Antarctica
— LILLIE, DENNIS G. - Caricature of Capt. Oates & Cecil H. Meares of Scott's Antarctic Expedition 1910-12; c.11.5 by 9.25 inches. In pencil & watercolor; captioned by Violet Oates. Framed. (89) £300
See also: Oates, Lawrence Edward Grace

Antheil, George, 1900-59
Autograph music, 1st Sonata, op.3; 1919. 26 pp & tp, 18 staves each, in 4to music composition book. Sgd twice & inscr to Constantine von Sternberg. (88) $2,800

Anthology
[A collection of verse, chiefly on affairs of state, [c.1669-91], c.40 pp, folio & 4to, sold at S on 20 July 1989, lot 36, for £250 to Quaritch.]
Ms, anthology of 8 verse & prose texts in Middle English & Latin. [England, 3d quarter of 15th cent]. 213 leaves, mostly vellum, 198mm by 136mm, in 17th- or early 18th-cent sheepskin over pastebds. In several forms of English cursive bookhands. With decorated initials throughout in deep blue with red penwork. Astor MS.A.2. (88) £20,000
— Ms, anthology of classical verse; Prudentius, Psychomachia; Galterius Anglicus, Fables of Aesop; & other texts, in Latin. [Northern France, Paris?, c.1250]. 124 leaves (1 blank) & flyleaf, vellum, 212mm by 136mm, in later limp vellum. In several small & regular gothic bookhands. With illuminated initial & many decorated initials. Robinson collection. (88) £18,000
— Ms, collection of 17 late 17th-cent poems, in at least 2 hands. (88) £500
— Ms, collection of texts including Leonardo Bruni, Vita Ciceronis; Marcus Terentius Varro, De Lingua Latina; Gaultier de Chatillon, Alexandreis; & others. [Florence?, c.1400 to 1480]. 145 leaves (12 blank), 286mm by 213mm, in contemp bdg of wooden bds incorporating earlier Mss. Written in 5 distinct sections. (90) £12,000
— Ms, collection of c.80 17th-cent poems, [c.1623 to 1711]. 150 pp, various sizes. Collected & partly copied by John Gibson of Welburn; including 3 autograph poems by Richard Graham, Viscount Preston. (91) £6,000
— Ms, Exempla, a collection of c.380 moral tales & fables, in Latin. [Northern? England, early 14th cent]. 129 leaves (some lacking) & 2 flyleaves,

ANTHOLOGY

vellum, 150mm by 104mm, in def contemp red lea over bevelled oak bds. In dark brown ink in a cursive bookhand. With decorated initials throughout for every tale. Worn. (90) £5,500

— Ms, Gerard of Vliederhoven, Tractatus de Novissimis; Heinrich of Weimar, Tractatus de Decem Praeceptis; & texts by Jacopo de Benevento & St. Bonaventura. [Germany, 15th cent]. 105 leaves, 206mm by 135mm, in 19th-cent mottled blue paper bds. In a small cursive bookhand. (90) £3,000

— Ms, miscellany of verse, drama & prose, [17th cent]. About 350 pp, 8vo, in def calf bdg. Comprising James Shirley's The Contention of Ajax and Ulysses for the Armour of Achilles, & poems by Robert Southwell, Walter Raleigh & others. In several hands. Various ownership inscriptions. Lacking some pages. (89) £5,500

— Ms, The [Francis] Rolfe Ms, 17th-cent verse miscellany, [chiefly c.1637]. About 70 pp, 8vo, in contemp calf. Comprising more than 50 poems by Thomas Randolph, Richard Crashaw, Walter Ralegh, John Harrington, & others, in 2 hands; with anr 15 poems added later. (88) £22,000

Anthony, Susan B., 1820-1906
ALs, 21 Sept 1890. (91) $350
— 15 July 1892. (90) $425
— 23 Jan 1897. (91) $750
— 31 Aug 1898. 2 pp, 4to. To Mrs. Holmes. About her new book, the Spanish-American War, & feminist issues. Byer collection. (90) $1,300
— [n.d.]. (88) $250

Ls, 8 Feb 1896. 2 pp, 8vo. To Adelaide Johnson. Expressing satisfaction that recipient was married by a woman & that her husband took her last name, & hoping that Congress will display busts of the originators of the women's suffrage movement. (90) $2,000

Autograph quotation, "Equal Rights for Women", [n.d.]. (91) $275

Autograph sentiment, sgd, 22 July 1900. (90) $325

Signature, [n.d.]. (90) $110

AMERICAN BOOK PRICES CURRENT

Anthony, Susan B., 1820-1906 —& Others
Signature, [c.Feb 1900]. (91) $140

Antigua
[Codrington Family. - 3 ledgers relating to their estates, 1775 - 1776, & 1881 to 1902, c.400 pp, folio, in marbled bds & purple mor, sold at S on 22 July 1988, lot 471, for £500 to Appelbaum.]

Ms, The Remonstrance of ... the inhabitants of the Iland Antigua. declaring the ... Reasons: that Enforced them to treat ... with the lord lefebure, de la bare, Lt Generall for the King of france, 9 Nov 1666. 4 pp, folio. Sgd by Bastion Bayer, President of the Council, & 23 other officers & inhabitants. (88) £2,800

Antiphoner
Ms, Antiphonal with Temporale & Sanctorale. [Southwest? Germany, 1430]. Of Dominican Use. 2 vols, 266 & 257 leaves, vellum, 323mm by 235mm & 330mm by 243mm, in contemp pigskin over red-painted wooden bds. With 10 lines each of text in black ink in a gothic textura & of music on 4-line red staves in square notation. With calligraphic initials throughout, 18 large initials on geometrically patterned ground & 4 very large initials with elaborate decoration of animals or flowers. Pease collection. (89) £30,000

— Ms, Antiphoner from the beginning of Advent to the 4th Sunday after Epiphany. (90) £1,000

— Ms, Antiphoner. (89) DM1,000

— Ms, Antiphoner. [Germany, 15th cent]. 17 leaves only, vellum, 380mm by 260mm. With 26 lines of text in a black textura & music on a 4- or 5-line stave. With large & 2 small penwork initials & 3 small initials depicting grotesque faces. (89) DM1,700

— Ms, Antiphoner. [Ghent or Bruges, early 16th cent]. 1 leaf only, vellum, 375mm by 268mm. With 7 lines of text in a gothic liturgical hand & of music on a 4-line red stave, full border of naturalistic trompe l'oeil pictures & very large historiated initial in burnished gold. Phillipps Ms. (88) £1,200

— Ms, Antiphoner. [Italy?, 15th cent]. 3 leaves only, vellum, 760mm by

520mm. With 10 initials, mostly in colors. (89) DM1,100
— Ms, Antiphoner. [Lombardy, c.1450-55]. Single leaf, vellum, 805mm by 535mm. With 5 lines each of text in a rounded gothic hand & of music on a 4-line red stave. With 5 penwork initials & very large historiated initial of St. Bernardinus attributed to the Master of the Budapest Antiphonary. (91) £10,000
— Ms, Antiphoner. [Northern Italy, late 14th cent]. 83 leaves only, vellum, 325mm by 245mm. Vellum bdg. With 34 lines of text in a rounded Gothic hand & music on a 4-line red stave. Somewhat def. (89) DM2,400
— Ms, Antiphoner. [Northern Italy, Bologna?, late 13th cent]. 3 leaves only, vellum, 53cm by 37cm. With 7 lines each of text in a rounded gothic hand & music on a 4-line red stave. With 3 large historiated initials. (88) £2,000
— Ms, Antiphoner. [Northern France, Paris?, late 13th cent]. 55 leaves only (2 later replacements), vellum, 256mm by 180mm, in vellum bdg of a 16th-cent Gradual leaf. With 11 lines each of text in a gothic liturgical hand & of music in small square neumes on a 4-line red stave. With c.45 large decorated initials in red or blue with marginal extensions. Somewhat def. (88) £2,000
— Ms, Antiphoner. [Rome, c.1550]. Single leaf, vellum, 690mm by 498mm. With 4 lines each of text & of music on a 5-line red stave; 21 lines on verso. With 4 border panels of putti & skulls, & miniature in ink & wash; drawings closely based on engraved designs. (90) £4,000
— Ms, Antiphoner. [South Germany or Austria, Tyrol?, c.1460-80]. 1 leaf only, vellum, 575mm by 390mm. With 6 lines of text in a very large compressed gothic liturgical hand & of music on a 4-line red stave. With very large historiated initial (cut out & replaced back) & 3-quarter illuminated border. Framed. (88) £6,000
— Ms, Antiphoner. [Spain, 18th cent]. 126 leaves (3 lacking), vellum, 590mm by 410mm, in massive wooden bds covered with lea. In dark brown ink in a large well-formed rounded gothic script. With c.180 large decorated or historiated initials in a variety of styles. (91) £1,300
— Ms, Antiphoner, [Spain, Toledo?, c.1490]. 1 leaf only, vellum, 702mm by 385mm. With 5 lines each of text in a rounded gothic hand & of music on a 5-line red stave, very large historiated initial & full broad floral border incorporating birds, grotesques, putti, angels, etc. Illuminated for Cardinal Pedro Gonzales de Mendoza, possibly by Benito de Cordova. (89) £11,000
— Ms, Antiphoner. (91) $400
— Ms, Antiphoner. [Switzerland? c.1500]. 133 (of 137) leaves, vellum, 520mm by 370mm, in contemp brown lea over wooden bds. With 5 lines each of text in a round italianate gothic hand & of music on a 4-line red stave. With c.323 large (7 very large) decorated initials, 34 with pen drawings of animals, putti or human figures. (91) £28,000
— Ms, Antyffony o Pyzichodu Bozjho Syna W Adwent. [Bohemia, c.1600]. 228 leaves, 210mm by 173mm. Comtemp mor over wooden bds. In red & black ink, with music on a 5-line stave. With numerous initials in red & blue, 9 large initials in gold & colors, & 9 elaborate illuminated borders encompassing birds, grotesques, etc. (90) DM3,800
— Ms, Beaupre Antiphoner, settings for the Gloria; [Beaupre Abbey, Flanders, 1290]. (89) £850
— Ms, [Bologna?, c.1300]. (90) £750
— Ms, [Bologna, c.1400]. Single leaf, vellum, 545mm by 370mm. With 8 lines each of text in a rotunda hand & of music on a 4-line stave. With large illuminated initial. (90) DM1,100
— Ms, [Bologna or Ravenna?, late 13th cent]. Single leaf, vellum, 533mm by 350mm. With 7 lines each of text in a rounded gothic hand & of music on a 4-line stave. With large historiated initial. Korner collection. (90) £28,000
— Ms, [Bologna or Siena?, 3d quarter of 13th cent]. 8 leaves only, vellum, 545mm by 373mm. Half brown mor gilt by Sangorski & Sutcliffe. With 7 lines each of text in a rounded gothic hand & of music on a 4-line red stave.

ANTIPHONER

With c.30 painted initials in red or blue with contrasting penwork, 2 large painted initials in leafy designs in colors & tracery, & 2 very large historiated initials. Korner collection. (90) £62,000
— Ms, [c.1450]. 2 conjoint leaves, vellum, 535mm by 360mm. With 8 lines each of text in a textura hand & of music on a 4-line stave. With historiated initial with penwork extensions & scrolling foliate border in lower margin. (90) DM3,000
— Ms, [Cologne, c.1510-20]. 258 leaves (some lacking), vellum, 430mm by 228mm. Remains of later cardboard wrap. With 10 lines each of text & of music. With 8 very large decorated initials & 3 historiated initials, 1 within full trompe l'oeil border, 2 with full-length bar extensions. Def. (90) £1,800
— Ms, [Eastern Switzerland, Lake Constance, c.1310]. Single leaf, vellum, 420mm by 292mm. With 8 lines each of text in a gothic liturgical hand & of music on a 4-line stave. With large historiated initial with full-length extension. Korner collection. (90) £16,000
— Ms, [Florence, c.1320-40]. Single leaf, vellum, 564mm by 406mm. With 6 lines each of text in a rounded gothic hand & of music on a 4-line stave. With large historiated initial with rich illuminated 3-quarter border composed of linked flowers & including 2 men & a child, very close to the style of Pacino da Bonaguida. Korner collection. (90) £32,000
— Ms, [Florence, c.1465]. 1 leaf only, vellum, 590mm by 420mm. Introducing vigils for vespers at Christmas. With 5 lines each of text & music on 4-line staves, large historiated initial, 3 large illuminated initials, & floral border. Attributable to the circle of Cosimo Rosselli. (89) £3,200
— Ms, [Italy?, 14th cent]. 3 leaves only, vellum, 75cm by 53cm. With 12 initials, 5 in colors. (88) DM1,100
— Ms, [Italy, early 16th cent]. Over 100 leaves, vellum, 20 by 15 inches, in contemp calf over wooden bds. With decorated initials. Incomplete. (90) £3,100

AMERICAN BOOK PRICES CURRENT

— Ms, [Italy or Spain, 18th cent]. (90) £650
— Ms, Mozarabic Antiphoner. [Spain, 13th cent]. 2 leaves only, vellum, 266mm by 215mm. With 7 to 8 lines of text in a large early gothic hand & of music on a 4-line red stave. With 4 large decorated initials & 2 very large historiated initials in brown ink & colored wash. Probably recovered from a bdg. (90) £1,300
— Ms, [Northern Italy, Siena or Ferrara?, c.1465-85]. Single leaf, vellum, 557mm by 406mm. With 6 lines each of text in a rounded gothic hand & of music on a 4-line stave. With 5 decorated initials & large historiated initial with 2-sided illuminated border. Mtd. (90) £5,000
— Ms, [Paris or Poissy?, early 16th cent]. (90) £850
— Ms, portable Antiphoner. [Northern? Italy, 15th cent]. 72 leaves & flyleaf from an earlier Ms, vellum, 171mm by 125mm. Modern black calf preserving remains of orig bdg. With 4 lines each of text in a rounded gothic bookhand & of music on a 4-line stave. With 58 large initials on calligraphic penwork ground, often incorporating grotesques. (90) £1,800
— Ms, portable Antiphoner. (88) £950
— Ms, [Prague, c.1405]. Single leaf, vellum, 562mm by 400mm. With 7 lines each of text in a very angular formal gothic liturgical hand & of music on a 4-line stave. With large historiated initial with long scrolling leafy extensions in colors & burnished gold in the style of the Master of the Golden Bull. Korner collection. (90) £58,000
— Ms, [Prague, c.1405]. Single leaf, vellum, 569mm by 402mm. With 7 lines each of text in a very angular formal gothic liturgical hand & of music on a 4-line stave. With large historiated initial with lush bursts of colored leaves in the style of the Master of the Golden Bull. Korner collection. (90) £45,000
— Ms, [Prague, c.1405]. Single leaf, vellum, 565mm by 397mm. With 7 lines each of text in a very angular formal gothic liturgical hand & of music on a 4-line stave. With large historiated initial with marginal extensions in

fluffy leafy designs in colors & burnished gold in the style of the Master of the Golden Bull. Korner collection. (90) £100,000

— Ms, [Rome, c.1550]. Single leaf, vellum, 690mm by 498mm. With 4 lines each of text & of music on a 5-line red stave; 21 lines on verso. With large historiated initial, 4 corner pieces depicting Evangelists, 4 painted panels, & miniature in ink & wash. (90) £8,000

— Ms, [Siena, 3d quarter of 14th cent]. Single leaf, vellum, 455mm by 327mm. With 10 lines each of text in a rounded gothic hand & of music on a 4-line stave. With 7 large initials in red or blue with contrasting penwork & historiated initial. Korner collection. (90) £15,000

— Ms, [Spain, 2d quarter of 16th cent]. Single leaf only, vellum, 842mm by 568mm; recto blank. With 5 lines each of text in a skilful huge rounded gothic hand & of music on a 5-line stave. With extremely large historiated initial. (90) £3,200

— Ms, [Spain, 2d quarter of 16th cent]. Single leaf only, vellum, 858mm by 575mm; recto blank. With 5 lines each of text in a skilful rounded gothic hand & of music on a 5-line stave. With enormous historiated initial & full border incorporating fish, eagles, cornucopiae etc. & roundels with the Holy Monogram & the Ara Coeli. (90) £5,200

— Ms, [Spain, 2d quarter of 16th cent]. 2 leaves only, vellum, 860mm by 578mm. With 5 lines each of text in a handsome rounded gothic hand & of music on a 5-line stave. With very large elaborate illuminated initial, & full illuminated border incorporating the arms of a bishop. (90) £1,700

— Ms, [Spain, early 16th cent & later]. 168 leaves, vellum, 440mm by 340mm, in contemp light brown lea over wooden bds with brass clasps. In red & black ink in a calligraphic Spanish rotunda, with music on 5-line staves. With hundreds of small & a few larger ornamental initials in colors. (90) DM10,000

— Ms, [Spain or Italy, early 16th cent].

(90) £310

— Ms, [Tuscany?, 2d half of 14th cent]. Single leaf, vellum, 587mm by 434mm. With 5 lines each of text in a rounded gothic hand & of music on a 4-line stave. With large historiated initial & 3-quarter border incorporating dragons, grotesques & human faces. Rubbed; trimmed. (90) £11,000

— Ms, [Tuscany?, late 13th cent]. Single leaf, vellum, 465mm by 369mm. With 6 lines each of text in a rounded gothic hand & of music on a 4-line red stave. With large historiated initial with scrolling leafy extension. (90) £3,500

Anton Ulrich, Herzog von Braunschweig-Wolfenbuettel, 1633-1714
ALs, 11 Jan 1705. 3 pp, 4to. To Matthias Johann von der Schulenburg. Congratulating him on a recent victory. (91) DM2,600

Ls, 7 Jan 1680. Kuenzel collection. (90) DM450

Antoninus Florentinus, Saint, 1389-1459
Ms, Confessionale; with Matthew of Cracow, Speculum Munditie Cordis; Bonaventura, Itinerarium Mentis; & other Franciscan texts. [Italy, c.1450]. 223 leaves (14 blank), vellum & paper, 117mm by 90mm, in 18th-cent calf gilt. By several scribes in a very small gothic bookhand. (90) £1,900

Apollinaire, Guillaume, 1880-1918
Autograph Ms, poem, Cortege, fragment; [1905-12]. 1 p, 8vo. Working draft; 19 lines. Including a doodle. On verso of ptd braodsheet advertising Vers et Prose, 2e annee. Mtd. (89) £1,400

ALs, 17 Dec 1913. (90) DM750

Appleton, Honor C.
Original drawings, (29), to illus Mrs. H. C. Cradock's Josephine's Happy Family, 1917. Various sizes. In ink & watercolor. Mostly sgd or initialled. (89) £6,000

— Original drawings, (30), to illus Mrs. H. C. Cradock's Josephine is Busy, 1918. Various sizes. In ink & watercolor. Mostly sgd or initialled. (89) £6,000

— Original drawings, (30), to illus Mrs. H. C. Cradock's Josephine's Christmas

APPLETON

Party, 1927. Various sizes. In ink & watercolor. Mostly sgd or initialled. (89) £1,600
— Original drawings, (30), to illus Mrs. H. C. Cradock's Josephine keeps House, 1931. Various sizes. In ink & watercolor. Mostly sgd or initialled. (89) £1,600
— Original drawings, (30), to illus Mrs. H. C. Cradock's Josephine's Pantomime, 1939. Various sizes. In ink & watercolor. Mostly sgd or initialled. (89) £1,600
— Original drawings, (31), to illus Mrs. H. C. Cradock's Josephine keeps School, 1925. Various sizes. In ink & watercolor. Mostly sgd or initialled. With related material. (89) £6,000
— Original drawings, (31), to illus Mrs. H. C. Cradock's Josephine goes Shopping, 1926. Various sizes. In ink & watercolor. Mostly sgd or initialled. With related material. (89) £3,200
— Original drawings, (32), to illus Mrs. H. C. Cradock's Josephine's Birthday, 1920. Various sizes. In ink & watercolor. Mostly sgd or initialled. (89) £6,000
— Original drawings, (33), to illus Mrs. H. C. Cradock's Josephine, John and the Puppy, 1920. Various sizes. In ink & watercolor. Mostly sgd or initialled. (89) £3,600
— Original drawings, (34), to illus Mrs. H. C. Cradock's Josephine and her Dolls, 1916. Various sizes. In ink & watercolor. Sgd or initialled. (89) £6,000

Arabic & Ottoman Manuscripts

Ms, album of calligraphy in concertina form. [Ottoman, early 18th cent]. 10 pp, 155mm by 234mm, in patterned paper bds. In thuluth & naskhi scripts by Abdullah al-Imam. Imperf at beginning. (90) £1,500
— Ms, album of calligraphy in concertina form. [Ottoman, A.H.1138/A.D.1725]. 6 pp, 167mm by 249mm. Green mor tooled in gold. In thuluth & naskhi scripts with 2 lines in rayhani by Isma'il al-Zuhdi, copied from an earlier album by Ibn al-Shaykh Hamdullah. (90) £2,200
— Ms, album of calligraphy. (90) £700
— Ms, album page of calligraphy, [Ottoman, A.H.1271/A.D.1854]. (88) £450
— Ms, Book of Prayers & selected Koranic Suras. [Ottoman, c.1625]. 189 leaves & 4 flyleaves, 198mm by 142mm. Contemp brown mor gilt. In naskhi script. With headings in white on gold ground within illuminated cartouche, 2 half-page illuminated headings & 2 double pages of illumination. (89) £5,500
— Ms, Firman of Sultan Ahmad II. (88) £800
— Ms, illuminated album page of calligraphy, Qajar, A.H.1277/A.D.1860]. (88) £650

Arabic & Persian Manuscripts

Ms, Al-Arba'in Hadith. [Persia, A.H.886/A.D.1481]. 9 leaves, 214mm by 124mm. Ottoman brown mor bdg tooled in gold. On gold-sprinkled colored paper in 2 sizes of nasta'liq script by Shah Muhammad al-Mashhadi. (89) £1,300
— Ms, Al-Arba'in Hadith. [Persia, c.1530]. 10 leaves & 2 flyleaves, 216mm by 143mm. Def brown mor tooled in gold & silver. In 2 sizes of nasta'liq script on pink paper by Selim al-Mashhadi. With richly decorated outer borders throughout. (89) £1,500
— Ms, Al-Arba'in Hadith. [Shiraz?, A.H.978/A.D.1570]. 9 leaves, 222mm by 137mm. Maroon mor gilt bdg. In nasta'liq script with interlinear Persian trans by Muhammad al-Qiwam al-Katib. Richly illuminated throughout, with illuminated headpiece. (90) £1,400
— Ms, album of calligraphy in concertina form. [Persia, 17th -19th cent]. 44 panels, 263mm by 165mm. Brown mor bdg. In various scripts by a number of calligraphers. (90) £2,000
— Ms, Book of Prayers. [Isfahan, A.H.1119/A.D.1707]. 80 leaves & flyleaf, 254mm by 162mm, in contemp floral lacquer bdg. In naskhi script within gold cloud-bands by Ahmad al-Nirizi. Partly with Persian interlinear trans in nasta'liq. (88) £1,900
— Ms, calligraphic scroll with Koranic verses & a Persian poem. (89) £300
— Ms, Min kalam-i Amir al-Mu'minin

Ali. (88) £550
— Ms, prayers, in safina form. (90) £180
— Ms, Prayers. (88) £260
— Ms, Sayings of Ali Ibn Abu Taleb. [Constantinople, A.H.977/A.D.1569]. 18 leaves, 171mm by 103mm. Rebacked marbled paper bds. On gold-sprinkled paper in 2 sizes of nasta'liq script by Abdul-Wahid al-Mashhadi. With illuminated headpiece. (89) £1,200
— ALI IBN ABI TALIB. - Selected verses. [Isfahan, A.H.1246/A.D.1830]. 16 leaves, 205mm by 135mm. Contemp limp red mor gilt. In black naskhi script with Persian interlinear glosses in red nasta'liq & 5 headings in gold thuluth on illuminated panels. (90) DM1,000
— ALI IBN ABI TALIB. - Selected verses. [Persia, 1st half of 19th cent]. 28 leaves, size not stated. Early 20th-cent lea bdg. In black naskhi script with Persian interlinear glosses in red nasta'liq. With half-page illuminated heading & double-page illuminated border. Interleaved. (90) DM1,000
— JAMAL AL-DIN HUSAIN AL-WA'IZ AL-KASHIFI. - Jawahir al-Tafsir. [Persia, c.1600]. About 869 leaves & 6 flyleaves, 349mm by 216mm, in fine contemp brown mor bdg, def. In naskhi script. With headings in white on gold polychrome floral ground within illuminated cartouche. Some leaves loose. (88) £12,000
— MUHAMMAD BAQIR BIN MUHAMMAD TAQI. - Zad al-Ma'ad. [Qajar, A.H.1206/A.D.1791]. 345 leaves, 241mm by 148mm, in rebacked contemp floral lacquer bdg. In naskhi script by Muhammad Mahdi bin Muhammad Ja'far al-Khavansari. Partly with interlinear Persian trans. (88) £500
— MUHAMMAD BAQIR BIN MUHAMMAD TAQI. - Zad al-Ma'ad. [Qajar, A.H.1261/A.D.1845]. 280 leaves, 250mm by 155mm, in contemp lacquer bdg. In naskhi script by Ibn Muhammad Taher Malik Muhammad al-Kavansari. With interlinear Persian trans & 16 illuminated headpieces. (88) £1,500
— MUHAMMAD BAQIR BIN MUHAMMAD TAQI. - Zad al-Ma'ad, prayers. [Qajar, 19th cent]. 313 leaves (9 blank), 234mm by 135mm. Floral lacquer bdg. In naskhi script with interlinear Persian trans in red. With illuminated headpiece. (89) £200
— MUHAMMAD TAQI. - Prayers. [Qajar, A.H.1220/A.D.1805]. 245 leaves, 155mm by 95mm. Floral lacquer bdg. In naskhi script by Ibn Muhammad Baqir Ahmad al-Musavi. With illuminated headpiece. (90) £220

Arabic & Turkish Manuscripts
Ms, Tabayan al-Salatin. (90) £160
— Ms, Waqfiyya of Shems Bey Fenarizade, with tughra of Sultan Selim I. [Ottoman, A.H.923/A.D.1517]. 123 leaves, 264mm by 171mm, in rebacked brown mor. In diwani script. (91) £8,000
— Ms, Waqfiyyah of Sokollu Mehmed Pasha, with tughra of Sultan Selim II in gold, [Ottoman, 1571-73]. 117 leaves, 244mm by 160mm. Contemp brown mor bdg with gilt lea onlay. In naskhi script. With illuminated headpiece. (89) £30,000

Arabic Manuscripts
Ms, 4 Prayer Books (1 written later). (88) £320
— Ms, Ad'iyat; Book of Prayers. (90) £800
— Ms, album of calligraphy in concertina form. (90) £380
— Ms, album of calligraphy. (91) £800
— Ms, Al-Burdah, & anr poem. (91) £200
— Ms, Al-Kashshaf. [Shiraz, A.H.655/A.D.1257]. 255 leaves, 24.8cm by 17.1cm. Def later brown mor bdg. In brown naskhi script by Ali Abu'l Hasan al-Khorasani. (89) £1,400
— Ms, Al-Sahifah al-Kamilah, prayer book. (89) £750
— Ms, Al-Shajarah al-Nabawiyah wa al-Tuhuf al-Hashimiyyah. [Ottoman, 17th cent]. 8 leaves, 342mm by 225mm. Marbled paper folder. In naskhi script. With diagrams in gold. (90) £2,600
— Ms, anthology of 3 astrological treatises. (88) £550
— Ms, Asma' al-Husna. [Turkey, 20th cent]. Scroll, 17.1cm by 1064cm. In

ARABIC MANUSCRIPTS

gold ornamental kufic on cream polished paper by Hibatullah bin Ahmad al-Ghaznavi. With various illuminated medallions. (91) £7,000
— Ms, Asma' Allah. [A.H.607/A.D.1211]. 30 leaves & 2 flyleaves, 33cm by 24.2cm. Later black mor bdg. In 2 sizes of naskhi script. Gold margins with rope-pattern design. (88) £5,000
— Ms, Awrad al-Usbu. [Ottoman, A.H.947/A.D.1540-41]. 9 leaves, 261mm by 180mm, in def brown mor. On gold-sprinkled paper mostly in alternating thuluth & naskhi scripts by Ahmed Qarahisari. With headings in gold on decorated panels, illuminated cornerpieces, decorated outer borders & 3 pages of illumination. (89) £40,000
— Ms, Awrad Uways bin 'Amer al-Qarni. (90) £200
— Ms, Book of Prayers. (89) £600
— Ms, Book of Prayers. [Ottoman, A.H.1202/A.D.1789-90]. 119 leaves & 3 flyleaves, 171mm by 114mm. Contemp brown mor bdg. In naskhi script by Ali al-Hasbi. With 10 double pages of illumination. (89) £2,200
— Ms, Book of Prayers. (88) £750
— Ms, Book of Prayers. (88) £700
— Ms, Book of Prayers. (90) £240
— Ms, calligraphy. [Ottoman, 20th cent]. 2 leaves, 127mm by 83mm. In gold thuluth. (91) £3,000
— Ms, charms attributed to various holy people, & Koranic passages. (91) $600
— Ms, collection of 3 poems in praise of 'Ali & the Imams. [Persia, A.H.1034-36/A.D.1624-26]. 44 leaves, 365mm by 260mm. Later red mor bdg. In 2 sizes of naskhi script on buff polished paper. With gold floral design on mauve borders, 3 illuminated headings, & 2 double pages containing miniatures. (90) £10,000
— Ms, Du'a al-Sayffi. (88) £850
— Ms, Fath al-Qarib. (89) £140
— Ms, Firman of Emperor Jalal-ad-Din Ali Jawhar Shah Alam II. (89) £500
— Ms, Firman of Sultan 'Abd al-Hamid. [Ottoman, A.H.1302/A.D.1884]. 1 p, 138.4cm by 81.3cm. Appointment for Tahir Pasha. In black & gold diwani script. Repaired. (88) £2,500
— Ms, Firman of Sultan Selim III. (89) £850
— Ms, Firman of Sultan Muhammad V Rashad. (90) £450
— Ms, Firman. (90) £220
— Ms, Hadith; fragment. [Ottoman, 16th cent]. 1 p, 15.2cm by 25.4cm. 2 lines in black & gold thuluth on buff paper, attributed to Ahmad al-Qarahisari. With authentication in naskhi script by Kamil [Akdik] on verso. Laid down. (89) £8,000
— Ms, Hadith. (89) £320
— Ms, Hadith. [Ottoman, A.H.1303/A.D.1885-86]. 3 leaves, 23.5cm by 31.1cm, in contemp brown mor. 8 calligraphic panels in black thuluth & naskhi scripts on buff ground by Hasan Rida. (89) £1,100
— Ms, Hadith. (88) £150
— Ms, Hilya. (89) £500
— Ms, Hirz-i-Aman. (88) £850
— Ms, Ijazatnameh scroll. [Ottoman, 19th cent]. 564cm by 20cm. In black naskhi script on gold floral ground. With illuminated heading. Issued by al-Shaikh Ibrahim al-Safi al-Rifa'i to initiate his successor into the Rifa'i order. (90) £1,900
— Ms, Ijazzah Mubarakah, genealogy of the Rifai family. [Aleppo, A.H.1315/A.D.1897]. Scroll, length 721cm. In nasta'liq script. With 2 illuminated headpieces. (91) £2,000
— Ms, Ijazzah Sharifah, genealogy of the Rifai family. (91) £1,000
— Ms, Kitab al Shifa (part XIII). (90) £1,000
— Ms, Kitab al-Ikhtiyarat 'ala ma-dalat 'alayh-i al-kawakib as-saba'. (89) £600
— Ms, Kitab al-Maghrib. [Near East, A.H.642/A.D.1244]. 351 leaves & 4 flyleaves, 190mm by 158mm. Brown mor bdg. In brown naskhi script on buff paper by Mustafa bin Muhammad bin Yusuf. (90) £3,200
— Ms, Kitab al-ta'widh. [Spain or North Africa, 12th or 13th cent]. 13 leaves, 8.75 by 6.25 inches. Brown lea wraps. In brown Andalusian script with marginal headings in nasta'liq. With a few diagrams & illuminated heading. (90) £7,500
— Ms, Kitab An-Namus Al-Muquaddas. [Homs, 4 Jan 1855]. 483 pp on pol-

ished paper, size not stated, in orig blindstamped red goatskin over pastebds. In naskhi script by Constantin Bin Al-Khouri Dawud. With 28 richly colored full-page calligraphic designs, 17 thuluth borders in gold, 8 mirror-script headpieces or tailpieces, & numerous marginal ornaments. (91) £6,000
— Ms, Kitab ul-ukar, 4 works on mathematics, astronomy & optics. [Persia?, A.H.575/A.D.1179 to A.H.673/A.D.1274]. 182 leaves & 6 flyleaves, 247mm by 165mm, in def red mor bdg. In naskhi script. With numerous diagrams. (88) £1,500
— Ms, Prayer Book. (90) $850
— Ms, prayer book. (90) £160
— Ms, prayer book. (88) £450
— Ms, prayer; calligraphic panel. (90) £400
— Ms, prayer scroll. [India or Turkey, A.H.1285/A.D.1868-69]. 218.9cm by 7.9cm. In naskhi script on buff ground with gold floral sprays & decorated borders. (91) £6,500
— Ms, prayer scroll. (89) £200
— Ms, prayer scroll. (90) £250
— Ms, prayers. (91) £600
— Ms, prayers. [Persia, A.H.1207/A.D.1792]. 21 leaves, 205mm by 135mm. Brown mor tooled in gold. In naskhi script in gold & silver on black paper by Ali al-Tabtaba'i. Interlinear Persian trans in red on silver throughout. (88) £1,600
— Ms, prayers. (91) £550
— Ms, prayers. (91) £300
— Ms, prayers. (91) £300
— Ms, prayers. [Qajar, A.H.1240/A.D.1824]. 12 leaves (3 blank), 206mm by 131mm, in worn brown mor. In naskhi script in alternating colors and gold on colored paper. With headings in red on illuminated panels & illuminated headpiece. Imperf. (91) £2,000
— Ms, Prayers. (88) £600
— Ms, Qa'ida. [Ottoman, A.H.1295/A.D.1878-79]. 8 leaves, 24.9cm by 31.1cm. Gilt-stamped brown mor bdg. 14 calligraphic panels each with 3 lines in thuluth & 2 lines in naskhi script. (89) £6,000
— Ms, Risalat Alwah al-Jawaher. (91) £950
— Ms, rules of grammar. [Persia, 17th cent?]. 48 leaves, 275mm by 180mm, in half mor box. In nasta'liq script. With half-page illuminated headpiece & gilt-sprinkled borders throughout. (90) DM1,250
— Ms, Sahifah al-Kamilah. (91) £800
— Ms, Sahifah Kamelah. (88) £160
— Ms, Sahifah Kamilah, prayer book. (89) £500
— Ms, Sahifah Sijaddiyah, book of prayers. (89) £180
— Ms, Salih. [Various dates & calligraphers from 1248 to 1432] In naskhi script in black ink with rubrics in red. 6 vols, leaf count not given, 280mm by 182mm, loose in old mor bdgs. (90) $1,800
— Ms, Shifa' as-Sharif. (89) £240
— Ms, Sifat Madina Rummiya. (91) £900
— Ms, Tashakurnama of Sultan Abdul-Aziz. (90) £200
— Ms, The Book of the Honorable Law & of the Shining Lamp. [Homs, northern Syria, 25 Apr 1876]. 213 leaves, 436mm by 295mm. Contemp red calf over bds. In naskhi script by the scribe Constantin, son of the priest Dawud al-Homsi. Richly decorated throughout, with 30 full pages in interlocking ornamental & zoomorphic designs, 25 carpet pages in dramatic designs often worked around calligraphic titles, & 36 large miniatures. (90) £6,000
— Ms, treatise on al-'Ulama. (90) £500
— Ms, treatise on theology. (91) £600
— Ms, Tughra of Sultan Selim II. [Constantinople, c.1567]. 357mm by 452mm. Drawn in lapis lazuli; elaborately decorated. Including 2 lines of text (1 fragmentary). (89) £27,000
— Ms, unidentified text. [North Africa, A.H.1286/A.D.1869]. 205 leaves (7 blanks), 223mm by 180mm, in contemp red mor gilt. In maghribi script. (88) £1,500
— Ms, unidentified text on jurisprudence. (89) £400
— Ms, Wasli. (90) £750
— 'ABD AL-MAJID KHWANASARI. - Jaushan-i-Kabir. [Persia, A.H.1338/A.D.1919-20]. Scroll, 238cm by 10cm. In naskhi script by Mirza Yusuf. (88)

ARABIC MANUSCRIPTS

£420
— ABDU'L BAQI TABRIZI. - Kitab-i Du'a. [Persia, 19th cent]. 176 leaves & 2 flyleaves. Contemp lacquer bdg in the style of Abu Talib al-Mudarris. In black naskhi script with Persian interlinear trans in red nasta'liq. With headings within illuminated cartouche & double page of illumination. Prince Muhammad Hasan Mirza Qajar Estate. (89) £450

— ABI ABDULLAH MUHAMMAD BIN ISMAIL AL-BUKHARI. - Al-Jami' al-Sahih. [Shiraz, A.H.758-760/A.D.1356-58]. 771 leaves in 4 vols, 320mm by 247mm, in marbled bds. In black naskhi script with headings in thuluth by Sain ma Shadah al-Isfahani. With 3 illuminated headings. (90) £19,000

— ABU AL-FADL 'IYAD IBN MUSA IBN 'IYAD AL-YAHSABI. - Kitab al-shifa' fi ta'rif huquq al-Mustafa. [Syria, 13 June 1337] In naskhi script in black with headings in dart red. 250 leaves, polished paper, 262mm by 175mm, in 15th or 16th cent mor. (90) $4,000

— ABU 'ALI AL-HUSAIN BIN 'ABDULLAH IBN SINA. - Al-Qanun fi at-Tibb, abridged version. [Persia, mid-16th cent]. 238 leaves, 215mm by 122mm. 19th-cent brown mor tooled in blind. In nasta'liq script on gold-sprinkled paper. With illuminated headpiece. (90) £800

— ABU 'ALI SINA. - Kitab al-Qanun, part V. [Near East, A.H.444/A.D.1052-53]. 82 leaves & 2 flyleaves, 21.2cm by 16.5cm. Later brown bdg. On brown paper in brown naskhi script. (89) £9,500

— ABU ISHAQ. - Ms, compilation of materials on the pilgrimage to Mecca & Medina. [North Africa, 19th cent]. 64 leaves, 250mm by 175mm. Def brown mor bdg. In maghribi script by Muhammad al-Madani bin Abdul-Wahhab. With illuminated diagram & illuminated headpiece. Waterstained. (89) £200

— ABU UMAR ABDUL-AZIZ BIN BADRADDIN ABU ABDULLAH MUHAMMAD BIN JAMA'A AL-SHAFI'I. - Kitab Manasil al-Hajj. [Egypt, A.H.753/A.D.1352]. 85 leaves, 190mm by 134mm. Brown

AMERICAN BOOK PRICES CURRENT

mor bdg. In naskhi script. (91) £1,100

— ABUL ABBAS AHMAD IBN RAJAB. AD-DURR AL-YATIM FI TASHIL SINA'AT AL-TAQWIM. [NORTH AFRICA, 19TH CENT]. 109 LEAVES (1 BLANK), 202MM BY 150MM, IN MODERN RED LEA GILT. IN NASKHI SCRIPT. WITH NUMEROUS TABLES. SOME WORMING. (88) £400

— ABU'L HASAN 'ABD AL-RAHMAN BIN 'UMAR AL-SUFI. - Kitab al-Kawakib. [Persia, 19th cent]. 187 leaves, 233mm by 171mm, in red mor. In naskhi script. With numerous tables & diagrams, & c.63 pp of illusts (some later replacements). (91) £7,000

— ABUL-QASIM IBN AHMAD AL-IRAQI (AS-SIMAWI). - Uyun al-Haqa'iq wa Idah al-Tara'iq. [Levant, 18th cent]. 44 leaves, 206mm by 145mm, in modern buckram bdg. In naskhi script, with numerous diagrams. Repaired. (88) £200

— ABU'L-QASIM MAHMUD AL-ZAMAKH-SHARI. - Al-Kashshaf 'an Haqaiq al-Tanzil. [Yazd, A.H.830/A.D.1427]. 983 leaves & 2 flyleaves, 356mm by 222mm, in later black mor. In naskhi script with headings in thuluth by 'Ubaidullah bin Fadlullah bin Muhammad known as Nasir al-Hafiz. With illuminated heading within illuminated cartouche & double page of illumination. (91) £4,000

— AHMAD AL-QALYUBI. - Risalat fi 'Ilm al-Waqt wa al-Qiblah. [Levant, 18th cent]. 18 leaves, 232mm by 165mm. Marbled paper bds. In cursive script by Abdul-Karim bin al-Shaykh Muhammad al-Maktabi. Some later glosses in margins. (88) £200

— AHMAD BIN 'ALI BIN MAS'UD. - Marah al Arwah. [Ottoman, A.H.947/A.D.1540]. 58 leaves & 4 flyleaves, 171mm by 118mm. Later black mor bdg. In naskhi script. With half-page illuminated heading. (88) £650

— AL-AFKARMANI. - Al-Ahadith al-Arba'un. [Ottoman, A.H.1251/A.D.1835]. 100 leaves, 250mm by 140mm, in green mor gilt. In nasta'liq script by Mir Yahya. (89) £450

— AL-BAIDAWI. - Anwar al-Tawil. [Istanbul, 25 Feb 1611] In naskhi script, in black & red on polished white & colored paper. 483 leaves, 240mm by

133mm, in orig mor covers. With illuminated headpiece with gold & blue background, red frame & silver, yellow, mauve & orange flowers. (90) $600

— AL-BUSAIRI. - al-Burda. [Ottoman?, c.1750]. 21 leaves & 4 flyleaves, 17.1cm by 10.7cm, in worn red mor. In elegant gold naskhi script within gold cloud bands by Muhammad Shukrullah Ibrahimabadi. (89) £1,200

— AL-FAIRUZABADI. - Al-Qamus al-Muhit wa al-Qabus al-Wasit. [Ottoman, 18th cent]. 418 leaves (1 later replacement), 330mm by 207mm, in worn brown mor. In naskhi script by Muhammad bin Ali al-Mahruqi. With illuminated headpiece. (91) £900

— AL-HUSAIN IBN 'ALI, EMIR OF MECCA. - Ls, A.H.1332/A.D.1914. 1 p, 902mm by 597mm. To Sultan Mehmed V Resad. Reporting on the successful completion of the Hajj. Framed. (91) £1,000

— ALI BIN ABU TALEB. - Arba'in Hadith. [Persia, mid-16th cent & later]. Length not stated, 270mm by 180mm. Detached 19th-cent red mor bdg. In nasta'liq script in gold on colored paper by Yari al-Bukhari Muddahib Sultani, with Persian trans in white & gold. With fine illuminated headpieces throughout. (91) £2,000

— ALI BIN SULTAN MUHAMMAD AL-QARI. - Al-Hizb al-'Azam wa al-Ward al-Afkham. [Ottoman, A.H.1176/A.D.1762]. 81 leaves, 164mm by 105mm. Red mor bdg. In naskhi script by Ahmad al-Nuri. With headings in white on illuminated panels & illuminated headpiece. (90) £300

— 'ALI IBN ABI TALIB. - Nahj al-Balagha. [Persia, A.H.1098/A.D.1687]. 193 leaves & 2 flyleaves, 33cm by 20.3cm. Brown mor gilt. In black & red naskhi script with interlinear Persian trans in red nasta'liq by Muhammad Mahdi Ibn Muhammad Baqir al-Husaini. With half-page illuminated heading. (88) £600

— ALI IBN ABU TALEB. - Nahj al-Balagha. [Persia, 19th cent]. 254 leaves only, 285mm by 155mm, in modern brown lea tooled in blind. In naskhi script. Imperf. (89) £280

— AL-JAZULI. - Dala'il al-Khayrat. [Ottoman, A.H.1198/A.D.1783-84]. 56 leaves & 7 flyleaves, 203mm by 127mm. Contemp brown mor bdg. In naskhi script by Muhammad bin al-Hajj Mustafa, known as Hafiz ul-Quran. With numerous illuminated panels, views of Mecca & Medina & 2 half-page illuminated headings. (89) £550

— AL-JAZULI. - Dala'il al-Khayrat. [Ottoman, A.H.1154/A.D.1741-42]. 100 leaves & 4 flyleaves, 190mm by 114mm. Contemp brown mor gilt. In naskhi script by Abu Bakr al-Zuhdi, illuminated by Muhammad Salih. With illuminated headings, views of Mecca & Medina, & 2 double pages of illumination. (89) £2,800

— AL-JAZULI. - Dala'il al-Khayrat. [Ottoman, A.H.1260/A.D.1845-46]. 99 leaves & 2 flyleaves, 127mm by 89mm, in contemp brown mor gilt. In naskhi script by Muhammad Nuri Efendi. With views of Mecca & Medina. (88) £650

— AL-JAZULI. - Dala'il al-Khayrat. [Persia, c.1800]. 133 leaves & 10 flyleaves, 197mm by 127mm, in contemp lacquer bdg. In black naskhi script on pale green ground, with Persian interlinear trans in red nasta'liq. With 8 illuminated double-pages. Doheny collection. (88) $3,800

— AL-JAZULI. - Dala'il al-Khayrat. [Northern Africa, early 19th cent]. 48 leaves, in def contemp lea. In maghribi script. With 20 pp of decoration. Incomplete. (90) DM540

— AL-JAZULI. - Dala'il al-Khayrat. [Ottoman?, early 18th cent]. 64 leaves, 198mm by 130mm. Contemp brown lea gilt. In naskhi script. With half-page illuminated headpiece & 2 full-page illuminated diagrams of the mosques at Mecca & Medina. (90) DM1,300

— AL-JAZULI. - Dala'il al-Khayrat. [Ottoman, 18th cent]. 96 leaves (2 blank), 155mm by 102mm, in contemp tooled red mor gilt. In naskhi script by Mustafa al-Rashid. With 2 illuminated drawings of Mecca & Medina. (89) £900

— AL-JAZULI. - Dala'il al-Khayrat. [Ot-

ARABIC MANUSCRIPTS

toman, 18th cent]. 96 leaves, 155mm by 102mm, in def brown mor gilt. In naskhi script by Abdullah known as Katibzadeh. With 2 illuminated diagrams of the interior of a mosque. Some gatherings detached. (89) £450

— AL-JAZULI. - Dala'il al-Khayrat. [Ottoman, A.H.1203/A.D.1788]. 137 leaves, 160mm by 105mm, in richly tooled brown mor gilt. In naskhi script by Abdul-Rahman al-Helmi. With gold-sprinkled outer borders & 2 illuminated drawings of Mecca & Medina. (89) £2,200

— AL-JAZULI. - Dala'il al-Khayrat. [North Africa, early 19th cent]. 244 leaves (6 blank), 105mm by 108mm, in contemp red mor tooled in gold. In maghribi script. With 13 pages of illumination. (89) £800

— AL-JAZULI. - Dala'il al-Khayrat. [Ottoman, A.H.1222/A.D.1807]. 86 leaves including 2 later vellum leaves, 173mm by 112mm, in red mor gilt. In small naskhi script by 'Ali al-Rashed. With illuminated headpieces & 2 full-page drawings of Mecca & Medina. (89) £300

— AL-JAZULI. - Dala'il al-Khayrat. [Ottoman, c.1738]. 92 leaves, 185mm by 116mm, in def red mor gilt. In naskhi script. With 3 illuminated headpieces & full-page drawings of Mecca & Medina. (91) £600

— AL-JAZULI. - Dala'il al-Khayrat, with prayers. [Ottoman, A.H.1195/A.D.1780]. 97 leaves (7 blank), 176mm by 104mm, in red mor gilt. In naskhi script by Mustafa bin Muhammad known as Shakeryaziji. With illiminated panels between suras, 2 illuminated headpieces, & 2 full-page illuminated drawings of Mecca & Medina. (91) £600

— AL-JAZULI. - Dala'il al-Khayrat. [Ottoman, A.H.1151/A.D.1738]. 85 leaves, 174mm by 110mm, in repaired brown mor gilt. In naskhi script by Muhammad known as Imamzadeh. With illuminated panels between chapters, 3 illuminated headpieces, & 2 full-page illuminated drawings of interiors of holy shrines. (91) £1,000

— AL-JAZULI. - Dala'il al-Khayrat. [North Africa, early 19th cent]. 191

AMERICAN BOOK PRICES CURRENT

leaves (18 blanks), 115mm by 110mm, in contemp red mor gilt. In maghribi script. With 2 illuminated diagrams. (88) £500

— AL-JAZULI. - Dala'il al-Khayrat. [Yawadud, Turkey, A.H.1225/A.D.1810]. 103 leaves, 172mm by 115mm. Contemp red mor gilt. In naskhi script by Ahmad, known as Na'ili. With headings in white on illuminated panels, 3 illuminated headpieces, & 3 drawings, 2 illuminated. Some prayers added later. (89) £600

— AL-JAZULI. - Dala'il al-Khayrat. [Ottoman, 18th cent]. 96 leaves, 182mm by 120mm. Marbled paper bds. In naskhi script. With illuminated headpiece & 2 full-page drawings of Mecca & Medina. Imperf. (90) £250

— AL-JAZULI. - Dala'il al-Khayrat. [Ottoman, A.H.1187/A.D.1773]. 87 leaves, 150mm by 95mm. Red mor bdg. In naskhi script by Sulayman. With 2 illuminated headpieces, illuminated panels intended for headings, & 2 full-page diagrams. (90) £550

— AL-JAZULI. - Dala'il al-Khayrat. [Ottoman, A.H.1204/A.D.1789]. 80 leaves, 182mm by 117mm. Marbled paper bds. In naskhi script by Muhammad Helmi. With 2 illuminated headpieces, 2 full-page illuminated drawings of Mecca & Medina, & full-page drawing of a rose. (90) £550

— AL-JAZULI. - Dala'il al-Khayrat. [Ottoman, early 19th cent]. 92 leaves, 158mm by 100mm. Red mor gilt bdg. In naskhi script. With illuminated headpiece & 2 full-page illuminated diagrams of Mecca & Medina. (90) £350

— AL-JAZULI. - Dala'il al-Khayrat. [Ottoman, A.H.1155/A.D.1742]. 79 leaves, 159mm by 98mm. Repaired red mor gilt bdg. In naskhi script by the scribe Mahmud. With illuminated headpiece & 3 full-page illuminated drawings. (90) £800

— AL-JAZULI. - Dala'il al-Khayrat. [Ottoman, A.H.1198/A.D.1793]. 86 leaves, 180mm by 116mm. Rebacked brown mor gilt bdg. In nasta'liq script on pink paper by Ahmad Rashid Ibn Muhammad Amin. With 3 illuminated headpieces & 2 full-page diagrams of

— Mecca & Medina. (90) £1,200
— AL-JAZULI. - Dala'il al-Khayrat. [Ottoman, A.H.1184/A.D.1770]. 109 leaves, 145mm by 95mm. Brown mor gilt bdg. In naskhi script by Dervish Mustafa al-Aghiribuzi. With 2 illuminated headpieces & full-page drawing of Mecca & Medina. (90) £1,200
— AL-JAZULI. - Dala'il al-Khayrat. [North Africa, 19th cent]. 255 leaves, 117mm by 115mm. Worn contemp red mor gilt. In maghribi script. With headings in gold on illuminated panels, full page of illumination, & 2 full-page illuminated diagrams. (90) £550
— AL-JAZULI. - Dala'il al-Khayrat. [Ottoman, A.H.1160/A.D.1747-48]. 47 leaves, 158mm by 110mm, in worn black lea gilt. In naskhi script by al-Sayyid 'Abd al-Karim al-Alataghi. With 2 illuminated headpieces & 2 miniatures of Mecca & Medina. (91) $650
— AL-JAZULI. - Dala'il al-Khayrat. [Ottoman, A.H.1160/A.D.1747-48]. 97 leaves, 160mm by 102mm, in brown mor gilt. In naskhi script by Mustafa Anis. With illuminated chapter headings & 2 miniatures of Mecca & Medina. (91) $850
— AL-JAZULI. - Dala'il al-Khayrat. [Ottoman, 19th cent]. 94 leaves, 170mm by 110mm, in brown lea bdg. In naskhi script. With 2 illuminated headpieces & 2 miniatures of Mecca & Medina. (91) $500
— AL-JULUKI. - Al-Durr al-Manthur. [North Africa, 19th cent]. 74 leaves (18 blanks), 223mm by 174mm, in modern green mor gilt. In maghribi script. (88) £400
— AL-QONUWI. - Sharh al-Shajarah al-Nu'maniyah fi al-Dawlah al-Uthmaniyah. [Levant, A.H.1308/A.D.1890]. 70 leaves, 205mm by 145mm, in modern buckram. In naskhi script. With numerous diagrams. (88) £110
— AL-SUFI. - Treatise of Fixed Stars, fragment. [India, 18th cent]. 20 leaves, 225mm by 152mm. Later patterned textile bdg. In naskhi script. With 26 colored drawings of constellations. Damaged. (89) £350
—— AL-YAHSUBI, ABU AL-FADL 'IYAD IBN MUSA IBN 'IYAD. - Kitab al-shifa bi-ta'rif-i Huquq al-Mustafa. [Morocco, 1790] In magribi script in black with headings & important words in colors. 196 leaves only, 340mm by 225mm, in lea. (90) $475
— AZ-ZAHRAWI. - Al-Tasrif, treatise on medicines. [North Africa, 19th cent]. 265 leaves, 276mm by 199mm. Faded green mor bdg. In maghribi script by different hands. (89) £300
— HAFIZ SHAMS AL-DIN ABU ABDULLAH MUHAMMAD BIN AHMAD BIN OTHMAN AL-DAHABI. - ?Kitab al Ma'ni. [Near East, A.H.817/A.D.1415]. 68 leaves & 1 flyleaf, 273mm by 184mm. Green bds. In black naskhi script with principal phrases in red by Ali bin Muhammad bin Da'ud bin Khizi. (88) £600
— IBN AL-FARA' AL-BAGHAWI. - Mu'allim al-Tanzil. [Near East, 15th cent?]. 210 leaves, 267mm by 178mm. Later brown mor bdg. In black naskhi script, with illuminated tp & some marginal notes in Arabic or Turkish. (90) £1,500
— IBN 'ARABI. - Kitab al-Dhakhir. [Near East, 17th cent]. 160 leaves & 2 flyleaves, 152mm by 102mm. Later black bdg. In black naskhi script with principal phrases in red by 'Umar bin Muhammad. (88) £380
— IBN SINA. - Al-Qanun, medicine; sections from book IV. [North India, A.H.1234/A.D.1818]. 258 leaves only, 242mm by 150mm. Worn black mor bdg. In nasta'liq script. With 3 illuminated headpieces. (89) £450
— IBRAHIM BIN MUHAMMAD 'ARAB SHAH. - Sharh Anwar al-Tanzil. [Istanbul, A.H.1084/A.D.1673-74]. 319 leaves, 273mm by 136mm. In Ottoman naskhi script by Ahmad Imamzadeh al-Istanbuli for presentation to Sultan Sulaiman bin Salim Shah bin Bayezid. Some leaves loose; lacking bdg. (88) £380
— IBRAHIM BIN MUHAMMAD BIN IBRAHIM AL-HALABI. - Multaqa al-Abhur. [Ottoman, A.H.1044/A.D.1634]. 170 leaves, 162mm by 100mm, in contemp decorated red mor bdg. In nasta'liq script by Abdul Qadir bin Ahmad bin Ramadan known as Sari Naib. (88) £200

ARABIC MANUSCRIPTS

— IMAM 'ALI BIN MUSA RIDA. - Risalat al-Dahabiyya fi'l Tibb, treatise on health & hygiene. [Persia, 18th cent]. 48 leaves & flyleaf, 130mm by 79mm. Contemp lacquer bdg. In gold naskhi script on buff polished paper by the author for al-Mamnun al-'Abbasi. (90) £4,200

— IYAD BIN MUSA AL-YAHSUBI. - Kitab as-sifa fi ta 'if huquq al-Mustafa. [Ottoman?, 1763]. 332 leaves, 8vo. Contemp lea gilt bdg. In naskhi script by Dahki Mustafa bin Muhammad. With illuminated headings & full page of illumination at end. (91) DM1,800

— JALAL AL-DIN MUHAMMAD BIN AHMAD AL-MAHALLI. - Tafsir al-Jalalayn. [Persia?, 18th cent]. 287 leaves & 2 flyleaves, 256mm by 152mm, in brown mor. In naskhi script. With 2 half-page illuminated headings. (91) £900

— JALINUS. - Treatise on diseases of the human body. [Levant, 18th cent]. 182 pp, 323mm by 220mm, in brown mor. In cursive script copied from a Ms by Muhammad bin Abu Shuja bin Muhammad bin Ali al-Katib, dated A.H.608/A.D.1211. Wormed, waterstained. (88) £1,000

— JAWDAT, MEHMED. - Ms, Hilyeh; sgd & dated A.D.1290/A.H.1873. 2 panels, 360mm by 260mm. In black naskhi script; illuminated. Framed. (89) £400

— KA'B IBN ZUHAIR. - Qasida Banat Su'ad. [Mamluk, A.H.878/A.D.1476]. 9 leaves & 4 flyleaves, 168mm by 120mm. Brown mor bdg. In naskhi script by Abd al-Latif bin 'Ala ad-Daula al-Sa'idi. (90) £1,100

— MAHMUD BIN AHMAD BIN ABU AL-HASAN AL-FARYABI. - Khalisat al-Haqayiq lima fihi min Asalib al-Daqayiy, vol 2 only. [Abbasid, early 13th cent]. 272 leaves, 253mm by 170mm, in modern green mor gilt bdg. In naskhi script; headings in bolder script. Wormed throughout. (88) £1,100

— MAHMUD BIN HUSAIN KNOWN AS AS-SADIQI AL-KAYLANI. - Fath al-Karim al-Munazzah 'an al-Masawi fi sahaif al-Baidawi. [Ottoman, 18th cent]. 642 leaves, 204mm by 140mm. Brown mor bdg with gilt lea onlay. In naskhi script. With illuminated headpiece.

AMERICAN BOOK PRICES CURRENT

(90) £400

— MAHMUD BIN MAS'UD AS-SHIRAZI. - Sharh Qanun Ibn Sina. [Mamluk, c.1385]. 196 leaves, 320mm by 240mm, in 19th-cent beige mor. In naskhi script. Dedicated to a Sultan. (91) £9,500

— MUHAMMAD AL-FIRUZABADI. - Al-Qamus al-Muhit wa al-Qabus al-Wasit, an Arabic dictionary. [Persia, c.1510]. 758 leaves, 295mm by 195mm. Worn shagreen bdg with green lea onlay. In naskhi script. With illuminated headpiece. Biographical note on the author added later. (89) £2,000

— MUHAMMAD BAQIR BIN MUHAMMAD TAQI. - Zad al-Ma'ad. [Safar, A.H.1264/A.D.1848]. 250 leaves & 4 flyleaves, 200mm by 124mm. Contemp floral lacquer bdg. In naskhi script by Abdu'l-Manla bin Muhammad Shafi' Tabrizi, occasionally with Persian interlinear trans. With double page of illumination. (90) £1,000

— MUHAMMAD BAQIR BIN MUHAMMAD TAQI. - Zad al-Ma'ad. [Shiraz, A.H.1219/A.D.1804]. 272 leaves, 210mm by 140mm. Floral lacquer bdg of A.H.1226/A.D.1811 by Mirza Baba. In naskhi script with interlinear Persian trans in shikasteh to certain chapters. With illuminated headpiece. (91) £950

— MUHAMMAD BIN ISMA'IL BUKHARI. - Sahih al-Bukhari, part VI. [Mamluk, 14th cent]. 239 leaves & flyleaf, 305mm by 216mm. Worn cloth bdg. In naskhi script with headings in gold & illuminated panel. Def. (90) £4,000

— MUHAMMAD BIN TALHAH. - Al-'Aqd al-Farid. [Levant, 19th cent]. 183 leaves, 191mm by 150mm, in modern marbled paper bds. In naskhi script. (88) £600

— MUHAMMAD IBN ABDUL-LATIF. - Al-Mafatih fi Sharh il-Masabih. [Ottoman, A.H.1050/A.D.1640-41]. 428 leaves & 13 flyleaves, 202mm by 148mm, in bds. In Ottoman naskhi script. Some leaves loose. (88) £280

— MUHAMMAD NURI. - Ms, panel of ghubari calligraphy, sgd & dated A.H.1222/A.D.1807. 550mm by 740mm. 4 lines of nasta'liq script, with Koranic verses in ghubari script. Waterstained. (89) £1,100

— MUSLIM[?] NISHAPURI. - Sahih al-Muslim, traditions of the Prophet Muhammad, part 1. [Samarqand, A.H.855/A.D.1451]. 232 leaves & 3 flyleaves, 350mm by 254mm, in later black cloth bdg. In naskhi script by Abdullah al-Haravi. Waterstained. (88) £650

— NAJM AL-DIN BAHA AL-SHARAF. - Sahifat al-Kamila. [Persia, A.H.1097/A.D.1685-86]. 144 leaves & 3 flyleaves, 197mm by 117mm. Contemp brown mor bdg. In naskhi script on gilt-sprinkled buff paper by Muhammad Riza bin 'Ali Riza al-'Abbasi. With half-page illuminated heading. (90) £1,600

— NAJM AL-DIN BAHA' AL-SHARAF ABU'L-HASAN MUHAMMAD AL-HUSAINI. - al-Sahifah al-Kamila. [Persia, A.H.1106/A.D.1694-95]. 179 leaves & 2 flyleaves, 184mm by 108mm. Floral lacquer bdg dated A.H.1223. In black & gold naskhi script with interlinear Persian trans in red nasta'liq & marginal commentary in black nasta'liq by Ibn Muhammad Amin Shirazi Muhammad Hadi. Opening double-page with half-page illuminated heading. (88) £800

— NASIR AL-DIN ABU SA'ID 'ABD ALLAH BIN 'UMAR AL-BAYDAWI. - Anwar al-Tanzil wa-Asrar al-Ta'wil, vol 1. [Persia, early 15th cent]. 308 leaves & 2 flyleaves, 178mm by 146mm, in def brown mor. In nasta'liq script. With illuminated panel & illuminated heading. (91) £1,400

— NASR-AD-DIN MUHAMMAD BIN MUHAMMAD AL-TUSI. - Kitab Tahrir al-Majisti (Ptolemy's treatise on astronomy). [Kashan, A.H.713/A.D.1313]. 132 leaves, 250mm by 180mm. Black mor bdg with gilt lea onlay. In naskhi script by Mahmud bin Muhammad Masud. With numerous tables & diagrams. (91) £35,000

— OTHMAN IBN SA'ID AL-DINI. - Al-Maqna' fi Ilm al-Qir'a. [Near East, A.H.823/A.D.1420-21]. 55 leaves, 170mm by 133mm. In naskhi script by Nizam al-din al-Hafiz ibn al-Imam Muhammad al-Katib. Lacking bdg. (88) £400

— RIOUW, RADJAH OF. - Courtesy letter to Capt. C. P. J. Eloret. [Indonesia?, A.H.1235/A.D.1819-20]. 1 p, 45cm by 36.8cm. Indonesian dialect. Gold flowers on buff ground & gold scrolling design. Framed. (88) £850

— UMAR BIN MUHAMMAD AL-NAFZAWI. - Treatise on love. [North Africa, A.H.1287/A.D.1870]. 54 leaves (2 blanks), 265mm by 200mm, in red mor tooled in blind & gilt. In maghribi script. Bookplate of E. C. Simpson. (88) £500

— WALI AL-DIN AL-TABRIZI. - Kitab Mishkat al-Masabih. [Turkey, A.H.1156/A.D.1743]. 343 leaves & 2 flyleaves, 184mm by 127mm, in contemp brown mor gilt. In naskhi script by Ahmad bin Khalil bin Mustafa. With numerous endorsements. (91) £1,000

— YAHYA BIN ALI AR-RIFA-I (TRANS). - Az-Zig al-Mu'arrab, trans of astronomical tables of Ulugh Beg. [Egypt?, A.H.1104/A.D.1694]. 59 leaves of text & 355 leaves of tables, 292mm by 198mm. 19th-cent red lea tooled in gold. In naskhi script, compiled by Mardawati Effendi[?]. Ownership inscr of Abdul-Rahman bin Hasan al-Gabarti. (89) £2,000

— ZAKARIYYA IBN MUHAMMAD AL-QAZWINI. - 'Aja'ib al-Makhluqat wa Ghara'ib al-Mawjudat, encyclopedia of cosmography & natural history. [Ayyubid, Syria?, 3d quarter of 13th cent]. 76 leaves (some lacking) & 43 unrelated 19th-cent leaves, 320mm by 230mm. Def early 19th-cent European half mor over marbled bds. In naskhi script. With 59 colored illusts of plants, birds & animals, some with gold. (90) £450,000

— ZAMAKHSHARI. - Al-Kashshaf. [Ottoman, 19th cent]. 582 leaves & 7 flyleaves, 222mm by 139mm. Repaired contemp brown mor bdg. In Ottoman naskhi script. With half-page illuminated heading. (89) £500

— ZAYN-AD-DIN AL-BASTAMI. - Miftah al-Jafr al-Jami' wa Misbah al-Nur al-Lami'. [Levant, 18th cent]. 70 leaves (2 later replacements), 200mm by 144mm, in red paper bds. In naskhi script, with numerous diagrams. (88)

ARAFAT

£280

Arafat, Yassir
Photograph, sgd, [c.6 June 1987]. (90) $65

Aragon, Louis, 1897-1982
ALs, 13 Sept [n.y.]. (91) DM380

Archipenko, Alexander, 1887-1964
Collection of ALs & autograph postcard, sgd, 20 Feb 1919 & 1 Feb 1920. (91) DM500

Architecture
[Carter, J. Coates & Seddon, John P. - A collection of c.260 plans & sketches by Carter & Seddon, c.1865 to 1910, including designs for churches in the South Wales area, sold at pn on 15 Nov 1990, lot 23, for £5,000 to the National Library of Wales.]
— PERRAULT, JEAN. - Autograph Ms, sgd, complete record for construction & expenditures for the dome of the Hotel des Invalides at Paris, 1 Dec 1690 to 23 Jan 1694. 330 pp, folio, in 18th-cent calf. With 39 drawings (some folding). Some staining; 2 wormholes. (88) $16,500

Arcioni, Angelo Maria, 1609-89
Ms, Oda Toscana, poem on the horoscope of Cardinal Prince Maurice of Savoy, in Italian. [Monte Cassino or Rome, c.1630-40]. 3 leaves, vellum, 200mm by 148mm. Contemp limp vellum gilt bdg. In a fine calligraphic hand. Probably dedication Ms; illuminated. Phillipps MS.4208 & Abbey collection. (89) £1,400

Arctic Exploration
— FORD, GEORGE JAMES. - His papers as carpenter on HMS Investigator during the Arctic Expedition, 1850 to 1854, including his diary, family papers, & related material, sold at S on 18 July 1991, lot 419, for £3,800 to Sawyer. 91

Ardenne, Manfred von
Autograph Ms, article, Der O 2-Selektor - ein Geraet zur Sauerstoffanreicherung in der Atemluft; sgd & dated 29 June 1981. (90) DM320
— Autograph Ms, scientific paper, Ein vorbereiteter weiterer Schritt der Sauerstoff-Mehrschritt-Therapie, 1979.

AMERICAN BOOK PRICES CURRENT

(90) DM260

Ardizzone, Edward, 1900-79
Original drawing, "The Regulars at the Hero", 2 men chatting with barmaid in a pub, to illus Maurice Gorham's Back to the Local, 1949. In ink. 194mm by 137mm; framed. Sgd E.A. (90) £1,400

Ariosto, Ludovico, 1474-1533
— STROZZI, ALESSANDRA. - ALs, 23 June [1529]. 2 pp, 4to. Recipient unnamed. Fragment, referring to man suffering from fever. (91) £500

Aristizabal, Gabriel de, 1743-1805
Ms, Extracto del Diario de la Navegacion hecha a Constantinopla, 1784. 45 pp, 540mm by 370mm, in velvet covered bds. Bound with 46 fine Ms charts, maps, views, etc., mostly in ink & watercolors. (91) £35,000

Aristophanes, 448?-380? B.C. —& Others
Ms, Aristophanes, Ploutos, & The Clouds; Euripides, Hecuba, & Orestes; Hesiod, Works and Days; in Greek. [Eastern Mediterranean, Crete?, 2d half of 15th cent]. 227 leaves (a few missing), 203mm by 135mm, in worn contemp Greek bdg of tooled dark brown tanned lea over wooden bds. In brown ink by several scribes in a Greek minuscule. (90) £80,000

Aristotle, 384-322 B.C.
Ms, Ethica, in the Latin trans of Leonardo Bruni. [Milan, 1456]. 173 leaves, vellum, 210mm by 145mm. Early 19th-cent English bdg of reddish brown mor gilt by Charles Lewis. In a small near cursive humanistic minuscule with some gothic features by Silvestro Balsamo. With 11 large illuminated white-vine initials & coat-of-arms. Phillipps MS.3349 & Abbey collection. (89) £36,000

Arkwright, Sir Richard, 1732-92
ALs, 2 Mar 1772. 4 pp, folio. To [Jedediah Strutt]. Describing the success of his spinning operations at Cromford. (91) £4,000

Armenian Manuscripts

Ms, Awetaran (Four Gospels). [Mewruk, Province of Siunik, 1659]. 344 leaves (4 lacking) & flyleaves, vellum, 133mm by 98mm. Contemp green velvet over wooden bds with metal ornaments, in mor slipcase. In black ink in a small neat bolorgir by the scribe Lukas. Lavishly illuminated with numerous decorated initials, marginal decorations, & 48 miniatures (20 full-page). Doheny collection. (88) £26,000

— Ms, Awetaran (Four Gospels). [Constantinople, 1682]. 274 leaves & 2 flyleaves of c.1200, vellum, 195mm by 152mm. Detached silver gilt repousse bdg. In black ink in a small bolorgir hand. With c.160 illuminated initials & marginal decorations in gold & colors, 2 full decorative borders, 8 pages with decorated canon tables, & 9 marginal & 4 full-page miniatures. (90) £65,000

— Ms, Four Gospels. [Sos, i.e. Julfa/Isfahan, Armenia, 1698]. 286 leaves, vellum, 135mm by 105mm, in contemp stamped calf over wooden bds. In black ink in a small regular Armenian minuscule or bolorgir hand by the scribe Ep'rem. With 10 pp of decoration, 4 half-page headpieces, & 4 full-page miniatures of the Evangelists. Worn & damaged. (90) £7,500

— Ms, Kiprianos (prayer scroll). (88) £400

— Ms, prayer scroll. [Constantinople, 1682]. 6050mm by 85mm, on glazed paper. In black ink in a regular bolorgir hand. With capitals in the form of zoomorphic initials, & 29 miniatures of various sizes. (90) £1,900

— Ms, prayer scroll containing extracts from the Gospels & writings of the saints, in Armenian. [Constantinople, 1641]. About 1800cm by 8cm. Written in black bolorgir for Lazar, son of Martiros. With 27 large miniatures. Last section from an earlier scroll. (88) £7,500

— Ms, Saraknoc; hymnal, with Calendar, doxologies, & chants. [Armenia, 1661-77]. 375 leaves, vellum, 120mm by 90mm, in new bds preserving covers of contemp bdg. In black ink in a very fine bolorgir minuscule by 4 scribes & the artist Yohan, with 2 flyleaves in 10th- or 11th-cent uncials. With zoomorphic initials throughout in colored inks, 138 marginal illusts, 9 small & 2 half-page headpieces, & 2 full-page miniatures. (90) £13,000

— Ms, Yaghas Khorhrdots arhasarak, catechism for the sacraments. (90) £280

— T'EODORUS, PATRIARCH OF JERUSALEM. - Ms, encyclical letter asking for funds, 25 Mar 1800. Scroll, in 6 sections (2 separated), 2660mm by 435mm. In black ink in a regular notragir hand, with initials in red. With extremely large & elaborate headpiece. (90) £2,000

See also: Gospel Manuscripts

Armitage, J. J., ("Ionicus")
Original drawings, (30), to illus Ogden Nash's Untold Adventures of Santa Claus, 1965. Archives of J. M. Dent & Son. (88) £300

Armstrong, John, 1755-1816. See: Indians, North American

Armstrong, John, 1758-1843
ALs, 6 Dec 1832. (91) $210
Ds, 16 Mar 1806. (89) $220
Franking signature, [13 Apr n.y.]. (88) $170

Armstrong, Louis, d.1791
Photograph, sgd & inscr, [1969]. (91) $250

Armstrong, Louis, .1971
Ptd photograph, sgd; [n.d.]. (90) DM280

Armstrong, Louis, d.1971
Autograph Ms, Scanning the History of Jazz. [Toronto, 1956] 11 pp, 4to. Sgd "Louis Armstrong, Satchmo." (91) $25,000

Typescript, mimeographed sheet of aphorisms entitled Satchmo Sez. (91) $275
ALs, 29 May 1949. (91) $400
Ls, 19 Jan 1942. 2 pp. To Walter Winchell. About the break-up of his marriage. (91) $1,500

Armstrong, Neil
Ls, 20 Dec 1972. (91) $450
— 11 Jan 1988. (91) $550
Photograph, sgd, [n.d.]. (91) $150
Photograph, sgd & inscr, [c.1969]. (91) $180

ARMSTRONG

— Anr, [n.d.]. (90) $110
Signature, [20 July 1969]. (91) $200
— Anr, [1969]. (91) $400
— Anr, on Memorial program held at the Houston Space Center after the Challenger disaster, 31 Jan 1986. (91) $275

Arnaz, Desi, 1915-86. See: Ball, Lucille & Arnaz

Arndt, Ernst Moritz, 1769-1860
Autograph Ms, Fuer Friedrich Hartmuth, instructions & admonitions to his son, 6 June 1843. (91) DM650
ALs, 12 May 1810. 2 pp, 4to. To [Georg Andreas Reimer]. Informing him that he will start teaching at Greifswald again, & mentioning problems with his parental estate. Albrecht collection. (91) SF1,200
— 14 Sept 1813. 4 pp, 8vo. Recipient unnamed. Asking for books in Swedish. Kuenzel collection. (90) DM1,600
— 22 July 1819. 3 pp, 4to. To [Freiherr von Hardenberg?]. Regarding the confiscation of his papers. (89) DM1,300
— 18 Dec 1829. (89) DM900
— 17 Feb 1842. (91) DM850
— 28 Aug 1842. 2 pp, 8vo. To an unnamed lady. Thanking for a Ms, but saying he is not editing an almanach. (89) DM1,450
— 12 Aug 1848. 4 pp, 8vo. To Karl Georg von Raumer. About the revolution in Germany. (91) DM2,200
— [late Sept] 1850. (90) DM700
— 3 Oct 1853. (91) DM800
— 9 Jan 1856. 2 pp, 8vo. To A. L. J. Michelsen. Expressing disappointment about the political situation. (91) DM1,350
— 28 Dec 1856. (91) DM650
— 15 Nov 1859. (91) DM800
A Ns s (2), 13 Aug 1840 & [n.d.]. (90) DM320

Arnim, Bettina von, 1785-1859
ALs, 22 Sept 1839. 1 p, 4to. To G. T. Fechner & H. Weisse. About her departure for Beerwalde & hoping they will review her husband's works. (91) DM2,000
— 25 June 1840. 1 p, 4to. To [Staatsminister von Werther]. Requesting permission for her son to take the Prussian foreign service exams. (90) DM1,300
— [24 July 1844]. 2 pp, 4to. To von Rudloff. Requesting his help in finding a new apartment. (91) DM1,700
— [after 1844]. 2 pp, 4to. To Adolf Mende. Praising his work & regretting she cannot help him. (91) DM2,300
— 22 Apr 1846. 2 pp, 4to. To Frau von Oelrichs. Fragment, concerning a sculpture by Steinhaeuser & relief for a needy man. (88) DM1,050
— 6 May [1850?]. Albrecht collection. (91) SF1,000
— [n.d.]. (89) DM300

Arnim, Ludwig Achim von, 1781-1831
Autograph Ms, poem, beginning "Wacht auf mit innern Sinnen", [pbd 1826]. 1 p, 4to. 3 (of 4) eight-line stanzas; sgd. Differing from ptd version. (89) DM3,400
— Autograph Ms, poem, Wenn ein Professor wird geboren. 32 lines, written for Friedrich Karl von Savigny on his birthday, 21 Feb 1825. 1 p, folio. (90) DM5,500
ALs, 24 Jan 1818. 2 pp, 4to. To Mohr & Winter. Concerning a reprint of Des Knaben Wunderhorn, vol 1. Albrecht collection. (91) SF2,100
— 31 May 1829. 4 pp, 8vo. To Schinkel. Recommending a young architect & mentioning Humboldt. (91) DM3,600
Autograph quotation, Ludwig Tieck's poem, Schau an umher das gruenende Land, sgd & dated 30 July 1801. 1 p, 8vo. 7 lines. (90) DM2,500

Arnold, Benedict, 1741-1801
Letter, 16 Sept 1780. 1 p, 4to. To George Washington. Retained copy, informing him about arrangements concerning Washington's projected journey. In the hand of Richard Varick. (91) $3,000
ADs, 26 Aug 1763. 1 p, 108mm by 174mm. Receipt to William Jepson for £10.10s in payment of olive oil. (90) $1,900
Ds, 1 July 1775. 1 p, 4to. Bond as security for payment of duties on a shipment of rum. Def. With related material. (90) $1,400
— 3 July 1786. 1 p, 4to. Complaint against Aaron Vanschaak, debtor to

Arnold. Also sgd by J[ohn?] Putnam. Fold break. (90) $1,700
— 7 June 1790. 1 p, 4to. Receipt in payment for legal action. (89) $1,400
— 30 Aug 1790. 1 p, 8vo, cut from larger sheet. Receipt to Colin Campbell in settlement of a debt. With related material. (90) $1,800
— AUSTIN, JOSHUA. - Ds, 22 May 1767. 1 p, 8vo. Receipt for payment for hay. Text in Arnold's hand; sgd by him in 3d person. With ALs by Benedict Arnold, Jr. to his father. (89) $850

Arnold, Matthew, 1822-88
Series of 6 A Ls s, 1884 to 1886. 33 pp, 8vo. To Charles Butler. Concerning his US tour. With related material. (88) $2,200
ALs, 4 Oct 1877. (90) $120
— 20 Sept 1884. (91) £170

Arnold, Thomas, 1795-1842
ALs, 31 Mar 1815. (91) £130

Arnoldus de Seehusen, fl.1411
Ms, commentary on the Sentences of Peter Lombard, in Latin. [Kulmbach Abbey?, Germany, 1413]. 493 leaves (4 blank), 300mm by 200mm, in wormed late medieval blindstamped bdg of pigskin over wooden bds. In cursive bookhands by "Johannes krizelmor de kulmach" & other scribes. With many large painted initials. (91) £7,500

Arp, Hans, 1887-1966
Ls, 22 Mar 1934. (90) DM700

Arrabal, Fernando
[A collection of 21 autographs, including 8 A Ls s, to Heribert Becker, 17 Oct 1971 to 8 Sept 1980, in French & Spanish, with related material, sold at star on 4 Oct 1989, lot 15, for DM1,700.]

Arrhenius, Svante, 1859-1927
ALs, 30 Aug 1900. (90) DM340

Artaud, Antonin, 1896-1948
Autograph Ms, essay about his life & work, dated 27 July 1946 & 13 Sept 1945. 23 pp, 4to. Written to Peter Watson. On paper taken from an exercise book, with numerous blots. With English trans & a partial transcription. (88) £1,700

Arthur, Chester A., 1830-86
ALs, 29 Nov 1873. (90) $400
— 30 Mar 1881. 3 pp, 8vo. To Gen. Joseph Bradford Carr. As Vice President, correcting a mistake in the name of an appointee. Was mtd. Rosenbloom collection. (88) $1,300
— 9 Oct 1881. 2 pp, 8vo. To Daniel G. Rollins. Requesting a private meeting. (90) $3,800
— 24 Apr 1882. 3 pp, 4to. To Edwin D. Morgan. Extending an invitation. Endorsed on verso. (89) $7,000
— 18 Mar 1884. 2 pp, 8vo. To Charles A. Dana. Promising to send a book. (90) $4,500
— 2 Nov 1884. 2 pp, 4to. To Daniel G. Rollins. Sending a paper from the State Department & inviting his comments. Sang collection. (91) $1,500
Collection of Ls & ANs, 25 Aug 1862 & 4 May [1885]. 5 pp, 4to & 8vo. To Erastus Corning, discussing troop movements. To Mr. Field, cancelling a dinner engagement. Pratt collection. (89) $1,200
— Collection of Ls & photograph, 13 July 1880 & [n.d.]. (89) $120
Ls, 21 June 1875. (89) $275
— 8 Jan 1880. (91) $250
— 8 Apr 1882. (89) $800
ANs, [after 29 May 1878]. (88) $200
— [n.d.]. (90) $375
ADs, 14 Nov 1860. (90) $170
Collection of Ds & Executive Mansion card, sgd, 7 Oct 1875 & [n.d.]. (90) $400
Ds, 13 May 1875. (91) $325
— 15 Oct 1881. (88) $300
— 3 July 1882. Byer collection. (90) $900
— 17 Jan 1883. (91) $450
— 11 May 1883. (88) $300
— [n.d.]. (89) $210
— 2 May 1884. (90) $550
— 26 May 1884. (90) $500
— 13 Feb 1885. 1 p, folio. Appointment of P. Henry Carpenter as Postmaster. (91) $1,200
Cut signature, [n.d.]. (90) $110
— Anr, [n.d.]. (90) $130
Executive Mansion card, [n.d.]. (91) $275

ARTHUR

— Anr, sgd, [n.d.]. (90) $425
— Anr, sgd, [n.d.]. (90) $240
Photograph, sgd, [10 Mar 1884]. Cabinet size. Hand-tinted. (90) $5,000
Signature, 18 Mar 1884. (91) $300
— Anr, [1884]. (91) $150
— Anr, [n.d.]. (91) $300
— Anr, [n.d.]. (90) $270
White House card, sgd, [3 June 1883]. (89) $300

Artmann, Hans Carl
Autograph Ms, poem, beginning "ich bin der tiefdunkle krug"; sgd, inscr & dated Mar 1982. (90) DM360

Ashby, Turner, 1828-62
Ds, 23 Dec 1861. (91) $550
— 31 Mar 1862. (88) $230

Askenase, Stefan, 1896-1985
Collection of ALs & 3 autograph postcards, sgd, 26 May 1979 to 7 July 1985. (88) DM250

Asquith, Lady Cynthia, 1887-1960
[A large collection of letters addressed to her, several hundred pp, with material relating to the rights to J. M. Barrie's plays, sold at S on 21 July 1988, lot 306, for £1,500 to Joseph & Sawyer.]
[A group of Mss & typescripts from her collection, including verses by G. K. Chesterton & K. Tynan, & autograph Mss by Arthur Machen & others, sold at S on 15 Dec 1988, lot 124, for £400.]
Autograph Ms, diaries, Oct 1914 & 15 Apr 1915 to 9 Nov 1919. About 2,330 pp in 10 different 4to vols. Some passages scored out. Mostly unpbd. (88) £15,000
— BAGNOLD, ENID. - 75 A Ls s & Ls s, 1931 to 1954; c.150 pp, 4to & 8vo. To Cynthia Asquith. About both their writings, friends, etc. (88) £800

Asquith, Herbert Henry, 1st Earl of Oxford & Asquith, 1852-1928
— ASQUITH, MARGOT. - 6 A Ls s, 8 Mar to 4 June 1928. 16 pp, 8vo. To R. A. Bennett. Regarding an article about her husband ptd in the magazine Truth, & giving her own assessment of her husband's qualities. In pencil. (88) £100

Asquith, Margot, Countess of Oxford & Asquith, 1864-1945. See: Asquith, Herbert Henry

Astaire, Fred
Ls, 21 Feb [19]35. (89) $250
Photograph, sgd, [n.d.]. (90) $65

Astaire, Fred —&
Rogers, Ginger
Group photograph, [n.d.]. (91) $225

Astor, John Jacob, 1763-1848
Ds, 25 Apr 1805. 1 p, 8vo. Affidavit regarding importation of tea from Canton. Corner def. (90) $1,100
— [n.d.]. (90) $300

Astor, John Jacob, 1822-90
ALs, 24 Feb 1868. (89) $450

Astor, William Waldorf, 1848-1919
[A collection of material relating to Astor's support of the Astor Foundation in Walldorf, Germany, c.1890, in velvet presentation album, sold at bba on 28 July 1988, lot 199, for £120 to Ramer.]

Astrid, Queen of Leopold III, King of the Belgians, 1905-35. See: Leopold III & Astrid

Astrological Manuscripts
Ms, Zael [i.e. Sahl ibn Bishr], Livre des jugemens de Astrologie; & Messehallach [Messalahus], Astrologien des coniunctions et receptions es investigations; 1349. 2 works in 1 vol, 52 & 36 leaves, vellum, 225mm by 160mm, in early 19th-cent English blue mor elaborately tooled. In pale & dark brown ink in a gothic bookhand, probably by 1 scribe. With calligraphic initals & historiated inital (1 removed). Trans & illuminated for Charles V of France. Borthwick collection. (88) £50,000
— BELLGRAVE, WILLIAM. - Autograph Ms, notebook recording his life's history in astrological terms, [17th cent]. 140 pp, 4to; disbound. Including various diagrams, horoscopes & tables. (89) £2,100

Astrology

Ms, Tesoro Genetliaco Di [Astrologia] Diviso in tre Parti..., [17th cent]. (89) £500

Astronauts

[The signatures of Judy Resnik & 5 crew members of shuttle flight STS 51, on a postal cover, 30 Aug 1984, sold at wa on 20 Oct 1990, lot 239, for $190.]

[The signatures of Greg Jarvis & 5 crew members of shuttle flight 51-G, on a postal cover, 17 June 1985, sold at wa on 20 Oct 1990, lot 238, for $325.]

[The signatures of 4 crew members of shuttle flight 51-D, & of 4 cosmonauts including the Soyuz 35 team, on postal cover with various US & USSR stamps, [1988], sold at wa on 20 Oct 1990, lot 241, for $210.]

[The signatures of Alan Shepard, Scott Carpenter, John Glenn, Walter Shirra, Donald Slayton & Gordon Cooper, on triple-cancelled postal cover, 1990, sold at wa on 20 Oct 1990, lot 240, for $110.]

[A group of 4 photographs, sgd & mostly inscr, by Alan Shepard, Sally Ride, Guion Bluford, & Mae Jemison sold at wa on 1 Oct 1988, lot 302, for $85.]

[Apollo 11. - The signatures of Buzz Aldrin, Neil Armstrong & M. Collins, on ptd card referring to them as honorary citizens of Appollo, Pa. sold at wa on 1 Oct 1988, lot 303, for $200.]

[A 12mo photograph of the U.S.S Hornet with Capsule next to ship, sgd by Neil Armstrong, Michael Collins & Buzz Aldrin sold at wa on 1 Oct 1988, lot 310, for $260.]

[Apollo 11. - 3 official NASA photographs, 4to, sgd by Michael Collins, Neil Armstrong & Edwin Aldrin sold at wa on 1 Oct 1988, lot 313, for $180.]

[Apollo 11. - The signatures of Neil Armstrong, Buzz Aldrin, Michael Collins & Capt. [Seirberlul?] on a framed clipped magazine leaf with 2 related color reproductions, [n.d.], 4to, sold at wa on 20 Oct 1990, lot 231, for $190.]

[The signatures of 10 astronauts & 9 cosmonauts on a NASA print of a painting of Apollo & Soyuz docking in space, [n.d.], 10 by 8 inches, sold at Dar on 4 Oct 1990, lot 64, for $300.]

[Apollo 11. - Photograph of quarantine mobile with astronauts aboard, [n.d.]. 4 by 5 inches. Sgd by Armstrong, Aldrin & Collins.] $170

Group photograph, official NASA composite port of 21 astronaut candidates at the Johnson Space Center, July 1980. (91) $110

— Anr, [n.d.]. (89) $240

— Anr, [n.d.]. (89) $140

— Apollo 11. - The signatures of Neil Armstrong, Buzz Aldrin, M. Collins & Richard Nixon, [n.d.], on a photograph of the plaque attached to the Apollo 11 Lunar Excursion Module, 8 by 10 inches, framed, sold at Dar on 7 Feb 1991, lot 36, for $750. 91

— Apollo 11. - A photograph of the Earth in the sky above the Moon, sgd by N. Armstrong, M. Collins & B. Aldrin, sold at Dar on 4 Oct 1990, lot 56, for $275. 91

— Apollo 11. - NASA photograph of crew of 5th Manned Apollo Mission, sgd by Neil Armstrong, Edwin E. Aldrin, Jr., & Michael Collins; 4to. Framed. (90) $290

— Apollo 11. - Photograph of B. Aldrin, N. Armstrong & M. Collins, next to capsule on a ship, [n.d.]. 10 by 8 inches. Sgd by all 3. (91) $450

— Apollo 11. - Photograph of President Nixon speaking with crew in quarantine, [1969]. 7 by 7 inches. Sgd by Nixon, N. Armstrong & B. Aldrin. (91) $700

— Apollo 11. - Photograph of Quarantine mobile for Apollo 11 team, [n.d.]. 3 by 5 inches. Sgd by Neil Armstrong, Buzz Aldrin & Michael Collins. (90) $160

— Apollo 11. - The signatures of Neil Armstrong, Buzz Aldrin & Michael Collins, on a philatelic cover, 29 May 1964, sold at Dar on 6 Dec 1990, lot 32, for $180. 91

— Apollo 11. - The signatures of Neil Armstrong, Buzz Aldrin & M. Collins, [n.d.], on a photograph of footprints on the Moon, 8 by 10 inches, sold at Dar on 7 Feb 1991, lot 37, for $450. 91

— Apollo 11. - The signatures of N. Armstrong, M. Collins & B. Aldrin, [n.d.], on a philatelic cover, sold at Dar

ASTRONAUTS

on 10 Apr 1991, lot 28, for $475. 91
— APOLLO 12. - Group photograph of crew, [n.d.]. 8 by 10 inches. Sgd by A. L. Bean, C. Conrad & D. Gordon; inscr by Bean. (91) $80
— APOLLO 14. - Group photograph of Alan Shepard & Edgar Mitchell on the moon, Feb 1971. 9 by 7 inches. Sgd by both; inscr by Shepard. (91) $250
— APOLLO 17. - Group photograph of crew, [n.d.]. 10 by 8 inches. Sgd by G. Cernan, J. Schmitt & R. Evans; inscr by Cernan. (91) $75
— APOLLO 17. - Photograph of surface of the Moon, Dec 1972. 102 by 9.5 inches, rolled. Sgd by H. H. Schmitt, R. Evans & G. Cernan. (91) $450
— CHALLENGER. - The signatures of D. Scobee, G. Nelson, J. van Hoften & T. Hart, on a Nasa envelope, [10 Apr 1984], sold at Dar on 4 Oct 1990, lot 60, for $80. 91
— CHALLENGER 41-B. - Group photograph of the 5 member crew, 1984. 8 by 10 inches. Sgd by Ron McNair, Bob Stewart, Robert L. Gibson, & Bruce McCandless. (91) $120
— CHALLENGER STS-13. - The signatures of the 5 man crew on a philatelic envelope, 1984, sold at Dar on 6 Dec 1990, lot 374, for $95. 91
— COLUMBIA SPACE SHUTTLE. - A photograph of the launch of the space shuttle, 9 by 8 inches, sgd by 8 shuttle astronauts, 1981 & 1982, each with assignment on mission, sold at Dar on 10 Apr 1991, lot 23, for $120. 91
— DISCOVERY. - Group photograph of crew, [n.d.]. 10 by 8 inches. Sgd by Judy Resnik, Michael L. Coats, Hank Hartsfield, Steven A. Hawley, Mike Mullane, & Charlie Walker. (91) $150
— MERCURY. - Photograph of capsule atop a rocket, [n.d.]. 8 by 10 inches. Sgd by orig Mercury astronauts A. Shepard, J. Glenn, S. Carpenter, W. Schirra, G. Cooper & D. K. Slayton. (91) $600
— PROJECT MERCURY. - The signatures of J. Glenn, D. K. Slayton, A. Shepard, W. Shirra, & S. Carpenter, on a philatelic envelope, 19 Mar 1964, sold at Dar on 6 Dec 1990, lot 31, for $200. 91
— PROJECT MERCURY. - Group photograph, [n.d.]. 11 by 14 inches. Sgd by all 7 orig Project Mercury astronauts; inscr to Iris [MacNabb] by Scott Carpenter. (91) $3,000
— RUSSIANS IN SPACE. - The signatures of 5 Russian astronauts on a philatelic envelope of the German Democratic Republic, 12 Apr 1964, sold at sg on 14 Mar 1991, lot 249, for $350. 91
— SPACE SHUTTLE. - Group photograph, [12 Apr 1989]. 4to. NASA photo showing crew & shuttle, sgd by John Young & Bob Crippen. (90) $170

Ataturk, Kemal, 1881-1938. See: Kemal Ataturk

Atchison, David Rice, 1807-86
ALs, 18 June 1852. (91) $300

Atkinson, Henry, 1782-1842
Autograph endorsement, on a letter to Gen. (89) $1,000

Atlan, Jean Michel, 1913-60
ALs, [n.d.]. (90) DM220

Atlas
Ms, Portolan Atlas of 4 charts covering the Barbary Coast, Western Europe as far north as Friesland, the British Isles, the Mediterranean & Black Seas. [Iberian, c.1560] Charts mtd back to back, principally in sepia outline, toponymy in black or red ink in a fine hand, with in the center of each chart a compass-rose with radiating rhumb lines in sepia or green ink. (90) £16,000

Attenhofer, Karl, 1837-1914
Autograph music, 4 songs for male choir, Op. 118; [n.d.]. 16 pp, 8vo. Sgd on tp. (88) DM1,050

Atwell, Mabel Lucy
Original drawing, two girls seated on a garden bench, for Mrs. (88) £880
— Original drawing, woman giving her niece breakfast in bed, for Mrs. (88) £950

Atwill, Lionel, 1885-1946
Ds, 4 June 1942. (91) $500

Auber, Daniel Francois, 1782-1871
Autograph music, Allegro, "Eh bien Suzanne vous ne me dites rien", for voice & piano; [n.d.]. (90) DM700
— Autograph music, fragment of an unnamed operetta, [n.d.]. (89) DM370
ALs, 4 Nov 1840. (89) DM240
— 24 Sept 1850. (90) DM230
— [n.d.]. (90) DM260

Auden, Wystan Hugh, 1907-73
[A group of 7 letters & cards, chiefly autograph, 3 Feb 1938 to 30 Oct 1950, to John Hayward, 1 written jointly with Isherwood, sold at S on 20 July 1989, lot 161, for £900 to Rota.]
Autograph transcript, Elegy for J. F. K[ennedy], [c.1964]. 1 p, 8vo. Sgd. (89) £1,200
Transcript, poem, A Shock, sgd; [n.d.]. (90) $110
Typescript, poem, Prologue at Sixty, [c.May 1967], later sgd & dated 18 Mar 1968. (89) £300
Typescript carbon copy, play, The Chase, [n.d.]. (89) £300
Collection of 4 A Ls s, 3 Ls s, autograph Ms, & 5 telegrams, 10 Mar [1959] to 30 Nov 1972. (91) £600
ALs, [postmarked 2 July 1935]. (91) $350
— 27 May 1965. (88) £180
— 20 Aug 1968. (90) DM450
— [n.d.]. (90) DM270
Autograph postcard, sgd, [n.d.]. (90) £350
Ds, 3 Nov 1964. (90) £800
Photograph, sgd, 1926. (89) £480

Auden, Wystan Hugh, 1907-73 —& Day-Lewis, Cecil, 1904-72
[An autograph poem by each, sgd, 8 Nov 1930 & [n.d.], in 8vo schoolboy's autograph book of Norman Wright, with related material, sold at C on 7 Dec 1988, lot 189, for £320 to Wilson.]

Audubon, John James, 1785-1851
Autograph Ms, Bay Breasted Warbler & Henslow's Bunting, pbd in Ornithological Biography, vol 1, 358 & 360; [c.1830/31]. 1 p, folio. Mtd. Martin collection. (89) $2,800
— Autograph Ms, episode "The Lost Portfolio" in Ornithological Biography, vol 1; [c.1830]. 3 pp, folio. With a few autograph revisions. In quarter mor gilt folding box. John F. Fleming Estate. (89) $2,500
— Autograph Ms, episode XV in Ornithological Biography, vol 1; [c.1830]. 5 pp, folio. With autograph revisions. In quarter mor gilt folding box. John F. Fleming Estate. (89) $2,800
— Autograph Ms, Great Horned Owl, pbd in Ornithological Biography, vol 1, 313-317; [c.1830/31]. 4 pp, folio. With autograph revisions; marginal pencil note by Elliott Coues. Martin collection. (89) $5,500
— Autograph Ms, Ivory Billed Woodpecker, pbd in Ornithological Biography, vol 1, 341-347; [c.1830/31]. 6 pp, folio. Heavily revised. Martin collection. (89) $8,000
— Autograph Ms, journal at sea & in Britain, 27 May to 29 Dec 1826. 214 leaves, 311mm by 197mm. Orig quarter brown sheep bdg, rebacked. Including 18 pencil drawings (12 full-page), & c.52 pp of retained copies of letters in secretarial hands, frequently sgd or initialled, & 2 leaves from an 1828-29 journal. Martin collection. (89) $200,000
— Autograph Ms, Red-Winged Starling, pbd in Ornithological Biography, vol 1, 348-352; [c.1830/31]. 3 pp, folio. Martin collection. (89) $3,250
— Autograph Ms, Swamp Sparrow, pbd in Ornithological Biography, vol 1, 331-332; [c.1830/31]. 1 p, folio. With several authorial corrections. Mtd. Martin collection. (89) $1,800
— Autograph Ms, The eccentric Naturalist, pbd in Ornithological Biography, vol 1, 455-460; [c.1830/31]. 5 pp, folio. With autograph emendations & pencil note by Elliott Coues. Martin collection. (89) $6,000
— Autograph Ms, The Ohio, pbd in Ornithological Biography, vol 1, 29-32; [c.1830]. 3 pp, folio. With autograph revisions; some pencil emendations by Elliott Coues. Martin collection. (89) $4,500
— Autograph Ms, The Rathbone Warbler, pbd in Ornithological Biography, vol 1, 333; [c.1830/31]. 1 p, folio. Martin collection. (89) $2,000
— Autograph Ms, White-eyed Flycatcher, pbd in Ornithological Biography,

AUDUBON

vol 1, 328-329; [c.1830/31]. 2 pp, folio. With several emendations. Martin collection. (89) $2,000

— Autograph Ms, Wild Pigeon, preliminary version of text pbd in Ornithological Biography, vol 1, 319-327; [c.1830/31]. 2 pp, folio. With autograph corrections & pencil note by Elliott Coues; 4 lines by Lucy Audubon on verso. Martin collection. (89) $5,500

ALs, 16 Jan 1827. Martin collection. (89) $700

— 1 Mar 1827. Martin collection. (89) $1,000

— 28 May 1827. 3 pp, 4to. To his wife Lucy Bakewell Audubon. Describing his first days in London. Seal tear. Martin collection. (89) $3,500

— 6 Dec 1827. 3 pp, 4to. To his wife Lucy Bakewell Audubon. Informing her about letters & parcels sent. Seal tear. Martin collection. (89) $1,300

— 22 Aug 1830. 3 pp, 4to. To Victor Audubon. About his itinerary in England, the revolution in France, & his work. With autograph postscript, sgd, on ALs by Lucy Audubon to their sons, 20 Apr 1836, 2 pp, 4to. Martin collection. (89) $1,600

— 29 Mar 1832. 2 pp, folio. To his wife & sons. Mentioning John Bachman & discussing subscriptions to his work. Integral blank def. Martin collection. (89) $2,500

— 16 May 1833. 3 pp, folio. To his wife. Describing preparations for his expedition to Labrador. Seal tear. Martin collection. (89) $2,500

— 31 Dec 1833. (89) £900

— 14 Jan 1835. (89) £1,000

— 5 July 1838. (89) £950

— 4 Feb 1842. 1 p, 4to. To Edward Harris. Mentioning his recent drawings, the construction of his new house, & hoping to see him. (88) $2,000

Auerbach, Berthold, 1812-82
Autograph Ms, Der Gevattersmann, [1845]. (88) DM850
ALs, 19 Jan 1876. (91) DM480

Augereau, Pierre Francois Charles, Duc de Castiglione, 1757-1816
Ls, [28 Oct 1797]. (88) DM340

August, Kurfuerst von Sachsen, 1526-86
Ls s (2), 21 Nov 1583 & 24 Feb 1584. (90) DM450
Ls, 10 Nov 1579. (89) DM400
Document, 26 Feb 1556. 17 pp, vellum, 4to. Statutes for 2 guilds. With large equestrian seal. (90) DM1,300

August, Prince of Prussia, 1779-1843
ALs, 29 Nov 1815. Schroeder collection. (89) DM200

August Wilhelm, Herzog von Braunschweig-Bevern, 1715-81
ALs, [3 Sept 1757]. (91) DM420

August Wilhelm, Prince of Prussia, 1722-58
Series of 5 A Ls s, Apr 1756 to 8 May 1758. 6 pp, 4to. To Viktor Amadeus Graf Henckel von Donnersmarck. Confidential letters regarding failures & successes during the war. Sgd Guille. (88) DM3,500

August Wilhelm, Prince of Prussia, 1887-1949
A Ls s (2), 7 & 12 Dec 1911. (90) DM340
ALs, Dec 1930. (88) $100

Augusta, Empress of Wilhelm I of Germany, 1811-90
ALs, 3 Aug 1832. (91) DM300
— 14 Aug 1832. (90) DM300

Auguste Viktoria, Empress of Wilhelm II of Germany, 1858-1921
Series of 9 A Ls s, 30 Dec 1895 to 22 Mar 1906. (91) DM900
ALs, 3 Jan 1883. Schroeder collection. (89) DM260
— 6 Apr [1919]. (90) DM250

Augustine, Saint, 354-430
Ms, Confessiones & other writings, including Liber exhortationis by Paulinus of Aquileia. [Northern Germany?, 13th cent]. 215 leaves, vellum, 293mm by 200mm. 18th cent lea bdg. In several hands. With 22 small & 5 larger initials in colors. Lacking 1 leaf. (88) DM42,000
— Ms, De Civitate Dei. (88) £700

— Ms, De Civitate Dei. [Milan, c.1430-50]. 341 leaves (4 lacking), vellum, 294mm by 210mm. 18th-cent French mottled calf bdg. In a regular rounded semi-humanistic gothic bookhand. With 23 very large illuminated initials, & miniature with full border. Illuminated for Giovanni Meizi by the Master of the Vitae Imperatorum. Ownership inscr of Montesquieu. (91) £55,000

— Ms, De Consensu Evangelistarum, in Latin. [Northeastern? Italy, late 14th cent]. 110 leaves, vellum, 275mm by 200mm. 18th-cent sprinkled calf. In brown ink in an accomplished rotunda script. With 2-line pen-flourished initials, 3 initials with partial or full borders, & unidentified coat-of-arms. Used as printer's copy. Doheny collection. (88) £6,000

— Ms, De Poenitentia (Confessions), in Latin. [France, c.1375]. 102 leaves, vellum, 31cm by 33cm. 18th-cent French calf gilt, rebacked. In a regular gothic hand. With penwork initials in red & blue with flourished borders & sprays. Doheny collection. (88) £10,000

— Ms, Enarrationes in Psalmos, 2:4 to 49:21. [England, c.1150]. 141 leaves only, vellum, 37cm by 36cm. Disbound. In brown ink by several scribes in minuscule scripts. With colored initials throughout, numerous large initials & 28 large decorated initials in colors. Margins of 4 leaves cut, 2 with text loss. (88) £7,200

— Ms, [H]omelie nvmero centvm uiginti qvatuor in Ewangelio secvndum Iohannem... [Northern Germany?, 13th cent]. 268 leaves, vellum, 313mm by 234mm. 18th cent lea bdg. In black & red ink in a large gothic hand by several scribes. With 124 initials in red & blue. Lacking 1 leaf. (88) DM19,400

— Ms, Sermones ad Fratres in Eremo Commorates. [Northern Italy, 2d half of 15th cent]. 100 leaves (2 blank), 215mm by 144mm. Contemp blindstamped brown goatskin, lacking upper cover. In brown ink in a small cursive bookhand with gothic features. With 42 small decorated initials & 4-line historiated initial. Some dampstains. (88) £1,500

— Ms, Soliloquia & Liber Contemplationis, with texts by St. Bernard of Clairvaux. [Northern Italy, Padua?, c.1450]. 86 leaves, vellum, 178mm by 120mm. Contemp blindstamped brown goatskin over bevelled wooden bds. In a fine semi-humanistic minuscule. With large painted initials throughout, some enclosing writing left white. (91) £8,000

— Ms, The Rule of St. (89) £750

Augustinian Nuns

Ms, [Constitution and Rules of the Nuns of Saint Augustine] [Italy, late 15th cent] 47 leaves & added leaf at front, vellum, 243mm by 177mm, in vellum gilt with lattice panel of cutwork over silk. Opening page of text with elaborate floriated initial in blue, red, mauve & green, heightened with gold & with marginal floral decoration on 3 sides. Manhattan College Ms (91) $2,200

Augustinian Order

Ms, Cartulary of the Augustinian Convent at Crema, Lombardy, issued by Giorgio Franciotus, vicar general of Cardinal Galeotto Francietti della Rovere. [Lucca, 1505]. 49 leaves (4 blank), vellum, 195mm by 134mm. Contemp limp vellum wraps using draft of a notarial document. In brown ink in a sloping gothic hand with calligraphic flourishes. With 34 illuminated initials & half-page armorial achievement with the arms of della Rovere, full border & gold roundel with half-length figure of St. Augustine. Astor MS.A.10. (88) £6,000

Augustus II, King of Poland, 1670-1733

Ls, 22 Sept 1685. (90) DM650

Ds, 16 Mar 1713. (90) DM750

— 18 Oct 1714. 11 pp, folio, in red velvet bds. Copy & ratification of the treaty between Augustus & Louis XIV of France, 20 Aug 1714, with copies of full powers of the negotiators. (91) £1,300

— 15 Oct 1717. Kuenzel collection. (90) DM380

— 13 Sept 1728. (90) £500

AUGUSTUS III

Augustus III, King of Poland, 1696-1763
ALs, 31 July 1754. (88) £300
Series of 7 Ls s, 1752 to 1762. (90) DM900
Ls, 24 July 1746. (90) DM440
— 31 Mar 1760. (91) DM400
Ds, 7 July 1756. (90) DM300

Auslaender, Rose, 1907-88
Autograph Ms, poem, Raum II, [n.d.]. (90) DM420
Autograph transcript, poem, Raum II; [n.d.]. (89) DM340
ALs, 8 Dec 1977. (88) DM320

Austen, Caroline Mary Craven, 1805-80
Autograph Ms (2), journal of a journey from Kippington to Marienbad made by members of Jane Austen's family, 1836 - 1837, & prayers, [c.1845 to 1876]. (91) £500

Austen, Jane, 1775-1815
Autograph Ms, novel, The Watsons, [1804-05]. About 75 pp, 8vo. With extensive autograph revisions. Lacking 1st 12 pp. (89) £90,000
— Autograph Ms, "Volume the Third", containing her 2 early novels Evelyn, & Catherine, or the Bower, sgd & dated 6 May 1792. About 125 pp (c.11 in anr hand), 4to, in vellum bds. Dedicated to Mary Lloyd & her sister [Cassandra]. Including some notes in other hands. (89) £120,000
ALs, 24 [- 26] Dec [c.1798]. 4 pp, 4to. To her sister Cassandra. About her brother's naval career, a ball, & mutual friends. Koch Foundation. (90) $18,000
— 4 Sept 1816. 1 p, 4to. To her sister Cassandra. Sending family news. (91) $7,500
— AUSTEN FAMILY. - Ms, 18th-cent recipe book, apparently once belonging to the family of Jane Austen. Over 200 pp, 4to, in 18th-cent reversed calf. Ownership inscr, sgd TK & dated 1793. (91) £1,400

Austin, Moses, 1761-1821
Ds, 7 June 1802. Alexander collection. (90) $750

AMERICAN BOOK PRICES CURRENT

Australia
[A group of 9 letters by Edward Bellamy & Caroline Gerard, 1840 to 1846, 36 pp, 4to, to Elizabeth & Francis Bellamy, reporting about their prospects in New South Wales, with related family letters, sold at S on 18 July 1991, lot 414, for £1,400 to Maggs.]
Ms, diary of an officer on the convict ship Guilford, 6 Mar to 25 July 1827. (88) £900
— Ms, Roll of foreign Accounts of the LV Year of King George the Third [for New South Wales], 1 Jan to 31 Dec 1813. Vellum roll, c.10 feet 8 inches by 11 inches. Accounts for Admiral William Bligh & officials & civil employees in the colony. Marked as examined [by the Treasury], 10 July 1820. (89) £1,150
Document, convict record of Thomas Matthews, 1842. (88) A$120
— 19 Dec 1844. (88) £110
— convict record of Francis Scott, 1844. (88) A$100
— APPLETREE, RICHARD. - ALs, 16 Apr 1810. 2 pp, folio. To his family in England. As a convict in Australia, about his pardon being granted. (88) £350
— BASKERVILLE, PERCEVAL. - Autograph Ms, logs of HMS Dromedary & HMS Bathurst (copy), 1819 to 1823; c.240 pp, folio, in contemp bds. Recording voyage to Australia & exploration of the Northern coast; with several pen-&-ink maps. (88) £5,500
— BODENHAM, FRANCIS. - ALs, 5 May 1857. 4 pp, 4to. To his sister. Describing his experiences in the gold rush. With related material. (90) £80
— FOSSETT, GEORGE. - ALs, 31 Dec 1848. 3 pp, 4to. To his sister. Describing his life on a South Australian sheep farm & a meeting with Aborigines. (88) £190
— FOWELL, NEWTON. - 13 Ls s (mostly autograph), 26 Nov 1786 to 31 July 1790. 75 pp, folio & 4to. To his father & [Capt.] George Ourry (1). Letters by a midshipman on the Sirius, flagship of the 1st convict fleet to New South Wales. With 6 letters & 2 documents relating to Fowell & Botany Bay, 11 pp, various sizes. (88) £96,000

— FRANKLIN, SIR JOHN. - Ds, 13 July 1840. Size not stated. As Lieut. Gov. of Van Diemen's Land, convict's remission for Margaret Christie. With related material. (88) £380

— GORDON, CAPT. JAMES. - Autograph Ms, journal kept during a voyage to Australia on the Eliza, 1832 to 1834; c.100 pp, 8vo, in brown calf. (88) £620

— LA TROBE, CHARLES JOSEPH. - Ds, land transfer for a block in Oakleigh, Melbourne, 1853. Size not stated. (88) A$150

— LYTTLETON, WILLIAM THOMAS. - Autograph Ms, court record kept as police magistrate & deputy chairman of Quarter Sessions at Launceston, 17 Aug 1833 to 24 Feb 1834. 450 pp, folio, in orig reversed calf. (88) A$6,000

— MORANT, THOMAS. - ALs, 16 June 1857. 3 pp, 4to. To his parents. About his life in Melbourne & some gold found at Ballarat. Written on no xii of the News Letter of Australasia, with woodcut view of "The Corroboree". (88) £450

— MORGAN, JOHN. - ALs, 11, 16 & 25 Aug 1829. 5 pp, folio; cross-written in 2 colors of ink. Describing the arrival of the 1st settlers in Western Australia & the foundation of Perth & Fremantle. (91) £3,000

— PRICE, JOHN. - 9 Ds s, 1839 to 1845. 8vo. Summonses. (88) A$200

— REIBEY, JANE. - ALs, 7 Feb 1823. 3 pp, 4to. To her cousin D. Hope. Expecting to visit "wild Caledonia". (88) £80

— TASMANIA. - Ms, Order for Garrison Guards, Hobart Town and Launceston, 17 July 1855. 23 leaves & blanks, 4to, in wraps. (88) £160

Austria

— BRAUNAU ON THE INN. - Ms, minutes of the Shoemakers' Guild, 1516 to 1854. 103 leaves & blanks, 4to. 16th-cent blindstamped lea bdg. Listing members, accounts, etc. (89) DM2,200

— CARINTHIA. - Document, [23 Apr] 1620. 1 p, vellum, 35cm by 61cm. Bill of sale for the manor of Sagritz to Hans Christoph Putz, sgd by 6 representatives of the province. With related material. (89) DM650

— COURT PROCEEDINGS. - A file containing the proceedings of the Landgericht at Pragstein in Upper Austria in the trial of Simon Enzendorfer for theft, 1768, 33 Mss, c.80 leaves, including the rope used by the hangman & the broken rod, sold at HK on 3 Nov, lot 17, for DM1,400. 88

— OSTERMIETING, ARCHDIOCESE OF SALZBURG. - Ms, Calendar of the Parish Church, in Latin. [Ostermieting, mid-15th cent]. 14 leaves, vellum, 350mm by 258mm, in 16th-cent blindstamped calf over pastebds formed of sheets of early ptg. In brown & red ink in a formal gothic liturgical hand. With many additions, including armorial shield of Egidius Puttnhaim. (88) £950

— VIENNA. - Document, Sept 1421. 1 p, 11.5cm by 14c. Receipt for quarterly wages paid to the watchmen on the tower of St. Stephen's by city treasurer Ulrich Bermann. (89) DM1,100

Ayckbourn, Alan

Autograph Ms, play, A Trip to Scarborough, draft; [1983 or earlier]. 54 pp, folio. With numerous revisions, & including 2 tabular plans showing disposition of characters. In pencil. With related material. (90) £1,900

Typescript, play, A Small Family Business, with autograph revisions; [1986]. (88) £350

Azanchevsky, Mikhail Pavlovich, 1839-1881

Autograph music, sketches for the song Sie frug die braune Zigeunerin, for voice & piano; [n.d.]. Heyer collection. (89) DM250

B

Baader, Franz, 1765-1841

ALs, 4 Aug 1811. (90) DM340
— 8 Jan 1831. (91) DM440

Bab, Julius, 1880-1955

Collection of 4 A Ls s & 2 autograph postcards, sgd, 21 Apr 1911 to 20 Apr 1919. Ernst Gottlieb collection. (88) DM380

Babbage, Charles, 1792-1871
ALs, 19 June 1824. 3 pp, 4to. To [Henry Thomas Colebrooke]. About his recently constructed calculating machine. (89) £15,500
— 24 Jan 1860. (88) £700

Bach, Carl Philipp Emanuel, 1714-88
ALs, 27 Jan 1785. 1 p, 4to. To Johann Joachim Eschenburg. Requesting his help in having his sonatas ptd. With contemp musical Ms, duet Parlami pur sincera svela, by Johann Christian Bach, 2 pp, 8vo; fragment. (88) DM19,000

Bach, Johann Christoph Friedrich, 1732-95
Autograph music, 2 movements from his oratorio Die Kindheit Jesu, scored for 4 voices, [1773 or later]. 13 pp, folio. (89) DM32,000

Bach, Johann Sebastian, 1685-1750
Autograph music, cantata, Auf Christi Himmelfahrt allein, BWV 128, full score; [before 10 May 1725]. 16 pp, c.34cm by 21cm. In brown/black ink on up to 22 hand-drawn staves per page; with numerous revisions. Marked by the ptr. Imperf. (90) £390,000

Ms, Basso Continuo of the Cantata "Herr Gott, dich loben alle wir" (BWV 130), fragment, [1724]. (88) £650

Ds, 5 June 1747. 1 p, 170mm by 201mm. Receipt for payment of a month's rent for a clavier. Contemp endorsement on verso. (89) £18,000

Bachmann, Ingeborg, 1926-73
ALs, 21 Dec 1957. 2 pp, 8vo. To an unnamed lady. Expressing thanks & hoping to see her in Munich. (88) DM1,600

Bacon, John H.
Original drawings, (13), to illus Charles Dickens' Dombey and Son, & Little Dorrit, 1901. (89) £500

Bacon's Rebellion
— MAITLAND, JOHN. - ALs, 14 Nov 1676. Length not stated. To his brother Charles, 3d Earl of Lauderdale. Mentioning news from Virginia & hoping for a "speedie end of that traitor Bacons rebellion". (88) $350

Baden-Powell of Gilwell, Robert S. S. Baden-Powell, 1st Baron, 1857-1941
Collection of 9 A Ls s & autograph postcard, sgd, 22 Feb 1901 to 5 Apr 1906. (89) £600
— Collection of ALs, Ls, & autograph Ms, Sept to Dec 1939. (89) £240

ALs, 28 July 1900. 3 pp, 8vo. To Miss Bridges. Sentting out some of his first ideas for what was to become the scouting movement. With related material. (91) £1,200
— 27 July 1903. (88) £90
— 8 Oct 1903. (90) £130
— 28 July 1907. 8 pp, 8vo. To Lucy Lyttelton. Announcing that he is putting his ideas to test in a boy scout camp. (91) £2,200
— 4 June 1936. (88) £100

Ls, 31 Oct 1933. (90) DM280

Photograph, sgd, 21 June 1901. (88) £160
— Anr, [c.1908]. (88) £170

Baer, Karl Ernst von, 1792-1876
ALs, 18 [Apr 1851]. (91) DM320

Baeumer, Gertrud, 1873-1954
Collection of 9 A Ls s & autograph postcard, sgd; 27 July 1948 to 15 May 1950 & [n.d.]. (89) DM380

Baeyer, Adolf von, 1835-1917
ALs, 10 June 1895. 4 pp, 8vo. To E. Bamberger. Discussing a scientific question & recipient's disagreement with Arthur Hanzsch. (91) DM1,100

Bahamas
— CAMERON, CHARLES. - Ms, letterbook kept as Governor of the Bahamas, 1805 to 1807. About 360 pp, 4to, in modern calf gilt. Over 340 letters, mostly to British officials; in the hand of his secretary Richard Roberts. (91) £800

Bailly de Monthion, Francois Gedeon, Comte, 1776-1850
Ls, 10 Oct 1813. (90) DM240

Bainbridge, Beryl
Typescript, short stories, Mum & Mr. (88) £400

Bainbridge, William, 1774-1833
Franking signature, [1827]. Alexander collection. (90) $110

Baird, John Logie, 1888-1946
Ls s (2), 1 Nov 1929 & 9 May 1930. (88) £220

Baird, John Logie, 1888-1946
Ls, 1 Nov 1929. (91) $600

Baker, Alpheus, 1825-91
ALs, 18 Apr 1864. (88) $240

Baker, Josephine, 1906-75
[A large collection of papers relating to her, including over 100 letters (mostly autograph) by her to H. Hurford Janes & his wife Peggy, 1943 to 1975, several thousand pages in 6 file boxes, sold at S on 15 Dec 1977, lot 180, for £6,800.]
Collection of ALs & 2 Ls s, July to Oct 1967. (91) $500
Ls, 25 June 1971. (91) $80

Baker, Sir Samuel White, 1821-93
Collection of 6 A Ls s & Ls s, 1867 to 1887. (90) £300

Bakst, Leon, 1866-1924
ALs, 29 Aug 1922. (88) DM240
— [n.d.], "Friday". (90) £200

Bakunin, Mikhail Aleksandrovich, 1814-76
ALs, 3 Mar 1843. 4 pp, 8vo. Recipient unnamed. Requesting a loan, mentioning Herwegh & Froebel, etc. In German. (89) DM2,800
— 20 Dec 1861/1 Jan 1862. 1 p, 8vo. To [Ivan] Turgenev. Hoping to see him in London. Was mtd. (89) DM1,800
— 3 Feb 1864. 3 pp, 8vo. To Karl Vogt. Informing him about his arrival in Florence & discussing the revolutionary movement in Italy. In French. (90) DM5,200
— [26 Sept 1873?]. 4 pp, 4to. To the editors of the Journal de Geneve. Open letter regarding his differences with Karl Marx. Sgd Michel Bakounine. In French. (88) DM4,500

Balakirev, Mily Alekseyevivh, 1837-1910
Autograph quotation, opening 8 bars of Islamey, 1895. On a card. Sgd. (91) £4,000

Balbi, Giovanni, d.1298
Ms, Catholicon. [Northeast Italy, c.1400]. 247 leaves & 2 flyleaves, 407mm by 285mm. In rebacked contemp wooden bds. In a small gothic bookhand. With decorated initials throughout & 2 very large illuminated initials (1 partly cut out). Incomplete at end. (91) £6,000

Balbo, Italo, 1896-1940
[A photograph of a port painting, 1933, 21.5cm by 15cm, sgd & inscr to Karl Schwabe, sold at star on 5 Apr 1991, lot 1509, for DM360.]
Photograph, sgd, [c.1933]. (88) $100

Balfe, Michael William, 1808-70
[A collection of some 500 pages relating to his arrangement of a Selection of Moore's Irish Melodies (some proof sheets dated 1858) sold at pn on 14 June 1989 for £400 to Maggs.]

Balfour, Arthur James, 1st Earl, 1848-1930
ALs, 20 Mar 1897. (91) $275
Ls s (2), 10 Dec 1924 & 8 Sept 1926. (91) $80

Ball, Lucille, 1910-89
Signature, [n.d.]. (91) $80

Ball, Lucille, 1910-89 —&
Arnaz, Desi, 1915-86
[A magazine cover reproducing a group photo of Ball & Arnaz with their children Desi IV & Lucy Desiree, sgd by all 4, [n.d.]., 4to; framed, sold at wa on 20 Oct 1990, lot 347, for $110.]
Group photograph, 1953. (91) $80
— Anr, [n.d.]. (91) $300

Ballantyne, Robert Michael, 1825-94
Autograph Ms, story, The Kitten Pilgrims, [pbd 1882]. 80 pp, 8vo; in fitted case. With proofs of 10 wood-engraved illusts. (89) £2,000
Original drawings, (5), pictorial tp for Erling the Bold & illusts for The Cannibal Islands & Hunting the Lions, [n.d.]. (89) £900

Ballin, Albert, 1857-1918
Collection of 2 A Ls s & 4 Ls s, 16 July 1904 to 28 Dec 1917. (89) DM700
ALs, 12 Dec 1897. 7 pp, 8vo. To Heinrich Wiegand. Suggesting a cooperation between their shipping lines. (91)

BALLIN

DM1,100
— 30 Sept 1916. (90) DM210
Ls, 19 Aug 1915. Schroeder collection. (89) DM220

Balshaw, John
Autograph Ms, drama in verse, beginning "Spectatours gallant that attend", 95 stanzas; [17th cent]. 11 pp, 150mm by 400mm. Sgd at end. Stitching def. (89) £5,600

Baltimore, Charles Calvert, 3d Baron, 1637-1715
Ds, 14 July 1679. 1 p, vellum, 4to. Grant of land in Baltimore County to James Ellis. Def. (89) $1,900

Baltimore, David
Ls, 6 Nov 1978. (90) DM270

Balzac, Honore de, 1799-1850
Autograph Ms, preface to his novel Pierrette, June 1840. 10 pp, folio, in a folder. With autograph revisions. Martin collection. (90) FF52,000
— Autograph Ms, Sur la destruction projettee du monument eleve au Duc de Berry, [31 Mar 1832]. 5 leaves, 4to. Rough draft, sgd. Barrett collection. (89) $4,000
Autograph transcript, extract from his novel Le Medecin de campagne, 21 lines; [n.d.]. 1 p, folio. Sgd. (89) £1,500
ALs, [Oct 1831]. 2 pp, 8vo. To Baron Gerard. Referring to La peau de chagrin, his Contes philosophiques, & sending a message for Mlle Godefroid. (88) £3,200
— 5 June [1834]. 1 p, 8vo. To Baron Gerard. Sending an inscr copy of 4 vols of his Comedie humaine. (88) £2,200
— [Feb 1835]. 2 pp, 8vo. To Baron Gerard. Letter of introduction for [Louis] Grosclaude. (88) £1,600
— [c.Nov 1840]. (91) £700
— [n.d.]. 1 p, 8vo. To °L°. Agreeing to the conditions offered for contributions to a magazine. Small tear. (88) DM1,350
— 3 Mar 1845. (90) $900
— [19 Feb 1849?]. 1 p, 4to. Recipient unnamed. Sending a book. Initialled. With related material. (90) DM2,800
— 8 June [n.d.]. 1 p, 8vo. To Morin. Informing him that he will not be able to finish a play as promised. (90) DM2,600
— [n.d.]. (89) £800
ANs, 5 June [n.y.]. (90) $450
Corrected proof, 1st gathering of Illusions perdues, [1837]. 16 pp, 4to. With substantial autograph revisions. Martin collection. (90) FF65,000
See also: Drouet, Juliette

Bamm, Peter, Pseud. of Curt Emmrich, 1897-1975
ALs, 26 Feb 1926. (89) DM360

Bancroft, George, 1800-91
ALs, 21 July 1863. (90) $75

Bankhead, Tallulah, 1902-68
Photograph, sgd & inscr, [n.d.]. (91) $300

Banks, Sir Joseph, 1743-1820
ALs, 18 Jan 1804. (90) £130
— 17 Dec 1807. (88) £150
— 25 May 1811. (88) £270
— 1 Feb 1814. (91) £720
— 20 Nov [n.y.]. (88) £150

Bantock, Granville, 1868-1946
Autograph music, Pagan Symphony, sgd GB & dated 20 June [19]28. (89) £950
Series of c.40 A Ls s, 1913 to 1926. (89) £550

Bantzer, Carl, 1857-1941
Collection of 13 A Ls s, 8 autograph postcards, sgd, 2 autograph Mss, & photograph, sgd & inscr, 1922 to 1941. 41 pp, mostly 4to, & cards. To Paul Heidelbach. Interesting letters about his pictures, his native Hesse, the concept of "Heimatkunst", etc. With related material. (89) DM1,200

Barbe-Marbois, Francois, Marquis de, 1745-1837
ALs, 13 Feb 1815. (91) $65
See also: Franklin, Benjamin

Barberini Family
— MAXIMO, MARIO, & OTHERS. - Ms, prose & poetry in praise of the Barberini Family & of the election of Urban VII to the Papacy, in Latin. [Rome or Bologna, 1623-28]. 14 leaves, vellum, 123mm by 150mm. Contemp armorial mosaic bdg richly gilt. In several calligraphic scripts. With il-

luminated tp. (91) £9,500

Barbey d'Aurevilly, Jules, 1808-89
Autograph Ms, Le Rideau cramoisi, from his collection Les Diaboliques, [c.1874]. 36 pp, folio, mostly laid down; in red mor bdg. In 3 colors of ink; with revisions. Some paper loss. Martin collection. (90) FF340,000
— Autograph Ms, Les Ecoles historiques du XIX Siecle, 2 reviews, each sgd; [n.d.]. 9 pp, folio. Some revisions. Ptr's copy. (90) DM3,600
ALs, 15 Mar [1885]. (90) DM360

Barbiere, Domenico del, c.1506-65?
ALs, 19 May 1542. (90) $450

Bardeleben, Adolf von, 1819-95
ALs, 17 May 1854. (91) DM480
— 11 Mar 1874. (91) DM250

Bardet di Villanova, Pietro
Ms, Modelli di cannoni ed altho per uso e studio di Pietro Bardet di Villanova. (91) £800

Bargiel, Woldemar, 1828-97
ALs, 11 Nov 1853. (91) DM420

Baring-Gould, Sabine, 1834-1924
Autograph transcript, hymn, Onward Christian Soldiers, sgd; [n.d.]. (88) £520

Barker, Cicely Mary
Original drawings, (14), cover designs for story books named after flowers or birds, 1922. 390mm by 290mm. In ink & watercolor. 12 initialled. (89) £9,500
— Original drawings, (6), to illus Our Darling's First Book, [1920s]. 355mm by 255mm. In watercolor. Initialled. (89) £5,000
— Original drawings, (7), to illus At the Window, [1920s]. 265mm by 190mm. In ink & watercolor. Initialled. (89) £6,000

Barlach, Ernst, 1870-1938
Autograph Ms, answer to an inquiry about the meaning of peace, [c.Dec 1933]. (89) DM460
— Autograph Ms, poem, beginning "Dieses ist herrjeh! Barlachs Selbstportrait...", [c.1903]. (91) DM900
Collection of 11 A Ls s & 3 autograph postcards, sgd, 1918 to 1936. 35 pp, 8vo. To Hans Franck. Dealing with private & professional matters. (89) DM7,000
Series of 17 A Ls s, 27 June 1914 to 1938. 62 pp, 4to & 8vo. To Arthur Moeller van den Bruck & his wife (1). Interesting letters covering a variety of personal & professional matters. (88) DM22,000
— Series of 5 A Ls s, 26 Oct 1932 to 12 Apr 1933. 12 pp, 4to. To Dr. Fritz Adler. Concerning designs submitted for a war memorial at Stralsund. (91) DM6,500
ALs, 18 Mar 1904. (91) DM1,000
— 7 Apr 1921. (88) DM700
— 22 Aug 1926. (91) DM650
— 9 Mar 1927. (88) DM600
— 6 Aug 1936. (90) DM500
Autograph postcard, sgd, 17 Mar 1893. (89) DM440
— [4 Apr 1893]. (90) DM430

Barlow, Robert H.
Collection of 1 ALs, 8 Ls s & 2 autograph postcards, sgd, 1934-38. (89) $325

Barnes, William, 1801-86
ALs, 7 Feb 1877. (91) £70
— 23 Jan 1880. (89) £120

Barnum, Phineas Taylor, 1810-91
Collection of 2 A Ls s & photograph, 21 [Jan?] 1861, 3 Mar 1866 & [n.d.]. Middendorf collection. (89) $550
— Collection of 5 A Ls s & Ls s, 26 May 1882 to 1 Nov 1889. 5 pp, 8vo. To A. D. Bartlett of the Royal Zoological Gardens. About the elephant Jumbo & other matters. With related material. (89) £1,400
ALs, [1860s]. (91) $350
— 19 Mar 1866. (91) $400
— 16 Sept [18]66. (89) $250
— 16 Sept 1873. (91) $280
— 22 July 1880. (88) $160
— 4 Mar 1882. (91) $550
— 11 Nov [18]82. (90) $600
— 23 Jan 1891. (91) $190
ANs, 16 May 1889. (88) $225
Ds, 1 May 1854. (91) $275
Signature, 22 Apr 1875. (90) $95
— Anr, 3 May 1877. (88) $75

Barr, Robert
Ds, 12 Apr 1839. 1 p, 4to. Appointment of Thomas Ward as Postmaster at Houston. (91) $1,700

Barraband, Jacques, 1767-1809
[Lots 215 to 266 of the Jeanson sale on 16 June 1988 at SM consisted of preparatory drawings by Barraband for Levaillant's ornithological works]

Barras, Paul, 1755-1829
Autograph Ms, views on Napoleon's return from Elba & the Restoration, [n.d.]. (88) £200

ALs, [19 Dec 1793]. (90) £340

— [19 Dec 1793]. (88) £250
See also: Lalande, Joseph Jerome de

Barraud, Allan
Original drawings, (20), to illus J. Archives of J. M. Dent & Son. (88) £500

Barrie, Sir James Matthew, 1860-1937
Autograph Ms, comedy, Dear Brutus, [1917]. 60 pp, 8vo. With many revisions, varying from ptd text. Including autograph dedication to Gerald du Maurier, 30 Jan 1918. With related material, in dark blue mor bdg. (88) £5,200

— Autograph Ms, essay, Cast Adrift, [c.1891]. 9 pp, 8vo. Comments on literary & social events. (89) £1,700

Typescript, comedy, The Twelve Pound Look, [c.1910]. 26 pp, 4to, in paper wraps. Including autograph title & revisions; differing from ptd version. (89) £1,150

Series of 7 A L s s, 1 May 1922 to 15 Apr 1926. (89) £650

ALs, 1 July 1892. (90) $80

— 4 May 1906. 3 pp, 8vo. To a young girl. Talking about Peter Pan. (90) £3,200

— 25 June 1908. (90) £160

— 7 July 1908. (90) $80

— 21 Jan 1909. (91) £600

— 22 Dec 1913. (91) $225

AL, 13 Mar 1923. (88) £260

Ls, 17 Apr 1923. (88) £85

Barrit, Thomas, 1743-1820
Autograph Ms, untitled treatise on archery. Manchester, 1782-84. 18 leaves, frontis, 5 watercolor drawings & 4 ink & wash drawings. 158mm by 102mm, in orig wraps. Sgd, 1782, but frontis & 1 other illust dated 1784. (91) $4,000

Barron, Clarence Walker, 1855-1928
[A collection of c.170 letters, cards & notes mostly addressed to him from business executives, politicians, & others, sold at CNY on 1 Feb 1988, lot 328, for $1,300 to Houle.]

Barron, James, 1769-1851
[A group of 4 letters addressed to Barron by Navy Commissioners, 1835 & 1836, concerning ship building, etc., sold at rf on 26 Nov 1988, lot 57, for $140.]

Barrow, Edward G., 1868-1953
Ls, 11 Apr 1944. (91) $200

Barrymore, John, 1882-1942
Ds, 9 Mar 1931. (91) $350

Barrymore, Lionel, 1878-1954
Ls, [n.d.]. (91) $65

Photograph, sgd & inscr, [n.d.]. (91) $75

Bartholomaeus Anglicus, fl.1230-50
Ms, Le livre des regions et des provins (De Proprietatibus Rerum XV), Le Tretiz de set mortens pechez, Les dis comandements, & 3 other texts, in Anglo-Norman. [England, c.1260]. 32 leaves, vellum, 203 by 145mm, in (contemp?) limp vellum. In brown ink in a neat early gothic bookhand. (90) £4,800

— Ms, Le Livre Propriete des Choses, in French, trans by Jehan Corbechon. [Nevers or Bourges, c.1472]. 352 leaves (c.17 lacking), vellum, 405mm by 275mm. Modern calf gilt over wooden bds. Written for Jehan Tenon in dark brown ink in a batarde script. With 26 four-line initials in gold & colors, 2 six-line initials with partial & full borders, & 11 miniatures. Doheny collection. (88) £30,000

— Ms, Livre de la Propriete des Choses, in French, trans by Jehan Corbechon. [Nevers or Bourges, c.1472]. 352 leaves (c.13 lacking), vellum, 400mm by

267mm. Modern calf gilt. Written for Jehan Tenon in dark brown ink in a batarde script. With 26 four-line initials in gold & colors, 2 six-line initials with partial & full borders, & 11 miniatures. Doheny collection. (90) £105,000

Bartlett, Josiah, Signer from New Hampshire
ALs, 16 July 1791. (90) $550
ADs, 9 Feb 1771. (90) $250
Ds, 31 Jan 1794. (91) $130

Bartok, Bela, 1881-1945
Autograph Ms (2), articles, The Peasant Music of Hungary, & Slovakian Peasant Music; [c.1902-04]. 10 pp, folio. Drafts, with corrections & a few musical notations; sgd. In German. In folding case with related material. Byer collection. (90) $5,250
Autograph Ms, inaugural speech for the Hungarian Academy of Sciences, draft; [1936]. 2 pp, folio & 8vo. Discussing Franz Liszt. With attached signature. (90) £1,800
ALs, [c.Apr/May 1905]. 2 pp, 8vo. To an unnamed lady. Inviting her to a charity concert. (90) DM1,800
— 27 Nov 1923. 2 pp, 8vo. To Frau Hentsch. Suggesting programs for concerts to be given with Jelly d'Aranyi. (91) £1,300
Ls, 23 June 1907. (88) £300
Autograph postcard, sgd, 14 Jan 1906. (91) £900
— 30 Aug [1920]. (90) DM620
— 14 May 1922. To Michel Dimitri Calvocoressi. Expressing his disappointment about the staging of his opera in Frankfurt. Was mtd. (88) DM1,250
— 9 Oct 1922. (88) £450
— 5 Oct 1923. (91) £420
— 1923. (91) £460
Autograph postcard, 6 Feb 1903. To Adila Aranyi. Regretting he cannot go to a concert. (90) DM1,500
Autograph quotation, 3 bars from his Rhapsody for piano, Op. 1, sgd & dated 6 Dec 1923. 1 p, 16cm by 20cm. Leaf also sgd by others. (90) DM3,800
— Anr, 8 bars from his Dance Suite, sgd; 31 Dec 1927. 1 p, 8vo. (91) $1,900

— Anr, 13 bars, sgd; [n.d]. (90) £950
Group photograph, [n.d.]. (91) £420
— Anr, [n.d.]. (91) $450
Photograph, sgd & inscr, 18 Dec 1937. 23cm by 17cm (image). Sgd on mount. (91) DM1,200

Bartolomeo da San Concordia, 1250-1347
Ms, Summa Casuum (here called Tractatus de Modo Legendi Iura et Leges). [Germany, 1456]. 215 leaves, 313mm by 210mm. Contemp calf over bevelled wooden bds. In a regular gothic bookhand by Iodocus Sparluezel. With large painted initials throughout. (90) £5,500
— Ms, Summa Casuum, with John of Fribourg's Confessionale. [Central Italy, late 14th cent]. 237 leaves, vellum, 221mm by 147mm, in modern mor gilt by Lortic. In dark brown ink in a small bookhand by the scribe Guilgelmus. With 22 large illuminated initials in leafy designs in full color & liquid gold with leafy extensions & 2 historiated initials. Ownership inscr of the Dominican convent of San Donato at Urbino. (88) £5,800
— Ms, Summa de casibus conscientiae [Summa Pisanella]; [Italy, early 15th cent]. 348 leaves, vellum, 165mm by 120mm, in later vellum bdg. With initials in red & blue. (90) £2,800
— Ms, Summa Pisana. [Italy, 1st half of 15th cent]. 200 leaves, 340mm by 240mm. Contemp blindstamped red lea over bevelled wooden bds. In a small gothic bookhand. (91) £3,800

Barton, Bernard, 1784-1849
ALs, 23 Oct 1824. (91) £260

Barton, Clara, 1821-1912
ALs, 4 Feb 1892. (88) $325
— 19 Oct 1909. Byer collection. (90) $325
Ls, 4 May 1900. (91) $800
Autograph sentiment, sgd, 4 Sept 1902. (90) $150
Ptd photograph, 21 Sept 1904. (91) $475

Baruch, Bernard M., 1870-1965
ALs, 23 Dec 1960. Byer collection. (90) $225
Collection of 2 Ls s & 1 Christmas card, sgd, [n.d.]. (91) $150
Ls, 19 Aug 1918. (90) $80

BARUCH

— 16 May 1958. (88) $60

Photograph, sgd & inscr, [n.d.]. (89) $55

Baseball

[NY Giants. - A 1936 Giants vs. Yankees World Series program, sgd by 25 members of the NY Giants, sold at CNY on 21 June 1989, lot 215, for $1,100.]

Document, 8 May 1951. (91) $200

— BROOKLYN DODGERS. - The signatures of 24 members of the team, 1952, 2 pp, 4 by 6 inches (card), sold at Dar on 10 Apr 1991, lot 54, for $110. 91

— NY GIANTS & BROOKLYN DODGERS. - Photograph, 3 Oct 1951, 10 by 8 inches, of Bobby Thomson; sgd by Thomson & 17 other members of both teams. (91) $475

— NY YANKEES. - The signatures of 31 members, on a color print picturing the team, 1961, 36 by 24 inches, in a tube, sold at Dar on 4 Oct 1990, lot 125, for $375. 91

— SCHNEIDER, L. E. - Orig drawing, giant baseball on holder with inscr referring to an annual dinner of the Baseball Writers Association, 31 Jan 1960. 16 by 20 inches. In ink. Sgd by 36 baseball players (including Ty Cobb) & notables. Framed. (91) $900

Basilius Valentinus

Ms, Chymische Schriften Soo veel alss daar van syn in twee delen verdeeld uyt het hoogduyts vertaalt..., [Netherlands, after 1677]. Over 750 pp, folio, in contemp calf bdg. In a single hand, with over 40 full-page water color plates of alchemical subjects & mumerous smaller illusts. (91) £22,000

Bassompierre, Francois de, 1579-1646

Ds, [n.d.]. (88) DM260

Bataille, Georges, 1897-62

ALs, 23 July 1948. (91) DM360

Bateman, Henry Mayo, 1887-1970

Original drawing, The colonel who found nothing in his Christmas pudding; possibly ptd in The Sporting and Dramatic, 16 Nov 1936. (90) £850

AMERICAN BOOK PRICES CURRENT

Bateman, Thomas, 1821-61

Autograph Ms, notebook relating to his excavations in Derbyshire, [c.Mar 1852 to Aug 1860]. (89) £500

Bates, Edward, 1793-1869

Franking signature, [24 Feb 1862]. Alexander collection. (90) $100

Bates, Katherine Lee, 1859-1929

Ls, 14 Jan 1924. Byer collection. (90) $300

Bates, Leo

Original drawings, (25), to illus R. Archives of J. M. Dent & Son. (88) £250

Bateson, William, 1861-1926

ALs, 17 Sept 1913. (88) $150

Bathory, Sophia, Princess, Consort of Gyoergi II Rakoczi of Transylvania, 1629-80

Ls, 13 June 1680. (89) DM720

Batsch, Karl Ferdinand, 1831-98

ALs, 8 Aug 1856. 4 pp, 8vo. Recipient unnamed. Reporting about military action after the landing of a naval unit on the coast of Morocco. (91) DM1,900

Batten, John Dickson, 1860-1932

Collection of ALs & orig drawing, [n.d.] & 1896. (90) £100

Battle of Waterloo

[Contemp copies of letters from Capt. Taylor & Lieut. Gen. Sir Henry Clinton, 21 & 23 June 1815, 33 pp, size not stated, describing the battle, sold at pn on 16 Mar 1989, lot 56, for £130 to Shutter.]

Letter, 15 July 1815. (90) £900

— BOULTER, SAMUEL. - ALs, 23 Sept 1815, 3 pp, folio. To his brother. Detailed description of the battle. Fold splits. Framed. (88) £580

— SOUTHEY, ROBERT. - Transcript, poem on the battle, illus with views in pencil. 50 pp, 8vo. Contemp calf. De Lancey bookplate. (89) £100

See also: Kempt, Sir James
See also: Nicolay, Sir William
See also: Peninsular War
See also: Sondes, George John Watson Milles

Baudelaire, Charles, 1821-67
Collection of ALs & ADs, 11 June 1864. 3 pp, 8vo. To Albert Collignon. Offering poems for print, & including a receipt for fees. (90) DM2,800

ALs, 16 Dec 1853. 4 pp, 8vo, in purple mor bdg. To Auguste Poulet-Malassis. Urgently requesting money so he can continue his trans of Poe. Martin collection. (90) FF85,000

— 16 Jan 1858. 1 p, 8vo. Recipient unnamed. Hoping for financial support from the government. Sgd C.B. (90) DM3,250

— 20 July 1859. 4 pp, 4to. To his mother Madame Aupick. Responding to her questions, complaining about his financial problems, etc. Spotted. (88) $2,000

— [early Nov 1859]. (89) £550

— 13 Mar 1860. 4 pp, folio, in a folder. To Auguste Poulet-Malassis. Sending the text of 2 poems & urging recipient to provide some publicity for Les Fleurs du Mal. Martin collection. (90) FF315,000

— 1 Jan 1864. 1 p, 4to. Recipient unnamed. Encouraging him to call on [Theophile] Gautier. (90) £1,300

— [c.21 May 1864]. (90) £800

— [6 July 1865]. (90) £600

— [n.d.], "Sunday". (90) £650

ADs, 21 July 1859. 1 p, 8vo. Receipt for fees for his contributions to Eugene Crepet's anthology. (88) DM1,600

— 13 Oct 1862. (89) £800

Baudouin, King of the Belgians
ALs, 10 June 1951. (90) DM700

Bauer, Andreas Friedrich, 1783-1860
ALs, 10 Feb 1836. (90) DM900

Bauer, Otto, 1881-1938
Ls, 26 July 1919. (89) DM600

Bauer, Wilhelm Sebastian Valentin, 1822-76
ALs, 1 Dec 1865. 4 pp, 4to. To Dr. Weber. Informing him that the Prussian admiralty is not interested in his submarine, & requesting support for projected experiments on Lake Constance. (90) DM5,500

Bauer, Wolfgang
Autograph Ms, poems, Das stille Schiff, 1 Nov 1967 to 13 Sept 1968. 75 pp, 4to, in sketchbook. Sgd twice on tp; poems mostly initialled. Including 36 pencil drawings, each sgd. With related material. (90) DM1,900

Bauernfeld, Eduard von, 1802-90
Autograph Ms, poem, An Oesterreich 1842; [n.d.]. (90) DM210

Baumeister, Willi, 1889-1955
Ls s (2), 12 Mar 1950 & 17 Oct 1954. (88) DM420

Ls, 16 Feb 1942. (88) DM240

— 25 May 1949. 2 pp, 8vo. To Hjalmar Westerdahl. Informing him about his recent work. (90) DM1,600

— 25 Apr 1954. (88) DM340

Baumhauer, Hans
Original drawings, (144), to illus books by Selma Lagerlof & Mary M. Archives of J. M. Dent & Son. (90) £360

Bause, Johann Friedrich, 1738-1814
ALs, 1 Mar 1788. (90) DM220

Bawden, Edward
Original drawings, (3), dust jacket designs for de Quincey's The English Mail Coach, & others. Archives of J. M. Dent & Son. (88) £500

Baxter, Doreen
Original drawings, (34), to illus New Fairy Tales, 1955. In ink & watercolor (5) or ink. Mostly sgd. Various sizes. Archives of J. M. Dent & Son. (88) £1,100

— Original drawings, (42), to illus Wonderland Tales, 1958. In ink & watercolor (5) or ink. Mostly sgd. Various sizes. Archives of J. M. Dent & Son. (88) £1,150

Baynes, Pauline
Original drawings, (13), to illus Christopher Tower's Oultre Jourdain, 1982. (90) £950

— Original drawings, (2), demon before archers, & horse & executioner, to illus The Enchanted Horse, by Rosemary Harris, 1982. (90) £460

— Original drawings, (2), gouache cover designs for Shadow on the Sun, by

BAYNES

Rosemary Harris, & anr book; [n.d.]. (90) £280
— Original drawings, (3), gouache cover designs for stories by George Macdonald, [n.d.]. (90) £320
— Original drawings, (3), to illus J. (90) £850
— Original drawings, (7), to illus Beatrix Potter's Little Mouse, ptd in Country Tales, 1987. (90) £580
— Original drawings, dust jacket design & alternative upper cover for Fairy Tales from the British Isles, [n.d.]. (90) £300
Original drawing, cover design for J. (90) £1,000
— Original drawing, oriental horseman fleeing from demon astride a black steed, to illus The Enchanted Horse, by Rosemary Harris, 1982. (90) £400
— Original drawing, oriental horseman riding through the night sky, to illus The Enchanted Horse, by Rosemary Harris, 1982. (90) £600
— Original drawing, servants carrying jewels to an elderly man, to illus The Enchanted Horse, by Rosemary Harris, 1982. (90) £280

Bazaine, Francois Achille, 1811-88
ALs, 7 Oct 1866. (91) DM700
— 7 Feb 1871. (90) DM360

Bazan, Alvaro de, 1526-88
ALs, [n.d., c.1565]. (88) £350

Beach, Amy Marcy Cheney, 1867-1944
Series of 4 A Ls s, 5 Nov 1934 to 23 Jan 1935. (90) $325
Autograph quotation, 6 bars from Grandmother's Garden, 15 July 1925. (91) $200
Photograph, sgd & inscr, Sept 1943. (90) DM280

Beale, Edward Fitzgerald, 1822-93
ALs, 23 July [1846]. (88) $800

Bealing, Richard
Typescript, Boadicea; or, The British Queen. A Tragedy. 1722. 69 leaves, 330mm by 206mm, in contemp mor gilt with vellum leaf mtd on rear pastedown bearing genealogical tree of author's family in gold & colors, sgd Tho. Harvey, 1730. Fleming estate.

AMERICAN BOOK PRICES CURRENT

(89) $1,300

Beardsley, Aubrey, 1872-98
Original drawing, artist in Renaissance costume painting at his easel while Death paints the artist from the other side, to illus Sydney Smith & Richard Brinsley Sheridan's Bons Mots, 1893. 93mm by 80mm. In pen-&-ink. Koch Foundation. (90) $3,000
— Original drawing, ink port of H[yppolyte] Taine, ptd in Pall Mall Budget, 9 Mar 1893. 251mm by 178mm. Captioned Henri Taine. (90) £1,200
— Original drawing, woman in long gown reaching for fruit in a bowl, ptd in The Early Work of Aubrey Beardsley, 1899. 270mm by 137mm. In ink. Framed. (90) £12,000
ALs, [c.Mar 1894]. 3 pp, 8vo. To John Lane. Insisting that he print a drawing of a fat woman resembling Whistler's wife, captioned A Study in Major Lines. Including ink self port pointing to a noose suspended from a gallows on 1st page. Koch Foundation. (90) $9,000
— [dated by recipient 10 Jan 1895]. 3 pp, 4to. To Mr. Thomas. Sending thanks fo the Autobiography & the printer's proofs. (91) $1,200
— [n.d.]. (89) £880
— JOHNSON, LIONEL. - ALs, 30 Mar 1898. 6 pp, 8vo. To Louise Imogen Guiney. Discussing Beardsley's conversion to Catholicism. With transcript. Doheny collection. (89) $3,800

Beasley, Reuben G.
Ls, 14 Feb 1812. (90) $200

Beatles, The
[3 photographs of the Beatles in the Star Club, [c.1962], 24cm by 31cm, sold at S on 12 Sept 1988, lot 146, for £620.]
[A Pound note & a photograph, 14cm by 17.5cm, each sgd by all 4 Beatles, 2 Nov 1963, sold at S on 12 Sept 1988, lot 162, for £350.]
[The television production script for "It's The Beatles!", recorded 7 Dec 1963, length not stated, 33cm by 20cm, sgd by all 4, sold at S on 12 Sept 1988, lot 178, for £800.]

1987 - 1991 · AUTOGRAPHS & MANUSCRIPTS — BEATLES

[A piece of paper sgd by all 4, c.1963, framed with an ad for their 1st albums, 15.5 by 11.5 inches, sold at P on 18 June 1988, lot 759, for $900.]

[A group of 10 Beatles signatures, 1963, on pages of 2 scrap albums & autograph album, sold at S on 12 Sept 1988, lot 137, for £450.]

[Their signatures, c.1963/64, on a piece of paper inscr in Ringo Starr's hand, framed with LP cover, 20 by 16 inches, sold at pnNy on 3 Dec 1988, lot 280, for $1,100.]

[A copy of the Clipper magazine, Jan - Feb 1964, sgd by all 4, with related material, sold at P on 18 June 1988, lot 615, for $700.]

[2 B.O.A.C. ticket portions each for George Harrison, John Lennon, & Paul McCartney, 1 June [19]64, 8.5cm by 20.5cm, sold at S on 12 Sept 1988, lot 179, for $550.]

[A souvenir program for A Hard Day's Night, Liverpool, 10 July 1964, sgd by all 4 & Brian Epstein, framed, 10.5 by 8 inches, sold at P on 18 June 1988, lot 768, for $3,250.]

[A Sept 1964 issue of Hit Parade, featuring autographed photo portraits of all 4 Beatles, with related material, sold at CNY on 21 June 1989, lot 441, for $900.]

[Their signatures, c.1967, individually mtd & framed with group photograph from LP sleeve, 18 by 26 inches, sold at pnNy on 3 Dec 1988, lot 271, for $1,700.]

[A program for the premiere of the film The Magic Christian, 11 Dec 1969, 28cm by 21.5cm, sgd by Ringo Starr, John Lennon & Yoko Ono, with related material, sold at S on 12 Sept 1988, lot 194, for £320.]

[A set of individual Beatles signatures, Lennon's with small facial caricature, each framed with a photograph, 12 by 16 inches, sold at pnNy on 3 Dec 1988, lot 241, for $750.]

[2 group photographs, various dates, 10 by 11 inches, each with 2 signatures & framed, sold at pnNY on 3 Dec 1988, lot 250, for $800.]

[Their signatures on individual photos, 10 by 8 inches, each inscr to Tony, sold at pnNY on 3 Dec 1988, lot 267, for $550.]

[Their signatures, n.d., on a piece of paper inscr to Wendy in Lennon's hand, framed with a group photograph, 15 by 23 inches, sold at pnNy on 3 Dec 1988, lot 282, for $2,200.]

[A card, sgd by all 4 & inscr by George Harrison, [n.d.], 3 by 2 inches, framed with a ptd group photograph, sold at Dar on 10 Apr 1991, lot 245, for $700.]

Ls, [n.d.]. Beatles Fan Club letter addressed to "Dear Mike"; sgd by all 4. Framed with a photograph. 19 by 29 inches. (88) $2,000

Note, [c.1964]. (88) £280

Ds, 1962. Salary receipt for DM2040 from the Star Club, Hamburg, sgd by Harrison. With related material. (89) £1050

Document, [c.24 Jan 1962]. 4 pp, 33cm by 21cm. Typescript carbon copy of contract with Brian Epstein; unsgd & undated. (89) £3,100

— [n.d.]. (88) $350

Christmas card, [c.1964]. (88) £220

— Anr, [c.1965]. (88) £190

Concert program, Star Matinee, 15 Oct 1961. (88) $750

— Anr, The Royal Hall, Harrowgate, 8 Mar 1963. (89) £500

— Anr, The Beatles Show, Bournemouth, Aug 1963. (88) £500

— Anr, Scottish Tour, Oct 1963. (88) £700

— Anr, Scottish Tour, Oct 1963. (88) £450

— Anr, Christmas Show 1963/64; size not stated. (89) £300

— Anr, The Beatles Show, [c.1963]. (88) £200

— Anr, [c.1963]. (88) £380

— Anr, 1963. (89) £550

— Anr, [c.1963]. (89) £800

— Anr, Dec 1964. (88) £200

— Anr, Beatles Christmas Show, [1964/65]. (88) £280

— Anr, Olympia Theatre, Paris, 1964. (89) £420

— Anr, [n.d.]. Sgd by all 4. 10.5 by 8 inches. (88) $1,400

Group photograph, [c.1963]. With anr. 2.25 by 5.75 inches & 4.25 by 5.25 inches. Both sgd by all 4 & framed. (88) $1,600

— Anr, [1963]. (88) £750

— Anr, [c.1963]. (88) £260

BEATLES

— Anr, 1964. (88) £280
— Anr, 1964. (88) £250
— Anr, [c.1964]. (88) £200
— Anr, [c.1964]. (88) £170
— Anr, [c.1964]. (88) £200
— Anr, [c.1964]. (88) £180
— Anr, [c.1964]. (88) £180
— Anr, [c.1964]. (88) £180
— Anr, [c.1964]. (88) £380
— Anr, [c.1965]. (88) £200
— Anr, [late 1960s]. (90) $950
— Anr, [n.d.]; John Lennon, Paul McCartney & George Harrison only. (88) $400
— Anr, [n.d.]. 5.25 by 4 inches. Sgd by all 4. Framed. (88) $1,100
— Anr, [n.d.]. (90) $450
Menu, 'Melody Maker' Poll Awards Winners' Luncheon, 10 Sept 1963. (89) £850
— Anr, Feb 1965. (88) £420
— Anr, 1965. (89) £280
— Anr, Supper Party following Royal World Premiere of 'Help!'; 1965. (89) £460
— Anr, 1965. (89) £350
— Anr, La Ronde Restaurant, [n.d.]. (89) £620
New Year's card, [c.1965]. (88) £230
Photograph, sgd, 1963. (89) £520
— Anr, [c.1965]. (89) £250
Photograph, sgd & inscr, 1964. (89) £220
— Anr, [c.1965]. (89) £220
Photograph, 1963, as used for record cover of "With The Beatles". (89) £550
— Anr, used for the album "Beatles for Sale"; 1964. (89) £900
— Anr, used for the album "Rubber Soul"; 1965. (89) 900
— Anr, 5 Beatles with instruments on a freight car, [n.d.]. (89) £500
Ptd photograph, [c.1963]. (88) $800
Signature, [c.10 July 1963]. (89) £250
— Anr, 1963. (88) £420
— Anr, [c.1963]. (89) £320
— Anr, in-flight position report, 10/11 June 1964; sgd by Paul McCartney, George Harrison & Jimmy Nichol. (88) £320
— Anr, 9 Oct 1964, by all 4 on front cover of The Beatles Monthly, June 1964. (88) £320
— Anr, [c.1964]. (88) £200
— Anr, [c.1964]. (88) £320
— Anr, 1964. (89) £260
— Anr, [c.1964]. (89) £250
— Anr, [n.d.]. (89) £200
— Anr, [n.d.]. (89) £380
— EPSTEIN, BRIAN. - ALs, [n.d.]. 26.5cm by 18cm. To "C". Contents not stated. Sgd Brian. On hotel letterhead. (89) £150
— MCCARTNEY, PAUL. - Autograph Ms, playlist for a charity show, [2 Dec 1963]. 1 p, 8 by 5 inches, on Grosvenor House letterhead. (88) £2,000
See also: Best, Pete
See also: McCartney, Paul

Beaton, Cecil, 1904-80
Original drawing, costume design for Barbra Streisand in Funny Girl, 1968. (89) $300
Collection of 24 A Ls s & Ls s, 1929 to 1971 & [n.d.]. About 50 pp, various sizes. To Stephen Tennant. About mutual friends, his work, etc. With related material. (89) £1,400
— Collection of 25 A Ls s & postcards, sgd, c.1937 to 1973. (88) £300
— Collection of c.100 A Ls s & postcards, sgd, [late 1940s to early 1970s]. (88) £700
A Ls s (2), [n.d.]. Koch Foundation. (90) $400
ALs, 19 July [n.y.]. Koch Foundation. (90) $350

Beatrice, Princess of Great Britain & Ireland, 1857-1944
[Her guest book containing c.100 pp with c.1,200 signatures mostly of the royal family & friends, 1873 to 1906, sold at sg on 9 Mar 1989, lot 190, for $2,600.]

Beauharnais, Eugene de, 1781-1824
[3 endorsements, sgd, on reports by the Director of Police at Milan & the Minister of Finance, 1811 & 1812, with related material, sold at star on 1 Dec 1988, lot 1036, for DM460.]
ALs, [9 Mar 1805]. (90) DM300
— 14 Feb 1818. (91) DM320
— 17 Apr 1819. (88) $140
Ls, 29 Sept 1805. (90) DM480
— 2 Mar 1808. (88) $140

— 20 June 1808. (90) DM230
— 23 July 1810. (91) $80
— 4 Dec 1817. (90) DM270
Endorsement, sgd, 8 Oct 1810. (88) DM400

Beauharnais, Hortense de, 1783-1837
ALs, 7 Nov 1819. (88) DM800
— 20 Mar 1826. (89) DM550
— 28 June 1835. (91) DM580
— 12 Mar 1829. (90) DM550
ADs, 30 Nov 1831. (90) DM440
Ds, 27 Jan 1815. (91) DM220

Beaulieu-Marconnay, Henriette von, 1773-1864
ALs, 27 Oct 1835. (90) DM420

Beaumarchais, Pierre Augustin Caron de, 1732-99
ALs, 27 Feb 1788. 2 pp, 4to. To Comtesse Fanny Beauharnais. Declining to print a satirical piece by Cubiere-Palmezeaux. (89) DM1,400
— [9 July 1796]. 1 p, 8vo. To Chalumeau. Informing him about his return from exile. Slightly def. (90) DM2,200
— [n.d.]. (91) DM720

Beaumont, Joseph, 1616-99
Ms, Annotationes in Epistolam S. (88) £600

Beauregard, Pierre G. T., 1818-93
ALs, 25 May 1861. 1 p, 4to. To C. H. Stevens. Confirming recipient's "valuable aid and services rendered°" at Fort Sumter. (91) $4,500
— 21 Feb 1862. 2 pp, 4to. To Major Gen. Earl Van Dorn. Informing him of arrangements for the defense of the Mississippi. (91) $6,000
— 25 July 1864. 1 p, 8vo. To an unnamed lady. About the bombardment of Fort Sumter. (91) $2,500
— 26 Feb [18]77. (88) $375
— 17 Apr [18]77. (88) $400
Autograph endorsement, sgd, 15 July 1863. Middendorf collection. (89) $750
Autograph telegram, sgd, 14 Apr 1865. 1 p, 100mm by 187mm. To Gen. Joseph E. Johnston. Informing him about Gen. Ferguson's problems in crossing the Yadkin River. (90) $4,200

Beauvoir, Simone de, 1908-86
Autograph Ms, dialogue with "Henri", from an unspecified work; [n.d.]. (90) DM420

Bebel, August, 1840-1913
Series of 7 A Ls s, 11 Nov 1889 to 27 Apr 1907. 17 pp, mostly 8vo. To Otto Adolf Ellissen. Mostly regarding recipient's biography of Friedrich Albert Lange. (89) DM10,500
ALs, 8 Nov 1879. 1 p, 8vo. To political friends in Philadelphia. Thanking for a donation for people deported from Berlin. On ptd appeal for contributions, 27 Oct 1879. (90) DM2,600
— 9 Nov 1888. (90) DM660
— 23 Feb 1891. (91) DM480
— 14 July 1896. 2 pp, 8vo. Recipient unnamed. Requesting information about an invention to produce gas for lighting a house. File holes. (88) DM1,050
— 6 Dec 1904. (88) DM550
— 28 Sept 1909. (90) DM750
Ls, 25 Mar 1869. (90) DM800
Collection of autograph postcard, sgd, & ADs, 1 Feb 1905 & 10 Oct 1911. 2 pp, 8vo. To Hermann Molkenbuhr, requesting some notes. Interpellation addressed to the German Chancellor regarding violations of the law on associations. With related material. (88) DM2,200
Autograph postcard, sgd, [18 Feb 1898]. (90) DM550
— STRUCK, HERMANN. - Lithographed port of Bebel, sgd; 1909. 58cm by 43.2cm. Also sgd by Bebel, in pencil. (90) DM520

Beccadelli, Lodovico, 1502-72
Ms, Vita del Card. Bembo. [c.1587]. 44 pp, 4to, in vellum. In humanist cursive script. (91) £1,100

Beccadelli Panormita, Antonius, 1394-1471
Ms, Alfonsi Regis Dicta et Facta Memoratu Digna. [Naples, c.1465-70]. 76 leaves, vellum, 220mm by 145mm, in 16th-cent vellum. With fine gold & vinestem border & 5 large illuminated initials. (91) £12,000

BECCARIA

Beccaria, Cesare Bonesana di, 1738-94
Ds s (2)3 Oct 1771 & 3 Apr 1774. (89) DM670
Ds, 3 July 1771. (90) DM380

Becher, Alfred Julius, 1803-48
ALs, 31 Mar 1847. (90) DM750

Bechstein, Ludwig, 1801-60
ALs, 8 June 1838. (88) DM600

Beck, Conrad
Autograph music, "Skizze zu einem Orchesterwerk", sgd, inscr & dated 1981. (90) DM340
Series of 7 A Ls s, 26 Aug 1927 to 2 June 1932. (90) DM550

Beck, Ludwig, 1880-1944
Collection of 7 A Ls s & AN, 1938 to 1941. 9 pp, 4to & 8vo. Recipients unnamed. About appointments, a book received, etc. (90) DM2,700

Beck, Maximilian Wladimir von, 1854-1943
ALs, 1 June 1906. (89) DM420

Beckerath, Alfred von
Autograph music, Kleiner Walzer (Capriccio) fuer Klavier, [n.d.]. (90) DM300

Beckett, Samuel, 1906-89
[His working rehearsal copy of the 1st Ed of En Attendant Godot, Paris, 1952, used for the orig production of the play in Paris, 1953, with numerous autograph annotations, additions, deletions & markings, sgd & inscr to John [Calder] & Bettina [Jonic], 31 Dec [19]64, sold at S on 13 Dec 1990, lot 209, for £30,000 to Quaritch.]
[4 ptd proof sheets of Stirrings Still with Beckett's autograph revisions, with 3 pp of typescript fragments of the work & further related material, 1988, sold at S on 13 Dec 1990, lot 215, for £1,200 to Gerard.]
[A collection of corrected & uncorrected proofs & publisher's Mss for various works sold at S on 18 July 1991, lot 276, for £1,200 to Mitchell.]
Typescript, play, Happy Days, sgd; [c.1961]. (90) £750
Collection of 2 A Ls s & autograph postcard, sgd, 10 Nov 1937, 2 Feb

AMERICAN BOOK PRICES CURRENT

1938 & [n.d.]. (90) £950
ALs, 20 Oct 1953. (90) DM550
ANs, 28 Dec 1983. (88) £160
Proof copy, All Strange Away, 1979, 8vo, in d/j. (91) £500

Beckford, William, 1760-1844
Collection of 353 A Ls s & A Ls, 4 Aug 1830 to 19 Oct 1834. Over 700 pp, 4to & 8vo. To George Clarke. "Extraordinary collection ... providing valuable insights into Beckford's avid collecting and his literary pursuits". Bradley Martin sale. (90) $140,000
— Collection of 3 A Ls s (2 initialled), 2 A Ls & AD, mostly 16 Mar 1843 to 31 Mar 1844. (88) £600
ALs, 7 Oct 1763. (89) $200

Beckmann, Johann, 1739-1811
ALs, 12 May 1791. (90) DM260

Beckmann, Max, 1884-1950
A Ls s (2), 5 Feb 1930 & 25 Mar 1931. (90) DM850
ALs, 6 May [19]13. (91) DM550
— 14 Jan 1922. (90) DM660
— 26 Sept 1927. (90) DM420
— [1927 or earlier]. (91) DM820
— 1 Nov 1947. (89) DM800

Becquerel, Antoine Cesar, 1788-1878
ALs, [n.d.]. (89) DM280

Becquerel, Henri, 1852-1908
Autograph Ms, notes regarding experiments with polonium & radium, with drawings; [n.d.]. (88) DM550

Beddington, Sir Edward, 1884-1966
Typescript, My Life. (91) £120

Bede, The Venerable, 673-735
Ms, De Natura Rerum; De Temporibus; & De Temporum Ratione; with Annales Laudunenses; Annales Trevirorum; & other scientific, cosmographical & historical texts. [Reims or Laon, 1st half of 9th cent]. 97 leaves, vellum, 260mm by 225mm. 18th-cent pigskin over medieval wooden bds with fragments of a 9th-cent Tours bible. Written by at least 4 scribes in a small Carolingian minuscule, with later additions. With 24 large or full-page diagrams including simplified world map, & full-length

contemp drawing of a man holding a branch. Ludwig MS.XII.3. (89) £560,000
— Ms, De Templo Salomonis, & 4 other texts. [Tournai, early 12th cent]. 75 leaves (1 lacking), vellum, 295mm by 205mm. 19th-cent blindstamped calf, rebacked. In brown ink in Caroline minuscule by at least 2 scribes. Some initials in red; 2 large decorated initials in colors. Doheny collection. (88) £50,000
— Ms, Expositio secundum Lucam et Actum Apostolorum. [Naples, c.1481]. 310 leaves (1 blank, 1 lacking), vellum, 379mm by 270mm, in later vellum over pastebds, rebacked. In red & black ink in a rounded semi-humanistic minuscule. With incipits & explicits in dark blue & burnished gold capitals, small illuminated initials throughout, & over 100 large & 7 extremely large illuminated floral initials. Written for the Royal Library at Naples by Venceslaus Crispus. Astor MS.A.26. (88) £26,000

Beebe, Lucius
Series of 4 Ls s [n.d.]. (91) $60

Beecham, Sir Thomas, 1879-1961
Autograph music, 2 songs, A Country Guy, sgd & dated 24 Aug 1898, & A Slumber Song, [n.d.]. (88) £200
Typescript, draft of introduction to a book about Frederick Delius, sgd; [n.d.]. (89) $375

Beer, Michael, 1800-33
ALs, 10 June 1831. 4 pp, 8vo. To Heinrich Heine. Thanking for a publication & making plans for joint holidays at Boulogne. (90) DM2,800

Beerbohm, Max, 1872-1956
Autograph Ms, draft of a review of B. (91) £900
Ms, drafts of a letter & notes concerning a biography of Brandon Thomas, [n.d.]. (91) £600
Typescript, review of Bertita Harding's biography of Duse, 31 Jan 1950. 5 pp, 4to. Including autograph revisions & directions to the ptr, & covering ALs to Leonard Russell. With related material. (90) £1,300

ALs, 18 May 1907. (91) $375
— 3 June 1914 [corrected to 1920 by recipient]. 4 pp, 8vo. To Thomas Moult. Denying that the character of Enoch Soames is based on Ernest Dowson. Koch Foundation. (90) $1,500
— 28 July 1928. (90) £190
— [n.d.]. Doheny collection. (89) $350
— [n.d.]. (91) $300
Series of 9 Ls s, 1954 to 1955. (88) £400
Caricature, pen-&-ink drawing of Oscar Wilde, sgd with monogram & inscr The House of Pomegranates by the Master; [c.1891]. 9 by 6.75 inches. With letter of authentication. (91) £2,000
— Anr, "Algernon Swinburne taking his great new friend Gosse to see Rossetti", in pencil & watercolor; sgd & dated 1916. 294mm by 300mm. 1st version of illus reproduced in Rossetti and his Circle, 1922. (88) £2,600
— Anr, Menage a Trois, Mussolini on a couch with a young girl, with man in uniform looking from window; sgd & dated Apr 1924. 384mm by 291mm. Framed. (89) £3,600

Beethoven, Ludwig van, 1770-1827
Autograph Ms, conversation, comment & shopping list from his conversation books, [c.Summer 1825?]. 4 pp, 8vo. 1 p in the hand of Carl Holz. (91) £11,500
— Autograph Ms, teaching notes dealing with counterpoint & double counterpoint, possibly written for Archduke Rudolf; [c.1805-1810]. 2 pp, folio. Including 10 bars of music. (90) £24,000
Autograph music, alterations & corrections for the 1st, 2d & last movements of the 9th Symphony, [late 1824 or early 1825]. 4 pp, folio; up to 16 staves per page. With [autograph?] mathematical calculations on last page; some annotations in Ferdinand Wolanek's hand. (88) £85,000
— Autograph music, leaf from an early sketchbook containing sketches for the 1st movement of his String Quartet in B-flat, Opus 18, No. 6. [late Spring-Summer 1800] 2 pp, oblong 4to. Czerny-Leschetizky-Zabriskie-Manhattan College

BEETHOVEN

Ms (91) $68,000
— Autograph music, sketch leaf for the 1st movement of his Cello Sonata in G minor, Op. 5 no 2, & 3 other pieces, [c.1796]. 2 pp, folio; 15 staves each. (89) $50,000
— Autograph music, sketches for Piano Concerto No 5, Op. 73, [early 1809]. 4 pp, 23.5cm by 30.5cm; 14 staves each. (88) DM110,000
— Autograph music, sketches for the overture to Koenig Stephan, Op. 117, & for no 6a of Die Ruinen von Athen, Op. 113, [1811]. 2 pp, 323mm by 226mm. Written in ink on recto on 16 staves, in pencil on verso on 7 staves. 3 stitch holes in inner margin. (88) £15,500
— Autograph music, sketches for the piano trio in B flat major, Op. 97 ("Archduke"), & the incidental music to Koenig Stephan, [1810 or 1811]. 2 pp, folio. Irregularly cut; stitch holes. With autograph inscr by Robert Schumann in margin. (89) £30,000
— Autograph music, sketches for the 1st movement of the 9th Symphony & for the song Ruf vom Berge; [c.1816]. 2 pp, folio. Inscr in a contemp hand. (90) £80,000
— Autograph music, sketch-leaf containing drafts for the string quartet in C major, Op. 29, & other works, c.April to Nov 1801. 2 pp, 220mm by 302mm, 12 staves each. Prinzmetal & Ammann collections. (88) $40,000
— Autograph music, sketch-leaf containing early ideas for the slow movement of Piano Sonata Op. 106 ("Hammerklavier"), [c.1818]. 2 pp, folio. Mostly in brown ink on 16 staves per page. With numerous revisions. Browned. (88) £20,000
— Autograph music, Sonata for Violoncello & Piano in A major, Op. 69, 1st movement; [c.1808]. 16 pp, folio. Working draft; sgd. Salzer collection. (90) £480,000
ALs, 15 Dec [1800]. 3 pp, 4to. To Franz Anton Hoffmeister. Offering 4 recent works for publication. (91) £40,000
— 8 Apr 1802. 4 pp, 4to. To [Franz Hofmeister]. Joking about the concordat with Napoleon, agreeing to write a sonata, & discussing the ptg of several works. (90) £44,000
— [c.1810]. 1 p, 4to. To [Joseph Anton Ignaz von Baumeister]. Requesting him to send a copy of the Sonata for Horn & Piano in F major to Baroness von Ertmann. Tipped to larger leaf. Barrett collection. (89) $26,000
— 10 Feb 1811. 3 pp, 4to. To Bettina Brentano. Praising Goethe & referring to his incidental music to Egmont, recipient's marriage, members of the Brentano family, etc. Salzer collection. (90) £86,000
— [c.1814]. 2 pp, 8vo. To Artaria & Co. Asking for the loan of the piano score of Fidelio. Salzer collection. (90) £9,500
— [c.1814]. 1 p, 4to. To Friedrich Treitschke. Announcing that he will start to work on the song [Germania], & complaining about the preparation of a concert. Salzer collection. (90) £20,000
— [summer 1815]. 3 pp, 8vo. To [J. Xaver] Brauchle. Announcing his visit as soon as his health improves & promising to bring 2 sonatas. (88) DM36,000
— 25 Feb 1817. 2 pp, 4to. To Moritz von Fries. About the publication of his arrangements of Scottish songs. (91) £12,000
— [1817/18?]. 1 p, 8vo. To [Joseph] Blahetka. Announcing his visit. Sgd B. Was mtd; repaired. (89) DM22,000
— [1817/18?]. 1 p, 8vo. To [Joseph] Blahetka. Announcing his visit. (91) DM18,000
— 5 Mar 1818. 3 pp, 4to. To Ferdinand Ries. About the possibility of visiting England, music & musicians in London, etc. (91) £22,000
— 28 Mar 1826. 3 pp, 4to. To his pbr B. Schott's Soehne. Informing them that the Prussian King has accepted the dedication of the 9th Symphony. Faded. (91) DM32,000
— [late Sept 1826]. 3 pp, 4to. To Ignaz Czapka. Suggesting that his nephew Carl should spend some time with him before joining the army. Seal tear. (89) £12,500
AL, [Jan 1818]. 2 pp & portion of conjugate leaf, 8vo. To [Nanette Streicher]. Fragment, complaining about his servants. (91) £4,800

— [c.1825]. 3 pp, 4to. To Johann van Beethoven. Requesting return of 2 scores for copying & revisions. Seal tear with loss of signature. (90) £8,000

Ls, 13 Oct [1]826. 1 p, 4to. To the pbr Adolf Martin Schlesinger. Important letter about the 9th Symphony, the string quartet Op. 135, the projected complete Ed of his works, etc. Text in the hand of his nephew Karl. Seal tear repaired. (89) £18,000

ANs, [before 26 Feb 1809]. 1 p, 8vo, cut from a larger sheet. To [Ignaz von Gleichenstein]. Probably regarding efforts to secure a stipend for him. Sgd with paraph. With English trans. (89) £5,200

— [early 1820s?]. 1 p, 70mm by 212mm. Recipient unnamed. Requesting that the pension for his nephew be paid to bearer. (89) $15,000

— [Apr 1825]. 1 p, 8vo, on conjugate leaf of recipient's letter addressed to him. To Ludwig Rellstab. Informing him that he is still very weak. Sgd B. In pencil. Also inscr in other hands. (90) DM7,000

AN, [c.1808]. 1 p, 8vo. Recipient unknown. 5 words, expecting recipient at an inn. (91) DM4,100

— [n.d., c.8 Aug 1826]. 1 p, 140mm by 229mm. To [Karl Holz]. Asking for the name of a police official, & mentioning that Karl was taken away by the police. In pencil. (88) £6,200

ADs, 1 Oct 1817. 2 pp, folio. Receipt for 600 florins from Prince Kinsky's treasury. With subsequent autograph correction of date; witnessed in anr hand. (91) £12,500

Ds, 26 June 1823. 1 p, 4to. Receipt for 20 ducats from the Dresden theater for the score of Fidelio; 3 autograph words. With contemp endorsements. Margin def. (88) DM30,000

Engraving, 1815. 17cm by 11cm. By Riedel after a port by Louis Letronne; sgd by Beethoven & inscr to von Molt. (91) £15,000

— FORGERY. - Musical Ms, [late 19th cent?]. 1 p, c.14.5cm by 21cm. Fragment; 14 bars on 6 staves. (89) DM420

— KALKBRENNER, FRIEDRICH WILHELM. - ALs, 26 Apr 1824. 2 pp, folio. To Ignaz Moscheles. About the reception of Beethoven's music in London. In French. With related material. (88) £300

— THOMAS BOOSEY & CO. - Ls, 24 Oct 1820. 3 pp, 4to. To A. M. Schlesinger. Discussing the publication of Beethoven's work in England & other publishing matters. Seal tear. (88) £800

Begin, Menachem
Photograph, sgd, [n.d.]. (89) $75
See also: Carter, James Earl ("Jimmy") & Others

Behmer, Marcus, 1879-1958
A Ls s (2), 15 May & 16 July 1950. (88) DM600

Behring, Emil von, 1854-1917
Autograph Ms, notebook containing scientific notes & programs, drafts of letters & lectures, reports, statistics & calculations, etc., 1895. 127 pp, 4to; disbound. (91) DM12,000

Collection of ALs & 2 autograph postcards, sgd, 9 to 29 Mar 1900. 3 pp, 8vo, & cards. To an unnamed colleague, & to Dr. F. Schaudinn. About scientific research regarding malaria. (89) DM1,700

ALs, 27 July 1896. (91) DM900

— 12 Jan 1900. 4 pp, 8vo. To Paul Ehrlich. Reporting about his experiments with diphtheria & tetanus bacteria. (91) DM4,000

Belcher, Jonathan, 1682-1757
ALs, 22 Nov 1718. (91) $220

— 16 Dec [1719]. (90) $300

Ds, 1720. (89) $55

— 1750. (89) $130

Belgium
— FYLER, GEORGE. - Autograph Ms, Journal of a Tour ... to Antwerp, Dec 1832. 150 pp, 8vo. Def half calf bdg. Contemp maps & engravings tipped in. (89) £200

Bell, Alexander Graham, 1847-1922
Ls, 8 Mar 1917. (90) $425

Signature, 15 Apr 1896. (91) $350

Bell, John, 1797-1869

Franking signature, [6 July n.y.]. Alexander collection. (90) $100

— Anr, [1 Sept, n.y.]. Alexander collection. (90) $95

Bellarmine, Roberto Francesco Romolo, Saint, 1542-1621

ALs, 5 Feb 1598. Doheny collection. (89) $800

AL, 30 Jan 1614. 1 p, folio. To Archduchesses Maria Christina & Eleonore. Draft, responding to their letter (on verso) requesting clarification of 2 conflicting papal briefs. In Latin. (88) DM1,400

Belliard, Augustin Daniel, Comte, 1769-1832

Ls, [4 Oct 1805]. (89) DM460

Bellini, Vincenzo, 1801-35

Autograph music, drafts of orchestral music for operas, including 2 substantial sketches, [c.1834]. 1 p, 17.5cm by 26cm, cut from larger sheet. (91) £3,800

— Autograph music, score for 2d oboe of a Tantum ergo in G major, [c.1820]. 5 lines on 1 p, c.23cm by 27.5cm. With name & title at head. (88) DM3,400

— Autograph music, sketches for operatic works & a piano piece in F major, [mid- to late 1820s]. 2 pp, folio; 16 staves each. Frayed. Note of authentication by Francesco Mantica at bottom. (89) £2,100

ALs, [Summer 1827?]. 1 p, 4to. To Felice Romani. Discussing the time for a meeting. Trimmed; laid down. (91) £1,200

— [1827-1833?]. 1 p, 16mo. To an unnamed composer [Mercadante?]. Regretting that he is unable to meet him as agreed. (91) £1,800

— 12 Nov [18]28. (90) £650

— 7 Oct [1834]. 4 pp, 8vo. To Felice Romani. Suggesting they resume collaboration after a long rift in their relationship. (91) £2,000

— 1 July [18]35. 3 pp, 8vo. To the singer Barroilhet. Interesting letter about I Puritani. Seal tear. (89) £2,600

— 11 May [n.y.]. (88) £1,000

Bellmer, Hans, 1902-75

ALs, 9 Jan 1951. (89) DM420

— 6 June 1951. (90) DM660

Belloc, Hilaire, 1870-1953

Autograph Ms, working drafts for his sonnet To Merivale Knight...; [n.d.]. (90) £160

Collection of 150 A Ls s & Ls s, 1924 to 1942. Over 550 pp, various sizes. To Lady Lovat. About his work, activities & opinions, mentioning other authors, sending poems & drawings (included), etc. (90) £8,000

Bellow, Saul

[An extensive & evidently complete collection of Mss, typescripts, galley proofs, correspondence & ancillary material for Mr. Sammler's Planet, c.1969, in 64 manila folders in 5 archive boxes, sold at P on 7 June 1988, lot 67, for $60,000.]

Bellows, George Wesley, 1882-1925

ALs, [c.1915]. (89) $425

— [c.1915]. (89) $325

Belmont, August, 1816-90

Collection of 6 A Ls s & Ls, 1852 to 1889. (89) $900

Beltrami, Giacomo Constantino, 1779-1855

Transcript, La decouverte des sources du Mississippi, [after 1824]. 286 pp, 302mm by 206mm. Fair copy. With Ms map by Ph. Giovannini, Carte des Sources du Mississippi, 381mm by 294mm. 19th cent half green mor. (88) $3,500

Belzoni, Giovanni Battista, 1778-1823

ALs, 12 July 1821. (89) £100

Bemelmans, Ludwig, 1898-1962

ALs, 17 Jan 1961. Byer collection. (90) $120

Bence-Jones, Henry

[A collection of papers of Dr. Bence-Jones, Secretary to the Royal Institution, several hundred items, sold at S on 15 Dec 1988, lot 180, for £1,800.]

Bendemann, Eduard, 1811-89
A Ls s (2), 2 Apr 1833 & 10 June 1834. (88) DM900
ALs, 11 Aug 1835. (90) DM280

Benedict, Saint, Abbot of Monte Cassino
Ms, La Regola del Sanctissimo Padre Benedecto. [North Italy, c.1450]. 74 leaves (1 lacking), vellum, 215mm by 157mm, in Italian limp vellum gilt of c.1600. In a large rounded gothic hand. With small penwork initials throughout & large historiated initial with scrolling leafy extensions. Lower cover set with 15th-cent cut historiated initial. (91) £6,000
— Ms, Regula beatissimi patris Benedicti Abbatis sanctissimi. [Milan, c.1430-1440]. 62 leaves, vellum, 170mm by 123mm, in early 19th-cent Italian blindstamped brown mor. In dark brown ink in a skillful rounded gothic hand. With 92 decorated initials with penwork & full-length extensions, & very large historiated initial by the Master of the Vitae Imperatorum within full border incorporating arms of the Venetian family of Loredano. Astor MS.A.25. (88) £19,000
— Ms, the Rule of St. Benedict, in Latin, with resolutions of the Salzburg chapter regarding rules for the province of Salzburg, 1275 & 1282. [Salzburg, late 13th cent]. 14 leaves, vellum, 143mm by 103mm. In black ink in a gothic textura. Some marginal defects. (89) DM3,200
— Ms, The Rule of St. Benedict, with the Privileges of the Order of Santa Justina in Padua & other texts, in Latin. [Padua, late 15th cent]. 134 leaves (1 lacking, 33 added later), 207mm by 155mm, in 19th-cent English russia gilt. In a formal rounded gothic hand with very many later additions in a variety of hands. With red & blue initials throughout. Phillipps Ms.16253. (91) £9,500
— Ms, the Rule of St. Benedict, in Latin & German, with office for admission to the Benedictine Order & Pontifical Mass. [Rhineland, Schuttern Abbey, 1593]. 182 leaves, 197mm by 150mm. Contemp blindstamped calf, rebacked. Latin text in a careful roman hand, German trans in a small cursive hand with headings & initials in large calligraphic gothic script. With c.200 large painted initials in 2 colors. (88) £1,100

Benedict, Sir Julius, 1804-85
[A group of 9 A Ls s addressed to Benedict by leading 19th-cent musicians, 1836 to 1864 & [n.d.], mainly 8vo, sold at S on 21 Nov 1990, lot 201, for £850 to Dr. Sam.]

Benedict XIV, Pope, 1675-1758
Ls, 4 Apr 1733. Byer collection. (90) $375
Document, 27 Apr 1745. (89) DM320
— 22 May 1749. (90) DM360
— [19 June] 1755. (88) DM400

Benedict XV, Pope, 1854-1922
ALs, 30 Aug 1918. 2 pp, 8vo (lettercard). To Giuseppe Sanfermo. About recipient's health, & sending money for masses. (90) DM1,100
Photograph, sgd, 30 Aug 1917. 23cm by 17.5cm (image). Sgd on mount, with benediction. (90) DM1,250

Benedictine Order
[A collection of 22 documents relating to the Benedictine Convent of Santa Croce in the Giudecca, Venice, 1435 to 1802, sold at CNY on 17 Oct 1988, lot 1061, for $8,000 to Salloch.]
Ms, precepts & dispensations; fragment. [Northern England, Durham?, early 15th cent]. 52 leaves only, 190mm by 130mm, disbound. In brown ink in a neat minuscule & cursive bookhand by 3 scribes. (89) £1,800

Benes, Eduard, 1884-1948
Photograph, sgd & inscr, 28 May 1937. (89) DM220
— Anr, [n.d.]. (90) DM280

Benet, Stephen Vincent, 1898-1943
ALs, 10 Mar 1940. Byer collection. (90) $325

Ben-Gurion, David, 1886-1973
ALs, 19 May [19]54. (90) $250
— 1 Mar 1955. 1 p, 8vo. To Shmuel Dayan. Stating "that war, possibly a decisive one, is imminent." (91) $2,000
— 10 Nov [19]63. (91) $225
— 8 Apr 1965. (88) $100
— 27 Jan 1966. (91) $160

BEN-GURION

— 23 Feb 1967. (91) $210
— 26 Nov 1967. (88) $260
— 19 Oct 1969. (88) $550
— 3 Jan 1970. (88) $275
— 6 Dec [19]70. (90) $230
— 19 Jan 1971. (90) $250
— 5 May 1971. (90) $260
— [n.d.]. (89) $230
Ls, 23 Apr 1955. (89) DM650
— 14 Jan 1956. (91) $600
— 29 Mar 1956. (91) $650
— 13 Apr 1956. (90) $600
— 15 May 1956. (91) $600
— 23 Sept 1956. (91) $700
— 22 Apr 1957. 1 p, 8vo. To Moshe Dayan. Congratulating him & his commanders on their victory in the Sinai. (91) $4,750
Group photograph, [July 1957]. (91) $190
Photograph, sgd, [1950s]. (91) $375
— Anr, [n.d.]. (91) $225
— Anr, [n.d.]. (88) DM240
Signature, on ptd typescript letter of Eliahu Epstein to President Truman, notifying him that "Israel has been proclaimed as an independent republic"; with typescript copy of Truman's statement recognizing the State of Israel below, 14 May 1948. (90) $950

Benjamin, Judah P., 1811-84
ALs, 21 Feb 1865. 2 pp, 4to. To Jefferson Davis. Offering to resign as Sec of State in Davis's cabinet. (89) $7,000
Ds, 23 Apr 1865. (88) $350

Benjamin, Walter, 1892-1940
Autograph Ms, compass-rose to determine the relationship between success & conviction, with Don Quichote in the center, 17 May 1932. 1 p, 4to. Sgd & inscr to Marietta Noeggerath. (91) DM6,500
ALs, 18 Nov 1930. 1 p, 4to. To Bernard von Brentano. About their plans to publish a literary journal. (91) DM2,400
— 26 Oct 1939. 2 pp, 8vo. To Bernard von Brentano. From internment camp, referring to his own & recipient's recent publications. In French. (91) DM4,000
Ls, 11 Oct 1930. 1 p, 4to. To Bernard von Brentano. Sending a review of a work by Kaestner. (91) DM1,500

Benn, Gottfried, 1886-1956
Autograph Ms, medical recipe, [n.d.]. (91) DM550
ALs, 9 May 1936. 1 p, 4to. To Alexander Amersdorffer. Referring to an unfavorable review of his poems in a Nazi publication. (91) DM2,600
— 2 Mar 1941. 1 p, 4to. To Alexander Amersdorffer. About Oskar Loerke's death. (91) DM4,200
— 26 Mar 1949. 1 p, 8vo. To Adolf Stier tom Moehlen. Asking to be informed about his work. With related material. (89) DM1,100
Ls, 14 Oct 1927. (88) £180
— 14 Oct 1927. 1 p, 4to. To the Ed of the journal Literarische Welt. Declining to review Paul de Kruif's book. (91) DM1,300

Bennett, Arnold, 1867-1931
Autograph Ms, essay on the art of writing for his column Books & Persons, 1 June 1929. (90) $160
Collection of 10 A Ls s & 17 Ls s, 22 Nov 1916 to 8 Sept 1921. (90) £720
— Collection of 2 A Ls s & 8 Ls s, 19 Mar 1927 to 24 Dec 1929. (88) £240

Bennett, William Sterndale, 1816-1875
Autograph music, 17 early compositions, 1829 to 1832 & [n.d.]. 28 pp & blanks, 14cm by 23.5cm, in brown half lea bdg. 4 works sgd at head; also sgd on flyleaf. (90) DM3,400

Benson, Edward Frederic, 1867-1940
[A collection of typescripts & galley proofs of short stories & articles, some with autograph corrections, 1901 & [n.d.], c.160 pp, 4to & folio, sold at S on 21 July 1988, lot 149, for £500 to Ferret Fantasy.]

Bentham, Jeremy, 1748-1832
A Ls s (2), 17 Oct 1803 & 10 Nov 1823. (91) £780
ALs, 21 Nov 1797. (89) £400

Bentley, Nicolas Clerihew, 1907-78
Original drawings, (21), to illus Stanley B. Archives of J. M. Dent & Son. (88) £100

Benton, Thomas Hart, 1782-1858
ALs, 23 Feb 1838. Alexander collection. (90) $100
— 13 Dec 1920. Alexander collection. (90) $90
Franking signature, [n.d.]. (88) $55
— Anr, [Feb 22, n.y.]. Alexander collection. (90) $75

Ben-Zvi, Itzhak, 1884-1963
Ls, 19 Feb 1946. (91) $150

Berard, Louis
Series of 94 A Ls s, 15 Dec 1706 to 7 Oct 1711. 185 pp, various sizes. To Thomas Osborne, Duke of Leeds. Reporting in detail about the European education of recipient's grandsons. (90) $2,000

Berdyaev, Nikolai Aleksandrovich, 1874-1948
Autograph postcard, sgd, 16 Jan [1925]. (90) DM240

Berg, Alban, 1885-1935
[A collection of papers relating to Berg, including ptd request for help for Schoenberg issued in Berg's name, Sept 1911, sold at star on 10 Mar 1988, lot 758, for DM650.]
[A collection of material relating to his opera Wozzeck, mostly ptd or typescript, with some autograph comments, sold at star on 10 Mar 1988, lot 760, for DM1,300.]
[A collection of 15 documents and receipts, mostly accomplished or annotated by Berg, 1933 & 1934, sold at S on 15 Nov 1988, lot 1759, for £350 to Schneider.]
Autograph Ms, copy of an article pbd in the Freiburger Tagespost, 16 May 1934, reporting about a conference denouncing Berg & others. (88) DM650
— Autograph Ms, draft for a tp for the musical journal 23, [winter 1931/32]. (88) DM550
Autograph transcript, Arnold Schoenberg. Stefan George-Lieder. Op. 15, [n.d.]. 4 pp, 33.5cm by 27cm; 14 staves each. Scored for voice & piano; some corrections. (89) DM9,500
ALs, 5 Oct 1919. 2 pp, 12mo (lettercard). To Gottfried Feist. Discussing the program of a concert. (88) DM4,400
— 5 Oct 1923. (90) £350
— 23 Oct 1931. 2 pp, 8vo. To [Robert Kolisko?]. About performances of Wozzeck at Zurich. (90) DM4,000
— 10 Nov [19]31. 3 pp, 8vo. To Robert Kolisko. Making plans to attend a production of Wozzeck at Zurich. (91) £1,800
— 27 Oct [1932]. 4 pp, 8vo. To Anny. Love letter, & deploring his miserable situation. Sgd A-. In pencil. (88) DM4,200
— 23 Mar [19]32. (88) £400
— [28 Mar 1932]. 4 pp, 8vo. To [Anny A.]. Love letter, & imploring her to write. Sgd Al. In pencil. (90) DM3,600
— 1 Apr [1932]. 2 pp, 8vo. To [Anny A.]. Hoping that she & her husband will come to Vienna for a music festival. (90) DM4,400
— 20 Apr [1932]. 4 pp, 8vo. To [Anny A.]. Explaining that their projected meeting in Vienna would be facilitated by her husband's presence. (91) DM3,200
— [n.d.], "Wednesday". (91) £800
AL, 30 July 1916. (89) £400
— 6 Jan 1932. 3 pp, 8vo. To [Anny A.]. Worrying about her situation & hoping to see her. In pencil. (89) DM4,200
— 23 Mar 1932. 6 pp, 8vo. To [Anny A.]. Assuring her of his love. In pencil. (89) DM4,200
— 28 Nov 1932. 1 p, 8vo. To Anny. Informing her that he will not be able to write her during a vacation with his wife. In pencil. (88) DM1,100
— [c.early Apr 1933]. 4 pp, 8vo. To [Anny A.]. Love letter, & rejoicing about a meeting. (90) DM3,600
Autograph postcard, sgd, 28 June [c.1920]. To Gottfried Kassowitz. About his summer plans, some concerts, & requesting return of a work. (90) DM1,250
— 28 June 1926. To Hermann Watznauer. Recommending Thomas Mann's Zauberberg. (90) DM2,200
— 15 June 1927. To Gottfried Kassowitz. Greetings from Leningrad. (88) DM1,800
— 19 Mar 1932. (90) DM650
— [10 Jan 1933]. To Hans Gal. Concerning a shipment of proofs. (91) DM1,300

BERG

ANs, 23 Sept 1931. 1 p, 8vo (on verso of photograph). To [Robert Kolisko?]. Praising recipient's sonata. Sgd Bg. (90) DM1,050

AN, [3 Jan 1927]. On verso of ptd visiting card. To Gottfried Kassowitz. Expressing thanks & inviting him to the premiere of a work. (89) DM1,100

Autograph endorsement, sgd, on typescript carbon copy of a letter by one of Berg's friends to the Ed of the Augsburger Postzeitung, 5 May 1930, 2 pp, 4to, regarding a performance of Wozzeck. (88) DM750

Autograph quotation, 4 bars from his song Regen, [1934]. 1 p, 20cm by 29cm, cut from larger sheet. Sgd & inscr to [David Josef] Bach. (91) £1,900

Photograph, sgd & inscr, 9 Feb 1935. 19cm by 14.5cm. Including 3-line musical quotation from Lulu on verso, inscr to Ludwig Schwab. (91) £3,800

Bergengruen, Werner, 1892-1964

[A collection of 23 letters & cards addressed to him & his wife by various writers, 1948 & later, sold at star on 30 Nov 1988, lot 21, for DM2,800.]

[A collection of letters, poems, etc., c.300 pp, mostly folio, addressed to him on his 60th birthday by numerous writers & artists, with related material, sold at star on 30 Nov 1988, lot 20, for DM6,500.]

Autograph Ms, fragment from his book Titulus, [n.d.]. (90) DM220

Collection of 2 A Ls s, 2 Ls s, & autograph postcard, sgd, 1946 to 1957. (90) DM650

Bergman, Ingrid

ALs, 11 May 1970. (88) $95

Photograph, sgd, [n.d.]. (91) $250

Playbill, sgd, for S. (88) $90

Bergman, Ingrid —& Hitchcock, Alfred, 1899-1980

[Their signatures on a magazine advertisement for the film Notorious, 1946, 10 by 13 inches, sold at Dar on 6 Dec 1990, lot 99, for $160.]

Bergner, Elisabeth, 1897-1986

Collection of 10 Ls s, 5 autograph postcards, sgd, 5 A Ns s & 2 Ns, 1978 to 1982. (88) DM1,000

Bergsma, Cornelis Adriaan, 1798-1859

Autograph Ms, Catalogus auctorum qui de thea scripserunt, [c.1824]. (88) $650

Berio, Luciano

Autograph music, draft of the central section of his Sequenza VI for solo viola, sgd & dated 1968. 3 pp, folio. With related Ls, 24 Feb 1970. (91) £3,800

Berkeley, John, 1st Baron Berkeley of Stratton, d.1678

Ds, 19 Feb 1662/63. 1 p, vellum, 16 by 25 inches. "Counterpart of Bargain and Sale between Lord Sterline's Right in New England" for £3,500. Mentioning Cape Cod, Long Island, Connecticut & Hudson Rivers, etc. Marquess of Downshire collection. (90) £7,000

Berlichingen, Goetz von, 1480-1562

ALs, [2 Jan] 1541. 1 p, folio. To his brother-in-law Hans Landeschat von Steynach. Discussing the redemption of a pawn & activities of Jewish moneylenders. (90) DM20,000

Berlin

[Akademie der Kuenste. - A group of papers, c.100 pp, [early 20th cent], relating to the work of the Academy, including applications for membership by Liebermann & Zille, sold at S on 17 Nov 1988, lot 159, for £950 to Davies.]

Berlin, Irving, 1888-1989

Collection of 2 Ls s & 2 telegrams, 1949. (91) $325

Series of 7 Ls s, 1942. To Walter Winchell. About the writing of I Threw a Kiss in the Ocean. (91) $1,600

Ls, 2 Mar 1932. (91) $425

— 20 Nov 1933. (91) $325

— 8 Aug 1942. (91) $250

— 24 July 1968. (91) $1,000

— 5 Jan 1971. (91) $350

— 26 Jan 1971. (90) $900

— 10 Feb 1971. (91) $250

— 8 Nov 1971. (91) $225

— 1 Dec 1971. (91) $300

— 16 Feb 1972. 2 pp, 4to. To Harry Ruby. Sending a John McCormick recording of God Bless America. (91) $1,200
— 26 Oct 1972. (90) $475
Autograph sentiment, sgd, 1979. (91) $120
— Anr, sgd, [1979]. (91) $375
Signature, [9 Aug 1948]. (91) $200

Berlioz, Hector, 1803-69
Autograph Ms, Feuilleton du Journal des Debats ... Premiere representation du Caid, opera bouffon en deux actes de M. Sauvage, musique de M. Ambroise Thomas, 7 June 1749. 27 pp, 8vo. Review, with extensive autograph revisions. (89) £5,500
— Autograph Ms, receipts & expenditures, Jan & Feb 1866. (90) DM480
Collection of ALs & ANs, [Summer 1848]. (91) £950
A Ls s (2), [n.d.]. (88) £500
ALs, 12 Apr 1831. (89) £800
— 19 [Jan 1833]. (91) £600
— [n.d.]. (89) £400
— [c.Nov 1836?]. 1 p, 4to. To Victor Hugo. Hoping to meet him at the theater. Salzer collection. (90) £1,200
— [c.Feb 1839]. 2 pp, 8vo. To Emile Deschamps. About the dramatic symphony Romeo et Juliette. (91) £1,200
— 21 Dec [1839]. 4 pp, 8vo. To his sister. Giving details about concerts. (91) $2,000
— [c.1840]. (89) £400
— 26 Sept [1842]. (91) £850
— 15 Mar [1843]. (91) £800
— 28 Jan 1844. 4 pp, 8vo. To Schlosser. Reporting about concerts & new compositions, complaining about Paris, etc. With ANs by Marie Recio at bottom. (90) £1,300
— 14 Feb [1848]. (91) £1,000
— 3 Oct [1850]. 1 p, 8vo. To Alexandre Batta. Inviting him to participate in a concert. (90) DM1,100
— 25 Apr [1851]. (90) £750
— 28 Jan 1852. (89) £700
— 11 Dec 1853. (91) £1,000
— 19 Dec 1854. 3 pp, 8vo. To Henry Chorley. Reporting about the 1st performance of L'Enfance du Christ. Repaired. (90) DM4,200
— [10 Mar 1855]. (90) £850

— "Sunday 18" [c.1855]. 1 p, 4to. To [Charles-Simon] Richault. Asking him to send the piano score of his song La Captive to Brussels. (91) DM1,900
— 2 Dec 1858. 2 pp, 8vo. To Melchior Rieter-Biedermann. About problems with a shipment of piano scores. (91) DM1,600
— 6 Feb 1859. 2 pp, 8vo. To an unnamed author. Commenting on words of praise in recipient's book. (90) DM2,200
— 2 Nov 1863. (90) £900
— 9 Oct 1864. 4 pp, 8vo. To Princess Sayn-Wittgenstein. Reporting about his meeting with Estelle Fornier. (91) £3,200
— [n.d.]. 1 p, 8vo. To Joseph Wieniawski. Requesting the return of a book. (88) DM1,300
— 29 June [n.y.]. (89) £220
— 12 Nov [n.y.]. (89) DM650
— [n.d.], "Tuesday". (91) $475
— [n.d.]. (91) $800
Autograph quotation, opening 4 bars of the overture Les francs-juges, sgd & dated 18 Mar [18]43. 1 p, 8vo. (90) £1,900
— Anr, 17 bars from Benvenuto Cellini, sgd & inscr to Adolphe Mueller, 18 Nov 1845. 1 p, 4to. Mtd. (91) £5,200
— Anr, Recitatif lent et solennel, from his L'Enfance du Christ; 14 bars, scored for voice. Sgd & dated 22 Feb [1855]. 1 p, 4to. (90) DM4,600
— Anr, 14 bars from his Symphonie Fantastique, [n.d.]. 1 p, 20.5cm by 27cm. On 3 hand-drawn staves; sgd. (91) £4,500
— Anr, 10 bars from the Ballade du pecheur, from Lelio; [n.d.]. 1 p, 8vo. Sgd. (89) £1,600

Bernadotte, Jean Baptiste, 1763-1844.
See: Charles XIV John, 1763-1844

Bernanos, Georges, 1888-1948
Autograph Ms, novel, Sous le soleil de Satan, part II; early draft of opening, [c.1926]. (88) £300

BERNARD

Bernard, Saint (Bernardus Claravallensis), 1091-1153
Ms, Homilies. [Northeast? Italy, 2d half of 15th cent]. 30 leaves, vellum, 205mm by 127mm. 18th-cent brown marbled paper over contemp wooden bds. In a regular cursive bookhand. With 9 large painted initials. (89) £2,000

Bernard, C. E. B.
Original drawings, (3), to illus The Cherry Tree Story Book (1) & The Pixie Alphabet Book, [n.d.]. (89) £850

Bernard, Sir Robert, 1739?-89
— LIBRARY CATALOGUE. - Ms, Catalogue of Books in the Library at Thorp Park; as they stood at the decease of Sir Robert Bernard, & Catalogue of the Books at Brampton Hall, 1789. 97 pp, folio; vellum bds. Listing c.1800 titles. (88) £600

Bernhard II Erich Freund, Herzog von Sachsen-Meiningen, 1800-82
ALs, 3 July 1866. (91) DM500

Bernhardt, Sarah, .1923
Photograph, sgd & inscr, 1896. (88) $325

Bernhardt, Sarah, d.1923
[An album containing letters addressed to Sarah & Maurice Bernhardt by noted cultural figures, with related material, sold at P on 14 Dec 1988, lot 56, for $2,000.]
Original drawing, lady in long dress with skeleton behind her; [n.d.]. (91) $110
Collection of ALs & ANs, 1882 & [n.d.]. (90) DM220
— Collection of ALs & autograph sentiment, sgd, [n.d.] & 1892. (88) $225
Series of 3 A Ls s, 31 Mar 1883 & [n.d.]. (91) £200
— Series of 3 A Ls s, [1915]. Koch Foundation. (90) $800
ALs, 1884. (91) $275
— [n.d.]. (91) $400
— [n.d.]. (89) DM320
— [n.d.]. (91) $95
ANs, 1912. (88) $200
— [n.d.]. (88) $200
Photograph, sgd, 1876. (90) $375
— Anr, 1918. (91) $160
Photograph, sgd & inscr, 1881. (90)

AMERICAN BOOK PRICES CURRENT

DM520
— Anr, 1909. (91) £150
— Anr, 1916. (91) $500
Ptd photograph, [1917]. (90) DM270
Signature, 1906. (91) $400

Berno of Reichenau, d.1048
Ms, Ratio Generalis, Dialogus, & other texts in Latin on the arrangement of the Liturgy. [Bavaria, Freising, mid-11th cent]. 21 leaves, vellum, 230mm by 170mm, in 19th-cent paper bds. In dark brown ink in a regular German Carolingian minuscule with some ligatures & words in late uncials; 17 lines written in red uncials; 7 large painted initials in red. "This is a superb example of Ottonian book production...." (90) £40,000

Bernoulli, Daniel, 1700-82
ALs, 20 Dec 1750. 3 pp, 4to. To Jean Jacques d'Ortous de Mairan. Discussing Leonhard Euler's disagreement with recipient's research on the aurora borealis. (90) DM7,000

Bernstein, Eduard, 1850-1932
ALs, 9 Sept 1915. (89) DM320

Bernstein, Leonard, 1918-90
Autograph quotation, 2 bars from his oratorio Jeremiah, 13 July 1978. (91) $325
Photograph, sgd & inscr, [n.d.]. (91) $110

Bernstein, Leonard, 1918-90 —& Others
Typescript, beginning of Act I of West Side Story, [n.d.]. (91) $350
Ds, 20 May 1954. (91) $450

Bernstein, Leonard, 1918-90 —& Copland, Aaron
Concert program, 13 Sept 1967. (91) $375

Bernstein, Leonard, 1918-90 —& Hellman, Lillian, 1905-84
Ds, 14 Jan 1955. (91) $200

Berryman, Jim
Original drawing, cartoon depicting District of Columbia as colonial gentleman being crushed by tidal wave of the President's Cup Regatta, sgd & dated 15 Sept 1939. (90) $50

Berryman, John, 1914-72
Collection of 10 A Ls s, 5 Ls s, & 3 autograph postcards, sgd, 1940 to 1971. 27 pp, 8vo & 4to. To Mark Van Doren. Wide ranging correspondence. With related material. (90) $6,400

Berthier, Alexandre, Prince de Wagram, 1753-1815
ALs, [16 Dec 1805]. (90) DM500
Series of 6 Ls s, [15 Dec 1799] to 30 Nov 1811. (88) £200
Ls, [21 Aug 1797]. (88) DM650
— [9 Apr 1801]. (88) DM300
— [18 Dec 1802]. (89) DM230
— [27 Nov 1803]. (90) DM320
— [28 Oct 1805]. (91) DM260
— 7 Nov 1806. (90) DM220
— 22 Aug 1809. (89) DM200

Bertram, Ernst, 1884-1957
Autograph transcript, 12 poems, Spruch-gedichte. An die Jugend, [n.d.]. 13 pp, 8vo. Sgd on tp. (88) DM1,100
— Autograph transcript, poems, Sieben Radierungen; [n.d.]. (89) DM650

Bertuch, Friedrich Justin, 1747-1822
Series of 3 A Ls s, 26 Jan 1789 to 3 Jan 1808. (88) DM600
ALs, 19 June 1789. Albrecht collection. (91) SF950
— 15 Jan 1794. (89) DM340

Berwald, Franz Adolf, 1796-1868
Ds, 22 Dec [1]846. (88) £400

Berzelius, Jons Jacob von, 1779-1848
ALs, 28 Jan 1827. Kuenzel collection. (90) DM800
— 10 Nov 1842. (91) DM320

Besant, Sir Walter, 1836-1901
[A group of 7 autograph Mss, including a novel, a play, & short stories, various dates, about 350 pp, mostly 4to, heavily revised & mostly sgd, sold at S on 20 July 1989, lot 163, for £1,700 to Rota.]
Autograph Ms, The Master Craftsman, complete working draft, [1895-96]. 380 leaves, 4to, in extra red levant gilt by Sangorski & Sutcliffe. Including autograph tp, sgd. (89) $2,250
Collection of 13 A Ls s & 3 Ls s, 1882 to 1900. (89) $250

— Collection of 11 A Ls s & 2 Ls s, 12 Jan 1888 to 19 Apr 1901. (90) £190
Series of 7 A Ls s, 20 May 1886 to 22 Jan 1892 & [n.d.]. (91) £100

Besenval, Pierre Victor, 1721-91
ALs, 13 Nov 1781. 2 pp, 4to. To Minister of War de Segur. Recommending M. de Caligny. (89) DM1,300

Bessel, Friedrich Wilhelm, 1784-1846
ALs, 29 May 1841. (91) DM360

Best, Pete
A Ls s (2), Sept & Oct 1960. (89) £400
ALs, Apr 1962. (89) £280
— May 1962. (89) £650
See also: McCartney, Paul & Best

Bestall, A. E.
Original drawings, (14), to illus Rupert Bear and the Baby Dragon. (88) £450

Bestiary
Ms, The Northumberland Bestiary, in Latin. [Northern? England, c.1250-60]. 74 leaves (2 lacking) & flyleaf, vellum, 210mm by 158mm, in mid-19th cent red mor by Francis Bedford. In dark brown ink in a small early gothic bookhand, possibly by 2 scribes. With penwork initials throughout & 112 miniatures (1 full-page, many half-page) in ink & colored washes. Alnwick Ms.447. (91) £2,700,000

Bethmann Hollweg, Theobald von, 1856-1921
ALs, 23 Oct 1914. (91) DM360
— 12 May 1915. Schroeder collection. (89) DM360
Ls, 13 Dec 1915. (90) DM220

Betjeman, Sir John, 1906-84
[A notebook containing Betjeman's own file copies of poems, more than 500 leaves, c.1946 to 1958, partly autograph but also including typescripts, carbon copies, galley proofs & clippings, some unpbd, sold at P (Bradley Martin sale) on 30 Apr 1990, lot 2624, for $16,000.]
[An archive of Mss & Typescripts containing various stages of drafts & variant versions for his poem Summoned by Bells, [n.d.], in 2 half mor folding cases, with copies of the 1st

BETJEMAN

English (sgd) & American Eds, sold at P (Bradley Martin sale) on 30 Apr 1990, lot 2623, for $8,000.]

[A large collection of autograph Mss & typescripts of poems, with related material, [n.d.], in mor folding case, including a number of unpbd poems, sold at P (Bradley Martin sale) on 30 Apr 1990, lot 2625, for $18,000.]

Autograph Ms, fair copies of 15 poems, most illus with drawings, [1948 & later]. 28 leaves, 4to, in half cloth. Sgd on front pastedown. With anr poem laid in. Bradley Martin Ms. (90) $9,000

— Autograph Ms, poem, Sir John Piers, 1938. 10 pp, 4to, on rectos only. Ptr's copy. 1 leaf repaired. With copy of 1st Ed & ANs. Bradley Martin Ms. (90) $2,250

Collection of ALs & 4 Ls s, 28 Apr 1933 to 8 Dec 1958. (88) £400

Series of 4 A Ls s, 1952 to 1966. (91) £500

Beuth, Peter Christian Wilhelm, 1781-1853

ALs, 9 Jan 1830. Albrecht collection. (91) SF400

Beuys, Joseph, 1921-86

[A collection of 5 lithographs, sgd, 1974 & [n.d.], 23cm by 16cm, autograph Ms, notes regarding economic problems of developing countries, with small drawing, sgd, [n.d.], 1 p, 4to, & 5 art postcards, sgd, sold at star on 9 Mar 1988, lot 606, for DM2,700.]

[A collection of 4 lithographs, sgd, 1974, 23cm by 16cm, autograph Ms, fragment, [n.d.], 2 pp, folio, & pencil sketch, sgd & inscr, c.105mm by 145mm, sold at star on 9 Mar 1988, lot 607, for DM3,400.]

[A collection of 2 lithographs, sgd & inscr, 1974 & [n.d.], 23cm by 16cm, & autograph Ms, sgd, [n.d.], 2 pp, 8vo, containing brief notes & a small sketch, sold at star on 30 Nov 1988, lot 565, for DM4,500.]

Autograph Ms, notes about European individualism; [n.d.]. 1 p, 8vo. Sgd & inscr later; including small drawing. In pencil. (90) DM7,500

— Autograph Ms, notes on a calendar leaf, 5 Apr [1982?]. 1 p, 8vo. With several entries, sgd. (90) DM1,200

AMERICAN BOOK PRICES CURRENT

Autograph postcard, sgd, 9 Dec 1973. (91) DM300

Autograph sentiment, [n.d.]. (88) DM450

— Anr, sgd, [n.d.]. (91) DM420

Bewick, Thomas, 1753-1828

ALs, 15 Feb 1819. 1 p, 4to. To William Bewick. About subscription fulfillment problems for The Fables of Aesop and Others.... (91) $1,200

Beyle, Marie Henri, ("Stendhal"), 1783-1842

ALs, [Oct 1804]. 2 pp, 4to. To his sister Pauline. About his new address, his problems with a young lady, & saying he is not associating with his old friends any more. (88) DM6,000

— [1807]. 4 pp, 4to. To his sister Pauline. Informing her about the young ladies he is seeing at Braunschweig. (90) DM5,500

— 7 Dec 1809. 4 pp, 4to. To his sister Pauline. Urging her to enlist the support of various relatives for his promotion. Sgd A. L. Lanvallere. (90) DM4,200

— "Wednesday" [1827]. 4 pp, 8vo. To Sophie Duvaucel. Describing his efforts to obtain a copy of Manzoni's I Promessi Sposi for her. (89) £1,400

— 15 May 1831. (89) £750

— [n.d.]. 3 pp, 8vo. To his sister Pauline. Asking her to obtain some money for him, & warning against interception of his letters. Sgd L. A. Chevallet. In French & English. (89) £1,300

AL, [18 Oct 1806]. 3 pp, 4to. To his sister Pauline. Informing her that he will be joining the Emperor with his cousin. (89) £1,600

— Dumas, Gen. Mathieu. - Ls, 14 Oct 1812. 2 pp, 4to. To Villeblanche, Intendant at Smolensk. Nominating Beyle as commissioner in charge of provisioning the army at Smolensk. Text in the hand of Beyle. (91) £1,600

Beyme, Karl Friedrich von, 1765-1838

A Ls s (2), 4 Aug 1814 & 1819. (90) DM240

ALs, 28 Oct 1809. (90) DM340

Bialas, Guenter
Autograph music, Neun Bagatellen, for wind instruments, strings & piano, 1985. (91) DM480
— Autograph music, part of his 5 Moments musicaux, [1976]. (90) DM380
— Autograph music, sketches for Neue Bagatellen, [c.1985]. (91) DM370

Bible Manuscripts, English
— HARDEY, JOSEPH. - Autograph transcript, The New Testament of our Lord & Saviour Jesus Christ. [London?, 1686]. 83 leaves (2 blank) & 3 flyleaves, 125mm by 65mm. Contemp London bdg of black mor gilt & painted. In black ink in an extremely small shorthand. Abbey collection. (89) £1,800

Bible Manuscripts, French
— Biblia Pauperum. [Northeastern France, c.1350]. Single leaf, vellum, 290mm by 200mm. With 4 miniatures, each with 3 to 5 lines of descriptive text in brown ink in a gothic bookhand, with red & blue initials & linefillers. Korner collection. (90) £16,000
— Bible Historiale, Old Testament only in the version by Guiart des Moulins from Peter Comestor's Historia Scholastica. [Paris, c.1410]. 479 leaves (3 lacking), vellum, 418mm by 305mm. 2 vols, modern red mor; earlier bdg preserved separately. In brown ink in a lettre batarde. With 102 large illuminated initials, & 93 large & 3 very large miniatures with ivyleaf borders. Part of 2d vol dampstained & restored. Doheny collection. (88) £260,000
— Bible Historiale. [Brittany, c.1470-85]. Opening leaf only, vellum, 312mm by 265mm. In brown ink in a cursive lettre batarde. With large miniature above very large illuminated initial & full border with the coats-of-arms of Arthur III, Duke of Brittany, & his wife Catherine of Luxembourg. (90) £1,300
Ms, Epitres et Evangiles de l'Annee, in the French trans of Jean de Vignay. [Paris, c.1360-70]. 134 leaves (2 lacking) & 3 flyleaves, vellum, 250mm by 165mm. Old limp vellum bdg. In an extremely fine compressed gothic liturgical hand. With small initials throughout in pale blue & burnished gold with high quality penwork, & 10 miniatures, each column-width & 10 or 11 lines high, painted in soft colors & liquid gold. Very waterstained throughout. (91) £11,000
— Ms, Epitres et Evangiles de l'Annee, in the French trans of Jean de Vignay. [Paris, c.1410-20]. 180 leaves (2 blank), vellum, 252mm by 175mm. 18th-cent French mor gilt bdg. In a well-formed lettre batarde. With small initials throughout in blue & burnished gold with red & blue penwork, & 6 miniatures of varying size drawn in grisaille in black ink shaded in grey & heightened with delicate touches of white, partially infilled with blue & grey-green wash, with frames in highly burnished gold; attributable to the workshop of the Apocalypse Master. (91) £65,000

Bible Manuscripts, German
Ms, compilation, Die 12 Maltzeitten Christi sampt der Schrieffft. [Southern Germany or Austria, c.1640]. 42 leaves, vellum & paper, 42mm by 51mm, in contemp enamelled gold bdg. With 13 very fine watercolors. (91) £65,000

Bible Manuscripts, Greek
— [Egypt, perhaps early Christian community at Fustat, late 3d cent]. Fragment of 1 leaf, vellum, 85mm by 111mm. Written in dark brown ink in a small late classical uncial script. Part of 14 lines of St. Paul's Epistle to the Romans, 4:23 - 5:3 (recto) & 5:8 - 13 (verso). Very def; enclosed between glass. "The earliest surviving Ms of the part of the text it contains." (88) £95,000

Bible Manuscripts, Latin
— [England, 1st half of 9th cent]. 1 leaf, vellum, 288mm by 198mm. In mor-backed buckram case. In dark brown ink in a formal insular minuscule. Containing Judges 10, vii to 11, xxvi. Recovered from a bdg; severely cropped. Doheny collection. (88) £24,000
— [Northwest France, c.840-850]. 42 vellum fragments (23 blank) of various

sizes, recovered from a bdg. Written in 3 columns in brown ink in a very elegant Carolingian minuscule. Cut from at least 7 leaves of a bible owned by the Abbey of St. Maximin, Trier. Partly mtd. Ludwig MS.I.2. (89) £18,000

— [Germany, end of 10th cent]. 2 conjoint leaves, vellum, c.480mm by 315mm. In brown ink in a fine regular caroline minuscule, with running titles, capitals & chapter nos in red. Recovered from a bdg. (90) £1,200

— [Tuscany, Siena?, c.1150-80]. 2 leaves only, vellum, 580mm by 410mm. In 2 sizes of a fine rounded romanesque minuscule, with explicits & headings in uncials. With 2 very large initials (1 historiated). Corner def. (90) £7,500

— [Florence, 3d quarter of 12th cent]. Single leaf, vellum, 410mm by 280mm. With headings in large decorative lombardic capitals in bright red & 2 very large initials in elaborate fretwork & interlaced designs filled with white vinestems on blue & green panel grounds. Lower edge trimmed. Korner collection. (90) £32,000

— [Northeastern? France, early 13th cent]. 479 leaves & flyleaf, vellum, 257mm by 174mm. 18th-cent French red mor gilt bdg. With Prologues attributed to St. Jerome & Interpretation of Hebrew Names. In dark brown ink by several scribes. With 191 large illuminated initials often formed of dragons etc. & 2 very large historiated initials. 3 leaves slightly later insertions. (88) £85,000

— [England, c.1210-20]. 479 leaves (1 blank), vellum, 257mm by 174mm. 18th-cent red mor gilt bdg. With prologues attributed to St. Jerome & Interpretation of Hebrew Names. In dark brown ink by several scribes. With 191 large illuminated initials, often formed of lions, dragons, etc., varying from 3 lines high to full height of the page, & 2 very large historiated initials. (90) £180,000

— [Paris, early 13th cent]. 1 leaf only, vellum, 220mm by 141mm. In fine gothic script. With 2 eight-line illuminated initials in highly burnished gold & colors, 1 historiated. Mtd. (88) £1,800

— [England, c.1230]. 244 leaves, vellum, 207mm by 150mm, in 18th-cent mor. Written in black ink in a minute early Gothic textura. With large initials in red blue & some green ink with pen flourishes; small initials in red or blue. Zabriskie-Manhattan College Ms (91) $29,000

— [Rome?, c.1230-50]. 506 leaves (4 lacking), vellum, 232mm by 148mm, in modern wooden bds. With Prologues, Capitula & Gospel Canon Tables. In dark brown ink in a very small rounded gothic bookhand. With 77 very large decorated initials with elaborate penwork & 4 pp of Canon tables in multiple arched compartments. A few 14th-cent additions. (90) £9,500

— [England, c.1240]. (88) £800

— [Paris, c.1250]. 613 leaves & 3 flyleaves, vellum, 143mm by 97mm, in early 19th-cent brown mor gilt. With Prologues, Interpretation of Hebrew names & [14th cent?] Calendar. In black ink in a small gothic rotunda. With decorated initials throughout, 79 large painted initials, many with long marginal extensions, & 2 historiated initials. (91) £17,000

— [England, c.1250]. 447 leaves (1 lacking), vellum, 195mm by 140mm. 18th-cent red mor gilt, rebacked, in calf slipcase. In dark brown ink in a small gothic bookhand. With Prologues attributed to St. Jerome, additional prologues & interpretation of Hebrew names. With numerous pen-flourished initials in red & blue, over 70 with pen-flourished sprays, 1 forming partial border. Doheny collection. (88) £17,000

— [England, mid-13th cent]. 337 leaves & 2 flyleaves, vellum, 235mm by 165mm, in late 16th-cent panelled calf gilt. With Prologue attributed to St. Jerome & Interpretation of Hebrew Names. Written by 2 scribes in dark brown ink in a small gothic bookhand. With c.80 large calligraphic initials with elaborate penwork decoration, some extending to form partial borders. (89) £30,000

— [Paris, 13th cent]. Single leaf, vellum, 201mm by 139mm. With capitals &

running titles in red or blue, & decorated & historiated initial. (90) £1,100

— [Northern France, c.1250]. 419 (of 420) leaves; lacking f.260. 145mm by 102mm, in 16th-cent bdg of calf over pastebd to an architectonic design gilt. Written in brown ink in a small gothic textura. With 34 large historiated initials with grotesques & dragon-pattern extension in colors & 45 illuminated initials without extensions. (91) £41,000

— [England or Northern France, c.1250]. 546 leaves, vellum, 160mm by 115mm, in 18th-cent mor gilt. In Black ink in a minute early Gothic textura. Large initials in red & blue with pen flourishes; smaller initials in red or blue. Psalms omitted. (91) $14,000

— [France, c.1250. Single leaf from the 2d Book of Esdras. 213mm by 152mm. Rubricated ini red & blue with historiated initial illuminated in colors & gold depicting a human figure wiith bucket & brush. (90) £1,100

— [Italy, c.1250]. 474 leaves & flyleaves, vellum, 170mm by 115mm, in 19th-cent Italian red-brown mor gilt. With Prologues, Interpretation of Hebrew Names, a treatise on miracles, & concordances. In brown ink in a very small gothic bookhand. With large initials at the start of every book & prologue with elaborate penwork & scrolling extensions, & many medieval sidenotes. (91) £9,000

— [England, Oxford?, mid-13th cent]. 532 leaves, vellum, 145mm by 97mm. Modern dark brown mor. With Prologues attributed to St. Jerome & Interpretation of Hebrew Names. In dark brown ink in a very small regular gothic hand. With 30 very large decorated initials, 51 very large painted initials, full-length illuminated Genesis initial & historiated initial attributable to William de Brailes. (88) £7,200

— [Paris, c.1250]. 534 leaves (some lacking), vellum, 138mm by 88mm, in English marbled calf of c.1800. With Prologues & Interpretation of Hebrew Names. In dark brown ink in an extremely small gothic hand. With c.60 large illuminated initials with long extensions in full colors with gold bezants & white tracery, & 7 large historiated initials. (90) £7,000

— [Paris, c.1250-75]. 602 leaves (1 lacking), vellum, 180mm by 122mm. Worn 17th-cent reversed calf. With Prologues attributed to St. Jerome & Interpretation of Hebrew Names. In dark brown ink in a very small gothic hand. With c.1,500 chapter initials in red or blue with penwork decoration, 71 large illuminated & 80 historiated initials. (89) £13,000

— [England, Salisbury?, c.1250-70]. 354 leaves & 3 flyleaves, vellum, 293mm by 206mm. Modern red mor by Riviere & Son. With Prologues. In a gothic bookhand. With 2-line initials throughout in red or blue with penwork, 42 large initials, & 64 historiated initials of varying size with branching extensions in full colors & burnished gold in the style of the Sarum Master. 6 initials cut out & replaced with skilful reconstructions. (91) £65,000

— [Paris, c.1250]. 729 leaves & 4 flyleaves, vellum, 170mm by 110mm. 18th-cent brown calf bdg. With Prologues, Interpretation of Hebrew Names, & lists of biblical readings. In a very small gothic hand. With 2-line chapter initials throughout in red or blue with full-length penwork, 57 large illuminated initials, & 85 historiated initials of varying size in the style of the Vie de Saint Denis atelier. (91) £35,000

— [England, mid-13th cent]. (90) £900

— [Paris, c.1250]. 692 leaves & 4 flyleaves, vellum, 150mm by 97mm. Medieval blindstamped calf over bevelled wooden bds. With Prologues attributed to St. Jerome, Calendar & Interpretation of Hebrew Names. In dark brown ink in a very small gothic hand by more than 1 scribe. With 2-line chapter initials throughout with full-length penwork, 113 large illuminated initials, & 14 historiated initials. (90) £38,000

— [Northeast Italy, Bologna?, c.1250-62]. 514 leaves, vellum, 275mm by 198mm. Oak bds with alum-tawed pigskin spine by Roger Powell, 1965. With Prologues, Interpretation of Hebrew Names, & Calendar. In dark brown ink in a neat rounded gothic

bookhand. With small initials with penwork extensions throughout, 112 mostly large historiated initials in full colors & burnished gold with elaborate bar borders, & c.87 separate marginal scenes & vignettes. Margins cropped with some loss of edges of illumination. Abbey collection. (89) £760,000
— [Northeast? Spain, c.1250]. 433 leaves (some lacking), vellum, 216mm by 172mm. 18th-cent mor gilt bdg. With Prologues & Interpretation of Hebrew Names. By several scribes in dark brown ink in early gothic bookhands. With c.77 large illuminated initials in highly burnished gold on blue & red grounds with white tracery. Some margins def. (89) £42,000
— [Paris, c.1250-60]. 614 leaves (3 blank), vellum, 125mm by 85mm. 17th-cent Italian red mor profusely gilt. With Prologues & Interpretation of Hebrew Names. In black ink in a very small gothic hand. With small initials throughout with full-length contrasting penwork, 60 large decorated penwork initials, 67 large illuminated initials in elaborate designs including dragons & lions' heads, & 16 large historiated initials. (89) £19,000
— [Paris, c.1250-60]. 591 leaves (c.15 lacking), vellum, 140mm by 92mm. Modern antique-style calf. With Prologues & Interpretation of Hebrew Names. In dark brown ink in a very small gothic hand. With small initials throughout with full-length penwork, 46 large & very large illuminated initials in leafy & dragon designs, & 78 historiated initials. Some leaves def. (89) £24,000
— [Italy, mid-13th cent]. New Testament only. 161 leaves, vellum, 127mm by 90mm, in 19th-cent vellum. In dark brown ink in a microscopic gothic bookhand. With decorated initials throughout & 17th-cent German miniature loosely enclosed. (88) £2,600
— [Paris, c.1250 - 1260). 686 leaves & 8 blanks, vellum, 138mm by 83mm. 17th-cent Scottish red mor gilt; mor box by Riviere. In black ink in a small gothic rotunda. With Prologues attributed to St. Jerome & interpretation of Hebrew names. With calligraphic initials throughout with full-length penwork decoration, 60 large decorated initials with branchwork or dragon patterns, & 79 historiated initials. Some pp cropped. Doheny collection. (88) £25,000
— [Tournai, c.1260-70]. (91) £800
— [Paris, c.1260]. Single leaf, vellum, 231mm by 159mm. In gothic script. With 4 small illuminated initials in colors & gold & 9-line historiated initial with leafy extension. (91) £1,300
— [Paris, c.1260-70]. 537 leaves (4 lacking), vellum, 157mm by 107mm. Modern calf bdg. With Prologues & Interpretation of Hebrew Names. In brown ink in a small fairly round italianate gothic hand. With 64 large illuminated initials extending up to 20 lines in height in colors & gold, & 78 large historiated initials. (89) £55,000
— [Paris, c.1265]. 560 leaves & flyleaf, vellum, 253mm by 165mm, in late 18th-cent French yellow-brown mor gilt. With Prologues, Interpretation of Hebrew Names & concordance. In dark brown ink in a well-formed gothic bookhand. With decorated initials with full-length borders throughout, 64 large illuminated initials in colors & burnished gold, & 81 historiated initials usually about 7 lines high. Attributable to the Bari workshop. (91) £145,000
— [Bologna, c.1270]. 534 leaves, vellum, 353mm by 240mm. Late 19th-cent blind-tooled mor bdg by Leighton. Vulgate version, with Prologue attributed to St. Jerome & interpretation of Hebrew names. In brown ink in a gothic rotunda script. With 74 historiated initials with extensions. Portions of text faded. Doheny collection. (88) £110,000
— [Paris?, c.1270]. 533 leaves, vellum, 358mm by 245mm. Antique-style blind-tooled mor bdg by Bedford. With Prologues attributed to St. Jerome & interpretation of Hebrew names. In brown ink in a small gothic rotunda script. With decorated initials throughout, 69 large illuminated initials, 78 historiated initials, many with extensions, & 3 full-length initials. Doheny collection. (88) £160,000
— [Northern France, Paris?, 2d half of

13th cent]. 457 leaves (some lacking) & 4 flyleaves, vellum, 140mm by 89mm, in 19th-cent dark blue velvet over wooden bds. With Interpretation of Hebrew Names, Calendar & abbreviated Missal. In dark brown ink in a microscopic gothic bookhand. With small initials throughout in blue or red with penwork, & large decorated initials at the start of every book & prologue. Many medieval marginal glosses. Astor MS.A.11. (88) £4,800
— [Paris?, c.1280-1300]. (90) £850
— [Paris, c.1280-90]. 519 leaves (many lacking), vellum, 300mm by 200mm, in [18th-cent?] vellum over pastebds. With Prologues & Interpretation of Hebrew Names. In black ink in a very fine formal gothic bookhand. With c.65 large or very large illuminated initials in designs of dragons & lions & leafy spirals with long ivyleaf extensions, 5 large historiated initials, & miniature inserted from anr Ms. 18 initials partially cut out & repaired. (90) £32,000
— [Northern France, late 13th cent]. 485 leaves (some lacking, some recent replacements), vellum, 213mm by 150mm. Repaired contemp blind-stamped brown lea over wooden bds. With Prologues. In a small rounded gothic liturgical hand. With numerous penwork initials in red & blue with full-length extensions. Dampstained. (91) DM12,000
— [France, late 13th cent]. 563 leaves & 3 flyleaves, vellum, 188mm by 115mm, in worn late 16th-cent English calf over wooden bds. With Prologues. In dark brown & black ink in a very small gothic hand. With large decorated initials throughout, 77 large historiated initials in full colors on burnished gold grounds, & many additions in medieval English hands. (90) £30,000
— [Paris?, late 13th cent]. 512 leaves (2 lacking, 25 facsimiles), vellum, 213mm by 147mm. Def 15th-cent blind-stamped calf over wooden bds. With Prologues & Interpretation of Hebrew Names. In dark brown ink in a small gothic hand by more than 1 scribe. With full-length borders beside every column throughout, & very large decorated initial for every Prologue & book of the Bible. (89) £3,500
— [France, 13th cent]. Over 300 leaves only, vellum, 234mm by 170mm; disbound. In a gothic hand. Def. (91) $6,750
— [Southern France, Bordeaux?, c.1300]. Single leaf, vellum, 332mm by 228mm. With 2 colored initials with full-length painted borders with purple penwork, & large historiated initial with full-length bar border. Phillipps Ms.2506. (91) £2,800
— [Italy, Naples?, early 14th cent]. 500 leaves (3 blank), vellum, c.310mm by 220mm, in 19th-cent lea. With Prologues & Interpretation of Hebrew Names. In dark brown ink in a regular rotunda by the scribe Phylippus. With 2-line initials throughout & c.100 large & very large illuminated initials with foliate extensions & grotesques. (90) DM100,000
— [East Anglia, Cambridge?, c.1345-48]. Single leaf, vellum, 447mm by 307mm. In brown ink in double column. With 2 historiated initials in the style of the Vienna Bohun Psalter, with full border surrounding the page & between columns of colored bars tied in elaborate knotwork patterns sprouting into sprays of colored leaves, & including a grotesque & a lion's face in central column. Korner collection. (90) £55,000
— [Bohemia, 1419] 515 leaves, vellum, 245mm by 168mm, in pigskin over wooden bds of the 15th cent. With 3- to 15-line initials in gold, blue, green & crimson at the beginning of each book, often with stylized penwork decoration in the same colors extending into the margins. Zabriske-Manhattan College Ms (91) $54,000
— [Germany, c.1450]. Single leaf, vellum, 440mm by 315mm. With large historiated initial in gold & colors & 3 small penwork initials. (89) DM2,200
— [Germany or Bohemia, c.1450]. Single leaf, vellum, 370mm by 267mm. With 11-line illuminated initial with fine leafy decoration on highly burnished punched gold ground & full-length border. Mtd. (91) £1,600
— [Austria or Bohemia, mid-15th cent]. 2 leaves only, vellum, 355mm by

BIBLE MANUSCRIPTS

245mm. In gothic script. With 2 large historiated initials in leafy designs on highly burnished ground within green faceted frames & with scrolling leafy borders. Framed. (88) £4,000

— [Southern Germany, 15th cent]. NT only, with prologues attributed to St. Jerome & list of liturgical readings with glossary. 260 leaves only, 318mm by 215mm, in contemp blindstamped calf over wooden bds. In a gothic hand in brown ink, with headings, initials, initial strokes & verse numbers in red. (90) $4,800

Ms, Bible exposition, with tables of words & readings, Exposition of Hymns, Legends of the Saints, & Homilies, [Low Countries, 2d half of 15th cent]. 170 leaves (50 vellum; 4 lacking), 285mm by 210mm, in contemp lea over wooden bds with brass bosses & clasps. In brown ink in a cursive bookhand. With large calligraphic initals throughout in red or blue. (88) £4,200

— Ms, New Testament. [Sicily?, late 12th cent]. 244 leaves, vellum, 193mm by 115mm, in oak bds by Douglas Cockerell, 1900. In brown ink in a small rounded late romanesque hand. With decorated initials throughout, 26 large illuminated initials in elaborate designs on burnished gold grounds, 2 large historiated initials & full-page miniature within full border incorporating 4 historiated roundels. Including some 13th-cent additions. (90) £55,000

— Ms, Old Testament from Genesis to Psalms, with Prologues ascribed to Saint Ambrose. [Bologna?, c.1265]. 159 leaves (17 lacking), vellum, 145mm by 101mm. Worn 17th-cent calf. In a neat gothic minuscule bookhand by a single scribe. With 6 decorated & 19 historiated initials. (90) £8,000

— Ms, Old Testament from Genesis to Psalms, with Prologues. [France, c.1250]. 198 leaves (some missing), vellum, 233mm by 156mm. Modern blindstamped calf bdg. In a well-formed early gothic hand. With 2-line initials throughout, some in burnished gold, a fine drawing of a queen in margin, & many early sidenotes. 1 initial cut out. (91) £9,000

AMERICAN BOOK PRICES CURRENT

See also: Cena Maletractati

Bible Manuscripts, Samaritan
Ms, Arhuta Qadishta, Exodus 29:1-14 & 30:34 to 32:6, [Nablus, c.1170-80]. (89) £500

Bickerstaff, Isaac, c.1735-c.1812
ALs, "Monday Evening" [Dec 1767]. (89) $325

Bickley, Francis
[A collection of c.190 A Ls s, Ls s & postcards addressed to him from numerous authors, historians, etc., with related material, sold at S on 21 July 1988, lot 206, for £500 to Rivlin.]

Biddle, Clement, 1740-1814
Ds, 21 Apr 1792. (88) $55

Biddle, John
ALs, [21 June 1828]. Alexander collection. (90) $90

Biddle, Nicholas, 1786-1844
Ds, 17 May 1831. (90) $100

Bienek, Horst
Autograph transcript, poem, beginning "Woerter, meine Fallschirme", sgd & dated 10 Oct 1977. (91) DM250

— Autograph transcript, poem, beginning "Woerter, meine Fallschirme", sgd & dated 20 Dec 1977. (90) DM280

Bierce, Ambrose, 1842-1914
Collection of 2 A Ls s & ANs, 10 Aug 1905, 5 June 1912 & 11 Apr [n.y.]. Kauffman collection. (88) $750

— Collection of ALs & letter, 11 Mar 1912 & [n.d., 1911?]. Kauffman collection. (88) $550

A Ls s (2), 1 & 26 May 1912. Doheny collection. (88) $800

ALs, 19 Jan 1899. (90) $300

— 19 June 1909. Doheny collection. (88) $380

— 5 Oct 1911. (90) $325

Big Painting Books
Original drawings, (102), for later vols in the Big Painting Books series, [after 1945]. (90) £600

— Original drawings, (240), to illus Big Painting Books, no 1 - 40, 1932 to 1944. (90) £520

Bill, Max
Ls, 11 Jan 1951. (88) £280

Billroth, Theodor, 1829-94
ALs, 9 Jan 1862. (91) DM800
— 23 Oct 1871. 4 pp, 8vo. To [Franz Stephani]. Regarding decorations conferred on doctors for work in field hospitals. (90) DM1,100
— 1888. Salzer collection. (90) £650
— 9 May 1890. (91) DM620
— 7 Feb 1892. (90) DM340

Binding, Rudolf Georg, 1867-1938
Autograph Ms, poem, Einholung; 5 four-line stanzas. (89) DM420
— Autograph Ms, poem, Herbstritt, sgd RG. (90) DM420
ALs, 23 June 1927. (90) DM260
— 23 July 1929. (89) DM320

Birk, Johannes, fl.1459-1494
Ms, Stifftung des gotzhauses Kempten und Sant Hyltgartn Leben. [Kempten Abbey, Swabia, 1499]. 147 leaves (2 lacking) & 2 flyleaves, 303mm by 202mm, in repaired remains of contemp bdg of wooden bds now covered with brown calf. In a cursive bookhand by Petrus Brack of Minderdorff. With 2 very large circular Calendar diagrams & 59 large colored drawings. (91) £190,000

Birnbaum, Uriel, 1894-1956
Collection of 2 A Ls s, 15 Ls s & autograph postcard, sgd, 30 Sept 1929 to 25 Oct 1932. (90) DM800

Biro, B. S.
Original drawings, (13), to illus John E. Archives of J. M. Dent & Son. (88) £150
— Original drawings, (51), to illus Frank L. Archives of J. M. Dent & Son. (88) £300
— Original drawings, (53), to illus Frank L. Archives of J. M. Dent & Son. (88) £300

Biron, Armand de Gontaut, Baron de, c.1524-92
ALs, 9 June [1581]. (88) DM500

Bischoffwerder, Johann Rudolf von, 1741-1803
ALs, 12 Feb 1788. Schroeder collection. (89) DM430

Bishop, Sir Henry R., 1786-1855 —& Moore, Thomas, 1779-1852
Autograph Ms, song, Here at Thy Tomb, musical arrangement for 2 voices; 1831-1835. (91) $600

Bismarck, Johanna von, 1824-94
ALs, 2 Sept 1888. Schroeder collection. (89) DM300

Bismarck, Otto von, 1815-98
Autograph Ms, [1862]. (88) DM700
— Autograph Ms, orders regarding the management of his estate, [n.d.]. (89) DM300
ALs, 25 Sept 1849. (89) £400
— 19 Jan 1851. (89) DM550
— 28 Aug 1851. (90) DM850
— 24 [Apr 1854]. (90) DM800
— 6 Apr/25 May 1862. (88) £420
— 18 May 1862. 2 pp, 8vo. To J. A. Fischer. Offering 2 bear cubs to the zoo in Berlin. (91) DM1,100
— 25 Apr 1863. (89) DM420
— 12 Dec 1868. 1 p, 4to. To a colleague in Saxony. Transmitting a letter by the King of Prussia. (88) DM1,300
— 1 Mar 1875. Schroeder collection. (89) DM450
— 1 Apr 1878. 2 pp, 4to. To Empress Augusta. Thanking for congratulations on his birthday. With related material. (88) DM6,000
Ls, 8 Apr 1859. Byer collection. (90) $400
— 24 Nov 1862. (89) DM440
— 24 Oct 1867. (90) DM480
— 24 Nov 1870. (90) DM900
— 16 Feb 1871. Schroeder collection. (89) DM750
— 26 Oct 1871. (90) DM500
— 11 Jan 1872. 4 pp, folio. To Kaiser Wilhelm I. Explaining why Prince Friedrich Karl's request to dispatch a ship to Constantinople cannot be granted. With related ALs by Prince Friedrich Karl, 30 Dec 1871, 3 pp, 4to, including autograph endorsement by Wilhelm I, 12 Jan 1872. Schroeder collection. (89) DM1,600
— 10 May 1876. (91) DM400

BISMARCK

— 31 May 1877. (88) DM550
— 5 Apr 1885. (88) DM500
— 4 Apr 1886. (89) DM240
— 5 June 1887. (90) DM440
— 9 Jan 1890. (89) DM290
— 7 Nov 1893. (90) DM550
— 5 Apr 1894. (91) DM380
— 3 Aug 1895. (89) DM250
— 27 Dec 1897. (91) DM400
AN, [Aug 1871?]. (88) DM380
ADs, 31 Mar 1869. (88) DM850
Ds, 31/19 Aug 1860. (89) DM210
— WERNER, ANTON VON. - Orig drawing, pencil port of Bismarck overlooking the battlefield at Sedan, sgd A.v.W. & dated 1890. 28cm by 21cm. With related material. (90) DM4,200

Bismarck, Otto von, 1815-98 —& Moltke, Helmuth, Graf von, 1800-91
[An ALs by Bismarck, 12 Jan 1864, 3 pp, 8vo, to Minister of War Albrecht von Roon, worrying that Austrian troops may reach the Schleswig territory earlier than Prussian troops, with related ALs by Moltke to Roon, 13 Jan 1864, 1 p, 4to, sold at star on 2 Dec 1988, lots 2204 & 2205, for DM8,000.]

Bismarck, Otto von, 1815-98. See: Roon, Albrecht & Bismarck

Bismarck, Otto von, 1815-98 —& Wilhelm I, Deutscher Kaiser 1797-1888
[An envelope, addressed to Wilhelm I in Bismarck's hand, & to Bismarck in Wilhelm I's hand, sold at star on 2 Dec 1988, lot 2231, for DM320.]

Bissett, Sir John, 1777-1854
Ms, retained copy letterbook, 15 May to 1 Sept 1812. (91) £300

Bissier, Julius, 1893-1965
Collection of 3 A Ls s & Ls, 2 Feb to 10 Apr 1948 & [n.d.]. (90) DM800
Ls, 24 June 1963. (89) DM200

Bizet, Georges, 1838-75
Autograph music, Prelude-Ouverture to L'Arlesienne, arranged for piano; [c.1872]. 4 pp, folio. Notated on up to 12 staves per page, with revisions. Including autograph tp, inscr to Mme Georges Bizet. (89) £18,000

AMERICAN BOOK PRICES CURRENT

ALs, 14 July 1871. 2 pp, 8vo. To Ambroise Thomas. Congratulating him on an appointment & praising his opera Hamlet. (90) £1,900
— [1871]. (90) £1,000
— [1873]. 3 pp, 4to. To [Vizentini]. Concerning rehearsals for Gounod's opera Jeanne d'Arc. (90) DM2,600
— [n.d.]. 3 pp, 16mo. To Paul Puget. Offering encouragement in his career. (91) £1,100
— [n.d.]. 2 pp, 8vo. Recipient unnamed. Expressing interest in his successes & misfortunes. (90) DM2,400
— [n.d.]. 1 p, 8vo. To his friend Leroy. Requesting him to forward papers relating to his opera [La jolie fille de Perth]. (89) DM2,000
— [n.d.]. 1 p, 8vo. Recipient unnamed. Regretting he is missing "cette occasion a vous applaudir". (88) DM2,200
ADs, 24 Feb 1869. (89) £550

Bjoernson, Bjoernstjerne, 1832-1910
A Ls s (2), 11 Jan [n.y.] & [n.d.]. (88) DM320

Blacher, Boris, 1903-75
Autograph music, "2 Ritornell", fragment from an unnamed work; [n.d.]. (89) DM440
— Autograph music, 8 bars from an unidentified work, in full score. (90) DM500
— Autograph music, sketches for a composition, c.140 bars; [c.1942]. (90) DM650
Photograph, sgd & inscr, 1969. (88) DM230

Black, Shirley Temple. See: Temple, Shirley

Blackman, John Lucie, c.1792-1815. See: Peninsular War

Blackmore, Richard Doddridge, 1825-1900
ALs, 10 Mar 1887. (88) £180

Blair, Eric Arthur, 1903-50. See: Orwell, George

Blair, Mary
Original drawings, (2), to illus Ichabod Crane, [n.d.]. (89) £80

Blair, Montgomery, 1813-83
Franking signature, [26 Sep 1861]. Alexander collection. (90) $270

Blake, James Hubert ("Eubie"), 1883-1983
ALs, 29 June 1973. (90) $80
Autograph quotation, 4 bars of music, entitled I'm Just Wild About Harry; [n.d]. (91) $140
Photograph, sgd, [n.d.]. (89) $50

Blake, Robert, 1599-1657
Ls, 23 Mar 1653/54. (90) £350

Blake, William, 1757-1827
ALs, 18 Jan 1808. 4 pp, 4to. To Ozias Humphry. Describing his painting The Last Judgment. With ALs from Humphry to Blake, 15 June 1806. Barrett collection. (89) $24,000
— [2 July 1826]. 1 p, 4to. To John Linnell. Postponing a visit on account of his health. Doheny collection. (89) $20,000

Blanc, Mel
Photograph, sgd & inscr, 26 July [19]76. (91) $130
— Anr, 30 May [19]87. (90) $130

Blasco Ibanez, Vicente, 1867-1928
Autograph Ms, novel, Canas y barro, Sept to Nov 1902. 456 pp, 4to. Complete working Ms, sgd. In purple ink. (88) $20,000

Blathwayt, William, 1649?-1717
Series of 13 A Ls, drafts, 15 July to 7 Nov 1701. 19 pp, folio. To Laurence Hyde, Earl of Rochester. Mostly written from Holland, informing Rochester of events during his attendance on William III, referring to Marlborough, affairs in Ireland & Jamaica, etc. With numerous revisions. Mtd in an album with 2 A Ls s & copies of 2 letters by Rochester, 1685 to 1705. Folio. Phillipps Ms. 8609 (88) £1,900

Blechen, Karl, 1798-1840
ALs, 22 Feb 1837. (91) DM850

Blei, Franz, 1871-1942
Series of 4 Ls s, 14 Aug 1912 to [19 May 1913]. (90) DM340

Blei, Franz, 1871-1942 —& Kubin, Alfred, 1877-1959
[An autograph Ms by Blei, poem, 3 stanzas beginning "Es drueckt dich keine Last", sgd & dated 18 July 1905, written below pen-&-ink drawing of a man by Kubin, c.35mm by 55mm, sgd & dated July 1905, sold at HN on 20 May 1988, lot 3267, for DM1,100.]

Blennerhassett, Harman, 1765-1831
ADs, 12 Sept 1806. (91) $220

Bleriot, Louis, 1872-1936
ANs, [n.d.]. (90) DM300

Blind, Karl, 1826-1907
ALs, 21 May 1876. (88) DM440

Blixen, Tania, 1885-1962. See: Blixen-Finecke, Karen

Blixen-Finecke, Karen, Baroness, 1885-1962
ALs, 20 Dec 1957. (89) DM460

Bloch, Ernest, 1880-1959
Autograph music, 2d String Quartet, full score, sgd & dated 28 Oct 1945. 54 pp, folio. In blue & black ink on 4 systems per page, 4 staves each. With autograph tp. (88) £1,600
— Autograph music, Annexe de l'Interlude du IIIe Acte de Macbeth, working Ms; sgd, dated 14 June 1938 & inscr to Alexandre Cohen. (88) £400
— Autograph music, Service Sacre, 1er Basson, [n.d.]. (90) DM700
— Autograph music, sketches based on compositions by Bach, 28 Dec [1947] to 13 Apr 1948. 31 pp, 32cm by 24cm. (90) DM1,700
— Autograph music, sketches based on Bach's Fugue IV, 29 Oct to 9 Nov 1940. 64 pp, 17.5cm by 20cm; 6 staves each. In spiral notebook. Mostly in pencil. (89) DM1,600
— Autograph music, sketches based on works by Bach, 12 Feb 1948 & [n.d.]. 13 pp, size not stated; 14 staves each. In spiral notebook. In ink & pencil. (89) DM1,200
— Autograph music, Violin Concerto,

BLOCH

complete draft in short score & sketches; 1933 to 1937. 196 pp, various sizes, in 2 annotated folders. Working Ms, sgd & dated in several places. Including some later autograph commentaries. (88) £3,600

Collection of 2 A Ls s & AL, 28 Sept 1934 to 9 Apr 1938. 8 pp, 4to. To Eleanor Foster. About performances of his works, his travels, current plans, etc. AL fragment. (90) DM1,100

Series of 8 A Ls s, 1933 to 1939. (88) £1,000

A Ls s (2), 24 May & 15 Nov 1932. (90) DM600

— A Ls s (2), 28 July 1949 & 5 Feb 1956. (89) DM620

ALs, 7 Nov 1931. (88) DM850

— 24 July 1936. (90) DM340

— 28 Jan 1949. (91) $275

— 5 May 1953. Byer collection. (90) $275

Ls, 9 Mar 1955. (91) DM440

Autograph quotation, 8 notes drawn diagonally, "the old fashioned major scale"; 5 Mar 1927. (91) $150

Bloch, Ernst, 1885-1977

Autograph Ms, beginning of a chapter of an unnamed philosophical treatise, numbered 18a; [n.d.]. (90) DM480

— Autograph Ms, comments on philosophy & nature, paginated 689a, possibly for his work Das Materialismusproblem; [n.d.]. (91) DM600

— Autograph Ms, leaf 5c of a treatise on social utopias, draft; [n.d.]. 2 pp, folio. 1st page typescript with numerous autograph revisions. (89) DM2,200

— Autograph Ms, section about Hegel's Phaenomenologie des Geistes, numbered 81a; [n.d.]. (90) DM500

ALs, 22 July 1960. (88) DM300

— 4 Jan 1961. 2 pp, folio. To Momi von Bendemann. Reminiscing about the past. With related material. (88) DM1,100

— [n.d.]. 2 pp, 4to. To [Else Ladenburg]. Inviting her to visit him in Maine. With related material. (89) DM1,050

AMERICAN BOOK PRICES CURRENT

Bloch, Iwan, 1872-1922
ALs, 26 Sept 1907. (91) DM440

Blodget, Samuel, 1757-1814. See: Washington, District of Columbia

Bloembergen, Nicolaas
Autograph Ms, Nonlinear Optics and Spectroscopy, draft for his Nobel lecture; 1981. (90) DM320

Blomberg, Wilhelm von, 1786-1846
ALs, 3 Sept 1806. Albrecht collection. (91) SF360

Bloomfield, Joseph, 1753-1823
Ls, 23 Mar 1805. (89) $65

Bloomfield, Robert, 1766-1823
ALs, 29 May 1804. (89) £500

Blos, Wilhelm, 1849-1927
ALs, 3 Mar 1924. (90) DM380

Blount, William, 1749-1800
Ls, 6 June 1793. 2 pp, 4to. To Gov. [Isaac] Shelby. Informing him about a delegation of Indians going to Philadelphia. (91) $1,200

Bluecher von Wahlstatt, Gebhard Leberecht, Fuerst, 1742-1819
[Horn, Johann Jakob von. - A collection of 14 letters addressed to him (partly while aide-de-camp to Bluecher), 1812 to 1820, with related material, sold at star on 10 Mar 1988, lot 1180, for DM800.]

Collection of 2 A Ls s & Ls, 1811 to 1817. 3 pp, 4to. To various recipients about different matters. (91) £1,100

A Ls s (2), 23 Aug 1811 & 13 Feb 1817. (89) £700

ALs, [1794]. 1 p, 4to. To Col. Ernst Hermann von Koelichen. Informing him that a French attack is to be expected the next day. (90) DM1,700

— 27 Oct 1799. 1 p, folio. To an unnamed relative. Promising to send horses, & reporting about the war in the Netherlands. Schroeder collection. (89) DM1,500

— 25 July 1806. 3 pp, folio. To Friedrich Wilhelm III, King of Prussia. Urging him to declare war on France & assuring him that the Prussian army will vindicate the honor of the country.

(90) DM8,000
— 25 Sept 1809. 2 pp, 4to. To his son Gebhardt. About troop movements & family news. (88) DM2,200
— 20 Sept 1813. 3 pp, 4to. To his wife. Expressing his opinion that the French will shortly abandon Dresden; says that their son Franz has been wounded & captured. (88) DM9,500
— 10 Feb 1814. 2 pp, 4to. To his wife. Reporting about the campaign in France & hoping for a speedy end of the war. (90) DM8,800
— 7 Mar 1815. 2 pp, 4to. To his son-in-law Count Asseburg. Family news, & saying he intends to retire & go to Silesia shortly. (88) DM2,600
— 26 July 1815. 3 pp, folio. To Staatsrat L'Abbaye. Expressing his annoyance about diplomats & politicians who ruin advantages won by the military. Repaired. Schroeder collection. (89) DM5,800
— 17 Feb 1817. 2 pp, folio. To his steward Schwenke. Discussing matters pertaining to his estate & the sale of Kunzendorff. (91) DM2,400
— 29 July 1819. 3 pp, 4to. To his cousin Count Bluecher at Altona. Inviting him for a hunt, & mentioning the Battle of Waterloo. (89) DM1,800
— [n.d.]. 1 p, 4to. To the military pay office. Protesting against a pay cut. Sgd B. Schroeder collection. (89) DM1,600
Ls, 7 Feb 1795. Schroeder collection. (89) DM650
— 25 Aug 1800. (90) DM850
— 23 June 1801. (89) DM650
— 1 Dec 1801. (88) DM600
— 18 Jan 1808. 4 pp, folio. To Marshall [Soult]. As military governor of Pomerania, discussing problems relating to the continental blockade & to income from taxes. In French. (91) DM1,400
— 15 Sept 1811. (88) DM1,000
— 4 Aug 1814. (90) DM450
— 25 Feb 1815. (89) DM700
— 16 Oct 1815. 3 pp, 4to. To the Prussian minister in London [von Jacobi-Kloest]. Expressing his disapproval of diplomatic blunders after the allied victory. With autograph subscription.

(90) DM3,600
— 25 Mar 1816. (88) DM700
— 18 Sept 1818. Schroeder collection. (89) DM600
ADs, 22 Sept 1812. (91) DM900
Ds, 4 Aug 1817. (90) DM550
Autograph endorsement, sgd, 14 Feb 1808. Schroeder collection. (89) DM750
See also: Napoleonic Wars

Bluecher, Hans, 1888-1955
Autograph Ms, essay, Friedrich Frhr. (90) DM500

Blum, Robert, 1807-48
ALs, 8 June 1843. (88) DM480
— 29 Oct 1844. (89) DM900
— 2 June 1847. (89) DM280

Blumauer, Alois, 1755-98
ALs, 4 Jan 1787. (91) DM800

Blumenbach, Johann Friedrich, 1752-1840
ALs, 1 Nov 1802. (90) DM600
— 22 Feb [1820]. (90) DM240
— 20 Jan 1822. (91) DM340
— 26 Apr [n.y.]. Albrecht collection. (91) SF280

Blumenthal, Leonhard, Graf von, 1810-1900
Series of 5 A Ls s, 4 to 9 Dec 1870. Schroeder collection. (89) DM950
ALs, 4 May 1859. Schroeder collection. (89) DM400

Blumentritt, Guenther, 1892-1967
A Ls s (2), 30 Mar & 12 June 1949. (90) DM550
ALs, 4 June 1949. (90) DM440
— 28 June 1949. (89) DM220

Blunden, Edmund Charles, 1896-1974
A Ls s (2), 8 Sept 1929 & 27 Sept 1965. (88) £120
See also: Sassoon, Siegfried & Blunden

Blunt, Anthony
ALs, [n.d.]. (90) $95

Bobrowski, Johannes, 1917-65
Autograph Ms, poem, Alexis Kiwi, 14 May [c.1961/62]. (89) DM620

Boccaccio, Giovanni, 1313-75
Ms, Des Cas des Nobles Hommes et Femmes, in the French trans of Laurent de Premierfait dedicated to Jean, Duc de Berry. [Paris, c.1470]. 508 leaves (some lacking), vellum & paper, 372mm by 260mm. Repaired 16th cent blindstamped pigskin over wooden bds. In dark brown ink in a distinguished lettre batarde. Illuminated; with 5 very large miniatures from the circle of Maitre Francois. (89) £68,000

Boccherini, Luigi, 1743-1805
Autograph Ms, thematic cat of compositions written c.1775 to c.1796, containing autograph incipits for 84 works; sgd & dated 21 Feb 1797. 6 pp, folio. Prepared for the pbr Ignaz Pleyel & incorporated within legal document. 2 pp in anr hand. Singed at edges. (89) £5,000

Bode, Johann Elert, 1747-1826
15 July 1822. (89) DM420

Bodelschwingh, Friedrich von, 1831-1910
Autograph Ms, notes for a religious service, 5 Aug [n.y.]. (89) DM320
ALs, 1 Oct 1898. (89) DM280

Bodenheim, Maxwell, 1893-1954
Series of 11 Ls s, [1930s]. (89) $450

Bodmer, Johann Jakob, 1698-1783
ALs, 18 June 1777. 1 p, 4to. To [Johann Martin Miller]. Sending his latest publications. (91) DM4,500

Bodoni, Giovanni Battista, 1740-1813
Autograph Ms, list of book supplied to Count Biffi, sgd; [c.1802]. (91) £900
A Ls s (2), 28 Apr & 2 Oct 1795. 3 p, 4to. To Cardinal De Nelis in Bologna. About sending him books. (91) $3,600

Boecklin, Arnold, 1827-1901
ALs, 6 Oct 1875. (88) DM1,000
Collection of Ls & photograph, sgd, 28 May 1896. (89) DM650
ADs, 27 June 1855. (88) DM470

Boehland, Johannes, 1903-64
Original drawings, (36), various musical instruments, to illus a book ptd for UNESCO. (89) DM220

Boehm, Hermann, 1884-1972
[His visitors' book, Oct 1933 to Aug 1939, c.80 pp, 4to, in lea bdg, containing the signatures of Hitler, Goering, Hess, Blomberg, Goebbels, Doenitz, etc., sold at star on 1 Dec 1989, lot 1427, for DM11,500.]

Boehm, Karl, 1894-1981
Collection of 2 A Ls s & 4 Ls s, [1970] to 1979. (90) DM720

Boell, Heinrich, 1917-85
Collection of 2 A Ls s, 11 Ls s, & 2 postcards, sgd, 1951 to 1985. 13 pp, 8vo, & cards. To Theodor Kleff. Concerning dates for lectures, the sale of his books, etc. (91) DM1,250
ALs, 31 Oct 1959. (91) DM650
— 22 Nov 1960. (91) DM400
Ls, 1 Sept 1969. (88) DM200
Autograph postcards (2), sgd, 13 Aug 1964 & 3 Mar 1966. (89) DM370

Boer War
[Four letterbooks containing transcripts of letters, 29 Oct 1899 to 11 Sept 1915, from Sergeants Leonard & Frank Adams to their mother, about their experiences in the Boer War, with related material, sold at S on 15 Nov 1988, lot 1718, for £340 to Maggs.]
[Vyvyan, Lieut. Col. Courtenay. - His papers, mostly relating to his duties as Town Commandant during the Siege of Mafeking, 1899 to 1901, over 2,000 pp, various sizes, sold at pn on 15 Nov 1990, lot 52, for £23,000 to Sawyer.]
Typescript, staff diary of the 3d Division of the South Africa Field Force, 21 Oct 1899 to 16 May 1901. (90) £130
— BARNETT, SGT. JOHN. - Autograph Ms, journal, 1 Oct 1879 to 1 June 1902. About 60 pp, 8vo. Describing action at Hussar Hill, Pieter's Hill, Bergendahl, evicting Boer families, etc. With related material. (89) £130
— BOTHA, GEN. LOUIS. - Ds, 8 May 1902. 1 p, folio. Pass through British lines issued to M. de Beer & others travelling to a meeting under flag of truce. Also sgd by Col. Hamilton. (89) £260
— BURN-MURDOCK, LIEUT. COL. J. F. - ALs, 9 Aug 1900. 8 pp, folio. To Kaiser Wilhelm II. Reporting about the battles of Colenso, Spion Kop, &

Springfield, & the relief of Ladysmith. Initialled & dated by Wilhelm II. (90) £300

— GIRDWOOD, LIEUT. ERIC STANLEY. - An album containing photographs of army life in the Boer War, army documents, & related material, c.1899 to 1914, 4to, sold at pn on 17 Sept, lot 533, for £400 to Bodily. 88

— KETSCHENDORF, CHARLES DE. - Autograph Ms, diary of the campaign at Ladysmith, Sept 1899 to July 1900. About 60 pp, 4to, in a notebook. Including newspaper clippings, etc. (89) £800

— MARKHAM, ALFRED. - ALs, 17 Dec [1899] to 17 Jan 1900. 15 pp, 8vo. Recipient unnamed. Reporting from the siege of Ladysmith. With related material. (90) £420

— MCCRACKEN, BRIG. GEN. F. W. N. - Autograph Ms, describing orders to seize a hill near Colesberg & the formation adopted for an attack on 1 Jan 1900, with related material; [n.d.]. 50 pp, folio. (90) £240

— ORPEN-PALMER, LIEUT. HAROLD. - Letterbook & journal, 23 Aug 1899-28 feb 1900. 57 pp plus blanks, 4to, syn. Includes 43 pp of reference to the Siege of Ladysmith; with a few cuttings & Ladysmith ephemera loosely inserted. (91) £600

— STOKER, CORPORAL G. - Autograph Ms, Diary Of The War, [n.d.]. 185 pp, 8vo, in def bdg. Describing action in the Transvaal. In pencil. (88) £200

Boerhaave, Hermann, 1668-1738
ALs, 9 Aug 1735. (91) £900

Boerne, Ludwig, 1786-1837
ALs, 26 July 1833. 1 p, 4to. To the bookseller Koenig. Offering his Briefe aus Paris for publication. (90) DM3,200

Ds, 6 Jan 1823. (90) DM550

Boettger, Adolf, 1815-70
Autograph Ms, poem, Bei Lesung von Heine's poetischem Nachlass, [1869]. Albrecht collection. (91) SF420

Boettger, Johann Friedrich, 1682-1719
Ds, 12 May 1716. 1 p, folio. Receipt for 5,000 pounds of white clay from Colditz. (91) DM7,000

Boetticher, Hans, 1883-1934. See: Ringelnatz, Joachim

Boettiger, Karl August, 1760-1835
ALs, 13 Oct 1823. (90) DM260

Bogardus, Abraham
Photograph, sgd, [n.d.]. (91) $220

Bogart, Humphrey
Ds, 12 Dec 1950. 8 by 5 inches. Preliminary Application for [Driver's] License. On State of California Department of Motor Vehicle form. Framed with a photograph. (89) $2,200

Cut signature, [n.d.]; in pencil. (88) $200
Photograph, sgd & inscr, [n.d.]. (91) $800
Signature, [1935], on portion of a program, 25mm by 75mm. (90) $400

— Anr, [n.d.]. On 1st music page of sheet music for As Time Goes By, from the film Casablanca. 2 sheets, 9 by 12 inches; incomplete. (91) $3,500

Bohr, Niels, 1885-1962
Ls, 13 May 1949. (88) DM400
Signature, [1945]. (91) $130

Boie, Heinrich Christian, 1744-1806
ALs, 5 Nov 1772. 3 pp, 4to. To Gottfried August Buerger. Interesting letter about friends & their literary work. Initialled. (89) DM3,600

— 3 Nov 1774. 2 pp, 8vo. To Johann Martin Miller. About a recent visit with Goethe, & mentioning Klopstock, Herder, & other literary friends. Albrecht collection. (91) SF3,000

— 5 July 1779. 1 p, 4to. To Philipp Erasmus Reich. Sending a corrected Ms by H. P. Sturz for publication. (90) DM1,300
See also: Hoelty, Ludwig Christoph Heinrich

Boieldieu, Francois Adrien, 1775-1834
ALs, [1824]. (91) DM200
— 19 Apr 1826. (91) £400
— 25 Nov 1833. (90) DM280

Boileau-Despreaux, Nicolas, 1636-1711
ALs, 19 May [1687]. Barrett collection. (89) $800

Boisseree, Sulpiz, 1783-1854
[An archive of papers, containing numerous drafts of letters & some letters addressed to him, 1810 to 1850, 140 pp, 4to & 8vo, waterstained, sold at star on 4 Apr 1991, lot 526, for DM10,000.]
ALs, 25 Mar 1820. (88) DM750
— 17 May 1828. 2 pp, 4to. To [C. W.] Coudray, Superintendent of Public Works at Weimar. Introducing Joseph Stieler who will paint Goethe for the King of Bavaria. Albrecht collection. (91) SF2,600

Boito, Arrigo, 1842-1918
ALs, [27 May 1915]. (89) DM340
— [27 May 1915]. (90) DM620
— 17 Jan [n.y.]. (90) DM440
— [n.d.]. (90) DM300

Bolger, Ray, 1904-87
Photograph, sgd & inscr, [n.d.]. (91) $100

Bolingbroke, Henry St. John, Viscount, 1678-1751
Ms, Copies of Mr Secretary St John's Letters to ... (89) £450

Bolivar, Simon, 1783-1830
ALs, 21 Dec 1827. 4 pp, 4to. To Jose Fernandez Madrid. Expressing his frustrations with economic problems, political divisions & territorial rivalries in the Republic of Colombia. (91) $6,500
Ls, 31 July 1817. 1 p, folio. To "Espanoles Europeos" in Guayana. As Head of the Venezuelan Republic, requesting them to support his cause. (90) £4,400
— 1 May 1818. 2 pp, size not stated. To Col. Wilson. Enquiring about his whereabouts. On ptd letterhead. In folio cloth case. Robinson collection. (88) £1,400
— 14 Feb 1819. 1 p, 4to. To James Hamilton. Inviting him to attend the session of the Congress of Venezuela the following day. With recipient's trans on verso & draft of reply on integral leaf. (91) £1,400
— 14 Sept 1819. 2 pp, folio. To the Governor General of the Province of Antioquia. Informing him about the recent successful campaign & discussing the lack of funds to buy arms & supplies. (90) $3,200
— 14 Dec 1819. 3 pp, size not stated. To Gen. John Devereux. Letter of congratulation after the liberation of Nueva Granada. On ptd letterhead. In folio cloth case. Robinson collection. (88) £1,600
— 5 Sept 1820. 2 pp, folio. To the Governor of Antioquia. Requesting him to raise money for the coming campaign. (91) $1,700
— 6 Sept 1820. 2 pp, folio. To the Governor of Antioquia. Repeating his order to raise money for the hiring of riflemen. (91) $1,500
— 2 July 1821. 3 pp, 4to. To Gen. La Torre. Offering to negotiate a peace treaty with Spain. (91) £9,000
— 3 Aug 1825. 3 pp, folio. To the President of the General Assembly of Bolivia. Accepting the leadership of the newly-born state of Bolivia. Margin def. (91) £13,000
— 15 Feb 1826. 2 pp, folio. To Andres Bello. Expressing surprise not to have received news from recipient in London. (90) £2,800
— 6 Apr 1827. 2 pp, folio. To Gen. Antonio Jose de Sucre. Offering him the Presidency of Bolivia. Margin frayed. (91) £16,000
— 8 Oct 1827. 1 p, 4to. To Feliz Blanco. Giving orders regarding payments to a congressional representative. Repaired. (88) DM2,600
Ds, 19 Nov 1817 & 20 Dec 1818. 4 pp, folio. 2 postscripts on Ms document, approving of funds for reparations & supplies for the city of Caracas. (91) $3,750
— 20 Sept 1822. 2 pp, folio. Military promotion for Pedro Antonio de la Pena. Also sgd by Jose Flores. (90) $1,400
— 1 July 1826. (90) $900
— [1828?]. 1 p, folio. Ship's papers; unaccomplished. (90) $1,200
— 16 Sept 1829. 3 pp, folio. Military promotion for Lieut. Vicente Javanes. (91) DM1,800

Bonaparte, Caroline, 1782-1839
ALs, 1 May [1813?]. (88) DM300
Ls, 30 July [after 1815]. (90) DM200

Bonaparte Family
[A collection of 2 A Ls s, 3 Ls s, & Ds by members of Napoleon's family, with 41 items relating to the Convention & the Napoleonic armies, sold at C on 22 June 1988, lot 7, for £1,400 to L'Autographe.]
[A collection of 10 letters & documents by various members of the Bonaparte family, 1800 to 1822, with a letter by Cambaceres, sold at S on 17 Nov 1988, lot 163, for £600 to Rye.]
[A collection of letters by members of the Bonaparte family, 1809 to mid-19th cent, with a description of Napoleon's will, together 38 pp, various sizes, with related material, sold at S on 26 Nov, lot 131, for £320 to Severi.]
[A collection of 12 autographs by Napoleon III & other members of the Bonaparte family, 19th cent, sold at S on 17 Nov 1988, lot 164, for £400 to Severi.]

Bonaparte, Jerome, 1784-1860
Collection of 2 A Ls s, AL & 3 Ls s, 1820 to 1831. 11 pp, 4to & 8vo. To Baron Gayl. About his financial situation, family news, etc. With related material. (89) DM2,600
ALs, 20 Sept 1814. (88) DM900
Ls, 11 Mar 1852. (89) DM240
ANs, [n.d.]. (91) $170
Ds, 6 Oct 1812. (90) DM420
— 2 Apr 1813. 1 p, folio. Confirmation of nobility for Hermann Werner von Lochausen. Including painting of the arms in gold & colors. (91) DM1,200

Bonaparte, Joseph, 1768-1844
A Ls s (2), 20 Dec 1830 & 21 Dec 1831. (89) $425
ALs, 23 Feb 1813. (88) DM600
Ls, 31 Oct 1807. Byer collection. (90) $300
— 18 Feb 1814. (90) DM320

Bonaparte, Louis, King of Holland, 1778-1846
ALs, [n.d.]. (88) DM400
Ls, [17 Jan 1805]. (88) $110

Bonaparte, Lucien, 1775-1840
ALs, 1 May 1818. (90) DM270
Ls, [10 Sept 1800]. Byer collection. (90) $225

Bonaparte, Maria Anna Elisa, 1777-1820
Ls, 12 June 1811. (90) DM250
— 18 May 1812. (88) DM360

Bonaparte, Maria Letizia Ramolino, 1750-1836
Ls, [1 June 1802]. Crawford Collection. (88) £500
— 4 Apr 1807. (90) DM720

Bonaparte, Napoleon Eugene Louis, son of Napoleon III, 1856-79
ALs, 31 Dec 1870. (90) DM380

Bonaparte, Pauline, 1780-1825
ALs, [25 Feb 1801]. (90) DM1,000
— 24 May 1813. (90) DM320
— 5 May 1816. (91) DM380
— 2 Feb [1823]. (89) DM260
— 13 May 1824. (88) DM380

Bonaventura, Saint, 1221-74. See: Speculum Beate Marie Virginis

Bone, Lady Gertrude Helena, 1876-1962
Collection of ALs & 3 autograph Mss, 18 Mar 1928 to 1933. (89) £70

Bone, Stephen, 1904-58 —& Adshead, Mary
Original drawings, (13), to illus their own Little Boys and their Boats, 1936. Archives of J. M. Dent & Son. (88) £750
— Original drawings, (24), to illus their own The Little Boy and his House, 1936. Archives of J. M. Dent & Son. (88) £850

Bonet, Paul, 1889-1971
[His papers, comprising letters to & from Bonet, accounts, a draft of his wartime diary, etc., 1930 to 1940, 120 pp, with related material, sold at S on 20 Nov 1990, lot 380, for £2,000 to Beres.]

Bonheur, Rosa, 1822-99
ALs, 27 July 1886. (90) $200
Signature, 27 July 1893. (91) $60

Bonhoeffer, Dietrich, 1906-45
ALs, 5 Mar 1942. 4 pp, 4to. To an unnamed lady. Expressing condolences on the death of her husband & explaining grief as a religious experience. (91) DM4,200

Boniface IX, Pope, c.1350-1404
Document, 5 Dec 1402. 1 p, vellum, 30cm by 48cm. Bull, granting revenues from the church in Riedhausen to the Hospital of the Holy Ghost at Ravensburg. With lead seal. (88) DM4,200

Boniface VIII, Pope, 1235?-1303
Ms, Liber Sextus Decretalium. [Italy, c.1300]. 2 separate leaves only, 406mm by 290mm. In a rounded gothic script. Comprising 1st leaf & opening of Book IX. With 2 large initials (1 historiated). (90) £1,800

— Ms, Liber Sextus Decretalium, with the Gloss of Giovanni d'Andrea. [Bologna, 3d quarter of 14th cent]. 130 leaves & flyleaf, vellum, 433mm by 292mm, in 19th-cent Italian calf. In various shades of dark brown ink in 2 sizes of a skillful rounded gothic bookhand. With decorated initials throughout with penwork infilling, over 150 large painted initials (4 incomplete), 6-line historiated initial, 4 column-width miniatures & very large double-column miniature with elaborate border. Astor MS.A.4. (88) £55,000

Bonizo of Sutri, c.1045-c.1095
Ms, Libellus de Sacramentis, & Liber de Vita Christiana. [Mantua?, c.1150]. 123 leaves (some lacking), vellum, 184mm by 115mm, in early 19th-cent English calf. By 2 main scribes in small rounded late romanesque scholastic bookhands. With over 400 large painted initials, mostly in red. (91) £15,000

Bonnard, Pierre, 1867-1947
ALs, [21 Feb 1903]. (89) DM440
— [n.d.]. (90) DM750

Bonomi, Joseph, 1796-1878
A Ls s (2), 30 June 1830 & 18 May 1832. (88) £350

Bonpland, Aime, 1773-1858
ALs, [18 Nov 1800]. 2 pp, 4to. Recipient unnamed. Giving an account of his stay with Indians in the interior of Venezuela. (91) DM4,500

Bonsels, Waldemar, 1880-1952
Series of 14 A Ls s, 12 Jan 1908 to 30 Sept 1913. (90) DM660

Bonstetten, Karl Viktor von, 1745-1832
ALs, [1787-92]. (90) DM520
AL, 9 Apr [1813]. (90) DM230

Boone, Daniel, 1734-1820
[A land grant, 1730, transferring title to the Pennsylvania farm on which Boone was born to his father Squire Boone, folio, sold at R on 17 June 1989, lot 208, for $600.]

ADs, 1 May 1780. 1 p, 4to. Receipt for £310 paid by Thomas Jameson for land. Also sgd by William Haye. Mathematical calculations & docket on verso. Margins def. (89) $3,000

— 1 May 1780. 1 p, 8vo. Receipt for £310 paid by Thomas Jameson for land located for him & others. Also sgd by William Haye. (89) $4,200

— 22 Dec [c.1782-1788]. 2 pp, folio. Survey of land from the estate of John Kennedy for Thomas Logwood; with plat drawing of bounds. On verso receipt for fees, sgd. Worn; silked & encased in Mylar. (88) $2,500

Ds, 23 Nov 1782. 1 p, 1.7 by 7.8 inches. Certificate that a horse was used in public service. Repaired. (88) $2,200

— [late Nov 1782]. 1 p, 2 by 8 inches. Certification "that a horse, the property of Benjamin Netherland was in Public Service for the use of my Company..." Mtd; repaired. (90) $4,000

— 8 Dec 1788. 1 p, oblong folio. Indenture involving Boone & Simon Kenton. (91) $5,500

Booth, Edwin, 1833-93 —&
Booth, John Wilkes, 1838-65
[A group of 4 items relating to them, including 2 playbills, & cut signature & ALs by Edwin, sold at sg on 11 Feb 1988, lot 18, for $225.]

Booth, Evangeline, 1865-1950

ALs, 1919. (90) $300

Booth, John Wilkes, 1838-65

Photograph, [n.d.]. (90) $550

— FORD, BLANCHE CHAPMAN. - Typescript, interview given to John Boos, 31 Dec 1912. 5 pp, 8vo. Describing the identification of Booth's body before burial. With holograph statement, sgd, confirming identification on verso of last page. (89) $2,200

— GILBET, C. C. - Autograph telegram, 15 Apr 1865. 2 pp, 8vo. To Capt. R. M. Clarke. Order to arrest John Wilkes Booth & M. W. Canning. Framed with a photograph of Booth. (90) $850
See also: Booth, Edwin & Booth

Booth, William, 1829-1912

Collection of ALs & Ls (partly autograph), 15 Dec 1905 & 18 May 1912. (88) £120

Photograph, sgd, [n.d.]. (90) £75

Borchardt, Rudolf, 1877-1945

Autograph Ms, poem, Eine Sestine von der Magnolie im Herbst; [n.d.]. (91) DM1,000

— Autograph Ms, poem, Seufzer im Neunreim, draft; [n.d.]. 1 p, 4to. 27 lines. (91) DM2,600

— Autograph Ms, poem, Tauben. [n.d.] 2 pp, 8vo. 15 lines; sgd later. (90) DM1,700

— Autograph Ms, sonnet, beginning "Der Stein bezeugt Lysipp", & 4 further poems, [n.d.]. 4 pp, 8vo. (90) DM3,200

Collection of 4 A Ls s, 6 autograph postcards, sgd, AN, & 2 photographs, sgd, 29 Mar 1912 to 10 Feb 1921. 8 pp, folio & 4to, & cards. To Walther Krug. Interesting letters about his experiences as a soldier, his literary work & private matters. With related material. (90) DM6,000

— Collection of 6 A Ls s & autograph postcard, sgd, 1935 to 1938. 10 pp, various sizes. To Joachim & Otto Stenzel. Aboput various matters relating to his or recipients' work. (91) DM2,400

B[orcken], E. F.

Ms, Reise, Durch Hog Vundt Nieder Teutschlandt, Schweitz, Italien, Sicilien, Sauoyen, Franckreich, Engellandt, Niederlandt..., [c.1650]. 460 pp & flyleaves, folio. Vellum bdg. Possibly incomplete. Some leaves def. [Ownership?] inscr Gabriel Lew on tp. (88) DM2,000

Borden, Gail, 1801-74

ALs, 20 Oct 1835. (91) $475

Borges, Jorge Luis, 1899-1986

[The Borges family archive of autograph Mss, drawings, juvenilia, association copies, photographs, etc., c.1878 to 1986, in 17 vols & unbound, sold at P on 14 Dec 1988, lot 61, for $20,000.]

Autograph Ms, short story, El muerto, [ptd 1949]. 13 pp, various sizes, in wraps. On graph paper from an exercise book, cut into strips of varying width. With extensive autograph corrections & autograph title on front cover. Probably ptr's copy. (90) £9,000

Typescript, short story, Emma Zunz, draft; [1940s]. (89) £1,000

ALs, [1925?]. (88) $500

Photograph, sgd, [n.d.]. (88) £80

Borgia, Francesco, Saint, 1510-72

ALs, 1 Nov 1557. 2 pp, folio. To [Queen Catherine of Portugal]. Explaining that he is sending Fathers Torres & Gonzales with a message. Sgd Franco. In Spanish. Doheny collection. (89) $1,100

Borglum, Gutzon de la Mothe, 1867-1941

[A photograph of Mount Rushmore being sculpted, sgd, dated 1938 & inscr to John E. Sloane, 11 by 14 inches, sold at sg on 21 Sept 1989, lot 56, for $275.]

ALs, [n.d.]. (90) $225

Ls, 15 Sept 1925. (91) $170

Borlaug, Norman Ernest

ALs, 31 July 1978. (88) DM320

BORMANN

Bormann, Martin

Ls, 3 Nov 1937. (91) $300

Autograph endorsement, 9 Sept 1943. On a letter addressed to him by Heinrich Heim, 2 pp, 4to & 8vo, requesting help for a projected museum. Disagreeing with the project; sgd with paraph. (90) DM1,600

Born, Max, 1882-1970

Collection of 4 A Ls s & Ls, 1 Feb 1962 to 31 Jan 1965. 6 pp, various sizes. To Horst Boerschmann, his wife & his mother. About a variety of matters. With related material. (89) DM1,200

Ls, 17 July 1964. (89) DM210

Autograph postcard, sgd, 27 Oct 1914. (88) DM550

— 27 Oct 1914. (91) DM420

Borodin, Aleksandr Porfirevich, 1834-87

ALs, 23 Oct 1884. 2 pp, 4to. To Ambroise Thomas. Applying for admission as a composer to the Societe des Auteurs, Compositeurs et Editeurs de Musique. In French. (90) £4,400

— 18 Jan 1885. 4 pp, 8vo. To Theodore Jadoul. Thanking for recipient's efforts in performing Borodin's 1st symphony in Belgium & promising to dedicate a work to him. In French. (88) DM9,000

— 25 Feb [18]86. 3 pp, 8vo. To an unnamed conductor. Asking him to lend his copy of the score of the B-minor Symphony to Edouard Colonne. (91) £3,800

Borris, Siegfried, 1906-87

Autograph music, sketches for the 2d movement of his Floetensonate Op.131; [n.d.]. (90) DM220

Borromeo, Carlo, Saint, 1538-83

Ls, 8 Oct 1572. Doheny collection. (89) $900

Borrow, George, 1803-81

Autograph Ms (2), fragments of verse, 4 & 12 lines, [n.d.]. 2 pp, 8vo. Doheny collection. (89) $1,800

AMERICAN BOOK PRICES CURRENT

Bosch, Robert, 1861-1942

ALs, 23 Aug 1922. (90) DM420

Bosschere, Jean de, 1881-1953

Original drawing, 10 people in exotic dress, sgd & dated 1920; to illus his own Weird Islands, 1921. In watercolor & gouache. 182mm by 155mm; framed. (90) £1,500

Bossuet, Jacques Benigne, 1627-1704

ALs, 7 Aug 1693. 4 pp, 8vo. To an unnamed lady. Giving spiritual advice. (91) DM2,300
See also: La Valliere, Louise Francoise de La Baume le Blanc

Boston Press Club

[2 4to vols containing Constitution & By-Laws, with members' signatures, in calf gilt, & a visitor's register, 1886 & later, in red mor, sold at rce on 28 July 1988, lot 562, for $700.]

Boswell, James, 1740-95

Autograph Ms, My Dream in the night ...; 6 Feb 1785. 1 p, 4to. Describing a dream visit from Dr. Johnson. Docketed on verso. Isham collection. (89) $38,000

— Autograph Ms, The Life of Samuel Johnson, fragment, foliated 384; [1785-90]. 1 p, 4to. Reporting a conversation at Gen. Paoli's, 15 Apr 1773. Isham collection. (89) $40,000

ALs, 23 Dec 1789. 3 pp, 4to. To the Countess of Rothes. Requesting information for his Life of Johnson. (88) £2,500

— 31 July 1790. 1 p, 4to. To Inigo Leighton. Requesting information about his brother. Doheny collection. (89) $2,800

— 31 July 1790. 1 p, 4to. To John Leighton. Requesting confirmation that his brother John is still alive. (91) £2,500

— 6 Aug 1792. 1 p, 4to. To Andrew Gibb. Giving instructions concerning his estate. Doheny collection. (89) $2,000

Corrected proof, The Life of Samuel Johnson, vol 1, pp 267 - 270, [1785-90]. 4 pp, 4to, on a single sheet of laid paper. With c.33 autograph corrections or revisions. Isham collection. (89) $24,000

Bosworth, Joseph, 1789-1876
ALs, 16 July 1839. (89) £150

Botanical Manuscripts
Ms, La culture des fleurs, tome second, representant la plus grande partie des fleurs que les curieux cultivent..., [c.1700]. 299 leaves. 4to, in contemp mottled calf. Including tp, preface, alphabetical index, & 279 watercolor drawings. Contemp armorial bookplate of Nicolaus Spycket. (88) £85,000

Boudin, Eugene, 1824-98
Collection of ALs & AL, 14 June 1867. (90) DM290
ALs, 31 Jan 1893. (89) DM360

Boudinot, Elias, 1740-1821
ALs, 11 Jan 1784. 3 pp, 4to. To Jacob Read. Thanking for Congressional news, & commenting about Washington's resignation. (90) $1,400
— [Mar 1797]. (91) $190
— 11 Nov 1819. (89) $120

Boughton, George H., 1833-1905
ALs, [n.d.]. (89) $55

Boughton, Rutland, 1878-1960
Autograph music, opera, The Immortal Hour, complete vocal score, 1912 & 1913. 223 pp, folio, in 2 vols of contemp bds. In blue ink on up to 12 staves per page. With autograph tp, numerous revisions, performance instructions, etc. Sgd in several places. (89) £3,000

Boulez, Pierre
Series of 3 Ls s, 3 Oct 1966 to 3 Aug 1972. (88) DM440

Boulton, Matthew, 1728-1809
ALs, 1789. (88) £680
— 22 June 1806. (91) £440

Bourdelle, Antoine, 1861-1929
Series of 13 A Ls s, 1908 to 1922. (90) DM550

Bouteville du Metz, Louis Guislain, 1746-1821
Ls, [9 Apr 1796]. (89) DM260

Bowen, Elizabeth, 1899-1973
[A collection of c.210 letters addressed to her & c.130 carbon copies of her own letters, with related material, 1945 to 1948, c.400 pp, 4to & 8vo, in a box file, sold at S on 21 July 1988, lot 151, for 1,800 to Maggs.]
A Ls s (2), [n.d.]. (89) £130

Bowie, James, 1796-1836
Ds, 27 Dec 1832. 1 p, folio. Power of attorney for Isaac Donoho & Thomas Gay. (90) $27,000
— 3 & 4 Nov 1834. 2 pp, folio. Manumission of his slave Maria & her children; sgd twice. Also sgd by others. (91) $28,000

Bowles, Paul
Ls s (2), 7 Sept 1958 & 3 Jan 1959. 3 pp, 4to. To Tennessee Williams. On his wife's illness & recovery & on various literary matters. (91) $1,100

Bowles, William Lisle, 1762-1850
Autograph sentiment, 29 Oct 1833. (89) £40

Boxall, d'Auvergne
Original drawings, (12), to illus Kath Ussher's Cities of Australia, 1928. Archives of J. M. Dent & Son. (88) £520

Boxer Rebellion
— KENDALL-BROWN, W. T. - Autograph Ms, A Personal Account of the Siege of Tientsin; with c.45 A Ls s, c.80 photographs & further related material. Length not stated. Report & family letters from a Marine serving aboard the U.S.S. Monocacy. (90) $5,000

Boxing
[A sheet of paper board, sgd in pencil by c.46 boxers & others, c.1937, framed, sold at R on 4 Mar 1989, lot 333, for $450.]

Boyd, Walter, 1754?-1837
[A collection of 88 letters addressed to the banking house of Boyd, Ker & Co. by members of the French & Belgian aristocracy, 30 Jan 1788 to 3 Jan 1798, c.110 pp, 8vo & 4to, stitched into later bds, referring to assets in France &

BOYD

problems during the Revolution, sold at C on 6 Dec 1989, lot 284, for £250 to Drury.]

Boyd, William
Autograph Ms, notebook containing revised drafts for Alpes Maritimes, Galapagos Affair, & Stars & Bars, 1984 to 1985. (88) £480

Boyd, William, 1898-1972
Collection of ANs & photograph, [n.d.]. (91) $80

Boyen, Hermann von, 1771-1848
ALs, 21 June [1815]. Schroeder collection. (89) DM420

Boyen, Leopold Hermann von, 1811-88
[A collection of 19 letters addressed to him by members of the nobility of Prussia & Kurland & others, Mar & Apr 1830, expressing congratulations on his engagement to Princess Fanny Biron, sold at star on 10 Mar 1988, lot 1183, for DM850.]

Boyle, Edmund, 7th Earl of Cork and Orrery
Ms, journal, "A Tour thro' Sicily and Malta, May 1770", with notes on travel in Italy & France & on reading. (88) $250

Boyle, Eleanor Vere, 1825-1916
Original drawing, children walking through a wood, in ink; sgd & dated 1850. (88) £700

Boyle, Kay
ALs, 25 Apr 1949. (89) $140
— 10 Dec 1965. (88) $175
Ls, 29 Mar 1979. (89) $60
Ns, 15 Dec 1935. (89) $60

Boyle, Robert, 1627-91
Series of 20 A Ls s, 17 Jan 1681/2 to 28 Nov 1685. 42 pp, 8vo & 4to, in 19th-cent album. To Dr. Narcissus Marsh. Mostly regarding the transcription & ptg of the Old Testament in the Irish language. With related material. (89) £16,000
ALs, 11 Nov 1665. 2 pp, folio. To his brother [Richard, 1st Earl of Burlington]. Sending news from the Court, referring to a new bridge, his Irish estates, etc. Endorsed by recipient. Mtd. (88) £1,100
— 20 Apr 1667. 1 p, 8vo. To his brother Richard. About an accident to his right hand, but says that nevertheless he writes to welcome him on his arrival in Yorkshire & to give news of imminent peace. (91) £1,400
Series of 20 Ls s, 17 Jan 1681/2 to 28 Nov 1685. 42 pp, 8vo & 4to, in 19th-cent album. To Dr. Narcissus Marsh. Mostly regarding the transcription & ptg of the Old Testament in the Irish language. With related material. (91) £8,200

Boyle, Roger, 1st Earl of Orrery, 1621-79
Ms, drama, Mustafa, in 5 acts; written in a late 17th-cent hand. (88) £170
— Ms, Mustapha. A Tragedy. 1669. 77 leaves, 187mm by 145mm, in contemp vellum, with 1 cover detached. (89) $1,200
ALs, 27 July 1665. (89) £45

Bozherianov, Nikolai Nikolaevich, 1811-76
Ms, Izobretenie y Nostenennoe Usovershenstvovanie Parovykh Mashin. [N.p., 1842 or 1849] 121 leaves, 365mm by 234mm, in modern mor with contemp lea covers laid down. With ink-wash frontis port of James Watt & 20 full-page technical drawings in ink & watercolors. (90) $7,000

Bradley, Katherine Harris, d.1914
A Ls s (2), 25 Oct 1906 & [n.d.]. (90) £65

Bradley, Omar, 1893-1981
Photograph, sgd, [n.d.]. (88) DM200

Bradshaw, John, 1602-59. See: Cromwell, Richard

Bradstreet, John, 1711-74
ADs, 12 Dec 1759. (89) $150

Bradstreet, John, c.1711-74. See: French & Indian War

Bradstreet, Simon, 1603-97
Autograph endorsement, sgd, 25 Sept 1663. (91) $500

Brady, Mathew B.
Photograph, sgd & inscr, 1864. About 6 by 4 inches. Brady's famous photo of U.S. Grant at Headquarters, Cold Harbor, Virginia. Inscr by Brady to J. E. Kelly. (91) $10,000

Bragg, Braxton, 1817-76
ALs, 15 June 1847. (90) $1,000
— 11 Jan 1850. Alexander collection. (90) $260
Autograph telegram, sgd, 5 Mar 1862. (91) $850

Brahe, Tycho, 1546-1601
Autograph sentiment, "Non sit vulgare quod optes", sgd & dated 6 Mar 1599. 1 p, 4to. Endorsed in anr hand at bottom. (91) DM12,000

Brahms, Johannes, 1833-97
[A group of 3 autograph envelopes, 29 Aug 1870 to 22 June 1889, with related material, sold at star on 10 Mar 1988, lot 773, for DM1,000.]
Autograph Ms, stylistic exercises in French & German, [n.d.]. (88) DM850
Autograph music, "Klavierstuecke", Op. 76, nos 5 - 8, [c.1878/79]. 10 pp, 25.4cm or 25.7cm by 32.9cm, & 26cm by 33cm; 12 or 10 staves each. In brown folder. Stichvorlage; with numerous revisions. (89) DM190,000
— Autograph music, song, In dieser Welt des Trug's und Schein's, to a text by Hoffmann von Fallersleben, scored for voice & viola; sgd & inscr to Emma Graedener, [spring 1858]. 1 p, 8vo. In Emma Graedener's album containing 35 entries in all; blindstamped black lea bdg. (90) DM18,000
Autograph transcript, song, In dieser Welt des Trugs und Scheins, to a text by Hoffmann von Fallersleben, [c.1859]. On 2 systems of 2 staves each. Sgd & inscr to Emma Graedener. In album belonging to Emma Graedener, 1858 to 1860. 35 entries, 4to. Contemp black mor gilt. (88) DM10,000
Collection of ALs & photograph, [n.d.]. 3 pp, 8vo. To an unnamed lady. Making arrangements for her to forward things he left behind. (91) £1,150
ALs, 3 Sept 1853. 4 pp, 8vo. To Arnold Wehner. Reporting enthusiastically about his journey along the Rhine & about new acquaintances. (91) DM22,000
— 2 Dec 1854. 4 pp, 8vo. To Robert Schumann. Thanking for Schumann's praise of his compositions, expressing admiration for Schumann & his wife, etc. (90) £6,200
— May 1855. 3 pp, 8vo. To Karl Graedener. In Clara Schumann's name, inviting him to stay during the forthcoming musical festival at Duesseldorf, & discussing the program. (90) DM8,000
— [19 Nov 1858]. 3 pp, 8vo. To an unnamed friend. Informing him about his musical activities in Detmold. (91) £1,900
— July 1860. 2 pp, 8vo. To Julius Otto Grimm. Asking him to forward his belongings, & mentioning Joseph Joachim & Albert Dietrich. (91) £1,300
— Dec 1868. 4 pp, 8vo. Recipient unknown. Discussing the possible publication of his works in France. (88) $1,800
— Dec [1873]. 3 pp, 8vo. To [Karl Reinecke]. Expressing reluctance to give a concert in Leipzig. (91) DM9,000
— Jan 1874. 2 pp, 8vo. Recipient unnamed. About forwarding the manuscripts or proofs of his Hungarian Dances. (91) $2,300
— Feb 1874. 2 pp, 8vo. To [August Schricker]. Declining to set a suggested text to music. (90) DM3,000
— July 1874. 1 p, 8vo. To Gottfried Keller. Sending a cantata for a wedding reluctantly composed at Keller's request. (88) DM5,500
— Mar 1875. 3 pp, 8vo. To Max Bruch. Regarding rehearsals for Bruch's Odysseus. (90) DM8,000
— [Sept 1875]. 3 pp, 8vo. To [Fritz Simrock]. About various publishing matters. Sgd J.Br. (89) DM4,800
— [n.d.]. (88) £600
— c.1875-1880?]. 3 pp, size not stated. To an unnamed young lady. About choral music in Vienna. (90) £1,800
— [1877]. (91) £950
— Feb [18]79. 3 pp, 8vo. To an unnamed violinist. Explaining that Joachim is in England with the Ms of his Violin

BRAHMS

Concert. (91) £3,400
— Mar [18]79. 3 pp, 8vo. Recipient unnamed. About a concert program, a cantata by Bach, his plans for the summer, Carl Riedel, etc. (90) £2,800
— [30 July 1882]. 3 pp, 4to. To his pbr Simrock. Regarding the score of his [2d Piano] Concerto. Salzer collection. (90) £2,400
— [21 June 1883]. 2 pp, 8vo. To Carl Reinecke. Explaining that he wishes to disassociate himself from a society. (90) £1,700
— [19 Feb 1884]. 3 pp, 8vo. To Fritz Simrock. Discussing a fee & publication matters. Sgd J.Br. (90) DM3,400
— [Sept 1884]. 2 pp, 8vo. To Marie Baumayer. About the performance of one of his concertos. Salzer collection. (90) £2,200
— [Oct 1884]. 4 pp, 8vo. To [Hans von Buelow]. Discussing the publication of works by Joachim Raff. (91) DM6,500
— [Jan 1886]. 4 pp, 8vo. To Robert Schnitzler. Accepting an invitation, & discussing a concert program. (90) DM7,500
— [Feb 1886]. 3 pp, 8vo. To [Hans Bronsart]. Promising to give a concert in Hannover. (90) DM5,800
— [21 July 1886]. 4 pp, 8vo. To his stepmother Karoline Louise Brahms. Family letter, inquiring about his brother's health, offering money, etc. (91) DM6,800
— [1886]. 3 pp, 8vo. To Frau von Januer. Thanking for a book. (91) DM3,900
— [11 June 1889]. 1 p, 8vo. To [Fritz] S[imrock]. Regarding changes in the score of his Fest- und Gedenksprueche, Op. 109. (89) DM4,600
— [6 Aug 1889?]. 3 pp, 4to. To [Fritz] S[imrock]. About his work for the Bach-Gesellschaft & other matters. (90) £1,350
— [n.d.]. 3 pp, 8vo. To Frau Breuer. Thanking for letters & chatting about his activities. (88) DM2,700
— [c.10 Apr 1894]. 3 pp, 8vo. To Fritz Simrock. Regarding a donation & his alleged birthplace. Including photograph of a house pasted in. Sgd JB. (90) DM3,400

AMERICAN BOOK PRICES CURRENT

— [12 Dec 1894]. 2 pp, 12mo. To Fritz Simrock. Requesting correction of a mistake in an advertisement. Sgd J.Br. (90) DM2,400
— [31 Oct 1895]. 4 pp, 8vo. To Mrs. Billroth. Thanking for a book & referring to discussions with her late husband. (91) £2,000
— [n.d.]. 4 pp, 12mo. To [Aloys Schmidt]. Discussing a proposed concert at Schwerin. Barrett collection. (89) $2,500
— [n.d.]. 1 p, 8vo. Recipient unnamed. Apologizing for a delay. (90) DM2,200
— [n.d.]. 2 pp, 8vo. Recipient unnamed. Inquiring about recipient's father. (91) DM3,400
— [n.d.]. 4 pp, 12mo. Recipient unnamed. Expressing thanks. Framed. (91) $1,900

Collection of autograph postcard, sgd & ANs, [12 Nov 1887] & [n.d.]. 1 p, 8vo, & card. To Bernhard Scholz, informing him that he will attend a concert. Recipient unnamed, accepting an invitation. (90) DM3,000
— Collection of autograph postcard, sgd, 2 A Ns s & AN, 15 Dec [18]88, 25 June [18]89 & [n.d.]. 5 pp, various sizes (2 visiting cards). To Josephine Oser. Expressing thanks, admitting her to rehearsals, sending greetings. (91) £1,350

Autograph postcard, sgd, 24 June [1873]. (91) £1,000
— 15 Dec 1877. To Georg Henschel. About the possibility of a performance of his symphony at Hamburg & Bremen. (89) DM3,400
— [1879]. (89) £750
— 21 Dec 1881. To Carl Reinecke. Requesting additional information regarding a concert at Leipzig. (88) DM1,600
— [18]84. (91) £800
— [10 Feb 1887]. (90) £600
— [Aug 1889]. Salzer collection. (90) £850
— 27 Jan 1897. (91) £750

ANs, [15 Oct 1873. 1 p, 8vo. To Fritz Simrock. Sending an enclosure for Joachim & requesting news about a performance. Sgd J. Br. (90) DM1,300
— [21 Apr 1889]. 1 p, 4to. To Helene Hecht. Sending greetings. At bottom

of ANs by Felix Hecht. (89) DM1,700
— [n.d.]. (90) DM1,000
Series of 3 A Ns, 1890 & [n.d.]. Salzer collection. (90) £950
A Ns (2), [1890 & n.d.]. Salzer collection. (90) £750
— A Ns (2), [n.d.]. Salzer collection. (90) £380
AN, [1889]. (90) DM650
— 2 Feb [18]94. Salzer collection. (90) £400
— [n.d.]. (90) £700
— [n.d.]. Salzer collection. (90) £400
— [n.d.]. Salzer collection. (90) £380
— [n.d.]. (90) DM400
Autograph quotation, last 3 bars of the Piano Quintet in F minor, Op. 34, in score; sgd, inscr & dated Oct [18]87. 1 p, folio. Related material on verso. (90) £4,800
— Anr, Nun, ihr Musen, genug!, 2 bars from his Neue Liebeslieder, Op. 65, [n.d.]. 1 p, 8vo. Sgd & inscr. (90) DM9,000
Photograph, sgd, [c.1885]. Cabinet size. Seated on a bench. Photo by R. Krzudanek. (89) £3,000
— Anr, [1895]. 163mm by 108mm. By Krziwanek. (91) DM5,000
Photograph, sgd & inscr, [c.1860]. Carte size. By Koenig. (91) £4,000
— Anr, Dec [18]81. 17cm by 11cm. By Friedrich Bruckmann. Inscr to Franz Schwab on verso. (91) £2,500
— Anr, Nov [18]86. 10cm by 6cm. Sgd & inscr on verso with autograph musical quotation. (89) £2,800
— Anr, 1894. 165mm by 105mm. Inscr to Emma Albani on verso, with autograph musical quotation from his Deutsches Requiem. (91) £3,500
Single sheet ptg, obituary for Brahms, issued by the Gesellschaft der Musikfreunde in Vienna, 4 Apr 1897. (88) DM320
— BRONSART, HANS VON. - ALs, 4 Mar 1886. 4 pp, 8vo. To Johannes Brahms. Agreeing to his request to postpone a concert in Hannover. (91) DM360
— BUSONI, FERRUCCIO. - Autograph music, cadenza for Brahms's Violin Concerto, sgd; 1913. 5 pp, size not stated. Stichvorlage, including partly autograph tp & scribal copy. (91) £1,500
— FRANZ, ROBERT. - ALs, 20 Dec [1853]. 3 pp, 8vo. To Theodor Twietmeyer. Giving an unfavorable account of a performance by Brahms of his Piano Sonata Op. 1. (91) £2,000
See also: Joachim, Joseph

Braine, John
[3 autograph Mss, drafts of articles (1 partly typed), with revisions, [n.d.], c.75 pp, 4to, sold at S on 15 Dec, lot 48, for £500.]

Branch, Lawrence O'Bryan, 1820-62
ALs, [n.d.]. (88) $200

Brandeis, Louis D., 1856-1941
ALs, 28 Oct 1925. (91) $550
— 8 Nov 1926. (89) $220
— 28 July 1940. (90) $380
Ls, 25 Feb 1913. (91) $325

Brandes, Georg, 1842-1927
ALs, 5 Sept 1901. (90) DM380

Brandt, Willy
Autograph Ms, instructions concerning a speech to be given at Kopenhagen, 9 Feb 1970. (91) DM850
— Autograph Ms, Neues Denken - Chancen fuer Europa und die Welt; 16 Oct 1989. (91) DM600
Ls, 30 Aug 1962. (90) DM240
— 22 Apr 1964. (88) DM320
See also: Ford, Gerald R. & Brandt

Brant, Joseph, 1742-1807
Ls, 19 June 1796. 2 pp, 4to. To T[homas] Morris. Trying to arrange a parley. (91) $1,900

Braque, Georges, 1882-1963
ALs, 1 June 1946. (88) £80

Brattain, Walter Houser
ALs, 31 July 1978. (89) DM280

Braun, Felix, 1885-1973
Autograph Ms, Erinnerung an Rainer Maria Rilke, from his autobiography Zeitgefaehrten, [n.d.]. (90) DM360
Collection of 5 A Ls s & autograph postcard, sgd, 15 Apr 1953 to 17 July 1969. (88) DM300

Braun, Wernher von, 1912-77
[An archive documenting the publishing history of his 1960 book, First Men to the Moon sold at sg on 22 Mar 1990, lot 25.] $15,000
Ls, 23 Apr 1959. (91) $300

Brecht, Bertolt, 1898-1956
[Typescripts of 3 poems (2 carbon copies), [1913-26], 4 pp, folio, with related material, sold at S on 17 Nov 1988, lot 179, for £1,200 to Rothenal.]
[3 typescripts of poems, Ballade auf vielen Schiffen, Die Geburt im Baum, & part of Ballade von der Freundschaft, [n.d.], 4 pp, folio, sold at star on 4 Apr 1991, lot 51, for DM3,500.]
Autograph Ms, Oratorium, [1916-17]. 4 pp, folio. Libretto for a proposed music drama. In ink & pencil; with revisions. (89) £3,500
— Autograph Ms, poem beginning "Mein Herz ist voller Glut", [n.d.]. 1 p, 8vo. 4 quatrains; some autograph corrections. Probably unpbd. (89) £2,800
— Autograph Ms, poem beginning "Bonnie Mac Sorel freite ...", sgd & inscr to Rosa Maria A; [1916?]. 2 pp, 4to. 5 quatrains with some autograph corrections. Probably unpbd. (89) £3,600
— Autograph Ms, poem beginning "Seine Musse zu geniessen ...", [1920-23]. 1 p, folio. 7 quatrains, written in 2 columns; some corrections. (89) £1,900
— Autograph Ms, poem, beginning "Eine kleine Weile wartet..."; [c.1918]. 1 p, 4to. 16 lines. (91) DM6,500
— Autograph Ms, poem, beginning "Mein lieber Bez..."; [c.1920]. 2 pp, 4to. 46 lines. (91) DM7,500
— Autograph Ms, poem, Das Lied von der Wolke der Nacht [here entitled Liebeslied fuer Orchester], sgd BB; [1913-26]. 1 p, folio. 2 five-line stanzas; in pencil. On verso of typescript carbon copy of his poem Ballade vom Mazeppa. (89) £1,600
— Autograph Ms, poem, Der Totenpflug, sgd; [n.d.]. 2 pp, folio. 10 quatrains; probably unpbd. (89) £3,800
— Autograph Ms, poem, Die Maenner der See, sgd & dated 1916. 2 pp, 4to. 4 five-line stanzas; probably unpbd. Edge torn. (89) £3,400
— Autograph Ms, poem, Liebeslied fuer Orchester; [n.d.]. 1 p, 4to. Sgd BB. On verso of typescript, Mazeppa; 8 four-line stanzas, sgd BB. (91) DM11,000
— Autograph Ms, poem, Lied der mueden Empoerer, sgd B & dated 22 Feb 1918. 2 pp, 8vo. 6 quatrains, with autograph revisions. (89) £1,900
— Autograph Ms, poem, Lied der mueden Empoerer, 22 Feb 1918. 2 pp, 8vo. 6 four-line stanzas; sgd B. (91) DM10,000
— Autograph Ms, poem, Nordlandsage [here entitled Nordlandschaft], [1913-26]. 1 p, folio. 9 lines. (89) £1,100
— Autograph Ms, poem, [Psalm], beginning "Eine kleine Weile wartet ...", [1917-19]. 1 p, 4to, torn from a notebook. 16 lines, differing from pbd version. (89) £2,000
— Autograph Ms, poem, Psalm II, sgd; [n.d.]. 2 pp, folio. 24 lines; probably unpbd. Fold splits. (89) £2,200
— Autograph Ms, poem, Tanzlied, [n.d.]. 1 p, folio. 3 eight-line stanzas; some autograph revisions. Probably unpbd. (89) £1,600
— Autograph Ms, poem, Tanzlied; [c.1918]. 1 p, folio. 3 eight-line stanzas. (91) DM9,000
— Autograph Ms, poem, Tod im Wald, sgd; [1918-19?]. 2 pp, folio. 8 stanzas. (89) £3,000
— Autograph Ms, prose drama, [Oratorium]; [c.1916/17]. 4 pp, folio. Including corrections. (91) DM11,000
Ms, 4 poems, Heider Hei, Der Himmel der Enttaeuschten, Rede an den Baum Green, & Der dicke Mann auf der Schiffschaukel singt, [c.1918]. 8 pp, 4to & 8vo. In an unidentified hand; subscribed B.B. an Lud Prestel. (89) £1,300
Typescript, poem, Die Legende vom toten Soldaten, [n.d.]. 2 pp, folio. 21 quatrains; probably unpbd. (89) £2,000
Collection of 21 A Ls s, 18 Ls s, 4 letters, 20 postcards, sgd (19 autograph), AN, 2 telegrams & typescript, [1923 to 1937]. 48 pp, various sizes, & cards. To Helene Weigel. Important letters dealing with a variety of professional & private matters. With related material. (90) DM35,000
ALs, [c.Feb 1924]. 1 p, folio. To Otto

Falkenberg & Benno Bing. About a performance of Marlowe's Edward II at Munich. (91) DM2,600

— 7 Jan 1956. 1 p, 4to. To Ruth Berlau. Thanking for a report. (91) DM2,700

Collection of 17 Ls s & Ds, 15 June 1945 to 14 Mar 1955. 27 leaves, various sizes. Mostly to Eric Russell Bentley. Discussing translations & productions of his works. Contract concerning productions of The Private Life of the Master Race. Including 3 autograph postscripts, 1 on Ls by Elisabeth Hauptmann. In English & German. (88) DM18,500

— Collection of 3 Ls s & AL (draft), 2 June 1950 to 14 July 1952. 4 pp, various sizes. To Joseph Noerden. Giving stage directions for Noerden's role in Hofmeister. 2 Ls s with file holes, AL mtd. With related material. (88) DM2,600

Series of 3 Ls s, Jan 1934 to 21 Apr 1956. 3 pp, folio. To Kurt Klaeber. Discussing literary & personal matters. Sgd b. (91) DM5,000

Ls, 30 May 1926. 1 p, 4to. To Hans Reisiger. Discussing a projected publication of Kipling's poems. (91) DM2,400

— [Nov 1947]. 1 p, 4to. To Ruth Berlau. About a financial matter, & praising her photographs. With autograph postscript, sgd b. (90) DM1,600

Autograph postcard, sgd, [17 May 1933]. (91) DM850

ANs, 1 May [1950]. (90) DM500

Breckinridge, John Cabell, 1821-75

Franking signature, [n.d.]. Alexander collection. (90) $190
See also: Beauregard, Pierre G. T.

Breguet, Abraham Louis, 1747-1823

ALs, [11 Nov 1805]. (89) DM550

Breitkopf, Johann Gottlob Immanuel, 1719-94

ALs, 29 Oct 1788. 1 p, 4to. To an unknown literary agent. Regarding the ptg of a Ms by Christian Bacmeister. (88) DM1,050

Breitkopf und Haertel

Ms, accounts detailing purchases of [Adolph Martin] Schlesinger, 8 Jan 1798. (88) £280

Series of 19 Ls s, 1798 to 1800 & 1861. 32 pp, mostly 4to. To Adolph Martin Schlesinger & his son. Regarding the publication of works by Mozart, Haydn, Hummel, Beethoven & others. (88) £1,800

— Series of 4 Ls s, 1850 to 1861. (88) £300

Brenner, Ernst, 1856-1911

ALs, 11 Jan 1908. (90) DM280

Brentano, Christian, 1784-1851

ALs, 5 Apr 1820. (91) DM700

Brentano, Clemens, 1778-1842

ALs, [8 Jan 1798]. 1 p, 4to. To Franz Brentano. Fragment, mentioning the possibility of a visit at Easter. (88) DM1,050

— [18?] Aug 1806. 1 p, 4to. To Joseph Mozler. Discussing a book order. (91) DM4,400

— [Dec 1808]. 3 pp, 4to. To his pbr Zimmer. Sending a rejoinder to a critical review of Des Knaben Wunderhorn by Johann Heinrich Voss, & mentioning Goethe & other literary figures. With full-page autograph postscript by Friedrich Karl von Savigny. Albrecht collection. (91) SF5,500

— 7 Feb 1830. 4 pp, 4to. To Hermann Joseph Dietz. Lively description of relief measures during the hard winter at Frankfort. (88) DM9,000

— 14 June 1832. 2 pp, 4to. To Joseph Hermann Dietz. Requesting his help in retrieving a stolen painting, mentioning his move to Regensburg & a donation for a cloister, etc. Albrecht collection. (91) SF8,000

— [c.1832/33]. 1 p, 4to. To Friedrich Overbeck. Introducing Herr Halenka & talking about various literary topics. Somewhat def. (89) DM4,600

Brentano, Lujo, 1844-1931

Autograph Ms, "Schluss der Gelegenheitsschrift zum 1. (88) DM400

Brereton, William, Sir, 1604-61. See: Fairfax, Thomas & Brereton

Bresgen, Cesar
Autograph music, draft of his opera Paracelsus; fragment of 1st act, [1944]. (88) DM280
— Autograph music, fragment from his opera Der Engel von Prag, Act II, [1977]. (89) DM260
— Autograph music, Maennerchor; [n.d.]. (90) DM240
— Autograph music, Skizze aus der Oper Der Engel von Prag, sgd & inscr later & dated 1977. (90) DM340
— Autograph music, songs, Die Schnecke im Winter, & Im D-Zug, & sketches; [n.d.]. (90) DM280
— Autograph music, Tanz aus Azerbeidschan (Erstschrift eines Tanzes), sgd & dated 1967. (90) DM270

Breton, Andre, 1896-1966
ADs, 1 July 1937. (90) DM200

Brett, Bernard
Original drawings, (15), to illus Ada Williams' Between the Lights, 1952. Archives of J. M. Dent & Son. (88) £180

Breuning, Carl G. F.
Ms, Tagebuch der Belagerung von Mainz 1793. 184 leaves, 180mm by 115mm. Contemp lea bdg. Describing the family of Franz Joseph Henner & the situation in Mainz during the siege by French troops. Including engraved map by G. J. Coentgen & anr etching. (89) DM1,900

Breviarium -- Latin Manuscripts
— [Salzburg, c.1150]. Single leaf, vellum, 293mm by 207mm. In brown ink in a late romanesque script, with opening words in red or in lombardic capitals & 47 lines of adiastematic musical notation. With 2 large historiated initials in brown & red ink colored with red, green & blue wash. Margin cropped, affecting text; recovered from a bdg. Korner collection. (90) £130,000
— [Southern Netherlands, c.1300]. Use of Rome. 436 leaves, vellum, 147mm by 108mm, in modern suede over old wooden bds. In black ink in a gothic minuscule bookhand. With numerous small initials, & 12 large initials in blue & red with elaborate penwork decoration & extensive marginal flourishes. (90) £3,800
— [Italy, 14th cent]. 274 leaves (incomplete), vellum, 175mm by 128mm, in medieval bdg of wooden bds sewn on 3 double thongs. In brown ink in a rounded gothic liturgical hand. With decorated initials throughout & 2 large painted initials in colors & white tracery with long leafy extensions. (91) £1,400
— [Rome?, 14th cent]. Use of Rome. 274 leaves, vellum, 270mm by 205mm. Early 19th-cent brown lea over wooden bds. In black & red ink in a rounded gothic hand. With 9 historiated initials in gold & colors & hundreds of red & blue initials with penwork extensions. (89) DM24,000
— [England, c.1400]. Use of Sarum. 138 leaves only, vellum, 175mm by 115mm. Disbound. In dark brown ink in a small anglicana bookhand. With initials throughout in red & blue. (88) £1,600
— [England, c.1400]. Use of Sarum. 229 leaves, vellum, 146mm by 94mm, in def 18th-cent red mor bdg. In brown ink in 2 sizes of a gothic minuscule hand. With eight 3- to 5-line initials with decorative blue borders & penwork embellishment. (90) £2,400
— [England, c.1425]. Use of Sarum. 244 leaves (4 lacking), vellum, 120mm by 85mm. 17th-cent half calf over medieval wooden bds. In brown ink by several scribes in varieties of anglicana bookhand. With initials throughout in red & blue. Including 6 flyleaves from 15th-cent English antiphoner with neumes on 4 staves. (88) £1,200
— [Northern Italy, Abbey of Cerreto?, c.1425]. Of Cistercian Use. 322 leaves & 2 flyleaves, vellum, 132mm by 98mm, in 4 vols of 19th-cent red-brown velvet. In a small rounded gothic hand including punctus flexus. With decorated initials throughout. Incomplete. (91) £1,500
— [Florence, c.1450] Proper of Saints & Common of Saints only. 186 leaves, vellum, 133mm by 95mm, in modern

mor. With large initials on gold grounds with stylized flowers & leaves extending into margins; full borders at beginning of Common & Proper. Zabriskie-Manhattan College Ms (91) $8,000

— [Italy, mid-15th cent]. Use of Rome. 388 leaves, vellum, 130mm by 100mm. Modern brown mor over wooden bds. In a small bookhand by a single scribe. With small colored initials & 6-line initials in red, yellow & green with spray extensions. (90) £3,400

— [Southern? France, 15th cent]. 382 leaves (some missing), vellum, 135mm by 91mm; lacking bdg. In dark brown ink in a very small gothic liturgical hand. With painted initials throughout in red or blue. (88) £1,500

— [Ferrara, c.1454-69]. The Llangattock Breviary. Single leaf only, vellum, 270mm by 200mm. In brown ink in a rounded gothic hand. With 6 two-line initials in burnished gold & 4 full-length borders. Possibly from the Breviary of Borso d'Este. (90) £1,300

— [Italy, c.1455-80]. Of Franciscan use. 175 leaves (c.15 lacking), vellum, 160mm by 108mm. 19th-cent Belgian armorial brown mor gilt. In dark brown ink in 2 sizes of a small gothic hand. With painted initials throughout. (89) £1,100

— [Lombardy, c.1460-80]. Of Franciscan use. 618 leaves, vellum, 127mm by 93mm. Late 16th-cent German bdg of pigskin over wooden bds with the arms of Wolkenstein. In dark brown ink in a small rounded gothic hand. With 23 large illuminated initials, 9 historiated initials, & full border. (89) £6,500

— [Ferrara, c.1460-70]. 1 leaf only, vellum, 270mm by 200mm. In a rounded gothic script with most of verso in red. With illuminated initial, 4 full-length illuminated borders & miniature in margin. Framed. (88) £1,300

— [Angers?, 2d half of 15th cent]. Of Carmelite use. 603 leaves (c.4 lacking), vellum, 158mm by 105mm. Contemp French panelled calf over wooden bds. In brown ink in a small lettre batarde. With numerous illuminated initials & 10 large initials with half borders of painted leaves & flowers. Outer margin of last 20 leaves cut. Doheny collection. (88) £5,500

— [Netherlands, last quarter of 15th cent]. 365 leaves, vellum, 175mm by 130mm, in early 16th-cent calf over wooden bds. Text preceded by a 6-page ptd calendar on paper from an early 16th office book. Written by 2 scribes in black ink in a gothic textura, with rubrics in red. With 1 large illuminated initials in red & blue with elaborate penwork floral decoration in red, gray & gold. (91) £6,000

— [Southern France, Rodez?, 2d half of 15th cent]. Use of Rome. 476 leaves (4 lacking), vellum, 124mm by 90mm. Def 19th-cent red pastebds. In brown ink in a small gothic hand. With 8 large illuminated initials with full-length borders. Worn. (89) £2,400

— The Boiardi Breviary. [Ferrara, c.1475-90]. Use of Rome. 422 leaves & later flyleaves, vellum, 247mm by 177mm. Contemp gilt-stamped goatskin over wooden bds, repaired. In dark brown ink in a fine regular rounded gothic liturgical hand. With decorated initials throughout, 83 large illuminated & 24 large historiated initials often with gold penwork in margins, & 4 full illuminated & historiated borders. Principal miniatures attributable to Fra Evangelista da Reggio. Abbey collection. (89) £190,000

— [Rome?, 2d half of 15th cent]. 429 leaves only, vellum, 116mm by 83mm. 19th-cent English blindstamped mor bdg. In dark brown ink in a small gothic hand. With painted initials throughout. (89) £1,900

— [Venice, 12 Oct 1479]. Use of Rome. 454 leaves including 32 blanks, vellum, 102mm by 67mm. Contemp Neapolitan dark brown mor gilt. In brown ink in a minute gothic bookhand. With 6-line illuminated initials with full-length floral extensions, & 3 pp with illuminated initials (2 historiated) & full borders. Doheny collection. (88) £7,500

— [Tuscany, c.1480-90]. Of Benedictine Use. 411 leaves only, vellum, 103mm by 70mm, in def 18th-cent mottled sheepskin bdg. In brown ink in a very

BREVIARIUM

small gothic hand. With decorated initials throughout with elaborate penwork & 80 large illuminated initials with full-length borders. 1 initial mostly cut out. Astor MS.A.8. (88) £4,200

— [Clermont-Ferrand, c.1486]. Use of Clermont. 535 leaves (4 lacking), vellum, 225mm by 150mm. Contemp French blindstamped calf over wooden bds. In brown ink in a secretary-influenced bookhand. With illuminated initials throughout, c.170 four-line initials with penwork sprays, 28 initals with decorated borders, 4 large historiated initials & large miniature with initial & full border. Doheny collection. (88) £19,000

— [Southern Germany, late 15th cent]. Of Benedictine Use. 285 leaves (of 294?), mostly vellum, 166mm by 285mm. Contemp red sheepskin over wooden bds. In black & red ink in a lettre batarde. With 3 large historiated & 15 decorated initials with borders in gold & colors. Rubrics & some passages in German. (89) DM27,000

— [Central France, c.1490]. 2 leaves, vellum, 141mm by 105mm. In very small script. With 6-line historiated initial, full borders, & 2 miniatures. (91) £2,000

— [Northeast Italy, late 15th cent]. 2 leaves only, vellum, 321mm by 238mm. In a rounded gothic script. With 13 small decorated initials with penwork in purple or red, & 4 historiated initials with illuminated borders. (90) £2,600

— The Monypenny Breviary. [Bourges, c.1490-95]. Use of Rome. 822 leaves (22 lacking), vellum, 232mm by 145mm. Very fine Parisian mosaic gilt bdg of c.1560 probably by Claude de Picques. In dark brown ink in 2 sizes of a small skillful lettre batarde. With small finely illuminated initials throughout, 20 fully illus Calendar pages incorporating several miniatures, 11 column-width miniatures with full borders, & 50 full-page miniatures or full-page illustrative schemes enclosing panels of text. Mostly illuminated by Jean & Jacquelin de Montlucon. Abbey collection. (89) £1,700,000

AMERICAN BOOK PRICES CURRENT

Brewer, David Josiah, 1837-1910
Corrected page proofs, 3 proofs of portions of court decisions, extensively revised in pencil, c.1904-05. (89) $175

Brian, W. Havergal, 1876-1972
Autograph music, Burlesque Variations on an Original Theme, full score; sgd & dated Sept 1903. (90) £850

Brice, Fanny, 1891-1951
Ls, 12 Apr 1950. (91) $150

Bridges, Robert, 1844-1930
Collection of ALs & Ls, 14 Jan 1895 & 2 May 1924. (88) £40
See also: Masefield, John & Bridges

Brigham, Asa, 1790-1844
Ds, 23 June 1836. (89) $130

Bright, John, 1811-89
ALs, 12 Dec 1868. (89) DM280

Bright, Richard, 1789-1858
ALs, 2 Nov [n.y.]. (90) £260

Brisbane, Thomas Makdougall, Sir, 1773-1860. See: William IV, 1765-1837

Briscoe, Ernest Edward
Original drawings, (18), to illus titles in the Storyland series & other books, 1929 to 1931. (89) £500

Britten, Benjamin, 1913-76
[A collection of c.80 photographs of Britten & his family, some inscr by Barbara Britten, c. 1912 to 1970, with 15 A Ls s by Robert Britten, sold at S on 22 Nov 1989, lot 36, for £400 to Macnutt.]
Autograph music, Canticle no III, "Still Falls the Rain", for Tenor, Horn & Piano, 27 Nov [19]54. 15 pp, folio. Working Ms, in blue ink on up to 18 staves per page. With autograph tp, sgd. (89) £5,000

— Autograph music, Kyrie Eleison from the Missa Brevis, draft, [1959]. 2 pp, folio. In pencil on 3 systems per page, 5 staves each. Tape remnants. (88) £1,400

— Autograph music, Six Metamorphoses for oboe solo, Op. 49, 1951. 15 pp, mostly folio. In blue ink on up to 16 staves per page. With autograph tp, sgd & inscr to Joy Boughton, &

alterations & annotations by Britten & Boughton. Some differences to pbd version. (89) £8,500
— Autograph music, song, Fairfield, [1955]. 3 pp, 4to, cut from larger sheets. On 8 systems, 2 staves each. Sgd & inscr; including autograph tp, sgd. (89) £2,700
Typescript, libretto, The Rape of Lucretia, [n.d.]. (90) £400
Collection of ALs & autograph postcard, sgd, 29 Sept 1942 & 1945. (90) £400
— Collection of 4 A Ls s & 2 Ls s, 18 June 1945 to 10 Jan 1974. (89) £500
— Collection of 11 A Ls s, 9 postcards, sgd, & photograph, sgd & inscr, 16 Sept 1963 to 21 Jan 1966. (91) £500
ALs, 6 Jan 1938. (91) £80
— 18 Sept 1942. (89) £360
— 20 Aug 1946. (90) DM780
— 16 Oct 1952. Byer collection. (90) $375
— [1970]. (90) DM390
Autograph postcard, sgd, 19 June 1923. (90) £520
See also: Forster, Edward Morgan & Britten

Britten, Benjamin, 1913-76 —&
Pears, Peter, Sir, 1910-86
[A large collection of A Ls s, Ls s, postcards, photographs, 117 items by Britten, 1937 to 1973, & 74 items by Pears, 1937 to 1980, written to John, Mary & George Behrend, referring to their work, private matters, social affairs, etc., sold at C on 9 Dec, lot 356, for £2,200 to Haas.]
Autograph postcard, sgd, [n.d.]. (90) £50

Broch, Hermann, 1886-1951
Ls, 12 Dec 1947. (91) DM900
Autograph postcard, sgd, [21 Dec 1938]. To Trude Geiringer. Complaining about fatigue. On verso autograph poem, Fuer ein Haus in der Fremde; 12 lines, with pen-&-ink sketch of Manhattan. (91) DM1,300

Brock, Charles Edmund
Original drawings, (10), to illus Thackeray's The English Humourists, 1903. In pencil (2) or ink. 9 sgd. Various sizes. With related material. Archives of J. M. Dent & Son. (88) £2,400
— Original drawings, (10), to illus Thackeray's Roundabout Papers, 1903. Archives of J. M. Dent & Son. (88) £450
— Original drawings, (11), to illus Thackeray's The Paris Sketch Book, 1903. Archives of J. M. Dent & Son. (88) £950
— Original drawings, (11), to illus William Cowper's John Gilpin, 1898. In ink. Mostly sgd or initialled. Various sizes. Archives of J. M. Dent & Son. (88) £1,100
— Original drawings, (118), to illus Charles Lamb's The Essays (& Last Essays) of Elia, 1900. In ink. Many sgd or initialled. Various sizes. Archives of J. M. Dent & Son. (88) £12,500
— Original drawings, (12), to illus W. Archives of J. M. Dent & Son. (88) £320
— Original drawings, (15), to illus Arthur Quiller-Couch's The Astonishing History of Troy Town, 1914. Archives of J. M. Dent & Son. (88) £350
— Original drawings, (15), to illus Frank Stockton's Rudder Grange, 1914. Archives of J. M. Dent & Son. (88) £750
— Original drawings, (15), to illus Mary Mitford's Our Village, 1904. In watercolor, sgd. 330mm by 230mm. Archives of J. M. Dent & Son. (90) £4,200
— Original drawings, (17), to illus George Eliot's Silas Marner, 1905. In watercolor, sgd. 370mm by 270mm. 2 discolored. With related material. Archives of J. M. Dent & Son. (90) £8,000
— Original drawings, (17), to illus Thackeray's Henry Esmond, 1902. In pencil (2) or ink. Sgd. Various sizes. With related material. Archives of J. M. Dent & Son. (88) £1,200
— Original drawings, (23), to illus Charles Lamb's Essays and Sketches, 1903. In ink. Sgd. Various sizes. With a copy of the book. Archives of J. M. Dent & Son. (88) £2,800
— Original drawings, (24), to illus Thackeray's The Newcomes, 1902. In pencil (2) or ink. Sgd or initialled. Various sizes. With related material. Archives of J. M. Dent & Son. (88) £1,700
— Original drawings, (29), to illus

BROCK

Thackeray's The Virginians, 1902. In pencil (6) or ink. Sgd. Various sizes. With related material. Archives of J. M. Dent & Son. (88) £2,000
— Original drawings, (3), to illus Elise de Pressense's Une Joyeuse Nichee. Archives of J. M. Dent & Son. (88) £270
— Original drawings, (3), to illus Thackeray's Samuel Titmarsh and the Great Hoggarty Diamond, 1903. Archives of J. M. Dent & Son. (88) £280
— Original drawings, (35), to illus Canon Atkinson's Scenes in Fairyland, 1892. Macmillan Archives. (90) £850
— Original drawings, (36), to illus James Galt's Annals of the Parish & The Ayreshire Legatees, 1894 & 1895. In ink; sgd. 310mm by 255mm. Macmillan Archives. (90) £1,700
— Original drawings, (4), to illus Thackeray's Denis Duval, 1903. Archives of J. M. Dent & Son. (88) £300
— Original drawings, (4), to illus Thackeray's Catherine, 1903. Archives of J. M. Dent & Son. (88) £280
— Original drawings, (4), to illus Thackeray's Rebecca and Rowena, & other stories, 1903. Archives of J. M. Dent & Son. (88) £260
— Original drawings, (6), to illus Charles Lamb's Poems, Plays and Rosamund Gray, 1903. Archives of J. M. Dent & Son. (88) £600
— Original drawings, (6), to illus Thackeray's The Book of Snobs, 1903. Archives of J. M. Dent & Son. (88) £850
— Original drawings, (7), to illus A. Archives of J. M. Dent & Son. (88) £300
— Original drawings, (7), to illus Thackeray's Vanity Fair, 1901. In pencil (3) or ink. Sgd. Various sizes. 2 framed. With related material. Archives of J. M. Dent & Son. (88) £1,100
— Original drawings, (7), to illus Thackeray's The Paris Sketch Book, 1903. Archives of J. M. Dent & Son. (88) £260
— Original drawings, (8), to illus E. Macmillan Archives. (90) £600
— Original drawings, (8), to illus E. Macmillan Archives. (90) £400

AMERICAN BOOK PRICES CURRENT

— Original drawings, (8), to illus Thackeray's Barry Lyndon, 1902. Archives of J. M. Dent & Son. (88) £350
— Original drawings, (87), to illus A. G. Gardiner's Pebbles on the Shore, 1917. In ink. 82 sgd or initialled. Some drawn 2 or 3 to a sheet. Various sizes. Archives of J. M. Dent & Son. (88) £3,000
— Original drawings, (96), to illus Thomas Hood's Humorous Poems, 1893. In ink; 93 sgd. Various sizes. Macmillan Archives. (90) £2,800

Brock, Henry Matthew
Original drawings, (13), to illus Ernest Rhys' The Old Country, 1917. Archives of J. M. Dent & Son. (88) £200
— Original drawings, (14), to illus M. Archives of J. M. Dent & Son. (90) £850
— Original drawings, (25), to illus J. F. Cooper's The Pioneers, 1897 (pbd 1900). In ink; sgd. About 285mm by 230mm. Macmillan Archives. (90) £1,200
— Original drawings, (27), watercolor portraits of authors, to illus books in The Wallet Library, [n.d.]. (89) £400
— Original drawings, (38), to illus Capt. Marryat's Jacob Faithful, 1894 & 1895. In ink; sgd. About 300mm by 250mm. Macmillan Archives. (90) £2,200
— Original drawings, (40), to illus Capt. Marryat's Japhet in Search of a Father, 1894. In ink; sgd. Various sizes. Macmillan Archives. (90) £4,600
— Original drawings, (50), to illus Oliver Wendell Holmes' The Poet at the Breakfast Table, 1902. In ink. Sgd; some initialled. Various sizes. Archives of J. M. Dent & Son. (88) £1,700
— Original drawings, (51), to illus Leigh Hunt's Essays, 1903. In ink. Sgd; some initialled. Various sizes. Archives of J. M. Dent & Son. (88) £2,500
— Original drawings, (56), to illus Oliver Wendell Holmes' The Autocrat at the Breakfast Table, 1902. In ink. Mostly sgd; 1 initialled. Various sizes. Archives of J. M. Dent & Son. (88) £2,200
— Original drawings, (7), to illus Lady J. Archives of J. M. Dent & Son. (88)

£800
— Original drawings, (8), Mr. (90) £80
— Original drawings, (8), to illus Charles Dickens' The Old Curiosity Shop, 1901. (89) £460
— Original drawings, (8), to illus Charles Dickens' Great Expectations, [c.1901]. (89) £600
— Original drawings, (9), to illus Charles Dickens' Bleak House, 1901. (89) £850

Brod, Max, 1884-1968
Autograph Ms, poem, An eine Frau, [n.d.]. (90) DM500
— Autograph Ms, poem, Der andre Blick, [n.d.]. (90) DM900
Collection of 16 A Ls s & 3 Ls s, 8 Aug 1949 to 20 May 1960 & [n.d.]. 34 pp, various sizes. To David Scheinert. Literary correspondence, especially regarding his works Galilei in Gefangenschaft & Der Meister. (88) DM4,200
ALs, 26 Aug 1907. (88) DM320
— 14 Sept 1916. (89) DM380
— 9 July 1932. (90) DM250
— 3 Mar 1963. (91) DM220

Broglie, Louis Victor, Prince de, 1892-1987
ALs, 20 Dec 1938. (88) DM340

Bromfield, Louis, 1896-1956
Collection of ALs & 3 Ls s, [1930s & 1940s]. (89) $90
Ls, 25 Jan 1948. (89) $150

Bromhead, Gonville, 1844-91. See: Zulu War

Brommy, Rudolf (Karl Rudolf Bromme), 1804-60
ALs, 14 May 1848. Schroeder collection. (89) DM550

Bronte, Anne, 1820-49
[Her copy of the 7th Ed of George Henry Noehden's A Grammar of the German Language, L, 1835, sgd & inscr on flyleaf, 14 Sept 1843, annotated throughout partly in miniature script, sold at S on 13 Dec 1990, lot 86, for £6,500 to Sellars.]

Bronte, Charlotte, 1816-55
Autograph Ms, poem, beginning "I've been wandering in the green woods", sgd & dated 14 Dec 1829. 2.75 by 3 inches (fragment of integral address leaf of a letter received). 4 four-line stanzas. Tipped to larger sheet. (89) $6,500
ALs, 6 Mar 1841. 1 p, 4to. To Ellen Nussey. About her employment as a governess. (91) $6,000
— [1845]. 3 pp, 16mo. To Ellen Nussey. Sympathizing with her for the suffering endured by her brother George. (91) £2,400
— 19 Jan 1847. 4 pp, 8vo. To Ellen Nussey. About the strange ways of society. (91) $6,500
— 24 Aug [18]47. 2 pp, 8vo. To Messrs Smith, Elder & Co. Sending them the Ms of Jane Eyre under separate cover. Sgd CBell. Koch Foundation. (90) $48,000
— 11 Mar 1849. 2 pp, 8vo. To W. S. Williams. Reporting about her sister's illness. (88) $3,750
— 19 Sept 1849. 1 p, 8vo. To [William Smith Williams?]. About proofs of a book & saying she lives "under no slavish fear of discovery". Koch Foundation. (90) $8,000
— 4 June 1850. 4 pp, 8vo. To her father, the Rev. Patrick Bronte. Reporting about her activities in London. John F. Fleming Estate. (89) $7,500
— 26 Sept 1851. 4 pp, 8vo. To her pbr W[illiam] S[mith] Williams. Stating that "Currer Bell" has nothing to publish at present. Sgd CB. (90) £8,500
— 18 Mar 1854. 1 p, 8vo. To T. C. Newby. Acknowledging receipt of a check. (89) £1,700
— [1 Apr 1854]. 2 pp, 8vo. To Ellen Nussey. Putting off her visit because Arthur Bell Nicholls is arriving on Monday. (91) $5,500
AL, 9 June 1838. 4 pp, 4to. To Ellen Nussey. Reporting about her health & the visit of Mary & Martha Taylor. (89) $12,000

Brooke, Leonard Leslie, 1862-1940
Original drawings, (7), to illus Thomas Nash's A Spring Song, 1898. Archives of J. M. Dent & Son. (88) £90

Brooke, Rupert, 1887-1915
ALs, [July 1908]. 6 pp, 8vo & 4to. To [Dudley Ward]. About arrangements for a holiday party in August. Koch Foundation. (90) $2,400
— 8 July 1910. 2 pp, 4to. To [Reginald Pole]. Discussing problems with a theatrical production of Dr. Faustus. Sgd Rupert. Some tiny fold holes. (88) $1,100
— [June 1911]. 2 pp, 4to. To [Dudley Ward]. Playfully referring to his activities & friends, giving advice about marriage, etc. (90) £1,300
Autograph postcard, sgd, [7 Mar 1911]. To Jacques Raverat. Sending his poem Dead Men's Love, 24 lines. Sgd R. Koch Foundation. (90) $2,400
— [3 Oct 1912]. John F. Fleming Estate. (89) $600

Brookner, Anita
Autograph Ms, A Friend from England; fragment. (88) £700

Brooks, Louise, 1906-85
Ls, 6 Feb 1965. (91) $375
— 5 Sept 1965. (91) $275
— [n.d.]. (91) $750

Brown, Arthur Whitten, Sir, 1886-1948.
See: Alcock, John William & Brown

Brown, Herbert Charles
Autograph Ms, scientific paper, A Remarkable Stereoselectivity in the Oxymercuration-Demercuration of Norbornene..., 1967. (88) DM320

Brown, John, of Osawatomie, 1800-59
ALs, 10 June 1848. 1 p, 4to. To Simon Perkins. Business letter regarding trade in wool. (90) $3,000
— 12 Apr 1851. 1 p, 4to. To his children. Family news, & informing them about his travels. Doheny collection. (89) $1,150
— 21 Apr 1851. 1 p, 4to. To his son John. About the importance of their causes. (91) $2,200
— 20 July 1852. 1 p, 4to. To his son John Brown, Jr. About the death of his infant son, the family's health problems, & his crops. Doheny collection. (89) $1,600
— 11 Oct 1856. 1 p, 4to. To the Rev. Samuel & Florilla Adair. Explaining his decision to leave Kansas. Repaired. Barrett collection. (89) $2,500
— 24 Nov 1859. 2 pp, 4to. To Rebecca Buffum Spring. From prison, discussing family matters, the education of his children, & his confinement. With related material. (91) $13,000
ADs, 21 Aug 1858. 1 p, 3 by 7 inches. As Agent for Nat. Kansas Committee, receipt. Alexander collection. (90) $1,050
Autograph sentiment, [8 Aug 1834?]. (91) $750

Brown, John F., Seminole Chief
Photograph, sgd & inscr, [c.1900]. (91) $180

Browne, Hablot K. ("Phiz"), 1815-82
Autograph Ms, Hunting Songs. L, [c.1860-70] 21 orig drawings (each sgd as Phiz) & a grouup of lyrics for 10 songs, the lyrics on 17 pp. 381mm by 270mm, in mor gilt. Schiff Ms (91) $7,500
See also: Dickens, Charles

Browning, Elizabeth Barrett, 1806-61
Autograph Ms, poem, Rogers, beginning "Thy song commended memory"; [c.1842?]. 2 pp, 16mo. Draft, 2 five-line stanzas, with 2 rewritten versions of 2d stanza. Bound into 1st vol of an extra-illus copy of Recollections of the Table-Talk of Samuel Rogers. L 1856, 2 vols. (90) $1,800
— Autograph Ms, poem, Song of the Rose, 13 lines; [n.d.]. 1 p, 8vo. Fair copy; including 2-line note by Robert Browning, sgd RB, at bottom. With covering ALs by Robert Browning, 24 Feb 1864, 1 p, 8vo, to Miss Griffith of the Brooklyn Sanitary Fair. (90) $7,500
— Autograph Ms, poems, Inclusions, Insufficieny, & Life and Love, [pbd 1850]. 3 pp, 8vo. Fair copies. (88) $3,000
Series of 101 A Ls s & fragments of 6 more, 22 Sept 1848 to 7 June 1861 & [n.d.]. About 600 pp, 8vo. To Sarianna

Browning, her sister-in-law. (91) $70,000
ALs, 10 June 1839. (91) £580
— [28 Mar 1858]. (89) £900
— Apr [1859]. 2 pp, 8vo. To [Frederic] Leighton. Criticizing his port of Robert Browning. (91) £1,300
— [n.d.]. (89) £620
AL, 19 Mar 1823. 5 pp, 4to, in half mor folder & box. To "My beloved Granny & Nippy". Recounting her 1st meeting with Hugh Stuart Boyd; unfinished. With later autograph endorsement on verso of final leaf. John F. Fleming Estate. (89) $7,000
See also: Browning, Robert & Browning

Browning, Oscar, 1837-1923
Collection of 4 A Ls s & letter, 1919-21. 8 pp, 4to. To Mr. Leftwich. Discussing the importance of "Greek love" to the Aesthetic Movement & commenting on Swinburne, Gosse, & Simeon Solomon. Torn & soiled. Koch Foundation. (90) $1,200

Browning, Robert, 1812-89
Autograph transcript, poem, Magical Nature, [n.d.]. 1 p, 8vo. 8 lines, sgd. Tipped to larger leaf. Barrett collection. (89) $1,500
Collection of 2 A Ls s & autograph transcript, sgd, 20 Feb 1887, 13 Mar [n.y.], & 27 May 1863. 11 pp, 8vo. To A. Wise, declining to be interviewed. To Dante Gabriel Rossetti, chatting about Mrs. Browning & John Ruskin. Poem, Porphyria's Lover, [pbd 1836], 60 lines. (88) $5,000
Series of 119 A Ls s, 1881-89. About 218 pp, various sizes. To Mrs. Skirrow & her husband. Each letter inlaid & bound in mor by Wallis. (91) $19,000
— Series of 3 A Ls s, 1 June 1883 to 26 June 1885. (88) £600
ALs, 5 Apr 1854. (91) £800
— 3 June 1859. (90) $900
— 19 July 1861. 3 pp, 8vo. To Sir Frederic Leighton. About his wife's death. Koch Foundation. (90) $6,500
— 9 Jan [18]62. (88) $900
— 10 June 1863. 3 pp, 8vo. To Alfred, Lord Tennyson. Asking him to meet Mercure Conway, & sending personal news. (90) £1,700
— 28 July [18]64. (91) $375
— 31 Dec 1865. (89) £380
— 13 Feb 1866. (91) £420
— 29 July 1868. (88) £580
— 20 Mar 1869. (89) £580
— 18 Dec [18]75. 1 p, 8vo. Recipient unnamed. Reporting his illness with a "vile cold". With ANs, in 3d person, by Elizabeth Barrett [Browning], 2 July 1844. (90) $1,200
— 6 June 1877. (90) £320
— 14 June [18]77. (91) $325
— 6 Feb 1878. (89) £320
— 5 Aug 1879. (91) £950
— 10 Nov 1881. Doheny collection. (89) $850
— 14 Feb 1882. (91) £800
— 11 July 1884. (88) £320
— 10 Dec 1884. (90) £600
— 15 Mar 1885. (89) $700
— 18 Dec 1886. (89) £260
— 21 Dec 1886. (88) £250
— 7 Jan 1887. 2 pp, 8vo. To Mr. Barnett Smith. Referring to an accompanying proof copy of his poem Parleyings with Certain People. Tipped onto flyleaf of the author's proof of the poem, 8vo. Brown crushed mor bdg. (88) £1,250
— 9 May 1887. (91) £500
— 26 June 1887. (91) £380
— 10 Dec 1888. (90) DM900
— [n.d.], "Monday". (91) $550
Autograph quotation, sgd, 24 May 1889. (91) $850
Photograph, sgd, 2 July 1888. (88) £480
Signature, [n.d.]. (91) $200
See also: Browning, Elizabeth Barrett

Browning, Robert, 1812-89 —&
Browning, Elizabeth Barrett, 1806-61
ALs, 27 Dec 1855. 1 p, 12mo. Recipient unnamed. Sending their autograph. In the hand of Robert; sgd by both. Tipped into Elizabeth Barrett Browning's Sonnets from the Portuguese. San Francisco, 1927; 2 vols, 12mo & folio. Doheny collection. (88) $1,100

BRUCE

Bruce, James, 1730-94

ALs, 12 Dec 1777. (89) £900

— 20 July 1790. (89) £800

— 12 Jan 1794. 3 pp, 4to. To Mrs. Riddel. About her husband's voyage to the West Indies, & asking for some specimens. (89) £1,200

Bruce, Stanley Melbourne, Viscount Bruce of Melbourne, 1883-1967

Ls, 14 Oct 1926. (89) £650

Bruch, Max, 1838-1920

Autograph music, Concerto for clarinet & viola in E minor, Nov & Dec 1911. 137 pp, folio, in half roan. Full orchestral score; presumably unpbd. (91) £15,000

Collection of ALs & autograph postcard, sgd, 18 Dec 1880 & 1896. (90) DM320

Series of 4 A Ls s, 1878 & 1879. 16 pp, 8vo. To Richard Peyton. About his works & projects, reviews of his music, the Birmingham Festival, etc. In German & French. (90) £1,600

— Series of c.29 A Ls s, c.1900 to 1919. About 60 pp (some on postcards), various sizes. To Paul Miche. About his life & works, politics, conductors, etc. (88) £1,200

A Ls s (2), 3 June 1863 & 18 Apr 1893. (90) DM800

ALs, 7 Aug 1855. 3 pp, 8vo. To Karl Breidenstein. About a journey to Frankfurt & his plan to play his new trio in a concert. With related material. (88) DM1,700

— 11 Jan 1863. 2 pp, 8vo. To Karl Breidenstein. Reporting about his compositions & a concert. (89) DM1,100

— 3 Nov 1866. (89) DM400

— 30 Nov 1866. (91) DM650

— 12 Mar 1895. (88) DM240

— 22 Jan 1904. (89) DM420

— 1 Feb 1912. (91) £800

— 2 Feb 1916. (88) DM320

— 28 Dec 1919. (89) £520

Autograph quotation, 3 bars from his 1st Violin Concerto, 10 Aug 1878. 1 p, 8vo. Sgd. (91) £1,100

AMERICAN BOOK PRICES CURRENT

Bruckner, Anton, 1824-96

Series of 6 A Ls s, 16 Apr to 19 Dec 1884. 19 pp, 8vo. To Arthur Nikisch. Discussing the 1st performance of his 7th Symphony. (89) DM46,000

— Series of 3 A Ls s, 25 Feb to 7 July 1885. 11 pp, 8vo. To Arthur Nikisch. About the success of his 7th Symphony & other works. (89) DM28,000

— Series of 3 A Ls s, [1 Jan] 1887 to 23 Nov 1888. 8 pp, 8vo. To Arthur Nikisch. Expressing New Year's wishes, & discussing a performance of his 7th Symphony at Berlin. (89) DM24,000

ALs, 30 Apr 1866. 4 pp, 4to. To [Simon Sechter]. About his 1st Symphony, Liszt, von Buelow, & Rubinstein, & enclosing a musical Ms; contrapuntal exercises written under recipient's supervision (present, 15 Nov 1861, 2 pp, folio). (90) £5,600

— 23 Jan 1870. 3 pp, 8vo. To J. B. Schiedermayr. Expressing his grief about the death of his sister. (88) DM6,000

— 30 May 1872. 2 pp, 4to. Recipient unnamed. Explaining that he will not be able to see him in his office. (91) DM12,000

— 15 Jan [1]885. 1 p, 8vo. To Alfred Stross. Saying he has been unable to find a pbr, & mentioning Prof. Winterberger. (88) £1,700

— [n.d.]. 1 p, 8vo. To Herr von Peraton. Describing disagreeable aspects of a port. Framed. Salzer collection. (90) £1,300

Autograph quotation, opening 5 bars of the 8th Symphony, in short score on 3 staves, sgd & dated 24 Jan [1]893. 1 p, folio. With related material. (90) £5,500

— Anr, 4 bars from the beginning of his 8th Symphony, [n.d.]. 1 p, 5cm by 20.5cm. Sgd. (90) DM6,500

Bruening, Heinrich, 1885-1970

Collection of ALs & 3 Ls s, 28 June 1949 to 28 Feb 1955 & [n.d.]. (89) DM320

Brugsch, Heinrich Karl, 1827-94
ALs, 19 Jan 1871. (91) DM400

Brummell, George Bryan, 1778-1840
ALs, 26 July 1823. Byer collection. (90) $500

Brunel, Isambard Kingdom, 1806-59
[A collection of 7 A Ls s addressed to Brunel by admirers & friends, 1841 to 1858, 13 pp, 4to & 8vo, with related material, sold at C on 9 Dec, lot 346, for £100 to Elton.]

Brunel, Sir Marc Isambard, 1769-1849
ANs, 9 May 1836, 1 p, 12mo. (90) $100
Signature, [n.d.]. (89) £340

Bruni, Leonardo, Aretinus, 1369-1444
Ms, Historie Fiorentine, in the Italian trans of Donato Acciaiuoli; with account of the conquest of Pisa by the Florentines in 1406. [Florence, 1476]. 267 leaves (2 blank), 330mm by 227mm. Old vellum over pastebds. Written for Bartolomeo di Leonardo de Bartoloni in a regular sloping humanistic cursive by [Domenico di Laurenzo?]. With 14 large initials (2 illuminated). (90) £11,500

Bryan, William Jennings, 1860-1925
Collection of ALs & 2 Ls s, 27 Aug 1913, 17 July 1923 & [n.d.]. (90) $190
ALs, 14 Dec [n.y.]. (91) $100
Ls, 16 June 1915. (91) $375

Bryant, Sir Arthur
[A collection of correspondence addressed to Bryant, c.80 items, by various literary figures, including T.S. Eliot, G. B. Shaw, etc., sold at C on 9 Dec, lot 290, for £1,300 to Wilson.]

Bryant, William Cullen, 1794-1878
Autograph Ms, poem, Ode for the funeral of Abraham Lincoln, [1865]. Doheny collection. (89) $250
— Autograph Ms, poem, To a Waterfowl, 1 Apr 1875. Doheny collection. (89) $800
Autograph transcript, poem, The Death of Lincoln, 28 June 1875. (89) $800
— Autograph transcript, poem, William Tell, 9 May 1864. (89) $300
ALs, 17 Nov 1843. 2 pp, 4to. To John Frost. Sending a trans (included) of a poem by Goethe for a journal. (89) DM1,050
— 31 Jan 1860. (90) $275
— 5 Apr 1862. (88) $60

Brychta, Alex
Original drawings, (25), to illus Helen Hoke's Eerie, Weird and Wicked, & Ghostly, Grim and Gruesome, 1976. Archives of J. M. Dent & Son. (88) £260

Buber, Martin, 1878-1965
Autograph Ms, essay, Schel Mahuta ha Tarbuth, [after 1938]. (91) DM620
A Ls s (2), 8 & 15 Aug 1952. (90) DM650
ALs, 19 Mar 1932. (90) DM330
— 21 Mar 1956. (89) DM420

Buch, Leopold von, 1774-1853
ALs, 11 Dec 1836. (90) £400

Buchan, John, 1875-1940
Typescript, novel, Sick Heart River, [1939]. About 280 pp, 4to, in cloth bdg. With extensive autograph insertions & revisions & autograph tp. (88) £4,000
Collection of c.50 A Ls s, Ls s, & cards, sgd, c.1910-35. (88) £650

Buchanan, James, 1791-1868
Collection of ALs & photograph, 1O Apr 1836 & [n.d.]. (89) $350
— Collection of ALs & cut signature, 1 Mar 1837 & 19 Apr 1858. (91) $550
Series of 3 A Ls s, 7 Dec 1836 to 7 June 1842. 4 pp, 4to. To Reah Frazer. Discussing political affairs. (88) $1,600
A Ls s (2), 1 July 1848 & 26 Feb 1851. 3 pp, 4to. To John Ritter & al., sending the text of a toast to be read at a dinner. To Robert J. Walker, planning a meeting. Pratt collection. (89) $1,700
ALs, 14 Apr 1819. (88) $110
— 3 Mar 1820. Byer collection. (90) $450
— 15 Mar 1828. (91) $475
— 7 Jan 1835. (90) $275
— 5 May [1836]. (91) $350
— 27 Oct 1836. (91) $900
— 19 Aug 1837. Doheny collection. (89) $550
— 21 Dec 1842. 3 pp, 4to. To James Ross Snowden. Discussing plans to present him as Presidential candidate, & explaining his stand on the tariff ques-

BUCHANAN

tion. (88) $1,400
— 21 July 1843. (88) $200
— 10 Apr 1846. (89) $700
— 22 July [18]47. (89) $450
— 2 Jan 1848. 3 pp, 4to. To B. S. Schoonover. Political letter expressing appreciation for the loyalty of Pennsylvania Democrats. (89) $1,600
— 10 Jan 1849. (90) $325
— 25 Feb 1850. 2 pp, 4to. To Robert Tyler. Sending news from Washington & discussing the sectional controversy over the admission of California. Sang collection. (91) $7,500
— 27 Nov 1850. 1 p, 4to. To Robert Tyler. Discussing the political situation in Pennsylvania. Doheny collection. (89) $1,500
— 22 May 1852. (88) £700
— 11 June 1852. 1 p, 4to. To Isaac G. McKinley. Commenting about Franklin Pierce as Presidential candidate. (89) $4,250
— 15 Mar 1853. 1 p, 4to. To Robert McClelland. Recommending that William W. King be continued as clerk in the General Land Office. (90) $1,400
— 20 Feb 1857. 2 pp, 8vo. To Jefferson Davis. About appointments & the mail system in Washington; declining a dinner invitation. (91) $2,000
— 13 June 1857. (88) $350
— 23 July 1857. 3 pp, 4to. To Richard Vaux. About the possibility of a removal of a post office, & requesting him to effect a reconciliation between groups of Democrats in Pennsylvania. (90) $2,000
— 14 July 1860. (91) $750
— 29 Aug 1861. (90) $380
— 20 Jan 1862. (88) $70
— 30 Mar 1863. Rosenbloom collection. (88) $450
— 26 Dec 1866. 2 pp, 4to. To James W. Wall. On politics and the need for Wall to take over the leadership of the Democratic Party in New Jersey. (91) $2,800
— [5 Apr n.y.]. (89) $300
Ls, 13 Feb 1823. (90) $150
— 23 Jan 1846. (90) $280
— 13 Apr 1846. (91) $220
— 18 Mar 1846. (91) $150
— 29 Apr 1857. (88) £300
ANs, [n.d.]. (89) $180
Ds, 6 Dec 1847. (88) $130
— 25 Jan 1849. (89) $290
— 2 Mar 1849. (89) $150
— 22 Apr 1857. (91) $500
— 1 June 1857. (91) $650
— 1 June 1857. (91) $260
— 1 Apr 1858. (90) $380
— 17 May 1858. (91) $280
— 18 Aug 1858. (88) $450
— 17 Dec 1858. (88) $250
— 15 Jan 1859. (90) $550
— 20 Aug 1859. (91) $700
— 21 Sept 1859. (90) $650
— 21 Sept 1859. Byer collection. (90) $700
— 26 Mar 1860. (90) $450
— 25 June 1860. (89) $200
— 10 Sept 1860. (90) $120
— 21 Dec 1860. (90) $375
— 18 Jan 1861. (91) $280
— 24 Jan 1861. (91) $290
Address leaf, 31 July [1839]. (88) $130
Autograph endorsement, sgd, 9 Aug 1816. (91) $200
Cut signature, [n.d.]. (91) $130
— Anr, [n.d.]. (90) $140
Franking signature, [3 Jan n.y.]. (88) $135
— Anr, [5 Apr n.y.]. (89) $170
— Anr, [22 Apr n.y.]. (88) $190
— Anr, [24 Dec n.y.]. Alexander collection. (90) $230
— Anr, [n.d.]. (91) $250
Photograph, sgd, 10 Nov 1862. Carte size. Inscr on mount. By E. Anthony from a Brady negative. (90) $4,000

Buchholtz, Alexander August von, 1800?-56
ALs, 22 Apr 1848. (88) DM500

Buck, Pearl S., 1892-1973
[A collection of 4 typescripts, each with holograph corrections, 17 Jan 1962 & [n.d.], 52 pp, with related material, sold at wa on 17 Oct, lot 16, for $95.]
[A collection of 6 carbon copies of typescripts on various subjects, [n.d.], 63 pp, 4to, each with a few holograph additions, sold at wa on 8 Mar 1990, lot 545, for $200.]
Ls s (2), 21 July 1944 & 30 Sept 1949. (89)

$120

Buckler, William, 1814-84

Original drawings, over 700 watercolors of various sizes for his The Larvae of the British Butterflies and Moths; [1857-84]. Mtd on or inlaid in c.240 leaves, 250mm by 200mm; 3 vols, 4to. (90) $6,000

Buddenbrock, Wilhelm Dietrich von, 1672-1757

Ls, 29 July 1755. (90) DM440

Buddhism

Ms, 18 paintings representing the Lohans with short poems on facing pages, [China, 18th or 19th cent]. 36 pp, native paper, 360mm by 365mm. In mahogany bds stitched within Middle Hill bds, def. Phillipps Ms.18055 & Robinson collection. (89) £1,050

Budge and Betty Series

[A collection of 129 ink drawings for the 2d series, c.1922, various sizes, with related material, sold at S on 2 June 1989, lot 581, for £450 to Lowery.]

[The complete set of 12 watercolor drawings for the 1st series, c.1927, c.270mm by 185mm, 1 sgd H.S., sold at S on 2 June 1989, lot 580, for £360 to Forsyth.]

[A collection of 19 ink & watercolor cover designs for reissues of the series, 1927 to 1932, c.320mm by 205mm, with related material, sold at S on 2 June 1989, lot 585, for £360 to Gaunt.]

[A collection of 164 ink drawings for the 3d series, c.1931, various sizes, with related material, sold at S on 2 June 1989, lot 583, for £450 to Ferrett Fantasy.]

[A collection of 12 watercolor drawings for the 3d series, c.1931, c.270mm by 190mm, sold at S on 2 June 1989, lot 584, for £450 to Ferrett Fantasy.]

Buechner, Alexander, 1827-1904

Collection of 46 A Ls s & autograph Ms, 1853 to 27 Jan 1902. (90) DM650

Buell, Don Carlos, 1818-98

ALs, 17 Jan 1862. (91) $1,000

Buelow, Bernhard, Fuerst von, 1849-1929

Collection of ALs & Ls, 17 July 1909 & 12 Jan 1911. (90) DM230

Series of 39 Ls s, 18 Sept 1902 to 15 Apr 1929. Over 80 pp, mostly 8vo. To Felix von Eckardt. Concerning articles pbd in the Hamburger Fremdenblatt, politicians, current affairs, etc. With related material. (89) DM2,700

Ls s (2), 8 Aug 1901 & 1907. (91) DM400

Ls, [May 1928]. (90) DM330

Buelow, Hans von, 1830-94

Collection of ALs & photograph, sgd & inscr, 14 June 1871. (91) DM360

— Collection of 10 A Ls s, 2 A Ns s, & AN, 1887 to 1892. 25 pp, 8vo & 12mo. To [Gustav Rassow]. Discussing theatrical & musical matters. (91) DM2,000

— Collection of ALs & photograph, sgd, [n.d.]. (90) DM430

Series of 5 A Ls s, 4 Dec 1857 to 26 May 1867. (88) DM800

— Series of 27 A Ls s, 1863 to 1869. Over 70 pp, 8vo. To Dr. Carl Gille. Informing him about his professional activities, talking about Liszt, Wagner, & others, etc. (89) £2,500

A Ls s (2), [9 Jan 1860] & 15 Apr 1862. (90) DM800

— A Ls s (2), 12 Aug 1862 & 20 June 1865. (90) £850

— A Ls s (2), 15 June & 2 Dec 1866. (88) £580

— A Ls s (2), 30 Apr 1889 & 18 Mar 1892. (88) DM950

ALs, 3 July 1858. (89) DM460

— 12 Feb 1865. 3 pp, 8vo. To Wendelin Weissheimer. About the situation in Bavaria & rumors that Wagner has incurred the King's displeasure. Including musical quotation. (91) DM1,500

— 17 Jan 1866. (90) DM430

— 23 Mar 1867. (90) DM320

— 11 Aug 1870. (90) DM540

— 18/30 Mar 1874. 7 pp, 8vo. To Bartholff Senf. Interesting report about his concert tour in Russia & Russian composers. Sgd in cyrillic letters. With anr, 24 Nov 1874. (88) DM2,600

— 11 Nov [1874]. (89) DM420

BUELOW

— 26 Nov 1883. (91) DM360
— 11 Apr 1884. 1 p, folio. To Graf von Schleinitz. Draft, sarcastic reply to disciplinary punishment for his criticism of the Royal Opera at Berlin. On verso of letter addressed to him. (89) DM1,100
— 8 Sept 1891. (90) DM800
— 8 Aug 1892. (88) DM420
Autograph postcard, sgd, 4 Mar 1885. (90) DM260

Buelow von Dennewitz, Friedrich Wilhelm, Graf, 1755-1816
ALs, 22 Apr 1809. Schroeder collection. (89) DM800
Ls, 6 Apr 1815. Schroeder collection. (89) DM440

Buerger, Gottfried August, 1747-94
Autograph Ms, poem, Der Bruder Graurock und die Pilgerinn, [c.1777/78]. 7 pp, 8vo. Sgd. (88) DM11,000
ALs, 2 Aug 1774. 8 pp, folio. To Adam Heinrich von Uslar. Discussing a court case & denying the necessity of a new plea. (90) DM2,600
— 29 Dec 1775. 4 pp, 8vo. To Leopold Goeckingk. Chatting about his family & their plan to start a ptg business. Albrecht collection. (91) SF2,200
— 23 June 1780. 2 pp, folio. To J. C. Dieterich. Chatting about unwanted visitors & the editing of the Musenalmanach. Sgd GAB. Corner def. (90) DM4,400
— 14 Apr [1781?]. 3 pp, folio. To the pbr J. C. Dieterich. Chatty letter discussing a horse sale & other matters. (89) DM2,600
— 20 Apr 1789. 4 pp, 8vo. To Heinrich Christian Boie. Inviting comments on the new Ed of his poems. (90) DM3,600
ADs, 23 Jan 1773. (89) DM320
Ds, 30 June 1773. (89) DM700

Buffon, Georges Louis Leclerc, Comte de, 1707-88
Ls, 17 Mar 1784. (90) DM270

AMERICAN BOOK PRICES CURRENT

Bultmann, Rudolf, 1884-1976
Autograph Ms, commentary on the Epistle to the Corinthians, fragment; [n.d.]. (89) DM400

Bulwer-Lytton, Edward, 1803-73
ALs, 10 Oct 1828. (89) £350

Bunche, Ralph J., 1904-1971
Collection of Ls, Photograph, sgd, & signature on philatelic envelope, 1969 & [n.d.]. (91) $250

Bunin, Ivan Alekseevich, 1870-1953
ALs, [n.d.]. (90) DM700

Bunker, Ellsworth, 1894-1984
Ls, 8 Feb 1984. (89) $60

Bunsen, Christian Karl Josias von, 1791-1860
Series of 3 A Ls s, 1828 & 1834. (90) DM250
— Series of 4 A Ls s, [1853], 17 May 1854 & [n.d.]. (90) DM360

Bunsen, Robert Wilhelm, 1811-99
Series of 3 A Ls s, 7 Apr 1848 to 7 Sept 1851. 10 pp, 4to. To Victor Regnault. Commenting on the political situation in France & Germany. (91) DM4,500
ANs, 7 May 1870. (91) DM320
Photograph, sgd, [n.d.]. (89) DM660

Bunting, Basil
Typescript, poem, The Spoils, 1951. (91) £500

Burdette, Robert Jones, 1844-1914
Autograph Ms, essay, The Christmas carols of a lunatic, sgd; [1880s]. Doheny collection. (89) $450

Burger, Warren. See: Ford, Gerald R. & Burger

Burgess, Anthony
Autograph music, Preludes for piano, 1964. (91) £400

Burgess, Gelett, 1866-1951
Series of 4 Ls s, 1937 to 1942. (89) $120

Burghley, William Cecil, 1st Baron, 1520-98
ALs, 21 May 1597. 1 p, folio. To the Earl of Essex. Referring to a financial matter concerning Sir Walter Raleigh.

(91) £1,600
Ds, Apr 1580. (89) £180
— 17 Apr 1590. (91) £140
— 15 Mar 1592/3. (88) £180

Burgoyne, John, 1722-92
ALs, 22 Mar 1778. 2 pp, 4to. To Major Gen. Wm. Heath. Referring to matters pertaining to his army. (91) $4,500
— 27 Mar 1778. 1 p, 4to. To Maj. Gen. William Heath. Prisoner of war arrangements with his captor. (91) $6,500

Burke, Edmund, 1729-97
A Ls s (2), 22 Aug 1768 & 19 Aug 1783. (90) £380
ALs, 26 Apr 1781. (90) $900
— 30 Jan 1788. (90) £460
— [c.1791]. 3 pp, 4to. To Sir William Fawkener. Congratulating him on his safe return from Russia & commenting about the French Revolution. (90) £1,200
— 16 Oct 1793. (89) $475
Letter, 29 July 1782. (89) $200

Burley, Walter, 1275-1345?
Ms, Expositio in Artem Veterem Porphyrii et Aristotelis. [Southern France, c.1435-50]. 120 leaves, 300mm by 217mm, in contemp wooden bds covered with later orange paper, rebacked with sheep. With 5 large decorated initials, coat-of-arms at foot of f.1, & 8 pp with diagrams. (89) £6,000

Burmese Manuscripts
Ms, Buddhist text. (89) £260
— Ms, contents not stated. (91) £220
— Ms, contents not stated. (88) £260
— Ms, Kammavaca (a Buddhist monk's ordination text). (91) £160

Burne-Jones, Sir Edward Coley, 1833-98
Series of 39 A Ls s, 1870 to 1888. About 120 pp, folio & 8vo. To G. F. Watts & his wife Mary. Letters to a close friend covering a variety of matters. Including 4 self-caricatures. With related material. (89) £6,500
— Series of 76 A Ls s, 1873-98. 279 pp, 12mo & 8vo. To his daughter Margaret & his son-in-law Jack Mackail (1). Covering a wide range of topics, & including c.60 sketches in 31 of the letters, mostly in pen-&-ink. With related material. Koch Foundation. (90) $19,000
— Series of c.300 A Ls s, Oct 1894 to Oct 1896. About 980 pp, 8vo. To Olive Maxse. Personal letters to a good friend, discussing a wide range of subjects. Including c.140 drawings. Some letters incomplete, some hinged into an album, 7 framed. (89) £160,000
ALs, [1882?]. 3 pp, 8vo. To [John Ruskin]. Paying tribute to him as his mentor, & mentioning Morris. With note of authentication. (89) £2,200
ANs, 3 Sept 1895. 4 pp, 8vo. To Violet Cecil. Sending "Four Little Messages of Extraordinary Affection For You", with 4 orig drawings of a bird. Sgd B-J. (89) £10,500
— Sept 1895. 1 p, 8vo. To V[iolet] C[ecil]. Sending "This Picture Of A Proud Mother" [a bird & her chick, below]. Sgd E B-J. (89) £3,800

Burnet, David Gouverneur, 1788-1870
Ds, 1 Jan 1841. (91) $250
— 1 Feb 1841. (91) $150

Burnett, Frances Hodgson, 1849-1924
ALs, 18 Jan 1903 [1904]. 4 pp, 12mo. To Kate Douglas Wiggin Riggs. Praising recipient's book Rebecca. Was mtd. Doheny collection. (89) $1,700

Burnett, Peter Hardeman, 1807-95
ALs, 20 May 1878. (91) $250

Burney, Frances, 1752-1840
Collection of ALs & AL, 1812 & 1829. (89) £350

Burns, George —&
Allen, Gracie, 1905-64
Photograph, sgd & inscr, 1937. (90) 140

Burns, Robert, 1759-96
Autograph Ms, A Hunting Song. [c.1788] 1 p, folio. Tipped to cardbd mt & bound with tp transcript & notes in mor gilt by Sangorski & Sutcliffe. (91) $4,000
— Autograph Ms, draft of New Year's Day. [c.1789] 2 pp, folio. (91) $5,500
— Autograph Ms, poem, Lesley Bailie; [n.d.]. 2 pp, 4to. 6 four-line stanzas, with explanatory postscript. (91) £1,400

BURNS

— Autograph Ms, poem, To Miss L-- With Beattie's Poems For A New Years Gift; 3 four-line stanzas, sgd, inscr to Susan Logan & dated 1 Jan 1787. On front flyleaves of a copy of James Beattie's Poems on Several Occasions. Edin., 1776. 8vo. John F. Fleming Estate. (89) $11,000

— Autograph Ms, song, The Bony Lass o'Ballochmyle, [c.1786]. 2 pp, folio. 5 eight-line stanzas & 4 variant lines. Silked. (91) £1,800

Original drawing, 2 crows beside the body of a knight, to illust the ballad The Twa Corbies; [n.d.]. 259mm by 438mm. In ink & watercolor; sgd with monogram. Framed. (90) £1,600

ALs, [19 Mar 1788]. 2 pp, 4to. To "Clarinda" [Agnes M'Lehose]. Love letter, & including a quotation from The Song of Solomon. With related material. (91) £3,400

— 3 May 1788. 2 pp, 4to. To Dugald Stewart. Enclosing some poems, & wishing him success on his visit to France. (91) £1,400

— 14 Feb 1791. 3 pp, 8vo, in red mor gilt by Sangorski & Sutcliffe. To Archibald Alison. Commenting on recipient's Essays on the Nature and Principles of Taste. (91) £2,300

— ALEXANDER, WILHELMINA. - ALs, 21 Mar 1826, 4 pp, 4to. Recipient unknown. Describing her encounter with Burns. With related material. (88) £220

Burnside, Ambrose E., 1824-81
ALs, 16 Feb 1861. Byer collection. (90) $275
Ls, 5 May 1862. (91) $850

Burr, Aaron, 1756-1836
Collection of ALs, 2 Ls s, & Ds, 15 July [1815], 18 Sept 1833, & [n.d.]. 5 pp, 8vo. To T. L. Ogden & H. M. Western (2), about legal matters. Legal brief in the case of Thomas Betts. All sgd A.B. (90) $1,500
ALs, 5 Apr 1786. (91) $325
— 3 Mar 1788. (90) $250
— 14 Jan 1795. (88) $280
— 4 Jan 1797. 1 p, 4to. To Peter Van Gaasbeck. About a financial matter & the Presidential election. Repaired. Doheny collection. (89) $4,200

— 25 Mar 1800. Middendorf collection. (89) $650
Ls, [12 May 1807]. (88) $250
ADs, 1 May 1788. 5 pp, folio. Articles of Agreement of the New Jersey Land Company. Also sgd by George Morgan & others. (89) $3,250
— 4 May [1818?]. (91) $275
Ds, 27 Dec 1835. Doheny collection. (89) $420
Check, sgd, 28 Dec 1789; 64mm by 165mm. (88) $225
— Anr, accomplished & sgd, 17 Mar 1800. (89) $225
— Anr, accomplished & sgd, 1 May 1800. (89) $175
Cut signature, [n.d.]. (90) $110
Franking signature, [n.d.]. (88) $200
— Anr, [13 Jan 1796]. Alexander collection. (90) $450
— Anr, [n.d.]. Alexander collection. (90) $210

Burroughs, Edgar Rice, 1875-1950
Ls, 27 Mar 1924. 2 pp, 4to. To W. K. Calvert. Responding to a request for information about his work, & commenting about Tarzan & the craft of fiction. (90) £1,150
— 9 June 1931. 1 p. To Mrs. E. R. Perry. About meeting Beatrice. (90) $1,600
ANs, 20 Feb 1937. On verso of a photograph of the copyright page of Burroughs' copy of the 1st Ed of Tarzan of the Apes. Telling Don that the photo will help him to determine which of Don's copies is a 1st. (90) $2,000

Burroughs, John, 1837-1921
Autograph Ms, book, Far and Near, [c.1904]. 142 pp, 8vo, on rectos only. With numerous revisions & 3 alternate beginnings; sgd. Doheny collection. (89) $3,500
— Autograph Ms, poem, 5 lines; sgd & dated 11 May 1906. (90) $60
Autograph transcript, poem, Waiting, Jan 1919. Doheny collection. (89) $480
Collection of 5 A Ls s & photograph, 19 Apr 1884 to 1921 & [n.y.]. Doheny collection. (89) $400

Burton, Adolphus William Desart. See: Crimean War

Burton, Sir Richard Francis, 1821-90
Autograph Ms, How a Woman was once made to tell the truth, to be pbd in his Vikram and the Vampire; [1860s]. 10 leaves, 4to. With many revisions. Incomplete; partly imperf. (91) £2,500
Series of 4 A Ls s, 21 June 1881 to 5 May 1883. (91) £800
ALs, [8 Feb 1872]. (91) £320
— [n.d.]. (88) £160

Busbecq, Augier Ghislain de, 1522-92
ALs, 25 May 1577. (89) DM270

Busch, Wilhelm, 1832-1908
Autograph Ms, poem, Die Uhren. Ein Sylvestercarmen, [n.d.]. 7 pp, 8vo. (88) DM5,500
Collection of 3 A Ls s, 2 A Ns s & AN, 29 Mar 1880 to 10 Apr 1882. 9 pp, various sizes. To Henriette Eller. Musing about various matters. Notes on verso of visiting cards & port photograph. (90) DM4,500
ALs, Feb 1878. 2 pp, 4to. To Paul Lindau. About recipient's play, an article about Busch, & other matters. Repaired. (90) DM1,900
— 29 Sept 1882. 1 p, 4to. To Marie Eller. Whimsical letter referring to his & her failure to write. (90) DM1,500
— 14 May 1898. 1 p, 8vo. To [August] Schwartz. Declining permission to print one of his works. (88) DM1,100
— 23 Jan 1907. (91) DM660
Autograph postcard, sgd, 30 Dec 1904. (91) DM460
ANs, [n.d.]. (91) DM360

Busch, Wilhelm, 1832-1908 —& Others
Group photograph, with Franz Lenbach & Paul Lindau, sgd by Busch & inscr to Henriette Eller on verso, 7 Apr 1880. (90) DM900

Bush, George
Ls, 10 Nov 1971. (91) $400
— 19 Aug 1974. (91) $225
— 24 Nov 1974. (91) $400
ANs, [n.d.]. (91) $110
Photograph, sgd & inscr, 22 Aug [19]74. (91) $170
— Anr, [n.d.]. (91) $180
— Anr, [n.d.]. (91) $130

Bush, George —& Others
[The signatures of Bush, Donald T. Regan & 8 members of Ronald Reagan's cabinet, 10 Apr [19]83, on photograph of south portico of the White House, sold at Dar on 6 Dec 1990, lot 120, for $160.]

Bush, George. See: Reagan, Ronald & Bush

Bush, George, 1796-1859
[A collection of c.50 letters written to him, with numerous references to the Abolitionist movement, sold at rf on 26 Nov 1988, lot 7, for $900.]

Bushman, Francis X., 1883-1966
Photograph, sgd & inscr, [n.d.]. (89) $90

Busoni, Ferruccio, 1866-1924
ALs, [n.d.]. (88) DM340
— 15 Mar 1923. (89) DM340
Autograph quotation, 7 bars from Souapina, inscr to Miss Marion; July 1915. (90) $325
Photograph, sgd, 1904 & 1914. (90) DM270
See also: Brahms, Johannes

Butenandt, Adolf
Autograph Ms, draft of a speech commemorating the 50th anniversary of the Max Planck-Gesellschaft, 11 Jan 1961. (90) DM400
Collection of Ls & autograph postcard, sgd, 28 Aug 1967 & 1969. (90) DM300

Butler, David
[His director's script from 20th Cent Fox's Pigskin Parade, 1st draft, dated 1 July 1936, 119 offset typewritten pages, annotated in pencil, with related material, sold at CNY on 21 June 1989, lot 351, for $300.]

Butler, Pierce, 1744-1822
ALs, 21 Oct 1795. (89) $90

Butler, Richard, 1743-91
ALs, 23 July 1780. (88) $600

BUTLER

Butler, Zebulon, 1731-95
[Butler/Murray Family. - A large collection comprising many hundreds of letters to & from the family & descendants of Butler & his granddaughter Gertrude Murray, 1795 to early 1900s, sold at R on 4 Mar 1989, lot 264, for $2,200.]

Butterfield, Francis
Original drawings, (19), to illus David Smith's Uncle Fred, 1952. Archives of J. M. Dent & Son. (88) £70

Byles, Mather, 1735-1814
Autograph Ms, working drafts of 8 sermons, c.1756 to 1764; c.80 pp, 8vo, chiefly sewn in separate gatherings. (88) £1,000

Byrd, Richard E., 1888-1957
[The typescripts of his books Dicovery, & Alone, 1935 & 1938, several hundred pages, folio, with autograph revisions & related material, sold at S on 15 Dec 1988, lot 161, for £2,800.]

Byron, George Gordon Noel, Lord, 1788-1824
[An envelope front, sgd & addressed in his hand to the Rev. Dr. G. Clarke, 16 Feb 1816, 5 by 3 inches, sold at Dar on 4 Oct 1990, lot 147, for $650.]

[A group of 4 letters written to his sister Augusta Leigh, [1840s & 1850s], partly regarding the purchase of Mss by Byron, with related material, sold at S on 15 Nov 1988, lot 1593, for £80 to Wise.]

Autograph Ms, poem addressed to Thomas Moore, [1816 & 1817]. 1 p, 4to. Repaired; in def red lea bdg. (91) $6,500

— Autograph Ms, poem, Maid of Athens, ere we part [here entitled Song. Athens 1810]; [1811]. 3 pp, 4to. Including 2 explanatory notes. Koch Foundation. (90) $34,000

— Autograph Ms, poem, On the death of Sir Peter Parker. [1814]. 3 pp, 224mm by 185mm, inlaid to large sheet & inserted in an extra-illus copy of Sir George Dallas's A Biographical Memoir of the Late Sir Peter Parker. Schiff Ms (91) $15,000

ALs, 2 Aug 1811. 3 pp, 4to. To Dr. [J. B. Pigot]. Informing him of the death of his mother. (88) £6,400

— 12 Feb 1812. 3 pp, 4to. To John Cowell. Requesting that he look out for Mr. Hanson's son at Eton. (91) £3,200

— 17 Nov 1813. 2 pp, 8vo. To Lord & Lady Mountnorris. Apologizing for the delay in answering a note & announcing a shipment of vases. Sgd Biron. Doheny collection. (89) $3,200

— 20 Nov 1813. 2 pp, 4to. Recipient unnamed. Responding to a request for information about his life & family. Repaired; tipped to larger leaf. Barrett collection. (89) $4,250

— [c.June 1815]. 1 p, 8vo. To Mrs. Bartley. Concerning the disposal of his box [at the Drury Lane Theater]. Trimmed; collector's stamp. (89) £1,500

— 27 Apr 1819. 3 pp, 4to. To the Ed of Galignani's Messenger. Denying authorship of The Vampire. Koch Foundation. (90) $30,000

— 28 Apr 1820. 2 pp, 4to. To Jean Antoine Galignani. Ordering copies of Shelley's Cenci & Thomas Moore's works, & questioning the ascription to him of Don Juan. Including postscript stating correct form of address for peers. Koch Foundation. (90) $22,000

— 9 Nov 1820. 2 pp, 4to. To Jean Antoine Galignani. About copyright matters & the pirating of his works. (91) $8,000

— 11 May 1821. 4 pp, 4to. To [Richard Belgrave] Hoppner. About the education of his daughter Allegra. (89) £4,600

— 21 Sept 1822. Length not stated. To Thomas Moore. Asking him to forward an enclosure to Mr. Galignani. Sgd N.B. (88) $2,500

— 24 Apr 1823. 3 pp, 4to. To John Hunt. About publishing matters. sgd with initials. (91) $8,500

AL, [n.d.]. (88) £560

Autograph check, sgd, 25 Oct 1811. (89) £1,000

Byron, Robert, 1905-41
Ls, 9 Dec [n.y.]. (90) £240

Byron, William, Lord, 1722-98
Ds, 11 June 1751. (91) $110

C

Caccini, Giulio Romano, c.1545-c.1618
Ds, 23 Dec 1610. 1 p, folio. Brokerage bill, listing 6 transactions. (90) £5,500

Caccini, Giulio Romano, c.1545-c.1618 —&
Peri, Jacopo, 1561-1633
— VAINI, ENEA. - 2 Ls s & Ds, 6 Aug 1603 & 6 Apr 1631. To Ferdinando I, Grand Duke of Tuscany, evaluating music & musicians under stipend at the Medici court, including Caccini & Peri. To Ferdinando II, contents not stated. (90) £8,000

Cadiz
— LANDMANN, GEORGE. - Ms, report on Cadiz, survey of the fortifications & recommendations on defense, 15 July 1809. 57 pp & blanks, 4to. Half calf bdg. Including 6 surveys in color (1 folding). With 2 further surveys loosely inserted. Surveys possibly holograph. (88) £420

Cadman, Charles Wakefield, 1881-1946
Autograph music, "Part of Pagaent score for Portland Pagaent [sic]", 1926. (91) $150

Caffyn, W. H.
Original drawings, (10), literary portraits, for titles by the authors in the Everyman series. Archives of J. M. Dent & Son. (88) £460
— Original drawings, (13), literary portraits, for titles by the authors in the Everyman series. Archives of J. M. Dent & Son. (88) £550
— Original drawings, (15), literary portraits, for titles by the authors in the Everyman series. Archives of J. M. Dent & Son. (88) £260
— Original drawings, (23), literary portraits, for titles by European authors in the Everyman series. Archives of J. M. Dent & Son. (88) £260
— Original drawings, (5), literary portraits, for titles by the authors in the Everyman series. Archives of J. M. Dent & Son. (88) £800

Cage, John —&
Stockhausen, Karlheinz
Group photograph, [n.d.]. (90) DM260

Cagliostro, Alessandro, Count, Pseud. of Giuseppe Balsamo, 1743-95
— NICOLAI, LUDWIG HEINRICH VON. - ALs, 6 July 1787. 8 pp, 4to. To Elisa von der Recke. Commenting on recipient's book & giving an account of Cagliostro. (91) DM550

Cagney, James, 1899-1986
Ds, 30 Apr 1957. (91) $650
Group photograph, [n.d.]. (91) $110
Photograph, sgd, [n.d.]. (91) $140
Photograph, sgd & inscr, [n.d.]. (90) $100

Caine, Sir Thomas Henry Hall, 1853-1931
[A collection comprising 6 autograph notebooks kept in Iceland, his corrected proof copy of Sonnets of Three Centuries, & further related material, sold at pn on 16 June 1988, lot 85, for £280 to Quaritch.]
Autograph Ms, four-act drama, The Christian; sgd, inscr to Isaac Henderson & dated 22 Mar 1898. 95 pp, 12mo, on rectos only. Tipped into 8vo half vellum book. With extensive revisions; apparently unpbd. Goetz collection. (89) $1,600
See also: Rossetti, Dante Gabriel

Calder, Alexander, 1898-1976
Original drawing, The Wild Boar, to illus A Bestiary, compiled by Richard Wilber; 1955. 12 by 11 inches. In ink; sgd. (90) 2,200
ALs, 26 July [19]42. (91) $250
— [n.d.]. (88) DM450
— 1 May [19]57. (91) $500

Caldwell, E.
Original drawings, (12), to illus Old Towler, 1886. (90) £100

Calendar
Ms, Calendarium ordinis Sancti Benedicti. (90) $600

Calhoun, John C., 1782-1850
Collection of ALs & cut signature, 16 Aug 1825 & [n.d.]. (90) $80
ALs, 1 Nov 1824. (89) $230
— 3 Dec 1844. (88) $100

CALHOUN

— 8 July 1847. 4 pp, 4to. To Pierre Soule. About party politics, the sectional crisis, & the need to establish a Southern proslavery newspaper in Washington. With franking signature. (89) $3,500

Ds, 19 July 1844. (88) $70

California

[A group of 21 documents relating to events in the northern provinces of New Spain, particularly California, 1767 to 1788, some concerning the Visitor General Jose de Galvez, about 110 pp, folio & 4to, in modern half vellum, sold at S on 26 Apr 1990, lot 339, for £18,000 to Joseph & Sawyer.]

[San Diego. - 2 documents, 19 Sept 1845 & 21 July 1846, 3 pp, 4to, to the Subprefect of San Diego & sgd by local officals, forwarding lists of male residents (not present), sold at sg on 22 Oct, lot 51, for $225.]

[A account book for a Boston food distributor, listing various ships sailing to California & items shipped on board, 1854, 20 pp, size not stated, sold at R on 4 Mar 1989, lot 271, for $120.]

[Nevada City. - A collection of 27 A Ls s & 2 poems by John Gibson to his family in Chicago, 23 Dec 1878 to 19 June 1881, discussing life in California, with related material, sold at sg on 22 Oct, lot 50, for $225.]

— BRADBURY, C. W. - ALs, 17 Dec 1858. 2 pp, size not stated. To his wife. About his experiences at Pilot Knob, Coloma. On illus letter sheet. (89) $350

— GOLD RUSH. - 2 A Ls s & retained copies of 3 letters in Pocket Letter Book issued by Gregory's Californian Express, from George Fawcett to his sister & uncle in England, 1850 to 1852, 8 pp, 4to & 48 pp, 8vo. Describing his voyage from Australia & the situation in California. (88) £580

— GOLD RUSH. - ALs, 20 Jan 1849, 3 pp, size not stated, of Charles Tyler to his brother & sister. Giving details of preparations for the ocean voyage around the horn to the gold fields. (90) $225

— GOLD RUSH. - ALs, 29 Sept 1849, 1 p, size not stated, of Luther Pearson to

AMERICAN BOOK PRICES CURRENT

Rufus Waterman. Referring to a shipment of pickaxes to be sold in California & to the Gold Rush. (90) $120

— GOLD RUSH. - ALs, 17 Mar 1850, 3 pp, size not stated, of D. R. Robinson to his father. About the overland journey, prices in the mines, & mining the Stanislaus River. (90) $325

— GOLD RUSH. - ALs, 30 June 1851, 3 pp, size not stated, of Charles [King] to his family in Maine. Reporting that he lost his store in a San Francisco fire & informing them of his plans to go to the mines. (90) $325

— GOLD RUSH. - Ms diary of an unnamed Bostonian aboard the ship Pharsalia sailing from Boston to San Francisco, 27 Jan-17 May & 6-23 July 1849. 44 pp, 4to & folio. (91) $1,400

— GOLD RUSH. - Ms, diary of Shubal W. Stowell, 27 Mar 1850 to 21 June 1851, travelling from Oswego to the gold fields & back. 2 small diaries, length not stated. In pencil. With related material. (91) $2,500

— GOLD RUSH. - Notes of Travel from New York to the Gold Region in California in the Year Eighteen Hundred and Forty-Nine. By Harvey Blunt. 5 Feb 1949 to 15 Jan 1852. 322 pp, 8vo, in orig bds, rebacked with calf. (89) $11,000

— GOODYEAR[?], WATSON. - ALs, 18 July 1866. 4 pp, size not stated. To his mother. Describing life in San Francisco. (90) $120

— HUGHES, BENJAMIN. - 5 A Ls s, 26 May 1850 to 21 Feb 1851. Size not stated. To his wife. Reporting from Los Angeles. (88) $1,400

— KING, ROBERT. - ALs describing the takeover of Monterey by the American forces on 7 July 1846. 21 July 1846. 3 pp. To his cousin William Muir in Philadelphia. (90) $2,750

— LIBBY, GRANVILLE M. N. - Autograph Ms, letterbook, & 28 A Ls s, 7 Mar 1852 to 2 Mar 1858. 40 pp, 16mo (letterbook), & 81 pp, 8vo & 4to. To his mother & brother in Maine. Describing life in a gold camp, etc. 2 letters on illus stationery. Doheny collection. (88) $8,000

— MCCLELLAN, JOSIAH T. - 5 A Ls s, 1 Aug 1851 to 12 Jan 1857. 14 pp, 4to.

To his family in Maine. Giving an account of his experiences in the gold prospecting areas of Calaveras County, & as farmer. With a letter to McClellan. Doheny collection. (88) $1,000
— NEWTON, R. C. - ALs, 17 Nov 1855. 4 pp, size not stated. To his aunt & uncle. Describing the beauties of California. (90) 160
— PENA, COSME. - ADs, 30 July 1836. 6 pp, 12.5 by 8.5 inches, sewn into wraps. To the Minister of Justice of Alta California. defending himself against the accusations of the Governor of California, Commandante general Don Mariano Chico. (91) $3,750
— REPUBLICAN PARTY. - Document, 8 Mar 1856. 2 pp, folio. Establishing the Republican Party of Sacramento, sgd by 22 Californians. Doheny collection. (88) $8,500
— SCAMMON, CHARLES MELVILLE. - ALs, written while off the coast of Brazil on the way to the Gold Fields of California. 16 Oct 1849. 5 pp. (90) $900
— VAN DYKE, JOHN. - Autograph Ms, diary, 25 Jan 1849 to 25 Nov 1850. 44 pp, folio. Detailing voyage from New York to California & work as a blacksmith. Some tears. (88) $1,800

Calixtus III, Pope, 1378-1458. See: Martin V & Calixtus III

Call, Richard Keith, 1791-1862
ALs, 24 June 1825. Alexander collection. (90) $100
— 5 May 1826. Alexander collection. (90) $500

Callas, Maria, 1923-77
ALs, 3 Nov 1950. 5 pp, 4to. To Dr. Leonidas Lantzounis. Personal letter informing him that Toscanini asked her to sing Lady Macbeth, comparing their lives, commenting on her family, etc. (90) $23,000
— 5 Feb 1963. 3 pp, 4to. To Dr. Leonidas Lantzounis. Recounting the problems her mother has created. (90) $7,000
— 18 July 1975. 2 pp, 4to. To Dr. Leonidas Lantzounis. Complaining about her workload & announcing she will stop singing. (90) $7,500

Collection of 2 Ls s & 2 Ds s, 14 Nov 1958 to 21 Sept 1961. 4 pp, 4to & folio. Recipient unnamed; responding to a suggestion that she sing Anna Bolena in NY. Contracts with the American Opera Society. With a photograph. (90) $5,000
Photograph, sgd & inscr, 1972. (88) $450

Calligraphy
[Nur Jahan. - A page of nasta'liq calligraphy [Mughal, A.H.1029/ A.D.1619-20], laid down on album page, 130mm by 72mm, sold at S on 10 Oct 1988, lot 141, for £1,100.]
[Mirza Muhammad Isma'il. - A page of nasta'liq calligraphy with religious illusts, [Qajar, 19th cent], laid down on album page, 497mm by 320mm, sold at S on 10 Oct 1988, lot 141, for £800.]
Ms, A Chosen Few, 1917. (89) £70
— Ms, address, To George Hudson Earle from the members of the Protestant Church at Ter Aa, July 1899. (88) £60
— Ms, Album of writing specimens using khatt-i nakhun technique, with text taken from the Sassanian ruler Khusrau Nurshirvan. Copied by pupils of the Lahore Government College for Dr. G. W. Leitner, in Lahore, 1861. 15 leaves, 273mm by 185mm, in lea gilt. Each page within illuminated borders of animals, birds & flowers painted in naive style on stippled colored background. (90) $1,200
— Ms, How Prince Geraint heard Enid sing the song of Fortune & her Wheel; 1914. (90) $425
— Ms, Prieres du matin et du soir, & De la sagrada Communion, 1740. 114 leaves, 197mm by 134mm, in contemp red mor with fleur-de-lys ornaments. In black ink in fine roman letter by Barth. Sampellegrini Placentinus. With 8 full-page pen-&-ink illusts & 12 tailpieces. Dedicated to Charles de Bourbon [Charles III of Spain]. Schiff collection. (90) £2,000
— Ms, Songs from the Idyll of the King by Alfred, Lord Tennyson. (91) $550
— Ms, The Ballad of Chevy Chase to which is added The Hontynge a'the Chyvyat. [England, 1855] 25 leaves, vellum, 8.5 by 7.24 inches, in mor gilt by Bedford. Illuminated in gold &

CALLIGRAPHY

colors. (91) $1,100
— Ms, The Tongue of Time. The Language of a Clock, [n.d.]. 26 leaves (3 blank), 280mm by 265mm, in extra metalwork-embossed brown mor bdg of c.1890. Illuminated; with various elaborate borders, full-page watercolor frontis & watercolor vignette on tp. Written on rectos only. Chevalier collection. (91) $2,000
— Ms, To the Reverend George Augustus Campbell, Master of Arts of Trinity College, Cambridge, Vicar of the Church of Saint Mary the Virgin at Loughton in the County of Essex & Diocese of Chelmsford, 1907-1918, Greeting...." [N.p., n.d.] 8 leaves plus 2 vellum flyleaves at each end, vellum, 250mm by 195mm, in mor gilt with upper cover lettered Saint Mary Loughton. (91) $300
— ADAMS, MARGARET. - Some well-known Birds of Britain. [Edgbaston, c.1960] 13 leaves plus 3 blanks, on vellum, 197mm by 125mm, in mor gilt. Inscr to Stuart B. Schimmel (91) $2,600
— BAYES, JESSIE. - The Gospel According to Saint Luke. [1948-57]. 112 pp, 4to, in red mor by Sangorski. Mostly in black ink. With numerous miniatures & initials. (89) £500
— BAYES, JESSIE. - Ms, Sonnets for the Months by Folgare da San Geminiano, trans by Dante Gabriel Rossetti, 1907 & 1908. 14 leaves (5 blank), 8vo, in vellum bdg. In an upright roman script. With 2 full-page miniatures & 11 historiated initials. (90) $1,000
— BAYES, JESSIE[?]. - 2 Mss, The Hound of Heaven by Francis Thompson, & a chapter from The Song of Songs, [c.1910], 14 leaves, vellum (partly purple-stained), in limp vellum bdg & oak bds, respectively. In an upright roman script & in capital roman letters, partly written in gold. With illuminated & decorated initials. (90) $550
— CALLANDIER, M. - Ms, Le Moyen Age, [France, mid-19th cent]. 19 leaves, folio, in cloth bdg. In a cursive hand. Including mtd vellum tp & mtd watercolor on vellum, & various medieval style borders. (90) $225

AMERICAN BOOK PRICES CURRENT

— CAMERON, SISTER MARY GERTRUDE. - Ms, Autumn Woods, by William Cullen Bryant; [c.1920]. 8 leaves & 2 flyleaves, vellum, 225mm by 187mm, in extra blue crushed levant mor by Riviere & Son. In an upright semi-roman cursive script. With 8 fine initials (4 historiated) with floral borders & 7 watercolor vignettes. Written on rectos only. Chevalier collection. (91) $4,000
— CHRISTIAENSSENS, B. - Gand et Flandre, chroniques inedites. [n.p., mid-19th cent]; c.50 pp, 580mm by 450mm, in contemp dark green mor with central cartouche. Illuminated throughout. (89) £2,100
— COLE, W. WILLOUGHBY T. - Ms, The Litany, 1860. 34 leaves & 6 flyleaves, vellum, 185mm by 137mm, in extra dark brown mor by Francis Bedford. In black & red ink in a semi-Gothic bookhand in French 14th-cent style. With numerous 2- & 3-line initials, full or 3-quarter borders throughout, & 4 large miniatures. Chevalier collection. (91) $2,500
— CROSS, HELEN REID. - Ms, The Lay of the Honeysuckle, by Marie de France, trans by Eugene Mason; [c.1910]. 8 leaves, vellum, 4to, in wraps. With floral borders, red & gold initials & 5 illuminated illusts. (91) £180
— GALLONDE, PH. CH. - Prieres pendant la Messe a l'usage de Madame de Montmartel, 1753. 33 pp, 138mm by 82mm, in contemp russet mor. In black ink in imitation of print. With ornate borders throughout. Doheny collection. (89) $1,800
— GREGORI, JOANNES. - Autograph Ms, album of calligraphy, [c.1745]. 35 leaves, 225mm by 360mm, in modern wraps. Including Chinese & Indian scripts, coats-of-arms & illusts of various topics. (90) DM2,300
— GROLIER SOCIETY. - Ms, The Raven, by Edgar Allan Poe, [c.1930]. 10 leaves & blanks, vellum, 180mm by 136mm, in extra blue levant mor by Sangorski & Sutcliffe. With illuminated initial, historiated miniature, & ornate borders. (90) $3,200
— HEWITT, GRAILY. - Holy Communion. [N.p., n.d.] 23 leaves plus 4 blanks,

123mm by 97mm, in mor gilt. In upright roman script, the line Our Father & 8 other 2-line initials in gold, many other 2-line initials in red & blue. Inscr by Loyd Haberly to his grandson Duncan (91) $3,500

— HEWITT, GRAILY. - Ms, Epistola Joannis, sgd & dated 1913. 1 leaf, 330mm by 423mm. Written entirely in gold in 5 columns. Framed. (88) £2,700

— HEWITT, GRAILY. - Ms, Georgina Burne-Jones' introduction to The Flower Book, 1905. 2 sheets, vellum, 327mm by 250mm. (88) £300

— HUTTON, DOROTHY. - Lines from The Passionate Shepherd by Nicholas breton. L, 1959. 4 leaves plus blanks at front & back, vellum, 135mm by 177mm, in half lea. Tp in blue, 5 pages in black ink in fine italic, opening initial in gold & 2 letters in blue, each page with watercolor drawings of British wildlife. Inscr to Stuart B. Schimmel, 14 May 1963. With related material. (91) $400

— INGLIS, ESTHER. - Ms, Octonaires sur la vanite et inconstance du monde, 1 Jan 1615. 54 leaves & blanks, 60mm by 43mm, in contemp embroidered bdg of dark red velvet over pastebds. In dark brown ink in several microscopic scripts; with 3 illuminated pages. 50 poems, written for the future Charles I of England. (90) £62,000

— JARRY, NICHOLAS. - Offices de la Vierge et du St. Esprit, in Latin & French. [Paris, 1647-49]. 48 leaves, vellum, 105mm by 67mm. Contemp French dark olive mor gilt. In a calligraphic roman hand for Latin, italic for French. With gold & red borders on each p, & 5 large decorated initials & floral headpieces. Doheny collection. (88) £4,500

— JOHNSTON, EDWARD. - Ms, Horace, Ad Torquatum (Odes IV:vii), dated 8 June 1927. 1 p, 237mm by 162mm; 35 lines. Written in red & black. (88) £130

— LAVELLI, MARTINO. - Ms, Caratteri et varie Cifre di Martino Lavelli, Scrittore et Maestro di Calligraphia in Pavia. [Pavia, 1788-89]. 124 leaves, 225mm by 343mm, in contemp half calf. In black ink in many varying styles of calligraphy, with many elaborate decorative details. (90) £4,200

— MORRIS, WILLIAM. - Ms, The Story of Frithiof the Bold, [trans by Morris & Eirikr Magnusson; c.1871 or 1873]. 22 pp & blanks, 391mm by 251mm, in turquoise straight grain mor by Thomas James Cobden-Sanderson. In brown-black ink in an upright roman script in double column. Written & profusely illuminated mainly by Morris, with 2 historiated miniatures & further illuminations by Charles Fairfax Murray, full-page border by Louise Powell, & gilding by Graily Hewitt. Some illuminations left unfinished. Doheny collection. (89) $120,000

— MORRIS, WILLIAM & GRAILY HEWITT. - Ms; Virgil, Aeneid, in Latin; [c.1874-75 & later]. 190 leaves (5 blank) & flyleaf, vellum, 335mm by 240mm. Blindtooled brown mor bdg by Leighton. In an upright open roman script; 177 pp by Morris, completed by Hewitt. Decoration begun by Morris & continued by Louise Powell. With opening lines of each book in gold capitals & full border after the Kelmscott Chaucer executed in gold by Hewitt, 11 half-page & 5 smaller historiated miniatures by Charles Fairfax Murray after drawings by Edward Burne-Jones, & page borders & initial letters by Powell. Some illumination left unfinished. Doheny collection. (89) $1,200,000

— OFFICINA PALAEOGRAPHICA OF THE ABBEY OF GROTTA FERRATA AT FRASCATI. - Hymns & Prayers, 1905. 27 leaves & flyleaves, vellum, 260mm by 167mm, in calf profusely gilt. 10 leaves in Greek in a fine minuscule, 17 in Latin in a gothic script. With initials throughout in burnished gold & colors in imitation of medieval styles. Interleaved in silk. (88) £800

— SANGORSKI & SUTCLIFFE. - Ms, The Rime of the Ancient Mariner, by Samuel Taylor Coleridge; [n.d.]. 30 leaves & 7 flyleaves, vellum, 330mm by 240mm, in extra jewelled blue levant mor by Sangorski & Sutcliffe. In an upright roman script. With full or partial borders on 12 pp, numerous initials in colors, & 7 miniatures (4 full-page). Chevalier collection. (91) $80,000

CALLIGRAPHY

— SANGORSKI & SUTCLIFFE. - Ms, Some Poems, by John Keats; [1912-14]. 21 leaves & 5 flyleaves, vellum, 330mm by 242mm, in extra jewelled dark purple levant mor by Sangorski & Sutcliffe. In an upright roman script. With 19 large illuminated initials, 10 full borders richly colored & gilt, 5 full-page miniatures by Ewan Geddes & 2 smaller miniatures. Executed for T. J. Gannon. Chevalier collection. (91) $150,000

— SANGORSKI & SUTCLIFFE. - Ms, Selections, by Henry Wadsworth Longfellow; [n.d.]. 16 leaves & flyleaf, vellum, 294mm by 209mm, in extra jewelled dark blue levant mor by Sangorski & Sutcliffe. With 14 scrollwork or brushwork borders & 6 miniatures, partly full-page. Chevalier collection. (91) $70,000

— SANGORSKI & SUTCLIFFE. - Ms, The Tragedy of Romeo and Juliet, by William Shakespeare; [c.1920]. 122 leaves & flyleaves, vellum, 259mm by 194mm, in 2 vols of extra crimson crushed levant mor by Sangorski & Sutcliffe. In an upright cursive script. With 26 large initials & other ornaments, mostly with borders, & 23 miniatures (4 full-page). Illuminated for the Grolier Society. Chevalier collection. (91) $40,000

— SANGORSKI & SUTCLIFFE. - Morte d'Arthur, by Alfred Lord Tennyson, [n.d.]. 17 leaves (5 blank) & 2 endleaves, vellum, 227mm by 117mm, in extra dark green crushed levant mor gilt with large central crowned armorial. In black & red ink. With large historiated initial & 3-quarter border on tp, 5 decorated initials in colors & burnished gold, 2 penwork initials & large watercolor vignette, framed in gold. Doheny collection. (88) $3,500

— SANGORSKI & SUTCLIFFE. - Ms, Lamia, by John Keats, [1913]. 39 pp, vellum, folio. Extra blue jewelled lev mor bdg. With full-page & 2 half-page miniatures & 20 large historiated or floriated capitals. Barstow collection. (89) $4,500

— SANGORSKI & SUTCLIFFE. - Ms, The Vision of Sir Launfal, by James Russell Lowell; 1908. 16 leaves, 258mm by 193mm, in extra full tan

AMERICAN BOOK PRICES CURRENT

crushed mor. With chapter headings in gold, 14 decorative initials, large miniature & 2 pp with full borders. (91) £2,400

— SANGORSKI, ALBERTO. - Ms, May-Day, by Ralph Waldo Emerson; 1914. 19 leaves & 2 flyleaves, vellum, 266mm by 208mm, in extra jewelled blue levant mor bdg by Riviere & Son. In a semi-gothic bookhand. With 18 finely illuminated large initials, 4 full borders, 3 miniatures (1 full-page), & port miniature of Emerson. Chevalier collection. (91) $15,000

— SANGORSKI, ALBERTO. - Ms, The Eve of St. Agnes, by John Keats; [1924/25]. 15 leaves & 2 flyleaves, vellum, 277mm by 232mm, in extra turquoise levant mor. In an upright semi-gothic bookhand. With 17 illuminated initials (1 historiated), 2 full-page miniatures, 7 vignettes, & tp with miniature port of Keats. Chevalier collection. (91) $17,000

— SANGORSKI, ALBERTO. - Ms, To Corinna, by Robert Herrick, [after 1910]. 10 leaves (1 blank), vellum, 215mm by 161mm, in extra green levant mor by Riviere & Son. With 2 watercolor vignettes & 10 illuminated initials. Christensen collection. (90) $7,000

— SANGORSKI, ALBERTO. - Ms, Lincoln's Gettysburg Speech & 2d Inaugural Address, & W. Whitman's poem Captain! My Captain!; 1928. 12 leaves (2 blank), vellum, 310mm by 261mm, in extra blue levant mor by Riviere & Son. With 5 watercolor miniatures (including portraits of Lincoln & Whitman), 9 illuminated initials & 12 ornamental borders. (90) $32,000

— SANGORSKI, ALBERTO. - Ms, The Raven & other poems by Edgar Allan Poe, 1929. 17 leaves (2 blank), vellum, 311mm by 254mm, in extra light blue levant mor by Riviere & Son. With 8 watercolor miniatures (including port of Poe), 23 ornamental initials in colors & gold & extravagant borders on 15 pp. Christensen collection. (90) $28,000

— SANGORSKI, ALBERTO. - Ms, Selected Poems by William Cullen Bryant, [c.1914]. 24 leaves including blanks, vellum, 263mm by 205mm, in extra maroon lev mor by Riviere & Son. With watercolor port of Bryant, full-page watercolor frontis, watercolor tailpiece, & numerous illuminated initials. Doheny collection. (89) $16,000

— SANGORSKI, ALBERTO. - Of Gardens, an Essay, by Francis Bacon; 1905. 17 pp, 4to, in orig limp vellum. With 7 watercolor drawings & 2 borders. (89) £3,000

— SANGORSKI, ALBERTO. - Of Gardens, an Essay. by Francis Bacon. 1906. 12 text leaves plus 11 blanks plus 4 miniatures in gold and colors, on vellum, in vellum bdg. (88) $3,300

— SCHUELLER, CASPAR LEO. - Ein Kussliches Betbuech warinnen Schoene Hertz erquickende Gebete auss Gottes; [Germany, Arnstadt, 1574]. 246 leaves (6 blank), vellum, 18cm by 15cm. Def bdg of calf over wooden bds. In dark brown ink in a very fine calligraphic compressed gothic hand; headings in red, blue, gold or silver. With 18 pp in bizarre calligraphic hands, mainly in mirror writing, 8 full-page calligraphic or illuminated pages, 10 pp with pictures & designs formed of micrographic writing, & 4 full-page miniatures showing members of the family of Hans Guenther, Graf zu Schwarzburg und Honstein. (88) £26,000

— TEARLE, JOHN H. - Ms, The Vision of Sir Launfal, by James Russell Lowell; [n.d.]. 22 leaves & 4 flyleaves, vellum, 230mm by 157mm, in blue mor gilt bdg in matching gilt folding box. In a semi-gothic bookhand. With large initial with 3-quarter border, 2 vignettes, 2 pictorial headlines, & full-page miniature. Chevalier collection. (91) $2,000

— WEBER, M. S. - Andachtsuebung, [c.1770]. 250 pp, 190mm by 115mm, in elaborately tooled 18th-cent olive mor gilt in contemp book-shaped calf slipcase. In a German gothic script with large intricately flourished initials in colors, 3 full-page & 10 smaller devotional drawings, & baroque-style frame borders throughout. (90) £2,000

— WIDEMAN, ENDRIS. - Ms, Ein christlicher lieblicher Trostbrief ... durch M. Leonhardum Jacobii Narthusianum, & Ein Vermanung von dem Heyligen Hochwirdigen Sacrament; [Augsburg, dated 5 Sept 1566 & 20 Jan 1567]. 44 leaves, vellum, 113mm by 74mm, in 19th-cent brown velvet. In brown ink in a fine small gothic hand. With 16 historiated gold rustic initials on colored ground & 3 large miniatures with floral borders. (89) £5,000
See also: Desportes, Philippe
See also: Jarry, Nicholas

Callinicus II, Patriarch of Constantinople
Document, Apr 1689. (89) DM500

Calve, Emma, 1858-1942
Photograph, sgd & inscr, 1896. (91) $120

Calvin, John, 1509-64
ADs, 18 Dec 1561. 7cm by 13.5cm, cut from a larger leaf. Receipt for salary received from the treasurer at Geneva. With a port. (89) DM11,000

Cambridge University
Ms, The Foundation of the Universitie of Cambridge..., compiled by W. Collection of Elizabeth, Dowager Duchess of Manchester. (88) £550

Camerer, Johann Caspar, 1772-1847. See: Hoelderlin, Friedrich

Cameron, Simon, 1799-1889
Ls, 21 May 1861. (88) $75

Cammell, Donald
Original drawings, (20), to illus Alice M. Archives of J. M. Dent & Son. (88) £100

Campan, Jeanne Louise Henriette, 1752-1822
Collection of 3 A Ls s & bust engraving, 16 May 1804, 19 Aug 1811 & [c.1812]. (90) $600

Campanella, Roy
Ls, 1 Sept 1966. (91) $300
Ds, 1 Sept 1966. (91) $300
Signature, [n.d.]. (91) $275

Campbell, Beatrice Stella ("Mrs. Patrick Campbell")
Photograph, sgd & inscr, 1892. (88) $175

Camus, Albert, 1913-60
ALs, 5 Jan [n.y.]. (89) DM450

Corrected page proofs, novel, La Peste, [early 1947]. 8vo, in green half mor gilt by P. L. Martin. With autograph tp, sgd, inscr to Lucien Sable & dated 16 May 1949, & extensive autograph revisions. The Garden Ltd. collection. (90) $32,000

Canada
— GORDON, ARTHUR CHARLES HAMILTON. - ALs, 11 Oct 1864. 23 pp, folio. To Edward, Viscount Cardwell. Retained copy, reporting about "the Conference summoned to consider the question of a Federal Union of the British North American Provinces". Fold tears. (90) $850

— HATT, C. DE S[ALABERRY?]. - Autograph Ms, diary of an overland journey from Fort Garry to Toronto, 7 June to 10 July 1870 [1871?]. 48 pp, 16mo. Including other notes. In pencil. With a photograph. In lea slipcase. With transcript. (88) C$400

— LA ROCHETTE, ALEXANDRE ROBERT D'HILAIRE DE [?]. - ALs, 6 Nov 1757. 4 pp, 4to. To Messrs. de Richemond & Demissi at La Rochelle. Reporting about the loss of their ship near Beaumont, Quebec. (88) C$600

Canby, Edward Richard Sprigg, 1817-73
Ls, 27 Jan 1864. (88) $75
— 23 Aug 1870. (88) $400

Canetti, Elias
A Ls s (2), 16 Mar & 5 Nov 1974. 2 pp, 4to. To Adolf Opel. Discussing a contribution to Opel's Anthology of Modern Austrian Literature. (88) DM1,100

Ls, 23 July 1970. (91) DM850

Canones Conciliorum
Ms, Canones Conciliorum, with Dionysius Exiguus, Symmachiana, & other early church documents. [Irish monastery in northern Italy, 3d to last quarter of 8th cent]. 94 leaves (some lacking), vellum, 223mm by 175mm. 19th cent brown mor by Lortic. By 3 different scribes in various pre-Caroline minuscules & half uncials. With many headings in red uncials, & many decorated capitals with penwork ornament. Ludwig MS.XIV.1. (89) £580,000

Canova, Antonio, 1757-1822
ALs, 29 Mar 1817. (89) DM380

Canteloube, Joseph, 1879-1957
Autograph music, Vocalise-Etude en forme de bourree, transcription for high voice, flute & piano; 1934. (91) £500

Capek, Karel, 1890-1938
ALs, 3 July 1937. (91) DM360
Photograph, sgd, 1921. (90) DM420

Capello, Bianca, Consort of Francesco de Medici, Grand Duke of Tuscany, 1548-87
ALs, 6 Mar 1573. (90) DM800

Capodistrias, Ioannis, 1776-1831
[A collection of Ms documents & letters relating to him, from the Blackmer Collection, sold at S on 12 Oct 1989, lot 452, for £3,800 to Constant.]

Capone, Alphonse ("Al"), 1899-1947
[A group of 5 items from Capone's file as a prisoner in the Eastern State Penitentiary, 1930, including a Ds, sold at Dar on 4 Oct 1990, lot 148, for $13,000.]

Ds, 18 Nov 1926. 1 p, 9 by 3 inches. Interest note for Loan No 6223 at the Lawndale National Bank; also sgd by Theresa & Mae Capone. Endorsed by all 3 on verso. (91) $3,500

— 18 Nov 1926. 1 p, 9 by 3 inches. Interest note, also sgd by Theresa & Mae Capone; also sgd by all 3 on verso. (91) $3,750

Signature, [20 Sept 1937]. On envelope addressed to Maj. K. T. Pietrzak. Sgd Alphonse Capone Alcatraz California 85. (88) $4,000

Capote, Truman, 1924-84
Autograph Ms, essay, Other Voices, Other Rooms: A Preface; 1969. On 27 note cards, 5 by 8 inches. In pencil & black ballpoint pen. Differing from ptd version. (90) $5,000

1987 - 1991 • AUTOGRAPHS & MANUSCRIPTS   CARNEGIE

Capp, Al
Ls s (2), 1946. (91) $425

Carco, Francis, Pseud. of Francois Carcopino-Tusoli, 1886-1958
Autograph Ms, Pour faire suite a La Boheme et mon coeur, 7 poems dedicated to Andre Rousseau; [n.d.]. (89) £100

Cardozo, Benjamin N., 1870-1938
ALs, 25 Sept 1923. (88) $350
— 24 Sept 1929. (88) $475
— 24 Oct 1937. (91) $400
Ls, 24 May 1929. (88) $225
— 29 Apr 1931. 1 p, 8vo. To Felix Frankfurter. Discussing colonial law. (90) $1,100

Carey, George R.
[An extensive archive including letters, drawings, documents, etc. relating to Carey & his inventions, 1870s to 1890s, sold at R on 17 June 1989, lot 106, for $2,800.]

Carleton, Sir Guy, 1st Baron Dorchester, 1724-1808
ALs, 23 Mar 1785. (89) £200

Carlos de Austria, Don, 1545-68
Ls, 29 Dec 1564. 1 p, folio. To Cardinal Carlo Borromeo. Responding to a letter interceding in favor of Pedro de Ulloa. (90) DM5,500

Carlota, Empress of Mexico, 1840-1927
[An allegorical port of her husband Emperor Maximilian after a painting by the Prince de Joinville, 103mm by 63mm, inscr to Dr. Jlek by Carlota, [1872], with authentication by Dr. Jlek on envelope, sold at CNY on 7 June 1990, lot 29, for $600.]
ALs, 6 July 1863. Koch Foundation. (90) $650
— 23 Dec 1865. 3 pp, 8vo. To her grandmother Queen Marie-Amelie of France. Describing the success of her visit to Yucatan. (90) $1,200
AL, 16 July 186[4]. (91) £120
ANs, [n.d.]. (91) DM400

Carlyle, Thomas, 1795-1881
Series of 3 A Ls s, 1844 to 1866. (89) £520
— Series of 16 A Ls s, 1857 to 1861. 56 pp, 8vo. To Charles Butler. About financial matters, his writing, politics, etc. 1 incomplete, 1 partly written by his brother J. A. Carlyle. With related material. (88) $7,250
ALs, 19 Jan 1837. 4 pp, 4to. To his sister Jenny Hanning. Announcing the completion of [The French Revolution] & giving advice about her health. Repaired. Doheny collection. (89) $2,200
— 10 Feb 1847. (90) $600
— 23 Oct 1851. (89) $325
— 26 Jan 1859. (90) DM220
— 30 June 1866. (88) £400
Ls s (2), 17 Nov & 10 Dec 1870. Doheny collection. (89) $420
Ls, 23 June 1872. 4 pp, 8vo. Recipient unnamed. Giving advice on a young man's spiritual struggle & commentong about "the general deluge of what calls itself 'Science'". Inlaid & bound in red mor gilt with a copy of privately ptd 1st Ed, Letter to a Young Man, Ed Clement K. Shorter, [London, n.d.]; one of 20 copies. Doheny collection. (89) $1,600
— CARLYLE. J. A. - 12 A Ls s, 1864 to 1873. 36 pp, 8vo. To Charles Butler. About financial matters, & giving detailed news about his brother Thomas. With related material. (88) $950

Carman, William Bliss, 1861-1929
Autograph Ms (2), poems, A Mountail Trail, & Venus, [n.d.]. Doheny collection. (89) $900

Carmichael, Hoagy, 1899-1981
Ls, [n.d.]. (91) $125
Autograph quotation, 4 bars from Stardust, sgd; [n.d.]. (90) $300

Carnarvon Papers. See: Herbert Family

Carnegie, Andrew, 1835-1919
Collection of ALs & ANs, 8 May 1907 & 6 Jan 1908. (90) $270
A Ls s (2), 3 Oct 1909 & 6 Jan 1910. (89) $300
ALs, 22 Dec 1902. (88) $110
— REICH, JACQUES. - Bust engraving of Carnegie, 1906. 11.5 by 15 inches. Sgd by Reich & Carnegie. (91) $250

121

CARNEGIE

See also: Clemens, Samuel Langhorne

Carnival Play
Ms, Unglickh Seelige Fassnacht der Jungen Goetter In Einem Sing Spill vorgestellt von dem Kost Haus S. Josephi Zu Dillingen, 1748. 20 pp, 4to, in modern bdg. Complete libretto of a musical comedy; 12 scenes involving Greek gods. (90) DM5,500

Carnot, Lazare, Comte, 1753-1823
ALs, [24 Jan 1794]. (90) DM500
— [18 Fructidor [n.y.]. (89) DM260
Ls, [13 June 1797]. (90) DM310
— [21 July 1800]. (90) DM350

Carnovsky, Morris
Collection of 7 A Ls s & 9 Ls s, [n.d.]. (88) $150

Caroline, Queen of George IV of England, 1768-1821
ALs, 3 June 1819. (89) $450

Carondelet, Francisco Luis Hector, Baron de, c.1748-1807
Ls, 8 May 1793. 2 pp, 8vo. To Dehault de Lassus. Mentioning the discovery of lead near Ste. Genevieve. Alexander collection. (90) $1,550

Carossa, Hans, 1878-1956
Autograph Ms, Ahnen-Lehre (Bruchstueck) Aus der Geschichte einer Jugend, [n.d.]. 11 pp, 4to. Sgd on tp & at end. Some corrections. Tp somewhat stained. (88) DM1,800
— Autograph Ms, poem, Krieg und Kunst, [n.d.]. (90) DM840
Autograph transcript, poem, Ein Stern singt, 5 four-line stanzas. 1 p, 4to. Sgd, inscr & dated 9 July 1928. (89) DM1,100
— Autograph transcript, poem, Vogelballade; [n.d.]. (90) DM900
Collection of 13 A Ls s & 3 autograph postcards, sgd, 19 Jan 1923 to 17 May 1937. 24 pp, 4to & 8vo, & cards. To Elisabeth Schaller-Lang. Literary correspondence. (91) DM2,600
A Ls s (2), 24 Mar 1940 & 12 Aug 1948. (90) DM550
— A Ls s (2), 20 Mar 1948 & 19 June 1952. (89) DM600
ALs, 25 Mar 1925. (90) DM600

AMERICAN BOOK PRICES CURRENT

— 2 Dec 1931. (91) DM250
— 22 Apr 1936. (91) DM440
— [5 Apr] 1942. (90) DM460
— 11 Sept 1948. (88) DM320

Carpenter, Humphrey
Typescript, book, Inklings; [c.1977]. (88) £250

Carradine, John, 1906-88
Ds, 12 Apr 1944. (91) $1,000

Carriere, Moriz, 1817-95
Series of 8 A Ls s, 14 Mar 1859 to 20 May 1874. (91) DM800
— Series of 3 A Ls s, 29 May 1870 to 12 Feb 1882. (90) DM700

Carrington, Leonora
[A collection of works by Carrington, including autograph Ms of a novel & typescript of a play in English, & typescripts of 2 short stories in French, 1940 & [n.d.], in all c.285 pp, folio & 8vo, sold at S on 15 Dec, lot 321, for £6,000.]

Carroll, Charles, Signer from Maryland
Autograph Ms, Latin exercise book kept at the College de St. Omer, 1752. 120 pp, 8vo, in contemp pink wraps. Sgd 3 times. (91) $3,500
ALs, 20 Aug 1786. 3 pp, 4to. To Daniel Carroll. Chatty letter regarding state politics & land. (90) $1,700
— 7 Apr 1823. 3 pp, 4to. To William Gibbons. Concerning the purchase of horses & the treatment of a new slave. Seal tear repaired. (88) $4,000
— 15 Feb 1827. 1 p, 4to. To [John Paca]. Returning a questionnaire (not present) & mentioning the Declaration of Independence. (90) $10,000
— 30 June 1829. Alexander collection. (90) $600

Carroll, Lewis, 1832-98. See: Dodgson, Charles Lutwidge

Carroll, Madeleine. See: Colman, Ronald & Carroll

Carson, Christopher ("Kit"), 1809-68
[2 signatures (C. Carson & Kit Carson), on a small slip of paper cut from a larger document, mtd with a port, sold at CNY on 1 Feb 1988, lot 201,

for $1,300 to Profiles in History.]

Carter, Allan
Original drawings, (25), to illus Aesop's Fables, [n.d.]. (89) £350

Carter, James Earl ("Jimmy")
[His business checkbook, 1956 - 1957, containing 59 check stubbs in the hands of Carter & his wife Rosalynn & 127 blank checks, sold at Dar on 4 Oct 1990, lot 149, for $600.]
Autograph Ms, speech to the International Chamber of Commerce at Disneyworld, 1 Oct 1978; draft. (88) $950
Ls s (2), 2 Sept & 2 Dec 1976. (88) $375
Ls, 9 Dec 1986. (90) $120
— 13 May 1988. (91) $90
Check, accomplished & sgd, 16 June 1960. (91) $150
— Anr, accomplished & sgd, 27 Sept 1960. (91) $150
— Anr, accomplished & sgd, 14 Oct 1960. (91) $100
— Anr, sgd, 5 Nov 1960. (91) $650
Franking signature, [19 Oct 1987]. (91) $350
Photograph, sgd, [n.d.]. (89) $55
Signature, on cover of Sept 1976 Citizens Telephone Co. (91) $200
— Anr, [20 Jan 1977]. (90) $50
— Anr, [n.d.]. (91) $130

Carter, James Earl ("Jimmy") —& Others
[A copy of The Egyptian-Israeli Peace Treaty, 23 Mar 1979, 4to, sgd & inscr on tp by Carter (twice), Sadat (in English & Arabic, 25 Feb 1981), & Begin (Apr 1981), sold at R on 28 Oct 1989, lot 317, for $3,000.]

Carter, James Earl ("Jimmy") —& Dukakis, Michael S.
Group photograph, [n.d.]. (91) $100

Carter, James Earl ("Jimmy") —& Ford, Gerald R.
[Their signatures on a 1968 philatelic cover sold at Dar on 6 Dec 1990, lot 340, for $80.]

Carter, James Earl ("Jimmy") —& Thatcher, Margaret
Group photograph, 7 leaders of the non-Communist world, [n.d.]. (91) $180

Carter, Rosalynn S.
[A collection of 10 checks, sgd, 1960, drawn on the Plains Mercantile Co. & made out to various people, sold at wa on 17 Oct, lot 120, for $100.]

Cartwright, Alexander Joy, 1820-92
ADs, 10 June 1867. (91) $700

Carus, Carl Gustav, 1789-1869
ALs, 8 July 1831. (90) DM650
— 9 Apr 1834. Albrecht collection. (91) SF750
— 8 Jan 1855. Albrecht collection. (91) SF800
— 31 Mar 1855. (89) DM320
— 13 Dec 1857. Albrecht collection. (91) SF600
— 9 Nov 1864. (91) DM280
— 23 Feb 1868. (91) DM270
ADs, 21 Jan 1862. (89) DM300

Caruso, Enrico, 1873-1921
[A group of 3 photographs, sgd & inscr, 1915, 1917 & [n.d.], various sizes, sold at S on 19 May 1989, lot 385, for £600 to Saggori.]
[5 items comprising 3 photographs, sgd, self-caricature & signature, 1915, sold at S on 17 May 1990, lot 80, for £1,900 to Horiuchi.]
Original drawing, head of a man with cigar, [n.d.]. (89) DM550
— Original drawing, India-ink caricature of F. (89) $475
— Original drawing, self port, sgd & dated 1909. (88) DM950
Collection of 17 A Ls s, postcards, visiting cards, & caricature, sgd, 1903 to 1915 & [n.d.]. 30 pp, mostly 4to & 8vo. To Costante Pignone. About his performances, his battles with the press, tickets, etc. (89) £2,300
— Collection of ALs & 2 autograph port postcards, sgd, 13 Nov 1911, 19 Mar 1913, & [n.d.]. To Meta Wulff. Expressing thanks for gifts & letters. (91) $1,200
Series of 17 A Ls s, 1903 to 1917. About 30 pp, various sizes. To Constante Pignone. Reporting about his success in Rigoletto in New York, & other tours. Including self-caricature. (90) £2,100
Collection of Ls & caricature, 5 June 1918

CARUSO

& [n.d.]. (88) $650
Ls, 16 Apr 1913. (91) $275
— 7 May 1913. (90) $200
Collection of 3 autograph postcards, sgd, & photograph, sgd, 8 & 12 Oct 1904, 17 June 1906 & [1910]. To Roberto Vittiglio. Contents not stated. (88) DM1,400
— Collection of autograph postcard, sgd, & photograph, sgd, 15 Sept 1911 & [5 Oct 1909]. (88) £150
Series of Ds s, 3 Ds s, [n.d.]. (89) £320
Ds s (2)20 July & 10 Aug 1899. (89) $750
Ds, 3 July 1899. 2 pp, 4to. Contract with the Bellini Theatre of Naples. Def. (89) $1,800
Caricature, lady with large hat; 7 Sept 1905. (91) $350
— Anr, sgd, 1910. (91) £900
— Anr, [n.d.]. (89) $350
— Anr, man with goatee; [n.d.]. (91) $225
— Anr, sgd, mustached man with a fat neck, identified on verso as Dr. (90) $300
Photograph, sgd, 1903. (89) £700
— Anr, 1905. (90) $550
— Anr, 1917. (90) DM360
— Anr, [n.d.]. (91) $475
Photograph, sgd & inscr, 1904. (91) £750
— Anr, 1917. (91) £650
— Anr, [n.d.]. (90) $500
Self-caricature, sgd, 1901. 1 p, 4to. Bust view, as Pagliacci. In India ink. Byer collection. (90) $2,600
— Anr, 1904. 27cm by 21.5cm. Facing left, in costume. In black ink; sgd. Framed. (90) £2,000
— Anr, sgd & dated 1914. (88) £360
— Anr, full-face; sgd & dated 1915. 20.5cm by 13.5cm. With photograph, sgd, 1917. (90) £1,700
— Anr, sgd & inscr, Feb 1920. 4to. On hotel letterhead. Matted with a photograph. (91) $1,800
— Anr, [n.d.]. (91) $850
— Anr, [n.d.]. (91) $900

Carvajal, Juan, Cardinal, c.1400-69
Ls, 17 May [14]98. (90) $325

AMERICAN BOOK PRICES CURRENT

Carver, George Washington, 1864-1943
Typescript carbon copy, A Message to Virginia Students, 22 Nov 1926. (91) $475
ALs, 25 Feb 1925. (91) $600
— 1 Dec 1934. (90) $375
— [n.d.]. (88) $220
Signature, [11 June 1940]. (90) $250

Casals, Pablo, 1876-1973
ALs, 6 Mar 1914. Byer collection. (90) $125
— 29 Jan 1920. (91) $80

Casanova de Seingalt, Giacomo Girolamo, 1725-98
ALs, 12 Feb 1789. 4 pp, 4to. To a nephew. Describing an eventful journey from Prague to Dux, & discussing his nephew's literary style. With German trans. (90) DM18,000
— [c.1795]. 1 p, 4to. To the Abbate de la Lena. In 3d person, requesting that 2 letters be forwarded to him, & stating his name & address. (90) $4,000

Casella, Alfredo, 1883-1947
Autograph music, Variations sur une Chaconne pour le Piano, [n.d.]. 9 pp, 35cm by 27cm, 14 staves each. (89) DM3,000

Cass, Lewis, 1782-1866
Ls, 2 July 1857. (89) $120

Cassatt, Mary, 1845-1926
ALs, 14 Dec [1891?]. (90) $900

Cassel, Sir Ernest Joseph, 1852-1921
[A Ls from Cassel to S. Loewe of the Maxim-Nordenfelt Gun & Ammunition Co., setting out the terms for a loan to the Chinese government, with related material, 1893 to 1896, 9 pp, 4to & 8vo, sold at pn on 16 Mar 1989, lot 25, for £80 to L'Autographe.]

Cassianus, Joannes, 360?-435?
Ms, Collations. [Northern France or Rhineland, c.1150]. Part of 5 leaves, vellum, 335mm by 235mm. In a very fine romanesque bookhand. With 14 very large decorated initials. Glued together to form a bdg wrap. (91) £2,200

Cassini, Giovanni Domenico, 1625-1712
Autograph Ms, notes on the motions of the satellites of Jupiter, [c.1692?]. (89) £1,000

Cassiodorus, Flavius Magnus Aurelius, c.487-c.580
Ms, Liber Humanarum Litterarum. [Abbey of St. Germain, Auxerre, 3d quarter of 9th cent]. 109 leaves, vellum, 243mm by 182mm. 18th-cent French mottled sheep bdg. In dark brown ink by more than 1 scribe in a slightly sloping Carolingian minuscule; headings & titles in uncials & half-uncials. With 39 ornamental diagrams & 10 pictorial drawings. Ludwig MS.XII.1. (89) £42,000

Castelli, Ignaz Franz, 1781-1862
Autograph Ms, poem, Auch eine Doebleriade, [n.d.]. (90) DM220

Castelnuovo-Tedesco, Mario, 1895-1968
Series of 10 A Ls s, 1950 to 1962. (89) £600

Castlereagh, Robert Stewart, Viscount, 1769-1822
Ls, 19 Feb 1820. (91) DM420
Franking signature, [after May 1815]. (90) $120

Castorano, Carlo Horatii da, b.1673
Ms, Parva elucubratio super quosdam Libros Sinenses. Ab illmo et Rmo D. Archiepo Myrensi de Nicolais relictor labore ac studio infrapti P. Auctoris. Rome, 6 Jan 1739. 537 pp, 4to, in a single scribal hand, in contemp mor gilt with small stamp of St. Francis. Sgd by Castorano in 3 places. (91) £5,000

Castro, Fidel
Ds, [n.d.]. (91) $275
Photograph, sgd, 30 May [19]76. (91) $550

Caswell, Richard, 1729-89
Ds, 30 Apr 1778. (90) $425

Catesby, Robert, 1573-1605
Ds, 1 May 1594. (90) £400

Cather, Willa S., 1873-1947
Autograph Ms, short story, Cecile; [n.d.]. (90) $375
Collection of 6 A Ls s & 3 Ls s, 1939 to 1945 & [n.d.]. (88) £140
ALs, [12 Nov 1929]. (89) $750
— 15 Oct [n.y.]. (91) $500
— [n.d.]. (89) $140
Corrected galley proof, 2 complete stories from Obscure Destinies, comprising pages 75 - 230; [1932]. 53 sheets, folio. With 20 autograph corrections. (90) $2,200

Catherine de Medicis, 1519-89. See: Charles IX & Catherine de Medicis

Catherine de Medicis, Queen of France, 1519-89
Ls, 26 Aug 1567. (89) $500
— 1 Jan 1569. 1 p, folio. To Bertrand de la Mothe-Fenelon, Ambassador to England. Suggesting he seek an audience with the Queen, & exhorting him to assist Mary Stuart. (90) £1,300
— 3 July 1571. Doheny collection. (89) $550
Ds, 1566. (90) $800
— 30 Dec 1577. (88) $350
— 22 Feb 1582. (91) £240

Catherine I, Empress of Russia, 1684-1727
Ds, 15 Sept 1726. 1 p, folio. Order to the Board of War regarding a request by Gen. Buturlin. (88) DM4,500
— 18 Sept 1726. 1 p, folio. Order regarding the sale of villages. (90) DM3,000

Catherine II, Empress of Russia, 1729-96
ALs, 7 Jan 1765. 1 p, 4to. To Count Muennich. Requesting his opinion about a letter by Gen. Braun. In French. (90) DM3,200
— [Oct/Nov 1772]. 1 p, 4to. To Count Muennich. Requesting him to translate a Russian comedy for Voltaire. In French. Repaired. (88) DM4,300
— 19 Aug 1792. 2 pp, 4to. To Markgraefin Amalie von Baden-Durlach. Discussing the projected stay of recipient's daughters at the Russian court. In French. (90) DM5,000
— 1 Nov 1792. 2 pp, 4to. To Markgraefin Amalie von Baden-Durlach. Inform-

CATHERINE II

ing her of the arrival of her daughters in Russia. (89) DM3,800
— 21 May 1795. 1 p, 4to. To Countess Lieven. Sending regards to her granddaughters, commenting on some visitors, etc. (91) DM8,000
— [n.d.]. 2 pp, 8vo. To Count Ostermann. Instructing him to respond to the complaint of the Swedish envoy about a newspaper article. (91) DM1,600
Ls, 22 Aug 1783. 2 pp, folio. To King Ferdinand of Naples & Sicily. Acknowledging the mission of his envoy the Duke of St. Nicolas. (88) DM1,600
— 17 Dec 1784. (88) £420
— 16 Sept 1790. 1 p, folio. To Prince Potemkin. Regarding payment for carpenters at Kherson. (90) DM1,700
— 7 Oct 1790. (88) £400
— 31 May 1792. 3 pp, 4to. To Landgraefin Ulrike von Hessen-Philippsthal. Criticizing her son who is serving in the Russian army. In French. (90) DM1,800
— 12 Oct 1793. 1 p, folio. To Herzog Karl II Eugen von Wuerttemberg. Notifying him of her grandson's marriage. (90) DM1,400
Ds, 28 July 1777. 1 p, folio. Military discharge for Lieut. Gen. Karl Kapcin. Countersgd by Potemkin. (90) $2,000
— 28 July 1777. (88) £650
— 29 Nov 1778. 5 leaves, vritten on vellum in gold, red & black, 430mm by 289mm, in gold brocade over bds with imperial seal in silver-gilt case (case by Clas Johann Elers & Evgraf Borovschikov). Illuminated nobility patent elevating the Alaskan explorer Sven Waxell & his 3 sons to hereditary baronetcy and granting the family a coat of arms. With Illuminated page borders in gold & colors incorporating a medallion port of Catherine surmounting the double-headed imperial eagle with the city arms of Moscow & the decoration of the order of St. Andrew; 23 oval miniatures; coats of arms of 30 Russian noble families; & newly granted Waxell arms. (91) $40,000
— 22 Sept 1786. (89) £450
— 23 Oct 1788. Byer collection. (90) $550
— 31 Dec 1793. (88) £650

Catherine of Aragon, Queen of Henry VIII of England, 1485-1536

ALs, 8 Feb 1534. 3 pp, folio. To Emperor Charles V. Entreating him to help her obtain justice from the pope & to save her & her daughter from captivity. In Spanish. With calligraphic tp, ptd transcription & English trans in scarlet mor gilt extra bdg by Sangorski & Sutcliffe. Huth Library (88) $38,000

Catherine of Austria, Duchess of Savoy, 1567-97

Ls, 30 June 1597. (90) DM260

Catherine of Braganza, Queen of Charles II of England, 1638-1705

Ds, 14 May 1689. (88) £300

Catlin, George, 1796-1872

Series of 3 A Ls s, 30 Oct [c.1814] to [1871]. To Steuben Butler. Regretting not being able to return to Wilkes Barre. Expressing pleasure about meeting Butler's son. With related ALs by Edward C. Butler to his father Steuben, 24 Nov 1871. (89) $1,100

Cavafy, Constantine P., 1863-1933

Autograph Ms (2), poems, The First Step, & Unfaithfulness; [c.1920]. 3 pp, folio. 26 & 25 lines; each sgd. In autograph folder. (89) £4,800

Autograph Ms, poem, Waiting for the Barbarians, [n.d.]. (88) £1,000

Cavalca, Domenico, 1270-1342

Ms, Lo Specchio della Croce, & other texts in Italian. [Florence, 1384]. 86 leaves (2 lacking) & flyleaf, 320mm by 230mm. Contemp goatskin over bevelled woodens bds; spine repaired. In brown ink in a round gothic bookhand by 2 scribes. With penwork initials with marginal extensions throughout, 2 very large illuminated initials & 3 (slightly later) miniatures, 2 full-page. Phillipps MS.12304 & Abbey collection. (89) £32,000
— Ms, Lo Spechio della Croce. [Tuscany, late 14th cent] 91 leaves, vellum, 190mm by 140mm, in calf over wooden bds. In black ink in an Italian textura. Zabriske-Manhattan College Ms (91) $10,000

Cavell, Edith, 1865-1915

[A collection of c.100 items, signatures, & letters addressed to Edith & Florence Cavell, mostly 1880, in def contemp half roan album, with related material, sold at C on 22 June 1988, lot 9, for £300 to Wilson.]

ALs, 19 Aug 1914. 2 pp, 8vo. To her mother & family. Reporting the imminent invasion of Brussels & making provision in case of her death. Bradley Martin sale. (90) $4,000

Cavour, Camillo, 1810-61

ALs, 3 Nov 1843. (88) £180

— [Feb 1853?]. 2 pp, 8vo. To [Conte Luigi Corti]. Concerning negotations for a loan. In French. (90) DM1,400

— [1855]. (89) DM950

— 13 Feb [n.y.]. (88) DM900

Celine, Louis Ferdinand Destouches, 1894-1961

Autograph Ms, draft of part of his autobiography, dealing with visits in Sigmaringen, Denmark & Meudon; [c.1956]. 24 pp, 4to, on rectos only. Including numerous revisions. (91) DM3,200

— Autograph Ms, draft of part of his autobiography, dealing with the last months of the war; [c.1956]. 18 pp, 4to, on rectos only. Including numerous revisions. (90) DM3,500

— Autograph Ms, fragment of novel, D'un chateau l'autre, early draft, [1954-57]. (88) £600

— Autograph Ms, fragment of novel, D'un chateau l'autre, early draft, [1954-57]. (88) £700

ALs, 17 May [n.y.]. (88) £100

— [n.d.]. (90) DM350

Series of 10 autograph postcards, sgd, 1921 to 1937. To Henri Mahe. Reporting about his travels. With related material. (90) DM2,200

Celsius, Anders, 1701-44

ADs, 20 Sept 1736. 1 p, folio. Receipt for pay as professor at Upsala University. At foot of pay order, sgd by Magnus Beronius. (91) DM4,200

Cena Maletractati

Ms, allegorical romance entirely made up of biblical quotations strung together to form a story, in Latin. [Northern France or Southern Flanders, c.1475]. 32 leaves (2 blank), vellum, 173mm by 120mm, in early 19th-cent quarter green sheep. In a regular lettre batarde. With 33 illuminated initials & 3-line initial with full border. (90) £4,800

Cerf, Bennett

Collection of 15 Ls s & Ns s, 1939 to 1961. (89) $150

Certificates

— BUTCHER'S CERTIFICATE. - Document, 4 July 1780. 1 p, 35cm by 63.5cm. Journeyman's certificate for Valentin Knatz, sgd by J. H. Helgenberg & J. H. Fuhrmann for the butchers' guild at Kassel, Hesse. With large painted coat-of-arms at head & a view of Kassel in lower margin. (91) DM1,600

— COOK'S CERTIFICATE. - Document, 22 Jan 1766. 1 p, folio. Attestation, sgd by Friedrich Anton Conrad Sommer & anr 22 master cooks at Dresden, that Johann Gottlieb Richter successfully completed his apprenticeship of 5 years in the Prince of Loewenstein's kitchen. With elaborate calligraphic decoration. (90) DM1,000

— GARDENER'S CERTIFICATE. - Document, 22 Feb 1727. 1 p, 360mm by 610mm. Journeyman's certificate for Johann Dietrich Deichmann, sgd by Georg Baumann at Arolsen, Principality of Waldeck. With 9 drawings in pen-&-ink & wash, including coat-of-arms of the Princes of Waldeck. (90) DM1,200

— GARDENER'S CERTIFICATE. - Document, 24 Apr 1824. 1 p, folio. Journeyman's certificate for Gottfried Teude, sgd by Christian Friedrich Klett at Schwerin. With painted coat-of-arms, 3 pen-&-ink drawings & seal in a silver box. (91) DM1,600

— GARDENER'S CERTIFICATE. - Document, 30 Nov 1730. 1 p, folio. Journeyman's certificate for Johann Georg Zinckher, sgd by Carl Ermann. With coat-of-arms of Johann Albrecht Reichsgraf von und zu Wallsee auf

CERTIFICATES

Wartenburg & vignettes with hunting scenes & falcons. (88) DM2,000
— GARDENER'S CERTIFICATE. - Document, 28 Oct 1772. 1 p, 29cm by 46cm. Journeyman's certificate for Franz Baumann, sgd by Norbert Schiffneder. With coat-of-arms of Fuerst Kaunitz & floral & ornamental borders. (88) DM700
— GARDENER'S CERTIFICATE. - Document, 1 June 1810. 1 p, 32cm by 51cm. Journeyman's certificate for Franz Sebastian Baumann, sgd by Franz Bollatschy. With coat-of-arms of Baden, floral & ornamental vignettes, & views of castle & landscape. With seal in ivory box. (88) DM1,100
— GARDENER'S CERTIFICATE. - Document, 1 Jan 1767. 1 p, 31cm by 57.5cm. Journeyman's certificate for Franz Baumann, sgd by Balthasar Seitz. With coat-of-arms of the Archbishop of Mainz & elaborate borders. (88) DM2,100
— GARDENER'S CERTIFICATE. - Document, Dec 1771. 1 p, 28.5cm by 44cm. Journeyman's certificate for Franz Baumann, sgd by Johann Georg Schreiber. With coat-of-arms of the Archbishop of Salzburg & elaborate floral & ornamental borders. (88) DM1,400
— GARDENER'S CERTIFICATE. - Document, 30 Oct 1754. 1 p, 29.5cm by 47cm. Journeyman's certificate for Cajetan Ovidera, sgd by Johann Matthias Trux. With coat-of-arms of the Counts Thun & elaborate borders. (88) DM1,100
— SMITH'S CERTIFICATE. - Document, 10 June 1805. 1 p, 44cm by 50cm. Journeyman's certificate for Johann Jacob Langenbach, issued at Prague. On sheet with engraved view of Prague. (90) DM460
— TAYLOR'S GUILD, KASSEL. - Document, 18 June 1793. 1 p, folio. Certificate of completion of apprenticeship for Johann Nikolaus Roettger. With ornamental borders & pen-&-ink sketch (view of Kassel) at bottom. Silked. (89) DM500

AMERICAN BOOK PRICES CURRENT

Cervantes Saavedra, Miguel de, 1547-1616
Ds, 6 Mar 1593. 1 p, folio. Fragment; legal agreement concerning a debt owed to Don Pasqual Sabagan by Gabriel de Viana; sgd as witness. Also sgd by 4 others. (88) $5,500

Cessolis, Jacobus de, fl.1290. See: Dante Alighieri & Cessolis

Cezanne, Paul, 1839-1906
ALs, 22 Nov [1903]. 2 pp, 8vo. To Octave Mirbeau. Recommending a young man from the Cevennes. (91) £3,200

Chabrier, Emmanuel, 1841-94
Autograph music, concluding section of a movement for string quartet in F major, [n.d.]. (89) £500
— Autograph music, transcription for piano of the Romance du roi from the opera Le roi malgre lui, [c.1887]. (89) $700

Chadwick, James, 1891-1974
Autograph Ms, a paragraph from his Nobel Prize lecture, [1935]. 1 p, 4to. Sgd. (91) DM1,200
ALs, 6 Dec 1967. (89) DM250

Chagall, Marc, 1889-1985
Collection of ALs, 4 Ls s & autograph postcard, sgd, 21 Apr 1946 to 6 May 1968. 6 pp, 4to & 8vo. To Alfred Werner. Regarding Werner's writings about Chagall, an exhibition, etc. With related material. (88) DM1,400
ALs, [n.d.]. (89) DM480
Ls, 25 Nov 1960. (91) $225
— 24 Apr 1967. (88) DM420
Photograph, sgd, [n.d.]. (91) $160
Ptd photograph, [n.d.]. (91) $150
Signature, on program for Ballet Russe Highlights, NY 1945. (91) $150
— Anr, on philatelic cover, 1963. (91) $300
— Anr, on 1st day cover, 17 Nov 1967. (89) DM280
— Anr, [17 Nov 1967]. (88) DM400
— Anr, [n.d.]. (91) $150

Chailly, Luciano
Autograph music, Abbozzi di strutture strumentali per il Kinder-Requiem, sgd at head & dated 1977. (90) DM320
— Autograph music, Concerto notturno

per voce recitante e 12 flauti, 1977. (88) DM850
— Autograph music, fragments of 5 different compositions, [c.1980]. (89) DM300
— Autograph music, Strutture per La cantatrice calva (testo di Ionesco); [n.d.]. (90) DM270

Chaliapin, Feodor, 1873-1938
Photograph, sgd, 1929. (90) DM350
Photograph, sgd & inscr, [Nov] 1923. (90) $140
— Anr, 1934. (90) DM280
Signature, [n.d.]. (89) $65

Cham, Pseud. of Amedee de Noe, 1819-79
Caricature, 2 Arabs having an argument, pen-&-ink; [n.d.]. (88) DM260
— Anr, gentleman in danger of drowning in an icy pond requesting his servant's help, pen-&-ink; [n.d.]. (88) DM340

Chamberlain, Houston Stewart, 1855-1927
Collection of ALs & ANs, 14 Dec 1887 & 3 Aug 1892. (89) DM270

Chamberlain, Neville, 1869-1940
ALs, 7 Jan 1937. (91) $130

Chambers, G. E.
Original drawings, (38), European scenes to illus works by Carlyle, Arthur Symons & Humbert Wolfe, 1928 to 1933. Archives of J. M. Dent & Son. (88) £950
— Original drawings, (50), English scenes to illus various works, 1931 to 1933. In pencil (4) or ink. Various sizes. Archives of J. M. Dent & Son. (88) £1,100
— Original drawings, (91), to illus M. Archives of J. M. Dent & Son. (88) £900

Chambers, John, 1780-1852. See: Indians, North American

Chamisso, Adelbert von, 1781-1838
Autograph Ms, poem, Ein Baal Teschuba, [1832]. 3 pp, 4to. 121 lines, with numerous revisions. (90) DM2,500
— Autograph Ms, poem, Im Traume; [Mar 1837]. 4 pp, 4to. 12 eight-line stanzas. (91) DM1,900
ALs, 27 Sept 1803. 1 p, 4to. To Queen Luise of Prussia. Presenting her with a literary work. In French. (91) DM1,700
— 2 Sept 1824. (91) DM1,000
— 4 Aug 1833. 2 pp, 8vo. To [G. A. Reimer]. About contributions to the Deutscher Musenalmanach. (91) DM1,400
— 20 Feb [1834]. (90) DM850

Champagny, Jean Baptiste de Nompere de, Duc de Cadore, 1756-1834
Ls, 27 Feb 1810. (89) $225

Champollion-Figeac, Jean Jacques, 1778-1867
ALs, [n.d.]. (88) DM340

Chandler, Raymond, 1888-1959
Ls s (2), [n.d.]. (88) $400
Ls, 7 Feb 1951. (88) $850

Chandrasekhar, Subrahmanyan
Autograph Ms, scientific paper, On the onset of relativistic instability in highly centrally condensed stars, [n.d.]. (89) DM440

Chaney, Lon, 1883-1930
Photograph, sgd, [n.d.]. (91) $500
Signature, [n.d.]. (89) $525
— Anr, [n.d.]. (91) $200

Chaney, Lon, 1907-73
Ds, 30 Sept 1955. (91) $200
— 11 Sept 1957. (91) $170
Photograph, sgd, [n.d.]. 8 by 10 inches. Sgd Creighton Chaney. (91) $1,100
Photograph, sgd & inscr, [n.d.]. (89) $210

Chaplin, Charles, 1889-1977
Ls, 5 Nov 1952. (90) $190
Ds, [1946]. 1 p, 8 by 5 inches. Preliminary Application for [Driver's] License, on California Department of Motor Vehicles form. Framed with a port. (89) $2,000
Menu, for a Luncheon in his honor at the Empress Club, London, 10 Oct 1952. (91) $450
Photograph, sgd, [n.d.]. (91) $300
Photograph, sgd & inscr, 1925. (90) £850
— Anr, [1950s]. (91) $200
Self-caricature, Sept 1921. (90) £525

CHAPLIN

Chaplin, Charles, 1889-1977 —& Chaplin, Oona

[Their signatures on a philatelic envelope, 1973, framed with a photograph of Charlie Chaplin, sold at Dar on 10 Apr 1991, lot 97, for $275.]

Chaplin, Charles, 1889-1977 —& Pickford, Mary, 1893-1979

[Their signatures on a ptd philatelic sheet honoring D. W. Griffith, [1975], 8.5 by 11 inches, sold at Dar on 7 Feb 1991, lot 9, for $110.]

[Their signatures, [n.d.], on a slip of paper, 6.5 by 1 inches, matted with related material, sold at Dar on 6 Dec 1990, lot 135, for $200.]

Chaplin, Oona. See: Chaplin, Charles & Chaplin

Chaplin, Sydney, 1885-1965

Collection of 70 A Ls s & Ls s, June 1930 to Feb 1956. Over 400 pp, 4to & 8vo. To R. J. Minney. Giving news of his activities & film projects, & referring to his brother Charles. With related material. (91) £1,200

Chapman, Arthur, 1873-1935

Autograph transcript, poem, Out Where the West Begins, sgd & dated Apr 1917. Doheny collection. (88) $180

Chaptal, Jean Antoine Claude, 1756-1832

ALs, [n.d.]. (89) DM220

— 10 June 1818. (90) DM200

Chapuis, Jean

Ms, Sept Articles de la Foi. [Paris, c.1470]. Single leaf, vellum, 288mm by 191mm, laid down on wooden panel. With full-page miniature attributed to Maitre Francois, incorporating a panel with 12 lines of text in a large lettre batarde & with 2-line initial. Retouched. (91) £12,000

Char, Rene

Autograph Ms (2), poems, Victoire eclair & Conversation avec une grappe, & essay, Note a propos d'une deuxieme lecture de La perversion essentielle, 1962 & 1965. (91) £650

AMERICAN BOOK PRICES CURRENT

Charcot, Jean Martin, 1825-93

A Ls s (2), [n.d.]. (90) DM900

Charles, Duke of Burgundy ("the Bold"), 1433-77

Ls, 10 Oct 1474. 1 p, folio. To his chamberlain. Informing him that the Emperor & German Princes are massing against his forces & urging him to send troops. (89) £2,600

— STEPHEN, BISHOP OF LUGANO. - Document, 16 May 1468. 580mm by 620mm, vellum. Official copy of declaration delivered as Papal Nuncio concerning dispensation granted by Pope Paul II for the marriage of Charles the Bold to Margaret of York. Including 10-line ratification by William, Bishop of London, & genealogical diagram. In buckram box. Doheny collection. (89) $4,500

Charles d'Orleans, 1394-1465

Ds, 6 May 1442. (91) £1,000

Charles Emmanuel I, Duke of Savoy, 1562-1630

Ls, 20 May 1586. (90) DM220

Charles I, King of England, 1600-49

Series of 3 A Ls s, [n.d.]. 3 pp, folio. To Prince Rupert. About matters pertaining to the Civil War. (91) £2,500

ALs, [c.1630]. (88) £1,000

— 31 Jan 1634/35. 1 p, folio. To his sister Elizabeth, Queen of Bohemia. Assuring her of his affection. (91) £1,600

— 4 Apr 1644. 1 p, folio. To Prince Rupert. Referring to the Yorkshire petitions & hoping he will be able to protect Oxford. (91) £2,100

Series of 4 Ls s, 19 to 26 Aug 1640. 5 pp, folio. To William Stanley, Earl of Derby, & James, Lord Strange. Ordering them to muster forces immediately [for the 2d Bishops' War]. (90) £3,100

Ls s (2), [17 July 1636 & 24 Oct 1637]. 2 pp, folio. To Sir John Bankes. Warrants concerning copperas. With related material. (89) £1,600

— Ls s (2), 17 Sept 1642 & 19 Jan 1642/43. 3 pp, folio. To James Stanley, Earl of Derby. Commissions of Col. Plaer & William Spottiswood under Derby's command. Including related material. (90) £1,050

— Ls s (2), 17 Jan 1642/43 & 28 Mar 1643. 2 pp, folio. To James Stanley, Earl of Derby. Discussing the military situation in Cheshire & Lancashire. (90) £2,000

Ls, 22 Dec 1632. (88) $550

— 24 July 1643. 1 p, folio. To Emperor Ferdinand III. Letter of State, acknowledging letters & the services of Ferdinand's envoy Francis de Lisola. In Latin, with trans. Byer collection. (90) $2,400

Ds, 1 May 1628. (91) £650

— 18 Mar 1642/43. (90) £450

— 20 Nov 1645. (88) £260

Document, 19 Apr 1642. 1 p, c.23 by 31.5 inches, vellum. Grant to Sir George Carteret of manors on Jersey for his service against the Turks. In Latin. With initial letter port, c.6 by 5.5 inches. (88) £1,400

— 28 Jan 1648. (89) £600

Endorsement, sgd, on a petition addressed to him by citizens of Oxford & tenants of Wolvercot, 23 Mar [1643-46], 1 large membrane of vellum, requesting that cattle belonging to the army be not allowed on common meadows until 25 July; granting petition. (89) £1,000

Charles II, King of England, 1630-85

Ms, draft, Project for a Treaty with Algiers, [1682]. 14 pp, folio. Sgd & initialled by Charles II. (89) £1,800

ALs, 14 May 1656. (88) £600

— 1 June 1660. (89) £920

Ls, 4 May 1646. (88) £420

— 20 May 1651. 1 p, folio. To William Berkeley. Requesting him to pay the debts of his deceased servant Charles Murray. (90) $1,500

— 30 Nov 1665. (91) £360

Ds, [Dec 1660]. (88) £750

— 3 Mar 1661. (91) $650

— 3 Mar 1661/2. Byer collection. (90) $750

— 30 Nov 1665. (90) £400

— 8 Sept 1672. (89) £720

— 9 May 1674. (88) £300

— 8 Mar 1679/80. 1 p, folio. Warrant to affix the Great Seal to a commission for Gabriel Sylvius to treat with Brunswick. (88) DM1,100

— 6 May 1682. (88) £260

— 25 Jan 1682/83. (90) £900

— 29 June 1683. (90) £550

Document, 13 May 1661. (89) £900

— 9 Jan 1673. 1 p, folio. Letters Patent, granting the prebendry of Westminster to John North. Including seal. Framed. (91) $1,500

— 5 Apr 1678. (89) £300

— 2 Apr [1682]. (88) $475

— KING'S REVENUE. - Ms, report prepared for the Speaker of the House of Commons listing the King's estimated income & expenses, 4 Sept 1660. 5 pp, folio. In a single hand, with marginal notations in 2 other hands. Byer collection. (90) $550

See also: Order of the Garter

Charles III, Duc de Lorraine ("The Great"), 1543-1608

Ls, 15 May 1577. (90) DM240

Charles III, King of Spain, 1716-88

Document, 6 May 1762. (89) £850

Charles IV, Emperor, 1316-78

Document, 26 Oct [1366]. 1 p, vellum, folio. Notification addressed to the magistracy at Cambrai that his brother Wenceslas will act as Viceregent during his absence in Italy. Including seal. (90) DM10,000

Charles IX, King of France —& Catherine de Medicis, 1519-89

[A bound vol containing 3 documents (2 sgd by Charles) & an Ls of Catherine, all concerning aid to Mary, Queen of Scots, sold at sg on 22 Mar, lot 42.] $6,250

Charles IX, King of France, 1550-74

Ds, [n.d.]. (88) $80

Charles of Lorraine, Governor of the Netherlands, 1712-80

Ms, instructions concerning the building of fortifications etc., addressed to Philipp von Harrsch; 30 June 1765. (90) DM220

Ls, 19 Sept 1743. (91) DM400

Charles V, Emperor, 1500-58
Ls s (2), 12 July & 23 Aug 1523. 4 pp, folio. To Antonio Adorno. Discussing the Turks, French plans to invade Italy, diplomatic negotiations, etc. Partly in cipher. Imperf. (90) £2,200
— Ls s (2), 26 June 1539 & 24 Apr 1545. (90) £1,000
Ls, 10 Oct 1516. (90) £1,000
— 18 Nov 1518. (88) £350
— 8 Oct 1520. 1 p, folio. To Kurfuerst Ludwig V von der Pfalz. Credentials for his envoys Maximilian von Berghe & Georg von Emershofen. Sgd Carolus. (90) DM4,200
— 29 Apr 1522. (88) £500
— 16 July 1522. 1 p, folio. To the Deputies of Valencia. Giving an account of his recent visit to England. (90) £2,200
— 24 Aug 1523. 1 p, folio. To the chaplains of the Chapel Royal in Granada. Ordering them to attend the annual memorial services for Ferdinand & Isabella. (90) £1,400
— 10 Sept 1523. 1 p, folio. To the Duke of Arcos. Reminding him of the necessity to send auxiliary troops. (90) DM1,400
— 12 Mar 1525. 1 p, folio. To the city of Loja. Informing the city officials of his victory over the French & the capture of Francis I. (90) £4,000
— 18 Sept 1525. Rua collection. (91) $650
— 16 Nov 1525. 1 p, folio. To the city of Loja. Announcing his betrothal to Isabella of Portugal. (90) £1,500
— 29 Nov 1526. 2 pp, folio. To the cities of Loja, Alhama & Alcala la Real. Informing them of the Turkish invasion of Hungary. (90) £4,200
— 29 Nov 1526. 2 pp, folio. To the city of Loja. Informing them of the Turkish invasion of Hungary. (90) £1,400
— 8 Oct 1527. 3 pp, folio. To Joerg von Wolmershausen & Willibald Pirckheimer. Giving instructions for negotiations with Nuernberg. Lower margin cut. (89) DM2,400
— 8 Feb 1528. (90) £600
— 10 Nov 1528. 1 p, folio. To the city of Loja. Announcing the French King's response to Charles's challenge to a duel. (90) £1,400
— 20 Feb 1529. 2 pp, folio. To the city of Loja. Announcing his probable departure for Italy & ordering that Empress Isabella should be obeyed as Regent. (90) £2,000
— 16 Apr 1529. 1 p, folio. To Pope Clement VII. Requesting him to renew an earlier brief regarding jurisdiction of the Inquisition. Imperf. (90) £2,200
— 28 July 1529. 2 pp, folio. To the city of Loja. About the peace treaty, his departure for Italy, & the appointment of the Empress as Regent. With related letter by Empress Isabella. (90) £1,500
— 7 Mar 1530. 1 p, folio. To the city of Loja. Announcing his coronation as King of Lombardy & Holy Roman Emperor. (90) £3,200
— 11 July 1532. 2 pp, folio. To the city of Loja. Announcing his determination to fight the Turks now threatening Vienna. (90) £2,500
— 9 May 1535. 2 pp, folio. To the city of Loja. Announcing he is gathering a fleet to fight the Turks in the Mediterranean. (90) £2,200
— 28 Jan 1539. (91) £600
— 13 Apr 1546. 1 p, 4to. To the magistracy at Trier. Giving instructions to allow Arnold Krutkremer back into the city after his acquittal. (90) DM2,200
— 31 May 1550. (90) £720
— 25 May 1552. 5 pp, folio. To the council of Regensburg. Urging them to remain loyal to himself & the Empire. (89) DM6,000
— 11 Sept 1552. (90) £600
— 30 July 1553. 4 pp, folio. To [Markgraf Albrecht Alcibiades?]. Explaining that he will not be able to pay him & his troops the next day since a shipment of money expected from Spain has not arrived. Dampstained. (90) DM3,800
Series of Ds s, 4 Ds s, 15 Aug 1518 to 19 July 1528. 12 pp, size not stated. In his own & his mother's name, authorization to the Constable of Castile to transfer the entail of Tovar, renewal of a grant, etc. (90) £1,500
— Series of Ds s, 7 Ds s, 17 Apr 1521 to 1 Jan 1554. 8 pp, folio. In Spanish, Latin & French, about a variety of matters. With several forms of signature. (90) £1,900
Ds s (2) 14 Sept 1526 & 17 May 1527. 9

pp, folio. Regarding a duel fought against 3 Moors by Gonzal Perez Gallegos & others. Including 2 related Portuguese documents. (90) £1,200

Ds, 19 Jan 1521. 1 p, folio. Granting Reinhard von Altdorff tithes at Dudenweyler. Countersgd by Card. Albrecht von Brandenburg. Seal lacking. (88) DM2,000

— 25 Mar 1521. 1 p, vellum, 340mm by 375mm. In his own & his brother Ferdinand's name, grant of feudal rights at Lagelheim to Jakob Villinger. (90) DM1,250

— 4 Feb 1526. 1 p, vellum, folio. Patent of nobility & grant of arms to Camillo Manino. Including painting of the arms. Somewhat def. (90) DM2,200

— 21 Mar 1530. 1 p, vellum, folio. Confirmation of privileges to the town of Brayde. Lacking seal. (90) DM1,500

— 30 Mar 1538. (91) £850

— 28 June 1539. (90) $850

— 4 Sept 1541. 1 p, folio. Confirmation of a patent issued to G. B. Visconti to buy & sell grains. (89) DM2,500

— 20 May 1545. 1 p, folio. Confirmation of a grant to an orphanage at Milan. (91) DM1,200

— 13 Mar 1554. 1 p, folio. Order addressed to Luis de Velasco, Viceroy of New Spain, to grant appropriate honors to Andres Ribero de Espinosa. (90) £1,400

Document, 28 Aug 1556. (88) DM600

Charles V, Emperor, 1500-58 —&
Isabella of Portugal, Empress of Charles V, 1503-39

[A group of 6 Ls s, including 2 Ls s by each to Pope Clement VII & 2 Ls s by Charles V to Spanish officials, 16 Apr 1519 to 29 July 1532, relating to negotiations with the Vatican, sold at S on 21 Nov 1989, lot 211, for £3,200 to Dominguez.]

[A group of 4 Ls s (2 by each), 11 Jan 1528 to 16 Jan 1531, 4 pp, folio, to the magistrates of Medina del Campo, regarding orders to grant land to some servants, sold at S on 21 Nov 1989, lot 220, for £700 to Charavay.]

[A group of 8 Ds s (1 by Charles V, 5 by Isabella, 2 with secretarial signatures), 25 May 1536 to 21 May 1542, 9 pp, folio, relating to fortifications at Fuenterrabia, sold at S on 21 Nov 1989, lot 221, for £1,600 to Porrua.]

Charles V, Emperor, 1500-58 —&
Juana, Queen of Spain, 1479-1555

Document, 22 Apr 1517. 24 leaves, vellum, 335mm by 245mm. Concerning taxes to be paid by the village of Salvaterra de Estremo near Montanchez. With 1 large & 11 small initials in gold & colors. (88) DM2,200

Charles VI, Emperor, 1685-1740

ALs, 1 Nov 1700. (89) DM700

— 28 Mar 1710. 1 p, folio. To Eusebia von Breuner. About his sisters. (90) DM1,100

— 27 June 1731. 4 pp, folio. To Count Neipperg. Confidential letter, partly concerning military matters. (91) DM1,400

— 17 July 1732. 2 pp, folio. To Count Wilhelm von Neipperg. Confidential letter discussing [his future son-in-law] Franz von Lothringen's performance as Governor of Hungary. (91) DM1,500

— 9 Oct 1734. 3 pp, folio. To Field Marshal Wilhelm Graf Neipperg. About the defeat at Guastalla, requesting further information about the state of the army, & discussing changes in command. (88) DM3,800

Ls, 31 Oct 1714. (89) DM380

— 12 Oct 1716. (88) DM650

— 7 Apr 1721. (88) £240

— 8 Oct 1721. (89) $300

— 29 Sept 1722. (90) DM220

— 17 Dec 1722. (89) DM300

— 3 Oct 1724. (88) DM220

— 31 May 1728. (90) DM250

— 26 July 1740. (90) DM250

Ds, 5 Feb 1712. 1 p, 60cm by 82cm. Patent of nobility & grant of arms for Balthasar & Adam Heintze. Including painting of the arms. Lacking seal. (90) DM1,100

— 26 Oct 1712. 1 p, folio. Patent of nobility & grant of arms for Martin Biro. With large painting of the arms in gold & colors & seal in woooden case. (90) DM1,200

— 7 July 1720. 21 p, 4to, in red velvet bdg. Patent of nobility & grant of arms

CHARLES VI

for Joseph Peter von Sermage. With full-page painting of the arms in gold & colors. (90) DM1,050
— 21 Nov 1722. (88) £150
— 27 Apr 1723. (88) DM240

Autograph endorsement, sgd, on a report by the Hungarian Chancellery concerning Jakob Saikl's petition for permission to organize a lottery, 1 Dec 1732, 4 pp, folio; denying petition. (90) DM360
— Anr, sgd, on verso of a report addressed to him & sgd by J. (91) DM360

Charles VII, Emperor, 1697-1745
Ls, 3 Jan 1739. (90) DM400
— 22 Oct 1741. Schroeder collection. (89) DM850
— 7 July 1744. (89) DM700
Ds, 6 [Oct?] 1727. (91) DM200
— 4 Jan 1743. (90) DM270

Charles X, King of France, 1757-1836
Ds, 25 Feb 1781. Byer collection. (90) $150
— 16 May 1825. (88) $100
See also: Louis XVIII & Charles X

Charles XII, King of Sweden, 1682-1718
Ls, 28 Aug 1699. (90) DM650
— 6 June 1703. 2 pp, 4to. To his commissariat. Giving orders to supply clothes to the servants of a regiment. (90) DM1,300
— 29 Mar 1705. (88) DM800
Ds, 8 Feb 1705. (90) DM650

Charles XIII, King of Sweden, 1748-1818
Ds, 18 Sept 1810. (89) $120

Charles XIV John, King of Sweden, 1763-1844
ALs, [2 May 1800]. (90) DM450
Ls, [13 July 1799]. (89) $375
— [12 Oct 1805]. (91) DM920
— 20 Sept 1809. (91) DM300
See also: Lalande, Joseph Jerome de

Charlotte Sophia, Queen of George III of England, 1744-1818
ANs, [1799 or after]. (88) $140

AMERICAN BOOK PRICES CURRENT

Charlotte Sophia, Queen of George III of England, 1744-1818
ALs, 7 Dec 1796. (91) £100

Chase, Salmon P., 1808-73
ALs, 7 Feb 1840. (88) $60
— 17 May 1860. 2 pp, 8vo. To Abraham Lincoln. Draft, congratulating him on his nomination as Presidential candidate. (89) $2,750
— 7 Dec 1863. (91) $85
— 10 Aug 1867. (91) $55

Chase, Samuel, Signer from Maryland
ALs, 23 Dec 1783. (91) $900
— 1 Feb 1805. (89) $800

Chase, William Merritt, 1849-1916
[A sgd & inscr photograph of a port of J. McNeill Whistler by Chase, 1886, sold at rce on 28 July 1988, lot 560, for $110.]

Chateaubriand, Francois Rene, Vicomte de, 1768-1848
ALs, 4 Feb 1823. (88) DM280
— 1 Apr 1826. (89) DM300
— 25 Oct 1828. (90) DM260
— 15 Apr 1829. (90) DM460
— 19 Apr 1840. (90) DM300
Ls, 6 Jan 1824. (91) $200

Chateau-Tournant, Allain
Ms, L'Effaut en Parabolle, in French verse. [France, Brittany?, early 16th cent]. 210 leaves & flyleaf, vellum, 321mm by 255mm. Contemp purple velvet over wooden bds. In a flamboyant calligraphic lettre batarde, with some words in gothic script. With c.100 very large colored calligraphic initials. Phillipps Ms.3621. (91) £13,000

Chatwin, Bruce, d.1989
[A collection of revised autograph & typescript working drafts on the theme of nomads & wandering, [c.1960?-1970], more than 700 pp, mostly folio, with related material, sold at S on 20 July 1989, lot 165, for £13,000 to Rota.]

Chauncey, Isaac, 1772-1840
Ls, 27 Mar 1834. (91) $50

Chauncy, Sir Henry, 1632-1719
Autograph Ms, Historical Antiquities of Herfordshire, fair copy; fragment. [Late 17th cent], 47 leaves, folio. Printer's copy. Professionally repaired & mtd. (88) £2,500

Chausson, Ernest, 1855-99
ALs, [n.d.]. (90) DM380

Chekhov, Anton, 1860-1904
ALs, 16 July 1896. 1 p, 8vo. To Vladimir Ivanovich. Coping with bureaucracy on behalf of a poor patient. (91) $6,500
Signature, 11 Apr 1900. 1 p, 8vo. (91) £2,800

Cheret, Jules, 1836-1932
ALs, 27 May 1909. (90) $225

Cherin, Louis Nicolas Hyacinthe, 1762-99
Ls, [4 June 1797]. (90) DM500

Cherubini, Luigi, 1760-1842
Autograph music, Canone Chiuso, a 8 Voci, to the text Non impedias musicam; sgd, inscr & dated 19 Aug 1811. (90) £850
— Autograph music, Solfege pour l'examen semestrier des classes au mois de juin 1836, 11 May 1836. 2 pp, 4to. Allegretto; 85 bars. (91) DM1,400
A Ls s (2), 3 May 1819 & 1 June 1829. Byer collection. (90) $500
ALs, 21 Nov 1823. (89) DM420
Ds, 4 Feb 1837. (91) DM200

Chesterfield, Philip Dormer Stanhope, 4th Earl of, 1694-1773
ALs, 5 Aug 1746. 6 pp, 4to. To Charles Guillaume Loys de Bochat. Discussing the education of his son. In French. With related material. (89) DM2,200
— 29 Sept 1747. 5 pp, 4to. To [Charles Guillaume Loys de Bochat]. Discussing his son's education. In French. (88) DM3,400

Chesterton, Gilbert Keith, 1874-1936
Autograph Ms (2), story, The God of the Gongs, [c.1913], 22 pp, sgd, & part of The Ballad of the White Horse, [c.1910], 10 pp (1 by his wife). With numerous revisions. In 4to ringfile.

(88) £2,700
Autograph Ms, essay, A Much Repeated Repetition, sgd; [n.d.]. 5 pp, 4to, on rectos only. In dark green mor gilt bdg with tp & typed transcript. Doheny collection. (89) $1,600
— Autograph Ms, poem, True Sympathy or Prevention of Cruelty to Teachers, 3 pp, 4to. (88) £178

Original drawings, sketches of various figures, in ink, pencil & colored crayons, [n.d.]. (89) £500

Typescript, one-act play, Tragic Women, a Tragedy, [1925]. (88) £180

Chiang Kai-shek, 1887-1975
Photograph, sgd, [n.d.]. (89) $55

Chicerin, Georgy Vasilyevich, 1872-1936
ALs, 27 May 1927. (89) DM950

Chilton, R. H.
A Ls s (2), 13 Nov [18]70 & 13 Feb 1871. (88) $450

China
[2 documents, Imperial rescripts, 1793, 2 scrolls, c.515mm by 1340mm, ordering food supplies for the embassy of George, 1st Earl Macartney, in black ink on decorated orange colored paper, repaired, sold at S on 22 Nov, lot 82, for £4,500 to Singer.]

Original drawings, (72), watercolors depicting animals, flowers, river craft, costume figures, etc., [China & Bengal, c.1780-1800]. On silk or paper, laid onto European paper, 535mm by 420mm. 19th-cent purple mor gilt bdg. Including 4 Bengali composite subjects. Phillipps MS.24024 & Robinson collection. (89) £28,000
— Original drawings, (8); houses, gardens & street scenes in watercolor & gouache, some heightened with gold, [China, c.1790]. 380mm by 380mm, in calf-backed bds. Including 3 woodblock prints in colors. Phillipps MS.18053 & Robinson collection. (89) £5,000

Ms, description of Court Costume of the Emperor Quianlong, from the Summer Palace at Peking, [c.1785]. 34 folios, 420mm by 409mm, in tan half mor box gilt. Comprising 67 leaves including 36 watercolor drawings of Court cos-

CHINA

tumes appropriate to an Empress-Dowager or Empress & 27 leaves of descriptive text; mtd. Phillipps MS.18054 & Robinson collection. (89) £80,000
— Ms, Di Wang Hou Lun, [On Emperors and Kings], [c.1790]. (89) £140
— Ms, extracts from Jesuit writings on aspects of Chinese life, presented to Lady Chambers by George Smith, Apr to May 1787. Phillipps MS.16867 & Robinson collection. (89) £700
— Ms, history of China & other countries in the Far East, probably compiled by a Jesuit, in Italian; [17th cent]. 400 pp, 8vo, in marbled bds. In a single hand, with table of contents in a later hand. Phillipps MS.5721 & Robinson collection. (89) £6,800
— CHINESE-LATIN VOCABULARY. - Ms, Vocabularium Sinico-Latinum, characteres circiter 1700 explicatos praebens, [early 19th cent]. About 100 pp, size not stated, in paper wraps. With phonetic transcription & index of Latin terms. Phillipps MS.7382 & Robinson collection. (89) £1,050
— HANGZHOU. - Ms, Relatione de la gran Citta del Quinsay, et del Re della China. Del Sr Cont'Ugo Contughi, 1583. 26 pp, 8vo. In a vol of "Relazioni" in a single italic hand, [late 16th cent], over 800 pp, in limp vellum. Phillipps MS.12248 & Robinson collection. (89) £2,200
— PAPER & INK. - Ms, Remarques touchant le papier de la Chine, Ecrit sur l'encre de la Chine, L'encre de la Chine, & De la maniere dont on imprime a la Chine, [18th cent]. 72 pp, folio, in bds. In a single hand, with footnotes & marginal notes. Partly copied from writings of the Jesuit Father d'Entrecolles. Phillipps MS.10129 & Robinson collection. (89) £600

Chinese Rites Controversy
[A collection of papers pertaining to the controversy & to the visit of Cardinal Maillard de Tournon to China, c.1705 to 1725, over 70 items, various sizes, sold at S on 22 Nov 1988, lot 20, for £4,500 to Loschiavo.]
[A collection of over 300 documents, oaths sworn by missionaries in accordance with Papal Bulls Ex Illa Die & Ex Quo Singulari, 1710 to 1759, over 300 pp, mostly folio, sold at S on 22 Nov 1988, lot 19, for £14,000 to Marsh.]

Ms, 370 paragraphs discussing the nature & limits of Papal authority & the authority of Papal Legates, [c.1709]. 162 pp, folio; unbound. In Latin. With related material. Phillipps MS.29734 & Robinson collection. (89) £1,100
— Ms, Compendium eorum que evenerunt in Sinis Ex.mo et Rev.mo D.D. Carolo Ambrosio Mediobarbe..., 26 Sept 1720 to 23 Mar 1721. About 80 pp, 4to, on Chinese paper. Stitched, in wraps. Day-by-day account of Patriarch Mezzabarba's visit to China from the Jesuit viewpoint. In a single hand. Phillipps MS.8104 & Robinson collection. (89) £3,500
— Ms, contemp copy of a letter instructing the superiors of the Dominican, Franciscan & Augustinian orders to observe the sentence of excommunication passed on the Bishop of Macao, 27 July 1707, & related material. Phillipps MS.8501 & Robinson collection. (89) £500
— Ms, Notizie all Santita di Nostro Signore P.P. Phillipps MS.13685 & Robinson collection. (89) £250
— Ms, Varia Scripta circa quosdam sinarum usus controversos ob Lata Sanctissimio Domino ... Innocentio P.P.XII et Sacrae Congreg[atio]ni Sancti Officii, 1697. About 290 pp, 4to. Contemp calf with the arms of Cardinal Balthasar Cenci. Copies of documents pertaining to the controversy, in a single scribal hand. Phillipps MS.5389 & Robinson collection. (89) £6,500
— LAURENTIUS DI S. MARIA, ARCHBISHOP OF GOA. - 9 Ls s, 9 Nov 1746. Each addressed to members of a different order. Requiring obedience to the Bull Ex Quo Singulari. Each sgd by c.40 missionaries who have sworn to obey the order. With a number of individual sworn oaths. About 50 pp, folio, in Middle Hill bds. Phillipps MS.22803 & Robinson collection. (89) £2,400
See also: Sala, Ilarione Bonaventura

Chirico, Giorgio de, 1888-1978
Typescript, essay, A proposito di Modernismo e di Biennale, [July 1950]. 4 pp, folio. With numerous autograph corrections; sgd. With covering ALs & English trans. (89) DM1,100
ALs, [n.d.]. (91) DM700
Autograph postcard, sgd, 8 June 1939. (88) DM380

Chisholm, Christine
Original drawings, (144), to illus Donald J. Dickie's Sent to Coventry, 1928. In ink. Various sizes. With related material. Archives of J. M. Dent & Son. (88) £1,900
— Original drawings, (49), to illus A. Archives of J. M. Dent & Son. (88) £100

Chladni, Ernst Florens Friedrich, 1756-1827
ALs, 23 July 1801. 1 p, 4to. To Rudolf Zacharias Becker. Regarding a fee to be used for charity. (90) DM1,050
— 12 Feb 1815. 2 pp, 4to. Recipient unnamed. Reporting about his losses in a fire & mentioning his scientific projects. (88) DM1,100

Chodowiecki, Daniel, 1726-1801
ALs, 3 Apr 1779. 3 pp, 8vo. To [Anton Graff]. Expressing condolences on the death of his father-in-law Georg Sulzer. (91) DM1,550
— 11 Sept 1797. 2 pp, 8vo. To Anton Graff. Requesting his port of Detmar Basse for an exhibition at the Berlin Academy. Albrecht collection. (91) SF1,800
— [n.d.]. (91) DM750

Chopin, Frederic, 1810-49
Autograph music, Berceuse for piano, Op. 57, [1843]. 2 pp, 22cm by 29cm, 14 staves each. Almost complete composition, with numerous revisions. Cortot collection. (89) DM150,000
— Autograph music, Czule serca, sketches for 2 Polish songs; 1847. 1 p, 21.8cm by 28.3cm; 14 staves. 11 bars in F minor & c.30 bars in G major. With contemp annotation by T. Kviatkovski at bottom. Repaired. (89) DM28,000
— Autograph music, Mazurka in F minor, Op. 7, no 3, sgd & dated 20 June 1831. 3 pp, 8vo; 8 staves each. Fair copy. (88) DM130,000
— Autograph music, opening 8 bars of the Etude in A flat major Op. 25, no 1, 10 May 1844. 1 p, folio. Notated on 2 systems, 2 staves each; sgd. (91) £21,000
ALs, 21 June 1838. 3 pp, 8vo. To Camille Pleyel. About pianos, his piano-playing, & an instrument ordered for [George Sand's house at] Palma. (89) £10,000
— 4 Oct [1839]. 3 pp, 8vo. To Julian Fontana. Inquiring about an apartment. Sgd Ch. In Polish with a few words in French. On George Sand's embossed stationery. Framed. With related material. (88) $9,500
— 5 Oct 1841. 3 pp, 8vo. To the Vienna music pbr, Pietro Mechetti. About the publication of various compositions. (91) $17,000
— 3 July 1842. 1 p, 4to. To Count Albert Grzymala. About Eugene Delacroix's stay at Nohant. Sgd Ch; in Polish. With autograph postscripts, sgd, by George Sand & her son Maurice. (90) DM35,000
— 31 Oct 1843. 2 pp, 8vo. To [Breitkopf & Haertel]. Sending "la petite feuille signee" & announcing new compositions. Kuenzel collection. (90) DM18,000
— [n.d., "Thursday"]. 1 p, 8vo. To an unnamed doctor. About an account, thanking for his assistance, & mentioning George Sand. (88) £6,000
— 5 Mar [1848]. 4 pp, 8vo. To [Solange Clesinger]. Informing her about his last meeting with her mother George Sand. Sgd Ch. (88) DM70,000
— [c.Apr - May 1848]. 1 p, 8vo. To [Marie de Rozieres?]. Draft, revealing his depressed mood at the suppression of the Poles. Sgd Ch. (90) £11,000
ANs, [c.1836?], "Thursday". 1 p, 8vo. To [Clara Wieck?]. Sending the Ms of his concerto as promised. With authentication by Arthur Hedley. (90) DM38,000
— [n.d.]. 1 p, 16mo, cut from larger sheet. To Mlle. de Rozieres. Informing her of an appointment. (91) £2,000
— [n.d.]. 1 p, 8vo. Recipient unnamed.

CHOPIN

"C'est bien." (89) DM4,800

Ds, [24 Nov 1836]. 1 p, 8vo. Selling the French rights to his Douze Etudes [Op. 25] to Maurice Schlesinger. With autograph note of approval. (88) DM7,000

— KWIATKOWSKI, T. - Orig drawing, port of Chopin, in pencil & colored washes; sgd twice & dated 17 Oct 1849. 28.5cm by 21.5cm; framed. (90) £1,600

— WINTERHALTER, FRANZ XAVIER. - Original drawing, port of Chopin, sgd & dated 2 May 1847. In pencil. Mtd; overall size 32cm by 25.5cm. With related material. (88) DM50,000

Chopin, Frederic, 1810-49 —& Others

[A 4to leaf, sgd by Chopin, 28 Sept 1835, also sgd & partly inscr by Chateaubriand, Meyerbeer, Canova, Ampere, Rachel, & others, 1835 to 1840, sold at S on 17 May 1991, lot 207, for £3,600 to Macnutt.]

Chouteau, Auguste, 1749-1829

ANs, 14 May 1807. Alexander collection. (90) $270

Ds, 2 May 1811. (88) $210

— 3 Dec 1823. (91) $250

Check, 18 Aug 1819. (88) $140

Chouteau, Auguste, 1749-1929. See: Slavery

Christian, Markgraf von Brandenburg-Bayreuth, 1581-1655

Ds, [c.3 June] 1593. Schroeder collection. (89) DM850

Christian Ernst, Markgraf von Brandenburg-Bayreuth, 1644-1712

Ls, 15 Dec 1675. (88) DM500

Christian IV, King of Denmark, 1577-1648

Ls, 22 Dec 1631. 1 p, folio. To Hans Georg von Arnim. Expressing satisfaction about recipient's good will. (91) DM1,200

Christian IX, King of Denmark, 1818-1906

Ds, 23 Mar 1875. Byer collection. (90) $275

AMERICAN BOOK PRICES CURRENT

Christian VIII, King of Denmark, 1786-1848

ALs, 12 May 1820 & 4 Mar 1828. (90) DM450

— 14 Dec 1822. (88) DM240

Christie, Agatha, 1891-1976

Autograph Ms (2), short story, An Episode of May 1st, sgd, 8 pp, 4to, in a Ms vol of The Monthly Magazine with 6 stories in other hands; & poem, L'Amitie, sgd, 29 June 1905, 3 pp, 8vo, in an album with other poems & illusts. (91) £1,300

ALs, 15 Sept [1958]. (91) $300

— 26 May [n.y.]. (90) $1,000

Ls, 31 Aug 1963. (90) £170

— 19 Feb 1975. (91) $350

— 19 Feb 1975. (90) $700

Christina, Queen of Sweden, 1626-89

ALs, 13 Oct 1652. (91) $110

AL, [spring 1687]. (89) DM1,000

Ls, 30 Aug 1645. Byer collection. (90) $600

— 22 June 1667. (91) £650

— 3 Oct 1685. 2 pp, 4to. To Conte Enea Silvio Caprara. Congratulating him on the capture of Neuhaeusel & recommending Count Marscian. (91) DM1,600

Ds, 4 June 1653. 2 pp, folio. Appointment of Du Plessis Saumaite as captain in her guard. In German. Orig conjugate leaf included, detached. (88) DM1,500

— 10 Mar 1654. (89) DM1,000

Christoph, Herzog von Wuerttemberg, 1515-68

Ls, 29 May 1554. 1 p, folio. To Count Ludwig von Oettingen. Suggesting changes to the draft of a letter submitted for his approval. (91) DM1,300

— 16 May 1564. 1 p, folio. To his treasury at Stuttgart. Giving instructions for transfer of funds to himself & his family. With related material. (89) DM1,600

Christy, Howard Chandler, 1873-1952

Collection of 11 A Ls s, Ls & 2 telegrams, 1935 to 1950. (88) $200

ALs, 8 Mar 1945. (88) $70

Photograph, sgd & inscr, 21 Aug [19]37. (88) $55

Chronicles
Ms, Les Grandes Chroniques de France. [Paris, c.1400-10]. 312 leaves in 2 vols (of 3), vellum, 409mm by 276mm. 18th-cent French mor gilt bdg. In a handsome lettre batarde. With 18 large illuminated initials with full-length bar borders & 10 miniatures by the Virgil Master, 3 in historiated initials. Many medieval sidenotes. (89) £150,000

Church, Frederick Stuart, 1842-1924
ALs, 16 Feb 1878. (91) $270
ANs, 17 July 1906. (91) $175

Churchill, Sir Winston L. S., 1874-1965
[2 memoranda by Churchill (1 autograph), initialled, with related memorandum sent to him, 8 June to 15 July 1919, 3 pp, folio & 4to, about regimental dress, sold at S on 20 July 1989, lot 274, for £1,400 to Fine Art Society.]
[A group of 3 memoranda as Secretary of State for War, 5 July to 22 Oct 1919, 5 pp, folio & 4to, regarding aliens & Col. Grigs's pay, including 2 autograph endorsements, sgd, sold at S on 20 July 1989, lot 272, for £1,000 to Fine Art Society.]
[An official file containing 17 minutes & memoranda relating to the military command of the London district, 1919 & 1920, 21 pp, various sizes, partly with autograph additions & initialled by Churchill, sold at S on 14 Dec 1989, lot 238, for £1,300 to Budden Books.]
[A group of 7 confidential memoranda relating to the Territorial Army, 1 Apr to 15 Aug 1920, 10 pp, various sizes, annotated & initialled by Churchill, sold at S on 14 Dec 1989, lot 239, for £800 to Budden Books.]
[2 typed memoranda, initialled, to the Secretary for Munitions, with related material, 22 to 24 July 1920, 7 pp, folio & 4to, regarding a delay in issuing revolvers to police in Ireland, sold at S on 20 July 1989, lot 276, for £2,800 to Fine Art Society.]
[2 memoranda (1 autograph), initialled, [1920], 2 pp, 4to & 8vo, complaining about the length of a paper, & requesting reasons, sold at S on 20 July 1989, lot 282, for £1,000 to Fine Art Society.]
[A collection comprising 3 port sketches (2 pencil, 1 chalk) sgd by the artist Swamy & Churchill, & photograph, sgd & dated July 1939, sold at C on 21 June 1989, lot 88, for £2,600 to Joseph.]
[A copy of an illuminated Ms of a script broadcast by the Egyptian State Broadcasting for Churchill's birthday in 1941, presented to the compiler Edith Howitt by the Marconi Company, 18 pp, folio, in calf bdg, sold at S on 19 July 1990, lot 253, for £400 to Houle.]
Original drawing, sketch of a pig, drawn blindfold, sgd & dated 12 July 1923. In the album of Sir Alfred Ewing, containing over 100 similar sketches, c.1922 to 1927. With related material. (88) £1,600
Typescript, memorandum about rioting in India & Egypt, addressed to the Military Secretary, 22 June 1919. 1 p, 4to. Initialled. (89) £1,400
— Typescript, memorandum, initialled, 24 Mar 1920, to H. (89) £600
Collection of ALs & Ls, 15 Mar 1901 & 23 Apr 1902. 5 pp, 8vo. To J. Travis-Clegg. About recommendations for the Leesfield Vicarage, & pledging to support him as Party Chairman at Oldham. (90) £1,500
— Collection of 2 A Ls s & Ls, 4 Apr 1902 to 12 Jan 1904. 10 pp, 8vo. To Mr. Strong, Librarian of the House of Lords. Requesting information on various subjects. (88) $3,500
— Collection of 27 A Ls s & 38 Ls s (1 partly autograph), 11 June 1902 to 9 June 1904; c.185 pp, 4to & 8vo. To J. Travis-Clegg, Chairman of the Oldham Conservative Association. Important letters chronicling his political problems as MP for Oldham. With related material, c.100 pp. (88) £35,000
— Collection of 2 A Ls s & Ls, 20 May 1908 to 20 Sept 1910. To C. D. O. Shakespear. Promising to look into the case of the ship Worcester, alluding to the election in South Africa, congratulating on his promotion, etc. With related material. (90) £2,600
— Collection of ALs & Ls, [c.1915-16] & 8 Jan 1921. (88) £540
ALs, 9 Sept [189]6. (88) £650
— 30 Oct 1899. 2 pp, 8vo. To Sir George

CHURCHILL

Allen. Putting off his series of letters for the Pioneer. (91) $4,800
— 20 Dec 1900. 2 pp, 8vo. To Major Pond. Discussing the possibility of cancelling lecture dates in America because of "low profits". (91) DM3,400
— 14 Oct 1907. 5 pp, 8vo. To his brother Jack. Expressing anxiety over his investments, & describing his travelling to Africa. (88) £1,700
— 4 Sept 1908. 1 p, 8vo. To [Lillie Langtry]. Thanking for a present. (89) DM2,700
— 9 Dec 1908. (89) £700
— 24 Sept [1910]. (88) £380
— 30 May 1911. 2 pp, 8vo. To King George V. Thanking for congratulations on the birth of his son. (88) £2,000
— 11 Aug 1914. 2 pp, 8vo. To Field Marshall Kitchener. Discussing the case of a man who should be courtmartialled. (89) £4,000
— 18 Aug 1916. (88) £350
— 27 Nov 1916. (88) £480
— 26 Sept 1917. (88) £1,000
— 13 Feb 1918. 1 p, 8vo. To Sir Robert Perks. Thanking him for a letter. (91) $2,200
— 31 July 1918. (88) £420
— 4 Sept 1918. (88) £450
— 27 Jan 1921. 4 pp, 8vo. To Clare Sheridan. Explaining his feelings about her trip to Russia. (91) £2,800
— 16 Dec 1921. 1 p, 8vo. To Tim Healy. Concerning a position for Capt. Freeman in the West African Customs Service. Matted with a port. (90) $1,600
— 17 Feb 1937. 2 pp, 8vo. To Pauline Astor (Mrs. Herbert Spender-Clay). Expressing condolences on the death of her husband. With a substantial collection of related papers. (88) £2,000

Collection of 3 Ls s & telegram, 1932 & 1933. Length not stated. To Lillian Calli. Thanking for her nursing care, discussing his health, etc. With a copy of 1st Ed of his Thoughts and Adventures, 1932, sgd & inscr to Nurse Calli. (89) £2,200
— Collection of 3 Ls s & telegram, 1946 to 1956. 3 pp, 4to, & telegram. To L. C. Graham-Dixon. Regretting his retirement, thanking for professional advice, urging him to accept an invitation. 1 Ls with autograph postscript. (89) £1,050
— Collection of Ls & photograph sgd, 26 Feb 1953 & [c.1940]. 1 p, 4to, & c.155mm by 110mm. To J. C. Findlater, expressing thanks & enclosing a photograph for the Legion of Frontiersmen. Photograph framed; Ls mtd on back. (91) £1,400

Series of 6 Ls s, 1 Jan 1904 to 27 Feb 1924. 12 pp, 4to & 8vo. To different recipients. About a variety of matters. With related material. (89) £3,400
— Series of 9 Ls s, [n.d.]. Length not stated. To A. L. Ball of Lloyd's Bank. Regarding financial matters. With related material. (88) £2,500

Ls s (2), 12 Dec 1948 & 13 Apr 1950. 2 pp, 4to. To Desmond Leslie. Thanking for a copy of his book, & declining a permission requested. (89) £1,200
— Ls s (2), 9 Dec 1958 & 1 Dec 1961. (88) £320

Ls, 11 June 1902. 14 pp, 8vo. To J. Travis-Clegg. Explaining his free trade principles & his opposition to the tariff reforms proposed by Joseph Chamberlain. (90) £1,600
— 22 Aug 1903. (88) £350
— 8 Oct 1903. (88) £350
— 9 July [1908-1910]. (90) £450
— 27 July 1910. 1 p, 4to. To King George V. Recommending 3 miners for an award. Endorsed by George V. With related material. (91) $1,600
— 10 Mar 1913. (88) £420
— 8 Dec 1917. (91) £340
— 11 Jan 1919. (91) £700
— 13 July 1919. (89) £1,000
— 25 Feb 1922. (89) £500
— [1922]. (88) £380
— 25 July 1923. (91) $900
— 4 Dec 1927. 1 p, 4to. To Curtis Brown. Informing him of his decision to write a 4th vol to The World Crisis. (91) £1,600
— 2 May 1929. (90) £400
— 10 June 1929. (88) £300
— 24 Nov 1929. (90) £500
— 16 Mar 1930. (90) £520

1987 - 1991 · AUTOGRAPHS & MANUSCRIPTS · CHURCHILL

— 14 Nov 1930. (88) £300
— 11 July 1931. (89) £1,000
— 24 Dec 1931. (89) £1,000
— 30 June 1932. 1 p, 4to. To Sir Treshem Lever. About the use of The World Crisis as a textbook at Sandhurst. (91) $2,200
— 15 Dec 1933. (88) DM950
— 20 Feb 1934. (88) £380
— 1 Mar 1934. (88) £420
— 11 Aug 1939. (88) £280
— 15 Oct 1944. 1 p, 4to. To Stalin. Draft, suggesting a meeting to discuss a solution of the "Polish troubles". With autograph revisions & subscription. (89) £16,500
— 18 Apr 1945. 1 p, 4to. To the Archbishop of Canterbury. Declining an invitation to his enthronement. (91) $2,600
— 15 Dec 1945. (89) £600
— 13 Sept 1946. (90) £600
— 21 May 1947. (91) £350
— 21 Nov 1947. (91) £480
— 10 Aug 1948. (88) £780
— 29 Oct 1950. (90) £440
— 18 Mar 1951. (89) £450
— 9 July 1952. (88) £450
— 4 Sept 1955. (90) £820
— 9 June 1962. (88) £380
— 24 Sept 1963. (89) $800

ANs, 26 Dec 1919. Isham collection. (89) $750

Ns, 31 Oct 1930. (88) $600

Ds s (2)[n.d.]. (88) £420

Ds, 19 Aug 1919. (89) £850
— 9 June 1938. 2 pp, folio. Contract with George G. Harrap for Europe since the Russian Revolution. Also sgd by Harrap. (91) £3,200

Autograph endorsement, initialled, 28 Apr 1920. On a memorandum sent to him by the Department of Munitions and Ordnance, 26 Apr 1920; 7 lines insisting that the garrison in Palestine should be reduced. 1 p, folio. With related memorandum on verso. (89) £3,000

Cut signature, 31 Jan 1895. (91) $350
— Anr, [n.d.]. (91) $550

Group photograph, [n.d.], 144mm by 197mm. Showing Churchill, George V, & Lords Portal, Alanbrooke, & Cunningham. Sgd by each. With anr, showing same group without Churchill. (88) £1,800
— Anr, on board ship with Dudley Pound, Viscount Cherwell, John Martin, & others, [c.1940-43]. 8 by 10 inches (image). Sgd on mount; also sgd by others. (91) £1,100
— Anr, sgd, [n.d.]. (90) £750

Menu, sgd, 23 Feb 1924. (89) £170
— Anr, sgd, 28 Jan 1925, for "Chingford Conservative and Unionist Association Complimentary Dinner" to Churchill. (89) £300

Photograph, sgd, [c.1895-99]. 7.5 by 4.75 inches; mtd, overall size 10.5 by 7.5 inches. Half-length; in uniform. (88) £2,000
— Anr, [1898]. 8 by 5 inches. In tropical uniform. (91) £2,400
— Anr, [c.1900]. 12cm by 8cm. Sgd on mount. (90) DM1,300
— Anr, [n.d.]. (88) £720
— Anr, [1912 or earlier]. 11.25 by 9 inches (image). Sgd on mount. In military uniform, wearing medals. (91) £2,400
— Anr, [c.13 Nov 1941]. (91) £880
— Anr, [1941]. (90) £600
— Anr, [26 July 1945]. (88) £800
— Anr, [Nov] 1945. (88) £620
— Anr, [c.1945]. 6.5 by 8 inches. Half length, seated. Sgd on mount. (90) $1,500
— Anr, 1948. 11 by 9.5 inches. On a horse. (91) £1,200
— Anr, [n.d.]. (88) £650
— Anr, [n.d.]. (88) £700
— Anr, [n.d.]. (91) £500
— Anr, [n.d.]. (91) £600
— Anr, [n.d.]. (91) $1,000
— Anr, [n.d.]. Framed; overall size 17.5 by 14 inches. Sgd on mount. (91) £1,400
— Anr, [n.d.]. Postcard size. Half-length, as young member of Parliament. (89) $1,500

Photograph, sgd & inscr, [1944 or later]. 200mm by 156mm. Inscr to Kay Summersby. (91) $6,000
— Anr, [n.d.]. 8.25 by 6 inches. Inscr to Alice [Keppel]. (91) £1,400

Ptd photograph, sgd, 1959. (91) $600

Signature, 1900. (89) £300

CHURCHILL

— Anr, 23 June 1915. (91) £300
— Anr, 1950. (90) £680
— Anr, on mount of a photograph of Frank Salisbury's port of Churchill & the "Panel of Praise" commemorating British fortitude in World War II; [n.d.]. (90) £700
— PRITCHETT, VICTOR SAWDON. - Autograph Ms, draft of his review of Randolph Churchill's biography of his father, [c.1966]. 7 pp, 4to. (88) £250
— SWAMY. - Orig drawing, brown chalk sketch of Churchill, [n.d.]. 285mm by 230mm. Sgd by both. (89) £1,200

**Churchill, Sir Winston L. S., 1874-1965
—& Others**
[The signatures of Churchill & over 40 others, including Roosevelt, Mountbatten, Anthony Eden, etc. at the Quebec Conference, Aug 1943, on flyleaf of a copy of William Hugh Coverdale's Tadoussac Then and Now. 1942, sold at S on 19 July 1990, lot 256, for £2,400 to Wilson.]
Signature, Dec 1944. (89) £700
— Anr, on illuminated calligraphic Ms by William Bromage, Sept 1945, entitled "The Child's Rights, The Declaration of Geneva...1924". Also sgd by Montgomery & Eisenhower. 12.25 by 16 inches; framed. (88) £3,200

**Churchill, Sir Winston L. S., 1874-1965
—&
Roosevelt, Franklin D., 1882-1945**
[A ptd souvenir card, c.9 by 7 inches, with Longfellow's verse "Sail on, o ship of state...", being Roosevelt's message to Churchill, Jan 1941, sgd by both, [Aug 1941], framed, sold at S on 15 Dec, lot 230, for £2,000.]

Churchill, Winston L. S., Sir, 1874-1965.
See: Roosevelt, Franklin D. & Churchill
See also: Wilhelm II & Churchill

Cicero, Marcus Tullius, 106-43 B.C.
Ms, De Amicitia, Paradoxica, De Senectute, & Somnium Scipionis. [Florence, c.1350-70]. 46 leaves & flyleaves, vellum, 249mm by 160mm, in contemp Florentine blindstamped bdg of dark brown goatskin over bevelled wooden bds. In dark brown ink in a regular humanistic minuscule with tall ascenders. With 4 large white-vine illuminated initials. Wormed. (88) £4,000
— Ms, De Officiis. [Florence, 1415-20]. 97 leaves, vellum, 230mm by 155mm, in contemp [Florentine?] blind-tooled panelled brown mor over wooden bds. In brown ink in a fine humanistic bookhand. With 6 large illuminated initials. Phillipps MS 12278. (89) £38,000
— Ms, De Senectute, De Amicitia, & Paradoxa. [Rome, c.1440-50]. 40 leaves (2 blank) & 2 flyleaves, vellum, 241mm by 171mm. Extra modern bdg by Jean de Gonay. In a slightly sloping humanistic cursive by 2 scribes. With 8 small illuminated initials, 4 large white-vine initials, & white-vine armorial panel. (91) £15,000
— Ms, De Senectute, De Amicitia, & other texts. [Verona, c.1470]. 60 leaves & 2 flyleaves, vellum, 203mm by 133mm. Contemp blindstamped brown tanned lea over thin wooden bds. In a slightly cursive humanistic minuscule. With 2 small illuminated initials & 3 large white-vine initials. (91) £15,000
— Ms, Epistolae ad Familiares. [Florence, c.1425-35]. 156 leaves, vellum, 345mm by 245mm. Contemp bdg of wooden bds later covered with vellum. In a fine regular round humanistic minuscule. With 13 very fine historiated whitevine initials in burnished gold including animals & putti. Some poems added in later hands. (89) £40,000
— Ms, Epistolae ad Familiares. (91) £500
— Ms, Epistolae ad Familiares. [Santa Vittoria in Matenano, 1454]. 91 leaves (some missing), vellum, 236mm by 166mm, in early 19th-cent French mor gilt in fitted case. In brown ink in a small slightly sloping mostly cursive humanistic bookhand by Bonifacio de Lazzareni. With large & very large illuminated white-vine initial & 1 full border. (88) £28,000
— Ms, In Verrem, with 3 texts about St. Jerome. [Northern Italy, c.1450 & c.1475]. 88 leaves, vellum, 285mm by 205mm. Old yellow-green velvet over

pastebds. In a semi-gothic script & a humanistic minuscule. (91) £3,800
— Ms, Pro Caecina, De Lege Agraria, Pro Rabirio Postumo, & Pro Rabirio Perduellionis. [Italy, Lombardy?, mid-15th cent]. 86 leaves, vellum, 276mm by 203mm, in modern mottled bds. In dark brown ink in a calligraphic humanistic minuscule. Spaces left blank for initials. (88) £4,000
— Ms, Tuscularum Disputationes. [Padua?, c.1451-63]. 129 leaves & flyleaf, vellum, 280mm by 183mm. Early 19th-cent red-brown velvet bdg. In a very skilful, rather joined near italic hand. With 5 small burnished gold initials, 5 extremely large white-vine illuminated initials, & panel border. Illuminated for Moses Buffarello, Bishop of Pola & Belluno. Abbey collection. (89) £65,000

Cimarosa, Domenico, 1749-1801
Autograph music, aria, Figlia cara benedetta, from his opera Il fanatico burlato; 46 bars in full score, [c.1787]. (90) £750
— Autograph music, fragment of an operatic scene, comprising an aria "Ojme! Che incendio!", in full score; [n.d.]. (89) £800
— Autograph music, fragment; quartet from an opera, beginning Oh Dio che affanno; [n.d.]. 2 pp, 22cm by 29.5cm, 10 staves each. (88) DM3,400
— Autograph music, opera, I traci amanti, fragment; [c.1793?]. 2 pp, 23cm by 28.5cm; 12 staves each. 11 bars from the sextet Guarda lieto soggiorno, in full score. (89) DM2,600
— Autograph music, scene & recitative, Che incanto e questo?, [n.d.] (91) £600

Cioran, Emile M.
Series of 8 A Ls s, 1981 to 1987. (91) DM600

Citroen, Andre, 1878-1935
Ls, 22 Oct 1923. (89) DM210

Civil War, American
[A series of 7 letters, 15 Oct 1860 to 11 Aug 1861, from a soldier's wife to her mother, mostly from New Mexico, sold at rf on 5 Dec, lot 10, for $425.]
[Smith, Watson. - A collection of 2 notebooks containing a biography & anr 29 items relating to Lieut. Commander Smith's career in the U.S. Navy, 1841 to 1864, sold at P on 26 Oct 1988, lot 63, for $1,600.]
[A soldier's letter, 30 Mar 1862, on illus letter sheet, Views of the Fair Grounds, St. Louis, Mo., sold at rf on 5 Dec, lot 57, for $80.]
[Confederate Prisoners of War. - An album kept by T. H. Huttory, containing more than 200 signatures of Confederate prisoners at Fort Warren, Mass., June & July 1862, 70 pp, 4to, in black lea gilt, sold at P on 31 Oct 1989, lot 48, for $5,500.]
[A collection of material containing muster rolls, receipts, returns of ordnance & stores, circulars, passes, etc., mostly 1862 to 1865, sold at pn on 17 Sept, lot 532, for £320 to Paper.]
[A collection of c.70 letters & documents relating to Union & Confederate forces sold at S on 21 Sept, lot 137, for £180 to Roppel.]
[A collection of 13 Union soldier's letters, some on patriotic letter sheets, sold at rf on 12 Mar, lot 4, for $150.]
[A collection of 28 Union soldier's letters, mostly from Arkansas, 1863 & 1864, sold at rf on 12 Mar, lot 5, for $350.]
[A collection of 33 carte size photographs of Union Generals sold at rf on 10 Sept 1988, lot 10, for $500.]
[2 A Ls s by Union Generals W. T. Sherman, 18 Aug 1880, & G. B. McClellan, 11 Oct 1871 sold at rf on 4 June 1988, lot 33, for $210.]
Ms, diary, Feb to 30 Oct 1864. (88) $270
Letter, 8 June 1865. (88) £300
Document, 27 Mar 1865. (91) $300
— 53D INFANTRY REGIMENT OF INDIANA VOLUNTEERS. - 30 documents, Aug 1861 to Sept 1864. Various sizes. Including commissions, discharges, requisitions, etc. (89) £400
— ABITT, COL. GEORGE. - Autograph Ms, diary written as officer of the 46th Virginia Regiment, Company B, 1863-64. Length not stated; faulty bdg. (90) $550
— BRADLEY, CAPT. THOMAS, & OTHERS. - 77 A Ls s, 1861 to 1867. Length not stated. To Sarah Kendall. Eloquent

descriptions of camp life & battles. (90) $2,500
— BROWN, WILLIAM J. - Autograph Ms, diary, 21 June to Aug 1863. Length not stated, 8vo. Recording his service with the Pennsylvania militia. (89) $450
— BURCKMYER, CAPT. - ALs, [c.Apr 1864]. 6 pp, size not stated. To his wife in Paris. Relating war news from Charleston, S.C. (90) $2,000
— BUTLER, GEORGE H. - Diary of member of 12th Wis. Vol. Infantry from Jan 1862 to Dec 1863. In orig mor wallet wrap. (91) $900
— CAMPBELL, CAPT. M. H. - ALs, 16 Dec 1862. 1 p, 8vo. To C. B. Johnson. Requesting supplies. Alexander collection. (90) $105
— CAMPBELL, JOHN PRESTON. - 45 A Ls s, 24 Jan 1863 to 5 June 1865. Length not stated. To his family. Letters from a Union soldier. (90) $1,100
— CHAMBERS, GEORGE W., JR. - Diary of a member of Company E of the 90th Regiment of Pennsylvania Volunteers. 1862-63. 124 pp, 8vo, in cloth. In pencil. (91) $1,800
— CHASE, LIEUT. J. B. - ADs, 30 Aug 1861. 1 p, 4to. List of Union soldiers turning in muskets for new arms at Chain Bridge near Washington, D.C. (89) $55
— DUNCAN, BLANTON. - ALs, 15 May 1861. 2 pp, 4to. To "Gen. Benjamin Franklin Butler, Viceroy of Lincoln for the Province of Maryland." Daring him to attack the Kentuckians under his command. With postscripts by Bradley E. Johnson & Duncan. In case. (88) $650
— EDMUNDSON, LIEUT. J. W. - Autograph Ms, Report of the wounded and sick federal prisoners of war, 9 May 1864. 3 pp, 4to. (90) $160
— FORBES, C.V.G. - Diary of member of Company G, New York Volunteers. May 1861-Apr 1862. 26 pp of short daily notations plus 27 pages listing members of the company. (91) $425
— FULSOM, R. W. - ALs, 2 Mar 1862. 1 p, 4to. To Chief Leflore. Regarding purchase of supplies. Alexander collection. (90) $80
— GRAY, FRED(?) P. - Autograph Ms, diary, Jan to Dec 1862. 149 pp, 5 by 3 inches, in full lea. Daily entries, recording thoughts & events in the field. Including 3 tintypes. (90) $230
— HARRIS, JUDGE J. W. M. - A large collection of correspondence, including c.100 letters to his wife, diaries, poems, letters to & from his brother Gen. Nathaniel Harris, etc., many items relating to the War, sold at rce on 28 July 1988, lot 565, for $9,500. 88
— HENRY, J. Y. - 16 A Ls s, 1861 to 3 Apr 1865. Length not stated. To Major D. S. Titus. Commenting about the war & politics from the vantage point of an Illinois railroad official. With related material. (90) $800
— HILL, JOHN R. - Autograph Ms, diary recording service in the 100th Infantry of NY Volunteers, 12 Feb to 27 Oct 1864. About 90 pp, 12mo, sewn into cloth covers. Mostly in pencil. Def. (90) $350
— IVIDAN [?], W. H. - ALs, 29 Mar 1861. 4 pp, size not stated. To a West Point classmate. Patriotic letter, & describing work on Fort Abercrombie in Dakota Territory. (88) $150
— JONES, ANNIE. - Ds, 16 Nov 1863. Size not stated. Parole issued by the District of Columbia; sgd below her statement. (89) $550
— KANNADY, LIEUT. COL. J. R. - ALs, 15 May 1861. 2 pp, size not stated. To John Ross. Asking if the Cherokee will support the Union or the Confederacy. Alexander collection. (90) $625
— LEAVENWORTH, FREDERICK. - ALs, 27 May 1861. 2 pp, size not stated. To his father, Rev. A. J. Leavenworth. Describing military preparations in Arkansas. (88) $240
— LEE'S SURRENDER. - A group of 4 items by Gen. J. G. Barnard & Mrs. Lucy Ord Mason referring to the scene at Lee's surrender sold at wa on 17 Oct, lot 213, for $150. 88
— LIBBY PRISON. - Ms, "Morning Report" for Nov 1864. 1 p, folio. Listing arrivals, transfers, etc. (91) $180
— MARSHALL, CHARLES. - A collection of material from his files, relating to R.E. Lee & the war, 1863 to 1901, sold at sg on 24 Mar 1988, lot 118, for $225. 88
— MARSHALL, CHARLES. - Autograph Ms, history of the Confederacy & its mil-

itary & political strategy, 3 Mar 1877. 75 pp, size not stated. Originally intended as draft of a letter to the Count of Paris. With related material. (88) $2,400
— McKendry, William. - 86 A Ls s, 1862 to 1865. To his wife & son. Reporting about his life on the U.S.S. Winona & other ships. With 50 A Ls s by Caroline (Caddie) McKendry to her husband, & further related material. (89) $2,000
— Miller, Henry J. - Fair copy, sgd, of a portion of a diary kept by Miller detailing th events of July 3-5, 1863, while Miller served as a medical steward in Company D, 142nd Regiment of Pennsylvania Volunteers. With extensive notes on the loss of life & the condition of wounded on the battlefield at Gettysburg. 7 pp, Folio. (91) $550
— Peck, Edward. - 42 A Ls s, 1861 to 1864. Length not stated. To his family in Bridgeport, Conn. Reporting from the Southern front. With related material. (90) $1,200
— Pendleton, Gen. William Nelson. - Ms, detailed account of the role of artillery in the campaigns of Lee's Army of Northern Virginia, [c.1865-69]. 30 pp (10 autograph), folio & 8vo. Sgd at end. (88) $1,100
— Reno, Marcus Albert. - ALs, 26 Aug 1864. 1 p, 8vo. To Brig. Gen. Custer. Instructing him to move his brigade to Shepherdstown. Carbon copy. (91) $650
— Roberts, William. - 17 A Ls s, 1862 & 1863. Length not stated. To his sister Annie in Maine. Reporting from camp, about a trip to Washington, war news, etc. (90) $550
— Scull, Capt. Gideon. - Ms, letterbook containing copies of letters sent as Union Supply Officer at Hilton Head, S.C., 17 Oct 1861 to 24 Oct 1862. Over 200 pp, 4to, in marbled covers. In a secretarial hand. (89) $200
— Seminole Indians. - ALs, 9 June 1865, 1 p, 4to, of Confederate States Seminole Agent J. S. Murrow to Col. C. B. Johnson, inquiring about the continuation of agreements with Seminole Indians in Oklahoma Territory. (91)

$450
— Shaw, Sergeant Francis M. - Ms, diary, 1864. 92 pp, 76mm by 122mm. Worn lea bdg. Recording experiences at Andersonville Prison & elsewhere. In pencil. (88) $650
— Sherwood, Frederick. - Autograph Ms, journal, 1 Jan 1863 to 1865. 240 pp, 8vo. Union soldier's diary. (90) $1,200
— Shiras, Alexander E. - ALs, 20 Oct 1864. 2 pp, 8vo. To "Patrick". Concerning recipient's accounts. (91) $100
— Skinner, Theodore Henry. - 9 A Ls s, 10 July 1864 to 16 Apr 1865. 50 pp, size not stated. To his family in England. Describing his service in the Army of Northern Virginia, etc. With related material. (88) £420
— Sorrel, Gilbert M. - ADs, 11 May 1862. 1 p, 4to. By command of Major Gen. Longstreet, special order addressed to Major Gen. D. H. Hill; drilling instructions. (90) $1,600
— St. John, Isaac Munroe. - ALs, 2 June 1876. 1 p, 4to. To Col. Charles Marshall. Transmitting 2 items concerning the Amelia incident. With related material. (88) $475
— Thompson, Brig. Gen. M. Jeff. - ALs, 27 Jan [18]62. 1 p, 4to. To Col. Ross. Requesting information about prisoners captured at Bloomfield. Alexander collection. (90) $525
— Thompson, M. Jeff. - ADs, 4 Oct [18]61. 1 p, 4to. Appointment for William Hall as Post Commissary at New Madrid. Repaired. (88) $325
— U.S.S. Hale. - 86 documents, 1863 to 1865. Length not stated. Various paymaster's Mss, including returns, invoices, requisitions, etc. (90) $220
— Vedder, Timothy. - Series of 43 A Ls s, 1861 to 1863. Mostly 8vo. Describing his service with a regiment of NY volunteers & the war in Virginia. With related material. (89) $1,000
— Walker, Col. Tandy. - 2 Ds s, 4 May 1862. Size not stated. Receipts for quilts for a Choctaw & Chickasaw regiment. Alexander collection. (90) $280
— White, James. - Series of 12 A Ls s, 1862 to 1864. Length not stated. To his family in Connecticut. Reporting

about his experiences in the Southern campaigns, his capture, imprisonment, etc. With related material. (89) $500
— WILLIAMS, GEORGE. - 106 A Ls s, Oct 1862 to May 1865. 8vo. To his sister Lillias. Letters by a musician in the 123d Ohio Voluntary Infantry. With a photograph & further related material. (89) $2,200

Clarence, Albert Victor, Duke of, 1864-92
ALs, 14 May 1872. (91) £100

Clark, Abraham, Signer from New Jersey
Ds, 18 Mar 1774. (89) $450

Clark, Frederick Scotson, 1840-83
Autograph Ms, journal, 9 May to 15 Sept 1872. (89) £100

Clark, George Rogers, 1752-1818
Ds, 23 Sept 1781. (90) $900
— 23 Sept 1781. (91) $900

Clark, Mark W., 1896-1984. See: Eisenhower, Dwight D. & Clark

Clark, William, 1770-1838
ALs, 6 Sept 1808. 4 pp, folio. To Sec of War Henry Dearborn. Reporting from his expedition to build a fort & trading post near the mouth of the Osage River. Imperf. Pforzheimer collection. (90) $22,000
— 24 Jan 1818. 3 pp, 4to. To [Sec of War John C. Calhoun]. Giving his ideas about Indian relations. Pforzheimer collection. (90) $4,250
— 25 July 1818. 5 pp, 4to. To Sec of War John C. Calhoun. Proposing a new scheme to improve Indian trade. Pforzheimer collection. (90) $8,000
Ds, [13 Aug 1814]. Alexander collection. (90) $700
— 7 July 1817. 3 pp, folio. Official transcript of an indenture. Clark, as Governor of the Missouri Territory, certifies the authoritiy of the 2 signing justices & Chief Justice C. Beebe, ordering that the territorial seal be affixed. (91) $1,100
— 16 Sept 1817. 2 pp, 4to. Deposition. (88) $1,400
— 7 May 1827. Alexander collection. (90) $750

Clarke, Harry
Original drawings, (3), preparatory ink cover designs for Lennox Robinson's Crabbed Youth and Age, and The Round Table, 1924. (90) £1,000
Original drawing, tailpiece for Goethe's Faust, 1925. (88) £450
— Original drawing, "The Last Hour of the Night", gaunt figure above buildings destroyed by fire; preparatory pencil drawing to illus Dublin of the Future, 1922. (90) £400
— Original drawing, to illus The Dying Patriot by James Elroy Flecker. 1920. 249mm by 190mm, in ink, sgd twice, framed. (88) £1,500
— Original drawing, to illus The Fidler of Dooney by W. B. Yeats. 249mm by 189mm, in ink, sgd, framed. (88) £2,200

Clarke, Henri Jacques Guillaume, Duc de Feltre, 1765-1818
ALs, 23 Feb 1807. (88) DM650
— 16 May 1807. (91) $80
Ls, 31 May 1812. (89) DM300

Clarke, Maud Umfreyville
Original drawings, (48), to illus her own Nature's Own Gardens, 1907. In watercolor. Initialled. Mostly 488mm by 304mm. Archives of J. M. Dent & Son. (88) £4,200

Clary, Desiree, 1777-1860. See: Desideria, King of Sweden, 1777-1860

Claudel, Paul, 1868-1955
Autograph Ms, poem, beginning "ami! encore un ideogramme", [n.d.]. (90) DM320
— Autograph Ms, poem, Nativite; [n.d.]. (89) DM400
ALs, 15 May 1930. (90) DM280

Claudia de Medicis, Archduchess of Leopold V of Austria, 1604-48
Ls, 25 Oct 1645. (89) DM220

Claudius, Hermann, 1878-1980
Autograph Ms, essay, Zwischen Frankfurt und Leipzig, [n.d.]. (90) DM270
Autograph transcript, poem, Urians Reise um die Welt 1915, [1915]. (88) DM440

Claudius, Matthias, 1740-1815
ALs, 25 Mar 1794. 1 p, 8vo. Recipient unnamed. Sending 6 copies of a work. (90) DM1,300
— 30 June 1804. 4 pp, 4to. To his son Friedrich. Advising him to study the Greek language, & sending family news. Sgd MC. With related material. (90) DM5,500
Autograph sentiment, 8 Oct 1814. (91) DM540

Clauren, Heinrich, Pseud. of Carl Heun, 1771-1854
ALs, 17 May 1794. (90) DM300

Clausewitz, Karl von, 1780-1831
ALs, 12 Nov 1831. 2 pp, 4to. To Prince August of Prussia. Sending his work about the Italian campaign of 1796. With related material. (90) DM4,400
Ls, 14 Mar 1816. 1 p, folio. To Graf von Borke. About a pension for a disabled soldier. Schroeder collection. (89) DM1,800
— 12 July 1819. 1 p, folio. To Minister of War von Boyen. Notifying him of the death of J. G. K. Chr. Kiesewetter. (91) DM1,300

Clay, Cassius Marcellus. See: Muhammad Ali

Clay, Clement Claiborne, 1816-82
ALs, 21 Aug 1865. (91) $500

Clay, Henry, 1777-1852
A Ls s (2), 25 Jan 1818 & 16 Mar 1820. Doheny collection. (89) $900
ALs, 18 May 1823. (88) $350
— 8 June 1829. (90) $450
— 17 Dec 1838. (88) $80
— 1 June 1840. (91) $250
— 7 June 1844. (89) $300
— 20 Oct 1847. (91) $275
— 3 Mar 1848. (91) $250
— 14 July 1851. (90) $225
Ls, 31 Dec 1851. 3 pp, 4to. To James Robb. On the importance of saving the Union. (91) $2,200
Ds, 1 Aug 1845. (91) $50
Franking signature, [5 Feb n.y.]. (90) $65

Cleaver, Reginald
Original drawings, (24), to illus Rudyard Kipling's Humorous Tales, 1931. Macmillan Archives. (90) £550

Clebsch, Alfred, 1833-72
ALs, 3 Jan 1872. (88) DM580

Cleghorn, Archibald S.
[An archive of c.54 diaries written in pencil, 1864-1910 by Cleghorn with related Hawaiian material sold at cb on 29 June 1989, lot 123, for $22,500]

Cleland, John, 1709-89
Series of 10 A Ls s, 1752 to 1762. 33 pp, 4to. To his mother's lawyer Edward Dickinson. Complaining about his poverty & his mother's refusal to grant him an allowance. With drafts of replies & 2 A Ls s by Mrs. Cleland. (90) £7,800
ALs, 6 Mar 1758. 5 pp, 4to. To his mother. Bitterly accusing her of acting towards him with "immortal hatred". (90) £3,800

Clem, John Lincoln
ALs, 11 June 1934. (88) $75
Autograph sentiment, sgd, [n.d.]. (91) $275

Clemenceau, Georges, 1841-1929
ALs, 15 May 1909. (89) DM600
ADs, 9 May 1865. (90) DM260
Ds, 19 Oct 1874. (91) DM240

Clemens August von Bayern, Erzbischof und Kurfuerst von Koeln, 1700-61
Ls, 25 July 1758. 1 p, folio. To Cardinal Oddi. Thanking for the notification of the election of Pope Clement XIII. In Italian. (91) DM1,100

Clemens, Samuel Langhorne, 1835-1910
[A group of 3 autograph Mss, An Open Letter to the (Hartford) City Government; The Science of Government; & To the Reader, 14 Oct 1888, 28 pp, 8vo, 1 sgd, all expounding his quarrel with Hartford's managers, sold at CNY on 21 Feb 1989, lot 1781, for $28,000 to Newman.]
[A galley proof for a page of A Connecticut Yankee in King Arthur's Court, [1889], including 2 A Ns s (initialled; 1 each on recto & verso) to his pbr & a pencilled note from his

pbr, discussing modifications fo a sentence, sold at CNY on 21 Feb 1989, lot 1782, for $3,500 to 19th Cent Shop.]
[A collection of 12 pieces relating to the 1901 copyright & trademark suits in which August Gurlitz represented Mark Twain & Rudyard Kipling was lot 382 at P on 11 Dec 1990.] $4,000
[A copper plate with etched self caricature & inscr, with affixed slip of paper sgd Mark Twain & inscr to David A. Munro, [n.d.], 5.25 by 3 inches, in lea wallet, sold at S on 15 Dec, lot 57, for £550.]
[A group of 3 brief autograph notes or memoranda, 1 sentence each, [n.d.], each c.35mm by 75mm, sold at CNY on 21 Feb 1989, lot 1776, for $700 to Heritage Bookshop.]
[A ptd port, [n.d.], 115mm by 190mm (image), inscr (recipient's name erased) & sgd as Twain, sold at sg on 8 Feb 1990, lot 207, for $900.]

Autograph Ms, A Family Sketch, [after 1897]. 65 pp, 8vo, mostly on rectos. With numerous autograph revisions. Orig title In Memory of Olivia Susan Clemens, 1872-1896, crossed out. In blue mor folding case. Doheny collection. (88) $85,000
— Autograph Ms, A Tramp Abroad, chapter 15, Down the River; [1879-80]. 33 pp, 8vo, on rectos only. With numerous revisions. In crimson mor bdg with ptd version of the chapter, removed from a copy of 1st Ed. (90) $30,000
— Autograph Ms, A Tramp Abroad, chapter 46 [1879-80]. 23 pp, 8vo, on rectos only; each tipped to larger sheet. Red mor gilt bdg. With many autograph revisions. Doheny collection. (89) $22,000
— Autograph Ms, An Incident, 11 Sept 1887. 7 pp, 8vo, on rectos only. Recounting "the largest & gratefullest compliment that was ever paid me." Doheny collection. (89) $8,000
— Autograph Ms, "Art Studies - First Pedestrian Tour", chapter 11 of A Tramp Abroad, [1880]. 29 pp, 8vo, mostly on rectos. Some revisions. In blue mor gilt bdg with a port & ptd text from Ed Hartford, 1880. Doheny collection. (88) $22,000

— Autograph Ms, comments on Gutenberg & the art of ptg; [c.1886]. 10 pp, 8vo, on rectos only. Working draft; possibly unpbd. Doheny collection. (89) $17,000
— Autograph Ms, elegy, In Memorian Olivia Susan Clemens, 18 Aug 1897. 4 pp, 4to, on rectos only. Some minor autograph corrections; probably printer's copy. With copy of ptd 1st Ed, [Lake Lucerne, Switzerland, 1897]; uncut & unbound. Doheny collection. (89) $20,000
— Autograph Ms, essay, Concerning the British Pirates, [ptd in The New Princeton Review, Jan 1888]. 61 pp, 8vo, mostly on rectos. Discussing the copyright problem; sgd Mark Twain. With numerous autograph revisions. 1 page repaired. In mor slipcase. Doheny collection. (89) $28,000
— Autograph Ms, Gilded Age, chapter 53, [c.1873]. 22 pp, 8vo, on rectos only, in red mor gilt box. Doheny collection. (89) $25,000
— Autograph Ms, In Memory Olivia Susan Clemens, 1872 - 1896; sgd & dated Jan 1902. 22 pp, 8vo, on rectos only. In mor gilt folder. With numerous autograph revisions; later incorporated into his Autobiography. Doheny collection. (89) $32,000
— Autograph Ms, notes for the dramatic version of Tom Sawyer, [c.1884-85?]. 3 pp, mostly 4to. In ink & pencil. Doheny collection. (88) $6,500
— Autograph Ms, notes; probably rough outline for a reading, in ink. 1 p. 8vo. On verso AL, draft, to unknown recipient, [c.1 Jan 1898?], in pencil. Doheny collection. (89) $1,600
— Autograph Ms, notes, "Vail's courtship", [Oct 1867]. Size not stated; cut from a larger leaf. 8 lines. Mtd. Barrett collection. (89) $1,300
— Autograph Ms, satirical parable, Adam's Expulsion, sgd; [1881]. 14 pp, 8vo, mostly on rectos. In pencil; some corrections in ink. Doheny collection. (88) $12,000
— Autograph Ms, speech attacking the teaching of religion at Girard College, [1889?]. 11 pp, 8vo, mostly on rectos. In pencil. Doheny collection. (89) $9,500

1987 - 1991 • AUTOGRAPHS & MANUSCRIPTS — CLEMENS

— Autograph Ms, table of contents for a collection of his humorous works, [1870s?]. 9 pp, 8vo, on rectos only. Possibly ptr's copy. Doheny collection. (89) $4,000

— Autograph Ms, The Gilded Age, chapter 8, [c.1873]. 32 pp, 8vo, on rectos only. With numerous revisions. In blue mor bdg with the ptd text, removed from a copy of the 1st Ed. (90) $25,000

— Autograph Ms, Unmailed Answer [to an anonymous critic, n.d.]. 4 pp, 8vo, on rectos only. Some revisions. Doheny collection. (88) $8,000

Autograph transcript, "From Soliloquy at Tomb of Adam", Nov 1870. 1 p, 8vo. Sgd as Clemens & as Twain. (91) $3,250

Typescript (duplicated), 1 ALs & 2 autograph postcards, sgd, 3-13 Dec 1900. To his lawyer, August T. Gurlitz. About a set of Kipling & trying to tie Kipling's suit to his continuing battle against Eli Perkins's literary piracy. (91) $2,250

Collection of 2 A Ls s, 6 letters, & ANs, 24 Feb 1882 to 6 July [1885]. 24 pp, various sizes. To Mr. & Mrs. Karl Gerhardt. About various artists, his new typewriter, the American black & the guilt of the white race, etc. 1 ALs initialled, 1 letter with autograph postscript, initialled. Doheny collection. (89) $10,000

— Collection of 4 A Ls s & AL, 20 Jan [1902] to [24 Sept 1903]. 10 pp, 12mo & 8vo. Family letters. Sgd Father, or Grenouille. Including postscript from Livy Clemens, 1 p. (88) $4,500

— Collection of 2 A Ls s & Ls, 5 & 12 Mar & 2 May 1907. 9 pp, 12mo & 4to. To Clara Clemens. Commenting about public speaking & performing, programs & his daughter's concert. Sgd Father. (88) $4,000

— Collection of ALs & autograph Ms, 14 Jan [1910]. 2 pp, 12mo, torn from larger sheet. To Albert Paine, regarding his autobiography. 2 four-line stanzas on verso, apparently attacking his former secretary. (90) $1,800

Series of 6 A Ls s, 5 Dec [1867] to 28 Feb 1905. 30 pp, 4to to 12mo. To Emma Beach (Thayer). Affectionate personal letters about a variety of matters. With transcripts, in gilt calf bdg. Doheny collection. (89) $19,000

— Series of 8 A Ls s, 2 Nov 1898 to 12 Nov 1899. 9 pp, 8vo & 4to. To James M.Tuohy. Regarding his story Wapping Alice & other works, & negotiating fees. In half mor bdg. Doheny collection. (89) $14,000

— Series of 3 A Ls s, 29 June & 1 Oct 1905 & 20 June 1906. 8 pp, 12mo & 8vo. To Clara Clemens. Chatting about his work & activities. Sgd Father. (88) $5,000

— Series of 6 A Ls s, 3 Aug [1905] to [7 June 1906]. 18 pp, 12mo & 8vo. To Clara Clemens. Family letters. Sgd Father. (88) $9,000

— Series of 5 A Ls s, [1 July 1906] to 24 Feb 1907. 12 pp, 12mo & 8vo. To Clara Clemens. Family letters. Sgd Father or Marcus. (88) $7,000

— Series of 3 A Ls s, 26 Nov & 6 Dec 1909, & 12 Mar 1910. 8 pp, 8vo. To Clara Clemens. Talking about his activities in Bermuda. Sgd Father or Marcus. (88) $5,500

A Ls s (2), 7 Dec 1892 & 9 Jan 1893. 4 pp, 8vo. To Clara Clemens. Sending Christmas greetings & messages. Complaining about pain under his shoulder blade. Sgd Papa. With autograph envelopes, 1 with initialled autograph postscript. (88) $1,800

— A Ls s (2), 30 & 31 July 1899. (91) £900

— A Ls s (2), 21-22 Dec 1900. 3 pp, 8vo & 4to. To his lawyer, August Gurlitz. Declaring war on literary pirate Eli Perkins. (91) $3,500

— A Ls s (2), 21 Nov 1905 & 26 Mar 1906. 4 pp, 8vo. To Asa Don Dickinson. Regarding the banning of his books from the children's sections of the Brooklyn libraries. With related material. (89) $23,000

— A Ls s (2), 30 June & 12 July 1907. 7 pp, 12mo & 8vo. To Clara Clemens. About an historical pageant at Oxford & his stay in England. Sgd Father. 2d letter on hotel letterhead. (88) $3,200

— A Ls s (2), 19 May & 20 June 1908. 6 pp, 8vo. To Clara Clemens. Refusing to buy an automobile. Describing his new home. Sgd Father or Marcus. (88) $2,500

ALs, 29 Dec 1868. 9 pp, 8vo. To Jervis

CLEMENS

Langdon. Defending his character to his future father-in-law. (91) $22,000
— 1 Jan 1869. 4 pp, 8vo. To the Rev. Joseph Hopkins Twichell. About Olivia Langdon & about staying with Mary Fairbanks while in Cleveland on a lecture tour. (91) $6,000
— 23 Jan 1869. 5 pp, 8vo. To the Rev. Joseph Hopkins Twichell & his family. About the wonderfulness of Olivia Langdon & about lecturing. (91) $3,000
— 1869. 3 pp, 8vo. To the Rev. Joseph Hopkins Twichell & his family. Announcing his engagement. (91) $4,500
— Apr 1869. 2 pp, 4to. To his sister Pamela. About his Livy & how he outrages her feelings. (91) $3,000
— 2 Jan [1872]. 2 pp, 8vo. To Mr. Redpath. About his lecture tour. (91) $1,800
— 13 Jan 1872. Doheny collection. (89) $850
— 12 Oct 1872. 3 pp, 8vo. To his wife. About the comfort of reading in bed. (91) $4,800
— 25-26 Apr 1873. 4 pp, 8vo. To his wife. Saying that The Gilded Age is finished. (91) $3,800
— 13 Apr 1877. 2 pp, 4to. To Miss Holmes. Commenting on his skill in drawing & sending a sketch of the President (not included). Sgd as Clemens & Mark Twain. (88) $1,500
— 12 Oct 1880. 6 pp, 4to. To his wife. Partly in pidgin German; describing the decorating of their home for a reception for former President Ulysses S. Grant. (91) $3,500
— [25 Aug] 1881. 2 pp, 8vo. To his wife Livy. Chatting about a train ride to Boston. On hotel stationery. In mor gilt case. Doheny collection. (88) $3,200
— 4 Dec 1881. 3 pp, 8vo. To his wife. About accepting an invitation from M. Frechette to a public dinner in Montreal; describes Canada. (91) $2,400
— 11 Aug 1885. 2 pp, 4to. Recipient unknown. Defending his opinion that Gen. Grant should be buried in NY. (90) $9,500
— 12 Nov 1885. 4 pp, 8vo. To James F. Glueck. Informing him about the writing & copying of Huckleberry Finn, & promising to send what is left of the orig Ms. Doheny collection. (88) $18,000
— 25 Aug 1886. 2 pp, 8vo. To George Standring. Inquiring about ptg costs, thanking for a book, etc. Sgd as Clemens & Twain. (90) $2,500
— 1 Sept 1886. 2 pp, 8vo. To [Mr. House?]. Fragment, incorporating 2 poems. Sgd Mark. (91) $1,800
— [19 June 1887]. 1 p, 8vo. To Mr. House. Expressing thanks. Sgd Mark. (91) $1,300
— 2 Dec 1887. 3 pp, 8vo. To Mary Halleck Forte. About his readings of Browning's poems. With related material. Doheny collection. (88) $6,500
— 2 Mar [18]89. 1 p, 8vo. To Mr. House. About a contract. Fold breaks. (91) $1,400
— 15 July 1889. 3 pp, 8vo, on rectos only. To Clara Clemens. Reporting about a railway tragedy. Sgd Papa. (88) $3,200
— 7 Sept 1889. 2 pp, 8vo. Retained draft of a letter to Nellie Bunce about her engagement to Archie Wetch. (91) $3,500
— 2 Feb 1890. 9 pp, 8vo. To [Daniel or Charles] Frohman. Strongly attacking [Abby Sage] Richardson's stage version of The Prince and the Pauper; unmailed. 1 p def. On hotel letterhead. Doheny collection. (88) $8,500
— [20 July] 1890. 3 pp, 8vo. To Clara Clemens. Expressing his disapproval of the dramatization of A Connecticut Yankee. Sgd Papa. (88) $2,800
— 12 June 1891. 2 pp, 8vo. To Clara Clemens. About animals & traveling. With related material. (91) $2,400
— [c.Oct 1891 to Feb 1892]. 4 pp, 8vo. To George Warner. Informing him of his family's unwillingness to agree to a proposed change of a river bed. (88) $1,800
— 27 Nov 1891. 2 pp, 16mo. Recipient unnamed. Replying to queries regarding Charles C. Jones' Negro Myths from the Georgia Coast. Repaired. Doheny collection. (88) $3,000
— 27 June 1892. 3 pp, 8vo. To his wife. About going to the dentist. (91) $1,900
— [15 Dec 1892]. 4 pp, 8vo. To [Clara Clemens]. Reporting about the family's activities in Florence. Sgd Papa.

Creased. (88) $2,800
— 26 Sept 1893. 6 pp, 8vo. To his publisher. About typesetting machines & about the family's black manservant, George, who has made large amounts of money by lending to waiters & members at the Union League Club. (91) $8,000
— 18 Oct 1893. 6 pp, 8vo. To his wife. Spelling out a scheme to rescue his stagnating publishing house. (91) $3,000
— 20 Oct 1893. 4 pp, 8vo. To his wife. About writing & about printing innovations. (91) $2,400
— 31 Oct 1893. 2 pp, 8vo. To Mary Mapes Dodge. Informing her of Clara's departure, & accepting a dinner invitiation for himself. Doheny collection. (88) $1,600
— 16 May 1894. 2 pp, 8vo. To his wife Livy. About his arrival in Europe & about Henry Huttleston Rogers's offer of financial support. (91) $3,000
— 28 Aug 1895. 3 pp, 8vo. To "Jack". Announcing that he will be celebrating recipient's birthday, & sending a copy of a poem (not present). With related material. (90) $4,250
— "Sunday" [c.1895?]. 2 pp, 8vo. To "Mrs. Susy". Thanking for offering her hospitality, & explaining his travel plans. (90) $2,800
— 26 Feb [18]96. (91) $750
— 10 Feb [1897]. 2 pp, 16mo. To [Robert] Barr. Explaining his desire to avoid publicity after his recent bereavement. (91) $3,200
— 2 July 1897. 3 pp, 8vo. To [Frank Fuller?]. Saying his wife will not consent to a projected lecture-tour. Sgd Mark. John F. Fleming Estate. (89) $2,800
— [4 July 1897]. (91) £1,000
— 28 Apr 1900. 1 p, 12mo. To [his pbr Harper & Bros.]. Postponing a decision on the Library of Humor. Doheny collection. (89) $1,500
— 21 May [19]01. (89) $500
— 30 May [1901]. (89) $500
— 14 Sept 1901. 3 pp, 4to. To August T. Gurlitz. Responding to a series of questions Gurlitz had sent him concerning an unauthorized Ed of Kipling's works. (91) $2,250
— 30 Nov 1902. 4 pp, 8vo. To his wife Livy. Recalling their wedding day & reporting about his birthday banquet in New York. Sgd Youth. With 3-line postscript & 3-line note to Clara Clemens at head. (88) $4,200
— 26 May 1904. 3 pp, 12mo. To Gov. Francis, Chairman of the St. Louis World's Fair. Regarding a port of Twain to be hung at the fair. (88) $3,000
— [11 June 1905]. 3 pp, 12mo. To Clara Clemens. Describing his writing output & expressing relief about her spiritual peace. Sgd Father. Fold tear. (88) $2,400
— [18] June 1905. 4 pp, 12mo. To Clara Clemens. Making plans for a publication of his letters & speculating about monarchy in the USA. Sgd Father. (88) $2,200
— 16 July 1905. 2 pp, 8vo. To Clara Clemens. About revising Adam's Diary. Sgd Father. (88) $1,600
— 3 Sept [1905]. 5 pp, 8vo. To Clara Clemens. Separately mailed postscript, discussing his musical taste & a wedding. 1 p lacking. Sgd Father. With enclosure of a "ghost autograph" with 5-line note on top, 1 p, 8vo. (88) $2,800
— 3 Oct [190]5. 2 pp, 8vo, on rectos only. To his daughter Clara. Postscript to a prior letter, describing autumn foliage & mentioning a reading "of the horse-story". Sgd Father. (88) $2,000
— 6 Oct 1905. 4 pp, 8vo. To Clara Clemens. About her health & his story A Horse's Tale. Sgd Father. (88) $2,200
— 15 Dec 1905. 2 pp, 8vo. To an unnamed recipient in Vienna. Thanking for a copy of his "cordial & complimentary appreciation" & explaining his pseud. (88) £1,300
— 7 May 1906. 6 pp, 8vo. To Otis Skinner. Angrily scolding him for firing an actress. Sgd Mark Twain. Doheny collection. (89) $4,500
— 3 Aug 1906. 4 pp, 8vo. To Clara Clemens. Discussing his Autobiography. (88) $3,800
— 2 [& 3] Oct 1906. 6 pp, 8vo. To Clara Clemens. Family news, & reporting about work on his Autobiography. Sgd

CLEMENS

Father. Last p, postscript, in pencil. (88) $2,000
— [9? Oct 1906]. 4 pp, 8vo. To Clara Clemens. Chatting about reading Henry Esmond & about Jean's carving things to sell. Sgd Father. (88) $2,000
— 1 Aug 1907. 4 pp, 8vo. To "Joy", an eight-year old admirer. Charming letter chatting about a variety of matters. Sgd as Twain. (90) £1,900
— 21-23 Feb 1910. 8 pp, 8vo. To Clara Clemens. Reflecting about his relationship with his daughters & commenting about the Catholic Church. Sgd Marcus. (88) $7,000
— 24-25 Mar 1910. 4 pp, 8vo. To Clara Clemens. Presumably last letter to his daughter, reporting about his illness. Sgd Marcus. (88) $5,500
— 9 Mar [n.y.]. 2 pp, 12mo. To Mr. Anthony. Commenting on the age of the Prince & Tom Canty in The Prince and the Pauper. Tipped into a copy of 1st American Ed of the book, 1882. (91) $2,500
— 10 Mar [n.y.]. 2 pp, 8vo. To Mr. McElroy. Declining to give a lecture. Corner def. (90) $1,100
— 14 May [n.y.]. (91) $950
— [n.d.], "Tuesday". Doheny collection. (89) $750
— [n.d.], "Sunday". (91) $850
AL, 20 May 1905. 7 pp, 12mo. To Clara Clemens. About Clara's health, a message from a family friend, & an idea for a proposed club. With initialled note on autograph envelope. (88) $2,000
Ls, 20 Dec 1873. (91) £360
— 8 Mar 1906. 2 pp, 8vo. To Alex C. Toncray. Informing him that the orig "Huckleberry Finn was Tom Blankenship." (91) $10,000
Letter, 12 Jan 1873. Doheny collection. (89) $320
Autograph postcard, sgd, [26 Sept 1873]. Doheny collection. (89) $450
— [11 Jan 1901]. (88) $325
Series of 4 autograph postcards, 15 Ju[ly 18]99. To Clara Clemens. Playful messages purporting to be from Henry M. Stanley, W. H. Lecky, F. Nansen & H. Campbell-Bannerman. Each with ptd color vignette on message side. (88) $2,800
Collection of ANs & photograph, [n.d.]. (89) $450
ANs, [22 Oct 1877]. 2 pp, 75mm by 130mm (card). To Charles W. Stoddard. Apologizing for not accompanying him to the station. Doheny collection. (89) $1,600
— 12 Feb 1893. (88) $550
— Feb 1900. 1 p, 8vo. To Alfred E. Mann. Advising him "never to do wrong when people are looking." Framed. (90) £1,200
— [n.d.]. Barrett collection. (89) $1,000
— 6 Jan [19]02. (91) $900
— 16 Jan [19]03. (91) $750
— 16 Jan 1903. Doheny collection. (89) $750
— 17 June [n.y.]. 1 p, 8vo. To Kate Riggs. Inviting her to a "Doe-Luncheon". (91) $1,700
— [n.d.]. (89) $750
Series of 3 A Ns s, 16-19 July 1877. 6 pp, 12mo. To his daughters. Whimsical notes about dolls named Hosannah Maria & Hallelujah Jennings and their doll children, Whoopjamboree & Glory Ann Jennings. (91) $4,800
Note, 26 Dec 1910. Doheny collection. (89) $480
Ds, 2 Apr 1863. Size not stated. Stock certificate for 10 shares in The Jackson Gold & Silver Mining Co., Unionville, made out to Clemens. Sgd on verso. (89) $5,750
Autograph endorsement, receipt for $2.00 from Archibald Henderson, sgd as Twain, at bottom of his ptd request for contributions to the building of a new library at Redding, 7 Oct 1908. 1 p, 4to. (90) $5,500
Autograph quotation, 22 Dec 1891. 1 p, 8vo. "Never put off till tomorrow what can be put off till day after tomorrow..."; sgd as Clemens & as Twain. (90) £1,550
Autograph sentiment, 2 Nov 1899. (89) £760
— Anr, sgd, 7 July 1900. On ptd Savage Club menu showing him making a speech. "Never waste a lie, for you never know when you may need one...." (91) £1,350
— Anr, sgd, Dec 1905. 1 p, 8vo. "Taking

the pledge will not make bad liquor good, but it will improve it." Unrelated autograph on verso. Byer collection. (90) $2,000
— Anr, sgd, 9 Dec 1907. Byer collection. (90) $1,000
— Anr, sgd; inscr to [Charles Dana] Gibson in the margin of a port lithograph of an unidentified man, [n.d.]. (90) $550

Group photograph, [c.1870s]. Cabinet size. With Routledge & Henry Lee; sgd by Clemens & Lee. (91) $1,200

Menu, 24 Sept 1907. 5 pp, 4to, in wraps. Program & menu of The Robert Fulton Monument Association Jamestown Exposition. Sgd & inscr to Mrs. Hugh Gordon Miller. (91) $1,600

Photograph, sgd, [n.d.]. (90) £750
— Anr, 27 Dec 1905. 13.5 by 10.5 inches. Half-length. Copyright note at lower right. Doheny collection. (88) $3,000
— Anr, [6 July 1907]. (90) £540

Photograph, sgd & inscr, 12 Aug 1895. 190mm by 116mm. Standing on a porch. Inscr to S. E. Moffet; sgd as Twain. On 4to sheet; captioned "Announcement Without Words". Repaired. Doheny collection. (88) $1,100
— Anr, 12 Dec 1899. 8 by 6 inches (image). Inscr to Mrs. Hinck on mount, as Clemens & as Twain. Framed. (90) £2,800
— Anr, [n.d.]. 9 by 11 inches. Sgd as Twain, on mount. Framed. (89) $1,500

Proof copy, Who was Sarah Findlay? With a Suggested Solution of the Mystery by J. Doheny collection. (88) $600

Signature, June [18]83. (91) $350
— Anr, 27 Nov [18]93. (88) $475
— Anr, [n.d.]. (91) $550
— Anr, [n.d.]. (91) $350
— Anr, [n.d.]. (91) $800
— Anr, [n.d.]. (90) $750
— Anr, [n.d.]. (88) $240
— Anr, [n.d.]. (90) $600
— BINNS, L. J. - Original drawing, sgd; pen-&-ink sketch of Clemens. 8vo. Sgd Mark Twain & inscr. With pen-&-wash caricature of Clemens by Binns. Barrett collection. (89) $2,000
— LANGDON, JERVIS. - ALs, 2 Mar 1870. 1 p, 8vo. Humourous letter to his son-in-law S. L. Clemens. Doheny collection. (89) $220
— WARNER, CHARLES DUDLEY. - Autograph Ms, portion of chapter 15 of The Gilded Age, [c.1873]. 8 pp, 16mo. Doheny collection. (89) $3,000
See also: Irving, Washington & Others
See also: Kipling, Rudyard

Clemens, Samuel Langhorne, 1835-1910 —&
Kipling, Rudyard, 1865-1936
[Their signatures on the ptd program for the convocation & awarding of honorary degrees at Oxford, 26 June 1907, sold at P on 11 Dec 1989, lot 156, for $1,600.]

Clemens, Samuel Langhorne, 1835-1910 —&
Warner, Charles Dudley, 1829-1900
[An autograph Ms by each, leaves from The Gilded Age, 2 pp, 8vo, on rectos only, [c.1873], paginated 1188 & 338, respectively, inlaid, sold at CNY on 8 Dec 1989, lot 143, for $2,000.]

Clemens Wenzeslaus von Sachsen, Kurfuerst & Erzbischof von Trier, 1739-1812
Ls, 2 Jan 1800. (88) DM380

Clement IV, Pope, d.1268
Document, [22 Aug] 1268. 1 p, vellum, 30cm by 42cm. Bull addressed to the Bishop of Rieti. Giving orders for a crusade against Conradin & his allies the Saracens at Lucera. With lead seal. (88) DM14,000

Clement IX, Pope, 1600-69
Ls, 18 Aug 1666. (89) $300

Clement VII, Pope, 1478-1534
Ls, 28 Aug 1515. (88) $500
— 28 Jan 1520. (88) $500

Clement VIII, Pope, 1536-1605
Ls, Dec 1599. (88) £100
— 30 May 1603. 1 p, 4to. To his treasurer. Instructing him to give permission for the sale of a castle near Assisi. (90) DM1,150

Document, 9 Aug 1594. (90) DM640
— 10 May 1597. (91) DM450

Clement X, Pope, 1590-1676
Ls, 23 July 1670. (89) $500

Clement XII, Pope, 1652-1740
Series of 120 Ls s, 1686 to 1725. Length not stated, folio. To several agents in Florence & Leghorn. Dealing with various business matters. (91) £3,200

Ds, [9 July] 1732. 14 pp, folio; vellum. Bull dealing with the return of church property after the conversion of the rulers of Saxony. Also sgd by c.30 cardinals. With elaborate calligraphic decorations. (90) DM3,800

— [9 July] 1732. 14 pp, folio; vellum. Bull dealing with the return of church property after the conversion of the rulers of Saxony. Also sgd by c.30 cardinals. With elaborate calligraphic decorations. (91) DM4,000

Clemente, Roberto, 1934-72
Photograph, sgd, [n.d.]. (91) $350

Clementi, Muzio, 1752-1832
ALs, 27 Jan 1816. 1 p, 4to. To Pierre Baillot. Regarding plans for concerts. (90) DM4,500

Clergy
Original drawings, (50), full-page miniatures of members of the clergy & of religous orders, with captions in French. [Southern Netherlands, 17th cent]. Vellum, 115mm by 87mm, in contemp calf gilt bdg. (91) £1,700

Cleveland, Frances Folsom, 1864-1947
Executive Mansion card, sgd; [n.d.]. (89) $60

Photograph, sgd, [c.1913]. (91) $75
See also: Cleveland, Grover & Cleveland

Cleveland, Grover, 1837-1908
Series of 3 A Ls s, 1884 to 1900. (89) $450
ALs, 5 June 1883. (88) $150
— 7 Jan 1884. (90) $175
— 27 July 1884. Rosenbloom collection. (88) $450
— 23 Oct 1885. 4 pp, 8vo. To Mr. [Bruce?]. Declining an invitation to stay with him at Buffalo. Pratt collection. (89) $1,200
— 4 Mar 1887. (91) $350
— 18 Aug 1887. 3 pp, 8vo. To Hampton L. Carson. Threatening to boycott the Pennsylvania Constitutional Centennial if expected to attend further functions. Pratt collection. (89) $1,400
— 25 Dec 1888. 3 pp, 8vo. To Postmaster Gen. Don M. Dickinson. Thanking for a Christmas present. With engraved port. (90) $1,200
— 23 Oct 1889. (88) $200
— 10 Feb 1890. (89) $350
— 7 Mar 1890. (89) $150
— 8 Feb 1892. (91) $275
— 15 July 1892. Rosenbloom collection. (88) $600
— 30 Mar 1896. (89) $650
— 16 Sept 1896. (90) $280
— 11 June 1897. (90) $100
— 24 Dec 1897. (90) $400
— 1 Mar 1898. (90) $150
— 14 July 1898. 11 pp, 8vo. To the manager of his farm, [Mr. Viram?]. Strongly disapproving of "the plan of taking the farm for a boy's school". Doheny collection. (89) $1,400
— 3 Feb 1900. (90) $325
— 30 Nov 1900. Byer collection. (90) $250
— 3 June 1901. (88) $130
— 20 Oct 1901. (91) $225
— 8 Feb 1902. (91) $180
— 13 Apr 1903. (88) $90
Collection of Ls, Ds, 2 photographs (1 sgd), & Executive Mansion card, sgd, 1861 to 1905. (89) $475
Ls, 31 July 1885. 1 p, 4to. To George W. Childs. Asking him to officiate as pall-bearer at Gen. Grant's funeral. (88) $3,000
— 15 Aug 1892. (89) $140
ANs, 21 May 1887. (88) $110
— 10 Dec 1904. (88) $125
Ds, 21 Jan 1862. (90) $200
— 10 July 1886. (90) $160
— 15 Mar 1887. (91) $325
— 7 Sept 1893. (90) $225
— 23 Nov 1896. (88) $250
— 26 Feb 1897. (91) $250
Bust engraving, sgd, 15 Nov 1888. (90) $150
Cut signature, [n.d.]. (90) $80
Engraving, oval port, sgd on mount, 30 June 1888. (90) $110
— Anr, sgd; 1894. (89) $210

— Anr, port, seated; sgd & inscr to J. (91) $200

Executive Mansion card, sgd, Oct 1894. (90) $160

— Anr, sgd, 13 Nov 1895. (90) $275

— Anr, sgd, [n.d.]. (91) $300

— Anr, sgd, [n.d.]. (90) $160

Franking signature, [20 Jan 1894]. (90) $400

Photograph, sgd, 22 Feb 1897. (90) $300

— Anr, 24 Feb 1897. (88) $300

— Anr, [n.d.]. (88) $350

— Anr, 30 Nov 1907. (91) $450

— Anr, 30 Nov 1907. (89) $300

Photograph, sgd & inscr, [24 Dec 1907]. (91) $250

— Anr, 24 Dec [19]07. (90) $400

Signature, 18 May 1891. (91) $160

White House card, sgd, [n.d.]. (89) $130

— Anr, sgd; [n.d.]. (89) $120

— Anr, sgd, [n.d.]. (91) $140

— REID, JACQUES. - Engraving, bust port of Cleveland, artist's proof no 9 of 24 impressions, [1906]. Sgd by Reid & Cleveland. Framed; overall size 24 by 29 inches. (91) $400

Cleveland, Grover, 1837-1908 —& Cleveland, Frances Folsom, 1864-1947

[2 White House cards, sgd, April 1894, sold at wa on 17 Oct, lot 122, for $150.]

[2 Executive Mansion cards, sgd (1 by each), [n.d.], both mtd on 8vo sheet, sold at sg on 21 Sept 1989, lot 75, for $175.]

Signature, 20 May 1887. (88) $120

Clifford, Thomas, 1st Baron Clifford of Chudleigh, 1630-73

Document, 1664. (89) £220

— TRADE. - Ms, A Breife of ye. whole Proiect of ye. East-India Company of france..., & covering letter by B. Worsley, Sec of the Council of Trade, to Sec of State Thomas Clifford, 8 May [1669], 9 pp, folio. (89) £420

Clifford, Thomas, 1st Baron Clifford of Chudleigh, 1630-73 —& Others

Document, 30 July 1665. Clifford Papers. (89) £85

Clift, Montgomery, 1920-66

Christmas card, sgd, [c.1940s?]. (90) $240

Clingan, William, d.1790

ADs, 9 July 1779. (91) $70

Clinton, DeWitt, 1769-1828

Ls, 9 Jan 1819. (88) $85

Ds, 13 Mar 1821. (90) $50

Clinton, George, c.1686-1761

ALs, 5 Dec 1745. Alexander collection. (90) $500

Clinton, George, 1739-1812

AL, [late Apr 1779]. (90) $250

Ls, 5 May 1789. 1 p, 4to. To the Governor of Connecticut. As Governor of NY, communicating an application [not included] of the Legislature to Congress for a Bill of Rights. (90) $3,750

Letter, 16 Feb 1780. Alexander collection. (90) $375

Ds, 4 Oct 1786. (91) $225

— 1 Nov 1786. (91) $100

— 13 Apr 1787. (91) $120

— 8 Sept 1787. (89) $300

Clive, Colin

Photograph, sgd & inscr, [n.d.]. (91) $190

Cloke, Rene

Original drawings, (12), to illus various annuals, 1931 to 1938. (89) £550

— Original drawings, (6), to illus various annuals, 1931 to 1935. (89) £800

— Original drawings, (8), to illus Our Kiddies' Gift Book, 1941-42. 290mm by 180mm. In ink & watercolor; sgd. (89) £1,200

Clymer, George, Signer from Pennsylvania

[2 checks (1 autograph), 8 & 29 Feb 1804, 57mm by 140mm, drawn on the Philadelphia Bank, sold at sg on 24 Mar 1988, lot 34, for $200.]

A Ls s (2), Apr & May 1803. (89) $250

ALs, 30 May 1791, 5 pp, 4to. (89) $500

— 29 July 1803. (88) $800

ADs, 14 Dec 1807. (88) $200

Ds, [n.d.]. (88) $100

Cobb, Howell, 1815-68
Ds, 22 Aug 1859. (88) $70

Cobb, Ty, 1886-1961
Collection of 2 A Ls s, AL & 3 telegrams, 5 Oct 1917 to 1918. 7 pp, 4to, & telegrams. To James Pollard. Relating to business & hunting. AL incomplete. With related material. (89) $2,000

ALs, 25 Jan 195[3]. 3 pp, 4to. To Gil Hodges. Offering advice on how to improve his baseball play. Including postscript, initialled. (91) $4,750

— 10 Apr 1959. 2 pp, 4to. To Mr. McDermott. Apologizing for the delay in responding to a request for his autograph. (91) $1,200

Ls, 4 Dec 1960. 1 p, 8vo. To "Al". Enclosing a sgd release & stating conditions. (90) $1,500

Check, accomplished & sgd, 22 June 1944. (91) $325

— Anr, sgd & accomplished, 15 Oct 1945. (89) $140

Ptd photograph, sgd, [n.d.]. (89) $210

Signature, [n.d.]. (91) $300

See also: Baseball

Cobbett, William, 1763-1835
Ms, On the conduct of the Westminster Rump..., Weekly Register, vol 34, issue 11; 5 Sept 1818. 42 pp, 4to, in later half mor gilt bdg. Partly autograph. (91) £1,300

ALs, 14 Feb 1802. (91) £260

— 27 Mar 1829. (89) £600

Cobbold, Richard, 1797-1877
Autograph Ms, journal of a tour in France, 13 June to 9 July 1817; c.50 pp, 4to, in red mor gilt. (89) £520

Cobden, Richard, 1804-65
Collection of 39 A Ls s & AL, 20 Apr 1839 to 14 May 1863; c.86 pp, 8vo & 4to, in brown mor album. To Sir Henry Cole (13) & other recipients. Supporting the introduction of the penny post, & discussing other political issues. With 2 engraved portraits. (88) £4,200

— Collection of 37 A Ls s & A Ns s, 24 Apr 1840 to 21 Mar 1865. (89) £1,000

Cochin, Charles Nicolas, 1715-90
ALs, 8 Jan 1772. (89) DM360

Cochran, Eddie
Ds, 21 May 1956. (89) £280

— 14 Jan 1957. (89) £350

— HUNT, BOB. - Orig drawing, oil port of Cochran used on front cover of Rockstar Records "Portrait of a Legend - Eddie Cochran"; [n.d.]. 18 by 18 inches. With record cover. (89) £300

Cochrane, Thomas, Lord, 1775-1860
ALs, 17 Feb 1818. (89) $65

Cockburn, Sir George, 1772-1853
Franking signature, [11 July 1842]. Alexander collection. (90) $75

Cockerell, Sir Sydney Carlyle, 1867-1962
Autograph Ms, account book kept as executor of the estate of William Morris, 1896 to 1935. About 250 pp, folio; vellum bdg. With related material. (89) £5,800

Series of 18 A Ls s, 1931 to 1951. (91) £600

Cocteau, Jean, 1889-1963
Autograph Ms, autobiographical sketch, Aug 1959. (90) DM480

— Autograph Ms, part of Les Maries de la Tour Eiffel, [c.1920-21]. (88) £480

Collection of 3 A Ls s, AL, autograph postcard & pencil diagram of a stage layout, Sept - Oct 1934 & [n.d.]. (88) $750

A Ls s (2), 11 Nov 1950 & 3 Sept 1953. (88) DM440

ALs, [18 Apr 1932]. (90) DM360

— 3 Nov 1952. (90) DM440

— 25 Nov 1952. (91) $130

— 3 Dec 1955. (88) DM420

— 8 Apr 1960. (89) DM260

— [n.d.]. (90) DM210

— [n.d.]. (89) DM280

— [n.d.]. (91) DM240

Autograph sentiment, 10 Aug 1950. Byer collection. (90) $850

Photograph, sgd & inscr, [after 1955]. 18cm by 13cm. Sgd & inscr on verso; including pen-&-ink sketch. (91) DM1,300

Codrington, Robert
Autograph Ms, The Memorialls of Queene Margaret, as trans by Codrington. [1640-41] 110 leaves, 4to, contemp mor gilt. (91) $2,750

Cody, William F. ("Buffalo Bill"), 1846-1917
A Ls s (2), 16 Mar 1890. (89) £650
ALs, 18 June [c.1900-1910]. (88) $400
— 3 Oct 1887. (91) $750
— 20 Dec 1890. (91) $1,000
— 16 May 1892. (88) £400
Cut signature, 30 Sept 1875. (90) $250
Photograph, [n.d.]. (90) $130
Signature, 6 May [18]74. (90) $325
— Anr, 19 Feb 1883. (90) $450
— Anr, 1900. (91) $550

Cody, William F. ("Buffalo Bill"), 1846-1917 —&
Edison, Thomas A., 1847-1931
[A lot of 5 items relating to Cody's invitation to Edison to join him for breakfast & a show in Paris, Aug 1889, with related material, sold at R on 4 Mar 1989, lot 340, for $1,500.]

Coghill, Nevill, 1899-1980. See: Vaughan Williams, Ralph & Coghill

Cogorno Family
Ms, Annals of the Counts of Cogorno, in Latin. [Gulf of Genoa or Nice, c.1535-40]. 56 leaves, vellum, 230mm by 163mm. Repaired 18th-cent green vellum over pastebds. In a rounded gothic hand & a sloping italic script. With 8 pp of full illus borders, some marginal illusts, double-page map & 2 full-page armorial frontispieces. Copies of privileges granted to the family & family history, 1080 - 1535; probably compiled by Count Giovanni de' Cogorno. Phillipps Ms.24782 & Abbey collection. (89) £4,500

Cohan, George M., 1878-1942
ALs, [n.d.], "Monday". (91) $170

Cohen, Vincent M.
Original drawings, (39), to illus Johanna Spyri's Heidi, 1951. Archives of J.M.Dent & Son. (88) £300

Cohn, Alfred A., 1880-1951
Typescript, preliminary outline of The Jazz Singer, 1927. 7 sheets, 9.5 by 9 inches. With handwritten corrections. With related material. (89) $1,200

Cohn, Ferdinand, 1828-98
ALs, 14 June 1888. (91) DM480

Coiter, Volcher, 1534-76
Original drawing, sheet of finished anatomical sketches in ink. 1 p, 17 by 11 inche, hinged to a larger sheet. (88) $2,000

Colbert, Claudette
ALs, [n.d., "Sunday"]. (88) $60

Colbert, Jean Baptiste, 1619-83
ALs, 13 June 1654. (90) DM750
— 28 Sept [1663]. 3 pp, 4to. To Louis XIV. Reproaching him for spending too much time & money on Versailles. (89) £1,800
Ls, 4 Mar 1683. (89) DM400

Colborne, Sir John, 1st Baron Seaton, 1778-1863
Series of 107 A Ls s, 1842 to 1863. (88) £250

Colden, Cadwallader, 1688-1776
ALs, 12 Dec 1763. (88) $175

Cole, Herbert
Original drawings, (16), to illus The Fairy Man & other titles, c.1914 to 1920. Archives of J.M.Dent & Son. (88) £700
— Original drawings, (19), to illus Froissart's Chronicles, 1908. In watercolor & ink (10) or ink. Mostly sgd or initialled. Various sizes. 2 mtd on 1 sheet. Archives of J.M.Dent & Son. (88) £1,600
— Original drawings, (22), to illus Edward Thomas' The South Country, 1909, & W. Archives of J.M.Dent & Son. (88) £600
— Original drawings, (31), to illus Winifred Hutchinson's The Sunset of the Heroes, 1911. In watercolor & ink (5) or ink. Mostly sgd or initialled. Various sizes. Archives of J.M.Dent & Son. (88) £1,500
— Original drawings, (34), to illus Walter Raymond's A Book of Simple Delights, 1912. Archives of J.M.Dent &

Son. (88) £170
— Original drawings, (44), to illus Christopher Hare's The Story of Bayard, 1911. In watercolor & ink (7) or ink. Sgd or initialled. Various sizes. Archives of J.M.Dent & Son. (88) £1,800
— Original drawings, (49), mostly to illus William Canton's The Child's Book of Warriors, 1912. In ink & watercolor (5) or ink. Mostly sgd or initialled. Various sizes. Archives of J.M.Dent & Son. (88) £1,900
— Original drawings, (55), mostly to illus Randall Williams' & Walter Rippmann's A Rapid French Course, & Continuation School French, 1917 & 1919. Archives of J.M.Dent & Son. (88) £250
— Original drawings, (94), to illus Ernest Rhys' Fairy-Gold, 1906. In watercolor & gouache (6) or ink. Mostly sgd or initialled. Various sizes. Archives of J.M.Dent & Son. (88) £3,800
— Original drawings, to illus his Heraldry and Floral Forms in Decoration, 1922. Archives of J.M.Dent & Son. (88) £950

Cole, Nat King, 1919-65
Signature, [c.1949]. (91) $200

Coleridge, Samuel Taylor, 1772-1834
Autograph Ms, philosophical notes, sgd, 13 May 1826. (89) £900
Autograph transcript, Sonnet addressed to Miss E. Bullock. 1 p, 8vo. Sgd & dated Nov 1817. Schiff Ms (91) $4,250
Transcript, contemp copy of his early poem "Absence: a Poem", [ptd 28 Oct 1793]. (90) £360
Series of 6 A Ls s, 17 Feb 1824 to 16 Feb 1828. 11 pp, 4to. To the Rev. George Skinner. Important letters dealing with his dreams & ailments symptomatic of his opium addiction, his philosophical & religious convictions, his works, etc. (90) £10,500
ALs, 12 May 1787. 4 pp, folio. To his brother [Luke Coleridge]. About his studies, & sending some of his poems (included, 54 lines). (91) £4,800
— [28 June 1793]. 4 pp, 4to. To his brother George. Giving an account of a drinking bout, & including a poem written on presenting a moss rose to a lady (present). (89) £4,000
— 2 Aug 1801. (88) £550
— 7 June 1816. (91) £650
— [19 Feb 1824]. (91) £650
— 4 Oct 1826. 4 pp, 4to. To Charles Augustus Tulk. Discussing theological issues. (88) £1,500
— [6 Mar 1829]. (89) £550
— [6 Mar 1829]. 1 p, 8vo. To William Pickering. Thanking for a parcel of books & asking him to borrow anr. (91) £1,050
ADs, [c.1830s]. (91) $500
Single sheet ptg, Prospectus of The Friend, [1808]. 2 pp, 372mm by 231mm. On conjugate leaf ALs, [n.d.], 1 p, folio, to John Broadhead; forwarding several prospectuses for distribution & explaining the object of The Friend. Seal tear. Folds strengthened. (88) £3,200

Coleridge-Taylor, Samuel, 1875-1912
Autograph music, 2 songs for 3 female voices, The Butterfly, to words by William Wordsworth & Isle of Beauty, to words by Thomas H. (89) £280
— Autograph music, full score of his Romance in G for Violin and Orchestra (Op. (89) £700
— Autograph music, Romance in G for violin & orchestra, Op. (91) £950
— Autograph music, The Corn Song, for voice, strings & harp, [n.d.]. (91) £550

Colette, Sidonie Gabrielle, 1873-1954
Autograph Ms, novel, La Chatte, [1933]. About 100 pp, folio. Complete working Ms. (91) £10,000
ALs, [before 1907]. (90) DM340
— [n.d.]. (90) $225
— MAJOR, HENRY. - Orig drawing, pencil study of Colette, sgd; [c.1930]. 343mm by 255mm. Sgd & inscr by Colette. (90) $500

Colfax, Schuyler, 1823-85
Autograph Ms, account of an overland journey to California & Vancouver Island, 1865. 41 pp, 4to, on 36 leaves; in red crushed levant mor gilt. Some pencilled revisions in anr hand. With related letter by Sec of War Edwin M. Stanton, 18 Apr 1865, bound in. Doheny collection. (88) $12,000

Coligny, Gaspard de, 1519-72
Ls, 26 Jan 1549. 1 p, folio. To King Henri II of France. About relations with the Count Palatine. (91) DM2,200

Collingwood, Cuthbert, 1st Baron, 1750-1810
Ls, 22 Oct 1805. 2 pp, folio. To the commanders of the fleet at Trafalgar, specifically Lieut. Cumby. Paying tribute to Nelson, & paising the conduct of all participants in the battle. (89) £3,800

Collins, Edward Trowbridge, 1887-1951
Ds, 8 Sept 1940. (91) $275
— 22 Jan 1946. (91) $200

Collins, Wilkie, 1824-89
Autograph Ms, 41 lines including a dialogue between Mr. (90) $700
— Autograph Ms, short story collection After Dark, fragment; [1856 or earlier]. 2 pp, 4to; numbered 36 & 37. Working Ms. (88) £1,500
— Autograph Ms, short story, She Loves and Lies, [1884]. About 40 pp, 4to. Contemp half calf bdg. Working Ms; inscr to A. P. Watt. (89) £12,500
— Autograph Ms, short story, The Girl at the Gate, [early 1880s]. 29 pp, 4to, in red mor gilt. Extensively worked draft. With ALs, 4 June 1887, & engraved port. (90) $14,000
Series of 42 A Ls s, 12 June 1885 to 8 Feb 1888. 115 pp, 8vo. To Annie Elizabeth ("Nannie") Wynne & her mother. Delightful series of letters to a child, giving a vivid picture of his life. (90) £6,500
ALs, 15 Feb 1861. (91) £150
— 12 Feb 1869. (90) DM340
— 22 Sept [1869?]. Doheny collection. (88) $600
— 17 Oct 1876. (89) £260
— 9 June 1880. (88) £70
— 30 Aug 1884. (88) £240

Collinson, Thomas, d.1803
Autograph Ms, journals describing his travels in France, Spain, Switzerland, Italy, Germany & Holland, 1789 & 1790. More than 1500 pp, 8vo, in 12 vols of limp calf. Including c.30 wash sketches. (89) £2,000

Colman, Ronald, 1891-1958 —& Carroll, Madeleine
Group photograph, 1936. (91) $160

Colt, Samuel, 1814-62
ALs, 22 Mar 1838. (91) $475
— 9 Oct 1840. 2 pp, 8vo. To Commodore John Nicolson. About selling arms to Commodore John Downes for the use of his squadron. (88) $1,100

Columbia Pharmaceutical Association
Ms, notebook containing the Constitution of the Association, list of officers, founders & members, 1871-72, & a register of poisons dispensed by a pharmacist, Aug 1880 to Oct 1895. (89) $175

Comer, George
Series of 15 A Ls s, 1879 to 1917. (89) $850

Commonplace Books
Ms, including passages about artists, America, taxation, & epigrams on Lady Waldegrave, [mid-18th cent]; c.250 pp, folio, in def calf bdg. (88) £70

Conde, Henri II de Bourbon, Prince de, 1588-1646. See: Henri II de Bourbon, 1588-1646

Conde, Louis II, Prince de, 1621-86. See: Louis II, 1621-86

Conder, Charles, 1868-1909
A Ls s (2), [c.1896-97]. (90) £750

Condorcet, Marie Jean Antoine Nicolas Caritat, Marquis de, 1743-94. See: Lavoisier, Antoine Laurent de & Condorcet

Congregation De Propaganda Fide
[A collection of Mss & ptd tracts pertaining to the Congregation, mostly reports & letters from Catholic minorites in various countries, 1654 to 1806, c.160 pp, folio & 4to, sold at S on 22 Nov 1988, lot 29, for £700 to Brill.]
[3 copies of a report on missions in China read before the Congregation on 23 Nov 1688, ptd 25 Aug 1690 & sgd by Domingo Diaz & 3 others, each 1 leaf, folio, in modern quarter mor cases, sold at S on 22 Nov 1988, lot 30, for £1,400 to Ad Orientem.]

CONGRESS OF BERLIN

Congress of Berlin
[A leaf bearing the signatures of the principal plenipotentiaries at the Congress of Berlin, including Bismarck & Disraeli, [c.13 July 1878], 1 p, c.13 by 8 inches, mtd, with related material, sold at S on 15 Dec 1988, lot 127, for £700.]

Congreve, William, 1670-1729
ALs, 10 Feb 1723/4. (91) £750

Congreve, Sir William, 1772-1828
ALs, 27 Mar [1820]. (88) $225

Connecticut
Ms, Debenture of the House of Representatives, Jan 1767. (90) $175

Conrad, Joseph, 1857-1924
Autograph Ms, story, Typhoon; dated "Midnight 10th-11th Jan 1901". 191 leaves, foolscap & 4to. Heavily revised working draft. With typescript, sgd, of Typhoon, 133 leaves, 4to, [1901]; final working draft. (90) $170,000

Collection of ALs & ANs, 8 Apr 1913 & 20 Apr 1915. 4 pp, 8vo & 12mo (card). To Sir Sidney Colvin, inviting him for the weekend. To Mr. Davis, thanking for a book. Doheny collection. (88) $1,500

— Collection of ALs & Ls, 10 June 1914 & 9 Apr 1896. 10 pp, folio & 4to. To the Ed of The Daily Express, draft, responding to criticism of his article The Lessons of the Collision. To Mr. Unwin, stating that he is beginning his 3d novel. (90) $7,500

Series of 12 A Ls s, 1893 to 1912. About 50 pp, mostly 8vo. To E. B. Redmayne. Covering a variety of personal & professional matters. (90) £3,600

ALs, 23 Sept 1889. (88) £540
— 23 Feb 1896. 8 pp, 8vo. To E. B. Redmayne. Enlarging upon his misgivings about the contemp world, announcing his marriage, etc. (90) £3,800
— 20 Jan 1900. 14 pp, 8vo. To Edward Garnett. Providing an analysis of his Polish literary roots, his immediate family, & commenting about Lord Jim. (91) £4,400
— 27 Feb 1914. (90) DM950
— 1 Apr 1916. 2 pp, 8vo. To Sir William Rothenstein. Promising to visit when he feels better. (88) DM1,900
— 27 Apr 1918. (90) £360
— 9 Apr 1919. (90) $550
— 29 Apr 1921. (90) $700
— 31 May 1924. 3 pp, 8vo. To Capt. Francis McCullagh. Thanking for a copy of his book about the Russian revolution. With newspaper clipping pasted in on verso. (90) DM1,400

Series of 6 Ls s, 3 May 1919 to 7 Apr 1923. 13 pp, 4to. To Elbridge L. Adams. Personal letters to his friend & biographer. With typed article by E. L. Adams, Joseph Conrad - The Man, fragment, 10 pp, 4to, annotated by Conrad, & further related material. In mor album. Doheny collection. (89) $7,000

Corrected page proofs, Nostromo: A Tale of the Seaboard. L, 1904; 8vo, in blue cloth. With autograph emendations on tp & occasionally throughout, & autograph list of works on verso of half-title. Sgd & inscr to J. B. Pinker. (90) $17,000

— Anr, Guy de Maupassant: Yvette, and Other Stories. Trans by A. G. With a preface by Joseph Conrad; L, 1904; 8vo, in contemp brown wraps. With Conrad's copious emendations in the preface, sgd, & throughout. End of preface completely rewritten. (90) $6,000

— PARTINGTON, WILFRED. - Autograph Ms, Joseph Conrad Behind the Scenes, sgd; [1927]. 17 pp, 8vo, on rectos only. In green mor bdg with copy of ptd article in The Bookman's Journal, vol 15, & further related material. Doheny collection. (89) $700

Conrad of Saxony. See: Speculum Beate Marie Virginis

Conradus de Brundelsheim, d.1321
Ms, Sermones de Sanctis, & other short texts. [Southern Germany, Buxheim Abbey?, c.1425]. Contemp bevelled wooden bds, with pastedowns from a 12th-cent Psalter & sewing-guards from an 11th-cent Breviary. By several scribes in cursive bookhands. (91) £5,500

Conring, Hermann, 1606-81
ALs, 27 Jan 1657. (88) $175
Ls, 28 Jan 1657. (90) DM540

Conscience, Hendrik, 1812-83
Photograph, sgd & inscr, 1866. (88) DM220

Constable, John, 1776-1837
ALs, 20 Mar 1821. 3 pp, 8vo. To William Bannister. Praising the work of Loutherbourgh & accepting an invitation. (89) £1,300
— 4 Feb 1825. (89) DM850
— [n.d.]. (88) £900

Constant de Rebecque, Benjamin Henri, 1767-1830
A Ls s (2), 21 July [n.y.] & [n.d.]. (88) DM200
ALs, 28 June [1823]. (89) DM240

Constantine, Grand Duke of Russia, 1779-1831
ALs, 20 June/2 July 1807. Schroeder collection. (89) DM400

Constantine I, King of Greece, 1868-1923
Ls, 25 Sept 1913. (89) DM450

Constantinople
[A series of 8 watercolor drawings depicting the costume of Constantinople in the 16th cent, captioned in German, sold as part of the Blackmer Collection at S on 11 Oct 1989 for £25,500]

Constantinus Africanus, c.1020-87
Ms, Viaticum, with glosses by Gerardus de Solo. [France, c.1350]. 67 leaves, vellum. 15th-cent red sheepskin over wooden bds. In 2 sizes of a gothic textura. Medical manual; with 8 penwork initials. Front pastedown incorporating 13th-cent document. (90) DM90,000

Constitution of the United States
[A collection of 37 autographs of 35 signers of the Constitution, 1760 to 1816, sold at CNY on 22 Feb 1989, lot 2164, for $8,500 to Scriptorium.]
— VIRGINIA CONSTITUTIONAL CONVENTION. - Document, proceedings of the Convention which ratified the Constitution & proposed the Bill of Rights, 25 to 27 June 1788. 14 pp, folio; sewn. Sgd by Edmund Pendleton, President of the Convention, & Sec John Beckley. Imperf. Sang collection. (89) $280,000

Continental Congress
[A group of 14 autographs, mostly A Ls s, by various members of the Continental Congress, 1754 to 1811, sold at CNY on 21 Feb 1989, lot 1785, for $2,800 to Lowe.]
Ms, extract from the Minutes, 12 Jan 1780. (89) $325
Letter, 27 Oct 1786. (89) $250
— 21 July 1787. (89) $250
Document, 16 Dec 1782. (89) $550

Cook, Capt. James, 1728-79
Autograph Ms, notes from a journal of his 2d Pacific Voyage, c.1772. 4 pp, 4to; detached from a notebook. Describing the manning & victualling of the ships, with list of provisions. Def. (89) £8,000
ALs, 1 Aug 1772. 1 p, folio. To Capt. William Hammond. From Madeira, reporting favorably on the performance of his ships & crew after the beginning of his 2d voyage. (90) £10,000

Cooke, Jay, 1821-1905
Series of 3 A Ls s, 1879 to 1900. (89) $650

Cooke, William Cubitt
Original drawings, (42), to illus Jane Austen's novels, 1893, & other titles. Archives of J.M.Dent & Son. (88) £190

Cookery Manuscripts
[2 19th-cent recipe books containing c.130 & c.100 mostly culinary recipes, folio & 4to, sold at bba on 28 July 1988, lot 197, for £60 to Ramer.]
Ms, [18th & 19th cent]; c.100 pp, 4to; some loosely inserted. (88) £140
— Ms, cookery & medical recipes, [18th cent]. (91) £260
— Ms, cookery, household & medical recipes, [17th cent]; c.180 pp, folio, in contemp calf bds. (88) £750
— Ms, cookery recipes, [early 18th cent]; c.150 pp, folio, in modern bds. (88) £140
— Ms, culinary & medicinal recipes, 1801. (88) £50

COOKERY MANUSCRIPTS

— Ms, culinary & medicinal recipes. (90) DM520
— Ms, culinary & medical recipes, [17th & late 18th cent]; c.130 pp & blanks, 8vo, in English 17th-cent extra red mor bdg by the Queen's binder B. In at least 3 hands. (88) £8,000
— Ms, culinary recipes & household remedies, [England, 1854]. (90) £110
— Ms, culinary recipes & household remedies, [England, late 18th cent]. (89) £160
— Ms, Ein Approbiert Gutes Koch-Buch, von vielerley kostbahren Sachen. (88) DM900
— Ms, Francis Egerton Her Book, 1727. (89) £180
— Ms, Kochbuch der Frau Maria Helena Weissin, [Muehldorf near Salzburg, 1796]. 426 pp & 23 index leaves, 205mm by 160mm. Contemp lea bdg. Culinary recipes & menus. (89) DM1,300
— Ms, The Contents of all manners of wines..., [England, late 17th cent]. (91) £600

Cookson, Catherine
Typescript, novel, The Parson's Daughter, 18 Oct 1982 to 9 Jan 1983. (88) £600

Coolidge, Calvin, 1872-1933
[2 checks, sgd (1 accomplished), 11 Jan 1913 & [1930s?], 85mm by 210mm, sold at sg on 25 Oct 1988, lot 44, for $200.]
ALs, 3 June 1901. (91) $325
— 12 Aug 1912. (90) $650
— 15 Mar 1921. Length not stated, 8vo. To Mr. Chapple. Suggesting changes for a magazine article regarding his election. On Vice Presidential stationery. (88) $1,200
— 19 Mar 1924. 1 p, 4to. To Herbert L. Pratt. Thanking for a letter from his former Amherst classmate. Pratt collection. (89) $3,250
Series of 8 Ls s, 1919 to Dec 1927. 8 pp, 4to. To C.W. Barron (6), Gen. Bancroft & Frank Leonard. Mostly expressing thanks for memoranda & support. With related material. Doheny collection. (89) $1,300
Ls s (2), 22 Nov 1924 & 31 Aug 1925. (91) $500

AMERICAN BOOK PRICES CURRENT

— Ls s (2), 7 Jan 1925 & 12 Mar 1927. (90) $450
Ls, 11 Jan 1917. (91) $130
— 20 Oct 1919. (91) $170
— 21 Jan 1920. (88) $110
— 17 Sept 1920. (90) $150
— 4 Nov 1920. (89) $110
— 8 Nov 1920. (91) $130
— 9 Aug 1923. (89) $220
— 27 Aug 1923. (88) $110
— 30 Aug 1923. (90) $275
— 18 Feb 1924. (90) $250
— 3 Mar 1924. (91) $275
— 10 May 1924. (91) $225
— 20 June 1924. Sang collection. (91) $600
— 8 Nov 1924. (90) $130
— 11 Nov 1924. Byer collection. (90) $275
— 25 Feb 1925. (88) $180
— 23 Apr 1925. (91) $325
— 27 Mar 1926. Pratt collection. (89) $600
— 16 Mar 1927. (88) $275
— 4 July 1927. (90) $190
— 26 Oct 1927. Middendorf collection. (89) $500
— 4 July 1927. (91) $190
— 11 Mar 1929. (88) $80
— 9 Apr 1931. (90) $140
Ns, 13 Feb 1925. (88) $275
Collection of Ds, White House card, sgd, & photograph, sgd & inscr, 13 June 1927, [n.d.], & 1924. (90) $350
Ds, 1 July 1924. (91) $130
— 5 Nov 1924. (89) $200
— 20 Dec 1924. (88) $120
— 20 June 1925. (90) $110
— 8 June 1926. (90) $100
Check, accomplished & sgd, 25 Dec 1912, for $1.00 payable to W. (89) $110
— Anr, sgd, 1 May 1916. (90) $160
— Anr, sgd, 2 May 1916. (91) $150
— Anr, sgd, 12 Jan 1927. (90) $400
— Anr, sgd, 29 Apr 1932; 76mm by 210mm. (88) $250
— Anr, sgd, 7 May 1932. (90) $180
— Anr, sgd, 28 May 1932. (89) $150
Photograph, sgd & inscr, [n.d.]. (88) $250
— Anr, [n.d.]. (88) $120
— Anr, [n.d.]. (91) $275
— Anr, [n.d.]. (90) $220

— Anr, [n.d.]. (89) $450
— Anr, [n.d.]. (90) $225
— Anr, [n.d.]. (89) $180
— Anr, [n.d.]. (90) $150
Signature, [21 Dec 1929]. (89) $170
White House card, sgd, [n.d.]. (89) $110
— Anr, sgd, [n.d.]. (88) $80
— Anr, sgd, [n.d.]. (90) $95
— Anr, sgd, [n.d.]. (91) $140
— Anr, sgd, [n.d.]. (91) $180
— Anr, sgd, [n.d.]. (91) $150
— Anr, sgd, [n.d.]. (90) $130
— Anr, sgd, [n.d.]. (90) $80
   See also: Taft, William Howard & Coolidge

Coolidge, Grace Goodhue, 1879-1957
Autograph Ms, poem, The Open Door, 7 July 1929. (91) $550
Ls, 24 Oct 1934. (89) $60
Photograph, sgd & inscr, 18 May 1954. (91) $120

Cooper, Gary, 1901-61
Ls, 6 Jan 1939. (91) $350
ANs, 1929. (91) $175
Photograph, sgd & inscr, [n.d.]. (91) $200

Cooper, James Fenimore, 1789-1851
   [2 checks, accomplished & sgd, 14 Mar 1836 & 30 Nov 1837, sold at sg on 9 Mar 1989, lot 39, for $225.]
   [A collection of 3 checks, sgd, 1837 to 1845, drawn on the Otsego County Bank at Cooperstown & payable to himself sold at wa on 17 Oct, lot 23, for $130.]
Autograph Ms, novel, The Headsman, fragments of chapters IX & XXIX; [pbd 1833]. 8 pp, various sizes. Including 2 notes of authenticity at head. Doheny collection. (89) $3,200
— Autograph Ms, novel, The Water-Witch, portion of beginning of chapter 8, [pbd 1830]. (90) $850
— Autograph Ms, The Bravo, closing paragraph of chapter VI; 16 June 1831. Sgd. (90) $1,300
Collection of ALs & ANs, [1832? & n.d.], 2 pp, 12mo. Doheny collection. (89) $500
A Ls s (2), [1846]. Byer collection. (90) $300
ALs, 19 Apr 1820. 2 pp, 4to. To Brig. Gen. Peter Gansevoort. Discussing political parties & the election in Westchester County. Doheny collection. (89) $1,900
— 14 May 1826. Byer collection. (90) $200
— 11 Dec 1826. (91) $800
— 5 Feb 1831. (89) £100
— 3 Jan 1836. 1 p, 4to. To Peter Gansevoort. Recommending Mr. Vicat, & discussing the need for naval preparedness. Doheny collection. (89) $1,700
— 14 June 1844. (89) $200
— 29 Apr 1847. 1 p, 4to. To President James K. Polk. Recommending Zephaniah Charles Foot for a lieutenancy. With autograph envelope, endorsed by Polk. Doheny collection. (89) $1,700
— [n.d.]. Doheny collection. (89) $850
Autograph check, sgd, 19 Sept 1834. Doheny collection. (89) $550
— Anr, sgd, 16 Feb 1848. (90) $150

Cooper, Peter, 1791-1883
Ls, 27 Jan 1866. (91) $80

Cooper, S.
Original drawings, (35), to illus W. Archives of J. M. Dent & Son. (88) £120

Cooper, Samuel, 1798-1876
Franking signature, [29 July 1835]. (89) $230
— Anr, [n.d.]. Alexander collection. (90) $105

Copland, Aaron
Ls, 20 Jan 1960. (90) $90
   See also: Bernstein, Leonard & Copland

Copleston Family
   [An album relating generally to the Copleston family, 18th & 19th cent, including autographs by Bishops Warburton & Heber, & George Canning, sold at S on 15 Nov 1988, lot 1674, for £180 to White.]

Copley, John Singleton, 1737-1815
Ls, 21 Aug 1783. (89) £380

Coptic Manuscripts

Ms, petitions for the clergy & the celebrant at the Mass, in the Sa'idic dialect of Coptic. (90) £900
— Ms, The Mississippi Codex, [Middle Egypt, Panopolis (now Achnim)?, 3d cent]. 52 leaves & fragments of anr 16, papyrus, 145mm by 153mm, preserved in 35 double sided glass mounts. Containing the Book of Jonah; Melito of Sardis, Peri Pascha; the story of the Jewish Martyrs from II Maccabees; & the 1st Epistle of St. Peter, all in the Sahidic dialect of Coptic. In black ink, mostly in double column. One of the earliest Mss in codex form, almost certainly the earliest with contemp pagination, & the earliest known complete texts of 2 books of the Bible. (89) £200,000

Corcoran, William Wilson, 1798-1888
ALs, 17 May 1848. (91) $95

Cordier, Benjamin
Ms, Livre contenant un plan general de la Forest de Saint Germain en Laye, [n.d.]. (88) £280

Corelli, Marie, Pseud. of Mary Mackay, 1855-1924
Series of 16 A Ls s, 1922 to 1925. (88) £140

Corfu
[A group of 21 items relating to the cession of Corfu & the setting up of a provisional government, May & June 1814, sold at pn on 16 Mar 1989, lot 70, for £200 to Army Museum.]

Corinth, Lovis, 1858-1925
ALs, 22 Nov 1917. (89) DM280
— 22 Sept 1923. 2 pp, 4to. To Max Liebermann. Explaining his reluctance to participate in an exhibition in Rome. (91) DM1,500
— 22 Mar 1925. (88) DM300

Corinth, Lovis, 1858-1925 —& Others
[A postcard addressed to Herr & Frau Groenwold, 10 Nov 1900, sgd by Corinth, Eleonore & Ludwig von Hofmann, Anna & Walter Leistikow, & others, sold at star on 27 June 1990, lot 676, for DM320.]

Cornelius, Peter, 1824-74
Autograph Ms, poem, Auf Hektor Berlioz, concluding 7 stanzas; [1866]. (90) DM380
Autograph music, song Das ist die schoenste Stunde to a text by Emil Kuh, [n.d.]. 4 pp, 28.2cm by 19.5cm; 12 staves each. Scored for voice & piano; sgd at head. (89) DM4,000
ALs, 1 Mar [1857]. (89) DM550
— [n.d.]. (91) DM800

Cornforth, John Warcup
Autograph Ms, What is biochemistry? Notes for a lecture, sgd at end & dated 26 May 1981. (90) DM250

Cornwallis, Charles Cornwallis, Marquis, 1738-1805
ALs, 2 July 1780. To Lt. Col Clarke. Discussing his strategic plans for the Southern states during the Revolutionary War. (91) £1,600
— 30 Apr 1786. (88) $400
— 16 Nov 1786. (91) $700
— 8 Nov 1801. (90) DM330
Ls, 9 Oct 1786. (88) $300

Coronation Street
Typescript (duplicated), television scripts for 5 episodes, 26 July to 5 Sept 1967. (91) £500

Corot, Camille, 1796-1875
ALs, 1 Apr 1859. (89) DM600
— 9 Aug [1864]. (90) DM540

Corso, Gregory
[A group of 11 whimsical autographs, sgd, mostly A Ls s, [1?] Apr 1977, 11 pp, 8vo, addressed to "Jonathan", with related material, sold at wa on 21 Oct 1989, lot 344, for $190.]

Cortes, Hernando, 1485-1547
Ds, 5 Jan 1528. 77mm by 207mm. Ordering payment for 2 sailors. Framed. (89) $12,000

Cortot, Alfred, 1877-1962
Series of c.20 A Ls s, 1938 to 1962. 50 pp, various sizes. To Arthur Hedley. Discussing various matters relating to Chopin. (89) £1,600
— Series of 6 A Ls s, 21 Sept 1958 to 15 July 1961. 9 pp, 8vo. To Madeleine T. at Loerrach. Letters to a young musi-

cian. (88) DM1,700
A Ls s (2), 19 May 1946 & 24 Apr 1962. (88) DM320
ALs, 2 Sept 1916. (90) DM250
— 25 June 1918. (90) DM220
— 29 Dec 1937. (89) DM320

Corvisart des Marets, Jean Nicolas, Baron, 1755-1821
AL, [11 Mar 1795]. (88) DM200

Corwin, Thomas, 1794-1865. See: Grant, Ulysses S.

Costa, Sir Michael, 1808-84
[A collection of c.60 A Ls s by Costa & letters addressed to him, 1833 to 1884, mostly relating to the London stage, with related material, sold at S on 21 Nov 1990, lot 70, for £1,200 to Palmer.]

Costa Rica & New Spain
[A group of 5 documents, 1567 to 1658, including a letter to the Viceroy, letters from the Town Council of Cartago & petitions, sold at bba on 15 Dec 1988, lot 96, for £350 to Bernard.]

Cotman, John Sell, 1782-1842
ALs, 9 Aug 1804. (90) £750
— 21 June 1826. (91) £280
— 30 Jan 1834. (91) £600
— 31 Mar 1834. (91) £300

Cottle, Joseph, 1770-1853
ALs, 14 July 1843. (90) £170

Coubertin, Pierre de, 1863-1937
Autograph postcard, sgd, 13 Sept 1905. (90) DM480

Coudray, Clemens Wenzel, 1775-1845
ALs, 6 June 1831. 3 pp, 4to. To Karl Christian Vogel von Vogelstein. Sending news from Weimar, mentioning David d'Angers's bust of Goethe, Goethe's health problems, etc. Albrecht collection. (91) SF1,100

Courbet, Gustave, 1819-77
ALs, [1877]. 2 pp, 8vo. To [A. G.] Chaudey. About his new exposition. (89) DM2,800
ANs, [n.d.]. (90) DM470
ADs, 2 Nov 1855. 1 p, 8vo. Receipt for final installment of payment for his painting Les Demoiselles de Village. With port photograph. (88) DM2,200

Courcy, Jean de, fl.1420
Ms, La Bouquechardiere, or Histoire Grecque et Romaine. [Paris or Loire Valley, c.1470-80]. 322 leaves (some lacking), vellum, 420mm by 294mm. 18th-cent French quarter mottled calf & pastebds. In brown ink in a regular lettre batarde. With 7 large illuminated initials & 5 very large miniatures with large initials & full illuminated borders. Phillipps MS.132 & Abbey collection. (89) £85,000

Coward, Noel, 1899-1973
ALs, [14 Feb 1929]. (91) $275
Ls, 28 Apr 1962. (91) $300
— 19 June 1964. (91) $130
— [c.1964]. (91) $300
Photograph, sgd & inscr, 1 June 1965. (90) $150

Cowper, Max
Original drawings, (18), to illus novels by Charles Dickens, [n.d.]. (89) £460

Cowper, William, 1731-1800
Autograph Ms, poem, In Memory of the late John Thornton Esqr., [Nov 1790]. 3 pp, 4to. 50 lines, with substantive revisions. (89) £2,800
— Autograph Ms, poem, The Acquiescence of Pure Love, draft of a trans from the poems of Mme Guyon; [n.d.]. (88) £700
— Autograph Ms, preface to his trans of Homer, [spring 1791]. (89) £600
Series of 19 A Ls s, 24 Mar 1782 to 25 July 1792. 34 pp, 4to. To William Bull. Important letters about his work & a variety of matters. Initialled; 1 signature removed. (89) £14,000
ALs, 22 June 1782. 3 pp, 4to. To William Bull. In verse, hymn to the goddess of tobacco; 73 lines. Sgd Wm.C. (89) £3,000
— 7 Mar 1783. 4 pp, 4to. To William Bull. About prospects for peace, & sending an epitaph on his hare (present, 11 stanzas). (89) £3,000
— 9 Feb 1790. (90) £950
— 6 Apr 1791. (88) £600
— 15 Apr 1793. (91) £500
— NEWTON, JOHN. - ALs, 1 Nov 1800. 4

pp, 4to. To Lady Hesketh. Describing Cowper's character, his attitude towards religion, his period of derangement, etc. (89) £1,100

Cox, E. Albert
Original drawings, (9), designs for dust jackets for titles pbd in The Wayfarer's Library, 1914 to 1920. Archives of J. M. Dent & Son. (88) £110

Cox, Palmer, 1840-1924
[An archive of letters, drawings, etc., various sizes, in a large fitted box, sold at P on 31 Jan 1990, lot 2340, for $3,750.]
Original drawings, (10), to illus The Brownies: Their Book, [pbd 1887]. Average size 240mm by 205mm. In pen-&-ink, sgd. Mtd on heavy card stock. Koch Foundation. (90) $8,500
— Original drawings, (29), mostly to illus The Brownies, their Book, [1887]. Sizes not stated. In ink. Martin collection. (90) $4,750

Cox, Sir Richard, 1650-1733
[An important collection of largely autograph literary Mss, notebooks & annotated books, nearly 1,600 pp, folio, in 6 vols, with related legal & estate documents, sold at S on 19 July 1990, lot 3, for £12,000 to Lyon.]

Coxe, Tench, 1755-1824
ALs, 30 Sept 1784. (88) $50

Crabbe, George, 1754-1832
Autograph Ms, poem, The Lady Frances, [1809 or later]. (89) £460
ALs, 30 Nov 1815. (91) £280

Craig, Edward Gordon, 1872-1966
[21 proof impressions of wood engravings, [1953], 8vo, in mor-backed bds, illusts for Robinson Crusoe [ptd 1979], sold at S on 18 July 1991, lot 30, for £650 to Meredith.]
Collection of 17 A Ls s & Ls s, 1892 to 1952. (88) £280
— Collection of c.35 A Ls s & cards, sgd, 1909 to 1931; c.150 pp, 8vo & 4to. (88) £720
— Collection of 14 A Ls & 2 autograph postcards sgd, 16 Nov 1924-23 Apr 1928 & 27 Feb 1950-21 Feb 1953. 44 pp, 8vo. To Lennox Robinson. (91) $1,200
— Collection of c.350 A Ls s & postcards, sgd, 1946 to 1965. More than 1200 pp, 8vo. To Janet Leeper. Interesting letters mostly concerning theatrical matters. With related material. (88) £3,500
A Ls s (2), 17 May 1913 & [n.d.]. (90) DM380

Craig, George
Original drawings, (24), to illus Edward de Bono's The Case of the Disappearing Elephant, 1977. Archives of J. M. Dent & Son. (88) £110

Craig, James, Viscount Craigavon, 1871-1940
[An important collection of his papers, chiefly relating to Irish affairs, & including letters by Eamon de Valera, Lloyd George, Kitchener, Asquith, etc., over 200 items, 1907 to 1940, sold at S on 19 July 1990, lot 271, for £14,500 to Sawyer.]

Craigie, Dorothy
Original drawings, (25), to illus The Scarecrows who Flew, [n.d.]. (89) £300

Cramer, Johann Baptist, 1771-1858
ALs, 23 May 1835. (89) DM700

Cramer, Rie
Original drawings, (11), to illus The Snow Queen, [c.1955]. Various sizes. In ink & watercolor. 9 sgd or initialled. (89) £2,200
— Original drawings, (32), mostly to illus Hansel and Gretel, & Goldilocks and the Three Bears, [c.1955]. Various sizes. In ink & watercolor. Mostly sgd. (89) £1,700
— Original drawings, (33), to illus The Little Mermaid, [c.1955]. Various sizes. In ink & watercolor. Mostly sgd or initialled. (89) £1,300
— Original drawings, (34), to illus Cinderella, [c.1955]. Various sizes, on 21 sheets. In ink & watercolor. 18 sgd. Some separated. (89) £1,700
— Original drawings, (34), to illus Thumbelina, [c.1955]. Various sizes. In ink & watercolor. Mostly sgd or initialled. (89) £1,900

Crane, Stephen, 1871-1900
ALs, 4 Jan [1896]. 2 pp, 8vo. To Corwin Knapp Linson. Asking him to forward a box of papers left in Linson's studio. Sgd S.C. With explanatory note by Linson at end. Doheny collection. (89) $2,200

Crane, Walter, 1845-1915
Original drawing, tp design for Eight Illustrations to Shakespeare's Tempest, 1893. Archives of J. M. Dent & Son. (88) £100
See also: Morris, William

Cranevelt, Francis, 1485-1564
[An important archive of 9 letters by Cranevelt & 108 letters addressed to him by leading humanists including Sir Thomas More, Erasmus, & others, 1520 to 1522, c.149 pp, mostly folio, dampstained, sold at C on 21 June 1989, lot 91, for £280,000.]

Crawford, Joan, 1908-77
Collection of Ls & photograph, [n.d.]. (89) $300
Photograph, [n.d.]. (89) $900

Crawford, William H., 1772-1834
A Ls s (2), 2 & 4 Mar 1811. (91) $375

Creed, Clara ("T. Pym")
Original drawings, (19), partly to illus Skipping Time (pbd 1887). (89) £850

Crescentiis, Petrus de, 1230?-1310?
Ms, Liber Ruralium Commodorum. [France, late 14th cent]. 36 leaves only, 335mm by 234mm, disbound. In dark brown ink in a large gothic bookhand. With decorated initials throughout & 4 very large initials with penwork extensions. Dampstained. (88) £3,200

Crimean War
[3 A Ls, sgd C. A. W., 26 Oct 1854 to 22 June 1855, 22 pp, 8vo, reporting about the Battle of Balaklava, the Charge of the Light Brigade, etc., sold at S on 15 Dec, lot 262, for £1,900.]
— BURTON, LIEUT.-COL. ADOLPHUS WILLIAM DESART. - Autograph Ms, diary describing the siege of Sebastopol, 1855, 8vo; & 8 A Ls s, 1854 to 1855, 42 pp, 8vo, to his sister Rosa or brother Charles; mostly from the Crimea.
With related material. (88) £420
— BUTTERS, THOMAS. - ALs, 14 May 1854. 2 pp, folio. To his cousin Ann Duffill. Describing the Turkish hospital, the inhabitants of Constantinople, etc. (89) £65
— GRAHAM, LIEUT. N. - 3 A Ls s, 7 June to 17 Aug 1855. 24 pp, 8vo. To his father. Describing life in the trenches, etc. With related material. (90) £240
— HAMMOND, MAX. - Series of 38 A Ls s, 2 Mar to 9 Oct 1854; c. 260 pp, 8vo. To his wife Rose. Reporting about the early stages of the campaign & the conditions in Scutari hospital. (88) £1,700
— HORN, PHILIP. - 90 A Ls s, 30 June 1853 to 23 July 1856. 250 pp, folio & 4to. To his brother & sister. Eyewitness account of the whole war by a Sergeant of the 11th Hussars [the Light Brigade]. (91) £2,400
— NOLAN, CAPT. LEWIS. - Autograph Ms, journal, 5 Sept to 12 Oct 1854. 97 pp, in 8vo notebook. With detailed accounts of the Battles of the Alma & Balaclava, discussing strategy, etc. (88) £11,000
— RIDLEY, MAJOR GEN. CHARLES WILLIAM. - 9 A Ls s, 15 Nov 1854 to 29 Dec 1855. About 90 pp, 8vo. To his cousin Maria. Describing his journey to the Crimea, the siege of Sebastopol, etc. (89) £480
— WHITE, HENRY DALRYMPLE. - Ms, memoirs, [c.1860s]; c.140 pp, 8vo, in cloth bdg. Dictated to his wife; covering his life from birth to 1861, & including account of his service in the Crimea. In pencil. (88) £350

Crippen, Hawley Harvey, 1862-1910
Series of 9 A Ls s, 5 to 26 Oct 1910. 34 pp, 4to. To Lady Henry Somerset. Letters from prison, expressing confidence in his acquittal. (91) £7,500
Ls, 11 Sept 1909. (91) £55
— 11 Sept 1909. (90) £110

Crockett, David, 1786-1836
ALs, 31 May 1830. 1 p, 4to. To William B. Lewis. Letter of recommendation for Thomas Graham. (90) $11,000
— 18 Dec 1832. 2 pp, folio. To Daniel Webster. Asking him to support the

CROCKETT

claim of the heirs of Col. Henry [Dyer] for relief. Fold splits. (89) $12,000
— 17 Jan 1834. 2 pp, 4to. To G. W. McLean. Informing him of his intention to publish his autobiography & denouncing Jackson. (89) $19,000

Ds, 14 Apr 1824. (91) $750

Franking signature, [11 Feb 1835]. On autograph address leaf. Alexander collection. (90) $6,250

Crofts, Freeman Wills, 1879-1957
Proof copy, detective story, Enemy Unseen, [1945]. (90) £260

Croissant-Rust, Anna, 1860-1943
Collection of 62 A Ls s & 9 autograph postcards, sgd, 11 Jan 1911 to 29 Oct 1927. Over 130 pp, mostly 4to, & cards. To her pbr Georg Mueller. Discussing the publication of her works. With related material. (90) DM1,100

Cromwell Family
— CROMWELL, HENRY. - Ds, 20 June 1600. Size not stated, vellum. Receipt for £3,800 from Edmund Anderson for the purchase of St. Neotts. Sgd Henrie Williams als. Cormwell of Godmanchester. Also sgd by others. Framed. (91) £190

Cromwell, Oliver, 1599-1658
Ls, 24 Aug 1649. 1 p, folio. To Sir John Wollaston. Order regarding pay for officers going to Ireland. Including receipt sgd by Paymaster Nath[aniel] Boyse, at bottom. (90) DM8,500
— 16 May 1654. 1 p, folio. To Col. Alured. Ordering him to surrender his command to Lieut. Gen. Fleetwood & to come to London. (90) £2,200

Ds s (2) 20 July 1649 & 28 Dec 1650. 2 pp, folio & 4to. Order to Sir John Wollaston to give Lieut. Col. Daniel Axtel £2,250 as pay for the troops going to Ireland, with Axtel's receipt at bottom of p. Order to his soldiers to allow Lady Polwarth to pass without molestation. Both matted. (88) $10,000

Ds, 25 Apr 1657. 1 p, folio. Appointment of Francis Brockhurst as Captain. (90) £1,800

Cromwell, Richard, 1626-1712
ALs, [n.d.]. 1 p, folio. To one of his children. Acknowledging receipt of a letter & expressing concern for his child's welfare. Sgd R.C. (89) £1,150
— BRADSHAW, JOHN. - Document, 11 Oct 1658. Size not stated, vellum. Exemplification of a verdict issued in the name of Richard Cromwell in the case of John Swain versus Peter Leicester. (89) £380

Cronin, Joseph E., 1906-84
Ds, 13 Sept 1948. (90) $100
— 2 Sept 1958. (91) $100

Crook, George, 1829-90
ALs, 3 Dec 1864. (91) $375
Ls, 17 Dec 1882. (91) $160

Crosby, Bing, 1904-77
Series of 10 Ls s, 1949 to 1976. (89) $500

Crowley, Aleister, 1875-1947
A Ls s (2), June 1936. (88) £140
ALs, [1932], 1 p, 8vo. (89) £85

Cruger, John, 1710-91
Ds, 10 Mar 1764. (91) $75

Cruikshank, George, 1792-1878
[A collection of correspondence with Bogue's & Bell's publishing houses & related material, including 37 A Ls s by Cruikshank, 1820 to 1872, over 100 items, sold at S on 18 July 1991, lot 269, for £2,800 to Pickering & Chatto.]
[An archive of letters by or to Cruikshank, autograph drafts, notes & sketches, [1850s to 1870s], 75 leaves, 4to or smaller, sold at P on 14 Dec 1988, lot 15, for $2,750.]
[A collection of watercolors, drawings & sketches, including pen-&-ink vignette for Cowper's Song of the Loss of the Royal George, 24 leaves, 4to & smaller, various dates, sold at P on 14 Dec 1988, lot 3, for $3,250.]

Autograph Ms, address book, [1840s to 1870s]. 139 pp, 12mo. Orig black crushed sheep bdg; def. In ink or pencil. (89) $3,000
— Autograph Ms, Day Book, sgd, 1810 to 1825. 63 pp, 315mm by 96mm, in orig vellum bdg. Account book recording dealings with numerous publishers.

(89) $5,000
Autograph sketchbook, 12 watercolors of views in Scotland, 1856, & other drawings. 31 leaves, 365mm by 252mm, in orig quarter dark-green sheep bdg. Mostly in pencil, sgd in 15 places. (89) $2,500
Original drawings, 13 character sketches, vignettes, & drawings for various works, [1833 to 1857]. 7 leaves, folio & smaller. In pencil or pen-&-ink, with watercolor. Sgd; 1 also inscr. Framed. David Borowitz collection. (88) $2,400
— Original drawings, [1830s to early 1850s]. 29 leaves, 4to or smaller. Drawings & sketches including illusts for works by Dickens & others. In pencil, watercolor, wash, or pen-&-ink; many sgd. Gough-Austin collection. (89) $8,500
— Original drawings, (2), preliminary sketches for Capt. Wolf collection. (89) £650
— Original drawings, (5), watercolor studies for illusts to Eccentric Tales by W. F. von Kosewitz, [1827]. 5 leaves, 8vo. (89) $1,800
— Original drawings, (7), to illus Freischuetz-Travestie, The Greatest Plague of Life, & Cinderella, [pbd 1824 to 1856]. 7 leaves, 8vo or smaller. In watercolor & pen-&-ink, or watercolor & pencil; sgd. (89) $2,750
Original drawing, man sitting on a barrel; [n.d.]. (90) $300
Collection of 2 ALs, AL, & 23 watercolor drawings, pencil sketches & prints, mostly sgd, 10 Feb 1831 to 22 Mar 1870 & [n.d.]. Various sizes, mtd on cards & bound in brown mor gilt album by Riviere & Son; 4to. Contents of letters not stated. Koch Foundation. (90) $4,500
— Collection of ALs & Ls, 28 Feb 1853 & 27 Nov 1877, 5 pp, 8vo & 12mo. Doheny collection. (89) $50
Series of 3 A Ls s, [1840?] to 9 Dec [18]71. 5 pp, 8vo & 4to. To Charles Dickens, regarding plates for [The Pic-nic Papers]; & draft, offering condolences on the death of his daughter. To Charles W. Kent, contents not stated. (89) $2,250
ALs, [c. Koch Foundation. (90) $300
Autograph sentiment, sgd, [10?] Oct 1859.

(91) $50
See also: Dickens, Charles

Cruikshank, Isaac Robert, 1789-1856
Original drawing, Red Riding Hood & the Wolf, surrounded by 4 smaller vignettes showing the main elements from Beauty and the Beast, [c.1825]. Koch Foundation. (90) $700

Crusades
[A collection of 10 vellum documents, 1191 to 1249, issued by Philip Augustus, King of France & other crusaders mostly during the siege of Acre & concerning loans of money from merchants of Genoa & Pisa, 4 with seals, sold at S on 20 June 1989, lot 29, for £29,000 to Beres.]

Csokor, Franz Theodor, 1885-1969
Collection of 5 A Ls s, 4 Ls s, & autograph visiting card, 1954 to 1968. 10 pp, 8vo & 4to. To Adolf Opel. About a variety of professional matters. With related material. (88) DM1,300

Cub Series
Original drawings, (238), for the 1st 12 titles in the Cub Series, by various artists, 1926 to 1928. Various sizes. With related material. (90) £1,100

Cui, Cesar, 1835-1918
ALs, 22 Oct [1908]. 4 pp, 4to. To Juliette Folville. About the use of bells in concerts, his Kapitanskaya dochka, & Pushkin's novella. Including small sketch. In French. (89) DM1,300

Cumberland, Richard, 1732-1811
ALs, 13 Sept 1785. (88) £450

Cummings, Edward Estlin, 1894-1962
Ds, 8 Feb 1960. (91) $100

Curie, Marie, 1867-1934
Series of 3 A Ls s, 12 Jan 1910 to 26 Feb 1911. 5 pp, 4to. To the Austrian Ministry for Public Works. Regarding the acquisition of uranium ore residues from the mines at St. Joachimsthal. Including instructions for the extraction of polonium. On Faculte des Sciences de Paris letterhead. Repaired. (89) DM28,000
ALs, 31 Jan 1904. 2 pp, 8vo. Recipient unnamed. Declining an invitation to

CURIE

lecture in Florence. (91) £2,600
— 20 Oct 1908. 1 p, 8vo. To Louis Frischauer. Regarding his wish to work in her laboratory. (90) DM8,000

Ls, Jan 1924. 1 p, 4to. To George Kunz. Thanking for congratulations on the 25th anniversary of the discovery of Radium. Byer collection. (90) $1,600

Ds, 29 Oct 1921. 1 p, 4to. Certificat No. 1737. Dosage de radium..., issued by the Laboratoire Curie. Accomplished in Curie's hand. (90) DM2,200

Curie, Pierre, 1859-1906
Autograph Ms, fragment from his diary, 25 July to 1 Aug [1905]. (89) £600

Curry, John Steuart, 1897-1946
Original drawing, [3 Dec 1941]. (88) $140

Curtis, Dora
Original drawings, (10), to illus Alicia Hoffmann's adaptation of Richard II, 1904. Archives of J. M. Dent & Son. (88) £150
— Original drawings, (10), to illus titles in The Wayfarer's Library, c.1914. Archives of J. M. Dent & Son. (88) £280
— Original drawings, (11), to illus Alicia Hoffmann's adaptation of Romeo and Juliet, 1905. Archives of J. M. Dent & Son. (88) £320
— Original drawings, (12), to illus Alicia Hoffmann's adaptation of As You Like It, 1905. Archives of J. M. Dent & Son. (88) £280
— Original drawings, (13), to illus Alicia Hoffmann's adaptation of The Merchant of Venice, 1904. Archives of J. M. Dent & Son. (88) £180
— Original drawings, (19), to illus The Little Duke, 1910. Archives of J. M. Dent & Son. (88) £270
— Original drawings, (31), to illus Beatrice Clay's Stories of King Arthur and the Round Table, 1905. Archives of J. M. Dent & Son. (88) £800
— Original drawings, (34), to illus Edward Hutton's Children's Christmas Treasury, 1905, & other titles. Archives of J. M. Dent & Son. (88) £260
— Original drawings, (4), to illus Jean Ingelow's Mopsa the Fairy, 1964. Archives of J. M. Dent & Son. (88) £180

AMERICAN BOOK PRICES CURRENT

Curtiss, Glenn Hammond, 1878-1930
Signature, [n.d.]. (91) $120

Curtius, Ernst, 1814-96
ALs, 28 Oct 1866. (89) DM260
— 28 July 1878. (91) DM230

Curzon, Robert, 1810-73
ALs, 20 Aug 1869. (90) £140

Cushing, Charles Goodwin
[An album containing more than 400 of his photographs, c.1949 to 1951, covering all aspects of American society, sold at sg on 24 Mar 1988, lot W123, for $1,100.]

Cushing, Harvey Williams, 1869-1939
Ls, 27 July 1935. (91) $350

Cushing, Thomas H., 1755-1822
Ls, 26 Sept 1809. (88) $80

Custer, Elizabeth Bacon, 1842-1933
Series of 3 A Ls s, 18 Jan 1887 & [n.y.]. (89) $160
ALs, 7 Jan [n.y.]. (90) $220

Custer, George Armstrong, 1839-76
ALs, 26 July 1863. 8 pp, 4to. To Judge Isaac Christiancy. Informing him about his promotion to brigadier general. Including postscript, sgd G.A.C. Imperf. (90) $12,000
— 26 Dec 1866. 4 pp, size not stated. To Sen. J. M. Howard. Assuring him that he has "never been a supporter of Mr. Johnson's policy". (91) $9,500
— [n.d.]. 1 p, 12mo. To Renie. Stating that Sam Wolf needs information concerning recipient's robe. Framed with related material. (91) $4,000
AL, 29 Oct 1863. 3 pp, 4to. To Judge Isaac Christiancy. Fragment, reporting about military action on the Virginia front. (90) $1,900
ADs, 10 July 1863. 1 p, 8vo. Receipt to William Miller for hay. In pencil. With related material. (89) $1,800
— 13 Dec 1863. Small size. Approval & forwarding something (not present). framed with a port. (91) $3,600
Group photograph, 9 Oct 1863. (89) $900
— Anr, 2 Jan 1865. 11 by 13 inches. With Gen. Philip Sheridan & his staff; by A. Gardner. Mtd; margin chipped. (89) $2,800

— Anr, [n.d.]. (89) $250
— Anr, [n.d.]. 6.5 by 8.5 inches. With Gen. Philip Sheridan & his staff; by Brady. (89) $3,500
Photograph, sgd & inscr, 3 Feb 1863. Carte size. As aide de camp of Gen. McClellan. Def. (90) $2,250
— Anr, 3 Feb 1863. Carte size. Sgd on verso; in pencil. (91) $1,400
Photograph, 8 Oct 1863. (89) $250
— Anr, 4 Dec [1863]. Carte size; by Brady. Inscr & dated in Custer's hand on verso. (89) $3,800
— Anr, [c.15 Feb 1864]. (89) $150
— Anr, [1872]. (89) $950
— Anr, Nov 1873. (90) $750
— Anr, [n.d.]. (90) $250
— Anr, [n.d.]. (89) $280
— Anr, [n.d.]. (89) $130
— Anr, [n.d.]. (89) $700
See also: Astor, John Jacob
See also: Remington, Frederic

Custine, Adam Philippe, Comte de, 1740-93
Ls, 16 Oct 1792. (91) DM360
Ds, 16 Nov 1792. (90) DM400

Cuvier, Georges L. C., Baron, 1769-1832
ALs, [n.d.]. (88) DM420

Cyril of Alexandria, Saint, c.375-444
Ms, Commentaria in Pentateuchum, in Latin trans. [Florence, c.1450-70]. 124 leaves (2 lacking), vellum, 164mm by 120mm, in early 19th-cent red mor gilt. In a small regular rounded humanistic minuscule. With 6 large white-vine illuminated initials & 2-sided white-vine border. (90) £3,800

Czartoryski, Adam Jerzy, Prince, 1770-1861
ALs, 13 July 1832. (90) DM450

Czermak, Johann Nepomuk, 1828-73
ALs, 10 July 1862. (91) DM700

Czerny, Carl, 1791-1857
Autograph music, 8 bars of a piano work in A flat major; [n.d.]. (91) £650
ALs, 23 Sept 1826. (91) DM750
— 29 Nov 1838. (90) £650
— 13 June 1842. (89) DM500
— 30 Jan 1852. (90) £650

— 20 May 1852. (88) DM380
— 9 Dec 1852. (91) £400
— 22 Oct 1853. 3 pp, folio. To the pbr Robert Cocks. Offering his Methode pour les enfants Op. 835 & a Fantasia on themes by Beethoven for publication. In English. (90) £1,200
— [n.d.]. (90) DM440
ADs, 16 June 1836. 1 p, 4to. Testimony recommending Leonhardt Maelzel's mechanism designed for the practice of trills, etc. Also sgd by Thalberg, Diabelli, Fischhof & others. (90) £1,200
Ds, 14 Sept 1855. (88) £380

D

Dadd, Frank
Original drawings, (3) to illus Guavas the Tinner by S. (88) £300

Dadd, Richard, 1817-86
Autograph Ms, poem, Elimination of a Picture & its Subject -- called the [Fairy] Feller's Master Stroke, sgd & dated Jan 1865. 24 leaves, 8vo, on rectos only. (89) £5,500

Daeubler, Theodor, 1876-1934
ALs, 25 Nov 1911. (90) DM750
— 1 July 1926. (91) DM380
— 13 Aug 1926. (89) DM340

Dahl, Roald
Autograph Ms, screen version of You Only Live Twice, 1st & 2nd drafts, sgd; 1966. Partly typescript. With related material. Together c.650 pp, in a file. (88) £2,200

Dahlmann, Friedrich Christoph, 1785-1860
Autograph Ms, motion submitted to the Frankfurt National Assembly to elect a ruling prince as head of state, [1848/49]. (91) DM520
A L s s (2), 8 Feb 1844 & 18 Mar 1847. (88) DM800
— A Ls s (2), 8 Feb 1844 & 18 Mar 1847. (90) DM850
— A Ls s (2), 21 Aug & 3 Sept 1849. 5 pp, 4to. To Christian Friedrich von Stockmar. Important letters discussing the political situation in Berlin, problems in Schleswig-Holstein, etc. (90)

d'Ailly, Pierre, 1350-c.1422. See: Henricus de Hassia & Petrus de Alliaco

Daingerfield, Elliott, 1859-1932
[His papers, including record book, c.200 pieces of correspondence, exhibition catalogues, periodicals, photographs, newspaper clippings, etc., sold at wd on 9 Dec 1987, lot 15, for $2,100.]

Dalai Lama
Letter, [late 19th or early 20th cent], 1 p, double folio. (89) £85

Dalberg, Karl, Reichsfreiherr von, Kurfuerst von Mainz, 1744-1817
Series of 4 A Ls s, 16 Dec 1806 to 27 Mar 1807 & [n.d.]. To Empress Josephine. Formal letters about a variety of matters. With related material. (89) DM5,500

ALs, 30 May 1796. 1 p, 4to. To Christoph Wilhelm Hufeland. Requesting advice regarding a young man's illness. (90) DM1,400

— 17 Sept 1799. 3 pp, 4to. To [Georg Karl von Fechenbach, Fuerstbischof von Wuerzburg]. About his activities at Erfurt & other matters. (88) DM2,800

Ls, 11 Jan 1812. (90) DM1,000
— 30 Mar 1813. (89) DM750

D'Albert, Eugen, 1864-1932. See: Albert, Eugen d'

Dale, Benjamin
Autograph music, full score of his Christmas Hymn for voices & orchestra, Before the Paling of the Stars, to words by Christina Rossetti. (89) £110

Dali, Salvador
Autograph postcard, sgd, [3 Feb 1937]. (88) £400

Dali, Salvador, 1904-89
Typescript, [n.d.]. (91) $160
Autograph postcard, sgd, [19 July 1936]. To Cecil Beaton. Sending greetings from Italy. With sketch of 2 figures looking at cloud-like apparition. (88) $1,100
Autograph sentiment, 4 lines, sgd, & small sketch, 1967. Inscr on flyleaf of Florent Fels, Dessins de Paris. Paris, 1966. (89) DM1,700
Group photograph, with Melina Mercuri, Vittorio de Sica & others, 1972. (91) $100
Photograph, sgd, [n.d.]. (91) $130
Signature, [n.d.]. (91) $140

Dallapiccola, Luigi, 1904-75
Autograph music, sketches "from 'Ulysses'...Study for the Scene of Hades", 1961. (88) DM480

Dalmatia
— SIBENIK. - Ms, Statuta della Confraternita religiosa di Santa Maria della Citta di Sebenico, 25 Nov 1437 to 2 Feb 1438. 16 leaves, vellum, 37cm by 27cm. 18th-cent wooden bds. In Venetian dialect, in black ink in a rotunda hand, with headings in red & numerous penwork initials. Some later additions. (90) DM9,000

Dalrymple, Sir Hew Whitefoord, 1750-1830
[His Peninsular War papers, comprising c.150 letters & dispatches received by him (c.50 from Viscount Castlereagh), letterbooks, draft of his address to the court of enquiry, etc., 1807 to 1809, c.1000 pp, in 5 vols & 2 unbound sheaves, sold at S on 22 July 1988, lot 386, for £5,000 to Quaritch.]

D'Alton, John, 1792-1867
[A collection of 123 letters addressed to him, 1828 to 1851, c.170 pp, including A Ls s by Thomas Moore, Walter Scott, Robert Southey, etc., mostly relating to D'Alton's work, sold at CNY on 17 Oct 1988, lot 1226, for $1,500 to Auerbach.]

Dalzell, Robert Alexander George, 1816-78
Autograph Ms, journals, 1834 to 1844. (90) £300

Dan Dare Series
Original drawings, 2 sheets of ink & watercolor illusts for the Dan Dare comic strip, vol 8; [n.d.]. (90) £450
— Original drawings, 2 sheets of ink & watercolor illusts for the Dan Dare comic strip, vol 8; [n.d.]. (90) £800
— Original drawings, 4 sheets of ink &

watercolor illusts for the Dan Dare comic strip, vol 10; [n.d.]. (90) £800
— HAMPSON, FRANK. - Orig drawings, 4 sheets of ink & watercolor illusts for the Dan Dare comic strip, vols 2 & 3; [n.d.]. Various sizes. 1 sgd. (90) £600
— HAMPSON, FRANK. - Orig drawings, 3 sheets of ink & watercolor illusts for the Dan Dare comic strip, vol 9; [n.d.]. Average size 400mm by 340mm. Sgd. (90) £950
— WATSON, KEITH. - Orig drawings, 3 airbrush illusts for the Dan Dare comic strip, vol 14; [n.d.]. 537mm by 380mm. Sgd. (90) £360

Dana, Richard Henry, Jr., 1815-82
Series of 4 A Ls s, 8 Dec 1858 to 28 Apr 1876. Doheny collection. (89) $420

Dandridge, Dorothy, 1923-65
Photograph, sgd & inscr, [n.d.]. (91) $300

Daniell, Thomas, 1749-1840
[An album containing 48 ink-&-watercolor drawings of Chinese costume, [China, c.1800], ascribed to Daniell but probably by a "follower of William Alexander", in silk covered bds, sold at S on 22 Nov 1988, lot 180, for £1,500 to MacTaggart.]

D'Annunzio, Gabriele, 1863-1938
Collection of ALs & photograph sgd, 13 Nov 1891. (90) £250
— Collection of 6 A Ls s & 3 photographs, 22 Feb 1922 to 24 Dec 1930. (89) $400
ALs, 14 Dec 1894. (89) DM450
— 25 Aug 1900. Doheny collection. (89) $450
— 17 Nov 1910. (88) DM260
— 30 Mar [1914?]. (90) £130

Dante Alighieri, 1265-1321 —& Cessolis, Jacobus de, fl.1290
Ms, De Monarchia, with Jacopo da Cessole, Ludus Scaccorum, & other texts. [Italy, late 14th cent]. 65 leaves & endleaf, vellum, 222mm by 147mm. 18th-cent sheep over pastebds. In a small neat rounded gothic bookhand. With 3 large initials & 13 miniatures. Phillipps Ms.16281. (91) £90,000

Danton, Georges Jacques, 1759-94
Ls, 31 Aug 1792. 2 pp, folio. To an unnamed "President". About a trial pending at Angers. (91) DM3,600
— [10 Sept 1792]. 1 p, folio. To [Jacques] Reverchon. As Minister of Justice, regarding an officer's petition for clemency. (89) DM4,400
Ds, 20 Aug 1792. 2 pp, 4to. Ptd decree regarding costs for a ceremony "pour honorer les manes des victimes du despotisme". Also sgd by Roland de la Platiere. (90) DM3,400
Autograph endorsement, sgd, 20 Aug 1792. At foot of a letter addressed to him by Guillaume Jacques Mollet, 2 pp, folio, asking for a position as surgeon; recommending Mollet to the Minister of War. Also sgd by others. (91) £1,500
— Anr, sgd, 21 Aug 1792. On a petition by Guillaume Jacques Mollet, 20 Aug 1792, 2 pp, folio, for employment as army doctor; supporting petition. With anr endorsement, sgd by 3 members of the convention, at bottom. With related material. (90) DM3,800

Danza della Morte
Ms, [Northeastern Italy?, c.1770]. 40 leaves, 8vo. Contemp mottled brown sheep gilt; ties lost. Containing 37 large allegorical miniatures, in gouache on laid card, with annotations & glosses in various Italian hands in cursive script. (88) $8,000

D'Aquino, Iva Toguri ("Tokyo Rose")
ANs, [c.Dec 1990]. (91) $100

Darley, Felix Octavius Carr, 1822-88
Autograph Ms, The Magpie, or the Maid?, [c.1841]. Calligraphic tp & 10 full-page drawings, sgd, with autograph legends; in pen & brown ink. In def contemp brown cloth bdg. (89) $2,250
Original drawings, (10), American historical & rural subjects, including tp design for Comstock's Phonetic Magazine, etc., [1840s to 1870s]. 7 leaves, folio & smaller. In pencil or ink wash; 6 sgd or initialled. (89) $1,600
— Original drawings, (13), to illus various works by Dickens, [n.d.]. 5 leaves, double folio or smaller. In pencil heightened with white. 2 matted. (89)

$2,250
— Original drawings, (16), to illus various humorous works pbd by Carey & Hart, 1844 to 1846. 16 pp, 8vo. In ink wash; sgd. (89) $3,500
— Original drawings, (3), to illus Scott's Ivanhoe & Sylvester Judd's Margaret, [c.1845 to 1848]. (89) $1,000
— Original drawings, (4), pencil studies for bank-note vignettes, [n.d.]. 3 leaves, 4to or smaller. Sgd on recto & verso. Mtd. (89) $1,100
— Original drawings, (61), to illus Cooper & other authors, [1840s to 1850s]. 57 leaves, mtd on 37 cards, in late 19th-cent half mor gilt bdg. In pencil or wash. 2 sgd, 16 initialled. (89) $7,000
— Original drawings, (9), American historical & rural subjects, including studies for Pioneers in the Settlement of America, [1860s & 1870s]. 7 leaves, 4to & smaller. In pencil; 5 sgd or initialled. (89) $3,000
— Original drawings, (9), to illus Evangeline & other works, [n.d.]. (89) $1,000

Darling, Sir Ralph, 1775-1858
Ds, 25 June 1831. (90) £200

Darre, Richard Walter, 1895-1953
Ls, 8 Feb 1936. (91) $85

Darwin, Charles, 1809-82
[An autograph envelope addressed to J. Paget, [4 June 1881], matted with a port, sold at Dar on 2 Aug 1990, lot 135, for $225.]
Autograph Ms, cat of fruit trees planted in his gardens, [n.d.]. 11 pp, 4to. (89) £1,800
— Autograph Ms, Fertilization of Orchids, sgd & dated 27 Feb 1877. 1 p, folio. Tipped to larger leaf. Barrett collection. (89) $4,000
— Autograph Ms, title page of The Effects of Cross and Self Fertilization in the Vegetable Kingdom. 1867. 1 p, 126mm by 209mm, sgd. With ALs of W. E. Darwin, forwarding the above. (91) $2,300
Collection of 2 A Ls s & AL, 8 Dec [1860] to 18 Sept [1861]. 19 pp, 8vo. To Henry Fawcett. Concerning the controversy over Darwin's On the Origin of Species. AL with signature cut. Bradley Martin Ms. (90) $13,000
— Collection of ALs & photograph, 22 Feb [n.y.] & [n.d.]. 4 pp, 8vo, & size not stated. To [Alexander Kowalewskij's brother]. Thanking for tea & reporting about his work. (91) DM3,600
A Ls s (2), 18 Dec 1856 & [n.d.]. 7 pp, 8vo. To John Maurice Herbert. Recommending bird-preservers, & postponing a meeting with Lieut. Blakinton. (91) $4,250
ALs, [1838]. 3 pp, 4to. To [John Stevens] Henslow. About birds & tortoises on the Galapagos Islands. (89) £12,500
— 8 Sept [1842]. (89) $850
— 25 Feb [1849]. 3 pp, 4to. To P. Simmonds. Commenting on the prospects of a settlement in Patagonia. Small tear. Mtd. (88) £1,900
— 22 June 1851. 3 pp, 8vo. To Albany Hancock. Thanking for assistance & requesting the return of his Ms. (89) £1,150
— 25 Feb [1858]. 3 pp, 8vo. To J. S. Bowerbank. Offering a selection of sponges from his collection. (91) £1,200
— 17 July [1869?]. 5 pp, 8vo. To William C. Tait. Discussing in detail "the case of the geranium" & offering to send one of his works. (90) £1,500
— 27 Aug [1869?]. 3 pp, 8vo. To William C. Tait. Gratefully declining the offer of more Drosophyllums. With related material. (90) £1,100
— 30 Nov [1870]. (90) £800
— 9 Dec [1870?]. 2 pp, 8vo. To St. George Mivart. Thanking for a work & expressing the wish to meet him. (88) £1,200
— [c.1870]. (89) £850
— 13 Jan [1871]. 7 pp, 8vo. To St. George Mivart. Discussing orchids, shells, & other cases relating to natural adaptation. (88) £2,400
— 21 Jan [1871]. 1 p, 8vo. To St. George Mivart. Thanking for Mivart's book & referring to his own [The Descent of Man]. (88) £1,050
— 23 Jan [1871]. 4 pp, 8vo. To St. George Mivart. Defending himself against the charge of dogmatism. (88) £2,300
— 26 Jan [1871]. 4 pp, 8vo. To St. George

Mivart. Stating his opinion that "belief in Evolution is infinitely more important for science than belief in Nat[ural] Selection. (88) £4,200
— 21 Apr [1871]. 4 pp, 8vo. To St. George Mivart. Criticizing Mivart's views on evolution. (88) £3,000
— 25 Apr [1871]. 4 pp, 8vo. To St. George Mivart. Referring to an article by Mivart, & discussing primates & the descent of man. (88) £3,200
— 8 Jan 1872. 4 pp, 8vo. To St. George Mivart. Expressing vexation at the spirit pervading Mivart's articles & saying he wants to drop their correspondence. (88) £2,400
— 11 Jan 1872. 6 pp, 8vo. To St. George Mivart. Pursuing their arguments about the origin of species, complaining about unfairness on Mivart's part & asking him not to write again. (88) £6,500
— 19 Apr [1872]. 1 p, 8vo. To Sir William Bowman. Returning a book about eye diseases. (90) DM3,000
— 9 Dec 1876. (89) £650
— 5 June 1878. (90) £700
— 31 Mar [1879]. 4 pp, 8vo. To his cousin. About Erasmus Darwin & Zoonomia. (91) £1,300
— 19 Apr [1879]. (91) £700
— 12 Feb 1880. 1 p, 8vo. To Ernst Haeckel. Thanking for a kind letter. (91) DM2,800
— 27 Apr 1880. (89) £750
— 5 Sept 1881. (88) £380
— 29 Nov 1881. 1 p, 8vo. To Dorothy Nevill. Expressing pleasure at her interest in his book on earth-worms. (91) DM2,200
— 3 Feb [n.y.]. (89) £480
— 18 Apr [n.y.]. 3 pp, 8vo. To Professor Kulliken. About some specimens sent & a memorandum. Repaired. Sang collection & John F. Fleming Estate. (89) $1,400
— 20 May [n.y.]. 3 pp, 8vo. To J. Jenner Weir. Requesting information about the migration of nightingales. Was mtd. Doheny collection. (89) $3,200
— 5 June [n.y.]. 5 pp, 8vo. Recipient unknown. Offering advice regarding recipient's research. (88) $5,200
— 6 Aug [n.y.]. 1 p, 8vo. To the sculptor Thomas Woolner. About Woolner's account of the Ourang. (89) £2,600
— 27 Sept [n.y.]. 2 pp, 8vo. Recipient unknown. Expressing thanks for mention in recipient's book. (89) $1,500
— [n.d.], "Tuesday". (89) £750
— "Sunday." 3 pp, 8vo. To George Waterhouse. Thanking him for his description of the natia ox; speaks of the peculiarity of the Galapagos fauna. (91) £3,500
— [n.d.]. (89) £700

AL, 28 Jan [1871]. (88) £600

Series of 4 Ls s, 1 Jan to 2 Sept 1875. 12 pp, 8vo. To [Ferdinand Cohn]. Discussing his own & recipient's work about insectivorous plants. (90) DM9,000

Ls, 18 Jan [1865]. (88) £520
— 7 Apr [1869]. 3 pp, 8vo. To William C. Tait. Reporting that his plants of Drosophyllum are recovering. Text in the hand of Emma Darwin. (90) £1,300
— 23 Jan [1871]. 8 pp, 8vo. To St. George Mivart. Defending his own position against Mivart's attacks. Including 9-line autograph postscript. With autograph draft of Mivart's reply. (88) £2,800
— 16 Feb 1871. (90) £850
— 5 Jan 1872. (88) £1,000
— 18 Feb 1874. (90) £800
— 25 Mar 1875. (88) £300
— 31 Mar 1875. (90) £800
— 8 Aug 1877. 4 pp, 8vo. To an unnamed German scholar. Responding to a letter concerning his son's research. With autograph postscript. (90) DM2,600
— 3 Jan 1878. 4 pp, 8vo. To an unnamed German scholar. Rejoicing about Robert Koch's discoveries, & talking about his son's research. (90) DM3,700
— 28 Jan 1878. (90) £700

Autograph postcard, sgd, 12 Jan 1880. To Dr. Alfred Krakauer. Thanking for scientific information. Repaired. (90) DM1,300

ANs, 18 Mar 1874. (88) $600

Ds, 23 Feb 1871. 1 p, 4to. Receipt for £630 from John Murray for the 1st Ed of his Descent of Man. Sgd Ch. R. Darwin, over revenue stamp. (88) £2,600

Check, sgd, 15 May 1879, drawn on the Union Bank of London. 1 p, 8vo. Ptd with autograph insertions. With related material. (89) DM1,150

Daudet, Alphonse, 1840-97
Autograph Ms, essay, Souvenirs de Jeunesse, [1893]; sgd at end. (90) DM950

Daumier, Honore, 1808-79
ADs, 30 Apr 1870. (88) DM1,000

Daun, Leopold, Graf von, 1705-66
Autograph Ms, Standt und Dienst Tabella, list of soldiers encamped at Pillau, 20 June 1741. (91) DM240
Ms, Kaiserlich-Koenigliches Exerzier-Reglement, [Darmstadt, 1768]. 622 pp, 185mm by 115mm, in 3 contemp red lea vols. Abbreviated version, probably in the hand of F. B. de Schmidburg. Including 55 illusts & several vignettes in pen-&-ink. (89) DM2,000
Ls, 16 Nov 1756. (90) DM520
— 31 Dec 1761. (89) DM260
— 6 Nov 1762. (89) DM450
— 24 Mar 1763. (88) DM340
— 11 Nov 1764. (88) DM300
— 24 Dec 1765. (90) DM440
— 9 Jan 1766. (91) DM550

Dauthendey, Elisabeth, 1854-1943
A Ls s (2), 2 Mar & 6 Apr 1909. (88) DM260

Dauthendey, Max, 1867-1918
Autograph Ms, poem, beginning "Zinkfarbene Nebel ueber der Stadt", [n.d.]. (90) DM620
Autograph transcript, poem, Atemloser August, [n.d.]. (88) DM600
ALs, 7 Aug 1910. (90) DM750
— 28 Oct 1913. 4 pp, 4to. To the pbr S. Fischer. Planning to return to Germany after a vacation in Italy & requesting an interview. (89) DM1,100
— [n.d.]. (91) DM500

David, Jacques Louis, 1748-1825
ALs, 5 Nov 1809. (90) DM800

David, Johann Nepomuk, 1895-1977
Autograph music, sketches for a score with 3 systems, sgd & dated 1977. 4 pp, 315mm by 235mm. In ink, with corrections in pencil. 3 lines pasted in. (90) DM2,000

Davies, M. Joyce
Original drawings, (26), to illus various titles, 1925 to 1935. 280mm by 200mm or 400mm by 280mm. In ink & watercolor; 19 sgd. (89) £1,200

Davies, Peter Maxwell
Autograph music, Organ Sonata, draft & extensive sketches; sgd & dated Jan 1982. 65 pp, various sizes. Mostly in pencil on up to 24 staves per page; with numerous revisions. (90) £5,000

Davis, Bette, 1908-89
Photograph, sgd & inscr, [1930s]. (90) $150

Davis, Jefferson, 1808-89
ALs, 1 Aug 1845. 2 pp, 4to. To his wife. About emotional upset. (91) $2,700
— 28 Feb 1846. 1 p, 4to. To President James K. Polk. Recommending A. S. Johnston. Middendorf collection. (89) $1,800
— 24 Oct 1847. (88) $500
— 21 June 1848. Middendorf collection. (89) $550
— 10 July 1861. 4 pp, 8vo. To Gen. J. E. Johnston. About troop shortages & transport problems. Sang & Middendorf collections. (89) $12,000
— 11 Nov 1861. 1 p, 4to. To [John L. Harrell?]. Informing him that [William] Yancey has long since been authorized to return home from Europe. Ruddy collection. (88) $2,000
— 23 May 1862. 2 pp, 8vo. To Gen. J. E. Johnston. Concerning military movements during the campaign against Richmond. Was mtd. (90) $3,500
— 13 July 1868. (91) $850
— 10 Dec 1872. Doheny collection. (89) $650
— 8 Dec 1877. 4 pp, 4to. To Gen. C. J. Wright. Considering his political career, the nature of the Union, & the problems of the South. (90) $10,000
— 8 Dec 1877. 4 pp, 4to. To Gen. C. J. Wright. About his political career, the nature of the Union & the problems of

the South within it. (91) $15,000
Ls, 21 Apr 1863. 1 p, 4to. To the Confederate House of Representatives. Transmitting reports (not present) regarding liability for the value of slaves impressed by the Government. Repaired. Ruddy collection. (88) $10,000
— 6 Aug 1863. 2 pp, 4to. To Gov. M. L. Bonham. Promising "to do all that is possible for the safety" of Charleston. (91) $8,000
Letter, 29 Jan 1887. (91) $300
— 21 July 1888. (89) $110
ANs, [n.d.]. (91) $550
Ds, 29 July 1864. 1 p, 4to. Pay order to the Confederate Sec of the Treasury for $12,000 payable to Sec of State Benjamin; partly ptd. Ruddy collection. (88) $2,000
— 1 Sept 1864. 1 p, 4to. Order to the Confederate Sec of the Treasury to pay $1,000 in gold to Sec of State Judah P. Benjamin for the Secret Service. (90) $3,750
Autograph endorsement, sgd, 18 Feb [18]65. (89) $350
Autograph telegram, sgd, 22 Nov 1864. 1 p, 8vo. To Gen. Braxton Bragg. Directing him to proceed to Georgia & "employ all available force" against Sherman. (90) $16,000
Cut signature, [n.d.]. (89) $200
Franking signature, [n.d.]. (91) $300
— Anr, [n.d.]. Alexander collection. (90) $270
Photograph, sgd, [Jan 1870]. Carte size. Bust image, by D. Day. Inscr in anr hand on verso. (90) $2,200
Signature, [n.d.]. (89) $275
— BEE, ANDREW. - Photograph, 1889. Cabinet size. "Captor of Jeff Davis" imptd on mat. (91) $50
See also: Hunter, Robert Mercer Taliaferro
See also: Pierce, Franklin & Davis

Davis, Jon
Original drawings, (19), to illus Len Collins's Rupert and the Wobbly Witch, 1986. (90) £840
— Original drawings, (22), to illus Len Collins's Rupert and the Yellow Elephant, 1986. (90) £850
— Original drawings, (22), to illus Len Collins's Rupert and the Trouble with Big Ben, 1986. In ink & watercolor. Average size 205mm by 210mm. With a copy of the book. (90) £1,100
— Original drawings, (22), to illus Len Collins's Rupert and the Nutwood Oilwell, 1986. In ink & watercolor. Average size 210mm by 215mm. (90) £1,300
— Original drawings, (23), to illus Len Collins's Rupert and the Bit of Magic, 1986. (90) £650
— Original drawings, (29), to illus Len Collins's Rupert and the Chocolate Buttons Gang, 1986. (90) £850
— Original drawings, 7 large & many smaller designs to illus Len Collins's Rupert's Sow 'n Grow Series, 1987. (90) £650

Davis, Katherine K.
Autograph music, The Carol of the Drum [The Little Drummer Boy], [c.1941]. 8 pp, folio. Sgd; with autograph annotations in pencil, under the Pseud. C. R. W. Robertson. With related material. (89) $11,000

Davis, Varina Howell, 1826-1906
ALs, [c.1855]. (89) $120

Davout, Louis Nicolas, Marshal of France, 1770-1823
Ls, [18 Dec 1805]. (90) DM220
— 10 Apr 1810. (91) DM220
— 25 Mar 1815. (89) DM220
— 21 Apr 1815. (88) DM240
Letter, 4 July 1815. (88) DM320

Davy, Humphry, 1778-1829
ALs, [1806]. (89) DM250
— 14 Sept [1815]. 3 pp, 4to. To Michael Faraday. Announcing his preliminary work on the problems of explosions in coal mines; including small pen-&-ink sketch. With related material. (89) £1,500
— [n.d.]. (88) DM220

Dawson, Gina
Original drawings, (8), to illus Marjorie Bowen's Strangers to Freedom, 1940. Archives of J. M. Dent & Son. (88) £70

Day, Benjamin, 1746?-94
Ds, May 1784. (88) $60

Day, Doris. See: Reagan, Ronald & Day

Day, Thomas
ADs, 25 Jan 1776. (91) £520

Day-Lewis, Cecil, 1904-72. See: Auden, Wystan Hugh & Day-Lewis

Dayton, Jonathan, 1760-1824
ADs, 8 Mar 1782. (89) $400

De Amicis, Edmondo, 1846-1908
A Ls s (2), 25 Aug 1888 & [n.d.]. (90) DM260

De Bodt, Jean, 1670-1745
Ls, 25 Nov 1744. (90) DM550

De Coster, Charles, 1827-79
Series of 3 A Ls s, 14 July 1866 to 9 Jan 1868. (88) DM620

De Coverly, Roger
ALs, 9 Oct 1886. 4 pp, 8vo. To T. J. Cobden-Sanderson. Saying that he is "proud of you as a pupil." (91) $2,600

De Forest, Lee, 1873-1961
Collection of Ls & photograph, sgd & inscr, 2 Dec 1958. (88) $450
Series of 3 Ls s, Feb & Mar 1956. (90) $425
Autograph sentiment, sgd, 10 Sept [1953?]. (91) $70

De Gaulle, Charles, 1890-1970
Typescript, "Discours du 15 Novembre 1941." 11 pp, folio. With numerous autograph revisions. (88) DM8,000
— Typescript, speech given at the Assemblee Consultative Provisoire in Algiers, 10 Jan 1944. 4 pp, 4to. Including numerous autograph revisions & additions. Differing from version ptd in Discours et Messages. Paris, 1946. (91) DM7,500
— Typescript, speech given at Metz after the liberation, [11 Feb 1945]. 2 pp, 4to. Saying the Rhine will be "une route francaise d'un bout a l'autre". Numerous autograph revisions. Not ptd in his Discours et Messages. Paris 1946. (90) DM7,500
Typescript carbon copy, speech given at Tunis, 27 June 1943. 4 pp, folio. With numerous autograph corrections. With related material. (88) DM5,500
ALs, 20 Oct 1938. 2 pp, 4to. To Lucien Nachin. Discussing the book La France et son armee in response to Nachin's criticism. (88) £1,800
— 17 Aug 1954. 2 pp, 8vo. Recipient unnamed. About the publication of his memoirs in America. (89) DM1,200
Ls, 3 July 1940. (91) $425
— 13 Nov 1947. Byer collection. (90) $225
— 26 Sept 1957. 1 p, 4to. To Lieut. Col. Coulet. Agreeing "que votre situation soit reglee comme vous le desiriez." With autograph postscript. (91) DM2,400
ANs, 17 Jan 1949. (88) £60
— [n.d.]. (89) $225

De Haviland, Olivia
Collection of ALs, 24 Ls s, & 2 photographs, sgd & inscr, 1944 to 1962. (89) $180

De la Cruz, Juana Ines, 1651-95
Ds, 18 Nov 1686. Contents not stated. In a sheaf of accounts of "autos" by Don Matheo Ortiz de Torres, superintendent of the convent of San Jeronimo, 1684 to 1688. 40 pp, folio. (89) £1,500

De la Hogue, Jean Baptiste, b.1786
[A collection of letters & documents relating to him, 1803 to 1815, including his Certificate of American citizenship issued in South Carolina, with related material, sold at C on 22 June 1988, lot 4, for £420 to L'Autographe.]

De la Mare, Walter, 1873-1956
Autograph Ms, 2 poems for his collection Flora, entitled "Come!" & "Crazed"; [n.d.]. (88) £70
Collection of 20 A Ls s, 11 Ls s, & 2 letters, 31 May 1920 to 12 Sept 1945. Bradley Martin sale. (90) $1,000
— Collection of 3 A Ls s & 7 Ls s, June 1921 to Apr 1928. (91) $650
— Collection of 10 A Ls s & Ls s, 1930 to 1952. (91) £800
— Collection of c.80 A Ls s & Ls s, 1935 to 1948; c.160 pp, 4to & 8vo. To Lady Cynthia Asquith. Covering a wide range of subjects. (88) £2,800
— Collection of 18 A Ls s & Ls s, 13 Feb 1938 to 23 Aug 1949. (88) £400

— Collection of 10 A Ls s & Ls s, 12 Aug 1947 to 10 Jan 1952. (90) £320
— Collection of 2 A Ls s & Ls, 1947 to 1951. (88) £160

De Mille, Cecil B.
Ls, 16 Oct 1945. (91) $125

De Paul, Vincent, Saint, 1581-1660
Collection of Ls & Ds, [10 Sept 1648] & [n.d.]. 9 pp, 4to & 105mm by 235mm. To [John Delorgny], fragment, commenting on the beliefs & propositions of Antoine Arnauld. Pay order. Doheny collection. (89) $8,000

De proprietatibus rerum moralizatae
Ms, description of fauna & flora, precious stones, etc., in Latin. [Franconia, 15th cent]. 42 leaves (5 vellum), 275mm by 200mm. Half cloth bdg. In black ink in a lettre batarde. (89) DM21,000

De Quincey, Thomas, 1785-1859
Autograph Ms (2), passage from Recollections of Grassmere, 3 Apr [1839], 43 lines on fragment of a folio leaf, & a short passage on the Justification of Novels, [n.d.], 1 p, 4to. (90) £900
Autograph Ms, Confessions of an English Opium-Eater, 1st part, as ptd in London Magazine, Sept 1821. Over 50 pp, 4to, in 19th-cent half mor. With extensive autograph revisions & notes to the pbr, some editorial revisions, & ptr's marks. (89) £26,000
— Autograph Ms, passage from Autobiographic Sketches, omitted from ptd version, [n.d.]. (88) £200
ALs, 1833. (89) $425
— 21 Nov 1839. (89) $350
— 6 Sept 1843. (89) $300
— 30 Jan 1846. Doheny collection. (89) $480
— [21 May 1846?]. (91) £220
— 13 Aug 1847. (89) £480
— 2 May 1851. (89) $425
— 13 Oct [1857]. 4 pp, 8vo. To John Sudlow. Worrying about his daughter Florence in India. (90) DM1,100
— 26 Dec 1857. (89) $100
— [n.d.]. (89) $60
ANs, 12 Dec [n.y.]. (91) $70
Corrected galley proof, The Confessions of an English Opium-Eater, 2d Ed,
[c.1856]. (89) £900

De Wette, Wilhelm Martin Leberecht, 1780-1849
ALs, 19 Dec 1839. (90) DM320

Dean, James, 1931-55
Ds, 10 June 1955. 1 p, 4to. Agreement with Warner Brothers, on Ls by C. H. Wilder; carbon copy. (91) $5,000
Autograph sentiment, sgd, [c.1954]. (89) $1,000
— Anr, sgd, 12 Feb [n.d.]. 3.5 by 2 inches. Dance ticket; inscr to Lindley. (91) $1,600

Dearborn, Henry, 1751-1829
ALs, 11 Oct 1808. (88) $120
Ls, 23 Jan 1805. (88) $55
— [3 July] 1807. (88) $125

Dearmer, Mabel, 1872-1915
Original drawings, (23), to illus Laurence Housman's The Story of the Seven Goslings, 1900. (89) £500

Debussy, Claude, 1862-1918
Autograph Ms, story, Chapitre ... ou il sera reparle d'Esther puis d'une maison de fous; [1900]. 4 pp, 8vo, on rectos only. (91) DM3,800
Autograph music, draft of a passage for violin & piano in G minor [for his Violin Sonata?], [c.1915-17]. 2 pp, 4to. Notated on 3 systems of 3 staves each. Including note of authentication by his daughter. (91) £3,800
— Autograph music, early version of part of the 1st movement of Iberia, [c.1905]. 1 p, c.19.5cm by 29cm, cut from larger sheet. 20 bars notated in brown ink on 2 systems of 4 staves. Differing from orchestral version. (90) £3,800
— Autograph music, eleven contrapuntal exercises, [n.d.]. 1 p, folio. In brown ink on 6 systems, 2 staves each. (90) £1,500
— Autograph music, sketches for Nocturnes, [c.1897]. 1 p, 8vo. 8 1/2 bars in short score, notated on 2 systems of 4 staves each. (89) $2,750
Collection of 3 A Ls s & signature, 17 Feb [19]10 & [n.d.]. 4 pp, various sizes. To various recipients. About a performance, travel arrangements, & an appointment. (91) £1,300

DEBUSSY

ALs, [c.1897]. (91) £600
— [n.d.]. 1 p, 8vo. To Pierre [Louis]. Expressing the wish to see him after a stay in the country. (88) DM1,600
— 23 Dec 1902. (89) £800
— 8 Feb 1906. (91) £1,000
— 27 Sept [19]07. (91) £650
— 24 Nov 1907. 1 p, 4to. Recipient unnamed. Explaining that he is too busy to see him. (89) DM1,500
— 4 Nov [19]08. (88) £1,000
— 15 Jan 1909. (90) DM850
— 12 July 1909. (90) DM980
— 2 Feb 1911. (90) £950
— 3 Dec 1911. (89) DM950
— 4 [Mar] 1912. (90) DM850
— 4 Oct 1912. 2 pp, 4to. Recipient unnamed. Protesting against a bill. (88) DM1,500
— 14 Mar 1914. Byer collection. (90) $850
— 2 June 1914. (90) £950
— [n.d.]. (88) $700
ANs, [c.1895]. (90) £400
— [after 1906?]. (90) £800
— 26 July 1907. (90) £750
— [c.1915]. (88) DM460
AN, [before 1900]. (90) £550
Autograph quotation, 1st 10 bars of his Prelude a l'apres midi d'un faune, in full score. Sgd, inscr to Eugene Ysaye & dated Jan 1908. 1 p, folio. Rosen collection. (89) $11,000
Proof copy, Nocturnes, 1st Ed, 1900. 11 pp, folio, in contemp bds. With autograph tp & extensive autograph annotations, some in anr hand. Sgd in several places. (89) $23,000

Debussy, Claude, 1862-1918 —& Others
[An album containing autograph musical quotations, sgd, by Debussy, Ravel, de Falla, Faure, & others, inscr to Mme Gaston Poulet, 1917 to 1939, 23 pp, 8vo, in lea bdg, sold at S on 17 May 1991, lot 220, for £6,500 to Lubrano.]

Decatur, Stephen, 1779-1820
ALs, 12 June 1807. Munson collection. (90) $1,000
Ds, 1801. (91) $250
Franking signature, [8 Oct n.y.]. Alexander collection. (90) $625

Declaration of Independence
[A collection of 16 autographs by 11 Signers, 1744 to 1823, sold at P on 26 Oct 1988, lot 186, for $1,900.]
[A collection of 4 items containing autographs of Benjamin Rush & George Clymer, George Taylor, Joseph Hewes, & Elbridge Gerry sold at pnNy on 10 Dec 1987, lot 79, for $2,000.]
See also: American Revolution

Degas, Edgar, 1834-1917
ALs, 4 Apr 1896. 1 p, 8vo. To M. Bracquemond. Indicating his excitement at the new Berthe Morisot exhibition. (90) $1,200
— 30 Apr 1899. (91) £220
— [n.d.]. (88) DM950
— [n.d.], "Friday". 4 pp, 8vo. Recipient unknown. Sending a poem about a play & talking about his work. Including small rough sketch. (89) £2,600
— [n.d.]. 1 p, 12mo. To an unnamed lady. Accepting an invitation. Framed with a port. (91) $1,500
— [n.d.]. 2 pp, 8vo. Recipient unnamed. Mentioning various engagements. (90) DM1,100
A Ls (2), [n.d.]. (90) DM750
AL, [n.d.]. 2 pp, 8vo. To [his sister]. Reporting about M. Blanche's visit & mentioning Ernest May. (90) DM1,400

Dehmel, Richard, 1863-1920
Collection of ALs & autograph postcard, sgd, [4 Aug] & 15 Sept 1906. (90) DM220
Series of 3 A Ls s, 4 Nov 1902 to 25 Apr 1903. (88) DM550
A Ls s (2), 31 Dec 1902 & 7 Jan 1903. (91) DM250
ALs, 29 Dec 1905. (89) DM420
— 18 Dec 1906. (89) DM250
— 24 Aug 1911. (91) DM220
Ls, 24 Feb 1910. (90) DM220

Dekyngston, Edward, Alchemist
Ms, commonplace book. L, c.1550-80. 399 leaves, folio, in 18th-cent calf-backed bds. Written in a number of secretary hands. With descriptions of his own experiments as well as old alchemical texts & recipes. (91) £24,000

Delacroix, Eugene, 1798-1863
Autograph Ms, partial French trans of Plato's dialogue Gorgias, [n.d.]. (88) £250
ALs, 28 Sept [1827]. 4 pp, 4to. To Ch. Soulier. Lively letter mentioning his paintings for a forthcoming exhibition & English plays in Paris. (90) DM3,000
— [11 Aug 1839]. (90) DM440
— 5 Aug 1857. (88) DM900
— 1863. (90) $300
— 1 Dec [n.y.]. (90) £350
— 7 Dec [n.y.]. (89) £400

Delamonce, Ferdinand Pierre Joseph, 1678-1753
Original drawings, (16), for an Ed of the works of Virgil, [n.d.]. In pen-&-ink & grey wash. In ink frames, 139mm by 82mm. Tipped to mounting sheets bearing engraver's name G. Scotin. Foxed. In quarter mor box. John F. Fleming Estate. (89) $3,000

Delbrueck, Max, 1906-81
Typescript carbon copy, table of contents & introduction to a review of Erwin Schroedinger's What is Life; [n.d.]. (89) DM900
ALs, Jan 1977. (91) DM300

Delbrueck, Rudolf von, 1817-1903
ALs, 23 Nov 1870. Schroeder collection. (89) DM220

Delibes, Leo, 1836-91
Series of 3 A Ls s, [n.d.]. (90) DM500
ALs, 17 Jan [n.y.]. Byer collection. (90) $175
— [n.d.], "Monday". (91) $425

Delius, Frederick, 1862-1934
[A postcard, sgd, 8 Jan 1910, text written by his wife, to Edwin Evans, about the pbr of Paris & a proof of Brigg Fair, sold at S on 27 Nov, lot 258, for £300 to Maggs.]
[A group of 8 letters by Jelka Delius & by Elise Delius, 19 Jan 1921 & [n.d.], referring to Frederick Delius, sold at S on 22 Nov 1989, lot 61, for £450 to Delius.]
A Ls s (2), Sept & 23 Dec 1916. (88) £900
ALs, [Jan 1900]. (88) £650
— 4 Nov 1904. 6 pp, 8vo. To Mrs. Norman. About recipient's separation from her husband, his own marriage, & performances of his works. (90) £1,200
— 27 Apr 1915. (90) £700
— [n.d.]. (90) £600
Ls, 14 Apr 1920. (89) DM420
Autograph postcard, sgd, [20 Nov 1907]. To John Coates. Offering tickets for a performance of Appalachia, & mentioning his opera. (90) DM1,100

Delvaux, Paul
ALs, [1964]. 1 p, 4to. To an unnamed collector. Sending a ballpoint drawing (present, on verso). (90) DM8,500

DeMille, Cecil Blount, 1881-1959
Autograph sentiment, 3 Mar 1955. (89) $450
Check, 30 Dec 1958. (89) $50

Demonology
Ms, Die alleredelste und allerhoechste Kunst und Meisterschaft, das ist Magia Universalis, Divina, Angelica ac Diabolica; [early 18th cent]. 492 leaves, 202mm by 165mm, disbound. With 23 diagrams & 7 very large illusts of various spirits. Including 2 related texts. (90) DM3,900

Dempsey, Jack, 1895-1983
Photograph, sgd, [n.d.]. (89) $60
Photograph, sgd & inscr, [n.d.]. (89) $50

Deng Xiaoping —& Schmidt, Helmut
Photograph, sgd, [1978]. (90) DM650

Denham, Joseph. See: Napoleonic Wars

Dent, Edward Joseph, 1876-1957
Series of 9 A Ls s, 1914 to 1916. (88) £450

Denver, James William, 1817-92
[A collection of 10 letters & 8 covers addressed to him, about a variety of subjects, sold at rf on 12 Mar, lot 8, for $190.]

Derain, Andre, 1880-1954
ALs, 27 Nov 1943. (88) DM320
— [n.d.]. Ammann collection. (90) DM380

Derfflinger, Georg, Freiherr von, 1606-95
Ls, 22 Feb 1677. 2 pp, folio. To Kurfuerst Friedrich Wilhelm of Brandenburg. Concerning missing letters. Schroeder collection. (89) DM1,300
— 24 Mar 1679. 2 pp, folio. To [Kurprinz Friedrich von Brandenburg?]. Informing him about army movements after the campaign against Sweden & the Great Elector's return to Berlin. (90) DM1,500
— [n.d.]. (91) DM650

Des Moulins, Guiart, c.1251-1313. See: Bible Manuscripts, French

Desbordes-Valmore, Marceline, 1786-1859
Autograph Ms, collection of poems, Les Pleurs, [c.1833]. 187 pp, folio, in dark blue mor by Marius Michel. 69 poems, lacking 5 from ptd Ed, but including others. Martin collection. (90) FF130,000

Descartes, Rene, 1596-1650
ALs, 15 Nov 1638. 11 pp, 4to. To Father Marin Mersenne. Discussing numerous aspects of physics & mathematics, & stating his philosphy regarding the scientific method. Including 3 diagrams. In modern vellum bdg, with a port. (89) £40,000

Desideria, Queen of Charles XIV John, King of Sweden, 1777-1860
ALs, [8 Sept 1804]. 2 pp, 4to. To Madame Faipoult. Giving news from Germany. Sgd Desiree Bernadotte. (88) DM1,600
— 30 May 1824. 4 pp, 4to. To "ma chere fanni". Confidential letter about her life in Sweden, etc. (89) DM1,200

Desmarest, Nicolas, 1725-1815
ALs, 19 Apr 1792. (89) £400

Desmoulins, Camille, 1760-94
Autograph Ms, leaf from a political commonplace book, [n.d.]. (88) £170

Desportes, Philippe, 1546-1606
[An illuminated cut-out book produced by Nicholas Gougenot for Anne d'Autriche, Prieres du Roy au Saint Esprit, [Paris, 1614], 72 leaves, 125mm by 85mm, in orig vellum covers within French 19th-cent red velvet bdg, in modern mor box, with 7 full-page decorated miniatures, from the Doheny collection, sold at C on 2 Dec, lot 180, for £130,000 to Kraus.]

Detmold, Charles Maurice, 1883-1908. See: Detmold, Edward Julius & Detmold

Detmold, Edward Julius, 1883-1957
Original drawing, 2 sailing ships foundering by a rocky island with a temple on top, illus for the Arabian Nights, 1922. 204mm by 145mm, in watercolor. (88) £1,800
— Original drawing, 3 men in turbans looking at a sea serpent, for The Arabian Nights, 1922. 204mm by 145mm, in watercolor. (88) £1,800
— Original drawing, Ali Baba entering a room full of treasure, for the 1922 Ed of The Arabian Nights. 204mm by 145mm, watercolor. (88) £5,500
— Original drawing, of an oriental archer on a white steed shooting from a gateway at a giant on a rearing horse with raised scimtar, illust for the 1922 Ed of The Arabian Nights. 810mm by 575mm, in ink & watercolor, sgd with monogram, framed. (88) £8,000
— Original drawing, procession of elephants, illus for the 1922 Ed of The Arabian Nights. 204mm by 145mm, watercolor. (88) £1,800

Detmold, Edward Julius, 1883-1957 —& Detmold, Charles Maurice, 1883-1908
Original drawings, (4; 2 each), to illus Pictures from Birdland, 1899. In ink & watercolor, initialled. 190mm by 140mm. Archives of J. M. Dent & Son. (90) £1,300

Deutscher Arbeiter-Saengerbund
[A file of 59 letters & cards addressed to the D. A. S. by musicians & composers, 1912 to 1932, with related material, sold at star on 10 Mar 1988, lot 750, for DM2,200.]

Dewey, George, 1837-1917
ALs, 12 Oct 1898. (89) $220
Ls, 19 Nov 1910. (90) $80

Dexter, Samuel, 1761-1816
Ds, 6 Jan 1801. (91) $85

Di Donato, Antonio, fl.1760-1800
Autograph music, Salve Regina, for 2 violins, basso continuo & soprano solo, sgd; [n.d.]. (88) £300

Diabelli, Anton, 1781-1858
Autograph music, song Im Wald und auf der Haide, for voice & piano, [n.d.]. 2 pp, 24cm by 30.5cm; 12 staves each. Some corrections; sgd at head. Stichvorlage. (89) DM1,600
— Autograph music, song, Nachtgebet, to a poem by Ignaz Franz Castelli, 6 Feb 1855. 2 pp, 28cm by 21cm. Sgd & inscr to Castelli. (91) DM2,600

Diaghilev, Sergei Pavlovich, 1872-1929
Ls, 15 Dec 1922. 1 p, 8vo. Recipient unknown. Acknowledging a letter relating to Nijinsky's will. (90) £1,100

Diaries
Ms, entries dated Nov 1623 to Mar 1637. (88) £460

Diaz, Francisco, d.1646
Ms, Diccionario de la lengua mandarina, [late 17th cent]. 400 pp, 4to, on Chinese & European paper, in 19th-cent russia gilt by Du Planil. In a neat hand in double columns. Phillipps MS.13944 & Robinson collection. (89) £6,500

Diaz, Juan
Ms, Itinerario del armata del Re Cat[oli]co in India verso la Isola de Jucatan del anno MDxviij, [Italy, c.1519]. 26 pp, folio, in 18th-cent gilt wraps. Account of Juan de Grijalba's expedition to Yucatan, differing somewhat from ptd version. (90) £9,000

Diaz, Porfirio, 1830-1915
Series of 14 Ls s, 10 Mar 1904 to 16 July 1911. (88) DM950
Series of Ds s, 7 Ds s, [n.d.]. (90) $250
Photograph, sgd, [1906]. (88) DM420

Dibdin, Charles, 1745-1814. See: Shakespeare, William

Dibdin, Thomas Frognall, 1776-1847
ALs, 5 Jan 1819. (90) DM260
— 25 Oct 1834. (90) £85

Dibelius, Otto, 1880-1967
Ls, 7 Aug 1940. (89) DM260

Dickens, Charles, 1812-70
[An album containing a collection of letters relating to Dickens, 1836 to 1898, 89 pp, various sizes, sold at S on 21 July 1988, lot 97, for £1,250 to Joseph & Sawyer.]
[An album containing 6 A Ls s by Dickens to Sir John Easthope, & ALs & Al (draft) by Easthope to Dickens, [1836] to 1844, 16 pp, 4to & 8vo, all relating to Dickens's work for The Chronicle, with related material, sold at S on 27 Sept 1988, lot 126, for £8,000 to Valentine.]
[An ALs each by his father-in-law George Hogarth & his sister-in-law Georgina Hogarth, 13 June [1844] & 17 Sept [1858], mentioning Dickens, sold at CNY on 17 Oct 1988, lot 1245, for $420.]
[An autograph envelope, sgd, addressed to the Rev. James White, [n.d.], sold at pn on 16 June 1988, lot 91, for £55 to Rivlin.]
[A cut signature with autograph address, & an autograph envelope with franking signature, 30 Dec 1852 & [10 Sept 1867], sold at C on 7 Dec 1988, lot 193, for £180 to Maggs.]
[An album containing 30 carte-sized photographs of Dickens, his house & family, with autograph address on visiting card, [n.d.]., sold at S on 20 July 1989, lot 93, for £1,400 to Holliman & Treacher.]
[His engraved visiting card, inscr by him with his new address, sold at pn on 19 Oct 1989, lot 127, for £120 to Knight.]
Collection of 2 A Ls s & check, sgd, 27 Apr & 10 June 1863, & 23 Apr 1866. (88) £320
— Collection of ALs & autograph quotation, sgd, 1 Apr 1867 & 16 Jan 1847. 2 pp, 8vo. To C. J. Rebton Turner, about recipient's dictionary. Quotation from The Battle of Life; laid down. With related material. (90) £1,900

DICKENS

Series of 21 A Ls s, [c.Apr 1832 to 1835]. 53 pp, 4to & 8vo. To Henry William Kolle. Containing important information about his early life, his courtship of Maria Beadnell, his work as parliamentary reporter, etc. Mtd in an album with related material. (89) £22,000

— Series of 15 A Ls s, 29 Dec 1835 to 12 Jan 1837. About 34 pp, 4to & 8vo. To John Pyke Hullah. Chronicling their collaboration on the comic opera The Village Coquettes. (89) £13,000

— Series of 4 A Ls s, 16 Apr to 3 May 1850. (88) £800

A Ls s (2), 13 Sept 1850 & 23 Oct 1852. 4 pp, 8vo. To Mrs. Poel, saying he will not emerge from solitude before finishing a book. To Hepworth Dixon, declining to become a patron of a benefit society. In red mor portfolio with related material. (88) $1,600

— A Ls s (2), 16 & 17 Aug 1865. (88) £750

ALs, 30 Jan 1837. (88) £480

— "Tuesday morning" [c.Apr 1837]. (88) £420

— 3 June 1837. (88) £420

— "Monday morning" [mid-Dec 1837]. (88) £400

— "Wednesday morning" [1837/38]. 4 pp, 8vo. To W. B. Archer. Commenting about a story concerning visions of the dead submitted by Archer to Bentley's Miscellany. Koch Foundation. (90) $6,500

— [16 Apr 1838]. (89) £600

— "Monday morning" [Apr 1838?]. (88) £420

— 29 July 1839. (89) £550

— "Monday morning" [Summer 1839]. (88) £420

— 10 Mar [1840]. (88) £500

— 25 June 1840. 2 pp, 4to. To George Chapman. Regretting that he cannot joint Chapman for a holiday because of the pressure of work. (91) £1,200

— 8 July 1840. Barrett collection. (89) $500

— 13 July 1840. Byer collection. (90) $750

— 13 Aug 1840. 2 pp, 8vo. To Samuel Rogers. Requesting permission to dedicate Master Humphrey's Clock to him. (88) £1,200

— 6 Jan [1841]. (90) $950

AMERICAN BOOK PRICES CURRENT

— 28 Jan 1841. (88) £400

— 27 July 1841. (88) £420

— 12 Sept 1841. 4 pp, 8vo. To George Cattermole. Giving instructions for illusts to Master Humphrey's Clock & Barnaby Rudge. Doheny collection. (88) $5,000

— 6 Dec 1841. 3 pp, 8vo. To David Macbeth Moir. Farewell letter before his visit to America. Doheny collection. (89) $3,800

— 24 Feb 1842. 3 pp, 8vo. To Dr. John Sherren Bartlett. Defending his advocacy of international copyright. Doheny collection. (89) $3,800

— 12 Mar 1842. 2 pp, 8vo. To Henry Clay. Sending petitions to be presented to the Congress. (90) $2,200

— 13 July 1842. (91) $900

— 6 Sept 1842. 2 pp, 8vo. To Dr. John Sherren Bartlett. About the copyright problem, & declining an arrangement proposed by Bartlett. Doheny collection. (89) $3,200

— 27 Nov 1842. 2 pp, 4to. To Edgar Allan Poe. Reporting that he has not been able to find a pbr for Poe's works in England. Martin collection. (90) $35,000

— 2 Jan 1843. (88) £800

— 15 Jan 1843. (88) £650

— 2 Mar 1843. (88) £420

— 3 July 1843. (88) $1,000

— 3 Apr 1844. (88) £600

— 12 Apr 1844. (90) $600

— 9 May 1844. (89) $650

— 16 Feb 1846. (88) £900

— 2 Mar 1846. 3 pp, 8vo. To William Locke. Requesting information on the Ragged Schools. Tipped to larger leaf. Barrett collection. (89) $1,400

— 22 Apr 1846. (90) $700

— 18 May 1846. (88) £500

— 25 Jan 1847. (88) £580

— 24 Feb 1847. John F. Fleming Estate. (89) $550

— [Mar/Apr 1847?]. (88) £520

— 27 June 1847. 2 pp, 8vo. To Moritz Feist. Regretting that he did not meet him. (90) DM1,500

— 28 Feb 1848. Barrett collection. (89) $950

— 29 Sept 1848. (90) £240

— 15 Dec 1848. 1 p, 8vo. To [James Arthur] Wilson. Sending "a little book that will not be published before next Tuesday." Matted with a port. (90) $1,300
— 15 Dec 1848. (88) £480
— 12 Aug 1850. 2 pp, 8vo. To Charles Black. Explaining that his health does not permit him to keep a dinner appointment. (88) DM1,200
— 22 Apr 1851. 2 pp, 8vo. To George Darbury. About a question propounded at a debating society. (91) $1,400
— "Friday" [c.Apr 1851]. (89) £250
— 5 Apr 1852. Doheny collection. (88) $750
— 13 July 1852. (88) £340
— 17 July 1852. Doheny collection. (88) $1,000
— 3 Dec 1852. (89) £520
— 10 May 1853. Doheny collection. (89) $950
— 6 July 1853. 1 p, 8vo. To Hablot K. Browne. Humorous letter expressing satisfaction with some sketches. In French & English. (89) $1,600
— 27 Sept 1853. 4 pp, 4to. To Baroness Burdett-Coutts. Giving an account of his current travels through Europe. Tipped to larger leaf. Barrett collection. (89) $7,500
— 18 Nov 1854. (90) £1,000
— 13 May 1856. (90) DM480
— 20 Sept 1856. (91) $1,000
— 8 Mar 1857. (91) £680
— 25 Apr 1857. (90) £950
— 4 Sept 1857. (88) £280
— 13 Oct 1857. (88) $850
— 8 Oct 1858. 1 p, 8vo. To William Logan. Inviting him to hear him read the Christmas Carol. (90) £1,700
— 19 July 1859. 2 pp, 8vo. To Thomas Adolphus Trollope. Sending payment for articles ptd, & praising Trollope's A Decade of Italian Women. Doheny collection. (89) $1,800
— 8 Apr 1860. 3 pp, 8vo. To Baroness Burdett-Coutts. Referring to personal problems. Sgd C.D. Barrett collection. (89) $4,500
— 17 Apr 1860. (89) $275
— 16 May 1860. (89) DM760
— 19 June 1860. (90) £750

— 5 Dec 1860. (88) £420
— 27 July 1861. (88) £350
— 8 Nov 1861. 1 p, 8vo. To Vera Watson. About his efforts to contact Lady Spencer & his readings from David Copperfield. Matted with a port. (89) $2,750
— 1 Apr 1862. (91) £400
— 20 May 1862. (88) £480
— 2 June 1862. 1 p, 8vo. To Eduard Hanslick. Sending a ticket for a reading of David Copperfield. (90) £1,600
— 13 June 1862. (89) £150
— 22 Apr 1863. 4 pp, 8vo. To Wilkie Collins. Regretting he did not see him before his departure & providing literary & theatrical gossip. (89) £3,000
— 26 June 1864. (91) £400
— 23 Sept 1864. (89) £200
— 28 Dec 1864. (89) £550
— 1864. (90) £450
— 27 Nov 1865. (91) £900
— 17 Dec 1865. (89) £280
— 23 Dec 1865. (91) DM950
— 29 May 1866. (89) $350
— 12 Nov 1866. (89) £480
— 6 Jan 1867. Doheny collection. (88) $500
— 30 Sept 1867. (89) £180
— 2 Oct 1867. (89) $300
— 13 May 1868. (89) £460
— 4 June 1868. (88) £300
— 21 Sept 1868. (88) £280
— 2 Apr 1869. (89) £600
— 10 Apr 1869. Doheny collection. (88) $500
— [n.d.], "Thursday". (89) £1,000
AL, 25 Dec 1845. (89) £150
Ls, 25 Feb [1842]. (90) $900
ANs, 14 Apr 1869. (89) £260
— 30 Apr 1869. Doheny collection. (88) $280
Autograph check, sgd, 30 July 1859, payable to Mr. (88) £240
— Anr, sgd, 3 Apr 1861. (89) £220
— Anr, sgd, 29 Jan 1866. (89) £170
— Anr, sgd, 26 July 1867, 1 p, 8vo. (88) £240
— Anr, sgd, 17 May 1869, payable to The St. (88) £220
— Anr, sgd, 27 May 1869, payable to Messrs. (88) £220

DICKENS

Check, 12 Feb 1839. (89) £220
— Anr, sgd, 21 Aug 1852. (91) £220
— Anr, sgd, 10 July 1861; 78mm by 180mm. Doheny collection. (88) $380
— Anr, sgd, 21 Mar 1865. (88) DM650
— Anr, sgd, 4 Sept 1865, payable to "House". (88) $250
Cut signature, [n.d]. (90) $250
— Anr, [n.d.]. (88) $200
Photograph, sgd, [n.d.]. Rawlins collection. (88) £720
Signature, 18 Mar 1861. (88) $170
— BROWNE, HABLOT K. ("PHIZ"). - Orig drawings (42), to illus Dickens's Little Dorrit; 1855 to 1857. Various sizes. In pencil, wash & ink. Mtd in 4 mor gilt vols by Riviere. (89) £26,000
— CLARKE, J. CLAYTON. - Orig drawings (39), illustrating David Copperfield; [n.d.]. Each 140mm by 88mm, mtd on larger sheets, in half mor bdg. In pen-&-ink & colors. Sgd Kyd. Doheny collection. (89) $4,200
— CRUIKSHANK, GEORGE. - Orig drawing, pencil port of Dickens, sgd & identified in Cruikshank's hand; [c.1835-1845]. 212mm by 162mm. Mtd. (91) $3,000
— CRUIKSHANK, GEORGE. - 25 proof impressions of the engraved plates for Dickens's Sketches by Boz, 2d series; [c.1836]. With 2 engravings; in folder. (89) £700
— DICKENS, JOHN. - ALs, 6 Sept [1850]. 2 pp, 8vo. To his physician. Sending payment for professional services during his wife's confinement. (90) £700
— KNOWLES, GEORGE SHERIDAN. - Orig drawing, port of Dickens, [n.d.]. 10.25 by 8.5 inches, oval. In pencil & watercolor, sgd. (89) £280
— PAILTHORPE, F. W. - Orig drawings (3), to illus The Posthumous Papers of the Pickwick Club; [n.d.]. 3 pp, 8vo. In pencil & watercolor. Unpbd. (89) £300

Dickinson, Emily, 1830-86
Autograph Ms, poem, beginning "But little Carmine..."; [c.1862]. 1 p, 8vo. 7 lines, sgd Emily. Addressed to Miss Whitney. (90) $13,000
Autograph transcript, poem, beginning "Heart not so heavy as mine," sgd; [c.1859]. 2 pp, 8vo (card). 5 four-line stanzas; 2 unpbd. Martin collection.

AMERICAN BOOK PRICES CURRENT

(90) $4,000
ALs, [21 Dec 1853]. 4 pp, 8vo. To Emily Fowler Ford. Expressing sadness about her friend's absence. With ALs by Lavinia Dickinson. (88) $7,500
— [13 Aug 1885]. 2 pp, 8vo. To William Jackson. Expressing grief & condolences on the death of his wife Helen Hunt Jackson. (89) $8,000
— [c.1885]. 2 pp, 8vo. To Eugenia Hall. Thanking for flowers. Martin collection. (90) $7,500
Autograph sentiment, sgd, [n.d.]. 1 p, 8vo. Portion of a poem, beginning "How dare a tear intrude..." (91) $6,200
— Anr, beginning "To be remembered what?...", sgd; [n.d.]. (89) $1,000

Dickinson, F. C.
Original drawings, (73), to illus various school or adventure stories & historical tales, 1930 to 1947. (90) £680

Dickinson, John, 1732-1808
Ds, 8 Apr 1783. (91) $150

Dickinson, Philemon, 1739-1809
ALs, 29 July 1778. (89) $350

Diderot, Denis, 1713-84
Autograph Ms, fragment beginning "Il y a des ames fortes et courageuses parmi les Barbares...", [1780?]. 2 pp, 4to. Discussing heroism & genius, Tacitus, literary originality, etc. Inlaid & pasted into a copy of Paradoxe sure le comedien, Ed by Ernest Dupuy, 1902. (90) £1,300

Diederichs, Eugen, 1867-1930
Collection of 3 A Ls s & 2 Ls s, 5 Apr 1899 to 13 Apr 1927. (90) DM260

Dienelt, Heinz-Erich, 1911-87
[A collection of c.100 letters & cards addressed or related to him, 1946 to 1956, mostly by other writers, sold at star on 30 Nov 1988, lot 73, for DM1,900.]

Diesel, Rudolf, 1858-1913
Autograph Ms, statement regarding the generation of heat by a motor, [n.d.]. 1 p, 8vo. Sgd. (90) DM7,000

Diesterweg, Friedrich Adolf Wilhelm, 1790-1866
Autograph Ms, note for the Berliner Nachrichten concerning scholarly lectures for women, 25 Oct 1851. (91) DM260

ALs, 13 Nov 1861. (90) DM360

Dietrich, Marlene
[3 photographs, sgd, [n.d.], 235mm by 300mm, sold at FD on 4 Dec 1990, lot 1280, for DM330.]

Diez, Friedrich, 1794-1876
Series of 6 A Ls s, 10 Mar 1869 to 28 June 1873. (90) DM260

Digby, John, 1st Earl of Bristol, 1580-1653
ALs, 6 Sept 1637. (91) DM410

Digby, Sir Kenelm, 1603-65
Ms, autobiographical romance, Loose Fantasies, [c.1665]. About 190 pp, folio, in contemp reversed calf. In a single scribal hand. (91) £2,500

Dighton, John
[The papers of John Dighton, containing correspondence, cuttings, scripts, certificates of Oscar nominations, 2 drawings by Ronald Searle, & material relating to his plays, sold at pn on 22 Mar 1990, lot 129, for £680 to Kelly.]

DiMaggio, Joseph Paul ("Joe")
ALs, 2 Feb 1971. (89) $130

DiMaggio, Joseph Paul ("Joe") —& Williams, Ted
Group photograph, [n.d.]. (91) $110

Dinesen, Isak, 1885-1962. See: Blixen-Finecke, Karen

Dinky Series
[The complete set of 87 ink & gouache drawings for 8 books in the series, [c.1942], c.325mm by 225mm, with related material, sold at S on 2 June 1989, lot 594, for £700 to Ash Rare Books.]
Original drawings, (172), to illus 16 titles in the Dinky Series, 1936 & 1938. (90) £800

Dinter, Christian Friedrich, 1760-1831
ALs, 6 Oct 1807. (89) DM210

Dinwiddie, Robert, 1693-1770
Ls, 25 Oct 1755. 1 p, 4to. To George Washington. About movements of the militia. (89) $1,800
Ds, 1754. (91) $180

Dirac, Paul Adrien Maurice, 1902-84
ALs, [n.d.]. (89) DM380

Disney Studios, Walt
[A color lobby card picturing the 7 dwarfs, 14 by 11 inches, sgd by artists Frank Thomas, Maurice Noble, Marc Davis, & Ollie Johnston, sold at Dar on 6 Dec 1990, lot 159, for $200.]
Original drawings, (2), Donald attempting to recover his rope, & Mickey making a vertical ascent, preparatory pencil drawings to illus The Alpine Climbers, 1936. (90) £550
— Original drawings, (2), Donald Duck & nephews, & nephews with storekeeper, in ink & gouache; [n.d.]. (89) £900
— Original drawings, (2), dwarfs crossing a bridge, & Bashful wading in a stream, preparatory drawings to illus The Seven Wise Dwarfs, 1941. (90) £650
— Original drawings, (2), Goofy as 1-man band, & young centaurette; preparatory pencil drawings for Mickey's Amateurs, 1937, & Fantasia, 1940. 2 pp, 230mm by 280mm; mtd. (90) £1,300
— Original drawings, (2), Mickey being congratulated, & being lassooed, preparatory pencil drawings to illus Mickey's Gala Premiere, 1933. 240mm by 303mm. (90) £2,500
— Original drawings, (2), Mickey dancing with a pig, preparatory pencil drawing to illus The Barn Dance, 1929, & Minnie seated at a piano. (90) £500
— Original drawings, (2), pencil studies of dwarfs, to illus Snow White; [n.d.]. (89) £550
— Original drawings, (2), preparatory pencil drawings for Touchdown Mickey, 1932, & Mickey's Mellerdrammer, 1933. (90) £850
— Original drawings, (3), preparatory pencil drawings of insects to illus Woodland Cafe, 1937. (90) £400

DISNEY STUDIOS

- Original drawings, (4), Mickey & Pluto in various scenes, preparatory pencil drawings to illus Society Dog Show, 1939. 254mm by 304mm. (90) £1,200
- Original drawings, (4), Mickey, Goofy & Donald in various scenes, preparatory pencil drawings to illus Mickey's Fire Brigade, 1935. (90) £800
- Original drawings, (6), depicting Bashful & Snow White, to illus Bashful's Birds, in ink & gouache; [n.d.]. (89) £360
- Original drawings, (7), dwarfs; preparatory pencil drawings for Snow White, 1938. 7 pp, 253mm by 304mm. (90) £2,400
- Original drawings, (7), ink & gouache illusts for Dopey's Funny Double; [n.d.]. (90) £350
- Original drawings, (7), preparatory pencil drawings of dwarfs, to illus Snow White, 1938. 252mm by 304mm. (90) £1,700

Original drawing, baby deer sheltering from shower, preparatory watercolor drawing to illus Bambi, 1942. 254mm by 303mm. (90) £1,800
- Original drawing, Captain Hook with hot water bottle on his head; preparatory pencil drawing for Peter Pan, 1953. (90) £420
- Original drawing, Goofy riding a horse; [c.1943]. (90) £300
- Original drawing, Mickey & Donald Duck as policemen; preparatory pencil drawing for The Dognapper, 1934. (90) £550
- Original drawing, Mickey as sorcerer's apprentice; preparatory pencil drawing for Fantasia, 1940. 205mm by 255mm; mtd. (90) £2,600
- Original drawing, Mickey as sorcerer's apprentice, preparatory drawing to illus Fantasia, 1940. (90) £1,000
- Original drawing, Mickey, Donald & Goofy paddling their canoe, preparatory drawing to illus Moose Hunters, 1937. (90) £1,000
- Original drawing, Mickey Mouse & friends playing in the snow, in ink & gouache; produced as endpapers for Donald Duck Annual, 1979. (89) £850
- Original drawing, Minnie serving lunch to Mickey from her cart; preparatory drawing for Building a Building, 1933. 235mm by 288mm; mtd. In blue crayon. (90) £1,800
- Original drawing, Pinocchio on a bird's perch; preparatory pencil drawing for Pinocchio, 1940. 230mm by 280mm; mtd. (90) £1,400
- Original drawing, Queen with poisoned apple, preparatory pencil drawing to illus Snow White, 1938. (90) £600
- Original drawing, Red Riding Hood, Grandma & 3 pigs, preparatory layout drawing for The Big Bad Wolf, 1934. In pencil & blue crayon. 240mm by 303mm. Annotations in lower margin. (90) £1,500
- Original drawing, Snow White standing; preparatory pencil drawing for Snow White, 1938. 177mm by 228mm; mtd. (90) £1,300
- Original drawing, Snow White waiving to the 7 dwarfs in a motorcycle combination & trailer, in ink & gouache; [n.d.]. (89) £500
- Original drawing, Snow White waving, preparatory pencil drawing to illus Snow White, 1938. (90) £400
- Original drawing, the queen as a witch offering an apple; preparatory pencil drawing for Snow White, 1938. (90) £750

Disney, Walter Elias, 1901-66

Original drawing, Mickey Mouse, sgd; [Nov 1946]. On back of British embarkation card, 152mm by 100mm. (89) £4,800

Autograph sentiment, inscr to Barbara Joyce, sgd, on mount of celluloid painting of Pinocchio, 168mm by 214mm. Framed. (89) £7,000
- Anr, inscr to Pat Hillyard, sgd, on mount of celluloid painting of Donald Duck, 200mm by 250mm. Framed. (89) £3,000
- Anr, inscr to David Sheldrick, sgd, on mount of celluloid painting of Captain Hook, 206mm by 282mm. Framed. (89) £4,200

Signature, [n.d.]. (91) $500
- Anr, [n.d.]. (91) $650
- Anr, [n.d.]. (91) $600
- Anr, [n.d.]. (91) $500
- Anr, [n.d.]. (91) $700
- Anr, [n.d.]. 6.5 by 6 inches. Including

sketch of cartoon figure. Mtd. (91) $2,000
— Anr, [n.d.]. (91) $475
— Anr, [n.d.]. (90) $375

Disraeli, Benjamin, 1st Earl of Beaconsfield, 1804-81
Collection of 22 A Ls s & A Ns s (some initialled), Jan 1869 to Feb 1881; c.50 pp, 8vo. To Henry Blagden, Vicar of Hughenden & his wife. Personal correspondence about a variety of matters. With letters relating to Disraeli's final illness, & autograph Ms by Henry Blagden, 8 pp, 16mo, reminiscences of Disraeli, & further related material. (88) £4,800
Series of 4 A Ls s, [7 Nov 1860] to 4 Nov 1865. 10 pp, 8vo. To the Rev. John Graves. Expressing invitations, & referring to Bradenham House, "the scene of my youth". With related material. (91) £1,400
A Ls s (2), 27 May & 1 June [n.y.]. (88) £350
ALs, 18 July 1842. (91) £600
— 20 Aug 1848. (91) £620
— 28 Jan 1854. (88) £700
— 24 Oct 1868. (89) £400
— 16 Feb 1870. 4 pp, 8vo. To Gen. Charles Grey. Reporting about his health. (88) DM1,200
— 3 May 1871. (88) £150
— 4 May 1872. 3 pp, 8vo. To Sir Thomas Grant. Regretting he will not be able to attend a meeting. (90) DM1,100
— 6 Feb [18]75. (88) $200
— 4 Oct 1880. (89) £420
AL, [c.20 July 1831]. 3 pp, 4to. To his sister Sarah. Announcing the death of her fiance William George Meredith; enjoins her to devote her life to her brother. (91) £1,500
Autograph sentiment, sgd D, [n.d.]. (91) $150
Franking signature, [n.d.]. (91) $170
— TREVELYAN, SIR GEORGE OTTO. - Autograph Ms, essay describing Disraeli's budget speech of 1852; 25 Mar 1927. 10 pp, folio & 4to. With related material. (91) £95
— TREVELYAN, SIR GEORGE OTTO. - Autograph Ms, essay describing Disraeli's budget speech of 1852; 25 Mar 1927. 10 pp, folio & 4to. With related material. (90) £90

D'Israeli, Isaac, 1766-1848
ALs, [n.d.]. (89) £220

Ditzen, Rudolf, 1893-1947. See: Fallada, Hans

Dix, Dorothea L., 1802-87
ALs, 3 Jan 1854. (88) $85

Dix, Otto, 1891-1969
ALs, 12 Aug 1952. (90) DM460
— [Dec 1959]. (88) DM370
— 6 Mar 1962. (90) DM600
— [n.d.]. (91) DM470

Dixon, Arthur A.
Original drawings, (48), to illus a series of Bible Stories, [c.1914]. (89) £450

Dmitrii Ivanovich, Saint, 1582-91. See: Lives of the Saints

Doddridge, Philip, 1702-51
ALs, 4 June 1748. (89) £90
— [n.d.]. (88) £60

Doderer, Heimito von, 1896-1966
Autograph Ms, poem, Das spaete Mittelalter [Fernes Fenster], [pbd 1957]. (89) DM360
ALs, 14 Nov 1964. (88) DM650

Dodgson, Charles Lutwidge, 1832-98
[Lutwidge Family. - A group of 3 Ms verse miscellanies compiled by members of the Lutwidge family of Holmrook Hall, [c.1758 to 1803], c.170 pp in 3 vols, 4to, sold at S on 21 July 1988, lot 100, for £350 to Rassan.]
Original drawing, ink drawing of Mabel & Alice Price, initialled & dated Mar 1871. 244mm by 176mm. In purple ink. (90) £4,800
Collection of 30 A Ls s, 3 A Ls, & photograph, sgd & inscr, 10 Dec 1877 to 6 Apr 1883. About 105 pp, 8vo, in 4to album. To Agnes Hull & her sister Jessie (1). Charming correspondence with a young child. With related material. (91) £115,000
— Collection of ALs & autograph postcard, sgd, 15 Sept 1893 & 1896. 1 p, 8vo, & card. To antiquarian booksellers. In 3d person, inquiring about

books, & contents not stated. (90) DM1,200
Series of 5 A Ls s, 12 Oct 1883 to 26 Dec 1886. 14 pp, 12mo. To Ruth [Dymes]. Charming letters to a child. 1 initialled; 1 signature removed. (90) £4,500
A Ls s (2), 1 & 15 May 1884. 5 pp, 12mo. To Ethel [Dymes]. Inviting her to a play. With related material. (90) £1,200
ALs, 10 Dec 1876. 2 pp, 8vo. To [Henry Morley]. Naming Mr. Pietrocola-Rossetti as a candidate for a lectureship. (90) DM1,700
— 25 Sept 1882. (91) £480
— 18 May [18]84. (88) $300
— 21 Aug 1891. 3 pp, 8vo. To Miss Brain. On behalf of a cousin, requesting advice about starting a boarding house for girls. (91) £1,200
— 1 Nov 1891. 3 pp, 8vo. To Nelly. Thanking for an antimacassar. Written backwards. Sgd CLD. (88) £1,300
— 24 Mar 1893. 4 pp, 12mo. To Alice Wilson-Fox. Informing her that the noise of a barrel-organ prevented him from visiting her. Doheny collection. (88) $1,800
— 3 July 1893. 4 pp, 8vo. To Mrs. Walton. Expressing good wishes for her marriage. (91) £1,300
— 19 Dec 1893. (89) £520
— 28 June [18]96. 2 pp, 96mm by 152mm. To Evelyn. Concerning the timing of a meeting. (90) $1,400
— 26 May [n.y.]. (89) £240
— [n.d.]. 2 pp, 8vo. To "Georgie". Discussing the publication of a forthcoming book. Was mtd. (88) £1,050
Autograph postcard, sgd, 14 Dec 1893. (89) £140
— ARGLES, AGNES & EDITH. - Ms, children's magazine, The Precincts Popgun, June to July 1868, c.60 pp, 8vo, in cloth wraps. In several hands, with some pen-&-ink illusts. (88) £450

Doeblin, Alfred, 1878-1957
Autograph Ms, essay about the writing of prose, sgd; [1920]. 6 pp, 4to. With covering ALs, 5 Nov 1920, to W. Schneider. (89) DM1,600
A Ls s (2), 11 Dec 1937 & 28 Mar 1938. 4 pp, 4to & 8vo. To Max Brusto. About the difficulty to find a publisher. With Ls from Doeblin to Brusto, 1947. (88) DM1,100
ALs, 14 Feb 1932. (90) DM400
— 30 Oct [19]36. (91) DM1,000
— [27 Jan 1938]. (91) DM650
— 2 Nov [19]38. (91) DM650
— 4 Dec [19]38. (91) DM650
— 3 Feb [19]39. 6 pp, 4to & 8vo. To Dr. Viktor Zuckerkandl. Giving details about his new work November 18. (91) DM1,300
— 4 June 1939. 5 pp, 4to & 8vo. To Mr. & Mrs. Rosin. Describing his return to Paris after his stay in America. 1st page written by Mrs. Rosin. (88) DM1,300
— 16 June 1939. (88) DM340
— 10 Oct 1940. 5 pp, 8vo. To Mr. & Mrs. Rosin. Reporting about his arrival in California & his impressions of Los Angeles. (88) DM1,200
— 18 Mar 1945. 8 pp, 8vo. To Dr. Viktor Zuckerkandl. Commenting on his life in America. (91) DM2,000
Autograph postcard, sgd, 19 Oct 1919. (90) DM360

Doellinger, Ignaz von, 1799-1890
ALs, 12 June 1871. (90) DM300

Doenitz, Karl, 1891-1980
Typescript, English trans of his Order of the Day to the Armed Forces, 1 May 1945. (90) $120
— Typescript, English trans of his broadcast to the German people on 1 May 1945, announcing his succession as head of state; sgd & dated 2 Feb [19]67. (88) $80
— Typescript, English trans of his assumption of power on Hitler's death, 1945, sgd at bottom & dated 2 Feb [19]67. (88) $150
— Typescript, instructions to Gen. (91) $190
— Typescript, instrument of capitulation, in the version sgd for the Russians, 8 May 1945. (89) $250
ALs, 11 May [19]69. (90) $90
Ls, 29 Sept 1944. (90) $100
Photograph, sgd, 29 Aug [19]75. (89) $65

Doernberg, Wilhelm Caspar Ferdinand, Freiherr von, 1768-1850
ALs, 6 July 1829. (90) DM480
— 9 Aug 1842. (89) DM450

Dohnanyi, Ernst von, 1877-1960
Autograph postcard, sgd, [20 June 1908]. (90) DM660

Dolmetsch, Arnold, 1858-1940
Collection of 11 A Ls s & Ls, 1914 to 1938. (89) £800

Domenech, Fra Jaume
Ms, History of the Ancient World, in Catalan. [Catalonia, Barcelona?, 26 May 1454 - 11 Jan 1455]. 649 leaves (1 lacking), vellum & paper, 280mm by 210mm, in 2 vols of 18th-cent Spanish limp vellum. In a rounded gothic bookhand. With 5 large historiated initials with full illuminated borders. Chester Beatty W.MS.180. (91) £45,000

Domenech y Montaner, Luis, 1850-1924
[A collection of Mss by & letters to Domenech, c.1881 to 1900, c.100 pp, 8vo, sold at S on 20 Nov 1990, lot 520, for £6,800 to Catalunya.]

Doniphan, Alexander William, 1808-87
ALs, 24 Feb 1849. Alexander collection. (90) $375

Donizetti, Gaetano, 1797-1848
Autograph music, aria, Odi d'un nom che muore, for voice & piano, 1826. 4 pp, size not stated. 33 bars. With autograph tp, sgd & inscr to Virginia Palmieri. (89) £1,200
— Autograph music, cavatina Un barbaro un ingrato, from this opera Zoraide di Granata, [c.1821]. 4 pp, folio. Draft, notated on up to 14 staves per page; in full score. (89) £1,600
— Autograph music, duet, a setting of lines from Metastasio's Adriano in Siria, for 2 sopranos & piano in E-flat major; [n.d.]. 8 pp, folio. Comprising 2 sections of 63 & 54 bars. Including autograph tp with note of authentication by B. Zanetti. (90) £2,550
— Autograph music, duet, Scarsa merce saranno, 4 July 1815. 19 pp, folio. Scored for soprano, tenor & piano on 3 systems of 4 staves each, with autograph tp, sgd, & some later sketches. (91) £6,500
— Autograph music, Ero e Leandro, for 2 soprano voices & piano in E-flat major; [n.d.]. 7 pp, folio. In brown ink on 3 systems per page, 4 staves each. Including authentication by B. Zanetti on tp. (90) £2,800
— Autograph music, fragment from an unnamed opera, containing 2 arias in full score, [c.1825/28]. 10 pp, 22cm by 29cm. (89) DM4,200
— Autograph music, fragment of aria, Dites avez vous connu Don[n]a Sabine, [c.1843]. (89) £1,000
— Autograph music, Irene e Dafni, duet for voices & piano; [n.d.]. 7 pp, size not stated. In brown ink on 4 systems per page, 4 staves each. Some corrections. Including authentication on tp. (90) £2,800
— Autograph music, movement in D minor, probably for violin & piano, [c.1840]. 6 pp, folio. Working Ms, on up to 15 staves per page. Including sketches for anr work on verso of last leaf. (89) £3,000
— Autograph music, part of an operatic scene, beginning "Sara, sara, La sposa felice amabile...", [n.d.]. 2 pp, folio. Over 100 bars on 22 staves; with revisions. (89) £1,100
— Autograph music, quartet, Rataplan, for 2 tenors, 2 basses & piano, [c.1841]. 5 pp, folio. In brown ink on 2 systems per page, six staves each. Working Ms. (89) £2,200
— Autograph music, section of the revised version of his opera Zoraide di Granata, Act I, scene 4; [c.1823]. (89) £500
— Autograph music, Studio duo for clarinet & bass, in C; [n.d.]. 7 pp, folio, in modern bds. In brown ink on up to 5 systems per page, 2 staves each. Working Ms, with autograph tp; sgd. Probably unrecorded. (89) £3,000
ALs, 3 May 1829. (88) £550
— 13 Aug 1833. 3 pp, 4to. To Giovanni Ricordi. Reporting about problems with impresarios, projects & prospects. (91) £4,000
— 9 Sept [18]34. 2 pp, 4to. To Rossini. Reporting the banning of his opera Maria Stuarda at Naples. (91) £5,000

DONIZETTI

— 16 July 1835. (89) £600
— 14 Apr 1836. 4 pp, 4to. To Antonio Pacini. Mentioning Lucia di Lammermoor, Rossini & other musicians in Paris, a string quartet by Cherubini, etc. Seal tear. (90) £1,800
— 12 Aug 1836. 1 p, 4to. To Paganini. Recommending Signore Desser. (91) £1,200
— [c.1839]. 1 p, 8vo. To Antonio Pacini. Informing him about his work on the French adaptation of his opera Belisario. With a port. (88) DM1,800
— 5 Jan 1843. (90) £550
— 17 Apr 1845. (91) £650
— [30 Aug 1845]. (89) £700
AL, [after 1841]. (89) £650
— SCRIBE, EUGENE. - Autograph Ms, discussion of Act II of Dom Sebastien, [c.1842]. 4 pp, 4to. Including related letter to Donizetti in anr hand on verso of 2d leaf. (89) £1,000

Doors, The

[The signatures of Jim Morrison, Robby Krieger, John Densmore & Ray Manzarek on LP cover Waiting for the Sun, inscr to Doug, [n.d.], framed, 15 by 15 inches, sold at pnNY on 3 Dec 1988, lot 326, for $1,500.]
Typescript, song, Light my Fire, sgd by Jim Morrison & Robby Krieger, [1968]. Framed with a group photograph, overall size 14 by 20 inches. (89) $2,100

Dorati, Antal

Autograph music, sketches for his string quartet, 1981. (89) DM300

Dore, Gustave, 1833-83

Collection of ALs & photograph, 16 Apr [c.1860?] & [n.d.]. (90) $150
ALs, 23 Aug 1869. (91) DM280
— 19 Oct [1877?]. (89) DM360

Dorn, Heinrich, 1804-92

ALs, 20 Jan 1836. (90) DM280

Dorothea, Kurfuerstin von Brandenburg, 1636-89

Ls, 4 Jan 1674. (91) DM460

Dorothea, Herzogin von Kurland, 1761-1821

ALs, 6 May 1814. (90) DM480

Dostoevsky, Fyodor, 1821-81

ALs, 3 Mar 1876. 1 p, 8vo. To an unnamed lady. Thanking for her kind words of admiration. (89) £10,500
— 18 June [i.e.July] 1880. 3 pp, 8vo. To Viktor Feofilovich Puzykovich. About his recent travels, his speech at the unveiling of the Pushkin memorial, his work on The Brothers Karamazov, etc. (90) DM75,000
Photograph, sgd & inscr, 1870. 16cm by 10cm; by Constantin Shapiro. Inscr to Jacob Bogdanovich on verso. (90) £6,000

Douglas, Lord Alfred, 1870-1945

Autograph Ms, draft of his introduction to the 2d Ed of his New Preface to the Life and Confessions of Oscar Wilde, sgd; Aug 1927. Koch Foundation. (90) $800
A Ls s (2), 8 & 16 June 1937. (90) DM360
ALs, 30 Mar 1894. (88) $200
— 13 Oct 1939. (91) £800

Douglas, Lord Alfred, 1870-1945 —& Harris, Frank, 1854-1931

[A collection of autograph & typed Mss & letters for The Second Preface to Harris's Life of Oscar Wilde, 1924 to 1926, 64 pp, 4to & 8vo, sold at S on 13 Dec 1990, lot 179, for £3,500 to Pickering & Chatto.]

Douglas, Claude Leroy

Typescript, Journalists & Journals of the Old West, [n.d.]. (88) $350

Douglas, Kirk

Ls, 18 Feb 1950. (89) $80

Douglas, Norman, 1868-1952

Ls, 1928. (90) £50

Douglas, Stephen A., 1813-61

ALs, 28 Dec 1843. Byer collection. (90) $275
— 22 Mar 1844. (90) $300
— 17 May 1852. (90) $200
Franking signature, [9 Nov 1859]. Alexander collection. (90) $105

Douglas, William O.
Ls, 12 Apr 1946. (91) $350

Douglass, Frederick, 1817-95
ALs, 13 Feb 1884. (89) $300
— 18 Mar 1884. (90) $950
Ds, 19 Oct 1881. (88) $65
— 19 Oct 1881. (88) $90
— 27 Oct 1881. (91) $110
— 22 Oct 1884. (90) $70
Autograph quotation, sgd, [n.d.]. (91) $950
Signature, 1877. (88) $60
— Anr, 1877. (88) $90

Doulton & Co.
Ms, Studioi Notes. (90) $800

Dove, Heinrich Wilhelm, 1803-79
Autograph Ms, comments on technical aspects of an apparatus to collect solar energy, [n.d.]. (91) DM370

Dowing, Lewis
ALs, 9 Sept 1862. Alexander collection. (90) $210

Dowsing, William, 1596?-1679?
[His annotated copy of The History of Polybius the Megalopolitan. L, 1634, in contemp rebacked calf, with his autograph notes on c.260 pp & a letter from Richard [Sleppore] to Dowsing, 23 Dec 1651, bound in, sold at S on 21 July 1988, lot 10, for £600 to Quaritch.]

Dowson, Ernest C., 1867-1900
Series of 19 A Ls s, [c.1895 to 1900]. 43 pp, 8vo. To Conal O'Riordan. Referring to a variety of matters "ranging from bacchanal activities and failing health to literary endeavors". With related material. Bradley Martin sale. (90) $5,500

Doyle, Sir Arthur Conan, 1859-1930
[His bank book, recording transactions of his account at the Capital and Counties Bank from 11 Feb 1904, 66 pp, 4to, sold at S on 21 July 1988, lot 167, for £1,200 to Rassan.]
Autograph Ms, description of his "Spirit Guide" Pheneas & of the mediumship of his wife, [n.d.]. 11 pp, in 4to notebook. With revisions. (88) £1,100
— Autograph Ms, "General Outlines of first Lecture", [n.d.]. (88) £500
— Autograph Ms, poem, A Forgotten Tale, sgd & dated 27 Nov [18]93. 3 pp, 8vo. 8 six-line stanzas. Printer's copy. (89) £1,600
— Autograph Ms, "Psychic Notes", [late 1920s]. 17 pp, in 8vo notebook. (88) £1,100
— Autograph Ms, Sherlock Holmes story, The Valley of Fear, [1913-14]. 176 pp, 324mm by 200mm; variously bound or disbound. Working draft; lacking epilogue. With related material. (90) $260,000
— Autograph Ms, story, The Adventure of the three Garridebs, sgd & dated June 1924. 22 pp, 4to, in white cloth. Including several autograph corrections. (90) £44,000
— Autograph Ms, "Swedenborg and Sp[iritualism] Notes", [n.d.]. (88) £700
Collection of ALs & 2 letters in the hand of a secretary, 15 Dec 1905, 23 Aug 1914 & [n.d.]. (88) £400
— Collection of 2 A Ls s & photograph, sgd, [n.d.]. (88) £520
Series of 5 A Ls s, 1921. (88) £1,000
A Ls s (2), 2 June 1893 & [n.d.]. (90) DM700
— A Ls s (2), 4 Mar & 8 Apr 1926. (89) £480
ALs, 10 Sept 1894. (89) £280
— [1894]. (88) £600
— [25 Nov 1896]. (91) £300
— [c.1914]. (90) £650
— 6 Jan 1916. (89) £380
— 23 Sept 1928. (90) £580
— 9 Aug [n.y.]. (91) £600
— [n.d.]. (90) $320
— [n.d.]. (89) £600
— [n.d.]. (89) $375
— [n.d.]. Byer collection. (90) $550
A Ns s (2), [n.d.]. (91) £220
ANs, 1894. (91) $250
Photograph, sgd & inscr, Dec 1921. (88) £400

D'Oyly Family
[A collection of papers of the D'Oyly & related families, 17th to 19th cent, hundreds of pages in a box, sold at S on 19 July 1990, lot 240, for £600 to White.]

Drabble, Margaret
[A box of working papers for her novel Realms of Gold, c.1974, c.250 items, sold at S on 15 Dec, lot 146, for £1,000.]

Drake, Sir Francis
Ms, inventory of the naval supplies for the last voyage of Drake & Sir John Hawkyns supplied by Queen Elizabeth I. [1596] 4 pp, folio, in half calf with early wraps bound in. Written in a fine calligraphic hand. (91) $4,000

Drake, Joseph Rodman, 1795-1820
Autograph Ms, poem, To Simeon DeWitt Esqr. Surveyor General, [10 Mar - 24 July 1819]. 3 pp, 4to. Sgd Croacker & Co. Addressed to the pbr of the NY Evening Post on verso. With 1819 Ed of Poems, by Croaker, Croaker & Co., & anr Ed, fragment, 1836. Martin collection. (90) $3,000

Dreiser, Theodore, 1871-1945
Collection of 2 A Ls s & 2 Ls s, 19 May 1909 to 14 Feb 1912. Doheny collection. (89) $500

ALs, 28 Jan 1918. (91) $90

— 12 Sept 1926. (91) $130

— 19 Jan 1945. (89) $150

Series of 4 Ls s, 1931. 7 pp, size not stated. To Harry Hansen. About his dispute with Paramount Pictures over the filming of An American Tragedy. With related material. (89) $1,900

Ls, Apr 1932. (89) $600

— 3 Aug 1933. (91) $100

— 7 May 1934. (91) $300

Drew, John, 1853-1927 —& Others
[A poster for a revival of A. W. Pinero's Trewlawny of the Wells at the Knickerbocker Theatre, [1925], 8 by 31 inches, sgd by Drew & 22 others, framed, sold at Dar on 4 Oct 1990, lot 11, for $80.]

Dreyfus, Alfred, 1859-1935
ALs, 25 May 1900. (90) DM660

— 10 Mar 1910. (88) DM750

— 1 July 1912. (89) £700

— [n.d.]. (89) DM850

Driesch, Hans, 1867-1941
Collection of 6 A Ls s & 5 autograph postcards, sgd, 25 Sept 1925 to 11 Dec 1938. (89) DM220

Drinkwater, John, 1882-1937
Autograph Ms, essay, The Poetry of London, [c.1924]. Doheny collection. (89) $380

Droste-Huelshoff, Annette von, 1797-1848
Autograph Ms, poem, beginning "Als diese Lieder ich vereint...", 15 Jan 1848. On verso of flyleaf of a copy of her Gedichte, Stuttgart & Tuebingen, 1844. 2 eight-line stanzas; sgd Die Verfasserin & inscr to Ludwig von Madroux, on recto. (89) £2,800

ALs, 14/17 Jan 1848. 3 pp, 8vo. To Ludwig von Madroux. Thanking for birthday presents & complaining about her health. (89) DM22,000

Drouet, Juliette, 1806-83
ALs, 20 Aug [1850]. (90) DM900

Droysen, Johann Gustav, 1808-84
ALs, 10 Nov 1843. (90) DM500

— 18 July 1883. (91) DM480

Drury Lane Theater
[2 items relating to Drury Lane Theater, memorandum of agreement by Thomas Greenwood to take Arthur Thiselton as apprentice, & ALs by G. Marinari, offering his services, 27 Oct 1814 & 6 Aug 1819, 3 pp, 4to, sold at S on 21 Sept, lot 17, for £100 to Sutherland.]

Du Barry, Jeanne Becu, Comtesse, 1743-93
Document, 6 Dec 1793. 1 p, 4to. Order for her execution on 7 Dec. (91) $5,500

Du Bois, William Edward Burghardt, 1868-1963
Ls, 20 July 1959. (91) $130

Du Bois-Reymond, Emil, 1818-96
Series of 4 A Ls s, 29 Mar 1874 to 11 Feb 1881. (91) DM550

ALs, 17 May 1851. 1 p, 8vo. To [Alexander von Frantzius?]. About several scholarly matters. (91) DM1,100

— 21 Aug 1883. (91) DM650

Du Maurier, Daphne, 1907-89
[The final shooting script for the film Rebecca, sgd & inscr to Du Maurier by David O. Selznick, 7 Sept 1939, 4to, in dark red mor bdg with 10 stills from the film, with related material, sold at pn on 22 Mar 1990, lot 130, for £2,000 to Reuter.]

Du Maurier, George, 1834-96
ALs, 20 Mar [n.y.]. (91) $190

Du Pont, Samuel Francis, 1803-65
ALs, 4 July 1863. (91) $275
Ds, Oct 1845. (91) $350

DuBarry, Emma
Photograph, [1852]. (90) $500

Dubuffet, Jean, 1901-85
ALs, 24 Mar 1975. (90) DM400
Ls, 14 Oct 1968. (91) $190
— 26 Sept [n.y.]. (89) DM750

Duchamp, Marcel, 1887-1968
Signature, on front cover of cat First Papers of Surrealism, NY, 1942; 4to. (88) DM1,200

Duckworth, Sir John Thomas, 1748-1817
Ms, letterbook, "Account of Despatches Sent and Received", 17 Oct 1798 to 30 Jan 1800. Wolf collection. (90) £950

Duerer, Albrecht, 1471-1528
Autograph Ms, transcript of a receipt issued by Emperor Maximilian, 8 Sept 1518. 1 p, folio. Tipped to larger leaf. Barrett collection. (89) $32,500

Dufour, Guillaume Henri, 1787-1875
ALs, 27 May 1847. (90) DM480
— 20 June [n.d.]. (91) DM850

Dufy, Raoul, 1877-1953
Ls, 22 Mar 1949. Byer collection. (90) $325
ANs, [n.d.]. (88) DM260

Dukakis, Michael S. See: Carter, James Earl ("Jimmy") & Dukakis

Dukas, Paul, 1865-1935
Autograph Ms, "2eme Version (Complementaire)", modifications to his ballet La Peri, sgd & dated 9 Feb 1935. (88) £360
Autograph music, overture to Goetz von Berlichingen, scored for orchestra; Oct 1884. 41 pp, folio. Working Ms, notated on up to 16 staves per page; sgd in several places. Including autograph tp. (90) £3,600
ALs, 17 Aug 1915. (90) £580
— 8 Jan 1917. (88) DM250

Dulac, Edmund
Original drawing, Snow Queen seated on her throne amid ice floes, to illus Andersen's Fairy Tales, 1911. In watercolor, sgd. 310mm by 248mm, framed. (90) £17,000
— Original drawing, young man reading to a girl seated on a settee, illus for My Lisette, an Old French Song in his Picture Book, 1914. Ink & watercolor, 307mm by 250mm, sgd & dated 1913, framed. (88) £3,500

Dumas, Alexandre, 1802-70
Autograph Ms (2), 2 scenes of an unnamed play, & fragment of a political essay, sgd; [n.d.]. 14 pp, folio & 4to. (90) DM1,100
Autograph Ms, literary text, Jules Rizzo; [n.d.]. (90) DM550
— Autograph Ms, M. (89) $450
— Autograph Ms, Montevideo, ou une nouvelle Troie, draft of 1st chapter; [ptd 1850]. (90) £480
— Autograph Ms, novel, Ange Pitou, [1851]. (91) £500
ALs, [8 June 1837]. (88) DM650
— 3 Jan 1848. (88) $175
— [n.d.]. (90) DM220
— [n.d.]. (90) DM220

Dumas, Alexandre, 1824-95
Autograph Ms, Un jour a vivre, sgd & dated 3 June 1853. 20 pp, 4to. With numerous revisions. Some repairs. (89) DM1,400
ALs, 8 Aug 1879. (90) DM240
— 8 Dec 1884. (91) $75
— [n.d.]. (90) DM260
— [n.d.]. (89) DM340
— [n.d.]. (90) DM280

Dumas, Jean Baptiste, 1800-84
ALs, 13 June 1869. (89) DM260

DUMONCEAU

Dumonceau, Jean Baptiste, Comte de Bergendael, 1760-1821
Ls, 10 Jan 1807. (88) DM280

Dumouriez, Charles Francois, 1739-1823
Series of 3 Ls s, 19 Oct 1820 to 29 Apr 1821. (91) DM550

Dunant, Henri, 1828-1910
ALs, 29 July [1892]. 1 p, 4to. To Wilhelm Sonderegger. Urgently requesting him to visit. (91) DM2,600
— 13/14 May 1901. (90) DM950

Dunbar, Paul Laurence, 1872-1906
Autograph transcript, poem, Life, [n.d.]. 1 p, 12mo. 2 five-line stanzas, sgd. Doheny collection. (89) $1,600

Duncan, Isadora, 1878-1927
ALs, 5 July 1905. (91) DM420
Autograph sentiment, 1905. (91) $900

Duncan, John
Original drawings, (4), to illus Myths of Crete, [n.d.]. 535mm by 365mm. In watercolor. (89) £2,200
— Original drawings, (8), to illus M. Archives of J. M. Dent & Son. (88) £320

Duncan, Ronald, 1914-82
[A large collection of letters addressed to him, various dates, in a suitcase, sold at S on 21 July 1988, lot 168, for £1,300 to Rota.]
See also: Pound, Ezra

Dunlap, John, 1747-1812
Ls, 28 Apr 1807. 1 p, 4to. To Gen. Charles Scott. Sending him "a little Tin case, which contains the life of 'our Washington...'." (91) $1,500

Dunne, Finley Peter, 1867-1936
Autograph Ms, sketch, Mr. Doheny collection. (89) $650

Dunsany, Edward Plunkett, 18th Baron, 1878-1957
Collection of 4 A Ls s, 6 Ls s, & 3 autograph postcards, sgd, 29 Jan 1921 to 23 June 1923. (89) £160
Series of 6 A Ls s, 1907 to 1922. (89) $475

AMERICAN BOOK PRICES CURRENT

Dupont, Gabriel, 1878-1914
Autograph postcards (2), sgd, 4 July 1904 & 31 Oct 1906. (90) DM320

Duras, Louis, Earl of Feversham, 1640?-1709
ADs, 7 July 1685. 1 p, 4to. Order to execute Monmouth's men at Weston, Bridgewater & Taunton; copy addressed to Sir John Guys. (91) £1,500

Duse, Eleonora, 1858-1924
ALs, 19 Sept [1889]. (91) $200
— 2 July 1913. (90) DM350
Photograph, sgd, [n.d.]. (90) DM380

Duse, Eleonora, 1859-1924
ALs, 4 Nov 1916. (88) $80

Duvall, Gabriel, 1752-1844
ALs, 26 Feb 1813. (91) $300

Dvorak, Antonin, 1841-1904
ALs, 30 Oct 1878. 1 p, 8vo. Recipients unnamed. Asking whether his Mss have been received. (90) DM1,900
— 7 July 1880. 1 p, 4to. To an unnamed lady. Sending a copy of his mazurkas. Repaired. (89) DM1,600
— [c.1880]. 1 p, 8vo. To Herr Doerffel. Assigning an opus number [to his Stabat Mater] & inquiring about the publication of his Ciganske Melodie. (91) £1,100
— 11 Aug 1885. (91) £900
— [Dec 1885]. 4 pp, 8vo. To Ferdinand Praeger. Describing his progress on the oratorio Saint Ludmila. (90) £1,800
— 12 Nov 1886. 4 pp, 8vo. To August Manns. Recommending works by several Czech composers. (91) DM3,400
— 2 Apr 1889. 3 pp, 8vo. To an unnamed conductor. Thanking for a successful performance of his Stabat Mater at Dordrecht. In German. (90) £1,700
— 18 Nov 1890. 1 p, 4to. To Heinrich Schwarz. Expressing thanks for playing one of his works in Munich. (88) DM1,600
— 27 June 1902. 1 p, 8vo. To Karel Kovarovic. About recommending a symphony by Drahlovsky to the Prague National Theater. (90) £2,000
AL, [Jan 1895]. 3 pp, 8vo. To Mr. Thurber. Draft, stating that he will return home unless the money owing

to him is paid immediately. (90) £1,700

Autograph postcard, sgd, 31 Mar 1882. To Alfred Doerffel at the Simrock publishing firm. Inquiring about the fees for a performance of his symphony at Prague. (88) DM1,200

— 27 Aug 1884. (91) £1,000

AN, 31 Dec 1895. (89) DM750

Autograph quotation, 16 bars from "Scherzo-Capriccio pro Orchestr", scored for violins, viola & cello, 24 Apr 1883. 1 p, 112mm by 201mm. Sgd. (88) £4,200

— Anr, 4 bars from the concert overture In Nature's Realm, sgd & dated 2 Oct 1894. 1 p, 7cm by 11.5cm, on verso of ptd visiting card. (90) £2,600

— Anr, theme from his V Prirode, Op. 91; 4 bars, sgd & dated 2 Oct 1894. 1 p, 7cm by 12cm, on verso of ptd visiting card. (90) DM4,800

— Anr, 7 bars from his Piano Quintet in A major, Op. 81, sgd & dated 25 Mar 1896. 1 p, 8vo (card). (90) £2,000

Photograph, sgd & inscr, 23 Dec 1897. Cabinet size. Inscr with 3 bars from his oratorio Ludmila, on verso. (90) DM3,600

— Anr, 1897. 16cm by 11cm. Inscr on verso with autograph musical quotation, Stabat Mater dolorosa. (88) £1,200

Dvorak, Antonin, 1841-1904 —& Others

Concert program, The Spectre's Bride; Birmingham Musical Festival, 27 Aug 1885. (91) £500

Dylan, Bob

Autograph Ms, song, Absolutely Sweet Marie, [n.d.]. 5 verses; working Ms. Framed with related material, 13.5 by 26.5 inches. (88) $7,000

— Autograph Ms, song, I Want You, 1966. 3 verses, with changes from released version. Framed with related material. 15.5 by 17.75 inches. (88) $8,000

Photograph, sgd & inscr, [n.d.]. (89) $100

Signature, [n.d.]. (89) $150

E

Eagels, Jeanne, 1890-1929

Photograph, sgd, [n.d.]. 13 by 10 inches. In black evening gown. Also sgd Strauss Peyton by photographer. (89) $1,100

Earhart, Amelia, 1898-1937

ALs, 20 Aug 1934. (89) $550

Ns, 5 Feb 1935. (91) $500

Photograph, sgd, 1937. (89) $900

— Anr, [n.d.]. (91) $450

— Anr, [n.d.]. Size not stated. Full length. (91) $1,800

— Anr, [n.d.]. (89) $475

Signature, 4 Feb 1933. (88) $210

— Anr, 24 Jan 1934. (88) $175

— Anr, on fold-out 8vo pamphlet by the Emergency Peace Campaign, c.1936. (88) $160

— Anr, 27 May [19]37. (90) $450

Earhart, Amelia, 1898-1937 —& Wilkins, Hubert, Sir, 1888-1958

[Their signatures on an airmail flight cover, 21 Apr 1928, also sgd by anr pilot, sold at sg on 25 Oct 1988, lot 16, for $550.]

Early, Jubal Anderson, 1816-94

A Ls s (2), 5 Apr 1876 & 14 May 1877. 6 pp, 8vo. To Col. Charles Marshall. About Lee's papers, Gen. Longstreet, Gettysburg & Chancellorsville. (88) $1,900

ALs, 23 Apr 1874. (88) $700

— 19 Mar 1883. 8 pp, 8vo. To Charles Marshall. Proving that Robert E. Lee's letters pbd in the NY Times are a forgery. (89) $1,200

— 19 Mar 1883. (88) $1,000

East India Company

[A group of 23 documents, mostly addressed to William Cornwallis, Commander-in-Chief in the East Indies, 1789 to 1804, relating to naval & shipping matters, sold at S on 20 July 1989, lot 332, for £650 to Maggs.]

Ms, letterbook of correspondence, 1752 to 1778, between officials of the East India Company & the Rajah of Tanjore; [c.1778]. (89) £750

— Ms, London. (88) £300

— BEGBIE, PATRICK. - Autograph sketch-

EAST INDIA COMPANY

book, containing pencil sketches of African & East Indian coastal profiles, etc., executed as purser on the ship Earl of Hertford; 1773 to 1779. 50 pp, c.11 by 4.5 inches, in def calf bdg. With related material. (89) £650

East India Trade
Ms, Invoyce of Goods Ship'd on Board the Lord North on Acct. (88) £650

Eastlake, Sir Charles Lock, 1793-1865
ALs, 25 Oct 1827. (89) £400

Eastman, Max, 1883-1969
Autograph transcript, poem, To Lenin; [n.d.]. (90) DM260

Eastwood, Clint
Ds, 5 Oct 1954. (91) $425

Eaton, John Henry, 1790-1856
Franking signature, [1831]. (90) $110

Ebbets, Charles H.
Ls, 16 Sept 1920. (90) $450

Eberhard III, Herzog von Wuerttemberg, 1614-74
Collection of Ls & 3 Ds s, 1634 to 1650. 4 pp, folio. To Bartholomaeus Marchthaler, ordering an investigation. Pay orders. With related material. (89) DM1,050

Eberhard IV Ludwig, Herzog von Wuerttemberg, 1676-1733
Ls, 2 Apr 1714. (91) DM520
— 12 Feb 1733. 4 pp, folio. To Herzog Karl Rudolf von Wuerttemberg-Neuenstadt. Regarding the sale of a forest for the use of a glass factory. With related material. (89) DM1,500

Eberl, Anton, 1765-1807
Autograph music, 1st movement of a concerto for violin, piano & orchestra in A major, fragment; [n.d.]. 2 pp, 23cm by 32cm. 21 bars in full score. Probably unrecorded. (90) DM2,600

Ebermayer, Erich, 1900-1970
Collection of 51 A Ls s, 13 Ls s & 13 autograph postcards, sgd, 23 Feb 1926 to 18 Jan 1934 & [n.d.]. (89) DM650

AMERICAN BOOK PRICES CURRENT

Ebert, Friedrich, 1871-1925
Signature, [18 Sept 1919]. (91) DM420

Ebner-Eschenbach, Marie von, 1830-1916
ALs, 24 Jan 1880. (90) DM300
— 22 June 1881. (89) DM440
Ls, 14 Oct 1905. (90) DM200

Eccles, Sir John Carew
Autograph Ms, scientific paper, Pain; 1980. 4 pp, folio. Sgd at head. (90) DM1,300

Echols, John, 1823-96
Ls, 22 Oct 1864. (88) $85
ADs, 27 Nov 1864. (89) $110

Eckardt, Felix von, 1866-1936
[A collection of 19 letters & cards addressed to him, with related material, sold at star on 1 Dec 1988, lot 1108, for DM650.]

Eckener, Hugo, 1868-1954
ANs, [n.d.]. (91) $130
Signature, 1 July 1931. (88) $110
— HERRIN, M. H. - Orig drawing, pencil bust port of Eckener, 27 Oct 1934. 9 by 12 inches. Sgd by both. (91) $180

Eckermann, Johann Peter, 1792-1854
ALs, 7 June 1843. (89) DM900
— 12 Apr 1846. 4 pp, 8vo. To Ulrike von Pogwisch. Thanking for Wolfgang von Goethe's play Erlinde. Albrecht collection. (91) SF1,500
— 30 Sept 1852. (88) DM650

Ede, Janina
Original drawings, (61), to illus Modwena Sedgewick's Matilda's Own Special Plate, 1969, & Bohumil Riha's Johnny's Journey, 1970. Archives of J. M. Dent & Son. (88) £150

Edgeworth, Maria, 1767-1849
Collection of 4 A Ls s & 2 A Ls, 17 Jan 1813 to 20 Dec 1816. (90) £260

Edison, Charles, 1890-1969
Collection of 7 A Ls s & A Ns s, [1920s & 1930s]. (90) $350
ALs, 18 Oct 1930. (90) $750
See also: Edison, Thomas A. & Edison

Edison, Thomas A., 1847-1931
[2 checks, accomplished & sgd, 8 Apr & 28 July 1876, for $15 & $10 payable to bearer, sold at sg on 9 Mar 1989, lot 61, for $600.]
[2 checks, accomplished & sgd, 26 Aug & 2 Sept 1876, 71mm by 200mm, sold at sg on 25 Oct 1988, lot 58, for $600.]
[A group of c.14 letters, photographs, etc., relating to Edison & his sons Thomas A. Jr. & William, 1909 to 1917, 5 with A Ns s by Edison, Sr. at head, with related material, sold at R on 4 Mar 1989, lot 341, for $2,000.]
[A group of 5 typed "Minutes of a Special Meeting of the Board of Directors of Thomas A. Edison, Incorporated", each sgd TAE & sgd or initialled by others, 1913 & 1914, sold at sg on 9 Mar 1989, lot 52, for $700.]
[Madeleine Sloane, nee Edison. - Her guest book, 1914 to 1950, 8vo, in def cloth bdg, containing signatures of her father Thomas A. Edison, Henry Ford, & others, with related material, sold at sg on 9 Mar 1989, lot 62, for $900.]
[A varied group of 13 sgd & unsgd items framed together, relating to Edison's association with Victor Young, sold at P on 25 Apr 1989, lot 50, for $1,500.]
[A group of 7 autograph items, 5 sgd, various dates, sold at sg on 9 Mar 1989, lot 60, for $2,600.]
[A family album with 83 photographs, mostly of Thomas Edison, with related material, sold at sg on 21 Sept 1989, lot 104, for $1,000.]
Autograph Ms, answers to 8 typewritten questions regarding politics, his rubber experiments, etc.; [16 Jan 1929]. (90) $170
— Autograph Ms, autobiographical notebook written for his biographers, 1908. 76 pp, 220mm by 150mm. With related ANs by Charles Edison. (89) $32,000
— Autograph Ms, list of chemical ingredients, from a laboratory book; [n.d.]. (91) $325
— Autograph Ms, notebook concerning synthetic rubber experiments, 1929. 158 pp, 105mm by 170mm, in leatherette bdg. (89) $15,000
Autograph sketchbook, Laboratory Notebook no 39, containing sketches of railroad cars, the phonograph, a telephonoscope, etc.; [1878]. 5 pp & blanks, 226mm by 300mm. With related material loosely inserted. (89) $5,000
Typescript, minutes of a meeting of the Board of Directors of the Edison Storage Battery Co., 7 June 1921. (90) $425
— Typescript, minutes of a meeting of the Board of Directors of the Edison Storage Battery Co., 10 Jan 1922. (90) $450
A Ls s (2), 1895. 7 pp, 4to. To [Mina Edison]. About labor difficulties at his brick manufacturing plant & other matters. Sgd TAE. Dampstained. (89) $2,000
ALs, 30 Apr 1878. 1 p, 4to. To Charles A. Cheever. About business dealings with the Western Electric Mfg. Co. & referring to his phonograph. With ANs by Cheever at bottom. Middendorf collection. (89) $3,800
— 30 Apr 1878. 1 p, 4to. To Charles A. Cheever. On the phonograph. (91) $3,000
— 10 Sept 1889. 1 p, folio. To M. Pirard. Expressing thanks & sending his autograph for Miss Frecinet. (90) DM3,000
— 8 Mar [c.1895]. 1 p, 4to. To [Mina Edison]. Reporting success with his mill. Sgd TAE. (89) $1,100
— [c.1895]. (90) $1,000
— [c.1895]. 4 pp, 8vo. To his wife. About X-rays, the free silver issue, & other matters. Sgd TAE. (90) $1,200
— 1 Dec 1898. 5 pp, 4to. To his wife. Expressing sorrow at his sister-in-law's death. In pencil. (91) $3,200
— 1898. (89) $550
— 5 Apr 1910. 3 pp, 8vo. To R. H. Beach. Discussing improvements for the electric-powered car. With related material. (91) $2,800
— 27 Jan 1914. (91) $800
— 7 Sept 1920. (89) $600
— [1923]. (89) $1,000
— [n.d.]. (91) $1,000
— [n.d.]. 4 pp, 8vo. To his wife. About difficulties with the brick manufacturing business, the silver issue, etc. Sgd

EDISON

- TAE. (91) $1,100
- — [n.d.]. (91) $850
- — [n.d.]. (89) $650
- — [n.d.]. (89) $550
- — [n.d.]. 4 pp, 8vo. To [Mina Edison]. About his work with phonograph records & an offer to buy batteries. Sgd TAE. In pencil. (89) $1,800
- — [n.d.]. 4 pp, 8vo. To his wife. Relating the success of the phonograph business. Sgd TAE. In pencil. (90) $1,200
- — [n.d.]. 4 pp, 4to. To his wife. Reporting about his day. Sgd TAE. (89) $1,100
- — [n.d.]. (89) $425
- — [n.d.]. 4 pp, 4to. To his wife. About cement manufacturing, & assuring her of his fidelity. In pencil. (91) $1,400
- — [n.d.]. 2 pp, 4to. To his wife. Asking her to visit him occasionally. In pencil. (91) $1,400
- — [n.d.]. 3 pp, 8vo. To his wife. Inquiring about their son's health. (91) $1,300
- AL, May 1917. (88) $450
- Ls, 22 May 1883. 1 p, 4to. Recipient unnamed. Fragment, reporting about plans to lighten small towns. (88) DM1,100
- — 23 May 1884. (90) $950
- — 16 Oct 1884. (89) DM650
- — 15 July 1903. 1 p, 4to. To Charles L. Edgar. Making suggestions about a charging station for electrical vehicles. (90) DM1,400
- — 1 July 1911. (91) $550
- — 31 Oct 1911. 1 p, 4to. To Harry V. Herrmann. Regarding recipient's response to his search for business partners. With 2 related secretarial letters & carbon copy of Herrmann's reply, Dec 1911. (89) $1,300
- — 14 June 1913. 1 p, 4to. To Jos. Platky. Advising him to keep his bonds. On ptd stationery. Doheny collection. (88) $1,500
- — 13 Nov 1914. 1 p, 4to. To Herman Bernstein. Stressing the influence of Jews on business & industries. (91) $7,500
- — 14 Sept 1915. (88) $650
- — 3 Aug 1918. (91) $450
- — 14 Feb 1922. (91) $850
- — 27 Feb 1922. (88) $750
- — 9 Jan 1929. (88) $150

AMERICAN BOOK PRICES CURRENT

- — 19 May 1931. (89) $400
- ANs, Oct 1906. (89) $900
- — 30 Oct 1916. (90) $550
- — 27 Aug 1924. (91) $700
- — [n.d.]. (90) $400
- AN, [Oct 1910]. (91) $190
- Series of Ds s, 3 Ds s, 3 Dec 1912 to 5 June 1918. (89) $350
- — Series of Ds s, 3 Ds s, 6 Jan 1914 to 5 Aug 1915. (89) $350
- Ds, lithographic plan of electrical machinery for the incandescent electrical light, to accompany his patent application for Bolivia, 7 June 1881. 1 p, 406mm by 558mm. Also sgd by 2 others. (91) $6,500
- — lithographic plan of electrical circuitry for the incandescent electrical light, to accompany his patent application for Bolivia, 7 June 1881. 1 p, 415mm by 568mm. Also sgd by 2 others. (91) $4,200
- — lithographic plan of electrical circuitry for the incandescent electrical light, to accompany his patent application for Bolivia, 7 June 1881. 1 p, 559mm by 405mm. Also sgd by 2 others. (91) $4,500
- — 7 June 1881. 44 pp, size not stated. Ptd patent application for the electric lamp, for submission to the Bolivian authorities. In Spanish. (90) $3,200
- — lithographic plan of the incandescent electrical light bulb, to accompany his patent application for Bolivia, 7 June 1881. 1 p, 402mm by 558mm. (90) $17,000
- — lithographic plan of electrical machinery for the incandescent electrical light, to accompany his patent application for Bolivia, 7 June 1881. 1 p, 408mm by 582mm. (90) $6,500
- — [1881]. 1 p, folo. Lithographic plan of electrical circuitry for the incandescent electric light. Also sgd by Charles H. Smith & George T. Pinckney. (91) $7,000
- — 8 Sept 1892. (91) $950
- — 13 June 1911. (89) $425
- — 19 Aug 1921. (91) $375
- — [n.d.]. 1 p, folio. Declaration that he is "in possession of an invention for Improvements in Phonogram Blanks". Barrett collection. (89) $1,500

Autograph quotation, sgd, 24 Feb 1906. 1 p, 8vo. "Everything comes to him that hustles while he waits." Byer collection. (90) $1,600

Autograph telegram, 4 Oct [n.y.]. (88) $375

Check, sgd, 17 Sept 1928. (91) $600

— Anr, 22 Nov 1928. (88) $140

Cut signature, [n.d.]. (90) $130

Group photograph, with 13 associates, preparing to watch the eclipse at Rawlins, Wyoming; 1878. 8vo. 8 participants identified in Edison's hand. (89) $2,600

— Anr, with his wife, Henry Ford, Luther Burbank & others in California, 1915. (89) $450

Photograph, sgd, [n.d.]. (91) $450

Photograph, sgd & inscr, [n.d.]. 322mm by 244m. With his wife. Inscr by Edison to their daughter Madeleine; sgd Father and Mother. (89) $2,400

— Anr, [n.d.]. 6.5 by 8.5 inches (image). Inscr to Edwin E. Witherby on mat. (91) $1,100

— Anr, [n.d.]. (88) $425

Photograph, [n.d.]. (89) $130

Signature, [c.1885?]. (88) $170

— Anr, [5 June 1929]. (91) $750

— Anr, [5 June 1929]. (89) $260

— Anr, [n.d.]. (91) $350

— Anr, [n.d.]. (91) $325

— Anr, [n.d.]. (88) $225

— EDISON, MADELEINE. - 3 autograph Mss, [c.1901 to 1906]. Various sizes. Diary of vacations taken by the Edison family. (90) $400

Edison, Thomas A., 1847-1931 —& Others
[A copy of Baby's Birthday Book, [c.1890s], 4to, owned by Madeleine Edison & sgd by Thomas A. Edison, a number of family members, & others, sold at sg on 14 Mar 1991, lot 75, for $350.]

Edison, Thomas A., 1847-1931. See: Cody, William F. ("Buffalo Bill") & Edison

Edison, Thomas A., 1847-1931 —& Edison, Charles, 1890-1969
Ds, 3 Mar 1916. (89) $500

Edmunds, Kay
Original drawings, (21), to illus W. Archives of J. M. Dent & Son. (88) £520

Edward Augustus, Duke of Kent, 1767-1820
Collection of ALs & 8 Ls s (1 fragment), 17 Mar 1792 to 15 Nov 1806. (91) DM550

Edward I, King of England, 1239-1307
[A collection of 5 vellum documents concerning his campaign against Scotland, 1306, & related wooden tally stick, sold at S on 1 Dec, lot 20, for £5,500.]

Edward IV, King of England, 1442-83
Document, 21 Dec 1461. 1 p, vellum, 125mm by 325mm. Letters Patent confirming appointment of Thomas Witham as Chancellor of the Exchequer. Including seal. (91) £2,000

— 26 Mar 1465. Phillipps Ms 32089. (89) £400

— 20 Nov 1468. (91) £250

Edward VI, King of England, 1537-53
Ds, 5 Apr 1547. 1 p, vellum, 12 by 22.5 inches. Letters Patent concerning the Royal Mint at Canterbury. Also sgd by the members of his Privy Council. Including seal. (89) £10,500

— 18 Dec [n.y.]. (91) £450

Edward VII, King of England, 1841-1910
[A collection of 18 greeting cards & other items inscr by Edward VII for Mrs. Alice Keppel, 1902 to 1910, sold at S on 18 July 1991, lot 380, for £1,600 to Browning.]

Collection of ALs & ANs, [n.d.] & [12 Oct 1909]. (89) £300

Series of 3 A Ls s, 21 Oct 1861 to 5 Dec 1862. (89) £240

— Series of 3 A Ls s, 2 Sept 1884 to [4 Mar 1909]. (88) £300

ALs, 16 June 1864. (90) £60

— 10 Jan 1882. (91) $425

— 8 Apr 1884. (88) $150

— 6 Aug 1885. Crohn Collection. (88) $450

— 8 Feb 1892. (89) DM320

— 13 Jan 1900. (90) £130

— 21 June 1905. (91) £500

— [n.d.] "Monday". (90) £500

EDWARD VII

— [n.d.], "Wednesday". (90) $160
— [n.d.]. (90) £220
Ls, 14 May 1878. Byer collection. (90) $120
Collection of ANs, Ds, & signature, 20 June [n.y.], [n.d.]., & 6 Dec 1903. (88) $180
Ds, 19 Mar 1901. (91) $170
— 23 Apr 1903. Byer collection. (90) $375

Edward VII, King of England, 1841-1910 —&
Keppel, Henry, Sir, 1809-1904
Group photograph, 1894. (91) £90

Edward VIII, King of England, 1894-1972.
See: Windsor, Edward
See also: Windsor, Edward & Windsor

Egloffstein, Henriette von, 1773-1864. See: Beaulieu-Marconnay, Henriette von

Egmont, Lamoraal, Count of, 1522-68
ALs, 25 July [1561]. 1 p, folio. To William of Orange. About deliberations to write to the King [Philip II of Spain] about their grievances. (90) DM6,000

Egyptian Manuscripts
Ms, Book of the Dead, chapters 130, 134 & 136; [Egypt, c.1080-746 B.C.]. Scroll, 215mm by 2,205mm; papyrus. Funerary payrus of Ankhef-en-Khonsu of Karnak, written in black & red ink in hieroglyphic & hieratic script. Richly illus in colors. Mtd on linen; framed. The Garden Ltd. collection. (90) $170,000

Ehrenburg, Ilya, 1891-1967
ALs, 19 Nov [1925]. (90) DM360
Ls, 5 Feb 1934. (91) DM240

Ehrenstein, Albert, 1886-1950
Autograph Ms, poem, Gottes Tod; [1917?]. 1 p, 4to. 16 lines, sgd. (91) DM1,300

Ehrlich, Paul, 1854-1915
Collection of 8 A Ls s & 16 Ls s, 11 Dec 1903 to 18 Apr 1913 & [n.d.]. 29 pp, 4to & 8vo. To Martin Freund. Scientific correspondence. File holes. (88) DM3,800
ALs, 29 Jan 1899. (91) DM460
— 6 Jan 1903. (90) DM650
— 5 Oct [n.y.]. 2 pp, 4to. Recipient unnamed. Discussing the toxicity of Salvarsan. Sgd PE. (89) DM1,200
— [n.d.]. 2 pp, 4to. To Moritz Oppenheim. Recommending Max Moszkowski's expedition to New Guinea. (89) DM1,400

Ls, 9 June 1904. (91) DM750

Eich, Guenter, 1907-72
Autograph transcript, poem, Aus Ryoanji; [c.1965]. (88) DM420
— Autograph transcript, poem, Weitgereist; [n.d.]. (89) DM740

Eichendorff, Joseph von, 1788-1857
Autograph Ms, 5 poems, [c.1810]. 2 pp, 4to. Drafts; 1 unpbd. (90) DM17,000
Autograph transcript, poem beginning "Das ist das Fluegelpferd"; sgd, inscr & dated 8 Apr 1853. 1 p, 4to. (89) DM7,000
ALs, 25 Oct 1835. 1 p, 4to. To F. A. Brockhaus. Promising a contribution for the next vol of Urania. (91) DM4,500
Autograph quotation, 4 lines beginning "Viele Boten gehn und gingen", sgd & dated 26 Aug 1856. 1 p, 8vo. (90) DM5,000
— Anr, 4 lines beginning "Viele Boten gehn und gingen", Apr 1857. 1 p, 8vo. Sgd. (88) DM6,000

Eichstaedt, Heinrich Karl Abraham, 1772-1848
ALs, 20 July 1842. Albrecht collection. (91) SF220
See also: Goethe, Johann Wolfgang von

Eiffel, Alexandre Gustave, 1832-1923
ALs, 25 Dec 1909. Byer collection. (90) $300

Eigen, Manfred
Autograph Ms, scientific paper, beginning "Is it possible to reconstruct precellular history..."; sgd & dated 17 Feb 1981. (88) DM340
— Autograph Ms, scientific paper, Das Gestaltkonzept, fragment; sgd later & dated Aug 1981. (90) DM440

Einem, Gottfried von
ALs, 30 Sept 1950. (91) DM800

Einstein, Albert, 1879-1955
[2 studio port photographs in sepia, sgd & dated 1931, 10 by 8 inches, sold at CNY on 1 Feb 1988, lot 552, for $4,500 to 19th Century Shop.]
[2 autograph mailing labels, in English, [n.d.], 3.5 by 7 inches & 3.5 by 4 inches, stating name & address of addressee, & return address with request not to bend, sold at ha on 8 Apr 1988, lot 16, for $200.]

Autograph Ms, abstracts & summaries of unidentified papers on the theory of distant parallelism, [1930s]. 4 pp, 4to & 8vo. In German. (89) $8,000
— Autograph Ms, calculations on the topic of unified field theory, [c.1932]. 2 pp, 4to. Working draft. In brown pen & pencil. (89) $5,500
— Autograph Ms, deliberations about his contract with Princeton, 7 Dec 1933. 1 p, 4to. Sgd. (88) DM5,000
— Autograph Ms, discussing relativity & the synchronising of clocks in different systems, [1927]. 1 p, c.20cm by 20cm, cut from larger leaf. Sgd E. With related material. (90) £1,400
— Autograph Ms, fragment of scientific paper, Die Feldgleichungen in erster Naeherung, [early 1930s]. 5 pp, 4to. Final section of unpbd article. (89) $20,000
— Autograph Ms, fragment of scietific paper referring to the 5-dimensional unified field theory, [probably for an article pbd 1929]. 1 p, 4to. Sgd. (89) $2,250
— Autograph Ms, fragments of scientific paper, Nachtrag zu der Abhandlung 'Die Kompatibilitaet der Feldgleichungen in der einheitlichen Feldtheorie', sgd; [mid-1930]. 8 pp, 4to. Presumably never completed. (89) $32,500
— Autograph Ms, on the theory of relativity, [1912?]. 72 leaves, written on rectos only. In brown & black ink; 17 lines in pencil. With numerous autograph revisions. Probably written for Marx's Handbuch der Radiologie, but never pbd. Earliest surviving (& longest) Einstein Ms on the subject. In new folding case. (88) $1,050,000
— Autograph Ms, poem concerning the creation of womankind, [c.1929-32]. (89) $800
— Autograph Ms, poem describing a stormy & rainy day, 11 Oct 1929. 1 p, 4to. 5 four-line stanzas, sgd. In German. (89) $3,500
— Autograph Ms, poem, expressing thanks for a gift of tobacco; 8 lines. Sgd & dated 7 Nov 1930. 1 p, 4to. With calculations on the unified theory on verso. Crudely repaired. (89) $2,200
— Autograph Ms, poem lauding Grete Lebach's baking skills, 27 July 1932. 1 p, 4to. 5 four-line stanzas, sgd. In German. Also sgd by Elsa Einstein & Rudolf & Ilse Kayser. (89) $4,250
— Autograph Ms, poem, thanking Frau Michanowsky for a book, [n.d.]. (89) $800
— Autograph Ms, poem, thanking Herr & Frau Biber for their hospitality, sgd & dated 9 Jan 1930. 1 p, 8vo. 16 lines. (89) $1,600
— Autograph Ms, scientific paper, Elementary Derivation of the Equivalence of Mass and Energy, [pbd 1935]. 2 pp, 4to. Fragment of draft, numbered (4) [cancelled] & (6). In German. (90) $12,000
— Autograph Ms, scientific paper, Einheitliche Feld-Theorie, [May 1929]. 19 pp, 4to & 8vo. Incomplete; sgd. Unpbd. (89) $75,000
— Autograph Ms, scientific paper, Zur einheitlichen Feldtheorie, [Feb 1929]. 19 pp, 4to & 8vo. Working draft, sgd. Unpbd. (89) $37,500
— Autograph Ms, scientific paper, Eine Ergaenzung des Systems der Feldgleichungen der einheitlichen Feldtheorie, sgd; [early 1930]. 1 pp, 4to. Unrelated autograph calculations & drawings on verso. (89) $8,000
— Autograph Ms, scientific paper, Einheitliche Theorie von Gravitation und Elektrizitaet, final section; [1931]. 7 pp, 4to. Some autograph corrections, some revisions in Walther Mayer's hand, & unidentified editorial markings. (89) $32,500
— Autograph Ms, series of algebraic equations demonstrating a theory of

energy, [1925]. (89) £950
— Autograph Ms, series of variable equations, small diagram & note regarding speed of light & the principle of relativity, [1925]. 1 p, folio. On headed paper of Bruno John Wassermann. Mtd. (89) £2,300
— Autograph Ms, speech at the California Institute of Technology, sgd; 25 Jan 1932. 6 pp, 4to. With numerous autograph revisions. In German. With English trans. Doheny collection. (88) $16,000
— Autograph Ms, various drafts dealing with a unified field theory based on a Hermitean metric tensor field in a space of 4 complex, or equivalently 8 real, dimensions, [c.1945]. 21 pp, 4to. In German. (89) $80,000

Original drawings, 2 pen-&-ink diagrams of electrical circuits & switching systems, [n.d.]. Paul Habicht papers. (88) £700

Typescript, explanation of a "paradox" on the basis of the theory of relativity, 2 pp, 4to. With autograph additions. In German. With covering letter, 6 Oct 1950, 1 p, 4to, to Robert Heppe, in English; & letter from Heppe to Einstein. (88) DM8,500
— Typescript, preface in German for the Czech trans of Ueber die spezielle und die allgemeine Relativitaetstheorie, [25 Sept 1922]. 1 p, folio. Sgd. (90) £2,800

Collection of ALs & Ls, 27 Mar & 8 June 1931. 2 pp, folio. To Harry Waldo Warner. Thanking for a copy of the work Einstein had played in Los Angeles. Declining to allow his name to be used for publicity purposes. (88) £1,050
— Collection of 12 A Ls s & 5 Ls s, 28 Sept 1937 to 15 June 1952. 20 pp, 4to & 8vo. To Otto Juliusburger & his daughter Erika (1). Important correspondence dealing with scholarly & political matters. (91) DM110,000
— Collection of ALs & Ls, 8 Nov 1940. 2 pp, 4to. To his cousin Lina Kocherthaler, regarding her son's plans to emigrate to the USA. To the US Consul at Montevideo, supporting Oscar Kocherthaler's application. (88) DM3,800
— Collection of 2 A Ls s & 4 Ls s, 26 June 1946 to 20 Mar 1953. 6 pp, 4to. To Hilde Pyteck (5) & her husband. Mostly about German artists in emigration. In German. With related material. (88) DM9,600
— Collection of ALs & group photograph, 16 Mar 1955 & [1955]. 1 p, 4to & 203mm by 252mm. To Dr. Frank G. Back. Discussing eclipses of the sun & atmospheric light. In German. Seated at a table, with Dr. Back & others. (90) $3,800

ALs, [Oct 1916]. 2 pp, 4to. Recipient unnamed. Urging him to acknowledge the paternity of a child. With draft of reply on integral leaf & related letter by Elsa Einstein. (91) £1,800
— [Oct 1916]. 2 pp, 4to. Recipient unnamed. Urging him to acknowledge the paternity of a child. With draft of reply on integral leaf & related letter by Elsa Einstein. (89) DM3,000
— [1921]. 1 p, 4to. To Carl Becker. Thanking for his decision in the case of G. F. Nicolai. (91) DM6,000
— 27 Mar 1922. 1 p, 4to. To Hermann Anschuetz-Kaempfe. Regarding a dispute about patent rights. (89) DM6,000
— 8 May 1922. 1 p, folio. To Paul Painleve. Sending 2 autograph sentiments as requested (included). (91) £2,400
— 18 June 1922. 1 p, 4to. To Hermann Anschuetz-Kaempfe. Making suggestions for the improvement of recipient's invention. (89) DM5,500
— 1 July 1922. 1 p, 4to. To Hermann Anschuetz-Kaempfe. About a visit to Kiel, a scientific problem, & the situation in Germany. (89) DM5,500
— 25 July 1922. 1 p, 4to. To Hermann Anschuetz-Kaempfe. Regarding the plan to provide him with a study in Kiel. (89) DM5,200
— 26 July 1923. 2 pp, 4to. To Hermann Anschuetz-Kaempfe. Asking him to intercede in a quarrel with his son. With related material. (89) DM3,800
— [Summer 1925]. 2 pp, 4to. To Hermann Anschuetz-Kaempfe. Mostly regarding improvements of the gyro-compass. (89) DM6,000
— 4 Aug 1925. 2 pp, 4to. To Hermann Anschuetz-Kaempfe. About his holi-

days in Kiel, his son, & a court case. With postscript in the hand of his son Albert. (89) DM3,600

— [n.d.]. 2 pp, 8vo, on rectos only. To Herr Muntz. Scientific letter including numerous mathematical equations. In German. Abrasion on 2d p affecting 1 word. (88) $2,700

— [n.d.]. 2 pp, 4to. To Mr. Jaifer. Discussing the origins of anthracite coal. In German. In green ink. (88) $3,500

— 6 June 1926. 1 p, 4to. To G. Y. Rainich. Discussing electron theories. (88) $7,000

— 12 Nov 1927. 1 p, 4to. To an unnamed lady. Regretting he is unable to accept an invitation to a concert. (89) DM2,400

— 9 Apr 1929. 1 p, 4to. To unnamed colleagues. Thanking for congratulations on his birthday. (90) DM7,500

— 6 May [19]29. 1 p, 8vo. To [Herman] Bernstein. Expressing thanks. (91) $2,200

— 17 Apr 1933. 1 p, folio. To Paul Painleve. Explaining why he is declining the offer of a chair at the College de France. (91) £1,700

— 1 Oct 1933. 1 p, 4to. To Dr. Jacob Klatzkin. Promising to help him find a pbr for his works. (91) DM3,800

— 5 July 1935. 2 pp, 8vo. To Paul Habicht. Reminiscing about their working together, describing his life in America, etc. Sgd A.E. In German. (88) £2,500

— 2 Sept 1935. 2 pp, 4to. To Paul Habicht. Discussing economics, communism, technological progress, etc. In German. In green ink. (88) £2,500

— 27 Jan 1947. (88) £1,000

— [1949?]. 2 pp, folio. To Leopold Infeld. Suggesting alternative ways of formulating an equation & admitting that Infeld's earlier suggestions for a joint work had not been correct. In German. (88) £2,200

— 11 Jan 1955. 1 p, 4to. To Hans Lindau. Responding to a scientific question. (90) DM5,000

— [n.d.]. (91) £1,000

Collection of AL & group photograph, [1950s]. 1 p, 4to & 200mm by 204mm. To Dr. Frank G. Back. Commenting on a scientific problem, with many equations. In German, on verso of typed scientific paper on optics [by Dr. Back?] in English. Seated at a table, with Dr. Back & anr man. (90) $2,000

Collection of Ls & postcard, sgd, 10 Feb 1920 & 21 Dec 1929. (88) DM1,000

— Collection of Ls & typescript, sgd, 2 Nov 1938 & [1938]. 2 pp, 4to. To Dr. A. S. W. Rosenbach, forwarding typescript. Preface for a charity auction to benefit European refugees, in German. With 2 related Ls s by Thomas Mann & auction cat, sgd by Einstein & Mann. John F. Fleming Estate. (89) $5,000

— Collection of Ls & photograph, sgd, 7 Jan 1943 & 1943. 1 p, 4to & 135mm by 100mm. To Barbara Lee Wilson. Encouraging her not to worry about her difficulties in mathematics. (89) $7,500

— Collection of Ls & group photograph, 2 Mar 1953 & [c.1955]. 2 pp, 4to & 120mm by 145. To Dr. Frank G. Back. Scientific letter discussing the perfection of lenses & the probability of flaws. In German. Seated on a porch with Dr. Back. (90) $5,800

Series of 3 Ls s, 16 May to 2 Aug 1944. 3 pp, folio. To Jechiel Hochermann of the National Labor Committee for Palestine. Expressing support, declining to give a radio address, & disapproving of dinners in his honor which he cannot attend. (89) £2,200

Ls s (2), 27 June & 8 Aug 1931. 4 pp, folio. To Meyer S. Frenkel. Discussing the conclusions of De Sitter & Walter Ritz, & defending his Special Theory of Relativity. Repaired. (89) £2,200

— Ls s (2), 30 Oct 1943 & 4 Jan 1944. 3 pp, 4to. To Emil Popper. Responding to queries relating to the problem of squaring the circle. With related material. (90) $9,000

— Ls s (2), 3 Dec 1947 & 28 Nov 1950. 2 pp, 4to. To Rudolf Ladenburg. Requesting advice in finding authors for a publication & in locating a lost paper. (89) DM2,600

— Ls s (2), 4 & 21 Feb 1949. 2 pp, 4to. To Dr. Alfred Werner. Declining to give an interview. Sending answers to questions (not included) & requesting to see the English trans before publica-

EINSTEIN

tion. In German. (88) DM1,800
— Ls s (2), 18 & 26 Aug 1949. 2 pp, 4to. To Jeanette van den Bergh von Dantzig. Regarding the publication of her Ms. Confessing his inability to understand her work. (88) DM3,600

Ls, 7 Dec 1921. 2 pp, folio. To Paul Painleve. Concerning an invitation to lecture in Paris, & responding to criticisms of the general theory of relativity. (91) £5,000
— 28 Aug 1922. 1 p, 4to. To [Dr. Pfister]. About an invitation to lecture in China. (91) DM2,400
— 24 Dec 1927. 1 p, 4to. To an Ed of the journal Der Montag-Morgen. Offering a remark for print hoping for a reduction of military spending. (90) DM1,600
— 24 Mar 1929. 1 p, 8vo (card). Recipient unnamed. Lithographed 18-line poem expressing thanks for congratulations on his birthday, with 2-line autograph addition. (90) $1,300
— 19 Oct 1931. (88) $850
— 30 Jan 1933. 1 p, 4to. To Hans Does. Saying he cannot help him & suggesting he write to Herr Frobenius at Frankfurt. (89) $1,900
— 1 Sept 1933. (89) £750
— 11 Jan 1934. 1 p, 4to. To Dr. Jacob Klatzkin. About letters of recommendation & the plight of refugees. (91) DM3,800
— 27 Apr [19]34. 1 p, 4to. To Herman Bernstein. Accepting "the friendly offer of Yeshiva College". (91) $1,400
— 17 June 1934. 1 p, 4to. To Herman Bernstein. Seeking employment for a Jewish journalist. (91) $2,000
— 2 Aug 1934. 1 p, 4to. To Dr. Erwin Beckhard. Responding to a proposal regarding newly arrived Jewish doctors. (91) $1,800
— 28 Dec 1935. 2 pp, folio. To Professor Lande. Discussing Lande's theories in the context of the general theory of relativity. In German. With an English trans. (89) £3,800
— 30 Mar 1936. 2 pp, 8vo. Recipient unknown (inked out). Soliciting support for "research in regard to the basic factors which determine the position of the Jew in the modern world." (91) $3,200

AMERICAN BOOK PRICES CURRENT

— 15 May 1936. 1 p, 4to. To Sigmund Schwartzenstein. Thanking for a publication. In German. Corner def. (89) $2,200
— 7 July 1936. (91) $750
— 21 Nov 1938. 1 p, 4to. To the German-American Aid Committee. Declining "in the present moment of direst need of the Jewish people" to aid the Spanish cause. (89) $3,000
— 2 Dec 1938. 1 p, 4to. To Dr. I. W. Held. Discussing Herr Ehrmann's attempts to leave Germany. Framed with related material. (90) $3,500
— 10 June 1939. 1 p, 4to. To A. E. Botthof. Expressing congratulations on her work done on behalf of Jewish refugees. (90) $3,800
— 10 June 1939. 1 p, size not stated. To Helen Greenbaum. Thanking for her work on behalf of Jewish refugees. On embossed letterhead. (88) $4,000
— 23 June 1939. 1 p, 4to. To Dr. Edward Barsky. Giving permission to add his name to the list of sponsors of the Medical Aid Committee of the Spanish Refugee Relief Campaign. With related material. (89) $1,200
— 11 July 1942. 1 p, 4to, at top left corner of a drawing sent to him. To Marvin H. Rubin. Responding to an inquiry about a geometry problem. With related material. (90) $4,000
— 7 Oct 1944. 1 p, 4to. To Mie Muenzer. Complimenting her on her artwork. In German. (88) $1,300
— 10 Jan 1946. 1 p, 4to. To Sammy Gronemann. Commenting on recipient's play. (91) DM1,500
— 29 Jan 1946. 1 p, 4to. To Robert P. Sharkey. About relinquishing his German citizenship, & the German problem after the war. (90) $4,000
— 28 Feb 1947. 1 p, 4to. Recipient unnamed. Requesting money for the task of teaching citizens " the simple facts of atomic energy and its implications for society." On Emergency Committee of Atomic Scientists letterhead. With related material. (90) DM2,000
— 14 June 1950. 1 p, 4to. To Paul Peltier. About the quantum theory, general relativity, & the state of modern physics. Silked. (91) $5,500

— 21 Aug 1951. 1 p, 4to. To Beatrice E. Bodenstein. Commenting on common sense. (91) $3,000
— 14 Apr 1952. (88) £580
— 30 Apr 1952. (88) £550
— 7 Sept 1953. 1 p, 8vo. To Ernst Johann Fischer. Giving permission to publish a letter; in German. Matted. With photograph, sgd, 12 Dec [19]36, with typed inscr to Sarah Brown. (88) $3,250
— 14 June 1954. (91) £1,000
— 1 Mar 1955. 1 p, 4to. To G. J. Martin of The National Drug Company. Arranging a meeting & commenting on Martin's Biological Antagonism (a copy present, sgd by Martin). (91) $1,500

Series of 3 autograph postcards, sgd, 22 July to 18 Sept 1921. To Hermann Anschuetz-Kaempfe. About a meeting & technical details of an invention. Including small sketch. (89) DM3,400

Autograph postcard, sgd, 12 Apr 1901. To Professor Paalzow. Applying for a position at Berlin. With related material. (89) DM7,500
— 20 Dec 1907. To Rudolf Ladenburg. Sending 3 copies of his work. (88) DM2,200
— 8 July 1925. To Professor A. Wiegand. Discussing the results of experiments conducted by Picard in Brussels. (90) £1,400

Ns, 8 Oct [19]21. (88) $400
— [n.d.]. (89) $400

Autograph sentiment, on the difference between the sexes, sgd & dated 1925. In 8vo brown mor album also containing signatures of Stravinsky, Thomas Beecham, Stefan Zweig, & others. (89) £1,100

Group photograph, in a boat with his wife & Gustav Bucky, 1934. 3 by 4.25 inches (image). Sgd & inscr to "Tomchen." (89) $1,100

Photograph, sgd, 1942. (90) $450
— Anr, [19]48. 175mm by 125mm. Seated in a chair. With related material. (90) £1,400
— Anr, [19]50. 5.5 by 4.5 inches. Seated by 2 microphones. Framed. (91) $1,100

Photograph, sgd & inscr, 1925. (90) £900
— Anr, 2 Feb 1933. 8 by 10 inches. Full length, standing at the seaside. Inscr to Mr. & Mrs. E. L. Doheny, 19 Feb [19]33, on mat. Doheny collection. (88) $3,500

Signature, [n.d.]. (88) £400
— Anr, 1931. Doheny collection. (88) $550
— Anr, on verso of a check for $50 payable to him, drawn on the First National Bank; 28 Mar 1950. Also sgd by Margot Einstein. (90) DM1,600
— BUETTNER, ERICH. - Engraving, sgd; Feb 1921. 30cm by 22cm. Proof copy of port of Einstein. Also sgd & inscr by Einstein, in pencil. Framed. (89) £8,200
— HERRIN, M. H. - Orig drawing, pencil bust port of Einstein, 20 Oct 1937. 9.5 by 11.5 inches. Sgd by both. (91) $3,000
— MAJOR, HENRY. - Orig drawing, pencil port of Einstein, sgd; [c.1930]. 305mm by 230mm. Also sgd by Einstein. Def; tipped to anr sheet. (90) $1,000
— PHILIPP, JOHN. - Engraving, port of Einstein, 1929. 29cm by 24cm (image). Sgd by both in facsimile & in pencil. (89) £3,000
— SEELIG, CARL. - ALs, 7 Ls s & 5 postcards, sgd, 30 Apr 1953 to 21 July 1960. 9 pp, 8vo, & cards. To Johann Jakob Laub. About his biography of Einstein. (91) DM4,000
— SWAMY. - Orig drawing, chalk sketch of Einstein, 1938. 235mm by 165mm. Sgd by both. (89) £2,800

Einstein, Albert, 1879-1955 —&
Anschuetz-Kaempfe, Hermann, 1872-1931
Ms, mathematical formulas (in Einstein's hand) & sketches (possibly by Anschuetz-Kaempfe) relating to the improvement of the gyro-compass, Aug 1921. 6 leaves, 4to. With photograph of both. (89) DM10,000

Einstein, Albert, 1879-1955 —&
Freud, Sigmund, 1856-1939
A Ls s (2), 28 July 1932 (Einstein) & 12 Sept 1932 (Freud). 4 leaves of graph paper & 14 folio leaves, respectively. Each leaf hinged on a window mat, each letter in a cloth folding case. About the nature of war & the possibility of preventing man from waging war [pbd in 1933 as Why War?]. At

EINSTEIN

end of each letter is an ANs of Leon Steinig, the League of Nations official who initiated the correspondence. (91) $150,000

Einstein, Albert, 1879-1955 —& Sommerfeld, Arnold, 1868-1951
[An autograph poem by Sommerfeld, sgd, & 2 additional lines in Einstein's hand, sgd, [n.d.], 1 p, 8vo, with related material, sold at HK on 11 Nov 1988, lot 3343, for DM2,000.]

Einstein, Alfred, 1880-1952
Series of 13 Ls s, 28 Feb 1951 to 22 Jan 1952. (88) DM900

Eisenhower, Dwight D., 1890-1969
[A typescript of his oath of office, 20 Jan 1957, 1 p, 8vo, sgd, matted with ptd photograph of Eisenhower being sworn in on the steps of the Capitol, 21 Jan 1957, sold at Dar on 13 June 1991, lot 136, for $650.]
[A philatelic envelope, postmarked the day of his funeral, 31 Mar 1969, sgd by his 12 honorary pallbearers, sold at Dar on 13 June 1991, lot 21, for $110.]
Transcript, final message as Supreme Commander of the Allied Expeditionary Forces to the Combined Chiefs of Staff, 13 July 1945. Sgd. (91) $12,000
Typescript, 1st Inaugural Address, [20 Jan 1953]. 9 pp, 4to, on rectos only. Sgd at head. Middendorf collection. (89) $1,600
Collection of ALs & Ds, 20 May & 21 Nov 1944. 4 pp, 4to. To Harry L. Hopkins, assuring him that his son "will be treated as a soldier, on a strictly official basis." Statement of recommendation for Robert Hopkins. (89) $8,500
ALs, 2 Mar [1943]. 3 pp, 4to. To his wife. About a carpet bought as a present for George C. & Mrs. Marshall. (90) $2,000
— 12 June [1943]. 3 pp, 8vo. To Vera McCarthy-Morrogh. Detailing Kay Summersby's severe depression over the death of her fiance. (91) $5,500
— 27 June [1943]. 2 pp, 8vo. To Vera McCarthy-Morrogh. Describing Kay Summersby's continuing grief over the death of her fiance. (91) $4,500
— [7 July 1944]. 1 p, 8vo. To Vera McCarthy-Morrogh. Thanking for her note & expecting his staff members to return the coming week. (91) $1,600
— 19 Sept [1944]. 2 pp, 4to. To his wife Mamie Doud Eisenhower. Family letter, & about the war. (88) $4,250
— 14 Feb [1946]. 1 p, 4to. To Kay Summersby. Thanking for her willingness to provide him with a copy of her diary kept as his aide. (91) $3,250
— [31 Oct 1952]. (90) $1,000
Collection of 2 Ls s & Letter, 18 Dec 1948 to 2 Jan 1952. (91) $1,000
— Collection of 7 Ls s & 2 Ds s, 1 Feb 1957 to 9 June 1966. 9 pp, various sizes. To Joe Lindholm. Regarding their mutual interest in cattle & horses, a visit, etc. Registration application & transfer report for a colt. With related material. (90) $4,250
Series of 3 Ls s, 18 Nov 1946 to 31 Oct 1963. (89) $275
— Series of 3 Ls s, 1 June to 30 Sept 1948. 3 pp, 4to. To Kay Summersby. About the publication of her war memoir. (91) $2,750
— Series of 3 Ls s, 1948. (89) $275
— Series of 3 Ls s, 12 Jan 1953 to 28 Apr 1958. McVitty collection. (90) $800
Ls s (2), 20 Oct 1953 & 19 Nov 1956. (90) $250
— Ls s (2), 13 Oct 1964 & 18 Oct 1965. (90) $320
Ls, 18 Feb 1943. 1 p. 4to. To Lt. Gen. Mark Clark. Thanking him for messages of congratulations on Eisenhower's promotion to four-star general. (90) $1,300
— 29 Mar 1944. 1 p, 8vo. To Kay Summersby. Presenting her with a fountain pen. (91) $1,800
— 9 Aug 1944. (90) $50
— 16 Mar 1945. (88) $140
— 9 Apr 1945. (88) DM600
— 25 Oct 1945. (88) $175
— 5 Nov 1945. (91) $250
— 8 Nov 1945. 2 pp, 4to. To Mrs. Lilian M. Stone. Explaining the modification of nonfraternization rules in Germany. (89) $4,250
— 30 Nov 1945. (90) $250
— 12 Feb 1946. Byer collection. (90) $275
— 17 Oct 1947. (90) $160

1987 - 1991 • AUTOGRAPHS & MANUSCRIPTS   EISENHOWER

— 7 Nov 1949. (90) $170
— 29 Oct 1951. (88) £300
— 19 June 1952. Alexander collection. (90) $160
— 16 Dec 1952. (90) $120
— 27 Jan 1953. (90) $375
— 16 Oct 1954. (90) $140
— 30 Oct 1954. (91) $250
— 15 Feb 1955. (91) $375
— 9 Mar 1955. (91) $350
— 25 Apr 1955. (90) $220
— 11 May 1955. (90) $300
— 21 Oct 1955. (90) $160
— 28 Mar 1956. (91) DM900
— 13 June 1956. (89) $210
— 8 Feb 1957. (91) $400
— 14 Oct 1957. (89) $250
— 1 Nov 1957. (91) $120
— 9 June 1958. (90) $175
— 13 Oct 1958. (88) DM400
— 18 Dec 1958. (89) $180
— 13 Aug 1959. (88) $350
— 31 Mar 1960. (88) $300
— 23 June 1960. (91) $350
— 5 Oct 1960. (91) $220
— 9 Nov 1960. (88) $200
— 22 Mar 1962. Byer collection. (90) $500
— 25 Sept 1963. (88) $170
— 11 Nov 1963. (89) $100
— 3 Feb 1964. (90) $300
— 4 Apr 1964. (90) $100
— 1 Sept 1964. (89) $120
— 3 Feb 1965. (89) £900
— 25 Oct 1965. (91) $250
— 14 Nov 1966. (91) $170
— 25 July 1967. (88) $400
— 16 Nov 1967. (90) $200

ANs, [15 or 16 Jan 1943]. 1 p, 4to. To Gen. George C. Marshall. Commenting on [Gen. Henry Maitland] Wilson. In pencil. Including 2 A Ns s by Marshall & ANs by Sir John Dill on same sheet. (91) $1,100

— [c.June 1944 - May 1945]. 1 p, 12mo. To [Kay Summersby]. Inviting her to "lunch, tea & dinner today". Sgd D. In pencil. (91) $11,000

Ds, 7 May 1945. 1 p, 4to. Copy No 37A of Special Cable 355, reading "The mission of this Allied Force was fulfilled at 0241 local time, May 7th, 1945." Sgd later & inscr to Kay Summersby. (91) $27,000

Autograph endorsement, 13 lines in the margin of a typed memorandum from Attorney Gen. Herbert Brownell, 10 Nov 1954; in pencil. Giving orders regarding Gen. Lawton's mission to South Vietnam. With related material. (88) $3,000

Autograph sentiment, [n.d.]. (88) $100

Check, accomplished & sgd, 4 Oct 1954. Drawn on Riggs Bank, Washington for $2.00 payable to M. F. Norling; using ptd check originally for Norling's account with a Denver bank. (89) $10,000

Cut signature, [n.d.]. (90) $95

Photograph, sgd, [5 Oct 1944]. (89) $300

— Anr, [c.1944]. (91) $300

Photograph, sgd & inscr, Apr 1943. (90) $450

— Anr, 14 June 1943. 226mm by 167mm. Inscr to Kay [Summersby]. (91) $3,750

— Anr, 1943. 179mm by 145mm. Inscr to [Kay Summersby] on mount. (91) $4,000

— Anr, [1944 or 1945]. 353mm by 280mm. Inscr to Kay Summersby. (91) $1,800

— Anr, [1945 or later]. 252mm by 199mm. Inscr to Kay Summersby. (91) $2,750

— Anr, [1953]. (91) $160

— Anr, [c.1960s]. (90) $130

— Anr, [n.d.]. (89) £130

Signature, in pencil, on 1st Day Cover commemorating Alaska's admission as state, 10 May 1959. (89) $110

— Anr, [n.d.]. (89) $270

White House card, sgd, [n.d.]. (90) $80

Eisenhower, Dwight D., 1890-1969 —& Others

Signature, in The 1915 Howitzer (Westpoint yearbook), on page with his port & biographical sketch; also sgd by Omar Bradley & James A. Van Fleet on their respective pages. 4to, in orig lea bdg, with bookplate of Jo Hunt Reaney. With related material. (90) $2,500

EISENHOWER

Eisenhower, Dwight D., 1890-1969 —& Clark, Mark W., 1896-1984
[Their signatures on a photograph of American troops marching up the Champs Elysees, 26 Aug 1945, 9.5 by 7 inches (image), framed, sold at Dar on 13 June 1991, lot 141, for $250.]

Eisenhower, Dwight D., 1890-1969 —& Eisenhower, Mamie Doud, 1896-1975
Group photograph, [n.d.]. (91) $80
— Anr, [n.d]. (91) $300

Eisenhower, Dwight D., 1890-1969 —& Nixon, Richard M.
[A card sgd by both, attached to an Inauguration ribbon & button, Jan 20-21, 1957, sold at rce on 28 July 1988, lot 590, for $300.]

Eisenhower, Mamie Doud, 1896-1975
Series of 14 Ls s, 1956 to 1974. (88) $220
Ls, 12 Feb 1953. (89) $50
— 20 July 1953. (90) $100
— 29 Mar 1956. (88) $55
A Ns s (2), [n.d.]. (90) $65
See also: Eisenhower, Dwight D. & Eisenhower

Eisenstecken, Joseph, 1779-1827
ALs, 23 May 1814. (88) DM750

Eisner, Kurt, 1867-1919
A Ls s (2), 23 Dec 1910 & [n.d.]. (90) DM850
Ls, 11 Feb 1915. 4 pp, folio. To Wolfgang Heine. Outlining his view of German politics during the war. (89) DM4,600

Elcock, H. K.
Original drawings, (11), to illus E. Archives of J. M. Dent & Son. (88) £300

Eleonora Gonzaga, Empress of Ferdinand II, 1598-1655
Ls, 28 Feb 1622. (90) DM200

Eleonore, Herzogin von Braunschweig-Lueneburg, 1639-1722
Ls, 14 May 1703. (90) DM530

Elgar, Sir Edward, 1857-1934
[A collection of 18 concert programs & handbills for concerts given by Elgar & members of his family, 1856 to 1921, sold at S on 21 Nov 1990, lot 96, for £950 to Macnutt.]

[3 proof scores of his Violin Concerto in B minor Op. 61, extensively annotated by Elgar, the Ed & engravers, incorporating revisions suggested by Fritz Kreisler, [Sept & Oct 1910], c.250 pp, folio, sold at S on 18 Nov 1988, lot 360, for £8,000 to Haas.]

Autograph music, Impromptu for piano, 7 bars; [Oct] 1932. (91) £950
— Autograph music, March in D major, Trio in G major & Coda, & Litany No 13; sgd & dated 5 Aug 1887. (88) £900
— Autograph music, opening 10 bars of the overture In the South, Op. 50; Jan 1904. 1 p, 32.5cm by 27.5cm (framed). Draft, notated in short score on 5 systems, 2 staves each. Sgd. (91) £1,800
— Autograph music, song, Inside the Bar, from The Fringes of the Fleet, in arrangement for solo bass, male chorus & piano, [1917]. (88) £750

Collection of 4 A Ls s, Ls & 2 postcards, 5 Feb 1903 to 14 May 1906. (89) £250
— Collection of 8 A Ls s & Ls, 1920 to 1933. (89) £650
— Collection of 15 A Ls s & Ls s, [c.1920] to 1933. 29 pp, various sizes. To Sir Edward German. Complimenting him on his music, offering to escort him to Buckingham Palace, etc. Partly initialled. With related material. (89) £1,200
— Collection of Als, 2 Ls s, & autograph postcard, sgd, 2 May 1927 to 1 May 1931. (88) £290
— Collection of 2 A Ls s & card, sgd, 25 Aug 1929 to 9 Dec 1933. (89) £150

Series of 8 A Ls s, 1893 to 1899 & 1931. (89) £850
— Series of 25 A Ls s, 1910 to 1933. 46 pp, various sizes. To W. H. Reed. About the composition of the Violin Concerto & a variety of professional & private matters. Including autograph musical quotation. 1 ALs incomplete. With related material. (90) £3,800
— Series of 3 A Ls s, 17 Feb 1914 & [n.d.]. (90) £420

ALs, 4 Feb 1901. (91) £400
— 20 Sept [19]02. (90) £525
— 20 May 1906. (88) £170
— 16 Dec 1907. (88) DM500
— 16 May 1909. (90) £260
— 26 Jan 1910. (88) £240

— 21 Mar 1912. (88) £150
— [n.d.], "Thursday". (91) £150
Autograph quotation, 2 1/2 bars from The Dream of Gerontius, scored for piano; sgd. (89) £480
Photograph, sgd & inscr, [26 July 1932]. (90) £500
Proof copy, 2d movement of his 2d Symphony, [1911]. (89) £360
— Anr, motet, Give unto the Lord, for four-part choir & organ, Op. (89) £400

Elgin, Thomas Bruce, 7th Earl, 1766-1841
ALs, 3 Nov 1789. (89) DM320
Series of 8 Ls s, 15 Jan 1800 to 30 Sept 1803. Wolf collection. (89) £600

Eliot, George (Mary Anne Evans Lewes), 1819-80
ALs, 6 Nov 1869. 3 pp, 8vo. To Mr. Browning. Thanking for slippers & referring to her health problems. Doheny collection. (89) $1,700
— 9 Aug 1873. (88) £420
— 17 May 1879. 1 p, 8vo. To Mr. Williams. Ordering a book to be sent to Charles Lewes. (90) DM1,150
ANs, [25 Feb 1875]. (91) £160
Ds, 2 June 1874. (91) $260

Eliot, John, 1604-90 —& Winthrop, John, 1588-1649
ADs, [before 8 Dec 1645]. 1 p, 4to. Will of Henry Dingham of Roxbury, in Eliot's hand & sgd by him as witness. With note of attestation at foot sgd by Winthrop. Repaired. Sang collection. (89) $4,250

Eliot, Thomas Stearns, 1888-1965
Typescript, revisions to The Waste Land, lines 257 - 321, [early 1950s]. 2 pp, 4to. With 2 holograph corrections; initialled. (91) $1,200
Collection of ALs, 17 Ls s & postcard, sgd, 1940 to 1964. Length not stated. To Mr. & Mrs. Montgomery Belgion. Mostly about social news. With related material. (89) £1,550
Collection of Ls & telegram, 30 May & 23 May 1945. (90) $190
Series of 3 Ls s, 31 Aug to 12 Sept 1922. 3 pp, 4to. To J. M. Robertson. Soliciting contributions for The Criterion. With related material. (89) £3,500

— Series of 3 Ls s, 1937-56. (88) $300
— Series of 10 Ls s, 1959 to 1963. (88) £1,000
Ls, 18 Oct 1932. (91) $175
— 1 May 1950. (89) $300
— 17 Nov 1954. (91) $160
— 24 Mar 1955. (90) DM350
— 1 Nov 1956. (91) $250
Ns, 26 Jan [19]45. (91) £340
Corrected galley proof, The Cultivation of Christmas Trees, 1954. (91) £750
Corrected page proofs, Four Quartets, 1st English Ed, sgd TSE; 1944. 8vo. Some minor corrections. (91) £2,400
— Anr, Notes towards the Definition of Culture, first gathering only, 1948, & Eliot's intro to J. (91) £420
— Anr, Poetry and Drama, 1st English Ed; 1951. (91) £340
Corrected proof, Poems, 1909-1925. New Ed, 1932. With a number of autograph corrections. Sgd with initials. (91) £4,200
Photograph, sgd & inscr, [25 Dec] 1930. 163mm by 117mm (image). Inscr to Virginia Woolf on mount. Koch Foundation. (90) $1,100
Photograph, [n.d.]. (91) £260
Proof copy, The Cocktail Party. (91) £100
— Anr, Collected Plays, 1962. (91) £650
— Anr, Poems written in Early Youth, 1st trade Ed, 1967. (91) £150

Eliot, Thomas Stearns, 1888-1965 —& Others
[The signatures of 32 participants of the John Lehmann Lunch at the Trocadero Restaurant, 15 Jan 1953, on Trocadero letterhead, 252mm by 198mm, framed, sold at S on 18 July 1991, lot 366, for £600 to Heinz.]

Eliot, Thomas Stearns, 1888-1965. See: Joyce, James

Elisabeth, Fuerstin von Hohenzollern-Hechingen, 1613-71
Ds, 4 Nov 1670. (89) DM650

Elisabeth, Princess of Braunschweig-Wolfenbuettel, 1746-1840
ALs, 11 Oct 1834. Schroeder collection. (89) DM350

ELISABETH

Elisabeth, Queen of Philipp IV of Spain, 1602-44
Ls, 29 Oct 1616. (90) DM320

Elisabeth, Queen of Frederick William IV, King of Prussia, 1801-73
ALs, 20 Jan 1827. (90) DM200
— 17 Aug 1833. (90) DM460
— 28 Jan 1869. Schroeder collection. (89) DM250
— 28 Jan 1869. (91) DM400

Elisabeth, Empress of Franz Joseph I of Austria, 1837-98
AL, [1889]. (88) DM700

Elisabeth, Queen of Carol I of Romania, 1843-1916. See: Sylva, Carmen

Elisabeth Alekseyevna, Empress of Alexander I of Russia, 1779-1826
ALs, 21 Sept 1813. (90) DM320

Elisabeth Charlotte, Kurfuerstin von Brandenburg, 1597-1660
ALs, 1 Sept [1616]. (90) DM1,000

Elisabeth Charlotte, Duchesse d'Orleans, 1652-1722
ALs, 29 May 1695. 1 p, 4to. To her stepsister Louise. Requesting her to forward an enclosure, & reporting about her activities. (90) DM2,800

Elisabeth Christine, Queen of Frederick II of Prussia, 1715-97
ALs, 1 Aug 1734. Schroeder collection. (89) DM420
— 21 Aug 1780. (90) DM650
— 28 May 1782. (91) DM580
Ls, 15 Jan 1763. Schroeder collection. (89) DM460

Elisabeth of Nassau, Duchesse de Bouillon, 1577-1642
ALs, 9 Aug 1626. (91) DM1,000

Elizabeth, Queen of George VI of England
ALs, 3 Dec 1972. (90) £80
Christmas card, sgd, 1960. (91) $160
Photograph, sgd, 1977. (91) $110

**Elizabeth, Queen of George VI of England —&
Anne, Princess of England**
Ds, 23 Mar 1977. (91) $600

AMERICAN BOOK PRICES CURRENT

**Elizabeth, Queen of George VI of England —&
Margaret, Princess of England**
Ds, 13 July 1976. (91) $350

Elizabeth, Queen of Bohemia, 1596-1662
ALs, [25 June 1636]. (90) £600
— [Aug 1660]. 1 p, 4to. To Lord Langdale. Informing him that her son Rupert will go to England as soon as possible. (91) DM4,600
— 17 Apr [n.y.]. 1 p, 4to. To the Lord Treasurer. Expressing her obligation for his kindness. (91) DM4,200
Series of 7 A Ls, 1655 to 1661 & [n.d.]. 19 pp, folio. To her son Prince Rupert. About her financial problems, family matters, & court news. (91) £1,300

Elizabeth I, Queen of England, 1533-1603
Ls, 16 July 1562. 1 p, double folio. To Catherine de Medicis, Queen of France. Complaining that some of her subjects have been maltreated by the French, & sending an envoy to discuss the matter. In French. (90) £13,500
— 6 Mar 1565/66. 1 p, folio. Recipient unnamed. Granting £500 to the inhabitants of Scarborough for the repair of the pier. (90) £3,800
— 18 June 1588. 2 pp, folio. To Roger, 2d Baron North. Announcing that the Armada is threatening England & requiring him to mobilize forces. (89) £40,000
— 4 Aug 1599. 2 pp, folio. To Roger North. Informing him about the possibility of a Spanish invasion, & instructing him to mobilize forces. Framed. (90) $18,000
Ds, 7 Sept 1562. 1 p, 8vo. Order addressed to Sir John Mason to pay Martyn Almayne for "dressing and curing of divers of o[u]r horses". (89) £2,200
— 31 Jan 1566. 1 p, vellum, 352mm by 212mm. Grant of a lease in lands worth £20 per year to William Vernon in reward of services. (90) $9,500
— 10 June 1574. 1 p, folio. Order addressed to Lord Burghley to grant to Richard Bunney a lease in reversion to the annual value of £26. (91) £3,800
— 20 Dec 1587. 4 pp, folio. Instructions to Charles Lord Howard as commander-in-chief of the navy for the

212

defense against the Armada. (91) £45,000
Document, 23 Jan [1563]. (88) £550
— 21 Nov 1567. (89) £600
— 21 Mar 1595. 1 leaf. Letters patent granting lands, etc, to William Lewyn & Robert Cranmer. On vellum. With Second Great Seal suspended by plaited black & white threads; framed. Includes fine initial letter portrait of Elizabeth. (90) £2,000
— 2 Sept 1601. (91) £800
— COURT OF THE EXCHEQUER. - Document, 19 Nov 1596. 1 p, vellum, 40cm by 52cm. Judgment in a dispute concerning the water-course of a corn-mill at Zeal in Devon, in English & Latin. (91) £160
— LEICESTER, ROBERT DUDLEY, EARL OF. - Ds, 16 July 1567. 1 p, folio. Acknowledging for the Queen a debt of £500 to the Earl of Kildare. Countersgd by William Cecil. With receipt by the Queen's agent at bottom. Nibbled by rodents. With transcript. (89) $550
See also: Pius V, 1504-72

Elizabeth II, Queen of England
Ds, 24 Oct 1957. (89) $550
— 19 Nov 1963. 1 p, folio. Appointment of Sir Francis Rundall as Ambassador at Tokyo. (90) $1,300
Christmas card, 1960. (90) $500

Elizabeth II, Queen of England —& Philip, Prince, Duke of Edinburgh
Christmas card, 1955. 7 by 8 inches. Sgd by both. Including family photograph. (91) $1,000
— Anr, 1968. 8vo. Sgd by both. Framed with related material. (90) $280
Group photograph, with unidentified people in front of a train, 1959. (89) $500

Ellery, William, Signer from Rhode Island
Autograph Ms, "Description of the Clan who wrote the Halifax Letter"; [Mar 1765]. 3 pp, folio. Discussing a political quarrel over Rhode Island's colonial government. 2d leaf torn. (90) $1,500
— Autograph Ms, journal of his journeys to & from Congress, 1776 to 1779. 102 pp, 8vo, in 5 notebooks (2 def). Including his accounts with the State of Rhode Island, an account of 4th of July observances, 1778, etc. (90) $80,000
— Autograph Ms, Minutes respecting the Declaration of Independence, 13 July 1818. 1 p, 4to. Sgd. With 10-line autograph docket, sgd, on verso. (90) $22,000
— Autograph Ms, Remarks on an infamous Publication in the R[hode] I[sland] Republican; [c.10 Apr 1810]. (90) $400
— Autograph Ms, transcription of the Body of Laws for Harvard College, [before 6 Sept 1743]. 33 pp & calligraphic tp, in contemp blue wraps. Sgd Gulielmus Ellery, 5 times. Including sgd endorsements by Edward Holyoke, President of Harvard, & 2 professors. (90) $2,500
Series of 9 A Ls s, 20 Jan 1812 to 17 May 1815. 24 pp, 4to. To his grandson George G. Channing. Affectionate correspondence about a variety of matters. (90) $11,000
ALs, 10 July 1776. 2 pp, 4to. To his brother Benjamin. Voicing his hopes & fears after the Declaration of Independence. (90) $110,000
— 1 Nov 1792. 4 pp, 4to. To his daughter Nancy. About her smallpox inoculation. (90) $1,500
— 19 July 1807. 3 pp, 4to. To William Stedman. Reminiscing about the Revolutionary War, & inquiring about politics in Washington & Burr's rebellion. (91) $2,800
— 1 Feb 1820. (90) $400
— REDWOOD, WILLIAM. - ALs, 22 Dec 1775. 2 pp, folio. To William Ellery. Discussing business affairs & the situation in Newport. Including 4-line docket in Ellery's hand, Jan 1776; sgd in text. (90) $7,500

Elles, Sir William Kidston
Collection of 44 A Ls s & Ms. (88) £400

Ellington, Duke, 1899-1979
Autograph music, unpbd full score inscr "(Title) To: Immaculately Attired Soft Speaking Gentleman", [n.d.]. 64 pp, folio. Mostly in pencil on up to 10 staves per page; with many blank staves. Partly lapsing into sketches. A few passages in other hands. (89)

ELLINGTON

$6,500

Photograph, sgd & inscr, [n.d.]. (91) $275

Elliot, Daniel Giraud, 1835-1915

Original drawings, (4), pencil drawings of American water-birds, to illus his Wild Fowls of the United States..., 1898. 4 pp, folio. Sgd & titled. Matted. (88) $2,000

Elliott, Robert Brown, 1842-84

ALs, 14 Aug 1880. (91) $180

Ellis, Havelock, 1859-1939

Collection of 25 A Ls s, Ls, & typescript, 1890 to 1938. (89) £700

Series of 3 A Ls s, Dec 1922 to Mar 1923. (90) £250

Ellis, Sir Henry, 1777-1869

[A collection of 82 A Ls s addressed to him by various antiquarians, scientists, historians & politicians, 1818 to 1854, sold at S on 22 July 1988, lot 526, for £160 to Quaritch.]

Ellsworth, Elmer Ephraim, 1837-61

Autograph Ms, "For the Journal. (91) $800

ALs, 12 June 1859. 1 p, 4to. To Adjutant Gen. Y. S. Mather. As commander of volunteer "cadets", complaining about equipment. (89) $2,500

ADs, [May 1861]. 1 p, size not stated. "Pass the bearer through camp Lincoln ...". Mtd. (89) $2,250

Ellsworth, Oliver, 1745-1807

Collection of 2 A Ds s & 2 Ds s, 1777 & 1778. (88) $60

ADs, 19 June 1776. (90) $65

— 20 Dec 1789. (88) $80

Ds, 5 July 1776. (91) $170

— 14 Jan 1777. (89) $75

Elsenhans, Ernst, 1815-49

ALs, 30 Apr 1846. (91) DM440

Elssler, Fanny, 1810-84

ALs, [1880] "89". (88) DM200

Eluard, Paul, 1895-1952

ALs, 14 Feb 1925. (89) DM440

AMERICAN BOOK PRICES CURRENT

Ember Press

[The archive of the poetry magazine Littack, together with material relating to New Headland, & The Village Review, comprising authors' Mss & typescripts, correspondence, etc., 1960s to 1980s, in 12 boxes, sold at S on 19 July 1990, lot 191, for £8,000 to Rota.]

Embury, Emma Catherine, c.1806-63

[An archive of c.60 items, mostly letters addressed to Mrs. Embury & her husband Daniel, with related material, 1808 to 1870, mtd on leaves of mor album, sold at P on 30 Jan 1990, lot 2033, for $6,000.]

Emerson, Ralph Waldo, 1803-82

Autograph Ms, early draft of the poem Monadnoc. 1845-46. 21 pp, 4to, each leaf inlaid to larger sheets & bound in mor gilt by Wallis, front cover detached. Schiff Ms (91) $14,000

— **Autograph Ms,** poem, The Chartists's Complaint, 8 couplets; [c.1858]. 1 p, 4to. Tipped to larger sheet; in mor bdg with related material. Doheny collection. (89) $1,100

Collection of ALs & autograph transcript, 24 Aug 1872 & [n.d.]. 5 pp, 8vo & 4to. To Anna M. Neil, thanking for a gift & reporting about the recent fire in his home. Poem, "Fable"; 19 lines. Barrett collection. (89) $1,100

ALs, 25 Jan 1842. (91) $350

— 21 June 1853. (90) $200

— 27 July 1857. (90) $220

— 14 Dec [1857]. (88) $270

— 27 May 1861. (88) DM320

— 20 Nov 1863. 8 pp, 8vo. To Maj. Gen. Ethan Allen Hitchcock. Discussing the question of retaliation for the starving of Union soldiers at Libby Prison. (89) $4,750

— 1 June 1869. 4 pp, 8vo, in folder by Sangorski & Sutcliffe. To Charles W. Upham. Discussing the raising of funds for Harvard. Sang & Middendorf collections. (89) $3,500

— 3 Aug 1875. Byer collection. (90) $375

ANs, 5 July 1849. (88) $160

Ds, 21 Jan [1856?]. (88) $110

— 6 Jan 1878. (88) $130

Autograph quotation, sgd; [n.d.]. (88) $140

214

Check, sgd, 12 May 1862. (91) £120

Emerson, William, 1701-82
ALs, 9 Dec 1778. (91) £120

Emma, Queen of The Netherlands, 1858-1934
ALs, 7 Sept 1886. (88) DM320

Emmett, Daniel Decatur, 1815-1904
Autograph music, I Wish I Was in Dixie's Land, [c.1860s]. 1 p, 4to. Transcript, sgd & inscr to Richard Wayne. Including verse. (88) $4,000

Emmett, Rowland
Original drawing, 2 soldiers & 3 groups of cows in the country, to illus Punch; later ptd in Sidings & Suchlike. (90) £1,000
— Original drawing, city businessmen leaving a train at Pentwiddle Cove, to illus Punch; later ptd in Sidings & Suchlike. In ink; sgd. 355mm by 292mm; framed. (90) £3,800
— Original drawing, outdoor performance of A Midsummer Night's Dream postponed until 25 Nov, to illus Punch; later ptd in Sidings & Suchlike. In ink & wash; sgd. 300mm by 292mm; framed. (90) £1,300

Encke, Johann Franz, 1791-1865
ALs, 8 Dec 1852. (91) DM380

Encyclopaedic Dictionary
Ms, compilation of notes on names, places, events & institutes from medieval times to the early 19th cent, [19th cent]. (89) £70

Endecott, John, 1589?-1665
Autograph endorsement, sgd, 13 Oct 1662. 1 p, folio. Witnessing the seal of Thomas Linkon on a deed dated 11 Oct 1662. Middendorf collection. (89) $2,200

Enesco, Georges, 1881-1955
ALs, 5 Oct 1910. (91) DM200
— 9 June 1954. (89) DM240

Engels, Friedrich, 1820-95
Autograph Ms, article analyzing a siege [of Sebastopol?], fragment; probably written for Allgemeine Militaer Zeitung, [Nov 1862]. 1 p, 8vo, on blue paper. (88) £2,600

ALs, 21 Oct 1876. 4 pp. 8vo. To Thomas Allsop. Analyzing the situation in Russia, the probability of a war with Turkey, & the consequences for Western Europe. (88) DM120,000
— 21 Oct 1879. 3 pp, 8vo. To [Thomas Allsop]. Reporting about the Marx family & discussing the European political situation. (90) DM60,000
— 22 Oct 1889. 1 p, 8vo. To Otto Adolf Ellissen. Responding to a request for letters by F. A. Lange. (89) DM45,000

Englaender, Richard, 1859-1919. See: Altenberg, Peter

England
[A group of 11 English land charters, c.1200 to 1500, sold at S on 5 Dec 1989, lot 59, for £1,500.]
[A group of 4 Ms charters on vellum, 13th cent to 1301, relating to lands in Lancashire & Dorset, sold at S on 21 June 1988, lot 42, for £300 to Brewer.]
[A collection of c.30 court rolls relating to Islington & some other places in Middlesex, 1423 to 1716, many of great length, detailing courts baron involving thousands of cases, sold at S on 19 July 1990, lot 285, for £1,400 to Quaritch.]
[A group of 5 vellum documents, 1493-94, 8 pp, folio, financial accounts probably kept for taxation & census, in Latin, sold at sg on 24 Mar 1988, lot 76, for $375.]
[Gloucestershire. - A large archive relating chiefly to the Manor of Mickleton & its occupiers since the time of Henry VIII, including the Porter, Graves & Hamilton families, [16th to 19th cent], thousands of pages, sold at S on 15 Dec, lot 247, for £4,800.]
[Wyatt Rebellion. - A group of 4 documents relating to the trial of the followers of Sir Thomas Wyatt after the collapse of his insurrection in Feb 1554, including Letters Patent by Queen Mary, sold at C on 21 June 1989, lot 128, for £600 to Quaritch.]
[Recusancy. - A collection of documents relating to Elizabethan Recusancy, from the papers of Sir Andrew Noel, including a letter sgd by members of the Privy Council & a ptd

broadside specifying duties of the Commissioners for Recusancy, 1591, sold at S on 15 Dec 1988, lot 135, for £3,600.]

[New River Company. - A collection of 12 documents, 1705 to 1713 & [n.d.], c.25 pp, folio, in buckram case, relating to the New River Company & the supply of water to various London districts, sold at C on 7 Dec 1988, lot 172, for £210 to Quaritch.]

[A group of 44 letters, mostly autograph, by the British Prime Ministers from Robert Walpole to Harold Macmillan, 1716 to 1953, sold at sg on 3 May 1990, lot 3787, for $7,500.]

[A collection of letters & documents relating to Blickling Hall & Joseph Bonomi's mausoleum for the 2d Earl of Buckinghamshire, 1729 to 1872, sold at S on 19 July 1990, lot 286, for £2,200 to Quaritch.]

[A collection of 132 letters & documents relating to Castle Durrow in the 18th & 19th centuries, c.260 pp, various sizes, sold at C on 20 June 1990, lot 278, for £400 to Ashbrook.]

[Wentworth Woodhouse, Yorkshire. - A series of 5 letterbooks, 1772 to 1805, c.750 pp, in quarter calf, containing copies of several hundred letters addressed to Earl Fitzwilliam & the Marquess & Marchioness of Rockingham by the steward of Wentworth Woodhouse concerning the running of the estate, sold at S on 20 July 1989, lot 270, for £2,600 to Dallas.]

[A volume of orig letters or documents of all the female sovereigns of England from Lady Jane Grey to Queen Victoria, embellished with miniatures on ivory, sold at sg on 22 Mar 1990, lot 172.] $37,500

Ms, account book, probably kept by Robert & Anne Eyre of Salisbury, 1638 to 1665. (91) £900

— Ms, Agenda Book, "In libro de Agendis in Custodia Rendatoris Thesaurarii a Curio remanen inter alia continetur ut Sequit", 1607. (88) £90

— Ms, Formulare Ecclesiasticum Iboracense for the reign of Edward VI; [c.1550]. (90) £280

— Ms, The Names of Certeine Personnes which weare atteinted in the tymes of Kings H.8th & E.6th & were restored to name & landes by parliament in the type of Quene Marye. (91) £450

— Ms, The Register of Writs, & the Statutes of England from Magna Charta, in Latin & Anglo-Norman. [London?, c.1350]. 216 leaves (1 blank) & 2 flyleaves, vellum, 158mm by 103mm. Def calf over pastebds. In brown ink in an English courthand. With c.60 illuminated initials & full-length bar border. (90) £7,000

— Ms, This Booke conteyneth a generall Collection of all the Offices of England with the fees and allowances belonging to them in the yngs gyft. (91) £550

— AYLSHAM, NORFOLK. - Ms, subscribers' list for the repair of the Aylsham fire engine, 1768. Length not stated. With related material. (91) £160

— BEDFORDSHIRE. - Ms, on the antiquities of Bedfordshire villages, [18th cent]. 526 pp, size not stated, in modern half calf. Including index. Pearl Assurance collection. (91) £160

— BERKSHIRE. - 13 documents, conveyances relating to land in Barkham & Finchamstead, 1328 to 1459, vellum, in 16th-cent box of lea over pastebds. (88) £550

— BRISTOL. - A large collection of papers of the Ward & related families of Bristol & elsewhere, late 17th cent to early 19th cent, hundreds of items in 2 boxes, sold at S on 21 Sept, lot 86, for £1,100 to Spake. 88

— CARTULARY. - Ms, transcription of charters from the Anglo-Saxon period & later relating to various abbeys & foundations; [late 16th cent]. 75 pp, folio, in vellum wraps. (90) £280

— COOPER, ANNE. - Autograph Ms, Journal of a Tour down the Wye, 1786, 39 pp of text & 22 sepia wash views (1 watercolor), 4to, in contemp bds. (88) £680

— CUSTOMS AND EXCISE, LONDON. - 8 large vols of official correspondence, orders, etc. relating to London customs & the East India Docks, 1814 to 1938, folio. (88) £350

— DECLARATORY ACT. - Ms, rough draft of the Declaratory Act of 18 Mar 1766. 1 p, 4to. Turner collection. (89) $1,800

— DERBYSHIRE. - Ms, account book of William Carrington relating to mining around Ashen Clough, 1711 to 1757. About 160 pp, size not stated, in calf bdg. Def. (89) £250

— DURHAM. - Ms, Minute Book for the dispensary at Stockton, 5 Oct 1789 to 29 July 1948. About 150 pp, folio. Def calf bdg. (89) £150

— ELY PRIORY. - Ms, contemp copy of Letters Patent, 18 Nov 1539 & 10 Sept 1541, dissolving the Benedictine Priory of Ely & establishing the secular Cathedral, with later material. Roll of 17 paper & 1 vellum leaves, 600cm by 28mm. (90) £850

— FLORDON, NORFOLK. - 28 documents, mid-13th cent to 1533. Vellum. Leases & conveyances of lands in the village of Flordon. (90) £1,600

— GODWINE. - Document, in Anglo-Saxon; charter granting to Leofwine the Red the swine pasture at Swithraedingden. [Canterbury, c.1013-20]. 1 p, vellum, 53mm by 258mm. 5 lines in a handsome skilful Anglo-Saxon minuscule. (89) £115,000

— HENRY DE BERBILAND. - Document, 8 Oct 1296. Vellum, 322mm by 328mm. Last will of a vicar in Exeter Cathedral, with detailed inventory of possessions. (91) £1,280

— HORSE BREEDING. - Document, 26 May 1584, 14.5 by 23 inches, sgd by Lord Burghley, the Earl of Leicester, Sir Christopher Hatton, & others. Warrant appointing Roger, Lord North & others as Deputies for the execution of Her Majesty's commission for the increase of horse-breeding. With a copy of the commission. (91) £1,800

— HOUSE OF COMMONS. - Ms, Journals of the Proceedings, transcription covering various periods between 8 Nov 1547 & 9 Nov 1703; [18th cent]. 10 vols, folio, in 19th-cent cloth. (91) $325

— HOUSE OF LORDS. - Ms, list of members of the House of Lords during the reign of Charles II. Vellum scroll, length not stated. Illuminated. (89) £240

— HOUSE OF LORDS. - Ms, scroll listing members of the House of Lords, c.1529. 2 skins of vellum, c.35 by 5 inches. Containing 81 illuminated coats-of-arms with names of each peer, notes on precedence, & other annotations. (89) £1,250

— HUNGERFORD, ROBERT, LORD MOLYNS & HUNGERFORD. - Ds, 10 July 1449. 1 p, 196mm by 355mm, vellum. Grant to Sir Philip Courtenay of an annual payment from 3 manors in Cornwall. Lacking seal. With related material. (88) $450

— IPSWICH, SUFFOLK. - Document, 10 Mar 1513. 2 membranes of vellum; size not stated. Exchange between William Hill & officials of Ipswich regarding a property near St. Thomas's Chapel. (90) £75

— KENT. - Document, 21 Apr 1803. Size not stated. Certificate no 15 of the Kent Fire Office, insuring the Bell Inn, Maidstone; sgd by 3 directors on 1st day of company's business. Framed. (91) £50

— LE BLUND, WILLIAM. - Document, 1321. 1 p, vellum, 8vo. Conveyance of land to William & Matilda Baneyr. In Latin. (91) $325

— LIVERPOOL. - Ms, autograph diary of Hugh Stowell Kewley, with a vol relating to railway legislation, 1849 to 1857. About 500 pp in 6 vols, 8vo. (91) £720

— LONDON. - Document, 13 Sept 1669. Size not stated. Agreement, sgd by Thomas Sharrow & others, referring to the Great Fire & granting Mary Clarke the right to make 2 windows. (90) £75

— LONDON. - Ms, memoranda book kept by members of the Dutch Church in London, 1 Oct 1615 to Oct 1642. 200 pp, 8vo, in contemp calf. (91) £400

— LONDON. - Ms, Poor Rate book for St. James's, Duke Place, sgd by the mayor & others, 1821 to 1822; c.75 pp, 8vo, in red mor. (88) £300

— NEDYRTONE, WAUTER. - Letter, presumably autograph, of the Chaplain to Isabelle de Claxtone reporting on negotiations over the Manor of Whetlaw. [England, late 14th cent] In French. 1 p, oblong folio. (90) £920

— NEWENT, GLOUCESTERSHIRE. - 2 documents, 25 Mar 1379 & 1393. 2 pp, vellum, 4to. Indentures pertaining to

property. (91) $350
— NORFOLK. - 14 documents, vellum, [mid-13th cent]. Conveyances of land in Methwold & Salle. (91) £1,500
— NORFOLK. - 22 documents, 1336 to 1395. Length not stated; vellum. Deeds relating to lands at Flordon, Braken & Hapton. (90) £1,350
— NORFOLK. - 30 documents, 1702 to 1798. Length not stated. Deeds relating to Brampton Hall, including the 1750 rental of Charles Townley. (90) £120
— NORFOLK. - 5 documents, 1321 to 1373. Length not stated; vellum. Deeds relating to lands at Flordan. (90) £360
— NORFOLK. - 7 Mss, manorial rentals for Buxton & Levisham, 1772 to 1802 & 1814 to 1860. 7 vols, size not stated. (90) £95
— NORTHAMPTONSHIRE. - Court Roll of the Manor of Raunds, 10 May 1756. 3400mm by 325mm, vellum. (88) £120
— NOTTINGHAMSHIRE. - Ms, notes taken by William Clay, Steward to the Archbishop of York in Southwell, 1640 to 1728, c.150 pp, 4to, in calf bdg. Comprising a register of will & testators, list of books, recipes, etc. (91) £500
— PARLIAMENT. - Ms, parliamentary journal, 17 Mar to 26 June 1628. 460pp, size not stated, in contemp vellum. Including some supplementary material. Marquess of Downshire collection. (90) £900
— PARLIAMENT. - Ms, journal of the Hon. Henry Grey Bennet, recording his activities in the House of Commons, 23 Jan to early July 1821; c.120 pp, 4to. Interspersed with newspaper cuttings. With related material. (88) £110
— PARLIAMENT. - Ms, A true Presentacon of forepast Parliaments to the review of present tymes and Posteritie, [c.1630]. About 285 pp, folio, in contemp vellum bdg. In a single professional hand. (88) £50
— PARLIAMENT. - Transcript, Journals of the House of Commons, 1653 to 1678. With a vol relating to the impeachment of Edward Hyde, Earl of Clarendon, 1667, & 2 vols of transcripts of parliamentary rolls for the reigns of Richard II & Edward IV, [late 17th cent]. Together c.4000 pp, folio, in 9 vols; in contemp calf, rebacked. (88) £500
— PHILIP DE BRADELEA. - Document, [late 12th cent]. Size not stated, vellum. Grant of lands at Frith to the Church of the Blessed Virgin Mary at Waverl[ey]. With large equestrian seal. With anr contemp document to the Church at Waverley. (88) £550
— PRIVY COUNCIL. - Letter, 15 July 1690, 1 p, folio, to the Earl of Macclesfield, ordering him to raise his militia in case of a threatened French invasion. (91) £240
— READING. - Document, 9 Jan 1582; 10.25 by 14 inches, vellum. Order of the Justices of the Peace, unsgd, providing that buyers, sellers & prices of cattle sold in the Borough of Reading should be recorded. Laid down & bound in modern half calf. (88) £300
— SHERRATT, ELIZABETH. - Ds, 28 Apr 1607. 1 p, 128mm by 445mm, vellum. Will. Also sgd by 6 witnesses. (88) $70
— SNARESTON, LEICESTERSHIRE. - Ms, school register, listing pupils, teachers, etc., 1719 to 1849. 150 pp, folio. (91) £420
— ST. MARTIN-IN-THE-FIELDS, LONDON. - Ms, Rate Book for Pall Mall & surrounding area for 1663, 30 pp, folio; worn. With rebuilding rate book for 1668 & further related material. (90) £300
— ST. PAUL'S SCHOOL. - Ms, survey of accounts listing rents, debts & payments, 1669 to 1670. 37 pp, 4to, in orig vellum. Dampstained. (89) £350
— STAPLE INN, LONDON. - Ms, admissions book, 12 May 1716 to 28 Feb 1881. About 150 pp, folio, in reversed calf. (90) £1,300
— SUFFOLK. - 13 Mss, court records of the Manors of Ulverston & Sackvills, with related material, c.1318 to 1936. 9 vols & 4 rolls, size not stated. (90) £720
— SUFFOLK. - 25 documents, 15th cent & later. Length not stated, vellum. Deeds relating to Sackvills, Ulverston, Ipswich & elsewhere, including will of Robert Joyne of Ipswich, 1540. (90) £240
— SUFFOLK. - Document, 1298. 1 p, vellum, 12mo. Grant of land in

Thorinton by John De Schinclinge to Robert, son of Augustine of Thorinton. (89) $190
— SUFFOLK. - Ms, A Rentall of all the Manno[rs] Lands and Tenements of Sr. Henry Wood..., 12 Dec 1671. 7 pp, folio. Stitched; in paper wraps. Listing estates at Whepstead & Brockley, Elmswell, Woolpit, etc. Clifford Papers. (89) £50
— SUSSEX. - 18 documents, [18th & 19th cent], deeds relating to property in Petworth & transactions by members of the Upton family. (88) £30
— SUSSEX. - Ms, recording cases brought before Justices of the Peace in the Rape of Hastings, 1819 to 1827. 1 vol, c.200 pp, 4to. (88) £200
— TOWER OF LONDON. - A collection of depositions, reports, etc. relating to Christopher Layer's plot to seize the Tower, 1722 to 1723, 13 pp, folio, sold at pn on 16 June 1988, lot 31, for £90 to Clark. 88
— TOWER OF LONDON. - Ms, "Demands of Sr. Wm. Balfour ... for the Diett of Prisoners...", 30 Sept to 25 Dec 1634, sgd by Balfour & others. 1 p, folio. Def. (88) £90
— WORCESTERSHIRE. - Ms, A Topographical Discription ... of the Mannor of Powde in the Parish of Church Honnyburne ... by mee Francis Allen. Estate plan, 1652. 80cm by 70cm, vellum. In ink & colors, with coat-of-arms. (88) £1,300
— YORKSHIRE. - Grant by Hugh de Neuville of land in Denby to Byland Abbey, [c.1250-75]. 1 p, vellum, 85mm by 233mm. With armorial seal. Phillipps Ms 36227. (88) £650
— YORKSHIRE. - Original drawings (c.100), working drawings belonging to a builder named Walker in the Bradford area, [mid-18th cent]. Mostly in pen-&-ink; with estimates, surveys, etc. (91) £5,500
— YORKSHIRE, WEST RIDING. - Ms, survey of John Arthington's land in Almondbury, by Dickinson, 1745. 1 p, 17 by 23 inches. (88) £240
— YORKSHIRE, WEST RIDING. - Ms, A Plan of Rogerthorp ... Belonging to Tho Ritchingman, by J. Fintoff, Sept 1760. 1 p, 17.5 by 21 inches. (88) £170

Englefield, Cicely
Original drawings, (17), to illus All Sorts of Dogs, [1930s]. (89) £420
— Original drawings, (24), to illus A Visit to the Farm, 1931, & other books. (90) £600

English, Thomas Dunn, 1819-1902
ALs, 14 Jan 1886. (89) $80

Ensor, James, 1860-1949
ALs, 14 Dec 1896. (88) DM550
Autograph postcard, sgd, 2 Apr 1925. (89) DM550

Entwistle, John
Autograph Ms, lyrics for the song Man on Run from Wife, for The Who album Who's Next; [n.d.]. (88) £300
— Autograph Ms, lyrics for the song Dr Jekyll And Mr Hyde, for The Who album Magic Bus; [n.d.]. (88) £450
— Autograph Ms, lyrics for the song Success Story, for The Who album Who by Numbers; [n.d.]. (88) £450
— HOUSTON POLICE DEPARTMENT. - Document, Prisoner Property Receipt, detailing property removed for safekeeping during Entwistle's stay in custody; 1975, 13cm by 20cm. (88) £110

Eon de Beaumont, Charles de, 1728-1810
Autograph Ms (2), autobiographical notes in 3d person, [n.d.], & description of the state of his health, 10 Jan 1791. (88) DM320
ALs, 20 June 1801. (91) $275

Epistles
Ms, Epistles of Saint Paul, with glossa ordinaria. In Latin. [Northern Italy?, early 12th cent]. 176 leaves, vellum, 21cm by 14cm. 19th-cent black mor gilt over wooden bds. In light brown, black & red ink in a minuscule bookhand. With interlinear & surrounding glosses & 10 large initials in colors with zoomorphic figures. (88) £6,600
— Ms, Epistles of Saint Paul, with preface of St. Jerome. In Latin. [Paris?, c.1515]. 118 leaves, vellum, 155mm by 90mm. Dark blue mor bdg by Derome, blue mor solander box by Riviere. In dark brown ink in a very fine cursive italic script in the style of Ludovico

degli Arrighi. With 96 two-line & 30 three- or four-line illuminated initials, & tp with design of fountain & landscape in ornamental frame. Doheny collection. (88) £27,000
— Ms, Epistles of St. Paul, with glossa ordinaria. In Latin. [Himmerode?, Eifel, late 12th cent]. 138 leaves, vellum, 215mm by 155mm. 16th-cent blindstamped calf over wooden bds. In brown ink in a well-formed minuscule bookhand. With 14 large decorated initials in red. Dampstained, repaired. Doheny collection. (88) £15,000

Epitres et Evangiles. See: Bible Manuscripts, French

Epstein, Jacob, 1880-1959
Series of 3 A Ls s, 1927 & [n.d.]. (88) £110
— Series of 17 A Ls s, 22 May 1940 to 21 May 1942. 26 pp, 4to. To S. Samuels & his wife (1). Mostly relating to recipient's purchase of Epstein's sculptures. With related material. Byer collection. (90) $1,700

Erasmus, Desiderius, 1466?-1536
[A copy of the Adagia. Basel: Froben, 1523, presented by Erasmus to Nicholas Cannius, heavily revised & annotated with material for the Ed of 1526 in at least 3 hands, including c.240 passages by Erasmus himself, sold at S on 20 Nov 1990, lot 397, for £450,000 to Israel.]

Erastus, Thomas, 1523?-83
ALs, 7 Mar [1572]. (88) £800

Erhard, Ludwig, 1897-1977
Photograph, sgd & inscr, Feb 1961. (88) DM550

Erich I, Herzog von Braunschweig und Lueneburg, 1470-1540
Ls, 29 Apr 1528. (90) DM650
Ds, [6 Apr] 1511. (89) DM400

Erichsen, Nelly
Original drawings, (18), to illus Susan E. Archives of J. M. Dent & Son. (88) £420
— Original drawings, (32), to illus Edmund J. Archives of J. M. Dent & Son. (88) £180
— Original drawings, (33), to illus J. Archives of J. M. Dent & Son. (88) £480
— Original drawings, (39), to illus T. Archives of J. M. Dent & Son. (88) £360

Ericsson, John, 1803-89
ALs, 25 Sept 1858. (91) $250
— 26 Dec 1860. (90) $400
— 28 Mar 1862. 2 pp, 4to. To Sen. James H. Grimes. Discussing the destructive power of the U.S.S. Monitor & his invention's importance for naval warfare. (90) $4,200

Erie Canal
— MOORE, HENRY M. - Series of 17 A Ls s, 1836 to 1838. 35 pp, folio & 4to. To Daniel Agnew. Describing his problems as engineering supervisor on the building of the Erie Canal. (88) $325

Erlach, Johann Ludwig von, 1595-1650
ALs, 17 June 1642. (91) DM750

Erni, Hans
Series of 3 Ls s, 11 July 1959, 27 Jan 1960 & [n.d.]. Byer collection. (90) $300

Ernst August, Kurfuerst von Hannover, 1629-98
Ls, 14 Apr 1663. Schroeder collection. (89) DM360

Ernst August II, King of Hannover, 1771-1851
ALs, 11 July 1837. Schroeder collection. (89) DM440
— 21 Feb 1838. (90) DM400
Ls, 30 June 1837. Schroeder collection. (89) DM260

Ernst, Heinrich Wilhelm, 1814-65
ALs, 29 Apr 1840. (90) DM580
Autograph quotation, 7 double bars of music, 9 May 1847. (91) $100

Ernst I, Herzog von Sachsen-Coburg, 1784-1844
Series of 7 A Ls s, 20 Aug 1831 to 24 Oct 1839. 39 pp, 4to & 8vo. To Christian Friedrich von Stockmar. Confidential letters, mostly about his sons' marital prospects. (90) DM2,400

Ernst, Max, 1891-1976
A Ls s (2), 14 Jan & 5 Apr 1936. (89) £230

Ervin, Sam J.
Typescript (duplicated), Some Personal Observations of Senator Sam J. (90) $75

Erzberger, Matthias, 1875-1921
ALs, 2 Sept 1913. (90) DM400
Ls, 26 June 1920. Schroeder collection. (89) DM380

Escher, Maurits Cornelis, 1898-1972
ALs, 11 Oct 1953. (90) DM850
— 8 Jan 1968. (91) DM550

Eschwege, Wilhelm Ludwig von, 1777-1855
Autograph Ms, Memoiren. Manuscript meiner Erlebnisse in der Alten und Neuen Welt ..., [c.1850-51]. 2350 pp, folio, in 10 vols. Modern red cloth. Describing his life in Brasil & Portugal. (89) DM64,000

Essex, Robert Devereux, 2d Earl of, 1567-1601
ALs, 24 Apr [1594]. 2 pp, folio. To [Maurice of Nassau?]. Stressing his desire to maintain himself in recipient's good graces, & mentioning his influence on the Queen. In French. (90) £3,000
Ls, 21 Sept 1588. 1 p, folio. To Richard Baggott. Appealing for aid in countering a court conspiracy. Partly autograph. (91) $2,400

Este, Alfonso II d', Duke of Ferrara, 1533-97
Series of 14 A Ls s, 2 Feb to 28 Dec 1586. 19 pp, folio. To Pope Sixtus V. Discussing various matters of state. With related material. (91) £2,000
Ls, 5 July 1582. (90) DM420
Ds, 18 May 1580. (89) DM440

Esterhazy, Paul, Prince, 1635-1713
Ds, 1 Oct 1700. (89) DM720

Esterhazy von Galantha, Emmerich, Prince, Archbishop of Gran
Ds, 27 May 1730. (89) DM250

Estienne, Antoine, 1592-1674
Ds, 3 May 1629. (91) $220

Ethiopic Manuscripts
[2 prayer scrolls, early 19th cent, vellum, each with 2 or 3 drawings & geometric ornamentation, sold at C on 21 June 1989, lot 46, for £380 to Fogg.]
[A collection of 3 magical prayer scrolls, [19th cent], vellum, each with 3 or 4 paintings & geometric ornamentation, sold at C on 7 Dec 1988, lot 50, for £300 to Fogg.]
[A collection of 3 magical prayer scrolls, [19th cent], vellum, each with 2 or 3 paintings & geometric ornamentation, sold at C on 7 Dec 1988, lot 51, for £200 to Craig.]
[A collection of 3 magical prayer scrolls, [19th cent], vellum, each with 2 or 3 paintings & geometric ornamentation, sold at C on 7 Dec 1988, lot 53, for £130 to Fogg.]
[A group of 3 magical prayer scrolls, [19th cent], vellum, each with 4 drawings & ornamentation, sold at C on 6 Dec 1989, lot 32, for £200 to Fogg.]
[A group of 3 magical prayer scrolls, [19th cent], vellum, each with 1 or 2 drawings & ornamentation, sold at C on 6 Dec 1989, lot 33, for £400 to Fogg.]
[A group of 4 magical prayer scrolls, [19th cent], vellum, each with 2 or 3 drawings & ornamentation, sold at C on 6 Dec 1989, lot 34, for £400 to Fogg.]
[A collection of 3 magical prayer scrolls, [19th or 20th cent], vellum, each with 3 paintings & geometric ornamentation, with 2 others, sold at C on 7 Dec 1988, lot 49, for £320 to Fogg.]
Ms, Amestu a'ema da mestir; prayer book. (90) DM530
— Ms, Four Gospels. [Ethiopia, 19th cent]. 110 leaves, vellum, 340mm by 284mm. Contemp bdg of wooden bds with remains of tooled lea; repaired. In black ink in several hands. With 8 full-page miniatures in black ink on backgrounds of colored wash. (89) £3,400
— Ms, Four Gospels. [Ethiopia, 1913]. 245 leaves, 265mm by 205mm.

ETHIOPIC MANUSCRIPTS

Contemp blindstamped red goatskin over wooden bds. In black ink in a regular square hand. With 4 elaborate half-page headpieces in bright colors, 4 miniatures of the Evangelists, & 3 full-page miniatures. (89) £1,400
— Ms, magical scroll, [Ethiopia, 19th cent]. (91) £110
— Ms, magical scroll. (90) £160
— Ms, Mary's Prayer. (89) DM1,000
— Ms, prayer book. [Ethiopia, 18th cent]. 150 leaves, vellum, 168mm by 115mm. Blindstamped brown lea over wooden bds. With 3 full-page miniatures in colors & several ornamental borders. (90) DM5,600
— Ms, prayer book. [Ethiopia, 19th cent]. 50 leaves, vellum, 100mm by 83mm. Contemp wooden bds. In black & red ink. Some annotations in a later hand. (90) DM1,400
— Ms, prayer book. (89) DM650
— Ms, prayer book. (89) DM600
— Ms, Synaxarium; Book of the Saints. [Ethiopia, Gondar?, c.1645-46]. 187 leaves, vellum, 385mm by 340mm. Contemp blindstamped tanned calf over wooden bds. With 33 large miniatures. Many erasures & alterations. Written for Emperor Fasilidas. (88) £8,000
— Ms, Synaxarium; Book of the Saints during winter months [Northern Ethiopia, Temamang, Gojam, 1st quarter of 19th cent]. 160 leaves, vellum, 340mm by 280mm. Massive orig wooden bds. With 36 miniatures in bright colors. Commissioned by Fitawrari Tedla & Guse Gebaz Aycheh. (89) £3,800
— Ms, Synaxarium; Book of the Saints from Sept to end of Nov. [Gondar, Ethiopia, 1709]. 135 leaves, vellum, 350mm by 270mm. Massive orig wooden bds, def. With 46 miniatures, 10 full-page. (89) £13,000
— Ms, T'amra Maryam; Miracles of the Virgin. [Gondar, Ethiopia, c.1730]. 87 leaves, vellum, 281mm by 245mm. Contemp blindstamped tanned calf over wooden bds. With 36 full- or nearly full-page miniatures in bright colors & sophisticated designs. (89) £14,000
— Ms, The Life & Acts of the Ethiopian

AMERICAN BOOK PRICES CURRENT

saint Takla Haymanot, in Ge'ez. [Gondar, Ethiopia, c.1800]. 129 leaves, vellum, 275mm by 230mm, in def contemp tanned lea over wooden bds. With 5 full-page miniatures. (91) £1,200
See also: Psalms & Psalters

Eugene of Savoy, Prince, 1663-1736

ALs, 27 Apr 1702. 1 p, folio. To an unnamed Prince. Giving instructions for troop movements. (91) DM4,500
— 1 July 1704. 3 pp, folio. To Margrave Ludwig Wilhelm von Baden. Informing him about the military situation in view of the French advance, & urging him to act. With related material. (90) DM11,000
— 22 Sept 1711. 5 pp, 4to. To the Duke of Marlborough. About recipient's victory at Bouchain, the burning of villages by the French commander, & the impending election [of Emperor Charles VI]. (90) DM6,000
Ls, 8 Jan 1709. (91) DM700
— 20 Nov 1710. 3 pp, folio. To the treasury at Milan. Transmitting an order to raise the pay of Liberato Rolandi. With related material. (89) DM1,500
— 21 Mar 1711. (91) DM600
— 4 Aug 1714. (88) DM550
— 9 July 1715. (91) DM600
— 4 Jan 1716. (90) DM600
— 24 Feb 1716. (90) DM450
— 3 Apr 1717. (91) DM1,000
— 11 Jan 1719. (91) DM550
— 1 May 1723. (90) DM950
— 23 Feb 1732. (89) DM600
— 28 July 1732. (91) DM700
Ds, 23 July 1718. (88) DM900

Eugenie, Empress of the French, 1826-1920

ALs, 17 Mar [1865/67]. (90) DM460
— 2 Jan 1885. (90) $130
— 12 July [1904?]. (90) DM280
Ls, 25 Feb 1856. (90) DM330
— 15 Feb 1860. (88) $180

Eugenius IV, Pope, 1383-1447
Document, 1 Aug 1431. Doheny collection. (89) $700

Eulenberg, Herbert, 1876-1949
Autograph Ms (2), poems, Dunkler Sommer, & Die Friedrichstrasse in Berlin, [n.d.]. (89) DM360

Eulenburg, August, Graf zu, 1838-1921
ALs, 17 Sept 1871. Schroeder collection. (89) DM750
— 19 Mar 1892. (91) DM280
— 15 June 1907. Schroeder collection. (89) DM250

Eulenburg-Hertefeld, Philipp, Fuerst zu, 1847-1921
ALs, 20 Aug 1878. (90) DM320
— 25 Apr 1900. (90) DM280
— 17 May 1916. Schroeder collection. (89) DM220

Euler, Leonhard, 1707-83
ALs, 30 Sept 1747. 1 p, 4to. To Pierre Louis Moreau de Maupertuis. Informing him of an attack on J. H. G. Justi's prizewinning essay. (91) DM3,300
— 25 June 1766. 1 p, 4to. To the Russian official Taubert. Regretting that he is unable to carry out recipient's wishes since his letter was received after his departure from Berlin. (90) DM5,500

Euripides, c.484-406 B.C. See: Aristophanes & Others

Evans, Dame Edith, 1888-1976
[A collection of her papers, comprising c.200 letters & cards sent to her, address books, autograph diary, typescripts, etc., with related material compiled by H. Hurford-Janes, sold at S on 21 July 1988, lot 245, for £600 to Applebaum.]

Evans, W. B.
Autograph Ms, diaries as schoolmaster in Hackney, Jan 1881 to Dec 1884 & Jan 1889 to Jan 1900. (90) £160

Everett, Edward, 1794-1865
Series of 3 A Ls s, 1848 to 1865. (88) $50
Franking signature, 1837. (89) $110

Everett, Major Edward
Autograph Ms, 6 Ms accounts of excursions to the Hawaiian volcanoes, 1890-95. 114 pp on 78 leaves, 8vo & 4to, with 2 Ms maps. With related material. (91) $2,200

Ewart, Gavin
[A collection of autograph Mss & typescripts of unpbd poems, [n.d.], 25 pp, folio & 4to, with covering letter, sold at S on 15 Dec, lot 148, for £380.]

Ewers, Hanns Heinz, 1871-1943
[A collection of c.212 A Ls s, Ls s, & postcards, sgd, mostly 1921 to 1924, to the publishing house of Georg Mueller, with related material, sold at star on 4 Oct 1989, lot 93, for DM4,000.]
ALs, 24 Oct 1907. (88) DM340
— 28 June 1908. (90) DM280
Ls, 15 Jan 1927. (89) DM340
— 15 Jan 1930. (91) DM280

F

Fabre, Jean Henri, 1823-1915
[An important archive comprising 27 autograph scientific notebooks, 19 watercolors, c.450 letters addressed to Fabre, 46 photographs, & further related material, 1855 to 1915, sold at S on 26 Apr 1990, lot 359, for £16,000 to Marizen.]

Fabricius, Johann, 1644-1729
ALs, 7 July 1714. (89) DM230
— 26 July 1725. (90) DM280

Fairbanks, Douglas, Jr.
Collection of 3 Ls s, 1 telegram & 1 photograph, 1937-67. (91) $250

Fairbanks, Douglas, 1883-1939 —& Griffith, David Wark, 1875-1948
Group photograph, 1927. (89) $380

Fairfax, Brian, 1633-1711
Autograph Ms, commonplace book containing autobiographical & family memoirs, some biblical quotations & poems; compiled for his sons, c.1683 to 1685. About 125 pp & blanks, 4to, in contemp calf. (88) £4,500

FAIRFAX

Fairfax, Thomas, 3d Baron, 1612-71 —& Brereton, William, Sir, 1604-61
Ls, 29 Jan 1643/4. 1 p, folio. To Gen. Monck. Reporting about their victory at Nantwich. (89) £2,800

Fairy Story Filmstrips
Original drawings, (186), gouache illusts for 5 fairy stories issued as filmstrips, [n.d.]. 248mm by 337mm. With related material. (90) £1,050

Fajans, Kasimir, 1887-1975
Collection of ALs & autograph postcard, sgd, 19 July 1969 & 24 May 1972. (88) DM380

Falla, Manuel de, 1876-1946
[A group of 2 autograph musical quotations & postcard photograph, all sgd & inscr, 1942, sold at S on 19 May 1989, lot 407, for £1,300 to Voerster.]
Autograph music, opening 5 bars of the Harpsicord Concerto, scored for harpsichord, violin & cello, with sketches for a vocal work; June 1927. (91) £800
Ms, Danza rituel del fuego, from El amor brujo; [mid 1920s]. 17 pp, folio. In the hand of the arranger Paul Kochanski; with autograph annotations & instructions by de Falla. With related material. (89) $1,400
Series of 7 A Ls s, 5 Apr to 2 June 1913 & [n.d.]. 11 pp, 4to & 8vo. To Michel Dimitri Calvocoressi. About his opera La Vida breve. In French. (88) DM2,200
ALs, 23 Mar 1911. (90) DM280
— 29 Apr [19]23. (89) £600
— 22 Nov 1929. (89) DM320
— Jan 1933. (89) DM270
Ls, 28 Sept 1933. (90) £500
— 26 Nov 1935. (90) £380
Autograph quotation, 2 bars from El retablo de Maese Pedro, sgd; [n.d.]. (91) £550
— Anr, 2 bars from El retablo de Maese Pedro, 1 Jan 1942. (88) £400
Photograph, sgd & inscr, 1939. (90) £400
— Anr, May 1940. (91) £500

AMERICAN BOOK PRICES CURRENT

Fallada, Hans, Pseud of Rudolf Ditzen, 1893-1947
Autograph Ms, novel, Der Jungherr von Stammin, dated 19 Jan 1943. 160 pp, folio & 2 pp, 8vo. Sgd on tp. Orig title Die Weizenballade deleted. Fair copy with some corrections. In orig folder. With typescript carbon copy of his Ein Mann haelt aus. Neuer Schluss - Seite 816 - 1067, in folder with autograph title. (88) DM2,800
Photograph, sgd & inscr, July 1935. (91) DM400

Fallmerayer, Jakob Philipp, 1790-1861
ALs, 10 Nov 1851. (90) DM900

Faneuil, Mary. See: Faneuil, Peter & Faneuil

Faneuil, Peter, 1700-43 —& Faneuil, Mary
[3 autographs by Peter or Mary Faneuil, 1726 to 1743, sold at rce on 28 July 1988, lot 571, for $80.]

Fantin-Latour, Ignace Henri Jean Theodore, 1836-1904
A Ls s (2), 22 June 1899 & [1904]. (89) DM270

Faraday, Michael, 1791-1867
Autograph Ms, part of an article on "Effect of Heat Upon the Magnetic Force of Bodies", [n.d.]. 1 p, folio. (91) $1,800
ALs, 27 May 1826. (89) DM440
— 11 Aug 1832. (90) £700
— 20 Mar 1851. (88) $110
— 19 Dec 1853. (88) DM900
— 14 May 1855. 2 pp, 4to. To Friedrich Woehler. Expressing thanks for a sample of aluminum. (90) DM2,200
— 2 Dec 1857. (88) DM500

Fargo, William George, 1818-81
Ds, 14 Feb 1869. (89) $230
See also: Wells, Henry & Fargo

Farina, Johann Maria
[A letter from the Cologne company, 12 Sept 1833, 3 pp, 4to, to Albert Franck, ordering forms, on letterhead with engraved vignette, with related material, sold at star on 10 Mar 1988, lot 1302, for DM300.]

Farleigh
[2 woodcuts on 1 sheet, 11.5 by 7.75 inches, cover designs for The Prefaces by G. B. Shaw, sold at Ck on 7 Dec 1988, lot 7, for £80.]

Farmer, Andrew
Original drawings, (15), to illus Nathaniel Harris' The Lawrences, 1976. Archives of J. M. Dent & Son. (88) £220

Farnese, Alessandro, Duke of Parma, 1545-92
Ls, 24 Sept 1578. (88) £70

Farouk, King of Egypt, 1920-65
Ls, 25 Jan 1940. (89) £650

Farragut, David G., 1801-70
Ls, 28 Oct 1862. 2 pp, folio. To Gen. Benjamin F. Butler. Thanking for supplies & discussing the defense of Galveston. (90) $2,900
— Jan 1866. (88) $150
Signature, [c.1866]. Beneath a mtd albumen port, 5 by 4 inches. (91) $1,100

Farrell, James T., 1904-79
Collection of 2 A Ls s & 4 Ls s, 1937 to 1949. (89) $375
ALs, 14 Jan 1966[?]. (91) $100
— 16 June 1966. (90) $160

Faulhaber, Michael von, Cardinal, 1869-1952
ALs, 21 Apr 1950. (89) DM400

Fauquier, Francis, 1704?-68
Ds, 16 Sept 1765. (88) $160
— 15 Dec 1767. (90) $750

Faure, Gabriel, 1845-1924
Autograph music, Morceau de lecture for flute & piano, 14 July 1898. 3 pp, folio. 19 bars, sgd, notated on 4 systems of 4 staves each. (91) £2,500
— Autograph music, motet, Ecce fidelis, full score; [n.d.]. 10 pp, folio. With autograph tp & a number of alterations. Double bass part in anr hand. (88) £2,700
A Ls s (2), [n.d.]. (90) DM550
ALs, [6 Mar 1905]. (90) DM220
— 17 Jan [n.y.]. (88) DM360
— [n.d.]. (91) DM300
Autograph quotation, 5 bars from the opening of his Violin Sonata in A major, sgd & dated 27 Dec 1908. (90) £850
Photograph, sgd & inscr, [c.1890]. (90) £450

Fechner, Gustav Theodor, 1801-87
ALs, 14 May 1835. (89) DM340

Feininger, Lyonel, 1871-1956
Series of 3 A Ls s, 4 Dec 1917 to 11 Feb 1918. 6 pp, 4to & 8vo. To [Frau Dr. Mayer]. Important letters dealing with his conception of art, various paintings, Bach's music, etc. (89) DM5,500
— Series of 10 A Ls s (1 incomplete), 1923 to 1936. 15 pp, various sizes. To Erich Scheyer. About his work & Scheyer's collection. 3 letters with woodcut headings. With related material. (88) £1,800
ALs, 19 Dec 1907. (88) DM750
— 16 May 1919. 1 p, 4to. To Fritz Schaefler. Expressing thanks, & sending a block for woodcuts. Including woodcut at head. Crudely repaired. (90) DM1,500
— 27 July 1926. (90) DM460
— 13 July 1932. 1 p, 4to. Recipient unnamed. Authorizing use of a painting to illus a book. With woodcut at head. File holes. (89) DM1,150
— 2 June 1954. (90) DM740
Ls, 7 Nov 1955. (91) DM450
Autograph postcard, sgd, 19 Nov 1919. (90) DM660

Felixmueller, Conrad, 1897-1977
Autograph Ms, essay "Ueber Kunst", Nov 1921. (89) DM700
ALs, [1923]. (91) DM420

Ferber, Edna, 1887-1968
Collection of 4 Ls s & Ns s, 1921 to 1947. (89) $375
Ls s (2), 25 Nov 1923 & 31 Oct 1952. (89) $275

Ferdinand, Herzog von Braunschweig-Wolfenbuettel, 1721-92
Collection of 3 A Ls s & Ls, 1783 to 1789. Schroeder collection. (89) DM420
A Ls s (2), 12 & 28 July 1789. (90) DM360

FERDINAND

Ferdinand, Herzog von Anhalt-Koethen, 1769-1830
ALs, 31 Aug 1807. (90) DM600

Ferdinand, Archduke, 1529-95
Ls, 8 July 1578. (89) DM620
— 3 May 1581. (90) DM260
Ds, 9 Nov 1585. (90) DM300

Ferdinand, Prince of Prussia, 1730-1813
Collection of 13 A Ls s & Ls, 30 Dec 1777 to 23 July 1803. 18 pp, 4to. To Viktor Amadeus Graf Henckel von Donnersmarck (2), his widow Ottilie (11) & Countess Neal. About a variety of matters. (90) DM2,200
A Ls s (2), 27 Apr & 5 Sept 1800. Schroeder collection. (89) DM750
ALs, 20 Dec 1770. Schroeder collection. (89) DM260

Ferdinand, King of Bulgaria, 1861-1948
Autograph transcript, poem, Tag des Gerichtes! Juengster Tag!; [n.d.]. (91) DM260
Ls s (2), 10/22 Jan 1897 & 20 Jan/1 Feb 1898. (90) DM360

Ferdinand, Herzog von Braunschweig-Wolffenbuettel, 1721-92
Ls, 17 Oct 1783. (88) DM550

Ferdinand I, King of Aragon, 1379?-1416
Ds, 30 Dec 1415. 1 p, folio. Order addressed to Sancho Monlon de Carmena to levy money from villages near Zaragoza. (90) £1,600

Ferdinand I, Emperor, 1503-64
Ls, 30 Mar 1530. (89) DM820
— 28 May 1563. (89) DM420
Ds, 11 Mar 1554. 1 p, folio. As Roman King, summons addressed to the knights of Franconia to meet at Mergentheim to decide measures against Albrecht Alcibiades von Brandenburg. (90) DM1,400
— 7 May 1560. (90) DM220
— 21 Oct 1561. (90) DM550
Document, 2 July 1528. (90) DM230
— 29 Apr 1539. (90) DM330

Ferdinand I, Emperor of Austria, 1793-1875
Ls s (2), 23 Nov 1837 & 22 Dec 1847. Byer collection. (90) $250
Ds, 23 May 1840. (90) DM700
— 29 July 1841. 4 leaves, 351mm by 270mm, in red velvet bdg. Patent of nobility for Golub Lazarovits. With ornamental borders throughout & achievement of the arms. (91) DM1,600
Autograph endorsement, sgd, 2 Mar 1835. (90) DM550

Ferdinand II, Emperor, 1578-1637
Ls, 29 Sept 1617. (89) DM800
— 30 Oct 1621. (88) DM800
— 28 Dec 1628. 2 pp, folio. To Franz Christoph von Khevenhueller. Concerning the conferral of a decoration on the Count of Dietrichstein. (91) DM1,800
— 1 Dec 1635. (90) DM900
Ds, 1 Feb 1621. 1 p, 42cm by 57.5cm. Ptd promulgation of the ban of the empire against Friedrich V, Elector Palatine [& King of Bohemia]. (91) DM2,200
— 1625. (91) DM500
— 20 July 1627. (90) £600
— 29 Apr 1628. (88) DM800
— 13 Nov 1628. (90) £80
— 15 Mar 1635. 1 p, 50cm by 60cm. Patent of nobility & grant of arms for Valentin Huniady. With painting of the arms in gold & colors. (89) DM1,500

Ferdinand III, Emperor, 1608-57
Ls, 8 Feb 1629. (90) DM400
— 10 June 1636. (89) DM600
— 7 Jan 1641. (89) $175
— 20 Apr 1644. (89) DM750
— 29 May 1652. (89) DM280
Ds, 3 Aug 1645. (90) DM1,000
— 20 Feb 1655. (90) DM750
Autograph endorsement, 29 Jan 1638. (90) DM400

Ferdinand IV, King of Castile & Leon, 1285-1312
Ds, [1304]. 1 p, vellum, 540mm by 430mm. Charter granting the estate of Deleytosa in Plascencia to Don Durant Sanchez & his heirs in lieu of the estate of Almazar; listing c.70 wit-

nesses. With illuminated Royal Seal painted in the center; leaden bulla detached. (90) £2,200

Ferdinand IV, Roman King & King of Bohemia, 1633-54
Ls, 7 Oct 1647. (89) DM450

Ferdinand V, King of Spain, 1452-1516
Ls, 18 Dec 1505. 1 p, 4to. To Amador de Aliaga. Instructing him to give a horse from the estate of Luis Tristan to Bartolomeo de Brizanos. With receipt by Brizanos on verso. (91) DM1,200
— 9 Feb 1508. 8 pp, folio. To the Cardinal Archbishop of Toledo. Requesting his opinion on 3 enclosures (included) relating to negotiations with France, Germany & Rome. (88) £1,050
— 19 Dec [1511?]. (91) £500
— 20 Jan 1515. (88) £520
Series of Ds s, 3 Ds s, 23 Dec 1486 to 30 Dec 1500. As King of Aragon, about different matters. (90) £1,500
Ds s (2) 30 Oct 1512 & 2 Dec 1515. 2 pp, folio. As King of Aragon, confiscation of the property of Anthon de Falces, & appointment for Miguel de Gurrea. (90) £1,200
Ds, 29 June 1476. 1 p, 4to. About regulations concerning Navarre. (91) $3,500
— 28 Apr 1498. 1 p, folio. Summons addressed to Don Miguel de Gurrea to attend the investiture of his daughter Isabella as successor to the throne of Aragon. In Latin. (90) DM1,600

Ferdinand V, King of Spain, 1452-1516 —&
Isabella I, Queen of Spain, 1451-1504
Ls, 1490. 1 p, c.300mm by 300mm. Recipient unnamed. On military matters. Doheny collection. (89) $3,800
Ds s (2) 2 & 20 Oct 1500. 3 pp, folio. Verdict in a dispute over tents surrendered by Moors, & order to stable horses; both addressed to the city of Loja. (90) £2,600
— **Ds s (2)** 2 & 20 Oct 1500. 3 pp, folio. Orders addressed to the city of Loja. (91) £1,800
Ds, 12 Feb 1475. (88) £1,000
— 13 May 1475. 1 p, folio. Order addressed to Enrique de Guzman to sequestrate the town of Gelves from Juan Tellez de Giron. (90) £1,300
— 25 Oct 1475. (90) £800
— 23 Mar 1480. 3 pp, 4to, vellum. Confirmation of an agreement between the constable of Castile & the marquess of Villena regarding the castle of Garcimunoz. (89) $3,250
— 23 Nov 1483. 1 p, 8vo. Informing Alonso de Monte Mayor that he will be receiving instructions from the Conde de Cabra. Cut from larger sheet. (89) £1,050
— 2 Oct 1492. 1 p, 210mm by 210mm. Authorization for the people of Cenete & Guadix to have communal rights for cutting wood & grazing cattle. (91) £2,600
— 7 Sept 1493. 1 p, 4to. Order to Juan de Ribera to raze the fortress at Cenicero. Tipped to larger leaf. Barrett collection. (89) $3,500
— 16 Oct 1496. 1 p, vellum, 308mm by 495mm. Ratification of the treaty renewing the Holy League. Middendorf collection. (89) $12,000
— 28 Feb 1503. 1 p, folio, in limp vellum bdg. Appointment of Diego Enriquez, Conde de Alba de Liste, as Alcalde of the fortress of Zamora. (91) $3,800

Ferdinand VI, King of Spain, 1713-59
Document, 11 Oct 1755. (89) £230

Ferdinand VII, King of Spain, 1784-1833
Ls, 2 Sept 1824. (91) $175

Ferdinand von Habsburg-Este, Archduke, 1781-1850
Series of 32 Ls s, 9 May to 1 Aug 1815. 70 pp, folio. To Prince Ferdinand von Hessen-Homburg, General in the Austrian army. Giving army orders & instructions about a variety of matters. With related material. (88) DM2,100

Fermi, Enrico, 1901-54
Signature, 1946. (91) $400

Fermor, Patrick Leigh
Autograph Ms, A Time of Gifts, [before 1977]. About 450 pp, mostly on rectos. Heavily revised. (88) £1,250

Fernow, Ludwig, 1763-1808
ALs, 18 Dec 1805. Albrecht collection. (91) SF500

Ferrari, Andrea Giacomo, Cardinal, Saint, 1850-1921
ALs, [8 Dec] 1920. (89) DM260

Ferreri, Bernardo
Ms, Last Will & Testament, & 8 other notarial documents, 1565 to 1572. [Palermo, Sicily, c.1572]. 87 leaves (27 blank), 305mm by 212mm. Contemp olive mor over pastebds profusely gilt. In Italian & Latin by several scribes in fine calligraphic sloping italic hands. Abbey collection. (89) £14,000

Ferrier, Kathleen, 1912-53
— GRUNWALD, HELEN. - Ms, In Praise of Kathleen Ferrier; [c.1953]. About 85 pp, 8vo, in def black mor. Memoir of the singer, illus with over 60 drawings, mostly in ink. (90) £350

Fesch, Joseph, Cardinal, 1763-1839
ALs, 24 June 1826. (89) DM400
Ls, [7 Feb 1805]. (88) DM200

Feuchtwanger, Lion, 1884-1958
ALs, 16 July 1919. (90) DM480
— [n.d.], "Whitsun". (90) DM260
Series of 5 Ls s, 2 Feb 1931 to 5 Sept 1938. (91) DM800

Feuerbach, Anselm, 1829-80
Autograph Ms, poem, El sospiros! (Der Seufzer), [n.d.]. (89) DM480
ALs, 1 Feb 1872. 2 pp, 8vo. To Henriette Feuerbach. Expressing satisfaction with his new painting & announcing his visit. (90) DM1,100
— [14 July 1872]. (91) DM480
— 30 Apr 1874. (90) DM400
Photograph, sgd, [n.d.]. (90) DM340

Feuerbach, Ludwig, 1804-72
ALs, 11 Jan 1842. 2 pp, 8vo. To an unnamed author. About the reception of his Vorlaeufige Thesen zur Reformation der Philosophie. (88) DM1,400
— 5 May 1866. (91) DM650

Fibich, Zdenek, 1850-1900
Autograph music, "Aus dem Cyklus 'Aus den Bergen". (90) DM550

Fichte, Hubert, 1935-86
Autograph Ms, draft of an interview, sgd & inscr later, 13 Apr 1980. (90) DM320

Fichte, Johann Gottlieb, 1762-1814
ALs, 10 June 1809. (88) £400
— 10 June 1809. 4 pp, 4to. To Freiherr von Altenstein. Discussing plans for the projected university in Berlin. Albrecht collection. (91) SF4,200
— [n.d.]. 2 pp, 8vo. To an unnamed pbr. Reminding him of an outstanding fee. (90) DM2,000

Fidus, Pseud. of Hugo Hoeppener, 1868-1948
Collection of 3 A Ls s & 2 autograph postcards, sgd, 4 Sept 1903 to 13 Feb 1942. (88) DM260

Field, Cyrus W., 1819-92
Check, sgd, 13 Feb 1878. (88) $60

Field, Eugene, 1850-95
[A collection of 5 Ms items by Field, including self-port, sgd, a Latin poem, sgd, etc., 1872 to 1894, with related material, sold at P on 26 Oct 1988, lot 75, for $1,100.] Barrett collection.
[3 autograph Mss of poems, A Paraphrase of Heine. (Lyric Intermezzo); Beranger's To My Old Coat; & Egyptian Folk-Song: Mother and Sphinx; 1889 & [n.d.], 8 pp, 4to, all sgd, sold at CNY on 7 June 1990, lot 45, for $400.]
Autograph Ms (2), poem, The Fisherman's Feast, 6 eight-line stanzas, [n.d.], & 1 eight-line stanza from Under the Greenwood Tree, 9 Jan 1889. Doheny collection. (89) $600
— Autograph Ms)2), poems, The Mole upon My Cheek & Over the Hills and Far Away, 4 Jan 1892 & 1894. 6 pp, 4to. Including colored drawing & ANs to Mrs. May. Both sgd; 1 tipped to newspaper clipping of ptd version. Koch Foundation. (90) $1,100
Autograph Ms, Extinct Monsters, [n.d.]. 3 pp, folio, on rectos only. Calligraphic text with 15 drawings. With note of authentication attached at end.

Doheny collection. (89) $3,000
— Autograph Ms, poem, Holly and Ivy. (91) $600
— Autograph Ms, poem, Little Boy Blue, 3 eight-line stanzas, sgd; [n.d.]. 1 p, 249mm by 99mm, tipped on card. In blue levant mor bdg by Riviere. Doheny collection. (89) $3,800
Autograph transcript, poem, Song and Heart, fair copy, sgd; Feb 1889. Doheny collection. (89) $550
— Autograph transcript, poem, The Old Story, fair copy, sgd; 17 Nov 1889. Doheny collection. (89) $950
Collection of 2 A Ls s & 3 A Ns s, 9 May 1889 to 2 Mar 1893. Doheny collection. (89) $420
ALs, 5 Nov 1892. Doheny collection. (89) $320

Field, Eugene, 1850-95 —& Wilson, Francis, 1854-1935
Group photograph, [1880s?]. (88) $175

Fields, W. C., 1880-1946
ALs, 17 Feb 1940. 4 pp, 8vo. To Miss Michael. Joking about various people. Sgd Boss-Head man-great man-Fieldsie Old boy. (91) $1,300

Fiesco, Eleonora Cibo, Marchesa di Massa, 1523-94
Ls, 2 Sept 1571. 1 p, folio. To Conte Francesco Durbeche. Recommending Benedetto di Bartolo to administer the church of Santa Christina at Papiano. (91) DM1,050

Figueroa, Jose
ADs, 20 June 1835. (89) $600

Fillmore, Millard, 1800-74
[An interleaved copy of the Constitution of the United States of America... Printed for the Use of the House of Representatives. Wash., 1853, in contemp mor gilt, sgd by Fillmore, 26 Feb 1853, 6 members of his cabinet, & 240 members of Congress, sold at CNY on 18 Nov 1988, lot 131, for $3,800.]
Autograph Ms (2), details of the Fillmore family genealogy, sgd & dated 29 Jan 1819 & 23 Aug 1853. 11 pp, folio & 4to. (89) $2,250
Collection of ALs & Ds, 11 Sept 1856 & 11 Feb 1853. 4 pp, 4to. To Henry S. Randall, thanking for information about Mr. Goodwin's request for money. Order to affix the US Seal. Sang collection. (91) $3,000
A Ls s (2), 24 Sept 1850 & 25 May 1852. 3 pp, 4to & 8vo. To J. L. Whitney, informing him of the sale of his land in Saginaw County. To Gov. Gibbs, regretting not having seem him. 1st ALs repaired. (89) $1,500
ALs, 9 Oct 1836. (90) $325
— 15 Jan 1839. (89) £750
— 27 Jan 1840. (91) $1,000
— 27 Dec 1840 [?]. (90) $900
— 26 Sept 1841. Byer collection. (90) $850
— 3 July 1842. (91) $300
— 4 Dec 1849. (91) $400
— 10 Dec 1849. (91) $550
— 18 July 1850. 1 p, 4to. To Messrs. W. H. Beebee & Co. Ordering a hat. With engraved port. (90) $1,500
— 8 May 1851. 2 pp, 4to. To John Bell. Responding to a complaint regarding an appointment & regretting he could not see him before his departure. Pratt collection. (89) $3,250
— 23 Oct 1852. (91) $900
— 8 Oct 1856. McVitty collection. (90) $600
— 29 Oct 1856. (88) £750
— 22 Feb 1860. (89) $275
— 26 June 1861. (91) $450
— 14 Apr 1865. (91) $320
— 13 Jan 1868. (88) $300
— 4 Oct 1870. (90) $650
— 31 Dec 1873. Whiton collection. (88) $750
AL, [n.d.]. (89) $120
Ls, 29 June 1852. 1 p, 4to. To Sec of the Interior A. H. H. Stuart. Suggesting closing the department because of Henry Clay's death. Rosenbloom collection. (88) $4,250
— 6 July 1852. (91) $425
ANs, [n.d.]. (89) $125
Ds, 27 Sept 1850. (91) $950
— 5 Sept 1851. (90) $650
— 2 Sept 1852. (89) $350
— 20 Sept 1852. (88) $150
— 4 Jan 1853. 1 p, 4to. Order to affix the Great Seal to a remission of penalties granted to James Garet & James A.

FILLMORE

Hooper. Fold splits repaired. Ruddy collection. (88) $1,900

Cut signature, 2 Sept 1852. (89) $180
— Anr, 27 Dec 1871. (91) $150
— Anr, [n.d.]. (90) $120

Franking signature, [5 Oct 1860]. (89) $220
— Anr, [1 Dec n.y.]. Alexander collection. (90) $160
— Anr, [22 Dec n.y.]. (89) $190
See also: Lincoln, Abraham

Finch, Daniel, 2d Earl of Nottingham, 1647-1730
Series of 7 A Ls s, 1692. (89) £65

Firbank, Ronald, 1886-1926
[A collection of letters & memorabilia relating to Firbank, including photograph, sgd & presentation copy of Santal, sold at S on 15 Dec 1988, lot 73, for £1,600.] £650

Collection of ALs & photograph, sgd, 17 Nov 1924 & 1917. 4 pp, 8vo, & 148mm by 100mm. To Montgomery Evans. Concerning a trans of Prancing Nigger into German, mentioning [Gertrude] Stein, etc. Koch Foundation. (90) $2,000

Ds, 23 Apr 1926. (91) $350

Firmian, Leopold Anton, Graf von, Archbishop of Salzburg, 1679-1744
Ds, 27 July 1737. (90) DM900

First Ladies of the United States
[A commemorative postal cover, 20 Aug 1987, sgd by Jacqueline Kennedy, Lady Bird Johnson, Betty Ford, Rosalynn Carter & Barbara Bush, sold at wa on 20 Oct 1990, lot 56, for $350.]
[A color photograph of the White House, 4to, sgd by Bess Truman, Mamie Eisenhower, Jackie Kennedy, Lady Bird Johnson, Betty Ford & Rosalyn Carter sold at wa on 1 Oct 1988, lot 129, for $260.]
See also: Presidents of the United States & First Ladies of the United States

Firth, W. P.
Series of 15 A Ls s, 1840 to 1889 & [n.d.]. (88) £380

AMERICAN BOOK PRICES CURRENT

Fischer, Johann Georg, 1816-97
ALs, 10 Dec 1866. (89) DM320

Fischer, Robert James ("Bobby")
Autograph Ms, composition book containing class notes, homework assignments & various drawings, 1956. (88) $600
— Autograph Ms, score sheet of a game with Rubinetti at the world championship in Buenos Aires, 9 Aug 1970. (88) $550

Typescript, My 60 Memorable Games, 1968. Over 400 pp, 4to; unbound. With numerous autograph corrections. (88) $5,500

Signature, [n.d.]. (91) $100

Fischhof, Joseph, 1804-1857
ALs, 11 Nov 1829. (90) DM350

Fisher, Vardis
Collection of 2 Ls s & ANs, 1934 to 1952. (89) $100

Fitchew, Dorothy
Original drawings, (262), to illus M. Archives of J.M.Dent & Son. (88) £400

Fitzgeffrey, Charles, 1575?-1638
ALs, 24 Mar 1633. (88) £200

FitzGerald, Edward, 1809-83
ALs, [5 Feb 1848]. Doheny collection. (89) $700
— 1 July [1862?]. (91) £300
— 25 Oct [n.y.]. Doheny collection. (89) $420

Fitzgerald, F. Scott, 1896-1940
ALs, 28 Dec 1920. (88) $1,000
ANs, [n.d.]. (91) $850
Check, sgd, 17 Nov 1936. (88) $350

Fitzherbert, Maria Anne, 1756-1837
Series of 5 A Ls s, [1830s]. (88) £700

Fitzroy, Robert, 1805-65
Series of 53 A Ls s, 13 Oct 1817 to 2 Oct 1836. 276 pp, 4to & 8vo. To his family, primarily his sister Fanny. Chronicling his training as midshipman & his service as captain of HMS Beagle. With related material. (91) $34,000

Fitzsimmons, Thomas, 1741-1811
ALs, 8 Aug 1800. Byer collection. (90) $175

Flagg, James Montgomery, 1877-1960
Series of 11 Ls s, 18 Nov 1947 to 7 Mar 1949. (88) $900

Flagg, James Montgomery, 1877-1960 —&
Hart, William Surrey, 1862?-1946
Group photograph, [n.d.]. (91) $130

Flaubert, Gustave, 1821-80
Autograph Ms, reading notes [for his novel Salammbo]; [before 1862]. 22 pp, folio. (90) £3,400

ALs, 14 Aug [1857]. 1 p, 4to, in goatskin bdg. To Charles Baudelaire. Asking for details of the charges brought against Baudelaire after publication of Les Fleurs du Mal. Koch Foundation. (90) $15,000

— [1863], "Wednesday". (90) £600

— 16 Nov 1866. Thorek collection. (88) $400

— [1869?]. (91) DM700

— [Mar 1874?]. 1 p, 8vo. To [Ivan Turgenev?]. Regarding seats for the premiere of his comedy Le Candidat. With related material. (90) DM1,100

— [Nov 1877]. (88) £600

— [n.d.]. 1 p, 8vo. Recipient unnamed. Referring to a disagreement. (90) DM1,100

Flecker, James Elroy, 1884-1915
Autograph Ms (2), poems, The Golden Journey to Samarkand, & Bryan of Brittany; [pbd 1913]. 8 pp, 4to. Drafts, with emendations; differing from ptd versions. Both sgd. With anr, The Ballad of Iskander, 1910. Bradley Martin Mss. (90) $3,250

Autograph Ms, poem, Santorin, [before 26 June 1912]. (90) £400

— Autograph Ms, poem, The Gates of Damascus; [c.1912]. (90) £700

Fleetwood, Charles, d.1692
ALs, 10 Sept 1650. (88) £450

Fleetwood, William, 1656-1723
Autograph Ms, sermons preached at various places, 1692-1720. (88) £750

Fleming, Sir Alexander, 1881-1955
Autograph Ms, script for a BBC radio broadcast, describing the discovery & development of Penicillin, Aug 1945. 7 pp, size not stated, on rectos only. With extensive autograph revisions. In folding case. (89) £13,500

Photograph, sgd, [n.d.]. (90) $600

Signature, [n.d.]. (91) $300

Fleming, Christopher le
[A collection of A Ls s & Ls s, sent to him Gerald Finzi, Elizabeth Poston, C, W. Orr, John Coates & others, sold at S on 6 May, lot 354, for £700 to Finzi.]

Fleming, Ian, 1908-64
Autograph Ms (2), diary containing cash accounts for 1923, & list of restaurants, names, books, etc., [c.1930]. 21 pp & blanks, in 2 small notebooks. 1 sgd. (89) £2,200

— Autograph Ms)2), notes for From Russia with Love, [n.d.]. 6 pp, folio; partly in notebook with initial leaves excised. (89) £8,800

Autograph Ms, article, Bang Bang. Kiss Kiss; [1956]. 5 pp, folio. Explaining how he began writing; with revisions. (89) £6,200

— Autograph Ms, notes for You Only Live Twice, [c.1961]. 39 pp & blanks, 6 by 4 inches (notebook). (89) £12,000

Photograph, sgd, [n.d.]. (91) £320

Fleury, Andre Hercule de, Cardinal, 1653-1743
Ls, 6 Jan 1738. (90) DM200

Flex, Walter, 1887-1917
Autograph postcard, sgd, 10 Jan 1917. (90) DM480

Fliess, Wilhelm, 1858-1928
Ls, 21 Nov 1916. (91) DM380

Flint, William Russell, 1880-1969
Original drawing, watercolor, man chasing Fortune on her wheel, sgd & dated 1912; to illus The Monk's Tale in Chaucer's Canterbury Tales, 1913. 275mm by 220mm; framed. (90) £4,300

Flint

Collection of c.70 A Ls s & autograph postcards, sgd, 6 Apr 1946 to 1 Dec 1969. (91) £450
Series of 16 A Ls s, 28 Mar 1939 to 8 Apr 1941. (88) £350
— Series of c.50 A Ls s, 1939 to 1965. (89) £950

Flora, Paul
Collection of ANs & orig drawing, [n.d.]. (91) DM430
Autograph sentiment, [n.d.]. (88) DM300
— Anr, sgd, 12 Aug 1980. (90) DM650
— Anr, [n.d.]. (90) DM380

Flores, Venancio, 1809-68
ALs, 2 Nov 1864. (91) $80

Florus, Lucius Annaeus
Ms, Epitoma de Tito Livio. [Milan, 2d quarter of 15th cent]. 33 leaves (4 lacking?), vellum, 285mm by 200mm. Def contemp green tawed skin over pastebds. In a small rounded gothic bookhand, with alternative readings in smaller script in margins. With large historiated initial. Dampstained. (90) £4,800

Flory, Paul John, 1910-85
Ls, 12 May 1977. (90) DM300

Flotow, Friedrich von, 1812-83
ALs, 11 Aug 1858. (89) DM620
— 14 June 1864. (90) DM900
— 4 May 1866. (90) DM870
— 8 Jan 1871. (88) DM800
— 17 Jan 1878. (88) DM950
— [n.d.]. (89) DM540
— [n.d.]. (91) DM800
Ls, 12 Jan 1853. (91) DM550

Flynn, Errol, 1909-59
Series of 10 A Ls s, 14 Apr to 18 May 1937. 47 pp, size not stated. To his wife Lili Damita. Discussing his work & their relationship. (90) $4,200
— Series of 5 A Ls s, 14 Oct 1938 to Nov 1939. 16 pp, mostly 8vo. About various subjects, his work, gossip, etc. (90) $2,000
— Series of 4 A Ls s, 1942 to 1944. Length not stated. To his son Sean. Contents not stated. With related material. (90) $2,000
A Ls s (2), 29 & 31 Mar [1937]. 8 pp, 8vo

& 16mo. To his wife Lili Damita. Reporting from the front during a visit to Spain. (90) $2,000
Ls, 23 Mar 1959. (91) $225
Photograph, sgd, [n.d.]. (91) $400
Photograph, sgd & inscr, [n.d.]. (90) $200
Signature, [n.d.]. (91) $110

Foch, Ferdinand, 1851-1929
[A "C Form" message sent to Field Marshal John French by Foch, 11 Nov 1918, 1 p, 8vo, announcing cessation of hostilities, marked as received from the Eiffel Tower at the Dublin Wireless G.H.Q., with related material, sold at pn on 22 Mar 1990, lot 63, for £200 to Doran.]
Autograph Ms, essay on Napoleon, sgd & dated 5 May 1921. (88) £420
ALs, 5 Aug 1923. (91) DM220

Foerster, Friedrich Wilhelm, 1869-1966
A Ls s (2), 15 Nov 1916 & 26 Mar 1917. (90) DM250

Foerster, Josef Bohuslav, 1859-1951
A Ls s (2), 25 Mar 1919 & 31 Oct 1920. (90) DM320

Foerster-Nietzsche, Elisabeth, 1846-1935. See: Nietzsche, Friedrich

Folkard, Charles
Original drawing, Gulliver in the sea, pulling 2 ships, in ink & watercolor; sgd & dated [19]10. (90) £500
— Original drawing, man being served refreshments in a garden, to illus Helena Nyblom's Jolly Calle and other Swedish Fairy Tales, 1912. (90) £800

Fontaine, Joan
Collection of 5 A Ls s, 5 Ls s, 4 autograph postcards, sgd, & 2 Christmas cards, [1940s to 1960s, & n.d.]. (89) $80

Fontana, Felice, 1730-1805
ALs, 8 Mar 1766. (91) $150

Fontane, Theodor, 1819-98
[An important collection of Mss, containing drafts for parts of Vor dem Sturm, Wanderungen durch die Mark Brandenburg, Effi Briest & Der Stechlin, c.140 pp, folio, sold at star on 30 Nov 1988, lots 90 - 93, for DM170.000.]

[A group of varied Mss, fragments of works, & literary drafts & sketches, c.1878 to 1886, about 35 pp, folio, including some mtd newspaper clippings, sold at star on 4 Oct 1989, lot 100, for DM16,000.]

Autograph Ms (2), fragments & drafts for his autobiographical works Meine Kinderjahre, & Von Zwanzig bis Dreissig; [c.1892-96]. About 68 pp on 53 leaves, mostly folio. Including 8 pp of drafts for other works. (90) DM44,000

Autograph Ms, 5 drafts & sketches outlining literary projects, [n.d.]. 21 pp, folio. (90) DM17,000

— Autograph Ms, 5 drafts of unfinished essays dealing with literary criticism or reviewing plays; [n.d.]. About 50 pp, folio. (90) DM17,000

— Autograph Ms, draft for an unpbd chapter about Potsdam for his Wanderungen durch die Mark Brandenburg, [n.d.]. 2 pp, folio. (90) DM5,000

— Autograph Ms, poem, beginning "Was noch fehlt ist eine Spritze", sgd Th:F., inscr to [his wife] E[milie] & dated 24 Dec 1858. 2 pp, 8vo. (90) DM3,800

— Autograph Ms, proverbs, poems or popular devotional songs, partly used in his novel Vor dem Sturm, 1878. 7 pp, folio. (90) DM4,500

— Autograph Ms, working draft for his novella Irrungen und Wirrungen, fragment; [c.1884]. 11 pp, folio. Newspaper clipping, Ludwig Pietsch's obituary for Theodor Storm, with some autograph lines by Fontane, mtd on verso. (90) DM13,000

Series of 3 A Ls s, 1 to 29 July 1862. 16 pp, 8vo. To his wife Emilie. Family letters. With related material. (89) DM12,000

— Series of 23 A Ls s, 23 Jan 1879 to 13 Mar 1890. 87 pp, 8vo. To Gustav Karpeles. Important literary correspondence, outlining projects, etc. (91) DM26,000

— Series of 3 A Ls s, 9 July 1891 to 11 Aug 1895. 12 pp, 8vo. To George von Graevenitz & his mother Julie (1). About recipient's literary work. (91) DM4,000

ALs, 12 Sept 1859. 4 pp, 8vo. To his wife Emilie. Family letter, & reporting about his work. (88) DM2,000

— 20 Sept 1859. 6 pp, 8vo. To his wife Emilie. About his travel plans, their financial situation, friends, etc. Corner chewed by rodents. (88) DM5,500

— 31 May 1861. 4 pp, 8vo. To his wife Emilie. Reporting about a trip to Rheinsberg & Ruppin. Corner chewed by rodents. (88) DM2,200

— 23 May 1862. 8 pp, 8vo. To his wife Emilie. Reporting in detail about his activities in her absence. (90) DM3,700

— 4 June 1862. 12 pp, 8vo. To his wife Emilie. Family letter, & reporting about his social life in Berlin. (88) DM6,000

— 10 June 1862. 10 pp, 8vo. To his wife Emilie. About his travel plans, George Eliot's novels, & other matters. Corner def. (89) DM6,000

— 17 June 1862. 8 pp, 8vo. To his wife. About travels for his book, friends, the purchase of a house, etc. (91) DM4,500

— 17 Aug 1864. 4 pp, 8vo. To Ferdinand von Quast. Making inquiries for a chapter in his Wanderungen durch die Mark Brandenburg. (90) DM1,600

— 10 Sept 1864. 3 pp, 4to. To his wife. Sending news about his journey to Copenhagen. Seal tear. (90) DM3,000

— 21 Aug 1865. 4 pp, 8vo. To the Ed [Rudolf von Decker]. Thanking for a fee & discussing the publication of Der Schleswig-Holsteinische Krieg. (89) DM3,200

— 28 Aug 1868. 8 pp, 8vo. To his wife Emilie. Chatting about his daily routine at Erdmannsdorf. (88) DM3,000

— 18 Oct 1868. 4 pp, 8vo. To his wife Emilie. Informing her about discussions regarding the admission of von Heyden to the Ruetli group, & family news. (90) DM4,600

— 24 Oct 1868. 8 pp, 8vo. To his wife Emilie. About her travel plans, & reporting about family & acquaintances. (89) DM8,600

— 25 Apr 1870. 8 pp, 8vo. To his wife Emilie. About her journey to London, his activities, their son Georg, etc. (89) DM6,200

— 4 May 1871. 4 pp, 8vo. To his wife Emilie. Reporting about his travels in France. In pencil. (90) DM6,500

FONTANE

— 9 Nov 1871. 3 pp, size not stated. To [Frau Brose?]. Giving names of art historians & architects. (88) DM1,400
— 11 Aug 1876. 2 pp, 8vo. To Christian Friedrich Scherenberg. Inviting him for dinner. Sgd Lafontaine Th. E. (89) DM1,600
— 30 Sept 1881. 1 p, 8vo. To an unnamed painter. About a date. (90) DM1,600
— 23 Apr 1884. 2 pp, 8vo. To J. Steinthal. Sending a poem (included, sgd). (90) DM2,200
— 6 June 1885. 4 pp, 8vo. To his son Friedel. Family letter, & comparing the coastal regions to Brandenburg. (91) DM3,600
— 30 Dec 1885. 4 pp, 8vo. To his son Friedrich. Family letter. Sgd Dein Alter. With postscript by Emilie Fontane. (89) DM4,000
— 3 Jan 1886. 2 pp, 8vo. To an unnamed lady. Thanking for congratulations on his birthday. (90) DM1,500
— 31 Aug 1888. 1 p, 8vo. Recipient unnamed. Thanking for a theater ticket. (90) DM1,050
— 20 Jan 1890. (91) £650
— 10 June 1890. 2 pp, 8vo. To [Johannes Proelss?]. Explaining why he cannot participate in a project, & discussing truth & beauty. (90) DM2,200
— 23 Apr 1891. 2 pp, 8vo. To Geheimrat [Max Jordan?]. Thanking for his support after being awarded the Schiller Prize. (88) DM1,700
— 18 Aug 1891. 2 pp, 8vo. To an unnamed lady. Sending congratulations on her birthday & talking about his trip to Amrum & Helgoland. (88) DM1,900
— 28 Feb 1894. 2 pp, 8vo. To Gustav Albrecht. Thanking for his book. (89) DM1,600
— 7 Sept 1896. 2 pp, 8vo. To Emil Moebis. Thanking for a book about Ferdinand Moehring. (90) DM1,700
— 17 Sept 1898. 1 p, 8vo. Recipient unnamed. Expecting to find some information in Riedel's Codex diplomaticus. (88) DM1,500
AL, [c.1876-87]. 1 p, folio. To Siegfried von Quast. Draft, discussing the publication of Bernhard Feldmann's Miscellanea historica. With related material. (89) DM2,200
Photograph, sgd, 26 Jan 1897; c.105mm by 65mm. Half-length; sgd on verso. (88) DM1,300

Forain, Jean Louis, 1852-1931
ALs, 23 Feb 1889. (90) DM320

Forcade, Friedrich Wilhelm von, 1699-1765
ALs, 26 Apr 1727. (90) DM250
— 24 Sept 1737. Schroeder collection. (89) DM620
— 5 Sept 1760. Schroeder collection. (89) DM650

Forchondt, Marcus
[A group of 6 letters written from Vienna to his brothers Willem & Justus at Antwerp, 1698 to 1708, 7 pp, folio & 4to, reporting about his commercial activities, mostly the sale of paintings & other artwork, sold at star on 4 Oct 1989, lot 689, for DM3,200.]

Ford, Betty. See: Ford, Gerald R. & Ford

Ford, Gerald R.
Autograph transcript, Presidential Oath of Office, 9 Aug 1974. Inscr & sgd on page following half-title (on verso of port) of the Public Papers of the Presidents of the United States. Gerald R. Ford, 1974, Wash., 1975. (91) $5,500
Typescript, statement regarding his Presidency, 9 Aug 1974. (90) $210
Ls s (2), 13 Dec 1950 & 30 Oct 1968. (90) $150
Ls, 6 Dec 1963. (91) $275
— 7 Dec 1965. (90) $350
— 27 Nov 1973. (90) $250
— 12 Feb 1976. (91) $550
— 11 June 1976. (91) $900
— 21 June 1976. (91) $225
— 19 Jan 1977. (90) $500
— 26 Apr 1977. (89) $225
— 31 Mar 1980. (90) $225
— 9 Feb 1981. (90) $150
— 14 June 1990. (91) $100
Group photograph, [n.d.]. (91) $85
— Anr, [n.d.]. (91) $75
Photograph, sgd, 27 Aug [19]74. (91) $350
— Anr, [n.d.]. (89) $55
Photograph, sgd & inscr, [n.d.]. (91) $100

Ptd photograph, sgd, [n.d.]. (89) $65
Signature, [9 Aug 1974]. (91) $130
— Anr, on cover of a copy of his speech at the Kennedy Center, 3 July 1976. (89) $70

Ford, Gerald R. —& Brandt, Willy
Group photograph, with Henry A. (91) $100

Ford, Gerald R. —& Burger, Warren
Group photograph, [n.d.]. (90) $350

Ford, Gerald R. See: Carter, James Earl ("Jimmy") & Ford

Ford, Gerald R. —& Ford, Betty
Christmas card, [n.d.]. (91) $85

Ford, Gerald R. See: Nixon, Richard M. & Ford

Ford, Harrison —& Others
Group photograph, Ford, Mark Hamill & Carrie Fisher, in the film Star Wars, [n.d.]. (91) $130

Ford, Henry, 1863-1947
Ls, 23 July 1927. 2 pp, 4to. To Herman Bernstein. Reiterating his apology for anti-Jewish articles pbd in the Dearborn Independent. (91) $10,000
Photograph, sgd, [n.d.]. 6.5 by 9 inches. Framed. (91) $1,100

Forel, Auguste, 1848-1931
ALs, 29 Mar 1887. (91) DM850
— 7 Jan 1904. (91) DM530

Forester, Cecil Scott, 1899-1966
Ls, 26 Dec 1924. (90) £160

Formey, Johann Heinrich Samuel, 1711-97
ALs, 13 May 1786. (91) DM900

Forrest, Nathan B., 1821-77
ALs, 24 Oct 1868. (88) $600
Ds, 1 Sept 1869. (91) $400
— 1 Sept 1869. (90) $250
Photograph, [c.1865]. (91) $800

Forster, Edward Morgan, 1879-1970
Autograph Ms, humorous verse on his gout, 14 July 1959. (91) £550
— Autograph Ms, radio talk on Proust [broadcast on 31 Mar 1943]. 9 pp, folio. Working draft. Koch Foundation. (90) $1,500
Series of c.49 A Ls s, 1907 to 1937. 125 pp, mostly 4to & 8vo. To Syred Ross Masood. Informative letters chronicling their friendship, discussing literature, general news, etc. With related material. (89) £10,000
— Series of 14 A Ls s, 1934 to 1957. (91) £1,000
A Ls s (2), 21 Feb & 11 Aug 1912. (89) $850
— A Ls s (2), 1 & 6 Sept 1936. (88) £650
— A Ls s (2), 29 Oct 1948 & 4 Apr 1949. (89) £150
ALs, 26 July 1942. (89) $425
— 6 Feb 1950. (91) £110
— 4 Apr 1950. (90) $210
Collection of 2 A Ls & postcard, [8 Sept 1934] & [n.d.]. (88) £130
ANs, 24 Nov 1961. (90) $130

Forster, Edward Morgan, 1879-1970 —& Britten, Benjamin, 1913-76
[The typescript (carbon copy) draft of Forster's libretto for Britten's opera Billy Budd, with extensive autograph alterations, some in Britten's hand, Aug 1949, 50 pp, folio, together with 3 A Ls s from Britten to Kenneth Harrison & further related material, sold at C on 7 Dec 1988, lot 196, for £11,500 to Haas.]

Forster, Georg, 1754-94
ALs, 11 Sept 1782. 4 pp, 4to. To J. K. Ph. Spener. Discussing various publication projects, criticizing his father, mentioning Lichtenberg, etc. (91) DM11,500
— 20 Feb 1791. 3 pp, 8vo. To Johann Wilhelm von Archenholtz. About a contribution to a publication & other matters. (90) DM5,500
AL, 5 May 1784. 10 pp, 8vo. To Georgine Heyne. About his recent engagement to her stepdaughter Therese Heyne & his travels. Incomplete. (91) DM3,200

Forster, Johann Reinhold, 1729-98
ALs, [c.1785]. (91) DM650

Forsyth, James W.
Photograph, sgd, 13 May [18]65. (89) $60

Fortner, Wolfgang, 1907-87
Autograph music, sketches for a composition for wind instruments & strings, sgd & dated 1979. (90) DM330
— Autograph music, sketches, sgd & dated 1978. (90) DM240
— Autograph music, "Skizze"; part of a score. (88) DM220

Fortnum, Peggy
Original drawings, (164), to illus 3 children's stories by Patricia Lynch, 1956 to 1959. Archives of J.M.Dent & Son. (88) £70

Foster, Marcia Lane
Original drawings, (80), to illus Roger Noakes' The Valley in the Woods, 1945, & other titles. Archives of J.M.Dent & Son. (88) £500

Fouche, Joseph, Duc d'Otrante, 1759-1820
ALs, [24 Nov 1794]. (89) DM500
— 9 Aug [1815]. (89) DM250
Ls, [23 Aug 1799]. (90) DM420
— [26 Aug 1799]. (90) DM380
— [30 Aug 1799]. (90) DM480
— [16 Feb 1800]. (88) DM400
— [2 June 1800]. (89) DM250
— [8 Feb 1802]. (91) $250
— [8 Aug 1804]. (91) DM570
— 5 Mar 1808. (91) DM240
— 27 July 1815. (91) DM380

Fouque, Friedrich de la Motte, 1777-1843
Autograph Ms, poem, Geburtstagsgruss, 9 Aug 1830. (91) DM550
Series of 11 A Ls s, 8 June 1822 to 6 Mar 1823. To Wilhelm Bernhardi. As his guardian, disagreeing with recipient's lifestyle, refusing to pay his debts, etc. (91) DM2,900
ALs, 4 Apr 1810. (90) DM600
— 1 June 1811. (89) £500
— 18 July 1816. (90) DM700
— 7 July 1817. (90) DM420
— 20 Dec 1818. (88) DM900
— 10 June 1819. (89) DM1,000
— 10 May 1822. (90) DM500

Fouque, Heinrich de la Motte, 1698-1774
Ls, 1 Aug 1759. (91) DM420

Fowell, Newton, 1768-90. See: Australia

Fox, Charles James, 1749-1806
ALs, 28 Aug 1783. 1 p, 4to. To William Cavendish Bentinck, Duke of Portland. In 3d person, informing him that the date has been set for signing the Treaty of Paris. (90) $3,250
— 19 Apr [n.y.]. (91) £90

Foxes of Harrow
[The original shooting script of the film, 1947, in lea binder, sold at pnNY on 3 Dec 1988, lot 7, for $170.]

Foxx, Jimmie, 1907-67
Photograph, sgd, [n.d.]. (91) $350

Foy, Eddie, 1856-1928
Autograph Ms, description of the "catastrophe at the Iroquois Theatre" on 5 Jan 1904. (90) $320

Francaix, Jean
Autograph music, Divertissement pour Violon, Alto et Violoncelle Soli avec accompagnement d'Orchestre, 10 Nov 1933. (91) £850
ALs, 25 Oct 1931. (90) DM420

France
[Ferroux, Etienne Joseph. - A series of 3 documents concerning his career, c.1780 to 1793, 3 pp, folio, sold at sg on 25 Oct 1988, lot 96, for $120.]
[Revolution. - A collection of 29 letters, ptd circulars, broadsides, etc., 1790 to 1794, various sizes, sold at sg on 9 Mar 1989, lot 83, for $700.]
[A file of records of the Revolutionary printing office, kept by the official Ducroix, 1793 & 1794, c.40 pp, folio, sold at sg on 21 Sept 1989, lot 129, for $675.]
[A group of 6 documents from the files of Marshall de Castries, 1794 to 1798, discussing the state of the world from the viewpoint of the exiled royalists, sold at sg on 21 Sept 1989, lot 130, for $1,400.]
[Revolution. - A letter from the Comite de Salut Public to Gen. Scherer, [28 July 1795], 2 pp, folio, sgd by Cambaceres & others, referring to

pay for soldiers, with related material, sold at star on 1 Dec 1988, lot 1137, for DM650.]

[Second Republic & Empire. - A varied collection of c.40 letters & documents, 19th cent, sold at S on 17 Nov 1988, lot 204, for £200 to Nicholas.]

Ms, Ordres et reglemens que le Roy veut estre observez Par les Capitaines et Officiers de ses Galeres Tires de l'Ordonnance du 15 mars 1548, [18th cent]. 569 pp & table of contents, folio, in red mor bdg with fleur-de-lys & royal arms. (88) FF58,000

Document, [19 Sept?] 1243. Byer collection & Philips Ms.36620. (90) $475

— ABBEY OF ST. MARTIN, TOURS. - Ms, rental. [Tours, c.700]. 2 leaves, vellum, 188mm by 283mm & 225mm by 194mm. In Merovingian cursive minuscule by 2 scribes. 1 leaf lined on blank verso with part of a leaf of a late classical papyrus codex in Greek uncials. Previously unrecorded. (89) £60,000

— DELAFOREST, A. - Autograph Ms, anecdotes relating to the 1st & 2d Empires, [19th cent]; c.100 pp, folio. Including pencil notes by Pierre Lafitte. With material relating to the Russian campaign. (88) £40

— DOCUMENT, 26 JULY 1789. 1 P, 4TO. STATEMENT OF NAMES & ADDRESSES OF ARTILLERYMEN WHO MANNED THE CANNON ON THE DAY THE BASTILLE WAS TAKEN; SGD BY SANTERRE. (90) £850

— HUGUE & FELICIE, COUNT & COUNTESS OF RETHEL. - Document, June 1218. 1 p, 4to, vellum. Receipt for the right of stationing their household in St. Agnan. In Old French. Later summary at upper right. (88) $300

— KIENLE, JULIE. - Autograph postcard, sgd, [11 Oct 1870]. To her father Georges Kienle. Sending family news from the siege of Paris. Mailed by military postal balloon. (90) DM600

— MARSEILLES. - Ls, 24 May 1565, 1 p, folio, from Pierre Bon to M. de Fourquevaux. About Turkish pirates on the French coast. (91) £700

— REVOLUTION. - ALs, 14 Aug 1793, 11 pp, folio, by the Comte de Moustier to Marshal de Castries. Analyzing the political situation with respect to the Revolutionary regime, England, Germany, Spain & the US. (91) $1,700

— REVOLUTION. - Document, [22 Apr 1794]. 2 pp, folio. Authorizing the requisitioning of horses & carriages; sgd by 4 members of the Comite de Salut Public. (90) DM700

— REVOLUTION. - Document, [6 May 1794]. 2 pp, folio. Statement of prices, sgd by Carnot, Collot d'Herbois & Lindet of the Comite du Salut Public. With related material. (90) DM560

— REVOLUTION. - Letter, [27 Feb 1794], 1 p, folio, from the Comite de Salut Public, sgd by Collot d'Herbois & Billaud Varenne. To the Commission de la Marine et des Colonnies. Requesting the names of committee members. (91) DM450

— REVOLUTION. - Letter, 23 June 1791. 5 pp, folio. To the National Assembly. Stressing the need for defense in view of the King's escape. Sgd by 30 officers & magistrates of the towns of Givet & Charlemont. (90) DM480

— REVOLUTION OF 1848. - A volume of c.34 A Ls s, 1848, c.250 pp, 8vo, in mor bdg, written by Florence Robinson at Paris to her brother Sir John Robinson, with related material, sold at pn on 10 Dec 1987, lot 502, for £280 to Bristow. 88

— RIBAUT, JEHAN, VISCOUNT OF MONTIVILLIERS. - Document, 21 July 1370. 1 p, 4to. Declaration that Capt. Jehennin le Brumen[t] of the ship Saint Sauveur has received supplies from Richard de Cornailles, victualler of Charles V. In Old French. (89) $550

— ROYAL FAMILY. - Ms, Table. Pour connoitre l'Etat present de la famille Royalle, des Princes du Sang, et des Princes legitimes; 1700. About 140 pp, 160mm by 210mm, in contemp lea. Including comments. (90) DM400

— TINDAL, R. - ALs, 24 July 1815. 4 pp, 4to. Recipient unnamed. Describing Paris after the fall of Napoleon. (89) £160

FRANCE

France, Anatole, 1844-1924
Autograph Ms, essay on the siege of Paris; [n.d.]. (90) £520
Autograph transcript, sonnet, Sur une signature de Marie Stuart, [ptd 1873]. (91) DM520
ALs, 19 Mar 1915. (88) DM420

Francis I, King of France, 1494-1547
Ls, 4 Sept 1539. (88) £180
— 27 June 1543. Doheny collection. (89) $700
Letter, 22 July [n.y.]. (91) DM400
Ds, 29 Nov 1518. (88) £210
— [1529?]. Byer collection. (90) $550
— 1540. (90) $600
— 16 Oct 1541. (91) £200
— 24 Nov 1543. (88) $350

Francis I, Emperor, 1708-65
[13 May 1740. 2 pp, 4to. Recipient unnamed. Regarding suggestions made by the Archduchess, & urging him not to lose hope.] DM550
ALs, 17 Oct 1741. (91) DM600
— 13 Nov 1755. 3 pp, 4to. To [Countess Ligniville]. Informing her about the birth of his daughter [Marie Antoinette]. In French. (90) DM1,700
— 21 Oct 1758. 2 pp, 4to. To [Countess Ligniville]. Reporting about the recent Austrian victory at Hochkirch. (91) DM3,000
— 10 Mar 1764. 4 pp, 4to. To Countess Beatrix de Ligneville. Inviting her to his son's wedding. Sgd with paraph. In French. (89) DM1,300
— [n.d.]. (89) DM650
— [n.d.]. (91) DM750
Ls, 20 Mar 1738. Byer collection. (90) $225
— 9 Jan 1740. (88) DM260
— 15 Apr 1741. (89) DM650
— 10 Mar 1742. (90) DM350
— 9 Oct 1743. (89) DM340
— 30 Mar 1746. Schroeder collection. (89) DM420
— 14 Aug 1754. (90) DM800
— 6 Oct 1759. (90) DM320
— 10 Mar 1760. (89) $100
— 8 Mar 1764. (89) DM280
— 4 Apr 1764. (90) DM440
ANs, [after 14 Oct 1758]. (91) DM320

AMERICAN BOOK PRICES CURRENT

Ds, 17 Oct 1749. 17 pp, 4to, in red velvet bdg. Patent of nobility & grant of arms for Jacob Reder. With full-page painting of the arms in gold & colors. (90) DM1,150
— 18 July 1760. (88) DM460
— 6 Oct 1763. (90) DM500
— 22 June 1765. (90) DM330
Autograph endorsement, sgd, on fragment (final page) of a letter addressed to him, 19 May 1765, 1 p, 4to, regarding a case to be decided by the Imperial Court of Chancery; expressing impatience. (90) DM360

Francis II, Emperor, 1768-1835. See: Franz I, 1768-1835

Franciscan Terciaries
Ms, Rules, in the form ratified by Nicholas IV; in French. [France, 15th cent]. 12 leaves (3 blank), vellum, 136mm by 100mm, in contemp tawed skin over pastebds. In a small lettre batarde by the scribe F. R. (91) £2,600
— Ms, Rules of the Thirde Order of Seynt Franceys..., in Middle English. [England, early 16th cent]. 19 leaves, vellum, 193mm by 132mm, in modern full dark brown mor. In an English cursive bookhand with some fine calligraphic cadels; some words in gothic script. With small illuminated initials throughout, large illuminated initial with border, & 3 full-page miniatures in arched compartments within full borders (repainted). Including account of the founding of the Order, in Latin. (91) £7,500

Franciscus de Mayronis, c.1285-after 1328
Ms, commentary on the Sentences of Peter Lombard. [Northeast Italy?, 15 July 1440]. 78 leaves, 296mm by 205mm, in old limp vellum. In brown ink in a small italianate bookhand by Iacobus Schonleip de Elbing. With c.180 large decorated initials in red or blue & full border. (91) £1,900
— Ms, Super Sententiarum IV, [Southern Germany?, 17 July 1440]. 78 leaves (2 lacking), 295mm by 210mm. Contemp limp vellum. In brown ink in a bookhand with humanist g by Iacobus Schonlap de Elbing. With c.176 large initials in colors. (88) £1,350

Franck, Cesar, 1822-90
Autograph music, "Choeur d. jeunes filles de Rebecca", scored for piano & 3 voices, 30 June 1887. 3 pp, 8vo; hand-ruled. Sgd & inscr to Olympia Nollet. (88) $2,800
— Autograph music, Menuet for piano & organ, transcribed from Bizet's L'Arlesienne, [n.d.]. 4 pp, folio. Notated on 4 systems of 4 staves each, sgd & initialled. (91) £1,600
ALs, 23 July 1884. (89) DM520
— 20 Dec 1884. (88) DM650
— [n.d.]. (90) DM570
— [n.d.]. (90) DM700
— [n.d.]. (91) DM870

Francke, August Hermann, 1663-1727
ALs, 28 Apr 1717. 1 p, 4to. To Herr Elers. Acknowledging receipt of letters & money. (90) DM1,100
— 15 Apr 1725. 1 p, 4to. To Herr Neubauer. Expressing thanks & sending wine. Partly in Latin. Collector's stamp erased. (89) DM1,100

Franckenberg, Abraham von, 1593-1652
Ms, Raphael Das ist Ein Heiliges Licht und Heilsamer Bericht von ... Der Menschlichen Kranckheit und darwieder geordneten Artzeney. [Germany, c.1700]. 23 leaves, 236mm by 186mm, in contemp lea bdg. Elaborate Ms in several scripts. (91) DM6,400

Franco, Francisco, 1892-1975
Ls, 28 June 1940. (91) £500
— 5 July 1940. (89) £850

Frank, Anne, 1929-45
Collection of ALs, autograph postcard, sgd, & photograph, 29 Apr 1940. To Juanita Wagner. Describing her family & interests. With ALs & photograph from her sister Margot to Betty Anne Wagner, 27 Apr 1940. Together 6 pp, & photographs. With related material. (89) $150,000
Autograph sentiment, sgd, 4 Mar [19]40. 2 pp, 165mm by 131mm; in linen album also inscr by 52 others. 4-line poem addressed to her childhood friend Henny, with lengthy autograph subscription & 2 paste-in chromolithographic stickers. (90) $32,000

Frank, Johann Peter, 1745-1821
ALs, 30 June 1787. (91) DM550

Frankel, Benjamin, 1906-73
Autograph music, Symphony No 5, Op.46; full score, [19]67. (90) £180

Frankfurter, Felix, 1882-1965
ALs, 20 July [1951?]. (91) $160
— [n.d.], "Labor Day". (91) $110
Ls, 16 Feb 1961. (91) $400

Franklin, Benjamin, 1706-90
ALs, 25 Oct 1750. 2 pp, 4to. To the Rev. Samuel Johnson. Returning recipient's Ms & sending a plan for a school in Philadelphia. (91) $30,000
— 3 Dec 1755. 1 p, 4to. To John Hunter. Referring to the recent act allocating funds for the defense of Pennsylvania. Including franking signature. Possibly unpbd. (90) £12,000
— 17 Mar 1756. 1 p, 4to. To James Balfour. Informing him about his travel plans. Including ANs on address panel. Possibly unpbd. (90) £10,000
— 27 June 1760. 2 pp, folio. To David Hall. Discussing business concerns & hoping to return to America next spring. Somewhat def. Doheny collection. (89) $13,000
— 11 Dec 1762. 1 p, 4to. To [Elias] Boudinot. Thanking for congratulations on his return home. With engraved port. (88) $6,500
— 9 May 1766. 1 p, folio. To Mrs. Hopkinson. Acknowledging receipt of a payment & mentioning Dr. [John] Morgan's new book. With franking signature. Prinzmetal collection. (88) $11,000
— 5 May 1773. 1 p, 8vo. To Arthur Lee. Informing him about a meeting with Lord Dartmouth [about the Hutchinson Letters]. (91) $26,000
Ls, 13 Feb 1787. 1 p, 4to. To Gen. Arthur St. Clair. Introducing M. De Chaumont. (91) $7,500
ADs, 27 June 1778. 1 p, 4to. Certification that Capt. Solomon Townsend took the oath of allegiance. Encapsulated. (90) $5,500
— 5 Dec 1787. 1 p, 118mm by 197mm. Order addressed to the Secretary of the Pennsylvania Council to issue a

FRANKLIN

commission to Matthew Clarkson & others. Christensen collection. (90) $5,000

Ds, 22 Sept 1764. 27 leaves, folio. Supplement to an act for erecting a lighthouse at Cape Henlopen. (91) $4,500

— 10 Apr 1782. 1 p, 4to. Promissory note for 1,500,000 Livres borrowed from the French Treasury. Ptd in French; accomplished in Franklin's hand. (91) $20,000

— 19 Oct 1785. 1 p, 4to. As President of the Pennsylvania Executive Council, pay order to Treasurer David Rittenhouse for interest due Gilbert Quirk. Framed with a port. (88) $2,800

— 16 Jan 1786. 1 p, double folio. As President of the Executive Council of Pennsylvania, grant of land to Thomas McKean. (91) $5,200

— 16 Mar 1786. 1 p, 4to. As President of the Pennsylvania Executive Council, pay order to Treasurer David Rittenhouse for interest due George Blakeley. Inlaid. (88) $3,500

— 12 May 1786. 1 p, 65mm by 202mm. As President of the Pennsylvania Assembly, ordering payment to Benjamin Brink. Doheny collection. (89) $5,000

— 20 Apr 1787. 1 p, 354mm by 404mm. As President of the Supreme Executive Council of Pennsylvania, land grant to Jeremiah Murray. (91) $3,800

— 8 June 1787. 1 p, 170mm by 207mm. As President of the Pennsylvania Assembly, recording deposition sworn by Robert Smith. With fragment of related document on verso. (90) $4,500

— 11 June 1787. 1 p, 336mm by 395mm. Land grant to Adam Good. (90) $4,000

— 27 June 1787. 1 p, 159mm by 200mm. As President of the Pennsylvania Assembly, pay order in favor of Evan Owen. With 3 engraved portraits. (90) $4,200

— 31 July 1787. 1 p, 4to. Order addressed to David Rittenhouse to pay Peter Muhlenberg's salary as member of the Council. Endorsed by Muhlenberg. (90) $4,500

— 14 Oct 1788. 1 p, folio. As President of the Supreme Executive Council of Pennsylvania, land grant to Absalom Fox. Doheny collection. (89) $4,500

— BARBE-MARBOIS, FRANCOIS, MARQUIS DE. - Ds, 1786. 1 p, 9 by 8 inches. Letter of recommendation for Franklin. (88) $175

— COSEY, JOSEPH. - Forgery of a purported Franklin payment authorization to David Rittenhouse. 1 p, oblong 4to. Sold with a port. (91) $400

— FORGERY. - Letter, 5 July 1775. 1 p, 4to. Purportedly in Franklin's hand, to Mr. Strahan. Announcing that they are now enemies. (90) $300

Franklin, Eleanor Anne, 1797?-1825. See: Franklin, Sir John

Franklin, Jane, Lady, 1792-1875. See: Franklin, Sir John

Franklin, Sir John, 1786-1847

— FRANKLIN, ELEANOR ANNE. - ALs, 18 Feb 1824. 4 pp, 4to. To [Mary Russell] Mitford. Describing preparations for her husband's next expedition, etc. Seal tear. (89) £240

— FRANKLIN, LADY JANE. - ALs, 31 Dec 1850. 3 pp, 8vo. To Mr. Dolland. Reporting about the last expedition to seek for her husband. (88) £65

— FRANKLIN, LADY JANE. - ALs, 29 Oct 1860. 4 pp, 8vo. To Mr. Willis. Sending a publication regarding the arctic, & discussing the project of a statue of her husband in Trafalgar Square. (90) DM420

See also: Australia

Franz Ferdinand, Archduke, 1863-1914

Series of 12 A Ls s, 1887 to 1897; c.30 pp, 8vo. (88) £900

ALs, 12 Feb 1897. 6 pp, 8vo. To Amy Ehrmann. Regretting he could not see her in Egypt & describing his voyage to Algiers. (88) DM1,300

— 3 Apr 1906. 5 pp, 8vo. To Count Karl Coudenhove. Inquiring about Eugen Czernin & stressing the necessity of putting his finances on a sound basis. (90) DM2,400

ANs, [26 Dec 1902]. (89) DM260

Franz I, Emperor of Austria, 1768-1835
ALs, [Dec 1795]. (90) DM600
— 17 Apr 1799. (89) DM350
— 7 Aug 1801. (88) DM750
— 5 May 1803. (90) DM520
— 17 July 1811. (89) DM950
Ds, 6 July 1797. (88) DM380
— 7 Aug 1801. (90) DM500
— 22 Jan 1817. (90) DM600
— 3 July 1825. (90) DM220
— 14 Sept 1827. 16 pp, 4to. Grant of arms to Georg Daniely. With full-page coat of arms in gold & colors. Lacking seal. (88) DM1,300
Autograph endorsement, sgd, 2 Apr 1831, on a proposal, sgd, by Prince Metternich, 1 Apr 1831, 2 pp, folio, reminding him that a present should be given to a Prussian diplomat; stating his agreement. (90) DM650

Franz Joseph I, Emperor of Austria, 1830-1916
ALs, [Apr 1864]. 1 p, 8vo. To Count Rechberg. Pointing out that he may have to delay his journey because of the burial of Archduchess Hildegard. Sgd with paraph. (90) DM1,900
— 11 Aug 1864. (91) $650
— 1 Oct 1887. 6 pp, 8vo. To Katharina Schratt. Complimenting her on her acting the previous evening. (91) DM5,500
— 21 Oct 1888. 4 pp, 8vo. To Katharina Schratt. Discussing her problems with the managers of the new Burgtheater & looking forward to a date. (89) DM3,200
— 14 Jan 1901. 2 pp, 8vo. To Katharina Schratt. About a meeting later in the day. (91) DM2,200
Ls, 9 Feb 1849. 1 p, folio. To Count Radetzky. Agreeing to the retirement of Major Gen. Georg von Schoenhals. (91) DM1,050
— 22 Feb 1852. Byer collection. (90) $350
— 2 June 1857. (90) DM520
— 30 Apr 1862. (90) DM320
— 17 Oct 1886. (91) $200
— 23 Sept 1894. (91) DM340
— 29 Mar 1908. (88) DM460
— 26 May 1916. (90) DM430
ANs, 22 Sept [1857]. (90) DM550
— 17 May [n.y.]. (88) DM220
Ds, 13 Jan 1859. (90) DM740
— 1867. 8 pp, 36.5cm by 27cm. Patent of nobility & grant of arms for Istvan Horner. Illuminated throughout; with full-page painting of the arms. Red mor bdg. (89) DM1,500
— 17 Feb 1871. (88) DM800
— 31 Jan 1875. 7 pp, size not stated, in extra contemp mor. Grant of arms to Jacob Levi. (90) £1,100
— 19 Feb 1889. (89) DM950
— 26 Oct 1899. (90) $275
— 22 Mar 1905. (90) DM750
— [29 Nov 1909]. (90) DM750
See also: Maximilian of Mexico & Franz Joseph I

Franz, Robert, 1815-92
Autograph music, song Es taget vor dem Walde, scored for choir. (89) DM250
— Autograph music, song, Wasserfahrt, for voice & piano, Op. 6, no 1, [1846]; after a poem by Heine. Sgd & dated 28 May 1881. 3 pp, size not stated. (88) DM2,400
ALs, 15 Apr 1873. (90) DM200

Fraser, Lady Antonia
Typescript, novel, Your Royal Hostage, with autograph revisions; 1985 to 1986. (88) £200

Fraser, Eric George, 1902-84
Original drawings, (10), dust jacket or cover designs for various titles. Archives of J. M. Dent & Son. (88) £380
— Original drawings, (12), to illus Gibbon's Decline and Fall of the Roman Empire; initialled. Archives of J. M. Dent & Son. (88) £280
— Original drawings, (2), to illus Eugene O'Neill's Mourning Becomes Electra, [n.d.]. (89) £170
— Original drawings, (2), to illus The Damnation of Faust, [n.d.]. (89) £200
— Original drawings, (21), dust jacket or cover designs for various classical titles. Archives of J. M. Dent & Son. (88) £850
— Original drawings, (22), dust jacket or cover designs for various titles. Archives of J. M. Dent & Son. (88) £440
— Original drawings, (22), to illus John Hamden's Ed of Sir William amd the Wolf, and other Stories, 1960. Ar-

FRASER

chives of J. M. Dent & Son. (88) £900
— Original drawings, (29), to illus a Radio 4 production of The Lord of the Rings, including cover design for The Radio Times, a map of Middle Earth, etc., Mar 1981. 12 by 14 inches & smaller. In watercolor or pen-&-ink. Mostly sgd. (89) £1,300
— Original drawings, (3), to illus works by Hendrik Ibsen, [n.d.]. (89) £320
— Original drawings, (3), to illus works by Thomas Hardy, [n.d.]. (89) £300
— Original drawings, (6), dust jacket or cover designs for various titles. Archives of J. M. Dent & Son. (88) £240
— Original drawings, to illus R. (89) £130
Original drawing, cover design for BBC, The Third Programme 10th Anniversary, 1956. (89) £130
— Original drawing, ink & watercolor dust jacket design for The Saga of Gisli; sgd. Archives of J. M. Dent & Son. (88) £220
— Original drawing, to illus Life Beyond the Veil, 1920. (89) £130
— Original drawing, to illus Moby Dick, [n.d.]. (89) £100
— Original drawing, to illus the Medea of Euripides, [n.d.]. (89) £80
— Original drawing, to illus The Waves, [n.d.]. (89) £60

Fraser-Simson, Harold, 1872-1944. See: Milne, Alan Alexander

Frazer, Sir James George, 1854-1941
ALs, 11 July 1889. (89) £200

Frederic, Harold, 1856-98
A Ls s (2), 11 Mar 1893 & [n.d.]. Doheny collection. (89) $150

Frederick Henry, Prince of Orange, 1584-1647
Ls, 13 Mar 1637. 1 p, folio. To Henry Rich, Earl of Holland. Thanking for horses & dogs. With autograph postscript. (91) DM5,200

Frederick I, King of Sweden, 1676-1751
Ls, 28 Apr [1744]. (90) DM320
— 11 Apr 1748. (91) DM750
Ds, 30 Jan 1729. (90) DM270

AMERICAN BOOK PRICES CURRENT

Frederick III, Emperor, 1415-93
Ls, [7 May] 1439. 1 p, folio. To the town officials of Wiener Neustadt. As Duke of Austria, notifying them of a grant of a plot to Peter von Poschikch. Sgd Praescripta recognoscimus. (89) DM12,000

Frederik VI, King of Denmark, 1768-1839
Ls, 23 July 1827. (90) DM330
Ds, 22 Feb 1822. Byer collection. (90) $200

Frederik VII, King of Denmark, 1808-63
Autograph Ms, autobiographical information, sgd at head as Crown Prince; [n.d.]. Kuenzel collection. (90) DM200

Frederik VIII, King of Denmark, 1808-63
Ds, 28 Aug 1862. (88) DM320

Freeman, Barbara
Original drawings, (15), to illus stories by the Brothers Grimm, [c.1950]. 303mm by 234mm or 403mm by 294mm. In ink & watercolor; sgd. (89) £1,500
— Original drawings, (17), to illus fairy tales by Hans Christian Andersen, [c.1950]. 304mm by 232mm or 398mm by 294mm. In ink & watercolor; 16 sgd. (89) £1,500
— Original drawings, (17), to illus The Gypsies, 1931. (89) £400

Freese, Hans, 1886-1966
Collection of 27 A Ls s & autograph postcard, sgd, 18 Nov 1947 to 18 Dec 1950. (88) DM300

Freiligrath, Ferdinand, 1810-76
ALs, 30 May 1837. (88) DM1,000
— [28 Aug] 1840. (89) DM900
— 31 Jan 1860. (91) DM380
— 23 Oct 1862. 4 pp, 8vo. Recipient unnamed. Responding to a linguistic inquiry. (90) DM1,250
— 23 Oct 1867. (89) DM600
— [1 Jan 1874]. (91) DM260
— 3 Oct 1875. (88) DM500
Photograph, sgd, 1871. (91) DM350

Freire, Dido. See: Renoir, Jean & Freire

Fremont, Jessie Benton, 1824-1902
ALs, 13 Oct [n.y.]. Alexander collection. (90) $110

Fremont, John Charles, 1813-90
ALs, 22 June 1850. Doheny collection. (88) $400
— 15 Feb 1859. (88) $240
— 25 July 1862. (90) $380
— 23 Jan 1879. Doheny collection. (89) $550
— 20 Nov [n.y.]. (90) $325
Ds, 2 Mar 1868. (88) $175
Autograph endorsement, note of approval, sgd twice, on ALs from Capt. (90) $375

French & Indian War
Single sheet ptg, resolves by the Connecticut General Assembly, 25 Oct 1756, ordering troops & supplies to be sent to Lake George. (89) $500
— ARMY ORDERLY BOOKS. - 5 Mss, recording orders, troop movements, court martials etc. in North America, 13 Mar 1758 to 23 Nov 1759. 5 vols, 8vo, in contemp wraps. (90) £5,000
— BRADSTREET, JOHN. - Ds, 24 June 1756. 1 p, 16mo. Certificate for amount due "for Riding at this great Carrying Place". Edges backed. (88) $200
— DELANCEY, JAMES. - ALs, 28 Mar 1758. 1 p, size not stated. To an unnamed Lieut. Colonel. Regarding troops to be raised near Onondaga. (89) $350
— FRYE, JOSEPH. - Autograph document, 24 Dec 1759. 1 p, 16mo. Daily signal orders for Fort Cumberland. (88) $200
— WILKINS, MAJ. - Ds, 6 Oct 1763. Size not stated. Certificate for hauling boats & provisions. Partially re-inked. (88) $190
See also: Newcastle, Thomas Pelham-Holles

Frerichs, Friedrich Theodor von, 1819-85
ALs, 14 Feb 1862. (91) DM550

Freud, Anna, 1895-1982
Collection of 60 A Ls s & Ls, 4 Jan 1950 to 10 Sept 1975 & [n.d.]. About 100 pp, folio & 8vo. To Paula Fichtl. Correspondence with the family housekeeper. (91) £3,000
ALs, 4 Oct 1938. (91) $800

Freud, Sigmund, 1856-1939
[An autograph envelope, addressed to Dr. P. Federn, [11 June 1927], sold at star on 9 Mar 1988, lot 435, for DM300.]
Autograph Ms, Meine individuelle Traumcharakteristik (Typische Traeume), [c.1903-1909]. 2 pp, folio. Description of his dreams. (89) £14,000
— Autograph Ms, scientific paper about migraine, [fall 1895?]. 4 pp, 4to. (88) DM24,000
Collection of ALs & autograph postcard, sgd, 21 & 23 Nov 1935. 2 pp, 8vo. To Percy Allen. Thanking for his books on Shakespeare, & requesting him not to publicize his views on the subject as yet. (90) £3,500
Series of 4 A Ls s, 31 July 1930 to 12 Nov 1933. 5 pp, 4to & 8vo. To Erik Carstens. Stating his fees, the possible duration of a training analysis, & his views of Wilhelm Reich. (91) £6,500
— Series of 4 A Ls s, 12 May to 8 Dec 1931. 6 pp, folio & 8vo. To Julius Tandler. Concerning Tandler's winter appeal for the needy. (88) £4,400
A Ls s (2), 21 Oct 1932 & 7 Mar 1934. 3 pp, 8vo. To an unnamed lady. Regarding presents of flowers & seeds, & commenting on political difficulties in Europe. On ptd letterhead. (88) $5,000
ALs, 20 Nov 1907. 2 pp, 8vo. Recipient unnamed. Commenting about recipient's Ms & his interpretation of dreams. File holes. With ALs by Anna Freud, 1962. (88) DM7,000
— 17 Apr [1909?]. 2 pp, 4to. To an unnamed lady. Warning her against reading one of his works pbd 3 years ago. (91) £1,600
— 16 Nov 1911. 2 pp, 8vo. To an unnamed colleague. Discussing revisions to recipient's lecture. (89) £1,900
— 30 Apr 1929. 2 pp, 8vo. To Walter Kluge. Hoping to meet him & mentioning criticism leveled against himself & his followers. (88) DM4,400
— 16 Aug 1930. 1 p, 8vo. Recipient unnamed. Replying to a question about his religious beliefs. Framed. (89) £3,500
— 12 Sept 1930. 2 pp, 8vo. To an unnamed professor. Commenting on criticism of his speech on Goethe &

FREUD

psychoanalysis. (91) DM8,000
— 8 July 1931. 2 pp, 8vo. Recipient unnamed. Expressing reluctance to participate in a congress. With port photograph, 1938. (88) DM4,400
— 13 Jan 1932. 1 p, 8vo. Recipient unnamed. Referring his correspondant to the Psychoanalytic Institute in Berlin or Dr. Watermann in Hamburg. (91) $4,500
— 20 Apr 1933. 1 p, 8vo. To Dr. Fritz Molenhoff. About a diagnosis. (91) $3,500
— 23 July 1933. 1 p, 8vo. Recipient unnamed. Sending birthday congratulations. (88) DM3,500
— 27 Oct 1935. 2 pp, folio. To Senor Paglione. Answering points made by recipient about the theory of dreams & the death instinct. (90) £4,400
— 7 Nov 1935. 2 pp, folio. To Percy Allen. Stating his belief that Shakespeare's plays were written by the Earl of Oxford. (91) £3,400
— 5 Dec 1935. 1 p, 8vo. To Percy Allen. Announcing that he is not convinced that Shakespeare's sonnets were addressed to the Earl of Oxford's son. (90) £2,800
— 1 Jan 1936. 2 pp, 8vo. To Percy Allen. Suggesting that Allen's theories [about Shakespeare] may gain acceptance sooner than his own. (90) £3,400
— 22 Jan 1937. 2 pp, folio. To Benjamin Mendelsohn. Discussing the case of a teacher accused of sexual abuse of pupils. With related material. (91) £5,400
— 25 Feb 1938. 1 p, 8vo. To Dr. King. Disagreeing with recipient's theory of the causes of restriction neurosis. (91) £2,000
— 8 June 1938. 2 pp, 8vo, on postcard. To Mrs. Gunn. Thanking for her kindness & promising to pass on her offer to Anna. With related material. (88) £1,300
— 22 June 1938. 1 p, 8vo. To [Janosch Plesch]. About his arrival in London. (91) DM5,500
— 3 Aug 1938. 1 p, 8vo. To his grandson, Gab. Sending belated birthday greetings. (91) $3,750
— 2 Nov 1938. 2 pp, 8vo (card). To an unnamed physician. Informing him

AMERICAN BOOK PRICES CURRENT

that he is recovering from his operation & will be able to see some gentlemen the following week. (90) £1,700
— 11 Mar 1939. 2 pp, 8vo. To [Dr. Adolf Sindler?]. Regretting his health does not allow him to set a date for a meeting. Repaired. (88) $3,000
— 11 Mar 1939. 2 pp, 8vo. To Dr. [Adolf Sindler]. Postponing a meeting on account of his health. (90) DM7,500
— 15 May 1939. 2 pp, 8vo. To Lady Reading. Regretting the impossibility "to partake in any activity to meet the needs of the Maccati Association". (88) DM3,800
— 29 May 1939. 1 p, 8vo. To an identified doctor. Noting that he cannot be of help to him. (91) $2,250
— 13 June 1939. 1 p, 8vo. To [Robert Neumann]. Informing him that he will accept an honorary membership in the Pen Club. (90) DM5,200
— [n.d.]. 1 p, 8vo. To an unnamed professor. Informing him that he is unable to attend a conference. Upper margin cut. (89) DM3,200
Ls, 9 Sept 1926. 2 pp, 8vo. To an unidentified doctor. Evaluating an article. (91) $3,250
— 15 Feb 1927. 1 p, 8vo. To Dr. Pierce Clark. Regarding translation of some some of his writings. Small rust stain from paper clip at top left corner. (91) $2,000
— 19 Feb 1934. 1 p, 8vo. To Dr. Edwin R. Eisler. Thanking him for support. (91) $2,500
Autograph postcard, sgd, 9 Jan 1921. To Dr. Oberholzer. Thanking for arranging Dr. de Saussure's visit. Framed. (89) $1,500
— 19 Oct 1938. To Benjamin Mendelsohn. Thanking for good wishes on his escape from Austria. (91) £1,500
ANs, 20 May 1929. 1 p, on personal lettercard. To an unnamed doctor. Thanking for a gift. (88) $1,625
— 11 Aug 1930. 2 pp, 8vo (card). To Dr. V. Rosenfeld. Requesting him to check a quotation. (88) DM2,600
— 28 Dec 1933. 1 p, oblong 8vo. To a patient named Doubek. In English, stating that he receives no patients. (91) $4,250

Ns, May 1936. 1 p, 128mm by 153mm (card). To Dr. Frank Alexander. Ptd card thanking for congratulations on his birthday; sgd & inscr. (90) $1,800

ADs, 9 June 1893. 1 p, 2.25 by 2.75 inches. Medical prescription. Patient's name cut off. (91) $2,200

— 13 Dec 1926. 1 p, 8vo. Customs declaration regarding a rug sent to him by his sister. (90) DM2,300

Photograph, sgd, [c.1936]. 7.5 by 10 inches. Bust pose. (91) $2,800

Photograph, sgd & inscr, Dec 1923. 6.4 by 8.75 inches (image). Bust pose, by Halberstadt. Sgd on mount. (90) $7,000

Signature, [25 Dec] 1930. Below engraving, sgd, by Oskar Pollak of Venice, Canale grande. (90) DM2,200
See also: Einstein, Albert & Freud

Freudweiler, Heinrich, 1755-95. See: Goethe, Johann Wolfgang von

Freund, Martin, 1863-1920
[A collection of c.450 letters addressed to him, mostly by colleagues & other scientists, including several Nobel Prize winners, sold at star on 9 Mar 1988, lot 436, for DM8,000.]
[A collection of c.200 letters addressed to him, mostly by physicians & patients, sold at star on 9 Mar 1988, lot 427, for DM750.]

Freytag, Gustav, 1816-95
ALs, 7 Jan 1852. (90) DM500
— 29 Oct 1852. (90) DM280
— 12 May 1862. (89) DM700

Frick, Wilhelm, 1874-1956. See: Schussen, Wilhelm

Frick, Wilhelm, 1877-1956
Ls, 3 Jan 1939. (90) $150

Friedell, Egon, 1878-1938
Collection of ALs & autograph postcard, sgd, [n.d.]. (88) DM500

Friederike Luise, Markgraefin von Brandenburg-Ansbach, 1714-84
ALs, 3 Oct 1760. (90) DM650

Friederike Luise, Queen of Frederick William II of Prussia, 1751-1805
ALs, [n.d.]. Schroeder collection. (89) DM320

Friedlaender, Max Jakob, 1867-1958
Series of 3 A Ls s, 30 Oct 1917 to 21 Jan 1938. (90) DM530

Friedlaender, Salomo ("Mynona"), 1871-1946
Autograph Ms, satire, Der totschicke Heiland, Nov 1920. 17 pp, 4to. Sgd Mynona. (90) DM1,700
Collection of 3 A Ls s, 19 Ls s, 16 postcards, sgd (3 autograph), & 3 A Ns s, 4 July 1919 to 26 Aug 1945. 28 pp, mostly folio & 4to, & cards. To Dr. Emil Tuchmann, interesting correspondence about a variety of matters; & to other recipients. With related material. (90) DM3,600

Friedman, Harold
Original drawings, (35), to illus Walter James' A Word Book of Wine, 1959. Archives of J. M. Dent & Son. (88) £60

Friedreich, Nikolaus, 1825-82
ALs, 29 July 1867. (91) DM420

Friedrich August, Herzog von Oldenburg, 1711-85
Ls, 16 Jan 1770. 2 pp, folio. To A. S. Struve. As Regent for Tsar Paul I, discussing the recall of a minister. (91) DM1,100

Friedrich August I, King of Saxony, 1750-1827
Ls, 14 Jan 1805. (90) DM900
Ds, 8 Oct 1800. (90) DM240

Friedrich August III, King of Saxony, 1865-1932
ALs, 1 Dec 1918. 5 pp, 8vo. To Gen. von Mueller. Expressing anger & disappointment about the recent revolution & his own abdication. (91) DM3,000

Friedrich, Caspar David, 1774-1840
ALs, 17 July 1835. 2 pp, folio. To his friend Roeder. Describing the effects of his recent stroke. Dampstained. (91) £2,800
Cut signature, "Friedrich Landschaftsmahler Schwedisch Pommern", [be-

FRIEDRICH

fore 1815]. (89) DM550

Friedrich Christian, Kurfuerst von Sachsen, 1722-63
ALs, 14 July 1748. (88) DM320

Friedrich Franz I, Grossherzog von Mecklenburg-Schwerin, 1756-1837
Ls, 14 June 1815. (90) DM440

Friedrich I, Kurfuerst von Brandenburg, 1371-1440 —&
Johann von Nassau, Kurfuerst von Mainz, 1360-1419
Document, [24 Aug] 1400. 1 p, folio; vellum. Joint decision (Friedrich as Burggraf von Nuernberg) in a quarrel between King Ruprecht & the Archbishop of Cologne regarding judicial rights at Bacharach. Schroeder collection. (89) DM6,500

Friedrich I, Herzog von Wuerttemberg, 1557-1608
Ls, 1 Nov 1597. 1 p, folio. To Gideon von Ostheim. Sending an essay about his mines in the Black Forest for publication. With related material. (89) DM1,600

Friedrich I, King of Prussia, 1657-1713
ALs, 11 Aug 1684. 2 pp, 4to. To his father, Kurfuerst Friedrich Wilhelm von Brandenburg. Requesting permission to marry [Sophie Charlotte von Braunschweig-Lueneburg]. (90) DM3,000
— 2 Aug 1698. 2 pp, 4to. To his sister Elisabeth, Duchess of Kurland. As Elector of Brandenburg, assuring her of his support in her problems with her brother-in-law Ferdinand. (90) DM2,600
— 1 Feb 1701. 2 pp, 4to. To his daughter Luise. Regretting that she could not attend his coronation. (91) DM2,500
— 27 Feb 1705. 1 p, 4to. To his sister Elisabeth, Markgraefin von Bayreuth. Thanking for condolences on the death of his wife. Schroeder collection. (89) DM1,800
— 24 Sept 1711. 1 p, 4to. To [his daughter-in-law Sophie Dorothea?]. Thanking for her letters. In French. (88) DM1,400
Ls, 29 July 1691. (91) DM540
— 27 May 1695. (90) DM800

AMERICAN BOOK PRICES CURRENT

— 26 Mar 1696. Schroeder collection. (89) DM450
— 28 Oct 1699. (90) DM250
— 29 Aug 1701. (90) DM520
— 17 Nov 1705. (90) DM750
— 19 June 1706. 1 p, folio. To his sister Elisabeth, Markgraefin von Bayreuth. Informing her about his son's engagement to marry Sophie Dorothee von Hannover. With autograph postscript. Countersgd by Count Wartenberg. (90) DM1,700
— 29 July 1706. Schroeder collection. (89) DM420
— 12 Nov 1707. (90) DM750
— 22 Nov 1707. (91) DM460
Ds, 15 Feb 1697. (90) DM360
— 4 Sept 1702. (89) DM340
— 12 July 1710. (88) DM800
— 10 Oct 1711. (88) DM240

Friedrich I, King of Wuerttemberg, 1754-1816
ALs, 8 Nov 1807. (90) DM380
— 23 May 1815. (90) DM220
Collection of Ls & Ds, 23 Dec 1797 & 23 May 1808. 2 pp, folio. To his revenue office, thanking for congratulations on his accession. Pay order. With related material. (89) DM1,600
Ls, 14 July 1795. (90) DM220
— 8 Oct 1803. (90) DM260
— 15 Nov 1806. (90) DM280

Friedrich I, Grossherzog von Baden, 1826-1907
Autograph Ms, congratulatory address on Kaiser Wilhelm I's birthday, [Mar 1877]. (90) DM950

Friedrich II, Landgraf von Hessen-Homburg, 1633-1708
ALs, 11 Oct 1698. (90) DM950
Ds, 30 Jan 1700. Schroeder collection. (89) DM450

Friedrich II, King of Prussia, 1712-86
Autograph Ms, Ode a mon frere Henry, 4 Oct 1757. 4 pp, 4to. 28 six-line stanzas, sgd; with some autograph revisions. Repaired. (91) DM18,000
ALs, 21 [no month, c.1735]. 1 p, 4to. To Wilhelm von Rohwedell. Sending a special messenger with a letter for "Truks". (90) DM1,900

— 16 Oct 1736. 2 pp, 4to. To his father Friedrich Wilhelm I. Reporting about the situation at Rheinsberg. With Ls, 24 Feb 1736, 1 p, 4to, from Friedrich Wilhelm I to his son Friedrich. (88) DM10,500

— 8 Feb 1737. 3 pp, 4to. To Voltaire. Discussing Christan Wolff's works & his own belief in a "supreme being". Albrecht collection. (91) SF13,000

— 14 May 1737. 3 pp, 4to. To Voltaire. Philosophical discussion about Christian Wolff's "parties indivisibles qui composent la matyere." Albrecht collection. (91) SF11,000

— 28 Mar 1738. 3 pp, 4to. To Voltaire. Commenting on Voltaire's works, recounting occurrences at the court of Tsar Peter the Great, etc. Albrecht collection. (91) SF6,500

— 24 July 1738. 2 pp, 4to. To Voltaire. Reporting about his journey across Westfalia. Albrecht collection. (91) SF8,200

— 18 July 1739. 1 p, 4to. To his wife Elisabeth Christine. Reporting about his travels in East Prussia & requesting that she procure a birthday present for his father. Sgd Federic. In French. (89) DM8,000

— 27 July 1739. 1 p, 4to. To his wife Elisabeth Christine. Reporting about his travels in East Prussia with his father. Sgd Federic. In French. (88) DM8,500

— 15 Apr 1740. 2 pp, 4to. To Voltaire. Thanking for a work, sending some of his own, & mentioning [John] Pine's intention to print an Ed of Virgil. Koch Foundation. (90) $4,500

— 2 May 1740. 1 p, 4to. Recipient unnamed. Expressing thanks. (90) DM2,400

— 17 May 1740. 1 p, 4to. To his wife Elisabeth Christine. Explaining a misunderstanding with her brother about the formation of a regiment. Sgd Federic. In French. (90) DM8,000

— 11 Aug 1740. 1 p, 4to. To his wife Elisabeth Christine. Suggesting that a building project be postponed until the next year. (91) DM6,500

— 17 Aug 1740. 1 p, 4to. To his wife Elisabeth Christine. Promising to attend to her requests after his return & reporting about his stay at Bayreuth. Albrecht collection. (91) SF3,400

— 22 July 1741. 4 pp, 4to. To Voltaire. Mostly in verse, about the current war & other matters. In French. (90) DM18,500

— 3 Feb 1742. 3 pp, 4to. To Voltaire. Lamenting the amount of time he is forced to devote to official duties, praising recipient's work, & commenting about the rulers of Europe. Including 2 lines of verse. Salzer collection. (90) £8,000

— [24 Apr] 1747. 3 pp, 4to. To Voltaire. Commenting about Voltaire's Semiramis & other works. Including 80-line poem. Sgd Federic. In French. Repaired. Schroeder collection. (89) DM18,000

— [c.1750]. 1 p, 4to. To P. L. Moreau de Maupertuis. About recipient's health, & thanking for a report regarding salt works. Sgd Federic. In French. Schroeder collection. (89) DM5,500

— [Nov 1753]. 1 p, 4to. To Michael Gabriel Fredersdorf. Worrying about recipient's health & agreeing to an experiment in alchemy. Sgd Fch. Schroeder collection. (89) DM16,000

— 18 Jan 1754. 1 p, 4to. To his brother Heinrich. Expressing congratulations on his birthday. In French. (89) $1,800

— 12 [Feb 1756]. 1 p, 4to. To [the Duc de Nivernois]. Welcoming pledges of goodwill from the King of France. (91) £1,700

— 11 Apr 1756. 1 p, 4to. To his sister Amalie. Wittily commenting on her inauguration as Abbess of Quedlinburg. Albrecht collection. (91) SF6,000

— 27 Oct 1759. 1 p, 4to. To his sister Amalie. Thanking for a present, & reporting about the war. (89) DM8,000

— 14 Apr [1762]. 1 p, 4to. To Henri de Catt. About the military & diplomatic situation & his current readings. Albrecht collection. (91) SF7,000

— 14 [July 1762]. 2 pp, 4to. To [Henri de Catt]. Complaining about the slow progress of the war & including 20 lines of orig verse. (91) £1,700

— 18 [July 1762]. 3 pp, 4to. To [Henri de Catt]. Sending 2 poems (included) & announcing that he has received some crushing news. (91) £1,700

FRIEDRICH II

— 18 [July 1762]. 3 pp, 4to. To Henry de Catt. Worrying about the news from Russia & the military situation, & sending 2 poems (included, 43 & 23 lines). (91) DM18,000

— 25 Nov 1762. 2 pp, 4to. To Henri de Catt. Sending a long poem (at head, 55 lines) about 16th-cent French church history, & expressing frustation about the military, political & financial situation. Albrecht collection. (91) SF9,700

— 5 Sept 1763. 1 p, 4to. To his sister [Queen Louisa Ulrika of Sweden?]. Recommending [Kaspar] von Saldern. In French. (90) DM5,500

— 3 July 1765. 1 p, 4to. To his sister Amalie. Responding to a request for money. In French. (91) DM5,600

— 25 Apr 1772. 1 p, 4to. To his brother Ferdinand. Asking that he take good care of his health & delay his travels. Sgd Federic. In French. With a port. (88) DM6,000

— 3 Aug 1779. 1 p, 4to. To his wife Elisabeth Christine. Expressing satisfaction about her brother's visit. Albrecht collection. (91) SF3,200

— 18 Jan 1784. 1 p, 4to. To his brother Heinrich. Expressing congratulations on his birthday. Sgd Federic. In French. (90) DM8,500

— 27 Feb 1784. 2 pp, 4to. To his brother Heinrich. Deliberating about human destiny, & referring to political problems in the Netherlands. (90) DM8,600

— 18 Jan 1786. 1 p, 4to. To his brother Heinrich. Expressing congratulations on his birthday. With engraved port. (91) DM6,500

— 20 Jan 1786. 1 p, 4to. To his brother Heinrich. Complaining about his failing health. Albrecht collection. (91) SF7,000

— 2 Apr 1786. 1 p, 4to. To his brother [Heinrich]. Informing him about his declining health. Sgd Federic. In French. (88) DM12,500

Collection of 14 Ls s & autograph endorsement, sgd, 1741 to 1770. 15 pp, folio & 4to. To various recipients. Orders & instructions regarding the admission of various students to the Joachimsthalsche Gymnasium at Berlin. With related material. (88) DM6,400

— Collection of 2 Ls s & Ds, 15 Apr 1744 to 25 Sept 1764. 6 pp, folio & 4to. To the Dowager Princess of Hesse-Homburg, concerning her son. To Baron Bielefeld, thanking for a report. Appointment of Simon Gorgier. Salzer collection. (90) £1,150

Series of c.90 Ls s, 30 May 1733 to 5 Aug 1780. About 250 pp, folio & 4to; 2 vols in 19th-cent limp bds. To Samuel von Marschall & members of his family. About a wide variety of military & financial matters. Various signatures; many autograph subscriptions; some endorsements in margins of memoranda. Including Ls by Friedrich Wilhelm I of Prussia. (89) £8,000

— Series of 4 Ls s, 17 Oct 1782 to 15 Apr 1785. 4 pp, 4to. To Christian von Massenbach. Thanking for a trans, referring to his wish to leave the Wuerttemberg army, fortifications, etc. (91) DM2,600

Ls s (2), 30 Mar 1751 & 17 June 1779. (91) £380

Ls, 30 May 1737. Schroeder collection. (89) DM750

— 17 Nov 1738. 1 p, 4to. To King Charles IV of Naples & Sicily. Requesting permission for Lieut. von Thoss to recruit soldiers in recipient's territories. (91) DM1,300

— 2 Feb 1739. Albrecht collection. (91) SF550

— 20 Sept 1739. (89) DM650

— 9 July 1740. 1 p, 4to. To Gen. Christian August von Anhalt-Zerbst. Concerning the supply of grain. Sgd Friderich. Fold tears repaired. (88) DM1,900

— 28 July 1740. (91) DM670

— 8 Apr 1741. Schroeder collection. (89) DM750

— 17 June 1742. 1 p, 4to. To Georg von Knobelsdorff. Discussing his building activities at Rheinsberg, Charlottenburg, & the Berlin Opera. Sgd Federic. With 11-line autograph postscript. In French. Verso used as address leaf at a later date. (88) DM8,500

— 18 Jan 1743. (90) DM800

— 27 May 1743. (88) DM650

— 13 June 1744. 1 p, folio. To King Charles of Naples & Sicily. Informing

him of his succession to the principality of East Friesland. Sgd Federic. In French. (88) DM1,300
— 3 Oct 1744. 1 p, folio. To King Charles of Naples & Sicily. Informing him of the birth of his nephew [the future King Friedrich Wilhelm II]. Sgd Federic. In French. (88) DM1,600
— 6 Nov 1744. 1 p, 4to. To Lieut. Gen. von Nassau. Concerning the war in Silesia. Sgd Friderich. With 6-line autograph postscript, sgd. Schroeder collection. (89) DM3,200
— 13 May 1747. (89) DM600
— 21 July 1747. (90) DM650
— 15 Apr 1749. Schroeder collection. (89) DM650
— 22 Apr 1750. (90) $425
— 1 July 1751. (90) DM800
— 27 Dec 1751. (88) £220
— 8 Oct 1755. (88) DM950
— 24 Nov 1756. (91) DM700
— 11 Jan 1757. Doheny collection. (89) $650
— 25 Feb 1765. (90) DM750
— 10 Apr 1765. 1 p, 4to. To his brother Ferdinand. About the illness of their sister Sophie & his own health problems. With autograph postscript, 2 lines. Sgd Federic. In French. (89) DM1,800
— 15 July 1765. (89) DM950
— 20 June 1767. 1 p, 4to. To Prince Wilhelm von Hessen-Kassel. Refusing his request to grant an extended leave to Baron Wulfen. In French. (90) DM1,100
— 10 Feb 1768. 1 p, folio. To his head office for postal administration. Giving instructions for the sale of the old post office at Wesel. (91) DM1,300
— 24 June 1768. (88) DM750
— 9 Oct 1770. (89) DM850
— 15 Apr 1771. (89) DM650
— 11 Nov 1771. (88) DM850
— 25 Nov 1771. (90) DM750
— 1 Sept 1772. 1 p, folio. To Empress Maria Theresa. Announcing the birth of a daughter of his nephew [the future King] Friedrich Wilhelm. (90) DM5,500
— 25 Feb 1773. (90) DM800
— 7 Sept 1773. (88) DM750

— 24 Feb 1774. 1 p, 4to. To his nephew [the future King] Friedrich Wilhelm II. Explaining his reluctance to discharge young officers. Sgd Friderich. (88) DM1,400
— 28 Oct 1774. (89) DM560
— 16 Jan 1775. 1 p, 4to. To Friedrich Christoph von Goerne. Discussing administrative matters. Sgd Frdch. With Ds, 1781. (90) DM1,100
— 17 Nov 1776. (89) DM700
— 23 Oct 1777. (89) DM450
— 8 July 1779. (89) DM700
— 17 June 1780. Schroeder collection. (89) DM650
— 4 Sept 1780. (91) DM1,000
— 29 Sept 1780. (89) DM700
— 24 Nov 1780. (90) $425
— 28 Nov 1780. (90) $450
— 7 Nov 1781. (91) $475
— 28 Jan 1782. (88) DM550
— 19 June 1783. (90) DM700
— 19 July 1785. Schroeder collection. (89) DM550
— 18 Jan 1786. 1 p, 4to. To his brother Heinrich. Expressing congratulations on his birthday. Sgd Federic. In French. Schroeder collection. (89) DM7,500

ANs, 11 Oct 1776. Salzer collection. (90) £450

ADs, 25 Sept 1770. 1 p, 4to. Pay order addressed to [his councillor] Buchholtz in favor of the brothers Jordan [for 2 snuff boxes]. With related material. Albrecht collection. (91) SF2,400

Ds, 25 June 1750. (90) DM750
— [n.d.]. (88) £280
— 4 Dec 1756. (90) DM800
— 25 May 1765. (90) DM750
— 24 Sept 1766. (90) DM800
— 15 Feb 1777. 3 pp, folio. Appointment of Christian Gottfried Schuetze as professor at Halle. (91) DM1,100
— 9 Sept 1781. (89) DM800
— 10 Feb 1784. (90) DM800
— 5 June 1786. Schroeder collection. (89) DM850

Autograph endorsement, sgd Fch, [1740?]. (88) DM680
— Anr, sgd Fch. 5 words on an inquiry regarding a subsidy for a manufacturer of silk, 11 Feb 1749. 1 p, folio.

FRIEDRICH II

(88) DM1,050
— Anr, sgd Fch. Schroeder collection. (89) DM700
— Anr, sgd Fr. On verso of a memorial by Baron Sweerts, 18 Mar 1754, 1 p, folio, concerning payment to Giuseppe Bibiena for theatre decorations. Allowing 300 ecus. (88) DM1,600
— Anr, sgd Federic, on a letter addressed to him by Johann Anton Calzabighi, 26 Nov 1765, 1 p, folio, notifying him of a payment. Note of acknowledgment, in French. (88) DM1,100
— Anr, sgd, on a report addressed to him, 5 Jan 1775, 1 p, folio, concerning buildings belonging to a clock manufactory; declining the sale of the buildings. (90) DM2,200
— Anr, [n.d.]. (89) DM330
See also: Friedrich Wilhelm I & Friedrich II

Friedrich II Eugen, Herzog von Wuerttemberg, 1732-97
Ls, 28 May 1795. (89) DM500
— 30 Jan 1797. (90) DM340

Friedrich III, Kurfuerst von Sachsen, 1463-1525
Series of Letters, 3 letters, 6 Jan 1513 to 29 Mar 1518. (90) DM470

Friedrich III, Deutscher Kaiser, 1831-88
Autograph Ms, comments in a conversation [with his sister Luise, 20 Feb 1888]. Schroeder collection. (89) DM460
— Autograph Ms, comments in a conversation with [Fuerst von Radolin?, 2 Apr 1888]. 1 p, 4vo. Referring to Bismarck, relations with Russia, & the possibility of his daughter's marriage to Alexander von Battenberg. Schroeder collection. (89) DM1,100
— Autograph Ms, comments in a conversation, complaining about lack of sleep, [1888]. (91) DM560
— Autograph Ms, general order addressed to the soldiers of the 3d army, 11 Aug 1870. 1 p, folio. Draft, expressing pride in the success of the German arms; sgd. Schroeder collection. (89) DM4,200
Series of 20 A Ls s, 20 Feb 1838 to Dec 1859. 34 pp, various sizes. To Christine Roessner. Early letters to his nurse.

With related material. (91) DM2,400
A Ls s (2), 21 Apr 1853 & 5 Nov 1863. (90) DM800
ALs, [March 1848]. 1 p, 4to. To Waldemar von Buelow. Informing him that his family will have to move to Potsdam, & requesting his immediate visit. (91) DM1,200
— 28 Oct 1856. Schroeder collection. (89) DM440
— 29 June 1857. (90) DM420
— 28 Mar 1858. (88) DM320
— 24 Oct [1861]. Schroeder collection. (89) DM420
— 9 Jan 1862. (88) DM1,000
— 28 Oct 1871. (89) DM380
— 24 Mar 1873. Schroeder collection. (89) DM220
— 5 June 1879. Schroeder collection. (89) DM550
— 8 June 1879. Schroeder collection. (89) DM550
— 28 Oct 1883. 4 pp, 4to. To Leonhard Graf von Blumenthal. Evaluating the talents of his son [later Emperor Wilhelm II], & thanking for congratulations on his birthday. Schroeder collection. (89) DM1,900
— 15 July 1884. (91) DM460
— 11 May 1885. (91) DM420
— 19 June 1885. Schroeder collection. (89) DM400
— 20 Mar 1888. (88) DM1,000
Ls, 28 Jan 1862. (91) DM360
— 7 June 1877. (88) DM550
— 17 Apr 1888. Schroeder collection. (89) DM700
— 24 May 1888. (91) DM900
ANs, 24 Jan 1872. (90) DM800
— 24 May 1888. (90) DM850
Ds, 24 Feb 1865. (91) $325
— 11 Apr 1888. Schroeder collection. (89) DM800
Autograph sentiment, sgd, 18 Oct 1851. Schroeder collection. (89) DM450
Autograph telegram, sgd, 29 Jan 1871. (90) DM650
— Anr, [30 June 1871]. (90) DM330
Photograph, sgd, 4/5 Sept 1886. 42cm by 25cm. In uniform. Sgd on mount. Schroeder collection. (89) DM1,300

Friedrich Karl, Prince of Prussia, 1828-85
ALs, 6 Apr 1868. (89) DM280
See also: Bismarck, Otto von

Friedrich Karl, Prince of Prussia, 1818-85
Autograph Ms, Rueckblicke am Silvesterabende 1848; tp & 9pp, folio. Account of the Revolution of 1848 in Berlin; sgd F.K. PvP. (90) DM1,300

Friedrich Karl, Prince of Prussia, 1828-85
A Ls s (2), 30 May & 1 June 1864. 8 pp, 4to. To Gen. von Moltke. Discussing preparations for a continuation of the war with Denmark. Endorsed by Moltke. (90) DM2,600
ADs, 7 June 1866. (91) DM380

Friedrich V, Kurfuerst von der Pfalz, 1596-1632
Series of 23 A Ls s, 13 Aug 1619 to 5/15 Nov 1632. About 50 pp, folio & 4to. To his wife Elizabeth, Queen of Bohemia. Discussing the political & military situation, family affairs, etc. (91) £13,000
ALs, 28 Nov 1620. (89) $425
Ls, 4/14 Feb 1621. 2 pp, folio. To the King of Denmark & the Dukes of Braunschweig, Mecklenburg & Saxony. Informing them that he is sending an envoy to their projected meeting at Segeberg. (91) DM14,000

Friedrich Wilhelm, Herzog von Braunschweig-Wolfenbuettel, 1771-1815
ALs, 27 Sept 1802. Schroeder collection. (89) DM480
— 30 Jan 1814. (90) DM450

Friedrich Wilhelm, Kurfuerst von Brandenburg ("The Great Elector"), 1620-88
ALs, 8 Feb 1662. 1 p, folio. To King Louis XIV of France. Sending an envoy to express congratulations on the birth of the dauphin. Geigy-Hagenbach collection. (90) DM8,500
Ls, 14 Jan 1654. (90) DM320
— 2 Apr 1661. (90) DM480
— 27 Oct 1662. (88) DM600
— 30 June/10 July 1663. (88) DM520
— 12 Feb 1664. (89) DM600
— 17 Nov 1664. (91) DM520
— 12 Nov 1666. (91) DM750
— 14 Sept 1672. (89) DM450
— 6 July 1683. (89) DM450

— 20 June 1684. Schroeder collection. (89) DM500
Ds, 16 Nov 1660. (90) DM500
— 12 Feb 1668. (88) £120
— 19 May 1681. (90) DM360

Friedrich Wilhelm I, King of Prussia, 1688-1740
ALs, [1718]. 1 p, 4to. Recipient unnamed. Providing for Gen. du Portail after his discharge. Schroeder collection. (89) DM2,500
— [18 May 1727]. 1 p, folio. To Graf von Seckendorff. Urging him to support a petition to the Emperor. (90) DM4,000
Collection of 8 Ls s & 56 autograph endorsements, sgd, 10 Oct 1722 to 11 Sept 1739. Nearly 100 pp, folio & 4to. To Samuel von Marshall. Letters to his Minister of State & comments & decisions in the margins of letters addressed to him by Marshall; including related material. (91) DM24,000
Series of c.60 Ls s, 10 Oct 1722 to 28 Aug 1739. About 240 pp, mostly folio, in 19th-cent limp bds. To Samuel von Marschall. Covering a wide variety of political concerns. Some initialled; some endorsements in margins of memoranda. (89) £3,000
Ls, 13 Mar 1713. Schroeder collection. (89) DM700
— 21 Mar 1714. Schroeder collection. (89) DM500
— 28 May 1717. (89) DM390
— 5 Aug 1719. (89) DM320
— 8 Nov 1719. (90) DM450
— 17 Jan 1721. (90) DM480
— 29 Aug 1721. 1 p, 4to. To his minister von Massow. Regarding preparations for his projected journey to East Prussia. With autograph postscript. Schroeder collection. (89) DM1,050
— 1 Feb 1722. (89) DM250
— 9 June 1723. (88) DM410
— 8 Dec 1725. (90) DM520
— 31 Oct 1726. Schroeder collection. (89) DM440
— 31 Aug 1730. (89) DM700
— 19 June 1733. Schroeder collection. (89) DM700
— 21 Sept 1734. (88) DM520
— 22 Mar 1738. (88) DM430

FRIEDRICH WILHELM I

— 31 Oct 1738. (91) DM650
Ds, 18 June 1721. Schroeder collection. (89) DM400
— 18 Oct 1731. Schroeder collection. (89) DM440
— 25 Feb 1736. (90) DM300
— 18 Nov 1737. (88) DM400
Autograph endorsement, sgd, 15 lines on a report addressed to him by a governmental agency, 5 Mar 1714, 2 pp, folio, regarding the lease of some meadows near Oranienburg; suggesting a lease to 9 families. (90) DM600
— Anr, sgd, 11 May 1724. (91) DM550
— Anr, sgd, 10 Dec 1728. (91) DM580

Friedrich Wilhelm I, King of Prussia, 1688-1740 —&
Friedrich II, King of Prussia, 1712-86
Series of Ds s, 11 Ds s, 1713 to 1740. (89) £1,000

Friedrich Wilhelm II, King of Prussia, 1744-97
ALs, 13 Jan 1793. 1 p, 4to. To an unnamed lady. Asking that she act as godmother to his daughter Julie. (91) DM2,000
Ls s (2), 19 Jan & 2 Aug 1782. (90) DM260
— Ls s (2), 8 July 1787 & 28 Nov 1794. (90) DM360
— Ls s (2), 31 Dec 1791 & 7 Jan 1794. (91) DM320
Ls, 27 Sept 1784. (91) DM330
— 19 Aug 1786. Schroeder collection. (89) DM260
— 19 May 1787. (88) DM330
— 24 July 1787. Schroeder collection. (89) DM200
— 12 Aug 1788. (89) DM360
— 28 Nov 1789. (90) DM230
— 30 Sept 1791. (90) DM450
— 26 Oct 1791. Schroeder collection. (89) DM220
— 15 Jan 1793. 3 pp, 4to. To August von Struensee. Giving instructions to negotiate loans in Amsterdam & Genoa & to coin new money. (90) DM1,500
Ds, 3 Jan 1797. Schroeder collection. (89) DM340
— Ritz, Johann Friedrich. - 3 A Ls s, 8 Dec 1789 to 11 Nov 1790. 3 pp, 4to. To Col. von Lange. Regarding payments to officers of recipient's regiment. (90) DM320

Friedrich Wilhelm II, King of Prussia, 1744-97 —&
Hardenberg, Karl August, Fuerst von, 1750-1822
[An important collection of Ls by Friedrich Wilhelm, 28 Oct 1791, & 19 A Ls s by Hardenberg, 1791 & 1792, 60 pp, 4to, to Markgraf Karl Alexander von Brandenburg-Ansbach und Bayreuth, with related material, regarding the sale of Karl Alexander's territories to Prussia, sold at star on 10 Mar 1988, lot 1441, for DM11,000.]

Friedrich Wilhelm III, King of Prussia, 1770-1840
Autograph Ms, 8 personal notes regarding the death of his wife Queen Luise, 18 July 1810 to 19 July 1816. 10 pp, 8vo & 4to. (89) DM8,500
ALs, 10 Feb 1791. (90) DM520
— 2 Dec 1795. (89) DM900
— 2 Oct 1823. (90) DM360
Ls s (2), 8 May 1788 & 19 Dec 1789. (88) DM300
— Ls s (2), 8 May 1788 & 19 Dec 1789. (90) DM280
— Ls s (2), 14 Dec 1810 & 12 Mar 1812. (91) DM550
Ls, 16 Mar 1802. (90) DM220
— 1 Apr 1802. (89) DM200
— 21 Dec 1802. (91) DM320
— 5 Mar 1806. (89) DM300
— 3 Aug 1807. (90) DM950
— 15 Feb 1808. (88) DM300
— 13 July 1808. Schroeder collection. (89) DM520
— 2 Aug 1809. (88) DM220
— 21 Nov 1809. Schroeder collection. (89) DM300
— 16 May 1810. Schroeder collection. (89) DM280
— 23 Mar 1813. Schroeder collection. (89) DM280
ANs, 10 June 1808. (91) DM600
Ds, 20 Mar 1798. (90) DM340
— 16 July 1798. (90) DM500
— 19 Mar 1805. (91) DM260
— 11 Dec 1811. (91) DM250
— 21 Dec 1828. (89) DM250
— 22 Aug 1831. 8 pp, folio, in red mor

bdg. Patent of nobility for Henriette Sontag von Lauenstein, Countess Rossi. Including large painting of the arms in gold & colors. (90) DM5,500
— 30 Mar 1832. (90) DM680

Friedrich Wilhelm IV, King of Prussia, 1795-1861
Original drawings, various ornaments & figures, [c.1850]. (90) DM220
Collection of ALs & 2 autograph Mss, [n.d.]. (90) DM950
Series of 3 A Ls s, 2 June to 4 July 1823. 4 pp, 4to & 8vo. To Friedrich Karl von Savigny. Regarding his brother Wilhelm's wish to marry Princess Elisa Radziwill. Schroeder collection. (89) DM1,600
— Series of 3 A Ls s, 5 Apr 1830 to 29 Dec 1837. Schroeder collection. (89) DM750
A Ls s (2), 31 Oct 1850 & 30 Apr 1852. 3 pp, 8vo & 4to. To Friedrich Karl von Savigny. Personal letters congratulating on the 50th anniversary of his examination for the doctorate, & sending condolences on the death of his son. Schroeder collection. (89) DM1,200
ALs, 24 Apr 1813. (90) DM900
— 6 June 1815. Schroeder collection. (89) DM460
— 2/4 Mar 1830. 5 pp, 4to. To his father Friedrich Wilhelm III of Prussia. Lively letter reporting about his visit in Dresden & his efforts to win Barthold Georg Niebuhr for a position in Berlin. Sgd Fritz. (90) DM2,200
— 16 Dec 1832. (88) DM520
— 12 May 1833. (90) DM440
— 17 Feb 1849. Schroeder collection. (89) DM420
— 17 Aug 1849. (89) DM300
Ls, 31 Oct 1823. (89) DM200
— 28 Dec 1825. (90) DM200
Ds s (2)4 Apr 1857. (91) DM360

Friesz, Othon, 1879-1949
ALs, [n.d.], "Tuesday". 6 pp, 4to. To an unnamed art dealer. Discussing the art market, the authenticity of works ascribed to Corot, etc. Including sketch of proposed painting. (91) $2,800

Friml, Rudolf, 1879-1972
Ds, 17 Apr 1936. (88) $70
Photograph, sgd & inscr, 16 Sept 1948. (91) $110

Friolus, Hieronymus, Doge of Venice
Document, 1559. Ducale appointing Pietro Delfino Governor of Monfalcone, in the province of Trieste. 24 leaves, vellum, 230mm by 165mm, in contemp mor gilt with Lion of St. Mark on upper cover & Delfino arms on lower cover. In cursive script in 2 hands. With full-page frontis of Justice conferring the appointment to Delfino. (91) $2,000

Frisch, Karl von, 1886-1982
Autograph Ms, draft of his Nobel Prize speech, p 11; [1973]. (91) DM250
ALs, 25 May 1975. (90) DM550

Frisch, Max
ALs, [n.d.]. (89) DM260

Fritchie, Barbara, 1766-1862
Ds s (2)3 Mar 1858 & 16 Sept 1861. 1 p, 4to, & size not stated. Power of attorney to Christian Steiner. Receipt for $170, sgd with her mark & witnessed by Harriet Yaner; inlaid with ptd verses of Whittier's poem. Sang collection. (90) $5,500

Fritsch, Werner, Freiherr von, 1880-1939
ALs, 10 July 1931. (90) DM680

Frobisher, Martin, Sir, 1535?-94. See: Burghley, William Cecil

Froebel, Friedrich, 1782-1852
ALs, 4 Apr 1843. 4 pp, 8vo. To Herr Scheider. Reflecting about life. Corner def. (89) DM2,200
— 27 July 1843. 4 pp, 8vo. To Friederike Schmidt. About an error in a list of donations, & about his aim to work for children. (91) DM1,400

Froebel, Julius, 1805-93
ALs, [c.late Oct 1842]. 1 p, 8vo. To [Karl Marx]. Sending an article for the Rh[einische] Z[eitung] & inquiring about Herwegh. (89) DM2,200

Froissart, Jean, 1333?-1400?

Ms, Chroniques; abridgement. [Rouen, c.1505-10]. 263 leaves, vellum, 500mm by 340mm. Massive 19th-cent bdg of thick wooden bds covered with red velvet & fitted with elaborate center & corner-pieces of silver gilt. In a very skilful large semi-gothic lettre batarde. With large illuminated initials throughout in elaborate classical designs, 194 column-width miniatures with borders in elaborate designs of colored flowers, fruit & acanthus leaves, including many animals & grotesques, & 4 full-page miniatures enclosing panels of text. Illuminated for Cardinal George d'Amboise, partly by the Master of Petrarch's Triumphs. (91) £1,250,000

Ds, 20 Nov 1369. 1 p, vellum, 3 by 11.25 inches. Pay order issued by Charles II, King of Navarre. Blank portion cut away. Tipped to larger leaf. Barrett collection. (89) $4,250

Fromentieres, Jean Louis de, Bishop of Aire, 1632-84. See: La Valliere, Louise Francoise de La Baume le Blanc

Froriep, Ludwig Friedrich von, 1779-1847

ALs, 15 Nov 1811. (91) DM210

Frost, Robert, 1874-1963

Autograph Ms, poem, Last October, sgd & inscr to G. B. Saul, 15 Mar 1939. On 2d front blank leaf of a copy of his Collected Poems. NY,1930. (90) $1,600

Collection of 6 A Ls s & 4 Ls s, 1930 to 1958. 12 pp, various sizes. To Paul Osborn. About personal matters & Osborn's writings. (90) $6,500

Series of 3 A Ls s, 1920-24. 5 pp, 8vo. To Julia Patton of Russell Sage College. About poetry readings at the school. With related material. (88) $1,600

A Ls s (2), 23 July 1921 & 23 Aug 1930. Doheny collection. (89) $900

ALs, 1 July 1936. (89) $250

— 1 Aug 1942. 2 pp, 4to. To Hervey Allen. Concerning Allen's visit & other personal matters. Burn hole. (90) $1,500

Autograph quotation, couplet, "We dance round in a ring..."; 1943. (91) $550

Froud, Brian

Original drawings, (10), to illus Margaret Mahy's The Wind between the Stars, 1975. In ink & watercolor, mostly 533mm by 761mm. Archives of J. M. Dent & Son. (88) £1,100

— Original drawings, (11), to illus Mary Norton's Are all the Giants Dead?; [n.d.]. Archives of J. M. Dent & Son. (88) £800

— Original drawings, (14), to illus Margaret Mahy's The Railway Engine and the Hairy Brigands, 1973. Archives of J. M. Dent & Son. (88) £500

Froude, James Anthony, 1818-94

Series of 39 A Ls s, 1873 to 1892. 161 pp, 8vo. To Charles Butler. About financial matters, English politics, literary projects, etc. With related material. (88) $3,200

Frundsberg, Georg von, d.1586

Ls, 14 Feb 1565. (90) DM340

Fry, Elizabeth, 1780-1845

ALs, 22 Aug 1823. (91) £400

Ds, [n.d.]. (88) £130

Fry, Roger, 1866-1934

ALs, 13 Nov 1926. (89) DM780

— 13 Jan 1927. (89) DM380

Fry, Rosalie

Original drawings, (137), to illus various of her own books, 1955 to 1959. Archives of J. M. Dent & Son. (90) £400

— Original drawings, (22), to illus her own The Mountain Door, 1960. Archives of J. M. Dent & Son. (88) £80

— Original drawings, (29), to illus Charles Kingsley's The Water Babies, 1963. Archives of J. M. Dent & Son. (88) £380

— Original drawings, (43), to illus the adventures of a mouse in 3 stories by Modwena Sedgewick, 1957 & 1959. Archives of J. M. Dent & Son. (88) £70

Frye, Joseph, c.1711-94. See: French & Indian War

Fugger Family
— UJLAKY, JOHN IV, BISHOP OF VAC. - Collection of 2 A Ls s, 5 Ls s & 2 Ls, 2 Aug to 17 Oct 1562. 17 pp, folio. To Jacob Sawrzapff, agent for the House of Fugger at Debrecen, & Stanislas Humhardt & Johann Jedelhauser, agents at Werecen. Regarding the transfer of the castle at Debrecen from the Fuggers to the King of Bohemia. In Latin. With draft of a letter from Sawrzapff to Ujlaky. (88) DM1,200

Fugger, Octavianus Secundus, 1549-1600
Ds s (2)3 June 1586 & [1598]. (89) DM850

Fugger, Oktavian, Freiherr von Kirchberg, 1549-1600
Ds, 1596. 1 p, 4to. Confirmation of a bill for paintings, etc. received from Heybrecht Caymor. With Caymor's receipt at bottom. (90) DM2,600

Fulda, Ida
[Her guest book, containing c.120 entries by German artists, musicians, literary personalities, etc., 1894 to 1915, 8vo, in half lea bdg, sold at HN on 30 Nov 1990, lot 1707, for DM2,700.]

Fuller, Melville Weston, 1833-1910
Collection of ALs, 4 A Ns s, 23 autograph documents, 5 typescripts, & 10 annotated printer's proofs, c.1903-05. (89) $300

Fuller, Roy
Autograph Ms, 20 lectures given at Oxford University, [n.d.]. (88) £300

Fulton, Robert, 1765-1815
ALs, 6 Sept 1806. 4 pp, 4to. To Capt. Thomas Johnson. Giving instructions for testing his submarine torpedo. Doheny collection. (89) $4,200
— 6 Aug 1811. 4 pp, 4to. To Mr. Colding. Discussing a suit against [John Stevens] for copying his steamboat. (91) $12,000
— 12 Mar 1812. 3 pp, 4to. To Oliver Evans. Retained draft, accepting a bet & doubting that Evans can build a successful steamboat. (90) $4,750
— 28 Dec 1813. 3 pp, 4to. To Peter Jay Monroe. Discussing the procurement of coal for his steamboats. Docketed.

(88) $2,200
— 23 Jan 1815. 1 p, 4to. To Soloman Etting. About money matters to pay for work on his submarine. (91) $2,000

Fundulus, Hieronymus
Autograph Ms, Lucia, comedia. Cremona, 1 Oct 1564. 50 leaves, 248mm by 177mm, in contemp mor gilt. Dedication copy presented to the bishop of Bergamo, Federigo Cornarus. Schiff Ms (91) $47,000

Funk, Casimir, 1884-1967
Typescript, autobiographical sketch of his career as biochemist, sgd; [29 Aug 1965]. (90) $550

Funk, Walther, 1890-1960
Ds, [1946]. (90) $170

Furniss, Harry, 1854-1925
ALs, 22 Mar 1919. (89) £140

Furtwaengler, Wilhelm, 1886-1954
Collection of 6 A Ls s, Ls, & 6 autograph postcards, sgd, 20 Jan 1920 to 4 Aug 1923 & [n.d.]. 9 pp, 4to & 8vo, & cards. To Benda Edenhofer. Mostly regarding concerts. With related material. (90) DM2,500
— Collection of ALs, 4 Ls s & 2 typescripts (carbon copies), 13 Jan 1946 to 12 Apr 1949. 30 pp, folio. To Willi Schuh, mostly about his attitude toward National Socialism. Typescripts, "Schlusswort am 17. Dezember 1946 - Berlin", & essay beginning "Als vor einiger Zeit in der Schweiz die Angriffe auf mich begannen..." (90) DM2,200
Series of 3 A Ls s, 7 Mar 1919 to 26 Sept 1939. 3 pp, various sizes. To a musician, regarding the possibility of her playing in concerts. To a friend, hoping to see him in Munich. (88) DM1,100
ALs, 4 July 1913. (90) DM550
— 5 June 1923. (88) DM500
Ls, 11 Sept 1926. (89) DM360
Autograph postcards (2), sgd, 7 Jan 1931 & [n.d.]. (89) DM550
Concert program, 16 Jan 1950. (88) $325
— DOHME, ENRIQUE GUILLERMO. - Engraved port of Furtwaengler, sgd; May 1950. 29.5cm by 19cm. Also sgd by

FURTWAENGLER

Furtwaengler. With related material. (90) DM950

Futurism

[An important collection of Futurist material, including Ms & typescript pentagrammatic poems by various authors, c.20 items, 1915 to 1935, sold at S on 18 May 1989, lot 247, for £5,000 to Libri.]

G

Gabelentz, Georg von der, 1868-1940
Signature, [c.1922]. (88) DM320

Gable, Clark, 1901-60
Check, sgd, 10 Mar 1945. (91) $225
— Anr, sgd, 13 Mar 1950. (89) $200
Photograph, sgd, [n.d.]. (91) $225
Photograph, sgd & inscr, [c.1940]. (90) $450
— Anr, [n.d.]. (90) $200
— HERRIN, M. H. - Orig drawing, pencil bust port of Gable, 1934. 8 by 11 inches. Sgd by both; inscr to Herrin by Gable. (91) $300

Gable, Clark, 1901-60 —&
Leigh, Vivien, 1913-67
[Their signatures, [n.d.], matted with a grouph photograph, overall size 14 by 14 inches, sold at Dar on 10 Apr 1991, lot 5, for $600.]

Gable, Clark, 1901-60. See: Lombard, Carole & Gable

Gaboriau, Emile, 1832-73
ALs, 9 Sept [n.y.]. (90) DM220

Gade, Niels Wilhelm, 1817-90
[A engraved port, inscr to A. Josephson, Apr 1847, 31cm by 26cm, laid down, with related material, sold at S on 6 May 1988, lot 262, for £200 to Kessler.]
Autograph music, sketches for the cantata Comala, sgd & dated Feb [18]46, containing c.230 bars for several sections of the work; & 3 autograph musical quotations inscr to J. (89) £600
ALs, 31 Jan 1848. (90) £450

AMERICAN BOOK PRICES CURRENT

Gagarin, Yuri, 1934-68
Photograph, sgd, [n.d.]. (91) DM340
Signature, [10 Jan 1964]. (91) $475
— Anr, on Russian stamp issued for his flight. (89) $230

Gage, Thomas, 1721-87
A Ls s (2), 4 Dec 1769 & 3 June 1772. (88) $350
Ls, 26 Mar 1764. (89) $350
— 19 Sept 1769. (88) $650

Gagern, Heinrich, Freiherr von, 1799-1880
ALs, 16 May 1843. (90) DM420
— 14 Feb 1849. 3 pp, 4to. To [Christian Friedrich von Stockmar]. Important letter discussing the political situation in Germany. With related material. (90) DM3,600

Gainsborough, Thomas, 1727-88
ALs, 15 Sept 1763. 2 pp, 4to. To James Unwin. Talking about his recent illness. (88) DM1,600
— 31 July [1787]. 2 pp, 4to. To his sister Mary Gibbon. Discussing a family problem. (88) $1,100

Gal, Hans
Autograph music, 2 songs, No 2 A Cradle Song (Thomas Dekker), & No 3 Youth and Cupid (Queen Elizabeth); [n.d.]. (91) DM750
— Autograph music, "3 Part Songs for female voices", fragment; [n.d.]. (89) DM550
— Autograph music, Divertimento fuer 3 Blockfloeten, Op. 98; sgd & dated 11 May 1969. 11 pp, 29.5cm by 23.5cm. Complete composition, with some corrections. (90) DM1,100
— Autograph music, "Meanders / Four Movements for Orchestra", Op. 69, complete Ms; 1955. Tp & 32 pp, 315mm by 235mm; 12 staves each. In ink & pencil. (88) DM1,100
— Autograph music, sketches for his Suite fuer Cello solo, Op. (90) DM900
— Autograph music, sketches for nos 2 & 23 of his 24 Preludes, Op. (90) DM550
— Autograph music, "Skizzen zu Op. (90) DM500
— Autograph music, song, Foolish Love, Op.51 no 4, scored for soprano; [n.d.]. (91) DM240

— Autograph music, Spaetlese, Lieder fuer Maennerstimmen, Op. 91; 1966 to 1969. 14 pp, 30.5cm by 24cm. Sgd twice. With Ls, 24 Aug 1976. (90) DM1,100
— Autograph music, Suite for Viola & Pianoforte Op. (91) DM500

Galilei, Galileo, 1564-1642
Transcript, contemp copy of his letter to Grand Duchess Christina, [1615], asserting inadmissiblity of theological interference in scientific matters; [n.d.]. 56 pp & tp, 4to, in vellum wraps. In Italian. (88) £2,200

Gall, Franz Joseph, 1758-1828
Ds, 16 Sept 1824. (89) DM300

Gallas, Matthias, Duke of Lucera, 1584-1647
ALs, [n.d.]. 1 p, folio. Recipient unnamed. Recommending members of the von Taubadel family. (90) DM1,400
Ds, 19 Jan 1647. 1 p, 4to. Safeguard for the town of Roth near Nuremberg. With related material. (89) DM1,400

Gallatin, Albert, 1761-1849
ALs, 21 Oct 1790. (91) $250
— 5 Oct 1802. (91) $225
— 15 Aug 1816. (89) $80
— 20 Dec 1845. (91) $130
Ls, [10 Sept] 1801. (88) $160
— 1 July 1812. (88) $70

Galle, Emile, 1846-1904
ALs, 3 Sept 1889. 2 pp, 8vo. To Henri Guerard. Discussing techniques to depict his vases. Including 4 pen-&-ink sketches. (90) DM4,200
Ls, 3 July 1894. (88) DM360

Galli-Curci, Amelita, 1882-1963
Photograph, sgd & inscr, 1918. (91) $200

Gallieni, Joseph Simon, 1849-1916. See: Madagascar

Gallini, Giovanni, 1728-1805
Ls, 24 Dec 1790. (88) £350

Gallizzi, G. E.
Original drawings, (17), to illus The Life and Death of John Falstaff, 1923. In watercolor (15) or ink. Sgd; c.425mm by 335mm. Archives of J. M. Dent & Son. (88) £2,800

Galloway, Joseph, 1731-1803
ADs, 27 July 1761. Byer collection. (90) $200

Gallup, George, 1901-84
Ls, 7 Dec 1940. (90) $200

Galsworthy, John, 1867-1933
Collection of ALs & 2 Ls s, 3 Dec 1930, 4 Feb [n.y.] & 26 Sept [n.y.]. Doheny collection. (89) $150
Series of 17 A Ls s, 24 Aug 1919 to 29 Oct 1925. 27 pp, 4to & 8vo. To John Middleton Murry. Referring to literary matters, Murry's work with The Adelphi, Katherine Mansfield, etc. Bradley Martin sale. (90) $2,250
A Ls s (2), 2 June & 17 Sept 1909. (88) £200

Galton, Sir Francis, 1822-1911
ALs, 18 Jan 1876. (89) DM240

Gambetta, Leon, 1838-82
ALs, 3 Sept 1874. (88) DM700

Gampp, Josua Leander
Series of 10 A Ls s, 24 Oct 1930 to 20 Apr 1935. (91) DM900

Gance, Abel, 1889-1981
Group photograph, with Cocteau & Ch. (89) DM210

Gandhi, Indira, 1917-84
Photograph, sgd, 1984. (90) $150

Gandhi, Mohandas K., 1869-1948
[A group of documents & letters relating to the foundation & management of the Phoenix Settlement, including an autograph draft deed expressing his intention to broaden the Phoenix Trust, with related material, 1905 to 1945, sold at C on 20 June 1990, lot 284, for £25,000 to Quaritch.]
[Polak, Henry S. L. - A large collection of his papers, mostly relating to Gandhi, c. 1906 to 1949, thousands of items in 5 boxes, sold at S on 22 July 1988, lot 316, for £22,000 to S. N. Rao.]
Autograph Ms, interview with the Rev. Norman Bennet conducted when under a vow of silence, [n.d.]. 4 pp, framed; overall size 12 by 18 inches.

GANDHI

Discussing his silence, matters in Lucknow, etc. Including explanatory note by Bennet. (88) £21,000

— Autograph Ms, school exercises in English & Sanskrit, [n.d.]. (91) DM650

Collection of 28 A Ls s & Ls s, 16 Aug 1895 to 10 Aug 1914. Nearly 100 pp (with enclosures), folio & 4to. To Sir Mancherjee Bhownaggree. Informing him about issues & developments relating to his civil rights campaign in South Africa. With related material. (90) £23,000

— Collection of 78 A Ls s, 5 A Ls, 45 Ls s, & 3 autograph postcards, sgd, 1905 to 1935. 469 pp, 8vo & 4to. Mostly to Henry Polak, some to his wife Millie. Important letters to a close associate & friend covering a wide range of subjects. With a substantial amount of related material. (90) £60,000

— Collection of c.80 A Ls s & Ls s, 1905 to 1941; c.280 pp, mostly 4to & 8vo. Chiefly to Henry & Millie Polak. Important letters to his legal partner, friend & disciple recording his activities, opinions, etc. With a substantial amount of related material. (88) £95,000

— Collection of 53 A Ls s & Ls s, & 18 autograph postcards, sgd, 1909 to 1947. 120 pp, various sizes. Mostly to Manilal & Sushila Gandhi. Setting out his precepts & giving advice concerning the running of the Phoenix Settlement. (90) £9,000

— Collection of 2 A Ls s & 3 autograph postcards, sgd, 22 Mar 1940 to 14 Oct 1941. 4 pp, 8vo, & cards. Recipient unnamed. Giving advice to a young follower. 1 sgd Bapu. (88) DM8,500

Series of 76 A Ls s, c.1900 to 1914. About 200 pp, 4to & 8vo. To his son Harilal & his wife Gulab (2). Remarkable letters dealing at length with his son's problems; "a litany of well-meaning criticism, reproach, and moral exhortation to reform." Mostly in Gujarati; with English trans. (90) £25,000

— Series of 5 A Ls s, 1914 to 1916. 16 pp, 8vo. To Willie Pearson. About Charlie Andrews & his own philosophy of passive resistance. With related material. (91) £3,500

— Series of 3 A Ls s, 20 Jan to 24 Sept

AMERICAN BOOK PRICES CURRENT

[1916?]. (90) £800

ALs, 9 Nov 1917. 2 pp, 8vo. To Annie Besant. Requesting information about her meeting with the viceroy, sending an address, etc. (91) DM1,900

— 20 Oct 1941. 2 pp, 8vo. To Abbasi. Threatening court action in case of publication of a libellous letter. (90) DM1,100

— "Monday". 1 p, 4to. To the Rev. Norman Bennet. Concerning the problem of prostitution in Lucknow. Framed. (88) £9,000

Collection of Ls & letter, 26 May 1931 to 21 Jan 1941. 3 pp, 4to & 8vo. To Amtul [Salam], expressing pleasure in hearing from her. To Amtul Salam's father, responding to an angry letter regarding his daughter's return home; retained copy on recipient's letter, docketed in Gandhi's hand. With a photograph. (89) £1,300

Ls, 30 Oct [n.y.]. 2 pp, 4to. To William Pearson. Expressing appreciation for his work. Silked. (89) $1,600

Autograph postcard, sgd, 28 May 1934. (89) £250

— Desai, Mahadev. - 3 A Ls s, 1937. 10 pp, 8vo. To Ronald Duncan. About Gandhi & Duncan's efforts for him, the Peace Pledge movement in England, etc. Dampstained. (88) £3,500

— Swamy. - Orig drawing, pencil sketch of Gandhi, Nov 1940. 250mm by 186mm. Sgd by both. (89) £650

— Swamy. - Orig drawing, pencil sketch of Gandhi, [n.d.]. 150mm by 110mm. Sgd by both. (89) £700

Ganghofer, Ludwig, 1855-1920

Collection of 10 A Ls s & autograph postcard, sgd, 6 Nov 1895 to 1 Apr 1899. 68 pp, 8vo. To Johannes Proelss. About his contributions to Die Gartenlaube & other professional matters. (90) DM1,400

ALs, 12 June 1897. (89) DM360

Gans, Eduard, 1798-1839

ALs, 23 Mar 1828. (91) DM480

Garbo, Greta, 1905-90

Collection of 9 A Ls s, A Ns s & autograph telegrams, 3 telegrams & photograph, inscr on verso, 19 Mar 1948 to 31 Oct 1950. Various sizes. To Allen Porter. Expressing thanks & referring to her health, her application for citizenship, etc. Sgd Brownie, Harry Brown, H.B., or unsgd. (89) $9,500

Autograph postcard, sgd, [n.d.]. To Lisa Fager. Birthday greetings to a school friend, sgd G.G. With ANs, 15 photographs, & further related material, c.1915 to 1930. (90) £2,500

Ds, 4 Sept 1941. 1 p, 4to. Carbon copy, addendum to her contract with MGM for Two Faced Woman. (91) $3,000

Autograph sentiment, [1930]. (89) $900

Autograph telegram, sgd, [n.d.]. 1 p, 4to. To Charles Feldman. Thanking for flowers. In pencil. (90) DM2,000

Cut signature, [n.d.]. (89) $550

Photograph, sgd, [4 May 1970]. 8 by 5 inches. Bust port from The Painted Veil. Note of authenticity on verso. With related material. (89) $3,800

— Anr, [n.d.]. 7.75 by 9.4 inches. With Lowell Sherman in The Divine Woman. Was mtd. (90) $1,500

Gardener, Gerald

Original drawings, (52), to illus Fred Kitchen's Jesse and his friends, 1945. Archives of J. M. Dent & Son. (88) £600

Gardner, Ava

Photograph, sgd & inscr, [n.d.]. (88) $130

Gareth, Benedetto, c.1450-1514

Ms, Endimion a la Luna, & other poems. [Naples, c.1490-1500]. 50 leaves, vellum, 205mm by 114mm. Old limp vellum bdg. In a round unright humanistic minuscule. With 7 large illuminated initials & full-page frontis. (91) £38,000

Garfield, James A., 1831-81

Autograph Ms, poem, beginning "When the days of youth are ended", 12 lines, sgd & dated Feb 1854. In autograph album of Mary L. Hubbell, 100 pp, 8vo. (91) $3,500

Collection of 3 A Ls s & 18 Ls s, 1875 to 1880. Length not stated, various sizes. Mostly to Henry Hubbard. Concerning federal funding for the harbor at Ashtabula, Ohio. With related material. (90) $3,000

— Collection of ALs & Ls, 25 Sept & 10 Nov 1880. (90) $800

ALs, 7 Jan 1861. Whiton collection. (88) $450

— 3 July 1862. 3 pp, 4to. To "Dear Wall". Discussing the war in Alabama, his health problems, & his candidacy for Congress. Sang collection. (91) $1,400

— 20 Oct 1862. 1 p, 4to. To Sec of War Stanton. Recommending the appointment of Edward Spear as paymaster. (89) $1,400

— 6 Aug 1865. (89) $300
— 6 Aug 1865. (88) £240
— 28 May 1866. (90) $600
— 14 July 1866. Byer collection. (90) $450
— 25 Sept 1869. Rosenbloom collection. (88) $550
— 31 July 1870. (91) $450
— 31 July 1870. (90) $350
— 5 Aug 1871. (89) $300
— 21 May 1873. (89) £800
— 17 June 1873. (88) $180
— 17 Feb 1875. (90) $600
— 12 Feb 1877. (91) $220
— 3 Sept 1878. (91) $200
— 28 Sept 1878. (91) $325
— 16 Nov 1878. (88) $400
— 25 June [18]80. (90) $280
— 30 June 1880. Pratt collection. (89) $1,000
— 3 July 1880. 1 p, 4to. To James M. Dalzell. Thanking for congratulations on his nomination as Presidential candidate. (88) $1,500
— 16 July 1880. (90) $550
— 20 Aug 1880. (89) $480
— 20 Sept 1880. Sang collection. (91) $800
— 1 Nov 1880. (90) $950
— [n.d.]. Doheny collection. (89) $800

Ls, 8 Feb 1869. (90) $400
— 18 Apr 1870. (91) $350
— 19 Jan 1877. (90) $350
— 27 Sept 1877. (90) $250
— 12 Oct 1878. (90) $250
— 31 Jan 1879. (90) $500

GARFIELD

— 7 Apr 1879. (90) $250
— 26 June 1880. (88) $220
— 13 Sept 1880. (89) $180
— 15 Sept [1880]. (88) $750
— 20 Nov 1880. (91) $600

Ds, 21 Mar 1881. 1 p, folio. Appointment of John Wesley Powell as Director of the US Geological Survey. Fold split. Ruddy collection. (88) $9,000

— 23 May 1881. 1 p, 16 by 20.5 inches. Appointment of Selah Merrill as U.S. Consul at Jerusalem. (89) £5,250

Autograph telegram, sgd, 18 Nov 1874. (91) $250

— Anr, sgd, [n.d.]. (88) $225
— Anr, 11 Feb 1879. (88) $175

Check, sgd, 2 June 1876. (89) $325
Cut signature, [n.d.]. (90) $140
Franking signature, [4 Feb n.y.]. (89) $300

— Anr, [24 May n.y.]. (89) $80
— Anr, [25 Sept n.y.]. (89) $210
— Anr, 22 Dec [n.y.]. (89) $175
— Anr, [n.d.]. (90) $120
— Anr, [n.d.]. (90) $125
— Anr, [n.d.]. (90) $150

Photograph, sgd, [n.d.]. (90) $1,000

— Anr, [n.d.] Cabinet size. Bust profile; by B. Frank Saylor. (90) $1,500
— Anr, [n.d.]. Cabinet size. Profile view. (90) $1,600

Signature, at bottom of ALs by Anson McCook, 23 Nov 1877, 1 p, 4to, to an unnamed recipient; sending autographs. (89) $160

— Anr, 16 Apr 1881. On card. (90) $2,500
— Anr, 25 Apr 1881. 8vo. (91) $2,750
— Anr, 12 May 1881. 8vo. (90) $1,600
— Anr, 8 June 1881. In an autograph album, 8vo. Also sgd by others. (91) $2,250
— Anr, [n.d.]. (91) $300
— Anr, [n.d.]. (91) $250

Telegram, sgd, 8 Aug [1863]. (88) $125

— GUITEAU, CHARLES. - ALs, 26 Nov 1881. 1 p, folio. To the public. Requesting funds for his defense. Doheny collection. (89) $4,500
— HEINLEIN, THOMAS W. - ALs, 8 Dec 1881. 2 pp, 8vo. To Frank Sherry. Reporting about his situation as juror on the assassination trial of Charles J. Guiteau. In pencil. (90) $95

Garfield, Lucretia R., 1832-1918
ALs, 7 May 1886. (90) $140
Check, accomplished & sgd, 18 Sept 1882. (91) $225

Garibaldi, Giuseppe, 1807-82
A Ls s (2), 4 June [1860] & 14 Dec 1871. (88) $500
ALs, 19 Aug 1874. (89) DM600
— 2 July 1875. (89) DM600
— 1 Jan 1879. (90) DM500
Ls, 16 Aug 1848. (89) £950
— 26 Jan 1863. (89) $900
— 23 Sept 1873. (90) DM620
— 5 Apr 1875. (90) DM380
— 14 Apr [18]75. (91) DM350
— 11 May 1875. (88) DM220
— 17 Aug 1878. (90) DM360

Garibay y Zamalloa, Esteban de, 1533?-99
Ms, Origen, y discursos de las Dignidades seglares destos Reynos de Espana, dated 6 Apr 1575. (88) $650

Garidel, Pierre Joseph, 1658-1737
Autograph Ms, Recueil des plantes qui naissent en Provence. [Aix-en-Provence, 1705] 2 vols. Folio, in contemp sheep. Containing 541 watercolor drawings of plants, painted on rectos of leaves only & interleaved with blanks. (90) £45,000

Garland, Judy, 1922-69
Ls, 30 July 1948. (91) $500
Photograph, sgd, [1965]. 8 by 10 inches. As Dorothy in The Wizard of Oz. (91) $1,100
Photograph, sgd & inscr, 25 June 1956. (89) $850
— Anr, [n.d.]. (90) $250

Garland, Judy, 1922-69 —& Others
— WIZARD OF OZ. - Group photograph from the film, [n.d.], size not stated. Framed with signatures of Garland, Ray Bolger, Jack Haley, & Bert Lahr on separate pieces of paper. (91) $425

Garner, John Nance, 1868-1967
Collection of 8 A Ls s & 6 Ls s, 1925 to 1955. (88) $240
Collection of Ls & cut signature, 10 Nov 1932 & [n.d.]. (90) $55
Autograph sentiment, sgd, 19 Oct 1933. (90) $55

Garnerin, Jean Baptiste Olivier, 1766-1849
ALs, 16 Sept 1793. (91) DM450

Garnett, David, 1892-1981
Corrected page proofs, Lady into Fox. John F. Fleming Estate. (89) $650

Garrett, Patrick Floyd, 1850-1908
ALs, 29 May [1898]. 1 p, 4to. To his wife. Informing her about his travel plans. (91) $2,250
— 14 May 1900. 1 p, 8vo. To his wife. Informing her that he has been detained on account of court business. (91) $1,900
Ds, 15 Mar 1900. 1 p, 4to. Location Notice filing claim to Big Copper Mine on the San Andres Canyon; accomplished & sgd. With related material. (90) $1,400
— 11 Aug 1900. (90) $1,000
Check, sgd, 8 Mar 1900. (90) $700

Garrick, David, 1717-79
[An acting copy of Shakespeare's Othello, 1773, 8vo, in def contemp calf, with numerous Ms notes, some possibly in Garrick's hand, & Garrick's bookplate on flyleaf, sold at C on 22 June 1988, lot 106, for £450 to Quaritch.]
Autograph Ms, ballad, beginning "O list To my Ditty", [n.d.]. (89) £750
ALs, 10 Mar 1758. (88) £500
— 2 Jan 1766. (88) £450
— 22 Apr [1767]. (91) £350
— 11 Jan [n.y.]. (88) £140
— 22 Sept [n.y.]. (91) £240
Autograph check, sgd by his mother, 24 Oct 1734. (89) £90

Garrison, William Lloyd, 1805-79
ALs, 30 Oct 1846. Byer collection. (90) $800
Autograph quotation, sgd, [n.d.]. (88) $50

Garside, John
Original drawings, (21), dust jacket designs for various titles in the Wayfarer's Library, 1914 to 1920. Archives of J. M. Dent & Son. (88) £900

Garson, Greer
[A collection of 31 various sgd items sold at wa on 1 Oct 1988, lot 295, for $65.]

Garvin, James Louis, 1868-1947
[An archive of over 4,000 letters addressed to him as Ed of The Observer, 1915 to 1925, with carbon copies of his replies, covering a wide range of political & social issues, sold at S on 20 July 1989, lot 453, for £6,500 to Rota.]

Gaskell, Elizabeth Cleghorn, 1810-65
Autograph Ms, fragment of Sylvia's Lovers, 11 lines, [n.d.]. (88) £280
ALs, 31 Aug & 1 Sept 1831. (89) £550
— 20 Oct 1831. (89) £550
— [before 30 Aug 1832]. (89) £550
— 6 Aug [1832]. (89) £550
— [1850], "Saturday". (91) £700
— 16 Jan [1865 or 1866]. (89) £550
— [n.d.]. (89) £520

Gaskin, Arthur J., 1862-1928
Original drawings, (5), to illus The Monk of Evesham, 1895. (89) £800
— Original drawings, (96), to illus stories by Charles Perrault & the Brothers Grimm, 1898 & later. Various sizes. Mostly in watercolor. Some initialled; some mtd. (89) £3,000

Gaskin, Georgie Cave
Original drawings, (12), to illus Isaac Watts's Divine and Moral Songs for Childrn, 1896. (89) £550

Gasser, Achilles Pirmin, 1505-77
Ms, Annales de vetustate origines, amoenitate situs, splendore aedificiorum, ac rebus gestis civium Reipublicae Augstburgensis; [c.1575]. 666 pp, folio, in contemp blue vellum. (90) DM6,800

Gates, Horatio, 1728-1806
ALs, 13 June 1779. (89) $750
Collection of 2 Ls s & Ds, 23 to 25 Dec 1777. 6 pp, folio. Concerning the release of Major John Dyke Acland & Lady Harriet Acland. With related material. (91) $3,000

Gaubil, Antoine, 1689-1759
[The almost entire archive of his A Ls s & Mss, especially his writings on Chinese astronomy & his letters to Father Souciet at Clermont, 1725 to 1751, more than 900 pp in 11 half mor vols, sold at S on 22 Nov 1988, lot 42, for £30,000 to Marsh.]

Gaufridus Babion, fl.1100 —& Hildebert of Lavardin, 1056-1133
Ms, Sermones Catholicorum. [East Anglia, 2d quarter of 12th cent]. 222 leaves (2 blank, some lacking), vellum, 284mm by 160mm. Medieval bdg of stout oak bds now stripped bare, rebacked in brown lea. In a spacious romanesque bookhand by 3 main scribes. With large multicolored initial on opening page & 75 large painted initials in colors. Abbey collection. (89) £20,000

Gauguin, Paul, 1848-1903
Original drawing, pen-&-ink sketch of a heart & a guitar on a photograph, mtd on 4to sheet; [n.d.]. Sgd PGo & inscr to Ida [Ericson-Molard]. (91) DM5,000

ALs, 22 Feb 1879. 1 p, 8vo. To Camille Pissarro. About measurements of a frame & his account with Mme Latouche. Framed with a port. (91) $7,000

— 17 Mar 1888. 3 pp, 8vo. To Emile Schuffenecker. Reporting about his situation at Pont Aven. Some fold tears. (88) DM12,000

— [c.early Oct 1890]. 4 pp, 8vo. To Emile Schuffenecker. About his financial problems before his departure for Tahiti, & other matters. (90) DM16,000

— [Mar 1891]. 2 pp, 8vo. To [Ary Renan]. Sending his official request to be sent on a government mission to Tahiti. (91) £3,800

— Dec 1902. 8 pp, 4to. To a police officer. Complaining about the corruption of the local police. With diagram. (89) £5,500

— [n.d.]. 2 pp, 4to. To Ambroise Vollard. Thanking for canvas & listing colors requested. Including sketch. (89) £4,500

Gauss, Karl Friedrich, 1777-1855
Autograph Ms, announcement of lectures at Goettingen University; [n.d.]. 1 p, 4to. In Latin; sgd at head. (90) DM1,500

ALs, 14 July 1820. 2 pp, 8vo. To Wilhelm von Struve. About a projected visit & various astronomical matters. (90) DM3,000

— 20 Jan 1833. 3 pp, 8vo. Recipient unnamed. Sending receipts for interest collected & several autographs. (91) DM2,000

— 15 July 1836. 3 pp, 4to. To Karl Kreil. Interesting letter regarding the observation of terrestrial magnetism. (89) DM8,500

— 31 Mar 1842. 1 p, 4to. To Friedrich Woehler. Requesting a report on a dissertation. (91) DM1,600

Gawsworth, John, Pseud. of Terence Ian Fytton Armstrong
[A large collection of autograph & typescript poems, c.1929 to 1963, over 300 pp in 5 vols or notebooks, sold at S on 15 Dec, lot 70, for £450.]

Gay, John, 1685-1732 —& Pope, Alexander, 1688-1744
ALs, 23 Sept 1725. 3 pp, 4to. To William Fortescue. Concerning the search for employment. Joint letter, 1st page in Gay's hand, sgd JG; continued by Pope. Repaired. (89) £3,000

Gay-Lussac, Louis Joseph, 1778-1850
ALs, 4 Mar 1817. (88) DM380
— 17 Oct 1837. (91) DM450

Gaynor, Janet
[2 sgd photographs, [n.d.], 10 by 8 inches, matted with related material, sold at pnNY on 3 Dec 1988, lot 24, for $50.]

Gaynor, Janet —& Taylor, Robert, 1911-69
[A group of 17 orig Clarence Sinclair Bull photographs from Small Town Girl, 1936, 11 by 14 inches, sold at pnNy on 3 Dec 1988, lot 65, for $400.]

Gayot, Francois-Marie
— LIBRARY CATALOGUE. - Ms, Catalogue des Livres de la Bibliotheque de Francois-Marie Gayot. [Strasbourg, 1762]. 302 leaves & 6 flyleaves, 399mm by 265mm. Fine contemp red mor gilt with the arms of Gayot. With 129 elaborate drawings in pen & wash by several artists. Abbey collection. (89) £38,000

Geheeb, Paul, 1870-1961
ALs, 3 June 1944. (89) DM340

Gehrig, Henry Louis ("Lou"), 1903-41
ALs, 16 Mar 1929. 1 p, 4to. To Mary Mahoney. Inviting her to a game in Pittsburg. With sgd envelope. (89) $8,500

Autograph postcard, sgd, [14 Mar 1930]. To Billy Drinnon. Stating that it "is a little hard to get a ball just now". (90) $3,800

Note, 14 Feb [19]41. (91) $75

Ds, 2 Mar 1935. 1 p, 4to. Legal release to William Esty & Reynolds Tobacco Company to use his name, port & dialogue for advertising Camel cigarettes. Imperf. (91) $4,000

Signature, 5 Dec 1934. (91) $400
See also: Ruth, George Herman ("Babe") & Gehrig

Gehrig, Henry Louis ("Lou"), 1903-41
Autograph Ms, notebook compiled while taken a statistics course at Commerce High School, NY; [c. 1920]. 37 pp, size not stated. In pencil. With related material. (89) $6,500

Geibel, Emanuel, 1815-84
Autograph Ms, 4 poems, Lieder der Heimkehr; [n.d.]. (89) DM380
— Autograph Ms, poem, beginning "Die Nachtigall auf meiner Flur..."; [n.d.]. (91) DM300
— Autograph Ms, poem, Tempora mutantur, [n.d.]. (88) DM370
— Autograph Ms, poem, Venedig. (91) DM460
— Autograph Ms, quatrain, beginning "Lass dich nicht irren von Kritikastern", [n.d.]. (90) DM560
Autograph transcript, poem, beginning "Verzaubert lag, verschollen...", sgd & dated Mar 1879. (90) DM350

A Ls s (2), 1 & 2 Sept 1876. (89) DM200
ALs, 17 Sept 1864. (89) DM280

Geldart, William
Original drawings, (9), to illus Joyce Stranger's The Fox at Drummers' Darkness, 1977. Archives of J. M. Dent & Son. (88) £100

Gellert, Christian Fuerchtegott, 1715-69
ALs, 1 July 1754. (89) DM420
— 17 Aug 1769. (90) DM580

Gemistus Plethon, Georgius, c.1355-c.1450
Ms, 24 works, including his comparison of Plato & Aristotle, his prayer to the One God, & commentaries on classical authors, in Greek. [Venice?, late 15th cent]. 142 leaves & 2 flyleaves, 207mm by 134mm, in contemp blindstamped brown goatskin over wooden bds. In dark brown ink in 2 sizes of a Greek minuscule. (90) £42,000

Genet, Edmond Charles, 1763-1834
ALs, 12 May 1826. (91) $100

Genet, Jean, 1910-86
Series of 6 A Ls s, [c.1952]. 9 pp, 4to & 8vo. To Lily Pringsheim. About her visit in Paris. (91) DM4,600
ALs, [n.d.], 2 pp, 4to. (88) DM800
Autograph postcard, sgd, 25 Nov 1953. (90) DM550

Gentz, Friedrich von, 1764-1832
ALs, 10 Aug 1813. 1 p, 4to. To Ludwig von Ompteda. Hoping that the new war with France will prove a blessing for Europe. Schroeder collection. (89) DM1,400
— [1813?]. (91) DM850
— 8 Sept [1815]. 8 pp, 4to. Recipient unnamed. Giving a detailed report about the peace negotiations in Paris & the situation in France. (90) DM1,500
— 14 Oct [n.y.]. (88) DM340
— [n.d.]. (89) DM200
ANs, [1827 or later]. (89) DM200
ADs, 21 Oct 1817. (90) DM550

Geoffroy du Lorroux, fl.1100. See: Gaufridus Babion & Hildebert of Lavardin

GEOFFROY SAINT-HILAIRE

Geoffroy Saint-Hilaire, Etienne, 1772-1844

Autograph Ms, lecture, Caracteres et causalites de la loi de succession et de la transmutation des especes, 8 Sept 1834. (91) £500

— Autograph Ms, Notice sur un squelette humain retire d'une momie Egyptienne; [1826]. (90) DM200

Geografia Moderna

Ms, Geografia Moderna, che contiene una veduta universale del globo terraqueo. (90) DM1,000

Georg I, Herzog von Sachsen-Meiningen, 1761-1803. See: Schiller, Friedrich von

Georg Wilhelm, Kurfuerst von Brandenburg, 1595-1640

ALs, 15 May 1618. 1 p, folio. To his father Kurfuerst Johann Sigismund. Reporting from a journey to East Prussia. Schroeder collection. (89) DM2,200

Ls, 30 Apr 1634. (90) DM750

— 2 Jan 1638. Schroeder collection. (89) DM800

Document, 21 Mar 1621. (91) DM400

George, Prince Consort of Queen Anne of England, 1653-1708

Ds, 6 Nov 1706. (89) £350

George I, King of England, 1660-1727

ALs, 12 Jan [n.y.]. 3 pp, 4to. To his daughter. Hoping to see her in the summer, discussing the marriage of the Prince of Saxe-Eisenach, etc. In French. Byer collection. (90) $1,300

Ls, 14 Sept 1700. (90) £900

— 22 Aug 1713. (89) DM550

— 9 Feb 1727. (89) £300

Ds, 11 Jan 1714/15. Byer collection. (90) $425

— 6 May 1715. 2 pp, folio. Licence to Bernard Lintott for the sole ptg of Pope's trans of the Iliad. (90) £1,900

— 2 Apr 1726. (88) £180

— 22 Dec 1726. (90) £400

Document, 26 Apr 1715. (91) £900

George I, King of Greece, 1845-1913

Autograph Ms, diary as cadet on board the corvette Heimdal, 15 May to 10 Aug 1860. 56 pp, 205mm by 170mm, in an exercise book. (90) £2,200

AMERICAN BOOK PRICES CURRENT

Series of 5 A Ls s, 13 Nov 1893 to 10 Oct 1905. (90) £240

ALs, 21 Apr 1895. (89) DM750

Ls, 22 July 1906. (90) DM210

George II, King of England, 1683-1760

Ls, 3 Feb 1756. Byer collection. (90) $500

Ds s (2) Privy Purse Cash Account Ledger, 2 leaves covering 3 July to 2 Aug & 2 Oct to 3 Nov 1758; folio. (88) £320

Ds, 23 Jan 1730/1. (88) £170

— 12 Aug 1737. Byer collection. (90) $350

— 17 Jan 1742/3. (91) £120

— 22 May 1751. (89) £220

— 24 May 1751. (91) $110

— 5 June 1754. (89) $275

— 13 Feb 1759. Byer collection. (90) $300

George III, King of England, 1738-1820

Autograph Ms, brief memoranda, [mid-1760s?]; on 6 pp (of 12) of pocket notebook, 96mm by 50mm. In pencil. In orig fitted box. John F. Fleming Estate. (89) $1,600

ALs, 10 May 1782. (88) £280

— 2 Sept 1786. Byer collection. (90) $700

— 18 Apr 1790. (91) $600

— 23 Oct 1798. (91) £180

— 12 Sept 1800. 1 p, 4to. To his son Frederick Augustus, Duke of York. Discussing the assignment of troops. Doheny collection. (89) $1,600

Series of Ds s, 3 Ds s, 1794 to 1808. (89) £400

— Series of Ds s, 5 Ds s, 1801 to 1807. (88) £650

Ds, 27 Oct 1760. (89) $475

— 27 Oct 1760. (89) DM210

— 15 May 1761. (90) $250

— 14 Mar 1765. (91) $550

— 21 Aug 1765. (88) £120

— 11 Sept 1767. 2 pp, folio. "Additional Instructions" to the Governor of New York Sir Henry Moore. Framed. Boone collection. (89) $2,750

— 23 Mar 1769. 2 pp, folio. Warrant addressed to Gen. Thomas Gage authorizing him to convene courts martial in the colonies. Also sgd by Hillsborough. Edge torn. (89) $1,200

— 16 July 1773. (88) $850

— 31 July 1789. (91) $400

— 20 Mar 1793. (89) $175

— 16 Apr 1794. (91) $120
— 25 July 1794. (90) DM300
— 30 Apr 1796. Byer collection. (90) $275
— 12 Dec [1798?]. (88) $130
— 9 Jan 1801. (91) $225
— 30 Oct 1801. (91) £1,000
— 21 June 1805. (88) $140
— 7 July 1809. (90) £800
— 21 Nov 1816. Byer collection. (90) $175
Document, 31 Oct 1790. (88) £300
Autograph endorsement, sgd, [n.d.]. (88) £400
Cut signature, [24 Dec 1791]. (91) $50
— Anr, [1798?]. (90) $75
— Anr, [n.d.]. (91) $140
— RYDER, DUDLEY, 1ST EARL OF HARROWBY. - ADs, 23 Dec 1810. 3 pp, size not stated. Report on George III's insanity. Docketed. (88) $180

George IV, King of England, 1762-1830
ALs, 17 July 1786. (90) £380
— 13 Jan 1809. 5 pp, 4to. To [Mrs. Fitzherbert]. Discussing the education of recipient's daughter Minney. (91) £2,400
— 5 Dec 1809. (88) £170
— 30 July 1811. (91) DM380
— 23 Dec 1818. (88) DM500
Series of Ds s, 3 Ds s, 7 Aug 1812 to 26 Jan [1821?]. (88) $400
— Series of Ds s, 3 Ds s, 12 May 1815 to 31 Dec [1820?]. (88) $400
— Series of Ds s, 3 Ds s, 10 July 1815 to 31 Dec [1820?]. (88) $1,000
— Series of Ds s, 3 Ds s, 13 Dec 1816 to 20 Nov [1821?]. (88) $400
— Series of Ds s, 6 Ds s, 1816 to 1823. (88) £500
— Series of Ds s, 3 Ds s, 24 Oct to 18 Dec 1818. (88) $400
— Series of Ds s, 3 Ds s, 9 & 18 Dec 1818, & 5 July [1824?]. (88) $650
Ds s (2) 24 July 1812 & 30 Nov 1813. (88) £240
— Ds s (2) 13 Dec 1816 & 5 July 1817. (88) $800
Ds, 13 Nov 1813. (90) £170
— 28 Jan 1814. (88) $35
— 31 Mar 1814. (90) £380
— 24 Dec 1814. (88) $550
— 27 Dec 1815. (90) £500
— 27 Dec 1815. (88) £170

— 27 Dec 1815. (89) DM320
— 16 Mar 1816. 15 pp, folio. As Prince Regent, warrant to affix the Great Seal to the ratification of the marriage treaty for Princess Charlotte Augusta & Prince Leopold of Saxe-Coburg. (90) £2,000
— 17 Oct 1817. (88) £190
— 21 Feb 1820. (88) £60
— 23 July 1829. Byer collection. (90) $120

George, Stefan, 1868-1933
ALs, 21 Jan 1897. 2 pp, 4to. To Richard M. Meyer. Regretting he cannot furnish copies of his early works. (90) DM4,200
Ls, 19 Apr [n.y.]. 3 pp, 4to. To his pbr Georg Bondi. Requesting advice concerning a charge brought against him by Ludwig Klages. With autograph postscript. (90) DM6,000
Autograph postcard, sgd, [15 Jan 1898]. To Theodor Dienstbach. Hoping to see him in a few days. (91) DM1,500
See also: Gundolf, Friedrich
See also: Wolfskehl, Karl

George V, King of England, 1865-1936
Autograph Ms, English dictation exercises, 1878. (91) £100
ALs, 1 Apr 1900. Byer collection. (90) $550
— 17 Apr 1904. 4 pp, 8vo. To Bishop Corfe. Commenting about the Russo-Japanese War. (89) £3,800
Ls, 26 Jan 1925. (90) $110
Ds, 29 May 1906. (90) £260
— 10 Apr 1929. (90) $140
— 9 Nov 1931. (90) DM260
Photograph, sgd, 1924. (91) $350
Signature, [n.d.]. (91) $120

**George V, King of England, 1865-1936
—&
George VI, King of England, 1895-1952**
[A Ds by each, 11 Sept 1931 & 25 Oct 1937, 2 pp, folio, letters of credence for P. H. Hubbard, sold at sg on 25 Oct 1988, lot 101, for $250.]

**George V, King of England, 1865-1936
—&
Mary, Queen of George V of England, 1867-1953**
[A collection of 4 photographs (1 of

George, 3 of Mary), sgd, 1895 to 1932, & ALs from Queen Mary to Lord Sandhurst, 29 June 1919, 3 pp, 8vo, sold at C on 22 June 1988, lot 30, for £450 to Solomon.]

George VI, King of England, 1895-1952
Collection of 2 A Ls s & photograph, sgd, 21 Dec 1915 & 4 July 1916. (88) £220
Ls, 13 Jan 1937. (89) $175
Ds, 29 Jan 1941. (90) $90
— 3 Sept 1942. (91) $80
Christmas card, 1922. Byer collection. (90) $200

George VI, King of England, 1895-1952 —& Others
Group photograph, [c.1947]. 11.5 by 8.5 inches. With Queen Elizabeth & daughters Elizabeth & Margaret; sgd by all 4 on mount. (91) $2,500

George VI, King of England, 1895-1952.
See: George V & George VI
See also: Windsor, Edward & George VI

Gerber, Ernst Ludwig, 1746-1819
ALs, 30 July 1781. (89) DM650
— WINTZIGERODA, L. G. E. VON. - Ms, biographical articles "C. M. Balthasar" to "William Bird", [c.1850]. 472 pp, 4to, in def half lea. Interleaved with columns 513 - 992 of Gerber's Historisch-biographisches Lexikon der Tonkuenstler, vol. 1, 1790/92. (89) DM1,100

Gere, Charles March, 1869-1957
Original drawings, (3) for the Ashendene Press Ed of Dante, 1909. (88) £500
— Original drawings, (7) to illus the House of the Wolfings by William Morris. Comprising 5 finished ink designs, 2 within ptd borders, & 2 preparatory sketches, 1 with annotations by Morris. (88) £2,000

Gerlach, Hellmut von, 1866-1935
A Ls s (2), 10 Oct 1934 & 8 July 1935. (90) DM330

Gerlach, Walther, 1889-1979
Collection of ALs & Ls, 1 Mar 1965 & 12 Sept 1966. (90) DM280
ALs, 10 Aug 1970. (89) DM400

Germain, George Sackville, 1st Viscount Sackville, 1716-85
ALs, 8 Jan 1778. (89) $200

Germaine de Foix, Queen of Ferdinand V of Spain, 1488-1538
Ls, 1 May 1516. (90) £550

German, Edward, 1862-1936
[A large collectionn of A Ls s by German & to him, with 16 autograph diaries, a draft scenario of an early libretto, autograph Mss of speeches, some musical notes, and further material, more than 1000 items in 6 boxes, c.1880 to 1936, sold at S on 6 May 1988, lot 370, for £1,500 to Cox.]
[A collection of A Ls s etc., c.100 items, sent to him by a number of contemp artists, critics, etc., including some replies by German, sold at S on 6 May 1988, lot 353, for £950 to May.]

Germany
[Frankfurt National Assembly. - The autograph diary of Otto Ungerbuehler as member of the Assembly, 1 May to 8 Sept 1848, 147 pp, 8vo, in 2 half lea vols, sold at star on 1 Dec 1988, lot 1120, for DM2,700.]
— AUSCHWITZ. - ALs from Auschwitz, 4 July 1943. 2 pp, 8vo. To the writer's mother. Contents not stated. (91) $400
— BAMBERG. - Document, [24 Mar] 1500. 1 folded leaf, vellum, 268mm by 568mm. Arbitral decision in the conflict between the village of Altendorf & the von Stiebar Family regarding the right of pasture. (89) DM1,100
— BAVARIA. - 4 Mss, 1729 & 1770. About 700 pp, folio, in contemp mottled calf (3). Account of the Bavarian Order of St. George, & inventories of the residences of Munich, Schleisheim & Fuerstenried (91) £3,200
— CARPENTER'S GUILD, RODA. - 3 Ds, 21 Mar 1660 to 1836. Statutes of the Carpenter's Guild for Saxe-Altenburg, particularly Roda, & later confirmations. 33 pp, folio, in calf-backed bds. (91) £300
— FRANKFURT NATIONAL ASSEMBLY. - 3 Mss, 1848. 5 pp, folio. Pamphlets discussing the political situation in Germany & Austria. With related material. (89) DM530

— HAMBURG. - Ms, Van ordineringe und geschick der hogesten oeueriheit desser erenntriken Stadt Hamborch. [Hamburg, 1570 - 1670]. 371 leaves (1 lacking, 149 blank), 305mm by 200mm. 16th-cent blindstamped lea over wooden bds; 2 clasps. In black & red ink in various hands. Listing rights & privileges of the city, magistrates, municipal regulations, etc. With full-page painting of the arms & 3 large drawings. (89) DM16,000

— IMHOFF FAMILY, AUGSBURG. - 9 documents, 1509 to 1800. 9 leaves (7 vellum), folio. Mostly letters of investiture. (90) DM1,400

— KOBLENZ. - Document, 7 July 1319. 1 p, vellum, 162mm by 271mm. Grant by Herman de Leye of property near the Jews' Gate at Koblenz to the Dean & Chapter of St. Florian. With municipal seal of Koblenz. (91) £700

— KOELLNBACH, BAVARIA. - Ms, Obernkhoellenpachisch Lehenpvech, 1565. 115 leaves, 210mm by 160mm. Contemp heraldic brown calf gilt bdg. In several hands. Listing feudal property of the von Ebeleben family in the vicinity of Moosburg. (89) DM6,600

— LOWER RHINELAND. - Document, [1 June] 1493. 1 p, folio. Marriage contract between Johann zu Elter [Autel] & Katharina von Palant. With names of bridegroom & witnesses on 16 attached vellum slips. (90) DM2,100

— NUERNBERG. - Ms, list of council members & magistrates, beginning c.1100; [c.1645]. 336 leaves (including blanks), 322mm by 204mm. Def 18th-cent half vellum bdg. In a very regular calligraphic gothic hand. With numerous painted coats-of-arms & 5 pen-&-ink illusts. Including continuations to c.1738. (89) DM7,500

— RODA, SAXE-ALTENBURG. - Ms, recordbook of the town administration, 1479 to 1559. 374 pp, 43cm by 14.8cm, in orig limp vellum bdg. (91) £500

— SATLER, JAKOB & KATHARINA. - Document, [26 July] 1434. 1 p, folio; vellum. Conveyance of a farm to the church & hospital at Neuoetting, Bavaria. (90) DM600

— SCHROEDER FAMILY, HAMBURG. - An extensive collection of papers pertaining to the merchant Octavio Rudolf Schroeder & his descendants, 1798 to 1935, sold at HN on 25 May 1991, lot 2020, for DM3,200. 91

— STRAEUB, JOHANN GEORG. - Document, 27 May 1667. 1 p, vellum, folio. As provost of the Prince-Bishop of Augsburg, release of Afra Bergkhmiller & Barbara Jeger from serfdom. (90) DM420

— SWABIA. - Ms, Acta betr. die beschreibung der Innhabern Bechenheim zue den Reichstaegen dess Viertels am Kocher..., 1577 to 1628. 135 leaves, size not stated; stitched. Collection of reports, letters, lists, etc. relating to meetings of the estates. (89) DM950

Gernatt, Mary
Original drawings, (22), to illus Kitty Barne's Admiral's Walk, 1953, & Primrose Cumming's Penny and Pegasus, 1969. Archives of J. M. Dent & Son. (88) £70

Gerning, Johann Isaak von, 1767-1837
ALs, 9 Apr 1801. Albrecht collection. (91) SF360

Gernsheim, Friedrich, 1839-1916
[An album kept by Gernsheim, 1851 to 1864, containing over 50 entries, including 29 musical quotations by Ignaz Moscheles & others, 4to, in contemp lea, sold at star on 10 Mar 1988, lot 834, for DM2,600.]

Gerok, Karl, 1815-90
Series of 4 A Ls s, 17 Aug 1852 to 10 July 1889. (90) DM550

Geronimo, 1829-1909
Photograph, sgd, [1904]. Cabinet size. By Murillo, St. Louis. Sgd on verso. With note of authenticity. (91) $4,500

Gerry, Elbridge, Signer from Massachusetts
[A passport issued to Gerry by the French Minister at The Hague, F. Noel, [23 Sept 1797], 1 p, 4to, sold at R on 4 Mar 1989, lot 317, for $600.]
ALs, [c.Jan - Feb 1792]. (90) $1,000
— 7 June 1813. 2 pp, 4to. To James Trecothic Austin. About the course

pursued by Massachsetts during the war, & expressing regard for President Madison. (91) $1,500
— 5 Sept 1814. 1 p, 4to. To John G. McDonald. Expressing relief that the records & files of the Senate are safe [after the British capture of Washington]. Including franking signature. (90) $1,900

Ds, 27 Aug 1810. (88) $210
— 23 May 1812. (91) $500
Franking signature, 1813. (90) $350

Gershwin, George, 1898-1937

Autograph music, notebook of songs, [1916] to 1922. 40 pp, 8vo. In various colored inks & pencil. 1 song sgd GG. Some lyrics in the hand of Ira Gershwin, 1 sgd IG. Blank interleaves. Dark red cloth wraps, with autograph paper label. (88) $110,000
— Autograph music, sketches for An American in Paris, [1927-28]. 4 pp, folio, 12 staves each. Some revisions. (88) $14,000
— Autograph music, trio, Where's Bess, Oh, Where's my Bess, from Porgy and Bess, Act III, [1934-35]. 8 pp, folio; 12 staves each. In pencil; unfinished. With check, sgd, 3 Dec 1933, & covering letter by Ira Gershwin, 23 July 1959. Prinzmetal collection. (88) $40,000

Original drawing, port of a young woman wearing a hat, in pencil & watercolor; [n.d.]. 380mm by 253mm. Sgd. Framed. (89) $3,500

ALs, [29 Sept 1918]. 2 pp, 8vo. To Max Abramson. Informing him of his plan to return to New York. (88) DM2,400
— [24 Aug 1928]. 1 p, 4to. To Margaret Mower. Promising to arrange a meeting with Ziegfeld. Rosen collection. (89) $1,800

Ls, 18 Nov 1929. 1 p, 4to. To Pamela. Hoping she will receive a scholarship. (91) $1,100
— 18 Mar 1933. (88) £380

Autograph quotation, 4 musical quotations & inscr to Mrs Kochanski, sgd, Dec 1923. On ptd sheet music for Virginia Don't Go Too Far, 5 pp, 4to. (90) $3,500

Check, sgd, 2 Feb 1932. (90) $1,000
— Anr, sgd, 14 Mar 1932. (91) $800
— Anr, sgd, 6 June 1932. (90) $950

Concert program, sgd, [n.d.]. (91) $850

Cut signature, [n.d.]. (91) $375

Photograph, sgd & inscr, Apr 1929. 8 by 10 inches. Seated at piano; inscr to William Vanden Burg. (90) $3,000
— Anr, Dec 1929. 20cm by 25cm. Inscr to Max [Abraham], with musical quotation from Rhapsody in Blue. (91) £3,100

Signature, [n.d.]. (91) $325

Gershwin, George, 1898-1937 —& Others

Signature, 26 Sept 1935. (91) $950

Gershwin, George, 1898-1937 —& Gershwin, Ira, 1896-1983

Collection of 8 A Ls s (3 from Ira), 4 Ls s & telegram, 1 Feb 1928 to 22 Mar 1938. 25 pp, 4to & 8vo. To Mrs. J. Van Norman. About her husband's music, Hollywood, concerts & other projects, etc. (88) $13,000

Ds, 24 May 1937. 1 p, 4to. Contract in the form of a letter, allowing RKO Radio Pictures to use their names in their Annual Sales Book. Carbon copy. (90) $2,500

Gershwin, Ira, 1896-1983

Typescript, lyrics for I Got Rhythm, sgd; [n.d.]. (90) $160

Ls, 28 Feb 1949. 1 p, 4to. To Albert Goldberg. Refuting recipient's assertion that Milhaud had influenced George Gershwin in his Rapsody in Blue. With copy of reply. (89) £1,200
See also: Gershwin, George & Gershwin

Gerson, Johannes, 1362-1428?

Ms, De theologia mystica speculativa & 2 other texts, with Petrus de Alliaco, De destructione in nocturnis pollutionibus compendiosa notabilia. [Paris?, early 15th cent]. 82 leaves, vellum, 150mm by 105mm. 19th-cent vellum bdg. In a gothic bookhand. (91) DM9,000

Gerstaecker, Friedrich, 1816-72

Autograph Ms, poem, Ein Nothschrei, Apr 1872. (88) DM550

ALs, 20 Apr 1851. (88) DM700
— 5 Aug 1862. (91) DM460
— 22 Sept 1865. (90) DM480

Gert, Valeska, Pseud. of Gertrud Samosch, 1892-1978
Collection of ALs & autograph postcard, sgd, 25 & 30 July 1977. (90) DM320

Gervinus, Georg Gottfried, 1805-71
Series of 5 A Ls s, 10 Aug 1848 to 25 May 1860. 14 pp, 4to & 8vo. To Christian von Stockmar. Important letters about politics in Germany. (90) DM1,900
ALs, [n.d.]. (90) DM200

Gesellschaft fuer Erdkunde
Ms, minutes of meetings of the Gesellschaft fuer Erdkunde in Berlin, 1855 to 1868. 280 pp, folio, in contemp lea bdg. In several hands. (91) DM3,000

Gessner, Salomon, 1730-88
ALs, 18 Dec 1776. 1 p, 4to. To Christian von Mechel. About their accounts, mentioning painters, etc. (90) DM3,800
— 17 Aug 1785. 4 pp, 4to. To his son Konrad. Commenting on his son's paintings. Amman collection. (88) DM3,800
— 17 July 1787. 2 pp, 4to. To his son Konrad. Fatherly advice for his stay in Rome. With postscript by his wife Judith. (89) DM5,000
— HEIDEGGER, JOHANN HEINRICH. - ALs, 3 Dec 1768. 5 pp, 4to. To Anton Graff. Hoping Gessner will illustrate 2 of his biographical sketches. Slightly def. (88) DM650
— HEIDEGGER, JOHANN HEINRICH. - ALs, 5 Mar 1788. 2 pp, 4to. To Anton Graff. Informing him of Salomon Gessner's death. (88) DM3,000

Giacometti, Alberto, 1901-66
ALs, 22 Sept 1933. 1 p, 8vo (lettercard). Recipient unnamed. Sending 6 sketches. (89) DM2,400

Giant Series
[A collection of 21 ink, watercolor, & gouache drawings for nos 45, 47 & 48 in the series, [c.1935], c.295mm by 210mm, with related material, sold at S on 2 June 1989, lot 591, for £300 to Gaunt.]
[A collection of 48 ink & watercolor drawings for 4 alphabet books in the series, [n.d.], c.350mm by 260mm, with related material, sold at S on 2 June 1989, lot 590, for £440 to Western.]
Original drawings, (241), by Madge Knight & other artists, for 22 books in the series; 1918 to 1927. Various sizes. With related material. (90) £1,100

Gibbings, Robert John, 1889-1958
[Proof impressions of 70 wood-engraved illusts for Coming down the Wye, & other titles, 1942 to 1957, mostly sgd or initialled, various sizes, 25 mtd in 5 frames, sold at S on 10 June, lot 752, for £1,300 to Powney.]

Gibbon, Edward, 1737-94
A Ds s (2), 1 Mar & 1 July 1789. (91) £750
Endorsement, 24 July 1787. (88) $400

Gibbon, Monk, 1896-1987
Series of 60 A Ls s, 1931 to c.1980. (88) £300

Gibraltar
— BOOTH, LIEUT. W. - Ms describing the armaments, dispositions & population of the Gibraltar garrison, including a discussion of powders, mortars, provisions, state of the garrison at the beginning of 1774 & list of inhabitants. 1770s. 82 pp, 8vo, in orig bds. (91) £500

Gibson, John, 1630-1711. See: Anthology

Gide, Andre, 1869-1951
A Ls s (2), 4 Dec 1908 & [24 May 1910]. (88) DM360
ALs, 1 Mar 1896. (90) DM440
— 9 June 1898. (90) DM400
— "Friday" [1908]. (88) $90
— [20 Mar 1914]. 2 pp, 4to, in mor bdg. To Marcel Proust. Retained draft, proposing that he publish the next vols of A la recherche du temps perdu with the N[ouvelle] R[evue] F[rancaise]. Koch Foundation. (90) $5,000
— 18 July [19]18. Byer collection. (90) $200
— 7 June 1919. (89) DM480
— 10 Mar [n.y.]. (91) DM450
— ROTHENSTEIN, WILLIAM. - Orig drawing, port of Gide, 1918. 22cm by 16cm. In red & white chalk; sgd W.R. Framed. (91) £950

Gide, Andre, 1869-1951 —&
Louys, Pierre, 1870-1925
Autograph Ms, poem, beginning "Quand je reparaitrait sous les etoiles pales"; 3 lines by each. (90) DM480

Gieseking, Walter, 1895-1956
A Ls s (2), 16 Aug 1943 & 9 June 1944. (89) DM600
ALs, 20 Aug 1954. (91) £600

Gigli, Beniamino, 1890-1957
[2 photographs, sgd, 1934, postcards, sold at star on 5 Apr 1991, lot 1073, for DM400.]
Photograph, sgd, 1939. (88) DM220
— Anr, 1957. (90) DM220
Photograph, sgd & inscr, 1935. (91) DM200

Gilbert, Sir Humphrey, 1539?-83
Ds, 6 June 1582. 13 pp, 4to; on rectos only. Grant of land & trading rights in America to George Peckham & Thomas Gerrard. Draft, with revisions possibly by Gilbert. Sgd by Gilbert, Peckham & Thomas Harris at end; individual leaves initialled by Gilbert. (89) £38,000

Gilbert, William Schwenck, 1836-1911
Series of 7 A Ls s, 21 Dec 1907 to 6 Sept 1908. 13 pp, 8vo. To Edward Bell. Concerning Bell's Ed of the Savoy Operas. (91) £1,300
ALs, 12 Aug 1876. (91) £240
— 2 Dec 1906. (91) $425
— 23 Mar 1909. Byer collection. (90) $650

Gill, Eric, 1882-1940
Collection of 19 A Ls s, Ls s, & postcards, sgd, c.1928 to 1935. 21 pp, various sizes. To Desmond Flower. About his work at the BBC headquarters, his literary activities, alterations in a publication, a review by D. H. Lawrence, etc. (89) £1,500
Series of 21 A Ls s, 1921 to 1940. About 40 pp, 4to & 8vo. To his daughter Betty. About family matters & his work abroad; partly with illusts. With related material. (91) £3,500
ALs, [25 Mar] 1932. 1 p, 324mm by 144mm. To David Jones. Calligraphic letter, sending Easter greetings & family news. Sgd with monogram.

Framed. (90) £1,500
Autograph postcard, sgd, 31 Dec 1926. (90) £75
Engraving, port of Dom Wilfrid Upson, [n.d.]. (90) £160

Gill, Eric, 1882-1940 —&
Pepler, Hilary
[An archive of autograph & typescript correspondence, memoirs & other related material, bearing on the disputes between Gill & Pepler & their professional association, 1918 to 1935, sold at wa on 8 Mar 1990, lot 561, for $10,500.]

Gilles, Werner, 1894-1961
Collection of 7 A Ls s & autograph postcard, sgd, 1950 to 1959. (89) DM440
ALs, 9 Nov 1929. (88) DM300
— 3 Apr 1952. (89) DM240

Gillet, Pierre Mathurin, 1762-95
ALs, [19 June 1795]. (88) £50

Ginger, Phyllis
Original drawings, (17), to illus Brooks & Cook's Modern French for Adults, & other titles. Archives of J. M. Dent & Son. (88) £75
— Original drawings, (21), to illus Madeleine Henrey's London, 1948, & other titles. Archives of J. M. Dent & Son. (88) £1,000

Ginsberg, Allen
ALs, 23 Mar 1974. Koch Foundation. (90) $250

Giono, Jean, 1895-1970
Autograph Ms, essay, beginning "Des diamants sur du velours noir...", draft. (90) DM550
Collection of ALs & photograph, sgd & inscr, 24 Oct 1965 & 24 Oct 1968. (90) DM380
ALs, 29 Jan 1933. (90) DM240

Giordano, Umberto, 1867-1948
Autograph music, Inno del Decennale, [1933]. 6 pp, 53cm by 38cm. Scored for orchestra; in pencil on up to 29 staves per page. Sgd on tp & at end. (89) £1,500
ALs, 19 July 1937. (90) DM550
— 29 Nov [1928?]. (90) DM430

Giovannini, Ph. See: Beltrami, Giacomo Constantino

Girard, Stephen, 1750-1831
Collection of Ls & 4 Ds s, 1796 to 1831. (89) $500

Girardi, Alexander, 1850-1918
Photograph, sgd & inscr, 19 May 1914. (91) DM550

Giraudoux, Jean, 1882-1944
ALs, 11 Feb [1928]. (91) DM220

Girdwood, Eric Stanley, Sir. See: Boer War

Gissing, George, 1857-1903
Collection of 3 A Ls s & 1 postcard, 5 Jan to 27 Dec 1889. (91) £850
— Collection of ALs (in 3d person), AL (fragment), 5 autograph postcards, sgd, & 3 Ds s (receipts), 1895 to 1901. (88) £480
ALs, 1 Sept 1872. (91) £550
— 26 Sept 1884. Doheny collection. (89) $650
— 3 Sept 1889. 4 pp, 8vo. To his sister Nelly. Commenting about Thomas Hardy as a writer. Initialled. Doheny collection. (89) $2,500
— 11 Jan 1901. (89) £190

Gist, Mordecai, 1743-92
ALs, 28 Apr 1777. (89) $220

Gladstone, William E., 1809-98
Autograph Ms, essay, British Poetry of the Nineteenth Century; [c.1890]. (90) £800
Series of 9 A Ls s, 1848 to 1898. (90) £220
Ls, 27 Jan 1874. (91) $75

Glasgow, Ellen, 1874-1945
Collection of 4 A Ns s & 6 Ns s, 1926 to 1943. (89) $350

Glasgow School of Art
[A collection of 16 A Ls s & Ls s, 1889 to 1931, mostly to F. H. Newbury, director of the Glasgow School of Art, sold at C on 9 Dec, lot 365, for £580 to Glasgow School of Art.]

Glassbrenner, Adolf, 1810-76
ALs, 20 Dec 1856. (90) DM240

Glazunov, Aleksandr Konstantinovich, 1865-1936
ALs, 25 Dec 1903. (91) £500
— 13 Apr 1905. (88) DM700
— 27 July 1918. (90) £600
— 7 Nov 1928. (90) £600

Gleichen-Russwurm, Emilie von, 1804-72
A Ls s (2), 2 Mar 1861 & 22 May 1871. (88) DM250

Gleim, Johann Wilhelm Ludwig, 1719-1803
Autograph Ms, minutes of a chapter meeting at Halberstadt cathedral, 26 Mar 1774. (90) DM240
ALs, 14 May 1795. (88) DM700
— 5 Nov 1797. 3 pp, 8vo. To Elisa von der Recke. Asking for her opinion about Goethe's Hermann und Dorothea. Albrecht collection. (91) SF1,900
— 15 Jan 1800. (89) DM680
— 23 Apr 1800. 4 pp, 8vo. To the pbr [G. J. Goeschen]. Imploring him to support a campaign against corruption of manners & morals in literature. (90) DM2,000

Gleizes, Albert, 1881-1953
ALs, 21 Feb 1936. (88) DM650

Glinka, Mikhail Ivanovich, 1804-57
ALs, 22 Sept [1832]. 1 p, 8vo. To Cerri. Requesting copies of the instrumental parts of his Serenata Brillanti on themes of Donizetti's Anna Bolena. (91) £3,800

Gluck, Alexander Johannes, 1683-1743. See: Gluck, Christoph Willibald

Gluck, Christoph Willibald, 1714-87
ALs, 31 Jan 1777. 1 p, 4to. To [Franz Kruthoffer]. About his plans to set Klopstock's Hermannsschlacht to music, his contract with M. Peters, etc. (89) DM48,000
— 31 Jan 1777. 1 p, 4to. To [Franz Kruthoffer]. About his plans to set Klopstock's Hermannsschlacht to music, his contract with M. Peters, etc. (91) DM42,000
AL, 28 Mar 1781. 1 p, 4to. To Franz Kruthoffer. Chatting about recipient's

GLUCK

trans, stage designs by Moreau, his own health, etc. (88) DM42,000

Ls, 1 May 1785. 2 pp, 4to. To M. Valadier. Regretting that his health will not permit him to contemplate setting recipient's libretto. In French. (91) £6,500

Letter, 30 Dec 1781. 1 p, 4to. To Franz Kruthoffer. Sending a port for Mme de La Frete. In the hand of his wife. (91) DM1,300

— GLUCK, ALEXANDER JOHANNES. - Ds, 9 Aug 1723. 1 p, 4to. Receipt for a shipment of pitch for the forestry office at Kamnitz. (91) DM360

— GLUCK, ALEXANDER JOHANNES. - Ds, 13 May 1723. 1 p, 4to. Order addressed to the forestry office at Kamnitz to deliver shingles. (90) DM250

Gneisenau, August, Graf Neithardt von, 1760-1831

ALs, 20 May 1807. 1 p, folio. To an unnamed French general. From the siege of Kolberg, concerning the treatment of prisoners of war. Schroeder collection. (89) DM3,800

— 13 May 1815. 1 p, folio. To Prince Hardenberg. Informing him that the military situation will prevent him from going to Aix-la-Chapelle as planned. (90) DM1,200

— 23 May 1815. (91) DM800

— 4 June 1815. (90) DM470

— 29 Jan 1820. (90) DM600

— 11 Dec [1820?]. (90) DM420

— 27 Dec 1822. 3 pp, 4to. To [Amalie von Helvig?]. Sending family news. (91) DM1,200

— 14 June 1825. (88) DM700

— 3 Sept 1826. (88) DM320

— 21 Mar 1828. Schroeder collection. (89) DM280

— 24 Apr 1829. (90) DM750

— 7 Sept 1830. (91) DM900

— 9 Aug 1831. 1 p, 4to. To [Herzog Eugen von Wuerttemberg]. About missing letters & the Polish-Russian War. Disinfection slits. Schroeder collection. (89) DM1,500

Ls, 6 Mar 1816. (91) DM460

— 28 Mar 1818. (91) DM850

AMERICAN BOOK PRICES CURRENT

Gobineau, Joseph Arthur, Comte de, 1816-82

ALs, 10 Feb 1867. (90) DM460

Godard, Benjamin, 1849-95

A Ls s (2), 6 Dec 1883 & 20 Feb 1884. (90) DM220

Godfrey, David

Original drawings, (14), dust jackets for works by Smollett, Trollope, Carlyle, & others, [n.d.]. Archives of J. M. Dent & Son. (88) £70

Godfrey, Edward

ALs, Dec 1896. (89) $280

Godwin, William, 1756-1836

ALs, 6 Feb [1834]. (91) £180

— 5 July [n.y.]. (91) £300

See also: Malthus, Thomas Robert

Goebbels, Joseph, 1897-1945

Ls, 22 Mar 1926. 1 p, 4to. To Eugen Munder. Carbon copy of circular letter, requesting contributions to a Nazi publication. (90) DM1,800

— [25 Dec] 1936. (89) DM380

— 30 Nov 1937. (91) $350

Autograph postcard, sgd, 13 Apr 1926. To Eugen Munder. Informing him of his projected arrival in Stuttgart. (90) DM1,100

— 28 June 1926. (90) DM1,000

Ns, 4 Dec 1934. (89) DM340

Photograph, sgd & inscr, [23 May] 1926. (90) DM1,000

— Anr, [25 Dec 19]29. (88) $400

Goerdeler, Carl Friedrich, 1884-1945

Collection of ALs & 2 Ls s, 7 Aug 1930 to 31 Dec 1938. 6 pp, folio & 8vo. To Karl Straube. About Bach's grave, recipient's work at Leipzig, & expressing New Year's wishes. With related material. (89) DM1,500

Ls, 15 Mar 1937. (91) DM700

Goering, Hermann, 1893-1946

Ls, 26 June & 2 July 1925. 8 pp, 4to. To Lieut. Lahr. From exile in Sweden, complaining about Hitler & his party. (89) DM8,500

Ds, 28 Mar 1944. (90) $500

Photograph, sgd, [1918]. (90) DM800

— Anr, [c.1943-45]. (88) $300

Goerres, Joseph von, 1776-1848
ALs, 5 Dec 1814. 3 pp, 8vo. To Friedrich Kohlrausch. Thanking for an essay about Hannover & commenting about Goettingen. (89) DM4,000

Goethe, August von, 1789-1830
ALs, [1817]. 1 p, 8vo. To Ottilie von Pogwisch. Informing her that he may be late for a meeting. Albrecht collection. (91) SF1,600

Goethe, Johann Caspar, 1710-82
Ds, 9 Aug 1775. 1 p, 8vo. Bill addressed to the Brothers Zahn for interest due the "Porcellanhoefer Creditorschafft". Including autograph receipt, 11 Aug 1775. (90) DM2,400

Goethe, Johann Wolfgang von, 1749-1832
[A file of the Theater Commission at the Weimar Court relating to a contract with T. Jannitsch & containing letters & drafts, with some endorsements by Goethe (2 autograph revisions), 17 Oct to 25 Dec 1799, 22 pp, 4to & folio, stitched, sold at star on 10 May 1991, lot 47, for SF3,200.]
[An autograph envelope, [c.1805-1815], 10cm by 12cm, addressed to [Friederike] Bethmann, sold at star on 10 May 1991, lot 58, for SF900.]
[An autograph envelope, addressed to Frau Meyer, [16 Sept 1826], 12cm by 14cm, sgd JWvG on verso, sold at star on 10 May 1991, lot 82, for SF1,600.]
[An autograph envelope addressed to Professor Zelter in Berlin, [27 Aug 1828], 11cm by 16.5cm, sold at star on 10 May 1991, lot 90, for SF1,700.]
[An autograph envelope, addressed to [Sara] von Grot[t]huss, [n.d.], c.97mm by 122mm, sold at star on 27 June 1990, lot 147, for DM450.]
[2 autograph envelopes, addressed to [Friedrich] von Mueller, [n.d.], 11.5cm by 13.5cm & 10cm by 12cm, sold at star on 10 May 1990, lot 96, for SF900.]
Autograph Ms, draft of an inscription in the Munich Botanical Gardens; [c.1811/12]. 1 p, 8vo. With Eckermann's note of authenticity on mount. (91) DM4,600
— Autograph Ms, poem, 4 lines beginning "Warum stehen sie davor", 1828. 2.2cm by 20cm. Sgd twice. Mtd on lower margin of an engraving of his house by L. Schuetze, 15.5cm by 21.7cm. (89) DM16,000
— Autograph Ms, poem, beginning "Willst du dir ein gut Leben zimmern", sgd & inscr to Regierungsrath Wittich, 25 Oct 1828. 1 p, 4to. 10 lines. (90) DM36,000
— Autograph Ms, poem, beginning "Der Deutsche ist gelehrt..."; 11 Apr 1818. 1 p, 4to. 8 lines. Albrecht collection. (91) SF7,500
— Autograph Ms, poem, beginning "Zarte, schattende Gebilde", 18 Apr 1818. 1 p, 8vo. Draft; 8 lines, sgd G. Albrecht collection. (91) SF7,000
— Autograph Ms, poem, Brautlied, [1810]. 1 p, 8vo. 1st 8 lines only. Light gray paper. Slightly differing from Sophien-Ed vol 16, p 231. Ott-Usteri & Stefan Zweig collections. (88) DM25,000
— Autograph Ms, poem, Den Reimkollegen, from Zahme Xenien VII; [n.d.]. 1 p, 8vo. 4 lines. Albrecht collection. (91) SF10,000
— Autograph Ms, poem, Eins geht nach dem andern hin, 8 lines, 1823; 1 p, 8vo. Pbd in West-oestlicher Divan. On verso inscr in anr hand. (88) £4,500
— Autograph Ms, poem from Zahme Xenien IV, "Wenn dir's nun nicht bei uns gefaellt...; [n.d.]. 1 p, 4to. 2 lines. Including authentication in anr hand. Albrecht collection. (91) SF4,000
— Autograph Ms, sonnet, Entsagen, beginning "Entwoehnen sollt ich mich vom Glanz der Blicke!"; [1807-1808]. 1 p, 4to. Albrecht collection. (91) SF24,000
— Autograph Ms, Ungedruckte Winckelmannische Briefe, announcement of his Ed of Winckelmann's letters, to be pbd in the Jenaische Allgemeine Literaturzeitung; [Feb 1804]. 2 pp, 4to. With related Ms in Wilhelm Schumann's hand with some additions by Goethe, describing contents of the letters; 9 pp, folio. Albrecht collection. (91) SF10,000

Original drawing, antique monument in a group of trees, [c.1770]. 20cm by 16cm. In pen-&-ink. Framed. (90) £7,000

Ms, essay on Dante, 9 Sept 1826. 6 pp, 4to

GOETHE

& folio. Sgd G in three places; 1 autograph revision. (91) DM16,000
— Ms, excerpts for Adele Schopenhauer's part [from the Festgedichte: Bei Allerhoechster Anwesenheit Ihro Majestaet der Kaiserin Mutter Maria Feodorowna in Weimar, 18 Dec 1818]; 13 pp, 4to, stitched. 144 lines in the hands of John & Krauter, with some additions in Goethe's hand & autograph inscr on tp, sgd. Albrecht collection. (91) SF6,000
— Ms, visiting card, [n.d.]. 5.7cm by 8.5cm. Oval borders. Slightly damp-stained. With engraved visiting card. (88) DM2,400
Collection of ALs & AL, [n.d.]. 2 pp, 4to. Recipients unnamed. Drafts, relating to a lithograph, initialled; & expressing thanks. (89) £1,050
Series of 4 A L s s, 14 Mar to 14 Aug 1804. 4 pp, 4to & 8vo. To Eichstaedt. About various literary matters pertaining to the Jenaische Allgemeine Literaturzeitung. With related material. Albrecht collection. (91) SF20,000
ALs, 16 Oct 1780. 4 pp, 4to. To Maria Antonia von Branconi. Thanking for her letter, promising to send a requested drawing soon, but postponing the copying of his letters from Switzerland. Albrecht collection. (91) SF26,000
— 2 Jan 1784. 1 p, folio. To [Karl Christian von Herda]. Returning New Year's wishes. With related material. (89) DM5,500
— 26 Apr 1784. 2 pp, 4to. To Maria Antonia von Branconi. Discussing the possibility of a meeting, & worrying about Lavater's health. Albrecht collection. (91) SF14,000
— 7 Oct 1785. 2 pp, folio. To [Johann Christoph Doederlein]. Responding to a complaint & regretting he was unable to see him at Jena. (91) DM12,000
— 5 Nov 1785. 2 pp, folio. To Christian Bernhard von Isenflamm. Inquiring about the possibility of performing an operetta in Vienna. Albrecht collection. (91) SF8,500
— 15 Aug 1787. 3 pp, 4to. To Georg Joachim Goeschen. Discussing the publication of his collected works. Sophien-Ed vol 8, no 2602. (88) DM38,000
— 24 July 1788. 4 pp, 4to. To Christian Gottlob Heine. Reporting about his concept of art & his travels in Italy. Albrecht collection. (91) SF19,000
— 16 Feb 1789. 1 p, 8vo. To Christian Gottlob Voigt. Requesting advice for Herr von Wedel. Sgd G. (90) DM4,500
— 10 Mar 1791. 2 pp, 4to. To Johann Friedrich Reichardt. Regretting his resignation as conductor in Berlin & asking for several compositions. Albrecht collection. (91) SF12,000
— [c.20 Nov 1795]. 2 pp, 8vo. To Christian Gottlob von Voigt. Discussing matters pertaining to the Ilmenau mines. Albrecht collection. (91) SF4,500
— [n.d.]. 1 p, 8vo. To an unnamed lady. Hoping to see her that day. (89) £1,700
— 17 July 1804. 1 p, 4to. To Friederike Unzelmann. Regretting being unable to meet with her & mentioning [Christiane Vulpius] & recipient's son Carl. Albrecht collection. (91) SF8,000
— 11 Aug 1804. 1 p, 8vo. To H. K. A. Eichstaedt. Sending reviews for the Allgemeine Jenaische Literaturzeitung. (90) DM5,500
— 25 Dec 1805. 1 p, 8vo. To Karl Ludwig von Knebel. About recipient's trans of Lucretius. Albrecht collection. (91) SF3,800
— 28 Mar 1811. 1 p, 4to. To the wine-merchant Ramann. Ordering wine. (88) DM4,600
— 20 [Sept] 1811. 1 p, 8vo. Recipient unnamed. Concerning the ptg of his list of autographs. Sgd G. (89) £2,800
— 13 Feb 1815. 1 p, 4to. To Herr Ramann. Ordering wine. (90) DM13,000
— 1 Apr 1815. 1 p, 4to. To Christian Gottlob von Voigt. Thanking for information. (90) DM5,500
— 18 Apr 1815. 1 p, 4to. To Christian Gottlob von Voigt. Returning a paper. (90) DM5,000
— 1 Aug 1815. 4 pp, 8vo. To Christian Gottlob von Voigt. Reporting about a meeting with vom Stein, a decoration conferred on him by the Emperor of Austria (with newspaper clipping pasted on), etc. Albrecht collection. (91) SF11,000

— 10 Apr 1817. 4 pp, 4to. To Christian Gottlob von Voigt. Discussing various matters pertaining to the university at Jena. Albrecht collection. (91) SF10,000

— 30 Aug 1817. 2 pp, 4to. To Christian Gottlob von Voigt. About Voigt's recovery, & expressing satisfaction about finding a lost collection of autographs. (89) DM14,000

— 7 Dec 1817. 1 p, 4to. To Christian Gottlob von Voigt. Sending an unspecified file for deliberation. Sgd G. (90) DM5,000

— 13 Apr 1818. 1 p, 4to. To H. C. W. von Lyncker. In the name of Grand Duke Karl August, inviting him for dinner. Albrecht collection. (91) SF3,600

— 5 Feb 1819. 1 p, 4to. To Voigt. Regarding the inscr discovered at Heilsberg. (90) DM10,000

— 1 Aug 1824. 4 pp, 4to. To Grand Duke Carl August. Mentioning Count Sternberg's visit, discussing meteorological research, etc. (89) DM18,000

— 2 Feb 1830. 2 pp, folio. To Grand Duke Karl Friedrich. Sending congratulations on his birthday & regretting his inability to attend the festivities. Repaired. (89) DM10,500

— [n.d.]. (91) £1,000

— [n.d.]. 1 p, 8vo. To H. C. A. Eichstaedt. Arranging for a date. Sgd G. (89) £1,100

— [n.d.]. 1 p, 8vo. To [Christian Gottlob von Voigt]. Announcing his visit to discuss administrative matters. Albrecht collection. (91) SF3,800

— [n.d.]. 1 p, 8vo. To [Karl Ludwig von Knebel?]. About a new Spanish play. Sgd G. (90) DM5,000

Ls s (2), 26 Dec 1806 & 17 Oct 1829. 2 pp, 4to. To Heinrich Luden, regarding a trans of one of his works. To Christian Ernst Friedrich Weller, about a list of books from the Jena library. (89) $2,500

Ls, 20 Aug 1781. 2 pp, folio. To Jenny von Voigts. Sending a Ms for her father & explaining the delay in sending a bust. (90) DM10,500

— 25 June 1783. 1 p, folio. To the Treasury at Weimar. By order of the Grand Duke, regarding an account. Also sgd by Christian Friedrich Schnauss. (90) DM2,600

— 12 Dec 1799. 1 p, 4to. To Herr Genast. Complaining about some people's behavior in the Weimar theater. Salzer collection. (90) £2,100

— 6 May 1801. 3 pp, 4to. To [Hans Heinrich Meyer?]. Thanking for a poem, & discussing a problem regarding a drawing by Hartmann. (90) £1,800

— 30 Dec 1801. 1 p, 8vo. To Schelling. Inviting him to the 1st performance of [Schlegel's] play Jon. Albrecht collection. (91) SF2,600

— [13 Oct 1803]. 2 pp, 8vo. To H. C. A. Eichstaedt. Commenting about the [Jenaische Allgemeine Literaturzeitung]. Sgd G. With related material. (89) £1,400

— 18 Jan 1804. 1 p, 4to. To Eichstaedt. Sending contributions to the Jenaische Allgemeine Literaturzeitung & discussing others. With 2 autograph lines. Albrecht collection. (91) SF4,000

— 15 Feb 1804. (89) £950

— 15 Feb 1804. 4 pp, 4to. To [H. C. A. Eichstaedt]. Commenting on a scientific work by Stuetz. Sgd G. (89) £1,900

— [15 Feb 1804]. 2 pp, folio. To Eichstaedt. Responding to his questions regarding reviews for the Jenaische Allgemeine Literaturzeitung. In the margin of Eichstaedt's letter addressed to him. Albrecht collection. (91) SF4,000

— 1 Aug 1804. 2 pp, 4to. To H. C. A. Eichstaedt. Regarding reviews in the Jenaische Allgemeine Literatur-Zeitung. With autograph postscript. (89) DM5,000

— 26 Jan 1805. 2 pp, 4to. To Eichstaedt. Sending reviews for the Jenaische Allgemeine Literaturzeitung. With autograph subscription & postscript. Albrecht collection. (91) SF5,500

— 11 May 1805. 2 pp, 4to. To Eichstaedt. About the death of Schiller, reviews for the Jenaische Allgemeine Literaturzeitung, etc. Albrecht collection. (91) SF6,500

— 28 Mar 1807. 2 pp, folio. To Duke Karl August. Regarding the actor [Friedrich] Haide's wish to leave Weimar & accept a contract in Vienna; also sgd by Franz Kirms. Including autograph

endorsements, sgd, by the Duke & by Goethe. Albrecht collection. (91) SF7,400
— 27 Dec 1808. 1 p, 4to. To [H. C. A. Eichstaedt]. Giving his opinion of Zacharias Werner's play Attila. Sgd G. (89) £1,300
— 12 July 1814. 1 p, 8vo. To Karl Duncker. Sending the concluding part of [Des Epimenides Erwachen]. Albrecht collection. (91) SF3,000
— 29 Jan 1815. 4 pp, 4to. To Hofrat Eichstaett. Commenting on a review of vol 3 of his Aus meinem Leben. With autograph subscription. Partly dampstained. Sightly differing from Sophien-Ed vol 25, no 7007. (88) DM9,500
— 25 Feb 1815. 1 p, 4to. To [F. J. Bertuch?]. Sending Capt. Hundeshagen's map of Mainz. (91) DM4,500
— 13 Apr 1815. 7 pp, 4to. To Konrad Levezow. Commenting on the recent premiere of his play Des Epimenides Erwachen. Albrecht collection. (91) SF8,000
— 18 Mar 1816. 1 p, 4to. To [Johann Wolfgang Doebereiner]. Inquiring about 2 scientific problems. Corners def. (91) DM2,800
— 19 Feb 1818. (91) £1,000
— 17 July 1818. 1 p, 4to. To the Duke of Weimar. Sending an article regarding the Academy library. Affixed to note of authenticity. (88) $1,500
— 4 Sept 1820. 3 pp, 4to. To his son August. Reporting about his current activities & about news from England concerning the reception of Faust; with autograph English quotation & postscript. Albrecht collection. (91) SF7,500
— 20 Sept 1820. 3 pp, 4to. To J. A. G. Weigel. Sending payment for engravings, mentioning his collection of autographs, etc. With autograph subscription. Repaired. (90) DM9,500
— 14 Jan 1821. 1 p, 4to. To Christian August Vulpius. Regarding affairs of the library at Weimar. Margin cut. (90) DM3,200
— 27 Mar 1822. 2 pp, 4to. To Hermann von Staff. Thanking for a sculpture & sending some of his works. Albrecht collection. (91) SF3,800

— 5 Dec 1822. 1 p, folio. To Karl August Schwerdgeburth. Referring to his appointment as engraver at the Weimar court. (91) DM2,800
— 11 Mar 1825. 1 p, folio. To Voigt. Refusing permission to use a collection of mineralogical samples. (91) £1,300
— 21 Apr 1825. 1 p, folio. To Miss Seidler. Sending orders regarding the upkeep of buildings belonging to the Grand Duke. Albrecht collection. (91) SF2,500
— 1 Nov 1825. 1 p, folio. To the Foreign Ministry of Hesse at Kassel. Expressing thanks for a charter forbidding a reprint of his works. With autograph subscription. Sophien-Ed vol. 40, no 108. (88) DM3,200
— 2 Jan 1826. 1 p, folio. To Franz Baumann. Granting permission to marry. Slightly dampstained. With related material. (88) DM2,800
— 24 June 1826. 1 p, 4to. To the ptr Frommann. Requesting a reprint [of his poem Sah gemalt, in Gold und Rahmen...]. Albrecht collection. (91) SF4,000
— 1 Sept 1826. 3 pp, 4to. To Clementine de Cuvier. Asking her to convey his thanks to her father for some of his works. With autograph subscription. (90) DM6,000
— 20 Dec 1826. 1 p, 4to. To Franz Baumann. Sending wheat seed brought back from Sicily. Sophien-Ed vol 41, no 225 (draft). (88) DM3,200
— 10 Jan 1828. 1 p, 4to. To Friedrich August Schmid. Notifying him that he has been granted permission to dedicate his Archiv fuer Berkwerkswissenschaften to the Grandduke. With autograph subscription. Sophien-Ed vol 43, no 166. (88) DM5,200
— 4 Mar 1828. 2 pp, 4to. To Wilhelm Reichel. Giving instructions for the ptg of the 2d part of Faust. Albrecht collection. (91) SF4,600
— 5 June 1828. 1 p, 4to. To Karoline Riemer. Inquiring about her husband's health. With autograph subscription. Margin cut; address leaf mtd. With engraved port. (90) DM4,200
— 13 June 1828. 1 p, 8vo. To Franz Baumann. Suggesting a change in a projected inscription. Including auto-

graph drawing of the script suggested. Albrecht collection. (91) SF3,000
— 15 Nov 1828. 2 pp, 4to. To F. F. H. Kuestner. Thanking for information about the price of platinum, & discussing the theater as a winter pastime. Albrecht collection. (91) SF5,000
— 4 Jan 1830. 2 pp, 4to. To Julius Adolf Voelkel. Acknowledging a grant for the Unmittelbare Anstalten fuer Wissenschaft und Kunst. With autograph subscription. (90) DM4,200
— 4 Jan 1831. 1 p, folio (tissue paper). To Frederic Soret. Duplicated copy taken from the orig letter, discussing the ptg of a work in German & French. Albrecht collection. (91) SF1,200
— 15 June 1831. 1 p, 8vo. To Frederic Soret. Acknowledging receipt of a book. (91) DM2,400
— [June 1831?]. 2 pp, 4to. Recipient unnamed. Asking him to forward books to Thomas Carlyle. (91) £1,600

Letter, 1 Oct 1796. (88) £650

ANs, 29 July 1804. 1 p, 8vo. To Demoiselle Blumau. Requesting her visit. Framed. (90) DM3,000
— 26 Apr 1809. 1 p, 8vo. To [Knebel]. Covering note, & hoping to see him. (91) DM2,200
— [1811-1816]. 1 p, 8vo. To [Christian Gottlob von Voigt]. Suggesting an advance payment to [Christian August] Vulpius. Albrecht collection. (91) SF3,200
— [Nov 1814 or 1825]. 1 p, 16mo (card). To [Karl Melchior Jakob] Moltke. Dinner invitation. (90) DM2,700
— 13 Jan 1817. 1 p, 4to. To Franz Krims. Responding to an inquiry (included, above) regarding guest performances at the Weimar theater. Sgd G. Salzer collection. (90) £2,000
— 20 May 1819. 1 p, 8vo. To [the future Grand Duchess] Maria Paulovna. Submitting material for her information. With [later] autograph address leaf. Albrecht collection. (91) SF2,000
— 28 June 1828. 1 p, 8vo. To the Weimar post office. Requesting the return of a package mailed to [Karl] von Holtei earlier in the day. Albrecht collection. (91) SF3,300
— 28 Feb 1831. 1 p, 8vo. To Frederic Soret. Asking for a meeting. Sgd JWvG. With ANs by Soret on autograph address leaf. (90) DM3,200
— [n.d.]. 1 p, 8vo. To [Johann Daniel Falk]. Inviting H. Schulze to visit him. Inscr by Falk at bottom. (90) DM3,200

AN, [Nov 1786]. 1 p, 8vo. [To his friends in Weimar]. Sending his address in Rome. Albrecht collection. (91) SF10,000
— 20 Apr 1796. 1 p, 8vo. Recipient unnamed. List of wood to be ordered. (88) DM1,400

Ns, [Aug 1827]. 1 p, 12mo. To Christian Wilhelm Schweitzer. Inviting him for lunch. Albrecht collection. (91) SF2,000

A Ds s (2), 12 Sept 1790. 2 pp, 8vo. Pay order in favor of Philipp Seidel, & pay order to Seidel in favor of [Christiane] Vulpius. With autograph receipt by Christiane Vulpius, 22 Sept [1790]. Albrecht collection. (91) SF13,000

ADs, 28 Mar 1804. 1 p, 8vo. Receipt for 50 thalers from Voigt for the Jena Anatomical Museum. (91) £1,100
— 26 May 1805. 1 p, 4to. Receipt to H. Cotta for payment for Winckelmann und sein Jahrhundert. With related material. Albrecht collection. (91) SF6,000
— [c.late Sept 1827]. (89) DM750
— [26 Nov 1828]. 1 p, folio. Receipt on shipping document for a box mailed to him from Strasbourg. (91) DM2,800

Ds, 1 Oct 1773. 2 pp, folio. Sale of a shop in Frankfurt by Frau von Voss to Catharina Moritz, sgd as witness. Albrecht collection. (91) SF8,000
— 24 Feb 1785. 1 p, folio. Ptd receipt for payment due for share no 429 in the Ilmenau mines. Also sgd by C. G. Voigt. (91) DM6,300
— 24 Feb 1786. 1 p, folio. Share certificate for the Ilmenau mining company issued to Mme Wieland; partly ptd. Also sgd by Voigt. Mtd. (88) £1,600
— 24 Feb 1786. 1 p, folio. Ptd receipt for payment due for a share in the Ilmenau mines. Also sgd by C. G. Voigt. (90) DM5,600
— 5 June 1791. 1 p, 8vo. Share certificate for the Ilmenau mining company. Also sgd by Voigt. (91) £2,200
— [c.1791]. 1 p, folio. Share certificate no

323 for the Ilmenau mining company; partly ptd. Also sgd by Christian Gottlob & Johann Karl Wilhelm Voigt. Unaccomplished. (90) DM14,000
— 19 Apr 1796. 1 p, 8vo. Ptd receipt for payment due for share no 277 in the Ilmenau mines. Also sgd by C. G. Voigt & J. G. Seeger. With related material. Albrecht collection. (91) SF3,300
— 27 Jan 1798. 1 p, 8vo. Ptd receipt for payment due for share no 748 in the Ilmenau mines. Also sgd by C. G. Voigt. (91) DM4,800
— 10 Nov 1803. (89) DM900
— 9 Dec 1803. 1 p, 4to. Receipt for 4 bottles of champagne. (89) DM3,200
— 25 May 1827. (90) £1,000
— 20 Apr 1828. (89) £950
— 16 May 1830. (89) DM900

Autograph endorsement, sgd, 28 Aug 1829; on ptd copy of the poem "Sah gemalt, in Gold und Rahmen...", [7 Nov 1825]. Repeating thanks. Repaired. (89) DM3,200
— Anr, sgd, 28 Aug 1831; on ptd copy of the poem "Des Menschen Tage sind verflochten...", [28 Aug 1826]. Repeating thanks. Margins cut. (89) DM5,400

Autograph quotation, quatrain, beginning "Zu unsres Lebens oftgetruebten Tagen...," sgd & dated 5 Oct 1806. 1 p, 8vo. (90) DM22,000
— Anr, "Was der August nicht thut Macht der September gut."; 1 Sept 1814. 1 p, 8vo. Sgd. Albrecht collection. (91) SF4,500
— Anr, poem, beginning "Liegt dir Gestern klar und offen"; 4 lines, sgd & dated 8 June 1828. 1 p, 8vo. (90) DM17,000
— Anr, poem, Buergerpflicht, 6 Mar 1832. 1 p, 12mo. 4 lines, sgd. Albrecht collection. (91) SF18,000
— Anr, 'Das noethigste zu erst." 2 July [18]96. 1 p, 8vo. Sgd. Albrecht collection. (91) SF3,800

Autograph sentiment, "Im Guten und Schoenen/ wie der Anfang so das Ende." Sgd & dated 24 Nov 1813. 1 p, 92mm by 183mm. Tipped to thick paper. (88) £1,900

Cut signature, 14 July 1816. (90) $550

Endorsement, sgd, 25 June 1824 [i.e. 1825]. On a letter by M. Kynaston, 1 p, 8vo, requesting permission to use the ducal library; granting request. (89) DM2,800

Signature, 7 Mar 1796. 1 p, 8vo. On list of cast for the play Der deutsche Hausvater. (91) DM2,600
— Anr, JWvG, on verso of envelope addressed to Cotta, [25 Sept 1823]. Albrecht collection. (91) SF900
— Anr, [n.d.]. Autograph visiting card, sgd Geheimer Rath/ von Goethe. 6cm by 9.7cm. Engraved borders. (88) DM5,800
— Anr, [1826]. On ptd copy of poem thanking for congratulations on his birthday, 1 p, 8vo. (91) DM4,800
— Anr, 15 Apr 1830. (91) £700

Single sheet ptg, poem, Sah gemalt, in Gold und Rahmen, sgd, inscr to [Ludwig Friedrich] von Froriep & dated 15 Sept 1819. 1 p, 8vo. Albrecht collection. (91) SF3,200
— Anr, poem, Sah gemalt, in Gold und Rahmen, sgd, inscr to Friedrich von Stein & dated 15 Sept 1819. 1 p, 8vo. Albrecht collection. (91) SF3,700
— Anr, poem, Des Menschen Tage sind verflochten..., 28 Aug 1826. 1 p, 8vo. Sgd. Albrecht collection. (91) SF3,800
— Anr, poem, Des Menschen Tage sind verflochten..., 28 Aug 1826. 1 p, 8vo. Sgd. Albrecht collection. (91) SF2,800
— Anr, poem, Sah gemalt, in Gold und Rahmen...; [1826]. 1 p, 8vo. Sgd. Albrecht collection. (91) SF3,400
— Anr, poem, Sah gemalt, in Gold und Rahmen...; [1826]. 1 p, 8vo. Sgd. Albrecht collection. (91) SF3,200
— Anr, poem, Sah gemalt, in Gold und Rahmen..., Jan 1832. 1 p, 8vo. Sgd. Albrecht collection. (91) SF2,400
— EICHSTAEDT, HEINRICH KARL ABRAHAM. - 22 Apr [1804]. 4 pp, 4to. To Goethe. Sending contributions for the Jenaische Allgemeine Literaturzeitung & requesting his comments. Including autograph endorsements by Goethe, 27 lines, 28 Apr 1804. Albrecht collection. (91) SF4,400
— FORGERIES. - A group of 5 varied Mss purporting to be autographs by Goethe sold at star on 10 May 1991, lot 98, for SF780. 91

— FREUDWEILER, HEINRICH. - ANs, [26 Nov 1779]. 1 p, 4to. To [Lisette Bachofen]. Referring to Goethe & Gellert. With pencil-&-ink drawing of a man dressed like Werther at head. (88) DM3,400

— KESTNER, CHARLOTTE, NEE BUFF. - ADs, 4 Oct 1821. 1 p, 8vo. Receipt. (89) DM620

— KNEBEL, KARL LUDWIG VON. - ALs, [c.1806]. 2 pp, 4to. To Riemer. Requesting the return of a book & expressing his wish to visit Goethe. (88) DM460

— KRAUSE, GOTTLIEB FRIEDRICH. - Autograph Ms, description of Goethe's last journey to Ilmenau in August 1831; 1832. 7 pp, 4to; stitched. Albrecht collection. (91) SF950

— KRAUSE, GOTTLIEB FRIEDRICH. - Autograph Ms, list of wine consumed in Goethe's household, Jan to 19 Mar 1832. 4 pp, folio. Sgd on cover. Albrecht collection. (91) SF1,900

— LODER, JUSTUS CHRISTIAN. - ALs, 13 Apr 1789. 2 pp, 4to. To Karl Ludwig von Knebel. Recommending a steward & talking about Goethe. (88) DM1,100

— VILLERS, CHARLES DE. - ALs, 6 Oct 1806. 1 p, 4to. To Goethe. Sending a publication. With autograph endorsement by Goethe. Albrecht collection. (91) SF950

— VULPIUS, CHRISTIAN AUGUST. - ALs, 9 Aug 1815. 1 p, 8vo. Recipient unnamed. Informing him that his letter has been forwarded to Goethe. (90) DM800

— VULPIUS, CHRISTIAN AUGUST. - ALs, 11 Dec 1801. 2 pp, 4to. To the winemerchant Ramann. Ordering "Erlauer" for Goethe. (88) DM420

— ZIX, BENJAMIN. - Orig drawing, profile port of Goethe, [20 Oct] 1806. 91mm by 84mm. In black lead pencil on cream colored paper. Mtd. (90) DM36,000
See also: Herder, Johann Gottfried von
See also: Riemer, Friedrich Wilhelm
See also: Stockmann, August Cornelius

Goethe, Katharina Elisabeth, 1731-1808
ALs, 12 May 1788. 4 pp, 4to. To K. W. F. Unzelmann. Deploring his departure & sending theater news from Frankfurt. Albrecht collection. (91) SF8,000

Ds s (2)1 & 6 Sept 1788. 6 pp, folio. Partial waiver of a loan granted to her sister Johanna Maria Melber; also sgd by others. Albrecht collection. (91) SF2,200

Ds, 30 Sept 1786. 1 p, 4to. Receipt for 40 guilders interest due for money invested with the Brothers Sanner. (90) DM1,800

Goethe, Ottilie von, 1796-1872
ALs, [13 Apr 1830]. Albrecht collection. (91) SF550
— 14 June 1853. (88) DM320
— 20 Aug 1869. (88) DM340
— [n.d.]. (90) DM280
— [n.d.]. Albrecht collection. (91) SF320
ANs, [Oct 1872]. 1 p, 4to. To Gustav Kuehne. Farewell message from her deathbed. With related material. Albrecht collection. (91) SF1,300

Goethe, Walther von, 1818-85
ALs, 8 June 1847. (88) DM700
— [n.d.]. Albrecht collection. (91) SF280

Goethe, Wolfgang von, 1820-83
ALs, 14 Nov 1873. (88) DM320

Goetz, Curt, 1888-1960
ALs, 14 Jan 1933. (90) DM850

Goetz, Hermann, 1840-76
Collection of ALs, 2 autograph postcards, sgd, & ANs, 30 May to 15 Oct 1876. 2 pp, 8vo, & cards. To Oskar Grohe. Responding to an inquiry about his compositions. ANs on visiting card. (90) DM1,700
ALs, 18 June 1875. (89) DM650
— 30 Sept 1875. 4 pp, 8vo. To an unnamed opera singer. Giving advice about the staging of his opera Der Widerspenstigen Zaehmung at Leipzig. (91) DM2,100

Gogol, Nikolai Vasil'evich, 1809-52
ALs, [mid-Sept 1845]. 2 pp, 8vo. To Anna Michailovna Wielgorskaya. Personal letter, asking her to take care of an ailing friend. Possibly unptd. (88)

GOLDBERG

DM160,000

Goldberg, Albert
[A large collection of A Ls s & Ls s addressed to Albert Goldberg, music critic of the Los Angeles Times, by numerous composers, artists, etc., with related material, sold at S on 19 May 1989, lot 468, for £2,800 to McNutt.]

Goldman, Emma, 1869-1940
ALs, 26 Dec 1905. (90) $375

Goldmark, Karl, 1830-1915
Autograph music, sketches for Die Koenigin von Saba, [Act II, Scene 4?]; [n.d.]. (91) £1,000

Gollwitzer, Helmut
Autograph Ms (2), Nachwort zu Argument/Reprint II, 1975, & Womit bekommt man zu tun, wenn man mit dem Evangelium zu tun bekommt, Apr 1969. (90) DM240

Autograph Ms, essay on Herbert Marcuse's 80th birthday, for the journal Akzente, June 1978. (88) DM340

Gone With The Wind
[A copy of Mitchell's book, sgd by the producer, director & cast of the film, Oct 1938, sold at CNY on 21 June 1989, lot 363, for $12,000.]
[The final shooting script of the film, 254 typed offset pages, in red mor bdg, inscr to Eric G. Stacey by David O. Selznick, [25 Dec] 1939, sold at CNY on 21 June 1989, lot 364, for $8,500.]

Gonzalez de Calvijo, Ruy, d.1412
Ms, Historia de el Gran Tamorlan... [c.1582]. About 200 pp, size not stated, in vellum wraps. Covering embassy sent by Henry II of Castile to Samarkand, & account of Tamerlaine by Pedro Meya. In 2 hands. Phillipps MS.21259 & Robinson collection. (89) £3,800

Goodall, John S.
Original drawings, (14), to illus Above and Below Stairs, [pbd 1983]. (89) £1,000
— Original drawings, (20), to illus Laurence Meynell's Bridge under the Water, 1954, & other titles. Archives of J. M. Dent & Son. (88) £150
— Original drawings, (3), to illus Lavinia's Cottage, [pbd 1982]. (89) £100

Goodchild, John
Original drawings, (17), to illus Mary E. Archives of J. M. Dent & Son. (88) £130

Goodyear, Charles, 1800-60
ALs, 22 Sept 1849. (90) $425
Check, sgd, 4 June 1860. (91) $550

Gookin, Daniel, 1612-87
ADs, 2 Aug 1652. (91) $650

Gorbachev, Mikhail Sergeyevich
Group photograph, sgd; [n.d.]. 4to. With Ronald Reagan. With related material. (90) $1,600
Photograph, sgd, [n.d.]. (90) $650

Gorcey, Leo —&
Hall, Huntz
Photograph, sgd, [n.d.]. (91) $180

Gorchacov, Alexander Mikhailovich, Prince, 1798-1883
ALs, [n.d.], "Monday". (91) $300

Gordimer, Nadine
Typescript, novel, Something out there, Dec 1982 to Jan 1983. 150 leaves, 4to. Working draft, with autograph revisions & notes, typescripts of alternative versions, etc. Sgd on autograph tp. (91) £2,600

Gordon, Arthur Charles Hamilton, 1st Baron Stanmore, 1829-1912. See: Canada

Gordon, Charles George, 1833-85
Autograph Ms, diary of his Chinese campaign, 18 Mar 1863 to [28] Aug 1864. 18 pp, folio. With related material. (89) £8,000
Series of 5 A Ls s, 20 Feb 1877 to 25 Jan 1884. (89) £650
A Ls s (2), 16 Mar [1878] & [n.d.]. (90) £380
ALs, [c.1874]. (90) $600
— 28 Mar 1877. (91) £340
— 27 Nov 1877. (88) $275
— 29 & 30 Mar 1878. (89) £500
— 14 Nov [18]81. (91) $450
— 1881. (88) £550
— 6 Mar 1884. (88) £60

**Gorges, Sir Arthur, d.1625 —&
Raleigh, Walter, Sir, 1552?-1618**
Ms, Gorges's Island Voyage, & Raleigh's appended Observations concerning the Royal Navy and Sea Service, [early 17th cent]. 170 pp, 4to, in contemp limp vellum. In a single professional hand; with dedicatory epistle. Robinson collection. (88) £4,000

Gorki, Maxim, 1868-1936
ALs, [Mar 1924]. (91) DM900
— 22 Feb 1925. 1 p, 4to. To W. Woitinski. Giving advice regarding problems with the publication of Russian books in foreign countries. (89) DM1,900
— [n.d.]. (90) £250
Ls, 2 May 1927. (90) DM750
Ds, 28 Dec 1922. (91) £600
Photograph, sgd & inscr, [n.d.]. (89) £600

Gospel Manuscripts
Ms, 4 Gospels, in Coptic & Arabic, with a concordance. (89) £550
— Ms, 4 Gospels, in Latin. [Milan?, c.1500]. 175 leaves (1 blank), vellum, 236mm by 155mm, in blindstamped pale brown mor bdg of c.1900. In dark brown ink in a very large rounded gothic hand. With 4 large historiated initials in elaborate classical & leafy designs with marginal extensions. (90) £4,400
— Ms, Die martel ihesu Cristi. [Southern Germany, c.1500]. 176 leaves, vellum, 175mm by 135mm. 18th-cent blindstamped brown lea over wooden bds. In black ink in an elegant gothic textura. The Passion of Christ in a series of episodes followed by homilies. With 22 large & 26 smaller initials in gold & colors with elaborate borders. (89) DM35,000
— Ms, Gospel according to St. Mark, with glossa ordinaria. [Central Italy, late 12th cent]. 100 leaves, vellum, 22cm by 15cm. 18th-cent Italian calf over bds, def. In brown ink in an uneven minuscule bookhand. With 3 decorated initials. Doheny collection. (88) £11,000
— Ms, Gospels in Arabic & Coptic. (90) DM1,000
— Ms, Gospels in Armenian. [Church of St. Vardan, Province of Mokk', Eastern Turkey, 1659]. 235 leaves, 250mm by 190mm, in contemp calf over wooden bds. In black ink in a regular bolorgir hand by the scribes Mxit'ar & Srapion for Vardanes & his wife. With 8 marginal drawings of saints, 10 decorated pages with the Eusebian Letter & Canon Tables, 4 half-page headpieces, & 20 full-page miniatures in full colors. (91) £15,000
— Ms, Gospels in Armenian. [Monastery of SS. Grigoris & Simon, K'art'man, Eastern Turkey, 1661]. 278 leaves (some lacking), 170mm by 115mm, in black lea over pastebds. In black ink in a regular bolorgir hand by the scribe Yarout'iwn for Hayrapet, his wife & son. With decorative zoomorphic chapter initials, 4 decorative headpieces & full-page miniature in full colors. (91) £2,400
— Ms, Gospels in Armenian. [Church of St. Minas at Marunan, Isfahan, 1703]. 272 leaves (some lacking), vellum, 175mm by 135mm, in contemp calf over wooden bds. In black ink in a regular bolorgir hand. With larger initials in zoomorphic & foliate designs, 4 decorative headpieces, & 4 full-page miniatures. (91) £6,000
— Ms, Gospels, in Church Slavonic. [Russia, 17th cent]. 165 leaves, 290mm by 180mm. Contemp blue velvet over wooden bds. In black & red ink. With 2 full-page colored pen-&-ink drawings & several initials & ornamental headpieces. Incomplete. (89) DM1,200
— Ms, Gospels, in Greek. [Constantinople, late 10th cent]. 309 leaves (lacking 3 canon leaves after f.7), vellum, 151mm by 115mm, in late medieval Greek bdg of lea over thick wooden bds, with thongs, blind-stamped & with spine raised alla greca. Written by a single scribe in a skilful Perlschrift. Purple capitals throughout. 14 pp in Alexandrian uncials; 4 poems in uncials with decorative red frames preceding each Gospel; 2 pp of Eusebian sections in purple uncials within ornamental illuminated frames; 4 full-page illuminated canon tables & 4 large initials & half-page illuminated headpieces preceding each Gospel. Phillipps Ms 7757. (88) £70,000
— Ms, Gospels, in Greek, with lists of

GOSPEL MANUSCRIPTS

Kephalaia. [Eastern Mediterranean, c.950]. 196 leaves (some missing), vellum, 155mm by 113mm. Remains of medieval bdg of thick wooden bds covered with lea. In brown ink in a very fine small Greek minuscule, with 6 pp in Alexandrian display script in red ink. With painted initials throughout, 3 decorative headpieces & 4 full-page miniatures (3 fairly recent, 1 c.11th cent). Worn; nibbled around edges. (91) £20,000

— Ms, Gospels, in Greek. [Eastern Mediterranean, c.1700]. 286 leaves (some missing), 103mm by 66mm. Modern French red mor bdg. In black ink in an extremely small, neat Greek cursive minuscule. With c.60 large illuminated initials in many different designs, 3 large illuminated headpieces & 2 full-page miniatures. Worn. (91) £1,100

— Ms, Gospels, in Greek, with Canon Tables & Kephalaia. [South Italy, 10th cent]. 285 leaves (some missing), vellum, 146mm by 113mm. Late medieval blindstamped bdg of tanned lea over wooden bds; def. In brown ink in a very regular Greek minuscule, with some pages written in red uncials. With painted initials throughout, 7 full-page Canon Tables in very elaborate architectural columns, & 9 small miniatures. Many medieval annotations. (90) £100,000

— Ms, Gospels, with Prologues & Capitulary (The Liesborn Gospels), in Latin. [Northwest Germany, 10th cent]. 169 leaves, vellum, 305mm by 238mm. Late 15th-cent bdg, upper cover carved oak board, lower cover lea. Written in brown ink in a Caroline minuscule by the Deacon Gerward for Berthild, Abbess of the nunnery of Saint Symeon at Liesborn in Westphalia. With 13 pp of canon tables in arcades & 5 pp with tituli & incipits decorated with leafy scrolls & interlace. Excellent condition. Doheny collection. (88) £380,000

— Ms, St. John's Gospel, in Greek. [Eastern or southern Mediterranean, Anatolia?, 3d cent]. Fragment of vellum leaf, c.50mm by 42mm (irregular), between glass sheets. In pale brown ink in well-spaced late classical Greek uncial script without word division.

Part of 5 lines, comprising St. John's Gospel 10:25-26, & 10:40. (90) £42,000

— Ms, Tetraevangelion, Gospel Book, in Church Slavonic. [Russia, 2d half of 16th cent]. 246 leaves (some lacking), 254mm by 170mm, in contemp wooden bds. In a semi-uncial hand. With 3 endpieces, 4 large decorated initials, 4 ornamental headpieces, & 3 full-page miniatures. Fekula Ms.419. (91) £5,000

— Ms, Tetraevangelion, Gospel Book, in Church Slavonic. [Russia, 2d half of 16th cent]. 274 leaves (some lacking), 295mm by 190mm, disbound. In a semi-uncial hand. With 4 illuminated headpieces, 1 roundel, & 3 full-page illuminated miniatures. Fekula Ms.420. (91) £24,000

— Ms, Tetraevangelion, Gospel Book, in Church Slavonic. [Russia, 2d half of 16th cent, with 19th-cent addition]. 261 leaves (some lacking), 295mm by 190mm, in 19th-cent embroidered textile cover over bds. In semi-uncial hands. With 4 tetratological initials, 4 decorative headpieces, & full-page illuminated miniature. Fekula Ms.421. (91) £4,000

— Ms, Tetraevangelion, Gospel Book, in Church Slavonic. [Ukraine, 1st half of 17th cent]. 126 leaves (48 lacking), 292mm by 205mm, loosely inserted in folder in 18th-cent calf bdg with the Russian Imperial arms. In a large, calligraphic semi-uncial hand. With decorative initial, half-page headpiece, circular vignette & full-page miniature. Fekula Ms.422. (91) £2,200

— Ms, Tetraevangelion, Gospel Book, in Church Slavonic. Fekula Ms.423. (91) £240

See also: Armenian Manuscripts
See also: Ethiopic Manuscripts
See also: Greek Manuscripts

Gotter, Friedrich Wilhelm, 1746-97

ALs, 25 July 1796. Albrecht collection. (91) SF380

Gotthelf, Jeremias, Pseud. of Albert Bitzius, 1797-1854

Ds, 5 May 1853. (90) DM750

Gottsched, Johann Christoph, 1700-66
ALs, 24 July 1746. 3 pp, 4to. To [Johann Heinrich Samuel Formey]. Offering an essay on Spinoza for print. (91) DM2,400
— 1 Sept 1748. 3 pp, folio. Recipient unnamed. Interesting letter about his collection of early German literary Mss. (90) DM4,600

Gougenot, Nicolas. See: Desportes, Philippe

Gough, Philip
Original drawings, (16), to illus Roger Lancelyn Green's Ten Tales of Adventure, 1972, & other titles. Archives of J. M. Dent & Son. (88) £250

Gould, Chester, 1900-85
Original drawing, bust profile of Dick Tracy, 18 Mar [19]78. (91) $325
ALs, 18 Nov 1972. (91) $325

Gould, Elizabeth, d.1841
[A lithographed trial plate for John Gould's A Monograph of the Ramphastidae, or Family of Toucans, [c.1830], 400mm by 352mm, with added pencil drawing & notes in ink, & pencil sketch of 2 birds on verso, sold at P on 11 Dec 1989, lot 18, for $4,250.]
Original drawing, Rose-Breasted Cockatoo, 1840, to illus The Birds of Australia. 538mm by 375mm. Watercolor over pencil sketching, sgd. Boone Estate. (89) $9,500
— Original drawing, Silvery-Gray Petrel, 1840, to illus The Birds of Australia. 383mm by 553mm. Watercolor over pencil sketching, sgd. Boone Estate. (89) $3,750
— Original drawing, Wandering Albatross, 1838, to illus The Birds of Australia. 380mm by 552mm. Watercolor over pencil sketching, sgd. Boone Estate. (89) $2,500

Gould, Jay, 1836-92
Collection of 2 A Ls s, ADs & Ds, 1856 to 1883. 7 pp, 8vo & 4to. Recipients unnamed, discussing financial matters. Land conveyance; stock proxy. (89) $1,100
— Collection of 3 A Ls s, Ls & cut signature, 1862 to 1891. (89) $1,000

Series of Ds s, 3 Ds s, Mar 1880. (89) $550
— Series of Ds s, 3 Ds s, Mar 1880. (89) $550
— Series of Ds s, 3 Ds s, Mar 1880. (89) $425
— Series of Ds s, 3 Ds s, Mar 1880. (89) $375
— Series of Ds s, 3 Ds s, Mar 1880. (89) $450
— Series of Ds s, 4 Ds s, Feb 1881. (89) $700
— Series of Ds s, 4 Ds s, 1881 to 1887. (89) $650
— Series of Ds s, 4 Ds s, 1883 to 1887. (89) $450

Gould, John, 1804-81
ALs, 9 Sept 1837. (89) £500
— 18 Feb 1842. (89) £1,000

Gould, S. Baring
Autograph quotation, sgd, [n.d.]. (91) $375

Gounod, Charles, 1818-93
Autograph music, Choeur de Chasseurs (no I) 1ere Basse; [1855]. (89) DM420
— Autograph music, Choeur des Chasseurs. (90) DM550
— Autograph music, Gloria for 4 voices, from an identified Mass. 13 pp, oblong 4to. (91) $1,100
— Autograph music, Hosanna (en Style fugue), for chorus & orchestra; [n.d.]. Rosen collection. (89) $700
— Autograph music, Hymne a Pie IX, reduction for piano for 4 hands, [n.d.]. 3 pp, folio, in paper bds. 56 bars, with ANs regarding the work's performance at end. John F. Fleming Estate. (89) $4,000
— Autograph music, "'Intermezzo' pour Violon avec Accomp[agnemen]t d'Orchestre", fair copy; [n.d.]. Tp & 9 pp, size not stated. Sgd on tp. In bds. Inscr to Paul Viardot erased. (88) DM3,200
— Autograph music, Psalm for 4-voice chorus & orchestra, [n.d.]. 16 pp, 4to, on hand-ruled staff paper. 154 bars, sgd. Including list of instruments & singers in anr hand. Dampstained; in cloth folding case. Doheny collection. (89) $3,000
— Autograph music, Stances de Romeo et Juliette, par Hectoir Berlioz; tran-

GOUNOD

scription for voice & harp, [n.d.]. Tp & 6 pp, c.35.5cm by 27cm. Margin def. (89) DM1,100
— Autograph music, working Ms of his unfinished opera George Dandin, comprising full orchestral draft of the overture & 8 scenes, sgd at end; [1873 or 1874]. About 215 pp, folio. Notated on up to 20 staves per page. Many pages sgd diagonally by Georgina Weldon. (90) £35,000

Collection of ALs & photograph, sgd & inscr, 7 May 1881 & 1865. (91) DM360

Series of 3 A Ls s, 25 Aug 1855 to 18 May 1890. Rosen collection. (89) $420

A Ls s (2), [c.1840] & [n.d.]. (90) DM320

ALs, [c.1840/42]. (90) DM270
— 14 June 1851. (89) DM280
— 15 Feb 1854. (89) DM260
— 24 May 1855. (91) $175
— [27 Nov 1856]. (88) DM420
— 23 July 1870. (91) $160
— [c.1871/74]. (88) DM220
— 4 June [18]73. Byer collection. (90) $300
— 15 Apr 1882. (88) £110
— 16 Aug 1893. (91) DM420
— [n.d.]. (90) DM260

Autograph quotation, 7 bars from the Ballade du Roi de Thule, scored for voice, sgd & dated 26 Oct 1879. (89) £160

Goya y Lucientes, Francisco Jose de, 1746-1828

[His death certificate, sgd by an assistant to the Mayor of Bordeaux as a true copy from the official register, 21 Apr 1828, 2 pp, folio, sold at S on 12 Nov 1989, lot 253, for £650 to Porrua.]

ALs, 29 July 1801. 1 p, 4to. To Don Pedro Cevallos. Acknowledging receipt of an order to make copies of portraits of the King & Queen. Written in right hand column, with draft of new order by Cevallos in left column. (89) £12,500
— 29 July 1801. 1 p, 4to. To Don Pedro Cevallos. Acknowledging receipt of the order of 26 July & repeating his unfavorable opinion about restoration work being undertaken. Written in right hand column; docketed in other hands in left column. (88) £21,000
— 30 July 1801. 1 p, 4to. To Don Pedro Cevallos. Acknowledging receipt of an order regarding the Queen's port. (89) £11,000

Ls, 7 Feb 1801. 4 pp, 8vo. To Pedro Cevallos. Disapproving of the practice of transferring paintings from one canvas to anr. (91) £15,000

Grabbe, Christian Dietrich, 1801-36

Autograph Ms, drama Hermannsschlacht, [n.d.]. 2 pp, 4to. Working Ms from an early draft, pp 75/76. (88) DM7,000
— Autograph Ms, fragment of an early draft of his Hermannsschlacht, [1835]. 2 pp, 4to. With numerous revisions. (90) DM6,500
— Autograph Ms, report about transactions of the military court at Detmold, 3 Jan 1827. 1 p, folio. Sgd. (91) DM2,400

ALs, 12 Jan 1829. (88) £480

ADs, 10 July 1828. 1 p, 8vo. Decision passed by the military court at Detmold. 1 sentence, in Latin; also sgd by anr. (90) DM1,100

Grace, Princesse de Monaco, 1929-82

ALs, 16 Oct 1972. 8 pp, 8vo. To Don Richardson. Chatting about her life & family. (91) $1,600
— [n.d.], "Sunday". (91) $225

Group photograph, with husband & children, [c.1968]. (91) $170

Photograph, sgd, [n.d.]. (89) $95

Photograph, sgd & inscr, [c.1952]. (91) $200

Signature, Sept 1979. (91) $100

Gradual

— [Tuscany?, c.1300]. Single leaf, vellum, 560mm by 357mm. With 5 lines each of text & of music on a 4-line red stave, & large historiated initial. (91) £1,400
— [Bologna?, c.1300]. (90) £800
— [Tuscany?, 1st half of 14th cent]. 2 leaves only, vellum, 513mm by 355mm. With 5 lines each of text in a rounded gothic hand & of music on a 4-line stave. With 2 large historiated initials. (90) £1,600
— [Tuscany?, 1st half of 14th cent]. Single leaf, vellum, 500mm by 355mm. With 5 lines each of text in a rounded gothic hand & of music on a 4-line stave.

With large historiated initial. (90) £3,000
— [Tuscany?, 1st half of 14th cent]. Single leaf, vellum, 514mm by 360mm. With 5 lines each of text in a rounded gothic hand & of music on a 4-line stave. With large historiated initial. (90) £1,500
— [Germany, Thuringia?, c.1330]. Single leaf, vellum, 433mm by 294mm. With 9 lines each of text in a gothic hand & of music on a 4-line stave. With small decorated initials & large historiated initial with scrolling leafy border including animals. (91) £2,600
— [Southern Germany, 3d quarter of 15th cent]. 1 leaf only, vellum, 465mm by 343mm. With 10 lines of text & of music on 4-line staves, historiated initial & historiated border. (90) £4,000
— [Netherlands, late 15th cent]. Of Dominican Use. 205 leaves, vellum, 477mm by 333mm, in 17th- or 18th-cent panelled calf over thick wooden bds with metal corner pieces, clasps & catches. With 8 lines each of text in a formal gothic liturgical hand & of music on a 4-line red stave. With calligraphic or painted initials throughout & 9 very large illuminated initials, 1 with 3-quarter illuminated border. (88) £8,000
— [Western Germany, 1496]. 158 leaves, vellum, & 6 later leaves, 40cm by 27cm, in yellow pigskin over wooden bds; lacking clasps. Written in textura with 8 lines of music on each page on 5-line staves. Lacking some leaves. Probably written for the church at Kond, near Cochem, Mosel. (88) DM8,600
— [Italy, c.1500]. (89) £320
— [Northern France, c.1520-40]. (91) £750
— [Southern Netherlands, Antwerp?, c.1520-30]. 2 leaves, vellum, 425mm by 292mm. With 11 lines each of text in a gothic liturgical hand & of music in Hufnagelschrift neumes on a 4-line black stave. With 5 calligraphic initials & 2 large historiated initials with panel borders in the Ghent/Bruges style with naturalistic flowers, birds, butterflies, etc. (90) £2,400
— [Spain, late 16th or early 17th cent]. Of Franciscan Use. 102 leaves (2 lacking), vellum, 560mm by 385mm, in lea over wooden bds with metal fittings. In 2 sizes of a rounded gothic hand. With large decorated initials throughout & 6 very large initials in colors. (88) £1,900
— [Bohemia?, 17th cent]. 292 leaves, 48cm by 32cm, in def contemp blind-stamped pigskin. In red & black ink, with 7 lines each of text in a calligraphic lettre batarde & of music on a 5-line stave. With c.500 ornamental initials in gold & colors, 29 larger initials decorated with vineleaves & borders, historiated initial, & colored engraving pasted in. (90) DM3,600
— [Germany, 18th cent]. (91) £300

Graefe, Albrecht von, 1828-70
Autograph Ms, orders regarding treatment of a patient, [1858]. (91) DM320
ALs, 29 Mar 1859. (91) DM850

Graf, Oskar Maria, 1894-1967
[An important collection of correspondence, including 4 A Ls s, 168 Ls s, 4 autograph Mss, etc., c.250 pp, 1945 to 1965, addressed to Max Radler & regarding the publication of his works in Germany, his financial concerns, post-war Germany, acquaintances, etc. sold at HK on 6 Nov, lot 3160, for DM23,000.]
Ls, 21 Feb 1967. (88) DM380

Grainger, Percy, 1882-1961
Autograph music, concert rag for piano, In Dahomey, 1909. 15 pp, size not stated. In black & red ink on up to 16 staves per page. With autograph tp; sgd & inscr to W. G. Rathbone. (89) £1,600
Series of A Ls s, [n.d.]. (89) £200

Granados, Enrique, 1867-1916
ALs, [n.d.]. (88) DM440
— 22 Oct 1911. 13 pp, 8vo. To Andre Mangeot. Giving a detailed analysis of his Liliana, with c.90 bars of music. (89) £1,250
Autograph quotation, Mar 1900. (91) $225

Granger, Gideon, 1767-1822
ALs, 1803. Alexander collection. (90) $100
Ds, 19 July 1809. (88) $65

GRANT

Grant, Cary
Photograph, sgd, [1937]. (91) $500
Photograph, sgd & inscr, [c.1945]. (91) $200
— Anr, [1940s]. (88) $50

Grant, Jesse R., 1794-1873. See: Grant, Ulysses S.

Grant, Julia Dent, 1826-1902
ALs, 12 May 1893. (90) $700
— 5 June 1895. (91) $400

Grant, Ulysses S., 1822-85
[3 ptd checks, accomplished & sgd by Grant, 22 Jan 1866 to 12 Mar 1868, various sizes, drawn on Jay Cooke & Co., sold at P on 16 Apr 1988, lot 69, fo $1,700.]
[A collection of 3 ptd checks, accomplished & sgd by Grant, 23 Jan & 5 Mar 1866, & 10 Nov 1873, sold at P on 23 Oct, lot 9, for $1,800.]
[3 ptd checks, accomplished & sgd by Grant, 24 Jan 1866 to 15 July 1869, various sizes, drawn on the Washington branch of Jay Cooke & Co., sold at P on 26 Oct 1988, lot 80, for $1,700.]
[A collection of 2 ptd checks, accomplished & sgd by Grant, 28 June 1867 & 30 Nov 1869, the second endorsed on verso by Julia Dent Grant, sold at P on 23 Oct, lot 11, for $1,000.]
[A collection of 2 ptd checks, accomplished & sgd by Grant, 6 Dec 1867 & 1 Sept 1869, sold at P on 23 Oct, lot 10, for $1,000.]
[3 ptd checks, accomplished & sgd by Grant, 21 Dec 1869 to 1 Dec 1873, various sizes, drawn on the First National Bank of Washington (1) & the National Metropolitan Bank, sold at P on 16 Apr 1988, lot 69, for $2,100.]
Autograph Ms, message to the US Senate asking for withdrawal of A. (91) $180
ALs, 30 Sept 1846. 1 p, 4to. To Maj. Gen. Thomas L. Jesup. Letter of transmittal. (91) $2,000
— 20 Sept 1861. 2 pp, 4to. To Major Gen. John C. Fremont. Reporting about matters pertaining to his command. (90) $4,000
— 21 Dec 1861. (90) $1,000
— 31 Dec 1861. 2 pp, 4to. To P[eter] Casey. Relating his wife's worries

AMERICAN BOOK PRICES CURRENT

about their son's stay in Kentucky & requesting that he be sent home. Repaired. (89) $3,000
— 22 Sept 1862. 2 pp, 4to. To Major Gen. W. S. Rosecrans. Suggesting that the army move towards Tupelo & that Confederate ships on the Yazoo be destroyed. (91) $7,000
— 21 Dec 1862. 2 pp, 4to. To Brig. Gen. Charles S. Hamilton. Giving orders for troops to move to Corinth. Rosenbloom collection. (88) $4,750
— 3 June 1863. 2 pp, 4to. To Admiral D. D. Porter. Asking him to transport troops up the Yazoo [during the siege of Vicksburg]. (91) $12,000
— 19 May 1864. 3 pp, 4to. To his wife Julia Dent Grant. Expressing confidence that he will defeat Lee's Army of Northern Virginia. (89) $14,000
— 22 Aug 1864. 1 p, 8vo. To Major Gen. Butler. Discussing troop movements. Repaired. With a photograph. (89) $2,600
— 14 Sept 1864. 1 p, 4to. To Major Gen. [George G.] Meade. Requesting information about Gen. Warren's reconnaissance. With engraved port. (90) $3,800
— 23 Sept [18]64. 1 p, 8vo. To E. B. Washburn. Assuring him that a dispatch has been sent to Gen. Halleck regarding a leave. (91) $1,700
— 12 Dec 1864. 1 p, size not stated. To Major Gen. Ord. Requesting him to telegraph news about Sherman. (89) $2,600
— 6 Apr 1865. 2 pp, 4to. To Col. T. S. Bowers. Reporting recent Confederate losses in the vicinity of Jetersville. Framed with engraved port. Sang collection. (90) $50,000
— 7 May 1865. 1 p, 8vo. To Sec of War Stanton. Recommending the sale of army horses. Endorsed by Stanton. Framed. (90) $4,000
— 13 Apr 1866. Byer collection. (90) $950
— 30 Mar 1868. (88) £250
— 23 May 1868. Byer collection. (90) $500
— 14 Aug 1868. 4 pp, 8vo. To his father Jesse R. Grant. Discussing Judge Levitt's letter. Sgd Ulysses. (90) $2,800
— 15 Jan 1870. 2 pp, 8vo. To his father.

Acknowledging his request for the appointment of Mr. Hay as postmaster. (89) £1,050
— 31 May 1873. 2 pp, 8vo. To his sister Mary Cramer. About their father's failing health & other family news. (90) $1,600
— 12 July 1873. (91) $750
— 11 Sept [18]77. (89) $500
— 26 May 1880. Pratt collection. (89) $500
— 19 Sept 1880. Pratt collection. (89) $900
— 6 Sept 1881. 2 pp, folio. To Mrs. George McClellan. Regretting he will not be able to attend a wedding. (90) $2,000
— 9 June 1882. (89) £700
— 28 Nov 1883. (89) $800
— 3 July 1884. (90) $1,000
— 9 Aug 1884. 2 pp, 8vo. To Robert Underwood Johnson. Concerning articles on the Civil War for the Century Magazine. Endorsed in anr hand. Sang collection. (91) $6,500

Ls, 22 Jan 1876. (88) £340
— 12 Dec 1883. (91) $450

ANs, 22 Oct 1861. 1 p, 4to. To Capt. Walker. Instructing him to convoy a steamer. Alexander collection. (90) $1,400
— [n.d.]. (88) $400

Ns, 1864. (91) $750

ADs, 7 Feb 1885. 2 pp, 8vo. Agreement to pay Adam Badeau $10,000 for assistance in preparing his Memoirs. Including ADs by Badeau, 2 Mar 1885; receipt for $250. Fold splits. Barrett collection. (89) $3,250

Collection of Ds & photograph, 17 Sept 1851 & [n.d.]. (91) $700
— Collection of Ds & photograph, 22 Feb 1871 & [n.d.]. (89) $750

Ds, 30 Sept 1862. (89) $900
— 4 Oct 1867. (89) $800
— 26 Mar 1869. (90) $280
— 5 Apr 1869. (91) $500
— 2 Mar 1870. (90) $450
— 21 Mar 1870. (88) $280
— 21 Mar 1870. (88) $230
— 3 May 1870. (89) $330
— 7 June 1870. (88) $350
— 7 Oct 1870. (91) $600
— 28 Oct 1870. (91) $800
— 13 Jan 1871. (89) $375
— 25 Jan 1871. (90) $380
— 20 Dec 1871. (91) $950
— 15 Jan 1873. (91) $500
— 7 Mar 1873. (88) $220
— 8 Aug 1873. (91) $500
— 30 Sept 1873. (91) $600
— 15 Oct 1873. (91) $450
— 3 Jan 1874. (88) $120
— 12 Feb 1874. (91) $600
— 19 June 1874. (89) $325
— 10 Aug 1874. 1 p, folio. Ship's paper for the barque Perry going on a whaling voyage. (91) $1,100
— 21 Aug 1874. (89) $320
— 7 Jan 1875. (89) $450
— 13 Jan 1875. (88) $300
— 11 Feb 1875. 1 p, folio. Appointment of William H. Clapp as Captain in the Infantry. Framed. (90) $1,400
— 12 Feb 1875. (91) $900
— 11 Aug 1875. (91) $425
— 16 Dec 1875. (88) $225
— 19 Jan 1876. (89) £500
— 7 Feb 1876. (89) $650
— 1 June 1876. (89) $475
— 27 June 1876. (90) DM420
— June 1876. (88) $450
— [n.d.]. 1 p, folio. Ship's passport; unaccomplished. (91) $3,200

Autograph endorsement, 30 Dec 1864. 12 lines, sgd, at foot of last page of a letter from Col. George H. Sharpe to Col. Theodore Bowers, 29 Dec 1864, suggesting a raid on Fredericksburg; agreeing with Sharpe. (89) $1,900
— Anr, sgd, 8 lines on integral leaf of ALs by Gen. (88) $375

Autograph telegram, 19 May 1863. 1 p, 4to. To [Maj. Gen. James B. McPherson]. Draft, informing him about preparations at Vicksburg. In pencil. Mtd with a signature, 22 Apr 1882. Whiton collection. (88) $1,200
— Anr, sgd, 3 Feb 1865. 2 pp, 4to. To Sec of War Stanton. Draft, suggesting changes of command in Tennessee & the Gulf Department. McVitty collection. (90) $7,500
— Anr, sgd, 28 Feb 1865. 1 p, 120mm by 196mm. To Sec of War Edwin M. Stanton. Regretting that "Lt. Foot was

GRANT

delivered to Rebel Authorities before the receipt of your dispatch". Christensen collection. (90) $2,000
— Anr, sgd, 14 Mar 1865. 1 p, 4to. To Major Gen. Henry Wagner Halleck. Giving instructions to order Gen. Benham to replace Gen. Kelley. (90) $2,000
— Anr, 24 Mar 1865. 2 pp, 4to. To Maj. Gen. Henry W. Halleck. Reply to false alarm about Lee's retreating south. (91) $4,750
— Anr, 14 June 1869. (91) $450
Cut signature, [before 31 July 1854]. (89) $240
— Anr, with closing, 13 June 1867. (91) $450
— Anr, 10 Aug 1882. (90) $250
— Anr, [n.d.]. (91) $300
Lithographed port, sgd, [n.d.]. 15 by 12 inches. By E. Bierstadt. (90) $3,000
Photograph, sgd, 5 Feb 1865. (90) $900
Photograph, sgd & inscr, [n.d.]. (88) $400
Photograph, [c.early 1870s]. Byer collection. (90) $150
— Anr, [n.d.]. (90) $400
Signature, [Apr 1875]. (90) $220
— Anr, 8 Dec 1876. (89) $425
— Anr, 27 Apr 1882. (90) $220
— Anr, 27 Apr [n.y.]. (91) $280
— Anr, [n.d.]. (91) $275
— Anr, [n.d.]. (91) $225
— Anr, [n.d.]. (91) $325
— Anr, [n.d.]. (90) $250
— CORWIN, THOMAS. - ALs, 16 Feb 1852. 1 p, 4to. To O. S. Seymour. As Sec of the Treasury, regarding a claim of Lieut. Grant. (88) $60
— GRANT, JESSE R. & HANNAH GRANT. - Ls, 5 Apr 1873. 1 p, 8vo. Recipient & contents not stated. Mtd with related material. (89) $75
— LAGOW, CLARK B. - ALs, 19 Sept [1862], 1 p, 8vo. To an unnamed general. Message sent by order of Maj. Gen. Grant regarding a dispatch from Rosecrans. (88) $60

Grant, Ulysses S., 1822-85 —& Others
— COURTNEY, EMMA. - Orig drawings (c.50), in def 8vo sketchbook kept on an excursion with the Grants & their party to Mexico, Feb & Mar 1880. Including portraits, sgd by Grant, Mrs.

AMERICAN BOOK PRICES CURRENT

Grant, Philip H. Sheridan, & others. (90) $2,000

Grapewin, Charley, 1869-1956
Photograph, sgd & inscr, [n.d.]. (91) $140

Grass, Guenter
Autograph Ms, notes about Heinrich Schuetz, for his novel Das Treffen in Telgte. (89) DM440
— Autograph Ms, sketches for his novel Das Treffen in Telgte. (91) DM650
— Autograph Ms, sketches for his play Die Plebejer proben den Aufstand, Act 1; [c.1965]. (90) DM420
Typescript, part of Ms (p 75) of his Das Treffen in Telgte. (90) DM460
— Typescript, part of Ms (p 92) of his Das Treffen in Telgte. (88) DM420

Grasse, Francois Joseph Paul, Comte de, 1722-88
ALs, 14 Mar 1781. 1 p, 4to. To the Comte de Langeron. Expressing his distress at the harsh treatment meted out to new naval recruits. (91) $1,300
Ls, 15 Aug 1783. (91) $900

Gratianus, the Canonist, d.c.1150
Ms, Decretum, glossed. [Paris, c.1290-95]. 2 conjoint leaves only, vellum, 470mm by 289mm. Written in double column, with gloss in a smaller hand. With 70 small initials in blue with red penwork, & miniature within a border of blue with white tracery & burnished gold above illuminated 3-line initial with branching ivyleaf border, attributable to Master Honore or his workshop. Korner collection. (90) £48,000

Gratz, Rebecca, 1781-1869
ALs, 26 July 1804. 5 pp, 4to. Recipient unnamed. Describing a trip to Coney Island & life in NY. (91) $2,200
— [n.d.]. (91) $850

Graun, Karl Heinrich, 1704-59
Ms, Cantata, Der Tod Jesu, full score; [2d half of 18th cent]. 135 pp, folio, in contemp half lea. In a scribal hand. Including ptd text, 16 pp, 8vo. (90) DM1,600

Graves, Alfred Perceval, 1846-1931
Collection of 3 A Ls s & autograph Ms, 11 Nov 1907 to 10 Jan 1908 & [n.d.]. (90) £110

Graves, Robert
[A collection of working papers for his book The Nazarene Gospel Restored, 1952 & 1953, c.430 pp, mostly folio, comprising autograph & typescript material, sold at S on 14 Dec 1989, lot 128, for £9,000 to Rota.]

Autograph Ms, 6 poems for Goliath and David, [1916]. 8 pp, folio. Some autograph revisions; some corrections in Siegfried Sassoon's hand. (91) £4,800

— Autograph Ms, poem, Limbo, [1916]. 1 p, 4to. 14 lines, differing from ptd version. (91) £1,100

— Autograph Ms, poem, The Corner Knot, [before 1926]. (91) £600

— Autograph Ms, radio program, Talk on Books, [1 Sept 1925]. 8 pp, folio. Including account of Lawrence of Arabia. (91) £1,900

Typescript carbon copy, novel, The Isles of Unwisdom, [1948]. 424 pp, size not stated. Including autograph revisions & notes in 2 other hands. With related material. (90) £7,000

ALs, 9 Aug 1916. 1 p, 8vo. To [Siegfried] Sassoon. About reports of his death; in verse, 31 lines. (91) £3,200

— 18 Aug 1916. 6 pp, 8vo. To Siegfried Sassoon. Sending some poems, discussing a joint project, etc. With related material. (91) £2,800

— [n.d.]. (89) £100

Corrected proof, Sergeant Lamb of the Ninth. 1940. Leaf count not given. With several corrections in red ink on nearly every page in Graves' hand. In wraps. Inscr to Ethel Hirdman. (91) £2,200

Proof copy, Goliath and David, [1917]. Length not stated; stitched. Corrections in the hand of Siegfried Sassoon. (91) £4,500

— Anr, Treasure Box, [1919]. Length not stated, 4to; stitched. With autograph corrections. (91) £1,600
See also: Lawrence, Thomas Edward

Gray, Norah Nielson
Original drawing, 3 girls on a hillside, to illus William Wordsworth's Recollections of Childhood, 1913. In watercolor; sgd. 350mm by 235mm, excluding margins. Archives of J. M. Dent & Son. (88) £1,400

Gray, Thomas, 1716-71
Autograph Ms, Habitations of our Kings, [n.d.]. (89) £500

ALs, 25 Aug 1757. 2 pp, 4to. To Richard Hurd. Commenting about the reception of his Pindaric Ode. (89) £2,800

Grayson, John B.
ALs, 28 Mar 1834. Alexander collection. (90) $160

Great Western Railway Temperance Union
Ms, testimonial to Viscount Cobham on his appointment as Railway Commissioner, Aug 1891. (88) £110

Greece
[A large & important archive of letters, documents, drafts, notes, memoranda, pamphlets, etc., comprising the political papers of Pericles Argyropoulos & Konstantin Schinas, c.500 items, c.1820 to 1865, documenting events in the 1st period of the newly-formed Greek state, sold at C on 6 Dec 1989, lot 286, for £16,000 to the Greek Embassy.]

— ATHENS. - Ms, Relation de la campagne de 1687. 15 leaves, small folio. Phillipps Ms 7338. Blackmer collection. (90) £1,500

Greek Manuscripts
[A collection of 8 Mss, c.18th & 19th cent, various sizes, including Thomas Gaisford's autograph copy of the 1526 Ed of Hephaestion from the Phillipps collection & religious works, sold at S on 21 Sept, lot 178, for £2,400 to Martinos.]

Ms, Catena Commentary on the Song of Songs by Theodoret of Cyrrhus, Gregory of Nyssa, Nilus the Ascetic, Maximus Confessor & Michael Psallus. [Eastern Mediterranean, 16th cent]. 158 leaves (2 blanks) & 2 flyleaves, 295mm by 205mm. Contemp Austrian red mor gilt bdg with the

GREEK MANUSCRIPTS

arms of Ferdinand Hoffmann von Gruenbuehel und Stechau, dated 1588. In dark brown ink in a regular professional Greek minuscule. (88) £3,500
— Ms, Gospel of St. John. [Egypt?, c.5th cent]. Single leaf, vellum, 67mm by 67mm. St. John 17: 1 - 4, in brown ink in a Greek uncial hand without word division. (91) £24,000
— Ms, hymns for major festivals, [Northern Greece, c.1800]. (89) £190
— Ms, Liturgy of St. (91) £800
— Ms, Menologion, for September. [Constantinople?, 11th cent]. 266 leaves, vellum, 320mm by 240mm. Modern blindstamped calf over wooden bds. In brown ink in a regular Greek Perlschrift; incipits in Alexandrian uncials in burnished gold. With 26 large illuminated headpieces mostly above elaborate gold initials. (89) £24,000
— Ms, Pseudo-Maximus, Loci Communes, florilegium of classical, biblical & patristic texts, [Eastern Mediterranean, late 11th cent]. 173 leaves, vellum, 223mm by 172mm. Def late medieval Greek blindstamped lea over wooden bds. In dark brown ink in a regular Greek minuscule. With illuminated headpiece & initials throughout in red. (89) £16,000
— Ms, Tetraevangelion [Four Gospels], [1271]. 165 leaves, vellum, 215mm by 150mm. 17th-cent sheep over wooden bds. In brown ink in a Greek minuscule by Georgios Kampnos. With chapter headings & marginal annotations in red & 4 simple headpieces in colors. 15 17th-cent paper leaves inserted at front. Doheny collection. (88) £13,000
See also: Gospel Manuscripts
See also: Lectionary

Greeley, Horace, 1811-72
Series of 5 A Ls s, 1842 to 1857. (91) $275
ALs, 26 Nov 1846. Doheny collection. (89) $800
— 27 Nov 1863. Christensen collection. (90) $150
— 14 Jan 1867. (89) $130
Photograph, sgd, [n.d.]. (90) $130

AMERICAN BOOK PRICES CURRENT

Green, Herbert
Original drawings, (6), to illus Roland Horne's The Lion of de Montfort, 1909. Archives of J. M. Dent & Son. (88) £300

Green, Julien
A Ls s (2), 27 Mar & 13 Apr 1939. (90) DM450

Green, Thomas J.
ALs, 13 Sept 1836. (91) $650

Green, William Pringle, 1785-1846
Ms, treatise describing experiments with lightning conductors, [c.1835]. (91) £600

Greenaway, Kate, 1846-1901
Autograph Ms, "Book No 2", 120 poems on various topics, supposedly by Greenaway herself; [n.d.]. 236 leaves, in 4to notebook. With related material. (90) £1,500
Autograph sketchbooks, (2), pencil sketches; mostly figure, costume or anatomical studies from life, [c.1890]. 127 & 140 pp, 127mm by 77mm & 128mm by 76mm. 1 stitched, 1 in blue mor bdg. (90) £3,200
Original drawings, (20), figure studies & decorative designs in pencil, including sketch of tp of Language of Flowers, [1884]. Various sizes, matted on 16 cards. In cloth folding box. Doheny collection. (89) $7,000
— Original drawings, (3), watercolors to illus Under the Window, [1878], & her Almanack for 1894. 3 pp, various sizes, in 2 frames. Doheny collection. (89) $2,400
— Original drawings, (48), in pen-&-ink & brushwork, mostly to illus her Birthday Book for Children, [1880]. Various sizes; framed. With a copy of the book, 1st Ed. Doheny collection. (89) $14,000
Original drawing, Old England's Annual Christmas 1896, in watercolor & gouache, 314mm by 219mm, on board. Design for a periodical cover, sgd K.G. Doheny collection. (89) $1,800
— Original drawing, to illus Robert Browning's The Pied Piper of Hamelin, [n.d.]. 191mm by 167mm. In ink & watercolor, initialled. Framed. (89)

£7,200
A Ls s (2), [25 Dec] 1895 & [24 Dec n.y.]. Doheny collection. (89) $480

ALs, 2 Sept 1895. 4 pp, 8vo. To Lady Tennyson. Thanking for her hospitality & sending gifts for her children. Byer collection. (90) $1,100

Greene, Graham, 1904-91

Autograph Ms, opening of an untitled story, [n.d.]. (91) £950

Typescript (duplicated), The Third Man, 2 June 1948. 126 pp, 4to. Early draft, including variants of the film & the pbd work. (91) £1,100

Collection of 5 A Ls s & Ls s, 1956 to 1969. 5 pp, 4to & 8vo. To Leonard Russell. About various articles, Nabokov's Lolita, & other matters. (90) £1,800

ALs, 4 July [n.y.]. (89) DM520

Document, [16 Mar 1984 & before]. (88) $800

— BOXER, MARC. - 2 orig drawings, pen-&-ink caricatures of Greene, sgd Marc, [n.d.], 13.75 by 10 inches, used to illus an interview in the New Yorker. (88) £400

Greene, Nathanael, 1742-86

ALs, 25 Oct 1783. 3 pp, folio. To William Ellery, Jr. Expressing reservations about a nomination as a commissioner to treat with the Indians. (90) $2,500

— 1 June 1785. (89) $500

— 1 June 1785. 2 pp, size not stated. To Lafayette. Letter of introduction for John McQueen. (91) $1,300

Ls, [10 Mar 1782]. 4 pp, folio. To Col. William Davies. Draft, stressing the necessity of continuing to support the war effort. (90) $2,750

Greenstreet, Sydney, 1879-1954

Photograph, sgd & inscr, [n.d.]. (90) $220

Gregorovius, Ferdinand, 1821-91

ALs, 4 Jan 1881. (89) DM280

Gregory, Augusta, Lady, 1852-1932. See: Gregory, Lady Isabella Augusta

Gregory I, Saint, Pope, 540-604

Ms, Cura Pastoralis, & Dialogorum Libri IV; with Adalerus, Liber de Studio Virtutum. [England, mid-13th cent]. 99 leaves (2 blank), vellum, 230mm by 158mm. Def old orange-red velvet over pastebds. In a small English gothic bookhand by several scribes. With decorated initials throughout & 2 late medieval drawings. (90) £4,500

— **Ms,** Homiliae super Evangeliis. [Germany, 3d quarter of 12th cent] 126 leaves, vellum, 322mm by 193mm, in 19th-cent half russia gilt. Written in black ink by 2 scribes in a fine late Romanesque German bookhand. With 22 Romanesque drawings in margins illustrating the text, including several highly finished & 1 colored in red & brown wash; also 1 later medieval drawing. (91) £60,000

— **Ms,** Homiliae XL in Evangelia, with Peter of Blois, Remediarum Conversorum, & Bernard of Clairvaux, De exhortationes & Cantica Canticorum. [Northern England, mid-13th cent]. 208 leaves, vellum, 300mm by 207mm, in old reversed calf over wooden bds, rebacked. In black ink in a small gothic rotunda. With 3 large illuminated & 19 historiated initials. Some leaves dampstained. (88) £42,000

— **Ms,** Moralia, in French. [Chimay, near Tournay, Feb 1388]. 184 leaves, vellum, 181mm by 125mm. Early 19th-cent French blue calf gilt. In brown ink in a secretary-influenced gothic bookhand. Large initials in red. Containing only the prologue & the 5 books comprising the 1st part. Doheny collection. (88) £4,000

— **Ms,** Moralia. [Merseburg?, 2d half of 10th cent]. 259 leaves, vellum, 345mm by 255mm. Modern dark brown mor in mor-backed case. In brown ink in Caroline minuscule script by 3 scribes. Initials in red. With prayer, Karoli Regis, & 2 further texts added on 1st 2 leaves in 13th or 14th cent hands. Some leaves missing; some repairs. Including earlier bdg preserved separately. Doheny collection. (88) £65,000

GREGORY

Gregory, Lady Isabella Augusta, 1852-1932
[Typescripts of 2 plays, Twenty Five, & Spreading the News, [1904-05], 39 pp, folio & 4to, with related material, sold at S on 20 July 1989, lot 184, for £1,600 to Rota.]

Gregory IX, Pope, d.1241
Ms, Decretals. [Northern France or Flanders, c.1450]. 69 leaves (many missing), vellum, 310mm by 230mm, in old vellum over pastebds. In a small regular lettre batarde. With small illuminated initials throughout & 3 larger illuminated initials. (90) £3,700

Gregory IX, Pope, d.1241
Ms, Decretales. [France?, c.1250]. 242 leaves, vellum, 179mm by 123mm. Modern dark brown mor bdg. In a small gothic hand, with marginal glosses in several hands. Rua collection. (91) $9,500
— Ms, Decretals, with the Gloss of Barnardo Bottoni. [Bologna, c.1330-40]. 291 pp, vellum, 425mm by 254mm. Very def medieval bdg of wooden bds. With 94 historiated initials & 5 large miniatures. (91) £9,000

Gregory X, Pope, 1210-76
Document, [9 June] 1274. 1 p, vellum, 18.5cm by 30cm. Bull confirming the privileges previously granted to the Abbey of St. Bertin at Saint-Omer. (89) DM11,000

Gregory XIII, Pope, 1502-85
Document, 16 Apr 1575. (91) $500

Gregory XVI, Pope, 1765-1846
Document, 7 Apr 1832. (89) DM250
Autograph endorsement, sgd, 20 Sept 1839. (89) $300

Greiffenhagen, Maurice, 1862-1931
Original drawings, (3); watercolor & gouache paintings; 2 possibly to illus W. (90) £400
— Original drawings, (4), to illus Egyptian Myth and Legend, [n.d.]. (89) £480

Greig, H. S.
Original drawings, (33), to illus novels of the Bronte sisters, 1893, & Madame de Stael's Corinne, 1895. Archives of J. M. Dent & Son. (88) £450

Grenada
[Lataste Estates. - A collection of documents, deeds of sale, letters, lists of slaves, accounts, etc., 18th to 19th cent, more than 100 items, in English & French, sold at S on 22 July 1988, lot 472, for £300 to Appelbaum.]
— MONTROSE ESTATE. - Ms, accounts prepared for Gen. David Graeme of Braco Castle, Perthshire, 1784 to 1796. 5 gatherings, folio. With related material. (90) £380

Grenfell, John Pascoe, 1800-69
[A large collection of his papers relating to Brazil, c.1839 to 1878, including 6 letterbooks of official & ministerial correspondence, sold at S on 22 July 1988, lot 376, for £1,200 to de Lago.]

Gretchaninoff, Alexandre, 1864-1956
Autograph music, song, Chto v' imyeni tyebe moyem, to a text by Pushkin; [c.1926]. (90) £550
ALs, 6 Nov 1934. (89) DM260
— 23 May 1942. (90) DM240
AL, [20 Oct 1910]. (88) DM850
Photograph, sgd & inscr, 15 Dec 1926. (88) DM280

Gretry, Andre Ernest Modeste, 1741-1813
ALs, [1792]. (91) DM850
— [3 July 1805]. (88) DM480
— 27 June 1810. (90) DM550

Greville, Sir Fulke, 1st Baron Brooke, 1554-1628
Ds, Feb 1618. (89) £100

Grey, Zane, 1875-1939
Autograph Ms, draft of article on his "first idea for a historical novel on the tragedy of the buffalo"; [n.d.]. (90) $750
— Autograph Ms, notebook recording visit to Flagstaff, Navajo vocabulary, etc., Apr & May 1908. (88) $950
Typescript, article, Sunfish, for an unidentified periodical, sgd; [n.d.]. Martin collection. (90) $1,000

— Typescript, Wolves of the Sea. (91) $550
ALs, 11 May 1917. Byer collection. (90) $375
— 19 Apr [n.y.]. (88) $275
Ds, [1932]. (88) $180

Grieg, Edvard, 1843-1907
Autograph Ms, recommendation for a "Pianino aus der Fabrik der Herrn Gebrueder Trau", sgd; 13 Dec 1883. (90) DM680
Autograph music, song, Blabaret, to a text by D. Gronwold, for voice & piano; sgd & dated 23 Aug [18]96. 23 bars. (89) $3,800
Collection of 2 A Ls s & autograph postcard, sgd, 26 Dec 1896 to 30 Oct 1900. (90) £750
ALs, 6 Oct 1882. (91) £740
— 1 Aug 1891. (90) DM800
— 20 Apr 1897. (88) DM740
— 5 Dec 1900. (91) £750
— 20 Aug 1901. (91) DM750
— 29 Apr [19]03. (90) £550
Autograph postcard, sgd, 17 Mar 1892. (91) DM660
— 3 June 1895. (91) DM370
— 12 Dec 1897. (90) DM600
— 27 Aug 1903. (89) DM750
ANs, 15 May 1875. (91) DM440
Autograph quotation, 4 bars from the Berceuse for piano, sgd, inscr & dated 28 Aug 1886. 1 p, 8vo. (89) $1,500
— Anr, 1st 2 bars of the piano piece Der var engang, from Lyrische Stuecke, Op. (88) £650
Photograph, sgd, [n.d.]. (90) £900
Photograph, sgd & inscr, [c.1890]; c.16cm by 11cm. (88) £480
— Anr, 28 Jan 1897. 167mm by 108mm. Inscr to Jenny Gertrud Schmidt, with musical quotation of 4 bars from Solveig's song from Peer Gynt. (91) DM4,000

Grieshaber, Helmut Andreas Paul ("HAP"), 1909-81
Series of 5 A Ls s, 9 Feb to 27 Sept 1967. (89) DM850
ALs, 1 Jan 1946. (88) DM800
Ls, 28 Aug 1951. (90) DM240
Series of 9 A Ns s, 1959 to 1967. 9 pp, various sizes. Recipients unnamed.

About a variety of subjects. 8 on woodcuts, 1 on the cover of a notebook. (88) DM2,100

Griffin, Cyrus, 1748-1810
Ds, 15 Sept 1774. (91) $350

Griffith, David Wark, 1875-1948
Ds, 8 Nov 1944. (90) $260
Signature, in booklet entitled "Souvenir Book D. (89) $110
See also: Fairbanks, Douglas & Griffith

Griggs, David, d.1989
Photograph, sgd & inscr, [n.d.]. (91) $80
Signature, on cover for 1st shuttle flight with Downey spaceship Columbia, [4 Dec 1981]. (90) $65

Grijalba, Juan de, 1480?-1527. See: Diaz, Juan

Grillparzer, Franz, 1791-1872
Autograph Ms, poem, Stabat Mater, beginning "Nun wohl, es ward euch dargebracht", [1842]. 3 pp, folio. 63 lines, sgd. (90) £1,400
ALs, 16 Feb 1866. 1 p, folio. To the tax office. Declaring his income for 1865. Repaired. (89) DM1,400
— 8 Feb 1870. 1 p, folio. To the tax office. Declaring his income for 1869. Endorsed. (90) DM1,500
ANs, [11 July 1863]. (88) DM650

Grimaldi, Joseph, 1779-1837
Autograph Ms, poem about musical instruments, music & money, sgd & dedicated to Tom Ellar; 20 Apr 1835. (90) $200

Grimm, Friedrich Melchior von, 1723-1807
ALs, 27 Apr 1782. (90) DM720

Grimm, Hans, 1875-1959
Collection of 13 Ls s & 3 postcards, sgd, 1946 to 1954. (88) DM480

Grimm, Hermann, 1828-1901
Series of 4 A Ls s, 7 to 20 Sept [1848]. 7 pp, 8vo. To his father Wilhelm Grimm. Commenting on the revolution in Berlin. (91) DM3,400
ALs, 1 Dec 1874. (88) DM380

Grimm, Jacob, 1785-1863

Collection of 2 A Ls s & AL, 2 Mar 1826 to 30 June 1836. 6 pp, 4to. To Friedrich Diez. Interesting letters about his own & recipient's research. AL def. (90) DM14,000

A Ls s (2), 6 Mar 1815 & 2 Apr 1845. (90) £750

ALs, [c.1809]. 2 pp, 4to. To a governmental official at Kassel. Concerning a demand to return books to the library. (91) DM1,900

— 7 Dec 1815. 1 p, 4to. To Dr. Thomas. Sending best wishes for his wife's recovery, & mentioning his itinerary & friends. (89) DM3,400

— 7 Dec 1832. (89) £750

— 7 Dec 1832. 2 pp, 4to. To the bookseller Reimer. Discussing the publication of Reinecke Fuchs. (90) DM5,000

— 31 Mar 1839. 1 p, 4to. Recipient unnamed. Declining to write a popular book about German mythology. (88) DM2,200

— 1 Aug 1843. 1 p, 8vo. To Heinrich Asmus. Commissioning a drawing for a book cover. (89) DM1,300

— 12 Feb 1859. 3 pp, 8vo. To August Raszmann. Responding to a rumor that a Ms of the Hildebrandslied has been found. Doheny collection. (89) $4,800

— 2 Feb 1861. (90) DM850

ANs, [after 1840]. (89) DM550

— 17 Aug 1857. (89) DM600

Grimm, Ludwig Emil, 1790-1863

Autograph Ms, interpretation of his drawing Der Sieg ueber den Tod, 12 July 1847. (90) DM480

Grimm, Wilhelm, 1786-1859

Collection of ALs & Ls, 15 Mar 1842 & 15 Jan 1843. 2 pp, 8vo. To Peter von Cornelius. Informing him that his brother's painting is being exhibited, & inquiring about an invitation originally declined. (90) DM1,400

ALs, 16 Mar 1825. 3 pp, 4to. To Professor Busching. Discussing runes & their significance. (89) £1,700

— 18 Mar 1836. 2 pp, 4to. To Albert Schulz. Commenting about his trans of Parzival. (88) DM2,600

— 12 Dec 1850. (91) DM480

— 4 Oct 1854. (90) DM650

ANs, 6 Mar 1851; c.65mm by 125mm. (89) DM550

Grimmelshausen, Hans Jakob Christoph von, c.1621-76

ADs, [1655]. 1 p, c.21cm by 6.5cm; cut from larger leaf. Statement of dues & receipt. (90) DM11,000

Gris, Juan, Pseud. of Jose Gonzales, 1887-1927

ALs, 15 Mar 1917. (88) DM750

— [n.d.]. Ammann collection. (90) DM950

Grock, Pseud. of Adrian Wettach, 1880-1959

Self-caricature, 16 Dec 1931. (89) DM400

Gropius, Walter, 1883-1969

ALs, [n.d.]. (90) DM320

— [n.d.]. (89) DM200

Ls, 26 Feb 1938. Byer collection. (90) $850

— 2 May 1938. (88) DM500

— 10 Nov 1960. (90) DM250

Gropius, Walter, 1883-1969 —& Others

[Schrammen, Eberhard. - A collection of 7 Ls & postcards addressed to him, 1926 to 1947, by Gropius, Oskar Schlemmer, Gerhard Marcks, & others, with related material, sold at S on 5 May 1988, lot 202, for £420 to Sotheran.]

Gross, Anthony

Original drawings, artwork for d/j of William Golding's Lord of the Flies, [1954]. (91) £900

Grossmann, Rudolf, 1882-1941

Autograph postcard, sgd, 14 Sept 1921. (88) DM750

Grosz, George, 1893-1959

[A collection of 8 Christmas cards designed by Grosz, 1930s, 1 sgd by him, 3 sgd (& inscr) in anr hand [his wife's?], with autograph envelope to Herrmann Vollmer & AN, 1941, sold at sg on 22 Oct, lot 120, for $100.]

Collection of 3 A Ls s & Ds, 29 July 1918 to 25 Feb 1920 & [n.d.]. (90) DM950

— Collection of 2 A Ls s, 6 autograph postcards, sgd, & autograph Ms, 13 Jan 1922 to [c.1948]. 9 pp, 4to & 8vo. To Mark Neven DuMont. Chatty notes, mostly concerning tobacco. Humorous poem. 3 cards with sketches (2 self portraits). With related material. (88) DM2,700

— Collection of 3 A Ls s & 2 Ls s, 29 Jan 1940 to 16 Jan 1950 & [n.d.]. 8 pp, folio & 4to. To Arthur Kaufmann. Reflecting on his life & art. (90) DM1,100

ALs, 31 Aug 1937. (89) DM200

— 27 Sept 1958. (88) DM300

Grosz, Karl
[A collection of letters addressed to him by fellow-practitioners, c.70 items, 1906 to 1939, mostly about medical & psychiatrical matters, sold at S on 5 May 1988, lot 285, for £1,500 to Maliye.]

Grotefend, Georg Friedrich, 1775-1853
ALs, 4 Jan 1850. 3 pp, folio. To an unnamed colleague. About deciphering cuneiform characters; with numerous examples in text. (91) DM4,000

Groth, Klaus, 1819-99
Autograph Ms, poem, Wenn die Lerche zieht, 19 July 1889. (91) DM900

Autograph transcript, poem, beginning "Ik gung int Holt in Duestern", sgd & dated 21 Nov 1866. (89) DM490

— Autograph transcript, poem, beginning "Mit de Bukunst fung de Welt mit an", 1873. (89) DM600

— Autograph transcript, poem, De Lurk treckt; [n.d.]. (90) DM550

— Autograph transcript, quatrain, beginning "Dat's swar to loeben un to lehrn"; sgd & dated 22 Jan 1894. (90) DM440

Series of 3 A Ls s, 5 Feb 1886 to 19 Mar 1895. 7 pp, 8vo. To [Albert & Margarethe Ladenburg]. About a private concert & personal news. (88) DM1,200

Gruelle, John Barton, 1880-1938
Original drawings, (15), preliminary watercolors & pencil drawings for a paper doll version of Mother Goose called The Scissors Mother Goose. Unpbd. Folio size, mtd. (90) $3,250

Grumbach, Conrad von. See: Julius Echter von Mespelbrunn & Grumbach

Grumbkow, Friedrich Wilhelm von, 1678-1739
ALs, 23 July [1733]. Schroeder collection. (89) DM360

Ls s (2), 30 May [1729] & 12 Feb 1734. (90) DM650

Ls, 20 Jan 1731. (91) DM360

Gruner, Justus von, 1777-1820
ALs, 20 Aug 1812. (90) DM340

Ls, 14 Sept 1815. (89) DM460

Grynaeus, Simon, 1493-1541
ALs, [n.d.]. Kuenzel collection. (89) DM1,000

Guarini, Giovanni Battista, 1538-1612
ALs, 29 Feb 1612. 1 p, folio. To Ludovico Ariosto. Discussing an epitaph for recipient's ancestor, the poet Ariosto. (90) DM2,600

Guericke, Otto von, 1602-86
ALs, 22 Feb 1646. 1 p, folio. To the magistracy at Magdeburg. Informing them about the itinerary of a messenger. (90) DM12,000

Guernsey
Series of Ds s, 9 documents, 3 Feb 1377 to 21 Mar 1512. (91) £1,000

Guerrieri, Gerardo, 1920-86
[A collection of c.25 letters addressed to him by Arthur Miller (5), Lucchino Visconti (3), Italo Calvino (6), Franco Zeffirelli & others, c.1959 to 1982, with related material, sold at S on 15 Dec, lot 182, for £500.]

Guetersloh, Albert Paris, Pseud. of Albert Konrad Kiehtreiber, 1887-1973
Collection of ALs & Ls, 2 July 1954 & [n.d.]. (91) DM500

Guichard, Karl Gottlieb, 1724-75
ALs, 22 Oct 1769. (88) DM550

Guillaume de Deguilleville, fl.1330
Ms, Le Pelerinage de la Vie Humaine, in the French prose trans of Jean Gallopes for Jeanne de Laval. [Anjou, c.1470-80]. 148 leaves (3 blank, 2

lacking), vellum, 290mm by 200mm, in late 18th-cent French mottled calf gilt. In a lettre batarde. With 3-line illuminated initials throughout, full-length border, 76 miniatures & achievement of arms. Written for Charlotte of Savoy, Queen of France. Phillipps Ms.228. (91) £22,000

Guillaumin, Armand, 1841-1927
ALs, 9 Sept 1906. (90) DM1,000

Guillotin, Joseph Ignace, 1738-1814
Ds, 9 June 1779. 1 p, 4to. Admission of Jean Paul Etienne Malgontier to the freemasons' lodge Le Grand Orient de France, sgd as president of the Chambre des Provinces. With decorative engraved borders. (89) DM2,200

Guiteau, Charles, c.1840-82. See: Garfield, James A.

Guitry, Sacha, 1885-1957
Autograph Ms, autobiographical reminiscences, "Si j'ai bonne memoire", abbreviated version; sgd & dated 12 Aug 1952. (90) £900

Guizot, Francois Pierre Guillaume, 1787-1874
Collection of 5 A Ls s & 2 Ls s, 12 June 1833 to 21 Mar 1853. (88) DM250

Gulbransson, Olaf, 1873-1958
Series of 25 A Ls s, 21 Oct 1924 to Sept 1935 & [n.d.]. 34 pp, mostly 4to. To Alexander Amersdorffer. Thanking for help, reporting about his activities, etc. Including numerous pencil sketches. (91) DM6,500

A Ls s (2), 21 Nov 1924 & [n.d.]. 3 pp, 4to. To Max Liebermann. Regarding an exhibition of his works. Including 3 orig drawings. (91) DM1,800

AL, [n.d.]. (91) DM370

Gundolf, Friedrich, 1880-1931
ALs, 18 Nov 1913. (90) DM900
— 22 Jan 1930. (89) DM420

Gungl, Joseph, 1810-89
Autograph quotation, 17 bars of music, sgd & inscr to Robert Weigelt, 18 May 1873. (91) $110

Gunther, John, 1901-70
Collection of 4 A Ls s & A Ns s, & 9 Ls s & Ns s, 1922 to 1962. (89) $80

Gurney, Ivor
Autograph music, song, Tarantella, for voice & piano, sgd, to a poem by Hilaire Belloc, [c.1920]. (88) £475
— Autograph music, song, The Penny Whistle, sgd, to a poem by Edward Thomas, [c.1919]. (88) £475

Gurney, Joseph, 1744-1815
Ms, account book recording payments made for shorthand reports in Parliament, etc., 1800 to 1807, c.160 pp, 4to, covers def. (88) £320

Gustav II Adolf, King of Sweden, 1594-1632
Ls, 20 May 1614. 1 p, folio. To an unspecified German prince. Requesting him to give permission to the bearer Col. von Arnim to recruit soldiers in his territory. With autograph subscription. In German. Address leaf def. (88) DM2,800
— 9 Oct 1622. 1 p, folio. To Count Philipp von Mansfeld. About recipient's release from Spanish captivity. In German. (90) DM1,700

Ds, 5 Dec 1612. 1 p, 4to. Confirmation of a grant to Reinhold Arep. (90) DM1,300

Gustav III, King of Sweden, 1746-92
ALs, 29 May 1785. (88) DM360
Ls, 12 Mar 1779. (89) DM220

Gustav IV Adolf, King of Sweden, 1778-1837
ALs, 1 Jan 1813. (90) DM260
Ds, Nov 1814. (89) £350

Gutzkow, Karl Ferdinand, 1811-78
Series of 19 A Ls s, 14 Jan 1845 to 12 Dec 1877. 38 pp, 8vo. To J. J. Weber. Discussing publication matters. (91) DM1,300

ALs, 15 Nov 1836. (91) DM260
Ls, 3 July 1855. Albrecht collection. (91) SF280

Guyton de Morveau, Louis Bernard, 1737-1816
Autograph Ms, instructions concerning the preparation of mineral waters, 24 Nov 1788. (89) DM850

Guzman, Gaspar de, Conde de Olivares, 1587-1645
Ls, 8 Nov 1616. (89) £130

Gwin, William McKendree, 1805-85
ALs, 29 Aug 1853. Alexander collection. (90) $180

Gwinnett, Button, Signer from Georgia —& Others
Ls, 12 July 1776. 1 p, folio. To John Ashmead. As Member of the Marine Committee of Congress, requesting him "not to go on the proposed expedition to the Jerseys". Text in the hand of Timothy Matlack; also sgd by John Hancock, Robert Morris, Francis Lewis, George Read & Arthur Middleton. Laid down; in mor folding case. Doheny collection. (89) $190,000

Gwinnett, Button, Signer from Georgia
Ds, 19 Feb 1773. 1 p, 8vo. Receipt for £4 2s from Levi Sheftall. Including 2 autograph lines. Silked. (90) $135,000

Gwynne, John, fl.1660
Ms, Military Memoirs of the Civil War, [late 17th cent]; over 200 pp, 8vo, in calf, gilt. (88) £500

Gye, Ernest. See: Albani, Emma & Gye

Gyrowetz, Adalbert, 1763-1850
Autograph music, 2 choruses for 2 sopranos & 2 altos, So lang, & Der Sturm, sgd twice & dated 1803. (88) £500

H

Haber, Fritz, 1868-1934
Collection of 5 A Ls s & 5 Ls s, 11 June 1905 to 21 Apr 1918. 17 pp, mostly 4to. To Martin Freund. About a position at Frankfurt & various scientific matters. (88) DM5,000
ALs, 28 July 1924. (88) DM550
— 28 July 1924. (91) DM950
— 28 July 1928. (89) DM400

Habersham, Joseph, 1751-1815
Ls, [21 Mar 1796]. (89) $140

Hackert, Philipp, 1737-1807
ALs, 30 July 1785. Albrecht collection. (91) SF900

Hader, Elmer Stanley, 1889-1973. See: Steinbeck, John

Hadfield, James
Autograph Ms, "The Old and and [sic] New Testament Contain", [n.d.]. (88) £60
— Autograph Ms, verses, sgd. (91) $300

Haeckel, Ernst, 1834-1919
Autograph Ms, review of the 2d Ed of Brehm's Thierleben, probably written for use as advertisement; 15 Nov 1876. (90) DM460
A Ls s (2), 23 Jan 1877 & 16 June 1900. (90) DM400
— A Ls s (2), 30 Sept 1890 & 11 Apr 1897. (91) DM600
ALs, 22 Dec 1901. (90) DM300
— 5 Nov 1905. (88) DM220

Haering, Wilhelm, 1798-1871. See: Alexis, Willibald

Haertling, Peter
Autograph Ms, poem, An ein Taubenpaar. (89) DM230
— Autograph Ms, poem, Gedicht mit Mond, 9 Mar 1982. (91) DM240
Autograph transcript, poem, Schlaflos; [n.d.]. (90) DM320

Hagedorn, Friedrich von, 1708-54
ALs, 28 Sept 1750. 4 pp, 4to. To Gottlieb Fuchs. Giving advice about contacting potential patrons. Repaired. Kuenzel collection. (90) DM1,700
— 15 Sept 1752. 3 pp, 4to. To [Gottlieb Fuchs]. Personal letter, & asking for his opinion about Klopstock's Messias. (88) DM1,900

Hagelstange, Rudolf, 1912-84
Autograph Ms, draft of an essay, beginning "Dem Volke aufs Maul schauen...", [n.d.]. (89) DM200
— Autograph Ms, poem, beginning "Die Rosen welk", 16 Oct 1942. (88) DM320
— Autograph Ms, poem, Torheit, sgd &

HAGGARD

dated 15 Nov 1979. (90) DM420

Haggard, Sir Henry Rider, 1856-1925
[An archive comprising over 70 letters by Haggard to his wife, c.300 family letters, a diary kept by Louisa Haggard, & further related material, 1880 to 1912, sold at S on 15 Dec 1988, lot 46, for £4,200.]

Autograph Ms, The Farmer's Year, sgd, dated 1 Feb [18]98 & inscr to William Carr, 15 Oct 1899. 33 pp, 4to, on rectos only. Draft, with several autograph corrections. (90) £7,500

Series of 27 A Ls s, 29 June 1905 to 18 Nov 1923. (90) £550

Corrected page proofs, Dawn. L, 1884. 3 vols, 8vo, in half mor gilt. With numerous autograph annotations & corrections; some Ms additions bound in. Bradley Martin Ms. (90) $25,000

Hahn, Otto, 1879-1968
A Ls s (2), 26 Jan & 4 Feb 1911. 4 pp, 8vo. To Martin Freund. Discussing a projected lecture at Frankfurt. Including draft of Freund's answer. (88) DM1,500

ALs, 12 Dec 1932. 3 pp, 4to. To Rudolf Ladenburg. About recipient's move to Princeton, plans to travel to America, etc. With postscript by Edith Hahn. (89) DM2,600

Collection of 4 Ls s & 8 autograph postcards, sgd, 20 Mar 1951 to Mar 1968. 7 pp, folio, & cards. To Fritz Weigel. Scientific correspondence. (88) DM2,200

Series of 3 autograph postcards, sgd, 14 Apr 1965 to Aug 1967. (91) DM650

Autograph postcards (2), sgd, 9 Dec 1953 & 7 Nov 1956. (89) DM320

Autograph postcard, sgd, [20 Sept 1897]. (91) DM200

Collection of ANs & AN, Mar 1967 & [n.d.]. (89) DM200

Photograph, sgd, 1964. (91) DM340

Hahn, Philipp Matthaeus, 1739-90
ALs, 4 Sept 1787. 4 pp, 4to. To Christian Adam Dann. Discussing theological questions. (90) DM2,400

AMERICAN BOOK PRICES CURRENT

Hahn, Reynaldo, 1875-1947
Autograph music, song, Reverie calme (D'une prison), for voice & piano, to a text by Verlaine, sgd & dated 29 Oct 1892. 5 pp, 355mm by 270mm, on rectos only. Cortot collection. (90) DM2,400

ALs, [14 June 1911]. (91) DM240

Hahn, Ulla
Autograph transcript, poem, beginning "Spuerest Du/Wenn der Tag sich neigt"; [n.d.]. (90) DM240

Hahnemann, Samuel, 1755-1843
ALs, 10 Jan 1823. 3 pp, 8vo. To [Adam Mueller]. About his problems at Leipzig, his move to Koethen & some new medical discoveries. (90) DM5,200

— 17 Nov 1825. 1 p, 8vo. To [Johann Friedrich Hennicke]. Sending a statement for print in the Allgemeiner Anzeiger der Deutschen. (90) DM1,100

— 31 July 1828. 1 p, 8vo. To [Jenny von Pappenheim]. Giving medical advice. (91) DM4,400

— HAHNEMANN, MELANIE. - ALs, 3 & 4 Nov 1841, 3 pp, 8vo. Recipient unnamed. Reporting about her husband. With 1-line subscription by Samuel Hahnemann, sgd. (88) DM1,600

Hahn-Hahn, Ida, Graefin von, 1805-80
Autograph Ms, story, Mein Traum, [1825?]. (89) DM300

Haig, Alexander
Series of 11 Ls s, 1973 to 1976. (89) $55

Haig, Douglas, 1st Earl, 1861-1928
ALs, 25 Apr 1898. 11 pp, 8vo. To an unnamed general. Giving an account of the campaign in the Sudan. With port postcard. (91) $1,100

Haile Selassie, Emperor of Ethiopia, 1892-1975
Ls, 27 Jan 1940. (88) £200
— 10 Aug 1942. (91) £800

Hailstone
Original drawing, Behind the Scenes in the Entertainment World, to illus Punch, 18 Dec 1935. (89) £60

Hale, Edward Everett, 1822-1909. See: Irving, Washington & Others

Hale, Nathan, 1755-76
— HASTINGS, MARY E. - ALs & ADs, 1 Jan 1927. 10 pp, 4to & 8vo. Giving details about the relationship between Hale & her great grandmother Alice Adams. (88) $225

Hale, Sarah Josepha, 1788-1879
Autograph Ms, poem, Mary's Lamb; 24 lines, sgd & dated 23 Jan 1865. 3 pp, 8vo, on rectos only. Repaired & matted; in slipcase. With related material. (89) $30,000

Hall, Huntz. See: Gorcey, Leo & Hall

Hallam, Arthur, 1811-33
ALs, 15 June [n.y.]. 4 pp, size not stated. To his fiancee Emily [Tennyson]. Mentioning Alfred Tennyson, society in London, various friends, etc. Partly cross-written. (90) £3,800

Halleck, Henry W., 1815-72
Autograph telegram, sgd, 16 Feb 186[2]. (91) $650

Haller, Albrecht von, 1708-77
Autograph transcript, excerpt from Johann Friedrich Merkel's letter addressed to him, 20 Aug 1752. (91) DM1,000

ALs, [c.1740]. 2 pp, folio. To his colleagues at Goettingen University. Requesting their opinion on several administrative matters. Endorsed by 4 colleagues. (91) DM1,600

— 17 Apr 1761. 2 pp, 4to. To Christian Gottlieb Ludwig. Thanking for a scientific work, mentioning his health problems, etc. In Latin. (90) DM1,700

— 8 Nov 1775. 1 p, 4to. To Marc Antonio Caldani. Sending some books & discussing other scientists. In Latin. (88) DM1,900

Halliburton, Richard, 1900-39
Ls, [1928]. (89) $375

Hallward, Patience
Original drawings, (51), preparatory ink or pencil drawings to illus Hans Andersen's The Little Mermaid, 1912. (90) £100

Halm, August, 1869-1929
Collection of 8 A Ls s & 2 autograph postcards, sgd, 4 Jan 1921 to 1 Oct 1928. (90) DM450

Hamann, Johann Georg, 1730-88
ALs, 23 May 1782. 1 p, 4to. To Johann Friedrich Reichardt. About the death of Reichardt's son. (88) DM15,000

Hamilton, Alexander, 1757?-1804
ALs, 28 July 1785. 1 p, 4to. To Richard Varick, Mayor of NY. Requesting him to name "persons to be inserted in the Commission in the Case of Wardrop and Macauley". Doheny collection. (89) $1,200

— 16 Aug 1791. 3 pp, 4to. To William Seton. Confidential letter discussing the national debt & giving instructions for purchases on behalf of the government. (90) $7,500

— 18 Mar 1794. 1 p, 4to. To President Washington. Providing information respecting the French debt. (89) $2,000

— 7 Oct 1794. 1 p, 4to. To Samuel Hodgdon. Complaining about the lack of supplies for troops in Pennsylvania. (90) $4,500

— 31 Dec 1794. (89) $400

Ls, 3 Oct 1789. 1 p, 4to. To Hodijah Baylies. Circular letter forwarding amendments to the "Act for registering and clearing Vessels...". (90) $1,800

— 4 Oct 1789. 3 pp, 4to. To Sharp Delany. Outlining duties of port collectors & requirements for securing statistics of port operations. Byer collection. (90) $4,800

— 21 May 1790. (89) $475

— 3 Sept 1790. (89) $650

— 23 Sept 1790. Doheny collection. (89) $1,000

— 7 Oct 1790. 1 p, 4to. To William Channing. Thanking for attending to a request. (90) $1,100

— 15 Dec 1790. 2 pp, 4to. To William Ellery, Jr. Giving instructions about duties & penalties to be paid by the ship Warren. Docketed by Ellery. (90) $3,000

— 21 Mar 1791. 6 pp, 4to. To Edward Carrington. Discussing the subdivision of the Virginia revenue service. (91) $5,500

HAMILTON

— 6 Apr 1791. (89) $1,000
— 30 May 1791. 2 pp, 4to. To William Ellery, Jr. Discussing the case of the ship Warren & Capt. Smith's "disposition to disregard the revenue laws". Including franking signature. (90) $2,000
— 30 May 1791. 1 p, 4to. To John Chester. Regarding a seal for stamping certificates. (91) $1,100
— 12 July 1791. 2 pp, 4to. To a port collector. Responding to inquiries concerning tea imports. (91) $1,700
— 6 Jan 1792. Alexander collection. (90) $950
— 21 June 1792. 1 p, 4to. To Sharp Delany. Asking him to recommend candidates for 3d mate on a revenue cutter. Byer collection. (90) $2,400
— 13 Aug 1792. (88) $450
— 3 Nov 1792. 1 p, 4to. To Jonathan Burrall. Sending funds for a Virginia lighthouse. Christensen collection. (90) $2,200
— 26 Mar 1794. 1 p, 4to. To William Ellery. Giving instructions for the enforcement of an embargo; mostly ptd. (90) $1,200
— 9 Sept 1794. 3 pp, 4to. To Gov. Thomas Mifflin. On behalf of the Sec of War, conveying Washington's request to mobilize the militia to suppress the Whiskey Rebellion. (90) $12,000
ANs, 24 Jan 1795. 1 p, 8vo. To Mr. Otis. Requesting him to return a report for a few days. (91) $1,400
ADs, 5 Feb 1782. 1 p, 8vo. Receipt to Jacob Cuyler. (91) $1,100
Collection of Ds & Ls, 17 Mar 1800 & 24 Oct 1792. 2 pp, 4to & folio. Pay order to Nathaniel Appleton for $3,883.14 to Benjamin Lincoln. Cancellation hole affecting signature. To Col. William Stephens Smith, regarding the resignation of Capt. Cole. With franking signature & covering letter by Smith on integral address leaf. Whiton collection. (88) $1,800
Ds, 29 Nov 1794. (91) $550
— 21 Nov 1801. (88) $450
Cut signature, 3 Sept 1785. (88) $400
— Anr, [n.d.]. (90) $320

AMERICAN BOOK PRICES CURRENT

Hamilton, Elizabeth Schuyler, 1757-1854
ALs, 10 Apr 1830. 1 p, 4to. To the Marquis de Lafayette. Introducing the Rev. Richmond & Mr. Goodhue. Doheny collection. (89) $1,100

Hamilton, Lady Emma, 1761?-1815
[A collection of 37 letters to & from Lady Hamilton after Nelson's death, 15 Dec 1807 to 21 Sept 1814, 105 pp, 4to & folio, sold at C on 20 June 1990, lot 263, for £2,200 to Wilson.]
Autograph Ms, anniversary prayer for her late husband, Lord Hamilton, & for Admiral Nelson at sea. [6 Sept 1803] 3 pp, 4to. (91) £6,500
— Autograph Ms, Day Account Book, 27 Oct 1784 to 21 Feb 1785. 19 pp & blanks, 4to, in orig marbled paper covers. Wolf collection. (90) £2,200
Ms, [Mar 1813]. Wolf collection. (90) £700
— Ms, petition, "The Memorial of Dame Emma Hamilton...", 1804. (88) £280
Collection of 15 A Ls s, 2 autograph transcripts, & 3 signatures, [n.d.]. 50 pp, mostly 4to. To various recipients. About social engagements, Merton, Sir William Hamilton's pension, etc. Copies of state papers. Signatures on ptd music. Wolf collection. (90) £1,800
ALs, 17 Jan 1807. 3 pp, 4to. To [Capt. Jonas Rose]. Saying she will send him some of Nelson's hair. With lock of hair & other related material. (88) £5,000
— 20 Sept 1811. 4 pp, 4to. To Sir Richard Puleston. About her visit to Nelson's sister, her move to a house in Bond Street, & her present circumstances. (88) £1,450
— [1814]. (88) £800
See also: Hamilton, William & Hamilton

Hamilton, Sir William, 1730-1803
[A collection of political correspondence from his years at Naples, 5 Jan 1765 to 15 Dec 1800, including 39 A Ls s & 3 autograph Mss by Hamilton, letters addressed to him, accounts, etc., c.487 pp, 4to & folio, sold at C on 20 June 1990, lot 266, for £3,800 to Genio.]
[A collection of correspondence to &

from Hamilton concerning antiquities & volcanoes, with related material, [n.d.], 131 pp, 4to & folio, sold at S on 20 June 1990, lot 269, for £5,000 to Kraft.]

Series of 3 A Ls s, 16 Jan 1783 to 4 May 1790. Wolf collection. (90) £250

— Series of 11 A Ls s, 1792 to 1797. (88) £400

— Series of 16 A Ls s, 31 July 1801 to 21 Jan 1803. 43 pp, 4to & folio. To Emma Hamilton. About social engagements, his fishing, his health, Nelson, etc. Wolf collection. (90) £1,200

— Series of 8 A Ls s, [n.d.]. 45 pp, 4to & folio. To Charles Greville. Discussing Emma Hart [the future Lady Hamilton] & other matters. 1 incomplete. Including related material. Wolf collection. (90) £3,800

ALs, 3 Mar 1778. (91) £200

— 30 May 1786. (91) £180

— 4 Sept 1793. (89) $700

Series of 14 A Ls, 14 Aug 1787 to 20 Apr 1798. (91) £700

Hamilton, Sir William, 1730-1803 —& Hamilton, Emma, Lady, 1761?-1815

[3 items, ALs by Charles F. Grenville, 1800, concerning Sir William; ALs by Sir William Bolton to Lady Hamilton, 1804, mentioning Nelson; & Lady Hamilton's accounts with 2 stores, 1802-03, sold at sg on 25 Oct 1988, lot 112, for $300.]

Hamilton, William Rowan, Sir, 1805-65. See: Wordsworth, William

Hamlin, Hannibal, 1809-91
Franking signature, [22 Mar 1864]. (89) $60

Hammarskjold, Dag, 1905-61
Ns, 11 Nov 1960. (90) $120

Hammerstein, Oscar, 1895-1960
Series of 3 Ls s, 1957 to 1960. (91) $250
Ls, 7 Dec 1949. (91) $160

Hammett, Dashiell, 1894-1961
[A group of 10 photographs or group photographs, 1934 to late 1940s, with related material, sold at CNY on 8 June 1990, lot 184, for $200.]
Typescript, detective story, A Knife Will Cut for Anybody, [n.d.]. (90) $500

— **Typescript,** plot outline & chapter summary for the 1st version of The Thin Man, [c.1930]. 2 pp, 4to. A few autograph additions. (90) $3,500

Ls s (2), 10 Sept 1946 & 10 Aug 1949. (90) $1,000

Hammond, Gertrude Demain
Original drawings, (16), to illus 2 works by Mrs Molesworth, 1907. Macmillan Archives. (90) £650

Hampton, Wade, 1818-1902
A Ls s (2), 6 Feb & 8 Mar 1871. (88) $650
— A Ls s (2), 11 May 1871 & 26 Feb 1877. (88) $400
ALs, 28 Mar 1871. (88) $700

Hamsun, Knut, 1859-1952
ALs, [c.1890/91]. 3 pp, 8vo. To [Bolette Pavels Larsen]. Thanking for her support & mentioning projected lectures. (89) DM1,300
— 25 July [c.1902]. (89) DM440
— 15 Dec 1934. (90) DM480
— 25 Aug 1940. (90) DM400
Ls, 2 Sept 1929. (88) DM300

Hancock, John, 1737-93
[A lot of 2 cut signatures, [n.d.], 5 by 4 inches & 6 by 3 inches, sold at R on 28 Oct 1989, lot 322, for $1,200.]
ALs, 21 Nov 1768. 1 p, 183mm by 111mm. To Joseph Jackson. Ordering a beaver hat to be delivered to Capt. Robert Ball. Mtd. Doheny collection. (89) $5,000

Ls, 10 Aug 1776. 1 p, folio. To Brig. Gen. James Clinton. Notifying him of his promotion. Repaired. (88) $2,000
— 5 July 1787. 2 pp, folio. To Gov. John Sullivan. Requesting permission for Massachusetts troops to pursue rebels into New Hampshire. (91) $13,000
Letter, 11 June 1776. (91) $550
Ds, 1 Sept 1767. 1 p, 8vo. Finding by the Selectmen of Boston with reference to the accounts of Paul Farmer, Master of the Alms. Sgd by Hancock as one of the Selectmen. (90) $1,600
— 1 Jan 1776. 1 p, 4to. Appointment of Charles Pond as 1st Lieutenant. Countersgd by Charles Thompson. Repaired. Doheny collection. (89)

HANCOCK

$4,500
— 19 Apr 1776. 3 pp, folio. Instructions to Indian Agent George Morgan, sgd as President of Congress. Repaired. (89) $12,000
— [Apr 1776 - Oct 1777]. Ptd Instructions to the Commanders of Private Ships or Vessels of War..., 3 Apr 1776. 1 p, folio. Sgd as President of Congress. (91) $9,000
— [Apr 1776 - Oct 1777]. Ptd Instructions to the Commanders of Private Ships or Vessels of War..., 3 Apr 1776. 1 p, folio. Sgd as President of Congress. (90) $10,500
— 21 Nov 1776. 1 p, 216mm by 290mm. Appointment of a Major, sgd as President of the Continental Congress. Countersgd by Charles Thomson. (91) $3,500
— 21 Nov 1776. 1 p, 4to. Commission for Jeremiah Van Rensselaer as paymaster, sgd as President of the Continental Congress. Countersgd by Charles Thomson. (90) $2,500
— 30 Dec 1776. 1 p, folio. Congressional resolution appealing to Spain for aid. Text in the hand of Charles Thomson. (91) $7,000
— [Apr 1776 - Oct 1777]. Ptd Instructions to the Commanders of Private ships or Vessels of War..., 3 Apr 1776. 1 p, folio. Sgd as President of Congress. (89) $7,500
— 12 Feb 1781. 1 p, 4to. As Governor of Massachusetts, pay order in favor of Hezekiah Smith. (90) $3,200
— 20 Oct 1781. 1 p, 395mm by 320mm. As Governor of Massachusetts, appointment for Johnson Moulton as sheriff. Fold tear. (90) $1,400
— 16 Mar 1789. 1 p, folio. As Governor of Massachusetts, confirmation of election results addressed to the selectmen of Pittsfield. Sgd twice. (91) $5,000
— 26 June 1789. 1 p, folio. As Governor of Massachusetts, commission for Jeremiah Powell as justice of the peace. Partly ptd. Framed. (89) $1,900
— 17 June 1790. (88) $1,000
— 9 May 1791. 1 p, folio. Appointment for Daniel Howard as senator from Plymouth County. (91) $3,000
— 13 July 1791. 1 p, size not stated.

Appointment for Charles Hastings as ensign in the militia. (91) $2,000
— 23 July 1792. 1 p, 315mm by 395mm. Appointment of Jonathan Thompson as lieutenant in the militia. Repaired. Doheny collection. (89) $3,000

Autograph endorsement, sgd, 25 June 1790. At bottom of a Court Martial sentence, 1 p, folio. Approving & ordering execution of sentence. Byer collection. (90) $2,200

Cut signature, [n.d.]. (88) $900
— Anr, [n.d.]. (88) $475
— HAAS, GEORGE. - Ds, receipt for "Oats for President Hancocks Horses", 24 Sept 1777. 1 p, 8vo. Docketed by Jeremiah Wadsworth. (88) $80

Hancock, Winfield Scott, 1824-86
ALs, 31 Dec 1864. (91) $400
— 14 Jan 1879. (90) $55

Handel, George Frederick, 1685-1759
Ms, Athalia, full score; [n.d.]. (88) £650
— Ms, Messiah, scored for strings & voices with figured bass, 1760. 258 pp, 4to. Contemp blue mor gilt. In the hand of Marmaduke Overend. (91) £3,200
— Ms, song, By the side of a murmuring stream, complete version including bass-line. (88) £800
— JENNENS, CHARLES. - ALs, 13 Dec 1733. 1 p, 4to. To John Ludford. Saying he has no need for the servant recommended, with postscript discussing Handel's difficulty in maintaining his Opera Company. (90) £4,200

Handke, Peter
ALs, 4 July 1974. (88) DM320

Handy, William Christopher, 1873-1958
Ls, 11 Dec 1945. (90) $190
— 6 Nov 1957. (88) $300

Autograph quotation, 1 bar from The Memphis Blues, sgd, inscr & dated 13 Feb 1946. (90) $475

Photograph, sgd & inscr, 21 Aug [19]52. (91) $150

Hansen, Harry
[An archive containing c.1,400 letters & notes sent to him as Ed of The Chicago Daily News, NY World, & NY World-Telegram, [1920s to 1960s], sold at sg on 23 Mar 1989, lot 305, for $4,600.]

Hansen, Karl-Heinz ("Hansen-Bahia"), 1915-78
Collection of ALs & Ls, 29 Jan 1970 & 6 Mar 1975. (88) DM240

Harbach, Otto, 1873-1963. See: Kern, Jerome & Harbach

Harburg, Edgar Yipsel, 1896-1981
Typescript, lyrics, Over the Rainbow, [n.d.]. (91) $100

Harden, Maximilian, 1861-1927
Collection of 5 A Ls s & 9 autograph postcards, sgd, 13 Sept 1907 to 22 May 1919. (90) DM700
ALs, 25 Oct 1916. (88) DM220
— 30 Nov 1916. (90) DM230

Hardenberg, Friedrich, Freiherr von, 1772-1801. See: Novalis, 1772-1801

Hardenberg, Karl August, Fuerst von, 1750-1822
A Ls s (2), 3 Jan & 8 June 1816. (91) DM600
ALs, 29 Mar 1797. (90) DM260
— 29 Jan 1800. Schroeder collection. (89) DM420
— 7 Sept 1800. (91) DM240
— 2 Feb 1806. (90) DM360
— 11 May 1808. (90) DM800
— 16 May 1820. (89) DM220
Ls, 17 Apr 1793. (90) DM300
— 21 Apr 1815. (91) DM250
Ds, 18 Mar 1813. (89) DM230
See also: Friedrich Wilhelm II & Hardenberg

Harding, Florence Kling, 1860-1924
Ls, 17 Aug 1923. (90) $150
Check, sgd, 15 Mar 1921, made out for $118.80 for income tax. (88) $65
— Anr, sgd, 19 July 1921, made out for $407.12 for June taxes. (88) $60
Franking signature, [4 Feb 1924]. Alexander collection. (90) $220

Harding, Warren G., 1865-1923
ALs, 5 Oct 1921. 1 p, 4to. To Herbert L. Pratt. Sending his autograph. Pratt collection. (89) $9,000
Collection of Ls & photograph, sgd & inscr, 5 Oct & 26 Apr 1922. (90) $600
— Collection of Ls, ADs, & photograph, sgd, 4 Jan 1923, 17 Nov 1913, & [n.d.]. 2 pp, 8vo, & 220mm by 172mm. To Edward L. Doheny, expressing thanks for the gift of an embassy site in Mexico City. As administrator of the estate of Mary C. Harding, receipt. With related material. Doheny collection. (89) $1,300
Ls, 29 Nov 1916. (91) $225
— 7 Feb 1917. (89) $220
— 9 May 1917. (90) $200
— 4 June 1920. (91) $300
— 20 July 1920. (90) $190
— 11 Dec 1920. (88) $200
— 26 Feb 1921. (90) $325
— 30 May 1921. (89) £800
— 29 Aug 1921. 8 pp, 4to. To Senator [Joseph] Medill McCormick. Draft, commenting about "the remarkable achievements of the extraordinary session of the Congress". Several emendations, some autograph; in pencil. (88) $2,700
— 30 Sept 1921. (89) $425
— 14 Nov 1921. 2 pp, 4to. To George Sylvester Viereck. Discussing the appointment of an ambassador to Austria. Sang collection. (91) $1,100
— 28 Nov 1921. (90) $200
— 16 Dec 1921. (90) $400
— 19 Dec 1921. (90) $425
— 8 Feb 1922. 1 p, 4to. To Charles C. Fisher. Discussing plans for the Marion centennial program. Sang collection. (91) $1,900
— 24 June 1922. (88) $1,000
— 25 Jan 1923. (90) $270
— 25 Apr 1923. 1 p, 4to. To John A. Stewart. Discussing the Prohibition issue in the forthcoming election campaign. With engraved port. (90) $3,000
— 4 May 1923. Byer collection. (90) $250
ADs, 17 Nov 1916. (91) $180
Ds, 24 Nov 1894. (91) $110
— 17 Apr 1897. (90) $140
— 13 Nov 1897. (88) $100

HARDING

— 13 June 1898. (88) $130
— 29 Jan 1899. (90) $200
— 2 June 1921. (89) $210
— 21 June 1921. (90) $110
— 17 Nov 1921. (88) $190
— 27 Jan 1923. (91) $140
— 28 Mar 1923. (91) $450
— [n.d.]. (90) $180
Cut signature, [n.d.]. (90) $110
Photograph, sgd, [n.d.]. (91) $400
— Anr, [n.d.]. (90) $250
Photograph, sgd & inscr, [n.d.]. (91) $550
— Anr, [n.d.]. (90) $280
— Anr, [n.d.]. (89) $450
— Anr, [n.d.]. (89) $330
— Anr, [n.d.]. (91) $110
Photograph, [n.d.]. (90) $450
Signature, 3 June 1900. (90) $85
White House card, sgd, [n.d.]. (88) $160
— Anr, sgd, [n.d.]. (89) $400
— Anr, sgd, [n.d.]. (90) $250
— REID, JACQUES. - Engraved port of Harding, 1922. 11 by 15 inches. Sgd by both. Framed. (91) $300

Harding, Warren G., 1865-1923 —& Others
Group photograph, Harding & his Cabinet seated around a table, [c.1921]. 6.75 by 9.25 inches (image). By Edmonston; sgd by all 12. (90) $4,200

Hardy, Oliver, 1892-1957
Photograph, sgd, [n.d.]. (88) $150
See also: Laurel, Stan & Hardy

Hardy, Paul
Original drawings, (8), to illus Tom Brown's Schooldays; [n.d.]. (90) £600

Hardy, Thomas, 1752-1832
[An important archive comprising the autograph Ms of Hardy's autobiography, letters to Hardy & material relating to his state trial, partly autograph, 1794 to 1831, c.100 pp, various sizes, sold at pn on 16 June 1988, lot 47, for £4,600 to Quaritch.]

Hardy, Thomas, 1840-1928
[A collection of proof sheets of A Call to National Service & other poems on the war, with 2 A Ls s & further related material, mostly 1917, 4to, in crushed mor bdg by Katherine Adams,

AMERICAN BOOK PRICES CURRENT

1918, sold at b on 20 June 1990, lot 82, for £9,000.]
Typescript, short story, On the Western Circuit, [c.1891-94]. 43 pp, 4to. With autograph revisions. Ptr's copy. (89) £26,000
Collection of ALs & autograph postcard, sgd, 31 May 1900 & 24 Nov 1911. (89) £520
— Collection of 2 A Ls s & ANs, 24 June 1914 to 17 Jan 1919. (88) £900
ALs, 10 Dec 1903. (88) £500
— 12 Nov 1905. (90) DM750
— 29 Nov 1908. (88) £400
Ls, 24 Dec 1912. (88) £300
— 20 Aug 1925. (91) $225
— 22 Nov 1926. (91) £120
— 2 Dec 1927. (90) £650
ANs, 23 Nov 1927. (90) £110
— HARDY, FLORENCE. - 4 A Ls s, 1920 to 1930. 10 pp, size not stated. To Siegfried Sassoon. Mostly about Thomas Hardy. (91) £650
— SASSOON, SIEGFRIED. - ANs, [n.d.]. 1 p, c.126mm by 95mm. On verso of mount of a photograph of his aunt Agatha Thornycroft, explaining that Hardy had her face in mind when writing Tess of the D'Urbervilles. Sgd with monogram. (91) £1,100
— SIMPSON, JOSEPH. - Orig drawing, pen-&-ink port of Hardy, sgd; [n.d.]. 7 by 5 inches, on thin paper. Mtd. (89) £260

Hardy, Sir Thomas Masterman, 1769-1839
Series of c.115 A Ls s, 1798 to 1839. About 325 pp, mostly 4to. To John C. Manfield (72), his brother Joseph Hardy (38) & others. Covering the whole span of his career & including frequent reports about Nelson. (89) £8,000
ALs, 24 Nov 1822. (89) £280

Hare, David
Typescript, screenplay, Wetherby, [1984-1985]. (91) £500

Haring, Keith
Signature, [6 May 1988]. (91) $325

Haringer, Jakob, 1898-1948
Autograph Ms, poems, Drei Oden und ein Lied fuer die tote Gespielin, [n.d.]. 6 pp, 8vo; stitched. Sgd on tp & on cover. In pencil. With ALs, [n.d.]. (90) DM1,200

Harlequinade
Autograph Ms, Harlequinade, drawn by John Hickson, 1753. Text & ink & watercolor illusts on folded sheet in 6 sections, each with 2 flaps to alter the illusts & continue the verses, folio. (88) £1,300

Harms, Friedrich, 1819-80
[A large collection of autograph notes for lectures given at the universities of Kiel & Berlin, 1850 to 1870, in 7 contemp folders, 4to, sold at HN on 9 Dec 1988, lot 3294, for DM1,000.]

Harrach, Johann Joseph Philipp, Graf von, 1678-1764. See: Neipperg, Wilhelm Reinhard & Harrach

Harradine, A. C.
Original drawings, (21), to illus D. Archives of J. M. Dent & Son. (88) £150

Harris, Frank, 1854-1931
ALs, 2 Apr [c.1925]. (90) £35
See also: Douglas, Alfred & Harris
See also: Shaw, George Bernard & Harris

Harris, Joel Chandler, 1848-1908
ALs, 2 Sept 1886. Doheny collection. (89) $350

Harris, John, 1756-1846
[A group of 22 ink & wash drawings, mostly children in various scenes, to illus titles in the series of Delightful Stories pbd by Harris, 1804 to 1806, sold at S on 30 Nov 1989, lot 355, for £300 to Schiller.]

Harrison, Anna Symmes, 1775-1864
ALs, 8 Apr 1847. 1 p, 8vo. To Clark Brodhead. Concerning the erection of an enclosure at her mother's grave. (90) $1,100
— 12 Oct 1850. (90) $650
— [26 Dec n.y.]. 1 p, size not stated. To Cleves Harrison. Family news. Including franking signature. (91) $1,200

Harrison, Benjamin, Signer from Virginia
ALs, 12 June 1783. 4 pp, folio. To John Dickinson. As Governor of Virginia, complaining about Pennsylvania's actions in a boundary dispute. Doheny collection. (89) $3,200
Ls, 16 Nov 1782. (89) $420
ADs, 5 May 1788. (88) $150
Ds, Dec 1782. (91) $325
Cut signature, [n.d.]. (91) $250
Franking signature, 30 Aug [c.1776]. (88) $525

Harrison, Benjamin, 1833-1901
A Ls s (2), 8 Aug 1887 & 20 Dec 1889. 2 pp, 8vo. To Hampton L. Carson, declining an invitiation. To George F. Edmunds, requesting an interview. Pratt collection. (89) $1,400
ALs, 10 Mar 1877. Byer collection. (90) $425
— 4 Oct 1881. (89) $475
— 11 Apr 1888. (89) $475
— 15 May 1889. 2 pp, 8vo. To Sec of State James G. Blaine. Informing him of 9 ambassadors' appointments. (91) $1,800
— 15 May 1889. (89) £600
— 28 Aug 1889. (90) $600
— 19 Mar 1890. (91) $650
— 5 Oct 1892. 1 p, 8vo. To Mrs. J. S. Clarkson. Reporting about his wife's illness. Mtd. Rosenbloom collection. (88) $1,400
— 17 Jan 1893. 1 p, 8vo. To his brother John Scott Harrison, Jr. Worrying about his brother's & granddaughter's illness. (89) $2,000
Ls, 21 Mar 1881. (91) $275
— 28 June 1888. (89) $150
— 2 July 1888. (90) $275
— 10 July 1888. (90) $250
— 13 Nov 1888. (88) $175
— 3 Jan 1891. (90) $325
— 1 Sept 1891. (89) $425
— 24 Feb 1894. (89) $275
— 30 Nov 1894. (91) $225
ANs, [n.d.]. (90) $800
ADs, 16 Apr 1855. (91) $300
Ds, 15 Mar 1889. (91) $900
— 19 Nov 1889. (88) $175
— 4 Jan 1890. (91) $250
— 30 Jan 1890. (88) $250

HARRISON

— 10 Jan 1892. (89) $280
— 5 Jan 1893. (90) $190
Autograph telegram, sgd, 29 Oct 1889. (90) $650
— Anr, sgd, [22 Feb 1890]. (91) $130
Cut signature, [n.d.]. (90) $140
Endorsement, sgd, on integral leaf of ALs by Capt. (88) $210
Photograph, sgd, [1864?]. 165mm by 107mm. In military uniform. (90) $1,800
— Anr, [n.d.]. (90) $900
Signature, [n.d.]. (91) $210
— Anr, [n.d.]. (90) $210
White House card, sgd, [n.d.]. (89) $150
— Anr, sgd, [n.d.]. (91) $200

Harrison, Benjamin, 1833-1901 —& Others
Ls, 21 Apr 1881. (91) $280

Harrison, Caroline Scott, 1832-92
ALs, 30 Sept 1891. 4 pp, 12mo. To Mrs. J. S. Clarkson. Complaining about press attacks on her family. (91) $1,700
— 25 Feb 1892. (90) $200

Harrison, Frederic, 1831-1923
Series of 19 A Ls s, 1880 to 1897 & [n.d.]. (90) £110

Harrison, George
Signature, [n.d.]. (89) $700

Harrison, Louise
[A collection of c.90 items, including letters, postcards, photographs, etc., mostly written to a friend in California, many mentioning George Harrison & the Beatles, sold at P on 18 June 1988, lot 627, for $700.]

Harrison, Mary Lord, 1858-1948
ALs, 9 Apr [1901]. (88) $70
Franking signature, [6 Dec 1932]. Alexander collection. (90) $100

Harrison, Rex
ALs, 3 Mar [n.y.]. (91) $110

Harrison, William Henry, 1773-1841
[An illus campaign lettersheet of 1840 with port & log cabin, sent as a letter to Boston, sold at rf on 26 Nov 1988, lot 18, for $80.]
ALs, 20 July 1795. (88) £800

AMERICAN BOOK PRICES CURRENT

— 17 June 1796. 2 pp, 4to. To Gen. James Wilkinson. About changes in his plans. (91) $1,800
— 29 Apr 1802. (88) $950
— 27 Sept 1812. 1 p, 4to. To Capt. Rowland. Giving marching orders for recipient's company. 6-line autograph postscript, sgd W.H.H., on verso. (91) $3,500
— 11 Oct 1812. 1 p, 4to. To Gen. John H. Platt. Giving orders to purchase flour. Including franking signature. (90) $1,600
— 4 Jan 1828. 1 p, 4to. To P. Benson. Concerning a transfer of money. Rosenbloom collection. (88) $1,700
— 7 Mar 1831. 2 pp, 4to. To Edward T. Tayloe. Discussing problems resulting from his mission to Colombia. (89) $3,000
— 1 Dec 1833. 1 p, 4to. To D. Campbell. Thanking for help relating to a publication. (90) $1,600
— 26 Jan 1836. 2 pp, 4to. To Lewis Cass. Content not given. (91) $1,600
— 13 Sept [c.1836]. (88) $950
— 13 Jan 1837. 1 p, 4to. To the "Committee of the Phrena Kosmian Society of the Pennsylvania College". Expressing thanks for his election as honorary member of the society. Pratt collection. (89) $3,000
— 4 Nov 1838. 3 pp, 4to. To J. F. Cox. Discussing his Presidential prospects. (90) $7,500
— 14 July 1840. 3 pp, 4to. To Moses B. Corwin. Defending himself against attacks regarding the Battle of the Thames. Repaired. (90) $1,200
— 26 Sept 1840. 3 pp, 4to. To Edward Curtis. Requesting help in a financial matter & commenting about his election campaign. 2 lines obliterated. Sang collection. (91) $3,250
Ls, 27 Sept 1812. 2 pp, 4to. To the commanding officer of a group of Virginia volunteers. Giving detailed instructions to proceed from Wooster to the rapids of the Miami. McVitty collection. (90) $2,500
— 18 Aug 1813. 2 pp, 4to. To Gov. Isaac Shelby. Making preparations for military operations against Upper Canada & accepting a higher number of Kentucky volunteers. With franking sig-

nature. Repaired. (89) $7,000
ADs, 4 Apr 1794. (91) $800
— 5 Apr 1794. (90) $600
— 7 Aug 1794. (91) $800
— 8 Aug 1795. (89) $500
— 9 Aug 1795. (90) $650
— 19 Sept 1796. (91) $650
— 2 Jan 1797. (91) $650
— 5 Feb 1802. (89) $600
Ds, 31 July 1795. (88) $750
— 4 Aug 1795. (88) $850
— 22 May 1802. 1 p, folio. Grant of land in Indiana Territory to Shadrack Bond. Framed. Byer collection. (90) $1,500
— 17 Dec 1816. 2 pp, 4to. As Governor of Indiana Territory, authorizing legislative acts. Doheny collection. (89) $1,100
— 16 June 1836. (91) $750
— [4 Mar - 4 Apr 1841]. 1 p, size not stated. Ship's papers for the brig Agate of New Bedford, issued 30 Apr 1841. Countersgd by Daniel Webster. Sang collection. (90) $80,000
Autograph check, sgd, 24 Mar [n.y.]. 2 by 6.5 inches. Drawn on the Bank of the U.S. at Washington for $10 payable to bearer. Imperf. (90) $1,400
Autograph endorsement, docket, 9 July 1835, sgd as Clerk of the Court of Common Pleas of Hamilton County, Ohio. (91) $400
Check, accomplished & sgd, 29 Apr 1815. (90) $700
— Anr, 1 Dec 1834. (88) $800
Franking signature, [24 July 1826]. As Senator from Ohio, on repaired cover to Richmond, Va. (88) $2,600

Harrison, William Henry, 1773-1841 —& Others
Ls, 14 Jan 1828. (91) $550

Harrison, William Henry, 1773-1841 —& St. Clair, Arthur, 1736-1818
Ds, 12 & 13 Feb 1799. (90) $1,000
— 13 Feb 1799. 1 p, folio. Territorial land grant, sgd by both. (89) $1,300

Hart, John, Signer from New Jersey
Ds, 25 Mar 1776. (89) $160

Hart, Neal
[An archive of material relating to his career sold at cb on 28 Apr 1989, lot 302, for $3,750]

Hart, William Surrey, 1862?-1946
ALs, 15 Jan [19]31. (90) $110
— 17 Feb 1936. (88) $150
Ls, 25 July 1924. (90) $110

Hart, William Surrey, 1862-1946
Signature, [n.d.]. (89) $65

Hart, William Surrey, 1862?-1946. See: Flagg, James Montgomery & Hart

Harte, Bret, 1836-1902
[A collection of autograph Mss, revised typescripts & corrected proofs of 7 poems, [c.1860s-1890s], 23 pp, various sizes, sold at S on 15 Dec 1988, lot 49, for £1,600.] £26,000
[A group of 7 autograph Mss, 6 sgd, c.1882 to 1888, 26 pp, bound together in a small notebook with related material, sold at CNY on 2 Feb 1988, lot 723, for $3000 to Neville.]
[An elaborate cut-out chromolithographed card, [n.d.], 16mo, sgd Bettit & inscr to his cousin Jessie on verso, in half red mor gilt slipcase, sold at CNY on 2 Feb 1988, lot 714, for $600.]
Autograph Ms, autobiographical essay, My First Book, 3 to 20 June 1893. 7 pp, 4to, on rectos only, each sheet composed of 2 8vo sheets pasted together. With numerous revisions. In folder with autograph label. Kauffman collection. (88) $2,200
— Autograph Ms, part of review of John Ruskin, The Queen of the Air, 1869. 4 pp, 8vo, on rectos only. Working draft; unfinished. Doheny collection. (88) $1,100
— Autograph Ms, poem, Por El Rey. (Northern Mexico) 1640; [n.d.]. 13 pp, 4to, on rectos only. 177 lines, sgd. In bright green crushed levant mor gilt by Riviere & Son. Doheny collection. (88) $2,500
— Autograph Ms, story, Ashore at Del Norte, [1890s]. Doheny collection. (88) $1,000

HARTE

— Autograph Ms, story, My Experiences as a Gold Digger, [pbd as How I Went to the Mines, 1900]. Sgd & dated 18-25 Nov 1897 on wrap. 9 pp, 4to, on rectos only. With partial typescript with autograph corrections, 7 pp, 4to. In blue folding case. Doheny collection. (88) $18,000

— Autograph Ms, story, Peter Atherly's Kindred, ptd as The Ancestors of Peter Atherly, 1898. 25 pp, 4to, on rectos only. With numerous revisions; sgd. In red mor folding case. Doheny collection. (88) $2,500

— Autograph Ms, story, The Ghosts of Stukely Castle, [pbd 1892]. 11 pp, 4to (each 2 8vo sheets pasted together). With many corrections & revisions; sgd. In mor folding case. Doheny collection. (88) $1,500

— Autograph Ms, story, The Youngest Prospector in Calaveras, sgd & dated 20 Aug 1896. 13 pp, 4to (each 2 8vo sheets pasted together), on rectos only. In cloth folding case. Doheny collection. (88) $4,000

— Autograph Ms, working draft of The Heir of the McHulishes. [c.1894] 39 leaves, 225mm by 174mm, in mor by Wallis. (91) $2,500

Typescript, story, Chu Chu, sgd, [c.1894]. 27 pp, 4to. With copious autograph revisions. (89) £1,200

— Typescript, story, Johnson's Old Woman, sgd, [c.1890-92]. 17 pp, 4to. With copious autograph revisions. Ptr's copy. (89) £1,200

— Typescript, story, Out of a Pioneer's Trunk, [c.1890-92]. (89) £800

— Typescript, story, The Bell Ringer of Angel's, fragment; [c.1890s?]. (89) £400

Collection of 2 A Ls s & photograph, sgd & inscr, [n.d.], 19 July 1887 & June [18]73. Doheny collection. (88) $700

— Collection of ALs & Ds, 22 Aug 1897 & 22 Sept 1863. Kauffman collection. (88) $420

Series of 20 A Ls s, 1871 to 1891. 54 pp, various sizes, each with typed transcription & tipped to leaf of brown mor album. To his sister Eliza (16), his son Griswold (2) & others. Mentioning his travels, his duties as US consul, family affairs, etc. Kauffman collection. (88) $6,000

— Series of 3 A Ls s, 19 Mar 1892, 16 May 1897, & [n.d.]. Kauffman collection. (88) $550

ALs, [1869?]. 8 pp, 8vo. To Ralph Keeler. Discussing Keeler's novel. Sgd F.B.H. In half red mor gilt bdg. Doheny collection. (88) $1,400

— 5 Mar 1871. 6 pp, 8vo. To Ambrose Bierce. Reporting about his reception & financial success in the East. With transcript. Doheny collection. (88) $4,500

— 28 Nov [18]84. (91) $150

— 7 July 1892. (91) $95

— [n.d.], "Sunday". (91) $85

Signature, [n.d.]. (91) $200

Hartford, George H., 1833-1917
Ds, 27 June 1916. (89) $110

Hartmann, Karl Amadeus, 1905-63
Series of 3 Ls s, 10 to 24 Aug 1961. (91) DM950

Hartrick, Archibald Standish, 1864-1950
Original drawings, (34), to illus Rudyard Kipling's Soldier Tales, 1896. Macmillan Archives. (90) £700

Harvey, William, 1578-1657
Ds, 4 Apr [1637]. 1 p, folio. Order to the Exchequer to pay for medicines for servants of the Royal household. Repaired. (88) $11,000

Haslinger, Tobias, 1787-1842
— ALTIERI, CARDINAL LUIGI. - Ls, 27 Sept 1839. 2 pp, 4to. Conferring a Papal decoration on Haslinger. With related material. (88) DM600

Haspinger, Joachim, 1776-1858
Autograph Ms, Curriculum vitae, 25 June 1835. 2 pp, folio. Sgd. Margin torn. (88) DM1,200

Hassall, Joan
Original drawings, (29), to illus Richard Church's Calling for a Spade, 1939. In ink. Mostly monogrammed. Various sizes. Archives of J. M. Dent & Son. (88) £1,200

Hassall, John
Original drawings, (107), to illus different books of nursery rhymes, [n.d.]. Various sizes. In ink; mostly sgd. (89) £1,150
— Original drawings, (52), to illus Swiss Family Robinson, [n.d.]. Mostly 290mm by 230mm, on 41 sheets. In ink; mostly sgd. With related material. (89) £1,700
— Original drawings, (6), to illus different books of nursery rhymes, [c.1905]. 400mm by 305mm. In ink & watercolor; sgd. (89) £1,500

Hassam, Frederick Childe, 1859-1935
ALs, 29 Jan 1908. (89) $225

Hassell, Ulrich von, 1881-1944
ALs, 6 Sept 1939. 3 pp, 4to. To Dora Sahm. Thanking for her hospitality in Oslo. (91) DM1,100

Hassenpflug, Hans Daniel, 1794-1862
Collection of Ls & Ms, sgd, 24 July & 16 Oct 1832. (89) DM220

Hastie, James, 1786-1826. See: Madagascar

Hastings, Warren, 1732-1818
Autograph Ms, notes in a def interleaved copy of James Steuart, The Principle of Money Applied to the Present State of the Coin in Bengal, 1772. Also containing notes by anr. (89) £3,500
ALs, 9 Sept 1800. (90) DM750
Ds, 23 Dec 1778. (90) $150

Hauer, Josef, 1883-1959
Autograph music, cantata, Der Menschen Weg, Op. 67, baritone solo from the 1st part, 20 Sept 1934. 1 p, 4to. Sgd at head & at end. (91) DM3,700
ALs, 2 June 1920. (91) £950

Hauff, Wilhelm, 1802-27
ALs, 16 July [June] 1826. 2 pp, 4to. To K. G. Th. Winkler. Sending an article for the Abendzeitung about Henriette Sontag's debut in Paris. (90) DM11,000

Haug, Friedrich, 1761-1829
[A collection of 5 autograph Mss, poems (2 initialled), 5 pp, 12mo & 16mo, dedicated to Emilie Zumsteeg, sold at star on 30 Nov 1988, lot 162, for DM740.]
Autograph Ms, poem, Fluechtigkeit des Lebens; [n.d.]. (90) DM550
ALs, 23 July 1808. (89) DM320

Hauptmann, Gerhart, 1862-1946
Autograph Ms, poem expressing thanks for congratulations on his birthday, addressed to Oswald von Hoyningen-Huene, [Nov 1940]. (91) DM440
A Ls s (2), [6 Jan 1900] & 2 Aug 1891. (89) DM260
ALs, 9 Sept 1887. (89) DM750
— 18 Sept 1899. (88) DM340
— 12 Dec 1899. (89) DM300
— 25 Jan 1908. (90) DM550
Ls, [6 Mar 1901]. (90) DM400
— 5 Apr 1908. (90) DM320
— 23 June 1914. (88) DM210
— 10 Dec 1928. (88) DM210
— 15 Jan 1941. (91) DM320
Photograph, sgd & inscr, Oct 1935. (90) DM320
— Anr, 1942. (90) DM650

Hauser, Kaspar, c.1812-33
[An autograph address leaf, 6 Dec 1831, 8vo, addressed to Professor Daumer, with attestation by Daumer, sold at star on 5 Apr 1991, lot 1475, for DM1,400.]
Autograph Ms, language exercises, Saetze mit Bindewoerter...; [1832]. 2 pp, 4to. Some corrections in anr hand. (90) DM2,000

Hausmann, Manfred, 1898-1986
Autograph Ms, essay about Oswald Spengler for his Im Spiegel der Erinnerung, 1st draft, [1974]. (88) DM210
— Autograph Ms, essay, Oswald Spengler, [n.d.]. (90) DM480
— Autograph Ms, sketches for his eaasy Wohin gehen wir?, 3 Oct 1965. (91) DM300
Autograph transcript, poem, Ende und Anfang. (89) DM370

HAWKER

Hawker, H. G. —& MacKenzie-Grieve, K. M.
Menu, for congratulatory luncheon at the Savoy Hotel; 30 May 1919. (90) $500

Hawkins, Sir Anthony Hope, 1863-1933
Autograph Ms, A Stage on the Road, sgd; [1890s?]. (89) $750

Hawkins, Sir John, 1719-89
Ls, 16 Feb 1782. (89) £350

Hawksmoor, Nicholas, 1661-1736
ALs, 14 Aug 1723. (88) £980

Hawthorne, Julian, 1846-1934
Autograph Ms (2), mystery story, Mrs. Doheny collection. (89) $950

Autograph Ms, article on Paris & the Paris Exposition, sgd & dated 18 Aug 1889. Doheny collection. (89) $500

— Autograph Ms, short story, Otto of Roses, [n.d.]. (89) £110

Hawthorne, Nathaniel, 1804-64
Autograph Ms, essay, Outside Glimpses of English Poverty, [ptd July 1863]. 35 pp, 4to, on 18 leaves; disbound. With autograph revisions. Ptr's copy. In quarter mor slipcase. John F. Fleming Estate. (89) $24,000

A Ls s (2), 10 Mar 1852 & 29 Dec [1855?]. 2 pp, 4to & 12mo. Recipients unknown. Sending his autograph, & acknowledging receipt of a watch-key. Doheny collection. (89) $1,300

ALs, 18 Apr [1843]. 1 p, 4to. To Zachariah Burchmore. About arranging a meeting. (91) $2,200

— 17 June 1846. 1 p, 4to. To Edgar Allan Poe. Suggesting that he review Hawthorne's latest book, & expressing reservations about Poe's critical writings. Martin collection. (90) $21,000

— 17 June 1856. (89) $350

Ds, 4 Nov 1853. (91) $425

— 14 May 1857. (90) $450

Hay, John Milton, 1838-1905
ALs, 12 Oct 1861. (88) $180

Franking signature, [11 Sept 1863]. (89) $110

— Anr, [27 Sept 1863]. Alexander collection. (90) $230

AMERICAN BOOK PRICES CURRENT

Haydn, Franz Joseph, 1732-1809
Autograph music, working Ms of the complete final chorus of the cantata Qual dubbio ormai, Hoboken XXXIVA, no 4; [Dec 1764]. 10 pp, folio; paginated 38 - 47. Notated in full score for 4-part chorus & orchestra. (91) £68,000

Transcript, oratorio, I ritorno di Tobia. (89) £780

ALs, 29 Mar [1]780. 1 p, 4to. To Artaria & Co. Expressing astonishment that the pbr Hummel in Berlin has received copies of his piano sonatas before he has. (91) £10,000

— 8 Apr 1784. 1 p, 4to. To his pbr Artaria. Asking him to deliver some songs to a lady. With postscript asking anr favor. Matted. (88) $8,500

— 16 Nov [1]788. 1 p, 4to. To the pbr Artaria. Thanking for arranging payment to Herr Schanz & promising 3 new sonatas. With a visiting card. (89) £10,000

— 19 Dec 1794. 1 p, 4to. To Giovanni Battista Viotti. Asking him to procure a ticket to hear the singer Brigida Banti. In Italian. With related material. (90) £11,000

— 24 July 1799. 1 p, 4to. To Franz Xaver Gloeggl. Thanking for subscribing to The Creation. (91) £12,000

— 10 Aug [1]799. 1 p, 4to. To [Karl Friedrich Moritz Paul von Bruehl?]. Thanking for subscribing to the publication of The Creation. Salzer collection. (90) £10,500

— 11 May [1]800. 1 p, 4to. To [J. J. Hummel?]. Acknowledging receipt of payment for the score of The Creation & reporting on progress on the score of The Seasons. (88) £10,000

Ds, 21 July 1801. 2 pp, 4to. Contract, ceding publication rights to his oratorio The Seasons to Breitkopf & Haertel. (90) DM38,000

— 26 May 1804. 1 p, 8vo. Receipt for 142 guilders from Breitkopf & Haertel [for an organ concerto, 2 arias & a sonata]. (91) DM15,000

Haydn, Franz Joseph, 1732-1809 —& Others
Ds, 5 Nov 1805. 1 p, folio. Attestation on behalf of the Vienna Tonkuenstler-Societaet, praising Joseph Mayseder as a violinist. Sgd by Haydn, Salieri, Albrechtsberger, & 3 others. (91) £14,000

Haydn, Michael, 1737-1806
Autograph music, Missa Sancti Gabrielis in C major, [n.d., written c.1758 to 1760]. Tp & 24 pp (16 autograph), 32cm by 21cm. Fair copy, scored for 4 voices, violin & organ. Tp in the hand of Marian Kaserer. (88) DM65,000
— Autograph music, Quartetto; a Violino, Corno Inglese, Violoncello, e Violone; [c.1795]. 2 p, folio. Opening 35 bars in score; sgd. (91) £5,000
ALs, 14 Mar 1803. 3 pp, 4to. To Georg Schinn. Expressing his gratitude for Schinn's "Abschiedskantate" but hoping to be able to stay in Salzburg. With Schinn's autograph musical Ms, Abschieds-Cantate, autograph poem by W. Rettensteiner, Abschiedslied, & Ms of Haydn's obsequies. Thorek collection. (88) DM20,000

Haydon, Benjamin Robert, 1786-1846
Collection of 3 A Ls s & AN, dates not stated. (88) £240
ALs, 22 July 1837. (91) £320

Hayes, Joseph
Typescript, novel, The Desperate Hours. (91) $275

Hayes, Lucy Webb, 1831-89. See: Hayes, Rutherford B. & Hayes

Hayes, Rutherford B., 1822-93
Series of 6 A Ls s, March 1870 to Aug 1873. 6 pp, 4to & 8vo. To his uncle Scott [Cook]. On genealogical matters pertaining to the Hayes & Cook families. (91) $1,100
— Series of 9 A Ls s, Dec 1870 to Sept 1876. 9 pp, 8vo. To his uncle Scott [Cook]. On varied personal matters. (91) $1,500
ALs, 4 May 1876. (90) $230
— 10 Aug 1876. (89) $400
— 26 May 1877. 2 pp, 4to. To Sec of the Treasury John Sherman. Regarding an investigation of the NY Customs House, & urging appointments on the basis of merit. Lower margins def. (89) $6,500
— 26 May 1877. (88) £700
— 11 July 1877. 1 p, 8vo. To Col. H. D. Shaw. Regarding a visit. (90) $1,200
— 14 Dec 1877. (91) $700
— 20 May 1878. Pratt collection. (89) $800
— 2 Aug 1880. Pratt collection. (89) $800
— 28 Aug 1883. Whiton collection. (88) $600
— 12 Dec 1883. (91) $275
— 7 Apr 1885. (89) $1,000
— 7 June 1885. (91) $325
— 3 July 1886. (91) $275
— 25 Aug 1886. (91) $300
— 26 Jan [18]89. (88) $375
— 15 Dec 1890. Rosenbloom collection. (88) $450
— Jan 1891. 1 p, 8vo. To Major George B. Davis. Responding to a request for official Civil War records in his possession. (89) $15,500
— Jan 1891. (90) $850
— 14 Apr 1892. (91) $325
Ls, 26 Jan 1880. (91) $150
ADs, 2 Apr 1866. (90) $250
Ds, 14 Aug 1855. (91) $110
— 27 Apr 1866. (90) $550
— 11 May 1877. (89) $275
— 14 June 1877. (88) $225
— 14 June 1877. (91) $170
— 23 June 1877. (89) $250
— 13 Nov 1877. (89) $310
— 6 Dec 1877. (89) $350
— 13 Dec 1877. (88) $200
— 28 June 1878. (91) $425
— 20 Dec 1878. (90) $180
— 1879. (91) $180
— 16 Jan 1880. (89) $250
— 5 Mar 1880. (90) $325
— 23 Sept 1880. (90) $300
— 6 Oct 1880. (89) £170
— 1 Feb 1881. (88) $180
— [n.d.]. (90) $140
Cut signature, [n.d.]. (91) $120
— Anr, [n.d.]. (91) $85
Executive Mansion card, sgd, [24 Apr 1880]. (91) $200
Photograph, sgd, 1886. Cabinet size. Bust

profile; by McKecknie & Oswald. (90) $1,200

Photograph, sgd & inscr, 21 Feb 1880. Cabinet size. Inscr to Thos. Donaldson. (90) $1,200

Signature, [n.d.]. (88) $70

— Anr, on ptd copy of his speech "at the Celebration of General Garfield's Election, Cleveland, Ohio", 4 Nov 1880. (91) $950

— Anr, 22 Mar 1884. (90) $110

— Anr, [n.d.]. (89) $95

Hayes, Rutherford B., 1822-93 —& Hayes, Lucy Webb, 1831-89

[Their signatures, 19 Apr 1881, 3.5 by 2 inches, sold at Dar on 2 Aug 1990, lot 205, for $100.]

Haymo, Bishop of Halberstadt

Ms, Commentarium in cantica canticorum. [Germany, 9th cent] 31 leaves, 175mm by 120mm, in early lea. In Carolingian miniscule in brown ink, on vellum. First leaf is from 11th cent with text of Missa de sancto Leonardo confesore. (90) $12,000

Hayne, Paul Hamilton, 1830-86

ALs, 21 June 1858. (91) $325

Hayward, Thomas, Signer from South Carolina

Ds, 27 Aug 1788. (90) $190

Haywood, Helen

Original drawings, (33), to illus British Wild Flowers, [n.d.]. (89) £850

Hayworth, Rita, 1918-87

Photograph, sgd & inscr, [n.d.]. (90) $280

Hayworth, Rita, 1918--1987. See: Welles, Orson & Hayworth

Hazard, Ebenezer, 1744-1817

ALs, 6 Apr 1781. (91) $225

— 19 Apr 1789. (91) $150

Hazlitt, William, 1778-1830

Autograph Ms, discussion of "Wit", [c.1820]. (88) $225

ALs, [20 Oct 1793]. (91) £850

Heaney, Seamus

Autograph Ms, poem, Remembering Malibu, drafts, [n.d.]. With 4 corrected typescripts & a carbon copy. Together 9 pp, folio & 4to. With a corrected typescript of an early version of A Drink of Water. (88) £2,400

Proof copy, Wintering Out [c.1972], & North [c.1975]. (88) £150

Hearn, Lafcadio, 1850-1904

[A collection of 33 photographs taken in Martinique & the Caribbean, [c.1887-88], various sizes, mostly captioned by Hearn, some initialled, sold at CNY on 8 Dec 1989, lot 227, for $3,900.]

Autograph Ms, article, After the War, sgd & dated 3 June 1895. 58 pp, 8vo, on rectos only. Speculating on Japan's military future. Including autograph tp. In mor slipcase. (90) $40,000

— Autograph Ms, essay about Japanese songs & poems, Out of the Street, sgd; 5 June 1896. 51 pp, 8vo., in red mor solander case gilt. Including ptr's marks. Martin collection. (90) $35,000

— Autograph Ms, short story, Illusion!, fair copy, sgd; [n.d.]. 3 pp, 4to. Supposedly unpbd. With 2 others. Martin collection. (90) $7,500

Collection of 25 A Ls s & A Ls, [16 June 1876] to 23 May 1896. About 130 pp, various sizes, in maroon buckram gilt. Mostly to Henry Watkin. Covering a wide range of personal & professional issues. Including 15 drawings. With related material. Martin collection. (90) $85,000

— Collection of ALs & ANs, [c.1891? & n.d.]. 3 pp, 8vo. To Elizabeth Bisland, lamenting his financial difficulties. To "Dear old Dad", stating that it is "soon going to take flight", with a drawing of a bird. Martin collection. (90) $4,250

Series of 18 A Ls s, [1887] to 23 Aug 1903 & [n.d.]. 93 pp, 12mo & 8vo, in half mor slipcase. To Elizabeth Bisland (Wetmore). Personal & literary correspondence, about his travels, etc. (90) $80,000

— Series of 6 A Ls s, [c.7 May 1889] to 13 July 1892. 18 pp, 8vo. To Joseph Tunison. Reporting about his travels.

In half mor bdg with related material. Martin collection. (90) $24,000
ALs, 2 May 1898. (91) $500
— [n.d.]. Doheny collection. (88) $900

Hearst, William Randolph, 1863-1951
Ls, 31 July 1923. 2 pp, 4to. To Herman Bernstein. Clarifying various interviews. (91) $1,100

Heath, William, 1737-1814
Ls, 28 Jan 1782. (90) $275
Ds, 23 Mar 1778. (91) $225
— 3 Apr 1778. (89) $100

Heath-Stubbs, John
[A collection of working papers for Artorius, The Labours of Artorius, & Palimpsest, [n.d.], c.100 pp, folio & 4to, partly autograph (28 pp), partly typescripts corrected in anr hand, sold at S on 15 Dec, lot 157, for £520.]

Hebbel, Christine, 1817-1910
ALs, 15 June 1834. (90) DM460

Hebbel, Friedrich, 1813-63
Autograph Ms, essay about the Austrian constitution, [1861]. 3 pp, 8vo. Including corrections. (91) DM3,600
— Autograph Ms, poem, Einem Freunde. 3 four-line stanzas, [n.d.]. Sgd. Cut from a larger sheet. With related material. (89) DM2,800
ALs, 1 Dec 1857. (90) DM950
— 5 May 1862. 2 pp, 8vo. To [Adolph Stern]. Thanking for a review of his Nibelungen & wondering whether his letter of 22 Mar has been received. (88) DM1,700

Hebel, Johann Peter, 1760-1826
ALs, 20 Feb 1806. 2 pp, 4to. To Ehrenfried Stoeber. Thanking for a copy of his almanach. (91) DM8,000

Hebra, Ferdinand von, 1816-80
ALs, 19 Sept [n.y.]. (91) DM700

Hebrew Manuscripts
Ms, Bible, comprising the Pentateuch, Greater & Minor Prophets, & Hagiographa, with the Masora Magna & Minora. [Iraq or Syria, perhaps Babylon, 9th or 10th cent]. 396 leaves (some lacking at each end), vellum, 352mm by 300mm, in modern brown mor. In dark brown ink in a large handsome oriental square Hebrew script with nikud, Masora Magna & Minora in very small unpointed square script. Repaired. One of the earliest Hebrew biblical Mss in book form. Sassoon Ms 1053. (90) £1,850,000
— Ms, Bible. [Germany, c.1100]. Bifolium, vellum, 344mm by 430mm. In a large formal Hebrew script. 1 leaf def; recovered from a bdg. (91) £1,300
— Ms, Bible. [Iraq or Syria, Babylon?, 9th or 10th cent]. 4 leaves, vellum, 387mm by 345mm. In dark brown ink in a large oriental square Hebrew script, with Masoretic rubrics in margins. (91) £13,000
— Ms, Bible. [Spain, c.1300]. Single leaf, vellum, 403mm by 278mm. In micrographic script shaped to form illusts of sacred vessels within elaborate borders of formal interlaced patterns within frames all formed of the Masoretic introduction to the Bible; verso blank. Recovered from a bdg. (91) £1,700
— Ms, Bible (The Rashba Bible). [Cervera, Spain, Sept 1383]. 476 leaves, vellum, 286mm by 220mm, in early 19th-cent red mor bdg. In dark brown ink in a regular elegant Spanish square Hebrew script with nikud, with Masora Magna & Minora in very small script. With 48 large illuminated initials, 54 illuminated floral borders, 36 column-width illuminated headpieces, 2 pages with elaborate micrographic borders with animals & flowers formed of minute script, 12 full-page illuminations of arcades, & 2 full-page miniatures. Written & illuminated for Ibn Astruc by the scribe Vidal ben Shaul Sartori. Sassoon Ms 16. (90) £750,000
— Ms, Bible, with commentary of Rashi & portions of the Haftoroth; [Germany, c.1200]. (91) £750
— Ms, Bible, with Targum-Onkelos & Masora; [Germany, c.1300]. (91) £650
— Ms, contents not stated. [15th cent]. Single leaf, vellum, 340mm by 22mm. Written in 3 columns on recto & verso. Recovered from a bdg. (89) DM1,100
— Ms, Haggadah. Meseritch, Moravia, 1730. In the hand of Nathan ben Shimson of Meseritch. 30 leaves, in

Hebrew & Yiddish block & cursive scripts, 295cm by 190cm, on vellum, in contemp calf gilt. Each leaf framed in gold; with fully illuminated tp, 6 half-page illusts & 36 miniatures. (91) $65,000
- Ms, Haggadah. Vienna, 1717. In the hand of Aryeh Juda Loeb ben Elhanan Katz of Trebitsch. 23 leaves, vellum, 190mm by 115mm, in contemp vellum tooled in silver & dated 1717 with owner's initials of Abraham Ulm. With fully illuminated tp & 44 vignettes framed in gold & executed in grisaille. (91) $70,000
- Ms, Ketubah. (90) $650
- Ms, Likutei Shirim. (90) $750
- Ms, Machzor Rome. [Pesaro, Apr 1480]. 421 leaves & blanks, vellum, 182mm by 125mm, in extra early 18th-cent Italian red mor. In dark brown ink in an elegant Italian square Hebrew & semi-cursive script. Illuminated throughout, with c.425 full-length bar borders & 23 three-quarter borders in designs of colored leaves & flowers sometimes including putti, & 12 full historiated borders. Written for Elijah ben Shlomo by the scribe Abraham ben Matatiah. Sassoon Ms 23. (90) £460,000
- Ms, Machzor. [Venice, c.1750]. Length not stated, 8vo. In a fine 18th-cent Italian-Jewish silver bdg. Lacking 3 leaves. (89) £5,500
- Ms, Megillah Esther, [late 18th cent]. Scroll of 3 vellum membranes (1 loose), c.600mm by 2670mm. (90) DM2,000
- Ms, Megillah Esther, [n.d.]. Scroll of 3 leaves stitched together, c.255mm by 1695mm. (90) DM1,200
- Ms, Megillah Esther, chapters 1:1 - 9:9 only; [n.d.]. (90) DM800
- Ms, Megillah Esther. [Amst., c,1659] 3 vellum membranes joined, 13cm by 213cm, in sq Sephardic script in sepia ink. The whole preceded by a cartouche borne by angels with trumptets; each column within an elaborately engraved arch, surmounted by an urn with flowers flanked by palm-bearing women in classical dress, the arches bedecked with flowers & foliate swags, each with a cartouche containing a landscape, the space between each major arch decorated with smaller floral arches, in which are situated various characters from the Book of Esther. (91) $45,000
- Ms, Megillah Esther. (90) $450
- Ms, Megillah Esther. (90) $350
- Ms, Seder Birchat Ha'mazon im Birchot Ha'nehenin Ve'im Tikunei Kriat Shma Al Ha'mitah. [Germany, 1728]. 21 leaves, vellum, 95mm by 71mm. Orig green velvet bdg. In Ashkenazi square Hebrew script with nikud. With 29 miniatures. (89) £40,000
- Ms, Seder Ha'mizmorim Mi'kol Ha'shanah. [Germany, 1760]. 15 leaves, 85mm by 62mm, in contemp green mor gilt. In sepia ink in a beautiful square Ashkenazi script with nikud by Levi Offenbach; decorated. (89) £2,500
- Ms, Seder Shirin Vetushbechan. (91) $220
- Ms, Seguloth Urephu'oth. [Poland, 18th cent] 27 pp, 145mm by 190mm, in modern half calf. In an Aschkenazic cursive script in black ink. (90) $3,600
- Ms, Seguloth Urephu'oth. [Italy, 17th cent] 48 leaves, in Italian cursive Hebrew with occasional use of "Angelic script," 105mm by 164mm, in contemp bds with later lea folding pouch. Collection of medical folk remedies & mystical prescriptions. (91) $3,000
- Ms, Sepher Leket Ya'akov. (91) $400
- Ms, Torah. [Europe, 18th or 19th cent]. Scroll on vellum, 57cm by 4315cm, on 2 wooden rollers; lacking handles. (91) DM5,800
- Ms, Torah. [Europe, 18th cent]. Scroll on vellum, 31cm by 1720cm, on 2 wooden rollers. Incomplete at beginning. (91) DM2,200
- Ms, Torah, Ketubim & Haftoroth (Pentateuch, Hagiographia & Haftoroth) [Seville, May 1468]. 436 leaves, vellum, 209mm by 156mm, in 19th-cent red mor bdg. In dark brown ink in a neat square Spanish Hebrew script with nikud. With the Masora throughout in a wide range of elaborate micrographic designs & pictures, 15 ornamental headpieces & 12 illumi-

nated carpet pages. Written for Abraham Siman Tov by the scribe Moshe ben Joseph. Sassoon Ms 487. (90) £240,000

— AVICENNA. - Ms, Canon. [Spain, 14th cent]. 17 fragments, 312mm by 212mm & smaller. In different sizes of Hebrew script. Presumably recovered from a bdg. (91) £1,100

— JOEL BAAL SHEM TOV & NAPHTALI KATZ. - Sepher Seguloth Murpheles Elokim. Ivachschatz, [c.1839]. 25 leaves, 110mm by 140mm, disbound. In Judeo-German written in Ashkenazi cursive script. (91) $3,200

— YITZHAK BEN ABBAMARE. - Sefer Ha'itur. [Southern France, late 13th cent]. 10 leaves only, vellum, 390mm by 240mm. In a rabbinic cursive, with some parts in Hebrew square script. Fragment from part 2. (91) £3,500

Hecht, Anthony
Autograph transcript, poem, Fifth Avenue Parade. (89) $60

Hecht, Ben, 1894-1964
Collection of 2 A Ns s & 5 Ns s, 1937 to 1953. (89) $400

Heckel, Erich, 1883-1970
Collection of ALs, autograph postcard, sgd, & postcard, sgd, with autograph postscript, 12 Feb 1946 to 18 Aug 1948. (88) DM320

— Collection of ALs, Ls, photograph, sgd & inscr, & picture card, sgd & inscr, 5 Jan 1952 to 1964. (88) DM400

— Collection of ALs & 2 postcards, sgd (1 autograph), [1952] & 9 Aug 1953. (90) DM550

ALs, 12 Apr 1925. (88) DM210

— 24 Sept 1927. (89) DM440

— 10 July 1944. (89) DM400

— 2 Feb 1947. (90) DM400

Hedin, Sven, 1865-1952
Collection of 2 A Ls s & ANs, 3 Dec 1931, 26 June 1932 & [n.d.]. (89) DM230

ALs, 31 Jan 1933. (91) DM300

Photograph, sgd & inscr, [n.d.]. (90) DM550

Heer, Oswald, 1809-83
Series of 6 A Ls s, 9 Nov 1877 to 2 Jan 1882. (88) DM580

Hegel, Georg Wilhelm Friedrich, 1770-1831
ALs, 3 Dec 1802. (89) £800

— 11 Sept 1818. 3 pp, 8vo. To Friedrich Frommann. Accepting his invitation to visit on his way to Berlin. Albrecht collection. (91) SF7,500

— 18 June 1827. 1 p, folio. To Freiherr von Altenstein. Asking for a date to submit a request. (91) DM4,200

— 1 Aug 1827. 1 p, 8vo. To "Herr Secretaer". Informing him that tickets have been arranged & urging him to visit. (89) £2,800

— 9 Aug 1829. 3 pp, 4to. To Philipp Guido von Meyer. Requesting him to talk to the bookseller Wesche about a new Ed of his Phaenomenologie des Geistes. (90) DM9,500

ANs, 3 Mar 1829. 1 p, 8vo. To [his students]. Stating that he will not be able to lecture. (91) DM1,100

ADs, 15 Nov 1824. 1 p, 12mo. Ticket of admission to his lectures for Candidat Heise. (90) DM1,600

— 1 Nov 1827. (89) DM520

Ds s (2)15 & 18 Mar 1830. 2 pp, folio. Certificates of good conduct & of studies for K. H. F. Hahn. 1 sgd as rector of the university at Berlin; 1 countersgd as government official. (89) DM2,200

Ds, 21 Oct 1830. 1 p, folio. Certificate of good conduct for Erich Gottlieb Neumann. (91) DM1,100

Heidegger, Johann Heinrich, 1738-1823
ALs, 28 Jan 1797. (89) DM650
See also: Gessner, Salomon

Heidegger, Martin, 1889-1976
Original drawing, sketch of Freiburg showing the way from the station to Reichsgrafenstrasse, [Spring 1946]. (90) DM260

Collection of 2 A Ls s & Ls, 16 July to 12 Aug 1935. 3 pp, 4to. To the district court at Bruchsal. Statements in a law case regarding support for 2 children. With related documents. (90) DM1,300

HEIDEGGER

— Collection of ALs & autograph postcard, sgd, 20 & 26 Oct 1937. (89) DM900
ALs, 10 Jan 1944. (88) DM440
— 7 May 1948. (88) DM660
Signature, [n.d.]. (89) DM230

Heiller, Anton, 1923-79
Autograph music, "Skizzenblatt aus dem 1953 komponierten Te Deum", later sgd, inscr & dated 12 Dec [19]77. (90) DM450

Heine, Heinrich, 1797-1856
Autograph Ms, Der Tannhaeuser -- Eine Legende, 3 stanzas of revised version [Apr 1838]. 2 pp, 8vo. With autograph corrections of & additions to the poem on a proof sheet (pp 265 - 279) of Der Salon, vol 3 [1837]. (89) DM22,000
— Autograph Ms, draft of 4 stanzas for chapter 26 of his epic poem Atta Troll, [1841/42]. 1 p, 4to. Heavily revised. (91) DM12,500
— Autograph Ms, draft of the preface of his Gestaendnisse, [1854]. 1 p, folio. Including revisions. (91) DM13,000
— Autograph Ms, poem, Bei des Nachtwaechters Ankunft zu Paris, 4th stanza only, beginning "Der Dom zu Collen wird vollendet"; [Winter 1841/42]. Repaired. (89) DM2,200
— Autograph Ms, poem, Nachtgedanken, [1843]. 3 pp, folio. 10 stanzas, numbered XXIV at head. Orig title Heimweh deleted. (89) £42,000
ALs, [23] May 1823. 4 pp, 4to. To Moses Moser. Important letter to a friend about his journey to Lueneburg, his identity as a Jewish author, etc. (90) DM42,000
— 14 Feb 1826. 2 pp, folio. To Moses Moser. Concerning the publication of Die Harzreise & the behavior of their friend Cohn. (89) £7,000
— 10 May 1827. 1 p, 8vo. To Mme Moscheles. Apologizing for being unable to dine with them. (89) £4,000
— 19 Nov 1843. 3 pp, folio. To [his wife Mathilde]. Asking her to purchase hats for his sister & niece. In French. (89) £7,000
— 17 May 1848. 1 p, 8vo. To Alexandre Gouin. Asking for payment of 500 francs promised by Giacomo Meyerbeer. In French. Endorsed by recipient. (90) DM9,500
— [28 May 1848]. 1 p, 8vo. To Alexander Weil. Informing him of his change of address & commenting about his health. In German, with French subscription. (89) $4,250
— 6 July 1852. 1 p, 4to. To his banker Homberg. Requesting him to send 1,000 francs. In German. (88) $2,100
Ls, 6 Nov 1851. 1 p, 4to. To his niece Anna Embden. Sending money for a present. (90) DM6,500
— 29 Dec 1852. 2 pp, 4to. To his mother Betty Heine & his sister Charlotte Embden. Chatty family letter. Sgd Harry Heine. (88) DM17,000
ANs, "Thursday morning" [c.Jan/Feb 1834]. 1 p, 8vo. To the Princess Belgiojoso. In 3d person, accepting an invitation to the theater. In French. (89) DM2,400
Autograph quotation, 4 lines from the Iliad, 28 Aug 1826. 1 p, 8vo. Sgd & inscr. Some notes in anr hand at foot. (91) DM18,000
— SELDEN, CAMILLE, PSEUD. OF ELISE KRINITZ. - ALs, 27 Jan 1884. 3 pp, 8vo. Recipient unnamed. Saying E. Rostand "se cache sous un pseudonyme". (91) DM600
See also: Beer, Michael

Heine, Thomas Theodor, 1867-1948
Series of 8 A Ls s, 6 June 1906 to 24 Dec 1907 & [n.d.]. (90) DM750
ALs, 20 Apr 1903. 2 pp, 4to. To Albert Langen. Discussing the political implications of the pardoning of Langen by the King of Saxony. (89) DM1,100

Heinefetter, Sabine, 1809-72
ALs, 21 Nov 1828. (90) DM320

Heinrich, Prince of Prussia, 1726-1802
ALs, 24 July 1777. Albrecht collection. (91) SF800
— 2 Feb 1784. (88) DM550
— 26 Dec 1785. Schroeder collection. (89) DM550
— [n.d.]. (90) DM800
Ls, 27 Oct 1766. (89) DM220
— 16 Mar 1779. (90) DM420

Heinrich, Prince of Prussia, 1862-1929
ALs, 3 Jan 1888. (90) DM350
Series of 3 Ls s, 18 Aug to 29 Dec 1919. 5 pp, 4to. To Gen. von Schwerin. Discussing the political situation in Germany. With anr, 1922. (90) DM1,400
Ls, 11 Dec 1922. (89) DM280

Heinrich III, Landgraf von Hessen, 1441-83
Document, 3 Mar 1471. (89) DM400

Heinse, Wilhelm, 1746-1803
ALs, 17 Apr 1774. 8 pp, 8vo. To Klamer Schmidt. About his departure from Halberstadt, his journey to Celle, Goethe's satirical essay about Wieland, etc. Albrecht collection. (91) SF9,000

Heinsius, Anthonie, 1641-1720
ALs, 4 Jan 1695. 4 pp, 4to. To [Eugene of Savoy]. Worrying about insufficient preparations for the war with France. (90) DM1,800

Heiseler, Bernt von, 1907-69
A Ls s (2), [16 May] & 5 June 1948. (88) DM220

Heisenberg, Werner, 1901-76
ALs, 4 Dec 1933. 3 pp, 4to. To the Ed of the D[eutsche] A[llgemeine] Z[eitung]. Requesting correction of their report about his alledged acceptance of a lectureship at Cambridge. (89) DM2,000
— 3 Apr 1962. (90) DM340

Heller, Stephen, 1813-88
Series of 34 A Ls s, 1843 to 1876. 73 pp, various sizes. To the pbr Heinrich Schlesinger. About the publication of his music, payments, titles, etc. With related material. (88) £1,300

Hellman, Lillian, 1905-84. See: Bernstein, Leonard & Hellman

Hellmesberger, Joseph, 1855-1907. See: Mahler, Gustav

Helmholtz, Hermann von, 1821-94
ALs, 13 Jan 1871. 4 pp, 8vo. To William Thierry Preyer. About their research on colors. (91) DM1,600
— 14 June 1873. (91) DM650
— 9 Mar 1880. (90) DM580
Photograph, sgd, [1881]. (91) DM360

Helvetius, Johann Friedrich, d.1709
Ms, Le veau dor que le monde adore... (91) DM800

Hemans, Felicia, 1793-1835
Autograph Ms, poem, Woman and Fame; [n.d.]. (91) £50

Hemingway, Ernest, 1899-1961
[A group of 120 photographs of & relating to Hemingway fishing in the Gulf of Mexico in the Summer of 1934, some captioned by Arnold Samuelson, sold at CNY on 20 May 1988, lot 246, for $1,000.]
Autograph Ms, list of 16 books a writer should have read, sgd, [Apr 1934]. 1 p, 4to. In pencil. (88) $7,000
Typescript carbon copy, log of his boat Pilar, 28 July 1934 to 2 Feb 1935. 95 pp, 4to. Typescript copy by Arnold Samuelson of handwritten log dictated by Hemingway to Samuelson. Some pages def. In cloth folding case with typed transcript. (88) $2,700
Collection of 2 A Ls s, 2 Ls s, & telegram, 6 Mar to 1 July 1952. 8 pp, 4to & 8vo. To Philip Young. Illustrating the controversy over the publication of Young's book about Hemingway. (90) $15,000
Series of 3 A Ls s, 29 Nov [19]56 to 24 May 1957. 8 pp, 4to. To Gianfranco Ivancich. Complaining about his publishers, describing his health problems, a trip to Spain, etc. Sgd Papa. On airmail paper. (88) £2,700
ALs, 27 Jan 1929. 2 pp, 4to. To Miss Sillcox. Responding to his election to the Authors' League. (91) $1,200
— [Oct 1929]. 1 p, 4to. To Charles & Lorine Thompson. Rejoicing about the success of [A Farewell to Arms] & planning to buy a boat. Gaiser collection. (89) $3,200
— [c.14 June 1930]. 1 p, 8vo. To [Charles Thompson]. On a train going to NY, about a variety of matters. Gaiser collection. (89) $1,900
— 19 Aug [1932?]. 2 pp, folio. To Charles Thompson. Describing a hunting & fishing trip to Wyoming. Fold tear. Gaiser collection. (89) $1,900
— [early 1930s]. Gaiser collection. (89) $380

HEMINGWAY

— [March 1934]. 1 p, 8vo. To Charles Thompson. Sending photographs from their safari. Gaiser collection. (89) $1,500
— 7 Sept [1934]. 2 pp, 12mo. To Arnold Samuelson. Giving instructions regarding the log of the Pilar. On hotel letterhead. (88) $1,200
— 31 July 1935. 2 pp, 4to. To Arnold Samuelson. Reporting about his summer in Bimini & expecting his book to come out in Oct. In pencil. (88) $1,800
— 28 Feb 1953. 3 pp, 4to, on rectos only. To Charles Poore. Commenting on Philip Young's book & Poore's review. In gray-black & blue ink. Paginated 2 - 4 by Hemingway, but complete. On Finca Vigia letterhead. Blank bottom half of 3d sheet cut away. (88) $3,200
Collection of Ls & Ds, 10 Mar 1930 & [n.d.]. 11 pp, 4to. To his daughter Carol. Informing her of a trust agreement (included, also sgd by Pauline Pfeiffer Hemingway). (91) $3,500
— Collection of 1 Ls & 2 telegrams, 1940. (91) $750
Ls, 26 Feb 1935. 1 p, 4to. To Arnold Samuelson. Chatting about some Mss, his boat, & plans to go to Bimini. (88) $1,500
— 6 Feb [1936]. 1 p, 4to. To Arnold Samuelson. About his boat, fishing, his work on a new book, & his hangover. (88) $1,300
— [7 Feb 1940]. 1 p, 4to. To Arnold Samuelson. Referring to his work on a new novel. Sgd in pencil. Fold tears. (88) $1,200
— 24 Apr 1942. 1 p, 4to. To Arnold Samuelson. Chatting about his family & improvements to his boat. (88) $1,600
— [19 May 1942]. 1 p, 4to. To Charles Thompson. About recipient's visit, fishing supplies, family news, etc. Sgd in pencil. Gaiser collection. (89) $3,000
— 26 May 1945. 1 p, folio. To Charles & Lorine Thompson. Chatting about the end of the war, a hurricane, fishing, etc. Gaiser collection. (89) $2,500
— 27 July 1949. 1 p, 4to. To his brother Leicester. About Irwin Shaw, who should be allowed to "fall of his own weight." (91) $2,800
— 23 Feb 1953. 1 p, 4to. To Charles Poore. Regarding a deadline for a book, & about critics, his work, Bill Faulkner & God. On personal letterhead. Bottom edge cut away by Hemingway. Tipped to 4to sheet. (88) $2,500
— 11 Mar [n.y.]. 1 p. To Walter Winchell. About his writings & about Cuba. (91) $6,000
Autograph postcard, sgd, [postmarked 5 Apr 1917]. 1 p, oblong 12mo. To his father. Sending news from a canoe trip. (91) $2,200
— 14 July [1929]. To Charles Thompson. About bull fights at Pamplona & their holidays in Spain. Gaiser collection. (89) $2,500
ANs, Dec 1925. (91) $800
— [Summer 1934]. (88) $750
Autograph sentiment, 27 Feb [19]56. (91) $750
Corrected galley proof, The Old Man & the Sea. Inscr "Okay to print E.H." Inscr to Phil Harris & with related material. (90) $15,000
Photograph, sgd & inscr, [c.1930s]. (91) $600
— Anr, [1935]. Photograph of Hemingway & Tom Heeney posing with 3 trophy marlin, the largest badly eaten by sharks. Inscr to Heeney by Hemingway. (91) $3,750
— SAMUELSON, ARNOLD. - Typescript, unfinished story about fishing in the Gulf with Hemingway, [c.June 1934]; 14 pp, 4to. Extensively revised by Hemingway, in pencil. (88) $5,000

Hemingway, Ernest, 1899-1961 —& Others

Ds, 2 Mar 1956. 2 pp, 4to. Amendment to orig distribution & financing agreements for The Old Man and the Sea; carbon copy sgd by Hemingway, Leland Hayward, Spencer Tracy, & Fred Zinnemann. (91) $3,500

Hemingway, Ernest, 1899-1961 —& Kennedy, John F., 1917-63

[A letter, sgd by a secretary, from Kennedy to Hemingway, 26 July 1955, 1 p, 4to, concerning Hemingway's definition of courage quoted in Kennedy's Profiles in Courage, & Hemingway's autograph draft reply, 17

Aug 1955, 1 p, 4to, sgd three times, twice EH, with comments about Senator McCarthy, etc., sold at P on 23 Oct, lot 13, for $13,000.]

Henckel von Donnersmarck, Viktor Amadeus, Graf, 1727-93
[A collection of 8 letters addressed to him, 1754 to 1788, sold at star on 10 Mar 1988, lot 1438, for DM480.]

Henckell, Karl, 1864-1929
ALs, 29 Nov 1914. (89) DM320

Henderson, Keith
Original drawings, to illus Stuart Piggott's Scotland before History, [n.d.]. (89) £60

Original drawing, watercolor cover design for Geoffrey Whitworth's Book of Whimsies, 1909. Archives of J.M.Dent & Son. (88) £90

Hendrix, James Marshall ("Jimi"), 1942-70
[His personal English checkbook from Martins Bank Ltd, containing 5 credit slips bearing his name & used checkstubs, 1967, sold at pnNY on 3 Dec 1988, lot 292, for $1,300.]
[A collection of 18 photographs, comprising 10 publicity photos, 10 by 8 inches, & 8 from his personal collection, sold at pnNy on 3 Dec 1988, lot 289, for $650.]

Autograph Ms, song lyrics, beginning "Is that the stars in the sky..."; [Nov 1966]. About 26cm by 20.5cm, on Hyde Park Towers headed paper. 5 lines in red ball-point pen. With caricatures by Hendrix & Cathy Etchingham on verso. Def; framed. (89) £3,600

Original drawing, watercolor, multi-colored psychedelic dreamscape, [n.d.]. Size not stated. Matted. (89) $1,500

ANs, [c.1968]. Recipient unnamed. Expressing thanks. Framed with a ptd photograph, 11.5 by 15.75 inches. (88) $2,750

Ds, 1966. International certificate of vaccination. Sgd James Hendrix inside front cover. (89) $1,500

— 1969. (88) $1,000

Concert program, sgd, 1967. (88) £460

Signature, [c.1968]. With inscr & small drawing of a heart. Framed with LP cover, 20 by 16 inches. (89) $1,500

Henley, William Ernest, 1849-1903
Autograph Ms (2), notebooks containing poetical collections & working drafts of his poems, 1872 to 1899. About 800 pp, 4to, in vellum & half roan. (91) £7,000

Autograph Ms, abstracts & quotations from works in Spanish, Italian, French, German & English, Jan 1874 to Mar 1875. About 800 pp in 6 notebooks, 8vo & 4to, in cloth bdg. (91) £2,500

Henley, William Ernest, 1849-1903 —& Stevenson, Robert Louis, 1850-94
ALs, 19 Feb 1885. (91) £600

Hennell Ltd.
Ms, Jewellery Order Books, 23 Feb 1899 to 6 Sept 1935. About 15,000 pp in 42 vols, 4to. Including the firm's Private Ledger, 1881 to 1897. (89) £1,500

Henri II de Bourbon, Prince de Conde, 1588-1646
ALs, 31 Mar [n.y.]. Byer collection. (90) $125

Henri III, King of France, 1551-89
ALs, [n.d.]. (88) $800
— [n.d.]. (89) £360
Ls, 27 May 1580. (91) £600
— 10 June 1586. (91) £650
— 17 Nov 1586. (91) DM750
— 8 Feb 1588. (88) £250
Ds, 17 Feb 1577. (91) DM300
— 1580. (90) $300
— [1589?]. (88) $160

Henri IV, King of France, 1553-1610
ALs, 29 July [1596]. Doheny collection. (89) $800
— 17 Aug [1597?]. 2 pp, folio. To [Montmorency], Constable of France. Urging him to do everything to ease financial difficulties, & discussing military matters. Margin def. (89) £2,500
— 16 June [1599]. 2 pp, folio. To "Monsr capysuchy general des armes an avygnon". Requesting him to cooperate with the Marquis d'Halincourt & to settle problems concerning M. de Gryllon's nephews. (90) DM2,200
— 25 Feb [n.y.]. 2 pp, folio. To Cardinal

HENRI IV

Francois de Joyeuse. Sending a special messenger & hoping to see him soon. Dampstained. (90) DM2,500

— 26 Mar [n.y.]. 1 p, 8vo. To "mr. de baumenyelle". Requesting to see him the next morning. Sgd Henry. Margins repaired. (88) DM1,650

— 28 June [n.y.]. 1 p, folio. To M. de St. Germain. Informing him that M. de Schomberg has been ordered to settle recipient's quarrels with the Sieur de St. Georges. (91) DM2,200

Ls, 3 May 1578. 1 p, 4to. To "Messrs de la Religion reformee de Ste Foy". Referring to the assassination of the Chevalier de Beauville. (91) DM1,100

— 24 June 1581. (91) £500

— 18 Feb 1591. 1 p, 4to. To M. de Dolot. Entrusting him with a mission to Venice. (90) DM1,350

— 19 May [1596]. (89) DM380

— 5 Nov 1599. 1 p, folio. To Cardinal Alfonso Visconti. Expressing pleasure that the Pope has decided in his favor regarding the dissolution of his marriage. (91) £2,600

— 8 Apr 1603. (91) £650

— 14 June 1609. (90) £360

Ds, 12 July 1590. (88) £180

— 1604. (88) $325

— Sept 1606. (90) DM480

— June 1609. Byer collection. (90) $550

— LE SIEUR DE COULON. - Le Soleil de l'Ame, Livre de la Journee du Roy. [Paris, c.1599]. 150 leaves (2 blank), 306mm by 204mm. Extra contemp olive mor over pastebds with crowned monogram of Henri IV. In a fine sloping italic hand. Illuminated. Satire by a political opponent; presumably unpbd. Phillipps MS.2650 & Abbey collection. (89) £55,000

Henricus de Bartholomaeis, d.1271

Ms, Summa de Titulis Decretalium. [Bologna, with miniatures added in Paris, c.1280-1300]. Single leaf, vellum, 430mm by 288mm. In a small gothic bookhand. With large historiated initial. Mtd. (91) £2,200

Henricus de Hassia, d.1397 —& Petrus de Alliaco, 1350-c.1422

Ms, Henricus, Speculum Anime; Petrus, Super Septem Psalmos Penitentiales; with Hours of the Cross & Prayers, in Latin. [Netherlands, Maastricht?, c.1450]. 143 leaves, vellum, 135mm by 95mm. Contemp calf over wooden bds, repaired. In textura script of varying formality by 2 scribes. With numerous initials in red & blue & 12 large decorated initials in colors. (88) £1,700

Henricus de Segusia, Cardinal, d.1271

Ms, Summa. [Paris, c.1250]. 2 leaves only, vellum, 340mm by 230mm. In a small gothic bookhand. With 2 large miniatures, showing tables of consanguinity & affinity, delicately painted in colors against pompeian red grounds within blue borders with white tracery; spaces left for initials. Versos blank. Korner collection. (90) £20,000

Henrietta Maria, Queen of Charles I of England, 1609-69

Ds, 5 June 1638. (88) £200

— 14 Aug 1655. (89) £520

— 13 Jan 1661/2. (88) $225

Henry Frederick, Prince of Wales, 1594-1612

Letter, 11 Sept 1604. 1 p, 362mm by 473mm. To the Tsarevich Feodor Borisovich. Requesting permission for James Cocks, a merchant of the Muscovy Company, to buy hawks in Russia. Illuminated. Framed. (89) £2,900

Ds, [31 Mar 1612]. (91) £550

Henry I, King of England, 1068-1135

Document, [c.1131-35]. 1 p, vellum, 45mm by 160mm. Writ to Randulf, Earl of Chester, confirming a grant to Calke Abbey. (89) £1,800

Henry II, Emperor, 973-1024

Ds, [28 Feb] 1003. 1 p, vellum, c.408mm by 653mm. Deed presenting the bishopric of Parma with Nonantola Abbey. Sgd with autograph mark in monogram. (90) DM94,000

Document, [7 Apr] 1019. 1 p, vellum, c.52.5cm by 52.5cm. Confirmation of an earlier grant & grant of an island near Absdorf to the Abbey at

Niederaltaich. With monogram & seal. Figdor collection. (89) DM320,000

Henry II, King of England, 1133-89
Document, [1157-58]. 1 p, vellum, 186mm by 164mm. Grant to William of Norwich of the manor of Blythburgh, Suffolk. Witnessed by Thomas Becket & 12 others. In a handsome romanesque charter hand. (91) £6,500
— FORGERY. - Document, purportedly c.1157/58, but late 12th or early 13th cent, 1 p, vellum, 470mm by 223mm. Confirmation to the Priory of Plessis-Grimoult of possessions granted by Bishops Richard & Philip of Bayeux. Purportedly attested by 5 witnesses with sign manual, including Thomas Beckett. (90) £4,500

Henry III, King of France, 1551-89
Ds, 17 Nov 1586. (88) $300

Henry IV, King of Castile, 1425-74
Ds, 18 May 1457. (88) £320
— 15 Sept 1474. (88) £280

Henry, Joseph, 1797-1878
ALs, 22 Aug 1862. (89) $70

Henry, Patrick, 1736-99
ALs, 30 Aug 1765. 1 p, 4to. To Archibald McCall. Informing him about his suit against Clevier Duke. Repaired. Whiton collection. (88) $2,500
— 8 Aug 1777. 2 pp, folio. To the Continental Congress. As Governor of Virginia, complaining about Lieut. Col. Edward Carrington. Including autograph postscript, sgd P.H. (90) $6,000
— 10 Dec 1777. 1 p, folio. To Gov. Thomas Johnson. Seeking assistance to repel a British attack. Address leaf detached. Middendorf collection. (89) $2,500
— 22 May 1779. 1 p, 4to. To the Speaker of the House of Delegates. Transmitting a letter from Brig. Gen. Allen Jones. (91) $5,500
— 15 Mar 1780. 1 p, 4to. To Thomas Madison. Requesting money due on recipient's bond. Doheny collection. (89) $3,000
— 26 Mar 1785. 1 p, 4to. Recipient unnamed. Letter of introduction for Albert Gallatin. (90) $2,600
— 14 Mar 1796. 1 p, 4to. Recipient unknown. Discussing the sale of his plantation. Doheny collection. (89) $1,300
— 31 Mar 1799. 1 p, 4to. To Phil. Payne. Discussing a land deal. (90) $3,000
AD, 1 Sept 1789. (91) $350
Ds, 9 June 1785. Christensen collection. (90) $700
— 2 Dec 1785. (88) $650
— 17 May 1786. (88) DM530

Henry VII, King of England, 1457-1509
Ms, Nova Statuta, opening leaf of the Statutes of Henry VII, [c.1490]. 1 leaf, vellum, 287mm by 194mm. In French & Latin. In brown ink in an English legal hand. With large historiated initial showing Henry VII with his courtiers & full illuminated border incorporating the royal arms of England. (89) £3,200
Ls, 1 Dec [n.y.]. 1 p, 4to. To Simound Stalworth. Requiring him to raise money for the invasion of Scotland. (89) £5,500
Ds, 16 Nov 1492. 1 p, vellum, folio. Laying charges of fraud against abbeys & parish churches in Warwickshire & other counties, & ordering an investigation. (90) £6,000
— 4 Apr [1498]. 1 p, vellum, 100mm by 230mm. Order to Sir Robert Litton to pay William Toll for expenses of the chapel. In mor case. Doheny collection. (89) $3,200
— 22 Mar [1506]. 1 p, vellum, 8vo. Warrant to deliver a coat-of-arms to Bennet Lamb. (89) $2,500
— 30 May 1506. 1 p, vellum, 196mm by 155mm. Warrant addressed to Andrew Windsor to deliver various gowns to Lord William of Devon & William de la Pole. Corner def. (90) $1,700
— [1506-07]. 2 pp, folio. Accounts for North Wales, Cheshire & Flint; sgd in upper margin. Endorsed possibly in Henry's hand. (89) £1,200

Henry VIII, King of England, 1491-1547
Ls, 3 July [1513]. 2 pp, folio. To George Talbot, Earl of Shrewsbury. Criticizing his conduct of the siege of Therouanne. (89) £6,000

HENRY VIII

— 7 July [1513]. 2 pp, folio. To George Talbot, Earl of Shrewsbury. Encouraging him to capture Therouanne & hoping for a withdrawal of German mercenaries from the French army. (89) £13,500

— [26 Mar 1517?]. 3 pp, folio. To Jehan de Thorroult, Jehan Dupuis, & Eloy de la Rue. Responding to complaints brought forth by the city of Tournai regarding contributions for the building of a citadel. Sgd twice. In French. Framed. (90) $12,000

— [c.1520/21]. 1 p, folio. Recipient unnamed. Announcing war against France, & requiring money for military preparations. (90) £10,500

— 1 Oct 1532. 1 p, double folio. To "Le seig[neu]r de Granvele premier maistre des Requestes et Conseill[e]r de L'emperor". Announcing that Dr. Hawkin will replace [Thomas] Cranmer as Ambassador to the Imperial Court. Marquess of Downshire collection. (90) £9,500

Ds, 28 June 1512. 1 p, vellum, size not stated. Warrant addressed to Sir Andrew Windsor to deliver material for wedding clothes to his tailor Stephen Jasper. (89) £4,600

— 3 Mar 1513. 1 p, folio. Signet letters addressed to Treasurer John Heron, allowing Richard Gresham to defer payment of a debt. Phillipps Ms 35570. (89) £4,500

— 16 July 1513. 1 p, 143mm by 202mnm. Pay order in favor of Guy de Portinaris. (91) $4,800

— 12 Feb 1526. 1 p, folio. Authorizing the appointment of Sir William Stanley as Sheriff of the county of Chester. Fold repaired. (89) $5,500

— 18 Apr 1536. 1 p, vellum, 243mm by 110mm. Pay order in favor of Richard Sampson. (90) $6,500

Document, 24 Feb 1539. (88) £420

— [1540]. 825mm by 470mm, vellum. Letters Patent granting the Manor of Denham, Buckinghamshire, to Edmund Peckham in consideration of a payment of £977 17s 8d. With initial letter port. With later related documents. (90) £1,200

— 21 Feb 1541. (88) £600

— 1 July 1542. 2 sheets of vellum, c.560mm by 870mm. Letters patent granting Nicholas & Katherine Fortescue the Chapel of St. Giles, the Priory of Cookhill, & other properties. With initial letter port & penwork decoration. (89) $1,500

Henschke, Alfred, 1890-1928. See: Klabund, 1890-1928

Hensel, Fanny, 1805-47
[Her album, 1817 to 1829, 140 pp (80 blank), 8vo, in contemp diced calf bdg, containing compositions by her brother Felix Mendelssohn-Bartholdy (2, presumably unpbd), Paganini, Moscheles, Zelter, & a number of others, as well as contributions by Friedrich Schlegel, Ludwig Uhland, & others, partly pasted in, sold at C on 26 June 1991, lot 391, for £80,000 to Haas.]

ALs, 19 Dec 1842. 4 pp, 8vo. To her sister-in-law Cecile Mendelssohn-Bartholdy. Relating the last hours & death of her mother Lea. (91) £4,200

— 10 June 1843. (88) DM900

Hensel, Wilhelm, 1794-1861
Autograph Ms, poem, An Tochter Julie, 1857. (89) DM600
ALs, 4 Nov 1853. (88) DM500

Hensoldt, Moritz, 1821-1903
ALs, 18 July 1868. (90) DM400

Henson, Jim, 1936-90
Ls, 18 Sept 1977. (91) $160
Photograph, sgd, [n.d.]. (91) $325

Hepburn, Katharine
Collection of 5 A Ls s, 4 A Ns s & 7 Ns s, [n.d.]. (88) $950
Ds, 29 Nov 1937. (89) $350
Photograph, sgd, [1946]. (90) $200
Photograph, sgd & inscr, [n.d.]. (88) $275
Playbill, for her appearance in Bagnold's A Matter of Gravity at the Broadhurst Theatre, NY; [n.d.]. (88) $110

Hepburn, Katharine —& Others
[A photograph of Nissa the Leopard, with over 50 signatures by the cast & crew members of the RKO film Bringing up Baby, 1939, including Hepburn, Cary Grant, & Howard Hawks, 8 by 10 inches, sold at CNY on 21 June

1989, lot 349, for $900.]

Heppe, Sopie von, 1836-97. See: Wilhelm von Hanau, 1836-1902

Heraldic Manuscripts

[2 grants of arms to William & Henry Brockman, 20 May 1588 & 3 June 1606, sgd by Robert Cooke & William Camden, Clarenceux Kings of Arms, each with illuminated large armorials, with related material, sold at C on 6 Dec 1989, lot 283, for £800 to Sabin.]

[An album containing 19 painted coats-of-arms (3 on vellum, 5 using engravings), 16th to 18th cent, in late 19th-cent half lea, sold at HK on 8 Nov 1988, lot 55, for DM800.]

[3 Ms vols containing extensive genealogical & heraldic collections begun c.1600 & augmented by later owners including Sir Isaac Heard, Garter King of Arms, until c.1820, c.1,500 pp, in 19th-cent blue mor, imperf, Philipps Ms.96, sold at S on 14 Dec 1989, lot 208, for £700 to Carroll Industries.]

[A collection of 10 English grants of arms, 1615 to 1862, all with painted coats-of-arms, sold at S on 22 July 1988, lot 326, for £1,300 to Heirloom & Howard.]

[2 illuminated grants of arms for James Higgford, 1825, & Higgford Burr, 1860, sold at pn on 8 Dec 1988, lot 49, for £95 to Argent.]

Ms, Alphabet of Arms, [17th cent]. (89) £180

— Ms, armorial. [Austria, c.1580-1600]. 49 leaves, 315mm by 210mm. Fragment, with c.1,000 coats-of-arms in pen-&-ink & watercolors. (90) DM1,800

— Ms, armorial. [Germany, 18th cent]. 135 leaves, 380mm by 230mm, in folder. Fragment, with 135 coats-of-arms of families with names beginning with B or P. (90) DM1,900

— Ms, armorial. [Germany?, early 19th cent]. 685 leaves in 3 vols, 185mm by 120mm. Contemp half lea. With more than 4,000 painted coats-of-arms. (90) DM3,400

— Ms, armorial history of the Burzaccarini family, 1747; c.50 leaves, 4to, in contemp red mor tooled in gilt. (88) $250

— Ms, armorial. (89) DM850

— Ms, armorial. [South Germany or Austria, 15th cent]. 34 leaves, 290mm by 210mm, disbound. With 136 emblazoned coats-of-arms. Repaired. (89) £2,200

— Ms, augmentation to a grant of arms to Robert Webb, sgd by Robert Cooke, Clarenceux King of Arms, 1 Aug 1591. (88) £220

— Ms, Book of c.800 English & Scottish coats-of-arms in color & a further c.300 in trick, with captions & an index. (90) £600

— Ms, Booke of Armorie otherwise called the Barrons Booke. [London, c.1603]. 100 leaves, 425mm by 280mm, in contemp limp vellum. With 532 armorial illusts. Executed for Sir William Stone. (90) £3,000

— Ms, Carta executoria de hidalguia in favor of Gabriel Ortis de Cagiguera, 1788. (89) £170

— Ms, Carta executoria de hidalguia in favor of Carlos Peres Mexia Lasso de la Vega, 5 Apr 1689. (90) £380

— Ms, Carta executoria de hidalguia in favor of Franco Anaya, Dec 1552. 36 leaves, 300mm by 215mm, in contemp vellum. With full-page miniature & half-page coat-of-arms. (91) DM1,050

— Ms, Carta executoria de hidalguia in favor of the Puente family, [2d half of 16th cent]. (89) DM650

— Ms, Carta executoria de hidalguia in favor of Pedro Martinez de Onate, 28 Aug 1585. (91) $425

— Ms, Carta executoria de hidalguia in favor of Balthasar Fernandez Polanco de Arauxo, 3 Nov 1671. 162 leaves (1 blank), vellum, 300mm by 205mm; disbound. With 2 full-page miniatures in gold & colors. (91) $1,400

— Ms, Carta executoria de hidalguia in favor of Sancho de Heredia, 21 Oct 1528. (88) $850

— Ms, Carta executoria de hidalguia in favor of Diego Larios de Portillo, 29 Apr 1604. (88) $700

— Ms, Carta executoria de hidalguia in favor of the Gallego, Mesa, & Monte Siguero families, [17th cent]. 4 leaves, vellum, 290mm by 210mm, in contemp tooled [Mexican?] mor over pastedbds; def. With 2 full-page

coats-of-arms. With related material. (88) $1,500
— Ms, Carta executoria de hidalguia in favor of the family of de la Barrera, 23 Nov 1576 & 5 Feb 1601; c.80 leaves, 302mm by 215mm, in contemp tooled Mexican lea over pastedbds; def. (88) $700
— Ms, certificate of arms & nobility in favor of Don Roque Perez de la Vega, issued by Don Manuel Joaquin Medina, King of Arms to King Charles IV, 6 Mar 1804. (88) £600
— Ms, confirmation of arms, nobility & genealogy in favor of Antonio Agustin Rodriguez de Alburquerque, sgd by Agustin de Loayssa, King of Arms to Ferdinand VI; 2 Oct 1747. (91) $500
— Ms, confirmation of arms issued by Juan Alphonso de Guerra Sandova for the Machin family, 1729. (89) £140
— Ms, confirmation of arms & nobility issued by Francisco Zazoy y Rosillo for the Canton, Guaza, Otero, Cascos & Villarmea families, 16 Dec 1753. (89) £240
— Ms, confirmation of nobility & genealogy in favor of the Manrique de Lara family; 2 Mss, [16th & 17th cent]. (88) $750
— Ms, confirmation of arms, nobility & genealogy in favor of the Lachruel, Caravallo, Retes, & Labastida families, 11 Mar 1726. (88) $275
— Ms, confirmation of arms, nobility & genealogy in favor of Pedro de Escuza y Lecanda, 29 Jan 1798. By Pasqual Antonio de la Rua, King of Arms to Charles IV. 43 leaves, vellum, 300mm by 202mm, in contemp red mor gilt. With 3 full-page miniatures, 4 coats-of-arms, 4 decorated headings, & 5 initials with landscape vignettes, all in colors & gold. (88) $1,600
— Ms, confirmation of arms, nobility & genealogy in favor of Ignacio Francisco Pedro Lopez de Herrera, [c.15 Oct 1726]. (88) $900
— Ms, Etat des officiers du regiment du Roy (infanterie) en 1748; c.40 pp, 8vo, in mor bdg by Riviere. (89) £340
— Ms, Executoria de Hidalguia in favor of Alonso Garcia Utrera de Vargas & Inigo de Vargas, 2 Aug 1588. (88) $550
— Ms, Executoria de Hidalguia in favor of Joseph Messia, 27 Apr 1627. 76 leaves (3 blank), 328mm by 210mm, in [contemp?] green velvet over wooden bds. With 3 full-page miniatures & headings in gold on red & blue ground with penwork decoration. (88) $1,300
— Ms, genealogical scroll of the Kings of England & France & the Dukes of Burgundy, [Flanders, c.1480]. On 2 membranes of vellum. In black ink in a lettre batarde. Decorated with columns & 84 interlinked cartouches in colors. Boone Estate. (89) $6,500
— Ms, Genealogy of William of Flanders & his wife Alice of Clermont. [Paris?, c.1500]. 25 leaves, vellum, 157mm by 114mm. 19th-cent French calf gilt. In a flourished lettre batarde. With illuminated initials throughout & 33 large miniatures of richly dressed noblemen & women with their arms in architectural interiors. (89) £18,000
— Ms, grant by Garter & Clarenceux Kings of Arms to George Ayton to adopt the name of Lee, 1773. (88) £150
— Ms, grant of arms to John Amson, sgd by Peter Le Neve, Norroy King of Arms, 3 Apr 1711. (88) £160
— Ms, grant of arms to Eric Dermot Bertrand von Dembinski, sgd by Clarenceux & Garter Kings of Arms, 1939. (88) £50
— Ms, grant of arms to Charles Heuret Edney, sgd by Clarenceux & Garter Kings of Arms, 1933. (88) £50
— Ms, grant of arms to Hubert Aloysius Leicester, sgd by Clarenceux & Garter Kings of Arms, 1933. (88) £50
— Ms, grant of arms to Reginald Engledow Harbord, sgd by Clarenceux & Garter Kings of Arms, 1951. (88) £35
— Ms, grant of arms to Eric Dermot Bertrand von Dembinski, sgd by Clarenceux & Garter Kings of Arms, 1940. (88) £80
— Ms, grant of arms to Carmen von Dembinska, sgd by Garter, Clarenceux & Norroy Kings of Arms, 1940. (88) £80
— Ms, grant of arms to Sir William Dansell, sgd by & with initial letter port of William Hervey, Clarenceux King of Arms, 4 Apr 1558. (88) £800
— Ms, grant of arms to Thomas Balle,

sgd by Robert Cooke, Clarenceux King of Arms, 20 June 1572. (88) £350
— Ms, grant of quarterings to John Michael Sweetman on taking the name of Powell in addition to his own, sgd by Ulster King of Arms, 1874. (88) £110
— Ms, Herald's notebook containing c.80 coats-of-arms borne by people called Browne, in a vol with "a Copie of Sir Willm Fayerfaxes Booke of Armes of Yorkshire", [early 17th cent], c.40 pp & blanks, folio. Phillipps Ms 1312b. (88) £240
— Ms, La Genealogie de treshaulte et puissante dame Madame Marguerite de Baux. [France, perhaps Fontevrault Abbey, c.1525]. 8 leaves, vellum, 250mm by 186mm, in modern embroidered brocade. In a very handsome lettre batarde. With full illuminated borders throughout & 4 pp of 4 achievements of arms each. Illuminated for Louise de Bourbon. (90) £9,500
— Ms, Ordinary of Arms in trick & blazon, [late 16th cent]. (90) £240
— Ms, patent of nobility for Don Gonzalo de la Lama y de la Zerda, Marques de Ladrada & his sons, 26 Mar 1733. (88) £280
— Ms, Principall Cataines, as well of Noblemen as of knightes ... (89) £420
— Ms, Venetian armorial of Bishops, Doges, & nobility, with list of nunneries. [Venice, c.1464 to 1785]. 37 leaves (3 blank) & flyleaf, vellum, 343mm by 232mm, in 19th-cent faded purple velvet. Written in many stages by many different scribes. With 44 illuminated coats-of-arms. (88) £7,500
— Austria. - Ms, armorial of the estates of Lower Austria, 1592 - 1602. 90 leaves, 193mm by 150mm. Restored contemp brown calf gilt. Including 54 watercolored coats-of-arms in gold, silver & colors. (89) DM8,500
— Carrington-Smith Family. - Ms, Heraldic Roll, The petigree of the Carringtons of the north partes of England, [16th to 18th cent]. Vellum, c.110 by 22 inches. Account beginning in 14th cent. With later roll on paper. (88) £300
— Counts of Pereira. - Ms, Genealogy of the Counts of Pereira, in Portuguese. [Evora, Portugal, 22 Feb 1534]. 6 leaves (1 blank) & flyleaf, vellum, 451mm by 328mm, in contemp decorated red velvet over pastebds. Profusely illuminated by Antonio de Hollanda with 38 half-length portraits with coats-of-arms, 4 very fine circular port miniatures of Ferdinand the Catholic, Emperor Charles V & others, c.160 paintings of birds & animals, & vast frontis with the arms of Pereira. Including attestation by the King-of-Arms of John III of Portugal. (90) £220,000
— Grenville, Denis. - Ms, illuminated genealogical scroll recording his family, 1066 - 1702; 23 June 1702. Vellum, 71 by 15.5 inches. (91) £500
— Lelij, W. van der. - Ms, Wapenen van zeer veele oude ende voorname familien...; [1728 & later]. 173 leaves (26 blank), folio, in contemp calf. Containing c.2100 coats-of-arms, mostly in full colors. (91) £1,400
— Nesle Family. - Ms, Histoire des Comtes de Neele, [late 15th & early 16th cent]. 32 leaves, vellum, 152mm by 105mm. 19th cent dark blue mor gilt. Genealogy beginning with King Charles (the Simple) of France. With 39 miniatures in gold & colors depicting members of the family with their coats-of-arms. (88) DM50,000
— Nuremberg. - Ms, armorial of the city. [Nuremberg, c.1605]. 290 leaves (23 blank) & flyleaf, 313mm by 200mm. Contemp brown mor over wooden bds with metal corner-pieces & the arms of the Gundlach family. In a very calligraphic high gothic hand. With c.120 emblazoned coats-of-arms. Phillipps MS.875 & Abbey collection. (89) £5,000
— Ordre de Saint Esprit. - Ms, Noms, surnoms, qualitez et armes des chefs, commandeurs, chevaliers & officiers de l'ordre et milice du St. Esprit, depuis son institution..., [Paris, c.1642]. 334 leaves, 428mm by 285mm, in contemp mottled calf. With ptd outlines of armorial shields & of cartouche borders on facing pages. (89) £10,000
— Osbaldeston Family. - Ms, Descent

of William Osbaldeston of Nunmanby..., 1682. Vellum roll, c.75 by 20.75 inches. Illuminated. With 77 coats-of-arms & autograph certification, sgd, by William Dugdale, Garter King of Arms. (88) £600
— SHELTON FAMILY OF NORFOLK. - Ms, armorial of the Shelton Family of Norfolk, [mid-17th cent]. About 85 pp, vellum, 4to, in contemp limp vellum. With 85 full-page coats-of-arms & preliminary unfolding watercolor of a moated house [Shelton Hall]. (89) £1,300
— SKELTON, BEVIL. - Ms, The Variation of the Armes and Badges of the severall Kings of England..., 1684 [continued to 1692]. 229 pp, folio, vellum. Contemp red mor gilt, bound for the author. Richly illuminated with 4 full-page coats-of-arms or miniatures, 16 large royal coats-of-arms & 507 smaller coats-of-arms of Knights of the Garter. (88) £14,000
— SKELTON, BEVIL. - Ms, A Catalogue of the Dukes, Marqueses, & Earles, with their Armes, Wives and Ishue since the Conquest. [England, c.1678]. 159 leaves & 3 flyleaves, vellum, 387mm by 307mm. Rebacked contemp red velvet over wooden bds. In black ink in a sloping cursive script or a rounded roman hand in imitation of ptd type. With c.480 emblazoned coats-of-arms. Possibly autograph or compiled for the author. Abbey collection. (89) £16,000
— VENICE. - Ms, Chroniche di tutte le Casate della nobil Citta di Venezia, con le Armi di tutti le Gentilhuomini..., [17th cent]. 626 leaves, c.25cm by 18cm, in contemp blindstamped calf over wooden bds. Alphabetical list of noble families, with their arms mostly in watercolor. In 2 hands. 8 leaves restored. Inscr on flyleaf to Mussolini, 11 Jan 1932. (88) £1,000
— VENICE. - Ms, Nomina et Insignia eorum, qui ab instituta Venetorum Republica Nobilitatis Dignitate claruerunt; in Italian. [Venice, c.1586]. 116 leaves & flyleaves, 332mm by 228mm. Extra contemp Venetian red mor over pastebds with the arms of Philippe Hurault, Comte de Cheverny & the royal arms of France. In black ink in a sloping italic cursive hand. With c.950 emblazoned coats-of-arms. Phillipps MS.875 & Abbey collection. (89) £9,500
See also: Order of the Garter

Herbal

Ms, in Latin & Greek. [Italy, c.1500]. 212 leaves (60 blank), 283mm by 215mm, in old limp vellum. Containing illusts of plants on 145 pp, identified in a later sloping humanistic cursive minuscule, with index in an italic Renaissance notarial hand & 6 impressions of plants made from nature. (90) £38,000

— PSEUDO-APULEIUS. - Ms, herbal, in Latin, with texts on cauterization & haemorrhoids. [Central or southern Italy, early 15th cent]. 32 leaves, 212mm by 140mm. Roman black mor gilt bdg of c.1540. In black ink in an Italian notarial hand. With 15 half-page sketches of doctors treating patients & 133 colored drawings of flowers & plants. (88) £10,000

Herbert Family

[The archive of the Herbert family, Earls of Carnarvon, c.1780 to 1880, comprising many thousands of letters, documents & papers in 16 boxes, sold at S on 18 July 1991, lot 384, for £18,000 to Quaritch.]

Herbert, Sir Henry, 1595-1673

Ls, 13 Oct 1660. 1 p, folio. To the Cockpit Theater in Drury Lane. Demanding a lowering of their rates & the right to censor their plays. Retained copy; with autograph endorsement. (89) £5,500

Herbert, Henry William

Autograph Ms, description of The Vale of Warwick. [c.1850-58] 14 pp, 8vo. (91) $1,300

— Autograph Ms, obituary for his friend Thomas Ward. 1 Feb 1854. 2 pp, 8vo. With letter of transmittal. (91) $2,250

Herbert, Stanley

Original drawings, (21), to illus Fitzwater Wray's The Visitor's Book, 1937. Archives of J. M. Dent & Son. (88) £150

Herbert, Victor, 1859-1924
Autograph quotation, 8 bars of music, entitled The Fortune Teller, sgd & dated Mar [18]99. (91) $225
— Anr, sgd, 4 Sept 1902. (91) $250
— Anr, 8 bars from Mlle. (90) $250
Photograph, sgd & inscr, Nov 1913. (91) $350

Herder, Johann Gottfried von, 1744-1803
Autograph Ms (2), 2 epigrams, Der gequaelte Prometheus in Bilde, & Das Eigenthum; [n.d.]. 2 small strips of paper, mtd on 8vo sheet. With autograph authentication by Goethe, sgd, Mar 1825, below. Albrecht collection. (91) SF6,000
Autograph Ms, 2 aphorisms, [n.d.]. (90) DM580
— Autograph Ms, 2 poems, Wunsch, & Lob des Gastfreundes; [ptd 1778]. 2 pp, 8vo. From the Greek; including revisions. Albrecht collection. (91) SF2,200
— Autograph Ms, essay about poets & their native tongue, fragment; [n.d.]. 2 pp, 8vo. Some revisions. (90) DM1,400
— Autograph Ms, Spanish poem beginning "De Ibero sagrado", with German trans; [n.d.]. 2 pp, 4to. 63 lines; incomplete. Slightly waterstained. (90) DM1,300
ALs, 25 Apr [17]83. 1 p, 4to. To Ph. E. Reich. Sending a title for insertion in a catalogue. (91) DM1,700
— 28 June 17[8]3. 1 p, 8vo. To [Johann Christoph Doederlein]. Sending his work on Hebrew poetry. (91) DM1,900
— 29 Jan [1787]. 1 p, 8vo. To Georg Joachim Goeschen. Announcing the receipt of the Ms of Goethe's Iphigenie auf Tauris. Albrecht collection. (91) SF1,200
— 11 June 1787. 2 pp, 8vo. To Georg Joachim Goeschen. Thanking for a copy of Goethe's works, & sending the addresses of some subscribers. Albrecht collection. (91) SF2,200
— [Feb 1797]. (91) DM1,000
— [c.Aug 1799]. 1 p, 4to. To [Garlieb] Merkel. Expressing reluctance to participate in a controversy involving Wilhelm Abraham Teller. Sgd H. (90) DM1,300
— [15 Nov 1799]. 2 pp, 8vo. To Emanuel [Osmund]. Expressing thanks for helping his son find a position. (91) DM1,400
— [n.d.]. (89) £750
— [n.d.]. (89) DM1,000
Autograph sentiment, Lob und Tadel, [n.d.]. (88) DM850

Herder, Maria Caroline von, 1750-1809
A Ls s (2), [1 Apr] 1804 & [n.d.]. (89) DM360
ALs, 15 Nov 1799. (90) DM600

Hermann, Ernest W. F.
[A group of c.25 letters relating to Hermann's attempts to market his patents for a flying machine, [c.1911 to 1917], sold at R on 17 June 1989, lot 75A, for $850.]

Hermes, Johann August, 1736-1822
ALs, 20 Jan 1774. 3 pp, 4to. To [E. Th. J. Brueckner]. Referring to disciplinary action taken against hinm by church authorities. (91) DM1,300

Hermine, Consort of Emperor Wilhelm II of Germany, 1887-1947
Series of 3 Ls s, 20 Dec 1924 to 17 Dec 1933. (90) DM320
Ls, 21 Dec 1934. (91) DM270

Herrick, Robert, 1591-1674
[Herrick, Nicholas. - A collection of 13 documents relating to the death & estate of Robert Herrick's father, c.1592-1611, with related 19th-cent letters & notes, sold at S on 15 Dec 1988, lot 18, for £8,000.]
[Herrick, Nicholas. - The post mortem inventories & accounts of the goods & chattels of Nicholas Herrick at his house & goldsmith's shop, [c.1593] to 26 July 1602, on 3 long vellum rolls, sold at S on 15 Dec 1988, lot 19, for £18,000.]
Ds, 25 Sept 1607. 1 p, vellum, c.5.5 by 10.25 inches. Indenture of apprenticeship to his uncle Sir William Herrick. (89) £9,500
— 28 Mar 1615. Receipt on Sir William Herrick's autograph account of a payment made to him, also recording other payments. 2 pp, top half of folio leaf, tipped into an album with related material. (89) £5,000

HERRICK

See also: Herrick, Sir William

Herrick, Sir William, 1562-1653

[The Exchequer Papers of Herrick, 1608 to 1623, over 2,300 documents & a series of ledgers in 28 vols, folio, including warrants sgd by Sir Francis Bacon, Fulke Greville & numerous others, & material relating to Sir Walter Raleigh, sold at S on 15 Dec 1988, lot 20, for £105,000.]

Autograph Ms, accountbook recording outgoing expenses, including payments to his nephew Robert Herrick, Sept 1601 to Apr 1637. About 250 pp, c.16.25 by 6.5 by 2.25 inches (ledger), in 19th-cent calf. With annotations by William Perry-Herrick on interleaves. (89) £12,000

Herrmann-Neisse, Max, 1886-1941

Collection of 4 A Ls s & 2 autograph postcards, sgd, 1 June 1925 to 21 July 1928. 9 pp, 4to & 8vo. To Mark Neven DuMont. About a public reading, George Grosz, economic problems, his health, etc. 1 letter including a poem, 1 a sketch (self port). (88) DM1,300

Herschel, Sir John Frederick William, 1792-1871

ALs, 16 June 1833. (90) DM220

Herschel, Sir William, 1738-1822

ALs, 24 May 1795. Byer collection. (90) $650

— 25 May 1804. (89) DM750

Hertz, Heinrich, 1857-94

Collection of 5 A Ls s, ANs & AN, 28 Apr 1891 to 12 Nov 1893. 14 pp, mostly 8vo (2 visiting cards). To Professor D. E. Jones. Discussing the trans of his work, Kelvin's intro, etc. With related material. (90) £2,200

Series of 3 A Ls s, 10 Mar to 26 July 1892. 8 pp, 8vo. Recipient unnamed. Responding to a request for advice in publishing a scholarly work. (89) DM5,500

ALs, [c.1880]. 3 pp, 8vo. To his brother Rudolf. Humorous family letter. (90) DM1,400

AMERICAN BOOK PRICES CURRENT

Hervey, James, 1714-58

Autograph Ms, working drafts of his Meditations among the Tombs, Reflections on a Flower Garden, & other works, [c.1740]; c.70 pp, folio. (88) £850

Herwegh, Georg, 1817-75

Autograph Ms, poem, Phylloxera ante portas; [n.d.]. (91) DM550

ALs, 13 Jan [1866]. (91) DM400

Herz, Henri, 1803-88

ALs, 4 Mar 1832. (90) DM320

Herz, Henriette, 1764-1847

A Ls s (2), 14 Nov 1834 & 12 Aug [n.y.]. 3 pp, 8vo. To Georg Andreas Reimer. Requesting help for 2 unfortunate people, & discussing a young lady's travel arrangements. (91) DM1,300

Herzberg, Gerhard

Ls, 12 Nov 1980. (88) DM360

Herzen, Alexander, 1812-70

ALs, 13 Feb 1862. (88) £250

Herzl, Theodor, 1860-1904

ALs, 21 Oct 1890. 2 pp, 8vo. To [Gustav Lewy?]. Informing him about negotations regarding the performance of a play in Berlin. (90) DM3,000

Hesiod. See: Aristophanes & Others

Hess, Johann Jakob, 1741-1828

ALs, 14 Apr 1811. (90) DM340

Hess, Rudolf, 1894-1987

Ls, 4 Feb 1927. 1 p, 8vo. To Eugen Munder. Informing him about Hitler's plan to visit Stuttgart. (90) DM1,200

— 24 June 1933. (90) $400

Photograph, sgd, [c.1940]. (88) $350

Hesse, Hermann, 1877-1962

[A group of 4 typescripts of poems, 2 sgd, 1929 to 1934, 4 pp, 8vo & folio, sold at HK on 11 Nov 1988, lot 3364, for DM900.]

[A collection of 4 typescripts of poems, 1 sgd, 2 sgd & inscr to Dr. O. Feilke, [n.d.], 5 pp, 4to, sold at HK on 6 Nov, lot 3182, for DM920.]

[A group of 6 photographs showing Hesse, probably taken by his son Martin, [c.1935], 12cm by 8cm, 4 inscr by Hesse, sold at S on 26 Apr 1989, lot 986, for £260 to Thon.]

[An archive containing 157 letters, pamphlets, photographs, news clippings, envelopes, etc., 1937 to 1962, to Mrs. Lotte Einstein, sold at sg on 12 Nov 1987, lot 104, for $3,000.]

Autograph Ms, horoscope, including astrological calculations, [n.d.]. 3 pp, folio. Sgd H.H. at head. Repaired. (91) DM4,000

— Autograph Ms, poem, beginning "Solang du nach dem Gluecke jagst", 11 lines; sgd. 1 p, 12mo. With small watercolor-&-ink drawing on integral leaf. Addressed to Lotte Einstein. (88) $2,200

— Autograph Ms, poem, Herbstgeruch, [c.1945]. 2 leaves, size not stated. With watercolored pen-&-ink sketch on tp. (90) DM1,300

— Autograph Ms, poem, Keine Rast, [n.d.]. 2 pp, 4to. Some corrections. With watercolored pen-&-ink sketch on tp. (89) DM1,800

— Autograph Ms, poem, Nachtlager, [19 Aug 1905]. 1 p, 8vo. 3 stanzas, sgd. On verso of an address leaf. (88) DM1,200

Original drawings, 6 sketches of villages in Ticino, [19]30 & 28 July [19]32. Various sizes; initialled. (88) £2,000

Original drawing, mountains in snow, in watercolor; [n.d.]. (89) DM550

— Original drawing, pen-&-ink sketch with watercolors, landscape with trees & lake, 17 Apr 1924, 4to. With authentication by Heiner Hesse, 29 May 1985, on verso. (88) DM7,000

— Original drawing, pen-&-ink sketch with watercolors, wreath of flowers, [n.d.]. (88) DM500

— Original drawing, trees & mountains in fall, in black crayon & watercolor; 1 Oct [19]22. 29cm by 23cm. Framed. With authentication by Heiner Hesse. (89) DM9,500

— Original drawing, watercolored pen-&-ink sketch, field & trees with mountains; sgd H.H. & dated [19]35. 11.5cm by 16.5cm. Framed. (90) DM4,600

— Original drawing, watercolored pen-&-ink sketch, house in mountainous landscape, 45mm by 62mm. On flypaper of his privately ptd Sommerbrief, 1959; 8vo. Autograph inscr, sgd HH, on tp. (88) DM1,500

— Original drawing, watercolored pen-&-ink sketch, landscape, 57mm by 21mm. (88) DM850

— Original drawing, watercolored pen-&-ink sketch, garden & houses with mountains, 1920. 178mm by 216mm. Sgd. (91) DM8,800

Autograph transcript, 12 poems, [1930-1931]. 13 double sheets, 4to, in vellum bdg. Sgd & inscr to Hans Fretz. With 13 watercolors. (91) DM18,000

— Autograph transcript, fairy tale, Piktors Verwandlungen; 1922. 16 pp, 4to, on rectos only; in paper wraps. Illus with 17 small watercolors & 2 decorated borders; inscr to Oskar Reinhart. (91) £7,500

— Autograph transcript, Piktor's Verwandlungen. Ein Maerchen, [early 1930s]. 16 leaves (2 blank), 8vo, in wraps. Including 16 watercolors. Inscr to Hans Fretz. (89) DM13,000

— Autograph transcript, poem, Kleiner Knabe, [n.d.]. 2 pp, 4to. Sgd. With watercolored pen-&-ink sketch on tp. (89) DM2,200

— Autograph transcript, poem, Leben einer Blume, [c.1930]. 2 pp, 4to. With watercolor of a carnation on tp. (88) DM2,000

— Autograph transcript, poem, Nachtlied, [n.d.]. 1 p, 8vo. Sgd. (89) DM1,300

— Autograph transcript, poem, Ski-Rast, [n.d.]. 2 leaves, size not stated. With watercolored pen-&-ink drawing. (89) DM2,200

— Autograph transcript, Zwoelf Gedichte, sgd & dated 1920. 27 pp, 4to. With 13 watercolors. (89) £4,500

— Autograph transcript, Zwoelf Gedichte, 1956. 13 double sheets, folio. Watercolored tp & 12 pen-&-ink sketches, with watercolors. Sgd twice. 1 fold tear. (88) DM26,000

Typescript, Drei Bilder aus einem alten Tessiner Park, fall 1937. 4 double sheets, 8vo. Sgd & inscr to Dr. O. Feilke. With 2 watercolored pen-&-ink drawings, 95mm by 80mm & 85mm by 85mm. (88) DM7,500

— Typescript, Ein paar Gedichte von Hermann Hesse, 12 poems illus with 13 watercolors, Aug 1918. 26 pp, 4to. Green calf gilt bdg. With autograph tp,

HESSE

sgd. (91) £2,800
- Typescript, poem, Alle Tode, sgd; [n.d.]. On double sheet, 8vo, with AL, initialled, to Dr. O. Feilke, requesting medicine, & watercolored pen-&-ink drawing, village with church in front of mountains. (88) DM3,600
- Typescript, poem, Ein Jugendgedicht von Josef Knecht, Feb [19]35. 1 p, 8vo. Sgd H.H., in pencil. With autograph title in watercolored vignette. Sent to Dr. Feilke. (88) DM1,300
- Typescript, poem, Ein Traum, fall 1958. 2 p, 8vo. Sgd. With watercolored pen-&-ink sketch at head. (88) DM1,800
- Typescript, poem, Ein Traum, sgd, inscr & dated Dec 1958. 2 pp, 8vo. 24 lines. Including small watercolor sketch at head. (90) DM1,400
- Typescript, poem, Floetenspiel, sgd, inscr & dated Mar 1940. (90) DM270
- Typescript, poem, Hoehe des Sommers, Aug [19]33. (89) DM900
- Typescript, poem, Morgenstunde, sgd & dated Feb 1959. 2 pp, 8vo. With a watercolored sketch at head. With anr. (89) DM1,300
- Typescript, poem, Seifenblasen, sgd, inscr & dated 14/16 Jan 1937. (89) DM400
- Typescript, poem, Spaetsommer 1929. 2 p, 8vo. Sgd. With watercolored pen-&-ink sketch on tp. Addressed to O. Feilke. (88) DM2,300
- Typescript, poem, Wache Nacht, Feb 1946. (90) DM250
- Typescript, poem, Zur Morgenlandfahrt, [1932-33]. 2 pp, 8vo. Including autograph tp with watercolored vignette; sgd & inscr. (91) DM1,600

Typescript carbon copy, poem, Seifenblasen, sgd, inscr to Carlo & dated Jan 1937. (90) DM280

Collection of 3 A Ls s & autograph postcard, sgd, [30 Aug 1904] to late Nov 1908. 10 pp, 8vo, & card. To Karl Lichtenhahn, 1 ALs to Mrs. Lichtenhahn. Private letters about living in Gaienhofen, family news, etc. (88) DM3,600
- Collection of ALs, 3 Ls s, & autograph postcard, sgd, 4 Mar 1907, 1934, & [n.d.]. 7 pp, various sizes, & card. To Hans Muehlestein. About a meeting, his work, his health problems, etc. (91) DM1,200
- Collection of 2 A Ls s & Ls, 17 Feb 1910, July 1928 & [n.d.]. 7 pp, 4to & 8vo. To Josef Hofmiller. About Hofmiller's Monatshefte, his own literary production, etc. 1st page of Ls def. (88) DM1,700
- Collection of ALs & autograph postcard, sgd, Apr 1914. 1 p, 8vo, & card. To H. F. S. Bachmair. Offering his story Anton Schievelbeyn for print. (91) DM1,150
- Collection of ALs, 8 Ls s, 2 autograph postcards, sgd, 4 typescripts (mostly carbon copies), & photograph, sgd, [1924?] to 1941. 20 pp, various sizes, & cards. To Willi Schuh, about his literary projects & other matters. Poems, sgd. With related material. (90) DM6,500
- Collection of ALs & 2 Ls s, Apr 1931 to Dec 1933. 3 pp, 8vo. To Dr. O. Feilke. Informing him about a journey & his work, & requesting him to forward copies of poems. (89) DM1,100
- Collection of 4 A Ls s & 2 Ls s, 1947, 1948 & [n.d.]. (91) £500
- Collection of ALs & Ls, 6 Oct 1952 & [n.d.]. 2 pp, 8vo. To H.-E. Dienelt. Commenting about recipient's poetry, & sending a poem (present, above; typescript carbon copy). With related material. (90) DM1,600
- Collection of ALs, Ls, 3 postcards, sgd (1 autograph), typescript (poem) & 2 privately ptd works, sgd & inscr, 1959 to 1961 & [n.d.]. To an unnamed lady in Munich. About his vacations in Switzerland, & contents not stated. With related material. (88) DM1,300

A Ls s (2), [25 Dec] 1932 & 1933. 6 pp, 8vo. To Joseph Englert. Describing the scene outside. Thanking for presents & sending New Year's wishes. Each with watercolor sketch at head. (88) £1,400
- A Ls s (2), [n.d.]. 5 pp, 8vo. To Joseph Englert. Thanking for presents. Each with watercolor sketch at head. (88) £1,350

ALs, [1930]. (88) DM380
- [1931]. 3 pp, 8vo. To Dr. O. Feilke. About his new house & his eye problems. Including sketch of his house, in

watercolor over pencil. (90) DM2,800
— [early Dec 1933]. (88) DM1,000
— [c.24 May 1936]. (90) DM380
— 26 May [19]36. (89) DM420
— [5 May 1938]. (90) DM320
— [c.10 Apr, "Easter"] 1955. 1 p, 8vo. To Dr. Michael. Thanking for books. With watercolored pen-&-ink sketch at head, landscape with tree. (88) DM1,600

Collection of 4 Ls s & 4 postcards, sgd (1 autograph), [31 Oct 1910] to 2 Feb 1914. 4 pp, 4to & 8vo, & cards. To the publishing house of Albert Langen. About various publication matters. File holes. (90) DM1,200

— Collection of Ls & autograph postcard, sgd, 9 May 1917 & 18 Sept 1919. (90) DM380

— Collection of Ls & postcard, sgd, [6 Feb 1934 & Feb 1936]. (89) DM420

— Collection of Ls & 2 postcards (1 sgd, 1 sgd in type), [c.Apr 1941 to c.1942/43]. (90) DM850

Series of 3 Ls s (1 initialled), 18 May 1929, 29 July 1932, & "Good Friday" [n.y.]. 6 pp, 4to & 8vo. To Joseph Englert. Sending greetings. About his drawings & the enthusiasm for Hitler. Talking about Gandhi. Each with watercolor sketch. (88) £1,500

— Series of 3 Ls s, [n.d.]. 6 pp, 8vo. To Joseph Englert. Discussing Steppenwolf. Contents not stated. Each with watercolor sketch. (88) £1,500

— Series of 5 Ls s (1 initialled), 10 Mar 1932, [25 Dec] 1940 & [n.d.]. 12 pp, 8vo. To Joseph Englert. About acquiring a taste for whisky, his literary plans, proofs of a new work, etc. With typed poem, Der Heiland. 4 Ls with watercolor sketches. (88) £2,500

Ls s (2), [16 Apr 1933 & 5 July 1934]. 2 pp, folio. To Dr. Feilke. Mentioning his own works & others, Thomas Mann, Andre Gide, etc. (89) DM1,600

— Ls s (2), [1939] & [25 Apr] 1943. (88) DM350

— Ls s (2), July 1942 & Sept 1945. (91) DM650

Ls, 29 Oct 1834. 2 pp, 8vo. To Dr. O. Feilke. Personal news, & complaining about a constant stream of visitors. Including watercolored pen-&-ink drawing. (90) DM2,400

— Dec 1923. (89) DM550

— 20 Dec 1928. 3 pp, 8vo. To Dr. O. Feilke. Thanking for a present, about F. Jammes, F. Timmermanns, his eye problems, etc. With watercolored pen-&-ink sketch at head, landscape with tree & village. (88) DM2,600

— 7 Mar 1929. 3 pp, 8vo. To Dr. O. Feilke. Acknowledging receipt of a prescription, & reporting about his health problems. With watercolored pen-&-ink sketch at head, mountains with 2 trees & sheds. (88) DM2,200

— [10 July 1929]. 2 pp, 8vo. To Dr. O. Feilke. Regarding his health problems & complaining he has no major literary plans at the moment. With watercolored pen-&-ink sketch at head, view from his apartment. (88) DM3,400

— [late Sept 1929]. 2 pp, 8vo. To Dr. O. Feilke. About leaving Montagnola at the end of the summer, & his son's visit. With watercolored pen-&-ink drawing at head, group of houses in the mountains. (88) DM3,000

— [27 Dec 1930]. 2 pp, 8vo. To Dr. O. Feilke. Thanking for a book, & saying he hopes to move into a house at Montagnola in the summer. With watercolored pen-&-ink drawing at head, tree & houses in the mountains. (88) DM2,400

— [1930]. 2 pp, 8vo. To Dr. O. Feilke. About his eye problems & the project to build a house. Including watercolored pen-&-ink sketch. (89) DM3,400

— [early July 1932]. 2 pp, 8vo. To Dr. O. Feilke. Complaining about financial problems & bad investments. With watercolored pen-&-ink drawing at head, house with a tree. (88) DM2,800

— [Dec 1932]. 2 pp, 8vo. To Dr. O. Feilke. Thanking for a present & recommending Musil's Mann ohne Eigenschaften & other books. Including watercolored pen-&-ink drawing. (90) DM2,400

— [Dec 1934]. (90) DM860

— [8 July 1935]. 2 pp, 8vo. To Dr. Feilke. About his activities around the house & Pueckler's books. With watercolored pen-&-ink sketch. (89) DM2,600

HESSE

— [2 Jan 1936]. (89) DM600
— [c.June 1940]. (90) DM200
— [n.d.]. 2 pp, 8vo. To Dr. Feilke. Informing him about his holidays & the state of his health. Including watercolored pen-&-ink sketch. (89) DM2,800
Collection of 2 autograph postcards, sgd & 2 photographs, sgd & inscr, 8 Dec 1914, 15 June 1946 & [n.d.]. (90) DM380
— Collection of autograph postcard, sgd & 2 postcards, sgd, 5 & 19 Apr [19]32 & [n.d.]. (89) DM320
Series of 3 autograph postcards, sgd, 1930 & 1931. (89) DM600
Autograph postcards (2), sgd, 2 Jan & 19 Apr 1934. (89) DM360
Autograph postcard, sgd, 12 July 1914. (90) DM420
— [Apr 1929?]. (88) DM320
— [3 Nov 1929]. (88) DM220
— 3 Aug 1950. (88) DM250
— [1958]. (91) DM320
— 22 Dec 1961. (88) DM620
— 22 Dec 1961. (88) DM500
Autograph postcards (2), 7 Sept 1928 & 11 Jan 1930. (88) DM400
Autograph sentiment, sgd, 1947. (89) DM520

Heuberger, Richard, 1850-1914
Collection of 4 A Ls s & postcard, sgd, 1878 to [n.d.]. (88) £200

Heuss, Theodor, 1884-1963
ALs, 16 July 1933. (91) DM650
— 11 Nov 1938. (91) DM1,000
— 29 Nov 1940. (90) DM800
Series of 5 Ls s, 21 Mar 1952 to 16 Nov 1962. (90) DM800
Ls, 7 Oct 1952. (88) DM220
Photograph, sgd, [1957]. (90) DM380

Hewes, Joseph, Signer from North Carolina
ALs, 20 May 1778. 1 p, 4to. To J. Searle & Sharp Delany. About lottery sales. Sgd Hewes & Smith. (91) $1,100

AMERICAN BOOK PRICES CURRENT

Hewes, Joseph, Signer from North Carolina —& Others
Ls, 5 & 11 Aug 1779. 3 pp, 4to. To Gov. Richard Caswell. About financial matters, & reporting about actions in Congress. Also sgd by John Penn, Thomas Burke, Cornelius Harnett & William Sharpe, delegates to the Continental Congress. Doheny collection. (89) $7,500

Hewes, Joseph, Signer from North Carolina. See: Hooper, William

Hewitt, Graily, 1864-1952
Series of c.70 A Ls s, 1939 to 1951. (89) £200
— Series of c.80 A Ls s, c.1940 to 1951. To Mrs Durnford. (91) $1,100
See also: Calligraphy

Heyse, Paul, 1830-1914
Autograph Ms, poem, Mondnacht, [n.d.]. (88) DM280
Series of 5 A Ls s, 6 July 1873 to 20 June 1888. (89) DM550
A Ls s (2), 1 Dec 1874 & 12 Jan 1887. (90) DM360
— A Ls s (2), 25 June 1906 & 4 June 1913. (90) DM260
ALs, 2 May 1857. (90) DM250
— 30 Sept 1889. (91) DM200

Heyward, DuBose, 1885-1940
Collection of 2 A Ls s & Ls, 1929 to 1939. (90) $250

Heyward, Thomas, Signer from South Carolina
Ds, 10 Jan 1785. (90) $170

Heywood, Thomas, 1574?-1641
Ms, verse trans, Ovid's De Arte Amandi or The Art of Love, [early 17th cent]; c.244 pp, 8vo, in contemp calf gilt. In a single, probably professional hand. (88) £2,800

Hidden Colour Painting Books
Original drawings, large collection of artwork for the series by various artists, 1924 to 1943. (90) £600

Higashikuni, Naruhiko
ALs, 23 May [1927]. (88) £300

Higden, Ranulf, d.1364
Ms, Polychronicon, in the Middle English trans of John of Trevisa. [London, c.1420]. 214 pp, 422mm by 285mm, Repaired 19th-cent russia bdg. In a fine English bookhand. In prose, with c.500 lines of verse. With over 300 illuminated initials, large historiated initial & very large miniature. (89) £36,000

Higginson, Stephen, 1743-1828
Ls, 3 July 1799. (88) $175

Hildebert of Lavardin, 1056-1133. See: Gaufridus Babion & Hildebert of Lavardin

Hilder, Rowland
Original drawings, (9), mostly to illus Monica Redlich's Five Farthings, 1937. Archives of J. M. Dent & Son. (88) £850

Hildesheimer, Wolfgang
Autograph Ms, comments about writing as an art; 1966. (89) DM320

Hill, Clara
[Her interleaved copy of E. Pauer's Birthday Book of Musicians and Composers, 1882, sgd by over 300 violinists, pianists, composers, singers, etc., each on their birthday, 1883 to 1934, 360 pp, 8vo, in green mor bdg, sold at star on 5 Apr 1991, lot 1090, for DM7,500.]

Hill, Sir Rowland, 1795-1879
ALs, 13 Oct 1855. (91) $190
Ls, 7 Oct 1859. Alexander collection. (90) $230

Hillary, Sir Edmund
Ls, 14 Mar 1973. (88) DM330
Photograph, sgd, [n.d.]. (89) $210

Hiller, Ferdinand, 1811-85
Series of 3 A Ls s, 11 Sept to 18 Dec 1853. (90) DM800
ALs, 13 Dec 1850. (89) DM380
— 23 Mar 1864. (88) DM440
— 23 July 1870. (88) DM250
— [n.d.]. (90) DM320

Hiller, Johann Adam, 1728-1804
Ms, opera, Die Jagd, [c.1800]. (90) DM850

Hiller, Kurt, 1885-1972
Collection of ALs & 3 Ls s, 2 June 1953 to 1957. (91) DM650
Autograph postcard, sgd, 8 Dec 1934. (91) DM300

Hilton, James, 1900-54
Ls, 30 Aug 1943. (91) $80

Himmel, Friedrich Heinrich, 1765-1814
ALs, 18 May 1811. (89) DM750

Himmler, Heinrich, 1900-45
Ls, 25 Feb 1939. 2 pp, folio. To Goering. Asking for the relocation of a projected airstrip on the Island of Sylt to save ancient burial mounds. (90) DM3,400
— 22 Apr 1943. 1 p, 4to. To [Joachim von] Ribbentrop. Transmitting a file concerning the shooting of Stalin's son during an attempt to escape from a prisoner of war camp. With file, 13 pp; carbon copy. (88) $4,600
Ns, Jan 1937. (89) DM360
— Jan 1938. (89) DM320
Ds, 1 Apr 1935. (90) $300
— Mar 1945. (90) $650

Hinchliff, Woodbine K.
Original drawings, 18 oil paintings to illus T. Okey's Venice and its Story, 1903. Some initialled. On wood panels, c.300mm by 220mm or 205mm by 205mm. Archives of J. M. Dent & Son. (88) £1,800
— Original drawings, 42 oil paintings to illus T. Okey's Paris and its Story, 1904. On wood panels, c.300mm by 230mm or 220mm by 320mm. 6 def. Archives of J. M. Dent & Son. (88) £4,600

Hinckle, Warren
Typescript, If You Have a Lemon, Make Lemonade. (91) $100

Hindemith, Paul, 1895-1963
[A varied group of material by Hindemith or relating to him, c.1946 to 1951, including autograph musical Ms, sold at S on 18 Nov 1988, lot 374, for £380 to Stargardt.]

HINDEMITH

Autograph music, 2 pieces for organ, 14 & 15 Aug 1918. 7 pp, 34cm by 27cm; 24 staves each. 86 & 53 bars; fair copies, 1 sgd at head. In pencil. (89) DM8,500
— Autograph music, notebook containing over 30 choral preludes & fugues, 1918. 48 pp, 4to. Mostly in pencil on up to 10 staves per page, mainly on systems of 3 staves. With autograph inscr, sgd, on label on outer cover. (89) £8,000

ALs, 6 Dec 1931. (89) DM900
— 19 Aug [19]47. Byer collection. (90) $425
— 13 July 1948. (91) DM750

Ls, 17 Jan 1946. (90) DM440
— [n.d.]. (90) DM220

Autograph postcard, sgd, [10 Apr 1925]. (88) DM550

A Ns s (2), 1952 & 1958. (90) DM380

Photograph, sgd & inscr, [n.d.]. (90) DM500

Hindenburg, Paul von, 1847-1934

Autograph Ms, declaration that he never advocated a peace without territorial annexations; 25 Feb 1918. 1 p, 4to. Sgd. (90) DM1,700

Ms, New Year's address to the army, [1932]. (90) DM750

ALs, 27 Sept 1876. (89) DM380
— 14 Nov 1892. (90) DM250
— 21 June 1895. 3 pp, 8vo. To Maj. von Wedderkop. Concerning the participation of the Grandduke of Oldenburg in a military commemoration. (88) DM1,050
— 31 Mar 1907. Schroeder collection. (89) DM380
— 22 July 1920. 3 pp, 4to. To Grossherzog August von Oldenburg. Commenting about the problems of the German nation. Schroeder collection. (89) DM2,600
— 10 Apr 1923. (89) DM280

Ls s (2), 30 Oct 1922 & 16 Oct 1925. (88) DM240
— Ls s (2), 26 Aug 1926 & 20 Feb 1933. (88) $175

Ls, 8 Feb 1919. (90) DM220
— 5 Sept 1929. (88) DM500

Ds, 20 June 1930. (89) DM650
— 11 July 1934. 1 p, folio. Permission to Joachim von Stuelpnagel to wear the uniform of a general of the 17th Regiment of Infantry. Countersgd by von Blomberg & von Fritsch. (91) DM1,300

Photograph, sgd, [c.1930]. (88) $110
— PETER, J. - Original drawing, port of Hindenburg, 1915. 28.4cm by 22.6. Sgd by Hindenburg. Mtd. (88) DM350

Hinz, Werner, 1903-85

[His album, containing c.335 entries by actors & other people connected with the theater, authors, composers & politicians, including B. Brecht, H. Hesse, Th. Mann, A. Gide, K. Hamsun, etc., 1921 to 1979, in lea bdg, sold at HN on 9 Dec 1988, lot 3313, for DM8,400.]

Hirohito, Emperor of Japan, 1901-89

Ls, 9 Apr 1928. 2 pp, folio. To the President of Argentina. Introducing his ambassador Dr. Masao Tsuda. Laid down. (90) £2,000
— 28 Aug 1931. 2 pp, folio. To Gabriel Terra, President of Uruguay. Congratulating him on his election to the Presidency. With French trans. (90) £8,500
— 13 Feb 1936. 2 pp, folio. To the King of the Hellenes. Expressing congratulations on his restoration to the throne. With French trans. (89) £30,000
— 14 July 1938. 2 pp, folio. To King George II of the Hellenes. Offering congratulations on the marriage of Crown Prince Paul. With French trans. (90) £11,000
— 24 May 1939. 2 pp, folio. To the King of the Hellenes. Expressing congratulations on the birth of Princess Sophie. With French trans. (89) £30,000
— 18 June 1940. 2 pp, folio. To King George II of the Hellenes. Offering condolences on the death of Prince Christopher. With French trans. (90) £9,800
— 24 June 1940. 2 pp, folio. Accrediting Antonio Luraschi as Italian Honorary Consul in Dairen. With French trans. (90) £13,000
— 24 Nov 1940. 2 pp, folio. To the King of the Hellenes. Expressing congratulations on the birth of Prince Con-

stantine. With French trans. (89) £2,600

His, Wilhelm, 1831-1904
ALs, 20 July 1885. (88) DM220
— 17 Oct 1887. (91) DM500

Histoire de Troye
Ms, L'Histoire de Troye le Grant, with extracts from the histories of the Fall of Thebes & of Theseus & the Minotaur. [France, mid-15th cent]. 118 leaves (1 blank), vellum, 325mm by 240mm, in mid-19th cent Parisian dark green mor by Thompson. In a very calligraphic lettre batarde with many decorative cadels & descenders. With painted initials throughout & blank spaces intended for 6 miniatures. Phillipps Ms.23240. (91) £19,000

Hitchcock, Alfred, 1899-1980
Original drawing, small self-port, sgd; [n.d.]. (89) $350
Ls, 12 Apr 1979. (91) $250
— 6 Sept 1979. (91) $200
Photograph, sgd, [n.d.]. (91) $250
— Anr, [n.d.]. (91) $275
See also: Bergman, Ingrid & Hitchcock

Hitler, Adolf, 1889-1945
[2 postcard photographs of Hitler, sgd, 23 June 1934, with related material, sold at S on 17 Nov 1988, lot 234, for £900 to Severi.]
ALs, 1 May 1924. 1 p, 4to. To an unnamed lady. From Landsberg Prison, about his political activities & thanking for a book. (88) DM18,000
Ls, 6 Dec 1935. 2 pp, folio. To the King of the Hellenes. Informing him of the recall of the German envoy Ernst Eisenlohr. (91) £1,500
— 6 Dec 1935. 2 pp, folio. To George II, King of the Hellenes. Notifying him of an ambassador's appointment. (89) £2,600
— 18 June 1940. 2 pp, folio. To George II of the Hellenes. Expressing condolences on the death of Prince Christopher of Greece. Countersgd by von Ribbentrop. (89) £1,900
Ds, 26 Feb 1935. (88) $850
— 19 Mar 1936. 1 p, folio. Commission for Aksel Holm as Consul in Norway. With commission for Holm sgd by von Hindenburg, 1932. (89) DM1,100
— 1 Sept 1935. 3 pp, 4to. 53 military & medical appointments. Countersgd by von Fritsch. File holes. (91) $1,600
— 18 Jan 1936. 9 pp, folio. Promotions for 157 army officers. Countersgd by von Blomberg & von Fritsch. (88) $1,400
— 12 Feb 1936. 2 pp, folio. Military directive on various topics. (89) $1,300
— 20 Feb 1936. (89) $1,000
— 19 Sept 1936. 2 pp, folio. Appointment for G. Albrecht as professor at Marburg. Countersgd by Goering. (89) DM1,100
— 30 Sept 1936. 1 p, folio. Discharge from active duty for Major Dahle. (90) $1,100
— 1 Apr 1938. 2 pp, folio. Act regarding tenure of worker's councillors. Also sgd by 3 others. (90) DM2,000
— 16 May 1941. (88) $950
— 24 June 1941. 1 p, folio. Directive assigning dates of rank to 2 generals. Countersgd by von Brauchitsch. (91) $1,200
— 15 Sept 1941. (89) $950
— 15 Oct 1941. (88) $800
— 7 Nov 1941. 1 p, folio. Promotion for Capt. Hartmann to major at the War Academy. Countersgd by von Brauchitsch. (90) $1,100
— 5 July 1942. 1 p, folio. Promotion for Gen. Lindemann as commander-in-chief of the 18th Army. Countersgd by Keitel. (90) $1,500
— 15 July 1942. 1 p, folio. Removal of Field Marshal von Bock as commander-in-chief of Army Group B. (88) $1,100
— 16 Nov 1942. 1 p, folio. Promotions for 5 lieutenant generals. Countersgd by Schmundt. (91) $1,300
— 13 Feb 1943. 1 p, folio. Assignment for Gen. von Vietinghoff-Scheel as commander of the 15th Army. (90) $1,300
— 11 Mar 1943. (88) $750
— Aug 1943. 2 pp, 4to. List of military promotions or transfers of generals. Countersgd by Rudolf Schmundt. (90) $1,200
— Oct 1943. 3 pp, folio. Promotions for 8 officers. Countersgd by Schmundt.

HITLER

(91) $1,200
— 9 Jan 1944. (88) $1,000
— 6 May 1944. 2 pp, folio. Promotions for 18 officers. Countersgd by Schmundt. (91) $1,200
— 27 June 1944. 1 p, folio. Military directive ordering 3 generals to new assignments. (90) $1,200
— 29 June 1944. (90) $850
— 5 July 1944. (89) $1,000
— 8 July 1944. 1 p, folio. Promotion for 6 generals. (90) $1,300
— 15 Aug 1944. (89) $950
— 28 Oct 1944. 4 pp, folio. Military promotion for 21 medical officers. Countersgd by Gen. Burgdorf. (88) $1,300
— 19 Jan 1945. 1 p, folio. Military directive reassigning generals. (88) $1,100

Autograph sentiment, sgd, 23 Dec 1925. On verso of port in vol 1 of his Mein Kampf. Munich: Eher, 1925; no 99 of 500 copies, sgd. (88) DM3,000

Photograph, sgd, 28 Apr 1935. 24.3cm by 18cm. In uniform. (88) DM1,150
— Anr, [13 June 1936]. 4 by 6 inches. With related material. (90) $1,600
— BARGATZKY, WALTER. - Ms, account of the plot of 20 July 1944 to assassinate Hitler, by one of the conspirators; 10 June 1945. 14 pp, folio. With English trans. (91) £6,500
— HITLER'S ADJUTANTS. - 6 port photographs, [1940s to 1960s], various sizes, all in uniform, 5 sgd on recto, 1 on mount. (88) $225
— HITLER'S CABINET. - 13 port photographs, sgd, [1930s to 1946], various sizes, mostly bust poses, many by Heinrich Hoffmann. (88) $425

Hoban, James, 1762-1831
Ds, 14 Aug 1822. (91) $130

Hoby, Sir Edward, 1560-1617
Autograph Ms, prayer book & other devotional matter, [late 16th cent]. About 65 pp, 4to, in contemp calf. In Latin with some pages in Hebrew; sgd. Dampstained. Marquess of Downshire collection. (90) £1,700

AMERICAN BOOK PRICES CURRENT

Hodges, C. Walter
Original drawings, (13), to illus A. Archives of J. M. Dent & Son. (88) £200
— Original drawings, (17), including ink & watercolor dust jacket designs for novels, 1934 to 1941, & the artist's dummy for Plain Lane Christmas, 1978. Archives of J. M. Dent & Son. (88) £220
— Original drawings, (18), to illus L. Archives of J. M. Dent & Son. (88) £320
— Original drawings, (39), to illus Mark Twain's Adventures of Tom Sawyer & Adventures of Huckleberry Finn, 1955 & later. Archives of J. M. Dent & Son. (88) £1,000

Hodges, William, 1744-97
ALs, 19 Aug 1794. (88) £550

Hoehn, Hermann Alfred, 1887-1945
Autograph music, theme & 14 variations for piano, [c.1905]. (90) DM400

Hoelderlin, Friedrich, 1770-1843
Autograph sentiment, sgd; comments about schools of philosophy, Mar 1795. 1 p, 8vo. In French & German. In album of Johann Caspar Camerer, containing c.100 entries; in vellum bdg. (89) DM32,000

Hoeller, Karl, 1907-87
Autograph music, Malinconia, from his Suite for piano, Op. (90) DM550

Hoelty, Ludwig Christoph Heinrich, 1748-76
Autograph Ms, 2 poems, An die Ruhe, & An eine Tobackspfeife, [n.d.]. 3 pp, 8vo. Sgd. On verso 3 poems by Heinrich Christian Boie in the hand of Johann Heinrich Voss. (90) DM13,000
ALs, 28 Nov 1774. 4 pp, 4to. To Johann Martin Miller. About his literary projects, travel plans, activities with friends, etc. (91) DM8,000

Hoeppener, Hugo, 1868-1948. See: Fidus, 1868-1948

Hofer, Andreas, 1767-1810
Ns, 14 Sept 1809. 1 p, folio. To the Directors of the Mines in Tirol. Stating that orders have been given to improve the supply of the mines with powder.

On 4th page of a letter addressed to him regarding the lack of powder for blasting. (88) DM1,900

ADs, 16 Nov 1809. 1 p, 7.5cm by 10cm. Order to provide lodgings for a young man. (91) DM3,500

Ds, 11 Sept 1809. 1 p, 4to. Appointment for Joseph Kirchberger as his deputy. With 3-line autograph postscript. (89) £1,800

Hofer, Karl, 1878-1955
A Ls s (2), 11 Nov 1932 & May 1933. (90) DM800

— A Ls s (2), 14 July [19]52 & Feb [19]53. (90) DM310

ALs, 12 Feb 1931. (91) DM470

— 22 June 1954. (89) DM360

Hoffa, James R., 1913-75?
Photograph, sgd & inscr, [n.d.]. (91) $275

Hoffmann, Ernst Theodor Amadeus, 1776-1822
ALs, 27 July 1814. 1 p, 4to. To Theodor Gottlieb von Hippel. Letter to a friend about being unemployed, his financial problems, etc. With engraved port. (88) DM9,500

— 10 May 1820. 1 p, 8vo. To Joseph Engelmann. Assuring him that he is now working on the promised contribution to his journal. Seal tear repaired. (90) DM8,500

— 25 Aug 1821. 1 p, 4to. To his pbr Wilmans. Offering his Meister Floh for publication. (90) DM30,000

ADs, 8 Dec 1817. 1 p, 8vo. Receipt to [Georg] Reimer for the fee for his fairy tale Das fremde Kind. (91) DM4,000

Hoffmann, Franz, 1804-81
Series of 11 A Ls s, 15 July 1877 to 24 July 1881. (88) DM420

Hoffmann, Friedrich, 1660-1742
Ds, 30 Nov 1726. (90) DM330

Hoffmann, Heinrich, 1809-94
Autograph Ms, poem, Wie geht's? 4 lines, [n.d.]. (90) DM650

ALs, 30 Sept 1860. (89) DM700

— 29 Sept 1877. (91) DM750

— 22 Jan 1886. (90) DM900

Autograph sentiment, quatrain expressing New Year's wishes, 30 Dec 1886. (90) DM850

Hoffmann, Ludwig, 1852-1932
[A large collection of material relating to the controversy about the building of museums in Berlin, 1910 to 1930, including correspondence, minutes of meetings, accounts, etc., sold at HH on 16 Nov 1989, lot 2473, for DM26,000.]

Hoffmann, Max, 1869-1927. See: World War I

Hoffmann, Peter Martinovich
Original drawings, (17), to illus [A Collection Worthy of Curiosity from the Realm of Plants, in Russian]. Moscow, 1797-1810. 17 leaves, 63.5cm by 49cm; disbound. 3 drawings with Ms descriptions in Russian; all waterstained. With Ms dedication leaf to Emperor Paul. (91) £12,500

Hoffmann von Fallersleben, August Heinrich, 1798-1874
Autograph Ms, poem, beginning "Kein Fruehling laesst uns Blumen spriessen"; [n.d.]. Albrecht collection. (91) SF460

— Autograph Ms, poem, Ein Herbsttag in Weimar, 1863. 2 pp, folio. 9 three-line stanzas, sgd HvF. Albrecht collection. (91) SF1,100

— Autograph Ms, poem, Zum 3. (88) DM620

— Autograph Ms, poem, Zum Geburtstage, 15 Dec [18]56. (91) DM580

Autograph transcript, poem, beginning "Wie Deine Schoenheit trat ans Licht der Welt", [n.d.]. (89) DM600

Collection of 3 A Ls s & AL, 11 Mar 1860 to 29 Mar 1870. 11 pp, 8vo. To Adolf Ellissen. About various literary matters. Sgd HvF. (90) DM1,500

— Collection of 5 A Ls s & 6 autograph Mss (5 sgd), 16 Oct 1871 to 22 July 1872 & [n.d.]. 18 pp, 4to & 8vo. Recipient unnamed. Sending poems & an essay for publication (included). 4 A Ls s sgd with paraph, 1 sgd HeutundImmer. (90) DM3,400

ALs, 25 Sept 1824. 3 pp, 8vo. To Eberhard von Groote. Thanking for Groote's Tristan, & mentioning Otfried Mss, Old German literature,

etc. (89) DM1,700
— 11 Sept 1835. (91) DM850
— 27 July 1852. (90) DM800
— 8 Aug 1852. 3 pp, 8vo. To [his pbr Carl Ruempler]. About a singing festival, a trip on the Rhine, a gathering of students, etc. Sgd HvF. (90) DM1,300
— 30 Nov 1852. 4 pp, 8vo. To Carl Ruempler. About the publication of Theophilus & his current work. (88) DM1,100
— 26 July 1855. (89) DM850
— 2 Feb 1857. (90) DM750
— 17 Apr 186[7]. (90) DM500
— [c.1871?]. (90) DM220
Autograph endorsement, sgd HvF, docket on Ls, 28 Nov 1811, 1 p, 4to, by Hans Graf Buelow to his father as mayor of Fallersleben, requesting a certification. Schroeder collection. (89) DM420

Hofmann, August Wilhelm von, 1818-92
ALs, 25 Aug 1877. (88) DM320
— 17 Aug 1888. (91) DM360
— 26 Nov 1891. (91) DM250

Hofmann, Josef Casimir, 1876-1957
[A collection of A Ls s, number, length & size not stated, 1955, to Albert Goldberg, with related material by Goldberg, sold at S on 19 May 1989, lot 427, for £900 to Spek.]

Hofmann von Hofmannswaldau, Christian, 1617-79
ALs, 1 May 1664. 1 p, folio. To Johann Hieronymus Imhof. Discussing the political situation & the campaign against the Turks. Sgd at head; in Latin. Seal tear repaired. Ammann collection. (89) DM1,900

Hofmannsthal, Hugo von, 1874-1929
Autograph Ms, libretto for the opera Der Rosenkavalier, 1st scene; [Mar 1909]. 5 pp, 4to. Sgd at head. Including musical sketches for the scene in the hand of Richard Strauss throughout. (91) DM40,000
Typescript, fragment of on early draft of Rosenkavalier; [n.d.]. 2 pp, folio; paginated 7 & 10. With revisions, partly in anr hand. (90) DM1,700
Typescript carbon copy, libretto for the 1st half of act I of the opera Die Frau ohne Schatten, [Dec 1913]. 24 pp, 4to. With autograph additions & musical sketches by Richard Strauss throughout. (91) DM24,000
Collection of 5 A Ls s, 4 Ls s, 2 autograph postcards, sgd, & telegram, 8 Apr 1909 to 8 Jan 1911. 24 pp, various sizes. To Otto Fuerstner. Mostly concerning the publication of Der Rosenkavalier. With copies of recipient's replies. (91) DM12,000

A Ls s (2), 13 Apr 1921 & [n.d.]. (88) £850
ALs, 22 Apr [1896]. 4 pp, 8vo. To Stefan George. Commenting on the latest issue of George's journal Blaetter fuer die Kunst. (90) £1,700
— 10 Feb [1899]. 4 pp, 8vo. To Otto Brahm. Discussing the premiere of 2 of his works. (90) DM2,400
— 26 May [1902]. 6 pp, 8vo. To his pbr S. Fischer. About his pantomime Der Schueler & Stefan George's refusal to translate D'Annunzio's Francesca da Rimini. (90) DM5,200
— [1905]. (90) DM650
— 6 May [1915]. (91) DM900
— 12 Apr 1918. 4 pp, 4to. To [Stefan] Grossmann. Discussing the 1st performance of Der Buerger als Edelmann. (90) DM2,200
— 15 Apr 1918. 2 pp, 8vo. To [Heinrich Gluecksmann?]. Explaining his intentions in using a Moliere play for a libretto set to music by Richard Strauss. (88) DM1,100
— 18 Nov 1920. (90) DM380
— 26 Oct [1922]. (89) DM680
— 10 Dec 1922. 2 pp, 4to. To Dr. Konrad Maril. Concerning the sale of movie rights to his plays & plans for a collected Ed of his works. (89) DM2,800
— 8 June 1926. (90) DM900
— [3 Feb 1928]. (89) DM320
— 7 Nov [n.y.]. (91) DM650
— [n.d.], "Sunday". (90) £950
— [n.d.]. (89) DM620
— [n.d.]. (90) DM380

Hofmannsthal, Hugo von, 1874-1929 —& Nostitz, Helene von, 1878-1944
[An important collection of correspondence, containing 78 A Ls s by Hofmannsthal (12 to Alfred von Nostitz) & 53 letters by Helene von

Nostitz, & further material, 1906 to 1928, sold at star on 9 Mar 1988, lot 179, for DM50,000.]

Hogarth, William, 1607-1764
Autograph Ms, segment from his vol Idle and Industrious Apprentices, 17 lines; [n.d.]. 1 p, 8vo. Working draft. Repaired & tipped to larger leaf. Barrett collection. (89) $1,800

Hogg, James, 1770-1835
Autograph Ms, poem, Love. (91) DM660
ALs, 17 Nov 1821. (91) £110

Hohenlohe-Ingelfingen, Friedrich Ludwig, Fuerst zu, 1746-1818
ALs, 12 Sept 1790. Schroeder collection. (89) DM260

Hohenlohe-Schillingsfuerst, Gustav Adolf, Prince, Cardinal, 1823-96
ALs, 18 Feb 1871. (89) DM360

Holbrooke, Josef, 1878-1958
Proof copy, Queen Mab, Op. (89) £400

Holiday, Billie, 1915-59
ALs, 22 June 1947. 2 pp, 4to. To Joe Guy. From prison, love letter, & worrying about his imprisonment. (89) $8,500
— 6 July 1947. 2 pp, 4to. To Joe Guy. Love letter, & about his & her own imprisonment. In pencil. (90) $6,500
— 12 July 1947. 2 pp, 4to. To Joe Guy. Love letter, about life in prison & her hope for better days. (90) $5,000
— 5 Aug 1947. 2 pp, 4to. To Joe Guy. Love letter from prison. (90) $3,500
— 16 Aug 1947. 2 pp, 4to. To Joe Guy. Love letter from prison, quoting a prayer from the Bible. (90) $3,000

Holladay, Ben, 1819-87
Check, sgd, 11 June 1870. (89) $350

Holly, Buddy
Photograph, 1958. (89) £280

Holly, Buddy —& The Crickets
[Their signatures on verso of Norman Petty's business card, 1958, 3.5 by 2 inches, with related material, sold at Dar on 4 Oct 1990, lot 241, for $1,600.]

Holmes, Oliver Wendell, 1809-94
Autograph Ms, poem, Sherman's in Savannah, sgd & dated 5 Jan 1865. Doheny collection. (89) $1,000
Collection of 2 A Ls s, photograph, & engraved port, 13 Mar 1879, 30 Apr 1880, & [n.d.]. 3 pp, 8vo, carte size, & size not stated, in folder by Sangorski & Sutcliffe. Recipients unnamed. Thanking for an introduction to Mr. Johnson. Comparing Jonathan Edwards & John Wesley. Middendorf collection. (89) $1,600
— Collection of 2 A Ls s & autograph Ms, sgd, 7 Aug 1888 to 18 Nov 1889. Doheny collection. (89) $550
ALs, 25 Sept 1856. (89) $95
— 16 Jan 1870. (88) $75
— 28 Jan 1885. (89) $275
— 6 Dec 1885. Doheny collection. (89) $750
— 19 Jan 1887. (89) $550
— 3 Apr 1887. (90) $100
— 8 Sept 1887. Byer collection. (90) $90
Autograph quotation, 3 Mar 1893. Byer collection. (90) $150
Signature, 10 Apr 1873. (90) $150
— Anr, 24 Mar 1887. (88) $60

Holmes, Oliver Wendell, 1841-1935
ALs, 4 Apr 1913. (88) $350
— 8 Nov 1926. (89) $260
— 31 May 1932. (91) $475
— 30 Apr [n.y.]. (90) $200

Holroyd, John Baker, 1st Earl of Sheffield, 1735-1821
Autograph Ms, drafts & working papers "On The Navigation and On The Political, Colonial, Manufacturing, Commercial and Agricultural Interests of The United Kingdom", [c.1808-1810]. About 750 pp, folio, in contemp portfolio. Including revision of his Observations on the Commerce of the American States. Some material in secretarial hands or ptd. With related material. (90) £5,200

Holst, Gustav, 1874-1934. See: Walton, William & Holst

HOLSTEIN

Holstein, Friedrich von, 1837-1909

Series of 4 A Ls s, 17 Feb to 20 Apr 1871. 34 pp, 8vo. Recipient unnamed. Important letters reporting in detail about the negotiations with France at Versailles. (91) DM10,000

— Series of 10 A Ls s, 28 Sept 1906 to 9 Jan 1907 & [n.d.]. 25 pp, 8vo. To Felix von Eckardt. Mostly relating to politics & the press. (89) DM2,600

A Ls s (2), 3 Sept 1906 & 8 Jan 1907. (90) DM750

ALs, [21 Mar 1892]. Schroeder collection. (89) DM800

Holtei, Karl von, 1798-1880

Autograph Ms, "postscript" to his Ed of Shakespeare's Much Ado About Nothing, [1849]. (91) DM380

Series of 31 A Ls s, 22 Oct 1864 to 30 Mar 1876. 114 pp, 4to & 8vo. To Karl Weinhold. Interesting letters to a good friend, covering a wide variety of matters. Signatures vary. (90) DM3,450

ALs, 23 July 1833. (91) DM250

— 28 Nov 1842. 4 pp, 4to. To [Tobias Gottfried Schroer]. Interesting letter about the political situation in Berlin, social life, the theater, acquaintances, etc. (89) DM1,900

Holten, Samuel, 1738-1816

ALs, [c.Mar 1785]. (90) $675

Holy League

Ms, The Records of the Holy League, in Latin & Italian. [Milan, c.1495]. 331 leaves (12 blank) & 5 flyleaves, vellum, 300mm by 222mm. Extra Parisian gold tooled bdg of c.1550. In a very fine sloping italic script. Official register of c.490 documents in the archives of the Dukes of Milan. Phillipps Ms.2175. (91) £80,000

Holz, Arno, 1863-1929

Autograph Ms, Zwoelf Liebesgedichte, [1926]. 66 pp, 8vo. In pencil; sgd on tp. Ptr's copy. In wraps. (90) DM4,000

ALs, 7 Feb 1904. (90) DM340

— 24 Apr 1915. (91) DM260

AMERICAN BOOK PRICES CURRENT

Homer, Winslow, 1836-1910

ALs, 12 Jan 1881. (90) $450

Hone, William, 1780-1842

[An important collection of books, papers & illustrative material of Hone, including c.200 letters to & from him, several autograph notebooks, etc., 1813 to 1842, sold at S on 20 July 1989, lot 124, for £12,000 to Quaritch.]

Honegger, Arthur, 1892-1955

Autograph music, Esquisse pour l'Adagio du II.d Quatuor; [n.d., after 1934]. 1 p, 34.8cm by 25.8cm. 37 bars in full score, sgd. (88) DM1,900

— Autograph music, Pacific (231) ... Reduction pour piano 4 mains, 1923. 11 pp, size not stated; 30 staves each. Sgd & inscr at head. Stichvorlage. (89) DM13,000

— Autograph music, part of Jeanne d'Arc au bucher, scene VIII, sgd; [n.d.]. (90) £950

— Autograph music, Petite Fanfare en l'honneur de l'Anniversaire de Madame van der Muehl, 28 Feb 1940. 1 p, folio. 8 bars scored for 3 trumpets, decorated with sketches of flowers; sgd. (90) £1,500

ALs, [19 May 1947]. (90) DM440

— 31 July [c.1947]. (88) DM260

ANs, [n.d.]. (90) DM340

Honey Mooners, The

Group photograph, [n.d.]. (89) $130

Honeymooners, The

[The signatures of Jackie Gleason, Audrey Meadows, Art Carney & Joyce Randolph on separate pieces of paper, [n.d.], framed with a group photograph, overall size 12 by 16 inches, sold at pnNy on 3 Dec 1988, lot 63, for $275.]

Hood, Samuel, Viscount, 1724-1816

ALs, 1805. (91) $100

Hood, Thomas, 1799-1845

Autograph Ms (2), humorous verses, The Logicians, & essay, On Reading; with covering ALs to R. John F. Fleming Estate. (89) $800

Autograph Ms, poem, beginning "No, not a cat's-paw here or there", [n.d.]. (88) £40

Hooghstraten, Antoon I van Lalaing, Count of, 1480-1540

Series of c.80 Ls s, May 1532 to 27 Sept 1534. About 200 pp, folio, in olive mor bdg. To Mary, Queen of Hungary, Regent of the Netherlands. As Governor of Holland, reporting on the state of his province, problems with the Estates, deteriorating relations with the Baltic states, Dutch trade, etc., (90) £8,000

Hooke, Robert

Document, [c.1660]. 1 p, folio. The King's Warrant for a Patent for Dr. Hookes Watches with Springs. Written in several hands & heavily revised in places. Docketed by Newton. (91) £21,000

Hooker, Joseph, 1814-79

Collection of ALs & Ls, 14 Jan & 16 Apr 1864. (89) $500

ALs, 12 May 1862. 3 pp, 4to. To Sen. Ira Harris. Criticizing Gen. McClellan. (89) $1,500

Hooper, William, Signer from North Carolina

Autograph Ms, record of a case heard in the Superior Courts of Justice, in which it was judged that John Parker took a horse belonging to Daniel Clary. (91) $900

ALs, 17 Apr 1776. 4 pp, folio. To Joseph Hewes. Analyzing the political & military situation in North Carolina. Def. John F. Fleming Estate. (89) $16,000

Letter, [c.1780]. (89) $950

ADs, 5 Mar 1768. (90) $900

Cut signature, [n.d.]. (91) $160

Hoover, Herbert, 1874-1964

Typescript, Address ... On the occasion of the dedication of The Harding Memorial at Marion, 16 June 1931. 4 pp, 4to. Sgd. (91) $1,500

ALs, 31 Mar 1909 [i.e.1910]. 1 p, 8vo. To Bewick, Moreing & Co. Requesting approval of his accepting directorships of 2 companies. (88) $1,300

— 31 Mar 1909. 1 p, 8vo. To Bewick, Moreing & Co. Requesting permission to accept the directorship of 2 companies. (89) $1,400

— 30 Oct 1929. 1 p, 4to. To Herbert L. Pratt. Sending his autograph. Pratt collection. (89) $14,000

— 2 Aug [n.y.]. (91) $220

Collection of 15 Ls s, autograph telegram, sgd, & signature, 20 Dec 1921 to 22 Oct 1958, 17 pp, mostly 4to. (88) $1,000

— Collection of 2 Ls s & 2 autograph telegrams, 23 & 29 June 1928, [c.15 July 1927], & [n.d.]. (90) $900

— Collection of Ls & photograph, sgd & inscr, 14 Mar 1929 & [Jan 1933]. (90) $550

— Collection of Ls & telegram, 24 Feb & 22 Jan 1940. 2 pp, various sizes. To Edward Lyman. Concerning use of the word "Hooverville" to describe shantytowns in Life Magazine. With related material. (90) $1,100

Series of 3 Ls s, 9 Oct & 19 Nov 1928, & 27 Nov 1956. (89) $150

— Series of 7 Ls s, 1928 to 1955. (88) $300

— Series of 6 Ls s, 23 Oct 1930 to Nov 1932. 6 pp, 4to. To Herman Bernstein, US Minister to Albania. On routine matters. (91) $1,200

— Series of 20 Ls s, 1933 to 1947. 20 pp, 4to. To Sarah B. Cope. About a variety of matters. With related material. (90) $1,900

— Series of 9 Ls s, 1936 to 1946. (90) $400

— Series of 15 Ls s, 1936 to 1949. (90) $550

— Series of 3 Ls s, 16 Nov 1938 to 14 July 1944. (90) $1,000

— Series of 3 Ls s, [1950s]. (89) $160

Ls s (2), 23 June 1920 & 3 Feb 1930. McVitty collection. (90) $700

Ls, 31 Mar 1920. (88) $75

— 28 Mar 1923. Byer collection. (90) $250

— 9 Dec 1927. (89) $60

— 15 Dec 1927. (90) $80

— 20 June 1928. (91) $110

— 21 June 1928. (90) $80

— 21 Apr 1929. (90) $350

— 24 May 1929. (88) $350

— 21 Feb 1930. (90) $170

— 8 May 1930. (88) $275

— 10 June 1930. (91) $100

— 17 June 1930. (91) $120

— 4 Sept 1930. (90) $225

— 22 June 1931. (91) $275

— 16 Nov 1932. (89) $325

— 19 Nov 1932. (88) $300

— 30 Nov 1932. Byer collection. (90) $475
— 2 Oct 1933. (90) $50
— 14 Aug 1934. (90) $80
— 17 Jan 1935. (91) $225
— 27 Nov 1935. (91) $100
— 10 Feb 1936. (91) $110
— 18 Sept 1936. (90) $85
— 29 June 1939. (91) $425
— 26 Feb 1947. (90) $90
— 17 Aug 1949. (89) $55
— 31 Oct 1949. (91) $75
— 31 Dec 1952. (91) $80
— 29 Oct 1953. (90) DM240
Ds, 5 Mar 1928. (91) $750
Photograph, sgd, [n.d.]. (89) $150
Photograph, sgd & inscr, 10 July 1930. (90) $120
— Anr, [c.1930]. (89) $500
— Anr, [n.d.]. (91) $275
— Anr, [n.d.]. (91) $110
— Anr, [n.d.]. (91) $100
— Anr, [n.d.]. (88) $180
— Anr, [n.d.]. (90) $150
— Anr, [n.d.]. (90) $150
— Anr, [n.d.]. (89) $80
— Anr, [n.d.]. (89) $110
— Anr, [n.d.]. (88) $230
Ptd photograph, front cover of the Globe-Democrat Sunday Magazine, 6 Aug 1961. (90) $55
Signature, [n.d.]. (89) $70
White House card, sgd, [n.d.]. (90) $120
— Anr, sgd, [n.d.]. (91) $120

Hoover, J. Edgar, 1895-1972
Ls, 23 Sept 1943. (88) $80
Photograph, sgd & inscr, 23 June [19]65. (91) $110

Hope, Anthony, 1863-1933. See: Hawkins, Sir Anthony Hope

Hope, Bob
Photograph, sgd & inscr, [n.d.]. (91) $125

Hopkins, Edward. See: Hopkins, Thomas & Hopkins

Hopkins, Esek, 1718-1802
ADs, 20 July 1780. 1 p, 16mo. Certification that he has requisitioned a blanket from Jonathan Whipple. (91) $1,200

Hopkins, Gerard Manley, 1844-89
Original drawing, Manor Farm, [Shanklin, Isle of Wight]; [n.d.]. (91) £950
ALs, 7 May 1862. 6 pp, 8vo. To Charles Noble Luxmoore. Giving an account of how he was nearly expelled from school. Including decorated salutation incorporating drawing of a rural scene. (91) £3,800

Hopkins, Samuel, 1753-1819
Ms, orderly book while engaged in the Indian campaigns in Indiana in 1812. 1 Oct-18 Dec 1812. 72 pp, 8vo, in orig half sheep. Includes 2 important mentions of Zachary Taylor. (90) $4,000

Hopkins, Stephen, Signer from Rhode Island
ALs, 5 June 1755. 2 pp, 4to. To Gov. William Shirley. 2 pp, 4to. Mobilizing for the ill-fated assaults on Niagara & Crown Point. (91) $3,200

Hopkins, Thomas —&
Hopkins, Edward
[An interesting collection of c.150 letters, about half addressed to Thomas Hopkins as secretary to Lord Sunderland (a few to Sunderland himself), c.1708 to 1710, the rest to Edward Hopkins, M.P., 1720s & 1730s, mostly concerned with personal & political gossip, with related material, sold at pn on 10 Dec 1987, lot 445, for £5,500 to Quaritch.]

Hopkinson, Francis, Signer from New Jersey
Ds, 1 Dec 1778. (90) $200
— 6 Feb 1779. (90) $250
— 25 Feb 1779. (90) $250
— 5 Oct 1780. (91) $380

Hopkinson, Francis, Signer from New Jersey
ALs, 26 Feb 1785. Doheny collection. (89) $220

Horace, 65-8 B.C.
Ms, Odes, Epodes, Carmen Saeculare, & Satires. [Northeast? Italy, 2d half of 15th cent]. 130 leaves (6 blank), 218mm by 122mm, in early 19th-cent English red mor. Written in 2 distinct humanistic bookhands. (90) £4,200

Horae B.M.V.

— [London or Oxford?, c.1280-90]. Use of Sarum. In Latin, with headings in Anglo-Norman. 110 leaves (13 lacking), vellum, 160mm by 110mm, in 19th-cent French mor gilt. In dark brown ink in 2 sizes of a gothic liturgical hand. With illuminated initials throughout with full-length bar borders, c.150 animals, dragons & grotesques in margins, & 2 colored drawings. (91) £36,000

— The Ghistelles Hours. [Flanders, 1299-1300]. 1 leaf only, vellum, 118mm by 82mm; mtd. In brown ink in 2 sizes of a gothic liturgical hand. With small historiated initial & 3-quarter border. (90) £1,200

— [Northern France, Paris?, c.1300]. Use of Paris. 72 leaves (some lacking), vellum, 137mm by 84mm, in early 16th-cent blind-tooled calf over wooden bds. In dark brown ink in a small gothic hand. With 2-line initials throughout in burnished gold, very elaborate & imaginative linefillers throughout, & 9-line initial with extensive penwork. (90) £7,000

— [Northwest Italy, Genoa?, or South East France, c.1340]. Use of Rome. In Italian, with Mass of the Virgin in Latin. 102 leaves (some lacking), vellum, 87mm by 63mm, in calf gilt bdg of c.1900. In dark brown ink in a rounded gothic hand. With c.85 large initials in colors with white tracery & burnished gold grounds with branching ivyleaf borders, & 4 large miniatures with historiated borders. Worn. (91) £9,000

— The Hours & Psalter of Elizabeth de Bohun. [East Anglia, Cambridge?, c.1340-45]. Of Dominican Use. 177 leaves (lacking c.6) & flyleaf, 294mm by 202mm, in early 19th-cent English russia profusely gilt; rebacked. In brown ink in 2 sizes of a gothic liturgical hand. With large illuminated initials & full-length borders with colored & burnished gold leaves, flowers, dragons, etc. throughout, & 18 extremely large illuminated initials with full borders, 8 historiated. Some later additions. Astor MS.A.1. (88) £1,400,000

— [London, c.1380-1400]. Use of Sarum. 132 leaves & flyleaf (a few lacking), vellum, 229mm by 158mm. Worn 15th-cent blindstamped Oxford bdg of tanned calf over bevelled wooden bds, probably by Thomas Uffington. In brown ink in a large calligraphic gothic liturgical hand by at least three scribes. With c.118 2-line initials in burnished gold with purple penwork extensions & 7 very large illuminated initials with full borders. Abbey collection. (89) £15,000

— [Netherlands, late 14th cent]. Use of Sarum. In Latin, with added prayers in Middle English verse. 90 leaves only, vellum, 190mm by 135mm. Contemp reversed calf over wooden bds, repaired. In brown ink in a textura script with additions in later hands. With illuminated initials throughout & 3 very large decorated initials with full borders. (88) £1,800

— [Paris?, late 14th cent]. Use of Paris. In Latin, with Calendar & some prayers in French. 198 leaves (2 lacking), vellum, 198mm by 135mm. 16th-cent dark green velvet. In dark brown ink by 2 scribes in textura script. With numerous illuminated initials, 14 small miniatures with partial borders & 14 large miniatures with 3-line initials & full borders. 8 leaves added c.1600 by Blanche de Soissons. (88) £34,000

— [Paris, c.1390-1400]. Use of Paris. In Latin, with Calendar in French. 104 leaves (3 blank), vellum, 166mm by 123mm. Old yellow-brown velvet over pastebds. In dark brown ink in a fine gothic liturgical hand. With 2-line initials throughout with full ivyleaf borders & 8 large miniatures. [Ownership?] inscr of Mary of Burgundy on last page. Badly waterstained. (88) £5,800

— [Rouen, c.1390-1400]. Use of Rouen. In Latin, with Calendar & prayers in French. 144 leaves (some lacking) & 3 flyleaves, vellum, 165mm by 112mm, in late 18th-cent English panelled mottled calf. In dark brown ink in 2 sizes of a gothic liturgical hand. With small initials throughout with marginal extensions, 20 large initials with cusped bar borders, & 5 full-page miniatures with ivyleaf borders. (90)

£13,000
— [Paris, c.1400]. Use of Paris. In Latin, with rubrics & prayers in French. 199 leaves (3 lacking), vellum, 167mm by 130mm, in 19th-cent English roan gilt. In a gothic textura. With Calendar with a series of 3 grisaille vignettes for each month, & 12 large miniatures (cut out & re-inserted) above 3-line illuminated initials within full borders. (91) £22,000

— [Avignon, c.1400]. Use of Rome. 121 leaves only, 165mm by 120mm, in 19th-cent blindstamped calf. In dark brown ink in a formal gothic hand. With small initials & linefillers throughout, 69 pp with partial baguette borders, many decorated with grotesques, birds & figures, & 46 initials in the litany each decorated with a minute port of the saint. Misbound; lacking miniatures. (89) £12,000

— [Paris, c.1500-10] Use of Rome. 141 leaves, vellum, 185mm by 130mm, in old damask over wooden bds. With 39 miniatures & 24 Calendar miniatures, 2 full-page miniatures, 2 full armorial pages & full-page illuminated inscr added c.1525; all miniatures in gilded architectural frames & all other pages with illuminated bands of leaves & flowers on gold grounds in the outer side borders. Ducal Library at Gotha —Manhattan College Ms (91) $75,000

— [Paris, c.1400-10]. Use of Paris. In Latin, with Calendar & some prayers in French. 113 leaves (2 lacking) & 4 added preliminaries, vellum, 165mm by 114mm, in late 16th-cent vellum gilt over pastebds, rebacked. In dark brown ink in a gothic liturgical hand. With small initials throughout in burnished gold on red & blue grounds with white tracery, & 9 large miniatures in the style of the Master of the Coronation of the Virgin above large illuminated initials within full borders. (91) £11,000

— [Paris, c.1400-10]. Use of Paris. In Latin, with Calendar, Quinze Joyes & Sept Requetes in French. 144 leaves, vellum, 179mm by 123mm, in [16th-cent?] dark green mor over pastebds. In dark brown ink in a gothic liturgical hand. With small initials throughout in burnished gold on red & blue grounds with white tracery, 8 large illuminated initials usually supporting full-length ivyleaf borders, & 6 large miniatures above large illuminated initials with full borders. (91) £17,000

— [Flanders, Bruges?, c.1400-10]. Use of Rome. 162 leaves (1 blank), vellum, 108mm by 73mm. Early 19th-cent vellum over pastebds. In brown ink in a small gothic liturgical hand. With 13 large illuminated initials with full ivyleaf borders & 6 full-page miniatures in soft colors within architectural frames. Borders partly cropped; worn. (88) £2,500

— [Paris or Burgundy, c.1400]. Use of Rome. In Latin, with Quinze Joyes & Sept Requetes in French. 176 leaves (3 blank) & 6 flyleaves, vellum, 145mm by 97mm. 18th-cent English calf. In brown ink in a small gothic liturgical hand. With small initials throughout in burnished gold on red & blue grounds, 17 very large initials with full-length ivyleaf borders & 4 large miniatures above 4 lines of text & with full ivyleaf borders. (88) £6,600

— [Bologna, c.1400-10]. 25 leaves only (2 blank), vellum, 237mm by 170mm. In dark brown ink in 2 sizes of a gothic liturgical hand. With c.50 small initials in highly burnished gold, 4 small historiated initials with partial borders, & large & very large historiated initials with 3-quarter borders. Probably illuminated by the Master of the Brussels Initials. (90) £6,000

— [Paris or Burgundy, c.1400]. Use of Rome. In Latin, with Quinze Joyes & Sept Requetes in French. 176 leaves (3 blank) & 6 flyleaves, vellum, 145mm by 97mm. 18th-cent English calf. In brown ink in a small gothic liturgical hand. With small initials throughout in burnished gold on red & blue grounds, 17 very large initials with full-length ivyleaf borders & 4 large miniatures above 4 lines of text & with full ivyleaf borders. (90) £8,000

— [London, c.1400]. Use of Sarum. 113 leaves (2 blank) & 3 flyleaves, vellum, 121mm by 85mm. Old limp vellum bdg. In a fine gothic liturgical hand. With small initials throughout in burnished gold on red & blue grounds, 5

large initials with 3-quarter illuminated borders, & 5 very large initials with full borders. (91) £4,000
— [Northern France or Southern Netherlands, c.1400]. Use of Tournai. In Latin, with rubrics in French. Single leaf, vellum, 177mm by 134mm. In brown ink in a small gothic liturgical hand. With historiated initial & 2 full-length bar borders. (90) £1,900
— [Paris or Lyons, c.1400 & c.1475]. Use of Paris. In Latin, with prayers in French. 275 leaves, vellum, 133mm by 90mm. Worn 15th-cent blindstamped tanned calf over wooden bds. In 2 sizes of a gothic liturgical hand by more than 1 scribe. With small initials with full-length borders throughout, & 3 large miniatures with full borders (2 added later). (89) £32,000
— [France, c.1400] 66 leaves only, vellum, 134mm by 92mm, in modern cloth over bds. In littera textura in brown ink. With 5 large initials in white on gold ground with ivy spray extensions; many 2-line initials in gold with white penwork on colored grounds. (91) $2,200
— [Bruges, c.1405-10]. Use of Sarum. 95 leaves & 4 flyleaves (at least 1 lacking), vellum, 203mm by 144mm. Repaired late 16th-cent English bdg of calf over pastebds. In dark brown ink in a compressed gothic liturgical hand. With small initials throughout in burnished gold on red & blue grounds, 13 very large illluminated initials with full borders, 16 full-page miniatures, & German etching of c.1470 loosely inserted. With Middle English recipe on flyleaf. Abbey collection. (89) £16,000
— [Paris, 1408]. 2 leaves, vellum, 175mm by 131mm. In a gothic liturgical hand. With full borders of formal ivyleaves on broad scrolling stems, large initial, & large miniature within 3-sided baguette by the Boucicaut Master or his workshop. Including colophon giving exact date. (91) £19,000
— [Paris, 1408]. Single leaf, vellum, 174mm by 130mm. In a gothic liturgical hand. With full borders of formal ivyleaves on broad scrolling stems, 12 illuminated initials (1 large), & large miniature within 3-sided baguette by the Boucicaut Master or his workshop. (91) £13,000
— [Paris, 1408]. 2 leaves, vellum, 175mm by 130mm. In a gothic liturgical hand. With full borders of formal ivyleaves on broad scrolling stems, small illuminated initials & linefillers, large initial, & large miniature within 3-sided baguette by the Boucicaut Master or his workshop. (91) £14,000
— [Paris, c.1408]. (90) £850
— [Paris, 1408]. 1 leaf only, vellum, 174mm by 130mm. In a gothic liturgical hand. With 10 illuminated initials, full borders, & large miniature showing St. Martin & the Beggar, from the workshop of the Boucicaut Master. Dampstained. Framed. (88) £18,000
— [Northeastern France, Amiens?, c.1410]. Use of Amiens. In Latin, with Calendar, Quinze Joies & Sept Requetes in French. 197 leaves (3 lacking), vellum, 172mm by 120mm. 18th-cent French calf. In brown ink in a gothic textura. With numerous initials & line-fillers in gold & colors, & 7 large & 2 full-page miniatures with full borders. Dampstained. (88) £8,000
— [Paris, c.1410]. Single leaf, vellum, 189mm by 133mm. With large miniature above illuminated initial & 5 lines of text, all within 3-sided baguette border & full border of blue flowers & gold bezants; from the workshop of the Boucicaut Master. (90) £12,000
— [Bruges?, c.1410-20]. Use of Rome. 190 leaves & flyleaves, vellum, 89mm by 68mm. Worn contemp Italian embroidered bdg. In dark brown ink in a very small gothic liturgical hand. With small initials throughout in burnished gold on red & blue grounds, 14 large initials in ivyleaf designs with full borders, 9 full-page miniatures, & full-page coat-of-arms of the Loredano family added at end. Abbey collection. (89) £40,000
— [Bologna?, early 15th cent]. Use of Rome. 285 leaves (1 blank), vellum, 103mm by 73mm, in def 18th-cent calf. In brown ink in a gothic rotunda. With 5 historiated initials in the style of Cristoforo Cortese with foliate &

floral ornamentation on gold ground, & 2 large miniatures. (89) £2,400

— [Paris, c.1415-20]. Use of Paris. In Latin, with Calendar, Quinze Joyes & Sept Requetes in French. 258 leaves (2 blank), vellum, 180mm by 125mm, in [16th-cent?] dark red velvet over pastebds. In dark brown ink in a gothic liturgical hand. With small initials throughout in burnished gold on red & blue grounds with white tracery, larger initials in ivyleaf designs on highly burnished gold grounds, 3-quarter illuminated borders throughout, & 15 large miniatures (13 by the Master of the Harvard Hannibal, 2 by the Boucicaut Master or his workshop) above large initials within broad illuminated baguettes in many styles. (91) £160,000

— [Paris, c.1415]. Use of Paris. Single leaf, vellum, 168mm by 123mm. In 2 sizes of a gothic liturgical hand. With large miniature from the workshop of the Boucicaut Master, above 4-line illuminated initial with 3-sided illuminated baguette & full border of burnished gold, colored flowers & acanthus leaves. Korner collection. (90) £7,000

— [Paris, c.1415]. Use of Paris. Single leaf, vellum, 169mm by 122mm. In a gothic liturgical hand. With large miniature from the workshop of the Boucicaut Master, above 4-line illuminated initial with 3-sided baguette border of interlinked scimitar-shaped leaves & full border of burnished gold, colored leaves & flowers. Korner collection. (90) £11,000

— [Paris, c.1415]. Use of Paris. Single leaf, vellum, 169mm by 122mm. In 2 sizes of a gothic liturgical hand. With large miniature from the workshop of the Boucicaut Master, above 4-line illuminated initial with 3-sided baguette border of alternate colored ivyleaves & full border of colored & burnished gold ivyleaves on hairline stems. Korner collection. (90) £6,000

— [Paris, c.1415]. Use of Paris. Single leaf, vellum, 168mm by 123mm. In a gothic liturgical hand. With large miniature from the workshop of the Boucicaut Master, above 4-line illuminated initial with 3-sided illuminated baguette border & full border of colored & burnished gold flowers & ivyleaves on hairline stems. Korner collection. (90) £6,000

— [England, c.1420]. Use of Sarum. 145 leaves (4 blank) & 4 flyleaves, vellum, 180mm by 130mm, in 19th-cent calf. In dark brown ink in a gothic textura. With many margins decorated with borders of gold ivy leaves & colored flowers, & 6 large initials on gold ground. Lacking miniatures. (89) £4,200

— [Paris, c.1420]. Use of Troyes. In Latin, with some prayers in French. 187 leaves (7 lacking), vellum, 175mm by 125mm. 17th-cent lea bdg. In black ink in a gothic textura. With numerous illuminated linefillers & initials, partly with full-length extensions, small miniature, & 10 large miniatures within full borders, with stylistic elements associated with the Egerton Master. (90) DM86,000

— [Brittany, c.1420-30]. 8 leaves only, vellum, 196mm by 140mm; stitched. In dark brown ink in a gothic liturgical hand. With small initials in burnished gold, 3- & 4-line initials in formal ivyleaf designs, & 11 very large miniatures within panel borders in designs of burnished gold leaves. (91) £8,500

— [Utrecht or Guelders, c.1420-30]. Use of Utrecht. In Dutch. 193 leaves & flyleaf, vellum, 132mm by 90mm, in late medieval blindstamped tanned lea over bevelled wooden bds. In dark brown ink in a small gothic hand. With 27 large illuminated initials supporting full-length bar borders, 4 very large illuminated initials (2 historiated) with full borders, & 3 full-page miniatures (worn) within full borders by the Master of Zweder van Culemborg or his workshop. (91) £4,200

— [Paris, c.1420-30]. Use of Paris. In Latin, with Calendar, Quinze Joyes & Sept Requetes in French. 133 leaves (some lacking), vellum, 170mm by 122mm. 16th-cent Parisian olive-brown mor gilt bdg. In 2 sizes of a gothic liturgical hand. With 2- & 3-line initials in ivyleaf designs on highly burnished gold grounds, some with partial borders of gold & colored leaves, 3-quarter illuminated borders throughout sprouting from full-length bar borders, & 14 large miniatures above large initials within full borders. Chester Beatty W.MS.100. (91) £95,000

— [Western France, c.1420-30]. 2 leaves only, vellum, 166mm by 121mm. In 2 sizes of a gothic liturgical hand. With 2-line initials with full-length bar borders & 4 miniatures. Korner collection. (90) £4,000

— [Paris, c.1420-30]. Use of Paris. In Latin, with Calendar, Quinze Joyes & Sept Requetes in French. 171 leaves, vellum, 179mm by 125mm. Modern full red mor gilt a la fanfare by Huser. In dark brown ink in a gothic liturgical hand. With panel borders throughout in outer margins in designs of colored & gold ivyleaves & flowers, & 14 large miniatures above large initials & 4 lines of text, all within elaborate borders. (89) £32,000

— [Paris, c.1420-30]. Use of Sarum. In Latin, with Calendar in French. 143 leaves only, vellum, 230mm by 160mm, in old red velvet over pastebds. In dark brown ink in 2 sizes of a fine gothic liturgical hand. With full floral & foliate borders on every page by several artists, sometimes incorporating animals, grotesques, etc., 1 large & 48 marginal miniatures from the workshop of or by the Bedford Master. Misbound & missing many leaves; dampstained. (88) £38,000

— The Hours of Margaret, Duchess of Clarence. [London, c.1421-30]. Use of Sarum. 120 leaves & flyleaf, vellum, 244mm by 171mm. Repaired [17th-cent?] red velvet over pastebds. In dark brown ink in a vertical formal gothic liturgical hand. With c.160 large illuminated & 2 very large historiated initials with full illuminated borders, & 11 half-page & 8 full-page miniatures. Dampstained. Abbey collection. (89) £260,000

— [Paris?, 1st half of 15th cent]. Use of Paris. In Latin, with prayers in French. 199 leaves (4 lacking), vellum, 160mm by 115mm. 17th-cent lea panels over wooden bds. In a textura script in a single hand. With small initials in gold, red & blue & decorated borders

throughout, historiated initial, 2 small & 10 large miniatures with full borders. (90) £11,000

— [France, 1st half of 15th cent]. Of unstated use. Over 500 leaves (some lacking), vellum, 85mm by 63mm, in 2 18th-cent red mor vols. In a textura script in a single hand. With small initials & linefillers in blue, red & gold. (90) £4,000

— [France, Burgundy?, c.1425]. Use of Rome. In Latin, with Calendar in French. 147 leaves (3 blank), vellum, 175mm by 128mm. 18th-cent English mottled calf bdg. In 2 sizes of a gothic liturgical hand. With small initials throughout in burnished gold on red & blue grounds with partial borders of flowers & ivyleaves, & 12 large miniatures above large initials supporting 3-sided baguette borders. (91) £9,500

— [Paris, c.1425]. Use of Rome. 12 leaves only, vellum, 102mm by 76mm, each mtd; in full green mor by Sangorski & Sutcliffe. In a gothic liturgical hand. With 12 large miniatures (1 full-page) attributable to the workshop of the Bedford Master, 11 above large illuminated initials & 3 lines of text within 3-sided baguette border & full illuminated border of delicate colored flowers & leaves. Korner collection. (90) £50,000

— [England, York?, 1st half of 15th cent]. Use of Sarum. In Latin, with additions in Middle English. 162 leaves & 8 flyleaves, vellum, 129mm by 85mm. Later vellum (re-used) over pastebds. In brown ink in a small gothic hand by Willelmus Watyr. With small initials throughout in dark blue with extensive penwork in red, & 16 large illuminated initials with full bar borders with clumps of lush acanthus leaves. (90) £8,500

— [Paris, c.1430-40]. Use of Paris. In Latin, with Calendar & prayers in French. 168 leaves, vellum, 215mm by 162mm, in 18th-cent French dark blue mor gilt. In a gothic textura. With initials throughout in gold on red & blue ground with white tracery, 3-quarter illuminated borders in every page, & 20 large miniatures with full borders by the Master of the Munich Golden Legend & his workshop. (91)

HORAE B.M.V.

£160,000

— [Utrecht, c.1430]. Use of Rome. In Latin, with Prayers in Dutch. 108 leaves (1 lacking), vellum, 162mm by 110mm. 15th & 17th-cent calf over wooden bds, def. In black ink in a gothic textura. With numerous illuminated initials partly with full foliate borders, & 15 full-page miniatures with full borders, 14 by the Master of Nicholas Brouwer. (88) £11,000

— [Paris?, c.1430]. Use of Paris. 197 leaves (4 lacking), vellum, 175mm by 118mm, in 19th-cent blindstamped calf. In brown ink in a gothic textura. With half borders throughout of flowers & gold ivy leaves & 11 large arched miniatures by a close follower of the Bedford Master with gold baguette frames & 3-line initials. (89) £65,000

— [Brittany, c.1430]. Use of Rennes. In Latin, with prayers in French. 170 leaves, vellum, 192mm by 146mm. Extra mid-16th cent French brown calf gilt. In black ink in a gothic textura. With numerous small & 7 four-line illuminated initials, 7 large historiated miniatures within full borders, & 4 full-page 16th-cent miniatures. (89) £19,000

— [Northern Netherlands, Utrecht?, c.1430-40]. Use of Utrecht. In Dutch. 176 leaves, vellum, 155mm by 110mm. 18th-cent mottled calf. In dark brown ink in a small gothic hand. With illuminated initials throughout, 7 very large initials with full borders & 2 full-page miniatures. Some signs of use. (88) £5,000

— [Flanders, Bruges?, c.1430-50]. Use of Sarum. In Latin, with additions in Middle English. 102 leaves (lacking c.8) & 6 flyleaves, vellum, 127mm by 85mm. 19th-cent calf inset with sides of 16th-cent French calf profusely gilt. In dark brown ink in a small gothic hand. With 7 large illuminated initials with three-quarter bar borders, 4 very large illuminated initials with full borders & 3 full-page miniatures (1 torn). Some edges nibbled by rodents. (88) £5,200

— [Besancon, c.1430-50]. Use of Besancon. In Latin, with Calendar, Quinze Joyes & Sept Requetes in French. 147 leaves, vellum, 167mm by 107mm. Def late 16th- or 17th-cent calf over pastebds. In black ink in a gothic liturgical hand. With panel borders on every page, initials throughout in burnished gold on red & blue grounds (1 with full-length border in inner margin), & 14 large miniatures (1 added in 16th cent; 1 tipped in from anr Ms). Worn throughout. (88) £5,500

— [France, c.1430-50, & Ghent or Bruges, c.1515]. In Latin. 1 leaf only, 208mm by 148mm. Opening leaf of the Hours of the Holy Ghost, in a gothic hand. With small initials in burnished gold & colors & white tracery, large illuminated initial & full broad Ghent/Bruges illuminated border of flowers, birds, butterflies, etc. (89) £1,200

— The Tarleton Hours. [Rouen?, c.1430-50]. Use of Sarum. Single leaf, vellum, 138mm by 103mm. In a flamboyant lettre batarde. With large miniature by a follower of the Rohan Master, above 3-line illuminated initial with 3-quarter illuminated baguette border; trimmed. Korner collection. (90) £6,500

— The Tarleton Hours. [Rouen?, c.1430-50]. Use of Sarum. Single leaf, vellum, 140mm by 102mm. In a flamboyant lettre batarde. With large miniature by a follower of the Rohan Master, above 3-line illuminated initial with 3-quarter illuminated baguette border formed of colored joined vases; trimmed. Korner collection. (90) £4,200

— The Tarleton Hours. [Rouen?, c.1430-50]. Use of Sarum. Single leaf, vellum, 140mm by 99mm. In a flamboyant lettre batarde. With large miniature by a follower of the Boucicaut Master, above 4-line illuminated initial with 3-quarter illuminated baguette border partly in complicated pattern of colored flowers on burnished gold ground; trimmed. Korner collection. (90) £5,000

— The Tarleton Hours. [Rouen?, c.1430-50]. Use of Sarum. Single leaf, vellum, 139mm by 102mm. In a flamboyant lettre batarde. With large miniature by a follower of the Boucicaut Master, above 3-line illuminated initial with 3-quarter illuminated baguette border of colored leaves sprouting from a colored bar on burnished gold;

trimmed. Korner collection. (90) £5,500
— The Tarleton Hours. [Rouen?, c.1430-50]. Use of Sarum. In Latin, with Calendar & Quinze Joyes in French. 125 leaves (44 lacking), vellum, 140mm by 103mm. 17th-cent English black mor. In a slightly sloping calligraphic lettre batarde by 2 main scribes. With 2-line illuminated initials throughout & 13 illuminated borders. Def. (89) £1,900
— [Bruges, c.1430-50]. Use of Dol. 72 leaves (1 facsimile), vellum, 192mm by 130mm. Worn 16th-cent calf over pastebds. With 3 very large initials with full borders of flowers & leaves with birds & grotesques, 7 large miniatures above large initials & within full borders, & 3 full-page miniatures, sgd with ptd artist's marks. (89) £19,000
— [Utrecht, c.1435]. Use of Utrecht. In Dutch, in the trans of Geert Groot. 142 leaves, vellum, 140mm by 96mm, in 16th-cent panelled calf over wooden bds. In dark brown ink in a gothic textura. With colored initials throughout, 21 small & 24 large initials in burnished gold with marginal flourishes, full border, & 3 full-page miniatures (worn). (90) £2,400
— [Paris or Troyes, c.1435-55]. The Hours of Marguerite de Valois. Use of Troyes. In Latin, with Calendar, Quinze Joyes & Sept Requetes in French. 141 leaves & flyleaf, vellum, 202mm by 135mm. In very fine Parisian orange-brown mor profusely gilt of c.1590. In dark brown ink in 2 sizes of a large gothic liturgical hand. With panel borders throughout including birds, leaves & flowers, & 15 large miniatures in colors & burnished gold within arched compartments above large initials & within full borders. Astor MS.A.13. (88) £50,000
— [Northern Netherlands, c.1435]. (90) £750
— [Utrecht?, c.1435]. 2 leaves, vellum, 147mm by 108mm. With 3 2-line initials, 5-line illuminated inital, 3-quarter border of colored & golden leaves, & 10-line historiated initial within full border including angels in the style of the Master of Zweder van Culemborg. (91) £1,600
— [Normandy, Coutances, c.1435-70]. Use of Coutances. 127 leaves (7 lacking, 1 blank), vellum, 160mm by 113mm. 16th-cent French calf gilt bdg. In a gothic liturgical hand. With small initials throughout in burnished gold, 2 large initials with partial borders, 6 large initials with 3-quarter borders, & small miniature. Worn. (91) £2,100
— [England, 2d quarter of 15th cent]. Use of Sarum. Single leaf, vellum, 201mm by 134mm. In 2 sizes of an English gothic liturgical hand. With large initial with full-length illuminated bar border, 3 coats-of-arms, & full-page miniature. Korner collection. (90) £9,500
— [Delft, c.1435 & Bruges, c.1460]. Use not stated. In Latin, Book of Hours & Prayerbook. 166 leaves, vellum, 122mm by 94mm. Modern calf over wooden bds incorporating parts of 16th-cent bdg. In dark brown ink in a small gothic bookhand. With elaborate & highly decorative penwork borders throughout, many including animals, epigrams, scriptural quotations, etc., 1 page made up entirely of penwork, 14 large or very large illuminated initials with full borders in several styles, & 13 full-page miniatures by the Master of Zweder van Culemborg; borders modified later. (89) £62,000
— [Utrecht?, c.1440]. Use of Utrecht. In Dutch. 176 leaves & 2 flyleaves, vellum, 155mm by 105mm, in brown mor over wooden bds. In a neat gothic littera textualis. With 27 four-line & 5 six-line initials in gold on red & blue ground with white tracery & outer baguette decoration with border of foliage. (91) £4,800
— [Bruges?, c.1440]. Use of Rome. In Latin, with Calendar in French. 348 leaves (some lacking), vellum, 152mm by 100mm, in 17th-cent Dutch calf gilt. In a gothic textura. With 28 three-line initials in gold on red & blue ground with white tracery & marginal extensions of gold ivy leaves. Lacking all miniatures & incipits. (91) £4,500
— [Rennes or Le Mans, c.1440]. Use of Le Mans & Rennes. In Latin. 113

HORAE B.M.V.

leaves (8 or 10 lacking) & 2 flyleaves, vellum, 202mm by 145mm. 15th-cent blindstamped French brown calf over wooden bds, rebacked; in mor solander box by Riviere. In brown ink in a gothic textura; 2 pp in anr hand. With initials in burnished gold on red & blue ground, many pp with outer panel borders, & 10 large miniatures in arched compartments with full borders. Doheny collection. (88) £19,000

— [Rouen or Paris, c.1440]. Use of Sarum. In Latin, with some rubrics in French & addition in English. 360 leaves, vellum, 102mm by 70mm. Early 20th-cent blindtooled mor over wooden bds, with earlier silver clasp. In brown ink in batarde script. With 207 pp with panel borders of gold ivy leaves & branchwork, 6 pp with full borders & decorated initials on gold ground, & 5 large miniatures within full borders by the Talbot Master. Doheny collection. (88) £20,000

— [Paris?, c.1440]. Use of Paris. In Latin, with prayers in French. 137 leaves (c.3 lacking) & 2 flyleaves, vellum, 183mm by 126mm, in extra mid-16th-cent brown mor gilt. In brown ink in an upright liturgical hand. With 10 three-line initials with branchwork decoration on gold ground with three-quarter foliate & floral borders, & 3 large miniatures with full borders & baguette frames. (89) £10,000

— [Bruges, c.1440]. Use of Rome. 135 leaves & 6 flyleaves, vellum, 157mm by 110mm, in 19th-cent blindstamped calf. In brown ink in a gothic textura. With 24 four- or five-line illuminated initials & 5 large miniatures in the style of the Master of the Golden Scrolls, all within three-quarter borders. (89) £13,000

— [Southern Netherlands?, c.1440]. (88) £900

— [Verdun, c.1440] 109 leaves, vellum, 178mm by 132mm, in 16th-cent calf gilt. With 2 full-page miniatrues on inserted single leaves by 2 identified artists; 10 large initials with 9 full borders. (91) $12,500

— [Utrecht?, c.1440]. In Dutch. 8 leaves only, vellum, 155mm by 112mm. In small gothic script. With 9 burnished gold initials with penwork in red & purple, & 14 large illuminated initials with full-length colored & bar borders. (90) £1,200

— [West central France, Rennes?, c.1440]. Use of Rome. In Latin, with prayers in French. 140 leaves (2 blank, 1 lacking) & 3 flyleaves, vellum, 216mm by 152mm. Modern dark red mor gilt by Zaehnsdorf. In dark brown ink in 2 sizes of a gothic liturgical hand. With 2-line initials with panel borders throughout, 3-line initial with 3-quarter border, & 13 large miniatures within full borders of colored & gold leaves. Illuminated by the Master of Marguerite de Willerval. Phillipps Ms.4216. (90) £78,000

— [Western France, c.1440]. 1 leaf only, vellum, 130mm by 101mm. In a lettre batarde. With 14 illuminated initials & line-fillers & large miniature of Christ carrying the Cross within 3-sided illuminated border. From the Tarleton Hours. Mtd. (88) £2,000

— [Southern Netherlands, Bruges?, c.1450]. Use of Rome. 134 leaves, vellum, 175mm by 130mm, in modern white mor. In a gothic textura. With 10 six-line historiated initials with 3-quarter borders & 13 large miniatures above 5-line initials within full borders. (91) £10,000

— [Southern Netherlands, Bruges?, c.1450]. Use of Rome. 111 leaves (a few lacking), vellum, 210mm by 145mm, in modern limp vellum. In a gothic textura. With 17 six-line decorated penwork initials, 9 six-line historiated initials with baguette extensions & 3-quarter borders, & 10 large miniatures (1 def) above large initials within full borders incorporating animals. (91) £17,000

— [Netherlands, Utrecht?, c.1450]. Use of Utrecht. In Latin. 156 leaves, vellum, 100mm by 65mm. Contemp dark brown calf over wooden bds. In brown ink in a small fere textura script. With 7 large flourished initials with full borders in gold & colors, 9 marginal paintings & 2 full-page miniatures. Front flyleaves detached. (88) £2,200

— [Flanders, c.1450]. Use of Rome. 116 leaves, vellum, 145mm by 100mm, in

17th-cent mor gilt, armorial bdg. Written in brown ink in a regular batarda, with rubrics in red & versals in gold or blue with penwork decoration. With 14 full-page miniatures with full borders; 14 5-line initials in blue on gold ground infilled with floral stems, each with full border of colored acorn leaves & flowers; 9 large historiated initials with half & three-quarter borders. (91) £12,000

— [France, c.1450]. Of unidentified use [Hainaut?]. 137 leaves, vellum, 168mm by 115mm. Lacking 1 leaf. Blind-stamped lea over wooden bds, lacking clasps. In brown & red ink. With ornamental borders throughout, numerous large & small initials, & 11 miniatures within full foliate borders, all in gold & colors. (88) DM57,000

— [Northern France, c.1450]. (89) DM720

— [France, 15th cent]. 2 leaves only, 135mm by 85mm. In a lettre batarde. With 27 small & 2 large initials, 2 floral borders, & 2 miniatures, all in colors & gold. Framed. (91) DM1,800

— [Burgundy or Franche-Comte, c.1450]. Of unrecorded Use. In Latin, with Calendar, Quinze Joyes & Sept Requetes in French. 150 leaves (2 blank) & 4 flyleaves, vellum, 173mm by 125mm, in contemp blindstamped tanned lea over wooden bds. In dark brown ink in a gothic liturgical hand. With small initials throughout in burnished gold on red & blue grounds with white tracery, panel borders on every page, & 21 large miniatures above large initials within full borders of colored acanthus leaves & gold ivyleaves. (91) £32,000

— [Bruges, c.1450-70]. Use of Sarum. In Latin, with additions in Middle English. 128 leaves (4 lacking), vellum, 210mm by 150mm, in late 19th-cent English red-brown mor gilt. In dark brown ink in a gothic liturgical hand. With small initials in burnished gold on colored grounds, 20 large historiated initials with partial borders, & 20 large miniatures above large illuminated initials within full borders. (91) £20,000

— [Bruges, c.1450]. Use of Rome. 121 leaves, vellum, 141mm by 102mm. Worn contemp panel-stamped calf over wooden bds. In dark brown ink in a small gothic liturgical hand. With 13 large illuminated initials in full colors & burnished gold with white tracery & full borders. Lacking miniatures. (88) £2,700

— [Bruges, c.1450-70]. Use not stated. In Latin, with sections in Dutch & French. 397 leaves (1 blank, 2 lacking), vellum, 156mm by 103mm. 19th-cent Parisian dark brown mor profusely gilt, by Niedree. In dark brown ink in a skilful gothic liturgical hand. With 32 large illuminated initials with full or partial borders, 13 very large initials with full borders including grotesque animals, & 5 full-page miniatures within full borders, in the style of Willem Vrelant. Unusual collection of Hours, but not including Hours of the Virgin. (88) £20,000

— [Paris, c.1450-75]. Use of Paris. In Latin, with Calendar, Quinze Joyes & Sept Requetes in French. 167 leaves, vellum, 130mm by 92mm. 19th-cent blindstamped vellum. In dark brown ink in a small gothic liturgical hand. With small initials throughout in burnished gold on red & blue grounds & 3 large illuminated initials with three-quarter illuminated borders. Some later additions. Lacking at least 15 leaves with all miniatures. (88) £1,800

— [Rouen, c.1450-70]. Use of Rouen. In Latin, with Calendar in French. 112 leaves (2 lacking), vellum, 174mm by 130mm. [16th-cent?] limp vellum, repaired. In dark brown ink in a gothic liturgical hand. With small initials in burnished gold on red & blue grounds, 5 large illuminated initials with three-quarter illuminated borders & 8 large miniatures in full borders. (88) £9,500

— [Paris?, c.1450]. (90) £850

— [France, c.1450]. (90) £850

— [Northeastern France, c.1450]. Use of Rome. In Latin, with Calendar in French. 161 leaves (3 lacking), vellum, 219mm by 140mm, in contemp blindstamped bdg of wooden bds. In dark brown ink in a compact upright gothic liturgical hand. With small initials throughout in burnished gold on red &

blue grounds, panel borders on every page in outer margins, & 12 large miniatures with full borders including foliage & birds. (90) £23,000

— [Northeastern France, Toul?, c.1450]. Use of Rome. In Latin, with Calendar in French. 301 leaves (7 lacking), vellum, 95mm by 67mm, in contemp blindstamped calf over wooden bds. By several scribes in brown ink in a large gothic liturgical hand. With 12 Calendar miniatures within panel borders, 14 large miniatures within full borders above large initials & 3 lines of text, 3 full-page miniatures & a full-page drawing. (90) £17,000

— [Northern Netherlands, c.1450]. Use of Utrecht. In Dutch. 134 leaves (c.8 lacking), vellum, 144mm by 105mm, in old vellum over pastebds. In dark brown ink in a small gothic hand. With 29 large illuminated initials with full-length borders. Worn. (90) £3,600

— [Flanders, c.1450, & France, c.1500]. Use of Rome. In Latin, with long sections in French verse. 141 leaves (2 lacking), vellum, 171mm by 120mm. Def 19th-cent blindstamped russia. In dark brown ink in a gothic liturgical hand in 2 distinct sections. With 9 large & 7 very large illuminated initials with partial or full borders. (89) £1,900

— [France, Paris?, c.1450]. Use of Paris. In Latin, with Calendar, Quinze Joyes & Sept Requetes in French. 151 leaves (15 lacking), vellum, 214mm by 148mm. 19th-cent French pale brown calf bdg. In a lettre batarde. With 2-line initials in floral designs in colors on highly burnished gold grounds, 4-line illuminated initial, & c.160 panel borders of acanthus leaves, flowers & fruit. (91) £9,000

— [Northern Netherlands, c.1450]. Use of Utrecht. In Dutch. 201 leaves (1 blank) & 6 endleaves, vellum, 131mm by 91mm. Contemp blind-stamped tanned lea over gently bevelled wooden bds. In a small angular bookhand. With 22 large blue initials with red penwork, 5 very large initials in divided red & blue with penwork surround in red & purple extending full height & sometimes into 3 margins. (91) £4,500

— [Southern Netherlands, c.1450]. Use of Sarum. With Psalter. 221 leaves (1 lacking, 1 replaced), vellum, 147mm by 102mm. 19th-cent English red mor gilt over wooden bds. In a small well-formed gothic liturgical hand. With 2-line initials throughout in burnished gold, 11 large illuminated initials with full borders, 26 historiated initials with 3-quarter illuminated borders, & 2 full-page miniatures in full borders. (91) £10,500

— [Northwest France, c.1450]. (90) £850

— [Southern Netherlands, c.1450]. Use of Rome. In Latin, with some Calendar tables & diagrams in Dutch. 227 leaves, vellum, 108mm by 70mm. 19th-cent vellum gilt bdg. In black ink in a very small gothic liturgical hand. With c.150 illuminated initials with partial borders, 62 large or very large initials with 3-quarter or full illuminated borders, & 5 pp of Calendar diagrams including 2 colored drawings. Lacking miniatures. Abbey collection. (89) £16,000

— [Southeast France, Valence?, c.1450]. Use of Rome & Paris. In Latin & French. 112 leaves (3 blank, c.13 lacking) & 3 flyleaves, vellum, 121mm by 83mm. 17th-cent French red mor gilt bdg. In dark brown ink in 2 sizes of a sloping lettre batarde. With small initials throughout in burnished gold on colored grounds, panel borders on every page, & 15 large miniatures within full borders. (90) £15,000

— [Artois, c.1450]. Use of Therouanne. In Latin, with Calendar in French. 93 leaves (9 lacking), vellum, 178mm by 134mm; disbound. In dark brown ink in a gothic liturgical hand. With small initials in blue & burnished gold with penwork of white tracery, & 14 large illuminated initials with full borders surrounding baguette borders in the style of the Master of Guillebert de Mets. 1 initial cut out; "all leaves apparently treated with some kind of oil and now rather greasy". (90) £3,400

— [Ghent, c.1450]. Use of Tournai. In Latin, with Calendar in Dutch. 79 leaves (2 blank) & 2 flyleaves, vellum, 139mm by 94mm. Worn late medieval blindstamped calf over wooden bds. In dark brown ink in a gothic liturgical hand. With 10 large initials in divided

red & blue & 3 full-page miniatures on inserted sheets. (90) £3,500
— [Paris?, c.1450]. (89) £550
— [Netherlands, c.1450]. (89) £400
— Northern Netherlands, Delft?, c.1450]. Use of Utrecht. In Dutch. 210 leaves (6 lacking), vellum, 176mm by 116mm. Repaired 18th-cent Dutch mottled calf bdg. In dark brown ink in a gothic hand. With 41 large decorated initials with penwork extensions, & 3 very large decorated initials with partial borders. (89) £4,000
— [Western France, Bayeux?, c.1450]. (88) £850
— [Netherlands, Delft?, c.1450]. In Dutch. 270 leaves (6 blank) & 4 flyleaves, vellum & paper, 141mm by 104mm, in def contemp blindstamped tanned calf over bevelled wooden bds. In dark brown ink in a small gothic bookhand. With 47 large decorated initials & 17 very large initials in a variety of styles, mostly with full borders. Astor MS.A.23. (88) £19,000
— [Northern Netherlands, Utrecht?, mid-15th cent]. Use of Utrecht. In Dutch. 271 leaves (1 blank) & 2 flyleaves, vellum, 187mm by 126mm, in 19th-cent English blindstamped brown mor. In dark brown ink in an angular gothic hand. With 12 large decorated initials with ornamental penwork extensions, 5 very large decorated initials with full borders, & 2 full-page miniatures within full borders. Dampstained. (88) £4,800
— [Rheims, mid-15th cent]. Use of Rheims. In Latin, with Calendar & prayers in French. 134 leaves (1 blank), vellum, 157mm by 105mm, in late 19th-cent brown mor gilt. In dark brown ink in a gothic liturgical hand. With 3 large contemp miniatures with full borders, 2 incorporating bas-de-page miniatures, & 7 large 16th-cent miniatures in architectural borders, all miniatures above very large illuminated initials. 1 leaf re-inserted. (88) £4,800
— [Paris, c.1455-70]. The Navarre Hours. Use of Paris. In Latin, with Calendar, Quinze Joyes & Sept Requetes in French. 244 leaves (1 blank) & flyleaves, vellum, 164mm by 110mm.

19th-cent brown velvet with silver filigree clasps. In dark brown ink in 2 sizes of a gothic liturgical hand. With three-quarter illuminated borders throughout, 24 Calendar roundels in borders, & 19 large miniatures within full borders incorporating historiated roundels. Some water damage; Calendar miniatures retouched; a few leaves bound out of sequence. Astor MS.A.15. (88) £34,000
— [Paris, c.1455-70]. Hours of the Passion & Office for the Crown of Thorns only. 52 leaves (1 blank), vellum, 117mm by 85mm. 18th-cent French red mor gilt. In a small well-formed gothic hand. With 2-line initials in leafy designs in colors on burnished gold grounds, c.40 panel borders, 8 small miniatures with 3-quarter or full borders, & large miniatare above 3 lines of text & with full border. (91) £10,000
— [Haarlem?, c.1460]. Use of Utrecht. In Dutch. 88 leaves & 5 flyleaves, vellum, 93mm by 62mm, in 17th-cent sheep over wooden bds. In a gothic littera textualis. With 13 two-line initials with marginal penwork decoration, 3 large historiated initials with 3-quarter border incorporating birds & beasts, & 2 large miniatures within full borders. (91) £3,200
— [Tours?, c.1460]. Of unidentified use. In Latin, with Calendar & prayers in French. 160 leaves, vellum, 170mm by 120mm, in 18th-cent French diced russia gilt. In brown ink in a gothic textura. With small initials throughout in burnished gold, 3-line initials on gold ground with outer panel borders, & 8 large miniatures within full borders in the style of the Follower of the Coetivity Master. Some spaces for miniatures left blank. Borthwick-Norton collection. (89) £26,000
— [Bruges?, c.1460]. Use of Rome. 250 leaves (2 blank), vellum, 163mm by 122mm, in 18th-cent French red mor gilt. In brown ink in a gothic textura. With 25 six-line illuminated initials, most pages with panel borders of gold ivy leaves, 23 pp with full illuminated borders, & 21 large miniatures with full borders, probably by William Vrelant or a Dutch collaborator.

HORAE B.M.V.

Lacking Calendar. Inscr by a Spanish censor on f.1, c.1600. (88) £70,000
— [Paris?, 1460-70]. Use of Langres. 186 leaves, vellum, 205mm by 140mm. Late 18th-cent red half mor bdg. In a calligraphic gothic hand. With small illuminated initials & baguette borders throughout, 8 large initials in blue or pink on polished gold ground with leafy extensions & 3-quarter borders, & 12 full-page miniatures in arched compartments above large initials & within full floral borders including birds & insects. (91) DM40,500
— [Paris?, c.1460]. Use not stated. In Latin, with prayers in French. 138 leaves, vellum, 194mm by 132mm. 19th-cent red velvet bdg. In black ink in a gothic textura. With 6 miniatures within full borders, 8 foliate & floral borders, & numerous small & large initials & linefillers in gold & colors. Ownership inscr of Marie Delasalle. (89) DM20,000
— [Flanders, c.1460-70]. Of unidentified use. 114 leaves, vellum, 145mm by 102mm. 17th-cent dark brown lea bdg. In a lettre batarde. With small initials in gold & colors throughout, 9 historiated initials, & 14 full-page miniatures within floral borders. (90) DM44,000
— [Paris, c.1460]. (91) £900
— [Rouen, c.1460-70]. Use of Coutances. In Latin, with Calendar in French. 147 leaves, vellum, 185mm by 135mm, in 18th-cent French red mor gilt. In black ink in a gothic liturgical hand. With 2-line initials with panel borders throughout, 18 very large initials with full borders (4 historiated), & 13 large miniatures in full borders. 1 leaf added later to correct a scribal error. (90) £65,000
— [Southern Netherlands, Bruges?, c.1460-80]. Use of Rome. 109 leaves, vellum, 97mm by 67mm, in old calf bdg. In dark brown ink in a small & careful gothic liturgical hand. With 14 large illuminated initials in floral designs on burnished gold grounds with full grisaille borders & full-page grisaille miniature (others removed) within full border. (90) £1,950
— [Troyes, c.1460-75]. Use of Troyes. In Latin, with Calendar in French. 99 leaves only, vellum, 177mm by 126mm. 18th-cent French mor. In black ink in a gothic liturgical hand. With 86 panel borders with colored flowers & leaves, 2 large original & 2 skillfully forged miniatures within full borders. (89) £5,800
— [Troyes or Langres?, c.1460-80]. Single leaf, vellum, 173mm by 123mm. With panel border & large miniature above large initial within full border of flowers & acanthus leaves on particolored liquid gold ground. (91) £1,700
— [Southern Flanders, Grammont?, c.1460-80]. Use of Rome. In Latin, with prayers in Dutch. 142 leaves (5 added later), vellum, 193mm by 129mm. Modern red-brown lea over medieval bevelled wooden bds. In a gothic liturgical hand. With 13 large or very large illuminated initials & 10 small & 6 full-page miniatures, all with 3-quarter or full illuminated borders of colored flowers & leaves, & full-page illuminated diagram. (91) £10,000
— [Loire Valley, c.1460]. Use of Paris. In Latin & French. 232 leaves (1 blank), vellum, 140mm by 95mm. 18th-cent French calf bdg. In a regular sloping lettre batarde. With 2- & 3-line initials throughout in red & blue on burnished gold grounds & infilled with colored ivyleaves, illuminated borders throughout on 3 sides of every page, & 19 large miniatures above 3 lines of text with full borders, some with little vignettes of animals, grotesques, etc. Some miniatures rubbed. (91) £20,000
— [Rouen, c.1460-70]. Use of Rouen. Single leaf, vellum, 173mm by 119mm. In a gothic liturgical hand. With 10 small illuminated initials & large miniature by the Master of the Geneva Latini, above 3-line illuminated initial with 3-sided illuminated baguette & full border of colored flowers, leaves & strawberries with a myriad of tiny gold leaves. Korner collection. (90) £6,000
— [Paris, c.1460-80]. Use of Rome. In Latin, with Calendar in French. 139 leaves (1 blank, 1 lacking) & 3 flyleaves, vellum, 124mm by 86mm. Mid 19th-cent English green mor gilt bdg. In dark brown ink in a very fine small lettre batarde. With small initials throughout in blue & burnished gold

with penwork, 9 large illuminated initials with 3-quarter illuminated borders, & 4 large miniatures within full borders in the style of Maitre Francois. (90) £7,000

— [Florence, c.1460-70]. Use of Rome. 182 leaves & 2 modern blanks, vellum, 113mm by 81mm. Late 19th-cent green mor gilt by Vickers & Son. In dark brown ink in a rounded gothic hand. With 2-line initials throughout with elaborate usually full-length penwork, 7 large illuminated initials, & 3 large historiated initials with full borders enclosing birds & putti. Borders cropped. (90) £4,800

— [Paris, c.1460]. (88) £900

— [Southern France, Clermond-Ferrand?, c.1460-80]. In Latin, with some prayers in French. 214 leaves (1 blank) & 6 flyleaves, vellum, 194mm by 134mm, in early 19th-cent calf gilt. In very dark brown ink in a gothic liturgical hand. With small illuminated initials throughout, panel borders on every verso in designs of acanthus leaves & other plants, some inhabited, & 18 large miniatures with full borders often enclosing grotesques, peasants, animals, etc. Astor MS.A.16. (88) £26,000

— The Great Hours of Galeazzo Maria Sforza. [Milan, c.1461-66]. Use of Rome. In Latin, with a few rubrics in Italian. 241 leaves (2 blank) & flyleaf, vellum, 350mm by 240mm, in 18th-cent Italian red mor gilt. In dark brown ink in a skilful humanistic minuscule with slight gothic traces. With principal headings in burnished gold capitals, small & 97 large illuminated initials throughout, 3 incorporating portraits, small historiated initial & 5 elaborate title-leaves with very large historiated initials & luxurious borders. Illuminated by the Hippolyta Master. Astor MS.A.6. (88) £700,000

— [Bruges, c.1465]. 234 leaves, vellum, 5.5 by 4 inches, in 19th-cent calf. 17 lines, in black ink in a gothic bookhand, rubricated. With 20 full-page miniatures in full borders, 10 fully colored & gilt, 10 in grisaille, touched with gold & with occasional use of blue. (90) £240,000

— [Flanders, c.1465]. Use of Sarum. 155 leaves, vellum, 213mm by 147mm, in repaired late 16th-cent sheep over wooden bds. In black ink in a gothic textura. With baguette borders on 126 pp, 193 three-line initials in colors & burnished gold, 22 six-line historiated initials with 3-quarter borders, & 24 full-page miniatures within full borders facing pages with similar borders & 5-line initials. (90) £35,000

— [Tours, c.1465-70]. Use of Rome. In Latin, with Calendar in French. 197 leaves (1 blank) & 2 flyleaves, vellum, 210mm by 148mm, in early 19th-cent English dark blue velvet by Hering. In dark brown ink in 2 sizes of a fine gothic liturgical hand. With small illuminated initials throughout, full borders surrounding every page incorporating animals, grotesques, angels, etc., 48 Calendar miniatures in roundels, & 18 large minatures (1 full-page) above large (sometimes historiated) initials. 2 miniatures attributed to the Master of Charles of France, 3 to the Master of the Geneva Boccaccio or his circle. (91) £250,000

— [Bruges, c.1465-80]. Use of Rome. In Latin. 131 leaves, vellum, 185mm by 130mm, in contemp wooden bds covered with early red velvet over orig blindstamped tanned lea. In black ink in a handsome, regular rounded gothic hand. With 2-line initials throughout in highly burnished gold, 13 very large illuminated intials with full borders, & 4 full-page miniatures (1 cut out & re-inserted). (91) £14,000

— [Northern or eastern France, 3d quarter of 15th cent]. Use of Rome. In Latin, with Calendar, Quinze Joyes & Sept Requetes in French. 178 leaves, vellum, 208mm by 143mm. 19th- or early 20th-cent blindstamped dark brown mor by Lucien Magnin. In dark brown ink in a gothic liturgical hand. With 2-line initials in red & blue on burnished gold grounds & large initial with three-quarter illuminated border. 1st leaf in modern facsimile on old vellum; lacking all miniature leaves. (88) £2,800

— [Rouen, c.1465]. (90) £1,000

— [Artois, Therouanne?, 3d quarter of 15th cent]. Use of Therouanne. In

HORAE B.M.V.

- Latin, with Calendar in French. 53 leaves (1 lacking), vellum, 182mm by 132mm, in late medieval bdg of calf over wooden bds. In dark brown ink in a gothic liturgical hand. With 6 large initials with 3-quarter borders, large initial with full border, & large miniature of the Annunciation above large initial & 6 lines of text, all within full border. (90) £3,000
- [Central? France, c.1465-85]. Of uncertain use. In Latin, with Calendar & prayers in French. 124 leaves (20 lacking), 125mm by 90mm, in modern red velvet. In dark brown ink in a small lettre batarde. With panel borders throughout, 22 Calendar roundels in outer margins, 17 small miniatures with 3-quarter borders, & 7 large miniatures with full borders. Very worn. (90) £12,000
- [Southern Netherlands, Burges?, c.1465-75]. Use of Sarum. 235 leaves (1 lacking) & 2 flyleaves, vellum, 84mm by 56mm, in old velvet over wooden bds. In brown ink in a very small gothic liturgical hand. With 25 large initials with full borders of leaves & flowers, 16 historiated initials with 3-quarter borders, & 14 full-page miniatures in full borders. (90) £14,000
- [Bayeux, 3d quarter of 15th cent]. Use of Bayeux. In Latin with prayers in French. 151 leaves (c.12 lacking), vellum, 157mm by 113mm. Modern blindstamped calf. In dark brown ink in a gothic liturgical hand. With small initials throughout with detailed penwork infilling & illuminated initial with 3-quarter foliate border. (89) £2,200
- [Utrecht, c.1465 & c.1510]. Use of Utrecht. In Dutch. 166 leaves (3 lacking, 3 blank) & 3 flyleaves, vellum, 180mm by 130mm. Late medieval bdg of blindstamped tanned lea over wooden bds; def. In a rather angular rounded gothic hand. With 10 half-page historiated initials with 3-quarter borders or full borders by the Master of Gijsbrecht van Brederode, & 17 small miniatures with partial or full borders & 7 full-page miniatures in the style of the Master of Cornelis Croesinck added c.1510. (91) £130,000
- [Bruges, 3d quarter of 15th cent]. Use of Sarum. 130 leaves (lacking c.3) & flyleaf, vellum, 197mm by 137mm. Early 19th-cent French mottled calf gilt. In dark brown ink in an upright contracted gothic liturgical hand. With 14 very large initials with full borders, 21 historiated initials, 8 half-page miniatures with full borders & 18 full-page miniatures on versos of inserted sheets. (90) £30,000
- [Flanders, 3d quarter of 15th cent]. Use of Rome. 56 leaves (some lacking), 157mm by 103mm. 19th-cent half black mor. In dark brown ink in a gothic liturgical hand. With 11 large illuminated initials with partial or full borders, & full-page miniature. Worn. (89) £1,800
- [Flanders, 3d quarter of 15th cent]. Use of Sarum. 201 leaves only, vellum, 105mm by 60mm, in 17th-cent English calf. In dark brown ink in a gothic liturgical hand. With 2-line illuminated initials throughout. Opening leaves of sections of the text missing. (88) £1,700
- [Rouen, c.1470]. Use of Rouen. 128 leaves (some lacking), vellum, 156mm by 110mm, in 18th-cent French red mor. In a gothic textura. With 5 large initials in blue & grisaille on gold ground with floral decoration, within 3-quarter border on partly liquid gold geometric ground, & panel borders on almost every page. Lacking all miniatures. (91) £4,000
- [Rouen, c.1470]. Of uncertain use, possibly Paris & Rouen. In Latin, with Calendar & Prayers in French. 127 leaves (lacking at least 6), vellum, 19cm by 14cm. In extra black crushed mor bdg by Stikeman. In dark brown ink in a gothic textura. With numerous illuminated initials, wide outer panel borders with painted fruits, leaves & flowers throughout, & 8 large miniatures with full borders. (88) £12,000
- [Northeastern France or Flanders, c.1470]. Use of Rome. In Latin. 221 leaves, vellum, 100mm by 77mm. 19th-cent black mor gilt. In brown ink in a rounded gothic bookhand. With 15 large illuminated initals with scrollwork decoration & full foliate borders, & 14 full-page miniatures within arched surrounds & full borders. (88)

£42,000
- [Northern Netherlands, c.1470]. Use of Utrecht. In Dutch. 200 leaves, vellum, 150mm by 110mm, in 18th-cent Durch mor gilt. In dark brown ink in a small gothic textura. With 36 large or very large illuminated initials & 6 full-page miniatures with foliate borders, many containing birds, angels & beasts. (89) £13,000
- [Brittany, Vannes?, c.1470]. Use of Paris. 102 leaves & 2 flyleaves, vellum, 143mm by 100mm, in 17th-cent calf gilt. In brown ink in a gothic textura. With calligraphic 2-line initials with penwork decoration & 4 large miniatures with full borders of flowers & ivy leaves. Some prayers inscr on flyleaves, 1524. (89) £2,800
- [Tuscany, Florence?, c.1470-80]. Use of Rome. 268 leaves & 2 orig flyleaves, vellum, 120mm by 85mm, in def 18th-cent black mor. In brown ink in a gothic rotunda. With 9 large initials in gold with penwork decoration & 5 historiated initials with elaborately decorated full borders in the style of the circle of Francesco d'Antonio del Cherico. With 18th-cent painted tp & inscr on front endpaper. (89) £9,000
- [Rouen, c.1470]. Use of Rouen. In Latin, with Quinze Joyes in French. 125 leaves (some lacking), vellum, 194mm by 140mm. Rebacked 16th-cent tooled calf gilt. In brown ink in a gothic textura. With c.140 small initials in colors on gold ground, illuminated panel borders throughout in outer margins, & 7 large miniatures by the Master of the Geneva Latini (smudged). (89) £4,200
- [Lower Rhine region?, c.1470]. Use not stated. In Dutch, in the trans of Geert Groot. 211 leaves, vellum, 128mm by 90mm. Later parchment over wooden bds. In brown ink in a gothic hand. With 32 three-line penwork initials in blue & red, & 5 very large calligraphic initials in colors with extensive marginal flourishes. (89) £4,000
- [Venice, c. 1470]. Use of Rome. 115 leaves of vellum stained purple, 140mm by 90mm. Modern black mor with silver clasps. In gold ink in a fine humanist hand. With 1 large & 7 three-line historiated initials in silver containing figures drawn in gold, probably by Belbello de Pavia. (89) £300,000
- [Northern France or Flanders, c.1470]. Use of Rome. 141 leaves, vellum, 90mm by 68mm, in 19th-cent blind-stamped calf. In brown ink in a small gothic rotunda. With 14 five-line initials in blue on gold ground & 3 large miniatures, all within full borders. Further miniatures removed. (88) £2,800
- [Tour, Angers or Le Mans?, c.1470]. Use of Rome. 212 leaves (2 lacking), vellum, 121mm by 86mm, in modern dark red mor over wooden bds. In brown ink in a lettre batarde. With painted borders throughout of gold & green foliage with fruits & flowers, inhabited by human figures, animals, grotesque creatures, etc., & 34 large miniatures by 4 different artists. (88) £68,000
- [Flanders, c.1470]. Use of Rome, in Latin, bound with Prayers & devotions of same date, in Dutch. 63 leaves & 62 leaves, vellum, 158mm by 113mm, in 18th-cent calf. 1st work illuminated, with 5 large miniatures with full borders (probably lacking 2), all apparently unfinished & colored later, often primitively. 2d work with penwork decoration. Both in brown ink, the first in a gothic textura & the 2d in a rounded gothic script. (91) £3,000
- [Lyons, c.1470] 163 leaves, vellum, 95mm by 70mm, in modern mor gilt. Written in ink in a French batarde. WIth 13 large miniatures & 1 later miniature. Zabriskie-Manhattan College Ms (91) $13,000
- [Utrecht?, c.1470]. Use not stated. In Latin, with prayers in Dutch. 138 leaves (2 lacking), vellum, 155mm by 110mm. 17th-cent vellum bdg. In a gothic liturgical hand by Henrich Pryem. With hundreds of small initials in gold & colors partly with penwork extensions, 16 larger initials with bar borders, & 13 large illuminated initials, mostly with full borders. (91) DM16,000
- [Besancon?, c.1470]. Use not stated. In Latin. 217 leaves (7 lacking), vellum,

105mm by 80mm. 16th-cent lea gilt. In black ink in a lettre batarde. With 13 miniatures, 2 illuminated borders & numerous initials in gold & colors, some with extensions. (89) DM13,000
— [Paris, c.1470-85]. Use of Paris. In Latin, with Calendar in French. 163 leaves & flyleaf, vellum, 175mm by 130mm, in early 20th-cent [English?] dark green mor over wooden bds. In dark brown ink in a gothic liturgical hand. With 10 large illuminated initials, often with faces or grotesques, & with panel or 3-sided borders, 20 small miniatures with partial illuminated borders, & 6 large miniatures. (91) £16,000
— [Southern Flanders, perhaps Picardy or Hainault, c.1470-90]. Of unidentified use. In Latin, with Calendar & Prayers in French. 162 leaves (2 blank, 2 lacking), vellum, 162mm by 118mm. 18th-cent sheepskin bdg. In dark brown ink in a gothic liturgical hand. With 13 large initials in color on burnished gold grounds (5 with full borders) & 2 small & 6 large or full-page miniatures. Last gathering loose. (88) £5,000
— [Bruges, c.1470]. Use of Rome. 17 leaves only, vellum, 157mm by 113mm. In black ink in a fine rounded gothic hand. With 6-line illuminated initial with full border of acanthus leaves & flowers. (90) £1,200
— The Montboissier Hours. [Paris, c.1470-80]. Use of Rome. 189 leaves (1 blank), vellum, 145mm by 92mm, in mid-17th-cent French armorial red mor gilt. In dark brown ink in a fluent gothic liturgical hand with some batarde features. With 2-line initials throughout in scrolling leafy designs in unusual colors, large historiated initial & 11 large miniatures all with full borders including birds & grotesques, & full-page frontis within fine architectural surround. Probably illuminated by Maitre Francois. (90) £60,000
— [Paris, c.1470]. Use of Rome. 151 leaves (c.3 lacking) & 2 flyleaves, vellum, 101mm by 76mm, in dark brown mor preserving parts of 16th-cent bdg. In black ink in a skilful slightly sloping lettre batarde. With linefillers & small initials throughout

in liquid gold on colored grounds, historiated initial, & 16 large or full-page miniatures within full borders of flowers & leaves with birds, insects or arms. Probably illuminated by Maitre Francois or his workshop. (90) £110,000
— [West Central France, Poitiers?, c.1470-80]. Of uncertain use. In Latin, with some prayers in French. 199 leaves (2 lacking) & 4 flyleaves, vellum, 136mm by 89mm, in worn 17th-cent French calf gilt. In dark brown ink in a regular lettre batarde. With panel borders throughout for every 2-line initial including putti, grotesques, animals, etc., 29 historiated initials, 21 Calendar miniatures in margins, & 18 large miniatures from the circle of the Jouvenal Master. (90) £24,000
— [Eastern Netherlands, Arnhem?, c.1470-90]. Single leaf, vellum, 146mm by 104mm. In Dutch. With historiated initial in colors on burnished gold ground & full length border with children climbing a tree as Death approaches a little girl below. (91) £4,500
— [Southern Netherlands, c.1470]. Use of Rome. 109 leaves & 2 flyleaves, vellum, 163mm by 113mm. Contemp blindstamped tanned lea over wooden bds; imperf. In a gothic liturgical hand. With 13 very large initials with full borders of grey & blue acanthus leaves, mostly including birds, & 12 full-page miniatures in full borders by a different illuminator. (91) £9,000
— [Northeast Italy, c.1470-80]. Use of Aquileia. 23 separate leaves, vellum, 108mm by 78mm. In dark brown ink in 2 sizes of a rounded gothic script. With 29 two-line illuminated initials with borders of flowers & bezants within brown penwork in the Ferrarese style. (90) £1,300
— [Rouen, c.1470]. (90) £850
— [Poitiers, c.1470-80]. Single leaf, vellum, 164mm by 105mm. In a gothic hand. With large miniature in an arched compartment above large initial, all within 3-sided border, by the Master of Adelaide of Savoy. Mtd. (90) £3,200

— [Bruges, c.1470-75]. Use of Rome. 152 leaves, vellum, 95mm by 67mm. 18th-cent French red mor profusely gilt. In dark brown ink in a very small skilful rounded gothic hand. With 21 large illuminated initials with full-length borders, 6 large initials with full borders, & 6 full-page miniatures within full borders by the Master of the Dresden Prayerbook. Abbey collection. (89) £85,000

— [Bruges, c.1470]. Use of Rome. 11 leaves only, vellum, 155mm by 110mm. In black ink in a fine rounded gothic hand. With 9 large illuminated initials in burnished gold on red & blue grounds, & 6-line illuminated initial with full illuminated border of flowers & leaves with strawberries. (89) £1,300

— [Lombardy, Milan?, c.1470-80]. Use of Rome. 172 leaves (2 blank) & 4 flyleaves, vellum, 125mm by 88mm, in 17th-cent tooled Italian olive-brown mor gilt. In pale black ink in a small rounded gothic bookhand. With small initials throughout with partial borders, 21 large illuminated initials with full-length borders & 19 full-page miniatures above bas-de-page vignettes & within full borders. Astor MS.A.7. (88) £160,000

— [Eastern Netherlands, Arnhem?, c.1470-80]. Of uncertain Use. In Dutch. 224 leaves (4 blank, 2 lacking), vellum, 133mm by 96mm, in 19th-cent black mor. In dark brown ink in a regular angular gothic bookhand with some calligraphic cadels. With 2-line initials with penwork extensions throughout, 23 large or full-page illuminated initials with 3-quarter or full illuminated borders by the Master of Margriet Uitenham, & 14 full-page miniatures by the Master of the Zwolle Bible. (88) £58,000

— [Southern Netherlands, c.1470-90]. Use of Utrecht. In Latin, with Calendar in Dutch. 128 leaves (many lacking), vellum, 165mm by 120mm, in very def contemp panel-stamped calf over wooden bds by Jan van der Lende of Bruges. In brown ink in a gothic liturgical hand. With c.100 2-line illuminated initials with marginal extensions & 2 full illuminated borders. (88) £3,000

— [Utrecht, c.1472]. Use of Utrecht. In Dutch. 141 leaves, vellum, 145mm by 110mm. 17th-cent embroidered silk over paper bds; silver clasp. In brown ink in a small gothic hand. With 16 three-line decorated initials. Lacking miniature leaves. (88) £1,050

— [Utrecht?, 2d half of 15th cent]. Use of Utrecht. In Dutch. 174 leaves, vellum, 134mm by 96mm. 16th-cent blindstamped calf over wooden bds. In brown ink in a small gothic bookhand. With 5 large decorated calligraphic initials & 6 miniatures, cut out & pasted onto blanks. Lacking 8 orig miniature leaves. (88) £5,000

— [France, 2d half of 15th cent]. Of unidentified use. In Latin. 134 leaves, vellum, 118mm by 84mm. 18th-cent vellum panelled in blind with fleur-de-lys tool. In dark brown ink in a small rotunda script. With numerous illuminated initials. Miniature leaves removed. (88) £2,600

— [Savoy?, c.1475]. Use of Rome. 189 leaves, vellum, 124mm by 82mm. 17th-cent blindstamped sheep. In brown ink in a gothic textura. With 8 three-line initials in colors on gold ground within 3-quarter borders, & 6 large miniatures with 3-line initials & full borders. (89) £2,400

— [Venice?, 3d quarter of 15th cent]. Use of Rome. 187 leaves, vellum, 133mm by 95mm, in 17th-cent mor gilt. In brown ink an an Italian gothic rotunda, with rubric in red & versals in gold or blue with penwork decoration & extensions. With 4 large historiated initials within painted floral borders. (91) £4,000

— [Rouen?, c.1475]. Use not stated. In Latin & French. 110 leaves, vellum, 170mm by 125mm. 17th-cent dark brown mor gilt. Mostly in black ink in a textura script. With illuminated initials & line-fillers throughout, 17 large initials & 8 miniatures within elaborate borders. With later coat-of-arms of the Dauzier family on flyleaf. (89) DM35,000

— [Southern Netherlands, Bruges?, c.1475-85]. Use of Rome. 153 leaves (4 lacking) & flyleaf, vellum, 175mm by

118mm. 17th-cent Italian red mor. In dark brown ink in a handsome lettre batarde. With small initials in burnished gold & panel borders throughout, 14 large illuminated initials with full borders, 24 calendar roundels & 11 full-page miniatures in arched compartments within full borders. Bradley Martin Ms. (90) $70,000

— [Northeast Italy, c.1470-80]. Use of Rome. 36 leaves only, vellum, 108mm by 77mm. In brown ink in 2 sizes of a rounded gothic script. With 47 small illuminated initials with partial or full-length borders, 4-line illuminated initial, & 2 five-line historiated initials within full borders. (90) £2,600

— [Northeast Italy, 2d half of 15th cent]. Use of Rome. 102 leaves, vellum, 138mm by 98mm, in repaired dark brown sheep over pastebds. In dark brown ink in a slightly clubbed round humanistic minuscule. With 19 illuminated initials with leafy extensions in full color & burnished gold, & 4 historiated initials (1 obliterated) with full borders. Worn throughout. (90) £2,000

— [Bruges? c.1475-85]. Use of Rome. 173 leaves, vellum, 129mm by 92mm. Contemp bdg by Thomas de Gavere of blindstamped calf over bevelled wooden bds; repaired. In dark brown ink in a rounded gothic hand. With small initials throughout in burnished gold heightened with white tracery, 16 three-quarter page illuminated borders of colored leaves, flowers & fruit, & 3 full-page miniatures within full borders. (89) £19,000

— [Florence, c.1475-85]. Single leaf, vellum, 137mm by 95mm; laid down. With very large historiated initial in colors & liquid gold on a burnished gold panel & full border of regularly scrolling stems incorporating coat-of-arms, attributed to Francesco di Lorenzo Rosselli. (91) £3,000

— [Northern France, Paris?, c.1475]. Use of Toul. In Latin, with Calendar in French. 234 leaves (1 lacking) & 8 flyleaves, vellum, 158mm by 110mm. Early 19th-cent English red mor bdg. In 2 sizes of a gothic liturgical hand, with some catchwords in a lettre batarde. With 2-line initials in leafy designs in colors on burnished gold grounds, c.140 panel borders, 24 small Calendar miniatures, & 17 large miniatures above large initials within full borders in the general style of Maitre Francois. (91) £10,500

— [Lyons?, 2d half of 15th cent]. Use of Lyons. 166 leaves (3 blank, 1 lacking), vellum, 99mm by 73mm. Def 16th-cent brown mor gilt. In dark brown ink in 2 sizes of a gothic liturgical hand. With small initials throughout in designs of liquid gold on colored grounds, 6 large initials with 3-quarter illuminated borders, & four large miniatures (retouched) in full borders. (90) £3,800

— [Northern Italy, 2d half of 15th cent]. Use of Rome. 226 leaves (1 lacking, some old replacements) & flyleaf, vellum, 68mm by 47mm. Old blind-stamped sheep over pastebds. In dark brown ink in a very small rounded gothic hand. With 2-line initials with elaborate penwork often extending the full height of the margins, & 9 large illuminated initials with partial borders. (90) £2,000

— [South or Southwest France, c.1475-85]. Use of Rome. 114 leaves (1 lacking), vellum, 156mm by 98mm. 18th-cent French olive-brown mor gilt. In dark brown ink in 2 sizes of a lettre batarde. With small initials throughout in liquid gold on colored grounds, & 14 large or full-page miniatures mostly with full borders enclosing animals, grotesques & people. (89) £7,500

— [Bologna?, 2d half of 15th cent]. Use of Rome. 220 leaves (1 lacking), vellum, 67mm by 47mm. 17th-cent Italian olive-brown mor gilt. In brown ink in a small rounded gothic hand. With 9 very large illuminated & 4 historiated initials with full borders sometimes including birds & dragons. (89) £22,000

— [Liege, c.1475-85]. Use of Utrecht. In Latin, with some rubrics in Dutch. 179 leaves & 2 flyleaves, vellum & paper, 101mm by 67mm, in worn contemp calf over wooden bds. In brown ink in a small gothic hand. With 2 large initials with 3-quarter borders, 4 very large initials in colors with full borders, & 2 circular Calendar diagrams.

(88) £18,000

— [Florence, c.1475-85]. Use of Rome. 203 leaves (4 blank), vellum, 113mm by 79mm, in 17th-cent calf profusely gilt with silver clasps & catches. In pale black ink in 2 sizes of a rounded gothic liturgical hand. With 2-line initials throughout in blue or burnished gold, 7 large illuminated initials with marginal extensions, & 5 full-page miniatures by the Master of the Sassetti Thucydides, with large historiated initals on opposite pages, all within full borders. (88) £7,000

— [France, c.1475]. Use of Rome. 146 leaves, vellum, 103mm by 71mm, in modern bdg. In black ink in a semi-gothic hand. With 2-line decorated initials throughout & 16 floral borders (shaved) with 4-line decorated initials in colors & gold. (91) $4,600

— [South Germany, Nuremberg?, 27 July 1480]. Of unidentified use. 240 leaves (1 lacking), vellum, 84mm by 62mm, in 17th-cent black mor. In black ink in a fine Gothic hand. With numerous penwork initials in colors. Ownership inscr of Hartmann Schedel. John F. Fleming Estate. (89) $14,000

— [Flanders, c.1480]. Use of Rome. 119 leaves & flyleaves, vellum, 182mm by 128mm. 18th-cent French mor gilt. In black ink in a gothic textura. With over 200 two-line initials in burnished gold on red & blue ground with white tracery, & 3 small & 14 full-page miniatures within full borders & facing page with similar borders & 5-line decorated initial. Illuminated in the style associated with the school of Willem Vrelant. (90) £28,000

— [Northern France, c.1480]. Use of Rome. 104 leaves (some lacking), vellum, 151mm by 98mm. 19th-cent blindstamped vellum bdg. In brown ink in a lettre batarde. With numerous small initials in liquid gold & colors, outer panel borders decorated with jewels & foliage throughout, & 6 large miniatures within full borders. (89) £1,600

— [Genoa, c.1480]. Use of Rome. 170 leaves, vellum, 120mm by 75mm. 17th-cent black mor gilt bdg. In brown ink in an elegant humanist hand. With c.125 two-line initials in gold on pink, blue & green ground with white tracery, & 11 large historiated initials with full borders of flowers & foliage containing putti. Lacking calendar. (89) £6,500

— [Veneto?, c.1480]. Use of Rome. 184 leaves, vellum, 112mm by 71mm. Late 18th-cent red mor gilt. In brown ink in a gothic bookhand. With numerous small initials in gold on colored ground & 11 large illuminated (2 historiated) initials in colors heightened with burnished gold. (89) £10,000

— [Bruges, c.1480]. Use of Rome. 188 leaves (5 blank), vellum, 90mm by 65mm. 18th-cent blue mor gilt. In brown ink in a rounded gothic textura. With 15 five-line gesso-like initials within full borders of naturalistic flowers, fruit, birds & insects on gold grounds, & eight-line historiated initial within 3-quarter border. Lacking miniatures. (89) £6,500

— [Paris or Eastern France, c.1480]. Use of Paris. In Latin, with prayers in French. 222 leaves (2 lacking), vellum, 170mm by 120mm, in 18th-cent red French mor gilt by Derome. In brown ink in a gothic bookhand. With illuminated small initials, & 6 small & 13 large miniatures within full borders of flowers & leaves on gold ground, decorated with animals & grotesque creatures. (88) £24,000

— [Rouen, c.1480]. Use of Rouen. In Latin, with Calendar in French. 123 leaves (at least 6 lacking), vellum, 150mm by 105mm, in early 20th-cent brown mor gilt by Riviere. In brown ink in a gothic bookhand by 2 scribes. With 10 pp with half or three-quarter panel borders, & 8 large miniatures (1 possibly later) within full painted borders of acanthus leaves with geometric panels containing flowers on gold ground. (88) £13,000

— [Florence, c.1480-90] 6 leaves, vellum, 131mm by 93mm, pasted onto modern vellum leaves with thin gold frames added to edges of orig leaves & extending onto modern mounts. With 3 full-page miniatures & 3 historiated initials by a different hand, all with full borders, 3 with bust-length ports & 1 with a bust-length crowned skeleton.

HORAE B.M.V.

Zabriskie-Manhattan College Ms (91) $11,000

— [Rouen, c.1480]. Use of Rouen. In Latin, with Calendar in French. 158 leaves (4 blank), vellum, 170mm by 125mm, in 17th-cent lea. In brown ink in a calligraphic textura. With small initials & decorative borders throughout, numerous larger illuminated initials, & 24 small & 15 very large miniatures. (90) DM43,000

— [Ferrara or Bologna, c.1480-90]. Use of Rome. In Latin. 198 leaves, vellum, 109mm by 74mm, in 19th-cent Parisian Jansenist plain black mor by Trautz-Bauzonnet. In dark brown ink in a regular rounded gothic hand. With illuminated initials throughout, 8 very large illuminated initials with full-length borders on pages entirely written in blue & red, & 4 large historiated initials with full historiated borders. (91) £18,000

— [Southwestern France, Poitiers?, c.1480]. Of unidentified use. 123 leaves (2 lacking), vellum, 160mm by 107mm. 18th-cent French red mor gilt. In dark brown ink in a small gothic liturgical hand; some rubrics in burnished gold. With 1- or 2-line illuminated initials throughout, 14 small miniatures in soft colors & liquid gold & 13 large miniatures (1 heraldic frontis) with elaborate borders. Prepared in 2 stages, probably by 3 artists. (88) £12,000

— [Delft, c.1480]. Use of Utrecht. In Dutch. 225 leaves (1 lacking), vellum, 186mm by 130mm. 18th-cent Dutch mottled calf bdg. In a compressed gothic liturgical hand. With c.70 large initials with 3-quarter red & blue Delft penwork borders, & 7 very large historiated initials with full borders of scrolling plant & acanthus stems including birds & animals. (91) £10,000

— The Wodhull-Haberton Hours. [Delft, c.1480-90]. Use of Utrecht. In Dutch. 245 leaves & 4 flyleaves, vellum, 185mm by 125mm. Contemp Dutch blindstamped pale brown tanned lea over bevelled wooden bds. In very dark brown ink in a small, well-formed gothic liturgical hand. With c.40 large initials with 3-quarter illuminated & often historiated borders, 8 very large illuminated initials with full borders, &

AMERICAN BOOK PRICES CURRENT

8 outstanding full-page miniatures in arched compartments within full borders. Abbey collection. (89) £520,000

— [Tours, c.1480]. Use of Poitiers & Paris. In Latin, with Calendar in French. 234 leaves & flyleaf, vellum, 110mm by 76mm. 19th-cent vellum over pastebds, gilt. In dark brown ink in 2 sizes of a fine lettre batarde. With 148 panel borders in designs of colored leaves & flowers, 6 large initials with full illuminated borders, & 16 miniatures (mostly very large or full-page) attributable to Jean Bourdichon, all within full borders or jewelled frames; worn. Abbey collection. (89) £70,000

— [Lower Rhineland, c.1480-90]. Use of Rome & Utrecht. 145 leaves & blanks, vellum, 162mm by 110mm. 19th-cent red mor with elaborate metal fittings. In dark brown ink in a regular small gothic liturgical hand. With 33 large illuminated initials, 4 extremely large initials merging with elaborate leafy & floral borders enclosing 5 lines of text, & 13 full-page miniatures by the Master of the Adair Hours partly with full illuminated borders incorporating animals & putti among colored foliage. Abbey collection. (89) £245,000

— [Paris?, c.1480-90]. Use of Paris. In Latin, with Calendar, Quinze Joyes & Sept Requetes in French. 138 leaves (11 lacking), vellum, 152mm by 105mm. 19th-cent blindtooled black mor. In black ink in a gothic liturgical hand. With small initials throughout, 4 large illuminated initials with partial borders, & 3 large miniatures with full borders of leaves & flowers on particolored liquid gold grounds. (89) £5,500

— [Tours, c.1480-1500]. Use of Tours. 96 leaves (2 lacking), vellum, 172mm by 113mm. Contemp blindstamped tanned calf over wooden bds. In black ink in a gothic liturgical hand. With 6 illuminated initials & 5 large miniatures with full borders. (89) £4,800

— [Rouen, c.1480]. Use of Rouen. In Latin, with Calendar in French. 88 leaves, vellum, 201mm by 153mm. Fine (Parisian?) dark mor gilt bdg of c.1570. In dark brown ink in 2 sizes of a lettre batarde. With panel borders throughout, 9 small miniatures or historiated initials with 3-quarter borders, & 4 large miniatures in arched compartments with full borders. (89) £19,000

— [Paris, c.1480-1500]. Use of Paris. In Latin, with Calendar in French. 155 leaves (c.30 lacking), vellum, 153mm by 103mm. 19th-cent French black mor gilt bdg. In dark brown ink in a well-formed lettre batarde. With panel borders throughout in designs of leaves & flowers, 6 small miniatures with 3-quarter illuminated borders, & 7 large miniatures with full borders. (89) £16,000

— [Tournai, c.1480-90]. In Latin, with Quinze Joyes & Sept Requetes in French. 82 leaves, vellum, 175mm by 122m. 18th-cent vellum gilt stamped with the arms of the city of Amsterdam. In dark brown ink in a gothic liturgical hand. With 14 small miniatures & 8 large miniatures in arched compartments above large initials & within full borders. Not including ordinary Hours of the Virgin, Calendar & Office of the Dead; possibly 2d part of a larger Ms. (89) £9,500

— [Burgundy, c.1480-90]. Use of Rome. In Latin, with Calendar in French. 126 leaves (2 blank) & 2 flyleaves, vellum, 232mm by 160mm, in 18th-cent French green mor gilt. In pale black ink in a gothic liturgical hand. With small initials throughout in liquid silver or liquid gold, 3 historiated initials & 14 full-page miniatures by the Master of the Burgundian Prelates, enclosing oblong panels with large illuminated initials & some lines of text. Astor MS.A.14. (88) £145,000

— [North Flanders, c.1480-1500]. Use of Rome. 100 leaves, vellum, 182mm by 128mm, in red mor bdg of c.1800. In dark brown ink in a gothic liturgical hand. With 2-line illuminated initials throughout, & 13 large illuminated initials, 17 small & 13 full-page miniatures with 3-quarter or full borders. (88) £12,000

— [Southern France, c.1480-90]. Use of Rome. In Latin, with Calendar & prayers in French. 165 leaves (1 later, c.3 lacking), vellum, 188mm by 127mm, in calf bdg of c.1800. In dark brown ink in a large lettre batarde with some calligraphic cadels. With 4 small miniatures & 14 large or full-page miniatures with borders including grotesques, dragons, monkeys, etc. Written for a man called Reymund. (88) £11,000

— [Venice, c.1480]. Use of Rome. 187 leaves (3 blank, at least 7 lacking) & flyleaf, vellum, 113mm by 79mm, in def 17th-cent Italian calf profusely gilt, lacking clasps. In dark brown ink in a rounded gothic hand. With 2- & 3-line initials throughout with full-length illuminated bar borders, 2 large historiated initals & 7 full, sometimes historiated borders in 2 distinct styles. (88) £4,500

— [Northeast Italy, c.1480-1500]. Use of Rome. 93 leaves, vellum, 112mm by 70mm, in 19th-cent black mor. In black ink in a rounded gothic hand, with 19th-cent additions in the hand of Edmund Waterton. With small initials throughout in blue or burnished gold, 6 large illuminated initials on faceted colored panels with gold tracery, & miniature & full border added in 19th cent. (88) £1,400

— [Barcelona, c.1485]. Use of Barcelona. In Latin, with rubrics in Catalan. 255 leaves including 4 blanks, vellum, 146mm by 110mm. Early 19th-cent red mor gilt elaborately tooled, with brass clasps. In brown ink in a gothic textura. With small calligraphic & illuminated initials throughout, 12 large initials on gold ground with floral ornamentation, 17 pp with elaborate borders on 3 or 4 sides, & 7 full-page miniatures painted in grisaille with full borders. Doheny collection. (88) £190,000

— [Paris?, last quarter of 15th cent]. Use of Paris. 128 leaves (c.20 lacking), vellum, 181mm by 119mm. Contemp green velvet over wooden bds. In brown ink in a gothic textura. With outer panel borders throughout, calendar pages with 3-quarter borders, 14 small miniatures & 12 calendar miniatures. (89) £5,500

— [Venice?, c.1485]. Use of Rome. In Latin & Italian. 206 leaves & 2 flyleaves, vellum, 97mm by 69mm, in 19th-cent black mor gilt. In brown ink in an Italian rotunda. With capitals in gold & blue, small initials with penwork decoration, 7 larger decorated initials on gold ground containing flowers & foliage, & 3 historiated initials within full floral borders. (90) £1,600

— [Paris, c.1485]. Use of Paris. In Latin, with Calendar in French. 162 leaves (2 lacking), vellum, 145mm by 100mm, in early 20th-cent olive mor. In brown ink in a gothic textura. With 1- & 2-line initials in burnished gold on blue & red ground with white tracery, outer panel borders throughout, & 10 large & 12 small miniatures within full borders. Doheny collection. (88) $14,000

— [Paris, c.1485-95]. Use of Rome. In Latin, with Calendar in French. 153 leaves & flyleaf, vellum, 167mm by 112mm, in early 19th-cent English red mor gilt. In dark brown ink in a regular small lettre batarde. With small initials throughout in designs of liquid gold, panel borders on every page, sometimes including animals & grotesques, 24 Calendar miniatures, 13 small miniatures within 3-quarter borders, & 15 large or full-page miniatures enclosing text panels. (91) £18,000

— [Bruges, c.1485-95]. Use of Rome. 219 leaves (1 lacking) & 6 flyleaves, vellum, 132mm by 93mm, in contemp blindstamped tanned calf over wooden bds. In dark brown ink in a very regular lettre batarde. With 10 full illuminated borders in a variety of designs, 71 small miniatures with 3-quarter borders, & 2 full-page miniatures in arched compartments in full borders. Illuminated by the Master of Edward IV & his workshop. (90) £95,000

— [Bologna, 2d half of 15th cent]. Use of Rome. 197 leaves (10 lacking), vellum, 82mm by 59mm. Def contemp blindstamped goatskin over thin wooden bds. In dark brown ink in a small rounded gothic hand. With 10 large illuminated initials in burnished gold with penwork infilling & blue surround. (90) £1,900

— [Paris, c.1485]. Use of Paris. In Latin, with Calendar in French. 155 leaves, vellum, 137mm by 100mm. Worn 18th-cent French red mor gilt. In dark brown ink in a gothic liturgical hand. With small illuminated initials throughout, 13 small & 13 large miniatures with partial or full borders. (89) £10,000

— [Bologna, c.1485]. Use of Rome. In Latin, with some rubrics in Italian. 157 leaves, vellum, 276mm by 186mm, in 19th-cent blindstamped calf over wooden bds. In dark brown ink in 2 sizes of a gothic liturgical hand. With c.275 small & 13 large illuminated initials with floral extensions or borders, & 5 very large historiated initials with full illuminated borders with very elaborate gold penwork swirling around colored flowers, vases, coats-of-arms, vignettes, etc. Astor MS.A.9. (88) £16,000

— [Chartres or Rouen, c.1490]. Use of Chartres. In Latin, with Calendar & prayers in French. 59 leaves, vellum, 215mm by 155mm. 19th-cent blue velvet bdg, def; in half mor case. In brown ink in a gothic textura. With 5 outer panel borders of leaves & flowers, 5 historiated initials, & 8 large miniatures within arched compartments & full borders. Doheny collection. (88) £9,500

— [Northern France?, late 15th cent]. Use of Rome. In Latin, with prayers in French. 120 leaves (c.7 lacking), vellum, 177mm by 119mm. 16th-cent French panelled calf over wooden bds with later clasps. In brown ink in a gothic textura. With 12 large unfinished miniatures; most initials left blank. (89) £3,200

— [Tours: Jean Poyet, c.1490]. Use of Rome, in Latin & French. 184 (of 188) leaves, vellum, 177mm by 125mm, in old wooden bds covered with velvet. With 17 smaller & 5 full-page miniatures, most by Jean Poyet of Tours. (91) £65,000

— [Bruges, c.1490]. 210 leaves, vellum, 97mm by 65mm, in 17th-cent mor gilt. From the workshop or circle of the Master of the Dresden Prayerbook. With 13 large miniatures with fine border, continued across the facing page; 24 roundels containing figurative scenes in lower margin; 15 6-line foliated initials with full borders in gold on blue or red ground & 1 large historiated initial with three-quarter border. (91) £65,000

— [Northern France, late 15th cent]. Hours of the Virgin & Horae Sancte Trinitatis only. 31 leaves (1 lacking), vellum, 125mm by 83mm. Early 16th-cent dark red velvet bdg. In a gothic liturgial hand, with 3 pp in a lettre batarde. With numerous small initials & linefillers in gold on red or blue grounds. (91) DM1,600

— [Rouen, c.1490-1500]. Use of Rouen. In Latin, with Quinze Joyes & Sept Requetes in French. 112 leaves, vellum, 163mm by 113mm, in 16th-cent lea gilt. In black ink in a lettre batarde. With hundreds of small initials in red & gold, 272 larger initials in gold & colors (3 historiated), ornamental borders on every page, 24 Calendar miniatures, & 14 large miniatures within architectural borders incorporating small miniatures. (90) DM85,000

— [Tours?, late 15th cent]. Use not stated. In Latin, 1 prayer in French. 95 leaves (5 lacking), vellum, 235mm by 172mm. Contemp blindstamped brown lea over wooden bds. In black ink in a gothic textura. With 2 (of 6) miniatures, 3 (of 6) illuminated borders & numerous initials & linefillers in gold & colors. (89) DM14,000

— [Northern France, late 15th cent]. Use not stated. In Latin. 74 leaves, vellum, 148mm by 113mm. Red mor gilt bdg of c.1920. In black ink in a gothic textura. With 13 miniatures, 26 foliate & floral borders, & 13 large & numerous small initials in gold & colors. Some 16th-cent prayers in French & Dutch. Ownership inscr of Jac. Dreis. (89) DM20,000

— [Northern France, Paris?, late 15th cent]. Use of Rome. In Latin, with Calendar in French. 92 leaves, vellum, 102mm by 70mm, in late 16th-cent brown mor gilt, tooled in blind. In brown & red ink in a calligraphic textura. With 14 large illuminated initials, partial or full borders inhabited by birds, dragons, etc. throughout, & 11 small & 14 large miniatures. Probably incomplete at end. (88) DM20,000

— [Flanders, late 15th cent]. 190 leaves & remmains of 2 others at front & 1 at end, vellum, 140mm by 908mm, in modern mor gilt by Zaehnsdorf. With 7-line initial depcting part skeleton with full border inhabited by birds, skull & angel; 5-line initials depicting saint, with full border including birds. Borders in blue, pink, green, red & gold. Some bomb damage. (90) £3,000

— [French Flanders, c.1490-1500]. Use of Rome. In Latin, with Calendar in French. 142 leaves (3 blank), vellum, 220mm by 157mm, in modern full dark red velvet. In brown ink in 2 sizes of a calligraphic lettre batarde. With 2-line initials thoughout in liquid gold on colored panels with tracery in liquid silver, 38 small miniatures with broad panel borders, & 15 large miniatures within full borders. (91) £70,000

— [Central or eastern France, late 15th cent]. Use of Rome. In Latin, with Calendar in French. 82 leaves (4 lacking), vellum, 157mm by 106mm. 19th-cent red velvet. In brown ink in a small lettre batarde. With 16 historiated initials, 91 small bas-de-page & Calendar miniatures, mostly with full-length borders, & 13 large miniatures with full camaieu d'or historiated borders. Worn throughout. Astor MS.A.18. (88) £6,000

— [Rouen, c.1490]. Use of Rouen. In Latin, with rubrics & prayers in French. 113 leaves only, vellum, 142mm by 98mm. 18th-cent mottled calf. In dark brown ink in 2 sizes of a lettre batarde. With initials throughout in gold & colors, full borders on every page & 3 large miniatures. Lacking numerous leaves; some misbound. Last gathering unilluminated early addition. (88) £2,500

— [Paris, c.1490-1500]. Use of Paris. In Latin, with Calendar in French. 168 leaves (7 lacking), vellum, 152mm by 100mm, in 19th-cent dark red velvet over pastebds. In grey-brown ink in a gothic liturgical hand. With panel borders throughout in designs of flowers & acanthus leaves, sometimes with people, animals or grotesques, 10 small miniatures with 3-quarter borders, 9 full-page miniatures with full borders above some lines of text, & 16th-cent full-page armorial frontis. (90) £21,000

— [Eastern France, Besancon?, late 15th cent]. Use of Rome. 102 leaves & 4 flyleaves, vellum, 187mm by 127mm, in embroidered 18th-cent Italian green silk over pastebds. In dark brown ink in a small regular gothic liturgical hand. With panel borders throughout of flowers, strawberries & acanthus leaves, 28 small miniatures within full borders, 14 large miniatures in full borders in arched compartments above large initials & several lines of text, & illuminated tp added later. (90) £125,000

— [Northern Italy, late 15th cent]. Use of Rome. 201 leaves (5 blank) & 2 flyleaves, vellum, 102mm by 73mm, in 19th-cent English russia gilt. In dark brown ink in 2 sizes of a rounded gothic hand. With 11 large illuminated initials in colors & white tracery on burnished gold grounds with marginal extensions, & large historiated initial with full border. (90) £2,000

— [Tours?, late 15th cent]. Use of Rome. In Latin, with Calendar in French. 94 leaves, vellum, 172mm by 115mm. Def 18th-cent French calf gilt. In dark brown ink in a regular lettre batarde. With small initials throughout in liquid gold, panel borders in outer margins of every page in elaborate designs of leaves, flowers & animals, & 19 large miniatures within architectural frames incorporating large initials. Including added full-page painting on textile. (89) £12,000

— [Rouen, late 15th cent]. Single leaf, vellum, 165mm by 113mm. With illuminated initials & linefillers, panel borders, & full-page miniature. Framed. (91) £1,800

— [Florence, c.1490-95]. Use of Rome. In Latin, with prayers in Italian. 213 leaves & 5 flyleaves, vellum, 97mm by 65mm. Old red velvet over pastebds with silver clasps. In 2 sizes of a rounded gothic hand. With 7 large illuminated initials with full-length borders, 6 very large initials (5 historiated) with full historiated borders, & full-page miniature within full border. Illuminated by Gherardo di Giovanni del Fora. (91) £38,000

— [Paris, late 15th cent]. Use of Paris. In Latin, with Calendar in French. 102 leaves (23 lacking), vellum, 178mm by 120mm. Old blue velvet over pastebds with baroque silver clasps. In a gothic liturgical hand. With small initials throughout in designs of liquid gold on blue or red grounds, panel borders throughout in designs of leaves & flowers on parti-colored liquid gold grounds, & 15 small & 3 large miniatures with 3-quarter or full borders. Def. (91) £8,500

— [Rouen, c.1490]. Use of Rouen. In Latin, with Calendar in French. 110 leaves, vellum, 178mm by 122mm. Rebacked calf bdg of c.1700. In a slightly backward sliding gothic liturgical hand. With 2-line initials throughout in wine-red heightened in white enclosing colored flowers on panels of liquid gold, & 13 large miniatures in the late style of the Master of the Geneva Latini within full borders including birds & grotesques. (91) £13,000

— [Northern France, Paris?, c.1490]. Use of Rome. 151 leaves (a few lacking), vellum, 170mm by 119mm. Worn 16th-cent French brown mor gilt bdg. In a large skilful lettre batarde. With small initials throughout in designs of liquid gold, panel borders on every page, 8 small miniatures, 14 tall narrow miniatures in margins, & 11 large or full-page miniatures within full borders. (91) £16,000

— [Paris?, late 15th cent]. (90) £850

— [Northeast Italy, Verona?, late 15th cent]. Use of Rome. 185 leaves & 2 flyleaves, vellum, 68mm by 50mm. Worn contemp blindstamped goatskin over thin wooden bds. In dark brown ink in a very small rounded gothic hand, with additions in a humanist cursive. With small illuminated initials throughout, & 14 large illuminated initials with borders, including 1 fully historiated & 2 with pictorial emblems. (90) £6,000

— [Northern France, late 15th cent]. (89) £300

— [Rouen, c.1490-1500]. Use of Rouen. In Latin, with Calendar, Quinze Joyes & Sept Requetes in French. 109 leaves

(1 blank, 1 lacking), vellum, 150mm by 108mm, in modern red silk over pastebds. In brown ink in a regular lettre batarde. With panel borders throughout in outer margins in designs of colored & grisaille leaves & flowers on liquid gold grounds, 24 Calendar miniatures & 13 large miniatures with full borders, 4 with bas-de-page miniatures. (88) £17,000

— [Florence?, c.1490]. Use of Rome. 144 leaves, vellum, 97mm by 68mm, in def 17th-cent sharkskin. In brown ink in a humanistic hand. With 2 four-line initials in gold & colors & 2 historiated initials with floral borders. (91) $7,500

— [Northern Netherlands, 1491]. Use of Utrecht. In Dutch. 149 leaves, vellum, 168mm by 115mm, in 17th-cent calf. In brown ink in a lettre batarde by Hugo Wouter die Bruyn's son. With 2 small & 8 large decorated illuminated initials in full color & liquid gold & 2 historiated illuminated initials, all with three-quarter borders of leaves with figures of animals, archers, etc. (88) £4,000

— [Bruges, c.1500]. Use of Sarum. 220 leaves, vellum, 90mm by 66mm, in 19th-cent red velvet. In dark brown ink in a rounded gothic textura. With numerous small initials in gold or colors, 22 small miniatures with 3-quarter borders of foliage & flowers, & 16 pp with full borders enclosing 5-line illuminated initials. Lacking full-page miniatures. (90) £3,800

— [Bruges, c.1500]. Use of Rome. 273 leaves, vellum, 94mm by 68mm, in 19th-cent blue velvet. In dark brown ink in a rounded gothic rotunda. With small initials throughout, 24 calendar pages with full-page marginal miniatures, 4 small miniatures with naturalistic scatterborders, 15 large miniatures in arched compartments mostly by the Master of the Prayerbooks of 1500, & text decorated throughout with c.1725 free-standing figures, grotesques, flowers & animals. (90) £280,000

— [Tours or Loire Valley?, c.1500]. Use of Rome. 114 leaves, vellum, 176mm by 103mm, in 16th-cent brown mor gilt. In brown ink in an elegant lettre batarde. With numerous 1-, 2- & 3-line initials in gold or in white on gold ground, decorated with tracery or floral ornamentation, & line-fillers in gold & colors. Lacking miniatures. (89) £3,200

— [Florence?, c.1500]. Use of Rome. 228 leaves, vellum, 122mm by 72mm. Extra 19th-cent gilt metal repoussé bdg. In brown ink in an Italian rotunda. With 7 five-line decorated initials on gold ground extended with painted foliage, & 5 large historiated initials each within a full border of flowers, foliage, urns & fruit, containing putti, faces & birds. Most outer margins cut. Illuminated for a member of the Attavanti family. (89) £13,000

— [Tour or Angers, c.1500]. Use of Tour or Angers. 194 leaves (4 blank, 1 lacking), vellum, 185mm by 125mm, in early 17th-cent calf gilt in mor box. In brown ink in a lettre batarde. With illuminated panel borders throughout, Calendar with panel miniatures on each page of the zodiac & labors of the month, & 32 small & 19 large miniatures with three-quarter or full borders. (88) £30,000

— [Bruges, c.1500]. Use of Rome. 222 leaves & old flyleaves, vellum, 128mm by 92mm, in sheep over wooden bds. With 20 large miniatures, including 4 full-page & all with borders of grisaille intertwined branchwork on grown ground with naturalistic flowers & fruit. (91) £17,000

— [Northern France, c.1500]. Use not stated. In Latin. 10 leaves only, vellum, 160mm by 105mm. Late 19th-cent red mor gilt. In black ink in a lettre batarde. With 6 large & 4 small miniatures, 10 borders & numerous initials in gold & colors. (89) DM12,000

— [Northern France, Paris?, c.1500]. Use not stated. In Latin. 148 leaves (2 blank), vellum, 165mm by 115mm. Early 19th-cent red velvet bdg with silver clasp. In black ink in a gothic textura. With 6 miniatures, 14 full or partial borders, 7 large historiated initials, & numerous initials & linefillers in gold & colors. Some prayers in French in a later hand. (89) DM26,000

HORAE B.M.V.

— [Rouen, c.1500] Use of Rouen. In Latin & French. 69 leaves only plus 2 flyleaves, vellum, 185mm by 125mm, in late 16th-cent mor gilt. In brown ink in 2 sizes of a strongly gothic lettre batarde. With 11 full-page miniatures within liquid gold frames & 24 calendar miniatures in rectangular compartments within full borders. (91) $28,000

— [Paris, c.1500]. Use of Paris. In Latin, with Calendar, Quinze Joyes & Sept Requetes in French. 125 leaves, vellum, 147mm by 99mm. In very fine Parisian brown mor profusely gilt of c.1595, made for Marie de Senicourt. In dark brown ink in 2 sizes of a small gothic liturgical hand. With illuminated initials throughout, 4 very large initials with three-quarter illuminated borders & 12 large miniatures in colors & liquid gold within arched compartments above large initials & within full borders. Astor MS.A.19. (88) £14,500

— [Eastern France, c.1500-1520]. Use of Toul. In Latin, with a few sections in French. 205 leaves (4 blank, 1 lacking) & 2 flyleaves, vellum, with 54 19th-cent blanks, 176mm by 112mm. In red velvet within elaborate 17th-cent North European silver gilt pierced covers. In black ink in a slightly clubbed round roman hand. With 2-line initials with colored flowers on gold ground throughout, 28 small miniatures with three-quarter illuminated borders, 19 large miniatures within full borders including animals & grotesques, & 4 full-page miniatures within architectural frames. Astor MS.A.17. (88) £68,000

— [Bourges or Tours, c.1500]. Use of Rome. 166 leaves (some lacking), vellum, 124mm by 76mm, in def 19th-cent red mor gilt. In dark brown ink in a regular lettre batarde. With small initials & linefillers throughout in designs of liquid gold & 9 full-page miniatures, mostly with text in a small panel inset, retouched. (90) £4,500

— [Paris, c.1500]. Use of Paris. In Latin, with Calendar, Quinze Joyes & Sept Requetes in French. 182 leaves (2 lacking), vellum, 170mm by 110mm. Modern brown mor incorporating 16th-cent Parisian gilt bdg. In dark brown ink in a gothic liturgical hand. With small initials throughout in burnished gold, panel border, historiated initial, 14 small & 13 large miniatures with partial or full illuminated borders. (89) £8,500

— [Paris, c.1500]. Use of Paris. In Latin, with Calendar in French. 172 leaves (1 blank, 3 lacking) & added frontis, vellum, 149mm by 105mm. Rebacked 18th-cent red mor gilt bdg. In a small late gothic liturgical hand by 2 scribes. With small illuminated initials throughout, panel borders on every page on parti-colored grounds with designs of leaves, flowers & fruit & some birds & grotesques, 4 small miniatures with 3-quarter borders, & 13 large miniatures with full borders. (91) £13,500

— [Southern Netherlands, Ghent?, c.1500]. Use of Rome. 123 leaves (1 blank), vellum, 200mm by 135mm. French red mor bdg of c.1800. In a gothic liturgical hand. With larger initials in scrolling acanthus designs in colors heightened with liquid gold, 8 full borders in the Ghent/Bruges style, naturalistically painted in full colors on broad liquid gold grounds, 28 small miniatures with 3-quarter illuminated borders, & 7 full-page miniatures within full borders. (91) £90,000

— [Bruges, c.1500]. 12 leaves only & 13 flyleaves, vellum, 141mm by 100mm. Early 16th-cent French brown mor gilt. In a fine lettre batarde. A full set of Calendar leaves, with 12 full-page miniatures enclosing panels of text, by the Master of the Prayerbooks. Korner collection. (90) £130,000

— [Paris, c.1500]. Use of Paris. In Latin, with Calendar in French. 131 leaves (3 lacking), vellum, 149mm by 100mm. 19th-cent blue velvet bdg. In dark brown ink in a gothic liturgical hand. With small initials throughout in designs of liquid gold on colored grounds, panel borders throughout of flowers & leaves on geometric & ornamental grounds, & 2 small & 10 large miniatures within full borders. Last leaves in 16th-cent hand; panel borders cropped. (90) £16,000

— [Artois, Arras?, c.1500]. Use of Rome.

In Latin, with Calendar in French. 144 leaves & 5 flyleaves, vellum, 157mm by 110mm. 18th-cent mottled calf bdg. In brown ink in 2 sizes of a gothic liturgical hand. With linefillers & small initials throughout in blue-grey or liquid gold, & 12 large miniatures within full Ghent/Bruges scatter borders including flowers, leaves, birds & insects. (90) £38,000

— [Amiens, c.1500-1515]. Use of Rome. In Latin, with Calendar in French. 121 leaves & flyleaf, vellum, 183mm by 123mm, in modern dark brown blind-stamped mor with pierced silver clasps & catches by Menard. In dark brown ink in a small lettre batarde. With illuminated initials throughout in highly burnished gold, large historiated initial, 13 small miniatures with panel borders, & 6 large miniatures with full borders inhabited by birds, animals, etc. Some prayers added later. (88) £9,500

— [Northern France, Paris?, 1504]. Use not stated. In Latin. 101 leaves (2 blank, 1 lacking), vellum, 158mm by 110mm. Red velvet bdg of c.1700. In black ink in a lettre batarde. With 16 full-page miniatures in architectural frames, 17 smaller miniatures, 12 calendar minatures, & numerous partial borders, initials & linefillers in gold & colors. (89) DM33,000

— [Rouen, Paris or Auxerre, c.1510-1520]. Use of Auxerre. 117 leaves, vellum, 215mm by 142mm, in re-backed 16th-cent calf gilt. In dark brown ink in a lettre batarde. With numerous small initials in gold on colored ground, c.230 larger foliate initials, 3 trompe-l'oeil borders, 26 small miniatures, & 12 large miniatures within architectural frames facing pages with full panel borders. Christensen collection. (90) £38,000

— [Paris?, early 16th cent]. Use of Paris. In Latin, with Calendar & prayers in French. 132 leaves (1 lacking), vellum, 184mm by 130mm. 19th-cent red velvet bdg. In brown ink in a regular lettre batarde. With small initials throughout in liquid gold on colored grounds, illuminated borders on every page incorporating leaves & flowers, 24 Calendar miniatures in margins, 8 very large space fillers in ornamental designs or enclosing miniatures, & 19 large or full-page miniatures within full borders. Abbey collection. (89) £24,000

— The Sainte-Chapelle Hours. [Paris or Burgundy, early 16th cent]. Use of Rome. 150 leaves, vellum, 197mm by 132mm. Worn old wooden bds covered with blue velvet. In brown ink in 2 sizes of a lettre batarde. With linefillers & small initials throughout in liquid gold on colored grounds, 32 small miniatures & 14 large or full-page miniatures with full borders mostly enclosing panels of text; 1 miniature showing the treasury of the Sainte-Chapelle in Paris. Illuminated by several artists in quite distinct styles. Abbey collection. (89) £160,000

— [Ghent or Bruges, early 16th cent]. Use of Rome. 155 leaves (1 lacking), vellum, 119mm by 83mm. Old vellum over pastebds. In black ink in a skilful small rounded gothic liturgical script. With small initials throughout in liquid gold on red or blue grounds, & 15 large initials with full borders strewn with naturalistic flowers, birds, insects & snails. (89) £17,000

— [Netherlands, early 16th cent]. Use of Utrecht. In Dutch. 215 leaves (8 lacking), vellum, 110mm by 76mm. Calf over early wooden bds; def. In dark brown ink in a small gothic hand, supposedly by Peter Claesen Soon. With illuminated initials throughout, c.110 floral panel borders in lower margins, c.70 borders in outer margins, & 9 very large initials with 3-quarter borders. (89) £4,000

— [Northern France, Rouen?, early 16th cent]. Use of Rome. 1 leaf only, vellum, 180mm by 116mm. In a small lettre batarde. With 14 initials in liquid gold on colored grounds, & large miniature in a full-page design above large initial & 5 lines of text on a trompe l'oeil scroll. Mtd. (88) £1,200

— [Paris, early 16th cent]. Use of Paris. In Latin, with Calendar, Quinze Joyes & Sept Requetes in French. 147 leaves (9 lacking), vellum, 191mm by 122mm, in later orange-red velvet over pastebds. In dark brown ink in a gothic liturgical hand by more than 1 scribe. With

panel borders throughout, each mirroring its design on its verso, & 16 small & 17 large or full-page miniatures within elaborate borders. Astor MS.A.20. (88) £35,000
— [Bruges, c.1510]. Use of Rome. 248 leaves, vellum, 73mm by 48mm, each inset into paper leaves, 166mm by 139mm, in early 19th-cent brown mor profusely gilt. In dark brown ink in a very small round italianate gothic hand. With historiated initial with 3-quarter border, 24 Calendar miniatures in margins of full architectural borders, 15 full borders, some including miniatures, & 15 full-page miniatures within full borders. (88) £24,000
— [Flanders?, early 16th cent?]. Of unstated use. 144 pp, vellum, 5 by 3.25 inches. Silver bdg richly ornamented with niello work. In an upright gothic script. With 18 borders of flowers, birds & insects on gold ground & 9 full-page miniatures. Martha L. Bulkley collection. (90) $300,000
— [Lower Rhine or Muenster, c.1515]. In Low German. 174 leaves, vellum (7 paper), 112mm by 75mm, in 16th-cent calf over wooden bds. In a gothic littera textualis. With 5 very large initials & 3 facing display-pages. (91) £3,800
— [France, after 1515]. (88) £800
— [France, Tours?, early 16th cent]. Use not stated. 92 leaves & 4 flyleaves, vellum, 37mm by 23mm. Late 17th-cent French mor gilt bdg. In a well-formed microscopic lettre batarde. With 2-line initials in pink or blue enclosing colored flowers & on panels of liquid gold, full borders on every page in liquid gold & red, & 8 full-page miniatures within elaborate classical architectural frames. "Possibly the smallest Book of Hours in existence, & one of the most miniature medieval Mss conceivable." (91) £28,000
— The Hours of Albrecht of Brandenburg. [Bruges, c.1522-23]. Use of Rome. In Latin, with some words in German. 2 vols, 294 & 298 leaves & flyleaves, vellum, 216mm by 145mm, in [18th-cent Dutch?] orange-red velvet over pastebds with elaborate gold clasps & catches. In black ink in a skilful rounded calligraphic mainly gothic hand. With illuminated initials & line-fillers throughout, 72 full broad illuminated borders 42 of which form full-page pictorial schemes enclosing the text, full-page coat-of-arms, & 51 very large miniatures (43 by Simon Bening) within full broad borders. Further miniatures removed. Astor MS.A.24. (88) £1.100,000
— [Tours?, c.1525]. Use of Rome. 80 leaves (3 blank), vellum, 81mm by 49mm, cut to oval format, in mid-17th-cent French black mor gilt, in later fitted case. In black ink in a very small rounded roman hand in imitation of ptd type. With illuminated initials throughout, 12 historiated initials, 3 small miniatures & 6 full-page miniatures within full architectural borders by the Master of the Doheny Hours. Illus with complete absence of human figures. (88) £85,000
— [Tours or Loire Valley, c.1528]. Use of Rome. 125 leaves, vellum, 185mm by 113mm. Parisian late 16th-cent red mor gilt bdg in the "Duodo" style. In brown ink in a fine roman hand, rubrics in red. With illuminated initials throughout, 13 pp with full borders of flowers, leaves, birds & insects on gold ground, & 14 large miniatures, 13 with full borders by the Doheny Master in a style previously associated with Geofroy Tory. Made for Henri Bonnet de Forez. Doheny collection. (88) £800,000
— [Toledo?, c.1530]. Use of Rome, with Calendar for Toledo. 194 leaves (lacking 1 leaf & 3 blanks), vellum, 86mm by 48mm. 17th-cent French red mor gilt, in mor-covered case. In black ink in a neat gothic rotunda, rubrics in red. With initials in gold on black ground or of foliate grisaille on gold-sprinkled ground, 18 leaves with black & gold ornamented borders, & 20 small & 13 large miniatures in grisaille. Made for Isabella of Portugal, wife of Emperor Charles V. Doheny collection. (88) £120,000
— [Rouen, c.1530-40]. Use of Rouen. In Latin, with prayers in French. 137 leaves, vellum, 170mm by 90mm, in contemp green velvet over wooden bds, in mor slipcase by Simier. In

brown ink in a lettre batarde. With wide gold frames throughout, & 1 small & 14 large miniatures within full architectural borders of liquid gold containing miniature vignettes. (88) £50,000

— [Bruges, c.1530]. Use of Rome. 166 leaves (14 lacking), vellum, 186mm by 125mm. 19th-cent diced calf gilt. In black ink in a fine calligraphic rounded gothic liturgical hand. With 7 large initials in brown & liquid gold on trompe l'oeil colored grounds, 4 very large initials with full illus borders in camaieu d'or on colored grounds, & 12 illus Calendar pages. From the workshop of Simon Bening. (88) £58,000

— [Genoa, 1568]. Use of Rome. 170 leaves, vellum, 98mm by 62mm. Late 19th-cent German silver bdg with repousse scenes. In black & red ink in a fine calligraphic sloping italic hand by Hieronymus Bordonius. With c.180 illuminated initials in imitation of ptd initials, full-page armorial title, & half-page & 11 full-page pen-&-ink drawings in imitation of engravings. (89) £9,000

— [Italy, early 17th cent]. Of unidentified use. 62 leaves (1 blank), vellum, 133mm by 92mm. 18th-cent russia gilt; red mor box by Riviere. In black ink in a small italic cursive hand. With margins of 39 leaves cut-out into a delicate imitation of lace forming border around text; 22 pp within full painted borders, 12 calendar & 15 larger miniatures, 1 full-page. Made for Marie de Medici. Doheny collection. (88) £75,000

— [Ilbenstadt, Diocese of Mainz, 1622-29]. Of Dominican Use. 151 leaves (1 lacking) & flyleaves, vellum, 182mm by 138mm, in rebacked contemp brown calf over wooden bds. In dark brown ink in a slightly backward sloping gothic liturgical hand. With elaborate illuminated borders throughout including 265 miniatures in lower margins & hundreds of other birds, animals, flowers, classical monuments, etc., 2 full-page illusts & tp with elaborate architectural surround. (90) £20,000
See also: Jarry, Nicholas

Horn, Gustav, Count, 1592-1657
ALs, 3 June 1641. 1 p, folio. To the Governor of Lorraine, du Hallier. As prisoner of war, asking for a speedy release in exchange for Gen. Johann von Werth. (90) DM1,850

Ds, 17 Mar 1655. (91) DM360

Horn, Karl Friedrich, 1772-1852. See: Karl August, 1757-1828

Hornsby, Rogers, 1896-1963
Signature, 1959. (91) $150

Horsburgh, James, 1762-1836
Ms, Chinese-Latin dictionary, [c.1800]. About 970 pp, folio, in red calf. Listing individual symbols & sentences. Phillipps MS.14874 & Robinson collection. (89) £1,600

Horse Furniture
Ms, Abrege des preceptes ou maximes de l'emboucheure, [late 17th cent]. 138 leaves, 398mm by 275mm, in contemp mottled calf. 68 full-page ink drawings alternating with text leaves. (90) £1,600

— Ms, Horse-bridles, & stable-marks, their uses & ownership, in Italian. [Prague, c.1550]. 60 leaves, 423mm by 290mm, in grey-brown paper over pastebds. Containing c.100 distinguishing marks used in the stables of Italian, French & Spanish aristocrats, & 59 drawings of bridles & mouthpieces, all in ink & pale blue wash. (91) £7,000

Horsley, Charles Edward, 1822-76
Autograph music, Three Pieces from "Euterpe" arranged for Florence Mary James, Feb 1871. (90) £130

Horticultural Manuscripts
Ms, notebook containing 24 designs for gardens & 15 lists of plants for decorative layout, [Italy, 1662 to 1665]. 42 pp, 4to, & blanks, in contemp wraps. (89) £1,900

Horticulture
— LEE, JAMES, JR., & KENNEDY, JOHN. - Ms, A Catalogue of Plants planted ... at Stow Hall the Seat of Thomas Hare Esqr., [after 1806]. 46 pp, 8vo. Red mor. (88) £1,600

Hosemann, Theodor, 1807-75
ALs, 14 Mar 1851. (89) DM270

Houdini, Harry, 1874-1926
[A large archive of personal files, including c.90 letters sent to him, carbon copies of replies, contracts, autograph Mss, etc., sold at sg on 11 Feb 1988, lot 146, for $7,600.]
Ls s (2), 21 Oct [19]11 & 2 June 1912. 2 pp, 4to. To Ira Davenport. Mentioning his travel plans, inviting recipient's brother to meet him after a performance, & sending photographs. Including 2 photographs. (90) $1,300
— Ls s (2), 19 Aug 1924 & 17 Feb 1926. 2 pp, 4to. To Regimus Weiss. Referring to mediums & tricks. With recipient's draft reply on verso of 1 Ls. (90) $1,200
Ls, 3 May 1910. (90) $600
— 8 May 1911. (90) $800
— 10 May 1918. (91) $600
— 20 Mar 1919. (91) $475
— 1 Mar 1920. (91) $475
— 28 Sept 1924. (91) $500
— [n.d.]. 1 p, 8vo. To John Anderson. Saying he "was nearly drowned in one of [his] escapades ... before the camera". (91) $1,400
ANs, [n.d.]. (91) $350
Photograph, sgd & inscr, [n.d.]. (90) $450

Houdon, Jean Antoine, 1741-1828
Autograph Ms, estimate for a statue of Diana in marble, [1774]. 1 p, 4to. (91) DM3,000

Houel, Nicolas
Ms, L'Ordre & Police gardez en l'institution de l'Appotiquairerye ... de la Charite Chrestienne, pour les pauvres honteux ... de Paris. [Paris, late 16th cent]. 22 leaves (1 blank), vellum, 225mm by 150mm. 18th-cent gilt paper bds. In a calligraphic italic hand with headings in a roman hand. With illuminated tp. Phillipps MS.2962 & Abbey collection. (89) £8,000

Hough, Emerson, 1857-1923
Typescript, article, Lo, the Poor Indian! Red Man vs. Doheny collection. (88) $400

Housman, Alfred Edward, 1859-1936
Autograph Ms, Miscellaneous Verses, chiefly educational, [n.d.]. 2 pp, folio. 6 short poems of various lengths. Probably unpbd. (89) £1,300
— Autograph Ms, poem, A Ballad of a Widower, [c.1884]. 4 pp, folio, on rectos only, in half mor folding box. 22 quatrains; fair copy. Imperf. John F. Fleming Estate. (89) $4,000
— Autograph Ms, poem, Amphisbaena or The Limits of Human Knowledge, [c.1906]. 1 p, folio, in quarter mor folding box. 42 lines in 2 columns. In ink; a few pencil revisions. John F. Fleming Estate. (89) $3,200
— Autograph Ms, poem, Aunts and Nieces or Time and Space, [n.d.]. 2 pp, folio. 52 lines. (89) £1,200
— Autograph Ms, poem, Inhuman Henry or Cruelty to Fabulous Animals, [n.d.]. 2 pp, folio. 13 four-line stanzas, with 2 drawings. Probably unpbd. (89) £1,200
— Autograph Ms, poem, Purple William or The Liar's Doom, [n.d.]. (89) £1,000
— Autograph Ms, poem, Thomasina and the Amphisbaena or Horrors of Horticulture, [n.d.]. (89) £1,000
Series of 17 A Ls s, [1881] to 1932. About 60 pp, 8vo. To his sister Katherine Symons. About a variety of matters. 1 ALs repaired. (89) £3,000
— Series of 11 A Ls s, 1920 to 1935. 16 pp, 8vo. To Donald Struan Robertson & his wife. Discussing academic & social matters. (89) £2,500
— Series of 3 A Ls s, 5 Oct 1923, 7 Nov 1925 & 6 Apr 1926. (91) $420
— Series of 19 A Ls s, 1929 to 1936. 67 pp, 8vo. To his sister-in-law Jeannie Housman. Family letters. (90) £2,500
A Ls s (2), 19 May & 21 June 1928. (90) $290
ALs, [1879]. 11 pp, 8vo. To his sister Kate. Doggerel verse letter; 245 lines. Illus with a sketch. (89) £1,200
— 13 Apr 1905. (88) £480
— 28 Oct 1922. (88) £350
— 30 Mar 1929. (88) £75
— 15 June 1930. (90) $300
Autograph postcard, sgd, 20 Dec 1934. (88) £50
Photograph, sgd, [n.d.]. (91) $800

Housman, Laurence, 1865-1959

Autograph Ms, play, A Settled Account; [n.d.]. Koch Foundation. (90) $600

— Autograph Ms, poem, Peace! Peace!; [n.d.]. (89) £95

Houston, Samuel, 1793-1863

ALs, 15 May 1828. 4 pp, 4to. To Col. John Campbell. As Governor of Tennessee, draft, referring to a controversy with Richard C. Johnson & the Presidential campaign. Stained. (90) $6,000

— 21 July 1847. 4 pp, 4to. To Col Thomas Ward. About the bill of costs for the case of Houston vs. Elisha Roberts, resolved in his favor by the Supreme Court. (91) $2,200

— 4 Oct 1848. 4 pp, folio. To Col Thomas Ward. Political letter about the coming election & Houston's frustration with the Polk administration. (91) $6,000

Ls, 10 Dec 1836. 1 p, folio. To the Texas Senate. As President of Texas, nominating F. Catlett as Secretary of Legation at Washington. (89) $2,250

— 4 Apr 1842. 2 pp, 4to. To Col Thomas Ward. The order which initiated the so-called Archives War. (91) $4,800

— 6 Sept 1842. 1 p, 4to. To Col. Thomas Ward. About the "Archives War." (91) $1,600

— 27 June 1846. 1 p, 4to. To President James K. Polk. Letter of recommendation for Stewart Newell. (90) $1,600

— 9 Feb 1855. (89) $900

Ds, 1 Nov 1838. (91) $400

— 6 Mar 1860. (91) $750

— 5 Nov 1860. (90) $550

— 24 Jan 1861. (88) $250

— 8 Feb 1861. (91) $475

— [n.d.]. Nelson Bunker Hunt collection. (91) $450

Cut signature, [n.d.]. (91) $425

Franking signature, [23 Sept n.y.]. Alexander collection. (90) $450

— Anr, [n.d.]. (89) $260

Howard, Charles, 1st Earl of Nottingham, 1536-1624

Ds, 27 June 1612. (89) £230

Howard, Henry J.

Original drawings, (45), mostly to illus D. Archives of J. M. Dent & Son. (88) £90

Howard, John, 1726?-90

[A group of 5 Mss relating to the Foundling Hospital, London, including documents relating to the erection of penitentiaries, 1779 & 1780, 20 pp, various sizes, sold at S on 14 Dec 1989, lot 295, for £1,600 to Quaritch.]

Howard, Leslie, 1893-1943

Telegram, [1930s]. 7 by 8 inches. To Jack Warner. Insisting that [Humphrey] Bogart play Mantee [in The Petrified Forest]. (89) $2,800

Howe, Julia Ward, 1819-1910

Autograph Ms, The Battle Hymn of the Republic, orig draft, 18-19 Nov 1861. 4 pp, 4to, in folding case by Sangorski & Sutcliffe. Sgd & inscr to Charlotte Whipple. Including 6th stanza discarded later. Middendorf collection. (89) $200,000

Autograph transcript, fair copy of The Battle Hymn of the Republic. 1 p, folio, mtd on card. Inscr to Charles C. McCabe & dated Sept 1904 at bottom. With presentation ALs. (91) $26,000

— Autograph transcript, poem, Battle Hymn of the Republic, 5 stanzas. Sgd & dated 21 Mar 1865. 2 pp, 4to. Doheny collection. (89) $18,000

— Autograph transcript, poem, Battle Hymn of the Republic, 1st & last stanza. Sgd & dated Jan 1907. 1 p, 4to. Doheny collection. (89) $3,500

ALs, 12 Mar 1871. (90) $180

— 18 Mar 1886. (91) $160

— 3 May 1894. (90) $95

— 9 July [n.y.]. (90) $80

Howe, Richard Howe, Earl, 1726-99

[A group of c.25 letters & documents relating to the career, family, & personal affairs of Howe, mostly autograph, [1741 to 1797], sold at P on 13 June 1991, lot 210, for $19,000.]

Ls, 12 Sept 1790. (89) $160

Howells, William Dean, 1837-1920
Series of 3 A Ls s, 6 July 1898 to 20 July 1918. Doheny collection. (89) $350
ANs, 15 June 1882. (89) $350

Hubermann, Bronislaw, 1882-1947
ALs, 27 Mar 1909. (91) DM370
— 24 Nov 1932. (90) DM280
Photograph, sgd & inscr, 12 Nov 1907. (90) DM700

Huch, Ricarda, 1864-1947
Autograph Ms, memoirs of her time at Trieste, [1944]. 8 pp, folio. With covering autograph postcard, sgd, 24 June 1944. (90) DM1,600
— Autograph Ms, poem, beginning "Ist dir nicht ein Voegelchen zugeflogen...", [n.d.]. (89) DM380
ALs, 31 Oct 1901. (90) DM220
— 20 June 1926. (90) DM260
Autograph postcards (2), sgd, 18 Aug 1909 & 2 June 1910. (89) DM200

Huchel, Peter, 1903-81
Autograph Ms, poem, Zeitspruch, Mar 1934. 1 p, folio. 5 lines, sgd. (91) DM1,700
Autograph transcript, poem, beginning "Unter der blanken Hacke des Monds". 1 p, folio. Sgd. (88) DM1,600
Ls, 11 Nov 1955. (91) DM480

Hudson, William Henry, 1841-1922
[The autograph Mss of 10 articles included in 3 of his collected works (The Book of a Naturalist; Birds in Town & Village; & A Traveller in Little Things), [1919 - 1921], 101 pp, 4to, each with some emendations, sold at P (Bradley Martin sale) on 30 Apr 1990, lot 2937, for $11,000.]
Autograph Ms, portions of 6 chapters of his book Far Away and Long Ago, [pbd 1918]. 100 pp, 4to, including 6 corrected page proofs. With some autograph emendations. 5 chapters sgd. Bradley Martin Ms. (90) $7,000
— Autograph Ms, story, Dead Man's Plack, including postscripts for Dead Man's Plack & An Old Thorn; [pbd 1920]. 132 pp, 4to. Working draft, with numerous revisons. Bradley Martin Ms. (90) $6,000
Collection of 60 A Ls s & AL, [Feb 1902?] to 14 May 1921. Total length not stated, mostly 8vo & 4to. To Edward Garnett. Important correspondence touching a wide variety of personal & professional topics. Bradley Martin sale. (90) $10,000
Series of c.250 A Ls s & 36 autograph postcards, sgd, [Mar 1897?] to 16 Aug 1922. Length not stated, 8vo & 4to. To Morley Roberts. Remarkable archive of letters to a friend, discussing personal & professional matters. Bradley Martin sale. (90) $17,000
ALs, 5 July 1917. (89) $400
— 6 Jan 1921. Bradley Martin sale. (90) $550

Hufeland, Christoph Wilhelm, 1762-1836
Ms, Vorlesungen ueber Therapia specialis, compendium of lecture notes in an unknown hand, begun 3 Nov 1798. (89) £260
ALs, 7 Jan 1791. (88) DM800

Hughes, Charles Evans, 1862-1948
Ls s (2), 16 & 20 Sept 1921. (91) $130
Ls, 15 June 1923. (88) $175
— 24 Dec 1945. (88) $60
Signature, [n.d.]. (91) $120
See also: Lindbergh, Charles A. & Hughes

Hughes, Howard, 1905-76
Menu, banquet at Houston, 30 July 1938. (91) $1,000
Signature, [n.d.]. (89) $500

Hugo de Folieto, fl.c.1140 —& William of Conches, d.c.1150
Ms, Hugo, De Avibus & Sermons; William, Moralium Dogma Philosophorum & Commentary on the Song of Songs. [Northern France?, c.1175]. 84 leaves only, vellum, 110mm by 75mm. 19th-cent blindstamped red velvet bdg, loose. In brown ink in a small gothic bookhand probably by one scribe. With over 50 initials & 10 miniatures. Lacking c.16 leaves. (88) £11,000

Hugo, Victor, 1802-85
Autograph Ms, poem, 5 lines; [n.d.]. Byer collection. (90) $900
— Autograph Ms, poem, Chanson, 22 May 1846. (88) £350
— Autograph Ms, political poem,

Quelqu'un, [10 Dec 1852]. (90) £900
Autograph transcript, Les chants du crepuscule, stanza XIV; [n.d.]. (91) £500
ALs, [July 1841]. (90) DM420
— [23 Apr 1853?]. (91) DM500
— 11 May 1858. (88) DM450
— 1 July [1860]. (89) DM500
— 22 May [n.y.]. (88) £110
— [n.d.], "Saturday". (91) $180
— [n.d.]. (90) DM320
— [n.d.]. (89) DM560
Photograph, sgd & inscr, [c.1865]. (88) DM950
See also: Drouet, Juliette

Hull, Isaac, 1773-1843
ALs, [n.d.]. (89) $220
Ls, 4 Jan 1830. (91) $300
— 15 June 1839. (91) $130
Ds, 3 Aug 1840. (89) $90

Humann, Karl, 1839-96
ALs, 23 Nov 1886. (91) DM440

Humboldt, Alexander von, 1769-1859
Autograph Ms, discussing experiments conducted by Eilhard Mitscherlich, sgd; 12 June 1849. 1 p, 8vo. With related material. (90) DM1,600
Original drawings, (16), pen-&-ink or pencil drawings of animals or details of animals, executed on his South American expedition, some sgd & dated 1800 or 1801. Various sizes. Some with descriptive text in Humboldt's hand. Including 1 drawing by Aime Bonpland & 1 in anr hand. Presented to J. J. von Tschudi, 1844. (90) DM15,000
Collection of 6 A Ls s & 2 orig drawings, [7 Aug 1844] to 15 Mar 1847. 6 pp, 4to & 8vo; 185mm by 235mm & 250mm by 135mm. To Johann Jakob von Tschudi. Sending 2 drawings of South American animals executed in 1802, discussing his own & Tschudi's studies on Peru, & expressing invitations. (90) DM3,600
Series of 11 A Ls s, [c.1816/17] to 26 Mar 1826. 19 pp, 4to & 8vo. To Count Andreossi. About Louis Gay-Lussac, his new address, scientists, etc. In French. (88) DM2,600
— Series of 5 A Ls s, 20 Sept 1844 to 16 May 1857. 5 pp, 8vo. To Francois Forster. About recipient's engravings, honors & decorations, a recommendation for the painter Duroque, etc. (91) DM6,300
A Ls s (2), 8 Apr & [12 May 1845]. (88) DM540
— A Ls s (2), 15 Apr & 1 May [1845]. (88) DM420
— A Ls s (2), [1858] & 28 Oct 1858. (88) DM500
ALs, 19 Apr 1798. 2 pp, 4to. To Eichstaedt. About his projected travels, & commenting on the political situation in France. (91) DM5,500
— 18 May 1809. (88) DM1,000
— [June 1814]. (90) DM460
— 12 July 1814. 2 pp, 8vo. To the pbr Thomas Norton Longman. Regarding the publication of his Researches concerning the Institutions & Monuments ... of America. In French. Albrecht collection. (91) SF1,300
— [7 Jan 1815]. (90) DM380
— [1815]. (88) DM420
— 3 Jan 1827. (88) DM550
— [26 Nov 1829]. (88) DM750
— [1830]. (90) DM280
— [19 Apr 1832?]. (90) DM940
— [c.8 Aug 1834]. (89) DM480
— [1836?]. (89) DM460
— 6 Apr 1837. 4 pp, 4to. To Geoffroy St. Hilaire. Discussing recipient's physiological findings. (91) DM2,200
— 26 Dec 1837. (90) DM850
— 2 Apr 1839. 2 pp, 4to. To C. G. Lorek. Thanking for his botanical work. (91) DM1,600
— 22 Feb 1840. (89) DM850
— 3 June 1841. 3 pp, folio. To Friedrich Wilhelm IV of Prussia. Reporting about his diplomatic mission to Paris. (91) DM1,800
— [22 Aug 1841]. (90) DM250
— 10 Oct 1841. 1 p, 4to. To Friedrich Wilhelm IV of Prussia. Expressing congratulations on his birthday. (91) DM1,200
— [Spring 1842]. (90) DM340
— [4 Aug 1844], "Sunday". (90) DM330
— 25 Oct 1844. (89) DM500
— 25 Oct 1844. 1 p, 8vo. To Baron Cotta. Recommending Rene Marjolin. (89)

HUMBOLDT

DM1,100
— 15 Apr 1846. (88) DM550
— 12 Mar 1848. (91) DM650
— 2 Jan 1849. 2 pp, 8vo. Recipient unnamed. Discussing meteors. (91) DM2,200
— 26 May 1850. (90) DM340
— [n.d.]. (88) DM360
— 27 Oct 1852. 2 pp, folio. To King Friedrich Wilhelm IV. Recommending the engineer & geographer Wolf & describing his work. Schroeder collection. (89) DM1,300
— 23 Dec 1852. (91) DM320
— 27 Nov 1854. 2 pp, 8vo. To Pauline Schelling. Expressing condolences on the death of her husband. (91) DM1,300
— 16 May 1857. (91) DM560
— 20 Apr 1858. (90) DM550
— [n.d.], "Thursday". (90) $175
— [n.d.]. (91) DM600
— [n.d.]. 1 p, 8vo. To [Charles Athanase de Walkenaer?]. Requesting a copy of some lines of a 1522 Ed of Ptolemy & pointing out that it was Waldseemueller who 1st used the name "America". (91) DM3,800
— [n.d.]. (89) DM360
— [n.d.]. (90) DM280
— [n.d.]. (89) DM320
— [n.d.]. (89) DM200
— [n.d.]. (91) DM250
— [n.d.]. (91) DM310
— [n.d.]. (91) DM260
— [n.d.]. (90) DM300
Ls, 4 July 1828. Schroeder collection. (89) DM260
Autograph sentiment, [1809]; inscr to Mr. (88) DM380
— Praetz, Theodor. - Orig drawing, watercolor of Humboldt in his study, 1856; sgd. 25cm by 36cm. With autograph attestation sgd by Humboldt on mount. Framed. (90) £6,000

Humboldt, Wilhelm von, 1767-1835
ALs, 15 Dec 1815. (89) DM1,000
— 18 Dec 1815. 2 pp, 4to. To Karl August von Hardenberg. About territorial negotiations at Frankfurt, the claims of Eugene Beauharnais, etc. In French. (90) DM1,700

— 2 Jan 1816. (88) DM680
— 27 Feb 1816. 1 p, 4to. To Prince Hardenberg. Informing him about diplomatic affairs at Frankfurt. (90) DM2,000
— 6 Mar 1816. 1 p, 4to. To Prince Hardenberg. Reporting about his negotiations at Frankfurt & making suggestions about territorial adjustments. (89) DM1,200
— 6 Apr 1816. 1 p, 4to. To Prince Hardenberg. Reporting about diplomatic negotiations at Frankfurt. In French. (88) DM1,700
— 21 Apr 1816. 1 p, 4to. To Prince Hardenberg. Commenting about the situation in France & forwarding a letter from his brother. In French. (88) DM1,800
— 28 Dec 1817. 2 pp, 4to. To Karl Freiherr von Altenstein. Concerning an exhibition of art treasures returned to Prussia after the war. (91) DM2,600
— 11 [May 1819]. (88) DM550
— 7 Sept 1819. (89) DM300
— 28 Mar 1829. Schroeder collection. (89) DM800
— 29 June [n.y.]. (90) DM700
Ls, 2 June 1810. (90) DM280
— 2 July 1832. 2 pp, 4to. To Friedrich von Mueller. Referring to Goethe's death, & sending a memorial lecture to be ptd in the journal Kunst und Alterthum. Albrecht collection. (91) SF2,400

Hume, David, 1711-76
Autograph Ms, "A Treatise of Fluxions By Mr George Campbell Professor of Mathematicks in Edinburgh", 1726; c.120 pp, 4to, in 19th-cent half calf. Lecture notes, sgd George Home on tp. (88) £8,500
ALs, [15 Oct 1754]. 1 p, 4to. To Messrs. Hamilton & Balfour. Stating conditions for a 2d Ed of the 1st vol of his History of Great Britain. (90) £6,500

Humes, William Y. C., 1830-82
Ls, 16 Jan 1865. (90) $140
Ds, 10 July 1871. (88) $100

Hummel, Johann Nepomuk, 1778-1837
Ls, 20 June 1831. (88) DM540
ADs, 18 Nov 1826. Albrecht collection. (91) SF460
— 6 Apr 1836. (89) DM380

Humperdinck, Engelbert, 1854-1921
Autograph music, sketches for Die heiligen Dreikoenige, from Buebchens Weihnachtstraum, [1906]. 2 pp, 35cm by 27cm. In pencil. With note of authenticity by Wolfram Humperdinck on verso. (90) DM4,500
A Ls s (2), 11 Jan & 12 Feb 1921. 5 pp, 8vo. To [Alexander Amersdorffer]. Inquiring about his pension. (91) DM1,500
ALs, 7 Sept 1896. (88) DM420
— 7 Feb 1903. (90) DM850
— 13 Dec 1910. (90) $115
Autograph postcard, sgd, [17 Sept 1896]. (91) DM460
Autograph quotation, 3 bars from Haensel & Gretel, with text; 22 Jan 1895. (91) $350
— Anr, sgd, [c.1890s]. (91) $300
— Anr, 4 bars from Haensel und Gretel, scored for piano; sgd & dated Oct 1898. 1 p, 8vo. (90) DM1,200

Humphreys, David, 1752-1818
ALs, 5 Aug 1780. (91) $600
— 10 Apr 1790. (90) $100

Humphreys, Joshua, 1751-1838
ALs, 14 May 1795. 1 p. To Sec of War Timothy Pickering. Enclosing ideas from William Rush for figureheads for the planned first 6 frigates of the fledgling United States Navy. (88) $1,250
— 14 May 1795. (88) $1,000

Hundred Years' War
Ms, account of proceedings of the Convocation des Trois Etats, 1356, & petition of the people of Rouen asking for peace between France & England, [c.1360]. [Bruges, c.1490-1500]. 44 leaves & flyleaves, vellum, 208mm by 147mm, in 17th-cent calf incorporating vellum bifolium of c.1400. In a very skilful lettre batarde. With 2 very large illuminated initials (1 historiated) with full borders of naturalistic flowers, strawberries, etc. Illuminated in the style of the Master of Edward IV. (90) £22,000

Hungerford, Robert, Lord Molyns & Hungerford, 1431-64. See: England

Hunt, Leigh, 1784-1859
Autograph Ms, poem, The Palfrey, fragment; [n.d.]. (89) £750
A Ls s (2), 9 June [n.y.] & 23 June [n.y.]. Doheny collection. (89) $600
ALs, 25 Jan [1840]. (91) £420
— 27 May [1853]. Doheny collection. (88) $180

Hunt, Rose Ward
Typescript, referring to Henry Ward Beecher, Lincoln, & the emancipation of slaves, 21 Oct 1927. (91) $300

Hunter, Andrew. See: Lee, Robert E. & Hunter

Hunter, Robert Mercer Taliaferro, 1809-87
Ls, 17 Feb 1862. 1 p, 4to. To Jefferson Davis. Resigning from the office of Sec of State of the Confederacy. Endorsed & initialled by Davis. Mtd. (89) $1,500

Huntington, Samuel, Signer from Connecticut
ALs, 22 Dec 1791. (91) $250

Huntington, Samuel, Signer from Connecticut
ALs, 15 Oct 1795. (91) $300
— [13 Mar 1806]. Alexander collection. (90) $800
Ls, 14 Mar 1780. (89) $500
— 28 Aug 1794. (91) $275
ADs, 10 May 1782. (90) $110
— [n.d.] 1 p, 12mo. (88) $80
Ds, 10 Oct 1774. (89) £140
— 1 Oct 1779. (90) $750
— [1779-81]. (90) $800

Hurry, J.
Autograph Ms, notebook kept by a watchmaker containing pen-&-wash illusts of movements, etc, [18th cent]; c.120 pp, 4to. (88) £180

HUSSEINI

Husseini, Haj Amin el, 1897-1974
Photograph, sgd, [19 Mar 1963]. (88) $100

Husserl, Edmund, 1859-1938
Autograph postcard, sgd, 15 Oct 1928. (90) DM500

Hutchinson, Edward, 1613-75
ADs, 6 Dec 1670. (90) $500

Hutchinson, Thomas, 1711-80
Ds s (2)2 Apr 1764. (89) $225

Hutten, Ulrich von, d.1522
ALs, [1 May] 1503. 1 p, 8vo. To Graf Wilhelm IV von Henneberg. Offering his help in a matter relating to Nuernberg. (90) DM1,100

Hutton, Barbara
Photograph, [n.d.]. (89) $250

Huxley, Aldous, 1894-1963
ALs, 12 May 1930. (89) £80
— 8 Oct 1951. 3 pp, 4to. To Mr. Ashworth & others. Responding to a question about war & conscientious objection. Byer collection. (90) $1,500
— [13 May 1959]. (89) DM380
Series of 3 Ls s, 1 Mar 1953 to 1 Feb 1955, 6 pp, folio. To Dr. J. R. Smythies. Describing his experiences with mescaline & other drugs, & sending a copy of The Devils of Loudun. With carbon copy of reply. (90) £1,500

Huxley, Andrew
Autograph Ms, "Explanation of early tension recovery in terms of elastic amd viscous components", 1975. (88) DM300
Typescript, fragment of a lecture on muscle contraction, [given Dec 1973]. (90) DM270

Huxley, Andrew F.
Autograph Ms, Notes for Nobel Lecture, 1963; sgd at head. (89) DM750

Huxley, Sir Julian, 1887-1975
Collection of 2 A Ls s & 2 Ls s, 10 Oct 1972 to 14 Apr 1973. (88) $200

AMERICAN BOOK PRICES CURRENT

Huxley, Thomas Henry, 1825-95
ALs, 20 May 1890. (89) £65

Hymnal
Ms, Hymnal. [France or England, c.1890] 75 leaves, vellum, 330mm by 237mm, in mor gilt by Gruel. In black & red ink & upright roman upper & lower case with gothic influence, without musical notation. With 2 full-page miniatures of Virgin & Child, 1 full-page miniatures of an enthroned saint & 131 borders containing scenes of religious subjects, birds, animals, etc. Manhattan College Ms (91) $9,500
— Ms, hymns, with versicles, responses & antiphons, for use of Franciscan nuns. (90) £650
— Ms, in Latin. (91) £250

Hyrtl, Joseph, 1810-94
ALs, 28 July [1845]. (91) DM250

I

Ibert, Jacques, 1890-1962
ALs, 20 Dec 1928. (88) DM480

Ibsen, Henrik, 1828-1906
Original drawing, watercolor depicting a fjord with mountains, [n.d.]. 145mm by 225mm. Authentication by Francis Bull on verso. (89) £2,300
Collection of 2 A Ls s, 2 A Ns s & AN, 1869 to 1871 & [n.d.]. 8 pp, 8vo, & 3 visiting cards. To Herr Bomhoff. About a variety of matters. (91) £1,700
— Collection of 2 A Ls s & photograph, sgd, 28 May 1887 & 25 Jan 1899. (89) £850
ALs, 4 Sept 1873. Doheny collection. (89) $700
— [n.d.]. (88) DM550
— 19 Sept 1878. (88) £550
— 12 June 1883. 4 pp, 8vo. To Georg Brandes. Discussing 3 of his works. (88) £2,850
— 25 May 1890. 2 pp, 8vo. To Bjorn Bjornson. Concerning the staging of Peer Gynt at the Christiania theatre. (89) £2,500
— 28 Oct 1894. Doheny collection. (89) $900
AN, 29 May 1891. (89) DM280
— 13 Feb 1900. (89) DM330

Photograph, sgd & inscr, 15 Dec [18]90. (89) £450
— Anr, 30 Aug 1892. (88) £240

Idaho
— HOLBROOK, E. D. - ALs, 17 Mar 1868. 2 pp, 4to. Recipient unnamed. About emigration to Idaho, & denouncing carpetbaggers, abolitionists, etc. (89) $55

Iffland, August Wilhelm, 1759-1814
ALs, 4 July 1805. Albrecht collection. (91) SF800
— 9 June 1808. (90) DM850
— 26 Apr 1812. (88) DM420
— IFFLAND, LUISE. - ALs, 23 July 1814. 3 pp, 8vo. To an unnamed lady. Informing her that her husband intends to consult a physician in Breslau, & requesting her to find lodgings. (90) DM320

Illinois
— CLARKSON, MATTHEW. - Ds, 31 Dec 1766. Size not stated. Sight draft on "account of your adventure to the Illinois", issued at Fort Chartres. (88) $600
— FINLEY, JOHN. - ALs, 22 Oct 1770. 2 p, size not stated. To Mr. Morgan at Kaskaskia. Listing goods shipped from Fort Chartres. (88) $600
— FORT CLARK, ILLINOIS TERRITORY. - Document, 23 Sept 1813. 2 pp, size not stated. Receipt for lines for laying off the fort, sgd by Robert C. Nickolas. Alexander collection. (90) $55

Imboden, John Daniel, 1823-95
Ds, 24 June 1860. (88) $140

Immelmann, Max, 1890-1916
Autograph postcard, sgd, [4 Feb 1916]. (88) DM550

Immermann, Karl, 1796-1840
Autograph Ms, poem, beginning "Ich siebe, wurstle, sichte nicht", [1833]. 1 p, 8vo. 3 four-line stanzas. Some revisions. Mtd. (88) DM1,600
ALs, 25 Oct 1835. 1 p, 4to. To J. G. Ch. Weiss. Announcing a change in the program of the Duesseldorf theater. Albrecht collection. (91) SF1,250
— 30 Aug 1838. 2 pp, 4to. To [Arnold Ruge?]. Discussing a possible contribution to recpient's new journal. (90) DM1,500

Inchbald, Elizabeth, 1753-1821
Autograph Ms, diary for 1782. About 50 pp plus accounts, 16mo, in calf. Written while employed at the Haymarket Theater in London & inDublin. (91) £2100

India
Ms, letterbook of military correspondence relating to Cawnpore, Dec 1807 to Mar 1808. (90) £420
— Ms, miscellany relating to Indian affairs, c.1798 to 1803. (89) £120
— HEARSAY, ANDREW WILSON. - Autograph Ms, journal describing the 2d Mysore War including British victories at Pollilur & Sholingarh, 1780 & 1781. 93 pp, in def 8vo notebook. (89) £500
— JONES, WILLIAM WYNNE. - Autograph Ms, diary, Jan to Feb 1825. 270 pp, 4to, in def calf. Describing voyage to India as army cadet & his stay at Benares & Lucknow. (89) £440
— MADDOCK, THOMAS H. - Ms, letterbook kept as Resident at Lucknow, 24 Mar to 30 Aug 1830. 340 pp, folio. Contemp half calf, def. Copies of letters sent & received regarding affairs in Oudh. (88) £480
— MORRIS, REV. THOMAS. - Autograph Mss, journals describing his voyage to India, the country, his missionary activities, etc., 1820 to 1829. More than 300 pp in 4 vols, various sizes. With related material. (88) £600

Indian Manuscripts
Ms, [19th cent]. (89) £85
— Ms, Bhagavata Purana. [India, c.1750]. Scroll, c.1400 by 5 inches, in red mor box gilt. In Sanskrit, with illuminated borders, elaborate headpiece & 33 large miniatures. The Garden Ltd. collection. (90) $9,000
— Ms, Bhagavata-purana (?). (88) DM1,000
— Ms, Kalpasutra. (89) £250
— Ms, Orissan Ms on palm leaf with 54 erotic illusts. (88) £280

Indians, North American

[A soldier's letter from Fort Union, New Mexico, 12 Mar 1858, discussing mail service & trade with the Indians, sold at rf on 22 Apr 1989, lot 10, for $110.]

Document, 16 Apr 1730. (89) $70

— ARMSTRONG, JOHN. - ALs, 10 July 1790. 1 p, size not stated. Recipient unnamed. Concerning trade with the Indians on the Mississippi. (88) $525

— BROWN, COL. C. - ALs, 23 Jan 1795. 2 pp, folio. To Col. Hogdon. Referring to Gen. Wayne's army & peace negotiations after the Battle of Fallen Timbers. (91) $650

— CHICKASAW BLUFFS. - Document, 14 Oct 1814. Length not stated. Receipt on verso of letter of Jacob Bowman regarding goods shipped to the U.S. Indian Factory. Alexander collection. (90) $105

— CONNECTICUT. - Document, 5 July 1744. 2 pp, 4to. Warrant for the arrest of an Indian man, sgd by a Justice of the Peace. Endorsed on verso by arresting person. Worm holes. (88) $180

— COOPER, DOUGLAS HANCOCK. - ALs, 10 June 1865. 1 p, 4to. To Johnson & Grimes. Requesting information about "the prospect of feeding the Reserve Indians." Alexander collection. (90) $550

— DAVIS, CHARLES L. - 4 A Ls s, 25 Mar 1862 to 29 Sept 1863. 11 pp, 4to & 8vo. To his father Asa Davis. About army life in Minnesota during the Sioux uprising. (91) $500

— FETTERMAN MASSACRE. - ALs, 29 Dec 1866, 6 pp, 16mo, from Thomas Mallony to "Friend Holman". Account of the massacre by a soldier at Fort Kearney. (90) $800

— JUMPER, JOHN. - ALs, 30 June 1865. 2 pp, 8vo. To Johnson & Grimes. Requesting supplies for the Seminole Indians. Alexander collection. (90) $270

— LECLAIRE, ANTOINE. - Ds, 22 Feb 1843. Length not stated. Receipt for payment for services as interpreter at a treaty with the Sacs & Foxes Indians, 29 Sept to 14 Oct 1842. Also sgd by John Chambers as Governor of the Iowa Territory. (91) $100

— MASSACHUSETT LANGUAGE. - 2 documents, 1715, 2 pp (single leaf), 311mm by 215mm; irregular. Certification of property rights in Gay Head on Martha's Vineyard, sgd by Joseph Josnin & others. In Massachusett Indian language. (91) $4,000

— MEXICAN INDIANS. - Ms, collection of sermons & prayers, [c.1615-22]. About 300 leaves, 8vo, in contemp vellum. Titles in Latin, with most text in a Latinized native Mexican language. In several hands. (88) $600

— NEW PLYMOUTH. - Document, 16 June 1685. 1 p, folio. Conveyance of land in New Plymouth by the Indian Scippeag to Elisha & John Bourn; sgd by Scippeag (with mark) & 5 others. (91) $1,900

— RAIZENNE, IGNACE. - ADs, 2 Aug 1817. 6 pp, folio, on 4 sheets. Agreement with 9 chiefs of the Iroquois & Algonkin at Lac des Deux Montagnes regarding maintenance of their reservations, prices for animals, etc. With signatures or marks of Indian chiefs & 3 others. (88) C$700

— RHODE ISLAND. - Document, 6 Mar 1661. 1 p, 8vo. Sale of 20,000 acres of land to Z. Rhodes & R. Rhoads, sgd by Sachem Tohomin & 2 other Indians (all with pictorial marks). True copy, attested by Simon Smith. (91) $700

— SARGENT, D. H. - ALs, 21 Oct 1835. 2 pp, 4to. To Suzen Sargent. Reporting about his life with the Indians at Fox River Prairie. (91) $400

— SCHWATKA, FREDERICK. - ALs, 27 Aug 1877. 2 pp, 8vo. To Mellie. About the Sioux in Nebraska. (91) $200

— SEMINOLE WAR. - Ms Journal of Amos B. Eaton of the US 1st Infantry while serving in the Seminole War. 24 Aug 1837-24 Aug 1838. 78 pp, 8vo, in pigskin wraps. Includes a transcript of a letter from Zachary Taylor reporting on an important engagement. (90) $2,600

— SIMMONS, WILLIAM. - Franking signature, 1809. As War Department Accountant, on letter to the Indian Factor at Chickasaw Trading House requesting receipt for a payment to the "King of the Chickasaws". Alexander

collection. (90) $350
— TEXAS. - ALs, 24 May 1871, 8 pp, 8vo, by H. W. Fox to his father. Reporting about an Indian attack on an army unit. (91) $375
— WARREN, ABEL. - ALs, 15 Jan 1844. 1 p, 4to. To Cherokee Agent J. M. Butler. Sending a white boy "purchased of the Comanches by Delaware Bob". (90) $120
See also: Civil War, American
See also: Morgan, George
See also: Thomson, Charles

Indy, Vincent d', 1851-1931
Autograph music, Istar. (88) DM540
Photograph, sgd & inscr, [n.d.]. (91) DM450

Infessura, Stefano
Ms, Diario della Citta di Roma ... Phillipps Ms.5921. (91) $900

Ingalls, Rufus
Ds, 12 Dec 1862. (91) $200

Inge, William, 1913-73
Typescript, play, Front Porch, [late 1947]. 77 pp, 4to. With numerous autograph revisions in pencil. 15 pp yellowed. With related material. (88) $5,000

Ingemann, Bernhard Severin, 1789-1862
ALs, 27 July 1838. (90) DM800

Ingenhousz, Jan, 1730-99
ALs, 7 Sept 1786. 3 pp, 4to. To Marsilio Landriani. Scientific letter discussing the physiology of plants. In French. Seal tear. (88) DM5,500

Inglis, Esther, 1571-1624. See: Calligraphy

Ingres, Jean Auguste Dominique, 1780-1867
A Ls s (2), 14 Dec 1860 & [n.d.]. (90) DM600
ALs, 26 Jan 1840. (89) DM270
— [30 June 1848]. (88) DM220
— 20 Oct 1848. 1 p, 4to. To Charles Blanc. Regretting that he will not be able to be on the jury for a competition. (90) DM1,300
— 20 Oct 1849. (91) DM550
— [1853]. 2 pp, 8vo. To [Albert Magimel]. Reporting about the work on his Apotheose de Napoleon I. (90) DM2,000
— [n.d.]. (90) DM950
Collection of Ls & Ds, 20 & 21 Jan 1861. 4 pp, 8vo. To Charles Blanc. Refusing to reduce the price of a painting. Receipt. With related material. (91) DM1,600
Ds, 31 Oct 1838. (88) $110
— BALTARD, VICTOR. - ADs, 31 Dec 1838. 1 p, 8vo. Receipt for travel expenses. Countersgd by Ingres. (91) DM620
— MOLE, LOUIS MATTHIEU, COMTE DE. - ALs, 1 Sept [1834]. 2 pp, 8vo. To Ingres. Inquiring about his port. (90) DM220

Innes, John
Original drawings, (31), to illus H. Archives of J. M. Dent & Son. (88) £100

Innocent IV, Pope, d.1254
Document, [25 July 1254]. 1 p, vellum, 470mm by 630mm. Bull dealing with financial arrangements concerning Bartholomeo Bontempi in Leon. (90) DM2,700

Innocent VIII, Pope, 1432-92
Document, Mar 1488. (88) $120

Innocent X, Pope, 1574-1655
ADs, 4 May 1641. (89) $300

Inquisition
Ms, Manual of the Inquisition, in Latin. [Italy, c.1270-80]. 52 leaves, vellum, 228mm by 163mm; lacking bdg. In neat rounded Italian gothic bookhands by several scribes. Last leaves def. (91) £32,000

Ionian Islands
Ms, Petition, sgd by 12 English merchants on the island of Zante, addressed to an unnamed English Lord, thanking him for his intervention with the Venetians. Blackmer collection (90) £550

Ireland, John, 1879-1962
Autograph music, 2 Mss of his song Sea Fever, both sgd, 1913 & [1915]. (88) £1,000
— Autograph music, song cycle, Marigold, 1913. (88) £450
— Autograph music, song, I have twelve Oxen, July 1918; sgd, & Psalm XXIII, unaccompanied setting for baritone, 1958; sgd & inscr to George Parker;

IRELAND

presumably unpbd. (88) £300

Series of c.70 A Ls s, 1913 to 1958; c.115 pp, various sizes. (88) £550

Iron Manufacture

— FRENCHAY IRON WORKS, BRISTOL. - Ms, Bought Book, 3 May 1776 to 15 Apr 1780. 360 pp, 4to. Vellum bdg. Detailed accounts of goods made & expenses. (88) £540

Irvine, William, 1741-1804

ALs, 17 Mar 1782. (91) $380
See also: McKean, Thomas & Irvine

Irving, Washington, 1783-1859

Autograph Ms, diary, 2 Aug to 1 Sept [1832]. 74 pp, in small orange mor notebook. Describing an excursion to Saratoga, the Lake Region, & Niagara Falls. In pencil. Including some small sketches & a clipping. Doheny collection. (89) $7,000

Collection of 2 A Ls s & ANs, 28 Jan 1835, 7 May 1857 & 20 Jan [n.y.]. Middendorf collection. (89) $750

ALs, 2 Jan 1831. (89) $150

— Apr 1831 ("Monday"), 1 p, 8vo. (88) $175

— 10 June 1835. (89) $150

— 19 Sept 1849. (90) $250

— 11 Feb 1850. (89) $850

— 15 Nov 1856. (90) $275

— 26 Jan 1857. Byer collection. (90) $600

— [n.d.]. (91) $190

ANs, 26 Dec 1854. (89) $275

— [n.d.]. (89) $90

— MURRAY, JOHN. - 5 A Ls s, 30 Jan to 14 Sept 1865. 11 pp, 8vo. To Col. Aspinwall. Concerning the publication of Irving's novels. With related material. (88) $140

Irving, Washington, 1783-1859 —& Others

ANs, 12 Sept 1848. 1 p, 4to. To Joseph R. Winchester. Sending his autograph. Including ANs by Samuel Langhorne Clemens, 12 Feb 1901, sgd Mark Twain, & ANs by Edward E. Hale, 19 Feb 1901, each sending his autograph, on integral leaf. With ALs by Irving & further related material. Barrett collection. (89) $1,900

Irwin, James B.

Photograph, sgd & inscr, [n.d.]. (91) $100

Isabella Clara Eugenia of Austria, Regent of the Netherlands, 1566-1633

Series of 4 A Ls s, 10 Mar 1625 to 23 Feb 1626. 18 pp, folio. To a member of the Spanish government. Regarding various political, military & personal matters. (90) £4,000

Series of 10 Ls s, 1612 to 1626. 10 pp, folio. Recipients unnamed. Regarding affairs of the Low Countries. With 3 Ls s by her husband Archduke Albert & further related material. (90) £4,000

Isabella I, Queen of Spain, 1451-1504

Ls, 15 Dec 1474. 1 p, folio. To Don Luis Lucas. Announcing the death of her brother & her proclamation as Queen. Margins trimmed. (90) £1,600

— 15 Dec 1500. 1 p, folio. To Sancho de Paredes. Ordering him to give 4 pounds of silk to her daughter Catherine's servant. Including receipt sgd by Francisco de Torres at foot. (90) £1,600

Ds, 16 May 1484. 1 p, folio. As Queen of Castile, urging her captains in Andalusia to keep up the war against the Moors. (90) £1,200

— 25 Sept 1499. (90) £1,000

— 4 Dec 1499. 1 p, folio. Pay order in favor of Sancho de Paredes for assorted expenses. (91) $2,600

— 15 Mar 1501. Rua collection. (91) $1,000

— 5 July 1500. 1 p, 4to. Order to her chamberlain, Sancho de Paredes, to pay 2,000 maravedis to Alonso de Camora. (91) $3,000
See also: Ferdinand V & Isabella I

Isabella of Portugal, Empress of Charles V, 1503-39

Ls, 9 July 1529. (88) £300

— 14 Nov 1529. (88) £450

— 7 July 1531. 2 pp, folio. To the city of Loja. Informing them that the Emperor has returned to Germany to deal with the Lutheran peril. (90) £1,200

Series of Ds s, 4 Ds s, 30 Apr 1529 to 12 Oct 1537. (90) £1,000
See also: Charles V & Isabella of Portugal

Isherwood, Christopher, 1904-86
[A large collection of correspondence & art work by Isherwood's family, including numerous references to him, sold at S on 15 Dec 1988, lot 87, for £800.]
Ls, 13 Nov 1937. (88) £180

Ismail Pasha, Khedive of Egypt, 1830-95
Series of 3 Ls s, 1887 to 1892. (88) DM340

Isolani, Johann Ludwig, Graf von, 1586-1640
Ls, [n.d.]. (90) DM550

Isouard, Nicolas, 1775-1818
ALs, [n.d.]. (90) DM360

Israels, Jozef, 1824-1911
Collection of 4 A Ls s & photograph, 22 July to 22 Nov 1881 & [n.d.]. (90) DM570

ALs, 23 June [n.y.]. Salzer collection. (90) £350

Italy
[Goldsmiths. - An extensive archive of Mss, drawings, etchings, ptd books, etc. relating to Italian goldsmiths, 15th to 20th cent, compiled by Sidney J. A. Churchill, sold at S on 18 May 1989, lot 277, for £38,000 to Stucki.]

[Risorgimento. - A collection of letters & documents relating to the unification of Italy, including autographs by Cavour, Garibaldi, Mazzini, & others, sold at S on 17 Nov 1988, lot 240, for £2,700 to Severi.]

Ms, journal of a tour of Italy & central Europe, [late 17th cent]. (88) £900

— Ms, rental listing rents due on property of the monastery of Santa Maria de Fontana [Fontevivo, Diocese of Parma?] & elsewhere, [Emilia-Romagna?, c.1350]. 16 leaves & wraps, vellum, 565mm by 392mm, in fitted case. In a round italic bookhand. With 14th- & 15th-cent additions in various hands. (91) £4,000

— Ms, Statuta et ordinaria de Tieboldo et de Agnedo. [Volviano on Lago di Garda?, 1445 & 1483]. 7 leaves, vellum, 205mm by 157mm, in contemp wooden bds. In brown ink in a semi-gothic hand by 2 scribes. (89) £1,800

— AREZZO. - Ms, account book of the Ospedale di S. Maria del Ponte, kept by Cristofano de Simone, 1 July 1438 to 27 Oct 1449. 147 leaves & blanks, 295mm by 220mm, in 18th-cent vellum bdg. Listing expenses. (90) DM2,200

— BRESCIA. - Ms, account book of a pawn shop (Monte de pieta) run by Franciscan monks to help impoverished citizens, 26 Dec 1513 to 27 Dec 1531. 192 leaves, in contemp blindstamped lea. (90) DM1,700

— BRESCIA. - Ms, compilation of privileges granted to the city of Brescia by the Doges of Venice, 22 June 1439 to 16 May 1470; [c.1470]. 16 leaves (1 blank) & 2 flyleaves, vellum, 255mm by 179mm. Contemp blindstamped goatskin over pastebds. In an upright humanistic minuscule. With 2 very large white-vine initials with long marginal extensions & large armorial panel. Phillipps Ms.4566. (91) £20,000

— CONFRATERNITY OF CORPUS CHRISTI. - Ms, Regula De la compagnia del corpo de Christo. [Northeastern Italy, 1512]. 10 leaves, vellum, 234mm by 155mm, in contemp calf over pastebds. In a regular rounded hand. With 30 illuminated initials, large historiated initial, illuminated border, & page-width miniature. (91) £2,800

— FERDINAND, PRINCE OF FRANCAVILLA. - Document, 8 June 1650. 1 p, vellum, 615mm by 820mm. As Grand Chamberlain of Sicily, confirmation of commercial privileges & tax exemptions granted by Frederick of Aragon, 1496. With 3-sided illuminated border incorporating coats-of-arms, & large vignette of a harbor scene. (91) £550

— FLORENCE. - Ms, accounts of the debtor's prison, 1422. 46 leaves (10 blank), 296mm by 220mm. Modern imitation lea. Written by Manio di Giovanni in an Italian notarial hand. (89) £2,600

— FLORENCE. - Ms, rules of the Scuola di San Giovanni Evangelista, in Italian. [Florence, c.1440]. 20 leaves & flyleaves, vellum, 250mm by 185mm. Contemp Florentine bdg of brown goatskin over wooden bds with tempera painting on vellum set under horn on lower cover. In brown ink in a large rounded gothic hand. With 17 large historiated initials, half-page miniature with full border, contemp archiepiscopal attestations & 16th- & 18th-cent additions. Abbey collection. (89) £90,000

— GUILD OF SHOEMAKERS, BOLOGNA. - Ms, Matricola, in Latin. [Bologna, c.1386]. Single leaf, vellum, 350mm by 245mm. In a large gothic hand. Divided into 3 parishes, with space left for additions. With full-length illuminated border & large miniature by Nicolo di Giacomo da Bologna. Korner collection. (90) £62,000

— GUILD OF SHOEMAKERS, BOLOGNA. - Ms, Matricola, in Latin. [Bologna, c.1386]. Single leaf, vellum, 350mm by 248mm. In a large gothic hand. Divided into 4 parishes, with space left for additions. With full-length illuminated border & large miniature by Nicolo di Giacomo da Bologna. Korner collection. (90) £32,000

— JEWS IN VERONA. - Ms, notarial copies of privileges granted the Jews by Maximilian II, 1566, & Bona & Giangaleazzo Sforza, 1479, with judgment given by Giustiniano Contareno in the trial of Joseph ben Abraham at Verona, 1603; [Verona, 1626]. 16 leaves (1 blank), vellum, 215mm by 155mm, in contemp limp vellum. (91) £2,600

— LEONARDI DI URBENERI, JOHANNES. - Ds, Mar 1344. 1 p, 166mm by 523mm, vellum. Will. Including signum comprising Star of David & Christian cross. In Latin. Docketed on verso in a 17th-cent hand. Wormed. (88) $275

— MILAN. - A group of 14 letters relating to the administration of the city or duchy of Milan, 1517 to 1844, 19 pp, folio, sold at star on 1 Dec 1988, lot 1202, for DM800. 89

— MILAN. - Ms, Archivo della ven. congregazione de' SS. quaranta Nobili crosesegnati privilegi si S. Pietro Martire eretta nella Chiesa di S. Eustorgio..., 1770. About 286 leaves (partly blank), size not stated, in red lea gilt. Church records. (90) DM1,100

— MODENA. - Ms, register of the household of Aldobrandino d'Este & Guido Baisio, Bishops of Modena, 1378 to 1380. 25 leaves (some blanks), 210mm by 140mm, in old soft paper bds. In brown ink in a notarial hand. Recording details of appointments, leases, household expenses, etc. (88) £1,000

— PADUA. - Ms, Stemmata quarundarum nobilium familiarum Patavinarum, [c.1625]. 22 leaves of genealogical family trees & 40 pp of indexes of names, 485mm by 380mm, in contemp vellum. (89) £1,100

— UNIVERSITY OF PERUGIA. - Document, 1735. 6 leaves, 243mm by 198mm. Vellum. Contemp brown mor gilt. Grant of a doctorate to Franciscus Felix Onesti. In black & gold ink, with full-page coat-of-arms. (88) DM600

— VERONA. - Document, 11 Nov 1093. 1 p, vellum, 522mm by 306mm. Exchange of lands between Donna Bricia, abbess of the Benedictine nunnery of San Michele di Compagna, & Benjamin, a resident of Verona. With various signatures. In a late Carolingian notarial hand. (90) £11,000

— VERONA. - Ms, terrier of Verona & surrounding districts, [c.1425]. 53 leaves (4 blank) & flyleaf, vellum, 287mm by 198mm, in contemp bevelled wooden bds. In a notarial hand, with headings in a larger gothic hand. Referring to earlier deeds or leases. (90) £4,200

— VICENZA. - 5 documents, 1337 to 1390, various sizes, vellum. Relating to Bernard de Portabarrada & Raymond de Villamontana. In Latin. Worn. Doheny collection. (89) $350

Ivan V, Emperor of Russia, 1666-96 —& Peter I, Emperor of Russia, 1672-1725

Document, 19 July 1682. (90) DM900

Ives, Joseph Christmas

Autograph Ms, record of his astronomical observations made along the Colorado River near the 35th parallel. California, 1861. In 3 vols. 8vo, contemp sheep. (89) $2,200

J

J. B. Nichols & Sons
["A Catalogue of Books relative to County Histories and the Antiquarian and Miscellaneous Books sold by J. B. Nichols & Sons", c.1850, c.50 pp, 8vo; excerpts from ptd catalogues pasted in with Ms notes of prices etc, in wraps, sold at pn on 10 Dec 1987, lot 446, for £170 to Marlborough.]

J. M. Dent & Sons
[The archive of the publishing firm, 1880s to 1980s, including readers' reports, correspondence, art work, ledgers, etc., many thousands of items in a large number of boxes, sold at S on 18 July 1991, lot 348, for £14,000 to Rota.]

Jackson, Andrew, 1767-1845
Ms, Annual Message to Congress, 5 Dec 1836. 81 pp, 4to & folio, mostly on rectos. Mostly in the hand of Andrew Jackson Donelson; with numerous revisions, some autograph. Marked by the ptr. In mor case. Doheny collection. (89) $2,800
ALs, 21 Nov 1805. (89) $500
— 13 Mar 1813. 3 pp, folio. To William B. Lewis. Criticizing the conduct of the war. Including franking signature. Imperf. (90) $6,500
— 25 Apr 1814. 1 p, 4to. To his wife Rachel. Informing her about the defeat of the Creek Indians. Doheny collection. (89) $9,500
— [25 Mar 1816]. 3 pp, size not stated. To Sec of War Crawford. About the defenses of Mobile, a letter from Gen. Smith, & the probability of an Indian war. Folds repaired. (88) $3,500
— 25 Jan 1819. 2 pp, 4to. To his wife, Rachel. Reporting on his arrival in Washington & his plans to defend his honor against a Congressional committee report condemning him. (91) $13,000
— 1820. 2 pp, folio. To Sec of War John C. Calhoun. Concerning the removal of intruders from Cherokee & Creek lands. (90) $10,000
— 11 Apr 1822. 2 pp, folio. To John McLemore. Giving instructions concerning his speculations in North Carolina lands. (90) $2,750
— 12 July 1823. 2 pp, folio. To the Rev. Hardy Cryer. Reporting about disciplining a slave. Folds split. (88) $4,750
— 9 Feb 1824. (90) $700
— 10 Mar 1824. 1 p, 4to. To Sec of War John C. Calhoun. As Chairman of the Senate Committee on Military Affairs, inquiring about lands needed for military purposes in St. Charles, Louisiana. Sang & Thorek collections. (91) $1,900
— 5 Apr 1824. 2 pp, 4to. To Andrew Jackson, Jr. Giving fatherly advice about his duties to his mother & his studies. With franking signature. Repaired. Rosenbloom collection. (88) $6,000
— 10 Sept 1824. 2 pp, 4to. To James Monroe. Letter of recommendation. (89) £1,100
— 30 June 1826. 1 p, 4to. To John H. Lewis. Regretting being unable to accept the invitation to a public dinner in Huntsville, Alabama. Whiton collection. (88) $2,600
— 1 Mar 1827. 1 p, 4to. To Hardy M. Cryer. Concerning plans for a public dinner in Sumner County. (88) $1,900
— [4 Oct 1829]. 1 p, 4to. To John C. McLemore. Requesting him to forward a letter to Gen. Coffee (not present). Including franking signature. (90) $2,000
— 8 Mar 1830. 2 pp, folio. To Sec of the Treasury Samuel D. Ingham. Discussing procedure in the handling of a complaint against the Customs Collector at New Orleans. (90) $4,500
— 18 Oct 1830. 4 pp, 4to. To Hardy M. Cryer. About the politics of his administration, the revolution in France, his horses, etc. (88) $9,000
— 24 June 1831. 4 pp, 4to. To Mrs. Stephen Decatur. Defending several recent appointments. Repaired. (90) $6,500
— 23 Apr 1832. 1 p, folio. To Andrew Jackson, Jr. Expressing sorrow at his son's departure. Repaired. (89) £2,800
— 31 May 1832. 3 pp, 4to. To Andrew Jackson, Jr. About family & business matters. (91) $9,000
— 25 Oct 1832. 1 p, 4to. To Sec of War

JACKSON

Lewis Cass. In 3d person, requesting a report about an office in the ordnance corps. (90) $1,800
— 8 Apr 1833. 1 p, 8vo. To Sec of War Lewis Cass. Introducing Mr. Campbell & insisting that missionaries may not be sent to the Indians without permission of the tribes. Christensen collection. (90) $3,000
— 14 Oct 1833. 1 p, 4to. To Henry Toland. Sending a check (not present) in payment of articles for the Hermitage & himself. Pratt collection. (89) $3,250
— 24 Apr 1835. 8 pp, 4to. To Joseph Conn Guild. Discussing party politics & his political principles. Postscript incomplete. Leaves separated at folds. (88) $6,500
— 6 Oct 1836. 1 p, 4to. To J. Miller. Stating conditions for his appointment as auditor. Marked "Private". (90) $2,500
— 28 Feb 1837. 2 pp, 4to. To Emma Yorke Farquhar Donelson. Making arrangements to meet her at Wheeling for the journey to Nashville. With franking signature. (89) $7,500
— 21 May 1840. 3 pp, 4to. To Col. Maunsel White. Explaining his failure to pay some debts & promising settlement. Including franking signature. (89) $4,250
— 14 Dec 1842. 1 p, 4to. To E. S. Johnson. Responding to a letter informing him about the Democratic victory in the Massachusetts election. With franking signature on detached address panel. Framed. (90) $3,250
— 28 Dec 1843. 3 pp, 4to. To R. W. Latham. Explaining the transactions leading to his son's failure to pay a bond. With franking signature. Repaired. (89) $2,500
AL, 11 Mar 1830. 1 p, 4to. To Sen. Littleton Tazewell. In 3d person as President, urging that the nomination of Col. Butler be acted upon. With ALs from Anthony Butler to Jackson, 26 Dec 1831, reporting about his negotiations in Mexico. (89) $1,500
Ls, 26 July 1814. 2 pp, 4to. To Samuel Justice. Remitting the death sentence passed on him for desertion & ordering him to return to his duties.

AMERICAN BOOK PRICES CURRENT

Framed. (88) £1,450
— 16 June 1830. (89) £650
— 13 Oct 1834. (89) $1,000
— 25 Apr 1835. (89) £1,000
— 25 June 1844. 5 pp, 4to. To Morven M. Jones. Discussing the Democratic nominating convention, the Texas question, & Polk's candidacy. In the hand of A. J. Donelson. Pratt collection. (89) $12,000
Collection of Ds & lithographed port, 1829 & [n.d.]. (90) $320
— Collection of 2 Ds s & ANs, 19 May 1830 to 20 Aug 1842. 3 pp, various sizes. Remission of fines & land grant. To Mr. Brown, sending money. Doheny collection. (89) $1,900
Ds s (2)6 & 7 Oct 1807. Byer collection. (90) $600
Ds, 2 Apr 1829. (91) $500
— 10 Apr 1829. Byer collection. (90) $500
— 1 Sept 1829. (88) $600
— 2 Nov 1829. (91) $375
— 1 Nov 1830. (88) $450
— 10 Nov 1830. (90) $650
— 15 Nov 1830. (91) $450
— 6 Dec 1830. (91) $700
— Dec 1830. (89) $420
— 1 Jan 1831. 1 p, folio. Land grant to Phenix Diskill. (91) $1,700
— 3 Jan 1831. (89) $425
— 8 Feb 1831. (90) $400
— 10 Feb 1831. (90) $700
— 11 Apr 1831. (88) $750
— 14 July 1832. (90) $850
— 1 Aug 1832. 1 p, folio. Appointment of Robert W. Burnet as 2d Lieutenant of Infantry. Conutersgd by Lewis Cass. Framed. (91) $1,100
— 30 Mar 1833. (91) $700
— Apr 1833. (89) $450
— 19 Nov 1833. (91) $1,000
— 6 Mar 1834. 1 p, folio. Ship's papers for the Nite of Portland. (90) $1,200
— 1 Nov 1834. (88) $1,000
— 1834. (91) $1,000
— 17 July 1835. 2 pp, on vellum, folio. Patent issued to John Moffett & Morton Saintor for the self heat retaining stove. (91) $1,800
— 25 Feb 1836. 1 p, folio. Suspension of execution of the death sentence for the slave John Arthur Bowen. Fold splits.

Ruddy collection. (88) $5,000
— 27 June 1836. 1 p, folio. Pardon for the slave John Arthur Bowen. Countersgd by Sec of State John Forsyth. Repaired. (90) $6,500
— 1 July 1836. (90) $750
— 14 Oct 1836. (88) $375
— 2 Dec 1836. 1 p, folio. Appointment of Andrew Jackson, Jr., as Sec of the General Land Office. Countersgd by John Forsyth. Repaired; framed with a port. (90) $1,400
— 17 Jan 1837. 1 p, folio. Appointment of John H. Wheeler as Superintendent of the Mint at Charlotte. (90) $1,700
— [n.d.]. (91) $750
— [n.d.]. (90) $650
Autograph endorsement, four lines, sgd A.J., on verso of an initialled note of recommendation from Susan Decatur, 28 May 1833, 1 p, 4to. (88) $200
— Anr, sgd A.J., June 1836. (90) $800
Check, 11 May 1835. Made out to himself & sgd, for $25. (91) $5,000
— Anr, accomplished & sgd, 6 June 1835. 65mm by 135mm. Drawn on the Bank of the Metropolis for $17 payable to John L. Brightwell. (89) $1,100
Cut signature, 19 Jan 1830. (90) $400
— Anr, 1 June 1830. (91) $425
Franking signature, [n.d.]. (88) $275
— Anr, [29 Mar n.y.]. (90) $500
— GLASSELL, J. M. - ALs, 20 Apr 1818. 1 p, size not stated. To Maj. Gen. E. P. Gaines. As aide-de-camp to Gen. Andrew Jackson, allowing application of Capt. Bee to be granted. (88) $1,200

Jackson, Andrew, 1767-1845 —& Others
Ls, 9 July 1817. 3 pp, 4to. To George Graham. Informing him about bribes to various Cherokees to obtain tribal consent to the cession of the Muscle Shoals reservation. Also sgd by Joseph McKinn & D. W. Meriwether. Including postscript, sgd by all 3. Sang collection. (91) $8,000

Jackson, Helen Hunt, 1830-85
Autograph Ms (2), poems, Parson Williams' Sabbath-Breaking, sgd, & The People's Voice, [n.d.]. Doheny collection. (88) $550

Jackson, James, Governor of Georgia
Ds, 19 Nov 1800. (91) $100

Jackson, Joe, 1889-1951
Cut signature, [Apr 1936]. 4 by 1.5 inches. On fragment of legal document. (91) $21,000

Jackson, Michael
Photograph, sgd & inscr, [c.1988]. (89) $200

Jackson, Thomas J. ("Stonewall"), 1824-63
Ms, account of the Battle of Fredericksburg, 30 Jan 1863. 17 pp, 4to. With autograph revisions. Possibly addressed to Robert E. Lee. (89) $7,000
ALs, 14 Dec 1861. 3 pp, 4to. To Gen. Joseph E. Johnston. Reporting about efforts to control the Chesapeake & Ohio Canal. Was mtd. (90) $9,000
— 14 Aug 1862. 1 p, 4to. To Gen. S[amuel] Cooper. Recommending Col. W. E. Jones to command the brigade formerly commanded by Brig. Gen Charles S. Winder. (89) $8,000
— 6 Jan 1863. 2 pp, 8vo. To an unnamed pastor. Providing a testimonial to the religious beliefs & bravery of Capt. Hugh A. White. (89) £2,000
— 11 Mar 1863. 1 p, 98mm by 165mm, mtd. To Robert E. Lee. Saying that he is too busy to report at the moment. (91) $17,000
Cut signature, [n.d.]. 1 by 2.5 inches. (91) $1,900

Jacob, Max, 1876-1944
ALs, 31 Dec 1918. (91) DM200

Jacobi, Friedrich Heinrich, 1743-1819
ALs, 3 Nov 1808. 1 p, 8vo. To Schelling. Sending letters by [Johann Georg] Hamann. Margin def. (90) DM1,300

Jacobs, Helen
Autograph sketchbooks, (9), containing numerous drawings. (90) £950
Original drawings, (101), to illus books by Stella Mead & Freda Collins, 1941 to 1948. (90) £680
— Original drawings, (2), to illus The Land of Never Grow Old; [n.d.]. 365mm by 242mm & 396mm by 264mm. In ink & watercolor; sgd. (90) £1,400

JACOBS

— Original drawings, (3); 1 to illus The Land where Dreams come True, 1932. Various sizes. In watercolor; sgd. (90) £2,300
— Original drawings, (5), partly to illus The Land of Never Grow Old, & Pains in Storyland, 1937. About 350mm by 230mm. In ink & watercolor; sgd. (90) £1,600
— Original drawings, (89), for various book projects; [n.d.]. 4to & folio. In ink, watercolor & pencil; some sgd. (90) £1,200
— Original drawings, (9), to illus Fairy Tales, [n.d.]. (89) £320

Jagemann, Caroline, 1777-1848
ALs, 17 May 1842. (90) DM280

Jagemann, Christian, 1735-1804
ALs, 24 June 1784. (89) DM340

Jago, Frederick William Pearce
Autograph sketchbook, Sketches ... (89) £220

Jahn, Friedrich Ludwig, 1778-1852
Autograph Ms, description of the view from a tower [at Neuenburg near Freyburg?], sgd; 5 Oct [1828]. (91) DM420
ALs, [1839]. 4 pp, 4to. To Friedrich Foerster. Complaining about his treatment by the Prussian government. Schroeder collection. (89) DM1,900
— 17 Dec 1847. (91) DM520
AL, [21 Oct 1848?]. (90) DM650

Jahnn, Hans Henny, 1894-1959
Collection of ALs, 9 Ls s & autograph postcard, sgd, 7 Mar 1948 to 21 Dec 1954. 12 pp, folio, & card. To Gustaf Gruendgens. Informing him about his work, hoping Gruendgens will stage one of his plays, & about private matters. With related material. (89) DM6,500
Ls, 5 Jan 1933. (88) DM600

James, Cyril Lionel Robert
Autograph Ms, autobiographical study, Beyond a Boundary [here entitled Who Only Cricket Know], with preparatory notes & further typescripts; [c.1957 - 1960]. (91) £800

AMERICAN BOOK PRICES CURRENT

James, Frank, 1843-1915
ALs, 5 Mar 1883. 2 pp, 4to. To his wife. Written from jail; sending news. (91) $3,500
— 14 Mar 1884. 2 pp, 4to. To his wife & son. From jail, about his forthcoming trial. (91) $4,000

James, Helen
Original drawings, (106), views of Italian towns to illus 4 vols in the Medieval Towns series, 1898 to 1904. Archives of J. M. Dent & Son. (88) £170
— Original drawings, (142), to illus 4 vols in the Medieval Towns series, 1898 to 1900. Archives of J. M. Dent & Son. (88) £190

James, Henry, 1843-1916
Typescript carbon copy, part of What Maisie Knew, numbered XVII; July [1897]. 18 pp, 4to, on rectos only, in quarter mor slipcase. With autograph revisions. Doheny collection. (89) $12,000
Collection of 7 A Ls s & 2 Ls s, 27 July 1888 to 17 June 1913. 51 pp, 8vo & 4to. To Robert Underwood Johnson. About publishing matters. Koch Foundation. (90) $8,000
— Collection of 3 A Ls s & ANs, 24 Feb to 10 June 1895. 20 pp, 8vo, & ptd calling card. To Arthur C. Benson. About a variety of matters. Koch Foundation. (90) $3,200
— Collection of 2 A Ls s & Ls, 2 June 1902 to 1913. 7 pp, 4to. To Basil Champneys. Thanking for recipient's book, sending The Wings of the Dove, & promising to support a candidate in a ballot at the Athenaeum Club. (90) £1,600
— Collection of ALs & 3 Ls s, 21 May 1903 to 2 Feb 1904. 14 pp, 4to. To his nephew William James Jr. Interesting family letters about a variety of matters. (88) $3,000
— Collection of 4 A Ls s & Ls, 18 June to 18 Nov 1906. (89) £900
— Collection of 2 A Ls s & 2 Ls s, 17 May 1912 to 28 Sept 1913. 33 pp, 8vo & 4to. To William James, & William & Alice James(1). About their newborn son, Sargent's port, & other matters. (89) $2,000

— Collection of 2 A Ls s & Ls, 2 Jan 1914 to 7 Mar 1915. 21 pp, 4to. To Alice James (2) & William & Alice James. About family matters & the war. (89) £1,300

— Collection of ALs & Ls, 20 & 31 Aug 1914. 16 pp, 4to. To Alice James & William James. Expressing dismay about the war. (89) $5,000

— Collection of 2 A Ls s & Ls, 20 May to 27 Aug 1915. 15 pp, 4to. To Alice James. Commenting about the war & his becoming a British citizen. With enclosures, 2 A Ls s from Burgess Noakes to H. James. (88) $2,800

Series of 4 A Ls s, 29 Feb to 29 Sept 1876. 17 pp, 8vo. To Arthur Sedgwick. Describing his activities & his work in Paris. 1 sgd H.J., jr. Koch Foundation. (90) $4,200

— Series of 4 A Ls s, 4 June 1901 to 24 Jan 1906. (89) £1,000

— Series of 5 A Ls s, 11 Sept 1902 to 14 Mar 1903. 28 pp, 4to & 8vo. To Alice H. Gibben James (1) & William James II. Interesting family letters about a variety of matters. (89) £1,300

— Series of 4 A Ls s, 15 Mar to 31 Dec 1903. 20 pp, 8vo & 4to. To William James Jr. About his nephew's studies, his own activities, his brother, etc. (89) $2,500

— Series of 4 A Ls s, 13 May 1904 to 12 Mar 1906. 16 pp, 4to. To William James Jr. About his travels, family news, Henry Adams, etc. (89) $2,000

— Series of 5 A Ls s, 9 May to 8 June 1906. 20 pp, 8vo & 4to. To William James Jr. About American visitors, travel plans, a visit to Wells, etc. (88) $2,500

— Series of 5 A Ls s, 16 May 1907 to 24 May 1908. 24 pp, 4to & 8vo. To William James II & Alice Runnells (1). Family letters about their & his own travels. (89) £1,700

— Series of 3 A Ls s, 16 Jan to 25 Feb 1907. (89) £1,000

— Series of 4 A Ls s, 24 Aug 1911 to 2 Jan 1912. 22 pp, 8vo & 4to. To Alice (Runnells) James. About a railway strike, her marriage to his nephew William, etc. (89) £1,100

— Series of 4 A Ls s, 19 Dec 1911 to 29 Feb 1912. 29 pp, 8vo & 4to. To William James II & his wife Alice. Family letters, & about plans for their honeymoon. (89) £1,050

— Series of 4 A Ls s, 15 Mar to 1 Apr 1912. 36 pp, 8vo. To William James Jr. About sitting for a port by John Singer Sargent & a coal strike. (88) $5,000

— Series of 3 A Ls s, 19 Mar to 9 Apr 1912. 17 pp, 4to & 8vo. To Alice James. Giving advice during their stay at Lamb House & mentioning his port by Sargent. (89) $2,200

— Series of 3 A Ls s, 17 Apr to 2 May 1912. 16 pp, 8vo. To William (1) & Alice James. Expressing dismay about the Titanic disaster, expecting their visit, & praising drawings by Alexander James. (89) $2,000

— Series of 6 A Ls s, 9 May to 3 June 1912. 38 pp, 4to & 8vo. To William & Alice James. About a variety of matters. With enclosures. (89) $3,200

A Ls s (2), 3 Feb 1885 & 7 Oct [1891]. 10 pp, 8vo. To George W. Smalley. Giving literary advice & discussing his play The American. With related material. Koch Foundation. (90) $1,500

— A Ls s (2), 16 Nov 1906 & Whitsunday 1912. 22 pp, 4to & 8vo. To his nephew Alexander Robertson James. Chatting about his dachshund & hoping he will come to visit. Commenting about his drawings. (88) $3,500

— A Ls s (2), 9 & 20 June 1907. 15 pp, 8vo. To William James Jr. About his travels in Italy, further travel plans, & his nephew's painting in the Louvre. (88) $1,800

— A Ls s (2), 1 Aug 1908 & [n.d.]. (89) £280

— A Ls s (2), 11 Sept & 27 Oct 1911. 22 pp, 8vo. To William James Jr. Sending congratulations on his engagement & advising him to travel before getting married. (88) $2,200

ALs, 29 June 1889. (90) $550

— [23 Feb 1892]. 12 pp, 8vo. To Mrs. Hugh Bell. Reviewing Oscar Wilde's Lady Windermere's Fan. Koch Foundation. (90) $6,000

— 15 Jan 1895. Koch Foundation. (90) $900

— 9 Feb [1895]. (88) £110

— 14 Dec 1895. 8 pp, 8vo. To Mrs. Bigelow. Discussing his recent travels

& current events. (88) $1,400
— [13 Oct 1896]. (88) £650
— 19 Nov 1897. (89) $800
— 15 May 1904. Doheny collection. (89) $750
— 1 Apr 1911. (89) $1,000
— 29 Sept 1911. (89) $250
— 2 May 1912. (91) DM600
— 16 July 1912. 10 pp, 4to. To William James Jr. & his wife Alice. Reporting about a visit to Oxford for the bestowal of an honorary degree. (88) $2,000
— 24 & 27 Aug 1913. 16 pp, 4to. To Alice James. Chatting about his life & social activities. (89) $2,200
— 16 Nov 1914. (90) DM400
— 4 May 1915. 6 pp, 4to. To Mabel & Bertie Jackson. Commenting about the war. (89) $2,200
— 21 May 1915. Doheny collection. (89) $1,000
— 25 Aug 1915. 2 pp, 4to. To William Butler Yeats. Thanking him for a contribution to a friend's anthology. Koch Foundation. (90) $3,800
— 15 June [n.y.]. Doheny collection. (89) $1,000
— 15 June [n.y.]. (88) £80
— 19 Aug [n.y.]. (91) £160
— 17 Oct [n.y.]. (90) £360
— 7 Nov [n.y.]. (91) £160
Collection of 2 Ls s & letter, 12 Oct 1912 to 29 Mar 1913. 28 pp, 4to. To William James Jr. & his wife Alice. Personal news, & protesting against plans to subscribe funds for him. Letter with secretarial signature. (88) $2,000

James I, King of England, 1566-1625
Ls, 9 May 1597. 1 p, folio. To Charles, Duke of Lorraine. As King of Scotland, letter of recommendation for Robert Crichton. In Latin. Byer collection. (90) $1,100
— 3 Oct 1604. 1 p, folio. To [William Keith]. Refusing to accept his excuses to be absent from discussions about a union of England & Scotland. With autograph postscript in margin. (89) £1,300
— 15 June 1605. 1 p, folio. To Ahmed I, Sultan of Turkey. Demanding the release of Sir Thomas Sherley. In Latin, written in a fine Roman bookhand, highlighted in gold. (89) £3,000
— 30 Jan 1607/08. (89) £650
— 5 May 1615. (90) £550
— 7 Jan 1615/16. (90) £700
— 7 June 1617. (89) £440
Letter, 31 July [n.y]. (88) £350
Ds, 28 Jan 1604. 1 p, 4to. Order to deliver an embroidered coat-of-arms. (90) $1,100
— 5 Jan 1606. (91) £500
Document, 1 July 1603. (88) £440
— 30 May 1616. (91) £400
— 24 May(?) 1620. John F. Fleming Estate. (89) $400
— [1620]. 1 p, vellum, size not stated. Letters Patent creating Francis Blundell a Baronet. Including colored initial letter port of James I, & decorative borders with the port of [the future] Charles I, mythical figures, animals, etc. Lacking 2d membrane. Marquess of Downshire collection. (90) £2,000
— 12 Feb 1620/21. (89) £200
— 30 Dec 1623. (89) £400

James II, King of Aragon, c.1264-1327
Ds, 18 June 1298. (90) £850

James II, King of England, 1633-1701
Transcript, contemp clerical copy of statement issued at Rochester, 22 Dec 1688, after his unsuccessful attempt to regain the throne. (91) $500
ALs, 16 May 1649. 3 pp, 4to. Recipient unidentified. Giving an account of a naval battle in the Bay of Banry. In French. Byer collection. (90) $1,300
— 22 - 23 May 1679. 1 p, 4to. To Samuel Pepys. Supporting his application for the Admiralty Commission & enclosing an ALs (present, 3 pp, 4to) to his brother King Charles II, recommending Pepys. In contemp folder. (88) £18,500
— 9 Dec 1688. 1 p, 4to. To Capt. Randal Macdonnel. Ordering him to take the Queen to France. (89) £5,000
— 22 July [n.y.]. (91) £350
Series of 6 Ls s, 8 Oct to 2 Nov 1664. 6 pp, folio. To Prince Rupert. Discussing naval affairs. 2 letters duplicates. (91) £1,600

Ls, 2 Apr 1692. 2 pp, folio. To Sir John Ernly. Urging his privy council to attend the birth of his new child [Louisa Mary]. Sgd & initialled. (89) £4,000

Ds, 8 June 1685. (88) £240
— 5 Apr 1687. (89) $650
— 22 May 1687. Byer collection. (90) $250
— 10 July 1688. 3 pp, folio. Order addressed to Lord Jeffreys to appoint Humphrey Borlace High Sheriff of Cornwall. Countersgd by Sunderland. With related material. (89) £1,050
— 1 Oct 1688. 1 p, folio. Order addressed to Capt. Davis to impress mariners for H.M.S. Resolution. Countersgd by Samuel Pepys. Byer collection. (90) $2,000

Document, 18 June 1686. (91) £300

James, Jesse, 1847-82
— FORD, ROBERT N. - Signature, [n.d.]. 3 by 1.5 inches (card). Framed with a port. (91) $425

James, P. D.
Typescript, novel, A Taste for Death, [c.1985], c.340 pp, size not stated; in folder. With extensive autograph revisions. (88) £1,200

James, Will. See: James, William Roderick

James, William, 1842-1910
A Ls s (2), 1903 & 1906. (88) £250
ALs, [Sept 1883]. (91) $210
— 3 Sept 1891. (88) DM380

James, William Roderick, 1892-1942
ALs, [n.d.]. (89) $425

Jameson, Sir Leander Starr, 1853-1917
ALs, [n.d.]. (91) $65

Jammes, Francis, 1868-1938
ALs, Jan 1908. (90) DM310

Janacek, Leos, 1854-1928
Autograph music, song, Koza bila, for soprano, clarinet & piano, [c.1925]. 4 pp, 4to. Slightly differing from ptd version. With copy of a French version. (88) DM16,000

ALs, [1893]. 1 p, 8vo. To an unnamed clergyman. Recommending Max Koblizek for the post of organist at Frydek. (90) £1,400

Autograph postcard, sgd, [26 Jan 1886]. To Frantisek Pivoda. Asking for a contribution to a journal. (89) DM1,900
— [Jan 1886]. To Frantisek Pivoda. Inquiring about a contribution [to his journal Hudebny Listy]. (90) DM1,900

Japan
Ms, Historia da Igreja do Japao, [17th cent]. 450 pp, folio, in calf wraps. Portuguese description of Japan & the work of St. Francis Xavier, 1549 to 1634, compiled by Jesuits living in Japan. In a single hand. Phillipps MS.3064 & Robinson collection. (89) £31,000

Japanese Manuscripts
Ms, Mahaprajnaparamita-sutra (Daihannyaharamitta kyo); [23 Mar - 1 Apr 730]. Scroll, 253mm by 8085mm. Written in Chinese characters in Dunhuang-style kaisho script for Lord Ashijima of Heguri-go; punctuated in red ink by Eion, [13th cent]. Vol 164 [of 600]. Restored & mtd on acrylic spindle; in wooden box. The Garden Ltd. collection. (90) $85,000

Jaques, Faith
Original drawings, (10), to illus E. (89) £360
— Original drawings, (20), to illus Mr. Buzz the Beeman, 1981. On 10 sheets, 266mm by 374mm. In ink & watercolor; sgd. (89) £1,600
— Original drawings, (32), pictorial dust jackets for Northanger Abbey, Middlemarch, & other titles. Archives of J. M. Dent & Son. (88) £300
— Original drawings, (44), to illus Mr. (89) £850
— Original drawings, (49), to illus Allison Uttley's Tales of Little Grey Rabbit, 1979 & 1980. (89) £800

Jaques, Robin
Original drawings, (8), mostly to illus Lynne Reid-Banks' Indian in the Cupboard, 1980. Archives of J. M. Dent & Son. (88) £170

Jaquotot, Marie Victoire, 1772-1855
Collection of ALs & autograph Ms, 6 May 1828. (89) DM660

Jarnach, Philipp, 1892-1982
Autograph music, sketches, "zum Quartett-Satz" & "Zwoelfton-Skizze". (88) DM200

Jarry, Nicholas, c.1615-70
Autograph transcript, Office de la Vierge Marie avec un Exercice Spirituel, in Latin & French. [Paris, 1654]. 169 leaves & 7 flyleaves, vellum, 113mm by 65mm. Extra green mor gilt bdg by Georges Trautz, c.1870. In dark brown ink in an extremely skilful small round roman & an elegant sloping italic hand. With gold frames throughout & 11 pp with large floral initials & headpieces of flowers & ribbons around crowned monograms. Schiff & Abbey collections. (89) £42,000

Jarry, Nicholas, c.1615-74. See: Calligraphy

Jarvis, Greg
Ls, [n.d.]. (91) $275
Signature, on First Day Cover below 8 Space Shuttle stamps, [21 May 1981]. (90) $210
— Anr, on shuttle flight cover, [17 June 1985]. (90) $280
— Anr, on envelope [cancelled later, 20 July 1986]. (90) $225
— Anr, [n.d.]. (89) $220

Jaspers, Karl, 1883-1969
Series of 5 A Ls s, 14 Oct 1960 to 24 Apr 1964. 5 pp, folio. To William Matheson. Regarding a publication. (90) DM1,200
ALs, 4 May 1922. 2 pp, 8vo. To [Alexander Amersdorffer]. Diagnosing a mental illness. (91) DM1,100

Jawlensky, Alexej von, 1864-1941
Series of 29 A Ls s, 1924 to 1937. 56 pp, folio & 8vo. To Erich Scheyer & his wife. About his pictures, reviews of his work, an exhibition, his lack of income, etc. With related material. (88) £2,200
ALs, 20 July 1934. 2 pp, 4to. To an unnamed lady. About his illness & her stay at Woerishofen. (90) DM1,500

Autograph postcard, sgd, 18 Sept 1927. To Mela Escherich. Thanking for a watercolor & asking her to mail some copies of the Fremdenblatt. Including small port sketch, sgd with monogram; also sgd & inscr by T. Kirchhoff. (90) DM6,200

Jay, John, 1745-1829
[A collection comprising 10 autograph draft letters or memoranda, & Ls, 17 Dec 1821 to 18 Mar 1826, documenting his term as President of the American Bible Society, with related material, sold at CNY on 18 Nov 1988, lot 194, for $3,200.]
Collection of ALs & Ds, 1 May 1765 & 17 Jan 1800. (88) £400
ALs, 19 Feb 1784. 1 p, 4to. To Elbridge Gerry. Regarding rumors about the USA circulating in Europe, the Order of the Cincinnati, & the Treaty of Peace. Address leaf def. (89) $13,000
— 20 Oct 1786. (89) £800
— 6 Sept 1787. 1 p, 4to. To George Washington. Expressing the wish of NY for "an occasion of giving you fresh Proofs of Esteem" for consenting to serve in the Constitutional Convention. Inlaid. Doheny collection. (89) $13,000
— 25 Mar 1791. 1 p, 4to. To Henry Remsen, Jr. Regarding payment of his salary. Endorsed by recipient. With 2 engraved portraits. (90) $3,500
— 23 Apr 1796. Christensen collection. (90) $550
— 27 Sept 1800. 1 p, 4to. To his son Peter. About the possibility of a new home & other family matters. (89) $1,200
— 18 Sept 1819. 1 p, 4to. To his son Peter. About family lands, expenses, the epidemic in NY, etc. Byer collection. (90) $1,100
AL, [c.May 1801]. 1 p, 4to. To the Mayor, Aldermen & Community of the City of Albany. Draft, expressing thanks for "conferring on me the Freedom of the City." With related Ds by Mayor P. S. Van Rensselaer, 11 May 1801. John F. Fleming Estate. (89) $1,400
Ds, [1778-79]. 1 p, folio. Ptd broadside of "Instructions to the Commanders of Private Ships or Vessels of War", dated 3 Apr 1776. Sgd as President of

the Congress. (90) $2,800
— [1778-79]. (88) £600
— [1778-79]. 1 p, folio. Ptd broadside of "instructions to the Commanders of Private Ships or Vessels of War", dated 3 Apr 1776. Sgd as President of the Congress. (89) $4,200
— 8 Mar 1797. (90) $550
— 13 Feb 1798. (88) $900
— 29 Mar 1798. (91) $550
— 29 Mar 1798. (91) $400
— 7 Feb 1800. (88) $650
— 31 Oct 1800. (91) $500
Autograph endorsement, sgd, 23 Sept 1785. (90) $300
— JAY, AUGUSTUS. - ADs, 26 Sept 1718. 8vo. Receipt to Robert Livingston, Jr. (89) $65

Jean Paul. See: Richter, Jean Paul Friedrich

Jeanneret, Charles Edouard, 1887-1965. See: Le Corbusier

Jefferies, Richard, 1848-87
Autograph Ms, notebook recording meditations about himself, life, religion, nature, etc., [n.d.]. 137 pp, 8vo, in black mor bdg. With related material. (89) £4,200

Jeffers, Robinson, 1887-1962
Autograph Ms (2), introduction to Sydney S. Alberts' A Bibliography of the Works of Robinson Jeffers, 1933, sgd, & 16 lines of his poem Saul, with unidentified fragments on verso; [n.d.]. 5 pp, 4to. With typed transcript of introduction, entitled "Remembered Verses". Koch Foundation. (90) $6,500
ALs, Aug 1957. (90) $475

Jefferson, Joseph, 1829-1905
Collection of ALs & group photograph, 31 Dec 1878 & [n.d.]. (91) $75
ALs, 20 Jan 1899. (88) $175

Jefferson, Joseph, 1829-1905 —& Others
[A group of 10 photographs, 8vo, in modern wraps, representing a type of program guide for C. B. Jefferson's & Joseph Brooks's production of Richard Sheridan's The Rivals, [c.1896], sgd by each of the 10 players including Joseph Jefferson, William Crane, etc., sold at sg on 8 Feb 1990, lot 199, for $150.]

Jefferson, Thomas, 1743-1826
Autograph Ms, fragment from his Farm Book, 1 p, 4to. Listing 67 servants for distribution of blankets, 1822 to 1827, in 3 columns. Lower margin def. Barrett collection. (89) $2,750
— Autograph Ms, latitudinal observations undertaken with his grandson T. J. Randolph, Oct & Nov 1811. 2 pp, 8vo. With 2 integral signatures Th: J. Mtd. Barrett collection. (89) $1,600
— Autograph Ms, "List of Balances", [mid-1790s]. 2 pp, 4to. Listing c.70 individuals with sums owed to Jefferson. Mtd. Barrett collection. (89) $3,250
— Autograph Ms, notes on sources for the history of Parliament, [1790s?]. 2 pp, 8vo. Mtd. Barrett collection. (89) $1,600
ALs, 20 Mar 1780. 1 p, 4to. Recipient unknown. As Governor of Virginia, giving instructions about supplying troops. With engraved port. (88) $8,600
— 8 Feb 1781. 1 p, 4to. To [George Washington]. Informing him that a British fleet has entered Cape Fear River. Sang collection. (91) $19,000
— 27 Mar 1783. 1 p, 4to. To Robert R. Livingston. Regarding his accounts for his appointment to the peace commission. Mtd. (88) $4,750
— 17 Aug 1786. 1 p, 4to. Recipient unnamed. Introducing Mme de Gregoire, going to America to reclaim lands in Maine. Recipient's name cut away. Byer collection. (90) $8,500
— 15 Dec 1786. 2 pp, 4to. To [Elizabeth] Trist. About his dislocated wrist, his stay in Paris, & friends in Virginia. Williams estate. (89) $16,000
— 15 Dec 1786. 2 pp, 4to. To Mrs. Trist. About his unease in living without a plan. (91) $17,000
— 4 Apr 1787. 2 pp, 4to. To Mazzei. About his journey in Southern France seeking specimens of fruits & plants for America. Repaired. (89) £3,200
— 9 Dec 1787. 2 pp, 4to. To C. w. F. Dumas. Explaining factors that might modify Congressional trade policy;

predicts revolution in France. (91) $23,000
— 16 June 1792. 2 pp, 4to. To the Marquis de Lafayette. Commenting about revolutionary France, political tendencies in America, the problems in Haiti, etc. Reid collection. (88) $23,000
— 7 Oct 1792. 1 p, 4to. To Henry Remsen. As Sec of State, inquiring about diplomatic instructions sent to Amsterdam. Rosenbloom collection. (88) $8,000
— 2 Mar 1801. 1 p, 4to. To The President pro tempore of the Senate. Setting the date for taking his Presidential oath. (91) $145,000
— 17 May 1801. 1 p, 4to. To George Clinton. Discussing new appointments in NY State. With franking signature. (88) $7,750
— 24 Dec [18]03. 1 p, 4to. To Gen. Muhlenberg. Requesting him to forward a shipment of sherry to Richmond. Including franking signature. (89) $7,000
— 31 Dec 1803. 1 p, size not stated. To George Clinton. About a libellous pamphlet, & discussing the political situation. With franking signature. (88) $12,500
— 5 June 1805. 1 p, 4to. To Thomas M. Randolph. Requesting help in finding a replacement for a hired man at Monticello. Christensen collection. (90) $7,000
— 3 Apr 1806. 1 p, 4to. To James Oldham. Informing him about a financial transaction. Def. With franking signature on detached address leaf. (90) $4,250
— 26 Sept 1807. 1 p, 4to. To James Madison. Retained copy, announcing his visit next Wednesday. McVitty collection. (90) $9,000
— 25 Oct 1807. 1 p, 4to. To Edmund Bacon, the farm manager of Monticello. About settling with Mr. Shoemaker & other farm matters. (91) $9,500
— 15 Mar 1808. 1 p, 124mm by 167mm. To Gen. [John] Shee. Inquiring about an overdue shipment. (91) $3,800
— 15 July 1808. 1 p, 4to. To [Christian Hendrik] Persoon. Thanking for a copy of his Synopsis [Plantarum]. Encased in gauze. (90) $4,700
— 29 Dec 1808. 1 p, 4to. To the Rev. Dr. [William] Bentley. Thanking for receipt of "a hortus siccus" & drawings by Miss Crowninshield. (89) £4,000
— 22 Aug 1809. 1 p, 4to. To Charles Willson Peale. Concerning settlement of accounts for his grandson's stay with the Peale family. (88) $7,000
— 18 Apr 1810. 1 p, 4to. To William W. Woodward. Giving directions concerning the bdg & shipping of a bible. Including franking signature. Pratt collection. (89) $13,000
— 4 Nov 1811. 1 p, 4to. To Charles Simms. Requesting his help in having goods shipped to Richmond. (91) $7,500
— 3 June 1812. 2 pp, 4to. To John Wayne Eppes. Content not indicated. (91) $10,000
— 21 Oct 1813. 1 p, 4to. To Mr. Gibson. Acknowledging receipt of funds & commenting on the price of flour. Mtd. (88) $4,200
— 30 Nov 1813. 3 pp, 4to. To [the Marquis de Lafayette]. Commenting on wool production, American manufactures, the war, & the situation in Latin America. Including postscript dated 14 Dec [1813]. Reid collection. (88) $23,000
— 6 Mar 1814. 1 p, 4to. To Henry M. Brackenridge. In 3d person, expressing thanks for a copy of his Views of Louisiana. With franking signature. Repaired. (88) $6,500
— 15 Aug 1816. 1 p, 4to. To Payne Todd. Thanking for a traveling thermometer, & sending a pair of pistols. Including franking signature. Framed. (90) $16,000
— 19 Sept 1816. 1 p, 4to. To James Fishback. Protesting against being misquoted in a statement about atheism in recipient's 4th of July oration. Def. (89) $13,000
— 10 Mar 1817. 1 p, 4to. To Gen. John Hartwell Cocke. Inviting him to a meeting of the Board of Visitors of the college to be founded near Charlottesville. With franking signature. Silked. (88) $28,000
— 11 Nov 1818. 2 pp, 4to. To Dr. [Andrew] Kain [Kean]. Inviting him to

join the faculty of the University of Virginia. Including franking signature. (90) $32,000
— 22 Sept 1819. 2 pp, 4to. To [Nathaniel] F. Moore. Discussing the pronunciation of the Greek language. Tipped into a copy of Julian P. Boyd's The Declaration of Independence. Princeton, 1945. (90) $22,000
— 11 May 1821. 1 p, 4to. To Dr. David Hosack. Thanking for a copy of his book & referring to political events in Spain, Portugal & Naples. Including franking signature. (91) $31,000
— 26 Jan 1822. 1 p, 4to. To Katherine Duane Morgan. Acknowledging receipt of her circular letter regarding domestic manufactures. (89) $13,000
— 9 Nov 1823. 1 p, 4to. To Gov. James Pleasants. Covering letter for a report about the University of Virginia (not included); retained copy. Splitting at folds. (88) $6,250
— 4 Jan 1824. 1 p, 4to. To Thomas M. Randolph. Suggesting books that should be read by future lawyers. With franking signature. Seal hole. (88) $8,000
— 3 Sept 1824. 1 p, 4to. To [the Marquis de Lafayette]. Retained copy; welcoming him to the USA & inviting him to Charlottesville. Margin def. Reid collection. (89) $21,000
AL, 12 Mar 1791. 3 pp, 4to. To William Carmichael. Draft, urging him to press the claims of Joseph Ste. Marie at Madrid & to demand an acknowlegment of the US right to navigate the Mississippi. Differing from version ptd in Boyd Ed, vol 19, 522-524. (89) $15,000
— 6 July 1805. 1 p, 4to. To William Jarvis. About a shipment of fruit & wine, Portugal & the European wars, & the Lewis & Clark expedition. Pratt collection. (89) $27,000
Ls, 31 Mar 1790. 1 p, 4to. To "The President of Philadelphia" [Thomas Mifflin]. Sending copies of acts concerning the census, naturalization & the budget. (91) $12,000
— 9 Mar 1792. 1 p, 4to. To Samuel Huntington. As Sec of State, transmitting acts of Congress, etc. Mtd. Doheny collection. (89) $8,500

— 6 Aug 1808. 1 p, 4to. To Messrs. Kerr, Moore, & Williams. Requesting them to alter their survey for the projected western road to include Washington, Pennsylvania. Sang collection. (91) $9,500
— 15 Aug 1821. 1 p, 4to. To Gen James Breckinridge. Planning the library of the University of Virginia. In the hand of his granddaughter, Cornelia Jefferson Randolph. A few letters missing & supplied in early ink facsilme. Framed with a port. (91) $9,500
— 30 Sept 1821. 2 pp, 4to. To Gen. James Breckinridge. Reporting about building costs of the University of Virginia & discussing the projected library building. Including franking signature. Def. McVitty collection. (90) $12,000
ANs, 20 Mar 1793. 1 p, 114mm by 194mm. To Capt. [Nathaniel] Cutting. In 3d person, informing him "that the President counts on him in the matter spoken of". (90) $2,400
ADs, 11 July 1803. 1 p, 133mm by 192mm. Pay order addressed to Mr. Barnes in favor of Mr. Lemaire. (90) $3,800
Series of Ds s, 3 Ds s, 2 Mar 1793. 2 pp, 380mm by 235mm. Broadsheet with 3 ptd Acts of Congress, each sgd by Jefferson as Sec of State. Small fold tear. (88) $4,000
Ds, 12 May 1780. 1 p, 4to. As Governor of Virginia, certifying that Mr. Beaumarchais' agent Lazarus Defrancey "has a Ballance due to him from the State of Virginia". (90) $8,000
— [c.10 Aug 1790]. 1 p, folio. As Sec of State, attestation on ptd copy of An Act ... to finish the Light-House, on Portland-Head. Matted with engraved port. (91) $5,000
— 12 Aug 1790. 2 pp, 4to. As Sec of State, attestation on ptd copy of An Act making Provision for the Reduction of the Public Debt. (90) $4,250
— [2 Mar 1791]. 2 pp, folio. An Act Giving Effect to the Laws of the United States within the State of Vermont; ptd broadsheet, sgd as Sec of State. (91) $18,000
— [after 23 Jan 1792]. 1 p, folio. Ptd Act of Congress "to extend the Time limited for settling the Accounts of the

JEFFERSON

United States with the Individual States." (90) $4,500
— [13 Apr 1792]. 2 pp, folio. As Sec of State, ptd Act for altering the times of holding the Circuit Courts. Docketed by Samuel Huntington as Governor of Connecticut. (91) $5,000
— 22 Feb 1793. 1 p, 4to. Ptd "Act to authorize the adjustment of a claim of Joseph Henderson"; sgd as Sec of State. Repaired. Whiton collection. (88) $2,100
— 16 Jan 1801. 9.25 by 14 inches. As President of the American Philosophical Society, certificate of election to membership of William Jones. Also sgd by 7 others. Mtd. (89) £2,400
— 14 Apr 1801. 1 p, folio. Ship's papers for the brig Fidelity of Portsmouth. (88) $2,900
— 22 May 1801. 1 p, on vellum, folio. Commission of Joshua Black as Lieutenant in the Navy. (90) $2,500
— 4 Nov 1801. 1 p, folio. Land grant to Andrew Buchanan. Countersgd by Madison. Framed. (91) $4,250
— 13 Apr 1802. Size not stated. Ship's papers in 4 languages for the schooner John of Baltimore. Countersgd by Madison. Small paper loss affecting signature. (88) $1,600
— 2 June 1802. 1 p, folio. Land grant to William Croghan. Countersgd by Madison. (89) $2,500
— 7 Dec 1802. 1 p, folio. Appointment of William Judd as General Commissioner of Bankruptcy in Connecticut. Countersgd by Madison. Stained. (90) $2,000
— 18 Jan 1803. 1 p, folio. Ship's papers for the Pyoningo of New York. Countersgd by Madison. Signature faded. Framed. (88) $1,800
— 23 July 1803. 1 p, 405mm by 485mm. Ship's papers in 4 languages for the brig The Adventure from NY. Countersgd by Madison. Christensen collection. (90) $4,000
— 24 Sept 1803. 1 p, folio. Mediterranean Pass for the Manchester of NY. Countersgd by Madison. Sang collection. (90) $3,250
— 23 Dec 1803. 1 p, folio. Ship's papers for the India Point. Countersgd by Madison. (91) $4,500

— 28 Apr 1804. 1 p, folio. Ship's papers in 4 languages for the sloop Patience of Philadelphia. Countersgd by Madison. Silked. Sang collection. (90) $2,000
— 28 May 1804. 1 p, 255mm by 304mm. Military land grant to Hezekiah Morton. Countersgd by Madison. (91) $4,000
— 28 Sept 1804. 1 p, folio. Ship's papers for the brig Sally of Boston. Countersgd by Madison. (89) $2,500
— 26 Dec 1804. 1 p, folio. Ship's paper for the Bristol Trader. Countersgd by Madison. (91) $3,500
— 7 Mar 1805. 1 p, 4to. Ship's papers in 4 languages for the schooner Lark. Fragment, English & Dutch parts only. Mtd. (89) $1,700
— 18 May 1805. 1 p, folio. Mediterranean passport for the ship Draper. Countersgd by Madison. Framed. (91) $4,000
— 22 June 1805. 1 p, folio. Ship's passport for the Mary of Charleston. Countersgd by Sec of State Madison. (88) $2,500
— 6 July 1805. 1 p, folio. Mediterranean Pass for the schooner Hiram of Marblehead. Countersgd by Madison. Sang collection. (90) $4,250
— 25 Oct 1805. 1 p, folio. Ship's passport for the brig Phoenix. Countersgd by Madison. (91) $2,600
— 4 Dec 1805. 1 p, folio. Mediterranean Pass for the schooner Ann of Marblehead. Countersgd by Madison. Later endorsements on verso. Signatures faded. (89) $3,000
— 23 Dec 1805. 1 p, folio. Mediterranean Pass for the brig Hope of Philadelphia. Countersgd by Madison. (88) $2,300
— 23 Dec 1805. 1 p, 26cm by 38cm. Ship's papers for the Little William of Philadelphia. Countersgd by Madison. (88) $2,800
— 24 Feb 1806. 1 p, folio. Appointment for Pierpont Edwards as Judge of the US District Court for Connecticut. Countersgd by Madison. (88) $3,000
— 23 Apr 1806. 1 p, folio. Mediterranean passport for the ship Jane. Countersgd by Madison. (91) $2,250
— 24 May 1806. 1 p, folio. Mediterranean Pass for the ship Active of Philadelphia. Countersgd by Madison. (89)

$3,250
— 14 July 1806. Ship's passport for the brig Fair America. Countersgd by Madison as Sec of State (ink light). (91) $4,000
— 26 Sept 1806. 1 p, folio. Land grant to Thomas Browder. Countersgd by Madison. (90) $3,500
— 23 Oct 1806. 1 p, folio. Ship's papers in 4 languages for the Hero of Portland. Countersgd by Madison. (90) $3,250
— 26 Oct 1806. 1 p, folio. Ship's papers in 4 languages for the Hero. Countersgd by Madison. Imperf. (90) $2,200
— 3 Nov 1806. 1 p, folio. Mediterranean Pass for the brigantine Alert of Newburyport. Countersgd by Madison. (90) $4,000
— 18 Nov 1806. 1 p, folio. Mediterranean Pass for the brig Sukey of Salem. Countersgd by James Madison. Wrinkled. (89) $2,400
— 29 Nov 1806. 1 p, folio. Mediterranean Pass for the schooner Mary of Marblehead. Countersgd by Madison. (89) $2,700
— 1 Jan 1807. 1 p, 8vo. Ship's papers; fragment. Countersgd by Madison. (88) $1,100
— 11 Feb 1807. 1 p, folio. Land grant to Duncan McArthur as assignee of James McNutt. Countersgd by Madison. Endorsed by Henry Dearborn on verso. (90) $2,600
— 25 Mar 1807. 1 p, folio. Ship's papers in 4 languages for the Ulysses of Savannah. Countersgd by Madison. (89) £2,100
— 30 May 1807. 1 p, folio. Ship's papers in 4 languages for the brig Friendship of Baltimore. Countersgd by Madison. (88) $1,850
— 17 June 1807. 1 p, folio. Ship's passport for the brig Elizabeth of Baltimore. Countersgd by Madison. (91) $3,200
— 28 July 1807. 1 p, 16.25 by 20.75 inches. Ship's papers in 4 languages for the Herald. Countersgd by Madison. (88) £1,500
— 20 Nov 1807. 1 p, 420mm by 525mm. Ship's papers in 4 languages for the Betsy. Countersgd by Madison. Repaired. (89) $2,600
— 30 Nov 1807. 1 p, folio. Patent to Simon Willard for a machine for cutting nails; countersgd by Madison & Caesar Rodney. (91) $4,000
— 5 Apr 1808. 1 p, folio. Military land grant to John Watts. Countersgd by Madison. Framed with portraits. (88) $1,900
— 26 Aug 1808. 1 p, folio. Land grant to Charles Deal. Countersgd by James Madison. (88) $2,600
— 26 Jan 1809. 1 p, 215mm by 370mm. Land grant to Samuel Stitt. Countersgd by Madison. (90) $2,200
— [c.1809]. 1 p, folio. Mediterranean Pass, sgd in blank. Countersgd by Madison. Sang collection. (90) $4,000
— [n.d.]. Size not stated. Ship's papers in 4 languages; unaccomplished. Countersgd by Madison. (88) $2,100
— [n.d.]. 1 p, folio. Ship's papers in 4 languages for the brig Eagle of New Bedford. Countersgd by Madison. (89) $3,000

Check, 13 July 1793. Payable to Mr. Petit & sgd. (91) $9,000

Cut signature, [n.d.]. Size not stated. (91) $1,800
— Anr, [n.d.]. Size not stated; mtd. With engraved port. (90) $1,500

Franking signature, [31 Mar 1791]. Alexander collection. (90) $2,300
— Anr, [1801-1809]. 1 p, 4to. On autograph address panel to Joseph Rapin. (90) $1,400
— Anr, [17 May n.y.]. (90) $800
— Anr, [n.d.]. On autograph address panel, 178mm by 253mm. (90) $1,600
— Anr, [n.d.]. With autograph address. (89) $1,450

Signature, [n.d.]. Matted with related material; overall size 15.5 by 12 inches. (91) $2,000

Jefferson, Thomas, 1743-1826 —& Others
Ls, 22 Sept 1784. 2 pp, folio. To M. de Pio, charge d'affaires of the King of Naples. Establishing diplomatic relations, & informing him of their powers to conclude a treaty of amity & commerce. Also sgd by John Adams & Benjamin Franklin. (88) £11,500

Jeffries, John, 1745-1819
ADs, 1769. Generales collection. (88) $110

Jenkins, Francis, 1650-1710
Ds, 13 Apr 1681. (88) $50

Jenner, Edward, 1749-1823
ALs, 10 Sept 1804. 4 pp, folio. To Louis Valentin. Discussing smallpox vaccination & requesting his help in securing the release of 2 prisoners of war. (91) £3,500

— 9 Mar 1808. 3 pp, 8vo. Recipient unknown. About recipient's publication, varieties of vaccination, organizational matters, etc. (88) $2,200

— 2 Apr 1815. (91) £550

— [26] Sept [n.y.]. (90) £230

— [n.d.], "Wednesday". (89) £850

Jennings, Al, 1864-1961
Signature, [c.1942]. (91) $110

Jensen, Wilhelm, 1837-1911
Collection of 5 A Ls s & 2 autograph postcards, sgd, 1907 to 1910. (89) DM370

Jeritza, Maria, 1887-1981
Series of 4 autograph postcards, sgd, & ANs, 12 Mar 1924 to 9 June 1929. Ernst Gottlieb collection. (88) DM410

Jersey
[A collection of 18 documents, 1720 to 1879, largely relating to the Dolbel & Cristin families, sold at S on 21 Sept, lot 62, for £150 to Stevens.]

Jerusalem, Johann Friedrich Wilhelm, 1709-89
ALs, 14 Sept 1784. (89) DM380

Jervis, John, Earl of St. Vincent, 1735-1823
Series of 21 A Ls s, 8 Nov 1763 to 12 Sept 1797. Wolf collection. (90) £900

— Series of 129 A Ls s, Aug 1785 to Apr 1803. 143 pp, various sizes. Mostly to Sir John Duckworth. Discussing a variety of naval matters. Wolf collection. (90) £2,400

Jesuit Relations
Ms, Avisi della Cina Cavati d'alcune lettere scritte al P[ad]re Generale della Compagnia di Giesu, 1583 & 1584. 10 pp, folio, in fitted box. Extracts from letters of the 1st Jesuits to enter China, in a single Italic hand. Phillipps MS & Robinson collection. (89) £12,000

Jesuits
— LOPEZ, GREGORIO. - Annua de la Provincia de Filipinas de la Compania de IHS del ano de 1607. Manila, 4 July 1608. 61 pp, on native paper, in contemp vellum. Stained & silked. (90) £21,000

Jimenez de Cisneros, Francisco, Cardinal, 1436-1517
Ds, 4 Sept 1508. (90) £500

Joachim, Abbot of Fiore, 1132-1202 —& Martinus of Troppau, d.1278
Ms, Joachim of Fiore, Vaticinia Pontificum, & Martinus, Cronicon Summorum Pontificum. [Eastern France, Savoy or northwest Italy, c.1450-75]. 57 leaves (4 blank) & 2 modern inserted blanks, vellum, 262mm by 190mm, in 18th-cent sheep. Written in a sloping lettre batarde by 2 scribes. With over 200 large painted initials & 30 almost full-page miniatures of prophetical scenes. (90) £50,000

Joachim Friedrich, Kurfuerst von Brandenburg, 1546-1608
ALs, 5 May 1578. 2 pp, folio. To [Joachim Ernst von Anhalt?]. Requesting the copy of a letter by Wilhelm von Hessen. Schroeder collection. (89) DM2,400

Ls, 24 Aug 1603. 3 pp, folio. To the University at Frankfurt on the Oder. Insisting on the payment of taxes. With related material. (90) DM1,200

Ds, [19 May] 1573. 9 pp, vellum, folio. Confirmation of the city of Magdeburg's sale of the estate at Neu-Gatersleben to Ludolf von Alvensleben. (90) DM1,050

Joachim I, Kurfuerst von Brandenburg, 1484-1535
Letter, [1 Dec 1515]. 1 p, folio. To Markgraf Friedrich V von Ansbach & Bayreuth. Sending the copy of a letter

by the Archbishop of Mainz concerning differences with Nuernberg. Schroeder collection. (89) DM3,200

Joachim II, Kurfuerst von Brandenburg, 1505-71
Ds, [31 Mar] 1559. 1 p, vellum, folio. Authorization for Hermann von Salza to cede his rights at Neuendorf to [the future Elector] Johann Georg von Brandenburg. (90) DM1,500
— [8 Apr] 1562. 1 p, folio; vellum. Investing Franz Sparre with the village of Kerckow. Margins cut. Schroeder collection. (89) DM1,300
— [8 Apr] 1562. 1 p, folio. Grant of feudal rights at Kerckow to Franz Sparre in consideration of a loan of 1,500 talers. (91) DM1,400

Joachim, Joseph, 1831-1907
Autograph music, 2 versions of a cadenza to a concerto in E minor by Pietro Nardini, Dec 1888. (91) £1,000
Collection of ALs & autograph quotation, sgd, 16 Apr 1852 & 1 Nov 1893. Salzer collection. (90) £800
— Collection of ALs & photograph, sgd & inscr, [n.d.]. (90) DM480
— Collection of 14 A Ls s & autograph postcards, sgd, [1886] to 1906. 22 pp, 8vo. To Esther Bright & her mother (1). Mostly about concerts & other musical matters. With related material. (91) £2,400
— Collection of ALs, group photograph, & signature, 30 Jan [1891] to 29 Apr 1903. (89) £300
— Collection of ALs, autograph postcard, sgd, 2 A Ns, & 2 A Ds s, [n.d.]. (90) DM380
Series of 13 A Ls s, 1848 & 1850s. 48 pp, various sizes. To Ferdinand David. Discussing German musical life. (88) £1,500
— Series of 4 A Ls s, [1858-1859]. 8 pp, 8vo. To Amalie Herstatt. About the death of one of his pupils & other matters. (91) DM1,100
ALs, [May 1844]. (89) £900
— [31 Dec 1856]. 11 pp, 4to. To Gisela von Arnim. Love letter, mentioning a performance of a play by [her future husband] Hermann Grimm. (91) DM1,900

— 6 Sept [1869]. (88) DM540
— 1 Oct 1874. 4 pp, 8vo. To [Richard Peyton]. About a proposed commission of a choral work by Brahms for a festival. (90) £1,600
— 1 Aug 1882. (90) DM340
— 26 Aug [n.y.]. (91) DM430
Collection of ANs & AN, [Feb 1905]. (88) DM360
Signature, 12 July 1902. (91) £450
— BRIGHT, ESTHER. - Autograph Ms, travel diaries, 1886 to 1903. Over 600 pp in 4 limp waxed cloth vols, 4to. Reporting about her work with Joachim, her travels, political events, etc. Including related letters. (91) £650
— ORLIK, EMIL. - Orig drawing, charcoal port of Joachim, sgd; 1906. 305mm by 240mm; framed. Also sgd by Joachim. (90) £1,600

Jodl, Alfred, 1890-1946
Ls, 21 Jan 1945. (90) $300

Johann, Archduke, 1782-1859
ALs, 17 Nov 1847. (90) DM550
— [n.d.]. (88) DM420
— 30 Aug 1855. (88) DM500
Ls, 31 July 1805. Schroeder collection. (89) DM260
Ds s (2)7 May 1849. 4 pp, folio. Appointment & orders for Moritz Briegleb as commissioner for Saxony. Countersgd by von Gagern. (91) DM1,400

Johann, King of Saxony, 1801-73
ALs, 19 Oct 1849. (91) DM220

Johann Adolf II, Herzog von Sachsen-Weissenfels, 1685-1746
Ls, 8 Mar 1735. (88) DM260

Johann Albrecht, Herzog von Mecklenburg-Schwerin, 1857-1920. See: Koch, Robert

Johann Albrecht von Brandenburg, Archbishop of Magdeburg, 1499-1550
Document, [27 Aug] 1546. (90) DM500

Johann Friedrich, Herzog von Wuerttemberg, 1582-1628
Ls, 14 Sept 1609. (89) DM850

JOHANN GEORG

Johann Georg, Kurfuerst von Brandenburg, 1525-98
Collection of Ls & 9 letters, 1572 to 1588. 16 pp, folio. To the University at Frankfurt on the Oder. Regarding taxes. (90) DM2,800

Ls, 2 Nov 1590. 2 pp, folio. To Eberhard von Dienheim, Bishop of Speyer, & the judges of the court of appeals at Speyer. Regarding a case pending between the town of Wernigerode & the Margrave of Baden. (90) DM1,500

— 19 Aug 1591. 2 pp, folio. To Queen Elizabeth of England. Concerning her differences with the Hanseatic League. Schroeder collection. (89) DM3,000

Ds, 3 Feb 1561. 2 pp, folio. Permission for an exchange of houses & the establishment of a brewery. (91) DM1,300

Johann Georg I, Kurfuerst von Sachsen, 1585-1656
Ls, 16 Sept 1620. (90) DM260
— 20 Mar 1636. (88) DM420

Johann Georg II, Kurfuerst von Sachsen, 1613-80
Ls, 9 June 1657. (91) DM330

Johann George II, Kurfuerst von Sachsen, 1613-80
Ls, 27 Nov 1650. (91) £500

Johann Salvator, Archduke, 1852-90?
ALs, 3 Jan 1886. (89) DM480

Johann Sigismund, Kurfuerst von Brandenburg, 1572-1619
Ls, 21 Jan 1608. 3 pp, folio. To Johann Georg, [later] Kurfuerst von Sachsen. Asking for a postponement of Daniel von Tettau's wedding. Schroeder collection. (89) DM1,500

— 21 Jan 1608. 3 pp, folio. To Johann Georg, [later] Kurfuerst von Sachsen. Asking for a postponement of Daniel von Tettau's wedding. Schroeder collection. (90) DM1,600

Ds, 5 Dec 1612. 1 p, folio. Cession of the village of Falkenau to Ludwig Rautter as security for a loan. Schroeder collection. (89) DM1,200

Johann von Nassau, Kurfuerst von Mainz, 1360-1419. See: Friedrich I & Johann von Nassau

AMERICAN BOOK PRICES CURRENT

Johann Wilhelm, Kurfuerst von der Pfalz, 1658-1716
Ls, 22 Sept 1695. (88) DM900
— 1 June 1706. (89) DM650

Johannes Chrysostomus, Saint, 345?-407
Ms, De eo quod Nemo Leditur, with De Verborum Copia [by Martin of Braga], here attributed to Seneca. [France, early to mid-15th cent]. 101 leaves, vellum, 126mm by 90mm. English red mor gilt of c.1800. In dark brown ink in a small regular lettre batarde. (88) £2,600

— Ms, Hiermologion, in Church Slavonic. [Balkan Peninsula, 15th cent]. 55 leaves (some lacking), vellum, 275mm by 187mm, disbound. In dark brown ink in a square cyrillic script. With painted initials throughout. Some leaves def. (89) £2,000

— Ms, Homiliae XXI de Statuis ad populum Antiochenum Habitae. (89) £850

— Ms, Opus Imperfectum in Mattheum; fragment of Homilies I - V. (88) £400

Johannes de la Verna
Ms, De gradibus animae. [Italy, c.1350-1400] 65 leaves, laid paper within vellum bifolia, 145mm by 102mm, in modern half vellum. In a humanistic hand in brown ink. (90) $2,400

Johannes de Utino, d.1363
Ms, Compilacio Historiarum Totius Biblie, [Italy, c.1360]. Roll of 11 membranes in concertina form, vellum, 555cm by 42cm. Early 19th-cent purple mor gilt. In brown ink in a small rounded bookhand. With 2 large illuminated initials, 8 large decorative elements in gold & colors & 12 large drawings & diagrams. Probably autograph. (88) £3,200

Johannot, Francois, c.1768-c.1830
ALs, 14 Jan 1794. (90) DM320

John, King of England, 1167?-1216
Ds, [c.1187-88]. 1 p, vellum, 130mm by 177mm. As Earl of Mortain, grant to Bertram de Verdun of land formerly belonging to William Peverell. With seal. (89) £9,500

John, Augustus Edwin, 1878-1961
Collection of 10 A Ls s & A Ns s, & 17 corrected galley proofs, 1958. (90) £1,000

John Climacus, Saint, c.570-649
Ms, Ladder of Paradise, in Church Slavonic. [Russia, early 16th cent]. 167 leaves only, 215mm by 140mm, in def half lea bdg. In a semi-uncial hand. With large miniature. Fekula Ms.741. (91) £2,500

John I, King of Aragon, 1350-95
Ds, 3 Feb 1392. 1 p, vellum, folio. Confirmation of a document of 1390 appointing a Procurador general to Queen Yolanda. In Catalan. (90) £1,200

John II, King of Aragon, 1397?-1479
Collection of 18 Ls s & Ds s, 28 Aug 1461 to 24 Dec 1478. Partly addressed to Pedro de Bach; several relating to the Catalonian Civil War. (90) £4,200

Ds, 26 Oct 1430. (90) £900

John II, King of Castile, 1405-54
Ls, 23 Dec 1449. (88) £300
Ds, 24 Feb 1427. (91) £700
— 12 July 1435. (89) $1,000

John II Casimir Vasa, King of Poland, 1609-72
Ds, 14 Nov 1665. (90) DM700

John of Austria, Don, 1547-78
Ls, 19 Aug 1572. 1 p, folio. To Gabrio Cerbellon. Announcing his intention to join with Marco Antonio Colonna at Corfu to form a united force against the enemies of the Holy League. (91) £2,000

— 16 Sept 1577. 1 p, folio. To Gaspar Schets de Grabbendonck. Discussing conditions for the removal of Spanish troops from Breda & s'Hertogenbosch. In French; sgd Jehan. (90) DM1,600

Ds, 24 Apr 1578. 1 p, folio. To the inhabitants of the Low Countries. Exhorting them to be loyal to King Philip & the Catholic faith. With related material. (90) £1,600
See also: Philip II & John of Austria

John of Austria, the Younger, Don, 1629-79
Ds, 27 Jan 1657. (91) $120

John Paul II, Pope
Ls s (2), [Easter 1970 & 1976]. (90) DM1,000
Photograph, sgd, [n.d.]. (91) $600
Signature, [n.d., c.late 1960s]. (89) $225
— Anr, 31 Jan 1981. (90) DM850

John Paul II, Pope —& Others
Group photograph, 19 Nov 1980. 12.7cm by 17.7cm (image). With the President of the Federal Republic of Germany & Mrs. Carstens; sgd by all 3, on mount. (90) DM1,600

John (XXIII), Antipope, d.1419
Document, [8 May 1413]. 1 p, folio; vellum. Bull addressed to the prior of the Abbey of St. Gregory's near Bologna regarding the transfer of a convent at Pontemaiore. Lacking seal. (90) DM2,100

John XXIII, Pope, 1881-1963
Photograph, sgd, 19 Mar 1962. 23cm by 17.5cm. (88) DM3,200
— Anr, 26 Aug 1962. 24cm by 18cm. (89) DM2,400

Johnson, Andrew, 1808-75
Autograph Ms, "Debt of the State", notes for a speech; [c.1874]. 2 pp, 8vo. In pencil. (91) $2,500

Collection of ALs & Ds, 11 Dec 1857 & 1 Feb 1867. 3 pp, 8vo & 4to. To T. H. Herbert, responding to a request for autobiographical information. Full Power for Edward M. McCook to negotiate a treaty with Hawaii. Sang collection. (91) $9,500

ALs, 22 May 1850. 1 p, 4to. To William M. Lowry. Informing him about efforts to remove him from the postmastership at Greenville. With franking signature. Repaired. (89) $3,000

— 24 May 1850. 1 p, 4to. To William M. Lowry. Hoping that he will be able to defeat John Bell's efforts to remove recipient as postmaster. With autograph postscript on verso. (90) $3,800

— 23 Jan 1858. 2 pp, 4to. To his son-in-law David T. Patterson. On political matters; speaks of the weakness of

JOHNSON

Buchanan & the cockiness of Douglas. (91) $6,000
— 6 Jan 1861. (89) £600
— 19 Jan 1861. (89) $550
— 1 Sept 1864. 2 pp, 8vo. To Schuyler Colfax. Content not given. (91) $1,200
Collection of Ls & Ds, 1 Nov 1866 & 24 Aug 1865. 3 pp, 4to. To Sec of War Edmund M. Stanton, instructing him to take measures to protect Washington in case of an insurrection; endorsed by Stanton. Appointment for Thomas Feran as Customs Commissioner ad interim. Pratt collection. (89) $13,000
Ls, 24 Nov 1864. (91) $750
— 7 Sept 1865. 1 p, 4to. To Sec of War Stanton. About revoking part of an order. (91) $1,700
— 2 July 1866. Whiton collection. (88) $750
— 30 Aug 1866. (90) $600
— 13 June 1868. 1 p, 4to. To Customs Collector H. A. Smythe. Recommending S. W. Harned for a "suitable situation". (90) $2,500
— 25 July 1868. (90) $800
— 21 Oct 1868. Rosenbloom collection. (88) $950
ANs, 19 Jan 1861. (90) $650
Collection of Ds & document, 20 Apr 1865 & 9 Apr 1866. (89) $750
Ds s (2)7 July 1865 & 26 Dec 1868. Doheny collection. (89) $850
Ds, 1 May 1854. (88) $300
— 31 July 1865. 3 pp, folio. Pardon warrant for B. P. Noland. Countersgd by Sec of State Seward. (91) $2,750
— 17 Aug 1865. (90) $1,000
— 11 Nov 1865. 1 p, folio, vellum. Address to the Blackfoot Chief Wa ma de k'tu, presenting 2 warriors with money & medals for rescuing 2 white women. With borders of red, white & blue ribbon. Waterstained. Ruddy collection. (88) $11,000
— 2 Dec 1865. (88) $375
— 15 Jan 1866. 1 p, folio. Appointment for Richard H. Dana as district attorney. Doheny collection. (89) $1,700
— 26 Jan 1866. (89) £420
— 3 Nov 1866. (89) $360
— 20 Nov 1866. (91) $900
— 28 Dec 1866. (88) $325
— 18 Mar 1867. (91) $450
— 15 Apr 1867. (91) $750
— 7 June 1866. (89) $400
Document, 25 Aug 1865. (90) $220
— 16 July 1866. (91) $160
Autograph endorsement, initialled, at bottom of an appointment of a Collector, 18 June 1868. (89) $180
Cut signature, [n.d.]. (91) $170
— Anr, [n.d.]. (91) $140
— Anr, [n.d.]. (90) $300
Franking signature, [n.d.]. (90) $300
— Anr, [25 Mar 1861]. Alexander collection. (90) $300
— Anr, [1861-62]. (91) $500
— Anr, [25 Mar n.y.]. (90) $325
— Anr, [26 Sept n.y.]. (91) $400
— Anr, [n.d.]. (89) $900
— Anr, [n.d.]. (89) $200
Photograph, sgd, [n.d.]. 101mm by 62mm. By Giers, with handcolored details. Sgd on verso. (90) $1,300
— Anr, [n.d.]. Carte size. By Gardner. (90) $2,200
Signature, 14 May 1868. (88) $210
— Anr, 26 Mar 1873. (90) $190
— Anr, [n.d.]. (91) $190
— Anr, [n.d.]. (90) $170

Johnson, Lady Bird. See: Johnson, Lyndon B. & Johnson

Johnson, Lionel, 1867-1902
Autograph Ms, poem, Hawker of Marwenstow, sgd & dated 1895. (88) £800
— Autograph Ms, poem, Hawthorne, initialled, 1889; with autograph orison written below, 1893. (91) £500
See also: Beardsley, Aubrey

Johnson, Lyndon B., 1908-73
Collection of Ls & 2 letters, 11 Oct 1961 to 8 Dec 1964. 3 pp, 4to. To Barry Goldwater, acknowledging a message of support. To Peter Hurd, expressing thanks. To Holmes Alexander, sending a memento of the 1964 campaign. Letters with autopen or secretarial signatures. Pratt collection. (89) $5,500
— Collection of Ls & photograph, sgd, 5 Oct 1966 & 14 Feb [19]69. 1 p, 4to, & size not stated. To George Jessel.

Commenting on an article about "American men of Jewish faith ... fighting ...on the battlefields in Vietnam". Framed. (90) $2,200
Ls s (2), 12 Apr 1956 & 14 Aug 1958. (90) $380
Ls, 13 Feb 1948. (91) $160
— 20 Apr 1949. (91) $150
— 8 May 1950. (91) $150
— 6 Apr 1954. (88) $70
— 23 June 1956. (91) $130
— 11 Nov 1957. (88) $80
— 30 July 1958. (91) $110
— 3 Jan 1959. (91) $110
— 13 July 1959. (91) $160
— 24 May 1960. (91) $200
— 7 July 1960. (91) $150
— 13 Nov 1960. (91) $120
— 15 Oct 1965. (88) $225
— 18 Sept 1967. 1 p, 8vo. To Mark Van Doren. Praising his eulogy at Carl Sandburg's memorial service. With related material. (90) $1,100
— 3 Apr 1968. (91) $850
— 24 June 1970. 3 pp, 4to. To Gen. Earle G. Wheeler. Requesting information about a plan for "Vietnamization" of the war supposedly submitted in 1968. (90) $2,500
ANs, [12 Oct 1965]. 1 p, 16mo (card). To Ernest [Gruening]. Hoping he is "doing well" [after an operation]. (91) $2,000
Ds, 22 Dec 1963. 2 pp, folio. Pardon issued to Theodore James Dvorak. Countersgd by Robert Kennedy. (91) $6,500
Group photograph, [1 Oct 1965]. (89) $325
— Anr, [n.d.]. (88) $110
— Anr, [n.d.]. (91) $100
— Anr, [n.d.]. 4to. Walking with Dean Acheson & others. Sgd by Johnson & inscr to Acheson. Framed. (89) $1,200
Photograph, sgd, [c.1968]. (89) $350
Photograph, sgd & inscr, [c.1952]. (89) $325
— Anr, [n.d.]. (90) $65
— Anr, [n.d.]. (88) $425
Ptd photograph, [n.d.]. (91) $110
Signature, 8 Dec 1966, on postal cover with ptd announcement regarding agreement to bar nuclear weapons from outer space, with small port pasted on; sgd twice. (89) $180
— Anr, [n.d.]. (91) $170

Johnson, Lyndon B., 1908-73 —& Johnson, Lady Bird
Photograph, sgd & inscr, on White House balcony on their daughter's wedding day. (88) $325

Johnson, Samuel, 1709-84
Autograph Ms, definition of the verb "to gain", 6 lines; [n.d.]. 1 p, 12mo. Repaired. Barrett collection. (89) $6,000
ALs, 9 Dec 1782. 2 pp, 4to. To the Rev. Dr. John Taylor. Discussing recipient's health. Repaired. (89) $6,000
— 2 Nov 1784. 1 p, 4to. To Mrs. White. Instructing her to request 3 guineas from Mr. Strahan. (91) £5,200
— BLICK, FRANCIS. - ALs, 22 July 1770. 1 p, folio. To Stephen Simpson. Referring to a message given to Johnson. (88) £360
— TROTTER, THOMAS. - Orig drawing, chalk port of Johnson at an advanced age, seated, wearing a full wig, [c.1782]. 12.75 by 10 inches. Almost certainly the original of an etching 1st pbd in 1786. (88) £6,500

Johnson, Uwe, 1934-84
Autograph Ms, excerpts from Luebecker General-Anzeiger, 1 to 20 Jan 1931. (89) DM650
Typescript, contribution to Die Zeit, dealing with people he meets in his daily activities; 22 Apr 1980. 2 pp, folio. With autograph corrections; sgd at head. Including related Ls, 12 June 1980. (91) DM1,600
— Typescript, essay for the magazine Die Zeit, 22 Apr 1980. 2 pp, folio. With autograph revisions; sgd at head. With Ls, 12 June 1980, 1 p, 4to. (88) DM1,300
— Typescript, response to a poll taken by Westermanns Monatshefte, fragment; [1961]. (90) DM380
Ls, 27 Sept 1963. (90) DM260
— 17 Feb 1967. (91) DM320
— 14 July 1972. (90) DM240
— 3 Mar 1977. (90) DM380
Corrected galley proof, Gespraeche ueber Jerichow, from Neue Rundschau 1972.

(89) DM340

Johnson, Walter Perry, 1887-1946

ALs, 14 Sept 1942. 1 p, size not stated. To Harry Ruby. Mentioning the World Series & hoping to see him. (88) $1,600

Collection of Ls & 2 photographs, sgd & inscr, 22 Apr 1925, 14 June 1931 & [n.d.]. 1 p, 4to; 12mo & 4to. Recipient & contents not stated. (89) $1,150

Signature, [1937]. (89) $950

Johnston, Albert Sidney, 1803-62

ALs, 4 June 1839. (88) $875

Ls, 26 Sept 1828. Alexander collection. (90) $575

Johnston, Harriet Lane, 1830-1903

ALs, 5 May 1857. (90) $160

Johnston, Joseph E., 1807-91

ALs, 6 Oct 1855. Alexander collection. (90) $260

Ds, 13 Jan 1866. (90) $110

Signature, [n.d.]. (91) $110

Telegram, 15 July [n.y.]. (91) $650

Johst, Hanns, 1890-1978

Collection of 29 A Ls s & Ls, 3 Mar 1949 to 19 June 1957. 64 pp, folio & 8vo. To Georg Wiessner. Interesting letters regarding his denazification, post-war Germany, & his literary work. With numerous carbon copies of Wiessner's replies. (88) DM1,400

Joliot-Curie, Frederic, 1900-58

Autograph Ms, draft of a ficticious interview, [ptd 21 Jan 1955]. 4 pp, 4to. Sgd in text. With ptd version. (91) DM1,450

Joliot-Curie, Irene, 1897-1956

ALs, 18 Nov 1942. (91) DM1,000

Jolly, Philipp von, 1809-84

Series of 4 A Ls s, 19 Apr 1852 to 28 Dec 1860. (91) DM580

Jones, Allen

ALs, [31 Mar 1970]. (90) DM400

Jones, Anson, 1798-1858

Ds, 10 Feb 1846. (89) $260

Jones, David

Original drawings, (26), to illus The Town Child's Alphabet. Various sizes, ink & wash, all captioned & many sgd. Lacking the letter C. With related material. (88) £15,000

Jones, David, 1895-1974

Series of 8 A Ls s, 29 Sept 1962 to 14 Nov 1964. 20 pp, folio. To Walter Shewring. About Desmund Chute & other members of the Ditchling community. (90) $2,200

Proof copy, In Parenthesis, dated 10 June 1937 on upper cover. (88) £520

Jones, John Paul, 1747-92

ALs, [13 Sept 1778]. 1 p, 4to [removed from larger leaf?]. To the French Minister of Marine, Sartine. Fragment, congratulating him on the successes of French ships & hoping that his projects will be adopted. Munson collection. (90) $9,500

— 26 Apr 1783. 3 pp, 4to. To Hector McNeil. Reporting about his voyage to the West Indies with the French fleet. (90) $18,000

Ds, 30 Oct 1777. 2 pp, folio. Power of attorney for Robert Morris & Joseph Hewes to manage his money from the sale of prizes. Munson collection. (90) $9,000

Document, 10 May 1776. 1 p, 73mm by 210mm. Appointment of Jones as Captain of the sloop Providence. In the hand of Samuel Lyon. (90) $3,600

Jones, Robert T. ("Bobby"), 1902-71

Ls, 27 Jan 1954. 1 p, 4to. To Totton P. Heffelfinger. Expressing satisfaction about "the creation of the Jones Award by the U.S.G.A." (91) $1,200

Photograph, sgd, 8 Oct 1930. (89) $525

Photograph, sgd & inscr, [1930s]. 7.5 by 9.5 inches. In golf outfit; inscr to Walter Schwimmer. (91) $1,400

Jones, William, 1760-1831

Ls, 29 Jan 1813. Alexander collection. (90) $170

Jordan, Charles Etienne, 1700-45
ALs, 12 Nov 1731. Schroeder collection. (89) DM300

Jordan, Dorothy, 1762-1816
ALs, [c.1812]. (88) £480

Jordan, Thomas, 1819-95
ALs, 24 Oct 1861. (89) $250
— 19 Dec 1862. (91) $325

Joseph, Chief of the Nez Perce Indians, c.1840-1904
Letter, [n.d.]. (88) $260

Joseph I, Emperor, 1678-1711
ALs, [Aug 1691]. 4 pp, 4to. To Herr Ayo. Rejoicing about the victorious battle against the Turks at Slankamen. (90) DM4,000
Ls, 15 Oct 1702. 2 pp, folio. To Markgraf Ludwig Wilhelm von Baden. About recipient's victory at Landau. (91) DM1,400
— 20 Oct 1706. (89) DM280
— 24 Apr 1709. (91) DM440
— 11 May 1709. (89) $280
Ds, 11 June 1707. (88) DM750
— 5 Mar 1708. 10 pp, 4to; vellum. Grant of privileges to the merchants at Breslau. (89) DM1,500

Joseph II, Emperor, 1741-90
Collection of 9 A Ls s & 18 Ls s, 5 May 1774 to 22 Apr 1784 & [n.d.]. 40 pp, 4to. To Ernst Gideon von Laudon. Important letters requesting advice & discussing a variety of military matters. 4 Ls s with autograph postscripts. (90) DM15,000
ALs, [c.1751?]. 1 p, 4to. To his mother, Empress Maria Theresa. Informing her that he paid good attention to the sermon & that his cough is better. In French, with postscript in German. Salzer collection. (90) £2,000
— 11 Mar 1767. 1 p, 4to. To a brother of Herzog Karl Eugen von Wuerttemberg. Promising to look into the case between the estates & the Duke of Wuerttemberg pending at the Imperial Court of Justice in Vienna. In French. (88) DM1,250
— 25 Sept 1768. (90) £520
— 24 May 1770. 2 pp, 4to. To Count Esterhazy. Complaining angrily about roads in Hungary & ordering repairs. (89) DM3,800
— 1 Jan 1777. (90) DM650
— [n.d.]. 1 p, 4to. Recipient unnamed. About financial problems. Margins cut; repaired. With engraved port. (90) DM1,050
Ls, 19 Aug 1765. (91) DM700
— 19 Aug 1765. (90) DM800
— 31 July 1766. (89) DM270
— 12 Mar 1767. (89) DM300
— 12 Mar 1767. (90) DM250
— 7 Aug 1769. (91) DM520
— 24 Mar 1770. (90) DM470
— 11 May 1771. (91) DM270
— 6 Jan 1773. (88) DM220
— 19 May 1779. (91) DM580
— 26 Mar 1780. 1 p, 4to. To Franz Anton von Khevenhueller. Requesting a report (included, 10 pp, with 11-line endorsement, sgd, by Joseph II) about a tax levied for a death certificate. (91) DM1,100
— 9 May 1785. Salzer collection. (90) £350
— 22 Jan 1787. (89) DM260
— 2 Aug 1788. (88) DM550
— 16 Jan 1790. Schroeder collection. (89) DM300
Ds, 7 June 1776. (89) DM1,000
— 23 Aug 1780. (89) DM900
— 30 May 1787. (91) DM320
— 12 Sept 1787. (91) DM340
— 14 Mar 1789. 13 pp, folio, in red velvet bdg. Patent of nobility & grant of arms for Johann Heinrich Bartholomaei. With full-page painting of the arms in gold & colors & large seal in brass box gilt. (90) DM1,900
— 3 Jan 1790. 10 leaves, 36cm by 25.5cm, in orig red velvet bdg. Patent of nobility & grant of arms for Vincenz Ignatz von Seydel & his wife Maria Barbara von Prosky. Including 2 full-page paintings of the arms & seal in brass case. (90) DM2,800

Autograph endorsement, sgd, on a petition by Johann Baptist von Puthon for the privilege of the foreign mercury trade, 19 Aug 1788, 2 pp, folio; ordering Count Kollowrat to report on the matter. (90) DM320

Josephine, Empress of the French, 1763-1814

ALs, [30 Nov 1796]. 1 p, 4to. To Barras. Letter of recommendation for Julien de la Drome. Repaired. (90) DM2,700
— [before 1799]. (89) £750
— [before 1799]. (91) £1,000
— 15 Dec [1806]. 2 pp, 4to. To Marshal Berthier. Expressing her anxiety for Napoleon during the current campaign & sending petitions. (91) £2,400
— 5 Feb [n.y.]. 1 p, 4to. To the Minister of Commerce. Recommending 2 merchants. (89) DM2,200
— 14 June [n.y.]. (91) £720
— [n.d.]. (88) $650
Ls, [1 Apr 1800]. (88) $550
— [29 Apr 1800]. 1 p, 4to. To an unnamed prefect. Requesting him to find a position for Citoyen Mouviel. Sgd Lapagerie Bonaparte. Mtd. (88) DM1,650
— [7 Jan 1801]. (89) £400
— [16 Mar 1804]. 1 p, folio. To Gen. Brune. Urging him to provide plants from the Levant for her garden at Malmaison. (91) £7,000
— 10 June 1809. 1 p, 4to. To [Comte Daru]. Thanking for his efforts to find rare plants for Malmaison, & suggesting he procure some kangaroos. (90) DM2,200
— [n.d.]. 1 p, 4to. To Gen. [Lefebvre]. Accepting his offer of some magnolias. (91) £1,100
Ds, 29 Jan 1811. (90) £800
— 22 Oct 1811. Doheny collection. (88) $750
Endorsement, sgd, 14 Nov 1810. (91) £850

Jouhandeau, Marcel, 1888-1979
Collection of ALs & autograph Ms, 9 Sept 1968 & [n.d.]. (90) DM250

Jourdan, Jean Baptiste de, 1762-1833
ALs, [11 Oct 1794]. 2 pp, folio. To Gen. Marceau. Giving instructions to send a detachment of troops to Gerolstein. Including autograph postscript. (90) DM1,700
— 30 July 1825. (90) DM240
Ls, [11 Oct 1795]. 1 p, folio. To Gen. Lefebvre. On the day of his defeat at Hoechst, giving orders for the destruction of bridges. With autograph postscript, 6 words. With elaborate engraved vignette on letterhead showing a montgolfier with the tricolor above a battlefield. (88) DM1,900

Joyce, James, 1882-1941
[Ogden, C. K. - A collection of 12 letters & postcard addressed to him, 1930 & 1931, mostly pertaining to Joyce's Anna Livia Plurabelle, including 2 letters & postcard written on behalf of James Joyce by Lucia Joyce & Georges Borach, sold at CNY on 20 May 1988, lot 317, for $1,200.]
[The mimeographed script of the screenplay for the Walter Reade, Jr. & Joseph Strick film Ulysses, 1967, 145 pp, 4to, with the script for the BBC program Portrait of James Joyce, Feb 1950, 78 pp, folio, & material relating to the film, sold at CNY on 20 May 1988, lot 321, for $1,600.]
Autograph Ms, Greek song & Irish song, both with English trans, [1918/19]. 3 pp, 4to. Including list of Greek words with English trans, the address of The Egoist, etc. (91) £7,500
— Autograph Ms, poem, G. O'Donnell, [1898]. 12 lines, in pencil, written on blank preliminary page of P. W. Joyce, A Concise History of Ireland. Dublin, 1894. 3d Ed, 12mo, in orig dark green cloth in half-mor slipcase. With related material. Halliday collection. (88) $28,000
Typescript, "Riverrun", opening episode of Finegan's Wake, sgd & dated 16 Dec 1926. 28 pp, 4to, on rectos only; interleaved, in green mor gilt. With numerous autograph revisions in ink & pencil; 1 addition in Harriet Shaw Weaver's hand. With autograph envelope addressed to Miss Weaver. The Garden Ltd. collection. (90) $90,000
Collection of 2 A Ls s & autograph postcard, sgd, 17 Jan to 7 Oct 1907. 2 pp, 8vo & folio, & card. To Elkin Mathews. Discussing the publication of Chamber Music & Dubliners. (89) £7,500
A Ls s (2), 17 Jan 1921 & 10 Feb 1922. 2 pp, 4to. To Maurice Martin du Gard. Discussing Helene du Pasquier's French trans of Araby, from Dubliners. Requesting anr copy of a trans of Eveline, from Dubliners. In French.

Halliday collection. (88) $3,500

ALs, 25 Apr 1917. 1 p, 4to. To Solomon Eagle. Thanking for a favorable review in The New Statesman. Repaired. Bradley Martin sale. (90) $5,000

— 17 May 1931. 1 p, 12mo. To C. K. Ogden. Suggesting G. B. Shaw may "be in just the right mood for trumpeting your scheme." Halliday collection. (88) $2,500

— 13 July 1931. 2 pp, 12mo. To C. K. Ogden. Requesting that copies of the Anna Livia Plurabelle recording be sent to John Dulany & Robert Lynd. Halliday collection. (88) $2,800

— 13 Oct 1931. Halliday collection. (88) $650

— 17 Oct 1931. 2 pp, 8vo. To C. K. Ogden. Returning notes on Ogden's trans of Anna Livia Plurabelle into Basic English. Halliday collection. (88) $3,200

— 23 Nov 1931. 1 p, 12mo. To C. K. Ogden. Informing him about a planned radio talk about him by Harold Nicholson. Halliday collection. (88) $1,600

— [May 1937]. 2 pp, 4to. To Carola Giedion-Welker. Hoping that his brother will be given permission to settle in Switzerland. (88) DM5,500

— 19 Jan 1940. 2pp, 8vo. To Padraic Colum. Asking him to see J. F. Byrnes & find out if his book has any merit. Halliday collection. (88) $4,200

Ls, 4 Feb 1930. 4 pp, 8vo. To C. K. Ogden. Strongly recommending John Sullivan as "the greatest dramatic tenor on the operatic stage". Halliday collection. (88) $3,200

Collection of autograph postcard, sgd, signature, & autograph envelope, 30 Dec [19]35 & [n.d.]. To [Lillian] Wallace, sending New Year's wishes. Endorsement on cheque made out to him by Lilian Wallace, 9 Aug 1935. Envelope addressed to Mrs. Wallace. Halliday collection. (88) $1,550

Autograph postcard, sgd, 10 Feb 1916. To Allan Wade. Informing him that his agent in London will give him the typescript of his play Exiles. Halliday collection. (88) $2,200

— 31 May 1933. Halliday collection. (88) $550

— [mid-1930s?]. Halliday collection. (88) $600

— 12 Aug 1937. Halliday collection. (88) $550

— [c.Oct 1937]. Halliday collection. (88) $650

Christmas card, [c.1930?]. Halliday collection. (88) $800

Corrected page proofs, Tales Told of Shem and Shaun: Three Fragments from Work in Progress. Paris, The Black Sun Press, 1929. 44 pp, 8vo & 4to. Corrections probably in the hand of Caresse Crosby. With 4 pp of pencilled notes by [C. K. Ogden?] for the preface, & a copy of the book. Halliday collection. (88) $28,000

Photograph, sgd & inscr, July 1933. Postcard size. "Taken by my wife/J.J." (91) $1,600

Photograph, 1927. 330mm by 255mm. Seated with hat & cane. Sgd by photographer Berenice Abbott, in pencil. Image scraped at edges; laid down. Halliday collection. (88) $2,200

Signature, on picture postcard, sgd & written by his wife Nora & daughter Lucia, 14 Apr 1931, to John Sullivan & his wife. Halliday collection. (88) $2,500

Telegram, 23 Dec 1929. Halliday collection. (88) $420

— ELIOT, THOMAS STEARNS. - Ls & autograph postcard, sgd, 30 June 1930 & 17 July 1931. 2 pp, 4to & 12mo. To C. K. Ogden. Requesting a copy of the record of Joyce reading from Anna Livia Plurabelle. Expressing his wish to talk to him about Anna Livia Plurabelle. Halliday collection. (88) $2,500

— MOZLEY, CHARLES. - 4 orig drawings, sgd, illustrating Ulysses, [n.d.]. 13 by 14 inches & 19 by 13 inches (3). In pencil (1) or ink. Pbd in John Ryder's Six on the Black Art. L, [1961]. Framed. With copy of the book, sgd; 1 of 400. Halliday collection. (88) $1,600

— SEARLE, HUMPHREY. - Autograph music, setting for voice & piano of Joyce's poem Goldenhair, from Chamber Music; sgd & dated 1935. 2 pp, 4to. 34 bars on 6 staves, with holograph tp. Halliday collection. (88) $160

— WEAVER, HARRIET. - Ls, 9 May 1921. 1

p, 4to. To James B. Pinker. Explaining difficulties concerning the publication of Ulysses. With related material. Halliday collection. (88) $2,800

Juana, Queen of Spain, 1479-1555. See: Charles V & Juana

Juana, Princess, daughter of Emperor Charles V, 1535-73

Ds s (2) 16 May 1556 & 8 Oct 1557. (90) £600

Juarez, Benito, 1806-72

Ls, 22 Apr 1863. 1 p, 4to. To Dr. Plumb. Commenting on "the triumphs of Mexican arms over the unjust invader". Encapsulated. (91) $2,400

— 1 May 1867. 1 p, 4to. To C. Sturm. Reminding him that his is the legitimate government of Mexico, with reference to Pavon's order for munitions. (91) $1,600

Juenger, Ernst

[A collection of 5 offprints, sgd, 4 with autograph inscr, 1947 to 1964, sold at star on 9 Mar 1988, lot 195, for DM1,000.]

Autograph Ms, travel account, Serpentara, 10 Mar to 19 Apr 1956. 36 pp, 4to, in folder. Including revisions. Sgd EJ on tp. (91) DM7,000

Collection of ALs, 11 Ls s, & 9 postcards, sgd (5 autograph), 26 Dec 1946 to 23 Sept 1948. 16 pp, 4to & 8vo, & cards. To Manfred Michler. Discussing the reception of his works. With related material. (89) DM3,400

— Collection of 2 A Ls s & 3 autograph postcards, sgd, 21 Feb 1948 to 18 Dec 1967. 3 pp, folio & 4to, & cards. To Manfred Michler. Regarding contributions to the journal Die Aussprache. With related material. (88) DM1,100

Juliana, Queen of The Netherlands

ALs, 10 Apr 1924. 3 pp, 8vo. To [a Princess of Erbach-Schoenberg?]. Reminiscing about time spent together; including 2 drawings. Sgd Juechen. In German. (90) DM1,400

Julius Echter von Mespelbrunn, Fuerstbischof zu Wuerzburg, 1545-1617 —& Grumbach, Conrad von

[An important exchange of letters, 10 Ls by Bishop Julius, 5 A Ls s by Grumbach & 1 related letter, 8 Oct 1582 to 10 June 1586, 22 pp, regarding the hiring of a Protestant preacher by Grumbach sold at HK on 3 Nov, lot 8, for DM2,400.]

Julius II, Pope, 1443-1513. See: Alexander VI & Julius II

Julius II, Pope, 1443-1513 —& Leo X, Pope, 1475-1521

Document, 26 July 1517. 1 p, 275mm by 190mm, vellum. Indulgence to raise money for St. Peter's basilica in Rome, offered by Julius II & renewed by Leo X; bought by Juhan Ferera. Ptd with Ms accomplishment; in Catalan. With woodcut initial; 5 holes affecting text. Framed. Doheny collection. (89) $8,500

Jung, Carl Gustav, 1875-1961

ALs, 5 Sept 1927. 3 pp, 4to. To Miss Morrison. Responding to an inquiry about the sexuality of a woman known to recipient. (91) $10,000

— 8 Apr 1952. 1 p, 4to. To Dr. J. Smythies. Expressing his perplexity in the face of extra-sensory phenomena. (90) £1,400

Collection of Ls & photograph, sgd, 24 Jan 1950 & [n.d.]. 1 p, 8vo, & size not stated. To Harriet Hardy. Giving general advice about how to find happiness. In English. Framed together. (90) $2,000

Ls, 3 May 1935. (90) DM860

— 12 Nov 1937. (91) $550

— 5 Dec 1951. 1 p, 4to. To Dr. J. Smythies. Describing his approach to the phenomenon of Synchronicity. (90) £1,400

— 29 Feb 1952. 4 pp, folio. To Dr. J. Smythies. Containing an essay on his psychical researches in the context of Einsteinian physics. Some autograph additions. (90) £2,800

Jung-Stilling, Johann Heinrich, 1740-1817
Original drawings, (2), sketch of the route from Heidelberg to Speyer, & plan of Speyer, drawn for Friedrich Matthisson, [Oct 1785]. (91) DM850

ALs, 14 Mar 1792. (91) DM1,000

— 25 Feb 1805. 1 p, 4to. To the Ed of the journal Der Freimuethige. Demanding the publication of his refutation of an insulting article. Albrecht collection. (91) SF2,000

Junkers, Hugo, 1859-1935
Ls, 29 Apr 1931. (90) DM280

Jury, Sir William, 1870-1944
[A collection of A Ls s, Ls s, & other items related to Sir William Jury's projects in the early days of the British film industry, c.1909 to 1927, c.300 items, 490 pp, sold at C on 9 Dec, lot 358, for £750 to the British Film Institute.]

Justi, Karl, 1832-1912
ALs, 13 Feb 1885. (90) DM240

Justinianus I, Emperor, 483-565
Ms, Institutiones, & Constitutiones. [Italy?, 2d half of 14th cent]. 172 leaves, vellum, 160mm by 115mm, in 18th-cent bdg. In a gothic textura. With 2 penwork initials. (90) DM12,000

Justinus, Marcus Junianus, fl.3d cent
Ms, Epitome delle Istorie Filippiche di Pompeo Trogo, in Italian. [Lombardy?, c.1470-90]. 97 leaves, vellum, 252mm by 170mm. Early 19th-cent English russia gilt bdg by Charles Lewis. In a regular humanistic cursive bookhand by Baldassare de Vigevano. With historiated initial & full historiated border. Phillipps Ms.3353. (91) £10,000

Juvenalis, Decimus Junius, 60-140
Ms, Satires. [Bologna or Ferrara, 1453]. 66 leaves (2 lacking), vellum, 250mm by 177mm. Early 19th-cent red mor gilt bdg. In a regular sloping humanistic minuscule. With 11 small whitevine initials & 4 very large initials with full historiated borders. (91) £80,000

K

Kabalevsky, Dimitri Borisovich
Collection of A Ls s, 3 Ls s, & photograph, sgd & inscr, 29 Apr 1951 to 8 Dec 1964. 5 pp, various sizes, & postcard. To Pavel & Eva Eckstein. Mentioning his works & projects. (91) DM1,400

Ls, 30 July 1957. (88) DM450

Kaestner, Abraham Gotthelf, 1719-1800
ALs, 2 Sept 1785. (91) DM320

Kaestner, Erich, 1899-1974
Ls, 7 Jan 1933. (90) DM290

Kafka, Franz, 1883-1924
Autograph Ms, novel, Der Prozess, including unfinished chapters ("Fragments"), [late July to late Dec 1914]. 316 pp, 4to, removed from exercise books. Working Ms, with numbering supplied by Max Brod. Including some typescript material. (89) £1,000,000

ALs, 14 July 1917. 1 p, 4to. To Rudolf Fuchs. Announcing his visit to Vienna. (88) £2,600

— [Dec 1917]. (88) £160

— [late Mar 1918]. 6 pp, 8vo. To Max Brod. About the performance of Brod's play in Dresden, the publication of his own short stories, & religious & philosophical concepts. (90) $9,000

— [n.d.]. 1 p, 8vo. To Johann Urzidil. Explaining he is unable to contribute to a journal at present. In tan goatskin folder. (88) £1,400

— [June 1921]. 7 pp, 8vo. To Robert Klopstock. Describing the state of his health, & discussing Kierkegaard. Sgd K. (90) $6,000

— [c.Oct 1921?]. 1 p, 8vo. To Ludwig Hardt. Regretting fever will prevent his attending a lecture. With a letter from Hardt to Imeken Gotzmann on verso. (90) DM13,000

Ls, [summer 1917]. (88) £900

Autograph postcard, sgd, 18 Aug 1917. To Rudolf Fuchs. Apologizing for the delay in forwarding his poems [to Buber?]. (88) £1,800

Corrected page proofs, collection of short stories, Ein Landarzt, 1919. Over 200 pp, 8vo & 4to. With numerous corrections in Kafka's, & some notations in anr hand. (90) $22,000

Kainz, Josef, 1858-1910
Autograph Ms, Leitfaden fuer Rollenstudium, [n.d.]. (89) DM200
A Ls s (2), 7 Mar 1900 & 8 Jan 1902. (89) DM440
ALs, 6 Dec 1892. (88) DM320

Kaiser, Georg, 1878-1945
Collection of 4 A Ls s & 23 Ls s, 29 Jan to 24 Nov 1941. 40 pp, mostly folio. To Paul Gordon. Describing his literary work, his difficult situation, & hoping for money to emigrate to New York. 3 letters in duplicate. With 6 telegrams. (88) DM1,300

Kalakaua, King of the Hawaiian Islands, 1836-91
ANs, [n.d.]. (88) $150

Kalb, Johann, 1721-80
ALs, 5 May 1779. 2 pp, 4to. To Mrs. Greaton. Asking for his servant to join him. (89) $1,600

Kalckreuth, Friedrich Adolf, Graf von, 1737-1818
ALs, 31 Jan 1806. (90) DM380
— 29 Aug 1815. (90) DM360

Kalkbrenner, Friedrich Wilhelm, 1788-1849. See: Beethoven, Ludwig van

Kalliwoda, Johann Wenzel, 1801-66
ALs, 18 Oct 1831. (89) DM550
— 3 Mar 1851. 3 pp, 4to. To the pbr Karl Boehme. Reporting about his life in retirement. (90) DM1,200

Kaltenbrunner, Ernst, 1903-46
Ls, 12 Oct 1944. (90) $500

Kaminski, Heinrich, 1886-1946
ALs, 10 May 1916. (88) DM280

Kandinsky, Wasily, 1866-1944
[A postcard, sgd, 23 May 1933, to the publishing house of Albert Langen, requesting information about a book, sold at star on 4 Oct 1989, lot 672, for DM440.]
A Ls s (2), 19 May & 23 June 1925. 2 pp, 4to. To the Ed of the journal Artwork. Regarding photographs of his works.

(88) DM1,750
ALs, [n.d.]. 2 pp, 4to. To [Leopold Graf von Kalckreuth]. Objecting to the election of Franz von Stuck as Vice President of the Deutscher Kuenstlerbund. (90) DM1,100
Autograph postcard, sgd, 18 Aug 1924. (89) DM650
— 30 Jan 1928. (90) DM650

Kanoldt, Alexander, 1881-1939
ALs, 6 Dec 1925. 6 pp, folio. To Franz Roh. Recommending Alexander Koch as pbr, & complaining about Oskar Moll, Otto Mueller, & the academy at Breslau. (90) DM2,400
— 5 Apr 1927. 6 pp, folio. To Franz Roh. Discussing his own work & a number of colleagues, expressing uneasiness with the Bauhaus, etc. (90) DM3,300

Kant, Immanuel, 1724-1804
ALs, 25 June 1787. 1 p, 4to. To Christian Gottfried Schuetz. About a mistake in a reference in the 2d Ed of the Critique of Pure Reason, & reporting about his work on the Critique of Practical Reason. (89) £7,000
— [after 1 Mar 1789]. 3 pp, 4to. To Jung-Stilling. Outlining the principles of a philosophy of law based on his Critik der Vernunft. (89) DM28,000
— 27 June 1799. 2 pp, 4to. Recipient unknown. Mostly about his health, & regarding a loan to his friend. (88) $6,500
— 28 Oct 1800. 1 p, 4to. To Christian Friedrich Jensch. Inquiring about a delivery of small turnips. Including recipient's answer at bottom, & autograph notes by Kant on verso. (90) DM8,500
ADs, 6 Sept 1795. 1 p, 8vo. Extension of terms of payment for a lecture fee due from the student Richter. (91) DM4,400
— 31 Oct 1800. 1 p, 4to. Receipt for 100 talers from Robert Motherby. (91) DM3,800

Kapodistrias, Ioannis Antonios, Count, 1776-1831
Ls, 5/17 Aug 1828. (88) DM350
— 1/13 May 1829. (90) DM420
Ds, 21 Aug/2 Sept 1828. (89) DM500

Karajan, Herbert von, 1908-89
Series of 3 A Ls s, 1955. 19 pp, folio & 8vo. To Mary Roblee. Expressing his love for her, his loneliness in America, describing his childhood, etc. (90) £6,500
A Ls s (2), 31 Jan 1947 & [June 1947?]. (88) DM950
ALs, [n.d.]. (90) DM950

Karamzin, Nikolai Mikhailovich, 1766-1826
ALs, 10 Mar 1814. (91) DM550

Karg-Elert, Sigfrid
Autograph music, organ work, Triptych (Op. (89) £380

Karl, Markgraf von Burgau, 1560-1618
Ls, 14 Apr 1615. (90) DM220

Karl, Archduke of Austria, 1771-1847
Ls, 6 June 1797. (88) DM380
— 27 Oct 1797. (90) DM380
— 24 June 1801. (91) DM210
— 30 May 1809. (91) DM480

Karl, Grossherzog von Baden, 1786-1818
Ls, 29 Sept 1812. 1 p, folio. Recipient unnamed. Announcing the birth of a son. (89) DM1,400

Karl, Prince of Prussia, 1801-83
Photograph, sgd & inscr, Sept 1872. Schroeder collection. (89) DM400

Karl, King of Wuerttemberg, 1823-91
ALs, 1 Feb 1874. (90) DM600

Karl Alexander, Grossherzog von Sachsen-Weimar, 1818-1901
Ms, commission report outlining the necessity of new barracks, sgd; 29 Mar 1847. (90) DM260

Karl August, Grossherzog von Sachsen-Weimar, 1757-1828
ALs, 18 June 1802. Albrecht collection. (91) SF520
— 29 Aug 1814. (88) DM440
— 22 May 1825. 3 pp, 4to. To Melanie de Montjoye. Giving news about life at Weimar & mentioning Goethe. (91) DM1,100
Ls, 21 Dec 1798. (90) DM600
Ds, 23 Oct 1818. Albrecht collection. (91) SF240

Autograph endorsement, initialled, on a report by the management of the court theater, 29 Mar 1818. (89) DM200
— HORN, KARL FRIEDRICH. - Autograph Ms, sgd, [1825/26]. 4 pp, folio. Report about the presentation of a congratulatory poem to Karl August. With 2 copies of the poem & further related material. (88) DM260

Karl Friedrich, Grossherzog von Sachsen-Weimar, 1783-1853
ALs, 6 May 1801. Albrecht collection. (91) SF950

Karl Friedrich, Grossherzog von Baden, 1728-1811
ALs, 23 Oct 1806. 1 p, folio. To Empress Josephine. Expressing congratulations after Napoleon's victory at Jena & Auerstedt. (89) DM1,100

Karl Friedrich Wilhelm, Markgraf von Brandenburg-Ansbach, 1712-57
ALs, 17 May 1735. Schroeder collection. (89) DM220

Karl I, Herzog von Braunschweig und Lueneburg, 1713-80
Ls, Dec 1735. (90) DM290
Ds s (2)3 Dec 1738 & 24 May 1753. (91) DM360

Karl I, Emperor of Austria, 1887-1922
Ls, 22 Nov 1916. (90) DM750
Ptd photograph, [c.1911]. (90) DM1,000

Karl I Alexander, Herzog von Wuerttemberg, 1684-1737
Ds, 14 Nov 1735. (89) DM580

Karl I Ludwig, Kurfuerst von der Pfalz, 1617-80
Series of c.50 A Ls s, 1632 to 1661 & [n.d.]. About 180 pp, folio & 4to. To his mother Elizabeth, Queen of Bohemia (7 to his brother Rupert). Reporting on diplomatic & political events. Partly in cipher. (91) £3,200
ALs, 14/24 Nov 1637. 1 p, folio. To Henry Rich, Earl of Holland. Hoping for his continued support. (91) DM2,200
— 20 May 1658. 2 pp, folio. To his [morganatic] wife Luise von Degenfeld. Love letter, & reporting about negotiations at Frankfurt. (91)

KARL I LUDWIG

DM3,400
— Luise von Degenfeld, Raugraefin. - ALs, 22 June 1678. 4 pp, 4to. To her son Karl Ludwig. Reminding him that he must write to his father. (91) DM1,100

Karl II, Herzog von Braunschweig und Lueneburg, 1804-73
ALs, 1 Jan 1863. (89) DM290

Karl II Eugen, Herzog von Wuerttemberg, 1728-93
Collection of 5 A Ls s & 131 Ls s, 7 Jan 1761 to 5 Oct 1793. 166 pp, 4to. To Christoph Dionys von Seeger. Mostly about the affairs of his academy (Karlsschule), giving detailed instructions about a variety of matters, mentioning Schiller's father, etc. With related material. (88) DM30,000
Ls, 21 Dec 1760. (88) DM380
— 20 Oct 1781. (91) DM300
ANs, [n.d.]. (90) DM350
Ds, 3 Dec 1751. 1 p, folio. Order to his revenue office to pay 6,000 guilders to his brother Friedrich Eugen. With related material. (89) DM1,200

Karl II von Steiermark, Archduke, 1540-90
Ls, 16 Jan 1567. (88) DM280

Karl III Philipp, Kurfuerst von der Pfalz, 1661-1742
Document, 6 Sept 1717. (90) DM360

Karl Theodor, Kurfuerst von Bayern, 1724-99
Ls, 8 Jan 1767. (90) DM300
— 3 June 1767. (91) DM750

Karl Wilhelm Ferdinand, Herzog von Braunschweig-Wolfenbuettel, 1735-1806
ALs, 25 Mar 1794. Schroeder collection. (89) DM420
Ls, 19 Feb 1788. (90) DM420
— 18 Apr 1795. (89) DM200

Karloff, Boris, 1887-1969
Ds, 22 Nov 1949. (91) $150
— 17 Aug 1951. 8 by 5 inches. Preliminary Application for [Driver's] License. On State of California Department of Motor Vehicles form. Framed with a port. (89) $1,400
Signature, [1950]. (91) $200

AMERICAN BOOK PRICES CURRENT

— Anr, [n.d.]. 16mo. Sgd as Karloff & as Frankenstein. In green ink. (91) $1,600
— Anr, [n.d.]. (91) $120
See also: Lugosi, Bela & Karloff

Karoline, Landgraefin von Hessen-Darmstadt, 1721-74
ALs, 20 Sept 1772. (90) DM520

Karoline, Queen of Maximilian I Joseph of Bavaria, 1776-1841
A Ls s (2), 13 June 1831 & [1832]. (89) DM300

Karpath, Ludwig, 1866-1936
[His visitor's book, 1905 to 1936, 74 pp, 4to, in brown mor bdg, "containing, in effect, a conspectus of Viennese musical and artistic life", including musical quotations by Richard Strauss, Alban Berg, Max Reger, etc., with related material, sold at P on 14 Dec 1988, lot 265, for $5,500.]

Karpis, Alvin
Typescript, report about his capture, entitled "Put the Cuffs on Karpis", 4 Sept 1975. (91) $250

Karsch, Anna Luise, 1722-91
Autograph Ms, poem, beginning "Wirttin die Du Deinesgleichen...", 29 Oct 1783. 2 pp, 8vo. 29 lines. Albrecht collection. (91) SF1,200
ALs, 2 Mar 1773. 3 pp, 4to. To the Rev. Plaen. Thanking for a present, & about his marital plans. Mostly in verse. (90) DM1,100
— 25 Apr 1777. 3 pp, 8vo. To Daniel Chodowiecki. 30 lines of verse, expressing disappointment that he refused a present of wine. Albrecht collection. (91) SF2,800

Kasack, Hermann, 1896-1966
Autograph Ms, poem, beginning "Wenn du waechst in deinem Leben", [n.d.]. (88) DM220
— Autograph Ms, poem, Stille. (90) DM320
Autograph transcript, poem, Lebensspruch; [n.d.]. (90) DM360

Kasavubu, Joseph, 1910?-69
Photograph, sgd, [n.d.]. (90) $50

Kaschnitz, Marie Luise, 1901-74
ALs, July 1932. (90) DM540

Kastler, Alfred, 1902-84
Autograph Ms, scientific article, Sur le rapport des intensites d'emission induite et d'emission spontanee, [ptd 1973]. (89) DM380
ALs, 1 Aug 1978. (90) DM850

Katharina, Queen of Westfalia, 1783-1835
Collection of 46 A Ls s, 6 A Ns s, & 4 A Ns, 1807 to 1813. 65 pp, 4to & 8vo. To Franziska de la Rochette. Letters to a confidante, chatting about life at the French court, personal matters, etc. (88) DM14,000
ALs, 21 Apr 1831. (89) DM320

Kauffmann, Angelica, 1741-1807
ALs, 6 Feb 1789. (89) £750
— 17 May 1790. Wolf collection. (90) £800
— ROMAGNOLI, FILIPPE. - Document, 25 Jan 1808. About 150 pp, 4to. Inventory of Kauffmann's house in Rome, with an Italian trans of sections of her will. Mostly in Italian. (90) £5,500

Kaunitz-Rietberg, Wenzel Anton, Fuerst von, 1711-94
Ls s (2), 15 Sept 1754 & 30 Sept 1761. (91) DM320
Ls, 28 Dec 1748. (91) DM750
— 10 July 1769. (90) DM550

Kautsky, Karl, 1854-1938
A Ls s (2), 25 Nov & 20 Dec 1889. (89) DM800
ALs, 13 June 1899. (90) DM320

Kean, Edmund, 1787-1833
ALs, [n.d.]. (88) £320
Ls, 12 Feb 1818. (88) $225
Check, accomplished & sgd, 1 Sept 1825. (89) £120

Kearney, Stephen Watts, 1794-1848
ALs, 7 Apr 1824. Alexander collection. (90) $400
— 18 Dec 1839. Alexander collection. (90) $650
— 18 Mar [18]45. (90) $300

Ds, 9 Apr 1848. (88) $375

Keaton, Buster, 1896-1966
Self-caricature, sgd, [n.d.]. Matted with framed port postcard. (89) $5,000

Keats, John, 1795-1821
[Charles Cowden-Clarke's annotated copy of Keats's Lamia, Isabella, The Eve of St. Agnes, and Other Poems. L, 1820, 1st Ed, with related material laid in, & ALs from Leigh Hunt to Cowden-Clarke, [1819?], 4 pp, 4to, referring to Keats, sold at CNY on 18 Nov 1988, lot 198, for $15,000.]
— FORGERY. - Letter (copy), 20 Nov 1817. 4 pp, 8vo. To B. R. ("H") Haydon. About Goethe & Dante. (88) £45

Keeping, Charles
Original drawings, (21), to illus R. L. Green's A Tale of Ancient Israel, 1969. In ink & watercolor (3) or ink. Various sizes. Archives of J. M. Dent & Son. (88) £1,300

Keffenbrink, Karl von, 1791-1809. See: Napoleonic Wars

Keitel, Wilhelm, 1882-1946
Ls, 18 June 1944. (91) $350
Ds, [n.d.]. (90) $140

Kekkonen, Urho Kaleva, 1900-86
Photograph, sgd & inscr, 30 Sept 1969. (90) DM320

Kekule von Stradonitz, August, 1829-96
Autograph Ms, announcing lectures at Bonn University, 1894. (90) DM620
ALs, 13 Oct 1861. 3 pp, 8vo. To Friedrich Woehler. Letter of recommendation for Theodor Swarts. (90) DM1,400

Keller, Gottfried, 1819-90
Autograph Ms, quatrain, beginning "Weil die Erkanntnus wir, der Wahrheit, nicht erleiden"; sgd & dated Feb 1884. 1 p, 8vo. Donated to the Leipziger Schriftstellergesellschaft for a lottery. (90) DM3,500
— Autograph Ms, story, Walliser Sage, 1885. 1 p, folio. Sgd. (91) DM5,200
ALs, 22 July 1845. 1 p, 8vo. Recipient unnamed. Letter of transmittal. (90) DM1,600

KELLER

— 23 [Feb] 1863. 1 p, 8vo. To [Alfred Hartmann]. Sending a contribution to the magazine Postheiri. (88) DM1,800
— 25 July 1882. 1 p, 8vo. To Dr. Proelss. Inquiring about the source of rumours concerning Keller's alleged authorship of a controversial article. (90) DM2,400
— 29 Apr 1884. 1 p, 4to. To the Richard-Wagner Society. Regretting that he will not be able to send a contribution for their publication. (90) DM1,700
— 6 May 1884. (88) £370
— 12 Sept 1886. 2 pp, 8vo. To the brothers Paetel. Reminding them of an unpaid fee. (90) DM4,000
— 4 Jan 1887. 2 pp, 8vo. To Dr. Proelss. Declining to write a contribution for a rifle-association's festival. (90) DM3,000

Keller, Helen, 1880-1968
Series of 3 Ls s, 22 Mar [1919] to 25 May 1925. 8 pp, 4to. To Mr. Sperry, permitting the introduction to Swedenborg to be ptd. To Mr. E. L. Doheny, on the work of the American Foundation for the Blind, & thanking for a contribution. With related material. Doheny collection. (89) $1,100
Ls, 24 Nov 1936. (88) $140
— 14 Jan 1938. Byer collection. (90) $250
— 2 Feb 1943. (91) $150
— 11 Feb 1944. (91) $325
— 24 Aug 1946. (89) $200
— 16 Aug 1947. (91) $300
— 26 Apr 1950. (91) $300
— 2 Sept 1958. (89) $225
— 27 Jan [n.y.]. (89) DM380
Photograph, sgd & inscr, May 1902. (91) $300
— Anr, 29 Oct 1921. (91) $250
Signature, [n.d.]. (89) $65

Kellermann, Francois Christophe, Duc de Valmy, 1735-1820
ALs, [2 Mar 1797]. (90) DM500
— 2 Dec 1812. (89) DM380
— 20 Jan 1813. (90) DM250
Ls, [2 Nov 1805]. (88) DM450
— 11 Apr 1808. (91) DM420
— 20 Nov 1808. (89) DM240
— 12 Mar 1813. (88) DM340
Ds s (2)28 Jan & 20 Apr 1814. (90) DM300
Ds, 9 Jan 1807. (90) DM260

Kelly, Emmett, 1898-1979
Photograph, sgd & inscr, 1973. (91) $150

Kelly, Grace, 1929-82. See: Grace, 1929-82

Kemal Ataturk, 1881-1938
Ls, [Oct 1919]. 2 pp, 8vo. To Rusen Esref. Informing him of the need to counter the pernicious propaganda emanating from Istanbul against Anatolia. With related material. (91) £1,500
— 1 Feb 1936. 2 pp, folio. To King George II of the Hellenes. Congratulating him on his recall to the throne. (90) £2,500

Kempt, Sir James, 1764-1854
ALs, 3 July 1815. (89) £420

Kemp-Welch, Lucy, 1860-1958
Original drawing, crowd gathering around a fallen horse & carriage, to illus Anna Sewell's Black Beauty, 1915. In watercolor; 295mm by 199mm. Initialled; framed. (88) £1,050
— Original drawing, man opening carriage door for a woman & child, to illus Anna Sewell's Black Beauty, 1915. In watercolor; 357mm by 261mm. Initialled; framed. (88) £1,250

Kennedy, John F., 1917-63
[A collection of autograph notes & memoranda relating to his Presidential campaign, May to Oct 1960, 101 pp, various sizes, sold at P on 16 Apr 1988, lot 93, for $35,000.]
[A ptd program for the Edward F. Foley Testimonial Dinner at Washington, 7 June 1961, 8 pp, 8vo, sgd & inscr to Ted Creen, sold at sg on 21 Sept 1989, lot 185, for $600.]
[An album containing c.50 items concerning Kennedy, mostly clippings but including sgd cards by Jacqueline Kennedy & Marina Oswald Porter, & Ls by Lyndon B. Johnson, sold at wa on 17 Oct, lot 280, for $350.]
[A press release, ptd as typescript, 28 Oct 1962, 1 p, 4to, sgd, announcing the end of the Cuban Missile Crisis, sold at Dar on 4 Oct 1990, lot 273, for $9,000.]

Autograph Ms, notes for a speech, [summer 1961]. 5 pp, 12mo (cards), on rectos only. (91) $2,000
— Autograph Ms, notes taken during a White House meeting, [c.July 1963]. 1 p, 4to, on verso of mimeographed minutes of the Harvard Board of Trustees, 1959. Including sgd sketch of farmyard & horse. (91) $4,500
— Autograph Ms, outlining American policy objectives regarding Germany, [late 1950s]. 1 p, 4to. On US Senate Committee on Foreign Relations letterhead. (90) $1,700
Typescript carbon copy, speech, The Political Integrity of Hiram Revels..., [6 May 1957]. 6 pp, 4to, on rectos only. With numerous autograph revisions. Powell collection. (89) $4,800
Typescript (duplicated), 20 Jan 1961. 3 pp, folio. Mimeographed copy of his Inaugural Address, sgd later. (88) $1,900
ALs, 26 Feb 1944. 2 pp, 4to. To [Francis E.] LaClive. Thanking for kind remarks in a letter. (90) $2,250
— [25 Oct 1951]. 4 pp, 4to. To Broke Mickey. Thanking for assistance in Karachi & discussing distribution of periodicals. Sgd Jack K. On hotel stationery. (89) $2,750
— [Aug? 1956]. 2 pp, 4to. To Burr Harrison. Thanking for support at the Democratic convention. Sgd Jack. (90) $2,750
— [Aug 1959]. 1 p, 4to. To [the doorman of 277 Park Avenue, NY]. Authorizing "Miss Desrosiers to use the Kennedy apartment." On ptd letterhead. (88) $2,400
Collection of Ls & check, accomplished & sgd, 15 June 1953. 1 p, 4to, & 66mm by 157mm. To Lewis Michaelson. Expressing thanks & returning money borrowed. Check uncancelled. (90) $6,000
— Collection of Ls & signature, 26 Feb 1955 & [n.d.]. (91) $400
Ls s (2), 13 Nov 1953 & 26 May 1954. 2 pp, 4to & 8vo. To Margaret Condon. Regarding the Social Security system. With 2 secretarial letters to Condon. (88) $2,000
Ls, 8 June 1951. (91) $700
— 18 June 1952. (90) $500
— [24 Nov 1952]. (90) $600
— 14 Apr 1953. (91) $350
— 28 Apr 1953. (88) $350
— 13 May 1953. (90) $750
— 17 June 1953. (88) $475
— 2 Apr 1954. (89) £400
— 15 Jan 1955. (90) £300
— 4 Aug 1955. (91) $300
— 4 Nov 1955. (90) $900
— 2 Dec 1955. (91) $700
— 25 Feb 1957. 1 p, 8vo. To [Paul] Buck. Announcing a statement on the Cyprus question. (91) $3,000
— 24 Jan 1958. (88) $650
— 14 Jan 1961. 1 p, 8vo. To Edward H. Foley. Thanking for work done on the Inaugural Committee. (90) $1,600
— 5 Apr 1961. 1 p, 8vo. To P. L. Prattis. About arrangements for Bob Weaver to attend a testimonial dinner. (91) $1,500
— 8 Sept 1961. 1 p, 4to. To Mark Van Doren. Hoping for a collaboration between government & the arts. (90) $3,100
— 10 Feb 1962. 1 p, 4to. To "Ralph E. Becker, Toastmaster". Commenting about the importance of Lincoln's Emancipation Proclamation. With related material. (90) $12,000
— 1 June 1962. 1 p, 4to. To Rose M. Diller. Expressing thanks for her role in the "Birthday Salute" at Madison Square Garden, 19 May 1962. (90) $2,000
— 3 June 1963. 1 p, 4to. To Mark Van Doren. Responding to a letter supporting a nuclear test ban treaty. (90) $6,200
— [c.July or August 1963]. 1 p, 4to. To Frank Aiken. Thanking for help during his tour of Ireland. Including autograph postscript. Framed with a photograph. (91) $3,000
— 14 Aug 1963. 1 p, 4to. To Mr. & Mrs. Robert Cramer. Thanking for condolences on the death of his son. (88) $3,000
— 15 Aug 1963. 1 p, 4to. To David L. Ladd. Accepting his resignation as Commissioner of Patents. (89) $2,000
— 19 Aug 1963. 1 p, 4to. To Barry Goldwater. Thanking for condolences on the death of his son. With autograph emendation in salutation. Pratt

KENNEDY

collection. (89) $8,500

— 7 Oct 1963. 1 p, 8vo. To Mark Van Doren. Thanking for his support of the partial nuclear test ban treaty. (90) $2,400

Ds, 29 Nov 1960. 1 p, 4to. Appointment of Edward H. Foley as Chairman of the Inaugural Committee. (90) $1,100

Autograph sentiment, inscr to Mrs. (88) $600

Cut signature, [n.d.]. (90) $550

— Anr, [n.d.]. (91) $450

Franking signature, [26 Feb 1944]. On autograph envelope addressed to Francis E. LaClive. (90) $3,000

Group photograph, 1961. (91) $500

Photograph, sgd, [n.d.]. (90) $320

Photograph, sgd & inscr, [n.d.]. (90) $900

— Anr, [c.1962]. 8 by 10 inches. Inscr to Paul Fay. (90) $1,100

Signature, on cover of program for the Jefferson-Jackson Banquet at Lewiston, Idaho, 20 May 1960. (90) $475

— Anr, on wrap of ptd program of annual dinner of the Alfred E. (89) $475

— Anr, [1960]. (91) $325

— ASSASSINATION. - A copy of the Report of the Warren Commission, NY, 1964, sgd on front flyleaf by Dr. Robert Shaw, John B. Connally, Henry Wade, Gerald R. Ford, & Ralph W. Yarborough, sold at Dar on 13 June 1991, lot 225, for $180. 91

— CABINET MEMBERS. - The signatures of 12 members of his cabinet, on a philatelic envelope, [29 May 1964], sold at Dar on 10 Apr 1991, lot 228, for $100. 91

— FAY, PAUL. - Orig drawing, ink profile bust port of Kennedy, sgd; [19]63. 8.5 by 11 inches. Sgd by Kennedy & inscr to Fay. (91) $1,400
See also: Hemingway, Ernest & Kennedy

Kennedy, John F., 1917-63 — & Truman, Harry S., 1884-1972

Photograph, sgd & inscr, 2 Nov 1960. (88) $120

AMERICAN BOOK PRICES CURRENT

Kennedy, Robert F., 1925-68

Ls, 17 Feb 1964. (88) $175

— [n.d.]. (90) $250

ANs, 25 Feb 1964. (90) $150

— [c.26 Feb 1964]. (91) $400

Photograph, sgd & inscr, Nov 1964. (90) $325

— Anr, [n.d.]. (91) $275

Kennedy, W. R., Admiral

Series of 23 A Ls s, c.1857 to 1860. (89) £45

Kent, James, 1763-1847

Ds, 1817. (89) $85

Kent, Rockwell, 1882-1971

ALs, 10 Dec 1939. (89) $225

Kenton, Simon, 1755-1836

Ds, 21 May 1810. (88) $300

Kepler, Johannes, 1571-1630

Autograph Ms, calculations of the relative velocity of Mars, the moon & the sun, & referring to the work of Copernicus; [n.d.]. 4 pp, 4to. In Latin; paginated 19 & 29. (89) £15,000

— Autograph Ms, discussion of movements of planets, including calculations; [after 1618]. 4 pp, 4to, on autograph address leaf addressed to his wife Barbara. (91) DM38,000

ALs, 6 Sept 1613. 2 pp, folio. To Emperor Matthias. Requesting a settlement of the pension granted him by Emperor Rudolf II. Repaired & tipped to larger leaf; with trans. Barrett collection. (89) $32,500

— 2 Jan 1625. 1 p, 4to. To his wife Susanna. Fragment, referring to money due from Hochkirchner & their projected meeting at Wallsee. With autograph astronomical calculations in margins & on verso. (90) DM35,000

— [Mar 1630]. 2 pp, folio. To Wallenstein. Petitioning for help in obtaining interest due him on Austrian bonds. (88) DM95,000

Autograph quotation, O curas hominum, o quantum est in rebus inane; sgd & dated 3 May 1612. 1 p, 8vo. (90) DM30,000

Keppel, Augustus, Viscount, 1725-86
Collection of 4 A Ls s & autograph Ms, 18 Sept 1777 to 7 May 1785 & [n.d.]. (89) £600

Keppel, Henry, Sir, 1809-1904. See: Edward VII & Keppel

Kerensky, Alexander Fyodorovich, 1881-1970
Ls, 18 Feb 1924. 1 p, 4to. Recipient unnamed. Begging recipient to save people accused of espionage in Russia. In English. (91) DM3,400

Kern, Jerome, 1885-1945
Ls, 31 Dec 1938. 1 p, 8vo. To Edna Ferber. Commenting on her autobiography. (91) $1,100
— 15 May 1944. (91) $150
— 15 Oct [n.y.]. 2 pp, 8vo. To Richard Gimbel. About the sale of his book collection. (91) $1,200
Photograph, sgd & inscr, Jan 1939. (91) $900

Kern, Jerome, 1885-1945 —& Harbach, Otto, 1873-1963
Ds, 25 Jan 1950. (88) $425

Kerner, Justinus, 1786-1862
Autograph Ms, poem addressed to the pianist [Lina Duncker], [c.1855]. 2 pp, 4to. Sgd. (90) DM1,300
ALs, 11 Jan 1810. 2 pp, 8vo. To Nikolaus Heinrich Julius. Expressing anger about Baggesen's almanach, & mentioning family & friends. With autograph postscript, sgd, by Karl August Varnhagen von Ense. (89) DM3,400
— [n.d.]. (88) DM320
— 10 Dec 1840. 2 pp, 4to. To Karl von Grueneisen. Giving information about old paintings to be found in the vicinity of Ulm. (91) DM1,600
— 5 Feb 1842. 2 pp, 4to. To the Rev. Hegler. Expressing best wishes on recipient's move to a new parish. (90) DM1,100
— 10 Jan 1843. (90) DM1,000
— 14 July 1844. 3 pp, 4to. To Karoline von Wolzogen. Referring to friends. (89) DM1,300
— [25?] Oct 1850. 4 pp, 4to. To Gustav Schwab. Praising Schwab's essay on Lenau, & worrying about his son.

Including a poem. (88) DM3,200
— 1850. 1 p, 4to. To Schelling. Introducing Frau von Suckow. (90) DM1,400
— 22 Nov 1852. (91) DM1,000
— 29 Mar [n.y.]. (90) DM1,000
ANs, 30 Aug 1838. (91) DM300

Kerouac, Jack, 1922-69
Collection of 3 A Ls s, 13 Ls s, & 13 postcards, sgd (6 autograph), 1959 to 1967. 37 pp, various sizes. To Lois Sorrells Beckwith. Describing his life, his work, his state of mind, etc. Including miscellaneous short notes, haikus, drawings, etc. (90) $7,000

Keroualle, Louise Renee de, Duchess of Portsmouth, 1649-1734
Ds, 23 Aug 1714. (91) $250

Kerr, Alfred, 1867-1948
ALs, [c.late Dec 1917]. (89) DM300
Ls, 30 May 1929. (90) DM220

Kerr, Deborah
Collection of 3 A Ls s & 2 Ls s, [n.d.]. (88) $70

Kesler, J. G.
Original drawings, (146), to illus tales from the Arabian Nights (11), Het Veenwijker Viertal by G. (88) £300

Kesselring, Albert, 1885-1960
A Ls s (2), 18 Jan & 30 May 1950. (90) DM800

Kesten, Hermann
Series of 3 A Ls s, 5 July 1946 to 10 Feb 1948. (88) DM420
Series of 12 Ls s, 23 July 1949 to 27 June 1955. (88) DM900.

Ketcham, Hank
Original drawings, (2), Dennis kneeling in prayer, to be ptd as Dennis the Menace cartoon, 12 Oct [n.y.]. (91) $160
Original drawing, Dennis the Menace, [n.d.]. (89) $65

Key, Francis Scott, 1779-1843
A Ls s (2), 20 Apr 1835 & 20 Feb 1840. Doheny collection. (89) $950
ALs, 22 Sept 1819. (88) $650
— 7 Apr 1823. (88) $330
Check, accomplished & sgd, 2 May 1808.

(91) $475
Cut signature, [n.d.]. (88) $100

Keynes, John Maynard, 1st Baron, 1883-1946
Collection of 3 A Ls s, Ls & ANs, 1920 to 1922. (89) $750
— Collection of 2 A Ls s, 3 Ls s, ANs, & 3 signatures, 1925 to 1937. (89) $850
— Collection of 2 A Ls s & 13 Ls s, 1931 to 1940. 21 pp, 4to to 16mo. To William Roberts. Discussing matters relating to art. (89) $2,600
ALs, 18 Dec 1919. (91) £850
Series of 4 Ls s, 1936 to 1946. 5 pp, 4to. To various recipients. About the Bank of England, the Babylonian Temple Bank, & other matters. With related material. (89) $1,200

Keyserling, Hermann, Graf von, 1880-1946
Series of 6 A Ls s, 13 Dec 1943 to 8 Feb 1946 & [n.d.]. 12 pp, 4to. To Corina Sombart. Hoping for a new beginning of his "Schule der Weisheit". (88) DM1,050
A Ls s (2), 22 Dec 1910 & 20 Feb 1928. (88) DM200
ALs, 8 Dec 1926. (89) DM270
— 26 June 1937. (89) DM420

Khachaturian, Aram, 1903-78
Autograph music, Allegro moderato, fragment from his 3d Symphony in full score, sgd & dated 1947. 1 p, 38cm by 26cm. Also sgd in Cyrillic. (90) DM6,000
Ls, 20 July 1959. (90) £600

Khevenhueller, Ludwig Andreas, Graf von, 1683-1744
Ls, 23 May [c.1742?]. (91) DM750

Khomeini, Ruhollah, Ayatollah, c.1900-89
Signature, [c.1986]. (90) $600

Khrushchev, Nikita Sergeyevich, 1894-1971
Ds, 1946. 2 pp, 8vo. Identity card as member of the Supreme Soviet, sgd in green ink. Including photograph. (91) £1,100

Kiddell-Monroe, Joan
Original drawings, (164), to illus 4 books by Patricia Lynch, 1943 to 1954. Archives of J. M. Dent & Son. (90) £400
— Original drawings, (180), to illus Aesop's Fables, 1961. Archives of J. M. Dent & Son. (88) £320
— Original drawings, (217), to illus Longfellow's The Song of Hiawatha, 1960. Archives of J. M. Dent & Son. (88) £110
— Original drawings, (30), to illus Tales from the Arabian Nights, 1937. Archives of J. M. Dent & Son. (88) £900
— Original drawings, (33), to illus Andrew Lang's The Adventures of Odysseus, 1962. Archives of J. M. Dent & Son. (88) £220
— Original drawings, (37), to illus Charles Kingsley's The Heroes, 1963. Archives of J. M. Dent & Son. (88) £280
— Original drawings, (48), to illus Roger Lancelyn Green's The Book of Myths, 1965. Archives of J. M. Dent & Son. (88) £280
— Original drawings, (51), to illus Elizabeth Coatsworth's The Cat who went to Heaven, 1949. Archives of J. M. Dent & Son. (88) £420

Kienzl, Wilhelm, 1857-1941
A Ls s (2), 10 & 17 Mar 1902. (88) DM320

Kilmer, Joyce, 1886-1918
Ls, 14 Sept 1916. (91) $175

Kilpinen, Yrjo, 1892-1959
ALs, [10 Nov 1932]. 4 pp, 4to. To Jo van Ammers-Kueller. Love letter. In German. (89) DM1,400
— 11 Jan 1956. (91) DM1,000

Kimball, Katherine
Original drawings, (30), to illus G. Archives of J. M. Dent & Son. (88) £110

Kind, Friedrich, 1768-1843
Autograph Ms, poem, Der Frau Doctor Schuetze, [n.d.]. (91) DM250
ALs, 4 Apr 1814. (90) DM400
— [mid-Jan 1833]. (88) DM320

King, Gordon
Original drawings, 4 watercolor & gouache designs for dust jackets, [n.d.]. Archives of J. M. Dent & Son. (88) £100

King, Jessie M.
Original drawing, frontis for L'Evangile de l'Enfance depicting a group of 5 girls. 298mm by 205mm, vellum, in ink. (88) £6,500

King, Martin Luther, Jr., 1929-68
Ls, 21 Apr 1961. 2 pp, 4to. To Dr. Martin Grossack. Commenting on the role that social psychologists have played in destroying myths about racial differences. (90) $1,800
— 30 Apr 1964. (89) $900
Signature, 25 Feb [1957]. (91) $550

King, Rufus, 1755-1827
ALs, 23 Apr 1786. (90) $420
Ls, 9 Nov 1797. 2 pp, 4to. To Sec of State John Jay. Copy, reporting on negotiations between Spain & France regarding the Louisiana territory. Entirely in coded cipher; with typed copy of deciphered text. (90) $3,500
Photograph, sgd & inscr, [n.d.]. (91) $425

King, Stephen
Autograph Ms, The Revelations of 'Becka Paulson. [c.1983]. First 10 pages, 8vo. Sgd on each page. Pbd in Rolling Stone in 1984. Inscr, 14 Jan 1985. With bottom portion of a King Ls in which he attests to the rarity of handwriten King material. (91) $5,100

King, William, 1768-1852. See: War of 1812

King, William Lyon Mackenzie, 1874-1950
Ls, 18 Oct 1926. (89) £90

Kingsley, Charles, 1819-75
Autograph Ms, essay, Heroism, [c.1874]. 28 pp, folio. Including extensive revisions; sgd. (91) £1,100
— Autograph Ms, poem beginning "Speak low, speak little", 21 Sept 1870. (89) £200
— Autograph Ms, sermon, Miracles and Simple Speech, 10 Mar 1872. (90) £350
ALs, [1853]. 6 pp, 8vo. To the pbr [John W.] Parker. Commenting on G. Whythe-Melville's Ms Digby Grand & the art of novel writing. With port & transcript. Koch Foundation. (90) $1,500

Kingsley, Mary Henrietta, 1862-1900
Series of 19 A Ls s, Oct 1896 to Sept 1898. (88) £620

Kinkel, Gottfried, 1815-82
ALs, 17 Sept 1847. 3 pp, 8vo. To G. M. Kletke. Sending 3 poems (at head, 7, 3 & 4 stanzas). (91) DM1,400
— 6 Sept 1852. (90) DM950
— 20 Apr 1872. (91) DM850
— 19 Nov 1874. (89) DM400
— 28 Oct 1880. (90) DM250
— KINKEL, JOHANNA. - ALs, 22 Apr 1847. 3 pp, 8vo. To Maximiliane von Arnim. Inquiring whether her mother [Bettina von Arnim] will reveive Gottfried Kinkel in Berlin. (91) DM1,300

Kinsman...
Ms, The Kinsman, An Opera In three Acts, [late 18th cent]. (89) £600

Kipling, John Lockwood, 1837-1911
Original drawings, (59), to illus Flora A. Macmillan Archives. (90) £600

Kipling, Rudyard, 1865-1936
[The page proofs for the unpdb English Ed of The Muse Among the Motors, 1904, 8vo, sold at S on 21 July 1988, lot 196, for £1,100 to Joseph & Sawyer.]
[The pbr's proof of Letters to the Family. Toronto 1908, 8vo, with bdg & preface but blanks in place of the main body of the text, with 2 leaves of page proofs for the preface, all with autograph corrections, sold at S on 21 July 1988, lot 193, for £550 to Joseph & Sawyer.]
[A collection comprising typescripts of 3 poems (2 sgd), various proof copies, & further related material, [c.1911 to 1919], sold at S on 20 July 1989, lot 204, for £2,600 to Gekoski.]
Autograph Ms, ballad, The Lost Legion (here entitled "A Banjo Song"); [1893]. 2 pp, 8vo, on rectos only. 6 stanzas & 4-line prose preamble, with brief deleted note, sgd RK, at head. Ptr's copy. Koch Foundation. (90) $7,000

KIPLING

— Autograph Ms, poem, Follow me 'ome; [n.d.]. 1 p, 4to. 37 lines, with autograph revisions. (91) £1,900
— Autograph Ms, poem, If, sgd, inscr to E. W. Bok & dated Sept 1913. 1 p, folio. Copied from memory; some differences to ptd version. Framed with accompanying card by Carrie Kipling. (88) $30,000
— Autograph Ms, poem, The Handiest Man; [n.d.]. Koch Foundation. (90) $500
— Autograph Ms, poem, The Spies' March, [1911]. 2 pp, 4to. Fair copy, written in his neat print hand; sgd. (90) £1,700
— Autograph Ms, story, Surgical & Medical; [1900]. 7 pp, 4to. Including revisions; sgd. (90) £4,500
— Autograph Ms, The Ballad of Mr Macgruder, [25 Dec] 1898. (91) £900
— Autograph Ms, With the Main Guard. [1888]. 16 pp, on rectos only, 8vo. (91) £4,800

Original drawing, pen-&-ink sketch of a naked devil, captioned "Leading Stoker-Devil: - 'More coals for the Admiral' R.K."; [c.1898]. 177mm by 112mm, on blue stationery of HMS Pelorus. Mtd. (88) $1,400

Autograph transcript, 3d verse of his poem, L'Envoi. (91) £220
— Autograph transcript, Recessional, 1st 2 stanzas; [n.d.]. (91) £500

Typescript, poem, beginning "So long as memory, valour and faith endure...", Nov 1934. (91) £220
— Typescript, poem, The Last Rhyme of True Thomas, [1894]. 7 pp, 4to. With autograph revisions throughout, including 2 stanzas at end. (91) £1,700
— Typescript, short story, Naval Manoeuvres, [n.d.]. 31 pp, 4to. With extensive autograph revisions; title deleted. Incomplete. (89) £4,200
— Typescript, story, Kaa's Hunting, for The Jungle Book, [1894]. 43 pp, 4to. With autograph revisions throughout & autograph 8-line poem on 1st page. (91) £10,000
— Typescript, story, Quiquern, for The Second Jungle Book, [1895]. 31 pp, 4to. With autograph revisions throughout, including 10 line-passage at end. (91) £8,000
— Typescript, story, Red Dog, for The Second Jungle Book, [1895]. 17 pp, folio. With numerous autograph revisions throughout. Incomplete. (91) £7,000
— Typescript, story, The King's Ankus, for The Second Jungle Book, [1895]. 25 pp, 4to. With autograph revisions & deletions; sgd RK at head. (91) £8,500
— Typescript, story, The Spring Running, for The Second Jungle Book, [1895]. 18 pp, 4to. With numerous autograph revisions throughout. (91) £8,000
— Typescript, story, The Visitation of the Sick, [n.d.]. 22 pp, folio. With autograph revisions & 10-line autograph poetical quotation on tp. (91) £3,500
— Typescript, story, The White Seal, for The Jungle Book, [1893]. 24 pp, folio. With autograph revisions & deletions. (91) £7,000
— Typescript, The Five Nations, 1903. 146 pp, folio. With autograph table of contents & Ms alterations & markings in other hands. (89) £2,700

Collection of ALs & ANs, 15 June 1894 & 19 Nov 1916. (88) £220
— Collection of 4 A Ls s & ANs, 3 June 1895 to 6 June 1908 & 14 Sept [n.y.]. 8 pp, 8vo & 12mo (card). To various recipients. About a variety of matters. Doheny collection. (88) $2,000
— Collection of ALs & autograph postcard, sgd, 23 Jan 1897 & [n.d.]. (88) £300
— Collection of ALs & 2 A Ns s, 11 & 25 Nov 1898 & [n.d.]. 6 pp, 8vo & 12mo. To Frank T. Bullen. Praising Bullen's The Cruise of the Cachalot. Doheny collection. (89) $2,000
— Collection of 2 A Ls s & Ls, 12 June 1901 to 21 Aug 1914. 3 pp, 4to & 8vo. To Sir Francis Champneys. About a date for a medical examination, & a request for permission to reprint his Recessional. 1 ALs fragment. (90) DM1,100
— Collection of 3 A Ls s, 3 Ls s & 7 letters, Oct 1901 to Nov 1928. 13 pp, various sizes. To Pilcher (2) & Harry Perry Robinson. About a variety of matters. 2 initialled; letters with secretarial signatures. With related material. (89) £2,400
— Collection of 3 A Ls s & 2 postcards,

sgd, 1902 to 1906. 7 pp, 8vo, & cards. To H. S. W. Edwardes. About the South African War, Nigeria, etc. (88) £1,500

— Collection of 6 A Ls s & cards, sgd, 10 Dec 1903 to 5 Oct 1918. 7 pp, chiefly 8vo. To Edward German. Discussing German's settings of Kipling's songs. (88) £1,400

— Collection of ALs & Ls, 7 Feb 1920 & 24 Jan 1924. (88) £180

— Collection of ALs & Ls, 15 May 1921 & [n.d.]. (88) £200

— Collection of ALs & Ls, 19 May 1930 & 15 Feb 1924. (90) £300

— Collection of 14 A Ls s & Ls s, 1931 to 1935. 17 pp, various sizes. To Col. Roland Gwynne. About dogs, invitations, his health, etc. With ALs by Carrie Kipling. (90) £1,700

Series of 3 A Ls s, 17 Sept 1904 to 19 Nov 1933. (88) £480

— Series of 6 A Ls s, 1905 to 1915 & [n.d.]. 9 pp, various sizes. To Lord Milner. About various matters. With related material. (89) £1,600

A Ls s (2), July 1895. (90) £600

ALs, 10 Feb 1895. 4 pp, 8vo. To the Rev. Mr. Wyatt. About his literary activities, recipient's recent appointment, & the people in Vermont. (90) £1,700

— 14 June 1895. (90) £600
— 7 Mar 1896. (89) £480
— 2 July 1896. (91) £550
— [5 May 1898]. (90) $450
— [n.d.]. (88) $300
— 21 Mar 1901. 2 pp, 8vo. Recipient unnamed. Requesting him to take photographs of soldiers' graves in South Africa. (90) DM1,100
— 6 May 1901. 3 pp, 12mo. To S. L. Clemens [Mark Twain]. Discussing cases of literary piracy. On personal letterhead. Doheny collection. (88) $3,800
— [1920s]. 4 pp, 8vo. To Claude Johnson. About the performance of his Rolls-Royce; muses on the automobile, the toilet & the Resurrection of the body. Illus with 1 large & 3 small sketches. (91) $2,000
— 1 Apr 1929. (90) DM360
— 27 June [n.y.]. 1 p, 12mo. To "Mowgli" [Anthony Hope]. Sending a souvenir "from the abode of the white Cobra." Sgd as Kaa. Koch Foundation. (90) $4,800
— [n.d.]. Doheny collection. (88) $900
— [n.d.]. 1 p, 8vo. To [W. E. Henley]. Humorous letter, passing on news & answers to queries. Sgd R. Including pen-&-ink cartoon. (91) £1,800

Collection of 12 Ls s & 2 typescripts, 4 June 1928 to 29 Sept 1928. 18 pp, various sizes. To Harry Perry Robinson. Regarding the War Graves Issue of the Times Supplement. Articles with autograph corrections; 9 letters initialled. With related material. (89) £3,000

Ls, 22 Sept 1903. (89) £350
— 9 Oct 1903. (90) £400
— 7 Mar 1918. (88) £200

Series of 2 A Ns s, photograph, & signature, 12 & 19 Dec 1898 & [n.d.]. (91) £600

Corrected galley proof, short story, In the Interests of the Brethren, [1918]. 3 long sheets, in double columns. With autograph corrections. (89) £1,500

Proof copy, Letters to the Family, 2d Ed. Toronto, 1910; 8vo, in orig wraps. With autograph corrections on c.45 pp. (88) £1,300

— Anr, Songs from Books, 1912. 239 pp (1 lacking), 8vo. With numerous autograph corrections. Marked by the ptr. (89) £3,000

— SPURRIER, STEVEN. - Orig drawing, caricature of Kipling in Indian costume, ptd in Bystander no 35, Aug 1904. In pen-&-ink with charcoal & white; sgd. 370mm by 272mm. Laid down. (88) $1,600

See also: Clemens, Samuel Langhorne & Kipling

Kipling, Rudyard, 1865-1936 —& Maurois, Andre, 1885-1967

Group photograph, [n.d.]. Doheny collection. (88) $550

Kippenberg, Anton, 1874-1950

Collection of 2 A Ls s, 4 Ls s, 4 autograph postcards, sgd, & 5 autograph endorsements, 1942 to 1950. (90) DM420

Series of 3 Ls s, 1941 to 1950. (88) DM320

Kircher, Athanasius, 1602-80
ALs, 6 Mar 1655. 1 p, 4to. To Barthold Nihus. Informing him that he has been able to procure the work requested. Endorsed by recipient. (91) DM10,500

Kirchhoff, Gustav Robert, 1824-87
ALs, 23 Feb 1878. (91) DM300
— 17 July 1883. (91) DM370

Kirchner, Ernst Ludwig, 1880-1938
[A collection of 40 photographic negatives mainly taken by Kirchner, 1928 & 1929, with prints made at a later date, mostly showing girls posing naked or dancing in the forest, sold at S on 18 May 1989, lot 280, for £5,000 to Thomas.]
ALs, 15 Feb 1914. 2 pp, 4to. To Eugen Diederichs. Sending some of his works & inviting comments. (88) DM1,250
— 16 Dec 1931. 4 pp, 4to. To Dr. Mardersteig. About his wife's operation, the Fischer collection, his loneliness, etc. (89) DM1,700

Kirsch, Sarah
Autograph transcript, poem, Maerz; [n.d.] (89) DM380
— Autograph transcript, poem, Maerz, [n.d.]. (88) DM350
— Autograph transcript, poem, Verwilderung; [n.d.]. (90) DM380

Kirst, Hans Hellmut, 1914-89
Autograph Ms, final pages of a novel; [n.d.]. (90) DM700

Kisling, Moise, 1891-1953
Series of 6 A Ls s (1 incomplete), 5 Jan 1920 to 4 Jan 1926. (88) £300
ALs, 31 Dec 1929. (90) DM260
— 3 Jan 1950. (90) DM240

Kissinger, Henry A.
Ls, 22 Aug 1969. (91) $250

Kitchener, Horatio Herbert, Earl Kitchener of Khartoum & of Broome, 1850-1916
Collection of ALs & photograph, sgd, 28 Apr 1907. (88) £85
ALs, 21 June [1898]. (89) £130
— 1 June 1913. (88) DM480
Ls, 18 Mar 1902. (89) $260

Klabund, Pseud. of Alfred Henschke, 1890-1928
Autograph Ms, novel, Rasputin, [1920s]. 57 pp, mostly 4to. With numerous revisions. In cloth folder. (90) DM3,000
— Autograph Ms, poem, Soldatenbegraebnis in Innsbruck, May 1915. (91) DM650
Typescript, account of his experiences as a prisoner, in letters to his parents, 18 Apr to 27 Apr 1919. 26 pp, 4to. Including some autograph revisions & orig drawing, sketch of prison cell. (90) DM1,400
Collection of ALs & 2 autograph postcards, sgd, [n.d.] & 1914. (90) DM400
Series of 4 A Ls s, 1924. 12 pp, 4to. To Konrad Lemmer. Discussing a literary project. In pencil. With related material. (89) DM1,050
ALs, 15 Oct 1916. (91) DM260
— 7 Nov 1918. (88) DM600
— 1 May 1924. (89) DM360
Collection of Ls & typescript, 4 Jan 1920 & [n.d.]. (90) DM400
Proof copy, Der Kreidekreis, 1st Ed. (88) £200

Kleber, Jean Baptiste, 1753-1800
ALs, [28 Nov 1793]. (90) DM1,000
Endorsement, sgd, at bottom of a petition, in French & Arabic, concerning contributions to be paid by an Arabian lady, [13 Sept 1799], 1 p, folio; referring petition to a financial official. (91) DM430

Klee, Paul, 1879-1940
[2 autograph envelopes, [20 Dec 1925] & [29 Oct 1929], addressed to Will Grohmann, sold at star on 9 Mar 1988, lot 658, for DM625.]
Collection of ALs & autograph postcard, sgd, 25 Mar & 18 May 1920. 4 pp, 8vo. To Waldemar Jollos. Inviting him to an exhibition, & concerning illusts for a publication. (90) DM1,600
Series of 5 A Ls s, 22 Dec 1929 to 15 May 1930. 5 pp, folio & 8vo. To Fraeulein Pines. Discussing matters pertaining to the sale of his works. (91) £2,800
ALs, 2 Dec 1918. 1 p, 8vo. To [Fritz] Schaefler. Discussing a possible consignment of prints. (90) DM2,400

— 25 Mar 1920. 3 pp, 4to. To Waldemar Jollos. Apologizing that pressure of work has prevented his writing a requested piece. (91) £1,900
— 15 Feb 1934. 1 p, folio. To R. Doetsch-Benziger. Requesting him to send payment to his Swiss address. (89) DM1,500
Autograph postcard, sgd, 7 Dec 1936. To Hermann Scherchen. Regretting he is not well enough to travel to Winterthur. (90) DM1,800

Kleiber, Erich, 1890-1956
ALs, 26 Aug 1934. (88) DM550
Photograph, sgd & inscr, Feb 1926. (91) DM320

Klein, Johann Adam, 1792-1875
Collection of 22 A Ls s & 4 autograph Mss, 21 Jan 1854 to 23 Aug 1861. 52 pp, 4to & 8vo. To Carl Jahn. Providing material for a cat of his engravings, discussing the sale of his collection, etc. With related material. (90) DM16,000

Kleist, Ewald Christian von, 1715-59
ALs, 6 Oct 1758. 4 pp, 4to. To Salomon Gessner. Interesting letter about his & Gessner's literary work & the war. (88) DM4,400

Kleist, Heinrich von, 1777-1811
ALs, 4 May 1808. 1 p, 4to. To Otto August Ruehle von Lilienstern. Discussing financial problems relating to the journal Phoebus. (90) DM42,000
— [n.d.]. 1 p, 8vo. To [Georg Andreas Reimer]. Requesting a book. With postscript. (88) £4,000

Kleist von Nollendorf, Friedrich, Graf, 1762-1823
ALs, 25 July 1811. (90) DM340
— 24 Nov 1811. Schroeder collection. (89) DM340
Ls, 4 Jan 1816. (91) DM250
— 20 Aug 1817. Schroeder collection. (89) DM280

Klemperer, Otto, 1885-1973
Collection of 3 A Ls s & 4 Ls s, 9 Sept 1910 to 7 June 1965. (90) DM850
— Collection of ALs & 2 Ls s, 25 Sept to [late Oct] 1926. (90) DM450

Series of 5 A Ls s, 9 June [1935] to 22 Nov 1938. 10 pp, mostly 4to. To Lonny Epstein. Interesting letters about a variety of professional & political matters. 1 ALs def. (90) DM1,600
— Series of 3 A Ls s, 28 Oct & 2 Dec 1938. (90) DM550
ALs, [1938]. (90) DM220
Ls s (2), 19 July 1958 & 1 June 1966. (90) DM200

Klenze, Leo von, 1784-1864
ALs, 6 Apr 1851. (91) DM220

Kletke, Hermann, 1813-85. See: Andersen, Hans Christian

Klimt, Gustav, 1862-1918
A Ls s (2), [n.d.]. 5 pp, 8vo. Recipient unnamed. Concerning recipient's port. (91) £2,600
ALs, 14 Mar 1890. 1 p, 8vo. To an unnamed lady. Declining an invitation. (91) £1,300
— 14 Mar 1890. 1 p, 8vo. To an unnamed lady. Declining an invitation. (90) DM1,500
— [n.d.]. 3 pp, 8vo. To Herr Wien. Discussing the price of his painting Sommerblume. (90) DM2,700
— [n.d.]. (89) £850
— [n.d.]. 3 pp, 8vo. Recipient unnamed. Requesting an early settlement of a bill. (91) £1,500
Autograph postcard, sgd, 27 Oct 1909. (89) £300
Autograph sentiment, greetings, sgd, on postcard from Franz Rumpelmayer to Anton Rogner, 29 Sept 1910. (90) DM550
Signature, [n.d.]. (88) DM900

Klingemann, August, 1777-1831
ALs, 17 Apr 1815. (91) DM1,000

Klingemann, Hermann A. L., d.1857
[A group of 3 autograph Mss, sgd, dealing with Mexican animals & plants & including numerous drawings in pencil & related material, 1846 to 1852, c.265 pp, 8vo, in German & Latin, sold at HN on 30 Nov 1989, lot 2212, for DM2,400.]

KLINGER

Klinger, Friedrich Maximilian von, 1752-1831
ALs, 30 Oct [11 Nov] 1790. 3 pp, 4to. To an unnamed bookseller. Concerning payment for books. Sgd Major Klinger. With postscript by an unnamed person. (88) DM1,200

Klinger, Max, 1857-1920
Collection of 5 A Ls s & autograph postcard, sgd, 1 May 1902 to 15 Dec 1907. 15 pp, folio & 8vo. To Karl Wittgenstein. About his sculpture & paintings, an exhibition in Weimar, etc. Salzer collection. (90) £2,200

Series of 11 A Ls s, 12 Oct 1892 to 14 July 1902 & [n.d.]. 14 pp, mostly 4to. To Rudolf Osius of the Kassel Society of Arts. Concerning exhibitions & the sale of works. (89) DM2,200

— Series of 3 A Ls s, 14 Nov 1904 to 25 June 1910. (90) DM460
— Series of 3 A Ls s, 3 Feb to 10 Oct 1914. (89) DM320
— Series of 3 A Ls s, 8 Sept 1917 to 20 Mar 1918. (91) DM750

A Ls s (2), 15 Feb & 20 Mar 1906. (90) DM240

ALs, [n.d.]. (88) DM380
— 1 May 1902. 2 pp, folio. To Karl Wittgenstein. Paying tribute to recipient's generosity. Including pen-&-ink drawing on verso. Salzer collection. (90) £2,400
— 7 June 1906. (88) DM440

Series of 4 autograph postcards, (2 sgd, 1 monogrammed), 1909-1916. (91) DM350

Klopp, Onno, 1822-1903
ALs, 23 Oct 1868. (91) DM420

Klopstock, Friedrich Gottlieb, 1724-1803
Autograph Ms, Greek trans of 1st stanza of his poem Die fruehen Graeber, sgd & dated 21 Aug [17]95. 1 p, 8vo. (90) DM2,400

ALs, 3 Sept 1754. 3 pp, 8vo. To Johann Josias Sucro. Chatting about friends & suggesting a picnic in the Harz Mountains. (91) DM5,000
— 21 June 1760. 1 p, 4to. To Johann Adolph Schlegel. Informing him about his travel plans. (91) DM3,200
— 27 Aug 1793. 4 pp, 8vo. To [Elisa von der] R[ecke]. Requesting her advice regarding the preparation of a new Ed of his odes. (90) DM10,000
— 23 Jan 1799. 3 pp, 4to. Recipient unknown. About a new Ed of Der Messias & the French threat to Germany. 2d leaf repaired. (89) £2,500
— 13 Feb 1799. 1 p, 8vo. To his pbr Goeschen. Regarding corrections for a new Ed of his works. (90) DM3,400
— 14 July 1799. 2 pp, 8vo. To Johann Joachim Eschenburg. Introducing [Antonio] Araujo, chatting about French emigrants, etc. (90) DM7,500

Knebel, Karl Ludwig von, 1744-1834
ALs, 8 Feb 1792. Albrecht collection. (91) SF350
— 17 Apr 1792. (91) DM460
— 4 Apr 1809. Albrecht collection. (91) SF900
— 12 June 1821. (90) DM360
— [n.d.]. (89) DM400
Ds, 11 Nov 1823. (89) DM300
See also: Goethe, Johann Wolfgang von

Kneipp, Sebastian, 1821-97
[A group of 3 photographs, 6 & 7 Sept 1890, 1 sgd & inscr with long autograph sentiment on verso, sold at star on 4 Apr 1991, lot 689, for DM850.]

Knigge, Adolf, Freiherr von, 1752-96
ALs, 18 Aug 1793. 3 pp, 4to. Recipient unnamed. Hoping for a reconciliation with Adam Weishaupt & mentioning his suit against [Johann Georg] Zimmermann. (90) DM6,000

Knight, Richard Payne, 1750-1824
Series of 7 A Ls s, 30 June 1791 to 24 Jan 1794. 24 pp, 4to. To Sir William Hamilton. Mostly concerning his collection of antiquities & art. Wolf collection. (90) £1,100

Knowles, Reginald L.
Original drawings, (21), decorative or pictorial ink designs for title-pages, bindings or dust jackets, 1900 to 1925. Archives of J. M. Dent & Son. (90) £520
— Original drawings, (69), ornamental or pictorial ink designs for title-pages, bindings or dust jackets, 1899 & later.

Archives of J. M. Dent & Son. (90) £500
— Original drawings, (c.160), ink designs for vignettes, initials, ornamental panels, tp designs, etc., partly for the Everyman's Library; 1 dated June 1944. Archives of J. M. Dent & Son. (90) £500

Knox, Henry, 1750-1806
Collection of ALs & Ls, 10 Apr 1784 & 26 Apr 1790. 4 pp, 4to & folio. To Gen. Nathanael Greene & Gen. Otho Williams. Concerning meetings of the Society of the Cincinnati. (89) $1,100
— Collection of ALs & 2 Ls s, 1785 to 1791. (90) $650
ALs, 7 Jan 1787. (89) $600
Series of 6 Ls s, 7 July to 27 Nov 1794. John F. Fleming Estate. (89) $500
Ls, 26 Feb 1786. Alexander collection. (90) $450
— 12 Apr 1792. (91) $250
— 15 Apr 1793. (89) $200
— 24 June 1793. (90) $280
— 10 Aug 1793. (89) $180
— 11 Sept 1793. (89) $150
— 11 Jan 1794. (89) $100
— 15 Apr 1794. (89) $350
— 7 Aug 1794. (91) $450
Ns, 7 Mar 1794. (89) $100
— 29 Mar 1794. (90) $70
ADs, 17 July 1782. (89) $325
— 29 Mar 1798. (88) $120
Ds, 31 Dec 1783. (91) $350
— 16 Feb 1792. (91) $100
— 13 Aug 1792. (89) $175
— 16 Aug 1792. (89) $150
— 27 May 1793. (89) $325

Kobell, Ferdinand, 1740-99
ALs, [1793?]. (89) DM300

Koch, Robert, 1843-1910
Series of 3 A Ls s, 13 June to 22 Nov 1888. 8 pp, 8vo. To Sir William H. Lindley. Discussing problems of sanitation in Frankfurt/Main. (91) DM3,500
ALs, 20 Oct 1885. 1 p, 8vo. Recipient unnamed. Regarding a specimen for microscopic research. Mtd. (88) DM1,500
— 26 June 1889. 2 pp, 8vo. Recipient unnamed. Suggesting he discuss his ideas about treatment of fever with more experienced doctors. (90) DM1,200
— 22 Dec 1889. 2 pp, 8vo. To an unnamed Ed. Denying rumors that he is about to publish a work on tuberculosis. (91) DM1,300
— 25 Jan 1904. (89) DM560
Ds, 16 June 1873. (89) DM800
— JOHANN ALBRECHT, HERZOG VON MECKLENBURG-SCHWERIN. - Ds, 10 Nov 1900. 1 p, folio. Conferral of a decoration on Koch. With related material. (89) DM240

Koch, Rudolf, 1876-1934
Collection of 9 A Ls s & 3 Ls s, 1916 to 1934. 29 pp, various sizes. Mostly to Professor Haupt. Referring to his work & projects. With some sketches, woodcuts, & other related material. (90) DM1,400

Kochanski, Paul, 1887-1934
[A collection of autograph Mss of violin works & arrangements by Kochanski, with a collection of Mss or ptd works written for or dedicated to him, more than 250 pp, folio, sold at P on 14 Dec 1988, lot 213, for $2,000.]

Kodaly, Zoltan, 1882-1967
Collection of 4 A Ls s & 2 autograph postcards, sgd, 1948 to 1950. 10 pp, various sizes. To Sir Ivor Atkins. Mostly regarding his Missa Brevis. Including 6 autograph musical quotations. With related material. (89) £1,050
Series of 4 A Ls s, 1928 & 1929. (89) £650
— Series of 6 A Ls s, 1 Nov 1949 & [n.d.]. 12 pp, various sizes. To Erno Balogh. About his travels in America & Europe. (90) DM2,600
ALs, 28 Jan [1931]. (89) DM850
— 15 Jan [1947]. (89) DM320
Autograph postcard, sgd, 27 Oct 1925. To M. D. Calvocoressi. About his work Hary Janos & the trans of his Psalmus Hungaricus. In French. (90) DM1,100
Photograph, sgd & inscr, 20/22 Oct 1934. (88) £260
— Anr, Dec 1950. (90) DM600

Koechlin, Charles, 1867-1950
Autograph music, Chant de Kala Nag, scored for piano, choir & tenor, [n.d.]. 33 pp, 35cm by 27cm. Sgd at head. Cortot collection. (90) DM2,000
— Autograph music, Partita, Op. (90) £300

Koehl, Hermann, 1888-1938 —& Others
Menu, 20 June 1928. (90) DM750

Koenig, Paul, 1867-1933
Collection of 3 A Ls s & 3 photographs (1 sgd), 14 Sept 1921 to 27 Nov 1932. (91) DM700

Koenig, Samuel, 1712-57
ALs, [n.d.]. (89) DM660

Koenigsmark, Otto Wilhelm, Graf von, 1639-88
Ds, 2 Sept 1686. (90) DM660

Koerner, Christian Gottfried, 1756-1831
ALs, 16 Feb 1795. (89) £700
— 19 Dec 1811. (88) DM220
ANs, 29 June 1816. Albrecht collection. (91) SF210

Koerner, Theodor, 1791-1813
Autograph Ms, fragment of a religious poem; [n.d.]. (90) DM200
— Autograph Ms, poem, Charade, [n.d.]. (88) DM400
— Autograph Ms, poem, Sehnsucht der Lily, [n.d.]. (89) £350
— Autograph Ms, trans exercises, in Latin & German; [c.1805]. (90) DM320
ALs, 25 Mar 1811. (90) DM800
Autograph sentiment, inscr to a fellow-student from Thuringia, expressing friendship; 30 Nov 1810. Albrecht collection. (91) SF1,000

Koestler, Arthur, 1905-83
Series of 3 Ls s, 28 June to 16 Aug 1966. (89) DM260
— Series of 5 Ls s, 3 Oct to 8 Dec 1966. (90) DM480

Kokoschka, Oskar, 1886-1980
Collection of 29 A Ls s & Ls, 1941 to 1956. About 80 pp, various sizes. To Jack & Minna Carney. About his work & the European political situation. In English. 2 letters with small pen-&-ink sketches; 1 on verso of a photograph of a painting; some written jointly with Olda Kokoschka. With 2 related letters. (88) £1,500
— Collection of c.100 A Ls s & postcards, sgd, 13 Mar 1953 to 3 Sept 1971. About 190 pp, 8vo. To Professor Edgar Horstmann. About his own work & contemp art. (89) £14,500
— Collection of c.20 A Ls s & postcards, sgd, 1953 to 1965. 40 pp, mainly 8vo. Mostly to Dr. August Mader. Relating to tapestry produced at the Gobelin workshop in Vienna. (89) £3,600
Series of 12 A Ls s, [c.1939 to 1945]. 25 pp, 4to. To Nelly Palache. Personal letters to a good friend, describing his situation after his emigration. With related material. (89) DM13,000
— Series of 3 A Ls s, 5 Sept to 28 Nov 1959. 3 pp, 8vo. To an unnamed pbr. Giving instructions for the reproduction of a painting. (90) DM1,400
— Series of 3 A Ls s, 16 June to 11 Oct 1963. (89) DM750
ALs, 5 June 1935. (90) DM750
— [n.d.]. (88) £120
— 28 Oct 1963. (90) DM780
— [n.d.]. (90) DM660
Autograph postcard, sgd, 7 June 1964. (89) DM280

Kolb, Annette, 1875-1967
ALs, 9 July 1943. (89) DM320

Kolbe, Johann Kasimir, Graf von Wartenberg, 1643-1712. See: Wartenberg, Johann Kasimir Kolbe

Kollwitz, Kaethe, 1867-1945
Collection of 3 A Ls s & autograph postcard, sgd, 6 Nov 1912 to [12 May 1917]. 9 pp, 4to & 8vo, & card. To Helene Voigt-Diederichs. Agreeing to meet recipient's niece, reporting about her current projects, etc. (91) DM3,700
— Collection of ALs & autograph postcard, sgd, 21 Feb & 28 July 1923. (91) DM850
— Collection of ALs & 4 autograph postcards, sgd, 10 Aug 1925 to 3 Mar 1929. 2 pp, 4to, & cards. To Konrad Lemmer. Recommending Kurt Vogel; giving advice about finding models; etc. (89) DM2,600

ALs, 24 Jan 1922. 4 pp, 4to. To Adolph Meyerdiercks. Informing him that she is working on woodcuts about the war. (88) DM1,400
— 22 July 1927. (90) DM420
— 25 Dec 1927. 4 pp, 4to. To Emil Ludwig. Thanking for a book & reminiscing about visits to Ascona & Moscow. (90) DM1,200
— 21 Sept 1934. (91) DM420
— 18 Sept 1935. (89) DM850
— 10 Aug 1940. (88) DM320
— 13 Oct 1941. 3 pp, 4to. To Walter Bauer. Thanking for his Tagebuchblaetter aus Frankreich. (90) DM1,400
— 28 May [n.y.]. (89) DM360

Koran

— [Abbasid?, 8th or 9th cent]. 1 leaf, red vellum, 167mm by 222mm. In kufic script with diacritics in white. Waterstained. (91) £5,200
— [Arabia, 8th/9th cent]. 10 leaves only, 175mm by 275mm, vellum. In disciplined kufic script with diacritics in red & red markers between verses. Frayed. (88) £5,000
— [Near East, 9th cent]. 8 leaves only, vellum, 178mm by 254mm. In gold kufic script outlined in brown. With blue rosettes between verses. Imperf. (91) £100,000
— [Near East, 9th cent]. 1 leaf, vellum, 229mm by 320mm. In brown kufic script with diacritics in red & green dots & illuminated marginal medallion. Framed. (90) £4,500
— [Near East, 9th cent]. 1 leaf, vellum, 178mm by 235mm. In brown kufic script with diacritics in red & green dots & gold rosettes between verses. Framed. (90) £1,100
— [Near East, 9th cent]. 2 leaves only, 229mm by 317mm, vellum. In brown kufic script with illuminated marginal medallions. (89) £4,200
— [Near East, 9th cent]. (89) £750
— [Near East, 9th cent]. (88) £800
— [Near East, 9th cent]. (90) £700
— [Iraq or Persia, 9th cent]. 9 leaves only, vellum, 178mm by 250mm. 15th-cent brown mor bdg. In gold kufic script outlined in brown, with diacritics in red, blue & yellow. With illuminated rosettes between verses & geometrical borders throughout interspaced with illuminated gold squares. (90) £160,000
— [Persia, 9th cent]. (91) £750
— [North Africa, 9th cent]. (91) £750
— [North Africa, 9th cent]. (88) £750
— [North Africa, 9th cent]. (88) £600
— [North Africa, 9th cent]. (88) £750
— [North Africa, 9th cent]. Single leaf, 210mm by 291mm, vellum. In kufic script with diacritics in red & red markers between verses. Waterstained, repaired. With anr. (88) £1,500
— [North Africa, 9th cent]. Single leaf, 210mm by 295mm, vellum. In kufic script with diacritics in red & sura heading in red on decorated panel. Waterstained, holed. With anr. (88) £1,500
— [North Africa, 9th cent]. (88) £800
— [Iraq or Persia, 9th cent]. 7 leaves only, 161mm by 239mm, vellum. In elegant kufic script with diacritics in red & sura headings in gold ornamental kufic. Parts of text retraced at a later date. (88) £1,200
— [North Africa, 9th cent]. (88) £450
— [North Africa, 9th cent]. (88) £500
— [North Africa, 9th cent]. 1 leaf, vellum, 155mm by 233mm. In kufic script with diacritics in red & green & gold markers between verses. (90) £1,300
— [North Africa, 9th cent]. 1 leaf, vellum, 185mm by 245mm. In kufic script with diacritics in red & green, & red roundels or green commas between verses. Imperf. (90) £1,200
— [North Africa, 9th/10th cent]. 1 leaf only, vellum, 317mm by 393mm. In brown kufic script with vowels in red. Def; framed. (90) £1,900
— [c.900]. 1 leaf only, vellum, 157mm by 226mm. In black kufic script with diacritics in red & sura heading in gold. (88) DM3,200
— [North Africa, 9th/10th cent]. 1 leaf only, 247mm by 342mm. In dispersed kufic script with diacritics in red & sura heading in gold. (89) £3,600
— [North Africa, 9th/10th cent]. 2 conjugate leaves only, 225mm by 315mm, vellum. In dispersed kufic script with diacritics in red & illuminated roundel. Badly frayed; framed. (88) £1,500
— [North Africa, 9th/10th cent]. Single

KORAN

leaf, 237mm by 306mm, vellum. In large kufic script with diacritics in red & decorated rosette. Holed, frayed. (88) £1,600
— [North Africa, 9th/10th cent]. (88) £650
— [North Africa, 9th/10th cent]. (88) £800
— [North Africa, 9th/10th cent]. Single leaf, 297mm by 367mm, vellum. In elongated kufic script with diacritics in red & 2 sura headings in red on colored panels. Damaged; framed. (88) £2,000
— [North Africa, 9th/10th cent]. (88) £320
— [North Africa, 9th/10th cent]. 1 leaf, vellum, 230mm by 335mm. In kufic script with diacritics in red & green, gold florets between verses & illuminated device in margin. Def. (90) £1,200
— [Qairawan, 10th cent]. 13 leaves only, vellum, 146mm by 203mm. In gold kufic outlined in brown. With illuminated rosettes between verses & illuminated marginal palmette. (91) £90,000
— [Qairawan, 10th cent]. 1 leaf, blue vellum, 286mm by 374mm. In gold kufic script with silver rosettes between verses. Part of Sura al-Baqarah. (90) £22,000
— [Near East, 10th cent]. 1 leaf only, 202mm by 282mm, vellum. In brown kufic script with clusters of gold discs between verses. (89) £3,500
— [Near East, 10th cent]. 1 leaf only, 254mm by 305mm, vellum. In brown kufic script with gold rosettes between verses. (89) £1,800
— [Near East, 10th cent]. 1 leaf only, 254mm by 308mm, vellum. In black kufic script with gold rosette between verses. Corner cut. (89) £4,200
— [Persia or Iraq, 10th cent]. 166 leaves (1 lacking), 7.3cm by 6 cm, vellum. Later floral lacquer bdg. In black Eastern kufic script with vowels in red, sura headings & verse numbers in gold ornamental kufic, illuminated marginal medallions & 2 double pages of illumination. Prince Muhammad Hasan Mirza Qajar Estate. (89) £160,000

AMERICAN BOOK PRICES CURRENT

— [Near East, 10th cent]. 1 leaf only, vellum, 190mm by 247mm. In brown kufic script with vowels in red & green dots. Framed. (90) £1,400
— [The Great Mosque, Quairawan, 10th cent]. Single leaf, 150mm by 210mm. In gold kufic script with diacritics in green, red & blue & illuminated markers between verses. (89) £6,500
— [North Africa, 10th cent]. (91) £850
— [North Africa, 10th cent]. (88) £600
— [North Africa, 10th cent]. (88) £800
— [North Africa, 10th cent]. (88) £900
— [The Great Mosque, Qairawan, 10th cent]. 1 leaf, vellum, 144mm by 202mm. In gold kufic script with diacritics in red & blue & illuminated sura heading. (89) £12,000
— [The Great Mosque, Qairawan, 10th cent]. 1 leaf, vellum, 146mm by 206mm. In gold kufic script with diacritics in green, red & blue, illuminated markers between verses & illuminated circular device in margin. Slight worming. (88) £11,000
— [North Africa, 10th cent]. 2 conjugate leaves, vellum, 144mm by 108mm. In kufic script with diacritics in green, red, blue & yellow, illuminated markers between verses, & illuminated device in margin. Repaired. (90) £3,400
— [The Great Mosque, Qairawan, 10th cent]. 1 leaf, vellum, 149mm by 210mm. In gold kufic script with diacritics in red, blue & green & gold florets outlined in blue between verses. (90) £7,000
— [North Africa, c.950]. 1 leaf, vellum, 305mm by 344mm. In elongated kufic script with diacritics in red & green. Lower part missing. (91) £1,600
— [North Africa, 10th cent]. 1 leaf, vellum, 194mm by 297mm. In bold kufic script with diacritics in green, red & yellow & illuminated device in margin. (91) £2,000
— [Persia, A.H.383/A.D.993]. 1 leaf, 240mm by 340mm. In eastern kufic script by Muhammad bin Ahmad bin Yasin. With diacritics in red, text interspersed with gold florets, illuminated devices in margins, & sura heading in gold on illuminated panel in green & gold. Trimmed. (90)

£22,000
— [Persia or Iraq, 10th or early 11th cent]. 70 leaves only & 2 flyleaves, 111mm by 85mm. Worn contemp brown mor bdg. In Eastern kufic script with diacritics in blue, & gold & green illuminated roundels between verses. Some leaves detached, 1 lacking. (90) £14,000
— [Ottoman, A.H.1021/A.D.1612]. (88) £900
— [Ghaznawid, 11th cent]. 262 leaves, 285mm by 178mm. Later black mor bdg. In black muhaqqaq script by Uthman bin al-Husain bin Abi Sahl al-Warraq al-Ghaznawi. With gold rosettes between verses, illuminated marginal medallions, sura headings in gold & double page of illumination. Some repairs; some leaves replaced. (90) £10,000
— [Persia, 11th or 12th cent]. 287 leaves only & 4 flyleaves, 127mm by 95mm. Brown mor bdg, def. In eastern kufic by Hasan bin Ali bin Muhammad bin Ali bin Musa. With sura headings in gold ornamental kufic & illuminated marginal devices. (88) £8,500
— [Spain or North Africa, A.H.534/A.D.1139-40]. 274 leaves & 9 flyleaves, 82mm by 70mm, in later red mor. In maghribi script on glazed cream paper, by Ahmad. With gold devices between verses, illuminated marginal medallions, sura headings in ornamental gold kufic, & 2 illuminated panels. (91) £65,000
— [Near East, 12th cent?]. 2 leaves only, 279mm by 19mm. In gold naskhi script on buff paper. With gold & red rosettes between verses & sura headings in gold outlined in red. Repaired. (91) £2,000
— [Near East, 12th cent?]. (90) £1,000
— [Near East, 12th cent?]. 2 leaves, 279mm by 190mm. In gold naskhi script on buff paper. With diacritics in red & blue, illuminated marginal medallions, & sura headings in gold outlined in red. Def; repaired. (90) £2,000
— [Persia, 12th cent]. (91) £600
— [Persia or Iraq, 12th cent]. 7 leaves only, 140mm by 105mm, vellum. In eastern kufic script with diacritics in blue, red & green & sura heading in gold within a panel with beadwork borders in gold. 4 leaves def. (88) £3,200
— [Persia or Iraq, 12th cent]. 2 conjugate leaves only, 127mm by 92mm, vellum. In eastern kufic script with diacritics in red & green & gold florets between verses. (88) £1,100
— [Persia, 12th cent]. Juz XXII only. 66 leaves, 147mm by 100mm, in 19th-cent blue lea. In eastern kufic script with diacritics in black, illuminated devices in margins, sura headings in ornamental kufic in gold, illuminated headpiece, & inscr mentioning Abu Sa'ad Muhammad bin al-Husain bin Ali. (88) £4,600
— [Abbasid, late 12th cent]. 59 leaves only, 210mm by 150mm, on light brown paper; in def 19th-cent North African brown mor bdg. In large naskhi script with illuminated roundels between verses, sura heading in gold on illuminated panel & 1 single & 2 double illuminated pages. (88) £22,000
— [Spain?, 12th or 13th cent]. Section containing almost the last ten juz. 142 leaves, 19cm by 17.8cm, vellum. Def brown mor bdg. In brown maghribi script with diacritics in orange, red & blue, illuminated marginal roundels & triangles, sura headings in gold ornamental Western kufic, & double page of illumination. (89) £75,000
— [North Africa or Andalusia, 13th cent]. (89) £1,000
— [Seljuk, 13th cent]. Juz XXVIII only. 51 leaves, 216mm by 158mm. Repaired 19th-cent brown mor tooled in blind. In gold thuluth with diacritics in gold, sura headings in gold kufic, & 2 illuminated panels. (89) £55,000
— [North Africa or Andalusia, 13th cent]. 1 leaf, vellum, 215mm by 200mm. In maghribi script with diacritics in green, blue & red, gold markers between verses & illuminated circular device in margin. (90) £1,700
— [North Africa or Andalusia, 13th cent]. 1 leaf, vellum, 215mm by 200mm. In maghribi script with diacritics in green, blue, red & yellow, & gold markers between verses. (90) £1,400
— [Anatolia, 13th cent]. 208 leaves (12

KORAN

later replacements), 324mm by 285mm. Repaired 19th-cent brown mor. In 2 sizes of naskhi script. With gold florets between verses, illuminated devices in margins, & sura headings in gold on illuminated panels. Crudely repaired throughout. (91) £12,000
— [Egypt, c.Dec 1313]. Single leaf, 340mm by 251mm. In naskhi script in gold by Shadhi ibn Muhammad ibn Ayyub for Sultan Al-Nasir Muhammad. With diacritics in blue, illuminated markers & sura heading in gold on illuminated panel in blue & gold. (88) £15,000
— [Persia, early 14th cent]. (91) £900
— [Persia, A.H.745/A.D.1344]. 57 leaves only, 430mm by 330mm, in brown mor. In naskhi script by Arghun bin Abdullah Kamili. With illuminated devices in margins, sura headings in gold on illuminated panels, & 2 pp of illumination. (91) £11,000
— [Mamluk, 14th cent]. 115 leaves & 2 flyleaves, 381mm by 279mm. Brown mor bdg. In naskhi script. With gold rosettes between verses & sura headings in gold outlined in black. Lacking last 6 suras. (90) £7,000
— [Mamluk, 14th cent]. (89) £1,000
— [Mamluk, 14th cent]. (89) £1,000
— [Mamluk, 14th cent]. 362 leaves, 35.5cm by 25.4cm. Repaired later black mor gilt. On cream paper in black naskhi script. With sura headings in red & double page of illumination with panels in white thuluth & text within cloud bands. (89) £3,500
— [Persia, 14th cent]. (91) £750
— [North Africa, 14th cent]. 2 conjugate leaves, 165mm by 155mm, vellum. In maghribi script with diacritics in green & yellow, gold markers between verses & sura heading in ornamental kufic in gold. Some defects. (88) £1,200
— [Anatolia, 14th cent]. (89) £750
— [Mamluk, 2d half of 14th cent]. Double page, 406mm by 319mm. In muhaqqaq script with diacritics in black, gold rosettes between verses & sura heading in white thuluth on illuminated panel in colors & gold. Margins repaired. (88) £1,800
— [Mamluk, 2d half of 14th cent]. (88) £800

AMERICAN BOOK PRICES CURRENT

— [Mamluk, 2d half of 14th cent]. 2 leaves only, 407mm by 317mm. In muhaqqaq script with diacritics in black, gold rosettes between verses & sura heading in white thuluth on illuminated panel in colors & gold. 1 leaf smudged. (88) £1,100
— [Mamluk, 2d half of 14th cent]. (88) £800
— [Egypt, c.1375]. 2 leaves, 407mm by 317mm. In muhaqqaq script. With significant words picked out in gold, & sura headings in white thuluth on illuminated panels in colors & gold. (91) £1,700
— [Mamluk, c.1400]. Juz X only. 38 leaves, 372mm by 259mm, in modern red mor gilt. In naskhi script. With illuminated tp & double page of illumination. Wormed; repaired. (91) £7,500
— [Persia, early 15th cent]. (88) £420
— [Herat, c.1420-30]. 1 leaf only; 184cm by 115cm. Sura VII, al-A'raf, verses 37-38; in monumental muhaqqaq script by Baysunghur bin Shah Rukh bin Timur. Gilt decoration added in 19th cent. Repaired. (89) £145,000
— [Herat, c.1420-30]. Fragment of single leaf, 71.5cm by 98.5cm. Part of sura XXIV, al-Nur; 3 lines in muhaqqaq & gold thuluth scripts by Baysunghur bin Shah Rukh bin Timur. Repaired. (89) £22,000
— [Syria or Anatolia, A.H.829/A.D.1425]. 298 leaves, 356mm by 260mm. Repaired brown mor tooled in blind. In naskhi script by Muhammad bin Ali bin Munshi. With illuminated circular devices in margins, sura headings in red, & double page of illumination. Crude repairs. (89) £4,000
— [Cairo, A.H.831/A.D.1427]. 229 leaves, 425mm by 210mm. 19th-cent brown mor bdg with painted central medallions. In naskhi script with diacritics in red, blue & black by Ahmad bin Yusuf al-Jushi. With glosses written diagonally in 2 shades of red, sura headings in thuluth in gold, & double page of illumination. (91) £95,000
— [Persia, 2d quarter of 15th cent]. About 380 leaves, 287mm by 225mm; in green mor gilt bdg. In muhaqqaq script by Hasan Kameli, with diacritics

in black, sura headings in gold thuluth & double page of illumination. Repaired throughout. (88) £3,000
— [Samarkand, A.H.851/A.D.1447]. 249 leaves & flyleaf, 36.2cm by 24.8cm. Def later brown mor bdg. In black naskhi script by Abdullah al-Harawi. With sura headings in gold within illuminated cartouche, illuminated marginal medallions & double page of illumination. (89) £5,500
— [Sultanate, 15th cent]. Juz XXI & part of Juz XXII. 22 leaves & 2 flyleaves, 279mm by 216mm, in brown mor bdg. In blue & gold thuluth. With illuminated discs between verses, sura headings in gold within illuminated cartouche, & 2 double pages of illumination. (91) £20,000
— [Sultanate, 15th cent]. (91) £1,000
— [Persia?, 15th cent]. 242 leaves & 6 flyleaves, 330mm by 254mm, in later brown mor. In naskhi & thuluth scripts. With gold & blue discs between verses, sura headings in blue thuluth, & double page of illumination. Repaired. (91) £2,500
— [Ottoman, 15th cent]. Bifolium, 342mm by 243mm. In naskhi script on buff polished paper, with interlinear trans in smaller script. With gold devices between verses & finely illuminated sura heading in flowing gold thuluth script on blue ground between scrolling arabesques in orange. From a Koran executed for Mehmed II. (90) £11,000
— [North Africa, 15th cent]. (89) £900
— [Egypt, 15th cent?]. 46 leaves only, 255mm by 185mm. Contemp blind-stamped lea bdg, wormed. In thuluth script. With full-page illuminated headpiece & numerous illuminated devices in margins. (88) DM10,000
— [Persia, 15th cent]. (89) £900
— [Persia, 15th cent]. 2 conjugate leaves, 522mm by 361mm. In muhaqqaq script with diacritics in black, interlinear Persian trans in red, decorated gold rosettes between verses & sura heading in white thuluth on illuminated panel. Wormed. (91) £1,500
— [Persia, 15th cent]. 2 conjugate leaves, 522mm by 365mm. In muhaqqaq script with diacritics in black, interlinear Persian trans in red, decorated gold rosettes between verses & sura heading in white thuluth on illuminated panel. Corner torn. (91) £1,700
— [Persia or Levant, 15th cent]. 20 leaves only, 436mm by 295mm, in modern red mor. In 2 sizes of naskhi script. With red & yellow markers between verses & sura headings in red. Repaired. (91) £2,400
— [Mamluk, 15th cent]. (91) £600
— [Mamluk, 15th cent]. (88) £380
— [Mamluk, 15th cent]. (89) £200
— [Timurid, 15th cent]. 574 leaves, 171mm by 120mm. Modern red bdg. In naskhi script with illuminated markers between verses, sura headings in white thuluth on illuminated panels & 2 double pages of fine illumination. Skilfully repaired. (89) £2,600
— [Anatolia, 15th cent]. Juz III only. 33 leaves, 300mm by 212mm. Repaired contemp brown mor tooled in blind. In large muhaqqaq script. With illuminated circular devices in margins, sura heading in thuluth, & double page of illumination. (89) £2,000
— [Anatolia, 15th cent]. Juz XVI only. 39 leaves, 298mm by 209mm. Repaired contemp brown mor tooled in blind. In large muhaqqaq script. With illuminated circular devices in margins & double page of illumination. (89) £2,600
— [Anatolia, 15th cent]. Juz XXIII only. 39 leaves, 297mm by 207mm. Repaired contemp brown mor tooled in blind. In large muhaqqaq script. With illuminated circular devices in margins, sura heading in gold thuluth, & double page of illumination. (89) £3,400
— [Sultanate, Jaunpur?, mid-15th cent]. 190 leaves only, 245mm by 160mm. Gilt-stamped red mor bdg. In large bihari script by Hasan. With interlinear Persian trans in red, glosses & illuminated devices in margins, & 11 double pages of illumination. Misbound. (89) £1,500
— [Mamluk, 15th cent]. (90) £850
— [Mamluk, 15th cent]. (90) £650
— [Timurid, Shiraz?, 15th cent]. (90) £550
— [Sultanate India, 15th cent]. 634 leaves, 360mm by 234mm. Brown mor bdg tooled in blind. In red & black bihari

KORAN

script, with Persian commentary written diagonally in borders. With sura headings in gold on illuminated panels & 33 double pages of illumination in colors & gold. (91) £2,500
— [Ottoman, A.H.859/A.D.1454]. 246 leaves (1 later replacement), 305mm by 233mm. Rebacked 19th-cent brown mor bdg. In naskhi script, with 1st & last lines in large muhaqqaq & central lines in gold thuluth, by Ahmad Ibn Abdullah at the instance of Muhammad Chelebi Ibn Sinan Beg. With gold rosettes with blue dots between verses & illuminated panels throughout with floral motifs. (91) £12,000
— [Persia or Anatolia, A.H.873/A.D.1469]. 282 leaves & 2 flyleaves (3 later replacements), 347mm by 255mm. Later Turkish bdg, def. In naskhi script by Yasin bin Muhammad al-Shafi'i. With Arabic glosses in red written diagonally in margins, sura headings in gold thuluth, & double page of illumination, partly repainted. (89) £4,000
— [Persia, c.1475]. 417 leaves, 190mm by 130mm, in modern black lea gilt. In naskhi script. With sura headings in gold on illuminated panels & 3 double pages of illumination preceded by a shamsa at beginning & end. (89) £1,350
— [Ottoman, 2d half of 15th cent]. 632 leaves, 218mm by 157mm, in repaired brown mor bdg. In naskhi script with interlinear Persian trans in nasta'liq, attributed to Yaqut al-Musta'simi. With gold discs between verses, sura headings in gold thuluth on illuminated panels, full-page illuminated panel, & double page of illumination. (91) £4,000
— [Persia, late 15th cent]. 572 leaves, 285mm by 180mm. Brown calf gilt with 18th-cent Indian floral lacquer inlay. In naskhi script with interlinear Persian trans in red throughout, attributed to Abdullah al-Tabbakh. With decorated gold discs between verses, sura headings in thuluth in gold, & double page of illumination. (91) £8,500
— [Persia, late 15th cent]. (88) £900
— [Mamluk or Ottoman, late 15th cent].

AMERICAN BOOK PRICES CURRENT

(89) £400
— [Persia, c.1500]. 637 leaves & 2 flyleaves, 324mm by 209mm. Fine contemp brown mor gilt bdg. In naskhi script on buff polished paper. With illuminated devices between verses, illuminated marginal medallions, sura headings in white on gold with polychrome floral pattern, & 3 double pages of illumination. (90) £15,000
— [Sultanate, c.1500]. 289 leaves & 2 flyleaves, 19cm by 13.4cm. Def brown mor bdg. In 2 sizes of black & gold naskhi script probably written by Muhammad 'Abdullah'. With sura headings in white on gold ground or gold on white ground within illuminated cartouches & def double-page of illumination. (88) £3,200
— [Persia, c.1500]. 239 leaves & 3 flyleaves, 17.2cm by 12cm, in Qajar gold & black lacquer bdg. In black naskhi script with sura headings in gold on blue ground & 2 double pages of illumination. (88) £6,000
— [Sultanate, c.1500]. 483 leaves & 5 flyleaves, 117mm by 76mm. Repaired later red mor bdg. In bihari script. With gold rosettes between verses, illuminated marginal medallions, & sura headings with gold & illuminated panel. (90) £2,000
— [Sultanate, 15th or 16th cent]. (90) £190
— [Ottoman, c.1500]. 24 leaves only, 230mm by 152mm, in rebacked brown mor bdg. In naskhi script, attributed to Shaykh Hamdullah. With gold florets between verses & illuminated headpiece in various shades of gold. (91) £11,000
— [Persia, c.1500]. (88) £800
— [Damascus, A.H.912/A.D.1506]. 325 leaves, 152mm by 107mm. Repaired brown mor tooled in blind. In naskhi script by Abdul-Rahman as-Salihi al-Dimashqi. With gold rosettes between verses, sura headings in gold thuluth, 2 double pages of illumination, & 3 illuminated circular medallions, 1 with dedication to a Mamluk prince. (89) £6,000
— [Persia, early 16th cent]. 50 leaves only, 250mm by 160mm, in modern brown mor gilt. In naskhi & muhaqqaq

scripts, [erroneously?] attributed to Yaqut al-Musta'simi. With sura headings in white thuluth on illuminated panels & double page of illumination. (91) £3,800

— [Ottoman, c.1510-20]. 20 leaves only, 240mm by 160mm. Repaired red mor bdg with stamped central medallions of gilt lea onlay. In naskhi script, attributed to Hamdullah ibn al-Shaykh. With gold discs decorated with red & blue dots & double page of fine illumination. (91) £1,300

— [Ottoman, c.A.D.1515]. 368 leaves, 210mm by 140mm. Contemp red mor gilt bdg. In naskhi script with diacritics in black by Hamdullah known as Ibn al-Shaykh. With gold florets between verses, illuminated devices in margins, sura headings in white or gold on illuminated panels, & double page of fine illumination preceded by 2 illuminated shamsa. (90) £270,000

— [Persia, c.1525]. 363 leaves & 4 flyleaves, 215mm by 152mm, in later green mor gilt bdg. On cream polished paper in blue & gold thuluth & black naskhi script. With sura headings in white on gold with illuminated cartouche & 4 double pages of illumination. (88) £12,000

— [Persia, A.H.943/A.D.1536-37]. 476 leaves & flyleaf, 162mm by 110mm. Contemp brown mor gilt bdg. In black naskhi script alternating with blue and gold thuluth by Muhammad al-Katib al-Shirazi. With gold discs between verses, gold margins, sura headings white on gold, & 2 opening double pages of illumination. (90) £22,000

— [Tabriz, c.1539]. 1 leaf only, 415mm by 285mm. On gold-sprinkled paper in nasta'liq script with diacritics in black; attributed to Shah Mahmud Nishapuri. With illuminated headpiece & Koranic verses in naskhi script in outer border. Framed. (89) £2,300

— [Tabriz, c.1539]. 1 leaf only, laid down, 460mm by 300mm. On gold-sprinkled paper in nasta'liq script with diacritics in black; attributed to Shah Mahmud Nishapuri. With Koranic verses in naskhi script in outer border. Framed. (91) £2,300

— [Mecca, A.H.947/A.D.1540]. 450 leaves & 2 flyleaves, 107mm by 76mm. Later brown mor bdg. In naskhi script. With gold dots between verses, marginal roundels in colors, sura headings in gold, & double page of illumination. (90) £1,100

— [Persia, 16th cent]. 257 leaves & 2 flyleaves, 356mm by 248mm, in contemp brown mor gilt. In naskhi & thuluth scripts on cream paper by Asadullah al-Kirmani. With illuminated cartouches & marginal medallions, sura headings in white on gold within illuminated cartouche, & double page of illumination. (91) £30,000

— [Ottoman?, 16th cent]. Juz VII only. 30 leaves & 2 flyleaves, 311mm by 222mm, in brown mor gilt. In elegant muhaqqaq script. With gold rosettes between verses, sura heading in white on gold within illuminated cartouche, & half-page illuminated heading. (91) £22,000

— [Persia, 16th cent]. 286 leaves & 2 flyleaves, 362mm by 254mm, in contemp brown mor gilt bdg. In black naskhi script on gilt-sprinkled ground. With sura headings in white on gold within illuminated cartouche & double page of illumination. (88) £5,500

— [Persia, 16th cent]. 334 leaves & 3 flyleaves, 330mm by 235mm. Contemp brown mor bdg. In black naskhi & thuluth scripts. With decorated panels to each side with gold floral designs, outer colored margins, illuminated marginal roundels, sura headings in gold within illuminated cartouche, & 3 double pages of illumination. (90) £13,000

— [Ottoman, 16th cent]. (89) £1,000

— [North Persia, 16th cent]. 220 leaves (1 later replacement), 299mm by 200mm, in contemp black mor with gilt lea onlay. In naskhi script in alternating blue & gold, with occasional Persian glosses in nasta'liq. With sura headings in gold on illuminated panels, 2 illuminated shamsas, & double page of fine illumination. (91) £30,000

— [Persia, c.1550]. 397 leaves, 258mm by 179mm; in modern brown mor tooled in blind. On gold-sprinkled paper in naskhi script by Maulana Jamal ad-Din Husain Fakhar. With diacritics in

black, sura headings in white thuluth on illuminated panels & 5 pages of illumination. Def & repaired. (88) £3,600
— [Safavid, c.1550]. 294 leaves, 370mm by 255mm. Richly decorated contemp lea bdg, repaired. In blue & gold muhaqqaq. With sura headings in white or gold on illuminated panels, 3 double pages of fine illumination, 2 illuminated shamsas within illuminated panels, incorporating Koranic verses in white thuluth, & verses from the Falnama in blue & white nasta'liq on last leaves. (89) £105,000
— [Ottoman, mid-16th cent]. 375 leaves, 197mm by 132mm. Brown mor bdg by Najm-ad-Din, A.H.1370/A.D.1950. In muhaqqaq script, attributed to Ahmed Qarahisari. With gold florets between verses, sura headings in white thuluth on illuminated panels, & 2 illuminated double pages, each with 2 illuminated central medallions & pendants. (89) £45,000
— [Persia & Turkey, A.H.963/A.D.1555]. 263 leaves, 492mm by 349mm. 19th-cent red mor bdg with gilt lea onlay. In black naskhi & gold muhaqqaq scripts by Maqsud al-Tabrizi; some commentary in nasta'liq. With gold discs with red & blue dots between verses, interlinear rules in gold throughout, illuminated circular devices in margins, sura headings in gold thuluth within cloud-bands on illuminated panels, & double page of fine illumination. (91) £145,000
— [Shiraz, c.1560]. 303 leaves, 362mm by 226mm. Def contemp brown mor gilt. In naskhi script on gold-sprinkled paper. With illuminated devices in margins, sura headings in white thuluth on illuminated panels, illuminated headpiece, & 4 pages of illumination. Repaired with fragments from a North African Ms. (89) £5,000
— [Persia, A.H.975/A.D.1567]. 343 leaves, 311mm by 212mm. Repaired contemp black mor gilt. In naskhi script by Abdullah Ibn Sultan Muhammad al-Haravi. With gold discs between verses, sura headings in white on illuminated panels, 2 illuminated shamsas, & double page of illumination. (89) £4,500

— [Ottoman, A.H.979/A.D.1571]. 19 leaves only, 352mm by 236mm. Contemp black mor gilt. In naskhi & gold thuluth scripts by Ali bin Muhammad bin Muqqadam. With inner borders with gold floral motifs throughout, illuminated circular devices in margins, sura headings in gold on illuminated panels, & illuminated headpiece. (89) £6,500
— [Mughal, 2d half of 16th cent]. 345 leaves, 330mm by 230mm; in brown mor bdg. On gold-sprinkled paper in muhaqqaq script by Ibn Ali Ahmad as-Sharif. With diacritics in black, 17 pp written in alternating black & gold, sura headings in white thuluth on illuminated panels, illuminated headpiece & 3 double pages of illumination. Repaired. (88) £15,000
— [Herat, 2d half of 16th cent]. 416 leaves, 282mm by 195mm; in repaired 18th-cent Indian bdg. In naskhi script by Nur ad-Din Muhammad bin Muhyi al-Haravi. With diacritics in black, sura headings in white on illuminated panels & double page of illumination. 18th-cent inscr stating provenance. (88) £4,200
— [Ottoman, A.H.984/A.D.1576]. 177 leaves, 373mm by 265mm. Modern brown lea bdg. In naskhi script. With illuminated circular devices in margins, sura headings in gold thuluth on decorated panels, double page of illumination, & later catchwords & inscr endowing Ms to the Sultan Ahmed Mosque in Istanbul. (89) £3,500
— [Mecca, A.H.987/A.D.1579]. (90) £700
— [Qazwin, A.H.995/A.D.1586-87]. 409 leaves & 2 flyleaves, 280mm by 184mm, in contemop brown mor gilt bdg. On cream polished paper in black thuluth & naskhi script by Ali Riza al-Abbasi. With sura headings mostly in white on gold with illuminated cartouche & 2 double pages of illumination. (88) £12,000
— [Persia, late 16th cent]. 347 leaves & 5 flyleaves, 235mm by 152mm, in repaired later red mor. In naskhi script by Fatima Sultan at the instance of Princess Sultan Begam. With sura headings in gold & double page of illumination. (89) £1,800

— [Persia, late 16th cent]. 354 leaves, 377mm by 255mm, in contemp black mor with gilt lea onlay. In muhaqqaq script by Sayyid Dervish Muhammad bin al-Hajj. With diacritics in black, gold discs between verses, illuminated devices in margins, sura headings in gold on illuminated panels & double page of illumination, repaired. (88) £6,500

— [Ottoman, late 16th cent]. 297 leaves, 45mm by 45mm, octagonal. Gilt lea bdg. In ghubari script. With yellow dots between verses, sura headings in red, & 2 double pages of illumination. (90) £3,600

— [Persia, late 16th cent]. Juz II only. 17 leaves, 345mm by 235mm. Contemp black mor bdg with gilt lea onlay richly decorated. In gold thuluth & black naskhi scripts. With illuminated panels decorated with floral motifs throughout, illuminated circular devices in margins, & illuminated headpiece. (91) £2,800

— [Safavid, A.H.1000/A.D.1591]. 378 leaves, 347mm by 205mm, in def 19th-cent lacquer bdg. In naskhi script by Nurallah Muhammad al-Lahiji al-Jilani. With diacritics in black, interlinear Persian trans in red nasta'liq throughout, sura headings in gold thuluth & double page of illumination. (88) £2,400

— [North Africa, A.H.1028/A.D.1618]. 232 leaves, 246mm by 185mm, in def brown mor. In maghribi script by Ahmed bin Abdul-Aziz bin Ali. With sura headings in ornamental kufic in gold & 3 pp of fine illumination. (91) £2,200

— [Tunis, A.H.1040/A.D.1630]. 200 leaves & 9 flyleaves, 263mm by 203mm, in def brown lea bdg. In maghribi script by 'Ubaidullah Ahmad bin 'Abd al-'Aziz. With illuminated devices between verses & sura headings in ornamental gold kufic or in gold maghribi, partly within illuminated cartouche. (91) £10,000

— [Shiraz, A.H.1042/A.D.1632]. (88) £700

— [Ottoman, A.H.1043/A.D.1633]. 149 leaves, 97mm by 65mm. Repaired contemp brown mor tooled in gold. In ghubari script by Sha'ban bin Muhammad. With gold dots between verses, cornerpieces in gold throughout, sura headings in gold & double page of illumination. Waterstained. (89) £1,200

— [Turkey, A.H.1055/A.D.1645-46]. (89) £1,000

— [Persia, 17th cent]. 321 leaves & flyleaf, 68mm by 49mm. Cloth cover. In naskhi script by Muhammad bin Abd al-'Aziz. With gold discs between verses, sura headings in gold, & double page of illumination. (90) £2,800

— [Persia, 17th cent?]. (88) £700

— [Persia, 17th cent]. (88) £600

— [Persia, 17th cent]. 179 leaves & 3 flyleaves, 47mm by 44mm, octagonal. In lea wraps stamped with Koranic verses; in later metal case. In black naskhi script. With gold discs between verses, sura headings in gold, & double page of illumination. (90) £3,000

— [Mughal, 17th cent]. (88) £650

— [Persia, 17th cent]. (91) £750

— [Safavid, A.H.1069/A.D.1658]. 341 leaves, 290mm by 190mm, in 19th-cent floral lacquer bdg. In naskhi script on gold-sprinkled paper. With gold discs between verses, sura headings in gold on decorated panels, & double page of illumination. (91) £4,000

— [Persia or India, A.H.1076/A.D.1665]. (89) £450

— [India, A.H.1079/A.D.1669]. (89) £400

— [Mughal, A.H.1081/A.D.1670]. (89) £320

— [Kashmir, A.H.1090/A.D.1679-80]. (90) £700

— [Persia, A.H.1094/A.D.1682]. (91) £850

— [Persia, A.H.1095/A.D.1683]. (91) £800

— [Persia, A.H.1096/A.D.1684-85]. 402 leaves & 4 flyleaves, 215mm by 152mm. Repaired Qajar lacquer bdg. In naskhi script on gilt-sprinkled buff leaf by Muhammad Riza al-Shirazi. With sura headings in gold & double page of illumination. (89) £1,300

— [Turkey, A.H.1061/c.A.D.1685]. 286 leaves, 270mm by 155mm. 19th cent lea gilt. In black & red naskhi script, headings in blue thuluth on gold

ground. With decorated borders throughout in gold & colors & double page of illumination. (88) DM3,600
— [Turkey?, A.H.1061/A.D.1685]. 286 leaves, 270mm by 155mm. Early 19th-cent lea gilt. In naskhi script with headings in blue thuluth on gold ground. With double page of illumination & 5 elaborate double-page borders. (89) DM4,300
— [India, late 17th cent]. (89) £650
— [Mughal, late 17th cent]. 437 leaves, 325mm by 205mm; contemp lacquer bdg. On gold-sprinkled paper in naskhi script. With diacritics in black, sura headings in white on illuminated panels & double page of illumination. Repaired throughout. (88) £15,000
— [Ottoman, late 17th cent]. (88) £380
— [Ottoman, late 17th cent]. (88) £800
— [Ottoman, late 17th cent]. 363 leaves, 240mm by 155mm. Repaired red mor bdg. In naskhi script. With gold discs between verses, occasional illuminated devices in margins, sura headings in white on illuminated panels, & double page of illumination. Trimmed. (90) £2,000
— [Qajar, A.H.1120/A.D.1708]. 286 leaves, 220 by 145mm. Floral lacquer bdg by Ibn Muhammad Ja'far Muhammad Yusuf. In naskhi script by Muhammad Hadi al-Isfahani. With Arabic glosses in margins, sura headings in gold thuluth on illuminated panels, 3 double pages of illumination, & 2 illuminated interleaves with text in minute nasta'liq. (89) £2,600
— [Persia, early 18th cent]. 282 leaves, 64mm by 40mm, in contemp black & brown mor gilt bdg. On thin gold-sprinkled paper in minute naskhi script with diacritics in black, margins ruled in red & gold, sura headings in gold thuluth & double page of illumination. Repaired. (88) £1,400
— [North Africa, early 18th cent]. 167 leaves, 256mm by 200mm. Contemp red mor tooled in gold. In maghribi script with diacritics in orange & blue, illuminated markers between verses, illuminated circular devices in margins, & sura headings in gold or white ornamental kufic on illuminated panels. (90) £3,000

— [Ottoman, early 18th cent]. 354 leaves, 53mm in diameter (octagonal). Brown lea bdg. In black naskhi script with headings in white & 4 pp of illumination. (91) $2,400
— [India, early 18th cent]. 431 leaves (1 blank), 145mm by 78mm, in brown mor with gilt lea onlay. In naskhi script on gold-painted paper. With illuminated markers between verses, sura headings in blue thuluth on illuminated panels, double page of illumination & 2 richly decorated borders. (91) £3,000
— [Ottoman, A.H.1214/A.D.1719]. 335 leaves, 174mm by 110mm, in contemp red mor tooled in gold, with slipcase. In naskhi script by Mustafa al-Hilimi. With diacritics in black, margins ruled in gold, sura headings in white on illuminated panels & double page of illumination. (88) £5,000
— [Persia, A.H.1132/A.D.1720]. 285 leaves & 2 flyleaves, 336mm by 215mm, in fine Qajar floral lacquer bdg. In naskhi script by Ahmad al-Nirizi. With sura headings in gold & double page of illumination in polychrome floral motifs with various tones of gold. (88) £4,500
— [Ottoman, A.H.1140/A.D.1727]. 384 leaves, 158mm by 105mm. Def contemp brown mor with richly decorated gilt lea onlay. In naskhi script by Ibrahim bin Suleyman. With gold discs between verses, catchwords, illuminated devices in margins, sura headings in white on illuminated panels, & double page of illumination. (89) £2,400
— [Persia, A.H.1151/A.D.1738]. (90) £800
— [18th cent]. (88) £230
— [India, 18th cent]. (89) £380
— [India, 18th cent]. 502 leaves, 167mm by 97mm, in repaired black mor gilt. In naskhi script. With sura headings in white on gold panels, 6 richly decorated outer borders & 2 double pages of illumination. Waterstained. (89) £1,400
— [Persia, 18th cent]. (91) £600
— [India, 18th cent]. About 250 leaves only, 41mm by 40mm; octagonal, in enamelled metal case. In ghubari

script. With sura headings in red. Imperf. (91) £1,300
— [North India, 18th cent]. 28 leaves only, 132mm by 80mm, in repaired floral lacquer bdg. In gold naskhi script on blue paper. With sura headings in while on gold panels & illuminated headpiece. (91) £1,400
— [Ottoman, 18th cent]. 280 leaves, 403mm by 290mm, in modern black lea gilt bdg. In naskhi script with diacritics in black, sura headings in red, double page of illumination & illuminated roundel painted at a later date. Repaired throughout. (88) £1,400
— [Persia, 18th cent]. (88) £300
— [North India, 18th cent]. 571 leaves, 320mm by 205mm, in def red mor bdg. In naskhi script with diacritics in black, extensive glosses in Arabic in margins, sura headings in red & double page of illumination. Small repairs. (88) £2,800
— [Arabic, 18th cent]. 174 octagonal leaves, 46mm by 46mm, in def contemp black shagreen painted in gold. In minute naskhi script with diacritics in black, margins ruled in gold, sura headings in red on gold panels & double page of illumination. (88) £1,400
— [India, 18th cent]. (88) £600
— [Persia, 18th cent & later]. 264 leaves, 160mm by 100mm, in black shagreen with gilt lea onlay. In small naskhi script with diacritics in black, occasional glosses in shikasteh in margins, sura headings in gold on illuminated panels, double page of illumination & 4 illuminated shamsas. Repaired. (88) £1,100
— [Ottoman, 18th cent]. (89) £800
— [North Africa, 18th cent]. 209 leaves, 271mm by 195mm. Contemp brown mor tooled in blind. In maghribi script with diacritics in red, yellow, green & blue, sura headings in gold ornamental kufic, & 2 double pages of fine illumination. Opening & last verses written in gold within illuminated panels. (89) £3,700
— [India, 18th cent]. 395 leaves, 243mm by 135mm. Worn brown mor gilt bdg. In thuluth & naskhi scripts. With panels decorated in gold throughout, illuminated circular devices in margins, sura headings in red, & double page of illumination; repaired. (90) £1,100
— [Turkey, A.H.1179/A.D.1765]. (89) DM1,000
— [Turkey, A.H.1179/A.D.1765-66, but probably A.H.1279/A.D.1862-63]. (91) $500
— [Persia, Zand, A.H.1188/A.D.1774-75]. 208 leaves & 11 flyleaves, 17.1cm by 10.3cm. Very fine contemp floral lacquer bdg. In black thuluth within gold cloud bands by Muhammad Hashim bin Muhammad Salih al-Isfahani. With sura headings in gold on blue with gold scrolling arabesques within illuminated cartouche & 3 double pages of fine illumination. Prince Muhammad Hasan Mirza Qajar Estate. (89) £55,000
— [Ottoman, A.H.1196/A.D.1781]. (91) £900
— [Galata, Constantinople, A.H.1196/A.D.1781]. 307 leaves, 212mm by 130mm. Contemp brown mor gilt bdg. In naskhi script by Ahmed known as Na'ili. With illuminated markers between verses, sura headings in white on illuminated panels, & double page of illumination. (91) £2,200
— [Persia, A.H.1195/A.D.1781?]. 148 leaves, 47mm by 40mm, in lacquer bdg of c.1875. In black ghubari script with titles in red by a calligrapher from Taliqan. With gold foliate designs in 2 borders & double page of illumination. (91) $3,000
— [Qajar, A.H.1200/A.D.1785]. (88) £350
— [Persia, A.H.1203/A.D.1789]. (89) £950
— [India, late 18th cent]. 280 leaves, 215mm by 135mm, in 19th-cent Persian lacquer bdg. In naskhi script possibly by Yaqut bin Abdullah. With interlinear gilt decoration, sura headings in white on gold panels, & double page of illumination. 1 leaf def. (91) £1,500
— [India, late 18th cent]. (88) £550
— [Kashmir, late 18th cent]. In naskhi script with Persian trans in ta'liq. 365 leaves, 235mm by 140mm, in lacquered papier-mache covers with paper onlays. With 8 full-page illu-

KORAN

minations. (90) $4,200
— [Persia, A.H.1207/A.D.1792-93]. 277 leaves & 2 flyleaves, 102mm by 63mm, in contemp floral lacquer bdg. In naskhi script within gold cloud-bands by Muhammad Hashim al-Lu'lu'i al-Isfahani. With sura headings in red on gold within illuminated cartouche & double page of illumination. (88) £4,800
— [Persia, A.H.1208/A.D.1793-94]. 437 leaves & 5 flyleaves, 82mm by 56mm, in contemp floral lacquer bdg. In naskhi script on gold ground by Muhammad Husain. With sura headings in red on gold within illuminated cartouche & 3 double pages of illumination. (88) £13,000
— [Qajar, A.H.1209/A.D.1794]. (91) £700
— Qajar, A.H.1210/A.D.1795]. (89) £1,000
— [Kashmir, c.1800]. 418 leaves & 4 flyleaves, 27cm by 17.5cm. Contemp floral lacquer bdg. In naskhi script with Persian interlinear trans in nasta'liq. With sura headings in red on gold within illuminated cartouche & 3 double pages of illumination. Some leaves detached. (89) £1,500
— [Kashmir, c.1800]. Juz V only. 21 leaves & 8 flyleaves, 229mm by 200mm. Contemp floral lacquer bdg. In naskhi script on gilt-sprinkled buff leaf, with Persian interlinear trans & commentary in nasta'liq. With corner cartouches with gold floral design, outer floral border between gold margins & double page of illumination. (89) £3,500
— [Kasmir, c.1800]. About 930 leaves & 2 flyleaves, 330mm by 202mm, in 19th-cent lacquer bdg. On gold-sprinkled paper in naskhi script by Nasr Hirati. With Persian interlinear trans & commentary in nasta'liq, sura headings in white on gold within illuminated cartouche & 3 double pages of illumination. (88) £2,800
— [Istanbul, 1800-1]. 77 leaves with selections of surahs 7 prayers only, 158mm by 102mm, in lea gilt. With 5 illuminated panels for chapter headings & 2 headpieces with floral decoration in colors. (90) $1,100
— [Persia, A.H.1217/A.D.1802-03]. (90) £800
— [Qajar, A.H.1220/A.D.1805]. (91) £350
— [Ottoman, A.H.1221/A.D.1806]. (91) £1,000
— [Qajar, A.H.1222/A.D.1807]. (88) £480
— [Ottoman, early 19th cent]. (90) DM800
— [Qajar, early 19th cent]. (88) £750
— [Qajar, early 19th cent]. (90) £600
— [Qajar, early 19th cent]. (90) £400
— [Kashmir, early 19th cent]. 664 leaves, 290mm by 175mm. Repaired floral lacquer bdg. In naskhi script. With c.52 lines written diagonally in outer borders of each page, sura headings in blue on illuminated panels, illuminated headpiece, 4 illuminated panels at beginning & end, & 7 double pages of illumination. (90) £2,200
— [Ottoman, A.H.1226/A.D.1811]. (90) £600
— [Ottoman, A.H.1229/A.D.1813-14]. 300 leaves & 3 flyleaves, 19cm by 11.4cm. Qajar floral lacquer bdg. In naskhi script by Sayyid Husain, a student of Mustafa Naili. With sura headings in white on gold within illuminated cartouche in 2 colors of gold & double-page of illumination. (88) £2,200
— [Qajar, early 19th cent]. (91) £750
— [Ottoman, early 19th cent]. (91) £500
— [Kashmir, early 19th cent]. (91) £800
— [Persia, A.H.1233/A.D.1818]. 217 leaves & 2 flyleaves, 222mm by 139mm, in def contemp floral lacquer bdg. In naskhi script between gold cloud-bands by Muhammad Kazim Shirazi for Haji Mirza Muhammad Hasan Khanazadeh. With Persian marginal commentary in nasta'liq, sura headings in blue on gold within illuminated cartouche & 2 double pages of illumination. (88) £2,800
— [Qajar, A.H.1235/A.D.1819]. (91) £850
— [Ottoman, A.H.1237/A.D.1821-22]. (90) £550
— [Isfahan, A.H.1237/A.D.1821]. 258 leaves, 200mm by 123mm, in fine floral lacquer bdg. In naskhi script by Abdullah. With diacritics in black, interlinear gilt decoration throughout, some marginal commentaries within gold cartouches, sura headings in gold

on illuminated panels & 3 double pages of illumination. (88) £5,500
— [Persia, A.H.1239/A.D.1823-24]. 383 leaves & flyleaf, 260mm by 165mm, in def floral lacquer bdg. In naskhi script by Muhammad Shafi' al-Tabrizi for Amir Gauhar[?] Khan Qajar. With Persian marginal commentary in diwani script, sura headings in gold on blue ground within illuminated cartouche & double page of illumination. (88) £1,400
— [Persia, A.H.1240/A.D.1825]. (89) £550
— [India, 1st half of 19th cent]. 1064 pp (incomplete), 67.5cm by 49cm, in contemp red mor. In naskhi script on colored paper, with interlinear Persian trans in red throughout. With occasional glosses in margins & sura headings in red. Imperf. (91) £40,000
— [n.p., A.H.1242/A.D.1826]. (89) £400
— [Qajar, A.H.1243/A.D.1827]. (89) £700
— [Ottoman, A.H.1245/A.D.1829-30]. 303 leaves & 4 flyleaves, 145mm by 89mm. Contemp green mor gilt. In elegant black naskhi script on green buff polished paper by Mir Hafiz Ibrahim, known as Afif the Mutawalli of the mosque of the Mother of the Sultan. With sura headings in white on gold within illuminated cartouches & double-page of illumination. (88) £1,800
— [Qajar, A.H.1245/A.D.1829]. (88) £800
— [Ottoman, A.H.1245/A.D.1829]. 152 leaves, 173mm by 105mm. Contemp brown mor bdg decorated in gold. In naskhi script by Yusuf Rifat. With sura headings in white thuluth on illuminated panels & double page of illumination in various shades of gold. Some leaves detached. (91) £2,400
— [Lahore, 1829-30]. (90) $325
— [Persia, A.H.1247/A.D.1831]. 279 leaves, 203mm by 136mm. Contemp floral lacquer bdg. In naskhi script with Persian interlinear trans in nasta'liq. With sura headings in gold thuluth on illuminated panels, illuminated marginal medallions, & 6 pp of illumination. (89) DM9,600
— [Ottoman, A.H.1249/A.D.1833-34]. (89) £600
— [Persia, A.H.1248/A.D.1833]. 273 leaves & 3 flyleaves, 17.8cm by 10.5cm. Contemp floral bdg. In black naskhi script by Saiyyid Sadiq bin Saiyyid 'Ali Musawi at the instance of Aqa Mirza Nasrullah. With sura headings in gold on blue with scrolling arabesques within illuminated cartouche, & double page of illumination. Prince Muhammad Hasan Mirza Qajar Estate. (89) £3,800
— [Persia, A.H.1249/A.D.1833-34]. 218 leaves & 3 flyleaves, 20.3cm by 12.7cm. Contemp floral lacquer bdg. In black naskhi script by Ghulam 'Ali Isfahani with the help of Muhammad Karin at the instance of Husain 'Ali Khan. With sura headings in red on gold within illuminated cartouche & 3 double pages of illumination. Prince Muhammad Hasan Mirza Qajar Estate. (89) £4,500
— [Qajar, A.H.1250/A.D.1834]. (91) £350
— [Qajar, A.H.1250/A.D.1834]. (88) £800
— [Qajar, A.H.1251/A.D.1835]. (89) £450
— [Ottoman, A.H.1253/A.D.1837]. 247 leaves, 202mm by 125mm, in brown mor tooled in gold. In naskhi script by Hasan Kashfi, illuminated by Ahmed Shaker. With diacritics in black, illuminated markers between verses, sura headings in white on illuminated panels & double page of illumination. (88) £1,400
— [Ottoman, A.H.1254/A.D.1838-39]. 303 leaves & 3 flyleaves, 120mm by 82mm. Contemp green mor finely gilt. In naskhi script on cream polished paper by Sayyid Husain bin Muhammad. With illuminated marginal medallions, sura headings in white on gold within illuminated cartouche, & double page of illumination. (89) £4,200
— [Qazwin, A.H.1257/A.D.1841]. (91) £350
— [Persia, A.H.1258/A.D.1842]. (88) £650
— [Qajar, A.H.1259/A.D.1843]. (91) £400
— [Ottoman, A.H.1264/A.D.1847]. 304 leaves, 180mm by 110mm. Green mor bdg. In naskhi script by Salih al-Sabri. With illuminated markers between verses, sura headings in white on illuminated panels, & double page & borders of 3 double pages richly il-

luminated in colors & gold. (90) £1,300
— [Ottoman, Shumni, A.H.1264/ A.D.1847]. 308 leaves, 188mm by 120mm. Contemp brown mor tooled in gold. In naskhi script by Isma'il Najib. With floral sprays in colors & gold, sura headings in white on illuminated panels, & double page of illumination. (91) £2,800
— [Ottoman, A.H.1266/A.D.1849]. 308 leaves, 171mm by 115mm, in def contemp green mor tooled in gold. In naskhi script by Muhammad Nuri. With diacritics in black, illuminated markers between verses, sura headings in white on illuminated panels & 5 double pages of illumination. (88) £4,500
— [Turkey, 1849-50]. (90) $325
— [Qajar, 19th cent]. 192 leaves, gazelle skin, 75mm by 41mm, in contemp lacquer bdg. In naskhi script. With illuminated marginal medallions & corner cartouches, sura headings in red on gold, & 3 double pages of fine illumination. (91) £6,500
— [Ottoman, 19th cent]. 303 leaves & 4 flyleaves, 168mm by 107mm, in contemp brown mor gilt. In naskhi script by Ahmad al-Nazifi. With gold discs between verses, sura headings in white on gold with illuminated floral spray beneath, & double page of illumination. (91) £1,500
— [Persia, 19th cent]. (90) £800
— [Persia, 19th cent]. 203 leaves & 5 flyleaves, 178mm by 102mm. Contemp floral lacquer bdg. In naskhi script. With gold discs between verses, sura headings in red & double page of illumination. (90) £1,300
— [Qajar, 19th cent]. 216 leaves & flyleaf, 254mm by 158mm. Fine contemp lacquer bdg. In naskhi script by Muhammad Ibrahim al-Qumi, with some marginal commentary in nasta'liq. With gold discs between verses, illuminated marginal medallions, sura headings in orange on gold within illuminated cartouche, & double page of illumination. (90) £6,000
— [Persia, 19th cent]. (90) £950
— [Persia, 19th cent]. 276 leaves & 3 flyleaves, 292mm by 184mm. Kashmir floral lacquer bdg. In naskhi script.

With sura headings in gold on blue & red within illuminated cartouche, illuminated marginal medallions, marginal commentary in nasta'liq, & 2 double pages of illumination. (89) £2,200
— [Persia, 19th cent]. 245 leaves, 235mm by 140mm. Contemp lacquer bdg. In naskhi script within gold cloud bands. With illuminated marginal medallions, sura headings in gold on blue or red ground within illuminated cartouche, & double page of illumination. (89) £2,000
— [Kashmir, 19th cent]. (89) £1,000
— [Ottoman, 19th cent]. Juz XVII - XVIII only. 31 leaves & 4 flyleaves, 349mm by 235mm. Fine 16th-cent Safavid brown mor gilt bdg. In muhaqqaq script. With sura headings in white on gold within illuminated cartouche & 2 half-page illuminated headings. (89) £2,500
— [Ottoman, 19th cent]. (89) £600
— [Persia, 19th cent]. Scroll, 531cm by 9.2cm, in lea wrap. In black & red naskhi script on buff polished paper. With finely illuminated heading, inner panels in geometric & floral designs & outer border with floral & lozenge design. (89) £8,000
— [Persia, 19th cent]. 203 leaves & 2 flyleaves, 11.7cm by 7.3cm. Contemp lacquer bdg. In black naskhi script with sura headings in gold & double page of illumination. Prince Muhammad Hasan Mirza Qajar Estate. (89) £1,100
— [Persia, 19th cent]. 251 leaves & 2 flyleaves, 120mm by 75mm, in contemp lacquer bdg. In naskhi script with sura headings in gold & double page of illumination. Some repairs. (88) £1,500
— [Persia, 19th cent]. 121 leaves & 2 flyleaves, 196mm by 95mm, in contemp floral lacquer bdg, dated A.H.1283. In naskhi script by Mirza 'Ala al-din Tabrizi. With sura headings in red on gold within illuminated cartouche & double page of illumination. (88) £1500
— [Persia, 19th cent]. 234 leaves & flyleaf, 107mm by 66mm. Contemp floral lacquer bdg. In naskhi script with

marginal Persian commentary in shikasteh by Abdullah bin Ashur. With illuminated marginal medallions, sura headings in gold on blue ground, interspaced with gold scrolling design within illuminated cartouche, & double page of illumination. (90) £10,000
— [Qajar, 19th cent]. 272 leaves in 2 parts, 44mm by 44mm, octagonal. Contemp floral lacquer bdg. In naskhi script. Lacking sura headings. (90) £2,000
— [Ottoman, 19th cent]. (88) DM800
— [Qajar, 19th cent]. (89) £550
— [Qajar, 19th cent]. (89) £900
— [Persia, 19th cent]. Scroll, 10.08 meters. In minute naskhi script with diacritics in black, geometric designs or calligraphic panels (1 later replacement), margins ruled in gold & sura headings in red. Some defects. (88) £1,600
— [South East Asia, 19th cent]. (89) £700
— [Qajar, 19th cent]. (89) £550
— [Qajar, 19th cent]. 265 leaves, 80mm by 50mm, in contemp floral lacquer bdg. On gold-sprinkled paper in minute naskhi script with diacritics in black, gold dots between verses, sura headings in red on illuminated panels & double page of illumination. (88) £2,200
— [Ottoman, 19th cent]. (90) £700
— [Kashmir, 19th cent]. 425 leaves, 258mm by 149mm. Repaired contemp floral lacquer bdg. In naskhi script with interlinear Persian trans in red nasta'liq by Mulla Ali Burujardi. With text interspersed with illuminated markers, sura headings in blue on illuminated panels, & double page of illumination. (90) £1,300
— [South East Asia, 19th cent]. 424 leaves, 316mm by 220mm. Contemp brown mor tooled in blind. In cursive script. With yellow or red discs between verses, sura headings in red, & 3 double pages decorated with arabesques & floral motifs in red, yellow & black. (90) £2,800
— [Kashmir, 19th cent]. (90) £650
— [Qajar, 19th cent]. (90) £400
— [Ottoman, A.H.1267/A.D.1850]. (91) £900
— [Qajar, A.H.1269/A.D.1852]. (91) £600
— [Qajar, A.H.1270/A.D.1853]. (88) £950
— [Ottoman, A.H.1274/A.D.1857]. 305 leaves & 2 flyleaves, 165mm by 114mm. Contemp brown mor gilt bdg. In naskhi script by al-Sayyid Hafiz Muhammad Kamil al-Wahbi. With illuminated devices between verses, illuminated marginal floral sprays, sura headings in white on gold within illuminated cartouche, & double page of illumination. (90) £1,100
— [Qajar, A.H.1277/A.D.1860]. 283 leaves, 290mm by 190mm, in fine floral lacquer bdg. In naskhi script by Ahmad al-Tabrizi. With diacritics in black, interlinear gilt decoration throughout, glosses in shikasteh within illuminated medallions, sura headings in gold on illuminated panels & 3 double pages of illumination. (88) £18,000
— [Ottoman, A.H.1277/A.D.1860]. Over 300 leaves, 153mm by 110mm, in red mor gilt. In naskhi script by Husain al-'Ashiqi. With diacritics in black, illuminated markers between verses, sura headings in white on illuminated panels & 3 double pages of illumination. (88) £2,200
— [n.p., A.H.1275/A.D.1861-62]. Doheny collection. (88) $900
— [Ottoman, Arzarum, A.H.1280/A.D.1863]. 365 leaves (1 blank), 243mm by 168mm, in modern red mor gilt. In naskhi script by Muhammad 'Asem bin Usman known as Khawajazadeh. With illuminated markers between verses, sura headings in white on illuminated panels, & double page of illumination. (91) £1,200
— [Ottoman, A.H.1280/A.D.1863]. (89) £400
— [Persia, A.H.1282/A.D.1865]. 255 leaves & 2 flyleaves, 108mm by 76mm. Contemp floral lacquer bdg. In black naskhi script with Persian marginal commentary in nasta'liq by Mahmud bin al-Sayyid Muhammad Hashim al-Musavi. With sura headings in red on gold within illuminated cartouche & 2 double-pages of illumination. (88) £1,400
— [Ottoman, A.H.1283/A.D.1866]. 327 leaves & 4 flyleaves, 228mm by 158mm. Contemp black mor bdg. In naskhi script within gold cloud bands

KORAN

by Sharifa Hafiza & Zulaikha Khatimi al-Sa'di. With illuminated marginal floral sprays, sura headings in white on gold, & double page of illumination. (90) £2,800
— [Ottoman, A.H.1283/A.D.1866]. (91) £200
— [Ottoman, A.H.1283/A.D.1866]. (88) £600
— [Qajar, A.H.1285/A.D.1868]. (90) £600
— [Ottoman, A.H.1287/A.D.1870]. (89) £600
— [Qajar, A.H.1287/A.D.1870]. 3 scrolls, c.300cm, cloth. In minute naskhi script by Ibn Mir Shihab ad-Din Ahmad. With diacritics in black, borders ruled in blue & gold, sura headings in red & 3 illuminated headpieces (2 repainted). 1 scroll waterstained. (88) £1,500
— [Persia, A.H.1289/A.D.1872-73]. 244 leaves & 5 flyleaves, 92mm by 57mm. Contemp lacquer bdg. In naskhi script between gold cloud bands by Ibn Ja'far al-Husaini Isma'il. With gold discs between verses, illuminated marginal medallions, & 5 pages of illumination (1 double-page). (90) £1,100
— [Ottoman, A.H.1289/A.D.1872]. (89) £800
— [Ottoman, A.H.1290/A.D.1873]. (89) £850
— [Qajar, A.H.1292/A.D.1875-76]. 223 leaves & 4 flyleaves, 54mm by 38mm. Contemp lacquer bdg. In naskhi script by Masih al-Talqani al-Dizani. With gold discs between verses, illuminated marginal medallions, sura headings in red on gold within illuminated cartouche, & double page of illumination. (90) £8,500
— [Qajar, 2d half of 19th cent]. (91) £900
— [Qajar, 2d half of 19th cent]. (90) £800
— [Persia, A.H.1293/A.D.1877-78]. 216 leaves & 4 flyleaves, 330mm by 202mm, in contemp floral lacquer bdg. In naskhi script by Sayyid Hasanbin 'Ali for presentation to Aqa Mirza Mahmud. With some marginal commentary in nasta'liq, sura headings in red on gold within illuminated cartouche & 2 double pages of illumination. Some repairs. (88) £3,800
— [Hamadan, A.H.1293/A.D.1876]. (91) £250
— [Kashmir, A.H.1302/A.D.1884]. 460 leaves, 372mm by 225mm. Contemp floral lacquer bdg. In naskhi script on gold painted paper, with commentary in outer margins & Persian trans in nasta'liq in outer borders, by Amir-ad-Din al-Kashmiri. With blue florets between verses, sura headings in white on gold panels, 4 illuminated panels at beginning & end, & 9 double pages of illumination. (90) £7,500
— [Kashmir, c.1885]. (90) £600
— [Qajar, A.H.1307/A.D.1889]. (91) £380
— [Provincial Ottoman, late 19th cent]. (90) £420

Ms, 5 selected suras. [Persia, 16th cent]. 83 leaves & 5 flyleaves, 19cm by 12cm, in contemp brown mor gilt. In black naskhi script within gold cloud bands. With sura headings in white on gold within illuminated cartouche & double page of illumination. (89) £3,000
— Ms, album page with surat al-Fatiha. [Mughal, c.1680]. 356mm by 221mm. In elegant nasta'liq script within cloud-bands, by Muhammad Rahim. With richly decorated borders in colors & gold. (91) £1,300
— Ms, calligraphic panel with Koranic verses. (90) £500
— Ms, calligraphic scroll, [North Africa, early 19th cent]. 475cm, on thin paper. In large ornamental kufic & ghubari scripts. Partly def. In metal carrying case. (89) £1,300
— Ms, Koranic phrase. (89) £650
— Ms, Koranic scroll. [Persia, A.H.1207?/A.D.1792-93?]. 509cm by 9.8cm. Red lea wraps. In black naskhi script by Muhammad 'Ali ibn Muhammad Sadiq al-Husaini, with sayings & couplets on the excellence of 'Ali & the names of the Imams in white. With cartouches interspaced with illuminated panels & illuminated heading (def). (90) £1,600
— Ms, selected Koranic verses. (89) £550

Koreff, Johannes Ferdinand, 1783-1851
ALs, [19 Jan 1827]. (91) DM700

Korngold, Erich Wolfgang, 1897-1957
ALs, 11 Feb 1920. (88) DM320
Autograph postcard, sgd, 18 Oct 1918. (90) $175

Kortum, Karl Arnold, 1745-1824
ALs, 11 Apr 1817. (88) DM800

Kosegarten, Ludwig Theobul, 1758-1818
ALs, 6 Aug 1798. (91) DM300

Kossel, Albrecht, 1853-1927
ALs, 26 Aug 1907. (88) DM650

Kossuth, Lajos, 1802-94
Ms, part of a speech delivered in Preston Corn Exchange, [1855?]. (88) £120
ALs, 9 Dec 1858. (91) $130
— 15 Jan [n.y.]. (91) $150
Ls, 24 Sept 1859. (90) £320

Kotzebue, August von, 1761-1819
Collection of 3 A Ls s & AL, 22 May to 24 Sept 1818. 6 pp, 4to & 8vo. To the bookseller Hoffmann. Regarding articles for the Literarisches Wochenblatt & orders for books. (90) DM1,600
ALs, 20 Jan 1787. (89) DM320
— 20 Aug 1790. (90) DM420
— 24 Dec 1790. (88) DM700
— 31 Dec 1818. (88) DM460

Krafft, Georg Wolfgang, 1701-54
ALs, 3 June 1753. 3 pp, 8vo. To Pierre Louis Moreau de Maupertuis. Agreeing with Maupertuis in his controversy with Samuel Koenig & Voltaire. (89) DM2,400

Krasin, Leonid Borisovich, 1870-1926
Ls, 5 Jan 1921. (89) DM1,000

Kraus, Karl, 1874-1936
Autograph Ms, poem, Dem Knaben Lenker, [1922]. 1 p, 12mo. 4 lines. (89) DM2,200
— Autograph Ms, poem, Volkshymne, [Nov 1920]. 1 p, 8vo. 5 stanzas. (88) DM9,000
ALs, 4 Nov 1898. 1 p, 8vo. To an unnamed Ed. Expressing the wish to see his work reviewed in recipient's journal. (90) DM1,200

Krause, Gottlieb Friedrich, 1805-60. See: Goethe, Johann Wolfgang von

Krauss, Clemens, 1893-1954
Photograph, sgd, 18 Jan 1926. (91) DM450

Krebs, Sir Hans Adolf, 1900-81
Autograph Ms, 4 contributions to a discussion about medical training & research, in German. (90) DM700
— Autograph Ms, lecture given at Marburg about German universities in an international context; sgd later & dated June 1977. (91) DM680
Typescript, part of scientific paper dealing with methionine, 10 & 11 Nov 1975. (90) DM550

Kreisler, Fritz, 1875-1962
Menu, sgd, 6 Apr 1901. (88) $80
Photograph, sgd, 23 Nov 1920. (90) $175

Krenek, Ernst
Autograph Ms, essay, Was ist, und wie macht man elektronische Musik, [n.d.]. (91) £780
Collection of 16 A Ls s, Ls, & 8 autograph postcards, sgd, 26 Aug 1933 to 27 Mar 1953. 34 pp, mostly folio, & cards. To Willi Schuh. Mostly concerning his professional activities in Switzerland. With related material. (90) DM3,200
— Collection of 3 A Ls s, Ls, autograph postcard, sgd, 3 A Ns s & autograph sentiment, sgd, 1941 to 1980. 9 pp, various sizes, & inscr copy. To Robert Breuer. About cultural standards in Europe & music during the war, his own work, etc. In English & German. With related material. (88) DM1,100
— Collection of 6 A Ls s & Ls s, 1950 to 1957. (89) £400
ALs, 12 Dec 1927. (91) DM320

Kreutzer, Konradin, 1780-1849
ALs, 18 May 1813. (90) DM550
— 9 Aug 1820. (88) DM950
— 20 Aug 1832. (91) DM1,000
— 9 Jan 1837. 2 pp, 4to. To Freiherr von Muenchhausen. About a fee, the theatre in Vienna, & his new opera. (90) DM1,100
— 19 Aug [1843]. (89) DM550

Kreymborg, Alfred, 1883-1966
Series of 14 Ls s, 1923 to 1945. (89) $110

Kriehuber, Josef, 1800-76
ALs, [n.d.]. (89) DM220

Krolow, Karl
Autograph Ms, poem, Durch die Strassen. (90) DM380
— Autograph Ms, poem, Vollstaendige Menschen; sgd & dated 5 May 1978. (89) DM300
Autograph transcript, poem, Erwachen, sgd & dated 16 Sept 1976. (90) DM260

Kropotkin, Petr Alekseevich, Prince, 1842-1921
ALs, 16 Jan 1890. (88) DM250
— 18 Feb 1904. (91) $130
— 8 July 1915. (88) DM800
— 9 Dec 1915. (89) DM300

Krug, Gustav, 1844-1902. See: Nietzsche, Friedrich & Krug

Kruger, Stephen Johannes Paulus, 1825-1904
Ds, 4 May 1900. (90) DM700
Photograph, sgd, 18 May 1900. (88) DM540

Krupp, Alfred, 1812-87
ALs, 1 Jan 1882. (88) DM340

Krupp von Bohlen und Halbach, Gustav, 1870-1950
ALs, 13 Sept 1915. 12 pp, 4to. To Gen. Otto von Lauenstein. Discussing the military situation & German war aims. With related material. (90) DM1,600
Ls, 19 July 1930. (90) DM350

Krupskaya, Nadezhda Konstantinovna, 1869-1939
ALs, [1923?]. (90) £250

Krusenstern, Adam Johann von, 1770-1846
ALs, 23 Apr 1815. (90) DM750
— [n.d.]. (91) DM330

Kubin, Alfred, 1877-1959
Collection of ALs, autograph postcard, sgd, & photograph, sgd & inscr, [31 Oct 1910], 27 Aug 1911 & [1917]. (90) DM900
— Collection of ALs & 3 autograph postcards, sgd, 16 Dec [1918] to 13 Apr 1930. (90) DM620
— Collection of 12 A Ls s & 4 autograph postcards, sgd, 23 Aug 1947 to 1 Apr 1950. 22 pp, folio & 8vo, & cards. To the Ed of the journal Thema. Concerning illusts for the journal. (91) DM3,500
Series of 11 A Ls s, 4 Mar 1930 to 5 Feb 1943. 22 pp, 4to & 8vo. To Gertrud Sentke. Interesting letters about his own & recipient's work, & a variety of matters. 1 ALs postscript to ALs by Hans Carossa. (89) DM6,500
ALs, [c.1922]. (91) DM350
— [1940]. (90) DM300
— 6 Oct 1942. (89) DM420
— 26 Apr 1943. (91) DM250
— 21 Feb 1949. (90) DM460
Autograph postcards (2), sgd, 22 Sept 1919 & 13 July 1922. (89) DM950
Collection of ANs & AN, 10 Apr 1942 & 10 Apr 1952. (89) DM440
ANs, 17 Aug 1942. (90) DM400
See also: Blei, Franz & Kubin

Kugler, Franz Theodor, 1808-58
ALs, 24 Dec 1849. (90) DM750

Kun, Bela, 1885-1939?
Ls, Aug 1924. 1 p, folio. To the headquarters of the German Communist Party. Requesting their cooperation in a project to improve control of the communist press. In German. (89) DM4,500

Kunert, Guenter
Autograph Ms, lecture, Was ist ein Gedicht?; sgd & dated 25 May 1981. (90) DM280
— Autograph Ms, poem, Selbsthass, 2 May 1982. (91) DM360

Kunz, George Frederick, 1856-1932
[An archive of correspondence addressed to him, containing 36 A Ls s & 59 Ls s, 21 retained copies of his own letters & related material, 1887 to 1936, dealing with numismatics, precious stones & various scientific matters, sold at sg on 8 Feb 1990, lot 181, for $650.]

Kunze, Reiner
Autograph transcript, poem, Dein kopf auf meiner brust; sgd & dated 11 Nov 1981. (90) DM370

Kussmaul, Adolf, 1822-1902
A Ls s (2), 24 Jan 1891 & 24 Mar 1891. (91) DM480
ALs, 15 Apr 1897. (91) DM230

Kutuzov, Mikhail Ilarinovich, 1745-1813
Ls, 16 June 1789. (89) £350

Kyburz, Abraham, d.1765
Original drawings, Historien-Kinder-Bet und Bilder-Bibel, comprising 291 wash drawings, [c.1730-1735]; to illus Catechitische Kinder-Bibel, 2 vols, 1744 & 1745. Mtd in folio album, with ptd French texts added later. (90) £2,500

Kyne, Peter B., 1880-1957
Series of 11 Ls s, 1915 to 1916 & 1925. (88) $325

L

La Condamine, Charles Marie de, 1701-74
ALs, 5 Feb 1772. (90) DM340

La Farge, John, 1835-1910
Collection of 3 A Ls s & Ls, 26 Feb 1908 to 24 Nov 1909. (89) $375

La Fontaine, Jean de, 1621-95
ALs, 28 Feb 1656. 1 p, 4to. To Claude Lamblet. Acknowledging receipt of a number of copies. Calculations in a later hand on verso. Tipped to larger leaf with trans. Barrett collection. (89) $4,250

Ds, 16 Apr 1663. 2 pp, folio. Dealing with a financial matter. Also sgd by 2 others. (90) DM2,500

La Genealogie des Contes de Boulogne
Ms, La Genealogie des Contes de Boulogne, 1531. 12 leaves (2 blank), vellum, 224mm by 154mm. 18th-cent red mor gilt. In a very skilful rounded roman hand resembling ptd type, probably by Geoffroy Tory. With full-page frontis with the crowned arms of Catherine de Medicis. Bradley Martin Ms. (90) $22,000

La Harpe, Frederic Cesar de, 1754-1838
ALs, [14 Apr 1804]. (90) DM420
— 6 Apr 1826. (89) DM550

La Roche, Sophie von, 1731-1807
Series of 3 A Ls s, 1784 to 27 Nov 1799. 12 pp, 4to & 8vo. To Countess Sophie zu Solms-Roedelheim. About private & literary matters, her visit with Wieland, etc. (91) DM4,000
— Series of 12 A Ls s, 29 July 1787 to 19 June 1799. 34 pp, 8vo & 4to. To Countess Sophie zu Solms-Roedelheim. About a variety of personal, literary & political matters. (89) DM8,000
— Series of 8 A Ls s, 13 Feb 1788 to 1 Aug 1798. 25 pp, 8vo. To Countess Sophie zu Solms-Roedelheim. Interesting letters about literature, politics, & private matters. (90) DM11,000
ALs, 9 Jan 1787. (89) £360

La Valliere, Louise Francoise de La Baume le Blanc, Duchesse de, 1644-1710
— FROMENTIERES, JEAN LOUIS DE, & BOSSUET, JACQUES BENIGNE. - Ms, Discours faits a la prise d'habit de Madame de la Valliere dans son Entree aux carmelites, & Discour Prononcee... a la Profession de Madame de la valliere..., [c.1675]. 64 leaves, 164mm by 110mm. In extra red-brown mor gilt bdg, [c.1720]. (88) DM1,700

Lachmann, Karl, 1793-1851
ALs, 3 Feb 1828. (90) DM650
— 19 Apr 1848. (91) DM520

Lachner, Franz, 1803-90
Autograph quotation, 5 double bars of music, sgd; 28 Aug 1847. (91) $120

Lachner, Vincenz, 1811-93
ALs, 30 May 1861. (88) DM340
Collection of ADs & photograph, sgd & inscr, 20 Aug 1853 & [n.d.]. (90) DM320

Lactantius, Lucius Caecilius Firmianus, c.240-c.320
Ms, Divinarum Institutionum Libri VII. [Florence, c.1420-30]. 125 leaves (1 lacking), vellum, 322mm by 228mm. Contemp Florentine blindstamped bdg of brown goatskin over wooden bds. In very fine well-formed early humanistic minuscule hands by 3 scribes, mostly by Guglielmino Tanaglia. With 3 small illuminated initials, 3-quarter illuminated border,

LACTANTIUS

& 6 very large illuminated white-vine initials by Filippo di Matteo Torelli. (91) £86,000

Ladd, Eugene F.
[A group of 8 presidential military commissions for Ladd, 8 July 1884 to 1914, sold at R on 4 Mar 1989, lot 254, for $3,200.]

Ladenburg, Albert, 1842-1911
[A collection of 29 letters & cards addressed to him & his wife Margarethe, with related material, sold at star on 9 Mar 1988, lot 491, for DM850.]

Ladenburg, Rudolf, 1882-1952
[A collection of 37 letters & cards addressed to him & his wife Else, with related material, sold at star on 9 Mar 1988, lot 492, for DM1,900.]

Laemmle, Carl, 1867-1939
Ls, 21 Apr 1932. (90) $120

Lafayette, Gilbert du Motier, Marquis de, 1757-1834
Series of 7 A Ls s, [1802-03 & n.d.]. 11 pp, 4to. To Citoyen Mascles. Commenting about French politics. In English. Mtd & in mor gilt bdg with transcripts. John F. Fleming Estate. (89) $2,500
ALs, 19 Mar 1778. 4 pp, 4to. To Gov. George Clinton. Regarding the transfer of cannon from Fort Ticonderoga & the settlement of accounts of British prisoners-of-war. Framed. (88) $5,500
— 8 Jan 1779. 1 p, 4to. To [Alexander] Hamilton. Requesting information on military & political affairs. In French. (90) $2,200
— 21 May 1781. 3 pp, folio. To Gov. [Thomas Sim] Lee. Requesting reinforcements from Maryland to help fight Cornwallis. Pforzheimer collection. (90) $5,000
— 25 July [1781]. 1 p, 4to. To Baron von Steuben. Informing him that Maj. Call will see him concerning an augmentation of the cavalry. (90) $3,000
— [Nov 1788]. (89) £280
— 1 June 1803. 3 pp, 4to. To James McHenry. Talking about his convalescence from a broken leg, the war between France & England, & the Louisiana Purchase. Seal tear. Was

AMERICAN BOOK PRICES CURRENT

mtd. (88) $3,200
— [6 May 1803]. Byer collection. (90) $550
— 23 Jan 1815. (91) $300
— 15 Aug 1818. (90) $650
— 14 May 1824. (91) $700
— 29 Aug 1824. (88) $700
— 5 Feb 1825. (91) $750
— 19 Oct [c.1825]. (88) £120
— 2 Nov 1825. (89) £400
— 16 June 1826. Pforzheimer collection. (90) $1,000
— 18 May 1827. (88) $350
— 4 Apr 1828. (90) $550
— 17 Sept 1829. 1 p, 4to. Recipient unknown. Commenting about French affairs & recommending Joseph Robert. In English. (90) $1,200
— 26 Aug 1830. (89) $325
— 15 Nov 1830. (91) $420
— 28 Mar 1831. (89) DM550
— 20 [?] 1831. (89) $450
— 14 July 1833. 1 p, 4to. To E. Lerminier. Requesting assistance for Jared Sparks & his Ed of Washington's correspondence. (90) $4,500
— 10 Feb [n.y.]. (90) $425
Ls, 6 Sept 1819. (89) DM450
— 20 Feb 1829. (89) $250
— 27 Nov 1832. (88) $130
ANs, [n.d.]. (91) $450
Ds, 9 Oct 1804. 1 p, folio. Attestation on clerical copy of his power of attorney to James Madison to locate & administer his lands in Louisiana. Including attestation by Fulwar Skipwith at bottom. (90) $11,000
Endorsement, 30 Aug 1791. (91) $325
Franking signature, [12 Apr 1780]. Alexander collection. (90) $800

Laforgue, Jules, 1860-87
Autograph Ms, Grains d'Aloes, [n.d.]. (88) £650

Lagerkvist, Paer, 1891-1974
ALs, 11 Oct 1922. (91) DM600

Lagerloef, Selma, 1858-1940
Series of 3 A Ls s, 31 Oct 1904 to 25 Jan 1905. (88) £850
ALs, 8 Oct 1919. (89) DM900
Autograph postcard, sgd, 11 Jan 1922. (91) DM330

Ds, 14 Oct 1898. (89) £600
Photograph, sgd & inscr, [n.d.]. (90) DM500

Lagrange, Joseph Louis, 1736-1813
ALs, [n.d.]. (91) DM950

Lagrenee, Louis Jean Francois, 1725?-1805
ALs, 7 Mar 1787. (88) DM550

Lajoie, Napoleon, 1875-1959
Signature, 28 Mar [19]50. (91) $250

Lake, Edward, 1641-1704
Autograph Ms, diary, 21 Oct 1677 to 23 Apr 1678. 23 pp & blanks, c.8 by 3.25 inches, in contemp vellum. Describing events touching the Duke of York's (James II) family, the marriage of William & Mary, Court & city news, etc. (89) £1,050

Lalande, Joseph Jerome de, 1732-1807
ALs, [17 Mar 1799]. (88) $250
— [May 1799]. (90) DM240

Lalo, Edouard, 1823-92
Series of 3 A Ls s, 1880 to 1885. (88) DM440
— Series of 3 A Ls s, 5 to 24 Nov 1884. (88) DM560
A Ls s (2), [c.1885]. (91) DM220
ALs, 31 Dec 1878. (89) DM800
— 13 Feb 1879. (90) DM520
— 22 May 1888. (90) DM260
— [n.d.]. (90) DM250

Lamarck, Jean Baptiste de, 1744-1829
ALs, [n.d.]. (90) DM440

Lamartine, Alphonse de, 1790-1869
Autograph Ms, poem, Une Loterie de Fleures peintes par Madame Pancoucke, 27 May 1847. (90) £150
ALs, 8 July [1822?]. (88) £500
— [12] Mar 1840. (90) DM320
— [c.1847/48]. (90) DM800
— 24 Jan [1848]. (90) DM550

Lamb, Lady Caroline, 1785-1828
Original drawings, 5 sketches, [n.d.]. In worn quarter-calf album, 4to, containing c.75 18th- & early 19th-cent drawings, mostly in watercolor. (89) £2,100
See also: Malthus, Thomas Robert

Lamb, Charles, 1775-1834
Autograph Ms, essay, The Praise of Chimney sweepers: a May day Effusion, [c.1821-22]. 6 pp, folio, in modern red mor gilt by Elizabeth Greenhill. With extensive autograph revisions. Sgd Elia, twice. (89) £22,000
ALs, [n.d., c.1804?]. (89) £650
— [11 July 1830]. 1 p, 8vo. To [Louisa Martin]. About his niece's visit & his health problems. Including 3 small drawings. Sgd CL. Barrett collection. (89) $1,200
— 11 Oct 1833. Doheny collection. (89) $420
— [29 Nov 1833]. 4 pp, folio. To Edward Moxon. Providing a detailed commentary on some of recipient's sonnets, & suggesting some changes for the ptd version. Bradley Martin sale. (90) $3,500
ANs, [n.d.]. (89) $375

Lamb, Lynton
Original drawings, (20) for William Mayne's A Grass Rope. (88) £300

Lamberg, Johann Maximilian, Graf von, 1608-82
ALs, 12 Sept 1641. (89) DM750

Lamennais, Felicite Robert de, 1782-1854
ALs, 25 Sept 1832. (90) DM650

Lameth Family
[An ALs each by Charles & Theodore de Lameth & Ls by Alexandre de Lameth, 1791 & 1793, sold at pn on 10 Dec 1987, lot 505, for £70 to L'Autographe.]

Lammers, Hans H., 1879-1962
Ls, 18 Nov 1939. (91) $110
— 9 Dec 1939. (91) $110

L'Amour, Louis
Photograph, sgd & inscr, [c.1983]. (88) $140

Lancaster, Joseph, 1778-1838
ALs, 25 Feb 1826. (90) £900

Landeck, Armin
Collection of 11 A Ls s, autograph Ms, & 3 autograph postcards, sgd, 1934 to [1946 & n.d.]. (90) $375

Landmann, George, 1779-1854. See: Cadiz

Landseer, Sir Edwin Henry, 1802-73
Collection of 6 A Ls s, 6 A Ls & 3 A Ns s, [c.1822 to 1824]. (88) £250

Lane, Sir Hugh Percy, 1875-1915
Collection of 8 A Ls s & autograph postcard, sgd, 12 Oct 1906 to 22 Nov 1907. (90) £75

Langdon, John, 1741-1819
Ds, 30 Sept 1806. (91) $95
— 1 May 1811. (88) $50

Langtree, Lillie, 1852-1929
[A collection of over 50 A Ls s & cards addressed to her, 1884 to 1929, c.120 pp, 4to & 8vo, with related material, sold at S on 21 July 1988, lot 248, for £600 to Joseph & Sawyer.]

Lanner, Joseph, 1801-43
ALs, [n.d.]. 1 p, 4to. To Johann Strauss (the Elder). Reporting about the accounts for a concert. (88) DM1,200
Ds, 22 Dec 1840. (89) DM700
— 23 July 1841. (88) DM900

Lannes, Jean, Duc de Montebello, 1769-1809
ADs, 27 [Dec 1806]. (89) £800

Laplace, Pierre Simon de, Marquis, 1749-1827
ALs, [19 Apr 1799]. (89) £650
Ds, [n.d.]. 1 p, 16mo. Attestation that he does not consider the project of a submarine worthy of the attention of the Academy of Sciences. Also sgd by A. M. Le Gendre. (91) $1,200

Larcombe, Ethel
Original drawings, decorative designs including title-pages for The Marsh-Kings Daughter, Mercury and The Woodman, The Studio, & others, [n.d.]. (89) £450

Larkin, Philip, 1922-85
Collection of 195 A Ls s & 24 Ls s, Aug [1938?] to 21 Jan 1952. About 1,160 pp, 4to & 8vo. To James Ballard Sutton. Letters to a close friend covering a variety of personal & literary matters & including 40 poems (or fragments), some blues lyrics, 2 watercolors of Jazz subjects, 114 drawings, & homemade greeting card. Some defects. (88) £31,000
— Collection of 8 A Ls s, 26 Ls s & ANs, 6 Sept 1971 to 18 Nov 1985. (91) £3,50

Lascaris, Janus, 1445?-1535
Ls, 28 June 1505. 1 p, 4to. To Pietro Soderini. Recommending Don Juan Henriquez. (91) £6,000

Lask, Berta, 1878-1967
ALs, 7 Mar 1918. (90) DM640

Laske, Oskar, 1874-1951
Series of 25 A Ls s, 1926 to 1951. 42 pp, various sizes. To various friends. Personal letters, each illus with 1 or more watercolor or crayon sketches. With related material. (89) DM2,400

Lasker-Schueler, Else, 1869-1945
Original drawing, self-port, in pencil; [n.d.]. 9cm by 5cm (image). Inscr Singale. (90) DM2,000
ALs, 8 Apr 1910. 4 pp, 8vo. To Max Brod. Proposing in florid terms to visit him in Prague. Sgd Tino von Bagdad. (91) £1,300
— 30 Oct [19]28. (90) DM370
Autograph postcards (2), sgd, 25 June & 9 Sept 1926. To Theodor Daeubler. Sending personal news & asking for his address. Sgd Prinz Jussuf. (91) DM2,000
Autograph postcard, sgd, [3 Apr 1917]. To "Leila". Mythical allusions, sgd Prinz. (90) DM1,300
— [2 Oct 1929]. (88) DM520

Lassalle, Ferdinand, 1825-64
ALs, [4 Mar 1860?]. 5 pp, 8vo. To Franz Duncker. Inviting him to the reading of an essay, & outlining his conception of history & politics. (90) DM1,900
— 26 Apr 1861. 2 pp, 8vo. To [Friedrich Karl von Savigny]. Sending his book Das System der erworbenen Rechte & expressing admiration for Savigny's work. With related material. (88) DM1,100
— [n.d.]. (90) DM650

Latham, Milton Slocum, 1827-82
Franking signature, [4 Apr n.y.]. Alexander collection. (90) $125

Laube, Heinrich, 1806-84
A Ls s (2), 3 Feb 1841 & 14 Mar 1868. (89) DM320
ALs, 12 June 1835. (91) DM420

Laud, William, 1573-1645
ALs, 13 Jan 1641/42. Marquess of Downshire collection. (90) £850

Laudermilk, Jerome
Original drawings, 3 pen-&-ink illusts for Lord Dunsany's The Secret of the Gods, [n.d.]. (88) £85

Laudon, Gideon Ernst, Freiherr von, 1717-90
Ls, 7 Apr 1790. (88) DM550

Laue, Max von, 1879-1960
ALs, 26 Oct 1942. (89) DM210
Autograph postcards (2), sgd, 9 Nov [1936] & 3 July 1951. (88) DM440
Autograph postcard, sgd, 18 Dec 1930. (90) DM280
— 20 Feb 1946. To Frau Woehler, nee Bathe. About his internment & his expected return to Goettingen. (90) DM3,800

Laurel, Stan, 1890-1965
Collection of 13 Ls s & cards, sgd, 1957 to 1964. (88) £500
Ls, 23 Nov 1927. (91) $200
— 29 Jan 1959. (91) $250
— 28 Nov 1959. (88) $225
— 11 Feb 1960. (91) $100

Laurel, Stan, 1890-1965 —& Hardy, Oliver, 1892-1957
[Their signatures, 1933, on an orange sheet of paper, 6 by 5 inches, inscr to Bob, sold at Dar on 13 June 1991, lot 232, for $110.]
[Their signatures, both with autograph sentiments, 1934, 1 p, 4 by 7 inches, sold at Dar on 10 Apr 1991, lot 234, for $350.]
[Their signatures, 3 Feb [19]42, in a scrapbook of newspaper clippings, 34 pp, 4to, inscr to Elsie in Laurel's hand, sold at Dar on 10 Apr 1991, lot 233, for $350.]

[Their signatures, [n.d.], on a single sheet, 4.5 by 3.5 inches, sgd diagonally, sold at Dar on 13 June 1991, lot 233, for $375.]
Photograph, sgd & inscr, [n.d.]. (89) $500

Laurencin, Marie, 1885-1956
ALs, [n.d.]. (88) £300
— 24 Aug [n.y.]. (90) DM220

Laurens, Henry, 1724-92
ALs, 20 June 1778. 1 p, folio. To Col. William Barton. War news, & inquiring about recipient's injuries. Middendorf collection. (91) $3,800
— 14 Feb 1780. 2 pp, 4to. To William Ellery, Jr. About the imminent British seizure of Charleston. (90) $10,000
Ds, [1 Nov 1777 - 10 Dec 1778]. (91) $450
— [1 Nov 1777 - 10 Dec 1778]. (90) $850
— [1 Nov 1777 to 10 Dec 1778]. 1 p, 4to. Ptd Instructions to the Commanders of Private Ships or Vessels of War, 3 Apr 1776; sgd at a later date as President of Congress. (89) $1,900
See also: Adams, John

Lavater, Johann Kaspar, 1741-1801
Autograph Ms, brief physiognomic analysis on an engraved port of a priest (Nicolaus von der Flue), sgd L. Albrecht collection. (91) SF250
— Autograph Ms, brief physiognomic analysis on a pen-&-ink drawing of Christ in front of Pilate, sgd L. Albrecht collection. (91) SF320
ALs, 4 Jan 1766. 2 pp, 4to. To [Prince Ludwig Eugen von Wuerttemberg]. About recipient's recovery from illness, a literary project, Rousseau, etc. (90) DM1,300
— 4 Dec 1770. (88) DM560
— 5 Apr 1776. (89) DM600
— 26 Aug 1777. (90) £400
— 29 May 1778. (89) £350
— 25 Nov 1786. (88) DM850
— 25 Oct 1788. 1 p, 4to. To the art dealer Spach. Offering to add texts to engravings. (90) DM1,100
— 7 Aug 1790. (89) DM360
— 1 Oct 1796. (90) DM320
ANs, 16 Mar 1788. (90) DM240
Single sheet ptg, poems, An eine lang leidende Schwester, & Am Ende einer schweren Leidenswoche, 13 & 15 Nov

1800. (89) DM700

Laver, James, 1899-1975
[A collection of over 600 letters & postcards addressed to him, c.1935 to 1965, with further material relating to theatrical productions etc., sold at S on 21 July 1988, lot 247, for £300 to Curtis.]

Lavoisier, Antoine Laurent de, 1743-94
ALs, 25 Jan 1785. (91) £850
— 23 Mar 1791. 1 p, 4to. To the manager of his estate at Villers-Cotterets, Paris. Regarding payment for an estate & discussing plans for further acquisitions. (90) DM3,000
— [3 Dec 1793]. 1 p, 4to. To an unnamed relative. Confirming receipt of money "en assignats". (91) DM2,400

Lavoisier, Antoine Laurent de, 1743-94 —&
Condorcet, Marie Jean Antoine Nicolas Caritat, Marquis de, 1743-94
Ds, 30 Aug 1791. 1 p, folio. Pay order for 3,950 livres for the building of a bridge. Also sgd by 2 other Commissaires de la Tresorerie Nationale. Partly ptd. (88) DM1,250

Law, John, 1671-1729
Ls, 22 Apr 1720. 2 pp, folio. To an unnamed prefect. Sending copies (1 included) of a royal decree relating to the issue of notes for fractions of the ecu. (88) £1,700
Ds, 29 Feb 1720. 1 p, folio. Order to pay a weekly sum of 2,500 livres to Thomas & Pierre Bourdon. (90) DM4,800

Lawrence, David Herbert, 1885-1930
[A collection of Mss & typescripts of his Studies in Classic American Literature, [1917 to 1922], over 900 pp, 4to, in 10 silk folding cases, largely autograph, sold at S on 19 July 1990, lot 176, for £26,000 to Beckett.]
Autograph Ms, fragment from his Apocalypse, [1929]. 4 pp, 8vo, numbered 13 - 16; torn from a notebook. Not included in ptd version. (91) $2,250
ALs, 12 Feb 1916. 1 p, 4to. To Mr. Pinker. Discussing negotiations with publishers. (88) DM1,600
— 3 Nov 1916. 2 pp, 8vo. To Friedel Schloffer. Requesting that letters be forwarded to Frieda von Richthofen's mother, & commenting on psychoanalysis. (90) DM1,200
— [30 Nov 1917]. (88) £300
— 21 June 1920. 2 pp, size not stated. To Miss Hubrecht. Contrasting the South with the North, & describing his life at Taormina. (90) £1,300
Ds, 1 Mar 1921. (88) £500
Proof copy, David, 1926; in bds. Some autograph annotations; inscr to Arthur S. Wilkinson. (91) £1,050

Lawrence, Gertrude, 1898-1952
[A photograph of Lawrence & anr woman, inscr, & a Christmas card with her likeness on front, inscr & initialled, sold at sg on 8 Feb 1990, lot 123, for $140.]

Lawrence, James, 1781-1813
Cut signature, [n.d.]. Size not stated. Framed with 2 newspaper obituary notices. (90) $2,000

Lawrence, Thomas Edward, 1888-1935
[A collection including a photograph of Erich Kennington's pastel drawing of Lawrence, 1921, 2 photographs of Kennington's bust of Lawrence, 1926, & 7 port photographs by Howard Coster, 1931, sold at CNY on 17 May 1989, lot 123, for $2,200.]
[The presumably only surviving portion of the copy of the 1922 Oxford Ed of Seven Pillars of Wisdom, comprising Book VII, very extensively revised by Lawrence for the Subscribers' Ed of 1926, 19 pp, [c.1923-24], with related material, sold at S on 14 Dec 1989, lot 146, for £36,000 to Maggs.]
[A collotype reproduction of an Augustus John charcoal drawing of Lawrence, 9 by 6.5 inches, sgd & inscr by Lawrence to Ian [Deheer] on a slip of paper pasted to mat, 1935, sold at CNY on 7 Dec, lot 58, for $3,500.]
Original drawings, (2), maps of Palestine & Upper Syria, traced from orig maps made by H. Pirie-Gordon in 1908; [1909?]. Later reproduced in Crusader Castles, 1936. Tovee collection. (91) $20,000
Typescript, trans of Book I of Homer's Odyssey, 1928. 6 pp, folio. A few autograph corrections. Differing from

ptd version. With related material. Isham collection. (89) $8,000

Series of 3 A Ls s, 5 Oct 1926 to 21 July 1927. 4 pp, 4to. To G. M. Sutcliffe, about the bdg of Seven Pillars of Wisdom. To A. Creswell, regarding a subscription to the book. Sgd TE Shaw. With related material. (89) £3,000

A Ls s (2), 19 Oct & [4 Dec 1914]. 8 pp, 16mo. To Mrs. [Winifred] Fontana. About the situation in Turkey, referring to smuggled arms, & reporting about his plans. Sgd T.E.L. & E.L. With related material. (88) £1,900

— A Ls s (2), 29 Jan 1924 & [1925]. Length not stated. To Col. M. V. Burrow Hill. Concerning recipient's subscription to The Seven Pillars of Wisdom. With related material, including a copy of the proof of the Introductory Book. (91) £2,300

— A Ls s (2), 18 Apr & 14 May 1929. 2 pp, 4to & 8vo. To Janet Hallsmith. Accepting an invitation & trying to arrange anr meeting. (90) £3,000

— A Ls s (2), 28 Oct 1929 & 10 June 1931. 2 pp, 4to. To Corporal Jack Harries. Responding to a request for books, & refusing to give a film interview. (90) £2,000

ALs, 1 Nov 1911. (88) £800
— 2 Sept 1920. (88) £950
— 23 Jan 1924. 3 pp, 8vo. Recipient unidentified. Explaining the subscription scheme for his Seven Pillars of Wisdom. With related material. Bradley Martin sale. (90) $10,000
— 4 & 14 April 1927. 2 pp, 4to. To [Apsley Cherry-Gerrard]. Commenting on Shaw's review of Revolt in the Desert. Including postscript. Tovee collection. (91) $8,000
— 1 June 1927. 4 pp, 4to. To "Pat". Expressing his "considered judgment" that the recently pbd Ed of The Seven Pillars of Wisdom is a "respectable, even important, failure." Sgd TES. Bradley Martin sale. (90) $8,000
— 19 Mar 1929. 1 p, 4to. To "Dear Gozlett". Regretting he did not see him in London. Sgd TEShaw. Small tears. (88) DM1,700
— 5 Jan 1933. 2 pp, 4to. To Wing Commander T. B. Marson. Giving his opinion on recipient's Ms on farming. Sgd T.E.S. Byer collection. (90) $2,000
— 9 Feb 1933. (88) £750
— 15 July 1933. 1 p, folio. To Capt. Robinson. Arranging for a meeting in Portsmouth. Tovee collection. (91) $1,800
— 4 Feb 1935. 4 pp, 4to. To R[obert] G[raves]. About the necessity to improve his income, the possibility of a film about himself, his contribution to boat design for the R.A.F., etc. Sgd TES. Alec Guinness collection. (88) £3,800
— 5 Apr 1935. 2 pp, 4to. To C. J. Greenwood. Defending James Hanley's novel against censorship. Sgd T.E.S. Middendorf collection. (89) $2,200
— 20 Apr 1935. 2 pp, 4to. To Ian [Deheer]. Reporting about his retirement. Tovee collection. (91) $3,000

Ls, 28 Jan 1915. (88) £680
— 22 Nov 1927. 2 pp, folio. To Lieut. Col. Ralph H. Isham. Important letter refusing to work for him, discussing books about himself, mentioning his own works & activities, etc. Sgd TEShaw. (89) $15,000
— 2 Jan 1927 [1928]. 1 p, folio. To Lieut. Col. Ralph H. Isham. Discussing the suggestion to translate Homer's Odyssey. Sgd TEShaw. With related material. (89) $11,000
— 10 Oct 1928. 1 p, folio. To Emery Walker & Wilfred Merton. Agreeing to translate the Odyssey. Sgd TEShaw. Isham collection. (89) $3,800
— 30 Oct 1931. (91) £1,000

Letter, 26 Feb 1931. 1 p, 4to. To T. B. Marson. About his trans of Homer, airforce duties, etc. Sgd T.E.S. in type. Tovee collection. (91) $1,200

Autograph postcard, sgd, 21 Aug 1929. Tovee collection. (91) $1,000
— GRAVES, ROBERT. - Autograph Ms, Addendum to 'Who was S. A.', pbd in the Saturday Review, 15 June 1963. 1 p, folio. Working draft; sgd. With related material. Tovee collection. (91) $1,200
— SLATTER. - Orig drawing, "El Sakhara", to illus the Subscribers Ed of Seven Pillars of Wisdom, 1926. In gouache. Tovee collection. (91) $5,500

Lawson, Sir Henry, 1859-1933
Series of c.90 A Ls s, 1880 to 1900 & [n.d.]. About 300 pp, mostly 8vo. To his mother & other family members. Covering his military career during the Suakin campaigns, the Sudan campaign & the Boer War; including related material. (89) £1,100

Le Cain, Errol
Original drawings, (2), 12 elves, & 12 robots, to illus Le Cain's Christmas 1993, or Santa's Last Ride, 1987. 119mm by 295mm & 119mm by 289mm. In ink & wash; sgd. Framed. (90) £1,100

— Original drawings, (2), elves in a corner, & Santa Claus seated on top of the world, to illus Le Cain's Christmas 1993, or Santa's Last Ride, 1987. (90) £350

— Original drawings, (2), elves stuck up with glue, & elves standing in a row, to illus Le Cain's Christmas 1993, or Santa's Last Ride, 1987. (90) £460

— Original drawings, (2), Santa Claus in despair, & elves trying to lift his thick passport, to illus Le Cain's Christmas 1993, or Santa's Last Ride, 1987. (90) £450

— Original drawings, (4), to illus Thomas Lewis's The Dragon Kite; [n.d.]. (90) £400

Original drawing, "And Christmas drifted slowly by"; Santa Claus & reindeer making their way home over skyscrapers, to illus Le Cain's Christmas 1993, or Santa's Last Ride, 1987. 410mm by 289mm. In watercolor; sgd. Framed. (90) £1,500

— Original drawing, "And modern-day technology is therefore not their cup of tea"; robot towering over 4 elves, to illus Le Cain's Christmas 1993, or Santa's Last Ride, 1987. 410mm by 287mm. In watercolor; sgd. Framed. (90) £2,900

— Original drawing, couples in 18th-cent costume dancing, sgd & dated [19]77; to illus The Twelve Dancing Princesses, 1978. 251mm by 336mm; mtd. In ink & watercolor. (90) £1,800

— Original drawing, "He found by travelling with the sun"; Santa Claus driving his sleigh past the sun, to illus Le Cain's Christmas 1993, or Santa's Last Ride, 1987. 409mm by 287mm. In watercolor; sgd. Framed. (90) £1,100

— Original drawing, "I didn't have to share the sky"; Santa Claus passing below a jumbo jet, to illus Le Cain's Christmas 1993, or Santa's Last Ride, 1987. 410mm by 290mm. In watercolor; sgd. Framed. (90) £1,400

— Original drawing, Santa Claus driving home, to illus Le Cain's Christmas 1993, or Santa's Last Ride, 1987. 408mm by 282mm. In watercolor; sgd. Framed. (90) £2,200

— Original drawing, "That was a sticky Christmas, too"; elves after the invention of glue, to illus Le Cain's Christmas 1993, or Santa's Last Ride, 1987. 408mm by 282mm. In watercolor; sgd. Framed. (90) £1,300

— Original drawing, to illus The Fox and the Stork. (88) £450

— Original drawing, "To set up bases round the world"; Santa Claus poring over a globe, to illus Le Cain's Christmas 1993, or Santa's Last Ride, 1987. 407mm by 288mm. In watercolor; sgd. Framed. (90) £2,400

Le Carre, John
Autograph Ms, The Good Soldier, with corrected typescripts, comprising 16 revised versions, & page proofs; 1990. Over 400 pp, 4to. (91) £1,600

Le Corbusier, 1887-1965
Autograph Ms, mock-up of his key plan for Buenos Aires, 1938 to 1940. 90 pp, folio. Each p with autograph text & rough drawings representing intended photographs. Mostly in pencil. (90) £25,000

ALs, 2 Sept 1930. (90) DM900
— 27 Jan 1934. (88) DM550

Le Gallienne, Richard, 1866-1947
Autograph Ms, essay, What is a Keat?, sgd; [n.d.]. (89) $275

Leacock, Stephen Butler, 1869-1944
Collection of 26 A Ls s, typescripts, corrected proofs, autograph Ms, etc., 1938 to 1942; c.75 pp, mostly 4to. Chiefly to James Keddie. Regarding articles & personal matters. Draft of article The Give and Take of Travel.

With related material. In solander box. (88) £2,000

Leadenhall Press
[A collection of more than 100 letters addressed to Andrew White Tuer & his wife, c.1879 to 1918, by writers, illustrators, etc., with related material, sold at S on 22 July 1988, lot 527, for £950 to Quaritch.]

Lear, Edward, 1812-88
Autograph Ms, 12 limericks each with accompanying ink drawing, [n.d.]. 6 pp, 145mm by 200mm, on cream or blue notepaper. (89) £18,000

Original drawing, Ger-woman talking to Ger-man at the side of a pond; ptd in Constance Strachey's Queery Leary Nonsense, 1911. 135mm by 198mm; mtd. In ink; captioned in German. (90) £3,200

A Ls s (2), 20 Dec 1876 & 7 Jan 1878. (88) £400

ALs, 29 Sept 1852. (90) £500

— 29 June 1869. 4 pp, 8vo. To Lady Wyatt. Describing his stay in Paris; including sketch of prevalent women's fashions. Byer collection. (90) $2,000

— 5 June 1878. (91) £500

— 28 Apr 1879. (90) £110

— 28 Apr 1879. (90) £130

— 3 Dec 1882. (90) £850

— 14 Nov 1884. (89) £380

Lear, Tobias, 1762-1816
Ls, 1 Aug 1815. (88) $50
See also: Washington, George

Leavenworth, Henry, 1783-1834
ALs, 22 Nov 1821. Alexander collection. (90) $260

Lebrun-Tondu, Pierre, 1754?-93
Ls, 18 Apr [1793]. (89) DM420

Lechter, Melchior, 1865-1937
A Ls s (2), 4 Jan 1906 & 3 Apr 1908. (91) DM440

L'Ecluse, Charles de, 1526-1609
Autograph endorsement, 1 Dec 1572. 6 lines on a letter addressed to him by G. Ruterius, 30 Nov 1572, 1 p, folio. (91) DM1,200

Lecocq, Alexandre Charles, 1832-1918
Autograph music, 3 Mss, Souvenir de Trianon, Gavotte, sgd; aria, Sous la verte ramure, from L'Egyptienne, vocal score; orchestral Ms of ballet music, Bataille et Final; [n.d.], 20 pp, folio. (88) £450

Lectionary
Ms, Evangelistary or Gospel Lectionary, in Church Slavonic. [Russia, 2d half of 15th cent]. 211 leaves, 255mm by 195mm, in 17th-cent maroon velvet over wooden bds. In a semi-uncial hand. With capital letters often with decorative flourishes, & opening decorative headpiece. Fekula Ms.442. (91) £8,000

— Ms, Evangelistary, or Gospel Lectionary, in Church Slavonic. [Russia, 2d half of 16th cent]. 467 leaves, 270mm by 185mm, in def bdg of wooden bds with remains of lea. In a semi-uncial hand. With large decorative initials throughout, 6 decorative headpieces, & 4 full-page miniatures. Fekula Ms.443. (91) £9,000

— Ms, Gospel Lectionary, in Greek. [Eastern Mediterranean, 13th cent]. 184 leaves (many lacking), vellum, 300mm by 227mm. Def ancient bdg of thick wooden bds covered with remains of red textile & tanned lea. In a large handsome Greek minuscule. With large decorated initials throughout. Some 14th-cent replacements. (90) £11,000

— Ms, Gospel Lectionary, in Greek. [Eastern Mediterranean, 12th or early 13th cent]. 158 leaves, vellum, 207mm by 138mm. In oak bds with spine of white alumed blindstamped pigskin by Sydney M. Cockerell, 1949. In a regular small Greek minuscule by 2 principal scribes. With over 190 decorated initials. Worn; repaired. Abbey collection. (89) £15,000

— Ms, in Greek. [Eastern Mediterranean, 1664/65]. 334 leaves, 363mm by 240mm, in contemp red velvet. In black ink in a flamboyant Greek minuscule by the scribe Ioasaph. With c.375 large decorated initials, 23 headpieces (9 large), & 4 full-page drawings of the Evangelists. (90) £4,500

— Ms, in Latin. [Bohemia, c.1480]. Single

LECTIONARY

- leaf, vellum, 342mm by 261mm. With large historiated initial with scrolling extension between columns & partial floral border. (90) DM5,500
- Ms, in Latin. [Bohemia, c.1480]. 2 conjoint leaves, vellum, 342mm by 261mm. With large historiated initial & partial floral border in gold & colors. Margin trimmed. (90) DM2,200
- Ms, in Latin. [Bologna?, 1st half of 15th cent]. 116 leaves only, vellum, 262mm by 195mm. Rebacked 19th-cent mottled calf gilt. In dark brown ink in a rounded gothic liturgical hand. With c.130 large decorated initials & 11 very large illuminated initials. Def. (89) £1,100
- Ms, in Latin. [Florence, 3d quarter of 12th cent]. 16 leaves only, vellum, 471mm by 332mm. Modern half red mor. In a handsome round late Carolingian minuscule, with headings in red uncials. With 16 large initials, partly by the First Master of the Pluteus Bible. Korner collection. (90) £30,000
- Ms, in Latin. [Northern France, c.1475]. Single leaf, vellum, c.272mm by 183mm. In a lettre batarde. With several small initials in gold & colors, historiated initial & half-length border. (90) DM1,300
- Ms, in Latin. [Northern France, c.1475]. Single leaf, vellum, c.272mm by 183mm. In a lettre batarde. With several small initials in gold & colors, historiated initial & half-length border. (90) DM1,300
- Ms, Old Testament Lections in the later Wycliffite version, in Middle English. [England, c.1400]. 16 leaves only, vellum, 215mm by 145mm. Modern wraps. In brown ink by one scribe in an anglicana script. With 50 initials in red & blue. (88) £15,000

Lee, Arthur, 1740-92
AL, 24 May 1782. (90) $160

Lee, Bruce —& Williams, Van
[Their signatures ("Kato" & "The Green Hornet"), [n.d.], on lined paper, framed with a photograph, sold at wa on 1 Oct 1988, lot 382, for $260.]

AMERICAN BOOK PRICES CURRENT

Lee, Charles, 1731-82
ALs, [c.1761]. (89) $750
— 1 Mar 1766. 3 pp, 4to. To his sister. Reporting about his travels to Constantinople in the service of the King of Poland. (90) $1,300
— 20 Sept 1779. 2 pp, folio. To his sister in England. Referring to the war, various British generals, & his court-martial. (91) $4,000
— 30 Apr [1780]. 4 pp, 4to. To Benjamin Rush. Appealing for support, & thinking of leaving the country. (91) $4,200

Lee, Fitzhugh, 1835-1905
Collection of ALs, Ls & photograph, 22 Feb 1893, 3 Apr 1889 & [n.d.]. (89) $250
ALs, 20 May 1870. (91) $500

Lee, Francis Lightfoot, Signer from Virginia
ALs, 8 Sept 1787. 2 pp, 4to. To Robert Carter. Giving agricultural advice. Tipped to larger sheet. Doheny collection. (89) $2,200

Lee, Henry ("Light-Horse Harry"), 1756-1818
ALs, 7 Nov 1780. (89) $1,000
— 23 July [1803]. (90) $250
— 10 Mar 1804. (89) $280
— 18 Apr [18]07. (89) $380
— 21 Mar 1808. (89) $320
ANs, 18 May 1794. (88) $180
Ds, 6 May 1793. Byer collection. (90) $300
— 5 May 1794. (88) $190
— 30 July 1794. (90) $85
Cut signature, [n.d.]. (91) $85

Lee, Mary Custis, 1806-73
ALs, 3 Dec 1870. (91) $900
— 6 Nov 1871. (89) $650
— 19 Dec [n.y.]. 6 pp, 8vo. To Charles Marshall. Describing her husband's decision to decline command of the Union Army, & related matters. (90) $3,000

Lee, Richard Bland, 1761-1827
Collection of ALs & 2 A Ds s, 2 Sept 1815, 1779 & [1815]. (90) $350

Lee, Richard Henry, Signer from Virginia
ALs, 2 June 1776. 3 pp, folio. To Landon Carter. Discussing the need for Independence. Including franking signature. Repaired. Doheny collection. (89) $20,000

— 19 June 1789. 1 p, folio. To his nephew Henry Lee. Forwarding a letter (not present) & expressing concern about the laziness of young people. Silked on verso. (89) $1,600
See also: Adams, John

Lee, Richard Nelson, 1806-72
Ms, The Life of a Fairy. (88) £80

Lee, Robert E., 1807-70
[A group of 2 letters & a telegram from Lee's files, 1863 to 1865, relating to troop movements etc. during the war, sold at sg on 24 Mar 1988, lot 107, for $1,100.]
[A group of 4 Ms war maps from Lee's papers, 1863 & later, various sizes, in India ink with red & blue on glazed linen, with related material, sold at sg on 24 Mar 1988, lot 108, for $3,200.]
Autograph Ms, 11 lines recapitulating his commands while in Confederate service, [n.d.]. 124mm by 203mm. With related material. (88) $4,200

ALs, 15 June 1831. 3 pp, 4to. To his cousin Molly [Custis]. Discussing arrangements for visits to Old Point. Torn. John F. Fleming Estate. (89) $1,800

— 25 July 1835. 4 pp, 4to. To his wife Mary Ann Custis Lee. About the expected birth of their 2d child, their wedding anniversary, & his situation in Michigan. (88) $5,250

— 7 Nov 1839. 4 pp, 4to. To Capt. John Mackay. Humorous letter describing his situation & military prospects. Alexander collection. (90) $4,750

— 1 Jan 1844. 1 p, 4to. To Adj. Gen. R. Jones. Enclosing instructions (not present) to Lieut. Benham regarding repairs at Fort Mifflin. (89) $2,000

— 1 Jan 1844. 1 p, size not stated. To Adj. Gen. R. Jones. Enclosing copy of instructions for Lieut. Benham regarding repairs at Fort Mifflin (not present). (88) $1,650

— 15 Sept 1857. 4 pp, 4to. To Major [Earl Van Dorn]. About a review of recipient's accounts, the high number of desertions, skirmishes with Indians, etc. Fold repaired. (89) $3,750

— 15 Sept 1857. 4 pp, 4to. To Earl Van Dorn. Referring to army accounts, desertions from units in the West, etc. (91) $4,500

— 21 June 1862. 1 p, 4to. To George Wythe Randolph. About Magruder's change of assignment. (91) $8,000

— 11 Jan 1863. 1 p, 8vo. To Gen. Thomas J. Jackson. Returning papers [not present]. (90) $5,750

— 20 Aug 1863. 1 p, 4to. To Gen. S. Cooper. Recommending Capt. William H. Rogers. Def. (89) $1,800

— 6 Jan 1864. 2 pp, 4to. To Kitty Stiles. Thanking for a Christmas gift & informing her of the death of his daughter-in-law. Including franking signature. (90) $11,000

— 16 Jan 1864. 3 pp, 4to. To Gen. James Longstreet. Discussing military movements, supply problems & Union strategy. Folds split. (89) $12,500

— 17 Feb 1864. 3 pp, 4to. To Gen. James Longstreet. Informing him about Sherman's movements & regretting he cannot send enough supplies & reinforcements. Def. (89) $10,000

— 24 June [18]65. 2 pp, 8vo. To Mr. Linman. Thanking for books. (91) $3,000

— 5 Oct 1865. 2 pp, 8vo. To the Hon. James Walter Wall. States his belief in education as the key to the restoration of the cultural fabric of the South. (91) $3,000

— 14 Nov [18]65. 2 pp, 4to. To Col. Charles Marshall. About the possibilities of marketing his memoirs. (88) $4,000

— 20 Nov 1865. 1 p, 4to. To Gen. Isaac R. Trimble. Informing him that he need not copy any of his pbd reports. Stained. Framed with engraved port. Sang collection. (90) $3,250

— 20 Dec 1865. 1 p, 8vo. To Maggie H. Thornton. Responding to a young admirer. Pencilled doodles on verso. Sang collection. (89) $4,500

— 4 Sept 1866. 2 pp, 4to. To Dr. C. S. Garnett. Describing a missing horse given to him by Gen. Stuart. (89)

$5,500
— 29 Oct 1867. 2 pp, 4to. To Gen. James Longstreet. Declining to endorse Republican policies. With ALs by G. W. C. Lee to Longstreet, 15 July 1879, concerning the campaign of 1864. (89) $15,500
— 31 Oct 1867. 2 pp, 4to. To Gen. Fitz John Porter. Responding to an inquiry about Confederate movements at the 2d Battle of Bull Run. Repaired. (90) $4,250
— 14 Mar 1868. 1 p, 8vo. To J. C. Underwood. Informing him that he will answer the summons to testify in the case against Jefferson Davis after the postponement ordered by the court. Byer collection. (90) $14,000
— 6 Jan 1869. 1 p, 8vo. To Gertrude S. Lowndes. Sending his photograph (not present). With reply. (88) $2,000
— 8 July 1869. 1 p, 8vo. To M. G. Harman. Hoping the Lexington Hotel will prove to be profitable under his direction. Doheny collection. (89) $4,200
— 7 Dec 1869. 1 p, 8vo. To William Preston Johnson. Inviting him for dinner. (90) $2,000
— 18 Feb 1870. 2 pp, 4to. To Gen. Fitz John Porter. Responding to a request for speculations on the "probable result" of hypothetical troop movements at the 2d Battle of Bull Run. Def; encapsulated. (90) $4,000
AL, 14 Apr 1866. (90) $400
Ls, 7 Apr 1862. 2 pp, 4to. To Gen. Benjamin Huger. Discussing the position of batteries on the Nansemond River. (91) $8,500
— 11 May 1862, 1 p, 4to. To Samuel L. Wilson. Regarding efforts to continue railroad communications. Silked. (88) $2,600
— 14 May 1862. 2 pp, 4to. To Gen. J. E. Johnston. Reporting on preparations for the defense of Richmond. Sang & Middendorf collections. (89) $8,500
— 18 May 1862. 2 pp, 4to. To Gov. Henry T. Clark. About shipments of arms. (89) $6,000
— 29 May 1862. 4 pp, 4to. To Gov. F. W. Pickens. Discussing the defense of Charleston. Signature faded. Encapsulated. (89) $6,000
— 28 June 1862. 1 p, 8vo. To Lieut. Col. Thomas S. Rhett. Ordering him to take charge of guns on the Chickahominy Road. (89) $2,800
— 19 July 1862. 1 p, 4to. To Col. W. Raymond Lee. Thanking him for "the care and attention of a humane and generous enemy." Was mtd. (89) $5,500
— 31 Aug 1863. 1 p, 4to. To Gen. James Longstreet. Urging that he prepare the army for an attack on Gen. Meade's forces. (89) $6,000
— 28 Apr 1864. 2 pp, 4to. To Sec of War James A. Seddon. Discussing the reorganization of a company of artillery. Endorsed by Seddon on verso. Middendorf collection. (89) $2,500
— 9 Apr 1865. 1 p, 4to. To Gen. Ulysses S. Grant. Duplicate, suggesting "a suspension of hostilities pending the discussion of the terms of surrender" at Appomattox Courthouse. Body of letter in the hand of Charles Marhall; in pencil. With autograph endorsement, sgd, by Gen. Edward O. C. Ord on lower half of leaf. (89) $200,000

Letter, 11 Jan 1865. (90) $500
— 13 June 1865. (88) $475
— [n.d.]. 4 pp, 4to. To Andrew Hunter. Retained copy, proposing use of Negroes as Confederate soldiers. (91) $2,000

ANs, 30 Apr 1864. 1 p, 8vo. To Gen. J. E. B. Stuart. 2 lines, asking to see him. (89) $3,500

Ds, [1838]. 1 p, 74mm by 197mm. Ptd confirmation that articles received were necessary for the improvement of the Mississippi. (90) $1,600
— [1838]. 1 p, 12mo; cut from larger leaf. Certification that charges for a room (not included) were incurred for "the Improvement of the Mississippi"; sgd as Captain. With a port. (90) $1,300
— [1838]. 1 p. Receipt certifying that the materials furnished were required for improvement of the Mississippi above the mouth of the Ohio. Apparently clipped from a manifest. (90) $1,200
— 10 Apr 1865. 1 p, folio. Copy of General Order No 9, addressed to Gen. W. H. Stevens. With related material. Middendorf collection. (89) $80,000

— 10 April 1865. 1 p, folio. "General Orders No: 9", drafted the day after Lee's surrender; later transcript, sgd. Fold split; silked. (88) $16,000
— 10 Apr 1865. 1 p, 4to. General Order No 9, drafted the day after his surrender; probably later transcript, sgd. On ruled paper. Matted. Martin collection. (90) $34,000
— [n.d.]. 1 p, 8vo. Membership certificate of the Southern Hospital Association for Disabled Soldiers; also sgd by J. B. Hood. Matted with engraved port. (91) $3,000
— [n.d.]. 77mm by 205mm; cut from larger account sheet. Certification that various articles were necessary for the "improvement of the Mississippi". (90) $1,200

Cut signature, [n.d.]. (89) $1,000
— Anr, [n.d.]. With ALs of Fitzhugh Lee supplying Miss Merriam with the signature she requested, 24 Sept 1874. (91) $1,300
— Anr, [n.d.]. (88) $950

Photograph, sgd, [1864]. Carte size. Photograph by J. W. Davis. (89) $1,900
— Anr, of Lee & his staff taken by Matthew Brady in Apr 1865. Image is 218mm by 178mm. Sgd on mount by Lee. (91) $26,000
— Anr, [c.1870]. 8.1 by 6.1 inches, oval; by Brady. Mtd & framed. (88) $1,600
— Anr, [n.d.]. Carte size. Bust pose, in civilian clothes. (90) $2,800
— LEE, G. W. C. - 2 A Ls s, 13 Mar 1871 & 16 Sept 1876. 5 pp, 4to & 8vo. To Col. Charles Marshall. About the final disposition of his father's papers. (88) $250
— LEE, G. W. C. - 5 A Ls s, 1870 to 1903. 10 pp, 4to & 8vo. To Col. Charles Marshall. Mostly about his father's papers. (88) $600
— LEE, G. W. C. - ALs, 24 Oct 1870. 8 pp, 8vo. To Col. Charles Marshall. About his father's last days & death. (88) $4,400
— LEE, MARY C. - ALs, 6 Feb 1871. 4 pp, 8vo. To Col. Charles Marshall. Transmitting copies of her father's letters to Winfield Scott & Simon Cameron (present). Worn. (88) $350
— LEE, MARY C. - ALs, "8th" [c.late 1870s]. 6 pp, 8vo. To Col. Charles Marshall. Concerning the genealogical history of her family. With related material. (88) $375
— LEE, MARY CUSTIS. - Autograph Ms, sketch of the life of Robert E. Lee prepared for Charles Marshall, [c.1870-73]. 7 pp, folio. (90) $1,900
— LEE, MARY CUSTIS. - ALs, [c.1870-73]. 2 pp, 8vo. To [Col. Charles Marshall]. Referring to attacks on her husband in the US Senate. Repaired. (90) $400

Lee, Robert E., 1807-70 —& Hunter, Andrew
[Contemp copies of an exchange of letters, 7 Jan & 11 Jan 1865, 10 pp, 4to, regarding employment of Negro troops & emancipation of the slaves, with related material, sold at sg on 24 Mar 1988, lot 106, for $1,000.]

Leech, John, 1817-64
Original drawing, "Although a young lawyer he could stump many of his friends on the question of bails"; [n.d.]. (90) £180
— Original drawing, "Mr. (89) $250

Lefebvre, François Joseph, Duc de Danzig, 1755-1820
[St. Albin. - A collection of notes on Lefebvre's life, including letter by Taponier, [early 19th cent], c. 50 items, various sizes, sold at pn on 10 Dec 1987, lot 506, for £55 to L'Autographe.]
Ls, 12 June 1806. (91) DM340

Legal Manuscripts
[A bundle of c.1000 writs returnable for the Octave of St. Hilary, 1548, sent to the Sheriffs of all counties in England & containing a wide variety of writ & action, in Latin, vellum, threaded on a length of catgut, sold at S on 20 July 1989, lot 263, for £1,500 to Fogg.]
Ms, anon formal letter instructing a student how to study, in particular the law, [mid to late 17th cent]. (89) £130
— Ms, Brevissima Summula super Decretalibus, & Decretum Abbreviatum. (88) £900
— Ms, court proceedings, 1620. (88) £550
— Ms, dictionary of English legal prec-

edents, [England, 17th cent]. 512 pp, 4to. Def contemp calf. Mainly in legal French. With colored marginal vignettes & decorated initials. (90) £4,000
— Ms, legal dictionary, [17th cent]. (88) £950
— Ms, legal dictionary, [16th cent]. Size not stated. In def blindstamped bdg. Bound with 13th-cent [& later] leaves on court proceedings. (88) £11,500
— Ms, legal formulary, in French. (88) £360
— Ms, legal miscellany. [England, mid to late 15th cent]. 178 leaves, vellum, 178mm by 95mm. Modern pigskin bdg. In a small anglicana cursive script with occasional textura headings. In Middle English, Law French, & Latin. Rua collection. (91) $8,000
— Ms, legal text book, with index. (88) £880
— Ms, legal vol arranged alphabetically. (88) £550
— Ms, notes on court cases, giving names of plaintiffs & defendants. (88) £320
— FLORENCE. - Ms, cartulary of a notary, 10 Oct to 23 Oct 1442. 50 leaves only, 298mm by 217mm. Modern imitation lea. In Latin & Italian, in a cursive notarial hand. (89) £500
See also: Canones Conciliorum

Leger, Alexis Saint-Leger, 1887-1975.
See: Perse, St-John

Leger, Fernand, 1881-1955
ALs, Aug [19]47. (90) DM850
— [n.d.]. (88) DM320

Legrand, Jacques Guillaume, 1743-1807
Autograph Ms, Galerie antique: Monumens de la Grece..., 1e division, vol. 1; [1807?]. 43 leaves, folio, disbound. With numerous pen-&-ink drawings; sgd. (91) $4,750

Legros, Alphonse, 1837-1911 —& Others
[The ledger of a firm of art dealers whose clients included Legros, Tissot, and Burne-Jones, 1875 to 1877, 163 openings, folio, in half calf bdg, sold at S on 17 Nov 1988, lot 255, for £1,400 to Sotheran.]

Lehar, Franz, 1870-1948
[A collection of nearly 100 port photographs, c.1870 to c.1940, various sizes, many sgd & inscr to Edith Windbichler, sold at S on 27 Nov, lot 289, for £1,600 to MacNutt.]
Autograph Ms, address to the union of employees at German theaters in Czechoslovakia, 2 May 1928. (89) DM240
Collection of ALs & autograph quotation, sgd, 1905 & 26 Apr 1929. (90) DM330
— Collection of c.40 A Ls s, postcards, visiting cards, musical quotations, & photographs, sgd, c.1925 to 1940. (88) £800
ALs, 25 Aug 1914. (91) $225
— 21 May 1944. (89) DM260
ANs, [n.d.]. (88) DM250
— 22 Sept 1942. (91) DM220
Autograph quotation, 7 bars of music, sgd & dated 12 Jan 1909. (91) $325
— Anr, 8 notes of music, sgd; [n.d.]. (91) $225
— Anr, 3 bars from The Merry Widow Waltz, sgd; [n.d.]. (90) $275
Photograph, sgd, [23 Oct 1948]. (90) DM290
Photograph, sgd & inscr, [n.d.]. (88) DM240
— Anr, [1927?]. (90) DM250
— Anr, 6 Apr 1936. (90) $200
— Anr, [n.d.]. (89) DM360
Proof copy, operetta, Friederike, 1928. (88) DM250

Lehmann, Lotte, 1888-1976
[An archive of letters written by & to Lehmann, c.200 items, 1927 to 1930, including 7 drafts of letters to Richard Strauss regarding the dispute about who should sing Die aegyptische Helena, sold at S on 19 May 1989, lot 527, for £2,100 to McNutt.]
Collection of 80 A Ls s & Ls s, 1948 to 1976. 90 pp, various sizes. To Albert Goldberg. Reminiscing about her stage career, commenting on other singers, offering opinions on directing opera, etc. Including some autograph caricatures. With related material. (89) £3,800

Lehmann, Rosamond
[Parts of the revised drafts of her novel A Sea-Grape Tree, [pbd 1976], 215 pp, with photocopy of part of final draft, 70 pp, folio & 4to, sold at S on 15 Nov 1988, lot 1656, for £100 to Mangle.]

Leibl, Wilhelm, 1844-1900
ALs, 19 Oct 1892. 2 pp, 8vo. Recipient unnamed. Discussing the possible sale of a painting. (91) DM1,600

Leibniz, Gottfried Wilhelm, 1646-1716
ALs, 5 Jan 1691. 2 pp, 4to. To Herzog Ernst August von Braunschweig-Lueneburg. Informing him about his work on the history of the Guelphs. In French. (90) DM10,000
— 30 Jan 1711. 2 pp, 8vo. To Johann Konrad Schwartz. Discussing recipient's work on the Helvetians & other scholarly works. In Latin. (91) DM9,800
Ls, 14 Jan 1712. 4 pp, 4to. To Johann Jacob Scheuchzer. Advising against applying for a position at Duisburg, & discussing Descartes, his own philosophical system, & recipient's studies. With autograph postscript. In Latin. (90) DM7,000
Autograph quotation, "Pars vitae, quoties perditur hora, perit"; [n.d.]. 1 p, 8vo. Sgd. (91) DM5,200

Leibowitz, Rene, 1913-72
Autograph music, Variations pour Piano sur un theme de Schoenberg ... (88) DM700

Leicester, Robert Dudley, Earl of, 1532-88
Ls, 26 Sept 1585. (88) £380
See also: Elizabeth I, 1533-1603

Leigh, Vivien, 1913-67
Collection of 6 A Ls s & 4 A Ns s, [n.d.]. 18 pp, 8vo & 4to. To Ludi Claire. Discussing news & stage work. (88) $1,300
Ls s (2), 9 Aug 1963. (91) $250
Ds s (2)26 Apr 1962. (91) $200
— Ds s (2)6 Aug 1963. (91) $225
— Ds s (2)4 Feb 1966. (91) $225
Ds, 23 May 1966. (91) $150
Playbill, for Tovarich at Boston's Colonial Theatre, Feb 1963. (91) $180
See also: Gable, Clark & Leigh

Leigh, Vivien, 1913-67 —&
Olivier, Laurence, Sir, 1907-89
Ptd photograph, [1936]. (91) $100

Leighton, Clare
Autograph Ms, diary. (91) $350

Leip, Hans, 1893-1983
Autograph Ms, poem, Lili Marleen; [n.d.]. (90) DM380

Leisewitz, Johann Anton, 1752-1806
ALs, 8 May 1805. (89) DM850

Leisler, Jacob, 1640-91
Ds, 31 May 1690. Byer collection. (90) $800

Lenau, Nikolaus, 1802-50
Autograph transcript, 15 couplets from his poem Johannes Ziska; [n.d.]. 2 pp, 4to. Sgd. (90) DM5,000
— Autograph transcript, poem, Herbstklage, 26 Dec 1834. 1 p, 8vo. 3 four-line stanzas, sgd. (91) DM5,000
ALs, [16 Oct 1844]. 1 p, 8vo. To Marie Behrends. Assuring her that he is well now. (90) DM4,800
Proof copy, Faust, 2d Ed, 1840. 8vo, in def contemp half lea bdg. With numerous autograph corrections, including 12 lines of verse. (91) DM6,400

Lenbach, Franz von, 1836-1904
Collection of 2 A Ls s, 5 A Ns s & photograph, sgd & inscr, Feb 1879 to 22 Feb 1889 & [n.d.]. (90) DM850

Lenin, Vladimir Ilyich, 1870-1924
ALs, [c.Aug 1915]. 6 pp, size not stated. Recipient unknown. Draft, discussing preparations for the Zimmerwald conference. (91) £20,000
— 21 Dec 1917/3 Jan 1918. 2 pp, 4to, in red mor gilt box by Sangorski. To Charles Dumas. Referring to their political differences & declaring that he has always fought against the "national defence trend". In French. (89) £24,000
— [1920/21?]. 1 p, 8vo. To Clara Zetkin. Agreeing to pursue the plan of a conference in spite of opposition. In German. (88) DM110,000
Autograph postcard, sgd, 21 June 1915. To Dr. Gregory Schklowsky. Complaining about hotel costs & praising the beauty

LENIN

of the Swiss mountains. With related material. (91) £12,000

ADs, 1 Oct 1914. Size not stated. Library callslip of Landesbibliothek Bern for a book by Ernst Jordi. Sgd Wl. Uljanow. In pencil. Mtd in 8vo album also containing other autographs. (88) DM50,000

Cut signature, 1920, 85mm by 140mm. Fragment of a document, sgd as President of the Council of People's Commissars. Also sgd by Georgi Vasilievich Chicherin. Mtd. (88) £2,200

Signature, [Oct 1908]. 1 p, folio. List of participants of the Interparliamentary Commission of an international meeting of Socialists in Brussels; also sgd by 21 others. (90) DM35,000

Lennon, John, 1940-80

[2 photographs, [n.d.], each framed, 52cm by 77cm, sgd by photographer Dezo Hoffmann, sold at S on 12 Sept 1988, lot 215, for £450.]

[His signature on an erotic lithograph, study of Yoko Ono, framed with a photograph, 10 by 8 inches (image), sold at pnNY on 3 Dec 1988, lot 249, for $500.]

Autograph Ms, Daily Howl, [c.1958]. 3 pp, 9 by 7 inches, on exercise book sheets. Comic poetry, prose & cartoon drawings. In black ink colored with crayon. With related material. (88) £12,000

— Autograph Ms, lyrics for the song Any Time At All, [1964]. 1 p, 20 by 8 inches. 4 verses & chorus; some alterations. (88) £6,000

— Autograph Ms, lyrics for the song If I Fell, [1964]. 1 p, 29cm by 29cm (folded Valentine card). Introduction & 3 verses. (88) £7,750

Original drawing, self port, sgd, inscr & dated 1965. (89) £520

ALs, [6 Sept 1967]. (88) £650

Autograph postcard, sgd, 9 Feb 1979. (88) $650

Document, 10 Oct 1962. 29cm by 23cm. Hire purchase agreement for a guitar. (89) £1,250

Caricature, cartoon of Lennon & Yoko Ono, entitled "Two Virgins were here"; [c.1969]. (89) £450

Photograph, sgd, [n.d] (91) $600

Photograph, [c.1960]. (89) £480

AMERICAN BOOK PRICES CURRENT

— Anr, 1965. (89) £320

Signature, on verso of Foyles Literary Luncheon place card, 23 Apr 1964. (88) £450

— Anr, [c.1974]. (89) £260

— Anr, [19]80. (89) $800

— CHAPMAN, MARK DAVID. - Signature, 1989. On 1972 philatelic cover. (91) $140

**Lennon, John, 1940-80 —&
Ono, Yoko**

[Their signatures on a "Look" magazine cover, 18 Mar 1969, framed, 20 by 16 inches, sold at pnNY on 3 Dec 1988, lot 279, for $850.]

[Their signatures on front cover of the LP Plastic Ono Band, inscr to Derek, framed, 15 by 15 inches, sold at pnNY on 3 Dec 1988, lot 259, for $425.]

Original drawing, facial caricature by Lennon, March 1969; sgd by both. Framed, 13.5 by 11.5 inches. With related material. (88) $2,750

Concert program, 10 Sept 1969. Sgd by both. Including 2 facial caricatures. Framed with a photograph; 14 by 18 inches. (89) $1,400

Group photograph, [1980]. Publicity Photograph for Double Fantasy; sgd by both. Framed with related material. 11.5 by 15.75 inches. (88) $1,400

— MACMILLAN, IAN. - 6 photographs, showing Lennon's face becoming Ono's face, used on record label for "Happy Xmas (War is Over)", [n.d.]. Size not stated. (89) £220

Lentulus, Rupert Scipio von, 1714-87

ALs, 3 Nov 1757. Schroeder collection. (89) DM520

Leo X, Pope, 1475-1521

Ls, 18 May 1504. 1 p, 4to. To Bernardo Micheloti. As cardinal, requesting him to induce the chapter of Santa Maria in Dominica at Florence to follow his instructions. (89) DM2,600
See also: Julius II & Leo X

Leo XI, Pope, 1535-1605

Collection of Ls & Ds, 8 Apr 1600 & 2 Oct 1601. Doheny collection. (89) $300

Leo XII, Pope, 1760-1829
Ls, 8 Aug 1797. Byer collection. (90) $275
Document, 10 May 1825. (90) DM320
— 19 Dec 1825. (88) DM360
— 22 Feb 1828. (89) DM300

Leo XIII, Pope, 1810-1903
ALs, 23 Apr 1857. (88) DM550
Ls, 25 Nov 1856. (91) DM420
— 26 Dec 1870. Byer collection. (90) $375
— 19 Feb 1883. (90) DM700

Leonardo da Vinci, 1452-1519
Ms, Trattato della Pittura, [Italy, 17th cent?]. (88) £120

Leoncavallo, Ruggiero, 1858-1919
Autograph music, song, Chitarretta, for solo bass voice & piano in A minor, sgd; [c.1893]. 4 pp, folio. Marked by the ptr; German text added in anr hand. Repaired. (90) £1,100
Collection of ALs & Ds, 17 & 23 Aug 1910. (91) £500
— Collection of ALs & autograph quotation, sgd, [n.d.] & 20 May 1911. (90) £400
ALs, 30 Sept 1894. (88) DM720
— 21 June 1904. (90) DM480
— 5 Mar 1905. (89) DM480
— 17 Mar 1913. (90) DM270
AN, [21 Mar 1892]. (88) DM300
Photograph, sgd & inscr, 14 Sept 1898. (90) DM550

Leopold, Fuerst von Hohenzollern-Sigmaringen, 1835-1905
ALs, 12 Dec 1870. Schroeder collection. (89) DM250

Leopold, Herzog von Braunschweig-Lueneburg, 1752-85
ALs, 2 Feb 1785. Schroeder collection. (89) DM420
Ds, 1 Apr 1784. (89) DM260

Leopold I, Fuerst von Anhalt-Dessau ("Der alte Dessauer"), 1676-1747
Ls, 22 Dec 1700. (91) DM380
— 23 Dec 1709. Schroeder collection. (89) DM370
— 30 Dec 1735. (90) DM550
— 23 Feb 1742. (90) DM700
— 2 Jan 1743. Schroeder collection. (89) DM550

Leopold I, Emperor, 1640-1705
Ls, 11 July 1662. (89) DM280
— 14 July 1667. (91) DM220
— 1 Dec 1668. (88) DM220
— 14 Oct 1670. (91) DM600
— 19 Aug 1674. (88) DM370
— 13 Sept 1681. (90) DM340
— 29 Apr 1687. (91) DM850
— 8 Dec 1687. (90) DM850
— 20 Nov 1697. (88) DM350
— 25 July 1701. (89) DM300
— 25 Jan 1702. (90) DM280
— 10 Dec 1703. (90) DM440
Letter, 17 Feb 1693. (91) DM210
Ds, 6 Jan 1665. (90) DM550
— 6 May 1686. (90) £500
— 30 Dec 1689. 1 p, folio. Order concerning the establishment of a commissary train. Countersgd by Ernst Ruediger von Starhemberg. (90) DM1,200
— VIENNA & THE TURKS. - 3 vols of Ms despatches sent from Constantinople by an agent of the Emperor, 1687 to 1695, c.700 pp, 4to, in vellum gilt bindings, reporting on events thoughout the Ottoman Empire, sold at S on 20 Nov 1990, lot 534, for £3,000 to Atabey. 91

Leopold I, King of the Belgians, 1790-1865
Collection of 11 A Ls s & A Ls, 21 Jan 1832 to 31 Mar 1848 & [n.d.]. 79 pp, 4to & 8vo. To Christian Friedrich von Stockmar. Confidential letters dealing with private & financial matters. Sgd L or unsgd. (90) DM4,400
ALs, 27 May 1827. (91) DM420
— 24 Aug 1833. (90) DM380
— 25 July 1848. (90) DM550
— 16 Mar 1854. (88) DM220
Ls, 24 July 1833. (89) DM280
— 8 Aug 1855. (90) DM200

Leopold II, Emperor, 1747-92
Ls, 1 Feb 1791. (89) DM330
— 9 Jan 1792. (90) DM800
Endorsement, sgd, on a report by Count Balassa, 22 Feb 1792, 1 p, folio; regarding the minutes of a meeting of his chancellery for Illyria. (90) DM650

Leopold II, King of the Belgians, 1835-1909
ALs, [May 1882]. (90) DM350
Ls, 9 Feb 1886. Byer collection. (90) $250

Leopold III, King of the Belgians, 1901-83 —&
Astrid, Queen of Leopold III, King of the Belgians, 1905-35
Photograph, sgd & inscr, 21/22 May 1932. (88) DM650

Leopold Salvator, Archduke of Austria, 1863-1931
Autograph Ms, diary listing military events, 1 Jan to 16 Sept 1918. 75 pp, 8vo, in stitched notebook. In pencil. (91) DM1,400

Lepsius, Richard, 1810-84
ALs, 1 Oct 1845. (91) DM380

Lermontov, Mikhail Yurievitch, 1814-41
Autograph Ms, poem, Predskazanie (eto mechta), [1830]. 1 p, 269mm by 180mm. Titel & 18 lines; some revisions. (91) £13,000

Lernet-Holenia, Alexander, 1897-1976
Autograph Ms, 2 poems by Giovanni Strozzi, in Italian & in Lernet-Holenia's German trans; 5 Apr 1941. (90) DM550

Lersch, Heinrich, 1889-1936
ALs, 18 Sept 1928. (90) DM370

Lersner, Kurt, Freiherr von, 1883-1954
ALs, 26 Mar 1925. Schroeder collection. (89) DM220

Les Voyes Chrestiennes
Ms, Treatise on virtues & vices, in French, with Ten Commandments, articles of the faith, Vision of St. John of the Apocalypse, etc. [Paris?, c.1415]. 22 leaves, vellum, 355mm by 265mm. Early 19th-cent russia gilt, interleaved with transcript. In brown ink in a lettre batarde. With calligraphic initials, illuminated 5-line initial, & 6 miniatures. Doheny collection. (88) £38,000
— Ms, Treatise on virtues & vices, in French, with Ten Commandments, articles of the faith, Vision of St. John of the Apocalypse, etc. [Paris?, c.1415]. 22 leaves, vellum, 355mm by 265mm. Early 19th-cent russia gilt. In brown ink in a lettre batarde. With calligraphic initials, illuminated 5-line initial, & 6 miniatures. Doheny collection. (90) £55,000

Lesseps, Ferdinand de, Viscount, 1805-94
ALs, 26 Aug 1855. (90) DM400
— 15 Sept 1857. (89) £650
— 2 Feb 1860. (89) DM260
— [n.d.]. (88) DM440
— 21 Apr 1880. (91) $375
— 18 Oct 1888. (89) DM430
ANs, [1885]. (91) $80

Lessing, Gotthold Ephraim, 1729-81
ALs, 30 Dec 1743. 1 p, folio. To his sister Dorothea. Protesting that she did not answer his letter & sending New Year's wishes. (90) DM30,000
— 20 Mar 1777. 1 p, 4to. To his sister Dorothea. About the death of his mother & his brother's expected visit. Ammann collection. (88) DM24,000
AL, [n.d.]. 1 p, 8vo, cut from larger leaf. Recipient unnamed. Fragment, asking recipient to return some silver shoe buckles. With signature pasted on. Note of authenticity at foot. (91) DM1,700
— TAUENTZIEN, FRIEDRICH BOGISLAW VON. - Ls, 23 Apr 1762. 1 p, folio. To [Ernst Wilhelm von Schlabrendorff?]. Forwarding a letter & giving orders for the Kings's visit. Letter in the hand of his secretary Lessing. (90) DM4,800

Lessmann, Daniel, 1794-1831
Collection of ALs & autograph Ms, 1 July 1825. Albrecht collection. (91) SF550

Lettow-Vorbeck, Moritz von
[An archive of documents & related material pertaining to Lettow-Vorbeck & his family, including 5 autographs by Emperors Wilhelm I (2) & Wilhelm II, sold at star on 1 Dec 1988, lot 1104, for DM2,600.]

Lettow-Vorbeck, Paul von, 1870-1964
ALs, 23 Feb 1930. Schroeder collection. (89) DM420

Leverett, John, 1616-79
Ds, 2 May 1663. (89) $450
— 28 Sept 1668. (89) $400

Levetzow, Ulrike von, 1804-99
ANs, 21 June 1880. (90) DM700

Levi, Hermann, 1839-1900
Series of 13 A Ls s, 4 Nov 1895 to 20 Oct 1898. 22 pp, 8vo. To Felix von Eckardt. About his translations of works by Anatole France & other matters. With related material. (89) DM1,400

Levy, Amy, 1861-89
[A collection of c.370 pp of varied autograph Mss, including stories, articles, drawings, juvenilia, etc., with related ptd articles & books, sold at S on 13 Dec 1990, lot 132, for £6,000 to Barton.]

Lewald, Fanny, 1811-89
ALs, 29 Oct 1845. (90) DM500
— 4 June 1851. (88) DM320
— 29 & 30 Dec 1874. (91) DM240

Lewis, Andrew, 1720-81
Ls, 3 June 1776. 2 pp, 4to. To [Major Gen. Charles Lee]. Informing him about the positioning of batteries on Gwin Island. (91) $1,400

Lewis, Francis, Signer from New York
ALs, 16 Feb 1761. (90) $800
— 5 Jan 1778. (89) $1,000

Lewis, Sir George Cornewall, 1806-63
[A large collection of his political papers, mostly relating to the Herefordshire election of July, 1852, hundreds of documents in a large deed-box, sold at S on 18 July 1991, lot 408, for £900 to Quaritch.]

Lewis, John, 1675-1747
Ms, A Collection made towards an Ecclesiastical Account of the Diocese of Canterbury..., [c.1740s]. (89) £440

Lewis, Meriwether, 1774-1809
ALs, 30 May 1808. 1 p, 4to. To Lieut. Whitlock. Concerning the purchase of horses. Def. Doheny collection. (89) $3,800
ADs, 20 Oct 1807. 1 p, 126mm by 199mm. As Governor of Louisiana, pay order in favor of George Divers, addressed to the President & Directors of the Bank of the United States. Duplicate. Doheny collection. (89) $4,800
AD, 1 Jan 1800. 1 p, 8vo. Receipt, sgd by Thomas Sheldon, for $8 from Lewis (sgd in text) for army expenses. (91) $2,200

Lewis, Sinclair, 1885-1951
Ls, 19 Oct 1925. (89) $275
— 3 Apr 1931. (90) DM360
Ns s, 16 Sept 1928 & 3 Dec 1931. (89) $275

Lewis, Sinclair, 1885-1951 —& White, William Allen, 1868-1944
Group photograph, July 1926. (89) $350

Lewis, Wyndham, 1884-1957
ANs, 27 July 1926. (89) $175

Lewisohn, Ludwig, 1883-1955
Collection of 7 A Ls s, 13 Ls s, 3 autograph Mss (1 sgd), 14 transcripts of poems (8 sgd), & related material, 1904 to 1955. (90) $550
Series of 4 Ls s, 1927 to 1930. (89) $110

Ley, Robert, 1890-1945
Ls, 10 Dec 1941. (90) $300

Leydig, Franz von, 1821-1908
Series of 5 A Ls s, 23 July 1873 to 10 Nov 1876. (91) DM700

Lhuyd, Edward, 1660-1709
ALs, 29 Mar 1697. (88) £400

Libby, Willard Frank
Ls, 15 Dec 1979. (89) DM300

Libero de Madonna Costanza
Ms, romance of Costanza, daughter of the Doge of Venice, in Italian; 13 cantos in ottava rima. [Florence?, 22 June 1433]. 117 leaves, 219mm by 145mm, in contemp red lea over wooden bds with vellum endleaves from a papal bull of c.1389-94. In a well-formed cursive bookhand by the scribe "mafro lion da veniexia". (90) £9,500

Library Catalogues. See: Bernard, Sir Robert
See also: Gayot, Francois-Marie
See also: Walpole, Horace

LIBRO D'ORE

Libro d'Ore
Ms, Libro d'Ore. [Florence, last quarter of 15th Cent]. 208 (of 212) leaves, 140mm by 94mm. Illuminated. (90) LIt6,500,000

Lichtenau, Wilhelmine, Graefin von, 1753-1820
ALs, 9 Sept 1796. Schroeder collection. (89) DM420
— 6 Nov 1806. (91) DM950

Lichtenberg, Georg Christoph, 1742-99
ALs, 16 Nov 1785. 2 pp, folio. To Christian Wilhelm Buettner. Thanking for recipient's book & requesting his opinion about 3 stones from Ceylon. (90) DM5,000
— 10 Nov 1786. 5 pp, folio. To [Franz Ferdinand] Wolff. Regarding experiments with electricity, English princes studying at Goettingen, etc. Including 3 sketches. (90) DM15,000
— 1 Mar 1788. 1 p, folio. To Karl Friedrich Kielmeyer. Inviting him for supper the next day. (91) DM2,600
— 14 Apr 1794. 3 pp, 4to. To Wattenbach. Discussing chemical experiments by Herr Scheier & the inadequacy of his own laboratory, & requesting some information. (90) DM4,000
— 27 May 1794. 3 pp, 8vo. Recipient unnamed. Commenting on Hogarth. (91) DM4,000
— 9 June 1797. 1 p, 4to. To Friedrich Bouterwek. Returning a book with critical comments. (90) DM4,000
ANs, [n.d.]. (91) DM550

Lichtwer, Magnus Gottfried, 1719-83
Autograph Ms, critical comments about some engravings; [n.d.]. (90) DM260

Liebermann, Max, 1847-1935
Autograph sketchbook, [c.1916]. 26 leaves (1 pasted in), 8vo. New cloth bdg. Containing 22 pp of sketches mostly for illusts to an Ed of Heinrich von Kleist & some self portraits in pencil & crayon, & pen-&-ink drawing. (91) DM14,000
Collection of 33 A Ls s & AN, 14 Mar 1911 to 20 Dec 1931. 51 pp, 4to & 8vo. To Hermann Mueller. Important letters about his works & the art

AMERICAN BOOK PRICES CURRENT

market. (91) DM80,000
Series of 3 A Ls s, 29 July 1896 & [n.d.]. (88) DM700
— Series of 3 A Ls s, 23 Dec 1910 to 8 Mar 1911. (89) DM900
— Series of 12 A Ls s, 1 July 1917 to 22 July 1934 & [n.d.]. To [Alexander Amersdorffer]. About his works, an exhibition, & matters pertaining to the Berlin Academy of Arts. (91) DM5,000
A Ls s (2), 29 Mar 1917 & 7 Nov 1920. (88) DM440
ALs, 7 July 1892. (90) DM480
— 16 Jan 1895. 1 p, 8vo. To an unnamed colleague. Expressing congratulations on his engagement & relating an anecdote about A. von Menzel. (91) DM2,000
— 7 Feb 1902. (90) DM320
— 23 Dec 1906. (90) DM360
— 20 July 1907. (90) DM950
— 13 Mar 1909. (88) DM250
— 5 May 1910. 3 pp, 8vo. To Bruno Cassirer. Suggesting that he meet Frank Wedekind's wish to leave Cassirer's publishing house. (91) DM2,000
— 28 Nov 1910. (89) DM600
— 1 Oct 1913. (88) DM700
— 21 Feb 1915. (90) DM700
— 4 May 1919. (88) DM300
— 5 Mar 1920. (89) DM700
— 11 May 1926. (90) DM340
— 23 Nov 1928. (90) DM300
Autograph postcards (2), sgd, 2 Feb 1895 & [3 Jan 1899]. (89) DM320
ANs, 24 Sept 1927. (91) DM270

Liebert, Gaston Ernest
[An archive of over 1,000 items, comprising his family & personal papers, with material relating to his service as French Consul General at Hong Kong, 1912-1913, & to preparations for the general insurrection in Indochina, sold at P on 27 June 1989, lot 61, for $1,100.]

Liebig, Henriette von, 1807-81
Series of 19 A Ls s, 27 Mar 1826 to 28 Feb 1871. 64 pp, 8vo. To Luise Vieweg. Family news. Including half-page postscript, sgd, by her husband Justus. (91) DM1,400

Liebig, Justus von, 1803-73
Series of 3 A Ls s, 17 Nov 1858 to 7 Nov 1859. 4 pp, 8vo. To [Friedrich Pauli]. Commenting on wine growing in the Palatinate area. (91) DM1,500
ALs, 10 June 1842. (90) £350
— 8 Feb 1845. 2 pp, 8vo. To Carl Vogt. Discussing experiences with the French & an academy election. (91) DM1,500
— 26 Apr 1850. (91) $950
— 21 Apr 1861. 4 pp, 8vo. Recipient unnamed. Concerning patent rights & the manufacture of mirrors at Doos. (89) DM1,300
— 18 May 1872. 1 p, 8vo. To Friedrich Woehler. Requesting him to analyze a sample of his meat extract. With ANs. (90) DM1,900
Ds, 15 Apr 1866. (91) DM600

Liebknecht, Karl, 1871-1919
ALs, 29 Aug 1901. 2 pp, 8vo. To Paul Loebe. Offering a date for a lecture at Breslau. (90) DM2,600
— 1 June 1906. 1 p, 8vo. To [Joseph Bloch]. Declining to write a review. (90) DM2,200
— 16 Nov 1918. 1 p, 4to. To a party member. Urgently requesting a meeting. (91) DM5,000
Autograph postcard, sgd, 24 Mar 1913. To [his nieces in Berlin]. About his travels in the Netherlands. Sgd Onkel Karl. In pencil. (89) DM1,100

Liebknecht, Wilhelm, 1826-1900
Collection of 2 A Ls s & autograph postcard, sgd, 3 Apr 1896 to 12 July 1899. 2 pp, 8vo, & card. To Max Quarck. About his son's law examinination, & promising to visit him in prison. With related material. (89) DM1,200
ALs, 28 May 1874. 2 pp, 8vo. To a friend in Switzerland. Thanking for support during his imprisonment & inquiring about a position for his daughter. (88) DM1,800
— 27 June 1882. (90) DM450
— 3 Sept 1894. (90) DM420
— 11 May 1898. (90) DM420
— 20 July 1900. (91) DM420

Liechtenstein, Anton Florian, Fuerst, 1656-1721
Ls, 10 Feb 1703. (88) DM440

Ligon, Thomas W.
A Ls s (2), 26 & 29 Sept 1856. (91) $950

Liliencron, Detlev von, 1844-1909
Autograph Ms, 3 epigrammatic poems, [n.d.]. (89) DM900
— Autograph Ms, 9 poems, 15 July 1891 to 18 Apr 1892. 43 pp, 4to, in half cloth notebook, numbered 43. Including numerous revisions. Each poem sgd D.v.L.; also sgd on front cover. (91) DM9,500
— Autograph Ms, poem, Einen Sommer lang; [Aug 1891]. 2 pp, 8vo. Fair copy. (90) DM5,000
— Autograph Ms, poem, Sehnsucht, [n.d.]. (89) DM700
Autograph transcript, poem, Der Kanarienvogel; [n.d.]. (88) DM750
Series of 8 A Ls s, 1891 & 1894. 25 pp, 8vo. To Louise Strebinger. Personal letters reminiscing about their meeting, expressing congratulations, recommending Gustv Falke, etc. (91) DM2,200
ALs, 22 June 1888. (91) DM440
— 1 Mar 1896. (90) DM200
— 1 Nov 1896. (88) DM220
— 13 June 1898. (90) DM440
— 9 Feb 1900. (91) DM380
— 18 Jan 1903. (90) DM340

Lilienthal, Otto, 1848-96
ALs, 13 Jan 1890. 3 pp, 4to. To August Platte. Discussing flight experiments & requesting a copy of recipient's work. (90) DM6,400
— 14 May 1890. 8 pp, 4to. To August Platte. Discussing diverging opinions about the mechanics of flight; including small drawings. (90) DM6,000
— 9 & 11 June 1890. 6 pp, 4to. To August Platte. Informing him about plans for a new experiment. Including postscript containing detailed description; sgd. (90) DM6,000
— 21 Jan 1891. 2 pp, 4to. To August Platte. Encouraging him to publish a paper about his theories on the mechanics of flight. (90) DM4,000
— 22 Aug 1895. 2 pp, 4to. To Capt.

Mensing. Discussing the construction of a machine. (91) DM4,200

Lillie, Gordon William, 1860-1942
ALs, 3 June 1916. (90) $170

Liman von Sanders, Otto, 1855-1929
ALs, 22 Feb 1914. Schroeder collection. (89) DM280

Lincoln, Abraham, 1809-65
[A letter, 8 May 1865, 8 pp, by an eyewitness describing Lincoln's funeral, with related material, sold at R on 4 Mar 1989, lot 235, for $550.]

Autograph Ms, draft instructions to a jury in a slander action [Campbell vs. Abraham Smith?], [1841?]. Def; repaired. Barrett collection. (89) $3,000

— Autograph Ms, fragment from a book for arithmetic lessons, bearing calculations & a poem, 5 lines; [c.1824-1826]. 2 pp on irregularly shaped oblong leaf, c.5.25 by 7.75 inches. With integral signature. Very def. Barrett collection. (89) $80,000

— Autograph Ms, fragment from his book for arithmetic lessons, with divisions & a doggerel quatrain; 1824 to 1826. 2 pp on irregularly shaped leaf, c.12.25 by 7.5 inches; between sheets of Plexiglas. Sgd 3 times. (91) $130,000

— Autograph Ms, [n.d., 1 July 1854-1859?]. 1 p, 4to. Rebuttal of arguments advanced by defenders of slavery. Repaired. Barrett collection. (88) $75,000

ALs, 7 May 1837. 2 pp, folio. To Mary Owens. About his situation at Springfield & suggesting that she "think seriously" before deciding to marry him. Separated at one fold. (88) $70,000

— 25 Feb 1847. 1 p, 4to. To Andrew Johnston. Agreeing to the publication of some poems sent in an earlier letter. (90) $130,000

— 13 Oct 1853. 1 p, 4to; cut from larger leaf. To Henry E. Dummer. Asking for a testimony in a suit arising from his father-in-law's estate. Repaired. (90) $14,000

— 14 Feb 1855. 4 pp, 4to. To Jesse O. Norton. Explaining his defeat for election to the US Senate. Somewhat def; encapsulated. With campaign badge. (89) $70,000

— 13 Sept 1857. 1 p, 4to. To Jesse K. DuBois. About enforcing banking laws. (91) $42,000

— 29 Jan 1858. 1 p, 4to. To John Olney. Expressing doubts that recipient's court case can be won. Repaired. (90) $24,000

— 15 May 1858. 2 pp, 4to. To J. F. Alexander. Declining to speak in Greenville, & commenting on the candidacy of Stephen A. Douglas. Silked & encapsulated. (88) $75,000

— 3 Sept 1858. 1 p, 4to. To "Dear Doctor". Informing him that he will speak at Danville the day after Douglas. Including postscript, initialled. Doheny collection. (89) $24,000

— 3 Mar 1859. 1 p, 4to. To Hayden Keeling. Advising him to drop a lawsuit. (91) $65,000

— 27 July 1860. 1 p, 4to. To Francis E. Spinner. Thanking for political advice & for some books. Sang collection. (91) $15,000

— 4 Sept 1860. 2 pp, 8vo. To John Coulter. Reviewing his early election performances against Peter Cartwright. Doheny collection. (89) $48,000

— 13 May 1861. 1 p, 4to. To "Whom it may concern" in the War Department. Referring James A. Sheahan's offer to raise a regiment of Baltimoreans to the Sec of War. (89) $6,500

— 20 Aug 1861. 1 p, 8vo. To Sec of War Stanton. Recommending Frederick A. Stamming for an appointment in the army. Def. (90) $9,500

— 18 Sept 1861. 1 p, 8vo. To Sec of State [Seward]. Asking for his comments on a Senator's proposal for a Secretary of Legation. (89) £1,700

— 18 Feb 1862. 1 p, 4to. To William A. Newell. Confirming that Newell advocated Col. Hatfield's appointment as brigadier general. Framed with a port. (89) $8,500

— 3 Mar 1862. 1 p, 8vo. To Sec of War Stanton. Requesting that Edward B. Jerome be appointed Lieutenant. (90) $14,000

— 8 Apr 1862. 1 p, 8vo. To Miss A. Lizzie Whipple. Responding to a request for his & his wife's autographs. Also sgd

by Mary Lincoln. Was mtd. Doheny collection. (89) $8,000
— 21 May 1862. 1 p, 4to. To [James Fowler] Simmons. Sending a "distressed girl" from his state looking for work. (90) $32,500
— 16 July 1862. 1 p, 4to. To Attorney Gen. [Edward Bates]. Asking for Samuel F. Miller's nomination as Justice of the Supreme Court & anr appointment. (90) $14,000
— 25 July 1862. 2 pp, 8vo. To Edwin M. Stanton as Sec of War. About the request of Lt. Shurtleff to be returned to his unit. (90) $13,000
— 7 Oct 1862. 1 p, 4to. To Gen. George McClellan. Suggesting that he see his family at his own discretion. McVitty collection. (90) $25,000
— 17 Oct 1862. 1 p, 8vo. To [Sec of War Edwin M. Stanton?]. Recommending the promotion of Lieut. Morgan Doheny. Doheny collection. (89) $4,600
— 22 Dec 1862. 1 p, 4to. To the Army of the Potomac. Expressing appreciation of their efforts in the battle of Fredericksburg. Draft; 5 autograph emendations. Fold splits. (88) $215,000
— 4 June 1863. 1 p, 8vo. To Sec of War [Edwin Stanton]. Suggesting the revocation of [Gen. Burnside's] order to suspend the Chicago Times. Pforzheimer collection. (90) $22,000
— 13 Jan 1864. 1 p, 8vo. To Attorney Gen. James Speed. Requesting him to prepare a pardon for Benjamin C. Robertson. Middendorf collection. (89) $6,500
— 14 Jan 1864. 1 p, 8vo. To Major Gen. [Benjamin F.] Fuller. Introducing Thomas Stackpole. Silked. Doheny collection. (89) $5,500
— 2 Feb 1864. 1 p, 8vo. To the Judge Advocate General. Asking for reports about the cases of Latshaw & Wilmon. (90) $10,500
— 7 Mar 1864. 1 p, 8vo. To the Sec of War. Ordering the appointment of Robert J. Stevens as additional paymaster. (88) $6,000
— 21 Mar 1864. 1 p, size not stated. To Sec of War Stanton. Discussing military appointments in Kentucky. (91) $32,000
— 24 May 1864. 1 p, 8vo. To the Sec of War. Ordering a military promotion. Laid down. (89) £2,600
— 18 June 1864. 1 p, 8vo. To Sec of War Stanton. Suggesting that Gen. E. A. Paine be assigned a command in Kentucky. Rosenbloom collection. (88) $11,000
— 13 Sept 1864. 1 p, 8vo. To Sec of the Interior [J. P. Usher]. Requesting him to prepare a paper in Mr. Allison's case. (91) $11,500
— 26 Oct 1864. 1 p, 8vo. To Mrs. George W. Swift. Responding to a poem requesting his autograph. With franking signature. Fold break. Doheny collection. (89) $22,000
Ls, 29 Oct 1860. 1 p, 16mo. To William R. Hull. Sending his autograph. (91) $2,800
— 8 Feb 1861. 1 p, 8vo. To Lewis J. Cist. Sending his autograph. Whiton collection. (88) $2,300
— 8 July 1861. 1 p, 8vo. To Sec of War Simon Cameron. Asking for formal nominations in cases of War Department appointments. (90) $4,000
— 9 Nov 1863. 1 p, 4to. To Robert B. Roosevelt, J. J. Astor, Jr., & others. About the nomination of Gen. John A. Dix for mayor of NY, & "declining to interfere with New York city politics". Marked "Private". With copy of communication by Roosevelt & others on integral leaf. Repaired. (89) $23,000
ANs, 5 Feb 1841. 1 p, 4to. To Thomas T. Gantt. Sending a payment. Encapsulated. (91) $3,250
— [c.10 Sept 1852]. 1 p, folio. To Ninian W. Edwards. Sending statement of costs in representing one of Edwards's clients. Including sgd docket in Lincoln's hand & anr Lincoln signature on address panel on verso, & ANs by Herndon below Lincoln's ANs. (89) $8,500
— 15 May 1862. 1 p, folio. To the Secretary of War. Requesting data to answer a resolution. On integral leaf of a Senate resolution concerning arrests in Kentucky. Byer collection. (90) $4,800
— 7 Feb 1863. 1 p, on envelope. To Sec of War Stanton & Gen. Halleck. Forwarding a letter recommending the

LINCOLN

appointment of Thomas D. Johns as Brigadier General (included). Endorsed by Halleck below Lincoln's note. (91) $5,000
— 12 May 1863. 1 p, 16mo (card). To Sec of War [Stanton]. Requesting that he "see Mr. Dole & others, about the first colored regiment." (91) $19,000
— 27 July 1863. 1 p, 45mm by 77mm. To the Sec of War. Requesting him to see Mr. Ordway. Mtd. (90) $2,600
— 2 Jan 1864. 4 lines on small card. To Postmaster Gen. [Montgomery Blair]. Requesting him to call. Was mtd. (89) $2,250
— 7 Sept 1864. 1 p, size not stated [cut from larger leaf?]. To Gen. Hitchcock. Requesting him to see Mrs. Ten Eyck. Framed with related material. (90) $3,250
— 22 Oct 1864. 5 lines on small card. To Sec of War Edwin Stanton. Requesting him to "give this man the proper direction to apply for leave to go home to vote." Was mtd. (88) $6,500
— 23 Nov 1864. 4 lines on a small oblong, cut from larger leaf. Order that a man "take the oath of Dec. 8, 1863, and be discharged." McVitty collection. (90) $3,000
— 8 Dec 1864. 2.5 by 3 inches, cut from a larger document. Asking the Sec. of war for an answer to an enquiry. Framed with Currier & Ives litho. Accompanied by a letter from Ben M. Plumb presenting the note to a friend, 7 Jan 1865. (91) $3,600
— 12 Jan 1865. Size not stated. Ordering that "these men take the oath of Dec. 8, 1865 [sic] & be discharged." Matted with related material. (91) $4,200
— 28 Jan 1865. 1 p, 16mo. Recipient unnamed. Stating he will see Mr. Bartlett. Sgd AL. Framed. (90) $1,500
— 16 Mar 1865. 2 lines on small card. Ordering a military discharge. Framed with a port. (89) $1,800
Ns, 12 Nov 1860. 1 p, 8vo. To Clement Haddock. Complying with request for his autograph. Text in the hand of E. E. Ellsworth. (88) $2,900
— 7 Feb 1861. 1 p, 4to. To William Hathaway. Sending his autograph. Pratt collection. (89) $3,250
ADs, 24 Sept 1835. 1 p, 4to. "Timber Lands Surveyed by A. Lincoln from Wm. Green to M. S. Marsh". Including plat drawing. Barrett collection. (89) $8,000
— [16 May 1839]. 1 p, 4to. Brief regarding the case of Kerr vs. Prickett; sgd Stuart & Lincoln. Inlaid. Doheny collection. (89) $4,200
— 2 Nov 1839. 3 pp, folio. Plea in the case of Kerr v. Constant & Francis, sgd Stuart & Lincoln (twice) & A. Lincoln. (90) $12,000
— [12 June 1840]. 1 p, 8vo. Plea in the case of Dunham v. Gray. Sgd Stuart & Lincoln. Fold breaks. (91) $2,600
— [c.1841]. 3 pp, folio. Petition & Summons in the case of Goodell v. Powell; sgd Logan & Lincoln. (91) $10,000
— [July 1842]. 1 p, folio. Declaration for the plaintiff in the case of William Dormady vs. Thomas Kavana [i.e. Cavanaugh]. Sgd Logan & Lincoln. Repaired. (89) $3,000
— [11 July 1843]. (88) £750
— [6] Mar 1844. 6 pp, 4to. Legal brief in the case of Johnson v. Wickersham. (91) $7,500
— [1844 or later]. 2 pp, 63mm by 196mm. Fragment of legal brief relating to the sale of a "Daguerrean Gallery". Sgd Lincoln & Herndon. (90) $4,500
— 8 Oct 1847. 3 pp, 4to. Legal brief in the case of Miller v. Miller; sgd Lincoln & Herndon. Framed with a port. (91) $10,000
— 26 Apr 1854. 2 pp, folio. Legal brief in the case of Coventry & Warwickshire Banking Co. v. William Whorrall. (91) $4,100
— [c.1 May 1855]. 1 p, 4to. 3 separate pleas, each sgd, in the case of Hitchcock v. Glasgow, filed with the Tazewell County Court. (89) $6,000
— 22 Jan 1864. 1 p. Ordering a stay of execution for Henry C. Fuller. With an ALs of Congressman Orlando Kellogg explaining the circumstances & a Brady carte-de-visite of Kellogg. (90) $6,000

AD, 9 Sept 1839. (89) $1,000
— [c.1839]. 1 p, folio. Affidavit of Abner Smith regarding a lost promissory note. Text in Lincoln's hand; sgd by Smith. Framed. (89) $2,750

1987 - 1991 · AUTOGRAPHS & MANUSCRIPTS   LINCOLN

— 17 June 1843. Byer collection. (90) $850

Ds, 19 June 1861. 1 p, oblong folio. Appointment of Franklin Webster as Consul at Munich. Countersgd by Seward, whose signature is slightly def. (91) $2,900

— 22 Mar 1861. 1 p, folio. Appointment for Rufus King as minister at Rome. Countersgd by Seward. Sang collection. (91) $4,000

— 25 Mar 1861. 1 p, folio. Commission for George Kyler as Register of the St. Louis Land Office. Framed. (90) $3,750

— 8 Apr 1861. 1 p, 276mm by 442mm, laid down on card. Appointment of William L. Adams as a collector of customs. (91) $2,600

— 13 Apr 1861. 1 p, folio. Appointment for Silas C. Booth as customs collector. (90) $4,200

— 18 Apr 1861. 1 p, 254mm by 375mm. Appointment of Robert Murray as Marshall for the Southern District of NY. Countersgd by William Seward. (90) $3,500

— 18 May 1861. 1 p, folio. Ship's paper in 4 languages for the ship Contest going on a whaling voyage. Countersgd by W. H. Seward. (91) $7,500

— 11 June 1861. 1 p, oblong folio. Appointment of Charles H. Richman as Consul at Cadiz. Countersgd by Seward, but short fold split through Seward's signature. (91) $3,000

— 19 June 1861. 1 p, bolong folio. Appointment of R. P. L. Baber as Consul at Matanzas. Countersgd by Seward. (91) $3,300

— 19 June 1861. 1 p, oblong folio. Appointment of Edward Trowbridge as Consul at Bermuda. Countersgd by Seward, whose signature is affected by smudges. (91) $3,100

— 22 July 1861. 1 p, double folio. Appointment of Robert B. Carnahan as U.S. Attorney. Countersgd by Seward. (91) $2,200

— 31 July 1861. 1 p, oblong folio. Appointment of Joseph G. Bowman of Indiana as Consul at Matanzas. Countersgd by Seward. (91) $3,600

— 5 Aug 1861. 1 p, folio. Commission of Thomas Y. Field as captain in the U. S. Marine Corps. Countersgd by Gideon Welles. (91) $2,600

— 9 Aug 1861. 1 p, 4to. Order to affix the US Seal to a pardon warrant. (90) $3,200

— 10 Aug 1861. 1 p, 19.5 by 15.75 inches. Appointment of Orville E. Babcock to the Corps of Engineers. Also sgd by Sec of War Cameron. (91) $3,800

— 10 Aug 1861. 1 p, folio. Appointment for Alexander McRae as captain. Countersgd by Sec of War Cameron. Framed with 4 portraits. (89) $2,750

— 15 Aug 1861. 1 p, folio. Commission for William B. Lowe as Captain in the 11th Infantry Regiment. (90) $2,250

— 6 Sept 1861. 1 p, oblong folio. Appointment of Norman M. Ross as Consul at Leipzig. Countersgd by Seward, whose signature has a fold split through it. (91) $3,300

— 7 Nov 1861. 1 p, folio. Credentials for William H. Seward to exchange ratifications of the treaty with Costa Rica sgd 2 July 1860. (91) $7,500

— 4 Apr 1862. 1 p, vellum, folio. Appointment of Daniel M. Skinner as an Assistant Surgeon in the U.S. Navy. Countersgd by Gideon Welles. (91) $3,800

— 3 May 1862. 1 p, folio. Commission for Edward O. C. Ord as Major General of Volunteers. (89) $8,500

— 7 May 1862. 1 p, folio. Appointment of H. J. Robinson as Assistant Quartermaster of Volunteers. Countersgd by Sec of War Stanton. Mtd. (89) $3,200

— 12 June 1862. 1 p, folio. Appointment of Zealous B. Tower as Brigadier General of Volunteers. (91) $5,000

— 19 July 1862. 1 p, 4to. Appointment of Walter J. Smith as Acting Sec of the Interior. Pratt collection. (89) $4,000

— 8 Aug 1862. 1 p, folio. Commission for Mark Howard as tax collector for the 1st District of Connecticut. Countersgd by Sec of the Treasury Salmon Chase. Framed. (89) $3,500

— 23 Aug 1862. 1 p, 4to. Appointment of Thomas G. Turner as Assessor of Taxes. Also sgd by Salmon P. Chase. Doheny collection. (89) $3,000

— 6 Sept 1862. 1 p, folio. Appointment of Cephas Brainerd as arbitrator under the treaty with England for suppres-

LINCOLN

sion of the slave trade. Countersgd by Seward. (91) $32,000

— 5 Nov 1862. 1 p, 4to. Order to affix the US Seal to a pardon warrant. Doheny collection. (89) $2,800

— 14 Nov 1862. 1 p, oblong folio. Appointment of William Whetten as Consul at Nassua, New Providence. Countersgd by Seward. (91) $3,700

— 31 Dec 1862. 1 p, folio. Military commission for James B. Turner. Mtd. (89) $2,200

— 1 Jan 1863. 1 p, 4to. Order to affix the Great Seal to [the Emancipation Proclamation]. Ruddy collection. (88) $175,000

— 26 Jan 1863. 1 p, folio. Commission for George S. Blake as Commodore in the Navy. (91) $4,250

— 21 Feb 1863. 1 p, 24.5 by 20.5 inches. Appointment for Abner Reed as Commander in the Navy. Countersgd by Gideon Welles. Framed. (88) £1,300

— 2 Mar 1863. 1 p, folio. Appointment of Thomas G. Turner as Tax Assessor. Also sgd by Salmon P. Chase. Doheny collection. (89) $3,800

— 5 Mar 1863. 1 p, 4to. Extension of a leave of absence. With autograph addition, 5 words. Pratt collection. (89) $4,500

— 6 Mar 1863. 1 p, folio. Appointment of Samuel J. Wright as Assistant Quartermaster of Volunteers. Countersgd by Stanton. Framed. (91) $4,250

— 6 Mar 1863. 1 p, folio. Appointment for Daniel W. Alvord as Revenue Collector. (90) $3,500

— 6 Mar 1863. 1 p, folio. Commission for Thomas McDill as Assistant Quartermaster. Countersgd by Stanton. (90) $2,800

— 6 Mar 1863. 1 p, folio. Appointment of Ralph Avery as Collector. Fold breaks. (89) $1,600

— 11 Mar 1863. 1 p, folio. Appointment of Edwin G. Eastman as consul at Cork. Silked. (90) $6,500

— 12 Mar 1863. 1 p, folio. Appointment of A. L. Dewey as assistant quartermaster of volunteers. Framed. (91) $4,000

— 13 Mar 1863. 1 p, folio. Appointment of George J. Marshall as assistant adjutant general of volunteers. (91) $3,750

— 13 Mar 1863. 1 p, folio. Appointment of Nathaniel C. Towle as Register of Deeds in Washington, D. C. Countersgd by Seward. (91) £2,300

— 13 Mar 1863. 1 p, 14 by 18 inches. Appointment of Nathaniel C. Towle as Register of Deeds in Washington, D.C.; countersgd by Seward. (89) £3,000

— 26 Mar 1863. 2 pp, folio. Pardon for John Doherty, convicted of rape. Countersgd by Sec of State Seward. (89) $2,500

— 13 Apr 1863. 1 p, vellum. Appointment of Hartman Buche as colonel in the Corps of Engineers. Countersgd by Stanton. (91) $3,800

— 2 May 1863. 1 p, folio. Commission for Henry B. Blood as Assistant Quartermaster of Volunteers. (91) $2,250

— 1 July 1863. 1 p, 278mm by 352mm. Appointment of O. Everett Webster as 1st Lieutenant in the Revenue Service. (91) $3,200

— 3 July 1863. 1 p, 8vo. Setting number of troops to be called up from Pennsylvania. Framed with port. (91) $7,000

— 24 July 1863. 1 p, 4to. Draft call for the 18th Pennsylvania District. (91) $7,500

— 27 July 1863. Size not stated. Summons for troops from Delaware. Partly ptd. Framed with a port photograph. (88) £1,500

— 10 Oct 1863. 1 p, 4to. Commuting a death sentence for desertion to confinement at hard labor. Text probably in the hand of Judge Advocate General Joseph Holt. Barrett collection. (89) $6,000

— 28 Nov 1863. 1 p, oblong folio. Appointment of Thomas Kirkpatrick as Consul at Nassau, New Providence. Countersgd by Seward, with fold split affecting Seward's signature. (91) $3,200

— 2 Mar 1864. 1 p, folio. Appointment of Stephen Longfellow as customs collector. Countersgd by Salmon P. Chase. Framed. (89) $3,000

— 1 Apr 1864. 1 p, folio. Appointment of James H. May as Lieut. in the infantry. Countersgd by Edwin M. Stanton.

(88) $2,100
— 6 Apr 1864. 1 p, folio. Commission for Edward Curtis as Assistant Surgeon in the Army. Countersgd by Sec of War Stanton. (89) $3,500
— 21 Apr 1864. 1 p, folio. Commission for John J. Read as a naval lieutenant. Countersgd by Gideon Welles. With 3 later naval commissions for Read. Framed. (88) $1,600
— 27 Apor 1864. 1 p, 4to. Appointment of George Harrington to act as Sec of the Treasury during the absence of Salmon P. Chase. (91) $3,500
— 24 May 1864. 1 p, folio. Appointment of Joseph C. Hays as Assistant Quartermaster of Volunteers. Framed with a port. (89) $2,800
— 1 July 1864. 1 p, folio. Commission as major for Anderson D. Nelson. (89) $3,500
— 6 July 1864. 1 p, folio. Appointment of W. W. McKim as assistant quartermaster of volunteers. (91) $3,250
— 15 July 1864. 1 p, folio. Appointment of Charles S. Bradley as 2d Lieutenant in the Signal Corps. Countersgd by Stanton. Framed with a port. (91) $5,000
— 26 July 1864. 1 p, 4to. Appointment of Rev. Isaac M. Ely as Chaplain of the US Hospital at Slough Barracks. (91) $3,500
— 1 Aug 1864. 1 p, folio. Appointment of a 1st Lieutenant in the Veteran Reserve Corp. Countersgd by Sec of War Stanton. (91) $1,600
— 24 Aug 1864. 1 p, folio. Ship's papers in 4 languages for the barque Laetitia. Tape repairs. (88) $4,000
— 23 Sept 1864. 1 p, folio. Appointment of James H. Causten as Consul of Ecuador at Washington. Also sgd by Sec of State Seward. Doheny collection. (89) $3,500
— 20 Oct 1864. 1 p, 347mm by 444mm. Recognizing Charles Frederick Adae as Consul for Bavaria. Countersgd by Seward. (90) $5,000
— 18 Nov 1864. 1 p, 4to. Order to affix the US Seal to the proclamation of a treaty with Belgium. Framed with a port. (89) $3,000
— 17 Dec 1864. 2 pp, folio. Pardon for David S. Everett; countersgd by Sec of State Seward. Framed & mtd on wooden stand with related material. (90) $20,000
— 17 Jan 1865. 1 p, 4to. Order to affix the U.S. Seal to a proclamation of a treaty with the Shoshonee Goship Bands of Indians of 12 Oct 1863. (91) $6,500
— 18 Jan 1865. (88) £550
— [1865?]. 1 p, folio. Ship's papers in 4 languages; sgd in blank. Countersgd by Sec of State Seward. (91) $6,500
— [1865?]. 1 p, folio. Ship's papers; sgd in blank. Countersgd by Sec of State Seward. Sang collection. (90) $7,000
— [n.d.]. 92mm by 280mm. Fragment of ship's papers, countersgd by Seward. (90) $2,800

Autograph endorsement, sgd, 10 Aug 1861. 4 lines on verso of last page of 4-page telegram from Gen. William S. Rosecrans recommending formal military training for West Virginia units; asking Gen. McClellan for advice. Barrett collection. (89) $2,750
— Anr, sgd, 29 Aug 1861. 13 lines on 8vo leaf, commenting on a letter from Gov. William A. Newell seeking a paymastership for his brother; suggesting appointment. Framed with Newell's letter & a port. (89) $4,250
— Anr, sgd, 4 Sept 1861. 11 lines on integral blank of a letter by Samuel Bowles, 23 Aug 1861, 3 pp, 4to, recommending William A. Hawley; supporting recommendation. Doheny collection. (89) $5,500
— Anr, sgd, 12 Mar 1862. On a small slip of paper. Asking Capt. Dahlgren to see the bearer. Framed with a port. Doheny collection. (88) $2,000
— Anr, sgd, 26 Mar 1862. Size not stated; cut from larger leaf. Submitting an unspecified matter to the Attorney Gen. (90) $2,500
— Anr, sgd, 27 Mar 1862. 3 lines on front of an envelope addressed to him. "Respectfully submitted to the War Department". Framed with a port. James Roosevelt collection. (89) $2,500
— Anr, sgd, 31 Mar 1862, on front of an envelope addressed to him. Submitting an unspecified matter to the Attorney Gen. (90) $2,250
— Anr, sgd, 2 May 1862, on integral

LINCOLN

blank of a petition from 7 Illinois Congressmen & a Senator, 2 pp, 4to, recommending the appointment of John Wesley Turner as aide to Gen. McClellan; submitting petition to the Sec of War. (89) $2,250

— Anr, sgd, 25 July 1862. 6 lines on an envelope containing ALs by Gov. William Sprague to Lincoln, 23 July 1862, regarding shipments of contraband to Richmond (present); requesting the Attorney Gen. to see bearer. (90) $3,500

— Anr, sgd, 10 Jan 1863. 4 lines on an envelope addressed to him, requesting the Surgeon General's opinion about an appointment. With Surgeon General's answer below. Doheny collection. (89) $3,800

— Anr, sgd, 28 Jan 1863. 9 lines on address leaf of a letter addressed to him by Brigadier Gen. Michael Corcoran, 26 Jan 1863, 1 p, 4to, recommending Lieut. Morgan Doheny; strongly supporting recommendation. Doheny collection. (89) $4,000

— Anr, sgd, 14 Apr 1863, on verso of letter from Brig. Gen. Benjamin F. Loan & others, 2 pp, 4to, recommending Dr. Richard A. Wells as surgeon; referring letter to the Secretary of War. (90) $3,250

— Anr, sgd, 19 May 1863. On a letter addressed to him by Millard Fillmore, 16 May 1863, 2 pp, 8vo, on behalf of his nephew. 7 lines, requesting the Judge Advocate General to report on the case. (91) $20,000

— Anr, sgd, 22 Oct 1863. 6 lines on verso of ALs addressed to him by Brigadier Gen. J. T. Boyle, 16 Oct 1863, 2 pp, 4to, recommending the release of Rev. Bristow's son; order to let him take the oath & be released. Doheny collection. (89) $4,500

— Anr, sgd, 23 Dec 1863. On ALs of Gen. John M. Schofield requesting Christmas leave. Approving the request. (91) $4,000

— Anr, sgd, 7 Mar 1864. 14 lines on verso of a telegram addressed to him by Major Gen. Frank Steele; requesting [Attorney Gen. Edward Bates] to prepare a special pardon for Willard M. Randolph. Pforzheimer collection. (90) $8,500

— Anr, sgd, 15 Aug 1864. 8 lines on 8vo leaf, removed from orig communication. Expressing approval of a "man who wishes to work", & suggesting he be employed at Cavalry Depot. With autograph endorsement, sgd, by W. H. Hay below. Framed. (89) $8,500

— Anr, sgd, 18 Oct 1864. 4 lines on verso of 2d leaf of a letter from Lieut. Col. James A. Hall recommending Edward Nugent for an appointment in the Treasury Department; endorsing recommendation. Imperf. With tintype port of Nugent. (90) $3,500

— Anr, sgd, 18 Nov 1864. 2 lines at bottom of a letter from William Peullen to William Orme, 2 pp, 4to, recommending James Scovel for a permit to trade at Memphis; supporting recommendation. (91) $3,800

— Anr, sgd, 7 Dec 1864. 2 lines at foot of Ls by C. A. Dana, Assistant Sec of War, giving Benson J. Lossing permission to visit the battlefields. Middendorf collection. (89) $4,500

— Anr, 4 Feb 1865. 1 p, 8vo. Commenting negatively on a suggestion regarding draft enrollment for 6 NY congressional districts. Sgd. With related letter addressed to Brig. Gen. J. B. Fry & ANs by Sec of War E. M. Stanton. Adlai E. Stevenson collection. (88) $6,000

— Anr, "Judge Advocate General", written across portion of 16mo document. (89) $220

Autograph telegram, sgd, 15 Mar 1864. 1 p, 4to. To Ulysses S. Grant. Suggesting that Frank Blair be assigned to command his old corps. Marked "Private". Framed with portraits of Lincoln & Grant. (89) $17,000

— Anr, 29 Mar 1865. 1 p, 4to. To Ulysses S. Grant. Requesting information about enemy movements. Mtd. Barrett collection. (89) $29,000

Check, sgd, 14 Mar 1860. Drawn on Springfield Marine & Fire Insurance Company for $24.00 payable to "Self". Ptd with autograph accomplishment. Cancellation cut affecting signature. (89) $5,750

— Anr, accomplished & sgd, 15 Nov

1864. 73mm by 193mm. Drawn on the Riggs Bank for $10.00 payable to the Christian Commission. (90) $6,000
— Anr, sgd, Feb 1865. 7.2 by 2.6 inches. Drawn on the Riggs Bank for $20.00 payable to John G. Nicolay. Attached to Ls by Robert Lincoln, 31 May 1916. (89) $6,000

Cut signature, [c.1860]. (88) $600
— Anr, [n.d.]. 38mm by 122mm. Cut from a document, also sgd by Sec of State Seward. With related material. (88) $1,500
— Anr, [n.d.]. 25mm by 100mm. Mtd on sheet with authentication sgd by John Hay. (91) $2,400

Endorsement, sgd, 22 June 1861. 1 p, 4to. About the removal of 3 land offices. (89) $2,500

Franking signature, [Dec 1846]. On envelope addressed to the Commissioner of Pensions. (90) $3,500
— Anr, [4 Apr 1864]. On front panel of autograph envelope addressed to Ambrose W. Thompson. (91) $2,000
— Anr, [10 June 1864]. On fragment of autograph cover addressed to James McAden. (90) $2,400
— Anr, [19 Sept 1864]. On autograph cover addressed to Dr. Zacharis. Alexander collection. (90) $5,250
— Anr, [n.d.]. On autograph envelope; repaired. (89) $2,800

Photograph, sgd, [n.d.]. Carte size; by Brady. Imperf. (90) $6,000
Photograph, 4 Oct 1859. Size not stated; oval. By S. M. Fassett. (91) $2,500
— Anr, [9 Feb 1864]. (91) $250
— Anr, 9 Feb 1864. Cabinet size. 3-quarter length, seated; by Anthony Berger. With Brady's imprint on recto & verso of mount. (90) $5,500
— Anr, [n.d.]. (89) $150
— Anr, stereoview, [n.d.]. (91) $800
— Anr, [n.d.]. Size not stated. Stereo view, by E. H. T. Anthony & Co. (90) $1,500
— Anr, [n.d.]. (90) $80
— BAKER, LIEUT. L. B. - Photograph, sgd, 1891. Cabinet size. Equestrian port, with portraits of Lincoln, Booth & Sergt. Corbett in corners. Sgd below ptd explanatory text on verso. (91) $300
— CORBETT, BOSTON. - ALs, 13 May 1865. 4 pp, 4to. To "Brother Eddy". Informing him about his wartime career & his shooting of John Wilkes Booth. (90) $8,000
— DAVIS, DAVID. - Ds, 14 June 1865. 1 p, 4to. "Affidavit of Decease and Names of Heirs" of Lincoln, filed with the Sangamon County Court. (90) $11,000
— GOURLAY, JEANNIE. - Autograph Ms, eyewitness account of Lincoln's assassination by an actress playing at Ford's Theatre, [n.d.]. 1 p, 4to. Sgd. (90) $1,000
— HUNTER, MAJOR GEN. DAVID. - Ds, 1865. 1 p, 2 by 3.25 inches. Pass to trial of the conspirators conducted by the Military Commission. (91) $450
— INAUGURATION, 1865. - An engraved invitation to the National Inauguration Ball, 4 Mar 1865, 1 p, 8vo (card), addressed to Miss C. L. Whetmore, sold at CNY on 22 Feb 1989, lot 2105, for $1,300 to 19th Cent Shop. 89
— KOONTZ, SAMUEL. - ALs, 24 Apr 1865. Length not stated. To William Weaver. Giving an eyewitness account of Lincoln's assassination. On Treasury Department letterhead. (89) $5,500
— NICOLAY, JOHN G. - Autograph Ms, essay, Lincoln's Literary Experiments, sgd; [n.d.]. 28 pp, folio, in crushed levant mor gilt with engraved portraits. Including 9 corrected galley proofs. Doheny collection. (89) $2,200
— PAINE, LEWIS. - Photograph, "Payne alias Wood alias Hall arrested as an associate of Booth in the conspiracy... by Alex. Gardner, 1865. Carte size. (89) $600
— PORTER, WILLIAM H. - Ms, statement describing Lincoln making his "Lost Speech" in Bloomington, 1856; sgd & dated 26 Oct 1932. With related material. (91) $85
— RANKIN, HENRY B. - Typescript, recollections of Lincoln's last visit to his Springfield law office, sgd & dated 7 Apr 1923. 2 pp, 8vo. (91) $120
— ROBINSON, MAJOR HENRY M. - Typescript, eyewitness account of the assassination by a guard assigned to Ford's Theatre; [c.1916]. 3 pp, 8vo. Sgd. (90) $600
— SALFORD, MOSE. - Als, 17 Apr 1865, to John Beatty. 4 pp, 8vo. Description by

an employee of the undertaking firm that cared for the remains. Tells how the President's shirt & buttons were distributed & sends a fragment of the shirt (present). (91) $11,000
— SIXBEY, LIEUT. HERMAN. - Autograph Ms, [n.d.], describing Lincoln's visit to Westfield, NY, in 1861. 1 p, 8vo. Sgd. (91) $300
— STEVENS, JOHN H. - Autograph Ms, [n.d.], eyewitness account of Lincoln's assassination. 2 pp, 8vo. Sgd. (91) $225
— TANNER, SGT. JAMES. - Ls, 3 Dec 1918. Length not stated. To J. E. Boos. About errors in an article referring to his report about what happened in the room where Lincoln died. (91) $130

Lincoln, Abraham, 1809-65 —& Others
[A salesman's sample book for J. T. Headley's The Great Rebellion, vol 1, 1863, with hundreds of signatures of subscribers including Lincoln, Winfield Scott, Edwin Stanton, Gideon Welles, William Seward, etc., sold at R on 17 June 1989, lot 319, for$3,800.]

[The signatures of Lincoln, the members of his cabinet, & Vice President Andrew Johnson, Apr 1865, 1 p, 241mm by 195mm, within an elaborate hand-drawn pen-&-ink oval border formed by American flags & laurel wreaths, sold at P on 22 May 1990, lot 58, for $24,000.]

Ms, sgd, of the proposed 13th Amendment, [1 Feb 1865 or later], 1 p, folio. Sgd by Lincoln, Hannibal Hamlin, Schuyler Colfax, & 148 Senators & Representatives. (91) $200,000

Ls, 20 July 1837. 3 pp, folio. To Gen. Thornton. Requesting him not to resign as President of the Board of Canal Commissioners. Also sgd by 73 others. With related material. (90) $11,000

Lincoln, Benjamin, 1733-1810
ALs, 28 Feb 1779. (89) $500
— 30 Dec 1789. (91) $120
— 3 May 1804. (90) $100
Ls, 14 Aug 1781. (89) $250
— 3 Mar 1785. (89) $85
Ds, 17 Aug 1807. (88) $60

Lincoln, Mary Todd, 1818-82
ALs, 29 June 1865. 2 pp, 8vo. To Mr. Williamson. Expressing sympathy for the country's widows & orphans. 1st leaf inlaid. Doheny collection. (89) $3,800
AL, [c.1869]. 4 pp, 4to. To [Sally Orne]. About her wish to obtain a federal pension, General Grant, & the death of Edwin M. Stanton. Repaired. (89) $2,500
Franking signature, [21 Aug n.y.]. With autograph address. (89) $3,500

Lincoln, Robert Todd, 1843-1926
ALs, 26 July 1896. (88) $140
Ls, 21 Jan 1911. (91) $90

Lind, Jenny, 1820-87
Series of 9 A Ls s, 1840 to 1847 & 1863. 32 pp, 4to. To Jacob-Axel Josephson. About various composers & her operatic roles. 1 repaired. With related material. (89) £3,500
— Series of 11 A Ls s, 1841 to 1877. Over 50 pp, 4to & 8vo. To J. A. Josephson. Reporting about performances, travels, operas, composers, etc. (88) £2,600
ALs, 14 Mar 1850. (91) DM650
— 27 Aug 1864. (91) $210
— 30 June [n.y.]. (90) DM260
Autograph quotation, sgd, Nov 1850. (91) $150

Lindberg, Anne Morrow
ALs, 2 Apr 1942. (89) $500

Lindbergh, Charles A., 1902-74
Autograph Ms, article, Air Speed Limited Only by Power and Streamline, [ptd 3 Feb 1929]. 3 pp, folio. Draft. (89) $4,000
ALs, 10 July 1933. (88) $650
— 11 Mar 1956. 5 pp, 8vo. To Emmett O'Donnell, Jr. Confidential letter discussing his appointment to the Board of Visitors to the Air Academy. (91) $2,000
Ls, 4 Nov 1929. (91) $600
— 29 June 1930. 1 p, 4to. To Peter Lamb. Responding to a request for permission to reprint some articles. (91) $1,700
— 21 Feb 1963. (91) $900
Autograph postcard, sgd, 3 Jan 1915. (90)

$225
Photograph, sgd, [11 June 1927]. (91) $720
— Anr, [c.1927]. 8 by 10 inches. In front of the Spirit of St. Louis. Inscr to Thomas A. Edison in anr hand. (89) $2,400
Signature, [15 Apr 1926]. (91) $650
— Anr, [n.d., late 1920s]. (88) $120
— Anr, [n.d.]. (91) $900
White House card, sgd; [n.d.]. (88) $275

Lindbergh, Charles A., 1902-74 —& Hughes, Charles Evans, 1862-1948
Ptd photograph, [n.d.]. (91) $350

Lindbergh, Charles A., 1902-74 —& Orteig, Raymond, 1870-1939
Group photograph, 16 June 1927. (89) $1,000

Lindbergh Kidnapping Case
[A group of 14 Ls s & related material, 1936 to 1940, various sizes, to Sarah Cope, including 2 Ls s by Anna Hauptmann & 10 Ls s by Gov. Harold G. Hoffmann, all pertaining to the trial & execution of B. R. Hauptmann, sold at sg on 21 Sept 1989, lot 198, for $1,400.]

Linde, Carl von, 1842-1934
ALs, 24 Oct 1923. (88) DM250

Lindley, Robert, 1776-1855
Ms, 1st & 2d violin parts of Tre duetti per due Violoncelli, [n.d.]. (89) £130

Lindpaintner, Peter Joseph von, 1791-1856
ALs, 16 Oct 1837. (90) DM800

Lindsay, Vachel, 1879-1931
Series of 3 A Ls s, 14 Sept 1921 to 29 Apr 1925. (89) $200

Lindsay, William Schaw, 1816-77
[A large archive comprising almost all the papers left by Lindsay to his family, c.1840s to 1877, many thousands of pages in a trunk & 4 boxes, comprising autograph journals, Mss, correspondence, etc., sold at S on 22 July 1988, lot 391, for £13,000 to Maggs.]

Linnaeus, Carolus, 1707-78
Ms, Geneologia plantarum, ovvero sistema delle piante, ordinato secondo la classificazione data loro da Linneo..., [Florence?, after 1767]. 121 folding tables, 430mm by 295mm, in worn contemp mottled calf. In pen-&-ink & watercolor. Dedicated to [the future Emperor] Leopold II. (90) $1,800

ALs, 16 Jan 1744. 1 p, 4to. To Francois de Sauvages. Informing him of his election to the Swedish Academy of Sciences. In Latin. With engraved port. (88) DM5,000

— [1744]. 4 pp, 4to. To Francois de Sauvages. Discussing a number of botanical problems, with 7 small sketches. In Latin. (88) DM8,500

— 13 Jan 1747. 4 pp, 4to. To Francois Boissier de Sauvages. Scientific letter covering a variety of matters. In Latin. (90) £5,000

— [early 1753]. 4 pp, 4to. To Francois Boissier de Sauvages. Announcing the publication of his Species plantarum, commenting on life in Sweden, etc. In Latin. (91) £3,000

— 13 May 1754. 3 pp, 4to. To Francois Boissier de Sauvages. Giving a list of animals which he knows to be poisonous. (90) £3,500

— 8 Jan 1760. 3 pp, 4to. To Francois de Sauvages. Discussing several plants & other scientific questions. In Latin. (88) DM7,500

— 26 Jan 1770. (88) £850

AL, 20 Feb 1767. 3 pp, 4to. To David Skene. Discussing his own & recipient's research concerning various kinds of worms. (90) DM5,000

Linnell, John, 1792-1882
Series of 4 A Ls s, 1838 & [n.d.]. (88) £75

Lipatti, Dinu, 1917-50
Autograph music, sketches & drafts for an organ concerto, July 1939. (89) £750

— Autograph music, Trois Danses pour deux pianos, 1937 to 1941. (89) £1,000

LISA

Lisa, Manuel, 1772-1820
Ds, 8 Dec 1798. Alexander collection. (90) $375

Lister, Joseph Lister, Baron, 1827-1912
ALs, 10 Feb 1874. 4 pp, 8vo. To Louis Pasteur. Regarding the antiseptic system of surgery. Bradley Martin Ms. (90) $25,000
— 23 Jan 1894. 8 pp, 8vo. To Richard Hamilton of the General Infirmary, Chichester. Giving detailed instructions on antiseptic procedures to be followed during operations. (91) £2,200
ANs, 12 Feb 1897. (91) $450

Liszt, Franz, 1811-86
[An autograph cover sheet, sgd, for Deux Allegri di Bravura, [1823?], 1 p, folio, & autograph music, Fragment de Minuet d'une Simphonie, 25 bars, & anr 5-bar fragment, 1 p, folio, with music on both versos in anr hand, in green mor bdg, sold at CNY on 13 Nov, lot 96, for $1,500.]
Autograph Ms, preface to his 2-piano Ed of 3 Beethoven piano concerti, 1881. 1 pp, 4to. In German & French; each sgd. Including autograph revisions. Middendorf collection. (89) $1,200
— Autograph Ms, protest that only the police require strangers to sign similar forms; [n.d.]. (90) DM420
Autograph music, 32 bars of the Feuilles d'album in A flat major; 28 May [18]44. 1 p, folio. Four systems of 2 staves each; sgd. (91) £3,200
— Autograph music, 9 bars to be inserted in an unknown work, possibly the piano score of an orchestral work; [n.d.]. 1 p, 24cm by 31.5cm. With authentication by Carl Gille at bottom. (90) DM1,600
— Autograph music, Allegro molto quasi presto [Scherzo for piano in G minor], 27 May 1827. 2 pp, folio. 85 bars on 6 systems of 2 staves each; sgd. Including autograph corrections. Inscr to Busoni by Frits Hartvigson at bottom. (90) £4,000
— Autograph music, choir of the pilgrims from Wagner's Tannhaeuser, scored for piano in E major, 16 bars; [c.1849]. 1 p, 19.5cm by 26.5cm, on a bifolium. (88) DM2,400
— Autograph music, Die heilige Caecilia, fragment of full orchestral score, [c.1874]. (89) $1,000
— Autograph music, early version of 17 bars of the 1st Ballade, in D flat major; [c.1845]. 1 p, 8vo. In brown ink on 5 systems, 2 staves each; sgd. (90) £7,500
— Autograph music, Fantasy on a Chansonette, for piano; complete working Ms, [1830s?]. 36 pp, folio, on 2 types of paper. Lacking a few bars on penultimate page. Apparently undocumented. (88) £65,000
— Autograph music, Orgie, from the Pastorale. Appel aux armes. Orgie, from Illustrations du Prophete de Meyerbeer, for piano, [c.1849]. 6 pp, folio. In brown ink on up to 12 staves per page. Some revisions. Marked for the ptr. (88) £2,800
— Autograph music, part of an arrangement of the song Le matin by Korbay, [n.d.]. 4 pp, folio. In black ink on up to 10 staves per page. 73 bars, sgd & inscr. (89) £1,400
— Autograph music, Rakoczy March, scored for 2 pianos, Aug [18]70. 10 pp, folio. Including corrections; sgd FL. (91) DM100,000
— Autograph music, sketch-book containing drafts for various [unidentified] works, 17 Aug 1830 & later. 30 pp & blanks, in half mor bdg. (91) £14,000
— Autograph music, Valse de Concert, piano transcription after Vegh's Suite en forme de Valse, [c.1882]. Parts of 2 pp, size not stated. 24 bars on 3 systems of 2 staves, with autograph heading, sgd. Laid down. (89) $2,500
Ms, Soirees de Vienne, Valse Caprice no 6, revised version; [c.1883?]. 26 pp, folio; stitched. Mostly in red & black ink, with autograph corrections. (91) £2,200
— Ms, song, Enfant, si j'etais roi, [c.1859]. 7 pp, folio. In a scribal hand on up to 12 staves per page, with numerous autograph annotations & corrections. (89) £2,400
— Ms, song, Le Matin by F. Korbay, "nouvelle version de F. Liszt" for tenor & piano, [n.d.]. 14 pp, size not stated. Some autograph additions. (89) DM1,400

— Ms, song, Oh! Quand je dors, [c.1859]. 8 pp, folio. In a scribal hand on up to 12 staves per page, with extensive autograph annotations. (89) £3,200

— Ms, Tre Sonetti del Petrarca for voice & piano, in Italian & German; [c.1881]. (88) DM900

Collection of 2 A Ls s & Ls, 6 Sept 1841 to 9 Feb 1853. 7 pp, 8vo & 4to. To Madame d'Ogareff, concerning money she gave him. To Manuel Garcia, sending a baritone to him for lessons. Recipient unnamed, declining an invitation to a festival of the Frankfurt Choral Society. (88) $1,400

— Collection of 2 A Ls s & signature, [n.d.]. (89) DM750

Series of 3 A Ls s, 25 July 1858 to 11 Feb 1861. 7 pp, 8vo. To Max Seifriz. Requesting a score for Dr. Damrosch, planning a visit in Loewenberg, & informing him about his journey to Leipzig. (90) DM3,000

A Ls s (2), 25 Mar 1849 & 18 Sept 1872. 5 pp, 8vo. To Carl Reinecke. Inviting him to visit at Weimar, & requesting him to respond to a circular from a professional organization. (91) DM2,200

— A Ls s (2), 21 Nov 1878 & 18 June 1879. 4 pp, 8vo. To Eduard Liszt, reporting about the completion of his oratorio Via Crucis. To [the pbr Spitzweg?], thanking for works of Hans von Buelow. (90) £1,400

ALs, [c.1829-30]. (88) $1,000

— 28 Feb 1834. 3 pp, 8vo. To Victor [Schoelcher]. Describing his sojourn in Britanny, his discussions with Lamennais, domestic arrangements, etc. (91) £1,200

— 1 Jan 1839. 6 pp, 4to. To Victor Schoelcher. About his musical career, his affair with Marie d'Agoult, Chopin, etc. (91) £3,200

— [6 Aug 1840]. (91) £750
— [6 Aug 1840]. (90) DM800

— [4 Aug 1841]. 4 pp, 4to. To Count Alberti. Reporting about his piano playing, his concert tours, & his operatic transcriptions. (90) £2,600

— 23 Jan 1844. 3 pp, 8vo. To Peter Lichtenthal. Thanking for comments in a musical journal & chatting about his plans. (88) DM1,600

— 24 Aug 1844. (90) £600
— [1844]. (91) £650

— 6 Oct 1849. 3 pp, 8vo. To Carl Reinecke. Making arrangements for his visit to Bremen. (90) £1,200

— 16 May 1850. 2 pp, 8vo. To [Prince Felix Lichnowsky?]. On ALs, 2 pp, 8vo, by Princess Carolyne Wittgenstein. Confidential letter regarding their personal situation & his musical projects. (88) DM2,400

— 4 Oct 1850. 7 pp, 8vo. To Siegfried Wilhelm Dehn. Expressing thanks, discussing the publication of a collection of music, mentioning E. T. A. Hoffmann, etc. (89) DM3,400

— 8 Oct 1850. 6 pp, 8vo. Recipient unnamed. Discussing the education of his daughters. (91) $3,000

— [n.d.]. (88) DM850

— 4 Feb 1851. 4 pp, 8vo. To his secretary Belloni. Discussing the publication of his book on Chopin. (90) £2,400

— 20 Aug 1851. 3 pp, 8vo. To Hector Berlioz. Making plans to stage Benvenuto Cellini at Weimar. With related material. (89) £2,400

— 18 Dec 1851. 6 pp, 8vo. Recipient unnamed. About performances at Weimar, Wagner, & Joachim. (91) £1,100

— 31 Oct [18]52. 3 pp, 8vo. To M. Ehrlich. Providing an assessment of 3 of Berlioz's works. (91) £2,700

— 2 Aug 1853. 4 pp, 8vo. To his daughters Cosima & Blandine. Hoping to send a young musician named Buelow to Paris next summer. (91) £1,800

— 27 Oct 1853. 3 pp, 8vo. To Carl Haine. Commenting on recipient's Loreley Fantasie. (91) £1,100

— [c.1854?]. 2 pp, 4to. To George Sand. About their long-term relationship, his travel plans, an article in the Revue des deux Mondes, etc. (88) £1,500

— 24 Oct [18]55. 4 pp, 8vo. To the mother of Hans von Buelow. About the possible marriage of Buelow & one of his daughters. (91) £2,400

— 9 Jan 1857. 7 pp, 4to. To Wilhelm Joseph von Wasiliewsky. Providing a biographical sketch of Schumann; including autograph musical quotation. (90) £16,500

LISZT

— 28 Feb 1857. (88) £320
— 1 May 1857. (88) £400
— [1 May 1857]. (89) £600
— 14 June [18]57. (91) £700
— 11 Dec [18]57. 4 pp, 8vo. Recipient unnamed. Giving news of his productions of Wagner's operas. (91) £1,800
— 28 Nov [18]58. (88) £800
— 23 Mar 1859. 3 pp, 8vo. To F. Burmeister. Sending a letter of introduction to Carl Haslinger. With related material. (90) DM1,600
— 12 May [18]59. (88) £900
— 18 Mar 1861. (91) $650
— 5 June [18]61. (91) £700
— 12 Apr 1862. 4 pp, 8vo. To Max Seifriz. Discussing musical affairs in Leipzig. (91) DM2,400
— 18 Nov 1864. 4 pp, 8vo. To a pbr at Leipzig. Concerning various publishing matters. (88) DM1,200
— 25 Oct 1867. (90) DM550
— 6 Sept [18]68. (89) £450
— 6 Sept [18]68. (88) £400
— 2 Dec 1868. 4 pp, 8vo. To Sigmund Lebert. Discussing a projected Ed of works by Weber & Schubert scored for piano. (90) DM2,000
— 26 May [18]69. (91) £750
— 5 Sept 1869. (90) DM650
— 28 Mar 1870. (91) DM850
— 2 July 1871. (91) DM600
— 12 Feb 1872. (88) DM750
— 19 May [18]72. (89) £400
— 15 Feb 1873. (90) £650
— 13 May 1873. (90) DM700
— 28 Sept [18]73. (91) £550
— 30 Apr 1877. (90) DM850
— 13 June [18]77. (91) £950
— 4 Apr [18]79. (91) DM900
— 6 July 1879. 2 pp, 8vo. To Berthold Kellermann. Advising him to change his situation. (88) DM1,200
— 18 Aug 1879. (90) £650
— 29 Oct 1879. 3 pp, 8vo. Recipient unnamed. Regarding an honor bestowed on [Ludwig] Nohl, & other matters. (89) DM1,500
— 22 Jan [18]80. (89) £700
— 16 May 1880. (88) DM1,000
— 26 May 1880. 2 pp, 8vo. To Sophie Menter. Informing her of his meeting with Boesendorfer in Frankfurt & enquiring about her travel plans. (90) £1,300
— 9 Jan 1881. (90) DM950
— 25 Nov 1881. 3 pp, 8vo. To his pbr [Adolf Fuerstner]. Asking him to send scores to Saint-Saens, & discussing the publication of his work Weihnachtsbaum. (90) £1,200
— 26 Jan 1882. (89) DM600
— 17 July 1882. 3 pp, 8vo. To Karl Riedel. Suggesting that Sophie Menter be reimbursed for hotel costs. (90) DM1,300
— 8 Dec [18]82. (91) £750
— 15 Nov 1883. 2 pp, 4to. To [Emperor Pedro II of Brazil]. Draft, about the 1st performance of Lohengrin at Rio de Janeiro. (91) DM2,000
— 24 Jan [18]84. (88) £700
— 18 June [18]84. 3 pp, 8vo. Recipient unnamed. Praising Wagner & his operas. (91) £1,300
— 5 July 1884. (90) DM700
— [n.d.]. (91) £200
— [n.d.]. (91) £600
— [n.d.]. (90) DM750
ANs, 6 Jan 1877. (89) DM460
— [n.d.]. (89) DM320
AN, [after 1865]. (91) DM420
— [n.d.]. (89) DM240
Ns, [n.d.]. (90) DM480
Ds, 28 Apr 1840. (90) $650
— 13 Jan 1875. (89) £1,000
— 13 Jan 1875. (88) £950
— 1 Sept 1875. (89) £900
— 1 Sept 1875. (88) £550
Autograph quotation, opening 4 bars of the 6th Etude transcendante, sgd & dated 5 June [18]38. 1 p, 8vo. (89) £1,200
— Anr, 8 bars from his Petite Valse favorite; sgd & dated 28 Mar 1840. 1 p, 8vo. (90) DM7,000
— Anr, 5 bars of a virtuosic work for piano, marked Preludio & Presto; sgd & dated 30 Aug 1840. 1 p, c.18cm by 21.5cm, cut from larger sheet. Notated on 2 systems of 2 staves each. (90) £3,000
Autograph sentiment, sgd, 22 July 1884. (89) £240
Corrected proof, Les Hugenots, [n.d.]. 31

pp & tp, 340mm by 273mm, in buckram slipcase. With extensive autograph corrections & alterations, including 4 pp of expanded substitute score. (89) £2,500
Group photograph, [n.d.]. (89) $550
Photograph, sgd, [c.1860]. 108mm by 60mm. Sgd by A. W. Gottschalg on verso. (90) DM1,900
— Anr, [1860s]. 10.5cm by 6cm. By Ghemar. Annotated in anr hand on verso. (91) £1,700
— Anr, [1872]. (91) $500
— Anr, [18]79. 15cm by 10 cm. Seated at a table, by Ferencz Kozmata. (90) £1,050
Photograph, sgd & inscr, May 1880. 21.2cm by 17.2cm (oval). Inscr to Julius Kniese on mount. (89) DM1,500
— Anr, Nov 1885. 165mm by 108mm. Inscr to Lina Schmalhausen, on verso. (90) DM1,200
— Anr, Apr 1886. (91) £550
— Anr, [n.d.]. Cabinet size. Inscr with biblical quotation. (90) DM1,800
Proof copy, Ungarischer Sturmmarsch, for full orchestra, [c.1876]. 40 pp, folio. Extensively annotated by Liszt. Lacking some bars at beginning & end. With related material. (88) £1,500
— Anr, Ungarischer Sturmmarsch, [c.1876]. 15 pp, folio. Revised version, for piano solo. With extensive annotations, partly autograph. (89) £1,600
— Anr, Reminiscences de Don Juan, for piano, 1877. 35 pp, folio. With extensive autograph annotations. (88) £3,000
See also: Saint-Saens, Camille

Liturgical Manuscripts
[2 single-sheet altarcards, [Paris, c.1690], 300mm by 220mm, vellum over wooden panels, each with 19 lines of text in brown ink in a rounded roman hand in imitation of ptd type, oblong miniature across the top & broad illuminated borders enclosing oval landscapes, by the artist of the choirbook of Louis XVI, sold at S on 6 Dec 1988, lot 18, for £1,200 to Schwing.]
Ms, Caeremoniale capellae pontificae. [Rome, c.1510]. 32 leaves, 22cm by 16cm. Contemp blindstamped brown calf gilt over wooden bds. In black ink in a humanistic cursive hand, with headings in red. Inscr to Cardinal Raphael Riario Galeotti by Paris Crassus, Papal Master of Ceremonies. (90) DM13,000
— Ms, Cantica Sacra, [Italy, c.1600]. (88) £350
— Ms, choirbook. [Bologna, c.1350]. Single leaf, vellum, 510mm by 340mm. With 7 lines each of text & of music on a 4-line red stave. With 3 large decorated initials & historiated initial. (91) £3,200
— Ms, Choirbook. [Bologna, c.1300]. Single leaf, vellum, 557mm by 379mm. With 6 lines each of text & of music on a 4-line red stave. With 2 initials in red & blue with penwork decoration, & large illuminated initial. (90) £1,200
— Ms, Choirbook. [Florence, early 14th cent]. Single leaf, vellum, 498mm by 359mm. With 6 lines each of text & of music on a 4-line red stave. With large historiated initial. (90) £1,350
— Ms, choirbook. (91) $225
— Ms, choirbook. (91) $325
— Ms, choirbook. [Lombardy, early 16th cent]. Single leaf, vellum, 580mm by 415mm. In a large rounded gothic hand. With large historiated initial on burnished gold panel. (91) £1,500
— Ms, Choirbook. [Southern Italy, c.1280]. Single leaf, vellum, 488mm by 356mm. With 7 lines each of text & of music on a 4-line red stave. With historiated initial. (90) £1,200
— Ms, choirbook. (91) $300
— Ms, Collectarium Sanctae Genovefae, in Latin. [Paris, Abbey of Ste-Genevieve, 1655]. 51 leaves (3 lacking) & 2 flyleaves, vellum, 360mm by 232mm. Contemp red velvet, in cloth slipcase. In brown ink in skilful roman & italic hands in imitation of ptd type by Jacobus Cousinet. With music on a 4-line red stave, burnished gold borders throughout, over 230 burnished gold initials filled with flowers in full color & 18 very large illuminated floral head- & tailpieces. (88) £4,200
— Ms, Epistolar. [Bologna?, c.1470]. 125 leaves (1 lacking), vellum, 260mm by 185mm. Contemp wooden bds. In black & red ink in a rounded gothic

script. With large initial in blue & colors & numerous small penwork initials in red, blue or violet. Written for a Dominican convent Sancti Floriani. (89) DM6,000
— Ms, Festal Menaion. [Russia, early 19th cent]. 338 leaves, 224mm by 177mm, in contemp blindstamped calf over wooden bds. With 9-11 lines each of text in a semi-uncial hand & of music in a single row of neumes above. With 10 large illuminated headpieces. Fekula Ms.625. (91) £4,000
— Ms, Hiermologion, Octoechos, & texts for Lent & Easter, in Church Slavonic. [Russia, 2d half of 17th cent]. 186 leaves (some missing), 150mm by 90mm, in rebacked contemp calf. In semi-uncial hands by 2 different scribes, with neumes in red. With full-page illuminated miniature. Fekula Ms.572. (91) £20,000
— Ms, Lenten & Festal Triodion, in Church Slavonic. [Russia, late 17th cent]. 114 leaves (some lacking), 205mm by 160mm, in rebacked contemp blindstamped calf over wooden bds. In a clear semi-uncial hand with musical notation in neumes. Fekula Ms.584. (91) £2,600
— Ms, Lenten chants. [Italy, c.1100]. 4 pp, vellum, 8vo. Containing sections of decorated monophonic chants, notated in diastematic neumes on up to 13 clef-less 3-line staves. Recovered from a bdg. (91) £1,600
— Ms, Litany & Nuptial Mass, in Latin, [Florence?, c.1475]. (88) £380
— Ms, Menaia for 1 July to 26 Aug, in Church Slavonic. [Russia, mid-16th cent]. 472 leaves (some missing), 285mm by 190mm, in contemp calf over wooden bds. In semi-uncial hands by 5 different scribes. With illuminated headpiece in Balkan style & quadripartite page with 4 illuminated miniatures. Fekula Ms.491. (91) £7,000
— Ms, Messes pour le Temps depuis Le Premier Dimanche de l'Avent iusques au Caresme. [Paris or Versailles, c.1670-80]. 114 leaves & flyleaf, vellum, 202mm by 140mm, in contemp black sharkskin with the arms of the Marquise de Montespan. In dark brown ink in a fine rounded roman hand in imitation of ptd type. With gold frames on every page, nearly 200 illuminated initials, 42 illuminated tailpieces or headpieces, & illuminated tp. (91) £24,000
— Ms, Order for the Reception of Novices; in Latin, with rubrics in Italian. [Florence, late 15th cent]. 68 leaves, vellum, 237mm by 170mm, in battered contemp decorated bdg of lea over wooden bds. In dark brown, red & blue ink in a large rounded gothic liturgical hand. With decorated initials throughout, 2 very large illuminated initials, 3 large historiated initials, & full border enclosing 2 contemp nielli. (88) £5,800
— Ms, Ordo ad communicandum infirmum. [Italy, 14th cent]. 27 leaves, vellum, 200mm by 145mm, in 15th-cent wooden bds. In black & red ink in an Italian rotunda, with music on a 4-line red stave. With numerous small penwork initials, partly with marginal extensions. (90) DM2,300
— Ms, prayers & antiphons for the canonical hours, in Latin. [Flanders, early 16th cent]. 100 leaves, vellum, 225mm by 165mm. Modern brown mor bdg. By a single scribe in a secretary hand. With small & large initials in gold & colors, 21 partial & 4 full illusionistic borders, & 18 small & 2 full-page miniatures. (90) £245,000
— Ms, Rituale, with Lectionary & Legendary. Use of Ghiemona. In Latin. [Ghiemona, Northeast Italy, c.1425]. 96 leaves, vellum, 215mm by 155mm. 17th-cent brown calf. In brown ink in a clear rotunda script. With over 70 2-line initials in red & some musical settings. Some pp repaired. Doheny collection. (88) £2,500
— Ms, service book, [France, c.1400]. (88) £170
— Ms, Sticherarion, in Church Slavonic. [Russia, mid-17th cent]. 141 leaves, 195mm by 150mm, in contemp gilt & blindstamped calf over wooden bds. With 16 to 18 lines each of text in a small semi-uncial hand & of music in a single row of neumes. With full-page illuminated miniature pasted in. Fekula Ms.626. (91) £4,800

— Ms, Sticherarion, with other material, in Church Slavonic. [Russia, early 17th cent]. 169 leaves, 148mm by 85mm, in contemp bdg of blindstamped calf over bds. With 13 lines each of text in a compressed semi-uncial hand & of music in a single row of neumes above. With illuminated opening page with headpiece & marginal decoration, & full-page miniature. Fekula Ms.603. (91) £11,000
See also: Greek Manuscripts

Lives of the Saints

Ms, Life of St. Fekula Ms.742. (91) £500

— Ms, Passio beatissimi Georgij martyris...; [Germany?, 14th cent]. Single leaf, vellum, 425mm by 320mm. In a gothic textura. With historiated initial. Margin trimmed, affecting text. (90) DM3,400

— Ms, Saints' Lives, in Church Slavonic. Fekula Ms.673. (91) £850

— Ms, Svyatsy, Book of Saints with short lives, in Church Slavonic, [Russia, Moscow?, 24 Mar 1831]. 196 leaves (34 blank) & flyleaves, 80mm by 59mm. Contemp red mor gilt. With elaborate decorated tp, 8 full-page tables & 29 full-page miniatures. (89) £2,600

— Ms, the legend of St. Sylvester, fragment, with 5 other religious texts. [Southwestern Germany?, 2d half of 12th cent]. 32 leaves, vellum, 235mm by 150mm. 19th-cent vellum bdg using 14th-cent liturgical Ms. In black ink in a gothic textura. (89) DM12,000

— Ms, Vitae Patrum, lives of the desert fathers. [Southern Germany, Buxheim Abbey?, c.1425]. 75 leaves, 300mm by 220mm. Contemp bevelled wooden bds covered with white skin; with sewing guards of an 11th-cent Breviary. In a cursive bookhand. (91) £26,000

— DMITRII OF MOSCOW. - Ms, The Life and Miracles of Saint Dimitrii of Moscow and Uglich and of all Russia. [Central Russia, mid-17th cent]. In Church Slavonic. 230 leaves, 330mm by 205mm, in contemp red velvet over wooden bds with engraved metal centerpiece. With 28 large & 94 smaller illusts. (89) £12,000

— SAINT JEROME. - Ms, Vita et Epistole di Santo Girolami. [Florence, c.1480]. 110 leaves (5 blank, 8 missing), 223mm by 158mm, in old limp vellum. In a small regular cursive minuscule. (90) £3,500

Livingston, Edward, 1764-1836

Ls, 28 Feb 1801. Alexander collection. (90) $80

Livingston, Philip, Signer from New York

Ds, June 1769. (91) $300

Livingston, Robert R., 1746-1813

ALs, 5 Feb 1807. (91) $400

Ds, 1795. (91) $150

Livingston, Walter, 1740-97

Franking signature, [2 Apr 1788]. (90) $160

Livingston, William, 1723-90

ALs, 2 Nov 1774. (88) $140

Livingstone, David, 1813-73

A Ls s (2), 6 Jan & 18 Apr 1857. (89) £480

ALs, 2 Dec 1841. 4 pp, folio. To John Naismith, Sr. Reporting about his journey into the interior of Africa. Initialled. Repaired. (89) £2,700

— 9 Aug 1847. (88) £900

— 31 Dec 1856. (88) £300

— 11 Feb 1858. (90) £220

— 6 Aug 1859. 4 pp, folio. To Edward Marjoribanks. Announcing his discovery of Lake Shirwa. (91) £3,000

— 7 June 1863. (89) £750

— 28 Nov 1864. (89) £550

— 23 May 1865. 6 pp, 8vo. To Angela Georgina Burdett-Scoutts. Recommending Horace Waller for missionary work in Borneo. (90) DM1,400

— 9 Aug 1865. (89) £300

— Nov 1870. 4 pp, 8vo. To R. Playfair & J. Kirk. Giving a detailed account of his experiences in central Africa. (89) £7,000

— 13 Mar 1872. 8 pp, folio. To Sir Roderick Murchison. Giving a report of his sufferings up to Stanley's arrival & affirming his determination to find the sources of the Nile. (89) £11,500

Autograph quotation, 18 June 1857. (88) £420

LLEWELLYN

Llewellyn, Richard, 1906-83
Proof copy, How Green was my Valley, [1939]. 8vo, in orig wraps. With autograph revisions; sgd. (89) £2,600

Lloyd George, David, 1863-1945
Autograph Ms, draft of a speech dealing with the British economy, [1908-1914]. (91) DM750
ALs, 28 July 1899. (88) £60
Ls, 31 July 1919. (90) £120
— 13 Dec 1920. (89) £800
Photograph, sgd, [n.d.]. (91) $150

Locke, John, 1632-1704
Autograph Ms, An Essay Concerning Human Understanding, draft, with extensive autograph revisions, sgd; 1671. In a notebook, 312 leaves (including 149 blanks), 295mm by 188mm, in contemp black calf. Including An Essay Concerning Toleration, draft in a secretarial hand with autograph revisions, 1667; Commonplace Book, mostly autograph notes in English, Latin & French, 1661 - 1700; & papers relating to the Council of Trade, in a secretarial hand, [c.1668-73]. The Garden Ltd. collection & Phillipps Ms.3877 (90) $825,000
Signature, on medieval vellum leaf of a glossed Latin text of the Institutes of Civil Law of Justinianus, [France, c.1300], presumably once part of a cover in his library, c.11.75 by 8.75 inches. (89) £420

Locker, Arthur, 1828-93. See: Locker-Lampson, Frederick & Locker

Locker-Lampson, Frederick, 1821-95 —& Locker, Arthur, 1828-93
[An album of humorous sketches, c. 1840s, in pen-&-ink or pen-&-wash, sgd F.L. or A.L., over 300 pieces attached to 108 pp, 4to, with autograph captions added c.1870 to 1883, in cloth-backed bds, sold at C on 9 Dec, lot 302, for £300 to Burn.]

Lockhart, John Gibson, 1794-1854
Series of 25 A L s s, [c.1824 to 1847], c.70 pp, various sizes. Mostly to Sir John McNeill & his wife Elizabeth. Discussing literary & political matters. With related material. (88) £1,300

AMERICAN BOOK PRICES CURRENT

Lockwood, Belva Ann Bennett, 1830-1917
Signature, [n.d.]. (90) $240

Loder, Justus Christian, 1753-1832
ALs, 10 Aug 1792. (89) DM320
See also: Goethe, Johann Wolfgang von

Lodge, Henry Cabot
[A group of 16 Ms & typed items mostly relating to the Vietnam War, comprising recollections, drafts of speeches, personal notes & memorandums, sold at R on 24 Feb 1990, lot 60, for $750.]

Lodge, Sir Oliver Joseph, 1851-1940
Photograph, sgd & inscr, Mar 1920. (90) DM260

Loens, Hermann, 1866-1914
Autograph Ms, essay, Im Moore; [n.d.]. 12 pp, 4to. Draft, with numerous revisions. (90) DM5,500
Autograph transcript, poem, Das bist du, sgd & dated spring 1912. On half-title of an inscr copy of his Da draussen vor dem Tore. Heimatliche Naturbilder. Warendorf, 1911. (89) DM1,300
Typescript, novel, Das zweite Gesicht, [1910/11]. 220 pp, folio. Printer's copy, with numerous autograph corrections & additions in ink & pencil. Some corrections in anr hand. (89) DM5,500
— Typescript, novel, Der Wehrwolf, [c.1910]. 180 pp, folio. With numerous autograph revisions, mostly in pencil; some corrections in a different hand. In cardboard cover with autograph title & signature. With related autograph Ms, 4 pp, 4to; sgd at head. (88) DM6,500
Series of 8 A L s s, 10 Feb 1910 to 28 Dec 1912. 36 pp, 4to & 8vo. To Lulu von Strauss und Torney. About his writings, the separation from his wife, etc. With related material. (88) DM5,500
ALs, 18 Nov 1905. (88) DM420

Loerke, Oskar, 1884-1941
Autograph Ms, poem, Deine Gestalten, 15 Nov 1937. 1 p, 8vo. 3 four-line stanzas, sgd & inscr to Gerhart Hauptmann. (91) DM1,300
Collection of 12 A L s s & 2 autograph

postcards, sgd, 22 Aug 1928 to 11 June 1940. 26 pp, 8vo & 4to, & cards. To Alexander Amersdorffer. About his professional situation & other matters. (91) DM3,800

ALs, 13 Jan 1920. (90) DM380
— 24 Jan 1926. (89) DM340

Loewe, Carl, 1796-1869

Autograph music, song, Der Liebesscheue, in G major, scored for voice & piano; [c.1815]. 3 pp, folio. (91) DM2,600

— Autograph music, song, Otto und Heinrich, Op. 121, for voice & piano, to a text by Heinrich von Muehler; [c.1855]. 4 leaves, 4to, in contemp cloth bdg. (88) DM3,500

— Autograph music, Weihnachts-Cantate, score for 2d horn. (89) DM550

ALs, [June 1824]. (90) DM580
— 20 Jan 1840. (88) DM380
— 5 Dec 1847. (89) DM580
— 24 Nov 1858. (88) DM900
— 7 Feb 1864. (91) DM800

Ds s (2)1 Apr 1868 & 15 Mar 1869. (91) DM400

Loewi, Otto, 1873-1961

ALs, [n.d.]. 2 pp, 4to. To Herr Raab. Responding to a philosophical question, & quoting Einstein. (91) DM1,300

Loewith, Karl, 1897-1973

ALs, 29 Aug 1942. (90) DM430

Log Books

— BOUVERIE, CAPT. DUNCOMBE PLEYDELL. - Autograph Mss (2), log books kept during his command of HMS Medusa in South American waters & elsewhere, 30 Mar 1807 to 27 Aug 1812. 325 pp, folio & 4to, in 2 notebooks. Including 3 inserted Ms charts, 2 coastal profiles & a plan of Montevideo. (89) £1,200

— "CHALLENGER". - Log kept by Lieut. A. Channer on the circumnavigatory scientific expedition of H.M.S. Challenger, 14 Sept 1873 to 31 Mar 1874. About 167 pp, 4to, in orig calf-backed cloth. Containing numerous pen-&-ink or pencil sketches. (89) £1,200

— "COMET". - Log Book of the Clipper Ship Comet kept by John C. Champion on a voyage from NY to San Francisco & back via Cape Horn, 1 Nov 1852 to 13 Mar 1854. 80 pp, 8vo, in quarter calf. (88) $550

— "DUCHESS ATHOL". - Log kept by Commander Edward Maxell Danniell on a voyage to Bombay, China & Hong Kong, 18 Nov 1829 to 16 Mar 1831. 176 pp, folio, in def reversed calf. (89) £200

— "EQUATOR". - Log of the Equator on a voyage from Boston to Hawaii & Manila, 10 Sept 1852 to 17 Mar 1853. 22 pp, folio, in bds. (90) $130

— FORBES, CAPT. CLEVELAND. - Ms, Journal of a Voyage fron New York to Panama... Onboard the US Mail Steam Ship California, 6 Oct 1848 to 23 May 1849. 63 pp, folio, in notebook in contemp half sheep bdg. Covering voyage to San Francisco & back to Panama. Doheny collection. (88) $3,800

— "GLASGOW". - Log of HMS Glasgow, covering Atlantic patrols, Sept 1814 to Aug 1815, in the hand of Midshipman Robert Hood. Including related material, 1809 to 1816. About 135 pp, folio. Contemp calf gilt; rebacked. (91) £1,800

— GOLDFINCH, LIEUT. HORACE E. - Autograph Ms, log kept as First Officer on HMS Pearl on a voyage from England to Australia, 1873 to 1876. 340 pp, folio, in half red calf. Recounting the ship's part in the annexation of Fiji & the death of Commodore Goodenough. Including maps & sketches. With related material. (90) £1,000

— "JANE". - Log kept by the boy apprentice George Hugh Haram on a voyage from Liverpool to Valparaiso & back, 1836-37. About 100 pp, folio. Limp bds; partly disbound. (89) £95

— "LIGHTNING". - Ms, log kept by the Acting Purser of the sloop Lightning during recovery of treasure & stores from the Thetis sunk off Cape Frio, 18 Jan 1831 to 8 Mar 1832. 90 pp, 8vo. Including some newspaper cuttings. (89) £650

— "MARION." - LOG OF THE U.S.S. MARION, 9 NOV 1839 TO 14 JUNE 1842. 227

LOG BOOKS

pp, folio, in contemp suede. In the hand of Midshipman George M. Ransom. (90) $950
— "Martha". - Log Book of the ship Martha kept by Capt. Philip Dumaresq on a trading voyage from Canton to Boston, 15 Jan to 7 May 1834. 110 pp, 4to, in worn orig half sheep bdg. (89) £200
— "Sampson". - Ms, Log of HMS Sampson on a mission from England to China & during the Arrow War, kept by George H. A. Cox; 16 Nov 1855 to 21 June 1858. 352 pp, folio, in rebacked half mor bdg. Including 23 ink & watercolor outline charts or plans, 10 watercolor views & 3 pencil drawings. (91) HK18,000
— "Taunton Castle". - Log book kept on a voyage from England to China via St. Helena, Rio de Janeiro & Malacca, Jan 1801 to Oct 1802. 250 pp, folio, in def bds. Including colored tables of signal flags. (89) £110
— "Vixen". - Log of HMS Vixen kept by J. C. D. Hay on a voyage from ports in China to Hong Kong & Singapore, 1844; c.48 pp, folio. With related material. (89) £80

Logan, James
Ds, 13 Sept 1714. (91) $70

Logan, Joshua, 1908-88
Ls, 16 Dec 1977. (91) $120

Lombard, Carole, 1908-42 — & Gable, Clark, 1901-60
Telegram, [n.d.]. (89) $320

Lombard, Johann Wilhelm, 1767-1812
Collection of 8 A Ls s & 4 A Ls, 3 Oct 1806 to 1809. 33 pp, mostly 4to. To his wife Dorothea. Mostly about the political situation in Prussia & the war. Some initialled; partly in French. With related material. Schroeder collection. (89) DM2,700

Lombardi, Vince
Ls, 6 Mar 1989. (90) $80

London, Charmian K.
[An archive of 13 A Ls s & 15 Ls s to Margaret Smith Cobb with related material, including a Jack London letter & a typed poem, sgd, by George Sterling sold at cb on 4 May 1989 for $3,250.]
Series of 1914-14. (89) $500

London, Jack, 1876-1916
[A collection of 38 photographs of London & his wife Charmian, c.1886 to 1916, various sizes, each tipped to 4to mounting card, sold at C on 20 May 1988, lot 215, for $1,300]
[A collection of 16 photographs of London & his wife Charmian, c.1886 & later, with c.120 clippings of photographs from magazines, various sizes, nearly all tipped to 4to sheets in half lea looseleaf binder, & photograph of Charmian London with Mrs [George] Sterling, sgd by Charmian, late 1920s, 18cm by 23cm, framed, sold at C on 20 May 1988, lot 216, for $1,300.]
[A group of 4 port photographs, 3 sgd & inscr, 1 with signature on separate card, various dates & sizes, each tipped to 4to mounting card, sold at C on 20 May 1988, lot 212, for $2,000.]
[A group of 3 port photographs, sgd, various dates & sizes, each tipped to 4to mounting card, sold at C on 20 May 1988, lot 213, for $2,000.]
[A group of 5 port photographs of London, 2 sgd, 2 port photographs of his wife Charmian, & photograph of both in foul weather gear, various dates & sizes, each tipped to 4to mounting card, sold at C on 20 May 1988, lot 214, for $350.]
[A large collection of material & clippings pertaining to London, mostly ptd, c.1897 to 1966, including c.50 letters addressed to Willard S. Morse, 1918 to 1921, & notes & bibliographical information on London's writings, sold at C on 20 May 1988, lot 183, for $3,400.]
Autograph Ms, carbon copy of report from the Manchurian front, titled "Actions of April 30 - May 1st" [1904]. (88) $800
— Autograph Ms, comparison of Chinese & American farming, sgd & dated 6 Oct 1916. (88) $950
— Autograph Ms, essay beginning "It was under the portals at Vera Cruz...", [1914?]. 8 pp, 8vo, on rectos only. With

numerous revisions. (88) $2,800
— Autograph Ms, short story, A Curious Fragment, sgd & dated 16 Apr 1907. 39 pp, 4to, on rectos only. Some revisions. In later reddish-brown mor. (88) $8,500
— Autograph Ms, short story, Flush of Gold, sgd & dated 18 May 1907. 68 pp, 4to, on rectos only. With numerous revisions. In half brown mor slipcase. Willard S. Morse collection. (88) $15,000
— Autograph Ms, short story, The Enemy of All the World, [1907 or 1908]. 63 pp, 4to, on rectos only. With numerous revisions; clipped signature pasted at end. In later reddish brown mor. Willard S. Morse collection. (88) $11,000
— Autograph Ms, story, Like Argus of the Ancient Times, sgd & dated 14 Sept 1916. 96 pp, 4to, on rectos only. With numerous revisions. In red crushed levant mor gilt bdg. (88) $20,000

Typescript, novel, The mutiny of the Elsinore; ptr's copy, with ANs to George Sterling, 28 Mar 1914, at head. 293 pp, 4to. With a few autograph corrections. 1st page def. In quarter calf slipcase. With a copy of 1st Ed. Kauffman collection. (88) $12,000
— Typescript, short story, Mauki, [c.1908]. 13 pp, 4to. Some minor pencil revisions. Marked by the ptr. 1 page cut in 2 & clipped together. Sgd on wrap. In quarter red mor case. (88) $2,400

Typescript carbon copy, resignation from the Socialist Party, 7 Mar 1916. (88) $350

Collection of 7 A Ls s, 6 Ls s & photograph, sgd & inscr, 27 Oct 1900 to 30 Oct 1906. 30 pp, 4vo; each leaf tipped into dark brown mor gilt album. To Charles Warren Stoddard. Interesting letters about the writing of his 1st novel & later works, private matters, etc. (88) $7,000
— Collection of ALs & check, sgd, 9 Nov 1902 & 17 Oct 1913. Doheny collection. (88) $800

ALs, 23 Aug 1903. 4 pp, 8vo. To Merle [Johnson]. Discussing The Call of the Wild. Fold tear. Doheny collection.

(88) $15,000
— 14 Oct 1903. 5 pp, 4to, on rectos only. To [Merle?] Johnson. Discussing questions concerning the editing of The Sea Wolf. (88) $1,600
— 2 Nov 1904. Doheny collection. (88) $750
— 6 Dec 1904. 6 pp, 4to. To Richard Watson Gilder. Delineating his plan for White Fang & offering it to Century Magazine. (88) $10,000
— 6 May 1905. 5 pp, 4to, on rectos only. To John Brisben Walker. Hoping the magazine Cosmopolitan will publish his article "Revolution". (88) $1,500
— 2 Dec 1905. 7 pp, 4to, on rectos only. To George Sterling. Discussing his relationship with Blanche [Bates], his decison to marry, & his current activities. Sgd Wolf. (88) $3,500
— 25 July 1907. 12 pp, 8vo, on rectos only. To George Sterling. Commenting on problems with [Col. Edwin] Emerson & reporting about his activities in Hawai. Sgd Wolf. (88) $2,600
— 27 Sept 1907. 3 pp, 4to, on rectos only. To George Sterling. Informing him about problems with Gene Fenelon & commenting on reviews of Sterling's book. Sgd Wolf. With autograph postscript. (88) $1,800
— 24 Nov 1907. (88) $650
— 17 Feb 1908. 6 pp, 4to, on rectos only. To George Sterling. Justifying his writing The Road, & mentioning proofs of a new novel. Sgd Wolf. With 2 brief A Ns s on sheets of navigational computations. (88) $2,000
— 31 Oct 1908. 9 pp, 4to, on rectos only. To George Sterling. Reporting about his adventures in the South Seas. Sgd Wolf. Last leaf torn. With related material. (88) $3,200
— 3 Mar 1909. 5 pp, 8vo, on rectos only. To George Sterling. Sending a sample of Australian wool, planning to return to California, & saying he does not care about the disapproval of the mob. Sgd Wolf. (88) $1,400
— 2 May 1909. 9 pp, 8vo, on rectos only. To George Sterling. Chatty letter about his activities on his voyage across the Pacific on a steamer. Sgd Wolf. With several lines added by Charmian London. 1st leaf torn. (88)

LONDON

$2,400
— 2 May 1909. 9 pp, 8vo, on rectos only. To [Herman Whitaker]. Commenting about the length of Whitaker's book, his own writings, royalties, his voyage on a steamer, etc. Tipped into blue mor album with related material. (88) $5,500

— 20 June 1910. 2 pp, folio, on rectos only. To [Merle] Johnson. Offering The Scarlet Plague for publication. Fold tear. (88) $1,800

— 21 Nov 1916. 1 p, 8vo. To George Sterling. Making plans for a meeting. Sgd Wolf. Probably last letter written by London. (88) $3,500

Ls s (2), 28 May & 1 June 1905. 4 pp, 4to. To George Sterling. Discussing a scheme to fund a Socialist journal, his plan to buy land for a home, & his finances. Sgd Wolf. (88) $1,600

Ls, 29 Mar 1906. (88) $600

— 22 Dec 1910. (90) $900

— 1913. (89) $750

— 1913. (89) $850

— 31 Aug 1915. (91) $550

— 31 Jan 1916. (90) $600

— 28 Aug 1916. (88) $900

Check, accomplished & sgd, 2 Oct 1910. (91) $350

Group photograph, [1900]. With his wife Bessie Maddern, standing in the water with bathing suits. Mtd; overall size 135mm by 160mm. With ANs, 31 July 1900, to [Charles] Warren [Stoddard] on verso of mount. Doheny collection. (88) $1,500
See also: Sterling, George

London, Jack, 1876-1916 —& Sterling, George, 1869-1926

[The typescript of Sterling's story The First Poet, [c.1910; ptd 1911 as London's work], 8 pp, folio, with 5 words added in pencil in London's hand, together with ALs by Sterling, 23 Aug 1924, 4 pp, 8vo, to [Charmian London?], confirming his authorship, sold at C on 20 May 1988, lot 207, for $1,200.]

AMERICAN BOOK PRICES CURRENT

Long, James E.
[A group of 5 albums kept by Long, including 3 photograph albums of the Mexican Revolution & trips to Europe & Mexico, his European diary, copies of letters, etc., [n.d.], sold at R on 28 Oct 1989, lot 160, for $650.]

Longfellow, Henry Wadsworth, 1807-82

Autograph Ms (2), poems, The Arrow and the Song, 3 stanzas, sgd & dated 15 Mar 1881, & It is Not Always May, 6 stanzas, sgd. With covering ALs, 15 Mar 1881. 4 pp, 8vo. Doheny collection. (89) $2,500

Autograph Ms, 4 lines beginning "All are architects of Fate," sgd & dated 13 Feb 1852. (90) $425

— Autograph Ms, diary, 1 - 2 Feb 1847. 1 p, 4to. Referring to Evangeline & the writing of poetry. Tipped to larger sheet. Doheny collection. (89) $2,800

— Autograph Ms, poem, Saga of The Skeleton in Armor, [1840]. 8 pp, 4to, in mor bdg by Riviere. 20 eight-line stanzas with added notes. Probably ptr's copy. John F. Fleming Estate. (89) $4,200

— Autograph Ms, poem, The Emperor's Bird's Nest, sgd; [n.d.]. 4 pp, 4to. 11 five-line stanzas. In mor folder. Doheny collection. (89) $2,000

— Autograph Ms, poem, To the Avon, 20 Jan 1876. Koch Foundation. (90) $1,000

Autograph transcript, poem, A Psalm of Life, sgd & dated 26 Aug 1845. 3 pp, 4to. In folder by Sangorski & Sutcliffe. Middendorf collection. (89) $6,500

— Autograph transcript, poem, The Children's Hour, [n.d.]. 4 pp, 4to. 10 stanzas, sgd. With related material. Martin collection. (90) $7,500

— Autograph transcript, poem, The Rainy Day, sgd & dated 27 Feb 1880. 1 p, 4to. 3 stanzas. Doheny collection. (89) $3,000

Series of 15 A Ls s, 15 Jan 1865 to 4 July 1880. 51 pp, 8vo. To Robert Ferguson. About his trans of Dante, his children, the Civil War, travels in Europe, etc. With 26 A Ls s by his daughter Edith to Ferguson, 2 Aug 1865 to 11 Apr 1883, & further related material. (88) £2,200

— Series of 3 A Ls s, 9 May 1877 to 20 June 1880. (90) $850

ALs, 1 Dec 1840. 4 pp, 4to. To Samuel Ward. Discussing Ward's sister Louisa & his own literary endeavors. Repaired. (89) $1,400

— 30 Nov 1841. (88) $110
— 12 Oct 1847. (89) £300
— 2 Mar 1852. (90) $250
— 14 Nov 1853. (89) DM550
— 25 Feb 1857. Byer collection. (90) $300
— 13 Aug 1857. (88) $130
— 24 Dec 1863. (90) $250
— 28 Mar 1864. (90) DM370
— 13 Oct 1869. (90) DM500
— 28 Feb 1875. 4 pp, 8vo. To an unnamed lady. Responding to an inquiry about his poem Victor Galbraith. Byer collection. (90) $1,200
— 20 Apr 1878. Doheny collection. (89) $800
— 27 May 1881. (88) $140

Longstreet, James, 1821-1904
ALs, 3 Apr 1856. Alexander collection. (90) $220
— 28 June 1861. 1 p, 4to. To Adjutant Gen. S. Cooper. Acknowledging receipt of his appointment as Brigadier Gen. Middendorf collection. (89) $12,000
— 20 Apr [18]75. 2 pp, 8vo. To Col. Charles Marshall. Denying knowledge of an order given by Lee at Gettysburg. (88) $1,800
— 14 May 1875. (88) $900

Lorca, Federico Garcia —& Others
[An autograph sentiment by Lorca, sgd, 1933, in the album of Sara Escrine, [c.1930-40], 70 pp, 8vo, also sgd by Stravinski, Respighi, Stefan Zweig, Artur Rubinstein, & others, sold at S on 16 May 1991, lot 76, for £500.]

Lorca, Federico Garcia, 1899-1936
Autograph Ms, essay, Las nanas infantiles, 1st draft; [c.1930]. With typed 2d draft, sgd; both with numerous autograph revisions. Together 35 pp, folio. (89) £30,000
Photograph, sgd, 1937. 16cm by 12cm. Mtd. (90) £1,300

Lorca, Federico Garcia, 1899-1936 —& Neruda, Pablo, 1904-73
[The typescript of 7 poems by Neruda, Paloma por dentro, o sea la mano de Vidrio, with autograph dedication to Sara Tornu de Rojas Paz, sgd, illus with 10 pen-&-ink drawings by Lorca, 7 sgd, 1 inscr, Apr 1934, 24 pp, 4to, disbound, sold at C on 6 Dec 1989, lot 342, for £36,000 to Dexeos.]

Loren, Sophia
[A collection of 96 original film stills, 33 sgd, from various films, sold at pnNy on 3 Dec 1988, lot 21, for $70.]

Lorentz, Hendrik Antoon, 1853-1928
ALs, 18 Oct 1921. 3 pp, 8vo. To Mr. Easton. About a speech to be given on the 25th anniversary of the discovery of the Zeeman effect. (91) DM2,400

Lorenz, Konrad, 1903-89
Ls, 27 Nov 1961. (90) DM460
— 19 Oct 1966. (90) DM600

Loring, William Wing, 1818-86
Ds, 31 Mar 1851. Alexander collection. (90) $125

Loriot, Pseud. of Vicco von Buelow
Ls, 23 Feb 1981. (88) DM240

Lorris, Guillaume de —& Meung, Jean de
Ms, Roman de la Rose. [Spain or Southwest France, mid-14th cent]. 185 leaves, vellum, 237mm by 170mm, in late 18th-cent French red mor gilt. In dark brown ink in a small gothic bookhand. With illuminated initials throughout, half-page miniature, 2 oblong miniatures across 2 columns, & 66 column-width miniatures. Astor MS.A.12. (88) £110,000

Lortzing, Albert, 1801-51
Ms, full orchestral score for his opera Hans Sachs; [c.1840]. (90) £750
ALs, 13 Nov 1840. 1 p, 4to. To an unnamed lady. Thanking for a libretto. (91) DM2,400
— 6 Oct 1843. 1 p, 4to. To Breitkopf & Haertel. Thanking for fees received & ordering texts of his Wildschuetz. (88) DM1,500
— 23 Nov 1848. 1 p, 4to. To [Raimund

LORTZING

Haertel]. Sending his opera Regina & speculating about a performance at Leipzig. (90) DM3,200
— 26 Feb 1850. 1 p, 4to. Recipient unnamed. Returning the play Nach Sonnenuntergang. Fold tears. (88) DM1,200

ANs, [n.d.]. (89) DM800

Ds, 26 July 1850. (89) DM900

Lothar, Mark, 1902-85
Autograph music, Abschieds-Festmarsch fuer die Familie Tessmer, sgd & dated 5 May 1934. (90) DM220
— Autograph music, fragment from his opera Rappelkopf, act I, scene 1; [n.d.]. (90) DM200

Loti, Pierre, Pseud. of Julien Viaud, 1850-1923
Series of 8 A Ls s, [26 Feb 1895 to 25 Oct 1908]. 21 pp, mostly 8vo. To Edmond de Pury & his wife. About his activities & a variety of matters. (90) DM1,100

Lotti, Antonio, c.1667-1740
Autograph music, cantata, Giac[c]he dovrai penar, for soprano & bass, partly for violin or violoncello; [n.d.]. 22 pp, 22cm by 29.5cm, 10 staves each. Note of authenticity by Georg Poelchau at head. (88) DM10,500

Louis Auguste de Bourbon, Duc du Maine, 1670-1736. See: Maine, Louis Auguste de Bourbon

Louis Ferdinand, Prince of Prussia, 1772-1806
ALs, 8 June 1792. 1 p, 4to. To Graf Lehndorff. Making plans for a night ride. Schroeder collection. (89) DM3,200
— 31 July 1795. (91) DM1,000

Ls, 15 Sept 1797. 3 pp, 4to. To King Friedrich Wilhelm II. Recommending 2 captains in his regiment. With autograph subscription. With related material. (89) DM1,200

Louis I, King of Hungary, 1326-82
Document, 12 July 1369. 20cm by 56cm, vellum. Order regarding a payment of 48 guilders. Seal def. (91) DM3,800

AMERICAN BOOK PRICES CURRENT

Louis II, Prince de Conde, 1621-86
ALs, 15 July 1644. (90) DM550
— [Aug 1654]. (90) DM520

Louis, Joe, 1914-81
Signature, [24 Oct 1946]. (89) $70

Louis Philippe, King of France, 1773-1850
[A collection of 34 letters & documents, sgd by Louis Philippe & members of his family, 1791 to 1884, 41 pp, various sizes, with related material, in an album, sold at C on 9 Dec, lot 270, for £300 to Schamb.]
[A group of 6 autograph Mss (5 sgd with paraph), brief comments & sketches executed in Council, 16 Dec 1838 to 1 Jan 1840, 6 pp, 8vo, sold at star on 1 Dec 1988, lot 1135, for DM460.]
ALs, 5 Nov 1800. (88) £100
— 1 July 1844. (91) DM240
Series of 4 Ls s, 31 Dec 1832 to 12 Sept 1847. (90) DM380
Ds, 8 July 1833. (88) $130
— 14 Dec 1840. (88) $140

Louis XI, King of France, 1423-83
Ds, 29 Mar 1468. 1 p, folio; vellum. Order addressed to his financial councillors to provide ransom money for Seigneur de Charny. (90) DM4,500
— 14 July 1477. (88) £580

Louis XII, King of France, 1462-1515
Ds, 2 July 1485. 1 p, vellum, 10cm by 27cm. Receipt to his treasurer Jacques Hunault for 6 ecus. (91) DM1,500
— 16 Nov 1495. (90) $600
— 16 Nov 1495. (89) $850
— 4 Nov 1506. (88) £280
— 1513. (88) $500

Louis XIII, King of France, 1601-43
Ls, 1 Feb 1619. (88) $275
Ds, 9 Apr 1628. (88) $75

Louis XIV, King of France, 1638-1715
[A collection of 9 items, sgd or with secretarial signature, 16 Jan 1654 to 8 Jan 1707, 9 pp, folio, relating to Michel & Charles de Bouteville (8), & announcing the birth of a son to the Duchesse de Bourgogne, mostly def, sold at HK on 6 Nov, lot 3211, for DM1,100.]

Autograph Ms, list of over 100 names of members of noble families, [n.d.]. (88) £600

ALs, 29 Feb 1660. Doheny collection. (89) $1,000

— 6 Aug 1682. 1 p, 4to. To Pope Innocent XI. Announcing the birth of his grandson [Louis, Duc de Bourgogne]. (90) £3,500

— 5 Sept 1698. 2 pp, folio. To the Mother Superior & the convent at St. Cyr. Insisting that 3 ladies recently expelled be barred from reentering the convent. With related material. (90) DM12,000

Ls, 19 Sept 1665. 1 p, 4to. To the Duke of Savoy. Informing him that the Marquis d'Ogliani is bringing news of the Queen Mother. (91) £1,500

— 29 Apr 1679. (88) £240
— 15 Feb 1696. (88) $475
— 13 Apr 1712. (89) £550
— 30 Jan 1713. Byer collection. (90) $400

Letter, 15 Dec 1676. (89) DM250

ADs, 22 Aug 1664. (88) $400

Series of Ds s, 3 Ds s, July 1703, 17 Sept 1707 & [n.d.]. (89) $800

Ds, 9 June 1682. (88) £140
— 4 Oct 1683. (88) £100
— 10 May 1708. (88) $50

— LUDRES, ISABELLE DE. - Autograph letter, [c.1681]. 4 pp, 4to. To Marie Louise, Queen of Spain. Retained copy, thanking for her letter & sending news from Paris. (91) DM5,500

Louis XIV, King of France, 1638-1715 — & Others

Ds, 17 Apr 1689. 32 pp, folio, stitched. Marriage contract of Maximilien P. F. N. de Bethune, Duc de Sully, & Madeleine Armande de Cambout, sgd by the King & numerous members of the royal family & French nobility. (91) DM7,000

Louis XV, King of France, 1710-74

ALs, [n.d.]. 1 p, 4to. To "Mon Cousin". Discussing the British threat to occupy Belle-Ile. (91) DM2,200

Ls s (2), 8 Nov 1732 & 17 May 1733. (90) DM400

Ls, 17 May 1733. (90) DM480

Letter, 5 Sept 1715. (90) DM430

— 26 Jan 1766. (89) DM200

Document, 24 Mar 1754. (89) DM260
— 12 Nov 1770. Byer collection. (90) $275
— PHILIP OF PARMA[?]. - ALs, 24 July 1744. 1 p, 8vo. To Louis XV. Announcing a victory over the Sardinian forces. (88) £75

Louis XV, King of France, 1710-74 — & Others

Ds, 17 Apr 1743. 22 pp, folio. Marriage contract of Charles F. G. d'Hallencourt & Marie Jeanne Ballet de la Chenardiere. Also sgd by Queen Marie & other members of the Royal family. With English trans, in extra bdg. (91) $3,200

Louis XVI, King of France, 1754-93

ALs, 25 Jan 1775. 1 p, 4to. To the Duc de La Vrilliere. Giving orders to buy horses. Seal tear. (90) DM3,000

Ls, 7 May 1782. (90) DM950
— 21 May 1792. (90) £900

ANs, [n.d.]. (91) £900

Ds, 3 Jan 1790. (88) £400
— 1 May 1791. (88) £380
— 7 July 1791. (88) $175
— 1 Sept 1791. (90) $400
— 6 Mar 1792. 1 p, folio. Pay order addressed to the Tresorier Tourteau de Septeuil. (89) DM1,050
— 10 June 1792. 1 p, folio. Pay order "pour achats de 5 916 545.3.6 de numeraire faite par le Caissier de la Tresorerie Nationale..."; with 6 countersignatures. (88) DM1,200

Document, 1 Feb 1785. (90) DM240

Autograph endorsement, [c.1790/91]. (90) DM800

Signature, on fragment (final page) of an account of a meeting of the Conseil Royal des Finances concerning taxation; 11 Dec 1787. (90) £400

Louis XVI, King of France, 1754-93 — & Marie Antoinette, Queen of Louis XVI of France, 1755-93

Ds, 18 Jan 1778. 27 pp, folio; stitched. Marriage contract of the Comte de Lordat & Mademoiselle de Tilly, sgd as witnesses. Also sgd by other members of the Royal family. With related material. (90) £4,200

— 9 Aug 1789. 11 pp, folio. Marriage contract of Gilbert Lemaitre & Char-

LOUIS XVI

lotte de Beraud. Also sgd by other members of the royal family. (89) £4,400

Louis XVII, King of France, 1785-95
— NAUNDORF, KARL WILHELM. - ALs, 8 Aug 1840. 3 pp, 4to. To Modeste Gruau de la Barre. Asserting that he is the legitimate heir to the French throne. Sgd Charles Louis Duc de Normandie. (89) DM950
— NAUNDORF, KARL WILHELM. - ALs, 14 Aug 1840. 2 pp, 4to. To Modeste Gruau de la Barre. About the publication of his Revelation sur les erreurs de l'Ancien Testament, the desertion of some of his followers, etc. Sgd Charles Louis Duc de Normandie. (90) DM650

Louis XVIII, King of France, 1755-1824
A Ls s (2), 1 Apr 1818 & 28 Mar 1822. (90) DM500
Ls, 13 May 1814. (91) DM270
Ds, 1 Jan 1793. (90) $250
— 21 Aug 1816. (91) DM330
Document, 25 Apr 1816. (90) DM330

Louis XVIII, King of France, 1755-1824 —&
Charles X, King of France, 1757-1836
Ds, 1 Mar 1792. (90) DM380
— 12 June 1792. (88) $425

Louisa Ulrika, Queen of Adolf Frederick of Sweden, 1720-82
ALs, 8 Sept 1744. Schroeder collection. (89) DM400

Louvois, Francois Michel Le Tellier, Marquis de, 1639-91
Ls, 3 Mar 1685. (90) DM220

Louys, Pierre, 1870-1925
Autograph Ms, essay, Plaidoyer Pour Romeo Et Juliette, [n.d.]. 12 pp, 4to, on rectos only, in half mor bdg. Sgd at end. Including newspaper cutting of ptd essay. (91) DM1,100
— Autograph Ms, Lectures antiques. (90) DM470
ALs, 26 Mar 1897. (89) DM260
— 7 Jan 1922. (90) DM240
See also: Gide, Andre & Louys

AMERICAN BOOK PRICES CURRENT

Love Letters
— SCHOENBRECHER, WERNER. - Series of c.260 A Ls s, 2 July 1841 to 21 May 1843. About 636 pp, 8vo & 4to. To Hedwig Guhrauer. In German; some in verse. In lea-backed bds. (89) £140

Lovecraft, Howard Phillips
ALs, 5 May 1934. (89) $250
— 13 May 1934. (89) $225
— 30 May 1934. (89) $250
— 19 June 1934. (89) $120
— 16 July 1934. (89) $275
— 29 July 1934. (89) $425
— 7 Sept 1934. (89) $250
— 7 Nov 1936. (89) $80
— 27 Dec 1934. (89) $120
Autograph postcard, sgd, 28 Apr 1934. (89) $90
— 7 Aug 1934. (89) $75
— 8 Aug 1934. (89) $90
— 30 Aug 1934. (89) $50
— 7 Sept 1935. (89) $85

Lovelace, Richard, 1618-58
Ds, 20 Mar 1647. 1 leaf on vellum, size not indicated. Power of attorney to Isaac Hunt to act for Lovelace in the sale of property specified in an accompanying indenture of John Mungeam of Smarden, Kent. With Lovelace's seal. Also sgd by his brother Dudley. (90) £3,600

Lovell, Mansfield, 1822-84
ALs, 30 Apr 1862. 4 pp, 8vo. To his wife. Interesting letter reporting about the campaign resulting in Confederate evacuation of New Orleans. With related material. (90) $1,800

Lowe, Sir Hudson, 1769-1844
Ls, 12 Oct 1816. 4 pp, folio. To Count Bertrand. Insisting that no financial transactions may take place with Napoleon & his entourage without his premission. (91) £1,300
— 28 Nov 1817. 1 p, folio. To Gen. Bertrand. Requesting him to communicate a memorandum to Napoleon. With memorandum, 3 pp, folio, regarding medical care for Napoleon. (88) DM2,200

Lowe, Thaddeus Sobieski Coulincourt, 1832-1913
Ds, 16 Oct 1862. (88) $350
— 15 Jan 1896. (88) $175
Signature, [n.d.]. (91) $85

Lowell, Amy, 1874-1925
Ns s, 7 July & 7 Aug 1920. (89) $60

Lowell, James Russell, 1819-91
Autograph Ms, poem, To H[enry] W[adsworth] L[ongfellow] on his birthday, sgd J.R.L. With covering ALs to C. T. Dunbar, 25 Feb 1867. 4 pp, various sizes, in mor case with 2 portraits. Doheny collection. (89) $3,000
Series of 4 A Ls s, 9 Mar 1860 to 19 Feb 1889. Doheny collection. (89) $600
ALs, 24 Jan 1882. (89) $55
— 5 Dec 1883. (89) $325
— 8 Dec 1883. (91) $80
— "29th" [1885?]. (88) $90
— 19 Jan 1886. (90) $55
— 17 July 1886. Byer collection. (90) $175

Lowell, John, 1743-1802
Collection of 5 A Ls s & 5 autograph Mss, 1762 to 1780s. (90) $800

Lowry, Laurence Stephen, 1887-1976
Series of 14 A Ls s, 22 Feb 1960 to 22 Sept 1965. (90) £500
— Series of 3 A Ls s, 23 Dec 1961 to 2 Apr 1963. (89) £150
ALs, [23 Dec 1961]. (90) £65

Lubbock, Francis Richard, 1815-1905
Ds, 1 Sept 1837. (89) $80

Lucan, Richard John Bingham, 7th Earl
Ls, 13 Sept 1964. (88) £90

Ludendorff, Erich, 1865-1937
Collection of ALs & ANs, [13] & 16 Feb 1914. (90) DM550
— Collection of ALs & photograph, sgd & inscr, [n.d.] & 1917. (89) DM550
— Collection of 6 A Ls s & Ls, 27 Dec [1920] to 19 Apr 1928. 10 pp, mostly 8vo. To Alfred Roth. About his & Roth's persecution, their fight against Freemasons, their nationalistic aims, etc. (88) DM3,300
— Collection of 2 A Ls s & Ls, 11 Mar 1937 & [n.d.]. (90) DM950

Series of 3 A Ls s, [spring 1919] to 8 Nov 1924. 3 pp, 4to & 8vo. To an unnamed lady. Expressing thanks. (89) DM1,100
— Series of 3 A Ls s, 6 Aug [1922] to 28 Dec [1925]. 3 pp, 8vo. To an unnamed lady. Responding to supportive letters. (91) DM1,300
ALs, 5 Jan 1916. Schroeder collection. (89) DM260
— 25 Jan 1922. (91) DM240
— 29 Dec 1924. (91) DM460
— 15 Jan 1937. (88) DM750
— 18 Mar [n.y.]. (91) DM320
— [n.d.]. (90) DM250
Series of 5 Ls s, 7 July to 13 Dec 1933. (88) DM700
— Series of 8 Ls s, 19 Jan 1934 to 2 Jan 1937. 8 pp, 8vo. To Anselm Bock. Expressing thanks & explaining his political opinions. With related material. (89) DM3,000
Ls s (2), 7 & 10 Mar 1934. (90) DM750
Ls, 8 Nov 1933. (90) DM650
— 15 Feb 1934. (90) DM460

Ludewig, Johann Peter von, 1668-1743
Ms, In Notitiam Bohemiae Austriae et Provinciarum Qua His Sunt Annexae Discursus. [Halle?, c.1720]. 391 leaves, 211mm by 184mm, in contemp vellum. In 2 hands. (91) DM1,200

Ludwig, Fuerst von Anhalt-Koethen, 1579-1650
ALs, 5 Oct 1627. 1 p, folio. To an unnamed prince. About negotiations with Wallenstein & the military situation in the north. (91) DM2,400

Ludwig, Markgraf von Brandenburg, Herzog von Bayern, 1315-61
Document, [14 Aug] 1345. 1 p, 8vo; vellum. Patent of indemnity issued to Frankfurt on the Oder. Schroeder collection. (89) DM4,500
— [23 Nov] 1348. 1 p, folio; vellum. Grant of tax exemption for the town of Frankfurt on the Oder. Repaired. Schroeder collection. (89) DM6,000

Ludwig, Herzog von Wuerttemberg, 1554-93
Ls, 29 July 1592. 1 p, folio. To Konrad Friedrich von Burgsdorff. Discharging him & promising full pay for 6 months. With related material. (89)

LUDWIG

DM1,600

Ludwig, Carl, 1816-95
Series of 3 A Ls s, 14 Oct 1877 to 12 Feb 1880. (91) DM420
ALs, 28 Oct 1849. (91) DM850

Ludwig, Emil, 1881-1948
[An archive of papers from his estate, comprising research material for his works, letters, Mss, etc., 1901 to 1946, c.800 pp, sold at S on 20 Nov 1990, lot 457, for £4,000 to Mytze.]
Autograph Ms, 2 essays about the situation in Germany, 3 May 1945. (90) DM550
ALs, 11 Sept 1941. (89) DM300
— 14 Apr [1948]. (91) DM350

Ludwig Eugen, Herzog von Wuerttemberg, 1731-95
Ds, 2 Mar 1795. (89) DM500

Ludwig Georg, Markgraf von Baden, 1702-61
Series of Ds s, 5 Ds s, 1730 to 1738. (90) DM500

Ludwig I, King of Bavaria, 1786-1868
Collection of 6 A Ls s, 6 Ls s (4 with autograph postscripts), 8 Ds s & document, 29 Jan 1828 to 8 June 1865. 30 pp, various sizes. To Graf Max von Marogna. About a variety of matters. (88) DM1,800
A Ls s (2), 8 Sept 1826 & 14 Sept 1845. 2 pp, 8vo. To Friedrich von Schelling. Granting his request to stay in Erlangen for anr year, & forwarding a book. With related material. (90) DM2,400
ALs, 31 July 1809. 1 p, 4to. To Hofrat Schlichtegroll. Requesting abvice about the acquisition of a collection of sculptures. (91) DM1,600
— 20 Apr 1818. (90) DM380
— 5 Aug 1818. (90) DM360
— 25 Nov 1825. (89) DM420
— 30 Aug 1831. (89) DM500
— 6 Mar 1841. 3 pp, 4to. To Friedrich Wilhelm IV of Prussia. Recommending Johannes von Geissel as Archbishop of Cologne. (90) DM3,200
— 22 Sept 1854. 1 p, 8vo. To Pauline Schelling. Expressing condolences on the death of her husband. (89)

AMERICAN BOOK PRICES CURRENT

DM2,000
Series of 4 Ls s, 6 Apr to 26 Oct 1841. 5 pp, 4to. To [Karl August] von Abel. Giving orders concerning repairs to public buildings, requesting construction plans, etc. (91) DM1,200
Ls, 3 Sept 1832. (91) DM1,000
— 3 Sept 1846. (91) DM360

Ludwig II, King of Bavaria, 1845-86
Collection of 3 A Ls s & 2 Ds s, 1868 to 13 May 1886. 6 pp, folio & 8vo. To Anton Ulsamer, summoning him to Hohenschwangau, discussing a position, new laws, etc. Appointments for Ulsamer. With related material. (88) £5,800
A Ls s (2), 3 Apr [n.y.] & [n.d.]. 3 pp, 8vo. To Karl Hesselschwert. Giving various instructions. (89) £2,600
ALs, 28 Nov 1861. 4 pp, 8vo. To Prince Heinrich von Hessen-Darmstadt. About his father's birthday & his own & his brother's army commissions. (90) DM3,500
— 1 July 1867. 1 p, 8vo. To his fiancee Sophie of Bavaria. Offering his own railway coach for her sister's journey to Munich. Sgd Dein treuer Heinrich. (91) DM8,500
— 28 May 1875. 4 pp, 4to. To [Grossherzog Peter II von Oldenburg]. Expressing condolences on the death of Queen Amalie of Greece. (89) DM3,200
— 19 Feb 1883. 12 pp, 8vo. To Friedrich Brandt. Grieving about recipient's move to Berlin & Wagner's death, & mentioning a ptd report about flight experiments (present). (90) DM20,000
— 12 Mar 1883. 8 pp, 4to. To Fritz Brandt. Regretting their separation & urging him to write. (90) DM7,500
— [n.d.]. (90) £900
Ls, 16 Dec 1864. 1 p, 4to. To Max von Neumayr. Conveying his mother's wish that Oktavia von Stein be appointed to a prebend at Bayreuth. (91) DM1,600
— 14 Oct 1865. 2 pp, 4to. To Max von Neumayr. Suggesting the acquisition of the newspaper Landbote. (91) DM2,600
— 31 Jan 1866. (91) £550
— 17 Aug 1874. (91) £400
— 1 Sept 1874. 1 p, 4to. To Paul von

Braun. Commending his work during the cholera epidemic. With related material. (89) DM1,200
— 9 May 1875. 1 p, folio. To King Karl I von Wuerttemberg. Notifying him of the death of Princess Alexandra Amalie. (88) DM2,000
Ds, 28 Feb 1874. 1 p, folio. Military commission for Luitpold von Poellnitz-Frankenberg. (90) DM1,500
— 18 Oct 1874. (91) $650
— 18 Oct 1874. 1 p, folio. Military commission for Friedrich Schoenlaub. (90) DM1,100
— 14 Oct 1880. (89) DM620
— 12 Sept 1883. 1 p, folio. Military commission for Johann von Geyer zu Lauf. (89) DM2,200
— 30 Dec 1884. (88) DM700
Endorsement, sgd, 13 July 1864. 1 p, folio. On a report from his Ministry of War, granting leave to Capt. von Heinleth. (90) DM1,100

Ludwig III, King of Bavaria, 1845-1921
Ds, 3 Jan 1914. (89) DM850
— 19 Nov 1916. (90) DM550

Ludwig Rudolf, Herzog zu Braunschweig-Lueneburg, 1671-1735
Ls, 5 Dec 1723. (88) DM280

Ludwig Wilhelm, Markgraf von Baden, 1655-1707
Ls, 20 Dec 1703. (91) DM950
— 19 Oct 1705. (90) DM850
Ds, 23 July 1703. (90) DM680

Luebke, Heinrich, 1894-1972
Ds, 5 May 1961. (90) DM440

Luedke, Friedrich Germanus, 1730-92
Series of 5 A Ls s, 28 Mar 1775 to 11 June 1777. (91) DM950

Luetzow, Adolph, Freiherr von, 1782-1834
Ds, 15 Nov 1814. Schroeder collection. (89) DM420
— 20 Nov 1815. Schroeder collection. (89) DM500

Lugard, Frederick, 1st Lord Lugard, 1858-1945
ALs, 9 Nov 1893. (91) £100

Lugosi, Bela, 1882-1956
Photograph, sgd, [n.d.]. (91) $650
Photograph, sgd & inscr, [n.d.]. (91) $650
Signature, [n.d.]. (91) $170
— Anr, [n.d.]. (89) $120

Lugosi, Bela, 1882-1956 — & Karloff, Boris, 1887-1969
[A signature by each, matted with 2 photographs as Dracula & Frankenstein, sold at wa on 21 Oct 1989, lot 409, for $325.]

Luise, Queen of Friedrich Wilhelm III of Prussia, 1776-1810
Series of 9 A Ls s, 3 June 1794 to 5 Feb 1797. 10 pp, 4to, in vellum bdg. To her father-in-law Friedrich Wilhelm II. Informing him about her uncle's death, & expressing thanks on various occasions. (91) DM8,400
ALs, [1786]. 2 pp, 8vo. To Hofrat Petermann. Charming letter promising to be good. (90) DM3,900
— 23 July 1794. 8 pp, 8vo. To her husband. Assuring him of her love, worrying about the war, etc. Albrecht collection. (91) SF12,000
— 29 Jan 1795. 1 p, 4to. To Graefin von Lusi. Thanking for a present of sweets, & reporting about her recent illness. In French. (90) DM1,250
— 9 Apr 1799. 2 pp, 4to. To Frau von Voss. Urging her not to return to court before she is fully recovered. (90) DM1,800
— 1 Apr 1802. 3 pp, 8vo. To Graefin Voss. Announcing her return to Berlin. In French. With a port. Schroeder collection. (89) DM2,300
— 2 Sept 1803. 3 pp, 8vo. To Frau von Berg. Personal letter about her family, her activities, etc. Mostly in French. (88) DM4,500
— [21 Feb 1804]. 1 p, 12mo. To Duchess Dorothea of Kurland. Inviting her to a dance. (90) DM1,200
— [24 Apr 1804]. 2 pp, 8vo. To Graefin Voss. Chatting about her activities & her family. (88) DM1,500
— 19 May 1807. 3 pp, 8vo. To Frau von Voss. Worrying about her daughter's illness. (91) DM1,900
— 20 June 1808. 4 pp, 8vo. To Johann George Scheffner. Returning copies of

LUISE

lectures by Professor Suevern & asking questions about European history. Schroeder collection. (89) DM6,500
Ls, 16 Apr 1804. (89) DM420
— 29 Apr 1805. (88) DM380
— Voss, Sophie Marie von. - ALs, 1 Nov 1808. 3 pp, 4to. To [Frau von Ompteda?]. Sending news from the court at Koenigsberg. (91) DM650

Luise, Queen of Friedrich Wilhelm III of Prussia, 1776-1810 —& Others
Signature, on a letter by Sebastian Ludwig Friedel, 4 Apr 1806, 1 p, folio, regarding reservations for a concert to be given at St. Peter's Church. Sgd by Luise ("La Reine") & 11 relatives & visitors at the court of Berlin. (90) DM1,700

Luise Henriette, Kurfuerstin von Brandenburg, 1627-67
Ls, 27 Mar 1649. (91) DM550
— 29 Jan 1667. (90) DM550

Luitpold, Prince Regent of Bavaria, 1821-1912
ALs, 22 Jan 1845. (88) DM600
Ds s (2)5 Mar 1892 & 13 Nov 1897. (90) DM300
Ds, 16 Oct 1892. (90) DM340
— 8 Mar 1906. (89) DM850
— 7 Dec 1910. 7 pp, folio. Patent of nobility for Joseph von Redwitz. With full-page illuminated coat-of-arms. (88) DM1,600

Lull, Ramon, 1235?-1315?
Ms, De Secretis Naturae seu Quinta Essentia. [Venice, 1498]. 183 leaves, 163mm by 115mm, in modern calf in a cloth case. In brown ink in a very small & regular upright cursive humanistic bookhand by Joannes Cycurius Theatinus. With 2 drawings of alchemical apparatus & 19 full-page or very large diagrams. Spaces left for large initials. (88) £7,500
— Ms, Liber de venatione sustantiae accidentis et compositi, De anima rationali, & Liber de natura; [Northeast? Italy, early 15th cent]. 154 leaves, vellum, 204mm by 140mm, in late medieval blindstamped calf. In a small gothic bookhand. With 2 large illuminated initials. The Garden Ltd.

AMERICAN BOOK PRICES CURRENT

collection. (90) $26,000

Lumley, Savile
Original drawings, (18), cover designs for various boys' & girls' annuals, 1927 to 1938. (89) £750

Lunacharski, Anatoli Vassiljevich, 1875-1933
ALs, 30 Sept [1927?]. 2 pp, 4to. To [Henri Barbusse?]. About a performance at the Maly Theatre. In French. (89) DM3,200

Lushington, Vernon, 1832-1912
[The papers of Lushington, comprising autograph drafts, notebooks, working papers, & other items, in 3 boxes, sold at S on 21 Sept, lot 148, for £480 to Joseph.]

Luther, Martin, 1483-1546
ALs, 29 July 1520. 1 p, 170mm by 216mm. To Johann Lang. Sending his sermon on the mass, denouncing his opponents & mentioning Melanchthon. In Latin. John F. Fleming Estate. (89) $60,000
— 28 May 1529. 1 p, 4to. To Gerhard Wiskamp. Thanking for his letter & presents, sending one of his works & offering to send other works upon request. In Latin. With related material stating provenance since c.1720. (90) DM24,000
— [15 Sept] 1530. 2 pp, folio. To Philipp Melanchthon. Advising him to break off his fruitless efforts to come to an understanding with the Catholics at Augsburg. In Latin. Margin cut. (90) DM75,000
— [27 June] 1538. 1 p, folio. To the representatives of the 7 reformed Swiss cities at Zurich. Trying to come to an agreement in the controversy about transubstantiation. (89) DM150,000
— 20 Mar 1545. 1 p, folio. To Johann Friedrich, Elector of Saxony. Discussing the appointment of a pastor at Altenburg. Repaired & tipped to larger leaf, with trans. Barrett collection. (89) $40,000
ADs, 1543. 3.5cm by 16cm, cut from larger leaf. Receipt for 25 florins as quarterly payment. With fragment of receipt by Melanchthon on verso. (91)

DM10,000
— LUTHER, PAUL. - Ls, [1586/89]. 2 pp, folio. To Kurfuerst Christian I of Saxony. Informing him that his commission must be executed before he can draw his salary. (91) DM660

L'vov, Alexey Fyodorovich, 1798-1870
ALs, 28 Mar 1847. (90) DM300

Lynch, Thomas, Signer from South Carolina
Ds, 31 Dec 1774. 1 p, 4to. Receipt for legal compensation for an executed slave belonging to his father. Doheny collection. (89) $19,000

Lyon, Nathaniel, 1818-61
ALs, 31 Oct 1850. (88) $150
— 27 Apr 1861. 6 pp, 4to. To Col. Thomas. About the mustering of troops in Missouri, etc. Including postscript, sgd. (91) $1,800
— 20 May 1861. (89) $650
Ls, 7 June 1861. (88) $400
Ds, [n.d.]. (91) $220

Lyons, Edmund, 1st Baron, 1790-1858
Series of 5 A Ls s, 3 Jan 1854 to 9 Jan 1855. (91) £90

Lyttelton, Charles, 1714-68
Autograph Ms, private accounts, 1 Jan 1751 to 13 Dec 1768. 310 pp, 4to, in 3 contemp vellum vols. Giving details of income & expenses. (89) £1,050

M

MacArthur, Douglas, 1880-1964
[A group of over 300 items from his personal military files, 1917 to 1919, sold at R on 17 June 1989, lot 251, for $3,500.]
Ls, 22 Jan 1953. (88) $130
A Ns s (2), 1953 & 1960. (89) $80
Menu, Annual Dinner of the National Association of Manufacturers, NY, 5 Dec 1952. (91) $160
Photograph, sgd, [n.d.]. (91) $400
— Anr, [n.d.]. (89) $210
Photograph, sgd & inscr, [n.d.]. (91) $375
Signature, on detached front page of the NY Journal American, 28 Dec 1941, headlining Japanese attack on the Philippines. (90) $85

Macartney, George, 1st Earl, 1737-1806
[An album from his collection containing 12 scenic views of South China in ink & monochrome, [c.1790s], folio, in early 19th-cent half mor, sold at S on 22 Nov 1988, lot 81, for £5,000 to Lack.]
Series of Letters, 5 letters, 25 Mar to 14 Apr 1793. (90) £1,000

Macaulay, Thomas Babington, 1st Baron Macaulay, 1800-59
Autograph Ms, review of [Francis] "Thackeray's History of the Earl of Chatham", [1834]. 122 pp, folio, in def mor bdg. With numerous revisions. John F. Fleming Estate. (89) $7,000

McAuliffe, S. Christa, 1948-86
Autograph sentiment, sgd, [c.31 Dec 1985]. (91) $400
Signature, [28 Jan 1986]. (91) $700

MacCarthy, Desmond, 1877-1952
Series of c.120 A Ls s, 1918 to 1952. More than 450 pp, 4to & 8vo. To Lady Cynthia Asquith. Letters reflecting their friendship, & discussing literary & dramatic subjects. (88) £1,200

McCartney, Paul
Autograph Ms, lyrics for "Love of the Loved", with guitar cords; [c.1961]. On a scrap of paper, 11.5cm by 18cm. (89) £1,700
— Autograph Ms, lyrics for the song Little Child, [c.1963]. 1 p, 23cm by 17cm. 2 verses & chorus. (88) £3,300
— Autograph Ms, notebook containing 2 draft letters regarding his deportation from Germany, pencil caricatures & guitar cord sequences; [c.1960]. Length not stated, 20.5cm by 16cm. (89) £4,000
Ls, 1969. (88) £260
— [n.d.]. To "Gwen". Fan letter about their new record, forthcoming tour, & birthdays. Also sgd by George Harrison. Framed with a photograph, 17.5 by 13.5 inches. (88) $1,200

McCartney, Paul —& Best, Pete
[4 documents relating to their deportation from Germany, Dec 1960, addressed to the Chief Officer of the Aliens Police at Hamburg, 4 typewritten sheets, 33cm by 20.5cm, sold at S on 12 Sept 1988, lot 281, for £2,000.]

McClellan, George B., 1826-85
ALs, 1869. (89) $120
— 9 Aug 1883. (88) $75
Ls, 16 Jan 1862. Middendorf collection. (89) $900
— DEMOCRATIC PARTY. - Letter, 8 Sept 1864. 4 pp, 4to. To Gen. McClellan. Notifying him of his nomination for the Presidency. Sgd by 11 members of the National Democratic Convention. Middendorf collection. (89) $420

McClellan, George R. W., Soldier
Ds, 30 Apr 1848. (88) $170

McCormick, Cyrus H., 1809-84
ALs, 10 Dec 1853. (91) $325
— 9 Jan 1876. (91) $600
Check, sgd, 5 Oct 1872. (89) $300

McCullers, Carson, 1917-67
Typescript carbon copy, The Mute, outline for The Heart Is a Lonely Hunter, 1940. 37 pp, 4to, on rectos only. Sgd & inscr. (91) $2,400

Macdonald, Etienne Jacques Joseph Alexandre, Duc de Tarente, 1765-1840
ALs, 14 Aug 1816. (88) DM210
Ls, 14 Dec 1830. (88) $275

MacDonald, James Ramsay, 1866-1937
Photograph, sgd, [n.d.]. (91) $100

Macdonough, Thomas, 1783-1825
— VAN RENSSELAER, PHILIPP. - Ds, 3 Oct 1814. 1 p, folio. Grant of land in the city of Albany to Macdonough for his victory on Lake Champlain, 11 Sept 1813; sgd as Mayor. (90) $550

MacDowell, Edward Alexander, 1861-1908
Collection of ALs, Ls & photograph, sgd, 8 Oct 1899, 6 Oct 1900 & [n.d.]. (89) $750
ALs, 1 June 1895. (91) $425

McDowell, Irvin, 1818-85
[2 ptd General Orders, sgd, No. 2, 28 Mar 1855, & No. 4, 9 May 1856, regarding protection of the Kansas frontier & troop movements on the Upper Mississippi, sold at rf on 5 Dec, lot 42, for $150.]
Ls, 8 June 1868. (91) $200

McFall, David
[A group of 4 autograph Mss, diaries kept as carpenter & stagehand in NY, 1872 to 1897, length not stated, sold at R on 24 Feb 1990, lot 179, for $100.]

MacFarland, J. E.
Autograph Ms, novel, Shenandoah or A Tale of the War, [1869]; c.450 pp, 4to. (88) £300

Macfarlane, J.
Original drawings, (18), to illus Charles Kingsley's The Water Babies, [n.d.]. In watercolor (15) & ink; 4 initialled. Mostly 228mm by 153mm. Macmillan Archives. (90) £1,300
— Original drawings, (32), to illus Thomas Hughes's Tom Brown's Schooldays, 1916. Macmillan Archives. (90) £800

McFee, William, 1881-1966
Collection of 2 A Ls s & 5 Ls s, 1926 to 1950. (89) $400

MacGregor (or Campbell), Robert ("Rob Roy"), 1671-1734
Ds, 21 Feb 1706. 1 p, folio. Bond for 1,000 marks; sgd Ro: Campbell. Also sgd by 4 others. In mor-backed slipcase. (88) $1,600

Machen, Arthur, 1863-1947
Autograph Ms, introduction to 1916 Ed of The Great God Pan, [c.1915-1916]. (88) $700
— Autograph Ms, Preface to Casanova's Escape from the Leads, [1925]. (88) $600

McHenry, James, 1753-1816
Ls, [Sept 1796]. Munson collection. (90) $700

Machiavelli, Niccolo, 1469-1527
ALs, 25 Dec 1521. 1 p, folio. To the Chief Magistrate. Intervening on behalf of Parigino, who has been threatened with a law-suit. Repaired. (88) £5,000

Letters (2), 24 July 1504. 2 pp, folio. To Guglielmo di Crona & Lutio Malvazio. Regarding the siege of Pisa after the rebellion. With autograph corrections. (89) £6,000

McIntosh, Lachlan, 1725-1806
ALs, 1 Sept 1778. 2 pp, folio. To Col. Lochry. Making plans for a militia company to assist "in making a Fort". With engraved port. (90) $1,100

Mack, Connie, 1862-1956
ALs, 20 May 1938. (88) $275
— 12 May 1949. (90) $600
Ds, 25 Nov 1943. (91) $450
Photograph, sgd & inscr, [n.d.]. (91) $300
Signature, [10 Oct 1930]. (91) $120

Mackay, Jack
AL, 18 July 1848. (91) $500

McKean, Joseph B., 1764-1826
ALs, 31 July 1802. (88) $180

McKean, Thomas, Signer from Delaware
Ds, 4 July 1794. (88) $110
— 2 Aug 1800. (89) $120
— 10 Sept 1806. (88) $150
Autograph endorsement, sgd, 8 Apr 1790. (91) $200

McKean, Thomas, Signer from Delaware —&
Irvine, William, 1741-1804
Ls, 23 Aug 1794. (90) $200

Mackensen, August von, 1849-1945
Series of 3 A Ls s, 11 Oct 1924 to 18 Oct 1930. (88) DM400
A Ls s (2), 10 Dec 1914 & 14 Mar 1920. Schroeder collection. (89) DM280
ALs, 23 June 1908. (91) DM200

Mackenzie, Sir Compton, 1883-1972
Autograph Ms, novel, Figure of Eight, dated 5 Feb 1936. Over 310 pp, folio, in blue buckram gilt. Working Ms, complete with dedicatory inscr, initialled. (90) £1,200

Mackenzie, Sir Morell, 1837-92
Ls, 11 June 1888. (90) DM420

McKenzie, Murdoch, 1743-1829
Ms, The Manuscript Works of the late Murdoch MacKenzie Esqr F.R.S..... (90) £400

MacKenzie-Grieve, K. M. See: Hawker, H. G. & MacKenzie-Grieve

McKinley, William, 1843-1901
Collection of ALs & Ds, 8 May 1898 & 26 Dec 1899. 2 pp, 8vo & folio. To Herrick, sending his autograph for Mr. Duncan's daughter. Appointment of Ernest M. Reeve as 2d Lieut. of Infantry; also sgd by Elihu Root. Doheny collection. (89) $2,200
— Collection of ALs & Ls, 23 Jan 1900 & 22 Jan 1897. 2 pp, 4to. Recipient unnamed, assuring him that there is no dress code for the White House. To Bishop John F. Hurst, thanking for suggestions. Pratt collection. (89) $6,000

ALs, 6 Feb 1884. (89) $375
— 29 May 1891. (90) $180
Collection of Ls, ANs & Ds, June 1871 to 25 July 1895. (89) $350
— Collection of Ls & Ds, 30 June 1896 & 14 July 1898. (89) $325
— Collection of Ls, ANs, & photograph, sgd & inscr, 14 Nov 1900, 2 July 1900 & [n.d.]. (90) $750
Series of 3 Ls s, 21 Jan to 11 Mar 1896. (88) $300
Ls s (2), 8 Aug & 19 Sept 1890. (90) $200
— Ls s (2), 2 Feb 1892 & 19 Mar 1896. (90) $200
Ls, 11 Mar 1886. (90) $200
— 13 Nov 1894. (91) $150
— 8 June 1895. (89) $95
— 11 July 1895. (91) $200
— 17 Apr 1896. (91) $300
— 31 Aug 1896. (91) $120
— 31 Aug 1896. (88) $150
— 14 Nov 1900. (90) $325
— [n.d.]. Christensen collection. (90) $100
Collection of ANs & Ls, 14 Jan 1878 & 10 Feb 1894. Rosenbloom collection. (88) $350
ANs, 9 Feb 1880. (88) $190
— 15 May [18]94. (88) $350

MCKINLEY

— [7?] Nov 1900. (88) $60
— 9 June 1901. 1 p, 8vo. To Garret A. Hobart. Reporting about his wife's illness. Probably draft for a telegram; in pencil. (89) $1,800
— 24 Aug [n.y.]. (89) $55
Ds, 6 Mar 1891. (88) $140
— 20 Mar 1894. (88) $150
— 15 Nov 1894. (89) $150
— 7 July 1897. (91) $275
— 24 May 1898. (90) $190
— 7 June 1898. (91) $220
— 24 Sept 1898. (88) $950
— 10 Nov 1898. (90) $160
— 17 Apr 1899. (91) $700
— 17 May 1899. (91) $225
— 29 Sept 1899. (88) $170
— 26 Dec 1899. (89) $210
— 8 Jan 1900. (88) $160
— 29 Jan 1900. (91) $350
— 6 June 1900. (89) $450
— 11 June 1900. (90) $130
— 16 Nov [1900]. (89) $90
— 20 Dec 1900. (91) $230
— 7 Mar 1901. (90) $160
— 27 May 1901. (89) $175
— 27 May 1901. Byer collection. (90) $175
Autograph endorsement, 6 Mar 1883. (91) $150
Autograph sentiment, sgd, 27 Oct 1898. (91) $325
Autograph telegram, [26 Sept 1892]. (88) $375
— Anr, sgd, 31 Mar 1897. (90) $250
— Anr, sgd, 31 Mar 1897. (90) $225
Check, sgd, 28 Feb 1898; for $48.05 payable to G.G.Cranwell & Son. (89) $280
— Anr, sgd, 31 Jan 1899. (89) $350
Endorsement, sgd, on ALs by W. (88) $275
Engraving, bust port from a photograph, etched by C. (90) $550
Executive Mansion card, [n.d.]. (89) $100
— Anr, sgd, [n.d.]. (91) $500
— Anr, sgd, [n.d.]. (90) $150
— Anr, sgd, [n.d.]. (90) $160
Menu, luncheon for McKinley & Party at the International Hotel, Niagara Falls, 6 Sept 1901 [the day he was shot]. (91) $400

AMERICAN BOOK PRICES CURRENT

Photograph, sgd, [1900]. (89) $850
Photograph, sgd & inscr, [n.d.]. (89) $550

McKinley, William, 1843-1901 — & Others
[A banquet program, 24 Aug 1897, 7 pp, 6 by 7 inches, sgd by McKinley beneath his photograph & by 13 others, including M. A. Hanna, R. A. Alger, etc., sold at Dar on 6 Dec 1990, lot 298, for $225.]

Mackreth, Sir Robert, 1726-1819
ALs, 27 June 1759. (90) £110

Mackworth, Sir Digby, 1789-1852
Autograph Ms, journal in Portugal, Spain & the Netherlands, 4 Apr 1809 to 15 Dec 1810 & 13 Mar to 18 June 1815. (91) £550

McLean, John, 1785-1861
ALs, 20 Mar 1829. (91) $95

MacLeish, Archibald, 1892-1982
Collection of 15 A Ls s & A Ns s, & 31 Ls s, 1945 to 1972. About 56 pp, various sizes. Mostly to Mark von Doren. About a variety of matters. With 3 autograph Mss & typescript; poems, sgd. (90) $3,500

McManus, George, 1884-1954
Original drawing, heads of Jiggs & a pal, with balloon; 1933. (91) $150

McNair, Ron, d.1986
Photograph, sgd, [n.d.]. (91) $200
Photograph, sgd & inscr, [n.d.]. (90) $85
Signature, [7 Feb 1980]. (91) $80

Macomb, Alexander, 1782-1841
ALs, 1823. (88) $130
— 1823. Alexander collection. (90) $105

McPherson, James Birdseye, 1828-64
Autograph Ms, Memoirs of a Military Reconaissance of the Coast... from San Francisco to Monterey..., June 1861. 23 pp, 4to. Draft, with numerous revisions. Mostly in pencil; probably lacking 4 pp. In half brown mor slipcase. With instructions issued to McPherson by Brig. Gen. James G. Totten, & further related material. Doheny collection. (88) $9,000
A Ls s (2), 31 Aug & 2 Sept 1863. (91) $800

Ls, 1 Sept 1862. 1 p 4to. To H. M. Woodward. Ordering platform freight cars. (91) $1,100

Macquarie, Lachlan
ALs, 18 Mar 1821. (91) £700

Macquarrie, Charles
[A box of trust papers of Lieut. Col. Charles Macquarrie of Ulva, Argyllshire, Scotland, 1830s to 1870s, several hundred items, sold at pn on 22 Mar 1990, lot 27, for £360 to Maggs.]

Macready, William Charles, 1793-1873
Series of 20 A Ls s, 1839 to 1859. (89) $600

Macrobius, Ambrosius Theodosius
Ms, Commentarii in Somnium Scipionis. [Southern Germany, 2d half of 10th cent]. 32 leaves (some lacking), vellum, 268mm by 193mm. 19th-cent blind-stamped sheep over pastebds. In dark brown ink in a slightly sloping late Carolingian minuscule with some Greek words in capitals. With 9 large painted initials, 4 marginal diagrams & 7 large or full-page illusts or diagrams, including a world map. Including an extract from Cicero's Somnium Scipionis. Ludwig MS.XII.4. (89) £320,000

Madagascar
[A small collection of material relating to King Radama & James Hastie, Civil Agent of the British Government to the King, 1825 & 1826, sold at S on 15 Dec, lot 259, for £250.]
— GALLIENI, GEN. JOSEPH SIMON. - Ls, 27 Feb 1897. 2 pp, folio. To Queen Ranavalona III. Sending her into exile after declaring Madagascar a French colony. With related material. (91) £280
— HASTIE, JAMES. - Autograph Ms, journal recording an expedition from Ovah to Manazari & Tamatave, 27 Oct to 23 Dec 1821; c.120 pp, 4to; vellum. Describing villages, local customs, agriculture, etc. With revisions throughout & autograph lists of cloth taken along for bartering. (88) £1,000

Madero, Francisco Indalecio, 1873-1913
Autograph quotation, sgd, [26 Oct 1912]. (91) $350

Madison, Dorothy Payne Todd ("Dolley"), 1768-1849
ALs, [n.d.]. (88) $400
— [n.d.] "Tuesday night". 2 pp, 8vo. To Miss Murray. Inviting her to a party & regretting she will be leaving Washington. Sgd DPM. Doheny collection. (89) $1,800
— 22 Feb 1841. 1 p, 4to. To Sec of the Navy J. K. Paulding. About Mrs. Paulding's & her sister's illness, the Ed of her husband's papers, etc. (89) $2,000
— 7 Dec [n.y.]. 2 pp, 4to. To her husband James Madison. Family news. Sgd DPM. With franking signature. Doheny collection. (89) $4,800
— [n.d.]. (91) $500
Ds, 23 Sept 1848. (90) $950
Autograph quotation, "Tis poor and not becoming proper gentry, to build their glories at their Fathers cost..."; sgd & dated 14 June 1848. (90) $600
Franking signature, [5 Oct n.y.]. Alexander collection. (90) $400
— TODD, CHARLES S. - ADs, 7 Mar 1849. 1 p, 4to. As chairman of a committee of officers of the War of 1812, address presenting their respects. (88) $120

Madison, James, 1749-1812
Ds, [c.1777-82]. 1 p, folio. As President of William & Mary, memorial to the Virginia House of Delegates, offering to trade slaves belonging to the college for land. Fold breaks. (91) $3,400

Madison, James, 1751-1836
[A ptd copy of his Message to Congress reporting about the War of 1812, 4 Nov 1812, 2 pp, 4to, sgd in type & addressed to Holland on attached blank, sold at rf on 5 Dec, lot 40, for $170.]
Autograph Ms, draft of essay addressed to John A. G. Davis, defending the right of Congress to encourage domestic manufactures by protective tariffs, 1832. 34 pp, 258mm by 100mm. With

MADISON

extensive revisions. (89) $40,000
- **ALs,** Aug 1791. 1 p, 4to. To John Dawson. Recommending Philip Freneau's projected journal. (91) $2,000
- 28 July 1802. 1 p, 4to. Recipient unknown. Responding to a recommendation for the position of consul at Barcelona. With related material. McVitty collection. (90) $4,000
- 6 Sept 1802. 4 pp, 4to. To Stephen Higginson & others. Regarding the capture of 2 ships & Charles Pinckney's negotiations in Spain. Sang collection. (91) $6,500
- 20 Feb 1803 [i.e.1804]. 1 p, 4to. To William Ellery, Jr. Reassuring him that there are no plans to turn him out of office. Including franking signature. (90) $3,800
- 17 July 1804. 1 p, 4to. To Messrs. Dudley & Porter. Advising them about proceedings in the case of a merchantman captured by the British. Including franking signature. (90) $1,800
- 1 Aug 1805. 1 p, 4to. Recipient unknown. Acknowledging receipt of money, & mentioning his wife's illness. Doheny collection. (89) $4,000
- 24 Nov 1805. 1 p, 4to. To Mr. Purviance. Sending a bank draft in payment of money advanced for importations. Doheny collection. (89) $1,900
- 22 July 1806. 1 p, 4to. To [Samuel Latham Mitchill]. Thanking for information that the testimony of the Cabinet will not be required [in the case against William S. Smith & Samuel G. Ogden]. (90) $6,500
- 10 Oct 1808. (90) $1,000
- 8 Dec 1810. 2 pp, 4to. To Peter Stephen Duponceau. Expressing thanks & commenting on his trans of Bynkershoek's [A Treatise on the Law of War]. (90) $13,000
- 20 Sept 1813. 2 pp, 4to. To Major Gen. [Henry] Dearborn. Discussing British war plans. Docketed by Dearborn. With engraved port. (88) $8,000
- 8 Sept 1815. 2 pp, 4to. To Attorney Gen. Richard Rush. Requesting him to confer with Sec of the Treasury Dallas about the need for a special session of Congress. Endorsed by Rush on integral address leaf. Pratt collection. (89) $6,500
- [27 Dec] 1815. (88) $750
- 1 Feb 1816. 1 p, 4to. Recipient unnamed. Giving assurances that he is seeking information regarding N[ew] O[rleans] & Gen. Lafayette's prospects. (89) £3,200
- 1 Jan 1817. 1 p, 4to. To Jeremiah Mason. Requesting his attendance in the Senate on 4 March. (90) $4,800
- 14 Nov 1817. 1 p, folio. To Tench Coxe. Thanking for his memoir on cotton wool & commenting on British trade policy. Christensen collection. (90) $2,800
- [7] Mar 1820. (88) £750
- 20 Mar 1820. 4 pp, 4to. To Tench Coxe. About a recommendation for recipient's son, colonization of freed slaves, domestic manufactures, etc. Pforzheimer Foundation. (90) $8,500
- 1 May 1824. 1 p, 4to. To Horatio Gates Spafford. About Spafaord's letter & his just published work. (91) $1,600
- 8 Mar 1827. 2 pp, 4to. To C. C. Cambreleng. Commenting on his speech on the tariff & analyzing American trade policy. Including franking signature. Pratt collection. (89) $11,000
- 14 Apr 1829. 1 p, 4to. To Benjamin Romaine. Thanking for 2 pamphlets & commenting on the "defects in the Constitution". With franking signature. Seal hole, waterstained. With related material. (88) $6,000
- 15 June 1829. 1 p, 4to. To Jean Guillaume, Baron Hyde de Neuville. Introducing William Cabell Rives, the newly appointed U. S. minister to France. With cut signature of Mrs. Madison. (91) $2,2500
- 5 Oct 1830. 2 pp, 4to. To Jared Sparks. Sending the draft of Washington's Farewell Address prepared in 1792 & commenting on authorship of the Federalist Papers. Sang collection. (91) $25,000
- 7 Nov 1831. 1 p, 4to. To Dr. John Wakefield Francis. Responding to questions about Monroe's & Livingston's negotiations with France & the Louisiana Purchase. With franking signature. Rosenbloom collection. (88) $24,000

Ls, 7 Jan 1804. (91) $550
— 11 June 1804. 2 pp, 4to. To James L. Cathcard of the Dept. of State. (91) $2,400
— 12 July 1805. (89) $650
— 29 May 1829. 2 pp, 4to. To Mr. Hunt. About recipient's American Annual Register. Text in the hand of Dolley Madison. (90) $2,500
— 15 Aug 1835. 2 pp, 4to. To Hubbard Taylor. Commenting on the state of the Union & the infirmities of old age. Including franking signature. Def. (90) $6,500

Ds, 1 Apr 1802. (91) $375
— 1 July 1805. (90) $1,000
— 1 July 1805. (89) $800
— 12 July 1805. (89) $550
— 20 Oct 1809. (89) $425
— 24 Oct 1809. (88) $350
— 7 Nov 1809. (88) $800
— 17 Nov 1809. (89) $800
— 7 Mar 1810. (88) $500
— 12 Mar 1810. (89) $700
— 8 Nov 1810. 1 p, 255mm by 382mm. Ship's passport for the schooner Lydia. Countersgd by R. Smith. (89) $2,600
— 7 Dec 1810. 1 p, folio. Mediterranean Pass for the brig Matilda. Countersgd by Sec of State Robert Smith. (90) $1,100
— 12 Dec 1810. (89) $850
— 27 Dec 1810. (89) $600
— 5 Jan 1811. (88) $450
— 28 Jan 1811. (88) $600
— 1 Feb 1811. 1 p, folio. Ship's papers in 4 languages for the brig Harvey Hyde. Framed. (91) $1,200
— 13 Feb 1811. (90) $550
— 13 Feb 1811. 1 p, 10 by 15 inches. Ship's passport for the Betsy. (91) $1,300
— 29 Nov 1811. (91) $1,000
— 1 Dec 1811. (90) $800
— 13 Dec 1811. (89) $550
— 13 Dec 1811. (89) $950
— 13 Dec 1811. (88) $650
— 16 Dec 1811. (88) $600
— 23 Dec 1811. (89) $650
— 28 Dec 1811. (90) $800
— 9 Jan 1812. (88) $900
— 18 Mar 1812. 1 p, folio. Mediterranean Pass for the schooner Fairy of New York. Countersgd by Monroe. (89) $1,250
— 21 Mar 1812. (89) $700
— 26 June 1812. (88) $850
— 3 July 1812. (89) $350
— 23 July 1812. (89) $700
— 30 July 1812. (88) $750
— 3 Aug 1812. (88) £200
— 31 Aug 1812. Byer collection. (90) $750
— 20 Oct 1812. (90) $450
— 5 Nov 1812. (88) $950
— 10 Nov 1812. (88) $800
— 21 Nov 1812. 1 p, folio. Letter of Marque for the brig Fox of Philadelphia. Countersgd by Monroe. (90) $1,500
— 14 Jan 1813. (88) $400
— 6 May 1813. (91) $400
— 11 May 1813. (90) $500
— 19 June 1813. (91) $425
— 30 July 1813. (90) $650
— 15 Dec 1813. (91) $750
— 22 Dec 1813. (88) $950
— 17 Mar 1814. (91) $300
— 1 Apr 1814. (90) $550
— 1 Jan 1815. (88) $625
— 20 Feb 1815. (89) $550
— 27 Mar 1815. (90) $500
— 14 Apr 1815. (88) $850
— 13 Nov 1815. (90) $600
— 21 Dec 1815. Whiton collection. (88) $900
— 16 Jan 1816. 1 p, folio. Appointment of Thomas D. Anderson as consul in Tunis. Countersgd by Monroe. (90) $1,100
— 29 Jan 1816. 1 p, folio. Ship's paper for the Belle of Charleston. Countersgd by Monroe. (91) $1,600
— 18 June 1816. (88) $700
— [n.d.]. (90) $950

Check, accomplished & sgd, 9 June 1813. (90) $850
— Anr, accomplished & sgd, 16 Nov 1814. Drawn on the Bank of Columbia for $600 payable to bearer. (91) $1,300
— Anr, accomplished & sgd, 29 Nov 1814. (90) $1,000
— Anr, accomplished & sgd, 9 Apr 1816. Doheny collection. (89) $850

Cut signature, [n.d.]. (90) $300

MADISON

Franking signature, [26 Apr 1806]. (90) $550
— Anr, [4 Mar 1812]. On letter addressed to Anthony Morris. (90) $1,250
— Anr, [8 Mar 1812]. (89) $475
— Anr, [n.d.]. (91) $500
— Anr, [n.d.]. (91) $375

Maeterlinck, Maurice, 1862-1949
Autograph Ms, "Marco"; sgd & dated 1 Sept 1911. (89) DM250

Magna Charta
Ms, Magna Charta & the Statutes of England, in Latin & Norman French. [Yorkshire?, c.1300-1325]. 182 leaves (6 blank) & 9 flyleaves, vellum, 100mm by 72mm, in def late medieval bdg of calf over wooden bds. In a small charter hand with headings in gothic script. With 25 illuminated initials & large historiated initial. Webster copy. (91) £15,000

Magnani, Anna, 1908-73 —& Others
[The signatures of Magnani, John Stride & Franco Zefirelli on a postcard addressed to Arnold Weissberger in Zefirelli's hand, [19 Aug 1965], sold at Dar on 10 Apr 1991, lot 254, for $100.]

Magritte, Rene, 1898-1967
Autograph Ms, album comprising reflections entitled Le Sens, & L'Habitude de Parler, 11 drawings, & a few smaller studies; [n.d.]. 14 pp & blanks, 4to, in limp brown calf. Sgd 5 times. (89) £3,500
Collection of 4 A Ls s & ANs, 16 June 1956 & [n.d.]. 5 pp, various sizes. To Edgard Brasseur. Discussing the fresco decorating project at the Palais des Beaux-Arts at Charleroi. (90) $1,500
— Collection of 15 A Ls s & postcards, sgd, 8 Apr 1963 to 6 July 1967. 20 pp, 8vo. To the art dealer Alexander Iolas. Concerning exhibitions, paintings, financial matters, etc. With related material. (90) £4,500
ALs, [n.d.]. (88) DM700
— 10 May 1964. (88) £250
Photograph, sgd & inscr, 16 Mar 1967. (90) DM460

AMERICAN BOOK PRICES CURRENT

Magruder, John Bankhead, 1810-71
Ds, [1859]. (90) $200

Mahan, Alfred T.
ALs, 12 Apr 1902. (91) $375

Mahler, Gustav, 1860-1911
[An etched port of Mahler by Emil Orlik, 1903, sgd by Mahler & inscr with 4 different musical quotations in margins, June 1907, 43cm by 33cm, framed, sold at S on 17 May, lot 35, for £16,000 to Horiuchi.]
Autograph Ms, Ballade, text of Das Klagende Lied, sgd & dated 27 Feb 1879. 10 pp, 8vo. Differing from pbd version. Repaired. (90) £9,000
Autograph music, draft of the 10th Symphony, 1910 & 1911. 108 pp, various sizes. In short score & in full score, with many alterations & revisions, & some personal notes to his wife Alma. (91) £350,000
— Autograph music, sketches for part of the 3d movement of his 9th Symphony, [1909]. 1 p, folio. 28 bars in D major in full & short score. (91) £11,000
— Autograph music, sketches for the last movement of his 2d Symphony, [early 1890s]. 1 p, folio. 2 sections, written in short score, with alterations. (90) £9,000
— Autograph music, song, Blicke mir nicht in die Lieder, for voice & piano to a text by Friedrich Rueckert; [1901]. 1 p, 26.5cm by 34.3cm, 20 staves each. Some corrections. (88) DM26,000
— Autograph music, song, Ich athmet einen linden Duft, to a text by Friedrich Rueckert, scored for voice & piano; 9 June [1901]. 1 p, 25cm by 33cm. Draft. (90) DM36,000
— Autograph music, song, In diesem Wetter, from the song-cycle Kindertotenlieder; [c.1901]. 2 pp, folio. Opening 11 bars, scored for voice & piano. Including autograph tp & list of titles of the 5 Rueckert Lieder. (91) £5,000
Autograph transcript, 4 musical quotations of themes from Beethoven's Overtures Leonora nos 2 & 3; [n.d.]. 2 scraps of paper, 7 cm by 11 cm. In pencil. Marill Estate. (89) $2,500
Collection of 4 A Ls s, AL & Ls, 7 Nov

1888 to 12 Feb 1889. 6 pp, mostly 4to. To Jacques Manheit. As Director of the Budapest Opera, negotiating a contract. AL def. With related material. (88) DM5,800
— Collection of ALs & autograph postcard, sgd, [c.1891 & after 1897]. 4 pp, 8vo & 12mo (cards). To Ludwig Karpath. About Karpath's newspaper & the appointment of performers. Marill Estate. (89) $1,600
— Collection of 2 A Ls s & autograph postcard, sgd, [n.d.]. 4 pp, 8vo & 12mo. To Ludwig Karpath. Concerning performers, rehearsals & meetings at the Vienna opera. Partly initialled. Marill Estate. (89) $1,700
Series of 3 A Ls s, 1897 [& later]. 3 pp, 8vo & 12mo. To Ludwig Karpath. Enclosing a ticket, arranging appointments, etc. Marill Estate. (89) $2,500
A Ls s (2), [3 & 23 Apr 1897]. 2 pp, 8vo. To Ludwig Karpath. Reporting on the confusion over his appointment at Vienna, & arranging meetings. Marill Estate. (89) $1,800
— A Ls s (2), 1898 & [n.d.]. 3 pp, 8vo. To Ludwig Karpath. Suggesting a notice celebrating the 25th anniversary of Schuch's appointment at Dresden, sending tickets, etc. Marill Estate. (89) $2,000
— A Ls s (2), [1900] & Dec 1903. 4 pp, 12mo (cards). To Ludwig Karpath. Regarding performances of Die Koenigin von Saba, & Merlin. Marill Estate. (89) $1,700
— A Ls s (2), [n.d.]. 3 pp, 8vo. To Eugen [Gruenberg]. Mentioning that he has applied for a post in Leipzig, & asking that a book be sent to von Weber. (91) £1,300
ALs, [Sept 1881]. 3 pp, 8vo. To Emil Freund. Reporting about his stay at Iglau. (90) DM4,200
— 26 Nov 1886. 2 pp, 8vo. To Max Staegemann. Inquiring about an announcement concerning the Leipzig production of Wagner's Ring des Nibelungen. (91) £2,200
— 26 Nov 1886. 2 pp, 8vo. To [Max Staegemann]. Requesting information about a newspaper report. (90) DM2,800
— [1886-1887]. 3 pp, 8vo. To his parents. Mentioning his financial affairs & conducting Die Meistersinger. (88) $2,400
— 16 Jan 1889. 1 p, 4to. To J. Wild. As director of the Budapest opera, requesting him to return a contract with Mila Kupfer-Berger's signature. (90) DM2,600
— [c.1892/94]. 2 pp, 8vo (lettercard). Recipient unnamed. About recipient's application for a position at Hamburg. (90) DM2,400
— 23 Dec 1896. 3 pp, 8vo. To Carl Goldmark. Expressing his desire to secure the post as Kapellmeister at the Vienna opera. Marill Estate. (89) $2,750
— 4 Jan 1897. 4 pp, 8vo. To Carl Goldmark. Discussing the prospects for his career & entreating him to promote his cause at Vienna. Marill Estate. (89) $3,000
— 12 Jan 1897. 4 pp, 8vo. To Carl Goldmark. About his wish to become conductor at Vienna & to perform Goldmark's operas. Marill Estate. (89) $2,500
— 14 Jan 1897. 1 p, 8vo. To Hermann Behn. Thanking for a loan, informing him about his journey to Dresden, & suggesting a meeting. (91) DM2,600
— [Mar 1897]. 4 pp, 8vo. To his sister Justine. About a concert in Munich, his songs & travels, etc. (90) £1,900
— [7 Apr 1897]. 1 p, 8vo (card). To Ludwig Karpath. Informing him of the imminent decision about the conductorship of the Vienna Opera. Marill Estate. (89) $1,400
— 11 Apr 1897. 3 pp, 4to. To Ludwig Karpath. Describing the circumstances of his appointment at Vienna. Marill Estate. (89) $3,000
— 15 Apr 1897. 1 p, 8vo. To Ludwig Karpath. Complaining about the treatment of his Vienna appointment in the local press. Marill Estate. (89) $1,500
— [Apr 1897]. 2 pp, 8vo. To Ludwig Karpath. Discussing the repertoire of the Vienna Opera at the beginning of his directorship. Marill Estate. (89) $3,000
— [c.1897]. 3 pp, 8vo. To Carl Goldmark. Thanking for congratulatory wishes & discussing the performance of Gold-

MAHLER

mark's operas. Marill Estate. (89) $2,750
— [after 1897]. (91) £1,000
— [25 May 1898]. 4 pp, 8vo. Recipient unknown. Discussing upcoming concerts & his plans for the next month. (88) $2,750
— [1 Aug 1898]. 2 pp, 8vo. To Nina Spiegler. Reporting that he has completed some songs to texts from Des Knaben Wunderhorn. (90) £1,400
— [c.1898]. 4 pp, 8vo. To [Carl Goldmark]. Discussing arrangements for the 1st performance of Goldmark's Die Kriegsgefangene. Marill Estate. (89) $1,900
— [n.d.]. (88) £900
— [after 1897]. 1 p, 8vo (lettercard). To Herr Schott. As Director of the Vienna Opera, returning a score. File holes. (88) DM1,200
— [6 Dec 1903]. Marill Estate. (89) $800
— [1904]. 1 p, 4to. To Alexander von Zemlinsky. Accepting the position of honorary president of the Vereinigung schaffender Tonkuenstler. (91) £1,300
— [1904]. 1 p, 4to. To Alexander von Zemlinsky. Accepting the position as honorary president of a society in Vienna. Ammann collection. (90) DM4,200
— 2 Mar 1905. 2 pp, 4to. To Ludwig Karpath. Explaining criteria used in selecting poems from Des Knaben Wunderhorn for musical setting. Marill Estate. (89) $3,250
— 7 Mar 1905. 2 pp, 12mo (card). To Ludwig Karpath. Angry reply to an article. Marill Estate. (89) $1,200
— [1907 or earlier]. 2 pp, 8vo (lettercard). To Max Kalbeck. Complimenting him on his new trans of a libretto. (91) DM2,600
— [8 May 1909]. 5 pp, 8vo. To Emil Freund. Requesting his help regarding a contract [with the NY Philharmonic Orchestra]. (88) DM4,200
— [c.Sept 1909]. 2 pp, 4to. To Emil Gutmann. Informing him about his travels & concert plans. (89) DM3,800
— 1 Jan 1910. 5 pp, 4to. To Guido Adler. Describing his activities in NY & his wife's important role in his life & career. (91) £4,000

AMERICAN BOOK PRICES CURRENT

— [n.d.]. 2 pp, 4to. To Ludwig Karpath. Acknowledging congratulations on his engagement to Alma Schindler. Marill Estate. (89) $1,400
— [n.d.]. 2 pp, 12mo (card). To Ludwig Karpath. Regarding his 5th, 6th & 7th Symphonies. Marill Estate. (89) $3,250
— [n.d.]. 2 pp, 8vo. To Franz Schalk. Informing him that he has engaged [Ferdinand?] Loewe. (90) £1,400
— [n.d.]. (90) £750
— [n.d.]. 2 pp, 8vo (lettercard). To Max Kalbeck. Hoping for closer relations. (90) DM2,400

Ls, 12 Mar 1889. Marill Estate. (89) $700

Autograph postcard, sgd, [29 Apr 1878]. (90) £550
— [15 Oct 1898]. To his sister Emma Rose. Sending congratulations on her birthday. (89) DM1,300
— 22 Feb [19]07. (88) £800
— [7 Oct 1907]. To his wife Alma. Greetings from Warsaw on his way to St. Petersburg. Sgd G. In pencil. (88) DM1,600

Collection of ANs & 3 autograph notes, [n.d.]. Marill Estate. (89) $800
— Collection of 2 A Ns s & autograph postcard, sgd, [n.d.]. 3 pp, 8vo. To Ludwig Karpath. Regarding appointments, etc. Partly initialled. Marill Estate. (89) $1,100

ANs, 18 June [18]97. Postscript on ALs by Natalie Bauer Lechner, 2 pp (card). To Ludwig Karpath. On operatic matters. With Ls by Mahler & ANs by Karpath. Marill Estate. (89) $1,700
— [n.d.]. 2 pp, 12mo. To Ludwig Karpath. Mentioning his 5th, 6th & 7th Symphonies. (90) $1,100
— [n.d.]. (90) £700

Series of 4 autograph notes, [n.d.]. Marill Estate. (89) $800

Ds, 28 Apr 1899. (89) £350
— 24 Jan 1902. 2 pp, folio. Contract with Edyth Walker, sgd as Director of the Vienna Opera. With related material. (88) DM2,000
— 21 Oct 1905. (90) £850
— 2 Mar 1906. (90) £950

Autograph quotation, O Roeschen roth, 3 bars from the 4th movement of his 2d Symphony, scored for voice & piano, [Apr 1899]. 1 p, 8vo. Sgd & inscr to

[Marcella Pregi]. (89) DM12,500
— Anr, opening 4 bars of his 5th Symphony, sgd & dated 11 Mar 1905. 1 p, 4to. (90) £7,500
Signature, [n.d.]. 55mm by 95mm (visiting card). (90) £1,800
— HELLMESBERGER, JOSEPH. - ALs, [Nov 1898]. 3 pp, 8vo. To Mahler. Explaining why he is leaving the Vienna Philharmonic Orchestra. (90) DM1,300

Mahler-Werfel, Alma, 1879-1964
Collection of 3 A Ls s & ANs, 1915 & 1916. (89) DM440
A Ls s (2), [c.1911]. (88) DM300
ALs, [1912]. (90) DM250
— [c.1930]. (89) DM500
— 6 May 1958. (89) DM280
Series of 5 autograph postcards, sgd, 21 Apr 1949 to 7 May 1960. (88) DM420
Autograph postcard, sgd, [n.d.]. (91) DM360

Maillol, Aristide, 1861-1944
ALs, [n.d.]. (88) DM550

Maine
[North Yarmouth. - A collection of 20 documents, 1745 to 1791, mostly relating to North Yarmouth, sold at rf on 12 Mar, lot 22, for $325.]

Maine, Louis Auguste de Bourbon, Duc du, 1670-1736
Ds s (2)19 Oct 1700 & 6 Apr 1705. Byer collection. (90) $120

Maintenon, Francoise d'Aubigne, Marquise de, 1635-1719
ALs, [3 Feb 1698]. (91) DM750
— 8 Oct [1716]. (88) $250
AL, [7 Dec 1660]. 5 pp, 4to. To her uncle de Villette. Reporting about her efforts to obtain a pension, mentioning a new comedy about the King's wedding, etc. Sgd with paraph. (90) DM1,350
Ds, 22 Apr 1713. (90) DM700

Maitland Family
[A box of 19th-cent trust & estate papers of Joseph & other members of the Maitland family of Barcaple & Valleyfield, Kirkcudbright, Scotland, several hundred items, sold at pn on 22 Mar 1990, lot 26, for £100 to Badman.]

Malcolm, Pulteney, Sir, 1768-1838. See: Napoleon I

Malesherbes, Chretien Guillaume de Lamoignon de, 1721-94
Collection of ALs, A Ls (drafts), & reading notes, [n.d.]. (88) £100

Malibran, Maria Felicia, 1808-36
ALs, 26 Mar 1829. (91) £500

Malipiero, Gian Francesco, 1882-1972
ALs, 8 Apr 1961. (90) DM320

Mallarme, Stephane, 1842-98
ALs, [n.d.]. (90) DM440

Mallory, Stephen Russell, 1813-73
ALs, 8 Feb 1854. (91) $60

Malraux, Andre, 1901-76
Collection of 17 A Ls s & Ls s, [c.1929] to 1932. (91) £850

Malta
— COMMISSION DES DOMAINES NATIONAUX. - Ms, letterbook, [31 July 1798 to 7 Feb 1800]; c.200 pp, folio, in modern bdg. Copies of proclamations & letters regarding Malta. (88) £200

Malthus, Thomas Robert, 1766-1834
ALs, 19 June 1815. 2 pp, 4to. To the pbr John Murray. Informing him that he may rewrite some chapters of his Essay on Population, & inquiring about prices in America. (89) £4,400
— 28 Nov 1816. 2 pp, 8vo. To Mrs. Smith. Inviting her daughters to a dance. (88) £1,350
— 23 Oct 1825. 4 pp, 4to. To Charles Butler. About the valuation of currency at different historical periods. (91) £8,000
— GODWIN, WILLIAM. - ALs, 15 Aug 1798. 1 p, 4to. To Thomas Robert Malthus. Discussing population. (91) £4,500
— LAMB, LADY CAROLINE. - 3 A Ls s, [n.d.]. 6 pp, 4to. To Malthus. Seeking his confidential advice on a novel & referring to Jane Austen's Pride and Prejudice. (91) £1,200

MAMET

Mamet, David
Typescript, screenplay, The Untouchables, Feb 1986. (91) £900

Mandelstam, Osip, 1891-1938
Autograph Ms, denunciation of the official Soviet writers' organization, draft; [c.1930]. 1 p, 8vo. Sgd. (91) £2,000

Manet, Edouard, 1832-83
ALs, [n.d.]. 1 p, 8vo. To an unnamed lady. Saying he has hurt his leg & hoping she will come to see him. (89) DM1,900
— [n.d.]. (88) DM750
— [n.d.]. 1 p, 8vo. Recipient unnamed. Asking to see him. (90) DM1,300
Ds, [after 1881]. (89) £550
See also: Zola, Emile

Mankiewicz, Herman J., 1897-1953
[Carbon copies of his scripts Citizen Kane, & The American, partly annotated, in 1 vol, [1940], 11 by 8.5 inches, with other scripts by Mankiewicz & further related material, sold at CNY on 21 June 1989, lot 369, for $21,000.]

Mankowitz, Wolf
[A large collection of c.100 working film scripts, with related material, 1954 to 1983, some thousands of pages in 8 boxes, sold at S on 19 July 1990, lot 326, for £4,200 to Rota.]
Typescript, working film scripts for Casino Royale, 1965 & 1966. About 900 pp, 4to. Partly cyclostyled; with autograph revisions. Including related material. (90) £2,200
— Typescript, working film scripts for Dr. No, 7 Sept to 1 Nov 1961. About 370 pp, 4to. Partly cyclostyled. Including related material. (90) £2,500
— Typescript, working film scripts for The Tragical History of Doctor Faustus, 14 Apr to 13 Aug 1966. (90) £500
— Typescript, working film scripts for The Millionairess, 8 May 1961 & later. (90) £400

Manley, Mary de la Riviere, 1663-1724
ALs, [2? Nov 1709]. (88) £980

AMERICAN BOOK PRICES CURRENT

Mann, Erika, 1905-69
ALs, [n.d.]. (90) DM280

Mann, Heinrich, 1871-1950
Autograph Ms, article dealing with his life & his concepts as an author, [c.1930]. 3 pp, 4to. Sgd. In French. (91) DM1,700
— Autograph Ms, lecture concerning "den Begriff des Europaeischen Denkens"; [n.d.]. 2 pp, 4to. Slightly stained. (88) DM1,100
— Autograph Ms, poem, Wegrast, 14 Aug [18]91. 2 pp, 8vo. 5 stanzas, sgd & inscr to his mother. (91) DM1,700
ALs, 18 Jan 1928. (89) DM280
— 19 June 1930. (90) DM320
— 14 Nov 1948. (88) DM700

Mann, Horace, 1796-1859
ALs, 28 July 1843. (91) $650
— 2 Mar 1844. (91) $130

Mann, Klaus, 1906-49
Typescript carbon copy, essay, Selbstmoerder. 5 pp, 4to. Sgd at head & dated 16 Sept 1930. Some autograph corrections. (89) DM1,100
Series of 3 A Ls s, 5 & 17 Mar 1926 & [n.d.]. (89) DM750
ALs, 21 Aug 1927. (89) DM480

Mann, Thomas, 1875-1955
Autograph Ms, broadcast to Germany, 15 Jan 1943. 2 pp, 4to. Sgd & inscr at end, 3 Apr 1943. (91) DM8,500
— Autograph Ms, essay on Franz Kafka's Das Schloss, sgd & dated June 1940. 10 pp, 4to, in folder. With numerous autograph revisions. Laughlin collection. (89) $30,000
Collection of ALs & autograph postcard, sgd, 6 June 1908 & 30 Nov 1910. (88) DM950
— Collection of ALs & ANs, 29 Jan & 5 Feb 1912. (90) £850
— Collection of ALs, ANs, telegram, & 2 autograph postcards, sgd, 24 Feb 1914 to 23 Nov 1919. 7 pp, 8vo. To Josef Hofmiller. Responding to Hofmiller's comments about Tod in Venedig, Tonio Kroeger, & Betrachtungen. Postcards to Hulda Eggart; contents not stated. (88) DM2,000
— Collection of 8 A Ls s & 4 autograph postcards, sgd, 17 Apr 1916 to 22 Nov

1919. 17 pp, 4to & 8vo, & cards. To Max Krell. Interesting letters about a variety of literary & political matters. (90) DM11,000
— Collection of 2 A Ls s, autograph postcard, sgd, & ANs, 23 Dec 1919 to 7 June 1925. 4 pp, 8vo, & 2 cards. To Wilhelm Schneider. Mostly concerning a contribution to an anthology. With related material. (89) DM2,800
— Collection of 7 A Ls s, Ls & postcard, sgd, 21 Apr 1933 to 15 June 1955. 15 pp, various sizes. To Willi Schuh. Interesting correspondence dealing with a variety of literary matters. (91) DM12,000
— Collection of 3 A Ls s & 2 Ls s, 19 Jan 1949 to 18 Mar 1952. 8 pp, folio & 8vo. To Hans Wolff. Interesting literary letters discussing his own & Wolff's work. (90) DM8,500

A Ls s (2), 28 Mar 1909 & 7 June 1910. (91) DM1,000
— A Ls s (2), 19 Mar & 16 May 1954. 4 pp, 8vo. To an unnamed young lady. About a radio version of Koenigliche Hoheit. Commenting on her Ms. (88) DM1,400

ALs, 3 July 1902. 1 p, 8vo. To an unnamed Ed. Inquiring about the publication of his novella Tristan. (90) DM2,200
— 5 Dec 1903. 4 pp, 8vo. To the pbr W. Opitz. Musing about letter writing in the past, & nmentioning Tonio Kroeger. (88) DM1,500
— 7 Oct 1909. 2 pp, 8vo. To Emil Grimm. Concerning the publication of a review of his novel Koenigliche Hoheit. (91) DM1,800
— 11 Mar 1910. 4 pp, 8vo. To Max Herrmann. Suggesting he approach a proper playwright for a play to be performed [on the centenary of the Berlin university]. (91) DM1,800
— 24 June 1910. (91) DM600
— 29 May 1919. 4 pp, 4to. To [Adolf] von Grolman. Referring to his literary projects & recipient's lectures about his works. (91) DM2,200
— 20 Sept 1924. 3 pp, 8vo. To [Jo van Ammers-Kueller]. Praising her Ms. (89) DM1,300
— 16 Aug 1926. 1 p, 8vo. To Hans Wolffheim. Commenting about an essay comparing himself & Stefan George. (89) DM1,400
— 4 Jan [19]27. (88) $250
— 22 Feb 1929. (89) DM460
— 26 Feb 1929. (88) DM500
— 17 Jan 1936. (90) DM420
— 20 Dec 1937. (88) DM480
— 29 July 1940. (89) DM950
— 20 Sept 1942. 1 p, 8vo. To Ernst Gottlieb. Returning a questionnaire & asking for copies of photographs. Initialled. With 37 photographs of the Mann family & further related material. (88) DM2,000
— 20 Oct 1945. 2 pp, 8vo. To Ernst Marx. About the impossibility to suit everybody, misprints in a Swedish Ed, etc. (88) DM1,600
— 17 Nov 1945. (89) $200
— 17 Nov 1946. 3 pp, 8vo. To Rudolf Schick. Praising Fritz von Unruh. (90) DM2,700
— 31 Mar [19]48. 2 pp, 8vo. To Professor S. Singer. Thanking for a trans & commenting on public affairs. (91) DM2,100
— 10 Oct 1950. 2 pp, 8vo. To Joachim Maass. About his lecture Meine Zeit, his meetings with Hermann Hesse, etc. (90) DM2,000
— 30 Oct 1950. 4 pp, 8vo. To Seiji Takahashi. Declining to write an article for Japanese journals, & suggesting an essay for trans. (89) DM2,800
— 27 Jan 1953. 2 pp, 4to. To William Matheson. Confirming arrangements for a meeting, & commenting about his handwriting; in 2 different scripts. (90) DM3,000
— 13 May 1953. 1 p, 8vo. To William Matheson. Commenting on a special Ed of a chapter of Bekenntnisse des Hochstaplers Felix Krull. (90) DM1,500
— 17 Apr [19]54. 2 pp, 8vo. To Ludwig Marcuse. Discussing Schopenhauer. (90) DM2,400
— 17 June 1954. 4 pp, 8vo. To Juergen Ernestus. Defending Death in Venice against the charge of immorality. (91) £4,400
— 8 July 1954. 2 pp, 8vo. Recipient unnamed. Responding to a reader's

MANN

comments on Buddenbrooks. With related material. (89) DM1,700
Collection of 2 Ls s & postcard, sgd, 22 July 1930 to 8 July 1936. (90) $350
Ls, 10 Jan 1926. (88) DM560
— 22 Aug [19]30. (90) $900
— 13 July 1931. (90) DM520
— 18 May 1932. (88) DM640
— 15 Nov 1932. (89) DM480
— 5 Nov [19]33. (90) $250
— 11 Nov [19]38. (91) DM950
— 15 Dec 1939. (91) DM420
— 23 Oct 1940. 2 pp, 4to. To Franz J. Horch. Concerning stage rights for his novel Lotte in Weimar. (90) DM1,050
— 14 Dec 1940. (90) $800
— 4 July 1947. (91) DM380
— 7 Nov 1947. (91) DM1,000
— 7 Dec 1949. (88) DM420
— 21 Dec 1954. (91) DM400
Collection of 2 autograph postcards, sgd & photograph, sgd & inscr, 10 Nov 1924 to 20 Nov 1926. Barrett collection. (89) $900
Autograph postcard, sgd, 20 Apr 1924. (91) DM600
— 3 Oct 1936. (89) DM380
ANs, 1 Jan 1948. 1 p, 8vo. To Professor S. Singer. Expressing thanks & praising recipient's work. On verso of photograph of his house. (91) DM1,100
— 9 Dec 1950. (91) DM420
Ns s, June 1935 & 8 June 1950. (90) DM320
Ns, 8 June 1950. (90) DM380
— [n.d.]. (91) $175
Ds, 27 July 1944. (88) DM380
Photograph, sgd, 1905. (90) DM750
— Anr, [n.d.]. (89) DM530
Photograph, sgd & inscr, [c.1930?]. (90) DM660
— MAJOR, HENRY. - Orig drawing, pencil sketch of Mann, sgd; [c.1930]. 190mm by 115mm. Also sgd & inscr by Mann. With anr. (90) $500
See also: Einstein, Albert

Mannerheim, Carl Gustaf Emil, Baron, 1867-1951
Ls, 13 Aug 1938. (88) DM400

Manning, Henry Edward, Cardinal, 1808-92
Series of 9 A Ls s, 16 Mar 1847, 6 Sept 1850 [& various dates]. 19 pp, 8vo. To the Rev. Arthur Baker & other recipients. Referring to the problem of Royal Supremacy, & about other matters. With related material. Doheny collection. (89) $1,100
— Series of 11 A Ls s, 6 Aug 1847 to 17 May 1891. 25 pp, 8vo. To Edward Walford (6) & other recipients. Acknowledging gifts & correspondence. Doheny collection. (89) $1,300

Mansfield, Jayne
Photograph, sgd & inscr, [c.1962]. (88) $110
Signature, [n.d.]. (90) $170

Mansfield, Joseph K. F., 1803-62
ADs, 22 Apr 1862. (91) $300

Mansfield, Katherine, 1888-1923
Collection of 14 A Ls s & 3 autograph postcards, sgd, 23 June 1921 to 3 Oct 1922. 34 pp, 4to & 8vo. To William Gerhardi. Providing advice & constructive criticism regarding recipient's novel Futility, but also referring to her own work. With related material. Bradley Martin sale. (90) $9,000
A Ls s (2), 30 [July?] & 21 [Aug?] 1821. 8 pp, 8vo & 4to. To J. Ruddick, thanking for 2 childhood photographs (included). To her sisters Chaddie & Jeanne, about Mr. Ruddick's photographs & describing her life in Switzerland; sgd K. With related material. (90) $1,800
— A Ls s (2), 18 Mar & 30 Sept 1922. 8 pp, 4to & 12mo. To her father Harold Beauchamp. About their relationship, her success as a writer, plans to continue her medical treatment in Paris, etc. Sgd Kass. With typed transcripts. (90) $2,800
ALs, 3 Jan 1908. 4 pp, 8vo. To her sister Vera. Expressing disappointment at her parents' refusal to allow her to live in London. Sgd K. With typed transcript. (90) $1,800
— 12 & 13 Mar 1908. 5 pp, 8vo. To her sister Vera. Deploring the lack of culture in New Zealand & reporting that she has finished a book. Sgd K.

1987 - 1991 • AUTOGRAPHS & MANUSCRIPTS

With typed transcript. (90) $1,800

**Mansfield, Katherine, 1888-1923 —&
Murry, John Middleton, 1889-1957**
[2 A Ls s by Mansfield, & 18 A Ls s & Ls by Murry, 1921 to 1929, 30 pp, to Orlo Williams, about her work, her health problems, his life with Mansfield, etc., sold at S on 13 Dec 1990, lot 271, for £2,000 to Silverman.]

Mansion, Colard, fl.1450-84. See: Penitence...

Manstein, Erich von Lewinski, 1887-1973
Collection of ALs & photograph, sgd, 18 Dec [n.y.]. (90) DM480

Manstein, Erich von Lewinski, 1887-1973
Collection of 6 A Ls s, 16 Ls s, & 8 postcards, sgd (3 autograph), 1952 to 1963. Length not stated, 8vo & 4to. To Adolf Spemann. Regarding the publication of his memoirs, books about the war, Hitler, Churchill, etc. With related material. (88) DM1,200

Manteuffel, Edwin, Freiherr von, 1809-85
ALs, 17 Apr 1870. Schroeder collection. (89) DM250

Manteuffel, Otto, Freiherr von, 1805-82
ALs, 13 Sept 1858. Schroeder collection. (89) DM220
— 15 Oct 1870. Schroeder collection. (89) DM220

Mantle, Mickey
Photograph, sgd, [n.d.]. (88) $225

**Mantle, Mickey —&
Stengel, Casey**
Group photograph, [n.d.]. (91) $400

Manuel I, King of Portugal, 1469-1521
Ds, 1502. 1 p, folio; vellum. Order to Don Diogno de Noronha to pay an annual pension to Don Diego Meneses. Slightly def. (89) DM1,400

Manutius, Paulus, 1512-74. See: Pius IV, 1499-1565

Manzoni, Alessandro, 1785-1873
ALs, 29 Apr 1859. (89) £700

MAPS & CHARTS

Maps & Charts
Ms, Atlas. [Korea, late 17th cent]. 15 leaves of mulberry rind paper in concertina form, 320mm by 200mm. With 14 double-page maps of the world, China, Japan, etc. in india ink, partly with colored wash. Mostly in Chinese, with some marginal comments in Korean. (90) DM14,000

— Ms, Atlas. [Korea, late 17th cent]. 13 leaves of mulberry rind paper, 360mm by 175mm. With 12 double-page maps of the world, China, Japan, etc. in india ink & colored wash. In Chinese. (90) DM13,000

— Ms, Atlas, Planos particulares que por jornadas representan a la larga, la direccion, y figura de la carretera de Andalucia nuevamente abierta asta Cadiz. [Spain, late 18th cent]. 12 sectional road maps in ink & colors, 26cm by 40cm, in contemp tree calf gilt. (91) £2,800

— Ms, chart covering the Arabian Gulf region from Syria to Yemen. [Ottoman, early 17th cent]. 8 double-folio sheets, joined in strip form, overall size 430mm by 3435mm. In inks & colors. Showing main caravan routes; not drawn to scale. Marquess of Downshire collection. (90) £16,000

— Ms, map of the Guianas region. [England, c.1596]. 335mm by 472mm, vellum, in sunk mount in mor gilt bdg by Riviere. In rich inks & colors. With large & small compass roses, coastlines in red or sepia, rivers & lake in blue, & mountains in sepia. (91) £35,000

— Ms, Plan de las Misiones Jesuitas y del paso por tierra de la California..., [Mexico, c.1760s]. Vellum, 370mm by 263mm. In ink & colors. (91) £32,000

— Ms, Plan du Champ de Bataille de Waterloo dit de la Belle Alliance. [N.d.]. 640mm by 970mm, linen-backed. (91) £2,000

— Ms, plan of Lake Como & the course of the River Adda from the Valtellina to Cassano. [Milan, 1st half of 17th cent]. 6 sheets, 460mm by 660mm each. In sepia ink & colors, the river accurately drawn with obstacles to navigation, & towns & hills in bird's eye perspective. (90) £6,000

— Ms, plan of the town & harbor of

Dover, incorporating proposal for sea defences, 22 Nov 1552. 2 joined sheets of vellum, maximum dimensions 670mm by 1650mm, in buckram cylinder by Sangorski. Bird's eye plan, in pencil, ink & colors. With accompanying 1-page petition from the town of Dover to Edward VI. (90) £8,500

— Ms, Portolan chart of Europe & North Africa. [Italy or Sicily, after 1564]. Vellum, maximum dimensions 580mm by 890mm. In black ink; coastlines in sepia. With 6 large compass roses, 3 scale bars, & 40 town vignettes. Skilfully restored. (89) £9,000

— Ms, portolan chart of the Mediterranean, including Atlantic Islands, British Isles, Black Sea & North Africa, [Genoa, c.1460-80]. 66cm by 120cm, vellum. With coastlines in brown, red or green, c.1,500 place names in a neat gothic rotunda script, 4 scale bars, rhumb-lines from 20 compass points, 8 colored wind disks & 10 town vignettes. Collection of the Counts of Maldeghem. (88) £260,000

— Ms, portolan chart of Western Europe & North Africa, [Netherlands, c.1580]. 89cm by 73cm, vellum. With coastlines in sepia ink & colors, 7 full or half colored compass-roses, rhumb-lines in green & red, 2 decorative scale bars, & 15 colored flags & shields. Small dampstains; tie holes. Collection of the Counts of Maldeghem. (88) £30,000

— Ms, portolan chart of the Mediterranean. [Venice, c.1460-70]. 355mm by 590mm, vellum. Divided into 6 small insets, each 143mm by 143mm, with double ruled borders & local scale-bars inset. With coastlines & minor place names in sepia, major ports in red; decorated with 31 flags & large town vignette of Venice. 5 small sections restored with modern vellum. (89) £17,000

— Ms, world chart on a Mercator-type projection. [England, 1615-1618?]. 400mm by 812mm, on a single sheet of vellum. With coastlines in green, red & orange, major place names mostly in Latin, equator & tropics rules in red. Possibly executed for Henry Percy, Earl of Northumberland. (91) £60,000

— Ms, Zhili sheng Yicang tu; 13 maps of the relief granaries in Zhili Province in ink & colors, each with facing text; [China, c.1800?]. Phillipps MS.10856 & Robinson collection. (89) £850

— AGNESE, BATTISTA. - Ms, Portolan Atlas, [Venice, 5 Feb 1544]. 16 leaves (7 bifolia & 2 blank leaves pasted together back to back), vellum, 293mm by 216mm. Contemp Venetian reddish-brown goldstamped mor over wooden bds, with compass under glass inset inside lower cover. In various colors of ink. With placenames in Latin, Italian & Spanish in a small humanistic minuscule. Containing 10 double-page maps, each with windrose in gold & colored ink. Doheny collection. (88) £600,000

— AGNESE, BATTISTA. - Ms, portolan atlas. [Venice, c.1535-38]. 7 double-page maps, each on a single double-paged sheet glued back to back, vellum, 398mm by 285mm. Repaired contemp Venetian dark brown goatskin over wooden bds. In various colors of ink, with placenames in brown & red by at least 2 scribes in a small gothic bookhand. Most maps with decorative compass rose; 2 city vignettes. Ludwig MS.XIII.15. (89) £230,000

— ALSOP, W. - Ms, Plan of an Estate Situate in Lowton in the Parish of Winwick [Lancashire]... the Property of H. Stirrup; [late 18th cent]. 11.75 by 16 inches, vellum. In pen, ink & gray wash; including cartouche. (90) £95

— [BECCARI, BATTISTA?]. - Ms, portolan chart of the Mediterranean, including Atlantic Islands, British Isles, Black Sea & North Africa. [Genoa, 2d quarter of 15th cent]. 66cm by 117cm, vellum. With coastlines in brown, red or green, c.1,500 place names in a neat gothic rotunda script, 4 scale bars, rhumb lines from 20 compass points, 8 colored wind disks & 10 town vignettes. (90) £240,000

— BOYM, MICHAL PIOTR. - Ms, Zhongguo Tu [Map of the Middle Kingdom, c.1652]. 5 joined sheets of paper, 1490mm by 1600mm, on roll. In ink & color, with Chinese characters probably in the hand of Andreas Che. Including 4 drawings. Phillipps MS.1986 & Robinson collection. (89)

£60,000
— BRANSBY, JOHN. - Ms, Plan of an Estate in Claydon, Suffolk. The Property of The Corporation of Ipswich...; 1813. 19.5 by 26 inches. In pen-&-ink, outlined in colored washes. With related material. (90) £100
— BRETTARGH, E. - Ms, A Plan of the Road from Rochdale to Edenfield [Lancashire] with the intended diversions for a turnpike, Oct 1793. 86 by 15 inches. In pen-&-ink. (90) £90
— CARNEGIE, DAVID. - Map Shewing Country North of Coolgardie including all the Mining Centres and Lake Darlot. 1895. 870mm by 610mm, on cloth with wooden rollers. With lakes marked in green & with red compass points. Sgd & dated by Carnegie. (89) £6,400
— CATTERMOLE, W. - Ms, Plan of an Estate at Scole in Norfolk, the property of John Ayton; 1832. 110cm by 113cm. In pen, ink & colors. Including 3 pencil vignettes. (91) £400
— CHAPMAN, ROBERT. - Ms, A map ... of the ... Estate belonging to Mr George Paman, situate in Wickhambrooke, Suffolk, 1758. 91cm by 113cm. In pen, ink & wash. With farms & houses in bird's-eye perspective, & decorative compass rose. (91) £400
— CHINA. - Ms, A Draft of the Ladroon Islands on the Coast of China near the Mouth of the River Canton. [England?, c.1680] 649mm by 972mm, hand-colored in wash & outline. (90) £3,200
— CONSAG, FERNANDO. - Ms, Seno de la Bahia de la Paz en la California..., [Mexico, June 1739]. 275mm by 275mm, in 18th-cent marbled bds. In inks & colors. (91) £17,000
— DARLINGTON. - Ms, plan of property belonging to the Friends in the Township of Darlington in the County of Durham, 1849, surveyed by J. Sowerby. 100cm by 132cm. In pen & watercolors. Linen-backed paper. (88) £900
— EVERENDEY[?], ANTHONY. - Ms, A Survay and ground plot of Cartaine Landes ... in the Parish of Mayfield ... and being Parcell of the Possessions of Mr St[e]phen Parker, 1640. Size not stated, vellum. Mtd. (89) £190
— GARGRAVE, GEORGE. - Ms, A Map of ... Listers Farm, near Leeds in Yorkshire, being part of the Estate of Nicholas Torre; 1741. 20 by 22 inches, vellum. In pen-&-ink with colored wash outlines. Dampstained. (90) £320
— HACK, WILLIAM. - Ms, maritime chart of Valdivia on the coast of Chile, sgd; [3 May 1694 - 1 Dec 1697]. 27 by 31.5 inches. In colored washes. Including sailing instructions; dedicated to William Trumbull as Secretary of State. Marquess of Downshire collection. (90) £22,000
— HARO, P. - Ms, Plan de las Misones de Jesuitas de Arizpe y de sus curatos en la Provincia de la Sonora..., [Arizpe, Sonora, 1755]. 255mm by 403mm, on tissue, tipped onto contemp paper. In inks & colors. (91) £6,000
— HUNT, C. - Ms, A Map of two Estates called Heathersomes and Palmers both in the Parish of Hartfield [Sussex], 4 Dec 1789. 30 by 41 inches. In pen-&-ink with colored washes. (90) £480
— JAMAICA. - Ms, Plan du Port Royal de la Jamaique old Harbour et ses environs. [France, c.1782?]. 3 joined sheets, 925mm by 1650mm. In ink & colors. (91) £3,000
— JONES, EDWARD. - Ms, plan of Cefn Manor, Denbighshire, Wales, 1841. 15 by 11.5 inches. (90) £40
— LATON, THOMAS. - Ms, portolan chart of England, the North Sea, Scandinavia & the Baltic, sgd & dated Danzig 1588. 52cm by 55cm, vellum. With coastlines in green & brown, 8 full or half compass-roses, rhumb-lines in red & green, 3 scale bars (2 with elaborate ornamentation), 8 flags & 3 armorial shields. Collection of the Counts of Maldeghem. (88) £52,000
— LEWIS, CAPT. G. - Coast of Africa from Table at the Cape of Good Hope to Saldanha Bay. [c.1799] 255mm by 710mm, ink & wash. (89) £3,000
— LEWIS, CAPT. G. - The Musenberg Mountains, Table Mountain & Devils Hill, as they appear from the middle of the Isthmus between Table Bay & Musenberg. 1799. 240mm by 1,120mm. Holed. (89) £1,300
— MACAO. - Ms, Plan contenant depuis

MAPS & CHARTS

les iles Sanchoam Macao jusques a l'isle de Leme avec l'entree de la bouche du Tigre pour aller a Canton, [c. 1760]. 54cm by 75.5cm. Coastal navigational chart; in watercolor. (91) HK15,000

— MARTINES, JOAN. - Portolan atlas. [Messina, c.1582-90]. 7 leaves (2 blank), vellum, comprising 1 half-page & 4 double-page maps; double-page sheet size 345mm by 560mm, in def wraps. With coastlines in black with maroon wash, islands in red, blue, green or gold, numerous compass roses heightened in gold, many flags, mountains, trees or animals, & 17 town vignettes. 2 sheets detached. (89) £38,000

— MUSSELBURGH, SCOTLAND. - Ms, Plan of Ground lying at Magdalene Bridge, Parish of Inveresk for J. Wanchope of Edmonstone 1809; c.21 by 13 inches. On linen-backed paper. (90) £110

— NORTHAMPTONSHIRE. - Survey of the Forest of Whittlewood... by Richard Davis, 1787. 79cm by 194cm. In pen & ink & watercolors. Linen-backed paper. (88) £800

— ROMANO, N. - Portolan chart of the Tyrrhenian Sea region of the Mediterranean. [Massa Lubrense?], 1576. 535mm by 743mm, on vellum, sgd & dated. In sepia, with blue, green, yellow, red & reddish brown. (90) £3,200

— ROSELLI, PETRUS. - Ms, portolan chart of Europe, North Africa & the Near East, sgd & dated 1469. 111cm by 66cm, vellum. With 18 radiating points with rhumb-lines of red & green, coastlines in various colors, emblazoned shields of many countries, 9 town views, 4 wind discs, 5 distance scales & thousands of placenames in a small gothic bookhand. 1 corner def. Framed. Ludwig MS.XIII.14. (89) £150,000

— ROUSSIN, AUGUSTIN. - Ms, portolan atlas of the Mediterranean, sgd & dated 1630. 3 sheets of vellum mtd on paper, 386mm by 575mm. With coastlines & rhumblines in sepia & red, islands in green, blue, red & gold, place names in a Provencal dialect, 5 large scale bars, 4 compass roses & 8 wind roses, & 12 town vignettes. 1 margin torn. (90) £23,000

— SHACKLETON, SIR ERNEST H. - Map of Antarctica, 1918. In blue & red crayon on paper, with several tracks relating to the expedition of 1914-1916. 1,415mm by 935mm. Inscr by Shackleton to D. D. Hirst, 27 Nov 1918. (91) £7,000

— SONGJIANG PREFECTURE. - Ms, Mappa Christianitatis Duarum Urbium In Provincia Nankinensi ..., [Sunkiang, 1661-1725]. 1340mm by 1390mm, in half mor box. In ink & colors on native paper. With legends in Chinese & annotations in a contemp European hand. Mtd. Phillipps MS.1986 & Robinson collection. (89) £15,000

— STAFFORDSHIRE. - Ms, A Map of the Autherley Estate in the Parish of Tetnall ... Surveyd by John Lewis 1773. 27 by 33 inches. In grey washes. (90) £220

— SURREY. - Ms, Plan of an Estate ... in the Parish of Streatham ... belonging to John Cross Crooke & others; surveyed by John Willock, 1780. 43 by 37 inches. With later survey, 1835. (90) £360

— SURREY. - Ms, plan of Blake Hall Farm in the Parishes of Streatham & Lambeth; surveyed by John Wollock, 1780. 21 by 25 inches. In 3 colors of ink. (90) £200

— SUSSEX. - Ms, A Map of a Farm called Boardright lying at Hartfield... the Property of Mrs. Anne Dyke; [late 18th cent]. 18 by 20 inches, vellum. In pen-&-ink. (90) £200

— TEIXEIRA ALBERNAZ I, JOAO. - Ms, portolan chart of the Americas, Africa & Europe, [Portugal, c.1620-80]. Sgd "Feita por [...] Alvernas". 765mm by 945mm, vellum. With coastlines in green & sepia heightened with gold, 5 colored compass-roses surmounted by decorative fleur-de-lys, 3 scale bars (2 with religious figures), 27 illuminated flags & shields, 4 views of trading posts & Golgotha, & area of South America filled with mountains, trees & rivers. Collection of the Counts of Maldeghem. (88) £300,000

— TEIXEIRA, LUIS. - Ms, portolan chart of Western Europe & North Africa, sgd

& dated 1578. 69cm by 61cm, vellum. With coastlines in sepia ink & colors, 5 colored & ornamented compass-roses heightened in gold, rhumb-lines in green & red, 3 decorative scale bars, & 14 colored flags & shields, 3 heightened in gold. Collection of the Counts of Maldeghem. (88) £130,000

— VERSAILLES. - 7 Mss, Plants de quelque Piesce de Trianon. [c.1720?]. 7 double pp, folio, in brown calf with the arms of Louis XV. Showing various parts of the park; in a single hand. (88) FF170,000

— VESPUCCI, GIOVANNI. - Portolan Chart of the Mediterranean & Atlantic Coasts of Europe. Seville, 1520. 670mm by 890mm, at maximum, on vellum, sgd & dated. Unrecorded. Extends from the Black Sea in the east to the Cape Verde Islands, Azores & the Baltic. Coastlines in Sepia & green wash; place names in red & black; islands in red, blue & gold; rhumblines in sepia, red & green. England, Scotland & Ireland decorated with heraldic arms. Cities in other places represented by a uniform stamp of a turreted town, colored in green & red; flags over Crimea, Madeira & the Canaries. (90) £130,000

— WALES. - Ms, pen-&-ink map of Wales, 1626. 26.5 by 29 inches, on 2 skins of vellum. Including illuminated coats-of-arms. (91) £340

— WATERS, STEPHEN. - Ms, plan of Wood Farm in the Parish of Cowden [Kent], belonging to Frances & Abigail Jordan; 1810. 18 by 18 inches, on wooden baton. In pen-&-ink & colored washes. (90) £260

— WHITPAINE, ROBERT. - Ms, A perfect Survay of Eiringham farme lying in the parish of Shoreham in the County of Sussex now belonging to Charles Tufton; sgd & dated 1687. 2 joined sheets of vellum, 138cm by 70cm. In ink & wash, with elaborate cartouche & compass rose. Decorated with shepherd & flocks, etc. (90) £1,050

— WILLIAMSON, JAMES. - Ms, trade album containing 16 orig watercolor & sepia specimen maps & plans of estates & towns in Ireland, 1785 to 1793, with calligraphic tp & 7 ornamental advertisements; 25 pp, 4to, in red mor gilt. With related material. (88) £6,000

— WILTSHIRE. - Ms, Admeasurement and Plan of Studley Farm situate in the Parish of Liddiard-Treygoze, 1807. 18 by 26 inches; canvas-backed paper. In pen-&-ink & colored washes; annotated in a later hand. (90) £140
See also: Lee, Robert E.
See also: William of Conches

Marat, Jean Paul, 1744-93

[663 parts of L'Ami du Peuple & 84 parts of Journal de la Republique francaise, with copious autograph annotations, & 21 political pamphlets, 1789 to 1794, in 12 early 19th-cent half green calf vols, 8vo, sold at S on 20 Nov 1990, lot 463, for £50,000 to the Bibliotheque Nationale.]

Autograph Ms, attack on the King's veto against decisions of the National Assembly; [1791]. 1 p, 8vo, cut from larger leaf. Def; silked. With a port. (90) DM3,200

ALs, [1779?]. 1 p, 4to. To [the secretary of the Academie des Sciences?]. Submitting his work Experiences sur le Feu. With related material. (91) £2,000

Marc, Franz, 1880-1916

Autograph postcard, sgd, 12 June 1912. To Walter Helbig. Sending pictures [for an exhibition]. (90) DM3,200

Marchesinus, Joannes

Ms, Mammotrectus. [Italy, early 14th cent]. 188 leaves, vellum, 125mm by 97mm, in [contemp?] limp vellum using a leaf of a canon law Ms. In brown ink in a small cursive bookhand. With c.36 large decorated initials & large historiated inital. (88) £3,500

— Ms, Mamotrectus expositorum vocabulorum super Bibliam. [Ansbach, Germany, c.1425]. 272 leaves, 422mm by 296mm. Extra blind-stamped contemp lea over wooden bds; somewhat def. In a regular early lettre batarde by Peter Burckhard. (89) DM105,000

MARCIANO

Marciano, Rocky, 1923-69
Autograph Ms, commonplace & address book, including thoughts on boxing; [c.1967]. 26 pp, 4to, in spiral notebook. (91) $4,000
— Autograph Ms, date book for 1967, 200 pp, 8vo. (91) $400
ALs, 28 Nov 1948. (91) $400
— [Dec 1948]. (91) $250
— [Summer 1949], "Thursday". (91) $650
— [Summer 1949]. (91) $300
— 7 Mar [1950]. 2 pp, 8vo. To Barbara Cousens. Referring to legal problems & requesting pictures for Life Magazine. (91) $1,600
— [1954?]. (91) $300
AL, [26 Dec 1949]. (91) $750
Autograph postcard, sgd, 4 Sept 1948. (91) $350
— 6 Aug 1949. (91) $300
— [31 May 1950]. (91) $160
Ds, 15 Sept 1964. (91) $750
— 28 Mar 1968. (91) $200
— 2 May 1968. (91) $625
— 27 May 1968. (91) $160
— 31 July 1968. (91) $160
— 25 Nov 1968. (91) $180
— 27 Jan 1969. (91) $400
— 24 Feb 1969. (91) $600

Marcks, Gerhard, 1889-1981
ALs, 27 Nov 1946. (90) DM350
Autograph postcard, sgd, 19 Nov 1948. (89) DM600

Marconi, Guglielmo, 1874-1937
[A collection of c.40 autograph radio messages sent from his yacht S.Y. Elettra, c.1931 to 1936, with numerous related items, mostly sgd, sold at S on 26 Apr 1990, lot 411, for £6,500.]
Ms, logbook for his yacht Elettra, June to Dec 1936. (91) £500
ALs, 28 Feb 1914. (89) $300
— 30 Aug 1920. (90) DM400
Ds, 21 Sept 1913. (90) $850
Photograph, sgd, 12 Dec 1901. (91) $750
— Anr, [6 Feb 1905]. (91) $225
Photograph, sgd & inscr, 30 Sept 1910. (88) £240
— Anr, [21 Jan 1930]. (89) $375
— Anr, July 1931. (91) $700
Ptd photograph, sgd & dated 23 Sept 1902.

AMERICAN BOOK PRICES CURRENT

(88) DM460
See also: Strauss, Richard

Marcuse, Herbert, 1898-1979
Autograph postcard, sgd, 28 July 1931. (90) DM600

Marescotti, Andre Francois
A Ls s (2), 8 Sept & 29 Nov 1960. (88) DM210

Margaret, Princess of England. See: Elizabeth & Margaret

Margaret, Duchess of Parma, Regent of the Netherlands, 1522-86
ALs, 21 Dec 1578. (91) £500
Series of 63 Ls s, 10 June 1551 to 9 Aug 1585. 83 pp, folio & 4to. To various agents in Rome & Florence. Giving instructions regarding political, administrative & financial matters. Some lines in code. 2 autograph postscripts. In Italian. (88) DM8,500
— Series of 21 Ls s, 10 May 1576 to 29 Nov 1579. 21 pp, 4to. To Martio Faralio. Regarding administrative & financial matters. (90) DM1,200

Margaret of Austria, Regent of the Netherlands, 1480-1530
Series of Ds s, 3 Ds s, 20 July 1498 to 20 Mar 1499. 3 pp, folio. Concerning various matters relating to the city of Loja near Granada. (90) £1,200

Marguerite de Valois, Duchesse de Savoie, 1523-74
ALs, 16 Sept 1578. 1 p, folio. To Mademoiselle Noblet. Regarding a payment of 50 livres. With 11-line endorsement at bottom. Repaired. (88) DM1,600

Marguerite de Valois, Queen of Henri IV of France, 1553-1615
Ds, 24 Apr 1575. (90) DM500

Maria Carolina, Queen of Naples, 1752-1814
ALs, 7 May 1811. (89) DM200
— 5 June 1811. (90) DM220
— 1 May 1812. (88) DM320

Maria Fyodorovna, Empress of Paul I of Russia, 1759-1828
ALs, 29 Sept 1810. (90) DM900
— 21 June 1815. (88) DM660
— 4 Oct 1821. (90) DM900
Ls, 10 Jan 1799. Byer collection. (90) $300

Maria Fyodorovna, Empress of Paul I of Russia, 1759-1828
ALs, 29 Sept 1821. (90) DM440

Maria Paulowna, Grossherzogin von Sachsen-Weimar, 1786-1859
ALs, 25 Apr/6 May 1825. (90) DM600
— 5 Jan 1836. Albrecht collection. (91) SF240
Ls, 19/31 July 1820. (90) DM300
— 28 Jan/9 Feb 1821. (91) DM270

Maria Theresa, Empress, 1717-80
Autograph Ms, brief notes pertaining to military matters [c.1760]. (91) DM750
— Autograph Ms, brief notes pertaining to military matters [c.1760]. (91) DM700
— Autograph Ms, brief notes pertaining to a report by Count Daun & the Elector of Cologne, [c.1760]. (91) DM400
— Autograph Ms, list of Hungarian nobles to be given appointments at court, [1758]. (90) DM520
ALs, [after 1768]. 2 pp, 4to. To her daughter Maria Carolina, Queen of Naples. Expressing sympathy. In French. Was mtd. (88) DM2,200
— 25 Aug 1779. (90) DM960
Collection of AL, 3 Ls s, & autograph endorsement, 1743 to 1768. (90) £700
AL, 10 Aug 1753. 2 pp, folio. To Graf Chotek. Draft, in the margin of Graf Chotek's letter to her; responding to his apology for being unable to act on her orders. Salzer collection. (90) £1,500
— [c.1756]. (91) DM680
Ls, 23 Mar 1744. (88) £140
— 2 June 1745. (89) DM580
— 6 June 1752. (88) DM600
— 16 Dec 1752. 10 pp, folio. To the magistrates of the Archduchy of Steyer. Giving orders concerning heretics. (91) DM1,150
— 23 Nov 1759. Byer collection. (90) $325
— 22 Jan 1761. Schroeder collection. (89) DM500
— 26 Jan 1762. (90) DM420
— 29 May 1762. (88) DM750
— 19 Aug 1765. 1 p, folio. To an unnamed prince. Informing him of the death of her husband. Def. With engraved port. (89) DM1,300
— 17 Aug 1769. 2 pp, 4to. To Gen. O'Donell. Commenting on his difficulties in Transylvania. With autograph postscript, 11 lines. (91) DM1,050
— 19 Oct 1770. (91) $275
— 28 Nov 1770. (89) DM260
— 24 Aug 1775. Schroeder collection. (89) DM1,000
ANs, 20 Oct 1755. 1 p, 8vo. To President of the Exchequer Rudolf Graf Chotek. Requesting extra funds. With autograph receipt at bottom. (89) DM2,000
Ds, 18 Aug 1746. 15 pp, folio, in reddish brown lea gilt. Patent of nobility & grant of arms for Paul Joseph Kozma. With full-page painting of the arms in gold & colors & elaborate calligraphic decoration. (90) DM3,200
— 16 Dec 1752. 10 pp, folio. To her representatives in Styria. Orders regarding the suppression of sectarianism & the arrest of Johann Hueber & his circle. (90) $1,100
— 14 June 1763. 12 pp, folio, in red velvet bdg. Patent of nobility & grant of arms for Georg Joseph Jeossich. In Latin. With full-page painting of the arms & large seal in wooden box. (90) DM2,000
— 5 Feb 1766. (90) DM700
— 31 May 1766. 21 pp, folio, in red velvet bdg. Patent of nobility & grant of arms for Joseph Ignaz Egger. With several pen-&-ink drawings & full-page painting of the arms in gold & colors. (91) DM2,200
— 31 July 1775. (90) DM420
— 1775. 12 leaves, 337mm by 248mm. Contemp red velvet bdg. Patent of nobility for Ladislaus Szepessy de Negyes. With illuminated tp, ornamental borders throughout, & full-page coat-of-arms. (91) DM1,400
— 18 Oct 1777. 22 pp, 4to. Patent of nobility & grant of arms for Johann

MARIA THERESA

Michael von Menghin und von Brunnenthal. With full-page painted coat-of-arms. Lacking seal. (88) DM1,300

— 28 May 1779. 19 pp, 4to, in red velvet bdg. Patent of nobility & grant of arms for Johann Le Fevre. With 9 large pen-&-ink drawings & full-page painting of the arms in gold & colors. (91) DM1,800

Autograph endorsement, sgd, 15 lines on a fragment of minutes of a meeting on religious customs, 17 Aug 1753, 1 p, folio; deciding that no changes should be made. Sgd with paraph. (90) DM1,050

— Anr, on "Resolutio" by her chancellery regarding taxes to be paid in Hungary, [1768], 1 p, 25.9cm by 12.1cm, cut from a larger sheet. (88) DM750

— Anr, sgd M, on a memorial addressed to her by Capt. Graf von Colloredo, 17 Aug 1778, 3 pp, folio, interceding on behalf of Lieut. Graf von Deym. Explaining at length that debtors in her guard have to be dismissed. (88) DM1,100

Endorsement, sgd, on a report by her treasury, 5 June 1762, 5 pp, folio; granting a compensation for clerks who issue death certificates. (90) DM900

— Anr, sgd, on a memorial by her accounting office, 19 Nov 1762, 6 pp, folio, concerning pay to troops in Hungary. (88) DM540

— Anr, sgd, at bottom of a letter addressed to her by Count Daun, 30 May 1764, 8 pp, folio, concerning a petition by a Jewish merchant for a deferment of taxes; requesting a report. (91) DM900

— Anr, sgd, on a memorial from the war council, sgd by Leopold von Daun, regarding the repair of army depots, 7 June 1764. 4 pp, folio. Consenting to repairs. (89) DM1,600

Marianne of The Netherlands, Princess of Prussia, 1810-83

ALs, 14 Mar 1842. (89) DM280

AMERICAN BOOK PRICES CURRENT

Marie, Queen of Ferdinand I of Romania
Photograph, sgd, [n.d.]. (90) $60

Marie, Queen of Maximilian II of Bavaria, 1825-89

ALs, 17 Sept 1845. 4 pp, 8vo. To a cousin. Thanking for congratulations on the birth of her son. (91) DM1,400

— 19 Apr 1864. (89) DM500

Marie Antoinette, Queen of Louis XVI of France, 1755-93

Ms, map of her wedding journey from Strasbourg to Versailles. Paris, drawn by Tonnet, [c.1770]. 10 sections mtd on silk & dissected to allow each section to fold into a fascicle of 184mm by 188mm, the front panel of each stamped with her arms marshalled with those of the Dauphin. In contemp mor case with the same combination of arms. Schiff Ms (91) $62,500

ALs, [n.d.]. 1 p, 8vo. To an unnamed lady. Expressing sympathy with her grief. Framed. (91) £3,600

AL, [c.1784]. 2 pp, 8vo. To her son [the 1st Dauphin]. Reprimanding him for disobeying his tutor. (90) £2,900

— [n.d.], "Monday". 1 p, 8vo. To the Comtesse d'Ossun. Informing her that the King has granted a pension to her mother. Docketed & sgd by 3 members of the Convent at bottom. (90) DM8,000

Letter, 31 Jan 1775. (89) DM400

Ds, 1 Apr 1786. 1 p, folio. Pay order for 200 francs to Jean Baptiste Henry. Doheny collection. (88) $2,000

Document, 1781. (89) £170

Cut signature, [n.d.]. (88) $250

See also: Louis XVI & Marie Antoinette

Marie de Cleves, Duchesse d'Orleans, 1426-86

Ls, 29 Apr [n.y.]. 1 p, 8vo. To Jean Le Sens. Granting an extension of time to Guillaume de Launay for payment of his debts. (88) DM1,100

Marie de Medicis, Queen of France, 1573-1642

ALs, 8 Aug 1622. 1 p, 8vo. To the Duke of Savoy. Thanking for his concern for her recovery. (91) £1,600

— 3 May 1629. 1 p, folio. To Cardinal de Richelieu. Letter of recommendation for [Antoine de Bourbon, Comte de Moret]. Was mtd. (89) DM1,600

Ls, 13 June 1638. Doheny collection. (89) $300

Ds, 2 Apr 1625. (88) $325

Marie Louise, Empress of the French, 1791-1847
ALs, 18 Oct 1807. (88) DM850
— 2 Jan 1813. (89) DM650
— 28 July 1813. (91) £800
— 2 Sept 1813. 1 p, 4to. To Cambaceres. Informing him about news from her husband. (91) DM1,050
— 22 Mar 1814. 1 p, 12mo. To [Napoleon]. Sending a copy of a letter to her father & hoping to hear from him. Sgd Louise. Doheny collection. (89) $1,600
— 27 May 1815. 2 pp, 4to. To Empress Elisabeth Alekseyevna of Russia. Thanking for her & her husband's help & friendship, declaring her determination not to return to France, & giving news of her son. (90) DM2,200
— 7 May 1832. 2 pp, 4to. To her son Wilhelm. Chatting about her stay at Milan, the theater, music, etc. Mostly in French. Byer collection. (90) $1,200

Ls, 25 May 1813. (91) £600
— 27 Feb 1814. (88) DM650

Ds s (2) 29 Dec 1812 & 10 Aug 1813. Doheny collection. (89) $320

Ds, 9 Dec 1812. (89) £240

Marinetti, Filippo Tommaso
Autograph Ms, Manifeste Collage Tapuscrit. 1924. (90) FF13,000

Marion, Elie
Autograph Ms, journal, 1716-38. (91) £150

Marion, Francis, c.1732-95
ALs, 26 Feb 1781. 1 p, 4to. To Capt. John Saunders. Concerning arrangements for an exchange of prisoners. Also sgd on address leaf. (91) $4,700
— 2 Aug 1785. 1 p, 4to. To Messrs. Blake & Bouquet treasurers, Charleston. On financial matters. (91) $8,000

Maris, Roger Eugene
Photograph, sgd, [n.d.]. (91) $100
Photograph, sgd & inscr, [n.d.]. (88) $120

Marlborough, John Churchill, 1st Duke, 1650-1722
ALs, 17 Sept 1705. (89) £480
AL, 15 July 1709. (89) £300

Ls, 16 July 1704. 2 pp, 4to. To an unnamed officer. Giving orders to requisition forage for horses from the subjects of the Elector of Bavaria. (91) DM1,100
— 22 Nov 1705. 3 pp, 4to. To Johann Wilhelm, Elector Palatine. Informing him that the Emperor is expecting him to furnish 6 batallions for the army in Italy. (91) DM1,500
— 22 Nov 1705. 3 pp, 4to. To Johann Wilhelm, Elector Palatine. Informing him about his mission to the Emperor. In French. (90) DM1,500

Ds, 20 May 1711. (89) £360
— [24 Dec] 1714. (89) £280
— 24 Dec 1714. Byer collection. (90) $450

Marlborough, Sarah Churchill, Duchess of, 1660-1744
Series of 3 A Ls s, 22 & 23 Apr 1703 & [n.d.]. (89) £250
ALs, 20 July [n.y.]. (89) £130

Marryat, Frederick, 1792-1848
ALs, 17 Feb [1833?]. (89) £500

Marschner, Heinrich, 1795-1861
A Ls s (2), 22 June 1840 & 8 Aug 1841. (90) DM700
ALs, 17 Mar 1830. (89) DM450
— 10 Apr 1843. (88) DM380
— 6 June 1855. (89) DM280
— 21 Aug 1855. (90) DM700
— 26 Aug [n.y]. (88) £100

Marsh, John, 1752-1828
Autograph Ms, autobiography & journal, covering his entire life; 1797 to 1828. About 6,500 pp in 37 white vellum vols, 4to. Final 14 pp in anr hand. (91) £26,000

Marshall, Charles, 1830-1902. See: Civil War, American

MARSHALL

Marshall, John, 1755-1835
ALs, 20 Sept 1800. 31 pp, 4to, in bds. To Rufus King. As Sec of State, giving instructions for negotiations with Great Britain concerning contraband of war & impressment. Pforzheimer collection. (90) $37,500
— 7 May 1833. 2 pp, 4to. To Humphrey Marshall. Commenting on recipient's pamphlet, analyzing federal relations & denouncing nullification. Barrett collection. (89) $11,000
— 14 Oct 1833. 3 pp, 4to. To his son James K. Marshall. Discussing plans to build quarters for himself next to his son's home. (90) $4,500
— [c.Feb 1834]. 1 p, 4to. To Benjamin Owen Tyler. Draft, replying to Tyler's letter (included, 11 Jan 1834; def), & complimenting him on his facsimiles. Sgd JM. Barrett collection. (89) $1,300
Ls, 4 Oct 1800. (88) $1,000

Marshall, Thomas Riley, 1854-1925
Ls, 1 Dec 1913. (91) $95

Martin du Gard, Roger, 1881-1958
A Ls s (2), 3 & 23 Apr 1938. (89) DM250

Martin, Frank, 1890-1974
Autograph music, "Fragment aus '3 Taenze' fuer Oboe, Harfe und Streichorchester", 1970. 4 pp, c.34cm by 25.5cm, 14 staves each. In pencil. Sgd later & dated Mar 1971. (88) DM1,400
ALs, 13 Nov 1936. (90) DM440

Martin I, King of Aragon, 1356-1410
Ds s (2) 4 Sept 1397 & 14 Dec 1409. 2 pp (1 vellum), folio. Permission granted to Bartolome de Villafranca to transport & sell wine. Appointment to the barony of Alcoy for Pere Joan. 1 def. (90) £1,800

Martin, James Green, 1819-78
Ds, [c.16 June 1856]. (89) $50

Martin, Luther, 1748-1826
ALs, 7 Feb 1781. (88) $225

Martin, Mary, 1913-90
Photograph, sgd & inscr, [n.d.]. (91) $100

AMERICAN BOOK PRICES CURRENT

Martin V, Pope, 1368-1431 —& Calixtus III, Pope, 1378-1458
Ms, transcript of 2 bulls addressed to German bishops, 2 July 1425 & 6 May 1455, [Germany, late 15th cent]. (88) £180

Martineau, Harriet, 1802-76
Autograph transcript, poem, "Set to music by Miss Flower in her 'Hymns & Anthems' 1842"; sgd & dated 1 Aug 1843. (90) $200

Martini, Giovanni Battista, 1706-84
ALs, 22 June 1732. 3 pp, folio. To Padre Giovanni Giacinto Sbaraglia. Incorporating a list of works by over 30 composers borrowed from the Convent library in Ferrara. (91) £2,800
— 22 July 1754. (90) DM600
— 6 Aug 1754. 2 pp, folio. To Anselmo Costadoni. Describing the notation of early music & recommending Guido d'Arezzo's Micrologus. (90) £4,200

Martinu, Bohuslav, 1890-1959
Autograph music, ballet, Spalicek, piano score; sgd & dated 20 Jan 1932. Tp & 84 pp, 34.5cm by 26.5cm, in half cloth bdg. With numerous corrections in red or blue pencil. Some texts in anr hand, in pencil. (88) DM14,000
— Autograph music, part of his Duo for Violin & Violoncello, [1926-27]. (91) £1,000
ALs, 20 Oct 1954. 1 p, 4to. To Marcel Mihalovici. Requesting to see the score of Wozzek. (90) DM1,500
Ls, [c.May/June 1959]. (88) DM650

Martinus of Troppau, d.1278. See: Joachim & Martinus of Troppau

Martius, Carl Friedrich Philipp von, 1794-1868
ALs, 24 July 1856. (90) DM340
— 22 Apr 1866. Albrecht collection. (91) SF220

Martyn, Thomas, fl.1760-1816
Ms, The English Entomologist, Exhibiting All the Coleopterous Insects...., L, 1791. 77 pp, vellum & paper, 345mm by 285mm. Crimson mor gilt bdg by Kalthoeber. With calligraphic tp & text, & 42 orig drawings by Martyn each showing a group of insects in ink

& gouache enclosed in gilt border. Executed for William Beckford. Bradley Martin Ms. (90) $21,000

Martyrologium Romanum
Ms, Martyrology, with Gospel Lections & Constitutions of the Dominican Order, [Florence?, c.1375]. (88) £900
— Ms, [Northern France, Lille?, late 12th cent]. 90 leaves [of c.94], vellum, 310mm by 225mm. 18th-cent vellum bgd. In black ink in a neat minuscule script. With 360 large decorated initials in colors. Some repairs. (88) £7,500

Marut, Ret, Pseud. See: Traven, B.

Marx, Adolph Bernhard, 1795-1866
ALs, 21 Mar [1831]. (88) DM320

Marx Brothers
[A group of separate signatures by Chico, Groucho, Harpo & Zeppo Marx, 1942 to 1978, sold at Dar on 4 Oct 1990, lot 301, for $300.]
Ls, 31 May 1949. 1 p, 4to. To the William Morris Agency. Confirming their understanding that the Agency will be paid by Kyle Crichton for negotiating an agreement with the Marx Brothers. Sgd by all 5. (91) $2,500

Marx, Chico
Ls, 7 Oct 1936. (91) $225

Marx, Groucho
Ls, 7 Oct 1936. (91) $300
— 14 Apr 1966. (91) $400
Ds, 1 Apr 1949. (89) $750
— 30 Nov 1950. (89) $800
Group photograph, with Harpo & Chico, [n.d.]. (91) $150

Marx, Harpo, 1893-1964
Ls, 7 Oct 1936. (91) $250
Photograph, sgd & inscr, [19]41. (90) $260

Marx, Karl, 1818-83
Autograph Ms, excerpts from 2 works dealing with Russian history, [c.1856/57]. 2 pp, 4to. (91) DM20,000
— Autograph Ms, excerpts from the works of English & French writers on political economy, with brief comments; [1844/45]. 48 pp, 4to; stitched. Including 10 pp with figures, calculations & a few lines of text. (90) DM140,000
— Autograph Ms, notes taken from Joseph Massie's Essay on the Governing Causes of the Natural Rate of Interest...; [n.d.]. 2 pp, 8vo. On blue paper. (88) £15,500
ALs, 4 Feb 1878. 3 pp, 8vo. To Thomas Allsop. Discussing English politicians, the war between Russia & Turkey, Bismarck, & the political order of Europe. (88) DM280,000
— 24 Jan 1879. 1 p, 8vo. To [the bookseller Hugo Heller]. About an order for the French Ed of "Capital", & asking for a verbatim copy of a quote. (89) DM50,000

Marx, Karl, 1897-1985
Autograph music, 2 Mss of songs, Auf eine kranke Rose & Auf Brummerhoff, 1936, & Sommerliches Land & Pfirsichbluete, 1953. (88) DM550
— Autograph music, 2 songs, Herbst to a text by F. (90) DM550
— Autograph music, sketches for the scherzo of his Op.73/2, [1978]. (91) DM500
— Autograph music, song, Ausgleich, to a text by Eugen Roth; 22 Dec 1953. (90) DM250
— Autograph music, song, Juchhe, der erste Schnee; [n.d.]. (90) DM400
— Autograph music, songs, Leicht verschwindet der Taten Spur, & Schmetterlinge, 20 Aug & 5 Sept 1976. (89) DM260

Marx, Wilhelm, 1863-1946
Ms, report about the political situation in the Rhineland, Dec 1928. (91) DM470

Mary, Queen of Scots, 1542-87
Ls, [10?] Jan 1565/6. 1 p, folio. To the Laird of [Glen Vorlich?]. Requiring his presence in Edinburgh during the visit of a French Ambassador. (89) £2,200
— 5 June 1567. 1 p, folio. To Robert Dudley, Earl of Leicester. Informing him that she has sent a messenger to Elizabeth I & asking him to promote amity between her & his Queen. Framed with a port. (90) $42,000
Document, 28 Apr 1564. (88) £200

MARY

Mary, Princess of Orange, 1631-60
ALs, 14 Dec [n.y.]. (89) £250

Mary, Queen of George V of England, 1867-1953
Christmas card, sgd, 1941. Crohn Collection. (88) $175
See also: George V & Mary

Mary I, Queen of England, 1516-58
Ls, 13 Dec 1557. 1 p, folio. To John Trelawnye. Requiring him to be speedy in returning sums collected in Cornwall. Def. (89) £2,200
Letter, 6 Aug 1556. 1 p, folio. To the Keeper of the Park at Nonesuch. Requiring him to deliver a buck to Jane Russell. With stamped signature. (90) £2,000
See also: Philip II & Mary I

Mary II, Queen of England, 1662-94
Ds, 30 Mar 1694. (90) £400

Mary of Burgundy, Consort of Maximilian I, 1457-82. See: Maximilian I & Mary of Burgundy

Mary of Castile, Queen of Alfonso V of Aragon
Ds s (2) 10 Sept 1426 & 29 Aug 1444. (90) £1,000

Mary of Guise, Queen of James V of Scotland, 1515-60
Ds, 9 July 1544. (89) £600

Mary of Modena, Queen of James II of England, 1658-1718
Ls, 13 Mar 1714. (88) £200

Maryland
[2 documents, 1802 & 1804, 2 pp, folio & 4to, each a finding by Frederick County, Md., against local liquor dealers, suspending sentence provided dealers pay the required liquor tax to support the University of Maryland, sold at BBC on 12 Feb 1990, lot 65, for $140.]

Masaryk, Jan Garrigue, 1886-1948
ALs, 7 June 1937. (90) DM420
Ls, 22 June 1945. (90) DM280

AMERICAN BOOK PRICES CURRENT

Masaryk, Thomas Garrigue, 1850-1937
Typescript (duplicated), Declaration of Independence of the Czechoslovak Nation by its provisional Government, 18 Oct 1918. 5 pp, 4to. Sgd later. File holes. (89) DM11,000
ALs, 30 Nov 1879. 1 p, 8vo. Recipient unnamed. Requesting a meeting with Mr. Heller about a Ms. (91) DM1,150
— 15 Feb 1899. 2 pp, 8vo. To Mr. Hlavac. About the use of money donated to a newspaper. (90) DM3,000
— 17 Oct 1929. (91) $500
— 7 Nov 1932. 2 pp, 4to. To Emil Ludwig. Requesting him to postpone his interviews until January. In German. (90) DM1,300
Ls, 25 Mar 1928. (90) $425
Photograph, sgd, 1935. (91) $160

Mascagni, Pietro, 1863-1945
Autograph music, Coro di Filatrici, from Pinotta, scored for 4-part mixed choir & orchestra, sgd & dated June 1884. (88) £850
— Autograph music, Invocazione alla Madonna, for chorus & organ, sgd & dated 6 Aug 1932. (88) £500
Collection of ALs & autograph quotation, sgd, 7 Oct 1899 & 6 Apr 1907. (90) £380
Series of 4 A Ls s, 29 Oct [18]89 to 27 Dec [18]90. (88) £450
— Series of 28 A Ls s, 1919 to 1939. 88 pp, various sizes. To his cousin Mario Mascagni. About his operas & a variety of matters. (88) £1,800
A Ls s (2), 24 May & 17 June 1918. (89) DM550
ALs, 25 Mar 1903. (89) DM600
— 19 Mar 1932. (88) £750
— [c.1934]. (88) £450
Autograph quotation, 2 bars from Cavalleria Rusticana, with lyrics; 31 Aug 1924. (91) $475
Photograph, sgd, 26 Apr 1898. (90) DM1,000
— Anr, 7 Aug 1935. (91) DM550
Photograph, sgd & inscr, 13 Oct [18]90. (88) £700
— Anr, 1 May 1901. Cabinet size. Inscr to [Leopold] Demuth. (88) DM1,550
— TABOR. - Orig drawing, charcoal port of Mascagni, sgd; [n.d.]. 315mm by

235mm; framed. Also sgd by Mascagni. (90) £700

Masefield, John, 1878-1967
[A collection of A Ls s & related material, 1956, 18 items, to Cicely Wise, sold at S on 15 Dec, lot 96, for £350.]
Collection of 4 A Ls s & Ls, 1918 to 1929. (90) $200
Autograph quotation, sgd & inscr, 16 Jan 1916. (89) $150

Masefield, John, 1878-1967 —&
Bridges, Robert, 1844-1930
Autograph Ms (2), verses written for the opening of the RADA Theatre, [n.d.]. (88) £45

Masereel, Frans, 1889-1972
Series of 17 A Ls s, 2 Mar 1967 to 17 Apr 1970. 26 pp, 8vo. To the pbr Karl Schustek. Dealing with exhibitions, his travels, editions of his works, etc. (91) DM1,400
A Ls s (2), 5 Dec 1952 & 29 Jan 1962. (89) DM250
ALs, 16 Feb 1921. (91) DM380
— 16 Nov 1932. (90) DM230
— 14 Sept 1942. (90) DM250

Mason, Alfred Edward Woodley, 1865-1948
Typescript, novel, The Dean's Elbow, [1930]. (89) £200

Mason, John, 1586-1635. See: Alexander, William & Mason

Massachusetts
Document, inventory of the estate of John Robie, prepared for Essex County Court hearing, 30 June 1691. (90) $75
See also: Indians, North American

Massena, Andre, 1758-1817
ALs, [24 Apr 1797]. (89) $160

Massenet, Jules, 1842-1912
Autograph music, Elegie, for voice, cello & piano, revised version; [after 1875]]. (90) £360
— Autograph music, L'aubade de Cherubin, transcription pour piano; [n.d.]. Tp & 6 pp, 35cm by 27cm; 12 staves each. Some corrections. (89) DM1,700

— Autograph music, song, Joie, for 2 voices & piano, Sept 1868 & 26 Aug 1870. 2 pp, 35cm by 27cm. In black & red ink; some revisions. (90) DM1,500
— Autograph music, Valse folle for piano in G major, [1898]. 10 pp, folio. Sgd & inscr to Raoul Pugno on tp. With related material. (90) £2,200
Collection of ALs & AN, [n.d.]. (90) $120
Series of 7 A Ls s, 21 Apr 1881 to 2 Mar 1884. (89) DM360
A Ls s (2), 5 July 1885 & 1 Jan 1889. (90) DM220
— A Ls s (2), [n.d.] & 2 Sept [n.y.]. (89) DM700
ALs, 15 Jan 1878. (91) DM220
— 19 Apr [18]81. (91) $300
— 20 June 1899. (91) $85
Autograph quotation, 6 bars from Esclarmonde, with lyrics; 5 May 1889. (91) $325
— Anr, 25 notes from Esclarmonde; 1892. (91) $275
— Anr, 3 bars from Manon, 24 Dec 1908. (91) $500

Masterman, Dodie
Original drawings, (6), to illus Jane Austen's Emma. (90) £480

Masters, Edgar Lee, 1869-1950
ALs, 26 Nov 1938. (91) DM220
Ls s (2), [10 Apr 1923] & 20 July 1926. (89) $175

Masterson, William Barclay ("Bat")
Ds, 12 Nov 1885. 2 pp, folio. Petition for change of venue on behalf of William T. Lane. Also sgd by 12 others. (91) $4,500

Mata Hari, Pseud. of Geertruida Zelle McLeod, 1876-1917
Collection of ALs & 5 photographs, [c.1905]. 2 pp, 8vo. To M. Bois. Reminding him of his promise to try for "un engagement aux Folies Bergeres" for her. With related material. (88) DM3,600
ALs, 8 Aug [1915]. 8 pp, 8vo. To her lawyer Hijmans. About problems with the furnishing of her house at The Hague. On hotel letterhead. (89) DM2,500
— [n.d.]. (91) £900

Matare, Ewald, 1887-1965
ALs, 9 Jan 1958. (91) DM360

Mather, Cotton, 1663-1728
Autograph Ms, comprehensive notes for a sermon, [n.d.]. (90) $700

ALs, 8 Sept 1722. 1 p, 8vo. To the Rev. Thomas Foxcroft. Discussing epitaphs. Middendorf collection. (89) $2,200

Matilda or Memoirs drawn from the History of the Crusades
Ms, historical novel, 1823; c.760 pp, 4to. (88) £70

Matisse, Henri, 1869-1954
Autograph transcript, Louise Labe's sonnet Baise m'encor, rebaise moy et baise...; [n.d.]. 1 p, folio. In black ink, with engrossed initial B & drawing of lips at foot. (90) £3,200

Collection of ALs & autograph postcard, sgd, [1910-1911]. 6 pp, 8vo. To Olga Merson. Reporting on his visit to Moscow, & referring to his London exhibition. (91) £1,700

ALs, 9 & 10 Dec 1911. (90) £700
— [1911]. (91) £800
— 7 Oct 1933. (88) £280
— [c.1945]. 2 pp, 8vo. To Andre Rouveyre. Asking him to call later that day; including drawing of a chastity belt on verso. Sgd HM. (90) £3,400
— 26 Apr 1946. (88) DM1,000

Matlack, Timothy, 1734-1829
ALs, 25 Mar 1779. (89) $160

Matthias, Emperor, 1557-1619
Collection of ALs & 2 Ls s, 29 Apr 1588 to 15 June 1602. 4 pp, folio. To Reichart Stein, discussing his new appointment in Prague. Recipients unnamed, about military matters. (90) £1,300

Ls, 29 Sept 1585. (89) DM650
— 6 Nov 1589. (90) DM1,000
— 29 June 1612. (89) £130
Letter, 22 May [1618]. (89) DM320
Ds, 25 Sept 1616. 1 p, vellum, 54cm by 63cm. Grant of arms for Benedict Burner. Including painting of the arms within architectural border. Signature stained. (90) DM1,300

Matthias I Corvinus, King of Hungary, 1443-90
Document, 25 Apr 1464. 53cm by 27cm, vellum. Confirmation of a court sentence listing property rights of Stephanus de Baijon. Including seal. (91) DM5,500

Matthisson, Friedrich von, 1761-1831
ALs, 10 Sept 1827. (90) DM750

Maude, Aylmer, 1858-1938
Collection of 13 A Ls s & 5 Ls s, 8 Jan 1922 to 6 Apr 1938. (90) £85

Maugham, William Somerset, 1874-1965
Autograph Ms, collection, The Casuarina Tree: Six Stories; [pbd 1926]. 319 pp, mostly on rectos only. In blue ink, with corrections in red. 3 pp typed. Sgd on tp. Mor bdg. Koch Foundation. (90) $45,000

Collection of 129 A Ls s & 16 Ls s, 1904 to 1962. 380 pp, various sizes. To Sir Gerald Kelly & Lady Kelly (10). Discussing recipient's painting & his own writing. (91) £4,500

— Collection of 2 A Ls s & Ns, 7 Sept 1926, 1 Mar 1945, & [n.d.]. (89) $350
— Collection of 3 A Ls s & Ls, 6 Feb [n.y.] to 14 Nov 1932. (90) £360
ALs, 23 July [1899]. (90) $650
— 6 June [n.y.]. (90) £260
— 20 Aug [n.y.]. (91) $70
— [n.d.], "Thursday". (90) $850
— [n.d.]. (88) DM200
Ls s (2), 1 Apr 1958 & 2 Feb 1965. (88) £85
ANs, 6 Nov [n.y.]. (91) $75
Photograph, sgd, [n.d.]. (90) $110

Maupassant, Guy de, 1850-93
ALs, 1 Sept 1874. (91) £850
— 14 May 1882. (88) DM800
— [c.1890]. 4 pp, 8vo. To an unnamed physician. Reporting about the state of his health. (89) DM1,700
— [n.d.]. (90) DM650
— [n.d.]. (91) DM650
— [n.d.]. (90) DM800

Mauriac, Francois, 1885-1970
Autograph Ms, article about Galeazzo Ciano, [n.d.]. (91) DM560

Maurois, Andre, 1885-1967
Collection of ALs & 8 Ls s, 1 Aug to 16 Dec 1962. (90) DM380
See also: Kipling, Rudyard & Maurois

Maury, Matthew Fontaine, 1806-73
ALs, 16 July 1858. (91) $325
Ls, 4 Dec 1852. (88) $150

Mauthner, Fritz, 1849-1923
Collection of ALs & Ls, 15 [?] & 18 Feb 1906. (88) DM480

Maxim, Sir Hiram Stevens, 1840-1916
Autograph Ms, contribution addressed to the Daily Mirror, discussing the influence of unions in London on production costs; 16 Nov 1905. (90) DM370

Maximilian, Prince of Baden, 1867-1929
ALs, 16 Oct 1903. Schroeder collection. (89) DM260
— 29 Jan 1919. (90) DM550

Maximilian I, Emperor, 1459-1519
Ls, [14]89. 1 p, 4to. To Albrecht, Duke of Saxony. Discussing negotiations with England. Trimmed. (89) £1,100
— 10 July 1509. 1 p, folio. To the magistracy at Enns. Informing them of a transfer of property. (90) DM3,200
— 12 Oct 1516. 1 p, folio. To Albrecht von Brandenburg, Kurfuerst von Mainz & Archbishop of Halberstadt. Stating conditions for repayment of 5,290 guilders due to Philipp Adler. (91) DM2,300
— 7 Nov [15]17. (89) £700
Ds, [10 Mar] 1497. 1 p, folio, vellum. Deed donating a house at Innsbruck to Mathis Paller. With seal, possibly from anr document. (88) DM3,000
— 12 Jan 1507. 1 p, vellum, folio. Letter of investiture for Lukas vom Graben. Repaired. (90) DM2,700
— 14 Feb 1508. 1 p, folio. Grant of arms for Hanns & Laurentz "die Sergannten gebrueder". With painting of the arms & seal. (91) DM3,400
— 14 Feb 1508. 1 p, 8vo. Pay order in favor of Lienhard Wallisser. Corner def. (90) DM2,200

— 28 Dec 1513. 1 p, vellum, 400mm by 600mm. Confirmation of a land grant by Maximilian Sforza to Ambros & Jason de Mayno. (91) DM1,700
— 31 Dec 1515. (90) £800
Document, 15 May 1515. 1 p, folio. Decree declaring Franz von Sickingen an outlaw. With facsimile signature. (89) DM2,700

Maximilian I, Emperor, 1459-1519 —&
Mary of Burgundy, Consort of Maximilian I, 1457-82
Document, 17 Sept 1481. 1 p, vellum, c.62cm by 68cm. Letter of investiture for "vrouwe van Ravestein" in recognition of her services. In Dutch. Including seal. Figdor collection. (90) DM9,500

Maximilian I, Kurfuerst von Bayern, 1573-1651
Ls, 12 Apr 1623. (88) DM420
— 16 Dec 1639. (90) DM420
— 23 Aug 1641. (89) DM960

Maximilian I Joseph, King of Bavaria, 1756-1825
ALs, 12 Oct 1809. 1 p, 8vo. To Lieut. Gen. von Wrede. Reassuring him in view of problems with the French generals & Napoleon. (88) DM1,300
— 23 July 1815. (89) DM480
— 11 Aug 1815. (89) DM600
Series of 4 Ls s, 1802 to 1809. (88) DM540
Ls, 10 Oct 1807. (88) DM450
— 26 Jan 1808. (89) $80
— 14 June 1814. (90) DM200
Series of Ds s, 3 Ds s, 23 Apr 1818 to 2 May 1820. (90) DM280
Ds, 28 Nov 1802. (90) DM430
— 16 Sept 1818. (89) DM420

Maximilian II, Emperor, 1527-76
Ls, 27 Nov 1550. (89) DM500
— 23 Oct 1563. (90) DM320
— 20 Nov 1573. (89) DM420
Ds s (2) 6 Aug 1573. (90) £550
Ds, 15 Aug 1565. (90) DM750
— 14 Oct 1568. (90) DM600
— 21 Oct 1569. 14 leaves, vellum, folio. Confirmation of patent of nobility for Lazarus von Schwendi. Including large painting of the arms in gold & colors.

MAXIMILIAN II

(90) DM1,500
— 26 Sept 1573. 1 p, vellum, folio. Grant of arms to the brothers Rapp. Including painting of the arms. In orig box. (90) DM1,300
— 26 June 1574. (88) DM750

Maximilian II, King of Bavaria, 1811-64
Series of 5 Ls s, 23 Sept 1845 to 31 Jan 1855. (88) DM360
Ls, 1 May 1861. (91) DM440
— 14 Dec 1861. (91) DM460
Ds, 17 May 1849. (90) DM280
— 16 Dec 1863. (90) DM220

Maximilian II Emanuel, Kurfuerst von Bayern, 1662-1726
Ls s (2), 31 Dec 1683 & 24 Dec 1688. (90) DM260
Ls, 12 Mar 1685. (89) DM800
— Sept 1694. (90) DM240

Maximilian of Mexico, Emperor, 1832-67
Collection of Ls & Ds, 6 May & 21 Aug 1865. (91) £190
Ls, 12 Sept 1860. (91) DM400
— 17 Oct 1863. Koch Foundation. (90) $700
— 28 Dec 1864. Koch Foundation. (90) $400
Ds, 22 Oct 1865. (91) DM650
— [1865]. (89) £700
— 20 Mar 1867. 6 pp, folio. Minutes of the council of war during the siege of Queretaro. Also sgd by others. (89) £1,300
Photograph, sgd, [1860s]. Koch Foundation. (90) $800
Telegram, 12 Feb 1865. 1 p, 4to. To Marshal Achille Francois Bazaine. Congratulating him on his recent victory. Text & signature ("Maximilian") in the hand of Empress Carlota. Koch Foundation. (90) $1,800

Maximilian of Mexico, Emperor, 1832-67 —&
Franz Joseph I, Emperor of Austria, 1830-1916
[A Ls by Maximilian, 22 Mar 1864, asking his brother for officers to accompany him to Mexico, with ANs by Franz Joseph, 8 Apr 1864, approving of his brother's request, 2 pp, folio, sold at CNY on 7 June 1990, lot 87, for $1,500.]

Maximilian zu Wied-Neuwied, Prince, 1782-1867
ALs, 10 Mar 1838. (91) DM320

May, Karl, 1842-1912
Collection of ALs & autograph Ms, 23 Feb 1877 & [n.d.]. 2 pp, 8vo. To Kaspar Braun, offering a contribution to a journal; possibly draft. On verso poem, 3 eight-line stanzas beginning "In Deines Auges reinem Blau"; draft. (88) DM4,800

Series of 5 A Ls s, 10 Dec 1906 to 16 May 1907. 7 pp, 4to & 8vo. To Leopold Gheri. Concerning a series of articles to be pbd in the journal Kunstfreund. (91) DM4,600
— Series of 3 A Ls s, 2 Mar to 18 Apr 1907. 8 pp, 4to & 8vo. To Leopold Gheri. Urging him to remain Ed of the journal Kunstfreund in spite of attacks. Sending a contribution. With picture postcard by Klara May. (88) DM3,800
A Ls s (2), 21 & 30 Apr 1907. 3 pp, 4to. To Leopold Gheri. Regarding publications in the journal Kunstfreund. (90) DM4,200
ALs, 9 Dec 1892. 1 p, 8vo. Recipient unnamed. Insisting that his stories are authentic. (90) DM6,800
— 4 Aug 1907. 3 pp, 8vo. To Leopold Gheri. Requesting information concerning a controversy. (90) DM3,000
Series of 6 autograph postcards, sgd, 1906 to 1908. To Herr Breitschmid. Sending greetings. Addresses in the hand of Klara May. With related material. (90) DM9,000
Photograph, sgd, [n.d.]. (89) DM550
Signature, 31 Mar 1909. (89) DM850

Mayenfisch zu Rappenstein, Carl, Freiherr von, 1803-77
[His passport, issued at Konstanz, 1 June 1843, with many stamps & endorsements by officials in a number of states in Europe & the Eastern Mediterranean, sold at star on 28 June 1990, lot 1068, for DM370.]

Mayer, Rupert, 1876-1945
Collection of Ls & typescript, 1 Feb 1933. (88) DM800

Mazarin, Jules, Cardinal, 1602-61
Autograph Ms, report about the political situation in Flanders, 20 May 1653. (91) £700
Ls, 21 June 1644. Byer collection. (90) $300
— 22 Oct 1649. (89) £380
— 23 July 1656. (88) £240
— 16 Feb 1657. (90) DM360
— 10 Nov 1658. (88) $425

Mazepa, Ivan Stepanovich, c.1644?-1709
Ds, 12 Sept [1687?]. 1 p, folio. Grant of feudal rights at Makova to Sadi Grigoriich. (91) DM1,300
— Nov 1699. 1 p, folio. To the commanding officer at Kiev. Order forbidding the sale of spirits at inns. (90) DM2,600

Mazzini, Giuseppe, 1805-72
Collection of ALs & autograph Ms, sgd, [8 Mar 1868] & [1847]. (88) DM520
Series of c.30 A Ls s, 1853 to 1865. About 60 pp, various sizes. To Giuseppe Dassi. Important political letters to a patriot active in Naples. (90) £5,100
— Series of 4 A Ls s, 7 Feb & 23 Sept 1869 & [n.d.]. (90) £320
ALs, 23 May 1849. (89) £800
— [n.d.]. (90) DM320
Series of 10 Ls s, 2 Aug 1859, 6 May 1863, & [n.d.]. 27 pp, mostly 4to. To various patriots in Italy. Important political letters discussing Garibaldi, advising against a monarchy, urging them to remove the Papacy, etc. (90) £4,300

McCartney, Paul. See: Beatles, The

McFarland, Spanky. See: Switzer, Alfalfa & McFarland

Measures
Ms, list of dry measures used for corn etc. in Amberg, Cham, Weiden & 26 other towns in the Upper Palatinate, [Germany, c. 1590]. 29 leaves & blanks, 20cm by 16cm. Contemp pigskin with blindstamped portraits of Luther & Melanchthon, 1593. (88) DM1,600

Meckel, Johann Friedrich, 1781-1833
ALs, 5 Jan 1833. (91) DM370

Medical Manuscripts

[A medical anthology from Bury St. Edmunds Abbey, containing 6 medieval texts written by 4 main scribes, [late 13th cent], 90 leaves & 4 flyleaves, vellum, 268mm by 200mm, in def [14th-cent?] bdg of bevelled wooden bds, sold at S on 23 June 1988, lot 50, for £44,000 to Quaritch.]

[A collection of medical Mss, mainly Italian, 17th to 19th cent, sold at S on 18 May 1989, lot 299, for £550 to Pampolini.]

Ms, Antidotarium. [Italy, 1st half of 13th cent]. 78 [of 80?] leaves, vellum, 195mm by 120mm. 19th-cent blindstamped brown lea over wooden bds. In black ink in a cursive script, with numerous glosses & marginal notes in a contemp & a later hand. Containing c.750 medical recipes. Margins uncut. (89) DM90,000

— Ms, Ein kostliches Undt Bewehrtes Artzney buchlein..., [Germany, late 16th cent]. (89) DM650

— Ms, Hie Inbegriff S[choe]ne Artznei Khinsst..., [Germany, 17th cent]. (89) DM650

— Ms, medical recipes in Latin. [Switzerland, late 8th cent]. 2 bifolia only, vellum, 220mm by 145mm. In dark brown ink by 2 scribes in a clear uncial hand with some letters in early minuscule; 40 headings in red uncials. Recovered from a bdg. Fuerstenberg collection at Donaueschingen. (88) £45,000

— Ms, pharmaceutical receipts, kept by a practitioner working in Devon & Dorset, [late 17th cent]. (88) £200

— GYE, DR. WILLIAM EWART. - ALs, 3 Apr [19]23. 3 pp, 4to. To Dr. Copher. Discussing his methods for preparing colloidal silica. (91) $200
See also: Constantinus Africanus

Medici, Carlo de, 1596-1666
Ds, 1637. (88) $95

MEDICI

Medici, Cosimo I de, 1519-74
Ls, 16 Apr 1569. (91) $600

Medici, Cosimo II de, 1590-1621
Ds, 1 July 1613. (88) $650

Medici, Ferdinando I de, 1549-1609
Ds, 2 Mar 1591. (90) £520

Mehay, I. P. J.
Ms, Essai de tableaux d'histoire naturelle, 1791 to 1794. 4 parts in 1 vol, 384 pp, 51cm by 36cm, in recent green half mor. With 4 title pages, 2 watercolor frontispieces, & numerous watercolor, pen-&-ink, & gouache drawings of birds, insects & animals from all parts of the world. (88) £18,000

Mehring, Franz, 1846-1919
ALs, 4 Dec 1888. (90) DM850
— 10 Feb 1908. (89) DM550

Mehring, Walter, 1896-1980
Autograph Ms, essay, Kuenstlerische Prophetie, [1925]. (90) DM850
Collection of ALs & autograph Ms, 21 Dec 1965. (90) DM270

Mehul, Etienne Nicolas, 1763-1817
Autograph Ms, Itineraire de rome a naples avec le detail de ce qui m'a paru de plus interessant dans la route, [n.d.]. (91) DM420
ALs, [1793]. (90) DM840
— [1800]. (88) DM420
— 17 June 1815. (89) DM360

Meid, Hans, 1883-1957
Collection of 2 A Ls s & Ls, 20 Oct 1945 to 6 Jan 1946. 6 pp, 4to & 8vo. To Alexander Amersdorffer. About the Berlin art scene & his own situation after the war. (91) DM1,200

Meidner, Ludwig, 1884-1966
Autograph Ms, essay, Von wahrer Kunst; [n.d.]. (90) DM950
— Autograph Ms, fragment from Gang in die Stille, [1926]. 7 pp, folio; stitched. Sgd at head & inscr to Hans Zeeck, Aug 1933. (90) DM1,700
A Ls s (2), 23 Sept 1931 & 9 Sept 1937. (91) DM500
ALs, 14 Aug 1918. (90) DM500
— 13 May 1920. (90) DM220
— 11 Oct 1920. 1 p, 4to. To an unnamed lady. Accepting an invitation. Including pen-&-ink self port. (90) DM2,200

AMERICAN BOOK PRICES CURRENT

Meir, Golda, 1898-1978
Ls, 1 Feb 1954. (91) $500
— 28 June 1954. 1 p, 8vo. To Prime Minister Moshe Sharett. Concluding that "our relationship with the U.N. has to be to respect it and suspect it". (91) $2,750
Photograph, sgd, [n.d.]. (91) $200
— Anr, [n.d.]. (89) $65

Meitner, Lise, 1878-1968
ALs, 22 June 1966. (90) DM700
Ls, 15 Oct 1957. (91) DM850
— 24 Feb 1960. (90) DM680

Melanchthon, Philipp, 1497-1560
ALs, [1555]. 8 pp, folio. To Joachim Camerarius. Suggesting ways to settle the difficulties with Leonhard Culmann in Nuremberg. (91) DM22,000
— [14 Apr] 1560. 3 pp, folio. To Jacob Runge. Commenting about a funeral sermon, anticipating his own death, & mentioning ecclesiastical developments. Repaired. (89) DM18,000
ADs, 1557. 1 p, 8vo. Receipt to Vincentio Hasen for "funff und sibenzig floren" for the 2d quarter of the year. Sgd at head. (88) DM1,500
— [1 Dec] 1559. 2 pp, folio. Receipt for 15 guilders from the village of Merschwitz, sgd by Melanchthon & Veit Oertel Winsheim as guardians for the heirs of Johann Velkirch. Margins def. (90) DM4,800
Ds, [late 1546]. 1 p, 4to. Receipt for salary at Wittenberg University; sgd in text. 2 receipts in other hands at bottom. (90) DM1,800
Autograph sentiment, discussion of prophecies regarding the end of the world, [June] 1559; sgd. On 5 pp of a copy of Ph. Melanchthon Heubartikel Christlicher Lere in latin genandt Loci Theologici Etwa von Doctor Justo Jona in Deutsche sprach gebracht... Wittenberg: V. Creutzer, 1558; in contemp calf richly tooled with portraits of Luther & Melanchthon. (88) DM8,000

Mellon, Andrew William, 1855-1937
Photograph, sgd & inscr, [n.d.]. (89) $95

Melville, Herman, 1819-91
[A collection of 12 letters & 2 documents relating to the publication of Melville's works in England, 1846 to 1852, including 8 A Ls s by Melville, sold at P on 31 Jan 1990, lot 2167, for $150,000.]
ALs, 6 June 1846. 3 pp, 4to. To Sec of War William L. Marcy. Appealing for financial help from the government on behalf of his deceased brother. Doheny collection. (89) $19,000
— 8 Jan 1852. 4 pp, 4to. To [Sophia] Hawthorne. Responding to her letter praising Moby Dick. Including autograph postscript. Martin collection. (90) $120,000
— 16 May 1854. 1 p, 8vo. To George P. Putnam. Regarding the publication of The Two Temples. Martin collection. (90) $7,500
— 12 Feb 1859. 2 pp, 4to. To W. H. Barry. Stating his terms for lectures at Lynn. Martin collection. (90) $7,000
— 12 July 1885. 1 p, 4to. To Laura M. Wachslager. Suggesting she read the sea-tales of W. Clark Russell. Martin collection. (90) $11,000
— 11 Dec [1887?]. 1 p, 8vo. To Rossiter Johnson. Declining a proposed writing assignment. Doheny collection. (88) $9,500
— 20 Feb 1888. 1 p, 8vo. To Edmund Clarence Stedman. Thanking for the loan of some books & inviting him to visit. Martin collection. (90) $6,000
— 9 Feb 1890. 2 pp, 8vo. To [W. Clark Russell]. Thanking for a set of recipient's An Ocean Tragedy. Martin collection. (90) $14,000
— 25 Feb [18]90. 2 pp, 8vo. To H. S. Salt. Thanking for his Life of James Thomson, & declining to authorize a new English Ed of Typee. Martin collection. (90) $7,000

Melzer, Moriz, 1877-1966
Collection of 31 A Ls s & autograph postcard, sgd, [July 1911] to 22 Feb 1919 & [n.d.]. 71 pp, mostly folio & 4to, & card. To Margarete Rosenberg. Covering a variety of subjects. Including collage. With related material. (90) DM5,500

Memminger, Christopher Gustavus, 1803-88
ALs, 26 June 1863. (90) $300

Mencken, Henry Louis, 1880-1956
[An amusing exchange of 3 letters involving Mencken, Ben Hecht & Katharine Adam, [n.d.], 4 pp, 8vo, sold at sg on 23 Mar 1989, lot 285, for $300.]
Typescript, A New Dictionary of Quotations on Historical Principles. (91) $1,000
— Typescript, article, The Triumph of the Have-Not, [1939]. (88) $500
Collection of 2 Ls s & photograph, sgd, 23 May & 23 Nov 1935 & [n.d.]. (90) $475
Series of 8 Ls s, 8 Dec 1924 to 22 June 1927. (90) $800
— Series of 3 Ls s, March to Dec 1936. (91) $950
— Series of 3 Ls s, [n.d.]. (91) $400
Ls, [1918]. (90) $200
— 27 Jan 1928. (89) $70
— 31 Oct 1929. (91) $90
— 12 Jan [n.y.]. (90) $80
Series of 16 Ns s, 1928 to 1948. 18 pp, 8vo. To Harry Hansen. Commenting on literary affairs. (89) $1,700

Mendeleev, Dimitri Ivanovich, 1834-1907
ALs, 4 Dec 1891. 3 pp, 8vo. To Vladimir Vladimirovich. Regarding contributions to a reference work. (91) DM4,000
Ls, 22 Jan/4 Feb 1902. 2 pp, 4to. To Etienne Jules Marey. Describing a shield to eliminate the influence of body temperature in scientific experiments. In French. (88) DM1,400

Mendelssohn, Arnold, 1855-1933
ALs, 20 June 1913. (90) DM370

Mendelssohn, Moses, 1729-86
ALs, 16 Oct 1766. Length not stated. To Christoph Friedrich Nicolai. Discussing the professional prospects of Herr Veist & asking Nicolai to help him. (88) $1,800
— 27 Aug 1773. 1 p, 4to. To Friedrich Nicolai. Discussing financial arrangements. Corner cut. (89) DM1,100

MENDELSSOHN

ADs, 20 Nov 1771. 1 p, 4to. Settlement of accounts with Friedrich Nicolai. Endorsed by Nicolai on verso. (88) DM1,100
— 1 Mar 1784. 1 p, 4to. Receipt to Kriegsrat Bauer for 500 talers in interest payments. Also endorsed by Bauer. (91) DM1,900
AD, [Aug 1772]. (88) DM420

Mendelssohn-Bartholdy, Fanny, 1805-47.
See: Hensel, Fanny

Mendelssohn-Bartholdy, Felix, 1809-47
[A draft for a concert program, 1835, 1 p, c.8.8cm by 20.4cm, fragment, addressed to Musikdirektor Rungenhagen in Mendelssohn-Bartholdy's hand, sold at star on 1 Dec 1988, lot 868, for DM240.]
Autograph music, 1st bass part of his Jagdlied, Op. 120 no 1; [c.1837?]. 1 p, folio. Notated on 6 staves. (91) £2,600
— Autograph music, 3 duets for 2 sopranos to texts by Heine & Uhland; [c.1836]. 5 pp, 30cm by 24cm. Sgd FMB on tp. (90) DM28,000
— Autograph music, 3 songs, Abschied, in F major; Volkslied, in E minor, & Gruss, in D major; [before 1834]. 3 pp, folio. Notated in brown ink on up to 4 systems per page, 3 staves each. Partly undocumented. Salzer collection. (90) £18,000
— Autograph music, 8 bars from an (unrecorded?) Adagio in A major for violin, violoncello & piano, sgd & dated 8 Sept 1839. 1 p, 4to. Written for the album of Gottfried Martin Meyer. (90) DM10,500
— Autograph music, Ave Maria, Op. 23, no 2, scored for organ, [1837]. 2 pp, size not stated; 16 staves each. Stichvorlage. (89) DM16,000
— Autograph music, Canone a 3, comprising 6 bars with 3-line verse; sgd & dated 14 Jan 1842. 1 p, c.20cm by 26.5cm. Framed. Salzer collection. (90) £6,000
— Autograph music, Gondel-Lied [Lied ohne Worte, Op. 62 no 5]; 11 Oct 1842. 2 pp, folio. Notated on 7 systems, 2 staves each; differing from ptd version. Sgd & inscr to Frau von Deutsch. (91) £16,000
— Autograph music, Piano Concerto no 2

AMERICAN BOOK PRICES CURRENT

in D minor, Op. 40, draft of piano part; [c.July 1837]. 19 pp, 4to, including tp. With extensive autograph revisions, partly on a paste-over. Inscr by J. A. Novello on wraps. (91) £50,000
— Autograph music, setting of a folksong text, Mein Vater ist ein Appenzeller, & 2 further musical quotations, with orig pen-&-ink drawing of an Alpine village; sgd, inscr & dated 21 Aug 1842 & 29 Sept 1842. 1 p, size not stated. Salzer collection. (90) £7,500
— Autograph music, song, Da lieg ich unter den Baeumen, sgd, inscr & dated 12 Oct 1844. 4 pp, folio. In brown ink on up to 3 systems per page, 3 staves each. With autograph tp. (89) £4,000
— Autograph music, song, Fruehlingslied, to a text by Heine, 22 Dec 1836. 3 pp, 8vo. Sgd on tp. (90) DM24,000
— Autograph music, song, Staendchen, for 2 tenor & 2 basses, sgd, inscr & dated 12 July 1841. 1 p, 4to. On 2 hand-drawn systems of 2 staves each. (89) $6,500
— Autograph music, songs Op. 57, no 1, 2 & 4, [c.1840]. 5 pp, size not stated. Sgd & inscr to Livia Frege. Some corrections in pencil. (88) DM28,000
Original drawing, view of Amalfi, in watercolor; [1839?]. 30cm by 37cm (framed). With [autograph?] initials attached to mount. (91) £12,000
— Original drawing, view of Amalfi, in watercolor; [1839?]. 18.5cm by 26.1cm. With [autograph?] initials attached to mount. (89) DM26,000
Transcript, 1st violin part of Elijah for the 1st half of the oratorio, with annotations by Mendelssohn in red crayon in some 20 places. 40 pp, 4to, unbound in 2 gatherings. (89) £1,200
— Transcript, full score of Elijah used by Henry Gauntlett as a performing score at the first performance of the oratorio at the Town Hall, Birmingham, on 26 Aug 1846. In the hand of Eduard Henschke, with holograph annotations by Mendelssohn in ink, pencil & red crayon in more than 200 places. About 500 pp, 4to, half mor, worn & broken. (89) £88,000
— Transcript, Hochzeits-Marsch [the

Wedding March] aus dem Sommernachtsraum von Shakspeare componirt und fuer Pianoforte zu 4 Haenden (Op. 61). 8 pp, 4to. With holograph tp & pencil annotations by Mendelssohn. (89) £5,000

— Transcript, Notturno from Shakespeare's Midsummer-Nights Dream composed & arranged as a Duet for 2 performers on the pianoforte (Op. 61). 8 pp, 4to. With hollograph tp & pencil annotations. (89) £3,200

— Transcript, organ part for Elijah, with holograph annotations by Mendelssohn in pen, red crayon & pencil in 10 places. 31 pp, 4to, sewn in 2 gatherings, disbound from brown stiff paper wrappings (89) £3,800

— Transcript, Scherzo from Shakespeare's Midsummers-Nights Dream composed & arranged as a Duet for 2 performers on the pianoforte (Op. 61). 20 pp, 4to. With holograph title in German & with annotations in pencil in Mendelssohn's hand (& 1 in red crayon). (89) £3,000

— Transcript, setting of Psalm 114 (Op. 51) bound with his second Symphony (Op. 52) in its first, unrevised version, the body of the score & the German text of both works in the hand of his copyist Eduard Henschke, & with the words of the English text of the 1st work added in pencil by Mendelssohn himself, with holograph revisions made to the scoring. About 250 pp, folio, in half mor gilt stamped Loggesang/ Full Score/ Mendelssohn. With note by Alfred Novello pasted into inside of upper cover saying that the Psalm setting was pbd 2 Dec 1840. (89) £32,000

Collection of ALs & AL, 29 Apr & 1 May [1832]. (88) £550

— Collection of 3 A Ls s, AL, & autograph Ms, 17 Mar & 24 Oct 1846 & [n.d.]. 6 pp, various sizes. To Ferdinand David. Regarding invitations, appointments, etc. Salary sheet for Gewandhausorchester & Caecilienverein, 1836. With related material. (89) $6,000

ALs, 11 Feb 1827. (88) $1,000

— 5 Mar 1827. 1 p, 8vo. To Carl Schlesinger. Returning the corrected piano score of the opera Oberon. (91) DM7,000

— [13 June 1829]. (91) £780

— 28 Nov [1830]. (88) £950

— [c.Sept/Oct 1831]. 1 p, 4to. To Heinrich Baermann. Suggesting a meeting. Sgd Isabelle, Prinzessinn von Trapezunt. (90) DM3,500

— 28 July 1832. 3 pp, 4to. To Mme Kiene. Reporting about his stay in London & the Berlin music scene, & criticizing Meyerbeer's music. Albrecht collection. (91) SF13,000

— [before 1832?]. (89) £800

— 17 June [1833]. (89) £900

— 30 May 1835. 1 p, 4to. To George Smart. Introducing Julius Benedict. In English. (91) £1,250

— 6 July 1835. 2 pp, 4to. To his aunt Henriette Mendelssohn. Informing her about his mother's illness. With postscript, dictated & initialled by his father Abraham Mendelssohn-Bartholdy. Seal tear. (89) DM5,200

— [1830s?]. (90) £900

— 27 Feb [18]37. 2 pp, 8vo. To the pbr F. Kistner. Inquiring about proof copies. (91) £1,300

— 17 Nov 1837. 4 pp, 4to. To Carl Klingemann. About his life in Leipzig, Handel's Messiah, the Novellos, visitors, etc. (91) £3,000

— 20 Nov 1837. 1 p, 4to. To Moritz & Leopold Ganz. Introducing Henri Vieuxtemps. (90) £1,500

— 23 Dec 1837. 1 p, 8vo. To Frau Karus. Thanking for a present & sending a score. (91) £1,300

— 13 Oct 1839. 1 p, 8vo. To [Karl] Voigt. Thanking for a port of his godchild, & hoping Mrs. Voigt will recover from her illness. (90) DM3,800

— 13 Jan 1840. 1 p, 8vo. To Friedrich Kistner. Inquiring about a soloist for a concert with the Gewandhaus Orchestra. (91) DM4,500

— 28 Feb 1840. 4 pp, 4to. To H. F. Chorley. Discussing plans for an oratorio, & mentioning friends. In English. Seal tears. (89) £1,600

— 15 Mar 1840. 2 pp, 8vo. To I. J. Hartknoch. Regarding the sale of some scores from a lady's collection of music. With related material. (88)

MENDELSSOHN-BARTHOLDY

DM4,200
— 15 Mar 1841. 4 pp, 4to. To Karl Klingemann. Interesting letter to a good friend, about the revision of his "Lobgesang" & various other matters. (90) DM9,000
— 28 Mar 1841. 1 p, 4to. Recipient unnamed. Acknowledging receipt of the overture to Goethe's play Jery und Baetely. Imperf. Salzer collection. (90) £1,300
— 27 Sept 1841. 1 p, 4to. To Professor Fischoff. Letter of introduction for M. P. Schlesinger. In gilt mor folder by G. Vauthrin. (89) $2,600
— 31 Oct 1841. 2 pp, 4to. To Siegfried Wilhelm Dehn. Refusing to publish anything about his own music. (88) DM4,600
— 9 Oct 1842. 4 pp, 8vo. To Madame Kiene. Paying tribute to the recently deceased composer Pierre Baillot. With related material. (91) £1,900
— 9 Oct 1842. 1 p, 8vo. To Rudolf Hirsch. Thanking for a dedication. Was mtd. With a port. (90) DM3,500
— 31 Mar 1843. 1 p, 8vo. To [Ferdinand Freiligrath]. Regretting he will not have time to set recipient's poem to music. (89) DM6,600
— 15 July 1843. 2 pp, 4to. To Robert Franz. Discussing the collection of songs Franz has sent him. (89) $3,750
— 31 May 1844. 1 p, 8vo. Recipient unnamed. Informing him that he will be unable to attend a rehearsal of his Trio. In English. (88) £2,100
— 11 Oct 1844. 1 p, 4to. To [J. A. Josephson]. Saying he has examined Josephson's songs & would like to discuss them personally upon his return. (88) £1,650
— 17 Feb 1845. (88) $1,000
— 30 Aug 1845. 2 pp, 4to. To Adolf Boettger. Complimenting him on his play & suggesting a suitable overture. Doheny collection. (89) $1,500
— 29 Nov 1846. 1 p, 4to. To Fritz Spindler. Giving his opinion of recipient's symphony. (91) £2,400
— 10 Feb 1847. 2 pp, 8vo. To Julius Benedict. Postponing an answer to an invitation extended by Thomas Mitchell. (88) DM3,600
— 28 Apr 1847. (91) £900
— "Friday", [1833]. (91) £900
Ds, 4 July 1835. (91) £500
Autograph quotation, Allegro vivace, 17 bars scored for piano, sgd, inscr & dated 5 Jan 1843. 1 p, 206mm by 276mm. Mtd. (90) $4,000
— Anr, 4 bars for piano in A flat major, sgd; 9 June 1844. 1 p, size not stated. Including autograph musical quotation by Julius Benedict at head. (91) £2,400
— Anr, Canone a 3, 9 bars; sgd & dated 8 July 1844. 1 p, 8vo. Mtd. (90) DM6,500
Concert program, Birmingham Musical Festival, 28 Aug 1846, sgd & inscr on cover. (89) £800
— BERGMANN, LEO. - Ms, Prolog zur Saecular Feier des Conzertvereins im Gewandhaussaale in Leipzig, [1843]. 3 pp, folio. With revisions & additions in Mendelssohn-Bartholdy's hand, in pencil. (88) DM1,600
— RIETZ, JULIUS. - Autograph music, piano reduction of Mendelssohn-Bartholdy's Athalie, [c.1846/47]. 61 pp, size not stated; 18 staves each. Stichvorlage. (89) DM3,200

Menger, Carl, 1840-1921
ALs, 9 Feb 1901. (89) DM300

Menotti, Gian Carlo
[A photographic copy of a Ms of The Saint of Bleecker Street, comprising a part of the 1st act, with autograph annotations & revisions, sgd & dated 1975, 58 pp, with a copy of the complete vocal score, sold at S on 22 Nov 1989, lot 133, for £550 to Lubrano.]

Menuhin, Yehudi
[A collection of contracts, letters, etc. concerning film work by Menuhin, late 1940s, especially his performance in the film Delirium, sold at pn on 8 Dec 1988, lot 78, for £180 to Stevens.]
ANs, 11 Aug [n.y.]. (88) DM260

Menzel, Adolph von, 1815-1905
[A proof impression of a reproduction of his painting Sankt Hubertus, [n.d.], c.25cm by 32cm, with autograph comments in margin, sgd A.M., sold at star

on 30 Nov 1988, lot 645, for DM440.]
Series of 4 A Ls s, 25 Jan 1859 to 3 Dec 1878. 12 pp, mostly 8vo. To different recipients about various professional matters. (90) DM1,400
A Ls s (2), 11 Aug 1861 & [n.d.]. (89) DM650
— A Ls s (2), 11 Nov 1889 & 9 Feb 1890. (88) DM620
ALs, 1 Nov 1837. 1 p, 8vo. To C. Schultz. Concerning an invitation. Including small drawing. (90) DM2,200
— 1 July 1847. (88) DM800
— 26 July 1861. 2 pp, 8vo. To his sister Emilie Krigar & her husband. Reporting about his vacation at Freienwalde. Including large pen-&-ink sketch. (90) DM5,500
— 18 Sept 1870. (91) DM380
— 5 Apr 1871. (90) DM320
— [n.d.]. (88) DM400
— 18 June 1877. (91) DM520
— 30 Oct 1877. 3 pp, 8vo. To Joseph Joachim. Inquiring about a ticket for recipient's concert with Clara Schumann. (91) DM1,300
— 17 Nov 1878. (90) DM400
— 24 Dec 1881. (91) DM380
— 24 Apr 1884. (91) DM900
— 15 Mar 1885. (90) DM300
— 30 Jan 1887. (91) DM330
— 19 Nov 1891. (90) DM480
— 13 June 1893. (89) DM380
— 12 Apr 1895. 3 pp, 4to. Recipient unnamed. Insisting upon his decision to resign from an academy. (89) DM1,100
ANs, [31 Dec 1848]. 1 p, 8vo (card). Recipient unnamed. Expressing New Year's wishes. Including pen-&-ink drawings on recto & on verso. (90) DM10,500
Photograph, sgd, [17 Nov 1898]. (90) DM330

Mercadante, Saverio, 1795-1870
ALs, [1 Nov 1847]. (90) DM220
— 3 Dec 1857. (90) DM260

Meredith, George, 1828-1909
[A collection comprising 3 A Ls s & ptd leaflet of verses by Meredith, & 10 letters by literary & theatrical figures seeking to attend his memorial service, 1908 & 1909, c.20 pp, 8vo, addressed to Israel Gollancz, sold at S on 21 July 1988, lot 209, for £1,150 to Joseph & Sawyer.]
Autograph Ms, poem, The Call, [pbd 1909]. (89) £500
Ms, poem, The Woods of Westermaine. [1910 or earlier] 18 leaves, on vellum, bound in mor by Charles Macleish, 1910. Calligraphic Ms in the style of Grailey Hewitt & with his ownership stamp. Tp & opening lines in gold. Full-page or double-page miniatures incorporating text. (90) £7,500
Series of 8 A Ls s, 1887 to 1892. (90) £280
— Series of 9 A Ls s, 1890-1908. 30 pp, 8vo. To Violet Maxse, Lady Edward Cecil. Personal letters about a variety of matters. Koch Foundation. (90) $2,500
ALs, 15 Oct 1868. (89) $350
— 19 June 1904. (91) DM300

Meredith, Goerge, 1828-1909
ALs, 28 Dec 1890. (88) £70

Merimee, Prosper, 1803-70
[A charcoal-&-crayon port of Merimee, 20 Nov 1866, 8.75 by 6.25 inches, sold at pn on 16 Mar 1989, lot 97, for £120 to Rota.]
ALs, 17 Aug [1840]. (90) DM1,000
— 3 Aug [1867?]. (90) DM240
— 12 Feb [n.y.]. (90) DM240

Merman, Ethel, 1908-84
Collection of ALs & signature, 5 Apr 1968 & [n.d.]. (91) $120

Merrick, Leonard, 1864-1939
Series of 8 A Ls s, 1 Feb 1925 to 12 Sept 1930. (89) £75

Merton, Thomas, 1915-68
Collection of 7 A Ls s, 11 Ls s & 5 postcards (4 autograph), sgd, 1959 to 1964. To Graham Carey & Mark Van Doren (3 Ls s). Literary correspondence. With much related material. (90) $7,700

Mesmer, Franz Anton, 1734-1815
Ds, 5 Apr 1784. 1 p, folio. Contract pledging himself to instruct the Marquis de Saisseral in the principles of animal magnetism, & stating condi-

MESMER

tions. Partly ptd; accomplished by Mesmer. (91) DM3,000

Messager, Andre, 1853-1929
ALs, 22 Oct [19]08. Byer collection. (90) $60
— 11 May 1921. Byer collection. (90) $90

Methfessel, Albert, 1785-1869
Autograph Ms, newspaper announcement of his move to Hamburg; 1 Jan 1823. (90) DM650
ALs, 11 May 1825. (91) DM700

Metternich, Klemens Wenzel Nepomuk Lothar von, 1773-1859
ALs, 9 Jan 1816. (90) DM1,000
— 2 Sept 1818. (90) DM900
— 18 June 1819. (88) DM420
— 20 July 1823. 5 pp, 4to. To [Aloys Graf von Rechberg?]. Analyzing the political situation in Europe after the failure of the Spanish revolution. In French. (89) DM1,700
— 1 Nov 1824. (91) $250
— 17 Apr 1826. (91) DM440
— 20 Mar 1835. 3 pp, 4to. To the Prussian envoy at Vienna. Assuring him that Austrian politics will not change with the new Emperor. (91) DM1,500
— 22 Sept 1839. (90) DM950
— 18 Jan 1845. (88) $450
— 6 Apr 1848. 3 pp, 8vo. To Josef Anton von Pilat. Analyzing the revolutionary movement. Sgd with paraph. (90) DM1,900
— 5 Dec 1848. 12 pp, 8vo. To Sir Travers Twiss. Answering questions about his assessment of the political situation in various parts of Europe. Sgd CM. In French. (89) DM2,500
— 29 Apr 1854. (90) DM1,000
— 12 Mar 1856. (91) $175
— 19 Jan 1858. (91) DM440
Ls, 16 Apr 1845. (90) DM550
Ds, [1835]. (90) DM650
See also: Schwarzenberg, Karl Philipp

Metternich-Winneburg, Franz Georg von, 1746-1818
ALs, 2 June [1772]. (90) DM300

Meung, Jean de. See: Lorris, Guillaume de & Meung

AMERICAN BOOK PRICES CURRENT

Meusel, Johann Georg, 1743-1820
ALs, 2 May 1816. (90) DM220

Mexican War
[A group of 4 letters & 2 covers from the correspondence of [James William] Denver, 1847 & [n.d.], 2 partially ptd circulars regarding recruiting, 2 sgd by M. L. Bonham, sold at rf on 12 Mar, lot 24, for $210.]
— GIBSON, GEORGE. - ANs, 19 May 1846. Length not stated. To Lieut. D. Ruggles, Army of Occupation, Texas. As Commissioner Gen. of Subsistence, contents not stated. With franking signature. Alexander collection. (90) $105
— WITMAN, W. C. - ALs, 3 Nov 1846. 4 pp, size not stated. To his nephew Henry O. Witman. Describing his "late tour to Mexico" as a soldier. (90) $100

Mexico
Ms, Declaration of the Prisoners ingaged in Megia's Expedition and Afterwards Shot. Tampico, 13 Dec 1835. 1 p, folio.. Sgd by the 29 condemned. (91) $3,200
— HACIENDA DE SANTA INES. - A Ms vol containing 14 groups of documents relating to property rights, livestock, etc., including 2 pen-&-ink drawings of the hacienda, 1st half of 18th cent, 250 leaves, folio, in contemp vellum, sold at sg on 3 Mar 1988, lot 167, for $1,900. 88
— MONASTERY & CONVENT OF LA CONCEPCION, MEXICO. - Ms, Libro de Memorias y Capellanias, [1567?]. 14 leaves, folio, in contemp vellum. 2 leaves loose. (88) $425
See also: California
See also: Indians, North American

Meyer, Conrad Ferdinand, 1825-98
Autograph Ms, poem, Da sitzt ein Pilgerim, 3 Sept 1888. 2 pp, 4to. Four 8-line stanzas. Fair copy, 1 correction; sgd. Lower margin cut. (88) DM8,000
— Autograph Ms, poem, Der todte Achill, sgd; [June 1882]. 2 pp, 4to. 50 lines, with revisions. Ptr's copy, but differing from ptd version. (90) DM12,000
ALs, [Sept 1852]. (90) £550

— 25 May 1891. 2 pp, 4to. Recipient unnamed. Declining a request for a contribution. (91) DM1,400
Autograph postcard, sgd, 30 [July] 1885. (90) DM800
AN, 2 Jan 1897. (91) DM550

Meyer, Heinrich, 1614-45
[His album, 1630 to 1638, containing 278 entries, 14 watercolors, 4 pen- &-ink drawings & 5 coats-of-arms, in contemp calf gilt, sold at HN on 20 May 1988, lot 3390, for DM12,000.]

Meyer, Johann Friedrich, 1772-1849
ALs, 3 Apr 1830. (91) DM520

Meyer, Johann Heinrich, 1759-1832
ALs, 14 June 1814. (89) DM650
— 27 Sept 1823. (91) DM1,000

Meyerbeer, Giacomo, 1791-1864
Autograph music, 10 bars for "Trompette en Fa"; [n.d.]. (88) DM600
— Autograph music, arrangement of the aria Lascia ch'io pianga from Handel's opera Rinaldo, full score of recitative & aria; [n.d.]. 5 pp, folio. Including revisions. Vocal line & text in the hand of a copyist. (91) £2,200
Collection of 5 A Ls s, 3 Ls s, AN, & autograph musical quotation, sgd, 1843 to 1863. 18 pp, various sizes. To various recipients about different matters. 8 bars of the overture to Struensee, inscr to A. de Beauchesne. (91) £1,300
— Collection of ALs & Ls, 9 Sept 1854 & 14 Apr 1864. (90) DM750
Series of 3 A Ls s, 7 June & 5 Nov 1862, & [n.d.]. (90) DM600
A Ls s (2), 21 Mar 1838 & 6 Nov 1841. (90) DM700
— A Ls s (2), 22 Nov 1851 & [n.d.]. (90) DM600
— A Ls s (2), 15 June 1855 & [Jan 1856]. (90) DM850
ALs, 21 Nov [18]31. 2 pp, 4to. To a conductor. On the day of the premiere of Robert le diable, expressing satisfaction at the standard of performance of the orchestra at the rehearsals. With autograph cast-list. (89) £1,300
— 4 June 1836. 2 pp, folio. To King Louis Philippe of France. Presenting him with the full score of his opera Les Huguenots. (88) DM1,200
— 20 Aug 1840. (88) DM400
— 23 Feb 1845. (90) DM600
— 5 Nov [1849]. (89) DM420
— [1849 or later]. (90) DM250
— [n.d.]. (88) DM440
— [n.d.]. (88) DM300
— 28 June 1854. (88) $120
— 7 May 1855. (91) £500
— 8 Aug 1855. Byer collection. (90) $200
— [1856 or earlier]. (91) DM420
— 13 May [n.y.]. (90) DM420
— [n.d.], "Thursday". (91) $150
— [n.d.]. (90) DM220
— [n.d.]. (90) DM240
Ls s (2), 7 Jan & 5 June 1846. (90) DM650
Ls, 14 Apr 1845. (91) DM700
ANs, [n.d.]. (89) DM300
A Ds s (2), 21 Nov 1831. 2 pp, 4to & 12mo. Cession of the German copyright for his opera Robert le Diable to Adolph Martin Schlesinger. Texts identical; 1 marked Duplicata; 4to sheet with 2 attestations, 1843. With related material. (90) DM2,800
— BEER, JACOB HERZ. - ALs, 9 July 1814. 1 p, 4to. To his son [Giacomo Meyerbeer]. Reporting about festivities planned for the King's return to Berlin. (90) DM1,200

Meyrink, Gustav, 1868-1932
ALs, 10 Oct 1917. (89) DM480
— 30 Jan 1920. (90) DM900
— 30 Oct 1921. (91) DM650

Michael Wisniowiecki, King of Poland, 1640-73
Ds, 5 Sept 1673. (88) £300

Michel, Louise, 1830-1905
ALs, [4 Mar 1882]. (90) DM250

Michel, Robert
[A folder with script & notes for Michel's film Raeder rasen, 1921, 14 pp, folio, sold at S on 5 May 1988, lot 191, for £420 to Sotheran.] £2,200

Michelangelo Buonarroti, 1475-1564
Autograph Ms, list of payments for marble purchased [for the facade of San Lorenzo], 24 Jan to 28 Mar 1519. 2 pp, folio. Tipped to larger leaf; with trans. Barrett collection. (89) $60,000

MICHELANGELO BUONARROTI

AN, [c.1523-25]. 1 p, 6cm by 20cm. To Giovanni [Spina]. Requesting him to pay 15 gold ducats to Antonio di Bernardo Mini. Margin torn. With 5 lines in a contemp hand on verso. (89) £4,600

ADs, 26 Oct 1521. 1 p, folio. Memorandum recording a payment; sgd in text. In red mor album by Riviere with Ds each by Pope Clement VII & Julius III. (89) £22,000

Micklewright, G. P.

Original drawings, (13), 3 large ink illusts & 10 large ink & gouache designs for dust jackets to adventure stories; [n.d.]. (88) £300

Middleton, Arthur, Signer from South Carolina

Autograph Ms, draft of a resolution in Congress referring to "the objection made by the Agents of Connecticut"; [1776-77?]. (90) $900

ADs, 25 Oct 1782. 1 p, 113mm by 212mm. Pay order in favor of John Reedle. Receipt sgd by Reedle on verso. (91) $3,000

Middleton, Arthur, Signer from South Carolina —& Others

Ds, 25 Mar 1776. 1 p, 255mm by 120mm. Certifying that Philip Will is Barrack-Master in Charleston. Also sgd by Thomas Heyward, Henry Laurens, & 4 others. Doheny collection. (89) $1,600

Miegel, Agnes, 1879-1964

Autograph Ms, short story, Das fremde Kind; [n.d.]. 15 pp, 8vo, on rectos only of detached leaves from an exercise book. (90) DM1,300

Collection of 10 A Ls s, Ls, & 4 autograph postcards, sgd, 26 Apr 1928 to 13 June 1934 & [n.d.]. (91) DM850

ALs, 26 Aug 1941. (88) DM320

Ls, 30 May 1944. (90) DM750

Mies van der Rohe, Ludwig, 1886-1969

Autograph Ms, notes for a lecture, beginning "Wirkungsvolle gegen wirkende Form...", [n.d.]. (90) DM650

AMERICAN BOOK PRICES CURRENT

Mifflin, Thomas, 1744-1800

ALs, [c.1776-82]. (88) $500
Ds, 15 Mar 1794. (88) $80
— 10 Sept 1794. Byer collection. (90) $150
— 2 Dec 1794. (88) $90
— 10 Oct 1796. (91) $300

Mihalovici, Marcel, 1898-1985

Autograph music, sketches for Alternamenti from his Symphonie pour un ballet; sgd twice & dated 25 Jan [19]57. (90) DM320

Milestone, Lewis

[His director's shooting script for the film Edge of Darkness, 1943, with annotations & related material, sold at CNY on 21 June 1989, lot 370, for $1,300.]

Milhaud, Darius, 1892-1974

Autograph music, song, Cimetiere basque, for voice & piano, to a text by Celine Laguarde, [n.d.]. 2 pp, 35cm by 27cm, 28 staves each. (88) DM2,400

Ms, Suite for piano, Op. 8, movements 4 & 5; sgd DM on tp & dated 1913. 16 pp, size not stated. With autograph revisions & comments, & inscr to Celine Laguarde. (88) DM1,100

Collection of 3 A Ls s & Ls, 1936, 1946 & [n.d.]. (88) £200

— Collection of 6 A Ls s & 2 Ls s, 10 Jan 1959 to 27 Jan [1969]. (88) DM600

Series of 6 A Ls s, 1913 to 1928. (88) £400

ALs, [7 Feb 1931]. (90) DM200
— 12 Aug [1945]. (90) DM360
— [July 1946?]. (90) DM220

Photograph, sgd, 1961. (90) DM270

Military Manuscripts

Ms, Rules Orders and Instructions for the future Government of the Ordnance in England, 1683 to 1702. (89) £95

— Ms, Theorie der wichtigsten Manoeuvers zur Bildung junger Officiers; [18th cent]. (90) £250

— ESCOFET, JUAN DE. - Ms, Tratado IV de la Fortificacion..., [Barcelona, 1753]. 260 pp, 4to, in old vellum bdg. In the hand of Joseph de Adrette y Medina. Including 13 folding plates showing fortifications. (89) £220

— GUNPOWDER. - Ms, Ein Buech ... wie ein Zeughaus sambt aller Monition

534

anhaimbisch gehalten werden soll ..., [Germany, 1617 or earlier]. About 600 pp, folio, in vellum bds. Treatise on preparation & use of gunpowder, organization of an arsenal, etc.; with numerous illusts. (89) £5,000
— PAGET, L. G. - Ms, A Course of Practical Artillery, 1843. 276 pp, 8 by 6 inches, in red half mor bdg. Some illusts. (89) £140
— PRENDERGARST, STEPHEN. - Autograph Ms, journal kept during the Napoleonic Wars, his service in India & retirement in England, 1794 to 1835. 250 pp, 4to, in contemp calf. (91) £300
— STAIN, BARON VOM. - Ms, Reglement u. Exercitium der Infanterie..., revised version, 1727. 66 leaves, 315mm by 210mm. Contemp bds; def. (89) DM520
— STAIN, CARL VOM. - Ms, Fortificazione regolare, e irregolare..., [Turin, 1745-46]. 71 leaves, 340mm by 240mm. Contemp limp lea. With numerous watercolors of fortifications. (89) DM850

Mill, James, 1773-1836
ANs, [26 Feb 1816]. (89) £300

Mill, John Stuart, 1806-73
A Ls s (2), 1855 & 1865. 8 pp, 8vo. To Mons. Anstide Guilbert, discussing politics. To John Watkins, about photographs of himself. (89) £2,200
ALs, 4 Sept 1830. 4 pp, 4to. To Edward Strutt. Inviting his comments on a Ms treatise. With related material. (91) £2,000
— 3 Apr 1848. 3 pp, 8vo. To [Sarah] Austin. Disagreeing with her husband's opinion about the situation in France. (91) £1,400
— 23 July 1871. (91) £800

Millais, Sir John Everett, 1829-96
Collection of A Ls s & corrected proof, 2 Aug 1846 & later. 5 pp, folio & 8vo. To the Hanging Committee of the Liverpool Exhibition, requesting it to consider his painting Pizarro Seizing the Inca of Peru. Essay, Painting a Big Picture; about the Pre-Raphaelite Brotherhood. With related material. (90) £1,500
— Collection of ALs & photograph, sgd, 4 Oct [1854] & [n.d.]. (90) DM250
ALs, 26 July 1853. (91) £200
— 29 July 1886. (90) DM220

Millar, H. R.
Original drawings, (13), to illus 2 works by Rudyard Kipling, 1935. Macmillan Archives. (90) £350
— Original drawings, (44), to illus Edith Nesbit's The Magic City, 1906 (pbd 1910). In ink; 42 sgd. Various sizes. Macmillan Archives. (90) £2,400

Millay, Edna St. Vincent, 1892-1950
Autograph Ms, poem, To S. (90) £600

Miller, Arthur —&
Monroe, Marilyn, 1926-62
[The signatures of Arthur & Marilyn Monroe Miller, 1 July 1956, on the sleeve of a phonograph recording, Arthur Miller speaking and reading from the Crucible..., inscr by Miller to Bob Goldburg, sold at sg on 25 Oct 1988, lot 167, for $2,000.]

Miller, Arthur. See: Monroe, Marilyn & Miller

Miller, Glenn, 1904-44
Autograph music, sketch of "I can't get started"; [early 1940s]. (90) £150

Miller, Henry, 1891-1980
Collection of 10 A Ls s & autograph postcard, sgd, 28 Nov 1949 to 24 Apr 1951. (88) £420
— Collection of c.300 A Ls s & Ls s, May 1960 to Apr 1970. About 700 pp, various sizes. To Renate Gerhardt. Partly love letters, & dealing with a wide variety of personal matters, his work, etc. (91) £16,000
— Collection of 65 A Ls s & A Ns s, 1974-79. 81 pp, 4to & 8vo. To Vearl Moody. (91) $3,000
ALs, 29 Dec 1957. (91) DM280
— 30 Oct 1974. (90) DM480
— 10 Feb 1976. (89) $95

Miller, Joaquin, 1839-1913
Collection of 18 A Ls s & 2 autograph Mss, 5 May 1885 to 10 May 1907. 22 pp, various sizes. To Howard Sutherland & other recipients. Mainly on literary & social affairs. Poem, The Old Country Road, 12 lines, & 6 lines

of verse, dated 23 Sept 1872. With postcard addressed to Miller. Doheny collection. (88) $1,800

Miller, Johann Martin, 1750-1814
ALs, 20 Feb 1773. 4 pp, 8vo. To Ernst Theodor Brueckner. Discussing Brueckner's Unschuldsidyllen & sending 3 of his own poems (included). (90) DM7,500
— 7 Oct 1773. 4 pp, small 4to. To Ernst Theodor Johann Brueckner. Deploring the departure of the brothers von Stolberg from Goettingen & sending a poem recited on the occasion (included). (88) DM7,500

Millet, Jean Francois, 1814-75
ALs, [n.d.]. (88) £300
— 27 June 1864. Doheny collection. (89) $350
— 11 June 1870. (89) DM650

Milloecker, Carl, 1842-99
Autograph music, orchestral polka, Frisch gelebt, sgd in several places & dated 5 June [1]876. 10 pp, folio. In black ink on up to 10 staves per page; including autograph tp. (90) £1,800

Milne, Alan Alexander, 1882-1956
Autograph Ms, anti-war polemic, Peace with Honour: An Enquiry into the War Convention, 1934. About 140 pp, 4to, in 2 vols; orig marbled bds. Revised throughout; with ANs, May 1942, on 1st leaf. (90) £2,600
— Autograph Ms, The Songs of Pooh, comprising the preface to each song, with incipits; [n.d.]. 17 pp, on rectos only, in 4to notebook. With related material. Koch Foundation. (90) $9,500
ALs, 11 Feb 1926. 2 pp, 8vo. To Peter. Responding to a young reader's letter. (89) £3,800
— 16 Feb 1949. 2 pp, 8vo. to Mrs. Bowden. About Pooh & Christopher Robin. (91) $3,000
— [n.d.]. (88) £300
Autograph postcard, sgd, [n.d.]. To Miss Smorley, who is ill. Referring to his photograph with Christopher Robin & Winnie the Pooh on verso & giving their ages. Koch Foundation. (90) $5,000

— FRASER-SIMSON, HAROLD. - Autograph music, songs from When We Were Very Young, mostly sgd, [c.1926]. 44 pp, folio. Mostly in blue ink on up to 12 staves per page. Working Ms, marked for the ptr. 1 title in Milne's hand. (88) £750
— FRASER-SIMSON, HAROLD. - Autograph music, songs from Toad of Toad Hall, [c.1930]. Over 120 pp, mostly folio. In blue ink on up to 12 staves per page. In full & short score. Working Ms, marked for the ptr. Including autograph poem by Milne, The Judge's Song, & further related material. (88) £500
— FRASER-SIMSON, HAROLD. - Autograph music, all 17 songs from The Hums of Pooh, sgd, [before 1929]. 31 pp, folio. In blue ink on up to 4 systems per page, 3 staves each. Working Ms, marked for the ptr. Some differences from ptd version. (88) £1,000
— FRASER-SIMSON, HAROLD. - Autograph music, songs from Now We Are Six, mostly sgd, [1927 & 1928]. 64 pp, folio. In pencil & blue ink on up to 12 staves per page. Working Ms, marked for the ptr. Some differences from ptd version. (88) £600

Milner, Alfred, Viscount, 1854-1925
[A collection of c.70 letters addressed to Milner, various dates, by C. J. Rhodes, Lords Roberts, Curzon, & Rosebery, Georges Clemenceau, & many others, sold at S on 20 July 1989, lot 297, for £500 to Strategic Developments.]

Milroy, Robert Huston, 1816-90
Collection of ALs & photograph, 17 Jan 1888 & [n.d.]. (91) $80

Milstead, Harris Glenn ("Divine"), d.1988
Photograph, sgd & inscr, [n.d.]. (89) $350
Photograph, [n.d.]. (89) $100

Milton, John, 1608-74
Transcript, copy of the Trinity Ms of Milton's Poems, copied by Arthur Young, 1792. About 60 pp, folio. Verbatim transcript, with deletions & revisions faithfully reproduced; containing text no longer extant in the orig Ms. (90) £2,600

Ds, 23 Jan 1657. 535mm by 660mm. Deed of mortgage of land in Reigate between John Woodman & George Caffey; sgd on verso as witness. With related material. Barrett collection. (89) $8,500

Cut signature, [25 Feb 1650]. (91) $950

Miquel, Johannes von, 1828-1901
Series of 6 A Ls s, 1 Jan 1866 to 1 Feb 1867. (90) DM650

Mirabaud, Jean Baptiste de, 1675-1760
Ms, Opinion des anciens sur les juifs, [c.1750]. 283 pp, 8vo, in contemp red mor gilt. In a scribal hand. (90) £1,100

Mirabeau, Honore Gabriel Victor Riqueti, Comte de, 1749-91
ALs, 28 Feb 1775. 2 pp, 4to. To his wife. Attacking her for failing to write to him more often. (90) DM1,800

— [July 1775]. 1 p, 8vo. Recipient unnamed. Promising to shoot some snipe the next day & requesting the return of some journals. (91) DM1,100

AL, 27 Mar 1787. 2 pp, 4to. To the Comte d'Antraigues. Complaining that he has fallen into disgrace & speculating about the King's displeasure. (90) DM3,600

Ls, 14 Aug 1783. 4 pp, 4to. To Gilbert Elliot. Informing him about his problems & seeking advice. With autograph postscript. (90) DM1,400

Miracle Plays
Ms, Ludi Sancti Nycholi; 8 miracle plays on the life of St. Nicholas. [Eastern France, Aubepierre?, early 15th cent]. 25 leaves (lacking c.5), 298mm by 105mm, in contemp wraps using a 1371 vellum document. In a neat cursive bookhand by probably 2 scribes. In French, with stage directions in Latin. (89) £105,000

Miranda, Francisco de, 1750-1816
[A collection of c.40 letters & documents to & from political figures in England, 1802 to 1806, with related material, sold at C on 21 June 1989, lot 106, for £3,000 to Van Wijck.]

Miro, Joan, 1893-1983
ALs, 25 Sept 1946. Byer collection. (90) $425

— 9 Apr 1947. (88) DM600

— 2 Aug 1962. (89) DM850

Mishima, Yukio
ALs, 25 Dec 1957. 4 pp, 8vo. In English, to Tennessee Williams. About Suddenly Last Summer & an 18th-cent Japanese short story called The Blue Turban. (91) $1,800

Missal
— [Middle Rhine, or possibly Erfurt, 2d half of 13th cent]. Adapted to Benedictine use. 326 leaves, vellum, 325mm by 225mm. 18th-cent calf. In dark brown ink in a gothic textura; ff 178 - 241 in an early 14th-cent hand. With extensive musical notation throughout, neumes on 4 staves, many large calligraphic initials, 5 large decorated initials, 7 historiated initials & 2 miniatures. Including a list of c.300 abbots & brothers of St. Peter's, Erfurt. Text on 12 leaves entirely, on others partly erased; some new text added over erasures. Doheny collection. (88) £90,000

— [Picardy, c.1315-25]. Single leaf, vellum, 350mm by 255mm. In a fine large gothic liturgical hand. With 2 two-line illuminated initials in ivyleaf designs with partial borders, & large historiated initial on burnished gold background with full-length bar border & ivyleaves extending around all 4 margins. (91) £9,000

— [Bologna, c.1350]. Single leaf, vellum, 367mm by 265mm. Settings of the Gloria, with music on a 4-line stave. With full-page miniature by Nicolo di Giacomo da Bologna; rubbed. (91) £12,000

— [Rhineland?, c.1400]. 260 leaves, vellum, 258mm by 180mm. Early 16th-cent blindstamped panelled calf bdg. In black ink in a regular gothic textura. With numerous small initials in blue & red & some calligraphic initials with extensive penwork flourishes. (89) £9,500

— [Southern Germany, c.1400]. 266 leaves, vellum, 233mm by 167mm. Contemp blindstamped red sheepskin

over wooden bds. In black & red ink. With painted initials in colors throughout & full-page miniature in gold & colors. (88) DM34,000
— The Missal of Anti-Pope John XXIII. [Bologna, c.1405-1410]. 277 leaves (1 lacking), 322mm by 240mm, in def 15th-cent Italian (Roman?) blind-stamped bdg of wooden bds bevelled on inner edges. In dark brown ink in 2 sizes of a rounded gothic liturgical hand; some pages with music in square neumes on a 4-line red stave. With decorated initials throughout in colors or burnished gold, 89 historiated initials within leafy surrounds, 24 Calendar miniatures, 8 large column-width miniatures, & 3 double-column miniatures with full richly illuminated & historiated borders. Illuminated for Cardinal Giovanni Meliorati probably by the Master of the Brussels Initials & adapted for Anti-Pope John XXIII. Astor MS.A.5. (88) £420,000
— [Northern Italy, early 15th cent]. About 120 leaves only, vellum, 330mm by 230mm; disbound. In brown ink in a rounded gothic hand. With small penwork initials in red & blue. (91) $1,700
— [Austria or Bohemia, mid-15th cent]. 1 leaf only, vellum, 370mm by 245mm. Introducing the Temporale. In a gothic bookhand. With large historiated initial & foliate three-quarter border. (89) £2,800
— [Southern Germany or Bohemia, 15th cent]. 212 leaves & 2 vellum flyleaves from an antiphoner, 300mm by 224mm, in contemp lea over thick wooden bds; lacking clasps. In black & red ink in a lettre batarde by several scribes. With small initials throughout in brown & red, 5-line initial, & full-page miniature of the Crucifixion. Worn throughout. (91) DM2,200
— [Lower Rhine, c.1450]. 288 leaves, vellum, 343mm by 245mm. 17th cent brown lea over wooden bds. In black & red ink in a gothic hand. With painted initials in red & blue throughout, 3 large & numerous smaller initials, & full-page miniature in gold & colors including coats-of-arms of the Morien & Borchorst families. (88) DM85,000

— [Germany, 15th cent]. (89) DM1,000
— [Veneto, c.1450]. 4 leaves only, vellum, 348mm by 262mm. In a rounded gothic script. With 38 small initials in red or blue with contrasting penwork, & 3 large historiated initials with full-length illuminated borders. (90) £7,000
— [Netherlands, 2d half of 15th cent]. Use not stated. 287 leaves, vellum, 185mm by 135mm. 18th-cent pink velvet bdg. In dark brown ink in a neat gothic bookhand. With 13 large historiated initials & full-page miniature. (88) £5,500
— [Southern Tyrol, c.1475]. 107 leaves (4 lacking) & flyleaf, vellum, 300mm by 213mm. Contemp tawed skin over bevelled wooden bds. In several sizes of a rounded gothic liturgical hand. With painted initials throughout up to 6 lines in height, some with penwork decoration. (91) £13,500
— The Missal of Etienne de Longwy. [Southern Burgundy, Macon, c.1490]. 285 leaves (3 blank) & 2 flyleaves, vellum, 344mm by 230mm. Parisian olive-brown mor bdg of c.1575 richly gilt. In several sizes of a formal calligraphic gothic liturgical hand. With 46 very large illuminated initials with full-length illuminated borders supporting panels across upper & lower margins with flowers, fruit & animals, 24 Calendar miniatures within full borders, 52 historiated initials with full borders & 2 full-page miniatures in elaborate architectural frames. (91) £110,000
— Pontifical Missal. [Northern Italy, late 15th cent]. 2 leaves only, vellum, 393mm by 281mm. In 2 sizes of a rounded gothic script, partly with music on a 3-line stave. With 22 decorated initials in red or blue with contrasting penwork, & 2 large historiated initials with illuminated borders. (90) £2,400
— Missale abbreviatum. [Bavaria, Diessen?, 1491]. 56 leaves, vellum, 238mm by 178mm. Contemp blind-stamped brown goatskin over wooden bds with clasps. In a gothic liturgical hand. With several large initials in red penwork. Dampstained. (91) DM7,000

— [Northern France, c.1500]. 105 leaves (2 blank, 1 lacking), vellum, 195mm by 130mm. 16th-cent green velvet over wooden bds. In black ink in an elegant lettre batarde. With 438 small & 3 large initials in gold & colors, & 23 small & 2 full-page miniatures; "in a remarkably fine state of preservation." (90) DM80,000

— [Italy, c.1500]. Single leaf, vellum, 403mm by 273mm. With large historiated initial & 3-quarter floral & foliate border. Framed. (90) DM2,400

— [Eastern France or Baden, early 16th cent]. Abbot's Missal. 3 leaves, vellum, 275mm by 183mm. In a lettre batarde. With 11 two-line initials in burnished gold & 3 historiated initials with partial borders. (91) £1,200

— Missal for the Funeral Mass. [Northern France or Southern Flanders, early 16th cent]. 25 leaves, vellum, 222mm by 165mm, in later limp vellum. By at least 2 scribes in a formal gothic liturgical hand. With 2 very large illuminated initials with partial borders, large historiated initial, & 6 pp with music on a 4-line red stave. (89) £1,500

— [Germany, Alsace?, 1518]. Votive Missal for Benedictine use. 77 leaves, vellum, 303mm by 200mm. Contemp blindstamped calf over wooden bds. In dark brown ink in 3 sizes of a regular gothic bookhand. With 170 two- or three-line initials in blue, red or white, a few with marginal extensions, & large contemp colored woodcut pasted in. (90) £4,000

— [Rome, 21 May 1539]. The Colonna Missal. 97 leaves (3 lacking), vellum, 370mm by 260mm. Contemp reddish-brown mor by Maestro Luigi. In black ink in a large gothic liturgical hand. With 36 pp containing musical notations, 266 illuminated initials, 33 decorated inhabited initials on gold ground with marginal decoration, 1 very large historiated initial & 1 miniature. Probably vol II of a set of 7 or 8 commissioned by Cardinal Pompeo Colonna. Doheny collection. (88) £55,000

— Pontifical Missal. [Antwerp, c.1846]. 96 leaves, 510mm by 350mm, in 19th-cent crushed mor by Gruyere. In a fine gothic hand by Joannes Josephus Waulers. With calligraphic & illuminated initials throughout, decorated borders on each page, & 11 full-page miniatures. (91) £1,900

Missouri
— SAINT CHARLES, TERRITORY OF LOUISIANA. - 2 documents, 28 Apr 1806 & 4 Feb 1809. Announcing an estate auction, & summons. Alexander collection. (90) $75

Mistral, Frederic, 1830-1914
A Ls s (2), 18 Jan & 2 Feb 1885. (90) £90

Mitchell, Janet Marshall —& Wilson, Thomas Epps
Group photograph, [c.1840s]. Daguerreotype, 5.75 by 6.5 inches. With anr, showing Janet Mitchell with child. (89) $1,900

Mitchell, John
Ms, A State of the Pay of the Army of Ireland. 28 Apr 1760. Leaf count not given, 168mm by 103mm, in contemp mor gilt by Parliamentary Binder B. (91) $3,250

Mitchell, Margaret, 1900-49
Ls, 5 Jan 1932. 5 pp, 4to. To her future mother-in-law. Chatting about the Christmas season. Sgd Peggy. (90) $1,500

— [late Nov] 1936. 1 p, 8vo. To Mrs. Fennel. Thanking for comments on her book. (91) $1,600

— 7 Jan 193[7]. 1 p, 4to. To Dr. Mayos. About letters received since the publication of her book. (91) $1,400

— 24 Feb 1937. 1 p, 4to. To Miss Gambrell. Declining to sign Confederate bills. (90) $1,600

— 17 June 1938. 1 p, 4to. To Dr. Mayos. Informing him about preparations for the film Gone With the Wind. (91) $4,000

— 15 Mar 1940. 2 pp, folio. To Walter Winchell. About problems she has had as the result of his printing an item saying that she got a bonus payment from Selznick & that he gave her his Oscar for Gone With The Wind. (91) $10,000

— 2 July 1941. (90) $800

— 26 Oct 1943. 3 pp, 4to. To Dr. Mayos. Chatting about a private viewing of Gone With the Wind. (91) $3,000
— [n.d.] "Wednesday". (90) $450

Mitford, Mary Russell, 1787-1855
[Substantial portions of 3 autograph Mss, revised throughout, comprising parts of her tragedies Julian & Charles I, & of an unidentified article, 164 pp, 4to & 8vo, sold at S on 20 July 1989, lot 133, for £450 to Meredith.]

Mitscherlich, Alexander, 1908-82
Autograph Ms, essay refuting H. (89) DM700
— Autograph Ms, fragment of a treatise about psychosomatic medicine; [n.d.]. (90) DM500
— Autograph Ms, notes about Freud's concept of psychoanalysis; [1971]. (90) DM320
— Autograph Ms, notes concerning the relationship between psychoanalysis & politics; [n.d.]. (88) DM750
Corrected galley proof, Psychoanalyse heute, sgd & dated 12 Mar 1964. (88) DM500

Mittermaier, Karl Joseph Anton, 1787-1867
ALs, 12 Dec 1848. (88) DM760

Mocenigo, Alvise, Doge of Venice
Document, 1702. 101 leaves, 215mm by 150mm, in contemp velvet. Appointment for Marcantonio Molin as administrator of Asola. With full-page miniature. (89) £1,800

Modersohn, Otto, 1865-1943
ALs, 4 July 1930. (88) DM420

Moedebeck, Hermann, 1857-1910
— Paulus, Kaethchen. - ALs, 16 Jan 1900. 2 pp, 4to. To Moedebeck. Responding to his inquiry about the construction of a paper balloon reinforced with "strips of percale". On personal letterhead with aeronautic vignette. (90) DM1,200

Moellendorff, Wichard Joachim Heinrich von, 1724-1816
A Ls s (2), [1792/93?]. (88) DM850
ALs, 22 Sept 1793. Schroeder collection. (89) DM400

— 6 Nov 1806. (90) DM500

Moeran, Ernest John, 1894-1950
Autograph music, 4 Mss of songs, Loveliest of Trees, June 1931; Oh fair enough, June 1931; Oh fair enough, revised version, 26 Dec 1934; & High Germany, [n.d.]. (88) £800
— Autograph music, 4 Mss of songs, Mantle of Blue, Tilly, Twilight, & Palm Sunday; Christmas 1934 & [n.d.]. (88) £750
— Autograph music, 4 Mss of songs, Loveliest of Trees, June 1931; Oh fair enough, June 1931; Oh fair enough, revised version, 26 Dec 1934; & High Germany, [n.d.]. (90) £600
— Autograph music, 4 Mss of songs, Mantle of Blue, Tilly, Twilight, & Palm Sunday; Christmas 1934 & [n.d.]. (90) £650
Series of 29 A Ls s, 1931 to 1941. (88) £550
— Series of 29 A Ls s, 1931 to 1941. (90) £850

Moerike, Eduard, 1804-75
Autograph Ms, poem, Scherz; [pbd 1856]. 1 p, 4to. 2 eight-line stanzas; fair copy. (90) DM6,200
Autograph transcript, poem, An Eduard Keller; [n.d.]. 2 pp, 8vo. Sgd. (89) DM9,500
ALs, "Saturday" [1856]. 1 p, 4to. To an unnamed Ed. Sending a poem for publication in the journal Salon. (90) DM2,800
— 23 May [1864?]. 1 p, 4to. To the booksellers Neff. Returning a book. (90) DM1,100
— 6 [Mar 1865]. 1 p, 4to. To Michael Bernays. Inviting him for coffee. (88) DM3,600
— 14 Apr 1871. 4 pp, 4to. To [Christian Kolb]. Personal letter about his failing health, the war, the death of friends, etc. (91) DM9,200
Autograph quotation, beginning "Alles Vortreffliche beschraenkt uns fuer einen Augenblick... (Goethe)", sgd & dated 15 Sept 1856. 1 p, 4to. With silhouette port by Luise von Breitschwert-Walther at head. In album kept by Mathilde Amman as student at the Katharinenstift, Stuttgart, con-

taining c.26 entries, partly with silhouettes. (90) DM8,000

Autograph sentiment, poem, 3 lines, referring to the postmaster F. A. von Scholl, [1869]. 1 p, 16mo. Including drawing of postillon's horn, in pen & pencil. With letter of transmittal by C. Hartlaub. (91) DM2,200

— SCHOENHARDT, KARL VON. - Autograph Ms, poem read at Moerike's funeral, 6 June 1875. 1 p, 8vo. Sgd. (90) DM450

Moeschinger, Albert, 1897-1985
Autograph music, sketches for his Fantasia 1944 for string orchestra, sgd & dated 10 July 1944. Ammann collection. (90) DM600

Moessbauer, Rudolf
Autograph Ms, notes for a lecture at the "Colloque Ampere, Ljublijana 1966". (89) DM320
— Autograph Ms, "orthogonality", calculations; [n.d.]. (90) DM340

Moffat, Robert, 1795-1883
ALs, 3 Feb 1843. (88) £50

Moholy-Nagy, Laszlo, 1895-1946
ALs, 25 Feb 1924. (88) DM520
— 10 Nov 1929. 1 p, 4to. To Franz Roh. Expressing satisfaction that a book is about to be pbd. Sgd m=n. (90) DM1,300
— 4 Dec 1929. 1 p, 4to. To Franz Roh. About a projected publication, comments about Picasso in a recent article, & an exhibition in Zurich. (90) DM3,200
— 5 Dec 1929. 2 p, 4to. To Franz Roh. Expressing gratification about recipient's approval, & musing about his reactions to criticism. (90) DM2,700
ANs, 21 Mar 1928. (88) £300

Moleschott, Jacob, 1822-93
Collection of 8 A Ls s & autograph Ms, 6 Oct 1864 to 21 Sept 1865. 22 pp, 8vo. To a pbr in Paris. Regarding the French Ed of his book Der Kreislauf des Lebens. Inquiries concerning copyright on translations. (91) DM1,100
ALs, 11 Jan 1891. (91) DM260

Moliere, Jean Baptiste Poquelin de, 1622-73
Ds, 20 June 1667. 1 p, folio. Stating he has given Claude Le Long power to collect a debt from Francois de La Court. Tipped to larger leaf, with trans. With related material. Barrett collection. (89) $28,000

Molnar, Ferenc, 1878-1952
Typescript, Thirteen chapters of Autobiographical Notes. 1947-1948. Remembrance of my Companion in Exile. Trans by Barrows Mussey..., 1948. 331 leaves, 4to. In black lea folder. With numerous autograph revisions. Inscr to Ben Raeburn, sgd & dated 1950. With sgd 1st Ed. (88) DM2,700
ALs, 10 Mar 1951. (91) DM240
Photograph, sgd & inscr, 1920. (90) DM220

Moltke, Helmuth, Graf von, 1800-91
ALs, 1 Aug 1856. (90) DM440
— 28 Sept 1857. 4 pp, 8vo. To his wife. Informing her about his journey from Thuringia to Koblenz. Schroeder collection. (89) DM1,100
— 21 Mar 1864. 3 pp, 4to. To Prince Adalbert of Prussia. Discussing troop movements & naval actions in the Baltic Sea. Margin cut; repaired. Schroeder collection. (89) DM6,000
— 19 June 1868. (89) DM320
— 27 Jan 1869. (89) DM300
— 30 Dec 1871. Schroeder collection. (89) DM750
— 15 Oct 1872. 2 pp, 8vo. Recipient unnamed. Giving biographical details about his youth. (90) DM1,200
— 14 Feb 1875. (89) DM460
— 15 Apr 1885. (88) DM500
— 3 Sept 1889. (88) DM700
— 6 Aug 1890. (91) DM310
— 29 Mar 1891. (90) DM800
Ls s (2), 30 Dec 1879 & 14 Jan 1880. (90) DM320
Ls, 5 Mar 1871. (89) DM280
— 29 Jan 1874. (90) DM260
ANs, [n.d.]. (88) DM270
See also: Bismarck, Otto von & Moltke

Moltke, Helmuth von, 1848-1916
Series of 11 A Ls s, mostly 1909 to 1915. 26 pp, 4to. To his niece Maria. Family letters, & reflecting on European & German politics & his role in the army. Schroeder collection. (89) DM1,300

Mommsen, Theodor, 1817-1903
Series of 8 A Ls s, 9 Nov 1889 to 2 Jan 1901. 19 pp, 8vo. To members of his family. About his work, the sale of his brother's library, etc. (91) DM1,100

A Ls s (2), 22 Dec 1895 & 6 June 1897. 8 pp, 8vo. To the Ed of the Deutsche Juristen-Zeitung. Refusing to review a report by Paul Hinschius & stating his opinion on the situation of unsalaried lecturers (Privatdozenten) at German universities. (91) DM1,400

ALs, 7 Dec 1861. (91) DM360
— 27 Aug 1865. (90) DM320
— 8 Sept 1884. (91) DM220
— 20 Oct 1890. (90) DM270
— 30 Jan 1903. (88) DM700
— [n.d.]. Kuenzel collection. (90) DM260

Monck, George, 1st Duke of Albemarle, 1608-70
Ls, 15 Nov 1659. (89) £950
— 18 Jan 1666/7. (89) £130

Mondrian, Piet, 1872-1944
A Ls s (2), 24 & 30 Sept 1928. 3 pp, 4to. To Professor Dorner. Regarding the sale of one of his paintings to the museum at Hannover. File holes. (89) DM2,400

— A Ls s (2), 3 Jan & 6 Oct 1941. 3 pp, folio & 4to. To Frederick John Kiesler. About settling down in New York, hoping to see him, & expressing thanks for words of appreciation. (90) DM3,000

Monet, Claude, 1840-1926
ALs, 9 July [1867]. (88) £650
— 17 Nov 1884. (88) £250
— 29 May 1889. 2 pp, 8vo. Recipient unnamed. Expecting the delivery of his paintings the next day. Framed with a photograph. (91) $3,000
— 2 June 1890. (88) £280
— 3 Aug 1897. 2 pp, 8vo. To Gustave Geffroy. Thanking for his new book & talking about his work. Byer collection. (90) $1,800
— 12 Feb 1899. 1 p, 8vo. Recipient unnamed. Announcing a consignment of pictures for an exhibition. (88) DM1,100
— 18 May 1900. (90) £240
— 16 Oct 1917. 3 pp, 8vo. Recipient unnamed. Thanking for port photographs & indicating the one he prefers. (90) DM1,900
— 1 Jan 1918. 2 pp, 8vo. To Charlotte Gyou (?). Sending New Year's wishes & hoping to see her. With related material. (89) DM2,000
— 12 Sept 1919. 2 pp, 8vo. Recipient unnamed. Informing him that his work makes it impossible for him to receive visitors. (90) DM1,900
— [9 Apr n.y.]. 1 p, 8vo. To Gauthier. Thanking for interceding with his aunt. (91) DM1,050

Mongolian Manuscripts
Document, [1837 or 1897]. Scroll, 254cm by 84cm, on yellow satin. Decree elevating the monk Mam-mkha'i-skar-ma to the rank of Er-rte-ni Mergen for support of the Buddhist religion & the Emperor of China. In dBu-med script. With colored illusts. (91) $4,000

Monroe, James, 1758-1831
Autograph Ms (2), draft regarding "the Jacobins", [7 Nov 1794], & account sheet "for Mr. (88) $225

A Ls s (2), 24 Apr 1821 & 11 Apr 1828. 4 pp, 4to. Recipient(s) unknown. Concerning debts incurred by an overseer, & the sale of slaves. (89) $2,500

ALs, 10 Nov 1790. (91) $600
— 3 June 1792. (90) $725
— 17 Jan 1795. 3 pp, 4to. To Thomas Pinckney. About the adverse effects of the Jay Treaty on his negotiations with the French. In blue mor folding case. Adlai E. Stevenson collection. (88) $6,000
— 15 July 1797. 1 p, 4to. To Alexander Hamilton. In 3d person, informing him of his arrival & suggesting a meeting. (88) $1,700
— 23 Mar 1798. 2 pp, 4to. To John Breckenridge. Discussing the sale of his bounty lands in Kentucky & rela-

— tions with France. Framed. (90) $4,800
— 23 Mar 1798. 2 pp, 4to. To John Breckenridge. About the necessity of selling his western lands, & commenting about news from Europe. Repaired. (89) $2,500
— 4 July 1802. 2 pp, 4to. To William B. Giles. Reporting on political events in Virginia, & asking for a loan. Seal hole repaired. Doheny collection. (89) $5,500
— 18 June 1803. 1 p, 4to. To Nathaniel [Cuttins?]. Hoping to see him in England in 2 weeks. Doheny collection. (89) $1,900
— 1 Mar 1805. (91) $700
— 20 June 1806. (89) £700
— [June 1806]. 2 pp, 4to. To John Pinkerton. Giving advice regarding revisions in recipient's book Modern Geography. Framed. (90) $1,100
— 12 May 1810. 1 p, 4to. To Mr. Everett. About his accounts with the government & his financial affairs. With bust engraving. (88) $2,200
— 15 Mar 1814. Christensen collection. (90) $800
— 22 Feb 1815. 2 pp, 4to. To [Sec of the Treasury Alexander J. Dallas]. As acting Sec of War, requesting his opinion on his proposed answer to the Senate regarding reduction of the army. Rosenbloom collection. (88) $2,250
— 26 Apr 1815. Whiton collection. (88) $650
— 28 May 1815. 4 pp, 4to. To A. J. Dallas. Reflecting on the state of the world & requesting legal advice regarding the sale of produce from the Virginia up-country. Sang collection. (91) $4,250
— 14 Sept 1815. (88) $850
— 10 Apr 1816. Christensen collection. (90) $500
— 13 June 1816. 1 p, 4to. To [H. P. Nugent?]. Sending material for the next Ed of [A. L.] Latour's war memoir. Inlaid. Sang collection. (91) $1,800
— 2 Apr [1817]. 2 pp, 4to. To Col. Samuel Lane. Offering to sell his own furniture, plate & china for use at the White House. Corner torn. (90) $7,000
— 23 Mar 1819. 2 pp, 4to. To Thomas Swann. Discussing legal action against Robert Swart for evading payment for land. Pratt collection. (89) $2,000
— 20 Oct 1819. (89) £650
— 2 June 1820. 1 p, 4to. Recipient unknown. Informing him about his arrival at Oak Hill & his intention to proceed to Albemarle. (90) $1,500
— 2 May 1821. 2 pp, 4to. To the House of Representatives. Content not given. (91) $2,400
— 13 June 1822. 2 pp, 4to. To [Peter Stephen DuPonceau]. Regarding his message on internal improvements & his political principles. Pratt collection. (89) $4,000
— 10 May 1823. 3 pp, 4to. Recipient unnamed. Explaining his withdrawal of the nomination of a member of the navy, & referring to affairs in South America. Names deleted. (89) £4,000
— 12 July 1824. 1 p, 4to. To William Lee. Concerning his problems in finding a passage to the US from Europe in 1797. (91) $2,800
— 16 Sept 1824. 2 pp, 4to. Recipient unknown. Referring to his return from Europe in 1797 & requesting a copy of the proceedings of the Hartford Convention. (91) $2,500
— 27 May 1825. 2 pp, 4to. To an unnamed banker. Asking for authorization to repay a loan in installments. (89) $1,500
— 19 May 1826. 4 pp, 4to. To an unidentified Congressman. Discussing strategies to obtain a settlement of his claims for expenses as envoy in Europe. (89) $3,750
— 11 Feb 1829. (90) $1,000
— 15 Aug 1830. 2 pp, 4to. To [James Madison]. Respecting inquiries by Jared Sparks about the negotiations for peace, 1782 & 1783. (90) $2,250
— 15 Apr 1831. 2 pp, 4to. To Gen. James Breckinridge. Informing him of his intention to sell his property in Virginia & to resign from the Board of Visitors of the University of Virginia. McVitty collection. (90) $4,250

Ls, 13 Oct 1812. (91) $1,000
— 14 Feb 1815. 2 pp, 4to. To Brig. Gen. Thomas Miller. As acting Sec of War, informing him about the peace treaty. (89) $17,000

Ds, 27 June 1800. (88) $240
— 2 Sept 1800. (88) $130
— 7 Apr 1801. (91) $300
— 17 June 1801. (89) $275
— [after 26 June 1812]. (88) $1,000
— 26 June 1812. (89) $600
— 28 Aug 1812. (89) $450
— 28 Aug 1812. (88) $450
— 7 Nov 1812. (90) $650
— 7 Nov 1812. (88) $650
— 7 Nov 1812. (88) $600
— 7 Nov 1812. (88) $525
— [c.1813]. Byer collection. (90) $750
— 6 Sept 1814. (90) $350
— 27 June 1817. (88) $220
— 16 July 1817. (91) $800
— 21 Jan 1818. (91) $400
— 17 Apr 1818. (90) $500
— 24 June 1818. (90) $600
— 29 June 1818. (89) $290
— 12 Oct 1818. (88) $350
— 26 Nov 1818. (91) $350
— 17 Nov 1818. (91) $850
— 4 Jan 1819. (88) $180
— 6 July 1819. (90) $175
— 23 July 1820. (90) $425
— 28 Aug 1820. (88) $650
— 29 Aug 1820. (90) $425
— 2 Oct 1820. (89) $300
— 2 Oct 1820. (91) $400
— 27 Nov 1820. (90) $250
— 28 Nov 1820. (90) $425
— 28 Mar 1821. (90) DM620
— 9 Apr 1822. (89) $300
— 17 May 1822. (88) $225
— 13 Nov 1822. (90) $350
— 3 Mar 1823. 1 p, folio. Appointment of Michael Hogan as Consul at Valparaiso. Countersgd by John Q. Adams. With decorative vignette. Framed. Byer collection. (90) $1,500
— 20 June 1823. (88) $350
— 11 July 1823. (90) $300
— 18 Aug 1823. (91) $550
— 10 Dec 1823. (90) $350
— 6 Jan 1824. (88) $325
Franking signature, [15 July n.y.]. (90) $650

Monroe, Marilyn, 1926-62
[A group of 4 photographs, [c.1947], with negatives, sold at CNY on 21 June 1989, lot 384, for $1,300.]
[A collection of material relating to her, 1 Apr 1957 to 16 Mar 1962, including 2 letters & a postcard sent to her, 5 photographs, hotel charge cards, pharmacy bills, & telephone messages, sold at S on 21 July 1988, lot 250, for £1,100 to Pedler.]
[2 autograph inscriptions, sgd, [n.d.], on small scraps of paper, sold at S on 15 Nov 1988, lot 1733, for £900 to Pervanas.]
Ls, 10 Aug 1957. 1 p, 8vo. To Rabbi Robert Goldburg. Thanking for a scarf. On Mrs. Arthur Miller letterhead. (89) $1,400
— 26 Feb 1958. Length not stated. To Milton H. Greene. Carbon copy, referring to the copyright of The Prince and the Show Girl. Sgd twice. (91) $3,250
Ds, 2 Mar 1949. 4 pp, 4to. Contract with the William Morris Agency. (91) $3,000
— 2 May 1950. 16 pp, 11 by 8.5 inches. Typed & mimeographed contract with Twentieth Century-Fox Film Corporation; also sgd by others. (90) $6,500
— 1 July 1956. 1 p, 4to. Certificate of Conversion to Judaism. Also sgd by Rabbi Robert Goldburg, Arthur Miller, & 2 others. (89) $6,500
Check, accomplished & sgd, 16 Oct 1948. Drawn on the Bank of America for $1.00 payable to the Hollywood Studio Club. (91) $2,500
— Anr, sgd, 19 Sept 1958. Payable to the NY Telephone Co; including her typed telephone no. (91) $2,250
Photograph, sgd & inscr, [c.1952]. (89) £600
— Anr, [n.d.]. (88) £700
— Anr, [n.d.]. (91) $600
— Anr, [n.d.]. 4to. Inscr to Reg, in white ink. Framed. (91) $1,500

Monroe, Marilyn, 1926-62 —&
Miller, Arthur
[Their signatures, in pencil, on a def program for Ralph Richardson in The Waltz of the Toreadors, [n.d.], sold at R on 4 Mar 1989, lot 353, for $500.]

Monroe, Marilyn, 1926-62. See: Miller, Arthur & Monroe

Montagu, Edward, 1st Earl of Sandwich, 1625-72. See: Pepys Family

Montagu, Elizabeth, 1720-1800
ALs, 8 Oct 1780. (88) £250

Montagu, John, 4th Earl of Sandwich, 1718-92
Ds, 31 Oct 1772. (91) $500
— 31 Mar 1775. (90) DM530

Monteagle, William Parker, 4th Baron, 1575-1622
Ds, 23 Oct 1596. (90) £140

Montecuccoli, Raimondo, 1609-80
Ls, 16 Apr 1671. (90) DM550

Montefiore, Sir Moses, 1784-1885
ALs, 26 May 1873. (91) DM320

Montesquieu, Charles de Secondat, 1689-1755
ALs, 11 Jan 1739. (90) £580

Montesquiou-Fezensac, Robert de, 1855-1921
Collection of 2 A Ls s & autograph Ms, 27 Apr 1909, 16 May 1909 & [1909]. (88) DM220

Montessori, Maria, 1870-1952
ALs, [c.Nov 1932]. 2 pp, 4to. To an unnamed lady. Discussing progress of her schools in Germany & Italy. (88) DM1,800

Montgelas, Maximilian, Graf von, 1759-1838
Ls, 14 Nov 1814. (90) DM650

Montgomery, Bernard Law, 1st Viscount Montgomery of Alamein, 1887-1976
A Ls s (2), 20 Dec 1948 & 23 Mar 1949. (88) £280
— A Ls s (2), 6 Oct & 6 Dec 1962. (90) DM600
ALs, 4 Feb 1950. (88) $65
— 25 May 1953. (91) $225
— 1 Jan 1961. (90) DM390
— 4 June 1964. (91) DM460
— 2 July 1965. (90) £160
Collection of 2 Ls s (carbon copies), 5 photographs, sgd, & signature on ptd message, 10 June 1944 to 1972. To 21 Army Group, congratulating on landings in Normandy. To the Sec of State for War, sending a dispatch. With related material. (89) £1,600
Autograph telegram, 11 Nov 1955. (88) £300

Montmorency, Anne, Duc de, 1493-1567
Ls, May 1559. (90) $90
— 4 Aug 1561. (91) DM430
— 30 Sept 1564. (90) $150

Moore, Clement Clarke, 1779-1863
ALs, 4 Dec 1812. Doheny collection. (89) $850

Moore, George, 1852-1933
Autograph Ms, novel, Esther Waters; fragment, [c.1894]. 5 pp, folio, on rectos only; numbered 6 - 10. Heavily revised. In cloth slipcase. Doheny collection. (89) $2,200
Typescript, play, The Peacock's Feathers [Elizabeth Cooper]; [1913 or earlier]. 116 pp, 4to, on rectos only. With autograph revisions. In cloth folding case. Doheny collection. (89) $3,000
Corrected galley proof, novel, Heloise and Abelard, [1920-21]. 266 galley pp, folio, mtd on guards. With extensive autograph revisions. In bds, with ptd tp. With 2 related Ls s. (89) £4,000

Moore, Henry, 1898-1986
ALs, "Sunday" [c.1919]. (89) £750
— 25 Jan 1929. 2 pp, 4to. Recipient unnamed. Describing the work on sculptures for the Underground Headquarters Building in London. With related material. (89) DM1,300
Ls, 13 Aug 1952. (89) DM260
— 20 Mar 1961. (91) DM400

Moore, Marianne, 1887-1972
Collection of ALs, Ls, 2 letters, & 3 postcards, sgd (2 autograph), 8 Feb 1957, 1 Nov 1959, & [n.d.]. (90) $260
Ls, 22 Jan 1929. (89) $100
ANs, 5 Feb 1952. (90) $55

Moore, Thomas, 1779-1852
Autograph Ms, poem, Thoughts on Soap, draft, [n.d.]. (88) £350
— Autograph Ms, song with music, Smile as you us'd to do, [Feb 1826]. (88) £150
— Autograph Ms, song with music, be-

MOORE

ginning "When the first summer bee...", [n.d.]. (89) £400
Series of 58 A Ls s, 6 May 1805 to 19 Nov 1846. 70 pp, 12mo to 4to. To John Wilson Croker. Literary correspondence. Some initialled. With 2 replies by Croker. Inlaid to larger sheets; in mor gilt bdg by Wallis. Doheny collection. (89) $11,000
ALs, 28 Nov 1816. (88) £300
— 15 Feb 1824. (91) DM320
— 24 Dec 1836. Doheny collection. (89) $350
— [n.d.]. (89) DM380
See also: Bishop, Henry R. & Moore

Morand, Joseph, Baron, 1757-1813
ALs, [20 July 1799]. (88) DM400

Moravia, Alberto, Pseud. of Alberto Pincherle
ALs, [n.d.]. (89) DM950

Mordaunt, Henry, 2d Earl of Peterborough, 1624?-97
ALs, 1 Mar [n.y.]. (90) £50

More, Sir Thomas, 1478-1535
Ds, 29 June 1533. 170mm by 400mm, vellum. Agreement confirming title to property in Oldford, Hackney & Stratford to Thomas Shaw. Also sgd by 2 others. With 3 seals on parchment tags. (89) £8,500

Moreau, Gustave, 1826-98
ALs, 1 Feb 1887. (90) DM360

Moreau, Jean Claude, Baron, 1755-1828.
See: Tirolean Uprising, 1809

Moreau, Jean Victor, 1763-1813
ALs, [15 Oct 1795]. (91) DM600
— [24 Nov 1795]. (90) DM680
— [Summer 1800]. (91) DM400
— 11 Feb 1813. 2 pp, 4to. To an unnamed count. Analyzing the political situation in Europe & the role of the Czar. With related material. (90) DM1,300

Morgan, Daniel, 1736-1802
ALs, 8 Mar 1786. (91) $450
— 22 Jan 1795. 1 p, folio. To Gen. John Neville, who was collector of the whiskey tax. About the whiskey rebellion. (91) $2,400

Morgan, George, 1743-1810
Ms, letterbook & journal, Apr to July & Sept to Nov 1776. 73 pp, folio; disbound. Retained copies of correspondence & memoranda as Indian agent, recording meetings with Indians at Fort Pitt, etc. Partly autograph. Def. (89) $10,000
— INDIANA COMPANY. - Ms, transcript of minutes of the proprietors of the Indiana Company, 21 Sept to 15 Nov 1775, 18 pp, folio; stitched. Sgd by Morgan as secretary. With related material. Somewhat def. (89) $2,250
See also: Hancock, John

Morgan, John Pierpont, 1837-1913
Ds, 30 June 1886. (91) $450
— 1886. (91) DM540

Morgenstern, Christian, 1871-1914
Autograph Ms, 2 poems, beginning "Es giebt noch Wunder, liebes Herz", sgd Chr.M., & "Ein Voeglein singt mich aus dem Traum"; Dec 1901. 2 pp, 8vo. Inscr to Robert Kahn. (90) DM1,800
— Autograph Ms, poem, Die beiden Flaschen, [n.d.]. 1 p, folio. (88) DM1,700
ALs, [1894]. (89) DM400
— 17 Oct 1903. (91) DM750

Moritz, Landgraf von Hessen, 1572-1632
Ls, 5 July 1603. 3 pp, folio. To King Henri IV of France. Discussing a variety of political matters. (91) DM2,700
ADs, 2 Apr 1617. (88) DM420
Ds, 25 Apr 1607. (89) DM440

Moritz, Karl Philipp, 1757-93
Autograph sentiment, dedication, sgd, on detached flyleaf of his novel Anton Reiser. Berlin, 1785. 8vo. Including tp & 1st page. (90) DM4,200

Morley, Christopher, 1890-1957
Collection of 7 A Ls s & 11 Ls s, 1926 to 1951. (89) $950

Mormons
[A letter, 20 Dec 1838, 3 pp, size, writer & recipient not stated, reporting about the killing of Mormons in Missouri, sold at rf on 5 Dec, lot 48, for $525.]

Morrell, Walter
Ms, Morrell's manufacture for the newe draperie Devided into Three Bookes..., 1616. 100 pp, 4to, in limp vellum gilt. Describing a woollen manufactury at Hatfield, Hertfordshire. Marquess of Downshire collection. (90) £4,200

Morris, Gouverneur, 1752-1816
ALs, 23 Nov 1784. (90) £170
— 12 Feb 1802. Byer collection. (90) $175
— 14 Feb 1809. (90) $300
— 10 Jan 1810. (91) $400

Morris, Lewis, Signer from New York
ALs, [c.1775]. (91) $500
— 3 Aug 1782. 1 p, 4to. To Aaron Burr. Congratulating him on his admission to the bar & his marriage, & hoping for an end of the war. (90) $1,100
— 9 July 1790. (91) $600
ADs, 26 Oct 1779. (89) $500

Morris, Robert, Signer from Pennsylvania
Collection of 2 A Ls s & Ls, 1779 to 1781. (89) $900
— Collection of ALs & Ls, 3 Nov 1787 & 21 Oct 1796. (89) $550
— Collection of 2 A Ls s & 2 Ds s, 13 Sept 1790 to 25 Feb 1795. (89) $550
A L s s (2), 18 May 1786 & 13 Nov 1792. (89) $800
ALs, 30 Nov 1788. (90) $800
— 30 July 1789. (91) $500
— 11 Apr 1793. (90) $400
— 12 Apr 1794. (89) $450
— 2 Dec 1797. 3 pp, 4to. To Israel Whelan. About fraud in a land transaction. (91) $1,300
— 6 Aug 1799. (89) $425
Ls, 27 Sept 1782. 5 pp, folio. To Benjamin Franklin. Discussing Franco-American relations. (89) $4,000
— 12 Feb 1784. 4 pp, 4to. To Benjamin Franklin. Urging him to pay the account of a commercial firm, & discussing the public debt. With related material. (89) $1,400
— 23 Jan 1787. (91) $280
ANs, 30 Oct 1799. (89) $280
Ds, 17 Nov 1774. (91) $700
— 2 Aug 1785. (88) $150
— 23 Apr 1793. (88) $70
— 18 Apr 1795. (89) $500
— 10 Nov 1795. (90) $325
— 17 July 1806. (91) $550
Signature, on verso of Ds by John Nicholson, 1 Nov 1794, 1 p, 8vo, regarding a payment to Morris. (91) $180

Morris, William, 1834-96
[A group of 47 letters & cards by Sydney Cockerell, Graily Hewitt, & others, 1934, thanking Estelle Doheny for a copy of the limited Ed of Anna Cox Brinton's A Pre-Raphaelite Aenid of Virgil ..., Being an Essay in Honour of the William Morris Centenary, Los Angeles, 1934; with a copy of the book, sgd by Doheny, Brinton & pbr Ritchie, sold at CNY on 19 May 1989, lot 2360, for $26,000 to Finch.]
Autograph Ms, humorous poem of 6 4-line stanzas about early morning games of tennis with the sister of an Essex friend. (91) $850
— Autograph Ms, notes for articles on various political subjects, [1880s?]. 6 pp, 4to, on rectos only. Inlaid & bound with a transcript in blue mor gilt by Riviere. Doheny collection. (89) $3,500
— Autograph Ms, novel, News From Nowhere, [1889-90]. 266 pp, folio, on rectos only. Working Ms, sgd at end. Some leaves pieced together from partial sheets. In Kelmscott-style bevelled oak bds. Doheny collection. (89) $75,000
Original drawings, (2), full-page border & capital initial, for The Well at the World's End, [1896]. 1 p, 266mm by 180mm. In indian ink over pencil, heightened with white. Anr initial removed. With note of authenticity by Sydney Cockerell in margin. Doheny collection. (89) $4,800
— Original drawings, 3-quarter border & 6 initials, designed for the Kelmscott Press, [c.1892]. Single sheet, overall size not stated. In indian ink over pencil, heightened with white. Inscr by Sydney Cockerell in margin. Doheny collection. (89) $6,000
— Original drawings, (8), initial capitals, [c.June 1893]. 3 sheets, size not stated. In indian ink over pencil, heightened with white. 1 sheet (containing 6 initials) inscr by Sydney Cockerell.

Doheny collection. (89) $3,250

Original drawing, 3-quarter page border, ptd in The Wood Beyond the World, May 1894. On a leaf from More's Utopia, [c.1893], height 170mm. In indian ink over pencil, heightened with white. With note of authenticity by Sydney Cockerell on verso. Doheny collection. (89) $2,500

— Original drawing, experimental drawing for an initial capital "A", [1896?]. 47mm by 47mm. In red, white & blue watercolor over pencil. Intended for the Kelmscott Press ptg of Laudes Beatae Mariae Virginis, but discarded. With note of provenance by Mrs. G. W. Millard on mount. Doheny collection. (89) $2,000

— Original drawing, full-page border, for the Kelmscott Chaucer, [1892-95]. 388mm by 267mm. In indian ink over pencil, heightened with white. Corner torn. With note of authenticity by Sydney Cockerell in margin. Doheny collection. (89) $25,000

— Original drawing, initial word "Now", for the Kelmscott Chaucer, [1892-95]. 81mm by 97mm. In indian ink over pencil, heightened with white. Some pencil sketches on verso. Doheny collection. (89) $2,200

— Original drawing, rejected tp design for The Golden Legend, [1892]. 182mm by 115mm. In indian ink over pencil, heightened with white. With inscr by Sydney Cockerell on verso. Doheny collection. (89) $4,800

— Original drawing, trial design (subsequently rejected) for the tp of The Earthly Paradise, [1896]. 230mm by 164mm. Ptd text & border with hand-drawn title panel. In indian ink over pencil, heightened with white. Inscr by Sydney Cockerell on verso. (90) $4,800

Ms, essay later pbd as A Note ... on his Aims in Founding the Kelmscott Press, 11 Nov 1895. 4 pp, folio. In the hand of Sydney C. Cockerell, sgd by Morris. With related material. Doheny collection. (89) $13,000

Series of 3 A Ls s, 8 July 1868, 26 Aug 1880, & [n.y.]. Doheny collection. (89) $650

ALs, 25 Nov [1872]. 6 pp, 8vo. To Aglaia Ionides Coronio. Complaining about the behavior of Dante Gabriel Rossetti [who was having an affair with Morris's wife]. Repaired. Koch Foundation. (90) $3,000

— 28 Feb 1885. 3 pp, 8vo. Recipient unnamed. Advising his correspondent to read Marx & Gronlund. (91) $1,400

— 27 Aug [1889]. (90) DM260

— 29 Feb 1892. (91) £160

— 4 June [n.y.]. (91) £220

Corrected page proofs, The Story of the Glittering Plain, [1891]. 72 leaves only, 4to, in brown mor bdg. Comprising 107 (of 188) pp of the 1st book ptd at the Kelmscott Press. Some leaves with autograph corrections by Morris; autograph note by Sydney C. Cockerell on front endpage. Doheny collection. (89) $9,000

— Anr, The Tale of King Coustans and of Over Sea, [1894]. 130 pp, 4to, on rectos only of thin proof paper. With numerous autograph corrections & shoulder notes by Morris & note of authenticity in the hand of Sydney Cockerell. In Kelmscott-style holland-backed bds. Doheny collection. (89) $13,000

Photograph, [1886]. 360mm by 293mm. With head supported on hand. Framed. (89) $1,900

Single sheet ptg, unused trial page for The Story of the Glittering Plain; "1st page printed at the Kelmscott Press, 31 Jan 1891". Doheny collection. (89) $800

— CRANE, WALTER. - Autograph Ms, sonnet on the death of Morris, sgd & dated 4 Oct 1896. 1 p, 12mo. Koch Foundation. (90) $1,000

— MURRAY, CHARLES FAIRFAX, ED. - 4 sets of page proofs for Girolamo Savonarola's Epistola de Contemptu Mundi, ptd by the Kelmscott Press, 1894. Each set 16 pp, 8vo, bound together in dark niger mor gilt by Katharine Adams. 1st set with extensive corrections, probably in Murray's hand. Doheny collection. (89) $3,000

See also: Calligraphy

Morrison, Blake

[The successive drafts of his poem Whinny Moor, partly autograph, partly corrected typescripts, with a covering letter, [n.d.], 18 pp, folio, sold at

S on 15 Dec, lot 162, for £150.]

Morse, Samuel F. B., 1791-1872
A Ls s (2), 16 Aug 1866 & 25 Jan 1870. 3 pp, 8vo. To Charles Butler. Mentioning the Atlantic cable, & contents not stated. (88) $1,100

ALs, 14 Aug 1843. 1 p, 4to. To Benjamin Silliman. Reporting about a long-distance test of his telegraph. (90) $4,500

— 20 May 1847. 2 pp, 4to. To Henry Rogers. Attacking attempts to "embarrass the operations of the Telegraph". (88) $2,000

— 14 Sept 1849. (88) $750

— 16 June 1865. Byer collection. (90) $450

— 26 Feb 1868. (91) $650

— 10 Oct 1868. (91) $350

— 19 Dec 1870. (90) $550

— 22 Feb 1871. 2 pp, 8vo. To G. W. Varnum. Suggesting that his experiment in electro-magnetism is not new. (91) $2,800

— 17 Apr 1871. 2 pp, 8vo. To Mrs. Botta. Sending an autograph copy, sgd, of the 1st despatch from Washington to Baltimore, 1844 (present, 14mm by 628mm). (90) $14,000

Autograph quotation, referring to the French motto "Faites bien, Laissez dire'; 2 Jan 1869. (90) $550

Cut signature, [n.d.]. (88) $140

Photograph, sgd & inscr, 1 Sept 1866. (88) DM730

— Anr, [n.d.]. 14.5 by 12.5 inches (image). Sgd & inscr to E. S. Sanford on mount. (90) $1,600

Mortimer, John
Autograph Ms, draft of Rumpole and the Blind Tasting, sgd; [n.d.]. (88) £260

Morton, John, Signer from Pennsylvania
ADs, [c.1767]. (89) $275
Ds, 1772. (90) $200

Mosby, John Singleton, 1833-1916
ANs, 18 Mar 1873. (90) $400

Moscheles, Ignaz, 1794-1870
Autograph music, Cadence, 11 bars in C major, scored for piano; sgd & dated 21 July 1845. (90) DM420

ALs, 9 Mar 1826. 3 pp, 4to. To Maurice Schlesinger. Offering a new composition for publication, mentioning Weber, etc. With postscript by Karl Schlesinger. (90) DM1,200

— 2 Feb 1841. (90) DM260

— 1 Sept 1853. (89) DM400

Autograph quotation, 6 double bars of music, sgd; 21 Nov 1844. (91) $200

Mosen, Julius, 1803-67
ALs, 10 July 1844. (91) DM230

— 12 Mar 1845. Albrecht collection. (91) SF320

Moser, Friedrich Karl, Freiherr von, 1723-98
ALs, 30 Oct 1775. (88) DM520

Moser, Koloman, 1868-1918
ALs, 27 Sept 1904. (89) DM650

Moses, Anna Mary Robertson ("Grandma"), 1860-1961
Christmas card, [n.d.]. (91) $300
Photograph, sgd, [n.d.]. (91) $190
— Anr, [n.d.]. (91) $225

Mosley, Sir Oswald, 1896-1980
ALs, 29 Mar 1969. (90) $100

Motion, Andrew
Typescript, poem, The Great Man, [n.d.]. (88) £350

Mott, Thomas Bentley, 1865-1952
[A carton of personal papers, family letters, photographs, etc., including a diary from a trip to Russia, 1904, sold at BBC on 12 Feb 1990, lot 99, for $110.]

[A file of typescripts & carbon copies of essays, reminiscences, etc. by Mott, with material regarding his imprisonment in a German concentration camp, sold at BBC on 12 Feb 1990, lot 100, for $75.]

[A large quantity of personal documents & carbon copies relating to Mott's military service sold at BBC on 12 Feb 1990, lot 101, for $150.]

Autograph Ms, recording his experiences

as aide-de-camp to Gen. (90) $220
Typescript carbon copy, reports no 12 - 35 on the allied efforts of the British, French & Italian armies in Italy, 11 Dec 1917 to 26 Feb 1918. (90) $230
A Ls s (2), 15 & 19 June 1917. (90) $400
See also: World War I

Moultrie, William, 1730-1805
Ls, 8 May 1794. (91) $380
Ds, 1 July 1793. (91) $120
— 17 July 1794. (88) $130

Mountbatten, Edwina, Countess Mountbatten of Burma, 1901-60. See: Mountbatten, Louis & Mountbatten

Mountbatten, Louis, Earl Mountbatten of Burma, 1900-79
Ls, 5 Sept 1949. (89) £140
— 13 June 1972. Byer collection. (90) $700
— 2 May 1974. (90) DM330
— 5 Sept 1974. (89) DM240

Mountbatten, Louis, 1st Earl Mountbatten of Burma, 1900-79 —&
Mountbatten, Edwina, Countess Mountbatten of Burma, 1901-60
[A collection of 6 Ls s by Edwina Mountbatten, 3 sgd port drawings of her by the artist Swamy, 14 Ls s by Louis Mountbatten, & 6 sgd photographs of both sold at C on 21 June 1989, lot 109, for £1,100 to Maggs.]

Mozart, Constanze, 1762-1842
Autograph transcript, [c.1830], of an ALs addressed to Leopold Mozart, 30 [May?] 1783. 1 p, 4to. Reporting on her husband's poor health & explaining that she is shortly to have a baby. (91) £15,000
ALs, 6 Sept 1837. 1 p, 4to. To Graefin Therese von Brunswick. Referring to recent events in Salzburg & her son's activities. Sgd Constanza Etates-Raethin Van Nissen Wittwe Mozart. (90) £10,050

Mozart, Leopold, 1719-87
Autograph music, copy of 2 cadenzas by his son Wolfgang Amadeus Mozart, K.624/626a, supplements C & K; [n.d.]. 2 pp, 18cm by 13.5cm. Some differences to other versions. (88) DM4,200

ALs, 10 July 1755. 2 pp, 198mm by 157mm. To his pbr Jakob Lotter. Concerning corrections in the proof-sheets of his Versuch einer gruendlichen Violinschule. Seal tear. (91) £7,000
— 28 July 1770. 3 pp, 4to. To his wife. About his foot injury, the libretto & list of singers for Mithridate, Re di Ponto, & 2 portraits. With autograph postscript by Wolfgang Amadeus Mozart to his sister, in Italian. Prinzmetal & Ammann collections. (88) $60,000
— 7 Sept 1778. 2 pp, folio. To an official of the Archbishop's Court in Salzburg. Seeking assistance in resolving legal problems after his wife's death in Paris. (90) £14,000
See also: Mozart, Wolfgang Amadeus & Mozart

Mozart, Wolfgang Amadeus, 1756-91
[An autograph address leaf, addressed to his father, [8 May 1784], 185mm by 115mm, cut from larger leaf, sold at S on 17 May 1990, lot 178, for £11,000 to Horiuchi.]
[An autograph address panel, addressed to his father, [n.d.], c.100mm by 115mm, irregularly cut, inscr in anr hand on verso, sold at S on 17 May 1990, lot 180, for £12,000 to Quaritch.]
Autograph music, 35 bars of a Quintet in B flat major for Oboe, Clarinet, Basset Horn, Bassoon & Piano, K.452a/Anh.54; [c.1783?]. 2 pp, folio. Notated on 3 systems of 6 staves each, with some corrections. Including notes of authentication by Nissen & Carl Mozart. (91) £45,000
— Autograph music, Adagio, K. A65, [1772-1775]. 1 p, 184mm by 240mm. 36 bars, scored for piano. Mtd. (90) DM60,000
— Autograph music, Adagio variee for piano in F major, K. Anhang 206a/A 65; [c.1773]. 1 p, c.18cm by 24cm. Notated on 7 systems, 2 staves each. (91) £35,000
— Autograph music, aria, Non tardar amato bene, comprising 29 bars of an early version of Susanna's aria in Le nozze di Figaro, Act 4; [1785 or 1786]. 4 pp, folio. Working Ms; laid out for full score, but only containing material for soprano & instrumental bass-line.

(90) £75,000
— Autograph music, aria, Schon lacht der holde Fruehling, for soprano & orchestra, K.580; 17 Sept 1789. 26 pp, size not stated. Working draft, notated on 12-stave paper, each system of 10 staves. Inscr in other hands. (89) £95,000
— Autograph music, arrangement for string quartet of the opening 20 bars of the 4th movement of Handel's 2d Suite for Keyboard, [c.1782]. 1 p, folio. In brown ink on 3 systems of 4 staves each; with autograph heading. Tp in the hand of Aloys Fuchs. Apparently unrecorded. (89) $33,000
— Autograph music, Fantasia for piano in C minor, K.475, & Sonata for piano in C minor, K.457; [1784 & 1785]. 18 pp (4 blank), folio, in wraps. Working Ms of the complete works. (91) £800,000
— Autograph music, fragment of a movement for piano duet in G major, K.357/497a, 98 bars; [c.1788]. 4 pp, folio. Notated on 3 systems per page, 4 staves each. A few alterations. Inscr by H. Henkel. (89) £38,000
— Autograph music, fugues in F major, K.375h, C minor & E minor, K.417b, [c.1782]. 2 pp, 22cm by 30cm. Possibly drafts for the Mass in C minor, K.427, notated on 2 & 3 systems of up to 5 staves each. Attestation by Nissen at head. (91) £40,000
— Autograph music, Minuets & Trios in G major, K. 130A (164) nos 5 & 6, [June 1772]. 2 pp, c.22cm by 30cm. In brown ink on 2 systems per page of 5 & 4 staves. (88) £40,000
— Autograph music, Notturni for 2 sopranos & bass, K.436 - 439 & 346/439a, [c.1787?]. 6 pp, size not stated. Notated on up to 4 systems per page, 3 staves each, with a number of autograph alterations & annotations. Inscr by von Nissen & Andre. (90) £75,000
— Autograph music, Rondo for piano in F major, K.494, [1786]. 3 pp, folio. 160 bars, notated in brown ink on 12 staves per page; working Ms. Salzer collection. (90) £87,000
— Autograph music, sketch of 16 bars in C Major, K. Anh. 109 g no 591, for string trio. Notated in brown ink on a system of 3 staves; [late 1780s]. 1 p, folio. With note of authenticity at bottom. (88) $16,000
— Autograph music, sketches for Sanctus, K.296c; [1778]. 1 p, 16cm by 21cm. 18 bars on 6 staves. (90) DM65,000
— Autograph music, Wind Serenade in E flat major, K.375, [c.July 1782]. 1 p, folio. Working draft of the opening 5 bars of the 1st movement. Including authentications by Nissen & Julius Andre. (91) £11,000

Ms, Andante fuer eine Walze in eine kleine Orgel, K.616; (1791). 3 pp, 23cm by 33 cm, 16 staves each. Contemp copy differing in parts from autograph version. With related material. (88) DM2,600

ALs, [c.2 Aug 1782]. 2 pp, 4to. To Baroness von Waldstetten. Suggesting he marry Constanze at once, since Frau Weber is threatening to have her fetched by the police. (89) £35,000

— 15 Feb 1783. 1 p, 4to. To Baroness Waldstaetten. Recounting his financial plight & imploring her for help. Sgd W: A: et C: Mozart. 1 corner torn; mtd. (88) DM170,000

— 15 Jan 1787. 4 pp, folio. To Gottfried von Jacquin. Reporting about his activities in Prague & the success of his Figaro. (90) DM220,000

— [8 Apr 1789]. 1 p, 6.5cm by 16cm. To his wife Constanze. Fragment, closing lines promising to write from Prague & sending his love. Tipped to larger sheet; with note stating provenance. (89) DM60,000
See also: Mozart, Leopold

Mozart, Wolfgang Amadeus, 1756-91 —& Mozart, Leopold, 1719-87

[An ALs by Leopold Mozart to his wife, & an ALs by Wolfgang Amadeus Mozart to his sister Nannerl on the same leaf, 21 Nov 1772, 2 pp, size not stated, reporting from Italy, sold at S on 17 May 1990, lot 42, for £70,000 to Horiuchi.]

Mozley, Charles
Original drawings, (12), to illus Bill Naughton's My Pal Spadger, 1978. (90) £400
— Original drawings, (44), to illus Erskine Childers's The Riddle of the Sands, 1970. (90) £450

Muecke, Hellmuth von, 1881-1957
Signature, [16 June 1915]. (88) DM280

Mueffling, Karl, Freiherr von, 1775-1851
ALs, 24 Aug 1817. (91) DM220
Ds, 27 Oct 1815. Schroeder collection. (89) DM220

Mueller, Adam, 1779-1829
ALs, 22 Jan 1810. (90) DM300

Mueller, Friedrich, 1749-1825
ALs, [c.1818]. 3 pp, 8vo. To Georg Brentano. Draft, discussing his difficulties with Herr von Schneider, & mentioning Goethe. With anr draft, to von Schneider. (89) DM4,200

Mueller, Friedrich von, 1779-1849
ALs, 24 Aug 1830. Albrecht collection. (91) SF1,000
— 7 Dec 1830. 3 pp, 4to. To [Alfred Nicolovius]. Reporting about Goethe's illness after the death of his son. Albrecht collection. (91) SF1,600
— 31 Mar 1832. Albrecht collection. (91) SF400
— 21 Oct 1845. Albrecht collection. (91) SF220

Mueller, Johannes Peter, 1801-58
Autograph Ms, Bemerkungen ueber die Metamorphose der Seeigel, 1848. 10 pp, various sizes. Ptr's copy for a revised Ed, incorporating 3 pp already ptd. Sgd at head. (91) DM1,500
ALs, 6 July 1847. (91) DM620
— 4 Nov 1853. (90) DM1,000
ANs, [c.1849]. (91) DM250

Mueller, Johannes von, 1752-1809
ALs, 1 May 1787. (91) DM550
— 7 Oct 1806. (88) DM360
— [n.d.]. (90) DM750

Mueller, Max, 1823-1900
ALs, 17 Nov 1867. (91) DM650

Mueller, Wilhelm, 1794-1827
ALs, 1 July 1817. (91) DM1,000
— 6 Mar 1822. (88) DM500
— 27 June 1826. (89) DM800

Muenchhausen, Boerries, Freiherr von, 1874-1945
ALs, 29 May 1919. (88) DM420
Ls s (2), 21 & 25 Jan 1938. (90) DM550

Muennich, Burchard Christoph, Graf von, 1683-1767
Ls, 25 Mar 1763. (91) DM550

Muhammad Ali
Collection of ANs & photograph, sgd & inscr, 8 Feb [19]84. (89) $65

Muhlenberg, John Peter Gabriel, 1746-1807
ALs, 17 Jan 1775. (89) $450
Ds, 20 Oct 1794. (89) $140

Muir, John, 1838-1914
ALs, 25 Mar 1903. (91) $1,000

Mumford, Lewis —&
Van Doren, Mark, 1894-1972
[A collection of 22 A Ls s, 3 Ls s & 2 autograph postcards, sgd, from Mumford to Van Doren, & 13 A Ls s & 2 autograph postcards, sgd, from Van Doren to Mumford, mostly 1963 to 1973, with related material, sold at wa on 8 Mar 1990, lot 538, for $1,600.]

Munch, Edvard, 1863-1944
Series of 4 A Ls s, 1909 to 1934. (88) £450
ALs, 18 July 1904. 2 pp, 8vo. To an unnamed German art dealer. Making arrangements for the transfer of some works for an exhibition. In German. File holes. (89) DM1,200
— [16 Dec 1908]. (89) DM550
— 15 Aug 1926. 2 pp, 4to. To Theodor Daeubler. Thanking for a work & announcing some engravings. (91) DM1,300
— [1 Aug 1929]. 2 pp, 8vo (lettercard). To Arthur Haseloff. Explaining that he is unable to visit an exhibition in Kiel. In German. (88) DM1,100

Munnings, Sir Alfred, 1878-1959
Series of c.100 A Ls s (1 Ls), [c.1943 to c.1958]. (88) £900

Munson, Thurman
Photograph, sgd & inscr, [n.d.]. (88) $225

Munthe, Axel, 1857-1949
Collection of 2 A Ls s & 2 Ls s, [n.d.]. (90) £50
Ls, [13 Dec 1938]. (90) DM320

Murat, Joachim, 1767-1815
ALs, 30 Dec 1808. (90) DM540
Ls, [17 July 1801]. (91) DM480
— 7 Feb 1809. (90) DM320
— 29 Aug 1810. (91) DM340

Murphy, Audie, 1924-71
Signature, [n.d.]. (90) $100

Murrow, Joseph Samuel, 1835-1929
ALs, 9 June 1865. Alexander collection. (90) $180

Murry, John Middleton, 1889-1957. See: Mansfield, Katherine & Murry

Musical Manuscripts
Ms, c.80 Italian arias by Handel, Scarlatti, Gasparini, Caldara, Marcello, & others, including scribal copy of Handel's Ho un non so che nel cor, with autograph annotation by Handel, & part of a lost opera by M. A. Ziani. [Venice, c.1700-1710]. 160 pp, 4to, in quarter calf. In several hands. (91) £15,000
— Ms, chamber & orchestral music by Pepusch, Gasparini, Torelli, Marini, Haym, & others, in score, [early 18th cent]. (88) £1,000
— Ms, collection of madrigals, [Italy, mid- to late 16th cent]. 53 leaves & blanks, size not stated, in contemp vellum. Comprising several groups of works, including settings of Petrarch. (89) £2,800
— Ms, collection of 332 dance movements and song arrangements for organ, [Germany, c.1650]. 350 pp, 4to. In German organ tablature in a scribal hand. (89) £5,000
— Ms, collection of 17th- & early 18th-cent clavecin music, [early 18th cent]. 90 pp, size not stated; vellum bds. In several hands. (88) £3,200

— Ms, collection of 17th-cent keyboard dances, [n.d.]. 179 pp, 8vo, in modern red mor bdg. In brown ink on 4 staves per page, each of six lines. Ownership inscr of Thurston Dart. (88) £3,800
— Ms, collection of keyboard & vocal music by Handel, Corelli, Purcell, & others, in several hands, [early 18th cent]. (88) £400
— Ms, contratenor parts of 2 settings of Gloria in excelsis Deo, & part of a ballade in French, [Monastery of Grottaferrata?, late 14th cent]. 2 pp, folio. In black & red ink by 2 scribes in Italian Ars nova notation. Trimmed; glazed. (89) £2,200
— Ms, Grund-Satz der Sing-Kunst. [Venice, c.1725]. About 360 pp, (7 leaves vellum), 120mm by 185mm. Contemp red mor gilt. In German & Italian. Containing an essay about the art of singing, & arias & cantatas. Including drawing in red chalk, sgd Angiola Concola. (89) DM1,400
— Ms, The Trumbull Lutebook, [c.1590s]. 33 leaves, folio. Anthology of music for 6-course & 7-course lutes by Dowland, Alfonso Ferrabosco, John Johnson, Anthony Holborne & others. (90) £24,000
— Ms, Yinyue pu [Book of Music, 17th cent?]. Phillipps MS.823 & Robinson collection. (89) £800
— STACKPOLE, WILLIAM A. - Autograph Ms, sailor's songbook, [c.1860]. 83 pp, 4to. 32 songs, with 21 illusts. (90) $500

Musil, Robert, 1880-1942
Ls s (2), 18 Jan & 18 Feb 1926. (88) £950
Ls, 18 Nov [19]38. 3 pp, 4to. To Dr. Viktor Zuckerkandl. After his emigration to Switzerland, about problems with his pbr in Vienna. (91) DM4,800
— 30 Nov 1938. 1 p, 4to. To Dr. Viktor Zuckerkandl. Referring to the Ms of his Mann ohne Eigenschaften. (91) DM2,800
— 9 Dec [19]38. 1 p, 4to. To Dr. Viktor Zuckerkandl. About financial problems & his work on Der Mann ohne Eigenschaften. (91) DM3,800
— 9 Jan 1939. 1 p, 4to. To Dr. Viktor Zuckerkandl. Discussing the publication of his Der Mann ohne Eigenschaften. (91) DM1,200

MUSIL

— 15 Jan 1939. 1 p, 4to. To Dr. Viktor Zuckerkandl. Hoping for a solution to his difficulties with his Vienna publishing house. (91) DM1,400
— 1 Feb 1939. 2 pp, 4to. To Dr. Viktor Zuckerkandl. About his work on Der Mann ohne Eigenschaften & expressing distrust of his pbr Bermann. (91) DM4,800
— 10 Feb [19]39. (91) DM800
— 22 June 1939. 2 pp, 4to. To Dr. Viktor Zuckerkandl. Expressing frustrations about his problems with Dr. Bermann. Including postscript, partly autograph. (91) DM6,000
— 9 July [19]39. 1 p, 4to. To Dr. Viktor Zuckerkandl. Making suggestions for a renewed cooperation with Dr. Bermann. (91) DM1,500
— 27 Oct [19]39. 1 p, 4to. To Dr. Viktor Zuckerkandl. Expressing good wishes for recipient's start in America & alluding to the transfer of European culture. (91) DM3,600
— 23 Dec 1940. 1 p, 4to. To Dr. Viktor Zuckerkandl. About his work on Der Mann ohne Eigenschaften, his financial problems, & his wish to publish his aphorisms in America. (91) DM4,200

Musset, Alfred de, 1810-57
ALs, [n.d.]. (90) DM900
— [n.d.]. (90) DM520

Mussolini, Benito, 1883-1945
[A bust photograph of a painting, sgd & dated May 1924, 7.5 by 9.5 inches, sold at sg on 14 Mar 1991, lot 202, for $475.]
[A collection of 49 photographs of Mussolini in Ethiopia, [c.1935 to 1936], 3.25 by 4.5 inches, with [related?] U. S. Customs receipt, sold at sg on 22 Oct, lot 191, for $80.]
ALs, [early 1908?]. 4 pp, 8vo. To [Salvatore Donatini?]. Discussing his plans for the future. (89) £1,300
— 22 Apr 1923. (90) $750
Ls, 2 May 1923. (89) DM420
— 20 Jan 1926. (88) DM600
— 24 May [1937]. (91) DM550
Ds s (2)2 Dec 1928 & 7 Jan 1939. (89) DM550
Photograph, sgd, [c.1922]. (88) $650
— Anr, [1923]. (90) DM500
— Anr, [1926]. (91) $450
— Anr, 5 Apr 1927. (90) $600
— Anr, 3 Aug 1933. (91) DM520
Photograph, sgd & inscr, Nov 1925. (89) £160
Signature, on reproduction of a port drawing, 1923. (90) £400
— Russel, Henri Tostel. - Typescript, article written after an interview with Mussolini, setting forth his ideas & ambitions; Nov 1930. 6 pp, 4to. Sgd by Mussolini as approval. With related material. (88) $1,300
See also: Heraldic Manuscripts
See also: Strauss, Richard
See also: Vittorio Emanuele III, 1869-1947

Muzio, Claudia, 1889-1936
Ds, [n.d.]. (91) $150

Myddleton Family
[A box of documents relating to the Myddleton Family of Chirk Castle, Wales, 17th & 18th cent, sold at pn on 22 Mar 1990, lot 43, for £90 to Quaritch.]

Mytton, Thomas, 1597?-1656
[The Civil War papers of Mytton, 11 items including letters by William Lenthal & John Bradshaw, 1643 to 1651, 11 pp, folio & 4to, sold at S on 15 Dec 1988, lot 141, for £3,500.]

N

Nabokov, Vladimir, 1899-1977
Ls, 20 Feb 1970. (88) $600

Nachtigal, Gustav, 1834-85
ALs, [after 1876]. (88) DM300

Nadar, Pseud. of Gaspard Felix Tournachon, 1820-1910
ALs, [n.d.]. (90) DM480

Naegeli, Hans Georg, 1773-1836
Autograph music, song, Des Wanderer[s] Trost; [n.d.]. 2 pp, folio. 52 bars, scored for voice & piano. (91) DM4,000
Series of 33 Ls s, 1795 to 1807. 57 pp, 4to. To Johann Andre. Concerning the publication of music by various composers, contracts, arrangements with

Clementi, etc. With related material. (88) £6,000

Nahl, Johann August, 1752-1825
A Ls s (2), 16 Aug & 2 Nov 1796. (89) DM250

Nansen, Fridtjof, 1861-1930
Autograph Ms, account of the 1st part of his expedition across Greenland, [1889]. (89) £1,000
Collection of ALs & Ls, 29 May & 10 July 1909. (90) DM530
A Ls s (2), 9 July 1892 & 12 June 1905. (89) DM440
ALs, 17 Feb 1907. (90) DM340
Ls, 6 May 1905. (90) DM420

Napoleon I, 1769-1821
[2 endorsements, sgd (1 autograph), on a letter addressed to him by Bertrand concerning costs of keeping a ship at the island of La Pinosa, 4 Oct 1814, 1 p, folio, giving orders regarding the ship, sold at S on 16 May 1991, lot 109, for £900 to Cosmatos.]
Autograph Ms, fragment of his love story Clisson et Eugenie, [before 1795]. 4 pp, folio. Including revisions. Crushed red mor bdg by Pomey. (91) £8,000
— Autograph Ms, memorandum, [19 Feb 1810]. (88) £750
— Autograph Ms, memorandum addressed to Montholon listing requested pieces of information, [1815 or later]. 1 p, 8vo. In pencil. (91) £1,050
— Autograph Ms, report on the defense of Ajaccio, [c.Apr? 1793]. 2 pp, folio. Crawford collection. (90) £4,500
Ms, orders for Gen. Bertrand regarding the siege of Graudenz; 21 Nov 1806. 1 p, 4to. Sgd. (90) DM1,100
ALs, [25 Sept 1797]. 1 p, folio. To Barras. Offering his resignation as Commander of the Army of Italy. Silked; in red mor gilt by Sangorski & Sutcliffe. (90) £13,000
— [12 Jan 1798]. (89) £650
— 30 Jan [1814]. 1 p, 12mo. Recipient unknown. Reporting on his recent victories & his health. Tipped to larger leaf. Barrett collection. (89) $7,000
AL, [c.1816]. (89) $550
— 3 Apr [1819]. 1 p, folio. To [Sir Hudson Lowe]. Draft, protesting against the form of address used in letters to him. Heavily revised. In pencil. With transcription. (88) £2,600
Collection of Ls & endorsement, sgd, [2 Nov 1798] & 1811. (88) £170
Ls s (2), [6 Dec 1795 & 8 Mar 1800]. (88) £900
— Ls s (2), [16 Aug & 15 Sept 1797]. (91) £1,000
— Ls s (2), 6 Apr 1808 & 20 Feb 1809. (91) £750
Ls, [17 Dec 1794]. (91) £650
— [4 Jan 1796]. 2 pp, folio. To Gen. Loison. Discussing action against brigands reported to be in the forests of recipient's district. (90) £1,200
— [10 Jan 1796]. (89) £650
— [June 1796]. (89) £580
— [21 Oct 1796]. (88) £500
— [9 Mar 1797]. 1 p, folio. To the administration of Mantua. Stating his intention to protect education & the arts in the city. (91) $1,400
— [1 June 1797]. (90) £750
— [1 June 1797]. (90) £900
— [4 July 1797]. (88) £450
— [12 Sept 1797]. (89) £420
— [6 Oct 1797]. (88) £600
— [8 Apr 1798]. (88) £45
— [14 May 1798]. (88) £450
— [18 Aug 1798]. 1 p, folio. To the Administrateur des Finances, Possielgue. Regarding the detection of coffee. Sgd Bonaparte. On ptd letterhead with woodcut vignette. (88) DM2,900
— [30 Dec 1798]. 4 pp, folio. To Ganteaume. Giving orders to explore the Suez area. (91) DM3,500
— [9 July 1799]. (88) £680
— [13 Feb 1800]. 1 p, 4to. To Minister of War Alexandre Berthier. Giving orders to recall Gen. Suchet from Italy. With vignette. Margin def. (89) DM1,400
— [9 Mar 1800]. (89) £150
— [19 Nov 1800]. 3 pp, 4to. To Minister of War Carnot. Giving instructions about various matters pertaining to the army. (90) DM2,100
— [19 Jan 1801]. 1 p, 4to. To Gen. Jourdan. Referring to the recent assault on Rue Nivaise. Mtd. (90)

NAPOLEON I

— DM1,700
— 25 Feb 1801. 3 pp, 4to. To Adm. Ganteaume. On the signing of the armistice with the King of Naples. (90) DM4,000
— [1 June 1801]. (90) £800
— [1 June 1801]. (90) £850
— 13 Sept 1801. (90) £800
— [30 Nov 1801]. (89) £1,000
— [15 Mar 1804]. 3 pp, 4to. To Gen. Brune. Informing him about his plans for an invasion of England. (89) £2,500
— [10 May 1805]. 1 p, 4to. To [Joseph] Prina. Concerning tariff regulations between France & Italy. (91) DM1,800
— [22 Aug 1805]. 1 p, 4to. To Admiral Ganteaume. Ordering him to rendezvous with Villeneuve & to set in train the invasion of England. (90) £2,000
— 30 Aug 1805. 2 pp, 4to. To Eugene de Beauharnais. Informing him of the abandonment of the invasion of England & the need to concentrate forces against Austria. (91) £3,200
— [2 Oct 1805]. 1 p, 4to. To [Eugene Beauharnais]. Informing him about the progress of his army in southern Germany. (89) DM4,000
— 29 Apr 1806. 1 p, 4to. To Mollieu. Discussing financial matters. Byer collection. (90) $1,100
— 11 Oct 1806. (88) £800
— [13 Oct 1806]. 1 p, 4to. To Capt. Drouot-Lamarche. Giving orders for troop movements on the eve of the Battle of Jena. (90) DM8,000
— 9 Nov 1806. 1 p, 8vo. To Gen. von Wrede. Urging him to get well since he is counting on him to fight Russia. (88) DM1,600
— 8 Jan 1807. 2 pp, 4to. To Maria Luisa, Queen of Etruria. Requesting her to join the Continental System against England. (90) DM1,600
— 28 Mar 1807. 1 p, 4to. To Gen. Compans. Informing him of his brother's appointment as Prefect of St. Gaudens. (91) DM1,050
— 19 Oct 1807. (90) £850
— 22 Oct 1807. 1 p, 4to. To Gen. Clarke. Giving instructions for the Armee de la Gironde & the reorganization of some German regiments. (91) DM1,350
— 24 Oct 1807. (91) $750
— 15 Jan 1808. 1 p, folio. To Cardinal Casoni. Assuring him of his good will. (91) DM2,200
— 8 Sept 1808. 3 pp, 4to. To Berthier. Criticizing Marshals Jourdan, Moncey & Bessieres, & their conduct of the Peninsular War. Including 4-line autograph postscript. (90) £1,800
— 29 May 1809. 2 pp, 4to. To Gen. Bertrand. Ordering the construction of pontoon bridges across the Danube. (90) DM3,600
— 26 June 1809. 1 p, 4to. To Eugene Beauharnais. Instructing him to send arms from Raab to Vienna. Sgd Nap. (88) DM1,100
— 31 July 1809. 1 p, 4to. To Gen. Bertrand. Regarding the defense of Klagenfurt. Sgd Nap. (88) DM1,600
— 12 Sept 1809. 1 p, 4to. To Comte Mollien. Requesting him to report about a letter. (90) DM1,400
— 26 Feb 1810. 1 p, 4to. To Eugene de Beauharnais. Announcing his forthcoming marriage to Marie Louise of Austria. (91) £3,400
— 3 Apr 1810. 1 p, 4to. To an unnamed King. Notifying him of his marriage to Archduchess Marie Louise of Austria. (90) DM2,200
— 2 Sept 1810. (89) £800
— 4 Sept 1810. (89) £600
— 1 Nov 1810. 1 p, 4to. To Gen. Clarke. Agreeing to postpone the evacuation of artillery from Magdeburg. (91) DM1,600
— 9 Nov 1810. 2 pp, 4to. To Eugene de Beauharnais. Pointing out deficiencies in a report & giving orders concerning troops in Italy. (91) £1,200
— 7 Dec 1810. 1 p, 4to. To Eugene Beauharnais. Insisting that the Continental System be observed in Italy. (91) DM1,500
— 15 Dec 1810. (90) £550
— 2 Jan 1811. (89) DM1,000
— 16 Jan 1811. (91) $1,000
— 8 Mar 1811. (88) $650
— 6 Aug 1811. (88) £200
— 9 Oct 1811. (88) £350
— 12 Nov 1811. (90) £850
— 14 Jan 1812. 2 pp, 4to. To G. J. Lacuee, Comte de Cessac. Giving

instructions about the purchase of supplies for his projected Russian campaign. (91) DM1,150
— 19 Feb 1812. 1 p, 4to. To Minister of War Clarke. Giving orders concerning the defense of Magdeburg. (89) DM1,050
— 27 Feb 1812. (89) DM1,000
— 13 June 1812. 3 pp, 4to. To Eugene de Beauharnais. Giving instructions for the provisioning of the army during the Russian campaign. (91) £2,000
— 1 Aug 1812. 1 p, 4to. To Eugene Beauharnais. Informing him of his order for the departure of a regiment of conscripts. Sgd Np. (88) DM1,400
— 20 Oct 1812. 2 pp, 4to. To [Eugene de Beauharnais]. Requesting information about return routes from Moscow & giving orders to build bridges. With autograph addition. (90) DM6,000
— 4 Dec 1812. 2 pp, 4to. To Maret, Duc de Bassano. Expressing dissatisfaction with the lack of support provided by the Confederation of the Rhine during his Russian campaign. (91) £1,300
— 11 Feb 1813. (88) DM800
— 6 Mar 1813. 3 pp, 4to. To Gen. Lauriston. Giving instructions regarding the defense of the Elbe at Wittenberg & Dessau. (89) DM1,400
— 17 Mar 1813. (90) DM1,000
— 19 Mar 1813. 1 p, 4to. To Gen. Clarke. About the occupation of Hamburg. (91) DM1,800
— 20 Mar 1813. (88) £280
— 5 Apr 1813. (88) DM750
— 28 Apr 1813. 2 pp, 4to. To Gen. Bertrand. Giving detailed instructions for troop movements. (90) DM1,700
— 11 June 1813. 3 pp, 4to. To Marshal Augereau. Giving orders for a demonstration of military strength at Wuerzburg. (90) DM1,800
— 14 June 1813. 1 p, 4to. To Eugene Beauharnais. Instructing him about troop movements. (89) DM1,500
— 3 Nov 1813. 3 pp, 4to. To Gen. Bertrand. Giving detailed instructions for the defense of Mainz & the Rhine area. Sgd Np. (88) DM2,700
— 21 Jan 1814. (91) £800
— 4 Apr 1814. 1 p, 4to. To Col. Wonsowicz. Expressing his appreciation of his services as interpreter. Sgd Nap. (88) DM1,500
— 6 Sept 1814. 1 p, 4to. To Bertrand. Giving orders regarding work to be done to a church. Some autograph revisions. Sgd Nap. (88) DM1,600

Ds, 4 Nov 1793. (91) £850
— [29 Dec 1794]. (88) $450
— [17 Jan 1796]. (88) £620
— [24 June 1797]. 1 p, folio. Military commission, countersgd by Berthier & Kilmaine. (90) DM1,350
— [13 Nov 1798]. (90) £700
— [6 Feb 1799]. 1 p, 4to. Contents not stated. In green straight-grained solander case by Sangorski & Sutcliffe. Doheny collection. (89) $1,300
— [c.1800]. 1 p, 4to. Contents not stated. With a port. (90) $1,200
— [4 Jan 1801]. (90) £340
— [16 Feb 1801]. (90) $1,000
— [15 July 1802]. (89) £550
— [26 Feb 1803]. (89) £700
— [9 May 1803]. (88) $50
— [7 June 1803]. (88) £700
— [11 June 1803]. (88) $350
— [17 Sept 1803]. (90) DM380
— 1803 [30 Fructidor an XI]. (88) $550
— 26 May 1806. (88) £260
— 21 Mar 1808. (88) $800
— 11 Aug 1808. 1 p, folio. Conferring the barony on Capt. Charles Buquet. With painted coat-of-arms. Countersgd by Cambaceres. (89) DM1,100
— 21 Dec 1808. (91) £1,000
— 20 May 1811. 9 pp, folio. Ratification of the Treaty of Paris with the King of Westfalia. (91) £2,000
— 5 Dec 1811. (91) £320
— 29 Apr 1812. (88) $350
— 11 July 1812. 1 p, folio. Licence for the ship Emmanuel to sail to England. (91) £1,600
— 11 Jan 1813. (88) £160
— 25 Mar 1813. (88) $700

Autograph endorsement, sgd, [1 Aug 1798]. 2 lines on verso of account submitted by Gen. Dupuy & pay order by Gen. Berthier, 1 p, folio; approving payment. With autograph receipt by Dupuy at bottom. (91) DM1,800
— Anr, 11 Dec [1806]. 5 lines, sgd, on a report addressed to him by Gen.

NAPOLEON I

Dejean, 29 Nov 1806, 1 p, 4to, regarding troop movements in Belgium; ordering a regiment to Wesel. Again endorsed by Dejean. (90) DM2,600
— Anr, sgd twice, on a letter addressed to him by Gen. (90) DM900
— Anr, sgd, 17 Mar 1808. (91) £320
— Anr, sgd Nap, in the margin of a report by Berthier, 8 Sept 1810, 1 p, folio, proposing leave for a wounded officer. (90) $800
— Anr, sgd, 7 Jan 1811, note of approval on a report addressed to him by Minister of War Berthier, 5 Jan 1811, 1 p, folio, regarding home leave for a wounded soldier. Crawford collection. (90) DM700
— Anr, note of approval, sgd Np, on a report by Bertrand, 31 Mar 1814, 1 p, folio, regarding a payment to his interpreter Col. Wonsowicz. Small tear. With related material. (88) DM1,100
— Anr, note of approval on a report addressed to him by Gen. (90) DM900
— Anr, sgd Np, on report from Gen. (88) $475

Endorsement, sgd, [8 Aug 1797]. (91) DM1,000
— Anr, sgd, at the foot of a letter addressed to him by Sheikh Sadat, [n.d.], 2 pp, folio, objecting to the terms of compensation offered to him. (88) £550
— Anr, sgd, on a report by Paymaster Gen. Esteve regarding contributions to be paid by the wife of Murad Bey, [17 Jan 1799]. 1 p, folio. Insisting on payment. (90) DM1,900
— Anr, sgd Bonaparte, in the margin of a letter addressed to him by 3 Captains in a regiment of Dragoons, complaining of unfair treatment, [23 Nov 1800]. (88) £350
— Anr, sgd, 5 Apr 1802, on a request for employment addressed to him by M. (89) DM950
— Anr, sgd, in the margin of a report by the Minister of War requesting that officers of a warship be allowed anr installment of their salary, 8 May 1811, 2 pp, folio; granting request. (90) £260
— Anr, sgd, on a report by the Minister of the Navy on the arrival of a ship at Bayonne, 8 May 1811. (88) $150
— Anr, sgd, 28 Aug 1811, in margin of a report from the Ministry of the Interior, 21 Aug 1811, 8 pp, folio, concerning plans to build warships at Bouc. (89) £210
— Anr, sgd, 9 Dec 1811. Crawford collection. (89) DM900
— Anr, sgd twice, on a report by Minister of War Clarke, 8 Apr 1812, 2 pp, folio, proposing transfers or appointments of officers; approving 5 of 6 names. (90) $850
— Anr, sgd, on a letter submitted by Gen. (90) £600
— Anr, sgd, 27 Mar 1815. (91) £600

Signature, at bottom of a letter addressed to him by the Duc de Feltre, 14 Apr 1813, 1 p, 4to; about funds for an artillery regiment. (88) $600
— Anr, on memorandum to Bertrand, 12 Dec 1817, authorizing payment of household expenditures. 1 p, 8vo, possibly torn from a larger sheet. Sgd N. (88) £1,400
— BLACKWELL, CAPT. THOMAS. - Diary of Capt. Blackwell of the 91st Regiment during his time in Ireland & as custodian of Napoleon's tomb on St. Helena. [1835-41] 11 pp & frontis in watercolor & 24 ink or watercolor maps & sketches; with mtd news cutting relating to the exhumation of Napoleon's body. (88) £500
— MALCOLM, SIR PULTENEY. - Autograph Ms, account of interviews with Napoleon on St. Helena, 20 June 1816 to 19 June 1817. 148 pp, folio. Covering a wide range of subjects. (88) £4,000
— O'MEARA, BARRY EDWARD. - Transcript, contemp copy of his letters to John Finlaison from St. Helena, 1815 to 1818. 750 pp, folio, in 2 vols; disbound. (89) £520
— ST. HELENA. - 2 documents, 28 Jan & 17 Feb 1816. 2 pp, 4to. Receipt, sgd by Marchand & Montholon, for expenses for Jan 1816, & statement of wages paid to members of Napoleon's household. (91) £600
— THOMAS, HENRY. - Autograph Ms, account of Napoleon's residence in Elba, 1814. 13 pp, folio. With related material. (88) £250
See also: Josephine, 1763-1814

See also: Pius VII, 1740-1823

Napoleon II, 1811-32
[A collection of 5 letters by members of his entourage, 1828 to 1841 & [n.d.], 7 pp, various sizes, sold at S on 21 Sept, lot 196, for £160 to Dr. Sam.]
Autograph Ms, exercise book containing letters, grammar rules, & an essay, La vraie felicite; Dec 1825. 16 pp, 4to. Including note of authenticity by the Chevalier de Foresti on final page. (90) DM5,500
— Autograph Ms, Second Cahier, [Dec 1825]. 16 pp, 4to. Notebook containing lessons in grammar & letter writing; with corrections in the hand of M. de Bartholemy. (89) $3,000
A Ls s (2), [n.d.]. (89) £300
AL, [n.d.]. (88) $575

Napoleon III, 1808-73
[A group of 8 autograph endorsements (6 sgd), on petitions & reports addressed to him, 1849 to 1862, 12 pp, various sizes, sold at star on 1 Dec 1988, lot 1238, for DM620.]
ALs, 17 July 1832. (88) $450
— [n.d.]. (88) $300
— 11 Apr [1860]. (90) DM450
— 22 Oct 1860. (90) DM420
— 21 May 1862. (88) DM460
— 2 Nov 1869. (89) DM300
Ls, 26 July 1850. (90) DM440
— 15 June 1856. (90) DM320
ANs, [n.d.]. (91) $70
ADs, 12 Oct 1839. (90) DM320
Autograph telegram, 24 Nov 1861. (91) DM250

Napoleonic Wars
[A collection of Mss by Napoleon & each of his 25 marshals, with engraved portraits, together 29 items, 1787 to 1824, sold at P on 14 Dec 1988, lot 147, for $5,000.]
[A collection of c.80 items relating to British troop movements in the Ionian Islands & Italy, & to Toulon, sold at S on 21 Sept, lot 107, for £150 to Burgess.]
[Battle of the Nile. - A collection of 5 letters & accounts by French naval officers, newspaper reports, broadsides, & an order in council, 14 Aug 1798 to 20 Feb 1799, 24 pp, various sizes, all relating to the Battle of the Nile, with related material, sold at C on 21 June 1989, lot 220, for £400 to Robson Lowe.]
[A collection of 12 letters & documents, mostly by Napoleonic Generals, c.1799 to 1825, sold at S on 17 Nov 1988, lot 274, for £400 to Severi.]
[A collection of 16 letters by Napoleonic Marshals, c.1799 to 1815, sold at S on 17 Nov 1988, lot 275, for £450 to Nicholas.]
[A group of ALs & 4 Ls s by various Napoleonic marshals, 1799 to 1829, sold at sg on 9 Mar 1989, lot 155, for $250.]
[A collection of 52 letters & documents, relating to the French Revolutionary & Napoleonic Wars sold at C on 7 Dec 1988, lot 158, for £1,000 to Smith.]
[Battle of Trafalgar. - A collection of 16 letters & Mss by various people, including Castlereagh, Admiral Collingwood, etc., 22 Oct 1805 to 10 Jan 1815, 31 pp, folio & 4to, concerning the Battle of Trafalgar, with related material, sold at C on 21 June 1989, lot 272, for £1,900 to Lindley.]
Ms, Campagne des Francais en Allemagne et en Italie en 1805. (89) £300
— Ms, journal kept by an English officer in the 3d Regiment of Guards, 1 Jan 1814 to June 1815. (89) £340
— BATTLE OF COPENHAGEN. - Ms, trans of the Danish Commander's account of the Battle of Copenhagen, 3 Apr 1801. 5 pp, folio. Including a map. With related material. Wolf collection. (89) £280
— BATTLE OF COPENHAGEN. - ALs, 14 Apr 1801, 4 pp, 4to, by James Stone to an unnamed friend. Eyewitness account of the battle. With related material. (90) £750
— BATTLE OF THE GLORIOUS FIRST OF JUNE. - ALs by Capt. William Parker, 13 June 1794, 3 pp, folio, to his wife Mary. Giving an acoount of the battle. Repaired. (89) £380
— BATTLE OF TRAFALGAR. - Ls, [Nov 1805], 3 pp, 4to, by a Spanish officer (Carrasco?) to Roberto de Herrera.

NAPOLEONIC WARS

Commenting on Spanish, French & English losses at Trafalgar & mentioning Nelson's death. (90) £350
— DENHAM, JOSEPH. - Series of 108 A Ls s, 23 Dec 1796 to 6 Feb 1798. Over 300 pp, 4to. To Sir William Hamilton. Giving a comprehensive account of Napoleon's invasion of Italy. With related material. (90) $3,500
— GROSVENOR, CAPT. L. - Autograph Ms, journal kept during the campaign in Holland, 25 Feb to 30 Apr 1793. About 80 pp, 12mo, in limp red calf. (89) £85
— ITALY. - A group of letters, documents, proclamations & broadsides relating to Napoleon's invasion of Italy, 61 items, 227 pp, 4to & folio, some ptd, sold at C on 20 June 1990, lot 277, for £850 to L'Autographe. 90
— KEFFENBRINK, KARL VON. - 3 A Ls s, 9 June & 16 Sept 1809. 6 pp, 8vo. To his mother Luise & his sister Friederike (1). Letter from prison, & farewell letters on the day of his execution, by an officer of Schill's Corps. (91) DM1,200
— PELLE, COMTE DE. - Ms, State of the Infantry Employed in the Grand Army, 1812. 8 pp, folio. Listing army corps, their composition, & their commanders. (91) $750
— SHAW, FREDERICK. - Autograph Ms, journal, 6 June to 5 July 1814. 22 pp, 8vo; partially disbound. Describing the army's march, fortifications & people in Southern France. (89) £170
— TREATY OF SAINT CLOUD. - Document, 3 July 1815. 7 pp, folio. Military convention ending hostilities, sgd by officers representing Great Britain, Prussia & France. With ratification, sgd, by Bluecher at bottom of last page, 4 July 1815. (89) £22,000

Nash, Ogden, 1902-71
Autograph quotation, "The cow is of the bovine ilk...", sgd & inscr to Harry Carl Henschkel; [n.d.]. (90) $275

Nash, Paul, 1889-1946
Original drawing, leaves, fruit & masonry by the seashore, preparatory study for Urne Buriall and Garden of Cyprus; [n.d.]. (89) £500
ALs, 28 Dec 1943. (90) DM210

Nasser, Gamal Abdel, 1918-70
Photograph, sgd & inscr, 16 Feb 1956. (90) $200

Nast, Thomas, 1840-1902
Original drawings, (11), pen-&-ink cartoons pertaining to the tariff reform, drawn for the NY Evening Post, 1888. Various sizes. All sgd. With related material. (89) $6,000

Naturforschende Gesellschaft
Document, 10 May 1803. (91) DM400

Naundorf, Karl Wilhelm, 1785?-1845. See: Louis XVII, 1785-95

Naval Manuscripts
[A group of 13 rolls of annual Navy Exchequer accounts by Edward Russell, Earl of Orford & 1st Lord of the Admiralty, 1688 to 1699, vellum, providing a highly extensive record of naval affairs & finances, sold at S on 14 Dec 1989, lot 229, for £2,000 to Garcy.]
[Low, Commander William W., U.S.N. - A group of 6 journals, 1841 to 1870s, mostly secretarial copies of letters to & from Low during his service on various ships, sold at R on 4 Mar 1989, lot 100, for $1,600.]
Ms, A List of their Ma[jes]ties Royall Navy with each Ships Dimension..., 19 Nov 1694. (91) £500
— Ms, album of c.200 dispatches received by Capt. (89) £150
— Ms, Mouvemens, ordres et signaux generaux de l'Armee du Roi, commandee par Monsr. Le Comte d'Orvilliers, Lieutenant General, en 1779. 82 leaves plus blanks, 238mm by 175mm, in contemp mor wallet bdg with brass clasp & lock. With c.350 small handpainted signal flags in colors. (90) $2,200
— Ms, Signals book, [after 1802]; c.100 pp, 16mo. (88) £480
— BARTON, ALFRED BOWER. - 2 autograph Mss, 3 Mss & typescript, journals kept as a ship's surgeon in the China seas, Crimea & elsewhere, 1853 to 1858. Over 800 pp, 4to, in roan & bds. Partly fair copies or transcript. (90) £750
— COCHRAN, GEORGE, U.S.N. - Auto-

graph Ms, private journal as Pay Inspector aboard the U.S. Steamer Congress on a voyage to Greenland, 1 July 1871 to 3 Feb 1872. 63 pp, 4to. Including uncancelled 1871 New Foundland stamp. (89) $600

— CORNWALLIS, CAPT. WILLIAM. - 2 Mss, Log book for H.M.S. Swift & Letters & Orders Received, 14 Oct 1762 to 31 May 1764, on duty in the Carribbean & off Florida. 149 leaves, 4to & folio, in 2 contemp vellum vols. (89) $2,500

— FOORD, EDWARD. - Autograph Ms, journal detailing 17 cruises in home waters, inspecting buoys & lights, 1847 & later; c.120 pp, 8vo, in blue mor bdg. (88) £75

— GALLEY, J. G. - Ms, journal kept during 2 surveys of the south-eastern coast of Africa on board the HMS Andromache & HMS Barracouta, 1822 & 1823. Over 170 pp, folio, in quarter calf. With related material. (90) £2,000

— HAWES, ABIGALL. - Ds, 13 Jan 1665. Length not stated. Bill of sale of a share of the new ship "named the Mary Ann of Woodbridge" to John Bass. Sgd by 2 witnesses on verso. (90) £85

— HMS PLANTAGENET. - Ms, Watch Bill of HMS Plantagenet under Capt. Robert Lloyd, [after 1811]. 43 pp, folio. Containing some hundreds of names of the ship's company set out in 3 or 4 columns to a page. Including 4 pen-&-ink vignettes & 6 watercolor illus. With related material. (89) £1,300

— KIRKHAM, MAJOR. - Autograph Ms, journal & notebook giving account of voyages to Turkey, in the Mediterranean & to the Baltic, c.1798 to 1816; c.235 pp, 4to, in def vellum bdg. Including over 50 watercolors. With related material. (88) £350

— LOUISBOURG EXPEDITION. - Ms, Log of H.M.S. Royal George & H.M.S. Namur, 16 Jan 1757 to 31 July 1758; c.25 pp, 4to, in vellum bdg. Including details of the landing of the British forces at Gabarus Bay, June 1758. (90) $4,500

— LOUISBOURG EXPEDITION. - Ms, Log of H.M.S. Royal George & H.M.S. Namur, 16 Jan 1757 to 31 July 1758; c.250 pp, 4to, in vellum bdg. Including details of the landing of the British forces at Gabarus Bay, June 1758. (88) £650

— MALONE, JAMES WILLIAM. - Ms, 75 precision scale drawings of engineering work carried out on ships (mainly warships), partly at Woolwich Naval Dockyard, with tables & explanatory notes; 26 Dec 1862. About 60 pp, 4to, in roan backed bdg. (91) £600

— PARKER, SAMUEL. - Ds, 11 Aug 1696. Length not stated. Bill of sale of a share of the new ship "Called the Prosperous Mary of Ipswich" to John Bass. Sgd by witnesses on verso. (90) £150

— ROYLE, CHARLES. - Autograph Ms, journal kept on board HMS Victory, Boscawen, Imaum & Termagant, on voyages to Halifax, Nova Scotia & the Caribbean, 1854 & 1855. 226 pp, 8vo, in half calf bdg. Including news from the Crimea. (88) £400

— "SEYMOUR". - Document, Mar 1742. 3 pp, folio. "To Sundry Accounts for the Cost and Outfit of Said Vessel", detailed list of expenses. (89) $100

— SMITH, LIEUT. COMMANDER WATSON. - A collection of Mss, documents & letters relating to his naval career, 1825 to 1864, including his service in the Civil War. (90) $1,200

— "SUFFOLK". - Ms, journal kept by [Lieut. Geast?] on a voyage to St. Lucia as escort to a merchant convoy, 6 Aug 1778 to 15 Aug 1780. 140 pp, 12mo, in def dark brown calf. (89) £320

— WHITING, HENRY. - Ls, 4 Nov 1848. 2 pp, 4to. To Capt. David Wood of USS Massachusetts. Sailing instructions, issued by the Assistant Quartermaster General's office. Tate collection. (91) $110

Nay, Ernst Wilhelm, 1902-68
A Ls s (2), 1 Sept 1929 to 7 May 1932. (88) DM450

Nazi Leaders
[The signatures of all 21 defendants in the Nuremberg trials, on 7 small sheets affixed to a manila folder, with a group photograph, 1946, sold at Dar on 10 Apr 1991, lot 287, for $1,000.]

NAZIMOVA

Nazimova, Alla, 1879-1945
Photograph, sgd, [n.d.]. (91) $180

Neander, Johann August Wilhelm, 1789-1850
ALs, 20 Aug 1831. (90) DM240
— 17 Apr 1848. (90) DM320

Necker, Jacques, 1732-1804
Ls, 24 June 1778. (88) DM400

Nees von Esenbeck, Christian Gottfried Daniel, 1776-1858
Series of 6 A Ls s, 12 Nov 1843 to 17 Nov 1845. (91) DM450
ALs, 3 Dec 1809. (90) DM220

Negri, Pola, Pseud. of Appolonia Chalupek, 1897-1987
ALs, 29 Jan 1929. (90) DM250

Neher, Caspar, 1897-1962
Autograph Ms, sketches for decorations & notes for the staging of Goethe's Faust, Goetz von Berlichingen & other plays; [c.1949]. 52 pp, 4to. In brown ink. (88) DM4,200
ALs, 25 Sept 1946. (89) DM220

Nehru, Jawaharlal, 1889-1964
Ls, 25 Dec 1938. (89) DM420
— 17 Sept 1962. (90) £110
— 17 Sept 1962. (90) DM320
Photograph, sgd, 1950. (89) £150
— Anr, 1959. (90) $200
— SWAMY. - Orig drawings (4), port sketches of Nehru, Nov 1949 to 1952, various sizes. Sgd by both. (89) £480

Neilson, Harry Bingham
Original drawings, (20), animals & birds, mostly to illus various annuals, 1929 to 1939. Mostly 310mm by 230mm. In ink & watercolor; 19 sgd. 1 torn. (89) £1,700

Neipperg, Wilhelm Reinhard, Graf von, 1684-1774 —&
Harrach, Johann Joseph Philipp, Graf von, 1678-1764
Ls s (2), 3 Dec 1755 & 28 May 1757. (88) DM340

AMERICAN BOOK PRICES CURRENT

Nelson Family
[A group of 8 letters & notes by various members of the Nelson family including the Rev. William Nelson & Lady Frances Nelson, 8 May 1802 to 15 May 1937, 20 pp, various sizes, about family matters, sold at C on 21 June 1989, lot 276, for 550 to Nash.]

Nelson, Horatia, 1801-81
A Ls s (2), 6 & 28 Mar 1815. Wolf collection. (89) £1,000

Nelson, Horatio Nelson, Viscount, 1758-1805
[A group of 8 letters from various Italian nobles, statesmen & soldiers, 28 June 1799 to 12 Jan 1802, 11 pp, various sizes, to Lord Nelson, about a variety of matters, sold at C on 21 June 1989, lot 250, for £300 to Fiske.]
[A group of 7 letters from various correspondents including Sir William Hamilton & Warren Hastings, 2 July 1801 to 15 June 1804, 16 pp, various sizes, to Lord Nelson, about a variety of matters, with a letter from Nelson in Emma Hamilton's hand, sold at C on 21 June 1989, lot 251, for £650 to Wilson.]
[2 autograph endorsements & 2 small autograph calculations on a group of 16 weekly household accounts for Merton, 21 June 1802 to 4 Apr 1803, 16 pp, folio, sold at C on 20 June 1990, lot 238, for £1,200 to Hayes.]
[A group of 6 notes & letters from various people including the Rev. William Nelson & Horatio Walpole, 2 to 6 Jan 1806, 6 pp, folio & 4to, concerning Nelson's funeral, with related material, sold at C on 21 June 1989, lot 273, for £300 to Laird.]
[A ptd pass for his funeral, sgd by the Dean of St. Paul's, 9 Jan 1806, sold at pn on 8 Dec 1988, lot 62, for £150 to Barlow.]
[A group of 6 letters & documents from various people, 15 Nov 1809 to 18 Feb 1847, 23 pp, folio & 4to, referring to Nelson, with related material, sold at C on 21 June 1989, lot 274, for £100 to Laird.]
Autograph Ms, address to the Senate of Palermo after having been made a citizen, [4 Mar 1799]. Wolf collection.

(89) £320
— Autograph Ms, brief draft memorandum concerning an order to various commanders, [1805?]. (90) £350
— Autograph Ms, directions to shipping for the approach to Porto Real, Cadiz; [1797?]. Wolf collection. (90) £350
— Autograph Ms, memorandum noting staff changes & recommendations after the Battle of Santa Cruz, [Aug 1797]. 1 p, 4to. Written in his left hand. Contemp endorsement on verso. Wolf collection. (89) £1,600
— Autograph Ms, notes listing recommendations for promotion, [n.d.]. Wolf collection. (89) £250
Ms, Detail of the Proceedings of the Expedition against the Town of Santa Cruz..., 27 July 1797. 5 pp, folio. Draft of a dispatch to Admiral Jervis; sgd in his left hand. Wolf collection. (90) £2,800
— Ms, letterbook containing copies of 32 naval orders from Nelson, & copies of orders from other captains of his fleet, with related material, 1793 to 1806. (90) £500
— Ms, Weekly acc[oun]t of the Rt. (90) £700
Transcript, Extract of a Private Letter from Lord Nelson of the Nile to Elgin dated Palermo 31 Mar 1800. Wolf collection. (89) £800
A Ls s (2), 23 Apr 1803 & [n.d.]. Wolf collection. (90) £220
— A Ls s (2), [n.d.]. Wolf collection. (90) £850
ALs, 28 Sept 1785. 2 pp, 4to. To Cuthbert Collingwood. Thanking for support in the matter of the controversial enforcement of the Navigation Laws. With engraved port. Wolf collection. (90) £1,600
— [n.d.]. Wolf collection. (89) £700
— 28 Feb 1790. 4 pp, 4to. To John R. Herbert. Discussing the bill for the abolition of slavery & reporting about his stepson. Seal tear. Wolf collection. (89) £1,200
— 2 Feb 1793. (91) £700
— 27 Sept 1793. 4 pp, 4to. To Sir William Hamilton. Apologizing for failing to return a butter pan & describing his activities off Leghorn. Wolf collection.

(89) £1,500
— 7 July 1794. 2 pp, 8vo. To Admiral Hood. Reporting about action at Monachesco on Corsica, & detailing casualties. Wolf collection. (90) £1,600
— 28 Oct 1794. Wolf collection. (90) £700
— 6 Feb 1795. 2 pp, 4to. To Thomas Pollard. Hoping to return to Leghorn soon. Including 2 postscripts, sgd HN, concerning "payment for my female friend", & ordering supplies. Wolf collection. (89) £1,200
— 21 Dec 1795. (90) £750
— 20 May 1796. 3 pp, 4to. To Sir William Hamilton. Discussing the implications of the Austrian defeat for Naples & Tuscany. Wolf collection. (90) £1,500
— 24 Sept 1796. 3 pp, 4to. To John Udney. Informing him of measures taken against Genoa for firing on a British flag. Wolf collection. (90) £1,100
— 27 May 1797. 3 pp, 4to. To Messrs. Marsh & Creed. About surgeon's expenses, & commenting on the blockade of Cadiz. (91) £1,200
— 15 June 1797. 3 pp, size not stated. To John F. Scrivener. Describing the situation of the fleet off Cadiz. Written with his right hand. Repaired. (88) £1,500
— 5 Apr 1798. 1 p, 4to. To Lady Frances Nelson. Inquiring about personal articles missed out of his packing for Lisbon. With related material. Wolf collection. (89) £1,400
— [summer 1798]. (91) £800
— 8 Aug 1798. 2 pp, 4to. To Sir William Hamilton. Announcing his Nile victory. Tipped to separate address leaf. Wolf collection. (89) £12,000
— 12 Aug 1798. 1 p, 4to. To Sir William Hamilton. Countermanding an order for wine & bread. Wolf collection. (90) £1,200
— 22 Dec 1798. Wolf collection. (89) £1,000
— 19 Jan 1799. Wolf collection. (90) £700
— 26 Mar 1799. 1 p, 4to. To Sir William Hamilton. Requesting that James Harryman should act as interpreter for Capt. Troubridge. Wolf collection. (90) £1,200
— 27 Mar 1799. 1 p, 4to. To Sir Charles

NELSON

Stuart. Informing him that supplies are loaded. Wolf collection. (89) £1,300
— 30 Mar 1799. Wolf collection. (90) £1,000
— 10 Apr 1799. 3 pp, 4to. To Lady Frances Nelson. About his situation in Palermo, & commenting on the death of his uncle. Wolf collection. (89) £2,800
— 19 May 1799. Wolf collection. (90) £850
— 20 May [1799]. 2 pp, 4to & 8vo. To Sir William Hamilton. Enclosing his order of battle for Lady Hamilton (present), & discussing the whereabouts of the French fleet. Wolf collection. (90) £2,000
— 28 June 1799. 1 p, folio. To Sir John Acton. Disapproving of affairs at Naples & urging the restitution of the King & Queen. With related material. Wolf collection. (89) £1,200
— 25 July 1799. 2 pp, 4to. To John Spencer Smith. Expressing admiration for his brother's part in raising the siege of Acre. Wolf collection. (89) £1,300
— 29 Nov 1799. Wolf collection. (90) £600
— 10 Jan 1800. Wolf collection. (90) £1,000
— 13 Feb 1800. 2 pp, 4to. To Emma Hamilton. Saying he misses her "house and company" & commenting on a note from Lord Grenville. Sgd Bronte Nelson. (88) $4,750
— 28 Feb 1800. 1 p, 4to. To Sir William Hamilton. Informing him about the treaty between France & Turkey. Wolf collection. (89) £1,900
— 28 Feb 1800. 1 p, 4to. To Sir William Hamilton. Informing him about the treaty between France & Turkey. Wolf collection. (91) £2,000
— 30 Mar 1800. 3 pp, 4to. To Sir William Hamilton. Complaining bitterly that French ships should have been allowed to return to Europe from Egypt. Wolf collection. (90) £2,000
— [17 Nov 1800]. 1 p, 4to. To Sir Isaac Heard. Announcing his intention to take his seat in the House of Lords. Repaired. Wolf collection. (90) £1,500
— 22 Nov 1800. Wolf collection. (89) £800

AMERICAN BOOK PRICES CURRENT

— [n.d.], "Saturday". 1 p, 4to. To Lady Hamilton. About William Locker's funeral. Wolf collection. (89) £2,200
— [n.d.]. 1 p, 4to. To Sir William Hamilton. Complaining that he is not kept informed. Wolf collection. (89) £1,100
— [n.d.], "Sunday". 3 pp, 4to. To [Lady Hamilton]. Declaring his indifference to society & damning Lady Abercorn. Wolf collection. (89) £3,800
— 25 Jan 1801. 2 pp, folio. To Lady Hamilton. Describing the anxiety of "Mr. Thomson" over "Mrs. Thomson's" condition. Wolf collection. (89) £7,000
— 26 Jan 1801. 3 pp, 4to. To Lady Hamilton. Expressing jealousy of the Prince of Wales's attentions to her, & mentioning "Mr. & Mrs. Thomson". Wolf collection. (89) £2,800
— 1 Feb 1801. 3 pp, 4to. To Lady Hamilton. Rejoicing about the birth of their daughter. Wolf collection. (89) £11,000
— 15 Feb 1801. 4 pp, 4to. To Lady Hamilton. Defending himself for retorting angrily to her accusations of infidelity. Wolf collection. (89) £3,200
— 17 Feb 1801. 3 pp, 4to. To Lady Hamilton. Sending naval gossip & talking of his child. Wolf collection. (90) £4,000
— 27 Feb 1801. 1 p, 4to. To Lady Hamilton. Expressing sorrow at parting & referring to "Mrs. Thomson's" child. Wolf collection. (90) £3,000
— [1801], "Wednesday". 3 pp, 4to. To Lady Hamilton. Criticizing her for entertaining the Prince of Wales. Wolf collection. (89) £5,000
— [1801]. 1 p, 4to. To Lady Hamilton. Sending "Mr. Thomson's professions of undying love". Wolf collection. (89) £2,400
— [n.d]. 2 pp, 8vo. To "Mrs. T." [Lady Hamilton]. Giving directions for the christening of the child. Wolf collection. (89) £7,000
— [n.d]. 3 pp, 8vo. To "Mrs. Thomson" [Lady Hamilton]. Conveying "Mr. Thomson's" intention to marry her, & sending money. Wolf collection. (89) £4,500
— 1 Mar 1801. 3 pp, 4to. To Lady Hamilton. Recommending the com-

pany of his mother & sister-in-law as protection against the Prince of Wales. Wolf collection. (90) £3,600
— 6 Mar [1801]. 4 pp, 4to. To Lady Hamilton. Warning her against the Prince of Wales. Sgd & initialled. Wolf collection. (89) £3,200
— 7 Mar [1801]. 4 pp, 4to. To Lady Hamilton. About 2 ladies visiting his ship, his opinion of Lady Hyde, & his wish to fly to her. Wolf collection. (90) £2,800
— 11 Mar 1801. 1 p, 4to. To Mr. Warmington. In 3d person, requesting him to forward a letter to Vienna. Repaired. (88) DM3,400
— [n.d.]. 1 p, 8vo. To "Mrs. Thomson" [Lady Hamilton]. On behalf of "Mr. Thomson", thanking for a present & talking about the christening of the child. Wolf collection. (90) £1,800
— 5 Apr [1801]. 3 pp, 4to. To Sir Thomas Warburton. Discussing a disagreement with Sir Hyde Parker. Wolf collection. (90) £1,500
— [24 May - 2 June 1801]. 4 pp, 4to. To Lady Hamilton. Hoping to be in London soon, & reporting about his situation in the Baltic. (89) £3,600
— 3 July 1801. (91) £700
— 7 July 1801. (88) $950
— 1 & 2 Aug 1801. 4 pp, 4to. To Emma Hamilton. Love letter, & referring to his search for the French fleet off Boulogne. (91) £4,200
— 5 Aug 1801. Wolf collection. (90) £1,000
— 14 Aug 1801. Wolf collection. (89) £950
— 14 Aug 1801. 2 pp, 4to. To Lady Hamilton. Saying he is in poor health, & requesting champagne to be sent. Wolf collection. (89) £1,800
— 15 Aug 1801. 3 pp, 4to. To Lady Hamilton. Asking her to find him a house. Wolf collection. (89) £3,800
— 11 Sept 1801. 4 pp, 4to. To Sir Evan Nepean. Discussing the plan to destroy the Dutch fleet at Goree. Wolf collection. (90) £1,200
— 20 Sept 1801. Wolf collection. (90) £650
— 24 Sept 1801. 3 pp (of 4), 4to. To Lady Hamilton. Expressing despair about the injuries suffered by Capt. Parker & his determination to quit the service. (90) £3,400
— 29 Sept 1801. 3 pp, 4to. To Lady Hamilton. Discussing the furnishings for Merton. Wolf collection. (90) £3,300
— 7 Oct 1801. 4 pp, 4to. To Lady Hamilton. Responding to news that Merton is not yet ready, & about other matters. Seal tear. Wolf collection. (89) £2,200
— 9 Oct 1801. 1 p, 4to. To Admiral Lutwidge. Thanking for news about the ratification of the peace, & expressing a desire to retire. (89) $2,000
— 14 Oct 1801. Wolf collection. (90) £1,000
— 14 Oct 1801. 2 pp, 4to. To James Tobin. Informing him of his failed efforts to obtain promotions for 2 men. (88) $2,100
— 21 Dec 1801. Wolf collection. (90) £900
— 7 Jan 1802. (88) £450
— 13 Feb 1802. Wolf collection. (90) £850
— 28 Apr 1802. Wolf collection. (90) £700
— 3 May 1802. 1 p, 4to. To William Marsh. Thanking for condolences on the death of his father, & discussing a financial matter. Wolf collection. (89) £1,100
— 19 May 1802. 2 pp, 4to. To Robert Barker. Regarding his panorama of the Battle of Copenhagen. Wolf collection. (89) £1,600
— 12 Oct 1802. 4 pp, 4to. To Sir William Stewart. Attacking Napoleon. (89) £11,500
— 31 Oct 1802. (88) £700
— 25 Dec 1802. Wolf collection. (89) £800
— 8 Apr 1803. Wolf collection. (90) £600
— 10 Apr 1803. (89) £950
— 13 Apr [1803]. (89) £800
— 7 May 1803. (90) £750
— 15 May 1803. Wolf collection. (90) £350
— [c.May 1803]. Wolf collection. (90) £500
— 9 July 1803. Wolf collection. (90) £850
— 11 July 1803. Wolf collection. (90) £800
— 12 July 1803. (88) £850
— 25 Aug 1803. (90) £700

NELSON

— 31 Dec 1803. 2 pp, 4to. To Major Gen. Villettes. Concerning his request for troops to retake some islands. Wolf collection. (90) £1,200
— [March 1804]. 3 pp, 4to. To [Lady Hamilton]. Worrying about her health & referring to their newborn child. Wolf collection. (89) £7,500
— 28 Apr 1804. 2 pp, 4to. To Lady Hamilton. Saying that the reign of Buonaparte will soon be over. Written on board the Victory. (91) $8,500
— 27 May 1804. Wolf collection. (90) £850
— 14 July 1804. 1 p, 4to. To John Hookham Frere. Thanking for forwarding a letter & referring to the French fleet. Wolf collection. (89) £1,300
— 27 Aug 1804. Wolf collection. (90) £900
— 6 Sept 1804. 1 p, 4to. To Sir Richard Bickerton. About observing the French fleet at Toulon. Wolf collection. (89) £1,300
— 19 Dec [1804]. 4 pp, 4to. To Sir John Acton. About Napoelon's designs on the Kingdom of Naples & related matters. (91) £2,800
— 11 Apr 1805. Wolf collection. (90) £750
— 2 Oct 1805. (90) £1,000
— 2 Oct 1805. (90) £800
— 6 Oct 1805. 4 pp, 4to. To George Rose. Informing him of the imminence of battle & hoping for reinforcements. Wolf collection. (89) £7,500
— 11 Dec [n.y.]. 1 p, 4to. Recipient unknown. Discussing the possibility of recipient's appointment as chaplain on Nelson's ship. With fragmentary postscript at top. Repaired. (88) $1,600
AL, 1 June [1801]. Wolf collection. (90) £250
— [c.29 Sept 1801]. 2 pp, 4to. To "Mrs. Thomson" [Lady Hamilton]. Expressing distress at their separation & Parker's death. Margin def. Wolf collection. (89) £2,800
— 10 June [1803]. 3 pp, 4to. To Lady Hamilton. Discussing his progress & the management of Bronte, & promising to send things from Malta. Wolf collection. (90) £1,600
— 7 June 1804. 7 pp, 4to. Wolf collection. (90) £850
— 29 Dec [1804]. Wolf collection. (90) £180
Ls, 24 Sept 1781. 1 p, 4to. To [The Lords Commissioners of the Admiralty]. Forwarding a letter (not present) from the Surgeon's Mate of the Albemarle. Contemp endorsements on verso. Wolf collection. (89) £1,300
— 29 Sept 1785. Wolf collection. (90) £850
— 23 Jan 1789. 1 p, folio. To [the future William IV]. Ordering the arrest of Lieut. Schomberg. Repaired. Wolf collection. (89) £1,300
— 10 Sept 1795. 3 pp, folio. To Francis Drake. Giving his views on the risks of escorting ships carrying provisions for towns near Genoa. With autograph subscription. (89) £1,200
— 14 Sept 1796. Wolf collection. (89) £850
— 9 Oct 1797. (88) £550
— 29 Nov 1798. (89) £600
— 1 Feb 1799. (88) £650
— 22 Mar 1799. (89) £700
— 11 July 1799. (91) £700
— 26 Oct 1799. Wolf collection. (90) £700
— 4 Dec 1803. (88) £650
— 15 Apr 1804. (91) £420
— 6 Apr 1805. (88) £650
— 11 Apr 1805. (89) £1,000
— 4 June 1805. (88) £600
ANs, 20 Dec 1798. Wolf collection. (89) £650
— 26 Dec 1800. Wolf collection. (90) £220
— [c.Jan 1801]. Wolf collection. (90) £500
— 3 Dec 1802. 1 p, 8vo. To Sir William North. Thanking for a note. Framed with a port. (88) $1,100
— 19 Sept 1803. 1 p, 8vo. To Lady Hamilton. Enclosing a letter for Mr. Vansittart (not present). Wolf collection. (90) £1,500
Ns, [1797 or earlier]. Wolf collection. (90) £400
ADs, 29 Oct 1794. (90) £750
— 17 Dec 1803. 4 pp, 4to. "Memorandum for Sir Richard Bickerton to carry into Execution at Malta"; orders. Wolf collection. (90) £1,300
Ds, 23 Sept 1785. Wolf collection. (89) £350

1987 - 1991 · AUTOGRAPHS & MANUSCRIPTS — NELSON

— [late July 1797]. 4 pp, folio. Demanding the surrender of the ship El Principe d'Asturias & the fort at Santa Cruz, addressed to the commanding officer at Santa Cruz. Sgd with his left hand; with autograph endorsement "Copy". With related material. Wolf collection. (89) £4,000

— [late July 1797]. 4 pp, folio. Demanding the surrender of the ship El Principe d'Asturias & the fort at Santa Cruz, addressed to the commanding officer at Santa Cruz. Sgd with his left hand; with autograph endorsement "Copy". With related material. Wolf collection. (91) £4,500

— 7 June 1798. 1 p, folio. Order of battle & sailing, addressed to Capt. Miller of HMS Theseus. (91) £1,100

— 13 Aug 1798. (88) $880

— 18 Sept 1798. (88) £360

— 12 Nov 1801. 2 pp, folio. Agreement with Thomas Bennett concerning the lease of barns at Merton. Also sgd by Sir William Hamilton. Wolf collection. (90) £1,400

— 30 May 1803. Wolf collection. (90) £500

— 31 July 1803. Wolf collection. (89) £1,000

— 1 Aug 1803. 1 p, folio. Orders for the lighting of ships in case of action by night, addressed to Capt. William Parker. Including pen-&-ink diagram. With related material. Wolf collection. (89) £1,400

— 1 Aug 1803. Wolf collection. (89) £900

— 22 Mar 1804. (88) $750

— 28 Apr 1804. 3 pp, folio. Orders addressed to Capt. Frank Sotheron to proceed to the Gulf of Frejus & keep watch on the French fleet at Toulon. (89) $2,200

— 27 May 1804. Wolf collection. (89) £950

— 10 June 1804. 1 p, folio. Instructions for private signals between British & Sicilian ships, addressed to Capt. William Parker. Wolf collection. (89) £1,100

— 8 July 1804. (88) £550

— 26 Sept 1805. 1 p, 4to. Instructions concerning paroles, addressed to Capt. Edward Codrington. Wolf collection. (89) £1,300

— 26 Sept 1805. 2 pp, folio. List of additional rendezvous locations, addressed to Capt. Edward Codrington. Wolf collection. (89) £1,800

— 26 Sept 1805. 1 p, 4to. Instructions concerning paroles, addressed to Capt. Nicholl Morris. (90) DM4,600

— 29 Sept 1805. 1 p, folio. Chart addressed to Capt. Robert Moorsom, showing pennants to be flown by British ships before Trafalgar. Including 21 small watercolor drawings of pennants. Lower margin def. With Ds by Cuthbert Collingwood & further related material. (90) £8,500

— 29 Sept 1805. 1 p, folio. "Order of Battle or Sailing", addressed to Capt. Edward Codrington. Wolf collection. (89) £3,200

— 29 Sept 1805. 1 p, folio. Chart showing 23 small watercolor drawings of pennants to be flown by ships before Trafalgar, addressed to Capt. Edward Codrington. Wolf collection. (89) £8,500

— 15 Oct 1805. 3 pp, folio. Order addressed to Capt. Edward Codrington to conduct an investigation into the health & fitness of some seamen. Wolf collection. (90) £1,500

— 17 Oct 1805. 1 p, 8vo. Additional rendezvous location, marked "Secret"; addressed to Capt. Edward Codrington. Wolf collection. (89) £1,500

Document, 21 Mar 1798. Wolf collection. (90) £650

— original grant that made him Duke of Bronte, 10 Oct 1799. 6 pp, vellum, folio, in contemp mor gilt with arms of King Ferdinand. Sgd by Ferdinand, King of the Two Sicilies & Infante of Spain & bearing his seal. (91) £30,000

Cut signature, 10 Oct 1805. 6.5 by 1.5 inches. Matted with bust print. (91) $1,100

Endorsement, sgd, on secretarial copy of a letter from Admiral Hood to Nelson, 24 July 1794, 2 pp, 4to, regarding supplies & personnel; certifying as true copy. Wolf collection. (90) £450

— BROMWICH, JOSEPH. - Autograph Ms, log kept on H.M.S. Albemarle commanded by Nelson, 16 Aug 1781 to 18 Feb 1783; c.93 pp, folio; in marbled

NELSON

covers. Covering convoy service in the North Sea, North America & the West Indies. (88) £600

— HAYLEY, WILLIAM. - ALs, 7 June 1806. 2 pp, 4to. To Lady Hamilton. Consoling her on the death of Nelson & sending a ptd poem (present). Sgd Your affectionate Hermit. (90) £500
See also: Elgin, Thomas Bruce

**Nelson, Horatio Nelson, Viscount, 1758-1805 —&
Others**

ALs, 1 June 1799. 3 pp, 4to. To Capt. Alexander Ball. About recipient's situation in Malta. Written jointly with Emma & Sir William Hamilton, a section written & sgd by each (William Hamilton's signature excised). Wolf collection. (89) £1,900

Nelson, Thomas, Signer from Virginia

ALs, 4 Jan 1776. 2 pp, 4to. To Mann Page. Saying that he does not fear the British but that their maritime force is formidable. In very poor condition. (91) $1,400

Ls, 7 Jan 1781. 1 p, 4to. To Baron von Steuben. On military matters. (91) $5,000

AN, 21 Sept 1776. (91) $700

Signature, [n.d.]. (91) $550

Nernst, Walther, 1864-1941

A Ls s (2), 2 May 1905 & 16 June 1908. (88) DM420

Neruda, Pablo

[A group of autograph Mss, typescripts, galleys, reviews, etc. relating to the play Fulgor y Muerte de Joaquin Murieta [1960s], c.72 pp & ptd material, sold at sg on 12 Nov 1987, lot 234, for $3,200.]

Neruda, Pablo, 1904-73. See: Lorca, Federico Garcia & Neruda

Nerval, Gerard de, 1808-55

A Ls s (2), [n.d.]. 2 pp, 8vo & 4to. To Messrs. Verteuil & Mirecourt. Requesting theater tickets. (91) DM1,200

AMERICAN BOOK PRICES CURRENT

Nesselrode, Karl Robert, Graf von, 1780-1862

ALs, 1 May 1804. Albrecht collection. (91) SF320

— 8 Feb 1814. (90) DM500

Ls, 22 Apr 1826. (88) DM420

Nestorian Christians

[A rubbing of the Syriac & Chinese inscr on the stele set up in 781 at Xian, recording the names of 67 Syriac Christians, in black on paper, size not stated, in cloth covered case, def, sold at S on 22 Nov 1988, lot 108, for £1,800 to Bjork.]

Nestroy, Johann Nepomuk, 1801-62

Autograph Ms, draft of a comedy, scenes 2 - 4, [n.d.]. 2 pp, 4to. With numerous revisions. With note stating provenance. (88) DM7,500

— Autograph Ms, drama, Friedrich Prinz von Korsika, pp 75 & 76; [1827]. 2 pp, 4to. (88) DM6,500

— Autograph Ms, introductory song from a comedy, fragment; [n.d.]. 2 pp, 4to (cut from a folio sheet). In pencil. (89) DM4,400

ALs, 5 Apr 1862. 3 pp, 8vo. To Carl Sluka. Asking him to forward a costume for a performance. (91) DM6,400

Ls, 12 Feb 1843. 1 p, 4to. To Charlotte Birch-Pfeiffer. About staging Einen Jux will er sich machen at Zuerich. (88) DM3,000

Netherlands, The

— MIDDELBURG. - Ms, Beschrijving van de Oost-kerk stande tot Middelburg in Zeeland... dor... Ian Bosdyk, 1800. 212 pp, 4to, in contemp half calf. Full account of the building of the church, with full-page drawing. (88) £160

Nettelbeck, Joachim, 1738-1824

Autograph Ms, dedication cut from his daughter's bible, [n.d.]. (89) DM900

ANs, [n.d.]. 1 p, 8vo. To an unnamed clergyman. About a financial matter. (90) DM1,600

Neuffer, Christian Ludwig, 1769-1839

Autograph Ms, poem, Die Hofnung [sic]; [n.d.]. (89) DM420

Neukomm, Sigismund, 1778-1858
ALs, 17 June 1815. (90) DM950

New, Edmund Hort, 1871-1931
Original drawings, (91), to illus W. Macmillan Archives. (90) £1,000

New Hebrides
[A series of c.80 letters written by Scottish missionaries (mostly Agnes & William Watt) on Tana in the New Hebrides, 1869 to 1880, describing the islanders, slave traders, their work, etc., with contemp photographs & ptd ephemera, over 400 pp, 4to & 8vo, sold at S on 19 July 1990, lot 299, for £3,000 to Quaritch.]

New Jersey
[A group of 12 legislative documents, drafts of acts, etc., some sgd, 1754 to 1785, with related material, sold at CNY on 22 Feb 1989, lot 2074, for $1,400.]

New Mexico
— MUNROE, JOHN. - ALs, 20 May 1850. 2 pp, 4to. To Gen. Jones. Transmitting a memorial from the inhabitants of Dona Ana complaining that Texas has claimed their property. Alexander collection. (90) $160
— SMITH, LIEUT. HENRY W. - ALs, 18 Jan 186[9]. 3 pp, 4to. To his mother. From Fort Stanton, reporting about mail riders being killed by Indians, military expeditions, etc. (90) $300

New York
[A collection of 23 letters & 1 Ds, 1679 to 1835, relating to the NY City area, sold at sg on 22 Oct, lot 198, for $150.]
[Brooklyn Bridge. - An engraved invitiation to the opening ceremonies, filled out to John G. Mayer, 24 May [1883], 1 p, 4to, with related material, sold at sg on 9 Mar 1989, lot 21, for $130.]
Document, 15 Oct 1765. Byer collection. (90) $110
— AMERICAN MUSEUM OF NATURAL HISTORY. - 48 documents, 1873 to 1885. Mostly 1 p each, various sizes. Invoices to & vouchers of the museum, sgd by Theodore Roosevelt, Sr., & others. With related material. (90) $175
— GENESEE COUNTY. - Ms, Field notes of the survey of a road from the village of Batavia to the village of Rochester..., by Samuel Foster, 1815. 64 pp, in 8vo notebook. Including fold-out watercolored drawing of the road. (91) $550
— MULFORD, GEORGE. - ALs, 17 Dec 1835. 2 pp, 4to. To his mother. Giving details of the great fire that broke out the previous evening. (91) $110
— ORANGE COUNTY. - 17 documents, 1791 to 1811, folio & 4to. Land conveyances of properties at Minnisink, Goshen or Wawayanda. 2 partly ptd. (88) $150
— ULSTER COUNTY. - Ms, A field book of surveys performed by Andrew Snyder in the County of Ulster..., 7 June 1792 & later. Length not stated; 8vo, in lea bdg. Including a few scale drawings. (91) $160

New York Herald
— G.M.D. - Ls, 6 Jan 1846, size not stated. Correspondent's report on proceedings of the House of Representatives regarding Texas & Oregon. (89) $100

New Zealand
— ABRAHAM, AUGUSTUS B. - Ms, letterbook (incoming) of correspondence to Robert Watkins from Abraham, 1850 to 1883. 120 pp, 4to, in repaired marbled bds. Describing affairs at the New Plymouth Settlement. (90) £380
— OTAGO GOLDFIELDS. - 3 Mss & 2 A Ls s, c.1864 to 1865, 84 pp, 8vo, by Allan Houston, describing the goldfields, the methods of the diggers, etc. With related material. (88) £1,700

Newberry, Percy Edward, 1869-1949
[A collection of over 50 letters addressed to him, relating to his work on the Theban tombs & other projects, 1892 to 1902 & [n.d.], c.100 pp, 8vo, sold at S on 22 July 1988, lot 410, for £600 to Maddalena.]

Newcastle, Thomas Pelham-Holles, Duke of, 1693-1768
[Notes of a meeting at Newcastle's home, 10 Apr 1755, 2 pp, folio, in an unknown hand, discussing the French answer to a British project, French

NEWCASTLE

military strength & British plans, sold at wa on 17 Oct, lot 94, for $210.]

Newman, Charles Alfred
Autograph Ms, journal describing his service in the 2d Chinese War of 1860. 39 pp, folio, in Indian wraps. With related material. (90) £1,400

Newman, Ernest, 1868-1959
[A collection of A Ls s written to him by Shaw, A. Schweitzer, Carl Orff, Rutland Boughton, Fritz Kreisler & others sold at S on 18 Nov 1988, lot 411, for £1,000 to Mandl.]

Newman, John Henry, Cardinal, 1801-90
Collection of 3 A Ls s & 8 Ds s, 4 Feb 1868 to 1888. Doheny collection. (88) $600

— Collection of 24 A Ls s & 3 Ls s, 30 Dec 1881 to 29 Jan 1890. 77 pp, mostly 8vo. To G. T. Edwards. Interesting letters about his religious development & theological questions; including 13-line verse, My Creed. 2 Ls s initialled. Doheny collection. (89) $6,000

Series of 3 A Ls s, 29 July 1840 to 7 Mar 1843. Doheny collection. (88) $550

— Series of 14 A Ls s, 26 June 1846 to 5 July 1879. 39 pp, 8vo & 12mo. To E. Walford (10), Father Lockhart (2) & Sister Mary Monica. About a variety of matters. Doheny collection. (89) $4,000

— Series of 11 A Ls s, 13 Dec 1853 to 7 Aug 1870. 32 pp, 8vo. To W. J. O'Neill Daunt. Discussing religious dogma & politics. With related material. Doheny collection. (89) $3,800

— Series of 12 A Ls s, 4 Oct 1862 to 19 May 1885. About 55 pp, mostly 8vo. To Lord Blachford (5), W. J. Daunt (3), & others. About various matters. In half-mor case. Doheny collection. (89) $5,000

— Series of 3 A Ls s, 9 Aug 1884 & [n.d.]. (90) £600

A Ls s (2), 3 Feb 1852 & 16 June 1878. Doheny collection. (88) $600

— A Ls s (2), 22 Dec 1866 & 25 Jan 1878. Doheny collection. (88) $400

ALs, 30 May 1871. (90) £430

— 20 Feb 1875. (89) $400

— 10 Sept 1881. (91) £60

AMERICAN BOOK PRICES CURRENT

— 18 Sept 1885. (90) £520

Autograph quotation, 2 quatrains of religious verse, sgd & dated 30 July 1875. (89) $450

Signature, 8 June 1881. (90) $110

Newton, Alfred Edward, 1863-1940
ALs, 3 Apr 1936. John F. Fleming Estate. (89) $420

Newton, Sir Isaac, 1642-1727
Autograph Ms, fragment relating to the Opticks. [late 1716] 2 by 5.25 inches, 7 lines. (88) $4,600

— Autograph Ms, notes on theology & history, [n.d.]. 4 pp, 4to. In Latin & Greek. Probably detached from a notebook. (89) £4,200

Ms, submitted to Newton & docketed by him 13 May 1710/11. On gravitational pull and the law of inverse squares, calculating the force necessary to put a satellite in orbit round the earth. 2 pp, c.5 by 6.5 inches. (91) £5,000

ALs, 10 Nov 1692. 1 p, 8vo. To N. Fatio de Duillier. Acknowledging the safe arrival of a receipt; parts that may be about mystical subjects have been censored, with 2 pieces having been torn out. (91) £3,800

AN, 19 Nov 1715. 1 p, 8vo. In 3d person, alluding to his birth & to a possible future Ed of the Principia. Written at foot of a transcript from a letter forwarded to Newton. (91) £4,000

Document, Draught of a Bill in Parliament for a Reward for finding Longitude. [Between 25 May & 3 July 1714] 2 pp, folio. Docketed by Newton. (91) £2,000

Autograph quotation, "Numero pondere et mensura Deus omnia condidit", 13 July 1716. 1 p, 8vo. Sgd. (91) DM9,500

Newton, John, 1725-1807. See: Cowper, William

Ney, Michel, Prince de la Moskowa, 1769-1815
Ls, [12 Sept 1804]. (89) $350

Endorsement, sgd, [Dec/Jan 1801/02]. (88) DM260

Nicholas I, Emperor of Russia, 1796-1855
ALs, 24 July 1831. (91) $650
Ls, 10 Aug 1843. (88) £65

Nicholas II, Emperor of Russia, 1868-1918
ALs, 12 Feb 1900. Size not stated. To [A. A. Mossolov?]. Giving instructions that a decoration be placed at his mother's disposal. Sgd N. (90) £1,300
— 19 May 1900. 1 p, size not stated. To Ilarion Ivanovich. Requesting that he come to see him. With related material. (90) £1,900
— 15 Feb 1902. 3 pp, 8vo. Recipient unnamed. Disapproving of his uncle's intentions to marry Olga von Pistohlkors. Repaired. (90) DM4,000
— [n.d.]. 2 pp, 8vo. To Mme Lannes de Montebello. Sending his travel book about Japan. In French. (89) £1,300
— [n.d.]. 3 pp, 8vo. To the Marquise de Montebello. Thanking for a photograph, & accepting an invitation. In French. (90) DM3,600
ANs, [c.20 Dec 1896]. 1 p, 4to. Recipient unnamed. Instructing him to circulate an enclosed order (not present). Sgd N. (90) DM1,700
— [1897]. 1 p, 8vo. To Ivan L. Goremykin. Instructing him to report [about Princess Hohenlohe's estates]. Endorsed by recipient. (91) DM1,300
— [n.d.]. Byer collection. (90) $800
Ds s (2)29 Jan 1903 & 18 Mar 1911. (88) £680
Photograph, sgd, Sept 1896. 11.5 by 7 inches. Mtd. (91) £1,700
Photograph, 1889. In silver-gilt & champleve enamel frame, overall height 366mm. By Levitsky. (90) £5,000

Nicholas II, Emperor of Russia, 1868-1918 —&
Alexandra Fyodorovna, Empress of Nicholas II of Russia, 1872-1918
Photograph, Apr 1894. 30cm by 19.5cm. Taken on the day their engagement was announced. (90) £1,600
— Anr, on upper balcony of a pavilion on Khodinko Field, acknowledging acclamation of the crowd, 20 May 1896. (90) £350

Nicholson, Ben, 1894-1982
Collection of ALs, autograph postcard, sgd, 4 A Ns, 3 postcards, inscr, & related material, 1958 to 1964. (88) £220

Nicolai, Friedrich, 1733-1811
ALs, 7 Feb [n.y.]. (89) DM440

Nicolai, Melchior, 1578-1659
Autograph sentiment, inscr to Johann Ulrich Ruemelin on detached flyleaf of one of his works, [n.d.]. (90) DM270

Nicolaus de Byard, d.1261
Ms, Distinctiones. [Northern Italy, mid 14th cent] 233 leaves, vellum, 245mm by 165mm, in contemp calf over wooden bd, modern rebacking. In black ink in an irregular & abbreviated Gothic textura. Zabriske-Manhattan College Ms (91) $6,500

Nicolaus de Dinkelsbuehl, c.1360-1433
Ms, De Tribus Partibus Penitentie, & other texts. [Southern Germany, Buxheim Abbey?, 1431]. 178 leaves (1 blank), 295mm by 213mm. Contemp bevelled wooden bds covered with white lea; with pastedown from a 12th-cent theological Ms. By several scribes in cursive bookhands. (91) £4,800

Nicolaus Salernitanus
Ms, Antidotarium; De Dosibus Medicinarum; & other texts. [France, 14th cent]. 40 leaves & 4 flyleaves, vellum, 247mm by 165mm. Repaired medieval bdg of tanned lea over bevelled wooden bds. In a gothic bookhand. With painted initials throughout. (89) £5,500

Nicolay, John G., 1832-1901
Franking signature, [1 Feb 1864]. (89) $105
See also: Lincoln, Abraham

Nicolay, Sir William, 1771-1842
Series of 4 A Ls s, 17 May to Oct 1815. (89) £180

Nicolle, Charles Jules Henri, 1866-1936
ALs, 3 Dec 1928. (88) DM320

Nicolovius, Alfred, 1806-90
ALs, 4 Dec 1825. 8 pp, 4to. To an unnamed uncle. Giving a detailed report about his stay with his granduncle Johann Wolfgang von Goethe. Albrecht collection. (91) SF4,800

Nider, Johann, d.1438
Ms, De Reformatione Status Cenobiorum. (91) £900

Niebuhr, Barthold Georg, 1776-1831
ALs, [n.d.]. (89) DM280
— 13 Apr [1822]. 1 p, 8vo. To Wilhelm von Humboldt. About Sanskrit Mss in Rome. (91) DM1,300
— 4 Dec 1828. Schroeder collection. (89) DM220
— [n.d.]. (90) DM250

Niebuhr, Markus von, 1817-60
ALs, 29 Mar 1848. 2 pp, 8vo. To his wife Anna. Reporting from Schleswig-Holstein after the annexation by the King of Denmark. (91) DM3,000

Nielsen, Kay, 1886-1957
Original drawings, (2), ink tp designs for In Powder and Crinoline, 1912, & Andersen's Fairy Tales, [n.d.]. (88) £420
Original drawing, a couple riding down an arch, in ink & watercolor; [n.d.]. (89) £700
— Original drawing, Hansel & Gretel walking towards the gingerbread house, to illus the Grimms' Hansel and Gretel and other Stories, 1925. In watercolor; sgd & dated 1924. 335mm by 247mm; framed. (90) £8,000
— Original drawing, man & woman in elaborate costume at a ball, in ink & watercolor, heightened with gold; to illus The Dancing Princesses in In Powder and Crinoline, 1912. 314mm by 276mm, sgd. Framed. (88) £10,500
— Original drawing, man in long gown on a quay, to illus The Reward of Virtue in R. (88) £350
— Original drawing, "The Lad in the Battle", to illus East of the Sun and West of the Moon, 1914. 366mm by 269mm. In pen-&-ink & brush-&-ink, with watercolor, heightened with gilt; sgd. Framed. (89) $11,000
— Original drawing, ugly man in elaborate costume, to illus King Uggermugger in R. (88) £380
— Original drawing, young Chinaman in costume, to illus Alladin in R. (88) £450
— Original drawing, young man & princess, to illus Rich Peter the Pedlar in R. (88) £750
— Original drawing, young man playing the whistle, to illus East of the Sun, West of the Moon; [n.d.]. 351mm by 258mm. In ink & watercolor; sgd. Framed. (89) £15,000

Niembsch, Nikolaus, Edler von Strehlenau, 1802-50. See: Lenau, Nikolaus

Nietzsche, Friedrich, 1844-1900
Ms, Hymnus auf die Freundschaft fuer Orchester und Chor von Friedrich Nietzsche, scored for 2 pianos, with autograph inscr to Gustav Krug, Sept 1874. 19 pp, 25.8cm by 36.5cm, in contemp red mor gilt. With related material. (90) DM9,000
ALs, [early Dec 1858]. 2 pp, 4to. To Wilhelm [Pinder]. About his wishes for Christmas, & suggesting a meeting at Almrich. Sgd Fritz. (89) DM7,800
— 16 Oct 1863. 1 p, 8vo. To [Max Heinze]. Expressing congratulations on his engagement to be married. With 2 notes of authentication. (91) DM10,500
— [c.20 Oct 1887]. 2 pp, 8vo. To Alfred Volkland. Sending his Hymnus an das Leben & inquiring about the possibility of a performance in Basel. (88) DM16,000
— [Oct or Nov 1887]. 1 p, 8vo. Recipient unnamed. Sending a correction for the score of his Hymnus auf das Leben. (90) DM6,500
— FOERSTER-NIETZSCHE, ELISABETH. - 2 Ls s, 26 & 28 May 1914. 3 pp, 8vo. To an unnamed musicologist. Concerning information about Nietzsche & access to material in the Nietzsche archives. (90) DM300
— FOERSTER-NIETZSCHE, ELISABETH. - Series of 9 Ls s, 28 Nov 1912 to 13 May 1931; c.27 pp, 8vo. To Felix von Eckardt. About Bernoulli's book Overbeck und Nietzsche, & other matters. With related material. (89) DM650

— FOERSTER-NIETZSCHE, ELISABETH. - Series of 6 Ls s, 7 Jan 1931 to 5 July 1934. 13 pp, 8vo. To Martha Erbs-Kuentzel. Praising her brother, the critical Ed of his works, & the National Socialists. With related material. (89) DM900

— FOERSTER-NIETZSCHE, ELISABETH. - Ls, 21 Feb 1912. 3 pp, 4to. To an unnamed lady. Declining an invitation to Leipzig. With autograph subscription. With anr Ls, 1921. (88) DM240

— FOERSTER-NIETZSCHE, ELISABETH. - Ls, 21 Apr 1899. 4 pp, 4to. To an unnamed lady. Praising her brother. (90) DM470

— FOERSTER-NIETZSCHE, ELISABETH. - 4 Ls, 1918 & 1919. 9 pp, 8vo. To Herr Mutzenbecher. About her brother, the Nietzsche-Archiv, & Eugen Diederichs. With autograph postscripts. (90) DM750

Nietzsche, Friedrich, 1844-1900 —& Krug, Gustav, 1844-1902
Autograph music, "Erscheinung eines Zauberbildes", 71 bars scored for piano; [c.1862/63]. 1 p, 34.8cm by 26.5cm. Mostly in the hand of Krug; bars 31 to 48 by Nietzsche. On verso excerpts from Schumann's Manfred & Wagner's Tristan und Isolde, in Krug's hand. Margins def. (90) DM9,000

Nightingale, Florence, 1820-1910
[An important collection of 160 A Ls s, sent to Nightingale by numerous correspondents including Prince Albert, William Gladstone, Sir William Jenner, Lord Palmerston etc., 1854 to 1870, c.470 pp, 4to & 8vo, a few with annotations by Nightingale, sold at S on 15 Dec, lot 224, for £3,000.]
Series of c.360 A Ls s, 1 May 1870 to 9 Apr 1902. About 1,600 pp, mostly 8vo. To her nephew & niece Frederick & Maude Verney. Giving a detailed picture of her activities. With replies by recipients & further related material. (89) £30,000
— Series of 4 A Ls s, 27 Feb 1883 to 17 Sept 1885. (88) £800
A Ls s (2), 16 July 1855 & 8 Dec 1856. (88) £180
ALs, 17 Dec 1850. (88) £170
— 3 Dec 1855. (91) £680

— 5 Jan 1856. (89) £500
— 7 Apr 1856. (88) £250
— [20 June 1857]. (88) £170
— 18 Mar 1861. (90) £340
— 31 July 1864. (89) £210
— 11 Feb 1880. (89) $425
— 18 Apr 1881. (88) £190
— 20 July 1884. (88) £150
— 20 July 1884. (90) £140
— 18 Feb [18]96. (91) $300
— [n.d.] "Thursday". (89) £240
— [n.d.]. (91) $170
Ls, 19 Dec 1888. Byer collection. (90) $500
ANs, 25 July 1884. (88) £75
Cut signature, 27 Apr [186]9. (91) $170
— Anr, [n.d.]. (90) $100

Nijinsky, Vaslav, 1890-1950
Autograph Ms, Diary, 1918 & 1919. 381 pp (including 31 blanks), 4to, in 3 vols; black wraps. In Russian; mostly in ink. Including 15 pp of dance notations & 10 pp of drawings, in pencil. Partly unpbd. The Garden Ltd. collection. (90) $130,000
Photograph, sgd, 1913. 165mm by 110mm. By Gerschel. (91) £1,050

Nimitz, Chester W., 1885-1966
ALs, 15 June 1942. (91) $450

Nin, Anais
Typescript, On Writing. (88) $425
— Typescript, untitled character sketches. (89) $120

Niven, David, 1909-83
Collection of 4 A Ls s & 7 photographs, 7 Mar to 10 June 1972. (91) $250

Nixon, Patricia
Ls, 3 Sept 1968. (90) $160
Photograph, sgd & inscr, [n.d.]. (88) $55

Nixon, Richard M.
Transcript, copy of his letter of resignation of 9 Aug 1974, addressed to the Secretary of State. 1 p, 8vo. (91) $3,800
Ls, 13 Feb 1950. (90) $950
— 13 Feb 1950. (90) $225
— 8 Mar 1951. (91) $120
— 11 June 1951. (91) $150
— 13 Aug 1951. (91) $150
— 27 Dec 1951. (91) $100

NIXON

— 3 Apr 1953. (91) $250
— 22 Dec 1953. (88) $120
— 14 June 1956. (89) $80
— 31 Oct 1956. (89) $160
— 29 Apr 1961. (88) $90
— 26 Mar 1968. (91) $110
— 15 July 1968. Byer collection. (90) $225
— 5 Dec 1970. (88) $85
— 22 Feb 1973. (88) $400
— 8 Feb 1980. (88) $160

Ds, car registration for a 1966 black Imperial leased from Chrysler Motors, Oct 1966. (91) $800

Group photograph, family port, [c.1965]. (91) $110

Menu, dinner given by the Lotus Club, 1964; 9 by 12 inches. (90) $140

Photograph, sgd, [n.d.]. (91) $250

Photograph, sgd & inscr, [c.1950]. (91) $110

Signature, 30 Sept 1954. (90) $50

— Anr, [20 Jan 1969]. (91) $130
— Anr, [24 July 1969]. (90) $70
— Anr, [24 May 1972]. (89) $100
— Anr, on ticket to the 1973 Inauguration Ceremonies; 4.5 by 2.5 inches. (91) $120
— Anr, on Inaugural Address pamphlet cover, 20 Jan 1973; 8vo. (90) $140
— Anr, [20 Jan 1973]. (89) $100
— Anr, [20 Jan 1973?]. (90) $65
— Anr, 30 Aug 1979. (89) $75
— Anr, [n.d.]. (91) $90
— Anr, [n.d.]. (90) $90

Nixon, Richard M. —& Others

Signature, on program for a "Testimonial Dinner to honor Republicans in Congress", 8 June 1959, 4 pp, 4to. (88) $475

Nixon, Richard M. See: Eisenhower, Dwight D. & Nixon

Nixon, Richard M. —& Ford, Gerald R.

[Their signatures on a philatelic envelope, [20 Jan 1973], sold at Dar on 4 Oct 1990, lot 316, for $200.]

AMERICAN BOOK PRICES CURRENT

Noailles, Anna Elisabeth, Comtesse de, 1876-1933

ALs, 7 Apr [n.y.]. (90) DM200

Nobel, Alfred, 1833-96

ALs, 26 Sept 1893. 3 pp, 8vo. To his brother Robert Nobel. Discussing their enterprises at Baku & the Standard Oil Company. Repaired. (90) DM4,200

Noe, Amedee de, 1819-79. See: Cham

Noel, Miriam

Typescript, My Life with Frank Lloyd Wright. [c.1928] 145 pp. Unpbd. (90) $3,200

Nolan, James F.

Ls, 12 July 1976. (91) $450

Nolan, Lewis, 1818-54. See: Crimean War

Nolde, Emil, 1867-1956

ALs, 29 Jan 1918. (88) DM580
— 19 June 1947. 1 p, 4to. To Clara Gans. Thanking for a food package & referring to his wife's death. (90) DM1,100

Ls, 24 Mar 1934. (91) DM800
— 10 Nov 1937. 1 p, 4to. To Herr Hebestreit. Informing him about the whereabouts of 2 paintings, & commenting on an exhibition in Munich. (90) DM1,300
— 27 Apr 1949. (90) DM600

Nono, Luigi, 1924-90

Autograph Ms, sketches for Prometeo; [n.d.]. (91) DM550

Autograph music, study for his work "no hay caminos...", sgd & inscr to The Limelight Society, 1987. (90) £400

ALs, [1962]. (88) DM550
— 26 Dec 1969. (89) DM250

Nordau, Max, 1849-1923

Autograph Ms, The Aims and Achievements of Socialism in Europe. (91) £620

ALs, 1 Nov 1881. (88) DM260
— 10 Feb 1882. (90) DM260
— 28 Apr 1882. (91) DM320
— 1 Dec 1893. (90) DM260

Norris, Frank, 1870-1902
ALs, 7 Dec 1899. Doheny collection. (88) $650

North, Marianne, 1830-90
Series of 13 A Ls s, [1875 to 1884?]. (89) £340

North, Oliver
Ls, 13 Apr 1990. (91) $120
Signature, [n.d.]. (89) $70

Northumberland, Hugh Percy, 2d Duke, 1742-1817
ALs, 26 June 1810. (89) $65

Noske, Gustav, 1868-1946
Ds, 24 Feb 1920. (90) DM1,000

Nossack, Hans Erich, 1901-77
Autograph Ms, draft of a movie script, [c.1966]. (89) DM220
Collection of 6 A Ls s, 7 Ls s, & 11 postcards, sgd (9 autograph), 4 Apr 1955 to 2 Jan 1977. 16 pp, various sizes, & cards. Recipient unnamed. Interesting letters about recipient's poems, his own work, other authors, etc. With related material. (90) DM2,400

Nostitz, Helene von, 1878-1944. See: Hofmannsthal, Hugo von & Nostitz

Novalis, Pseud. of Friedrich Freiherr von Hardenberg, 1772-1801
Autograph Ms, poem, Balsora, [c.1789]. 1 p, folio. 9 lines, sgd. (91) DM26,000
— Autograph Ms, poem, Kenne dich Selbst; sgd & dated 11 May 1798. 1 p, 8vo. 16 lines. (90) DM44,000
ALs, [2 May 1794]. 1 p, 4to. To his brother Erasmus. Merrily inviting him to a reunion at Leipzig. Including postscript by [Friedrich Wilhelm von] Kommerstedt. (90) DM30,000

Novello, Ivor, 1893-1951
[A collection containing brief autograph musical Mss, some autograph verse, numerous photographs & related material, collected by his mother, c.240 items in a box, sold at S on 19 July 1990, lot 335, for £2,000 to Mackenzie.]

Novello, Vincent, 1781-1861
[Novello's autograph album, of c.100 pp plus blanks, containing autograph music by Mozart, Beethoven, Haydn, Mendelssohn, Paganini, Liszt, Donizetti, Rossini & others, sold at pn on 14 June 1989 for £62,000 to Otto Haas.]

Nursery Series
Original drawings, (34), to illus Our pets in Fancy Dress, 1931, & A Visit to the Circus. (90) £600

O

Oates, Lawrence Edward Grace, 1880-1912
Series of 13 A Ls s, 2 Jan to 24 May 1902. About 40 pp, 8vo & 12mo. To his mother. Reporting his experiences in the Boer War. (90) £1,400

Oates, Lawrence Edward Grace, 1880-1912
Series of 7 A Ls s, 15 June to [Nov] 1910. 30 pp, mostly 8vo. To his mother. Describing the early stages of Scott's Antarctic Expedition. (91) £4,500

O'Brien, Flann, Pseud. of Brian O'Nolan, 1911-66
Proof copy, The Dalkey Archive, 1964. In orig wraps. With autograph corrections. (88) £1,200

O'Brien, Richard, c.1758-1824
Ls, 10 Mar 1800. 4 pp, 4to. To Sec of State Timothy Pickering. As consul at Algiers, reporting about problems with the stipulated "annuity" of goods to Algiers. (90) $1,300

Observations sur ... la Politique de France
Ms, Observations sur le Traite de la Politique de France. [France, late 17th cent]. 101 leaves & blanks, 226mm by 165mm, in contemp red mor profusely gilt with devices of Louis XIV. With penwork initial. Proposal for administrative reform. Astor MS.A.22. (88) £13,000

O'Casey, Sean, 1880-1964
Autograph Ms, play, The Plough and the Stars, full 1st draft, [1924-25]. In ink & pencil, with numerous alterations, 3 pen-&-ink sketches of the flag, 2 pencil sketches of stage sets, & several doodles. 72 pp, in a 4to school exercise book together with autograph Ms of parts of chapters 1 - 3 of Rose and Crown, 1st draft, being part of vol 2 of his autobiography; 36 pp. In ink, with 3 small caricatures of G. B. Shaw. Most pages crossed through with colored crayon. (88) £35,000

ALs, 9 June 1956. (91) $375

Ls, 27 Nov 1957. (91) $150

Occult Manuscripts
Ms, Oraculum Salomonicum Kabalisticum. [Italy, mid-18th cent]. 24 leaves (2 blank) & 2 large folding tables, vellum, 165mm by 117mm, in contemp red mor gilt. Illuminated. (91) £1,200

— Ms, The Lady Witch or Pythagoras's Oracle of the Future, [c.1850]. (90) £190

— BENEDICTIS IN LOVERBERG, ANTON FERDINAND. - Saeculum cabalisticum, ab anno MDCC usque ad annum MDCCC. [Innsbruck?, c.1750]. 46 leaves, 325mm by 205mm. Contemp lea bdg. (91) DM2,200

Ochoa, Severo
Autograph Ms, "Fragment of a rough draft of a paper published several years ago...", [n.d.]. (90) DM300

Ochs, Peter, 1752-1821
ALs, 25 May 1802. (90) DM550

Ochs, Siegfried, 1858-1929
Collection of 17 A Ls s, 3 Ls s, 4 autograph postcards, sgd, & autograph musical quotation, sgd, 1 Jan 1916 to 28 Sept 1928. 38 pp, mostly 4to, & cards. To Hans Tessmer. Discussing musical matters, his own & recipient's work & publications, etc. With related material. (91) DM2,200

O'Connell, Daniel, 1775-1847
ALs, 9 June 1843. (89) $650

O'Connor, Flannery
Collection of 3 A Ls s & Christmas card, sgd, 7 Aug 1961 to 22 June 1962. (90) $950

Ls s (2), 11 June 1955 & 11 May 1956. (89) $1,000

Ls, 10 Jan 1960. (91) $800

O'Connor, William Douglas, 1832-89. See: Whitman, Walt

Odle, Alan
Original drawings, a collection of prelim pencil sketches for Candide, [n.d.]. (90) £1,000

Oehlenschlaeger, Adam, 1779-1850
Collection of ALs & autograph Ms, 1 Oct 1806 & [n.d.]. (91) DM850

ALs, 10 Nov 1844. (90) DM650

Oersted, Hans Christian, 1777-1851
ALs, 5 Nov 1834. (91) DM550

— 14 Oct 1840. (90) DM680

— 16 Jan 1841. 2 pp, 4to. To Friedrich Woehler. Describing his invention of a platinum battery. Including small drawing. (90) DM3,000

Ls, 20 Apr 1847. (91) DM220

Oeser, Friederike, 1748-1829
ALs, [n.d.]. Kuenzel collection. (90) DM220

O'Faolain, Sean
Autograph Ms, The Boy Genius; [n.d.]. 45 leaves (3 pp not holograph), 4to, in black mor gilt bdg. With numerous revisions. With related material. (90) $3,800

Offenbach, Jacques, 1819-80
Autograph music, 2 orchestral Entr'actes in C major & A major, & deleted sketch of a movement in G major, [n.d.]. (89) $600

— Autograph music, Bourgmestre's aria; [n.d.]. 4 pp, 27cm by 35cm. 31 bars scored for voice & piano, with blanks for orchestration. Probably sketch for the projected operetta Les Musiciens de l'Orchestre. (89) DM1,700

— Autograph music, Derniere pensee de Weber for orchestra, in full score, [n.d.]. 12 pp, folio. Written on up to 14 staves; sgd in pencil. With ALs, 17 Dec 1873, 4 pp, 8vo, to an unnamed

conductor. (90) £2,500
- Autograph music, sketches for an unspecified work, [n.d.]. Size not stated. On 6 staves. (90) DM1,600
- Autograph music, sketches; [n.d.]. (89) DM550
- Autograph music, sketch-leaf with themes & ideas, 12 staves; [n.d.]. (89) £200
- Autograph music, song, "pas du tres haut c'est toi qui t'agitais...", [n.d.]. (88) DM950

Ms, Le Reveil, Partition - Parties de choeurs et Quatuor, [n.d.]. 141 pp, folio. Including autograph tp, autograph corrections throughout, & c.10 autograph pages of music. (91) DM11,500

Series of 4 A Ls s, [n.d.]. (89) £420

A Ls s (2), 25 Mar 1872 & [n.d.]. 5 pp, 8vo. Recipients unnamed. Insisting that his contract with the theater Bouffes-Parisiens be annulled; & expressing thanks. (90) DM1,300

ALs, 25 Oct 1852. (90) DM460
- 17 Nov [1857]. (89) DM500
- 24 July 1862. 4 pp, 8vo. To an unnamed pbr. Concerning the sale of his operettas. (91) DM2,400
- 26 Nov 1867. (90) DM950
- [1869]. 4 pp, 4to. To Colla. Discussing a libretto. (91) DM1,300
- [1873/75]. 3 pp, 8vo. Recipient unnamed. Responding to the offer of a play for Offenbach's theater. (91) DM1,300
- 26 Dec 1875. 4 pp, 8vo. To his daughter Pepita. Reporting about his stay in Vienna. (90) DM2,800
- 29 June [n.y.]. (88) DM400
- [n.d.], "Sunday". (91) $600
- [n.d.]. (90) DM550
- [n.d.]. (91) DM500

Officium

Ms, Book of Offices for use in a Dominican convent, in Latin & German. [Southern Germany, Bamberg?, c.1460]. 307 leaves, vellum, 119mm by 92mm, in 16th-cent blindstamped pigskin over wooden bds. In brown ink in a gothic textura. With numerous small initials in red & blue, c.20 with decorative penwork, black initials in the Office of the Dead, & 7-line historiated initial. (90) £4,800
- Ms, in Latin. Officium B.M.V., with calendar & psalms. [Italy, late 15th cent]. Use of Rome. 248 (of 251) leaves, vellum, 107mm by 87mm. Early 19th-cent vellum bdg. In black ink in a rounded gothic hand. With 2 large historiated initials with full borders, & 7 large & 207 small initials with ornamental extensions in gold & colors. (89) DM9,500
- Ms, lection from St. John 6:54-65 used at Corpus Christi. [England, c.1050]. 1 leaf, fragment, vellum, 144mm by 106mm. 17 lines in dark brown ink in 2 sizes of a square English Carolingian minuscule, with part of 2 headings in uncials. With 4 large initials, faded. Recovered from a bdg. (90) £4,200
- Ms, Office of the Dead, with Calendar & Suffrages. [Flanders, c.1450]. In Latin & Flemish. 63 leaves & flyleaf, vellum, 149mm by 95mm, in 19th-cent black calf gilt. In brown ink in a gothic textura. With small illuminated initials, 4- & 5-line inital on gold ground, 6 large historiated initials with three-quarter borders, & full-page miniature. (89) £4,200
- Ms, Office of the Passion & the Fifteen O's of St. Bridget, in Latin. [Florence, 1510]. 182 leaves, vellum, 171mm by 112mm. Mid-18th cent Spanish red mor profusely gilt with the arms of Ferdinand VI. In black ink in a well-formed rounded gothic liturgical hand. With small initials throughout in raised burnished gold on colored grounds, 7 large decorated initials in colors & gold with partial borders, 5 historiated initials with partial or full illuminated borders, & 2 full-page miniatures with full borders, possibly by Stefano di Tommaso Lunetti. Executed for Pope Julius II. Abbey collection. (89) £100,000
- Ms, Offices for Russian Saints, in Church Slavonic. [Russia, late 15th cent]. 262 leaves (some lacking), 205mm by 140mm, in rebacked contemp plain calf over wooden bds. In 2 different semi-uncial hands. With full-page miniature. Fekula Ms.502. (91) £7,000

OFFICIUM

— Ms, Offices for Selected Feasts & Saints, in Church Slavonic. [Russia, early 19th cent]. 278 leaves, 285mm by 210mm, in [earlier?] blindstamped calf over wooden bds. In a semi-uncial hand, with neumes in red. With very large initial, 15 illuminated headpieces, 16 floral endpieces, & illuminated tp. Fekula Ms.604. (91) £2,800

O'Hara, John, 1905-70

[The uncorrected galley proofs of his A Rage to Live. NY, 1949, in wraps, sold at sg on 12 Nov 1987, lot 242, for $400.]

Ls, [late 1930s]. (89) $200

O'Higgins, Bernardo, 1776?-1842

Ds, 4 Sept 1822. (90) DM370

Endorsement, sgd, 13 July 1821, on a petition of the chapter of the cathedral of Santiago for remission of taxes, 2 pp, folio. (89) DM500

Ohm, Georg Simon, 1789-1854

ALs, 8 Nov 1833. 4 pp, folio. To the directors of a military academy at Berlin. Explaining his reasons for accepting a position at Nuernberg. (88) DM4,400

O'Keeffe, Georgia

Series of 10 A Ls s, 10 Mar 1960 to 3 Aug 1971. 14 pp, 4to & 8vo. To Anita Young. Arranging for a visit, discussing exhibitions, mentioning her painting, etc. (90) $4,250

Ls, 20 Feb 1973. (91) $375

O'Kelly, Dennis, 1720?-87

[An album containing 10 letters & documents relating to O'Kelly, 1786 to 1814, in extra bdg by Riviere & Son with cameo bust attributed to Tassie inlaid in upper cover, sold at P on 2 Dec, lot 110 for $1,600.]

Oken, Lorenz, 1779-1851

Ms, advertisement announcing the publication of the magazine Isis, addressed to the Augsburger Allgemeine Zeitung, 12 Jan 1832. (91) DM650

Ls, 31 Jan 1831. (88) DM300

— 14 May 1835. (90) DM400

ANs, 26 Apr 1832. (90) DM280

AMERICAN BOOK PRICES CURRENT

Okopenko, Andreas

Autograph Ms, school essay, Not entwickelt Kraft; 5 Aug 1944. (90) DM260

Oland, Warner, 1879-1938

Photograph, sgd, [n.d.]. (88) $80

Oldenbarnevelt, Jan van, 1547-1619

Ls, 6 June 1597. 1 p, folio. To [Johann van Wassenaer]. Requesting information about the number of Dutch ships, & asking him to report in person to the Prince of Orange. With autograph subscription. With engraved port. (90) DM3,200

Olga Nikolaievna, Grand Duchess of Russia, 1895-1918

ALs, 4/17 Apr 1918. Length not stated. To Dalechka. Describing her family's activities in Tobolsk. Sgd O. (90) £1,500

Oliphant, Margaret, 1828-97

Series of 4 A Ls s, [n.d.]. (89) £40

Olivares, Gaspar de Guzman, Conde de, 1587-1645. See: Guzman, Gaspar de

Olivier, Sir Laurence, 1907-89

Photograph, sgd, [n.d.]. (90) $300

Ptd photograph, [n.d.]. (91) $75

— RICHTER, W. D. - Typescript (duplicated), filmscript of Dracula, Sept 1978. 120 pp, 4to. Extensively annotated in Olivier's hand (playing the part of Van Helsing). (91) £1,100

See also: Leigh, Vivien & Olivier

O'Meara, Barry Edward, 1786-1838. See: Napoleon I

Onassis, Aristotle, 1906-75

Signature, [c.10 July 1941]. (91) $70

Onassis, Jacqueline Bouvier Kennedy

Ls, 18 Dec 1963. (90) $235

Group photograph, sgd, [14 Apr 1963]. (91) $180

O'Neill, Carlotta Monterey

ALs, 11 Dec 1951. (91) $400

O'Neill, Eugene, 1888-1953
Series of 3 A Ls s, 22 Feb to 18 Nov 1920. 7 pp, 8vo. To St. John Ervine. Thanking for a note of appreciation, & talking about recipient's & his own work. John F. Fleming Estate. (89) $4,000

ALs, [22 Jan 1924]. 1 p, 4to. To his son Eugene. Arranging for him to see a Strindberg play. Sgd Father. Doheny collection. (89) $1,800

— [n.d.]. (89) $450

Collection of Ls & ANs, 10 Dec 1926 & 7 June [n.y.]. (88) $400

Autograph postcard, sgd, 15 Dec 1932. (91) $275

— 15 Dec 1932. (89) $400

Check, accomplished & sgd, 30 Mar 1920. (90) $280

Onizuka, Ellison
Photograph, sgd & inscr, [n.d.]. (91) $130

— Anr, [n.d.]. (90) $120

Signature, [31 Oct 1977]. (91) $100

— Anr, [5 Nov 1980]. (91) $150

— Anr, 16 Jan [19]81. (91) $80

— Anr, [16 Nov 1981]. (89) $80

Ono, Yoko. See: Lennon, John & Ono

Onslow, Georges, 1784-1853
ALs, 11 Apr 1830. (90) DM300

Oosterhuis, H. P.
Original drawings, (24), to illus works by G. (88) £420

— Original drawings, (47), to illus Johannes Hazeu's Onderwijzende Gedichtes, 1828, & other works. (88) £300

Opitz, Georg Emanuel, 1775-1841
ALs, 14 Apr 1827. (90) DM220

Oppenheim, Meret, 1913-85
A Ls s (2), 8 June 1978 & 6 Nov 1985. (90) DM480

Oppenheimer, Julius Robert, 1904-67
Signature, [n.d.]. (91) $300

Oppermann, Heinrich Albert, 1812-70
Series of 3 A Ls s, 17 Jan 1860 to 23 Aug [1867]. 9 pp, mostly 8vo. To Adolf Ellissen. About literary & personal matters. (90) DM1,250

ALs, 10 Feb 1864. (90) DM320

Orbison, Roy, 1936-88
Photograph, sgd, [n.d.]. (91) $100

Orczy, Emmuska, Baroness
ALs, 3 Sept 1934. (90) £170

Order of the Garter
Ms, illuminated armorial, with the arms of the Knights of the Garter from its foundation until 1603; [England, 17th cent]. 38 leaves & flyleaves, vellum, 249mm by 191mm. Contemp calf gilt, rebacked. With 375 coats-of-arms. (90) £7,500

— Ms, Statutes and ordinances of the most noble order of St. George named the Garter..., [c.1672]. 32 pp, folio, in black mor gilt by Samuel Mearne with the arms of Charles II. Ownership inscr of William Russell, 1st Duke of Bedford. Phillipps MS.4351. (90) £1,100

— Ms, The Statutes of the Most Noble Order of the Garter, [1673-75]. 37 pp, folio, in contemp dark blue turkey gilt by Samuel Mearne with the arms of Charles II. With full-page illuminated arms of the Order & of Charles Fitzroy, Earl of Southhampton. (89) £2,500

— Ms, The Statutes of the Most Noble Order of the Garter, [c.1670-80]. 26 leaves & 2 flyleaves, 257mm by 178mm, in contemp dark blue turkey lea gilt [by Samule Mearne] with the arms of Charles II. Opening words in gold capitals. Astor MS.A.3. (88) £2,400

— Ms, The Statutes of the most Noble Order of the Garter. (89) $1,000

Order of the Golden Fleece
Ms, Livre de lordre du thoison d'or, comprising names & armorials of all members of the Order, 1429 to 1559, with extracts from the Statutes in Spanish; [Bruges or Ghent, c.1562]. 68 leaves, paper, & 6 full-page miniatures on vellum, 295mm by 195mm, in modern red mor gilt by Weckesser preserving covers of orig bdg with arms of Philip II. In a neat humanistic bookhand. With 6 full-page & 237 quarter-page armorials; 6 miniatures depicting grand-masters of the order.

ORDER OF THE GOLDEN FLEECE

Middendorf collection. (89) £60,000
— Ms, Statutes of the Order of the Golden Fleece, in French. [Bruges or Brussels, c.1491]. 36 leaves, vellum, 253mm by 185mm. Contemp Flemish calf over wooden bds, tooled in blind. In brown ink in a large cursive lettre batarde. With 70 illuminated initials & 2 large armorials in gold & colors. Made for Jean, Count of Egmont. (89) £5,000

Orff, Carl, 1895-1982
Collection of 5 A Ls s & 7 Ls s, 2 Dec 1947 to 18 Nov 1975. 22 pp, folio & 8vo. To Willi Schuh. About Richard Strauss, his own works & projects, etc. (90) DM4,000
ALs, 21 Dec 1947. (88) DM320
— 24 Oct 1970. (90) DM450
Ls, 29 Feb 1956. (88) DM220

Orlik, Emil, 1870-1932
Collection of ALs & orig drawing, 21 Dec 1929 & 1921. (91) DM950
ALs, 6 Nov 1911. (89) DM700
— 28 Apr 1913. (90) DM260
Photograph, sgd & inscr, Oct 1930. (90) DM220

Orlov, Nikolai Alekseyevich, Prince, 1827-85
ALs, 28 July 1876. (88) DM240

Ornitological Manuscripts
Ms, General Essay on a naturall History (A.) of ... (88) £130

Oroz, Pedro, d.1597
Ms, alphabetical dictionary of Canon Law & its application to the conversion of the American Indians. [Mexico, c.1572]. 67 leaves, 188mm by 144mm; disbound, in fitted cloth case. In dark brown ink in a small rounded calligraphic hand; possibly autograph. In Spanish. (88) £4,800

Orpen, Sir William, 1878-1931
Autograph sketchbooks, (2), [c.1889-1895]. (88) £500
Series of 9 A Ls s, 1907 to 1917 & [n.d.]. (89) £600
— Series of 95 A Ls s, 18 Feb 1920 to 20 Aug 1928. 114 pp, various sizes. To Cara (Charlotte) Copland, 1 to Lord

AMERICAN BOOK PRICES CURRENT

Beaverbrook. Vividly describing his life in Paris. Including 45 sketches. (88) £3,000

Ortega y Gasset, Jose, 1883-1955
Typescript, contribution to a festschrift for Karl Jaspers, [c.1952]. 55 pp, mostly 4to. With autograph revisions. In Spanish. (88) DM1,050

Orteig, Raymond, 1870-1939. See: Lindbergh, Charles A. & Orteig

Orth, Johann, 1852-90?. See: Johann Salvator, 1852-90?

Orwell, George, 1903-50
Typescript, school play, King Charles II, [1932]. 15 pp, folio & 4to. In blank verse. Partly carbon copy, partly roneoed; some autograph pencil sidenotes. With related photograph. (89) £4,000
Collection of ALs, 14 Ls s, & Letter, 15 Feb 1945 to 14 Nov 1947. 18 pp, 4to & 8vo. To Roger Senhouse of Secker & Warburg. About the publication of Animal Farm & other books. With related material. (91) £14,000

Oscar I, King of Sweden, 1799-1859
ALs, 10 Dec 1822. (90) DM300

Oscar II, King of Sweden & Norway, 1829-1907
ALs, 7 May 1867. (89) DM250

Osgood, Samuel, 1748-1813
Franking signature, [20 June c.1785]. Alexander collection. (90) $180

Oshima, Hiroshi, 1886-1975
Ls, 17 Feb 1942. (90) DM380

Osler, Sir William, 1849-1919
ALs, [n.d.], "16th". (91) $600

Ossietzky, Carl von, 1889-1938
Ls, 30 Oct 1930. 1 p, 8vo. To Walter Zadek. As Ed of the Weltbuehne, returning a Ms. Sgd in pencil. (90) DM2,200

Ostwald, Wilhelm, 1853-1932
Autograph Ms, lecture about the high school system, deploring the lack of scientific instruction & the uselessness of language teaching, [n.d.]. (91) DM750

ALs, 12 Sept 1897. (90) DM260

Oswald, Lee Harvey, 1939-63
Autograph sentiment, [1954 or 1955]. 1 p, 105mm by 152mm. 4 lines of doggerel verse, sgd, in the autograph book of Ivan Hurlstone, compiled at Beauregard Junior High School at New Orleans; 52 vari-colored leaves, in bds. (90) $3,200

Others. See: Gropius, Walter & Others
See also: Nelson, Horatio Nelson & Others
See also: Windsor, Edward & Others

Otis, Harrison Gray, 1765-1848
Autograph Ms, speech in the Massachusetts Senate, 31 Jan 1811. Sang collection. (89) $120

Otis, James, 1725-83
Ds, 29 Oct 1768. (90) $200

Otis, Samuel A., 1740-1814
ALs, 17 Mar 1777. (88) $325
— 12 May 1802. (90) $80

Otto, King of Greece, 1815-67
Series of 4 Ls s, [c.1837 to 1867]. (88) £600
Ls, 17/29 Dec 1842. (88) DM500
— 17/29 Nov 1853. (90) DM280
— 18/30 June 1859. (89) DM260

Oughton, Sir James Adolphus Dickenson, 1719-80
Autograph Ms, journal & memorandum book, including a trans of part of Alain Manesson Mallet's Les traveaux de Mars, poems, autobiographical material, etc., c.1734 to 1743; over 100 pp, folio, in contemp calf. (88) £400
— Autograph Ms, journal covering his service in the Flanders Campaign, 10 June 1742 to 4 Oct 1743; c.100 pp, 4to, in def contemp calf. (88) £350
— Autograph Ms, memorandum book of military history, compiled from various sources, c.1740s to 1773; c.270 pp, folio, in def contemp calf. (88) £400

Our Animal Friends at Home
[The complete set of 17 drawings for the book, [1930s], mostly 380mm by 270mm, in ink & watercolor, with related material, sold at S on 2 June 1989, lot 606, for £700 to Brunner.]

Outram, Benjamin, 1764-1805
ADs, 15 June 1802. (88) £70

Overbeck, Christian Adolf, 1755-1821
ALs, 24 Feb 1781. (91) DM410

Overbeck, Johann Friedrich, 1789-1869
ALs, 1 Feb 1859. (88) DM380

Overbury, Sir Thomas, 1581-1613
[A contemp Ms account of the divorce of Lady Frances Howard & the Earl of Essex & proceedings in the case of Overbury's murder, c.150 pp, 4to, in contemp sheep, Phillipps Ms.3969, sold at pn on 22 Mar 1990, lot 110, for £380 to Knowles.]

Ovid (Publius Ovidius Naso), 43B.C.-17?A.D.
Ms, Metamorphoses, with Gloss, Medicamina Faciei Femineae, & other Pseudo-Ovidian texts. [France, Paris?, c.1250]. 156 leaves, vellum, 240mm by 177mm. 18th-cent mottled sheep over pastebds. In a small scholastic bookhand, with glossing in a smaller more cursive hand. With 15 large decorated initials in red & blue with extensive penwork. Final bifolium probably slightly earlier. Phillipps MS.6912 & Abbey collection. (89) £55,000
See also: Heywood, Thomas

Owen, Robert, 1771-1858
Ms, Report to the County of Lanark..., [n.d.]. (90) £300

Owens, Jesse, 1913-80
Photograph, sgd & inscr, [19]36. (91) $275
Signature, on First Day Cover, Olympic Games, 17 Aug 1972. (89) $55
— Anr, on 1st Day Cover, Olympic Games 1980. (90) $130

Oxenstierna, Axel, Count, 1583-1654
Ls, 23 Mar 1632. (90) DM700
— 7 May 1632. 1 p, folio. To administrative officers of Johann II of Zweibruecken. Requesting the immediate delivery of bread for the Swedish soldiers. (91) DM1,700
Ds, 2 Jan 1645. (90) DM550

P

Pabst, Waldemar, 1885-1967
Ls, 23 May 1930. (89) DM220

Paca, William, Signer from Maryland
Ds, 5 Dec 1782. (90) $300

Packer, Fred Little, 1886-1956
Original drawing, cartoon, Look Who's Talking, to illus the NY Daily Mirror, 1952. (90) $80

Paderewski, Ignace Jan, 1860-1941
Autograph Ms, list of recital pieces, sgd; [n.d.]. (88) $225
ALs, 8 Feb 1891. (90) DM470
— 26 Mar 1904. (90) DM400
— 28 Mar 1931. (90) DM460
— 3 Apr 1931. (91) DM400
Ls, 8 May 1941. (91) $150
Autograph quotation, 4 bars from Sonata op. (88) £70
Autograph telegram, sgd, [1914?]. (91) $175
Menu, sgd, for a dinner in his honor at the Lotus Club, 8 Apr 1893. (88) DM380
Photograph, sgd, [n.d.]. (88) $225
— Anr, [n.d.]. (90) $275
Photograph, sgd & inscr, 14 Feb 1892. (91) $300

Paganini, Nicolo, 1782-1840
[A ptd visiting card, inscr P.P.C. in anr hand, sold at star on 10 Mar 1988, lot 983, for DM1,600.]
Autograph music, 58 bars in A minor, scored for viola; [n.d.]. 1 p, folio; on 8 (of 18) staves. With a port. (89) DM6,000
— Autograph music, drafts of compositions for guitar; [n.d.]. 2 pp, folio. Over 200 bars in all. Including note of authentication by Andrea Paganini. (90) £5,000
ALs, [1818]. 2 pp, size not stated. To Luigi Germi. Fragment, discussing marriage, Canova & music. (89) £1,300
— 14 Dec 1819. 1 p, 4to. To Luigi Guglielmi Germi. Inquiring about a quartet, mentioning recent compositions, etc. Imperf. (90) £1,500
— 3 Apr 1829. (90) £1,000
— 3 Apr 1829. 1 p, 8vo. To Herr Beer. Concerning a concert in Berlin. (89) DM2,000
— 16 Nov 1831. 2 pp, 8vo. To [Dr. Billings]. Expressing his gratitude for marks of friendship, & describing his forthcoming journey. (90) £1,500
— 12 July 1832. 1 p, 8vo. To an unnamed lady. Apologizing for missing an appointment. (88) DM2,300
— 14 Feb 1833. 1 p, 4to. Recipient unnamed. About his decision to retire from public performance. Framed with contemp port in pencil & wash, & playbill. (91) £5,500
— 23 Feb 1833. (88) £900
— 22 Nov 1833. 1 p, 8vo. To his sister Paola Domenica. Promising to find husbands for her daughters after his return to Italy. Mtd. (91) DM3,200
— 17 Nov 1837. 3 pp, 8vo. To Lazzaro Rebizzo. Explaining his involvement in the Casino Paganini affair. (90) £2,500
Ls, 5 July 1831. 1 p, 4to. To S. Willis. About arrangements for concerts in London. Seal tear. Mtd with a Spanish trans. (90) £1,250
— 16 Aug 1831. 3 pp, 4to. To J. Vetten. Describing his success in England & complaining about the Parisian press. Sgd twice. (91) £1,400
— 18 Feb 1839. 2 pp, folio. To Hector Berlioz. Congratulating him on the success of his opera & suggesting concerts to be performed at Marseille. With autograph subscription. (89) £3,200
ANs, 27 June 1831. (90) £520
Autograph quotation, Preludio [for violin], 2 May 1831. 1 p, 105mm by 155mm. Notated on 3 staves; sgd. (91) £3,500
— Anr, Preludio, on 2 staves; sgd & dated 8 Jan 1834. 33.5cm by 26cm. (90) DM7,500

Paine, Robert Treat, Signer from Massachusetts
Ds, 24 Dec 1771. (91) $50

Paine, Thomas, 1737-1809
Autograph Ms, address to "Brothers and fellow Citizens of the World." [c.1791-92] Fair copy, 2 pp, 4to. Commending the French for the Glorious Revolution. (91) $30,000

— Autograph Ms, Letter of Thomas Paine to Camille Jourdan ... occasioned by this report on the priests, the worship and the bells, [1797]. 14 pp, folio. 1 corner torn. With letters stating provenance. (89) £11,000

— Autograph Ms, newspaper article, To the People of New York, sgd; [ptd 21 Aug 1807]. 4 pp, 4to. Discussing the defense of New York harbor. (90) $29,000

ALs, [28 Dec 1797]. 1 p, 4to. To "Citizen President". About his prosecution in England, & sending memoranda. With autograph endorsement by Paul Barras at head. Including contemp trans. (89) £5,000

— 9 July 1804. 1 p, 4to. To John Fellows. Inviting him for a visit. Mentions Deism. (91) $13,000

— 12 July 1806. 1 p, 4to. To Thomas Rickman. About mutual acquaintances & about a man firing into Paine's house. (91) $14,000

— 4 May 1807. 2 pp, 4to. To George Clinton. Requesting his help in regaining the right to vote, & referring to the political situation during the Revolution & his Common Sense. With autograph draft of Clinton's reply on verso. (88) $13,750

AL, [1790s]. 1 p, 8vo. In 3d person. To R. B. Sheridan. Requesting an interview. (91) $3,500

Paisiello, Giovanni, 1740-1816
Ls, 5 Oct 1811. 1 p, folio. To the Minister of the Interior at Naples. As President of the Academy of Fine Arts, reporting progress on Mattioli's painting. (90) DM1,300

Palin, Nicki
Original drawing, knights passing below hilltop castle; cover design for Sharon Penman's Fall of the Shadow. (90) £400

— Original drawing, riders looking at sailing ships in a bay; cover design for Dorothy Dunnett's Spring of the Ram, 1987. (90) £500

Pallas, Peter Simon, 1741-1811
ADs, 9 Sept 1782. (88) DM440

Palmer, Nathaniel Brown, 1799-1877
Check, sgd, 4 Sept 1870. (88) $75

Palmer, Samuel, 1805-81
A Ls s (2), 23 Oct 1854. (90) £850

Palmerston, Henry John Temple, 3d Viscount, 1784-1865
ALs, 9 Mar 1834. (90) DM280
— 15 July 1855. (90) DM380
— 22 Dec 1861. (90) DM280

Panama Rail Road Company
Document, 1 June 1872. Alexander collection. (90) $85

Panizza, Oskar, 1853-1921
Autograph Ms, satire, Auf vielseitiges Verlangen, 14 July [19]03. 2 pp, 4to. (90) DM1,800

ALs, [n.d.]. 3 pp, 8vo. To List & Francke at Leipzig. Ordering antiquarian books. With AN, 1900. (90) DM1,100
— 17 Nov 1903. (91) DM680

Panizzi, Sir Anthony, 1797-1879
Ls, 22 Jan 1839. (88) £85

Pankhurst, Dame Christabel Harriette, 1880-1958
Ls, 19 Mar 1908. (89) £50

Pankhurst, Emmeline, 1858-1928
Collection of ALs & 2 Ls s, 8 July 1913 to 15 July 1920. (89) £300
Photograph, sgd, [n.d.]. (91) £90

Pankhurst, Sylvia, 1882-1960
Autograph Ms, article on Soviet Communism, [1922]. 90 pp, 4to. With revisions; incomplete. In pencil. (91) £1,800

Pannwitz, Rudolf, 1881-1969
ALs, 27 Oct 1929. (91) DM250

Paoli, Betty, Pseud. of Barbara Elisabeth Glueck, 1814-94
ALs, 9 Apr 1847. 3 pp, 8vo. To [Adalbert Stifter]. Discussing Annette von Droste-Huelshoff & George Sand. Sgd BP. (90) DM1,600

Paoli, Pasquale, 1725-1807
Ls, 6 May 1792. (89) £750

Papacy
[3 vols of 17th-cent transcripts, diplomatic & other, relating to 17th-cent Papacy, in Italian, in contemp half calf, sold at DN on 26 Apr 1988, lot 236, for £400.]

Papadiamantes, Alexandros, 1851-1911
Autograph Ms, short story, O Alibanistos, [c.1903]. 26 pp (3 lacking), 8vo. Sgd. With related material. (90) £7,500

Pape, Frank C.
Original drawings, (8), to illus Bernard Falk's The Naked Lady, 1934. (90) £850

— Original drawings, (8), to illus Ethel Reader's The Story of the Little Merman, 1909. In ink; sgd. 355mm by 252mm. Macmillan Archives. (90) £2,800

Papen, Franz von, 1879-1969
ALs, 11 Dec 1935. (91) $120

— 11 Apr 1938. 1 p, 4to. To Hitler. Expressing congratulations on the Austrian referendum. (89) DM8,000

Ls, 25 Aug 1934. (91) $700

— 23 May 1938. (90) $170

Photograph, sgd & inscr, [1932]. (88) $200

Papermaking
— PHIPPS, JOHN. - Ds, [17 June 1790]. 2 pp, folio. Petition for a patent for an invention. Docketed. (88) £140

Papini, Giovanni, 1881-1956
ALs, 30 Apr 1907. (90) DM240

Pappenheim, Gottfried Heinrich, Graf von, 1594-1632
ALs, 26 Oct 1623. 1 p, folio. To an unnamed prince. Informing him that his troops have been ordered to march through recipient's territory without delay. With related material. Kuenzel collection. (91) DM4,800

— 7 June 1631. 1 p, folio. To Prince [Christian II von Anhalt-Bernburg]. Informing him that Tilly's troops are about to depart, & hoping to see him the next day. (90) DM3,200

Ls, 15 Oct 1629. 1 p, folio. To the magistracy of an unnamed town. Credentials for Lieut. Hans Jakob Losacker. Kuenzel collection. (90) DM1,050

— [29 Jan 1632]. (88) DM700

Pappenheim, Martin
Collection of 15 Ls s & postcards, sgd (1 autograph), 1933 to 1934. (88) £450

Paraguay
— JESUIT & FRANCISCAN MISSIONS. - Ms, Manifiesto del P[adre] Fr[ay] Miguel Vargas Muchuca, [1st half of 18th cent], 135 pp, folio. Defending Paraguayan missions against their detractors. (89) £1,500

— JESUIT MISSIONS. - A group of 23 documents relating to the Jesuit Missions among the Guarani Indians, 1636 to 1767, c.400 pp, folio, sold at S on 18 May 1989, lot 307, for £5,500 to Special Collections. 89

Paris, Gaston, 1839-1903
[A collection of 51 autographs comprising letters, postcards & notes, 1884 to 1903, addressed to Heinrich Morf & dealing mostly with scholarly questions, with related material, sold at star on 4 Oct 1989, lot 551, for DM260.]

Parish, Mitchell
Ms, essay on songwriters & their lack of complete control of their work. (91) $600

Parmentier, Antoine Augustin, 1737-1813
ALs, 11 Dec 1784. (90) DM460

Parnell, Charles Stewart, 1846-91
Autograph Ms, appeal "To the Irish People of America", [c.1886]. 2 pp, folio. With autograph revisions; sgd. (89) £6,400

— POWELL, CROXDEN. - Orig drawing, pen-&-ink sketch of Richard Pigott reading his forgery of a letter by Parnell; [21 - 22 Feb 1889]. 7.75 by 6.5 inches. Sgd & inscr by Powell. Framed. (90) £800

Parr, Samuel, 1747-1825
Series of 4 A Ls s, 19 Dec 1810 to 20 June 1811. (90) £65

Parrish, Maxfield, 1870-1966
ALs, 15 Nov 1900. (90) $350
Ls, 25 Mar 1927. (90) $220
— 2 Mar 1940. (90) $325

Parry, Sir William Edward, 1790-1855
ADs, 1820. (89) £100

Paschen, Friedrich, 1865-1947
Series of 3 A Ls s, 27 Dec 1914 to 24 Jan 1915. (91) DM600

Paskevich, Ivan Fyodorovich, Prince of Warsaw, 1782-1856
ALs, 12/24 Apr 1818. (90) DM320
Ls, 11/23 Sept 1836. (90) DM240

Pasquinade
Ms, Dialogo Di Marforio, e Di Pasquino Nel quali s'esaminani i disegni Spagnuoli alla Monarchia universale..., 1620. (88) DM800

Passy, Frederic, 1822-1912
Ls, 11 Sept 1902. (88) DM340

Pasternak, Boris, 1890-1960
Autograph Ms, poem, Winter Night, from Dr. Zhivago; [n.d.]. 2 pp, 8vo. 8 quatrains, sgd. (91) £2,600
Collection of 2 A Ls s & photograph, sgd & inscr, 14 & 15 Feb 1959. 2 pp, 4to, & photograph. To a correspondent at Heidelberg University. Thanking for a book & regretting he misplaced a letter. With related material. (91) DM2,600
ALs, 27 Oct 1957. (91) $800
— 20 Nov 1959. (88) £500

Pasteur, Louis, 1822-95
Collection of 4 A Ls s & 2 Ls s, 25 June 1863 to 10 July 1875. 16 pp, 8vo. To [Edmond Terrel des Chenes]. Discussing his findings regarding the making & improvement of wines. 1 tear, fold splits. (88) £2,100
ALs, [n.d.]. (88) $550
— 12 Jan 1859. (88) $800
— 19 May 1877. 2 pp, 8vo. Recipient unknown. Discussing his efforts to search for the cause of anthrax. (91) $4,000
— 11 Feb 1881. 1 p, 8vo. Recipient unnamed. About rabbits infected with rabies. (91) DM2,400
— 20 Oct 1882. Doheny collection. (89) $450
— 12 Oct 1883. 3 pp, 8vo. Recipient unnamed. Discussing his efforts to develop a vaccine for swine fever. (90) $4,000
— 7 Feb 1884. (89) £600
— [n.d.]. (90) $450

Pater, Walter, 1839-94
ALs, [9 May 1889]. 2 pp (card). To Arthur Symons. Thanking for his sonnets, & offering to write a note of introduction for him. Koch Foundation. (90) $1,200

Paterius, Saint, d.606
Ms, Liber de Expositione Veteris ac Novi Testamentii. [Swabia, Ochsenhausen?, early 12th cent]. 271 leaves, vellum, 320mm by 215mm. Modern brown mor in half mor slipcase. In brown ink in neat Caroline minuscule script by 2 scribes. With large initials throughout in red, some in red & yellow with foliate scroll design, or bird or dragon decoration; some drawings of animals in margins. 2 smaller leaves of hymns bound in front; sermon added on endleaves. Doheny collection. (88) £55,000

Patmore, Coventry, 1823-96
ALs, [n.d.]. (89) £350

Paton, Allan
[A group of 3 autograph Mss comprising Instrument of Thy Peace, sgd, [1967 - 1968], Hope for South Africa (with typed carbon copy), [late 1950s], & A Drink in Peace, [n.d.], sold at P on 13 June 1991, lot 74, for $8,000.]
Autograph Ms (2), autobiograhikal works, Towards the Mountain, 26 Sept 1974 to 7 Mar 1979, & Journey Continued, 2 Mar 1984 to [1986]. 927 leaves, 4to, & 37 pp of revisions. Working drafts. (91) $13,000
— Autograph Ms)2), Kontakion for You Departed, complete working draft, 16 Dec 1967 to 21 May 1968; & Salute to my Greatgrandchildren, 2 drafts (1 partly typed), [1952]. About 190 pp, mostly folio. (91) $8,500
Autograph Ms, biography, Hofmeyr, [1962 - 1963]. 1510 leaves, foolscap. Complete working draft, including

PATON

appendix & revised text for 2 chapters. (91) $9,000

— Autograph Ms, novel, Ah, But Your Land is Beautiful, 29 Oct 1979 to 22 Aug 1980. 337 leaves, 4to. Complete working draft. (91) $32,500

— Autograph Ms, novel, Cry, the Beloved Country, 25 Sept to 29 Dec 1946. 335 leaves, various sizes. Heavily revised working draft of complete text. (91) $120,000

— Autograph Ms, novel, Too Late the Phalarope, 3 Apr 1951 to 2 Dec 1952. 494 pp, various sizes. Complete working draft. (91) $62,500

Patton, George S., 1885-1945

[An autograph envelope, sgd twice & addressed to Suzanne Miner, [26 Apr 1943], with photocopy of orig ALs, sold at Dar on 7 Feb 1991, lot 240, for $900.]

Ls, 24 Feb 1919. 1 p, 4to. To Gen. Conner. Farewell letter on his return to Washington. (91) $2,000

— 17 Dec 1944. 1 p, 4to. To Gen. Conner. Describing his strategy trying to break through German lines. (91) $26,000

— 13 Mar 1945. 1 p, 4to. To Major General Fox Conner. About taking Trier and the Rhine. (91) $16,000

Ds, 25 Jan 1940. 1 p, 4to. Army discharge of William R. Finks. (91) $1,100

Signature, [25 Jan 1943]. (91) $650

— Anr, [16 Nov 1943]. (91) $750

— Anr, [26 Dec 1943]. (91) $500

— Anr, [2 Dec 1944]. (91) $500

— Anr, [20 Apr 1946]. (91) $650

Paul I, Emperor of Russia, 1754-1801

ALs, 15/26 Mar 1776. 2 pp, 4to. To Quartermaster Gen. [Bauer]. Hoping to talk to him about the contents of a lost letter. In French. (90) DM1,100

Ds, 21 Dec 1798. (88) £180

— 13 July 1799. (88) DM620

Paul II, Pope, 1417-71

Document, 1 Dec 1465. (91) £420

Paul of the Cross, Saint, 1694-1775

ALs, 24 Dec [1769?]. Doheny collection. (89) $800

AMERICAN BOOK PRICES CURRENT

Paul V, Pope, 1552-1621

ALs, 4 Oct 1619. 1 p, 4to. To King Louis XIII of France. Regarding offenses committed by Frenchmen in Rome. In Italian, with address in Latin. With engraved port. Fillon collection. (89) DM6,500

Ls, 16 July 1605. (89) $450

Paul VI, Pope, 1897-1978

ALs, 15 June 1941. 2 pp, 4to. To an unnamed Cardinal. Informing him that the Pope has granted permission for him to officiate at a wedding. (90) DM1,100

Ls, 2 Oct 1942. (90) DM850

— 5 July 1950. Byer collection. (90) $275

— 2 July 1954. (89) DM550

Ns, 14 Dec 1954. (91) $700

Photograph, sgd, 3 Mar 1964. 14.5cm by 10.5cm. Sgd on mount, 35.5cm by 23cm. (88) DM1,600

Pauli, Wolfgang, 1900-58

Series of 6 A Ls s, 22 Nov 1944 to 22 June 1957. 10 pp, 8vo & 4to. To Isaac Rabi. Discussing various scientific questions, publications, meetings, etc. With related material. (90) DM6,500

ALs, 14 Nov 1922. 2 pp, 4to. To Rudolf Ladenburg. Sending information about forthcoming publications by Niels Bohr. (88) DM1,300

Pauling, Linus C.

Autograph Ms, 6 exercises, [n.d.]. (88) DM220

— Autograph Ms, chapter from a scientific work, The [alpha]-Helix and the Pleated Sheets; n.d. (90) DM550

— Autograph Ms, introduction to scientific paper, Ascorbic Acid and Cancer. (89) DM550

— Autograph Ms, scientific paper about the structure of combinations of phosphorus & oxygen, [n.d.]. (88) DM240

Pavlov, Ivan Petrovich, 1849-1936

ALs, 14 June 1906. 3 pp, 8vo. To Armin Tschermak. Expressing congratulations on his appointment to a professorship in Vienna. (91) DM5,500

Pavlova, Anna, 1882-1931
Photograph, sgd, [n.d]. (88) £150
— Anr, [n.d.]. (88) £200
— Anr, [1920s]. (91) $425
— Anr, [n.d.]. (88) $325
— Anr, [n.d.]. (89) $320
Photograph, sgd & inscr, 28 Jan 1908. (91) $275
— Anr, 1928. (88) $200
— Anr, 1929; c.8.5 by 6.5 inches. (88) £200
Ptd photograph, sgd, 1924. (91) $225

Pax Mundi
[A collection of over 1,000 autograph Mss, sgd, by leading figures of the early 20th cent, each discussing his view of peace, compiled by the World League for Peace, 1925 to 1932, with Ds by Maria of Aragon, 29 July 1426, sold at P on 2 Dec, lot 44, for $22,000.]

Payne, John Howard, 1791-1852
Autograph Ms, letterbooks, Jan 1842 to Dec 1850. 6 vols, 4to. Some letters excised, some notes & cuttings inserted. (89) £2,500

Payne, Roger, 1739-97
A Ds s (2), [n.d.]. (91) $650

Payne, William Henry
ALs, 3 Dec [1880s?]. 4 pp, 4to, on rectos only. To Eugene Shurgait Mayor. Recounting his war service. Middendorf collection. (89) $1,100

Peake, Mervyn, 1911-68
Original drawings, (2), mouse with tiny shoes, & Tom Thumb in a field of boulders, to illus Paul Britten Austin's The Life and Adventures of Tom Thumb, [1950s]. (90) £500
— Original drawings, (2), Tom Thumb avoiding a huge foot, & walking around rim of a drum, to illus Paul Britten Austin's The Life and Adventures of Tom Thumb, [1950s]. (90) £500
— Original drawings, (2), Tom Thumb crouching on a man's shoulder, & seated on 2 books, to illus Paul Britten Austin's The Life and Adventures of Tom Thumb, [1950s]. (90) £400
— Original drawings, (3), to illus Paul Britten Austin's The Life and Adventures of Tom Thumb, [1950s]. In ink. Various sizes. (90) £1,050
— Original drawings, (3), to illus Paul Britten Austin's The Life and Adventures of Tom Thumb, [1950s]. (90) £400
— Original drawings, (3), to illus Paul Britten Austin's The Life and Adventures of Tom Thumb, [1950s]. (90) £450
— Original drawings, (3), to illus Paul Britten Austin's The Life and Adventures of Tom Thumb, [1950s]. (90) £680

Original drawing, girl looking at minute figure of a man bowing at her from a piece of furniture, to illus Paul Britten Austin's The Life and Adventures of Tom Thumb, [1950s]. In ink. 285mm by 196mm. (90) £1,050
— Original drawing, piper followed by a procession of young boys, to illus Paul Britten Austin's The Life and Adventures of Tom Thumb, [1950s]. (90) £750
— Original drawing, Tom Thumb giving after-dinner speech to a group of mice, to illus Paul Britten Austin's The Life and Adventures of Tom Thumb, [1950s]. In ink; sgd & dated [19]53. 290mm by 223mm. (90) £1,050
— Original drawing, Tom Thumb in a birdcage before a judge, to illus Paul Britten Austin's The Life and Adventures of Tom Thumb, [1950s]. In ink. 230mm by 196mm. (90) £1,050

Peale, Rembrandt, 1778-1860
A Ls s (2), 8 Nov 1854 & July 1860. 2 pp, 16mo & 8vo. To A. Wilson, informing him he is sending a port of Washington. To G. H. Martin, giving information about his portraits of Washington & copies made. (90) $3,200

Peale, Rubens
ALs, 20 Aug 1814. (90) $500

Pears, Peter, Sir, 1910-86. See: Britten, Benjamin & Pears

Peary, Robert Edwin, 1856-1920
ALs, 18 Jan 1904. (91) $150

Pechstein, Max, 1881-1955
ALs, [22 July 1930]. 1 p, 4to. To [Alexander] Amersdorffer. Concerning his wish to teach at the Prussian Academy of Arts. (91) DM1,200

Autograph postcard, sgd, [3 Jan 1931]. To Irmgard Hasenbach. Sending New Year's wishes; with pen-&-ink sketch, c.12.5cm by 10cm. (88) DM1,600

Peckham, John, 1292. See: Sacrobosco, Johannes

Peddie, T. H.
Original drawings, (55), to illus the Old & New Testaments, 1950 to 1952. (89) £600

Pedro I, Emperor of Brazil, 1798-1834
ALs, 22 Feb 1831. (91) DM850
— 10 June 1832. 3 pp, 8vo. To his daughter Januaria. Regretting that he had to leave her, his family, & his home in Brazil. (91) DM2,000

Pedro II, Emperor of Brazil, 1825-91
ALs, 14 Jan 1874. (90) DM280
— 2 Oct 1875. (90) DM240
Ls, 29 Dec 1860. (88) £85

Peel, Sir Robert, 1788-1850
Series of 11 A Ls s, 1845 to 1846 [7 n.y.]. (88) £520
ALs, 11 Dec 1834. Byer collection. (90) $175
— 24 Nov 1838. (90) DM220
— 14 Jan 1849. (88) DM1,000
— 29 Oct [n.y.]. (91) £50
— 14 Dec [n.y.]. (91) $100

Pegram, Fred
Original drawings, (33), to illus Benjamin Disraeli's Sybil, 1895 (pbd 1896). Macmillan Archives. (90) £500
— Original drawings, (37), to illus Capt. Macmillan Archives. (90) £600
— Original drawings, (38), to illus Capt. Macmillan Archives. (90) £600
— Original drawings, (40), to illus Capt. Macmillan Archives. (90) £600
— Original drawings, (8), to illus Charles Dickens' Martin Chuzzlewit, [n.d.]. (89) £360

Pegram, John, 1832-65
Ds, 12 Dec 1862. Size not stated. Return of military personnel in his cavalry brigade. (90) $1,300

Peirce, Waldo
ALs, 14 July 1947. (91) $75

Pelham Family
[A collection of papers relating to the Pelham family, c.1738 to 1849, including 3 A Ls s by & 12 letters to Thomas Pelham-Holles, Duke of Newcastle, papers of Thomas Pelham, 2d Earl of Chichester, etc., sold at pn on 17 Sept, lot 488, for £260 to Quaritch.]

Pelham-Holles, Thomas, Duke of Newcastle, 1693-1768. See: Newcastle, Thomas Pelham-Holles

Pellico, Silvio, 1789-1854
Ms, English trans of Le mie prigioni, by James Claridge, Feb 1833; c.200 pp, 4to. (88) £90
ALs, 2 Jan 1838. (89) DM320

Pendleton, Edmund, 1721-1803
Ls, 10 Apr 1792. (91) $350

Pendleton, William Nelson, 1809-83. See: Civil War, American

Peninsular War
[Wilson, Sir Robert. - A large collection of Ms copies of letters, 1808 to 1811, addressed to Lord Castlereagh & others, with copies of letters addressed to Wilson, [mid-nineteenth cent?], c.550 pp, folio, sold at C on 9 Dec, lot 281, for £200 to Duran.]
[An ALs, 25 June 1811, 3 pp, 4to, by an unnamed Lieut. Col. in Gen. Nightingall's Brigade to the Hon. Charles Stuart, reporting about Wellington's moves etc., with related material, sold at pn on 17 Sept, lot 525, for £70 to Rankin.]
Ms, journal kept by an engineer with the 47th Regiment, Jan 1813 to 1814. (89) £430
— BLACKMAN, JOHN LUCIE. - Series of 104 A Ls s, 20 Jan 1811 to 15 June 1815. Mainly to his parents. Describing his activities in the Peninsular War, & awaiting the Battle of Waterloo. With related material. In an album, c.200

pp, 4to. (88) £1,050
— POULDEN, RICHARD. - Ms, letter book as Resident Agent of Transports, Lisbon, 18 Aug 1810 to 6 Mar 1813. 390 pp, 4to. Vellum bdg. To various correspondents; some replies. Mostly autograph. With watercolor port & Ms account of Poulden's naval career. (88) £540
— PRINCE, CAPT. JOHN. - 20 A Ls s, 1809 to 1815. 70 pp, 4to & folio. To Samuel, Sarah & William Hibbert. Describing his experiences as a member of the Coldstream Guards in Wellington's army & the victory ball in Paris. (91) £900
See also: Cadiz

Penitence...

Ms, La Penitence Adam. Dedicated to Louis de Gruuthuuse. [Bruges, c.1475-80]. 37 leaves (1 blank), vellum, 282mm by 200mm. 19th-cent dark red mor bdg. In a fine calligraphic lettre batarde, written by or in the workshop of Colard Mansion. With 184 illuminated initials & paragraph marks in highly burnished gold on red & blue grounds, & large illuminated initial with 2-sided border of acanthus leaves & naturalistic flowers. (91) £105,000

Penn Family

[A document, c.1737, 4 pp, 4to, interrogatory drawn up by Fernand John Paris as legal counsel for the Penn Family in the dispute with the Calvert Family over the Pennsylvania-Maryland boundary line & the ownership of the Lower Counties, sold at R on 9 Mar 1991, lot 81, for $600.]

Penn, John, Signer from North Carolina

ALs, 22 Sept 1780. 1 p, folio. To Brig. Gen. Sumner. Discussing military strategy. Doheny collection. (89) $4,800
— 22 Sept 1780. 1 p, folio. To [Gen. Butler or Gen. Sumner]. Giving instructions about troop actions. Including franking signature. (91) $6,000

Ds, [n.d.]. (88) $120

Penn, John, 1729-95

Ds s (2)19 Oct 1773. (88) $150

Penn, William, 1644-1718

ALs, 28 July 1683. 7 pp, folio. To Robert Spencer, Earl of Sunderland. Reporting about Pennsylvania, the progress of his colony, Indians, etc., & enlisting his aid. Silked. Martin collection. (90) $50,000
— 18 Aug 1700. (88) $750
— 16 Jan 1701/02. 1 p, folio. To [James Logan?]. Requesting him to forward an enclosure. (91) $2,300
— [7 July] 1702. 3 pp, folio. To James Logan. Introducing Henry Child. Including postscript. Repaired. (90) $7,500
— 5 Mar 1704. 3 pp, 4to. To Capt. [John] Evans. Worrying about his arrival in America, & instructing him about the governing of Pennsylvania. Corner torn. (89) $6,500

Ds, 6 Sept 1681. 1 p, folio. Indenture. Repaired. (90) $1,500
— 11 Sept 1681. 1 p, 8 by 12 inches. Deed for land in Pennsylvania sold to Thomas Harriot. (90) $2,000
— 23 Mar 1681/82. 1 p, vellum, 26.5 by 21 inches. Sale of 5,000 acres of land in Pennsylvania to Robert Turner for £100. Also sgd by others. (90) £1,400
— 12 Apr 1684. 1 p, vellum, folio. Grant of land in Philadelphia County to John Gilbert. (91) $2,200
— 29 May 1684. 1 p, size not stated. Permission to John & Francis Day to exchange their lands granted previously for lands in Philadelphia. (91) $4,000
— 6 Aug 1684. 1 p, folio. Appointment of Robert Jurner as Justice of the Peace in Philadelphia County. Mtd. (89) $1,500
— 22 Mar 1685. 1 p, folio. Indenture to John Dwight for 500 acres in Pennsylvania. Framed. (90) $3,000
— 10 Mar 1701. 1 p, folio. Appointment of an [unnamed] agent for "the Incouragement of trade". (91) $2,000
— Aug 1701. 1 p, 13 by 15 inches, vellum. Deed for land in Plimouth Township. Seal detached. (88) $1,200
See also: Charles II, 1630-85

PENN

Penn, William, Sir, 1621-70. See: Pepys, Samuel & Penn

Pennsylvania
[A group of 5 land indentures, 1685 to 1801, 5 pp, folio, 1 mentioning George Clymer, sold at sg on 24 Mar 1988, lot 138, for $350.]

Penzoldt, Ernst, 1892-1955
ALs, [1930s]. (90) DM420

Pepler, Hilary. See: Gill, Eric & Pepler

Pepys Family
[A collection of papers relating to the Pepys Family, chiefly early 19th cent, some relating to Samuel Pepys's estates, Mss, etc., others to Samuel Pepys Cockerell, sold at S on 22 July 1988, lot 348, for £250 to Tarling.]
— MONTAGU, EDWARD, 1ST EARL OF SANDWICH. - Ds, 15 Mar 1653. 1 p, 14.25 by 11.25 inches. Award & judgment concerning differences between William Hetlie & Robert Pepys of Brampton. (88) £1,000

Pepys, Samuel, 1633-1703
[A collection of 10 documents relating chiefly to Pepys's property at Brampton, 1 with autograph endorsement, 1643 to 1704, sold at S on 22 July 1988, lot 347, for £1,700 to Maggs.]
[A series of financial accounts & memoranda sgd by Thomas Trice (11) & Capt. Robert Pepys (3), 1 on verso of autograph address leaf by Samuel Pepys, anr with his autograph endorsement, 1654 to 1662, 14 pp on 9 leaves of varying size, sold at S on 22 July 1988, lot 338, for £4,200 to Quaritch.]
[2 albums containing Ms notes, letters, pamphlets, press-cuttings etc, partly relating to the preparation of a new Ed of his diary, c.1853 to 1935, about 140 pp, 4to, sold at S on 22 July 1988, lot 350, for £500 to Maggs.]
Autograph transcript, "A copy of my promise to Mr. Tho. Trice about letting him have 4 acres of Land " [at Brampton], sgd & dated 17 Nov 1663. 2 pp, 4to. With autograph endorsement, initialled. (88) £3,500
Ms, "Generall State & Terrer of my Brampton Lands", July 1681. (88) £1,000
Ls, 21 Aug 1669. (89) £500
— 18 May 1671. (89) £500
— 24 Jan 1677. Doheny collection. (89) $800
— 6 May 1679. 8 pp, folio. To James, Duke of York [later James II]. Summarizing his career & requesting support for his application to become an Admiralty Commissioner. Retained copy, sgd with initials. (88) £14,500
— 17 Apr 1761. (90) $1,000
Letter, 9 June 1679. 2 pp, folio. To James, Duke of York [later James II]. Written from the Tower, informing James of his problems. Retained copy, in a secretary's hand. (88) £1,800
Ds, 16 June 1663. (88) £550
— June 1667. Byer collection. (90) $950
— 29 Mar 1669. (89) £800
— 27 Jan 1671. (89) £700
— 2 Dec 1696. 1 p, 12.25 by 15.5 inches. As tenant of the manor of Brampton, declaration of uses to be made of lands surrendered to the Lord of the Manor. 3 countersignatures. (88) £1,800
— TRICE, THOMAS. - ALs, 17 Dec 1664. 1 p, 4to. To Pepys. Demanding remainder of money due to him. With Pepys's autograph draft answer subscribed in shorthand. (88) £3,200
— WORDEN, SIR JOHN. - Ls, 15/25 Apr 1679. 2 pp, folio. To Pepys. Informing him of Capt. Saunders's arrival in Flanders & the Duke of York's voyage across the Channel. With retained copy of Pepys's answer, 5 May 1679, 1 p, folio, in a secretary's hand. (88) £1,000
See also: Charles II, 1630-85
See also: James II, 1633-1701

Pepys, Samuel, 1633-1703 —&
Penn, William, Sir, 1621-70
Ds, 9 Feb [16]61. (88) £260

Peralta, Manuel Maria de
[A collection of 26 A Ls s & Ls s addressed to him at Paris, 1874 to 1920, with a group of autograph verses by Peralta, 1868 to 1881, sold at bba on 15 Dec 1988, lot 109, for £400 to Amero.]

Percy, Hugh, Sir, 2d Duke of Northumberland, 1742-1817. See: Northumberland, Hugh Percy

Percy, Thomas, 1729-1811
ALs, 7 Feb 1785. (89) £380

Perelman, Sidney Joseph, 1904-79
Typescript carbon copy, essay, Garnish Your Face with Parsley and Serve, [ptd 1 Apr 1944]. (90) $750

Perez de Mesa, Diego
Ms, Tratado de astrologia por ellicenciado, [c.1595]. 458 leaves, 300mm by 205mm, in contemp limp vellum. With astrological tables & diagrams. Probably lacking c.10 leaves. (89) £2,000

Pergolesi, Giovanni Battista, 1710-36
Ms, Stabat Mater, full score; [18th cent]. 135 pp, 22cm by 31cm, in old bds. (90) DM1,100

Peri, Jacopo, 1561-1633. See: Caccini, Giulio Romano & Peri

Perkins, Maxwell
Ls, 11 Feb 1943. (89) $150

Peron, Juan Domingo, 1895-1974
Ls, 10 Mar 1957. (91) $425
— 2 Nov 1957. (91) DM440
Ds, 9 Oct 1946. (88) $90

Perrault, Charles, 1628-1703
ADs, 31 July 1672. 1 p, 8vo. Receipt for payment for materials for a banquet hall. Bradley Martin Ms. (90) $1,500

Perry, Matthew Calbraith, 1794-1858
Ls, 12 Oct 1833. (91) $350
— USS POWHATAN. - Ms, broadside announcing performance of The Comedy of The Lawyers aboard Perry's flagship in Japan, Apr 1854. 1 p, 310mm by 500mm. (91) $2,200

Perry, Matthew Calbraith, c.1821-73
Autograph Ms, Journal of Cruises in the U. (91) $375

Perry, Oliver H., 1785-1819
ALs, 20 Sept 1817. 1 p, 4to. To Commodore William Bainbridge. Sending a list of "Med[iterranea]n memo[rialis]ts" [not present]. Encapsulated. Munson collection. (90) $1,400

Ls, 15 May 1818. 1 p, 4to. To William Ellery, Jr. Informing him that a gun boat has been ordered to Block Island as requested. 8-line docket in Ellery's hand on verso. (90) $4,000

Perse, St John, Pseud. of Alexis Saint-Leger Leger, 1887-1975
Series of 10 A Ls s, 1954 to 1960. 24 pp, 8vo. To Carl Haverlin. About a variety of professional matters. Sgd Alexis Leger. With related material. (88) £1,500

Perse, St-John, Pseud. of Alexis Saint-Leger Leger, 1887-1975
ALs, 26 Sept 1952. (90) DM320

Pershing, John J., 1860-1948
Collection of 2 A Ls s & 4 Ls s, 4 Oct 1907 to 26 Feb 1926. (89) $800
ALs, [3 Oct 1915]. (91) $325
— [c.1923]. (90) $85
Ls s (2), 8 Feb 1932 & 12 Aug 1940. (88) $80
Ls, 6 May 1918. (90) $65
— 11 Sept 1921. (91) $325
— 10 Sept 1924. (91) $70
ANs, 14 Sept 1918. (90) $80
Photograph, sgd & inscr, [n.d.]. (90) $125

Persian Manuscripts
Ms, 2 calligraphic panels forming a rhyming couplet in praise of Nasir al-Din Shah Qajar. (89) £400
— Ms, album of calligraphy in concertina form, [Persia, 19th cent]. (89) £420
— Ms, album of calligraphy in concertina form. [Persia, A.H.960/A.D.1552]. 24 pp, 335mm by 227mm. Brown mor bdg. In nasta'liq script by Shah Muhammad al-Mashhadi. With illuminated headpiece. (90) £1,600
— Ms, anthology of poetry. (89) £400
— Ms, anthology of poetry. (91) £1,000
— Ms, anthology. (91) £1,000
— Ms, aphorism; calligraphic panel. (90) £200
— Ms, Baburnama. [Mughal, c.1590]. Single leaf, 285mm by 175mm. Including full-page miniature by Jamshid Chela. (91) £15,000
— Ms, Chang. [Persia?, c.1550]. 35 leaves & 2 flyleaves, 222mm by 152mm, in

contemp lacquer bdg. In nasta'liq script by Khwaja Mahmud Ishaq. From the Library of the Mughal Emperors; ownership inscr of Nizamal-din Nazar Muhammadi & Nur al-din Jahangir. (88) £3,800
— Ms, Diwan. [Northwestern India, 1711]. 272 leaves, 188mm by 116mm. Contemp lacquer bdg. In nasta'liq script by Maz-am-ud-Din. With 3 pages of illumination & 17 very large miniatures. (90) DM5,500
— Ms, Firman of Nasir al-Din Shah Qajar. (88) £400
— Ms, genealogy of the Prophet, Caliphs & Kings. (88) £800
— Ms, Hamla-i-Haidari. (88) £380
— Ms, history of Bhopal in poetry. [Bhopal, A.H.1310/A.D.1892]. 56 leaves, 346mm by 240mm, in modern green bds. In nasta'liq script. With 16 ink drawings. (91) £1,900
— Ms, Kitab Hamlat-i Haidari. (91) £300
— Ms, Layla va Majnun; [late 19th cent]. (88) £180
— Ms, Layla va Majnun. [Isfahan, A.H.1000/A/D.1591]. 99 leaves (some lacking), 220mm by 140mm. Worn green mor bdg. In nasta'liq script by Sahifi al-Jawhari al-Farsi. With 9 miniatures. Dedicated to Abul-Muzaffar Shah Abbas al-Husaini. (90) £1,500
— Ms, Min Maqalat al-Sultan Abul Ghazi Sultan Husain. [Herat, c.1507]. 32 leaves only, 257mm by 170mm, in 19th-cent red mor gilt bdg. In nasta'liq script. With richly decorated colored borders throughout & 1 page of illumination. Waterstained; some leaves detached. (88) £1,200
— Ms, Munazarat al-Hayawan. [Lucknow, A.H.1269/A.D.1852]. 450 pp, 207mm by 132mm. Brown lea tooled in gold. In cursive script. With 91 colored drawings of animals, figures & landscapes, 12 full-page. (89) £1,200
— Ms, Persian poem. (89) £180
— Ms, poem. [Ottoman, late 16th cent]. 4 leaves, 242mm by 150mm; in paper folder. In nasta'liq on gold-sprinkled paper. With illuminated headpiece. (90) £2,000
— Ms, poetry & prose. [Delhi, 19th cent]. 62 leaves of pink-tinted paper, 307mm by 190mm, in bds with calf spine. Including 6 Mughal miniatures mtd on blanks. (91) £1,200
— Ms, poetry. (91) £550
— Ms, prayer scroll. [Qajar, 2d half of 19th cent]. 200cm by 9cm, gazelle skin. In cursive script, with text forming various shapes of Imans, animals, etc. (91) £1,500
— Ms, Qasida dar Manqabat. (88) £650
— Ms, rhyming couplets. [Mughal, 16th cent]. 1 p, 413mm by 279mm. In elegant nasta'liq on buff paper by Muhammad Husain Kashmiri. Interspaced with fine studies of birds & gold floral sprays. (91) £1,500
— Ms, Sekandar. [Afghanistan, A.H.1254/A.D.1838]. 141 leaves, 200mm by 120mm. Contemp lacquer bdg. In nasta'liq script. With half-page illuminated headpiece & 9 miniatures in gold & colors. (90) DM1,800
— Ms, Treatise on Astronomy. (88) £320
— Ms, unidentified historical work in prose. [Qajar, A.H.1224/A.D.1809]. 218 leaves, 300mm by 195mm, in damaged painted lacquer covers. In nasta'liq script by Muhammad Quli called Mulla Kuchik bin Muhammad Husain. With 20 miniatures. Repaired. (89) £1,100
— Ms, unidentified historical Ms. [Mughal, c.1590]. Single leaf, 355mm by 237mm; mtd. Script "verging on naskhi". Including full-page miniature in gouche & gold. (91) £60,000
— Ms, Wasli. (90) £400
— Ms, Wasli; poetry. (90) £500
— Ms, Wasli; quadruplet. (89) £400
— Ms, Wasli; rhyming couplets. (90) £380
— Ms, Wasli; rhyming couplets. (90) £400
— Ms, Wasli; rhyming couplets. (90) £1,000
— Ms, Wasli; rhyming couplets. (89) £500
— Ms, Wasli; rhyming couplets. (90) £500
— Ms, Zakhira Iskandari. [Isfahan?, mid-17th cent]. 25 leaves, 193mm by 115mm. Decorated green mor bdg. In naskhi script. With 29 small miniatures representing a variety of creatures. (90) £4,500
— ABDUL RAHMAN JAMI. - Haft Awrang. [Persia, 15th cent]. 351 leaves & 3 flyleaves, 209mm by 139mm, in

contemp brown mor gilt bdg. In 4 columns of nasta'liq; text within cloud-bands. (88) £1,600

— ABDUL RAHMAN JAMI. - Diwan-i-Jami. [Persia, A.H.892/A.D.1486-87]. 342 leaves & 4 flyleaves, 209mm by 143mm, on pink paper. Later dark brown floral lacquer bdg. In black nasta'liq by Sultan Muhammad Nur. With double page of illumination. (90) £8,000

— ABDULLAH BIN FAZLALLAH. - Tarikh-i Vassaf. [Qajar, A.H.1248/A.D.1832]. 456 leaves, 362mm by 225mm. Def richly decorated lacquer bdg. In nasta'liq script by Zayn-al-'Abidin al-Hamadani. With 5 illuminated headpieces. From the library of Ehtisham ad-Daulah. (90) £2,000

— ABDUL-RASHID AL-HUSAIN AL-MADANI AL-TATARI. - Muntakhab al-Lughat. [Mughal, Delhi, A.H.1110/A.D.1698]. 258 leaves, 301mm by 190mm. Modern brown bdg. In nasta'liq script. With illuminated headpiece. (91) £140

— ABUL-HASAN BIN MIRZA MUHAMMAD SHIRAZI. - Hairatnama, journal as ambassador to England, 1809 & 1810. [Qajar, 1st half of 19th cent]. 144 leaves, 290mm by 170mm. Modern black lea. In nast'liq script with headings in red. (89) £1,500

— AHLI SHIRAZI. - Poetry; complete work. [Persia, 18th cent]. 344 leaves & 2 flyleaves, 254mm by 146mm. Brown mor gilt bdg. In nasta'liq script. With 3 miniatures & 6 double pages of illumination. (90) £600

— ALI QULI KHAN. - Diwan. [Persia, A.H.1162/A.D.1748]. 294 leaves, 188mm by 110mm. In nasta'liq script with extensive glosses in margins & 3 double pages of illumination. (88) £420

— AMIR HUMAYUN. - Ghazals. [Persia, A.H.97(0)/A.D1562]. 45 leaves, 250mm by 165mm, in extra lacquer bdg. On gold-sprinkled blue paper in nasta'liq script by Shah Mahmud Nishapuri. With double page of illumination. (88) £2,600

— AMIR KHUSRAU DIHLAVI. - Diwan. [Tabriz, c.1540-50]. 202 leaves, 202mm by 125mm. Repaired red mor bdg with sunken central medallions. In nasta'liq script. With illuminated headpiece & 3 miniatures. (89) £1,100

— AMIR KHUSRAW. - Laila wa Majnum. [India, A.H.1099/A.D.1687-88]. 89 leaves & 6 flyleaves, 158mm by 102mm. Contemp brown mor bdg. In nasta'liq script, occasionally written diagonally. With 39 miniatures & half-page illuminated heading. (90) £480

— ARIFI. - Guy u Chaugan. Herat, dated A.H. 925/ A.D. 1519. In nasta'liq script. 13 leaves, 191mm by 125mm, in mor gilt. With illuminated headpiece in colors & gold. (91) $9,500

— ARIFI. - Guy u Chaugan. [Persia, A.H.942/A.D.1535]. 22 leaves, 187mm by 119mm. 19th-cent green lea gilt bdg. On gold-sprinkled paper in 2 columns of nasta'liq script by Muhammad 'Ali bin al-Mahmud al-Munajim. With illuminated headpiece. (91) £500

— ARIFI. - Guy u Chaugan. [Persia, A.H.950/A.D.1543]. 23 leaves, 230mm by 146mm. 19th-cent maroon sheepskin gilt. On gold-sprinkled paper in 2 columns of nasta'liq script by Mahmud al-Katib. With illuminated headpiece. (91) £1,000

— BAHA' AL-DIN AMILI. - Nan-i-Halwa, & Shir-i-Shakar, 2 narrative verses with mystical themes. [Persia, A.H.1310/A.D.1892-93]. 32 leaves & 3 flyleaves, 127mm by 78mm. Brown mor bdg. In nasta'liq script. With half-page illuminated heading. (90) £150

— FARID AD-DIN 'ATTAR. - Mantiq al-Tayr, Ilahi-nama, & Musibat-nama. [Shiraz, A.H.1024/A.D.1615]. 216 leaves, 270mm by 170mm, in 19th-cent brown lea. In nasta'liq script by Mahmud bin Hajji Muhammad. With 5 miniatures. Repaired. (89) £1,000

— FIRDAUSI. - Shahnama. [Tabriz, c.1530]. 1 leaf only, 47cm by 31.7cm; f.179 from the Houghton Shahnameh. With gilt-sprinkled buff border & large miniature attributed to Painter D ('Abd ul-'Aziz?), supervised by Mir Musavvir. (89) £42,000

— FIRDAUSI. - Shahnama. [Tabriz, c.1530]. 1 leaf only, 47cm by 31.7cm; f.45 from the Houghton Shahnameh. With gilt-sprinkled buff border & large

PERSIAN MANUSCRIPTS

miniature possibly designed by Mir Musavvir; colored by Painter B (Qasim son of 'Ali?). (89) £38,000

— FIRDAUSI. - Shahnama. [Tabriz, c.1530]. 1 leaf only, 47cm by 31.7cm; f.221 from the Houghton Shahnameh. With gilt-sprinkled buff border & large miniature attributed to Painter A (Qadimi?). (89) £38,000

— FIRDAUSI. - Shahnama. [Tabriz, c.1530]. 1 leaf only, 47cm by 31.7cm; f.295 from the Houghton Shahnameh. With gilt-sprinkled buff border & large miniature attributed to Mirza 'Ali. (89) £230,000

— FIRDAUSI. - Shahnama. [Tabriz, c.1530]. 1 leaf only, 47cm by 31.7cm; f.84 from the Houghton Shahnameh. With gilt-sprinkled buff border & large miniature attributed to Painters A & C (Qadimi? & 'Abd ul-Vahab?). (89) £45,000

— FIRDAUSI. - Shahnama. [Tabriz, c.1530]. 1 leaf only, 47cm by 31.7cm; f.218 from the Houghton Shahnameh. With gilt-sprinkled buff border & large miniature attributed to Painter B (Qasim?) under the direction of Mir Musavvir. (89) £45,000

— FIRDAUSI. - Shahnama. [Tabriz, c.1530]. 1 leaf only, 47cm by 31.7cm; f.308 from the Houghton Shahnameh. With gilt-sprinkled buff border & large miniature attributed to Dust Muhammad. (89) £20,000

— FIRDAUSI. - Shahnama. [Tabriz, c.1530]. 1 leaf only, 47cm by 31.7cm; f.77 from the Houghton Shahnameh. With gilt-sprinkled buff border & large miniature attributed to Painter D ('Abd ul-'Aziz?) under the direction of Sultan Muhammad. (89) £78,000

— FIRDAUSI. - Shahnama. [Tabriz, c.1530]. 1 leaf only, 47cm by 31.7cm; f.436 from the Houghton Shahnameh. With gilt-sprinkled buff border & large miniature attributed to Painter C ('Abd ul-'Vahhab?) under the direction of Aqa Mirak. (89) £52,000

— FIRDAUSI. - Shahnama. [Tabriz, c.1530]. 1 leaf only, 47cm by 31.7cm; f.553 from the Houghton Shahnameh. With gilt-sprinkled buff border & large miniature attributed to Muzaffar 'Ali. (89) £13,000

AMERICAN BOOK PRICES CURRENT

— FIRDAUSI. - Shahnama. [Tabriz, c.1530]. 1 leaf only, 47cm by 31.7cm; f.32 from the Houghton Shahnameh. With gilt-sprinkled buff border & large miniature attributed to Sultan Muhammad, assisted by Painter D ('Abd ul-'Aziz?). (89) £50,000

— FIRDAUSI. - Shahnama. [Tabriz, c.1530]. 1 leaf only, 47cm by 31.7cm; f.328 from the Houghton Shahnameh. With gilt-sprinkled buff border & large miniature attributed to Painter E (Bashdan Qara?). (89) £42,000

— FIRDAUSI. - Shahnama. [Tabriz, c.1530]. 1 leaf only, 47cm by 31.7cm; f.124 from the Houghton Shahnameh. With gilt-sprinkled buff border & large miniature attributed to Painter C ('Abd ul-Vahhab?) under the direction of Mir Musavvir. (89) £115,000

— FIRDAUSI. - Shahnama. [Tabriz, c.1530]. 1 leaf only, 47cm by 31.7cm; f.513 from the Houghton Shahnameh. With gilt-sprinkled buff border & large miniature attributed to Aqa Mirak. (89) £80,000

— FIRDAUSI. - Shahnama. [Shiraz, A.H.945/A.D.1539]. 1 leaf only, 36.2cm by 20.9cm. In black nasta'liq [by Mushid al-katib al-Shirazi]. With very fine miniature on recto, 20.9cm by 12.7cm. (89) £8,000

— FIRDAUSI. - Shahnama. [North India, A.H.1255/A.D.1839]. About 672 leaves, misbound, 291mm by 180mm, in def brown lea tooled in blind. In 4 columns of nasta'liq script. With 96 miniatures. (89) £3,000

— FIRDAUSI. - Shahnama. [Persia, A.H.980/A.D.1572]. 338 leaves only, 340mm by 250mm, in worn contemp black mor. In nasta'liq script. With 2 illuminated headpieces. Illus leaves removed. (91) £340

— FIRDAUSI. - Shahnama (Indian version). [North India, 19th cent]. 539 leaves, 441mm by 275mm, in def bds. In nasta'liq script. With 41 miniatures & illuminated headpiece. Repaired. (91) £1,000

— FIRDAUSI. - Shahnama. [North India, Punjab?, A.H.1227/A.D.1812]. 559 leaves, 420mm by 275mm, in red mor gilt. In nasta'liq script by Muhammad Mehdi. With 179 miniatures. (91)

£6,000
— FIRDAUSI. - Shahnama, 3d book only. [North India, 19th cent]. 320 leaves, 285mm by 180mm. Written in 4 columns of nasta'liq script. With 33 miniatures. Seal impressions of Sayyid Muhammad Nuh, A.H.1293/A.D.1876. (88) £500
— FIRDAUSI. - Shahnama. [Bukhara, c.1600]. 547 leaves (25 later replacements), 325mm by 214mm, in 19th-cent red Indian lacquered bdg with gilt lea onlay. In four columns of nasta'liq script. With 2 illuminated headpieces (1 later), 41 miniatures & small 14th-cent miniature mtd in margin. (88) £4,800
— FIRDAUSI. - Shahnama. [North India, 19th cent]. 617 leaves, 301mm by 188mm, in rebacked contemp floral lacquer bdg. In 4 columns of nasta'liq script with sura headings in red on illuminated panels, 4 illuminated headpieces & 105 miniatures. (88) £1,000
— FIRDAUSI. - Shahnama. [Sub-Imperial Mughal, early 17th cent]. 572 leaves (some 19th-cent replacements), 258mm by 163mm. Def shagreen bdg. In nasta'liq script. With 5 illuminated headpieces & 18 miniatures (2 replacements). (90) £3,000
— FIRDAUSI. - Shahnama (to the death of Rustam, with part of the Garshasp Nama). [Persia, A.H.1251?/A.D.1835]. 281 leaves, 415mm by 265mm. Floral lacquer bdg. In 4 columns of nasta'liq script by Safar Ali Qajar. With 2 illuminated headpieces & 31 miniatures. (91) £4,000
— HAFIZ. - Diwan. [18th cent]. 230 leaves, 175mm by 105mm. Contemp half lea & lacquer bdg, def. In nasta'liq script on gold-sprinkled paper. With double page of illumination, 24 very large miniatures & numerous illuminated borders. (88) DM3,600
— HAFIZ. - Diwan. [India, c.1750]. 211 leaves, 186mm by 104mm. Contemp painted Indian bdg. In 2 columns of nasta'liq script. With decorative floral headpiece. (91) £200
— HAFIZ. - Diwan. [Kashmir, A.H.1191/A.D.1777]. 217 leaves, 132mm by 75mm. Rebacked contemp floral lacquer bdg. In nasta'liq script on gold-sprinkled paper. With illuminated cornerpieces throughout, illuminated headpiece, & 42 miniatures. Some gatherings detached. (89) £1,200
— HAFIZ. - Diwan. [Persia, c.1580]. 295 leaves & 4 flyleaves, 330mm by 216mm. Very fine contemp brown mor gilt bdg. In nasta'liq script on gilt-sprinkled buff paper by Muhammad al-Qiwami al-Shirazi. With 2 miniatures & 10 double pages of illumination. (90) £18,000
— HAFIZ. - Diwan. [Persia, A.H.1233/A.D.1817-18]. 180 leaves & flyleaf, 12.7cm by 8.2cm. Chipped contemp floral lacquer bdg. In black shikasteh by Muhammad Hadi bin Muhammad Riza. With half-page illuminated heading. Prince Muhammad Hasan Mirza Qajar Estate. (89) £1,400
— HAFIZ. - Diwan. [Persia, A.H.[9?]56/A.D.1549?]. 203 leaves & 3 flyleaves, 241mm by 152mm, in brown mor bdg. On gilt-sprinkled brown paper in nasta'liq script by Muhammad Husain. With numerous illuminated panels. (88) £3,800
— HAFIZ. - Diwan. [Persia, early 16th cent]. 186 leaves, 207mm by 123mm, in modern European bdg. In nasta'liq script. With illuminated headpiece. (91) £700
— HAFIZ. - Diwan. [Persia, early 17th cent]. 173 leaves, 254mm by 157mm, in worn brown mor. In nasta'liq script. With 2 illuminated headpieces & full page of illumination. (91) £160
— HAFIZ. - Diwan. [Persia, 1st half of 16th cent]. 145 leaves, 244mm by 155mm, in rebacked Ottoman mor gilt bdg. In 2 columns of nasta'liq script. With six 16th-cent miniatures, illuminated headpiece & double page of illumination. Some defects. (88) £2,200
— HAFIZ. - Diwan. [Shiraz, c.1540]. 189 leaves, 252mm by 142mm, in 19th-cent lacquer bdg. In 2 columns of nasta'liq script. With 2 illuminated headpieces & double-page miniature. (88) £500
— HASAN BIN HUSAIN SABZAVARI. - Bahjat al-Mabahij. [Shiraz, A.H.955/A.D.1548]. 427 leaves, 310mm by 180mm. Richly decorated contemp black mor bdg. In nasta'liq script by Murshid al-Katib as-Shirazi. With il-

luminated headpiece. (90) £4,500
- HILALI. - Diwan. [Persia or Turkey, A.H.885/A.D.1480]. 102 leaves, 270mm by 170mm. 16th-cent Ottoman lacquer bdg. In nasta'liq script on gold-sprinkled paper by Sultan Muhammad. With headings in white on gold panels & later illuminated headpiece. (89) £1,000
- HILALI. - Sifat al-'Ashiqin. [Shiraz, c.1570]. 54 leaves, 217mm by 135mm, in repaired contemp bdg. On gold-sprinkled paper in 2 columns of nasta'liq script. With 3 single pages & 1 double page of illumination (1 contemp). (88) £500
- HUSAIN BIN ALI UL-VA'IZ KASHIFI. - Anvar-i Suhaili. [Qajar, A.H.1230/A.D.1814]. 250 leaves, 289mm by 190mm, in contemp floral bdg. In naskhi script. With 166 miniatures. (88) £1,400
- HUSAIN BIN ALI AL-VA'IZ KASHIFI. - Anwar Suhaili. [Multan, A.H.1206/A.D.1791]. 357 leaves, 315mm by 212mm. Rebacked brown mor tooled in blind. In nasta'liq script for Muzaffar Khan. With double page of illumination & 109 miniatures. Crude repairs. (89) £9,000
- HUSAIN BIN ALI AL-VA'IZ AL-KASHIFI. - Tuhfat al-Salawat. [Herat?, A.H.899/A.D.1493]. 170 leaves, 177mm by 125mm. Beige mor bdg. In naskhi script, with an inscr by the author himself. With illuminated headpiece & later seal impressions of Sultan Iskandar. (90) £3,000
- IBN ISKANDAR ZAYN A-'ABIDIN SHIRVANI. - Bustan-al-Siyahah. [Qajar, A.H.1251/A.D.1835]. 392 leaves (1 blank), 304mm by 200mm. Worn beige mor gilt bdg. In naskhi script by Ahmad bin Muhammad Ali. With illuminated headpiece. (90) £400
- IBN MUHAMMAD AHMAD (KAZI AHMAD GHAFFARI). - Nigaristan. [Shiraz, A.H.1071/A.D.1660]. 223 leaves, 239mm by 135mm, in brown buckram bdg. In nasta'liq script by Mir Salman valad Sayyid Muhammad Hamadani. Some repairs. (88) £180
- IMAD AL-HUSAINI. - Ms, album of calligraphic exercises, sgd; [early 17th cent]. 7 leaves, 133mm by 215mm. Lacquered brown mor bdg. 2 lines per page in elegant nasta'liq on gold-sprinkled paper. With richly decorated borders & illuminated headpiece. (89) £5,000
- ISKANDAR KNOWN AS MUNSHI. - Tarikh-i 'Alam Arai, 1 vol only. [Persia, A.H.1025/A.D.1616]. 312 leaves, 293mm by 182mm. Green mor tooled in blind. In nasta'liq script. With illuminated headpiece. (89) £650
- ISKANDAR KNOWN AS MUNSHI. - Tarikh-i 'Alam Arai. [Persia, A.H.1025/A.D.1616]. 1 vol only, 313 leaves, 293mm by 182mm. Green mor bdg. In nast'liq script. With illuminated headpiece. (91) £400
- JALAL AD-DIN RUMI, KNOWN AS MAULAVI. - Mathnavi Ma'navi. [17th cent]. 348 leaves, 270mm by 165mm. Contemp black mor gilt bdg. In nasta'liq script on gilt-sprinkled paper. With 6 double pages of illumination. (90) DM10,500
- JALAL AD-DIN RUMI. - Mathnavi Ma'navi. [Afghanistan, A.H.1032/A.D.1622-23]. 335 leaves, 275mm by 165mm. Contemp blindstamped lea bdg. In nasta'liq script. With 8 large ornamental headpieces in gold & colors. (90) DM1,300
- JALAL AD-DIN RUMI. - Mathnavi Ma'navi. [Afghanistan?, late 17th cent]. 815 leaves, 278mm by 158mm. Contemp blindstamped lea bdg. In nasta'liq script. With 18 large ornamental headpieces in gold & colors & double-page of illumination. (90) DM2,200
- JALAL AD-DIN RUMI, KNOWN AS MAULAVI. - Mathnavi Ma'navi. [A.H.876/A.D.1472]. 292 leaves, 237mm by 150mm. Contemp lea gilt, def. In black ink in a combination of naskhi & nasta'liq scripts, headings in red thuluth. With illuminated headpiece & 9 full-page miniatures in gold & colors. (88) DM9,500
- JALAL AD-DIN RUMI. - Mathnavi. [Anatolia?, A.H.798/A.D.1395]. 215 leaves, 257mm by 176mm. 19th-cent brown mor bdg. In naskhi script by Ibrahim bin Ishaq bin Ibrahim as-Sarayi. With 5 illuminated headpieces, double page of illumination, & illu-

minated shamsa. (90) £20,000

— JALAL AD-DIN RUMI. - Mathnavi. [Persia, c.1580]. 263 leaves, 300mm by 200mm. Worn black shagreen bdg with gilt lea onlay. In nasta'liq script. With 5 illuminated headpieces & double page of illumination. (90) £1,700

— JALAL AL-DIN RUMI. - Mathnavi. [Persia, A.H.1124/A.D.1712]. 409 leaves & 37 flyleaves in 6 parts, 248mm by 139mm, in lacquer bdg & lacquer slipcase by Muhammad Kazim. In nasta'liq script. With 6 illuminated headings. (91) £3,000

— JALAL AL-DIN RUMI. - Mathnavi. [Persia, A.H.1027-29/A.D.1617-19]. 468 leaves & 17 flyleaves, 21.5cm by 12.7cm. Contemp brown mor gilt. In black naskhi script on gilt-sprinkled buff leaf by Safi bin Karim bin Ibrahim. With 3d column written diagonally in outer border & 8 finely illuminated double pages. (89) £11,000

— JALAL AL-DIN RUMI. - Mathnavi. [Persia. A.H.895/A.D.1490]. 609 leaves & flyleaf, 202mm by 140mm, in contemp black mor bdg. In 3 columns of nasta'liq by Mun'im al-din ibn Ibrahim ibn Mas'ud al-Awhadi. Principal words & phrases in gold. (88) £1,400

— JALAL AL-DIN RUMI. - Mathnavi. [Persia, A.H.1079/A.D.1668-69]. 387 leaves & 2 flyleaves, 164mm by 95mm, in later blue cloth & red mor bdg. On gilt-sprinkled buff leaf in naskhi script by Muhammad Sadiq al-Tabatabai al-Shirazi. (88) £450

— JALAL AL-DIN RUMI. - Mathnavi. [Persia, A.H.1244/A.D.1828-29]. 278 leaves & 4 flyleaves, 197mm by 127mm, in contemp floral lacquer bdg. In nasta'liq script by Vasal al Shirazi. (88) £3,800

— JALAL AL-DIN RUMI. - Mathnavi. [Kashmir, 19th cent]. 362 leaves & 4 flyleaves, 30.5cm by 19cm, in 19th cent lacquer bdg. In nasta'liq script. (88) £550

— JALAL AL-DIN RUMI. - Mathnavi, book 1, with an extract from Al-Ghazzali. [Persia?, 19th cent]. 47 leaves, 260mm by 164mm, in def brown lea bdg. In black & red nasta'liq script. Including Qajar miniature pasted in. (91) $350

— JAMI. - Haft Aurang. [Persia, late 16th cent]. 193 leaves, 331mm by 203mm. Repaired shagreen bdg with gilt paper onlay. In nasta'liq script. With headings in white on illuminated panels, 7 illuminated headpieces, & 3 miniatures. (89) £650

— JAMI. - Haft Awrang. [School of Bihzad, Herat, A.H.911/A.D.1505/6]. 228 leaves, 323mm by 210mm, in old European vellum. In four columns of nasta'liq script by Abu Tahir al-Haravi. With 8 illuminated headpieces & 13 miniatures. Seal impression of Mughal Emperor Shah Alam, 1707. (88) £20,000

— JAMI. - Iskandarnama. [Bukhara, A.H.994/A.D.1585]. 84 leaves, 276mm by 180mm. Repaired black mor bdg with gilt lea onlay. In nasta'liq script on gold-sprinkled paper by Muhammad Salah Ibn Muhammad Ali. With double page of fine illumination. (90) £2,000

— JAMI. - Kulliyat. [Persia, late 16th cent]. 508 leaves & 3 flyleaves, 330mm by 202mm, in later green lacquer bdg by Muhammad Ali. In nasta'lic script by Mir ibn Muhibb 'Ali Rashidi. (88) £2,200

— JAMI. - Silsilat al-Dahhab. [Safavid, A.H.952/A.D.1545]. 249 leaves, 219mm by 125mm, in contemp dark green mor with stamped medallions of gilt lea onlay. In 2 columns of nasta'liq script. With 3 illuminated headpieces. 1st gathering loose. (88) £900

— JAMI. - Yusuf u Zulaykha. [Qajar, A.H.1234/A.D.1818]. 116 leaves (1 blank), 198mm by 120mm, in lacquer bdg of A.H.1230/A.D.1814 by Muhammad Hadi. In shikasteh script written horizontally & diagonally by Sayyid Ali-al-Husaini. With illuminated headpiece & 2 decorated borders. (91) £3,200

— JAMI. - Yusuf va Zulaykha. [Shiraz, c.1540-50]. 177 leaves, 215mm by 130mm. Contemp Safavid bdg. In nasta'liq script. With double page of illumination & 5 miniatures. Some repairs. (89) £1,300

— JAMI. - Yusuf va Zulaykha. [Shiraz?, c.1570]. 89 leaves only, 200mm by 120mm. [18th-cent?] Turkish red mor

gilt. In nasta'liq script on gold-sprinkled paper. With headings in white on illuminated panels & 3 miniatures (1 def). (89) £550
— KHAWAJAH 'ALA-UD-DIN 'ATA MALIK BIN BAHA-UD-DIN MUHAMMAD JUVAINI. - Tarikhi-Jahankushai. [Persia, A.H.697/A.D.1297]. 164 leaves, 270mm by 185mm. Modern brown lea gilt. In naskhi script by Mubarak Shah bin al-Haji al-Hasan. With double page of illumination. Repaired throughout. (91) £4,200
— MINA KHUBAN. - Kabutarnama, treatise on pigeons. [India, A.H.1202/A.D.1788]. 22 leaves, 254mm by 152mm. Later half-calf bds. In nasta'liq by Sayyid Muhammad Musavi. With illuminated headpiece & 13 miniatures. Wormed; repaired. (89) £3,000
— MIR 'ALI SHIR NAWA'I. - Diwan. [Persia, 17th cent]. 96 leaves & 2 flyleaves, 20.2cm by 13cm. Brown mor gilt. In nasta'liq script. With 6 miniatures & half-page illuminated heading. (88) £380
— MIRKHAWAND. - Raudat al-Safa, vol IV. [Persia, A.H.1045/A.D.1635]. 304 leaves, 359mm by 217mm. Contemp black mor bdg with gilt lea filigree. In nasta'liq script. With double page of illumination & illuminated shamsa with dedication to Shah Safi I & Abu al-Muzzafar Mu'iz al-Daulah. (90) £1,800
— MUHAMMAD ALI MUSAVI (SHIKIB AL-ISFAHANI). - Gulshan-i-Jamal. [Persia, A.H.1230/A.D.1814-15]. 49 leaves, 285mm by 178mm. Contemp lacquer bdg. In nasta'liq script. With 3 miniatures & half-page illuminated heading. Holograph copy. (88) £800
— MUHAMMAD IBN KHAWAND SHAH IBN MAHMUD MIRKHWAND. - Rawzat al-Safa. [Persia, late 17th or early 18th cent] In Ta'liq script, with poetry written diagonally in cursive in margins. 212 leaves, 350mm by 245mm, modern mor. With 5 large archaistic miniatures painted over text in 20th century. (90) $550
— MUZAFFAR IBN MUHAMMAD QASIM QUNABADI. - Tenbihat-i Munajjimin. [Persia, 17th cent]. 289 leaves (2 blank), 175mm by 134mm, in 19th-cent brown lea. In nasta'liq script on pink & cream-colored paper. (89) £350
— NASIR AL-DIN TUSI. - Zij-i-Ilkhani. [Persia, Maraghah, A.H.672/A.D.1274]. 136 leaves & 2 flyleaves, 26cm by 18cm, in red mor bdg dated A.H.1260. On brown polished paper in naskhi script by Hamid bin Mahmud bin Muhammad Bad'i Shams Fakhri. With numerous astronomical tables & marginal annotations, some autograph. (88) £95,000
— NIZAMI. - Khamsa. [Qazwin?, c.1560]. 300 leaves & flyleaf, 265mm by 178mm, in contemp brown mor gilt. In nasta'liq script. With 4 illuminated half-page headings, double page of illumination, & 22 contemp miniatures by several artists. (91) £6,000
— NIZAMI. - Khamsa[?]. [Shiraz?, late 16th cent]. 197 leaves, 208mm by 140mm. Contemp blindstamped black lea. In 2 columns of nasta'liq script. With illuminated headpiece & 4 large miniatures in gold & colors. (90) DM1,900
— NIZAMI. - Khamsa. [Safavid, A.H.1043/A.D.1633]. 376 leaves, 305mm by 177mm, in def Qajar floral lacquer bdg. In nasta'liq script by Haji Muhammad ibn Mulla Sultan Muhammad. With 4 later miniatures. Dampstained, repaired. (88) £150
— NIZAMI. - Khamsa. [Qajar, A.H.1258-59/A.D.1842-43]. 330 leaves, 304mm by 196mm, in black shagreen with gilt lea onlay. In 4 columns of shikasteh script by Muhammad Ibrahim al-Husaini for Mehr Ali Khan-e Nuri Shuja' ul-Mulk. With 21 miniatures. (88) £9,500
— NIZAMI. - Khamsa. [Ahmadabad, A.H.1029/A.D.1619]. 367 leaves, 280mm by 177mm. Def Persian floral lacquer bdg. In nasta'liq script by Muzaffar Husain Badakhshi by order of Muhammad Latif Beg Badakhshi. With 6 illuminated headpieces & 5 late 19th-cent double-page miniatures. (89) £2,000
— NIZAMI. - Khamsa. [Qajar, A.H.1249/A.D.1834]. 302 leaves, 220mm by 115mm. Contemp floral lacquer bdg. In 4 columns of nasta'liq script by

Muhammad Hasan at the instance of Hasan. With illuminated headpiece at beginning of each poem & 35 miniatures. (91) £3,800

— NIZAMI. - Khamseh. [Shiraz, A.H.906/A.D.1501]. 383 leaves & 2 flyleaves, 305mm by 178mm, in contemp brown mor bdg by Taj Muhammad. In nasta'liq script by Pir Husain. With 29 miniatures. (88) £4,000

— NIZAMI. - Khusrau u Shirin. [Mughal, c.1590]. 29 leaves, 225mm by 150mm, in modern bds. In 4 columns of nasta'liq script. With illuminated headpiece & 4 contemp miniatures. Waterstained. Bound with 2 poetical Mss. (89) £2,500

— NIZAMI. - Khusrau u Shirin, & Layla wa Majnun. [Shiraz, c.A.H.1032/A.D.1622; colophon tampered with to read A.H.932/A.H.1525]. 148 leaves only, 263mm by 145mm, in repaired brown mor gilt. In nasta'liq script. With 11 miniatures. Imperf. (89) £550

— NIZAMI ARUDI. - Chahar Maqala. [Persia, A.H.1293/A.D.1876-77]. 71 leaves & flyleaf, 15.8cm by 9.8cm, in later red mor gilt. In black shikasteh by Muhammad Husain Shirazi. With illuminated heading. Prince Muhammad Hasan Mirza Qajar Estate. (89) £1,200

— QASIM AL-ANWAR. - Diwan. [Persia, A.H.879/A.D.1474]. 292 leaves & 4 flyleaves, 17cm by 12.7cm. Later brown Ottoman bdg. In nasta'liq script by Muhammad Nizam al-Din. With illuminated headings. A few leaves detached. (89) £1,000

— QASIMI. - Anis al-'Arifin. [Persia, 15th cent]. 82 leaves, 197mm by 122mm, in 19th-cent mor gilt. In 2 columns of nasta'liq script with headings in gold thuluth & illuminated headpiece. (89) £500

— QAZWINI. - Aja'ib al-Makhluqat. [Shiraz, c.1560-70]. 461 leaves, 280mm by 180mm, in marbled paper bds. In nasta'liq script. With double-page frontis & 65 small miniatures. Wormed. (88) £4,000

— SA'DI. - Bustan. [Herat?, c.1500-1525]. 146 leaves & flyleaf, 22.2cm by 14cm. 18th-cent Ottoman brown mor bdg. In black nasta'liq by Muhammad Qasim bin Shadishah. With double-page of illumination; 4 miniatures added later. (89) £8,500

— SA'DI. - Bustan. [Persia, 17th cent]. 165 leaves, 248mm by 160mm, in black lea with sunken central medallions. In nasta'liq script with borders of orange colored paper sprinkled in gold, & illuminated headpiece. (88) £900

— SA'DI. - Gulistan. [Qajar, A.H.1279/A.D.1862]. 61 leaves, 152mm by 100mm, in fine contemp floral lacquer bdg. In shikasteh script written horizontally & diagonally. With double page of illumination. (88) £500

— SA'DI. - Gulistan. [Shiraz, c.1560]. 217 leaves, 236mm by 140mm. Repaired contemp bdg of stamped panels of gilt lea onlay. In nasta'liq script on gold-sprinkled paper by Muhammad al-Katib al-Shirazi. With 11 miniatures & double-page frontis. (91) £1,800

— SA'DI. - Gulistan. [Qajar, A.D.1257/A.D.1841]. 46 leaves, 163mm by 197mm. Black shagreen with gilt lea onlay. In shikasteh script. With illuminated headpiece. (91) £260

— SA'DI. - Intikhab-i Bustan. [Qazwin, A.H.902/A.D.1496]. 29 leaves, 345mm by 240mm, in 19th-cent red mor gilt. In nasta'liq script on gold-sprinkled paper by Muhammad Badakhshi al-Husaini. With seal impressions of Sultan Bayezid II. (91) £13,000

— SA'DI. - Kulliyat. [Herat?, A.H.901/A.D.1496]. 382 leaves & 2 flyleaves, 305mm by 176mm. Contemp buff mor. In fine nasta'liq on cream polished paper by Muniml-Din al-Awhadi. With double-page of illumination & 4 illuminated sectional headings. (88) £2,500

— SA'DI. - Kulliyat. [Persia, A.H.1254/A.D.1838-39]. 295 leaves & 3 flyleaves, 24.1cm by 15.2cm. Contemp floral lacquer bdg. In black shafi'a script by Abdul Husain Shikasta Raqam Isfahani. With 3d column written diagonally in outer border & 5 illuminated double pages with half-page headings. Prince Muhammad Hasan Mirza Qajar Estate. (89) £3,000

— SA'DI. - Kulliyat. [Persia, 16th cent]. 444 leaves (54 later replacements), 205mm by 122mm, in repaired red

PERSIAN MANUSCRIPTS

mor. In nasta'liq script. With double page of illumination & 8 illuminated headpieces. Hagop Kevorkian collection. (89) £500
— SA'DI. - Kulliyat. [Qajar, A.H.1236/A.D.1820]. 242 leaves (3 blank), 292mm by 181mm. Contemp floral lacquer bdg. In shikasteh-nasta'liq script. With 14 illuminated headpieces. (89) £700
— SA'DI. - Kulliyat. [Qajar, A.H.1246-48/A.D.1830-32]. 336 leaves, 228mm by 140mm. Rebacked contemp floral lacquer bdg. In nasta'liq script by Ibn Muhammad Karam Ali al-Isfahani. With 16 illuminated headpieces. (89) £600
— SA'DI. - Kulliyat. [Qajar, 19th cent]. 333 leaves, 224mm by 140mm, in rebacked floral lacquer bdg. In nasta'liq script with extensive glosses in margins, headings in red on illuminated panels & illuminated headpiece. (88) £120
— SA'DI. - Kulliyat. [Shiraz, c.1600-05]. 362 leaves (some later replacements), 166mm by 85mm (text area). 19th-cent brown lea bdg. In nasta'liq script, partly written diagonally in outer margins. With 9 illuminated headpieces & 5 miniatures. (90) £800
— SA'DI. - Poetry & prose. [Aleppo, A.H.1004/A.D.1595]. 13 leaves (incomplete), 291mm by 184mm, in richly decorated lacquer bdg. In nasta'liq script by Imad al-Husaini. With borders of colored paper with fine drawings in gold & silver in the hands of several artists [partly Tabriz, 2d quarter of 16th cent]. (91) £36,000
— SHAH TAHMASP. - Ms, double-page illuminated frontis with nasta'liq calligraphy, sgd & dated A.H.970/A.D.1562. 320mm by 370mm; framed. (89) £1,400
— SHAMS TABRIZI. - Diwan. [Ottoman, A.H.1248/A.D.1832]. 109 leaves, 220mm by 127mm, in red mor. In nasta'liq script with illuminated headpiece, some illuminated cornerpieces & colored drawing of a rose. (88) £220
— TAQI-I KASHI. - Khulasat al-Ashar wa Zubdat al-afkar, biographies of poets; vol 2 only. [Kashan, A.H.999/A.D.1590]. 415 leaves only, 243mm by

AMERICAN BOOK PRICES CURRENT

190mm. Def brown mor bdg. In nastaliq script, copied by the author. (89) £600
— TIMUR. - Tusukat. [Afghanistan?, A.H.1192/A.D.1778]. 354 leaves, 300mm by 200mm. Contemp lacquer bdg. In nasta'liq script within cloud bands on golden ground. With half-page illuminated headpiece, 3 full borders in gold & colors, & thousands of floral devices in blue & gold in corners. (90) DM14,000
— URFI SHIRAZI. - Diwan. [Ottoman, 18th cent]. 228 leaves, 235mm by 130mm. Def red mor gilt bdg. In naskhi script. With 5 illuminated headpieces. (90) £1,000
— XAVIER, GERONIMO. - Mir'at al-Quds. [Mughal, early 17th cent]. Single leaf, 262mm by 143mm. In nasta'liq script. Including full-page miniature in gouache & gold. (91) £9,500

Perthes, Friedrich Christoph, 1772-1843
ALs, 10 Dec 1815. (91) DM440
— 21 May 1839. (89) DM440

Peru
— FALCON, FRANCISCO. - Ms, petition to the church authorities describing the Inca system of government & criticizing Spanish exploitation of Indians; [16th cent]. 34 pp, folio; stitched. In a single hand. (91) £2,500

Perutz, Max Ferdinand
Autograph Ms, description of his joint research with J. (91) DM520
— Autograph Ms, paper, Evolution of Allosterin Regulation of Crocodile Haemoglobin by Bicarbonate Ion; [n.d.]. 4 pp, folio. Sgd. (90) DM1,100
— Autograph Ms, scientific paper, Structure and Function of Haemoglobin, [n.d.]. (90) DM650
— Autograph Ms, scientific paper, A Three-dimensional Fourier Synthesis of Dioxyhaemoglobin of Horse..., [c.1965]. (89) DM800

Pestalozzi, Johann Heinrich, 1746-1827
Autograph Ms, draft of a proclamation written for the Helvetic Republic, fragment; [May 1798]. 2 pp, 8vo. (88) DM6,500
— Autograph Ms, draft of a treatise on

elementary education, fragment; [n.d.]. 8 pp, 4to. 4 pp in anr hand. (89) DM4,000
— Autograph Ms, drafts for Lienhard und Gertrud, [c.1787-90]. 10 pp, various sizes. Partly autograph, partly in the hand of Anna Pestalozzi with autograph revisions. Some defects. With related material. (88) DM8,000
— Autograph Ms, early draft of his Nachforschungen, fragment, dealing with relations between government & the people; [n.d.]. 2 pp, 4to, & 10 small correction slips. (89) DM9,000
— Autograph Ms, fragment from his Industrieschriften; [c.1807/08]. 1 p, 54mm by 183mm. (90) DM2,400
ALs, [c.1805?]. 1 p, 4to. To his sister Barbara Grosse. Letter of introduction for the Rev. Schinz. (91) DM5,500
— 22 Apr 1826. 1 p, 4to. To a pastor. Sending his speech. (89) £1,600
ADs, 20 Jan 1803. 1 p, 8vo. Receipt issued to Paul Usteri. (90) DM2,200

Peter Friedrich Ludwig I, Herzog von Oldenburg, 1755-1829
ALs, 6 Jan 1788. (90) DM380

Peter I, Emperor of Russia, 1672-1725.
See: Ivan V & Peter I

Peter I, Emperor of Russia, 1672-1725
ALs, 23 Mar [1696]. 2 pp, 4to. To [Prince Fyodor Yurievich Romodanovsky]. Reporting about the construction of ships & mentioning visitors. Sgd Piter; salutation in Dutch. (88) £2,700
— 31 Dec 1720. 1 p, 4to. To his Board of War. Naming 3 officers for promotion. (88) DM15,000
Ls, 15 Sept 1715. 1 p, 4to. To Lieut. Col. Gennin, superintendent of foundries in Carelia. Ordering him to produce guns for ships. (90) £2,000
— 25 July/5 Aug 1716. 1 p, 4to. To an unnamed duke in Holstein. Notifying him of the death of his sister. (89) DM4,500
— 14 Feb 1721. 1 p, 4to. To Hetman Koronnyi. Consenting to the marriage of Prince Menshikov's daughter with Sapjeha's son. With related material. Unrelated French letter on verso of mount. (89) DM3,600
— 7 May 1721. (88) £170

Ds, 8 May 1711. 1 p, 33cm by 38cm. Proclamation to the Christian peoples of the Balkans to rise against the Turks. (91) £7,000
— 28 Dec 1724. 1 p, 25cm by 37.2cm, vellum. Grant of a yearly salary of 2,000 rubles & further privileges to Professor Jacob Hermanns. Repaired. In black mor portfolio. (88) $1,300

Peter I Karageorgevich, King of Serbia, 1844-1921
Collection of 19 A Ls s & AL, 22 Apr to 31 Oct 1873. 64 pp, 8vo. Mostly to Dr. Victor Trotter. About his financial troubles & his efforts to obtain money from his father or the estate of his mother. In French. With related material. (88) DM5,000
Ls, 30 Sept 1913. (90) DM250

Peter IV, King of Aragon, 1319-87
Ds, 24 Feb 1356. (90) £400

Peter Owen Ltd.
[A part of the publisher's archive, 1955 to 1990, comprising Mss & typescripts, proofs, correspondence & other publishing material, some thousands of pages in 8 large boxes, sold at S on 18 July 1991, lot 350, for £5,000 to Reece.]
[The archives of the publishing firm of Peter Owen Ltd, comprising Mss, typescripts, proofs, & correspondence by & relating to many writers pbd in the 1980s, some thousands of pages in 6 boxes, with copies of some books, sold at S on 14 Dec 1989, lot 160, for £8,500 to the University of Reading.]

Peters, Carl, 1856-1918
ALs, 14 Oct 1885. (88) DM380
— 1 Oct 1890. (91) DM440
Ls, 28 Nov 1891. (90) DM220

Petrarca, Francesco, 1304-74
Ms, Africa. [Northeast Italy, Vicenza?, c.1415]. Single (opening) leaf, vellum, 337mm by 251mm. In dark brown ink in a rounded gothic hand. With very large historiated initial of Petrarca & illuminated border extending around 4 margins incorporating armorial cartouche. (91) £18,500
— Ms, Canzoniere e Trionfi. [Florence, before 1469]. 178 leaves, vellum,

140mm by 90mm. 18th-cent red mor gilt, in modern red mor solander box. In brown ink in a small roman script by Antonio di Francesco Sinibaldi. With over 370 small decorated initials, 7 historiated initials, 2 with eleborate decorated borders, & small miniature. With added colophon, dated 16 May 1370, mentioning Franciscus Antonius Petri Bartoli & the scribe Stephanus Canossa. Doheny collection. (88) £18,000

— Ms, Canzoniere e Trionfi. [Florence, c.1460]. 198 leaves, vellum, 260mm by 168mm. Contemp blindstamped Florentine bdg of goatskin over wooden bds. In dark brown ink in a rounded humanistic minuscule, possibly by Antonio Sinibaldi. With painted initials throughout, 5 small illuminated initals & historiated initial with full-length whitevine border, attributed to the Master of the Riccardina Lactantius. (89) £25,000

— Ms, Trionfi e Canzoniere. [Northeast? Italy, 2d half of 15th cent]. 144 leaves, vellum, 211mm by 141mm. Red flock velvet over pastebds, with some sewing-guards formed of vellum strips of a 9th- or 10th-cent Ms. In dark brown ink in a slightly backward sloping humanistic minuscule. Some headings & versal initials in red. (88) £8,000

— Ms, Trionfi. [Florence, c.1470]. 53 leaves & flyleaf, vellum, 198mm by 131mm. Contemp Florentine blindstamped dark brown goatskin over wooden bds. In a fine regular humanistic minuscule. With 13 small illuminated initials, & very large historiated & whitevine initial with full historiated border, attributable to Antonio di Nicolo di Lorenzo. (91) £28,000

— Ms, Trionfi. James Wardrop collection. (88) £500

Petrus Comestor

Ms, Historia scholastica. [Germany, c.1200]. 142 leaves [of 186?], vellum, 297mm by 220mm. Rebacked contemp vellum over wooden bds. In dark brown ink in a late romanesque minuscule bookhand by a single scribe. With c.580 pen flourished & 4 illuminated initials. (89) £15,000

Petrus de Alliaco, 1350-c.1422. See: Henricus de Hassia & Petrus de Alliaco

Petrus de Rosenheim, d.1440?

Ms, Roseum memoriale. [Germany or Austria, mid-15th cent]. 79 leaves (2 blank), 206mm by 130mm, in 19th-cent quarter black mor & mottled bds. In dark brown ink in a regular gothic bookhand. With painted initials throughout in red. Ownership inscr of the Augustinian Abbey of Rouge-Cloitre near Brussels. (88) £2,400

Petrus Lombardus, 1100?-c.1160

Ms, Great Gloss on the Psalms, in Latin. [Paris, c.1200-1215]. 204 leaves, vellum, 279mm by 202mm. Old red velvet over massive medieval wooden bds set with 12th-cent metal fittings & a 15th-cent painting; enamel corner plaques removed. In a regular early gothic hand by more than 1 scribe. With multiple outer columns, small penwork initials throughout, 18 large illuminated initials & 2 historiated initials. Abbey collection. (89) £95,000

— Ms, Sententiae. [Central? France, c.1180-90]. 1 leaf only, vellum, 318mm by 234mm. In brown ink in a well-formed late romanesque or very early gothic bookhand. With large historiated initial (St. John the Evangelist?) on flat burnished gold ground with blue surround. Mtd. (90) £38,000

Petrus Riga, c.1140-1209

Ms, Aurora. [Spain, early 13th cent]. 56 leaves only, vellum, 222mm by 150mm, in 18th-cent green mor bdg in cloth slipcase. In dark brown ink in a regular early gothic bookhand. With decorated initials throughout in red or purple with penwork. (88) £5,200

Pettenkofer, Max von, 1818-1901

ALs, 4 Feb 1859. 2 pp, 4to. To Friedrich Woehler. Discussing a chemical experiment. (90) DM1,100

— 21 Sept 1875. (91) DM380

— 13 July 1894. (90) DM330

Pettigrew, James Johnston, 1828-63
ALs, 22 May 1863. 6 pp, 4to. To Gov. Zebulon Baird Vance. Discussing desertions from the Confederate Army & public opinion. Middendorf collection. (89) $2,500

Pettit, Charles, 1736-1806
Ls, 7 Feb 1798. (88) $50
ADs, 8 Nov 1780. (91) $350

Pettus, Edmund W., 1821-1907
ALs, 2 Dec 1855. (88) $140

Peurbach, Georg
Ms, Movable illusts to Novae Theoricae Planetarum. [Padua, c.1530] 39 leaves, 288mm by 214mm, in contemp mor tooled in silver-gilt. With 75 full-page & 1 double-page astronomical drawings in pen & brown & red ink, 9 with yellow wash, 25 with volvelles & other movable parts. Honeyman copy (91) £32,000

Pevsner, Sir Nikolaus
Collection of ALs & 4 Ls s, 21 Mar 1935 to 20 Oct 1948. (90) £65

Pfeffel, Gottlieb Konrad, 1736-1809
Ls, 12 Feb 1797. (91) DM600

Pfitzner, Hans, 1869-1949
ALs, 26 Dec 1915. (90) DM800
— 31 Oct 1925. (91) DM350
— 24 Apr 1945. (88) DM750

Pfuel, Ernst von, 1779-1866
ALs, 16 Apr 1822. Schroeder collection. (89) DM240

Pharmacology
[2 documents, diplomas in pharmacology, Venice 1701 & 1740, 9 leaves, 280mm by 200mm & 215mm by 150mm, disbound & in contemp brown mor, illuminated & with full-page miniatures, sold at C on 7 Dec 1988, lot 42, for £1,100 to Denniston.]
Ms, Artznej Buechlein, compilation of medical recipes. [Germany, c.1599]. 234 leaves, 170mm by 116mm, in contemp blindstamped lea over wooden bds. Additions at end in various hands. (91) DM1,800
— Ms, Artzneu buech, compilation of medical recipes. [Germany, 1617]. 111 leaves, 318mm by 224mm, in half vellum bdg. In several hands. (91) DM1,100
— Ms, Artzney Buch, compilation of medical recipes. (91) DM1,000
— Ms, compilation of medical recipes. [Germany, 17th cent]. Length not stated, 211mm by 162mm, in contemp blindstamped lea. Hundreds of recipes. (91) DM1,200
— Ms, compilation of medical recipes. [Germany, c.1720-30]. 587 pp, 310mm by 202mm. Contemp vellum bdg. In German throughout. Some leaves missing. (91) DM1,200
— Ms, compilation of medical recipes. [Germany, 1st half of 17th cent]. 115 leaves, 200mm by 168mm. Half vellum bdg. In German throughout. (91) DM1,200
— Ms, compilation of medical recipes, with some cookery recipes. [Germany, early 18th cent]. 506 pp & 32 index leaves, 162mm by 110mm, in contemp vellum bdg. In a single hand. Ownership inscr of Herrmann Gotthelf Sticke, 1737. (91) DM1,200
— Ms, Dispensatorium Pharmaceuticum Viennense, medical reipes. [Vienna, 1764]. 427 pp, 320mm by 211mm, in half vellum bdg. By 2 scribes. (91) DM1,800
— Ms, Handt Biechl, Darinen begriffen manicherlay volkomne Probierter Wundt und Leib Artzney... [Germany, 1630]. 202 leaves, 150mm by 68mm, in contemp lea bdg. By 2 scribes; sgd A.M. & AH. (91) DM1,500
— Ms, Wie die Apoteckher sollen beschaffen sein... [Germany, late 16th cent]. 8 leaves, 208mm by 165mm, in contemp wraps. Rules & regulations for pharmacies. (91) DM1,200

Document, 4 Jan 1752. 6 leaves, vellum, 223mm by 155mm. Contemp pink lea bdg. Privilegium in arte aromataria for Joannes Baptista Pipamariana, issued in Venice. With 4 full-page watercolors & illuminated tp. (91) DM2,600
— POETE, PIERRE. - Ms, Petit recueil cont. plusieurs remedes tires de divers bons autheurs... [Sassenage, Dauphine?, 1763-67]. 523 pp & 3 index leaves, 235mm by 158mm, in contemp lea bdg. With some painted initials. (91)

PHILADELPHIA

DM1,400

Philadelphia
Ms, survey of Philadelphia's principal streets, 1795 to 1802. (90) $675

Philidor, Andre Danican, c.1647-1730
Autograph music, La Princesse de Crete Comedie Heroique meslee d'Entrees de Ballet, 1688. 250 pp, 8vo, in contemp red mor gilt. In black ink on up to six staves per page; numerous revisions. Almost certainly autograph; vol 53 from the Collection Philidor. Bookplate of Mortimer L. Schiff. (88) £4,200
Ms, Nouvelle analyse du jeu des echecs..., [19th cent]. (91) £850

Philip, Prince, Duke of Edinburgh. See: Elizabeth II & Philip

Philip I, Landgraf von Hessen, 1504-67
Ls, 8 Mar 1557. 4 pp, 4to. To Landgraf Wilhelm IV von Henneberg. Requesting the arrest of a fugitive robber. (90) DM3,200

Philip II, King of Spain, 1527-98
[A collection of royal & official documents, mostly transcripts, granting titles & privileges to Don Fernando de Torres y Portugal, Conde de Villar, including material relating to his appointments in Peru, c.1577 to 1586, over 40 pp, folio, in contemp limp vellum bdg, sold at S on 5 May 1988, lot 268, for £1,000 to Camus.]
Series of 3 Ls s, 22 Nov 1544 to 28 Sept 1575. 3 pp, folio. To Juan Nunez de Olozaga. Regarding troops at Fuenterrabia. Corners def. (90) £1,200
— Series of 3 Ls s, 11 Feb 1560 to 13 July 1566. (88) £800
Ls, 2 June 1555. (91) £900
— 19 Aug 1555. 1 p, folio. To the Duke of Alba. As King of England, recommending Alexander Olcraph. (91) £1,800
— 10 Jan 1567. 1 p, folio. To his mother-in-law Catherine de Medicis, Queen of France. Interceding in favor of the Jesuits in France. With autograph subscription. (90) DM2,800
— 22 Jan 1568. 1 p, folio. To Ottavio Farnese, Duke of Parma. Informing him of the arrest of his son Don Carlos. (88) DM11,000
— 23 Jan 1568. 1 p, folio. To King Charles IX of France. Letter of credence for F. de Alava, dispatched to inform him about the arrest of Don Carlos. (90) DM2,900
— 27 July 1568. 1 p, folio. To the inhabitants of the city of Loja. Informing them of the death of Don Carlos. (91) £1,200
— 7 Oct 1568. (91) £1,000
— 7 Oct 1568. 1 p, folio. To the inhabitants of the city of Loja. Announcing the death of his wife Elizabeth of Valois. (90) £1,500
— 6 Oct 1573. (88) £250
— 31 Mar 1575. (88) £550
— 9 Mar 1578. 2 pp, folio. To the inhabitants of the Low Countries. Urging them not to desert the Catholic faith & to recognize Don John of Austria as Governor. In French; sgd phpe. Repaired. (90) £1,300
— 13 Jan 1579. 2 pp, folio. To M. de Mourbecque. Encouraging him to uphold the Catholic faith in the Netherlands. (91) £1,200
— 16 June 1579. Doheny collection. (89) $400
— 16 June 1579. (90) £450
— 26 Sept 1586. (89) DM900
— 5 Feb 1588. (90) DM1,000
— 12 Oct 1588. 1 p, folio. To the Abbot of Benifaza. Thanking for the prayers of his monks during the voyage of the Armada. (90) £3,000
— 9 June 1590. (88) DM650
— 24 Mar 1593. 1 p, folio. Recipient unnamed. Informing him that the Inquisitor General has seen fit to show mercy to the converted Jews. Imperf. (90) £4,000
Ds s (2)31 Aug 1546 & 15 Apr 1553. (90) £1,000
Ds, 12 Nov 1594. (89) $900
Document, 15 May 1557. (90) £900
— 2 Mar 1564. (88) £900
— 26 Aug 1566. (88) £260
— 25 Nov 1566. (91) £950
— 17 Oct 1572. 26 leaves, vellum, 315mm by 212mm, in fine contemp pale brown mor gilt. Carta executoria de hidalguia in favor of Juan Gutierrez. With 27 illuminated headings & large

historiated initial. (89) £3,000

— 22 Dec 1572. 47 leaves, vellum, 311mm by 229mm, in contemp brown mor gilt. Carta executoria de hidalguia in favor of Sebastian de Lampresa. With illuminated initials in liquid gold on red panels, 4 full borders, 2 large historiated initials, & achievement of the arms. (91) £2,000

— 20 May 1584. (88) £700

Philip II, King of Spain, 1527-98 — & John of Austria, Don, 1547-78

[A Ms vol containing c.30 documents relating to the revolt of the Moriscos in Granada, 1569 to 1576, including 4 Ls s by King Philip & 7 Ls s by Don John of Austria, sold at S on 21 Nov 1989, lot 229, for £7,000 to Spain.]

Philip II, King of Spain, 1527-98 — & Mary I, Queen of England, 1516-58

Ds, 4 Apr [1555]. 1 p, 4to. As King & Queen of England, passport for Henry Knolles. (91) $2,700

Philip III, King of Spain, 1578-1621

Ls, 23 July 1611. (91) £500

Ds s (2)20 Apr 1601 & 3 Dec 1605. (90) £400

Ds, 8 July 1610. (89) $475

— 30 Jan 1618. (89) $400

Document, 1604. (90) £600

— Nov 1606. (90) £600

— 1 July 1610. (89) £580

— 30 May 1612. 67 leaves, on vellum, 306mm by 212mm, in contemp velvet over bds. Carta executoria de hidalguia in favor of Alvaro Lopez de Cangas. With 3 full-page miniatures & 18 large illuminated initials, including 11 historiated with ports of saints; half-page port at end. (90) $3,600

— 24 Dec 1620. 54 leaves & 2 flyleaves, vellum, 334mm by 225mm, in contemp roll-tooled red-brown mor over pastebds profusely gilt. Carta executoria de hidalguia in favor of Lorenco de Tejada. With port of Philip III & 2 full-page miniatures. Abbey collection. (89) £3,200

Philip IV, King of Spain, 1605-65

[An important collection of c.140 letters relating to Don Antonio de Zuniga y de la Cueva, Marques de Flores-Davila, c.1631 to 1651, including c.70 Ls s by the King, concerning the government of Spain's North African forts, c.280 pp in modern calf fitted box, sold at S on 5 May 1988, lot 253, for £11,000 to Camus.]

Ds, 8 Oct 1628. (91) $250

— 4 Aug 1632. 296 pp, vellum, folio. Contemp red velvet over wooden bds. Sale of feudal rights & revenues attached to 20,000 subjects in order to raise funds for the treasury. Rua collection. (91) $3,500

— 2 May 1636. (90) DM330

Document, 1634. 72 leaves, 275mm by 195mm. Brown calf gilt bdg. Carta executoria de hidalguia in favor of the Ruiz del Sotillo Family. With full-page achievement of the arms in gold & colors. (91) DM2,000

— 8 Aug 1641. 24 leaves, 351mm by 250mm, in orig velvet over wooden bds. Carta executoria de hidalguia in favor of Diego de Sanjvan y Paraquedello. With 4 full-page miniatures within richly illuminated full borders (some historiated). (90) £4,000

Philip V, King of Spain, 1683-1746

ALs, 7 Sept 1709. (90) DM650

Philipp I, Landgraf von Hessen, 1504-67

Ls, 24 June 1562. (88) DM950

Philipp Ludwig, Pfalzgraf zu Neuburg, 1547-1614

Ls, 27 Aug 1607. (91) DM700

Philippine Charlotte, Herzogin von Braunschweig und Lueneburg, 1716-1801

Ds, 7 Apr 1790. (90) DM270

Philippine Elisabeth, Herzogin von Sachsen-Meiningen, 1686-1744

ALs, 23 Aug 1732. (90) DM240

Philippines

— CEREZO SALAMANCA, DON JUAN. - Ms, contemp copy of his report about his predecessor Juan Nino de Tavora's period of office as governor, 1633. More than 1,000 pp, folio, in vellum wraps. (90) £2,100

PHILIPPINES

— GADNANG, INOCENCIO. - Ms, notebook, sgd, containing detailed information on tribal life, natural resources, etc., with 6 pencil drawings & ALs transmitting the report to Manila, 14 Aug 1902. 26 pp, 4to. (88) $200

Philips, Ambrose, 1675?-1749
ALs, 31 May 1710. (88) £100

Phillips, William, 1731?-81
ALs, 10 Aug 1779. (89) $280
Ls, 20 June 1778. (89) $220
— 3 July 1778. (90) $140

Piaf, Edith, 1915-63
Photograph, sgd & inscr, [n.d.]. (89) $240

Picard, Jacob, 1883-1967
Series of 3 A Ls s, 5 May to 13 Nov 1912. (90) DM420

Picard, Max, 1888-1965
ALs, 21 Aug 1920. (89) DM340

Picasso, Pablo, 1881-1973
Ls, 20 May 1930. 1 p, 4to. To the pbr Albert Skira. Agreeing to provide 15 more illusts for an Ed of Les Metamorphoses & stating conditions. With 4-line autograph postscript, sgd. Byer collection. (90) $4,800
Autograph postcard, sgd, 22 Oct 1920. (88) £450

Piccinni, Niccolo, 1728-1800
ALs, [after 1783]. (90) £900

Piccolomini, Enea Silvio, 1405-64. See: Aeneas Sylvius Piccolomini, 1405-64

Piccolomini, Ottavio, 1599-1656
Ls, 19 Apr 1649. 1 p, 4to. To unnamed officials. Requesting use of funds for his journey to Nuernberg in the Emperor's service. (90) DM1,300
— 17 Sept 1654. (88) DM750

Pichegru, Charles, 1761-1804
Ls, [8 Oct 1794]. (89) DM550
— [17 Mar 1795]. (90) DM420

Pichler, Karoline, 1769-1843
ALs, [n.d.]. (89) DM220

AMERICAN BOOK PRICES CURRENT

Pickering, Timothy, 1745-1829
ALs, 19 May 1785. (90) $120
— 20 Nov 1797. (89) $100
— 2 Jan 1798. (89) $700
Ls, 16 Nov 1799. (91) $650
— 20 Dec 1799. (88) $50
Franking signature, 19 Oct [1795]. (88) $95
— Anr, [12 Jan 1798]. Alexander collection. (90) $105

Pickford, Mary, 1893-1979
Typescript, replies to questions asked her by Thomas L. (91) $300
Collection of 2 Ls s & 2 photographs, sgd & inscr, 17 May 1923 to 15 Feb 1928 & [n.d.]. (89) $400
Ls, 16 Feb 1942. (88) $350
See also: Chaplin, Charles & Pickford

Pierce, Franklin, 1804-69
[An interleaved copy of the Constitution of the United States of America... Printed for the Use of the House of Representatives. Wash. 1852, in contemp mor, sgd by Pierce, 5 members of his cabinet, & 315 members of Congress, sold at CNY on 7 Dec 1990, lot 245, for $7,000.]
ALs, 18 Mar 1838. 4 pp, 4to. To the Rev. D. W. Burroughs. Responding to a letter attacking his views on slavery. Pratt collection. (89) $6,500
— 15 May 1841. Byer collection. (90) $500
— 6 Apr 1847. 2 pp, 4to. To Caleb Cushing. Commenting on the Mexican War & opposition in New England. Sang collection. (91) $3,250
— 25 May 1848. Byer collection. (90) $425
— 19 Jan 1849. (91) $750
— 20 Oct 1852. Rosenbloom collection. (88) $600
— 26 Apr 1854. 1 p, 4to. To Postmaster Gen. James Campbell. Letter of introduction for Joel H. Angier. (89) $1,900
— 17 Oct 1854. 1 p, 8vo. To the Sec of the Treasury. Introducing Dr. Sanders. (90) $1,300
— 2 Jan 1855. (91) $750
— 8 Jan [1855]. 1 p, 8vo. To Sam Houston & Thomas J. Rusk. Inviting them to a reception for soldiers of the War of

1812. (89) $2,250
— 20 Jan 1855. (88) £800
— 2 Oct 1855. 3 pp, 4to. To J. Glancy Jones. Discussing party politics in Pennsylvania. (89) $2,000
— 29 Sept 1856. (90) $850
— 2 Jan 1858. 4 pp, 4to. To George Mifflin Dallas. Commenting on American politics. Ink showing through. McVitty collection. (90) $5,000
— 11 Apr 1860. (89) £500
— 28 May 1860. (89) $350
— 22 Aug 1864. (91) $475
Ls, 31 Dec 1853. (90) $800
— 29 Nov 1854. (88) £350
Ds s (2)[n.d.]. (90) $850
Ds, 23 Feb 1854. (89) $250
— 1 Nov 1854. (90) $850
— 29 Oct 1855. (88) $425
— 12 Nov 1855. (90) $450
— 31 Dec 1855. (91) $300
— 12 Feb 1856. (88) $275
— 27 June 1856. (91) $280
— [1857?]. 1 p, folio. Ship's papers in 4 languages; sgd in blank. Countersgd by Sec of State Marcy. (91) $1,100
— [n.d.]. (88) $180
Address leaf, [n.d.]. (88) $175
Cut signature, 25 Apr 1853. (91) $100
— Anr, [n.d.]. (91) $200
— Anr, [n.d.]. (90) $160
Franking signature, [4 Jan n.y.]. Alexander collection. (90) $230
— Anr, [10 Aug n.y.]. (89) $200

Pierce, Franklin, 1804-69 —& Others
Ls, 17 Jan 1835. (91) $190

Pierce, Franklin, 1804-69 —& Davis, Jefferson, 1808-89
[An autograph endorsement, sgd, by each, 18 Jan 1856, on integral leaf of a letter by Col. A. K. Craig, 2 pp, 4to, regarding charges made against a military storekeeper, recommending & ordering that proceedings be suspended, sold at sg on 3 May 1990, lot 230, for $1,500.]

Pierce, Jane, 1806-63
ALs, 14 Feb 1839. Byer collection. (90) $550
— 5 Sept [1855]. (91) $250
— [n.d.]. (91) $250

Pierson, Henry Hugo, 1815-73
Series of 4 A Ls s, 1860 to [1863]. (91) £450

Pijper, Willem, 1894-1947
Ms, opera, Halewijn, piano score; [1933]. 147 pp, size not stated. Marbled bds. In blue ink on up to 20 staves per page; with autograph annotations by Pijper, 1 sgd WP. Working text used probably for 1st peformance. (88) £1,200
Series of 3 A Ls s, 22 Dec 1921 to 22 Dec 1924. (90) DM800

Pike, Zebulon Montgomery, 1779-1813
ALs, 14 Dec 1812. (90) $325
ADs, 9 Jan 1813. (89) $350
Ds, 31 May 1809. (91) $650
— 4 Sept 1810. (88) $250

Piloni, Giorgio
Ms, Historia nella quale oltre le molte cose degne, avvenute in diverse parti del mondo ... (90) DM900

Pinckney, Charles, 1757-1824
Ds, 20 Apr 1807. (88) $230

Pink Floyd
[Mason, Nick. - An autograph message in large bubble lettering, "Pink Floyd, Los Angeles, Dec 1987", sgd, 11 by 8.5 inches, on hotel letterhead, matted, sold at pnNy on 3 Dec 1988, lot 395, for $100.]
[A group of autograph or annotated Mss relating to music by Pink Floyd sold at S on 12 Sept 1988, lot 91, for £580.]
[An album cover, Dark Side of the Moon, sgd by all 4 members of the group, with a photograph, sgd, each of Jimmy Page & Robert Plant, sold at pnNy on 3 Dec 1988, lot 415, for $325.]

Pinter, Harold
Typescript, play, Landscape, 1st draft; 1967. (88) £600

Pinuela, Pedro de la
Ms, Relacion sumaria de lo acontecido a Frai Pedro de la Pinuela desde que en este Reino entro..., [c.1690]. Phillipps MS.6069 & Robinson collection. (89) £1,000

Piontek, Heinz
Collection of 8 A Ls s, Ls, & 3 autograph postcards, sgd, 13 Oct 1976 to 29 July 1981. (90) DM800

Piozzi, Hester Lynch Thrale, 1741-1821
ALs, 15 Nov 1773. (90) £300
— 8 Dec 1790. 4 pp, 4to. To [Charlotte?] Lewis. About Mrs. Siddons; praises Edmund Burke. Sgd H.L.P. Seal hole. John F. Fleming Estate. (89) $2,800
— 22 July [1812?]. Doheny collection. (89) $250

Piper, John
Original drawings, (4), to illus Walter de la Mare's The Traveller, [1946]. 4 sheets, 31cm by 39.5cm. In watercolor & gouache. With related material. (91) £8,000

Piringer, Ferdinand, 1780-1829
[His album, containing 91 compositions & musical quotations mostly by musicians in Vienna, including Beethoven, Moscheles, Paganini, Schubert & Carl Maria von Weber, 1820 to 1829, 304 pp, 4to, in later lea box, sold at star on 10 Mar 1988, lot 987, for DM220,000.]

Pissarro, Camille, 1830-1903
ALs, 30 Jan 1888. (89) DM600
— 13 Jan 1891. 3 pp, 8vo. To his wife Julie. Reporting about his health & family matters. (90) DM1,350
— 30 June [18]91. (90) DM550
— [n.d.]. 4 pp, 8vo. To Esther Isaacson. About the artistic creations of his children. Including 2 small sketches. (89) $3,200

Pitcairn Island
— GARDNER, GEORGE H. - Autograph Ms, A Short Account of Pitcairn's Island, South Pacific Ocean Visited by Her Majesty's Ship Curacoa, Aug 1841. 30 pp, 12mo, in detached paper covers. Giving details of the history & topography of the island, with reference to the descendants of the mutineers of H.M.S. Bounty, & including 3 topographical drawings. (91) £5,500

Pitt, William, 1st Earl of Chatham, 1708-78
Ls, 4 Feb 1757. 3 pp, folio. To Gov. [Robert Dinwiddie]. Sending orders to raise troops for the war against France. (91) $8,500
— 31 Mar 1757. 5 pp, folio. To Gov. William Henry Lyttelton. Informing him that troops have been dispatched for the defense of Charleston & the Southern Colonies. (91) £1,900
— 7 Mar 1758. 3 pp, folio. To Gov. William Henry Lyttelton. Discussing plans to attack French settlements on the Mississippi & in Alabama. (91) £1,900

Pitt, William, 1759-1806
Cut signature, 31 Dec 1784. (91) $90
— Anr, 20 Jan 1790. (91) $85

Pitter, Ruth
Collection of c.30 A Ls s & cards, sgd, 1963 to 1979. (88) £180

Pius II, Pope, 1405-64. See: Aeneas Sylvius Piccolomini, 1405-64

Pius IV, Pope, 1499-1565
Ls, 27 Dec 1535. (89) $550
Document, [May 1561]. 1 pp, 4to. Contract for Paulus Manutius to set up his press in the Vatican, made out for Pius IV & the Apostolic Camera; sgd by Cardinal Morone. (90) £9,500

Pius IX, Pope, 1792-1878
ALs, 4 Jan 1831. (88) $200
Ls, 23 June 1864. (89) $300
Ds, 7 Apr 1860. (89) DM360
Document, 27 Feb 1857. (90) DM260
— 3 Aug 1857. (90) DM640
Autograph endorsement, sgd, 19 Dec 1862. Byer collection. (90) $225
Autograph sentiment, blessing, sgd, on a petition for his benediction, [n.d.]. (89) DM520

Pius V, Pope, 1504-72
Single sheet ptg, Sententia declaratoria contra Elisabeth praetensam Angliae Reginam; papal bull excommunicating Queen Elizabeth, 25 Feb 1569 [1570]. 1 p, 455mm by 335mm. Inscr & stamped by the Papal agent. (91) £13,000

Pius VI, Pope, 1717-99
Document, [19 Feb 1795]. (89) DM700
— 17 Apr 1798. (90) DM500
Endorsement, sgd, 13 Apr 1785. (89) $325

Pius VII, Pope, 1740-1823
Ls, 13 Dec 1786. (91) DM360
— 22 June 1791. (91) DM500
— 6 Aug 1792. (89) $325
Ds, 10 June 1809. 1 p, folio. Excommunicating [Napoleon & the French] army of occupation. (89) £7,000
Document, 28 Apr 1815. (89) DM300
— [16 Mar] 1817. (88) DM340

Pius VIII, Pope, 1761-1830
Autograph endorsement, 22 Aug 1816. (89) DM240

Pius X, Pope, 1835-1914
Autograph Ms, address to Hungarians having erected a monument on the tomb of Sylvester II; [1910]. 3 pp, 4to. Draft. (89) DM2,700
Ds, 24 Sept 1892. 1 p, folio. As Bishop of Mantua, permission to a priest to read the mass. (88) DM1,200
Autograph endorsement, sgd, 9 Apr 1908. On address leaf of a petition addressed to him by Francesco Morelli, 3 Apr 1908, 1 p, folio, requesting employment beyond the official age limit; granting petition. (90) DM1,300
— Anr, sgd, 4 Apr 1914. On a petition by the parish priest of Santa Maria delle Grazie at Montepulciano, 25 Jan 1914, 2 pp, 4to, requesting an indulgence for visitors of the church; granting petition. Also endorsed by the Bishop of Montepulciano. (90) DM1,300
Photograph, sgd & inscr, [n.d.]. 145mm by 125mm. Sgd & inscr on mount. (90) DM2,000

Pius XI, Pope, 1857-1939
Ds, 4 Oct 1927. (91) $450
Photograph, sgd, 1936. 16.5cm (round; image). Sgd on mount, under a petition for his benediction. (90) DM1,300
— Anr, [n.d.]. 14cm by 10cm (image). Sgd on mount. (89) DM1,100

Pius XII, Pope, 1876-1958
Ls, 14 Oct 1928. 1 p, 4to. To Prince Alfons of Bavaria. Referring to his recent visit in Speyer. (91) DM1,500
— 4 Jan 1930. (88) DM480
Ds, 12 Aug 1944. (90) $350
Document, 11 June 1947. (91) DM640
Photograph, sgd, [n.d.]. (88) $700
Signature, [1928/29]. (88) DM330
— Anr, as Cardinal, on a brief by his predecessor Pius XI, 22 Dec 1931, 1 p, folio; appointment of a prothonotary. (90) DM750
— Anr, under a petition for his benediction, 20 Dec 1949. 1 p, folio. With floral border including his port. (88) DM1,750
— Anr, under a petition for his benediction, [c.1950]. (90) $300

Planck, Gottlieb, 1824-1910
Collection of 4 A Ls s & Ls, 21 Dec 1865 to 1901. (90) DM380

Planck, Max, 1858-1947
Collection of 4 A Ls s & autograph postcard, sgd, 1921 to 1932. 6 pp, 4to & 8vo. To [Richard von Mises]. Concerning a dissertation, an examination, & relief for relatives of deceased colleagues. With 2 visiting cards with autograph inscriptions. (88) DM2,800
A Ls s (2), 27 June & 4 Oct 1943. 4 pp, 8vo. Recipient unnamed. About a lecture to be given at Kassel. (89) DM1,900
ALs, 17 June 1908. (88) DM850
— 17 June 1908. 3 pp, 8vo. To Albert Ladenburg. Expressing condolences on the death of his son. Repaired. (91) DM1,700
— 26 May 1917. 2 pp, 8vo (lettercard). To Pastor Priebe. Thanking for the funeral service for his daughter. File holes. (89) DM1,100
— 9 Dec 1924. (91) DM800
— 24 Mar 1927. 1 p, 4to. To [Carl Stumpf?]. Correcting a mistake regarding the year of Schubert's death. (88) DM1,100
— 31 Jan 1937. 1 p, 4to. To Rudolf Stumpf. Concerning the return of his deceased father's Pour le Merite insignia. (90) DM1,400
— 7 July 1939. (90) DM650

PLANCK

— 6 Feb 1942. 2 pp, 8vo. Recipient unnamed. Regarding a lecture engagement in Vienna. (90) DM1,700
— 23 Feb 1944. 1 p, 8vo. Recipient unnamed. Agreeing to conduct a committee meeting in the house of recipient's father, since his own house has been destroyed by a bomb. (91) DM1,200
— 10 June 1946. 1 p, 4to. To Luise Zimmermann. Thanking for a food package. With related material. (90) DM1,100
Autograph postcards (2), sgd, 28 Oct 1906 & 16 June 1936. (89) DM700
— Autograph postcards (2), sgd, 31 Jan & 5 May 1944. (88) DM750

Plantagenet-Harrison, George, 1817-90
Autograph Ms, The History of Yorkshire, [c.1879]. (90) £800

Plassard, Philibert
Ms, Secreti Eccelentissimi ... Huomini del Mundo...[Italy or France, c.1600]. 129 leaves, 277mm by 206mm, in contemp Parisian red mor profusely gilt for Henri IV. In dark brown ink in a fine calligraphic sloping italic hand. Profusely illus throughout. Containing pharmaceutical & quasi-medical recipes. Astor MS.A.21. (88) £28,000

Platen, August, Graf von, 1796-1835
Autograph Ms, 13 poems, Epigramme aus Venedig; [1829 to 1832]. 6 pp, 8vo. (89) DM6,500
— Autograph Ms, 3 poems, Neujahrsgesaenge, [1823]. 4 pp, 4to. (90) DM3,600
— Autograph Ms, brief guide to sights in Verona, Vicenza, Padua & Venice, [n.d.]. 6 pp, 8vo. With related material. (90) DM3,000
— Autograph Ms, poem, An die Brueder Frizzoni in Bergamo, [1835]. 4 pp, 8vo. 12 five-line stanzas. (91) DM2,000
— Autograph Ms, poem, beginning "Von einem Apfel soll ich singen"; [1824?]. 1 p, 8vo. 3 four-line stanzas. (90) DM2,400
Autograph transcript, poem, Bilder Neapels, [1827]. 4 pp, 4to. Inscr to [Pauline] Schelling at head. (89) DM4,200
ALs, 2 June 1823. 1 p, 4to. To F. A. Brockhaus. Requesting the return of some poems but offering his Prolog an Goethe for print in an almanac. Albrecht collection. (91) SF1,500
— 14 June 1825. 2 pp, 8vo. To the publishing house F. A. Brockhaus. Sending a poem for publication & insisting that his spelling be retained. Foxed; margin repaired. With a port. (88) DM2,100
— 18 Mar 1828. 3 pp, 4to. To Georg Friedrich Puchta. Commenting on Goethe's Faust & quoting from his own comedy Der romantische Oedipus. Sgd P. (90) DM3,800
— 8 Mar 1829. 2 pp, 4to. To Konrad Schwenck. Outlining his literary projects. (91) DM2,600
— 27 Jan 1831. 1 p, 4to. To Eduard Gerhard. Asking him to forward some vols of Goethe's works to Naples. Albrecht collection. (91) SF1,700

Platter, Felix, 1536-1614
Ds, 13 Feb 1593. 1 p, folio. Receipt for 15 gold crowns from Michael Zekher, treasurer for Wuerttemberg. (91) DM1,400

Plimsoll, Samuel, 1824-98
ALs, 28 Sept 1876. (90) $95

Plinius Secundus, Gaius, 23-79
Ms, Panegyricus Traiano imperatori dictus. [Naples?, c.1465]. 68 leaves, vellum, 255mm by 155mm. Contemp blindstamped brown lea gilt over wooden bds with 2 brass clasps. In an elegant rounded humanistic hand. With illuminated tp, large & small illuminated initial with elaborate borders in gold & colors, & coat-of-arms of the Sanseverino family. (89) DM95,000

Plomer, William, 1903-73
Autograph Ms, address to the English Society at Oxford, on modern Japanese literature, [c.1930]. (90) £380

Plutarch, 46?-120?
Ms, De la Fortune des Romains, in the French trans of Arnauld Chandon. [Paris or Fontainebleau?, c.1530-40]. 28 leaves, vellum, 218mm by 152mm. 19th-cent mor incorporating sides of contemp Parisian black mor profusely

gilt with crowned cipher of Francois I. In a calligraphic lettre batarde with pronounced humanist features. With large illuminated initial. (90) £30,000

Pocci, Franz, Graf von, 1807-76
ALs, 10 Feb 1865. (91) DM200

Poe, Edgar Allan, 1809-49
Autograph Ms, Marginalia [9th series, no 2], sgd & dated 7 Nov 1846. 3 leaves joined to form a roll, 19 by 4.75 inches. Written for Graham's Magazine, Dec 1946. Martin collection. (90) $30,000
— Autograph Ms, poem, Elizabeth; [1829?]. 1 p, 4to. Acrostic for his cousin Elizabeth Rebecca [Herring]; sgd Edgar. Inlaid; in red mor bdg. Martin collection. (90) $18,000
Series of 3 A Ls s, 7 June 1836 to 9 Aug 1848. 3 pp, 4to. To John Pendleton Kennedy, requesting a loan. To Sarah J. Hale, responding to her request for an article. To Thomas W. Field, agreeing to a personal interview. Inlaid; in mor bdg. Martin collection. (90) $47,500
ALs, 30 Dec 1840. 1 p, 4to. To Lewis J. Cist. Informing him that publication of his projected magazine will be delayed. In mor bdg with related material. Martin collection. (90) $15,000
— 6 Jan 1841. 1 p, 4to. To Nicholas Biddle. Requesting him to "lend me the influence of your name in a brief article" for a proposed magazine. Tipped to larger sheet. (89) $28,000
— 21 Sept 1843. 1 p, 4to. To Elwood Evans. Sending Mr. Dana's address. Doheny collection. (88) $14,000
— 10 Jan 1846. 1 p, 16mo. Recipient unnamed. Responding to a request for his autograph. Doheny collection. (89) $8,500
— 16 Apr 184[6]. 2 pp, 4to. To Philip Pendleton Cooke. Discussing a variety of literary matters, fees, projects, etc. Corner def. Martin collection. (90) $22,000
— 31 Aug 1847. 1 p, 4to. To Robert Taylor Conrad. Requesting an answer respecting 2 articles submitted to him. Seal hole repaired. Doheny collection. (89) $19,000
— 17 Jan 1848. 2 pp, 8vo. To H. D. Chapin. Asking for a loan to arrange a lecture. Repaired. (89) £7,000
— 20 Nov 1848. 1 p, 12mo. To J. Bayard Taylor. Asking him to print an enclosure (not present) in a magazine. Doheny collection. (89) $17,000
— Cosey, Joseph. - Forgery of an ALs of Poe, 7 Apr 1849. 2 pp, 8vo. To Dr. N. C. Brooks. Transmitting (on verso) a transcript of his poem Annabel Lee. With related material. (89) $325
— Forgery. - Signature, purportedly Feb 1844, by Joseph Cosey forging Poe's hand. On front wrap removed from The Rover magazine, 3 Feb 1844. 1 p, 4to. (91) $120
See also: Dickens, Charles
See also: Hawthorne, Nathaniel

Poellnitz, Karl Ludwig von, 1692-1775
ALs, 17 Apr 1751. (90) DM460
— 13 Jan 1756. (89) DM320

Poetry
Ms, 16 lines, beginning "Yf conscience be grieved...", [Scotland?, mid-16th cent]. (88) £160
— Ms, Poems on Several Occasions By W[illiam] E[yre of Grays Inn], 26 Nov [16]96. 1 vol, size not stated. (88) £1,100
— [Garrow, George?]. - Ms, The Joys of Sex, dated 1846 to 1852. 200 pp, 4to, in def calf. "A vol of bawdy & extremely salacious verse", supposedly in the hand of Selina Upton. (89) £350
— Love, Stephen. - Autograph Ms, 27 orig verses, 5 sgd or initialled, 1760 to 1780. 71 pp, folio, disbound. Many poems on religious subjects. With copies of poems by other writers, riddles, etc. Some leaves def. (88) £260

Pogany, Willy, 1882-1956
Original drawing, Bellerophon astride Pegasus, to illus A Wonder Book, [n.d.]. (90) £800
— Original drawing, frontispiece for Heine's Atta Troll, trans by Scheffauer; [n.d.]. (90) £50
— Original drawing, Nude woman startled by a bird in flight, to illus The Picture of Dorian Gray, [n.d.]. (89) $130
— Original drawing, roses embracing a violin, to illus Sonnets from the Por-

tuguese, [n.d.]. (89) $325

Poggendorff, Johann Christian, 1796-1877
ALs, 26 Sept 1853. (88) DM440
— [n.d.]. (91) DM220

Poincare, Henri, 1854-1912
Autograph Ms, scientific paper, Sur la Theorie Cinetique des Gaz, [n.d.]. 41 pp, 4to. Sgd at head. (91) DM2,100

Pole, Reginald, Cardinal, 1500-58
Ls, 28 Oct 1544. (90) £1,000
— 28 Oct 1544. 1 p, folio. To Antoine Perrenot de Granvelle, Bishop of Arras. Requesting him to intervene with the Emperor to expedite payment of his pension. In Italian. (90) £1,050

Polgar, Alfred, 1875-1955
Autograph postcards (2), sgd, 23 July 1930 & 25 June [1931]. (90) DM300
Ds, 27 Feb 1913. (89) DM260

Polk, James K., 1795-1849
ALs, 22 Mar 1826. 2 pp, 4to. To William Polk. Reporting from Washington. Including franking signature. Pratt collection. (89) $2,750
— 14 June 1833. (90) $800
— 24 Oct 1834. (90) $800
— 1 Mar 1838. (91) $450
— 7 Aug 1838. 1 p, folio. To J. E. Edwards of the War Department. Regarding a pension for Henry Goodnight. Doheny collection. (89) $1,200
— 29 Mar 1839. 2 pp, 4to. To Dr. James S. Young. Regarding efforts to obtain a War Department appointment for Young & Polk's projected tour of Tennessee. Repaired. (89) $1,900
— 8 June 1844. 1 p, 4to. To Henry Horn. Acknowledging congratulations on his nomination as Presidential candidate. Pratt collection. (89) $3,500
— 8 July 1844. 1 p, 4to. To Samuel H. Laughlin. Discussing the refutation of charges that his grandfather was a Tory sympathizer. Rosenbloom collection. (88) $4,000
— 18 July 1844. (88) £900
— 2 Oct 1844. (90) $600
— 12 June 1845. 1 p, 4to. To Vice President George Mifflin Dallas. Letter of introduction for Col. Joseph H. Talbot. McVitty collection. (90) $1,700
— 13 Aug 1845. 1 p, 4to. To Henry Horn. Expressing interest in acquiring his port painted by Thomas Sully. Including franking signature. Pratt collection. (89) $4,250
— 1845. 1 p, 4to. To Sec of the Treasury Robert J. Walker. Requesting papers relating to a collector's appointment. Whiton collection. (88) $1,600
— 18 Feb 1846. 1 p, 8vo. To the Secretary of War. Content not given. (91) $1,600
— 1 Sept 1846. 1 p, 4to. To Midshipman Thomas B. Childress. Urging him not to think of resigning from the Navy. (90) $2,500
— 11 Sept 1846. 1 p, 4to. To John Y. Mason. Inviting him to a cabinet meeting. (91) $2,000
— 31 Oct 1846. 2 pp, 4to. To Vice President George Dallas. Asking for a reference in the Madison papers. (91) $1,900
— 6 Mar 1847. 1 p, 4to. To Adjutant Gen. [Roger Jones]. Requesting a list of army officers. (90) $2,250
— 14 May 1847. 1 p, 4to. To Sec of War Marcy. Transmitting copies of Congressional resolutions concerning Zachary Taylor's victory at Monterey. (89) £4,500
— 27 Nov 1847. 1 p, 4to. To Sec of the Treasury Robert J. Walker. Letter of recommendation for M. M. Smith. Sang collection. (91) $4,250
— 26 Mar 1848. 1 p, 4to. To Sec of the Treasury Robert J. Walker. Requesting recipient's views on the tariff & the state of the finances for his Annual Message. Sang collection. (91) $3,000
— 30 July 1848. 1 p, 4to. To the Sec of War. Requesting information in order to answer resolutions of the House of Representatives. (89) £2,800
Ls, 19 May 1828. (89) $650
Ds, 26 Sept 1839. (91) $700
— 12 Jan 1841. (88) $475
— 12 Jan 1841. (88) $450
— 4 Apr 1845. Byer collection. (90) $800
— 30 June 1846. (90) $850
— 3 Feb 1848. (91) $700
— 25 Aug 1848. (90) $750
— 25 Nov 1848. (90) $950
Autograph endorsement, sgd, 12 Mar

1847. (91) $400
— Anr, sgd, 24 Apr 1847. (91) $450
— Anr, initialled, 28 July 1847. (89) $350
Cut signature, [1846]. (90) $260
Endorsement, [1847]. (90) $65
Franking signature, [n.d.]. (89) $800
— Anr, [n.d.]. Alexander collection. (90) $400

Polk, Leonidas, 1806-64
ALs, 12 July 1862. 4 pp, 8vo. To Gen. Van Dorn. Concerning a command for Capt. A. S. Stewart. (89) $1,200
— CRAWFORD, A. A. - ALs, 26 Jan 1862. 1 p, 4to. To Maj. Gen. Polk. Requesting a hardship leave. Alexander collection. (90) $170

Polk, Sarah Childress, 1803-91
Collection of ALs & signature, 7 Apr 1888 & 25 Oct 1887. (91) $450

Pollexfen, Sir Henry, 1632?-91
Transcript, defense of the City of London's charter (Rex v City of London), 1682. (89) £95

Pollini, Francesco, 1762-1846
Autograph music, Capriccio per Arpa, [n.d.]. 7 pp, folio; 12 staves each. Fair copy, sgd at head. (89) DM1,900

Pomare IV, Queen of Tahiti
ALs, 3 Aug 1843. (88) £300
Ls, 16 Feb 1844. (90) $750

Pompadour, Jeanne Antoinette, Marquise de, 1721-64
AL, 23 June 1762. 2 pp, 4to. To her brother, the Marquis de Marigny. About his letter to the Duc de Choiseul, & informing him about deliberations in council. Seal tear. (89) DM3,500

Ponchielli, Amilcare, 1834-86
Autograph music, scena & duet Innanzi a miei passi, for tenor, bass & keyboard to a text from Cammarano's Ines de Castro; [n.d.]. 12 pp, folio, in modern bds. Some stage directions; numerous revisions. Sgd. (90) £2,000
Series of 4 A Ls s, 14 Dec 1854 to 3 Dec 1868. 7 pp, 8vo & 4to. To Giacomo Vietti (3), about the publication of a composition & a shipment of books. To Cesare Confalonieri, about the death of Rossini. (90) £1,100
ALs, 20 Apr 1868. (90) £650
— 28 Sept 1868. (90) £480
— 8 Apr 1876. (91) £600
Autograph postcard, sgd, 23 July 1883. (91) DM380

Poniatowski, Joseph, Prince, 1763-1813
Ls, 5 Jan 1810. (89) £450
Ds, 10 July 1792. (88) £750

Ponsonby, Sarah, 1745?-1831
ALs, 28 Aug 1831. (88) £120

Pontano, Giovanni, 1426-1503
Ms, De Principe. [Central Italy, c.1480-90]. 58 leaves & 2 flyleaves, vellum, 180mm by 110mm, in contemp blind-stamped dark brown mor over thin wooden bds. In a fine rounded slightly clubbed humanist minuscule by Federico Veterano for Ambrogio Landriano. With illuminated opening page with large initial & 3-quarter border incorporating coat-of-arms. (91) £12,000

Pontelli, Baccio, c.1450-95?
ADs, 13 Aug 1481. (91) £700

Pontifical
Ms, [Bologna?, late 14th cent]. 283 leaves, vellum, 275mm by 195mm. 19th-cent English calf panelled in gilt; def. In red & brown ink in a clear gothic rotunda. With musical notation in red & brown ink on 84 pp, 2 calligraphic Greek & Roman alphabets, numerous small & 28 large initials in gold & colors, 26 large miniatures & full-page miniature of the Crucifixion. Doheny collection. (88) £90,000
— Ms, in Latin. [Southwestern France?, c.1495]. 417 leaves (1 blank, 4 lacking), vellum, 285mm by 195mm. 19th-cent green mor over wooden bds tooled in gold & blind, by Hering. In brown & red ink in a gothic textura. 244 pp with music on a 4-line red stave. With illuminated initials throughout with floral decoration, 30 large initials with coats-of-arms, 1 full border & 26 pp with partial borders of painted leaves, flowers & birds. Spaces for historiated initials left blank. Doheny collection. (88) £14,000

PONTIFICAL

— Ms, Pontifical Benedictions of William Durandus, Bishop of Mende, in Latin. (91) £900
— Ms, The Pontifical of Salomo I, Bishop of Constance. [Reichenau Abbey, 2d quarter of 9th cent]. In Latin. 116 leaves (c.6 lacking), vellum, 228mm by 165mm. 14th-cent chained bdg of tawed skin over bevelled wooden bds, rebacked. In dark brown ink in an extremely fine Carolingian minuscule, with rubrics & headings in red uncials. With initials throughout in red usually set out in margins & infilled with yellow. Donaueschingen Ms.192. (90) £580,000

Ponto, Antonino

Ms, Rhomitypion. [Southern Italy, Cosenza?, 1523]. 58 leaves, 210mm by 141mm. Contemp gilt bdg of calf over pastebds with arms of the bishop of Cosenza. In black ink in a slightliy sloping italic hand. With 3 large illuminated initials & half-page coat-of-arms. Description of Rome; dedication Ms presented to Giovanni Ruffo de Theofoli, Archbishop of Cosenza. Phillipps Ms.887 & Abbey collection. (89) £7,000

Pope, Alexander, 1688-1744

Autograph Ms, Pastorals, including An Essay on Pastoral, 1704 [- 1706]. 37 pp on 19 leaves, 193mm by 130mm, in early 19th-cent calf gilt. In calligraphic script in imitation of ptd type, with many erasures & autograph revisions in his regular cursive hand. The Garden Ltd. collection. (90) $90,000

Collection of ALs & ADs, [22 Mar 1742/43] & 25 Mar 1743. Houghton collection. (90) £450

ALs, 8 Aug 1707. 2 pp, 4to. To [Anthony Englefield]. Thanking for his letter, reporting about his present state of idleness in the country, praising recipient's genius, etc. Marquess of Downshire collection. (90) £1,200
— 13 Sept 1714. (90) £950
— [c.1 Nov 1716]. Houghton collection. (89) $800
— 25 Oct [1718?]. 2 pp, 4to. To Thomas Dancastle. Expressing thanks, & chatting about his stay in the country. Houghton collection. (89) $2,800

AMERICAN BOOK PRICES CURRENT

— 16 Dec 1718. (90) £600
— 26 Feb 1719/20. 1 p, 4to. To Jabez Hughes. Expressing condolences on the death of recipient's brother. Repaired. Houghton collection. (89) $1,900
— [Aug 1723?]. 2 pp, folio. To [Charles Mordaunt, Earl of Peterborough & Monmouth]. Musing about recipient's absence, & about writing "voluminous Treatises about Nothing." Corner torn. Houghton collection. (89) $5,000
— [c.1724]. 2 pp, 4to. To Jacob Tonson. Regarding the index to his Ed of Shakespeare. Inlaid. Houghton collection. (89) $3,500
— [June 1734?]. 1 p, 4to. To George Fortescue. Trying to arrange a meeting. Houghton collection. (89) $1,400
— [6 May 1735]. 1 p, 4to. To [William] Duncombe. Thanking for a present & sending his new book. Margin def. Houghton collection. (89) $1,200
— 4 Dec 1735. 2 pp, 4to. To Jacob Tonson. Sending condolences & hoping for a meeting. Houghton collection. (89) $3,200
— [c.1735]. 1 p, 8vo. To Jonathan Richardson. Confirming arrangements for a portrait sitting. (91) $1,200
— 31 Oct [1739]. (90) £1,000
— 12 Dec 1739. 2 pp, 4to. To George, Baron Lyttleton. Reporting about his stay in Bath & musing about his life. John F. Fleming Estate. (89) $2,500
— [6 Dec 1740]. (90) £800
— [Apr 1741?]. 1 p, 4to. To William Warburton. Assuring him he will be at home in May & June. Houghton collection. (89) $1,800
— [April or May 1742]. 1 p, 4to. To George Arbuthnot. Requesting him to examine a receipt in Mr. Lintott's books. Seal hole. Houghton collection. (89) $4,200
— [c.July 1742]. Houghton collection. (90) £450
— "Thursday" [1742?]. 1 p, 8vo. To Jonathan Richardson. Arranging for a meeting. Houghton collection. (89) $1,500
— 8 Feb 1743/44. 1 p, 4to. To Slingsby Bethel. Discussing a financial matter. Address leaf detached. Houghton col-

lection. (89) $1,800
— 14 Feb [n.y.]. 1 p, 4to. To James Eckersall. About lottery orders. Inlaid. Houghton collection. (89) $1,500
— 6 Mar [n.y.]. (90) £950
— [n.d.], "Tuesday". (88) $1,000
— [n.d.], "Monday". Houghton collection. (90) £500
— [n.d.], "Wednesday". (90) £600
— [n.d.], "Saturday". Houghton collection. (90) £950
— [n.d.]. (88) £150
AN, [1742]. 1 p, 12mo. To [William] Warburton. Requesting him to point out errors for a new Ed of his Homer. Houghton collection. (89) $1,100
See also: Gay, John & Pope

Pope, Alexander, 1688-1744 —& Walsh, William, 1663-1708
Autograph Ms, Alterations to the Pastorals, [1706?]. 4 pp, 185mm by 150mm; bifolium. About 125 lines from the Pastorals in Pope's hand, with c.25 lines of comments and suggestions by Walsh. The Garden Ltd. collection. (90) $17,000

Pope, John, 1822-92
Ls, 21 Aug 1862. (91) $550

Porphyrius, c.234-c.305
Ms, Eis ta harmonika Ptolemaiou hypomnema, [Spain or Italy, c.1560-80]. 242 leaves, 290mm by 200mm, in contemp blindstamped tanned lea over wooden bds. In a regular Greek cursive hand. Including diagrams. The Garden Ltd. collection & Phillipps Ms.3877 (90) $12,000

Porter, Cole, 1893-1964
Autograph Ms, lyrics for the song Taxes, [n.d.]. 2 pp, 4to. Working Ms. With related material & authentication. (91) $3,750
Ls, 29 Mar 19[5]1. (91) $350
— 2 May 1951. (90) $400
Collection of AN & signature, [c.1955]. (91) $250
Autograph quotation, 2 bars from Night & Day. On small sheet. Sgd. (91) $1,600
Photograph, sgd, [n.d.]. (91) $250
Signature, [1962]. (91) $350

Porter, David, 1780-1843
ADs, 2 Jan 1821. (91) $110
Franking signature, [28 Aug n.y.]. Alexander collection. (90) $80

Porter, David Dixon, 1813-91
Ms, The Island of St. (91) $450
Ls, 13 Dec 1863. Alexander collection. (90) $210

Porter, Endymion, 1587-1649. See: James I, 1566-1625

Porter, Fitz-John, 1822-1901
ALs, [n.d.] (88) $130
— 11 June 1869. (91) $750
— 22 Jan [18]70. (88) $400
— 24 Jan [18]82. (88) $475

Porter, Katherine Anne, 1890-1980
Collection of Ls & photograph, sgd & inscr, 15 Jan 1976. (89) $210
Series of 4 Ls s, July to Sept 1960. (90) $300
Ls s (2), 10 June 1937 & 6 June 1940. (89) $225

Porter, William Sydney, ("O. Henry"), 1862-1910
ALs, 2 Oct [1909?]. Doheny collection. (88) $900

Portraits des Fondatrices
Ms, Portraits des Fondatrices de tous les differents Ordres Religieuses. (91) $400

Portugal
Ms, Livro dos prestimonios, igreijas, alcaidarias mores, lugares deletras officios, dejustica e fazenda..., 1665. 58 leaves, 400mm by 275mm, in contemp mottled calf. Very finely lettered & decorated throughout. Listing Royal patrimonial properties under the governorship of Simao de Vasconcellⅼo. (91) £6,000
— BROOKE, MAJ. GEN. WILLIAM. - Ms, journal of a journey through Portugal, 16 July to 6 Nov 1812. 16 pp, 4to. (88) £110

Postal Service
Document, Oct 1671. Byer collection. (90) $350
— LAUD, WILLIAM, & OTHERS. - Ds, [1635]. 2 pp, folio. Warrant, sgd by the

Privy Council & addressed to Attorney Gen. [Sir John Bankes], appointing Thomas Witherings as Postmaster Gen. of England, & giving details of conditions of the office & related regulations. (89) £5,200

— STRATFORD-UPON-AVON. - Ms, working drafts of a petition by the inhabitants of Stratford to the Postmaster General concerning poor service to London, with related papers; 1821 to 1841. 18 pp, folio & 4to. (90) £400

Postl, Karl Anton, 1793-1864. See: Sealsfield, Charles

Potemkin, Grigori Aleksandrovich, Prince, 1739-91
ALs, [n.d.]. 1 p, 4to. To [Friedrich Wilhelm Bauer?]. Promising to report about enemy movements & requesting 2 further batallions. (91) DM1,300

Ls, [summer 1776]. 3 pp, 4to. To [Prince Heinrich von Preussen?]. Thanking for & expressing compliments. With autograph subscription. In French. (90) DM1,300

Pott, Percivall, 1714-88
Ms, extracts from his lectures at St. (89) £500

Potter, Beatrix, 1866-1943
Original drawings, 3 pencil drawings relating to Christopher Le Fleming's Peter Rabbit Music Books, [c.1935], c.110mm by 165mm. With autograph Ms, 4 A Ls s to Le Fleming, & further related material. (88) £5,000

Original drawing, frog hopping through the rushes; rejected drawing for The Tale of Jeremy Fisher, 1906. In watercolor. 112mm by 92mm. (90) £7,500

— Original drawing, of Aunt Petitoes with the piglets drinking buckets full of milt, from The Tale of Pigling Bland. [c.1913]. Ink & watercolor, 8 by 6.5 inches. (88) £5,000

Collection of 4 A Ls s & Christmas card, sgd, 1917 to 1936. (88) £850

ALs, 28 Oct 1913. (88) £220

— 9 Jan 1924. 4 pp, 12mo. To Sir Alfred Tripp. Promising a contribution to support the Invalid Children's Aid Association. (91) $1,800

— 14 Mar [19]29. (88) £200

Poulden, Richard. See: Peninsular War

Poulenc, Francis, 1899-1963
[A ptd program of a meeting of "The Bohemians", 25 Jan 1950, 1 p, 4to, sgd by Poulenc & 2 others, sold at sg on 22 Oct, lot 214, for $350.]

Series of 4 A Ls s, [14 Sept 1931 & n.d.]. (90) £700

— Series of 4 A Ls s, [n.d.]. (90) £500

A Ls s (2), 5 May & 19 June 1927. (88) £600

— A Ls s (2), 9 June [1958] & 19 Jan 1963. (89) £500

ALs, [1920]. (89) £400

— 1 Jan [1941]. (90) £500

— 10 Sept [n.y.]. (91) DM300

Autograph quotation, 2 bars from Les Biches, inscr; [1950s]. (91) $700

Pound, Ezra, 1885-1972
Collection of 3 A Ls s, 41 letters, ANs, 2 Ns, & autograph fragment, 15 Dec 1949 to 23 June 1959 & [n.d.]. 50 pp, various sizes. To Raymond Hughes & Henry Swabey of the journal Four Pages. Expressing his views on art, poetry, theater, economics & politics. Initialled where sgd. With related material. (89) £7,500

— Collection of 5 A Ls s, 3 Ls s, 17 Ls, 3 autograph postcards, sgd, ANs, 3 notes, & 2 postcards, [mostly 1950s]. 34 pp, various sizes. To Elizabeth Winslow. Commenting on a variety of matters. Initialled where sgd. With related material. (89) £4,200

ALs, [1913 or 1914]. (90) £850

— [28 Dec 1917]. (90) DM540

— 11 July [1949]. (91) $250

— 10 Jan 1950. (89) $140

Collection of Ls & ANs, 24 Feb 1928 & [n.d.]. (90) $500

— Collection of 18 Ls s & Letters, 13 Oct 1954 to 16 Apr 1958. 20 pp, various sizes. To John Mavrogordato. Complimenting him on his works, & airing his views on poetical translation. (91) £1,050

Ls s (2), 12 Jan 1927 & 12 Feb 1929. 2 pp, 4to. To Harry Hansen. Correcting comments by Hansen. Suggesting that Mr. Sumner be arrested. 1 sgd E.P. (89) $1,200

— Ls s (2), 30 Mar 1930. (89) $600

Ls, 21 Mar [c.early 1930s]. (88) $300
— 13 Nov 1957. (89) DM850
Ns, 28 Mar 1931. (90) £120
— DUNCAN, RONALD. - Autograph Ms, A Memoir of Ezra Pound, sgd & dated 2 July 1979. 53 pp, in folio notebook. With related material loosely inserted. (88) £1,300

Pousseur, Henri
Autograph music, sketches for 6e Vue sur les Jardins interdits, scored for strings, 30 July 1982. (91) DM500
— Autograph music, Variations - Caprice, for flute & harpsichord, [1983]. (91) DM300

Powell, Cecil Frank, 1903-69
Autograph Ms, draft of a lecture, Why we study high-energy physics; [1964]. (90) DM220

Powell, John Wesley, 1834-1902. See: Garfield, James A.

Power, Tyrone, 1914-58
Photograph, sgd & inscr, [n.d.]. (91) $80

Powers, Hiram, 1805-73
ALs, 1 Jan 1833. (88) $85

Powys, John Cowper, 1872-1963
Series of 13 A Ls s, 19 Sept 1948 to 15 Oct 1951. (90) £650
ALs, 23 Feb 1940. (89) £120

Powys, Theodore Francis, 1875-1953
Series of 3 A Ls s, 12 Jan 1930 to 15 Feb 1932. (89) £200

Prayer Books
Ms, Andaechtige Gebet, prayers for the Profession of Novices & other occasions, in German. (88) £750
— Ms, Betrachtungen und Gebeter. (88) DM700
— Ms, Christliches und Catholisches HandBuechlein..., [Germany, 1755]. More than 500 pp, 8vo, in contemp black mor. With numerous illusts, partly full-page. Initials M.E. on cover. (90) £1,100
— Ms, collection of prayers, in German & Latin. [Upper Rhine, 1437?]. 230 leaves (some lacking), c.110mm by 75mm, in 17th-cent lea over wooden bds. In black ink in a lettre batarde by several scribes. (90) DM5,800
— Ms, collection of prayers, in German. (90) DM800
— Ms, collection of prayers, with sections on astronomy & astrology, in German & Latin. [Nordhausen, Germany, 1483]. 389 leaves, 107mm by 75mm. Worn contemp blindstamped bdg elaborately tooled. In dark brown ink in a Germanic cursive bookhand. With painted initials throughout & 4 large circular diagrams. (89) £3,400
— Ms, Commendation of Souls & other prayers, in Latin. [London, c.1430-50]. 38 leaves only, vellum, 147mm by 94mm. Repaired 18th-cent English calf. In brown ink in 2 distinct gothic hands. With large historiated initial with full border & many small illuminated initials. Extracted from a larger vol. (89) £1,400
— Ms, Der Geheiligte Seelenweker... [Germany, 1809]. 129 pp, 157mm by 95mm. Contemp lea bdg. In a single hand. With watercolored frontis, 5 chapter headings with floral decoration in colors, & several small vignettes. (91) DM1,600
— Ms, devotional readings & moral precepts, in Low German. [Netherlands, 2d half of 15th cent]. 134 pp & 2 flyleaves, 194mm by 135mm, in contemp limp vellum with 14th-cent pastedowns. In brown ink in a regular lettre batarde. With 37 two-line initials in red. (90) £6,000
— Ms, Hours of the Holy Ghost & prayers for Holy Week, for use in England. [Bruges, c.1516]. 155 leaves, 90mm by 64mm, in brown mor gilt by Riviere. In brown ink in a fine Roman hand. With 15 full-page miniatures each with full border of naturalistic flowers, fruit & insects on gold ground, facing pages with similar borders. (89) £15,000
— Ms, Illuminiertes Gebetbuechlein..., in German; [Oberammerthal, Upper Palatinate, c.1820]. (90) DM340
— Ms, in Dutch. (89) £700
— Ms, in Dutch. [Northern Netherlands, Leiden?, c.1500]. 153 leaves, vellum, 132mm by 90mm. 17th-cent vellum bdg. In brown ink in a square gothic hand. With 52 large fine colored wash

PRAYER BOOKS

drawings, each within gold arched frame, by the Master of Hugo Janszoen van Woerden. (89) £35,000
— Ms, in Dutch. (89) £700
— Ms, in Dutch. [Northern Netherlands, Utrecht?, late 15th cent]. 63 leaves & 4 flyleaves, vellum, 131mm by 92mm, in contemp or very early bdg of wooden bds covered with green velvet. In dark brown ink in a gothic liturgical hand. With 9 large illuminated initials with white tracery & full-length bar borders, 2 large initials with full borders, & 6 full-page miniatures from other Mss pasted onto inserted vellum leaves. (90) £4,200
— Ms, in Dutch. [Northern Netherlands, c.1450]. 212 leaves (4 blank, a few lacking) & flyleaf, vellum, 146mm by 100mm, in old calf over pastebds. In dark brown ink in a small gothic bookhand. With small initials throughout, 44 large or very large decorated initials with extensive or full-length penwork, & large illuminated initial. (90) £4,500
— Ms, in Dutch. [Northern Netherlands, c.1500]. 92 leaves (some lacking), vellum, 139mm by 88mm. Contemp blindstamped calf over wooden bds. In dark brown ink in a gothic liturgical hand by more than 1 scribe. With over 60 decorated initials, & 3 large initials (1 historiated) with partial or full borders. (89) £1,150
— Ms, in Flemish. [Northern Belgium, July 1546]. 273 leaves, 172mm by 120mm. Gilt stamped calf bdg with 2 clasps, 1601. In black & red ink in a skilful lettre batarde. With 6 large initials in penwork & colors. Including 17 colored engravings [15th & 16th cent] pasted on vellum leaves. (88) DM54,000
— Ms, in German & Latin. [Southern Germany, c.1450]. 188 leaves, 160mm by 109mm. Contemp suede over wooden bds. Of Dominican use. In black ink, with some headings & initials in green. (90) DM3,600
— Ms, in German. [Cologne?, c.1500]. 357 (of 363) leaves, 172mm by 109mm. Contemp lea with 2 clasps. In red & black ink. With numerous initials in red & blue. Including many prayers for indulgences. (89) DM6,700
— Ms, in German. [Nuremberg?, early 16th cent]. 297 leaves, vellum, 118mm by 87mm. Red velvet bdg over old wooden bds. In black ink in an extremely fine calligraphic germanic gothic hand. With c.100 large illuminated initials in leafy designs, 31 large historiated initials with full or partial borders often including animals, grotesques, hunting scenes, etc., 9 full-page or almost full-page miniatures, & full-page coat-of-arms, probably of the Huber family. Abbey collection. (89) £160,000
— Ms, in German. [Rhineland?, 3d quarter of 15th cent]. 197 leaves (2 lacking), vellum, 100mm by 79mm, in vellum over wooden bds. In brown ink in a German batarde hand. With 6 large illuminated initials in gold & colors with scrolling foliate & floral borders. (89) £11,000
— Ms, in German. [Rhineland, Cologne?, late 15th cent]. 197 leaves (5 blank) & 2 13th-cent flyleaves, vellum, 98mm by 74mm, in modern vellum over wooden bds. In dark brown ink in a German cursive bookhand. With 5 large illuminated initials with floral borders. (91) £2,800
— Ms, in German. (89) DM650
— Ms, in German. [South Germany or Austria, 2d half of 15th cent]. 165 leaves, vellum, 118mm by 90mm. Old pastebds covered with part of a leaf from a Ms choirbook. In a neat Germanic slightly cursive bookhand. With c.50 large illuminated initials in a variety of styles, 3 historiated initials, 5 full-page miniatures, & 15th-cent votive miniature pasted inside front cover. Ownership inscr of Marx Holer, 1492. (91) £7,000
— Ms, in Latin & Spanish. [Spain, 2d half of 15th cent]. 172 leaves, vellum, 110mm by 80mm, in old limp vellum. In dark brown ink in a skilful rounded gothic hand. With 56 finely decorated initials, 25 large illuminated initials with partial borders, 3 very large initials with full borders, & full-page miniature. (90) £2,400
— Ms, in Latin. James Wardrop collection. (88) £500

— Ms, in Low German. (89) £1,000
— Ms, Liber amicorum consisting of Suffrages & Memoria, in Latin. [Southern Germany, Augsburg?, late 16th cent]. 160 leaves, vellum, 91mm by 51mm, in early 18th-cent French red mor gilt. In brown ink in an Italianate bookhand. Listing 185 saints in the Suffrages, with 127 miniatures in gold & colors below crimson bands, many inscr with names of friends. (89) £6,500
— Ms, meditations on the life of Christ & of the Virgin Mary, beginning "Iesus Maria Anna: A meditation of the blessed virgin Maries conception; [3d quarter of 17th cent?]. (90) £90
— Ms, Orazione Divote da Praticarsi in varie parti del Giorno. (90) £480
— Ms, prayers in Flemish. [Oost-Malle, Belgium, 1554]. 228 leaves, vellum, 144mm by 103mm. Contemp blindstamped brown lea over wooden bds. In black ink in a lettre batarde by "Suster adriaenke van gheele". With 3 miniatures & hundreds of small initials in gold & colors. (89) DM10,000
— Ms, prayers in Latin & German. [Upper Rhine, late 15th cent]. 309 leaves (6 lacking), 148mm by 100mm. Contemp blindstamped brown calf over wooden bds. In black ink in a lettre batarde. With numerous small & larger penwork initials in colors, 9 pp of music on a 4-line stave, & 3 woodcuts pasted in. Ownership incr of Sister Anna Maria Staeffelin. (89) DM74,000
— Ms, prayers in Latin & Old French. (88) £480
— Ms, prayers on the Passion of Christ, in German. [Germany, early 16th cent]. 4 leaves, vellum, 177mm by 132mm. In gothic script. With 9 large miniatures & 3-quarter borders on every leaf including birds, animals, grotesques, & a knight in armor. (90) £1,800
— Ms, Preces selectae usui Excell. ac Grat. Dni Hermanni Werneri L. B. d'Asseburg. [Germany, c.1780]. 50 leaves & 7 blanks, 184mm by 120mm. Contemp red mor gilt bdg. With 16 engravings pasted in. (91) DM1,200
— Ms, Prieres de la Messe. [Paris, early 18th cent]. 46 leaves, vellum, 112mm by 67mm, in 19th-cent red velvet. In dark brown ink in a fine regular rounded roman hand in imitation of ptd type. With illuminated initials & illuminated full borders throughout, elaborate tailpieces, & 10 small & 5 full-page miniatures. Attributable to Jean Pierre Rousselet. Some dampstaining. (88) £16,000
— Ms, Rosarium, with a prayer in Dutch. [Burges?, early 16th cent]. 33 leaves, 91mm by 66mm, disbound. With 2 pp of text in a small gothic bookhand & 60 full-page miniatures (2 later) for meditation on the life of Christ. (91) £8,000
— Ms, The Commendation of Souls, in Latin. (90) £700
— Ms, The Imhof Prayer Book, in Latin & Flemish. [Antwerp, 1511]. 329 leaves & 11 flyleaves, vellum, 90mm by 62mm, in contemp red velvet over wooden bds with elabotare contemp silver clasp & catch. In black ink in a fine calligraphic lettre batarde with many decorative cadels. With 15 very small miniatures, 12 Calendar miniatures in roundels in panel borders, 17 full illuminated or historiated borders, & 8 small & 11 full-page miniatures within full borders by Simon Bening (1 by anr artist). (88) £700,000
— Ms, The Prayer Book of Alessandro Farnese, in Latin & Spanish. [Antwerp, 1591]. 43 leaves (1 lacking), vellum, & paper flyleaves & 2 engravings, 118mm by 75mm. In 19th-cent purple velvet bdg with black mor slipcase. In black ink in a calligraphic italic hand with many flourishes; last 2 pp in smaller script by Luicas de Vergara [Brussels, 1597]. With 34 illuminated initials & 3 very fine pen-&-ink drawings by Johan Wiericx. Astor MS.A.27. (88) £11,500
— Ms, The Prayerbook of the Anti-Pope Clement VII. [Avignon, c.1378-83]. 75 leaves, vellum, 146mm by 110mm. 19th-cent English calf bdg. In an extremely skilful small compact gothic liturgical hand. With 3 tiny historiated initials, illuminated borders throughout in branching ivyleaf designs, 16 borders including people or angels or bas-de-page scenes, many large illu-

minated initials (2 historiated), & 15 large miniatures. (91) £200,000
— GROOT, GERHARD. - Ms, [Getijdenboek], in Dutch. [Netherlands, 15th cent]. 128 leaves (some lacking), vellum, 132mm by 100mm, in vellum bdg. In brown ink in a lettre batarde. With numerous small & 13 larger initials in colors, some with marginal extensions. (90) DM3,200
See also: Calligraphy
See also: Hoby, Sir Edward

Prelog, Vladimir
Autograph Ms, essay about his earlier article (with R. (90) DM450

Prescott, Oliver, 1731-1804
Ds, 17 Sept 1779. (90) $300

Prescott, William Hickling, 1796-1859
A Ls s (2), 10 July 1841 & 4 Nov [1847]. (88) $50
— BENTLEY, RICHARD. - 8 A Ls s, 16 May to 7 June 1843. 13 pp, size not stated. To Col. Aspinwall. Concerning the publication of Prescott's latest work. (88) $160

Presidents of the United States
— A collection of 33 Presidential signatures, from Washington to Eisenhower (A Ls s, Ls s, A Ds s & Ds s) sold at CNY on 18 May 1991 (91) $32,000
[A complete set of Presidential autographs from Washington to Carter, in 2 archival albums with related material, sold at R on 28 Oct 1989, lot 261A, for $16,000.]
[The Doheny collection of 36 autographs of 32 Presidents from Washington to Truman, mostly A Ls s, mostly inlaid, each with a port, in extra red levant mor by Riviere & Son inlaid with 5 port miniatures, sold at CNY on 22 Feb 1989, lot 2144, for $65,000 to 19th Cent Shop.]
[A collection of 40 Presidential signatures from Washington to Bush, mostly sgd cards or photographs & cut signatures, sold at R on 17 June 1989, lot 285, for $10,000.]
[Freeman, William H. - A series of 8 Marine Corps commissions for Freeman, 17 Aug 1812 to 21 Mar 1837, sgd by Presidents Madison, Monroe, Jackson & Van Buren, sold at P on 26 Oct 1988, lot 157, for $5,000.]
[A copy of The Constitution of the United States, NY, 1976, sgd by Presidents Nixon, Ford (with autograph quotation), Carter, & Reagan, including note of authentication by Senator Mark O. Hatfield, sold at Dar on 7 Feb 1991, lot 247, for $1,800.]
[The signatures of Presidents Nixon, Ford, Carter, Reagan & Bush on a card with ptd Presidential Seal & Oath of Office, 8.5 by 11 inches, Reagan's signature dated 17 Sept 1988, sold at Dar on 2 Aug 1990, lot 299, for $2,250.]
[A complete set of 39 Presidential signatures from Washington to Reagan, each framed with a Presidential medal & a port, sold at CNY on 1 Feb 1988, lot 261, for $14,000.]
[A vol of 31 clipped signatures of Presidents from Washington to F. D. Roosevelt, each mtd with a port, with signatures by Harry & Bess Truman & TLs by Eisenhower laid in, sold at CNY on 8 Dec 1989, lot 76, for $14,000.]
[An album of Presidential autographs from Washington to Franklin D. Roosevelt, mostly cut signatures, each mtd with a port, in 19th-cent French red mor gilt, presented to Franklin Roosevelt by Pierre C. Cartier & inscr by Roosevelt to his son James, 1941, sold at P on 22 May 1990, lot 107, for $24,000.]
[A reproduction of The Great Seal of the US, 7.5 by 8.5 inches, sgd by Presidents Nixon, Ford & Carter, sold at Dar on 6 Dec 1990, lot 339, for $450.]
[The signatures of Presidents Nixon, Ford, Carter & Bush, with autopen signature of President Reagan, on a White House photograph, [n.d.], 13 by 16 inches, sold at Dar on 10 Apr 1991, lot 316, for $700.]

Group photograph, Presidents Reagan, Carter, Ford & Nixon in the White House, 8 Oct 1981. 6 by 9 inches. Sgd by all 4. (91) $1,800
— Anr, Presidents Reagan, Ford, Carter & Nixon in the White House, Oct

1981. 8 by 10 inches. Sgd by all 4. (91) $1,800
— Anr, 8 Oct 1981; 4to. Richard Nixon, Gerald Ford, Jimmy Carter & Ronald Reagan; in the White House before Sadat's funeral. Sgd by all 4. Framed. (89) $3,000
— Anr, Presidents Reagan, Carter, Ford & Nixon in the White House, Oct 1981. 8 by 10 inches. Sgd by all 4. (91) $2,500
— Anr, Presidents Reagan, Ford, Carter & Nixon in the White House, Oct 1981. (91) $1,000
— Anr, Presidents Reagan, Carter, Ford & Nixon in the White House, Oct 1981. 8 by 10 inches. Sgd by all 4. (90) $2,000
— Anr, Presidents Reagan, Carter, Ford & Nixon in the White House, Oct 1981. 8 by 10 inches. Sgd by all 4. (91) $2,600
— Anr, Presidents Ford, Nixon, Carter, with Reagan speaking at lectern, 1981. (91) $800
— Anr, Presidents Reagan, Ford, Carter & Nixon in the White House, 1981. 8 by 10 inches. Sgd by all 4. (91) $1,800
— Anr, Presidents Reagan, Ford, Carter & Nixon in the White House, 1981. (91) $350

White House card, [n.d.]. (91) $160

Presidents of the United States —& First Ladies of the United States

[The signatures of Bess Truman, Mamie Eisenhower, Lady Bird Johnson, & Presidents Reagan & Ford, on a 1969 White House photograph, sold at Dar on 10 Apr 1991, lot 150, for $150.]

[The signatures of George & Barbara Bush, Ronald & Nancy Reagan, James E. & Rosalynn Carter, Gerald & Elizabeth Ford, Richard & Patricia Nixon, Claudia T. Johnson, Jacqueline Kennedy, Mamie Eisenhower & Bess Truman, mostly with wedding dates, on a 4to sheet, sold at Dar on 7 Feb 1991, lot 251, for $3,750.]

Presley, Elvis, 1935-77
[2 photographs, [c.1963], 25 cm by 20 cm, 1 sgd, inscr & mtd, sold at S on 12 Sept 1988, lot 24, for £260.]
[His Black Belt Karate Degree, issued by Kang Rhee Institute of Taekwondo, 16 Sept 1974, with a photograph, sold at CNY on 21 June 1989, lot 398, for $1,000.]
Ls, 18 Sept 1956. 1 p, 4to. To Special Projects, Inc. Notifying them that he may sue "unauthorized users and imitators" of his name & style. (91) $2,500
ANs, [19]77. (89) £300
Ds, [n.d.]. 2.5 by 4 inches; laminated card with color photograph. Concealed Weapons Permit, issued by the Denver Police Department. (89) $1,500
Menu, sgd & inscr, [n.d.]. (89) $450
Photograph, sgd, [n.d.]. (88) $170
Photograph, sgd & inscr, [n.d.]. (89) $220

Prien, Guenther, 1908-41
Photograph, sgd, 22 Feb 1941. (88) $275

Priestley, Joseph, 1733-1804
ALs, 25 June 1770. (91) £440
— 24 Aug 1794. 4 pp, folio. To the Rev. Theophilus Lindsey. Discussing his initial impressions of America, his literary pursuits, & Thomas Paine. Seal tear. (89) $1,500
— [n.d.]. (91) $500

Prior, Matthew, 1664-1721
ALs, 18 Sept [1697]. (88) $425
— 17 Oct 1697. (88) £270
— 12 Oct 1714. (89) £300
Ls, 17 Jan 1706/07. (89) £280

Pritchett, Victor Sawdon. See: Churchill, Sir Winston L. S.

Processional
— [East Anglia, c.1350]. 118 leaves (some lacking) & 2 flyleaves, vellum, 171mm by 118mm, in 19th-cent black mor gilt. In brown ink by at least 4 scribes. With numerous colored initials with penwork flourishes, some with grotesques. Including four 15th-cent leaves. (90) £3,400
— [Germany, c.1475]. 60 leaves, vellum, 167mm by 125mm, in contemp sheep over wooden bds. In brown ink in a

gothic liturgical hand; last 5 pages in a later hand. With music throughout in square black notation on 4 red staves & large calligraphic initials. (89) £2,200
— [Northern France?, c.1500]. Of Dominican use. 101 leaves, vellum, 188mm by 125mm. 17th-cent mottled calf. In brown ink in a late, uneven textura with musical neumes on 4-line staves. With over 60 calligraphic initials. (88) £1,700

Proclus, Diadochus, 410?-85
Ms, Eis ten Platonos theologian, book 5, & 2 other works; [Spain, c.1560-80]. 234 leaves, 197mm by 140mm, in 18th-cent English russia gilt. Possibly in the hand of Andreas Darmarios. The Garden Ltd. collection & Phillipps Ms.8276. (90) $31,000

Prokofiev, Sergei Sergeevich, 1891-1953
Autograph music, Cinq Melodies pour violin et piano, Op. 35b; 1925. 17 pp, folio. Reworking of earlier ptd version for voice & piano, with extensive alterations. Some annotations probably by Paul Kochanski. (90) £1,800
Collection of 4 A Ls s, 6 Ls s, & AN, 29 Sept 1920 to 9 Feb 1934. Length not stated. To Paul & Zosia Kochanski. Discussing various compositions & other professional matters. (88) $9,500
Ls, 11 July 1929. Byer collection. (90) $950
Autograph quotation, 2 bars from his 2d Piano Concerto, 1931. 11cm by 17cm (card). Sgd. (91) £1,100
— Anr, 4 bars from his ballet Romeo and Juliet; sgd & dated 1947. 1 p, 8vo. (90) DM4,600
— Anr, 6 bars from the last movement of his 3d Piano Concerto, sgd; [n.d.]. 1 p, 8vo; cut from larger sheet. (90) £1,200
Proof copy, Skazki staroy babushki (Grandmother's Tales) Op. 31, 7 Apr 1921. 11 pp, folio; interleaved. With autograph annotations; sgd. (91) £1,400

Prokosch, Frederic
[3 typescripts, The Captive (no 2 of 2 copies), 1931; The Man at the White Cape (no 1 of 3 copies), 1931; & The Flamingoes (1 of 3 copies), 1933; 8vo, in worn bds, all inscr to Siegfried

Sassoon & including 10 orig illusts, sold at S on 18 July 1991, lot 105, for £500 to Reece.]

Proudhon, Pierre-Joseph, 1809-65
ALs, 23 June [1860]. 4 pp, 4to. To P. Ch. A. Rolland. Discussing acquaintances & their political ideas. (90) DM1,500

Proust, Marcel, 1871-1922
Autograph Ms, account of a dinner at the Daudets' with Reynaldo Hahn & others; [c.1895?]. 5 pp, 4to. Some notes in anr hand. Torn & repaired. Martin collection. (90) FF32,000
Series of 24 A Ls s, [c.1895 to 1916; 1 later]. More than 100 pp, 4to & 8vo. To Maria de Madrazo, sister of his friend Reynaldo Hahn. Covering a wide range of topics. (90) £12,000
— Series of 7 A Ls s, Apr to July 1921. 52 pp, 4to. To Jacques Boulanger. Literary correspondence, discussing reactions to his work, Robert de Montesquiou, etc. Martin collection. (90) FF90,000
ALs, 23 Sept [1890]. 4 pp, 8vo. To his father. Asking about his meeting with Maupassant, complaining he cannot concentrate, etc. Martin collection. (90) FF11,000
— [2 Jan 1899]. 1 p, 12mo. To Anatole France. Praising him for his stance in the Dreyfus Affair. File holes. Sang collection & Koch Foundation. (90) $2,500
— [14 Aug 1902]. 5 pp, 8vo. To his mother. Mostly about his health. (90) DM2,800
— [c.Mar 1906]. 1 p, 8vo. To Robert [de Billy]. Informing him that he is staying at Versailles. (91) DM1,500
— [c.Sept 1906]. 4 pp, 8vo. To Georges de Lauris. About his health problems, & requesting him to postpone his visit. (91) DM3,000
— [May 1907]. (91) £600
— [Feb 1910]. (91) £1,000
— [Aug 1910?]. Koch Foundation. (90) $1,000
— [25 July 1911]. (91) £700
— [n.d.]. 4 pp, 8vo. To Mme Catusse. Commenting on the illegibility of his handwriting, & mentioning his current work & the war. (88) $1,200

— [n.d.]. 3 pp, 8vo. To [Rene Peter]. Thanking him for recommending an acquaintance. Small fold tear. (88) DM1,250

— [c.23 to 30 May 1919]. (88) £800

— [Sept 1919]. 16 pp, 8vo. To Jacques Porel. Contrasting the reception of A l'ombre des jeunes filles en fleurs with that of Du cote de chez Swann. (89) £3,500

— [c.22 Aug 1920]. (88) £800

— [Aug 1920]. 8 pp, 4to. To the Princess [Soutzo]. Regretting he did not find her at home to discuss a misunderstanding, & about other matters. (89) DM4,200

— [17 June 1921]. 8 pp, 4to. To Paul Souday. Responding to a review of his Guermantes II. Martin collection. (90) FF15,500

— [28 Feb 1922]. 15 pp, 8vo. To the Princess [Soutzo]. Interesting letter about his inability to read E. R. Curtius's book in German, his relations with Paul Morand, invitations to balls, etc. (88) DM9,000

— [8 June 1922]. (88) £700

— [23 or 24 Sept 1922]. 5 pp, 8vo. To Jacques Riviere. Concerning the publication of Albertine disparue & his feeble state of health. (89) £1,400

— [c.1 Nov 1922]. 1 p, 8vo. To Jacques Riviere. Reminding him of a book for M. Zavie. (88) DM1,400

— 2/3 Jan [n.y.]. 4 pp, 4to. To Reynaldo Hahn's mother. Thanking for news about her son. (90) DM4,000

— [n.d.] "Monday". (89) $600

— [n.d.], "Wednesday". 11 pp, 4to. To the Princess [Soutzo]. About his efforts to find the name of her hotel, & responding to her letter. (90) DM3,500

— [n.d.]. 6 pp, 8vo. To Lucien Daudet. Sending news of his poor health. Koch Foundation. (90) $1,500

— [n.d.]. (91) £700

AL, [n.d.]. (90) DM400

Photograph, sgd & inscr, [n.d.]. Reproduction of a painting showing Proust in his youth, 4.5 by 5.6 inches. Sgd & inscr to Paul Brach on mat, 7.75 by 1.1 inches. Mtd on heavy board. (88) $1,700

Prudhomme, Rene Francois Armand, 1839-1907. See: Sully Prudhomme, 1839-1907

Prutz, Robert Eduard, 1816-72
Series of 15 A Ls s, 25 Jan 1845 to 14 Aug 1857. (91) DM450

Psalms & Psalters
Ms, Ferial Psalter, with alternate verses in Latin & French. [France, c.1435]. 359 leaves (some lacking), 143mm by 98mm. Old green vellum over pastebds. In black ink in a current lettre batarde. With illuminated initials (14 large) & linefillers for every verse. (90) £2,800

— Ms, in Coptic, Psalter. [Upper Egypt, White Monastery near Sohag?, 4th - 6th cent?]. Fragment of 7 very def leaves & 2 tiny scraps only, vellum, 200mm by 157mm, in green folders. In dark brown ink in a handsome large upright Coptic uncial script. With at least one large calligraphic initial. (88) £15,000

— Ms, in Ge'ez, Psalter. (91) £380

— Ms, in German, Psalter. [Nuremberg? 20 Jan 1378] 110 leaves, 146mm by 100mm, in 15th-cent wooden bds with pink sheep back, upper cover detached. Written in brown ink in a rounded gothic bookhand, with rubrics & initials in red. (91) £17,000

— Ms, in Latin & French, Psalter, with Calendar & Book of Hours. [Brabant, c.1280]. 213 leaves, vellum, 169mm by 118mm, in rubbed vellum over pastebds gilt of c.1600. In black ink in a small gothic liturgical hand. With c.320 illuminated initials in highly burnished raised gold usually with long marginal extensions on panelled grounds, 21 large historiated initials with partial or full bar borders including faces & animals, 24 Calendar roundels, & 4 full-page miniatures, each formed of 8 pictures. (90) £360,000

— Ms, in Latin, Ferial Psalter, [Archdiocese of Cologne, late 13th cent]. 133 leaves (some lacking), vellum, 113mm by 81mm, in worn old sheep over wooden bds. In brown ink in 2 sizes of a gothic hand. With 10 very large decorated initials with elaborate

PSALMS & PSALTERS

penwork & long marginal extensions. With some headings in German. Imperf. (91) £2,800
— Ms, in Latin, Ferial Psalter & Breviary. Of Bridgettine use. [Marienwater Abbey?, Brabant, 15th cent]. 285 leaves, vellum, 183mm by 130mm. Contemp blindstamped tanned calf over wooden bds. In black ink in a regular angular gothic liturgical hand. With 20 large & very large decorated initials in colors. (88) £8,800
— Ms, in Latin, Ferial Psalter, with Calendar & Canticles. [Flanders, Grammont Abbey, 15th cent]. 149 leaves (4 blank), vellum, 121mm by 83mm. 19th-cent blindstamped dark brown mor. In dark brown ink in 2 sizes of a small lettre batarde. With 8 large initials with penwork in red & blue & 11-line initial with full penwork border. (88) £1,900
— Ms, in Latin, Ferial Psalter. [Florence, c.1450-80]. 286 leaves (1 blank), vellum, 139mm by 95mm. Full modern dark red mor by Katharine Adams with orig gilt edges elaborately gauffered & lettered. In black ink in a regular rounded gothic liturgical hand. With 6 large illuminated initials, 1 with 2-sided borders of leaves & flowers, & half-page historiated initial with colored leafy design on burnished gold ground & full-length illuminated border. (88) £4,800
— Ms, in Latin, ferial Psalter & Book of Hours. [Florence, c.1480-90]. 227 leaves & 2 flyleaves, vellum, 158mm by 107mm, in contemp blindstamped Florentine bdg of brown goatskin over wooden bds. In black ink in a regular rounded gothic hand. With 2-line initials throughout, 8 large illuminated initials & 9 six-line historiated initials all with full-length illuminated borders, & opening leaf with large historiated initial & full border including coat-of-arms. (90) £14,000
— Ms, in Latin, Ferial Psalter & Breviary of Dominican Use. [Switzerland?, Schoensteinach Abbey?, c.1320]. 355 leaves & flyleaves, vellum, 143mm by 97mm. Medieval blindstamped white lea over bevelled wooden bds. In a small gothic bookhand. With 11 large illuminated initials in burnished gold

AMERICAN BOOK PRICES CURRENT

with leafy terminals with branching red penwork often extending into margins. (90) £16,000
— Ms, in Latin. [Germany, c.1450]. 2 conjoint leaves, vellum, 390mm by 290mm. In a textura hand. With 6 penwork initials & historiated initial with marginal extension. (90) DM2,600
— Ms, in Latin, Penitential Psalms & Litany. (88) £650
— Ms, in Latin, Penitential Psalms & Litany. (88) £700
— Ms, in Latin, Psalter. [England, Glastonbury Abbey, c.1400]. 253 leaves, vellum, 108mm by 75mm. 19th-cent calf bdg. In brown ink in a fere textura script by Jon Taunton. With musical neumes on 4 staves in red & initials in blue & red throughout. (88) £6,200
— Ms, in Latin, Psalter, with Calendar, Canticles, Litany & Office for the Dead. Use of Sarum. [London?, c.1455]. 133 leaves & 2 flyleaves, vellum, 290mm by 205mm. 19th-cent English mor tooled in blind. In black & brown ink in a gothic textura. With illuminated initials throughout & 8 large historiated initials with full foliate borders. Doheny collection. (88) £52,000
— Ms, in Latin, Psalter. [Paris?, c.1270]. 1 leaf only, vellum, 140mm by 98mm. Introit to Psalm 26. In a gothic minuscule. With 12-line & six 1-line illuminated initials. Framed. (89) £1,500
— Ms, in Latin, Psalter, with Hymnal for the Temporal & Sanctoral. [Paris?, c.1300]. 350 leaves, vellum, 180mm by 123mm. Early 19th-cent green mor gilt. In dark brown ink in a gothic bookhand. With penwork initials (30 four-line) throughout, & 371 pp with rectangular musical notation on four-line red staves with text below. 3 leaves torn. Phillipps MS.1312. (89) £8,000
— Ms, in Latin, Psalter, with Canticles, Litany & Hymnal. [Brescia, late 15th cent]. Of Dominican use. 141 leaves (some lacking), vellum, 204mm by 152mm. 16th-cent blindstamped panelled calf over wooden bds. In a fine Italian liturgical hand. With music with black square notation on 4-line red staves throughout, numerous cal-

ligraphic initials with penwork decoration, & 32 historiated initials partly with page-length bar extensions. (89) £30,000

— Ms, in Latin, Psalter, with Hours of the Virgin & Office of the Dead. [Paris or Northern France, c.1400]. 225 leaves (3 lacking), vellum, 145mm by 105mm, in modern blindstanped calf over wooden bds. In brown ink in a gothic textura. With 6 seven- & 1 six-line initials in blue on burnished gold ground, & 1 full border of gold cusped baguettes. (88) £3,400

— Ms, in Latin, Psalter, with Hymns, Canticles, Litany, Prayers & Breviary. [Northern France, late 13th cent]. 234 leaves, vellum, 178mm by 116mm. Dark blue velvet bdg, c.1900. In a small gothic hand. With 20 historiated initials in gold & colors & elaborate foliate borders. Some later musical notations. (88) DM34,000

— Ms, in Latin, Psalter with Antiphons. [Northern Italy, c.1500]. 166 leaves, vellum, 175mm by 140mm. Late 16th-cent Italian calf tooled in gilt. Of Dominican use. In a rotunda hand by a single scribe. With music in brown & red ink on a 4-line stave, flourished initials throughout, historiated initial with full border & small miniature. (90) £3,200

— Ms, in Latin, Psalter, of 2d Dominican Use. [Italy, late 15th cent] 140 leaves, vellum, size not indicated, in late 19th-cent mor gilt. Historiated initial D of David with border; pen-flourished initials in purple, red, green & blue. (90) £2,800

— Ms, in Latin, Psalter. (91) £500

— Ms, in Latin, Psalter, with Canticles & Calendar. [Lower Rhineland, c.1240 & England, c.1400]. 189 leaves (7 lacking) & flyleaf, vellum, 147mm by 114mm, in def contemp bdg of oak bds re-covered with tanned lea, c.1500. In dark brown ink in a small early gothic hand. With illuminated initials throughout, 7 very large illuminated initials in designs of burnished gold on panelled grounds, & 6 full-page miniatures. Calendar added in England. Worn. (91) £18,000

— Ms, in Latin, Psalter, with Canticles, Litany & Prayers. [England, Oxford?, c.1450]. 116 leaves (3 blank) & flyleaf, vellum, 197mm by 128mm. Early 16th-cent (London) panel-stamped calf, repaired. In dark brown ink in a rounded gothic hand with humanist features. With large illuminated initials throughout & 5 very large illuminated or historiated initials with 2-sided illuminated borders. Many antiphons added in lower margins. (88) £9,500

— Ms, in Latin, Psalter. [Flanders, 2d half of 13th cent]. 2 leaves only, vellum, 177mm by 131mm. In gothic script. With illuminated linefillers including 7 drawings of animals extending into margins, & 5 four-line historiated initials in colors & highly burnished raised gold. (90) £4,400

— Ms, in Latin, Psalter, with Canticles & prayers. [Southern England, c.1450]. 124 leaves only, vellum, 272mm by 174mm, in 19th-cent English brown calf. In dark brown ink in a large compressed gothic liturgical hand. With c.150 two-line illuminated initials in burnished gold, 4 larger initials with partial borders with ivyleaf sprays extending into margins, & 5 very large initials with full borders. (90) £14,000

— Ms, in Latin, Psalter, with Calendar & Office of the Dead. [Picardy or South Flanders, late 13th cent]. 283 leaves (2 lacking), vellum, 108mm by 75mm. Worn 18th-cent mottled calf bdg. In dark brown ink in a small upright gothic liturgical hand. With initials throughout in raised burnished gold with full-length bar borders, 12 Calendar roundels & 7 large historiated initials with three-quarter illuminated borders. With copy of a letter by J. M. W. Turner in the hand of John Ruskin inside lower cover. Dampstained. (89) £45,000

— Ms, in Latin, Psalter, with Canticles & Litany. [Southern England, London?, c.1320-30]. 112 leaves (incomplete), vellum, 168mm by 120mm. Worn 16th-cent English calf gilt over wooden bds. In a gothic liturgical hand. With c.1,240 linefillers including an endless variety of animals & grotesques in red & blue penwork, 2-line illuminated initials throughout in burnished gold with full-length penwork,

& 5 historiated initials. 4 16th-cent paper leaves added at end. (91) £12,000

— Ms, in Latin, Psalter. Of Benedictine Use adapted to Cistercian Use. [Muenster, Westfalia, c.1400]. 250 leaves (4 later replacements), vellum (a few paper), 160mm by 108mm. 16th-cent tanned calf over wooden bds. In a gothic liturgical hand & a smaller bookhand; 15th-cent additions in a current bookhand. With 9 very large initials in red & blue with penwork infilling. (91) £2,200

— Ms, in Latin, Psalter, with Calendar & Book of Hours. [Tongres, Belgium, c.1252]. Use of Tongres. 232 leaves (3 lacking) & 2 flyleaves, vellum, 193mm by 130mm. Medieval bdg of wooden bds covered with tanned lea. In dark brown ink in 2 sizes of a gothic liturgical hand. With 3-line penwork initials throughout, 27 large illuminated initials on burnished gold ground (13 historiated), & 6 full-page miniatures. Abbey collection. (89) £120,000

— Ms, in Latin, Psalter. [Paris?, late 14th cent]. 21 leaves only, vellum, 199mm by 122mm. Modern blindstamped vellum bdg. In brown ink in a small gothic liturgical hand. With 37 large illuminated initials. 2 leaves with modern illuminated borders based loosely on medieval models. (89) £1,600

— Ms, in Latin, Psalter. [Diocese of Seville, early 13th cent]. 1 leaf only, vellum, 137mm by 94mm. In black ink in a small gothic hand. With large historiated initial in shades of red & green on an unraised gold ground & very large gold capitals. Mtd. (88) £2,000

— Ms, in Latin, Psalter. [Eastern France or Rhineland, late 13th cent]. 1 leaf only, vellum, 177mm by 137mm. Part of prayers & canticles. In 2 sizes of gothic script. With 4 large historiated initials in colors & burnished gold & 12 decorated line-fillers including a penwork dragon & a grotesque with a double face. Mtd. (88) £1,600

— Ms, in Latin, Psalter, with Canticles & Litany. [Flanders, c.1300]. 227 leaves (2 blank, c.31 missing) & 2 flyleaves, vellum, 110mm by 78mm, in 17th-cent dark red-brown mor gilt, repaired; in slipcase. In dark brown ink in a small gothic hand. With illuminated initals & 3-quarter bar borders for every psalm & canticle, c.50 small & 7 large historiated initials, 8 calendar miniatures, & c.116 marginal miniatures including men, animals & grotesques in a wide variety of activities. (88) £65,000

— Ms, in Latin, The Barningham Psalter, with Canticles, Litany & prayers. [Southern England, perhaps London or Bury St. Edmunds, c.1460-80]. 183 leaves & 2 flyleaves, vellum, 300mm by 225mm, in contemp bevelled wooden bds covered with white tawed lea & purple velvet. In black ink in a very large skilful formal gothic liturgical hand. With c.170 fine illuminated initials with 2-sided foliate borders, & 9 large illuminated initials with full borders in a variety of styles. Including Middle English medical recipe on flyleaf. (90) £140,000

— Ms, in Latin, The Du Boisrouvray Psalter, with Calendar, Canticles, Litany & prayers. [Amiens, c.1260]. 212 leaves (1 blank), vellum, 173mm by 122mm, in red-brown velvet over old wooden bds. In dark brown ink in a gothic liturgical hand. With linefillers throughout in elaborate geometric & ornamental designs, large illuminated initials for every psalm & canticle, 8 large historiated initials in full colors on highly burnished gold grounds with long leafy extensions in margins, 24 Calendar roundels, & 8 full-page miniatures, each divided into 2 compartments within ornamental frames. (90) £680,000

— Ms, in Latin with some additions in German, Ferial Psalter & Litany. Of Dominican use. [Middle Rhineland, 2d half of 13th cent]. 274 leaves, half-leaf & flyleaf, vellum, 99mm by 64mm. Upper cover contemp bevelled wooden board covered with red lea; lower cover modern board. In dark brown ink in a small gothic hand. With 8 large decorated initials & 2 contemp & 1 15th-cent full-page miniatures. 15 leaves 15th-cent additions. (88) £8,000

— Ms, in Latin, with additions in Middle English, Psalter. [Flanders or Artois, c.1250]. 208 leaves (5 lacking, 12 added later) & 2 flyleaves, vellum, 120mm by 90mm. 18th-cent blindstamped calf bdg. In a small gothic liturgical hand by 2 scribes. With c.180 illuminated initials in thickly raised burnished gold on red & blue grounds, often with full-length bar borders, 6 Calendar miniatures & 9 large historiated initials. (91) £26,000

— Ms, in Latin, with a few words in German, Psalter, with Calendar, Litany, Hours of the Trinity, Hours of the Virgin, Office of the Dead, & prayers. [Flanders, Brussels?, c.1250-75]. 316 leaves (1 lacking), vellum, 131mm by 95mm. 19th-cent green mor gilt bdg. In dark brown ink in several sizes of a regular gothic liturgical hand. With 13 historiated initials with decorative borders, 12 Calendar miniatures, & 7 full-page miniatures, each formed of 2 pictures. Fuerstenberg collection. (89) £400,000

— Ms, Octoechos & Psalter, in Church Slavonic. [Russia, late 18th cent]. 102 leaves (1 lacking), 195mm by 150mm, in def contemp blindstamped calf over bds. In a semi-uncial hand; partly with music. With 9 ornamental headpieces in neo-Byzantine style. Fekula Ms.602. (91) £2,200

— Ms, Penitential Psalms (7), with litany & prayer to Saint Apollonia. In Latin. [Portugal, 2d half of 16th cent] 45 leaves, 115mm by 220mm, in 18th-cent red velvet album of blank leaves. With fine cut-work text, decorative borders & ports unbound on later colored-paper backgrounds. (91) £7,000

— Ms, Psalter. [Braunschweig?, c.1239]. Single leaf, vellum, 224mm by 155mm. In dark brown & red ink in a small early gothic hand. Calendar for December, with miniature & 2 vignettes, all on burnished gold ground, & large gold monogram on blue ground. With multicompartmented polygon on verso, incorporating 6 miniatures, all in full color. Framed. (91) £240,000

— Ms, Psalter, with Appendices with various Offices, in Church Slavonic. [Russia, c.1600]. 580 leaves, 182mm by 135mm, in repaired late 17th-cent blindstamped calf over wooden bds. In semi-uncial & cursive hands by at least 5 different scribes. With illuminated headpiece & full-page illuminated miniature. Fekula Ms.785. (91) £8,000

— Ms, The Psalter of Joan of Navarre, in Latin. [Paris, c.1220-25]. Single leaf, vellum, 259mm by 167mm. In black ink in a handsome early gothic liturgical hand. With 30 very fine versal initials & linefillers & 3 large historiated initials with colored marginal extensions. (90) £11,000

— Ms, The Psalter of Francois de Dinteville, in Latin; ferial Psalter. [Auxerre or Paris?, c.1525]. 181 leaves & flyleaf, vellum, 273mm by 176mm. Blindstamped black mor bdg by Riviere & Son, c.1900. In black ink in a skillful rounded roman hand in imitation of ptd type. With small illuminated initials throughout, 9 large miniatures in colors & gold within frames inscr with scriptural texts, & 9 achievements of arms, altered in 16th cent. Abbey collection. (89) £90,000

— Ms, The Psalter of Maria Plettenberg, in Latin. [Cologne, 2d half of 15th cent]. 198 leaves, vellum, 134mm by 93mm. Blindstamped dark red pigskin over wooden bds, dated 1598. In dark brown ink in a small gothic bookhand. With 4 very large painted initials with full-length penwork & 3 very large illuminated initials with full or 3-quarter illuminated borders. Including many late 16th-cent additions on 32 paper leaves. (90) £10,000

— SPANISH FORGER. - Ms, Psalm 77, [early 20th cent]. Bifolium, vellum, 181mm by 112mm. With illuminated miniature & four-line historiated inital within 3-quarter baguette border. Framed. (89) £400

Pseudo-Euclid. See: Sacrobosco, Johannes

Puccini, Giacomo, 1858-1924
Autograph Ms, plan for the Canzona di Doretta from La Rondine, [c.1912]. (88) £420

— Autograph Ms, poem, 20 lines beginning "...Il sor Doman Barducci", [n.d.]. (88) £300

— Autograph Ms, poem, 28 lines referring to the librettist Adami & the recently begun war, 13 Nov [1]914. (88) £300

Autograph music, collection of 17 early marches, waltzes, organ works & sketches, [c.1875], 36 pp, folio. Apparently unpbd. Some incomplete or annotated in anr hand, possibly by Carlo della Nina. (89) £10,000

— Autograph music, draft of part of Act 2, Scene 2 of Madama Butterfly, [1902 or 1903]. 1 p, c.34cm by 27cm. 12 bars in short score, notated in pencil on 10 staves; with revisions. (90) £8,000

— Autograph music, draft of the opening of the Flower Duet in Madama Butterfly, Act 2; [1902 or 1903]. 1 leaf, 34cm by 27cm; trimmed. 9 bars, notated on 3 systems of 3 & 4 staves. In pencil. (91) £7,000

— Autograph music, opening 13 bars of La fanciulla del West, sgd, inscr & dated May 1908. 2 pp, folio. Working draft in piano score, notated on 3 systems per page, 3 staves each. (89) $17,000

Collection of 2 A Ls s, AL, & 7 telegrams, [c.1895] to 1918. (90) £500

— Collection of ALs & autograph quotation, sgd, 5 Aug 1905 & 1913. 2 pp, 8vo & 9cm by 7.5cm (card). To Sig. Mola, commenting on a work submitted. 2 bars from Mi chiamano Mimi. (90) £1,300

— Collection of ALs & ANs, 1 Oct 1924 & [n.d.]. (88) £600

Series of 3 A Ls s, 31 July [18]99 to [12 Oct 1909]. 6 pp, 8vo. To Cosimo Pavone. Reporting the imminent completion of Tosca, ordering whisky & sweaters, etc. Including 2 ink sketches. (91) £1,100

— Series of 12 A Ls s, 1903 to 1922. 16 pp, various sizes (3 on visiting cards). To Attilio Bisio. About the success of La Fanciulla del West in New York, boats, motorcars, etc. With anr. (88) £2,100

A Ls s (2), 21 Feb [19]19 & 21 Oct [19]24. (88) £520

ALs, 14 Oct 1893. 3 pp, 8vo. To "Carissimo Floridin". About the German Ed of Manon Lescaut & the 1st performance scheduled for 1 Nov at Hamburg. (88) DM1,500

— 10 Aug [18]98. (88) £450
— [n.d.]. (88) $275
— 17 Sept 1903. 4 pp, 8vo. To Carlo Paladini. About Madama Butterfly, a quarrel with the librettist Giacosa, the pain in his leg, etc. (90) £1,500
— 14 Mar 1904. 1 p, folio. To Pavone. Requesting writing paper, & mentioning the failure of his Madama Butterfly at Milan. (90) DM1,850
— 9 Mar 1905. 1 p, 8vo. To G. Marcout. Congratulating him on a performance of Tosca. (91) $1,300
— 9 Mar 1905. 1 p, 8vo. To Giovanni Marcoux. Expressing pleasure about the success of Tosca at The Hague. (88) DM1,400
— 26 Dec [19]06. (88) £480
— 25 Mar 1907. (91) $850
— 29 Jan 1909. To Sybil Seligman. About the "Doria Affair." (91) $2,750
— 28 June 1909. (90) DM600
— 15 Mar 1911. (90) £400
— 26 May [19]11. (91) £800
— 19 Aug [19]11. (88) £300
— 27 Feb [19]17. (88) £220
— 17 May 1921. (88) $290
— 22 Mar [19]23. (88) £380
— 5 Oct [n.y.]. (91) DM650
— [n.d.]. (91) $400

AL, 14 Nov 1913. (90) DM650

Autograph postcard, sgd, 3 Nov 1900. (88) DM450
— 25 Dec 1907. (89) DM430
— [n.d.]. (89) DM560

AN, 16 July 1900. (89) DM420

Autograph quotation, 2 bars of Mi chiamano Mimi, sgd & dated 6 Oct [18]96. (88) £800

— Anr, 2 bars of Mi chiamano Mimi, sgd & dated 14 Aug [18]97. 1 p, 20cm by 13.5cm. (91) £2,000

— Anr, 5 bars from La Boheme, 25 Mar 1898. 1 p, 4to. Sgd & inscr to Maria Rovinazzi. (90) DM4,000

— Anr, 2 bars from Mi chiamano Mimi, sgd ; 7 July 1904. (91) £1,000

— Anr, 2 bars from the love duet of La Boheme; sgd, inscr to Sig. Weber & dated 1 Nov [19]07. 1 p, 8vo. (89) $3,000

— Anr, 3 bars from La Boheme, 31 May 1911. 1 p, 8vo. Sgd & inscr to M.

Reynolds. Framed with a port. (91) $2,000
— Anr, 2 bars from La Fanciulla del West, sgd & dated 1913. (88) £800
— Anr, 2 bars of Mi chiamano Mimi, sgd & dated 1916. 7cm by 11cm (card). (90) £1,500
— Anr, 3 bars from the aria "Senza Mamma" in Suor Angelica, sgd & dated 1919. (90) £900
— Anr, 3 bars, idea in un pomeriggio, [n.d.]. (91) DM500

Photograph, sgd, [c.1890s]. (91) $800
— Anr, Dec 1904. (88) DM950
— Anr, [1905]. (91) £550
— Anr, [5 Aug 1915]. 25cm by 17cm. Inscr to Francesco Branda in anr hand. Mtd. (90) £1,200
— Anr, [n.d.]. (91) £160
— Anr, [n.d.]. (89) £450

Photograph, sgd & inscr, 14 Sept [18]97. (90) £500
— Anr, 20 June [18]98. 16cm by 10.5cm. Inscr to Mme Artot Padilla. (91) £1,300
— Anr, 14 Aug [1]905. (90) £550
— Anr, 16 Aug [1]905. (90) £950
— Anr, Mar 1907. 19cm by 15cm (including mount). Lighting a cigarette. Inscr to Sybil Seligman. (91) £4,200
— Anr, June 1907. 28cm by 22cm. Inscr to Sybil Seligman, with 4 musical quotations on mount. (91) £3,800
— Anr, 1907. 15cm by 10.5cm. Inscr to Selma Kurz. (89) £2,300
— Anr, 24 Feb 1910. 145mm by 98mm. Half length; inscr to Frau Storch. (90) DM1,400
— Anr, 1918. (91) £160
— Anr, Jan 1919. (91) £725
— Anr, 1920. Postcard. Full length; inscr to Fanny Basch-Mahler. (90) DM1,150
— Anr, [n.d.] 20cm by 15cm. (89) £420

Ptd photograph, 1907. (88) $425
— Anr, [n.d.]. (90) DM900
— CICIOLO, R. O. - Orig drawing, charcoal & pencil port of Puccini, 1908. 14cm by 9cm (postcard). Sgd & inscr by Puccini. (91) £550
— MOEKERK, HERMANN. - Orig drawing, charcoal port of Puccini, 1921. 28cm by 21cm. Sgd by Puccini. Framed. (89) £700
— TOSTI, FRANCESCO PAOLO. - ALs, 28 Jan 1909. 2 pp, 8vo. To Giulio Ricordi. Discussing the effects of Doria Manfredi's suicide on Puccini. (89) DM450

Puccini, Giacomo, 1858-1924 —& Others
[The signatures of Puccini & the cast of the 1st production of La Fanciulla del West, including Caruso & Toscanini, 10 Dec 1910, on a copy of the 1st Ed of the vocal score, with related material, sold at S on 21 Nov 1990, lot 208, for £5,000 to What.]

Puccini, Michele, 1864-93
Autograph music, collection of varied drafts of songs, suites for piano, studies in harmony, counterpoint, etc., some sgd; [c.1881-84]. (91) £500

Pueckler-Muskau, Hermann, Fuerst von, 1785-1871
ALs, [June 1855?]. (88) DM340
— [n.d.]. (91) DM200
— [n.d.]. (90) DM220

Pugin, Augustus Welby Northmore, 1812-52 —& Others
Original drawings, 78 Gothic architectural studies of Thornbury, Glastonbury & Wells, 12 sgd by Pugin, 1831 & 1832. On folio sheets, in half-calf bdg. Mostly in pencil & pen-&-ink. Executuded in connection with A. C. Pugin's Examples of Gothic Architecture. (88) £1,900

Pulaski, Casimir, Count, c.1748-79
ALs, 18 June 1778. 1 p, folio. To Col. Hoppe. Asking that courtesy be shown to Mr. Couch, Colonel of his legion. (91) $7,000

Pullman, George Mortimer, 1831-97
ALs, 8 May 1866. 2 pp, 4to. To Gilbert, Brest & Co. Ordering 2 railroad cars & specifying terms. (91) $2,200

Punto, Giovanni, Pseud of Johann Wenzel Stich, 1746-1803
Autograph sentiment, "Frauend die Hoerner sind besser zu Hoern, alss die selbe zu Tragen...", sgd & dated 8 Dec 1799. 1 p, 8vo. Inscr in a contemp hand. (90) DM4,000

PURCELL

Purcell, Henry, 1659-95

Autograph music, transcription of a canon Miserere mei, Domine, in 10 parts by Dr. John Bull, [c.1680]. 2 pp, folio. In brown ink on 2 systems each of 10 staves. In Ms also containing music by Orlando Gibbons, John Coprario & Monteverdi; in all 27 pp, in limp vellum wraps. (88) £16,000

Purrmann, Hans, 1880-1966

Collection of 2 A Ls s & Ds, 24 Nov 1956, 2 Feb 1964 & [n.d.]. (88) DM540

ALs, 28 Oct 1946. 4 pp, 4to. To Mr. Rosin. Reflecting about the war, the collective & individual guilt of Germans, friends & acquaintances, & current problems. (88) DM1,800

— 18 Apr 1947, 4 pp, 4to. To Mr. Rosin. About an invitation to NY, problems concerning the reception of his work, etc. (88) DM1,900

— 7 Dec 1954. (90) DM1,000

— 18 Apr 1955. 5 pp, 4to. To Mr. Rosin. Commenting on contemp art & artists in Germany. (90) DM2,200

Ls, 6 Oct 1947. 3 pp, 4to. To Mr. Rosin. Commenting about the German state of mind, Hermann Hesse, Matisse, & others. (88) DM1,400

Purvis, Melvin H.

Collection of ALs & check, sgd, 9 Feb 1944 & [n.d.]. (91) $150

Check, sgd, 4 Aug 1939. (91) $60

Pusey, Edward Bouverie, 1800-82

Autograph Ms, discourse on virginity, referring to Hebrew & Arab writings; [n.d.]. (91) $110

Pushkin, Aleksandr Sergyeevich, 1799-1837

Autograph Ms, poem, beginning "On the hills of Georgia", [1829]. 1 p, 4to. 8 lines. (91) £34,000

Original drawing, city policeman & street sweeper, [c.1813 - 1814]. 1 p, 4to. In pencil, sgd. (91) £26,000

ALs, 20 July [1834]. 1 p, folio. To Alexandre Vattemare. Informing him of Zagoskin's reply concerning performances in Moscow. In French. (89) £30,000

AMERICAN BOOK PRICES CURRENT

Putnam, Israel, 1718-90

Ls, 12 Jan 1779. (89) $950

Ds, 10 Jan 1766. (88) $210

— 1 Feb 1777. (89) $500

See also: Connecticut

Putnam, Rufus, 1738-1824

ALs, 18 Nov 1790. (89) $850

Ds, 1 Feb 1779. (91) $450

— 17 Apr 1797. (90) $320

— 29 Mar 1800. (91) $100

Puvis de Chavannes, Pierre, 1824-98

Series of 6 A Ls s, [5 Apr 1892] to Feb 1898, & [n.d.]. (90) DM460

Pyle, Howard, 1853-1911

ALs, 13 Mar 1881. (91) $425

Autograph sentiment, sgd, inscr to Angel de Cora, 2 Sept [18]98. (90) $150

Q

Quaglio, Domenico, 1787-1837

ALs, 23 Oct 1833. (90) DM280

Quakers

[Shackleton Family. - A collection of several hundred letters written by & to members of the family, mostly c.1710 to 1843, chiefly written from Ireland & Northern England, about family & local news & religious affairs, sold at S on 15 Dec, lot 281, for £6,000.]

Document, 18 July 1760. (91) $55

Quarto Toys Series

Original drawings, (207), in ink, watercolor & pencil, by various artists, for 34 titles in the series; 1918 to 1924. (90) £550

R

Raabe, Wilhelm, 1831-1910

[A group of autograph Mss, 16 pp, 4to & 8vo, including sketches for his story Das Odfeld, [1886/87], a list of his works, etc., sold at star on 4 Apr 1991, lot 347, for DM2,600.]

Autograph Ms (2), transcripts of the Dutch version of 2 poems from his novel Die Leute aus dem Walde; 29 Apr & 3 May 1869. (90) DM900

Autograph Ms, notes recording receipt of

proofs for his work Der Daeumling, 24 May to 19 Nov 1871. (90) DM320
— Autograph Ms, poem expressing congratulations to Herr & Frau Mueller, 21 Feb 1884. 1 p, 8vo. 18 lines, sgd in text. Including pen-&-ink sketch. (90) DM1,500
— Autograph Ms, preface to Der Heilige Born, 2d Ed; Feb 1891. 3 pp, 8vo. Sgd at end. Ptr's copy. (90) DM1,700
Collection of ALs & 2 autograph postcards, sgd, 4 Oct 1910, & 1909 & 1910. (89) DM760
ALs, 12 Sept 1869. 2 pp, 8vo. Recipient unnamed. Saying his latest work is too serious to appeal to readers of the "Album". (88) DM1,300
— 7 Nov 1872. (90) DM750
— 20 Sept 1878. (91) DM800
— 25 Jan 1880. 2 pp, 8vo. To [the pbr Westermann]. Discussing the fee for Das Horn von Wanza. (90) DM1,600
— 10 Feb 1880. (89) DM900
— 27 Nov 1903. (91) DM650
Series of 3 autograph postcards, sgd, 31 Dec 1884 to 31 Dec 1888. (90) DM650
Photograph, sgd & inscr, 11 Apr 1864. (90) DM700
Signature, 1880. (90) DM280

Rabener, Gottlieb Wilhelm, 1714-71
ADs, 19 Aug 1763. (90) DM340

Rabi, Isaac, 1898-1988
Autograph Ms, scientific paper, The Moments of the Light Nuclei, [n.d.]. 10 pp (1 typescript), 4to. With related material. (90) DM3,200

Rachel Felix, Elisa, 1821-58
ALs, 7 July 1842. (91) DM860
— 15 June 1848. (91) $200
— 15 Jan 1852. (91) $110
— [n.d.]. (90) DM300

Rachmaninoff, Sergei, 1873-1943
Autograph music, arrangement for violin & piano of the "Gopak" from Mussorgsky's Sorochintsy Fair, sgd S. R. & dated 13 Mar [1925]. 6 pp, folio. In black ink on up to 12 staves per page. With several revisions; some annotations in the hand of Paul Kochanski. (89) $21,000
ALs, Mar 1899. (90) £700

— 22 Sept 1908. 1 p, 8vo. To [a German musical society?]. Giving details of the scoring & timing of his [2d] Symphony. In German. (90) £1,700
Ls, 25 Jan 1934. (90) DM480
— 24 Aug 1934. Byer collection. (90) $425
— 19 Nov 1937. (91) $350
— 22 Apr 1940. (89) DM760
— 22 Apr 1940. (90) DM750
— 1 Nov 1940. (90) £550
Autograph quotation, opening of his 2d Symphony, sgd; 7 Nov 1908. 8vo. In an album also sgd by Casals, Ysaye, Kubelik & others, [c.1907-19]. (91) £1,200
— Anr, Prelude pour Piano Op. 3, opening 2 bars; sgd & dated 9 Nov 1908. 1 p, 8vo. (90) £1,400
Concert program, Boston, 22 Feb 1919. (91) $475
— Anr, Mrs. (89) DM280
— Anr, sgd, for a performance at Baltimore Lyric Theatre, 21 Mar 1928. (88) $130
Photograph, sgd & inscr, 1927. (90) $650
— Anr, 1929. (88) £180
Signature, [n.d.]. (89) DM850

Racine, Jean Baptiste, 1639-99
ALs, 4 Mar 1660. 2 pp, 8vo. To his sister. About his failure to write & the purchase of a muff. (89) £7,500
— 4 Mar 1698. 5 pp, 4to. To Mme de Maintenon. Defending himself against suspicions of Jansenism & asking her to intervene with the King on his behalf. Endorsed by recipient. (90) £40,000
— 15 Aug [n.y.]. 1 p, 8vo. To Nicolas Boileau-Despreaux. Arranging a meeting. Tipped to larger leaf, with trans. Barrett collection. (89) $4,500
AL, 28 Sept [1683]. 2 pp, 8vo. To his sister Marie Riviere. Announcing his visit. (91) £4,500

Rackham, Arthur, 1867-1939
Original drawings, (3), to illus Stories of the Table Round, ptd in Little Folks, 1902. 3 pp, 244mm by 176mm. In ink & watercolor; sgd. Framed together. (90) £26,000
Original drawing, a sprite pulling at the ear of an ugly monster, to illus The Tempest in Lamb's Tales from Shake-

speare; [1927]. 159mm by 93mm. In ink & watercolor; sgd. Framed. (90) £2,800
— Original drawing, animals & birds standing at a doorway, to illus Aesop's Fables, 1912. In ink & watercolor; sgd. 224mm by 170mm; framed. (90) £12,000
— Original drawing, boy seated on the bough of a tree, for the 2d Ed of Peter Pan in Kensington Gardens. 256mm by 353mm, ink & watercolor, sgd & dated 1912, framed. (88) £2,800
— Original drawing, cat sitting in the road, to illus The Bremen Town Musicians from the Grimms's Fairy Tales, [before 1900]. (88) £420
— Original drawing, girl covered in pitch, to illus Mother Hulda in the Grimms' Fairy Tales, 1900. 216mm by 402mm. In ink; sgd. Framed. (89) £2,400
— Original drawing, girl greeted by a young man, to illus Ashenputtel in the Grimms' Fairy Tales, 1909. Sgd; framed. (88) £2,500
— Original drawing, girl in ragged clothes, to illus Tattercoats in English Fairy Tales, 1918. 210mm by 174mm. In ink & watercolor; sgd. Framed. (89) £3,600
— Original drawing, man protecting a girl from a dragon, to illus Cesarino and the Dragon in The Allies Fairy Book, 1916. 248mm by 188mm. In ink & watercolor; sgd. Framed. (89) £8,500
A Ls s (2), 26 Oct 1898 & 7 Feb 1905. (89) £280
ALs, 5 Dec 1907. (91) £280
— 24 Feb [19]13. 8 pp, 8vo. To the pbr Crowninshield. Discussing drawings for a children's book. (91) $1,200

Radetzky, Josef, Graf von, 1766-1858
ALs, 27 Apr 1835. (90) DM360
— 30 Sept 1842. (91) DM420

Radetzky, Joseph, Graf von, 1766-1858
ALs, 6 Jan 1845. (90) DM520
— 1 Mar 1853. (88) DM620
Ls, 14 Jan 1839. (90) DM220
Ds, 15 Mar 1849. (88) DM360

Radziwill, Elisa, Princess, 1803-34
ALs, 12 Aug 1823. Schroeder collection. (89) DM700

Radziwill, Franz, 1895-1983
ALs, 12 Apr 1960. (90) DM220

Radziwill, Luise, Princess, 1770-1836
ALs, 1 Sept 1787. (90) DM320

Raeder, Erich, 1876-1960
Collection of ALs & photograph, sgd, 6 Nov 1957. (90) DM520
Ls, 28 Nov 1936. (90) $200

Raemaekers, Louis, 1869-1956
Original drawings, (2), 1 to illus The Great War. (90) £480

Raft, George. See: West, Mae & Raft

Raimund, Ferdinand, 1790-1836
Autograph Ms, poem, Rhapsodie, 54 lines; [n.d.]. (88) £550
— Autograph Ms, poem, Rhapsodie; [n.d.]. 4 pp, 4to. Sgd. (90) DM4,700

Rainey, William
Original drawings, (29), mostly to illus novels by Charles Dickens, [n.d.]. (89) £450

Rain-in-the-Face
Photograph, sgd, [1893]. (89) $650

Rains, Claude, 1889-1967
Photograph, sgd, [n.d.]. (88) $55

Raleigh, Carew, 1605-1666
Ds, 15 Feb 1659. (89) £60

Raleigh, Walter, Sir, 1552?-1618. See: Gorges, Arthur & Raleigh

Rameau, Jean Philippe, 1683-1764
ALs, 10 Jan 1740. 1 p, 4to. To M. Bazin. Acknowledging receipt of 5,000 livres for the sale of his family home. (90) £16,000
Ds, 29 Oct 1753. 2 pp, 4to. Signature as receipt under a pay order by the [Paris] Bureau de la Ville, sgd by de Bernage, 22 Sept 1753, for 2,400 livres payable to Rameau for a revision of his opera Castor et Pollux. With related material. (90) DM15,000

Ramin, Guenther, 1898-1956
A Ls s (2), 5 Jan 1928 & 27 Apr 1936. (90) DM460

Ramler, Karl Wilhelm, 1725-98
ALs, 16 Feb 1776. (91) DM460
— 24 Apr 1787. 3 pp, 4to. To an unnamed pbr. About putting Salomon Gessner's Idyllen to verse. (88) DM2,800
— 25 Feb 1791. (89) DM420
— 25 Feb 1791. (90) DM300

Ramsay, Andrew Michael, 1686-1743
ALs, 30 Mar [1728]. (90) $400

Ramsay, Sir William, 1852-1916
ALs, 16 Mar 1895. (89) DM340
— 24 Aug 1911. (91) DM280

Ramuz, Charles Ferdinand, 1878-1947.
See: Stravinsky, Igor & Ramuz

Randolph, Edmund, 1753-1813
ALs, 24 July 1794. Alexander collection. (90) $400
Ds, 9 Dec 1786. (88) $70
— [1794]. (89) $110
Franking signature, [21 Aug 1794]. Alexander collection. (90) $160

Randolph, George Wythe, 1818-67
Ls, 28 July 1862. (90) $325

Randolph, John, 1773-1833
ALs, 31 Mar 1806. Alexander collection. (90) $250
ADs, 2/14 Sept 1830. (90) $200

Randolph, Peyton, c.1721-1775
ADs, 7 Feb [n.y.]. (91) $900

Ranke, Leopold von, 1795-1886
Autograph Ms, fragment from a work about German emperors; [n.d.]. (91) DM270
ALs, 9 Oct 1825. (90) DM650
— 10 Jan 1829. 4 pp, 8vo. To Bartholomaeus Kopitar. Reporting about his archival studies in Venice. Slightly def. (89) DM1,400
— 12 Apr 1831. (88) DM440
— 1 May 1838. (91) DM200
— 15 Feb 1853. (91) DM800
— 28 Feb 1853. 1 p, folio. Recipient unnamed. Requesting him to forward a letter to the King of Bavaria & explaining his reasons for declining an offer to teach in Munich. With related material. (89) DM1,100

Ransom, Thomas
ALs, 22 May [1863]. 1 p, folio. To Brigadier-Gen. McPherson. Written during the height of the battle of Vicksburg & describing it. (91) $5,600

Ransome, Arthur, 1884-1967
Corrected page proofs, biography, Oscar Wilde. (91) £700

Rantzau, Gerhard von, 1558-1627
Ds, 14 May 1613. 1 p, folio. Passport for Karsten [Eucke?]. (91) DM2,200

Rantzau, Heinrich von, 1526-98
Ds, 7 Apr 1589. 1 p, folio. Passport for Luetke & Hanns Johansen. (91) DM3,500

Rantzau, Josias, Marshal of France, 1609-50
ALs, [Feb 1642?]. 2 pp, 4to. To [Richelieu?]. Petitioning for his protection. In French. (90) DM2,500

Raphael, Frederic
Typescript, novel, Glittering Prizes, fragments; [n.d.]. (88) £300

Rasputin, Grigory Efimovich, 1872?-1916
Autograph quotation, proverb, 4 lines; sgd. 8vo. (88) $7,000
Autograph sentiment, sgd, [c.1914]. 1 p, 8vo. "Bright light does not come from the dark coffers". With note of authentication. (91) £2,600

Rathbone, Basil, 1892-1967
Signature, [n.d.]. (91) $120

Rathenau, Walther, 1867-1922
ALs, 27 June 1915. (90) DM500
Ds, Oct 1920. 1 p, folio. Certificate for 39,000 shares of preferred stock of the Allgemeine Electricitaets-Gesellschaft, Berlin, sgd as board member. Cancellation affecting signature. (90) DM1,200

Rauch, Christian Daniel, 1777-1857
ALs, 30 Oct 1828. 3 pp, 4to. To Alfred Nicolovius. Reporting about his recent visit with Goethe in Weimar. Albrecht collection. (91) SF2,800
— 2 Nov 1833. (88) DM500

RAUCH

— 22 Jan 1844. (91) DM360
— 2 Sept 1847. (89) DM560
— 13 Dec 1855. (90) DM380
— 6 May 1857. (89) DM350

Raumer, Friedrich von, 1781-1873
ALs, 5 Mar 1844. (90) DM530
— 23 July 1848. (91) DM220

Ravel, Maurice, 1875-1937
Autograph music, Pavane pour Mimie et Jean Godebski, comprising an early version of Pavane de la Belle au Bois dormant, from Ma mere l'oye, 20 Sept 1908. 2 pp, folio. Scored for piano duet, with unpbd autograph fingering. Sgd. (91) £19,000
Collection of 2 A Ls s & autograph postcard, sgd, 30 Nov 1902 to 8 Aug 1933. 6 pp, 8vo. To Marie & Jane Gaudin. About his exams, driving his truck in the War, his medical problems, etc. (90) £1,200
— Collection of ALs & autograph postcard, sgd, [1906 & 1908]. (89) £750
— Collection of 2 A Ls s & autograph postcard, sgd, 16 Dec 1910 to 7 Apr 1932. 4 pp, various sizes. To Mme Grunwaldt, about a meeting. To Hans Fisher, sending greetings to the Cercle amical franco-allemand. To M. Gil-Marcheux, requesting help in a financial matter. Rosen collection. (89) $1,600
ALs, [c.1896-1900]. (91) £650
— [c.1904]. (91) £800
— 27 Feb 1906. 4 pp, 8vo. To the pbr Demets. Giving instructions about complimentary copies of his work Miroirs & related matters. Ammann collection. (90) DM2,400
— 7 Mar 1906. 2 pp, 8vo. To Jane Bathori. About the postponement of a concert. (89) DM1,050
— 27 July 1906. 2 pp, 8vo. Recipient unnamed. Requesting him to set anr date for the signing of a document. (88) DM1,200
— 14 Sept [19]07. (91) £800
— 2 Jan 1912. 4 pp, 8vo. Recipient unnamed. Discussing the staging of Ma Mere l'Oye. (90) DM2,900
— 4 Jan 1912. (89) £500
— 18 Mar [19]15. (88) £800
— 12 June [19]16. 3 pp, 8vo. Recipient

AMERICAN BOOK PRICES CURRENT

unnamed. Offering congratulations on his marriage, sending 2 musical quotations, mentioning medical complaints, etc. (91) £1,700
— 18 Feb [19]17. (88) £600
— 17 Sept [19]29. (88) £440
— 26 June 1923. (90) £800
— 3 Oct 1924. (90) £800
— 11 Dec 1925. 1 p, 8vo. To Zdenka Duschwitz. Expressing thanks, & regretting he did not meet her. (88) DM1,400
— 22 Apr 1926. (91) £725
— 7 Nov 1927. (90) £900
— 22 Jan 1929. 2 pp, 8vo (lettercard). To an unnamed friend. Regretting his illness makes it impossible to see him before his departure. (88) DM1,200
— "Thursday 26" [n.y.]. (89) £320
— [n.d.]. (90) £450

Ls, 23 May 1929. (88) £280

Collection of autograph postcard, sgd, & photograph, 31 Dec [19]27 & 1 Jan [19]28. (91) £600
Autograph postcards (2), sgd, [3 Aug 1905] & 13 July 1906. To Mme Delage. About his holidays, & referring to her husband's "lignes desesperees". (90) DM1,100
Autograph postcard, sgd, 27 Sept 1924. To [Helene] Jourdan-Morhange. Saying he will see her on Oct 15. (89) DM1,050
Autograph quotation, 4 bars from Ma mere l'Oye, Mar 1919. 1 p, 17.5cm by 20cm. Sgd & inscr to Pierre Bourdillon. Scored for string quartet. (91) £1,500
Concert program, 3 May 1922. 3 pp, 8vo. Including ptd caricature of Ravel, sgd & inscr with autograph musical quotation; 2 bars. With related material. (90) £1,600

Signature, Nov 1923. (90) $225

Rawlins, John Aaron, 1831-69
Ls, 12 Mar 1869. (88) $65

Ray, James E.
Ls, 21 Apr 1980. (90) $80

Raymundus de Penaforte, c.1185-1275
Ms, Summa de Casibus Poenitentia, with the Gloss of Guillaume de Rennes. [Paris?, late 13th cent]. 406 leaves, vellum, 168mm by 113mm. Late 15th-cent panel-stamped bdg by Anthony van Gavere. In a regular gothic hand. With 5 illuminated initials in colors & gold with white tracery. (89) £17,000

Read, George, Signer from Delaware
ADs, 22 July 1784. (88) $175

Reagan, John Henninger, 1818-1905
ALs, 19 Nov 1882. (91) $85

Reagan, Nancy. See: Reagan, Ronald & Reagan

Reagan, Ronald
Typescript, radio program, Youth Employment, [1980]. (89) $110
— Typescript, story, The Bear Who Wasn't There, [n.d.]. (91) $700

A Ls s (2), 28 Apr & 13 Nov 1948. 3 pp, 4to. To Doris Lilly. Chatty letters regretting he cannot see her. Sgd Ronnie. With 4to photograph of Reagan & Lilly in a nightclub. (89) $4,000
— A Ls s (2), 12 July & 16 Nov 1967. (88) $600

ALs, 31 Jan [1955]. (91) $450
— 7 June [1958]. (90) $500
— 10 July [1961]. 2 pp, 4to. To Miss Merced. Discussing an article by Drew Pearson, explaining his views on public aid for medical costs, & disclaiming intention to seek public office. On misptd personal letterhead with autograph correction. (88) $2,800
— 23 July [1961]. 2 pp, 4to. To Miss Merced. About libel laws & the difficulties in demanding corrections from the press. On misptd personal letterhead with autograph correction. (88) $1,600
— 1 June 1967. 1 p, 4to. To George Catkin. As Governor of California, explaining his views on China. Draft; sgd R.R. (89) $1,800
— 14 June 1967. 1 p, 4to. To the 1st Grade at St. Elizabeth's School in Van Nuys. Draft, trying to explain his views about abortion. Sgd RR. (88) $1,600
— 27 Nov [19]67. (89) $225
— [3 Jan 1968]. (90) $250
— 20 Feb 1968. 1 p, 4to. To Dwight D. Eisenhower. Draft, sending a memorandum (not present) & joking about a golf game. Sgd Ron. (89) $2,000
— 7 June 1968. (89) $800
— 10 July 1968. 1 p, 4to. To Spruille Braden. Draft, expressing concern about Communism. Sgd Ron. At foot of Braden's letter addressed to him, 24 June 1968. With secretarial notations. (89) $1,400
— 30 Aug 1968. (90) $325
— 16 Sept 1975. 1 p, 4to. To Brad Wilde. Responding to an inquiry about his concept of the Presidency. (89) $11,000
— 3 Sept 1977. 1 p, 4to. To Jeffrey Benziger. Responding to an inquiry about his favorite TV show. (91) $1,400
— [1984]. 1 p, 8vo. To "Dear Spencer". Thanking for a record of the music for the film Kings Row & saying it "remains the best picture I ever played in." On Air Force One letterhead. With autograph sentiment sgd, [1984], 2 lines, on cardboard jacket of the record. (88) $12,000
— 22 Oct [n.y.]. (91) $400

Collection of Ls & photograph, 31 Jan 1968. (91) $170

Ls, 6 Nov 1945. (91) $550
— 14 June 1967. 1 p, 4to. To Gary Lorenz. Responding to a letter suggesting that he seek the Republican Presidential nomination. Framed with a photograph. (90) $2,200
— 27 Feb 1974. (91) $1,000
— 26 Feb 1980. (91) $500
— 25 July 1980. (88) $170
— 2 Aug 1983. (91) $600
— 10 June 1986. (88) $350
— 20 Feb 1987. (91) $500
— [n.d., but as President]. 1 p, 4to. To David Miller. About George Armstrong Custer. (91) $4,000

ANs, 13 June 1967. 1 p, 4to, removed from a larger leaf. To Doreen Fassio. Replying to a joke about birth control. Draft; sgd R.R. Stapled to fragment of envelope with Miss Fassio's communication. (89) $1,400

Autograph sentiment, [n.d.]. (91) DM300

REAGAN

Check, accomplished & sgd, 15 July 1948. (91) $800

Franking signature, [20 Jan 1981]. On postmarked, unaddressed Inauguration Day envelope. Including authentication by Tip O'Neill. (91) $1,200

Photograph, sgd & inscr, [2 Oct 1941]. (90) $180

— Anr, [n.d.]. (91) $170
— Anr, [n.d.]. (91) $130
— Anr, [n.d.]. (91) $140
— Anr, [n.d.]. (90) $300

Signature, on reproduction of 4 bust drawings of Reagan by Norman Rockwell ptd in Saturday Evening Post, 1968. (91) $425

— Anr, [20 Jan 1981]. (91) $100
— Anr, [20 Jan 1981]. (91) $180
— Anr, [21 June 1983]. (91) $500
— Anr, 30 Sept 1986. (91) $275
— Anr, [n.d.]. (91) $80

Reagan, Ronald —& Others

Group photograph, [1981]. 9.5 by 8.5 inches. With members of the Supreme Court on the day Sandra O'Connor became a Justice; sgd by all 10 on mat. (91) $2,500

Reagan, Ronald —& Bush, George

Group photograph, on a stage with their wives, [1980]. (91) $400

Reagan, Ronald —& Day, Doris

Group photograph, [n.d.]. (91) $180

Reagan, Ronald —& Reagan, Nancy

[Their signatures, 23 Sept 1982, on a philatelic envelope [20 Jan 1981], sold at Dar on 4 Oct 1990, lot 351, for $450.]

Group photograph, [n.d.]. (91) $80

Reaumur, Rene Antoine Ferchault de, 1683-1757

ALs, 21 May 1748. 4 pp, 4to. Recipient unnamed. Thanking for a flamingo. (91) DM1,200

— 19 May 1753. (88) DM650

AMERICAN BOOK PRICES CURRENT

Recamier, Julie, 1777-1849
ALs, [n.d.]. (91) DM340

Recke, Elisa von der, 1756-1833
ALs, 16 Dec 1819. Albrecht collection. (91) SF420

Redding, John M., d.1965
[A collection of documents & letters by Presidents Truman, Kennedy & Johnson & other political leaders, together with clippings, photographs, etc. relating to Redding's career sold at P on 23 Oct, lot 31, for $1,800.]

Redgrave, Richard, 1804-88
Series of 9 A Ls s, 1836 to 1869. (88) £450

Redon, Odilon, 1840-1916
ALs, 19 Dec 1909. (90) DM570

Redoute, Pierre Joseph, 1759-1840
Original drawing, Allium tartaricum/Ail de Tartarie, to illus Les liliacees, part 17, plate 98, [1804]. 477mm by 344mm. Watercolor over pencil; sgd. With ptd text leaf. The Garden Ltd. collection. (90) $6,500

— Original drawing, Amaryllis aurea/Amaryllis doree, to illus Les liliacees, part 11, plate 61, [1804]. 476mm by 341mm. Watercolor over pencil; sgd. With ptd text leaf. The Garden Ltd. collection. (90) $33,000

— Original drawing, Anthericum aloides/Antheric a feuilles d'aloes, to illus Les Liliacees, part 48, plate 283; 1810. 471mm by 328mm. In watercolor over pencil, sgd. Framed. (90) $8,000

— Original drawing, Antholyza cunonia/Antholyse papiplionacee, to illus Les liliacees, part 2, plate 12, [1802]. 481mm by 346mm. Watercolor over pencil; sgd. With ptd text leaf. The Garden Ltd. collection. (90) $14,000

— Original drawing, Colchicum autumnale/Colchicum d'automne, to illus Les Liliacees, part 38, plate 228; 1808. 460mm by 316mm. In watercolor over pencil, with 6 fine grisaille detail drawings in pencil; sgd. Framed. (90) $27,000

— Original drawing, Galaxia ixiaeflora/Galaxia fleur d'Ixia, to illus Les liliacees, part 7, plate 41, [1803].

480mm by 342mm. Watercolor over pencil; sgd. With ptd text leaf. The Garden Ltd. collection. (90) $14,000
— Original drawing, Hypoxis stellata/Hypoxis etoilee, to illus Les Liliacees, part 29, plate 169; 1807. 460mm by 328mm. In watercolor; sgd. Framed. (90) $4,500
— Original drawing, Iris foetidissima/Iris fetide, to illus Les Liliacees, part 59, plate 351; 1812. 471mm by 328mm. In watercolor over pencil, with 2 watercolor & 2 pencilled grisaille detail drawings; sgd. Framed. (90) $17,000
— Original drawing, Rosa damascena aurora, to illus Les roses, part 15; 1820. 388mm by 267mm. In watercolor over pencil; sgd. (90) $24,000
— Original drawing, Rosa damascena italica, to illus Les roses, part 23; 1821. 387mm by 268mm. In watercolor over pencil; sgd. (90) $25,000
— Original drawing, Scilla patula/Scille etalee, to illus Les Liliacees, part 38, plate 225; 1808. 460mm by 316mm. In watercolor over pencil, sgd. Framed. (90) $11,000
— Original drawing, Tulipa suaveolens/Tulipe odorante, to illus Les Liliacees, part 19, plate 111; 1805. 460mm by 316mm. In watercolor; sgd. Framed. (90) $10,000

Reed, E. T.
Original drawings, (61), cartoons & illusts for Punch's Holiday Book & other publications, [n.d.]. (88) £500
— Original drawings, (7), to illus Tails with a Twist, Mr. (88) £300

Reed, Joseph, 1741-85
ALs, [19 Dec 1780]. (90) $170
— 25 Oct 1784. (91) $160

Reeves, George, 1914-59
Photograph, sgd & inscr, [n.d.]. (91) $550
Signature, [n.d.]. (91) $475

Regenstein
Document, 4 Aug 1346. 1 p, vellum, 185mm by 377mm. Contract regarding the feud between Count Albrecht II von Regenstein & others, & Bishop Albrecht II of Halberstadt. In Low German. With 11 seals. (88) DM1,800
— 21 Sept 1370. (88) DM400
— 3 Mar 1425. 1 p, vellum, 193mm by 403mm. Contract between Count Ulrich von Regenstein und Blankenburg & the town of Blankenburg concerning a transfer of property. In Low German. With 6 seals. (88) DM1,400

Reger, Max, 1873-1916
Autograph music, song, Der Tod, das ist die kuehle Nacht, to a text by Heinrich Heine, [n.d.]. 3 pp, 4to. Scored for voice & piano; sgd at head. Tp & text in anr hand. (91) DM9,000
Collection of 8 A Ls s & 17 autograph postcards, sgd, 30 Dec 1903 to 14 Apr 1916. 30 pp, 8vo, & cards. To Ossip Schnirlin. Planning concerts, discussing & explaining bis works, etc. With related material. (91) DM7,500
ALs, 10 Sept 1901. (88) DM560
— 16 Sept 1901. (88) £100
Autograph postcard, sgd, [16 May 1903]. (89) DM420
— [30 Nov 1905]. (90) DM340
— [17 Sept 1910]. (90) DM380
Photograph, sgd, [n.d.]. (91) DM650
Photograph, sgd & inscr, Feb 1895. (90) DM420
— Anr, 21 May 1907. (90) DM450

Reger, Max, 1873-1916 —& Others
Menu, dinner at Essen for the final full rehearsal of his Sinfonietta, Op. (90) DM270

Rehfues, Philipp Joseph von, 1779-1843
ALs, 17 Jan 1826. (88) DM240

Reich, Wilhelm, 1897-1957
Ls, 18 Oct 1937. 1 p, 4to. To unnamed young political friends. Trying to give advice about their work. File holes. (89) DM1,300
— 8 Apr 1938. (89) DM680
— 16 Nov 1938. 2 pp, 4to. To Oskar & Mrs. Bumbacher. Commenting about the political situation. (88) DM1,900

Reichard, Georg, b.c.1600
— MATTHAEI, LAURENTIUS. - ALs, 26 July 1645. 3 pp, folio. To the Hannover town council. Requesting money to enable Reichard to have more of his visions ptd. (88) DM500

REICHARD

Reichard, Heinrich August, 1751-1828
ALs, 28 June 1777. (90) DM850

Reichardt, Johann Friedrich, 1752-1814
ALs, 27 Aug 1787. 2 pp, 4to. To Georg Joachim Goeschen. About his compositions of texts by Goethe. Albrecht collection. (91) SF1,600
— 27 Apr 1805. 3 pp, 8vo. To Karl Friedrich Zelter. Inviting him to visit, & worrying about Goethe's illness. Albrecht collection. (91) SF1,500

Reichenbach, Heinrich Gottlieb Ludwig, 1793-1879
ALs, 27 Oct 1849. (91) DM500

Reichenbach, Karl von, 1788-1869
ALs, 7 Apr 1837. (89) DM800
— 1 Nov 1865. (90) DM600

Reichstein, Tadeusz
Autograph Ms, scientific paper, Die Konstitution von Adynerin; [n.d.]. (90) DM400
— Autograph Ms, scientific paper, Die Struktur der Sarmentoside; [1960 or later]. (89) DM460
— Autograph Ms, scientific paper, Diploides Asplenium obovatum Viv.; [1962]. (91) DM360
— Autograph Ms, scientific paper, Chemische Rassen von Strophantus samentosus; [n.d.]. (90) DM320

Reid, Forrest, 1875-1947
[2 typescripts with autograph revisions, comprising scenes from a pastoral play & a piece entitled "Criticism", [n.d.], 26 pp, 4to, sold at S on 15 Dec 1988, lot 101, for £360.]

Reid, Wallace
Autograph sentiment, 31 Jan [19]20. (91) $80

Reimann, Aribert
Autograph music, sketches for his opera Melusine, sgd later & dated 25 Aug 1981. (91) DM500

Reinhard, Karl Friedrich, Graf von, 1761-1837. See: Talleyrand-Perigord, Charles Maurice de

AMERICAN BOOK PRICES CURRENT

Reinhardt, Max, 1873-1943
A Ls s (2), 23 July 1901 & 23 Sept 1923. (88) DM500
ALs, 29 Mar 1922. (91) DM580
— [n.d.]. (90) DM370

Remak, Robert, 1815-65
ALs, 6 May 1853. 1 p, 8vo. To [Heinrich Meckel]. Promising to look into a problem & requesting research material. With related material. (90) DM1,300

Remarque, Erich Maria, 1898-1970
Collection of ALs & 2 autograph postcards, sgd, 3 Oct 1966 to 28 Dec 1969. (90) DM400

Remington, Frederic, 1861-1909
[An extensive collection of clippings of Remington's works extracted from periodicals, c.1885 to c.1906, with related material, compiled by Willard S. Morse with the assistance of Merle Johnson, sold at CNY on 1 Feb 1988, lot 269, for $2,500 to Rosenstock.]
A Ls s (2), 5 July 1895 & 1 Dec [n.y.]. 2 pp, 4to. To A. T. Gurlitz, sending a sketch of his sculpture The Bronco Buster (included). To Mr. Caplan, refusing to be a party to a suit. (91) $13,000
— A Ls s (2), [n.d.]. (88) $700
— A Ls s (2), [n.d.]. 2 pp, 8vo. To "My dear Russell". Thanking for a Christmas present. Forwarding a statement. Doheny collection. (88) $1,200
ALs, 15 June [n.y.]. (91) $450
— [n.d.]. 3 pp, 8vo. To Julian Ralph. Commenting on a reference to him in Collier's Magazine. Including full-page sketch. With postscript, sgd R. Doheny collection. (88) $4,000
— [n.d.]. (91) $700
— [n.d.]. 2 pp, 8vo. To Elizabeth Custer. Regarding a statue [of George A. Custer]. (89) $1,500
Autograph endorsement, sgd, 19 Sept 1899. (90) $325
Signature, [n.d.]. (89) $800
— Anr, [n.d.]. (89) $700
— DAVIS. - Orig drawing, sgd; pen-&-ink port of Remington; [n.d.]. 5 by 4 inches. Probably used to illus Century Magazine. (89) $300

Remizov, Aleksei Mikhailovich, 1877-1957
Series of 4 A Ls s, 1950. (91) £500

Renn, Ludwig, Pseud. of Arnold Vieth von Golssenau, 1889-1979
ALs, 17 Dec 1936. (90) DM750

Renner, Karl, 1870-1950
ALs, 30 May 1906. 2 pp, 4to. To Franz Klein. Thanking for approval of his book & his political ideas. (89) DM2,000

Renner, Willy, 1883-1955
[A collection of 48 postcards & 2 letters addressed to him by various correspondents including Wilhelm Backhaus & Max Reger, with related material, sold at star on 10 Mar 1988, lot 1000, for DM950.]

Rennie, Michael
Autograph sentiment, sgd, [n.d.]. (91) $110

Reno, Jesse Lee, 1823-62
ALs, 21 May 1847. (91) $750

Reno, Marcus Albert, 1834-89. See: Civil War, American

Renoir, Jean, 1894-1979 — & Freire, Dido
Series of 52 Ls s, 13 Sept 1941 to 1 Nov 1959. 65 pp, mostly 4to. To Dudley Nichols. Giving detailed news about their life & his current work. Partly by Renoir or his wife separately, partly sgd together. (90) £2,700

Renoir, Pierre Auguste, 1841-1919
ALs, 29 Feb 1908. 2 pp, 8vo. To [Georges Riviere]. About a visit, expecting news about a nomination, etc. (91) DM1,200
— [Feb 1908]. (88) DM1,000
— [n.d.]. 1 p, 8vo. Recipient unnamed. About an expected decision of a military commission for the area of Cagnes. Framed with a photograph. (91) $1,500

Repnin, Nikolai Vasilyevich, Prince, 1734-1801
Ls, 14/25 Jan 1764. (90) DM250

Resnik, Judith A., 1949-86
ALs, 23 May 1984. (91) $225

Respighi, Ottorino, 1879-1936
[A collection of autograph musical Mss, 53 pp, folio, with proof copy of Cinque liriche with autograph alterations, & inscr copies of Pini di Roma, Deita Silvane sold at S on 27 Nov, lot 380, for £1,500 to Nestle.]
Autograph music, No 3 Contrasto, to a text by Carlo Zangarini, fragment; 1905. 1 p, 28cm by 24cm. 8 bars scored for voice & piano; sgd. With additions in anr hand. (90) DM1,100
Collection of c.130 A Ls s & 15 telegrams, mostly 1913 to 1921. Over 325 pp, various sizes. To Chiarina Fino Savio (a few to Giuseppe Fino). About the composition & performances of his works, colleagues & friends, & complaining about being apart from her. (88) £5,000
— Collection of 2 A Ls s & autograph postcard, sgd, 6 Mar to 26 July 1915. (88) DM900
ALs, 20 Sept 1914. Byer collection. (90) $150
— 27 July 1935. (89) DM320

Reuter, Fritz, 1810-74
Autograph Ms, poem, beginning "In der grossen Wasserpfuetze", [n.d.]. 1 p, 8vo. 25 lines, sgd. (91) DM1,300
Collection of ALs & AL, 19 Oct 1870 & [n.d.], 3 pp, 8vo & smaller. To D. C. Hinstorff & Ludwig Reinhard. Fragments (postscripts), regarding a copyright problem, & humorous remark. With related material. (89) DM1,100
ALs, 6 Apr 1868. 1 p, 8vo. To Detloff Carl Hinstorff. Thanking for a shipment of smoked fish & saying he needs more time to get settled in his new house. (89) DM1,200
— 9 Sept 1868. (91) DM950
Ls, 14 Oct 1868. (88) DM420
— 6 Mar 1870. (88) DM680
Letter, 17 Apr 1871. (88) DM260
— REUTER, LUISE. - 4 A Ls s, 3 Jan 1864 & [n.d.]. 6 pp, 8vo. To Ludwig Reinhold Walesrode. Expressing invitations in her husband's name, & worrying about her husband's health. 1 ALs in verse. With anr. (90)

REUTER

DM1,300

Reuter, Gabriele, 1859-1941
Series of 5 A Ls s, 26 July 1915 to 28 Dec 1918. (89) DM900

Reuter, Luise, 1817-94. See: Reuter, Fritz

Reutter, Hermann, 1900-85
Autograph music, sketches for his Hamlet, Scenes 1 & 2; [n.d.]. (89) DM400

Revere, Paul, 1735-1818
ADs, 8 Oct 1779. 1 p, 8vo, removed from larger leaf. As Lieut. Colonel of Artillery in the militia, receipt for rations. (90) $7,000

Revolution Society. See: Society for the Commemoration of the Glorious Revolution (Revolution Society)

Reynolds, J.
ALs, [n.d.], "Saturday". 2 pp, 8vo. To John Liston. Suggesting improvements to his stage costume. Repaired. Doheny collection. (89) $1,600

Reynolds, John Hamilton, 1796-1852
[A collection of 11 items, letters & Mss relating to Reynolds, 1844, 1847 & [n.d.], sold at C on 22 June 1988, lot 122, for £75 to Bristow.]

Reynolds, Sir Joshua, 1723-92
ALs, 17 June 1782. (89) £600
AL, [n.d.]. (89) £500

Reznicek, Emil Nikolaus von, 1860-1945
Autograph Ms, essay about the future of the opera; [n.d.]. (90) DM360
ALs, 10 Sept 1927. (89) DM550

Rezzori, Gregor von
Autograph Ms, fragment (p 23) of an unidentified work; [n.d.]. (89) DM220

Rhead, Louis, 1857-1926
Original drawings, (2), to illus The Yellow Dwarf & Prince Cherry in Dinah Maria Mulock's The Fairy Book, 1922. (90) £150

Rhodes, Cecil John
ALs, [n.d.]. (88) £300

AMERICAN BOOK PRICES CURRENT

Ribbentrop, Joachim von, 1893-1946
Ds, [1946]. (90) $200
See also: Stalin, Joseph & Ribbentrop

Ricardo, David, 1772-1823
ALs, 6 Dec 1812. 5 pp, 4to. To Leonard Horner. Discussing bullion, the circulation of currency & exchange rates. (91) $14,000
— 13 Mar 1823. (88) £550
AL, 3 Mar 1813. (91) £980

Ricardo, John Lewis, 1812-62
Autograph Ms, diary, 23 Jan 1847 to 22 May 1858. (91) £750

Rice Family
[A collection of correspondence & papers of the Rice family, [c.1750 to 1839], over 600 pp, containing references to Mrs. Thrale & Johnson, sold at S on 15 Dec 1988, lot 31, for £2,100.]

Rice, Grantland, 1880-1954
— HERRIN, M. H. - Orig drawing, pencil port of Rice, 24 Feb [19]42. 9 by 12 inches. Sgd by Rice. (91) $300

Richard III, King of England, 1452-85
Document, 1 June 1485. 1 p, vellum, 263mm by 527mm. Licence for Margaret Clifford to grant the advowson of the church of Belton, Lincolnshire, to the convent of St. Leonard at Esholt. In a handsome charter hand, with very large historiated initial & painting of the nuns kneeling in prayer. Seal def. (90) £21,000

Richards, Henry Brinley, 1819-85
Autograph music, 10 songs in draft & final versions, mostly sgd or initialled; [n.d.]. (89) £400

Richardson, Israel Bush, 1815-62
ALs, [3 July 1845]. Alexander collection. (90) $180

Richardson, S. T.
[A group of 2 Mss, Family Annals by Road and Rail, by Flood and Field, [after 1873], & Our Drive to Albalanda, 1896, illus with 71 & 24 orig drawings, respectively, sold at S on 7 June 1990, lot 461, for £900 to Temperley.]

Richardson, Samuel, 1689-1761
ALs, 9-10 Apr 1753. 3 pp, 4to. To Hester Mulso. About faults in Sir Charles Grandison. (91) $2,000
AN, [n.d.]. (89) £280

Richelieu, Armand-Jean du Plessis, Cardinal de, 1585-1642
ALs, 1 Nov 1636. (88) $600
Ls, [1638?]. (88) $700
Ds, 26 May 1624. (90) $200
— [1634?]. Byer collection. (90) $550
Cut signature, [n.d.]. (89) $250

Richter, Jean Paul Friedrich, 1763-1825
Autograph Ms, appeal for donations for Bayreuth citizens who lost their property in a recent fire, sgd; 17 Nov 1804. 3 pp, folio. With list of contributions & 2 related A Ns. (91) DM4,000
— Autograph Ms, dedication of his Daemmerungen fuer Deutschland to Grand Duke Karl Friedrich von Sachsen-Weimar & his consort Maria Paulowna, final part; sgd & dated 17 Nov 1809. 2 pp, 8vo. (90) DM2,200
— Autograph Ms, description of a dream about a graveyard scene; for Herbst-Blumine, vol 3, early draft, [1794]. 4 pp, 4to. Working Ms, pp 79 - 82, numbered in anr hand. Partly foxed. (88) DM6,500
ALs, [Aug 1796]. 1 p, 8vo. To Renate Otto. Sending a book containing one of his essays. Sgd R. (90) DM1,300
— 18 Apr 1798. 3 pp, 8vo. To Louise [Reim]. Expressing congratulations on her birthday. (90) DM7,500
— 24 Aug 1801. 3 pp, 8vo. To Henriette von Schlabrendorff. Referring to his journey to Bayreuth & mentioning various friends. Sgd R. (90) DM2,500
— [24 June 1808]. 1 p, 4to. To Emanuel [Osmund]. Sending birthday presents. Margin cut. (90) DM3,800
— 30 Aug 1817. 1 p, 8vo. To the bookseller Enslin. Promising a contribution to his sister-in-law's almanach. (89) DM3,600
— 8 May 1819. 4 pp, 8vo. Recipient unknown. Informing him about the safe arrival of proofs. (90) £1,500
— [1819?]. 1 p, 8vo. To [Lorenz Heinrich] Wagner. Asking for red ink to correct a Ms. With related material. (89) DM3,000
— 17 Jan 1820. 2 pp, 8vo. To his brother. Thanking for the gift of a guitar. (89) £1,200
— 29 May 1822. 1 p, 8vo. To Maria Therese von Velthusen. Referring to a projected journey. (91) DM2,900
AL, 26 Apr 1799. 2 pp, 8vo. To Josephine von Sydow. Fragment, replying to her letter telling the story of her life & hoping to meet her some time. In Roman script; some corrections. (88) DM3,600
— KALB, CHARLOTTE VON. - 5 letters, 16 Apr to 16 Oct 1830 & [n.d.]. 14 pp, 4to & 8vo. To Emanuel Osmund. Written in her name, requesting not to include her letters to Jean Paul in the Ed of his papers, expressing the wish to send some money to Jean Paul's widow, etc. With related material. (90) DM650
— RICHTER, CAROLINE. - 2 A Ls s & AL, [Dec 1803] to 12 July 1804. 10 pp, 8vo. To Emanuel [Osmund]. Sending news about her husband Jean Paul, their move to Bayreuth, etc. (90) DM700
— SCHWENDLER, HENRIETTE. - ALs, 4 Dec 1802. 4 pp, 8vo. To Emanuel [Osmund]. Expressing regrets about Jean Paul's projected move to Coburg. (90) DM340

Richter, Ludwig, 1803-84
A Ls s (2), 30 Dec 1857 & 9 Feb 1858. (88) DM650
ALs, 8 Mar [1847]. (89) DM400
— 1 Oct 1853. (90) DM280
— 30 Dec 1871. (89) DM380
AL, 30 Sept 1870. (90) DM380

Richthofen, Manfred, Freiherr von, 1892-1918
[A collection of 6 typed reports sgd by R.A.F. officers, some later victims of von Richthofen, describing air combats, 1916 to 1918, with related material, sold at S on 15 Nov 1988, lot 1729, for £250 to Burton.]
Autograph postcard, sgd, 12 Apr 1917. To an unnamed recipient in Tirol. Expressing thanks. On verso port. With related material. (88) DM3,300

Rickenbacker

Rickenbacker, Edward Vernon, 1890-1973
[2 checks, sgd, 23 Jan & 28 Feb 1969, sold at Dar on 4 Oct 1990, lot 355, for $130.]
Ls, 17 Oct 1935. (90) $80
— 22 July 1947. (88) $60
— 12 Dec 1968. (91) $300
— 15 July 1970. (90) $130
Photograph, sgd & inscr, [n.d.]. (90) $60

Rickenbacker, Edward Vernon, 1890-1973 —& Others
[A program for a dinner in honor of Arthur Godfrey, 4 Dec 1952, 4 pp, 4to, sgd by Rickenbacker, Hoyt S. Vandenberg, & 6 others, sold at Dar on 10 Apr 1991, lot 41, for $100.]

Rickey, Wesley Branch, 1881-1965
Ls, 15 Oct 1947. (89) $275

Rickover, Hyman
Ls, 3 Dec 1964. (91) $150
— 24 Mar 1969. (90) $350

Ricoldo da Montecroce, c.1243-1320
Ms, Libellus contra legem Saracenorum. [Bologna, 9 Apr 1442]. 30 leaves (6 blank) & 2 flyleaves, 222mm by 145mm. Worn contemp blindstamped tanned lea over wooden bds. In a neat cursive bookhand. (91) £10,000

Ricord, Philippe, 1800-89
ALs, 19 July 1849. (89) $100

Ricordi, Giovanni, 1785-1853 —& Others
[A collection of 6 letters and documents from the publishing house of Ricordi, mostly to the publishers Schlesinger & Haslinger, regarding works by Donizetti, Lanner & Verdi, 1836 to 1877, 10 pp, various sizes, with related material, sold at star on 10 Mar 1988, lot 1002, for DM2,600.]

Riehl, Wilhelm Heinrich von, 1823-97
Autograph Ms, novella, Abendfrieden; [Jan 1867]. (90) DM480

Riemann, Bernhard, 1826-66
ADs, 25 Oct 1855. (89) DM750

Riemer, Friedrich Wilhelm, 1774-1845
Autograph Ms, [n.d.]. (89) DM330
A Ls s (2), 28 & 30 Jan 1830. Albrecht collection. (91) SF480
ALs, 19 Nov 1803. (90) DM220
— 21 May 1825. (88) DM320
— 6 Dec 1825. Albrecht collection. (91) SF520

Riesser, Gabriel, 1806-63
Series of 3 A Ls s, 2 Oct 1850 to 15 July 1856. (88) DM380
ALs, 1 June 1849. 2 pp, 4to. To Adele Haller. Justifying his political principles & actions. (90) DM1,800

Rigby, T. R.
Original drawing, pencil & watercolor illus for The Rime of the Ancient Mariner; [n.d.]. (90) £120

Riley, James Whitcomb, 1849-1916
[A collection of 6 autograph poetical Mss, partly sgd, [c.1888 to 1897], 13 pp, 4to & 8vo, with related material, sold at P on 7 June 1988, lot 48, for $2,750]
Autograph transcript, poem, There Little Girl Don't Cry; [n.d.]. (91) $225
Collection of 2 A Ls s, 3 autograph transcripts, autograph quotation, sgd, & photograph, sgd & inscr, July 1891 to 1 Dec 1904. Doheny collection. (89) $800
ALs, 17 July 1882. 2 pp, folio, on rectos only. To Robert J. Burdette. Thanking profusely for his letter; with 6-line verse & 2 sketches at head. In mor bdg with a port. Doheny collection. (89) $1,300
Autograph quotation, sgd, [1 Jan] 1908. (88) $70

Rilke, Clara, 1878-1954
ALs, 12 Nov 1899. (89) DM800
See also: Rilke, Rainer Maria

Rilke, Rainer Maria, 1875-1926
Autograph Ms, 2 dialogues in verse, Zwei Spiele; sgd on tp, dated [25 Dec] 1916 & inscr to Hertha Koenig. 12 pp, 4to, in vellum bdg. (90) DM11,000
— Autograph Ms, poem, beginning "Leben heisst es und geniessen", May 1891. 1 p, 8vo, in an album kept by Christian Gellinek. 16 lines, sgd Rene

Rilke. Possibly Rilke's earliest known poem; presumably unpbd. (91) DM17,000

Autograph transcript, 3 poems, Duineser Elegien, 5th & 6th elegies, & Sonette an Orpheus, II,13; 7 Mar 1922. 12 leaves, 225mm by 179mm, in marbled wraps & blue mor folding case gilt by Sangorski & Sutcliffe. The Garden Ltd. collection. (90) $18,000

— Autograph transcript, Der Tod Moses, excerpt from Herder's poetical works, [c.1914]. 4 pp, 8vo. (91) DM2,400

— Autograph transcript, poem, Auferstehung; [n.d.]. 1 p, 4to. 15 lines. (90) DM3,000

— Autograph transcript, poem, Das Lied von den Lilien, 20 Nov 1904. 2 pp, 8vo. Sgd & inscr to Stinta Frisell. (88) $1,800

— Autograph transcript, poem, his German version of Les Vivants et les Morts by Anna de Noailles; 23 four-line stanzas. Tp & 9 pp, 4to. Sgd & inscr to Princess Sophie von Oettingen, Sept 1918. Stitched. (89) DM9,500

Series of 3 A Ls s, 19 Apr 1906 to 29 Mar 1908. 10 pp, 4to & 8vo. To S. Fischer. About Rodin & Shaw, his literary projects, his contract with Fischer, etc. (91) DM7,200

— Series of 3 A Ls s, 13 May 1915 to 5 Mar 1918. 9 pp, 4to. To Augusta Hartmann-Rauter. About Schoenberg's Orchesterlieder to texts from Rilke's Stundenbuch, & mentioning various artists & friends. (90) DM6,500

— Series of 6 A Ls s, [20 Nov 1918] to 11 Feb 1921. 15 pp, 4to & 12mo. To Else Hotop-Guembel. About a variety of personal matters. With 4 replies. (91) DM4,500

A Ls s (2), 16 Jan 1919 & [n.d.]. 3 pp, 4to. To May Purtscher. Discussing a date for a meeting, & refusing to sit for anr port. (90) DM2,000

— A Ls s (2), "Wednesday" [c.1919?]. (90) DM1,000

ALs, [c.Oct 1902]. 3 pp, 8vo. To Ignacio Zuloaga. Expressing admiration for his work & the wish to see him. (90) DM2,600

— 6 Mar 1903. (90) £650

— 2 Oct 1906. 4 pp, 8vo. To Axel Juncker. Returning proofs & discussing the ptg of his Cornet. (90) DM4,200

— 15 Nov 1909. (88) £400

— 8 Mar 1913. (90) DM850

— 24 Oct 1913. 4 pp, 4to. To an unnamed lady. About his return to Paris & a meeting with Claudel. Repaired. (89) DM3,400

— 22 Dec 1913. 4 pp, 4to. To Hedwig Fischer. Season's greetings, & reporting about his recent activities. (88) DM1,800

— 25 Aug 1915. (88) DM1,000

— 12 Sept [19]15. 1 p, 8vo. To Marie Helene Krell. Thanking for an invitation & inquiring about Freddie Doehle-Lee. (91) DM1,300

— [Oct 1915]. (91) DM1,000

— 5 Oct 1916. 4 pp, 8vo. To Loulou Albert-Lazard. Commenting on an exhibition of Franz Marc's paintings. (90) DM3,500

— 5 Aug 1918. 3 pp, 4to. To Wilhelm Fliess. Praising recipient's work [Das Jahr im Lebendigen]. (90) DM1,900

— 21 Aug 1919. (90) DM1,000

— 27 Feb 1923. 2 pp, 4to. To an unnamed Ed. About a French Ed of his Aufzeichnungen des Malte Laurids Brigge. In French. (91) DM1,300

— [1924]. (90) £400

— "Tuesday", [early Feb 1925?] 1 p, 8vo. To [Christine von Hofmannsthal]. Hoping for a meeting. (89) DM1,850

— [after 1923]. 4 pp, 4to. To Otto Frommel. Responding to an inquiry about the influence of religion on his poetry. (90) DM4,200

ANs, 3 Sept 1812. (90) £300

— RILKE, CLARA. - ALs, 17 Jan 1904. 4 pp, 4to. To Rudolf von Poellnitz. Reporting about their stay at Paris, & mentioning Rodin. (88) DM750

See also: Rodin, Auguste

Rimbaud, Arthur, 1854-91

Autograph Ms, essay, Boileau. (Satires et Art poetique); [n.d.]. 14 pp, 4to. Some holes along folds. Koch Foundation. (90) $6,500

ALs, 15 Jan 1885. 4 pp, 4to. To his family. Reporting about his life in Aden, his financial situation, & his wish to travel. Koch Foundation. (90) $9,000

RIMSKI-KORSAKOV

Rimski-Korsakov, Nikolai Andreevich, 1844-1908

ALs, 5 Oct 1903. 3 pp, 8vo. To Wassili Ilyich. Informing him about his Homer Cantata, Op. 60. (88) DM6,500

— 2/15 May 1905. 1 p, 8vo. To an unnamed friend. Asking him to provide a trans of his opera Sadko. (90) £1,300

— 18 May 1908. 2 pp, 8vo. To Mikhail Osipovich. Thanking for newspaper articles about the Snow Maiden, & mentioning his illness. (90) £1,600

Ls, 2/14 July 1899. 2 pp, 8vo. To Joseph Dupont. Postponing the decision about a projected concert at Brussels. In French. (90) DM1,700

Autograph postcard, sgd, 7 Feb 1903. To his son Andrei. About a performance of his opera Kashchey Bessmertniy. (89) £2,400

Ringelnatz, Joachim, Pseud. of Hans Boetticher, 1883-1934

Autograph Ms, poem, Cassel/Die Karpfen Wilhelmstrasse 15; [n.d.]. (90) DM750

Ls, 6 Feb 1926. (90) DM210

— 20 Sept 1928. (91) DM460

Autograph postcards (2), sgd, 2 Mar 1919 & [22 Sept 1922]. To Fritz Otto. Poem about his dog & his situation in Freyburg. About his illness & the death of his father-in-law. Sgd Specht. With related material. (89) DM1,150

— Autograph postcards (2), sgd, [5 Nov] & 25 Dec 1922. (88) DM600

Autograph postcard, sgd, [3 Apr 1923]. (91) DM850

Ringling, John, 1866-1936

Ls, 20 Sept 1932. (91) $150

Ritter, Karl, 1779-1859

ALs, 21 Feb 1850. (91) DM320

— 9 Oct 1855. (91) DM380

Rivera, Diego, 1886-1957

Photograph, sgd & inscr, 1949. (88) $325

Rivington, James, 1724-1802

ALs, 8 Jan 1784. (91) $190

AMERICAN BOOK PRICES CURRENT

Robert, Ludwig, 1778-1832

ALs, 22 May 1822. Albrecht collection. (91) SF1,000

— [10 June 1823]. Albrecht collection. (91) SF950

Robert, Nicolas, 1614-85

[Lots 80 to 159 of the Jeanson sale on 16 June 1988 at SM consisted of works by Robert or by his workshop in watercolor & gouache on vellum]

Roberts, David, 1796-1864

Series of 3 A Ls s, 7 May 1849 to 5 July 1861. (90) £400

Robeson, Paul, 1898-1976

Photograph, sgd, [n.d.]. (91) $150

Robespierre, Augustin Bon Joseph, 1763-94

ALs, [1793?]. 3 pp, 4to. To his brother Maximilien. Sending news from Arras, reporting about the founding of a Jacobin club, requesting papers from Paris, etc. (90) DM1,900

Robespierre, Maximilien, 1758-94

AL, 23 July 1789. 12 pp, 4to. To A. J. Buissart. Giving a detailed report about the beginning of the Revolution & the situation in Paris. With 2 contemp engraved portraits. (88) DM130,000

Ds, 2 Feb 1793. (91) £750

— 26 Aug 1793. (91) £1,000

— [12 May 1794]. (90) £800

Robespierre, Maximilien, 1758-94 —& Others

Ds, [2 June 1794]. (90) £700

Robin, Louis

[His papers, comprising a large quantity of correspondence & ephemeral publications, [mid-20th cent], hundreds of items in 2 tin boxes, mostly relating to African wildlife, sold at pn on 8 Dec 1988, lot 55, for £160 to Way.]

Robinson, Bill ("Bojangles"), 1878-1949

Photograph, sgd & inscr, 1935. (88) $210

— Anr, 1941. (91) $350

Robinson, Charles
Original drawings, (123), to illus Walter Jerrold's The Big Book of Fairy Tales, 1911. Various sizes; some drawn 2 to a sheet. In ink, mostly with wash or crayon shading. (89) £4,000
Original drawing, cherub on the branch of a tree, to illus Percy Bysshe Shelley's The Sensitive Plant, 1911. In watercolor, sgd. 468mm by 309mm. Framed. (88) £3,500
— Original drawing, man in oriental dress gazing at crystal ball, to illus Oscar Wilde's The Happy Prince, 1913. In ink & watercolor, sgd. 345mm by 257mm. Framed. (88) £3,000
— Original drawing, sailing ship filled with figures of small children, to illus When the Great Ship Cometh, a Mystery, ptd in The Tatler; [n.d.]. 509mm by 399mm. In watercolor; inscr To Phyllis. (90) £3,700

Robinson, Edward G., 1893-1972
Photograph, sgd, [n.d.]. (91) $55

Robinson, Henry Crabb, 1775-1867
ALs, 27 Sept 1812. (88) £400
— 12 Feb 1847. (91) £80

Robinson, Jackie, 1919-72
Signature, [23 Feb 1951]. (91) $170

Robinson, Sugar Ray
Photograph, sgd & inscr, [n.d.]. (90) $130

Robinson, Thomas Heath
Original drawings, (4), to illus St. (90) £140
— Original drawings, (6), to illus The Mill on the Floss, 1924. (90) £150
— Original drawings, (75) to illus the 1935 Ed of Of the Imitation of Jesus Christ by Thomas a Kempis. (88) £850
Original drawing, man with a cigarette at the zoo, 1931. (90) £180
— Original drawing, of a medieval procession for the 1935 Ed of Of the Imitation of Jesus Christ by Thomas a Kempis. (88) £380

Robinson, William Heath, 1872-1944
Original drawing, elderly fairy floating past trees, sgd & captioned Elfin Mount, to illus Andersen's Fairy Tales; [n.d.]. (90) £700
— Original drawing, man playing a concertina to a young child, to illus his own Bill the Minder, 1912. In watercolor; sgd. 355mm by 258mm; framed. (90) £5,000

Rochambeau, Jean Baptiste Donatien de Vimeur, Comte de, 1725-1807
Ds, 16 Jan 1776. (91) $250
Autograph endorsement, sgd, on a petition by Chevalier de Saint Louis, 25 Sept 1788. (90) $200

Rockefeller, John D., 1839-1937
Ls, 17 July 1925. (90) $600
— 25 Feb 1927. (91) $700

Rockne, Knute Kenneth, 1888-1931
Ls, 19 Nov 1928. (91) $800
Ds, 1915. (91) $1,000

Rockwell, Norman, 1894-1978
Collection of Ls & autograph sentiment, sgd, 24 Aug 1976. (90) $110
Ls, 2 Mar 1976. (89) $70
Collection of ANs & photograph, sgd & inscr, [n.d.]. (89) $180
Ns, [n.d.]. (91) $300
Photograph, sgd & inscr, [n.d.]. (91) $350
Signature, [16 Nov 1973]. (90) $75
— Anr, [n.d.]. (89) $260

Roda Roda, Alexander, Pseud. of Sandor Friedrich Rosenfeld, 1872-1945
Collection of 3 A Ls s, 3 Ls s, & 3 autograph postcards, sgd, 1893 to 1918. (90) DM550

Rodgers, John, 1773-1838
Franking signature, [10 Oct 1815] On letter addressed to U.S. (89) $80

Rodgers, Richard, 1902-79
Ls, 9 Dec 1943. (91) $120
— 29 Jan 1957. (88) $90
— 22 Aug 1966. (91) $200
Photograph, sgd & inscr, [n.d.]. (91) $100

Rodin, Auguste, 1840-1917
Collection of ALs & photograph, sgd & inscr, [18 Oct 1908] & [n.d.]. (90) DM650
A Ls s (2), 8 Jan 1908 & [n.d.]. Salzer collection. (90) £420
ALs, 28 Apr 1886. (90) DM750
— 29 Aug 1893. (90) $275

RODIN
— [1898]. (88) DM450
— 17 Apr 1913. (88) $425
— [n.d.]. (91) DM300
— [n.d.]. (90) DM500
Ls, 9 Nov 1905. 2 pp, 8vo. To Gustave Geffroy. Expressing thanks; with postscript proposing a meeting. In the hand of Rainer Maria Rilke. (89) DM3,800
— 22 Feb 1906. (91) $190
— 24 Oct 1909. (91) DM420
— 20 Nov 1910. (88) DM220
— 17 May 1912. (91) $200
— RILKE, RAINER MARIA. - ALs, 10 Apr 1906. 3 pp, 8vo. To Gustave Geffroy. As secretary for Rodin, regarding the unveiling of a statue. Sgd R.M.Rilke pour M. Rodin. (88) DM4,200

Rodney, Caesar, Signer from Delaware
ALs, 4 July 1776. 1 p, 4to. To his brother Thomas Rodney. Referring to the adoption of the Declaration of Independence. In mor case. Doheny collection. (89) $400,000
Ds, 15 Mar 1776. (91) $525

Rodney, George Brydges, 1718-92
Ds, 1 Jan 1780. (88) £80
— 12 July 1781. (88) £90

Rodrigo, Joaquin
Ms, Concierto de Aranjuez for guitar & orchestra, [c.1939]. 75 pp, folio; unstitched. Scored for solo guitar & piano. (91) £3,500

Roe, Sir Thomas, 1581?-1644
Ls, 12 Mar 1624. Byer collection. (90) $1,000

Roebling, Washington Augustus, 1837-1926
Ds s (2)1 Sept 1922. (90) $130

Roemer, Friedrich von, 1794-1864
ALs, 19 June 1859. (90) DM450

Roentgen, Wilhelm Conrad, 1845-1923
A Ls s (2), 5 July 1903 & 8 Oct 1906. 3 pp, 8vo. To Rudolf Ladenburg. About a research opening in a laboratory. Offering comments about a paper. (88) DM2,200
ALs, 17 Apr 1908. 2 pp, 8vo. To Walter Lissauer. Insisting that some important point must be clarified before his work can be ptd. (91) DM3,600

Roettingen (Lower Franconia)
— DIEMER, NICLAUSS. - Ms, Roettingen die Stadt Mit deren Rechten, und Gerechtigkeiten, 1662. 203 leaves, 320mm by 210mm. Contemp vellum bdg. Extracts from the muniment book. Lacking 1 leaf; some leaves loose. With related material. (88) DM1,300

Rogers, Ginger
Collection of c.40 A Ls s, Ls s & Ns s, 1969 to 1983. (89) £1,000
See also: Astaire, Fred & Rogers

Rogers, Will, 1879-1935
Photograph, sgd, 1921. (89) $850
Signature, [25 Oct 1930]. (90) $300

Rogers, Woodes
ADs, 29 Mar 1732. (91) $120

Roh, Franz, 1890-1965
[A typed postcard, sgd, [n.d.]., to Raoul Hausmann, with witty comments about Max Ernst, Hans Arp, & life in general, sold at HH on 16 Nov 1989, lot 2612, for DM1,300.]

Rohan, Henri, Duc de, 1579-1638
Ls, 2 June 1619. (91) DM750
Ds, 31 Mar 1607. (89) DM300

Rohan, Rene, Vicomte de, 1550-86
Ls, 13 Oct 1578. (91) DM740

Rohlfs, Christian, 1849-1938
ALs, 31 Dec 1928. (90) DM550

Rokeby, Sir Thomas, 1631?-99
Autograph Ms, diary recording his activities & expenses as Judge on Circuit, Mar 1688 to Aug 1697; c.150 pp, size not stated, in contemp panelled calf. (88) £800

Roland, Jeanne Marie Phlipon, 1754-93
A Ls s (2), 16 Feb 1776 & 8 Oct 1788. (88) £180

Rolfe, Frederick William, 1860-1913
Collection of 123 A Ls s, ANs, & autograph postcard, 13 Nov 1895 to 25 Nov 1906. About 175 pp, various sizes, mtd & bound in 4 vols & boxed with a

copy of Without Prejudice, specially bound in mor gilt. To John Lane & members of his staff, & to Grant Richards (1). Covering the gamut of his relationship with his pbr. Various signatures. Koch Foundation. (90) $38,000

Series of 4 A Ls s, 21 Oct 1902 to 16 Jan 1909. 13 pp, 8vo. To Mrs. [Gleeson] White. About his struggle as an artist, college work at Oxford, a stay in Venice, etc. (90) £2,800

Rolland, Romain, 1866-1944
[An important collection of over 40 A Ls s & Mss by Rolland, 1906 to 1936, c.80 pp, to a variety of recipients covering a number of subjects sold at S on 17 Nov 1988, lot 288, for £8,800 to Motramm.]

Autograph Ms, article, Un Appel aux Europeens par Georg Fr. Nicolai, sgd & dated 20 Oct 1918. 6 pp, mostly 4to. With related autograph postcard, sgd, 5 Nov 1918. (90) DM1,100

Collection of ALs & autograph quotation, sgd, 29 May 1930 & 5 May 192. (89) DM400

Series of 4 A Ls s, 15 May 1899 to 15 July 1909. (90) DM420

A Ls s (2), 25 June 1930 & 2 July 1934. 6 pp, 8vo. To Ernst Wurm. Reflecting about poetry & the mission of an artist. Contents not stated. 1 letter foxed. (88) DM1,100

ALs, 3 Feb 1906. (91) DM220
— 2 Feb 1913. (88) DM250
— 9 Sept 1924. (91) DM250
— 22 Mar 1932. (89) DM200
— 10 Dec 1942. (90) DM360

Photograph, sgd & inscr, Mar 1928. (90) DM300

Rolling Stones, The
Ns, [c.1965]. (88) $1,000
— JAGGER, MICK. - ALs, [n.d.]. Fan letter. Framed with related material, 11.5 by 24 inches. (88) $950

Rolls, Charles Stewart, 1877-1910
Series of 4 A Ls s, 28 to 31 Oct 1901. (88) £520

ALs, 5 June 1907. (88) DM270
— 4 Feb 1909. 10 pp, 4to. To Frederick Henry Royce. Discussing in detail their cars, their sales strategy & their aero-engines, & sending photographs of the Wright Brothers' aeroplanes (present). (90) £17,500

Roman Catholic Church
Ms, Decretti della Congregazione de' Vescovi, e Regolari dell' Anno 1582, fino 1619. Phillipps Ms.10179. (91) $475

Romayne, Nicholas, 1756-1817
Series of 9 A Ls s, 10 Feb to 12 May 1797. 18 pp, folio & 4to. To William Blount. About political matters, foreign affairs, the need to confer privately, etc. With related material. (88) $1,100

Romberg, Bernhard, 1767-1841
Autograph music, Andante con Moto for violoncello & bass, notated on 6 systems of 2 staves each; [n.d.]. (91) £525

Rommel, Erwin, 1891-1944
Ls, 3 Apr [19]33. 1 p, 4to. To his publishers Mittler & Son. Discussing the schedule for completion of his book on infantry tactics. Retained carbon copy, sgd in pencil. Margins trimmed. (88) $1,200
— 22 Nov 1940. 1 p, 4to. To Barth. Thanking for birthday congratulations. (91) $2,000
— [1942]. (89) DM650
— [n.d.]. 1 p, 4to. To Dr. Launsky. Ptd letter acknowledging a message of support. Including typed postscript. (90) DM3,600

Autograph postcard, sgd, 9 Sept [19]39. Recipient unnamed. Thanking for congratulations on his promotion & expressing satisfaction about the military situation in Poland. (89) DM1,600
— 1 Jan 1941. (88) DM1,000

Ds, certificate for [the future Gen.] Johannes Mayer, issued by the military academy at Potsdam; 23 Aug & 24 Oct 1938. 2 pp, folio. Partly ptd; sgd twice. (90) DM2,200
— 21 July 1940. 1 p, 8vo. Conferral of a decoration on Lieut. Melchior. (89) DM1,400

Photograph, sgd, [n.d.]. Postcard size. Sgd in indelible pencil. In uniform, with decoration. (88) DM1,050

Romney, George, 1734-1802
ALs, 8 July 1775. (89) £800

Romulo, Carlos P., 1899-1985
Ls, 9 Sept 1969. (91) $160

Rooke, Sir George, 1650-1709
Collection of 3 A Ls s & AL, 9 July to 24 Aug 1701. (88) £440

Roon, Albrecht, Graf von, 1803-79
ALs, 7 Sept 1868. (91) DM850
— 26 May 1872. Schroeder collection. (89) DM220
— 16 May 1876. Schroeder collection. (89) DM260
Autograph postcard, sgd, 4 Aug 1870. Schroeder collection. (89) DM550

Roon, Albrecht, Graf von, 1803-79 — & Bismarck, Otto von, 1815-98
[An ALs by Roon, [13 Nov 1864], 1 p, 4to, to Bismarck, with ALs by Bismarck to Roon at bottom, discussing the plan to appoint Prince Friedrich Karl Governor of Schleswig & Holstein, sold at star on 5 Apr 1991, lot 1683, for DM5,200.]

Roosevelt, Edith Kermit, 1861-1948
ALs, 24 Feb 1920. (89) $65
— [n.d.]. (89) $55
Ns, [31 Jan 1941]. (89) $90
Franking signature, [7 Aug 1932]. Alexander collection. (90) $85

Roosevelt, Eleanor, 1884-1962
Collection of 4 Ls s, photograph, sgd & inscr, & 2 signatures, 26 Jan 1939 to 28 Oct 1945. (90) $800
Series of 6 Ls s, 1948 to 1953. (90) $300
Ls s (2), 4 Aug 1937. (90) $50
— Ls s (2), 14 Apr & 19 May 1938. (88) $140
— Ls s (2), 24 June 1945 & 17 Sept 1953. Byer collection. (90) $550
Ls, 25 Jan 1941. (91) $375
— 22 Oct 1945. (91) $450
— 2 July 1947. (91) $425
— 13 Oct 1949. (90) $275
— 18 Sept 1950. (91) $550
— 24 Oct 1958. (88) $50
See also: Roosevelt, Franklin D. & Roosevelt

Roosevelt, Franklin D., 1882-1945
[A group of 7 autograph draft Mss, sgd pseudonymously ("Callaghan"), 19 - 27 Feb 1939, length not stated, press releases issued during his cruise coinciding with Navy maneuvers in the Caribbean, with related material, sold at P on 22 May 1990, lot 105, for $8,500.]
[Elfenbein, Julien. - A pen-&-ink bust port of Roosevelt, 1944, 475mm by 370mm, sgd by Roosevelt & Elfenbein, sold at sg on 24 Mar 1988, lot 163, for $325.]
Transcript, Address ... Accepting the Democratic Nomination for President of the United States, 27 June 1936. 5 pp, folio. Typescript copy, sgd. With letter of transferral, 11 Aug 1936. (89) $2,500
Typescript (duplicated), The Log of the Cruise of President Franklin D. Roosevelt to Dry Tortugas", 29 Nov - 6 Dec 1937. 23 pp, size not stated; mimeographed. Sgd & inscr to Harry Hopkins on tp. (88) $2,300
Collection of 2 A Ls s, 15 Ls s, autograph endorsement, sgd, & 4 telegrams, 16 Apr 1913 to 18 Apr 1934. Length not stated. To Eckford DeKay. Mostly about matters of naval interest. With 6 secretarial letters & 10 carbon copies of DeKay's replies. (89) $6,500
— Collection of ALs & telegram, [30 Mar - 7 Apr, & 28 May 1927]. 1 p, 4to, & telegram. To Eugene Van Nest. Accepting an invitation to deliver the Memorial Day address at Rhinebeck, NY. Wiring he will not be able to arrive in time. With copies of 4 letters from Van Nest to Roosevelt. (89) $1,500
ALs, 18 Nov 1927. (91) $500
— [19 Nov 1927]. (91) $850
— 19 Nov [19]27. (91) $650
Collection of 3 Ls s & 2 Ds s, 2 Feb 1920 to 11 Oct 1933. (89) $900
— Collection of Ls & group photograph, sgd, 19 Aug 1937 & [n.d.]. (90) $600
Series of 3 Ls s, 9 Jan 1929 to 17 June 1932. (90) $650
— Series of 5 Ls s, 13 Nov 1929 to 30 Dec 1931. (88) $400
— Series of 4 Ls s, 14 May 1930 to 13 Oct 1932. (88) $375

1987 - 1991 • AUTOGRAPHS & MANUSCRIPTS   ROOSEVELT

— Series of 3 Ls s, 8 Jan 1935 to 9 Nov 1936. (88) $650
— Series of 3 Ls s, 24 May 1937 to 28 Oct 1938. 4 pp, 4to. To Archibald R. Watson. About an "interpretation" suggested by Watson, & discussing the cataloguing of historical records by the W.P.A. & the possibility of publishing NY City records. (89) $1,200
Ls s (2), 6 Dec 1917 & 17 June 1929. McVitty collection. (90) $700
— Ls s (2), 1 & 30 Aug 1932. (88) $175
— Ls s (2), 23 Jan & 21 Feb 1933. (88) $600
— Ls s (2), 26 June & 24 July 1935. (89) $1,000
— Ls s (2), 26 Sept 1935 & 10 Oct 1938. 2 pp, 4to. To Harold Jacobi of the United Jewish Appeal of NY. Regarding a benefit performance, & extending greetings. (90) $1,100
Ls, 8 Sept 1914. (91) $150
— 19 June 1916. (91) $400
— 16 Oct 1917. (91) $225
— 16 Mar 1918. (88) $250
— 9 May 1918. (90) $120
— 23 May 1924. (88) $120
— 13 Jan 1927. (89) $120
— 26 July 1927. (91) $750
— 19 Oct 1927. (91) $100
— 31 July 1928. (91) $180
— 19 Aug 1930. (90) $425
— 13 Nov 1930. (90) $200
— [n.d.]. (88) $100
— 5 May 1931. (88) £160
— 5 May 1931. (90) $120
— 19 June 1931. Byer collection. (90) $425
— 7 Dec 1931. (91) $130
— 8 Feb 1932. (90) $180
— 23 Mar 1932. (89) $425
— 18 July 1932. (91) $110
— 22 Aug 1932. (91) $375
— 20 Nov 1932. (90) $210
— 1 Feb 1933. (89) $220
— 3 June 1933. (91) $275
— 1 Nov 1933. Rosenbloom collection. (88) $600
— 6 Nov 1933. (89) $210
— 22 Nov 1933. (91) $180
— 9 Jan 1934. (91) $100
— 13 June 1935. (91) $600
— 26 Aug 1935. (90) $450
— 30 Jan 1936. (89) $140
— 30 Apr 1936. (88) $425
— 24 Aug 1936. (88) $220
— 22 Apr 1938. (90) $250
— 16 Sept 1939. (88) $350
— 2 Oct 1940. (90) $260
— 29 Nov 1940. (89) $250
— 3 Feb 1942. (91) $400
— 9 Feb 1942. (91) $300
— 2 Apr 1943. (89) £380
— 28 Dec 1943. (91) $175
— 25 Jan 1944. Byer collection. (90) $800
— 11 Dec 1944. (91) $200
Series of 5 A Ns s, [18 - 27 Feb 1939]. 5 pp, 4to. To Stephen Early (2), Henry Morgenthau, Cordell Hull, & Gov. Lawrence Kramer. Draft telegraph messages about various matters, sent from his cruise in the Caribbean. With related material. (90) $8,000
ANs, [n.d.]. (88) $190
Ns, 2 July 1936. (89) $150
Collection of Ds & photograph, sgd, [n.d.]. (90) $850
Ds s (2) 1 Jan 1929 & 1 Jan 1932. (89) $210
Ds, 1916. (91) $250
— 1 Feb 1927. (91) $600
— 17 Apr 1931. (88) $90
— 25 Feb 1932. (88) $110
— 7 July 1933. (88) $110
— 19 Jan 1934. (88) $130
Autograph endorsement, docket, sgd FDR, on insurance bill from the William Hart Insurance Office, 1 Jan 1927. (90) $160
Check, accomplished & sgd, Sept 1927. (90) $500
— Anr, accomplished & sgd, 17 Oct 1927. (91) $600
— Anr, accomplished & sgd, 10 Jan 1928. (90) $600
— Anr, accomplished & sgd, 3 Mar 1928. (91) $500
Engraving, 18 Feb 1933. (91) $400
Executive Mansion card, sgd as Governor of NY; [n.d.]. (89) $220
Group photograph, [1936?]. (90) $950
— Anr, sitting at long meeting table with Vice President John Nance Garner & his entire cabinet, c.1938. 4to. Sgd on image by all. (90) $2,750

649

ROOSEVELT

— Anr, with Basil O'Connor, [late 1930s]. (91) $550
Menu, dinner given in his honor by the National Press Club, Washington, 22 Nov 1932. (90) $200
— Anr, dinner of the Inner Circle at the Hotel Astor, 18 Feb 1933. (90) $200
Photograph, sgd, [early 1930s]. (89) $400
— Anr, [c.1932]. (88) $325
— Anr, [n.d.]. (91) $375
Photograph, sgd & inscr, [c.1929]. (89) $230
— Anr, [n.d.]. (90) $300
— Anr, [n.d.]. (90) $220
— Anr, [n.d.]. (90) $500
Signature, [n.d.], on Masonic membership certificate, 12 Sept 1918. (88) $140
— Anr, on engraved 8vo bust port by J. (88) $175
— Anr, 28-29 Nov 1941, on mimeographed White House agenda for his official trip to Warm Springs, Georgia; 2 pp, folio. (90) $450
White House card, sgd; [n.d.]. (90) $300
— Anr, sgd, [n.d.]. (90) $300

Roosevelt, Franklin D., 1882-1945 —& Churchill, Winston L. S., Sir, 1874-1965
Group photograph, seated on the deck of the U.S.S. Augusta, with aides in background; [c.12 Aug 1941]. 4to. Sgd by Roosevelt, Churchill, E. J. King, George Marshall, J. E. Dill & H. R. Shark. Framed with related material. (90) $16,000

Roosevelt, Franklin D., 1882-1945. See: Churchill, Winston L. S. & Roosevelt

Roosevelt, Franklin D., 1882-1945 —& Roosevelt, Eleanor, 1884-1962
[Their signatures, 19 Apr 1934, 5 by 6.5 inches, with related material, sold at wa on 21 Oct 1989, lot 292, for $270.]

Roosevelt, Franklin D., 1882-1945 —& Roosevelt, James
[5 typed memoranda prepared & initialled (4) by James Roosevelt as White House Secretary, 10 Feb to 22 Oct 1937 & [n.d.], all with his father's autograph endorsements, sgd FDR, sold at P on 26 Oct 1988, lot 176, for $1,400.]

AMERICAN BOOK PRICES CURRENT

Roosevelt, Hilborne L., 1849-86
ALs, 28 Aug 1878. (90) $180

Roosevelt, James
[A collection of 2 brief A Ns s ("Pa") by Franklin D. Roosevelt, & 1 Ls each by Harry S. Truman, 13 Feb 1964, & Dwight D. Eisenhower, 30 Sept 1967, all addressed to James Roosevelt, sold at P on 26 Oct 1988, lot 168, for $1,200.]
See also: Roosevelt, Franklin D. & Roosevelt

Roosevelt, Theodore, 1858-1919
[A family photograph, with Roosevelt's head affixed from anr photograph, 2 July 1903, 13 by 10 inches, sgd by all 8 members of his family, framed, sold at Dar on 4 Oct 1990, lot 366, for $6,000.]
[A photogravure port, sgd, 1 p, 4to, from the limited, sgd Ed of his Big Game Hunting in the Rockies and on the Great Plains, sold at pnNy on 10 Dec 1987, lot 73, for $325.]
Autograph Ms, article, Riding to Hounds on Long Island. [Pbd July 1886] 20 pp, folio, in mor gilt by Stikeman. With a copy of the pbd version. (91) $13,000
Collection of ALs & Ls, 23 May 1887 & 21 July 1905. (89) $600
— Collection of ALs & typescript, sgd, 12 Nov 1893 & [n.d.]. 4 pp, 8vo & 4to. To Joseph E. Brown, declining an invitation to speak. Transcription of remarks about Lincoln, sgd. (90) $2,750
— Collection of ALs, 11 Ls s & letters (some by secretaries), autograph Ms, typescript, & 2 telegrams, 27 June 1910 to 23 July 1918. To Sen. Elmer J. Burkett. Concerning a speaking engagement at Omaha, 2 Sept 1910, including Ms & typescript of his speech, & later attempts to arrange a reunion. With related material. (89) $1,100
ALs, 28 Dec 1883. 2 pp, 8vo. To [Philip] Garbutt. Hoping for recipient's vote [in the NY Assembly's Speakership contest]. (91) $1,700
— 21 Feb 1884. (91) $500
— 27 Nov 1889. 1 p, 8vo (card). Recipient unknown. Replying to an inquiry & stating that "a politician can be a christian". Rosenbloom collection.

(88) $1,900
— 14 Nov 1890. (89) £400
— 26 Dec [18]91. (88) $500
— 19 July 1904. (90) $900
— 8 Sept 1909. 2 pp, 4to. To Carl Akeley. Offering an elephant "for your group in the American Museum at New York". (90) $3,250
— 13 Sept 1909. 2 pp, 4to. To Carl Akeley. Concerning the skin & skeleton of an elephant for the American Museum. Sgd in pencil. Including 1-line postscript in anr hand. (90) $2,750
— 2 Feb 1910. 2 pp, 4to. To Carl Akeley. Thanking for photographs & mentioning hunting "nine white rhino". In pencil. (90) $3,000
— 5 Feb 1910. 3 pp, 8vo. To Mr. Everhart. Offering antelope skulls to a museum. In pencil. With related material. (89) $1,550
— 16 Aug 1915. (89) $750
— 10 July 1916. 4 pp, 4to. To Edwin A. Van Valkenburg. Analyzing the demise of the Progressive Party. With related material. (90) $4,750
— 15 July 1916. (91) $500
— 6 Jan 1917. (88) $550

Collection of 3 Ls s & 2 Ds s, 23 Dec 1898 to 10 Nov 1911. (89) $650
— Collection of Ls & photograph, sgd & inscr, 29 Oct 1901 & 15 Aug 1912. Size not stated, & 6.5 by 4.25 inches. To Sen. William P. Frye, informing him of an appointment. Photograph inscr to John A. Ordway. Framed. (90) $1,800
— Collection of Ls & Ds, 4 June 1902 & 30 Apr 1904. Doheny collection. (89) $800
— Collection of Ls & ANs, 14 & 27 July 1906. 2 pp, 4to, & White House card. To Howard Allen Bridgman & Mary North Bryant Bridgman. Complimenting him on a recent editorial, & sending his autograph. McVitty collection. (90) $2,400
— Collection of 4 Ls s & letter, 9 Nov 1911 to 2 Feb 1912. 5 pp, 4to. To Edwin A. Van Valkenburg. About various political issues. With related material. (90) $1,600
— Collection of 2 Ls s & letter, 16 July to 28 Aug 1912. 4 pp, 4to. To Edwin A. Van Valkenburg. About matters pertaining to his Presidential nomination. With related material. (90) $4,750
— Collection of 3 Ls s, letter, & ANs, 22 Jan 1913 to 11 Dec 1914. Length not stated. To Edwin A. Van Valkenburg. About various matters pertaining to Progressive Party politics. With related material. (90) $5,000
— Collection of 3 Ls s, letter & ANs, 20 May 1913 to 19 Sept 1918. (90) $1,000
— Collection of 4 Ls s & 3 A Ns s, 12 Jan to 8 Dec 1916. Length not stated. To Edwin A. Van Valkenburg. About various domestic issues, speeches, etc. With related material. (90) $2,250
— Collection of Ls, letter, & 2 A Ns s, 23 Apr to 24 Dec 1918. 7 pp, 4to & 8vo. To Edwin A. Van Valkenburg. About newspaper articles, his son's death, his health, etc. 1 ANs initialled. With related material. (90) $3,000

Series of 3 Ls s, 8 Nov 1907 to 10 Mar 1909. 3 pp, 4to. To Carl Akeley. Thanking for gifts & making plans for his African expedition. With carbon copy of Akeley's letter to Roosevelt, 5 Feb 1909. (90) $1,800
— Series of 3 Ls s, 7 to 28 July 1911. (90) $800
— Series of 6 Ls s, 15 Jan to 3 Sept 1915. 6 pp, 4to. To Edwin A. Van Valkenburg. About various political matters. With related material. (90) $3,250
— Series of 10 Ls s, 25 Jan to 25 Oct 1917. 10 pp, 4to. To Edwin A. Van Valkenburg. About his activities during the war, speeches, etc. 2 letters with secretarial signatures. With related material. (90) $1,700

Ls s (2), 8 June 1906 & 18 Aug 1908. 3 pp, 4to. To Sen. Elmer J. Burkett. Stressing the importance of the meat-inspection bill. Approving of the 1907 emergency currency law. With related material. (89) $2,250
— Ls s (2), 27 & 28 Nov 1906. 2 pp, 4to. To John W. Burgess. Disapproving recipient's recent remarks on the Monroe Doctrine in Berlin. Sang collection. (91) $1,500

Ls, 21 May 1895. (90) $350
— 1 July 1895. (91) $180
— 2 Dec 1896. (90) $140

ROOSEVELT

— 14 Apr 1898. (88) $300
— 20 Feb 1899. (91) $150
— 9 Nov 1901. (91) $950
— 8 Dec 1902. 1 p, 4to. To Edward North Buxton. Commenting about Buxton's book & hunting. Laid into a copy of book. (89) £1,400
— 24 Dec 1903. (91) $400
— 1 Sept 1904. 1 p, 4to. To the Civil Service Commission. Accepting their reasoning regarding a petition & suggesting ways of addressing him. With photo of drawn port. (89) $1,600
— 7 Nov 1904. (89) $180
— 6 Mar 1905. (91) $650
— 12 July 1905. (90) $350
— 29 Aug 1905. (89) $750
— 12 Feb 1906. (91) $750
— 10 Dec 1907. 1 p, 4to. To Fairfax H. Wheelan. About the application of recipient's half-brother for a position under the Canal Commission. McVitty collection. (90) $1,100
— 5 Feb 1908. (90) $300
— 15 May 1908. (91) $950
— 4 Dec 1908. (89) $550
— 22 Dec 1908. (91) $275
— 11 Feb 1909. (89) $800
— 14 June 1911. 2 pp, 4to. To Edwin A. Van Valkenburg. Complaining about the faking of news by Associated Press. With related material. (90) $2,250
— 27 June 1911. 3 pp, 4to. To Edwin A. Van Valkenburg. Insisting that he never pledged himself to support President Taft's renomination. (90) $2,250
— 7 June 1912. (88) $75
— 6 Feb 1913. (91) $110
— 25 Mar 1913. (89) $160
— 23 Nov 1914. 2 pp, 4to. To Edwin A. Van Valkenburg. Outlining party strategy after the lost election. (90) $4,750
— 17 Dec 1914. 3 pp, 8vo. To Chester H. Rowell. On Progressive party politics. With ink annotations. (89) $1,600
— 12 Apr 1915. 2 pp, 4to. To Herman Bernstein. Explaining his policy of toleration for all religions & national origins. (91) $4,400
— 29 June 1915. 2 pp, 4to. To Edwin A. Van Valkenburg. Commenting on plans to support a League for International Peace. (90) $4,750
— 24 Sept 1915. (90) $175
— 8 May 1916. (90) $200
— 17 Aug 1916. (89) $170
— 2 Sept 1916. 2 pp, folio. To Chester H. Rowell. About the Judge Ben Lindsay incident & about his puzzlement about what to do about California. With ink annotations. (89) $1,500
— 5 Sept 1916. (90) $130
— 5 Sept 1916. 3 pp, 4to. To Edwin A. Van Valkenburg. Analyzing his political failures & successes. (90) $7,500
— 4 Jan 1917. (91) $425
— 1 May 1917. (91) $950
— 18 May 1917. 1 p, 4to. To Edwin A. Van Valkenburg. Commenting on recipient's editorial on Wilson & the war. Including 2-line autograph addition. (90) $2,250
— 13 Aug 1918. (89) $140
— 14 Aug 1918. 1 p, folio. To Chester H. Rowell. Criticizing Woodrow Wilson & comparing Wilson's differences in theory & in practice to the Bolshevists. (89) $5,000
— 14 Aug 1918. 2 pp, 4to. To John Burroughs. About his wounded sons & the war. Some autograph additions. Doheny collection. (89) $6,500
— 18 June [n.y.]. (88) $110

Letter, [n.d.]. 6 pp, 4to. To Ernest Brucken. Typed draft with extensive autograph additions; about Americanism & patriotism, & charging him with an attempt to create a German-American voting block. In mor bdg with related material. Byer collection. (90) $4,600

ANs, 23 Nov 1904. Size not stated. To Col. Stone. Thanking for a letter. (89) $1,600
— 13 June 1906. 2 pp, 16mo (White House Card). Recipient unnamed. Requesting help for Mr. Davenport. (90) $1,800

Ns, 3 Feb 1897. (88) $250

Collection of Ds & engraving, 2 May 1906 & 11 Nov 1908. (90) $350

Ds s (2) 19 & 25 Apr 1906. 3 pp, folio, on rectos only. Typed proclamations regarding aid for the victims of the San Francisco earthquake. With autograph corrections. Doheny collection. (88)

$8,000
Ds, 5 May 1896. (91) $80
— 26 Dec 1901. (91) $550
— 3 Mar 1902. (89) $300
— 14 Mar 1902. (91) $100
— 12 Apr 1902. (89) $300
— 14 May 1902. (91) $500
— 28 June 1902. (91) $450
— 28 June 1902. (88) $275
— 16 July 1902. (91) $300
— 3 Nov 1903. (91) $400
— 13 Nov 1903. (90) $475
— 30 Nov 1903. (91) $475
— 23 Jan 1904. (88) $325
— 23 Apr 1904. (90) $250
— 12 Dec 1904. (91) $475
— 20 Dec 1904. Byer collection. (90) $900
— 21 Dec 1904. (88) $260
— 2 June 1906. (88) $190
— 28 June 1906. (91) $500
— 10 Jan 1907. (91) $500
— 19 July 1907. (91) $220
— 19 Dec 1907. (90) $220
— 19 Dec 1907. (90) $325
— 7 Jan 1908. (89) $600
— 21 Mar 1908. (89) $500
— 23 Dec 1908. (88) $260
— 15 Jan 1909. (89) $130
— 15 Jan 1909. (88) $150
Autograph sentiment, Nov 1892. (88) $120
Photograph, sgd, 1898. (91) $85
— Anr, [n.d.]. (90) $300
Photograph, sgd & inscr, 22 Oct 1904. (91) $400
— Anr, 21 Dec 1904. Inscr to Mrs. L. S. Hungerford. Oval format, ptd on 8.5 by 12 inch sheet. (91) $1,400
— Anr, 26 Mar 1905. (89) $600
— Anr, 19 Aug 1905. (89) $425
— Anr, 30 Mar 1907. (90) $320
— Anr, 30 Apr 1908. (91) $650
Photograph, [n.d.]. (90) $140
Signature, [3 June 1899]. (91) $140
— Anr, 3 June 1899. (91) $65
— Anr, 7 Feb 1902. (91) $300
— Anr, 31 Mar 1903. (91) $425
— Anr, [n.d.]. (90) $100
White House card, sgd, [n.d.]. (90) $260
— Anr, sgd; [n.d.]. (90) $190
— ROOSEVELT, ETHEL CAREW. - Series of 88 A Ls s, 1908 to 1913. To Josephine Osborn. Describing her travels with her father, etc. With related material. (89) $700
See also: Clemens, Samuel Langhorne

Root, Charlie, 1899-1970. See: Ruth, George Herman ("Babe") & Root

Rops, Felicien, 1833-98
Collection of ALs & ADs, 1 Jan 1887 & [n.d.]. 3 pp, 8vo. To Adolphe [Popp], about missing a meeting; with pencil sketch at head, 12cm by 13cm. Humorous promissory note to Mme Popp, with satirical etching; on official stamped paper. With small watercolor, sgd F.R., & 2 small etchings. With material relating to his student Armand Rassenfosse. (88) DM1,600

ALs, [1859]. (89) £500

Roscoe, William, 1753-1831
ALs, 28 July 1826. (89) £40

Rosegger, Peter, 1843-1918
Autograph Ms, story, Das Verbrechen; [n.d.]. 4 pp, 4to. With numerous additions; sgd at head. (90) DM1,500

Collection of ALs & photograph, sgd & inscr, 28 Mar 1896 & [n.d.]. (91) DM240

A Ls s (2), 2 & 24 Oct 1877. (88) DM280
ALs, 11 Oct 1878. (89) DM280
— 17 July 1888. (90) DM220

Roselius, Ludwig, 1874-1943
ALs, 9 Mar 1908. (91) DM850

Rosenberg, Alfred, 1893-1946
Ds, 23 Dec 1940. (91) $140
— [1946]. (90) $120
Photograph, sgd, [c.1940]. (88) $200

Ross, George, Signer from Pennsylvania
Ds, July 1750. (88) $130
— 14 May 1761. (91) $220

Ross, John, 1790-1866
ADs, 6 Mar 1857. (89) $500

Ross, Sir John, 1777-1856
Ls, [c.1812]. (88) $50

Ross, Sir William Charles, 1794-1860
[A collection of c.100 letters addressed to him and to members of his family, many regarding arrangements for his portraits of members of the Royal family, c.1832 to 1855, sold at S on 22 July 1988, lot 535, for £550 to Maggs.]

Rossetti, Christina Georgina, 1830-94
Autograph quotation, poem, Up-Hill, 1st stanza; [n.d.]. (89) £190

Rossetti, Dante Gabriel, 1828-82
Autograph Ms, poem, The Five from Trafalgar, 21 Oct 1880. Wolf collection. (89) £850
— Autograph Ms, sonnet, Place de la Bastille, Paris; [c.1880]. (91) $800
Series of 11 A Ls s, 1863 to 1865. 30 pp, 8vo. To W. H. Clabburn & Mrs. Clabburn. Discussing his painting Magdalene purchased by recipient. 2 A Ls s torn. (89) £1,800
ALs, 2 Jan 1850. 8 pp, 8vo. To William Bell Scott. Sending a copy of the 1st issue of The Germ & inviting contributions. Koch Foundation. (90) $6,000
— 20 Nov 1863. Byer collection. (90) $150
— 15 Dec 1863. (89) $375
— [Feb 1865]. (91) £220
— 10 Mar [n.y.]. (90) DM450
— CAINE, HALL. - Proof copy, Recollections of Rossetti; 1882. Annotated by William Michael Rossetti, Theodore Watts, & Caine. With related material. (88) £1,700

Rossi, Bruno
Ls, 29 July 1976. (91) $200

Rossini, Gioacchino, 1792-1868
Autograph music, Andante for piano in G minor, 7 Sept 1844. 1 p, 16.5cm by 27cm. 11 bars, sgd. Possibly unrecorded. (91) £2,800
— Autograph music, song, Mi lagnero tacendo, 30 Mar 1855. 1 p, 8vo. 9 bars in B flat major, scored for voice & piano; sgd. (91) £2,500
— Autograph music, song, Un Rien, for mezzo-soprano & piano in G major, 6 Oct 1862. 3 pp, 8vo. Sgd & inscr to Mme J. Cohen. Some corrections. (91) £2,800
— Autograph music, song, Un rien, sgd, inscr to Mme Robin & dated 1860. 2 pp, folio. Including fine ptd borders. (90) £3,500
Collection of ALs & photograph, sgd & inscr. (88) $850
A Ls s (2), 26 Jan & 15 Mar 1846. (88) £750
ALs, 22 Aug 1830. 2 pp, 4to. To Sig. Severini. Requesting recipient's support for [Giovanni] Tadolini. (90) DM1,800
— 10 Feb 1834. 1 p, 4to. To Donizetti. About the lack of success of Donizetti's opera in Paris & the advantages of the theatrical life of the city. (89) £5,800
— 9 May 1841. 3 pp, 4to. To the Marquis de las Marismas. Describing his health problems. In French. (89) DM2,400
— 9 May 1841. 3 pp, 4to. To the Marquis de las Marismas. Describing his health problems. In French. (90) DM2,900
— 30 Aug 1841. 1 p, 4to. To Francesco Pasetti. Introducing Conte Regoli. (91) DM1,500
— 29 Dec 1841. 2 pp, 4to. To Giovanni Ricordi. Informing him about the dispute over publishing rights to his Stabat Mater. Repaired. (91) £3,200
— 14 Mar 1843. 1 p, 8vo. To Donizetti. Letter of introduction for Marietta Alboni. (89) £2,800
— 16 Nov 1845. (91) £900
— 25 Jan 1848. (89) £550
— [n.d.]. (88) £300
— 25 Mar 1851. 2 pp, 4to. To his banker Della Ripa. Expressing dissatisfaction & disgust with Bologna & the Bolognese. (91) £1,050
— 9 Feb 1853. (88) DM900
— 23 Sept 1853. 1 p, 4to. To Count Giulio Litta. Recommending the singer Rosine Stoltz. (90) £1,200
— 31 Dec 1853. (89) £350
— 31 Dec 1853. (91) £850
— 25 July 1858. 1 p, 8vo. To Prince Carlo Poniatowski. Requesting his help in a search for teachers for a conservatory at St. Petersburg. (88) DM1,200
— 17 Jan 1859. (91) £750
— 25 Mar 1861. (88) £450
— 16 June 1861. 1 p, 4to. To his friend d'Ancona. Sending his port. (89) DM1,100
— 15 July 1864. (88) £650

— 28 May 1866. 1 p, 4to. To Michele Costa. Thanking for a gift of a Cheddar cheese, & mentioning Adelina Patti. (91) £1,200
— 24 Apr 1868. (91) £850
— [n.d.]. (89) £500
Photograph, sgd & inscr, 1860. 17cm by 12cm; framed. Inscr to Mme Falk. (90) £1,700
— Anr, 19 Aug 1866. 60cm by 49cm. Inscr to Adolphe Danhauser. Framed. (89) £2,800

Rostand, Edmond, 1868-1918
ALs, [n.d.]. (91) DM260

Rostopchin, Fyodor Vasilyevich, Count, 1763-1826
ALs, 13 July 1799. (91) DM800
— [n.d.]. (90) DM440

Roth, Alfred, 1879-1969
[A collection of 75 letters & cards addressed to him by politicians, authors, generals, etc., 1910 to 1945, mostly relating to the radical national movement in Germany, with related material, sold at star on 10 Mar 1988, lot 1222, for DM2,500.]

Roth, Eugen, 1895-1976
Autograph Ms, play, Der Dom; 1923. 75 pp, folio. Half vellum bdg. Complete text. Fair copy; sgd on tp. (90) DM1,100
Photograph, sgd, [n.d.]. (89) DM390

Roth, Joseph, 1894-1939
Collection of 2 A Ls s & autograph postcard, sgd, 6 Feb 1929 & [n.d.]. 2 pp, 4to, & card. To Efraim Frisch. About recipient's financial security & the situation in Germany. (90) DM2,300
Series of 3 A Ls s, 3 July 1924, 3 Jan 1925 & [n.d.]. 3 pp, 4to & 8vo. To Eugen Kirchpfening. Asking him to write. 1 with postscript by his wife Friedl. With related material. (90) DM1,700
ALs, 17 Sept 1922. 1 p, 4to. To Emil Faktor. Explaining his reasons for quitting the staff of the Berliner Boersen-Courier. (91) DM4,200
— 22 Nov [1925]. 2 pp, 8vo. To Max Krell. Thanking for reviews & reporting about a visit with Rowohlt. (91) DM2,400
— 27 Dec 1927. 1 p, 8vo. To Georg Heinrich Meyer. Mentioning his book Die Flucht ohne Ende, & hoping Meyer will write his memoirs. (90) DM1,700
— 1 June 1928. 1 p, 4to. Recipient unnamed. Thanking for words of praise. (90) DM1,550
Ls, 28 Feb 1939. (88) DM900
ANs, 26 May 1931. (91) DM850

Rothenstein, Sir William, 1872-1945
Series of 68 A Ls s, 4 July 1905 to 20 Dec 1940. (88) £300

Rothschild, Amschel Mayer, Freiherr von, 1773-1855
ALs, 10 Oct 1815. (90) $500
Series of 5 Ls s, 27 Aug 1816 to 15 Apr 1846. 6 pp, folio & 4to. To different recipients about a variety of financial matters. (90) DM4,000
Ls, 6 Jan 1828. (90) DM1,000

Rothschild, James, Freiherr von, 1792-1868
Ls, 19 Dec 1860. (88) DM280

Rotteck, Karl Wenzeslaus Rodecker von, 1775-1840
A Ls s (2), 24 Aug 1827 & 5 Sept 1839. (90) DM280

Rouault, Georges, 1871-1958
Autograph Ms, Le Gand Pan, [n.d.]. (89) DM320
ALs, [n.d.]. Byer collection. (90) $200
ANs, 21 Jan 1924. (91) $325
— [n.d.]. (90) $110

Rouget de Lisle, Claude Joseph, 1760-1836
Autograph Ms, narrative poem, Comal et Galvina, [n.d.]. (88) £150
ALs, [4 Mar 1796]. 2 pp, folio. To Minister of War Petiet. Explaining his determination to quit military service. (90) DM1,400
— 28 Dec 1830. 2 pp, 4to. To Hector Berlioz. Admiring his talents & suggesting a meeting. (89) £2,400
— 30 [Oct 1831]. (90) DM700
— 11 June [1834]. (91) DM800

ROUSSEAU

Rousseau, Jean Jacques, 1712-78
Autograph Ms, about marriage & divorce, compilation for Mme Dupin's projected work on the history of women; [c.1746-51]. 6 pp, 4to, in wrap. (90) £1,300
— Autograph Ms, about the education of women, [c.1760s]. (88) $550
— Autograph Ms, essay about the art of translating & Tacitus, fragment; on verso various notes, crossed out; [n.d.]. 2 pp, 8vo. Fold brittle; stained. (88) DM2,800
— Autograph Ms, excerpt from Fleury's Histoire ecclesiastique, describing events of 1119; [n.d.]. 3 pp, 4to. (89) DM1,050
— Autograph Ms, excerpts from the Rec[ueil] gen[er]al des Ab[bayes] de Fr[ance], [n.d.]. (91) DM950
— Autograph Ms, excerpts from various works about learned women; [n.d.]. 12 pp, 4to. (90) DM4,500
Autograph transcript, excerpt from Fleury's Histoire ecclesiastique, vol 8, p 417. (90) DM650
ALs, 26 Nov 1762. 2 pp, 4to. To Jacques Francois De Luc. Responding to a proposal that he travel to Geneva, & complaining about his political tribulations. Repaired & tipped to larger leaf, with trans. Barrett collection. (89) $4,250
— 7 June 1764. 3 pp, 4to. To Jean Andre De Luc. Suggesting changes to De Luc's dedicatory epistle to the Academy & agreeing to sit for a port. (88) £4,500
— 30 June 1765. 2 pp, 4to. To the bookseller Duchesne. Ordering books & complaining about delays in receiving consignments. Doheny collection. (89) $2,200
— 18 Mar 1766. 3 pp, 4to. To [his pbr Pierre Guy]. Returning proofs, & recommending the son of his landlord Mr. Pulleyn. (89) £4,000
— 16 May 1770. 1 p, 4to. To [William Constable]. Expressing thanks for a pamphlet, & promising to visit soon. Including quatrain at head. (90) DM5,200
ADs, 15 Apr 1765. 1 p, 8vo. Pay order drawn on his pbr Duchesne for 1,200 Livres payable to M. Roguin. Endorsed by Duchesne; cancellation marks. 3 endorsements on verso. With a port. (88) DM3,000

Rousseau, Theodore, 1812-67
ALs, [n.d.]. (88) DM550
— 28 May 1861. (91) DM750
— [n.d.]. Byer collection. (90) $110

Roussel, Albert, 1869-1937
ALs, 16 Jan 1922. (89) DM400

Royal Academy
[A collection of c.400 items, letters, cut signatures, engravings, etc, compiled by Henry Howard, Secretary to the Academy, [1st half of 19th cent], mtd in 2 19th-cent half calf albums, sold at C on 22 June 1988, lot 166, for £150 to Bristow.]

Rubens, Peter Paul, 1577-1640
ALs, [n.d.]. 1 p, 4to. To M. de los Allve. Explaining his delay in completing a painting. In French. Tipped to larger leaf, with engraved port. Barrett collection. (89) $11,000

Rubinstein, Anton, 1829-94
Autograph Ms, program for "2d Recital" in Liverpool, Manchester & Birmingham, [1886]. (91) $75
Autograph music, Etudes for piano Op. 23, nos 1, 3, 4 & 5, [c.1860]. 15 pp, folio, unbound. On 8 & nine staves per page; some alterations. Marked by the ptr. (89) £3,500
— Autograph music, Melodie [in F], for piano; [n.d.]. 2 pp, folio. Name added in anr hand; edges frayed. (90) £5,000
— Autograph music, Violin Concerto in G major, Op. 46, full score; [c.1857]. 102 pp, folio. Notated on up to 16 staves per page, with numerous alterations. Sgd & dedicated to Henri Wieniawsky. Tp repaired. (89) £7,500
Collection of ALs & autograph quotation, sgd, 5 Apr 1863 & 18 May 1881. (90) £650
ALs, 19 Aug 1855. (88) DM650
Autograph quotation, 8 bars from an unidentified work, sgd; 9 Mar 1876. (90) $225

Rudolf, Archduke of Austria, Cardinal, 1788-1831

Ls, 23 Mar 1823. (90) DM280

Rudolf, Archduke, 1858-89

A Ls s (2), 6 Jan & 5 Feb 1885. 4 pp, 8vo. To the court painter Angeli. Asking him to paint his & his wife's portraits for the Antwerp exhibition. With a photograph. (88) £1,600

ALs, 19 Mar 1878. 7 pp, 4to & 8vo. To Alfred Edmund Brehm. About his grandfather's death, & sending a Hungarian eagle. (91) DM2,200

— 29 Feb 1880. (90) £900

— 26 Mar 1880. 6 pp, 8vo. To the Austrian ambassador in Brussels [Graf von Chotek]. Thanking for his help, & mentioning his forthcoming marriage to Princess Stephanie. (90) £1,800

— 26 Mar 1880. (90) £900

— 5 Apr 1880. (90) £1,000

— 27 Jan 1881. (91) £700

— 16 June 1881. (88) DM1,000

— 25 May 1882. (91) £380

— [May 1883]. 3 pp, 8vo. To an unnamed Marquis. About a meeting, & making plans for a hunt. (91) DM1,700

— 26 Aug 1886. 4 pp, 8vo. To Prince Wilhelm of Prussia [Kaiser Wilhelm II]. Thanking for a heron, sending a book, & looking forward to a visit. (89) DM1,600

— 26 June 1887. (91) £700

— 1 Jan 1888. (89) $325

— 13 Sept 1888. (89) £350

— [n.d.]. 2 pp, 8vo. To Count Roman Potocki. Sending antlers of deer shot on recipient's estates. (90) DM1,100

Autograph telegram, sgd, 6 Mar [1880]. 1 p, 4to. To his father. Stating that he has seen the princess [Stephanie, his future bride] at dinner. (90) £1,400

Photograph, sgd, July 1877. (90) £950

Rudolf II, Emperor, 1552-1612

Ls, 1 Jan 1582. (88) DM800

— 2 Oct 1586. (90) DM900

— 29 Oct 1594. (90) DM320

— 6 Dec 1602. (89) DM480

— 12 Jan 1604. (89) DM550

Ds, 22 Oct 1576. (90) DM480

— 20 Aug 1608. 1 p, vellum, 590mm by 640mm. Patent of nobility & grant of arms for Thomas & Ludwig Blingony. With painting of the arms in gold & colors. (90) DM2,700

Rudolf IV, Duke of Austria, 1339-65

Ds, [17 Dec] 1361. 1 p, 8vo. Order addressed to the mayor & magistracy of an unknown town to exempt the monastery at Rain from taxes. Repaired; was mtd. Figdor collection. (89) DM8,000

Rueckert, Friedrich, 1788-1866

Autograph Ms, poem, 2 quatrains, beginning "Lass deinen Arm nicht schlapp am Leibe niederhangen; [n.d.]. (91) DM650

— Autograph Ms, poem, beginning "Was haelt den Vogel, der in Lueften schwebt, ein Band", [n.d.]. (89) DM650

— Autograph Ms, poem, beginning "Das Bisschen Dichterruhm...", [n.d.]. (88) DM700

— Autograph Ms, poem, Die nackten Weisen; [n.d.]. (90) DM850

— Autograph Ms, poem, Die Schoene von Basra, [n.d.]. 1 p, 8vo. 24 lines, sgd. Fragment of address on verso. (90) DM1,600

ALs, 20 May [1820]. (91) DM550

— 24 June 1835. 1 p, 4to. To Schelling. Letter of recommendation for Eduard Closter. Address leaf def. (90) DM1,200

— 23 Mar 1838. (88) DM700

ADs, 20 Aug 1832. (90) DM550

Ruest, Anselm, Pseud of Ernst Samuel

Series of 3 A Ls s, Jan 1937 to Sept 1938. 18 pp, 4to & 8vo. To Paul Zech. About political & literary matters & the situation of writers in emigration. Including fragments of anr 4 A Ls (1 sgd). (90) DM1,100

Ruffus, Jordanus, fl.1240

Ms, De medicina equorum, in Italian. [Italy, c.1490]. 129 leaves, 245mm by 175mm. Contemp lea over wooden bds. (91) DM9,000

Ruge, Arnold, 1803-80
Autograph Ms, essay, Aus der deutschen Emigration, [1877 or later]. (91) DM850
A Ls s (2), 8 Sept 1839 & 16 Jan 1840. (91) DM550
ALs, [c.1 Jan 1865]. 2 pp, 8vo. To a friend in NY. Commenting on the Civil War in America, public opinion in Germany, political journals, etc. (91) DM1,050

Rugendas, Georg Philipp, 1666-1742
Ms, Der Harnisch von seinem Entstehen bis zu seinem Wiedervergeh, 1714. 23 pp, 325mm by 205mm. Including 14 fine watercolors of armor. Interleaved with English trans, & bound with related material. (90) $8,500

Ruggles, Daniel, 1810-97
ALs, 22 Feb 1862. (91) $350
Ls, 24 Apr 1863. (88) $85

Rundstedt, Gerd von, 1875-1953
ALs, 5 Apr [19]16. (88) $150
— 8 Aug 1916. (91) $100
Autograph postcards (2), sgd, 11 June & 24 Aug 1941. (90) DM440
— Autograph postcards (2), sgd, 6 Apr 1942 & 1 July 1943. (91) DM950

Rungenhagen, Karl Friedrich, 1778-1851
Series of 3 A Ls s, 1 Mar 1844 to 20 Nov 1846. (89) DM220

Runyon, Damon, 1880-1946
ALs, [c.1932]. (90) £280

Ruppert, Jacob, 1867-1939
Cut signature, 25 Mar 1924. (91) $110

Rupprecht, Crown Prince of Bavaria, 1869-1955
Photograph, sgd, 23 Feb 1915. (90) DM550
— Anr, 1939. (89) DM210

Rush, Benjamin, Signer from Pennsylvania
ALs, 22 May 1787. (88) $700
— 23 May 1788. (91) $200
— 24 Apr 1790. 3 pp, 4to. To James Madison. Sending Madison a pamphlet & a sermon by Dr. Richard Price. Docketed by Madison. (91) $7,500
ADs, 17 Feb 1797. 1 p, folio. Certificate that Samuel Taylor attended medical lectures at the Pennsylvania Hospital. With related material. (91) $4,000
Ds, 17 Apr 1786. (90) $800
— 17 Apr 1786. (89) $500
— 8 Mar 1796. (89) $700

Ruskin, John, 1819-1900
Autograph Ms, draft of 2 fragments of The Queen of the Air. (91) £85
Original drawings, 3 pencil sketches of Venetian architecture, with accompanying notes, [n.d.]. (89) £260
Collection of ALs & AL, [n.d.], 4 pp, 8vo. (88) $250
Series of 8 A Ls s, [n.d., 30 Aug 1855, &] 29 Aug 1856. 27 pp, mostly 8vo. To Mrs. Hewitt (6), discussing personal issues. To Elizabeth A. Solt, giving advice on drawing. To Robert Browning, chatting about doing "nothing this summer but vegetate". (88) $3,500
— Series of 6 A Ls s, 16 May to 14 Aug 1858. 7 pp, 4to. To his father. All illus, written from France, Switzerland & Italy. With a portion of a 7th letter. Koch Foundation. (90) $6,000
— Series of 40 A Ls s, [Apr 1864] to 2 Aug 1881. 145 pp, 8vo. To Mrs. Cowper Temple. About his obsession with Rose La Touche. With 5 letters by Rose La Touche & further related material. (91) £15,000
— Series of c.30 A Ls s, 1871 to 1875. 50 pp, 8vo. To Mary Spence. Discussing drawing techniques & private matters. (91) £2,400
— Series of 30 A Ls s, 1880 to 1887. (89) £550
— Series of 7 A Ls s, 1882 to 15 Dec 1882. (88) $1,000
— Series of 6 A Ls s, 1885 to 1887 & [n.d.]. (89) £420
A Ls s (2), 17 Feb 1878 & [n.d.]. (90) £320
— A Ls s (2), 24 Nov 1880 & 19 Dec 1884. Doheny collection. (89) $350
— A Ls s (2), 26 May 1882 & [n.d.]. (89) $350
ALs, [1848]. (91) £120
— 24 Apr 1849. (90) £300
— 25 Aug 1852. (88) £160
— [c.1858]. (88) £230
— 15 June 1863. Doheny collection. (89) $800

— [Feb 1867]. (88) £120
— 4 Apr [18]77. (88) $100
— 16 Apr 1884. (89) DM260
— 5 May 1886. (89) £130
— 4 Mar 1887. (91) $140

Russell, Bertrand, 3d Earl, 1872-1970
Collection of c.1000 A Ls s & Ls s, 1915 to 1968. 4to & 8vo. To his pbr Allen & Unwin, mostly to Sir Stanley Unwin. Discussing his writing activities & other matters. With carbon copies of replies & related material. (91) £18,000
— Collection of 3 A Ls s & autograph Ms, 7 June 1916 & [n.d.]. 7 pp, 8vo & 4to. To Catherine Marshall. Letters to a fellow pacifist. Memorandum regarding the activities of the No Conscription Fellowship. (89) DM1,150
ALs, 23 May 1937. (89) £380
— 7 July 1937. (90) $900
Ls, 15 July 1933. (90) $800
— 9 June 1964. (88) £260
Photograph, sgd, [n.d.]. (90) DM260
— HERRIN, M. H. - Orig drawing, pencil bust port of Russell, 14 Mar [19]40. 9 by 12 inches. Sgd by Russell. (91) $100
— SWAMY. - Orig drawings (4), port sketches of Russell; [n.d.]. Various sizes. Sgd by both. (89) £700

Russell, Charles Marion, 1864-1926
Original drawing, "The Hoss that Con Bought", [n.d.]. In pen-&-ink, 9cm by 18cm. In cloth folder with Ns by H. P. Raban giving story of the drawing. In mor case. Doheny collection. (88) $4,500
Ms, story, The Ghost Horse, [pbd 1927]. 26 pp, 4to, in Russell's (?) & Percy Raban's hand. Including pencil sketch of mtd Indians on a butte. With related material. In red mor gilt slipcase. Doheny collection. (88) $4,000
Typescript, story, Longrope's Last Guard, [pbd 1927]. 10 pp, folio & 4to. Sgd; with autograph corrections. In mor slipcase. Doheny collection. (88) $3,200
ALs, 23 July 1925. 1 p, 4to. To Percy Raban. Letter of invitation. On verso ALs from Nancy Russell to Albertine Raban. With 2 group photographs. In cloth folder & mor slipcase. Doheny collection. (88) $2,200
— 14 May [n.y.]. 3 pp, 8vo. To "Friend Pony". About working on the range in Montana, & saying he cannot "make a living painting". At head sgd ink drawing of cowboys driving a herd of horses. Doheny collection. (88) $8,000
Ds, 1 Nov 1921. 4 pp, folio. Contract for collaboration on the book Back-Trailing on the Old Frontiers, also sgd by H. P. Raban & W. W. Cheely. Doheny collection. (88) $2,500
Photograph, sgd, [c.1897]. 140mm by 97mm. Seated, 3-quarters length. Sgd on mount. Framed. Doheny collection. (88) $3,500
— Anr, [c.1900]. 8.1 by 6.1 inches, by Louis Heyne. Sgd by Russell in ink, by Heyne in pencil. Framed. (88) $3,000
Photograph, [c.1900]. (88) $500

Russell, Edward, Earl of Orford, 1653-1727
ALs, 6 Aug 1692. (88) £50

Russell, Gerald Walter, 1850-1925
Series of 85 A Ls s, 1861 to 1882. (90) £360

Russell, John, Earl Russell, 1792-1878
Series of c.50 A Ls s, c.1852 to 1871. (88) £280

Russell, Lillian, 1861-1922
Photograph, sgd, 1893. (89) $150
Photograph, sgd & inscr, [n.d.]. (89) $110

Russell, Willy
Typescript, script of Educating Rita, with additional autograph material, [n.d.]. 130 pp, folio. (91) £1,300

Russian Imperial Family
[A group of 3 photographs of Alexander II & his consort, 2 of his sons, & his grandson Nicholas II, with further photographs of Russian national types, sold at S on 5 Apr 1990, lot 11, for £1,000.]
[A collection of 21 photographs, including 7 group photographs of Nicholas II & family members, 1889 to 1928, & 14 mtd photographs of St. Petersburg, sold at S on 5 Apr 1990, lot 22, for £2,600.]
[An album of 14 photographs of a shoot at the Imperial hunting lodge of Belovejhsk, 1900, dedicated to Nikolai

RUSSIAN IMPERIAL FAMILY

Georgievich, Prince of the Hellenes, 355mm by 470mm, sold at S on 5 Apr 1990, lot 29, for £1,300.]
[A group of 75 photographs, 2 showing members of the Imperial Family, 1909 & 1912, 35 taken by an army officer during the war, & 38 recording peasant life, 1911 to 1915, sold at S on 5 Apr 1990, lot 30, for £1,000.]
[The signatures of Nicholas II, his wife, 4 daughters, & Grand Duchess Maria Pavlovna, on the occasion of the consecration of a church in Tsarskoe Selo, 1916, in an album also sgd by others, sold at C on 26 June 1991, lot 361, for £3,200 to Rosenthal.]
[4 photographs recording the life of the Imperial Family in Tobolsk, 1917, various sizes, possibly taken by Pierre Gilliard, sold at S on 5 Apr 1990, lot 34, for £700.]
[A lea album containing family photographs, reproductions of photographs & postcards, compiled by Grand Duchess Xenia Alexandrovna, c.1900 to 1928, sold at S on 5 Apr 1990, lot 23, for £16,000.]
[A photograph showing the Imperial Regalia & other works of art belonging to the Imperial Family, spread on a table before the Bolshevik committee organized to value & partially dispose of them, with related material, sold at S in 5 Apr 1990, lot 36, for £9,500.]
Group photograph, 1896. 28cm by 39cm. Nicholas II & Empress Alexandra at Ilinskoe after the coronation with 10 guests & family members. (90) £1,900
— GILLIARD, PIERRE. - 10 photographs taken by him of the Imperial Family at Tsarskoe Selo & Tobolsk, 1917, each c.85mm by 85mm. (90) £3,000
— HENDRIKOVA, COUNTESS ANASTASIA VASILIEVNA. - 102 photographs collected by her, mostly dating from her time as maid-of-honor in attendance on the Empress Alexandra, 1912 to 1916. Each c.85mm by 85mm. (90) £10,000
— SOKOLOV, NIKOLAI ALEXEEVICH. - 6 vols of evidence compiled by Sokolov, the official investigator of the murder of the Imperial Family, all with typewritten depositions by witnesses & plans of the place of murder, each

AMERICAN BOOK PRICES CURRENT

document marked as a copy & sgd by Sokolov. (90) £4,000

Russian Manuscripts
Ms, Compass of the Wise, History of a Masonic lodge. Fekula Ms.873. (91) £1,000
— Ms, Polemic for Orthodoxy and against Catholicism, & Kamen' soblazna, The Stone of Temptation, compiled by Ivan Lushkov. Fekula Ms.724. (91) £160

Ruth, George Herman ("Babe"), 1895-1948
ANs, [c.1914]. 1 p, 12mo (on verso of ptd card). To Orie Poller. Valentine greetings. (91) $2,250
— [1940s]. (89) $1,000
Ds, 16 Oct 1940. 1 p, 4to. Certificate from the Academy of Sports at the NY World's Fair, issued to Howard Good. Also sgd by others. (90) $1,900
Menu, New Haven Base Ball Dinner, 26 Jan 1923. 4 pp, 8vo. Sgd by Ruth & 3 others. (89) $1,500
Photograph, sgd, [n.d.]; size not stated. With signature on card, 2 Aug 1948. Both mtd in his book The Babe Ruth Story, 1948. (90) $1,600
— Anr, [n.d.]. (88) $425
Photograph, sgd & inscr, 1932 World Series photograph, 9 by 7 inches. Sgd & inscr to Bernadette Brown, 1948. (88) $2,700
Signature, on program for Lawn Fete, 8 & 9 June 1923, at Iona School, New Rochelle, NY. (89) $350
— Anr, [10 Oct 1930]. (91) $540
— Anr, [5 Nov 1935]. (91) $1,000
— Anr, [n.d.]. (91) $500
— Anr, [n.d.]. (89) $425
— Anr, [n.d.]. (89) $310
— Anr, [n.d.]. (90) $425
— FOSTER, E. J. - Typescript, 40-line poem entitled "Babe Ruth"; [n.d.]. On 4to sheet. Sgd by Ruth. Framed with related material. (91) $2,000

Ruth, George Herman ("Babe"), 1895-1948 —&
Gehrig, Henry Louis ("Lou"), 1903-41
[Their signatures on a card, [n.d.], framed with related material, sold at wa on 21 Oct 1989, lot 363, for $1,000.]

Ruth, George Herman ("Babe"), 1895-1948 —&
Root, Charlie, 1899-1970
[Their signatures on a creased light brown paper, [n.d.], framed with photographs, overall size 26 by 20 inches, sold at Dar on 13 June 1991, lot 333, for $600.]

Rutherford, Ernest, Lord Rutherford of Nelson, 1871-1937
ALs, 7 Jan 1931. (89) DM650

Rutledge, Edward, Signer from South Carolina
ADs, 1 July 1777. (91) $325

Ryder, Dudley, 1st Earl of Harrowby, 1762-1847. See: George III, 1738-1820

S

Sacher-Masoch, Leopold von, 1836-95
Collection of ALs & photograph, sgd, 1 Oct 1873 & [n.d.]. (90) DM440
Series of 7 A Ls s, 5 Jan 1871 to 10 July 1874. 8 pp, 8vo. To the Ed of the Illustrirte Zeitung at Leipzig. Concerning the reception of some of his works, etc. (91) DM1,100
ALs, 19 Jan 1874. (91) DM360
— 25 Jan 1885. (89) DM360

Sackville-West, Victoria, 1892-1962
Autograph Ms, essay, Outdoor life, for The Character of England, Ed by Ernest Barker, draft; [n.d.]. With corrected typescript & further related material; together c.68 pp, various sizes. (88) £1,200
Series of 3 A Ls s, 12 Mar 1946 to 18 July 1950. (88) £320

Sacrobosco, Johannes
Ms, Algorismus, Tractatus de Sphera, & Computus Lunaris. [Paris, late 13th cent]. 27 leaves (some lacking), vellum, 186mm by 139mm. Modern vellum bdg. In a well-formed gothic bookhand. With 15 red or blue initials with contrasting penwork, 2 large illuminated initials with full-length extensions, & 9 large scientific & astronomical diagrams. (90) £9,000
— Ms, Tractatus de Sphera, & Computus Lunaris, with John Peckham, Perspectiva Communis, & Pseudo-Euclid, Catoptrica. [Italy, early 14th cent]. 70 leaves & a half-leaf, vellum, 187mm by 135mm. Limp vellum bdg. In professional rounded gothic bookhands by several scribes. With 4 full-page tables in red & black & 56 pp with diagrams. (88) £24,000

Sadat, Anwar El, 1918-81. See: Carter, James Earl ("Jimmy") & Others

Sade, Donatien Alphonse Francois, Marquis de, 1740-1814
ALs, [Dec 1773]. 1 p, 4to. To M. [Rayolle?]. Asking if he will work for him. Tipped to larger leaf. Barrett collection. (89) $1,100
— [3 Nov 1799]. 2 pp, 4to. To his lawyer Gauffridi. Regarding attempts to have the sequestration lifted from his property. (89) £1,150
AL, 3 Aug [1793]. 4 pp, 4to. To Charles Gaufridi. About the political situation in Paris, problems regarding his castle, etc. Seal tear. (89) DM4,200
— 3 Aug [1793]. 4 pp, 4to. To Charles Gaufridi. About the political situation in Paris, problems regarding his castle, etc. Seal tear. (90) DM4,500
Ls, [10 Feb 1795]. (91) £700

Sage, Russell, 1816-1906
Collection of 8 A Ls s, ADs, 6 Ds s, photograph, sgd, & 4 signatures, 1854 to 1886. To various recipients. Mostly concerning financial matters. (89) $2,000
ALs, 26 Feb 1900. (91) $85

St. Clair, Arthur, 1736-1818
ALs, 6 Aug 1796. (91) $550
ADs, 13 June 1801. (90) $320
Ds, 10 July 1799. (88) $350

Sainte-Beuve, Charles Augustin, 1804-69
ALs, [n.d.]. (89) DM220

Saint-Exupery, Antoine de, 1900-44
Original drawings, 5 small sketches for the Petit Prince, [n.d.]. (89) £850
Original drawing, Le Petit Prince watering his flower. 112mm by 146mm, ink & watercolor, sgd. (88) £3,000
— Original drawing, Le Petit Prince protecting his flower with a screen. 102mm by 133mm, ink & watercolor,

SAINT-EXUPERY

sgd. (88) £3,800
— Original drawing, Le Petit Prince placing a cloche over his flower. 113mm by 146mm, ink & watercolor, sgd. (88) £2,000
— Original drawing, of a boa constructor about to swallow his prey, for Le Petit Prince, 1945. 128mm by 178mm, ink & watercolor, sgd. (88) £2,100
— Original drawing, Petit Prince talking to the snake, in pencil, ink & watercolor; [n.d.]. 24cm by 18cm. Sgd on mount. (89) £3,500
— Original drawing, small figure proffering a bunch of flowers in a landscape reminiscent of the Petit Prince's planet, in pencil; [n.d.].1 p, folio. (89) £700
Typescript carbon copy, Le Petit Prince, complete draft, differing somewhat from ptd version; [1943-44]. 74 pp, folio, in cardbord folder. With numerous autograph revisions. Including 2 pencil sketches of the Little Prince. With related material. (89) £15,000
— SAINT-EXUPERY, CONSUELO DE. - Ls, 21 Nov 1945. 1 p, 4to. To Harry Hansen. Inviting him to a memorial mass in honor of her husband. With ptd invitation. (89) $80

Saint-Just, Antoine Louis Leon de, 1767-94

Ds, [5 June 1794]. 2 pp, folio. Authenticated copy of a decision of the Comite de Salut Public revising an earlier decision about rations for army horses; also sgd by Billaud-Varenne & Lindet. (90) DM1,700
— [24 July 1794]. (91) $800

Saint-Just, Antoine Louis Leon de, 1767-94 —& Others

Ds, [10 July 1794]. 1 p, folio. As member of the Comite de Salut Public, pay order in favor of Citoyen Haindel. Contemp copy, also sgd by Collot d'Herbois & Billaud-Varenne; with scribal signatures of others. Margin cut. (90) DM1,400

Saint-Pierre, Bernardin de, 1737-1814

ALs, [3 June 1797]. (90) DM250

Saint-Saens, Camille, 1835-1921

Autograph Ms, article, Liszt pianiste, sgd; [1911]. 8 pp, 4to. Written in celebration of the 100th anniversary of Liszt's birth. (90) £1,900
Autograph music, full score & choral score of his oratorio The Promised Land (Op. 140. About 320 pp & about 120 pp, both folio, the full score in half mor & the choral score in wraps. (89) £5,000
— Autograph music, Prelude pour piano in G minor, sgd & dated Oct 1866. 6 pp, size not stated; 14-stave paper. Including autograph tp. With ALs. (90) £2,500
Collection of 6 A Ls s & autograph musical quotation, 1898 to 20 Apr 1907 & [n.d.]. (90) $1,000
Series of 4 A Ls s, 18 Nov 1895 to 12 Aug 1897. (90) DM1,000
ALs, 2 Jan 1887. (89) DM220
— 8 July 1905. (89) DM340
— 9 May 1909. (90) DM420
— 11 Mar 1913. Byer collection. (90) $175
— 14 Nov 1917. (88) DM210
— 27 Nov 1917. (91) DM280
— [n.d.]. (91) £520
Photograph, sgd & inscr, 1890. (90) DM320

Saint-Simon, Claude Henri de Rouvroy, Comte de, 1760-1825

Autograph Ms, draft of a lecture concerning political science & progress, fragment; [n.d.]. (89) DM550

Saint-Simon, Louis de Rouvroy, Duc de, 1675-1755

ALs, 1 Apr 1738. 1 p, 4to. To M. de Chiron. Recommending Sieur de l'Orme. (90) DM1,800

Sala, Ilarione Bonaventura

Ms, a collection of papers, partly autograph, pertaining to the Chinese rites controversy, including 2 A Ls s to his mother, [c.1705 to 1710]. 350 pp, mostly rice paper, folio & 4to, in contemp vellum bds. (89) £4,000
Series of 12 A Ls s, 1702 & 1703. About 190 pp, 4to. To his mother & brother. Giving a detailed account of his journey from Italy to China via Brazil. Phillipps Ms.6069 & Robinson collec-

tion. (89) £3,000

Salieri, Antonio, 1750-1825
Collection of ALs & autograph music, 27 Mar 1803. 3 pp, 8vo. To [Mathias?] Stegmayer. Sending "le petit changement dont j'ai eu hier le plaisir de vous entretenir." Musical Ms, opera, Die Hussiten in Naumburg, final bars of 2 pieces in full score. (88) DM3,200

ALs, 9 Jan 1816. 3 pp, 4to. To an unnamed Baron. Explaining the importance of simplicity in music & including 6 musical canons as examples. (91) £2,500

— 19 May 1819. 1 p, 4to. Recipient unnamed. Responding to an inquiry about a monument to Mozart & Haydn. (90) £2,800

Salinger, Jerome David
Collection of 2 Ls s & corrected galley proof, 7 & 15 Nov 1962. 3 pp, mostly 4to. To John E. Woodman of Little, Brown & Co. Regarding the publication of Raise High the Roof Beam, Carpenters; and Seymour - An Introduction. With pbr's dummy of the book. (90) $3,750

Ls, 19 July 1957. 2 pp, 4to. To Don Herbert. Explaining his negative attitude towards screen & stage rights for The Catcher in the Rye. Repaired. (89) $3,750

Sallustius Crispus, Gaius, 86-34 B.C.
Ms, De Coniuratione Catilinae, & De Bello Jugurthino. [Florence, c.1460-70]. 88 leaves & flyleaf, vellum, 210mm by 137mm. Contemp Florentine blind-stamped dark brown goatskin over wooden bds. In humanistic minuscule scripts by 2 scribes. With large illuminated initial & large white-vine initial with 2-sided border. (91) £15,000

Salten, Felix, Pseud. of Siegmund Salzmann, 1869-1945
Collection of ALs & 3 Ls s, 11 Feb 1929 to 29 Dec 1934. (90) DM320

Salwowski, Mark
Original drawing, 4 young men & women standing outside a village below a galazy of stars, cover desicn for John Wyndham's The Midwich Cuckoos.
(88) £350

— Original drawing, cloaked figure on steps leading to a fantastic tower; cover design for Philip Mann's Master of Paxwax. (90) £500

— Original drawing, coach travelling towards a large castle; cover design for Barbara Hambly's The Silicon Mage. (90) £600

— Original drawing, cover design for Michael Moorckck's The Chronicles of Corum, showing a man riding through the snow away from a castle. (88) £350

— Original drawing, girl standing in front of a huge winged monster with a human head & arms, cover for Threshold by David R. (88) £500

— Original drawing, solitary figure on the wheel of a large war machine; cover design for Barbara Hambly's Handful of Darkness. (90) £500

— Original drawing, two girls in a rocky lagoon watching 3 horsemen, cover design for Sarah Brown Agen's The Trolls' Grindstone. (88) £400

— Original drawing, young man floating naked above a lake bordered by crystaline rocks & the monument of a horned figure, for the cover of Tom o' Bedlam by Robert Silverberg. (88) £350

Samuel, Patriarch of Constantinople
Ds, Sept 1763. (90) DM850

Samuelson, Arnold, 1912-81. See: Hemingway, Ernest

San Martin, Jose de, 1778-1850
Series of 7 Ls s, 1 Oct 1817 to 14 June 1820. 7 pp, folio. To the Government & the Ministry of War. Regarding various military matters. (90) DM4,400

— Series of 18 Ls s, 11 Feb to 21 Dec 1820. 18 pp, folio. To Bernardo O'Higgins & Jose Ignacio Zenteno. Mostly regarding preparations for the liberation of Peru. Edges trimmed. (89) £1,500

Ls, 3 Feb 1821. 2 pp, 4to. To Joaquin de Echevarria. Informing him about negotiations for the independence of Peru. Somewhat def. (88) $1,900

— 21 [May or June] 1822. 2 pp, folio. To Gen. Jose de Lamar. Expressing his

SAN MARTIN

suspicions of Bolivar; in cipher. With key to cipher, sgd by San Martin, on separate sheet. (91) $5,000
Ds s (2) 10 Feb & 23 Mar 1816. 5 pp, 4to. Letters of promotion. Both def. (88) $1,100
Ds, 27 Dec 1821. (91) $300

San Pasqual, Agustin de
Autograph Ms, Noticias de la Mission Serafica en China desde ... 1687, sgd & dated 4 Oct 1690. 36 pp, folio. Treatise on Franciscan missions in China, with revisions. Phillipps Ms.6069 & Robinson collection. (89) £3,000

Sanchez, Francisco, c.1550-c.1623
Ms, Doctoris Sanctij Liber I D. (90) DM300

Sancroft, William, 1617-93
Series of 37 A Ls, 12 Sept 1680 to 27 Sept 1692. 38 pp, 4to. To William Lloyd, Bishop of Norwich. Dealing with ecclasiastical & political problems. With related material. (91) £3,200

Sand, George, Pseud. of Amandine, Baronne Dudevant, 1804-76
Autograph Ms, Autour de la table, 7 articles numbered 1 - 6 & 8, each sgd; 6 June to 15 Oct 1856. About 250 pp, 8vo, stitched; in half mor case. Heavily revised. Martin collection. (90) FF36,000
— Autograph Ms, Preface d'un roman inedit. Fragments [La Mare au diable], 1845. 11 pp, 8vo, in half mor bdg. Sgd. Martin collection. (90) FF48,000
Original drawing, watercolor, hilly landscape, [c.1870]; c.10.5cm by 13.5cm. Sgd gs, in pencil. Mtd. (89) DM1,600
— Original drawing, watercolor, trees on a hill, [c.1870]; c.11cm by 15cm. Sgd gs. (89) DM1,300
Series of 3 A Ls s, 1853 & [n.d.]. (89) £800
— Series of 6 A Ls s, 9 Jan 1857 to 6 Mar 1868. 13 pp, 8vo & 4to. To different correspondents. About the actress Rachel & various literary & personal matters. (90) £2,000
ALs, 29 Apr 1842. (89) $700
— 22 Apr 1848. Barrett collection. (89) $800
— 2 May 1862. (91) $500
— [1865]. Doheny collection. (89) $420

AMERICAN BOOK PRICES CURRENT

— 29 Nov 1867. (88) $125
— 13 June 1870. (89) DM550
— 8 Dec 1871. (90) DM950
— 30 Mar 1872. (91) $300
— 29 May 1875. (88) DM550
— 4 Sept [n.y.]. (88) £180
— 4 Dec [n.y.]. (91) DM540
— [n.d.], "Friday". (90) £750
AL, 11 June 1861. (88) DM500
— 6 to 8 July 1874. 6 pp, 8vo. To [Gustave Flaubert]. Complaining about old age, commenting about the insignificance of criticism, etc. Martin collection. (90) FF7,500

Sandburg, Carl, 1878-1967
Autograph transcript, poem, Cool Tombs, [n.d.]. (89) $1,000
Typescript, The Long Shadow of Lincoln, [c.1950s]. (91) $200
Collection of 13 A Ls s & A Ns s, & 11 Ls s & Ns s, 1928 to 1959. (89) $1,000
Ls, 20 Mar 1948. (88) $80
— 10 May 1961. (91) $85
Photograph, sgd, 1965. (91) $200

Sandwich, John Montagu, 4th Earl, 1718-92. See: Montagu, John

Sandys, Frederick, 1829-1904
Series of 35 A Ls s, [c.1903-04]. (90) £750

Santa Anna, Antonio Lopez de, 1794-1876
Transcript, contemp English trans of his proclamation to his troops, 3 Aug 1829. (90) $140

Santander, Francisco de Paula, 1792-1840
ALs, 29 Dec 1823. (89) DM320

Santayana, George, 1863-1952
Series of 3 A Ls s, 19 Jan 1951 to 13 Jan 1952. (88) $175
ALs, 22 Jan 1934. Byer collection. (90) $300
— 16 June 1936. (91) $250
— 13 May 1937. (91) $175
— 23 Nov 1946. (91) $110
— 31 Jan 1950. (88) $600
— 12 Oct 1950. (88) $600

Santos-Dumont, Alberto, 1873-1932
Original drawing, India-ink drawing of an airship, sgd & dated 26 Nov 1901; 95mm by 95mm. (88) $120

Saphir, Moritz Gottlieb, 1795-1858
[A collection of 4 autograph Mss, 1 sgd at head, 15 pp, 4to, mostly def, containing fragments of a poem, of 2 essays & a review, sold at star on 9 Mar 1988, lot 288, for DM850.]
Autograph Ms, poem, Die guten und die schlechten "S" der Liebe; 20 Mar 1845. Albrecht collection. (91) SF270
ALs, 28 Mar 1826. (91) DM360

Sarg, Tony, 1880-1942
ALs, 21 Mar [n.y.]. (90) $400

Sargent, John Singer, 1856-1925
Collection of 4 A Ls s & ANs, 1914 & 1915. (90) $275
Series of 5 A Ls s, 1911 to 1915. (89) £280
— Series of 3 A Ls s, [n.d.]. (89) £520
ALs, 3 July 1899. (89) $225
— [n.d.]. (89) $500
— [n.d., "Monday"]. (88) $110

Saroyan, William, 1908-81
Collection of ALs, 6 Ls s & autograph postcard, sgd, 1934 to 1937. (89) $900
ANs, 2 May 1935. (89) $50

Sartre, Jean Paul, 1905-80
Autograph Ms, 16 lines of dialogue from Les Mains Sales, [1948]. (91) $90
— Autograph Ms, Individu et Societe. Kafka; [n.d.]. 7 leaves, 4to. Philosophical essay. (90) DM2,050
— Autograph Ms, notes on the development of bourgeois & peasant mentality in France, [n.d.]. (88) £250
— Autograph Ms, notes taken during a stay at Rome, 13 & 23 Sept [n.y.]. (88) DM1,000
— Autograph Ms, working draft of preface & conclusion to his Question de methode (initial section of his Critique de la raison dialectique), [before 1960]. About 120 pp, 4to. One section with dedication to Simone de Beauvoir ("Au Castor"). (89) £2,300
ALs, 2 Oct 1945. (91) DM900
— [c.1958]. 4 pp, 4to. Recipient unknown. Commenting on a meeting to discuss the war in Algeria. (88) DM2,200

Sassoon, Siegfried, 1886-1967
[A vol of press-cuttings & reviews largely for The Old Huntsman & Counter-Attack, compiled & annotated by Sasson, with some inserted letters, c.90 pp, 1917 to 1919, sold at S on 18 July 1991, lot 115, for £1,800 to Reece.]
[A group of 5 poetical Mss, 1937 & [n.d.], 5 pp, 8vo & 16mo, with related material, sold at S on 18 July 1991, lot 120, for £2,200 to Rota.]
[A collection of 72 letters addressed to Sassoon by a variety of literary personalities sold at S on 18 July 1991, lot 93, for £2,000 to Sawyer.]
[A vol of press-cuttings & letters, compiled & annotated by Sassoon, relating to his statement against continuation of World War I, his military career, & his support for Philip Snowden, sold at S on 18 July 1991, lot 116, for £3,500 to Imperial War Museum.]
[A collection of c.25 letters & cards addressed to him by various women writers, including Virginia Woolf & Willa Cather, sold at S on 18 July 1991, lot 151, for £1,450 to Fergusson.]
Autograph Ms, account of the background of his anti-war statement, 22 Aug 1954. 1 p, 8vo. (91) £1,200
— Autograph Ms, Aids to Reflection, notebook containing quotations mainly about poetry, in different colored inks. Initialled & dated 21 Apr 1933. 3 pp, 8vo; in wraps. With autograph tp addressed to Stephen Tennant. (88) £2,400
— Autograph Ms, hunting diaries, 1909 to 1914. About 240 pp, written in 3 vols of Bailey's Hunting Directory & 2 vols of The Hunting Diary; 8vo. With related material. (91) £6,000
— Autograph Ms, poem, [At Daybreak], 2 six-line stanzas; [n.d.]. (88) £320
— Autograph Ms, poem, December Stillness, initialled. (88) £900
— Autograph Ms, poem, To the Red Rose, draft; [n.d.]. (88) £500
Series of 9 A Ls s, 1929 to 1964. (88) £700
— Series of 11 A Ls s, 1934 to 1965. (91) £450
— Series of 4 A Ls s, 1963 to 1966. (88) £400

SASSOON

A Ls s (2), 19 Mar & 8 Apr 1920. (88) $225
— A Ls s (2), 1930 & 1951. (88) £1,000
ALs, 2 Sept 1944. (88) £160
Series of 8 autograph postcards, sgd, c.1929 to 1933. (88) £280
Autograph postcards (2), sgd, 14 & 19 Dec [1932]. (88) £260
Proof copy, Memoirs of an Infantry Officer, 1st limited Ed, 1930; 8vo. In orig wraps. With c.180 autograph alterations. Covers decorated with cut-out parrots, presumably by Stephen Tennant. (88) £3,400
— FREEDMAN, BARNETT. - Orig drawing, watercolor-&-ink design for the dustjacket of Sassoon's Memoirs of an Infantry Officer, 1931. 14.5 by 22.5 inches. (88) £2,300

Sassoon, Siegfried, 1886-1967 —&
Blunden, Edmund Charles, 1896-1974
[Autograph Mss of Sasson's poem April Birthday, & of Blunden's poem Avon or Acre, [n.d.], 2 pp, 4to, laid down on recto & verso of a single sheet, sold at S on 15 Oct 1987, lot 862, for £300.]

Sassoon, Siegfried, 1886-1967. See:
Hardy, Thomas
See also: Sitwell Family

Satie, Eric, 1866-1925
ALs, [7 July 1915]. 1 p, 8vo. To Valentine Gross. Declining an invitation. With calligraphic initials. (89) DM1,800

Satie, Erik, 1866-1925
ALs, 29 Feb 1912. 1 p, 4to. To Roland-Manuel. Declining an invitation by recipient's parents & mentioning Ravel. Sgd ES. (88) DM2,300
— 2 Oct 1915. 2 pp, 8vo. To Valentine Gross. Welcoming her on her return to Paris, asking about Varese, etc. Sgd ES. (90) £1,100
— 24 Nov 1915. (90) £800
— 15 May [19]16. (88) £600
— [1916]. (88) £780
— 18 Feb 1918. 1 p, 8vo. To Monsieur Roux. Relating to criminal proceedings against him for insulting a critic. Sgd ES. (88) DM2,000
— 10 May 1920. (90) £700
Autograph postcard, sgd, [16 Mar 1916].

AMERICAN BOOK PRICES CURRENT

(90) £420

Sauckel, Fritz, 1894-1946
Ls, 5 Dec 1939. (90) $190

Sauerbruch, Ferdinand, 1875-1951
ALs, 26 Sept 1916. (91) DM850

Saumaise, Claude de, 1588-1653
Ls, 9 Apr 1650. 2 pp, 4to. To Nicolas de Flecelles, Vicomte de Bregy. Acknowledging a letter & informing him about the [Swedish] Queen's illness. (90) DM2,200

Sauter, Rudolph H.
Original drawings, to illus "Harvest", [n.d.]. (89) £100

Savigny, Friedrich Karl von, 1779-1861
ALs, 11 Oct 1812. (88) DM550
— 25 Apr 1856. (91) DM580
— 24 Feb 1860. Schroeder collection. (89) DM400
— 4 July 1860. (89) DM450
See also: Brentano, Clemens

Savigny, Karl Friedrich von, 1814-75
ALs, 27 July 1866. (91) DM700

Sayers, Dorothy L., 1893-1957
Ls, 3 Jan 1937. (91) $275
— 19 Oct 195b [sic]. (90) £180

Schacht, Hjalmar, 1877-1970
Ls, 7 Aug 1931. (90) $120

Schadow, Johann Gottfried, 1764-1850
ALs, 26 Jan 1813. (90) DM480
— 25 Aug 1832. (91) DM440
— 11 May 1835. (90) DM360
— 9 Apr 1848. (91) DM550
— 5 Dec 1849. (91) DM320
ADs, 21 Dec 1795. (88) DM380

Schall von Bell, Adam Johann, 1591-1666
Autograph Ms, Discurso com que se conclue a Relacao da China, 11 Nov 1638. 3 pp, folio, in half mor. Appendix to an unrecorded work on the Chinese missions. Final paragraph in Latin. Margins trimmed. Phillipps Ms.17214 & Robinson collection. (89) £3,000
ALs, 1 Sept 1634. 8 pp, folio, in half mor. To Manuel Dias, Vice-Provincial of China. Duplicate, discussing the re-

form of the Chinese calendar & methods used in establishing Chinese chronology. In Latin. Phillipps Ms.17214 & Robinson collection. (89) £10,000

Scharf, Sir George, 1820-95
[An album containing c.85 letters & notes addressed to him by various recipients including Charles Dickens, C. Kean, G. B. Shaw, etc., mostly 1830s to 1860s, sold at S on 15 Nov 1988, lot 1672, for £800 to Wilson.]

Scharnhorst, Gerhard von, 1755-1813
Autograph Ms, report concerning a petition by the Jew Mendel Wolf for permission to manufacture saltpeter, 15 July 1808. (91) DM1,000
— Autograph Ms, review of an artillery manual, sgd; 3 Dec 1812. 3 pp, folio. Repaired. Schroeder collection. (89) DM1,050

A Ls s (2), 19 Mar 1810. 3 pp, 4to. To King Friedrich Wilhelm III of Prussia. Official letter resigning his position as head of the War Department, & covering letter discussing the King's wish to keep him as acting head. (90) DM4,000

ALs, 24 Apr 1798. 1 p, folio. To Lieut. Preuss. Requesting him to collect topographical information about Westfalia. Schroeder collection. (89) DM1,100
— 2 Apr 1805. (90) DM580
— 18 Apr 1810. 2 pp, 4to. To Karl von Altenstein. Making plans for the recruiting of soldiers. (89) DM1,500

Ls, 23 Dec 1808. Schroeder collection. (89) DM560
— 16 May 1809. (88) DM540

Schaukal, Richard von, 1874-1942
ALs, 9 Oct 1933. (88) £260

Scheer, Reinhard, 1863-1928
ALs, 2 Dec 1918. 6 pp, folio. To Admiral von Levetzow. Commenting about the revolution in Germany & explaining his resignation from the navy. With related material. Schroeder collection. (89) DM4,800

Scheerbart, Paul, 1863-1915
Autograph Ms, story, Die Nussbaumtorte; [n.d.]. 22 pp, 4to, in bds. Complete text. (90) DM3,500
— Autograph Ms, story, Die Weltschaukel, [n.d.]. 12 pp, 4to, on rectos only. Complete text, sgd at head. (91) DM6,000

ALs, 2 Sept 1906. (88) DM260
— 18 Aug 1908. (90) DM750

Schefer, Leopold, 1784-1862
Autograph Ms, poem, Prometheus und der Nachtwaechter; [n.d.]. (90) DM300

Scheffel, Joseph Victor von, 1826-86
Autograph Ms, poem, Sommerfrische am Bodensee, sgd & dated 26 Aug 1871. 6 four-line stanzas. With related material. (89) DM1,300

Collection of 16 A Ls s, 22 autograph postcards, sgd, & autograph sentiment, sgd, Feb 1872 to 17 Dec 1884. About 20 pp, 8vo, & cards. Mostly to his nephew, the bookseller Adolf Mehl. Concerning business affairs & private matters. With related material. (89) DM1,400

Series of 11 A Ls s, Nov 1856 to July 1875. 34 pp, 8vo & 4to. To various friends & to his mother (1). Covering a wide range of topics. (90) DM3,000

Scheffer, Thassilo von, 1873-1951
Collection of 14 A Ls s, 32 Ls s, 14 autograph cards, sgd, & 3 typescripts, sgd, 18 Oct 1947 to 26 June 1951. 105 pp, 8vo & 4to. To Thea Leymann. Regarding his personal situation, his work, poetry, problems with his pbr, etc. With related material. (91) DM2,500

Scheler, Max, 1874-1928
ALs, [1915/16]. (88) £160

Schelling, Friedrich Wilhelm Joseph von, 1775-1854
Collection of ALs & AL, 11 & 14 Nov 1843. (90) DM1,000
ALs, [Apr 1819]. (91) DM750
— 16 Mar 1844. (91) DM550
— 18 May 1848. 2 pp, 4to. To the pbr [Perthes]. Regarding an advertisement for his son's book. Margin def. (89)

SCHELLING

DM1,700
A Ls (2), [Dec 1853]. (90) DM550
AL, 13 Oct 1853. (90) DM900
Ds, 21 Nov 1818. (90) DM220
— STROEHLIN, FRIEDRICH JAKOB. - ALs, 2 Nov 1795. 4 pp, 4to. To Josef Friedrich Schelling. About the position as tutor with the Riedesel family for recipient's son Friedrich Wilhelm. (90) DM580
— WILHELM, PRINCE OF PRUSSIA. - ALs, [late Mar 1848]. 1 p, 8vo. To Schelling. Commenting on the abdication of the King of Bavaria. (90) DM240

Schelling, Joseph Friedrich, 1737-1812
ALs, 14 July 1806. (90) DM260

Schelling, Pauline, 1786-1854
Collection of ALs & autograph transcript, 17 Oct 1844 & [n.d.]. (90) DM320

Schenkendorf, Max von, 1783-1817
ALs, 8 May 1816. (89) DM480

Scherffenberg, Gotthard von, d.1634
Ds, 27 Nov 1631. (88) DM300

Schetky, John George, 1776-1831
Ms, Duo pour Flute & Violoncello, in D major; [n.d.]. (89) DM650

Schicht, Johann Gottfried, 1753-1823
ALs, 16 Jan 1802. (90) DM250

Schiele, Egon, 1890-1918
Autograph Ms, poem, Abendland, sgd & dated 1910. 1 p, folio, on cartridge paper. 12 lines, written in majuscules. In indelible pencil. (88) £4,000
— Autograph Ms, poem, Ahrenfeld, sgd & dated 1910. 1 p, folio, on cartridge paper. 8 lines, written in majuscules. In pencil. On verso notes about the Wittek family in anr hand. (88) £3,000
— Autograph Ms, poem, Anarchist, sgd & dated 1910. 1 p, folio, on cartridge paper. 11 lines, written in majuscules. In pencil. (88) £5,500
— Autograph Ms, poem, Anarchist - Sonne, sgd & dated 1910. 2 pp, folio, on cartridge paper. 21 lines, written in majuscules. In pencil. (88) £4,000
— Autograph Ms, poem, Dame im Park, sgd & dated 1910. 1 p, folio, on cartridge paper. 7 lines, written in majuscules; 1 revision. In pencil. (88)

AMERICAN BOOK PRICES CURRENT

£3,800
— Autograph Ms, poem, Das Portraet des stillbleichen Maedchens, sgd & dated 1910. 1 p, folio, on cartridge paper. 11 lines, written in majuscules. In indelible pencil. (88) £3,800
— Autograph Ms, poem, Ein Selbstbild, sgd & dated 1910. 1 p, folio, on cartridge paper. 14 lines, written in majuscules. In pencil. (88) £4,000
— Autograph Ms, poem, Ein Selbstbild, sgd & dated 1910. 1 p, folio, on cartridge paper. 12 lines, written in majuscules. In indelible pencil. (88) £3,800
— Autograph Ms, poem, Kuenstler, sgd & dated 1910. 1 p, folio, on cartridge paper. 4 lines, written in majuscules. In pencil. (88) £3,000
— Autograph Ms, poem, Landstrasse, sgd & dated 1910. 1 p, folio, on cartridge paper. 5 lines, written in majuscules. In indelible pencil. (88) £3,000
— Autograph Ms, poem, Musik beim Ertrinken, sgd & dated 1910 & 22 July 1910. 1 p, folio, on cartridge paper. 8 lines, written in majuscules. In pencil. (88) £3,000
— Autograph Ms, poem, Nasser Abend, sgd & dated 1910. 1 p, folio, on cartridge paper. 13 lines, written in majuscules. In indelible pencil. (88) £3,000
— Autograph Ms, poem, Staatsmann, sgd & dated 1909. 1 p, folio, on cartridge paper. 3 lines, written in majuscules. In pencil. (88) £2,400
— Autograph Ms, poem, Tannenwald, sgd & dated 1910. 1 p, folio, on cartridge paper. 9 lines, written in majuscules. In indelible pencil. (88) £3,200
— Autograph Ms, poem, Visionen, sgd & dated 1910. 2 pp, folio, on cartridge paper. 44 lines, written in majuscules. In indelible pencil & pencil. (88) £6,800
— Autograph Ms, poem, Weisser Schwan, sgd & dated 1910. 2 pp, folio, on cartridge paper. 6 lines, written in majuscules. In indelible pencil. (88) £3,200
— Autograph Ms, poem, Zwei Chleriker, sgd & dated 1910. 1 p, folio, on cartridge paper. 13 lines, written in

majuscules. In indelible pencil. (88) £4,000

ALs, "Sunday" [1910]. 1 p, 4to. To Otto Wagner. Requesting a loan to go to Vienna. (89) £3,800

— 18 Aug 1912. 4 pp, 4to. Recipient unnamed. "Virtually a literary manifesto". In pencil. Small tear. (88) £4,000

— 23 Nov 1914. 2 pp, 8vo. To his mother. About his sister's wedding. (89) £4,000

— 28 Sept 1918. 1 p, 4to. To Johannes Fischer. Sending drawings, & inquiring about books & 2 pictures. (89) £2,500

— 30 Sept 1918. 1 p, 8vo. To Dr. Schneider. Declining his invitation to collaborate on a project. (89) £1,800

— 25 Oct 1918. 3 pp, 4to. To Anton Kolig. Informing him that he has been unable to send the money for Kolig's drawing because of medical expenses for his wife. (90) £5,000

Autograph postcard, sgd, 1917. (89) £700

ADs, [n.d.]. (89) £700

Schill, Ferdinand von, 1776-1809

ALs, 31 July [1808]. 3 pp, folio. To Capt. von Oppen. Protesting against a reprimand. Schroeder collection. (89) DM3,000

Ls, 11 Nov 1808. (90) DM800

Schiller, Charlotte von, 1766-1826

Series of 12 A Ls s, 6 Apr 1806 to 5 Jan 1815; c.60 pp, various sizes. (88) £500

ALs, 6 June 1789. (89) £350

— 21 Dec 1822. Albrecht collection. (91) SF700

Schiller, Friedrich von, 1759-1805

[A collection of 2 documents, 1 sgd by Georg Wilhelm zu Schaumburg-Lippe, 9 Dec 1826, 1 sgd by Ernst I von Sachsen-Coburg, 20 Dec 1826, 4 pp, folio, guaranteeing the copyright to Schiller's works to his children, sold at star on 9 Mar 1988, lot 293, for DM1,600.]

Autograph Ms, outline for the tragedy Die Maltheser, [n.d.]. 2 pp, 4.5cm by 20cm, cut from larger leaf. Fragment. (91) DM3,400

— Autograph Ms, part of the draft for Act II, scene 2 of this trans of Phaedra, [n.d.]. 2 pp, c.7.7cm by 21.3cm; cut from a larger sheet. Was mtd. (89) DM6,500

Ms, fragment of the stage Ms prepared for the 1st performance of Wilhelm Tell, 1804, with autograph corrections; with autograph list of dramatis personae, [June 1804], inscr in Goethe's hand with names of actors [for the performance of 21 Dec 1805]. 64 pp, c.18.5cm by 16cm. Def; rescued from the fire of the Weimar theater, 1825. Albrecht collection. (91) SF55,000

ALs, 13 Sept 1785. 3 pp, 4to. To Friedrich Kunze. Assuring him of his friendship, & referring to his medical studies. Albrecht collection. (91) SF16,000

— 4 Apr 1786. 1 p, 4to. To Georg Joachim Goeschen. Discussing the ptg of Don Carlos. Postscript removed. (90) DM16,500

— 26 July 1788. 1 p, 4to. To his pbr Crusius. Regarding the Ms for his Geschichte des Abfalls der vereinigten Niederlande. (89) DM15,000

— 1 Oct 1788. 4 pp, 4to. To Christian Gottfried Koerner. Reporting about his recent work & reflecting about his writing. Sgd S. (89) £7,500

— 15 Apr 1790. 2 pp, 8vo. To Georg Joachim Goeschen. Requesting an advance on his fee for a calendar, offering a new Ms for an Ed of Thalia, mentioning Goethe's Faust, etc. Albrecht collection. (91) SF17,000

— 30 Nov 1790. 3 pp, 4to. To Kriegsrath [Bertram]. Responding to an inquiry about the Ms of his Fiesco. (89) £8,000

— 9 Oct 1794. 3 pp, 4to. To Christian Gottfried Koerner. Informing him about his joint literary plans with Goethe. Albrecht collection. (91) SF18,000

— 23 Jan 1795. 1 p, 8vo. Recipient unnamed. Expressing thanks & promising to send a copy of Die Horen. (88) £4,200

— 5 Feb 1795. 4 pp, 4to. To Christian Gottfried Koerner. Suggesting improvements to an essay. (89) £7,500

— 3 July 1796. 2 pp, 4to. To Christian Gottfried Koerner. Praising Goethe's novel Wilhelm Meisters Lehrjahre, & sending Mss for publication. With

SCHILLER

Koerner's reply, 8 July 1796, analyzing differences between Goethe & Schiller. Albrecht collection. (91) SF25,000
— [25 Jan 1798]. 2 pp, 4to. To Christian Gottfried Koerner. About his health problems & efforts to complete his Wallenstein. Repaired. (91) DM15,000
— 1 May 1800. 2 pp, 4to. To [Friedrich von] Schelling. Concerning Schelling's controversy with C. G. Schuetz & the Allgemeine Literatur-Zeitung. (89) DM28,000
— 16 June 1800. 4 pp, 4to. To Christian Gottfried Koerner. Informing him about the successful premiere of Maria Stuart & promising to send some of his works. Sgd Sch. (90) DM28,000
— 3 [i.e.4] Sept 1800. 4 pp, 8vo. To Christian Gottfried Koerner. Sending a copy of his poems, mentioning Goethe & Humboldt, etc. Sgd Sch. Kuenzel collection. (90) DM28,000
— 11 Feb 1802. 2 pp, 4to. To Siegfried Lebrecht Crusius. Reporting that he bought a house at Weimar & asking for an advance on forthcoming payments. Was mtd. (88) DM40,000
— 16 July 1804. 3 pp, 4to. To Carl Friedrich Zelter. Commenting on recipient's proposed essay to Hardenberg & discussing the relationship between art & religion. (91) £11,000

Autograph sentiment, "Das Leben ist kurz, die Kunst ist lang", 4 Mar 1801. 1 p, 8vo. Sgd. (90) DM12,000
— FORGERY. - Letter, 9 Sept 1795, 1 p, 4to, by Gerstenbergk, forging Schiller's hand, to an unnamed recipient. Requesting the return of a journal. Albrecht collection. (91) SF320
— FORGERY. - Ms, 2 poems [by Gerstenbergk], Das weibliche Ideal, & Die schoenste Erscheinung, [n.d.]. 2 pp, 4to. Sgd Schiller. (89) DM360
— GEORG I, HERZOG VON SACHSEN-MEININGEN. - Ds, 5 Jan 1790. 2 pp, folio. Appointment of Schiller as Court Councillor. Albrecht collection. (91) SF2,200

Schiller, Johann Kaspar, 1723-96
ALs, 22 Dec 1794 to 2 Jan 1795. 4 pp, 4to. To his daughter Christophine Reinwald & her husband Wilhelm. Sending New Year's wishes, & discussing his horticultural activities. With engraved port. Albrecht collection. (91) SF3,600
ADs, 18 Jan 1779. (89) DM700

Schiller, Karl von, 1793-1857
Autograph endorsement, sgd, on a document regarding a theft in a forest, [spring 1852]. (90) DM300

Schinkel, Karl Friedrich, 1781-1841
ALs, 18 May 1821. 3 pp, 4to. To Baron von Altenstein. Pointing out that an interesting estate near the Botanical Gardens in Schoeneberg is for sale. Albrecht collection. (91) SF1,600
— 25 Sept [18]29. (90) DM650
— 6 Oct 1835. (91) DM850
— 14 Dec 1837. (90) DM950

Schirach, Baldur von, 1907-74
Ls, 14 June 1967. (90) $140

Schlaf, Johannes, 1862-1941
Autograph Ms, poem, Meernacht, sgd & dated 1 Jan 1907. (89) DM260
Autograph transcript, 3 poems, Das einsame Haus, Erwachen, & Yggdrasil, [n.d.]. (88) DM380

Schlatter, Adolf, 1852-1938
Autograph Ms, essay, Die Kirche, wie Jesus sie sah; Dec 1935. (88) DM380
— Autograph Ms, essay, Ist Jesus ein Suendenbock?, [n.d.]. (90) DM350

Schlegel, August Wilhelm von, 1767-1845
Autograph Ms, information concerning access to the Museum of Antiquities at Bonn, [n.d.]. (89) DM900
Autograph transcript, of a letter addressed to him by August Wilhelm Iffland, [c.Feb/Mar 1802], 1 p, 8vo, concerning Schlegel's play Jon. Albrecht collection. (91) SF400
Series of 4 A Ls s, 26 Feb 1831, 13 Feb 1836 & [n.y.]. 5 pp, 8vo. To Friedrich Diez. Discussing various philological questions. Slightly def. (90) DM2,200
ALs, 12 Feb 1796. 3 pp, 8vo. To the pbr of the journal Erholungen. Offering a trans of Mary Wollstonecraft's Letters Written ... in Sweden, Norway and Denmark. With engraved port. (88) DM2,200
— 15 July 1798. 8 pp, 8vo. To Gottlieb Hufeland. About Goethe, Schelling,

Iffland, various literary matters, & contributions to journals. Including postscript by his wife Caroline. Albrecht collection. (91) SF5,000
— [spring 1816]. 1 p, 8vo. To [Friedrich Wilken]. Asking him to locate a medieval Ms in Rome. (89) DM1,200
— 21 Oct 1824. (90) DM850
— 23 Oct 1826. (91) DM950
— 8 Dec 1830. 1 p, 4to. To Guillaume Guizot. Letter of recommendation for M. de Ribbentrop. In French. (90) DM1,100
— 28 Jan 1832. (88) DM500

Schlegel, Friedrich von, 1772-1829
Autograph Ms, fragment of his preface to Johann Peter Silbert's Dom heiliger Saenger; [1819/20]. (90) DM1,000
— Autograph Ms, notes for his lectures "Philosophie des Lebens" at Vienna, [spring 1827]. 1 p, 4to. Somewhat def. Including note of authenticity. (88) DM1,100
Collection of ALs & autograph Ms, [n.d.]. (90) DM320
ALs, 24 Nov 1801. (90) DM350
— [29 Oct 1802]. 1 p, 8vo. To M. Noel, inspecteur general des etudes. Applying for a professorship in Paris. Was mtd. (89) DM1,300
— 29 Nov 1805. (91) DM680
— 5 May 1811. 4 pp, 8vo. To Georg Andreas Reimer. Hoping to be able to write his projected study of Charles V in the near future. Albrecht collection. (91) SF1,050
— 25 Feb 1828. (88) DM650
— [n.d.]. (90) DM460
— [n.d.]. (89) DM420
Ls, 6 Apr 1813. 3 pp, 4to. To J. G. G. Buesching. Letter of recommendation for [Joseph von] Eichendorff. In the hand of Dorothea Schlegel; with 14-line autograph postscript, sgd. Corner def. (90) DM3,500

Schlegel, Johann Adolf, 1721-93
ALs, 20 Mar 1766. (90) DM250

Schlegel-Schelling, Caroline, 1763-1809
ALs, 23 Sept 1799. 4 pp, 8vo. To [Wilhelm Gottlieb Becker]. Recommending Sophie Tieck's novel for publication in recipient's almanac. (90) DM6,500

Schleich, Carl Ludwig, 1859-1922
ALs, 1 May 1920. (91) DM360
— 28 Jan 1921. (90) DM520

Schleicher, Kurt von, 1882-1934
Ds, 27 Jan 1933. (89) DM900

Schleiermacher, Friedrich, 1768-1834
Autograph Ms, Ueber den Unterschied zwischen Naturgesetz und Sittengesetz, 6 Jan 1825. 8 pp, 4to, in contemp bds. Marked for the ptr; sgd. (91) DM7,500
ALs, 31 Aug 1802. 6 pp, 8vo. To [Georg Reimer]. Hoping for Eleonore Grunow's divorce, reporting about his work, requesting books, etc. (90) DM3,000
— 30 Dec 1806. 3 pp, 8vo. To Hofrat [Eichstaedt]. Sending a review of Fichte's Grundzuege des gegenwaertigen Zeitalters & commenting about the political situation. (88) DM1,200
— 6 Dec 1808. 1 p, 4to. To Schelling. Expressing thanks to the Munich Academy of Arts for his nomination as corresponding member. (90) DM1,300
— 25 Mar 1809. 3 pp, 8vo. To "lieber Schulz". About the Prussian Government, efforts to obtain a position for Schulz, & his wedding plans. (88) DM1,200
— 1 Oct 1823. (91) DM700
— 14 July 1830. 1 p, 4to. To Ludwig Tieck. Introducing Ehrenfried von Willich & discussing Friedrich Schlegel. Kuenzel collection. (90) DM3,000
— [n.d.]. (91) DM320
Ds, 26 Sept 1817. (90) DM300
— 23 Aug 1820. (89) DM220

Schlesinger, Adolph Martin, d.1838
[A contract between Mechetti & Schlesinger regarding Mendelssohn-Bartholdy's First Symphony, 8 Apr 1834, & 2 letters from Peter Simrock to Schlesinger, 27 Dec 1818 & 5 July 1819, in all 3 pp, 4to, sold at S on 27 Nov, lot 346, for £350 to Berlin.]

SCHLESINGER

Schlesinger, Moritz
— 016 9 A Ls s, May to Sept 1829. To his father Adolph Martin Schlesinger (5) & his brother Carl Schlesinger. Reporting on musical life in Paris, the premiere of Rossini's William Tell, & about publishing matters. 1 written jointly with his brother Carl. With ALs from Carl Schlesinger to his father & incomplete letter from anr pbr. Together 32 pp, 4to. (88) £2,000

Schlick, Moritz, 1882-1936
Collection of 61 A Ls s & 4 A Ls (3 fragments), 6 June 1917 to 2 Feb 1936. Over 250 pp, mostly 4to & 8vo. To a younger friend (Gerda). Important letters touching private & scholarly matters. (89) DM20,000

Schlieffen, Alfred, Graf von, 1833-1913
ALs, 28 Feb 1908. Schroeder collection. (89) DM240

Schliemann, Heinrich, 1822-90
ALs, 14 Mar 1874. 1 p, 8vo. To [Gustav Wittmer]. Saying he has asked his pbr to send him his Troianische Alterthuemer. (89) DM1,200

— 3 Dec 1875. (91) DM750

— 4 Mar 1877. 3 pp, 4vo. To Herr Schell. Detailed refutation of an article criticizing his interpretation of his finds at Troy & Mycenae. (91) DM5,100

— 27 Feb 1881. 1 p, 8vo. To A. Woldt. Sending a description of his house & mentioning his excavations at Orchomenos. (89) DM1,100

— 22 Aug 1882. (91) DM700

— 19 Oct 1885. 2 pp, 8vo. To Jakob Maehly. About his forthcoming publications & his brother-in-law. In Greek. (88) DM1,700

— 1 May 1887. 1 p, 8vo. To Ferdinand Duemmler. Reporting about problems with his projected excavations in Crete. Sgd at head. In Greek. (90) DM2,400

— 16 Mar 1890. 1 p, 8vo. To the bankers L. von Hoffmann & Co. Declining to think about financial matters at this point. (91) DM1,100

AMERICAN BOOK PRICES CURRENT

Schlosser, Friedrich Christoph, 1776-1861
ALs, 15 Nov 1856. (89) DM240

Schmid, Carlo, 1896-1979
Autograph telegram, sgd, [Nov 1964]. (91) DM650

Schmidt, Helmut. See: Deng Xiaoping & Schmidt

Schmidt-Rottluff, Karl, 1884-1976
ALs, 5 Dec 1936. (88) DM750

Autograph postcard, sgd, 13 Sept 1920. (88) DM320

Schmitt, Carl, 1888-1985
Collection of 35 A Ls s, 2 Ls s, 3 autograph postcards, sgd, AN & 2 typescripts, 29 Jan 1947 to Aug 1979. 60 pp, 4to & 8vo. To Nicolaus Sombart. Interesting letters discussing personal & professional matters. 2 poems, sgd. With related material. (88) DM8,000

— Collection of 7 A Ls s, 2 autograph postcards, sgd, & 2 A Ns s, 24 Oct 1950 to 27 July 1968. (88) DM540

Schneider, Friedrich, 1786-1853
Series of 3 A Ls s, 21 Jan 1811 to 30 Apr [1818]. (90) DM380

ALs, 5 Mar 1843. (90) DM380

Schneider, Reinhold, 1903-58
Typescript, review of Kurt Ihlenfeld's Huldigung fuer Paul Gerhardt, sgd. (89) DM220

Collection of 2 A Ls s, Ls & postcard, sgd, 11 May to 29 Dec 1957. (89) DM760

Ls, 11 June 1954. (91) DM420

Schnittke, Alfred
Autograph music, draft of part of an orchestral work scored for a large ensemble, [n.d.]. (90) £950

Schnitzler, Arthur, 1862-1931
Autograph Ms, notes for chapter 8 of his story Doktor Graesler, [1917]. (91) DM360

Series of 3 A Ls s, 18 July 1897 to 2 Nov 1919. 14 pp, 4to & 8vo. To Georg Hirschfeld. About literary & personal matters. (91) DM1,600

— Series of 3 A Ls s, 22 July 1922 to 1927. (91) $90

A Ls s (2), 12 Nov 1896 & 7 May 1905.

(90) DM800

ALs, Mar 1902. (90) DM700
— 5 Apr 1903. (88) DM440
— 25 May 1903. (90) DM270
— 1 [Dec?] 1922. (91) DM380
— 14 Apr [1925?]. (91) DM250

Collection of Ls & letter, 29 Apr & 12 July 1920. (90) DM500

Ls s (2), 25 May 1920 & 29 Mar 1928. (91) DM780

Corrected proof, Buch der Sprueche und Bedenken, [c.1927]. 49 galleys & 12 pp. With numerous corrections, partly autograph. Marked by the ptr. (89) £1,800

Schoeck, Othmar, 1886-1957

Autograph music, song, Der Mond ist aufgegangen, from his Wandsbecker Liederbuch, Op.52; [1936/37]. 1 p, folio. 7 bars, scored for voice & piano. Sgd at head. Collector's stamp. (90) DM5,500

— Autograph music, song, [Gekommen ist der] Mai, Op. 17 no 5, to a text by Heine; sgd & dated 1904. 4 pp, folio. Notated on 4 systems per page, 3 staves each. Some alterations. Including draft of anr song. (89) £1,150

Ms, song, Lebewohl, to a text by Lenau, scored for voice & piano; 1905. (90) DM900

— Ms, song, Vergangenheit, to a text by Lenau, scored for voice & piano; [n.d.]. (90) DM620

AL, [c.20 Sept 1945]. (90) DM260

Corrected proof, song, Die Kindheit, to a text by Hermann Hesse, 1921. (90) DM900

Schoenbein, Christian Friedrich, 1799-1868

ALs, 1 Nov 1846. 4 pp, 4to. To an unnamed French official. Insisting that gun cotton is his invention, not M. Morel's. In French. (90) DM1,300

Schoenberg, Arnold, 1874-1951

Autograph Ms, essay, Parsifal und Urheberrecht, 5 Feb 1912. 9 pp, folio. Extensively revised draft; sgd. (91) £6,000

ALs, 20 May 1922. 1 p, 8vo. To Ossip Schnirlin. Granting permission to use some of his music in a teaching manual for violin. (91) DM1,100

— 11 May 1931. 1 p, folio. To Georg Wolfsohn. Sending his address at Territet near Montreux. (88) DM1,050

— 15 Apr 1932. 2 pp, 8vo. To Josef Rufer. About his stay in Barcelona, a performance of his choirs Op. 35, the progress of his opera, etc. Including postscript by his wife Gertrud. (88) DM3,200

— [n.d.]. (91) £650
— [n.d.]. (89) DM800

Ls s (2), 3 Oct 1944 & 16 Sept 1949. 2 pp, folio. To Willi Reich. Ptd letters of thanks for congratulations on his birthday, with autograph salutations & subscriptions. With related material. (88) DM1,050

Ls, 2 June 1934. 1 p, 4to. To the Victor Record Corporation. Protesting against a recording of one of his compositions without compensation. (88) DM1,050

— 3 Oct 1944. (88) DM660
— 3 Oct 1944. (91) DM850
— 16 Jan 1946. (88) $300
— 4 June 1947. 2 pp, 4to. To the pbr J. Aelberts. Sending a Ms about Webern & Berg, & mentioning his Trio, Op. 45. In French. (88) DM1,550

— 3 Oct 1950. 1 p, folio. To Georg Wolfsohn. Complaining about the lack of interest in his work in Israel. (88) DM1,900

— 24 Apr 1951. 1 p, folio. To Peter Gradenwitz. About Wolfsohn's birthday, records of his works, & the book Style and Idea. Some autograph additions. (88) DM1,400

— 1 May 1951. (89) DM750
— 22 May 1951. (90) £700

AN, [n.d.]. (90) £360

Autograph quotation, "So les man mich in Toenen", 4 bars; sgd & dated 1 Mar 1920. (90) £850

— Anr, 4 bars from his Fuenf Orchesterstuecke, Op. 16, no 2, sgd & dated 21 Mar 1920. 1 p, 8vo. (90) DM3,400

— Anr, 2 bars from Das Buch der haengenden Gaerten, sgd, inscr in French & dated Mar 1924. (88) £550

See also: Berg, Alban

SCHOENBORN

Schoenborn, Lothar Franz, Freiherr von, Kurfuerst von Mainz, 1655-1729
Ls, 1 Sept 1708. (90) DM440

Schoenhardt, Karl von, 1833-1916. See: Moerike, Eduard

Schoenlein, Johann Lukas, 1793-1864
Autograph Ms, medical report, 8 May 1843. (91) DM500
ALs, 21 Aug 1831. (91) DM650

Scholten, Albert, 1749-1822. See: Album

Scholz, Wilhelm von, 1874-1968
ALs, 12 Apr 1918. (88) DM260

Schopenhauer, Adele, 1797-1849
Autograph Ms, Ueberblick ueber die Schriftsteller unserer Zeit, [n.d.]. 6 pp, 4to. Reviewing current literary trends; written as a letter to her cousin, sgd. (90) DM1,700

Schopenhauer, Arthur, 1788-1860
[A copy of J. E. Bode's Kurzer Entwurf der astronomischen Wissenschaften. Berlin, 1794, with Schopenhauer's bookplate & his marks or marginal comments on c.30 pp, sold at star on 30 Nov 1988, lot 533, for DM5,000.]
[A volume containing treatises by J. A. H. Reimarus, J. Purkinje, M. Klotz & E. M. [A. Loewis?], with Schopenhauer's bookplate, 3 marginal comments & several pencil marks, with related material, sold at star on 30 Nov 1988, lot 534, for DM5,000.]
Autograph Ms, Ueber Gelehrsamkeit u. Gelehrte, for his Parerga und Paralipomena, vol 2, chapter 21; complete working draft, [1851]. 12 pp, folio. Some differences to ptd version. (88) DM60,000
— Autograph Ms, working draft of part of his Parerga und Paralipomena, vol 2, chapter 6; [1851]. 12 pp, folio. With numerous revisions. (90) DM58,000
ALs, 3 Jan 1821. 2 pp, 4to. Recipient unknown. Regarding errors in a work to be ptd in recipient's paper. Tipped to larger leaf, with trans. Barrett collection. (89) $3,250
— 4 Nov 1858. 2 pp, 4to. To David Asher. Commenting about recipient's publication & other works, & advising

against marriage. Partly in English. (90) DM8,500

Schopenhauer, Johanna, 1766-1838
ALs, [c.1826/28]. (89) DM460
— 19 Sept 1829. Albrecht collection. (91) SF950
— 4 Jan 1832. 2 pp, 4to. To Karl von Holtei. Complaining that the outbreak of the cholera prevented her from going to Weimar. Margins def. Was mtd. (88) DM1,600

Schrattenbach, Sigismund, Graf von, Archbishop of Salzburg, 1698-1771
Ds, 15 Aug 1758. (90) DM850

Schreker, Franz, 1878-1934
ALs, 23 Mar 1909. (90) DM320
— 4 Oct 1913. (91) DM750
— 18 May 1917. (89) DM400
— 20 June 1919. (90) DM380
Ls, 5 Mar 1921. (88) DM320
— GOTTSELIG, H. - Engraving, port of Schreker; [n.d.]. 24cm by 18cm (image). Sgd by Schreker, in pencil. (91) DM300

Schrimpf, Georg, 1889-1938
ALs, 8 Dec 1924. 4 pp, 8vo. To Franz Roh. About an art exhibition in Leipzig, the sale of a painting, his current projects, etc. (90) DM2,400
— 7 Mar 1925. 4 pp, 8vo. To Franz Roh. Discussing technical problems of his work, an exhibition in Munich, etc. (90) DM2,600

Schroeder, Nicolaus Wilhelm, 1721-98
Ms, Observationes in librum Psalmorum, dated 19 June 1764. (89) £110

Schroeder, Rudolf Alexander, 1878-1962
Autograph Ms, 2 quatrains, Gedenkvers, & Ein andrer; [n.d.]. (90) DM360
— Autograph Ms, poem, Vorm Walde, [n.d.]. (91) DM450
ALs, 11 Jan 1925. (88) DM420

Schroeder-Devrient, Wilhelmine, 1804-60
ALs, 9 Jan 1835. Kuenzel collection. (91) DM600
— 1 June 184[8]. 2 pp, 4to. To her lawyer. Concerning her separation from her husband. Albrecht collection. (91) SF1,300

Schroedinger, Erwin, 1887-1961
ALs, 24 Feb 1949. 2 pp, 4to. To G. von Frankenberg. Explaining the basic ideas expounded in his work What is Life? (90) DM3,200
Ls, 5 May 1932. (88) DM350

Schubart, Christian Friedrich Daniel, 1739-91
ALs, 4 June 1790. 2 pp, 4to. To Johann Martin Miller. Letter of introduction for Mr. Petersen, a trans from Denmark. With engraved port. (88) DM2,200

Schubert, Franz, 1797-1828
Autograph music, 2 songs, Der Abend, D. 221, & Geist der Liebe, D. 233, to texts by Kosegarten, [1815]. 2 pp, folio. Marked for & by the ptr. (91) £32,000
— Autograph music, 2 songs, Geist der Liebe, & Der Abend, scored for voice & piano; [1815]. 2 pp, size not stated. Fair copies. Some marginal notes in anr hand. (89) DM75,000
— Autograph music, Canon a tre, Dreyfach ist der Schritt der Zeit, to a text by Schiller, 8 July 1813. 2 pp, 12cm by 31cm, cut from a larger sheet. Fragment (last line) on recto; complete text & composition on verso, sgd. (90) DM32,000
— Autograph music, finale of the "Fantasie" for piano duet in G/C major, D. 1, 8 Apr to 1 May 1810. 8 pp, folio. In brown ink on up to 12 staves per page, with some alterations. Including autograph tp, sgd. Marked by the ptr. (88) £30,000
— Autograph music, Magnificat in C major, D.486, full score; sgd & dated 25 Sept 1816. 48 pp, folio, in bds. Working Ms. (90) £135,000
— Autograph music, octet, Gesang der Geister ueber dem Wasser, Op.167, to a poem by Goethe; Feb 1821. 19 pp, 24cm by 29.5cm. In full score; sgd at head. Stichvorlage. Albrecht collection. (91) SF260,000
— Autograph music, Overture in D major D. 556, May 1817. 39 pp, folio. Working Ms in full score; sgd. Marked for the ptr. (91) £130,000
— Autograph music, Overture "in the Italian Style" in D major, D. 590; full score, [1817]. 50 pp, folio. Working Ms, written in brown ink on up to 12 staves per page. Some annotations in pencil, mostly in anr hand. (88) £120,000
— Autograph music, song, Als ich sie erroethen sah, in G major, D.153; sgd & dated 10 Feb [1]815. 4 pp, folio; 4 systems of 3 staves each. 65 bars (lacking final 14). Stichvorlage. (90) £35,000
— Autograph music, song, An die Sonne, to a text by Johann Peter Uz; sgd & dated June 1816. 11 pp, 24cm by 31 cm, 16 staves each. Full score for mixed choir & piano; some revisions. (88) DM100,000
— Autograph music, song, Lebenslied, D.508; fair copy of 18 bars. In brown ink on 4 systems of 3 staves each, sgd & dated Dec 1816. 2 pp, folio. On verso autograph draft of Rondo for piano in E major, D.506, bars 57 to 87. (88) $18,000
— Autograph music, song, Vergebliche Liebe, to a text by J. K. Bernard, scored for voice & piano; 6 Apr 1815. 2 pp, size not stated; 12 lines each. Sgd at head. Margin cut. (90) DM60,000
— Autograph music, String Trio in B flat major, D. 581, Sept 1817. 19 pp, folio. Complete draft in score of all 4 movements; sgd. Marked by the ptr. (91) £100,000
ALs, [1822]. 1 p, c.13cm by 18.5cm, cut from a larger sheet. To [Josef Huettenbrenner]. About corrections to the score of his opera & enquiring about his accounts with Diabelli. (88) £10,500
— 30 Nov 1823. 4 pp, 4to. To Franz von Schober. Expressing sorrow at the disintegration of his circle of friends, mentioning his compositions, Weber's Euryanthe, etc. Salzer collection. (90) £65,000
— 19 Sept 1827. 1 p, 4to. To Franz Selliers de Moranville. Apologizing for not being able to keep his word. (90) DM32,000

Schubert, Gotthilf Heinrich von, 1780-1860
Series of 4 A Ls s, 9 Oct 1836 to 11 Apr 1837. 17 pp, 4to. To Schelling. Reporting about his journey to Palestine.

SCHUBERT

(90) DM3,300
ALs, 12 Oct 1842. (88) DM500

Schuecking, Levin, 1814-83
A Ls s (2), 7 Aug 1856 & 15 Feb 1875. (88) DM360
ALs, 23 Apr 1845. (91) DM900
— 26 Nov 1875. (89) DM260

Schuetz, Christian Gottfried, 1747-1832
ALs, 3 Mar 1791. (90) DM220

Schuetze, Stephan, 1771-1839
Autograph Ms, essay, Die Gesellschaft der Hofraethin Schopenhauer in Weimar, [ptd 1840]. 20 pp, 4to, stitched. Including revisions. With related material. Albrecht collection. (91) SF2,200

Schulenburg-Kehnert, Friedrich Wilhelm von der, Graf, 1742-1815
Ds, 5 Jan 1792. Schroeder collection. (89) DM380

Schulhoff, Jules, 1825-98
[An extensive collection of autograph music by Schulhoff, over 50 items, c.1845 to 1860, including sonatas dedicated to Chopin & Liszt, working Mss, Stichvorlagen, etc., sold at S on 27 Nov, lot 253, for £1,400 to Faure.]

Schulze, Ernst, 1789-1817
ALs, 31 Oct 1812. (91) DM780

Schulze-Delitzsch, Hermann, 1808-83
ALs, 11 June 1877. (90) DM440

Schumacher, Heinrich Christian, 1780-1850
ALs, 16 Apr 1844. Kuenzel collection. (90) DM360

Schuman, Robert, 1886-1963
Series of 7 A Ls s, 24 Nov 1946 to 6 May 1958. 11 pp, 8vo. To Herbert Muellenmeister, a comrade during World War I. About the situation after World War II, his activities, a meeting, etc. In German. With group photograph, 1916. (88) DM1,150

Schumann, Clara, 1819-96
Autograph music, song, Der Mond kommt still gegangen, to a text by E. Geibel, sgd & dated Nov 1891. 2 pp, folio; 3 systems of 3 staves each. Including fine ptd borders. With autograph quotation, sgd; 4 bars from Beethoven's 5th Piano Concerto. (90) £1,400
Collection of ALs & 5 Ls s, 1862 to 1893. (88) £320
— Collection of ALs & Ls, 11 & 16 Feb 1873. (88) DM560
— Collection of 2 A Ls s, 4 Ls s, 2 autograph postcards, sgd, ANs & autograph document, sgd, 2 May 1877 to 22 Nov 1893. 18 pp, mostly 8vo, & cards. To Theodor Mueller-Reuter. Mostly regarding recipient's studies & career as musician, including certificate. With related material. (90) DM3,400
— Collection of ALs & Ls, 12 July 1883 & 9 June 1884. (90) DM850
— Collection of 8 A Ls s & Ls s, [c.1884 & later]. 25 pp, 8vo. To Marie Baumayer. Discussing her piano repertoire, her concerts, friends, etc. Including related material. Salzer collection. (90) £2,200
A Ls s (2), 9 Dec 1870 & 7 Aug 1890. (89) DM550
— A Ls s (2), 24 July 1879 & 19 Mar 1895. (88) DM700
ALs, 22 Nov 1841. 2 pp, 4to. To Emma Meyer. Discussing household matters & informing her about her concert tour. (91) DM1,100
— [late Nov 1841]. (88) DM600
— 6 Feb 1847. 3 pp, 8vo. To an unnamed lady. After the family's return from Vienna & Prague, expressing thanks. (90) DM1,400
— 23 July 1850. 4 pp, 8vo. To an unnamed lady. Encouraging her to practice composition, & talking about recent professional events. (90) DM2,000
— 14 July 1852. 4 pp, 8vo. To Joseph von Wasielewski. In her husband's name, making plans for a meeting & sending a composition. (91) DM2,000
— 10 Apr 1854. 6 pp, 8vo. To an unnamed lady. Reporting about her husband's illness. (90) DM9,000
— 4 Nov 1855. 4 pp, 4to. To an unnamed lady. Giving news about her husband & making plans for concerts. (91) DM2,500
— 15 Sept 1856. (89) DM550
— 7 Dec 1858. (91) DM750
— 9 Apr 1863. (91) DM550

— 5 Sept 1869. 8 pp, 8vo. To her son Felix. Advising against choosing music as a profession. (91) DM2,500
— 18 Aug 1870. 4 pp, 8vo. To Friedrich Wieck. Expressing congratulations on his birthday & commenting on the Franco-Prussian war. (90) DM1,600
— 27 Feb 1872. (89) DM850
— 6 Mar 1873. 4 pp, 8vo. To Johannes Brahms. Congratulating him on the success of his music in London, & reporting about her own concerts. (90) DM5,000
— 7 May 1884. (90) DM260
— 10 June 1884. (90) DM850
— 23 Oct 1884. (88) DM380
— 21 Dec 1895. (90) DM750
Ls, 10 May [1875]. (90) DM360
Autograph postcard, sgd, 30 Sept 1887. (90) DM420
ANs, 29 July [18]92. (91) DM300
Autograph quotation, 5 bars from Robert Schumann's 2d Symphony, 9 Feb 1860. 1 p, 8vo. Sgd. (91) DM1,100
— Anr, 5 bars from Robert Schumann's Schlummerlied, Op. 124 no 16; sgd, inscr & dated 24 Mar 1866. 1 p, 17cm by 33cm. (90) DM1,900
Lithographed port, inscr to Wilhelm Wieck, Jan 1863. 207mm by 154mm (image). By Hanfstaengl. Sgd in facsimile on mount, 385mm by 285mm. (90) DM2,800
See also: Schumann, Robert & Schumann
See also: Wieck, Friedrich

Schumann, Robert, 1810-56
Autograph Ms, list of pieces in Album fuer die Jugend, Op.68; [c.1848]. 1 p, 4to. Differing from sequence finally pbd. (91) £2,800
Autograph music, Faschingsschwank aus Wien, Op. 26, 31 bars from the middle section of the 1st movement; [1839]. 1 p, 8vo. Working Ms. (90) £9,500
— Autograph music, Piano Concerto in A minor, Op. 54, full score; June & July 1845. 192 pp, folio, in contemp half calf. Working Ms. Some parts in other hands (including Clara Schumann's), with autograph revisions. Sgd several times. (90) £800,000
— Autograph music, song, Die Blume der Ergebung for voice & piano in A major, Op. 83 no 2, to a text by Friedrich Rueckert; [c.1850]. 6 pp, folio. Notated in brown ink on up to 3 systems per page, 3 staves each. Including autograph tp. Salzer collection. (90) £26,000
— Autograph music, song, Die Nonne, 16 bars on 3 systems of 3 staves; sgd, inscr & dated 25 Apr 1843. 1 p, folio. (90) £5,500
ALs, 15 July [18]35. 1 p, 4to. To Ignaz von Seyfried. Letter of introduction for Herr Wille. (90) £1,600
— 2 July 1836. 2 pp, 4to. To Anton Wilhelm von Zuccalmaglio. About recipient's contributions to the Neue Zeitschrift fuer Musik, Mendelssohn, his own music, etc. Repaired. (90) DM7,000
— 24 July 1836. 2 pp, 4to. To A. W. von Zuccalmaglio. Expressing sorrow about Friedrich Wieck's opposition to his marriage, & mentioning a meeting with Mendelssohn. With ALs by Clara Schumann, 1895. (91) £2,800
— 14 Feb 1837. 1 p, 8vo. To [Gustav Adolf Keferstein]. Discussing matters pertaining to his Neue Zeitschrift fuer Musik, & an advertisement in the journal Caecilia. (90) DM3,600
— 23 Jan 1838. 2 pp, 8vo. Recipient unnamed. Asking him to review a concert by Adolf Henselt & the Neue Zeitschrift fuer Musik. (89) DM4,200
— 8 May 1838. 3 pp, 8vo. To Joseph Fischhof. Discussing the publication of his Kreisleriana, mentioning other works, & inquiring about Clara Wieck. Salzer collection. (90) £6,000
— 10 May 1839. (88) £720
— 18 June 1839. 1 p, 4to. To Herr Hofmeister. Responding to a complaint that his articles are slow to appear in the Neue Zeitschrift fuer Musik. (91) £1,400
— 7 Feb 1840. 1 p, 8vo. To F. Moeller. Introducing Clara Wieck & her mother, & referring to his marriage plans. (91) £1,700
— 4 July 1840. (88) £750
— 16 July 1841. 2 pp, 4to. Recipient unnamed. Concerning contributions for the Neue Zeitschrift fuer Musik & his plans to write an opera. (89) DM8,000

SCHUMANN

— 7 Sept 1843. 1 p, 4to. To Robert Franz. Discussing the publication of Franz's songs by Haertel. Inlaid. Doheny collection. (89) $1,500
— 12 Dec [18]44. 2 pp, 8vo. To the pbr Boehme. Offering a piano trio for publication. (90) £3,400
— 10 Nov 1845. 3 pp, 8vo. To August Ambros. Expressing interest in his writings & informing him about his own work. Seal tear. (89) £2,100
— 15 Feb 1846. 1 p, 8vo. To his pbr. About the ptg of his Overture. (91) £1,900
— May 1846. 1 p, 8vo. To Eduard Hanslick. Expressing thanks, & regretting he is too ill to write more. Framed. (90) $3,000
— 22 Nov 1846. 1 p, 8vo. To J. A. Josephson. Enquiring about the possibility of dedicating his 2d Symphony to the King of Sweden. (88) £1,050
— 10 Apr 1848. 3 pp, 8vo. Recipient unnamed. Commenting on recipient's score & hoping to find a pbr. (88) £1,300
— 14 Sept [18]48. 2 pp, 8vo. To Carl Reinecke. Announcing that he has finished his opera, discussing the publication of Reinecke's songs, etc. (90) £3,000
— 11 Nov 1848. 2 pp, 4to. To [Julius Rietz]. Discussing particulars of a proposed performance of his opera Genoveva. With English trans. (89) £2,600
— [Jan 1849]. 1 p, 8vo. To Karl Gottschalk. Protesting that the copying of his works must not be delayed any longer. Sgd R.Sch. (90) DM3,800
— 1 May [18]49. 2 pp, 8vo. To Carl Reinecke. Describing his Piano Trio in F major & commenting on Reinecke's songs. Sgd R.Sch. (90) £3,500
— 6 July 1849. 2 pp, 8vo. To [Julius Rietz]. Asking for a copy of his opera Genoveva & discussing Bach. (91) DM6,000
— 17 Nov 1849. 2 pp, 8vo. To Fritz Spindler. Discussing recipient's symphony. (91) £1,800
— [Spring 1850]. 1 p, 4to. To an unnamed musician. Hoping to finish a score in time for a concert. Was mtd. (90) DM3,800

— 4 Apr 1850. 2 pp, 8vo. To his pbr C. F. Peters. Sending the piano arrangement of his overture to Genoveva, & discussing publication matters. (91) £2,200
— 22 July 1850. 1 p, 8vo. To the pbr C. F. Peters. Enclosing drafts for a tp for his opera [Genoveva]. (90) £1,800
— 9 Aug 1850. 2 pp, 8vo. To his pbr C. F. Peters. Requesting the speedy return of the revision of Act 1 of Genoveva. (90) £3,000
— 16 Aug 1850. Length not stated. To the pbr C. F. Peters. Discussing in detail the publication of his opera Genoveva. (91) £3,000
— 18 Oct 1850. 1 p, 8vo. To the pbr C. F. Peters. Discussing the ptg of Genoveva. (90) £2,300
— 4 Dec 1850. 2 pp, 8vo. To his pbr C. F. Peters. Announcing he has sent the last section of his opera Genoveva, & requesting an extra copy as Christmas present for his wife. (90) £2,800
— 19 Jan 1851. 2 pp, 8vo. To Richard Pohl. Declining to set Schiller's Braut von Messina to music, & discussing other possible librettos. (90) DM7,000
— 22 Feb 1851. 1 p, 8vo. To F. Heuser of Cologne. Saying the instrumental parts of the [3d] symphony should be in his hands the next day, & referring to the programmatic nature of the work. Small tear. (88) £1,100
— 22 Feb 1851. 1 p, 8vo. To F. Heuser. Referring to the programmatic nature [of his 3d Symphony]. (91) £1,900
— 24 Mar 1851. 3 pp, 8vo. To his pbr. Enclosing the score of Die Braut von Messina & discussing publication matters. (90) £2,800
— 3 Apr 1851. 2 pp, 8vo. To the pbr C. F. Peters. Enclosing proofs & discussing the piano score of his opera Genoveva, & mentioning payment for Die Braut von Messina. (91) £2,200
— 3 Apr 1851. 1 p, 8vo. To W. Zirges. Giving advice about a concert. (91) DM4,000
— 9 June 1851. 2 pp, 8vo. To [his pbr C. F. Peters]. Enclosing Act 3 of Genoveva & discussing proofs of various works. (90) £3,800
— 13 Aug 1851. 2 pp, 8vo. To the pbr C. F. Peters. Sending the Ms of the 4th

act of his opera Genoveva, & enquiring about proofs of Die Braut von Messina. (91) £2,200

— 22 Aug 1851. 1 p, 8vo. To Richard Pohl. Informing him about his return to Duesseldorf. Was mtd. (89) DM3,200

— 22 Jan 1852. 2 pp, 8vo. To Dr. Plifke. About Herr Teuwitz & music teaching in Duesseldorf. (91) £1,500

— 9 June 1852. 1 p, 8vo. To [Carl Montag]. Sending the text of his Manfred for Liszt's use & inviting comments about the work. (90) DM4,500

— [n.d.]. 6.5cm by 21cm. To [Raimund Haertel]. Fragment, sending tickets for a concert. (91) DM2,300

AL, 14 Mar 1852. (90) DM520

Letter, 22 July [n.y.]. (90) DM1,000

Autograph quotation, 2 bars from the opening of his 2d Symphony, sgd, dated 17 Nov 1846 & inscr to A. Josephson. 1 p, folio. With autograph musical quotation by Clara Schumann on verso. (88) £3,800

Proof copy, 3d Symphony, Op. 97, 1st Ed of the full score, [1850]. 211 pp, 8vo, in orig blue wraps, repaired. With extensive autograph annotations & alterations. (88) £9,500

Schumann, Robert, 1810-56 — & Schumann, Clara, 1819-96

Ms, unidentified piano piece by Robert Schumann; fair copy by Clara Schumann, sgd, dated Dec 1856 & inscr to E. Jibone. 3 pp, 8vo. 48 bars. Doheny collection. (89) $3,800

Schurz, Carl, 1829-1906

ALs, 4 Aug 1869. (89) DM460

— 23 Jan 1875. (90) DM520

— 1 Jan 1889. (90) DM440

— 7 Apr 1891. (90) DM390

— 26 May 1894. (91) DM650

— 15 Feb 1897. (88) DM500

— 9 Feb 1899. (89) DM370

— 26 Nov 1901. (88) DM300

— 14 Mar 1906. (89) DM370

Ds, 28 Oct 1879. (90) DM550

Schussen, Wilhelm, Pseud. of Wilhelm Frick, 1874-1956

Autograph Ms, story, Teufel Theodor Trukenmiller, [n.d.]. (91) DM400

Schwab, Gustav, 1792-1850

Autograph Ms, sonnet, beginning "Nimm, Freund, zurueck dein maechtig Strausseney", sgd, inscr to D. (90) DM650

ALs, 15 July 1835. (88) DM480

Schwarzenberg, Adam, Graf zu, 1584-1641

Autograph endorsement, comments on a report addressed to him concerning the defense of the Brandenburg territory, 4 Apr 1622. (89) DM700

Schwarzenberg, Karl Philipp, Fuerst zu, 1771-1820

ALs, 29 Aug 1813. Schroeder collection. (89) DM850

Ds, 2 June 1813. (88) DM640

Schweinfurth, Georg, 1836-1925

ALs, 7 Feb 1898. (91) DM600

Schweitzer, Albert, 1875-1965

Autograph Ms, comments about the program of Schweitzer's concert in Zurich, 23 Oct 1921. (88) DM520

Collection of 3 A Ls s & ANs, 30 Mar 1922 to 13 Apr 1936. 8 pp, 8vo & 4to. To Willibald Gurlitt. Interesting letters about his activities & plans, organ concerts, etc. ANs as postscript to a letter by his secretary Mathilde Kottmann. (89) DM1,500

— Collection of 13 A Ls s & 13 autograph postcards, sgd & photographs, sgd, 9 July 1923 to 9 July 1965. 29 pp, 8vo. To Julie Schlosser. Mostly brief notes to a good friend, enclosures to longer letters (present, 46 pp) by Emmy Martin & Mathilde Kottmann, reporting about Schweitzer & Lambarene. (90) DM9,000

— Collection of 4 A Ls s & autograph postcard, sgd, 2 Feb 1926 to 10 Jan 1933 & [n.d.]. 11 pp, 4to & 8vo, & card. To Gustav Giemsa. Regarding research to find cures for African diseases. With related material. (89) DM1,600

— Collection of 8 A Ls s & 5 Ls s, 1934 to 1958. (91) £900

SCHWEITZER

— Collection of ALs, ANs & ptd photograph, sgd & inscr, 20 Apr & 3 May 1961. (90) DM680

A Ls s (2), 23 Apr 1961 & 18 Nov 1964. 3 pp, 8vo. To an unnamed Polish author. Remembering Stephan Zweig. Regretting that he does not have time to write about Bach & religion. (88) DM1,300

ALs, 16 Apr 1928. (91) $500

— 29 Dec 1952. (91) DM680

— 21 May 1958. (90) DM500

— 10 June 1958. (91) DM800

— 29 May 1962. (88) DM400

— 17 Oct 1962. (90) DM480

— [n.d.]. (91) $225

Ls, [Apr 1958]. (91) DM700

Autograph postcard, sgd, 30 Aug 1921. (88) DM260

ANs, 30 July 1927. (90) DM270

— 21 Sept 1930. (88) $400

— 24 Mar 1947. (91) DM500

Signature, [n.d.]. (89) $65

Schwerdgeburth, Karl August, 1785-1878
ALs, 26 Jan 1807. (91) DM450

Schwerin, Friedrich Albrecht, Graf von, 1717-89
ALs, 29 Jan 1762. Schroeder collection. (89) DM540

Schwerin, Kurt Christoph, Graf von, 1684-1757
ALs, 11 Aug 1756. 2 pp, 4to. To Ludwig Wilhelm von Muenchow. Reporting about diplomatic activities. With related material. Schroeder collection. (89) DM1,600

Ls, 17 Mar 1757. (91) DM1,000

Schwerin von Krosigk, Johann Ludwig, Graf, 1887-1977
Typescript carbon copy, Staatsbankerott - Das Reichfinanzministerium von 1920 - 1945, [ptd 1974]. (91) DM900

Schwimmer, Max, 1895-1960
A Ls s (2), 20 Nov 1937 & 26 Apr 1938. (88) DM950

ALs, 22 Nov 1949. (91) DM650

Schwind, Moritz von, 1804-71
ALs, 4 Dec 1836. (88) DM750

— 4 Jan 1855. (89) DM500

Schwitters, Kurt, 1887-1948
Typescript carbon copy, poem, Nr. (88) DM800

ALs, [n.d.]. 2 pp, 8vo. To Herr Schorer. Informing him about the publication of a poem by Raoul Hausmann. (91) DM2,200

Autograph postcard, sgd, 31 July 1919. To Adolf Allweber. Mentioning "Anna Blume". With reproduction of his Arbeiterbild on verso. (89) DM3,200

Scobee, Dick
Photograph, sgd, [n.d.]. (91) $130

Photograph, sgd & inscr, [16 Jan 1978]. (91) $100

— Anr, [n.d.]. (91) $225

Signature, [19 Nov 1975]. (89) $90

— Anr, on memorial cover, [30 June 1977]. (90) $65

— Anr, on philatelic envelope, [13 Apr 1984]. (90) $80

Scotland
[Neill Family of Barnwell. - The estate papers of the Neill family, 16th to 20th cent, several hundred items in 2 tin trunks, sold at S on 15 Dec 1988, lot 137, for £400.]

[A box of documents & letters relating to the Wardrop & other families, 17th & 18th cent, sold at S on 15 Nov 1988, lot 1712, for £210 to White.]

Ms, journal of a tour of Scotland, July & Aug 1810, by a member of a London family. (88) £85

— Ms, Scotichronicon, history of Scotland from the earliest times to c.1515. [Edinburgh?, c.1515-20]. 223 leaves & 2 flyleaves, 195mm by 137mm. Contemp blindstamped calf over wooden bds. In a current lettre batarde. With large red initials throughout. (90) £38,000

— ARGYLLSHIRE. - An archive of documents relating mainly to A. Allan of Aros House & Hugh MacLaine of Killunline, 19th cent, sold at pnE on 3 Oct 1990, lot 178, for £300. 91

— EDMONSTON HOUSE. - Ms, plan of Edmonston House & grounds, with

notes regarding proposed new garden walls, etc., [c.1800]. 1 p, 19 by 15 inches; linen-backed paper. Torn. (90) £65
— FORT GEORGE. - Ms, account book for building & repairs, & other matters, 1767 to 1771. 350 pp, folio. (90) £500
— GLASGOW. - A group of 46 documents regarding the partnership of Glasgow merchants George Carmichael, Thomas Hopkirk, John Cochran Carmichael & Matthew Guthell, 1731 & 1751, sold at pnE on 3 Oct 1990, lot 171, for £50. 91
— LEICHE, ANDREW. - Ds, 3 Jan 1556/7. Size not stated, vellum. As Prior of the Friars Preachers of Aire, lease of land to John Pollock. (91) £120
— LINLITHGOWSHIRE. - A group of 11 plans of various buildings, 1861 & [n.d.], sold at pnE on 3 Oct 1990, lot 173, for £70. 91
— MCCRAE FAMILY, EDINBURGH. - An archive of trust documents & papers of the McCrae Family, mid-19th cent, in a tin trunk, sold at pnE on 3 Oct 1990, lot 177, for £150. 91
— NEWTON, MIDLOTHIAN. - Ms, Ground Plan for the New Church of Newton... drawn by John Birrell, Oct 1742. Size not stated. In ink & color wash. (91) £50
— ORMISTON CHURCH, HADDINGTONSHIRE. - Ms, An exact plan of the Church of Ormiston..., [late 17th cent]. Size not stated. In ink & grey color wash. (91) £100
— ROSS AND CROMARTY. - An extensive collection of documents concerning Capt. Donald McKenzie of Newhall, c.1800 to 1840, in a tin trunk, sold at pnE on 3 Oct 1990, lot 179, for £150. 91

Scott, Charles, 1739-1813
Ls, [10 Feb 1811]. Alexander collection. (90) $180

Scott, Sir Giles Gilbert, 1880-1960
Ls, 27 Nov 1933. (89) £50

Scott, Sir John, 1585-1670
Ms, The staggering state of the Scottish statesmen, from anno 1550 till anno 1650, [17th cent]. (89) £320

Scott, Robert Falcon, 1868-1912
[His commission as a Sub Lieutenant, 2 Jan 1889, c.12 by 13.25 inches, with related material, sold at S on 15 Dec 1988, lot 159, for £800.]
Autograph Ms, log kept as a midshipman on H.M.S. Euphrates, Boadicea, Royal Adelaide, Monarch, & Rover, 8 Sept 1883 to 5 Aug 1887, with additions to 1895. About 450 pp, folio, in black half roan bdg. Including c.20 hand-drawn charts & c.45 small drawings & watercolors. (89) £4,200
Series of 21 A Ls s, 17 Dec 1901 to 30 Oct 1911. Nearly 50 pp, 4to & 8vo. To his sisters & his brother-in-law Willy Macartney (1). Family letters, partly written from his Antarctic expeditions. With related material. (90) £5,500
— Series of 6 A Ls s, 11 Feb 1903 to 23 Nov [1904]. 18 pp, 4to & 8vo. To Mrs. Wilson Noble. Chiefly written on board the Discovery, commenting on the expedition. (90) £2,600
— Series of 6 A Ls s, 1905 to 1910 & [n.d.]. (88) £850
A Ls s (2), 22 & 24 Aug 1908. (89) £400
ALs, 18 Feb 1896. (90) £450
— 6 July 1910. (90) $800
— 16 Mar [1912]. 4 pp, 8vo. To Sir Edgar Speyer. Farewell letter later found with his body. On sheets extracted from his diary. (89) £34,000
Collection of 6 autograph postcards, sgd & 2 photographs, sgd, 1901 to 1910. To his sisters Kitty Brownlow & Ettie Macartney. Partly mailed at the start of his last Antarctic expedition. With further material relating to his expeditions & to the Scott family. (90) £2,400

Scott, Sir Walter, 1771-1832
Autograph Ms, poem, Helvellyn; 1805. 2 pp, 4to. 5 eight-line stanzas & introduction. In green mor album by Riviere with 3 A Ls s & 2 fragments. (91) £2,400
Collection of ALs & autograph Ms, 4 Mar [1806] & [n.d.]. 5 pp, 8vo & 4to. To Miss Smith, saying he has ordered a copy of Marmion sent to her. Poem, Bridal of Trierman, 26 lines; endorsed by J. Ballantyne on verso. Was mtd. (88) $1,200

SCOTT

A Ls s (2), 20 May 1814 & 21 Apr [n.y.]. 4 pp, 4to & 12mo. To John Bell, acknowledging a diploma & recommending the collecting of popular rhymes. Recipient unknown, cancelling a meeting. Doheny collection. (89) $1,700

ALs, 22 Oct 1796. 2 pp, 4to. Recipient unnamed. Sending a copy of his trans of German ballads. (89) £1,200

— 27 Mar 1802. 3 pp, 4to. To Messrs. Cadell & Davies. Offering them the copyright of The Minstrelsy of the Scottish Border. (90) £2,600

— 16 Nov 1804. (91) £160

— 18 Sept 1811. Byer collection. (90) $200

— 22 Dec 1811 & 5 Jan [1812]. 7 pp, 4to. To Matthew Weld Hartstinyen. Thanking for books & commenting on literary works. Including postscript. (91) $1,300

— Apr 1816. (89) $250

— 25 Apr 1818. (90) £400

— 9 Dec 1822. (91) £260

— 24 June [1823]. (91) $800

— 4 Mar 1831. (89) $175

— 31 Jan [n.y.]. (89) $150

— 5 Mar [n.y.]. (89) DM220

— [n.d.], "Saturday". (91) DM660

Ds, 29 Jan 1814. (91) £150

Scott, Winfield, 1786-1866

ALs, 6 Apr 1822. (89) $110

Franking signature, [n.d.]. Alexander collection. (90) $65

Photograph, sgd, [c.1861]. (89) $250

Scriabin, Alexander, 1872-1915

ALs, 11 July 1909. 3 pp, 8vo. Recipient unnamed. Answering an inquiry about the Editions Russes de Musique. (89) DM13,000

Photograph, sgd, [n.d.]. (89) £950

Scribe, Eugene, 1791-1861

ALs, [n.d.]. (90) DM650
See also: Donizetti, Gaetano

Seaborg, Glenn Theodore

Series of 6 Ls s, 1961 to 1969. (91) $80

Sealsfield, Charles, Pseud. of Karl Anton Postl, 1793-1864

ALs, 14 Sept 1846. (90) DM220

Searle, Ronald

Original drawings, (2), ink caricatures of Sacha Guitry & Ronald Shiner, to illus the theater column in Punch. (90) £600

— Original drawings, (44), ink & wash illusts for a cartoon strip version of The Odyssey, ptd in Punch Almanack, 1955. 4 sheets, 65cm by 47cm; framed. 1 sgd. (90) £2,200

Original drawing, pencil port of T. (90) £950

— Original drawing, "Playing with lethal weapons, a boy of your age", Cupid crying as girls take his bow & arrows; 1st ptd in Lilliput Magazine, Apr 1950. 11 by 8.75 inches. In pen, brush & ink; sgd & captioned. (90) £3,000

— Original drawing, St. Trinians Soccer Song, to illus The St. Trinians Story, 1959. 6 by 8 inches. In pen & brown ink; sgd. (90) £1,700

Caricature, ink drawing of Donald Wolfit & Robert Harris, pbd in Punch, 1955. (89) £360

— Anr, ink drawing of Donald Wolfit as Sigismondo Malatesta, pbd in Punch, 1957. (89) £360
See also: Dighton, John

Sechter, Simon, 1788-1867

Autograph Ms, 25 aphorisms about arts & sciences, written for Ignaz Castelli; [1860/61]. (88) DM750

Seckendorf, Friedrich Heinrich, Graf von, 1673-1763

Ls, 3 Jan 1760. Schroeder collection. (89) DM240

Seeckt, Hans von, 1866-1936

ALs, 14 Aug 1913. (88) DM550

Seeger, Christoph Dionys, Freiherr von, 1740-1808

Series of c.500 A Ls s, c.1793 to 1806. Over 1,000 pp, 4to & 8vo. To his son Karl Christian, & to his wife. Family letters chronicling his activities & developments in Wuerttemberg. With related material. (88) DM11,000

Seeger, Karl Christian, Freiherr von, 1773-1858
Series of c.300 A Ls (some A Ls s), 1791 to 1801. Over 1,000 pp, 4to & 8vo. To his father Christoph Dionys & his mother. Giving full details of his activities. Some letters probably by his brothers. With a large archive of material relating to the Seeger family & Seeger's collection of maps & charts. (88) DM18,000

Seewald, Richard, 1889-1976
Collection of 4 A Ls s & postcard, sgd, 8 Oct 1967 to 27 Aug 1974. (91) DM780
Collection of 3 Ls s & 9 autograph postcards, sgd, 23 Dec 1965 to 3 Aug 1974. (90) DM500

Seidel, Heinrich, 1842-1906
Autograph Ms, poem, Der Fliederbusch, [n.d.]. (89) DM340
ALs, 4 Mar 1886. (90) DM240

Seidel, Ina, 1885-1974
Autograph Ms, outline & 2 stanzas of her Grosse Werk- oder Arbeitsballade; [1946]. (90) DM250

Selby, Prideaux John
[An archive of 277 of the orig drawings for Selby's Illustrations of British Ornithology, formerly owned by H. Bradley Martin, sold at P on 8 June 1989, for a total of $1,482,085, though 68 were bought in. Of the drawings, 217 were by Selby himself, 55 were by Robert Mitford, 4 were by Sir William Jardine & 1 was by Edward Lear. The Lear Great Auk brought the high price of $60,000, with Selby's Purple Heron bringing the second-highest price at $55,000.]

Sellers, Peter, 1925-80
Ds s (2)5 Aug 1963. (91) $100

Selznick, David O., 1902-65
Ls, 8 Dec 1958. (91) $450
Ds s (2)18 Feb 1937. (91) $475
Check, sgd, 27 May 1941. (91) $200

Semenov, Nikolai Nikolayevich, 1896-1986
Ls, 22 Sept 1978. (90) DM200

Semler, Johann Salomo, 1725-91
A Ls s (2), 27 Aug 1774 & 9 Jan 1779. 8 pp, 8vo. To E. Th. J. Brueckner. Returning recipient's old promissory note (included), & explaining his theological position. (91) DM1,100

Semper, Gottfried, 1803-79
ALs, 8 June 1857. (91) £450

Senancourt, Etienne Pivert de, 1770-1846
Autograph Ms, Annotations encyclopediques elementaires, Nov 1795 to [c.1840]. About 500 pp, folio, in vellum bds. Alphabetical notes covering a wide range of subjects; unpbd. Martin collection. (90) FF170,000
ALs, [c.1840]. 3 pp, 8vo. To George Sand. Thanking for her interest in his work & describing the nature of his religious inspiration. Mtd; in half mor folder with related material. Martin collection. (90) FF7,000

Senior, Nassau William, 1790-1864
ALs, "Sunday 23". (89) £150

Sentences...
Ms, Les Sentences Conseil & Bons Enseignemens des Sept Sages de Grece. [France or England], 1573. 29 (of 30) leaves, vellum, 112mm by 84mm, in 18th-cent mor gilt. Written a very fine italic script, with prose explanations in an equally fine upright batarda. Calligraphic title illuminated in gold; drawing in ink & gold paint on verso of tp showing crossed quill pens, a crown & scroll; borders of interlace ornament on the 1st page of each remaining quire; double frame of gold paint & brown ink round every page. (91) £19,000

Sermons
Ms, Sermons on the Deadly Sins, & other sermons including some of Jacobus de Voragine, in Latin. (90) £1,000

Servius Honoratus, Marius, fl.4th cent
Ms, commentaries on the Eclogues & Georgics of Virgil, in Latin. [Lombardy, c.1450]. 110 leaves & flyleaves, 268mm by 198mm. Early 18th-cent blindstamped vellum over pastebds. In a cursive bookhand with pronounced humanistic elements. With large il-

SERVIUS HONORATUS

luminated initial & full illuminated border. (91) £10,000
— Ms, Ratio Litterae, a commentary on Donatus. [Northeast? Italy, 2d half of 15th cent]. 5 leaves, 200mm by 137mm, in modern wraps. In a small slightly sloping humanistic cursive. (90) £2,400

Sette of Odd Volumes
[A collection of papers relating to the bookmen's club, 1920 to 1925, with related material, sold at S on 15 Nov 1988, lot 1744, for £130 to Wilson.]

Seume, Johann Gottfried, 1763-1810
ALs, [c.1805?]. 1 p, 4to. To [Friedrich von Matthisson]. Sending his latest work. (91) DM2,200
— 30 Mar 1809. 1 p, 8vo. To his pbr Hartknoch. Asking him to return his comments about Plutarch which he wants to have ptd. (88) DM2,800

Seuse, Heinrich, 1295?-1366. See: Suso, Heinrich

Severini, Gino, 1883-1966
Collection of 15 A Ls s, autograph postcard, sgd, ANs, & 2 typescripts, 2 Oct 1934 to 4 Feb 1965. 40 pp, 4to. To Bernard Wall. About his work, art in the postwar years, sending an article, introducing Luisa Manfredi, etc. Articles about modern art. With related material by Renato Guttoso & Eugenio Montale. (88) £1,050

Sevier, John, 1745-1815
Ds, May 1802. 1 p, 8.5 by 8 inches. Bill to the State of Tennessee for travel expenses as commissioner to determine the boundary with Virginia. (91) $1,250
— 7 June 1809. (91) $750

Sevigne, Marie de Rabutin-Chantal, Marquise de, 1626-96
ALs, 22 Oct [1661]. 3 pp, 8vo. To Gilles Menage. Thanking him & M. de Scudery for defending her in the Fouquet affair. (89) £3,500
Ls, 20 Dec [n.y.]. 3 pp, 8vo. To the [Abbe de Coulanges?]. Worrying about his health. With autograph postscript, 8 lines. (91) DM3,700

AMERICAN BOOK PRICES CURRENT

Sewall, Samuel, 1652-1730
ALs, 21 Jan 1723/24. (90) $600
ADs, 3 Jan 1698/99. Byer collection. (90) $250

Seward, Anna, 1742-1809
[Her autograph letterbooks & a vol of her sonnets, 1784 to 1807, 13 vols in early 19th-cent calf bdg, including some related material, with the pbd 1st Ed of the Letters of Anna Seward, 6 vols, Edin., 1811, sold at S on 15 Dec 1988, lot 29, for £34,000.]
ALs, 29 Dec 1809. (89) £220

Seward, William Henry, 1801-72
Ls, 7 Nov 1861. (89) $90
ADs, 13 Mar 1862. (90) $85
Ds s (2)29 June 1864. (91) $650
Ds, 8 Nov 1842. (89) $130

Sexton Blake Library
Original drawings, (54), watercolor & gouache cover designs for stories in the Sexton Blake Library series; [mid-1940s]. (90) £1,000

Seydlitz, Friedrich Wilhelm von, 1721-73
Ds, 13 May 1768. 1 p, folio. Military discharge for Capt. von Eneroth; partly ptd. Schroeder collection. (89) DM2,200

Seymour, Sir George Francis, 1787-1870
Autograph Ms, Memoirs, 1815 to 1836. (88) £240

Seyss-Inquart, Arthur, 1892-1946
Ds, [1946]. (90) $150

Sforza Family
[A collection of Ds s or Ls s by various members of the House of Sforza, 1475 to 1558, sold at S on 18 May 1989, lot 335, for £1,800 to Sam.]

Sforza, Ludovico, Duke of Milan, 1452-1508
Letters (2), 25 June [n.y.] & 15 Apr 1491. (91) £800

Shackleton, Sir Ernest Henry, 1874-1922
ALs, [n.d.]. (91) $250

Shaffer, Geneve
[A collection comprising 19 letters to Shaffer by Van M. Griffith, 1910 to 1913, & a photograph album assembled by her, all relating to the early days of aviation, with further material related to Shaffer, sold at R on 17 June 1989, lot 74, for $7,500.]

Shakers
[A collection comprising an autograph book kept by Maggie Gill, 1883 to 1922, 2 postcards, 12 photographs of shakers, & related material, sold at R on 4 Mar 1989, lot 275, for $1,400.]

Shakespeare Memorial Committee. See: Shaw, George Bernard & Shakespeare Memorial Committee

Shakespeare, William, 1564-1616
— BETTY, HENRY. - His promptbook of Hamlet, L, 1839, interleaved & extensively annotated, [c.1844], with additions in other hands. (89) £550
— DIBDIN, CHARLES. - Autograph Ms, poem, four 11-line stanzas supposedly written by Shakespeare to Anne Hathaway, with related note, [n.d.].; 3 pp, 4to. Mtd in half mor album, folio. (88) £180

Sharpe, Horatio, 1718-90
Ds, 13 Apr 1764. (90) $50

Sharpe, Tom
[Early typescript drafts of his 1st novels, Riotous Assembly (here titled ELS), & Indecent Exposure, 340 & 342 pp, 4to; carbon copies with a few Ms corrections, sold at bba on 28 July 1988, lot 189A, for £220 to Ferret Fantasy.]
Autograph Ms, notebook containing two-thirds of an unpbd novel about the adventures of Arthur Fluke, [n.d.], c.50 pp, folio. (88) £500

Shaw, George Bernard, 1856-1950
[A copy of The Intelligent Woman's Guide to Socialism and Capitalism (Popular Ed), 1929, with Shaw's autograph revisions & corrections on c.25 pages & including a typed reworked passage tipped in, sold at S on 14 Dec 1989, lot 162, for £2,200 to Gekoski.]

[An autograph envelope addressed to J. A. Edgcumbe, [6 Feb 1930], matted with ptd caricature of Shaw, sold at Dar on 2 Aug 1990, lot 338, for $140.]
[A copy of the 1st Ed of Wilfred Partington's Forging Ahead. The True Story of the Upward Progress of Thomas James Wise. NY, [1939], with extensive autograph comments & notes by Shaw on flyleaves & in margins, sgd & initialled, 16 July 1940, & related AN to Alan Kee laid in, sold at CNY on 18 Nov 1988, lot 313, for $6,500.]
[A group of 4 autograph checks, sgd, 1946 to 1948, payable to Dr. T. C. Probyn, sold at pn on 16 June 1988, lot 107, for £108 to Reuter.]
Autograph Ms, comments on Stalin & World War II, written in answer to a questionnaire by Hubert Humphreys, 19 Nov 1940. On the back of calendar pages, pasted on 2 sheets, 4to. (91) £1,400
— Autograph Ms, reply to a typed question on state-regulated marriages, [n.d.]. 1 p, 4to. (91) $1,200
— Autograph Ms, Scheme for the Elgar Book, sgd G.B.S. & dated 17 Aug [19]34. 3 pp, folio. Written for Elgar's biographer W. H. Reed & discussing the symphony from Haydn to Elgar. In pencil. (89) £3,800
Original drawing, sketch of Napoleon & the oracle, illustrating Back to Methusaleh, Act II, Part IV. (88) £600
Transcript, humorous pronouncement commending views of town clerks, sgd & inscr to John L. (88) £220
Typescript, "Connective Tissue" for a radio broadcast of Back to Methuselah, [1934]. 2 pp, 4to. With autograph revisions & further revisions by the producer Cecil Lewis. With accompanying autograph note, 19 Nov 1934, on compliments slip. (88) £2,200
— Typescript, Democracy and The Apple Cart, 1st version of the preface to his play The Apple Cart as submitted to the Week End Review, with autograph revisions; 9 Mar 1930. 5 pp, 4to. With covering ALs & corrected galley proofs. (90) £4,000
— Typescript, essay, Equality of Income. To the Editor of The Nation, [pbd 17

SHAW

May 1913]. 6 pp, 4to, on rectos only; in mor bdg. With numerous autograph revisions. Goetz collection. (89) $3,800
— Typescript, essay, Neglected Aspects of Public Libraries, with autograph postscript, sgd; 4 Feb 1949. (91) £700
— Typescript, prose sketch, The King, the Constitution and the Lady: Another Fictitious Dialogue; sgd, inscr & dated 5 Dec 1936. 4 pp, 4to. On the crisis caused by King Edward VIII's impending marriage. Isham collection. (89) $2,000
— Typescript, radio talk on Boots, Socks, and Schools, 23 June 1937. (91) £600

Typescript carbon copy, The Garden of Eden [In the Beginning]. (89) $200
— Typescript carbon copy, with holograph revisions of a remarkable letter to Frank Harris occasioned by Harris's biography of Oscar Wilde, 7 Aug 1916. 17 pp, 4to. With covering letter to Carlos Blacker asking for comment, 22 Sept 1916, 2 pp, 8vo. Koch Foundation. (90) $13,000
— Typescript carbon copy, working prompt-book for the orig production of Arms and the Man. With autograph revisions of text & with prompt & stage directions; used by producer & actress Florence Farr; [Apr 1894]. About 75 pp, 4to. Koch Foundation. (90) $38,000

Collection of ALs & autograph postcard, sgd, 31 May 1889 & 12 Aug 1904. Doheny collection. (89) $650
— Collection of 2 A Ls s & 2 autograph postcards, sgd, 1890 to 1894. 5 pp, 3to, & cards. To C. Thomas. Giving reasons for leaving his post as music critic for The World, etc. (89) £1,000
— Collection of 15 A Ls s & A Ns s, & 8 Ls s, 1894 to 1928. 34 pp, various sizes. To Mr. & Mrs. Arnold Dolmetsch. Mostly about musical matters. 2 Ls s in the hand of Mrs. Shaw, 1 carbon copy. Tipped to larger sheets; in blue mor bdg by Riviere. Doheny collection. (89) $19,000
— Collection of 22 A Ls s & Ls s, 22 Jan 1900 to 6 July 1950. 30 pp, various sizes. To Hubert & Gertrude Humphreys. Discussing political & theatrical matters. With related material. (91) £12,500

AMERICAN BOOK PRICES CURRENT

— Collection of c.120 A Ls s & Ls s, 1913 to 1939. About 165 pp, various sizes. To Charles Macdona. Discussing the production of his plays. With related material. (88) £13,500
— Collection of 6 A Ls s, 12 Ls s, 2 A Ns s & 3 autograph postcards, sgd, 14 Jan 1914-6 Feb 1930. About 30 pages, various sizes. To the publishing firm of Bernhard Tauchnitz. With related material. (91) $14,000
— Collection of 29 A Ls s, Ls s, cards & telegram, chiefly 1923 to 1934. To Cecil Lewis. Mostly concerning film production. With retained copies of 39 letters from Lewis to Shaw, 7 transcripts of letters from Shaw to Lewis, & further related material. Over 100 pp in all. (88) £9,000
— Collection of ALs & ANs, 3 Mar 1926. 2 pp, 4to, & card. To Edyth Goodall. Giving last minute advice on the 1st performance of [Mrs. Warren's Profession]; sgd GBS. Expressing congratulations on her performance. (90) £1,800
— Collection of 4 A Ls s & Ls s, 1927 & 1931. 7 pp, 4to & 8vo. To Mr. Hieatt of the St. Alban's District Council. Complaining about a refuse dump. Filing holes. (88) £2,800
— Collection of 3 A Ls s & 2 letters, 1934 to 1936. 6 pp, various sizes (2 on cards). To W. H. Reed. About T. E. Shaw & Reed's biography of Elgar. Letters incomplete. With related material. (89) £1,100
— Collection of 9 A Ls s, AL, 11 Ls s, 10 autograph postcards, sgd, & 2 A Ns s, 3 Nov 1936 to 29 Aug 1943. 37 pp, 4to. To Hugh Beaumont. Commenting & advising on the production of his plays. In half green mor album. (91) £9,000
— Collection of 2 A Ls s, Ls & autograph postcard, sgd, 2 Aug 1949 to 1 Aug 1950. (88) £750

A Ls s (2), 10 Feb & 9 Mar 1937. (90) £900

ALs, 28 Apr 1888. 2 pp, 8vo. To Harry Furniss. Defending his criticism of recipient's exhibition. (91) $1,500
— 14 Oct 1895. 1 p, 8vo. To an unnamed lady. About the importance of "expressive pantomine" for operas. Some

stains. (88) DM1,800
— 3 June 1896. 2 pp, 12mo. To Clement Scott. About the writing of criticism. (91) $2,200
— 23 Sept 1896. (91) £250
— 13 May 1904. (88) £240
— 11 Dec 1904. (90) $380
— 3 - 17 Jan 1905. 54 pp, 4to. To Archibald Henderson. Answering a series of biographical questions. Including extensive autograph corrections & alterations. With related ANs. (90) £31,000
— 16 Apr 1905. 4 pp, 4to. To J. H. Morgan. Responding to an article about social reform. Annotated by recipient. (89) £1,700
— 7 Sept 1905. 2 pp, 4to. To [Sydney] Olivier. About the chairmanship of the Stage Society, a production of As You Like It, & his own Major Barbara. Koch Foundation. (90) $1,600
— 30 Apr 1907. (89) £550
— 18 Nov 1907. (91) $500
— 14 Nov 1913. (88) £680
— 8 May 1916. (90) $500
— 30 Nov 1921. 1 p, 116mm by 177mm. To F. Day Tuttle, Jr. Giving advice to a Yale undergraduate. (90) $2,800
— 29 May 1924. (91) £320
— 20 Aug 1931. (90) £820
— 30 Mar 1936. 2 pp, 8vo. To Chockalingam Pillai. Apologizing for not having read his book yet, & theorizing about politics. (90) £1,300
— 13 Aug 1940. (90) £160
Collection of Ls & autograph Ms, 31 July 1945. 2 pp, 8vo & 4to (cut from larger sheet). To Michael Takla Guirguis. Discussing recipient's projected biography of Shaw in Arabic. Reply to personal questions, written as annotations on a paragraph cut out from Guirguis' letter. With related material. (90) £1,700
Ls s (2), 5 May & 2 June 1932. (89) £700
Ls, 28 July 1909. 2 pp, 4to. Ptd circular letter to colleagues, asking them to give evidence before a Select Committee on Stage Plays in order to fight censorship. Byer collection. (90) $1,600
— 8 Oct 1909. (90) £750
— 16 Jan 1915. 7 pp, 4to. To James F. Muirhead. Justifying his controversial

Commonsense about War. With autograph corrections & postscript. (88) £1,800
— 12 Oct 1928. (91) $200
— 5 Aug 1935. (90) £140
— 7 Oct 1935. (88) £600
— 15 Nov 1935. 1 p, 4to. To W. H. Reed. Making suggestions for recipient's biography of Elgar. (89) £1,100
— 1 Jan 1936. (89) £900
— 28 Apr 1940. (88) £450
— 21 July 1946. (88) £680
Collection of 2 autograph postcards, sgd, & ANs, 1939 to 1941. (88) £500
Autograph postcards (2), sgd, 10 Dec 1935 & 10 May 1944. (89) £400
— Autograph postcards (2), sgd, 5 & 17 Dec 1945. (91) $200
Autograph postcard, sgd, 15 Dec 1897. (89) £160
— 19 Sept 1907. (90) £150
— 18 Mar 1908. (91) $180
— [1908]. (90) $425
— 13 Jan 1910. (90) $225
— 6 Jan 1913. (90) $300
— [4 Aug 1915]. Doheny collection. (88) $160
— 10 July 1920. Doheny collection. (88) $420
— 22 Oct 1920. (88) £180
— 23 Jan [19]21. (91) $300
— 23 Nov 1921. (90) DM400
— [1925]. (91) $325
— 12 Nov 1927. (88) £150
— 23 Dec 1929. (89) £280
— 29 Apr 1930. (90) £340
— 18 July 1932. (89) £320
— 3 July 1935. (90) £220
— 20 Nov 1937. (88) £60
— 31 Oct 1938. (91) $750
— 22 Oct 1941. (89) £150
— 25 Mar 1942. (88) £90
— 24 Dec 1946. (89) $525
— 3 Feb 1950. (88) £320
— 5 Mar 1950. (88) £450
— [n.d.]. (88) £60
A Ns s (2), 22 Apr 1919 & 18 Dec 1924. (91) £700
ANs, 14 June 1906. (88) $175
— 27 Aug 1912. (89) $300
— 22 Apr 1914. (88) £250
— 8 July 1918. (89) DM740

SHAW

— 22 June 1925. (89) DM400
— 4 Feb 1928. (89) $500
— 11 July 1928. (88) £160
— 1 Dec 1936. (89) $250
— 25 Mar 1937. (88) £130
— 25 June 1946. (90) £280
— 24 May 1948. (89) $325
— 12 Nov 1949. (90) £320
— [n.d.]. At foot of ALs by John F. Tucker, 1 p, 8vo. Responding to an invitation to a dinner in his honor. Framed with ptd photograph. (91) $1,100

Ds, 5 Oct 1911. (88) £190

Autograph endorsement, [14 Sept 1924]; on Ms of a sonnet, 1 p, 4to, by L. (89) £550

Check, sgd, 3 Nov 1937. (89) $200
— Anr, 15 Nov 1945. (88) $175

Corrected proof, Autobiographer's Apology, pbd in Shaw gives himself away, 1939. (88) £550
— Anr, of Marie Stopes's verse drama Oriri, annotated throughout by Shaw. 30 July 1940. 8vo, in orig wraps. About 120 words of correction. (91) £1,100

Photograph, sgd & inscr, 1944. (88) £95
— Anr, 19 Aug 1949. (89) £400

Ptd photograph, sgd & inscr, [n.d.]. (89) $400

Proof copy, Too True to be Good: a Collection of Stage Sermons, 5th Rough Proof; sgd, inscr & dated 19 July 1933. 84 pp, 8vo, in orig wraps. With autograph annotations for the Polish trans. Isham collection. (89) $2,800
— GILL, COLIN. - Orig drawing, crayon port of Shaw, 17.5 by 14.5 inches. Sgd & inscr by Shaw, 21 Oct [19]22. Framed. (91) £1,600
— SWAMY. - Orig drawings (2), pencil sketches of Shaw, dated by Shaw 14 Mar & 30 Sept 1938. Various sizes. Sgd by both; 1 inscr by Shaw. (89) £600
— SWAMY. - Orig drawing, chalk sketch of Shaw, [n.d.]. 270mm by 220mm. Sgd by both; initialled & inscr by Shaw on attached sheet. With related material. (89) £450
— SWAMY. - Orig drawings (2), pencil sketches of Shaw, dated 30 Sept 1938 & 23 June 1947 by Shaw. Various sizes. Sgd by both; 1 inscr by Shaw.

(89) £1,100
— SWAMY. - Orig drawings (2), port sketches of Shaw, 1 inscr & dated 29 June 1946 by Shaw. Various sizes. Sgd by both. With related material. (89) £800

Shaw, George Bernard, 1856-1950 —& Harris, Frank, 1854-1931
[The autograph revised Ms of parts of Harris's Oscar Wilde: His Life and Confessions, with orig typescript with autograph revisions of Shaw's related Memories of Oscar Wilde & tp annotated by Harris, c.1916, over 50 pp, 4to, in mor bdg, sold at S on 15 Dec, lot 121, for £15,500.]

Shaw, George Bernard, 1856-1950 —& Shakespeare Memorial Committee
[The minute books of the Committee, May 1909 to July 1912, 2 vols, 4to, sgd 5 times by Shaw, with 2 related autograph cards by Shaw & a sheet sgd by 15 members of the Executive Committee, 20 Oct 1908, sold at S on 21 July 1988, lot 221, for £1,800 to Pearson.]

Shaw, George Bernard, 1856-1950. See: Sullivan, Edmund Joseph

Shaw, Henry Wheeler, 1818-85
ALs, 27 Nov [c.1872]. Doheny collection. (89) $900

Shaw, Nathaniel, 1735-82. See: American Revolution

Shelby, Isaac, 1750-1826
Ds, 3 July 1804. (91) $120

Sheldon, Ralph, 1537-1613
Ms, account book, 1586 to 1588; c.220 pp, folio, in contemp vellum bdg. Sgd twice. Mostly in the hand of his servant Robert Jones. Recording hundreds of disbursements (some receipts) relating to every aspect of the manufacturer's life. (88) £11,000

Shelley, Mary Wollstonecraft, 1797-1851
Series of 7 A Ls s, [Feb to Apr 1828]. 14 pp, 8vo & 16mo. To her pbr John Bowring. About the principles observed in her reviews, Byron's letters, & her research on Spain. 3 initialled. (91) £7,000

A Ls s (2), 14 May [1838] & [n.d.]. 5 pp, 16mo. To Dionysius Lardner. About the ptg of her lives of Pascal, La Fontaine, & others. (91) £1,100

ALs, 27 May [n.y.]. (89) £400

Shelley, Percy Bysshe, 1792-1822
[A group of 31 letters, drafts, copies, etc., relating to the friendship between Shelley & Thomas Jefferson Hogg, their expulsion from Oxford, their correspondence with the Rev. G. S. Faber, etc., mostly addressed to John Hogg, with related material, 1810 to 1812, over 100 pp, sold at pn on 15 Nov 1990, lot 113, for £20,000 to Quaritch.]

[Shelley, Bysshe. - A solicitor's copy of the settlement of the estate of the poet's grandfather, 1819, including transcript of the settlement made on 20 Aug 1791, 74 pp, 4to, in a calf vol of settlements, c.155 pp in all, sold at S on 15 Dec 1988, lot 60, for £200.]

ALs, 13 July 1809. 1 p, 4to. To an unnamed pbr. Discussing terms for the publication of a work. Repaired. (89) £8,000

— 7 Nov 1812. 3 pp, 4to. To John Williams. Reporting about his efforts to raise funds for the works at Tremadoc. Repaired. (88) £5,800

— 24 Dec 1812. 4 pp, 4to. To Clio Rickman. Ordering a long list of books (included). Endorsed by recipient. (89) £4,500

— 25 Sept 1816. 2 pp, 4to. To an unidentified bookseller. Ordering 5 books. (89) £3,200

Ls, 6 May 1815. (90) £140

— 10 May 1815. 1 p, 4to. To William Whitton. Ordering him to pay debts to moneylenders. (90) £1,900

ADs, 21 Feb 1817. Pay order addressed to his bankers in favor of Mr. Ducroz. Cancellation affecting signature. (91) $1,100

Autograph check, sgd, 26 Mar 1816. 1 p, 70mm by 185mm. Drawn on Messrs. Brookes & Co. for £6.00 payable to Mrs. Clairmont. Repaired. Doheny collection. (89) $1,200

Check, accomplished & sgd, 11 Apr 1816. 90mm by 185mm. Drawn on Messrs Brooks, Son & Dixon for £34 payable to himself. Doheny collection. (89) $1,600

— Anr, sgd, 2 Mar 1818. (88) £750

Cut signature, [14 Oct 1815?]. (91) £190

— FORMAN, HARRY BUXTON. - The Ms & annotated text for his 1892 Aldine Ed of Shelley, comprising 197 pp in autograph, & ptd leaves of 1882 Reeves & Turner Ed heavily revised on interleaves, in all 430 leaves in 5 8vo cloth vols, sold at CNY on 22 Feb 1989, lot 2162, for $3,200 to Ximenes. 89

— HOGG, THOMAS JEFFERSON. - Ds, 19 July 1816. Passport; also sgd by the French Ambassador. With dockets by officials in Paris, Brussels & Amsterdam. (91) £130

Shenstone, William, 1714-63
A Ls s (2), 20 Apr 1748 & 10 Aug 1758. (90) £750

ALs, 25 Oct 1753. (88) £400

Shepard, Alan B.
ALs, 29 Nov 1969. (91) $650

Photograph, sgd & inscr, [n.d.]. (91) $85

Shepard, Ernest Howard, 1879-1976
Original drawing, 'Handsome bell rope, isn't it?' said Owl, to illus Winnie-the-Pooh, 1926. 10.5 by 8 inches. In pencil, pen & black ink; sgd. (90) £17,000

— Original drawing, Making the Gun Barrel, to illus Richard Jeffries' Bevis, 1932. (90) £240

— Original drawing, Pooh seated on a stone in the middle of a stream, to illus The House at Pooh Corner, 1928. 185mm by 221mm; framed. In ink; sgd. (90) £16,000

— Original drawing, Tigger Comes to the Forest, [n.d.]. 10.5 by 10 inches. In pencil, pen, & black ink; sgd. (90) £17,000

— Original drawing, Tiggers Can't Climb Trees, [n.d.]. 14.5 by 10.5 inches. In pencil, pen, & black ink; sgd. (90) £19,000

Sheridan, Philip Henry, 1831-88
[A military carbon dispatch, sgd, 4 Apr 1865, 1 p, 8vo, to Maj. Gen. Meade, reporting about enemy movements, with autograph postscript, sgd, on verso, sold at CNY on 18 Nov

1988, lot 319, for $800.]

Sheridan, Richard Brinsley, 1751-1816
ALs, 12 July 1780. (88) £350
— [1796]. (90) $190
— [c.1799]. (90) £200
— 1816. (89) $130
— [n.d.], "Monday". (91) $325
— [n.d.]. (88) £200

Sherman, James S., 1855-1912
Ls, 8 Feb 1910. (89) $65

Sherman, Roger, Signer from Connecticut
ALs, 1 Sept 1758. (89) DM620
— 16 Nov 1781. (88) $170
— 6 Mar 1790. 3 pp, 4to. To Gov. Samuel Huntington. Informing him about Congressional business, the national debt, etc. (90) $8,500
ADs, 16 May 1787. (91) $275
Ds, 19 Dec 1777. (91) $275

Sherman, William Tecumseh, 1820-91
Collection of 6 A Ls s & AL, 3 May to 2 Nov 1862. 26 pp, 4to. To Thomas (1) & Philemon Ewing. About the Battle of Shiloh, the occupation of Memphis, & other matters pertaining to the Civil War. AL incomplete. (89) $8,500
— Collection of ALs, photograph, & signature, 1 June 1863 & [n.d.]. 2 pp, 4to, 101mm by 61mm, & visiting card. To Generals McClernand & McPherson. Informing them about troop positions around Vicksburg. (90) $12,000
— Collection of 2 A Ls s & AL, 28 July to 24 Oct 1863. 14 pp, 4to. To Philemon Ewing. Describing his camp on Big Black River, reflecting about the War, mourning his son & analyzing his relationship with Grant. AL incomplete. (89) $3,000
Series of 7 A Ls s, 4 Mar 1832 to 4 Apr 1862. 4to. To Thomas (6) & Philemon Ewing. About his appointment to West Point, & his career at the beginning of the Civil War. With ALs by his mother Mary Sherman & his West Point report for Feb 1839. (89) $4,750
— Series of 5 A Ls s, 16 Jan [1863] to 14 June 1863. 32 pp, 4to. To Thomas Ewing. Describing his efforts to take Vicksburg & his battles with the press. (89) $6,000
— Series of 5 A Ls s, 21 Apr 1864 to 29 Jan 1865. 26 pp, 4to. To Philemon Ewing. Describing the movements of his army in Georgia & South Carolina, & reflecting about the War & his own role. (89) $11,000
ALs, 7 July 1841. (88) $160
— 1 Sept 1851. (88) $230
— 11 Dec 1863. 4 pp, 4to. To Major Gen. Grant. Reporting about his movements in Georgia & discussing strategy. In pencil. Doheny collection. (89) $7,000
— 28 Mar 1864. 3 pp, 8vo. To Gen. R. M. Sawyer. Giving orders to pursue Gen. Forrest after the Fort Pillow Massacre. (90) $25,000
— 31 Mar 1864. 1 p, 4to. To Gen. John M. Schofield. Requesting him to send a pontoon bridge. (91) $2,800
— 19 July 1864. 1 p, 4to. To Gen. George H. Thomas. Setting up troop movements. (91) $4,500
— 20 July 1864. 2 pp, 8vo. To Gen. James B. McPherson. Informing him about troop movements around Atlanta. (91) $5,500
— 21 Feb 1867. 4 pp, 4to. To Anna Chase at Tampico. About the Mexican revolution, Maximilian & Juarez. (91) $3,000
— 9 Jan 1869. (89) £70
— 30 Sept 1874. (89) $190
— 16 Jan 1882. (88) $85
— 17 Aug 1882. (90) $750
— 27 Dec 1884. (91) $375
— 27 Dec 1884. (91) $550
— 17 Apr 1889. Byer collection. (90) $225
Franking signature, [17 Aug n.y.]. (88) $70
Photograph, sgd & inscr, 13 July 1889. (91) $650
Signature, [n.d.]. (91) $175

Shields, Frederic James, 1833-1911
[A Ms journal of an [unidentified] companion of Shields written during a trip to Italy, 7 Sept to 10 Oct [n.y.], 65 pp, 4to, in vellum bdg, illus with a number of pen-&-ink sketches, sold at S on 13 Dec 1990, lot 449, for £400 to Bristow.]

Shirley, William, 1694-1771
ALs, 24 Mar 1755. (91) $250

Shostakovich, Dimitri, 1906-75
Autograph Ms, draft of a radio speech on "Ten Choral Poems by Revolutionary Poets." 25 Oct 1951. 2 pp, 8vo. (91) $2,500

Autograph music, 10th movement of his Symphony no 14, 25 Sept 1972. 4 pp, folio. Draft of 72 bars in full score; sgd twice. (91) £16,000

— Autograph music, Aphorismes for piano, Op. 13, sgd twice & dated Feb to Apr 1927. 14 pp, folio. Complete working draft, notated on up to 14 staves per page; with titles in Russian & French. Marked by the ptr. (89) $40,000

— Autograph music, Ophelia's song for the film Hamlet, Op. 116; 1st 11 bars, scored for voice & violoncello. 1 p, size not stated. Sgd twice, inscr to Miss J. H. A. Verhagen & dated 15 July 1968. (88) DM4,500

ALs, 12 Dec 1929. 1 p, 8vo. To Nikolai Malko. Regarding a dispute over the payment of royalties. (90) £2,400

— 13 Dec 1946. (91) £850

— 17 July 1974. 1 p, folio. To A. P. Mitchell. Giving his views on tempo markings in his 1st Symphony. In Russian. (91) £3,000

— [n.d.]. (90) £600

Photograph, sgd, 28 May 1958. (91) £800

Photograph, sgd & inscr, 31 Oct 1966. (88) DM660

— Anr, 7 July 1974. 145mm by 95mm. Seated. (90) £1,050

Shostakovich, Dimitri, 1906-75 —& Others
Ls, 27 Feb 1957. (90) £800

Sibelius, Jean, 1865-1957
Autograph music, Polonaise for piano, Op. 40, no 10, complete score; 6 July 1916. 7 pp, folio. Fair copy, sgd twice. Corner torn, affecting 5 bars. (90) £7,500

— Autograph music, Suite mignonne Op. 98 no 1, for 2 flutes, violin, viola, cello & bass; full score, [1921]. 41 pp, folio. Written in black ink on eleven staves per page, with numerous autograph revisions. Including autograph tp, sgd. File holes. (88) £26,000

Series of 5 A Ls s, 8 Sept 1910 to 26 Jan 1917. 5 pp, 8vo & 4to. To [Raphael Ahlstroem]. Asking for a loan & referring to problems with repayments. (91) £1,300

ALs, 18 Oct 1903. 3 pp, 8vo. To an unnamed professor. About his 2d Symphony. In German. (90) DM3,000

— 19 Mar [19]05. (88) £480
— 5 May 1905. (89) £600
— 30 June 1905. (89) £800
— 12 July 1905. (89) £600
— 3 Oct 1905. (89) £600
— [c.1905]. (89) £750
— 26 June 1906. (89) £1,000
— 28 Aug 1906. (91) £700
— 24 Sept 1906. (89) £500
— 21 Dec 1906. (89) £700
— 1 Feb 1907. (91) £850
— 11 Oct 1907. (91) £750
— 22 Oct 1907. (91) £750
— 6 Dec 1907. (89) £600
— 16 Dec 1907. (91) £800
— 29 Apr 1908. (89) £1,000
— 17 Feb 1909. (89) £440
— 27 Nov 1910. (91) £1,000
— 8 Sept 1923. (91) $475
— 17 Feb 1924. 1 p, 4to. To Herbert Wright. Thanking for interest in his work. In English. (88) DM1,500
— 2 May 1930. (88) £400
— 18 Dec 1931. (91) $350

Ls, 7 May 1943. (90) £700
— 9 Dec 1946. (89) £400

Autograph quotation, 3 bars from The Swan of Tounela, [n.d.], sgd & inscr. (89) £800

Photograph, sgd, [n.d.]. 23.3cm by 17cm. Sitting, by Pietinen. (90) DM1,600

Signature, [n.d.]. (90) $250

Sibley, George Champlain, 1782-1863
Ds, 31 Mar 1818. Alexander collection. (90) $210

Sibley, Henry Hastings, 1811-91
ALs, [2 Feb 1841]. Alexander collection. (90) $650

Sibley, Henry Hopkins, 1816-86
Ds, 27 Aug 1852. (88) $170

Sibley, Solomon, 1769-1846
ALs, [4 Aug 1821]. Alexander collection. (90) $220
— 18 Nov 1822. Alexander collection. (90) $115

Sickingen, Franz von, 1481-1523
Letter, [14 Sept] 1519. 1 p, folio. To Heinrich von Schwarzenberg. Requesting him to intercede with the Duke that no harm be done to the village of Merxheim. With secretarial signature. Bovet collection. (90) DM3,100

Siddons, Sarah, 1755-1831
ALs, 26 July 1794. (90) £500
— 2 July 1827. (91) £280
— 4 June [n.y.]. (89) £200
Series of Letters, c.325 letters, 1785 to 1802. About 350 pp, 8vo, in 3 notebooks. To Elizabeth Adair, Mrs. Soame & Miss Wynne. Copies of letters to close friends providing insights into her professional & private life; in the hand of Elizabeth Adair. (89) £1,400

Siebold, Karl Kaspar, 1736-1807
Ls, 19 June 1790. (90) DM430

Siege of Vienna
Ms, Relation or diary of the Seige of Vienna. [c.1683-84] 72 leaves, folio, in contemp mor gilt with monogram of James II as duke of York. Written in a calligraphic hand. (91) $6,000

Siemens, Werner von, 1816-92
ALs, 17 Dec 1839. (91) DM750
— 17 Feb 1872. (91) DM550
— 31 Jan 1880. (88) DM650

Sierra Leone
— WALSHE, CAPT. HOLWELL. - Ms, letterbook, 1862 to 1874, 250 pp, folio. Kept as Commandant in Sierra Leone & as Police Magistrate in Singapore. (91) £500

Sigel, Franz, 1824-1902
ALs, 22 Mar 1889. (88) DM210
— 7 Apr 1890. (90) DM250
— 3 Aug 1893. (89) DM240

Sigismund, Markgraf von Brandenburg, 1592-1640
Ls, 26 Oct/5 Nov 1629. (90) DM700

Signac, Paul, 1863-1935
ALs, [1925 or later]. (90) DM550
— [1934]. (89) DM360
— [n.d.]. (90) DM450
ANs, 15 Sept [n.y.]. (90) DM240

Sikorsky, Igor I., 1889-1972
Typescript, list of Sikorsky's honors & awards; [n.d.]. (91) $80
Photograph, sgd & inscr, 2 May 1962. (90) DM400
Signature, 19 June 1940. (91) $85
— Anr, 2 Oct 1947. (91) $150
— Anr, 21 Apr 1972. (90) $100

Silliman, Benjamin, 1779-1864
ALs, 14 Sept 1852. (88) $100

Silliman, Benjamin, 1816-85
ALs, 10 Feb [18]70. (90) $120

Silvestre de Sacy, Antoine Isaac, 1758-1838
ALs, 12 Feb 1818. (89) DM550

Sime, Sidney H.
Original drawing, cover design for The Lunatic at Large. (88) £750

Simenon, Georges, 1903-89
ALs, Mar 1978. (91) DM250
Ls, 16 Dec 1959. 3 pp, 4to. To [Marcel Achard]. Explaining the role of judges in French courts of inquiry. Including 8-line autograph postscript. Margin def. (90) DM1,800

Simeon, Charles, 1759-1836
Series of 3 A Ls s, 27 Apr 1825 to 16 Jan 1830. (89) £90

Simmons, Aloysius Harry ("Al"), 1903-56
Check, sgd, 10 July 1952. (91) $120

Simon de Tournai
Ms, Homilarius. [N.p., early 13th cent] 219 leaves, vellum, 148mm by 105mm, in modern vellum bdg. In semi-cursive gothic hand in brown ink. (90) $5,200

Simpson, Louis
Collection of 5 A Ls s, 10 Ls s, autograph postcard, & 2 typescripts, sgd, 1943 to 1964 & [n.d.]. (90) $600

Simrock, Karl, 1802-76
Autograph Ms, report about a visit to an educational establishment at Wiesbaden in 1838, sgd & dated 14 Aug 1855. (88) DM460

ALs, [5 June] 1838. (88) DM280

— [c.1855]. (91) DM320

— 20 Apr 1868. (91) DM250

Sinatra, Frank
Photograph, sgd & inscr, 1948. (91) $450

Sinclair, Sir John, 1754-1835
ALs, 29 Oct 1819. (89) £620

Ls, 22 Jan 1797. (88) £95

Sinclair, Upton, 1878-1968
Typescript, chapter 10 from No Pasaran!, [n.d.]. (90) DM550

Collection of ALs & 18 Ls s, 9 Aug 1944 to 16 May 1962 & [n.d.]. 20 pp, 4to & 8vo. To Robert Breuer. Mostly concerning Breuer's reviews of his works. 6 Ls s with autograph additions. Some small tears. (89) DM1,500

ALs, 24 Sept [n.y.]. (89) $55

Collection of 4 Ls s & ANs, 1928 to 1939. (89) $175

Singer, Isaac Bashevis, 1904-91
— ROSENTHAL, JACK. - Typescript, film script for Yentl, Mar 1982. 167 pp, folio. With autograph revisions & additional material. (91) £500

Sintenis, Renee, 1888-1965
Collection of 6 A Ls s & 2 Ls s, 4 Oct 1953 to 10 Feb 1956. (89) DM600

Sisler, George Harold, 1893-1973
ALs, [n.d.]. (91) $170

Sisley, Alfred, 1839-99
ALs, [n.d.]. (88) DM400

Sismondi, Jean Charles Leonard Simonde de, 1773-1842
ALs, [n.d.]. (88) DM440

— 18 Feb 1838. (90) DM240

Sitting Bull, 1834?-90
Ptd photograph, sgd, [19 Apr 1887]. Oval; mtd on cardboard, 3 by 4.5 inches. Note of authentication on verso. (91) $5,500

Signature, [late 1880s?]. 12mo. Sgd in pictograph & in script. (91) $3,100

— Anr, [n.d.]. 3.5 by 2 inches. Matted with ptd group photograph. (91) $3,500

Sitwell, Dame Edith, 1887-1964
[Her autograph notes in the margins & on half-title of John Malcolm Brinnin's Dylan Thomas in America. L, 1956, 8vo, sold at S on 15 Dec 1988, lot 111, for £450.]

Autograph Ms (2), working notebooks for Gold Coast Customs, [1928]. About 240 pp, folio, in marbled bds. Both inscr to Siegfried Sassoon. With related material. (91) £6,000

Collection of 30 A Ls s & AN, 18 Mar 1949 to 25 Nov 1958. 256 pp, 4to & 8vo. To Zosia Kochanski. Chatty letters discussing her writing, friends, & current events. With 45 A Ls s & Ls s by Osbert Sitwell to Kochanski & further related material. (88) $6,000

— Collection of 3 A Ls s & 2 autograph Mss, [n.d.]. (88) £340

Series of c.40 A Ls s, [n.d.]. About 110 pp, 4to & 8vo. To Leonard Russell, Roger Senhouse, John Lehmann, & others. About a variety of matters. With related material. (90) £1,400

ALs, 5 Apr 1920. (88) $140

Concert program, sgd & inscr, 19 May 1952. (90) £200

Sitwell Family
— SASSOON, SIEGFRIED. - 118 caricatures of Sir Osbert, Edith, & Sachaverell Sitwell, in pencil, watercolor & ink; [c.1925]. In 4to vol. (91) £8,000

SITWELL

Sitwell, Sir Osbert, 1892-1969
Collection of 4 A Ls s, 4 postcards, sgd, & autograph Ms, 1918 to 1949. (91) £500

Sitwell, Sir Sacheverell
Autograph Ms, poem, Opus Anglicanum, 24 Jan 1972. (89) $300

Sixtus IV, Pope, 1414-84
Document, 31 Aug 1474. Doheny collection. (88) £450

Sixtus V, Pope, 1521-90
Document, 26 June 1585. (88) DM380

Skelton, Bevil, d.1692. See: Heraldic Manuscripts

Skinner, Theodore Henry. See: Civil War, American

Skorzeny, Otto, 1908-75
[2 ptd Christmas & New Year's cards, [c.1950s], both sgd, with handwritten additions in English, sold at sg on 22 Oct, lot 246, for $120.]
Ns, 21 Jan 1943. (91) $500

Slavery
[Jamaica. - A collection of 54 Mss relating to slavery in Jamaica & the estates of the Dehany family of London, 1701 to 1884, including a plan of Point Estate, 1786, with related material, sold at C on 22 June 1988, lot 71, for £620 to Burgess & Browning.]
[Tennessee. - A collection of 21 letters, 1844 to 1852, 67 pp, folio & 4to, from members of the Gilbert family at Athens to Rev. & Mrs. Gottlieb Bassler, containing many anti-slavery references, sold at sg on 22 Oct, lot 247, for $400.]
[A group of 15 Mss mostly relating to slavery in Missouri, including bills of sale for slaves & items regarding a runaway slave, etc., [n.d.]., sold at rf on 22 Apr 1989, lot 23, for $800.]
Transcript, poem, The Negro's Hymn, beginning "If Pity in thy Nature dwell"; 1792. (90) $65
Letter, 1844. (89) $450
Ds, 7 Dec 1833. (88) $50
— 7 Dec 1833. (88) $85
— 25 May 1855. (88) $160
Document, 13 June 1829. Alexander collection. (90) $200
— 16 Jan 1850. (90) $50
— JAMAICA. - Ms, Return of slaves in Parish of Manchester in possession of Edward Owen, 1817 to 1829. 226 entries on 9 pp, folio. Sgd by Thomas Amyot, Registrar of Colonial Slaves in Great Britain, 1832. (88) £90
— LAGOS, WEST AFRICA. - Ms, ledger recording accounts for the Lagos Factory, listing slaves acquired & sold, etc., 1802 to 1803. 47 pp, folio, & 5 pp later childish exercises. Orig bds, def. (88) £520
— LANIER, ANN. - Ds, 24 Mar 1841. 4 pp, 4to. Last Will & Testament, bequeathing slaves to her daughter & grandsons, & providing for the emancipation of an old servant. (90) $200
— TAUNSTEN, JAMES. - ALs, 29 Sept 1820. 1 p, folio. To Dabney Minot. Informing him that his runaway slave has turned himself in. Endorsed by Minot. (90) $100
— TEXAS. - 2 documents, 1841 & 1848, bill of sale for a slave boy, sgd by N. Townsend, & warranty for a slave girl, sgd by W. Wells, sold at rf on 22 Apr 1989, lot 27, for $130. 89

Slavonic Manuscripts
Ms, Acathists for the Annunciation & Dormition. Fekula Ms.432. (91) £280
— Ms, Apocalypse, with Commentary of Andrew of Caesarea. [Russia, mid-18th cent]. 190 leaves, 200mm by 162mm, in contemp blindstamped calf over wooden bds. In a semi-uncial hand imitating typographical script. With ornamental tp & full-page miniature. Fekula Ms.650. (91) £1,300
— Ms, Apostol, with Commentaries. [Russia, c.1500]. 393 leaves (some lacking), 285mm by 205mm, in 19th-cent blindstamped calf over wooden bds. In a semi-uncial hand. With 4 very fine illuminated initials & headpieces, very elaborate calligraphic headpiece & initial, & full-page illuminated miniature of 18 medallions of Saints. Fekula Ms.651. (91) £52,000
— Ms, Canon for Prophets & Martyrs for Saturdays & Exapostinaria. (91) £950
— Ms, compilation of various biblical, moral & religious texts. [Russia, 18th cent]. 153 leaves (some lacking),

165mm by 110mm, in contemp calf over wooden bds. In cursive & semi-uncial hands by 10 different scribes. With 25 full-page miniatures. Fekula Ms.674. (91) £1,600
— Ms, Hiermologion [The Book of Eight Tones]. (90) £400
— Ms, Life of St. John the Divine & Apocalypse, with Commentary of Andrew of Caesarea. [Russia, mid-16th cent]. 283 leaves, 185mm by 130mm, in later calf gilt. In a very elegant semi-uncial hand. With 4 illuminated ornamental headpieces, 3 line drawings in colored washes, & full-page illuminated miniature. Fekula Ms.743. (91) £9,000
— Ms, Liturgicon or Missal. [Serbia, early 15th cent]. 109 leaves (some lacking), 210mm by 140mm, in very def bdg with contemp colored sewing-threads. In a small, formal semi-uncial hand with later additions. Fekula Ms.477. (91) £1,100
— Ms, Mesyataa iunia v 26 den, Prazdnuem Yavlenie Preblagoslovennoj Vladychitsy Nashej Bogoroditsy i Prisno Devy Marii na Prechestnoy Ikone Tikhvinskoy. (90) £380
— Ms, miscellany, including the story of Barlaam & Josephat attributed to St. John Damascene. [Serbia, early 15th cent]. 173 leaves (some lacking), 285mm by 205mm, in 19th-cent gilt-stamped half calf. In a semi-uncial hand. Fekula Ms.653. (91) £24,000
— Ms, miscellany including psalms, hymns, stichera, etc. [Serbia, 17th cent]. 197 leaves, 150mm by 100mm, in elaborately gilt & painted bdg. In a semi-uncial hand. With 33 colored & illuminated initials, 20 illuminated headpieces, & half-page opening headpiece. (91) £2,600
— Ms, Paschalia, Computus. [Russia, early 18th cent]. 60 leaves (some lacking), vellum, 70mm by 45mm, in contemp calf over paper bds. In a semi-uncial hand. With 2 illuminated decorative headpieces & full-page miniature. Fekula Ms.505. (91) £2,600
— Ms, Prologue, accounts of the feasts of the Church year for the period 20 Apr to 15 Aug. [Russia, c.1590]. 349 leaves (some lacking), 280mm by 185mm, in 18th-cent blindstamped calf gilt over wooden bds. In a very regular semi-uncial hand. With 3 illuminated headpieces & fine full-page illuminated miniature. Fekula Ms.783. (91) £13,000
— Ms, Ruchnaya Paskhaliya, Computus. [Russia, c.1685]. 363 leaves (some lacking), 151mm by 90mm, in rebacked contemp blindstamped calf. In several colors of ink. With over 350 diagrams & calendrical computations in various forms, many representations of hands for finger-computation, & a radiating sphere with the signs of the zodiac. Fekula Ms.506. (91) £9,500
— Ms, Siya Kniga Sobryanie Sloves' i Deyanii. [Russia, c.1820]. 104 leaves & blanks, 335mm by 205mm, in canvas-backed floral cloth. In a regular semi-uncial church slavonic hand. With 4 ornamental headpieces, 3 title-pages with full-page decoration, & 70 large illusts in ink & watercolors. (90) £7,500
— Ms, Triod Tsvetnaia [Festal Triodion]. (90) £500
— Ms, Triodion of Dionysius the Wonderworker, [Russia, 14th cent]. 107 leaves (some lacking), vellum, 260mm by 200mm, in contemp calf over wooden bds. In a regular uncial hand. With 2 interlaced initials, very fine decorative teratological headpiece, & 16th-cent inscr recording that Ms belonged to Dionysius of Sosnovets. Fekula Ms.551. (91) £22,000
— Ms, Typicon for the liturgical year. [Russia, late 14th cent]. 214 leaves, 270mm by 190mm, in 17th-cent blindstamped calf over wooden bds. In a semi-uncial hand. With fine ornamental headpiece. Fekula Ms.810. (91) £24,000
— JOHN DAMASCENE, SAINT. - Ms, The Book of Heaven, with St. John Chrysostom, Homilies. [Russia, 1st half of 17th cent]. 210 leaves, 330mm by 210mm, in rebacked contemp calf gilt over wooden bds. In semi-uncial hands by 2 different scribes. With elaborate opening page with headpiece & full-page miniature. Fekula Ms.676. (91) £2,000
— PROKOPOVICH, FEOFAN. - Ms, Catechism. [Grabovec Monastery, Hunga-

ry, 21 Mar 1744]. 119 leaves, 145mm by 90mm, in contemp gilt-stamped calf. In a cursive hand, with headings in a typographical semi-uncial script, by Hierodeacon Daniil. Fekula Ms.666. (91) £160
See also: Gospel Manuscripts
See also: John Climacus, c.570-649
See also: Lectionary
See also: Liturgical Manuscripts
See also: Lives of the Saints
See also: Officium
See also: Psalms & Psalters

Slevogt, Max, 1868-1932
Series of 4 A Ls s, 5 Dec 1927 to 9 Sept 1931. 6 pp, 4to & 8vo. To Alexander Amersdorffer. Concerning matters pertaining to the Prussian Academy of Arts. (91) DM1,800
Autograph postcard, sgd, 17 Aug 1932. To Paul Lewy. Quatrain, referring to his studio. Including pen-&-ink self port. (90) DM2,000
ANs, [Oct] 1928. 1 p, 8vo (card). Recipient unnamed. Thanking for birthday greetings. With small humorous self port on verso. (90) DM1,520

Slezak, Leo, 1873-1946
[His album, 1903 to 1906, with over 100 entries mostly by musicians, singers, etc., with notes about his concerts, 1901 to 1918, & further related material, sold at star on 28 June 1990, lot 981, for DM3,300.]
Collection of 9 A Ls s & 7 Ls s, 23 Oct 1921 to 18 May 1927. 27 pp, 4to & 8vo. To F. A. Broetz. Witty letters about his financial affairs. With related material. (90) DM1,300

Sloan, John, 1871-1951
ALs, 19 Mar 1928. (88) $80
— 17 May 1928. (91) $275

Sloane, Sir Hans, 1660-1753
ALs, 18 Sept 1705. (91) £220
— 17 Aug 1736. (88) $350

Smetana, Bedrich, 1824-84
ALs, 29 Mar 1857. 4 pp, 4to. To Alexander Dreyschock. Informing him of his decision to remain in Gothenburg. (91) £4,800
— 18 Apr 1859. 3 pp, 4to. To Alexander Dreyschock. About the impending death of his wife. (91) £2,200
— 8 Mar 1874. 3 pp, 8vo. To Breitkopf & Haertel. Offering 4 orchestral works for publication. (91) DM11,000
Autograph quotation, 8 bars from the opera Certova stena, sgd & dated 10 Apr 1882. 112mm by 196mm. (88) £3,400
Photograph, sgd & inscr, 1881. 10cm by 6.5cm. Inscr in Czech, on verso. (89) £5,500

Smetana, Friedrich, 1824-84
ALs, 8 July 1875. 2 pp, 8vo. To [Emanuel] Stary. Discussing the ptg of the score of Libussa. (89) DM11,000

Smidt, Johann, 1773-1857
Series of 6 A Ls s, 22 Sept 1848 to 14 Feb 1849. 17 pp, 4to & 8vo. To Christian Friedrich von Stockmar. Important letters informing him about political discussions & plans at the Frankfurt National Convention. (90) DM2,000

Smith, Adam, 1723-99
ALs, 21 Jan 1790. 1 p, 4to. To Henry Herbert. Inviting him to take up residence at his house. Integral address leaf def. (88) £8,500

Smith, Florence Margaret ("Stevie"), 1902-71
Autograph Ms, poem, The Deathly Child, [ptd 1937]. (90) £360
— Autograph Ms, poem, To the tune of the Coventry Carol, [ptd 1937]. (90) £420

Smith, Francis
Ls, 3 June 1771. (91) $380

Smith, Jessie Willcox
Original drawings, Sketchbook. [c.1883-84] 62 pp, 263mm by 182mm, in half cloth with paper label on upper cover with Jessie W. Smith in black ink. (91) $3,250

Smith, Madeleine Hamilton, 1835-1928
Series of 3 A Ls, [Feb 1857]. (88) £800

Smith, Robert, 1757-1842
ALs, 11 June 1810. (90) $160
Ls, 7 Apr 1802. Alexander collection. (90) $65

Smith, Samuel, 1752-1839
Ls, 30 Sept 1814. Alexander collection. (90) $550

Smith, Samuel F., 1808-95
Autograph Ms (2), 4 stanzas of America, & account of the writing of the poem, 7 Nov 1893. 5 pp, 8vo, inlaid. Both sgd. In presentation folder. (91) $3,500
Autograph Ms, "Century Hymn for the Baptist Church Festival in Livermore, Me, Sept 1893"; 1 p, 4to. (88) $275
Autograph transcript, 1st stanza of America. Sgd & dated 13 Dec 1864. 1 p, 8vo. With related ALs. (91) $1,100
— Autograph transcript, 1st stanza of America, sgd; 18 Feb 1893. (91) $425
— Autograph transcript, 4 stanzas of America, sgd. 2 pp, 8vo, on rectos only. In dark blue mor gilt bdg, with a cabinet photograph. (90) $1,800
— Autograph transcript, 4 stanzas of America, 11 Feb 1892. (91) $500
— Autograph transcript, 4 stanzas of America, sgd & dated 15 Oct 1885. (89) $600
— Autograph transcript, 4 stanzas of America, sgd & dated Feb 1884. (88) $850
— Autograph transcript, 5 stanzas of America, sgd twice; 24 Dec 1894. 2 pp, 4to & 8vo. Framed with a port. (91) $3,500
— Autograph transcript, falir copy of America. 2 pp, 8vo, tipped to a blank & bound in mor gilt with a cabinet photo of Smith. Sgd & dated 1832-1880. (91) $1,500
— Autograph transcript, lyrics of My Country Tis of Thee, 1884. (89) $500
ALs, 31 Mar 1846. (88) $70

Smith, Sir Sidney, 1764-1840
ALs, 26 May 1809. (88) £100
AL, 16 July 1814. (90) DM300

Smith, Watson, 1825-64. See: Civil War, American

Smith, William
ALs, 26 Mar 1782. (89) $110
— 4 July 1792. (91) $300

Smith, William, 1460?-1514
Ds, 26 Apr 1510. (90) £190

Smuts, Jan Christian, 1870-1950
Photograph, sgd & inscr, 1949. (89) DM380

Smyth, Dame Ethel, 1858-1944
Typescript, article, Delirious Tempi in Music, [c.1932]. (90) £500

Smythe, Emily Anne, Viscountess Strangford, d.1887
Autograph Ms, journal of a voyage in the Eastern Mediterranean & the Levant, 1859-60. (89) £380

Snow, Charles Percy, Baron, 1905-80
Collection of 20 A Ls s & Ls s, 1948 to 1972. (90) £550

Sobieski, James Louis, Prince, son of John III Sobieski of Poland, 1667-1734
ALs, 7 Jan 1718. (90) DM400

Societe du Commerce...
Document, 1 Oct 1781. 1 p, folio. Receipt for 250 guilders issued to M. van Pruyssen for the 1st quarter of his share in the Societe du Commerce d'Asie & d'Afrique. Partly ptd. With 3 similar receipts below. (91) DM1,600

Society for the Commemoration of the Glorious Revolution (Revolution Society)
Ms, Minute Book, 16 June 1788 to 4 Nov 1791. (88) £900

Society of the Cincinnati
[A collection of 13 letters, documents & Mss relating to the early years of the Society, mostly 1783 & 1784, sold at P on 26 Oct 1988, lot 187, for $7,500.]

Soemmerring, Samuel Thomas von, 1755-1830
ALs, 4 Nov 1806. (90) DM520
— 30 Oct 1826. (91) DM750

Sohn, Karl Ferdinand, 1805-67
ALs, 20 Mar 1852. (90) DM360

Solf, Wilhelm, 1862-1936
Ls, 24 Dec 1911. Schroeder collection. (89) DM220

SOLGER

Solger, Karl Wilhelm Ferdinand, 1780-1819
ALs, 31 Oct 1809. (89) DM900

Somerset, Edward Seymour, 1st Duke of, 1506?-52
Ls, 29 Mar 1548/9. (89) £400

Sommerfeld, Arnold, 1868-1951
ALs, 22 Jan 1915. (91) DM380

Collection of Ls & autograph postcard, sgd, 10 Feb 1925 & [n.d.]. (88) DM420

— Collection of Ls & autograph postcard, sgd, 10 Feb 1925 & [n.d.]. (91) DM280
See also: Einstein, Albert & Sommerfeld

Sondes, George John Watson Milles, 4th Baron Sondes, 1794-1874
Autograph Ms, journal as lieutenant in the Royal Horse Guards, 27 Apr 1815 to 9 Feb 1816; over 60 pp, in 8vo notebook. Including account of the Battle of Waterloo. (88) £1,500

Sonnenberg, Franz, Freiherr von, 1779-1805
Autograph Ms, draft of his work Donatoa, fragment; [1804/05]. (90) DM320

— Autograph Ms, poem, An Lida, sgd & dated 2 Mar 1803. (90) DM500

Sonnenfels, Joseph, Freiherr von, 1733-1817
ALs, [n.d.]. (90) DM700

Sontag, Henriette, 1806-54
[A group of 11 A Ls s & 4 other letters, 1826 to 1852, 24 pp, 4to & 8vo, to various recipients, sold at S on 21 Nov 1990, lot 275, for £1,500 to Meister.]

A Ls s (2), 13 May 1840 & 10 Apr 1846. (88) DM450

— A Ls s (2), 25 July 1849 & [n.d.]. (91) DM550

Sophie, Kurfuerstin von Hannover, 1630-1714
Ls, 20 Jan 1712. 2 pp, 4to. To Abraham Stanyan. Thanking for support of the Protestant church at Hameln. In French. (90) DM1,100

AMERICAN BOOK PRICES CURRENT

Sophie Charlotte, Queen of Frederick I of Prussia, 1668-1705
Ls, 7 May 1701. 2 pp, folio. To an unnamed Prince. Responding to congratulations on her coronation as Queen. (90) DM1,100

Sophie Dorothea, Queen of Friedrich Wilhelm I of Prussia, 1687-1757
Ls, 18 Jan 1732. Schroeder collection. (89) DM650

Sor, Fernando, 1778-1839
Ms, Fantaisie in D minor for solo guitar, dedicated to Miss Houze; [after 1830]. 12 pp, 4to; stitched. Partly a working Ms, in 3 parts; probably autograph. Including tp. (91) £3,500

Sorabji, Kaikhosru, 1892-1988
Autograph music, passacaglia for piano, 1929. 41 pp, folio. Notated on up to 16 staves per page; unfinished. (89) £2,000

Sotheby, John, 1740-1807
Series of Ds s, 1792-1804. (89) £520

Soubise, Benjamin de Rohan, Seigneur de, 1583-1642
ALs, 25 Nov 1637. (91) DM720

Soubise, Charles de Rohan, Prince de, 1715-87
ALs, 4 Aug 1762. (90) DM300
Ls, 7 Mar 1762. (88) DM360

Soult, Nicolas Jean, Duc de Dalmatie, 1769-1851
Ls, 25 June 1815. (89) £110

Sousa, John Philip, 1854-1932
Photograph, sgd & inscr, [n.d.]. (91) $300
Signature, 1916. (91) $160

Sousa, John Philip, 1859-1932
Collection of Ls & photograph, sgd & inscr, 20 Jan 1925 & 27 Mar 1922. (90) $375

Autograph quotation, 2 bars from The Diplomat, sgd; 1905. (88) DM750

South Africa
— HENDRIE, JAMES H. - Transcript, typed by Margaret E. Meyer, 1965, 167 pp, 4to, of 56 letters, 29 June 1879 to 31 Jan 1886, to his father & brother. Dealing with diamond mining. (89)

$150
— RANDALL, WILLIAM. - 16 A Ls s, 1875 to 1881. 60 pp, 8vo. To his sister & brother-in-law. Describing the Zulu & 1st Boer War. With related material. (89) £350

South Carolina
— COLLOTON COUNTY. - Document, 4 Apr 1683. 1 p, 4to. Land grant to John Smyth & his wife, authorized by Gov. Joseph Norton & sgd by Surveyor Gen. Matthew [Malhou?]. (89) £180

Southey, Robert, 1774-1843
[His copy of John Lyly's Euphues and his England, & The Anatomie of Wit, 1606 to 1607, in 19th-cent cent calf, 4to, marked for recording in his commonplace book, sold at S on 21 July 1988, lot 119, for £550 to Quaritch.]
Autograph Ms, compilation of sources concerning famous poets; [n.d.]. (91) $120
— Autograph Ms, fragment of chapter 42 of his [History of the Peninsular War], [n.d.]. (89) £150
Ms, album verses, 1831 to 1837. 50 pp, 8vo, in green roan gilt. In the hand of his daughter Katharine & including autograph poem by Southey, sgd & dated 9 Sept 1831. (89) £3,400
— Ms, play, Wat Tyler [here attributed to Coleridge], [late 18th or early 19th cent]. (90) £350
Series of 6 A Ls s, 7 Feb 1821 to 10 Sept 1833 & [n.d.]. (88) £410
A Ls s (2), 15 Mar & 10 May 1816. (89) £380
ALs, 22 Sept 1806. Doheny collection. (89) $450
— 27 Dec 1811. (91) £200
— 11 July 1826. (89) $400
— 23 June 1830. (88) £50
See also: Battle of Waterloo

Soutine, Chaim, 1894-1943
ALs, [n.d.]. (90) DM420

Spain
[A Ms vol containing c.50 reports by the Inquisition & Royal letters relating to the converted Moors in the Kingdom of Valencia, 1542 to 1610, c.350 pp, in blindstamped black calf, sold at S on 21 Nov 1989, lot 381, for £27,000 to Smith.]
— AVILA. - Ms, survey detailing 610 properties belonging to the diocese or the bishop of Avila, 6 July 1250. 1 p, vellum, 630mm by 418mm. In brown & red ink in a small gothic hand. (91) £550
— CONVENT OF THE HOLY GHOST, GRANADA. - A collection of copies of deeds relating to the properties Burgales & Mari Sanchez, sgd by Luis Diaz, 1578, 202 pp, 4to, bound in vellum leaf from antiphoner, sold at pn on 10 Dec 1987, lot 512, for £60 to Jacobs. 88

Spalatin, Georg, 1484-1545
ALs, [early Sept] 1528. 2 pp, folio. To Martin Luther. Discussing a case involving a promise of marriage. In Latin. With postscript, in German. (90) DM3,200
— [7 Oct] 1528. 1 p, folio. To Heinrich von Einsiedel. Discussing a case involving a promise of marriage. (91) DM2,300

Spallanzani, Lazzaro, 1729-99
ALs, 22 July 1768. 1 p, 4to. To his pbr Fortunato Mandelli. Concerning a new Ed of 2 of his works. Seal tear. (89) DM1,100
Ds s (2) 31 July & 31 Oct 1792. (89) DM750
Ds, 31 May 1792. (90) DM330

Sparks, Jared, 1789-1866
ALs, 5 Sept 1833. (88) $50

Speckbacher, Joseph, 1767-1820
Ds, 5 Sept 1814. (88) DM600

Speculum...
Ms, Speculum puritatis et munditie. [Italy, 12th-13th cent] 56 leaves, vellum, 110mm by 95mm, in early vellum over bds. In a book hand in brown ink, with headings & paragraphs in red. (90) $5,500

Speculum Beate Marie Virginis
Ms, [Northeastern France or Flanders, late 13th cent]. 251 leaves & 6 flyleaves, vellum, 120mm by 85mm. German 15th-cent blind-tooled calf over wooden bds, rebacked. In black & brown ink in a small neat gothic rotunda. With 6 full-page miniatures, 9

inhabited & 4 historiated initials, & 52 decorated initials, all with full-length marginal extensions. Attributed to Bonaventura or Conrad of Saxony. Doheny collection. (88) £210,000

Spee, Maximilian, Graf von, 1861-1914
ANs, 15 Apr 1912. Schroeder collection. (89) DM550

Speke, John Hanning, 1827-64
ALs, [1860]. 6 pp, 4to & 8vo. To Christopher Rigby, Consul at Zanzibar. Giving an account of the progress of his expedition. (89) £3,600

Spencer, Sir Stanley, 1891-1959
Collection of 73 A Ls s & 2 autograph postcards, sgd, 5 May 1932 to 19 Feb 1959 & [n.d.]; c.265 pp, mostly 8vo. To Mary & John Louis Behrend. Interesting letters concerning his murals for the Chapel at Burghclere & later works. 1 letter containing 2 small pen-&-ink sketches. With a letter by his wife. (88) £1,400

— Collection of 29 A Ls s & 2 telegrams, 12 Jan 1950 to 29 June 1959. 95 pp, 4to & 8vo. To Sheila & Robert Brygman. Commenting on several of his works, explaining the representation of Christ in modern social settings, & giving personal news. (90) £3,800

ALs, 25 Sept 1958. (89) £40
See also: Scott, Sir Giles Gilbert

Spender, Stephen
Autograph Ms, draft of an essay on Edward Upward; Jan 1987. (90) £250

— Autograph Ms, notebook containing drafts of various literary works & projects, 30 May 1967 & [n.d.]. About 75 pp, folio. With 33 pp (partly typescript) loosely inserted. (88) £1,400

Typescript, speech, The Poetic Image of Venice in the English Mind, [1983]. (88) £200

Collection of 10 A Ls s & Ls s, 1944 to 1961. 11 pp, 4to & 8vo. To Vernon Watkins. About recipient's poetry, Dylan Thomas, publishing matters, etc. (90) £1,300

Spener, Philipp Jacob, 1635-1705
ALs, 18 Oct 1688. (90) DM850

Spenser, Edmund, 1552-99
Ms, A Vewe of the present state of Ireland discoursed by waie of Dialogue betweene Eudoxus & Irenius; [1st half of 17th cent]. About 70 pp, folio, in wraps. In a single scribal hand. Marquess of Downshire collection. (90) £10,000

Sperrle, Hugo, 1885-1953
Ds, 24 June 1941. (90) DM280

Spielhagen, Friedrich, 1829-1911
Autograph Ms, autobiographical outline, 1862. (91) DM320

Spinner, Francis Elias, 1802-90
A Ls s (2), 15 Dec 1846 & 28 Feb 1858. (89) $175

Spitteler, Carl, 1845-1924
ALs, 16 Nov 1906. (89) DM300

Spitzweg, Carl, 1808-85
ALs, 6 June 1869. 2 pp, 8vo. Recipient unnamed. Refusing to paint a 2d version of a picture, but promising to offer a similar one. (90) DM3,200

Spock, Benjamin
ALs, 2 Sept 1978. (91) $300

Spode, Josiah, 1754-1827 —& Others
Ls, 24 Oct 1789 & 25 June 1790. 6 pp, folio. To William Strutt. Soliciting a concerted effort to counteract the danger threatened by a Danish spy illegally collecting plans of machines. Also sgd by others, including Josiah Wedgwood & Matthew Boulton. (91) £1,100

Spohr, Louis, 1784-1859
Autograph music, sketch for a song, Trostlos, for tenor & piano, [n.d.]. (89) DM1,000

— Autograph music, song, Maria, Op. 139 no 2; May 1842. 4 pp, folio. Notated on 4 systems of 3 staves each; sgd on tp. (91) £1,600

A Ls s (2), 8 Dec 1856 & 30 Mar 1857. (88) £400

ALs, [c.1810/12]. (91) DM850

— 17 Oct 1825. 2 pp, 4to. To Gottlieb Wiedebein. Reminiscing about the

days of their youth & promising a copy of his opera Faust. (88) DM1,300
— 14 Oct 1826. 3 pp, 4to. Recipient unnamed. Informing him of his decision to publish his new oratorio himself. (89) DM1,100
— 28 July 1828. (90) DM900
— 5 July 1830. (90) DM650
— 22 Mar 1831. 3 pp, 4to. To his mother. Announcing his visit to attend a wedding. (90) DM1,200
— 15 Oct 1854. (88) DM800
— [1858]. (88) DM600

Spontini, Gaspare, 1774-1851
Autograph music, 23 brief compositions for 4 voices, 7 to 10 bars each; [c.1793-95]. 16 pp, 22cm by 28.5cm. Fair copy. Stitched. (89) DM1,700
— Autograph music, song, L'Impatience, scored for voice & piano; [n.d.]. 2 pp, 34cm by 25cm. Sgd at head & inscr to Mme de Witzleben. (90) DM1,800
ALs, 6 July 1812. (88) DM450
— 7 Oct 1823. (90) £400
— 1 Jan 1831. (90) DM750
— 4 May 1836. (88) DM420
— 10 Dec 1837. (88) DM500
— 12 May 1840. (91) DM450
— 3 July [1842]. Albrecht collection. (91) SF500
— 9 Mar 1846. (91) £500
— [n.d.]. (90) DM250
— [n.d.]. (89) DM320

Sporck, Johann, Graf von, 1601-79
Ls, 20 Dec 1666. 1 p, folio. To Prince Wenzel Eusebius von Lobkowitz. Expressing good wishes for Christmas & the new year. (91) DM1,350

Spranger, Eduard, 1882-1963
Collection of 14 A Ls s, 11 Ls s, & 3 postcards, sgd (1 autograph), 20 Dec 1947 to 23 Aug 1960. 35 pp, various sizes, & cards. To Wilhelm Weischedel. About his own & recipient's work, university news, etc. (90) DM1,700

Springsteen, Bruce
[Orig "C-Type" photographic prints showing uncut pose for the LP Darkness on the Edge of Town, 18 by 14 inches, framed, sold at pnNY on 3 Dec 1988, lot 303, for $225.]
Autograph Ms, lyrics for his song Slow Fade, [n.d.]. 1 p, yellow legal pad paper. With list of sequence for his album The River [1980] below. (89) $1,800
— Autograph Ms, lyrics for his song Sweet Lady, [c.1971]. (89) $750
— Autograph Ms, lyrics for unpbd song Full of Love, [early 1970s]. (89) $950
— Autograph Ms, lyrics for unpbd song Still Here, [c.1974]. (89) $750
— Autograph Ms, Poem for Clarence, [n.d.]. 1 p, size not stated, on lined notepaper. Creased. (89) $1,600
Photograph, sgd, [n.d.]. (89) $500
Signature, [n.d.]. (89) $450

Sprinzenstein, Ferdinand Max, Graf von, 1625-78
Ls, 4 Dec 1656. (89) DM640

Spurr, Barbara
Original drawings, (17), to illus Winken-Blinken & Nod in the Nursery Series, 1931. (89) £600
— Original drawings, (19), to illus various annuals & children's books, 1930 to 1960. (90) £680
— Original drawings, (22), cover designs for titles in the Storyland series & various annuals, 1930 to 1945. (89) £750

St. Clair, Arthur, 1736-1818. See: Harrison, William Henry & St. Clair

St. John, Isaac Munroe, 1827-1880. See: Civil War, American

Stael, Nicholas de, 1915-55
ALs, 29 July 1950. (91) £500

Stael-Holstein, Anne Louise Germaine, Baronne de, 1766-1817
Collection of 3 A Ls s & AL, 6 June to 21 Sept [1815]. 9 pp, 4to & 8vo. To Comte Gaetan de Larochefoucauld. Discussing the military & political situation. With related material. (90) DM2,400
ALs, [1805]. (88) DM420
— [c.16 Dec 1807]. 1 p, 8vo. To Schelling. Inviting him for dinner. (90) DM1,800
— 18 Apr 1814. (89) DM350
— [3 June 1814]. (88) DM420
— [1814 or later]. (89) DM280

STAEL-HOLSTEIN

AL, [1792/97]. (90) DM450
— 23 Jan 1814. 6 pp, 4to. To [Benjamin Constant]. Praising his De l'esprit de conquete but doubting the wisdom of criticising France when the country is threatened. Including 6-line note in the hand of Albertine de Stael. Mtd; in mor case. Martin collection. (90) FF28,000
Ls, 14 Jan 1814. (91) DM750

Stalin, Joseph, 1879-1953

[A group of 5 photographs of Stalin by the photographer Petrov, [n.d.], postcard size, sold at S on 20 Nov 1990, lot 519, for £600 to Franks.]
ALs, [c.1930]. 1 p, 8vo; torn from notebook. To Klimenti Voroshilov. Commuting the death sentence of Andrei Snesaryev to 10 years' imprisonment. In pencil. With related material. (90) £13,000
— [c.1930?]. 1 p, 4to. To Klimenti Voroshilov. Asking to see him at the theater. In pencil. With related material. (90) £4,500
Ds, 1943. 7 pp, folio, in fitted box. Ptd certificate issued to Jakobi Vassilievich Marusov, winner of the Stalin Prize. Also sgd by Chadaev. (91) £4,800
Photograph, sgd & inscr, [c.1932]. Postcard size. Inscr to Comrade Malishkin. With related material. (89) £7,000

Stalin, Joseph, 1879-1953 —& Ribbentrop, Joachim von, 1893-1946

Group photograph, 28 Sept 1939. 27.5cm by 22cm. Shaking hands [on the day of the signing of the German-Russian treaty]. Sgd by both. (89) DM38,000

Standish Family

— DUXBURY, LANCASHIRE. - Ms, register of accounts of overseers of the poor, 1653 to 1830; c.285 pp, long narrow ledger in worn calf bdg. Containing signatures of various members of the Standish family, possibly related to Myles Standish. (88) £1,050

Stanford, Sir William, 1509-58

[A family notebook, [1480s - 1650s], c.170 pp, in 15th-cent blindstamped calf, containing entries & accounts by Stanford & earlier & later members of the family, sold at S on 14 Dec 1989, lot 213, for £6,500 to Fogg.]

Stanhope, Lady Hester Lucy, 1776-1839

ALs, 12 May - 4 June 1814. 84 pp, 4to. To Michael Bruce. Describing her life in Lebanon after his departure. Tipped into def 19th-cent letterbook, together with transcript in anr hand. (89) £2,800

Stanislas I Leszcynski, King of Poland, 1677-1766

ALs, 3 Nov 1733. (88) DM1,000
— 24 Jan 1748. (90) $300

Stanislas II Augustus Poniatowski, King of Poland, 1732-98

Ls, 22 Jan 1772. (89) DM540

Stanley, Sir Henry Morton, 1841-1904

[A collection comprising c.40 letters, with photographs & other related material, mostly 1882 & 1893, concerning Stanley's expeditions in Africa, sold at S on 19 July 1990, lot 305, for £700 to Apfelbaum.]
Autograph Ms, memorandum addressed to Alfred Cox outlining specifications for 3 boats for his 2d African expedition, with related material; [summer 1874] to 27 Sept 1877. 6 pp, folio & 4to. (90) £1,850
Collection of 2 A Ls s & 7 photographs, 17 Aug & 16 Sept 1877, & [n.d.]. 8 pp, 4to, & c.80mm by 144mm each. To Edward Levy, regarding money to pay his men's wages, & noting attacks made on him in the press. With related material. (89) £1,600
ALs, 15 Aug 1875. 2 pp, 4to. To Edward Levy. Announcing the safe arrival of his expedition in Uganda & his need for more guns. (91) £1,050
— 23 Oct 1878. (90) $300
— 8 Apr 1885. (90) DM470
— 9 July 1892. (89) $130
— 16 Mar 1895. (91) DM650
— 31 Dec 1895. (91) £60
— 6 Mar 1896. (88) £140
Ls, 20 Feb 1890. Byer collection. (90) $200

Stanton, Edwin M., 1814-69

ALs, 24 Sept 1865. (89) $180
— 25 Apr 1866. (91) $80
— 29 Mar 1867. (91) $200

Starhemberg, Ernst Ruediger, Graf von, 1638-1701. See: Leopold I, 1640-1705

Staricius, Johann, fl.1641
Ms, Neu vermehrter Helden-Schatz. Das ist Natur Kuendliches gedencken Uber und bey Uulcanischer auch Natuerlich m[a]gischer Fabrifaction und zubereitung der waffen des beruehmten Helden Achillis, [c.1720]. 405 pp, 8vo, in modern lea bdg. Including 14 pen-&-ink drawings. Medical recipes, instructions for fireworks, arms, etc. (91) DM3,400

Stark, John, 1728-1822
Cut signature, [n.d.]. (91) $160

Starr, Ringo
Document, 1961. (88) $400

Stawell, John, 2d Baron Stawell of Somerton, c.1669-92
Autograph Ms, The Fruits of a Toleration Being the Dissent[e]rs Creed, [c.1680s]; c.60 pp & blanks, in fine contemp London bdg of red mor gilt. (88) £450

Steele, John, 1764-1815
Ls, 6 Oct 1799. Alexander collection. (90) $60

Steele, Sir Richard, 1672-1729
ALs, 28 Mar 1708. (88) £440

Steffens, Henrik, 1773-1845
ALs, 22 Sept 1804. (90) DM900

Steidele, Raphael Johann, 1737-1823
ADs, 20 Mar 1771. (89) DM300

Stein, Charlotte von, 1742-1827
[A place card or visiting card inscr Frau von Stein in elaborate border sold at star on 30 Nov 1988, lot 147, for DM420.]
ALs, 11 Feb 1826. 2 pp, 12mo. To [Karl Ludwig von Knebel]. Reporting about her failing health. (90) DM3,200

Stein, Friedrich ("Fritz"), Freiherr von, 1772-1844
Autograph Ms, autobiographical essay, Mein Leben. An meine Kinder; [n.d.]. 11 pp, folio. Incomplete, but including a description of his stay in Goethe's household. Albrecht collection. (91) SF4,000

Stein, Gertrude, 1874-1946
— ROSE, SIR FRANCIS. - 4 orig pen-&-ink drawings for The Gertrude Stein First Reader, 1946. 4 sheets, 180mm by 115mm; each framed. With a copy of 1st Ed of the book. (90) $800

Stein, Karl, Freiherr vom und zum, 1757-1831
Autograph Ms, memorandum discussing the role of Prussia, Austria & Russia in the Napoleonic Wars, 9 Sept 1808. 7 pp, 4to. Sgd. (89) DM5,500

Series of 6 A Ls s, 3 Mar [1777] to 14 Apr 1778. 29 pp, 4to. To Franz von Reden. Interesting letters about his acitivities at Wetzlar, Mainz, Mannheim, planning a journey with recipient, etc. Sgd Charles de Stein. In French. (89) DM10,000

ALs, 27 Aug 1786. 4 pp, 4to. To Graf Johann Eustachius von Goertz. Confidential letter recommending [Ernst von] Gemmingen & discussing politics after the death of Friedrich II of Prussia. In French. (90) DM1,500

— 9 Oct 1807. 2 pp, 4to. To Johann G. Scheffner. Thanking for a congratulatory poem. Kuenzel collection. (90) DM2,200

— 12 May 1815. (91) DM550

— 8 June 1827. (91) DM860

— 15 Aug 1827. 1 p, 4to. To Friedrich Gottlob Welcker. Recommending his nephew & announcing a shipment of books. Repaired. Schroeder collection. (89) DM1,600

— 11 Apr 1829. 3 pp, 4to. To Gneisenau. Forwarding a letter by Kapodistrias, & commenting about literary & political progress in Europe. Schroeder collection. (89) DM4,500

— 11 Dec 1829. (90) DM1,000

— 22 Dec 1829. 3 pp, 4to. To the bookseller Broenner. Ordering books & requesting that 2 corrections be included in a work. (91) DM1,100

AL, 6 Sept 1808. 4 pp, 4to. To Friedrich Wilhelm von Goetzen. Draft for a letter in cipher, informing him about negotiations with France, the situation in Prussia, etc. Schroeder collection. (89) DM4,600

Steinbeck, John, 1902-68

[A group of 4 carbon copies (3 typescripts, 1 autograph) from his The Acts of King Arthur and His Noble Knights, 16 May & July 1959 & [n.d.], 347 pp, folio & 4to, partly with holograph corrections, sold at CNY on 18 Nov 1988, lot 329, for $7,000.]

Typescript carbon copy, screenplay for Cannery Row; [1940s]. (88) $750

Collection of ALs & AL, [c.1955-56]. 22 pp, folio. To "Mack and Jim Pope", making plans to attend the party conventions & to write about them. To "Richey", detailing tactics he recommends for the Democratic Party. In pencil. John F. Fleming Estate. (89) $8,000

A Ls s (2), 21 July 1963. 4 pp, 4to & 8vo. To Robert Wallsten. About his eye problems, & giving advice on recipient's work on Judith Anderson's autobiography. Covering letter. (90) $3,250

ALs, 20 Sept 1961. 1 p, 4to. To [Robert] Wallsten. About Dag Hammarskjold's death & family activities in London. (91) $2,500

— 20 Sept 1961. 1 p, 8 by 10 inches. To [Robert] Wallsten. About Dag Hammarskjold's death & family activities in London. (90) $1,200

— 9 Jan 196[2]. 2 pp, 4to. To Robert & Cynthia [Wallsten]. Informing them about problems with the pbr concerning the last section of Travels with Charley. (90) $2,250

— 10 Feb 1962. 2 pp, 4to. To Robert & Cynthia [Wallsten]. Chatting about their stay in Capri & quoting Oscar Wilde. (90) $2,750

— 24-25 Feb [1962]. 2 pp, 4to. To Robert [Wallsten]. About various literary projects & family matters. (91) $1,200

— [27 Feb 1962]. 2 pp, 4to. To [Robert & Cynthia Wallsten]. Giving instructions for cleaning a taperecorder. (90) $1,100

— [2 Mar 1962]. (90) $1,000

— 18 Mar 1966. 1 p. Recipient unnamed. Declining an invitation to visit the Bohemian Club. (91) $1,100

— 23 June [n.y.]. 2 pp, 4to. To [Robert & Cynthia Wallsten]. Discussing methods to lock the hood of a car; including 3 small sketches. (90) $1,200

Autograph postcard, sgd, 1 Mar 1960. (90) $800

— [n.d.]. (90) $225

— HADER, ELMER STANLEY. - Orig drawing, to illus the dustjacket of The Grapes of Wrath, 1939. In watercolor & pen-&-ink over light pencil sketching. 383mm by 567mm. (89) $24,000

Steinberg, Saul

Caricature, Pablo Casals playing the cello with tears falling from his left eye; in brush & ink; [n.d.]. 33cm by 25cm, on staved paper. Sgd. (88) $1,500

Steiner, Rudolf, 1861-1925

Autograph postcard, sgd, [9 Jan 1898]. (91) DM800

— 7 May 1902. To Lotte Gubalke. Inviting her to read from her works at a meeting of Die Kommenden. With related material. (89) DM1,500

Steinhardt, Jakob, 1887-1968 — & Steinhardt, Minni

Series of 7 Ls s, 22 Feb 1956 to 25 Feb 1968. (88) DM600

Steinhardt, Minni. See: Steinhardt, Jakob & Steinhardt

Steinmetz, Charles P., 1865-1923

Check, sgd, 12 May 1904. (91) $80

— Anr, sgd, 14 Sept 1904, drawn on Schenectady Trust Company. (88) $60

— Anr, accomplished & sgd, 23 May 1905. (91) $100

— Anr, sgd, 1 July 1907. (89) $75

Stelluti, Francesco, 1577-1651

Ms, Questiones astromicae, [early 17th cent]. About 70 pp, 8vo, in later marbled bds. Mainly in the hand of Giovanni Battista Stelluti; 7 pp autograph. Supposedly unpbd. (89) £1,100

Stendhal. See: Beyle, Marie Henri

Stengel, Casey. See: Mantle, Mickey & Stengel

Stephan, Heinrich von, 1831-97
Collection of ALs & 3 Ls s, 17 Dec 1891 to 23 Oct 1896. 10 pp, 4to & 8vo. To a forester. About hunting, his travels, an application of recipient's nephew for a position with the postal service, etc. With related material. (89) DM1,400

ALs, 21 Oct 1890. (88) DM850

Ls, 11 Oct 1879. (88) DM650

— 4 Oct 1894. (90) DM380

Stephanie, Crown Princess of Austria, 1864-1945
ALs, 6 Mar 1940. (90) DM300

Stephen, Sir Leslie, 1832-1904
Autograph Ms, notebook containing "Memoranda end 1900," with 1 entry written in the month of his death, Feb 1904. (89) $1,000

Stephens, Alexander H., 1812-83
A Ls s (2), 21 Feb 1863 & 1 Aug 1865. (90) $700

ALs, 3 Apr 1858. (89) $175

— 31 Aug 1862. (88) $600

— 9 June 1865. (90) $400

— [n.d.]. (90) $150

Franking signature, [n.d.]. (90) $100

Stephens, James, 1882-1950
[A varied collection of A Ls s, pencil notes, typescripts, etc., [c.1944 to 1948], 42 pp, 8vo & 4to, sold at S on 15 Dec 1988, lot 112, for £500.]

Typescript, poem, Theme and Variations, [ptd 1930]. Doheny collection. (89) $850

Stephenson, George, 1781-1848
ALs, 30 Jan 1828. (88) £260

— 31 Jan 1828. 4 pp, 4to. To his son Robert. Making technical suggestions for the design & manufacture of his locomotive. Seal tear repaired. (89) £3,200

— 26 Oct 1835. 1 p, 4to. To Frederick Swannick. Informing him that he will leave for Birmingham to inspect railroads. With a port. (90) DM1,600

Signature, [n.d.]. (90) $200

Stephenson, Robert, 1803-59
ALs, 23 Aug 1848. (90) DM440

— 11 Oct 1851. (91) DM440

Sterling, George, 1869-1926
[4 poems, sgd, including 2 autograph Mss, typescript, & typescript carbon copy, 19 Oct 1915 & [n.d.], 7 pp, 4to, tipped into album, sold at CNY on 2 Feb 1988, lot 968, for $280 to Hartnoll.]

[4 autograph Mss, sgd, 3 poems & checklist of his books to 1925, with ANs, autograph postcard, sgd, & 2 signatures with address, various dates, sold at CNY on 20 May 1988, lot 223, for $120.]

[9 autograph Mss of poems, sgd, [n.d.], 13 pp, mostly 4to, fair copies with a few corrections, mostly in folders with transcripts, sold at CNY on 20 May 1988, lot 224, for $200.]

[31 typescript carbon copies of poems, sgd, [n.d.], 35 pp, mostly 4to, fair copies, 9 in folders with transcripts, sold at CNY on 20 May 1988, lot 225, for $150.]

[16 typescripts of poems, sgd, [n.d.], 16 pp, 4to, fair copies with a few corrections, some in folders with transcripts, sold at CNY on 20 May 1988, lot 226, for $120.]

[2 typescript carbon copies of the poem Strange Waters, sgd, [n.d.], 12 & 6 pp, 4to, with some corrections, 1 with holograph insertion of 2 lines, with ptd copy of 1st issue, 1926, 10 pp, 12mo, corrected throughout by Sterling, sold at CNY on 20 May 1988, lot 217, for $180.]

Autograph Ms (2), dramatic poem, Lilith, Act 1, Scenes 1 & 2, [pbd 1919]; & poem, The Black Hound Bays, [n.d.]. Doheny collection. (88) $480

Typescript, dramatic poem, Lilith, [pbd 1919]. (88) $450

Typescript carbon copy, poem, A Wine of Wizardry, [1907]. Doheny collection. (88) $850

— Typescript carbon copy, poem, Yosemite, inscr to Fenner Hale Webb, sgd & dated 28 June to 8 July 1915. (88) $250

Collection of 4 A Ls s, autograph Ms, & 3 typescript carbon copies, 19 Mar 1910

to 27 June 1926. 12 pp, 4to & 8vo. To H. L. Mencken & other recipients. About a variety of matters, & sending poems. Poems, sgd. Doheny collection. (88) $1,500
— Collection of 26 A Ls s & 3 A Ls, [Nov 1920] to 4 Dec 1925. 105 pp, 8vo. To Marie Parmelee Nuese. Love letters. With related material. (88) $3,500
A Ls s (2), 20 Jan & 9 Oct 1916. (88) $600
See also: London, Jack & Sterling

Stern, Otto, 1888-1969
ALs, 28 June 1921. (88) DM800

Sterne, Laurence, 1713-68
AL, 24 May 1766. 1 p, 4to. To Mrs. "Tutte" [Tuting?]. In 3d person as Tristam Shandy, sending his respects. On verso of portion of a letter [by Sally Tuting?] to her mother. Silked. Bradley Martin sale. (90) $3,750

Steuben, Friedrich Wilhelm von, 1730-94
Ls, 23 Aug 1783. 4 pp, 4to. To George Clinton. Reporting about the failure of his mission to Canada. (90) $6,500

Stevens, Clement Hoffman, 1821-64
Ds, 19 Jan 1853. (91) $300

Stevens, Isaac Ingalls, 1818-62
Franking signature, [18 Jan 1858]. Alexander collection. (90) $260

Stevens, John, 1749-1838
ALs, 20 Apr 1791. 1 p, 4to. To Henry Ramsen. Referring to his competition with Fitch & Rumsey in the building of a steamship. (91) $1,600

Stevenson, Adlai E., 1900-65
[An archive of A Ls s & Ls s, 1955 to 1961, 28 pp, 4to & 8vo, to Mrs. Clara Urquart, about American politics & world problems, with related material, sold at sg on 22 Oct, lot 250, for $550.]

Stevenson, Carter L., 1817-88
ALs, 13 Aug 1861. (88) $140

Stevenson, Robert Louis, 1850-94
Autograph Ms, 3 stanzas of his poem The Lamplighter, [n.d.]. 1 p, 8vo. 16 lines. (91) £2,000
— Autograph Ms, Analytical contents, Part I. The Marquesas, [c.1890]. 2 pp, folio. Working Ms, draft for his In The South Seas, summarizing contents of 12 sections. (91) £2,800
— Autograph Ms, poem, beginning "A great while ago the world began", Jan 1876. (91) £1,000
— Autograph Ms, poem, Madarigal, [pbd 1895]. 1 p, folio. Six 4-line stanzas; fair copy. (88) $1,600
Original drawing, castle in mountainous landscape, [n.d.]. 80mm by 135mm. Pencil sketch, sgd. Pasted to front advertisement leaf of 1st Ed of his Catriona: a sequel to "Kidnapped". L, 1893. Doheny collection. (89) $1,300
Ms, The History of Moses, Nov & Dec 1856. 31 pp, 8vo. Dictated to his mother Margaret Stevenson, & including 8 pp of watercolor sketches by himself; sgd R. L. B. Stevenson. With related material. "Stevenson's very earliest known literary composition." (91) £13,000
Series of 3 A Ls s, 10 July 1893 to 9 June 1894. 3 pp, 8vo. To Mr. & Mrs. Cusack-Smith. About Samoan matters. With related photographs. (91) £1,500
ALs, [2?] Dec 1863. 3 pp, 8vo. To his mother. Enquiring about her activities & chatting about a party. Doheny collection. (89) $3,000
— 27 June 1870. 4 pp, 8vo. To his mother. Describing a Sunday outing. Doheny collection. (89) $3,200
— [late summer 1878]. 1 p, 8vo. To his mother. Suggesting she send his allowance & reporting about his stay in France. (88) $2,500
— 15 Apr 1879. 8 pp, 8vo. To W. E. Henley. Discussing their unfinished play Old Glory. (91) £2,700
— 6 Aug [1884]. Doheny collection. (89) $800
— [Oct 1887 - Apr 1888]. (89) £750
— [after 1890]. 1 p, 8vo. To "dear Lewis". Offering a shipment of pineapples from his plantation. Some stains. (88) DM1,300
— 1894. (89) £300
— 17 July [n.y.]. (88) £400
— [n.d.]. Doheny collection. (88) $900
— [n.d.]. (88) £450
Ls, [c.1889-90]. (91) £900
Note, ptd invitation to a dance on 21 Feb

[n.y.], 3 by 4 inches (card). (88) £180
Ds, 24 Mar 1892. (90) £550
Check, accomplished & sgd, 13 Apr 1887. (90) $350
Photograph, [n.d.]. Doheny collection. (88) $180
See also: Henley, William Ernest & Stevenson

Stewart, Alexander, Duke of Albany, 1454?-85
Ds, 27 Mar 1482. (90) $225

Stewart, Charles, 1778-1869
ALs, 9 Aug 1804. (88) $425

Stewart, Jimmy
ANs, [n.d.]. (91) $150

Stiegel, Henry William, 1729-85
Ds, 12 Feb 1774. (90) $450

Stieler, Joseph, 1781-1858
ALs, 5 May 1838. Albrecht collection. (91) SF800

Stifter, Adalbert, 1805-68
Autograph Ms, fragment, c.280 words of an early version of the beginning of Witiko, book 4; [n.d.]. 1 p, 4to. Cut by Stifter to make an envelope; addressed to Gustav Heckenast on verso. (90) DM9,000
— Autograph Ms, thoughts about the relationship between passion & the arts, 18 Apr 1855. 1 p, 8vo. Sgd. (91) DM8,000
ALs, 26 May 1856. 1 p, 4to. Recipient unnamed. Agreeing to meet him. (91) DM3,000
— 21 Dec 1864. 1 p, 4to. To Friedrich & Theresia von Jaeger. Offering congratulations on their golden wedding. Also sgd by Amalie Stifter. (88) DM4,200

Stinnes, Hugo, 1870-1924
A Ls s (2), 25 Sept & 8 Dec 1918. Schroeder collection. (89) DM650

Stobbs, William
Original drawings, (16), to illus The House that Jack Built, 1983. (90) £600
— Original drawings, (40), to illus Marcus Crouch's The Whole World Story Book, 1983. (90) £500
— Original drawings, (46), to illus Marcus Crouch's Ivory City, [n.d.]. (90) £500

Stockhausen, Karlheinz
[A collection of 3 autograph Mss (2 musical sketches), 3 pp, with photograph, sgd, & signature, [n.d.], sold at star on 1 Dec 1988, lot 948, for DM420.]
Autograph Ms, "Plattentext", [late 1969]. (90) DM360
Autograph music, "Einschub DKM1", correction to be inserted in a score, 1 bar on a system of 16 staves; [n.d.]. (90) DM440
See also: Cage, John & Stockhausen

Stockmann, August Cornelius, 1751-1821
[His album, 1770 to 1776, 8vo, in contemp marbled calf gilt, containing autograph sentiments, sgd, by Goethe, Wieland, & 47 others, sold at star on 4 Apr 1991, lot 145, for DM24,000.]

Stockmar, Christian Friedrich, Freiherr von, 1787-1863
Series of 15 A Ls s, 7 Aug 1828 to 23 July 1846. 81 pp, 4to & 8vo. To Busso von Alvensleben. Confidential reports dealing with European politics, King Leopold I of the Belgians, his activities in London, etc. 1 def. (90) DM3,200
— Series of 3 A Ls s, 4 Mar [1830] to 9 Apr 1840. (90) DM900

Stockton, Robert Field, 1795-1866
ALs, 9 July 1838. (89) $55

Stoddard, Charles Warren, 1843-1909
Series of 15 A Ls s, 11 Jan 1900 to 18 Mar 1905. Doheny collection. (88) $800

Stoker, Bram, 1847-1912
Autograph Ms, essays on witchcraft, Cagliostro, Mesmer, & John Law's Mississippi Scheme, draft; 31 May to 24 June [19]10. (88) £700
ALs, 16 Sept 1889. (88) $130
— 4 Feb 1890. (91) $200

Stokowski, Leopold, 1882-1977
Series of 3 Ls s, 1966 to 1969. (88) $110

Stolberg, Auguste Luise, Graefin zu, 1753-1835
ALs, 15 Nov 1776. 4 pp, 8vo. To her friend Emily. Chatting about their friendship, her activities, etc. (89)

STOLBERG

DM2,600

Stolberg, Christian, Graf zu, 1748-1821
ALs, 23 Dec 1820. 4 pp, 4to. To Georg Philipp Schmidt von Luebeck. Complimenting him on his recently pbd poems. With engraved port. Kuenzel collection. (88) DM2,400

AL, 29 Mar [1787]. 1 p, 4to. To Georg Joachim Goeschen. Sending the tp for his trans of Sophocles. (91) DM1,800

Stolberg, Friedrich Leopold, Graf zu, 1750-1819
ALs, 28 Dec 1779. 4 pp, 8vo. To [Dr. Stein]. Reminiscing about his youth, & mentioning his recently pbd poems. (91) DM2,400

— 4 Oct 1791. 4 pp, 4to. To Johann Martin Miller. Describing his impressions during a stay in Switzerland. Albrecht collection. (91) SF5,000

— 26 Oct 1799. 4 pp, 8vo. To [Dietrich Wilhelm Soltau]. Commenting about his trans of Don Quixote. Including postscript, 28 Oct 1799. (89) DM2,400

— [c.4 July 1818]. 1 p, 4to. To Adam Mueller. Fragment, talking about his family. (88) DM1,300

Ds, 3 Dec 1787. (91) DM320

Stoltze, Friedrich, 1816-91
ALs, 30 July 1884. 8 pp, 8vo. To his daughter Lyde. Family news. With related material. (89) DM1,200

— 12 Nov 1885. (88) DM950

Stone, Harlan Fiske, 1872-1946
Ls, 15 July 1924. (89) $70

Stone, Michael Jenifer, 1747-1812
ALs, 20 July 1790. Alexander collection. (90) $85

Stoppard, Tom
Autograph Ms, fragment of film script for The Empire of the Sun by J. (89) £550

— Autograph Ms, play, Dalliance, adapted from A. Schnitzler's Liebelei; 25 to 30 Dec 1985. 44 pp, 4to. Draft, with revisions. (91) £1,100

— Autograph Ms, screen play, The Human Factor, after Graham Greene's novel; June to Aug 1978. About 150 pp, folio. With revised typescript, 171 leaves, 4to. (88) £1,800

Storm, Theodor, 1817-88
Autograph Ms, early draft of part of his novella Eine Halligfahrt; [1870]. 13 pp, 8vo, paginated 13 to 25. In modern bds. With revisions. (90) DM35,000

A Ls s (2), 8 Jan & 20 Apr 1845. 2 pp, folio & 4to. To Fritz Stuhr. Requesting help in a legal matter, & sending a contribution to an almanach. (91) DM1,900

ALs, 9 Dec 1832. 2 pp, 4to. To Fritz Stuhr. Describing pranks directed against a teacher at his school at Husum. (91) DM6,400

— 15 Feb 1864. 6 pp, 8vo. To the pbr Johann Jakob Weber. Reporting about his election as Landvogt at Husum & about the fairy tales he is writing now. (88) DM5,500

— 28 to 30 [Dec] 1867. 4 pp, 8vo. To his son Hans. Reporting about Christmas activities & their plans to let part of their house. (91) DM5,000

— 23 June 1868. 3 pp, 8vo. To Mr. & Mrs. Delius. About the death of their son & his wife, & describing his current situation. (91) DM3,800

— 17 Sept 1876. (90) £800

— 25 Sept 1878. (89) DM700

— 8 Oct 1884. 2 pp, 8vo. To his son Karl. Requesting him to write. With related material. (90) DM3,600

— 10 May 1885. 3 pp, 8vo. To Anna Biebendt. Giving literary advice. (91) DM2,800

— 20 Sept 1887. 2 pp, folio. To a group of ladies at Kiel. Thanking for a birthday present. (88) DM2,000

— [c.Oct 1887]. 2 pp, 8vo. To Frau Toennies. Thanking for birthday presents. (90) DM1,900

Autograph postcard, sgd, 19 Dec 1882. (88) DM520

ANs, [n.d.]. (88) DM800

Stosch, Albrecht von, 1818-96
ALs, 2 Nov 1875. Schroeder collection. (89) DM230

Stout, Rex, 1886-1975
Ls, 13 Nov 1944. (89) $175

Stowe, Harriet Beecher, 1811-96

Autograph Ms, poem, beginning "I would not ask dear child for thee", 8 lines. (88) $325

— Autograph Ms, short story, The Tea Rose. Prefaced by ANs, 28 Oct [1841]; covering note to Louis Godey. 8 pp, 4to, mtd together as a booklet. With autograph sentiment, sgd; 2 lines on card. Barrett collection. (89) $5,000

Collection of 2 A Ls s & photograph, sgd, 12 Feb 1875, 16 Sept 1878 & [n.d.]. Doheny collection. (89) $850

ALs, 25 Sept [1852?]. 3 pp, 4to. To the Rev. J. C. Webster. Describing her sources for Uncle Tom's Cabin. Doheny collection. (89) $26,000

— 2 Jan 1858. (89) £650

— 26 Sept [1873]. (90) $950

— 7 Feb 1882. (90) $350

— [c.1890]. (91) $600

— 8 Dec [n.y.]. (91) $450

— [n.d.]. (90) $500

Autograph quotation, sgd, 30 July 1880. (88) $80

— Anr, "Trust in the Lord and Do good." Sgd & dated 3 May 1892. (88) $200

— Anr, sgd; [n.d.]. (89) $250

Cut signature, 1 Nov 1875. (89) $75

Strachan, John, 1778-1867

Single sheet ptg, lithographed letter, 12 June 1850. (88) C$320

Strachey, Sir Henry, 1736-1810

[His papers relating to the American War of Independence & the Treaty of Paris, comprising official correspondence & related drafts, instructions & other documents, letters to his wife, autograph diary, draft of Sir William Howe's defense of his conduct of the war, etc., 1776 to 1783, c.480 pp, in mor fitted case, sold at S on 23 June 1988, lot 109, for £160,000 to D. Sloan.]

Strachey, Lytton, 1880-1932

[A group of 3 autograph Mss, 2 sonnets & a poem, 27 May 1916 & [n.d.], 4 pp, 4to & 8vo, sold at C on 28 Nov 1990, lot 218, for £300 to Rota.]

Strangford, Emily Anne, Lady, d.1887

See: Smythe, Emily Anne

Strassburg

Ms, inventory of the Bishop's Palace, 9 Mar 1630. (89) £400

Strasser, Gregor, 1892-1934

ALs, 8 Jan 1926. 2 pp, 8vo. To Eugen Munder. Agreeing to attend a meeting. (90) DM1,200

Ls, 5 May 1926. 2 pp, 4to. To Eugen Munder. Congratulating him on a successful convention of the National Socialists in Wuerttemberg. (90) DM1,100

— 5 Oct 1926. 5 pp, 4to. To Eugen Munder. Expounding the theory of National Socialism & the aims of the party. (90) DM2,000

Strassmann, Fritz, 1902-80

Ls, 23 Mar 1974. (91) DM700

Stratz, Carl Heinrich, 1858-1924

[A collection of 5 autograph Mss, diaries, notebooks, etc., 1873 to c.1916, with related material, sold at HN on 5 Dec, lot 4199, for DM660.]

Autograph sketchbooks, (3), 1887 to 1892. (88) DM520

— Autograph sketchbooks, (7), 1876 to 1908. (88) DM460

Original drawings, 78 (of 79) pen-&-ink drawings for a manual for midwives, Leitfaden der Geburtshilfe..., [n.d.]. (88) DM320

Straub, Joseph Ignatz, 1773-1850

ALs, 6 Sept 1809. (88) DM800

Straus, Oscar, 1870-1954

— MAJOR, HENRY. - Orig drawing, pencil port of Straus, sgd; [c.1930]. 345mm by 243mm. Also sgd by Straus. With anr. (90) $150

Strauss, David Friedrich, 1808-74

Series of 4 A Ls s, 14 Feb 1857 to 18 Oct 1870. (90) DM950

ALs, [1832?]. (91) DM300

— 28 Feb 1848. (91) DM440

— 22 July 1858. (89) DM270

— 27 Jan 1860. (90) DM600

STRAUSS

Strauss, Franz Josef, 1915-88
Ls, 30 Sept 1976. (90) DM550

Strauss, Johann, 1804-49
Autograph music, fragment of his Mode-Quadrille, Op. 138; [1842]. 2 pp, 4to. Full score, notated on 15 staves; sgd. (91) £3,000
ALs, 25 Dec 1847. (89) £420

Strauss, Johann, 1825-99
Autograph music, 5 sketches, written on part of a handbill for the "Techniker-Ball" on 24 Jan 1895, c.11cm by 18cm. (88) £500
— Autograph music, drafts & sketches for the comic opera Ritter Pazman, [1891]. 25 pp, folio. On up to 24 staves per page, with numerous revisions. Title-pages in anr hand. (88) £8,000
— Autograph music, duet, Zum ersten Mal mit dir allein, from Prinz Methusalem, Act 1, in full score, [1876]. 32 pp, folio. In brown ink on up to 24 staves per page. 10 pp in anr hand. Many autograph revisions throughout. (89) $7,000
— Autograph music, Klaenge aus der Raimundzeit, Op.479; [May 1898?]. 17 pp, folio. Working Ms of the full orchestral score, incorporating music by his father, Lanner, Kreutzer, & others. (91) £13,500
— Autograph music, sketches for vocal & instrumental works, c.70 bars, in pencil; [1899]. (90) £1,000
— Autograph music, sketch-leaf containing drafts for marches & other works, [n.d.]. 2 pp, folio. Polychromatic Ms, eight staves per page. Numerous alterations. In brown ink & various colors of pencil. (88) £1,500
— Autograph music, sketch-leaf containing c.40 sketches & drafts for waltzes, polkas, & other works, [c.1870?]. 2 pp, folio. Polychromatic Ms, 12 staves per page. With numerous revisions. Edge repaired with tape. (88) £1,900
— Autograph music, waltz, An der schoenen blauen Donau, Op.314, 25 July [n.y.]. 1 p, 4to. Scored for piano; sgd. (91) DM12,000

A Ls s (2), 27 Mar & 4 July [n.y.]. (89) DM520
ALs, [n.d.]. 3 pp, 8vo. To an unnamed conductor. Making suggestions regarding the directing of a piece. (88) DM1,300
— 16 Jan [1892]. (90) £500
— 23 Oct [18]97. 2 pp, 8vo. To [Gustav Mahler]. Expressing pleasure that Mahler wishes to perform his Fledermaus. Salzer collection. (90) £1,900
— [n.d.], "Wednesday". 4 pp, 8vo. Recipient unnamed. About the collection of fees & his current work. (91) DM1,950
— [n.d.]. (91) £520
— [n.d.]. (89) DM900
— [n.d.]. (91) DM900
Ls, 26 Apr [n.y.]. (88) DM700
AN, 27 Oct 1894. (90) DM260
Autograph quotation, 16 bars from Kuenstlerleben, Op. 316, no 5, sgd, inscr to Emanuel Wehner & dated 14 Aug 1871. 1 p, 215mm by 285mm. (90) DM6,400
— Anr, 4 bars from G'schichten aus dem Wienerwald, sgd & inscr; [n.d.]. (88) £1,000
— Anr, 8 bars from the Emperor Waltz, sgd & dated 26 May [18]95. 1 p, c.22cm by 24cm. Framed. Salzer collection. (90) £1,900
— Anr, 4 bars of music, sgd & inscr; [n.d.]. 1 p, 12mo. (91) $1,700
— Anr, 4 bars, Ja das Alles auf Ehr, sgd; [n.d.]. (90) £400
— Anr, 4 bars from his G'schichten aus dem Wienerwald, sgd & inscr, [n.d.]. (89) £480
— Anr, waltz in D major, [n.d.]. 1 p, 8vo. Sgd. Possibly unpbd. (91) DM2,700
Cut signature, [n.d.]. (90) $250
Photograph, sgd, [1870s]. 10cm by 6.5cm. By Fritz Luckhardt. (91) £1,100
Photograph, sgd & inscr, [Summer 1872]. 17cm by 11cm. Inscr to Herr Hillmann. By Gurney & Son. (91) DM2,400
— Anr, [1886]. (89) $850
— Anr, [n.d.]. 10cm by 6cm. Inscr to Emilie Tolentino on verso, with autograph musical quotation. (90) £1,300

Strauss, Richard, 1864-1949
[A photograph, sgd & inscr with a musical quotation, 11 Nov 1920, 26cm by 32cm, with a menu, 15 Sept 1934, sgd by Strauss, Mussolini & Guglielmo

Marconi, sold at S on 17 May 1990, lot 255, for £1,900 to Horiuchi.]

Autograph Ms, essay, Kunst, Kunstgeschichte, Geschichte, 19 July 1945 to 4 July 1946. Length not stated; in gray notebook. (91) DM9,500

— Autograph Ms, sketch of the libretto of Die Aegyptische Helena, part of Act 2; [c.1927 or 1928]. (91) £800

Autograph music, draft of part of Die Donau, 12 Jan 1942. 1 p, folio, cut from larger sheet. 16 bars in short score on 2 systems of 4 staves each. Sgd & inscr to Fritz Meinl. (90) £2,800

— Autograph music, Duett Concertino fuer Clarinette und Fagott mit Streichorchester und Harfe, 29 Nov 1947. 27 pp, folio, in half brown mor. In short score; sgd twice. (91) £28,000

— Autograph music, Fanfare zur Eroeffnung der Musikwoche der Stadt Wien, Sept 1924. Tp & 6 pp, folio, 32 staves each. Scored for brass & timpani, sgd in several places & inscr to D. Bach, 9 Sept 1824. (89) $15,000

— Autograph music, Improvisationen und Fuge fuer Pianoforte zu 2 Haenden Op.15, [1884?]. 17 pp, folio & 8vo, in contemp bds. Notated on up to 6 systems per page, with revisions. Including autograph tp, sgd & inscr to Hans von Buelow. (91) £18,000

— Autograph music, Instrumentations Skizze zu Ruhe meine Seele, sgd & dated 4 June [19]48. 1 p, 4to, cut from larger sheet. 4 bars, scored for 7 string instruments. (90) DM2,400

— Autograph music, Lied der Saengerin, I Scene, sketch for Ariadne auf Naxos; [c.1912]. 1 p, 8vo. With anr sketch on verso. (91) DM2,400

— Autograph music, notebook containing extensive drafts for the Concerto for Oboe & Orchestra, the 2d Sonatina for wind instruments, & the song Im Abendroth, [1945-46]. 90 pp, 3 by 5 inches. Autograph inscr, sgd & dated 4 Apr 1948 on flyleaf. (88) $40,000

— Autograph music, sketch for a song to Goethe's poem Naehe des Geliebten in A flat major, sgd & inscr to Hans F. Schade, 22 Sept 1930. 1 p, folio, in bds. 30 bars in pencil; incomplete. (91) £2,200

— Autograph music, sketch leaf for his work Muenchen, bars 109 - 123; [1938?]. 2 pp, 12cm by 8cm. In short score on 4 systems of 3 staves each. Sgd later, inscr with Christmas greetings & dated 1945. With autograph Ms, list of 13 of his works, 2 pp, 8vo. (90) £1,600

— Autograph music, sketches for Elektra, Aegisth's dying scene, [1908]. 2 pp, 12.5cm by 16.5cm; 10 staves each. In pencil. (89) DM6,500

— Autograph music, sketches for his opera Elektra, duet Elektra-Orest; [1908]. 2 pp, 12.5cm by 16.5cm. In pencil. (88) DM14,000

— Autograph music, sketches for his opera Die Liebe der Danae, [1938/39]. 40 pp, 8vo, in blue wraps. Sgd & inscr to [George] Georgescu, 23 May [19]39. (90) DM30,000

— Autograph music, sketches for his opera Elektra, 33 bars; [c.1907]. 2 pp, 12.5cm by 17cm. In ink & pencil. (90) DM5,200

— Autograph music, sketches for Rosenkavalier, Act 2; [1909]. 99 pp, 8vo, in notebook. (91) DM85,000

— Autograph music, sketches for the 3d act of his opera Die schweigsame Frau, [c.1933]. 2 pp, folio. Sgd. (91) DM10,000

— Autograph music, sketches for various [unidentified] compositions, [n.d.]. 9 pp, folio. In pencil. (91) DM7,500

— Autograph music, Sonata in B minor for Piano Op.5, 15 Feb 1881. 21 pp, folio. Notated on up to 12 staves per page, with revisions. Including autograph tp, sgd & inscr to Josef Giehrl. (91) £22,000

— Autograph music, song, Alphorn, to a text by J. Kerner; [c.1877]. 6 pp, folio. Scored for voice, French horn & piano. Sgd & inscr to his father on tp; sgd & inscr to [Manfred & Maria] Mautner at end. (91) DM25,000

— Autograph music, song, Die sieben Siegel, to a text by Friedrich Rueckert; [c.1899]. 2 pp, folio. About 120 bars; working draft, sgd. (90) £3,500

— Autograph music, song, Waldseligkeit, Op.49 no 1, to a text by Richard Dehmel, [n.d.]. 2 pp, folio. Half cloth bdg. Fair copy, scored for soprano & piano. Inscr to Willi Schuh by Franz

STRAUSS

Strauss. (91) DM22,000
— Autograph music, waltzes & other sketches for his opera Arabella, [c.1931]. 4 pp, folio. Sgd twice & inscr to Willi Schuh. (91) DM13,000
— Autograph music, Walzerpotpourri aus Rosencavalier [Der Rosenkavalier; erste Walzerfolge], sgd & dated 26 Oct [19]44. 13 pp, folio. Draft of the complete work. (90) £42,000
Collection of 11 A Ls s & photograph, sgd, 1901 to 1907 & [n.d.]. 12 pp, 8vo. To Gustav Rassow. Mostly regarding organizational questions, music festivals, recommendations, etc. (91) DM7,200
— Collection of 3 A Ls s & autograph postcard, sgd, 3 July 1905 to 24 June 1925. 3 pp, 8vo & 12mo, & card. To Dr. Walter Kuelz. Inviting him, thanking for a present, etc. With related material. (89) DM1,100
— Collection of ALs & Ls, 9 Oct 1912 & 8 Feb 1925. (89) DM900
— Collection of 5 A Ls s, Ls & 2 A Ns s, 28 Sept 1922 to 7 Apr 1930 & [n.d.]. 10 pp, 4to & 8vo. To Ida Strauss. Inviting her to performances of his works, etc. With related material. (90) DM2,600
— Collection of 167 A Ls s, 5 Ls s, 26 postcards, sgd (25 autograph), 2 telegrams, autograph Ms, & typescript, 12 June 1936 to 11 July 1949. About 330 pp, various sizes. To Willi Schuh. Important correspondence dealing with his life, his compositions, other composers, etc. Including 4 port postcards. With related material. (91) DM85,000
— Collection of A Ls s, ANs & photograph, sgd & inscr, 1936 to 10 Mar 1947. (89) £400
— Collection of 3 A Ls s & autograph postcard, sgd, 1946 & 1947. (91) £800
Series of 4 A Ls s, 22 Mar to 2 Dec 1933. 11 pp, 8vo. To Max Brockhaus. Recommending Eugen Papst to succeed Bruno Walter as conductor of the Gewandhausorchester. (90) DM6,000
A Ls s (2), 4 May [18]94 & 26 Dec [19]46. (91) £750
— A Ls s (2), 9 Feb 1906 & 23 Apr 1925. (90) £600
— A Ls s (2), 1924 & 1936. (90) £500
— A Ls s (2), 24 May 1934 & 19 May 1936. (88) DM900
ALs, 28 July [1888]. (91) £280
— 27 Aug [1889]. 8 pp, 8vo. To Hans von Bronsart. Giving a detailed account of performances at the Bayreuth Festival. (91) £1,800
— 2 Sept [18]90. Salzer collection. (90) £600
— [Dec 1895], "Monday". 2 pp, 8vo. To Fritz von Ostini. About the publication of his song Wenn... [Op.1 no 2] in the journal Jugend. (91) DM1,100
— 15 Feb 1898. (88) DM450
— [7 Apr 1902]. (88) DM680
— 10 Mar 1903. 2 pp, 8vo. To his musical agent Gutmann. Protesting against the publication of a confidential letter. On hotel letterhead. (88) DM1,700
— 11 Sept 1908. 3 pp, 8vo. To Ernst von Schuch. Discussing arrangements for the 1st performance of his opera Elektra. (90) DM3,000
— 17 Nov 1908. (90) £450
— 3 Jan [19]09. (91) $175
— 28 Dec 1910. 3 pp, 4to. To [Willy Levin]. Chatting about his vacation in Switzerland. Sgd Ihr treu ergebener Saeugling. (89) DM2,400
— 14 Mar 1911. 3 pp, 8vo. To Princess Charlotte of Sachsen-Meiningen. Recommending Theodor Mueller-Reuter for a position at Meiningen. With ANs by recipient's husband at bottom. (90) DM1,300
— 10 May [19]11. (91) £550
— 26 May 1913. (88) £420
— 29 May 1916. 4 pp, 8vo. Recipient unnamed but probably Count Seebach, Director of the Dresden Opera. On operatic matters. (91) $1,300
— 5 June 1919. (89) £260
— 29 Aug [19]19. (88) £400
— 26 Oct 1922. (89) $750
— 25 Oct 1923. Byer collection. (90) $425
— 29 July 1924. 2 pp, 8vo. To Heinrich Koehler. Thanking for congratulations on his birthday. (90) DM1,300
— 25 Dec [19]24. (89) £1,000
— 21 Jan [19]25. (89) £400
— 2 Dec [19]25. (89) £400
— 23 Feb [19]28. (90) £480
— 9 Apr [19]28. 2 pp, 8vo. To Lotte

1987 - 1991 · AUTOGRAPHS & MANUSCRIPTS — STRAUSS

Lehmann. Praising her performance in Rosenkavalier in Vienna. (89) £1,700
— 16 June [19]28. (89) £400
— 19 July [19]28. 4 pp, 8vo. To Lotte Lehmann. About Die aegyptische Helena & the rivalry between Lehmann & Maria Jeritza. With draft of reply. (89) £1,700
— 11 Aug [19]28. 4 pp, 8vo. To Lotte Lehmann. Attempting to clarify who should sing Die aegyptische Helena in Budapest. (89) £1,400
— 6 Sept [19]28. (89) £1,000
— 13 Sept [19]28. 4 pp, 8vo. To Lotte Lehmann. Discussing the solution to the dispute over Die aegyptische Helena. (89) £1,200
— 15 Sept [19]28. 3 pp, 8vo. To Lotte Lehmann. Stating he has heard she will not sing the role of Helena in October, comparing roles, etc. (89) £1,300
— 16 Jan 1929. (88) DM950
— 16 Sept 1932. (89) DM420
— 22 June 1939. (90) DM800
— 12 Apr 1941. (88) DM300
— 6 May 1941. 2 pp, 4to. To the manager of the theater at Chemnitz. Thanking for a report about a performance of Die Frau ohne Schatten. (90) DM1,100
— 8 May 1944. (90) DM650
— 26 July 1944. 4 pp, 8vo. To Clemens Krauss. Asking for his opinion about his new opera Die Liebe der Danae. (90) DM2,200
— 21 Mar 1947. (88) £480
— [n.d.], "Tuesday". (89) £480
Collection of 2 Ls s & 4 autograph postcards, sgd, 27 June 1907 to 16 June 1924. 2 pp, 4to, & cards (1 port postcard). To Herr Kuelz. About meetings, his travels, etc. With related material. (91) DM1,500
Ls, 29 June 1912. (90) $175
— 9 Apr 1921. (91) $250
— 7 Aug 1933. (91) DM360
Autograph postcard, sgd, 16 May 1894. (90) DM450
— 30 Aug 1918. (88) DM440
— 22 Mar 1941. (91) DM500
— 10 Nov 1943. (89) DM240
ANs, 29 Aug 1894. (88) $300

A Ds s (2), 1 & 4 Aug 1920. (90) £1,000
Autograph quotation, 3 bars from the theme of his Ein Heldenleben, sgd & dated 20 Feb 1901. 1 p, 8vo. (90) DM2,700
— Anr, first 4 bars from his opera Salome, sgd, 25 Feb 1907. 1 p, folio. (90) DM3,600
— Anr, 2 opening bars of Der Rosenkavalier, sgd; 28 May [19]23. 1 p, 8vo. (90) £1,200
— Anr, 4 bars from his opera Arabella, [n.d.]. (91) DM850
— Anr, 2 bars from Till Eulenspiegels lustige Streiche, Op. 28; [n.d.]. 1 p, 8vo. Sgd. Mtd. (90) DM1,300
Autograph sentiment, inscr to [Hans Esdras] Mutzenbecher, 25 Mar 1935, on flyleaf of ptd full score of his opera Ariadne auf Naxos, 250 pp, folio, in def half lea bdg. (88) DM850
Concert program, sgd below port, 5 Oct 1947. (90) DM250
Photograph, sgd, [c.1904]. (88) DM600
— Anr, [c.1930s]. (90) $325
— Anr, 27 Oct 1938. (90) DM850
Photograph, sgd & inscr, 2 July 1894. (90) DM900
— Anr, 1902. Cabinet size. Sgd in lower margin; autograph musical quotation on verso. (89) DM2,000
— Anr, 10 Apr 1911. 24cm by 16cm. Inscr to Paul Redl. With Ls. (90) £1,300
— Anr, 29 Jan 1916. (89) £400
— Anr, [25 Dec] 1916. 25cm by 20cm. Inscr to Selma Kurz on mount. (89) £1,150
— Anr, 11 Nov [19]20. Mtd; overall size 28cm by 22.5cm. Inscr with musical quotation. With ALs, 1917. (90) £1,200
— Anr, 11 Nov [19]20. 23cm by 32cm, mtd. Inscr to Augusto Senez with musical quotation. (91) £1,200
— Anr, 29 Oct [19]27. (88) £150
— Anr, 16 Mar 1947. 24cm by 19cm. Sgd on image; with 3 musical quotations, sgd & inscr to Kurt Bothorn on verso. (90) £1,100
— Anr, 14 Nov 1948. (88) DM560
See also: Hofmannsthal, Hugo von
See also: Lehmann, Lotte

STRAVINSKY

Stravinsky, Igor, 1882-1971
Autograph music, Les Noces, sketches for a version for "Pleyela", [c.1923]. 24 pp, various sizes. In pencil. Some additions in anr hand. (88) DM32,000
— Autograph music, Scherzo a la Russe, 1943 - 1944. 14 pp, 4to. Complete score, notated on 2 systems of up to 5 staves each. Including some autograph revisions; sgd & initialled. (91) £8,500
— Autograph music, Sonata for 2 pianos, 1943 - 1944. 41 pp, 4to, in cloth folder. Working score, notated on 2 systems of 4 staves each; sgd. (91) £13,500
Ms, violin part of the Suite from Pulcinella, comprising Overture, Gavotta, & Tarantella, with some autograph annotations, & anr copy in the hand of Paul Kochanski; [n.d.]. 20 pp, 4to. (90) $1,300
— Ms, violin part of the Suite from L'histoire du Soldat, [c.1919]. (89) £600
Collection of ALs & Ls, [22 Nov 1915] & 2 Apr 1968. (90) £400
A Ls s (2), 1 Dec [19]38 & 15 June [19]47. (89) £650
ALs, 22 May 1911. 2 pp, 8vo (lettercard). To Michel Dimitri Calvocoressi. Correcting an erroneous statement about The Firebird, & inviting him to the premiere of Petroushka. (90) DM2,000
— 5 July 1911. 1 p, 4to. To [Michel Dimitri Calvocoressi]. About Petroushka, the possibility of a collaboration, & his intention to move to Paris. (90) DM1,900
— 11 Apr 1912. 1 p, 4to. To Michel Dimitri Calvocoressi. About "notre pauvre ami Steinberg", Petroushka & Le Sacre du Printemps. Including musical quotation. (88) DM3,200
— 11 Dec 1912. 1 p, 4to. To Princesse [Edmond de Polignac]. Discussing a concerto to be performed at one of her private concerts. (91) DM1,900
— 28 Oct 1917. 3 pp, 4to. To Edwin Evans. Saying he is enclosing a copy of his Etude pour Pianola [not included] & discussing publication problems. In pencil. In French. (89) £2,200
— 7 May [19]18. 1 p, 4to. To Edwin Evans. About his composition Ragtime & Evans's visit to Switzerland. With autograph envelope. (90) £2,200
— 19 Nov 1918. 4 pp, 4to. To Edwin

AMERICAN BOOK PRICES CURRENT

Evans. Concerning terms of publication for his Histoire du Soldat & other works. In pencil. (90) £2,700
— 15 June 1922. (90) DM650
— 14 Aug [19]22. (89) £750
— 26 Dec 1925. (91) £450
— 8 June 1932. 2 pp, 8vo. To Paul Hirsch. Thanking for congratulations & planning a meeting in Frankfurt. (91) DM1,400
— 17 June [19]39. (89) £500
Ls, 6 Feb 1959. (90) $450
Autograph postcard, sgd, 17 Oct 1913. (88) £480
— 17 Dec [19]13. To Alfredo Casella. Explaining how to keep people quiet in concerts & promising to send photographs when he is famous. (91) £1,300
— 26 July 1919. To Misia Sert. Objecting to Diaghilev's plan to perform Les Noces at the Paris opera. (90) DM2,400
ANs, [24 Dec 1952]. (91) $650
— 14 June 1954. (90) £450
— 31 Jan [19]60. (91) $400
Autograph quotation, 6 bars "de la IVeme Pribaoutka", scored for voice & 5 instruments; 1 Oct 1919. 3 pp, folio (bifolium). Sgd & inscr to [Jean Aubry] on tp & at end. (90) DM5,200
— Anr, 2 bars, sgd & dated 1924. On caricature, sgd, by E. Kochanski, depicting Stravinsky on podium with puppets dangling from his music stand; 33cm by 19.5cm. Was mtd. With 3 autograph postcards, sgd, & AN from Stravinsky to Paul & Zosia Kochanski. (88) $4,500
— Anr, April 1940. (88) $500
Corrected proof, Illumina nos, from Sacrae cantiones by Carlo Gesualdo, with sextus & bassus parts supplied by Stravinsky, 21 May 1957. (88) £600
Group photograph, with Willem Mengelberg, Feb 1926. 23cm by 16.5cm. Sgd & inscr by Stravinsky. (91) DM1,200
Photograph, sgd, 1926. 23cm by 17cm. Sgd on mount, 41cm by 28cm. Half-length, by Vajda, Budapest. (90) DM3,200
— Anr, 1926. 23cm by 17cm (image). Sgd on mount. By Vajda. (91) DM1,800
— Anr, 22 Feb 1934. 9cm by 14cm. Seated at piano, by Lipnitzki. (91)

£1,100
— Anr, 1965. (89) DM700
Photograph, sgd & inscr, 21 May 1914. 19cm by 22cm. Inscr to Jean Aubry on mount. (90) £2,400
— Anr, 23 Nov 1924. 12.5cm by 17.5cm. Playing the piano. Corners def. (88) DM2,200
— Anr, 10 Aug 1932. (89) £600
— Anr, May [19]36. (91) £1,000
— Anr, 26 Mar 1937. (90) $500
— Anr, 1937. (89) £300
— Anr, Aug 1951. (89) £400
— Anr, Jan 1961. (90) DM400
— Anr, 1964. (91) $200
— Anr, 1964. (90) $850
Proof copy, Les noces, vocal score, 1922. 180 pp, folio, in brown wraps. With autograph corrections in red ink; sgd. (91) £1,500
— Anr, ballet, Jeu de Cartes, 1st Ed of full score, [Nov - Dec 1936]. 101 pp, 4to, in later gilt-stamped calf. With autograph corrections in red ink & pencil. (91) £3,200

**Stravinsky, Igor, 1882-1971 — &
Ramuz, Charles Ferdinand, 1878-1947
Group photograph,** 1929. (88) £300

**Stresemann, Gustav, 1878-1929
Collection** of 3 Ls s & autograph postcard, sgd, 23 Dec 1924 to 14 June 1926. (89) DM850
Ls s (2), 23 & 29 Jan 1917. Schroeder collection. (89) DM210
Ls, 10 Mar 1924. (90) DM320
Photograph, sgd & inscr, 25 Feb 1919. (90) DM350

**Strindberg, August, 1849-1912
Autograph Ms** (2), draft of statement, sgd, addressed to a court at Berlin, & draft of an outline of contents, both dealing with his work En Dares Foersvarstal, 26 Sept 1893 & [n.d.]. 2 pp, folio & 8vo. (91) DM1,700
Autograph Ms, Gold-Synthese, 3 Sept 1896. 8 pp, 4to, on rectos only. Describing 2 experiments to prove that gold can be made from iron; sgd. (91) DM3,600
Series of 6 A Ls s, 19 Aug 1888 to 9 Mar 1906. 9 pp, 8vo. Mostly to Herr Brausewetter. Regarding the trans & performance of his plays in Germany. (89) £4,000
ALs, [20 Oct 1881]. 1 p, 8vo. To Robert Haglund. Mentioning his comedy Gillets hemlighet. With related material. (89) DM2,600
— 1 Dec 1892. 2 pp, 8vo. To Stanislaw [Przybyszewski]. Complaining about "la divine misere de l'amour". (91) DM1,800
— 24 Dec 1892. 2 pp, 8vo. To [Maximilian Harden]. Asking him to appoint a date for a meeting. In German. (91) DM1,400
Autograph postcard, sgd, 15 Oct 1892. To Ernst Brausewetter. Confirming receipt of a drama & the Ms of a novel. In Swedish. (88) DM1,900

Stroheim, Erich von
ALs, May 1940. (91) $200

Stuart, Charles Edward ("The Young Pretender"), 1720-88
ALs, 25 Nov 1776. (89) £680

Stuart, Gilbert, 1755-1828
ANs, [1797?]. 1 p, in pencil. Announcing that Chief Little Turtle is with him and suggests bringing a "Segar" to "smoke a whiff with him." (88) $1,500

Stuart, James Ewell Brown, 1833-64
ALs, 24 Apr 1862. 1 p, 4to. To George Wythe Randolph. About Union offensives. (91) $6,000
ANs, 29 Mar 1856. 1 p, 8vo. Recipient unnamed. Reply at foot of letter addressed to him requesting contract price of rations. Alexander collection. (90) $2,200
— 22 May 1862. 1 p, 4to. To [Gen. J. E. Johnston?]. Forwarding an ALs from Col. B. H. Robertson (on verso) regarding defenses around Richmond. In pencil. (90) $6,000

Stuart, James Francis Edward ("The Old Pretender"), 1688-1766
ALs, 24 Apr 1714. (89) £520
Ls, 31 Jan 1761. (91) $175

Studebaker, John Mohler, 1833-1917
Photograph, sgd, 1914. (88) $450

Sturges, Preston, 1898-1959 —& Vallee, Rudy
[3 scripts of films directed by Sturges, 1942 & 1948, 2 sgd by Vallee, 1 annotated by him on front cover, sold at pnNy on 3 Dec 1988, lot 43, for $400.]

Su Hua Ling Chen, 1904-90
[Her papers, including series of letters addressed to her by Julian Bell, Virginia Woolf, Vanessa Bell, Vita Sackville-West, & others, with related material, sold at S on 18 July 1991, lot 363, for £17,000 to Rota.]

Suckling, Sir John, 1609-42
Ms, A Discours wrytten ... To ye Earl of Dorsett..., [c.1640]. Tp & 28 pp, folio. With 3 other tracts on state affairs & religion in different hands, 37 pp, in 17th-cent limp vellum bdg. Houghton collection & John F. Fleming Estate. (89) $1,100

Sucre, Antonio Jose de, 1795-1830
Collection of 15 A Ls s & Ls s, 12 Apr 1825 to 30 Dec 1827. 18 pp, 8vo & 4to. To Gen. Francis Burdett O'Connor. Official letters relating to the liberation, creation & development of the Republic of Bolivar. With related material. (88) $21,000

Series of 5 A Ls s, 7 Apr 1825 to 11 Feb 1828. 8 pp, 8vo & 4to. To Francis Burdett O'Connor. Regarding troop movements & territorial boundaries. With related material. (90) $3,000

A Ls s (2), 20 June 1822 & 25 Mar 1823. 2 pp, 4to. In 3rd person, detailing a mission of Jose Barba. To the commanding officer of the department at Quito, ordering the replacement of Pedro Gonzalez. Trimmed; was mtd. (88) $1,600

ALs, 1820. (90) £700

Ls, 18 Dec 1824. 1 p, folio. To Simon Bolivar. Speculating on the problems in stabilizing the liberated territories [after the Battle of Ayacucho]. (91) $1,500

Sue, Eugene, 1804-57
Autograph Ms, novel, Les sept peches capitaux, chapter 34; [1847]. (91) DM750

Series of 7 A Ls s, [n.d.]. (89) £140

Suess-Oppenheimer, Joseph, 1698-1738
Ds, 19 Apr 1735. 1 p, folio. Voucher for payment of 10,633 guilders to Jakob Ullmann for military supplies. With related material. (89) DM2,600

Suetonius Tranquillus, Caius, c.70-140
Ms, Vitae XII Caesarum. [North-East Italy or Austria, c.1470]. 169 leaves, 240mm by 163mm, in late 19th-cent blue mor gilt by Lortic. In dark brown ink in a square slightly sloping humanistic minuscule. With 12 large illuminated initials. (88) £12,000

Sugar and Spice Series
Original drawings, (236), to illus 15 titles in the Sugar and Spice Series, 1932 to 1947. (90) £700

Suhr, Christoffer, 1771-1842
ALs, 8 May 1812. (89) DM450

Suhrkamp, Peter, 1891-59
Series of 3 Ls s, 22 June 1933 to 17 Dec 1937. (91) DM420

Sullivan, Sir Arthur, 1842-1900
Autograph music, 9 songs, including 1 from his lost opera, The Sapphire Necklace, 1857-1885. About 50 pp of music plus titles, folio & 4to. With some holograph revisions. (89) £3,400

— Autograph music, collection of hymn-tunes, including his setting of Onward, Christian Soldiers. 12 pp, 4to, with holograph revisions. Fold tears. (89) £9,500

— Autograph music, full score, Symphony in E [first performed 1866; pbd by Novello, 1902]. About 240 pp, 4to, in half calf. Some stains & wear. With revisions & marked up for conducting in blue crayon. (89) £17,000

— Autograph music, song, Sea-side Thoughts, for Alto, 2 Tenors & Bass, to a text by Bernard Barton, sgd; Aug 1857. 4 pp, folio; 3 systems of 4 staves each. Some corrections. (90) £1,400

Series of 6 A Ls s, 1880 to 1897. (88) £800

ALs, 28 Nov 1873. (89) $350

— 4 Dec 1875. Byer collection. (90) $400

— [n.d.]. (88) DM520

Autograph quotation, 4 bars from the song Sweet day, so cool..., sgd, inscr to Miss Harding & dated 28 Aug 1867. (90) £750

Sullivan, Edmund Joseph, 1869-1933

[A large collection of preparatory drawings for various works & cartoons, partly in 3 disbound sketchbooks also containing autograph drafts of letters & notes, sold at S on 7 June 1990, lot 501, for £500 to Forsyth.]

Autograph sketchbook, series of studies of George Bernard Shaw, 17 Jan 1929, & other drawings. 50 pp, 4to, in bds. In pencil & pen-&-ink. Including 8 port studies of Laura Knight. (89) £2,000

Original drawings, (17), to illus Nathan Bone's Skeletons, 1900, & other works. (90) £360

— Original drawings, (20), to illus R. Macmillan Archives. (90) £380

— Original drawings, (35), to illus Capt. Macmillan Archives. (90) £600

— Original drawings, (5), cartoons depicting Lloyd George & others in various situations. (90) £380

— Original drawings, (56), to illus Thomas Hughes's Tom Brown's Schooldays, 1896. Macmillan Archives. (90) £900

— Original drawings, (7), World War I cartoons depicting various subjects. (90) £400

— Original drawings, (8), cartoons depicting various political or military figures. (90) £400

Original drawing, pen-&-ink study of George Bernard Shaw for his etched port, 20 Dec 1929. (89) £680

Proof copy, etched port of George Bernard Shaw, 1st trial proof, [1930]. (89) £420

Sullivan, John, 1740-95

ADs, Feb 1768. (91) $250

Ds, 4 July 1778. (88) $65

Autograph endorsement, sgd; [n.d.]. (88) $55

Sully Prudhomme, Pseud. of Rene Francois Armand Prudhomme, 1839-1907

ALs, 20 Mar 188[?]. (90) DM370

Sully, Thomas, 1783-1872

ALs, 27 Jan 1845. (89) $250

Sulzer, Johann Georg, 1720-79

ALs, 27 June 1755. 1 p, 4to. To Philipp Erasmus Reich. About a dog presented to recipient. In French. With a port. (90) DM3,400

Summers, Montague, 1880-1948

Autograph Ms, book, The Restoration Theatre, [c.1933-34]. (89) £950

Series of c.40 A Ls s, Feb 1913 to Mar 1921. About 80 pp, 4to & 8vo. To A. H. Bullen & his assistant Miss Lister. Discussing Summer's Ed of Aphra Behn & other publication matters. (91) £1,100

Sumner, Charles, 1811-74

A Ls s (2), [c.1860s & n.d.]. 4 pp, 8vo. To Frederick Douglass. Hoping to talk with him "about the Republican party & its perils", & correcting an interview. (91) $1,600

ALs, 1 to 12 May 1871. (91) $260

Sumner, Jethro, 1733-85

ALs, 25 Feb 1781. (91) $600

Sumula seu Breviloquium super Concordia Novi et Veteris Testamenti. See: Theological Manuscripts

Supervielle, Jules, 1884-1960

Autograph Ms, poem, Terre, [n.d.]. (88) £40

Suppe, Franz von, 1819-95

Autograph music, vocal part of his arrangement of Johann Strauss's waltz Fruehlingsstimmen, [n.d.]. (88) £120

ALs, 8 June 1871. (91) DM340

Surtees, Robert Smith

Autograph Ms, unpbd autobiography. 264 pp, various sizes, each page hinged to larger sheets & bound in half mor. (91) $3,500

Suso, Heinrich, 1295?-1366
Ms, Der Ewicher Wisheit Boich, [Cologne, 1472]. 56 leaves, 28cm by 21cm. 19th-cent half calf, def. In brown ink in a secretary-influenced bookhand. With 14 large penwork initials in colors. Dampstained. (88) £2,900

— Ms, L'Horloge de Sapience, in French trans made in 1389. [France, mid-15th cent]. 263 leaves (lacking 3), vellum, 230mm by 156mm. 18th-cent mottled calf gilt. In dark brown ink in a lettre batarde; some names & headings in red. With c.40 large illuminated initials & calligraphic tp in fanciful gothic script. (88) £5,000

Sutcliffe, G. M.
[A collection of c.45 letters addressed to Sutcliffe by various writers & artists, [c.1918 to 1930s], relating to bookbinding matters, sold at S on 20 July 1989, lot 449, for £1,050 to Silverman.]

Sutherland, Graham, 1903-80
Collection of 2 A Ls s & Ls, 2 May & 24 July 1973 & [n.d.]. (90) DM260
ALs, [n.d.]. (90) DM320

Sutras
Ms, Diamond Sutra, [China, c.1800]. 46 pp, 330mm by 200mm, in modern half mor box. Including 22 gouache paintings on leaves of the pipal tree with facing text in gold, mtd on double-page blue ground, & double-page of the Heart Sutra. Phillipps MS & Robinson collection. (89) £2,500

Sutter, John A., 1803-80
ALs, 4 May 1848. 2 pp, folio. To Heinrich Thommen. Reporting about the beginning of the Gold Rush. In German. Repaired & silked. In mor case. Doheny collection. (88) $22,000
— 17 Sept 1852. 2 pp, 4to. To James L. L. F. Warren. Regretting being unable to participate in a fair & speaking of problems with his crop. (91) $1,600

Suttner, Bertha von, 1843-1914
ALs, 25 Nov [18]90. (90) DM270
— 7 May 1896. (91) DM460
Ls, 23 Oct 1900. (91) DM240

Swan, Caleb
Ls, [28 Apr] 1806. (88) $55

Swanson, Gloria, 1899-1983
Photograph, sgd & inscr, [n.d.]. (91) $200
Photograph, [n.d.]. (89) $400

Swedenborg, Emanuel, 1688-1772
Ls, 15 Sept 1740. 4 pp, folio. To the Royal Board of Trade. About a petition by J. Synnerberg for the refunding of duties. Als sgd by 6 other commissioners of the General-Tull-Arrende Societet. Was mtd. (89) DM1,700

Swieten, Gerard van, 1700-72
ALs, 2 Dec 1757. 1 p, 4to. To M. Graafenhueber. Inquiring about Marshal Daun. (91) DM1,600
— 22 Sept 1761. 1 p, 4to. To Gabriel Brotier. About his position as director of the Vienna Court Library, & forwarding a note by [Adam Franz] Kollar (present). (90) DM2,200

Swift, Jonathan, 1667-1745
ALs, 12 Dec 1734. 3 pp, 4to. To the Rev. Doctor Clerk of Trinity College, Dublin. Commenting about a discourse concerning the condition of Trinity College sent to him. Houghton collection & John F. Fleming Estate. (89) $6,500
AL, 7 June 1713. 1 p, 4to. To Charles Ford. Jocular letter touching a variety of matters. (90) £3,200

Swinburne, Algernon Charles, 1837-1909
[A collection of letters, 46 pp, c.1866 to 1909, mostly to Swinburne (some to D. G. Rosetti) sold at S on 15 Dec, lot 31, for £2,000.]
[Galley proofs & ptd copies of 7 poems for his Poems and Ballads, 1866, 5 with autograph revisions, bound with a charcoal & chalk port, sgd, by Charles Fairfax Murray & inscr by Swinburne on mount, in mor gilt folio album by Riviere, sold at CNY on 18 Nov 1988, lot 340, for $3,000.]
Autograph Ms, ballad, A Reiver's Neck-Verse, [n.d.]. (90) £900
— Autograph Ms, essay, John Webster. [1885-86] 44 leaves, folio, in mor gilt by Sangorski & Sutcliffe, cover detached (91) $4,250

- Autograph Ms, poem, An Autumn Vision, 19 & 31 Oct 1889. 10 pp, folio. With revisions. Houghton collection & John F. Fleming Estate. (89) $4,000
- Autograph Ms, poem, beginning "All heaven, in every baby born...", [n.d.]. (88) $525
- Autograph Ms, poem, On the South Coast, [n.d.]. (89) £780
- Autograph Ms, poem, Prologue to The Duchess of Malfy. (91) £500
- Autograph Ms, poem, Quam Multum Amavit, [c.1871]. John F. Fleming Estate. (89) $450
- Autograph Ms, poem, The Garden of Cymodoce, [1876-80]. 16 pp, folio, on rectos only. 343 lines, with revisions. Interleaved; in modern green mor gilt. (89) £3,500

Series of 8 A Ls s, 6 Mar 1874 to 13 Jan 1877. 30 pp, 8vo. To John H. Ingram. Discussing recipient's efforts to counter slanders of Edgar Allan Poe's biographer R. W. Griswold, acknowledging publications, etc. With related material. Bradley Martin sale. (90) $3,750

- Series of 7 A Ls s, 1876 to 1884. 20 pp, 8vo, mtd in red mor album by Riviere. To Theodore Watts-Dunton & Mr. MacColl (1). About Charles Lamb's interleaved copy of George Wither & other matters. Including related letter by Alfred Ainger to Swinburne. (88) £1,500

ALs, 14 Mar [1878]. (88) £120
- 8 Dec 1878. (90) DM850
- 20 Jan 1880. Doheny collection. (89) $400
- 21 July 1885. Doheny collection. (89) $150
- 7 May 1893. (88) £580
- 28 Nov 1907. (88) DM750
- [n.d.]. (90) DM620

Autograph postcard, sgd, 2 Apr [1898]. (91) $225

Group photograph, [n.d.]. (89) £600

Swinnerton, Frank
Autograph Ms, novel, The Chaste Wife, [1915 - 1916]. (91) £700

Collection of 5 A Ls s & Ls, 1925 to 1934. (89) $140

Swinnerton, James
Original drawing, Mr. (89) $200

Switzer, Alfalfa, 1926-59 —& McFarland, Spanky
[Their signatures, [1930s], on a 12mo sheet, sold at Dar on 10 Apr 1991, lot 7, for $150.]

Switzerland
- ZURICH. - Document, 14 Nov 1642. 1 p, vellum, 31cm by 65cm. Decision by 4 magistrates of the city in a controversy concerning a right of way. (90) DM290

Sylva, Carmen, Pseud. of Elisabeth, Queen of Carol I of Romania, 1843-1916
Autograph Ms, poem, Was die Karpathenfee dazu meinte, 17 July 1882. (88) DM360

Collection of ALs & photograph, sgd & inscr, [n.d.]. (91) DM680

ALs, 7 Oct 1888. (90) DM650

Symington, James Ayton
Original drawings, (112), to illus titles by G. Archives of J. M. Dent & Son. (90) £750
- Original drawings, (12), to illus Marryat's The Little Savage, 1901. Archives of J. M. Dent & Son. (90) £400

Symmes, John Cleves, 1780-1829
Ls, 10 Apr 1818. (88) $425

Symonds, John Addington, 1840-99
Autograph Ms, The History of Blank Verse; [c.1878]. (90) £750

Symons, Arthur, 1865-1945
Autograph Ms, trans of Baudelaire, The Artificial Paradises: Opium and Hashish; [c.1925]. 119 pp, 4to. Sgd on tp. With a typescript & extensive related material. Koch Foundation. (90) $2,500

Syriac Manuscripts
Ms, 3 treatises on grammar & spelling. (91) DM1,000
- Ms, Gazza; hymns for the 2d half of the year. [Northern Iraq, Haraba, 1 June 1723]. 213 leaves (1 lacking), 320mm by 215mm. Contemp dark brown lea over wooden bds. In black & red ink by the priest Hormez from

SYRIAC MANUSCRIPTS

the village of Garbaye. With 8 ornamental paintings in colors & numerous birds & animals in margins. (91) DM10,000

— Ms, Gospels. [Northern Iraq, Alqos, 21 Aug 1742]. 103 leaves (3 lacking), 460mm by 310mm. Contemp dark brown lea over wooden bds. In black & red ink with headings in yellow by the priest Hanna for the Monastery of St. Quryaqos at Sabina. With circular ornaments in borders, several painted borders, numerous small decorative paintings, & 2 very large miniatures. (91) DM12,000

— Ms, wedding rituals. (91) DM1,000

Szigeti, Joseph, 1892-1973

Collection of 23 A Ls s & Ls s, 1936 to 1967. Over 40 pp, 4to & 8vo (some on postcards). To Spike Hughes. Giving news of his life as recitalist & performer, including anecdotes of composers, etc. (89) £1,350

Szold, Henrietta, 1860-1945

Typescript, interoffice memorandum regarding the appointment of Elsa Pikard as clerk, 29 Feb 1940. (91) $200

Szyk, Arthur, 1894-1951

[A set of proofs for illusts, decorated text, doublures & subscription form for the book Haggadah. L, 1939, together 52 items, 4to, mostly mtd & initialled by Szyk, sold at CNY on 7 June 1990, lot 125, for $7,500.]

Original drawing, man & woman on a horse flying through the air, to illus The Ebony Horse for an Ed of the Arabian Nights tales, [19]48. 160mm by 122mm. In watercolor; sgd. Framed. (89) £2,400

— Original drawing, Sindbad clasping the leg of Roc, to illus an Ed of the Arabian Nights tales, [19]48. 160mm by 122mm. In watercolor; sgd. Framed. (89) £2,400

Signature, 1949, on color reproduction of tp for The United States of America. (88) $60

AMERICAN BOOK PRICES CURRENT

Szymanowski, Karol, 1883-1937

Autograph music, arrangement of the Bauerntanz from his ballet Harnasie, 3 Mar 1931. 10 pp, folio. Notated on up to four systems per page, 3 or 4 staves each. Some revisions. (89) $4,250

— Autograph music, arrangement of Roxane's aria from King Roger, a Danse Sauvage, & a work in F sharp minor, all for violin & piano; 1920 & [n.d.]. 20 pp, folio. Mostly autograph ; some parts written out or revised by Paul Kochanski. (89) $4,000

— Autograph music, arrangements for violin & piano of Paganini's Caprices nos 23, 24 & 25; [c.1918]. 21 pp, folio. With numerous alterations. Some annotations probably in the hand of Paul Kochanski. (89) $4,000

— Autograph music, La berceuse d'Aitacho Enia for violin & piano, Op. 52; [1925]. 4 pp, folio. Notated on up to 4 systems per page, 3 staves each. Some alterations in pencil. With related material. (89) $2,250

— Autograph music, Mazourka (N.1 de l'op. 52); [n.d.]. 3 pp, size not stated; 12 staves each. Sgd on tp. (89) DM7,000

— Autograph music, Tarantella for violin & piano, Op. 28 no 2, sgd; [1915]. 16 pp, folio. Notated on up to 4 systems per page, 3 staves each. Some annotations probably in the hand of Paul Kochanski. (89) $5,500

— Autograph music, Violin Sonata in D minor, Op. 9, score & separate violin part; 1903. 43 pp, folio. Notated on up to 4 systems per page, 3 staves each. With many autograph revisions; some annotations in the hand of Paul Kochanski. (89) $6,000

ALs, [16 Sept 1921]. (91) DM1,000

— 24 Sept 1924. 3 pp, 4to. To an unnamed professor. Giving information about his String Quartet Op.37. (91) DM3,000

— 29 Sept 1925. 4 pp, 4to. To an unnamed singer. About his cantata Demeter & the musical scene in Warsaw. (90) DM2,000

— 27 Sept 1927. (88) £500

— 5 Sept [1]932. (89) £350

— [n.d.]. 2 pp, 4to. To an unnamed lady. Sending tickets for a concert & refer-

ring to a disagreement. (90) DM1,100
Autograph quotation, Air de Raxou from his opera Le Roi Roger, 2 bars; sgd & dated 8 Aug 1926. 1 p, 4to. (90) DM2,000

T

Taft, Helen H., 1861-1943
Photograph, sgd, [n.d.]. (88) $90

Taft, William Howard, 1857-1930
[2 autograph endorsements, sgd, & autograph notes & memoranda, 11 & 15 Jan 1911 & [n.d.], 7 pp, 4to & 8vo, concerning immigration & emigration questions respecting Jews in Russia, sold at S on 15 Dec 1988, lot 204, for £2,000.]
Collection of ALs & typescript, 27 July 1920. 28 pp, 4to. To Jacob G. Ullery, letter of transmittal. Article, [On Getting On], with 3 substantial autographic insertions. With ptd pamphlet. (89) $1,100
— Collection of ALs, Ls & photograph, sgd, 9 Apr 1921 to 2 Feb 1926. (89) $240
ALs, 12 June 1887. (91) $700
— 14 July 1904. (89) $260
— 16 Dec 1912. 1 p, 8vo. To the Utica Public Library. Sending his autograph. (89) $1,300
— 25 July 1915. (88) $200
— 4 Sept 1915. (91) $250
— 12 Sept 1921. (89) $320
Collection of Ls & check, sgd, 30 Nov 1908 & 1 Dec 1917. (90) $400
— Collection of 2 Ls s, ANs & photograph, sgd & inscr, 28 Jan 1911 to 23 Sept 1917. Doheny collection. (89) $800
Series of 3 Ls s, Sept to Nov 1899. (89) $425
Ls s (2), 2 Mar 1900 & 16 Apr 1908. (90) $250
— Ls s (2), 6 Feb 1904 & 19 Oct 1906. (89) $180
— Ls s (2), 12 Apr & 26 June 1912. (89) $350
— Ls s (2), 24 Jan 1915 & 28 Jan 1917. (89) $190
— Ls s (2), 22 Aug 1922 & 30 Aug 1929. (90) $300

— Ls s (2), 1924 & 1927. (89) $325
— Ls s (2), 12 Jan & 3 Feb 1925. (89) $300
Ls, 28 June 1905. (89) $75
— 9 Jan 1906. (91) $600
— 21 Feb 1908. (91) $375
— [Summer 1908]. (88) $75
— 10 Dec 1908. (88) $120
— [1908]. (88) $70
— 17 Feb 1909. (89) $200
— 10 Apr 1909. (90) $160
— 27 Nov 1909. (89) $110
— 9 Feb 1910. (90) $275
— 29 Aug 1910. (88) $90
— 28 Jan 1911. (90) $160
— 1 Mar 1911. (88) $300
— 28 Mar 1911. 4 pp, 4to. To Talcott Williams. Giving detailed confidential information about the Mexican situation. (91) $5,500
— 25 Apr 1911. 1 p, 4to. To the Rev. J. Wesley Hill. Regretting that his many engagements will not allow him to visit the Hadley Rescue Mission. With autograph memorandum, sgd, by Hill, 12 Nov 1918, on verso of integral blank, stating Taft visited the Mission at midnight. Rosenbloom collection. (88) $1,300
— 20 May 1914. (90) $95
— 14 May 1917. (90) $95
— 19 Apr 1918. (91) $225
— 11 Oct 1919. (89) $60
— 17 Dec 1919. (91) $100
— 14 Mar 1921. (89) $65
— 23 July 1921. (91) $375
— 10 Aug 1921. (90) $150
— 27 July 1926. Byer collection. (90) $225
Collection of Ds & photograph, sgd & inscr, 6 June 1911 & 4 June 1912. (90) $550
Ds, 16 June 1904. (89) $170
— 5 Aug 1909. (89) $190
— 13 Nov 1909. (90) $300
— 21 Dec 1909. (91) $650
— 21 May 1910. Byer collection. (90) $450
— 15 July 1910. (91) $375
— 14 Jan 1911. (89) $70
— 14 Jan 1911. (88) $75
— 10 Feb 1911. (88) $200
— 13 Apr 1911. (88) $220
— 26 May 1911. (91) $160

TAFT

— 7 June 1911. (88) $135
— 29 June 1911. (90) $130
— 12 Aug 1911. (90) $200
— 22 Dec 1911. (90) $130
— 1 Feb 1912. (91) $300
— 31 Dec 1912. (88) $200
— 1 Mar 1913. (91) $500
— [c.1910s]. (90) $100

Engraving, port by unidentified artist, pbd by Wm. (88) $110

— Anr, port by [J. (88) $130

Photograph, sgd & inscr, 26 Sept 1907. (90) $200

— Anr, [c.1908]. (90) $250
— Anr, 2 Apr 1910. (90) $375
— Anr, 14 Oct 1911. (91) $700
— Anr, 28 Mar 1924. (91) $180
— Anr, 14 May 1929. (88) $160
— Anr, [n.d.]. (90) $350

Ptd photograph, sgd, [n.d.]. (90) $55
Signature, 19 Jan 1913. (88) $80
White House card, sgd, [n.d.]. (90) $100

— Anr, sgd, 24 Feb 1913. (90) $225

Taft, William Howard, 1857-1930 —& Others

[The signatures of Taft, Calvin Coolidge, Arthur J. Balfour, & 20 others, mostly with autograph address, [c.Feb 1922], 2 pp, 8vo, sold at wa on 20 Oct 1990, lot 94, for $130.]

Taft, William Howard, 1857-1930 —& Coolidge, Calvin, 1872-1933

[3 Ls s & ANs from Taft to Sen. Elmer J. Burdett, 1 Sept 1908 to 21 Aug 1911, & Ls from Coolidge to Burdett, 28 Dec 1923, with retained carbon copies of Burdett's letters & further related material, sold at P on 26 Oct 1988, lot 190, for $2,000.]

Tagliacozzi, Gaspare, 1545-99

Document, Libellus supplicatorium, 18 Dec 1576. 1 p, folio. Request for admission to the Colleges of Medicine & Philosophy at Bologna, sgd & subscribed by Ovidio Giubetti & 2 others. (89) £2,800

Tagore, Rabindranath, 1861-1941

Collection of 115 A Ls s & Ls s & 59 autograph Mss, 1904 to 1938. 460 pp, mostly 8vo & 4to. To Charuchandra Bandyopadhay. Dealing with literary matters & sending Mss for print (included, poems, songs, dance-drama). Including a few pieces possibly not in Tagore's hand. (91) £26,000

ALs, 5 Dec 1930. (90) DM230
Photograph, sgd & inscr, 12 Nov 1926. (90) DM470

Tait, Archibald Campbell, 1811-82

Series of 12 A Ls s, 18 June 1853 to 2 Mar [18]63. (88) £40

Talbot, Elizabeth, Countess of Shrewsbury ("Bess of Hardwick"), 1518-1608

Ds, 3 Oct 1605. (90) $200

Talbot, William Henry Fox, 1800-77

ALs, [n.d.]. (89) £340

Talleyrand-Perigord, Charles Maurice de, 1754-1838

Series of 5 A Ls s, [c.1834-1835]. (91) £850
ALs, 24 Nov 1795. (89) £420
— [21 Dec 1801]. (89) DM880
— 15 Dec [1806]. 1 p, 4to. To an unnamed lady. Informing her that a pension for her father can only be granted by the Emperor. (88) DM1,100
— 12 Apr 1807. (89) £300
— 26 Aug 1815. (91) $200
— [c.1830]. (91) $120
— 30 brumaire [n.y.]. (88) $300

AL, [n.d.]. (90) £300
Ls, [27 June 1801]. (89) $225
— 11 Aug 1802. (89) $200
— [8 Sept 1803]. (90) DM470
— [28 Dec 1803]. (88) DM320
— [28 Apr 1804]. (91) DM360
— 5 Aug 1804. (90) DM750
— 13 June 1807. (91) DM320

Letter, [29 Sept 1800]. (90) DM450
Ds, [1803]. (89) DM380
— [1805]. (91) DM380

Tandler, Julius

[A collection of letters addressed to him by prominent figures in literature, art or medicine, c.30 items, 1918 to 1929, on medical & civic matters, sold at S on 5 May 1988, lot 286, for £2,400 to Maliye.]

Taney, Roger B., 1777-1864
Ls, 2 Nov 1832. (91) $170
Ds, 15 Feb 1834. (90) $55

Tansley, Eric
Original drawings, (37), to illus his own Birds of the Field and Woodland, [1948]. (89) £700

Tansman, Alexander
Autograph music, Mazurka pour la Guitare, [1926]. (90) £550
— Autograph music, Sonata for Violin & Piano, score & separate violin part; sgd & dated July 1919. (89) $800

Tarin, Jaime
Ms, Relacion y breve noticia de la Fundacion de la Yglesia de S. Antonio de Padue..., 1687. About 50 pp, Chinese paper, folio; disbound. Account of Franciscan attempts to found churches in the Province of Canton. Repaired. Phillipps Ms.6069 & Robinson collection. (89) £2,000

Tarkington, Booth, 1869-1946
ALs, 6 Aug 1917. Koch Foundation. (90) $420

Tartini, Giuseppe, 1692-1770
Ms, concerto in F major for 4 violins, viola & bass; full score, [mid- to late 18th cent]. (89) £250

Tasso, Bernardo, 1493-1569
ALs, 24 July 1557. 1 p, folio. Recipient unnamed. Informing him that he may have to travel to Rome. Repaired. (89) DM3,500
Ls, 3 Oct 1559. (91) £550

Tasso, Torquato, 1544-95
Autograph Ms, dialogue, Agostin da Sessa, e Cesare Gonzaga [later: Il Gonzaga overo del Piacere Onesto], [May 1580?]. 60 pp, folio, in modern limp vellum wraps. With extensive revisions. Lacking some leaves. (89) £26,000
— Autograph Ms, madrigal, Perche pur me saetti, [c.1586]. 3 pp, 8vo. With note of authenticity. (91) £4,100
— Autograph Ms, sonnet to be delivered to Donna Francesca Maria della Rovere by Forza Santinello di Pesaro, sgd; [early 1570s]. 1 p, 4to. Small paper losses. Tipped to larger leaf, with trans. Barrett collection. (89) $3,250
ALs, 15 May 1593. 1 p, folio. To the Abate Francesco Polverino. Sending copies of his Lagrime, & complaining about misprints in the Brescia Ed of his Rime. (89) DM27,000

Tate, Allen, 1899-1979
Collection of 30 A Ls s, 12 Ls s, & 11 postcards, sgd (10 autograph), 1940 to 1972. 55 pp, 8vo & 4to, & cards. To Mark & Dorothy Van Doren. Wide ranging personal correspondence. With related material, including autograph poem by Mark Van Doren. (90) $4,500

Tauber, Richard, 1891-1948
Autograph Ms, essay, Kuenstlerferien, 3 Aug 1925. (90) DM450

Tauentzien, Friedrich Bogislaw von, 1710-91
Ls, 11 Sept 1771. (90) DM360
See also: Lessing, Gotthold Ephraim

Tauentzien von Wittenberg, Bogislaw, Graf, 1760-1824
ALs, 8 Dec 1812. (89) DM550
Ls, 2 Oct 1814. (88) DM600

Taylor, George, 1772-1851
Autograph Ms, Index Idoneorum. (88) £100

Taylor, George W.
Ms, Private Letters. (91) £170

Taylor, Robert, 1911-69. See: Gaynor, Janet & Taylor

Taylor, Zachary, 1784-1850
Collection of ALs & AL, 3 May & 4 Nov 1820. 8 pp, 4to. To his brother Hancock Taylor. Reporting about his activities, the military road to Nashville, the sale of his slave & the death of his daughters. Def. (89) $1,200
— Collection of ALs & 3 A Ls, 22 May 1823 to 3 Aug 1829. 15 pp, 4to. To his brother Hancock Taylor. About his plantation in Louisiana, family news, his father's estate, etc. Def. (89) $3,500
ALs, 22 Mar 1820. 3 pp, 4to. To his

TAYLOR

brother Hancock Taylor. About moving his family to Louisiana, the sale of a slave, & Louisiana's general prospects. With 1-line autograph postscript, sgd Z.T. Def. (89) $2,250
— 3 June 1823. 4 pp, 4to. To Dr. Thomas Lawson. Chatting about his command at Baton Rouge, a court martial, his family & friends. (88) $5,500
— 1 Oct 1825. 1 p, 4to. To Col. Roger Jones. Transmitting copies of estimates for supplies [not present]. Whiton collection. (88) $1,600
— 31 Aug 1838. 1 p, 4to. Recipient unknown. Explaining an error concerning his Indian accounts. With engraved port. (90) $1,200
— 17 Feb 1846. (89) £1,000
— [c.1846/47]. (88) $300
— 28 May 1846 [i.e.1847]. 4 pp, 4to. To Jefferson Davis. Cordial letter referring to Davis's return home after being wounded at Buena Vista, events of the Mexican War, etc. Repaired. Pratt collection. (89) $13,000
— 5 Aug 1848. 1 p, 4to. To Henry C. Wiley. Sending his autograph. Byer collection. (90) $1,900
— 26 Sept 1848. 7 pp, 4to. To Robert C. Wood. Discussing his Presidential campaign. Including postscript, initialled. Sang collection. (91) $7,500
— 14 June 1850. 1 p, 8vo. To Adonirum Chandler. Content not given. (91) $4,400

Ls, 10 Jan 1830. (88) $525
— 25 Nov 1847. 1 p, 4to. To Charles Reynolds. Responding to a young admirer who has requested a sword & epaulettes. Sang collection. (91) $2,250
— 13 Dec 1848. 1 p, 4to. To Benson Lossing. Enclosing a pen-&-ink sketch of his residence (present; 4to). Both silked. Rosenbloom collection. (88) $6,500
— 17 Apr 1849. 2 pp, 4to. To Sec of the Interior Thomas Ewing. Requesting that William R. Hackley be appointed District Attorney. (89) $4,000
— 12 Oct 1849. 2 pp, 4to. To Joseph Grinnell. Regretting that he will not be able to visit New Bedford. (90) $4,000
— 1 June 1850. 3 pp, 4to. To Gov. George N. Briggs of Massachusetts. About visiting Massachusetts. (91) $2,250

ADs, 30 June 1835. 1 p, folio. Account of Mary Ann Lowry with the Indian Department for services as teacher, & pay order. Including receipt, sgd, by Mrs. Lowry; at bottom. (90) $2,500

Ds, 26 July 1813. (88) $600
— Jan 1814. (89) $750
— Dec 1832. (88) $600
— Feb 1834. (88) $400
— 31 Mar 1836. (89) $700
— 25 Apr 1847. (88) $950
— 19 Aug 1848. 1 p, 4to, cut from larger leaf. Recommendation of Sergeant Porter for an army appointment. McVitty collection. (90) $1,100
— 16 Mar 1849. 1 p, folio. Commission for Theodorus Bailey as Commander in the Navy. Countersgd by Sec of the Navy Preston. (88) $3,000
— 21 July 1849. 1 p, 4to. Appointment of Nathaniel P. Prickett as Midshipman. (91) $4,250
— 2 Aug 1849. 1 p, folio. Commission for John C. Clark as Auditor of the Treasury. Countersgd by Sec of State John M. Clayton. (89) $3,500
— 18 Jan 1850. 1 p, 4to. Order to affix the US Seal to a letter of congratulation addressed to the King of Hannover. On blue paper. (90) $2,800

Cut signature, 26 Sept 1849. (89) $950
— Anr, 4 Feb 1850. (89) $650
— Anr, [n.d.]. (90) $500

Endorsement, sgd, 13 Oct 1847. Note of approval on verso of ALs by Lieut. J. Kellogg to President Polk, resigning his commission. Also endorsed by Roger Jones & Sec of War Marcy. Framed. (91) $1,100

Franking signature, [27 Dec 1814]. (90) $1,000
— Anr, [8 May 1850]. (91) $500
— Anr, [4 July n.y.]. As President. (89) $2,000
— Anr, [n.d.]. (91) $400

Tchaikovsky, Peter Ilyich, 1840-93
ALs, 6/18 Sept 1877. 4 pp, 8vo. To a friend in Vienna. Asking him to find a piano teacher for his sister's children. In French. (88) DM7,500
— 21 Dec 1877/2 Jan 1878. 1 p, 4to. To [Robert de Thal]. Informing him about

his arrival in Paris to participate in the deliberations of the Imperial commission for the forthcoming international exhibition. With related material. (90) DM4,600

— 25 Dec [1878]. 3 pp, 8vo. Recipient unnamed. Introducing a young Polish-Russian musician. With port postcard mtd on integral blank. (91) £2,600

— 22 July 1879. 3 pp, 8vo. Recipient unnamed. Providing an autobiographical sketch for a projected work. In French. (90) DM19,000

— 17 Sept [18]79. 3 pp, 12mo. To Edvard Frantsevich Napravnik. Requesting his opinion about his opera Vakula the Smith. Including autograph postscript. With related material. (90) $4,200

— 22 Jan 1882. 1 p, 8vo. Recipient unknown. Introducing Mr. & Miss Burmester, 2 young musicians. In French. Doheny collection. (89) $3,500

— 4 May [1882]. 4 pp, 12mo. To Adolphe Davidovich Brodsky. About the success of his violin concerto in London. Rosen collection. (89) $7,500

— 11/23 Mar 1884. 3 pp, 4to. To "Monsieur le President" [Alfred Bruneau?]. Regarding recipient's wish to have a work by Tchaikovsky performed at the Festival de l'Union Internationale. (90) DM6,000

— 26 Mar [1884]. 4 pp, 4to. To Edvard Napravnik. Informing him that he has completed 3 revisions to his opera Mazeppa. (90) £4,800

— 19 June [18]86. (88) £850

— 8 July 1886. 4 pp, 8vo. To an unnamed French composer. Discussing piano transcriptions of his works. In French. (90) £3,000

— 7 Oct 1886. 1 p, 8vo. To Eduard Napravnik. Asking for a box for recipient's opera Harold. (91) £3,000

— 7 Oct 1886. 1 p, 8vo. To Eduard Napravnik. Requesting a ticket for a performance of recipient's opera Harold. (91) £1,600

— 25 Sept [1887]. 3 pp, 8vo. To [E. F. Napravnik]. Apologizing for mistakes in recipient's copy of a score. (91) £2,800

— 16 Nov 1887. 4 pp, 12mo. To E. F. Napravnik. Informing him about Erdmannsdorf's refusal to discuss a program. (91) £1,900

— 17 Apr 188[8?]. 4 pp, 8vo. To Lucien Guitry. Suggesting that he appear as Hamlet or Romeo, & offering to arrange music for a performance. (91) £4,000

— 8 Nov 1888. 2 pp, 8vo. To E. F. Napravnik. Commenting on the poor state of his health & arranging a meeting. (91) £2,200

— 31 Aug/12 Sept 1889. 3 pp, 8vo. Recipient unnamed. Concerning recipient's wish to give a concert in Moscow. In French. (89) DM6,200

— 8/20 Jan 1890. 2 pp, 8vo. To R. Bignell. Promising to help him find a position in Russia. In German. Repaired. (88) DM4,400

— 19 June/1 July 1890. 4 pp, 8vo. To an unnamed conductor. About Dvorak's reception in Russia, his own new opera, recipient's concert, etc. In French. (90) £4,800

— 19/31 Jan 1891. 4 pp, 4to. To Louis Gallet. Discussing the possibility of arranging a production of Pique Dame for the French stage. (91) £3,500

— 24 Mar/5 Apr 1891. 1 p, 8vo. To Katerina Ivanovna Laroche. Informing her about the ship on which he is travelling. (90) £2,000

— 22 Sept [18]92. 4 pp, 8vo. To Anton Door. Discussing arrangements for a cancelled concert in Vienna. (91) £3,000

— 18 Oct [18]92. 4 pp, 8vo. To [Napravnik?]. Discussing rehearsals for his opera Yolanta. (90) £2,500

— [n.d.]. 2 pp, 4to. Recipient unnamed. Concerning his visit to London & rehearsals at the Royal College of Music. (91) £2,100

ADs, 9 Feb 1888. 1 p, 7.3cm by 21.5cm. Testimonial for the singer Aline Friede after a concert with the Berlin Philharmonic Orchestra. Was mtd. (89) DM1,400

Autograph quotation, 3 bars marked "Moderato", sgd & dated 25 Apr 1885. 1 p, 8vo. (90) £1,800

— Anr, 5 bars marked "Andante", sgd & dated 22 July 1888. 117mm by 198mm. Inscr to Jos. Wilimu. (88) £4,200

— Anr, 7 bars from his String Quartet in D major, Op. 11, notated on 2 sys-

TCHAIKOVSKY

tems; sgd & dated 12 Feb 1889. 1 p, 8vo. Was mtd. (90) DM13,000
— Anr, 4 bars from his Cradle Song, Op. 16 no 1, sgd & dated 10 June 1893. 1 p, 8vo. (90) DM9,000
— Anr, 4 bars from the Suite no 3 in G, sgd; [n.d.]. 9cm by 12.5cm. (91) £2,800
Photograph, sgd & inscr, [9 Feb 1888]. Cabinet size. Inscr to Aline Friede. (89) DM5,000

Tchelichew, Pavel, 1898-1957
ALs, 2 Aug 1956. (88) £140

Teasdale, Sara, 1884-1933
ALs, 8 Feb 1918. (88) $50

Tegner, Esaias, 1782-1846
ALs, 30 Apr [1841]. 1 p, 4to. To [Gottlieb Mohnike]. Thanking for his hospitality & informing him about his return to Sweden. (90) DM1,300

Telfair, Edward, c.1735-1807
ALs, 1 Mar 1788. (91) $280

Teller, Edward
Transcript, The Secret of Los Alamos, [n.d.]. (89) $210
Collection of ALs & photograph, sgd, 19 Sept 1977. (89) DM550
Collection of Ls & photograph, sgd, 8 Dec 1959 & [n.d.]. (90) DM550
Photograph, sgd, [n.d.]. (89) $85

Temple, Shirley
Signature, [19 Sept 1939]. (88) $55
— Anr, [n.d.]. (89) $60

Ten Broeck, Abraham, 1734-1810
Ds, 27 Apr 1779. (91) $140

Tennant, Stephen
[A large collection of typescript & autograph writings & drawings by Tennant, c.7,500 pp, with related material, sold at S on 15 Oct 1987, lot 909, for £6,000.]
Original drawings, Favourite Fairy Tales Illustrated by Stephen Tennant 1916; 14 pp, folio. (88) £320
Series of 12 A Ls s, [n.d.]. (88) £400
See also: Whistler, Rex

AMERICAN BOOK PRICES CURRENT

Tenniel, Sir John, 1820-1914
Original drawing, "You go first", 2 oriental figures with daggers on a pier near a boat called Europa; pbd in Punch, 20 Mar 1897. (90) £260

Tennyson, Alfred, Lord, 1809-92
Autograph Ms (2), poem, The Eagle, sgd & dated 30 Oct 1849, & poem beginning "Here on this Terrace fifty years ago", [n.d.], with cut signature affixed. Barrett collection. (89) $1,000
Autograph Ms, poem, Come not when I am dead, [1847]. (91) £1,000
Collection of ALs & photograph, sgd, [n.d.] & [1884]. (88) £280
ALs, 18 Feb 1846. (91) $180
— [n.d.]. (88) £140
— 22 Apr 1868. (90) DM300
— [26 Jan 1874]. (89) £300
— 27 Apr 1876. (90) £200
— [n.d.]. (91) £90
ANs, 18 June 1828. (89) $125
— 27 July 1870. (88) $80
Autograph check, sgd, 14 Sept 1870. (90) $220
Photograph, sgd, [3 June 1869]. (88) £600
Signature, [n.d.]. (90) $150
— HERKOMER, SIR HUBERT VON. - Orig drawing, prelim version of Tennyson's port, [c.1878]. 20 by 16 inches. In brush, ink & white. Initialled. Framed. (89) £500

Terentius Afer, Publius, 185-159 B.C.
Ms, Comoediae. [Florence, c.1440-50]. 117 leaves, vellum, 243mm by 160mm. Late 18th-cent red mor gilt bdg. In a regular rounded humanistic hand with strong gothic features. With 2-line initials throughout in dark blue & 8 large white-vine initials. (91) £19,000

Tereshkova, Valentina
Signature, [6 June 1978]. (91) $120

Tergolina, Vicenzo, Count
[A patent granted to him for improvements in the construction of bits for horses, 1872, size not stated, sold at pn on 10 Dec 1987, lot 464, for £100 to Ephemera.]

Terry, Alfred Howe, 1827-90
ALs, 20 Jan 1873. (91) $100

Terry, Ellen, 1847-1928
Collection of c.100 A Ls s, Ls s, & card, sgd, 1908 to 1923 & [n.d.]; c.200 pp, various sizes. (88) £580

Tesla, Nikola, 1857-1943
Autograph sentiment, sgd, 22 Nov 1904. Byer collection. (90) $950

Tettenborn, Friedrich Karl, Freiherr von, 1778-1845
ALs, [1836]. (88) DM240

Texas
[A varied group of 8 letters & documents relating to Texas, 1833 to 1878, sold at rf on 22 Apr 1989, lot 25, for $350.]
[A letter, 22 May 1836, 3 pp, size not stated, reporting news of Texas & the arrival of Gen. Houston at New Orleans, sold at rf on 5 Dec, lot 68, for $300.]
— FISHER, GEORGE. - Ls, 27 Nov 1843. 2 pp, size not stated. To the Sec of State of Mississippi. Transmitting (not present) a copy of a document regarding the annexation of Texas. (89) $105
— HAYS COUNTY. - Ms, Minutes of Witness Accounts, 1 Mar 1886 to 16 Mar 1889. 184 pp, folio, in lea bdg. (90) $300
— MILLER, THOMAS R. - Ds, 24 Dec 1833. 2 pp, 4to. Deed of one lot of land in Gonzales to William W. Arrington; retained copy. Also sgd by Arrington, George W. Davis, & J. B. Patrick. (91) $500

Texas Rangers
— PRICE, JOHN T. - Ds, 8 June 1846. 1 p, size not stated. Return for forage for 7 horses. Sgd twice. (88) $130

Thacher, Thomas
ALs, 16 Aug 1676. (89) $225

Thackeray, William Makepeace, 1811-63
Autograph sketchbook, pen-&-ink studies & sketches, [n.d.]. 38 pp & blanks, 150mm by 98mm. Half mor gilt, in mor case by Riviere & Son. Koch Foundation. (90) $6,000

Collection of 2 A Ls s & 2 A Ns s, 18 May 1860, 28 Oct & 28 Nov [n.y.], & [n.d.]. Doheny collection. (89) $450
— Collection of ALs & orig drawing, [n.d.]. (91) £90
Series of 5 A Ls s, 10 Mar [1860] to 4 May [1862]. (91) £380
ALs, 20 Mar 1840. (89) £150
— 20 Feb 1851. (90) £300
— [13 May 1858]. (90) £130
— 22 June [1860]. (91) £90
— [27 Mar 1863]. (89) £550
— 4 Feb [n.y.]. (91) £90
— 30 June [n.y.]. Byer collection. (90) $150
— 14 Oct [n.y.]. (91) £90
— [n.d.]. (89) £110
ANs, 5 Nov [c.1846]. (91) $60
Signature, [n.d.]. (89) $80

Thai Manuscripts
Ms, Buddhist text. (89) £400
— Ms, Buddhist text. (91) £700

Thalberg, Sigismund, 1812-71
ALs, 29 Mar 1839. (89) DM460

Thatcher, Margaret. See: Carter, James Earl ("Jimmy") & Thatcher

Thayendanegea, 1742-1807. See: Brant, Joseph

Thayer, Sylvanus, 1785-1872
ADs, 27 June 1820. (91) $130

The Crickets. See: Holly, Buddy & The Crickets

Theodore of Studios, Saint, 759-826
Ms, Catechesis Minor. [Monastery of Chortaites near Thessalonica, c.1100]. 181 leaves, vellum, 330mm by 223mm. Red mor bdg by Birdsall & Son, [1894]. In dark brown ink in a large elegant Greek minuscule by the scribe Ambrosius. With c.70 large decorated initials. Abbey collection. (89) £30,000

Theological Manuscripts
[A collection of 6 theological Mss, comprising vellum vol with notes on the scriptures, 3 June 1621 & later, & 5 calf vols with texts for sermons (1 dated 1660), sold at DN on 26 Apr 1988, lot 234, for $85.]
Ms, 47 sermons for Lent, in Latin.

THEOLOGICAL MANUSCRIPTS

[Eastern France, 15th cent]. 90 leaves, 281mm by 205mm, in contemp bdg of wooden bds rebacked in vellum. In dark brown ink in a regular clear gothic bookhand with cursive features; biblical lemmata in gothic script. With c.50 painted initials. (90) £2,200

— Ms, A comfortable Companion for Afflicted Souls being a threefold discorse collected out of scripture by a woman ..., 1684. (90) £90

— Ms, A Treatise upon Heaven, with revisions & ownership inscr of John Archer, & Mr Jeffery, his sermons upon the Psalms preached at Trinity Church Cambridge, 1619. (88) £170

— Ms, anthology of texts attributed to Petrus Pictor, Innocent III, Petrus Pulka, & others, in Latin & German. [Germany, Bavaria?, 15th cent]. 182 leaves (1 blank), 210mm by 145mm. Modern wooden bds; with sewing guards from a vellum Ms in Hebrew. In gothic cursive bookhands by Georg Hereberstorff & other scribes. (91) £7,000

— Ms, dictionary, comprising expositions of biblical & theological terms, [1st half of 16th cent]. 62 leaves (lacking at least 4), in early 17th-cent blind-stamped calf. With calligraphic initials & penwork. 14th-cent Ms guard strips. (88) £2,100

— Ms, discussion on demons & on the nature of Christ. [Italy, 9th cent]. 4 leaves only, vellum, 280mm by 380mm. Part of 27 lines in a Carolingian minuscule, with c.30 small initials in red. Recovered from a bdg. (90) £2,800

— Ms, Exempla, c.40 moral tales, in Latin. (88) £550

— Ms, Expositio Passionis, with St. Augustine, Meditationes. [Southern Germany, Buxheim Abbey?, c.1475]. 112 leaves (7 blank), 221mm by 158mm. Contemp blindstamped white pigskin over bevelled wooden bds; with sewing guards from a 12th-cent Breviary. By several scribes in cursive bookhands. (91) £20,000

— Ms, extract against Papists in Ireland, & texts for sermons, some dated 22 Oct 1618 & 21 Mar 1623. (88) £170

— Ms, Histoire de la Passion, with La Beaute de l'Ame Raisonnable, & Sermon d'Amour Espirituelle, by Robert Sybole. [Paris, c.1470-85]. 162 leaves, vellum, 295mm by 217mm, in 19th-cent English half russia & watered cloth. In a regular lettre batarde. With small illuminated intials throughout, 20 very large illuminated initials with partial borders, & 10-line historiated initial with 3-quarter illuminated border. (91) £8,500

— Ms, Il Male della Natura, devotional Ms dealing with life & the inevitability of death, inscr to Marino Carracciolo, Prince of Avellino. [Naples, 1 Dec 1752]. 100 leaves, 167mm by 108mm. Contemp red brown mor gilt. With pen-&-ink frontis. (91) DM1,200

— Ms, La Somme des Vices et des Vertus. [France, Paris?, mid-14th cent]. 57 leaves (lacking c.11), vellum, 307mm by 225mm, in def late 18th-cent marbled bds. In brown ink in a gothic bookhand. With c.185 small & 8 large illuminated initials. Dampstained. (88) £1,900

— Ms, monastic sermon collection in Latin, readings from the Church Fathers & Seneca's Liber de Formula honesti viri, [2d half of 15th cent]. (90) £300

— Ms, Prophetia Hussi, excerpts from various authors, mostly in Czech; copied by Matthias Zaborszky, Jan 1708. 515 pp, 138mm by 80mm. Contemp blindstamped lea. (90) DM2,200

— Ms, Pseudo-Bernard, Stimulus Amoris (here ascribed to Henricus de Balma); Speculum Peccatoris; & anr meditative text. [Belgium, 2d half of 15th cent]. 231 leaves (some blanks), vellum, 115mm by 75mm. 19th-cent calf gilt incorporating sides of earlier bdg. In a small well-formed lettre batarde. With small & 4 very large illuminated initials. (90) £5,500

— Ms, sermons by James Durhame & others, c.1651 to 1678. (88) £220

— Ms, sermons, [late 15th cent?]. 107 leaves, 8vo, in later bds. In Latin, with extensive contemp annotations; initials in red. (88) $2,200

— Ms, sermons preached in East Anglia by various preachers, 1656 to 1658;

more than 200 pp, 8vo. (88) £160

— Ms, Sumula seu Breviloquium super Concordia Novi et Veteris Testamenti, preceded by 122 lines of verse prophecies by a follower of Joachim de Fiore. [Italy, c.1460]. 76 leaves & flyleaf, vellum, 280mm by 197mm. Late 18th-cent Italian half sheep bdg. In brown ink in a fine humanist bookhand. With 2 historiated initials with extensions & 67 illusts in wash & tempera. Doheny collection. (88) £105,000

— Ms, The Lay Folks' Catechism, The Abbey of the Holy Ghost, & 8 other theological texts in Middle English prose & verse. [Norfolk, 1st half of 15th cent]. 43 leaves (some lacking), vellum, 193mm by 131mm, in old limp vellum wraps using legal document dated 9 Dec 1659. In brown ink in a small English cursive bookhand by Willelmus Hallys. With c.50 decorated initials. Most texts apparently unrecorded. (90) £75,000

— Ms, Treatise on the Mass, with prayers; in French & Latin. [Northern France, c.1520]. 37 leaves (1 lacking), vellum, 162mm by 98mm, in early 20th-cent red mor bdg. In brown ink in a well-formed lettre batarde. With half-page miniature & full border incorporating coat-of-arms. (90) £1,300

— Ms, Ung Petit Devys et Recreation Devoste, conversations on the stories of the Old Testament, in French. [North Central France, c.1530]. 153 leaves, 188mm by 129mm, in 19th-cent mottled bds. In dark brown ink in a curious calligraphic hand like a sloping disjointed mannered lettre batarde. (90) £1,500
See also: Legal Manuscripts

Theroux, Paul

Typescript, short story, Dengue Fever, sgd at head; Dec 1974. (88) £400

Thielicke, Helmut, 1908-86

Autograph Ms, draft of a sermon, Nov 1942. (88) DM380

Thiess, Frank, 1890-1977

Collection of ALs, Ls, & 3 autograph postcards, sgd, 1924 to 1928. (89) DM480

Thiroux d'Arconville, Marie Genvieve

Autograph Ms, Pensees et Reflexions Morales. (91) £320

Thirty Years' War

— GOETZ, JOBST FRIEDRICH VON. - Ls, 6 Dec 1646. 1 p, folio. To [the pastor at Lembeck]. Insisting that a contribution be paid & threatening military action. (90) DM550

Thoeny, Wilhelm, 1888-1949

Series of 177 A Ls s (6 fragments), 1932 to 1949. About 480 pp, 8vo & 4to. To Eva Hermann. Discussing his life & the times, & covering a wide range of private & professional matters. Including 35 pen-&-ink drawings, (6 colored, 19 on separate leaves). (91) DM74,000

Thoma, Hans, 1839-1924

Autograph Ms, essay, Kukuksuhr, [1913]. (89) DM480

ALs, [9] Aug 1895. (90) DM400

Ls, 14 Oct 1924. (90) DM260

Series of 3 autograph postcards, sgd, 11 to 23 Nov 1919. (91) DM350

Thoma, Ludwig, 1867-1921

ALs, 16 Oct 1902. (88) DM750

— 1 Nov 1906. 4 pp, 8vo. To 'Dearest girl". Reporting about his work & his visitors during his imprisonment. (90) DM1,200

— 10 Feb 1912. (90) DM480

— [n.d.]. (91) DM820

Thomas a Kempis, Saint, 1380-1471

Ms, De Imitatio Christi, in the Italian trans of Lorenzo Giustiniani. [Venice?, c.1460-80]. 75 leaves, vellum, 177mm by 126mm, in vellum over pastebds of c.1800. By 2 scribes in a small slightly sloping bookhand. With small initials throughout & 4 very large illuminated initials (1 with full-length bar border). (91) £4,200

THOMAS

Thomas, Ambroise, 1811-96
Autograph Ms, notes regarding his opera Francoise de Rimini, & other matters; [n.d.] & June 1891. 44 pp, 12mo, in red bds. In pencil. (90) DM1,500

Thomas de Celano, c.1190-1260
Ms, Vita Sancte Clare. (88) £1,000

Thomas, Dylan, 1914-53
Autograph transcript, passages from 3 poems by D. (88) £200
A Ls s (2), 23 Oct & [29 Dec] 1939. 3 pp, 8vo. To Ithel Davies. Explaining his conscientious objection to war. (90) £2,500
ALs, 15 Sept 1950. (90) £700
Proof copy, The Doctor and the Devils, 1st issue of proofs, 1947. In orig wraps, 8vo. Some pencil notes. (88) £1,550
Signature, on oval port by an unknown artist, in red chalk heightened with blue. (88) £180

Thomas, Edward, 1878-1917
Series of 9 A Ls s, 3 Jan to 3 Mar 1896. 60 pp, 8vo. To James Ashcroft Noble. Discussing his literary endeavors, his state of mind, efforts to have his articles pbd, etc. With 28 A Ls s by Noble to Thomas, 1895 & 1896. Bradley Martin sale. (90) $13,000
— Series of 74 A Ls s, 1901 to 1917. Over 100 pp, 4to & 8vo. To Jesse Berridge. About his earliest poems, his prose writing, his military training, etc. Including pencil draft of a poem. (90) £6,800

Thomas, Isaiah, 1750-1831
ALs, 10 June 1791. (91) $350

Thomas, Lorenzo
Photograph, sgd, [n.d.]. (91) $325

Thomas, Ronald Stuart
Series of 30 A Ls s, 2 July 1957 to 23 Feb 1972 & [n.d.]. (88) £320
A Ls s (2), 1964. (90) £300

Thomas, Rufus
Signature, [n.d.]. (89) $50

AMERICAN BOOK PRICES CURRENT

Thompson, William, 1736-81
ALs, 1 Feb 1774. (91) $120

Thomsen, Christian Juergensen, 1788-1865
ALs, 23 July 1852. (91) DM400

Thomson, Charles, 1729-1824
ALs, 28 Mar 1785. 2 pp, folio. Recipient unknown. Sending a report dealing with forged certificates for settling army accounts. (91) $2,000
— 26 May 1788. 2 pp, folio. To William Ellery, Jr. Sarcastic letter denouncing the Anti-Federalists' opposition to ratification of the Constitution. (90) $13,000
Ds, 22 June 1779. (89) $300
— [after 21 Jan 1785]. 7 pp, 4to. Treaty of Fort McIntosh with representatives of the Wyandot, Delaware, Chippewa, & Ottawa nations; clerical copy attested by Thomson. Probably prepared for Indian Agent George Morgan. With related material. (89) $1,800
— 12 July 1787. (90) $300
Autograph check, sgd, 28 Aug 1821. (88) $80

Thomson, Hugh, 1860-1920
Original drawings, (13), to illus Bret Harte's A Ship of '49, ptd in the English Illustrated Magazine, 1885. Macmillan Archives. (90) £500
— Original drawings, (19), to illus D. Macmillan Archives. (90) £800
— Original drawings, (40), to illus Joseph Addison's Days with Sir Roger de Coverley, ptd in the English Illustrated Magazine, 1885 & 1886. In ink. Various sizes. Macmillan Archives. (90) £2,800
— Original drawings, (55), to illus Coridon's Song and other Verses from Various Sources, ptd in the English Illustrated Magazine, 1887 to 1889. In ink; some sgd. Various sizes. Macmillan Archives. (90) £3,000
— Original drawings, (7), ink illusts for the English Illustrated Magazine, June 1884. Macmillan Archives. (90) £550
— Original drawings, (9), to illus Austin Dobson's The Squire at Vauxhall, ptd in the English Illustrated Magazine, Dec 1884. Macmillan Archives. (90) £520

— Original drawings, (9), to illus Basil Field's angling anecdotes, ptd in the English Illustrated Magazine, Oct 1885 to July 1887. Macmillan Archives. (90) £600

Original drawing, man on horseback greeting a party in a coach, to illus Thackeray's The History of Samuel Titmarsh and the Great Hoggarty Diamond, 1902. (88) £650

— Original drawing, "When I went to make a bow, I popt my bald head into Mrs. Frizzle's face", to illus Oliver Goldsmith's She Stoops to Conquer, 1912. 320mm by 255mm. In pen & watercolor. Mtd. (91) $3,600

Thomson, Sir Joseph John, 1856-1940
ALs, 18 June 1908. (88) DM320
— 18 June 1908. (91) DM450

Thomson, Virgil
ALs, 29 Apr 1968. Byer collection. (90) $140

Thomson, William, 1st Baron Kelvin of Largs, 1824-1907
Autograph Ms, regarding the transatlantic cable just completed, sgd & dated 5 Dec 1866. (89) $200

Collection of 64 A Ls s, 8 Ls s & 21 autograph postcards, sgd, 20 May 1888 to 20 Dec 1906. About 323 pp, mostly 8vo & 4to. To David Reid & James Kean. Referring to his inventions & giving instructions for the manufacture of scientific instruments. Including many small diagrams & related material. (89) £4,500

ALs, 28 Apr 1894. (89) DM220
— 17 Nov 1896. (90) DM220
— 17 Nov 1901. (89) DM360

Thoreau, Henry David, 1817-62
ALs, 15 Nov 1850. 1 p, 4to. To [Franklin Forbes]. Suggesting a date for a lecture. Backed. Doheny collection. (89) $4,000
— 2 Feb 1855. 2 pp, 4to. To Franklin B. Sanborn. Regarding a review essay of Walden for the Harvard Magazine, & inviting him to Concord. Barrett collection. (89) $6,500
— 1 Jan[?] 1859. 8 pp, 4to. To Mr. [Harrison G. O.?] Blake. Defending his love for solitude, mentioning Alcott & Emerson, & describing his vision of society. Sgd H.D.T. Koch Foundation. (90) $11,000
— 8 Mar 1857. 2 pp, 8vo. To [Mary] Brown. Sending & explaining a pressed botanical specimen (present). Sang & Middendorf collections. (89) $5,000

ADs, 11 Sept 1854. 1 p, 340mm by 352mm. Survey of woodlot in Concord belonging to Daniel Shattuck. Framed. Middendorf collection. (89) $5,500

Autograph sentiment, sgd, [n.d.]. 5 by 4.5 inches. "How many preparations are necessary before the sour plum begins to sweeten." (91) $5,500
See also: Greeley, Horace

Thornton, Edward Parry, 1811-93
[A collection of c.130 letters & documents to & from colleagues in India, primarily relating to the Indian Mutiny of 1857, with related material, sold at C on 21 June 1989, lot 101, for £1,700 to Maggs.]

Thornton, William, 1759-1828
ANs, [1790s?]. (90) $100

Thorpe, James Francis, 1888-1953
Signature, 2 Feb 1951. (91) $600

Thorpe, Rose Hartwick, 1850-1939
Autograph transcript, Curfew Must Not Ring Tonight, sgd & dated Apr 1932. Doheny collection. (89) $400

Thorvaldsen, Bertel, 1768?-1844
Letter, 24 July 1814. (90) DM700
Ds, 29 Apr 1825. (90) DM600

Thou, Francois Auguste de, 1607-42
Ds, 3 Mar 1637. (89) DM290

Three Stooges
[Their signatures, [1936], size not stated, framed with 4to photograph, sold at wa on 21 Oct 1989, lot 446, for $550.]

[The signatures of Moe Howard, Larry Fine, & Curly Howard, framed with 4to double port, sold at wa on 1 Oct 1988, lot 413, for $600.]

THUBRON

Thubron, Colin
Autograph Ms, book, Mirror to Damascus, [n.d.]; c.350 pp, 4to. (88) £650

Thuemmel, Moritz August von, 1738-1817
ALs, 20 Aug 1775. Kuenzel collection. (88) DM900
— 13 Sept 1781. (91) DM800

Thurber, James, 1894-1961
Original drawing, entitled "Art and Marriage", [n.d.]. 7 by 10.5 inches, on brown paper. In pencil, sgd. On verso sketch of woman's profile. Matted with a Christmas card sgd & inscr on verso, with variant sketch of the Art and Marriage drawing at bottom, dated 1939. Small tear. (88) $1,600
— Original drawing, entitled "Marriage is made in Heaven", [n.d.]. In pen-&-ink; 9 by 14 inches. Sgd & inscr to Charles Laughton. (88) $2,800
— Original drawing, pencil sketch of a husband spurning his wife's advances; [n.d.]. (91) $950
Ls, 31 July 1951. Byer collection. (90) $325

Thurloe, John, 1616-68
ALs, 27 Jan 1652[/53]. (90) £160

Thurlow, Edward, 1st Baron, 1731-1806
ALs, 18 Oct 1784. (91) DM320

Thurn und Taxis, Maximilian Karl, Fuerst von, 1802-71
Ds, 21 Feb to 19 Sept 1831. 27 pp, folio, in red velvet bdg. Family compact, changing the previous compact of 1776 & regulating various financial matters. Sgd twice; also sgd by 6 other members of the family. With related material. (90) DM4,000

Thurston, Samuel R.
Franking signature, [n.d.]. Alexander collection. (90) $230

Thurzo, Gyoergy, 1567-1616
Ls, [1597]. 1 p, folio. To Archduke [later Emperor] Matthias. Discussing hereditary succession & claims in Transylvania. (89) DM3,200

AMERICAN BOOK PRICES CURRENT

Thurzo, Szaniszlo, 1576-1625
Ls, 31 May 1624, 2 pp, folio. To Count Meggau. Discussing an amnesty after a rebellion in Hungary, territorial questions, etc. (89) DM1,600

Thwaites, Christine
Original drawings, (3), to illus The Wind in the Willows for a set of Royal Doulton collectors plates, [n.d.]. (89) £220
— Original drawings, (4), to illus The Wind in the Willows for a set of Royal Doulton collectors plates, [n.d.]. (89) £350
— Original drawings, (4), to illus The Owl and the Pussycat for a set of Royal Doulton collectors plates, [available 1989]. (89) £420

Thyssen, August, 1842-1926
Series of 7 A Ls s, 23 May to 18 Sept 1915. 20 pp, 8vo. To Gen. Otto von Lauenstein & his wife. Regarding invitations, commenting about the war & expressing his hope for territorial acquisitions. (90) DM3,200

Tibet
[2 documents issued by the 7th Dalai Lama & Pho-lha-nas bSod-nams-stobs-rgyas as representative of temporal authority, privileges granting free preaching of the Christian faith in Tibet, 1741, on 2 pieces of yellow silk, size not stated, in 19th-cent box, sold at S on 22 Nov 1988, lot 140, for £24,000 to Rosenthal.]

Tieck, Dorothea, 1799-1841. See: Tieck, Ludwig & Tieck

Tieck, Friedrich, 1776-1851
ALs, 18 Mar 1827. (91) DM360

Tieck, Ludwig, 1773-1853
Autograph Ms, poem, Einsamkeit; [pbd 1802]. (90) £1,000
— Autograph Ms, prologue to his comedy Kaiser Octavianus, [1804]. 2 pp, 4to. 40 lines, 2 differing from ptd version. (91) DM2,500
ALs, 1839. (89) £500
— 20 Sept 1842. (88) DM480
— 14 May 1846. (89) DM420
— 23 Apr 1847. (89) DM1,000
— 13 Aug 1850. (88) DM440

— [n.d.]. (90) DM400

**Tieck, Ludwig, 1773-1853 —&
Tieck, Dorothea, 1799-1841**
[An autograph Ms trans of the 1st two of Shakespeare's sonnets by Ludwig Tieck, 2 pp, 4to, tipped into a vol containing autograph translations of 137 Shakespeare sonnets by Dorothea Tieck, 186 pp, 8vo, in contemp bds, [c.1825], sold at C on 6 Dec 1989, lot 343, for £7,000 to Quaritch.]

Tiedge, Christoph August, 1752-1841
ALs, 16 Sept 1803. (91) DM300
— 28 May 1805. Albrecht collection. (91) SF1,000

Tiffany, Louis Comfort, 1848-1933
Original drawing, Lily Pach Motife 3 in. (91) $1,000

Tilden, William Tatem ("Big Bill"), 1893-1953
Signature, [10 Oct 1930]. (91) $100

Tilly, Johann Tserclaes, Graf von, 1559-1632
Ls, 20 June 1624. (88) DM650
— 10 July 1624. 2 pp, folio. To Philipp Adolf von Ehrenberg, Bishop of Wuerzburg. Responding indignantly to an inquiry concerning soldiers' pay. (89) DM2,200
— 12 Oct 1625. 1 p, folio. To Johann Aldringen. Suggesting that he meet with Wallenstein at the village of Eyersshausen. (91) DM1,400
— 14 Oct 1625. 1 p, folio. To the magistrate of Hildesheim. Ordering bread for the arrival of his army. (88) DM1,700
— 28 Sept 1626. 1 p, folio. To the magistracy at Marburg. Requesting their assistance for Lorenzo de Medici. (90) DM1,300
— 5 Apr 1627. 1 p, folio. To the magistracy at Hildesheim. Concerning the storage of grain bought for his army. (90) DM3,600
— 4 Sept 1631. 1 p, folio. To the mayor & magistracy of Lingen. Declining to reduce requisitions. (89) DM1,800
Ds, 7 Dec 1625. 1 p, folio. Passport for Liborius & Friedrich von Wrisberg. Partly ptd. (89) DM1,600
— 3 Dec 1626. 1 p, folio. Letter of protection for Gambach & other villages in Hesse. (90) DM1,100

Tilney, Frederick C.
Original drawings, (16), to illus the Fables of Aesop & of La Fontaine, 1913. Archives of J. M. Dent & Son. (90) £520

Timlin, William M.
Original drawing, large building, to illus The unfinished Palace in Timlin's The Ship that Sailed to Mars, 1923. In watercolor; sgd. 221mm by 270mm. Framed. (88) £2,000

Tinbergen, Jan
Autograph Ms, essay, The Relevance of Economic Policy and Informatics to Health Care, [n.d.]. (90) DM260
— Autograph Ms, review of Charles E. (89) DM220

Tinworth, George, 1843-1913
ALs, 16 June 1890. (90) £150

Tippett, Sir Michael
Autograph music, sketches for an unspecified work; [n.d.]. (90) DM450

Tirol
— PETLINER, DOMENICUS. - Document, 27 July 1681. 1 p, folio. Bond acknowledging feudal rights of the heirs of Matthias Mayr von Mayrheim in a farm acquired by him. (90) DM320

Tirolean Uprising, 1809
— GEN. SEVEROLI, COMTE. - Ls, 20 Dec 1809. 3 pp, 4to. To [Gen. Baraguay d'Hilliers, Commander of the French troops in Tirol]. Requesting instructions concerning captive rebels. With related material. (88) DM320
— MOREAU, GEN. JEAN CLAUDE. - Ls, 4 Dec 1809. 2 pp, folio. To Gen. Baraguay d'Hilliers, Commander of the French troops in Tirol. Sending papers found on a prisoner & informing him about arrests. (88) DM380

Tirpitz, Alfred von, 1849-1930
A Ls s (2), 5 Mar & 23 Apr 1908. 6 pp, 8vo. To Heinrich Wiegand. About the recent loss of a ship of the North German Lloyd off the coast of Sardinia. (91) DM2,500

ALs, 14 Apr 1915. 4 pp, 8vo. To his son, a prisoner of war in England. Assuring him that the German people remain unshaken. Sgd Dein Vater. (90) DM1,900

Ls s (2), 26 Feb & 9 Apr 1925. (88) DM450

Tischbein, Johann Heinrich Wilhelm, 1751-1829
ALs, 3 Aug 1806. 3 pp, 4to. To his brother Johann Heinrich Tischbein. Reporting about his travels in Holstein. Seal tear. (89) DM1,900

— 28 May 1807. 1 p, 4to. To A. H. F. Schlichtegroll. Regretting his early departure & introducing Arthur Schopenhauer. (88) DM1,800

Tischendorf, Konstantin von, 1815-74
ALs, 4 Oct 1856. (90) DM320
— 26 Nov 1860. (91) DM320

Titanic Disaster
Ms, Certificate of Clearance of the ship at Queenstown, 11 Apr 1912; official Board of Trade copy. 1 p, folio, on blue paper. Ptd with Ms insertions. Related letter by W. D. Harbinson mtd on verso. Framed. (88) £1,700

Proof copy, transcript of hearings on the loss of the Titanic, 3 May to 3 July 1912; sgd & marked by W. (89) £750

— BUTTERWORTH, JACK. - ALs, 12 Apr 1912. Length not stated. To his "Darling Girl". Written on board the ship at Queenstown; describing near-accident with the New York. (88) £600

— JOHNSTON FAMILY. - A group of letters relating to the Johnston family, steerage passengers on the Titanic, 1912, 27 pp, with newscuttings, sold at S on 18 July 1991, lot 441, for £900 to Fine Art Society. 91

— TAYLOR, LEONARD. - 3 A Ls s & postcard sgd, [n.d.] & 9 Apr 1912. 10 pp, 8vo. To his parents. Describing conditions on board. Postcard showing Titanic. (88) £2,200

— WOOLNER, HUGH. - ALs, 10 Apr 1912, 4 pp, 8vo, on Titanic letterhead. To Kit. Describing the ship & giving an account & sketch of the near-collison at Southampton. With newspaper cuttings. (91) £2,600

Tobacco
[A group of 3 official documents concerning the importation of tobacco & the tobacco monopoly in England, June 1634 to 1636, 4 pp, various sizes, sold at S on 20 July 1989, lot 440, for £600 to Shapero.]

Tobin, James
Autograph Ms, essay dealing with the economical development of the United States, draft; sgd later & dated Aug 1982. (90) DM210

Tocqueville, Alexis de, 1805-59
ALs, 29 July 1834. (89) $350
— 15 July 1855. (90) DM290
— [n.d.]. (90) DM330

Togo, Heihachiro, Marquis, 1847-1934
Photograph, sgd, [n.d.]. (89) $500

Toklas, Alice B.
Collection of 36 A Ls s & 7 autograph postcards, sgd, 1952-63. About 45 pp, 8vo & 12mo. To Lloyd Frankenberg & his wife, Loren Maciver. (89) $4,800

Toler, Sidney, 1874-1947
Ds, 18 Jan 1946. (91) $800

Tolkien, John Ronald Reuel, 1892-1973
Collection of 7 A Ls s & Ls, 1954 to 1959. 16 pp, mostly 8vo. To Patricia Kirke. About The Lord of the Rings, his Catholicism, his opinions on Oxford, etc. (91) £2,600

A Ls s (2), 2 & 19 May 1955. (91) £700
ALs, 11 Mar 1949. (91) £1,000
— 4 Dec 1963. (90) £800
— 19 Nov 1968. (88) £200

Ls, [25 Apr 1954]. 7 pp, 4to. To Naomi Mitchison. Giving a detailed description of the Westron & Elvish languages used in The Lord of the Rings. With related material. (89) £3,200

— 22 June 1957. (90) $800

Autograph postcard, sgd, 7 July 1946. (88) £200

Toller, Ernst, 1893-1939
Collection of ALs & Ls, 16 Jan 1921 & 22 Apr 1930. (90) DM850
Ls s (2), 3 & 13 Dec 1934. (91) DM1,000

Tolstoy, Leo, 1828-1910
Ms, fragment (p 46) from a philosophical treatise, with extensive autograph revisions; [n.d.]. 1 p, 4to. (89) DM8,500
ALs, 2 Feb [1881?]. 1 p, 8vo. To the Ed of the Boersenblatt fuer den Deutschen Buchhandel. Sending a statement for print. (90) DM1,500
— 15 Nov 1893. 2 pp, 8vo. To [Sophie Behr]. Sending an essay for trans. (88) DM2,800
— 17 Oct 1895. 2 pp, 8vo. Recipient unnamed. Commenting on the labor movement & the "whole social reformation movement". In English. (91) £1,600
— 25 Nov [1898]. 3 pp, 8vo. To Aylmer Maude. Discussing the trans of his works into English. In limp brown mor gilt bdg with a trans & engraved port. Barrett collection. (89) $3,500
— 24 Mar / 5 Apr 1892. 1 p, 8vo. To Francis Garrison. Thanking for money. In English. (89) DM1,300
— 6 Nov 1908. 4 pp, 8vo (torn from notebook?). To Roman Stanislavovich. Warning him that being "in love" is a harmful emotion & not the same as love. With English trans. (90) £3,200
— 20 May 1910. 2 pp, 8vo. To [Menarul Tsapuzeria]. Discussing his views on Christianity & attitudes to life. In French. (90) £2,000
Ls, 4/16 Nov 1891. 4 pp, 8vo. To [T. Fisher Unwin?]. About measures to alleviate the famine in Russia. In English; with autograph subscription. (88) £1,100
ANs, 20 Mar/1 Apr [n.y.]. (89) $1,000
Ns, 20 July 1910. (91) £200
Photograph, sgd, [n.d.]. Postcard. (91) DM1,200
Ptd photograph, sgd, [n.d.]. Postcard. Mtd. (91) DM1,250
Signature, July 1896. (89) DM580
— Anr, 23 May 1908. (88) DM460

Tomasek, Vaclav Jan, 1774-1850
ALs, 5 Jan 1813. (88) DM600

Toombs, Robert Augustus, 1810-85
ALs, 4 Sept 1854. (88) $90
Franking signature, [24 June n.y.]. Alexander collection. (90) $85

Torberg, Friedrich, 1908-79
Collection of ALs & 4 Ls s, 24 Feb 1946 to 9 Nov 1947. (88) DM620
ALs, Nov 1977. (90) DM200
Series of 4 Ls s, 28 Mar to 5 May 1974. (90) DM300

Torelli, Giuseppe, 1721-81
Collection of 5 A Ls s & autograph Ms, [n.d.]. Phillipps MS 2911, vol 3. (88) £50

Toscanini, Arturo, 1867-1957
ALs, 20 Mar 1950. (90) DM460
Autograph quotation, sgd, 10 Feb 1942. (88) $300
Autograph sentiment, referring to popular taste in music, 16 Apr 1908. (91) $600
Concert program, 8th concert in series at Carnegie Hall for The Philharmonic Society of NY, sgd & dated 4 Feb 1928. (90) $130
Photograph, sgd & inscr, 16 Dec 1930. (90) $750
Photograph, [n.d.]. (90) $250
Ptd photograph, 28 Apr 1936. (88) $300
— Anr, [n.d.]. (91) $130
Signature, [n.d.], on reproduction of a charcoal port by Lupas, 3.5 by 5.5 inches. (90) $190
— Ahrens, Dorothy A. - Orig drawing, pencil port of Toscanini, 1950. 197mm by 267mm. Bust view, sgd by Toscanini. (91) $400

Toulouse-Lautrec, Henri de, 1864-1901
Autograph Ms, description of a bohemian wedding, [n.d.]. 2 pp, 4to. With extensive autograph corrections & pen-&-ink sketches of cattle, soldiers & women. (89) £4,500
— Autograph Ms, Recit de la premiere croisade, [n.d.]. 4 pp, 4to. Including 11 small pen-&-ink sketches. (88) DM10,500
ALs, [c.1892-94]. 2 pp, 8vo. To the art pbr Marty. Complimenting him on the ptg of drawings, particularly of Yvette

TOULOUSE-LAUTREC

Guilbert. In purple ink. (88) £1,400
— [27 June 1894]. 4 pp, 8vo. To his mother. Commenting about the presidential election & the delay in the ptg of his lithographs. Sgd H. (90) DM6,500
— [n.d.]. 2 pp, 12mo (lettercard). To the art dealer Portier. Asking for 100 francs to be given to bearer & requesting an account. (90) DM2,500
— WEBER, LOUISE ("LA GOULUE"). - Autograph postcard, 3 Jan 1925. To Mme Seuse. Informing her about a new program at the Moulin [Rouge]. (91) DM950

Townsend, F. H.
Original drawings, (9), to illus Rudyard Kipling's They, 1905. Macmillan Archives. (90) £380

Tracy, Spencer, 1900-67
Ls, 24 Feb 1956. (91) $100

Trakl, Georg, 1887-1914
Autograph Ms, poem, Entlang; draft, in pencil. On verso of postcard addressed to him by the pbr of Die Fackel, 6 Aug 1913, regarding a meeting with Karl Kraus. (90) £3,200

Travel
Ms, artist's travel journal through the Low Countries, 4 to 11 Sept 1793. About 130 pp, 4to, in contemp vellum bdg. Including over 25 annotated drawings after Rubens, Van Dyke & others, in pen, pencil & ink wash. Describing Rubens's paintings in Antwerp before their removal by French troops. (90) £5,500
— Ms, journal of an English gentleman on the Continent, 1 May to 24 Sept [1700]; c.210 pp, 8vo, lacking covers. (88) £850
— Ms, Souvenirs de Voyages 1875 - 1877. (89) £300
— KENNEDY, LANGFORD. - Ms, Diary of a Journey through Holland, Belgium, Germany, Switzerland, Italy, Savoy and France, 1832 & 1833. 2,100 pp, 8vo, in 6 half mor vols. (89) £100
— MARSH, JOHN HENRY. - Ms, Journal of a Tour through England & Scotland to the Western Isles, 1830. 70 pp, 4to, in contemp half calf. Illus with 40 engravings, pencil sketch & 2 watercolors. (89) £280
— PARKINSON, JOHN. - Autograph Ms, diaries of his tours of Russia, Northern Europe, Switzerland, The Netherlands & parts of England, 1781 to 1794. About 1,700 pp, 4to, in 10 early 19th-cent quarter calf vols. (90) £3,200

Traven, B., Pseud., 1890?-1969
[A large collection of autograph Mss, typescripts, letters addressed to him, & further material related to Ret Marut/B. Traven, 1901 to 1919, sold at HN on 25 May 1989, lot 2962, for DM62,000.]

Travies, Edouard, 1809-65
[Lots 363 to 392 of the Jeanson sale on 16 June 1988 at SM consisted of watercolor over pencil drawings by travies, some made in connection with his Les Oiseaux Les Plus Remarquables....]

Trcka, Adam Erdmann, Count, 1599-1634
ALs, 1 June [1633]. 1 p, folio. To Gen. Hans Georg von Arnim. Writing upon Wallenstein's orders, & requesting safe-conduct for meeting with him. (89) DM8,000

Treitschke, Friedrich, 1776-1842
ALs, 4 Dec 1834. (89) DM400

Treitschke, Heinrich von, 1834-96
ALs, 22 June 1857. (91) DM280
— 1 Oct 1864. (88) DM220
— 22 June 1870. (90) DM240

Trelawney, Edward John, 1792-1881
Series of 3 A Ls s, 19 Mar to June 1875. 12 pp, 8vo. To Clare Clairmont. About Shelley & her Shelley letters. With related material. (88) £1,800
ALs, 27 Aug 1877. (91) £170

Trenholm, George Alfred, 1807-76
Ls, 9 Jan 1865. (91) $750

Tresilian, Stuart
Original drawings, (36), to illus Mazo de la Roche's The Sacred Bullock, 1939. Macmillan Archives. (90) £600
— Original drawings, (6), dust jacket designs for Enid Blyton's The Island of Adventure & its 5 sequels, 1944 to

1950. In ink & watercolor or gouache; sgd. Average size 340mm by 510mm. Macmillan Archives. (90) £3,800
— Original drawings, (7), to illus Rudyard Kipling's Animal Stories, 1932. In watercolor; sgd. 325mm by 235mm. Macmillan Archives. (90) £2,600

Trevelyan, George Otto, Sir, 1838-1928.
See: Disraeli, Benjamin

Troekes, Heinz
Series of 3 A Ls s, 29 Feb to 9 July 1952. (90) DM440

Trollope, Anthony, 1815-82
Autograph Ms, travel account, North America, 1862. 1,166 pp & tp, 4to, in 2 red mor vols by Riviere & Son. With numerous revisions. Ptr's copy. (90) $75,000
Series of 6 A Ls s, 4 May 1865 to 28 Oct [1879]. (91) £550
ALs, 20 Feb 1873. 2 pp, 8vo. To an unnamed lady. About his plans to move house. With related material. (90) DM1,100
— 7 June 1878. (91) £440
— 22 Sept 1878. 8 pp, 8vo. To Mr. Buxton. Defending opinions expressed in his book South Africa. (91) £1,400
— 10 May 1881. (90) £800

Trommsdorff, Johann Bartholomaeus, 1770-1837
Autograph Ms, 12 Oct 1834. (88) DM240

Trotsky, Leon (Lev Davydovich Bronstein), 1879-1940
Ls, 29 Dec 1929. (88) £800

Trotsky, Leon (Lev Davydovich Bronstein), 1879-1940
Typescript, address "To the Conference of the Young People's Socialist League", 24 July 1938. 2 pp, 4to. Sgd. (89) DM5,500
ALs, Jan 1918. 1 p, 4to. To Comrades Lenin & Stalin. Outlining the formula which was later adopted at the peace negotiations at Brest-Litovsk. (90) $25,000
Ls, 29 Dec 1929. (89) £480
— 12 Apr 1933. 1 p, 4to. To [Max Eastman]. Hoping for permission from American authorities for "an incognito journey in America." (89) DM2,800
— 24 Nov 1935. (88) £520
— 18 July 1938. (91) £700
Ds, 27 Oct 1917. 1 p, folio. Letter of protection for Vera Nikolajevna Machrova; partly ptd. (90) DM4,000
— 2 Apr 1929. 4 pp, folio. Contract with the pbr Carl Reissner, in Reissner's hand. Sgd twice. In German. (90) DM2,000
Photograph, sgd & inscr, 3 Apr 1929. Postcard size. Inscr to Harry Schumann on verso, in German. With inscr in Cyrillic, 18 July 1928, crossed out. (90) DM1,700
Signature, 6 Dec 1925. On ptd invitation to the inauguration of a power plant, 4 pp, 8vo. Also sgd by 3 others. (90) DM1,400

Trudeau, Gary B.
Signature, [n.d.]. (90) $55

Truman, Bess Wallace
A Ls s (2), [15 & 17 Oct 1948]. (88) $175
Ls, 5 July 1951. (90) $200

Truman, Harry S., 1884-1972
[2 checks, accomplished & sgd, 3 July 1925, 12mo, drawn on the City Bank of Kansas City, sold at sg on 25 Oct 1988, lot 227, for $375.]
[2 checks, accomplished & sgd, 3 July & 4 Aug 1925, 12mo, drawn on the City Bank of Kansas City, sold at sg on 25 Oct 1988, lot 228, for $375.]
[2 checks sgd as Commissioner of Jackson County, Missouri, 30 Mar & 20 Apr 1934, with cancellation affecting signatures, sold at wa on 1 Oct 1988, lot 207, for $260.]
[2 checks, sgd as judge, 30 Mar & 4 Apr 1934, 90mm by 204mm, drawn on the treasrer of Jackson County, Missouri, with bust engraving, sgd & inscr, 29 Oct [19]59, sold at sg on 25 Oct 1988, lot 229, for $400.]
[A typescript of his oath of office, 12 Apr 1945, 1 p, 5 by 6 inches, sgd, matted with a photograph of the ceremony, sold at Dar on 13 June 1991, lot 366, for $1,000.]
[A Jubilee Program, 14 Apr 1965, 4 leaves, 4to, sgd & inscr by Truman, sold at sg on 22 Oct, lot 264, for $200.]

TRUMAN

Typescript (duplicated), mimeographed Message to Congress, 7 Jan 1953. (90) $550

ALs, 1 July 1962. 1 p, size not stated. To Robert Lovett. Remembering that they "went through a lot of hell together". File holes. (91) $1,800

Collection of 2 Ls s & photograph, sgd, 10 Dec 1958, 14 Dec 1959 & 29 May 1946. (90) $300

Series of 6 Ls s, 21 Jan 1946 to 30 Apr 1951. 6 pp, 4to. To Harry H. Woodring. Responding to communications on various political issues. (89) $3,750

Ls s (2), 21 Jan 1935 & [n.d.]. (88) $200

— Ls s (2), 28 Feb 1945 & 4 Mar 1946. 2 pp, 4to. To Mrs. Ollie Hafner, responding to a letter regarding her son. To Gov. Dwight H. Green, inviting him to a conference on traffic safety. (89) $2,250

— Ls s (2), 7 Oct 1949 & 1 Dec 1951. (90) $450

Ls, 24 Jan 1945. (91) $485

— 12 Apr 1945. 1 p, 4to. To J. F. T. O'Connor. Thanking for comments on a speech. Including 3-line autograph postscript, [13 Apr 1945], referring to Roosevelt's death. Explanatory note by recipient at bottom. (91) $22,000

— 26 Apr 1945. (90) $250
— 2 May 1945. (91) $600
— 8 May 1945. (88) $550
— 9 May 1945. (90) $275
— 9 May 1945. Sang collection. (91) $800
— 28 June 1946. 1 p, 4to. To Emil Hurja. Thanking for a historical document & commenting on [Harold] Ickes. (91) $7,000
— 28 Mar 1947. Sang collection. (91) $600
— 9 Feb 1948. 1 p, 4to. To Frank Buchanan. Regarding the United Nations & the settlement of the Palestinian question. Rosenbloom collection. (88) $3,250
— 8 Sept 1948. (88) $325
— 12 Nov 1948. (91) $350
— 23 Nov 1948. Byer collection. (90) $450
— 12 May 1949. (89) $550
— 14 Sept 1949. (88) $350
— 21 Sept 1949. (89) $210
— 5 June 1950. (89) $250

AMERICAN BOOK PRICES CURRENT

— 9 Nov 1950. (90) $275
— 20 Nov 1950. 1 p, 4to. To Dwight R. G. Palmer. Sending a message to be read at a National Democratic Dinner in NY. Was mtd. (88) $2,900
— 25 July 1951. (89) $600
— 9 Nov 1951. (91) $400
— 22 Nov 1951. (90) $450
— 6 Mar 1952. (91) $250
— 6 June 1952. Byer collection. (90) $425
— 14 Nov 1952. (91) $300
— 16 Dec 1952. 1 p, 4to. To Chester Lang. Commenting about the end of his Presidential term. With related material. (88) $2,900
— 14 Jan 1953. (90) $350
— 20 Jan 1953. 1 p, 4to. To Robert V. Fleming. On his last day in office, returning some bank forms. (91) $8,000
— 27 Feb 1953. (88) $250
— 14 Mar 1953. (88) £110
— 21 Apr 1953. (88) $250
— 30 Oct 1953. (91) $130
— 27 Nov 1953. (91) $425
— 24 May 1955. (91) $280
— 20 Dec 1955. 1 p, 4to. To Leonard Lyons. Concerning his daughter's appearance on a radio program. With autograph postscript. (89) $1,200
— 7 Apr 1956. 1 p, 4to. To Harry Hansen. Indicating the proper numbering of Presidential terms. (90) $1,700
— 11 July 1956. (88) $60
— 2 Mar 1959. Alexander collection. (90) $100
— 24 Sept 1959. (89) $140
— 23 May 1960. (91) $100
— 11 Apr 1961. (90) $130
— 11 Apr 1962. (90) $130
— 27 Apr 1962. (90) $90
— 27 Nov 1962. 1 p, 4to. To Howard J. McGrath. Contents not stated. With autograph postscript & envelope with franking signature. (89) $1,800
— 7 Oct 1965. (88) $90
— 28 Oct 1970. (91) $500

ANs, Mar 1951. (90) $500

Series of 6 Ns s, 1965 to 1970. (90) $600

Ds, 12 Dec 1943. (88) $150
— 7 Feb 1946. (88) $200
— 7 June 1946. Byer collection. (90) $750

— 2 Feb 1949. (91) $350
— 27 Sept 1949. (91) $800
— [c.1949-50]. 1 p, 280mm by 355mm. As President of the American National Red Cross, citation awarded to Dwight D. Eisenhower for "service during the 1949 Fund Campaign". (90) $1,600

Check, sgd, 3 Oct 1924. (88) $130
— Anr, sgd, 28 Apr 1925. (90) $100
— Anr, sgd, 21 Aug 1925. (88) $140
— Anr, sgd, 2 Apr 1934. (90) $250
Group photograph, 24 Aug 1949. (91) $170
Photograph, sgd, [n.d.]. 8 by 10 inches. Photographic reproduction of news picture showing Truman holding up a copy of the Chicago Daily Tribune with headline "Dewey Defeats Truman", Nov 1948. (89) $1,600
— Anr, 11 Dec [19]68. (91) $130
— Anr, [n.d.]. (88) DM380
Photograph, sgd & inscr, 15 Apr 1952. (88) $120
— Anr, showing Truman holding 3 Nov 1948 issue of Chicago Daily Tribune with headline "Dewey Defeats Truman"; dated 14 June [19]60 & inscr "President to the Tribune for 24 hours". 4to. (89) $13,000
— Anr, 27 Jan [19]64. (89) $175
— Anr, [n.d.]. (91) £140
— Anr, [n.d.]. (90) $600
— Anr, [n.d.]. (89) $200
— Anr, [n.d.]. (88) $85
— Anr, [n.d.]. (88) $180
— Anr, [n.d.]. (90) $270
Ptd photograph, 3 Jan 1961. (91) $250
Signature, [n.d.]. (91) $75
White House card, sgd & inscr to Kenneth Lee Geist, 9 May [19]47. (89) $240
— Anr, sgd, [n.d.]. (90) $260
See also: Kennedy, John F. & Truman

Trumbull, John, 1756-1843
ALs, 20 Mar 1823. (89) $70
ADs, [c.1822]. 1 p, 160mm by 305mm. Account with the US government for 3 historical paintings [now in the Capitol Rotunda]. (91) $8,500

Trumbull, Jonathan, 1710-85
ALs, 25/26 Jan 1777. 2 pp, folio. To Gov. Nicholas Cooke. Reporting about Washington's victories at Trenton & Princeton. Middendorf collection. (89) $4,500
Ds, 24 Apr 1782. (89) $60
Franking signature, [25 Jan 1777]. Alexander collection. (90) $675

Trumbull, Jonathan, 1740-1809
ALs, 22 Mar 1802. (91) $200

Trumbull, Sir William, 1639-1716
Autograph Ms (2), legal commonplace books, in Latin & English; [late 17th cent]. (91) £600
Autograph Ms, legal commonplace book, in Latin & English, with inserted documents & letters, partly in other hands; [late 17th cent]. 1400 pp, folio, in contemp reversed calf. (91) £3,400

Truxtun, Thomas, 1755-1822
Series of 16 A Ls s, 13 Jan to 27 July 1807. 1 to 4 pp, 4to. To Commodore Thomas Tingey. Disclaiming rumours of being an associate of Aaron Burr. With contemp copy of a letter from Truxton to Charles Biddle, 11 July 1807. (88) $5,500
ALs, 9 July 1808. Munson collection. (90) $750

Tschechowa, Olga, 1897-1980
Collection of 4 A Ls s & 4 autograph postcards, sgd, 29 Apr 1922 to 16 Sept 1924. (90) DM450

Tsvetayeva, Marina Ivanovna, 1892-1941
Series of 4 A Ls s, 9 Jan to 5 Feb 1940. 14 pp, 4to & 8vo. To Liudmila Vassilievna Veprizkaia. Highly expressive personal letters. (91) DM4,000

Tucholsky, Kurt, 1890-1935
Ls, 1 Apr 1926. 1 p, 4to. To Willy Haas. Sending a review for the journal Literarische Welt. File holes torn. (88) DM1,400

Tucker, John F., of New Bedford
Autograph Ms, Notes of a Traveler. [1860s]. About 140 pp, folio, loose in half cloth. About travels to the Azores; & other places; includes 29 pp of Nantucket genealogy. (91) $1,300

Tuerckheim, Anna Elisabeth von, 1758-1817
ALs, 11 July 1799. 1 p, 4to. To her brother Friedrich Schoenemann. Expressing relief about her son's recovery from an illness, & conveying a request by her daughter. Albrecht collection. (91) SF2,000

Tuerheim, Ulrich von. See: Ulrich von Tuerheim

Tunnicliffe, Charles Frederick, 1901-79
Original drawing, racehorses in training, to illus his own & Sidney Rogerson's Both Sides of the Road, 1949. (90) £200

Tupac Amaru (Jose Gabriel Condorcanqui), 1742?-81
Ls, 22 Dec 1779. 3 pp, folio. To Don Antonio de Arriaga. As leader of the towns in the province of Tinta, arguing for permission to build mills for the Indians. Sgd ThupaAmaru Inga. In an official file of documents relating to the dispute about mill rights, 16th cent to 1780, c.33 pp in all, in modern marbled bds. (88) £3,500

Turenne, Henri de la Tour d'Auvergne, Vicomte de, 1611-75
Autograph Ms, discussion of the relationship of Spain & Portugal, & French policy, [n.d.]. (88) £250
ALs, 7 July 1654. (90) DM650
— [n.d.]. (89) DM270
Ds, 15 Dec 1648. (88) DM550

Turgenev, Ivan, 1818-83
ALs, 28 Mar 1865. 4 pp, 8vo. To Princess Troubetskoy. Criticizing Tolstoy's War and Peace. In French. Koch Foundation. (90) $5,500
— 5 Aug 1865. 1 p, 8vo. To Nikolai Vasilevich Shtcherban. Inviting him for breakfast after his arrival in Paris. (90) DM1,300
— 15 Aug 1866. (91) DM750
— 18 June 1869. (89) £900
— 6 May 1871. (88) DM540
— [n.d.]. (89) DM440
— 12 Feb 1877. (89) £350
— 31 Aug 1878. 2 pp, 8vo. To the pbr Henry Holt. About missing shipments of books & the success of his works outside Russia. In English. (89) DM2,200
— 25 Oct [18]79. (91) DM750
— 22 Feb [18]81. (88) £180
— [n.d.]. 3 pp, 8vo. Recipient unnamed. Commenting on recipient's literary production. In French. (91) DM1,600
ANs, 1 Nov [18]81. (89) £150

Turkey
Ms, Memoire touchant les revenues et les depenses de l'Empire Ottoman..., sgd Girardin & dated 15 Apr 1688. 166 pp, folio, in brown calf with the arms of Louis XV. (88) FF30,000

Turkish Manuscripts
Ms, Baza'at al-Mubtadi. (90) £100
— Ms, Berat of Sultan Abdul-Majid I. (88) £850
— Ms, Berat of Sultan Abdulhamid II. [Constantinople, A.H.1303/A.D.1885]. 119cm by 79cm. In black & gold Celi diwani script; tughra in gold. Repaired; framed. (88) £2,600
— Ms, Berat of Sultan Mustafa III, issued to Niccolo Franco. (91) £1,000
— Ms, calligraphy. (91) £800
— Ms, calligraphy. (91) £850
— Ms, Firman of Sultan 'Abd al-Hamid I (Nishan-i Alishan). (88) £600
— Ms, Firman of Sultan 'Abd al-Hamid I (Nishan-i Alishan). (88) £550
— Ms, Hilyeh. [Ottoman, late 17th cent]. 1 p, 570mm by 360mm. In elegant naskhi script by Usman. Richly decorated in colors & gold. Repaired. (91) £3,200
— Ms, Hilyeh. [Ottoman, 18th cent]. 710mm by 360mm. Richly illuminated, with diagrams incorporating decoupee calligraphy in gold. In def frame. (91) £1,800
— Ms, horoscope of Sultan Abdul-Hamid II. (90) £240
— Ms, Maktubat Imam Ahmed al-Faruqi as Saramandi. [Ottoman, A.H.1163/A.D.1749]. 2 vols, 297 & 276 leaves (including blanks), 335mm by 205mm, in red mor gilt. In nasta'liq script. With 2 illuminated headpieces each. (91) £1,200
— Ms, Muqadamat-i Ibn Khaldun. (89) £400
— Ms, Nishan & Tughra of Sultan Mus-

tafa III. [Ottoman, A.D.1757-58]. 1 p, 109.2cm by 52cm. Grant of a garden to Saliha Sultan. In red & gold diwani script on gilt-sprinkled buff paper; tughra in gold. Lacking last lines. (89) £3,200
— Ms, Safinat al-Fatawi. (90) £300
— Ms, Seyahatnama. (91) £850
— Ms, survey of history. (90) DM900
— Ms, Tawarikh-i Khayr-ud-Din Pasha. (89) £900
— Ms, Tughra & Firman of Sultan 'Abd al-Aziz (Nishan-i Alishan). [Constantinople, A.H.1290/A.D.1873]. 1 p, 66cm by 45cm. Granting Sharif Abdilah Pasha a decoration. In gold & black diwani script. Framed. (88) £1,200
— Ms, Tughra & Firman of Sultan 'Abd al-Hamid II (Nishan-i Alishan). (88) £750
— Ms, Tuhfat al-Kibar fi Asfar al-Bihar. [Ottoman, A.H.1067/A.D.1656]. 58 leaves, 275mm by 172mm. Worn brown mor gilt bdg. In diwani script by Mustafa, known as Hajji Khalifah. With illuminated headpiece. (89) £1,900
— Ms, waqffiyah of al-Sayyid Khalil 'Abduh. (90) £250
— Ms, Waqfnameh [Deed of Endowment] & tughra of Muhammad Shah bin Ibrahim Khan. (89) £280
— ABDUL-HAQ MULLA. - Tarikh-i Liva. [Ottoman, A.H.1248/A.D.1832]. 99 leaves, 240mm by 152mm. Contemp red mor gilt. In diwani script. With illuminated headpiece. Account of Sultan Mahmud's residence in military quarters during the Russian war, 1828 to 1830. (89) £320
— 'ASHIQ PASHA. - Gharibnama. [Turkey, A.H.850/A.D.1446-47]. 329 leaves & 4 flyleaves, 254mm by 165mm. Later brown mor bdg, repaired. In naskhi script. With half-page illuminated heading, repainted. (88) £650
— FUZULI BAGHDADI. - Hadiqa as-Sa'ada. [Ottoman, A.H.1008/A.D.1599]. 277 leaves, 276mm by 171mm (text area). Repaired contemp brown mor with gilt lea onlay. In nasta'liq script. With illuminated headpiece & 13 miniatures in the Ottoman court style. Repaired throughout. (90) £11,000
— HUSAIN WA'IZ KASHIFI. - Tafsir ul-Mawahib. [Safar, A.H.1254/A.H.1838]. 345 leaves & 4 flyleaves, 355mm by 241mm, in brown mor bdg. In naskhi script by Saiyyid 'Ali Ridza ibn Ibrahim Wazif. (88) £750
— IBRAHIM HAKKI. - Ma'rifatname, encyclopaedia. [Ottoman, A.H.1251/A.D.1835]. 371 leaves & 4 flyleaves, 295mm by 197mm. Contemp brown mor bdg. In naskhi script by Hafiz 'Umar Khulusi. With numerous tables & astrological diagrams & 2 half-page illuminated headings. (90) £2,000
— MAKKI. - Diwan. [Ottoman, 19th cent]. 32 leaves (2 blank), 178mm by 116mm. Marbled paper bds. In naskhi script. With illuminated headpiece. (90) £100
— MEHMED SUBHI. - Poem in praise of Sultan Selim III. [Ottoman, c.1800]. 4 leaves, 222mm by 150mm, in black bds tooled in gold. In nasta'liq script. With illuminated headpiece. (91) £260
— MUHAMMAD YAMANI. - Kitab Qasa'id al-Makkah wa al-Madinah wa al-Quds. [Jerusalem, A.H.849/A.D.1445]. 174 leaves, 245mm by 170mm. Def brown mor bdg. In naskhi script by Muhammad bin Muhsin bin Hasan. With illuminated headpiece & illuminated medallion with dedication to al-Zahir Abu Sa'id Muhammad. (90) £2,400
— MURAD V & ABD-UL-HAMID II. - 2 letters (1 each), [June & Oct] 1876, 2 pp, 4to. To Grand Duke Nikolaus Friedrich Peter II of Oldenburg. Informing him of their accession to the throne. (89) DM420
— NIZAMI. - Layla va Majnun. [Azerbaijan, 1900] In nasta'liq script in black with Persian headings in red. 92 leaves, 193mm by 115mm, in lea. With 45 large miniatures in a naive late Qajar style. (90) $425
— QASIM BIN MUHAMMAD. - Tarjamat Tanbihat al-Munajimin. [Ottoman, 19th cent]. 202 leaves, 225mm by 145mm. Rebacked brown mor bdg. In diwani script. With illuminated headpiece. (90) £100
— SULTAN ABDULHAMID II. - A Tauqi. [A.H.1314/A.D.1896]. 1 p, 819mm by 565mm. Letter to Mufti Maulana al-

TURKISH MANUSCRIPTS

Hajj Mustafa Hilmi Efendi regarding the grant of nishan i Humayuni. In diwani script on buff polished paper. With illuminated tughra. (90) £1,200

Turner, Dawson, 1775-1858
Series of 10 A Ls s, 1798 to 1816, c.30 pp, 4to. (88) £160
A Ls s (2), 12 Jan 1845 & 16 Feb 1848. (91) £80

Turner, Joseph Mallord William, 1775-1851
ALs, 4 Nov 1815. (88) £780
— [Dec 1837]. 2 pp, 4to. To Mrs. Wheeler. Hoping he will be able to accept her invitation. (90) DM1,300
— 31 May 1840. (88) DM850
— "Tuesday 1841". (88) £800
— [n.d.], "Tuesday". (89) £450
— [n.d.], "Sunday". (89) £700

Turner, Lana
Series of Ds s, 3 Ds s, 1937 to 1947. (91) $350

Turpin, Ben, 1874-1940
Photograph, sgd, [Oct 1919]. (90) $325
Photograph, sgd & inscr, [n.d.]. (89) $400

Twain, Mark, 1835-1910. See: Clemens, Samuel Langhorne

Tweed, William Marcy, 1823-78
Ds, 27 Mar 1863. (90) $80
— 1867. (91) $100
— March 1871. (88) $70

Twiggs, David E., 1790-1862
ALs, 13 Nov 1845. (90) $120

Two Guns White Calf, Chief
Photograph, sgd, [n.d.]. (90) $650
— Anr, [n.d.]. (91) $550

Tyler, John, 1790-1862
Collection of ALs & franking signature, [14 Jan 1843] & [12 June 1853]. (90) $400
ALs, 13 [Apr] 1832. 1 p, 4to. To R. F. Graves. Sending his speech on the tariff & commenting on Senate business. McVitty collection. (90) $1,400
— 30 Jan 1833. 1 p, 4to. To H. St. George Tucker. Forwarding newspapers containing obituaries of Hugh White. (90) $1,300

AMERICAN BOOK PRICES CURRENT

— 28 Sept 1841. (89) £500
— [c.1843]. (91) $550
— 14 Sept 1844. (88) $600
— 4 Oct 1844. 3 pp, 4to. To his daughter Mary Tyler Jones. Discussing arrangements for his return to Virginia. (90) $3,750
— 16 Feb 1845. (91) $700
— 6 Nov 1845. (90) $750
— 14 Feb 1848. 1 p, 4to. To Nahum Capen. Acknowledging receipt of his "prospectus for publishing a statistical journal". Including franking signature. Pratt collection. (89) $1,300
— 19 Feb 1850. (88) £1,000
— 27 Oct 1857. (90) $250
— 14 July 1858. 3 pp, 4to. To his son Robert. On political matters; says that he thinks that he is the last of the Virginia Presidents. (91) $3,250
— 8 Sept 1858. (90) $350
— 1 Oct 1860. Doheny collection. (89) $700
— 12 Oct [n.y.]. (90) $160
— [n.d.]. Rosenbloom collection. (88) $350
Ls, 30 Mar 1843. (88) £450
— 10 Oct 1843. 2 pp, 4to. Recipient unknown (deleted). Discussing trade relations with Europe & hoping for recipient's election. (91) $2,100
— 24 June 1844. Byer collection. (90) $950
ANs, [n.d.]. (89) $230
Ds, 1837. (89) $210
— 31 Oct 1841. (90) $600
— 14 May 1842. (89) $375
— 27 May 1842. (90) $400
— 22 June 1842. (91) $650
— 1 Sept 1842. (91) $800
— 26 Nov 1842. (91) $700
— 30 Jan 1843. (88) $425
— 29 July 1843. (91) $950
— 28 Aug 1843. (88) $450
— 6 Oct 1843. (91) $500
— 6 Nov 1843. (88) $200
— 9 Jan 1844. (91) $400
— 27 Nov 1844. (91) $550
— 1 Aug 1845. (91) $650
Franking signature, 25 Jan [1848]. (89) $300
— Anr, [13 Feb 1850]. (90) $170

— Anr, [10 Jan n.y.]. (90) $115
— Anr, [8 Feb n.y.]. (90) $250
— Anr, [9 Feb n.y.]. (90) $300
— Anr, [30 Mar n.y.]. Alexander collection. (90) $130
— Anr, [13 July n.y.]. (90) $300

Tyler, John, 1790-1862 —& Others
[The signatures of Tyler, 5 members of his cabinet, Winfield Scott, & 135 members of the 27th Congress, [1842], 66 pp, 7.5 by 8.5 inches, bound, sold at Dar on 4 Oct 1990, lot 338, for $1,000.]

Tyler, Julia Gardiner, 1820-89
ANs, 15 May 1889. (91) $320

Tzara, Tristan, 1896-1963
Series of 3 A Ls s, Feb to Mar 1928. 7 pp, 4to. To [Louis Marcoussis]. Complaining about his pbr, an article about Apollinaire, etc. (91) £1,200

U

Ubbelohde, Otto, 1867-1922
Collection of 8 A Ls s & 6 autograph postcards, sgd, 13 Oct 1902 to 15 Aug 1914. 11 pp, 8vo, & cards. To Dr. Walter Kuelz. Touching private & legal matters. With related material. (89) DM1,700
— Collection of ALs & autograph postcard, sgd, 9 Feb 1908 & 8 July 1913. (89) DM550

Udet, Ernst, 1896-1941
Photograph, sgd & inscr, 4 Sept 1934. (91) DM650

Uhland, Ludwig, 1787-1862
ALs, 14 Dec 1834. 2 pp, 4to. To Max Goetzinger. Requesting him to buy an old collection of songs for him at a forthcoming auction. Margin slightly def. (88) DM1,300
— 7 Feb 1859. (91) DM600
— 24 Apr 1859. 2 pp, 8vo. To H. H. Pierson. Regretting that he is unable to read Pierson's music to his Ich hatt einen Kameraden. With ALs by his father, 1820. (88) DM1,300
A Ns s (2), 22 Oct 1832 & [19 Feb 1834]. (89) DM350
AN, [1831]. (90) DM200
Ds, 27 Jan 1830. (90) DM320

Autograph sentiment, "Wann hoert der Himmel auf zu strafen mit Albums und mit Autographen?"; [n.d.]. (90) DM700

Ujlaky, John IV, Bishop of Vac, d.1578.
See: Fugger Family

Ulfeldt, Corfiz, Count, 1606-64
ALs, 17 June 1647. 2 pp, folio. Recipient unnamed. Recommending the son of Bernard de Vieilletard. In Italian. (91) DM1,800

Ulrich, Herzog von Wuerttemberg, 1487-1550
Ds, 11 May 1548. 1 p, folio. Receipt for money sent from Stuttgart by Wilhelm Khun & Wolff Bonackher. With related material. (89) DM2,400

Ulrich von Tuerheim
Ms, Rennewart, lines 12883 - 13172. [Southern Germany, early 14th cent]. 2 pp, 354mm by 225mm, vellum. With 3 initials. Recovered from a bdg. (88) DM7,000

Undset, Sigrid, 1882-1949
Collection of ALs & Ls, 13 & 22 June 1931. (89) DM240
Ls, 11 Jan 1930. (88) DM320

Ungaretti, Giuseppe, 1888-1970
Autograph Ms, trans of Shakespeare's Sonnett 128 into Italian, [n.d.]. (91) £420

Ungerer, Tomi
Autograph sentiment, sgd, [n.d.]. (90) DM320

Ungnad, Hans, Freiherr zu Sonnegg, 1493-1564
Ls, 23 Mar 1547. 2 pp, folio. To the Diet of Lower Austria & the County of Goerz. Protesting that his pay as Feldhauptmann is overdue. (91) DM1,650

United States
[Attorneys General. - The signatures of John W. Mitchell, William P. Rogers, Ramsey Clark, Richard Kleindienst, Herbert Brownell & Nicholas Katzenbach, on the cover of a copy of the Constitution of the United States, Wash., 1968, sold at sg

UNITED STATES

on 25 Oct 1988, lot 9, for $175.]
[Supreme Court. - The signatures of 8 Supreme Court Justices on the cover of a booklet, The Constitution of the United States of America. Wash, 1972, sold at wa on 1 Oct 1988, lot 88, for $160.]
[Supreme Court. - A collection of 11 signatures of members of the Burger Court, 2 on Supreme Court cards, & 9 sgd portraits in 8vo booklet, The Supreme Court of the United States, [c.1972], sold at wa on 1 Oct 1988, lot 89, for $190.]
[Supreme Court. - The signatures of Chief Justice Burger & 8 justices, c.1972, in booklet, The Supreme Court of the United States, 20 pp, 8vo, sold at wa on 1 Oct 1988, lot 410, for $160.]
— Cantonment Belle Fontaine. - 5 documents, 1813 to 1829. Length not stated. From the 1st military post west of the Mississippi River, about various matters. Alexander collection. (90) $450
— Election of 1880. - Document, 8 Dec 1880. 3 pp, 4to. Electoral votes of the State of Georgia, cast for Winfield S. Hancock & William H. English; sgd twice by each elector. (91) $400
— General Land Office. - Ms, Annual Report of the General Land Office For 1868. 950 pp in 3 vols, folio. Sgd several times by Commissioner Joseph S. Wilson. Including 19 pp of foldout charts. (89) $1,500
— Supreme Court. - The signatures of Chief Justice Warren & 8 Justices, [c.1968], on 1966 U.S. Bill of Rights first day cover, sold at Dar on 6 Dec 1990, lot 388, for $325. 91
— Supreme Court. - The signatures of all 9 members, 7 Oct 1946, on ptd sheet with their photographs & biographies, 5.5 by 8.5 inches, sold at Dar on 13 June 1991, lot 355, for $225. 91
— Supreme Court. - The signatures of Chief Justice Rehnquist & Justices Marshall, O'Connor, Stevens, Brennan, White, Blackmun & Powell, on a philatelic envelope, [17 Dec 1981], sold at Dar on 13 June 1991, lot 356, for $110. 91
— Supreme Court. - Group photograph, [c.1981-86]. 13 by 10 inches. Sgd by all 9. (91) $750
— Supreme Court. - Supreme Court card, 4 by 3 inches, sgd by Chief Justices Charles E. Hughes & Harlan F. Stone; [n.d.]. (90) $120
— Supreme Court. - Group photograph of the entire Court, [1965/66]. 13.25 by 9.5 inches. Sgd by all 9 on mount. (91) $500
— Supreme Court. - Ptd group photograph, from a publication, [c.1935]. 1 p, 6 by 10 inches. Sgd by the full Hughes Court. Mtd. (88) $550
— Supreme Court. - Ptd group photograph, from a magazine, [c.1940]. 1 p, 6 by 9 inches. Sgd by 7 members of the Hughes Court; 1 name added in anr hand. With related material. (88) $325

Unruh, Fritz von, 1885-1970
Collection of 22 A Ls s, 44 Ls s, 9 postcards, sgd (partly autograph), & 2 telegrams, 15 May 1947 to 18 May 1970. 71 pp, various sizes, & cards. To his friend Robert Breuer. Personal letters touching literary & political topics. With 12 letters & cards by his wife Friedrike & further related material. (88) DM4,200
ALs, 12 Jan 1924. (90) DM650
— 12 June 1936. (90) DM850

Upshur, Abel Parker, 1791-1844
Franking signature, [12 Oct n.y.]. Alexander collection. (90) $55

Urban VIII, Pope, 1568-1644
Document, 9 Mar [1624]. (90) DM750
— 30 Nov 1630. (88) DM650

Ursuleac, Viorica, 1894-1985
Ds, 4 Nov 1934. (91) DM950

Urzidil, Johannes, 1896-1970
A Ls s (2), 7 May 1932 & [n.d.]. (90) DM300

Usedom, Guido, Graf von, 1805-84
Series of 15 A Ls s (10 carbon copies), 23 Oct 1848 to 13 Nov 1858. (90) DM850

Uspensky, Gleb Ivanovich, 1843-1902
ALs, 15 Mar 1888. 8 pp, 8vo. To Anna Mikhailovna Evreinov. Blaming censorship for the dullness of literary journals. (89) DM4,600

Usuardus
Ms, Martyrology, in Latin. [Ravenna, c.1460-80]. 157 leaves (2 blank) & flyleaf, vellum, 223mm by 160mm, in 16th-cent blindstamped bdg of brown goatskin over wooden bds. In dark brown ink in a regular gothic bookhand. With decorated initials throughout, historiated initial & full illuminated border. (88) £11,000

Utrillo, Maurice, 1883-1955
ALs, 7 Nov 1919. (89) DM850
— 1 Feb 1928. (90) DM1,000
— 4 Jan 1936. (88) £300
Signature, 15 Jan 1952. (91) $450

Uvarov, Sergei Semoyonovich, Count, 1786-1855
Ls, 1/13 May 1845. (90) DM270

Uz, Johann Peter, 1720-96
ALs, 10 Apr 1793. (90) DM650

V

Vail, Alfred, 1807-59
Ds, 26 Apr 1843. (89) $100

Valentino, Rudolph, 1895-1926
[A collection of 3 photographs, sgd, c.14.5 by 11.75 inches, in 18th-cent costume, sold at S on 21 Sept, lot 121, for £500 to Reuter.]
ANs, [n.d.]. (91) $375
Photograph, sgd & inscr, 1922. (88) £400
— Anr, [n.d.]. (89) $300
— Anr, [n.d.]. (90) $950
Photograph, [early 1920s]. (90) $650
— Anr, [n.d.]. (89) $100

Valery, Paul, 1871-1945
Collection of 10 A Ls s & postcards, sgd, 1924 to 1929 & [n.d.]. 13 pp, 8vo. To Mme Revelin. Reflecting his depressed state of mind. (88) £2,000
— Collection of 40 A Ls s & autograph postcards, sgd, & 8 photographs, 1925 to 1939 & [n.d.]. 48 pp, 8vo. To Madame Revelin. Mostly reporting from his travels throughout Europe. (91) £6,000
Series of 18 A Ls s, 3 Feb 1893 to 1921. 30 pp, 8vo & 12mo, mtd in half mor vol. To Eugene Rouart. Personal letters about his own & recipient's work, friends & family. Koch Foundation. (90) $6,000
ALs, 5 Apr 1937. (90) DM240
Ls, [1933]. (90) DM240

Valignani, Alessandro, 1538-1606
Ms, Principio y progresso de la Relegion christiana en Japon, [late 17th cent]. About 300 pp, folio, in calf wraps. Describing the Jesuits' mission in Japan, 1542 to 1570. Phillipps Ms.3065 & Robinson collection. (89) £34,000

Vallee, Rudy
[His personal script for the film The Bachelor and the Bobby-Soxer, 1947, written by Sidney Sheldon, sold at pnNY on 3 Dec 1988, lot 64, for $100.]
See also: Sturges, Preston & Vallee

Vallisneri, Antonio, 1661-1730
ALs, 30 Dec 1726. (90) DM360

Valtan, Pierre Louis de, d.1518
Ms, Super Qualibet Dictione Symboli Apostolici [A Commentary on the Apostles' Creed], [Tours, c.1500]. 24 leaves (1 blank) & flyleaf, vellum, 235mm by 160mm. Contemp red velvet over wooden bds. In a formal rounded humanist minuscule, possibly by the author. With small initials throughout, 72 trompe-l'oeil scrolls, & 12 large miniatures by Jean Poyet within full-page frames. Dedicated by the author to Queen Isabella of Spain. Bradley Martin Ms. (90) $450,000

Van Buren, Martin, 1782-1862
Series of 3 A Ls s, Mar to Sept 1847. (89) $600
A Ls s (2), 29 Oct 1830 & 30 Sept 1852. (89) £400
ALs, 1 Aug 1821. (90) $350
— 4 May 1822. (90) $220
— 10 Dec 1825. Christensen collection. (90) $400
— [c.Mar - Apr 1833]. Pratt collection. (89) $900
— 9 Mar 1834. Sang collection. (91) $700
— 5 July 1834. (89) $190
— 16 Feb 1836. (88) $250
— 8 Mar 1836. (90) $275
— 7 Sept 1840. (91) $500
— 21 Oct 1841. 2 pp, 4to. To Thomas W.

VAN BUREN

Gilmer. Hoping that he will join the Democratic Party. Sang & Thorek collections. (91) $2,500
— 2 May 1845. (91) $550
— 10 June 1856. Rosenbloom collection. (88) $450
— 22 Dec 1857. (91) $400
— 9 May 1858. (91) $200
— 13 Sept 1860. (91) $220
— [n.d.]. (91) $650
— [n.d.]. (89) $160
AL, 30 Oct 1852. (89) $95
Ls s (2), 15 Nov 1830 & 17 Feb 1831. (88) DM950
ANs, 7 [May?] 1857. (90) $300
— [n.d.]. (89) $95
Collection of 8 A Ds s & 42 Ds s, Nov 1816 to Oct 1818. 1 or 2 pp each, folio & 4to. As Attorney Gen. of NY, bonds, judgments & dockets in Supreme Court cases. (88) $1,800
ADs, 6 Apr 1817. (89) $250
— 3 Aug 1829. (90) $250
Series of Ds s, 41 Ds s, Oct 1817. 82 pp, mostly folio. As Attorney Gen. of NY, bonds issued to defendants in Supreme Court actions. Partly accomplished by Van Buren. (88) $1,300
Ds, 16 Sept 1809. (91) $400
— 9 May 1838. (91) $650
— 10 June 1838. (90) $700
— 10 July 1838. (90) $650
— 23 July 1838. (91) $700
— 26 July 1838. (91) $500
— 1 Apr 1839. (89) $600
— 1 May 1839. (91) $190
— 13 June 1839. (91) $500
— 22 July 1840. (91) $260
— 29 Aug 1840. Byer collection. (90) $450
Cut signature, [n.d.]. (88) $95
Franking signature, [1822]. Alexander collection. (90) $200
— Anr, [n.d.]. (91) $80

Van Buren, Martin, 1782-1862 —& Others
[The signatures of Van Buren, Daniel Webster, Henry Clay, John C. Calhoun, & 5 other politicians, [n.d.], on an 8vo sheet, sold at Dar on 7 Feb 1991, lot 24, for $475.]

AMERICAN BOOK PRICES CURRENT

Van Cantelbeeck, Henri Jean
Autograph Ms, Logica bipartita; Physica Aristotelis; Physica bipartita, & other lecture notes, 1669 to 1670. (89) £700

Van Dam, Rip, 1660-1749
ALs, 11 Apr 1716. (89) $80

Van de Velde, Henry, 1863-1957
Collection of 2 A Ls s & 2 Ls s, 1922 to 1957. (89) DM900
ALs, [28 Sept 1899]. (89) DM550
— 13 Jan 1910. (88) DM280

Van Dieren, Bernard, 1884-1936
[An archive containing several thousand pages of autograph & scribal scores by van Dieren, including some of his most important pieces, sold at pn on 13 Oct 1988, lot 45, for £3,600 to Nosk.]

Van Dine, S. S., Pseud. of Willard Huntington Wright, 1888-1939
— HERRIN, M. H. - Orig drawing, pencil bust port of Van Dine; 1934. 9 by 12 inches. Sgd by Van Dine. (91) $160

Van Dongen, Kees, 1877-1968
ALs, 10 Oct 1917. (89) DM300
— [n.d.]. (90) DM200
— [n.d.]. (90) DM360

Van Doren, Mark, 1894-1972
Autograph Ms, 57 poems, 13 May 1968 to 1 Dec 1972. (90) $600
See also: Mumford, Lewis & Van Doren

Van Halen
[A sheet with a sgd doodle by each member of the band, [n.d.], 11 by 14 inches, matted, sold at pnNy on 3 Dec 1988, lot 150, for $150.]
[The orig cover proof slick for Van Halen album 5150, sgd by all 4 members of the group, [n.d.], framed, sold at pnNY on 3 Dec 1988, lot 384, for $50.]

Van Heusen, James, 1913-90
[2 autograph musical quotations, sgd, [n.d.], on one sheet, 9.5 by 7 inches, sold at Dar on 10 Apr 1991, lot 393, for $250.]

Van Laureten, Melchior
[His Liber Amicorum, [Southern Netherlands, 1574-83], 383 leaves (303 blank), 158mm by 100mm, in contemp calf gilt, with 71 pp of illuminated armorial shields, 42 pp of colored drawings, & 44 pp of text, mainly French verse, sold at C on 7 Dec 1988, lot 34, for £11,000 to Desmet Germain.]

Van Loon, Hendrik Willem, 1882-1944
ALs, [n.d.]. (88) $55

Van Vechten, Carl, 1880-1964
Series of 4 Ns s, 1924 to 1933. (89) $200

Vancouver, George, 1757-98
Ls, 6 Sept 1794. 3 pp, folio. To Manuel Alaba. Requesting supplies & inquiring about dispatches. (89) $7,000

Ds, Feb 1795. 2 pp, 4to. "Account of the Expense of Gunner's Stores on board His Majestys Sloop Discovery". Doheny collection. (88) $15,000

Vanderbilt, Cornelius, 1843-99
ALs, 11 Mar 1880. (91) $60

Vanderbilt Family
[A collection of 19 items, mostly A Ls s & Ls s, 1823 to 1915, by various members of the Vanderbilt Family sold at sg on 25 Oct 1988, lot 236, for $950.]

Vansittart, Nicholas, 1st Baron Bexley, 1766-1851
[A collection of c.100 letters & documents to & from collegues & family, including a few A Ls s, various dates, 432 pp, various sizes, sold at C on 26 June 1991, lot 372, for £800 to Shutter.]

Varese, Edgard, 1883-1965
Series of 3 A Ls s, 1955 & 1956. 3 pp, 8vo. To a French musicologist. Sending information about the American premiere of Deserts, commenting on an article, etc. (89) £1,300

— Series of 3 A Ls s, 1956 & 1957. (90) £450

ALs, 11 Mar 1928. (89) DM750

— 6 June 1930. (90) DM300

Autograph postcard, sgd, [18 July 1930]. (90) DM260

Vargas, Jose, 1786-1854
ALs, 2 May 1844. (91) $100

Varick, Richard, 1753-1831
ALs, 14 Apr 1782. (89) $700

ADs, Aug 1796. (91) $80

Varnhagen von Ense, Karl August, 1785-1858
Series of 6 A Ls s, 15 Dec 1840 to 9 Apr 1843. 19 pp, 8vo. To Luise zu Stolberg-Stolberg. Personal & literary correspondence. (91) DM2,200

A Ls s (2), 5 Dec 1842 & 5 Mar 1844. (89) DM950

ALs, 4 Mar 1834. (90) DM440

— 3 Mar 1835. 3 pp, 8vo. To [Hermann Scheidler]. About his wife Rahel, & criticizing Bettina von Arnim's Goethe's Briefwechsel mit einem Kinde. With related material. Albrecht collection. (91) SF1,400

— 29 Apr 1841. (91) DM650

— 24 Mar 1844. (90) DM650

— 8 Feb 1846. (89) DM250

— 2 June 1849. 4 pp, 8vo. To [M. Sougey-Avisard]. Analyzing the political situation in Germany after 1848. Was mtd. (88) DM1,800

— 20 July 1849. 4 pp, 8vo. To [M. Sougey-Avisard]. Commenting about the political situation. (89) DM1,400

— 27 July 1849. (88) DM650

— 31 Mar 1851. 5 pp, 8vo. Recipient unnamed. Thanking for a shipment of autographs & commenting about autographs & character studies. (90) DM2,800

— 18 Apr 1853. (90) DM600

— 25 Nov 1853. (90) DM320

See also: Kerner, Justinus

Varnhagen von Ense, Rahel, 1771-1833
ALs, 29 Apr 1814. 3 pp, 8vo. To "liebste Jeny". Introducing Auguste Brede & rejoicing about the end of hostilities. Sgd R: Robert. (90) DM2,600

— 10 Mar [1816]. 2 pp, 4to. To Henrik Steffens. Fragment, expressing her friendship & her wish to protect him. (91) DM1,100

VARNHAGEN VON ENSE

— 3 Feb 1830. 2 pp, 4to. To [Amalie von Helvig]. About her failing health. (91) DM3,600

AL, 25 Apr [1832]. 3 pp, 4to. To Capt. von Willisen. Criticizing a novella by Ludwig Tieck & sending journals. With related material. Albrecht collection. (91) SF2,200

ANs, [1806]. 2 pp, 8vo. To [Regina Frohberg]. Hoping to see her the next day. Sgd RL. With related ALs by Karl August Varnhagen von Ense, 9 Oct 1839. (90) DM3,000

— MARWITZ, ALEXANDER VON DER. - ALs, 26 June 1809. 4 pp, 4to. To Rahel [Varnhagen von Ense]. Describing [her future husband] Karl August Varnhagen. (91) DM540

Varo y Guerrero, Francisco, 1627-87
Ms, Chinese grammar, [late 18th or early 19th cent]. About 100 pp, 4to, in Middle Hill bds. With Chinese characters in pencil. Phillipps MS.25708 & Robinson collection. (89) £3,200

Vasarely, Victor de
Photograph, sgd, [n.d.]. (90) DM200

Vatel, Jean
Autograph Ms, L'art de L'Escuyer Tranchant utile a Tous Les Gentilshommes..., 1665. 26 pp, 4to, in 19th cent bds. Bound with port drawing & 32 engravings from Pierre Petit's L'Art de trancher. With related material. (90) DM12,000

Vauban, Sebastien Le Prestre de, 1633-1707
Ls, 29 Nov 1703. (90) £400

Vaughan, Richard, 2d Earl of Carbery, 1600?-86
Ms, Rental for his manors in Wales, 29 Dec 1671. 250 pp, 4to, in vellum bdg. Sgd at foot of most pages. (91) £1,600

Vaughan Williams, Ralph, 1872-1958
Autograph music, song, How can the Tree not wither, [c.1920?]. (88) £520

Collection of 22 A Ls s & Ls s, 1920s to 1940s. (89) £950

— Collection of 14 A Ls s, Ls s, & secretarial letters, [1930s & 1940s]. (88) £360

— Collection of 29 A Ls s & Ls s, [c.1935

AMERICAN BOOK PRICES CURRENT

to 1956]. (88) £700

ALs, 11 May [1918]. (91) £300

— 13 Nov 1938. (89) £350

— 16 Nov [n.y.]. Byer collection. (90) $275

Ls, 27 Oct 1952. (91) £130

Ds, 13 July 1914. (90) $175

Vaughan Williams, Ralph, 1872-1958 —& Coghill, Nevill, 1899-1980
[A collection of A Ls s & Ls s by Vaughan Williams (1) & Coghill (c.25) mostly to Hal Burton, relating to the 1st performance of The Pilgrim's Progress, including Coghill's ideas for costume designs, Burton's stage designs, & further related material, 1950 & 1951, sold at S on 18 Nov 1988, lot 476, for £1,000 to Macnutt.]

Vauvenargues, Luc de Clapiers, Marquis de, 1715-47
Autograph Ms, reflections on literary matters, Sur Fontenelle, Sur l'ode, & Sur la poesie et l'eloquence; [n.d.]. (88) £800

Vega, Georg von, 1756-1802
ALs, 13 Oct 1795. (89) DM850

Vegesack, Siegfried von, 1888-1974
Autograph Ms, collection of poems, Geliebte Erde; [1953]. (90) DM340

Vegetius Renatus, Flavius
Ms, De Re Militari; On the Art of Warfare, in a Middle English trans. [London?, 2d quarter of 15th cent]. 104 leaves, vellum, 274mm by 173mm. Modern blindstamped red mor by Riviere. In a regular English bookhand. With c.125 decorated initials (3 very large) with elaborate penwork extensions. (89) £42,000

Veit, Philipp, 1793-1877
ALs, 6 Apr 1856. (89) DM480

— 8 Jan 1870. (88) DM360

Venezuela
— MORILLO, PABLO. - 2 Ds s, 26 & 27 Nov 1820. 8 pp, folio. Contemp certified copies of treaties between Spain & the new republic of Colombia [later Venezuela], sgd 25 & 26 Nov 1820. (91) £2,000

— PAEZ, JOSE ANTONIO. - Ds, 21 Apr

1822. 1 p, folio. Proclamation addressed to the inhabitants of Puerto Cabello to surrender to the army of liberation. (91) £5,400

Venice
Ms, record book of the galleon Foscarini trading between Venice & Candia (Crete), 1574. About 120 pp, folio, in vellum bdg. Containing records of bills, consignments, expenses, etc. Waterstained. (89) £1,400
— PISANO, ALVISE, DOGE. - Document, 23 Apr to 22 June 1739. 320 pp, 8vo. Contemp brocade covered bds. Instructions addressed to Gierolemo Bolini, Venetian Bailo in Corfu, with decrees issued by the Council of Ten. With illuminated frontis. (91) £300
— RENIER, DOGE PAOLO. - Ms, dogale granted to Anzolo Barbaro di Niccolo of Friule, 3 Apr 1788. 101 leaves, vellum, 225mm by 160mm, in contemp Venetian silver repousee bdg with silver seal of Doge Ludovico Manin, 1791. In brown ink in a scribal hand. With full-page miniature & heading in gold capitals. (88) £3,500

Venus, Sylvia I.
Original drawings, (17), to illus By Candlelight, [1930s]. (89) £400
— Original drawings, (20), to illus various annuals & titles in the Treasure and Storyland Series, 1926 to 1935. (90) £550

Verdi, Giuseppe, 1813-1901
[An autograph visiting card, [25 May 1877], size not stated, sold at star on 1 Dec 1988, lot 972a, for DM700.]
Autograph Ms, libretto, Il Ballo in Maschera, complete working Ms of 3d version of text; [1858]. 52 pp, 8vo. 3d act in Giuseppina Verdi's hand with autograph annotations; some in anr hand. (89) £80,000
Autograph music, chorus, O virtu che provvidente; [c.1840-45]. 2 pp, folio. 27 bars for 2-part chorus of sopranos & cembalo; working draft, sgd. Supposedly unpbd. (90) £20,000
— Autograph music, I due Foscari, Act 2, scena for Jacopo; [c.summer 1844]. 2 pp, folio. Draft of 69 bars in short score; sgd. Differing from final version in words & music. (90) £20,000
— Autograph music, opera, Giovanna d'Arco, Act 3, working draft of the duet Amai, ma un solo instante; [1844]. 4 pp, folio, in modern half-calf. 88 bars in short score. (90) £40,000
Ms, libretto of Il Trovatore, [1852]. 39 pp, 4to. In a scribal hand, with extensive annotations & revisions in Verdi's hand. (89) £88,000
Collection of ALs & AN, 2 July 1895. (90) £620
Series of 51 A Ls s, 1843 to 1865. 120 pp, 8vo. To Francesco Maria Piave. Important collection covering the entire period of their collaboration & dealing with a variety of professional & some private matters. (90) $140,000
A Ls s (2), 25 June 1880 & [n.d.]. (90) £750
— A Ls s (2), 12 July 1884 & 6 Mar 1898. (88) £620
— A Ls s (2), 18 July 1885 & 7 June 1889. (89) £650
— A Ls s (2), 10 Sept 1888 & 24 May 1889. (88) £850
— A Ls s (2), [27 Feb 1898] & [n.d.]. (91) £600
ALs, 15 Aug 1844. 1 p, 8vo. To Luigi Tollagni. About a performance of Ernani at Bergamo, performances at La Scala, & a new libretto. (90) $2,600
— 18 Oct 1848. 2 pp, 8vo. To F[ilippo] Colini. Explaining that he is not in a position to offer him a part in his new opera Il corsaro. (90) £1,800
— 25 Dec 1852. 1 p, 8vo. To Emanuele Muzio. Hoping that Il trovatore will be successful in Rome, & expressing New Year's wishes. (91) £1,400
— [c.1850-60]. (88) £600
— 21 May 1862. (88) £800
— 3 May 1864. (89) £420
— 17 July 1864. 1 p, 4to. To M. Beule. Thanking for his nomination to the Academie des Beaux-Arts. In French. Mtd. (88) $1,100
— 11 Aug 1864. (88) £500
— 12 Sept 1864. (89) £420
— 1868. 2 pp, 8vo. To Count Opprandino Arrivabene. Praising Cremonese biscuits & commenting on the favorable astrological stars. (89) £1,500
— 22 Jan 1869. 1 p, 8vo. To Achille Montuoro. Declining to interfere in a

dispute with the management of La Scala concerning the production of La forza del destino. (91) £1,700
— 5 Nov 1869. (88) £350
— [c.1869]. (90) £500
— [5?] Oct 1872. 3 pp, 4to. To Antonio Ghislanzoni. Instructing him on changes to the libretto of Don Carlos, incorporating a draft of c.20 lines of poetry. (91) £10,000
— 7 Sept 1873. (89) £750
— 7 Dec 1873. 1 p, 8vo. To [Giulio Carcano?]. Declining to give a judgment on recipient's biography of Manzoni. (90) £1,600
— 20 May 1876. 1 p, 8vo. To Mauro Corticelli. Giving instructions. With related material. (88) DM2,400
— 14 July 1882. (89) £450
— 23 May 1884. (89) £450
— [25 June 1884]. (88) £400
— 3 Oct 1884. (89) £500
— 31 Dec 1884. 3 pp, 8vo. To Antonio Ghislanzoni. Arguing against modernist symphonic tendencies in music. Imperf. (91) £2,200
— 1 Dec 1885. (88) £420
— [19 Mar 1886]. (90) £540
— 2 Apr 1886. 4 pp, 8vo, framed. To Giulio [Ricordi]. Comparing the Paris Opera with La Scala, discussing preparations for the premiere of Otello, & mentioning La Traviata. With framed postcard photograph. (90) £17,000
— [15 May 1887]. (88) £600
— 5 June 1887. (88) £420
— 7 Sept 1887. (90) £500
— 22 Sept 1887. (89) £420
— [23 Oct 1887]. (88) £380
— 11 May 1888. (88) £450
— 23 June 1888. (89) £420
— 17 [Sept 1888]. (89) £450
— 23 Sept 1888. (89) £480
— 8 Nov 1888. (91) £480
— 19 Mar 1889. (90) £520
— 29 May 1889. (90) £550
— 24 June 1889. (89) £480
— 28 Aug 1889. (88) £400
— 6 May 1890. 3 pp, 8vo. To Giulio [Ricordi]. Requesting him to speed up the delivery of a journal. 2 lines of text set to music. (90) DM9,000
— 18 June 1890. (89) £450
— 24 July 1890. (89) £450
— 3 Aug 1890. (89) £450
— 21 Oct 1890. (91) £700
— 21 Oct 1890. (91) £680
— 1 May 1891. (88) £380
— 5 May 1891. (88) £600
— 22 May 1891. 2 pp, 8vo. To Monsieur Sauchon. Concerning copyright proceedings on his works. In French. (88) $1,500
— 23 Nov 1891. (89) £480
— 6 Mar 1892. (90) £550
— 18 Oct 1892. (90) £480
— 20 Oct 1892. (88) £500
— 11 June 1893. (88) £480
— 21 Nov 1893. (90) £480
— 21 Feb 1894. (90) £550
— 3 Mar 1894. (91) £450
— 13 June 1894. (88) £470
— 21 July 1894. (90) £480
— 5 Mar 1895. (90) £500
— 15 May 1895. (88) £520
— 11 Nov 1895. (89) £450
— 11 Feb 1896. (90) £550
— 12 Feb 1896. (90) £550
— 25 June 1896. (89) £480
— 28 June 1896. (91) £450
— 15 Aug 1896. (90) £480
— [19 Aug 1896]. (88) £380
— 19 May 1897. (89) £480
— 26 May 1897. (89) £480
— 4 Feb 1898. (88) £620
— 23 Feb 1898. (89) £500
— 7 May 1898. (90) £550
— 10 June 1898. (90) £480
— 11 July 1898. (90) £510
— [9 Aug 1898]. (90) £550
— 4 Sept 1898. (90) £420
— [31 Dec] 1898. (90) £550
— 30 July 1899. (88) £340
— 2 Sept 1899. (90) £650
— 16 Sept 1899. (90) £500
— 17 Oct 1899. (90) £450
— 10 Feb 1900. (89) £550
— 27 May 1900. (88) £740
— 15 Mar [1844]. 1 p, 8vo. To Francesco Pasetti. Informing him about the successful 2d performance of his opera Ernani. (91) DM4,400
— 31 Dec [n.y.]. (88) £350
— [n.d.] "Friday". (89) £420

— [n.d.]. (91) £420
— [n.d.]. 1 p, 8vo. To Giovanni Maloberti. Asking whether he can recommend a coachman. With AN on visiting card, 1 word. (89) DM1,150
AL, 29 Sept 1846. 3 pp, 8vo. To Alessandro Lanari. Giving instructions regarding the production of his opera Macbeth. 2 words & flourish only on 3d page. (90) £6,000
— 20 Aug 1865. 2 pp, 8vo. To Vincenzo Luccardi. Fragment, about his plans to visit Paris. With cut signature. (88) DM2,100
— [c.1873]. 2 pp, folio. Recipient unknown [Tito Ricordi?]. Draft, expressing doubts about the wisdom of performing Aida in Germany. (90) £5,000
Autograph postcards (2), sgd, 20 May 1895 & [8 June 1897]. (88) £520
Autograph postcard, sgd, [n.d.]. (90) £650
Collection of ANs & 4 A Ns, [1886 to 1900]. (89) £650
A Ns s (2), [6 June 1887 & 23 June 1892]. (89) £750
— A Ns s (2), 20 Mar 1892 & 20 July 1895. (89) £800
ANs, [20 July 1871]. (90) $650
— [n.d.]. (91) $900
Series of 5 A Ns, 1884 & [n.d.]. (90) £750
— Series of 7 A Ns, [c.1888-1900]. (90) £850
AN, [n.d.]. 1 p, 54mm by 87mm, on ptd visiting card. Note of thanks & good wishes. (88) DM1,100
Autograph quotation, 10 bars from Lo spazzacamin, for voice & piano, sgd & dated 25 Apr 1846. 1 p, 16.5cm by 25cm. Differing from ptd version. Unrelated musical quotation on verso. (89) DM8,500
— Anr, 9 bars from Arrigo's aria, La brise souffle au loin, from Les vepres siciliennes; with lyrics. Sgd & dated 8 July 1855. 1 p, folio. (89) $5,000
— Anr, 4 bars from Les vepres siciliennes, 23 July 1855. 1 p, 8vo. Sgd. (91) £2,800
— Anr, part of Gremont's aria Di Provenza il mar, from La Traviata, 18 Apr 1858. 1 p, 21.5cm by 28cm. Vocal score, notated on 5 systems of 2 staves each; sgd. (91) £10,500
— Anr, 10 bars from Simon Boccanegra, sgd & dated 7 Sept 1858. 1 p, 8vo. Framed with a photograph. (91) $8,000
— Anr, 2 bars in C major, sgd, June 1862. 1 p, 8vo. With musical quotations, sgd, by Davide, Silas & Martin on same page. (89) £2,300
— Anr, 6 bars from his Requiem, with vocal line & orchestral parts reduced to 2 staves; 22 May 1874. 1 p, folio. Sgd. With unrelated musical quotation on verso. (91) £5,500
— Anr, 10 bars from his Requiem, scored for tenor & piano, 23 May 1877. 1 p, folio. Sgd & inscr to Heinrich Seligmann. (90) £5,400
— Anr, theme from his opera Falstaff, Tutto nel mondo e burla; sgd & dated 20 Apr 1895. 1 p, 8vo. (90) DM9,000
Group photograph, 5 Apr 1900. Mtd, overall size 30cm by 20cm. Arm-in-arm with Francesco Tamagno; dated by Verdi, sgd by both. (89) £8,200
Photograph, sgd, [c.1855]. 28cm by 20cm. By Disderi. (91) £3,800

Verdi, Giuseppe, 1813-1901 —& Verdi, Giuseppina

ALs, 27 Jan 1880. (88) £650

Verdi, Giuseppina. See: Verdi, Giuseppe & Verdi

Vergennes, Charles Gravier, Comte de, 1719-87

Ds, 18 July 1784. (90) $180

Vergilius Maro, Publius, 70-19 B.C.

Ms, Aeneis & Bucolica. [Italy, 15th cent] 204 (of 208) leaves, vellum, 250mm by 175mm, in early blind-tooled calf over wooden bds with 3 (of 10) brass bosses. Lacking first 2 leaves & penultimate leaf; last leaf imperf. In a book hand in brown ink. With 16 divisional initials in gold with penwork decoration in colors. (90) $18,000
— Ms, Opere. [Southern Italy, c.1460]. 1977 leaves only; lacking the Bucolica & all of the Aeneid after line 1,543 in 12th Book. On vellum, 225mm by 160mm, in 19th-cent vellum. (90) LIt5,000,000

VERHAEREN

Verhaeren, Emile, 1855-1916
Autograph transcript, poem, beginning "L'absurdite grandit comme une fleur fatale", [n.d.]. (88) DM560
Series of 10 A Ls s, 1915 to 1919. (89) £450
A Ls s (2), [11 & 24 Nov 1912]. (90) DM240

Verlaine, Paul, 1844-96
Autograph Ms (2), 2 poems, Invectives, working draft of 10 quatrains & fair copy of 5 quatrains, respectively; [n.d.]. 3 pp, 8vo. With 2 caricatures by F. Bac. (91) £2,600
Collection of 9 A Ls s & 16 Mss (12 autograph, 4 with autograph corrections), 1893 to 1895 & [n.d.]. About 70 pp, 8vo, in green mor gilt. To the pbr Heinemann, concerning payments for poems. Article, Les momes monocles, & poems. Including letters & articles on Verlaine by others. Martin collection. (90) FF115,000
ALs, [13 Apr 1886]. (91) DM520
— 20 June 1893. (88) DM500
— 7 Dec 1894. (90) DM900
— 4 Oct 1895. 3 pp, 8vo. Recipient unknown. About the publication of Rimbaud's Poesies. Including self port, lounging on a sofa. Koch Foundation. (90) $2,000
— 10 Nov 1895. (88) £230
Autograph postcard, sgd, 1 June 1894. (89) DM360
Proof copy, Les poetes maudits. Paris, 1884. 12mo, in light brown mor by Marius Michel. With numerous typographic corrections & autograph revisions in red ink. Martin collection. (90) FF210,000

Verne, Jules, 1828-1905
Autograph Ms, science-fiction tale, Une fantaisie du docteur Ox, sgd; 29 Sept 1871. 27 pp, folio, in half mor folding box. Including autograph emendations in red ink. Koch Foundation. (90) $45,000
ALs, 19 Dec 1868. (90) DM450
— 24 Oct [18]89. (91) $850
— 14 Jan 1897. (88) DM500
— 6 Jan 1902. (90) DM550
Autograph postcard, sgd, 24 May 1903. (91) DM750

AMERICAN BOOK PRICES CURRENT

ANs, [n.d.]. (91) DM450

Verona
Ms, Storia municipale e statuti della citta di Verona. [Verona, end of 15th cent] 28 leaves, folio. (90) LIt650,000

Veronese, Paolo Caliari, 1528-88
ALs, 4 Jan 1578. 1 p, folio. To Marcantonio Gandino. Inviting him to stay on his next trip to Venice. Corner repaired. (89) £4,500
— 4 Aug 1578. (91) £800
— 19 Dec 1578. (88) £1,000

Verri, Pietro, 1728-97
ALs, 29 Aug 1769. (90) £300

Vespucci, Amerigo, 1454-1512
Ms, Von der New Gefundenen Innsel der Nakhendenn Leutt [On the New-Found Island of Naked People]. [Germany or Bohemia, c.1505]. 5 pp, 188mm by 137mm. Early 20th-cent orange mor bdg. In a calligraphic gothic bookhand, with 1st line in a gothic display script. (90) £24,000

Vetch, James, 1789-1869
[His own extra-illus copy of his Inquiry into the Means of Establishing a Ship Navigation between the Mediterranean and Red Seas, 1843, 2 vols, 4to, in def marbled bds, containing his Ms notes, maps, & articles by others, sold at S on 22 July 1988, lot 406, for £250 to Drury.]

Veterinary Manuscripts
Ms, Vermehrte undt koestliche Artzney vor allerley gebrechen, und Kranckheiten der Pferde; cures for diseases of horses. (91) DM1,000

Vetterli, Friedrich, 1822-82
ALs, 5 June 1872. (88) DM240

Victoria, Empress of Friedrich III, 1840-1901
ALs, 21 Aug 1895. Schroeder collection. (89) DM280

Victoria, Duchess of Kent, 1786-1861
ALs, 2 Oct 1846. (90) DM260

Victoria, Queen of England, 1819-1901
[A visitor's book, believed to have originated from Windsor Castle, 4 May 1874 to 7 July 1883, 4to, mor bdg, sgd by members of nobility, diplomats, etc., sold at pn on 17 Sept, lot 497, for £150 to Lyons.]
[An album of 22 photographs of the royal family, recording the "Tableaux Vivants" at Balmoral Castle, 5 & 6 Oct 1888, with ALs by Queen Victoria presenting the album to Emma Albani, sold at S on 18 July 1991, lot 374, for £1,500 to Goldschmidt.]
Series of 3 A Ls s, 1 Dec 1893 to 17 June 1896. (90) £600
A Ls s (2), 13 June & 4 Oct 1842. 8 pp, 4to. To King Friedrich Wilhelm IV of Prussia. Sending Lord Hardwicke to accompany him to Russia, commenting about recent events, her reception in Scotland, etc. (90) DM2,200
ALs, 16 Aug 1826. 2 pp, 4to. To the Duke of York. Offering congratulations on his birthday. (91) £1,300
— 25 May 1827. (88) £400
— 7 July 1837. (88) £500
— 29 Jan 1840. Doheny collection. (89) $700
— 8 May 1851. (88) £350
— 9 Apr 1855. (91) £140
— 4 June 1877. 15 pp, 8vo. To Mrs. Drummond. Discussing in detail the emotional & spiritual problems of the Dean of Westminster & other matters. (90) £1,050
— 22 June 1882. (91) DM440
— 4 June 1884. (90) DM750
— 28 Sept 1889. (91) DM550
— 13 Apr 1900. 3 pp, 8vo. To Lord Kitchener. In 3d person, sending a medallion (present) & commenting about the war. (89) £1,200
— [n.d.], "Tuesday". Byer collection. (90) $550
AL, 8 Feb 1849. (89) $275
— 8 Mar 1862. (91) £500
— 30 July 1873. (91) £300
— 10 June 1878. (91) £280
— 14 Dec 1878. (91) £320
— 6 June 1883. (91) £440
— 28 Aug 1883. (91) £480
— 1 Jan 1891. (91) £120
— 26 Jan 1891. (89) £250
— 12 Apr 1892. (90) £250
— 26 May 1898. (89) £130
Ls, 28 July 1840. (91) DM850
— 5 Oct 1847. (88) $350
— 3 Mar 1869. (88) DM460
ANs, 29 June 1897. (90) $225
Series of Ds s, 8 Ds s, 1849 to 1853. (88) £400
— Series of Ds s, 13 Ds s, 1851 to 1888. (88) £280
— Series of Ds s, 9 Ds s, 1853 to 1889. (88) £280
— Series of Ds s, 16 Ds s, 1854 to 1882. (88) £380
Ds s (2) 20 Oct 1851 & 13 June 1854. Doheny collection. (88) $450
— Ds s (2) 29 Mar 1853 & 13 Dec 1888. (88) £380
Ds, 29 Aug 1837. (91) $175
— 9 May 1838. (89) £350
— 16 Feb 1839. (91) $250
— 18 Mar 1840. (90) $300
— 1 Dec 1842. (90) DM250
— 28 Aug 1843. (91) $200
— 10 July 1848. (91) $200
— 21 Jan 1854. (91) $200
— 11 Dec 1854. (90) £250
— 23 June 1869. (91) £95
— July 1870. (91) £60
— 11 Aug 1871. Sang collection. (88) $900
— 11 Aug 1871. (90) £720
— 9 Jan 1872. (89) $150
— 26 Feb 1880. (90) £850
— 2 Feb 1886. (88) £80
— 1 July 1886. Byer collection. (90) $300
— 1 Feb 1888. (89) £100
— 11 May 1894. (89) DM420
— 2 Aug 1895. (88) £65
— 26 Aug 1898. (89) £280
— 2 Nov 1899. (88) £1,000
— [n.d.]. (91) £80
— [n.d.]. (89) $240
Franking signature, [n.d.]. Alexander collection. (90) $55
Photograph, sgd, 1899. (91) £700
Photograph, [c.1875]. (88) £80
— CROFT, GEORGE. - ALs, 7 Mar 1840. 4 pp, 4to. To his brother. Describing a Court Levee & Prince Albert's investiture with the Order of the Garter. With related material. (88) £120

VICTORIA

— THOMSON, ANDREW. - Autograph Ms, journal kept as dancing master at Balmoral, 1849. 33 pp, 8vo. Bound in a folder with 4 A Ls s from Thomson to James Kay & ALs by Edward VII to his father, 1849. (88) £520

Victoria, Queen of England, 1819-1901 —&
Albert, 1819-61, Prince Consort of Victoria of England
Ls s (2), 7 Dec 1844 & 13 June 1846. (88) £200

Victoria, Empress of Friedrich III, 1840-1901
Series of 4 A Ls s, 16 June to 13 Aug 1895. (91) DM700
ALs, 1 Aug 1870. 12 pp, 8vo. To "Dear Cousin". Discussing the war with France, the need for England & Germany to draw together, national feelings in Germany, etc. (91) DM1,700
— 27 June 1877. (89) £220
Ds, 10 Oct 1888. (90) DM260

Vigee-Lebrun, Marie Louise Elisabeth, 1755-1842
ALs, [16 Dec 1822]. (89) DM550

Vignolle, Martin, Comte de, 1763-1824
Ls, [5 Nov 1797]. (90) DM550

Vigny, Alfred de, 1797-1863
Autograph transcript, 44 lines from his poem La maison du berger, sgd & dated Oct 1854. 3 pp, folio. Martin collection. (90) FF1,800
— Autograph transcript, 70 lines from his poem La maison du berger, sgd & dated 1844. 4 pp, folio, in half mor bdg. Martin collection. (90) FF3,800
A Ls s (2), 30 Nov 1845 & 7 Feb 1857. (90) £260
ALs, 19 Sept 1862. (90) DM400

Villa Lobos, Heitor, 1887-1959
ALs, 3 June 1955. (88) DM320
Photograph, sgd & inscr, 4 June [19]35. (90) DM240
— BERKE, BERENICE. - Orig drawing, pencil bust port of Villa Lobos, [c.1950]. 205mm by 257mm. Sgd by both. (91) $90

AMERICAN BOOK PRICES CURRENT

Villers, Charles de, 1765-1815. See: Goethe, Johann Wolfgang von

Villon, Jacques, Pseud. of Gaston Duchamp, 1875-1963
ALs, 2 Sept 1924. (89) DM270

Vinson, Frederick Moore, 1890-1953
Ls, 6 Aug 1940. (91) $275

Viotti, Giovanni Battista, 1755-1824
ALs, 16 Aug 1821. (88) DM550

Viozzi, Giulio
Autograph music, Trio per flauto, violoncello e pianoforte, 15 Nov 1960. (88) DM260

Virchow, Rudolf, 1821-1902
Autograph Ms, notes about a discussion of church-related questions in the Prussian House of Representatives, [n.d.]. (88) DM260
— Autograph Ms, notice for examination candidates, sgd & dated 22 Nov 1892. (90) DM550
ALs, 30 Aug 1846. (90) DM1,000
— 20 Nov 1863. 2 pp, 8vo. To Otto Gruendler. Discussing parasites found in pork. (90) DM1,700
— 12 Feb 1865. (91) DM900
— 28 Jan 1874. (90) DM500
— 5 Jan 1877. (89) DM520
— 14 May 1882. (88) DM800
— 9 Dec 1893. (91) DM520
Autograph postcard, sgd, 14 Mar 1876. Schroeder collection. (89) DM600

Virginia
— AYRE, GEORGE S. - Ms, farm book containing inventory of slaves, records of payments, & daily records for Rose Hill Farm in Loudoun County, Jan to Apr 1854. In ptd book, Plantation and Farm Instruction, Regulation, Record, Inventory and Account Book... Richmond, 1852. 136 pp, 4to. Worn. With related material. (89) $350
— BRANDT, SEBASTIAN. - ALs, 13 Jan 1622. 3 pp, folio. To Henry Hovener. Reporting about the situation in Virginia & ordering supplies from England. (91) $19,000
— BRANDT, SEBASTIAN. - ALs, 13 Jan 1622. 3 pp, folio. To Henry Hovener. Reporting about his situation in Vir-

ginia & mining prospects, & requesting supplies. (88) £6,000

Vischer, Friedrich Theodor, 1807-87
ALs, 17 Jan 1849. (90) DM640
— 11 Apr 1860. (88) DM300
— 9 Feb 1862. (91) DM700

Vittorio Emanuele III, King of Italy, 1869-1947
Ls, 2 Aug 1900. (90) DM460
— 27 Feb 1936. (90) £400
— 28 July 1939. (91) DM800
Series of Ds s, 6 Ds s, 4 Jan 1920 to 22 Dec 1938. 10 pp, folio. Orders relating to the Opera Nazionale per i Combattenti. 4 countersgd by Mussolini. (89) DM1,200
Photograph, sgd & inscr, 1940. (89) DM380

Vivaldi, Antonio, 1678-1741
Ms, aria, Leon feroce che avvinto freme; [c.1725?]. 4 pp, folio. With autograph inscr, annotations & corrections. Bound with 13 contemp musical Mss. (91) £24,000

Vladimir Alexandrovich, Grand Duke of Russia, 1847-1909
Photograph, [n.d.]. (90) £800

Vladislas II, King of Bohemia & Hungary, 1456-1516
Document, [11 Aug] 1471. (90) £480

Vlaminck, Maurice de, 1876-1958
ALs, [n.d.]. (90) $200
— [n.d.]. (89) DM360

Vogel, Eduard, 1829-56
Ls, 22 Feb 1854. (90) DM500

Vogel, Wladimir, 1896-1984
Autograph music, Nature vivante. Quartre morceaux poetiques pour piano; 1917 to 1921. 7 pp, 34cm by 27cm. Sgd on tp. (90) DM3,000

Vogeler, Heinrich, 1872-1942
A Ls s (2), 26 Nov & 20 Dec 1920. (91) DM460
ALs, 10 Nov 1912. (88) DM380
Series of 3 autograph postcards, sgd, 1921 & 1922. (89) DM300

Vogt, Karl, 1817-95
Collection of 2 A Ls s & ANs, 25 Nov 1859 & [n.d.]. (91) DM450
A Ls s (2), 23 Mar 1866 & 15 Feb 1871. (89) DM260
— A Ls s (2), 23 Mar 1866 & 15 Feb 1871. (91) DM480

Vollmoeller, Karl Gustav, 1878-1948
Autograph Ms, poem, beginning "Und unsre Schuhe sind besohlt mit Eisen"; sgd & dated 4 Apr 1922. (90) DM220

Volta, Alessandro, 1745-1827
Autograph Ms, notes & drawings for his electrophore, [1775]. 4 pp, folio. (90) £9,500
Series of 5 A Ls s, 5 Feb to 30 July 1776. 5 pp, folio. To Canon Francesco Fromond. About various matters of scientific interest. (90) £6,800
ALs, 31 July 1775. 1 p, folio. To Canon Francesco Fromond. Inquiring about recipient's attempts to construct an electrophore. (90) £2,000
— 3 Aug 1775. 2 pp, folio. To Canon Francesco Fromond. Describing improvements he has made to the composition of the resin in his electrophore. (90) £2,000
— 12 Aug 1775. 2 pp, folio. To Canon Francesco Fromond. Promising to send a copy of his letter to Joseph Priestley & reporting about his latest experiments. (90) £2,000
— 20 May 1816. 1 p, folio. Recipient unnamed. Proposing Luigi Monti as his substitute as Deputy for the commune of Lazzate. Collector's stamp. (88) £1,400
ADs, 15 Mar 1808. 1 p, folio. Receipt for salary from the University of Pavia. (91) DM1,250

Voltaire, Francois Marie Arouet de, 1694-1778
Autograph Ms, comedy, Therese, [before 1743]. 8 pp, 4to, in modern red mor bdg. Comprising scenes 3, 4 & 5 of the 1st act; including revisions. (91) £3,000
Collection of 20 A Ls s & AL, [c.Feb 1751] to 3 Oct 1752 & [n.d.]. 27 pp, 4to & 8vo. To M. Le Baillif. During his stay at the Prussian court, covering a wide range of subjects. 19 sgd V. In red mor bdg, with related material.

VOLTAIRE

(90) DM36,000
— Collection of ALs & ANs, 25 Apr 1777 & [n.d.]. 1 p, 8vo, & visiting card. To M. de Frenoi, giving him power of attorney. Recipient unnamed, concerning a dinner meeting. (91) £1,400

ALs, 13 May 1740. 3 pp, 4to. To Dr. James Jurin. About his advocacy of the Newtonian system, & announcing he is sending a Ms. In English. (89) £7,200
— 16 Mar 1751. 1 p, 8vo. To his pbr G. C. Walther. Suggesting a text to advertise the new Ed of his works, & ordering books. Sgd V. Bestermann no 3839. (90) DM2,800
— [1751]. 1 p, 4to. To Algarotti. Quoting Virgil, requesting the return of a paper, etc. In Latin, Italian & French; sgd V. (90) £1,800
— 23 Oct [1754?]. (88) £700
— 18 Apr [1757]. 1 p, 8vo. To d'Alembert. Sending a book to pass on to Briasson & praising d'Alembert's work. Sgd V. Foxed. (88) DM4,400
— 17 June 1760. 1 p, 4to. To Louis Gaspard Fabry. Asking him to give orders concerning necessary road repairs at Pregni. Was mtd. Bestermann no 8236. (88) DM3,000
— 23 May [1763]. 3 pp, 4to. To Francois de Chennevieres. Referring to letters written to M. de Varenne & a financial problem to be decided by the parliament. Sgd v. (89) DM2,500
— 14 Dec [1767]. 1 p, 12mo. To [Sebastien Dupont]. Sending an official letter (not included) regarding money due him from the Wuerttemberg treasury. Sgd V. (90) DM2,000

AL, [1762/63]. 1 p, 8vo. To his pbr Gabriel Cramer. Concerning corrections to a publication. (89) DM3,600

Ls, 25 Feb [1752]. 4 pp, 4to. To Charles Jean Francois Henault. Responding to questions about his Siecle de Louis XIV & talking about his stay at Potsdam. With autograph subscription. Sgd V. Bestermann no 4213. Sacha Guitry collection. (88) DM2,800
— Nov 1757. 4 pp, 4to. To Jean Baptiste Francois de La Michodiere, intendant of the Auvergne. Discussing methods of calculating the population of a town from baptismal registers or from the recorded number of hearths. Bestermann, Vol 102, D7420. (90) £1,350
— [c.10 Dec 1759]. 2 pp, 4to. To Francois Guillet, Baron de Monthoux. About a financial transaction. With related material. (90) DM3,400
— 24 Apr 1764. (90) DM950
— 25 Dec 1775. 2 pp, 8vo. Recipient unnamed. Sending a letter from M. Turgot concerning his taxes. Byer collection. (90) $1,100

Von der Schulenburg Family

[A collection of letters & documents, 1712 to 1727, 183 leaves, stitched, regarding a dispute about hunting rights between the Von der Schulenburg family at Altenhausen & Bodendorff in Saxony & the Prussian forest administration sold at HK on 8 Nov 1988, lot 93, for DM700.]

Von Stiebar Family

[A collection of 9 documents relating to the Von Stiebar family at Buttenheim & their property in Franconia, 1701 to 1770, folio, with related material, sold at HK on 8 Nov 1988, lot 95, for DM650.]

Vonnegut, Kurt

Ls, 16 Aug 1978. (90) $110
— 22 Apr 1981. Byer collection. (90) $110

Voragine, Jacobus de, 1230?-98?

Ms, Legenda aurea. [Southern England, London?, c.1315-20]. 2 conjoint leaves, vellum, 282mm by 318mm. In dark brown ink in a small formal gothic hand. With 9-line historiated initial by the circle of the Master of the Queen Mary Psalter. Margin cut; recovered from a bdg. (90) £6,500

Vordemberge-Gildewart, Friedrich, 1899-1962

Collection of 16 Ls s & postcards, sgd, mostly 1934 to 1935. Length not stated, mostly folio. To Eduardo Westerdahl. Concerning articles about his painting to appear in the Gaceta de Arte. With related material. (88) £1,250

Vorlaender, Karl, 1860-1928
Collection of 59 A Ls s & 130 autograph postcards, sgd, 11 Jan 1899 to 26 Feb 1927. 190 pp, mostly 8vo, & cards. To Otto Adolph Ellissen. Interesting political correspondence. Partly initialled or sgd with pseudonyms. (90) DM2,600

Voss, Heinrich, 1779-1822
Series of 3 A Ls s, 23 Nov 1818 to 6 July 1819. 21 pp, 8vo. To Friedrich Diez. Interesting letters about Shakespeare translations & other literary matters. (90) DM1,800

Voss, Johann Heinrich, 1751-1826
Autograph Ms, epigram, Der allzufriedene Urtheiler; [n.d.]. (89) DM360

ALs, [May 1784]. 2 pp, 8vo. To Heinrich Wilhelm von Gerstenberg. Discussing recipient's situation, suggesting that he move to Eutin, & mentioning several friends. With related material. (90) DM4,200
See also: Hoelty, Ludwig Christoph Heinrich

Vulpius, Christian August, 1762-1827
Autograph Ms, poem, das Jahr 1803. (88) DM300

ALs, 8 May 1797. (89) DM360

— 16 Nov 1803. (90) DM210

— [1807]. (91) DM360

— 4 Apr 1822. Albrecht collection. (91) SF550
See also: Goethe, Johann Wolfgang von

Vyshnegradsky, Ivan, 1893-1979
[A collection of letters addressed to him sold at S on 21 Sept, lot 220, for £70 to McCann.]

W

Wackenroder, Wilhelm Heinrich, 1773-98
ALs, [after 20] Jan 1793. 9 pp, 8vo. To Ludwig Tieck. Commenting on Tieck's works & informing him that his Ode an die Zeit will be pbd under a pen name. Sgd W.H.W. Kuenzel collection. (88) DM28,000

Wadham, Percy
Original drawings, (51), to illus F. Macmillan Archives. (90) £650

Wadsworth, Jeremiah, 1743-1804
ALs, 15 Nov 1778. (91) $140

Waggerl, Karl Heinrich, 1897-1973
Autograph Ms, poem, Salbei, Feb 1966. (90) DM270

— Autograph Ms, story, Jahrmarkt 2, fragment, dated 21 Dec 1940 / 21 Jan 1941. (89) DM500

Typescript, novel, Brot, 1929. (89) DM750

A Ls s (2), [c.1950]. (90) DM240

ALs, [n.d.]. (91) DM230

Wagner, Cosima, 1837-1930
Collection of 4 A Ls s & 2 Ls s, c.1860-1925. Length not stated. To various recipients. About Wagner & Liszt. With related material. (91) £1,500

— Collection of 4 A Ls s & AL, 3 June 1868 & [n.d.]. 15 pp, 8vo. To Isidora von Buelow-Bojanowski. Interesting letters about her life, family & acquaintances. 1 ALs & AL def. (90) DM1,800

A Ls s (2), 28 Feb 1872 & 2 May 1873. (91) DM700

ALs, 19 Oct 1858. (91) $850

— 27 May 1862. (91) $225

— 10 Nov 1865. (88) DM680

— [before 1870]. (90) DM300

— 25 July 1878. (88) DM400

— [20 Aug 1880]. (90) DM380

— 22 Dec 1893. (89) DM200

— [n.d.]. (89) DM220

Ls, 25 Aug 1902. (90) DM380

Wagner, Ernst, 1769-1812
ALs, 5 Mar 1811. (90) DM480

Wagner, Friedrich, 1803-76
[A collection containing 3 autograph poems, sgd or initialled, correspondence with C. S. Zindel, copies of his poems in Zindel's hand, & further related material, stitched, sold at HK on 11 Nov 1988, lot 3443, for DM550.]

WAGNER

Wagner, Johann Martin von, 1777-1858
ALs, 2 Aug 1837. (90) DM650

Wagner, John Peter ("Honus"), 1874-1955
Photograph, sgd, 1948. (88) $250
Signature, [n.d.]. (91) $210

Wagner, Minna, 1809-66
Series of 13 A Ls s, [c.1855] to 1861. 60 pp, various sizes. To Emma Herwegh. About her husband, his works & problems, her own life, acquaintances, etc. 1 incomplete. (91) £3,600
ALs, 25 Apr 1865. (88) £400

Wagner, Richard, 1813-83
[Bayreuth Festival, 1958. - A print, Die Mitwirkenden der Bayreuther Festspiele 1958, 52 pp, 8vo, with 92 portaits (87 sgd), sold at star on 10 Mar 1988, lot 1098, for DM550.]
Autograph Ms, angry reaction to a devastating review of his opera Rienzi, [Feb 1843]. 4 pp, 4to. Written for Ferdinand Heine as a draft for his rejoinder. Including 6 musical quotations, 36 bars in all. (90) DM19,000
— Autograph Ms, text of Hans Sachs's song, from Die Meistersinger von Nuernberg, Act 2; [n.d.]. 2 pp, folio. Fair copy. (91) DM5,000
Autograph music, 1st 22 bars of the overture to his opera Lohengrin, scored for 2 violins; [May 1853]. 1 p, 334mm by 249mm. (90) DM15,000
— Autograph music, composition sketch of the Wedding March & the love duet from Lohengrin, [1846]. 2 pp, c.39cm by 29cm. In brown ink on 19 & 29 hand-drawn staves, with extensive revisions. Marked "15" at head. With ALs by Siegfried Wagner presenting Ms. (89) £30,000
— Autograph music, Das Liebesmahl der Apostel, complete 1st draft, 14 May to 16 June [1843]. 12 pp, folio, in modern box. In brown & red ink & pencil on up to 31 hand-drawn staves per page. With numerous revisions, showing different layers of working. (91) £85,000
— Autograph music, opera, Der fliegende Hollaender, Act II, final part of Senta's song; 16 bars in full score, 1841. 1 p, 35.5cm by 25cm, 22 staves.

AMERICAN BOOK PRICES CURRENT

A few corrections. (88) DM16,000
Ms, Das Rheingold, full score; [before 1873]. 437 pp, size not stated. Wagner's signature removed. Presumably used by Heinrich Porges at Bayreuth, 1876. (91) £7,000
Series of 3 A Ls s, 9 Dec 1874 to 27 Feb 1878. 3 pp, 8vo. To the pbr Ernst Schmeitzner. About the publication of a new music journal, & complaining about ptg errors. With related material. (91) DM6,000
ALs, 15 Mar 1839. 2 pp, 4to. To Heinrich Dorn. Suggesting that he resign the position of conductor offered to him at Riga in Wagner's favor. With explanatory ANs by Dorn at bottom. (90) DM6,000
— 18 Mar 1841. 3 pp, 4to. To Ferdinand Heine. Discussing his opera Rienzi. Was mtd. (88) $2,750
— 12 Sept 1841. 3 pp, 8vo. To his mother. Reviewing his past misfortunes & his life in Paris, & hoping for a successful performance of Rienzi in Dresden. (90) DM9,000
— 19 Dec 1842. 1 p, 4to. To Ferdinand David. Apologizing for having troubled him with the search for a score. Repaired. (88) DM2,200
— 10 Nov 1843. 2 pp, 4to. To Moritz Hauptmann. Requesting information about a performance of his Liebesmahl der Apostel at Leipzig. (89) DM2,400
— 19 Nov [18]50. (89) £900
— 4 Apr [1851?] 3 pp, 8vo. Recipient unknown. Thanking for a port medallion & mentioning finishing a part of Die Nibelungen. Doheny collection. (89) $1,600
— 9 May [18]51. 3 pp, 8vo. To Gottfried Semper. Mentioning his theoretical writings & work on Der Ring des Nibelungen. (91) £4,400
— 28 May [18]51. 4 pp, 8vo. To Gottfried Semper. Announcing the completion of his work Oper und Drama, & mentioning work on Der Ring des Nibelungen. (91) £3,400
— 31 Jan [18]52. 4 pp, 4to. Recipient unnamed. Describing his medical problems & giving news of his work on Der Ring. (91) £4,200
— 12 Nov 1852. 2 pp, 8vo. To Ferdinand

Fuerstenau. About Tannhaeuser, & sending an autograph. (88) DM3,600
— 16 Feb 1853. 2 pp, 4to. To Louis Schindelmeisser. Discussing ideas for the performance of Tannhaeuser. Strip of 4 10-rappen stamps on integral address leaf. (89) £3,600
— 21 Apr 1853. (91) £750
— 31 May 1853. 2 pp, 8vo. Recipient unnamed. Declining a position in Bremen & recommending Rudolf Schoeneck. (90) DM4,600
— 20 Sept 1853. 1 p, 8vo. Recipient unnamed. Discussing Herr Engel's idea to give a concert-performance of Tannhaeuser in Berlin. (89) £1,500
— [mid-1850s]. 2 pp, 4to. To Heinrich Szadrowsky. Discussing performances of works by Donizetti & others, & explaining the best placing of the orchestra in an opera pit; with 2 autograph diagrams. Sgd RW. (88) £2,200
— 18 Nov [18]56. (88) £750
— [1856]. 4 pp, 4to. To [Heinrich Szadrowsky]. About the program & his requirements for the orchestra for his projected concert at St. Gallen. Sgd RW. (88) £1,050
— 23 Dec [18]58. 8 pp, 8vo. Recipient unnamed. Describing his progress on Tristan und Isolde, & complaining about financial problems. (90) £8,000
— 23 Nov 1859. 7 pp, 8vo. To [Johann Hoffmann?]. Discussing possible alternatives for the 1st performance of Tristan. Small repairs. (88) DM6,000
— 10 Dec 1859. 2 pp, 8vo. To Julius Stockhausen. Asking for advice concerning the formation of a male choir. (89) DM2,200
— 11 Apr 1860. (89) £900
— 13 June [c.1860]. 1 p, 4to. Recipient unnamed. Expressing surprise at being asked to repay 3,000 francs. In French. (90) £1,200
— 25 Feb 1861. 2 pp, 8vo. To Eugene Cormon of the Paris opera. Demanding a change of decorations for the 3d act of Tannhaeuser. (89) DM3,600
— [c.Feb 1861]. 7 pp, 8vo. To [Pauline von Metternich]. Requesting her help in averting unreasonable demands regarding the performance of Tannhaeuser in Paris. (90) DM7,000

— 21 Mar 1861. (89) £800
— 16 June 1861. 2 pp, 8vo. To Wilhelm Kalliwoda. Discussing a possible move to Karlsruhe. (90) DM4,000
— 25 July 1861. 4 pp, 8vo. To Malvida von Meysenbug. Informing her about his last days in Paris as a house-guest of the Prussian Minister & about his projected travels. (90) DM5,200
— 13 Sept 1861. 3 pp, 8vo. To Malwida von Meysenbug. Telling her about his recent endeavors. With related material. (91) £1,800
— [c.1861]. 1 p, 8vo. To Herr Flaxland. Requesting his help with a delivery of musical scores. (89) £1,300
— [c.1861]. (91) £900
— 22 Nov 1862. 3 pp, 8vo. To Wendelin Weissheimer. Requesting scores & reporting about his activities in Vienna. Sgd RW. (88) DM3,400
— 17 July 1863. 1 p, 8vo. To Wilhelm Kalliwoda. Asking him to forward a letter to the Grand Duke of Baden. (91) DM3,800
— 16 Oct [1863]. (91) £1,000
— 31 Oct [18]63. 4 pp, 8vo. To Hans von Bronsart. Discussing a concert program. (91) £3,100
— 16 Dec 1863. 2 pp, 8vo. To Pauline Tichatschek. Sending money for his wife Minna & discussing various old debts. (88) DM2,400
— 29 Feb 1864. 2 pp, 8vo. To [Pauline von Schoeller]. Asking for financial help. With related material. (88) DM3,200
— 11 Apr 1866. 4 pp, 8vo. To Julius Froebel. Discussing the immaturity of Ludwig II of Bavaria & his own situation. (89) $4,500
— 7 Mar 1867. 1 p, 8vo. To Franz [Mrazek]. Discussing arrangements for his visit to Munich, & sending a letter for the king. (90) £1,600
— 8 Aug 1867. 3 pp, 8vo. Recipient unnamed. Discussing problems about casting the role of Hans Sachs, complaining about musical standards, etc. (91) £3,600
— 25 Sept 1867. 2 pp, 8vo. To Hans von Bronsart. Describing the voice of Malvina Schnorr von Carolsfeld & discussing the casting of Die Meister-

WAGNER

singer. (91) £4,200
- 2 Aug 1868. 3 pp, 8vo. To Hans von Bronsart. Discussing the 1st production of Die Meistersinger at Munich. (91) £3,200
- 16 Jan 1869. 2 pp, 8vo. To Anton Mitterwurzer. Discussing the forthcoming production of Die Meistersinger at Dresden. (89) £1,650
- [Jan 1869?]. 3 pp, 12mo. To Mme Flaxland. About a music box to be sent as a present for his wife. In French. (90) DM1,650
- 14 Apr 1869. 3 pp, 8vo. To [Franz Mrazek]. Criticizing the shipment of his household effects. Sgd & initialled. (89) DM2,800
- 9 Aug 1869. 1 p, 8vo. To Caecilie Avenarius. Looking forward to her visit. (91) DM1,900
- 23 Nov 1869. 4 pp, 8vo. To [Hans von Buelow?]. Protesting against plans to postpone a performance of Die Meistersinger. (91) $7,500
- 19 Dec 1869. 1 p, 8vo. To the ptr G. A. Bonfantini. Agreeing to conditions for the ptg of his autobiography. (91) DM3,500
- 13 Apr 1872. 1 p, 8vo. To Karl Hill. About the prospect of using Hill in a performance. (91) $2,250
- 28 May 1872. (91) £600
- 28 Jan 1873. 2 pp, 8vo. To the pbr E. W. Fritzsch. Inquiring about proofs, stating conditions for concerts, etc. (91) £1,800
- 2 Feb 1873. 1 p, 8vo. To Julius Stern. Discussing times for rehearsals. (88) DM1,500
- 29 Mar 1873. 1 p, 8vo. Recipient unnamed. Discussing a financial matter. (89) DM2,400
- 5 May 1873. 1 p, 8vo. To Carl Voltz. Stating terms for the performance of his operas in Mannheim & Wiesbaden. (89) £1,300
- 13 Dec 1873. (88) £750
- [c.1873]. 1 p, 8vo. To Herr Wolffel. Arranging an appointment on the site where his house is to be built. (90) $1,200
- 18 July 1874. 3 pp, 8vo. To Herr Voltz. Discussing payment for performances. (91) $3,200
- 17 Dec 1874. 3 pp, 8vo. To Amalia Materna. Discussing preparations for the 1st Bayreuth Festival & for her performance of a scene from Goetterdaemmerung at Vienna. (89) £4,000
- 15 Mar 1875. 1 p, 8vo. To Georg Stuffler. Ordering writing paper. (90) DM1,600
- 18 June 1875. 1 p, 8vo. To Franz Betz. Expecting him for rehearsals for Der Ring des Nibelungen. (90) £2,200
- 4 Oct 1875. 2 pp, 8vo. To Karl Eckert. Regarding the cast for performances of Tristan in Berlin. (88) DM4,500
- 21 Dec 1875. 2 pp, 8vo. To [Hermann] Zumpe. Discussing his request about Der fliegende Hollaender, & mentioning Anton Seidl's misfortunes. (88) £1,600
- 19 Mar 1876. 1 p, 8vo. To an unnamed pbr. Declining to edit Liszt's music pbd by Kistner. (91) £1,600
- 28 June 1877. 2 pp, 4to. To Hans von Bronsart. Regretting that plans to perform the Ring des Nibelungen at Hannover have come to nothing, & recommending Anton Seidl. (91) £2,600
- 27 Oct 1877. 1 p, 4to. To [Lorenz Duefflipp?]. Inquiring about arrangements for a performance of Siegfried in Munich. (91) £1,600
- 24 Feb [18]78. 3 pp, folio. To the manager of a German opera house. Discussing terms & giving advice for a possible staging of Der Ring des Nibelungen. (90) £2,000
- 17 July 1878. (88) £800
- 20 Feb 1880. 1 p, 8vo. Recipient unnamed. Complaining about problems with the collection of fees. (90) DM3,300
- 10 Dec 1882. 1 p, 8vo. To an unnamed theater director. Giving instructions concerning fees for Tristan und Isolde. (90) DM3,200
- [n.d.]. 2 pp, 8vo. To Richard Lindau. About his own & Lindau's financial problems. (89) $1,500
- [n.d.]. (91) £500
- [n.d.]. 1 p, 8vo. Recipient unnamed. Dinner invitation. (90) DM1,300

AL, 3 Sept 1859. 4 pp, 8vo. To Joseph Tichatschek. Expressing his disappointment about cuts in Lohengrin & stressing the need for his own opera house; incomplete. (91) £1,400

Ls, 18 May 1870. 3 pp, 8vo. Recipient unnamed. Informing him that he lives in seclusion & is not in a position to write a recommendation. In French. Text in Cosima Wagner's hand. (90) DM2,100

— 25 May 1875. 2 pp, 4to. To Court Musician Hieber in Munich. Offering terms for participation in the Bayreuth orchestra; body of letter ptd. (88) £1,500

ANs, [1871]. (88) DM650

— [12 Sept n.y.]. 1 p, 7cm by 11.3cm. To Otto Zacher. Answering an inquiry about the Ms of Tannhaeuser. Sgd RW. (89) DM1,100

— [n.d.]. (89) DM650

Ds, [c.Aug 1847]. 1 p, 4to. As conductor at Dresden, certificate for the singer Wenzel Dressler. In the hand of & also sgd by Karl Gottlieb Reissiger. (91) DM1,100

— 21 Nov 1849. 2 pp, 4to. Power of attorney, ceding rights to Rienzi, Der fliegende Hollaender, & Tannhaeuser to Julius Schirmer. (91) £1,200

Autograph endorsement, statement that he directed Beethoven's Eroica at St. Gallen on 23 Nov 1856, sgd. On engraved score of the Eroica, [c.1830], 251 pp, 8vo, in contemp marbled bds. With 4 contemp drawings of Liszt in rehearsal for this joint concert with Wagner, in pencil on flyleaves, sgd & annotated by Heinrich Szadrowsky. (88) £3,000

Autograph quotation, Fuer deutsches Land das deutsche Schwert..., from his opera Lohengrin; sgd & dated 7 Aug 1852. 1 p, 4to. 9 bars, scored for voice & piano. (90) DM10,500

— Anr, 7 bars on a system of 2 staves, sgd & dated 16 Oct 1860. 180mm by 236mm. (89) £6,000

Engraving, port by J. Lindner. Sgd by Wagner & inscr to the Pasinelli Family with a musical quotation, 8 Aug 1871. Folio. (91) DM2,600

Menu, dinner in Wagner's honor at the Grand Hotel de Rome, 10 May 1881. (91) £400

Photograph, sgd, [c.1865]. 10.5cm by 6cm. By Hanfstaengl. (91) £3,800

— Anr, 1876. 10.5cm by 6cm. By Hanfstaengl, Munich. (90) DM8,500

— Anr, [c.1880?]. 16cm by 10.5cm. By J. Albert. (91) £4,800

Photograph, sgd & inscr, [c.1867]. 9.5cm by 6cm. By Pierson. Inscr to Rosalie Wagner on verso. (91) £2,000

Signature, [n.d.]. On visiting card, 6.8cm by 10.9cm. Also sgd "Herr und Frau von Buelow" in Cosima (von Buelow-) Wagner's hand. (89) DM1,100

— DOEPLER, CARL EMIL. - Autograph Ms, sgd; 24 Nov 1876. 16 pp, 8vo. Detailed description of costumes for the 1st complete production of Der Ring des Nibelungen. With 43 contemp photographs. (91) £4,200

— JOUKOVSKY, PAUL VON. - ALs, 21 Feb/4 Mar 1884. 4 pp, 4to. To [Henry Thode]. Expressing congratulations on his engagement to Wagner's stepdaughter Daniela von Buelow. (90) DM480

— NIEMANN, ALBERT. - ALs, 21 Apr 1872. 1 p, 8vo. To Richard Wagner. Accepting an offer to sing at Bayreuth. (88) DM650

— THODE, DANIELA, NEE VON BUELOW. - Collection of 13 A Ls s, 25 postcards, sgd, & 3 A Ns s, 1927 to 1935. 37 pp, mostly 8vo, & cards. To Evelyn Faltis. Commenting about her life at Bayreuth, her family, the political situation, etc. With related material. (90) DM600

— TICHATSCHEK, JOSEPH. - ALs, 5 Feb 1855. 4 pp, 8vo. To Wagner. Informing him about rehearsals & projected performances of Lohengrin & Tannhaeuser. (91) £500

— WAGNER FAMILY. - A large collection of letters, Mss, documents & memorabilia relating to Wagner's sister Rosalie & other members of the family, c.1819 to 1929, sold at S on 21 Nov 1990, lot 445, for £3,500 to Haas. 91

— WOLZOGEN, HANS VON. - Collection of 4 A Ls s, 2 autograph postcards, sgd, autograph sentiment, & photograph, sgd, 9 Sept 1917 to 9 Dec 1924 & [n.d.]. 10 pp, 4to & 8vo. To Karl Haller. Concerning contributions to the Bayreuther Blaetter, & other matters. (90) DM250

WAGNER

See also: Buelow, Hans von
See also: Semper, Gottfried

Wagner, Siegfried, 1869-1930

Collection of 23 A Ls s & Ls s, & 71 postcards, sgd (mostly autograph), 1914 to 1930. 55 pp, 4to & 8vo, & cards. To Evelyn Faltis. Mostly relating to singers at the Bayreuth Festivals. With related material. (90) DM4,500

Wagner von Jauregg, Julius, 1857-1940

ADs, 13 Aug 1935. (90) DM220

Wagner, Winifred, 1897-1980

Collection of 3 A Ls s, 11 Ls s, 4 autograph postcards, sgd, & 3 A Ns s, 1923 to 1935. (90) DM850

— Collection of 3 A Ls s & 4 Ls s, 24 June 1939 to 24 June 1974. (90) DM440

Ls s (2), 6 Nov 1930 & 3 Mar 1934. (90) DM220

Ls, 30 Jan 1933. (88) DM240

Photograph, sgd & inscr, [n.d.]. (88) DM360

Wagner-Regeny, Rudolf, 1903-69

Autograph music, sketches for a composition for voice & piano, [n.d.]. (90) DM320

ALs, 1 June 1941. (90) DM240

Wagner-Warmbronn, Christian, 1835-1918

ALs, 16 Sept 1893. 4 pp, 8vo. To an unnamed Ed. Offering 3 poems for print (included). (91) DM3,800

Waiblinger, Wilhelm Friedrich, 1804-30

ALs, 29 Dec 1826. 1 p, 4to. To Gustav Schwab. Giving an enthusiastic account about his first weeks in Rome & his further plans. Seal tear. (88) DM19,000

Walbach, J. De B.

Franking signature, [20 May c.1814]. Alexander collection. (90) $140

Waldeyer, Wilhelm, 1836-1921

ALs, 14 Feb 1889. (91) DM240

— 24 Jan 1903. (88) DM300

AMERICAN BOOK PRICES CURRENT

Waldo, Lawrence

ALs, 15 May 1840. (89) $130

Wales

— RICHARD DE GLANVILLE. - Document, [c.1130]. 1 p, vellum, 380mm by 138mm. Grant of land in Wales near Neath Castle to the Abbey of Holy Trinity at Savigny in Normandy. In fine romanesque script. Imperf. (91) £3,800

Walker, James A., 1832-1901

ALs, 30 June 1886. 4 pp, 4to. Recipient unnamed. Describing how Stonewall Jackson got his name at the Battle of Manassas. (91) $2,000

Wallace, George C.

Ls, 14 Apr 1964. (91) $450

Wallace, Lew, 1827-1905

Series of 4 A Ls s, 6 July 1886 to 12 Dec 1888. Doheny collection. (89) $600

Ls, 27 Mar 1889. (90) $65

Wallace, Susan Arnold Elston, 1830-1907

Autograph Ms, poem, The Patter of Little Feet, 1858. (88) $50

Wallenstein, Albrecht von, Herzog von Friedland & Mecklenburg, 1583-1634

[An autograph address ("Herren Keplero zu zustellen"), cut from larger sheet, [3 Jan 1629?], 8cm by 10cm, with authentication by Otto von Struve on verso, sold at star on 28 June 1990, lot 1571, for DM950.]

Ms, list of provisions to be given to officers & soldiers, sgd; 13 Feb 1630. 1 p, folio. (89) DM2,200

ALs, 10 Feb 1624. 1 p, folio. To [Otto von Nostitz], Vice Chancellor for Bohemia. Asking him to support his request for a conversion of his Bohemian estates to Imperial fiefs. Sgd AFzuFrd. (90) DM4,600

— 11 Nov 1627. 1 p, folio. To Hans Georg von Arnim. Informing him about negotiations with the Duke of Mecklenburg & requesting horoscopes of the Kings of Sweden & Poland. (90) DM6,000

— 27 Feb 1628. 1 p, folio. To Hans Georg von Arnim. Sending a letter for the Duke of Pomerania & discussing the siege of Stralsund. (91) DM7,200

— 1 Apr 1628. 1 p, folio. To Capt. [Hans Georg von Arnim]. Giving instructions in case of opposition in Mecklenburg. (89) DM7,000

— 23 Aug 1628. 1 p, folio. To Franz Christoph Khevenhueller, Graf von Frankenburg. Describing his victory at Wolgast. Repaired. (88) DM14,500

Ls, 14 June 1626. 1 p, folio. To the commanding officer at Bernburg. Summoning him to a meeting the next day. (88) DM2,000

— 4 July 1626. 1 p, folio. To an unnamed prince. Responding to a complaint about Capt. Brandtstein, & promising redress. (90) DM3,300

— 28 July 1626. (89) £600

— 27 Oct 1626. 3 pp, folio. To Col. Adam Wilhelm Schelhardt von Dornwerdt. Reprimanding him for spoliations caused by his troops & ordering him to return to headquarters. (90) DM4,500

— 21 Oct 1627. 1 p, folio. To Hans Georg von Arnim. Informing him about complaints by the Duke of Pommerania. Repaired. (88) DM3,800

— 4 June 1630. (90) £1,000

— 11 May 1631. 1 p, folio. To Otto Heinrich Stosch von Kaunitz. Requesting him to send a letter to von Tieffenbach. (88) DM1,700

Ds, 11 Dec 1628. 1 p, 60.5cm by 39cm. Ptd army orders regulating affairs at winter quarters in Mecklenburg. Fold tears. (88) DM3,400

— 14 July 1632. 1 p, folio. Appointment of Lorenz von Merode as Colonel. (91) DM2,100

— ARNERI, CAPT. GEROLAMO. - 3 Ls s, Oct to 14 Nov 1634. 3 pp, folio. To the magistracy of Roth in Franconia. Demanding contributions. (89) DM550
See also: Trcka, Adam Erdmann

Waller, Thomas ("Fats"), 1904-43

Autograph music, song, There's a Little Good in Me, [n.d.]. (91) $750

Menu, College Inn Panther Room, Sept 1, [19]39. (91) $275

Wallington, John

ALs, 31 Dec 1795. (88) $190

Wallnoefer, Adolf, 1854-1946

Autograph music, Flammen-Lieder, Op. (89) DM550

Walpole, Horace, 4th Earl of Orford, 1717-97

ALs, 28 Aug 1734. (91) £650

— 18 Aug 1773. Wolf collection. (90) £900

— 19 July 1785. Doheny collection. (89) $450

— LIBRARY CATALOGUE. - Ms, Catalogue of the Library of Mr. Horace Walpole at Strawberry-hill, 1763. About 160 pp & blanks, folio, in contemp calf. With autograph tp with engraved vignette pasted in, autograph additions & additions in anr hand. Phillipps Ms.11792. (90) £42,000

Walpole, Sir Robert, 1st Earl of Orford, 1676-1745

ALs, 27 Aug 1728. (88) £150

Ds, 25 Feb 1720/1. (88) £80

Walrond Family

[2 Ms account books pertaining to Bradford House, Devon, 1740 to 1795, c.200 pp, folio, vellum bdg, with details of the estate, prescriptions, etc., in several hands, sold at C on 9 Dec, lot 268, for £200 to Bristow.]

Walser, Martin

Autograph Ms, book review, "Bregenz, beneidenswert"; 9 Mar 1984. (91) DM900

— Autograph Ms, essay, Maerzsaetze und Musik, [n.d.]. 15 pp, folio, on blank versos of proofs. Sgd twice. (89) DM1,400

— Autograph Ms, trans of Shaw's Mrs. (88) DM750

Walser, Robert, 1878-1956

Autograph Ms, Schreiben an ein Maedchen, [ptd in Neuer Merkur, June 1920]. 4 pp, 4to, on rectos only. Sgd at head. With covering ANs on verso. (90) DM12,000

Walsh, Edward Augustine, 1881-1959
Ptd photograph, [n.d.]. (91) $120

Walsh, William, 1663-1708. See: Pope, Alexander & Walsh

Walshe, F. W. H., d.1931
[His papers as a Colonel during the Allied Intervention in Russia, 1919 & 1920, comprising c.100 documents & reports, sold at S on 18 July 1991, lot 427, for £1,600 to Maggs.]

Walsingham, Sir Francis, 1530?-90
Ls, 14 May 1578. (88) £200

Walter, Bruno, 1876-1962
Autograph Ms, radio speech, Bruno Walter spricht zu Deutschland, [1940/41]. 2 pp, folio. Including autograph English trans on verso. (89) DM1,100
Collection of ALs & 4 Ls s, 5 Nov 1941 to 18 Nov 1961. (89) DM800
— Collection of ALs & 33 photographs, 25 Dec 1947. (88) DM560
ALs, 26 May 1929. (90) DM320
— 30 Oct 1931. (88) DM500
— 26 Dec 1931. (90) DM660
— 16 Sept 1933. (88) DM220
— 31 Aug 1943. (91) DM600
— 30 Aug 1960. (88) DM380
Ls, 5 Sept 1949. (90) DM240

Walther, Philipp Franz von, 1782-1849
ALs, 8 Nov 1844. (90) DM350

Walton, George, Signer from Georgia
ALs, 14 June 1784. Doheny collection. (89) $350
ANs, [c.1775]. (91) $140
Ds, April [n.y.]. (91) $160

Walton, Izaak, 1593-1683
Ds, 25 Oct 1659. (91) £950

Walton, Sir William, 1902-83
Autograph music, A Lyke-wake Song, for voice & piano to a text by Swinburne, July 1918. 5 pp, folio. Fair copy, sgd at head. Apparently undocumented. Including anr autograph Ms of the opening 28 bars of the song. (90) £1,800
— Autograph music, Child's Song, for voice & piano to a text by Swinburne, July 1918. 3 pp, folio. Fair copy, sgd at head. Apparently undocumented. (90) £2,200
— Autograph music, Song, beginning "Love laid his sleepless head", for voice & piano to a text by Swinburne, July 1918. 3 pp, folio. Fair copy. Apparently undocumented. (90) £1,500
— Autograph music, The Bear. (90) DM550
Autograph quotation, 2 bars from the polka in Facade, 18 Feb [19]77. (91) $140

Walton, Sir William, 1902-83 —& Holst, Gustav, 1874-1934
[A collection of 6 A Ls s by Holst, 1922 & later, & 4 A Ls s by Walton, [1940s], to Sir Ivor Atkins, mostly regarding professional matters, sold at S on 18 Nov 1988, lot 487, for £650 to Rankin.]

Wandrei, Howard
Collection of 187 Ls s. [Various dates] To his parents. (89) $2,250

Wangenheim, Karl August, Freiherr von, 1773-1850
ALs, [25 Dec] 1810. (89) DM550

War of 1812
[A soldier's letter, 21 Sept 1812, 3 pp, size not stated, from Fort Wayne, talking about an invasion of Canada, sold at rf on 5 Dec, lot 82, for $260.]
[A soldier's letter, 12 July 1813, size & recipient not stated, requesting assistance regarding a trunk & commenting on the hardships of the war sold at rf on 5 Dec, lot 77, for $230.]
[A letter from Fort Washington, 30 July 1813, 3 pp, size not stated, to Maj. Gardner at the War Department, seeking to remove officers for incompetence, sold at rf on 5 Dec, lot 79, for $110.]
[A soldier's letter, 13 Oct 1813, 3 pp, size not stated, from Fort Defiance, mentioning trip to the Turtle Village, sold at rf on 5 Dec, lot 81, for $200.]
[A letter written by an American prisoner of war, 8 Mar 1814, 2 pp, size not stated, describing his situation in Puerto Rico, sold at rf on 5 Dec, lot 74, for $525.]
[A letter, 21 Sept 1814, size not stated,

containing a copy of a letter from a prisoner of war & commenting on the difficulty of exchanging prisoners sold at rf on 5 Dec, lot 76, for $110.]

[A document, sgd by a British Assistant Quartermaster General, 1 p, folio, "return for 165 days Forage Money" for officers in the expeditions against Washington & Baltimore, sold at rf on 5 Dec, lot 71, for $850.]

[A letter, 12 Feb 1815, 1 p, 4to, by the Captain of H.M.S. Favorite at New York to Gen. Scott, requesting supplies to return to England, sold at rf on 5 Dec, lot 75, for $200.]

[Battle of New Orleans. - A soldier's letter, 25 Feb [1815], 2 pp, size not stated, reporting about the battle, sold at rf on 5 Dec, lot 73, for $950.]

— FLEISCHMAN, MIDSHIPMAN HENRY P. - Ms journal recording naval events of the War of 1812. 13 Dec 1812-1 June 1813. 105 pp, folio, in contemp half calf. (89) $3,600

— HAWKINS, LIEUT. COL. SAMUEL. - ALs, 22 July 1813. Size not stated. Recipient unnamed. Commenting about "national disaster and disgrace". (88) $120

— HILLS, ELEZUR. - ALs, 2 Sept 1814. 3 pp, 4to. To Hart Forbes. About the burning of Washington & the defenseless state of Savannah. (91) $325

— KING, WILLIAM. - ALs, 6 Dec 1812, 5 pp, size not stated. To Sec of War William Eustis. Stating arrangement with volunteers for protection from the British. (88) $130

— MACHIAS, MAINE. - Document, 12 Sept 1814, 1 p, folio. Parole of civil officers & citizens at Machias by which they surrender to British forces, sgd by John Cooper, Sheriff of Washington County, Jeremiah O'Brien & 17 others. (88) £250

— MACHIAS, MAINE. - Document, 12 Sept 1814, 1 p, folio. Parole of civil officers & citizens at Machias by which they surrender to British forces, sgd by John Cooper, Sheriff of Washington County, Jeremiah O'Brien & 17 others. (89) $130

— MASCALL, CAPT. - ALs, 27 Jan 1815. Size not stated. Written on H.M.S. Asia, informing recipient of his safety after the attack on New Orleans. (88) $550

Ward, Artemas, 1727-1800
Ds, 7 Sept 1767. (89) $180
— 26 June 1776. (91) $200
— 3 Jan 1777. (89) $650
— 6 Sept 1787. (91) $110

Ward, William
Series of 14 A Ls s, 1807 to 1846 & [n.d.]. (88) £140

Warhol, Andy, .1987
[2 signatures, on Campbell's Soup color postcards, [n.d.], sold at wa on 1 Oct 1988, lot 93, for $160.]
Photograph, sgd, [n.d.]. (89) $120
Signature, on colored WFUNA print, 8.5 by 11 inches, no. (89) $240

Warhol, Andy, .1987 —& Others
[A Rain Dance Benefit poster, designed & sgd by Warhol, Roy Lichtenstein, Yoko Ono, & others, 1985, 30 by 21.5 inches, framed, sold at CNY on 21 June 1989, lot 433, for $600.]

Warhol, Andy, d.1987
Photograph, sgd, [n.d.]. (90) DM850
Signature, [1964]. (91) $180
— Anr, [1964]. (91) $150
— Anr, on poster picturing his port of Russell Means, Mar 1977, 36 by 54 inches. (91) $180
— Anr, [9 Mar 1979]. (91) $130
— Anr, [9 Mar 1979]. (90) $260
— Anr, March 1979. (91) $150
— Anr, [9 May 1979]. (90) $55
— Anr, [14 Jan 1981]. (90) $75
— Anr, [n.d.]. (91) $250
— Anr, [n.d.]. (91) $250
— Anr, [n.d.]. (91) $70
— Anr, [n.d.]. (91) $140

Warner, Charles Dudley, 1829-1900. See: Clemens, Samuel Langhorne
See also: Clemens, Samuel Langhorne & Warner

Warren, Earl
Ls, 10 Dec 1943. (89) $60

WARREN

Warren, James, 1726-1808
ADs, 28 June 1769. (88) $180

Warren, Joseph, 1741-75 —& Others
Ls, 4 June 1775. 2 pp, 4to. To the NY Provincial Congress. Describing their gunpowder shortage & urgently requesting help. Also sgd by Artemus Ward & Moses Gill. (90) $18,000

Wartenberg, Johann Kasimir Kolbe, Graf von, 1643-1712
ALs, 22 Dec 1708. Schroeder collection. (89) DM250

Wartensleben, Alexander Hermann, Graf von, 1650-1734
Ls, 18 June 1695. Schroeder collection. (89) DM420

Warwick, E. A.
Original drawings, (119), to illus Fairy Star's Annual, 1925. (89) £400

Washington, Booker T., 1856-1915
Ls, 12 Oct 1898. (90) $200
— 15 May 1900. (91) $200
— 25 Feb 1901. (91) $200
— 19 Nov 1907. (90) $200
— 17 Mar 1910. (88) $100
Ds, 30 May 1912. (90) $100

Washington, District of Columbia
[A group of 4 documents, [19th cent], mostly deeds, with signatures by William Thornton, W.W. & James Corcoran, & Albert Fairfax, sold at wa on 17 Oct, lot 312, for $100.]
[A group of 4 documents, [19th cent], mostly deeds, with signatures by William Thornton, W.W. Corcoran, & others, sold at wa on 17 Oct, lot 313, for $100.]
— BLODGET, SAMUEL. - Ds, 25 Feb 1792. 1 p, folio. Sale of a lot of land in the Jamaica district of Washington to John Dewhurst. (90) $375

Washington Family
[2 documents, sgd by various members of the Washington family & others, 1 June 1785 & 14 Aug 1817, 5 pp, folio, concerning the sale of land & George Washington's estate, sold at R on 24 Feb 1990, lot 40, for $600.]

AMERICAN BOOK PRICES CURRENT

Washington, George, 1732-99
[An autograph address leaf, [25 July 1781?], 6 by 3 inches, addressed to John Parke Custis, sold at Dar on 6 Dec 1990, lot 406, for $950.]
Autograph Ms, "From the York Papers", statement about British troops designed for America; [c.1794/95]. 1 p, 8vo. With autograph docket on verso. Tipped to larger sheet with related material. (90) DM4,200
— Autograph Ms, instructions for recording his Farewell Address in his letterbooks, [c.19 Sept 1796]. 23 lines on tp of a copy of Claypole's American Daily Advertiser, 19 Sept 1796, containing the Address. With 3-line notation by Jared Sparks on verso. Worn, silked; in olive green case. Fleming collection. (90) $25,000
— Autograph Ms, "Remarks", account of his experiences in the French & Indian War & of Braddock's defeat, [c.1786-89]. 11 pp, folio. In 3d person, prepared as addition to a draft biography by David Humphreys. Partly reinforced with tissue. John F. Fleming Estate. (89) $280,000
ALs, [7] Dec 1773. 1 p, folio. To [James Mercer]. Requesting copies of deeds & court proceedings regarding the estate of George Mercer. Def; framed. (90) $6,000
— 28 Nov 1775. 1 p, 4to. To Lieut. Col. George Baylor. Giving instructions for meeting Mrs. Washington on her journey to Cambridge. Repaired. Armstrong collection. (88) $8,500
— 10 Mar 1779. 1 p, 4to. To Capt. [John] McQueen. Requesting him to deliver letters (not present) to Lafayette. Imperf. (90) $10,000
— 15 Aug 1780. 2 pp, folio. To Nathanael Greene. Testimonial praising his services as Quartermaster General. With endorsement on detached integral blank. Pratt collection. (89) $21,000
— [7-8 Sept 1781]. 1 p, 4to. To Maj. Gen. Benjamin Lincoln. Instructing him to send the corps of sappers & miners with the 1st troops embarking for Virginia. Trimmed. Presumably unpbd. (89) $23,000
— [c.June 1782]. 1 p, 191mm by 312mm. Recipient unknown. Referring to a

proposed invasion of Jamaica. Repaired. (88) $7,750
— 12 Mar 1783. 1 p, 8vo. To Henry Knox. Hoping to talk to him the next day [about an anonymous call for officers to desert]. Framed with bust engraving. (91) $19,000
— 10 July 1783. 3 pp, 4to. To George Augustine Washington. Family letter, & commenting on the mutiny at Philadelphia. Possibly unpbd. Wine stains; repaired. (90) $10,000
— 23 Oct 1783. 1 p, folio. To Col. [Richard] Varick. Forwarding papers. (89) $5,000
— 24 Mar 1784. 1 p, 4to. To Thomas Jefferson. About delivery of silver plate from France to Mount Vernon; puts off the matter of whether he will interrupt his retirement long enough to oversee construction of the proposed Potomac Canal. (91) $23,000
— 27 Mar [17]8[4]. 2 pp, folio. To [Gen. Nathanael Greene]. Urging him to attend a meeting of the Society of the Cincinnati. (89) $6,000
— 15 Mar 1785. 2 pp, folio. To Col. Frederick Weissenfels. Expressing regrets about his financial problems & promising to write a recommendation after receipt of the necessary papers. Silked & framed. (90) $16,000
— 26 Nov [17]85. 1 p, 4to. To Col. John Fitzgerald. Regarding a petition & bill drawn up by Mr. Johnson. With postscript, sgd GW. Seal tear repaired. (88) $9,000
— 20 Jan 1788. 2 pp, 4to. To John Jay. Asking him to forward letters, & discussing the ratification of the Constitution. Dampstained. Chetwynd collection. (89) $32,000
— 27 Nov 1788. 2 pp, 4to. To Thomas Jefferson. Letter of introduction for Gouverneur Morris. (88) DM45,000
— 5 Feb 1789. 3 pp, 4to. To Samuel Powel. Speculating on the composition of the new Congress & commenting on George III's insanity. (91) $90,000
— 30 June 1790. 2 pp, 4to. To Messrs. Duchesne, de Barth, Thiebaud & Associates in the Scioto Settlement. Assuring them of governmental protection for their settlement. (91) $19,000
— 3 Oct 1790. 1 p, 4to. To Sec of the Treasury Alexander Hamilton. Thanking for a report [regarding the Nootka Sound Controversy]. (88) $14,000
— [12 Dec 1790?]. 1 p, 4to. To [James Madison). Sending dispatches received from Gouverneur Morris. Framed with related material. (90) $11,000
— 20 Feb 1818. 1 p, 4to. To M. LeRaydechaumont. Content not given. (91) $15,000
— 17 Feb 1793. 1 p, 4to. To William A. Washington. Requesting his help in procuring a supply of oyster shells for Mount Vernon. Mtd with a port. Rosenbloom collection. (88) $16,000
— 26 July 1793. 1 p, 4to. To his nephew Robert Lewis. Rebuking him for letting "Major Harrison's land slip through [his] fingers". With postscript informing him of Mrs. Lear's death. Repaired. (90) $28,000
— 8 Nov 1793. 1 p, 4to. To the Earl of Buchan. Introducing his secretary Lear going to Scotland to study manufactures. With autograph endorsement by Buchan on address panel. (89) £4,000
— 24 Nov 1793. 2 pp, 4to. To Col. Burgess Ball. About purchasing buckwheat & his renting of a house in Germantown; retained draft, sgd G. W--n. (88) $4,400
— 16 Mar 1794. 2 pp, 8vo. To Col. Burgess Ball. About a shipment of clover seed to Alexandria & the breeding of horses. With related material. (88) $8,250
— 29 Apr 1794. 2 pp, 4to. To John Jay. Offering him the position of US Minister in London. (88) £14,000
— 6 Oct 1794. 1 p, 4to. To Major John Clark. About preparations to take the field to suppress the Whiskey Rebellion; declines Clark's offer to serve as his aide. (91) $24,000
— 15 Feb 1795. 3 pp, 4to. To John Jameson. Regarding his share in the Dismal Swamp Land Company. Framed. (90) $9,000
— 7 Sept 1795. 1 p, 4to. To a [Committee of towns in Suffolk County, NY]. Responding to their letter & defending Jay's Treaty. Repaired. (89) £13,000
— 28 Feb 1796. 1 p, size not stated. To George Clinton. Draft, informing him

about Mr. [William] Cooper's desire to purchase land managed by Clinton. Pforzheimer collection. (90) $16,000
- 10 Aug 1796. 1 p, 4to. To John Marshall. Requesting information about a letter forwarded to Gen. Pinckney. Including franking signature. Pratt collection. (89) $18,000
- 22 Dec 1796. 1 p, 4to. To Rufus King. Requesting him to forward a letter to Count Rumford. Repaired. (90) $13,000
- 30 Sept 1798. 3 pp, 4to. To Sec of War James McHenry.About his distrust of the Democratic Societies & the possiblity of war with France. (91) $30,000
- 11 Aug 1799. 3 pp, 4to. To Sec of War James McHenry. Discussing political problems, William Duane's attacks on the government, President Adams, etc. Framed. With related material. (91) $23,000

AL, 22 Mar 1776. 1 p, 4to. To Dr. John Morgan. In 3d person ("The General"), declining a horse captured from a Tory. Prinzmetal collection. (88) $11,000

Ls, 6 Apr 1776. 1 p, 4to. To Maj. Gen. Artemas Ward. Concerning money requested by Mr. Parke & other matters. Cropped. (88) $7,000
- 16 May 1777. 2 pp, folio. To Gen. [Alexander] McDougall. Concerning the lack of clothing of Massachusetts troops & a change in command. (89) DM21,000
- 19 May 1777. 1 p, 4to. To [Lieut. Col. Edward Antill]. Assigning a French volunteer to Col. Hazen's regiment. Doheny collection. (89) $11,000
- 21 Oct 1778. 1 p, folio. To Henry Laurens. Letter of introduction for the Chevalier Du Plessis. Framed. (89) $12,000
- 30 Jan 1779. 2 pp, folio. To Gen. William Phillips. Giving information about arrangements made in Virginia for British prisoners of war. (89) $18,000
- 11 Feb 1779. 1 p, folio. To George Clinton. Stressing the need "to secure a communication between forts Schuyler and Schenectady." (90) $18,000

- 22 Apr 1779. 1 p, 4to. To William Ellery, Jr. Informing him that the "Arrangement of the two Rhode Island Regiments has been settled". Including franking signature. (90) $16,000
- 11 May 1779. 1 p, folio. To George Morgan. Setting a date for a meeting with a party of Delaware chiefs. Silked. (89) $12,000
- 24 May 1779. 1 p, 4to. To Gen. James Clinton. Ordering him to join Major Gen. Sullivan's command. With postscript listing troops under Clinton's command. Text in the hand of Alexander Hamilton. Framed with a port. (90) $12,000
- 20 July 1779. 2 pp, 4to. To Gen. Arthur St. Clair. Instructing him to secure his position at Fort Putnam. Text in the hand of Alexander Hamilton. Repaired. (88) $9,000
- 24 Oct 1779. 1 p, folio. To Col. Sylvanus Seely. Acknowledging an intelligence report. Also sgd on integral address leaf. (89) $9,500
- 12 Jan 1780. 3 pp, folio. To David Ariel[?]. Discussing a suit brought against him as executor of Thomas Colvill. Repaired. (91) $5,000
- 14 Mar 1780. 4 pp, folio. To Col. Daniel Brodhead. Discussing a variety of military matters relating to the fort at Pittsburgh. Def; silked. (90) $6,000
- 2 July 1782. 1 p, 4to. To Lieut. Col. [George] Reid. Authorizing the defence of Fort Plain, NY. Margin def. (89) $8,000
- 10 Oct 1783. 2 pp, size not stated. To Col. [William Stephens] Smith. Thanking for a glass & some information, & inquiring about missing letters. (90) $10,000
- 16 Oct 1783. 2 pp, 4to. To Marinus Willett. Discussing military arrangements on the Mohawk frontier. Including recipient's draft reply on integral blank. (91) $10,000
- 13 Mar 1787. 1 p, 4to. To Charles W. Peale. Sending an ornithological specimen. (89) $8,500
- 18 June 1788. 1 p, 4to. To Brig. Gen. Henry Knox. Making an appointment. (91) $5,500
- 8 June 1789. 2 pp, 4to. To Gov. John

Hancock. Circular letter enclosing resolutions of Congress (present). Pratt collection. (89) $20,000
— 13 Dec 1791. 1 p, 4to. To Congress. Communicating "the plan of a City" in the proposed District [of Columbia]. Barrett collection. (89) $90,000
— 14 Nov 1798. 1 p, 4to. To Sec of War James McHenry. Concerning the supply of rations for the troops. Wormed; mtd. (89) $5,750
ADs, 5 Apr 1750. 1 p, 4to. Survey of land in Frederick County for Edward Kinnison. Inlaid. Sang & Middendorf collections. (89) $15,000
— 18 Apr 1751. 2 pp, 4to. Land survey for John Thomas, including plat drawing. (89) $13,000
— 25 Apr 1751. 1 p, folio, in folder by Sangorski & Sutcliffe. Survey of land along the Potomac for Daniel Pursley. Middendorf collection. (89) $13,000
— 23 Mar 1752. 1 p, 4to. Survey of land in Frederick County for William Warden. Folds reinforced. Middendorf collection. (89) $11,000
— 22 June 1769. 3 pp, 4to. Purchase of land in Maryland from Robert Alexander, contingent upon Mrs. Alexander's consent. Also sgd by R. Alexander. (91) $32,000
— 1 Jan 1789. 1 p, 4to. Certificate of military service for Major E. Haskell. Fold tear. (90) $14,000
AD, [after July 1773]. 1 p, 4to. "State of the Acct. with Capt. Crawford for Surveying 1773", recording debits & credits. Sang & Middendorf collections. (89) $3,000
— 22 Mar 1785. (88) £500
— map of lands in Kentucky surveyed by John Saunders, with explicit captions; [after 2 Dec 1785]. 1 p, 4to. Sang & Middendorf collections. (89) $6,000
Ds, 1768. 1 p, size not stated. Ticket for the Mountain Road Lottery. In extra-illus copy of Henry M. Brooks, Curiosities of the Old Lottery. Bost., 1886. 4to, modern sprinkled calf gilt. Extra-illus with 18 lottery tickets, mostly 18th cent; anr 14 lottery tickets loosely inserted. (88) $2,750
— 28 Oct 1773. 1 p, 4to. Bond of Washington & G. W. Fairfax to Charles West for £202.10s. Accomplished by Washington; also sgd by Fairfax, R. Burwell & J. Fitzhugh. Sang collection. (91) $18,000
— 25 Jan 1774. 1 p, 12mo. Account with John Kincaid. With endorsement, sgd, on verso. Middendorf collection. (89) $4,800
— 14 Feb 1779. 1 p, 4to. Authorization of the delivery of clothing to Burgoyne's captured army. (91) $7,500
— 24 Mar 1781. 1 p, folio. Testimonial to the military service of Adam Hubley. Sang collection. (91) $8,500
— [5?] June 1783. 1 p, 4to. Military discharge for Hezekiah Vandoren. Def; silked. (90) $4,500
— 7 June 1783. 1 p, folio. Military discharge for Griffen Jones. With related documents on verso. Doheny collection. (89) $4,000
— 7 June 1783. 1 p, 4to. Army Discharge for Daniel Mulliken. (91) $9,500
— 8 June 1783. 1 p, folio. Military discharge for Bove. With related document on verso. Doheny collection. (89) $5,500
— 8 June 1783. Size not stated. Military discharge for Corporal William Tolbert. Countersgd by Jonathan Trumbull. Framed with a port. (88) $4,000
— 9 June 1783. 1 p, folio. Military discharge for Benjamin Brayman [Braymer]. With related material. Whiton collection. (88) $5,250
— 9 June 1783. 1 p, 4to. Soldier's discharge. Repaired; silked. (88) $4,000
— 8 May 1784. 1 p, folio. Diploma of Brig. Gen. John Crane as member of the Society of the Cincinnati. Countersgd by Henry Knox. (90) $8,000
— 24 May 1784. 1 p, folio. Membership certificate in the Society of the Cincinnati for John Ross. (90) $6,000
— 1784. 1 p, folio. Certificate of membership of Samuel Cliff in the Society of the Cincinnati. Framed. (90) $3,900
— 26 Sept 1785. 1 p, 8vo. Contents not stated. Also sgd by others. Def. (89) $1,100
— 31 Oct 1785. 1 p, folio. Membership certificate in the Society of the Cincinnati for Percival Butler. Also sgd by

WASHINGTON

- Henry Knox. (88) $8,000
- 10 Dec 1785. 1 p, 360mm by 495mm. Membership certificate in the Society of the Cincinnati for Joseph Hardy. Also sgd by Henry Knox. (90) $9,500
- [n.d.]. 1 p, folio. Mediterranean Pass, sgd in blank. Countersgd by Pickering. (89) $8,500
- 18 Oct 1787. 1 leaf, 8vo. Countersignature on verso of receipt for £25 3s 3d from William Hartshorne, sgd by Richard Stuart, 17 Nov 1786. (89) £2,200
- 26 Sept 1789. 1 p, folio. Appointment for Pierpont Edwards as US District Attorney for Connecticut. (88) $6,750
- 7 Aug 1790. 1 p, 4to. Appointment of William Skinner as Commissioner of Loans in North Carolina. Countersgd by Jefferson. Framed. (91) $8,000
- 5 Aug 1791. 1 p, folio. Appointment of Matthew Clarkson as Marshal of NY. Countersgd by Jefferson. (90) $9,000
- 8 Mar 1792. 1 p, 320mm by 408mm. Appointment of Thomas Benbury as Inspector of the Revenue. Countersgd by Jefferson. (91) $10,000
- 3 May 1793. 1 p, 4to. Ship's papers in 3 languages for the schooner Betsey of Alexandria. Countersgd by Jefferson. Matted with a port. (90) $6,200
- [before 29 June 1793]. 2 pp, folio. Ship's papers in 3 languages for the brig Fanny of Salem. Sgd twice & countersgd twice by Jefferson. (89) $15,000
- 7 Nov 1793. 1 p, 10.5 by 13 inches. Ship's papers in 3 languages for the brig Richmond. Countersgd by Jefferson. (88) £3,000
- 14 Nov 1793. 1 p, folio. Ship's papers in 3 languages for the brig Recover of New London. Countersgd by Thomas Jefferson. Repaired. (88) $4,250
- 12 Dec 1793. 1 p, 330mm by 407mm. Ship's papers in 3 languages for the brig Clarissa. Countersgd by Jefferson. (88) $5,400
- 14 Dec 1793. 1 p, c.305mm by 410mm. Ship's papers in 3 languages for the Hiram. Countersgd by Jefferson. (89) $9,500
- 24 Dec 1793. 1 p, folio. Ship's papers in 3 languages for the schooner Rurina. Countersgd by Jefferson. (89) $11,000
- [Dec 1793]. 2 pp, folio. Ship's papers in 3 languages for the schooner Polly. Sgd twice. Countersgd twice by Thomas Jefferson. (88) $10,000
- 16 Jan 1794. 1 p, folio. Ship's papers in 3 languages for the schooner Phoebe. Countersgd by Jefferson. (89) $9,000
- 17 Jan 1794. Size not stated. Ship's paper in 3 languages for the schooner Sally of Boston. Countersgd by Jefferson. (89) $8,750
- 1 Feb 1794. 1 p, folio. Ship's papers in 3 languages for the schooner Polly of Salem. Countersgd by Jefferson. (89) $9,500
- 6 Feb 1794. 1 p, folio. Ship's papers in 3 languages for the schooner Three Brothers. Countersgd by Jefferson. (88) $7,000
- 27 Mar 1794. 1 p, folio. Ship's paper in 3 languages for the ship Hamilton. Countersgd by Jefferson. (91) $9,500
- 26 May 1794. 1 p, folio. Ship's paper for the brig Virginia. Countersgd by Jefferson. Def. (89) $2,500
- 3 Sept 1794. 1 p, folio. Ship's papers in 3 languages for the brig Leonard. Countersgd by Edmund Randolph. Framed. (90) $8,000
- 20 May 1795. 1 p, folio. Ship's paper in 3 languages for the brigantine Young James of Norfolk. Countersgd by Edmund Randolph. (89) $5,000
- 26 July 1795. 1, folio. Ship's papers in 3 languages for the schooner Industry. Def. (90) $6,500
- 20 Feb 1796. 1 p, folio. Grant of land north-west of the River Ohio to Nathaniel Massin & John Graham. Endorsement, sgd by Sec of War James McHenry, on verso. (91) $6,500
- 2 June 1796. 1 p, folio. Ship's papers in 3 languages for the brig The Drake. Countersgd by Timothy Pickering. Repaired. (88) $4,200
- 30 Jan 1797. 1 p, folio. Ship's papers for the Leopard. Countersgd by Pickering. With engraved port. (90) $5,500
- 14 Oct 179[?]. 1 p, 4to. Fragment (2 of 4 columns); ship's papers for the brigantine Sally of NY. Countersgd by Edmund Randolph. Christensen collection. (90) $4,500

Autograph endorsement, sgd, 12 Jan 1795. On ALs by Tench Coxe to Alexander

Hamilton, 11 Mar 1794, 2 pp, 4to, recommending appointment of a lighthouse keeper at Cape Fear; appointing Henry Long. With ANs by Alexander Hamilton pasted beneath. With engraved port. (90) $6,000
— Anr, sgd, at bottom of Ds by James Ross, [3 Mar 1795], 2 pp, folio, concerning money paid to Washington by Israel Shreve; confirming payment. Framed. (91) $7,000
— Anr, "A/c Jno Waring, June 1798", docket on address leaf of ALs addressed to him by Francis Dickens; 2 pp, 4to. (89) $225

Cut signature, 1768. Framed with related material. (91) $2,800
— Anr, [n.d.]. 1 p, 70mm by 115mm. Cut from a Presidential document. Countersgd by Thomas Jefferson. Inlaid. (88) $4,600

Franking signature, [17 July 1780]. On address leaf with his seal. Alexander collection. (90) $4,500
— Anr, [June 1781]. On autograph address leaf from secretarial letter to Charles Petit. (90) $3,800
— BERRY, JOSEPH. - ADs, 24 Aug 1742. 1 p, 4to. Survey of George Washington's birthplace Wakefield. With related material. (89) $5,000
— CHAMPLIN, GEORGE. - ALs, [12 Dec] 1792. Length not stated. To Benjamin Bourne. Regarding the 1st electoral college vote for Washington & Adams. (90) $300
— LEAR, TOBIAS. - Autograph Ms, journal, 23 Oct 1786. 12 pp, 8vo, in def notebook. Giving a verbatim version of Washington's memories of Benedict Arnold's treason. (89) $8,500
— LEWIS, LAWRENCE. - ALs, 8 Aug 1800. 1 p, 4to. To Clement Biddle. About collection of funds due Washington's estate. (88) $120
— WASHINGTON, BUSHROD. - ALs, 29 July 1818. 4 pp, 4to. To William P. Lunell. Describing his uncle's habits & attitudes, & sending autographs by George Washington & others (not present). Pforzheimer Foundation. (90) $2,250
— WASHINGTON'S CABINET. - A group of 7 autographs of members of Washington's cabinet, 20 Jan 1790 to 15 Sept 1800, sold at CNY on 8 Dec 1989, lot 92, for $2,800. 90
See also: Mifflin, Thomas

Washington, John Augustine
ALs, 28 Feb 1776. (90) $500

Washington, Martha Dandridge Custis, 1731-1802
ALs, 24 Sept 1794. 2 pp, 4to. To her sister Becky. Regretting she will not see her before leaving for Philadelphia. Margin def. In red mor bdg with engraved portraits. Doheny collection. (89) $19,000

Wassermann, Jakob, 1873-1934
Autograph Ms, poem, beginning "Weil im Dunkel geboren"; [n.d.]. (91) DM800
Series of 4 A Ls s, 19 July to 5 Sept 1919. (88) DM420
— Series of 14 A Ls s, 17 Dec 1919 to 12 June 1928. 17 pp, 8vo & 4to (5 lettercards). To Emmy & Egon Wellesz. About his & Egon Wellesz's work, his stay in America, personal news, etc. (88) DM3,000
ALs, 15 July 1900. (88) DM650
— 10 Apr 1902. (91) DM250
— 10 Dec 1910. (89) DM220
Ls, 7 Dec 1932. (90) DM200
Photograph, sgd & inscr, [25 Dec] 1921. (88) DM280

Waterhouse, Benjamin, 1754-1846
ALs, 7 Sept 1813. (88) $210

Waterton, Charles, 1782-1865
Autograph Ms, notes on P. B. Du Chaillu's claims about his discovery of the Gorilla, [1861]. 13 pp, various sizes. With 13 related letters addressed to Waterton by various naturalists. (90) £1,500

Watie, Stand, 1806-71
ALs, 12 July 1863. 1 p, 6 by 15 inches. To his wife. Informing her about a recent battle. Repaired. Alexander collection. (90) $4,750

Watkins, Vernon Phillips, 1906-67
[A collection of page proofs & typescripts of various poems & collections, mostly corrected by the author, with some A Ls s, Ls s, & related material, some hundreds of pages, sold at S on

WATKINS

14 Dec 1989, lot 170, for £400 to Quaritch.]

Watkins-Pitchford, D.
Original drawings, (119), to illus 4 Eds of fairy tales, 1952 to 1965. Various sizes. In ink or watercolor (22); mostly sgd or initialled. (90) £1,700

Watson, A. H.
Original drawings, (56), to illus Mazo de la Roche's Beside a Norman Tower, 1934. Macmillan Archives. (90) £1,000

Watt, James, 1736-1819
ALs, 31 Oct 1787. (89) £800
— 20 Dec 1791. 1 p, 4to. To Fermin de Tastet & Co. Inquiring about drawings & directions for an engine mailed some time ago. Sgd Boulton & Watt. (91) DM2,000
— 10 Oct [1808?]. (90) £600
— 15 Nov 1808. (91) £820
— 25 Apr [1816]. (91) £220
— 19 Feb 1818. (89) £400

Watts, Arthur
Original drawings, (3), cartoons to illus Winter's Pie, 1927; The Sketch, 1928; & Punch, 1930. (90) £150

Watts-Dunton, Walter Theodore, 1832-1914
Collection of 27 A Ls s, Ls, & Ms, 1 Oct 1906 to 13 Aug 1913. (90) £420

Waugh, Evelyn, 1903-66
[A collection of 2 autograph programs, with photographs, for a musical & theatrical performance at Underhill, 26 Aug 1916, 6 pp, 12mo, & 3 further items relating to Evelyn & Alec Waugh & the Fleming children, sold at C on 22 June 1988, lot 135, for £500 to Maggs.]
Autograph Ms, novel, Vile Bodies; [1929]. 142 pp, mostly folio & on rectos only, in dark brown mor by Sangorski & Sutcliffe. Inscr to Brian & Diana Guinness & with Brian Guinness's inscr to Jonathan Guinness. With inscr proof of d/j design laid in. Koch Foundation. (90) $100,000
Typescript carbon copy, The Pistol Troop Magazine, Ed by Evelyn Waugh, [1912]. Including his short story, Multa Pecunia, 4 pp, an autograph frontispiece, & contributions by his brother Alec, his father Arthur Waugh, the Fleming children, & other friends. Together 82 pp, 4to, in red mor bdg. (88) £5,000
ALs, 28 July 1925. (91) £440
— [n.d.]. (90) £340

Wayne, Anthony, 1745-96
Ms, orig letter books, 12 Apr 1792 to 4 Oct 1794; 536 pp, folio, in 3 vols. Incoming & outgoing letters relating to his Ohio Valley campaign; partly autograph. Sgd in many places. 89 leaves removed, 8 loosely inserted. John F. Fleming Estate. (89) $33,000
ALs, 12 July 1781. 3 pp, 4to. To Robert Morris. Defending his tactics & describing his escape at the Battle of Green Spring. Middendorf collection. (89) $8,500
— 20 May 1789. 3 pp, 4to. To James Wilson. Congratulating him on his appointment to the Supreme Court. (91) $5,500
Ds, 6 June 1793. (88) $750
— DELANY, T. - ALs, 24 Aug 1793. Length not stated. To Gen. Wayne. Discussing Citizen Genet & hoping for peace with the Indians. (89) $240

Wayne, John, 1907-79
Photograph, sgd, [1942]. (91) $375
— Anr, [n.d.]. (91) $200
Ptd photograph, 1973. (91) $200

Webb, Clifford
Original drawings, (3), to illus different works, 1934 to 1965. (90) £600

Weber, Bernhard Anselm, 1766-1821
A Ls s (2), 13 [Aug] & 23 Sept 1814. 13 pp, 4to. To August von Kotzebue. About difficulties with his commission to set Goethe's Des Epimenides Erwachen to music. Albrecht collection. (91) SF1,700

Weber, Carl Maria von, 1786-1826
Autograph music, 11 bars in full score from the incidental music to A. Rublack's play Lieb um Liebe, [1818]. 2 pp, folio; 12 staves each. (90) £4,000
— Autograph music, sketches for various works, [c.1816]. 2 pp, 22cm by 8cm. (88) DM4,000

ALs, 13 Nov 1811. 1 p, 8vo. To Regina Lang. Sending an aria written for her. (88) DM2,800

— 14 Feb 1812. 3 pp, 4to. To Friedrich Rochlitz. Describing his concert tour to Gotha & Weimar & a meeting with Wieland. (89) £2,600

— 1 Oct 1812. 2 pp, 4to. To the recorder of Stuttgart. Sending 20 ducats to pay off his debts. (89) DM5,400

— 12 Oct 1812. 1 p, 4to. To his pbr [Ambrosius Kuehnel]. Sending letters for Louis Spohr, referring to some of his works, etc. (90) DM2,800

— 25 [July 1814]. 2 pp, 8vo. To Caroline Brandt. Love letter, & hoping for reassurance. (91) DM4,000

— 17 Oct 1817. 2 pp, 4to. To his fiancee Caroline Brandt. About preparations for their wedding. With authentication by Max Maria von Weber at bottom, 1868. (90) DM4,500

— 17 Sept 1819. 1 p, 4to. To Herr Teichmann. Responding to an inquiry about Konrad Kocher's opera Der Elfenkoenig. (90) DM3,200

— 3 Mar 1820. 1 p, 4to. To the pbr C. F. Peters. Recommending Christian Frederick Barth & mentioning his opera Die Jaegersbraut [Der Freischuetz]. (89) DM3,800

— 17 Dec 1820. 1 p, 4to. To "Licentiat Weber". Referring to his birthday & a forthcoming concert. Seal hole. Doheny collection. (89) $1,400

— 22 Mar 1821. 2 pp, 4to. Recipient unnamed. Discussing the musical education of his pupil Julius Benedict. (91) £1,400

— 25 Mar 1821. 2 pp, 4to. Recipient unnamed. Interesting letter discussing additions to Der Freischuetz. (90) £2,600

— 17 Dec 1821. 3 pp, 8vo. Recipient unnamed. About his work on the opera Euryanthe. (91) DM4,600

— [14 May 1822]. 1 p, 4to. To the pbr C. F. Peters. Regarding recipient's belated response to an offer to print several works. (88) DM3,400

— 19 June 1822. 2 pp, 4to. To the director of the Munich Court Theater, Stich. Regretting not to be able to attend a performance of Freischuetz. Silked. (88) DM5,500

— 18 Dec 1822. 2 pp, 4to. To friends in Berlin. Thanking for birthday wishes & quoting Der Freischuetz. Inscr by Hinrich Lichtenstein. (88) £1,600

— 5 Dec 1823. (91) £700

— 23 Jan 1826. 1 p, 4to. To Ferdinand Schimon. Thanking for a port, & mentioning Euryanthe. (90) DM3,600

— 20 May 1826. (89) £950

— 31 May 1826. 1 p, 8vo. To Eliza Aders. Reporting on his poor health, announcing his imminent departure & thanking for help. (91) £1,500

— 1 Mar 1826. 1 p, 4to. To Sir George Smart. Informing him about a delay in his arrival in London. In English. With related material. (90) DM3,600

Autograph endorsement, sgd, 4 lines on a letter addressed to him by Carl Christian Boenisch, 1 Apr 1823, 3 pp, 4to, requesting payment of a tailor's bill incurred in 1806; referring letter to his lawyer. (90) DM1,200

Autograph sentiment, "Das Leben ist ernst - die Kunst ist heiter", 3 Feb 1812. 1 p, 8vo. Sgd. (91) DM1,600

— Anr, sgd, 9 Nov 1824. (91) £300

Signature, on ticket for his last concert, 26 May 1826. (91) £800

Weber, Friedrich Wilhelm, 1813-94

Autograph Ms, prescription for Kammer-Gerichts-Raethin Rohden, sgd & dated 2 Sept 1866. (90) DM200

Weber, Karl Julius, 1767-1832

ALs, 19 Dec 1824. (89) DM360

Weber, Louise ("La Goulue"), 1870-1929.
See: Toulouse-Lautrec, Henri de

Weber, Max, 1864-1920

ALs, 8 Apr 1915. (91) DM600

Weber, Wilhelm, 1804-91

ALs, 5 Aug [1848]. 2 pp, 4to. To Friedrich Woehler. Informing him about negotiations regarding his return to Goettingen. (90) DM3,400

— 24 Oct 1858. (91) DM380

— 19 Dec 1876. (90) DM1,000

Webern, Anton von, 1883-1945

Ms, Zwei Lieder, Op. 8; [c.1925]. 10 pp, mostly folio. Full score, including autograph corrections & autograph note specifying alterations. Sgd twice. (91) £1,800

ALs, 18 Feb 1912. 1 p, folio. To Gerhard Tischer. Concerning the fee for an article about Schoenberg. (88) DM1,500

— 6 Sept 1917. 2 pp, 8vo. To "lieber Paul". About Schoenberg's being drafted into the army & enlisting his help to assist Schoenberg to emigrate, mentioning Berg & Alma Mahler. (88) £1,500

— 7 Dec 1918. (91) £600
— 25 July 1921. (91) £400
— 11 Sept 1928. (91) £700
— 20 Jan 1932. (90) £600

— 7 Jan 1939. 2 pp, size not stated. To Else Cross. Enquiring about the performance of his music in London. (90) £3,200

— 17 Mar [19]39. 2 pp, folio. To Else Cross. Advising her about her professional career, & giving news of his latest compositions. (90) £2,600

— 30 June [19]39. 2 pp, folio. To Else Cross. Announcing the publication of his String Quartet, enquiring about acquaintances, etc. (90) £2,600

— 20 Oct 1939. 2 pp, 4to. To Willi Reich. Complaining about his current situation, suggesting suitable works for performances of his music, etc. Sgd W. (91) £1,800

— 9 Feb 1940. 2 pp, size not stated (card). To Else Cross. Describing a performance of his Passacaglia in Wintherthur, asking about exiled friends, etc. (90) £1,800

Autograph postcard, sgd, 25 Jan 1936. (88) £700

Webster, Daniel, 1782-1852

ALs, 13 Apr 1838. (88) $175
— 13 Nov [18]40. (90) $100
— 8 Feb 1841. Christensen collection. (90) $550
— 20 June 1841. (90) $300
— 27 Apr 1843. (88) $225
— 17 Jan 1849. (88) $110
— "Tuesday", [June 1849]. (89) $200

Ls, 17 Apr 1840. (89) $750
Ds, 29 Mar 1837. (91) $250
— 2 July 1852. (91) $550

Franking signature, [1824]. Alexander collection. (90) $75
— Anr, [2 Apr 1837]. Alexander collection. (90) $130

Photograph, [1848]. (90) $550

Webster, Harry Tucker

Original drawings, "The 18 year old office boy who collects autographs", for his strip Life's Darkest Moments; 3 Feb [n.y.]. (91) $550

Webster, John White, 1793-1850

ALs, 22 July 1847. Byer collection. (90) $425

Webster, Noah, 1758-1843

Autograph Ms, definitions of 12 words (Bestain - Bestorm) for his An American Dictionary; [before 1828]. 1 p, 4to. (90) $6,000

— Autograph Ms, definitions of beanfly, bear & other words, part of the Ms for his American Dictionary of the English Language, pbd 1828. 2 pp, 4to. Framed. (91) $5,250

— Autograph Ms, draft of definitions of 7 words (blobber - blomary) for his dictionary; [n.d.]. 2 pp, 4to. Framed. (90) $4,500

ALs, 17 July 1786. 1 p, 4to. To his publishers. About his Grammatical Institute of the English Language. (91) $2,600

— 23 May 1788. 1 p, 4to. Recipients unnamed. Regarding business matters. Doheny collection. (89) $1,200

— 8 Mar 1797. 2 pp, 4to. To Francis Childs. Regarding the purchase of ptg types, financial matters, & the sale of his books in England. (91) $1,700

Wedekind, Frank, 1864-1918

ALs, 6 Aug 1894. (91) DM430
— 15 Nov 1905. (88) DM440
— 8 Dec 1909. (89) DM750
— 2 May 1910. (91) DM700
— 29 May 1910. (91) DM370
— 26 May 1911. (90) DM460
— 15 Jan 1913. (90) DM220
— 11 Oct 1913. (89) DM300

Wedgwood, Josiah
ALs, 22 Apr 1765. 2 pp, folio. To Erasmus Darwin. Enlisting his help in the promotion of the Grand Trunk Canal. (91) £1,600

— 10 July 1765. 3 pp, folio. To Erasmus Darwin. Pleading for his help in designing the Queen's Service. (91) £1,800

Wehner, Herbert, 1906-89
Autograph Ms, draft of a speech given to members of German trade unions, [1963]. (90) DM450

Weigl, Joseph, 1766-1846
ALs, 5 Oct 1835. (90) DM400

Weill, Kurt, 1900-50
Autograph music, song, The Saga of Jenny, to a text by Ira Gershwin, 1943. 2 pp, folio. Notated on 6 systems, 3 staves each. Sgd. (91) £4,000

Typescript, essay, Kulturreaktion in Deutschland, [c.1930]. 3 pp, 4to. With covering ALs to Walter Zadek of the Berliner Tageblatt. (91) DM1,700

ALs, 14 Aug 1925. 2 pp, 4to. To Herr Kastner. Asking him to return the score of a violin concerto. (91) DM1,600

— 15 Mar 1935. (91) £180

Ls, 13 Aug 1945. 2 pp, 4to. To David Ewen. Listing his major works & explaining his beliefs as a composer. (90) $1,800

— 29 Sept 1946. 2 pp, 4to. To David Ewen. Offering corrections & comments on a biographical sketch. (90) $1,500

Weinberger, Jaromir, 1896-1967
Autograph music, Meditations (Three Preludes for Organ), 30 Nov 1953. 14 pp, 34cm by 27.5cm. Sgd & inscr on tp. With related material. (90) DM1,100

— Autograph music, opera, Valdstejn, complete working Ms in full score, sgd & dated 21 Nov 1936. 615 pp & over 100 additional pp, folio, in 6 folders. In pencil on up to 28 staves per page, with piano reduction on last 2 staves. (88) £3,500

Weinheber, Josef, 1892-1945
Autograph postcard, sgd, 22 Dec 1936. (88) DM360

Weiser, Johann Conrad, 1696-1760
ADs, 7 Sept 1759. (89) $450

Weishaupt, Adam, 1748-1830
[A collection of 14 autograph Mss containing biographical & philosophical notes in English, French or German, [n.d.], 13 pp, 8vo, & 9 notesheets of various sizes, sold at star on 30 Nov 1988, lot 552, for DM2,500.]

Weiss, Peter, 1916-82
Autograph Ms, "Notizblatt zum Stueck 'Hoelderlin'", Feb 1971. (89) DM460

Weizmann, Chaim, 1874-1952
Collection of c. 130 A Ls s & Ls s, & 3 cards, sgd, 23 Mar 1910 to 16 May 1943. About 205 pp, 4to & 8vo. To Harold Davies. Detailed correspondence about their work in chemistry. (89) £30,000

— Collection of 5 A Ls s, 4 Ls s, letter & 5 telegrams, 7 Feb 1928 to 26 May 1931. 25 pp, 4to & 8vo. To Lieut. Col. F. H. Kisch, Chairman of the Palestine Zionist Executive. Discussing matters related to the Zionist cause. (90) £4,000

Ls, 7 Apr 1930. (91) £340

— 20 Aug 1949. 1 p, 8vo. To Minister of Transportation David Ramaz. Congratulating him "on the arrival of the first Hebrew train to Jerusalem". (91) $2,500

Weizsaecker, Heinrich, 1862-1945
Series of 19 A Ls s, 15 Apr 1904 to 24 Jan 1914. (88) DM750

Weizsaecker, Julius, 1828-89
Series of 5 A Ls s, 30 Apr 1880 to 11 Nov 1881. (88) DM240

Weizsaecker, Marianne von
Ls, 21 May 1949. (90) DM550

Welles, Gideon, 1802-78
Autograph Ms, attack on Benjamin F. (91) $550

Ls, 13 Nov 1861. (91) $280

— 30 May 1864. (88) $150

— 10 Oct 1864. (88) $250

WELLES

— 20 July 1867. (89) $55

Welles, Orson
Typescript, introduction to Arnold Weissberger's book of photographs, sgd; [n.d.]. (91) $400
Ls, 17 Aug 1938. (91) $225
— 21 Jan 1943. (90) $140
— 5 Aug 1974. (91) $500
Ds, 21 Jan 1957. (91) $475
— KOCH, HOWARD. - Typescript, radio adaptation of H. G. Wells's The War of the Worlds; [1938]. 46 pp, 4to. Final working draft, with numerous revisions by Welles & CBS censors. With photocopy of the actors' script. (89) $130,000

Welles, Orson —&
Hayworth, Rita, 1918--1987
Ls, 20 Sept 1945. 1 p, 4to. To The Haig Corporation. Carbon copy, stating terms for a contract for the film The Lady from Shanghai. (91) $1,400

Wellesz, Egon, 1885-1974
A Ls s (2), 30 Aug 1946 & 12 Mar 1948. (91) DM500
— A Ls s (2), 8 July & 3 Aug 1966. (90) DM600

Wellington, Arthur Wellesley, 1st Duke, 1769-1852
Collection of 27 A Ls s (6 in 3d person) & Ls, 21 May 1816 to 25 Mar 1848. (88) £850
Series of 3 A Ls s, 25 Feb 1809 to 10 Oct 1840. (89) $375
A Ls s (2), 27 Feb 1826 & 13 July 1836. (89) £90
ALs, 6 Aug 1801. (88) £100
— 25 Feb 1805. 1 p, 4to. To Lieut. Stephens. Sending the copy of an admiral's letter praising Stephens' merits as a soldier. Including autograph Ms, 1 p, 4to; letter copy, sgd A.W. (88) DM1,050
— 28 May 1807. (90) $400
— 29 Nov 1814. (88) £250
— 9 July 1816. (91) $300
— 24 Aug 1817. (90) DM450
— 22 Feb 1818. (90) $90
— 7 May 1820. (91) $120
— 7 Aug 1824. (90) DM450
— 12 Oct 1830. (90) DM950

AMERICAN BOOK PRICES CURRENT

— 26 Nov 1831. (89) £350
— 18 Jan 1834. (88) £320
— 1 Oct 1834. (91) £280
— 1 Oct 1834. (90) £300
— 3 Sept 1837. (91) DM480
— 15 Aug 1840. (89) DM450
— 8 June 1844. (89) £380
— 6 June 1846. (91) $160
Ls, 8 May 1809. (90) $100
Ds, 18 Aug 1851. (90) $250
— ALAVA, MIGUEL DE. - 5 A Ls s, 22 Oct 1814 & [n.d.]. To Lady Dalrymple & Lady Hamilton. Discussing the political situation in Europe & referring to Wellington. Including retained copy of Wellington's letter to the King of Spain protesting Alava's arrest, 1814. With related material. (88) £250

Wellington, Arthur Wellesley, 1st Duke, 1769-1852 —& Others
Ds, 31 Jan 1820. 1 p, 4to. Addressed to the Mayor of York, proclaiming George IV as King & requiring the Mayor to publish the proclamation within his jurisdiction. Also sgd by Sidmouth, Canning, Melville, & other members of the Council. Byer collection. (90) $1,100

Wells, Henry, 1805-78
Ds, 1 May 1866. (88) $170

Wells, Henry, 1805-78 —&
Fargo, William George, 1818-81
Ds, 11 Sept 1861. (88) $350
— 9 June 1864. (91) $700
— 15 July 1864. (90) $475

Wells, Herbert George, 1866-1946
Autograph Ms, open letter to Germans, Austrians & Hungarians, sgd; [c.1914]. (88) £450
— Autograph Ms, The First Horseman, part III of A Story of the Stone Age, from Tales of Time and Space, 1899; sgd. 17 pp, 4to. Working draft. (88) $4,750
Typescript, Character in Guatemala, review of Rose Macaulay's Staying with Relations; [c.1930]. (90) £300
Typescript carbon copy, novel, Marriage, 1912. About 550 pp, folio. With Ms revisions entered in anr hand. Printer's copy. (88) £2,200

ALs, [n.d.]. (88) £400
— 21 Oct 1920. (91) £110
— 6 Aug 1933. (90) $90
ANs, [18 Jan 1921]. (91) £500
— GURNEY, ALEX. - Orig drawing, pencil port of Wells, sgd; [n.d.]. 8.5 by 5.75 inches. Also sgd by Wells. (89) £200
— HERRIN, M. H. - Orig drawing, pencil bust port of Wells, 4 June 1940. 9 by 12 inches. Sgd by both. (91) $225

Welti, Albert, 1862-1912
ALs, 10 Jan 1910. (91) DM250

Welty, Eudora
Ns, 26 July 1939. (89) $225

Wenceslaus, German King & King of Bohemia, 1361-1419
Document, [30 Nov] 1367. 1 p, folio; vellum. Assent to annuities settled on his sister by her husband Otto von Brandenburg. Schroeder collection. (89) DM7,500

Wentworth, John, 1719-81
Ls, 7 Feb 1774. 3 pp, 4to. To the Speaker of the House of Representatives of Connecticut. Acknowledging receipt of their resolves & assuring cooperation "in the glorious cause of Liberty". (89) $2,800

Wentworth, Sir Peter, 1592-1675
[A collection of 11 letters, c.1616 to 1652, c.16 pp, folio & 4to, addressed to Wentworth by various correspondents, about militia, public news, the invasion of Scotland, etc., sold at S on 21 Sept, lot 69, for £680 to Arygil.]

Wentworth, Thomas, Earl of Strafford, 1593-1641
Series of 10 A Ls s, 30 Apr 1634 to 22 Apr 1639. To Lady Anne Rushe & her mother (1). Referring to arrangements for her marriage to his brother. With related material. (91) £2,800
Ds, 14 Oct 1632. (89) £450

Werdenberg, Johann Baptist von, d.1648
ALs, 14 Sept 1632. 3 pp, folio. To Franz Christoph von Khevenhueller. Reporting about Wallenstein's victory at Fuerth. (88) DM1,800

Werfel, Alma, 1879-1964. See: Mahler-Werfel, Alma

Werfel, Franz, 1890-1945
Autograph Ms, poem, Der Weltfreund versteht nicht zu altern, [n.d.]. 1 p, 4to. 5 four-line stanzas, sgd. (91) DM1,400
— Autograph Ms, poem, Mensch und All, 1938. 1 p, 4to. Sgd. (90) DM1,300
— Autograph Ms, poem, Romanze einer Schlange, [n.d.]. (88) DM650
Collection of 14 A Ls s, 12 autograph postcards, sgd & ANs, [June] 1916 to [June] 1917. 40 pp, 4to & 8vo, & cards. To Alice Gerstel. Personal letters. (91) DM3,500
ALs, 27 Sept 1928. (88) DM420
— 10 Dec 1937. (90) DM500
— [n.d.]. (91) DM650
Ls, 10 July 1939. (91) DM400
Letter, 3 July [1925]. (90) DM200

Werner, Anton von, 1843-1915
ALs, 10 Mar 1878. (88) DM240
See also: Bismarck, Otto von

Werner, Zacharias, 1768-1823
Autograph Ms, sonnet, An Iffland's Geist, sgd W. (89) DM850
ALs, 13 Okt 1798. (88) DM650

Wesenbeck, Matthaeus von, 1600-59
Ls, [early 1648]. (89) DM550

Wesley, Charles, 1707-88
Series of 21 A Ls s, 1778 to 1784, c.50 pp, mostly 4to. To John Langshaw. Important letters about Methodism & musical life in London. With 5 A Ls s by Charles Wesley, Jr., & ALs by Samuel Wesley to members of the Langshaw family. (89) £8,000

Wesley, John, 1703-91
ALs, 27 Mar 1771. 2 pp, 4to. To Joseph Pilmoor. Mentioning a scandalous report about chapels in America & requesting information. Framed. (88) £2,000
— 12 Feb 1773. 2 pp, 4to. To Eliza Bennis. Commenting about religious matters, sending messages for various people, & encouraging her to trust in God. (90) $1,500
— 13 Dec 1776. (88) £800
— 14 Mar 1789. (88) £320

WESLEY

— 15 June 1789. (88) £450
— 19 Jan 1791. (88) £520

Wesselenyi, Ferenc, Count, 1605-67
Ls, 28 Apr 1656. (88) DM800
— 18 June 1659. 2 pp, folio. To Emperor Leopold I. Discussing political problems in Hungary. With autograph endorsement by Leopold. (91) DM2,600

West, Benjamin, 1738-1820
ALs, 18 Dec 1798. (91) $700

West Florida
— MARTIN, JOHN ALLEN. - Ds, 4 Apr 1769. 2 pp, folio. Power of attorney to Ezra Collins of Boston. With confirmation sgd by John Eliot, Captain-General & Governor-in-Chief of West Florida, 4 Apr 1769. Including Great Seal of West Florida. (91) £800

West Indies
[Pinney Family. - A large collection of account books, journals, ledgers & other business documents relating to the Pinney Family of Bristol & their sugar plantation on the Island of Nevis, [early 17th to mid-19th cent], 17 vols & ledgers, & c.100 documents, sold at S on 15 Dec, lot 261, for £2,400.]
[Barbados. - A collection of c.90 documents, chiefly relating to the Newton Family of Bramley Hall & their sugar plantation on Barbados, 1666-1738, sold at S on 20 July 1989, lot 306, for £1,100 to Wilson.]
[Grenada. - A vol containing the oath of allegiance to George III & of abjuration of the supremacy of the Pope & the claims of James III, sgd by c.1,200 inhabitants, with contemp annotations, 1765 to 1777, 22 pp & blanks, folio, in vellum bdg, sold at pn on 10 Dec 1987, lot 514, for £1,000 to Fletcher.]
— BARBADOS. - A collection of c.86 letters & documents, chiefly relating to the Newton Family of Bromley Hall & their sugar plantation in Barbados, 1660-1738. (90) £1,100
See also: Willoughby, Francis

AMERICAN BOOK PRICES CURRENT

West, Mae, 1892-1980
Autograph sentiment, [n.d.]. (91) $80
Photograph, sgd, [n.d.]. (88) $100

West, Mae, 1892-1980 —& Raft, George
Group photograph, [1932]. (91) $150

West, Rebecca, 1892-1983
Collection of 17 A Ls s & Ls s & typescripts, 1944 to 1967. About 95 pp, 4to & 8vo. To Leonard Russell. Discussing articles & other literary & political matters. Revised typescripts of her articles on Sen. McCarthy. With related material. (90) £1,200

Westerdahl, Eduardo
[A collection of letters addressed to him by various artists & galleries, relating to articles pbd in the Gaceta de Arte, with related material, c.60 items, 1932 to 1933, sold at S on 5 May 1988, lot 270, for £900 to J. Wilson.]

Westmacott, C. M.
Ms, The three Royal Secretaries of George the Fourth..., [n.d.]. John F. Fleming Estate. (89) $400

Wetzel, Friedrich Gottlob, 1779-1819
ALs, [1812/13]. 2 pp, 8vo. To Friedrich August Koethe. About friends & literary projects. Margin def. (90) DM4,400
— 14 Oct 1815. 2 pp, 4to. To Hofrat [Eichstaedt]. Offering to review books for the Jenaische Allgemeine Literatur-Zeitung. (90) DM3,000

Wetzel, Justus Hermann, 1879-1973
Autograph music, song, Das laechelnde Roesslein, to a text by Carl Spitteler, scored for voice & piano; [1967]. (90) DM300

Whaley, John, 1710-45
Collection of 7 A Ls s & autograph Ms, 27 Aug 1735 to 4 Dec 1744. (91) £550

Whaling Manuscripts
[A group of 3 letters, 1843, 1844 & [n.d.], written on board whaling ships, sold at rf on 12 Mar, lot 30, for $350.]
Ms, journal of the bark Rajah of New Bedford, 8 June 1839 to 28 May 1841, on a voyage to the New Zealand

whaling grounds, & of the ship William Baker, 29 Oct 1843 to 28 June 1845, on a voyage to the Northwest Coast. 1 vol, length not stated. Including some pencil drawings. (89) $2,200

— Brayley, Samuel T., Master of the Arab. - Voyage accounts on a sperm & right whale voyage to the Indian Ocean, 17 Nov 1849 to 8 July 1853. 51 pp. (91) $400

— Chase, Joseph C., Master of the Clarkson. - Journal of a whaling voyage that ended badly in Talcahuano, Chili, when the ship was pronounced to be in unseaworthy condition & sold, 15 Sept 1842 to 5 Jan 1846. 173 pp, folio, in cloth. With later business records & Civil War data following the journal. (91) $2,400

— John A. Hawes Company of Fairhaven MA. - Invoice & letter copy book for this sperm candle & oil manufacturing firm, 11 Dec 1821 to 6 Dec 1823. Folio, in half calf. (91) $400

— McFall, David. - Autograph Ms, journal of a whaling voyage aboard the bark Fanny, 18 Aug 1860 to 7 Jan 1864. 179 pp, 4to, in cloth bdg. Documenting a whaling voyage in the Atlantic, Pacific & Arctic oceans & the Okhotsk Sea. (90) $2,500

— McFall, David. - Autograph Ms, journal of a whaling voyage aboard the bark Fanny & the bark Martha, 1 Sept 1864 to 24 Apr 1868. 288 pp, folio, in cloth bdg. Documenting whaling voyages in the Atlantic, Pacific & Arctic oceans. (90) $4,000

— McFall, David. - Ms, The Whaling Voyage of David McFall aboard the Bark Java, 22 Oct 1857 to 10 Apr 1860. 227 pp, folio, in cloth bdg. Documenting a whaling voyage in the Atlantic, Pacific & Arctic oceans. Text in the hand of Robert Nathaniel Houghson. (90) $6,000

— Pierce, Capt. Abraham W. - 14 A Ls s, c.1850 to 1853. Length not stated, 4to. To Henry Thomas. Reporting about the voyage of the whaleship Kutusoff to the Pacific & Arctic oceans. With 3 Hawaiian bills of exchange. (90) $1,700

— Pierson, Elihu M., First Officer of the Splendid. - Whaling log of a North Pacific voyage from 27 Oct 1848 to 15 Mar 1851. 175 pp, folio, in orig half calf. (91) $2,400

— Snell, Capt. Otis H. - Ms, A J[o]urnal of A Voyage From Nantucket to the Pacific Ocean On Board the Ship Richard Mitchell, 22 July 1829 to 3 Sept 1831. 161 pp & blanks, in folio journal book in def contemp quarter calf & marbled paper bds. Daily entries, with 81 ink & watercolor whale stamps of varying size & some drawings of island profiles. (88) $4,200

— Wheeler, James John. - Autograph Ms, log of the whaler Eclipse on a voyage to Timor, 1837 to 1841; c.200 pp, folio, in vellum bds. Daily entries. With Ms of a poem inserted. (88) £2,000

Wharton, Edith, 1862-1937
ALs, 5 Jan 1919. (90) $375

Wharton, Thomas, 1735-78
Ls, 14 Oct 1776. (91) $950
Ds, 25 Oct 1777. (89) $380

Wharton, Sir Thomas
— Wharton, Lady. - Ms, Some short observations on the Life of ... Sir Thomas Wharton, second son to the Right Honorable the Lord Wharton, [18th cent]. 16 pp, 8vo, in modern half mor. Written for their daughters. (89) £140

Wheelhouse, Mary V.
Original drawings, (8), to illus Jan of the Windmill; [n.d.]. 15.5 by 10.5 inches & smaller. In pen, black ink & watercolor; sgd. (90) £1,600

Whelen, Israel
ALs, 12 Feb 1801. Alexander collection. (90) $170

Wherwood, Sir Thomas, d.1684
Autograph Ms, memoranda, financial records, details of purchases, wages, etc., frequently sgd or initialled, on c.65 interleaved pages of his copy of Wharton's Calendarium Carolinum or a New Almanack... (88) £400

Whistler, James Abbott McNeill, 1834-1903

Autograph Ms, "Correspondence", letter to Henry Labouchere, 21 Aug [1886], [later "The Commercial Travellers of Art", ptd in The Gentle Art of Making Enemies]. 3 pp, folio, on rectos only. Discussing English art. Sgd, & with butterfly device. Printer's copy; repaired. In mor bdg by Riviere & Son, with a port. Doheny collection. (89) $10,000

Collection of ALS & ANs, [n.d.]. Doheny collection. (89) $750

Series of 4 A Ls s, 30 Mar to 22 May 1887 & [n.d.]. (88) £550

— Series of 5 A Ls s, [n.d.]. (90) £700

A Ls s (2), [10 Feb 1896] & Apr 1898. (88) $850

ALs, [n.d.]. (88) $325

— 6 Nov 1889. (90) $350

— [5 Nov 1890]. (90) $450

— 19 May 1896. Doheny collection. (88) $160

— [n.d., 1899?], "Thursday". 3 pp, 8vo. To "dear Pauling". Discussing the bdg of [Eden versus Whistler]. Some words underlined in sepia chalk. Was mtd. Doheny collection. (89) $1,400

— [n.d.]. (88) DM800

— 7 May [n.y.]. (90) $300

— 30 May [n.y.]. (91) $300

— [n.d.], "Saturday". (91) $260

— [n.d.]. (90) $200

— [n.d.]. (90) $325

Letter, 24 Dec [1867]. (90) £300

Series of 5 A Ns s, [n.d.]. (89) £650

Signature, [n.d.]. (91) $250

Whistler, Laurence

Series of 15 A Ls s, c.1947 to 1970. (88) £150

Whistler, Rex, 1905-44

Autograph Ms, story, The Four Kichelles, Apr 1925. 37 pp, in def 8vo notebook. Illus with 20 pen-&-ink & wash drawings by Whistler & Stephen Tennant. 3 separate drawings by Whistler & Tennant loosely inserted. (88) £3,000

Original drawings, (26), to illus Gulliver's Travels, 1929 & 1930. Various sizes. In ink; mostly sgd. With related material. (89) £65,000

— Original drawings, (3), various Edwardian figures, in ink & watercolor; [n.d.]. 3 leaves, 240mm by 165mm. Inscr by Siegfried Sassoon. (91) £2,000

— Original drawings, (4), in wash, pencil, ink & crayon, 1928 & 1942. Various sizes. Inscr by Siegfried Sassoon. (91) £2,200

— Original drawings, (5), to illus a humorous story for a child [George Sassoon?]; [n.d.]. (91) £600

— Original drawings, (7); pen-&-ink & watercolor drawings of the Vlasto family home at Henley; [1920s]. 7 pp, 10.5 by 7.25 inches. 2 sgd; captioned on verso by Mrs. Vlasto. (90) £2,300

Original drawing, A merrie Christmas, in pen-&-ink & watercolor. Sgd twice, inscr & dated 25 Dec 1923. 6.5 by 9.5 inches. Mtd on card with calendar beneath. (90) £1,750

— Original drawing, design for The Listener, Christmas 1941. 13 by 10 inches. In pen, brush & ink. (89) £4,000

Collection of 20 A Ls s, 8 illus envelopes & hand-drawn Christmas card, 1924 to [1936?]. About 65 pp, various sizes. To Stephen Tennant. Chatty letters about a variety of subjects, with drawings & vignettes. 4 letters incomplete. (88) £5,800

Series of 11 A Ls s, Apr 1925 to Apr 1927. (90) £1,000

ALs, 1923. (88) $350

— 4 Feb [1925]. (88) £450

— [21 Jan 1930]. (91) £700

— [1943]. (91) £420

White, Edward H., 1930-67

Signature, [8 Apr 1964]. (91) $375

White, Henry Dalrymple, 1820-86. See: Crimean War

White, Henry Kirke, 1785-1806

Autograph Ms, poem, A Ballad, [1803]. (89) £250

White, Sir John Chambers, 1770-1845

[His naval letter- & order-books relating to HMS Sylph, Renown, Foudroyant & Centaur during the Napoleonic Wars & the War of 1812, Aug 1795 to Oct 1814, including transcripts from HMS Victory, 1803, nearly 1,500 pp in 10 vols, folio & 4to, with related

White, Patrick, 1912-90
Autograph Ms, Memoirs of Many in One, [1985 - 1986]. 200 pp, folio. In blue ballpoint, with revisions in red. Sgd on tp. (91) £11,500

White, Peregrine, 1620-1704
Ds, 8 Mar 1697/98. 1 p, 12 by 15 inches. Indenture by Lieut. John Whitmarsh, granting land to Ephraim Hunt; sgd as witness. Def; mtd. (91) $1,100

White, William Allen, 1868-1944. See: Lewis, Sinclair & White

White, William S.
Autograph telegram, 28 Nov 1864. Written from 4 miles west of Big Buckhead Church to Gen. Braxton Bragg. Reporting on the fight with Gen. Hugh J. Kilpatrick. Body may be in the hand of a clerk. (91) $1,100

Whitehead, William, 1715-85
Autograph Ms, poem, beginning "On him, whose very Soul was here", 1782. (88) £50

Whitelocke, Bulstrode, 1605-75
Ms, journal & letterbook relating to the Parliamentary Commission to the King at Oxford, 1 Feb to 13 Apr 1643; c.130 pp (51 autograph), 8vo, in bds. Bdg def. (88) £5,400
Ls, 9 Dec 1652. (90) £190

Whitman, Walt, 1819-92
[A ptd proof sheet of his poem Patroling Barnegat, 1 p, 16mo, with last 4 lines pasted together from verso, inscr "Harpers' April '81" in Whitman's hand, sold at CNY on 22 Feb 1989, lot 2203, for $300 to Carnegie Book Shop.]
[Forgery. - Letter, 22 May [n.y.], 2 pp, 8vo, purportedly by Whitman to "Pete". About a visit & his medical situation. Sgd Walt.] $50
Autograph Ms, "Ah Not for nothing you gay fields of battle...", unpbd version of closing lines of stanza 10 & 1st two sections of stanza 11 of By Blue Ontario's Shore; [1865-67]. 1 p, 349mm by 200mm, composed of 3 joined sections. With numerous revisions. The Garden Ltd. collection. (90) $8,000
— Autograph Ms, "As I sat alone by Ontario's shores...", revisions of the 1st stanza for the 1867 Ed of Leaves of Grass,; [1865-67]. 1 p, 209mm by 128mm, composed of 2 joined sections. With numerous emendations. The Garden Ltd. collection. (90) $8,000
— Autograph Ms, autograph Ms, article, Walt Whitman in Denver, [n.d.]. 4 pp, 4to. Ficticious interview, with revisions; in pencil. With covering ALs to the Ed of the Denver Tribune, 17 June 1880; 1 p, 4to. Doheny collection. (89) $5,500
— Autograph Ms, "Chant me a poem for Poets...", fair copy of unpdb version of the phantom's address from the 1st stanza of By Blue Ontario's Shore; [1865-67]. 1 p, 114mm by 197mm. The Garden Ltd. collection. (90) $2,250
— Autograph Ms, draft for an advertising circular for his works, fragment; [1882]. 3 pp, 4to. With instructions to the ptr in anr hand. (89) $5,500
— Autograph Ms, extract from Johann Wolfgang von Goethe, taken from George Lewes's Life of Goethe; [n.d.]. 1 p, folio. Giving a definition of the poet's nature. In pencil. Doheny collection. (89) $3,000
— Autograph Ms, Impromptu memorandum, preface to D. Doheny collection. (89) $500
— Autograph Ms, poem, Montauk Point, draft; [c.25 Feb 1888]. 1 p, 4to, on envelope addressed to Whitman. Mtd with a signature. With ADs, [19 Apr 1886]; receipt. (89) $2,750
— Autograph Ms, poem on the death of Ulysses S. Grant, [May 1885]. 1 p, folio (2 sheets pasted together). Working draft, sgd; including 4 lines later deleted. With letter, 20 Apr 1885, requesting his autograph, on verso. Doheny collection. (89) $11,000
Autograph transcript, poem, The Sobbing of the Bells, 19/20 Sept 1881. 1 p, 4to. Including pencil instructions to the ptr. With photograph, sgd, & engraved port, sgd & framed. (89) $3,000

Collection of ALs & autograph Ms, 29 Aug [1879]. 3 pp, 8vo & 4to. To John Burroughs, sending a Ms for possible use in an essay. Ms describing himself as a nature poet. Doheny collection. (89) $2,500

ALs, 6 [May 1864?]. 2 pp, 16mo. To his mother. Reporting rumors about Grant's campaign in Virginia. Doheny collection. (89) $5,000

— 26 Aug 1865. 4 pp, 4to. To "Byron". About his work in Washington, Southerners seeking pardons, & President Johnson. Fold tears. Doheny collection. (89) $4,200

— 5 June [1874]. Doheny collection. (89) $700

— 24 Feb 1878. 2 pp, 8vo. To John Burroughs. Agreeing to give a lecture on the anniversary of Lincoln's death. Doheny collection. (89) $1,200

— 12 Dec [1878]. 2 pp, 12mo. To John Burroughs. Talking about various publications, letters & friends. Doheny collection. (89) $1,100

— 20 Aug [1879]. 2 pp, 8vo. To John Burroughs. Reporting about his summer & enclosing letters. Was mtd. Doheny collection. (89) $1,100

— 2 Jan 1880. 2 pp, 8vo. To John Burroughs. Acknowledging a present & announcing his return from St. Louis. With engraved vignette of Mississippi River Bridge. Doheny collection. (89) $1,200

— 26 Nov 1880. 1 p, 8vo. To John Burroughs. Sending a carbon copy (present, 2 pp, 4to) of a protest against an unauthorized Ed of Leaves of Grass, & requesting his help. Doheny collection. (89) $1,600

— 29 Mar [1882]. 1 p, 4to. To John Burroughs. Giving his opinion about "the Carlyle proof". Doheny collection. (89) $1,400

— 13 Aug [1882]. 2 pp, 8vo. To John Burroughs. About the publication of a new Ed of Leaves of Grass, & Specimen Days. Doheny collection. (89) $3,000

— 11 Oct 1884. Doheny collection. (89) $750

— 13 Oct [1884]. Doheny collection. (89) $800

— 14 Dec 1884. 2 pp, 8vo. To Talcott Williams. Declining an invitation to meet [Ellen] Terry & [Henry] Irving. Doheny collection. (89) $2,200

— 18 Mar 1886. 2 pp, 4to. To John Burroughs. Returning books, & informing him about his writings & other activities. With related material. Doheny collection. (89) $6,500

— [8 Apr 1886?]. 1 p, 4to. To "T D". Regarding a date. (90) $1,400

— 31 July 1888. 1 p, 8vo. To John Burroughs. Forwarding a letter, & mentioning his health problems & his forthcoming book. Doheny collection. (89) $1,300

— [1878-1884?], "Thursday". 1 p, 8vo. To Alma Calder Johnston. Sending a "queer little book ... I spoke about some weeks since." The Garden Ltd. collection. (90) $2,250

AL, 26 July 1886. (88) $150

Series of 3 autograph postcards, sgd, 17 Mar 1881 to 28 Feb 1889. To John Burroughs. Mentioning his new book Specimen Days & Carlyle. Doheny collection. (89) $2,800

Autograph postcard, sgd, 13 June 1887. To his brother Thomas J. Whitman. About his health & immediate affairs. Margin cut. (90) $1,200

— 14 Jan 1888. Doheny collection. (89) $350

Collection of ANs & photograph, [n.d.]. (90) $280

ANs, [25 Dec] 1875. (91) $850

Autograph sentiment, 27 Oct 1866. (91) $650

— Anr, [n.d.]. (88) $850

Photograph, sgd, Sept 1886. 93mm by 122. Seated by a window. Sgd on mount. Doheny collection. (89) $1,500

— Anr, [15 Apr 1887]. 235mm by 178mm; by George Cox. Sgd on mount. Dampstained. Doheny collection. (89) $2,200

Signature, 8 Apr 1891. (88) $300

— O'CONNOR, WILLIAM DOUGLAS. - Collection of 18 A Ls s & 3 A Ns s, 4 May 1876 to 2 Aug 1885. 156 pp, 8vo & 12mo, in brown mor-backed case. To John Burroughs & R. M. Bucke (1). Defending Leaves of Grass against censors, & about other literary matters. With related material. Doheny collection. (89) $2,200

Whitney, Eli, 1765-1825

ALs, 15 Mar 1804. 1 p, 4to. To J. M. Hopkins "Armky at Law." About a lawsuit for patent infringement. (91) $2,400

Whittier, John Greenleaf, 1807-92

[A group of 8 autograph letters by "Harriet", 1832 to 1836, 28 pp, 4to, to Elizabeth Parrott, containing frequent references to Whittier, sold at sg on 22 Oct, lot 283, for $450.]

Autograph Ms, address & account book, 1853 to 1881. Doheny collection. (89) $900

Series of 4 A Ls s, 21 Oct [1838] to 23 Jan 1884. 8 pp, 8vo & 4to. To Theodore D. Weld, requesting his attendance at an anti-slavery meeting. To [Lucy Larcom?], about various matters. Doheny collection. (89) $1,300

A Ls s (2), 6 Nov 1875 & [n.d.]. (89) $150

ALs, 12 Dec 1860. (89) $190

— Dec 1873. Doheny collection. (89) $1,000

— 2 Jan 1890. Byer collection. (90) $250

Autograph quotation, sgd, [n.d.]. (89) $110

Photograph, sgd & inscr, 20 Jan 1877. (91) $250

Who, The

[A ptd facsimile of the lyrics of "My Generation", sgd by all 4, framed with a group photograph, sold at P on 18 June 1988, lot 728, for $1,400.]

[A piece of paper inscr Best Wishes from the High Numbers, sgd by all 4 (John Entwistle as John Allison), framed with 2 ptd photographs, 10.5 by 13.5 inches, sold at P on 18 June 1988, lot 729, for $900.]

[An album cover, Who's next, sgd by all 4 members including Keith Moon, [n.d.], framed, sold at pnNY on 3 Dec 1988, lot 404, for $550.]

Wichern, Johann Hinrich, 1808-81

Series of 27 A Ls s, 31 May 1854 to 20 Oct 1876 & [n.d.]. 38 pp, 8vo. To Carl Moenckeberg. Dealing with various Protestant organizations. (91) DM2,500

Widmann, Joseph Viktor, 1842-1911

Autograph Ms, review of vol 4 of Hans von Buelow's works; [c.1898]. (90) DM640

Widor, Charles-Marie, 1844-1937

Autograph Ms, essay, Les sept premiers secretaires perpetuels de l'Academie des Beaux-Arts; sgd & dated 6 Nov 1914. (90) DM210

ALs, 23 July 1918. (89) DM260

Wiechert, Ernst, 1887-1950

Collection of 17 A Ls s, AL, & 12 autograph postcards, sgd, 10 Jan 1924 to 29 Mar 1925. 28 pp, 4to, & cards. To his publishers Habbel & Naumann. Mostly about his novel Der Totenwolf. File holes. AL fragment. (90) DM1,800

— Collection of 29 A Ls s, 59 Ls s, & 124 postcards, sgd (107 autograph), 28 Oct 1936 to 18 Sept 1944. About 90 pp, 4to & 8vo, & cards. To the publishing house Langen-Mueller. About a variety of literary, political & private matters. (90) DM3,200

— Collection of ALs & autograph postcard, sgd, 11 & 15 Jan 1937. (91) DM200

— Collection of 5 A Ls s & Ls, 14 July [1947] to 24 May 1948. (90) DM750

Series of 6 A Ls s, 17 July 1939 to 3 Apr 1944. (91) DM700

ALs, 12 [Aug?] 1936. (88) DM360

Collection of 4 Ls s & postcard, sgd, 1948 to 1950. (89) DM320

Wieck, Friedrich, 1785-1873

ALs, 15 June 1838. (91) £900

— 7 Nov 1863. (90) DM550

ADs, 31 May 1873. (90) DM550

Wiegand, Theodor, 1864-1936

Collection of 7 A Ls s & Ls, 29 May 1904 to 20 Sept 1906. 39 pp, 4to & 8vo. To Heinrich Wiegand. About his research & excavations in Greece & the Near East. With related material. (91) DM1,700

Wieland, Christoph Martin, 1733-1813

Autograph Ms, brief comment regarding his accounts with the bookseller Hoffmann for 1788, [c.Jan 1789]. (88) DM320

ALs, 26 May 1763. 3 pp, folio. To Orell,

WIELAND

- Gessner & Co. Discussing terms for the publication of his Geschichte des Agathons. (91) £2,000
- 28 July 1770. 3 pp, 4to. To Prof. Clodius. Recommending Wilhelm Heinse. (89) £2,400
- 12 Mar 1773. 1 p, 4to. To Philipp Erasmus Reich. Thanking for copies of Alceste, & sending some Mss. (91) DM6,600
- 16 Apr 1773. 1 p, 4to. To Arnold Ebert. Thanking for praise of his new journal & promising to print a contribution. Albrecht collection. (91) SF4,200
- 3 July 1778. 1 p, 4to. To Johann Heinrich Merck. Chatting about recipient's travels with the Duchess of Saxe-Weimar, Jacobi's failure to send a contribution to a journal, etc. Albrecht collection. (91) SF11,000
- 7 May 1781. 1 p, 8vo. To Johannes von Mueller. Thnaking for a contribution to his journal Merkur. Albrecht collection. (91) SF4,000
- [Jan 1787]. 4 pp, 8vo. To Gleim. Affectionate letter to a friend about a variety of matters. (89) £2,500
- [May 1788]. 1 p, 8vo. To an unnamed lady. Accepting an invitation. Sgd W. Repaired. (91) DM1,500
- 28 Oct 1799. 4 pp, 8vo. To his son-in-law Karl Leonhard Reinhold. Discussing his family, his estate at Ossmannstedt, Sophie La Roche, etc. (90) DM13,000
- 17 Aug 1801. 1 p, 4to. To the winesellers Ramann at Erfurt. About a financial transaction. (90) DM2,200
- 22 May 1807. (91) DM900
- 22 Apr 1808. 1 p, 4to. To the wineseller Ramann. Expressing satisfaction with a shipment of wine. (90) DM1,100
- 7 Dec 1809. 4 pp, 8vo. To Henriette von Knebel. Requesting her help in finding a buyer for an engraving to support a poor artist. Fold repaired. (88) DM8,500
- 20 Oct 1811. 2 pp, 8vo. To Friedrich Justin Bertuch. Insisting that he cannot possibly accept the wine sent to him as a present. (90) DM3,000

Autograph endorsement, 3 lines on verso of account with Heinrich Gessner, bookseller at Zurich, 5 July 1806. (88) DM750

See also: Stockmann, August Cornelius

Wien, Wilhelm, 1864-1928
Autograph Ms, appeal to German scientists to cease collaborating with English colleagues in response to a wartime declaration by British scientists, [Dec 1914]. (91) DM650

Wieners, John
Autograph Ms, notebook filled with poems, prose pieces & notes, etc. [c.1971] About 170 pp, 8vo. Inscr to Louisa. (91) $1,500

Wieniawski, Henri, 1835-80 —&
Wieniawski, Joseph, 1837-1912
A Ls s (2), (1 each), 19 July 1853. (88) DM560

Wieniawski, Joseph, 1837-1912. See: Wieniawski, Henri & Wieniawski

Wiessner, Georg. See: Wiessner, Lily & Wiessner

Wiessner, Lily —&
Wiessner, Georg
[Their visitor's book, containing c.100 entries by Kandinsky, Carl Vossler, & others, with numerous illusts, 1921 to 1934, over 100 pp, folio, in purple cloth, sold at S on 26 Apr 1989, lot 994, for £220 to Cohan.]

Wigner, Eugene Paul
Autograph Ms, scientific paper, The Use and Ultimate Validity of Invariance Principles; 7 Sept 1983. (91) DM470

Wilberforce, William, 1759-1833
A Ls s (2), 1 Oct 1805 & 30 Jan 1824. (88) £300
ALs, 26 Jan 1798. Byer collection. (90) $550
Ls s (2), 27 Dec 1810 & 5 Feb 1824. (90) $200

Wilde, Constance, d.1896
[The autograph book of Constance Wilde, containing a poem & a maxim by Oscar Wilde & entries by Pater, Mark Twain, Whistler, Swinburne, Browning & others, 1886 to 1896, 49 pp & 2 pp of loosely inserted items, 4to, in contemp roan, sold at S on 15

Dec, lot 36, for £13,000.]

Wilde, Oscar, 1854-1900
[An interleaved copy of his play Vera, 1882, 8vo, with extensive autograph deletions, additions & emendations, imperf, sold at S on 13 Dec 1990, lot 151, for £4,600 to Maggs.]
[A def envelope addressed to Elkin Mathews, [28 Apr 1892], "bearing two and a half examples of Wilde's signature," sold at pn on 24 Mar, lot 55, for £130 to Rivelin.]

Autograph Ms, notes sent to [Sir Edward Tyas] Cook of The Pall Mall Gazette in defense of his review of Harry Quilter's Sententiae Artis; [18 - 23 Nov 1886]. 6 pp, folio, on rectos only. With related material. (90) £3,000
— Autograph Ms, poem, Serenade, 1st stanza, 11 Jan [n.y.]. 1 p, 4to. 8 lines, sgd. (91) £2,000
— Autograph Ms, poem, The Harlots House; [c.1883]. 1 p, folio. 33 lines, including revisions. Koch Foundation. (90) $18,000

Autograph transcript, 4 stanzas from his poem Ave Imperatrix, sgd & dated 12 Feb [1882]. 1 p, 4to. Tipped to larger leaf. Barrett collection. (89) $5,000
— Autograph transcript, 5 lines from his poem Ave Imperatrix, sgd; [Apr 1882]. 1 p, 8vo. On verso of hotel letterhead. With signature. (89) £1,100
— Autograph transcript, poem, In the Garden, sgd & dated Jan 1891. 1 p, folio. (89) £3,200

Collection of 11 A Ls s & postcard, sgd, June to Oct 1897. 36 pp, 4to & 8vo. To Ernest Dowson. Important letters dealing with his readjustment to society, his loneliness & financial problems, his new poem [The Ballad of Reading Gaol], etc. Bradley Martin sale. (90) $62,000

ALs, [c.4 Dec 1880]. (91) £700
— [c.May 1883]. (90) £1,000
— [c.May 1883]. 1 p, folio. To [Edward Pinches]. Requesting a ticket for a dinner in honor of Henry Irving. Mtd; with related letters on verso. (90) £1,450
— [Jan 1885]. 3 pp, 8vo. To Walter Herries Pollock. Thanking for a book of poems. With autograph fragment. (90) £2,000
— [c.early 1885]. 3 pp, 8vo. To [George Webb] Appleton. Regarding a lecture. With related material. Koch Foundation. (90) $1,100
— [c.May 1886]. 4 pp, 8vo. To Henry E. Dixey. Praising his acting. With related material. Koch Foundation. (90) $2,600
— 7 Oct 1887. 2 pp, 8vo. To Fenwick Miller. Asking for a biographical contribution to the journal Woman's World. (90) DM2,600
— 14 Nov 1887. 4 pp, 8vo. To Mrs. Singleton. Accepting an invitation. (90) £2,400
— [n.d.]. 3 pp, 8vo. To Philip Robinson. Sending a ghost story (not present) for publication. (89) £1,600
— [16 Jan 1888]. 2 pp, 8vo. To Philip Robinson. Sending a review by Haddon Chambers (not present). (89) £1,300
— [1888]. (91) £950
— [c.1888]. 4 pp, 8vo. To "Phil". Accepting her idea for an article on decorative art in Ireland. (90) £1,500
— [c.1887-89]. (91) £900
— [c.June 1890]. 4 pp, 8vo. To Sir George Douglas. Expressing gratitude for his appreciation of The Picture of Dorian Gray. (91) £3,000
— [1890]. 4 pp, 8vo. To [Charles Ricketts]. Praising his design for The Picture of Dorian Grey. Koch Foundation. (90) $4,000
— [Dec 1891]. 4 pp, 8vo. To Robert [Sherard]. Commenting on a draft of a biographical notice sent to him. In French & English. (91) £1,100
— [May 1892]. (91) £700
— June 1893. 4 pp, 8vo. To Charles Ricketts. Returning proof of The Sphinx. (91) $5,000
— [July 1894]. (91) £900
— 22 Sept 1897. 5 pp, 8vo. To his pbr Leonard Smithers. Discussing the publication of [The Ballad of Reading Goal]. On hotel letterhead. Doheny collection. (89) $17,000
— 23 Nov 1898. 2 pp, 4to. To Leonard Smithers. Concerning the publication of The Importance of Being Earnest. Koch Foundation. (90) $5,500

WILDE

— [n.d.]. 1 p, 8vo. To Mrs. Morgan. Thanking for a poem about Sarah Bernhardt. (89) £1,100
— [n.d.]. (89) £350
— [n.d.]. Doheny collection. (89) $380
— [n.d.]. (91) £500
— [n.d.]. (91) £500
— [n.d.]. (91) £550
— [n.d.]. 4 pp, 8vo. To Violet Fane [Mrs. Singleton]. Discussing vegetarianism. (90) £2,800
— [n.d.]. (88) £650
— [n.d.]. 4 pp, 12mo. To a doctor. Submitting partial payment of a bill for the doctor's care of Wilde's wife & saying that the balance will have to wait until after Christmas. (89) $1,400
— [n.d.]. 1 p, 4to. To "My Dear Little". Accepting an invitation. (90) DM1,200

Collection of ANs & autograph sentiment, [18 June 1892 & n.d.]. (91) £600
— Collection of ANs & photograph, [n.d.]. (90) £400

ANs, [n.d.]. (90) £500

Autograph quotation, sgd, [23 Jan 1882]. 1 p, 8vo. Quoting Keats. Inscr to Miss Meigs in anr hand. Tipped into def copy of his Poems, 4th Ed. (89) £1,500

Photograph, sgd, May [18]92. 6.5 by 4.25 inches. By Alfred Ellis. (91) £2,700

Photograph, sgd & inscr, [n.d.]. 9.5 by 7.25 inches. Inscr to Bobbie; sgd OW. (91) £1,500

— DUPOIRIER, J. - 11 documents, 10 Mar to 1 Dec 1900. 15 pp, 8vo. Accounts, giving lists of food, drinks & services provided for Wilde [Sebastian Melmoth] at the Hotel d'Alsace, Paris. With related material. (91) £4,500
— MAISON HELBIG, PARIS. - Document, bill for flowers ordered by Robert Ross for Wilde's funeral, 2 Dec 1900. 2 pp, 12mo. (91) £800
— SHERARD, ROBERT HANBOROUGH. - Ls, 8 May 1935. 7 pp, 8vo. Tp [Arthur] Symons. Mostly about Wilde's sexual preferences & syphilis. (91) £2,000
— SHERRARD, ROBERT H. - 16 Ls s & 4 postcards, sgd, 7 May 1938 to 16 Feb 1939. To Walter Armytage. Angry correspondence regarding biographies of Wilde by Boris Brasol & Frank Harris. With related material. (90) £220

— TUCKER, MAURICE A COURT. - Document, 5 Dec 1900. 1 p, size not stated. Physician's account for 68 visits & consultations during Wilde's illness after 27 Sept 1900. (91) £650
See also: Beerbohm, Max
See also: Douglas, Lord Alfred
See also: Ransome, Arthur

Wilder, Thornton, 1897-1975

Collection of 9 A Ls s, 1 Ls, 3 autograph postcards sgd & 1 Christmas card sgd, [1950s-60s]. (88) $800
— Collection of 13 A Ls s, autograph postcard, sgd, 5 autograph Mss, & 2 telegrams, 1959 to 1974. 36 pp, 8vo & 4to. Recipient unnamed, mostly with private news. Mss dealing with various literary questions. With related material. (90) DM2,400
— Collection of 4 A Ls s & autograph postcard, sgd, 21 Nov 1960 to 14 June 1973. 7 pp, 4to, & card. To Otto Klemperer. Interesting correspondence about literary & musical matters. With a copy of his The Eighth Day, 1967, inscr to Klemperer & including over 100 autograph annotations, & further related material. (90) DM2,600

Series of 8 A Ls s, 1947 to 1956. (90) $600

A Ls s (2), 14 Mar & 19 Apr 1938. (90) $400
— A Ls s (2), 28 Nov 1939 & 29 Oct 1964. (90) $475

ALs, 14 Dec 1927. (91) $160

Wilhelm, Prince of Prussia, 1783-1851.
See: Schelling, Friedrich Wilhelm Joseph von

Wilhelm, Crown Prince of Germany, 1882-1951

ALs, 16 June 1921. (90) DM380
— 9 Nov 1921. Schroeder collection. (89) DM320

Collection of Ls & photograph, sgd, 30 June 1905 & 1936. (90) DM360
— Collection of Ls & photograph, sgd, 8 May 1935. (90) DM220

Ls, 3 July 1925. (91) DM220

Wilhelm I, Herzog von Berg, d.1408
Letter, [3 Mar 1406]. 1 p, 4to. To his son Gerhard. Informing him about efforts for the release of his son Wilhelm imprisoned by Heinrich von Oer. (89) DM2,600

Wilhelm I, King of Wuerttemberg, 1781-1864
Collection of ALs, Ls & autograph Ms, [n.d.], May 1816, & 27 Sept 1842. (90) DM480
ALs, 17 May 1845. (88) DM380
— [n.d.]. (90) DM260
Ls, 11 Sept 1818. 1 p, folio. To his Ministry of Finance. Concerning expenses for the visit of his mother-in-law [Maria, Empress of Russia]. With related material. (89) DM1,600
Ds, 4 Mar 1849. (90) DM250

Wilhelm I, Deutscher Kaiser, 1797-1888
[A list of 99 signatures of Prussian officials, generals, envoys, etc. present at a reception given by Friedrich Wilhelm von Hessen-Kassel at Berlin on Kaiser Wilhelm's birthday, 22 Mar 1884, sold at star on 2 Dec 1988, lot 2252, for DM250.]
Original drawing, Die Capelle auf dem Zobtenberg, [c.1810]. (91) DM550
Collection of ALs & AN, 9 Aug 1876 & 10 Jan 1878. (89) £400
Series of 4 A Ls s, 29 June 1859 to 20 May 1860. 8 pp, 8vo & 4to. To his brother Carl. Discussing a court case. Sgd W. (90) DM1,300
ALs, 6 Feb 1814. 3 pp, 8vo. To his brother Carl. Reporting about the war in France. (90) DM1,800
— 26 & 27 Feb 1821. 8 pp, 4to. To Ludwig von Wolzogen. Personal letter about von Wolzogen's marriage, his own thoughts about matrimony, politics in Prussia, etc. Repaired. Schroeder collection. (89) DM1,600
— 8 Jan 1829. (90) DM800
— 5 Nov 1833. Schroeder collection. (89) DM650
— 14 June 1846. Schroeder collection. (89) DM420
— 14 Dec [1847]. Schroeder collection. (89) DM270
— 15 Apr 1848. 4 pp, 8vo. Recipient unnamed. Commenting about the revolution in Germany. Sgd PrinzvPreussen. (90) DM1,100
— 15 Apr 1852. (91) DM580
— 11 Mar 1856. Schroeder collection. (89) DM320
— 9 Aug 1856. Schroeder collection. (89) DM340
— 27 Feb 1860. Schroeder collection. (89) DM340
— 10 July 1870. 4 pp, 8vo. To Gen. Bernhard von Werder. About the Russian army in Poland, the Spanish succession, & relations with France. Schroeder collection. (89) DM9,000
— 12 Mar 1871. 2 pp, 8vo. To Gen. von Herwarth. Referring to the recent victory & the peace treaty. (90) DM3,800
— 2 Mar 1872. (88) DM550
— 30 Mar 1879. Schroeder collection. (89) DM520
— 14 Apr 1880. (88) DM650
— 9 Feb 1882. (88) DM600
— 5 Dec 1884. 4 pp, 4to. To [Bernhard von Werder]. Discussing the Duke of Cumberland's claims to the succession in Brunswick. Schroeder collection. (89) DM1,500
Series of 3 Ls s, 19 Feb 1878 to 24 May 1883. (89) DM300
Ls, 17 Jan 1871. 2 pp, folio. To Grossherzog Peter II von Oldenburg. Formally accepting the Imperial crown. With autograph subscription. With related material. Schroeder collection. (89) DM9,500
— 18 Oct 1877. (90) DM270
— 22 Mar 1884. 1 p, 4to. To Graf Moltke. About the conferral of a decoration on the Russian Foreign Minister von Giers. Countersgd by Bismarck. Schroeder collection. (89) DM2,400
— 15 Jan 1888. Schroeder collection. (89) DM320
ANs, 22 Feb 1869. (89) DM360
Series of Ds s, 4 Ds s, 21 Apr 1868 to 14 May 1887. (90) DM460
Ds, 4 Oct 1861. (90) DM240
— 4 Jan 1864. (91) DM200
— 23 Jan 1864. (88) DM580
— 1 Dec 1872. (88) DM750
— 8 May 1877. (90) DM700
— 31 Jan 1881. Schroeder collection. (89)

WILHELM I

DM650
— 25 Nov 1884. (89) DM210
— 9 July 1886. (90) DM220
Autograph telegram, sgd, [1885?]. (89) DM300

Wilhelm I, Deutscher Kaiser, 1797-1888 —& Others
Group photograph, 29 July 1878. 36.5cm by 50cm. With son Friedrich Wilhelm, daughter Luise & granddaughter Viktoria in the park at Babelsberg. Sgd by all 4 on mount. Schroeder collection. (89) DM3,200

Wilhelm I, Deutscher Kaiser, 1797-1888.
See: Bismarck, Otto von

Wilhelm I, Deutscher Kaiser 1797-1888.
See: Bismarck, Otto von & Wilhelm I

Wilhelm I, Deutscher Kaiser, 1797-1888.
See: Lettow-Vorbeck, Moritz von

Wilhelm II, Deutscher Kaiser, 1797-1888 —&
Churchill, Winston L. S., Sir, 1874-1965
Group photograph, Sept 1906. (89) £850

Wilhelm II, King of Wuerttemberg, 1848-1921
Autograph postcard, sgd, 25 Apr 1920. (90) DM370

Wilhelm II, Deutscher Kaiser, 1859-1941
[A heliography, a knight guarding the temple of peace, drawn by H. Knackfuss after a sketch by Wilhelm II, 59cm by 42.5cm, initialled by Wilhelm II & dated 30 Sept [18]96, in pencil, sold at star on 10 Mar 1988, lot 1218, for DM850.]
[A collection of 8 autograph telegrams, sgd, 7 July 1898 to 2 Aug 1899, 9 pp, 4to, to the Empress Auguste Viktoria, with related material, sold at star on 1 Dec 1988, lot 1096, for DM1,500.]
[A group of 3 autograph telegrams, sgd, 12 July 1898, 2 Aug 1899 & [n.d.], 3 pp, 4to, to various recipients, sold at star on 1 Dec 1988, lot 1097, for DM800.]
[A postcard, sgd, 27 Jan 1935, thanking for congratulations on his birthday, with autograph postscript & related material, sold at star on 2 Dec 1988, lot 2317, for DM280.]

AMERICAN BOOK PRICES CURRENT

Autograph Ms, comments & sketch to illus a poem, [c.1896?]. Schroeder collection. (89) DM320
— Autograph Ms, exposition of German relations with France in historical perspective; [c.early 1930s]. (90) $550
— Autograph Ms, ptr's copy of his work Meine Vorfahren, sgd at end & dated 20 May to 9 Sept 1928. 172 pp, 4to. In indelible pencil. With numerous revisions & differences from ptd version. In autograph envelope addressed to K. Fr. Nowack. (90) DM11,000
Typescript, "Comparative definition of so-called 'masculine" and so-called 'feminine" Culture according to Professor Frobenius", [n.d.]. (88) DM210
— Typescript, "Extract from a letter of H.I.M. (88) $100
— Typescript, Hints for Students of Raciology and Ethnology, sgd & dated 10 Jan [19]28. (90) $190
— Typescript, trans of an article by Maj. (89) $325
Collection of ALs & Ms, 26 June 1883. (90) DM550
— Collection of ALs & autograph postcard, sgd, 19 Nov 1905 & [n.d.]. (91) DM660

ALs, [c.1870]. (90) DM400
— 31 Dec 1880. (91) DM700
— 21 Nov 1887. 3 pp, folio. To Field Marshal Moltke. Sending a memorandum regarding the relationship of the military establishment & the emperor, & requesting his advice. (91) DM2,000
— 10 Oct 1898. (90) DM850
— 1 Dec 1898. 3 pp, 8vo. To Grossherzog Karl Alexander von Sachsen-Weimar. Reporting about his travels in Palestine. (90) DM3,800
— 4 Jan 1907. 4 pp, 8vo. To Philipp Graf zu Eulenburg. Concerning the marriage of recipient's daughter to a commoner. In pencil. Schroeder collection. (89) DM1,500
— 1 June 1928. (89) DM950
— 1 Jan 1933. 1 p, 8vo, on verso of picture postcard. To Magnus von Levetzow. Disagreeing with his opinions about Hitler. (90) DM2,000
— 13 Mar 1940. 4 pp, 4to. To [Marianne] Geibel. Outlining his views about God

& the world, nature, history & the war. With port photograph, sgd, 1 Aug 1939. (88) DM1,900

Collection of Ls & Ds, 27 Jan 1890 & 16 June 1909. (89) DM260

Series of 3 Ls s, 22 May 1889 to 29 Dec 1900. (90) DM350

— Series of 3 Ls s, 28 Apr 1897 to 25 June 1900. (90) DM420

— Series of 4 Ls s, 1 Dec 1903 to 6 July 1904. (91) DM900

Ls, 30 June 1889. Schroeder collection. (89) DM260

— 10 Apr 1901. (90) DM220

ANs, 21 June 1904. Schroeder collection. (89) DM750

Series of Ds s, 3 Ds s, 31 Aug 1890 to 18 July 1902. (90) DM800

Ds s (2) 20 Sept 1890 & 15 Dec 1900. (90) DM240

— Ds s (2) 27 Jan 1896 & 19 Dec 1907. (89) DM200

— Ds s (2) 4 Mar 1904 & 10 Sept 1910. (90) DM320

Ds, 27 Jan 1889. (88) £85

— 19 Jan 1902. (91) $110

— 6 Sept 1903. (91) $250

— 18 Jan 1905. (90) DM440

— 21 Jan 1907. (88) DM340

— 12 Apr 1910. (89) £50

— 14 Jan 1911. (90) DM270

— 30 July 1911. 11 pp, folio. Codicil to his last will. Docketed on autograph envelope. (89) DM6,000

Autograph telegram, sgd, 21 July 1898. 2 pp, 4to. To the Foreign Office at Berlin. Giving orders to prevent the sale of property at Cuxhaven to an English merchant. In pencil. (89) DM1,100

— Anr, 14 July 1899. (90) DM400

Endorsement, sgd, 18 Mar 1888. Schroeder collection. (89) DM220

— Anr, comments, sgd, on a typed Ms, Extracts from an Article on China by Major Mossdorf, [c.1927]. (88) $175

Group photograph, [1 Jan] 1905. (89) DM300

Photograph, sgd, 27 Jan 1898. Schroeder collection. (89) DM600

Photograph, sgd & inscr, 10 Apr 1930. (88) $250

Telegram, sgd, 27 Jan [n.y.]. (91) $130

See also: Lettow-Vorbeck, Moritz von

Wilhelm Ludwig, Herzog von Wuerttemberg, 1647-77

Ls, 24 June 1676. (90) DM600

Ds, 18 July 1676. 1 p, folio. Order to tax collectors in Suebia to transfer money to quartermasters. (89) DM1,100

Wilhelm V, Herzog von Bayern, 1548-1626

ALs, 19 Nov 1590. 2 pp, folio. To Cardinal Petrochini de Montelbaro. Concerning recipient's order that Frater Alfonso de Yela return to Spain. In Latin. (91) DM1,500

Wilhelm von Hanau, Fuerst, 1836-1902

— HEPPE, SOPHIE VON. - Series of 210 A Ls s, 1 Jan to 27 Dec 1857. 8vo. To Wilhelm von Hanau. Love letters. With related material. (90) DM1,800

Wilhelmina, Queen of The Netherlands, 1880-1962

ALs, 17 Dec 1896. (88) DM850

Ls, 15 June 1909. (90) DM320

Photograph, sgd & inscr, 19 Oct [n.y.]. (89) DM550

Wilhelmine, Markgraefin von Bayreuth, 1709-58

ALs, 19 Dec 1750. 3 pp, 4to. To her brother Friedrich II of Prussia. Regretting her departure from Berlin & relating 2 tragic love stories. Albrecht collection. (91) SF2,800

Ls, 10 Jan 1758. Schroeder collection. (89) DM650

Wilkes, John, 1727-97

ALs, 19 Apr [1768]. 2 pp, 4to. To Jean Baptiste Suard. About events during the recent election, his plans, books he is sending, etc. (90) £1,200

AL, 9 Dec 1768. (91) £80

— 19 Sept [1777]. (89) £300

Wilkins, Hubert, Sir, 1888-1958. See: Earhart, Amelia & Wilkins

Wilkinson, Sir Geoffrey

Autograph Ms, Acceptance speech of honorary degree, University of Granada Spain, 6 Mar 1976. (90) DM220

— Autograph Ms, First Mond Lecture given to the Chemical Society, 2 Dec 1980. (90) DM250

WILKINSON

— Autograph Ms, scientific paper, The Chemistry of Rhenium Alkyls, Part III... (91) DM300

Wilkinson, James, 1757-1825
ALs, 27 Nov 1800. Alexander collection. (90) $230
— 25 Sept 1801. Alexander collection. (90) $230
Ds, 21 Dec 1792. (88) $650

Willard, Aaron. See: Willard, Simon & Willard

Willard, Frances E., 1839-98
ALs, [n.d.]. (90) $110

Willard, Simon, 1753-1848 —& Willard, Aaron
[1 ADs each by Simon Willard, 25 Aug 1829, order for books, & Aaron Willard, 5 Sept 1817, receipt for Bedford Meeting House clock, 2 pp, 8vo, framed with a photo of the clock, sold at rce on 28 July 1988, lot 607, for $170.]

Wille, Bruno, 1860-1928
Collection of 52 A Ls s & 9 A Ns s, 10 Jan 1901 to 11 Apr 1907. About 210 pp, various sizes. To Carl Hauptmann. Literary correspondence with a friend. (88) DM1,700

Wille, Johann Georg, 1715-1808
ALs, 9 Mar 1765. (88) DM420
— 25 Aug 1776. (89) DM260

Willemer, Marianne von, 1784-1860
ALs, 13 Nov 1855. 3 pp, 8vo. To Sophie Schlosser. Sending news from Frankfurt. Albrecht collection. (91) SF1,250

William I, Prince of Orange, 1533-84
Ls, 31 May 1576. 2 pp, folio. To Robert Beale. In 3d person, responding to British demands to release English merchant ships. (90) DM3,700

William I, King of The Netherlands, 1772-1843
ALs, 14 May 1814. (90) DM1,000

William I, King of Prussia, 1797-1888. See: Wilhelm I, 1797-1888

AMERICAN BOOK PRICES CURRENT

William II, King of The Netherlands, 1792-1849
ALs, 5/17 Mar 1817. (89) DM300
— 13/25 Aug 1817. (90) DM340
— [n.d.]. (90) DM240

William III, King of England, 1650-1702
ALs, 10/20 Dec 1695. (90) £350
— 17/27 Mar 1696. (89) £650
Ls, 1 Mar 1688[/89]. 2 pp, folio. To an unidentified sovereign (inked out). Announcing his accession to the throne. In Latin. Byer collection. (90) $1,400
— 23 Aug 1694. (88) £250
— 30 Dec 1694. (88) $600
Ds, 23 Feb 1673. (90) $400
— 25 Feb 1692. Byer collection. (90) $800
— 1692. 60 pp, folio. Establishment Book of the Royal Forces, listing rates of pay, rank, allowances, rewards, etc. Sgd 18 times by William III; countersgd ten times by the Earl of Nottingham. In contemp red mor gilt with the royal arms. (89) £4,200
— 10 June 1693. (90) £380
— 28 Jan 1697. (88) £350
— 14 Mar 1698. (88) £90
Document, 6 May 1692. 2 membranes, c.26 by 32 inches. Letters Patent granting John Conyers & Theophilus Colladon £600 per year from a grant by Charles II. Illuminated; with initial letter port. With Great Seal. In orig calf box. (89) £4,800
— 6 May 1697. 1 p, c.25 by 29 inches, vellum. Letters Patent, sgd by Gov. Benjamin Fletcher of New York, confirming an earlier grant by Gov. Andros to Col. Lewis Morris of land & a lordship of the manor in The Bronx. With engraved initial letter port. (88) £1,800
— FLEMING, MICHAEL. - ALs, 30 July [16]93. 3 pp, folio. To his father Sir Daniel Fleming. Giving a detailed account of the Battle of Neerwinden. (88) £380

William III, King of The Netherlands, 1817-90
ALs, 17 June 1849. (90) DM320

William IV, King of England, 1765-1837
ALs, [11 Oct 1790]. (90) $200
— [6 July 1800]. Crohn Collection. (88) $100
— 14 Jan 1804. (88) £900
— 10 Sept 1818. (91) DM380
— 8 May 1819. (90) DM460
— [n.d.]. (90) DM420
Document, 1836. 2 rolled sheets, 23 by 32 inches & smaller. Letters patent creating Sir Thomas Makdougall Brisbane hereditary baronet; with marginal portraits of King William & Queen Adelaide. With seal; in mor covered wooden case. (88) A$6,000

William of Conches, d.c.1150
Ms, Dragmaticon philosophiae. [Germany, 2d half of 12th cent]. 2 conjoint leaves only, vellum, 145mm by 195mm. In a gothic textura, in 2 columns; outer columns heavily trimmed. With 2 drawings in colored inks, showing a map of the world & an eclipse of the sun. Recovered from a bdg. (90) DM7,000
See also: Hugo de Folieto & William of Conches

Williams, Roger, 1603?-83
ALs, 7 June [16]40. 1 p, folio. To Gov. John Winthrop. Regarding hostages held by the Connecticut Indians. Sang collection. (89) $20,000

Williams, Samuel M., 1795-1858
A Ls s (2), 10 Mar & 1 July 1834. (89) $130

Williams, Ted. See: DiMaggio, Joseph Paul ("Joe") & Williams

Williams, Tennessee, 1911-83
[An interesting collection of 44 letters, postcards, documents, etc., including 12 A Ls s, c.1920 to 1958, written to his family, with family photographs & correspondence from other members of his family & acquaintances & further related material, sold at P on 11 Dec 1989, lot 160, for $13,000.]
[An autograph Ms, poem "To Anna Jean", 14 Sept 1931, & a typescript, "Madrigal (to A.J.)", sgd Tom, [n.d.]; each 1 p, 4to, with a photograph showing Williams & Anna Jean O'Donnell, [c.1931], sold at sg on 12 Nov 1987, lot 320, for $1,200.]
Autograph Ms, poem, Home Remedy, sgd; 3 Feb [19]54. 3 pp, 8vo. With holograph revisions. 1 stanza dictated by Williams to the dedicatee & written in the latter's hand. Koch Foundation. (90) $1,200
Typescript, A Playwright's Prayer. [1960s] 3 pp, 4to. With 35 words of holograph revisions. (91) $1,200
Series of 5 Ls s, 13 May to 17 Aug 1960. 5 pp, 4to. To Frank Corsaro. About the production of The Night of the Iguana. Sgd "Tenn" or "10"; in pencil. (90) $6,000
— Series of 4 Ls s, 11 Feb 1966 to 29 Dec 1980. 6 pp, 4to. To his cousins Stell &/or Jim Adams. Mainly about his sister Rose. With related material (91) $1,100
Ls, [c.Jan 1959]. 4 pp, 8vo. To Elia Kazan. About his view of the production of Sweet Bird of Youth and Kazan's direction of it. Sgd "1". (91) $1,600
— 18 Mar 1959. (91) $420
— 20 Mar 1959. (91) $750
— [c.1959]. (91) $750
— 22 June 1963. 3 pp, 8vo. To Edward Albee. About the dangers that come with being a sudden Broadway success. (91) $1,400
— [1963]. 1 p, 4to. To Geraldine Page. Asking her and her husband (Rip Torn) to read Summer and Smoke as a possible vehicle. (91) $2,200

Williams, Tennessee, 1911-83 —& Others
[A clipped advertisement for the film Cat on a Hot Tin Roof, [n.d.], 11 by 9 inches, sgd by Williams & actors Elizabeth Taylor, Paul Newman, & Burl Ives, framed, sold at wa on 20 Oct 1990, lot 331, for $450.]

Williams, Van. See: Lee, Bruce & Williams

Williams, William, Signer from Connecticut
ALs, 25 Nov 1785. (91) $250
ADs, 25 Dec 1780. (91) $120
Cut signature, 2 Feb 1779. (90) $80
See also: Connecticut

Williamson, Henry, 1895-1977
Typescript, A Summer Day on Dunkerry, [n.d.]. (88) £350
Collection of c.50 A Ls s, Ls s & cards, 1928 to 1970; c. 100 pp, 4to & 8vo. To his bookseller Robert Harper. Expressing hopes for Tarka the Otter, ordering books, talking about Hitler, etc. With related material & a quantity of 19th & 20th-cent letters by other authors. (88) £1,250
— Collection of c.40 A Ls s & Ls s, 1931 to 1973. 70 pp, 4to & 8vo. To Elsie Alderton. Discussing her emotional problems, his difficulties, friendships, books, etc. Some unsgd; some on postcards. (89) £1,050
— Collection of 10 A Ls s & Ls s, 2 Jan 1962 to 21 Dec 1963. (91) £850
ALs, 31 July 1923. (91) £70
— 14 June 1927. (91) £500
Ls, 26 Mar 1961. (90) £300

Willis, Nathaniel Parker, 1806-67
ALs, [1850]. (88) $100

Willkie, Wendell Lewis, 1892-1944
Menu, 6 Nov 1940. (91) $120

Willoughby, Francis, 5th Baron, 1613?-66
Ds, 7 June 1664. (90) £950

Willstaetter, Richard, 1872-1942
ALs, 27 Apr 1915. (88) DM630

Wilmot, David, 1814-68
ALs, 3 Mar 1848. (91) $200

Wilson, Dooley, 1894-1953
Signature, [n.d.]. (91) $1,000

Wilson, Edith Bolling, 1872-1961
Autograph Ms, beginning of the preface to My Memoir; [pbd 1939]. (91) $300
— Autograph Ms, fragment from My Memoir (p 176); [pbd 1939]. (91) $225
Series of 4 A Ls s, 16 Dec 1924 to 10 Nov 1930. (91) $150
ALs, [n.d.]. (90) $90

Wilson, Ellen A., 1860-1914
ALs, 10 Oct 1910. (91) $300
— 19 Nov 1910. (91) $375

Wilson, Francis, 1854-1935. See: Field, Eugene & Wilson

Wilson, George, 1808-70
[An archive of letters addressed to him as chairman of the Anti-Cornlaw League & about other matters, with family letters by Wilson, 1830s to 1860s, sold at pn on 16 Mar 1989, lot 22, for £1,050 to Rota.]

Wilson, James, Signer from Pennsylvania
Ds, 14 Mar 1791. (89) $200
— 13 Sept 1797. (90) $325

Wilson, Robert, Sir, 1779-1849. See: Peninsular War

Wilson, Thomas Epps. See: Mitchell, Janet Marshall & Wilson

Wilson, Woodrow, 1856-1924
[Cobb, Frank. - An archive of 26 A Ls s & Ls s addressed to Cobb, 1914 to 1921, concerning the Wilson administration & the war, sold at sg on 24 Mar 1988, lot 209, for $175.]
Typescript, speech commemorating the 50th anniversary of the Battle of Gettysburg, draft; sgd & dated 4 July 1914. 7 pp, 8vo. Including autograph corrections. (90) $2,800
ALs, 29 Nov 1898. 1 p, 4to. To James P. Munroe. Disagreeing with the demands of the Anti-Imperialist League. (90) $5,000
— 20 May 1911. (91) $700
— 4 Apr 1912. (91) $800
— 24 Feb 1914. 1 p, 4to. To Herbert L. Pratt. Hoping his autograph collection may "be made available for the inspection of scholars". Pratt collection. (89) $9,500
Collection of Ls & Ds, 27 Apr 1905 & 25 Feb 1913. (89) $275
— Collection of Ls & White House card, sgd, 3 July 1913 & [n.d.]. (90) $450
— Collection of Ls & photograph, sgd & inscr, 23 Feb 1915 & [n.d.]. (90) $450
Series of 5 Ls s, 14 Dec 1921 to 15 Sept 1923. 1 or 2 pp, 4to. To Dr. Francis Dercum. About a variety of matters. With ALs by Edith Wilson & correspondence relating to Wilson's illness, 1919 - 1920. (90) $1,800
Ls s (2), 12 Apr & 9 Aug 1916. Doheny collection. (89) $450
Ls, 15 July 1909. (89) $95
— 14 Dec 1909. (89) $175

1987 - 1991 • AUTOGRAPHS & MANUSCRIPTS   WINDSOR

— 17 June 1910. (89) $200
— 19 Sept 1910. (91) $250
— 8 Feb 1911. (91) $275
— 16 Mar 1911. (90) $180
— 23 Mar 1911. (90) $200
— 7 Sept 1912. (90) $180
— 23 Oct 1912. (91) $170
— 9 Nov 1912. (88) $225
— 12 Nov 1912. (89) $140
— [n.d.]. (89) $140
— 21 Jan 1913. (88) $275
— 21 Jan 1913. (88) $150
— 29 Apr 1913. (89) $400
— 19 May 1913. (90) $250
— 1 Nov 1913. (90) $275
— 9 Dec 1913. (91) $160
— 29 June 1914. (88) $475
— 1 Jan 1916. (88) $250
— 8 June 1916. (88) $200
— 5 Dec 1916. (90) $180
— 13 Dec 1916. (90) $250
— 2 Mar 1918. (91) $250
— 13 May 1918. (91) $275
— 9 Sept 1918. 1 p, 4to. To Edward N. Hurley. Stating his position about shipping negotiations with England. Byer collection. (90) $1,100
— 6 July 1922. (89) $240
— 29 Nov 1923. (91) $350
ANs, [6 Aug 1914]. On White House correspondence card. To Vice President Thomas R. Marshall. Regarding his wife's illness. (89) $2,250
Ns, 26 July 1909. (88) $70
Ds, 10 June 1913. (91) $175
— 10 June 1913. (91) $160
— 14 July 1913. (90) $250
— 22 Oct 1913. (91) $500
— 22 Apr 1915. (91) $225
— 7 June 1915. (91) $110
— 17 Feb 1916. (88) $150
— 17 Feb 1916. (90) $80
— 15 May 1916. (91) $225
— 27 July 1916. (88) $160
— 17 Aug 1916. (90) $190
— 26 Sept 1916. (91) $275
— 5 Jan 1917. (91) $220
— [n.d.]. (91) $250
Cut signature, 14 Sept 1904. (90) $100
Group photograph, [n.d.]. (89) $250
Photograph, sgd, [n.d.]. (90) $400

— Anr, [n.d.]. (89) $210
— Anr, [n.d.]. (91) $200
Photograph, sgd & inscr, [n.d.]. (88) $250
— Anr, [n.d.]. 4to. Inscr to Mr. Clemenceau. Photograph by Harris & Ewing. Framed. (89) $2,250
Ptd photograph, [n.d.]. (91) $190
Signature, 12 Oct 1910. (91) $190
— Anr, [c.1919], on photograph of the U.S.S George Washington. (89) $325
— Anr, [n.d.]. (91) $180
White House card, sgd, 10 Apr 1913. (90) $200
— Anr, sgd, [n.d.]. (90) $180
— Anr, sgd; [n.d.]. (90) $500

Wilson, Woodrow, 1856-1924 —& Others
[A program for a performance of Beaucoup Joie by the crew of USS George Washington, 21 Feb 1919, 4 pp, 8vo, sgd by Wilson, his wife Edith, & Franklin D. & Eleanor Roosevelt, with related photographs, sold at P on 13 June 1991, lot 247, for $1,000.]

Winchell, Walter, 1897-1972
[archive of clippings, letters & notations used in his effort to discredit her with reference to her law suit against him. This sold at b&b on 12 Dec 1990 for $550]

Winckelmann, Johann Joachim, 1717-68
ALs, 4 Jan 1764. 1 p, 4to. To his pbr Georg Konrad Walther. Requesting him to change the dedication of his Geschichte der Kunst des Alterthums. (90) DM9,500
— 12 July 1766. 1 p, 4to. To Johann David Michaelis. Providing information about his works. Albrecht collection. (91) SF13,000
Autograph quotation, Durum: sed leuis fit patientia... (Horace), sgd & dated 25 Sept 1742. 1 p, 8vo. Sgd & inscr by J. D. Ballin on verso. (91) DM2,700

Windsor, Edward, Duke of, 1894-1972
ALs, 8 May 1911. (89) $175
— 19 Nov 1911. Crohn Collection. (88) $175
— 27 Mar 1914. Crohn Collection. (88) $550
— 31 Dec 1914. Crohn Collection. (88) $800

WINDSOR

— 27 Mar 1915. Crohn Collection. (88) $700
— 25 June 1915. Crohn Collection. (88) $650
— 15 Oct 1915. Crohn Collection. (88) $650
— 19 Dec 1915. Crohn Collection. (88) $300
— 4 July 1918. 2 pp, 8vo. To Capt. Faussett. Reporting about the war & his official duties in Italy. Punch holes. Crohn Collection. (88) $1,100
— 28 Oct 1921. (89) $300
— 1 June 1922. (89) $800
— 25 June 1922. Crohn Collection. (88) $250
— 28 June 1922. Crohn Collection. (88) $550
— [after 1922]. Crohn Collection. (88) $200
— 19 Mar 1923. (90) $200
— 28 June 1923. Crohn Collection. (88) $300
— [30 Oct 1925]. (90) $200
— [late 1928]. (90) $200
— 22 Dec 1932. (88) £260
— 6 Sept 1944. Crohn Collection. (88) $550

Ls, 18 June 1923. (89) $200
— 5 May 1925. Crohn Collection. (88) $250
— 26 Sept 1927. (89) $225
— 10 May 1936. 2 pp, 4to. To the King of the Hellenes. As King of England, informing him of the death of George V. (91) £2,400
— 22 June 1937. Crohn Collection. (88) $200
— 21 Apr 1939. (90) $850
— 15 Feb & 23 Mar 1943. 3 pp, 4to. To Philip Guedalla. About a variety of matters, his situation in the Bahamas, etc. On Government House letterhead. Mtd. Crohn Collection. (88) $1,300
— 8 Nov 1946. Crohn Collection. (88) $650
— 18 Sept 1950. (89) $375
— 10 Feb 1952. (88) $325
— 24 May 1967. (90) $275

ANs, [3 July 1904]. Crohn Collection. (88) $350
— 16 Feb 1913. Crohn Collection. (88) $250

AMERICAN BOOK PRICES CURRENT

Ds, July 1915. (89) $275
— 3 June 1918. Crohn Collection. (88) $150
— 17 Apr 1928. (88) $100
— 20 Jan 1936. 1 p, 305mm by 403mm. As King, appointment for Anthony Douglas as Officer in the Land Forces. With affixed seal of George V. Crohn Collection. (88) $1,200
— 15 June 1936. Crohn Collection. (88) $800

Christmas card, sgd, 1925. Crohn Collection. (88) $350

Group photograph, 1970. 9.5 by 7.75 inches. Standing behind a table; sgd by both. Crohn Collection. (88) $1,600

Photograph, sgd, Mar 1911. Crohn Collection. (88) $350
— Anr, 1911. Crohn Collection. (88) $300
— Anr, 1912. Crohn Collection. (88) $150
— Anr, 1914. Crohn Collection. (88) $275
— Anr, Aug & Oct 1919. Crohn Collection. (88) $225
— Anr, 1921. Crohn Collection. (88) $400
— Anr, 1925. Crohn Collection. (88) $300
— Anr, [c.1925-30?]. Crohn Collection. (88) $300
— Anr, 1939. (91) £280

Signature, 24 Feb 1925. Crohn Collection. (88) $100
— Anr, [n.d.]. Crohn Collection. (88) $375
— Anr, 17 Feb [19]53. Crohn Collection. (88) $325
— POYNDER, CAPT. FREDERICK. - An album compiled by him, containing 109 photographs relating to the visits of Edward (as Prince of Wales), the Duke of Connaught, & the Crown Prince of Sweden, to India, 1 sgd by Edward, 1921-22, sold at sg on 24 Mar 1988, lot W121, for $750. 88
— RAND, SALLY. - Ls, 18 Apr 1941. 1 p, 4to. Recipient unnamed. Speaking of a performance & subsequent invitation from the Duke & Duchess of Windsor. Crohn Collection. (88) $200

Windsor, Edward, Duke of, 1894-1972 — & Others
[The signatures of the Duke of Windsor, Ben Hogan & Bing Crosby, on verso of a Seminole Golf Club tournament admission tag, [n.d.], 3 by 4 inches, sold at Dar on 10 Apr 1991, lot

170, for $250.]

Windsor, Edward, Duke of, 1894-1972 —& George VI, King of England, 1895-1952
[A picture postcard of Sandringham Church, sgd Edward, & Albert, & dated Christmas 1904, addressed in an unknown hand, sold at sg on 24 Mar 1988, lot W2, for $425.]

Windsor, Edward, Duke of, 1894-1972 —& Others
[An album containing c.130 photographs of members of the Royal family, various dates, many with ptd wire service captions, sold at sg on 24 Mar 1988, lot 122, for $375.]
Group photograph, "Drill Photograph at York Cottage, 1906", 3 by 4 inches, showing Edward with sister Mary & brothers Albert & Harry. Crohn Collection. (88) $850

Windsor, Edward, Duke of, 1894-1972 —& Windsor, Wallis Simpson, Duchess of, 1896-1986
[A group of 7 ptd & partly ptd luncheon & dinner invitations, 16mo & 12mo, with date & time added in the Duchess's holograph, sold at sg on 24 Mar 1988, lot W99, for $250.]
[A group of 19 telegrams sent by the Duke or Duchess to American friends, 1953 to 1965, sold at sg on 24 Mar 1988, lot W98, for $500.]
[Their signatures on an engraved card, [c.1950s], 90mm by 135mm, sold at sg on 8 Feb 1990, lot 66, for $350.]
[Their signatures on a 1st day cover, [16 Mar 1966], sold at sg on 9 Mar 1989, lot 67, for $275.]
[Their signatures on a card, [n.d.], 12mo, sold at Dar on 7 Feb 1991, lot 119, for $400.]
Christmas card, [n.d.]. (91) £160
Group photograph, 3 June 1937. 11.5 by 9.5 inches. Wedding day photograph, sgd by both. Sgd by photographer Soper on mount. Crohn Collection. (88) $2,200
— Anr, 1940-42. Crohn Collection. (88) $800
— Anr, [c.1950?]. Crohn Collection. (88) $600
Signature, [c.1940-44]. (88) $200

Windsor, Wallis Simpson, Duchess of, 1896-1986
Collection of 3 A Ls s, autograph postcard, & ANs, 2 Aug 1958 to 9 Jan 1960 & [n.d.]. (90) $800
Series of 4 A Ls s, 3 Jan 1955 & [n.d.]. Crohn Collection. (88) $400
ALs, 6 Jan [1936]. Crohn Collection. (88) $300
— 8 Jan [1937]. 3 pp, 4to. To Mrs. James Dunn. Discussing the abdication of Edward VIII. (89) $1,300
— 12 Jan 1958. Crohn Collection. (88) $150
— 16 Feb 1965. (89) $300
— 10 Apr [1965]. (89) $110
— 26 Jan [n.y.]. Crohn Collection. (88) $150
— 5 Feb [n.y.]. Crohn Collection. (88) $400
— 28 Dec [n.y.]. Crohn Collection. (88) $200
Collection of Ls & 2 autograph postcards, sgd, 1952 to 1958. Crohn Collection. (88) $100
ANs, [n.d.]. 1 p, size not stated. To [Judy Garland]. Brief poem stating she is being missed [at a dinner party]. Also sgd by the Duke of Windsor & others. On restaurant letterhead. Framed with photographs. (89) $2,200
Photograph, sgd & inscr, 1947. Crohn Collection. (88) $600
See also: Windsor, Edward & Windsor

Winnig, August, 1878-1956
Autograph Ms (2), fragment of a story, & part of an autobiographical work; [n.d.]. (90) DM660

Winslow, Edward, 1595-1655
ALs, 13 Apr [16]43. 1 p, 4to. To John Winthrop. Informing him about votes on the New England Confederation, & discussing cattle. Integral address leaf def. Sang collection. (89) $7,500

Winthrop, John, 1588-1649. See: Eliot, John & Winthrop

Wirt, William, 1772-1834
ALs, 26 Sept 1823. (88) $90

Wirz, Henry, Commandant of the Andersonville Prison
ALs, 24 Oct 1865. (91) $800

Wise, Henry Alexander, 1806-76
Autograph endorsement, sgd, [n.d.]. (88) $50

Witch Trials
[A large file containing proceedings of witch trials at Benshausen & related documents, Nov 1596 to Apr 1598, 400 leaves, in contemp limp vellum, mostly in the hand of Conrad Alphey, some sgd by Friedrich Wilhelm, Elector of Saxony.] DM18,000

[2 files recording witch trials at Grossen-Buseck in Hesse, 1655 & 1656, 26 pp, folio, sold at star on 28 June 1990, lot 1284, for DM11,000.]

Wittgenstein, Ludwig, 1889-1951
Autograph Ms, series of childish exercises in writing, partly in mirror-writing; [n.d.]. (89) £1,000

Collection of 4 A Ls s & Ls, 1932 & [n.d.]. 13 pp, folio & 4to. To Moritz Schlick. Accusing Rudolf Carnap of plagiarizing his work, & about other matters. Including typescript carbon copy of a letter to Carnap. (89) £5,000

Series of 8 A Ls s, 1915 to 1939 & [n.d.]. 21 pp, folio & 4to. To W. Eccles. Interesting letters relating to his life & work. (89) £8,000

A Ls s (2), 29 May & 20 Oct 1908. 8 pp, 8vo. To his sister Hermine. Describing his life & work at the experimental station in Derbyshire. (89) £3,000

ALs, [1936]. (89) £800

— 16 Dec 1948. (89) £800

— 17 Apr 1951. 3 pp, 8vo. To his sister Margarete Stonborough. Agreeing that a meeting between them may not be right. (89) £2,500

Autograph postcard, sgd, 31 Mar 1918. (89) £550

— SCHLICK, BLANCHE. - 2 A Ls s, 17 May & 26 July 1953. 6 pp, folio. To F. A. Hayek. Giving reminiscences of Wittgenstein for a biographical sketch. With related material. (90) £400

Wittgenstein, Paul, 1887-1961
ALs, [n.d.]. (90) DM650

Witton, Philip Henry
Autograph Ms, workbook, illustrating utensils in canalwork for the Warwick & Birmingham canal. [c.1797] 83 leaves, 4to, modern half calf. Most leaves with ink & watercolor engineering drawings or relevant diagrams. (91) £2,900

Wizard of Oz
[A Wizard of Oz continuity script, dated 8 Jan 1939, 110 pp, 11 by 8.5 inches, with MGM label, sold at CNY on 21 June 1989, lot 353, for $2,000.]

[A def copy of The New Wizard of Oz, 1930, sgd & inscr to Diane Catherine [Selser] by Judy Garland & other cast members of the 1939 MGM film, sold at CNY on 21 June 1989, lot 354, for $19,000.]

Wladyslaw IV Vasa, King of Poland, 1595-1648
Ls, 25 July 1625. 1 p, 4to. To Cardinal Farnese [?]. Letter of introduction for Bernardo Pandolfini. In Italian. (91) DM2,000

Wodehouse, Pelham Grenville, 1881-1975
[The draft of his story Life with Freddie, [pbd 1966], 67 pp, 4to, part autograph Ms, part typescript with extensive autograph revisions, in half mor box, sold at C on 6 Dec 1989, lot 330, for £7,500 to Rosenthal.]

Collection of 4 A Ls s & Ls s, 7 Feb 1933 to 5 Apr 1956. (90) £850

— Collection of ALs & 2 Ls s, 1967 to 1973. (88) $250

Series of 3 Ls s, 11 Sept 1967 to [Mar 1974]. (91) £900

Ls s (2), 29 Apr to 4 May 1954. (91) $225

Ls, 14 Dec 1952. (89) £450

— 20 May 1962. (90) £650

Photograph, sgd, [n.d.]. (88) £130

Woehler, Friedrich, 1800-82
[An archive of over 100 letters addressed to Woehler by numerous scholars & scientists, 1829 to 1882, dealing with academic & scientific matters & partly annotated by Woehler, sold at star on 4 Apr 1991,

lot 895, for DM11,000.]
Series of 8 A Ls s, 23 Oct 1867 to 24 May 1879. 10 pp, 8vo. To Karl Albert Ludwig von Seebach. About a variety of university matters. (91) DM3,800
ALs, [6 June 1861]. (89) DM850
— 16 Mar 1875. (91) DM550

Woellner, Johann Christoph von, 1732-1800
ALs, 18 Oct 1792. Schroeder collection. (89) DM340

Wolcot, John, 1738-1819
ALs, 19 Feb 1796. (89) $425

Wolcott, Oliver, Signer from Connecticut
ADs, 24 Sept 1781. (91) $60
— 2 July 1787. (91) $120
Ds, 28 Dec 1775. (88) $190
— 8 Dec 1796. (91) $550

Wolcott, Oliver, 1760-1833
Ls, 26 Dec 1800. Alexander collection. (90) $105

Wolf, Hugo, 1860-1903
Autograph Ms, draft of a concert program listing c.25 songs, singers, etc; [after 1 Apr 1891]. (90) £950
Autograph music, song, Alle gingen, Herz, zur Ruh, from the Spanisches Liederbuch, [1889]. 2 pp, folio, in bds. Notated on up to 4 systems per page, 3 staves each; sgd. (91) £8,500
— Autograph music, song, In dem Schatten meiner Locken, from his Spanisches Liederbuch, [1889]. 3 pp, folio. Fair copy; scored for voice & piano. Sgd at head. (91) DM22,000
— Autograph music, song, Wer that deinem Fuesslein weh?, to a text by Emanuel Geibel, scored for voice & piano; [after 5 Dec 1889]. 4 pp, 44cm by 26cm. Stichvorlage; sgd at head. (90) DM22,000
Autograph transcript, poem beginning "Wie der Mond sich leuchtend draenget" by Heinrich Heine, 20 lines; [n.d.]. (90) £450
Collection of ALs & AN, 1 Feb [1]889 & [n.d.]. (90) £550
ALs, 25 Apr [1]883. 3 pp, 8vo. To Heinrich Koechert. Explaining his abrupt departure from recipient's house on the previous evening. (90) £1,300
— 10 June 1884. 3 pp, 8vo. To Therese Preyss. Expressing his wish to stay at her boardinghouse. (88) DM2,400
— 6 July 1887. (91) £700
— 9 Sept [1]887. 6 pp, 8vo. To Heinrich Koechert. Thanking for hospitality, explaining his drunkenness, & reporting about his stay at Arnfels. (90) £1,300
— 20 Dec [1]888. (90) £450
— 3 June [1]890. (90) £750
— [after 1890]. (90) £560
— 29 Jan [1]891. (89) £1,000
— 10 Apr [1]891. (90) £900
— 2 May 1891. 4 pp, 8vo. To Oskar Grohe. About a meeting with Weingartner, & commenting on various singers. (91) DM2,800
— 10 Jan [1]894. 4 pp, 8vo. To [Oskar Grohe]. Reporting about a concert of his songs in Berlin. (89) £1,200
— 8 June 1894. (90) £400
— 6 July 1894. 6 pp, 8vo. To Melanie Koechert. Reminiscing about entries in his diary & mentioning his difficulties with the orchestration of a work. (90) £1,500
— 26 Aug [1]895. (90) £220
— 26 Mar 1896. 2 pp, 8vo. To an unnamed lady. Expressing condolences on the death of her mother. (89) DM1,500
— 27 July [1]897. 1 p, 8vo. To Heinrich Potpeschnigg. Expressing enthusiasm about Mahler's appointment in Vienna, hoping for a performance of his opera, & discussing a libretto. (90) £2,400
— 4 Dec [n.y.]. 1 p, 8vo. To [Karl & Rosa Mayreder?]. Expressing thanks for flowers, in verse. Sgd Woelflein. (90) DM1,500
Autograph postcard, sgd, [23] Dec 1890. To Oskar Grohe. Worrying about missing scores. (90) DM1,100
— 31 Oct [1]895. (90) £400
AN, 19 July 1897. (91) £400
Autograph quotation, 9 bars from Der Corregidor, in short score; 5 Sept [1]895. 1 p, folio. Sgd & inscr to Oskar Grohe. 2 bars of an ensemble in vocal score on verso. (90) £3,500

Wolfe, James, 1727-59
ALs, 24 Aug 1754. (90) £1,000
— 7 Feb 1758. 10 pp, 4to. To [Lord George Sackville]. Discussing the military situation, the forthcoming Louisburg campaign, the condition of troops, etc. Including long postscript. Martin collection. (90) $16,000
Ds, 27 June 1752. 32mo. Authorizing payment to Robert Finlay. (91) $3,000

Wolfe, Thomas, 1900-38
ALs, 2 June 1938. (89) $800
Ls, 2 June 1934. 1 p, 4to. To Harry Hansen. Giving permission to enter his story Boon Town in the O'Henry competition. (89) $1,200
— 21 Feb 1938. (91) $900

Wolff, Bernhard, 1799-1851
ALs, 13 Oct 1844. (89) DM260

Wolff, Christian, Freiherr von, 1679-1754
ALs, 20 Oct 1734. 3 pp, 4to. Recipient unnamed. Thanking for recipient's intention to write a pamphlet in his defense, & mentioning his current projects & the King of Prussia's offer to return to Halle. In Latin. (91) DM1,500

Wolff, Christian, Freiherr von, 1679-1754
ALs, 28 Aug 1740. 2 pp, 4to. Recipient unknown. Informing him of the terms of his appointment as Professor at Halle. (88) DM2,000

Wolf-Ferrari, Ermanno, 1876-1948
[A collection of autograph Mss & working papers, including autograph librettos, annotated typescript carbon copy of a letter to Mussolini, drawings (some possibly by his father), etc., 32 items, c.200 pp, various dates, sold at S on 27 Nov, lot 426, for £750 to Schneider.]
ALs, [1899]. (88) DM650
— 13 Feb 1945. (90) DM340
— [n.d.]. (89) DM480

Wolfram von Eschenbach, c.1170-c.1220
Ms, Willehalm, fragment; 56 lines from Book IV. [West central Germany, 2d half of 13th cent]. Single leaf, 243mm by 188mm. Written in double column in a large compressed gothic hand. With large illuminated initial & full-page miniature within broad red border. Recovered from use as a wrapper around a bdg. Miniature worn. (89) £32,000

Wolfskehl, Karl, 1869-1948
ALs, [11 Mar 1898]. (89) DM320
— [n.d.]. (88) DM280
— 27 Apr [n.y.]. (90) DM600

Wols, Pseud. of Wolfgang Schulze, 1913-51
Autograph Ms, [shopping?] list, 7 lines; [1948?]. 1 p, 4to. With 2 pen-&-ink drawings below, self port & abstract composition. (89) DM1,400

Wolzogen, Karoline von, 1763-1847
ALs, 20 Feb 1835. (88) DM240

Wood, John, fl.1596
ALs, [c.1585-90]. (88) $1,000

Wood, Owen
Original drawings, (11), ink drawings to illus Blue and Green Wonders, and other Latvian Tales, 1971. (88) £800
— Original drawings, 2 double-page illusts for a French Ed of Wind in the Willows, 1967. (88) £350
— Original drawings, (2), Rat talking to swallows & Toad escaping down a rope, to illus the French Ed of Wind in the Willows, 1967, & the English Ed, 1985. (90) £100
— Original drawings, (2), Toad at the wheel of a car & rowing under a bridge, to illus the French Ed of Wind in the Willows, 1967, & the English Ed, 1985. (90) £150
— Original drawings, (21), to illus Answer Me That, 1969. 240mm by 190mm or 240mm by 410mm. In ink; sgd. (90) £1,800
— Original drawings, (5), to illus the French Ed of Wind in the Willows, 1967, & the English Ed, 1985. (90) £100
Original drawing, 2 men supporting a dish with a naked girl, to illus Plexus, 1967. (90) £100
— Original drawing, 3 girls dressing up in military uniforms, to illus Plexus, 1966. (90) £100
— Original drawing, crowd celebrating the launching of the sieve, to illus

Edward Lear's The Jumblies, 1986. (90) £350
— Original drawing, man kneeling at feet of a woman in medieval dress, d/j design for Balzac's Droll Stories; [n.d.]. (90) £180
— Original drawing, naked girl with scorpion's claws, to illus Harpers' Bazaar, 1967. (90) £100
— Original drawing, naked woman reclining on a bench & other classical figures, d/j design for the works of Catullus, 1966. (90) £80
— Original drawing, onlookers watching the approach of the sieve & its crew, to illus Edward Lear's The Jumblies, 1986. (90) £550
— Original drawing, oval watercolor drawing of a man with scientific instruments suspended from a balloon, with panel enclosing text, to illus There was an Old Man of the Hague, in Edward Lear's The Owl and the Pussy-Cat, 1978. (88) £420
— Original drawing, sieve & crew weathering the storm, to illus Edward Lear's The Jumblies, 1986. (90) £300

Woodhull, Nathaniel, 1722-76
ALs, 27 Aug 1776. 1 p, folio. To the NY State Convention at Harlem. About the defense of Long Island & his precarious position. (88) $2,250

Woodroffe, Paul
Original drawing, Prospero, with Ferdinand & Miranda playing chess, for an Ed of The Tempest, 1908. (90) £1,000

Wool, John Ellis, 1784-1869
Franking signature, [3 Mar n.y.]. Alexander collection. (90) $55
Photograph, [c.1847]. 1/2 plate daguerreotype. Bust pose. In push button case. (89) $4,000

Woolf, Virginia, 1882-1941
ALs, [n.d.]. (89) $375
Ls, 2 Feb 1928. 1 p, 8vo. To Max Rychner. Agreeing to a trans of one of her short stories for the Neue Schweizer Rundschau. (91) DM1,300
— 20 Mar 1929. 2 pp, folio. To her nephew Quentin Bell. Chatty letter, saying she wants to write "an entirely new kind of book". With autograph conclusion. Sgd Virginia. Koch Foundation. (90) $1,400
— 18 Oct 1938. (88) $750
— 31 Oct 1940. (89) £400
— PARSONS, TREKKIE. - ALs, 11 Dec 1980. 2 pp, 8vo. To Berthold Wolpe. Enclosing a box of steel pen nibs (present) used by Virginia Woolf. (91) £130

Wooster, David, 1711-77
ADs, 20 Aug 1765. (91) $190

Wordsworth, Christopher. See: Wordsworth, William & Wordsworth

Wordsworth, Mary
A Ls s (2), 6 Sept & 26 Nov 1852. (89) $475

Wordsworth, William, 1770-1850
Autograph Ms, 1st stanza of his version of Chaucer's The Cuckoo and the Nightingale, sgd & dated 27 Nov 1819. 1 p, 4to. Differing from ptd version. (90) £2,000
— Autograph Ms, fair copy of his poem, The Longest Day, Addressed to my Daughter, Dora. Written in the commonplace book & album of Elizabeth Watson of Calgarth Park, Windermere, Rydal Mount, 5 September 1817. 5 pp, 4to, in contemp mor gilt. (91) $9,500
— Autograph Ms, poem, beginning "To be a Prodigal's Favorite", sgd & dated 20 Apr 1842. (89) £850
— Autograph Ms, poem, beginning "Let other Bards of Angels sing", sgd & dated 1 Oct 1826. 1 p, 4to. 4 four-line stanzas; differing from ptd version. Framed. (89) £5,000
— Autograph Ms, quatrain, beginning "Doubt not that there are holy powers", 26 Mar 1841. 1 p, 8vo. Sgd. With visiting card, sgd. (91) £1,400
Autograph transcript, 2-line verse epigram: License they mean when they cry liberty,/ For who loves that must first be wise and good. (91) £420
— Autograph transcript, poem, [The Portrait], 28 Nov 1832. (89) £1,000
— Autograph transcript, sonnet, Adieu Sweet Maid. 15 Aug 1843. 1 p, 12mo. With accompanying ALs to Mrs. S. L. Minstanly. (89) $1,600

WORDSWORTH

— Autograph transcript, sonnet, [Before the Picture of the Baptist by Raphael], sgd; contained in ALs, [n.d.], 3 pp, 4to, to [Laura] Carr [later Rolfe]. Laid in a copy of his Poetical Works, sgd & inscr to Laura Rolfe, 15 Nov 1845. (88) £1,400

A Ls s (2), 17 Dec 1819 & [n.d.]. 2 pp, folio & 4to. To Francis Wrangham. About efforts to raise money on behalf of the family of the late Rev. William Stevens, & thanking for a contribution to a fund for orphans. (88) £2,200

ALs, 10 Oct 1828. 3 pp, 4to. To R. Money. Responding to verses sent to him, & discussing the conditions necessary for the composition of poetry. (89) £3,600

— 20 May 1839. (89) $400

— [c.Oct 1842]. (91) £800

— 21 May 1846. 4 pp, 8vo. To William Boxall. About painting, John Ruskin, & J. M. W. Turner. (90) £3,200

— 12 Dec 1848. (88) £680

— 7 Sept [n.y.]. Doheny collection. (88) $850

AL, 10 June 1828. (89) $140

Ls, 9 Jan [1838]. 4 pp, 8vo. To Thomas Powell. Requesting help in finding a school for a nephew, mentioning a question of copyright, etc. In Mary Wordsworth's hand. Doheny collection. (89) $1,200

— 26 Jan 1840. (89) $400

— 1 Apr [n.y.]. (89) $375

Autograph quotation, 6 lines beginning "If Thought and Love desert us", sgd & dated 3 Dec 1840. (88) £800

Autograph sentiment, sgd, 6 Sept 1841. (88) £200

— Anr, sgd, 19 Jan 1843. (91) $750

— HAMILTON, SIR WILLIAM ROWAN. - ALs, 30 July 1830. 4 pp, 4to. To his sister Sydney Hamilton. Reporting on a visit to Wordsworth. Seal tear. (88) $300

— WORDSWORTH, DORA. - Autograph sketchbook, kept when accompanying her father on his last visit to Sir Walter Scott, 1831. About 25 views in all, some double-page, folio, in quarter mor marbled bds. Mostly in pencil. (90) £4,600

Wordsworth, William, 1770-1850 —& Wordsworth, Christopher

Ds, 3 Feb 1817. (88) £350

World War I

[Battle of Jutland. - A group of 9 A Ls s or Ls s by British admirals, Nov 1932 to Apr 1933, 22 pp, 8vo, to Thomas Brock, replying to an inquiry concerning sources for the history of the battle, with related material, sold at S on 15 Nov 1988, lot 1715, for £320 to Hofstra.]

— BORRADAILE, CAPT. COLIN. - Series of 30 A Ls s, Nov 1914 to Nov 1917. Length not stated. Mostly to his mother. Family letters, & about his experiences at the Front. With related material. (89) £90

— HMS WARSPITE. - Typescript, account by an unnamed officer of the Warspite of the Battle of Jutland, 1917. 34 pp, on rectos only, 8vo, in contemp cloth. Tate collection. (91) $310

— HOFFMANN, GEN. MAX. - Autograph Ms, diary kept during the Battle of Tannenberg, 24 Aug to 1 Sept 1914. 93 pp, 8vo, in lea wraps. In pencil. With related material. (90) DM1,300

— LUSITANIA. - ALs by Frederick MacMonnies, [n.d.]. 3 pp, 8vo, on Lusitania stationery. Looking forward to his voyage. (91) $100

— MENIN GATE. - Document, 28 July 1922. 7 pp, folio. Contract between the Imperial War Graves Commission & Sir Reginald Blomfield to design & supervise the erection of the Menin Gate Memorial at Ypres, Belgium; sgd by Sir Fabian Ware for the Commission. (90) £280

— MOTT, THOMAS BENTLEY. - Ms carbon copy, translator's memorandum of a meeting between Generals Pershing & Foch regarding the use of American troops in the war, 28 Apr 1918. 11 pp, 4to, in wraps. With related material. (90) $400

— PEACE OF BUCHAREST. - Menu, 6 May 1918, 8vo, of a dinner given by Gen. Field Marshal von Mackensen on the eve of the signing of the peace; sgd by vom Mackensen, the Foreign Ministers of Austria & Bulgaria, 2 Turkish & 4 Romanian delegates. (91) DM500

— ROYAL FLYING CORPS. - Ms, copies of observers' reports of France, Aug to Sept 1914. 49 pp, in folio notebook. Including carbon copies of 7 related letters. (89) £180

World War II

[Operation Menace. - A collection of c.80 pp of correspondence, maps & reports relating to the Gen. Spears Mission in the event of a Franco-British landing at Dakar, 1940, sold at S on 21 Sept, lot 111, for £60 to Spake.]

[Royal Air Force. - A collection of secret zone maps for Frankfurt, Hamburg, Luebeck & Dresden, with related photographs & reports, sold at S on 21 Sept, lot 112, for £100 to Domenico.]

[Ferebee, Major Thomas. - 3 photographs, sgd, 8 by 10 inches, showing the Enola Gay B29 Bomber, its crew, & Ferebee, with related material, sold at wa on 1 Oct 1988, lot 59, for $85.]

[Tibbets, Paul. - 2 signatures on photographs relating to the dropping of the 1st Atomic Bomb, 1 also sgd by Jacob Beser, sold at wa on 1 Oct 1988, lot 316, for $130.]

Transcript, Declaration of War on Germany, 11 Dec 1941. (89) $120

— ATOMIC BOMB. - Document, [n.d.]. 11 by 9 inches. Certification that John L. Priest participated in the production of the Atomic Bomb, with facsimile signature of Sec of War Stimson. Sgd by Edward Teller & by 5 crew members. (91) $650

— ENOLA GAY CREW. - Group photograph, [n.d.]. 4to. Sgd by Paul Tibbets, Tom Ferebee, Jacob Beser & George R. Caron. (91) $110

— FEREBEE, THOMAS. - 10 signatures, [n.d.]. Each on ptd card commemorating the Hiroshima bombing. (91) $95

— HIROSHIMA. - ALs, [n.d.], 1 p, 4to, by George R. Caron, Tail Gunner of the Enola Gay, describing the explosion of the atomic bomb. (91) $475

— HIROSHIMA. - Group photograph of 11 man crew in front of the Enola Gay, [n.d.]. 8 by 10 inches. Sgd by 6. (91) $225

— HIROSHIMA. - Group photograph of the crew in front of the Enola Gay, [n.d.]. 10 by 8 inches. Sgd by 7 crew members. (91) $275

— HIROSHIMA. - Photograph of the crew of the Enola Gay, [n.d.]. 8 by 10 inches. Sgd by 6 crew members. (91) $400

— HONG KONG. - Document, instrument of surrender of Hong Kong by the Japanese armed forces, sgd by Maj. Gen. Mekichi Okada & Vice Admiral Ruitaro Fujita, 16 Sept 1945. 1 p, folio. Framed. (89) £7,500

— JAPANESE SURRENDER. - A $1 bill, sgd by Eisenhower & 15 other allied military figures, mostly on USS Missouri in Tokyo Bay, 2 Sept 1945, sold at CNY on 7 Dec 1990, lot 276, for $6,500. 91

— NAGASAKI. - Group photograph of 10 man crew in front of Bock's Car, [n.d.]. 8 by 10 inches. Sgd by 6. (91) $150

— NAGASAKI. - Group photograph of the crew of Bock's Car, [n.d.]. 10 by 8 inches. Sgd by 9 crew members, with assignments on flight. (91) $225

— NAGASAKI. - Photograph of the crew of Bock's Car, [n.d.]. 8 by 10 inches. Sgd by 7 crew members. (91) $190

— STALAG IVB PRISONER OF WAR CAMP. - Prisoner of War "magazines" produced under editorship of W. J. Pitt, Cymro, 7 issues (of 8), & 20 Bees Buzz, 2 issues, May 1944 to 14 Jan 1945; c.70 pp, large broadsheets & 4to. With numerous watercolors & pen-&-ink cartoons; 2 pp in Welsh. Each leaf in transparent casing. (88) £1,000

— TOGURI, IVA ("TOKYO ROSE"). - New Year's card, [n.d.]. 8vo. Recipient unnamed. Sgd & inscr. (91) $75

Worsley, John

Original drawings, (31), to illus Black Beauty; sgd & dated 1974. (90) £1,000

Wrage, Klaus

Collection of 36 A Ls s & 8 autograph postcards, sgd, 1923 to 1974. (90) DM1,000

Wrangel, Carl Gustav, Graf von Salmis, 1613-76

Ds, 27 Sept 1643. (91) DM500

Wrangel, Friedrich Heinrich Ernst, Graf von, 1784-1877
ALs, 24 Feb 1848. Schroeder collection. (89) DM500
— 22 June 1849. (91) DM400
— 21 Feb 1856. 2 pp, 8vo. To P. J. Lenne. Inviting him to Steglitz, & expressing admiration for parks planned by him. Schroeder collection. (89) DM1,200
— 22 Sept 1872. (90) DM260
— 10 Nov 1876. Schroeder collection. (89) DM220
Autograph telegram, [20 Feb 1864]. 2 pp, 8vo. To the King of Prussia. Draft, requesting further instructions after the [unauthorized] occupation of Kolding. In pencil. (91) DM2,200

Wrede, Karl Philipp, Fuerst, 1767-1838
Ls s (2), 12 May 1815. (89) DM650

Wren, Sir Christopher, 1632-1723
[A series of 6 papers, including Ls by Wren, regarding the reconstruction of St. Paul's Cathedral, 1675 to 1718, 9 pp, folio, with related material, sold at S on 15 Dec 1988, lot 244, for £3,000.]
Ds, 19 Jan 1710. 2 pp, folio. Account leaf from one of the Books of Works for Greenwich Hospital, sgd as member of the board of directors. Also sgd by Vanburgh, Hawksmoor, & others. Wormed; framed. (90) £2,600
— 19 Jan 1709/10. 2 pp, folio. Accounts for Greenwich Hospital for Mar 1707. Also sgd by others. Framed. (90) £2,000

Wright, Anna
ALs, 2 June 1919. (90) $400

Wright, Basil
[A collection of c.90 letters addressed to him (a few to other recipients) by various writers & actors, sold at bba on 15 Dec 1988, lot 181, for £550 to Mandl.]

Wright, Frank Lloyd, 1869-1959
Autograph Ms, 1st draft of his Autobiography, Books I & II, [1926-27]. 166 pp, 4to. Heavily revised throughout. With typescript & typescript carbon copy, prepared under Wright's direction, 108 pp, 4to. Some corrections in Wright's & an unidentified hand. (90) $25,000
— Autograph Ms, aphorisms & observations on art & life, [c.1926?]. 2 pp, folio, on rectos only. 1 p def. (90) $1,800
— Autograph Ms, Bowie Knives and cutlasses, [c.1926?]. (90) $600
— Autograph Ms, Bowie Knives and cutlasses, [c.1926?]. (90) $950
— Autograph Ms, The Fly Symphony, [c.1926?]. 1 p, folio. Anecdotal account of an invasion of the Wright residence by a swarm of flies. With revisions. (90) $1,300
ALs, 23 Aug 1912. 2 pp. To D. D. Martin. About some dealings with Mr. Sanderson. (90) $1,600
— 11 June 1919. To Miriam Noel. 2 pp, 4to. About gifts he has sent her. (90) $1,600
— 15 July 1919. 3 pp, 4to. To Miriam Noel. Discussing a trip he has taken to Nikko & a telegram from Aline Barnsdall. (90) $1,300
— Summer 1919. 7 pp, 4to. To Miriam Noel. About why he is not coming to Ikao now. With 2 A Ls s of Miriam Noel. (90) $3,800
— Summer 1919. 4 pp, 4to. To Miriam Noel. About Mme Krynska & Miriam's unjustified anger & jealousy over her. (90) $2,000
— Summer 1919. (90) $1,000
— [1920s]. 3 pp, 8vo. Without salutation, but apparently to Miriam Noel. About his poor financial situation. (90) $1,400
— [1920s]. (90) $1,000
— [11 July, n.y.]. (90) $900
— [1925]. 2 pp, 8vo. To Miriam Noel. Discussing grounds for divorce & their meetings with attorneys. With a holograph card to her. (90) $2,000
— 9 July 1927. 2 pp, 4to. To Maud & Owen Devine. About his financial difficulties & revealing his bitterness towards a friend who failed to contribute to the corporation organized to support him. (90) $3,800
Ls, 11 Mar 1930. 2 pp, 4to. To Mrs. Helen Raab. About his inability to assist Miriam Noel. (90) $1,500
— 9 Nov 1946. 1 p. To Herman Breitenbach. About a bridge at the Wisconsin Dells. (90) $1,700

ANs, 20 Apr 1914. To Faye Barnes. About her possible employment in Wright's Studio. Framed with her photo & envelope. (90) $1,100
— [1919]. (90) $800
— [early 1920s]. 1 p, 12mo. To Beth Cary. Writing her about Miriam Noel. (90) $1,100
Ns, 25 Jan 1956. (90) $850
Ds, 1 May 1912. 1 p. Promissory note to Darwin D. Marin. Also sgd by Catherine Wright (90) $1,400
— WRIGHT, OLGIVANNA. - Collection of 25 A Ls s & autograph postcard, sgd, 3 Dec 1926 to 29 Mar 1931. 112 pp, various sizes. To Maude E. Devine. Chronicling her husband's financial problems, his activities & plans. (90) $4,000

Wright, Marcus Joseph, 1831-1922
Typescript, General Officers of the Confederate Army. 157 leaves, 4to, in mor. With related material. (89) $3,200
ALs, 3 Aug 1880. (88) $250

Wright, Orville, 1871-1948
Collection of Ls & photograph, sgd & inscr, 20 Feb 1930 & [n.d.]. 1 p, 4to & 173mm by 244mm. To Henry S. Rorer. Describing the photograph of their 1st flight (present) & explaining their sister's contribution. (90) $17,000
Ds, [c.1920s]. (89) $310
Check, accomplished & sgd, 15 Nov 1940. (90) $450
Photograph, sgd & inscr, 15 Dec 1925, but depicting their 1st flight at Kitty Hawk, 17 Dec 1903. 173mm by 244mm. Inscr to George A. Gray. (90) $3,500
Signature, [19 Aug 1940]. (90) $500

Wright, Orville, 1871-1948 —& Others
Autograph sentiment, inscr to Little Fred on flyleaf of Mother Goose's Nursery Rhymes, Ed by Walter Jerrold. NY, [c.1910]. Sgd by Orville, Wilbur & Katharine Wright; inscr by Orville, Christmas 1911. (91) $4,800

Wright, Wilbur, 1867-1912
Ls, 5 Feb 1904. 2 pp, 4to. To the Ed of the Independent. Protesting strongly against the publication of "a forged signed article." (90) $8,500

Wright, Willard Huntington, 1888-1939.
See: Van Dine, S. S.

Wunderlich, Paul
Autograph sentiment, sgd, [n.d.]. (89) DM300

Wundt, Wilhelm, 1832-1920
ALs, 26 July 1884. (89) DM220
— 9 [Dec] 1913. (91) DM300

Wyatt, Sir Thomas, 1503?-42
— VAUX, THOMAS, 2D BARON VAUX OF HARROWDEN. - Ds, 10 Mar [1535]. 1 p, vellum, 11 by 5 inches. Receipt for £280 from Roger Cholmeley for the manor of Newyngton Luces. With names of Thomas Wyatt, Thomas Poynings & Humfrey Bouchier as witnesses on verso. Bradley Martin sale. (90) $5,500

Wyeth, Andrew
ALs, 5 Mar 1965. (91) $180

Wylie, Elinor, 1885-1928
ALs, 6 Mar 1928. (89) $100

Wyndham, Madeline Caroline Frances Eden
Original drawings, Coloured Designs & Patterns &c &c &c Labyrinths and Mazes, [n.d.]. Over 40 pp, 4to, in cloth bdg. Pencil drawings & watercolors; chiefly mtd & annotated. Some loose insertions. (88) £2,000

Wynn, Ed
Collection of 1 ALs, 3 Ls s & 3 telegrams. (91) $125

Wyse, Sir Thomas, 1791-1862
Series of 15 A Ls s, 26 Sept 1816 to 2 July 1822. (91) £460

Wythe, George, Signer from Virginia
ADs, 31 Aug 1789. (88) $350
— 24 May 1799. (91) $750
Ds, 16 May 1769. 2 pp, folio. Copy of the resolutions adopted by the Virginia House of Burgesses claiming exclusive right of taxation, etc., sgd as Clerk of the House. Separated at folds. (88) $35,000

Wyther, George, Signer from Virginia
ADs, [after 1772]. Doheny collection. (89) $450

Y

Ye Sette of Odd Volumes. See: Sette of Odd Volumes

Yeats, William Butler, 1865-1939
[A collection of 37 items, including 21 A Ls s by Yeats, 1889 to 1937, c.50 pp, 8vo & 4to, to various correspondents, about personal & literary matters, with related material, sold at C on 9 Dec, lot 316, for £4,500 to Rogers.]
[An autograph working draft for the revised version of his poem At Algeciras - A Meditation upon Death, written in a presentation copy of the poem's 1st ptg in A Packet for Ezra Pound, 8vo, sgd by Yeats & inscr to Edith Sitwell, Aug 1929, sold at S on 13 Dec 1990, lot 302, for £1,300 to Maggs.]
Autograph Ms, journal, 11 July 1898 to 31 Mar 1902. 128 pp, 4to, in 2 vols; orig vellum over bds. Recording his dream-life, his visions, his spiritual marriage to Maud Gonne, etc. Including 6 pp of visionary drawings by George Russell & some enclosures by Maud Gonne. (90) £54,000
— Autograph Ms, poem, beginning "Where nobody gets old and godly and grave", sgd; 15 Mar 1920. Inscr on flyleaf of his The Hour-Glass and other Plays. NY, 1906. (90) DM1,100
— Autograph Ms, poem, His Dream [here untitled]; [3 July 1908]. 1 p, 4to. Working draft; c.30 lines. Inscr by Lady Gregory at head. Koch Foundation. (90) $4,500
— Autograph Ms, "The Great Vellum Notebook", containing working drafts for poetry & prose, 23 Nov 1930 to Summer 1933. 387 pp, folio, in contemp vellum over bds. Sgd in many places. (90) £180,000
Typescript carbon copy, More Memories [later The Tragic Generation], from The Trembling of the Veil, [1922]. 141 pp, 4to, in green cloth bdg. With extensive autograph revisions. Doheny collection. (89) $15,000

Collection of ALs & 2 Ls s, 4 Sept 1911, 31 Mar 1912 & [n.d.]. (88) £650
— Collection of ALs & 2 Ls s, 26 Mar 1924 to 27 Nov 1935. (88) £380
— Collection of ALs & autograph postcard, sgd, [n.d.] & 31 July 1932. (90) £360
— Collection of ALs & AN, 19 June [n.y.] & [n.d.]. (91) $425
Series of 3 A Ls s, [27 Dec 1908] to 7 Aug [1909]. To his father John Butler Yeats. Reporting about his work & literary views. (88) £1,500
— Series of 4 A Ls s, [29?] Apr to 30 July [1933?]. 5 pp, 4to & 8vo. To Capt. Dermot A. MacManus. Sending information requested, inviting him to a meeting, discussing censorship, mentioning Lady Chatterley, etc. With a collection of MacManus's family papers. (88) £2,400
ALs, 12 June 1913. (88) £700
— 4 Oct [1914]. (88) £750
— 16 Aug [c.1917]. (90) £500
— 25 July [n.y.]. (90) DM480
— 5 Dec [n.y.]. (88) £90
— 21 Dec [n.y.]. (91) $750
— [n.d.]. Doheny collection. (88) $500
— [n.d.]. (90) $200
— [n.d.]. (90) DM520
Ls, 11 Feb 1909. (89) £480
ANs, 5 May [n.y.]. (89) $150
Photograph, sgd & inscr, May 1905. (88) £900

Yevtushenko, Yevgeny Aleksandrovich
Autograph Ms, poem, in Russian; [n.d.]. (90) DM950

Yonge, John, 1467-1516
Ds, [1515]. (91) $300

Yorck von Wartenburg, Ludwig, Graf, 1759-1830
ALs, 5 Jan 1815. 1 p, 4to. To Gen. von Boyen. Informing him about the military situation in Poland. With cut signature, 1814. Schroeder collection. (89) DM1,050
Ls, 1 July 1808. (90) DM450
— 23 Mar 1812. (90) DM450
— 21 Feb 1813. (90) DM800
— 1 Sept 1813. (91) DM600
— 2 Apr 1814. Schroeder collection. (89)

DM520
— 8 June 1815. Schroeder collection. (89) DM460

Young, Ann Eliza, b.1844. See: Young, Brigham & Young

Young, Art, 1866-1943
Original drawing, L'Enfant Terrible, to illus Life, 11 Sept 1912. (90) $300

Young, Brigham, 1801-77
Ls, 1 Apr 1864. (91) $475
Ds, 20 Apr 1876. Byer collection. (90) $650
Cut signature, [Apr 1875]. (90) $260
— Anr, [n.d.]. (91) $225
— Anr, [n.d.]. (91) $170
Signature, [n.d.]. (88) $175
— Anr, 4 May [18]73. (91) $300

Young, Brigham, 1801-77 —&
Young, Ann Eliza, b.1844
[A lot of 4 items, a calling card, sgd, by each, & a photograph of each, carte size, 29 June 1874 & [n.d.], sold at R on 17 June 1989, lot 260, for $300.]

Young, Rida Johnson, 1875-1926
Autograph transcript, poem, Mother Macree, sgd & dated 20 Sept 1920. Doheny collection. (89) $750

Young, Thomas, 1773-1829
Ls, 6 Aug 1801. (88) DM800

Young, Whitney M., 1921-71 —& Others
[A philatelic card honoring Booker T. Washington, [5 Apr 1956], 6.5 by 5 inches, sgd by Young, A. Philip Randolph, & Thurgood Marshall, sold at Dar on 13 June 1991, lot 80, for $225.]

Z

Zacchi, Gasparo, d.1474
Ms, Bononiensium Res Publica. [Rome or Tivoli, 1471]. 10 leaves & flyleaves, vellum, 152mm by 94mm. Early 19th-cent French citron mor gilt bdg by Simier. In a skillful upright formal humanistic bookhand; a few autograph corrections. With large illuminated white-vine initial & full-page coats-of-arms of Bologna & the author. Phillipps MS.864 & Abbey collection. (89) £8,500

Zach, Franz Xaver von, 1754-1832
Collection of 5 A Ls s, 1 AL (fragment), & 2 autograph Mss, 9 Aug 1787 to 13 May 1798. 17 pp, 8vo & 4to. To Herzog Ernst II von Sachsen-Coburg-Gotha. Concerning the Seeberg observatory, astronomical instruments & observations, etc. 2 letters def. (88) DM1,250
Series of 5 A Ls s, 1790 to 1799. (89) DM520
ALs, 30 June 1790. (90) DM260

Zachariae, Just Friedrich Wilhelm, 1726-77
ALs, 14 Jan 1773. (89) DM540

Zacharias Chrysopolitanus
Ms, In unum ex quatuor. [Southern England, c.1175]. 179 leaves (lacking c.14), vellum, 328mm by 222mm. Contemp wooden bds covered with deerskin. In brown ink in a small minuscule bookhand by 2 scribes. With numerous (2 large) decorated initials in colors, early gothic capitals throughout, & 4 large historiated initials. Doheny collection. (88) £1,200,000

Zador, Eugene, 1894-1977
Collection of 38 A Ls s, Ls, & 2 autograph postcards, sgd, 22 Nov 1968 to 29 Sept 1976. 58 pp, 4to & 8vo, & cards. To Robert Breuer. Interesting letters about his own works & other composers. Mostly in German. (90) DM1,100

Zaehnsdorf Ltd.
Ms, Minute Book No 1, 7 May 1913 to 17 Nov 1947. (91) £850

Zangwill, Israel, 1864-1926
Ls s (2), 30 June 1919 & 1 Mar 1920. (88) £120

Zech, Paul, 1881-1946
Autograph Ms, poem, S.M.S. (89) DM520
— Autograph Ms, Vortragsbuch I, containing various poems & a short story; [n.d.]. 41 pp, 8vo, in half cloth bdg. Sgd on tp. (91) DM3,200
Typescript, play, Der unbekannte Kumpel, [c.1936]. (89) DM850

ZECH

— Typescript, play, Die drei Gerechten, sgd & dated Nov 1945. 130 leaves, 4to, in bds. With some autograph corrections. Probably unpbd. (89) DM1,600

Zeeman, Pieter, 1865-1943
ALs, 19 Apr 1914. (88) DM530

Zelter, Karl Friedrich, 1758-1832
Autograph Ms, ceremonies at the introduction of new members of the Liedertafel, 4 Mar 1828. (90) DM750
Autograph music, canon for 3 voices, beginning "So waelz ich ohne Unterlass", 22 Aug [18]10. (90) £1,000
ALs, 10 Jan 1803. 2 pp, 4to. To Johann Nikolaus Forkel. Thanking for his biography of Bach & stressing Bach's importance as a composer. Albrecht collection. (91) SF4,800
— 10 Feb 1811. (88) DM650
— 26 July 1816. 2 pp, 8vo. Recipient unnamed. Thanking for his hospitality & informing him about his travel plans. (89) DM1,800
— 12 July 1823. 1 p, 8vo. To an unnamed lady. Recommending the singer Nina Cornega. (88) DM2,000
ANs, 2 July 1831. (89) DM300

Zemlinsky, Alexander von, 1871-1942
ALs, [n.d.]. (90) DM850

Zenger, John Peter, 1697-1746
Ds, 2 Nov 1731. 1 p, folio. Declaration by Johann David Wolff concerning claims to property in Germany, sgd as witness. Also sgd by 8 others. With copy of German deed attached. Sang collection. (89) $4,000

Zeppelin, Ferdinand von, 1838-1917
ALs, 9 Nov 1907. (88) DM580
— 25 Apr 1910. 3 pp, 4to. To Mueller, Adjutant Gen. of the King of Saxony. Explaining his plans for a flight from Vienna to Dresden. (91) DM1,200
— 14 Aug 1912. (91) DM540
Photograph, sgd & inscr, 16 Aug 1912. (89) DM1,000

Zieten, Hans Joachim von, 1699-1786
Ls, 25 Nov 1755. (90) DM750
— 20 May 1765. Schroeder collection. (89) DM680
Ds, 25 May 1765. 1 p, folio. Death certificate for Johann Andreas Tugend. (91) DM1,300
— 13 Jan 1780. (90) DM950

Zille, Heinrich, 1858-1929
Original drawing, pen-&-ink self port, sgd & inscr to Frau Else; with signature & address on separate card, 27 Aug 1928. (89) DM500
ALs, 23 June 1915. (90) DM600
— 31 Dec 1917. (90) DM280
— [1927]. (91) DM280
— [n.d.]. 1 p, 8vo. To [Hermann Frey?]. Fragment, mentioning recipient's play & other matters. Including pen-&-ink sketch. (90) DM1,700
— [n.d.]. (89) DM340
Autograph postcard, sgd, 10 Nov 1926. (91) DM300

Zimmermann, Eberhard August Wilhelm von, 1743-1815
A Ls s (2), 31 Mar & 8 Apr 1788. (89) DM220

Zimmermann, Johann Georg, 1728-95
ALs, 1 June 1754. 6 pp, 4to. To [Albrecht von Haller]. Requesting material for his biography of von Haller & reporting about his work as physician. (90) DM1,200
— 18 July 1759. (88) DM380

Zingarelli, Niccolo Antonio, 1752-1837
Autograph music, final 29 bars of an aria, scored for voice & piano, [n.d.]. (91) DM250
— Autograph music, working scores of 3 late sacred choral works; 1810 & [n.d.]. 13 pp, folio. 1 sgd & inscr. (91) £3,300
ALs, 14 Dec [1819]. (90) DM260

Zinoviev, Grigorii Avseevich, 1883-1936
Photograph, sgd, [c.1920]. (90) DM650

Zinzendorf, Nikolaus Ludwig, Graf von, 1700-60
ALs, 26 Mar 1728. 3 pp, 8vo. To [Daniel] von Buchs. Making arrangements for the payment of his debts. With anr, 5 Dec 1741; def. (89) DM1,150

Zola, Emile, 1840-1902
Ms, article on Taine, [1878]. (88) £880
Collection of ALs & autograph Ms, 4 Mar 1880 & [n.d.]. 8 pp, 8vo. To Paul Lindau, sending a Ms (included). Essay, Balzac; sgd. (90) DM4,500
A Ls s (2), 19 Jan 1880 & 1 Feb 1890. (90) £380
— A Ls s (2), 13 & 29 Apr 1888. (90) DM800
— A Ls s (2), 8 Jan & 23 Mar 1892. Barrett collection. (89) $550
ALs, 19 Sept 1871. (89) DM400
— 21 May 1877. (88) DM420
— 30 Mar 1878. (89) £420
— 19 Jan 1880. (89) DM320
— 2 Dec [18]81. (90) DM300
— 24 May 1884. (90) £320
— 15 June 1885. (88) DM280
— 3 Mar 1886. (90) $250
— 28 Apr 1887. (89) DM460
— 26 July 1887. (88) £300
— 23 Nov 1892. (90) $450
— 24 June 1893. 3 pp, 8vo. Recipient unnamed. Responding to a request to comment on Victor Hugo. (91) DM1,900
— 13 July 1895. (89) £200
— 13 Dec [18]97. Byer collection. (90) $250
— 12 July 1899. (90) DM460
— [n.d.]. (90) DM520
Ds, 23 Feb 1870. 1 p, 8vo. Attestation that a duel was fought between [Edouard] Manet & [Edmond] Duranty. Also sgd by 3 others. (89) £1,100

Zollicoffer, Felix K., 1812-62
Cut signature, [n.d.]. (89) $95

Zopello, Michele
Ms, Liber Litterarum Simulationis et Dezifris, in Latin & Italian. [Rome, 1455-58]. 20 leaves, vellum, 223mm by 147mm. Contemp blindstamped bdg of red-brown mor over wooden bds. In a regular upright round humanistic bookhand. With 10 small illuminated initials, & very large initial with full whitevine border incorporating the arms of Pope Calixtus III, illuminated by Gioacchino di Giovanni de Gigantibus. Dedication copy. (89) £160,000

Zschokke, Heinrich, 1771-1848
A Ls s (2), 11 June 1814 & 28 Mar 1815. (89) DM900
ALs, 22 June 1796. (90) DM420
— 30 Jan 1797. (88) DM800
— 30 May 1801. 2 pp, 4to. To Heinrich Gessner. Discussing political developments in Switzerland. (90) DM1,300
— 1 May 1833. 3 pp, 4to. To his pbr Creuzbauer. Outlining his plans for his work Die klassischen Staetten der Schweiz. (88) DM1,600
— 14 Nov 1836. (91) DM500
— 28 July 1840. (89) DM220

Zuccalmaglio, Anton Wilhelm von, 1803-69
ALs, 30 Jan 1868. (91) DM350

Zuckmayer, Carl, 1896-1977
Collection of ALs, 2 autograph postcards, sgd, ANs, & autograph Ms, 1930. 28 pp, 4to & 8vo, & cards. To Erika Dernburg. Hoping to see her as Minna von Barnhelm, & contents not stated. Poems; 28 stanzas in all, mostly written in pencil; supposedly unpbd. (90) DM3,600
— Collection of 4 A Ls s, 2 autograph postcards, sgd, & ANs, 14 Jan 1938 to 7 Mar 1967. 14 pp, 4to & 8vo. To Hanna Thimig. Personal letters, about their relationship & his marriage, announcing his visit, reminiscing, etc. Postcards sgd with paraph. (90) DM1,600
— Collection of ALs & Ls, 9 June 1959 & 29 Dec 1961. (88) DM220
ALs, 30 Nov 1918. 2 pp, 4to. To Ludwig Bamberger. Voicing his frustrations. (91) DM1,200
— 15 July 1955. (91) DM240
— 5 July 1961. (89) DM440
— 9 Apr 1967. (91) DM320
Collection of 2 Ls s & typescript, 11 & 17 Aug 1957. (88) DM420
Series of 4 Ls s, 7 Jan to 8 Oct 1961. (89) DM400
Ls s (2), 22 Mar & 12 July 1974. (88) DM360
Ls, 10 Oct [19]38. (91) DM300
— 10 June 1942. (91) DM360
— 8 Jan 1955. (90) DM320
— 21 Sept 1955. (90) DM320

Zukofsky, Louis

Collection of 11 A Ls s, 3 autograph postcards, sgd, 2 autograph Mss & 3 typescripts, 1947 to 1957. About 69 pp, various sizes. To Mark Van Doren, personal letters. 2 pieces of music with verse; essay; & 2 poems. With related material. (90) $1,600

Zulehner, Georg Carl, 1770-1841

ALs, 9 Jan 1835. (91) DM750

Zuloaga, Ignacio, 1870-1945

A Ls s (2), 25 Jan & 24 Feb 1906. (90) DM200

ALs, 24 Feb 1925. (90) DM210

Zulu War

— BROMHEAD, LIEUT. GONVILLE. - Als, 3 Feb 1879. 2 pp, 8vo. To his sister. Reporting about the Battles of Isandhlwana & Rorke's Drift. (88) £2,800

Zweig, Arnold, 1887-1968

[A group of 4 typescripts (1 carbon copy), presented at various times to Sigmund Freud, comprising 3 essays & draft of an unpbd novel, 41 pp, folio, sold at C on 21 June 1989, lot 166, for £1,200 to Farber.]

Autograph Ms, essay, Ueber alte juedische Gedichte, 1923. 7 pp, 4to in a Russian notebook of 1834. Sgd & inscr to Sina Grosshut, 26 Oct 1945. (91) DM1,600

Ms, Empfindsame Geschaeftsreise, [11 Jan 1911]. (90) DM650

Collection of 76 A Ls s, 22 Ls s, & 9 autograph postcards, sgd, 18 Mar 1927 to 9 Sept 1939. 240 pp, mostly 4to & 8vo. To Sigmund Freud. Discussing his writing, psycho-analysis, private & political matters, etc. With related material. (89) £4,800

A Ls s (2), 16 July 1910 & 16 Nov 1917. (90) DM360

ALs, 20 Nov 1937. (90) DM340

Ls, 8 June 1959. (90) DM350

— 17 Feb 1960. (88) $140

Series of 3 autograph postcards, sgd, 6 Oct 1921 to 16 Feb 1922. (90) DM270

Zweig, Stefan, 1881-1942

Autograph Ms, description of Rio de Janeiro, fragment from his book Brasilien; [c.1940]. (91) DM820

— Autograph Ms, poem for Emil Lucka on his birthday, 11 May 1917. 8 pp, 4to. Sgd on tp. (90) DM3,800

— Autograph Ms, poem, Matkowskys Othello, [after 16 Mar] 1909. (88) DM650

Typescript, article, Kleine erlebte Lektion ueber Vergaenglichkeit, [n.d.]. 7 pp, 4to. With autograph corrections; 2 pp autograph. (89) DM2,300

Collection of 10 A Ls s, 2 Ls s & 18 autograph postcards, sgd, [c.1904] to 22 Aug 1931. Length not stated, 4to & 8vo. To Erwin O. Krausz. About a variety of professional, personal & social matters. Some items initialled. Ernst Gottlieb collection. (88) DM6,000

— Collection of 24 A Ls s, 12 Ls s & 10 postcards, 3 Nov 1920 to 14 Sept 1929. 57 pp, 4to & 8vo, & cards. To Sigmund Freud. About his writings, their situation as refugees, etc. With 10 postcards. (89) £5,500

— Collection of 26 A Ls s & Ls s, & 8 autograph postcards, sgd, 1932 to 1941. About 40 pp, various sizes. To Desmond & Newman Flower at Cassell's. About the publication of his books & his autograph collection. (90) £4,000

— Collection of ALs, Ls & autograph postcard, sgd, 30 May to 31 July 1935. 2 pp, folio, & card. To Willi Schuh. About Othmar Schoeck, the 1st performance of Die schweigsame Frau, & a performance of Falstaff with Toscanini. (90) DM2,600

ALs, 23 Nov 1908. (89) DM300

— [Jan 1913]. (88) DM300

— 9 Mar 1917. (88) DM850

— 2 Jan 1929. (88) DM650

— 31 Dec 1933. (91) DM1,000

— 21 Dec 1939. 2 pp, 8vo. To Mr. Maudslay. Commenting about the war. (90) DM1,100

— [1939]. (90) DM850

— [29 Feb 1940]. (89) DM360

— [n.d.]. (88) DM300

— [n.d.]. (90) DM600

Series of 4 Ls s, 30 Nov 1929 to 26 May 1931. (91) £400
— Series of 6 Ls s, 21 Dec 1929 to 10 Dec 1936. 9 pp, 4to. To Jo van Ammers-Kueller. Mostly about his own & her literary work. (90) DM2,400
— Series of 3 Ls s, 14 June 1932 to 27 Jan 1934. (90) DM780
Ls, 3 Nov 1920. (91) DM340
— 11 Mar 1925. (89) DM220
— 14 Dec 1928. (91) DM400
— 18 Apr 1929. (91) DM320
— 28 June 1936. (91) DM600
— 10 July 1936. (91) DM360
— 19 July 1936. (91) DM320
— 31 Oct 1936. (91) DM600
Series of 3 autograph postcards, sgd, 16 Mar 1907 to 11 Nov 1908. (90) DM580
Autograph postcard, sgd, 24 Aug 1904. (90) DM280
— [30 Aug n.y.]. (90) DM540
Collection of ANs & autograph quotation, sgd, [n.d.]. (89) DM420
Corrected galley proof, Begegnungen mit Menschen, Staedten, Buechern, 1937. Complete set of galleys, folio, in half mor bdg. With extensive autograph corrections; sgd & inscr to Lord Carlow. (91) £3,500

PART II

Books

ATLASES, BOOKS, BROADSIDES, AND MAPS & CHARTS ARE REPORTED IN THIS SECTION

A

A la Gloire...
— A la Gloire de la Main. Paris, 1949. One of 164. 4to. (90) $350

A., M.B.A. See: Beyle, Marie Henri ("Stendhal")

Aa, Abraham Jacob van der, 1659-1733
— Aardrijkskundig woordenboek der Nederlanden. Gorinchem, 1839-51. 13 parts & supplement in 14 vols. (89) HF650

Abbadie, Jacques, 1654?-1727
— L'Art de connoitre soy-meme.... Rotterdam: Vander Slaat, 1693. 12mo. (88) $90
— The History of the late Conspiracy against the King and Nation.... L, 1696. 8vo. (90) £80

Abbatius, Baldus Angelus
— De admirabili viperae natura.... Nuremberg, 1603. 4to. (89) £580

Abbe, Dorothy
— The Dwiggins Marionettes, a Complete Experimental Theatre in Miniature. NY, [1970]. Folio. (91) $65, $100, $100

Abbe, Elfriede
— Plants of Virgil's Georgics. Ithaca, NY, [c.1975]. One of 50. 4to. (90) $425

Abbey Collection, John R.
— The Italian Manuscripts in the Library of Major J. R. Abbey. L, 1969. 4to. (90) £55; (91) $150
— Life in England in Aquatint and Lithography. L, 1953. One of 400. 4to. (88) $475, £270, £380, £380, £440; (89) £400, £320; (90) £330, £420, £500; (91) £650

ALs to Biddulph presenting the book, 5 Nov 1959, inserted. (89) £400

L, 1972. 4to. Reprint of the 1953 Ed. (88) $275, $325, £240; (89) £190, £200; (90) $230, £220, £230; (91) $110, $250, $350, £100, £180, £220

— [Sale Catalogue] Catalogue of Valuable Printed Books and Fine Bindings. L, 1965-78. 10 vols. 4to. (88) £240; (91) $225

7 vols in 4. 4to. (88) $80

Parts 1-4 only. (91) $90

Parts 1-9 in 6 vols. (90) £220; (91) £140

— Scenery of Great Britain and Ireland in Aquatint and Lithography. L, 1952. One of 500. 4to. (88) $400, $450, £270, £380, £400; (89) $400, $450, £340, £480; (90) £350, £380, £450; (91) £500, £200

Bound in 2 vols. 4to. (91) $425

L, 1972. 4to. Reprint of 1952 Ed. (88) $250, £270; (89) £170, £200; (90) £240, £280, £320; (91) £375, £160

— Travel in Aquatint and Lithography. L, 1956-57. One of 400. 2 vols. 4to. (88) $800, $850, £550, £700; (90) £620, £700

One of 400. (89) $700, £550; (91) $950, £420

Vol II only. (90) £180

L, 1972. 2 vols. 4to. Reprint of 1956-57 Ed. (88) $500, £460; (89) £380, £440, £450; (90) £400, £500; (91) £150, £320

Abbey, Edward
— The Monkey Wrench Gang. Phila.: J. B. Lippincott, [1975]. (91) $60

Abbildungen...
— Abbildungen Osterreichischer Rindvieh-Racen. Herausgegeben im Auftrage des K. K. Ministeriuims des Innern. Vienna, 1859. Oblong folio. (90) £800

811

ABBOT

Abbot, George, 1562-1633
— A Briefe Description of the Whole Worlde.... L: for John Browne, 1608. 4to. (89) £150
— The Case of Impotency as Debated in England.... L, 1719. 2 vols. 12mo. (88) £120

Abbot, Henry L.
— Report upon Experiments and Investigations to Develop a System of Submarine Mines.... V.p., 1881-92. 5 parts in 2 vols, including addenda. 4to. Abbot's working set, with holograph corrections & related material. (90) $1,100

**Abbot, John —&
Smith, Sir James Edward, 1759-1828**
— The Natural History of the Rarer Lepidopterous Insects of Georgia.... L, 1797. 2 vols. Folio. (89) £9,000; (90) $16,000, $17,000; (91) £7,500
Martin copy. (90) $14,000

Abbott, Berenice
— The World of Atget. NY, [1964]. 1st Ed. 4to. (88) $70

**Abbott, Berenice —&
McCausland, Elizabeth**
— Changing New York. NY, 1939. 4to. (91) $325

Abbott, Charles D.
— Howard Pyle, a Chronicle. NY, 1925. 1st Ed. (89) $60
Inscr & with Ls. (91) $250

Abbott, George
— Views of the Forts of Bhurtpoore & Weire. L, 1827. Folio. Colored copy. (90) £850

Abbott, Henry
— Antiquities of Rome.... L, [title watermarked 1822]. Folio. (91) £300

Abbott, John
— Exposition of the Principles of Abbott's Hydraulic Engine. Bost., 1835. 8vo. (88) $100

Abd Ullah ibn Umar
— A Chinese Chronicle. L: William Clarke, 1820. 8vo. De Guignes—Phillipps —Robinson copy. (89) £220

Abdalla of Beyza. See: Abd Ullah ibn Umar

A'Beckett, Gilbert Abbott, 1811-56
— The Comic Blackstone. L, 1844-46. Vol I only. 8vo. (88) $80
— The Comic History of England. L, 1846-48. Illus by John Leech. 1st Ed in orig 20/19 parts. 8vo. (88) $400

AMERICAN BOOK PRICES CURRENT

1st Ed in orig 20/19 parts. 8vo. (88) $400; (89) $50; (90) $480; (91) $210
1st Ed in Book form. L, 1847-48. 2 vols. 8vo. (89) $160; (90) $55, $120
L, [1849]. 2 vols. 8vo. (91) £70
L, [c.1850]. Illus by John Leech. 2 vols in 1. 8vo. (91) $120
L, 1880. 4 vols. 4to. (90) $250
— Rome. L, [1851-52].. ("The Comic History of Rome.") 1st Ed. Illus by John Leech. 8vo. (90) $60
L, [1852]. 8vo. (91) $150
L, [1860s]. 8vo. (90) $70; (91) $70

Abeel, David, 1804-46
— Journal of a Residence in China.... soiled & worn; spine dulled. 1st Ed. 12mo. (91) $100
NY, 1834. 12mo. (91) $150

Abeille, Louis Paul, 1719-1807
— Principes sur la liberte du commerce des grains. Paris: Desaint, 1768. 8vo. (88) FF7,000

Abel, Clarke
— Narrative of a Journey in the Interior of China.... L, 1818. 1st Ed. 4to. ALs tipped in. (91) $1,200
L, 1819. 4to. (88) £400
NY, 1971. 4to. Reprint of L, 1818 Ed. (91) $65

Abel, Gottlieb Friedrich. See: Reitter & Abel

Abel, Thomas
— Subtensial Plain Trigonometry, Wrought with a Sliding Rule.... Phila., 1761. 1st Ed. 8vo. (90) £340

Abela, Giovanni Francesco, 1582-1655
— Della Descrittione di Malta. Malta, 1647. 4 parts in 1 vol. Folio. (90) $4,250

Abelard & Heloise
— Letters of Abelard and Heloise. L, 1815. Illus by George Cruikshank. 12mo. (88) $140
L, 1925. One of 750. (89) £50

Abelin, Johann Philipp, d.c.1634
— J. L. Gottfridi historische Chronica, oder Beschreibung der fuernehmsten Geschichten.... [Frankfurt]: Merian, 1674. Bound in 2 vols. Folio. (90) £350
Folio. (91) DM3,300
— Newe Archontologia Cosmica. Frankfurt, 1646. Folio. (91) $6,500
— Newe Welt und Americanische Historien.... Frankfurt, 1655. 2d Ed. Folio. (89) £2,600

Abelin, Johann Philipp, d.c.1634 —& Others

— Theatrum Europaeum, oder aussfuehrliche und warhafftige Beschreibung...aller und jeder denckwuerdiger Geschichten.... Frankfurt, 1635-1738. Vol I only. Folio. (91) £850
  Vol XI only. Folio. (88) DM1,900
  Vols I-III, V-VI, VIII-XI, XIII-XIV & XVI-XX. 16 (of 21) vols. Folio. (91) £13,500

Abell, William —& Kilvert, Richard

[-] The Copie of a Letter sent from the Roaring Boyes in Elizium.... L: Brought over by the Same Messenger, 1641. 4to. (91) £650
— A Dialogue or Accidental Discourse betwixt Mr. Alderman Abell, and Richard Kilvert.... L, 1641. 4to. (91) £650
— The Last Discourse betwixt Master Abel and Master Richard Kilvert.... L, 1641. 4to. (91) £550

Abel-Remusat, Jean Pierre, 1788-1832

— Elemens de la Grammaire chinoise.... Paris: l'Imprimerie Royale, 1822. 8vo. (89) £450
— Memoire sur les livres chinois de la Bibliotheque du Roi.... Paris: Le Normant, 1818. 8vo. Extracted from Annales Encyclopediques. Robinson copy. (89) £100

Abels, Niels Henrik

— Oeuvres. Christiania, 1881. 2 vols. 4to. (89) £180

Abercrombie, John, 1726-1806. See: Mawe & Abercrombie

Abercrombie, Lascelles, 1881-1938

— Lyrics and Unfinished Poems. See: Gregynog Press

Abercromby, Patrick

— The Martial Atchievements of the Scots Nation. Edin., 1711-15. 2 vols. Folio. (90) £95

Abernethy, John, 1764-1831

— Surgical Observations on the Constitutional Origin and Treatment of Local Diseases.... L, 1809. 1st Ed. 8vo. (91) £160

Abert, James W.

— Message from the President of the United States...Report of an Expedition...on the Upper Arkansas.... Wash., 1846. 8vo. (88) $275
— Report and Map of the Examination of New Mexico. [Wash.], 1848. 1st Ed. 8vo. Senate Exec. Doc. 23, 30th Congress, 1st Session. (88) $300; (90) $275

ABRAHAM BEN ME'IR IBN EZRA

Sgd & with inked textual corrections. Extracted from Emory's Notes on a Military Reconnoissance and bound with the reports of Cooke & Johnston which also appeared in the larger work. (91) $800
— Report of the Secretary of War, communicating...a Report and Map...of New Mexico.... Wash., 1848. 8vo. (91) $400
— Through the Country of the Comanche Indians.... [San Francisco], 1970. 4to. (89) $50, $60; (90) $55; (91) $50
— Western America in 1846-1847. San Francisco, 1966. Folio. (88) $50; (89) $55

Abney, Capt. William de W.

— Thebes and its Five Greater Temples. L, 1876. 4to. (88) £180; (89) $325; (90) $650

Abolition Societies

— Minutes of the Proceedings of a Convention of Delegates from the Abolition Societies. Phila., 1794-97. 1st-4th Conventions in 4 vols. 8vo. (91) $375

Abracadabra

— Abracadabra. Manchester, 1946-88. Vol I, No 1 through Vol 86, No 2230 plus Colley's index to Vols 1-85. (91) £450
  Manchester, 1946-73. Vols 1-55. (90) $600

Abraham a Sancta Clara, 1644-1709

— Etwas fuer Alle, das ist: Eine kurtze Beschreibung allerley Stands- Amkbts- und gewerbs-Personhen.... Wuerzburg, 1699. 8vo. (88) DM5,000
— Mala gallina, malum ovum; das ist... Hundert Ausbuendinger Naerinnen... moralisch vorgestellt. Nuremberg & Vienna, [c.1710-12?]. 4to. (88) $420
— Neu-eroeffnete Welt-Galleria, worinnen... kommen allerley Aufzeug und Kleidungen.... Nuremberg: C. Weigel, 1703. Folio. (88) DM6,400; (91) $2,200, £12,000

Abraham ben Me'ir ibn Ezra, 1092-1167

— De nativitatibus. Venice: Erhard Ratdolt, 24 Dec 1485. Bound with: Firminus de Bella Valle. Opusculum Repertorii Prognosticon in mutationes aeris.... Venice: Erhard Ratdolt [before 4 Nov] 1485. 4to. 30 leaves; Goff A-7. 50 leaves; Goff P-1006. Abrams copy. (90) £12,000
  Bound with: Firminus de Bella Valle. Opusculum Repertorii Prognosticon in mutationes aeris.... Venice: Erhard Ratdolt [before 4 Nov] 1485. (91) £7,000

813

ABRAHAM ELEAZAR

Abraham Eleazar
— Uraltes chymisches Werk.... Erfurt: Crusius, 1735. 2d Ed. 2 vols in 1. 8vo. (91) DM4,800

Abraham, James Johnston
— Lettsom: His Life, Times, Friends and Descendants. L, 1933. 4to. (91) $220

Abramovitch, Raphael
— Die Farshvundene Velt—The Vanished World. NY, 1947. Oblong 4to. (89) $325
— Die Farshvundene Velt/ The Vanished World. NY: Forward Association, 1947. Oblong 4to. (89) $325

Abravanel, Judah, d.1535
— Philosophie d'Amour. Lyons: Guillaume Rouille, 1551. 8vo. Samuel Putnam Avery copy. (89) $900

Abrizzi, Isabella, Countess
— The Works of Antonio Canova in Sculpture and Modelling.... L, 1824. 2 vols. 4to. (91) $120, £150

Abstract...
— An Abstract, of Certain Acts of Parliament, of certain her Majesties Injunctions, of certain Canons.... L, 1583. Bound with: Cosin, Richard. An Answer to the two first and principall Treatises of a certeine factious libell.... L, 1584. With some underscoring & marginalia & old institutional rubberstamp. 2 vols in 1. 4to. STC 10394 & 5819.5. (90) $600
— An Abstract of the Evidence...on the Part of the Petitioners for the Abolition of the Slave Trade. L, 1791. 1st Ed. 8vo. (88) £50, £90

Abu Bakr Muhammad ibn Zakariya al-Razi. See: Rhazes

Abul Hasan al Muchtar ibn Botlan. See: Elimithar, Elluchasem

Academia Medico-quirurgica
— Ensayo para la materia medica Mexicana.... See: Puebla de Los Angeles

Academie...
— L'Academie des dames. [Paris, c.1750]. 8vo. (88) £1,200
— Academie universelle des jeux, contenant les regles des jeux de cartes permis, celles du billard.... Amst., 1786. 3 vols. 12mo. (91) £100

AMERICAN BOOK PRICES CURRENT

Academie des Inscriptions et Belles Lettres, Paris
— Histoire et memoires. Paris, 1717-86. For 1663-1779. Vols 1-43. 4to. (88) FF26,000

Academie des Sciences, Paris
— Histoire et Memoires. Paris, 1702-91. For 1699-1788. 102 vols. 4to. (88) FF60,000
For 1666-69. Paris, 1733-34. 12 vols, comprising the table alphabetique. (88) FF13,000
— Machines et inventions approuvees par l'Academie.... Paris, 1735-77. 7 vols in 3 & 3 vols of plates, together 6 vols. 4to. (88) FF32,000
— Memoires de mathematique et de physique.... Paris, 1750-86. 11 vols. 4to. (88) FF12,000
— Recueil des pieces qui ont remporte les prix de l'Academie, 1720-72 9 vols. 4to. (88) FF11,500

Academie Royale des Sciences
— Histoire et Memoires de.... Paris, 1719-1809. About 123 vols. 4to. (88) $2,700

Academy of Natural Sciences of Philadelphia
— Journal. Phila., 1847-63. Second Series, Vols 1-5. 5 vols. 4to. Martin copy. (90) $400

Accademia del Cimento. See: Saggi...
— iSaggi di naturali esperienze. See: Saggi...
— Saggi di naturali esperienze. See: Saggi...

Accademia della Crusca
— Vocabolario degli Accademici della Crusca.... Florence, 1729-38. Folio. (88) £340
Venice, 1741. Folio. (90) £240
Naples, 1746-48. 6 vols. Folio. (91) $475

Accademia Ercolanese
— Delle Antichita di Ercolano. Naples, 1757-92. 8 vols. Folio. (89) £300

Accademici di Bianchi
— Apologia de gli Academici de Bianchi di Roma contra M. Lodovico Castelvetro da Modena.... Parma: Seth Viotto, 1573. 2d Ed. 2 parts in 1 vol. 8vo. (88) £120

Accolti, Pietro, fl.1625-42
— Lo Inganno de gl'occhi, prospettiva pratica.... Florence, 1625. Folio. (88) £550; (90) £1,300

Account...
— Account of an Expedition from Pittsburgh to the Rocky Mountains. See: James, Edwin
— An Account of the General Nursery, or Colledg of Infants.... L: R. Roberts, 1686.

Variant of Wing A294. 4to. (88) £1,200
— An Account of the New-York Hospital. NY, 1820. 8vo. (89) $130
— Account of the Terrific and Fatal Riot at the New-York Astor Place Opera House.... NY, 1849. 1st Ed. 8vo. (88) $50; (89) $80, $80; (90) $70; (91) $70, $140
— An Account of the European Settlements in America. See: Burke, Edmund

Accum, Friedrich Christian, 1769-1838
— Culinary Chemistry; Exhibiting the Scientific Principles of Cookery. L: R. Ackermann, 1821. 12mo. (88) £250; (91) £155, £170
— A Treatise on Adulterations of Food.... L, 1820. 1st Ed. 8vo. (90) $275; (91) £220 Cambr., 1953. Reprint. (90) $65

Acerbi, Giuseppe, 1773-1846
— Travels through Sweden, Finland, and Lapland, to the North Cape.... L, 1802. 1st Ed. 2 vols. 4to. (88) $50, £120; (91) £380

Acharisio, Alberto
— Vocabolario, grammatica, et orthographia de la lingua volgare. Cento, 1543. 4to. (90) £480

Acharius, Erik, 1757-1819
— Lichenographiae Svecicae prodromus. Linkoping, 1798. 8vo. (88) $120

Achdjian, Albert
— A Fundamental Art, the Rug.... Paris, 1949. Ltd Ed. 4to. In French & English. (89) $70

Acherley, Roger
— The Britannic Constitution; or, The Fundamental Form of Government in Britain. L, 1727. Folio. (89) $50

Achilles Tatius
— The Love of Clitophon and Leucippe. Oxford: Shakespeare Head Press, 1923. One of 498 on Batchelor's Kelmscott handmade paper. Trans by Wm. Burton. 4to. (91) $60

Achterberg, Gerrit, 1905-62
— Meisje. Groningen: In agris occupatis, 1944. One of 10. (88) HF1,000; (89) HF1,000

Ackerman, Phyllis. See: Pope & Ackerman

Ackermann Publications, Rudolph—London
[A uniformly bound set of Oxford, Cambridge & Winchester, Eaton & Westminster, without the Founders plates, sold at S on 29 Nov 1990] £9,000
— Cambridge. 1815. ("A History of the University of Cambridge.") 2 vols. 4to. (88)

ACKERMANN PUBLICATIONS

£2,000, £2,000, £2,200; (90) $3,600
Without Founders' ports. (88) £1,500
Vol I only. (91) $675
— Engravings after the Best Pictures of the Great Masters. [N.d.]. Folio. (90) $200
— Ghost-Stories, collected with a Particular View to Counteract the Vulgar Belief in Ghosts.... 1823. (88) £250
— The History of the Abbey Church of St. Peter's Westminster.... 1812. 1st Ed, 2d Issue. 2 vols. 4to. (89) £130; (91) £70
Issue not specified. (88) £160, £180; (89) £80, £170; (90) £480, £140, £450, £500; (91) £250, $550, £105, £380
Vol II only. 4to. (90) £130
Later Issue. 2 vols. 4to. (91) $190
— LeBrun Travestied; or, Caricatures of the Passions. 1800. 4to. (90) $1,100
— The Microcosm of London. 1808-10. 3 vols. 4to. (88) $4,200, $5,500, £2,600, £3,000, £3,000, £3,200, £3,400; (89) $5,000, £3,200, £5,500; (90) $4,200, £1,700, £2,800, £3,800; (91) $5,000, $6,500, £4,300, DM11,500
Doheny copy. (88) $4,500
Martin copy. (90) $6,500
[watermarked 1821]. 3 vols. 4to. (91) £2,000
— Oxford. 1814. ("A History of the University of Oxford.") 2 vols. 4to. (88) £1,200, £1,200, £1,400, £1,400; (90) $2,800, £1,700, £1,900; (91) £1,600
Extra-illus with 49 plates. (91) $2,100
Schiff copy. (91) $3,000
Subscriber's copy. (91) £2,200
Without the Founders' ports. (88) £1,200; (89) £2,100
One of 25 colored L.p. copies. (89) £1,500, £2,300
Doheny copy. (88) $6,200
— Poetical Sketches of Scarborough. 1813. 1st Ed. Illus by Thomas Rowlandson. 8vo. (88) £250, £280
— The Repository of Arts, Literature, Commerce.... L, 1809-28. Series 3, Vols VII-XII only, bound in 3 vols. (88) £700
Series 1 & 2. 20 vols. 8vo. (88) £3,000
Vol IV, Nos 20-24. 1817. Bound in 1 vol. (90) $250
— Winchester, Eton & Westminster. 1816. ("The History of the Colleges of Winchester, Eton, and Westminster....") 4to. (90) £1,500; (91) £1,700
Doheny copy. (88) $1,600
Eton only. 4to. (91) £650
1st Ed. ("The History of the Colleges of Winchester, Eton & Westminster....") 1st Issue. 4to. (91) £1,600
L, 1816. ("The History of the Colleges of Winchester, Eton, and Westminster....") 4to. (88) £1,080, £1,100; (89) £1,200

Acosta, Cristoval
— Aromatum & medicamentorum in Orientali India nascentium.... Antwerp: Plantin, 1582. 8vo. (91) £500
— Trattato di Christoforo Acosta...della historia, natura, et virtu delle droghe medicinali.... Venice: F. Ziletti, 1585. 4to. (88) DM1,400

Acosta, Jose de, 1539?-1600
— De natura novi orbis, libri duo.... Cologne, 1596. 8vo. (90) $500
— De temporibus novissimis libri quatuor. Rome: Jacobus Tornerius, 1590. 4to. (88) £90
— Histoire naturelle et moralle des Indes.... Paris, 1606. 8vo. (89) $175
— The Naturall and Morall Historie of the East and West Indies.... L, 1604. 1st Ed in English. Trans by Edward Grimstone. 4to. (91) $275, $1,800
  Fleming copy. (89) $1,100

Acosta, Manuel, 1540-1604
— Rerum a Societate Iesu in Oriente.... Dillingen: Sebald Mayer, 1571. Trans by Giovanni Pietro Maffei. 2 parts in 1 vol. 8vo. Phillipps-Robinson copy. (89) £4,500

Acquaviva, Claudio. See: Jesuit Relations

Acrelius, Israel, 1714-1800
— Beskrifning om de Swenska Forsamlingars.... Stockholm, 1759. 1st Ed. 4to. (91) $170

Acta...
— Acta Eruditorum. Leipzig, 1682-1731. 62 vols. 4to. (88) $4,600
  Leipzig, 1683-94. 14 vols. 4to. (88) $1,200
  Leipzig, 1701-7. 7 vols. 4to. (88) $1,800

Actius, Thomas
— De Ludo Scacchorum in legali methodo tractatus.... Pesaro, 1583. 4to. (88) £450

Acton, Eliza, 1799-1859
— The English Bread-Book for Domestic Use. L, 1857. 8vo. (90) $80

Acton, Harold
— Five Saints and an Appendix. L: Robert Holden, 1927. 1st Ed. Inscr to Walter Chapman with 32-line poem. Bradley Martin copy. (90) $550

Acton, John
— An Essay on Shooting, containing the Various Methods.... L, 1791. 8vo. (88) £80; (90) $250

Actuarius, Joannes
— De urinis libri septem.... Utrecht, 1670. ("De urinis libri VII.") 2 parts in 1 vol. 8vo. (88) $150

Acuna, Christoval, 1597-1676?
— Nuevo Descubrimiento del gran rio de las Amazonas. Madrid, 1641. 4to. (88) £14,000
— Relation de la riviere des Amazons.... Paris, 1682. 4 parts in 2 vols. 8vo. (88) FF11,000; (89) FF45,000
— Voyages and Discoveries in South America. L, 1698. 8vo. (88) £1,000
  Tixall Hall copy. (91) £600

Adagia...
— Adagia sive proverbia graecorum ex Zenobio. See: Schottus, Andreas

Adair, James, 1709?-1783?
— The History of the American Indians.... L, 1775. 1st Ed. 4to. (89) $375; (90) $1,100; (91) £500, £750

Adalbert, Prince of Prussia, 1811-73
— Travels in the South of Europe and in Brazil. L, 1849. 2 vol. 8vo. (89) £55

Adam, Albert
— Voyage pittoresque et militaire de Willenberg en Prusse jusqu'a Moscou.... Munich, 1827-28. 2 vols in 1. Folio. (88) DM2,000

Adam, Lambert Sigisbert
— Recueil de sculptures antiques grecques et romaines. Paris: Daumont, [c.1754]. Folio. Blackmer copy. (90) £1,000

Adam, Robert, 1728-92
— Ruins of the Palace of the Emperor Diocletian at Spalatro in Dalmatia. L, 1764. Folio. (88) £500, £1,300; (90) £1,800
  Blackmer copy. (90) £4,500
  "In remarkably fresh condition." Martin copy. (90) $160,000
  Kissner copy. (91) £1,800

Adam, Robert & James
— A Book of Mantels. NY, [1915]. Folio. (89) $175
— The Decorative Work.... L, 1901. Folio. (88) £55, £60; (89) $225

Adam, Robert Borthwick, 1833-1904
— The R. B. Adam Library relating to Samuel Johnson and his Era. Buffalo, 1929-30. 4 vols. Inscr. (90) $375
  Inscr & with ALs to Charles Biron mtd on front pastedown. (91) $400

4 vols. 4to. Inscr. (88) $500
Vols I-III only. (89) $400
Inscr & with ALs & Ls. (88) $400
Martin copy. (90) $600

Adam, Victor
— Collection des costumes militaires, armee Francaise.... [Paris, 1840]. Oblong 4to. (88) $900

Adam, William, d.1748
— Vitruvius Scoticus; being a Collection of Plans, Elevations and Sections of Public Buildings. Edin.: A. Black, [1810]. Folio. (89) £4,500

Adams, Andrew Leith
— Field and Forest Rambles.... L, 1873. 8vo. (89) £55; (90) $90
Inscr. (88) £65
— Wanderings of a Naturalist in India.... Edin., 1867. 8vo. Proof copy annotated & corrected by Sir William Jardine. Martin copy. (90) $800

Adams, Andy, 1859-1935
— The Log of a Cowboy. Bost., 1903. Illus by E. Boyd Smith. 8vo. (89) $90; (90) $60, $95

Adams, Ansel Easton
— Born Free and Equal. NY, 1944. Sgd, 1981; also sgd by the dedicatee, Ralph Palmer Merritt. (89) $300
— The Four Seasons in Yosemite National Park. [Los Angeles, 1936]. 1st Ed. 4to. (88) $65
2d Ed. [Yosemite National Park, 1937]. 4to. Sgd, 1971. (89) $110
— Images 1923-1974. NY, 1974. Folio. (88) $130, $550; (91) $110
One of 1,000 with orig print. (89) $1,500
NY, 1981. Folio. (89) $65
— The Islands of Hawaii. [N.p., 1958]. Text by Edward Joesting. Oblong 4to. (91) $190
— Making a Photograph.... L & NY, 1935. (91) $85
— My Camera in Yosemite Valley. Yosemite National Park & Bost., 1949. 1st Ed. Folio. Sgd on tp. (89) $180
— My Camera in the National Parks.... Yosemite National Park & Bost., 1950. 4to. (89) $170
Sgd. (89) $325; (91) $130, $190, $200, $275, $325
— The Pageant of History in Northern California.... San Francisco, [1954]. Text by Nancy Newhall. 4to. (88) $55
— Photographs of the Southwest. Bost.: NY Graphic Society, [1976]. Essay by Lawrence Clark Powell. Oblong 4to. Sgd, 1978. (89) $90
— The Portfolios of Ansel Adams. NY, [1977].
Sgd, 1978. (89) $85
— Sierra Nevada: The John Muir Trail. Berkeley: Archetype Press, 1938. One of 500. Folio. (88) $550; (90) $950
— Taos Pueblo. See: Grabhorn Printing
— Yosemite and the Sierra Nevada: Selections from the Works of John Muir. Bost., 1948. 4to. (89) £120
— Yosemite and the Range of Light. Bost.: New York Graphic Society, 1979. Intro by Paul Brooks. Oblong 4to. Sgd on half-title. (89) $140
Special Ed, with mtd ptd label sgd by Adams. Bost.: New York Graphic Society, 1979. Oblong 4to. (89) $105; (91) $110
Sgd on half-title. (88) $200

Adams, Ansel Easton —& Newall, Nancy
— This Is the American Earth. San Francisco: Sierra Club, [1960]. Folio. (88) $50

Adams, Ansel Easton & Virginia
— Illustrated Guide to Yosemite; the Valley, the Rim, and the Central Yosemite Sierra, and Mountain Photography. San Francisco, 1940. (89) $90

Adams, Frederick B., Jr.
— Radical Literature in America. Stamford, Conn., 1939. One of 650. (89) $55, $65; (90) $75, $90; (91) $55

Adams, George, 1720-73
— A Treatise Describing and Explaining the Construction and Use of New Celestial and Terrestrial Globes.... L, 1766. 1st Ed. Dedication by Samuel Johnson. 8vo. (88) £515

Adams, George, 1750-95
— Astronomical and Geographical Essays. L, 1790. 2d Ed. 8vo. (88) £150; (91) £200
— An Essay on Electricity.... L, 1784. 12mo. (90) $425
2d Ed. L, 1785. 8vo. (90) £100
3d Ed. L, 1787. 12mo. (88) £75
— An Essay on Vision.... L, 1792. 2d Ed. 8vo. (88) £170
— Essays on the Microscope. L, 1787. 2 vols in 1. 4to. (91) £820
Plate vol only. (91) £170, £300
Vol I only. 4to. (89) £440
— Geometrical and Graphical Essays. L, 1797. 2d Ed. 2 vols in 1. 8vo. (89) £225
— Micrographia Illustrata, or, the Microscope Explained.... L, 1746. 8vo. (88) $600
4th Ed. L, 1771. 8vo. (88) £240

Adams, Henry, 1838-1918
— The Education of Henry Adams. Wash.: Pvtly ptd, 1907. 1st Ed, One of 100. 4to. Doheny copy. (89) $4,800
See also: Limited Editions Club
— A Letter to Teachers of American History. Wash., 1910. Inscr to James Laughlin. (90) $425
— Memoirs of Arii Taimai E Marama of Eimeo Teriirere.... Paris, 1901. 4to. (90) $1,400
— Mont Saint Michel and Chartres. Wash., 1904. 1st Ed. 4to. (89) £200

Adams, Henry Gardiner
— Humming Birds, Described and Illustrated. L, [1856]. 8vo. (90) £75

Adams, Herbert Mayow
— Catalogue of Books Printed on the Continent of Europe, 1501-1600, in Cambridge Libraries. Cambr., 1967. 2 vols. 4to. (88) £220, £220; (89) $450, $500, £240, £340; (90) £280, £450; (91) $300, $600, £300

Adams, John, Riding Master
— The Analysis of Horsemanship.... L, 1805. 3 vols. 8vo. (88) £100

Adams, John, 1735-1826
— A Defence of the Constitutions of Government of the United States of America. L, 1787. 12mo. (89) $475; (91) $425
Phila., 1787. 12mo. Talleyrand copy. (89) $550
Phila., 1797. 3 vols. 8vo. (89) $190

Adams, Capt. John, d.1866
— Sketches taken during Ten Voyages to Africa.... L, [1822]. 8vo. (90) £280

Adams, John Quincy, 1767-1848
— Oration on the Life and Character of Gilbert Motier de Lafayette.... Wash., 1835. 8vo. Inscr "Poquonock Library Company from John Quincy Adams". (88) $800

Adams, Ramon F.
— Cowboy Lingo. Bost., 1936. (89) $55
— The Rampaging Herd: a Bibliography. Norman, Okla., [1959]. 1st Ed. (88) $50, $100; (89) $70
— Six-Guns & Saddle Leather: a Bibliography.... Norman, Okla., [1954]. 1st Ed. (89) $80; (91) $50
Inscr by Loring Campbell, the dedicatee. (91) $90
Sgd by Adams & inscr by the dedicatee, Loring Campbell. (89) $55
Norman, Okla., [1969]. (88) $100

Adams, Ramon F. —& Britzman, Homer E.
— Charles M. Russell: The Cowboy Artist. Pasadena, 1948. (88) $85; (91) $80

Adams, Randolph G.
— The Passports Printed by Benjamin Franklin at his Passy Press. Ann Arbor, 1925. One of 505. (91) $800

Adams, Richard, Novelist
— Watership Down. L, 1972. 1st Ed. (88) £240; (89) £85
L, 1976. One of 250 specially bound in mor gilt. Illus by John Lawrence. Sgd by both author & artist & with watercolor drawing of a rabbit at the foot of a tree. (90) £380

Adams, Robert, Sailor
— The Narrative of Robert Adams, a Sailor, who was Wrecked on the Western Coast of Africa. L, 1816. 1st Ed. 4to. (88) £55

Adams, Samuel, 1722-1803
— An Appeal to the World.... L: by the Direction of Dennys de Berdt, 1769. 1st English Ed. 8vo. (88) £700
— The Writings. NY, 1904-8. 1st Ed, One of 750. Ed by Harry A. Cushing. 4 vols. (90) $450

Adams. William, M.A.
— The Modern Voyager and Traveller.... L, 1828. 4 vols. 8vo. (88) DM700; (90) £240
Vol I only. (90) $90

Adams, William Henry Davenport, 1828-91
— The History, Topography and Antiquities of the Isle of Wight. L, 1856. 4to. (89) £110; (91) £100

Adams, William Taylor
See also: Ashton, Warren J.
— The Boat Club, or the Bunkers of Rippleton, by Oliver Optic. Bost., 1855. 1st Ed. 8vo. Martin copy. (90) $250

Adamson, John
— The Muses Welcome to the High and Mighty Prince James.... Edin: T. Finlason, 1618. Bound with: Planctus & vota musarum. Edin.: Andreas Hart, 1618. Folio. STC 141, 142. Huth-Abbey-Martin copy. (90) $5,500

Adamson, William Agar, 1800-66?
— Salmon-fishing in Canada.... L, 1860. 8vo. (89) A$220

Adamus, Melchior
— The Life and Death of Dr. Martin Luther. L, 1641. 1st Ed in English. 4to. (90) $325

Adanson, Michel, 1727-1806
— Histoire naturelle du Senegal.... Paris, 1757. 1st Ed. 4to. (88) FF24,000

Addison, Charles Greenstreet, d.1866
— Damascus and Palmyra. L, 1838. Illus by Wm. Makepeace Thackeray. 2 vols. 8vo. (88) $90, £130, £260; (90) $190; (91) £400 Blackmer copy. (90) £600

Addison, Joseph, 1672-1719
— The Campaign.... L, 1705. 1st Ed, Issue with ads on verso of last leaf. Folio. (90) £380
— The Free-Holder, or Political Essays. L, 1761. 4to. (91) $50
— The Miscellaneous Works in Verse and Prose.... L, 1765. 4 vols. 8vo. L.p. copy. (88) £550
— Remarks on Several Parts of Italy. L, 1705. 1st Ed. 8vo. (89) $225, £65; (90) £65 L, 1718. 12mo. (88) £35
— The Spectator. See: Spectator...
— Works. L, 1721. 4 vols. 4to. (88) £80; (90) $110
3d Ed. L, 1741. 4 vols. 4to. (89) $200
Birm.: Baskerville, 1761. 4 vols. 4to. (88) $225; (89) $80; (90) £85
L, 1761. 4 vols. 4to. (88) £280; (89) $130, $300, £120; (90) £340; (91) $700, £180, £200
L, 1804. 6 vols. 8vo. (88) (91) $130
NY, 1811. 6 vols. 12mo. (89) $200

Addison, Lancelot
— West Barbary, or, a Short Narrative of the Revolutions of the Kingdoms of Fez and Morocco. Oxford, 1671. 8vo. (88) $150

Addison, Thomas, 1793-1860
— On the Constitutional and Local Effects of Disease of the Supra-Renal Capsules. L, 1855. 1st Ed. 4to. (88) $6,500

Ade, George, 1866-1944
— The Old-Time Saloon. NY, 1931. Ltd Ed. (88) $70

Adelung, Johann Christoph, 1732-1806
— Versuch einer Geschichte der Cultur des menschlichen Geschlechts. Leipzig, 1782. 8vo. (88) $110

Adept, An. See: Johnstone, Charles

Adhemar, Jean
— Toulouse-Lautrec: his Complete Lithographs and Drypoints. NY, [1965]. 4to. (89) $150; (90) $90; (91) $250, $250

Adler, Rose
— Reliures. Paris, [1930]. Folio. (89) SF400

Adolphus, John, 1768-1845
— The History of England.... L, 1805. 2d Ed. 3 vols. 8vo. (91) £220

Adrianus Carthusiensis
— De remediis utriusque fortunae. [Cologne: Ulrich Zel, c.1470]. 4to. 160 leaves. Goff A-54. Abrams copy. (90) £1,700

Adrichomius, Christianus, 1533-85
— A Briefe Description of Hierusalem.... L: P. Short for T. Wight, 1595. Trans by Thomas Tymme. 4to. (88) £80; (89) £130
— Theatrum terrae sanctae et biblicarum historiarum. Cologne, 1590. Folio. (90) £1,200; (91) £1,500
Cologne, 1600. Folio. (89) £350; (90) DM1,900
[Cologne, 1628]. Folio. (89) £800, £1,800

Adventurer...
— The Adventurer. L, [1753]-54. Ed by John Hawkesworth. 140 nos in 2 vols. 8vo. Doheny set. (89) $2,000
L, 1794. 3 vols. 8vo. (91) £100

Adventures...
— The Adventures of a Silver Penny.... L: Newbery [1787?]. 1st Ed. Ed by Richard Johnson. 32mo. Martin copy. (90) $650
— The Adventures of Thom Thumb, the Little Giant and Grumbo the Great Giant.... L, 1795. 32mo. (89) £950
— The Adventures of Doctor Comicus.... L: B. Blake, [1815]. 8vo. (91) $130
— The Adventures of Huckleberry Finn. See: Clemens, Samuel Langhorne
— The Adventures of Tom Sawyer by Mark Twain. See: Clemens, Samuel Langhorne

Advertisement...
— An Advertisement Concerning the Royal Fishery of England.... L, 1695. Bound with: A Discourse Concerning Fishery within the British Seas. L, 1695. 4to. (88) £350

Advertiser's ABC
— The Advertiser's ABC. T. B. Browne's Directory. The Standard Advertisement Press Directory. L, 1901-2. 4to. (88) $130

Advertising Agencies' Service Company
— Type Faces for Advertising. the Specimen Book of.... NY, [c.1940]. Folio. (88) $60

Advice...
— Advice to a Son. See: Osborne, Francis

AEFFERDEN

Aefferden, Francisco de
— El Atlas abreviado, o compendiosa geographica del mundo antiguo y nuevo.... Madrid, 1709. 8vo. (88) £950
Antwerp, 1725. 8vo. (91) £480

Aelfric Grammaticus, Abbot of Eynsham, 955-1020
— A Testimonie of Antiquitie.... L: J. Day, [1567]. Issue with the preface paged & the errata corrected. 8vo. (88) £480

Aelian (Aelianus Tacticus)
— De militaribus ordinibus instituendis. Venice, 1552. 4to. (91) $750

Aelianus, Claudius
— Aelian on Fly Fishing. Berkeley: Poole Press, 1979. One of 250. 64mo. Handset, ptd, bound & sgd by Maryline P. Adams & sgd by J. R. Adams. (90) $50
— Variae historiae libri XIII.... Rome, 1545. 4to. (88) £325
Leiden: J. du Vivie & I. Severinus, 1701. 2 vols. 8vo. (91) £350

Aelianus Tacticus. See: Aelian (Aelianus Tacticus)

Aeneas Sylvius, Pope Pius II, 1405-64
— Breve (Ad apostolicae dignitatis apicem), 21 Aug 1461, to Adolf of Nassau, confirming election as Archbishop of Mainz. [Mainz: Johann Fust & Peter Schoeffer, after 21 Aug 1461]. Single sheet, 280mm by 419mm. Goff P-655. Doheny copy. (88) $44,000
— De duobus amantibus Euryalo et Lucretia. Rome: Stephan Plannk, 15 July 1485. 8vo. 25 (of 26) leaves; lacking final blank. Goff P-681. (88) £1,000
— Epistola ad Mahumetem. [Cologne: Ulricus Zell, 1469-72]. ("Pius papa secundus eloquentissimus q obijt....") 4to. 53 (of 54) leaves; lacking 1st blank. Goff P-697. Abrams copy. (90) £6,500
[Rome: Bartholomaeus Guldinbeck, c.1477]. 4to. 54 leaves. Goff P-701. (89) £2,800
— Epistolae familiares. [Nuremberg: Anthon Koberger, 17 July] 1486. ("Familiares epistolae ad diversos....") 4to. 246 leaves. Goff P-719. (91) $2,200
— Secundi Pontificis Maximi: ad illustrem Mahumetem turcorum imperatorem epistola. Treviso: Gerardus de Lisa de Flandria, 12 Aug 1475. 4to. Blackmer copy. (90) £3,500

AMERICAN BOOK PRICES CURRENT

Aeronautical Annual...
— Aeronautical Annual. Bost. & L. [1894-1910]. Nos 1-3 with the Epitom. (88) £220

Aeronautics...
— Aeronautics: A Complete Guide to Civil and Military Flying. L: George Newnes, [c.1935]. 4 vols. (91) $50

Aeschines, 389-314 B.C. —& Demosthenes, 385?-322 B.C.
— Orationes. Basel: Joannes Oporinus, [1553]. 4 vols in 2. 8vo. (90) £50
— Orationes de Falsa Legatione. Cambr., 1769. Ed by John Taylor. 2 vols. 8vo. L.p. copy. Beckford copy. (91) £250

Aeschylus, 525-456 B.C.
— Agamemnon. Cambr.: Rampant Lions Press, [1969]. One of 250. (88) £500
— Opera. Venice: Aldus, 1518. ("Tragoediae.") 8vo. In Greek. (89) £580; (91) £1,600
Paris: Adriani Turnebi, 1552. 8vo. In Greek. (90) £85; (91) £220
Glasgow, 1795. Folio. (89) $175
— The Oresteia. See: Limited Editions Club
— The Oresteian Trilogy. Greenbrae: Allen Press, 1982-83. One of 140. (90) $160

Aesop, c.620-560 B.C.
See also: Miniature Books
— The Fables.... See: Fore-Edge Paintings
— Fables. See: Gregynog Press; Limited Editions Club
— The Subtyl Historyes and Fables. See: Grabhorn Printing
— 1492, 27 Mar. - Vita Esopi. Venice: Manfredus de Bonellis de Monteferrato. 4to. 40 (of 42) leaves; lacking frontis & D2, which are supplied in facsimile. Goff A-110. (88) £800

Fables
— [c.1480]. - Vita et Fabulae. Milan: Bonus Accursius. 3 parts in 1 vol. 4to. 167 (of 168) leaves; lacking final blank. Goff A-98. The Garden copy. (90) $90,000
168 leaves. Goff A-98. Rylands copy. (88) £65,000
— 1485, 13 Feb. - Naples: Francesco del Tuppo. Folio. In Latin & Italian. 166 (of 168) leaves. Goff A-155. (89) £100,000
— 1501. - Appologi sive mythologi.... Basel: Jacob Wolf of Pforzheim. 2 parts in 1 vol. Folio. (91) DM120,000
2 parts in 2 vols. Sussex-Huth-Jeudwine-Abrams copy. (90) £46,000
— 1505. - Vita et fabellae.... Venice: Aldus. Folio. (90) £220

AESOP

— 1524. - Fabellae. Basel. Bound with: Euripides. Tragoediae duae.... Basel, 1524. 8vo. (88) £320
— 1538. - Fabulae Graece et Latine. Basel: J. Hervagius. 8vo. (89) £35; (91) £180
— 1541. - Basel: J. Hervagius. 8vo. (91) £900
— 1549. - Fabulae cum aliis quibusdam opusculis. Paris: Petrum & Io. Mariam. 8vo. (91) £70
— 1557. - Esopus constructus moralizatus & hystoriatus.... Genoa: Antonius de Bellonis. 4to. Fairfax-Murray copy. (91) £9,000
— 1567. - Aesopi et aliorum fabulae. Antwerp: Plantin. 16mo. (89) $210
— 1589. - Fabulae. Leipzig: Johannes Steinmann. 12mo. (90) $225
— 1617. - Fabularum Aesopiarum libri V. Paris: R. Estienne. 4to. (90) $60
— 1665. - Fables. Paraphras'd in Verse. L. Folio. (88) £300
— 1666. - Fables.... L. Folio. In English, French & Latin. (88) DM2,000
— 1668. - The Fables. L. Bound with: Aesopics, or a Second Collection of Fables. L, 1668. 2 parts in 1 vol. 2d Ed of 1st part; 1st Ed of 2d part. Paraphrased in verse by John Ogilby. Folio. (90) £200
2d Ed. Paraphrased in verse by John Ogilby. Folio. (91) £500
— 1678. - Paris: chez Sebastien Mabre-Cramoisy. Folio. (88) £80
— 1687. - Fables.... L: H. Hills for Francis Barlow. Folio. In English, French & Latin. (89) £550, £2,500
— 1692. - Fables of Aesop and Other Eminent Mythologists. L: R. Sare, etc.. Ed by Roger L'Estrange. Folio. (88) £50
Library markings. (90) £50
— 1694. - Fables. L. Folio. (91) $250
— 1699. - Fables of Aesop and other Eminent Mythologists. L. Ed by Sir Roger L'Estrange. 2 vols. Folio. (89) £65
— 1701. - Fabularum Aesopiarum.... Amst. 4to. (90) $2,750; (91) £160
Institutional stamp on title. (90) $275
— 1701. - Fabularum Aesopiarum libri V. Amst.: Franciscus Halma. 4to. (91) £300
— 1701. - Liberti fabularum Aesopiarum, libri V. Amst. Illus by Jan van Vignen. 4to. (89) $220
— 1737. - Fables of Aesop and Others. L. 8vo. (89) $80
— 1745. - Phaedri fabularum Aesopiarum libri quinque. Leiden: S. Luchtmans. 8vo. (88) £65
— 1757. - Phrygis, et aliorum fabulae. Venice: Ex Typographia Remondiniana. 12mo. (88) £90
— 1761. - Select Fables of Esop and other Fabulists. Birm.: Baskerville. 8vo. (88) $55, $110, £200; (90) $180
— 1792. - Phila.: Benjamin Johnson. 12mo. (91) £55
— 1793. - Fables. L: John Stockdale. (88) £85, £260
2 vols. (89) £400
2 vols. 8vo. (89) $400; (90) $450; (91) £160; (88) $165, £250; (89) £220
— c.1800. - Fables d'Esope. Paris: chez Jean. Folio. (89) £600
— 1813. - Select Fables of Esop and Other Fabulists.... Gainsborough: Henry Mozley. 8vo. (90) $160
— 1818. - The Fables of Aesop and Others. Newcastle. Illus by Thomas Bewick. 8vo. (88) $180, $500, £60, £90, £380; (89) £75, £240, £620; (90) $400, £260, £450
L.p. copy. (88) £520
With thumb-mark receipt. (91) £260
One of 500 in imperial 8vo. (89) £370; (90) £500; (91) £170
— 1823. - Newcastle. 8vo. (89) £110
Tipped-in receipt with Bewick thumb print. (88)
— 1848. - Fables: a New Version.... L. Illus by John Tenniel. 8vo. (89) $110
— 1857. - The Fables of Aesop and Others. L. Illus by Charles H. Bennett. 4to. (89) $70, £180
— 1871. - Bewick's Select Fables of Aesop and Others. L: Bickers. 8vo. (88) $80
— 1886. - L: Bickers. 8vo. (91) $100
— 1887 [1886]. - The Baby's Own Aesop. L. Illus by Walter Crane. 4to. (88) $80
— 1909. - Fables. L. Illus by Edward Detmold. 4to. (88) $175; (89) £90
One of 750. (88) $425; (89) £280; (90) £80; (91) $750, £420
— [c.1910]. - L. Illus by E. J. Detmold. 4to. (91) £110
— 1912. - L. One of 1,450. Illus by Arthur Rackham. (89) $150; (90) $800, $1,000, £200, £220, £900, A$550; (91) $100, $325, £650, £280, £380
4to. (89) $270
With orig ink-and-watercolor drawing by Rackham, sgd & dated 1912, bound in. (89) $4,600
Trans by V. S. Vernon Jones; illus by Arthur Rackham. (90) A$130
One of 1,450. (88) $400, $475, $1,900, £260, £280, £420; (89) $200, £170
— 1928. - Twenty Four Fables.... L: Alcuin Press. One of 50. Ed by Sir Roger L'Estrange. 4to. (89) $175
— 1936. - Fables. L. One of 525. Trans by Sir Roger L'Estrange; illus by Stephen Gooden. (88) £300, £400, £420; (89) £350, £350; (90) £280, £350, £380

AESOP

Inserted are an Ls & an autograph postcard sgd, both by Stephen Gooden to R. Hamilton Brown & a sgd pencil drawing given by Gooden to Brown. (89) £1,500 Review copy. (90) £300
— 1968. - L. One of 250, sgd by the artist. Illus by Elizabeth Frink. Folio. (90) £340
— 1973. - The Fables: The First Three Books of Caxton's Aesop. Verona: Officina Bodoni. One of 160. 2 vols. (91) $1,850
— 1976. - History and Fables...translated and printed by William Caxton, 1484. L. One of 50. 4to. Facsimile of the copy in the Royal Library, Windsor. (91) $325
— 27 Aug 1567. - De warachtighe Fabulen der Dieren. Bruges: Pieter de Clerck. 4to. (88) £8,000

Afbeeldinge...
— Afbeeldinge van de Verscheyde Vergrootinge van Amsterdam.... [Amst., c.1662]. Oblong 8vo. (88) HF550

Affiches...
— Les Affiches etrangeres illustrees.... Paris, 1897. 4to. (88) $750; (90) $1,500

Africa
— Proceedings of the Association for Promoting the Discovery of the Interior Parts of Africa. L, 1790. 4to. (91) $225

African...
— African Wild Life. Johannesburg, 1946-87. 41 vols. (88) R300

Africanus. See: Leo, Johannes

Agassiz, Louis, 1807-73
— Bibliographia Zoologiae et Geologiae. A General Catalogue.... L, 1848-54. Ed by H. E. Strickland. 4 vols. 8vo. (89) $175
— Contributions to the Natural History of the United States.... Bost., 1857-62. 1st Ed. 4 vols. 4to. (88) $80; (89) £170
— Etudes sur les glaciers. Neuchatel, 1840. 1st Ed. Atlas vol only. (91) £2,400
— Histoire naturelle des poissons d'eau douce. Neuchatel, 1839-42. 2 parts in 1 vol, including Vogt's Embryologie des Salmones but lacking 8vo text vol. Oblong 4to. (90) $1,400
— Iconographie des Coquilles Tertiaires. Neuchatel, 1845. 4to. (89) $60
— Lake Superior. Bost., 1850. 8vo. (88) $110; (90) $300
— Memoires sur les moules de molusques vivans et fossiles. Neuchatel, 1839. Part 1 only. Folio. Offprint from Vol II of the Memoires de la Societe des Sciences Naturelles de Neuchatel. (90) $60

AMERICAN BOOK PRICES CURRENT

Agate, James Evershed, 1877-1947
— Ego [Ego 2-9]. An Autobiography [complete set]. L, 1935-48. 1st Ed. 9 vols. (88) £65
— A Shorter Ego. L, 1946. One of 110, sgd. 2 vols. (91) £60

Agathias
— De bello Gotthorum.... Augsburg: Sigismund Grimm, 20 Sept 1519. 1st Ed. 4to. (91) $175

Agee, James, 1909-55
— A Death in the Family. NY, [1957]. (89) $80; (90) $80
— Four Early Stories. West Branch: Cummington Press, 1964. One of 285. 4to. (90) $130
— Let Us Now Praise Famous Men. Bost., 1941. Illus by Walker Evans. 4to. (91) $85
— The Morning Watch. Bost.: Houghton Mifflin, 1951. (89) $50

Aglio, Augustine
— Antiquities of Mexico. See: Kingsborough, Edward

Agnesi, Margarita Gaetana Angiola Maria, 1718-99
— Instituzioni analitiche.... Milan, 1748. 1st Ed. 2 vols. 4to. (91) £340
— Traites elementaires de calcul differentiel et de calcul integral. Paris: Chardon for Claude Antoine Jombert fils aine, 1775. 8vo. (91) $150

Agnew, Georgette
— Let's Pretend. L, 1927. One of 160, sgd by author & artist. Illus by E. H. Shepard. 4to. (88) $80; (91) $110

Agocchie, Giovanni dall'
— Dell'arte di scrimia libri tre.... Venice: Giulio Tamborino, 1572. 4to. (88) £110

Agop, Joannes
— Puritas haygica seu grammatica armenica.... Rome: Sacra Congregatio de Propaganda Fide, 1675. Nerssesian 42. Bound with: Puritas linguae armenicae. Rome, 1674. Nerssesian 40. And: Grammatica ltaina armenice explicata. Rome, 1675. Nerssesian 43. 4to. With signature of Anquetil-Duperron on tp. (91) £3,600
Nerssesian 42. Bound with: Puritas linguae armenicae. Rome, 1674. Nerssesian 40. And: Grammatica latina armenice explicata. Rome, 1675. Nerssesian 43. (91) £3,600

Agostini, Antonio
— Dialoghi sopra le medaglie.... Rome, 1698. Folio. (88) £250

Agostini, Giovanni degli
— Notizie istorico-critiche intorno la vita, e le opere degli scrittori Viniziani. Venice, 1752-54. 2 vols. 4to. (88) $110

Agostini, Leonardo
— Gemmae et sculpturae antiquae. Franeker: Leonardum Strik, 1694. 2 parts in 1 vol. 4to. (89) $275
 Blackmer copy. (90) £400
— La Gemme antiche figurate. Rome, 1657. 2 parts in 1 vol. 4to. (89) £230
— Le gemme antiche figurate di Leonardo Agostini. Rome, 1657-69. 2 vols. 4to. (90) $4,750
— Le Gemme antiche.... Rome, 1686. 2 vols. 4to. Kissner copy. (91) £300

Agricola, Daniel
— Passio domini nostri Jesu Christi secundum seriem quatuor evangelistarum. Basel: Adam Petrus de Langendorff, Feb 1519. 4to. (90) £850

Agricola, Georg Andreas, 1672-1738
— The Experimental Husbandman and Gardener.... L, 1726. 2d Ed. 4to. (89) £320

Agricola, Georgius, 1494-1555
— Berckwerck Buch: darinn nicht Allain alle Empter, Instrument, Bezeug und alles so zu diesem Handel gehoerig..... Frankfurt: Peter Schmidt in Verlegung Sigismundt Feyrabendts, 1580. Folio. (88) £1,500
— De l'arte de metalli. Basel: Froben & Bischof, 1563. Folio. (89) £600
— De ortu & causis subterraneorum.... Basel, 1546. Folio. (88) $3,200
 De Bure-Horblit copy. (89) £3,200
 Basel, [1563]. Folio. (88) £2,400
— De re metallica. Basel: Froben, 1556. 1st Ed. 4to. (88) DM33,000; (90) DM19,500; (91) £340
 Doheny copy. (89) $11,000
 Basel, 1561. Folio. (90) £4,400
 L, 1912. Trans by Herbert C. & Lou Hoover. Folio. (88) £240, DM650; (89) $350, £220; (90) £220; (91) $130
 Inscr on behalf of both Hoovers by Lou Hoover. (88) $500
 Inscr to Whitelaw Reid II by Herbert Hoover. (88) $700
 Library markings. (89) $275
 With Ls from Herbert Hoover, 1923, tipped in, Doheny copy. (88) $650
— Vom Bergwerck XII Buecher. Basel: J. Froben, 1557. Folio. (88) £2,200, £2,500; (91) DM10,000

Agricola, Rudolphus
— De inventione dialectica libri tres.... [Cologne: F. Bieckmann?], 1528. 4to. (88) £420

Agrippa, Camillo
— Trattato di scientia d'arme. Rome: Antonio Blado, 1553. 4to. Dyson-Perrins—Abrams copy. (90) £2,000
 Venice, 1604. ("Trattato di scienza d'arme....") 4to. (90) $550
— Trattato di trasportar la guglia in su la piazza di San Pietro.... Rome: Zanetti, 1583. Bound with: Sixtus V, Pope. Ordo dedicationis obelisci.... Rome, 1586. And: Pigafetta, Filippo. Discorso s'intorno all'historia della aguaglia, et alla ragione del muouerla. Rome, 1586. And: Familiaris quaedam epistola e Roma in Hispaniam missa.... Rome, 1586. 4to. Kissner copy. (91) £2,200

Agrippa, Henricus Cornelius, 1486?-1535
— De occulta philosophia liber primus. Paris: Christian Wechel, 1531. Folio. (90) £1,200
— De occulta philosophia libri tres. [Cologne: Johannes Soter], July 1533. Folio. (88) (89) £200; (91) $1,600
 Bound with: Muenster, Sebastian. Organum Uranicum. Basel: Henricus Petrus, 1536. (91) £16,000
— Three Books of Occult Philosophy *His Fourth Book of Occult Philosophy. L, 1651-55. 2 vols. 4to. Wing A-789 & A-785. (91) £750
— Three Books of Occult Philosophy. L, 1651. 8vo. (88) $550; (91) £550

Aguecheek, Andrew
— The Universal American Almanack...1764. See: Almanacs

Aguiar, Vasco Jose de
— Viagem ao interior da Nova Hollanda.... Lisbon, 1841. 3 vols. 8vo. (90) £110

Aguiar y Acuna, Rodrigo de
— Sumarios de la Recopilacion general de la Leyes.... Mexico, 1677. Folio. (89) $425

Aguilar, Pedro de
— Tractado de la Cavalleria de la Gineta. Seville: Hernando Diaz, 1572. 4to. (89) $1,300

Aguilar y Santillan, Rafael, 1863-1940
— Bibliografia Geologica y Minera de la Republica Mexicana. Mexico City, 1898. Folio. Inscr to Antonio Penafiel. (91) $225

AGUILLON

Aguillon, Francois d'
— Opticorum libri sex. Antwerp: Plantin, 1613. Folio. Honeyman copy. (90) $5,000

Aguilo y Fuster, Mariano, 1825-97
— Catalogo de Obras en Lengua Catalana impresas desde 1474 hasta 1860. Madrid, 1923. 4to. (91) $200

Agustin, Antoine
— De Emmendatione Gratiani, dialogorum libri duo.... Paris: Pierre Chevalier, 1607. 2 parts in 1 vol. 4to. (89) £700

Agustin, Antonio, Archbishop of Tarragona
— Dialoghi...sopra le Medaglie, Iscrizioni, e altre Antichita.... Rome, 1698. Folio. (90) $110; (91) LIt420,000

Ahmad ibn Mohammad ibn Kathir, al-Farghani. See: Alfranganus

Aikin, Charles Rochemont, 1775-1847
— A Concise View of all the most Important Facts...Concerning Cow-Pox. Charlestown, 1801. 18mo. (89) $70

Aikin, John, 1747-1822
— A Description of the Country from Thirty to Forty Miles round Manchester. L, 1795. 4to. (88) £160; (89) £220; (91) £240, £240
— England Delineated; or, a Geographical Description.... L, 1790. 8vo. (89) £80, £85; (91) £110
  4th Ed. L, 1800. 8vo. (89) £100
— Essay on Song-Writing, with a Collection of...English Songs.... Warrington, 1774. 2d Ed. 8vo. (88) £100; (91) $70

Aikin, John, 1747-1822 —&
Enfield, William, 1741-97
— General Biography; or Lives, Critical and Historical.... L, 1799-1815. 10 vols. 4to. (88) £160

Aimoinus, Monachus Floriacensis
— De regum procerumque Francorum origine gestisque clarissimis.... [Paris]: Johannes Parvus & Badius Ascensius, 1514. Folio. (91) $325

Ainsworth, Edward
— The Cowboy in Art. NY: World, [1968]. One of 100. Foreword by John Wayne. (89) $60, $80
  One of 1,000. With ink sketch of a mountain man on horseback, sgd Wieghorst. Inscr by Ainsworth's wife. (90) $750
  NY & Cleveland, 1968. (88) $70
— Golden Checkerboard. Palm Desert, [1965]. (88) $60; (90) $70; (91) $70

AMERICAN BOOK PRICES CURRENT

Inscr. (89) $55
— Painters of the Desert. Palm Desert, CA, 1960. 1st Issue. 4to. (90) $75
  1st ptg. (90) $150
  Palm Desert, CA, 1961. 2d ptg. 4to. (89) $160
  Inscr to Amy Brown O'Toole. (91) $75

Ainsworth, Henry
— Annotations upon the Five Books of Moses.... L: M. Parsons for John Bellamie, 1639. Folio. STC 220. (90) £75, £75

Ainsworth, Robert
— The Most Natural and Easy Way of Institution.... L: Christopher Hussey, 1698. 4to. Dedicatee's copy, with the bookplate & signature of Sir William Hustler. (88) £1,300

Ainsworth, William Harrison, 1805-82
— Guy Fawkes: or, the Gunpowder Treason. L, 1857. Illus by George Cruikshank. 8vo. (89) $185
— Jack Sheppard. L, 1839. 1st Ed. Illus by George Cruikshank. (91) $110, $200
— The Lord Mayor of London. L, 1862. 1st Ed. 3 vols. 8vo. (88) $50
— Merry England; or, Nobles and Serfs. L, 1874. 1st Ed. 3 vols. 8vo. (89) $110
— The Miser's Daughter.... L, 1842. 1st Ed. Illus by George Cruikshank. Bound in 1 vol. 8vo. Extracted from Ainsworth's Magazine. (88) $85
— The Tower of London. L, 1840. 1st Ed in Book form. Illus by George Cruikshank. 8vo. (91) $1,200
  Inscr to William Beckford & with ALs to an unidentified recipient. Bradley Martin copy. (90) $1,700
— Windsor Castle. L, 1843. 8vo. (90) $110; (91) $225
— Works. Phila.: Barrie, [c.1900]. ("Historical Romances.") One of 250 L.p. copies on japan. 25 vols. 4to. With plates in 3 states. (89) $400
  Windsor Ed. L, 1901-2. 20 vols. 8vo. (91) £140

Ainsworth, William Harrison, 1805-82 —&
Aston, John Partington
— Sir John Chiverton, a Romance. L, 1826. 12mo. (90) £140

Aircraft...
— Aircraft Yearbook. Wash., etc., 1929-40. For 1929-40. 12 vols. 8vo. (91) uS160

Airy, Osmund, 1845-1928
— Charles II. L, 1901. One of 300 on japanese paper. 4to. (90) £70 One of 1,250. (89) $70, $375; (91) $225

Aiton, William, 1731-93
— Hortus Kewensis. L, 1810-13. 5 vols. 8vo. (89) £85

Aiton, William, 1760-1848
— General View of the Agriculture of the County of Ayr. Glasgow, 1811. 4to. Inscr. (91) £60

Akenside, Mark, 1721-70
— The Pleasures of Imagination. See: Fore-Edge Paintings
— The Poems. L, 1772. 1st Collected Ed. 4to. (88) £40

Akerman, John Yonge, 1806-73
— Remains of Pagan Saxondom. L, 1855 [1852-55]. 4to. (88) (91) £190

Akropolites, Georgios, 1220-82
— Georgii Acropolitae magni logothetae historia, ioelis chronographia compendiaria.... Paris, 1651. Bound with: Doukas, Michael. Ducae Michaelis Ducae nepotis historia Byzantina.... Paris, 1649. Blackmer copy. (90) £5,800

Akurgal, Ekrem —& Others
— Treasures of Turkey. Geneva: Skira, [1966]. (88) $70

Alabama
— Ordinances and Constitution of the State of Alabama.... Montgomery, 1861. 8vo. (90) $175

Alabaster, William
— Roxana. L: Gulielmus Jones, 1632. 8vo. (89) £150

Aladdin...
— Aladdin and the Wonderful Lamp. Chicago: Reilly & Britton, [1915]. Illus by John R. Neilla. (91) $55

Alain-Fournier, Henri, 1886-1914
— Le Grand Meaulnes. Paris, 1913. 12mo. Inscr to Thomas Hardy. Martin copy. (90) FF26,000
Paris, 1946. One of 15 with an additional suite of illusts. Illus by Madeleine Melsonin. 4to. (90) £120

Alaman, Lucas
— Decreto del soberano congreso mexicano para las eleciones.... Mexico, 17 June 1823. Folio. (88) $120

Alamanni, Luigi, 1495-1556
— La Coltivatione. Paris: Estienne, 1546. 1st Ed. 8vo. (89) £280; (90) £120; (91) £90, LIt850,000
— Gyrone il cortese. Paris, 1548. 1st Ed. 4to. (88) £75; (90) LIt425,000; (91) LIt320,000, LIt850,000
— Opere Toscane. Venice: Peter Schoeffer for the heirs of Lucantonio Giunta, 1542. 8vo. (88) £110

Alanus de Insulis
— Doctrinale altum seu Liber parabolarum. [Leipzig: Conrad Kachelofen, c.1490]. 4to. 30 leaves. Goff A-180. (91) $13,000

Alarcon, Pedro Antonio de
— The Three-Cornered Hat. NY, 1944. One of 500. Illus by Fritz Kredel. (91) $65

Alaska
— Alaskan Boundary Tribunal. Wash., 1904. Complete Atlas in 3 vols. Folio. 58th Congress, 2d Session, Senate Exec Doc 162. (88) $290
— The Official Guide to the Klondyke Country and the Gold Fields of Alaska. Chicago: W. B. Conkey, 1897. 8vo. (90) $200

Alastair. See: Voight, Hans Henning

Albani, Giovanni Girolamo
— Liber pro oppugnata Romani pont. dignitate et Constantini donatione adversus obtrectatores. Rome: Antonio Blado, 17 Sept 1547. 4to. Abrams copy. (90) £550

Albanis de Beaumont, Jean Francois, Viscount, 1753?-1811?
— Travels from France to Italy through the Lepontine Alps.... L, 1800. Folio. Kissner copy. (91) £1,300
2d Ed. L, 1806. Folio. (91) £750
— Travels through the Rhaetian Alps. L, 1792. Folio. (90) £550; (91) £300, £1,400
Kissner copy. (91) £800
L.p. copy. (89) £1,300
Penrose copy. (91) £1,150
— Travels through the Maritime Alps from Italy to Lyons. L, 1795. Folio. (88) R620; (90) £1,500

Alberoni, Giulio, Cardinal, 1664-1752
— Cardinal Alberoni's Scheme for Reducing the Turkish Empire to the Obedience of Christian Princes. Dublin, 1736. 8vo. Blackmer copy. (90) £100

ALBERS

Albers, Josef
— Interaction of Color. New Haven, 1963. 2 vols. 4to. (88) $1,500, $1,600; (89) $1,600

Albert, Consort of Victoria, Queen of England, 1819-61
[-] The National Memorial. To His Royal Highness the Prince Consort. L, 1873. Folio. (90) $225

Albert d'Ailly, Michel Ferdinand, Duc de Chaulnes. See: Chaulnes, Michel Ferdinand d'Albert d'Ailly

Albert, Heinrich
— Acht Theil der Arien, Theils Geistlicher zu Christlichen Leben Weltlicher.... Koenigsberg, 1650-54. 8 parts in 1 vol. Folio. (91) $4,000

Albert, Joseph
— Die Bayerischen Koenigs-Schloessen. Neuschwanstein. Munich, [c.1870]. Folio. (90) $375

Albertanus Causidicus Brixiensis
— Ars loquendi et tacendi. Cologne: [Heinrich Quentell], 1497. 4to. 12 leaves. Goff A-209. (91) £900
— De arte loquendi et tacendi. Antwerp: Gerard Leeu, June 1485. 12 leaves. Goff A-197. Bound with: Mensa Philosophica. Louvain, c.1481. 82 leaves. Goff M-492; And: Adelardus bathoniensis. Quaestiones naturales. Louvain: Johannes de Westfalia, c.1475. 50 leaves. Goff A-50. And: Ferrariis, Albertus de. De horis canonicis. Louvain: Johannes de Westfalia, 1485. 32 leaves. Goff T-471. Folio. Myres copy. (90) £15,000

Alberti, Giuseppe Antonio
— I Giuochi Numerici fatti arcani.... Venice, 1788. 3d Ed. 12mo. (90) $2,200
4th Ed. Venice, 1795. 12mo. (89) $275; (90) $500

Alberti, Johann Christoph Ludwig, 1768-1812
— Description physique et historique des Caffres sur la Cote Meridionale de l'Afrique. [Amst., 1811]. Folio. (88) R750

Alberti, Leandro, 1479-1552
— Descriptio totius Italiae.... Cologne: Theodorus Baumius, 1567. Bound with: Irenicus, Franciscus. Totius Germaniae descriptio. Folio. (88) £200
— Descrittione di tutta Italia. Bologna: A. Giaccarelli, Jan 1550. 1st Ed. Folio. Kissner copy. (91) £800
Venice: P. & N. de Sabbio, 1551. 8vo. (89) £120; (91) LIt320,000

AMERICAN BOOK PRICES CURRENT

Venice: Giovanni Maria Leni, 1577. 2 parts in 1 vol. 4to. (88) $140

Alberti, Leon Battista, 1404-72
— L'Architecture et art de bien bastir. Paris: R. Massellin for J. Kerver, 2Aug 1553. Folio. (88) FF15,000
— The Architecture...Painting...Statuary. L, 1726. 3 vols, including Supplement. Folio. (89) £500
L, 1755. Folio. (89) £90; (91) £130, £400
— L'Architettura. Venice, 1565. 4to. STC 489. Inscr by Nicholas Stone. (91) £650
— Della Architettura...Della Pittura...Della Statua. Londra: Tommaso Edkin, 1726. Folio. (88) £160; (89) £650
Bologna, 1782. Folio. (89) £180, £180
— I Dieci libri di architettura. Venice: V. Valgrisi, 1546. 8vo. (88) £350; (91) LIt1,600,000
Rome, 1784. 4to. (89) $350
Dedication copy. (91) £1,700

Alberti, Rafael
— Gedicht. Frankfurt: Edition Lieder, 1982. One of 15. Illus by Barbara Fahrner. (91) DM520
— Picasso: Le Rayon Interrompu. Paris: Cercle d'Art, [1974]. Illus by Pablo Picasso. Folio. (88) $80

Alberti, Romano
— Trattato della nobilta della pittura. Rome: Francesco Zannetti, 1585. 1st Ed. 4to. (89) $80

Albertinus, Franciscus
— Opusculum de mirabilibus novae & veteris urbis Romae.... Rome: Jacobum Mazochium, 7 Feb 1510. 4to. Kissner copy. (91) £2,000
Rome: Jacobum Mazochium, 1515. 4to. Kissner copy. (91) £800
Basel: Thomas Wolff, 1519. 4to. Kissner copy. (91) £750
Lyon: Marion for Morin, 1520. 4to. Kissner copy. (91) £800

Alberts, Sydney Seymour
— A Bibliography of the Works of Robinson Jeffers. NY, 1933. One of 487. (91) $85

Albertus Magnus, 1193?-1280
— Les Admirables secrets d'Albert le Grand.... Lyons: Heirs of Beringos, 1791 [but Avignon, Offray aine, c.1850]. 16mo. (88) $80
— Compendium theologicae veritatis. Venice: Gregorius Dalmatinus & Jacobus Britannicus, 1 Apr 1483. 4to. 97 (of 98) leaves; lacking first blank. Goff A-236. (91) £3,000
— Mariale. [Strassburg: Johann Mentelin, not after 1473]. Bound as issued with the De laudibus Mariae. Folio. Formerly attrib-

uted to Albertus Magnus. 66 leaves; Goff A-272. 213 (of 215) leaves; lacking final 2 blanks. Goff A-247. This copy bears the rubrication date 1473. Abrams copy. (90) £7,000
— Secreta Mulierum et Vivorum.... Lyons, 1512. 5 parts in 1 vol. 8vo. (91) £90
— Secreta mulierum et virorum. Amst., 1643. ("De secretis mulierum item de virtutibus herbarum lapidum et animalium.") 12mo. (88) $800; (91) $200

Albin, Eleazar, fl.1713-59
— Birds. L, 1731-38. ("A Natural History of Birds.") 3 vols. 4to. (89) £5,000; (91) £5,000 One of 89 sets ptd & hand-colored for orig subscribers; Vol I, 1st Issue, Vols II & III, 2d Issue. Bradley Martin copy. (89) $17,000
  L, 1738-40. 3 vols. 4to. (91) £3,400
  Thomas Forster's copy. (90) £1,600
— Histoire naturelle des oiseaux. The Hague, 1750. 3 vols. 4to. (89) £3,800
— Insects. L, 1720. ("A Natural History of English Insects.") 4to. (89) £900, £1,600
  2d Ed. L, 1724. 4to. (90) $4,000; (91) $2,600
  L, 1749. 4to. (91) £1,100
— Songbirds. L, 1741. ("A Natural History of English Songbirds....") 2d Ed. 8vo. (88) £35
— Spiders. L, 1736. ("A Natural History of Spiders.") 4to. (91) £350

Albinus, Bernard Siegfried, 1697-1770
— Anatomical Tables of the Bones, Muscles, Blood Vessels.... L, 1827. Folio. (91) £1,700
— Explicatio tabularum anatomicarum Bartholomaei Eustachii.... Leiden, 1744. Folio. (89) $1,200; (90) $1,150; (91) £750
— Historia musculorum hominis. Leiden, 1734. 4to. (89) HF500
— Tables of the Skeleton and Muscles.... L, 1749. With 28 plates plus 12 outline plates. Bound with: The Compleat System of the Blood Vessels and Nerves. With 7 plates & 4 outline plates. Folio. (90) £1,300
— Tabulae ossium humanorum. Leiden, 1753. Bound with: De uteri gravidi. Leiden, 1748. And: Tabula ossis chyliferi. Leiden, 1757. Folio. (91) LIt2,400,000
— Tabulae sceleti et musculorum corporis humani. L, 1749. Folio. (91) £3,200

Albinus, Petrus
— Meissnische Land und Berg-Chronica. Dresden: Gimel Bergen, 1589-90. 2 parts in 1 vol. Folio. (88) DM1,700, DM2,000

Albizzi, Antonio degli, 1547-1626
— Principium christianorum stemmata. Augsburg: Typis Christophori Mangi, 1608. Folio. (89) $1,900; (90) $8,000

Albizzi, Bartolomeo da Pisa. See: Bartholomaeus degli Albizzi de Rinonichi

Albrecht, Kurt
— Nineteenth Century Australian Gold and Silver Smiths. Melbourne, 1969. (88) A$130

Albrizzi, Girolamo
— L'Origine del Danubio. Venice, 1685. 12mo. Kissner copy. (91) £380

Albucasis
— Chirurgia. Graz, 1979. One of 960. Folio. Facsimile of the Orig Ms. (88) $350
— De Chirurgia. Oxford: Clarendon Press, 1778. 3 vols in 1. 4to. L.p. copy. (88) $2,200

Album...
— L'Album: Aquarelles et Dessins Inedits. Paris: Tallandier, [1902]. 4to. (90) $550
— L'Album: Les Maitres de la Caricature. Paris, 1902. 4to. (88) HF550
— Album of the Finest Birds of All Countries. Phila.: Weick & Wieck, [c.1870]. Oblong 4to. Martin copy. (90) $1,500
— Album pintoresco de la Republica Mexicana. Mexico: Michaud y Thomas, [c.1850]. Oblong folio. (88) £3,800
— Album pittoresque de Stockholm. [Stockholm: A. Bonniers, c.1840]. Oblong folio. (90) £300
— Album Rebusov, Sharad, Anagramm, Zagadok, i Proch. St. Petersburg, 1883. Folio. (90) $225
— Al'bum Revoljutsionnoj Rossii...Album of Revolutionary Russia. [N.p., 1919]. Oblong 4to. (91) $300

Albumasar, 805-886
— De magnis conjunctionibus. Augsburg: Ratdolt, 31 Mar 1489. 1st Ed. Ed by Johannes Angelus. 4to. 118 leaves. Goff A-360. (89) $6,500

Alcala, Pedro de
— Arte para ligeramente saber la lengua aravica.... Granada: Juan Varela de Salamanca, 5 Feb 1505. 2 parts in 1 vol. 4to. (88) £17,000

Alcalde, Antonio de, 1736-1812
— Elogios funebres con que la santa iglesia catedral de Guadalaxara.... Guadalajara, 1793. 4to. (89) $140

ALCAROTTI

Alcarotti, Giovanni Francesco
— Del viaggio di Terra Santa. Novara: Appresso gli Heredi di Fr. Sefalli, 1596. 4to. Blackmer copy. (90) £1,700

Alcedo y Herrera, Dionisio de
— Relacion de los meritos, servicios y circunstancias de.... Madrid, 1768. Folio. Bound with Ms, sgd, Duplicado del Aviso historico, politico y geographico con las noticias mas particulares de la America Meridional en las Indias Occidentales.... 592 pp. (88) £8,000

Alchabitius
— Libellus Isagogicus. Venice: Erhard Ratdolt, 1485. 4to. 95 (of 98) leaves; lacking 2a7 & 8 & 2f8. Goff A-363. (88) £220

Alciatus, Andreas, 1492-1550
— Diverse imprese accommodate a diverse moralita.... Lyons: M. Bonhomme, 1549. 8vo. (88) £500; (90) LIt1,000,000
Lyon: G. Rouille, 1579. 8vo. (89) £420
— Emblematum.... Lyon: Mathias Bonhomme, 1550. ("Emblemata....") 8vo. (89) £400; (90) $1,500
Lyons: M. Bonhomme, 1551. 8vo. (88) £300
Frankfurt: G. Raben for Feyrabend & S. Huter, 1567. 8vo. Johannes Stephanus's copy, used as an album amicorum by him, with 17 watercolor coats-of-arms & emblematic paintings & with dedicatory inscrs, etc. (91) $3,400
Paris: H. de Marnef, viduam G. Cavellat, 1583. ("Omnia emblemata....") 8vo. (88) £70
Paris, 1589. ("Emblemata....") 8vo. (89) $375
Leiden: Plantin, 1591. 8vo. (88) $250
Paris: Francois Gueffier for Jean Richer, 1608. ("Omnia emblemata....") 8vo. (91) £380
Padua: Tozzi, 1618. 8vo. (91) LIt850,000
Padua, 1621. ("Emblemata.") 4to. In Latin. (90) £260; (91) $475
Padua, 1661. 4to. (88) $275
— Les Emblemes. Lyons: G. Roville, 1549. 8vo. (88) £400
— Lyon: Mathias Bonhomme, 1550
— ("Emblemata.") 8vo. (88) £1,000

Alciphron
— Lettres grecques.... Amst.: Nyon, 1785-84. 3 vols. 12mo. Blackmer copy. (90) £350

AMERICAN BOOK PRICES CURRENT

Alcocer y Martinez, Mariano
— Catalogo razonado de obras impresas en Valladolid, 1481-1800. Valladolid, 1926. 4to. (91) $120

Alcock, Charles William
— Famous Cricketers and Cricket Grounds.... L, [1895]. 18 parts in 1 vol. Folio. (90) $55

Alcoforado, Mariana
— Las Cartas Portuguesas. [Buenos Aires: Osvaldo F. Colombo, 1968]. One of 20 on japon. Illus by Raul Russo. (88) £1,600

Alcoholics Anonymous
— Alcoholics Anonymous: The Story of How More than Fourteen Thousand Men and Women Have Recovered from Alcoholism. NY: Works Publishing, 1945. 1st Ed, 8th Ptg. (91) $150

Alcott, Louisa May, 1832-88
— Flower Fables. Bost.: George W. Briggs, 1855. Greenhill-Martin copy. (90) $2,250
— Little Men. Bost., 1871. 1st American Ed, 1st Issue. 12mo. (90) $90; (91) $70, $70
— Little Women. Bost., 1868. With: Little Women...Part Two. Bost., 1869. 1st Eds. 8vo. (91) $400
With: Little Women...Part Two. Bost., 1869. Martin copy. (90) $5,000
L: Sampson Low, Son, & Marston, 1869. 2 vols. 8vo. (88) $130

Alcott, Ten, Pseud. —&
Gems, Talismans & Guardians: Their Sentiment and Language.... —& NY, 1887 Oblong 4to. (88) $480

Alcyonius, Petrus
— Legatus de exsilio. Venice: Aldus, Nov 1522. 8vo. (88) £550
— Medices legatus de exsilio. Venice: Aldus, Nov 1522. 8vo. Doheny copy. (89) $3,000

Aldam, W. H.
— A Quaint Treatise on "Flees...." L, 1876. 4to. (88) $1,100, £320, £420, £450, £500, £500; (89) $375, A$900; (90) $600, $950, $1,500; (91) $700

Alden, John
— European Americana: A Chronological Guide. See: Brown Library, John Carter

Aldenhoven, Ferdinand
— Itineraire descriptif de l'Attique et du Peloponese. Athens: L'Ami du Peuple, 1841. 8vo. Blackmer copy. (90) £200

Aldin, Cecil, 1870-1935
— Old Inns. L, 1921. One of 380. 4to. (89) $100
— The Twins. L: Hodder & Stoughton, [1910]. 4to. (91) £100

Aldine...
— The Aldine: A Typographic Art Journal. NY, 1873. Vol V, No 1 to Vol VI, No 12, bound in 2 vols. Folio. (91) $55

Aldington, Richard, 1892-1962
— Death of a Hero. L, 1929. Inscr & with Ls inserted. (89) £260
Paris, 1930. One of 300. 4to. (89) £130; (91) $400
— The Eaten Heart. Chapelle-Reanville, Eure: The Hours Press, 1929. 1st Ed, One of 200. 4to. (88) £60
— Ezra Pound & T. S. Eliot. A Lecture. [L]: The Peacock Press, 1954. 1st Ed, One of 10 trial copies on azure hand-made paper. (91) $130
— Last Straws. Paris: Hours Press, 1930. 1st Ed, Revue copy. (88) £65

Aldini, Giovanni
— Essai theorique et experimental sur le galvanisme.... Paris, 1804. 2 vols. 4to. (88) $800
2 vols in 1. 4to. (88) $900

Aldis, Harry Gidney, 1863-1919
— A List of Books Printed in Scotland before 1700. Edin., 1904. 4to. (91) $80

Aldrich, Henry, 1647-1710
— Elementa architecturae civilis ad Vitruvii.... Oxford, 1789. 1st Ed. 2 parts in 1 vol. 4to. Myres copy. (90) £100

Aldrich, Thomas Bailey, 1836-1917
— Friar Jerome's Beautiful Book. Bost, 1881. Sgd on half-title & dated Feb 1882. (91) $90
— Prudence Palfrey, a Novel. See: Clemens's copy, Samuel Langhorne
— The Story of a Bad Boy. Bost., 1870. 1st Ed in Book form, 1st Issue. 12mo. Martin copy. (90) $1,300
— Works. Cambr., Mass., 1897-98. One of 250 L.p. copies, sgd. 10 vols. 8vo. (88) $900; (91) $175

Aldrovandi, Ulisse, 1522-1605
— De animalibus insectis libri septem.... Bologna, 1638. Folio. (89) HF2,000; (91) DM3,100
— De piscibus libri V et de cestis lib. unis. Bologna, 1613. Folio. Heber-Britwell Court-Howard copy. (90) $14,000
— De quadrupedibus solidipedibus. Bologna, 1616. 1st Ed. Folio. (88) £360; (89) £380

— De reliquis animalibus exanguibus libri quatuor.... Bologna: Ferroni fuer Bernia, 1654. Folio. (91) DM2,200
— Monstrorum historia.... Bologna, 1642. Folio. (88) £1,700
— Opera. Bologna, 1599-1668. 13 vols. Folio. Jeanson copy. (88) FF190,000
— Ornithologiae. Bologna, 1599-1603. 1 vol (of 3) only. Folio. (88) DM1,300
3 vols. Folio. Inscr to the Ipswich Literary Institution by Thomas Clarkson. (89) £2,200
Martin copy. (90) $2,750
— Serpentum et draconum historiae libri duo. Bologna, 1640. 1st Ed. Folio. (91) £150

Alechamps, Jacques d'. See: Dalechamps, Jacques

Aleman, Mateo, 1547?-1610?
— The Rogue: or the Life of Guzman de Alfarache. L, 1623. 1st Ed in English, 2d Issue dated 1623. 2 parts in 1 vol. Folio. (89) £175
Houghton-Fleming copy. (89) $600
3d Ed in English. L, 1634. 2 vols in 1. Folio. (90) £50
STC 291.5. (91) £95

Alembert, Jean le Rond d', 1717?-83
See also: Diderot & Alembert
— An Account of the Destruction of the Jesuits in France. L, 1766. 8vo. (91) £50
— Elemens de musique theorique et pratique. Lyon: Jean-Marie Bruyset, 1766. 8vo. (91) $425
— Essai d'une nouvelle theorie de la resistance des fluides. Paris, 1752. 4to. (89) $500, £280
— Traite de dynamique.... Paris, 1743. 4to. (89) £280

Alembert, Jean le Rond d', 1717?-83 —& Others
— Nouvelles Experiences sur la resistance des fluides. Paris, 1777. 8vo. (89) £220

Aleph. See: Harvey, William Henry

Alexander Aphrodisaeus
— In Topica Aristotelis Commentarii [in Greek]. Venice: Aldus, Sept 1513. Folio. Spencer-Rylands copy. (88) £6,500
— Quaestiones naturales, morales, et de fato. Venice, 1541. 8vo. The Garden copy. (90) $31,000

Alexander Benedictus
— Diaria de bello Carolino. Venice: Aldus, after 27 Aug 1496. 4to. 68 leaves. Goff A-389. Spencer-Rylands copy. (88) £5,000

ALEXANDER

Alexander, Boyd, 1873-1910
— From the Niger to the Nile. L, 1907. 1st Ed. 2 vols. (88) £50

Alexander de Ales
— Summa theologica. Pavia: Franciscus Girardengus & Johannes Antonius Birreta, 1489. 4 vols. 4to. 1,568 leaves. Goff A-384. (90) £2,800
Part 3 (of 4) only. 4to. 350 (of 360) leaves. Goff A-384. (90) £350

Alexander de Villa Dei
— Doctrinale. [Utrecht: Ptr of the "Speculum," c.1463-70]. 2 (of 42) leaves. Ffs. 29,30. Folios 29 & 30. Goff A-417. Doheny copy. (88) $15,000
Strassburg: Martin Flach, 1490-91. 4 parts in 1 vol. 4to. 326 leaves. Goff A441 & A450. Doheny copy. (88) $18,000

Alexander, George William
— Letters on the Slave-trade, Slavery, and Emancipation.... L, 1842. 8vo. Inscr to Lord Ashburton. (89) £110

Alexander, Hartley Burr, 1873-1939
— Sioux Indian Painting.... Nice, [1938]. One of 400. Folio. In French & English. (91) $1,600

Alexander II, Emperor of Russia, 1818-81
[-] Giostra Corsa in Torino addi XXI de Febbraio MDCCCXXXIX nel Passaggio de sua Altezza Imperiale e Reale Alessandro.... Turin, 1839. Folio. Inscr by King Carlo Alberto to Vicomte de Cholette. Schiff copy. (91) $3,750
— Opisanie svashchenn'shago koronovia ikh' Imperatorskikh' velichestv' gosudaria imperatora Aleksandravtorago i gosudariyii imperatirtritsi Mariyaliksandrovna vsei Rossii. Folio,. orig half mor (89) £13,000; (90) $9,500

Alexander III, Emperor of Russia, 1845-94
[-] Description du Sacre et du Couronnement de leurs Majestes Imperials...Alexandre III...Marie Feodorovna. St. Petersburg, 1883. Foliio. (88) £1,300 Folio. (91) DM3,200

Alexander, Sir James Edward, 1803-85
— Excursions in Western Africa.... L, 1840. 2d Ed. 2 vols. 8vo. (88) £160
— Narrative of a Voyage of Observation among the Colonies of Western Africa. L, 1837. 1st Ed. 2 vols. 8vo. (89) £75, R650
— Salmon-Fishing in Canada, by a Resident. L, 1860. Ed by Alexander. 8vo. (89) £60; (90) $50; (91) $110, $175
— Transatlantic Sketches, comprising Visits to the most interesting Scenes in North and South America.... L, 1833. 1st Ed. 2 vols. 8vo. (90) $55
— Travels from India to England. L, 1827. 4to. (91) £400
— Travels to the Seat of War in the East.... L, 1830. 2 vols. 8vo. (88) £120; (89) £160; (91) £150

Alexander, Kirkland Barker
— The Log of the North Shore Club. NY, 1911. (90) $50

Alexander, L.
— Alexander's Hebrew Ritual, and Doctrinal Explanation.... L, 1819. 8vo. (90) £80

Alexander, Russell George
— The Engraved Work of F. L. Griggs. Stratford, 1928. One of 325. Folio. (88) £60

Alexander the Great
[-] The Romance of Alexander. A Collotype Facsimile of Ms. Bodley 264. Oxford, 1933. Ed by Montague Rhodes James. Folio. Doheny copy. (88) $650

Alexander VI, Pope, 1431?-1503
— Copie de la bula del decreto y concession que hizo el papa Alexandro sexto al Rey y a la Reyna nuestros senores de las indias.... [N.p., c.1540]. Single sheet, 308mm by 248mm (orig a full chancery sheet). Doheny copy. (89) $70,000

Alexander VIII, Pope
— Carlo Magno. Festa Teatrale. Rome, 1729. Folio. Kissner copy. (91) £3,000

Alexander, William, Earl of Stirling, 1567?-1640
— A Paraenesis to the Prince. L, 1604. 4to. Hoe-Huntington-Clawson-Bradley Martin copy. (90) $1,900
— Recreations with the Muses. L, 1637. 1st Ed. 2 parts in 1 vol. Folio. (89) $1,200 Folio. (88) $50, £100; (89) £130

Alexander, William, 1767-1816
— Austrians. L, 1813. ("Picturesque Representations of the Dress and Manners of the Austrians.") 4to. (91) £260
— Chinese. L, 1814. ("Picturesque Representations of the Dress and Manners of the Chinese.") 4to. (91) £320
L, 1814 [plates watermarked 1829]. 4to. (89) £350
L, 1825 [plates watermarked 1829]. 4to. (91) £280
L, 1814 [plates watermarked 1829]. 4to. (91) £440
— The Costume of China. L, 1805. 4to. (88) £550, £620; (89) £500, £780; (91) £650,

LIt1,000,000
- Engravings with a Descriptive Account...of the Egyptian Monuments, in the British Museum.... [L: Longman, 1805-7]. Oblong folio. Blackmer copy. (90) £1,800 [Longman, 1805]. Part 1 only: 4 color plates. Blackmer copy. (90) £200
- Russians. L, 1814. ("Picturesque Representations of the Dress and Manners of the Russians....") 8vo. (91) $725
  L, [c.1823]. 8vo. (88) £190
  L, [c.1830]. 8vo. (91) $600
- Turks. L, [c.1828]. ("Picturesque Representations of the Dress and Manners of the Turks.") 8vo. (91) $600

Alexander, William DeWitt, 1833-1913
- History of the Later Years of the Hawaiian Monarchy.... Honolulu: Hawaiian Gazette, 1896. 8vo. (88) $120; (91) $110

Alexandre, Arsene
- L'Art decoratif de Leon Bakst. Paris, 1913. Folio. (88) £460, £550; (89) £600; (91) £300
- The Decorative Art of Leon Bakst. L, 1913. Notes by Jean Cocteau. Folio. (90) $500
- Jean-Francois Raffaelli, peintre, graveur.... Paris, 1909. 4to. (88) $325; (89) $150

Alexandro, Alexander ab
- Genialium dierum libri sex.... Paris, 1579. 8vo. (91) $150

Alexis of Piedmont. See: Ruscelli, Girolamo

Aleyn, Charles, d.1640
- The Historie of that Wise and Fortunate Prince, Henrie...the Seventh. L, 1638. 1st Ed. 8vo. (88) £130

Alfonso de Cartagena
- Doctrina e instruction de la arte de cavalleria. Burgos: Juan de Burgos, 6 May 1497. Folio. 130 leaves. Goff A-537. (88) £11,500

Alfonso X, King of Castile & Leon
- Lapidario del Rey D. Alfonso X.... Madrid, 1881. 4to. (88) $1,100 Folio. (88) £95; (90) £120; (91) £130
- Libros del saber de astronomia. Madrid, 1863-67. Ed by Manuel Rico y Sinobas. Vols I-V, Part 1 (all pbd). Folio. (88) £120
- Las Siete Partidas del Sabio Rey don Alonso el nono.... Salamanca: Andreas de Portopariis, 1565. 7 parts & index in 3 vols. Folio. (88) $400
- Tabulae astronomicae. Venice: Petrus Liechtenstein, 1521. 4to. (89) £500
- Tabule & L. Gaurici...Theoremata. Venice: Giunta, 1524. 2 parts in 1 vol. 4to. (90) £280

Alford, Joseph
- The Souls Dispensatorie. Or a Treasure for True Believers. L, 1649. 12mo. (88) £500; (91) £650

Alford, Lady Marianne Margaret
- Needlework as Art. L, 1886. 8vo. (91) £280

Alfranganus
- Elementa astronomica.... Amst., 1669. 4to. (89) £460

Algarotti, Francesco, 1712-64
- Il Newtonianismo per le dame.... Naples, 1737. 4to. (90) $425
- Sir Isaac Newton's Philosophy Explain'd for the Use of the Ladies. L, 1742. ("Sir Isaac Newton's Theory of Light and Colours....") 2 vols. 12mo. (89) £95
  2 vols in 1. 12mo. (88) £75

Alger, Horatio, 1832-99
- Bertha's Christmas Vision. Bost., 1856. 8vo. Swann-Greenhill-Martin copy. (90) $1,300
- Grand'ther Baldwin's Thanksgiving, with Other Ballads and Poems. Bost.: Loring, [1875]. 8vo. Martin copy. (90) $500
- Ragged Dick; or, Street Life in New York with the Boot-Blacks. Bost.: Loring, [1868]. 1st Ed, 1st Issue. 8vo. (89) £750; (90) $1,400; (91) $300

Alhoy, Maurice —& Haurt, Louis
- Les Cent et un Robert Macaire. Paris, 1839-40. Illus by Honore Daumier. 2 vols. 4to. (88) DM1,800; (90) £280, £600

Ali Bey, 1766-1818
- Travels of Ali Bey in Morocco, Tripoli, Cyprus, Egypt.... L, 1816. 2 vols. 4to. (91) £2,000
  Blackmer copy. (90) £4,600

Ali Sharaf Al-Din
- The History of Timur-Bec. L, 1723. 2 vols. 8vo. (89) $250; (90) £250

Ali-Bab, Pseud.
- Gastronomie pratique.... Paris, [1928]. 6th Ed. (91) $70

Alibert, Jean Louis, 1766?-1837
- Description des maladies de la peau.... Paris, 1833. ("Clinique de l'Hopital Saint-Louis....") Folio. (91) £600

Aligny, Theodore
- Vue des sites les plus celebres de la Grece antique.... Paris, 1845. Folio. Blackmer copy. (90) £1,900

ALISON

Alison, Sir Archibald, 1792-1867
— History of Europe from the Commencement of the French Revolution in 1789 to the Restoration of the Bourbons.... Edin. & L, 1849-50. 14 vols. 8vo. (88) $130; (90) £340 Millard Fillmore's sgd copy. (90) $1,600
— History of Europe from the Commencement of the French Revolution in 1789 to the Restoration of the Bourbons...[to the accession of Louis Napoleon in MDCCCLI]. Edin. & L, 1852-60. 23 vols including Index to 2d series. 8vo. (89) £380
— Travels in France, during the Years 1814-15. L, 1815. 2 vols. 12mo. William Beckford's annotated copy. Bradley Martin copy. (90) $800

Alistair. See: Voight, Hans Henning

Alix, Alexandre Louis Felix
— Precis de l'histoire de l'Empire Ottoman. Paris: Didot, 1822-24. 3 vols. 8vo. Blackmer copy. (90) £110

Alkemade, Cornelius van
— De Goude en Zilvere Gangbaare Penningen der Graaven en Graavinen van Holland. Delft, 1700. Folio. (88) $50

**Alkemade, Cornelius van —&
Schelling, Pieter van der**
— Beschryving van de Stad Briele, en den Lande van Voorn. Rotterdam, 1729. Folio. (89) HF1,100

Alken, Henry, 1784-1851
— The Analysis of the Hunting Field.... L, 1846. 8vo. (89) £120
— The Beauties and Defects in the Figure of the Horse.... L, [1816]. 8vo. (89) £55; (90) $350; (91) £70
— A Collection of Sporting and Humourous Designs.... L: Thomas M'Lean, 1824. 3 vols. Folio. (89) £14,000; (90) £30,000
— Driving Discoveries. L, 1817. Oblong 4to. (89) A$2,200
L, 1817 [but last plate watermarked 1821]. Oblong 4to. Schiff copy. (91) $2,000
— The Grand Steeple Chace over Leicestershire on the 12th of March, 1829. L: Ackermann, 1830. Oblong folio. Schiff copy. (91) $8,500
— How to Qualify for a Meltonian: addressed to All Would-be Meltonians. By Ben Tally-Ho. L, 1819. Oblong 4to. Schiff copy. (91) $3,250
L, 16 July 1819. (91) £1,400
— Hunting Discoveries. L, 1817 [but 1 plate watermarked 1819]. Oblong 4to. Schiff copy. (91) $2,250
— Illustrations for Landscape Scenery. L, 1821. Oblong 8vo. (91) £100

AMERICAN BOOK PRICES CURRENT

— Illustrations to Popular Songs. L, 1822. 1st Ed. Oblong folio. (89) $525
L, 1823. Oblong folio. (90) £60
— Indispensible Accomplishments; or Hints to City Gentlemen. L, 1824. Oblong folio. Schiff copy. (91) $3,500
— Involuntary Thoughts. L, 1823-24. Oblong 4to. (91) $300
— Moments of Fancy. L, 1823. Oblong folio. (91) $650
— The National Sports of Great Britain. L, 1820. ("National Sports of Britain.") Parts 1-3 bound in 1 vol. Folio. Alfred Barmore Maclay copy; "probably the only surviving copy issued in parts." Schiff copy. (91) $11,000
1st Ed. L, 1821. Folio. (91) £5,400
2d Issue, with colored title dated 1821. (89) £6,500, £6,800
Martin copy. (90) $9,000
L, 1825. Folio. (88) £300; (89) £2,400; (90) £7,000
L, 1903. Folio. (90) £650; (91) £750
L, 1904. Folio. Facsimile of the 1823 Ed. (90) $850
— Qualified Horses and Unqualified Riders. L, 1815 [but 2 plates watermarked 1821]. 1st Ed, 2d Issue. Oblong folio. Schiff copy. (91) $2,250
— Scenes in the Life of Master George. L, 1823. ("Progressive Sports (Numbers 1 and 2): A Graphic Description of the Rise and Progress of a Sporting Lad.") 2 vols. Oblong 4to. Widener-Bement-Schiff copy. (91) $3,500
— Scraps from the Sketch-Book. L, 1821. 4to. (90) £800
L, 1823. Oblong folio. (89) £440; (91) $650
— Shakespeare's Seven Ages of Man. L, 1824. Oblong 4to. (89) £420; (91) £300
Doheny copy. (88) $750
L, 1799 [but watermarked 1826]. Oblong 4to. (89) $425
— Some Do, and Some Do Not. L, [1821]. Issue not given. Oblong folio. Schiff copy. (91) $3,000
— Some Will, and Some Will Not. L, 1821. Oblong 4to. Schiff copy. (91) $2,750
— Sporting Discoveries. L, [2 plates watermarked 1820]. Oblong 4to. Schiff copy. (91) $2,500
— Sporting Scrap Book. L, [1824]. 8vo. (88) £200
— Sporting Sketches. L, [1817-19]. Oblong folio. (91) $850
— Studies of the Horse. L: R. Ackermann, 1830. Oblong 4to. (90) $250
— Symptoms of Being Amused. L, 1822. Vol I (all pbd). Oblong folio. (90) £280; (91) $650, $200, $250
— A Touch at the Fine Arts. L, 1824. 4to.

(89) £280; (91) $200
— Tutor's Assistant. L, 1823. Oblong 4to. Wilmerding copy. (91) $475

Alken, Samuel
— Sixteen Views of the Lakes in Cumberland and Westmorland. L, [plates dated 1794-95, but after 1807]. 4to. (88) £260

All...
— All the Year Round. L, 1859-1864. 10 vols. Conducted by Charles Dickens. 8vo. (89) £50
Vols 1-17. L, 1859-1867. 8vo. (88) £70

Allaeus, Franciscus
— Astrologiae nova methodus.... Rennes: ex typis Juliani Herbert, 1654. Folio. (88) £1,500

Allan, John Harrison
— A Pictorial Tour in the Mediterranean. L, 1843. Folio. (88) £200, £260; (91) £400
Blackmer copy. (90) £700
Kissner copy. (91) £750
2d Ed. L, 1845. Folio. (91) £220

Allard, Abraham
— Toutes sortes d'oiseaux, tant de pais etrangers que de Hollande.... Leiden: P. Vander Aa, [1710?]. Oblong folio. MacGillavry-Martin copy. (90) $3,250

Allard, Roger
— Les Elegies martiales. Paris: Camille Bloch, 1917. One of 5 on japon a la form des manufactures imperiales with a suite of the illusts on chine. (90) £1,200

Allason, Thomas, 1790-1852
— Picturesque Views of the Antiquities of Pola, in Istria. L, 1819. 1st Ed. Folio. (90) £260
Kissner copy. (91) £350
L.p. copy. Blackmer copy. (90) £1,000

Allemagne, Henry Rene d'
— Les Anciens Maitres serruriers et leurs meilleurs travaux. Paris, 1943. One of 600. 2 vols. Folio. (88) £130
— Les Cartes a jouer du XIVe au XXe siecle. Paris, 1906. 2 vols. 4to. (91) $1,500
— Du Khorassan au pays des Backhtiaris. Paris, 1911. 4 vols. 4to. (88) $800
— Histoire des jouets. Paris, 1902. 4to. (88) $700
— Histoire du luminaire depuis l'epoque romaine.... Paris, 1891. 4to. (89) £120
One of 1,000. (89) $200
— La Maison d'un vieux collectionneur. Paris, 1948. 2 vols. 4to. (88) $110
— Musee le Secq des Tournelles a Rouen. Ferronerie Ancienne. Paris, 1924. 2 vols.

4to. (88) $380; (89) $375
— La Toile imprimee et les indiennes de traite. Paris, 1942. One of 100. 2 vols. 4to. (91) $700

Allen...
— The Allen Press Bibliography. [Greenbrae, 1981]. One of 140. Folio. (88) $800
· San Francisco: Book Club of CA, 1985. Folio. (91) $900
One of 750. (88) $110
Folio. (88) $90, $750; (89) $65; (90) $75, $100, $120, $850; (91) $100, $110, $130

Allen, A. J.
— Ten Years in Oregon. Ithaca, NY, 1848. 1st Ed, 2d Issue. 8vo. (90) $70; (91) $60

Allen, Albert H. See: McMurtrie & Allen

Allen, Charles Dexter, 1865-1926
— American Book-Plates. A Guide to their Study.... L, 1894. Ltd Ed. 8vo. (91) $90
Inscr to Dewitt Miller. (88) $140
— Ex Libris. Essays of a Collector. Bost., etc., 1896. Ltd Ed on hand-made paper, sgd by author & pbr. 8vo. Inscr to T. L. De Vinne. (90) $130

Allen, Edward B.
— Early American Wall Paintings, 1710-1850. New Haven, 1926. 4to. (90) $50

Allen, Fred Hovey
— Masterpieces of Modern German Art. Bost., 1884. 2 vols. Folio. (91) $50

Allen, Grover M.
— The Mammals of China and Mongolia. NY, 1938-40. 2 vols. 4to. (90) $300

Allen, Hervey, 1889-1949
— Anthony Adverse. NY, 1933. 1st Ed, one of 105. (90) $200
See also: Limited Editions Club

Allen, Ira
— The Natural and Political History of the State of Vermont. L, 1798. 8vo. (88) $750

Allen, Jay
— All the Brave. See: Quintanilla, Luis

Allen, John, Riding Master
— Principles of Modern Riding for Gentlemen. L, 1825. 8vo. (90) $300

Allen, John Romilly, 1847-1907 —& Anderson, Joseph, 1832-1916
— The Early Christian Monuments of Scotland. L, 1903. Ltd Ed. 2 vols in 1. 4to. (91) $600

ALLEN

Allen, Lewis M.
— Printing with the Handpress. Kentfield, Calif.: Allen Press, 1969. One of 140. (89) $1,100, $1,300; (90) $1,150; (91) $1,100

Allen, Paul, 1775-1826
— A History of the American Revolution.... Balt., 1819. 1st Ed. 2 vols. 8vo. (90) $85

Allen, Thomas, 1803-33
— The History and Antiquities of London. L, 1827-28. 4 vols. 8vo. (90) $100
— Lancashire Illustrated. L, 1832. 4to. (88) £140, £160; (89) £280
— A New and Complete History of the County of York. L, 1828-31. 3 vols. 4to. (88) £240; (90) £140
— The Picturesque Beauties of Great Britain: Kent. L: George Virtue, [c.1830]. 4to. (90) £250
  L: George Virtue, [c.1832?]. 4to. (89) £300
  L: Virtue, 1833. 4to. (88) £180

Allen, William. See: Titus, Silas

Allen, William, Cardinal, 1532-94
— An Apologie and True Declaration of the Institution and Endevours of the two English Colleges, the one in Rome, the other now resident in Rhemes. Mounts in Henault [i.e., Rheims: Jean Foigny], 1581. Bound with: Allen. A Defense and Declaration of the Catholike Churchies Doctrine.... Antwerp: John Latius, 1565 8vo. (89) £300

Allen, William, 1793-1864
— Picturesque Views in the Island of Ascension. L, 1835. Folio. (90) £480
— Picturesque Views on the River Niger.... L, 1840. Oblong folio. (88) £360; (91) £900

Allen, William, 1793-1864 — & Thomson, Thomas Richard Heywood
— A Narrative of the Expedition sent by Her Majesty's Government to the River Niger.... L, 1848. 2 vols. 8vo. (89) £150, £180, £220; (90) £180

Allen, William A.
— Adventures with Indians and Game.... Chicago, 1903. 8vo. (89) $275; (91) $200

Allenby, Edmund Henry Hymnam, 1st Viscount, 1861-1936
— Proclamation of Martial Law in Jerusalem. Jerusalem, Dec 1917. Single sheet. Folio. Inscr by Sir Ronald Storrs to Ralph H. Isham. With related material. (89) $4,500

AMERICAN BOOK PRICES CURRENT

Allers, C. W.
— Die Silberne Hochzeit. Hamburg, 1890. Folio. (90) £60

Allerton, Reuben G.
— Brook Trout Fishing. NY, 1869. 8vo. (90) $90, $650; (91) $450

Allestree, Richard, 1619-81
— The Art of Contentment. Oxford, 1677. 8vo. (89) $350
— The Causes of the Decay of Christian Piety. L, 1667. 1st Ed. 8vo. (90) £50; (91) $75
  L, 1671. 8vo. (90) £300
— The Government of the Tongue. Oxford, 1674. 8vo. (90) £500
  Oxford, 1675. 8vo. (88) £45
— The Ladies Calling. Oxford, 1673. 1st Ed. 8vo. (88) £80
  See also: Fore-Edge Paintings
— The Whole Duty of Man.... L, 1675. 8vo. (89) £480; (91) $90
  L, 1682. 12mo. (91) £250
— Works. L, 1703-4. 2 parts in 1 vol. Folio. ESTC 102260. (91) £55

Alley, Ronald
— Francis Bacon. L, [1964]. Intro by John Rothenstein. 4to. (91) £600

Allezarg, Jean Joseph
— Recueil de 163 des principaux plans des ports et rades de la Mediterranee. Livorno: Joseph Gamba, 1817. 8vo. (91) £600

Allgemeine...
— Allgemeine Geschichte der Laender und Voelker von Amerika. See: Schroeter, J. F.

Allgemeines...
— Allgemeines Teutsches Garten-Magazin. Weimar, 1804-7. Jahrgang I-IV. 3 vols. 4to. (91) £1,100

Alliaco, Petrus de
— Concordantia astronomiae cum theologia.... Augsburg: Erhard Ratdolt, 2 Jan 1490. 4to. 55 (of 56) leaves. Goff A-471. (89) £520
  56 leaves. Goff A-471. Horblit-Abrams copy. (90) £5,500
  56 leaves. Goff A-471. (91) £4,000

Allibone, Samuel Austin, 1816-89
— A Critical Dictionary.... Phila., 1859-71. 1st Ed. 5 vols including Supplements, 1897. 4to. (91) £50
  Phila., 1874-91. 3 vols. 4to. (88) £110
  3 vols plus 2-vol Supplement by J. F. Kirk. Together, 5 vols. 4to. (89) £110
  Phila., 1877-92. 5 vols, including Supplements. 4to. (90) £110

1987 - 1991 • BOOKS

Phila., 1899. 5 vols, including 2-vol Supplement. 4to. (90) $130
Phila., 1902. 5 vols, including Kirk's Supplement. 4to. (88) $130
Detroit, 1965. 5 vols, including Supplement. (91) $80

Allies'...
— The Allies' Fairy Book. L, [1916]. Illus by Arthur Rackham. (88) $50
One of 525. (91) $650
1st Ed Deluxe (88) $110, $300, $300, £280; (89) $300, £380; (90) £220; (91) $375

Allingham, Helen
— Happy England, as Painted by Helen Allingham. See: Huish, Marcus Bourne

Allingham, William, 1824-89
— In Fairyland.... L, 1870 [1869]. 1st Ed. Illus by Richard Doyle. 4to. (88) £260, £320; (89) £850; (90) £420
1st American Ed. NY: Appleton, 1870. Folio. (90) £140; (91) £220, £240
2d Ed. L, 1875. Folio. (88) £60; (89) £60, £250, £300; (90) $850; (91) £200
— Rhymes for the Young Folk. L: Cassell, [1887]. 4to. (91) £110
— Sixteen Poems. See: Cuala Press

Allioni, Carlo, 1725-1804
— Flora Pedemontana. Turin, 1785. 3 vols in 1. Folio. (88) FF17,000

Alliot, Hector
— Bibliography of Arizona. Los Angeles, 1914. One of 500. Inscr. (89) $275

**Allison, Antony Francis —&
Rogers, David Morrison**
— A Catalogue of Catholic Books in English Printed Abroad or Secretly in England, 1558-1649. Bognor Regis, 1956. 2 vols. 4to. (91) $70

Allman, George James
— A Monograph of the Gymnoblastic or Tubularian Hydroids. L: Ray Society, 1871-72. 2 parts in 2 vols. Folio. (88) £50; (91) £60

**Allom, Thomas —&
Reeve, Emma**
— Character and Costume in Turkey and Italy. Paris, [1839]. Folio. (88) £450

Allom, Thomas, 1804-72
— The Counties of Chester, Derby, Leicester, Lincoln, and Rutland. Illustrated. L, 1836. 4to. (88) £120
— Views in the Tyrol. L, [1836]. 4to. (88) £60, £120, £130; (89) £110, £140, £160; (90) $225, £90; (91) £170, £170

ALMANACS

— Westmorland, Cumberland, Durham, and Northumberland. See: Rose, Thomas

Allott, Robert, fl.1600
— Englands Parnassus. L, 1600. 1st Ed, Issue with dedication leaf to Mounson sgd "R.A.". Ed by Allott. 8vo. STC 378. Sykes-Huntington-Bishop-Bradley Martin copy. (90) $20,000
— Wits Theater of the Little World. [L] by J. R. for N. L., 1599. 1st Ed, Issue with dedication unsgd. 8vo. Houghton-Fleming copy. (89) $1,000

Almack, Edward, 1852-1917
— A Bibliography of the King's Book or Eikon Basilike. L, 1896. 4to. (91) £50
One of 150. (91) $50
— Fine Old Bindings. L, 1913. One of 200. Folio. (88) £240; (89) $300
One of 200, sgd by pbrs. (88) £360

Alman, Pseud.
— A Letter to John Barrow, Esq. F.R.S. on the late extraordinary and unexpected Hyperborean Discoveries. L: W. Pople for private perusal only, 1826. 8vo. Lansdowne copy with Lansdowne House stamp on tp. (88) £800

Almanacs
See also: Miniature Books; Partridge, John; Thomas, Robert Bailey
— Almanach des Muses.... Paris, [1792]. ("Almanach des Muses, 1793") 12mo. Contains 1st ptd in Book form of the Hymne des Marseillois. (89) £280
— Almanach Imperial, pour l'annee M.DCCC.XIII. Paris, [1813]. 8vo. (88) FF19,000
— Almanach pacifique ou l'ecole de la vertu tire des plus beaux endroits de l'Ecriture Sainte. Paris: chez Janet, [1793]. 32mo. (89) £700
— Almanach royal. [Paris, 1699]. 8vo. (88) $225
Paris, 1739. 12mo. (89) SM45,000
Paris, 1745. 12mo. (91) FF52,000
Paris, 1758. 12mo. (89) FF20,000
Paris, [1761]. 8vo. (89) £160; (91) £150
Paris, 1762. 12mo. (88) FF6,000
Paris, 1763. 8vo. (89) FF6,500
Paris, 1764. 8vo. (88) FF5,000
Paris, 1766. 8vo. (88) FF8,500
Paris, 1767. 8vo. (88) FF9,000
Paris, [1769]. 8vo. (89) £360
Paris: Le Breton, [1772]. 8vo. Martin copy. (90) $22,000
Paris, [1773]. 8vo. (89) FF15,000
Paris, [1775]. 8vo. (88) FF42,000
Paris, [1776]. 8vo. (88) FF19,000

ALMANACS

Paris, [1777]. 12mo. (88) FF8,500
Paris, [1778]. 8vo. (88) FF32,000
Paris, 1784. 8vo. (89) FF25,000
Paris, [1787]. 12mo. (90) £190
Paris, [1788]. 8vo. (89) £120
Paris, [1825]. 12mo. (91) £500
— Australian Almanack.... Sydney, 1830. ("Australian Almanack, for the Year of Our Lord 1830.") 8vo. (89) A$2,200
— Elliston's Hobart Town Almanack and... Van Diemen's Land Annual for 1837. Hobart Town, [1837]. 8vo. (90) A$1,100
— English Bijou Almanac. See: Miniature Books
— The Hobart Town Almanack..... Hobart Town, [1830]. ("The Hobart Town Almanack, for the Year 1830.") 24mo. (88) £320; (90) A$1,000
Hobart Town, [1832]. ("The Hobart Town Almanack for the Year 1832.") 24mo. (90) A$650
Hobart Town, [1833]. ("The Van Dieman's Land Anniversary and Hobart-Town Almanack....") 24mo. (90) A$500
— ("The Van Dieman's Land Annual and Hobart-Town Almanack....") 8vo. (90) A$550
Hobart Town, [1834]. 8vo. (90) A$500
Hobart Town, [1835]. ("Hobart Town Almanack and Van Dieman's Land Annual....") 8vo. (90) A$750
Hobart Town, [1836]. 8vo. (90) A$375
Hobart Town, [1838]. 8vo. (89) A$260; (90) A$1,100
— Koenigl. Gross-Britannischer und Churfuerstl. Braunschweig-Lueneburgscher Staats-Kalendere auf das Jahr 1803. Lauenburg: in der Berenbergschen Druckerey, [1802]. 8vo. Andrews-Bishop-Martin copy. (90) $3,250
— The London Almanack. See: Miniature Books
— Nautical Almanac and Astronomical Ephemeris for 1773.... L, 1771. Compiled by Nevil Maskelyne. 8vo. (89) $50
— Peacock's Polite Repository or Pocket Companion. L, [c.1802]. 12mo. (90) $120
— Le Petit Almanach de poche pour l'an de grace de notre Seigneur MDCCXLII. Liege: Everard Kings, [1742]. 95mm by 35mm. Doheny copy. (88) $1,100
— Poor Richard's Almanack, for the Year of our Lord 1784. NY: Morton & Horner, [1783]. 12mo. Drake 5913. (88) $80
— The Quebec Almanac, and British American Royal Kalendar. Quebec, [1835]. For 1836. 12mo. (91) $80
— Rider's British Merlin for MDCCXII. L, [1712]. 12mo. (88) $2,100
— Rider's British Merlin for the Year of Our Lord God 1754. L, 1754. 12mo. (90) $175;

AMERICAN BOOK PRICES CURRENT

(91) $250
— San Francisco Almanac. 1859. See: California
— Schloss's English Bijou Almanac. See: Miniature Books
— The Van Dieman's Land Pocket Almanack, for...MDCCCXXIV. Hobart Town: Andrew Bent, [1824]. 12mo. (90) A$3,200
— The Van Diemen's Land Almanack. Hobart Town: Henry Melville, 1833. ("The Van Diemen's Land Almanack for the Year 1833.") 8vo. (90) A$550

For 1834. Hobart Town: Henry Melville, [1834]. ("Van Diemen's Land Annual for the Year 1834.") 8vo. (90) A$650

For 1836. Hobart Town: Henry Melville, [1836]. ("Van Diemen's Land Annual for the Year 1836.") 8vo. (90) A$400

— Van Diemen's Land Royal Kalendar, and Almanack.... Launceston, 1847. ("Van Diemen's Land Royal Kalendar, and Almanack, 1847.") 12mo. Inscr by the compiler, James Wood. (90) A$280

For 1848. Launceston, 1848. ("Van Diemen's Land Royal Kalendar, and Almanack, 1848.") 12mo. (90) A$650

Launceston & Hobart Town, 1849. ("Van Diemen's Land Royal Kalendar, and Almanack, 1849.") 8vo. (90) A$280

— Walch's Tasmanian Almanack and Guide to Tasmania for 1863. Hobart Town, [1862]. 12mo. (90) A$220

— Walch's Tasmanian Almanack and Guide to Tasmania for 1867. Hobart Town, [1866]. 12mo. (90) A$240

— Walch's Tasmanian Guide Book: a Handbook of Information.... Hobart Town, 1871. 8vo. (90) A$300

— Wood's Tasmanian Almanack.... Launceston, 1856. ("Wood's Tasmanian Almanack for 1856.") For 1856. 12mo. (90) A$160

For 1857. Launceston & Hobart, [1857]. ("Wood's Tasmanian Almanack for 1857.") 8vo. (90) A$180

— AGUECHEEK, ANDREW. - The Universal American Almanack...1764. Phila., 1763. 16mo. (89) $700

— SHARP, ANTHONY. - The Continental Pocket Almanac...1781. Phila., [1780]. 32mo. (89) $250

Almeida, Christoval de
— Sermones Varios. Madrid: Mateo de Espinosa y Arteaga, 1675. 4to. (88) $50

Almosnino, Moses ben Baruch
— Regimiento de la vida.... Amst., [1729]. 4to. (89) £2,000

Alnander, Joannes Olaus
— Historiola artis typographicae in Svecia. Upsala, [1722]. 8vo. (88) £70

Alpenlandschaften...
— Alpenlandschaften. Ansichten aus der... Oesterreichen und Schweizerischen Gebirgswelt. Leipzig, [c.1890]. 2 vols. Folio. (88) DM500

Alphabet...
— Alphabet of Trades. [N.p., c.1830]. 115mm by 1,830mm. (89) £850

Alphabetum...
— Alphabetum brammhanicum, seu indostanum universitatis Kasi. Rome, 1772. Ed by Giovanni Cristoforo Amaduzzi. 8vo. (89) £55
— Alphabetum divini amoris. [Cologne: Ulrich Zel, c.1466-67]. 1st Ed. 4to. 28 leaves. Goff A-524. Sometimes attributed to Johannes Gerson or Johannes Nider. Goldwater-Abrams copy. (90) £7,200

Alphand, Jean Charles Adolphe
— Les Promenades de Paris.... Paris, 1867-73. 2 vols. Folio. (89) £290

Alpheraky, Sergius
— The Geese of Europe and Asia. L, 1905. 4to. (89) £180

Alphonsus de Spina
— Fortalitium fidei. Nuremberg: Anton Koberger, 10 Oct 1485. 4to. 160 leaves. Goff A-541. Doheny copy. (88) $3,000

Alpinus, Prospero, 1553-1617
— Historiae Aegyptis Naturalis.... Leiden: Gerard Potvliet, 1735. 2 vols. 4to. Blackmer copy. (90) £180

Alpinus, Prosperus, 1553-1617
— De medicina Aegyptiorum. Paris, 1645. 2 parts in 1 vol. 4to. (89) £200
  Leiden, 1745. ("Medicina Aegyptiorum accessit....") 4to. (91) $230
— De medicina methodica, libri tredecim.... Leiden, 1719. 4to. (91) $120
— De praesagienda vita, et morte aegrotantium libri septem.... Leiden, 1733. 4to. (88) $80
  Venice, 1735. 4to. (89) $50
— The Presages of Life and Death in Disease.... L, 1746. 2 vols. 8vo. (88) $80

Alpoym, Jose Fernandes Pinto
— Exame de Bombeiros. Madrid, 1748. 4to. (89) $550

Alsop, Richard
— Narrative of the Adventures and Sufferings of John R. Jewitt. NY, [c.1815]. 12mo. (90) $350

Alston, J. William
— Hints to Young Practitioners in the Study of Landscape Painting. L, [1801]. 8vo. (90) $80
  L, [1804]. 8vo. (89) $50, £60
  Library copy. (91) $50

Alt, Rudolf & Franz
— Album von Wien. Vienna: E. Hoelzel, [1873]. Oblong folio. (91) £750

Altamirano, Diego Francisco de
— Breve Noticia de las Missiones de Infieles, que tiene la Compania de Iesus de esta Provincia del Peru en las Provincias de los Moxos. See: Jesuits

Alter, J. Cecil
— James Bridger. Salt Lake City, [1925]. Ltd Ed, sgd. (88) $150; (89) $140, $190, $225; (91) $120, $140
  Sgd. (90) $130
  Enlarged Ed. Columbus, 1951. One of 1,000. (89) $190

Alternance
— Alternance. Paris, 1946. One of 340. 4to. (90) £900

Al'tman, Natan
— Lenin. Petersburg, 1920. (89) £250

Altmann, Johann, 1695-1758
— L'Etat et les delices de la Suisse. See: Etat...

Alto, Giovanni. See: Splendore....

Altschul Collection, Frank
— COOLIDGE, BERTHA. - A Catalogue of the Altschul Collection of George Meredith in the Yale University Library. [N.p.]: Pvtly ptd, 1931. One of 500. 4to. (91) $50

Alunno, Francesco, d.1556
— Le Ricchezze della lingua volgara.... Venice: Sons of Aldus Manutius, 1543. 4to. (88) $700
  Sold w.a.f. (90) $175
  2d Ed. Venice: Sons of Aldus Manutius, 1551. 4to. (89) £1,000

Alvares, Francisco, c.1465-1541
— The Prester John of the Indies. Cambr., 1961. 2 vols. (88) $50

ALVAREZ DE COLMENAR

Alvarez de Colmenar, Juan
— Les Delices de l'Espagne et du Portugal. Leiden: P. Vander Aa, 1707. 1st Ed. 5 vols in 4. (91) £750

Alverdes, Paul
— Schlupp der boese Hund. Potsdam: Ruetten & Loening, [c.1942]. Illus by Wolfgang Felten. (91) DM280

Alvord, Thomas G.
— Paul Bunyan, and Resinous Rhymes of the North Woods. See: Derrydale Press

Alyon, P. P.
— Cours de Botanique.... Paris, [1787]. 4 parts only. (90) £5,000

Alzate, Joseph Antonio
— Descripcion de las antiguedades de Xochicalco. Mexico, 1791. 4to. (89) $225

Amadis de Gaul
— The Fifth Book of the most Pleasant and Delectable History of Amadis de Gaule. L: T. J. for Andrew Kemble, 1664. 4to. (88) £3,000
— Le Sinqiesmi Livre d'Amadis de Gaule. Paris: Estienne Groulleau, 1550. 8vo. (90) £550
— Le Thresor des douze livres d'Amadis de Gaule. Paris: Jean Longis & Robert le Mangnier, 1559. 8vo. (91) £360

Amadon, Dean. See: Brown & Amadon

Amaduzzi, Giovanni Cristoforo, 1740-92. See: Venuti & Amaduzzi; Venuti & Amaduzzi

Amalteo, Cornelio, 1530-1603
— Protheus. Hoc poemmate auctor multo ante pugnam navalem ad Echinadas.... Venice: Onofri Farre, 1572. 4to. Blackmer copy. (90) £800

Amana Society
— A Selection of Fruits of America...lithographed and colored by J. and G. Prestele. Amana IA: Amana Society, 1861. 4to. Martin copy. (90) $9,000

Amantius, Bartholomaeus. See: Apianus & Amantius

Amat di San Filippo, Pietro, 1826-95 —& Others
— Studi Bibliografici e Biografici sulla Storia della Geografia in Italia. Rome, 1875. 4to. (91) $130

Amateur, An. See: Egan, Pierce; Specimens...

Amateur Angler. See: Marston, Edward

AMERICAN BOOK PRICES CURRENT

Ambassades...
— Ambassades memorables de la Compagnie des Indes Orientales des Provinces Unies, vers les Empereurs du Japon. See: Montanus, Arnoldus

Ambrose, Daniel Leib
— History of the Seventh Regiment, Illinois Volunteer Infantry. Springfield, 1868. 12mo. Coulter 5. (91) $175

Ambrosius, Saint, 340?-397
— De officiis. Milan: Christophorus Valdarfer, 7 Jan 1474. 4to. 128 leaves. Goff A-560. Heber-Broxbourne-Abrams copy. (90) £6,000
Milan: Uldericus Scinzenzeler for Philippus de Lavagnis, 17 Jan 1488. 4to. 140 leaves. Goff A-561. Kane-Newton-Doheny copy. (88) $2,400
— Expositio in evangelium S. Lucae. Augsburg: Anton Sorg, 1476. 1st Ed. Folio. 159 leaves. Goff A-554. Doheny copy. (88) $2,800
— Hexameron [De paradiso liber, & other works]. [Milan: Antonius Zarotus, not before 1475]. Folio. (89) £1,700

Amedeo, Luigi, of Savoy. See: Luigi Amedeo of Savoy

Ameilhon, Hubert Pascal, 1730-1811
— Eclaircissemens sur l'inscription grecque du monument trouve a Rosette. Paris: Baudouin, 1803. 4to. (90) £600

Amelot de la Houssaie, N.
— Histoire du gouvernement de Venise.... Amst.: Pierre Mortier, 1695. 4 parts in 3 vols. 12mo. (91) £2,600
— The History of the Government of Venice. L: H. C., 1677. 8vo. Library copy with numbers on title. (88) £352

American...
— American Academy of Arts and Sciences: Memoirs. Bost., 1785. Vol I. 4to. (89) $110
— The American Agriculturalist. [V.p.], 1843-1906. Vols 2-77. 4to & 8vo. (88) $230
— American and British Chronicle of War and Politics.... L, [1783]. 1st Ed. 8vo. (91) $450
— American Architecture of the Twentieth Century, NY, [1927]. Ed by Oliver Reagan. 7 parts in 5. Folio. (88) $80
— American Art Review. Bost., 1880-81. One of 500, each part with extra portfolio of proof plates on mtd india paper. First & second Series in 4 parts. (89) $800
Vol I. Bost., 1880. Folio. (89) $290
— The American Artisan and Tinner and House Furnisher. [Chicago, 1884-1906]. Vols 7-52. 4to. (88) $2,100
— American Book Prices Current. NY, 1925-

74. Indexes for 1916-70. Together, 10 vols. (89) $300
Indexes for 1955-83. NY, 1925-84. 12 vols. (90) $800
Vols 31-46. NY, 1925-40. (88) $160
Indexes for 1940-83. NY, 1946-84. 11 vols. (89) $750
Vols 59-83, lacking Vols 62-63. Together, 23 vols. NY, 1953-78. (90) $170
Index vols of 1955-60 & 1960-65. NY, 1961-68. (91) $110
Vols 72-76. NY, 1969-73. (88) $110
Vols 74-85. NY, 1971-79. (88) $350
Vols 76-82. NY, 1973-78. (88) $150
Index vol for 1965-70. NY, 1974. 2 vols. (88) $95; (90) $80, $275; (91) $70, $150
Vols 81-92. NY, 1975-86. 12 vols. (90) £280
Vols 83-93 & Index (1980-84). Together, 12 vols. NY, 1975-87. Martin copy. (90) $700
Index 1970-75. NY, 1976. (88) $300; (91) $90, $95
2 vols. (90) $110; (91) $90, $120
Vols 82-93 & 1970-75 Index. NY, 1976-87. (89) £450
Vols 83-93. NY, 1977-87. (91) £200
Vols 83-91. NY, 1978-86. (88) £190
Vols 84-88. NY, 1979-82. (88) $230, $350; (91) $170
Vols 84-92. Together, 9 vols. NY, 1979-86. (89) $500
Index for 1975-79. NY, 1980. 2 vols. (88) $250, $325; (90) $325; (91) $130
Vols 86-92. NY, 1980-86. 7 vols. (90) $400
Vols 89-93. NY, 1983-86. 5 vols. (90) $300
Index for 1979-83. NY, 1984. 2 vols. (88) $300; (90) $350, $400; (91) $200
Vol 90. NY, 1985. (91) $70
Vols 90-92. NY, 1985-86. (88) $275; (90) $160
Vols 90-94. NY, 1985-89. 5 vols. (90) $450
Vol 92. NY, 1986. (88) $80
Vol 93. NY, 1987. (91) $110
Vols 93-94. NY, 1987-89. (90) $160
Index for 1983-87. NY, 1988. 2 vols. (90) $400, $425; (91) $400
Vol 94. NY, 1989. (91) $100
Vols 94-95. NY, 1989-90. (91) $250
Vols 95-96. 2 vols. (91) £120
— American Journal of Science and Arts. New Haven, 1834. Vol 26, No 1. 8vo. Sgd by Charles Babbage. (89) $90
— American Journal of the Medical Sciences. Phila., 1841-47. New Series, Vols 1-13. (90) $90
— The American Mercury: A Monthly Review. NY, 1924. Vol I, No 1, One of 200 L.p. copies. Ed by H. L. Mencken. (88) $130
Vol I, No 1-Vol III, No 12. 12 issues. 8vo. (90) $90
— The American Monthly Microscopical Journal. NY & Wash., 1880-1902. Vols 1-23, but lacking Vol 22. 8vo. (88) $300
— American Museum, or Repository of Ancient and Modern Fugitive Pieces.... Phila.: Mathew Carey, 1787-91. Vols I-III, V, VII, IX-X. 8vo. (90) $550
— American Philosophical Society: Transactions. Phila., 1818-43. New Series, Vol 1. (91) $250
— The American Pioneer, a Monthly Periodical Devoted to the Objects of the Logan Historical Society. Cincinnati, 1842-43. Ed by John S. Williams. 2 vols (all pbd). 8vo. (88) $275
— American Poems, Selected and Original. Litchfield, [Conn.], 1793. Vol I (all pbd). 8vo. (91) £200
— The American Review: a Whig Journal. NY, 1845. Vol I, Nos 1-6. 8vo. (88) $400; (90) $425
Vol I, Jan-Dec. 8vo. (91) $250
— American Spectator: a Literary Newspaper. NY, 1932-34. Vol I, No 1. (89) $175
— American Statesmen: A Series of Biographies. Bost., 1898-1916. One of 500 L.p. sets. Ed by John T. Morse, Jr.. 40 vols. (90) $850
Bost., 1898-1900. Out of series L.p. set. 32 vols, 1st Series. 8vo. (88) $800
— American Turf Register and Sporting Magazine.
— ("Balt. & NY, 1829-37") Vols I-VIII. 8vo. (88) $375
— American Type Founders Company: American Specimen Book of Type Styles.... Jersey City, N.J. [1912]. 4to. Carl Purington Rollins' copy, sgd & with Supplements 1 & 2, each sgd by him. (89) $60

American, An. See: Child, Lydia Maria

American Bibliopolist
— The American Bibliopolist. NY, 1869-75. Vol I, No 1 to Vol VII, No 78, bound in 7 vols. (91) $90

American Game Fishes. See: Shields, George Oliver

American Geographical Society
— Catalogue of Maps of Hispanic America. NY, [1930-33]. 4 vols. (91) $200

American Magician
— The American Magician [originally The Boy Magician]. NY, 1909-12. Nos 1-39 (complete) in 1 vol. (90) $850

AMERICAN MUSEUM

American Museum, or Repository...
— American Museum, or Repository of Ancient and Modern Fugitive Pieces.... Phila.: Mathew Carey, 1787. Vol II, No 3. 8vo. First magazine ptg of the Constitution of the United States comprises pp. 276-84. (88) $3,000

American Revolution
— Advertisement. The Committee of Correspondence in New-York...proceeded to the Nomination of five Persons to go...General Congress at Philadelphia. See: Broadside

American Type Founders Company. See: History...

Amerique...
— L'Amerique du Nord pittoresque. Paris, 1880. Ed by Wm. Cullen Bryant; trans by B. H. Revoil. 4to. (90) $70

Amery, Leopold C. M. S.
— The Times History of the War in South Africa. L, 1900-9. 2d Ed. 7 vols, including Index. 8vo. (88) $110

Ames, Fisher
— An Oration on the Sublime Virtues of General George Washington. [Bost.: Young & Miles, 1800]. 8vo. (91) $70, $110 From the library of Robert Treat Paine with an 18th-cent document addressed to Paine. (88) $130

**Ames, Joseph, 1689-1759 —&
Herbert, William, 1718-95**
— Typographical Antiquities. L, [1810]-19. Ed by Thomas Frognall Dibdin. Vols I-IV (all pbd). 4to. (88) $80; (90) £500 Fleming copy. (89) £750

Ames, Richard
— A Farther Search after Claret. L, 1691. 4to. Wing A-2977. (89) £500
— The Last Search after Claret in Southwark.... L, 1691. ("The Search after Claret....") 4to. Wing A-2989. (89) £500 Wing A-2985. (89) £500
— A Search after Wit.... L, 1691. 4to. (89) £500

Amherst College
— Amherst Collegiate Magazine. Amherst, 1854-57. Vols I-IV in 2. 8vo. (88) $100

Amhurst, Nicholas, 1697-1742
— The Craftsman. L, 1731-37. 14 vols. 8vo. (91) £340
— Terrae-Filius; or, The Secret History of the University of Oxford. L, 1726. 8vo. (90) $80

AMERICAN BOOK PRICES CURRENT

Amici, Domenico
— Raccolta delle principali vedute di Roma. Rome, 1841. Oblong folio. (88) $300
— Raccolta delle vedute dei Contorni di Roma. Rome, 1847. Folio. (88) $375

Amicis, Edmondo de, 1846-1908
— Spain and the Spaniards. NY, 1875. Guadalquiver Ed, One of 600. (91) $225

Amico, Bernardino
— Trattato delle piante & immagini de sacri edifizi di Terra Santa. Florence: Pietro Cecconcelli, 1620. Plates engraved by Jacques Callot. 4to. (91) £1,000 Blackmer copy. (90) £6,000

Amillet, Paul
— La Maison de Danses. Paris, 1928. Unique copy for Henri Chanee with 3 orig drawings bound in, all inscr & a 2d vol containing 5 suites of the etchings. Illus by Almery Lobel-Riche. 8vo. (90) $3,200

Amiot, Joseph Marie
— Art Militaire des Chinois.... Paris: Didot, 1772. 4to. (88) FF7,500; (90) £750

Amis, Kingsley
— Lucky Jim. L, 1953. 1st Ed. Dedication copy, inscr to Philip Larkin. (90) £3,600

Amman, Johannes, 1707-41
— Stirpium rariorum in Imperio Rutheno sponte.... St. Petersburg, 1739. 4to. (88) £335

Amman, Jost, 1539-91
— Habitus praecipuorum populorum, tam virorum quam foeminarum singulari arte depicti. Trachtenbuch.... Nuremberg: Hans Weigel, 1577. Folio. (90) DM14,000
— Kuenstliche Wolgerissene New Figuren von allerlei Jag und Weidtwerck.... Frankfurt: Martin Lechler for Sigmund Feyerabends, 1582. 4to. Beaufort-Schwerdt-Schiff copy. (91) $13,500
— Kunst und Lehrbuechlein fuer die anfahenden Jungen. Frankfurt: S. Feyerabend, 1580. Part 1. 4to. (88) £8,000
— Kunstbuechlein. Frankfurt, 1599. 4to. (91) £550
— Neuw Jag und weydwerck Buch. Prague: Caspar Wussin, 1699. ("Adeliche Weydwercke, das ist, ausfuehrliche Beschreibung vom Jagen.") 4to. (90) £1,200

Ammianus Marcellinus
— Rerum Gestarum Qui de XXXI supersunt, Libri XVIII. Leiden: P. Vander Aa, 1693. Ed by Jacobo Gronovio. 4to. (88) $150, £60

Ammirato, Scipione, 1531-1601
— Gli Opuscoli. Florence: Marescotti, 1583. 1st Ed. 8vo. (91) LIt500,000

Ammonius the Grammarian
— Commentaria in librum peri Hermenias.... Venice: Aldus, June 1503. Bound with: John of Alexandria. In posteriora resolutoria Aristotelis commentaria. Venice: Aldus, Mar 1504. Folio. Spencer-Rylands copy. (88) £22,000

— In quinque voces Porphyrii commentarii. Venice: Zacharias Callierges for icolaus Blastos, 23 May 1500. Bound with: Simplicius of Cilicia. In Aristotelis categorica scholia Simplicii. Venice: for Nicolaus Blastos, 27 Oct 1499. Folio. 38 leaves, Goff A-565 & 168 leaves, Goff S535. Spencer-Rylands copy. (88) £65,000

Amoreux, Pierre Joseph
— Memoire sur les haies destinees a la cloture des pres.... Paris, 1787. 8vo. (91) $110

Amortti, Luigi
— De naturali et artificiali perspectiva: Bibliografia.... Florence, 1979. 8vo. Mar 1979 issue of Studi e Documenti de Architettura, No 9-10. (91) $120

Amory, Thomas, 1691?-1788
— The Life of John Buncle, Esq. L, 1756-66. 1st Ed. 2 vols. 8vo. (91) $150
L, 1770. 4 vols in 2. 12mo. (91) $140

Amos, William
— Minutes in Agriculture and Planting.... Bost., 1804. 4to. (91) £180

Amours...
— Les Amours d'Anne d'Autriche.... Cologne, 1730. 12mo. (89) $275
— Amours des dames illustres de nostre siecle. Cologne, 1700. 12mo. (89) £85

Ampere, Andre Marie, 1775-1836
— Recueil d'observations electro-dynamiques. Paris: Crochard, 1822. 8vo. (88) £700
— Theorie des phenomenes electro-dynamiques uniquement deduite de l'experience. Paris, 1826. 1st Separate Ed, Issue with pp. 85-92 correctly numbered. 4to. (88) £1,200

Ampudia, Pedro de
— El Cuidadano General Pedro de Ampudia ante el tribunal respetable de la Opinion Publica.... San Luis Potosi: Imprenta del Gobierno, 1846. 8vo. (88) $475

Amsden, Charles Avery
— Navaho Weaving: its Technic and History. Santa Ana, 1934. 8vo. (88) $200, $225; (89) $180; (90) $130, $200
Albuquerque, 1949. 8vo. (90) $175

Amsinck, Paul
— Tunbridge Wells, and its Neighbourhood. L, 1810. 4to. (88) £85; (89) £90

Amstel, Cornelis Ploos van. See: Ploos van Amstel, Cornelis

Amsterdam
— Le Guide ou nouvelle description d'Amsterdam, enseignant aux voyageurs, et aux negocians. Amst.: Paul de la Feuille, 1722. 12mo. (88) $170

Amtmann, Bernard
— Contributions to a Short-Title Catalogue of Canadiana. Montreal, 1971-73. 5 vols. 4to. (89) $150

Amuchastegui, Axel
— Some Birds and Mammals of South America. L, 1966. One of 250, sgd. Text by Carlos Selva Andrade. Folio. (91) £200, £200
Out-of-series copy. (89) £160
— Some Birds and Mammals of North America. L, 1971. One of 505. Text by Les Line. Folio. (91) £110, £320

Amundsen, Roald, 1872-1928
— The South Pole: an Account of the Norwegian Antarctic Expedition in the "Fram." L, 1912. 2 vols. (88) £75, £220, £260; (89) £280; (91) £400
2 vols. 8vo. (88) £260
L & NY, 1913. Trans by A. G. Chater. 2 vols. (91) $375
— "The North West Passage": Record of a Voyage of Exploration on the Ship "Gjoa...." NY, 1908. 2 vols. (88) £120; (89) £120; (91) $250, $275

Amusement...
— Amusement for Winter Evenings. L, [c.1800]. 12mo. (90) $4,000
— Amusement for Good Children. See: C, G. S.

Amyntor. See: Belknap, Jeremy

An de la Vie...
— Un An de la Vie d'une Jeune Fille, Roman Historique en XVII Chapitres, ecrits par son Confident.... Paris, 1824. Illus by E. Wattier. Folio. (91) $550

ANACREON

Anacreon, 572?-488? B.C.
— Odes...traduites en vers.... See: Fore-Edge Paintings
— Poems. See: Nonesuch Press
— 1554. - Odae. Paris: Estienne. Bound with: Anacreontis... odae. Latin translated by Elie Andre. 24 leaves. Paris: Thomas Richard, 1555. (88) $650
  Bound with: Anacreontis... odae. Latin translated by Elie Andre. 24 leaves. Paris: Thomas Richard, 1555. Dampier-Chatsworth copy. (90) $950
  4to. (90) £230
— 1785. - Odaria. Parma: Bodoni. 4to. (88) HF750
— 1791. - Parma: Bodoni Press. 8vo. (88) $140; (89) £95; (90) £190; (91) £120
— 1800. - Odes. L. 4to. Extra-illus with c.70 plates. (88) $375
— 1810. - Paris. 8vo. (89) £70
  Grau copy. (89) FF20,000

Anacreon, 572?-488? B.C. —& Others
— Oeuvres. Paphos, 1773. 8vo. (89) SM25,000
  Esmerian copy. (89) £850
  Paris: Le Boucher, 1773. 8vo. (89) FF24,000

Analectic...
— Analectic Magazine. Phila., Nov 1814. Vol IV. 8vo. Contains 1st magazine appearance of The Star-Spangled Banner, here called Defence of Fort M'Henry. (90) $250

Anales...
— Anales de Ciencias, Agricultura, Comercio y Artes, por Don Ramon de la Sagra. Havana, 1827-28. 12mo. (88) $225

Anania, Giovanni Lorenzo d'
— De natura daemonium libri III. Venice: Aldus, 1581. 8vo. (90) £900

Ananoff, Alexandre
— L'Oeuvre dessine de Jean-Honore Fragonard. Paris, 1961-68. One of 650. Vols I-III (of 4). 4to. (89) $425

Anbruch...
— Der Anbruch. Berlin, 1919-21. Vol II & 1st 2 Nos of Vol I. 14 nos bound in 1 vol. Folio. (91) $2,000

Anburey, Thomas
— Travels through the Interior Parts of America. L, 1789. 1st Ed. 2 vols. 8vo. (91) £400
  L, 1791. 2 vols. 8vo. (88) £110; (90) £160
— Voyages dans les parties interieures de l'Amerique. Paris, 1790. 2 vols. 8vo. (89) $225

AMERICAN BOOK PRICES CURRENT

Ancestor...
— The Ancestor: A Quarterly Review of County and Family History.... L, 1902-5. Vols I-XII (all pbd) with the 56-page Index. (88) $70
  Vols I-XII (all pbd). (89) $95

Ancient...
— The Ancient and Renowned History of Whittington and his Cat. L, 1812. Bound with: The Pleasures of Piety in Youth Exemplified. Edin., 1805. 12mo. (88) $90
— Ancient Spanish Ballads, Historical and Romantic. See: Lockhart, John Gibson

Ancillon, Charles
— Eunuchism Display'd, Describing all the different Sorts of Eunuchs.... L, 1718. 8vo. (88) £140; (91) £220
— Traitie des Eunuques.... [Berlin?], 1707. 12mo. (91) £60, £160

Ancona, Peolo d'
— La Miniature Fiorentina (Secoli XI-XVI). Florence, 1914. 2 vols. Folio. Doheny copy. (88) $1,700

Ancora, Gaetano d'
— Guide du voyageur pour les antiquites...de Pouzol. Naples, 1792. 8vo. (89) £150

Anczel, P. See: Celan, Paul

Anderdon, John Lavicount
— The River Dove... L, 1847. 8vo. K. D. Coleridge copy. (88) £35

Andersen, Hans Christian, 1805-75
— The Complete Andersen.... See: Limited Editions Club
— Contes Danois. Tours, 1853. 8vo. (89) $60
— Danish Fairy Legends and Tales. L, 1846. 8vo. (91) £200
— Danish Fairy Tales and Legends. L: Bliss, Sands and Co., 1897. Illus by W. Heath Robinson. 8vo. (91) £95
— Digte. Copenhagen, 1830. Bound with: Phantasier og Skizzer. Copenhagen, 1831. 12mo. (91) £750
— Eventyr og Historier. Copenhagen: Reitzel, 1862-63. 1st Collected Ed. 2 vols. 8vo. (88) $150
— Fairy Tales. L, 1872. Trans by H.L.D. Ward and Augusta Plesner; illus by E.V. Boyle. 4to. (91) $140
  L: Hodder & Stoughton, 1913. One of 100. Illus by W. Heath Robinson. 4to. (91) £190
  L, [1916]. Illus by Harry Clarke. 4to. (90) £60
  One of 125. (91) £850

Out-of-series copy, sgd by Harry Clarke. (91) $350
L, [1924]. Illus by Kay Nielsen. 4to. (88) $130, $250, £150, £2,400; (89) $130; (90) £110; (91) £85
One of 500. (88) £500; (89) $90, £2,100, £2,400; (90) $1,900; (91) $1,800, £550
With orig ink drawing, inscr by Nielsen to Margaret Ewans. (89) £2,400
NY, [1924]. 4to. (91) $200, $275
L, [1932]. Illus by Arthur Rackham. 4to. (88) $110, £110; (89) $80
One of 525. (89) £500; (90) £500; (91) $850
One of a few copies specially bound by Sangorski & Sutcliffe, containing a sgd ink & watercolor drawing. (90) £5,200
1st Ed Deluxe. L: Harrap, 1932. One of 525. 4to. (88) $600, $750, £900
Phila., [1932]. 4to. (88) $90, $90
L, 1935. ("Fairy Tales and Legends.") One of 150. Illus by Rex Whistler. (90) A$170
— Historier. Copenhagen, 1855. 16mo. (91) £95
— The Ice Maiden, and other Tales.... L: Richard Bentley, 1863. 1st Ed in English. Trans by Mrs. Bushby; illus by Pearson after J. B. Zwecker. 4to. (91) $130
1st American Ed. Phila., 1863. 4to. (88) $50; (91) $90
— The Improvisatore, or Life in Italy. L, 1845. 1st Ed in English. Trans by Mary Howitt. 2 vols. 8vo. (89) £20
2 vols in 1. 8vo. Kissner copy. (91) £80
— In Spain.... L: Bentley, 1864. Trans by Mrs. Bushby. 8vo. (91) $60
— Neue Maerchen. Hamburg: Kittler, 1846-48. Vol I trans by Dr. Le Petit; Vol II trans by H. Zeise. 2 vols. 8vo. (88) DM3,600
— Old Lukoie, Eventyr-Comedie i tre Acter. Copenhagen: Reitzel, 1850. 1st Ed. 12mo. (90) £340
— A Picture-Book without Pictures.... L: David Bogue, 1847. Trans by Meta Taylor from the German trans of De la Motte Fouque. 8vo. (90) $80
— A Poet's Bazaar. L, 1846. 1st Ed in English. 3 vols. 12mo. (91) $100
— La Reine des Neiges.... Paris: H. Piazza, [1911]. One of 500. Illus by Edmund Dulac. 4to. (88) $65
— Stories. L, 1911. ("Stories from Hans Andersen.") Illus by Edmund Dulac. 4to. (88) $130; (90) A$300; (91) $60, $80, $130
One of 100. (88) £450
One of 750. (88) $175, £100; (89) £400, £720; (90) £85, £250, £360, £420, £550; (91) $350, $1,400
— Stories and Fairy Tales. L, 1893. One of 300. Illus by Arthur Gaskin. 2 vols. 8vo. (88) £65, £150; (91) £220

— The True Story of My Life. L: Longmans, 1847. Trans by Mary Howitt. 12mo. (89) $110
— Wonderful Stories for Children. L: Chapman & Hall, 1846. Trans by Mary Howitt. 16mo. (91) £1,700

Andersen, Troels. See: Malevich, Kazimir Saverinovich

Anderson, Adam, 1692?-1765
— An Historical and Chronological Deduction of the Origin of Commerce.... L, 1764. 2 vols. 4to. (88) £400; (90) £460
L, 1787-89. 4 vols. 4to. (91) £95
Dublin, 1790. 6 vols. 8vo. ESTC 014947. (91) £420

Anderson, Aeneas, fl.1802
— A Narrative of the British Embassy to China. Dublin, 1796. 8vo. (91) $130

Anderson, Andrew A.
— Twenty-Five Years in a Waggon in the Gold Regions of Africa. L, 1887. 2 vols. 8vo. (89) R460

Anderson, David, Merchant
— Canada: or, a View of the Importance of the British American Colonies. L, 1814. 1st Ed. 8vo. (88) C$100

Anderson, Frank J.
— German Book Illustration Through 1500: Herbals Through 1500. NY: Abaris, [1983]. Part 1 only. 4to. Vol 90 of The Illustrated Bartsch. (91) $55

Anderson, Frederick Irving
— Adventures of the Infallible Godahl. NY, [1914]. (89) $90

Anderson, George William
— A Collection of Voyages round the World.... See: Cook, Capt. James
— A New, Authentic, and Complete Collection of Voyages round the World.... L: Alex. Hogg [1784-86]. 2d Ed. Folio. (88) $425; (89) A$2,000; (88) £720; (89) £280, £480, £800; (90) £240, £280, £850; (91) £240, £550, £700
L: Alex. Hogg, [c.1800]. 6 vols. 8vo. (91) $950

Anderson, James
— The New Practical Gardener. L: William Mackenzie, [1872-74]. 8vo. (89) £82; (91) £75

ANDERSON

Anderson, James, 1662-1728
— Selectus diplomatum et numismatum Scotiae thesaurus. Edin., 1739. Folio. (88) £150

Anderson, James, 1680?-1739
— The Constitutions of the Free-Masons.... L, 1723. 4to. (90) £750
  Cashiobury House copy. (91) £1,500
— Constitutions of the Antient Fraternity of Free and Accepted Masons. L, 1738. ("The New Book of Constitutions.") 4to. (91) £550
  Dublin, 1751. 4to. (91) £850
  L, 1756. 4to. (88) £70
  L, 1767. 2 vols, including the Appendix, 1776. 4to. (91) £700
  4to. (91) £900
  L, 1784. 4to. (88) £600; (89) £400; (91) £280
— The Constitutions of the Free-Masons.... See: Franklin Printing, Benjamin
— Royal Genealogies.... L, 1736. Folio. (88) $75

Anderson, James, 1739-1808
— The New Practical Gardener and Modern Horticulturist. L, [c.1875]. 4to. (91) £90, £110
— Observations on Slavery. Manchester, 1789. 8vo. (91) $200

Anderson, Johann, 1674-1743
— Histoire naturelle de l'Islande, du Groenland.... Paris: Sebastien Jorry, 1750. 2 vols. 8vo. (88) FF7,500

Anderson, John
— Political and Commercial Considerations Relative to the Malayan Peninsula.... Prince of Wales Island [Penang], 1824. 4to. (88) R9,500

Anderson, John, 1833-1900
— Anatomical and Zoological Researches... Two Expeditions to Western Yunnan.... L, 1878 [1879]. 2 vols. 4to. Martin copy. (90) $4,250

Anderson, John, b.1854
— The Unknown Turner. NY, 1926. One of 1,000. Folio. Inscr. (89) $100

Anderson, John Corbet
— To India and Back by the Cape. By a Traveller. Croydon, 1859. 4to. (91) £560

Anderson, John Henry
— The Fashionable Science of Parlour Magic.... L, 1843. 12mo. (90) $600
  L, [c.1850]]. 12mo. (90) $550

AMERICAN BOOK PRICES CURRENT

Anderson, Joseph, 1832-1916. See: Allen & Anderson

Anderson, Joseph, 1832-1916 —& Drummond, James, 1816-77
— Ancient Scottish Weapons. L, 1881. One of 500. 4to. (88) £65

Anderson, Lawrence Leslie
— The Art of the Silversmith in Mexico.... NY, 1941. 2 vols. Folio. (88) $175

Anderson, Poul
— The Fox, the Dog, and the Griffin. Garden City, [1966]. (91) $100
— Three Hearts and Three Lions. Garden City, 1961. (89) $130

Anderson, Poul —& Dickson, Gordon
— Earthman's Burden. NY: Gnome Press, [1957]. (88) $70

Anderson, Sherwood, 1876-1941
— Alice and The Lost Novel. L, 1929. One of 530. (90) $60; (91) $80
— Dark Laughter. NY, 1925. One of 350. (89) $90
  With etched port of Anderson by Richard Hood, sgd by both. (91) $225
— Marching Men. L, 1917. 1st Ed. Inscr to Alice Henderson. (89) $550
— Nearer the Grass Roots. See: Grabhorn Printing
— Notebook. NY, 1926. 1st Ed, One of 225, sgd. (91) $80
— Tar: a Midwest Childhood. NY, 1926. 1st Ed, one of 350 L.p. copies. (89) $55
— The Triumph of the Egg. NY, 1921. 1st Ed, 1st Issue. (89) $375
— Winesburg, Ohio. NY, 1919. 1st Ed, 1st Ptg. Doheny copy. (89) $6,500
  Ptg not stated. Inscr. (89) $240
  Sgd. (91) $400

Anderson, William, 1805-66
— The Scottish Nation. Edin., 1870. 3 vols. 4to. (91) $110

Anderson, William, 1842-1900
— The Pictorial Arts of Japan.... Bost., 1886. Artist Proof copy. 4 parts. Folio. (89) $300
  L, 1886. Folio. (88) £180

Anderson, Winslow
— Mineral Springs and Health Resorts of California.... San Francisco, 1892. 8vo. (91) $65

Andersson, Charles John, 1827-67
— Lake Ngami, or Explorations and Discoveries.... L, 1856. 8vo. (88) £50; (89) £80, R400
  1st American Ed. NY, 1857. 8vo. (91) $55, $100
— Notes of Travel in South Africa. L, 1875. 8vo. (89) R950

Andersson, Johan Gunnar. See: Nordenskiold & Andersson

Andrada, Jacinto Freire de
— The Life of Dom John de Castro, the Fourth Vice-Roy of India. See: Freire de Andrada, Jacinto

Andrade Library, Jose Maria
— [Sale Catalogue] Catalogue de la riche bibliotheque.... Leipzig & Paris, 1869. 8vo. (89) $60

Andrade, Manoel Carlos de
— Luz da liberal e nobre arte da cavallaria. Lisbon, 1790. 2 parts in 1 vol. Folio. (88) £950, £2,000

Andrae, Walter
— Coloured Ceramics from Ashur. L, 1925. Folio. (89) $120

Andrasy, Mano
— Hazai vadaszatok es sport Magyarorszagon. Budapest: Armin Geibel, 1857. Folio. Schiff copy. (91) $6,500

Andrasy, Mano, Count —& Others
— Les Chasses et le sport en Hongrie. Pest, [1857]. Folio. (90) £3,000; (91) £4,500 Schiff copy. (91) $11,000

Andre, Albert —& Elder, Marc
— L'Atelier de Renoir. Paris, 1931. One of 500. 2 vols. Folio. (91) $750

Andre, Jacqueline
— La Creation et l'histoire d'Adam et d'Eve. Paris, 1926. One of 1,500. Illus by Henri Cote. Folio. Inscr by Dorothy Canfield Fisher to Dorothy Lathrop. (91) $130

Andre, John, 1751-80
[-] Andreana. Containing the Trial, Execution and various Matters Connected with the History of Major John Andre.... Phila., 1865. One of 100. 8vo. (91) $65
— Andre's Journal. Bost., 1903. Ed by Henry Cabot Lodge, One of 487. 2 vols. 4to. (88) $110; (91) $100
  Ed by Henry Cabot Lodge. Extra-illus with 9 ports, maps, & various illusts. (91) $4,000

Andre, Peter. See: Chapman & Andre

Andreae, Johannes
— Super arboribus consanguinitatis, affinitatis.... Nuremberg: Friedrich Creussner, [not after 1476]. ("Lectura arboris diversis....") Folio. 10 leaves. Goff A-602. Broxbourne-Abrams copy. (90) £1,400
  Additional contemp diagram in brown ink bound in. 10 leaves. Goff A-602. Huth-Hofman-Abrams copy. (90) £2,400

Andreas, Alfred Theodore, 1839-1900
— Illustrated Historical Atlas of the State of Iowa. Chicago, 1875. Folio. (88) $750

Andreas, Johannes Bononiensis
— Novella super tertio decretalium. [Trino: Giovanni Giolito de' Ferrari, 1512]. Folio. (89) $400
— Quaestiones mercuriales super regulis iuris. [Strassburg: Heinrich Eggestein], 1475. Folio. 129 (of 130) leaves; lacking final blank. Goff A-635. (90) £4,500; (91) $11,000

Andree, R. John
— A Vocabulary in Six Languages.... L, 1725. 1st Ed. 8vo. (89) £140

Andreini, Giovanni Batista
— L'Adamo, sacra rapresentatione. Milan, 1613. 4to. (88) £900

Andrelinus, Publius Faustus
— Epistolae proverbiales & morales. Strassburg: M. Schurer, 1508. 4to. (91) $225

Andreossi, Antoine Francois, 1761-1828
— Constantinople et le Bosphore de Thrace. Paris, 1828. 2 vols. including Atlas. 8vo & folio. (90) £2,200
— Histoire du canal du Midi, ou canal de Languedoc. Paris, 1804. 2 vols. 4to. (90) £400
  Inscr. (91) £200

Andrewes, Lancelot, 1555-1626
— A Manual of the Private Devotions. L, 1648. Bound with: Andrewes. A Manual of Directions for the Sick. L, 1648. 24mo. Penrose-Fleming copy. (89) $600
— The Pattern of Catechistical Doctrine at Large.... L, 1650. "2d" Ed. Folio. (88) £70; (90) £70

Andrews, Frederick Henry
— Wall Paintings from Ancient Shrines in Central Asia. L, 1948. 2 vols. 4to. (90) $500; (91) £550
  Plate vol only. 4to. (88) £75

ANDREWS

Andrews, Henry C., fl.1799-1828
— The Botanist's Repository, for New, and Rare Plants. L, 1797-[1813?]. 10 vols. 4to. (90) £12,000; (91) £1,150
— Coloured Engravings of Heaths. L, [1794]-1802-9. Vols I-III only. (88) £3,400
— Geraniums: or a Monograph of the Genus Geranium. L, 1805. 1 vol (of 2) only. 4to. (91) £1,800
Sold w.a.f. (89) £2,500
Vol I (of 2). 4to. (88) £1,250
— The Heathery, or a Monograph of the Genus Erica. L, 1804-7. Vols I-IV. (90) £1,000
L, 1804-6. Vols I-V (of 6). 8vo. (90) £850
L, 1845. 6 vols. 8vo. (89) £2,000

Andrews, Israel de Wolf
— Report on the Trade and Commerce of the British North American Colonies.... Wash., 1853. Map vol only. 8vo. Senate version. (90) $70

Andrews, James, 1801?-76
— Flora's Gems or the Treasures of the Parterre. L, [1830]. Folio. (90) $2,000, £580
— Lessons in Flower Painting. L, [c.1835]. Oblong 4to. (88) £200
— The Parterre, or Beauties of Flora. L, 1842. Folio. (89) £900; (90) £1,700

Andrews, John —&
Dury, Andrew
— A Map of the Country Sixty-Five Miles round London. L, [1774-77]. Folio. (90) £800
L, [1777-78]. Folio. (90) £800
— A Topographical Map of Hartford-Shire. L, [1766]. Folio. (90) £550
— A Topographical Map of Wiltshire. L, 1773. Folio. (91) £360

Andrews, John, Geographer
— A Collection of Plans of the most Capital Cities of Every Empire...in Europe. L, [1792]. 4to. (91) $1,600

Andrews, John, 1736-1809
— History of the War with America, France, Spain, and Holland.... L, 1785-86. 4 vols. 8vo. (88) £180; (91) £650

Andrews, Lorrin, 1795-1868
— A Dictionary of the Hawaiian Language.... Honolulu, 1865. 8vo. (88) $200; (90) $100
— Grammar of the Hawaiian Language. Honolulu: Mission Press, 1854. (88) $130; (91) £80

AMERICAN BOOK PRICES CURRENT

Andrews, Mottram
— A Series of Views in Turkey and the Crimea. L, 1856. Folio. (88) £180
Kissner copy. (91) £750

Andrews, Roy Chapman
— The New Conquest of Central Asia.... NY, 1932. Inscr; also sgd by Walter Granger. (88) $180; (89) $110

Andrews, William Loring, 1837-1920
— An English XIX Century Sportsman, Bibliopole, and Binder of Angling Books. NY, 1906. One of 125. (88) £110; (90) $225
— Gossip about Book-Collecting. NY, 1900. One of 125. 2 vols. 8vo. (88) $65
— The Heavenly Jerusalem: a Mediaeval Song.... NY, 1908. One of 5 on imperial japan. (89) $210
— The Iconography of the Battery and Castle Garden. NY, 1901. One of 135. (90) $100
— James Lyne's Survey.... NY, 1900. One of 170. 8vo. (89) $80
— Jean Grolier de Servier, Viscount d'Aguisy: Some Account of...his Famous Library. NY, 1892. One of 140. 8vo. (91) $1,200
— The Old Booksellers of New York.... NY: Pvtly ptd, 1895. One of 142. Plates engraved by E. D. French. 8vo. (91) $70
— Roger Payne and his Art.... NY, 1892. One of 120. 8vo. (88) $250; (89) $300
— Sextodecimos et infra. NY, 1899. One of 140. 8vo. (88) $95; (91) $275

Andries, Jodocus
— Perpetua crux, sive Passio Iesu Chriisti.... Antwerp: Cornelius Woons, 1649. Bound with: Altera perpetua crux. Antwerp, 1649. And: Perpetuus gladius reginae martyrum. Antwerp, 1650. And: Necessaria ad salutem scientia. Antwerp, 1654. 12mo. (90) $2,100

Andriessen, Andreas
— Plegtige injulding van zyne doorlugtigste Hoogheidt Willem...Prinse van Oranje en Nassau...als Markgraaf van Vere. See: Huet, Daniel Theodore

Androuet du Cerceau, Jacques, fl.1549-84
— De architectura.... Paris, 1559. 1st Ed. Folio. (90) £220
— French Chateaux and Gardens in the XVIth Century.... L, 1909. Folio. (91) $110
— Livre d'Architecture. Paris, 1582. Folio. (90) £150
Paris, 1615. Folio. (90) £140
— Petites Habitations ou logis domestique. Paris, [c.1540-45]. Folio. (89) £920
— Le Premier [Second] Volume des plus excellents bastiments de France. Paris, 1607. 2d Ed. 2 vols in 1. Folio. (91) £2,700

— Le Premier Volume des plus excellents bastiments de France. Paris, 1576-79. 1st Ed. 2 vols in 1. Folio. (88) FF15,000

Andry de Boisregard, Nicolas
— L'Orthopedie ou l'art de prevenir et de corriger dans les enfans.... Paris, 1741. 2 vols. 12mo. (89) £2,000

Andry, Nicolas, 1658-1742
— An Account of the Breeding of Worms in Human Bodies. L, 1701. 8vo. (89) £90

Anecdotes...
— Anecdotes chinoises, japonoises, siamoises, tonquinoises, &c., dans lesquelles on s'est attache principalement aux moeurs, usages, coutumes & religions de ces differens peuples de l'Asie. Paris: Vincent 1774. Compiled by J. Castillon. 8vo. Phillipps-Robinson copy. (89) £750

Anesaki, Masaharu
— Buddhist Art in its Relation to Buddhist Ideals.... Bost. & NY, 1915. 1st Ed. 4to. (90) $50

Anet, Claude
— Notes sur l'amour. Paris: G. Cress, [1922]. Illus by Pierre Bonnard. 4to. (89) $150 With plates in 2 states. (88) FF2,000

Angas, George French, 1822-86
— Australia, a Popular Account of its Physical Features.... L, [1855]. 12mo. (89) A$140
— The Kafirs Illustrated.... L, 1849. Folio. (90) A$8,000
— The New Zealanders Illustrated. L, 1847. Folio. (88) £3,800; (90) £2,600; (91) £3,600 L, 1966. Folio. Facsimile of the 1847 Ed. (90) A$225
— A Ramble in Malta and Sicily. L, 1842. 8vo. (91) £300
— Savage Life and Scenes in Australia and New Zealand. L, 1847. 2 vols. 8vo. (88) £120; (91) £180 2 vols. Folio. (89) A$320
— South Australia Illustrated. L, 1847. Folio. (89) £14,000; (91) £3,000, £6,000 Sydney, 1967. Ltd Ed. Folio. Facsimile of the 1847 Ed. (89) A$440; (90) A$375

Angelis, Paulus de
— Basilicae S. Mariae majoris.... Rome, 1621. Folio. Kissner copy. (91) £850

Angell, Samuel, 1800-66 — & Evans, Thomas
— Sculptured Metopes Discovered amongst the Ruins of the Temples of the Ancient City of Selinus.... L, 1826. Folio. Blackmer copy. (90) £450

Angelo, Domenico, 1717?-1802
— L'Ecole des Armes, avec l'explication generale.... L, [1763]. Oblong folio. (88) £980; (89) £1,300; (91) $1,700
— The School of Fencing.... L, 1765. 1st Ed. Oblong folio. (91) £750 L, 1787. Oblong 8vo. (88) £260, £300, £320; (89) £400 Facsimile of the 1765 Ed. L, 1968. Oblong folio. (88) $130

Angelo, Henry
— Angelo's Pic Nic; or, Table Talk. L, 1834. Illus by George Cruikshank. 8vo. (88) $80

Angelo, Michael. See: Johnson, Richard

Angelo, Valenti
— Valenti Angelo: Author + Illustrator + Printer: A Checklist.... Bronxville: Press of Valenti Angelo, 1970. One of 55. (91) $225
— Valenti Angelo: Author, Illustrator, Printer. San Francisco: Book Club of Calif., 1976. One of 400. Folio. (88) $225, $325; (89) $225, $275, $300, $325; (90) $190, $300; (91) $170, $250

Angelus a Sancto Josepho
— Gazophylacium linguae persarum. See: Labrosse, Joseph

Angelus de Clavasio, 1411-95?
— Summa angelica de casibus conscientiae. Chivasso: Jacobinus Suigus, de Suico, 13 May 1486. 1st Ed. 363 leaves (of 388). 4to. 388 leaves. Goff A-713. (88) $550 3d Ed. Venice: Nicolaus de Frankfordia, 30 Oct 1487. 4to. 414 leaves. Goff A-715. Dunn-Doheny copy. (88) $2,400 Strassburg: Martin Flach, 1 Dec 1491. Folio. 369 (of 370) leaves; lacking last blank. Goff A-721. (89) £1,000 Nuremberg: Anton Koberger, 10 Feb 1492. Folio. 312 leaves. Goff A-722. (89) $3,600 Venice: Paganinus de Paganinis, 7 June 1499. 8vo. 476 leaves. Goff A-729. (88) DM950 Lacking initial blank, g3-9 & colophon leaf. Goff A-729. (90) $650

Angelus, Johannes
— Astrolabium planum. Augsburg: Erhard Ratdolt, 1488. 4to. 175 (of 176) leaves. Goff A-711. (89) £6,000 Venice: Johannes Emericus de Spira for Lucantonio Giunta, 9 June 1494. 4to. 173 (of 176) leaves. Goff A-711. (91) £950 174 (of 176) leaves; lacking final blanks. Goff A-711. (90) $3,000
— Esoptron astroligikon. Astrologicall Opticks. L: for John Allen & R. Moon, [1655]. 8vo. Wing E-737. (91) £360

ANGHIERA

Anghiera, Pietro Martire d'. See: Martyr, Peter

Angiolieri, Cecco
— Sonette. Verona: Officina Bodoni, 1944. One of 165. (90) £320

Angler, An. See: Davy, Sir Humphry

Anglerius, Petrus Martyr. See: Martyr, Peter

Angler's...
— The Angler's Note-Book and Naturalist's Record. L, 1884. Ed by Thomas Satchell. 8vo. (91) $60
— The Angler's Pocket-Book, or Complete English Angler.... L, 1805. 3d Ed. 8vo. (89) A$200

Anglers' Club of New York
— The Anglers' Club Story. Our First Fifty Years, 1906-1956. NY: Pvtly ptd, 1956. One of 750. (88) $110
4to. (89) $85, $90; (90) $150
— The Best of the Anglers' Club Bulletin 1920-1972. NY, 1972. One of 1,000. (90) $100

Anglo-Saxon...
— An Anglo-Saxon Gnomic Poem. San Francisco: Grabhorn-Hoyem, 1968. One of 400. (88) £300

Angstrom, Ander Jonas
— Recherches sur le spectre solaire. Upsala, 1868. 2 vols, including Atlas. 4to & oblong folio. (90) £850

Anguillara, Maria Madalena
— Vita di Santa Francesca Romana.... Rome: heirs of Corbelletti, 1691. 4to. (91) £2,500

Angus, William, 1752-1821
— The Seats of the Nobility and Gentry.... L, 1787. Oblong 4to. (88) $200, £120; (89) $200, £130, £170, £190, £200, £220, £320, HF750; (90) $290, $280; (91) $240, £220, £260

Aniante, Antonio
— Les Merveilleux Voyages de Marco Polo. Cannes: Atelier a'Art Ryp, 1963. One of 5 with an orig gouache and a suite in green; lacking the hors-texte encadre. Illus by Jean Gradassi. Folio. (88) FF4,500

Anianus, Magister
— Computus cum commento.... Lyons: Claude Nourry, 1504. 4to. (90) £460

Animal...
— Animal A.B.C. A Child's Visit to the Zoo. Chicago, 1905. 1st Ed. Intro by L. Frank Baum. 16mo. Baughman 72c. (91) $60

AMERICAN BOOK PRICES CURRENT

Anker, Jean Thore Hojer Jensen
— Bird Books and Bird Art. Copenhagen, 1938. 4to. (88) $400; (90) $450; (91) $425

Anley, Charlotte
— The Prisoners of Australia. L, 1841. 12mo. (89) A$230

Annabel, Russell
— Tales of a Big Game Guide. See: Derrydale Press

Annales...
— Annales de l'Industrie Nationale et Etrangere, ou Mercure Technologique. Paris, 1820-26. Vols 1-22 & Index. 8vo. (88) $700
— Annales des Arts et Manufacturers.... Paris, 1800-15. Vols 1-56. 8vo. (88) $850
— Annales des voyages, de la geographie et de l'histoire. Paris, 1808-13. Ed by Conrad Malte-Brun. Vols 1-20 (of 24). 8vo. (90) $140
— Annales d'horticulture et de botanique, ou flore des jardins du Royaume des Pays-Bas.... Leiden, 1858-62. 5 vols. 8vo. (89) £650
— Annales romantiques.... Paris, 1825-36. 10 vols. 16mo. Martin copy. (90) FF4,200

Annales de Chimie
— Annales de Chimie; ou Recueil de Memoires Concernant la Chimie et les Arts qui en dependent. Paris, 1789-1815. Vols I-XVIV. 8vo. (88) $400

Annals...
— Annals of Medical History. NY, 1917-42. First Series, Vols I-X; New Series, Vols I-X; Third Series, Vols I-IV [all pbd]. Index vol. Together, 25 vols. (89) $1,100
NY, 1927-37. Nos 33-90 [that is, Vol 9, No 1 to New Series Vol 9, No 2]. 4to. (88) $120
— The Annals of Sporting and Fancy Gazette. L, 1822-28. 13 vols. 8vo. (88) $2,400; (90) $2,000, £3,000; (91) £3,300
13 vols (all pbd). 8vo. Lacking final number. (91) $1,200
Vols 5-10. L, 1824-26. 8vo. (88) £240

Annals of Electricity...
— Annals of Electricity, Magnetism, and Chemistry. L 1837-43. Vols I-X. 8vo. (88) $750

Annan, Thomas
— The Old Country Houses of the Old Glasgow Gentry. Glasgow, 1870. One of 225. 4to. (88) $550
— Photographic Views of Loch Katrine.... Glasgow, 1877. Descriptive notes by James M. Gale. Oblong 4to. (88) $1,500

Anne, Consort of William IV, Prince of Orange
[-] Convoi-funebre de son altesse Anne, Princess Royale de la Grande Bretagne.... The Hague, 1761. With 16 plates. Bound with: Description de la chambre et lit de parade sur lequel le corps de Son Altesse Royale Anne.... The Hague, 1759. With 4 plates. Folio. (89) £250

Anne, Queen of England & Ireland
— The Life and Reign of...Queen Anne.... L, 1738. 8vo. (91) £85

Anne, Saint
[-] Hec est quedam rara et ideo cara legenda de sanctam Anna.... Strassburg: Kysteler, 1501. 4to. (90) £660
[-] L'Histoire de Madame Saincte Anne.... Antwerp: widow of Heyndrick Peeterson van Biddelburch, [c.1555]. 8vo. Firmin-Didot copy. (91) £2,600

Annenberg, Maurice
— Type Foundries of America and their Catalogs. Balt., 1975. One of 500. 4to. (91) $300

Annesley, George, Viscount Valentia & Earl of Mountmorris
— Voyages and Travels to India, Ceylon.... L, 1809. 3 vols. 4to. (88) £450, R1,000; (90) £420, £800; (91) £900
2d Ed. L, 1811. 4 vols. including Atlas. 8vo & 4to. (89) £160
Atlas vol only. 4to. (88) £100; (89) £160; (90) £280

Annesley, James
— Memoirs of an Unfortunate Young Nobleman, Return'd from a Thirteen Years Slavery in America where he had been sent by the Wicked Contrivances of his Cruel Uncle. L, 1743. 2 vols. 12mo. (88) $250

Annual...
— The Annual Register; or, a View of the History, Politics.... L, 1758-1852. Vols 1-94, lacking Vols 55-61, & 2 vols of Indexes covering 1758-92. Together, 90 vols. 8vo. Sold w.a.f. (88) £280
For 1758-97. L, 1791-85-1800. 39 vols. 8vo. (88) £1,200

Anonymous
— A Journal of a Voyage Round the World, in his Majesty's Ship Endeavour.... See: Cook, Capt. James

Anouilh, Jean
— Le Bal des voleurs. [Paris, 1952]. One of 40 with an additional suite of plates. Illus by T. Schmied after R. Peynet. 4to. (90) $90

Anquetil, Louis Pierre
— A Summary of Universal History. L, 1800. 9 vols. 8vo. (91) £260

Ansaldo, Matheo
— Empleos Apostolicos, y religiosas virtudes del fervoroso P. Joseph Xavier de Molina.... [Mexico, 1743]. 4to. Doheny copy. (88) $850

Ansei.....
— Ansei kemmon-shi. [Japan, c.1858]. Illus by Utagawa Kuniyoshi. 3 vols stitched together. 8vo. Sorimachi 607. (90) £650

Anselm, Saint, 1033-1109
— Opera. Nuremberg: Caspar Hochfeder, 27 Mar 1491. Folio. 182 leaves. Goff A-759. (91) $14,000
— Theologia. Rome, 1688-89. 2 vols. Folio. (88) $150

Anselme de Sainte-Marie, Pere
— Le Palais de l'honneur, contenant les genealogies historiques.... Paris, 1664. 4to. (90) $300

Anselme de Sainte-Marie, Pere —& Du Fourney, Honore Caille, Sieur
— Histoire genealogique et chronologique de la maison royale de France.... Paris, 1726-33. 9 vols. Folio. (88) FF26,000
3d Ed. 9 vols. Folio. (88) £380

Anslijn, Nicholaas, 1777-1838
— Abbeeldingen van Nederlandsche Dieren. Leiden: D. du Mortier en Zoon, 1838. 2 vols. 8vo. Martin copy. (90) $1,500

Anson, George, 1697-1762
— Des Herrn Admirals, Lord Ansons Resise um die Welt. See: Walter, Richard
— Viaggio attorno al mondo.... Livorno, 1756. 4to. (89) $175
— Voyage autour du monde. Geneva, 1750. 4to. (90) $300; (91) $150
Amst. & Leipzig, 1751. 4to. (91) £380
— A Voyage Round the World.... L, 1748. 1st Ed. 2 vols. 4to. (89) £340
4to. (88) £160; (89) £350, £600, £190, £200, £340, £650, £1,700; (90) £220, £220, £250, £340, £360, £600; (91) £600, $1,200, $1,500, £300, £420, £600, £650
Richard Rawlinson's copy. (90) £600
4th Ed. 4to. (91) $110
L, 1749. 4to. (88) £450; (90) $475
L, 1753. 4to. (88) £60
9th Ed. L, 1756. 4to. (88) £320
12th Ed. L, 1767. 4to. (88) £300; (89) £100, £150

ANSPACH

Anspach, Elizabeth Fitzhardinge, Margravine of, 1750-1828
— Modern Anecdote of the Ancient Family of the Kinkvervankotsdarsprankengotchderns: A Tale for Christmas, 1779. L: Pvtly ptd, [1779?]. 8vo. (88) $85

Ansted, David T.
— The Ionian Islands in the Year 1863. L, 1863. 8vo. (91) £150
Blackmer copy. (90) £300; (91) £200

Anstis, John, 1669-1744
— The Register of the Most Noble Order of the Garter. L, 1724. 2 vols. Folio. (91) $175

Anstruther, George Elliot
— The Bindings of To-morrow. L, 1902. One of 500. 4to. (89) $375; (90) £340; (91) £275

Answer...
— Answer of the Company of Royal Adventurers of England. See: Company of Royal Adventurers
— An Answer to a Pamphlet, entitled Taxation no Tyranny. L, 1775. 8vo. (91) $275
— An Answer to the late K. James's Last Declaration. See: Defoe, Daniel

Antes, Horst
— Radierungen zu 17 Gedichten von Cesare Pavese. Munich: Galerie Stangl, [1964-65]. One of 21. Folio. (91) DM6,200

Antes, John
— Observations on the Manners and Customs of the Egyptians. L: John Stockdale, 1800. 4to. Blackmer copy. (90) £140

Anthing, Friedrich
— Collection de Cent Silhouettes de Personnes illustres et celebres dessinees d'apres les originaux. Gotha: J. Perthes, 1793. (91) $3,800

Anthologie...
— Anthologie poetique. Paris, 1943. One of 999. 4to. (88) £160

Anthonisz, Cornelis
— The Safeguarde of Saylers, or Great Rutter.... L, 1671. 4to. (91) £650

Anthony, Edgar Waterman
— A History of Mosaics. Bost., [1935]. One of 50, inscr. (91) $80

Anthony, Gordon
— Ballet: Camera Studies.... L, 1937. 4to. (89) $60
— Russian Ballet: Camera Studies. L, 1939. 4to. (89) £60

AMERICAN BOOK PRICES CURRENT

Antigonus, Carystius
— Historion paradoxeon synagoge.... Leipzig, 1791. 4to. (88) $175

Antiguedades...
— Antiguedades Mexicanas.... Mexico, 1892. Plate vol only. Folio. (88) £700

Anti-Jacobin...
— The Anti-Jacobin; or, Weekly Examiner. L, 1797-98. Nos 1-36 (all pbd). 4to. (91) £160

Antiphoner
— Antiphonarium de tempore et de sanctis... secundum usum Cisterciensis ordinis. Troyes: Nicole Paris, 1545. 2 parts in 1 vol. Folio. (90) $1,500

Antique...
— Antique Gems from the Greek and Latin. Phila., [1901-2]. One of 12 on japan with duplicate impresssions of the vignette illusts finished in watercolors. 13 vols. (88) $1,200

Antiquites...
— Antiquites mexicaines, relation des trois expeditions du Capitaine Dupaix. Paris, 1834. 2 parts text in 1 vol plus Atlas. Folio. (90) £2,800; (91) £2,000, £4,200

Antoine, F.
— Die Coniferen nach Lambert, Loudon und anderen. Vienna, 1840-41. 11 parts. Folio. (88) £650

Antommarchi, F.
— Planches anatomiques du corps humain.... Paris, [c.1825]. Atlas vol only. Folio. (89) £850

Antonini, Annibale, 1702-55
— Dizionario Italiano, Latino e Francese.... Lyons, 1770. 2 vols. 4to. (91) $80

Antonini, Carlo
— Manuale de vari ornamenti tratti dalle fabbriche e trammenti antichi. Rome, 1781. 2 vols. Folio. Kissner copy. (91) £160
2 vols in 1. Folio. Earle-Kissner copy. (91) £750
Rome, 1781-90. Vol I only. (89) $150
Vols II & IV in 1 vol. (91) £800

Antoninus, Brother. See: Psalms & Psalters

Antoninus, Brother. See: Everson, William

Antoninus Florentinus, Saint, 1389-1459
— Chronicon. Nuremberg: Anton Koberger, 31 July 1484. ("Summarium primi voluminis partis hystorialis.") 3 vols. Folio. 768 (of 772) leaves; lacking 2 leaves of table in Vol I & f.122 in Vol III. Goff A-778. (90)

850

£3,800
— De censuris et de sponsalibus et matrimonio. Venice: Johannes de Colonia & Johannes Manthen, 23 Sept 1474. 4to. 135 (of 136) leaves. Goff A-776. (90) £2,500
— Summa confessionum. Cologne: Printer of the Historia S. Albani, [not after 1472]. 4to. 143 (of 144) leaves; lacking final blank. GKW 2085. Pirckheimer-Arundel copy. (91) £4,000
Strassburg: Johann Grueninger, 4 Dec 1490. ("Tertia pars summe.") Part 3 (of 5) only. Folio. 374 (of 376) leaves. Goff A-877. (91) £1,500
— Summa theologica. Venice: Leonardus Wild, 1480. Vol III. Folio. 210 leaves. Goff A-873. (90) DM6,400
Strassburg: Johann (Reinhard) Grueninger, 24 Apr-4 Sept 1496. Parts 1 & 2 only (of 4) bound with index in 1 vol. Folio. 485 (of 486) leaves; lacking last blank of Part 2. Goff A-878. (89) $1,200
— Tractatus de instructione seu directione simplicum confessorum. Mainz: Peter Schoeffer, [before 1475]. 4to. 143 (of 144) leaves; lacking final blank. Goff-801. (91) £6,000

Antonio, Nicolas
— Bibliotheca Hispana vetus. Rome, 1672. ("Bibliotheca Hispana siva Hispanorum qui usquam....") 2 vols. Folio. (91) £170
— Bibliotheca Hispana vetus [Hispana nova]. Madrid, 1788. 2d Ed. 4 vols. Folio. Library stamps. (91) $600

Antonius de Vercellis
— Sermones quadragesimales de xii mirabilibus Christianae fidei excellentiis. Venice: Joannes & Gregoriis de Forlivio, 16 Feb 1492. 4to. 268 leaves. Goff A-918. (91) $900

Antonius Nebrissensis, Aelius, 1444-1522
— Vafre dicta philosophorum. [Salamanca: Ptr of Nebrissensis Grammatica, c.1498]. 4to. 30 leaves. Goff A-911. "One of four copies." Abrams copy. (90) £9,000

Anville, Jean Baptiste Bourguignon d', 1697-1782
— Antiquite geographique de l'Inde.... Paris, 1775. 4to. (88) FF2,800
— Atlas and Geography of the Antients. L, 1815. Folio. (88) £65, £90
— Atlas generale. Paris, 1743-60. 2 parts in 1 vol. Folio. (88) £800
— Compendium of Ancient Geography. L, 1791. 2 vols. 8vo. (88) £110
— A Complete Body of Ancient Geography. L: Robert Sayer, [1771?]. Folio. (89) £70
L, 1775. Folio. (88) £90
L, 1785. Folio. (91) £260
L, 1801. Folio. (89) £90
— Eclaircissemens geographiques sur l'ancienne Gaule.... Paris, 1753. 12mo. Library stamps. (89) $175
— Nouvel Atlas de la Chine.... The Hague, 1737. Folio. (89) £1,000; (90) £1,900; (91) $3,100

Apel, Johann August
— Der Freischuetz. Travestie.... L, 1824. Illus by George Cruikshank. 8vo. (91) $250

Apianus, Petrus, 1495-1552
— Astronomicum Caesareum. Leipzig, [1967]. One of 750. Folio. (88) DM750
NY, 1969. 2 vols with commentary. Folio & 8vo. Facsimile of 1540 Ed. (91) $1,200
— La Cosmographia. Antwerp: Jean Bellere, 1575. 4to. (88) £600, £900; (89) $1,100; (91) £850, £1,300
— Cosmographicus liber. Ingolstadt, 1529-32. ("Cosmographiae introductio: cum quibusdam geometriae....") 8vo. Tomash copy. (91) £600
Antwerp: A. Berckman, 1540. ("Cosmographia....") 4to. (88) £420; (89) £800; (90) £600
Antwerp: G. de Bonte, 1545. 4to. (89) £120; (91) $500
Antwerp: G. Bontius, 1553. 4to. (89) £380
Antwerp, 1564. 4to. (88) £700
Cologne: Heirs of A. Birckmann, 1574. 4to. Sold w.a.f. (91) £250
— Cosmographie oft Beschrijuinghe der gheheelder Werelt.... Antwerp: Jan Werwithagen, 1573. 4to. Gillis Speelman's copy. (89) £650
Amst.: C. Claesz, 1609. 4to. (89) £150
— Instrument Buch.... Ingolstadt, 1533. Folio. (88) DM7,400; (90) DM5,700; (91) £900
— Instrumentum sinuum, seu primi mobilis. Nuremberg: Johannes Petrus, 1541. 2 parts in 1 vol. Folio. (89) £180
— Libro dela cosmographia.... Antwerp: Gregorius Bontius, 1548. 4to. (89) £1,400

**Apianus, Petrus, 1495-1552 —&
Amantius, Bartholomaeus**
— Inscriptiones sacrosancte vetustatis.... Ingolstadt: P. Apianus, 1534. Folio. (88) $1,600, £850
Kissner copy. (91) £2,000

Apicius Coelius, fl.14-37 A.D.
— Cookery and Dining in Imperial Rome: A Bibliography. Chicago, 1936. One of 500. Folio. (88) $60
— De re coquinaria libri decem. Zurich: Froschouer, 1542. ("De opsoniis et

APICIUS COELIUS,
condimentis....") 4to. (89) £400
Amst., 1709. 8vo. (89) £100

Apollinaire, Guillaume, 1880-1918
— Alcools. Paris, 1913. 1st Ed. With frontis by Pablo Picasso. With ANs to Leon Deffoux tipped in. (88) FF39,000
— Calligrammes. Paris, 1918. 8vo. Martin copy. (90) FF7,000
— L'Enfer de la Bibliotheque Nationale. Paris, 1913. 1st Ed. (91) $300
— Ombre de mon amour.... Geneva: Pierre Caillier, 1947. 1st Ed, one of 150. 12mo. Tipped in are 2 autograph postcards, sgd, to Louise de Coligny. (88) FF35,000
— Poemes secrets. Paris, 1967. One of 135 on Arches blanc. Illus by Salvador Dali. Folio. (88) FF11,000
— Le Poete assassine. Paris, 1916. 12mo. (88) FF3,000
Paris, 1926. One of 20 with 2 suites of lithos, 1 on chine & 1 on japon & with hand-coloring by Dufy. Illus by Raoul Dufy. 4to. (91) FF300,000
— Sept Calligrammes. Paris, 1967. One of 8 hors commerce. Illus by Osip Zadkine. (89) $1,500, FF18,000
One of 75. (88) FF7,200
— Si je mourais la-bas. Paris, 1962. One of 150. Illus by Georges Braque. Folio. (88) FF58,000

Apollo...
— Apollo. A Journal of the Arts. L, 1925-82. Vols 1-116 (lacking Vols 33-34). Bound in 107 vols. 4to. (91) £1,200

Apollodorus Atheniensis
— Bibliotheces, sive de deorum origine.... Rome, 1555. 1st Ed. 8vo. (90) £220
Lamoignon copy. (91) LIt650,000

Apollonius of Tyre
— Historia. See: Golden Cockerel Press

Apollonius Pergaeus
— Conicorum libri IV. 1675. See: Archimedes

Apollonius Pergaeus, fl.225 B.C.
— Conicorum.... Bologna: Alexander Benacius, 1566. Ed by Federicus Commandinus. 2 parts in 1 vol. Folio. (89) £75

Apollonius Rhodius, 240-186 B.C.
— The Argonautic Expedition. See: Fore-Edge Paintings
— Argonautica. Florence: [Laurentius (Francesci) de Alopa, Venetus], 1496. 1st Ed, One of 5 recorded copies on vellum. 4to. 171 (of 172) leaves; lacking final blank. Goff A-924. MacCarthy-Spencer-Rylands copy. (88) £80,000

AMERICAN BOOK PRICES CURRENT
1st Aldine Ed. Venice: Aldus, Apr 1521. 8vo. (88) £600; (91) £800, £1,300
Basel: [J. Oporini, 1550]. ("Argonauticorum libri quatuor.") 8vo. (90) £260
[Geneva:] H. Estienne, 1574. ("Argonauticon libri IIII.") Folio. (90) £60, £85
Martin copy. (90) $1,100

Apperley, Charles J., 1777?-1843
— Hunting Reminiscences. L, 1843. 1st Ed. 8vo. (88) £100, £60, £180; (89) £270
— The Life of a Sportsman; by Nimrod. L, 1842. 1st Ed. 8vo. (88) £700; (90) £700
1st Issue. (89) £700, £750
L, 1874. 8vo. (88) £200, £280; (89) £320
L, 1905. 8vo. (89) £240
L, 1914. (89) £100, £95
— Memoirs of the Life of the Late John Mytton, Esq. L, 1835. 1st Ed. Illus by Henry Alken. 8vo. (88) £480; (90) £460
2d Ed. L, 1837. 8vo. (88) £60, £200, DM1,200; (89) £320; (91) £200, £380
Doheny copy. (89) $350
3d Ed. L, 1851. 8vo. (88) $275, £200, £260, £420; (90) $325, $325, £100, £280; (91) $250, $300
4th Ed. L, 1869. ("The Life of John Mytton.") (88) £165; (90) £180
5th Ed. L, 1870. 8vo. (89) £130; (90) $190; (91) $160, £80
Benz copy. (91) $1,100
L, 1877. 8vo. (88) £120; (90) £130; (91) £195
L, 1899. One of 50. Illus by Henry Alken. 8vo. (90) £120
— Memoirs of the Late John Mytton. See: Fore-Edge Paintings
— Nimrod's Hunting Tours.... L, 1903. (88) £150; (89) £140; (90) £50; (91) £120
One of—50. (88) $250
Editor's copy. Inscr by the Ed, Joseph Grego, to T. J. Barratt. (88) £130
— Sporting; Embellished by Large Engravings and Vignettes Illustrative of Field Sports.... L, 1838. 4to. (88) £120, £130

Appert, Nicholas, 1750-1841
— The Art of Preserving all Kinds of Animal and Vegetable Substances for Several Years.... L, 1811. 1st English Ed. 8vo. (90) £200

Appian of Alexandria
— De bellis civilibus. [Venice]: Vindelinus de Spira, 1472. Folio. 146 (of 148) leaves; lacking first & last blanks. Goff A-931. (90) £3,800
— Historia Romana. Venice: Bernhard Maler, Erhard Ratdolt & Petrus Loeslein, 1477. 2 vols. Folio:. 131 (of 132) & 211 (of 212) leaves; lacking 1st blank in each vol. Goff A-928. Broxbourne-Abrams copy. (90)

£20,000
Venice: Bernhard Maler & Erhard Ratdolt & Petrus Loeslein, 1477. Part 2 only. 212 leaves. Goff A-928. (88) $1,200
Venice: Bernhard Maler, Erhard Ratdolt & Petrus Loeslein, 1477. Vol II (of 2) only: De civilibus bellis. Folio. 211 (of 212) leaves. Goff A-928. (91) $1,300
Paris: J. Petit, 1521. ("De bellis civilibus.") 12mo. (88) £95
— The History.... L, 1679. Trans by John Davies. Folio. (89) £130; (91) $140
— Rom. historiarum.... Paris: Stephanus, 1557. Folio. (91) £280
— Romanarum historiarum celtica. Paris: Charles Estienne, 1551. ("Romaikon Keltike....") Folio. (88) £350; (90) £400, £450
Doheny copy. (89) $1,900

Appier, Jean, called Hanzelet
— La Pyrotechnie.... Pont a Mousson, 1630. 4to. (91) £1,200

Appier, Jean, called Hanzelet —& Thybourel, Francois
— Recueil de plusieurs machines militaires et feux artificiels pour la guerre, & recreation. Pont-a-Mousson, 1620. 1st Ed. 7 parts in 1 vol. 4to. John Evelyn's copy. (90) $8,500

Appleton & Co., Daniel
— Appleton's Cyclopaedia of American Biography. NY, 1887-89. Ed by J. G. Wilson & John Fiske. 6 vols. 4to. (88) $210; (89) $225; (91) $160
NY, 1888-89. 6 vols. 4to. (90) $130, $160
NY, 1891. 6 vols. 4to. (88) $70
Detroit, 1968. 7 vols, including Supplement. Facsimile of 1888-1901 Ed. (88) $90
— Appleton's Dictionary of Machines, Mechanics, Engine-Work, and Engineering. NY, 1852. 2 vols. 4to. (89) $250; (90) $95
4to. (88) $90, $100, $140
— Mechanics: A Dictionary of Mechanical Engineering and the Mechanical Arts. NY, 1880. 2 vols. 8vo. (88) $100

Appleton, Nathaniel, 1693-1784
— How God Wills the Salvation of All Men.... Bost., 1753. 8vo. (91) $150

Aprentices...
— The Aprentices Advice to the XII. Bishops. See: Taylor, John

Apres de Mannevillette, Jean Baptiste N. D. d'
— Le Neptune Oriental.... [Paris, c.1775]. Folio. (91) $1,200
[Paris: Depot Generale de la Marine, c.1820]. Folio. (88) £600; (89) £1,200

Apuleius, Lucius
— L'Amour de Cupido et de Psiche. Paris: Jean de Marnef for Denis Janot, 15 Sept 1546. 2 parts in 1 vol. 8vo. In French & Italian. (90) £5,500
— L'Apulegio tradotto in volgare.... Venice: Bartholomeo detto l'imperadore & Francesco Vinitano, 1549. 8vo. (88) £200
— Apuleo volgare tradotte per il magnifico conte Mattheo Maria Boiardo. Venice: N. Zoppino & V. de Paolo, 1518. 8vo. (90) £2,000
— De Cupidinis et Psyches amoribus. L: Vale Press, 1901. One of 310. Illus by Charles Ricketts. Folio. (89) $130
— The Excellent Narration of the Marriage of Cupide and Psyches. L: Vale Press, 1897. One of 210. Illus by Charles Ricketts. 8vo. (91) £2,600
— The Golden Ass. NY: Pvtly ptd at Chiswick Press for the Scott-Thaw Co., 1904. One of 210. Folio. (89) $65; (91) $140
— The Golden Asse. See: Ashendene Press
— Der goldene Esel. Darmstadt, 1972. 2d Issue, one of 50. Illus by Eberhard Schlotter. (91) DM2,000
— The Marriage of Cupid & Psyche. See: Limited Editions Club
— Metamorphose, autrement l'asne d'or. Lyon: Jean de Tournes & Guillaume Gazeau, 1553. 16mo. Sold w.a.f. (90) £55
— Les Metamorphoses; ou, L'Asne d'Or. Paris, 1648. 2 parts in 1 vol. 8vo. (89) $200
— Opera. Venice: Aldus, May 1521. ("Metamorphoseos, sive lusus asini libri XI.") 8vo. (88) £190, £650; (91) LIt700,000
Florence: Giunta, 1522. 8vo. (91) LIt250,000
Rome: Sweynheym & Pannartz, 28 Feb 1569. Folio. 177 (of 178) leaves; lacking final blank. Goff A-934. La Valliere—Spencer-Rylands copy. (88) £39,000
— The XI Bookes of the Golden Asse. See: Golden Cockerel Press

Aquila...
— Aquila. Annales Instituti Ornithologici Hungarici. Budapest, 1894-1947. 19 vols. Martin copy. (90) $300

Aquila, Joannes
— Opusculum enchiridion appellatum de omni ludorum genere. Oppenheim: [Jacob Koebel], 1516. 4to. (90) £650, DM8,000

Arabian Nights
— 1802. - The Arabian Nights L. Edward Forster's trans. 5 vols. 4to. L.p. copy. (91) £1,150

ARABIAN NIGHTS

5 vols. 8vo. (91) $80
— 1839-41. - The Thousand and One Nights L. Edward William Lane's trans. 3 vols. 8vo. (88) $325; (89) £50; (90) $210, £80, £130, £170
The Garden copy. (90) $1,300
— 1885-88. - The Book of the Thousand Nights and a Night, with Supplemental Nights. Benares: Kamashastra Society. One of 20. Sir Richard F. Burton's trans. 16 vols. 8vo. (90) $900
— 1886. - Lady Burton's Edition of her Husband's Arabian Nights. Prepared for Household Reading.... L. Sir Richard F. Burton's trans. 6 vols. 8vo. ALs inserted in Vol I. (89) £60
— 1894-[97]. - The Book of the Thousand Nights and a Night, with Supplemental Nights. L. Sir Richard F. Burton's trans. 12 vols. 8vo. (90) £65; (91) £420
— 1897. - Kamashastra Society Ed. L. 12 vols. 8vo. (91) $350
Library Ed. 12 vols. 8vo. (89) $825, £550; (90) £110, £170; (91) $450, £145
W. K. Bixby's copy, with titles replaced with those of the Benares Ed of 1885-88. (88) $260
12 vols plus Letchford's 1897 vol of illusts. 8vo. (88) £160
— 1899-1904. - Le Livre des mille nuits et une nuit. Paris. J. C. Mardrus's trans. 16 vols. 8vo. (88) $100; (89) £190
— 1900-1. - The Book of the Thousand Nights and a Night, with Supplemental Nights. [Denver: Burton Society]. One of 1,000. Sir Richard F. Burton's trans. 16 vols. 8vo. (90) $210; (91) $375
— 1907. - Contes des mille et une nuits. Paris. Illus by Edmund Dulac. 4to. (91) £90
— 1907-8. - Die Erzaehlungen aus den Tausend und ein Naechten. Leipzig: Insel-Verlag. 12 vols. (91) £130
— [1908]. - Contes des mille et une nuits. Paris. Illus by Edmund Dulac. 4to. (88) £55; (91) $140
One of 300. (91) $300
— 1908-12. - Le Livre des Mille Nuits et une Nuit. Paris: Eugene Fasquelle. Unique set, embellished with c.450 watercolors by Rina Vasarri. 4to. (91) $1,600
— 1919. - Conte des 1001 Nuits. Paris: Les Editions de la Sirene. One of 200. Illus by Kees Van Dongen. 4to. (89) $650
— 1923. - The Book of the Thousand Nights and One Night. L. E. Powys Mathers's trans from Mardrus's version. 16 vols. Ltd Ed. (89) $80, £100, A$480; (90) £210; (91) $150
— 1926. - Le Livre des mille nuits et une nuit. Paris. Illus by Leon Carre. 12 vols. 4to. (88) FF5,000

AMERICAN BOOK PRICES CURRENT

— 1926-32. - Paris. J. C. Mardrus's trans. 12 vols. 4to. (88) $275; (91) $800
— [1934]. - The Book of the Thousand Nights and a Night. NY: Heritage Press. Trans by Sir Richard F. Burton; illus by Valenti Angelo. 6 vols. 4to. (91) $60
— 1959. - Les Mille et Une Nuits. Grenoble: Roissard. One of 974. Illus by Poucette. 24 vols. 4to. Inscr to Diane by Poucette, 21 Nov 1959. (89) $650
— [n.d.]. - The Book of the Thousand Nights and a Night, with Supplemental Nights. L: Burton Club. One of 250. Sir Richard F. Burton's trans. 17 vols. 8vo. (91) $950
One of 1,000. (88) $60, £60; (89) £95; (90) $90, £85, £170; (91) $750, £190
— [n.d.]. - The Book of the Thousand Nights and a Night. L: Burton Club. One of 1,000. Trans by Richard F. Burton. 17 vols. 8vo. (91) £60
— [n.d.]. - Racconti delle Mille e Una Notte. Bergamo: Istituto d'Arti Grafiche. Illus by Edmund Dulac. 4to. (88) $80

— The Adventure of Hunch-Back, and the Stories connected with it.... L, 1814. Illus by Wm. Daniell after Robt. Smirke. Folio. (90) $325
— Aladdin; or the Wonderful Lamp. Phila, 1847. 8vo. (88) $60
— Histoire d'Aladdin et de la Lampe Magique. Paris, 1914. One of 570. Trans by J. C. Mardrus. 2 vols. 4to. Ptd in Peking. (89) $275
— The Magic Horse. L, 1930. One of 495. Illus by Ceri Richards. 4to. (88) £52
— Persian Stories from the Arabian Nights. Kentfield, CA: Allen Press, 1980. One of 140. Folio. (88) $200
— Princess Badoura. Retold by Laurence Housman. [L, 1913]. Illus by Edmund Dulac. 4to. (88) $140; (90) A$100; (91) $130
One of 750, sgd by artist. (88) £280, £340; (90) £170; (91) $50, $65, £240
— Sinbad der Seefahrer. Potsdam: Muller, [c.1920]. Illus by Edmund Dulac. (91) $65
— Sinbad the Sailor. L, [1911]. Illus by Edmund Dulac. 4to. (89) $50
L, [1914]. 4to. (91) $120
— Tales from the Thousand and One Nights. NY: Stewart, Tabori & Chang, [1985]. One of 250. Illus by Antonio Lopez. (91) $55

Arago, Jacques Etienne Victor, 1790-1855
— Narrative of a Voyage Round the World.... L, 1823. 4to. (88) £180; (89) £180, £1,200, A$1,200
— Promenade autour du monde.... Paris, 1822. 3 vols. 8vo & folio. (88) £1,100; (89) £750,

1987 - 1991 • BOOKS

A$3,500
Atlas vol only. (88) £400; (89) £200; (91) £250
— Souvenirs d'un aveugle, voyage autour du monde. Paris, 1839-40. 5 vols, including Supplement. 8vo. (89) A$1,900
Paris, [1843]. 2 vols. 8vo. (89) $300; (91) £220

Aragon, Louis
— Henri Matisse: A Novel. L, 1972. 2 vols. (90) £75; (91) £90
— Persecute Persecuteur. Paris: Editions Surrealistes, 1931. One of 100 hors commerce on green paper. 4to. Inscr by Benjamin Peret on half-title. (91) $400
— Les Poetes. Paris: NRF, 1960. One of 30. 4to. (88) SF18,000
— Le Reoman inacheve. Paris, 1956. One of 96 on velin pur fil. 8vo. (90) £1,800
— Shakespeare. NY, 1964. One of 1,000. Illus by Picasso. Folio. (90) $80
Paris, 1965. Folio. (88) $55; (89) $100; (90) $75

Arata, Giulio Ulisse
— L'Architettura Arabo-Normanna e il Rinascimento in Sicilia. Milan, [1925]. Folio. (90) $75

Aratus of Soli, c.315-c.245 B.C.
— Syntagma Arateorum. Leiden: Officina Plantiniana apud Christophorum Raphelegium, 1600. Ed by Hugo Grotiuis. 4to. (90) $1,500

Arber, Agnes
— Herbals. Their Origin and Evolution. Cambr., 1938. (88) $60; (89) $80; (91) $175
Cambr., 1953. (89) $60

Arber, Edward, 1836-1912
— The Term Catalogues, 1668-1709. L, 1903-6. 3 vols. 4to. (89) $50; (90) £260; (91) $50

Arcadian...
— The Arcadian Princesse. See: Silesio, Mariano

Archaeologia....
— Archaeologia Cantiana, being Transactions of the Kent Archaeological Society. L, 1858-98. Vols 1-23. (89) £75

Archenholtz, Johann Wilhelm von, 1743-1812
— The History of the Pirates, Free-Booters or Buccaneers of America. L, 1807. 8vo. (88) $180; (91) $110

ARCHIVES DE L'ELECTRICITE.

Archer, Sir Geoffrey Francis —& Godman, Eva M.
— The Birds of British Somaliland and the Gulf of Aden.... L, 1937-61. 4 vols. 4to. (88) £500; (91) £280, £350
L, 1961. Vols 3 & 4 only (of 4). 4to. (91) $90

Archer, John Wykeham, 1808-64
— Vestiges of Old London. L, 1851. Folio. (88) £95; (89) £130; (91) £80

Archer, William George
— Indian Paintings from the Punjab Hills. L, 1973. 2 vols. 4to. (89) £100; (90) $110

Archimedes, 287?-212 B.C.
— Arenarius, et dimensio circuli. Oxford, 1676. 8vo. (89) $650
— De iis quae vehuntur in aqua libri duo. Bologna: Benacius, 1565. Bound with: Commandinus, Federicus. Liber de centro gravitatis solidorum. Bologna, 1565. 4to. (89) £550
— Opera. Basel: J. Hervagius, 1544. Folio. (88) FF28,000; (90) £1,800
Spencer-Rylands copy. (88) £5,000
Venice: Aldus, 1558. 2 parts in 1 vol. Folio. (90) £750
Paris, 1615. Ed by David Rivault. Folio. (88) DM600; (90) $550; (91) £2,600
Greek text & Latin transl. (88) $750
L, 1675. Bound with: Apollonius Pergaeus. Conicorum libri IV. L, 1675. And: Theodosius. Sphaerica. L, 1675. 4to, vellum 3 parts in 1 vol. 4to. (89) $450
— Tetragonismus.... 1503. See: Tetragonismus...

Archipelagus...
— Archipelagus Turbatus, oder dess Schoenen Griechen-Lands.... Augsburg, 1686. 8vo. Blackmer copy. (90) £1,000

Archipenko, Alexander
— Alexandre Archipenko. Berlin, 1923. 4to. (88) $225

Architectural...
— The Architectural Review and American Builders' Journal. Phila., 1869-70. Vols I-II. 8vo. (88) $425
— Architectural Forum: Frank Lloyd Wright. NY, 1938. Vol 68, No 1. 4to. (90) $300

Archives de L'Electricite.
— Archives de L'Electricite. [Paris, 1841-45]. Vols I-V. 8vo. (88) $140

Arcos, Rene
— Medardus. Leipzig, 1930. One of 50 on japon. Illus by Frans Masereel. (88) DM1,000

Arctic...
— Arctic Bibliography. Wash. & Montreal, 1953-59. Vols 1-6. (91) $130
Wash. & Montreal, 1953-69. Vols I-VI. (89) $250
Vols 1-16. Wash. & Montreal, 1953-75. (91) $650
Vols 1-2 only. Wash. & Montreal, 1953-69. (91) £50
Vols 1-3 only (91) $120
Vols 1-7 only (89) $425; (91) $475
— Arctic Explorations: The Second Grinnell Expedition in search of Sir John Franklin. See: Kane, Elisha Kent
— The Arctic World: Its Plants, Animals, and Natural Phenomena. L, [1876]. 4to. (90) £70

Arctic Blue Books
— Additional Papers Relative to the Arctic Expedition under the Orders of Captain Austin and Mr. William Penny. See: England

Arden, George
— Latest Information with Regard to Australia Felix.... Melbourne, 1840. 8vo. (89) A$22,000

Aremberg, Carolus de
— Flores Seraphici...sive Icones.... Cologne, 1642. Folio. (88) £400

Arenas, Pedro de
— Vocabulario manual de las lenguas Castellana, y Mexicana. Los Angeles, 1793. 8vo. Doheny copy. (88) $650

Arents Collection, George, Jr.
— Tobacco: Its History Illustrated in the...Library. NY, 1937-52. By Jerome E. Brooks. One of 300. 4to, cloth. With Supplementary Catalogue, Parts I-VII, compiled by Sarah A. Dickson & Parts VIII-X compiled by Perry H. O'Neil. 4to, orig cloth. (90) £1,200
By Jerome E. Brooks. 5 vols. 4to. With Supplementary Catalogue, Parts I-VII, compiled by Sarah A. Dickson & Parts VIII-X compiled by Perry H. O'Neil. (89) $1,200
One of 300. With Supplementary Catalogue, Parts I-VII, compiled by Sarah A. Dickson & Parts VIII-X compiled by Perry H. O'Neil. (91) £2,000
Vol IV only. (88) $150

Aresta...
— Aresta amorum cum erudita Benedicti Curtii Symphoriani explanatione. See: Martial de Paris

Aretaeus
— Libri septem nunc primum e tenebris eruti a Iunio Paul Crasso.... Venice: Giunta, 1552. 4to. (91) $4,200
— Medici insignis ac vetustissimi libri septem.... Venice: Junta, 1552. 4to. (91) LIt1,100,000
— Works. L: Sydenham Society, 1856. Ed & trans by Francis Adams. 8vo. (89) $150

Aretino, Pietro, 1492-1556
— Del Primo Libro de le lettere. Paris, 1609. 6 vols. 8vo. (91) £170
— Lettere scritte al Signor Pietro Aretino. Venice: Francesco Marcolini, 1551. 2 vols. 8vo. (91) £600
— The Ragionamenti or Dialogues. Paris, 1889-90. 6 parts. 4to. (89) $100
6 vols in 3. 4to. (89) $120; (90) £50
— Ragionamento nel quale M. Pietro Aretino figura quattro suoi amici.... Venice: Francesco Marcolini, 1538. 2d Ed, 1st Issue. 8vo. (91) £4,800

Arevalo, Rodriguez Sanchez de, 1401-70. See: Rodericus Zamorensis

Arfwedson, Carl David, 1806-81
— The United States and Canada in 1832, 1833, and 1834. L, 1834. 1st Ed. 2 vols. 8vo. (91) $80

Argalus & Parthenia. See: Quarles, Francis

Argellata, Petrus de, d.1423
— Cirurgia. Venice, 12 Sept 1499. Folio. 131 (of 132) leaves; lacking final blank. Goff A-954. (89) £3,400

Argens, Jean Baptiste de Boyer, Marquis d'
— The Jewish Spy: Being a Philosophical, Historical and Critical Correspondence.... L, 1739-40. 5 vols. 12mo. (88) £120
— Lettres juives, ou correspondence philosophique.... The Hague, 1738. 6 vols. 8vo. (88) $110

Argensola, Bartolome Leonardo y, 1562-1631
— Conquista de las Islas Malucas. [Madrid: Alonso Martin, 1609]. 4to. Phillipps copy. (88) £3,800
— The Discovery and Conquest of the Molucco and Philippine Islands. L, 1708. 1st Ed in English. 4to. (90) £1,500; (91) $2,400
— Histoire de la conqueste des isles Moluques.... Amst., 1706-7. Mixed Ed. 3 vols. 12mo. (88) $300; (91) £360

Argenti, Philip Panteles
— The Costumes of Chios. L, 1953. One of 500. 4to. (90) £325; (91) £280, £320

Argolus, Andreas, 1570-1657
— Ptolemaeus parvus in genethliacis junctus Arabibus. Lyons, 1659. 4to. (91) £70

Argote de Molina, Gonzalo, 1549-90
— Libro de la Monteria que mando escrivir...Rey Don Alonso de Castilla.... Seville: A. Pescioni, 1582. Folio. Jeanson 1540. Schiff copy. (91) $16,000

Argument...
— An Argument in Defence of the Exclusive Right Claimed by the Colonies to Tax Themselves. L, 1774. 8vo. (91) $250

Arguments...
— Arguments and Materials for a Register of Estates. L: for Samuel Lowndes, 1698. 4to. (88) £150

Arias Maldonado, Jose
— Dirige me in veritate tua & doce me, ex David Psal. 24. Por la Provincia de la Sagrada Religion de la Compania de Jesus de las Islas Filipinas.... [Mexico: widow of B. Calderon, c.1670]. Folio. Robinson copy. (89) £900

Arias Montanus, Benedictus, 1527-98
— Benedictus Antiquitatum Judaicarum libri IX. Leiden: Officina Plantiniana, 1593. 4to. (91) £600
— Dictatum Cristianum. Antwerp: C. Plantin, 1575. 16mo. (89) HF600
— Humanae salutis monumenta. Antwerp: Plantin, 1571. 8vo. (89) DM3,200

Aricivita, Juan Domenigo
— Chronica apostolica, y seraphica de todos los colegios de propaganda fide de esta Nueva Espana.... See: Espinosa, Isidro Felix de

Ariel...
— The Ariel Poems. [L, 1927-54]. 1st Series: Nos 1-38. Three Things sgd by Yeats at end. (91) £170

Aries, Robert S. —& O'Hana, Jacques
— Mane-Katz: The Complete Works. L, 1970-72. Out-of-series copy. 2 vols. Folio. (91) $550

Arif Pacha, Mushir
— Les Anciens Costumes de l'Empire Ottoman. Paris, [1863]. Vol I (all pbd). Folio. Blackmer copy. (90) £13,000

Aringhus, Paulus
— Roma subterranea novissima. Rome, 1651. 2 vols. Folio. (91) LIt1,500,000
Kissner copy. (91) £4,200
Paris, 1659. 2 vols in 1. Folio. Kissner copy. (91) £750

Ariosto, Ludovico, 1474-1533
— La Cassaria. Venice, 1560. 12mo. (90) $120
— Opere. Venice, 1730. 2 vols in 1. Folio. (91) LIt750,000
— Orlando furioso. Venice: Aldus, 1545. 2 parts in 1 vol. 4to. Renouard-Holford-Doheny copy. (89) £6,500
Venice: G. Giolito, 1550. 3 parts in 1 vol, 8vo. (89) £200
Lyon: Rouille, 1556 [1555]. 4to. (89) £250
Lyons: J. Faure for S. Honorat, 1556. 8vo. (88) £140; (89) £170; (91) LIt850,000
Venice: Vincenzo Valgrisi, 1562. 4to. (88) $450; (89) £140; (90) £750; (91) LIt750,000
Venice: Valgrisi, 1568. 2 parts in 1 vol. 4to. (91) £140, £420
Venice: V. Valgrisi, 1572. 4to. (91) $275
Venice: Francesco & Franceschi Senese, 1584. 2 parts in 1 vol. Folio. (91) £350
Venice: Felice Valgrisi, 1587. 8vo. (88) £180
Venice: Valgrisi, 1587. Ed by Girolamo Ruscelli. 4to. (89) £300
1st Ed in English. L: Richard Field, 1591. 4to. Houghton copy. (89) £34,000
Venice, 1603. 4to. (88) $225; (89) £250; (90) $275; (91) LIt650,000
L: R. Field for J. Norton & S. Waterson, 1607. Folio. (88) £400
L, 1634. English trans by Sir John Harington. Folio. (89) $220, £450; (91) $180, £400
STC 748. (91) £750
L, 1755. 4to. (91) £470
Venice: Zatta, 1772-73. 4 vols in 2. 4to. (88) £420; (91) £1,500
Birm.: Baskerville, 1773. 4 vols. 4to. (88) $475, £80; (89) $275; (90) £700, DM1,400
Paris, 1795. 4 vols. 4to. (90) £480
Pisa, 1809. 5 vols. Folio. (89) £75
See also: Fore-Edge Paintings
— Roland furieux. Paris, 1775-83. 4 vols. 8vo. (89) £200
— Le Satire, in terza rima, di nuovo stampate. Ferrara, June 1534. 8vo. (91) £600

Aristarchus
— De magnitudinibus, et distantiis solis et lunae.... Pesaro: C. Franciscanus, 1572. 4to. (90) £850

ARISTOPHANES

Aristophanes, 448?-380? B.C.
— Comoediae undecim.... Amst.: J. Fritsch, 1710. Folio. (88) $80
— Die Froesche. Frankfurt, [1968]. Ltd Ed. Illus by Oskar Kokoschka. Folio. (88) DM5,200
— Komodiai ennea. Comoedia novem. Venice: Aldus, 15 July 1498. Folio. 341 (of 348) leaves. Goff A-958. (91) $2,800
346 (of 348) leaves; lacking 2 blanks. Goff A-958. (90) $18,000
347 (of 348) leaves. Lacking final blank. Goff A-958. (90) £6,000; (91) £10,000
348 leaves. Goff A-958. Spencer-Rylands copy. (88) £15,000
348 leaves. Goff A-958. (90) £8,500; (91) £34,000
Florence: Haeredes Philippi Iuntae, 1525. 4to. In Greek. (90) £360
Basel: A. Cratandrum & J. Bebelium, 1532. 4to. (91) £380
Franfurt: Johann Spies, 1597. ("Nicodemi Frischlini Aristophanes veteres comoediae....") Bound with: Callimachus. Hymni et epigrammata.... Basel: L. Osten, 1589. 8vo. Adams A-1719 & C-236. (91) £280
Frankfukrt: Johann Spies, 1597. Bound with: Callimachus. Hymni et epigrammata.... Basel: L. Osten, 1589. 8vo. Adams A-1719 & C-236. (91) £280
— Lysistrata. Sydney: Fanfrolico Press, 1926. One of 725. Trans by Jack Lindsay; illus by Norman Lindsay. Folio. (91) $300
L, 1927. One of 750. Illus by Aubrey Beardsley. 4to. (88) $80; (89) $70
Paris: Le Livre du Bibliophile, [1928]. One of 40 on japon imperial with a suite of 12 of the illusts & an additional suite in black only. Illus by Carlegle. 4to. (91) £220
N: Three Sirens Press, [1930s]. Illus by Norman Lindsay. (90) $120
See also: Limited Editions Club
— Lysistrate. Paris, 1911. One of 100 on japan imperial with 2 extra suites of the illustrations, plain and colored. Illus by Francois Kupka. 4to. (91) $1,800
One of 100 on japan imperial with plates in 3 states. With 30 orig watercolor drawings in margins. (89) SF13,000
— Women in Parliament. L: Fanfrolico Press, 1929. One of 500. Trans by Jack Lindsay; illus by Norman Lindsay. Folio. (91) $200

Aristotle, 384-322 B.C.
— De animalibus. Venice: Johannes de Colonia & Johannes Manthen, 1476. Folio. 252 leaves. Goff A-973. (88) $22,000 "Intended to receive elaborate illumination, which remained at an unfinished stage." 252 leaves. Goff A-973. Honeyman-The Garden copy. (90) $105,000

AMERICAN BOOK PRICES CURRENT

— De caelo et mundo. Venice: Gregorius & Joannes de Gregoriis, 31 Oct 1495. Ed by Hermann de Virsen. Folio. 72 leaves. Goff A-979. Doheny copy. (88) $4,500
— De rhetorica seu arte dicendi, libri tres.... L, 1619. 4to. (88) £60; (91) £160
— L'Ethica. Florence, 1550. 8vo. (91) LIt380,000, LIt500,000, LIt500,000
— Expositiones textuales in libros de caelo et mundo... Cologne: Heinrich Quentell, 22 Sept 1497. Folio. 245 (of 246) leaves; lacking final blank. Goff A-967. (90) £1,300
— Logica.... Lyons: G. Rouilium, 1584. 8vo. (91) £135
— Logica nova: Copulata totius nouae logicae Aristotelis. [Cologne: Heinrich Quentell, c.1488]. Folio. 199 (of 200) leaves; lacking tp. Goff A-999. (91) $4,000
— Oeconomica. [Leipzig: Martin Landsberg, c.1499]. Folio. Not written by Aristotle. 12 leaves. GKW 2438. (89) $1,400
— Opera. Venice: Aldus, 1495-98. 1st Ed in Greek. 5 vols. Folio. 1,852 leaves. Goff A-959. (90) £220,000
5 vols in 6. Folio. 1,521 leaves. Goff A-959. Doheny copy. (88) $120,000
1,521 leaves. Goff A-959. The Garden copy, formerly the Clive-Kalbfleisch-Kettaneh copy. (90) $165,000
1,850 leaves. Goff A-959. Spencer-Rylands copy. (88) £110,000
— ("Opera. Part 1, Organon.") Folio. 234 leaves. Goff A-959. The Garden copy. (90) $5,000
Venice: Joannes & Gregorius de Gregoriis de Forlino, for Benedictus Fontana, 13 July 1496. Folio. 508 leaves. Goff A-966. (88) £1,700
Venice: Aldus, 29 Jan 1497. Part 4 (of 5) only. Folio. 170 (of 520) leaves. Goff A-959. Sold w.a.f. (90) £850
292 (of 520) leaves. Goff A-959. Lacking pp 1-227. (91) £5,400
Basel, 1538. Folio. (88) £300
Geneva, 1605. Folio. (91) £60
— Politicorum et oeconicorum libri. See: Fore-Edge Paintings
— Politicorum Libri VIII. Leiden: Elzevir, 1621. 8vo. (89) £65
— Politics & Poetics. See: Limited Editions Club
— Rettorica, et Poetica. Florence: L. Torrentino, 1549. 4to. (91) LIt380,000
— La Rhetorique d'Aristote. Paris, 1675. 12mo. Ownership inscr of Edmund Waller. (89) £50
— Sepher Hamidoth. Berlin, 1790. 4to. (89) $150

Arithmetique...
— L'Arithmetique et maniere de apprendre a chiffrer & compter.... Lyons: Thibault Payen, 1548. 8vo. (88) £1,800

Arkansas
— The Hot Springs of Arkansas. America's Baden-Baden.... St. Louis: St. Louis Iron Mountain & Southern Railway Co., 1877. 8vo. (91) $60

Arkham...
— The Arkham Sampler. Sauk City: Arkham House, 1948-49. 8 issues from Spring 1948 to Winter 1949. (88) $130

Arkwright, William
— The Pointer and his Predecessors. L, 1902. One of 750. 4to. (88) £300
Out-of-series copy. (91) £230

Arland, Marcel
— Antares. Paris, 1944. Out-of-series copy. Illus by Marie Laurencin. 4to. (90) £1,400
— Avec Pasca. Paris, 1946. One of 1,150. Illus by Georges Rouault. (91) $100
— Maternite. Paris, 1926. One of 60 on verge d'Hollande, but this copy lacking the extra suite of plates. Illus by Marc Chagall. (88) $850
One of 960. (88) £600; (89) $1,200
Martin copy. (90) $1,500

Arlen, Michael, 1895-1965
— Hell! Said the Duchess; a Bed-Time story. L, [1934]. Inscr. (88) $60

Arlequi, Joseph
— Chronica de la provincia de N.S.P.S. Francisco de Zacatecas.... Mexico: Joseph Bernardo de Hogal, 1737. 4to. (89) £300
Doheny copy. (88) $1,700

Arlington, Lewis Charles
— The Chinese Drama from the Earliest Times Until Today. Shanghai, 1930. 4to. (91) $225
One of 750. (91) $180

Arlt, Carl Ferdinand von
— Die Krankheiten des Auges.... Prague, 1851-56. 3 vols. 8vo. (90) £400; (91) £260

Armchair...
— The Armchair Detective. White Bear Lake, 1967-75. Ed by Allen J. Hubin. Vol I, No 1 through Vol 8, No 4 in 5 vols. Inscr by Hubin. (88) $170

Armand, Alfred, 1805-88
— Les Medailleurs Italiens de XVe et XVIe siecles. Paris, 1883-87. 3 vols. 4to. Inscr. (91) $200

Armand-Dunaresq, Charles Edouard
— Uniformes de l'Armee Francaise en 1861. Paris: Lemercier, 1861. Folio. (91) £1,100

Armee...
— Armee Francaise d'Orient 1915-1917. En Macedoine. Paris, 1917. Unique copy on papier du japon avec fonds en couleur et remarques, made for Gen. Auguste-Clement Gerome. Illus by Lobel Riche. Folio. (88) £750

Armengaud, Jean Germain Desire
— Les Tresors de l'art. Paris, 1859. Folio. (90) $90

Armengaud, V —& Others
— The Practical Draughtsman's Book of Industrial Design. L, 1853. Trans by William Johnson. 4to. (90) £80

Armenini, Giovanni Baptista, 1540-1609
— De veri precetti della pittura. Ravenna, 1587. 1st Ed. 4to. (89) $650; (91) £600

Armes, George A.
— Ups and Downs of an Army Officer. Wash., 1900. (89) $130

Armiger, Charles
— The Sportsman's Vocal Cabinet. L, 1830. 12mo. (88) $60

Armitage, Albert Borlase
— Two Years in the Antarctic. L, 1905. 1st Ed. Inscr. (88) £300

Armitage, Merle
— George Gershwin. NY, 1938. 4to. Inscr by Armitage on front flyleaf. (88) $60

Armour, George Denholm
— Humour in the Hunting Field. L, 1935. Folio. (90) £180

Arms, Dorothy Noyes
— Churches of France. NY, 1929. 4to. (89) $275; (90) $175

Armstrong, Sir Alexander, 1818-99
— A Personal Narrative of the Discovery of the North-West Passage.... L, 1857. 8vo. (89) £110
Inscr. (90) £380

Armstrong, Edmund Archibald
— Axel Herman Haig and his Work. L, 1905. 4to. L.p. copy. (89) $130
L.p. copy. With a sgd orig etching by Haig. (89) $60

Armstrong, Elizabeth
— Robert Estienne: Royal Printer. Cambr., 1954. 4to. (91) $60, $110

Armstrong, John, of Minorca
— The History of the Island of Minorca. L, 1752. 1st Ed. 8vo. (88) £60; (90) £110
2d Ed. L, 1756. 8vo. (88) £70, £110

Armstrong, John, 1709-79
— The Art of Preserving Health: a Poem. L, 1744. 4to. (89) £50
— Miscellanies. L, 1770. 2 vols. 8vo. (91) £60

Armstrong, Col. John, Engineer
— The History of the Antient and Present State of the Navigation of the Port of King's Lynn. L, 1725. Folio. (91) £300

Armstrong, Martin Donisthorpe
— Saint Hercules and Other Stories. L: Curwen Press, [1927]. One of 310. Illus by Paul Nash. 4to. (89) £70; (90) £160; (91) $110, £130, £150
Out-of-series copy. (89) $90

Armstrong, Mostyn John
— An Actual Survey of the Great Post-Roads between London and Edinburgh. L, 1776. 8vo. (89) $80, £150, £220; (91) £170
L, 1783. 8vo. (88) £190
— A Scotch Atlas; or Description of the Kingdom of Scotland. L, 1787. 4to. (88) £380; (91) £520
L, 1794. 4to. (89) £300

Armstrong, Robert Bruce
— Musical Instruments. Part 1: The Irish and the Highland Harps. Part 2: English and Irish Instruments. Edin., 1904-8. One of 180. 2 vols. 4to. (91) £260

Armstrong, Sir Walter, 1850-1918
— Sir Henry Raeburn. L, 1901. Folio. (89) £65
— Sir Joshua Reynolds: First President of the Royal Academy. L & NY, 1900. Folio. (89) $50; (91) $190
— The Thames from its Rise to the Nore. L, [1886-87]. 2 vols. 4to. (88) £65; (89) £55
— Turner. L, 1902. One of 350. 2 vols, including portfolio of extra suite of plates. 4to. (88) £50

Arnaldi, Enea, Count, b.1716
— Idea di un teatro nelle principali.... Vicenza, 1762. 4to. (91) £500

Arnaldus de Villa Nova
— Le Tresor des Poures. Rouen: Estienne Dasne, 27 Oct 1529. 4to. Yemeniz copy. (89) £3,800

Arnaud, Francois, 1718-1805
— Lamentations de Jereme. Odes dediees a la reine de Pologne. Paris: la veuve Lottin, 1757. 8vo. (89) £700

Arnauld, Antoine, 1612-94
— Mysterion tes Anomias. That is, Another Part of the Mystery of Jesuitism. L, 1664. Issue not indicated. 8vo. (88) £130

Arnauld, Antoine, 1612-94 —& Nicole, Pierre, 1625-95
— Logic; or, The Art of Thinking.... L, 1685. 1st English Ed. 2 parts in 1 vol. 8vo. (91) £260

Arnauld, Pierre
— Trois Traitez de la philosophie naturelle non encore imprimez.... Paris: Guillaume Marette, 1612. 4to. (88) £950

Arnault de Nobleville, Louis Daniel, 1701-78
— Aedologie, ou traite du rossignol franc, ou chanteur. Paris: Dubure, 1751. 8vo. Martin copy. (90) $600

Arndt, Johann, 1555-1621
— Of True Christianity. L: Joseph Downing, 1720. Vol I only. 8vo. (91) £500
— Sechs Bucher von Wahren Christenthum.... Phila., 1832. 2 parts in 1 vol. 4to. (91) $60
— Vom Wahren Christenthum.... Nuremberg, 1762. 4to. (91) $140, LIt1,700,000

Arnigio, Bartolomeo
— Prima Canzone...nella quale si celebra la gloriosissima vittoria della christiana lega in mare contra l'armata turchesca. Venice: Giorgio Angelieri, 1572. 4to. Blackmer copy. (90) £600

Arnim, Mary Annette, Countess von
— The April Baby's Book of Tunes. L, 1900. 1st Ed, 2d impression. Illus by Kate Greenaway. Oblong 4to. (89) $70

Arnkiel, Trogillus
— Aussfuerliche Eroeffnung. Hamburg: Thomas von Wiering, 1703. 4 parts in 1 vol. 4to. (88) £480; (89) £150

Arnobius Afer, fl.290
— Disputationum adversus gentes libri octo. Rome: Franciscus Priscianensis, 1542. Folio. (90) £360

Arnold Arboretum
— Catalogue of the Library of.... Cambr., Mass., 1914-33. Compiled by Ethelyn Maria Tucker. 3 vols. 4to. (91) $550

Arnold, Christian Friedrich
— Der herzogliche Palast von Urbino. Leipzig, 1857. Folio. (89) £180

Arnold, Edwin
— Poems Narrative and Lyrical. Oxford, 1853. Inscr. (88) $80

Arnold, Josias Lyndon, 1768-96
— Poems. Providence, 1797. 12mo. (91) £80

Arnold, Matthew, 1822-88
— Cromwell: a Prize Poem Recited in the Theatre, Oxford.... Oxford, 1843. 1st Ed. 8vo. Hayward-Bradley Martin copy. (90) $1,200
— Empedocles on Etna, and Other Poems. L, 1852. 1st Ed. 8vo. (91) £100
Inscr by the 1st Earl of Lytton to Mrs. Petre. Newton-Fleming copy. (89) $450
— Essays in Criticism. L & Cambr., 1865. 1st Ed. 8vo. Inscr to Lord Granville. (89) $80
— Poems. L, 1888-90. 3 vols. 8vo. (88) £1,400
L, 1895. 3 vols. 8vo. (90) $200, $350
— The Strayed Reveller, and Other Poems. L, 1849. 1st Ed. 8vo. (90) £130; (91) £160
Inscr for W. S. Landor. Hugh Walpole—Carroll Wilson—Bradley Martin copy. (90) $700
— Works. L, 1898. 12 vols. 8vo. (91) £50
L, 1903-4. One of 750. 14 (of 15) vols. (91) $280
15 vols. (88) $550

Arnold, Thomas, 1795-1842
— Introductory Lectures on Modern History.... See: Fore-Edge Paintings

Arnold, Sir Thomas Walker, 1864-1930 —& Grohmann, Adolf
— The Islamic Book. L, 1929. One of 375. 4to. (88) $325; (89) £260

Arnold, William Harris, 1854-1923
— A Record of Books & Letters. NY, 1901. One of 145. (88) £55

Arnoldus de Villa Nova, 1235?-1312?
— Regimen sanitatis. Das ist ein Regiment der gesuntheit.... Strassburg: M. Hupfuff, 1513. 4to. (90) £800

Arnot, Hugo, 1749-86
— The History of Edinburgh. Edin., 1779. 1st Ed. 4to. (88) £120; (89) £130
Edin., 1788. 4to. (91) $120

Arnott, James Alexander —& Wilson, John
— The Petit Trianon, Versailles. L, 1907-8. 3 vols. Folio. (89) £70

Arnout, Jean Baptiste & Louis Jules
— Paris et ses Souvenirs. Paris: Veith et Hauser, [1837]. Folio. (90) £1,500

Arnoux, Charles Albert d'
— The Communists of Paris 1871. L, [1873]. 4to. (88) $120, £45; (89) $150; (91) £80

Arntzen, Etta —& Rainwater, Robert
— Guide to the Literature of Art History. Chicago, 1980. Folio. (91) $120

Aronson, Boris
— Marc Chagall. [Berlin], 1923. 4to. In Russian. (88) $175; (89) $425
— Sovremyennaya Evreiskaya Grafika. Berlin, 1924. One of 300. Folio. (89) $1,000

Arp, Jean (or Hans), 1887-1966
— Behaarte Herzen, 1923-1926; Koenige vor der Sintflut, 1952-1953. [Frankfurt, 1953]. One of 100. 4to. (88) $275
— Dreams and Projects. NY, [1951-52]. One of 320. 4to. (90) $1,200; (91) $1,000
— I, rue Gabrielle; douze eaux-fortes originales. Paris, 1958. One of 60. Preface by Michel Seuphor. Oblong 4to. Lydia Winston Malbin's copy. (90) $2,000
— On My Way. NY, 1948. 4to. (88) $50
— Vers le blanc infini. Lausanne & Paris, 1960. One of 600. 4to. (89) SF850
— Le Volier dans la foret. [Paris:] Louis Broder, [1957]. One of 130. 4to. Extra-illus with a pencil sketch of 3 interlocking abstract shapes, sgd. (91) £850
— Weisst du schwarzt du. Zurich: Pra Verlag, 1930. One of 250. With 5 illusts by Max Ernst. (88) $225

Arp, Jean (or Hans), 1887-1966. See: Lissitzky & Arp

Arphe y Villafane, Juan de
— Varia commensuracion para la escultura y arquitectura. Madrid, 1795. 7th Ed. Folio. (91) $125

ARRIANUS

Arrianus, Flavius
— Arriani & Hannonis Periplus [& other works]. Basel: Froben & Episcopius, 1533. 4to. (90) £400
— De expeditioni sive rebus gestis Alexandri. Amst.: Jansson, 1668. ("De expedit. Alex. Magni, historiarum libri VIII.") Folio. (91) £1,200
— De i fatti del Magno Alessandro... Venice: Michele Tramezzino, 1544. 8vo. (90) DM2,400
— De rebus gestis Alexandri regis.... Pesaro: Hieronymus Soncino, 9 June 1508. Folio. Adams A-2011. (91) £700
— Les Faicts & conquestes d'Alexandre le Grand. Paris: Frederic Morel, 1581. 4to. (90) $650

Arrighi Vicentio, Ludovico degli. See: Vicentio, Ludovico degli Arrighi

Arrillaga, B. J. See: California

Arrillaga, Jose
— Recopiliacion de Leyes, Decretos, Bandos.... See: California

Arrington, Alfred W.
— The Rangers and Regulators of the Tanaha: or, Life Among the Lawless. NY: Robert M. De Witt, [1856]. 1st Ed, 1st Issue. 8vo. Sabin 2108a. (91) $150

Arrowsmith, Aaron
[An atlas comprising the large World map & the 4 continents in edge-bound, largely uncut sheets, each hand-colored in outline, c.1800-4, sold at S on 5 Nov 1987 for £3,200] £3,200
— Atlas to Thompson's Alcedo or Dictionary of America.... L, [1795-1811]. Folio. (90) £2,600
— Orbis Terrarum. A Comparative Atlas of Ancient and Modern Geography.... L, 1828. Folio. (88) £95, £170; (89) £110 Sold w.a.f. (89) £80

Arrowsmith, Aaron —& Lewis, Samuel
— A New and Elegant General Atlas.... Phila.: 1804. 4to. (91) $475
Bost., 1812. 4to. (91) $475

Arrowsmith, Aaron, the Younger
— Outlines of the World. L, 1828. 4to. (88) £240

Arrowsmith, H. W. & A.
— The House Decorator and Painter's Guide.... L, 1840. 4to. (88) £420

AMERICAN BOOK PRICES CURRENT

Arrowsmith, John, 1790-1873
— The London Atlas of Universal Geography. L, 1834. Folio. (90) £1,600
L, 1838. Folio. (91) £1,100
L, 1842. Folio. (89) £2,000

Arrowsmith, Joseph
— The Reformation, a Comedy. L, 1673. 4to. (89) $275

Ars...
— Ars Orientalis. The Arts of Islam and the East. Wash.: Freer Gallery, 1954-79. Vols 2-9 & 11. 4to. (90) $325
— Ars Typographica. NY, 1918-34. Vol I, Nos 1-4. Ed by Frederic W. Goudy. Bound in 1 vol. Folio. (90) $70

Ars Memorandi
— Memorabiles evangelistarum figurae. Pforzheim: Thomas Anshelm, 1502. 4to. (91) $16,000

Ars Moriendi
— Speculum artis bene moriendi.... [Cologne: Heinrich Quentell, c.1493]. 4to. 16 leaves. Goff A-1097. (88) $1,900

Arsene de Paris
— Derniere Lettre du Reverend Pere Arsene de Paris.... Paris: Jean Nigaud, 1613. 8vo. Harmsworth copy. (88) £12,000

Art...
— Art and Australia. Sydney, 1976-87. Vol 13, No 4 - Vol 25, No 1. Together, 45 issues. (89) A$200
— L'Art de voyager dans les airs, ou les ballons.... Paris, 1784. 8vo. (90) $450
— L'Art decoratif francais, 1918-1925. Paris, 1925. Folio. (91) $300
— L'Art et science de arismetique moult utile et prouffitable a toutes gens. Paris: A. Lotrian for Pierre Sergeant, [c.1540]. 8vo. Fairfax Murray—Kenney-Honeyman copy. (88) £1,800
— Art in Australia. Sydney, 1916-42. 85 of orig 100 parts; lacking Third Series, Nos 17, 19, 20, 23, 25, 28-32, 40, 48, 70, 74 & 79. (88) A$7,500
Sydney, 1916-24. First Series, Nos 2, 3, 4, 5 & 7. (88) A$220
Series I-III. Sydney, 1916-40. Together, 98 issues; lacking the 1st 2 nos of Series IV. (88) A$8,000
First Series, No 5; Third Series, Nos 3, 4 & 11. Sydney, 1918-25. (88) A$230
Sydney, 1920. Special No on Tasmania. 4to. (90) A$120
Third Series, Nos 6, 9 & 11. Sydney, 1922. (88) A$85
Third Series, No 27. Sydney, 1924. (88) A$32

Third Series, No 13 (Etching). Sydney, 1925. (89) A$140

Third Series, No 22. Sydney, 1927. (88) A$50

Third Series, No 24. Sydney, 1928. (88) A$60

Third Series, No 25. One of 40 with orig etching. (89) A$1,100

Third Series, No 40. Sydney, 1931. (88) A$160

Third Series, No 44. Sydney, 1932. (88) A$25

Third Series, Nos 72-75 & 77. Sydney, 1938-39. (88) A$260

— Art in California.... San Francisco: R. L. Bernier, 1916. (88) $650; (89) $300, $475

— Art in Federal Buildings: an Illustrated Record of the Treasury Department's New Program in Painting and Sculpture. Wash., 1936. Vol I: Mural Designs. Oblong folio. (89) $80

— The Art Journal. L, 1849-1908. 20 vols only. 4to. Sold w.a.f. (90) £1,000

Vols XI-XVIII. L, 1849-56. 4to. (90) £520

— The Art Journal Illustrated Catalogue: The Industry of All Nations. See: Great...

— The Art of Conjuring Made Easy.... Davenport, [c.1840]. 12mo. (90) $550

— The Art of Manual Defence.... L, 1789. 8vo. (90) £580

— L'Art: Revue Hebdomadaire illustree. Paris & L, 1875-80. 7 vols only. Folio. With c.125 etchings and engravings from other vols. Sold w.a.f. (90) $3,000

— Art Work of Baltimore.... [N.p.]: Gravure Illustration Company, 1899. 1st Ed in orig 12 parts. Folio. (88) $250

— Art-Gout-Beaute, Feuillets de l'Elegance feminine. Paris, Feb 1922. 4to. Sample copy. (91) $60

Nos 29-52. Paris, 1923-24. 24 issues. 4to. (88) £5,000

Art Amateur

— The Art Amateur. A Monthly Journal Devoted to the Cultivation of Art in the Household. NY, 1882-94. Vols 7-31 plus 4 Supplement vols. 4to. (88) $1,500

Art, Gout, Beaute...

— Art, Gout, Beaute: Feuillets de l'elegance feminine. Paris, July 1923. Vol III, No 35 only. Folio. (88) $100

Arte...

— Arte y vocabulario en la lengua general del Peru.... [Lima], 1614. 8vo. (90) £850

Arthur, King of Britain

— The History of the Valiant Knight Arthur of Little Britain. L, 1814. 4to. (89) $150
One of 25 L.p. copies. (89) £190
One of 175. (89) £460; (91) £350

— The Most Ancient and Famous History of the Renowned Prince Arthur. L, 1634. 3 parts in 1 vol. 4to. (88) £1,300

Arthur, Joshua. See: Brandon & Arthur

Articulen...

— Articulen van Vrede ende Verbondt [Treaty of Breda]. The Hague, 1667. 1st Ed. 4to. (91) £160

Artillery...

— Artillery-Vollenkommene Unterweisung wie Raketen, Feuer-Wasser Strum-Kugeln.... Osnabrueck: Johann Georg Schwanders Tilman, 1660. 2 parts in 1 vol. Folio. (91) £1,400

Artistes...

— Les Artistes du livre. Paris: Henry Babou, 1928-33. Ltd Ed. 24 vols (complete set). 4to. (88) FF8,800

Artistic...

— Artistic Houses; being a Series of Interior Views.... NY, 1883-84. One of 500. 2 vols in 4. Folio. (90) $4,800

Artist's...

— The Artist's London. As Seen in Eighty Contemporary Pictures. L, 1924. Ltd Ed. 4to. (88) £70, £90

Artizan

— The Artizan. A Monthly Journal of the Operative Arts. L, 1844-70. Vol 1 - 4th Series, Vol 4. 4to. (88) $1,000

Arundale, Francis, 1807-53

— Illustrations of Jerusalem and Mount Sinai. L, 1837. 4to. (91) £200, £400, £520
Blackmer copy. (90) £950

Arundel Collection, Thomas Howard, Earl of

— Marmora Arundelliana.... L, 1628. 1st Ed. 4to. (89) £180
STC 823. Blackmer copy. (90) £750

Arundell, Francis Vyvyan Jago

— Discoveries in Asia Minor. L, 1834. 2 vols. 8vo. Blackmer copy. (90) £500

Arundell, Francis Vyvyan Jago, 1780-1846
— A Visit to the Seven Churches of Asia.... L: J. Rodwell, 1828. 8vo. Blackmer copy. (90) £250

Arvers, Felix
— Mes Heures perdues, poesies. Paris, 1833. 8vo. Martin copy. (90) FF1,400

Arvieux, Laurent d'
— Travels in Arabia the Desart. L, 1718. 8vo. (90) £110; (91) £300

Asbjornsen, Peter Christen, 1812-85 —& Moe, Jorgen I, 1813-82
— East of the Sun and West of the Moon. NY: Doran, [c.1913-14]. Illus by Kay Nielsen. 4to. (88) $100; (91) $110
L, [1914]. 4to. (88) £250, £50; (89) £140, £420, £1,400, £4,200; (90) £120; (91) $1,400
One of 500. (88) $150; (89) $50, $2,600; (90) £480
NY, [c.1914]. 4to. (91) $120
1st American Trade Ed. NY, [1914]. 4to. (91) $170
L, [n.d.]. 4to. (91) $140
— A l'Est du Soleil et a l'Ouest de la Lune.... Paris, 1919. One of 1,500. Illus by Kay Nielsen. 4to. Inscr by Nielsen, 1923. (89) £700
— East of the Sun and West of the Moon. NY: Doran, [1927?]. Illus by Kay Nielsen. (88) $100, $140

Asbury, Francis
— The Journal.... NY, 1821. 3 vols. 8vo. (88) $120

Asbury, Henry, 1810-96
— Reminiscences of Quincy, Illinois.... Quincy, 1882. 8vo. Inscr. (89) $50
Quincy: D. Wilcox, 1882. 8vo. Inscr. (89) $50

Ascham, Roger, 1515-68
— Disertissimi viri Rogeri Aschami, Regiae liam Majestati a Latinis Epistolis, familiarium Epistolarium libri tres.... L: Francisco Coldocko, 1581. 8vo. STC 828. (91) £85
— The English Works. L, 1761. 1st Ed, 1st Issue. 4to. (88) $200
— The Scholemaster.... L: John Daye, 1570. 1st Ed. 4to. (88) £4,000; (89) £600
Bradley Martin copy. (90) £11,000
L: A. Jeffes, 1589. ("The Schoolemaster. Or, Playne and Perfit Way of Teaching....") 4to. (88) £650
L, 1711. ("The Schoolmaster....") 8vo. (88) £75
— Toxophilus. L: Edward Whitchurch, 1545. 4to. STC 837. Huntington-Clawson-Bradley Martin copy. (90) $15,000
L: Thomas Marshe, 1571. 4to. (88) $500
L: A Jeffes, 1589. 4to. (88) £350; (91) £1,000
L, 1788. 8vo. (88) $150

Asconius Pedianus, Quintus
— Commentarii in orationes Ciceronis [& other works]. Venice: Johannes de Colonia & Johannes Manthen, after 2 June] [1477. Folio. 184 leaves. Goff A-1154. Doheny copy. (88) $5,000
184 leaves. Goff A-1154. Spencer-Rylands copy. (88) £9,500

Aseev, N.
— Zor. Moscow, 1914. One of 20. (91) $375

Ash, Edward C.
— The Practical Dog Book. See: Derrydale Press

Ash, Edward Cecil
— Dogs: their History and Development. L, 1927. 2 vols. 4to. (88) $175

Ashbee, Charles Robert
— American Sheaves and English Seed Corn.... L: Essex House Press, 1901. One of 300. 4to. (88) £80; (89) £65
— An Endeavour towards the Teaching of John Ruskin and William Morris. L & Chipping Camden: Essex House Press, 1901. One of 350. (89) $175; (90) $140; (91) £110, £140, $200
Doheny copy. (89) $420
— The Essex House Song Book. L, 1904. One of 205. 2 vols. 4to. (91) $150
— The Last Records of a Cotswold Community. L: Essex House Press, 1904. One of 75. (91) £160
— The Masque of the Edwards of England. L & NY, 1902. One of 300. Illus by Edith Harwood. Oblong folio. (91) $150
— Modern English Silverwork. L, 1974. One of 1,000. 4to. (90) £500
— Peckover: The Abbotscourt Papers, 1904-1931. L: Curwen Press, 1932. One of 350. Folio. (88) £60

Ashbee, Henry Spencer, 1834-1900
— Bibliography of Prohibited Books. NY, 1962. 3 vols. (90) $60
— Catena Librorum Tacendorum: Being Notes...by Pisanus Fraxi. L, 1877. One of 250. 4to. (91) £105
— The Encyclopedia of Erotic Literature. NY, [c.1962]. 3 vols. (89) $120
— An Iconography of Don Quixote, 1605-1895. L, 1895. 4to. (91) $130
— Index Librorum Prohibitorum. L, 1877. 1st Ed, One of 250. 4to. (91) $1,300, £100
— Index Librorum Prohibitorum. Centuria

1987 - 1991 • BOOKS

Librorum Absconditorum. Catena Librorum Tacendorum. L, [1960]. One of 395. 3 vols. Facsimile reprint of the L, 1877-85 Ed. (88) $100

Ashbery, John —&
Schuyler, James
— A Nest of Ninnies. NY, 1969. Inscr. (88) $100

Ashby, H. See: Hodgkin & Ashby

Ashby, Thomas Almond
— The Valley Campaigns, being the Reminiscences of a Non-Combatant...during the War of the States. NY, 1914. (91) $110

Ashe, Thomas, 1836-89
— Travels in America.... Newburyport, 1808. 1st American Ed. 12mo. With numerous contemp marginalia vilifying Ashe and his portrayal of American domestic manners. (89) $175
  American Ed. 3 vols. 12mo. (88) $130

Ashendene Press—London
  [The Ashendene Press collection of Stuart Schimmel, including books, emphemera, related works & 16 A Ls s of H. St. J. Hornby, sold at CNY on 17 May 1991 as lot 241] $170,000
— The Boke of the Revelacion off Sanct Jhon the Divine. 1901. One of 54. (89) £480; (91) $550, $1,600
— A Book of Songs and Poems from the Old Testament and the Apocrypha. 1904. One of 150. (88) £400; (89) £240; (90) £400; (91) $700, $800
  Doheny copy. (88) $550
— A Chronological List, with Prices of the Forty Books... 1935. Dampstain to covers & internally. (91) $90
— A Descriptive Bibliography of the Books... 1935. One of 390. (88) £850, £900; (89) £850, £850; (90) $1,200, £1,050; (91) $130, £650, £1,200
  Doheny copy. (88) $2,400
  The Garden copy. (90) $2,200, $2,400
  1976. One of 375. Reprint of 1935 Ed. (91) $80
— [Ecclesiasticus] The Wisdom of Jesus, the Son of Sirach... 1932. One of 25 ptd on vellum. (89) £6,000; (90) $9,000
  One of 328. (88) £880, £1,000, £1,050; (89) £500, £650, £850, £1,400; (90) £750, £1,300; (91) $1,900, £800
  Doheny copy. (88) $1,800
  The Garden copy. (90) $2,500
— A Hand-List of the Books Printed at the Ashendene Press MDCCCXCV-MCMXXV. 1925. (89) £90
— Hymns and Prayers to be Sung and Said at the Marriage of St. John Hornby and

ASHENDENE PRESS

Cecily Barclay. 1897. (89) £100
— Hymns and Prayers for Use at the Marriage of Michael Hornby and Nicolette Ward. 1928. (89) £130
  One of 250. (90) £90
— The Song of Songs which is Solomon's. 1902. One of 40. Ptd on vellum. (89) £12,500
  Illuminated by Valenti Angelo. (91) $60
— The Song-Story of Aucassin and Nicolete.... 1901. One of 40. (89) £260
— The Story without an End.... 1909. One of 6 on vellum. Trans from the German by Sarah Austin. Inscr by St. John Hornby to his sister-in-law, Charlotte Barclay. (91) £4,800
  One of 30 on Japanese paper. Presentation copy from Diana Hornby, the dedicatee. (89) £750
— Three Elegies. Lycidas by John Milton. Adonais by Percy B. Shelley. Thyrsis by Matthew Arnold. 1899. One of 50. (89) £90; (90) £350
— APULEIUS, LUCIUS. - The Golden Asse. 1924. One of 16 on vellum. The Garden copy. (90) $11,000
  One of 165. (88) £300, £320; (89) £320; (90) £400
— BERNERS, DAME JULIANA. - A Treatyse of Fysshynge wyth an Angle. 1903. One of 25 ptd on vellum. (90) £1,000
  One of 150. (88) £260, £260, £320; (89) £200
— BOCCACCIO, GIOVANNI. - Il Decameron. 1920. One of 105. (89) £380, £680, £700
  Bookplate of John Henry Nash Library. (88) $900
— BRIDGES, ROBERT. - Poems Written in the Year MCMXIII. 1914. One of 85. (89) £450
— CERVANTES SAAVEDRA, MIGUEL DE. - Don Quixote. 1927-28. One of 225. 2 vols. (88) £1,050; (89) £650, £1,200; (90) $2,200; (91) £1,000
  ALs of St. John Hornby to subscriber John Charrington laid in. (89) £800
  Doheny copy. (88) $2,800
  Martin copy. (90) $2,300
— DANTE ALIGHIERI. - La Divina Commedia. 1902-4-5. One of 14, 20 & 20. 3 vols. The Garden copy. (90) $23,000
  One of 135 & one of 150. (88) £2,300
  Mosher-The Garden copy. (90) $6,000
  Lo Inferno only. 1902. One of 135. Doheny copy. (88) $600
— DANTE ALIGHIERI. - Tutte le Opere di Dante Alighiere Fiorentino. 1909. One of 6 on vellum. St. John Hornby's own copy. The Garden copy. (90) $77,500
  One of 105. (88) £4,500; (89) £2,700

865

ASHENDENE PRESS

Doheny copy. (88) $10,000
The Garden copy. (90) $10,500
— DANTE ALIGHIERI. - La Vita Nuova. 1895. One of 45 on Japanese vellum. (89) £650
— FRANCIS OF ASSISI. - I Fioretti... 1922. One of 240. (88) £380; (89) £320; (90) $350
— FRANCIS OF ASSISI. - Un Mazzeto scelto dei fioretti... 1904. One of 25 on vellum. (88) £2,200
One of 125. (89) £200; (90) £100
Doheny copy. (88) $650
— H., B. - The Children's Garden. 1913. One of c.150. (89) £160
— HORACE. - Carmina Alcaica. 1903. One of 150. (89) $300
One of 25 on vellum with initials painted in 3 colors by Graily Hewitt. Doheny copy. (89) $3,000
— HORACE. - Carmina Sapphica. 1903. One of 25 on vellum. (89) £950
One of 150. (89) £480
— LONGUS. - Les Amours pastorales de Daphnis et Chloe. 1933. One of 20 on vellum. (88) £11,500
One of 290. (88) £450, £500; (89) £360; (90) £600; (91) £420
— LUCRETIUS CARUS, TITUS. - T. Lucreti Cari de rerum natura libri sex. 1913. One of 80. (89) £850
— MALORY, SIR THOMAS. - Le Morte Darthur. 1913. One of 145. (88) £1,550; (89) £1,600
Doheny copy. (88) $3,200
With ALs from C. H. St. John Hornby, 9 Dec 1913, tipped in. (89) £1,200
— MILTON, JOHN. - Three Poems of John Milton. 1896. One of 50. (89) £550
Doheny copy. (88) $1,400
— MORE, SIR THOMAS. - Utopia. 1906. ("A Fruteful and Pleasaunt Worke....") One of 100. Doheny copy. (88) $1,500
— OMAR KHAYYAM. - Rubaiyat. 1896. One of 50. St. John Hornby's own copy, with related material inserted. (88) £1,800
— SPENSER, EDMUND. - The Faerie Queene. 1923. One of 180. (88) £850; (89) £800; (90) £800
— SPENSER, EDMUND. - Minor Poems. 1925. One of 200. (88) £55; (89) £650, £650, £240; (90) £280, £300; (91) £280
— THUCYDIDES. - The History of the Peloponnesian War. 1930. One of 17 on vellum. (88) £10,000
One of 260. (88) £850; (89) £900, £1,300; (90) $1,600, £800; (91) £750
Doheny copy. (88) $1,500
The Garden copy. (90) $1,200
— TOLSTOY, LEO. - Where God is Love Is. 1924. One of c.200. Trans by Louise & Aylmer Maude. (89) £140; (91) $400
— VERINO, UGOLINO. - Vita di Santa Chiara Vergine. 1921. One of 236. (88) £250; (90) £140; (91) £200, £250

AMERICAN BOOK PRICES CURRENT

One of 286. (89) £170
Doheny copy. (88) $350
— WILDE, OSCAR. - Four Tales. 1924. One of 65. Inscr to John Galsworthy "from his friend, the Printer. October 31, 1924". (90) $800
— WILDE, OSCAR. - The Young King. L, 1924. One of 65. Inscr to John Galsworthy "from his friend, the Printer. October 31, 1924". (91) $750

Asher, Adolf, 1800-53
— A Bibliographical Essay on the Scriptores Rerum Germanicarum. L, 1843. 4to. (91) $175

Ashik, Anton
— Vosporskoe tsarstvo s' ego paleograficheskimi i nadgrobnimi pamyatnikami.... Odessa: T. Neyman, 1848-49. 3 parts in 1 vol. 4to. From Tsarkoe Selo with the armorial bookplate of Nicholas I. Blackmer copy. (90) £3,500

Ashley, Clifford Warren
— Whaleships of New Bedford. Bost. & NY, 1929. One of 1,000. 4to. (89) $175; (91) $160
— The Yankee Whaler. Bost. & NY, 1926. 1st Ed. 4to. (88) $185, $210; (89) $100; (91) $175

Ashley, William H. See: Morgan, Dale Lowell

Ashmole, Elias, 1617-92
— The Antiquities of Berkshire. L, 1719. 3 vols. 8vo. (91) £320
— The Institution, Laws & Ceremonies of the Most Noble Order of the Garter. L, 1672. 1st Ed. Folio. (88) $425; (90) $1,100; (91) £210, £520
— Memoirs of the Life of that Learned Antiquary.... L: for J. Roberts, 1717. Issue with the price 1/6 on half-title. 12mo. (91) £220
— Theatrum chemicum Britannicum.... L, 1652. 1st Ed. Part 1 (all pbd). 4to. (91) £3,200

**Ashmole, Elias, 1617-92 —&
Lilly, William, 1602-81**
— The Lives of those Eminent Antiquaries Elias Ashmole...and Mr. William Lilly, Written by Themselves.... L, 1774. 8vo. (89) $250, £100

Ashton, John
— Chap-Books of the Eighteenth Century. L, 1882. 8vo. (89) $50; (90) $110; (91) $55
L, 1885. 8vo. (91) $175
— A History of English Lotteries.... L, 1893. 8vo. (90) $120; (91) $100, £50

Ashton, Warren J., Pseud.
— Hatchie, the Guardian Slave.... Bost., 1853. 8vo. Martin copy. (90) $225

Ashworth, Thomas
— The Salmon Fisheries of England.... L, [1868]. 8vo. (90) $100

Asimov, Isaac
— David Starr: Space Ranger. Garden City, 1952. (89) $110
— The End of Eternity. Garden City, 1955. (90) $65; (91) $65
  Inscr. (89) $80
— Foundation. NY: Gnome Press, 1951. (88) $110; (89) $225
— Foundation and Earth. NY, 1986. One of 300. (89) $90; (90) $65
— The Gods Themselves. Garden City, 1972. (91) $50
  Sgd. (90) $55
— Lucky Starr and the Oceans of Venus. Garden City, 1954. (89) $160
— The Naked Sun. Garden City, 1957. (89) $160, $170
— Robots and Empire. West Bloomfield MI: Phantasia, 1985. One of 35 specially bound. Sgd. (90) $500
  One of 650. (89) $55
— The Robots of Dawn. Huntington Woods MI: Phantasia Press, 1983. One of 750. (89) $70
  Ltd Ed. Huntington Woods MI: Phantasia Press, 1983. (88) $75
— The Stars, Like Dust. Garden City, 1951. (91) $80

Askew Library, Anthony
— [Sale Catalogue] Bibliotheca Askeviana.... L, 1775. 8vo. (89) £140; (90) £300

Aspin, Jehoshaphat
— Cosmorama: a View of the Costumes and Peculiarities of all Nations. L: J. Harris, [1827]. 12mo. (89) £55
— The Naval and Military Exploits.... L, 1820. 1st Ed. 12mo. (88) £550, £620; (90) (91) £450
— A Picture of the Manners, Customs...Inhabitants of England.... L, 1825. 1st Ed. 12mo. (88) $70

Asplund, Karl
— Anders Zorn, his Life and Work. L, 1921. 4to. (89) $100; (90) $80; (91) $110
— Zorn's Engraved Work. Stockholm, 1920. One of 300. 2 parts in 2 vols. 4to. (89) $700

Asquith, Cynthia
— This Mortal Coil. Sauk City: Arkham House, 1947. (89) $75

Assay Office, Birmingham
— Catalogue of Books in the Library. See: England

Asiento...
— The Asiento; or Contract for Allowing to the Subjects of Great Britain the Liberty of Importing Negroes into the Spanish America. L, 1713. 1st Ed. 4to. (89) £260

Assiette...
— L'Assiette au beurre. Paris, 1903. No 137. 4to. (90) $80

Assize of Bread...
— The Assize of Bread: with Sundry Good and Needful Ordinances for Bakers, Inholders, Victuallers.... L, 1684. 4to. (88) £420

Astell, Mary, 1668-1731
— An Essay in Defence of the Female Sex....
  L, 1696. 8vo. (90) £240
  L, 1698. 8vo. (88) £150
— A Serious Proposal to the Ladies.... L, 1695. 12mo. (88) £260
  L, 1697. 2 parts in 1 vol. 12mo. (88) £130
— Some Reflections upon Marriage.... L, 1700. 8vo. (88) £600

Astesanus de Ast
— Canones poenitentiales. [Vienna: Johann Winterburg, c.1496]. 4to. 6 leaves. Goff A-1159. (90) DM4,400
— Summa de casibus conscientiae. [Strasbourg: Johann Mentelin, not after 1469]. Folio. 235 (of 443) leaves; lacking all after leaf 235. Goff A-1160. (89) $3,200
  Venice: Leonardus Wild for Nicolaus de Frankfordia, 28 Apr 1480. Folio. 522 (of 554) leaves; lacking a1 & y12, both blank. Goff A-1169. (91) $3,200

Astle, Thomas, 1735-1803
— The Origin and Progress of Writing. L, 1803. 2d Ed. 4to. (88) £150, £250; (89) £80, £130, £320; (91) £500, £140
  L, 1876. Folio. (88) $190

Astley, Philip
— Astley's System of Equestrian Education. L, [1801]. 3rd Ed. 8vo. (90) $150

Astley, Thomas
— A New General Collection of Voyages and Travels.... L: Thomas Astley, 1745-47. 4 vols. 4to. (88) £500, £1,500, R1,300; (90) $600; (91) £300, £650

ASTLEY

Vols I-II only. (91) £180
Vols I-III, 2d Ed; Vol IV, 1st Ed. L: Thomas Astley, 1754-47. 4 vols. 4to. (88) £320

Aston, John Partington. See: Ainsworth & Aston

Atget, Eugene
— A Vision of Paris. NY, 1963. Text by Marcel Proust. 4to. (88) $55, $100; (89) £70; (91) $200

Athanasius, Saint
— Opera. Strasburg: J. Knoblouchum, 1522. Folio. (91) £340
Cologne: Melchioris Novesiani, 1548. Folio. (91) $160
Cologne, 1686. 2 vols. Folio. (88) £65

Athenaeus
— Deipnosophistarum. Venice: Aldus, Aug 1514. 1st Ed in Greek. Folio. (90) £4,000
Spencer-Rylands copy. (88) £4,500
Lyons: Antoine de Harsy, 1583. Folio. Sgd "Larochefoucauld" on tp. (88) FF5,000

Athenby, Edward. See: Whyte & Athenby

Athenian...
— The Athenian Gazette: or Casuistical Mercury. L, 1691-97. Vols 1-10 (of 20). Folio. (88) £140
Vols 1-20. Bound in 1 vol. Folio. (91) £340
— Athenian Letters or the Epistolary Correspondent of an Agent to the King of Persia.... L, 1741-43. 4 vols. 8vo. (88) £100

Athens
— Athenes moderne. Athens: M. P. Vreto, 1861. Folio. Blackmer copy. (90) £1,800
— Athens moderne, ou description abregee de la capitale de la Grece.... Athens, 1860. 8vo. Blackmer copy. (90) £170
— Vera, e distinta relatione dell'acquisto della citta, e fortezza d'Athene fatto dall'armi della Serenissima Republica di Venetia.... Venice: Antonio Pinelli, 1687. 4to. Blackmer copy. (90) £600

Atherton, Gertrude
— The Conqueror. Being the True and Romantic Story of Alexander Hamilton. NY, 1902. 1st State. Inscr to Mrs. Bridgeman. Parsons-Fleming copy. (89) $190
— The Splendid Idle Forties.... Kentfield: Allen Press, 1960. One of 150. Folio. (89) $175, $225, $225, $375
— What Dreams May Come: A Romance. Chicago, [1888]. 1st Ed. 8vo. Sgd on tp, 1934. (91) $275

AMERICAN BOOK PRICES CURRENT

Atherton, John
— The Fly and the Fish. NY, 1951. Inscr & with ALs to Joseph Bates. (90) $320
One of 222. (88) $60; (90) $400; (91) $200
Inscr to the Darbees. (88) $210
With 2 A Ls s to Joseph Bates laid in. (90) $750

Atherton, William
— Narrative of the Suffering and Defeat of the North-Western Army.... Frankfort, Kentucky, 1842. 1st Ed. 16mo. (90) $120

Atistotle, 384-322 B.C.
— De arte rhetorica libri tres. Paris: Gerard Morrhius, 1530. 8vo. (88) $325

Atkins, John, 1685-1757
— A Voyage to Guinea, Brasil, and the West-Indies.... L, 1735. 8vo. (90) £220; (91) £110, £160, £340
L, 1737. 8vo. (91) £200

Atkins, Samuel Eliot —& Overall, William Henry
— Some Account of the Worshipful Company of Clockmakers of the City of London. L, 1881. 8vo. (89) $70, £160
Front endpaper inscr "With the compliments of the clerk to the Company April 1929". (88) $125

Atkins, Thomas
— The Wanderings of the Clerical Eulysses.... Greenwich, [1859]. 1st Ed. 8vo. (90) A$650
Malvern, 1869. ("Reminiscences of Twelve Years' Residence in Tasmania and New South Wales....") 8vo. (90) A$200

Atkinson, Geoffroy
— La Litterature geographique francaise de la renaissance. Paris, 1927. One of 550. 4to. (88) $70, $90

Atkinson, George Francklin
— The Campaign in India. L, 1859. Folio. (88) £150, £230; (90) £300; (91) £240
— "Curry & Rice" on Forty Plates.... L, [1859]. 4to. (91) £95

Atkinson, Herbert, d.1936
— The Old English Game Fowl. L: Fanciers Gazette, [1891]. One of 100. 4to. (91) £200

Atkinson, J. C.
— A Glossary of the Cleveland Dialect. L, 1868. 4to. With 2 A Ls s to the ptrs pasted in at beginning. (90) £60

Atkinson, James, of Oldbury
— An Account of the State of Agriculture...in New South Wales. L, 1826. 8vo. (89) A$44,000

Atkinson, James, 1780-1852
— Sketches in Afghaunistan. L, [1842]. Folio. (88) £600; (89) £380

Atkinson, John Augustus, 1775-1831
— Sixteen Scenes Taken from the Miseries of Human Life. L, 1807. Oblong 4to. (91) $400

Atkinson, John Augustus, 1775-1831 —& Walker, James, 1748-1808
— A Picturesque Representation of the Manners...of the Russians. L, 1803-4. 3 vols. Folio. (89) £300
  3 vols in 1. Folio. (91) £580
  Vols II & III only, bound in 1 vol. (89) £160

Atkinson, Sophie
— An Artist in Corfu. L, 1911. (91) $200

Atkinson, Thomas Witlam, 1799-1861
— Oriental and Western Siberia. L, 1858. 8vo. (89) £120; (91) $50, £60
— Travels in the Regions of the Upper and Lower Amoor. L, 1860. 1st Ed. 8vo. (89) £50, A$210; (91) $475, £60

Atkinson, William B., 1832-1909
— The Physicians and Surgeons of the United States. Phila., 1878. 1st Ed. 8vo. (91) $300

Atkyns, Richard
— The Kings Grant of Privilege for Sole Printing Common-Law-Books, Defended.... L: John Streater, 1669. 4to. (88) £550
— The Original and Growth of Printing.... L, 1664. 4to. Bridgewater-Doheny copy. (89) $1,200

Atkyns, Sir Robert, 1647-1711
— The Ancient and Present State of Gloucestershire. L, 1768. 2d Ed. Folio. (88) £1,800; (89) £2,600, £2,600; (90) $5,000, £3,800; (91) £3,800

Atlantic...
— Atlantic Monthly. Bost., 1857-1916. Vols 1-56 & 59-115. (88) $80

Atlantic Charter
— CHURCHILL, SIR WINSTON L. S. & ROOSEVELT, FRANKLIN D. - Atlantic Charter August 12th 1941. Amst.: Busy Bee (De Algemeene Vrije Illegale Drukkerij), [c.1944]. One of 100. 16mo. (90) £750

Atlas
[A composite atlas with c.1847 maps in 33 large volumes, from the Bibliotheque du Chateau de La Roche-Guyon, sold at SM on 8 Dec 1987] FF1,800,000
[The Doria Atlas, a 16th-cent Italian composite with 17th-cent additions, originally comprising 104 Italian maps & views, 1535-70 & including a unique woodcut wall map of Spain by Vincentus Corsulensis dated 1551, sold at S on 27 Sept 1988 for £225,000 to Israel]
See also: Faden, William
— The American Gazetteer.... L, 1762. 3 vols. 12mo. (90) $80; (91) $3,250
— The American Military Pocket Atlas. L, [1776]. 8vo. (88) $6,250, £2,600; (91) $5,750, $6,000
— Asher & Adams' New Topographical Map of the State of New York. NY, [1869]. Folio. (88) $100
— Asher & Adams' New Topographical Atlas and Gazetteer of New York.... NY, [1870]. Folio. (90) £230
  NY, [1871]. Folio. (89) $100, $120; (90) $130
— Asher & Adams' New Commercial, Statistical and Topographical Atlas.... NY, [1872]. Folio. (88) $180
— Atlas Celeste, or the Celestial Atlas. L, 1786. Compiled by John Bevis. Oblong folio. (91) £4,000
— Atlas de toutes les parties connues du globe terrestre. [Geneva, 1780?]. 4to. (88) $325, $800
— Atlas minor ad usum serenissimi Burgundiae ducis. Amst.: Carel Allard, [c.1700-5]. Folio. Composite made for presentation to the dauphin Louis, duc de Bourgogne. Martin copy. (90) $37,500
— Atlas of Russia made up of 19 Special Maps representing the Russian Empire [title in Russian]. St. Petersburg, 1745. Folio. (90) £3,800
— An Atlas of the United States of North America, Corrected to the Present Period.... L & Phila., 1832. 4to. Franklin D. Roosevelt's copy, sgd by him. (90) $850
— Atlas of the Philippine Islands. Wash., 1900. 8vo. Special Publications of the U. S. Coast and Geodetic Survey, No. 3. (88) $60
— Atlas portatif pour servir a l'intelligence de l'histoire philosophique et politique des establissemens et du commerce des Europeens dans les deux Indes. Amst., 1773. 4to. (89) HF2,500
— Atlas portatif a l'usage des colleges, pour servir a l'intelligence des auteurs classiques. Paris: Jean, [1790 or later]. 2 vols. 4to. (91) £450

ATLAS

- Atlas Russicus. St. Petersburg, 1745. Folio. (89) £800; (90) £2,400
- Atlas to Accompany 2d Report of the Railway Commissioners Ireland 1838. Dublin & L: Hodges & Smith, Gardner, [1839]. 1830mm by 1480mm. (88) £120
- Atlas to Accompany the Official Records of the Union and Confederate Armies. Wash., 1891-95. 2 vols in 1. Folio. (90) $700
  Vol III only. (89) $180
- Atlas topographique et militaire, qui comprend Les Etats de la Couronne de Boheme & la Saxe Electorale.... Paris, 1758. Folio. (90) £50
- Bradley's Atlas of the World. NY, 1884. Folio. (91) $300
- Colton's Atlas of the World. NY, 1856. 2 vols. Folio. (88) $550, £1,700
  NY, 1856-57. 2 vols. Folio. (90) $1,100
- Colton's General Atlas.... NY, 1857. Folio. (89) £1,300; (91) $750, £460
  NY, 1858. Folio. (88) $550
  NY, 1859. Folio. (88) $850
  NY, 1861. Folio. (88) $900; (90) £600; (91) £600
  NY, 1866. Folio. (89) £1,100
  NY, 1868. Folio. (88) $210
  NY, 1877. Folio. (91) $550
  NY, 1881. Folio. (91) $850
- Colton's Octavo Atlas of the World. NY, 1856. (88) $325
- The Edinburgh Imperial Atlas. Edin., [1850]. Folio. (90) £100
- Il Gazzettiere Americano contenente un distinto regguaglio di tutte le parti del Nuovo Mondo.... Livorno, 1763. 3 vols. 4to. (90) £1,500; (91) $1,700, £1,800, LIt5,500,000
- A General Atlas, being a Collection of Maps of the World and Quarters. See: Wilkinson, Robert
- Gray's Atlas of the United States. Phila., 1873. Folio. (91) £700
  Phila., 1874. Folio. (91) $475, $475
  Phila., 1878. Folio. (90) $425
- Johnson's New Illustrated Family Atlas. NY, 1865. Folio. (88) $500
  NY, 1866. Folio. (90) $650
  NY, 1867. Folio. (89) $475; (91) $375
  [NY, c.1869]. Folio. (89) $375
  NY, 1869. Folio. (91) $550
  NY, 1872. Folio. (89) $230, $350
  NY: Johnson & Ward, 1872. Folio. (89) $400
  NY, 1873. Folio. (89) $500
- Leigh's New Pocket Atlas of England and Wales.... L, 1834. 8vo. (91) £100
- Lett's Popular Atlas. L, 1883. Folio. (90) £130
- Letts's Popular County Atlas. L, 1884. Folio. (89) £100
- Lizars' Edinburgh Geographical General Atlas. Edin., [c.1842]. Folio. (89) £320
- Magnus's Commercial Atlas of the World. NY, 1856. Folio. (91) $325
- Malby's Telescopic Companion or Celestial Globe-Atlas. L, 1848. Folio. (91) $1,100
- Mappamundi: The Catalan Atlas of the Year 1375. Zurich, 1978. One of 790. Ed by Georges Grosjean. Folio. (91) $950
- Maps and Plans, Showing the Principle Movements, Battles and Sieges in which the British Army was Engaged during...1808-1814. L, [1840]. Folio. (89) £350; (91) £600
- Mitchell's New Universal Atlas. Phila., 1862. ("Mitchell's New General Atlas.") Folio. (90) $550; (91) $550
  Phila., 1863. Folio. (89) £440; (91) $550, $550
  Phila., 1864. Folio. (88) $400, $400
  Phila., 1865. Folio. (91) $650
- Mitchell's New General Atlas.... Phila., 1866. 4to. (91) $50
  Phila., 1867. Folio. (88) $500
- Mitchell's New Universal Atlas. Phila., 1869. ("Mitchell's New General Atlas.") Folio. (88) $550
  Phila., 1871. Folio. (90) $425
  Phila., 1872. Folio. (88) $100; (89) $200
  Phila., 1874. Folio. (88) $400; (89) $350; (90) $425
  Phila., 1880. Folio. (91) $400
  Phila., 1882. Folio. (91) $475
  Phila., 1887. Folio. (90) $225
- The National Atlas Containing Elaborate Topographical Maps of the United States and the Dominion of Canada. Phila., 1875. Folio. (91) $400
  Phila., 1888. Folio. (89) $250; (91) $400
- Le Neptune francois. See: Neptune...
- New General Atlas.... Phila., 1860. Folio. (89) £380
- New Topographical Atlas of the County of Hampden Massachusetts. Springfield, 1894. Folio. (88) $160
- Procli De Sphaera Liber I. Cleomedis de Mundo sive circularis inspectionis metorum. Arati Solensis Phaenomena...una cum Io. Honteri Coronensis de Cosmographiae.... Basel: Heinrich Petri, 1561. 5 parts in 1 vol. 12mo. (88) £880
- The Royal Illustrated Atlas of Modern Geography. L & Edin.: Fullarton, [c.1862]. Folio. (89) £450; (91) £660
  L & Edin.: Fullarton, [1864]. Folio. (90) £800
- Stanford's London Atlas of Universal Geography. L, 1887. Folio. (89) £75; (91) £70
- Tabulae geographicae, quibus universa geographia vetus continetur. Padua: Stamperia del Seminario [Vescovile], 1699-

1702. 4 parts in 1 vol. Folio. (90) £3,000
Extra-illus with 5 double-page maps, 1701-2, by Giovanni Battista Canali. (89) £3,800
— West Point Atlas of American Wars, 1689-1953. NY, [1959]. Ed by Vincent J. Esposito. 2 vols. Folio. (88) $50, $60; (91) $55
Inscr. (91) $80
NY, 1960. 2d ptg. 2 vols. Folio. (91) $50

Atwater, Caleb
— Remarks made on a Tour to Prairie du Chien.... Columbus, Ohio: Jenkins & Glover, 1831. 12mo. (90) $120

Atwood, George, 1746-1807
— A Treatise on the Rectilinear Motion and Rotation of Bodies.... Cambr., 1784. 8vo. (89) £400

Aubert du Petit-Thouars, Abel, 1758-1831
— Voyage autour du monde sur la Fregate la Venus.... Paris, 1840. 4 parts in 2 vols. 8vo. (89) $375
Paris, 1840-46. Atlas de zoologie only. Folio. Martin copy. (90) $4,500
Paris: Gide, 1841. Folio. (88) $5,800; (90) £3,200
Paris: Gide, 1846. 2 Atlas vols bound in 1. Folio. (91) £2,200
— Voyage autour du monde sur la fregate La Venus: Album historique. [Paris: Arthus Bertrand, c.1845]. Folio. (90) £7,000

Aubert, Marcel
— Notre-Dame de Paris: Architecture et Sculpture. Paris, [1928]. Folio. (88) $55

Aubin, Nicolas
— Dictionnaire de marine contenant les termes de la navigation.... Amst.: Pierre Brunel, 1702. 4to. (91) £900
Amst.: Jean Covens & Corneille Mortier, 1736. 4to. (91) £170
Alan Moore's copy, with pencilled notes. (88) £420

Aublet, Jean B. C. Fusee
— Histoire des plantes de la Guiane francoise.... L, 1775. (91) $2,000

Aubrey, John, 1626-97
— Miscellanies. L: for Edward Castle, 1696. 8vo. (90) £850

Aubry, Charles
— Histoire pittoresque de l'equitation ancienne et moderne. Paris, 1833. Folio. (88) $225; (89) $150; (90) HF1,700

Aubry, Octave
— Napoleon. [Paris, 1936]. 4to. Extra-illus with 96 plates, 9 hand-colored. (89) £110

Aubry, Roger
— L'Epreuve Photographique. Premiere Serie. Paris: Librairie Plon, [1904]. Preface by Emile Dacier. Folio. (89) $2,200

Aubusson, Louis Magaud d'
— Les Oiseaux de la France...Premiere monographie Corvides. Paris: A. Quantin, 1883. 4to. (88) FF4,000
Martin copy. (90) $500

Aucassin & Nicolette
— Aucassin & Nicolete.... L: David Nutt, 1887. One of 63 on japan with frontis in 2 states. Trans by Andrew Lang. 8vo. (91) £190
— Of Aucassin and Nicolette: a Translation in Prose and Verse. L, 1925. One of 160. Trans by Laurence Housman. Sgd by Housman. (89) $55

Aucher-Eloy, Remi, 1793-1838
— Relations de voyages en Orient.... Paris, 1843. 2 vols. 8vo. Blackmer copy. (90) £350

Auction...
— Auction Prices of Books: a Representative Record. See: Livingston, Luther Samuel

Auctores...
— Auctores octo cum glossa. Lyons: Mathias Huss, 9 June 1494. 4to. 21 leaves. GKW 2790. (89) £850

Auctoritates...
— Auctoritates Aristotelis et aliorum philosophorum. [Cologne: Johann Guldenschaff, c.1490]. 4to. 60 leaves. Hain 1921. Abrams copy. (90) £2,200

Audebert, Jean Baptiste, 1759-1800
— Histoire naturelle des singes et des makis. Paris, 1799-1800 [An VIII]. 1st Ed. Folio. (89) £3,000
Martin copy. (90) $7,000

Audebert, Jean Baptiste, 1759-1800 —& Vieillot, Louis Jean Pierre
— Oiseaux dores ou a reflets metalliques. Paris, An XI [1802]. 4to Ed, with plate captions ptd in black. 2 vols. (89) $3,250, £3,400
Folio Ed, with plate captions ptd in gold. 2 vols. (89) £10,000
Bradley Martin copy. (89) $40,000
Jeanson copy. (88) FF200,000

AUDEN

Auden, Wystan Hugh, 1907-73
— Another Time: Poems. NY, 1940. 1st Ed. Caroline Newton's copy with each poem marked by Auden with the place & date of composition & with accompanying proof copy. (89) £750
— The Double Man. NY, [1941]. 1st Ed. Inscr to Caroline Newton. Fleming copy. (89) $800
— On This Island. NY: Random House, [1937]. Sgd. (91) $75
— The Platonic Blow. NY, 1965. One of 300. (89) $175
— Poems. L: S.H.S. [Stephen Spender], 1928. 1st Ed. 16mo. Inscr to C. Day Lewis & with holograph corrections. Bradley Martin copy. (90) $17,000
1st Trade Ed. L, 1930. 4to. (88) £130; (89) $150, £100, £260; (90) £230, £80; (91) $150, £105
Inscr to Stephen Spender with 4-line autograph verse. (90) £7,000
Sgd by Mary Moffat (Auden's governess). (90) £75
With ALs to Frederic Prokosch, 1935, inserted. (90) £350
L, 1933. Inscr to Elinor Loring, Nov 1933. (91) £110
NY: Random House, [1934]. Sgd by Auden, Louis MacNeice & Christopher Isherwood. (91) $160
NY, 1937. 3d impression. With Auden's holograph revisions in pencil throughout. Caroline Newton's copy. (89) £450
Edition B, this 1 of 10 hors commerce copy with an additional suite of 4 plates, all numbered & sgd in pencil. L: Petersburg Press, 1974. Illus by Henry Moore. Folio. (90) £1,600
— Spain. L, 1937. 2d impression. Inscr to D. M. Prince. (91) £70
— Three Songs for St. Cecilia's Day. [NY]: Pvtly Ptd, 1941. One of 250. (90) $350, £190
— Two Songs. NY, 1968. One of 26. Oblong 8vo. Sgd. (89) $275

Auden's copy, W. H.
— HROSWITHA. - The Plays of Roswitha. L, 1923. Sgd on front free endpaper by Auden. (91) $175

Audin,—
— Favole heroiche, contenenti le verre massime della politica et della morale.... Venice: Giacomo Hertz, 1667-69. 2 vols in 1. 12mo. (91) £290

Audin, M. See: Laurent-Vibert & Audin

AMERICAN BOOK PRICES CURRENT

Audin, Marius
— Histoire de l'imprimerie par l'image. Paris, 1928-29. 4 vols. 4to. (88) £110

Audouit, Edmond, d.1859
— L'Herbier des demoiselles.:.. Paris, 1847. 8vo. Inscr. (89) £110

Audsley, George Ashdown, 1838-1925
— The Art of Organ-Building. NY & L, 1905. 2 vols. 4to. (88) $70; (90) $100; (91) £120
— The Ornamental Arts of Japan. L, 1882-[85]. 2 vols. 4to. (88) £1,000, £1,050; (89) £480; (91) £600
2 vols in 4. 4to. (88) $425; (89) $500; (90) £320
4 vols. 4to. (89) £420
NY, 1883-84. One of 500. 2 vols in 4. 4to. (88) $85
— The Practical Decorator and Ornamentist. Glasgow, [1892]. 15 orig parts. Folio. (90) £500; (91) $480
Folio. (88) £500

Audsley, George Ashdown, 1838-1925 —& Audsley, William James, b.1833
— Polychromatic Decoration as Applied to Buildings in the Mediaeval Styles. L, 1882. 1st Ed. Folio. (88) $200; (89) $200; (90) £160; (91) $90, $150, £75, £100, £110

Audsley, George Ashdown, 1838-1925 —& Bowes, James Lord, 1834-99
— La Ceramique japonaise. Paris, 1880. 2 vols in 1. Folio. (91) $150
— Keramic Art of Japan. Liverpool & L, 1875-[80]. 2 vols. Folio. (89) £600; (90) $700; (91) $500, $550
Dampstained ex-library copy. (91) £40
7 parts. Folio. (88) $160
L, 1881. 4to. (88) A$170; (89) $50; (90) $90, $200, £90

Audsley, William James, b.1833. See: Audsley & Audsley

Audubon, John James, 1785-1851
— The Birds of America. L, 1827-38. 4 vols. Elephant folio. Yorkshire Philosophical Society—Reed—Deerfield Academy copy. (90) £1,600,000
4 vols in 5. Elephant folio. "A magnificent set in exceptionally fine condition." John Heathcote's subscriber's copy. Bradley Martin copy. (89) $3,600,000
1st 8vo Ed. NY & Phila., 1840-44. 7 vols. (88) $12,000, $14,000; (89) $15,000, $17,000, $19,000, £8,000; (90) $16,000, $19,000, $19,000; (91) $12,000, $13,000
ALs laid in. (89) $11,000
Bradley Martin copy. (89) $17,800

AUDUBON

Jeanson copy. (88) FF100,000
98 (of 100) orig parts; lacking Parts 89 & 92. Bradley Martin copy. (89) $16,000
Vols I-IV only. (91) $6,750
Mixed Ed. NY & Phila., 1840-55. 7 vols. (88) $16,000
NY, 1856-57. 7 vols. 8vo. (88) $9,000; (89) £4,000; (90) $8,000; (91) £4,800
NY, 1859-60. 7 vols. 8vo. (90) $7,500
2d Folio Ed. NY, 1860. With text of 8vo Ed of c.1870 Ed of this title. (90) $40,000
Vol II only. (89) $1,700
NY, 1861. 7 vols. 8vo. (89) $5,500; (91) $10,000
NY, [1870-71]. 8 vols. 8vo. (89) $6,000, £4,800
Title stamped. (91) $8,500
Vols I-VII. (88) $3,000
NY, 1889. 8 vols. 8vo. (91) £3,800
NY, 1937. Text by Wm. Vogt. Folio. (90) $55
NY & Amst., 1971-72. One of 250. 4 vols. Folio. (91) $12,000
Folio. (89) $18,000; (90) $13,000; (91) £5,500
Amst., 1972-73. 2 vols. Folio & 8vo. (89) £9,000

— The Birds of America: A Selection of Plates. L: Ariel Press, 1972-73. 2 vols. Folio. (88) £950
Folio. (88) £300
One of 1,000. 2 vols. Folio. (89) £700, £750; (90) $65
Vol I only. (88) £400

— Birds of America. NY: Abbeville Press, [1981]. Folio. (89) $300; (90) $65, $200
Sgd by R. T. & V. M. Peterson. (90) $175

— The Original Water-Colour Paintings by John James Audubon for the Birds of America. NY & L, 1966. 2 vols. 4to. (88) $50, $110, £45, £45; (89) $80, $100, $110, £60; (90) $50, $70, $150, £80; (91) $50, $130, $150, $325

— Ornithological Biography.... Edin., 1831-39. 5 vols. 8vo. (88) $500; (89) £750
Harwood copy. (90) $3,250
Inscr to John Greig on half-titles of 4 vols. Bradley Martin copy. (89) $5,000

— A Synopsis of the Birds of North America. Edin., 1839. 1st Ed. 8vo. Inscr by Audubon to Joseph C. Delano. Bradley Martin copy. (89) $1,200
Inscr by M. R. Audubon to George C. Dean & with her ALs. (91) $425

Audubon's copy, John James

— GOULD, JOHN. - The Birds of Australia.... L, 1837-38. 2 parts in 1 vol. Folio. Audubon's copy, with facsimile of a typed statement of authenticity sgd by Leonard B. Audubon pasted inside front cover. (91) £35,000

Audubon, John James, 1785-1851 — & Bachman, John, 1790-1874

— The Viviparous Quadrupeds of North America. NY, 1845-48. 1st Ed. 3 plate vols only. Folio. "A clean set with bright coloring". (90) $110,000
NY, 1849-51-54. ("The Quadrupeds of North America.") 3 vols. 8vo. (88) $2,750, $3,600, $3,750; (89) $3,250, $4,200
NY, 1849-54. 31 parts. 8vo. "A made-up set...comprising the 150 plates from the 1845-48 first folio edition...and five of the six plates from the rare 1854 folio supplement to that work.". (88) $2,500
NY, 1849-51-54. Orig 31 parts. 8vo. (88) $6,000; (89) $5,000; (91) $5,000
Bradley Martin copy. (89) $12,000
Vols I & II only. (89) $2,250
1st 8vo Ed. NY, 1849-54. 3 vols. (90) £2,000; (91) $4,000, £2,400
31 orig parts. (91) $7,000
Mixed Ed. NY, 1849-56-54. 3 vols. 8vo. (89) $2,800
NY: Lockwood, [c.1850]. 3 vols. 8vo. (88) $1,700; (89) $2,750, $3,200
NY, 1851-56-56. 3 vols. 8vo. (90) $3,200
NY, 1852-54-54. 3 vols. 8vo. (88) $3,250
L, 1854-54-[n.d.]. 3 vols. 8vo. (89) $2,000, $3,500; (90) $2,800, $5,000
Mixed Ed. L, 1854-51-[n.d.]. Vols I & II only. (88) $1,600
NY, 1854. 3 vols. 8vo. (91) £1,800
NY: George R. Lockwood, [1870]. 3 vols. 8vo. Titles stamped. (91) $3,250

Audubon, John Woodhouse, 1812-62

— The Drawings of John Woodhouse Audubon Illustrating his Adventures Through Mexico.... San Francisco: Book Club of California, 1957. One of 400. (91) $180, $190

— Western Journal, 1849-1850. Cleveland, 1906. (90) $110; (91) $90, $125, $125

— The Drawings of John Woodhouse Audubon Illustrating his Adventures Through Mexico.... San Francisco: Book Club of California, 1957. One of 400. (88) $110; (89) $95, $110, $120, $200

— Western Journal, 1849-1850. Cleveland, 1906. (88) $175, $190

Audubon, Maria R.

— Audubon and his Journals. NY, 1897. 2 vols. 8vo. (89) $75; (91) $80
L, 1898. 2 vols. 8vo. Library copy. (91) $80

AUENBRUGGER

Auenbrugger, Leopold, 1722-1809
— Inventum novum.... Vienna & Leipzig, 1922. Facsimile of the 1761 Ed. (89) $110
— Nouvelle Methode pour reconnaitre les maladies internes de la poitrine.... Paris, 1808. 8vo. (89) $800

Auer, Alois, 1813-69
— Die Entdeckung des Naturselbstdruckes oder die Erfindungen.... Vienna, 1854. 1st Ed. Folio. (88) £1,000

Augustin, J. J.
— 300 Jahre Buchdrucker in Glueckstadt. Glueckstadt, 1932. One of 750. 4to. (90) $275

Augustine, Saint, 354-430
— Confessiones. [Strassburg: Johann Mentelin, not after 1470]. Folio. 143 (of 144) leaves; lacking final blank. Goff A-1250. Doheny copy. (88) $32,000 Milan: Johannes Bonus, 21 July 1475. 4to. 164 leaves. Goff A-1251. (91) $6,000
— Confessions.... L, 1620. 8vo. STC 910. Bradley Martin copy. (90) $16,000 L, 1900. (88) $1,000
— Confessionum libri X. Cologne, 1646. 12mo. (90) £150
— La Cuidad de Dios. Antwerp: Henrico & Cornelio Verdussen, 1710. Folio. (88) $150
— De anima et spiritus.... [Lauingen: Ptr of Augustinus, "De consensu evangelistarum"], 9 Nov 1472. 4to. Bound with 6 other tracts, all pseudo-Augustine. 75 (of 76) leaves; lacking first blank. Goff A-1224. Abrams copy. (90) £17,500
— De arte praedicandi [Book IV of De doctrina christiana]. [Mainz]: Johann Fust [& Peter Schoeffer, before Mar] 1467. Folio. 22 leaves. Goff A-1227. Sexton-Abrams copy. (90) £20,000
— De arte praedicandi. [Germany, c.1475]. Bound after: Bruni, Leonardo. Epistolae. Ms on 60 paper leaves. [Germany, c.1475] Folio. 22 leaves. Goff A-1227. (91) £14,000
— De civitate Dei. Rome: Conradus Sweynheym & Arnoldus Pannartz, 1468. Folio. 271 (of 274) leaves; lacking 1st & last 2 blanks. Goff A-1231. Broxbourne-Abrams copy. (90) £80,000 273 (of 274) leaves; lacking final blank. Goff A-1231. Terry-Doheny copy. (88) $70,000 Rome: Sweynheym & Pannartz, 1470. Folio. 291 (of 294) leaves; lacking 3 blanks. Goff A-1232. Spencer-Rylands copy. (88) £18,000 Venice: Johannes & Vindelinus de Spira, 1470. One of 8 recorded copies ptd on vellum. Folio. 271 (of 274) leaves; lacking 3 blanks. Goff A-1233. MacCarthy-Spen-

AMERICAN BOOK PRICES CURRENT

cer-Rylands copy. (88) £45,000 Mainz: Peter Schoeffer, 5 Sept 1473. Folio. 364 (of 365) leaves; lacking final blank. Goff A-1240. Doheny copy. (88) $19,000 364 (of 365) leaves; lacking final blank. Goff A-1240. Doheny-Abrams copy. (90) £20,000 Venice: Gabriele di Pietro, 1475. Folio. 306 leaves. Goff A-1236. Doheny copy. (88) $8,000 306 leaves. Goff A-1236. Abrams copy. (90) £4,000 Naples: Mathias Moravus, 1477. Folio. 295 (of 298) leaves. Goff A-1237. (88) £1,300 Venice: Bonetus Locatellus for Octavianus Scotus, 18 Feb 1489. Folio. 264 leaves. Goff A-1245. Doheny copy. (88) $3,000 Basel: Froben, Sept 1522. Folio. (91) £200 See also: Bremer Press
— De consensu evangelistarum. Lauingen, 12 Apr 1473. Folio. 106 (of 108) leaves; lacking initial & final blanks. Goff A-1257. Doheny copy. (88) $15,000
— De la cita di Dio. [Venice: Antonio di Bartolommeo, not after 1483]. Folio. 324 leaves. Goff A-1248. (91) £2,200
— De trinitate. Venice: Paganinus de Paganinis, 12 Nov 1489. Goff A-1344. Bound with: Hilarius. De trinitate contra Arianos. Venice: Paganinus de Paganinis, 1489. Goff H-270. 4to. 169 (of 170) leaves. (91) DM2,000
— De vita christiana. [Mainz]: Peter Schoeffer, [c.1470-75]. 4to. 17 (of 18) leaves; lacking final blank. Goff A-1356. Morgan-Heyer copy. (91) $5,000 [Cologne: Bartholomaeus de Unkel, c.1480-82]. Bound with: De Doctrina Christiana. And: De Disciplina Christiana. And: De Moribus Ecclesiae Catholicae. And: Voragine, Jacobus de. Tractatus super libros sancti Augustini. 8vo. 27 leaves (lacking initial blank); Goff A1358. 100 leaves; Goff A1262. 10 leaves; Goff A1261. 34 leaves; Goff A1296. 28 leaves; Goff A1296. (89) £2,500
— Explanatio psalmorum. Basel: Johannes Amerbach, 1489. 2d Ed. 3 vols. Folio. 548 (of 550) leaves; lacking 2 blank in Vol I. Goff A-1272. Doheny copy. (88) $3,500
— Libri quatuor. De Praedestinatione & Gratia. De Praedestinatione sanctorum. De Bonae Preservantiae. De Praedestinatione Dei. Venice: Giovanni Padovano & Venturino Ruffinelli, 1534. 8vo. (90) £900
— Meditationes. Venice: Andreas de Bonetis, 23 July 1484. 4to. From the Buxheim Charterhouse. 288 leaves. Goff A-1217. (91) £3,800
— Of the Citie of God.... L, 1610. Folio. (88)

$300; (89) $550
Doheny copy. (88) $650
STC 916. (91) $900
STC 916. Bradley Martin copy. (90) $1,700
2d Ed in English. L, 1620. Folio. (89) £200

— Opera. Venice, 1551. ("Quintus tomus operum.") 4to. (91) £3,700

— Opuscula.... Strassburg: Martin Flach, 11 Aug 1491. Folio. 271 (of 274) leaves; lacking tp & last 2 leaves. Goff A-1221. (89) £220
Paris: Jean Alexandre & Jean Petit, [1502]. Vol II only. 4to. (89) $375
Paris: Jean Petit, 1521. 4to. (90) £240

— Sermones. Basel: Johann Amerbach, 1494. 7 parts in 2 vols. Folio. 617 leaves. Goff A-1308. Doheny copy. (88) $4,000

— Sermones ad heremitas. Brescia: Jacobum Britannicum, 5 Jan 1486. 8vo. 172 leaves. Goff A-1313. (91) £1,600
Florence: Antonio di Bartolommeo Miscomini, 28 June 1493. 8vo. 34 leaves. Goff A-1322. (91) $3,800

— Soliloquia. Winterberg: Johannes Alakraw, 1484. 4to. 30 leaves. Goff A-1236. (91) $18,000
Florence: [Lorenzo Morgiano & Johannes Petri], 10 Nov 1[4]91. ("Soliloquii di Sancto Augustino vulgari.") 4to. In Italian. 44 leaves. Goff A-1329. (91) £920
Florence: Lorenzo Morgiano & Johannes Petri, 18 June 1496. ("Soliloquii del divo padre Sancto Augustino volgari....") 4to. 34 leaves. Goff A-1331. Galletti—de Landau —Cherry Garrard—Abrams copy. (90) £5,500

— Soliloquia; Speculum Peccatoris. [Augsburg: Guenther Zainer, before 5 June 1473]. Folio. 28 leaves. Goff A-1333 & A-1337. Doheny copy. (88) $2,100

Augustinian Order. See: Universis...

Augustinus de Ancona
— Summa de potestate ecclesiastica. Augsburg: [Johann Schuessler], 6 Mar 1473. Folio. 470 leaves. Goff A-1363. Doheny copy. (88) $8,000
470 leaves. Goff A-1363. (91) £5,200
3d Ed. Rome: Francisci de Cinquinis, 20 Dec 1479. 4to. 327 (of 328) leaves; lacking blank. Goff A-1365. Doheny copy. (88) $1,700

Augustinus, Venetus
— Inlustrium Viror ut exstant in urbe expressi vultus caelo Augustini Veneti. Rome: Antonio Lafreri, 1569. Folio. Kissner copy. (91) £850

Auk...
— The Auk: A Quarterly Journal of Ornithology. Lancaster & Wash., 1884-1984. 101 vols in orig issues. Martin copy. (90) $900

Auldjo, John, d.1857
— Journal of a Visit to Constantinople.... L, 1835. Illus by George Cruikshank. 8vo. (91) £110, £180
Blackmer copy. (90) £350
— Narrative of an Ascent to the Summit of Mont Blanc. L, 1828. 4to. (89) £380
L.p. copy. Inscr. (88) £650
— Sketches of Vesuvius.... Naples, 1832. 8vo. (88) £75; (91) £380
L, 1833. 8vo. (89) £170, £180

Aulnoy, Marie Catherine de la Mothe, Comtesse d', 1650?-1705
— A Collection of Novels and Tales.... L, 1721. 3 vols. 12mo. (90) £900
— Les Contes des fees * Nouveaux Contes des fees. Amst., 1717-19. 5 vols in 2. 12mo. (90) £700
— The Diverting Works of the Countess of D'Anois. L, 1707. 8vo. (89) £2,700
— The History of Fortunio. Bost.: Isaiah Thomas, 1812. 32mo. (88) $90
— The History of the Earl of Warwick, Sirnam'd the King-Maker...by the Author of the Memoirs of the English Court.... L, 1708. 8vo. (91) £50
— The History of the Tales of the Fairies. L, 1758. 12mo. (91) £750
— Hypolitus Earl of Douglas. Containing Some Memoirs of the Court of Scotland,... Amst., 1708. 3 parts in 1 vol. 8vo. ESTC 053966. (91) £260
— Nouveaux contes des fees. Amst., 1708. 2 vols in 1. 12mo. (89) £700
— Works. L, 1715. ("The Diverting Works....") 8vo. ESTC 003321. (91) £600

Aunay, Alfred d'. See: Liebert, Alphonse

Aurbach, Johannes
— Summa de sacramentis. Augsburg: Gunther Zainer, 1469. Folio. 49 leaves. Goff A-1381. Doheny-Fleming copy. (89) $10,000
49 leaves. Goff A-1381. Sexton-Abrams copy. (90) £6,500

Aurel, Marco
— Libro primero, de arithmetica algebraica.... Valencia: J. de Mey, 1552. 4to. Honeyman copy. (88) £950

Aurelius Augustinus. See: Augustine

Aurelius Victor, Sextus
— Historiae romanae breviorium. Antwerp: C. Plantin, 1579. Bound with: De vita et moribus imperatorum romanorum. Antwerp: C. Plantin, 1579. 8vo. Colbert copy. (90) £340

Aurora...
— Aurora Australis. East Antarctica [pbd at the Winter Quarters of the British Antarctic Expedition] 1908. Ed by Sir Ernest H. Shackleton; illus by George Marston. 4to. (89) A$40,000
Inscr by Shackleton to Mrs. Lysaght, Feb 1910. (91) £19,000
Inscr by Shackleton. (91) £22,000
Antarctica: Ptd at the Sign of the Penguins by Joyce & Wild, 1908. One of c.100 copies. Ed by Ernest Shackleton. 4to. Inscr by Shackleton to G. Wyatt Truscott, Lord Mayor of London. (91) £3,500
Bluntisham: Paradigm, 1986. One of 58. Ed by Sir Ernest H. Shackleton; illus by George Marston. 4to. Facsimile reprint. (88) $750

Ausbund...
— Ausbund, das ist, eitliche schoene Christliche Lieder.... Germantown: Leibert & Billmeyer, 1785. 8vo. (88) $1,300

Auslaender, Rose
— Inventar. Duisburg: Guido Hildebrandt, 1972. One of 300. Illus by Otto Piene. (91) DM420

Ausonius, Decimus Magnus
— Opera. Venice: Aldus, 1517. 8vo. (88) $275
Venice: Aldus, Nov 1517. 8vo. (88) £240; (90) £380
Geneva: Jacob Stoer, 1588. 16mo. Doheny copy. (89) $1,700
Paris, 1730. 2 parts in 1 vol. 4to. (88) £400
— Patchwork Quilt: Poems. L: Fanfrolico Press, [1930]. One of 400. Trans by Jack Lindsay. (89) £65

Austen, Jane, 1775-1817
— Emma. L, 1816. 1st Ed. 3 vols. 8vo. (89) $2,600, £320, £700, £1,100, £1,700, £2,200; (90) $3,400, £1,000, £4,000
Bradley Martin copy. (90) $5,500
Doheny copy. (88) $3,500
— Mansfield Park. L, 1814. 1st Ed. 3 vols. 12mo. (89) £950, £1,250; (90) $3,600, $4,200, £2,000, £3,200
Bradley Martin copy. (90) $8,000
2d Ed. L, 1816. 3 vols. 12mo. (91) £190
— Northanger Abbey and Persuasion. L, 1818. 1st Ed. 4 vols. 12mo. (89) £1,200; (90) $2,200, $3,000; (91) £1,600
Bradley Martin copy. (90) $6,000, $7,000
Copy with half-titles. (88) £1,250
— Pride and Prejudice. L, 1813. 1st Ed. 3 vols. 12mo. (89) £3,500; (90) $1,500, £580, £6,800, £7,000; (91) £5,500
A. E. Newton—Bradley Martin copy. (90) $15,000
Bradley Martin copy. (90) $17,000
Hogan-Doheny copy. (89) $45,000
Made-up copy with 2d Ed titles & half-titles & 1st Ed sheets. 3 vols. 12mo. (91) £290
— Sense and Sensibility. L, 1811. 1st Ed. 3 vols. 12mo. (89) £9,500
Bradley Martin copy. (90) $11,000
2d Ed. L, 1813. 3 vols. 12mo. (89) £650; (90) $8,500
3 vols in 1. 12mo. (88) £650
— Three Evening Prayers. San Francisco: Colt Press, 1940. One of 300. (91) $55
— Works. L, 1892. One of 150 L.p. copies. 10 vols. (91) £250
8 (of 10) vols. (88) £85
L, 1898. ("Novels.") Ed by R. B. Johnson; illus by C. E. & H. M. Brock. 10 vols plus the 1912 Letters in 2 vols. 8vo. (88) £150
Edin., 1906. 10 vols. (88) £80; (91) £140
Winchester Ed. Edin., 1911-12. 12 vols. (88) £125; (89) £360; (91) £150
Oxford, 1923. One of 1,000 L.p. copies. Ed by R. W. Chapman. 5 vols. (88) £130
L, 1957-63. 7 vols. (90) £70

Austin, A. B.
— An Angler's Anthology. L, 1930. One of 100, sgd by author & artist. Illus by Norman Wilkinson. 4to. (91) $300

Austin, Benjamin, Jr.
— Constitutional Republicanism.... Bost., 1803. 8vo. (90) $55

Austin, Gabriel
— The Library of Jean Grolier... See: Grolier Club

Austin, J. B.
— The Mines of South Australia.... Adelaide, 1863. 1st Ed. 8vo. (91) £220

Austin, John G.
— A Series of Lithographic Drawings of Sydney and its Environs. Sydney, 1836. Oblong 8vo. (89) £3,200

Austin, Mary Hunter, 1868-1934
— The Flock. Bost., 1906. (88) $90
— The Land of Little Rain. Bost & NY, 1903. 4to. (88) $80, $100; (91) $120
  4th Impression. Sgd on tp. (88) $150
  Bost., 1950. Illus by Ansel Adams. 4to. (88) $85, $100; (89) $110; (91) $55, $65, $70
  Sgd by Adams on half-title. (89) $160
— Mother of Felipe and other Early Stories. San Francisco: Book Club of Calif., 1950. One of 400. (88) $70
— Taos Pueblo. See: Grabhorn Printing

Austin, Sarah
— The Story without an End. L, 1868. Illus by Eleanor Vere Boyle. 8vo. (89) $55

Austin, William, of Lincoln's Inn
— Haec Homo; Wherein the Excellency of the Creation of Woman is Described.... L: R. O. for R. M. & C. G., 1639. 12mo. (88) £130

Austin, William, 1587-1634
— Devotionis Augustinianae Flamma. L: for I. L. & Ralph Mab, 1635. Folio. (88) £85, £120; (90) £130

Australia
[The Ms journal of Pierre-Bernard Milius, on the official French Expedition to Australia Commanded by Nicolas Baudin, 1800-4, 259 pp, in contemp mor-backed bds, along with a collection of 76 orig drawings sold at C on 16 Oct 1988, lot 80] £70,000
— 14 Views of Old Adelaide from Sketches in 1840-49.... [Adelaide]: E.S. Wigg & Son [1850s?]. Illus by S. T. Gill, F. R. Nixon, S. Calvert & O. Korn. Oblong 4to. (89) A$450
— The Australian Irrigation Colonies on the River Murray. L, 1888. Folio. Ferguson 17976. (89) £100, A$160
— Copies of the Royal Instructions to the Governors of New South Wales, Van Diemen's Land, and Western Australia, as to the Mode to be adopted in disposing of Crown Lands. L, 1831. Folio. (88) £75
— Historical Records of New South Wales. Sydney, 1892-1901. 7 vols in 8 plus the 4to vol of chart facsimiles. 8vo. (88) A$1,050
— The New South Wales Calendar and General Post Office Directory. Sydney, 1834.

  8vo. Hobill Cole copy. (89) A$1,400
— Photographs of Some of the Principal Buildings in the City of Sydney.... Sydney: Charles Potter, 1890. 4to. Inscr by Potter. (90) $425
— Views in Sydney & Melbourne. Sydney: Sands & Kenny, [plates dated 1853]. 4to. (89) £500
— ELIZABETH RETREAT FOR FEMALE EX-PRISONERS. - First [to Fifteenth] Annual Report. Melbrone or Prahan, 1886-1900. Bound in 1 vol. (91) £380
— SPENCER, SIR WALTER BALDWIN. - Report on the Work of the Horn Scientific Expedition to Central Australia. L & Melbourne, 1896. 4 parts in 3 vols. 4to. Martin copy. (90) $3,800
  4 vols in 2. 4to. (88) A$600

Van Diemen's Land
— Hobart Town Directory, and General Guide. Hobart Town, July 1852. 8vo. (90) A$350

Australian...
— Australian Ex Libris Society Bookplate Artists. Sydney, 1933. Number One, Adrian Feint, One of 150. (88) A$360
— The Australian Journal. Melbourne, 1865-66. Vol 1, Nos 1-52, in 1 vol. 4to. (89) £130
  Melbourne, 1865-68. Vols I-III. 4to. (88) A$380
— Australian Men of Mark. Sydney, [1889]. Series 4. 2 vols. 4to. (89) A$160

Austria
— Constitutio criminalis Theresiana, oder der...Maria Theresia Erzherzogin von Oesterreich.... Vienna, 1769. Folio. (88) DM1,300; (91) DM2,500
— K. K. Oesterreichische Armee nach der neuen Adjustirung.... Vienna, [1837-48]. 7 parts numbered to VI in 1 vol. Folio. (89) £3,200
  Folio. (88) £6,800

Austro-Turkish War
— Das zwar hochmuetig aber Gedemuethigte Tuerckische Hunds Gemarr.... [N.p., c.1690]. 4to. Blackmer copy. (90) £600

Authentic...
— Authentic Memoirs of the Little Man and the Little Maid. L: E. Wallis, [n.d.]. 12mo. (88) $200
— An Authentic Narrative of Four Years' Residence at Tongataboo. See: Vason, George
— Authentic Papers relating to the Expedition against Carthagena.... L, 1744. 8vo. (91) $500
— Authentic Papers from America. L, 1775. 8vo. (91) $350

Author of the Memoirs of the English Court.
See: Aulnoy, Marie Catherine LaMothe

Author's Club. See: Liber...

Autocar
— The Autocar. L & Coventry, 1901-65. Vols 6-123. 4to. (88) $3,700

Auton, Jean d'
— Histoire de Louys XII, Roy de France.... Paris, 1620. 4to. (91) $90

Aux Bibliophiles...
— Aux Bibliophiles: Ultima, Notes et Chroniques. Paris, 1891. One of 300. Ed by D. Jouaust. 8vo. Inscr by Jouaust. (90) £50

Auzebi, Pierre
— Traite d'odontalgie, ou l'on presernt un systeme nouveau sur l'origine & la formation des dents.... Lyon, 1771. 8vo. (91) £320

Avedon, Richard
— Avedon Photographs 1947-1977. NY: Farrar, Straus & Giroux, [1978]. Intro by Harold Brodkey. Folio. (89) $70; (91) $100 Inscr. (91) $55
— Nothing Personal. NY, 1964. Text by James Baldwin. (88) $90; (91) $75, $200 Inscr by Avedon. (91) $350
— Observations. NY, [1959]. Text by Truman Capote. Folio. (88) $110; (89) $110; (90) $75, $175; (91) $225, $300

Aveiro, Pantaleao d'
— Itinerario de Terra Sancta, e todas suas particularidades. Lisbon: Antonio Pedrozo Galram, 1732. 4to. Kissner copy. (91) £200

Avenarius, Tony
— Historischer Festzug Veranstaltet bei der Feier der Vollendung des Koelner Domes am 16 October 1880. [Cologne, 1881]. Oblong folio. (90) $700

Aventinus, Joannes, 1477-1534
— Annalium Boiorum libri septem. Ingolstadt: A. & S. Weissenhorn, 1554. Folio. (90) DM3,400
Basel: Perna, 1580. Folio. (90) DM1,800

Averill, Charles
— A Short Treatise on Operative Surgery.... Phila.: H. C. Carey & I. Lea; Bost.: Wells & Lilly, 1823. 1st American Ed. 12mo. (89) $150

Avery, Clara Louise
— American Silver of the XVII and XVIII Centuries: a Study based on the Clearwater Collection. NY, 1920. (89) $60

Avery Library
— Catalogue of the Avery Architectural Library. NY, 1895. One of 1,000. 4to. (89) $80, $350; (91) $400

Avery, Milton
— Paintings. 1930-1960. NY & L, [1962]. One of 90. Intro by Hilton Kramer. Folio. (90) $1,300

Avery, Samuel Putnam, 1822-1904
— Catalogue Raisonne: Works on Bookbinding.... NY: Pvtly ptd, [1903]. One of 100. 12mo. Inscr to James W. Ellsworth. (89) $300

Avezac de Castera de Macaya, Marie
— Note sur une Mappemonde turke du xvie siecle conservee a la Bibliotheque de Saint-Marc a Venise. Paris: E. Martinet, 1866. 8vo. Arvanitidi copy. (91) £130

Avicenna, 980-1037
— Canon Medicinae. Louvain: Hieronymus Nempaeia, 1658. 2 vols in 1. Folio. (91) $130
— Liber canonis. Lyons: Johannes Trechsel, completed by Johannes Clein, 24 Dec 1498. ("Fen prima quarti canonis Avicenne principis....") Parts 2/1 & 4 (of 4) in 1 vol. 293 leaves. Goff A-1428. (88) $1,400
[Venice: Paganinum de Paganisis, 1507]. ("Liber canonis Avicenne, revisus....") 4to. (90) $750

Avicultural...
— The Avicultural Magazine: Being the Journal of the Avicultural Society.... L, 1895-1927. Vols 1-82 & Vol 83, No 2 & Index. 8vo. (88) £800

Avila, Juan de, 1494?-1569
— The Audi Filia, or a Rich Cabinet Full of Spirituall Jewells.... [St. Omer], 1620. 1st Ed in English. 4to. (89) $200

Aviler, Augustin Charles d', 1653-1700
— Cours d'architecture.... Paris, 1691-93. Mixed Ed. 2 vols in one. 4to. (89) £190
Paris: Nicolas Langlois, 1691. 2 vols. 4to. (88) £500
— Cours d'architecture qui comprend les ordres de Vignole.... Paris, 1720. 2 vols. 4to. (88) FF6,000
— Cours d'architecture. Paris, 1738. 4to. (91) £380

Paris, 1750. 4to. (91) £240

Avity, Pierre d'
— Description generale de l'Asie [-l'Afrique] [-l'Amerique] [l'Europe]. Paris, 1660-61. 4 vols. Folio. (91) £600
— The Estates, Empires, & Principallities of the World. L, 1615. 1st Ed in English. Folio. (89) £160; (91) £400

Avogadro, Amedeo, 1776-1856
— Fisica de' corpi ponderabili.... Turin, 1837. 4 vols. 8vo. (88) $2,200

Avril, Philippe, 1654-98
— Voyage en divers etats d'Europe et d'Asie. Paris, 1693. 12mo. (88) £100
  Blackmer copy. (90) £520

Axe, John Wortley
— The Horse: Its Treatment in Health and Disease. L, 1906. 9 vols. 4to. (88) £90; (90) $50, £65

Ayer Collection, Edward Everett
— A Bibliographical Check List of North and Middle American Indian Linguistics in the Ayer Collection. Chicago, 1941. 2 vols. 4to. (88) $95
— Narratives of Captivity among the Indians of North America. Chicago, [1912]. (89) $60
  Chicago, [1912-28]. 2 vols. including 1st Supplement. (91) $200

Ayers, John G.
— Chinese Ceramics. See: Baur Collection

Aylmer, John, Bishop of London
— An Harborowe for Faithfull and Trewe Subjects.... [L: J. Daye], 1559. 8vo. (90) £280

Ayme, Jean Jacques, ("Job"), 1752-1818
— Deportation et naufrage.... Paris, [1800]. 8vo. (90) £50

Ayme, Marcel
— La Fosse aux peches. [N.p.], 1946. Unique copy with plates replaced throughout with watercolor drawings & with the plates present as a separate suite. Illus by Robert Naly. 4to. With 2 sheets of prelim sketches & the 4-page autograph Ms of the text, inscr by Ayme. (89) £1,100

Ayres, Atlee Bernard
— Mexican Architecture. NY, 1926. Folio. (88) $60; (91) $80

Ayres, Philip, 1638-1712
— Cupids Addresse to the Ladies.... L, 1683. 8vo. (90) $1,300
  Martin copy. (90) $4,000
— Emblems of Love.... L: for John Wren, [1683]. 8vo. In English, Latin, Italian & French. Wing A-4309. (91) £360

Ayres, W. P.
— The Gardeners' Magazine of Botany. See: Gardeners'...

Ayrton, William
— The Adventures of a Salmon in the River Dee. L: Whittaker & Co., [1853]. 12mo. (90) £200

Ayton, Richard, 1786-1823. See: Daniell & Ayton

Aytoun, William Edmondstoune
— Lays of the Scottish Cavaliers.... Edin., 1865. 4to. (89) $8,500

Azara, Felix de, 1746-1811
— Apuntamientos para la historia natural de los Paxaros del Paraguay y Rio de la Plata. Madrid: la Viuda de Ibarra, 1802-5. 3 vols. 8vo. Martin copy. (90) $3,000
— Voyages dans l'Amerique meridionale.... Paris, 1809. 4 vols plus Atlas. 8vo & folio. (90) £600

Aznar de Polanco, Juan Claudio
— Arte nuevo de escribir.... Madrid, 1719. 1st Ed. Folio. (89) £380

B

B., A.
  See also: Britaine, William de
— Gloria Britannica; or, the Boast of the British Seas. L: E. Smith & George Harwar, 1690. 1st Ed, later Issue. 4to. (88) £150

B., H. See: Doyle, John

B., J.
  See also: Bullokar, John
— A Letter from a Citizen of Glasgow to his Friend at Edinburgh. L, 1700. 4to. (88) £550

B., R.
  See also: Crouch, Nathaniel
— Coral and Steel: A Most Compendious method of Preserving and Restoring Health. L: for the Author, sold by S. Miller, [1660?]. 12mo. (88) £500

B., W.
— The Elephant's Ball and Grand Fete Champetre. L. 1807. 1st Ed. 16mo. (89) £170

Baardt, Pieter
— Deugden-spoor; in de ondeughden des werelts affgebeeldt.... Leeuw.: H. W. Coopman, 1645. 8vo. (88) HF1,000

Babbage, Charles, 1792-1871
— A Comparative View of the Various Institutions for the Assurance of Lives. L, 1826. Bound with: Reflections on the Decline of Science in England.... L, 1830. And: On the Economy of Machinery and Manufactures. L, 1832. 8vo. Final work with Ms note by Babbage's son, saying that 3,000 copies were sold within 2 months. (91) £1,800
— The Ninth Bridgewater Treatise. A Fragment. L, 1838. 2d Ed. 8vo. Inscr to Professor Oersted. (90) £600

Babcock, Amos G.
— Journal of a Young Man of Massachusetts.... Bost., 1816. 1st Ed. 12mo. (89) $130; (91) $110

Babcock, Havilah
— Tales of Quails 'n Such. NY, [1951]. One of 299. Illus by William Schaldach. Inscr. (90) $200

Babcock, Philip H.
— Falling Leaves: Tales from a Gun Room. See: Derrydale Press

Babel, Isaak
— Drei Welten. [Cologne, 1964]. One of 100. Illus by Emilio Vedova. 4to. (90) $175

Babelon, Jean
— La Bibliotheque Francaise de Fernand Colomb. See: Bibliotheca Colombina

Babes...
— The Babes in the Wood. [L]: George Routledge, [c.1880]. Folio. (89) $65

Babeuf, Francois Noel. See: Gracchus Babeuf

Babin, Jacques Paul
— Relation de l'etat present de la ville d'Athenes.... See: Jesuits

Babington, John
— Pyrotechnia or, a Discourse of Artificiall Fire-Works. L 1635. Folio. (89) £160

Babinski, Henri. See: Ali-Bab, Pseud.

Bablet, Denis
— The Revolutions of Stage Design in the 20th Century. Paris: Leon Amiel, [1977]. (88) $250, £70; (90) $200

Babo, Lambert J. L. von —& Metzger, Johann
— Die Wein- und Tafeltrauben der deutschen Weinberge und Gaerten. [Mannheim, 1836-38]. Atlas only. Oblong folio. (91) £2,600

Babson Collection, Grace K.
— A Descriptive Catalogue of the...Collection of the Works of Sir Isaac Newton. NY, 1950. One of 750. (89) $80; (91) $90
2 vols, including Macomber's 1955 Supplement, one of 450. (88) $220; (89) $130

Babylonian...
— A Babylonian Anthology. North Hills, Pa.: Bird & Bull Press, 1966. Trans by William White, Jr. 4to. (88) $100; (90) $150

Baca, Manuel C. de
— Vicente Silve & his 40 Bandits. Wash., 1947. One of 300. (91) $55

Bacci, Andrea, d.1600
— De naturali vinorum historia.... Rome: Nicholaus Mutius, 1596 [1597]. Folio. (88) £1,200
— De thermis, libri septem.... Venice: Valgrisi, 1571. Folio. Kissner copy. (91) £750
— Del teuere libri tre. Venice: [Aldus], 1576. 4to. Colbert-Westbury-Kissner copy. (91) £450
Kissner copy. (91) £180

Bache, Richard
— Notes on Colombia, taken in the Years 1822-3.... Phila., 1827. 8vo. (89) $140

Bacheller, Irving Addison, 1859-1950
— Eben Holden. Bost., [1900]. 1st Ed, 1st State. 12mo. Inscr to Mark Twain. Doheny copy. (89) $1,100

Bachhofer, Ludwig
— Early Indian Sculpture. NY, [1929]. 2 vols. 4to. (88) $225; (91) $50, $170

Bachman, John, 1790-1874. See: Audubon & Bachman

Bachman, Richard. See: King, Stephen

Back, Sir George, 1796-1878
— Narrative of the Arctic Land Expedition.... L, 1836. 8vo. (88) £70, £90
L.p. copy. (90) £600
— Narrative of an Expedition in H.M.S. Terror. L, 1838. 1st Ed. 8vo. (90) £220; (91) $550

Back, Howard
— The Waters of Yellowstone with Rod and Fly. NY, 1938. 8vo. (90) $250

Backer, Augustin de & Alois de
— Bibliotheque de la Compagnie de Jesus.... Louvain, 1960. 12 vols. 4to. Reprint of 1890 Ed. (90) £780
Vols I-X & XII. 4to. (88) $1,200

Backhouse, Edward, Jr.
— Original Etchings of Birds. Ashburne, 1840. Folio. Martin copy. (90) $700

Backhouse, James, 1794-1869
— Extracts from the Letters of James Backhouse.... L, 1842 [Part titles dated 1838-41]. 10 parts in 2 vols. 8vo. (90) A$280
— A Narrative of a Visit to the Australian Colonies. L & York, 1843. 8vo. (88) £130; (90) £200, A$650; (91) £170
Martin copy. (90) $500
— A Narrative of a Visit to the Mauritius and South Africa. L, 1844. 8vo. (88) R110
Inscr. (88) £200

Backhouse, James, 1794-1869 —& Tylor, Charles
— The Life and Labours of George Washington Walker of Hobart Town, Tasmania. L & York, 1862. 8vo. (90) A$100

Backmanson, H.
— L'Empereur Nicolas Alexandrovitch en tenue de 10 regiments dont sa Majestie est Chef. St. Petersburg: E. J. Marcus, 1896. Folio. (88) £550

Bacon, Sir Francis, 1561-1626
— Baconiana, 1679. 1st Ed, Issue with the imprimatur at A4 verso. 8vo. (91) $200
— Certaine Miscellany Works. L, 1629. 1st Ed. 4to. (91) £360
— A Charge Given by the most Eminent and Learned Sir Francis Bacon...for the Verge.... L, 1662. 4to. (88) $100
— Considerations Touching a Warre with Spaine. L, 1629. 1st Ed. 4to. STC 1126. (91) £600
— De Sapientia Veterum.... L, 1634. 12mo. (89) £75
— A Declaration of the Practices & Treasons Attempted and Committed by Robert late Earle of Essex.... L, 1601. 1st Ed. 4to. (88) $275
— The Elements of the Common Lawes of England. L, 1630. 1st Ed. 2 parts in 1 vol. 4to. (91) £360
STC 1136; Gibson 195. (89) $300
L, 1636. 2 parts in 1 vol. 4to. Gibson 194. (91) £275
— The Essaies.... L, 1612. 8vo. Hoe-Huntington-Bradley Martin copy. (90) $18,000

— The Essayes or Counsels, Civill and Morall. L, 1625. 1st Ed, 1st Issue. 4to. (89) £1,400
Gibson 13; STC 1147. Bradley Martin copy. (90) $3,750
Hogan-Doheny copy. (89) $3,500
The Garden copy. (90) $3,250
2d Issue. Doheny copy. (88) $800
L, 1639. 4to. (89) $200; (91) $150
L, 1798. One of 6 L.p. copies. 8vo. Gosford copy. (90) £550
See also: Cresset Press
— The Essays. See: Bremer Press
— The Essays or Counsels.... See: Limited Editions Club
— The Historie of the Raigne of King Henry the Seventh. L, 1622. Bound with: Godwin, Francis. Annales of England. L, 1630. Folio. (91) £325
1st Ed. Folio. Gibson 116a; STC 1159. (88) £190, £220; (89) £250, $300
Gibson 116a; STC 1159. Bradley Martin copy. (90) $1,100
Gibson 116a; STC 1159. (91) $160
STC 1160. Doheny copy. (88) $550
L, 1629. Bound with: Annales of England, containing the Reigns of Henry the Eighth.... L, 1630. Folio. (90) £130
L, 1641. Folio. (91) £160
— Letters...written during the Reign of King James the First. L: B. Tooke, 1702. Ed by Robert Stephens. 4to. (89) $425; (91) £160
— Neuf livres de la dignite et de l'accroissement des sciences.... Paris, 1632. 4to. (88) $325
— [Novum organum] Instauratio magna. L, 1620. 1st Ed. 2d Issue. Bound with: Sylva Sylvarum.... L, 1662-24. 2 vols in 1. Folio. (88) $2,000
1st Ed, 1st Issue, without the errata. Folio. Horblit-The Garden copy. (90) $29,000
2d Issue. 2 vols in 1. Folio. (89) $2,200
Bradley Martin copy. (90) $6,000
Doheny copy. (89) $10,000
Folio. (89) £2,400
— Opera. L, 1730. 4 vols. Folio. (89) $140; (90) $250
— The Philosophical Works. L, 1733. 3 vols. 4to. (90) £95
— Resuscitatio.... L, 1671. 2 parts in 1 vol. Folio. (91) $250
— Saggi Morali del Signore Francesco Bacono.... L: John Bill, 1618. 8vo. (88) $175
— Sylva Sylvarum. L, 1626. 1st Ed, 1st Issue. 2 parts in 1 vol. Folio. Gibson 170. (89) £600
2d Ed. L, 1628. Folio. (88) £90
L, 1639. Folio. (90) £100
STC 1172. (91) £190
6th Ed. L, 1651. Folio. (89) $200
8th Ed. L, 1664. 4 parts in 1 vol.

BACON

Folio. (88) £70
9th Ed. L, 1670. Folio. (88) £50
11th Ed. L, 1685. Folio. (91) £160
— The Twoo Bookes of Francis Bacon. Of the Proficience and Advancement of Learning.... L, 1605. Bound with: The Charge of Sir Francis Bacon Knight...touching Duells.... L, 1614. 4to. STC 1164 & 1125. (91) £900
1st Ed. 4to. (88) £400; (89) £250; (91) $1,900, £360
Doheny copy. (89) $1,300
L.p. copy. The Garden copy, formerly the Heber-Britwell Court-Horblit copy. (90) $26,000
L.p. copy. The Garden copy. (90) $28,000
Rabinowitz copy. (89) £450
STC 1164. (90) $750
Stockhausen-Bradley Martin copy. (90) $2,750
2d Ed. L, 1629. 4to. (89) $450
— ("The Two Bookes of the Proficience and Advancement of Learning.") (89) £200
3d Ed. Oxford, 1633. 4to. (88) £160; (90) £130
1st Ed in English of the Expanded Ed. Oxford, 1640. ("Of the Advancement and Proficience of Learning....") 2d Issue with colophon dated 1640. Folio. (88) $200, $700, £550; (89) $150, $450; (90) $200, $275, £300
Huggins-Musgrave copy. (88) $800
STC 1167.3. Bradley Martin copy. (90) $1,600
STC 1167.3. Sold w.a.f. (91) $120
STC 1167.3. (91) £80
Later Issue with Colophon dated 1640. (91) $120
L, 1674. Folio. (88) £90, £160; (90) £140; (91) £110
— Works. L, 1740. 4 vols. Folio. (88) $200; (89) £95
L, 1753. 3 vols. Folio. (90) £80
L, 1765. Ed by Thomas Birch. 5 vols. 4to. (88) £270, £420
L, 1778. 5 vols. 4to. (89) £220; (91) £230
L, 1788. 5 vols. 4to. (90) £480
L, 1803. 10 vols. 8vo. (88) £60; (91) £600
L, 1825-36. 17 vols. 8vo. (90) £400

Bacon, Sir Francis, 1561-1626 —& Godwin, Bishop Francis, 1562-1633
— The History of the Reigns of Henry the Seventh, Henry the Eighth, Edward the Sixth and Queen Mary. L, 1676. 2 parts in 1 vol. Folio. (88) £50; (91) £200

AMERICAN BOOK PRICES CURRENT

Bacon, Mary Ann
— Flowers and their Kindred Thoughts. L, 1848. Illus by Owen Jones. 8vo. (90) £50
— Winged Thoughts. L, 1851. Illus by Owen Jones. 8vo. (91) $150

Bacon, Nathaniel
— An Historical and Political Discourse of the Laws and Government of England.... L, 1760. 4to. (90) $275

Bacon, Roger, 1214?-94
— The Cure of Old Age, and Preservation of Youth.... L, 1683. 1st Ed in English. 2 parts in 1 vol. 8vo. (88) £150; (90) £260
Myres copy. (90) £240
— De his que mundo mirabliliter eveniunt.... Paris: Simon de Colines, 1542. 2 parts in 1 vol. 4to. (90) £5,000

Bacqueville de la Potherie, Claude Charles Le Roy, b.c.1668
— Histoire de l'Amerique septentrionale.... Paris, 1722. 4 vols. 12mo. (88) £750

Badcock, John
See also: Hinds, John
— Conversations on Conditioning.... L, 1829. 12mo. (90) £75

Badcock, William
— A Touch-Stone for Gold and Silver Wares. L, 1677. 8vo. (90) $70

Baddeley, John Frederick
— The Rugged Flanks of Caucasus. Oxford, 1940. 1st Ed. 2 vols. 4to. (88) £220, £380; (90) £150
— Russia, Mongolia, China. L, 1919. One of 250. 2 vols. Folio. (89) £700; (90) £750; (91) £900

Badeau, Adam
— Military History of Ulysses S. Grant from April 1861 to April 1865. NY, 1881. 3 vols. 8vo. (91) $140

Baden-Powell of Gilwell, Robert S. S. Baden-Powell, 1st Baron, 1847-1941
— Sketches in Mafeking and East Africa. L, 1907. 1st Ed. Oblong folio. (91) $70

Badeslade, Thomas —& Toms, William Henry
— Chorographia Britanniae, or a Set of Maps of all the Counties in England and Wales.... L, 1742. 8vo. (88) £450; (89) £360, £420, £440, £480, £550; (90) £650; (91) £450, £550, £550
L, [c.1744]. 8vo. (88) £390; (89) £700
L, [1749]. 8vo. (90) £780

Badger, Mrs. C. M.
— Floral Belles from the Green-House and Garden. NY, 1867. Folio. (89) £650
— Wild Flowers. NY, 1859. 4to. (91) $900

Badger, George Percy, 1815-88
— The Nestorians and their Rituals. L, 1852. 1st Ed. 2 vols. 8vo. Blackmer copy. (90) £425

Badham, Charles David
— A Treatise on the Esculent Funguses of England. L, 1847. 1st Ed. 8vo. (91) $130
 L, 1863 [but c.1869]. 8vo. (89) $70

Badia y Leblich, Domingo. See: Ali Bey

Badius, Jodocus
— Stulifere navicule seu scaphe fatuarum mulierum. Strassburg: Johannes Pruss, 1502. 4to. (89) £1,800

Badminton...
— Badminton Magazine of Sports and Pastimes. L, 1895-99. Vols 1-8. 8vo. (88) £60

Baedeker, Friedrich Wilhelm Justus
— Die Eier der europaeische Voegel nach der Natur gemalt. Leipzig, 1855-63. 2 parts in 1 vol. 4to. Martin copy. (90) $1,600

Baedeker, Karl, Publishers
— Russia, with Teheran, Port Arthur, and Peking.... Leipzig, 1914. (88) $300, £180; (89) £220
— La Russie. Manuel du Voyageur. Leipzig, 1902. (90) £50

Baer, Elizabeth
 See also: Fowler & Baer
— Seventeenth Century Maryland: a Bibliography. Balt., 1949. One of 300. 4to. (90) $150; (91) $110

Baer, Elvira
— Trau keinem Fuchs auf seiner Heid und keinem Jud bei seinem Eid. Nuremberg, 1936. Oblong 4to. (91) $750

Baer, Nicholas
— Ornithophonia. Sive harmonia melicarum avium.... Bremen: Johann Wessel, 1695. 4to. (88) FF8,000

Baerle, Kasper van
— Blyde inkomst der allerdoorluchtig Koninginne, Marie de Medicis, t'Amsterdam.... Amst., 1639-42. 2 parts in 1 vol. Folio. (88) HF1000

Baers, Johannes
— Kabinet der Schrifjkonst. Amst.: A. Meyer, 1761. 2 vols. Oblong 4to. (88) £80

Bage, Robert, 1728-1801
— Hermsprong; or Man as he is Not. L, 1796. 1st Ed. 3 vols. 12mo. Sadleir-Bradley Martin copy. (90) $650

Bagehot, Walter, 1826-77
— Lombard Street. L, 1873. 8vo. (90) £1,300; (91) £460

Baglione, Giovanni
— Le Vite de' pittori, scultori.... Naples, 1733. 4to. (90) LIt900,000; (91) LIt700,000

Baglivius, Georgius, 1669?-1707
— De fibra motrice et morbosa nec non de experimentis.... Perugia, 1700. 4to. (88) $450
 Bound with: Pascoli, Alessandro. Il Corpo-Umano.... Perugia, 1700. (91) £650
— Opera. Antwerp, 1715. 4to. (88) $140
— The Practice of Physick Reduc'd.... L, 1704. 8vo. (91) $125

Bagrow, Leo
— History of Cartography. L, 1964. Revised by R. A. Skelton. 4to. (88) $50, $75; (89) $100, $150; (90) $100
— A. Ortelii Catalogus Cartographorum. Gotha, 1928-30. 2 vols in 1. 4to. Inscr. (91) $275

Bahr, A. W.
— Old Chinese Porcelain and Works of Art in China.... L, 1911. 1st Ed. (88) $65; (89) $65; (90) $50, $1,100

Baif, Lazare de, d.1547
— Annotationes in legem II de captivis, et postliminio reversis. Basel: Froben & Episcopius, 1541. 4to. Kissner copy. (91) £80
 Paris: R. Estienne, 1549. 4to. Kissner copy. (91) £420, £750
 Sion College copy. (89) £180
— De re navali commentarius. Basel, 1537. 8vo. (88) $260
— Opus de re vestimentaria.... Basel: Froben & Episcopius, 1531. 2 parts in 1 vol. 8vo. (88) $200
 [Venice: Giovanni Antonio de Nicolini de Sabio, 1535]. 8vo. Kissner copy. (91) £150

Baigell, Matthew
— Thomas Hart Benton. NY: Abrams, [1973]. Oblong folio. (91) $70

BAIGENT

Baigent, William
— A Book on Hackles for Fly Dressing. [N.p., n.d.]. 2 vols, including box of specimens. 4to. (88) £900; (89) A$2,100
  [Newcastle upon Tyne, c.1941. 2 vols, including box of specimens. 4to. (88) £1,400; (89) £1,250

Baikie, William Balfour
— Narrative of an Exploring Voyage up the Rivers Kwo'ra and Bi'nue.... L, 1856. 1st Ed. 8vo. (89) £110, £125

Bailey, David. See: Evans, Peter

Bailey, Florence Merriam
— Birds of New Mexico. Santa Fe, 1928. 8vo. (91) $55

Bailey, Henry
— Local Tales and Historical Sketches. Fishkill Landing, 1874. 8vo. (91) $70
— Travel and Adventures in the Congo Free State.... L, 1894. 8vo. (91) £160

Bailey, Liberty Hyde, 1858-1954
— Cyclopedia of American Horticulture. NY, 1900-2. 4 vols. 8vo. (90) $80
  NY, 1906. 6 vols. 8vo. (89) $50; (91) $60

Bailey, Nathan, d.1742
— Dictionarium Britannicum. L, 1770. Folio. (91) £170
— An Universal Etymological English Dictionary. L, 1755. ("A New Universal Etymological English Dictionary.") Folio. (88) £100

Bailey, Percival. See: Cushing & Bailey

Bailey, Robert G.
— River of No Return.... Lewiston, 1935. 1st Ed. (90) $75

Bailey, Rosalie F.
— Pre-Revolutionary Dutch Houses and Families in Northern New Jersey and Southern New York. NY, 1936. One of 334. 4to. (88) $110

Bailey, Samuel
— A Critical Dissertation on the Nature, Measures and Causes of Value. L, 1825. 8vo. (91) £840

Bailey, Vernon Howe
— Empire State; a Pictorial Record of its Construction. NY, 1931. Folio. (89) £190; (90) $175, $350

AMERICAN BOOK PRICES CURRENT

Baillet, Adrien
— The Life of Monsieur Des Cartes.... L, 1693. 8vo. Wing B451A. (90) $300

Baillet, Adrien, 1649-1706
— Auteurs deguizez. Sous des noms etrangers.... Paris, 1690. 12mo. (91) $375
— La Vie des Saints.... Paris, 1701. 12 vols. 8vo. (88) $70

Baillie, Granville Hugh
— Watches: Their History, Decoration and Mechanism. L, 1929. (89) $80
  Inscr to Lady Lewis. (88) $120
— Watchmakers and Clockmakers of the World. L, 1929. (89) $50; (91) $60

Baillie, Marianne
— First Impressions on a Tour upon the Continent.... L, 1819. 8vo. (90) £50
— Lisbon in the Years 1821, 1822 and 1823. L, 1824. 1st Ed. 2 vols. 16mo. (90) £70

Baillie, Matthew, 1761-1823
— A Series of Engravings Accompanied with Explanations which are Intended to Illustrate the Morbid Anatomy of...Parts of the Human Body. L, 1812. 2d Ed. 4to. (91) £260

Baillie-Grohman, William Adolph
— Sport in Art. L, [1913]. 1st Ed. 4to. (88) £50
— Sport in Art: an Iconography.... L, [1919]. 4to. (89) $50

Bailliere, F. F.
— Bailliere's South Australian Gazetteer and Road Guide.... Adelaide, 1866. 8vo. (88) A$1,000

Bailly, Jean Baptiste
— Ornithologie de la Savoie.... Paris: Clarey, 1853-[55]. 4 vols text & Atlas in 4 parts. 8vo. Martin copy. (90) $1,600

Bailly, Jean Sylvain, 1736-93
— Essai sur la theorie des satellites de Jupiter. Paris, 1766. 1st Ed. 4to. (88) £80; (90) £280
— Histoire de l'astronomie ancienne.... Paris, 1781. 4to. (89) £70

Baily's Magazine...
— Baily's Magazine of Sports and Pastimes. L, 1878-85. Vols 32-43. Together, 12 vols. 8vo. (91) $120

Bainbridge, George Cole
— The Fly Fisher's Guide.... Liverpool, 1816. 1st Ed. 8vo. (88) £160; (89) £220; (90) £270; (91) $400
  4th Ed. L, 1840. 8vo. (88) £90

Bainbridge, Henry Charles
— Peter Carl Faberge.... L, 1949. One of 350 on handmade paper. 4to. (89) £180
One of 1,000. (90) £60; (91) $65

Baines, Edward, 1774-1848
— The History, Directory, and Gazetteer, of the County Palatine of Lancaster. Liverpool, 1824-5. 3 parts in 3 vols. 8vo. (88) £180
— History of the Wars of the French Revolution. L, 1817. 2 vols. 4to. (89) $425
— The History of the County Palatine and Duchy of Lancaster. L, 1836. 4 vols. 4to. (88) £160; (89) £210
L, 1888-93. 5 vols. 4to. (88) £85

Baines, Thomas, 1806-81 —& Fairbairn, William
— Lancashire and Cheshire, Past and Present.... L, [1868-69]. 2 vols in 4. 4to. (89) £95

Baines, Thomas, 1822-75
— The Birds of South Africa.... Johannesburg, 1975. 4to. (89) R820
One of 500. (88) R380
— Explorations in South-West Africa. L, 1864. 8vo. (89) R1,600; (91) $250, £240
— The Gold Regions of South Eastern Africa. L, 1877. 8vo. (88) R130; (91) $200
— The Victoria Falls Zambesi River.... L, 1865. Folio. (88) R7,500; (91) £1,300, £2,200
Bulawayo, 1969. Folio. Facsimile. (88) £70

Baird, Joseph Armstrong
— California's Pictorial Letter Sheets 1849-1869. See: Grabhorn Printing

Baird, Robert, 1798-1863
— View of the Valley of the Mississippi.... Phila., 1834. 12mo. (88) $80

Baird, Spencer Fullerton, 1823-87
— Birds of the Boundary. Wash., 1857. 4to. (89) $80
Extracted from William H. Emory's United States and Mexican Boundary Survey. (88) £260; (90) $600

Baird, Spencer Fullerton, 1823-87 —& Others
— The Birds of North America. Phila., 1860. 2 vols. 4to. (91) $1,100; (88) $1,100; (90) $1,800
Martin copy. (90) $1,600
Text vol only. 4to. (90) $90
— A History of North American Birds. Bost., 1874. 1st Ed. 3 vols. 4to. (91) $230
Martin copy. (90) $600
— A History of North American Birds: Land Birds. Bost., 1875. 3 vols. 4to. (91) $650

— The Water Birds of North America. Bost., 1884. 2 vols. 4to. (90) $250, $250; (91) $900
Martin copy. (90) $900

Baja...
— Baja California Travel Series. Los Angeles: Dawson's Book Shop, 1965-86. 48 vols. (88) $450

Baja California Travels Series. See: Dawson's Book Shop

Baker...
— The Baker Street Journal. NY, 1946-48. Vol I, No 1 to Vol III, No 4. (89) $60
Vols I-II. NY, 1946-47. 8 parts in 2 vols. (91) $130

Baker, Caroline Horwood. See: Horwood, Caroline

Baker, Charles Henry Collins
— Crome. L, 1921. 4to. (88) £80
— The Gentleman's Companion. See: Derrydale Press
— Lely and Stuart Portrait Painters. L, 1912. One of 375. 2 vols. 4to. (90) $160

Baker, David Erskine, 1730-69
— Biographia Dramatica: or, a Companion to the Playhouse.... L, 1764. ("The Companion to the Play-House....") 2 vols. 8vo. (88) $175, £110
3d Ed. L, 1812. 3 vols in 4. 8vo. (88) £60
4 vols extended to 6. 8vo. Extra-illus with illumination on vellum as frontis, 14 orig watercolors & c.400 mtd views & ports. (91) £480

Baker, Edward Charles Stuart
— The Birds of British India, including Ceylon and Burma. L, 1922-30. 2d Ed. 8 vols. 8vo. (88) £110
— The Game Birds of India, Burma and Ceylon. Calcutta, 1879-[81]. 3 vols. 8vo. (89) £260
L, 1921-30. 3 vols. (88) £180, £280
— The Indian Ducks and their Allies. L, 1908. 8vo. (88) £105, £220, £280; (89) £175, £220, £220; (91) £220

Baker, George Percival
— Calico Painting and Printing in the East Indies in the XVIIth and XIIIth Centuries. 2 vols, including portfolio. Folio. (88) £2,000

Baker, Henry, 1698-1774
— An Attempt towards a Natural History of the Polype.... L, 1743. 8vo. (88) $150
— The Microscope Made Easy. L, 1744. 3d Ed. 8vo. (88) £110; (91) $150
— Original Poems: Serious and Humorous. L,

1725. 8vo. (89) £300

Baker, Humphrey
— The Well-Spring of Sciences, which Teacheth the Perfect Worke and Practise of Arithmeticke.... L, 1631. 8vo. (88) £300

Baker, J.
— A Complete History of the Inquisition.... Westminster, 1736. 4to. (88) $90

Baker, Lafayette Charles, 1826-68
— History of the United States Secret Service. Phila., 1867. 1st Ed. 8vo. (91) $200

Baker, Oliver
— Black Jacks and Leather Bottells. Stratford, [1921]. Ltd Ed, sgd. 4to. (89) £70; (91) $150

Baker, Sir Richard, 1568-1645
— A Chronicle of the Kings of England.... L, 1665. Folio. (89) £100
  6th Ed. L, 1674. Folio. (88) £100
  L, 1679. Folio. (89) £60
  L, 1733. Folio. (91) $100

Baker, Richard Thomas
— Building and Ornamental Stones of Australia. Sydney, 1915. 4to. (88) A$140
— Cabinet Timbers of Australia. Sydney, 1913. 8vo. (89) A$450
— Hardwoods of Australia and their Economics. Sydney, 1919. 4to. (89) A$80, A$150 Presentation copy. (90) £70

Baker, Sir Samuel White, 1821-93
— The Albert N'yanza. L, 1866. 1st Ed. 2 vols. 8vo. (88) £180; (91) £50, £170 Inscr to Lady Wharncliffe. (88) £550 L, 1867. 2 vols. 8vo. (90) £130
— Eight Years' Wanderings in Ceylon. L, 1855. 1st Ed. 8vo. (91) $130
— Ismailia. L, 1874. 1st Ed. 2 vols. 8vo. (88) £65, £100, £100; (89) £100; (90) £60 Blackmer copy. (90) £160 Paris, 1875. Trans by Hippolyte Vattemare. 8vo. (88) £80
— The Nile Tributaries of Abyssinia. L, 1867. 1st Ed. 8vo. (89) £120, £180; (90) £80 Inscr. (88) £220; (89) £90 Hartford, 1868. 8vo. (89) $55; (91) $80 2d Ed. L, 1868. 8vo. (89) £60
— Wild Beasts and their Ways. L, 1891. 8vo. (91) $150

Baker, Thomas, 1625?-90
— The Geometrical Key.... L, 1684. 4to. (88) $1,100; (89) $250

Bakewell, Robert, 1768-1843
— Travels, Comprising Observations made during a Residence in the Tarentaise...the Grecian and Pennine Alps.... L, 1823. 1st Ed. 2 vols. 8vo. Sion College copy. (89) £90

Bakker, R. See: Ollefen & Bakker

Bakst, Leon, 1866?-1924
— The Designs of Leon Bakst for The Sleeping Princess. See: Levinson, Andre
— The Inedited Works. NY: Brentano's, 1927. One of 600. Oblong folio. (90) $850; (91) $350, $500
— L'Oeuvre de Leon Bakst pour la belle au bois dormant. See: Levinson, Andre

Balashev, —
— Risunki obmundirovaniia k istorii leibgvardii kirasirskago ego velichestva polka. St. Petersburg, 1872. Folio. (88) £750

Balbinus, Bohuslaus Aloysius
— Vita S. Joannis Nepomuceni. Augsburg: J. A. Pfeffel, 1730. 4to. (91) £100

Balbus, Joannes
— Catholicon. Mainz: [Johann Gutenberg], 1460. Single leaf. Folio. (88) £1,250; (89) £800; (90) $1,300
  3d Issue. Folio. 373 leaves. Goff B-20. "A fine unpressed copy." Hopetoun-Linlithgow copy. (89) £120,000
  Augsburg: Guenther Zainer, 30 Apr 1469. In 2 vols. Folio. 522 leaves. Goff B-21. Chatsworth-Abrams copy. (90) $55,000
  3d Ed. [Strassburg: R-Press type 2 (Johann Mentelin & Adolf Rusch), not after 1475]. Folio. 399 (of 400) leaves; lacking final blank. Goff B-22. Deckel-Abrams copy. (90) £48,000
  Venice: Bonetus Locatellus for Octavianus Scotus, 20 Nov 1495. Folio. 312 leaves. Goff B-33. (88) £850

Balch, Herbert E.
— Wookey Hole. L, 1914. 4to. (89) £50; (90) £55; (91) £50

Baldacchino, Filippo
— Predica damore bellissima composta per el digno poeta Baldoino Cortonese. [Florence?, 1510?]. 8vo. (91) £1,400

Baldaeus, Phillippus, 1632-72
— Naauwkeurige beschryvinge van Malabar en Choromandel. Amst., 1672. Folio. (88) HF3,000; (89) £850; (90) £950
— Wahrhaftige ausfuehrliche Beschreibung der beruehmten Ost-Indischen Kusten Malabar und Coromandel, als auch der Insel Zeylon.... Amst: J. Waesburge & J. Soneren, 1672. Folio. (90) £410

Baldi, Bernardino, 1553-1617
— Cronica de matematici.... Urbino, 1707. 1st Ed. 4to. Horblit copy. (89) $425

Baldinucci, Filippo, 1624-96
— Cominciamento, e progresso dell'arte dell'intagliare in rame.... Florence, 1686. 4to. (89) $550
Florence, 1767. 4to. (90) LIt500,000

Baldner, Leonhard
— Vogel-, Fisch- und Thierbuch. Stuttgart, [1974]. 4 vols. Oblong 4to. Facsimile of the Cassel copy. (88) $50

Balduinus, Benedictus
— Calceus antiauus et mysticus.... Leiden, 1711. 2 parts in 1 vol. 12mo. (91) $175
— De Calceo Antiquo, et jul. nigronus de caliga veterum.... Amst.: Andreae Frisl, 1667. 2 vols in 1. 12mo. (88) $175; (91) $50

Baldung, Hieronymus
— Aphorismi compunctionis theologicales. [Strassburg:] Johann Grueninger, 6 Jan 1497. 1st Ed. 4to. 39 (of 40) leaves; lacking final blank. Goff B-36. Abrams copy. (90) £4,500

Baldus de Ubaldis de Perusio
— Lectura super i parte digesti veteris. Venice, 17 Nov 1488. Folio. 249 (of 294) leaves; lacking final blank & all before F3, including initial blank, but with register leaf unknown to Hain & Pellechet. Hain 2303. (91) £900

Baldwin, Edward. See: Godwin, William

Baldwin, James
— Go Tell It on the Mountain. NY, 1953. (88) $250; (89) $60

Baldwin Locomotive Works
— Illustrated Catalogue of Locomotives. Phila., [1872?]. 8vo. (89) £240; (90) $600; (91) $200
Phila., 1881. 8vo. (90) $475

Baldwin, Thomas, of Chester
— Airopaidia. Chester, 1786. 1st Ed. 8vo. (90) £700

Baldwin, William, fl.1547
— A Myrrour for Magistrates. L: Thomas Marshe, 1559. ("A Myrroure for Magistrates.") 1st Ed. 4to. STC 1247. Fauconberg-Steevens-Bradley Martin copy. (90) $55,000
2d Ed. L: Thomas Marsh, 1563. 4to. STC 1248. Chew-Bemis-Greenhill-Bradley Martin copy. (90) $5,500
L: Felix Kingston, 1609-10. 4to. STC 13446. Sykes-Perkins-Greenhill-Bradley Martin copy. (90) $2,000

Baldwin, William Charles
— African Hunting from Natal to the Zambesi.... L, 1863. 2d Ed. 8vo. (88) R480; (89) R600; (91) £100
3d Ed. L, 1894. 8vo. (88) $70

Bale, John, 1495-1563
— A brefe Chronycle concerning the Examination and Death of...Sir John Oldecastell.... [Antwerp: A. Goinus, 1544]. 1st Ed. 8vo. STC 1276. Huth-Greenhill-Bradley Martin copy. (90) $7,500

Balen, Matthys
— Beschryvinge der Stad Dordrecht. Dordrecht, 1677. 4to. (88) £200

Balestier, Wolcott. See: Kipling & Balestier

Balfour, Alice Blanche
— Twelve Hundred Miles in a Waggon. L, 1895. 8vo. (91) $70

Balfour, J. O.
— A Sketch of New South Wales. L, 1845. 8vo. (89) A$250
Inscr on tp. (89) A$150
Martin copy. (90) $300

Ball, Charles. See: Stafford & Ball

Ball, James Moores
— Andreas Vesalius, the Reformer of Anatomy. St. Louis, 1910. 4to. Ls to M. H. Spielmann laid in. (91) $140

Ball, John, 1818-89
— Peakes, Passes, and Glaciers. L, 1859. 8vo. (89) £70
Series I-II. L, 1859-62. 3 vols. 8vo. (88) £340

Ball, Katherine M.
— Bamboo: Its Cult and Culture. Berkeley: The Gillick Press, 1945. One of 500. (88) $110
— Decorative Motifs of Oriental Art. L & NY, 1927. 4to. (88) $110; (90) $150; (91) $150

Ball, William
— Tractatus de jure regnandi...The Sphere of Government.... L, 1645. 4to. (91) $150

Ballantyne Press
— The Ballantyne Press and its Founders, 1796-1908. Edin., 1909. 8vo. (90) $60

BALLANTYNE

Ballantyne, Robert Michael, 1825-94
— The Coral Island, a Tale of the Pacific Ocean. L, 1858. 1st Ed, 1st Issue. 8vo. Ewing-Martin copy. (90) $3,500

Ballard, Ellis James
— Catalogue Intimate and Descriptive of my Kipling Collection. Phila., 1935. One of 120. (91) $130

Ballard, George, 1706-55
— Memoirs of Several Ladies of Great Britain.... L, 1775. 8vo. (91) $150

Ballard, J. G.
— News from the Sun. L: Interzone, 1982. One of 20. (88) $80

Ballard Collection, James Franklin
— Illustrated Catalogue and Description of Ghiordes Rugs of the Seventeenth and Eighteenth Centuries. St. Louis, [1916]. One of 100. 4to. Inscr. (90) $200

Ballonius, Gulielmus
— Opera omnia. Geneva: De Tournes, 1762. 4 parts in 2 vols. 4to. Bullock copy. (88) $850

Ballu, Roger
— L'Oeuvre de Barye precede d'une introduction de M. Eugene Guillaume. Paris, 1890. Folio. (89) £150

Bally, Francois Victor —& Others
— Histoire medicale de la fievre jaune.... Paris, 1823. 8vo. (89) £150

Balmer, Edwin, 1883-1959. See: MacHarg & Balmer

Balston, Thomas
— The Cambridge University Press Collection of Private Press Types. Cambr., 1951. One of 350. (91) $150

Baltard, Louis Pierre
— Paris et ses monumens.... Paris, 1803-5. 2 vols in one. Folio. (89) £1,050

**Baltard, Victor —&
Callet, Felix Emmanuel**
— Monographie des halles centrales de Paris.... Paris, 1873. 2 parts in 1 vol. Folio. (89) £650; (91) £900

Balthasar, Juan Antonio
— Carta del Juan Antonio Balthasar, en que de noticia de la exemplar vida.... [Mexico, 1752]. 4to. Doheny copy. (88) $1,500
— Catalogus personarum & domiciliorum.... Mexico, 1751. Oblong 4to. Doheny copy. (88) $3,000

AMERICAN BOOK PRICES CURRENT

Baltimore
— City Atlas of Baltimore Maryland and Environs. Phila: G. M. Hopkins, 1876. LeGear L1543. (91) $350
— Souvenir of Baltimore, 1911. Compliments of The Old Town Booming Committee of The Old Town Merchants and Manufacturers' Association. [Balt., 1911]. 4to. (91) $160
— HYMNAL. - The New Baltimore Hymn Book: Intended to Aid the Devotion of Christians of Every Denomination. Balt., 1813. 16mo. S & S 29275. (91) $55

Baltimore, Frederick Calvert, Baron. See: Calvert, Frederick

Baltimore Museum of Art
— 2000 Years of Calligraphy. Balt., 1965. 4to. (90) $90; (91) $150

Balzac, Honore de, 1799-1850
— L'Anonyme, ou ni pere ni mere..... Paris, 1823. 3 vols. 12mo. Martin copy. (90) FF2,400
— L'Art de mettre sa cravate. Paris, 1827. 3d Ed. 12mo. Martin copy. (90) FF4,000
— Beatrix ou les Amours forces.... Paris, 1839. 2 vols. 8vo. Martin copy. (90) FF19,000
— La Bourse. Paris, 1853. 12mo. Martin copy. (90) FF1,800
— Les Cent Contes drolatiques. Paris, 1832-37. 1st Ed. 3 vols. 8vo. Martin copy. (90) FF15,000
With ALs. (88) FF20,000
5th Ed. Paris, 1855. ("Les Contes drolatiques.") Illus by Gustave Dore. 12mo. (88) FF5,000
— Le Centenaire ou les deux Beringheld...par M. Horace de Saint-Aubin. Paris, 1822. 4 vols. 12mo. Martin copy. (90) FF6,500
— Le Chef-d'oeuvre inconnu. Paris, 1931. One of 65 on japon imperial, with a suite of plates on Rives. Illus by Picasso. 4to. (89) SF92,000
One of 240. (88) FF120,000
— Les Chouans ou la Bretagne en 1799. Paris, 1834. 2 vols. 8vo. Martin copy. (90) FF42,000
— Clotilde de Lusignan ou le beau Juif.... Paris, 1822. 4 vols in 2. 12mo. Martin copy. (90) FF12,000
— Code des Gens honnetes.... Paris, [1825]. 18mo. Martin copy. (90) FF4,500
— Code du commis-voyageur. Paris, 1830. 12mom. Martin copy. (90) FF1,100
— La Comedie humaine. Phila., [1885-86]. Water-Color Ed, one of 10. Trans by Katharine Prescott Wormeley. 40 vols. 8vo. (89) $2,000

[N.p.]: Renaissance Society, 1902. One of 6, this copy for S. Jennie Sorg, the colorist. 33 (of 40) vols; lacking Vols 1-6 & 13. (89) $1,200
— Contes Bruns. Paris, 1832. 8vo. Martin copy. (90) FF2,800
— Le Cure de Tours. Tours, 1947. One of 1,000. Illus by Georges Pichard. (89) SF200
— Un Debut dans la vie. Paris, 1844. 2 vols. 8vo. Martin copy. (90) FF8,500
— Le Dernier Chouan ou la Bretagne en 1800. Paris, 1829. 1st Ed. 4 vols. 12mo. Martin copy. (90) FF32,000
— La derniere fee.... Paris, 1823. 2 vols in 1. 16mo. Martin copy. (90) FF11,000
Paris, 1836. 2 vols. 8vo. Martin copy. (90) FF16,000
— La derniere incarnation de Vautrin. Brussels, 1847. 16mo. Martin copy. (90) FF1,400
Paris, 1848. 3 vols. 8vo. Martin copy. (90) FF15,000
— Les deux freres. Brussels, 1841. 12mo. Martin copy. (90) FF1,200
— Les deux Hector ou les deux familles bretonnes. Paris, 1821. 2 vols. 16mo. Martin copy. (90) FF12,000
— Discours de la girafe au chef de six osages.... Paris, 1827. 12mo. Martin copy. (90) FF6,000
— Un Drame dans les prisons. Paris, 1847. 2 vols. 8vo. Martin copy. (90) FF6,000
— Droll Stories. See: Limited Editions Club
— Etudes de moeurs au XIX3 siecle.... Paris, 1834-35. 4 vols. 8vo. Martin copy. (90) FF1,800
— Eugenie Grandet. Paris, 1911. One of 20 on chine with suites of plates & a watercolor on half-title. Illus by Auguste Leroux. 4to. (89) SF1,100
— La Fille aux Yeux d'Or. Paris: Briffaut, [1923]. One of 450. Illus by Lobel-Riche. Folio. (88) SF1,100
— Une Fille d'Eve. Paris, 1839. 1st Ed. 2 vols. 8vo. Martin copy. (90) FF6,000
— Die Frau Konnetable. Berlin, 1922. One of 380. Illus by Lovis Corinth. Folio. (88) DM540
Inscr by Corinth to his daughter. (88) DM3,000
— Un Grand Homme de province a Paris. Paris, 1839. 1st Ed. 2 vols. 8vo. (88) FF3,800
Martin copy. (90) FF2,800
— The Hidden Treasures.... Kentfield: Allen Press, 1953. Illus by Malette Dean. (89) $150
One of 160. (89) $150; (90) $180
— Histoire de Napoleon contee dans une grange par un vieux soldat. Paris, 1833.

4to. Supplement extraordinaire au Bons Sens , 21 July 1833. Martin copy. (90) FF9,000
— Histoire des treize. Brussels, 1833. 12mo. Martin copy. (90) FF1,100
— Histoire des parents pauvres.... Brussels, 1846. 4 vols. 12mo. Martin copy. (90) FF6,000
Paris, [1849]. 4to. Martin copy. (90) FF3,000
— Histoire intellectuelle de Louis Lambert. Paris, 1832. 8vo. Martin copy. (90) FF9,500
— Honorine. Paris, 1845 [1844]. 2 vols. 8vo. Martin copy. (90) FF6,000
— Le Livre mystique. Paris, 1835. 2 vols. 8vo. (91) $800
Martin copy. (90) FF20,000
— Louis Lambert, Suivi de Seraphita. Paris, 1842. 12mo. Inscr to E. Dupaty. Martin copy. (90) FF8,000
— Le Lys dans la vallee. Paris, 1836. 1st Ed. 2 vols. 8vo. (89) FF4,500; (91) $650
Inscr to the Comte Sclopis by Balzac & by Sclopis to the Countess of Baldisee. (91) £3,500
Martin copy. (90) FF12,000
— Das Maedchen mit den Goldaugen. Leipzig, 1904. One of 500. Illus by Marcus Behmer. 4to. (88) DM550
— Le Medecin de campagne. Paris, 1834. 4 vols. 12mo. Inscr to Emanuel Arago. Martin copy. (90) FF18,000
— Memoires de deux jeunes mariees. Brussels, 1842. 2 vols. 16mo. Martin copy. (90) FF4,200
— Modeste Mignon. Paris, 1845. 4 vols. 8vo. Martin copy. (90) FF14,000
— Notes remises a MM. les Deputes composant la Commission de la Loi sur la Propriete Litteraire. Paris, 1832. 8vo. Martin copy. (90) FF3,800
— Nouveaux Contes philosophiques. Paris, 1832. 1st Ed. 8vo. Hoe copy. (89) FF3,500
— Oeuvres. Paris, 1856-59. 42 vols. 12mo. (90) £60
Paris, 1868-69. 20 vols. 8vo. (88) £440
Paris, 1869-76. 24 vols. 8vo. (89) FF6,500
Paris, 1877. ("La Comedie humaine.") 20 vols. 8vo. (88) FF6,000
Paris, 1912-40. Vols 1-39 (of 40). (91) £160
— Les Parents pauvres. Paris, 1847-48. 12 vols. 8vo. Martin copy. (90) FF2,800
— Les Paysans, scenes de la vie de campagne.... Paris: L. de Potter, [1855]. 5 vols. 8vo. Martin copy. (90) FF2,800
— Le Peau de chagrin.... Paris, 1831. 1st Ed. 2 vols. 8vo. (89) FF13,000
— La Peau de chagrin.... Paris, 1831. 1st Ed. 2 vols. 8vo. (90) FF2,800

BALZAC

Exhibition copy. Martin copy. (90) FF35,000
3d Ed. 2 vols. 8vo. Dedication copy, inscr to Nacquart. Martin copy. (90) FF160,000
— Le Pere Goriot. Paris, 1835. 2 vols. 8vo. Inscr to Nacquart. Martin copy. (90) FF160,000
1st Ed. 2 vols. 8vo. Gabalda copy. (88) FF70,000
— Physiologie du mariage.... Paris, 1834. 2d Ed. 2 vols. 8vo. Martin copy. (90) FF4,500
— Pierrette. Paris, 1840. 2 vols. 8vo. Martin copy. (90) FF10,000
1st French Ed. 2 vols. 8vo. (88) FF2,800
— Le Provencial a Paris. Paris, 1847. 2 vols. 8vo. Martin copy. (90) FF6,500
— Les Ressources de Quinola. Souverain, 1842. 8vo. Martin copy. (90) FF6,000
— Romans et contes philosophiques. Paris, 1831. 2d Ed. 3 vols. 8vo. Martin copy. (90) FF6,000
— Scenes de la vie privee. Paris, 1832. 4 vols. 8vo. Martin copy. (90) FF1,800
— Les Trois Amoureux. Paris: Arnaud de Vresse, [1844]. 4 parts in 3 vols. 8vo. Martin copy. (90) FF4,500
— Ursuel Mirouet. Paris, 1842. 2 vols. Martin copy. (90) FF13,000
— Le Vicaire des Ardennes.... Paris, 1822. 4 vols. 12mo. Martin copy. (90) FF36,000
— Works. L, 1895-98. ("Comedie humaine.") Ed by G. Saintsbury. 40 vols. 8vo. (90) £25
One of 50 for sale in England. (90) $2,000
Phila., [1895-1920]. One of 300. 53 vols. 8vo. (89) £2,200
Definitive Ed. Phila., [1895-1900]. One of 1,000. 53 vols. 8vo. (89) $150
Phila., 1899-1900. ("The Human Comedy.") 33 vols. 8vo. (91) $60

Balzac, Jean Louis Guez, Sieur de, 1597?-1654
— Oeuvres. Paris, 1665. 2 vols, including 2 parts in Vol II. Folio. (88) FF3,200
— Le Prince. Paris, 1631. 4to. L.p. copy. The De Backer copy, presented by Balzac to the Earl of Exeter. (88) £1,000

Bances Candamo, Francisco Antonio de, 1662-1704
— La Gran Comedia de la Restauracion de Buda. Madrid: Sebastian de Armendariz, [1686?]. 4to. (91) $150

Bancroft, Edward
— An Essay on the Natural History of Guiana.... L, 1769. 1st Ed. 8vo. (88) £120; (91) $550
— Experimental Researches concerning the Philosophy of Permanent Colours.... L, 1794. Vol I (all pbd). 8vo. (89) £85

AMERICAN BOOK PRICES CURRENT

Bancroft, George, 1800-91
— History of the United States.... Bost., 1876. 6 vols. 8vo. (91) $110

Bancroft, Hubert Howe, 1832-1918
— The Book of the Fair. Chicago, 1895. Folio. (90) $150
— History of Alaska, 1730-1885. San Francisco, 1886. (91) $50
— History of California. San Francisco, 1886-90. 7 vols. With: California Pastoral, 8 vols. (91) $200
Santa Barbara: Hebberd, [1963-70]. 7 vols. (88) $160; (89) $75, $100, $110; (90) $110, $110, $200
Santa Barbara: Hebberd, [1963]. 7 vols. (91) $110
Santa Barbara: Hebberd, [1963-70]. 7 vols. (91) $150, $180
— History of Oregon. San Francisco, 1886 & 1888. 2 vols. 8vo. (90) $65
— History of the North Mexican States and Texas. San Francisco, 1884. 2 vols. (91) $70
— History of Utah, 1540-1887. San Francisco, 1890. 8vo. (88) $200
— The Native Races of the Pacific States of North America. NY, 1874-76. 5 vols. 8vo. (89) $80; (91) $230
— Works. San Francisco, 1883-90. 39 vols. 8vo. (88) $350, $850; (89) $450
Sold w.a.f. (91) $275
San Francisco, 1886-91. Vol XXXIII only. (90) $75
Vols 18-24 (of 39). Together, 7 vols. (90) $120

Bancroft, John
— Henry the Second. L, 1693. 1st Ed. 4to. (89) £240

Bancroft, Laura. See: Baum, L. Frank

Bancroft, Squire B. & Marie W.
— Mr. and Mrs. Bancroft: On and Off the Stage. L, 1888. 2 vols. 8vo. (88) $210; (89) $70

Bandelier, Adolph Francis, 1840-1914
— A Scientist on the Trail: Travel Letters.... Berkeley: Quivera Society, 1949. One of 500. (89) $80; (90) $60
— The Unpublished Letters.... NY, 1942. One of 295. (88) $200

Bandello, Matteo, 1480?-1562
— Continuation des histoires tragiques.... Paris, 1560. 8vo. (89) $425
— La Prima [-quarta] parte de la novelle. L [Italy ptd], 1740. 4 vols in 3. 4to. (90) £360
— La Prima [-quarte] parte de la novelle. Lyons: Alessandro Marsilii per Pietro Roussino, 1554-73. 4 vols. 4to & 8vo.

Renouard-Vernon-Holford copy. (91) £4,500

Bandini, Angelo Maria, 1726-1803
— Catalogus codicum latinorum bibliothecae medicae Laurentianae. Florence, 1774-78. 5 vols. Folio. (88) FF7,000
— Vita e lettere di Amerigo Vespucci. Florence, 1745. 1st Ed. 4to. (91) £160

Bandini, Ralph
— Veiled Horizons... See: Derrydale Press

Banduri, Anselmo
— Imperium orientale sive antiquitates Constantinopolitaniae.... Paris: J. B. Coignard, 1711. Folio. Blackmer copy. (90) £800
— Numismata imperatorum Romanorum a Trajano decio ad Palaeologos Augustos. Paris, 1718. 2 vols. Folio. (88) DM800

Bangs, E. Geoffrey
— Portals West: A Folio of Late Nineteenth Century Architecture in California. San Francisco: California Historical Society, [1960]. One of 1,000. (91) $65

Bangs, Mary Rogers
— Jeanne d'Arc: The Maid of France. Bost.: Houghton Mifflin, [1910]. Inscr by Ingrid Bergman. (90) $55

Bangs, Outram. See: Thayer & Bangs

Banier, Antione
— The Mythology and Fables of the Ancients.... L, 1739-40. 4 vols. 8vo. (91) £160

Bank of England
— Rules, Orders and By-Laws; for the Good Government of the Corporation.... [L, 1697]. 4to. (88) £680

Bankes, Thomas —& Others
— A New Royal Authentic and Complete System of Universal Geography. L, [c.1790]. 2 vols. Folio. (89) £620
2 vols in 1. Folio. (88) £400; (89) £520, £750, A$130; (90) £240, £480; (91) £370, £380, £550, £550
— ("A Most Authentic and Complete System of Universal Geography.") Folio. (91) £650
Vol I only. (88) £330

Banks, Iain M.
— Consider Phlebas. L: Macmillan, [1987]. One of 176. (88) £160; (89) £90

Banks, Sir Joseph, 1743-1820
— The Endeavour Journal of Joseph Banks 1768-1771. Sydney, 1962. Ed by J. C. Beaglehole. 2 vols. 8vo. (89) A$190, A$360; (90) A$220; (91) $70
— The Journal of.... Guildford: Genesis Publications, 1980. One of 500. 2 vols. (88) $250, £280; (89) A$400
Facsimile of orig Ms. (91) $260

Bannerman, David Armitage
— Birds of the Atlantic Islands. Edin., 1963-68. 4 vols. (88) £280
L, 1963-68. 4 vols. (88) £240; (90) £280
— The Birds of Tropical West Africa. L, 1930-51. 8 vols. (88) £290; (89) £220, £280, £420, £420; (90) £180, £400; (91) £250, £380, £400
— The Birds of West and Equatorial Africa. Edin., 1953. 2 vols. (88) £70, £260; (91) $75, $275

Bannerman, David Armitage —& Bannerman, Winifred Mary
— Birds of Cyprus. L, 1958. (91) $175, £90

Bannerman, David Armitage —& Lodge, George E.
— The Birds of the British Isles. Edin. & L, 1953-63. 12 vols. (88) £105, £110, £220, £270; (89) £130, £130, £140, £220, £220, £240, £250; (90) £300, £900; (91) £200
L, 1953-63. Vols 6-11 only. (91) £70

Bannerman, Helen
— The Story of Little Black Sambo. L, 1899. 1st Ed. 16mo. (89) $950; (91) £1,400
NY: Stokes, [c.1901]. (89) $225; (91) $375
Animated Ed. Garden City, [1933]. Illus by Kurt Wiese & A. V. Warren. (91) $275, $375

Bannerman, Winifred Mary. See: Bannerman & Bannerman

Bannet, Ivor
— The Amazons. See: Golden Cockerel Press

Banning, Kendall, 1874-1944
— Pirates! or, the Cruise of the Black Revenge.... Chicago: Brothers of the Book, 1916. Illus by Gustave Baumann. 4to. (88) $175
One of 525. (90) $110

Banting, Sir F. G. —& Best, C. H.
— The Internal Secretion of the Pancreas. St. Louis, Feb 1922. 4to. In: The Journal of Laboratory and Clinical Medicine, Vol 7, No 5, pp. 251-66. (90) $1,000

BANTYSH-KAMENSKII

Bantysh-Kamenskii, Dmitri Nikolaevich, 1788-1850
— Biograffii Rossiiskikh General-Issimusov i General-Feldmarshalov. St. Petersburg, 1840-41. 4 vols in 2. 8vo. (88) £300

Banville, Theodore de, 1823-91
— Les Cames parisiens. Pincebourde, 1866. 8vo. From the library of Princess Mathilde with an AMs poem bound in. (90) FF44,000
— Diane au bois. Paris, 1911. One of 50 on velin with 2 extra suites of the lithos. (88) $9,000; (89) SF13,500
One of 200 with 2 extra suites of the plates, 1 colored. 4to. (91) £80
— Les Exiles. Paris, 1867. 1st Ed. 12mo. Inscr to Stephene Mallarme. Martin copy. (90) FF32,000
— Petit Traite de poesie francaise. Paris: Bibliotheque de l'Echo de la Sorbonne, [1872]. 12mo. Martin copy. (90) FF2,200
— Les Poesies, 1841-1854. Paris, 1857. 1st Collected Ed, Ltd Ed on papier verge. 12mo. With ALs of Docteur Fleury to Jules Janin. Martin copy. (90) FF4,800
— Les Princesses. Paris, 1874. 18mo. Inscr to Princesse Mathilde on half-title. Martin copy. (90) FF6,800
Paris, 1904. One of 130. 4to. With an orig watercolor by Rochegrosse. (91) FF20,000
One of 20 with illusts in 3 states & with orig watercolor. (91) £650

Baptist Association, Philadelphia
— A Confession of Faith. Phila., 1743. 8vo. (89) $225

Baptista Mantuanus, Carmelite
— De patientia. Brescia: Bernardinus de Misintis, 30 May 1497. 4to. 116 leaves. Goff B-76. (91) £1,600
Basel: Johann Bergmann, de Olpe, 17 Aug 1499. 4to. 118 leaves. Goff B-79. (90) £4,400
— Parthenice prima sive Mariana. Bologna: Franciscus (Plato) de Benedictis for Benedictus Hectoris, 17 Oct 1488. 4to. 70 leaves. Goff B-58. (91) $700
— Parthenice secunda. Paris, Michiel Tholoze, [c.1500]. 4to. (90) £180

Bar, Jacques Charles, 1740-1811
— Recueil de tous les costumes des ordres religieux et militaires. Paris, 1778-[89?]. 6 vols in 3. Folio. (89) £2,400

Bara, Jerome de
— Le Blason des armoiries.... Paris, 1628. Folio. (90) $200

AMERICAN BOOK PRICES CURRENT

Baratta, A.
— Constantinopoli effigiata e descritta.... Turin, 1840. 4to. (88) $200

Baratteri, Giovanni Battista
— Architettura d'acque. Piacenza, 1656-63. 2 vols. 4to. (89) £300

Barba, Alvaro Alonso, fl.1640
— Arte de los metales.... Madrid, [1729]. 4to. (88) $350
Madrid, [1770]. 4to. (89) $110, $300
— Berg-Buchlein.... Hamburg, 1676. 8vo. (88) DM1,300
— A Collection of Scarce and Valuable Treatises upon Metals, Mines and Minerals. L, 1738. Trans by the Earl of Sandwich. 12mo. (88) £110
L, 1739. 8vo. (89) $375
— The First Book of the Art of Mettals. L, 1674. 2 parts in 1 vol. 8vo. (90) £520

Barbarigo, Giovanni Francesco, Cardinal
— Numismata virorum illustrium ex Barbadica gente. Padua, 1732 [but not pbd until 1760]. 3 vols in 2, including 2 supplements. Folio. Kissner copy. (91) £1,700

Barbarities...
— Barbarities of the Enemy, Exposed in a Report of the Committee of the House of Representatives...and the Documents. Worcester, 1814. 12mo. (90) $110

Barbaro, Daniele
— Exquisitae in Porphirum commentationes. Venice: Aldus, Mar 1542. 4to. (90) £1,150

Barbauld, Anna Laetitia Aikin, 1743-1825
— Hymns in Prose, for Children. Newburyport, 1813. 12mo. (88) $60

Barbault, Jean, 1705?-66
— Denkmaeler des Alten Roms. Augsburg, 1782. Folio. (90) $750
— Les Plus Beaux Monuments de Rome ancienne.... Rome, 1756. Folio. Thomas Thistlethwaite's copy. (89) £420
Rome, 1761. Folio. (89) £920
Kissner copy. (91) £1,200, £2,000
— Vues des plus beaux restes des antiquites romaines.... Paris: Bouchard et Gravier, 1770. Folio. Kissner copy. (91) £3,800

Barbeau, Charles Marius
— Totem Poles. Ottawa, [1950]. 4to. (88) $80

Barber & Baker
— Sacramento Illustrated. Sacramento, 1855. Folio. Streeter 2777. (89) $1,100
Sacramento, 1950. One of 300. Reprint of 1855 Ed. (91) $50

Barber, Joel D.
— 'Long Shore. See: Derrydale Press
— Wild Fowl Decoys. NY, [1934]. (88) $80; (89) $110; (91) $110, $200

Barber, John Warner, 1798-1885
— Connecticut Historical Collections.... New Haven, 1836. 8vo. (89) $80; (90) $55
— History and Antiquities of New Haven.... New Haven, 1831. 1st Ed. 12mo. (88) $80; (91) $70

Barber, John Warner, 1798-1885 —& Howe, Henry, 1816-93
— Historical Collections of New Jersey.... New Haven, 1868. 8vo. (91) $120

Barber, Mary
— Poems on Several Occasions. L, 1734. 1st Ed. 4to. (88) £60; (90) $70

Barber, Thomas
— Picturesque Illustrations of the Isle of Wight. L, [1834]. 8vo. (88) £65

Barber, William
— Farm Buildings.... L, 1802. 4to. (88) £180

Barberini, Maffeo
— Poemata. See: Urban VIII

Barberino, Francesco, 1264-1348
— Documenti d'amore. Rome: Vitale Macardi, 1640. 4to. (90) $2,250; (91) LIt700,000

Barbey d'Aurevilly, Jules, 1808-89
— Amaideem Poeme en prose.... Paris, 1890. 12mo. Martin copy. (90) FF1,200
— L'Amour impossible, chronique parisienne.... Paris, 1841. 8vo. Martin copy. (90) FF1,800
— La Bague d'Annibal. Paris, 1843. One of 15. 12mo. Martin copy. (90) FF17,000
— Les Bas bleus. Paris, 1878. 12mo. With autograph ticket to M. Bourdillat. (90) FF1,800
— Le Chevalier des touches. Paris, 1864. 1st Ed. 12mo. Martin copy. (90) FF4,500
— Les Diaboliques. Paris, 1874. 1st Ed. 12mo. (88) FF19,000; (89) FF7,500 With ANs tipped in. (88) FF19,000 Paris, [1910]. Illus by M. Lobel-Riche.
  — (88) FF7,500
  One of 300. (89) $275
  One of 120 on vellum with a triple suite of all the illusts and a suite in 3 states. (88) FF4,800
— Les Diaboliques, Les Six Premieres. Paris, 1921. One of 16 on papier de chine. Illus by Gaston Pastre. (90) $130
— Du Dandysme et de G. Brummell. Paris, 1845. 16mo. Martin copy. (90) FF3,000

— L'Ensorcelee. Paris, 1855. 2 vols. 8vo. Martin copy. (90) FF2,800
  Paris, 1922. One of 10 hors commerce on japon imperial. Illus by G. Pastre. 8vo. Unique copy with the 33 orig drawings bound in. (90) $2,000
— Goethe et Diderot. Paris, 1880. 12mo. Inscr to Armand Haym. Martin copy. (90) FF4,500
— Laocoon, a Forgotten Rhyme.... Paris, [1857]. 16mo. Martin copy. (90) FF1,800
— Lea. Paris, 1832 [1907]. One of 90. 16mo. Martin copy. (90) FF1,800
— Memorandum. Caen, [1856]. 16mo. Martin copy. (90) FF1,800
— Notice sur J. M. Audin.... Paris, 1856. 8vo. Martin copy. (90) FF2,800
— Le Pacha, rhythme oublie. Caen, [1869]. 16mo. Martin copy. (90) FF5,800
— Un Page d'histoire. Paris, 1886. 16mo. Inscr to Edmond de Goncourt. (90) FF14,000
— Poesies. Caen, 1854. One of 36 on holland. 8vo. Inscr to his editor, Trebutien. (90) FF7,000
— Poesies de Barbey d'Aurevilly commentees par lui-meme. Brussels, 1870. One of 72. 8vo. Martin copy. (90) FF4,500
— Un Pretre marie. Paris, 1865. 2 vols. 12mo. Martin copy. (90) FF16,000
— Les Prophetes du passe. Paris, 1851. 16mo. Martin copy. (90) FF2,800
— Le Theatre contemporain. Paris, 1887. One of 90. 12mo. Martin copy. (90) FF2,800
— Une Vieille Maitresse. Paris, 1851. 1st Ed. 3 vols. 8vo. Martin copy. (90) FF42,000

Barbie du Bocage, Jean Denis
— Maps, Views. See: Barthelemy, Jean Jacques

Barbier, Antoine Alexandre, 1765-1825
— Dictionnaire des ouvrages anonymes. Paris, 1822-27. 2d Ed. 4 vols. 8vo. (89) $60
  Paris, 1872-89. 4 vols. 8vo. (89) $120, $400
  5 vols, including Supplement. 8vo. (89) HF500
— Dissertation sur soixante traductions francaises de l'Imitation de Jesus-Christ.... Paris, 1812. 8vo. (91) $110

Barbier, Georges
— Designs on the Dances of Vaslav Nijinsky.... L, 1913. One of 400. 4to. (88) £240, £450; (91) £360
— Dix-Sept Dessins sur le Cantique des Cantiques. Paris: La Belle Edition, 1914. One of 25 with an extra suite of illusts. 4to. (91) £900
— Falbalas et Fanfreluches. Paris, 1921-24.

BARBIER

(88) DM5,200
3 vols only. (91) £1,600
— Falbalas et Fanfreluches...pour 1924. Paris, [1923]. (90) $750
— Falbalas et Fanfreluches: Almanach des modes presentes, passees et futures. Paris, 1925. (89) SF1,100; (90) $750
— La Guirlande des Mois. Paris, 1917-21. Bound in 1 vol. 16mo. (91) £1,200
Vol II only. 16mo. (91) £260
Vols II-IV only. 16mo. (88) DM5,800
Paris, 1920. 16mo. (88) DM460; (90) £200

Barbier, Stephen
— An Expedient to Pay the Publick Depts with a Letter to the King. L, 1719. 4to. (88) £110

Barbieri, Carlo
— Direction pour les Voiageurs en Italie. Bologna, 1779. 8vo. (89) £100

Barbieri, Giovanni Francesco. See: Guercino, Il

Barbosa Machado, Diego
— Bibliotheca Lusitana Historica, Critica e Cronologica. Lisbon, 1741-47. Vols I & II (of 4). Folio. (91) $175

Barbour, Thomas
— The Birds of Cuba. Cambr., Mass., 1923. 4to. Nuttall Ornithological Club, Memoir No. VI. (90) $200
— Cuban Ornithology. Cambr., 1943. 4to. Watkinson Library deaccession. This copy with some discoloration. (90) $70
Watkinson Library deaccession. (90) $110

Barbusse, Henri, 1873-1935
— L'Enfer. Paris: Albin Michel, [1921]. One of 355. Illus by Edouard Chimot. Folio. (89) FF5,000

Barbut, Jacques
— The Genera Insectorum of Linnaeus. L, 1781. 4to. (88) £140, $300; (91) £350
Bound with: The Genera Vermium. Part 1 (of 2). L, 1783 (91) £650
— The Genera Vermium of Linnaeus. L, 1783-88. 2 parts in 1 vol. 4to. (89) £340
Part 1 only. 4to. (91) £250
— Les Genres des insectes de Linne. L, 1781. 4to. (88) £260

Barcia, Andres Gonzales de. See: Gonzalez de Barcia, Andres

Barckley, Sir Richard
— A Discourse of the Felicitie of Man. L: for W. Ponsonby, 1598. 4to. STC B1381. (91) £700

AMERICAN BOOK PRICES CURRENT

Barclay, Andrew
— Life of Captain Andrew Barclay of Cambock.... [Edin.: Pvtly ptd by Thomas Grant, 1854]. One of 30. Ed by Thomas Scott. (90) A$275

Barclay, James
— A Complete and Universal Dictionary of the English Language. Bungay, 1813 [but later]. ("The Bungay Edition of Barclay's Dictionary.") 4to. (89) £100
L, [c.1840]. ("A Complete and Universal English Dictionary....") 4to. (88) £105, £240, £500, £500, £560, £600
— ("A Universal English Dictionary....") (91) £820
L, [1848?]. 4to. (88) £420, £575, £580; (89) £650; (90) £50, £650; (91) £650
L, [1851]. 4to. (88) £650

Barclay, John, 1582-1621
— Argenis: or, the Loves of Poliarchus and Argenis. L, 1625. Trans by Kingsmill Long. Folio. (89) £100
L, 1636. 4to. (88) £160; (89) £85; (91) £110
— Euphormio's Satyricon. See: Golden Cockerel Press
— The Mirrour of Mindes. L, 1631. 1st Ed. 2 parts in 1 vol. 12mo. (88) $325

Barclay, Robert, 1648-90
— The Anarchy of the Ranters, and other Libertines.... See: Franklin Printing, Benjamin
— An Apology for the True Christian Divinity.... L, 1703. 8vo. (90) £50
8th Ed. Birm.: Baskerville, 1765. 4to. (89) $175; (90) $180; (91) £150
— Robert Barclays Apologie oder Vertheidigungs-Schrift.... Germantown: Saur, 1776. 8vo. (91) $75

Barclay, William
— De regno et regali potestate adversus Buchananum, Brutum, Boucherium.... See: Donne's copy, John

Barclay-Smith, Phyllis
— British & American Game-Birds. See: Derrydale Press

Barde, Frederick S.
— Life and Adventures of "Billy" Dixon.... Guthrie OK, [1914]. (89) $225

Bardi, Giuseppe. See: Pagni & Bardi

Bardi, Lorenzo
— Nuova Raccolta delle piu interessante vedute della citta di Firenze.... Florence, [n.d.]. Oblong 4to. (89) £1,000
— Vedute Principali della Citta di Firenze. Florence, 1818. Oblong 4to. (91) £420

Bardi, Luigi
— L'Imperiale e reale Galleria Pitti.... Florence, 1837-42. 4 vols. Folio. (91) LIt3,400,000

Bardsley, Samuel Argent
— Medical Reports of Cases and Experiments.... L, 1807. 8vo. (90) $70

Bardswell, Minoca. See: Tristram & Bardswell

Barduzzi, Bernardino
— A Letter in Praise of Verona (1489). Verona: Officina Bodoni, 1974. One of 150. (90) £220

Baret, John, d.1578?
— An Alvearie or Quadruple Dictionarie.... L: Henry Denham, 1580. Folio. (88) £650

Baretti, Giuseppe Marc' Antonio, 1719-89
— An Account of the Manners and Customs of Italy. L, 1769. 2d Ed. 2 vols. 8vo. (88) £110; (91) £150
— An Introduction to the most useful European Languages. L, 1772. 8vo. (88) £400
— A Journey from London to Genoa.... L, 1770. 3d Ed. 4 vols. 8vo. (88) £170; (89) £380, £2,000

Bargagli, Girolamo
— Dialogo de' giuochi che nelle vegghie sanesi.... Venice: Alessandro Gardane, 1581. 8vo. (91) LIt420,000

Bargagli, Scipione, d.1612
— Dell' impresse. Venice: F. de' Franceschi Senese, 1594. 4to. (89) £260; (91) LIt1,000,000

Barham, Henry
— Hortus Americanus; containing, an Account of the Trees.... Kingston, Jamaica: Alexander Aikman, 1794. 8vo. (89) £240

Barham, Richard Harris, 1788-1845
— The Ingoldsby Legends. L, 1840-42-47. 1st Ed. 3 vols. 8vo. (90) £90; (91) £450
Inscr to Sergeant Talfourd. Bradley Martin copy. (90) $900
L, 1876. 2 vols. 8vo. (89) £200
L & NY, 1907. Illus by Arthur Rackham. 4to. (88) £60, £85; (89) £250; (91) £70, $110, $130
One of 560, sgd by Rackham. (89) £200, £300, £850; (90) £110, £480; (91) £400, $425
L, 1909. 4to. (89) £150
L, 1912. 4to. (91) £50
L, 1913. 4to. (90) £50
L, 1922. Later ptg. 8vo. (89) $210
See also: Fore-Edge Paintings
— The Jackdaw of Rheims. L, 1913. One of 100. Illus by Charles Folkard. Folio. (88) £65

Barillet, J.
— Les Pensees, histoire, culture, multiplication, emploi. Paris: J. Rothschild, 1869. One of 200. 4to. (88) £420

Baring-Gould, Sabine, 1834-1924
— Iceland: its Scenes and Sagas. L, 1863. 8vo. (89) $90; (90) $180; (91) £110

Barker, Benjamin
— English Landscape Scenery. Bath, 1843. Oblong folio. (88) £460

Barker, Benjamin —&
Fielding, Theodore Henry, 1781-1851
— The Fine Arts. Forty-Eight Aquatint Colored Engravings...Views in and Near Bath. Bath, 1824. Oblong 4to. (88) £380; (89) £420; (91) £140
Sold w.a.f. (88) £300, £380

Barker, Bligh. See: Crocker & Barker

Barker, Clive
— Books of Blood. L: Sphere Books, [1984-85]. 1st Ed, 1st Issue. 6 vols. (88) $75
Each vol sgd. (89) $130
Vols 1 & 2 (of 6) in 1 vol. Sgd. (89) $85
L: Weidenfeld & Nicolson, [1985-86]. One of 200. 6 vols. (88) $425
Each vol sgd. (89) $425
Trade Issues. (90) $225; (91) $250
Santa Cruz: Scream Press, 1985. One of 250. (88) $85
— Cabal. NY: Poseidon, [1988]. One of 750. (90) $70
— The Damnation Game. L: Weidenfeld & Nicolson, [1985]. Inscr. (89) $70
Sgd. (90) $70
One of 250. (88) $130
— Weaveworld. L, 1987. One of 526. (91) $140
L: Collins, 1987. (91) $160
NY: Poseidon Press, [1987]. (91) $60
One of 500. (91) $60
Uncorrected proof. (89) $80
Inscr with a drawing of a monster, 9 Oct 1987. (89) $65

Barker, James N., 1784-1858
— Sketches of the Primitive Settlements on the River Delaware. Phila., 1827. 8vo. (88) $65

Barker, Jane
— Poetical Recreations: consisting of Original Poems, Songs.... L: for Benjamin Crayle, 1688. 8vo. (88) £220; (89) £380

BARKER

Barker, Lucy D. Sale
— Kate Greenaway's Birthday Book for Children. L, [1880]. 1st Ed. 16mo. (88) $53

Barker, Matthew Henry, 1790-1846
— Greenwich Hospital. L, 1826. Illus by George Cruikshank. 4to. (88) £80, £S380; (89) £350; (90) $300, $350, $500, £200, £240, £260; (91) $200, $400, $425, £120 Doheny copy. (89) $2,800

Barker, Nicolas
— Bibliotheca Lindesiana. See: Roxburghe Club
— The Publications of the Roxburghe Club, 1814-1962. See: Roxburghe Club
— A Sequel to an Enquiry. See: Carter & Pollard

Barks, Carl
— The Carl Barks Covers of Walt Disney's Uncle Scrooge. See: Disney Studios, Walt

Barlach, Ernst, 1870-1938
— Der Findling.... Berlin, 1922. Folio. (90) £100

Barlaeus, Caspar, 1584-1648
— Blyde inkomst der allerdoorluchtig Koninginne, Marie de Medicis, t'Amsterdam.... Amst., 1639-42. 2 parts in 1 vol. Folio. (90) $2,500
— Marie de Medicis.... Amst., 1638. Folio. (89) £260
— Rerum per octennium in Brasilia et alibi nuper gestarum.... Amst.: Blaeu, 1647. Folio. (88) £9,000; (89) £9,000; (90) $19,000 Barlow-American Antiquarian-Wormser-Strathallan copy. (90) $100,000
2d Ed. Cleves, 1660. 8vo. (89) £1,000

Barlandus, Hadrianus
— Hollandiae comitum historia et icones.... Leiden: Christopher Plantin, 1584. 2 parts in 1 vol. Folio. (88) HF750

Barlas, John Evelyn
— Yew Leaf and Lotus-Petal, Sonnets. New Jersey: Oriole Press, 1936. One of 10 on japon. Illus by John Buckland Wright. (90) £900

Barlet, Annibal
— Le Vray et methodique cours de la physique resolutive vulgariement dite chymie.... Paris, 1653. 1st Ed. 4to. (88) £2,400

Barlow, Edward, b.1642
— Barlow's Journal of his Life at Sea in King's Ships.... L, 1934. One of 100. 2 vols. Ls from pbrs loosely inserted; with pencilled Ms notes by Alan Moore. (88) £85
— An Exact Survey of the Tide. L, 1717. 2 parts in 1 vol. 8vo. Horblit copy. (91) £600
— Meteorological Essays concerning the Origin of Springs.... L, 1715. 8vo. (91) £105

Barlow, Francis
— Livre de plusieurs animaux.... Paris: De Poilly, [c.1675]. Oblong 4to. (89) £1,550
— Severall Wayes of Hunting, Hawking and Fishing.... L: John Overton, 1671. Illus by Wenceslas Hollar. 4to. Schiff copy. (91) $7,500
— Various Birds and Beasts Drawn from Life. L, [1710?]. Oblong 4to. Martin copy. (90) $1,800

Barlow, Jane, 1860-1917
— The End of Elfintown. L, 1894. One of 50 L.p. copies. Illus by Laurence Housman. 8vo. (91) £320

Barlow, Percival
— The General History of Europe and Entertaining Traveller. L, [c.1790]. Folio. (88) £150, £400; (89) £600

Barlow, William, d.1613
— An Answer to a Catholike Englishman.... L, 1609. 4to. (89) $450

Barlow, William, d.1625
— A Briefe Discovery of the Idle Animadversions of Marke Ridley.... L: Edward Griffin for Timothy Barlow, 1618. 4to. Horblit-Fleming copy. (89) $4,000
— Magneticall Advertisements.... L, 1616. 1st Ed. 4to. (89) £700

Barman, Christian
— The Bridge.... L & NY, 1926. One of 125. Illus by Frank Brangwyn. 4to. (90) $130

Barnaby, Andrew, 1734-1812
— Travels through the Middle Settlements in North-America.... L, 1775. 8vo. (90) £85

Barnard, George, 1807-90
— The Theory and Practice of Landscape Painting in Water-Colours. L, 1855. 8vo. (88) $110

Barnard, George N.
— Photographic Views of Sherman's Campaign. NY, [1866]. 2 vols. Text, 8vo; Atlas, oblong folio. (89) $29,000

Barnard, John Gross, 1815-82 —& Barry, W. F.
— Report of the Engineer and Artillery Operations of the Army of the Potomac. NY, 1863. 8vo. Inscr by Gen. Barnard. (91) $325

Barnard, Osbert H. See: Biorklund & Barnard; Biorklung & Barnard

Barnard, Thomas, M. A., of Leeds
— An Historical Character Relating to the Holy and Exemplary Life of...Elisabeth Hastings. Leeds, 1742. 1st Ed. 12mo. (89) £50

Barnes, Djuna
— Ladies Almanack showing their Signs and their Tides.... Paris: Pvtly ptd, 1928. One of 1,000 on Alfa paper. 4to. (89) $130
— Nightwood. L, [1936]. (89) $195 1st Ed. Inscr. (88) £66
— Ryder. NY, 1928. (88) $130

Barnes, James M.
— Picture Analysis of Golf Strokes.... Phila., [1919]. 4to. (91) $130

Barnes, John Sanford
— Submarine Warfare.... N.Y., 1869. 8vo. (91) $280
NY, 1902. 8vo. (91) $110

Barnes, Joseph K.
— The Medical and Surgical History of the War of the Rebellion. Wash., 1870-88. 2 vols in 6. 4to. (90) $1,300
With envelope sgd by Sherman. (91) $325
Part I, Vol II: Surgical History. 4to. (91) $160
Part I, Vol II: Surgical History. Wash., 1870-79. 4to. (89) $110
Vol II, Parts 1-3 (of 6 vols) only. Wash., 1870-83. 4to. (89) £240

Barnes, William, 1801-86
— Hwomely Rhymes: A Second Collection of Poems in the Dorset Dialect. L, 1859. 12mo. (90) £65; (91) £100

Barnes, William C.
— Western Grazing Grounds and Forest Ranges.... Chicago, 1913. (89) $75

Barnestapolius, Obertus. See: Turner, Robert

Barnett, Percy Neville
— Australian Book-Plates, and Book-Plates of Interest to Australia. Sydney: Pvtly ptd, 1950. One of 200. 4to. (88) A$350; (89) A$450, A$450; (90) A$280
— The Bookplate in Australia, its Inspiration and Development. Sydney, 1930. (89) A$260; (91) A$100
— Figure Prints of Japan. Sydney, 1948. One of 40. Folio. (91) A$800
— Hiroshige. Sydney, 1938. One of 200. Inscr to his daughter. (91) A$900
— Japanese Colour-Prints. Sydney, 1936. One of 65. 4to. Inscr by G. W. Lambert.

(89) A$600

Barney, George Murray
— Everett Hosmer Barney. His Family Connections. Springfield: Pvtly ptd, 1912. 4to. (89) $180; (91) $110

Barney, Joshua
— Report of the Survey, Estimates, etc.; of a Route from St. Louis to the Big Bend of the Red River. [Wash., 1853]. 8vo. 32nd Congress, 1st Session, Sen. Exec. Doc 19. (88) $90

Barney, Stephen
— Minutes of the Proceedings of the Court-Martial Held at Portsmouth, August 12, 1792, on The Persons Charged with Mutiny on Board His Majesty's Ship the Bounty.... See: Bligh, William

Barnivelt, Esdras. See: Pope, Alexander

Barnum, Phineas T., 1810-91
— Barnum the Yankee Showman.... L, [1855]. 8vo. (88) $50
— Life of P. T. Barnum. Written by Himself.... Buffalo, 1888. 8vo. (91) $190

Barocci, Luigi
— Collezione di quaranta Sacre Ceremonie usate principalmente in Roma.... Rome, [1841-50]. Oblong folio. Doheny copy. (88) $1,100

Barocius, Franciscus. See: Barozzi, Francesco

Baronius, Caesar, Cardinal, 1538-1607
— Annales ecclesiastici. Antwerp: Plantin, 1612-29. With: Bzovius, Abrahamus. Annalium ecclesiasticum post...Caesarem Baronium. Cologne: A Boetz, 1621-30. 7 vols. Together, 19 vols. (91) £3,500

Barozzi, Francesco, 1528-1612
— Cosmographia in quator libros distributa.... Venice: G. Perchacini, 1598. 8vo. (91) £260
— Il Nobilissimo et Antiquissimo Giuoco Pythagoreo nominato rythmomachia.... Venice, 1572. 4to. (88) £400; (89) £230

Barozzi, Giacomo, called Vignola, 1507-73
— Le Due Regole della prospettiva practica.... Rome: Zanetti, 1583. 1st Ed. Folio. (88) £1,000; (89) £240
Rome, 1611. Folio. (88) £170, £350
Rome, 1644. Folio. (91) $600
Bologna, 1682. Folio. (90) $550
— Livre nouveau ou regles des cinq ordres d'architecture.... Paris, 1767. Folio. (89) £1,250
— Der neue Vignola; oder, Elementar-Buch der Baukunst. Leipzig, 1818. Folio. (88)

BAROZZI

$130
— Oeuvres. Paris, 1815. Folio. (89) $550
— Panseron. Grand et nouveau Vignole.... Paris, [c.1780]. Folio. (89) $650
— Regles des cinq ordres d'architecture. Paris, [c.1800]. 4to. (89) $175
— Regola delli cinque ordini d'architettura. Amst.: William Ianssz, 1617. Folio. (88) £150; (90) £110
 Rome, [c.1620]. Folio. (91) £260
 Siena, [c.1635]. Folio. (91) £150, £400
 Amst.: Ian Janz & Jan van Hilten, 1642. Folio. (91) £550
 Rome, [c.1710]. Folio. (91) £120
 Rome, [1779]. Folio. (88) £110
 Naples: presso Vincenzo Orsini, 1795. Folio. (90) £280
 Rome, [c.1800]. Folio. (89) $200
 Verona: Mainardi, 1811. ("Gli Ordini di architettura....") Folio. (91) LIt320,000
— The Regular Architect, or the General Rule of the Five Orders of Architecture. L, 1669. Folio. (89) £800
— Il Vignola illustrato proposto da Giambattista Spampani.... Rome, 1770. Folio. (91) £300
— Il Vignola illustrato proposto da Carlo Antonini. Rome, 1828. Folio. (91) £450
— Vignola Revived. L, 1761. Folio. (89) £180; (91) £150

Barr, Alfred H.
— Matisse; his Art and his Public. NY, [1951]. 4to. (88) $50; (90) $700
 One of 495. (90) $650

Barr, Louise Farrow
— Presses of Northern California and their Books. Berkeley, 1934. One of 400. (88) $55; (91) $140

Barr, Robert
— Triumphs of Eugene Valmont. L, 1906. (88) $130

Barratt, Francis
— The Magus.... L, 1801. 4to. (88) £320; (89) £150, £190

Barratt, Thomas James
— The Annals of Hampstead. L, 1912. One of 550. 3 vols. 4to. (88) £150, £260; (89) £110; (90) £180

Barraud, Charles Decimus —& Travers, William T. L., 1819-1903
— New Zealand Graphic and Descriptive. L, 1877. Folio. (89) £550, £650

AMERICAN BOOK PRICES CURRENT

Barrault, Jean, 1705?-66
— Recueil des vues des plus beaux monumens antiques de Rome.... Rome: Pierre Piale, [c.1770]. Oblong folio. (88) £350

Barre, Joseph, d.1794
— Histoire generale d'Allemagne, depuis l'an de Rome 648.... Paris, 1748. 10 parts in 11 vols. 4to. (88) FF6,000

Barre, Louis, 1799-1857
— Herculaneum et Pompei. Paris, 1872. Musee secret vol only. 8vo. (91) $50

Barre, Richard, Lord Ashburton
— Genealogical Memoirs of the Royal House of France.... L, 1825. Folio. L.p. copy. (89) £750

Barre, William Vincent, 1760?-1829
— History of the French Consulate, under Napoleon Buonaparte. L, 1804. 8vo. (91) £170

Barreda, Augustin de
— Oracion evangelica y funebre predicada en la Nueva Capilla de Maria Santissima de la Soledad.... Lima, 1674. 4to. (88) £500

Barrelier, Jacques, 1606-73
— Plantae per Galliam, Hispaniam et Italiam observatae. Paris, 1714. Folio. (88) $850; (91) £900

Barrere, Albert Marie Victor —& Leland, Charles Godfrey, 1824-1903
— A Dictionary of Slang, Jargon and Cant. L, 1889-90. One of 675. 2 vols. 8vo. (90) £95

Barrere, Pierre, 1690-1755
— Nouvelle Relation de la France equinoxiale.... Paris, 1743. 12mo. (88) £150

Barres, Maurice, 1862-1923
— Un Jardin sur L'Oronte. Paris, 1927. Hors commerce copy. Illus by Sureda. 4to. (88) £75
 One of 475. (90) $130
— La Mort de Venise. Lyon: Cercle Lyonnais du Livre, 1936. One of 120 on Vidalon, with a corrected copy of the signature comprising pages 33-34 & 39-40. Illus by Henry de Waroquier. 4to. Chevalier copy. (91) $10,000

Barret, Robert
— The Theorike and Practike of Moderne Warres.... L: William Ponsonby, 1598. Folio. STC 1500. (91) £950

Barrett, Charles Golding
— The Lepidoptera of the British Islands. L, 1892-1907. 11 vols plus index. 8vo. (88) £520

Barrett, Charles Leslie
— Across the Years. The Lure of Early Australian Books. Melbourne, 1948. (88) A$120

Barrett, Charles Raymond Booth
— The 7th Queens Own Hussars. L, 1914. 2 vols. 4to. (89) £130

Barrett, Ellen C.
— Baja California: A Bibliography.... Los Angeles, 1957-67. One of 550. 2 vols. (89) $110, $150; (90) $190

Barrett, Timothy
— Nagashizuki: the Japanese Craft of Hand Papermaking. North Hills, Pa.: Bird & Bull Press, 1979. One of 300. (89) $300

Barrett, W. P.
— LV. Book Plates Engraved on Copper. L, 1900. One of 260. 4to. (90) £70

Barrett, William, 1733-89
— The History and Antiquities of the City of Bristol. Bristol, [1789]. 4to. (89) £90

Barri, Giacomo
— The Painters Voyage of Italy. L, 1679. 8vo. (91) £170
Kissner copy. (91) £350

Barrie, Sir James Matthew, 1860-1937
— The Admirable Crichton. L, [1914]. Illus by Hugh Thomson. 4to. (89) $50
One of 500. (88) £95, £150; (91) $175
— Auld Licht Idylls. L, 1888. 8vo. (91) $130
— The Greenwood Hat. Being a Memoir of James Anon, 1885-1887. [Pvtly ptd, 1930. One of 50. Inscr to Florence Hardy, Christmas 1930. Fleming copy. (89) $1,400
— The Little Minister. L, 1891. 1st Ed in Book form. 3 vols. 8vo. (89) $80
With ALs y Barrie, 22 Dec 1907. (88) $200
With ANs, 10 May 1896. (88) $250
— Margaret Ogilvy. L, 1896. 8vo. Inscr to George Meredith, 3 Dec 1896. Fleming copy. (89) $1,300
— Peter Pan in Kensington Gardens. L, 1906. Illus by Arthur Rackham. 4to. (88) $120, £50, £80, £85; (89) £170, £800; (90) £180; (91) $175, $300, £180
Inscr. (90) $850
One of 500. (88) $750, £700; (89) £850, £950; (90) $1,400, £800; (91) $1,600, $1,800
Out-of-series copy. (89) $950

L, 1907. 4to. (90) £90
L, [1912]. 4to. (88) £110; (89) $250, £150, £160; (90) £360, A$320; (91) $120, £170, £220, £750
ANs by Rackham laid in. (91) $400
— Piter Pan dans les Jardins de Kensington. Paris, 1907. One of 250. Illus by Arthur Rackham. 4to. (88) $350; (89) $450
— Quality Street. [L, 1913]. Illus by Hugh Thomson. 4to. (88) $425
One of 1,000. (88) $130, $250, £150; (89) £65, £75; (91) $50, $175
Doheny copy. (88) $150
— Scotland's Lament: Robert Louis Stevenson. L, 1918. One of 25. 4to. (91) $225
— When a Man's Single. L, 1888. 8vo. (91) $55
— Works. NY, 1896-1911. ("The Novels, Tales and Sketches.") Author's Ed. Vols I-XI. (88) $300
Kirriemuir Ed. L, 1913. One of 1,000. 10 vols. (90) £110
L, 1929-31. One of 1,030. 14 vols. (88) £260; (90) $150
With ALs laid into Vol I. (89) $180
— Zuleika Dobson. L, 1911. Fleming copy. (89) $2,000

Barriere
— Les Oiseaux de volieres et de parcs. Bordeaux: A. Bellier, 1886. 4to. Martin copy. (90) $300, $400

Barriere, Dominique, d.1678
See also: Falda & Barriere
— Villa Aldobrandina Tusculana.... Rome, 1647. Folio. (89) £1,900; (91) £3,000
— Villa Pamphilia, eiusque palatium sum suis prospectibus.... Rome: Giovanni Giacomo de Rossi, [c.1660]. Folio. (91) £1,500

Barriffe, William
— Military Discipline. L, 1643. 4to. (89) £220

Barrington, Daines, 1727-1800
— Miscellanies. L, 1781. 1st Ed. 4to. (89) £420
ALs laid in. (89) £700
— The Possibility of Approaching the North Pole Asserted. L, 1818. 8vo. (88) $60; (90) £150

Barrington, George, 1755-c.1840
— An Account of a Voyage to New South Wales. L, 1795. ("A Voyage to New South Wales.") 8vo. (89) A$29,000
L, 1803. 8vo. (88) £130; (89) A$900; (90) £200
Martin copy. (90) $800
With: The History of New South Wales including Botany Bay. Together, 2 vols. 8vo. (88) A$1,850

BARRINGTON

L, 1810. 8vo. (89) A$1,000
— The History of New South Wales.... L, 1802. 1st Ed. 8vo. (88) £260; (89) $210, A$900; (90) £160, A$450
Martin copy. (90) $800
— The Memoirs of George Barrington.... L, [c.1790]. 8vo. (90) A$650
— A Sequel to Barrington's Voyage to New South Wales.... L, 1800. 8vo. (88) $450
— A Voyage to Botany Bay. L: C. Lowndes, [c.1800]. Bound with: A Sequel to Barrington's Voyage.... L: C. Lowndes, 1801. 8vo. (90) £260

Barrington, Jonah, 1760-1834
— Personal Sketches of his own Times. L, 1827-32. 3 vols. 8vo. (90) $150

Barron, Capt. Richard
— Views in India.... L, 1837. Folio. (90) £6,500

Barros, Joao de, 1496-1570
— Asia.... Lisbon, 1552-53. 2 parts in 1 vol. Folio. (88) £6,000
2 parts in 2 vols. Folio. (90) $1,800
— L'Asia.... Venice: Vincenzo Valgrisi, 1561. 4to. (91) £800
Venice, 1562. 2 parts in 1 vol. 8vo. (88) £220; (91) LIt700,000

Barrough, Philip
— The Method of Physick. L: T. Vautroullier, 1583. ("The Methode of Phisicke....") Folio. (88) $1,500
L: G. Miller, 1634. 7th Ed. 8vo. Bound with: Stephens, Phillip & William Brown. Catalogues Horti Botanici Oxoniensis. (89) £650

Barrow, Albert Stewart, 1746-1848
— More Shires and Provinces. L, 1928. Illus by Lionel Edwards. 4to. (88) £170; (91) £120
One of 100, sgd by author & artist. (88) £240, £260; (90) £300; (91) £300
— Shires and Provinces. L, 1926. Illus by Lionel Edwards. Folio. (89) £250; (91) £110, £120
One of 100. 4to. (88) £280

Barrow, Isaac, 1630-77
— Lectiones XVIII.... L, 1669. Bound with: Barrow. Lectiones geometricae. L, 1670. 2 vols in 1. 4to. Rigaud-Horblit copy. (91) $100

Barrow, J. H. See: Landseer & Barrow

AMERICAN BOOK PRICES CURRENT

Barrow, John, fl.1735
— A New and Impartial History of England. L, 1763. 10 vols. 12mo. (91) £150

Barrow, John, fl.1756
— Abrege chronologique ou histoire des decouvertes faites par les Europeens.... Paris, 1766. 12 vols. 12mo. (89) £70

Barrow, Sir John, 1764-1848
See also: Alman
— An Account of Travels into the Interior of Southern Africa. L, 1801-4. 1st Ed. 2 vols. 4to. (88) £170; (89) £420, R900; (90) $225
2d Ed. L, 1806. ("Travels into the Interior of Southern Africa.") 2 vols. 4to. (88) £140, R1,000; (89) £190; (91) £350
— A Chronological History of Voyages into the Arctic Regions. L, 1818. 1st Ed. 8vo. (88) £110; (89) £175, £160; (91) £200
— Nouveau Voyage dans le partie meridionale de l'Afrique. Paris, 1806. 2 vols. 8vo. (89) £60
— Travels in China. L, 1804. 1st Ed. 4to. (88) £320, £380; (90) £700, £220
2d Ed. L, 1806. 4to. (88) £200, £150; (91) £60, £105
— A Voyage to Cochinchina.... L, 1806. 4to. (88) £300, £400, £650; (89) £200, £320; (90) £450; (91) £120, £450, £700
— Voyages of Discovery and Research within the Arctic Regions.... NY, 1846. 8vo. (90) £150

Barrows, John R.
— Ubet. Caldwell, 1934. Sgd. (89) $100

Barrucand, Victor
— Le Chariot de terre cuite. Paris, [1921]. One of 135 on japon imperial with a suite in black & an orig aquarelle sgd by Carre. Illus by Leon Carre. 4to. (89) SF4,500

Barry, Sir Edward, 1696-1776
— A Treatise on the Three Different Digestions, and Discharges of the Human Body.... L, 1759. 1st Ed. 8vo. (88) $90

Barry, George
— History of the Orkney Islands. Edin., 1805. 4to. (90) £75

Barry, Henry
— The General Attacked by a Subaltern. NY, [1775]. 8vo. (91) $375
NY: James Rivington, [1775]. 8vo. (91) $700

Barry, Martin, 1802-55
— Ascent to the Summit of Mont Blanc....
 Edin. & L, 1836. 8vo. (89) £220; (91) £460

Barry, Theodore Augustus, 1825-81 —& Patten, B. A.
— Men and Memories of San Francisco.... San Francisco, 1873. 12mo. (88) $80; (89) $120, $160; (90) $110; (91) $50, $110

Barry, W. F. See: Barnard & Barry

Barrymore, John
— Confessions of an Actor. Indianapolis: Bobbs-Merrill, [1926]. Inscr to Carmel Meers. (90) $340

Bartalini, Biagio, 1746-1822
— Catalogo delle piante che nascono spontaneamente intorno all citta' di Siena. Siena, 1776. Folio. (89) £85

Bartell, Edmund
— Hints for Picturesque Improvements in Ornamental Cottages. L, 1804. 8vo. (89) £170; (91) £220

Bartels, Max & Paul. See: Ploss & Bartels

Barth, Heinrich, 1821-65
— Travels and Discoveries in North and Central Africa. L, 1857-58. 5 vols. 8vo. (88) £350; (89) £320, £580; (91) £580
 Vols I-IV (of 5). (89) £50

Barthelemy, Jean Jacques, 1716-95
— Abrege de l'histoire grecque. Paris, 1793. 8vo. Arvanitidi copy. (91) £200
— Dissertation sur une ancienne inscription grecque.... Paris, 1792. 4to. Blackmer copy. (90) £130
— Travels of Anacharsis the Younger in Greece.... L, 1791. 7 vols (without Atlas). 8vo. (91) £120
 8 vols, including Atlas. 8vo & 4to. (88) £40
 8 vols, plus atlas ("Maps, Views....by M. Barbie du Bocage"). Together, 8 vols. 8vo & 4to. (88) £40; (89) £425
 Phila., 1804. 4 vols. 8vo. (91) $150
 L, 1806. 8 vols. 8vo & 4to. (89) £70; (90) £260
 L: J.J. & G. Robinson, 1896. 5 vols in 4, including Atlas. 8vo. (89) £85
— Voyage du jeune Anacharsis en Grece. Paris, 1788. Bound in 5 vols, including Atlas. 4to. (91) £1,900
 With 2 other works bound in. Blackmer copy. (90) £1,800
 Paris, 1789. ("Recueil de cartes geographiques...de l'ancienne Grece....") 4to. (91) £275
 3d Ed. Paris, 1790-92. 10 vols, including Atlas. 8vo & 4to. (91) LIt320,000

Paris, 1790. 8 vols, including Atlas. 8vo & 4to. (89) £120
 Amst., 1799. 8 vols, including Atlas. 4to. (88) £130
 Paris, 1822. Atlas vol only. (91) £300
 Paris, 1836. Atlas vol only. 4to. (88) £95

Barthelemy-Lapommeraye, Christophe Jerome. See: Jaubert & Barthelemy-Lapommeraye

Barthema, Lodovico. See: Varthema, Ludovico di

Bartholdy, Jakob Ludwig Salomon, 1779-1825
— Voyage en Grece. Paris: Dentu, 1807. 8vo. (91) £360
 Blackmer copy. (90) £520

Bartholin, Caspar, of Malmo, 1585-1629
— Institutiones anatomicae. Leiden, 1641. 8vo. (91) £250

Bartholinus, Caspar, 1650-1705
— De inauribus veterum syntagma.... Amst., 1676. 12mo. (88) $110
— De tibiis veterum, et earum antiquo usu libri tres. Amst., 1679. 12mo. (88) $250

Bartholinus, Thomas, 1616-80
— Anatomia, ex Caspari Bartholini parentis institutionibus.... Leiden, 1673 [1674]. ("Anatome, ex omnium veterum recentiorumque observationibus....") 8vo. (89) £170
 Leiden, 1677. ("Anatome quartum renovata....") 8vo. (88) $225
 Leiden: F. Hackius, 1691. 8vo. (88) £80
— De usu flagrorum in re medica et veneria, lumborumque et renum officio. Frankfurt, 1670. Bound with: Colin, Sebastian. Declaratio Fraudum et Errorum apud Pharmacopoeos commissorum. Authore Lisseto Benacio [pseud.].... 8vo. (88) $190; (90) £75
— Differatio de cygni anatome.... Copenhagen: Daniel Paulli, 1668. 8vo. Martin copy. (90) $700

Bartholomaeus, Anglicus, fl.1230-50
— Batman uppon Bartholome, his Booke De Proprietatibus rerum. L: Thomas East, 1582. Folio. (88) £250
— De proprietatibus rerum. Nuremberg: Anton Koberger, 20 June 1492. Folio. 197 (of 200) leaves; lacking tp, f.94 & final blank. Goff B-141. (91) $650
 199 (of 200) leaves; lacking last blank. Goff B-141.. (90) DM5,200

BARTHOLOMAEUS DE CHAIMIS

Bartholomaeus de Chaimis
— Interrogatorium seu confessionale. [Strassburg: Printer of Henricus Ariminensis type 1, c.1475]. Folio. 137 (of 138) leaves; lacking initial blank. Goff B-153. Doheny copy. (88) $4,000

Bartholomaeus de Pisa. See: Bartholomaeus degli Albizzi de Rinonichi

Bartholomaeus degli Albizzi de Rinonichi
— Opus aurea & inexplicabilis bonitatis & continentie. Milan: Joannes de Castelliono, 1513. Folio. (89) £500
— Opus aurea & inexplicabilis bonitatis & continentie. Conformitatum. Milan: Joannes de Castelliono, 1513. Folio. (89) £900

Bartholomew, Valentine
— A Selection of Flowers Adapted Principally for Students. L, [1821]-22. Folio. (90) £2,800

Barthou Library, Louis
— [Sale Catalogue] Bibliotheque de M. Louis Barthou. Paris, 1935-36. 4 vols. 4to. (90) $100

Bartisch, Georg, 1535-1607?
— Ophthalmodouleia, das ist Augendienst. [Dresden: Matthes Stoeckel], 1583. Folio. (91) £6,500

Bartlett, A. W.
— History of the Twelfth Regiment New Hampshire Volunteers. Concord, 1897. 8vo. (91) $130

Bartlett, Edward
— A Monograph of the Weaver-Birds.... [Maidstone, 1888-89]. Parts 1-5 (all pbd) in 1 vol. 4to. (89) £550
Martin copy. (90) $600, $4,250

Bartlett, Edward Everett
— The Typographic Treasures in Europe. NY & L, 1925. One of 585. Folio. (90) $50; (91) $50

Bartlett, Elisha, 1804-55
— An Essay on the Philosophy of Medical Science. Phila., 1844. 1st Ed. 8vo. (88) $120; (89) $150
— The History, Diagnosis, and Treatment of Typhoid and of Typhus Fever. Phila., 1842. 1st Ed. 8vo. (88) $120; (89) $80

Bartlett, Henrietta Collins —& Pollard, Alfred William
— A Census of Shakespeare's Plays in Quarto...(1594-1709). New Haven, 1916. 4to. Inscr by A. S. W. Rosenbach to Charles W. Clark. Fleming copy. (89) $175

AMERICAN BOOK PRICES CURRENT

Bartlett, John, 1820-1905
— A Collection of Familiar Quotations. Cambr., 1855. 1st Ed. 12mo. (89) $140
Inscr "from the author". (89) $225

Bartlett, John Russell, 1805-86
— Personal Narrative of Explorations and Incidents in Texas.... NY, 1854. 1st Ed. 2 vols. 8vo. (88) $110, $180, $375, $475; (90) $425; (91) $150

Bartlett, Thomas
— New Holland: its Colonization, Productions & Resources.... L, 1843. 8vo. (89) A$160

Bartlett, Vernon. See: Sherriff & Bartlett

Bartlett, William Henry, 1809-54. See: Beattie, William

Bartlett, William Henry, 1809-54
— Canadian Scenery. See: Willis, Nathaniel Parker
— Forty Days in the Desert. NY: Arthur Hall, [1856]. "5th" Ed. 8vo. (89) £30
— Gleanings Pictorial and Antiquarian on the Overland Route. L, 1851. 8vo. (88) $100; (91) £90
— The History of the United States of North America. NY, [1856]. 3 vols. 8vo. (89) $350
— The Nile Boat.... L, 1850. 8vo. (88) £70, £85; (91) £50, £300
NY, 1851. 8vo. (90) $140; (91) $55
L, 1852. 8vo. (90) $80
L, 1861. 8vo. (88) £45
— Pictures from Sicily. L, 1862. 8vo. (89) £70
— The Ports, Harbours, Watering-Places and Coast Scenery of Great Britain. See: Finden, William
— La Suisse pittoresque. See: Beattie, William
— Switzerland Illustrated. See: Beattie, William
— Walks about the City and Environs of Jerusalem. L, [c.1845]. 2d Ed. 4to. (88) £45; (89) £90; (91) £80
3d Ed. L, [c.1847]. 4to. (91) £60

Bartley, Nehemiah
— Australian Pioneers and Reminiscences. Brisbane, 1896. Ed by J. J. Knight. 8vo. (88) A$95
— Opals and Agates; or, Scenes Under the Southern Cross.... Brisbane, 1892. 8vo. (88) A$55

Bartoli, Cosimo, c.1503-72
— Del modo di misurare le distantie, le superficie, i corpi, le piante.... Venice, 1564. 1st Ed. 4to. (91) LIt1,500,000

Venice, 1614. 4to. (89) £120

Bartoli, Daniello, 1608-85
— Del ghiaccio e della coagulatione. Rome, 1681. 4to. (89) $110
— Del suono de' tremori armonici e dell' udito. Rome, 1679. 4to. (91) £200

Bartoli, Pietro Santi & Francesco
— Picturae antiquae cryptarum Romanorum. Rome: S. Michaelis & Hieronymi Mainardi, 1737. Folio. Kissner copy. (91) £250
Rome: Geronimo Mainardi, 1738. Folio. (91) £450
Rome, 1750. Folio. Kissner copy. (91) £380
Rome, 1791. Folio. Kissner copy. (91) £600

Bartoli, Pietro Santi, c.1635-1700
— Admiranda Romanarum antiquitatum ac veteris sculpturae vestigia. Rome, [c.1690]. 1st Ed. Oblong folio. Kissner copy. (91) £600
Rome, 1693. Oblong folio. (88) £150, £240; (89) $275, £110
Bound with: Bartoli. Colonna Traiana. Rome, 1673. (91) £420, £450
Kissner copy. (91) £1,400
— Le Antiche Lucerne sepolcrali figurate. Rome, 1691. 3 parts in 1 vol. Folio. (88) £170
Kissner copy. (91) £150
Rome, 1729. Folio. (89) £85
— Gli antichi sepolcri, ovvero mausolei Romani.... Rome, 1697. Folio. (90) $650
Rome, 1727. Folio. (88) £220
Bound with: Le Antiche lucerne sepocrali figurate.... Rome, 1729. Kissner copy. (91) £850
Rome, 1768. 4to. (88) £110; (90) £110
— Colonna Traiana..... [Rome, 1673]. Oblong folio. (88) $275, £150, £220; (89) £140, £240; (90) £260; (91) $400, £300
Issue on papier fort. Kissner copy. (91) £1,400
— Columna Antoniniana. Rome, [1672]. Oblong folio. (88) £260
— Columna cochlis M. Aurelio Antonino Augusto dicata.... Rome, 1704. Folio. (88) £160
Kissner copy. (91) £900
— Medailles de Grand et Moyen Bronze du Cabinet de la Reine Christine. The Hague, 1742. Folio. Kissner copy. (91) £350
— Museum Odescalchum, sive Thesaurus antiquarum gemmarum. Rome, 1751-52. 2 vols. Folio. (89) $325; (90) £750
Kissner copy. (91) £220

2 vols in 1. Folio. (89) $325
2 vols in one. Folio. (90) $225
2 vols in 1. Folio. (90) $425, £400
— Picturae Antiquissimi Virgiliani Codicis Bibliothecae Vaticanae. Rome: Monaldini, 1782. 4to. (90) $150
— Recueil de peintures antiques. Paris, 1783-87. Bound in 2 vols. Folio. (88) £13,000
Vols I-II. Folio. (88) FF115,000

Bartolommeo dalli Sonetti, Zamberto
— Isolario. [Venice: Gulielmus Anima Mia Tridensis?, c.1485]. Single leaf only, with hand-colored woodcut views of Tine & Micone. Goff B-183. (91) $1,500

Bartolozzi, Francesco —& Others
— Eighty-Two Prints.... L, [c.1800]. 2 vols in 1. Folio. (91) £1,800

Barton, Benjamin Smith, 1766-1815
— Elements of Botany. L, 1804. 8vo. (89) £40
— Fragments of the Natural History of Pennsylvania. Phila., 1799. Folio. Martin copy. (90) $1,000, $1,600

Barton, Benjamin Smith, 1766-1815 —& Castle, Thomas, c.1804-38
— The British Flora Medica. L, 1877. 8vo. (88) £100

Barton, Charlotte
— A Mother's Offering to her Children. See: Bremer, Lady J. J. Gordon

Barton, Clara, 1821-1912
— History of the Red Cross. Wash., 1883. Bound following: The Work of Humanity in War. NY, 1870. 4to. Inscr to the Loyal Legion, Commandery of Massachusetts. With ALs. (90) $1,200

Barton, Rose
— Familiar London. L, 1904. One of 300. 4to. Inscr to Mrs. Bill, Dec 1904. (89) £350
Out-of-series copy with Ms note Plate Printers Copy. (88) £800

Barton, William Paul Crillon, 1786-1856
— Compendium Florae Philadelphicae; containing, a Description of...Plants.... Phila., 1818. 2 vols in 1. 12mo. (89) $110
— A Flora of North America. Phila., 1821-23. 1st Ed. 3 vols. 4to. (90) $3,000
Vol I only. (88) $350, £350
Vols I-II. (91) $475
— Vegetable Materia Medica of the United States; or, Medical Botany.... Phila., 1825-19. 2d Ed of Vol I, 1st Ed of Vol II. 2 vols. 4to. (91) $225

BARTRAM

Bartram, William, 1739-1823
— Travels through North and South Carolina, Georgia.... Phila.: James & Johnson, 1791. 1st Ed. 8vo. Martin copy. (90) $6,250
Dublin, 1793. 8vo. (89) $500
L, 1794. 8vo. (88) £140

Bartsch, J. Adam von, 1757-1821
— Catalogue raisonne de toutes les estampes qui forment l'oeuvre de Rembrandt.... Vienna, 1797. 2 vols in 1. 4to. (88) £160
— Le Peintre graveur. Vienna, 1803-21. 21 vols in 17. 8vo. (89) £300
Vols 1-20 (of 21). 8vo. (89) $850
Leipzig, 1843-76. 21 vols in 16 plus 1 supplementary vol. 8vo. (88) £120
Leipzig, 1854-76. 21 vols. 8vo. (91) $300
Hildesheim & Nieuwkoop, 1970. 23 vols in 4. 8vo. Small-format reprint of the 1920-22 Ed. (90) $150; (91) LIt380,000

Baruch, Hugo Cyril K.
— Jack Bilbo. An Autobiography. L, 1948. Folio. (88) $75; (90) $150, $150
Inscr. (90) £55

Barudartius, Wilhelmus, 1565-1640
— Les Guerres de Nassau. Amst.: Michel Colin, 1616. 2 vols in 1. Oblong 4to. (91) £2,000

Basan, Pierre Francois, 1723-97
— Dictionnaire des graveurs anciens et modernes. Paris, 1767. 2 vols. 8vo. (88) DM460
2d Ed. Paris, 1789. 2 vols. 8vo. (88) £120; (89) £85
— Recueil d'estampes gravees d'apres les tableaux du Cabinet de Monseigneur le Duc de Choiseul. Paris, 1771. 4to. (89) £380; (90) £720

Baschet, Armand. See: Feuillet de Conches & Baschet

Bashutskii, Alexandr Pavlovich, 1801-76
— Nashi Spisannie s Natury Russkimi. St. Petersburg, 1841. 8vo. (88) £150

Basil the Great, Saint, c.330-379
— Opera. Cologne: E. Cervicorni, 1531. Folio. (88) £85
Basel: Froben, 1551. Folio. (91) £150
In Greek. (91) £380

Basil the Great, Saint, c.330-379 —& Gregory of Nazianzum, Saint, 329-389
— Epistolae graecae. Hagenau, 1528. 8vo. (91) £240

AMERICAN BOOK PRICES CURRENT

Basile, Giovanni Battista, c.1575-1632
— Stories from the Pentamerone. L, 1911. Illus by Warwick Goble. 4to. (88) $55; (89) $80; (90) A$110

Basilius Valentinus
— The Last Will and Testament. L, 1671. 8vo. (88) £380

Baskin, Leonard
— Ars Anatomica: A Medical Fantasia. NY, [1972]. Folio. (88) $70; (89) $100, £50; (90) $100, $110, $175; (91) $100, $110
One of 300 with an extra suite of plates. (91) $140, $250
— Birds & Animals. Northampton: Gehenna Press, 1977. One of 50. Oblong 4to. (88) $1,900
— Birds and Animals. Northampton MA: Gehenna Press, [1974]. Oblong 4to. Inscr to Becky, 1986. (91) $2,300
— Demons, Imps & Fiends. Northampton: Gehenna Press, 1976. One of 450. 4to. (91) $140
— Terminalia from Ovid's Fasti. Northampton MA: Gehenna Press, 1972. One of 35. 4to. (89) $1,500
— "To Colour Thought." New Haven, 1967. One of 300. (89) $50, $200; (90) $110, $175, $210

Baskin, Robert Newton
— Reminiscences of Early Utah. Salt Lake City, 1914. (89) $50
Salt Lake City: Tribune-Reporter Printer Co, 1914. 8vo. (89) $50

Basnage, Jacques, 1653-1725
— Annales des Provinces-Unies. The Hague, 1719-26. 2 vols. Folio. (88) FF3,500
— Histoire du Vieux et du Nouveau Testament. Amst., 1704. Illus by Romeyn de Hooghe. 2 parts in 1 vol. Folio. (91) £340
— The History of the Jews.... L, 1708. Trans by Thomas Taylor. Folio. (90) $550
— 't Groot waerelds tafereel en met vaersen verrykt d. A. Alewyn. Amst., 1721. Folio. (89) $175

Basoli, Antonio
— Collezione di varie scene teatrali.... Bologna, 1821. Oblong folio. (91) £3,800
— Raccolta de prospettive serie, rustiche, e di paesaggio.... Bologna, 1810. Oblong 4to. (91) £900

Bassi, Agostino
— Del mal del segno calcinaccio o moscardino malattia.... Lodi, 1835-36. 2 vols. in 1. 8vo. ANs inserted. (90) £1,150

Bassi, Martino
— Dispareri in materia d'architettura et perspettiva. Milan: Giuseppe Galeazzi, 1771. 4to. (89) £200

Basta, George, d.1607
— Il Governo della cavalleria leggiera. Oppenheim, 1616. Folio. Kimbolton Castle copy. (90) £750

Bastard d'Estang, Henri Bruno, Vicomte de, 1798-1875
— Recherches sur Randan, ancien Duche-Pairie. Riom: Thibaud, 1830. 8vo. (88) FF7,500

Bastelaer, Rene van
— Les Estampes de Peter Bruegel l'ancien. Brussels, 1908. 4to. (89) $100

Bastiat, Frederic
— Sophismes economiques. Paris, 1846-48. First & Second Series. 2 vols in 1. 16mo. (88) £180

Baston, Thomas
— Twenty-Two Prints of Several Capital Ships.... L: T. Bowles, [c.1721]. Folio. (90) £4,000

Batchelor, S.
— The Cabinet of Gems or a Vocabulary of Precious Stones.... L, 1829. (88) $550

Bate, George, 1608-69
— Elenchi motuum nuperorum in Anglia.... L, 1685. 3 parts in 1 vol. 8vo. Extra-illus with 5 ports. (89) $250
— Pharmacopeia Bateana, or Bate's Dispensatory. L, 1694. 1st Ed in English. 8vo. (90) £110

Bate, John
— The Mysteries of Nature and Art. L, 1635. 2d Ed. 4to. (91) $900

Bateman, James, 1811-97
— The Orchidaceae of Mexico and Guatemala. L, [1837]-43. One of 125. Folio. (90) $42,000
   Doheny copy. (88) $52,000
— A Second Century of Orchidaceous Plants. L, 1867. 4to. (88) $160

Bateman, John Frederic la Trobe
— History and Description of the Manchester Waterworks. Manchester, 1884. 4to. (90) £110

Bateman, Thomas, 1778-1821
— A Practical Synopsis of Cutaneous Diseases.... Phila., 1824. 2d American Ed. 8vo. (89) $70

Bates, George Washington
— Sandwich Island Notes. By a Haole. NY, 1854. 12mo. (89) $80

Bates, Herbert Ernest
— Flowers and Faces. See: Golden Cockerel Press
— A German Idyll. See: Golden Cockerel Press
— The House with the Apricot.... See: Golden Cockerel Press
— Mrs. Esmond's Life. [N.p.: Pvtly Ptd, 1931]. One of 50. 4to. Leaf of orig Ms bound in. (88) $175

Bates, Joseph D.
— Atlantic Salmon Flies and Fishing. Harrisburg: Stackpole, [1970]. One of 24 for presentation. Inscr to Henry Siegel. (90) $1,900
   One of 600. (88) $320
— The Atlantic Salmon Treasury. Montreal: Atlantic Salmon Association, 1975. One of 1,000. (90) $275
   Bates's copy. (90) $210
— Streamer Fly Tying and Fishing. Harrisburg, [1966]. Ltd Ed. Inscr to Henry Siegel. (90) $275
   Sgd, with Als to Darbee inserted. (88) $230
   One of 10 for presentation. Inscr to Henry Siegel. (90) $2,500
   One of 600. Author's copy. (90) $200

Bates, Paulina
— The Divine Book of Holy and Eternal Wisdom.... Canterbury NH, 1849. 8vo. (88) $60

Bates, Samuel P.
— History of Pennsylvania Volunteers, 1861-5.... Harrisburg, 1869-71. 5 vols. 4to. (90) $290

Bates, William, 1625-99
— The Harmony of the Divine Attributes.... L: J. Darby, 1674. 4to. (89) $550
— The Soveraign and Final Happiness of Man.... L, 1680. 8vo. (88) $70

Bates, William, d.1884
— George Cruikshank.... L & Birm., 1879. 2d Ed. 4to. Extra-illus with over 90 plates & with Cruikshank Ls. (91) $550

Bateson, Edward —& Others
— A History of Northumberland. Newcastle-on-Tyne, 1893-1940. 15 vols. 4to. (88) £260; (89) £280

Bathe, Henry de
— The Charter of Romney-Marsh. L, 1686. 8vo. (89) £60

Batier, —
— La Theorie pratique de l'escrime.... Paris, 1772. 8vo. (91) £400

Battely, John, 1647-1708
— Antiquitates Rutupinae. Oxford, 1745. 2d Ed. 4to. (89) £50

Batteux, Charles
— Les Quatre Poetiques: d'Aristote, d'Horace, de Vida, de Despreaux. Paris, 1771. 2 vols. 12mo. (88) $275

Battie, J.
— The Merchants Remonstrance.... L: Ric. Cotes for William Hope, 1648. 4to. (88) £500

Battles...
— Battles of the Civil War 1861-1865. A Pictorial Record. [Little Rock: Pioneer Press, 1960]. Oblong folio. (88) $130

Batty, Elizabeth Frances
— Italian Scenery. L, 1820. 4to. (88) £90, £150, £160, £190, £190; (89) £150, £280; (90) £240, £250; (91) £320, £380, £400

Batty, Robert, d.1848
— Campaign of the Left Wing of the Allied Army in the Western Pyrenees.... L, 1823. 4to. (88) £120, £200
— French Scenery. L, 1822. 4to. (88) £110; (89) $130, $230, $375, £120, £130; (90) $185, £300
— German Scenery.... L, 1823. 4to. (88) £1,100, £1,300, DM2,800; (89) £850, £950, £1,300
Folio. L.p. copy. (90) £2,000
— Hanoverian and Saxon Scenery. L, 1829. Folio. (88) £1,300, £1,300; (89) £1,400; (90) £1,200, DM5,500
Inscr to Robert Walsh by S. C. & A. M. Hall. (91) £1,150
With monogram of George, 2d Duke of Cambridge, on tp. (90) £1,200
— Scenery of the Rhine, Belgium and Holland. L, 1826. 4to. (89) £500, £600
— Select Views of Some of the Principal Cities of Europe. L, 1832. Folio. (90) £240
L, [c.1832]. Folio. (90) £400
L, 1832. Folio. (91) £420, £420

With ALs to John Barrow, 26 Oct 1848, presenting the book to him, & with 4 orig pencil sketches by Batty loosely inserted. (90) £700
— Welsh Scenery. L, 1823. 4to. L.p. copy. (89) £160
L, 1825. 4to. (88) £60

Bauchart, Ernest Quentin. See: Quentin-Bauchart, Ernest

Baud-Bovy, Daniel —& Boissonnas, Frederic
— Des Cyclades en Crete au gre du vent. Geneva, 1919. One of 160. Folio. Blackmer copy. (90) £1,500
— En Grece par monts et par vaux. Geneva, 1910. Folio. (88) £850

Baud-Bovy, Daniel —& Boissonas, Fred
— En Grece par monts et par vaux. Geneva, 1910. Folio. Blackmer copy. (90) £850

Baudelaire, Charles, 1821-67
A set of 5 Poe translations done by Baudelaire & pbd by Michel Levy, 1857-65, uniformly bound in half mor & inscr in 3 of the vols to Charles Asselineau, sold in the Bradley Martin sale at SM on 16 Oct 1990. (90) FF295,000
— De l'Essence du Rire.... Paris, 1925. One of 500. Folio. (89) $50; (90) $60
— Les Fleurs du mal. Paris, 1855. 8vo. In: Revue des Deux Mondes, XXV annee. (89) £400, £500; (91) £250
Bound in 4 vols. 8vo. In: Revue des Deux Mondes, XXV annee. (91) £110
Paris, 1857. 12mo. Martin copy. (90) FF130,000
With ALs to Asselineau, 24 Feb 1859. (88) FF56,000
1st Issue. (88) £1,700; (91) £4,800
The Garden copy. (90) $13,000
8vo. (91) DM3,800
Copy on hollande with frontis on chine. 12mo. With proof of the poem "le reniement de Saint-Pierre' with 2 holograph corrections. Inscr to Charles Asselineau. Martin copy. (90) FF250,000
One of 50. (89) $175
2d Ed. Paris, 1861. 12mo. (88) £140
Paris: Pour les Cent Bibliophiles, 1899. One of 115, this copy for Guillaume de Montozon, with a drawing for Les Femmes damnees sgd & inscr & tipped to a guard at front. Illus by Armand Rassenfosse. 4to. Chevalier copy. (91) $8,500
Paris, 1910. One of 80 on japon imperial. Illus by Georges Rochegrosse. 4to. (91) $800

Paris, 1916. One of 200 on velin d'Arches. Illus by Emile Bernard. 4to. (90) £240
Paris, 1920. One of 450 on papier velin. 8vo. (89) SF620
Paris: G. Cress, 1923. One of 840. 4to. With letter from the binder detailing creation of the bdg. (90) £2,900
Paris: Covone, 1928. Unique copy on vellum, with a suite of 33 hand-colored lithos on vellum, sgd by the artist. Illus by Mariette Lydis. (88) £1,200
— Fleurs du mal in Pattern and Prose. L, 1929. One of 500. Illus by Beresford Egan. 4to. (89) £100; (90) £160
— Les Fleurs du mal. Paris, 1945. One of 150. 4to. Lacking all but 1 of the 20 lithos by Roger Schardner but illus in mixed media by an unknown hand. (90) £55
Paris, 1947. One of 320, sgd by Matisse. Illus by Matisse. (89) SF5,000
Paris, 1948-52. One of 200. Illus by Edouard Goerg. 2 vols. 4to. (88) FF6,000, FF8,000
Paris: Editions de L'Etoile Filante, 1966. One of 425. Illus by Georges Rouault. Folio. (88) FF45,000
See also: Limited Editions Club
— Flowers of Evil. NY, 1936. Trans by George Dillon & Edna St. Vincent Millay; preface by Millay. 8vo. Inscr by Millay to Frank Crowninshield, Mar 1936. Fleming copy. (89) $550
— L'Homme et la mer Poeme, Saint Cast. Paris, 1962. One of 125 on Arches. Illus by Bernard Buffet. (89) SF8,800
— Intimate Journals. NY & L, 1930. One of 50 specially bound & sgd by T.S. Eliot. Trans by Christopher Isherwood; intro by T. S. Eliot. (90) £260
— Lettres 1841-1866.... Paris, 1906. One of 84 on hollande. 8vo. Martin copy. (90) FF2,000
— Notice sur P. Dupont. Paris, 1851. 8vo. Martin copy. (90) FF5,500
— Oeuvres posthumes et correspondances inedites.... Paris, 1887. 8vo. Martin copy. (90) FF2,000
— Les Paradis artificiels.... Paris, 1860. 1st Ed. 12mo. (91) £1,000
Martin copy. (90) FF9,500
With ALs. (88) FF10,000
Paris: Editions Vialetay, 1955. "Exemplaire d'Artiste," sgd by Mariette Lydis. Illus by Mariette Lydis. 4to. (89) $325
One of 16 on Rives with an orig drawing, the plates in 4 states. (89) £400
— Petits poemes en prose. Paris, [1926]. ("Le Spleen de Paris.") One of 75 on velin. Illus by Edouard Chimot. 4to. (89) FF3,800
Paris, 1934. One of 148. Illus by M. Alexeieff. 4to. (89) $300
— Poemes. Paris, [1933]. One of 15 on japon.

Illus after Charles Despiau. 4to. Inscr by Despiau. (88) FF6,000
Paris, [1946]. Out-of-series copy with an additional suite of plates. 4to. (90) $60
— Les Poetes de l'amour. Paris, 1850. 32mo. Martin copy. (90) FF17,000
— Richard Wagner et Tannhaeuser a Paris. Paris, 1861. 12mo. (88) FF1,600
Martin copy. (90) FF6,500
— Salon de 1845. Paris, 1845. 1st Ed. 12mo. Martin copy. (90) FF32,000
— Salon de 1846. Paris, 1846. 1st Ed. 12mo. Martin copy. (90) FF12,000
— Selections from Les Fleurs du Mal. [N.p.], 1967. One of 30. Illus by John Muench. Folio. (90) $90
— Le Spleen de Paris. Paris, 1921. One of 30 on japon imperial with 3 states of plates & an orig drawing. Illus by Lobel-Riche. Inscr by Lobel-Riche to Denis Soulier. (91) FF18,000
Paris, [1922]. One of 30. Illus by Louise Hervieu. (90) $130

Baudelot de Dairval, Charles Cesar
— De l'Utilite des voyages.... Paris, 1686. 1st Ed. 12mo. (91) £170

Baudement, Emile
— Les Races bovines au concours universel agricole de Paris en 1856.... Paris, 1861. 2 vols. Oblong folio. (88) £800, £800
Paris, 1862. Oblong folio. (88) £700

Baudier, Michel, 1589?-1645
— Inventaire de l'histoire generalle des Turcz.... Paris: Sebastien Chappelet, 1617. 8vo. Blackmer copy. (90) £1,150

Baudoin, Jean
— Recueil d'emblemes divers.... Paris, 1638-39. 2 vols. 8vo. (91) £160

Baudot, Anatole de —&
Perrault-Dabot, Alfred
— Archives de la Commission des Monuments Historiques.... Paris, 1855-72. 3 vols. Folio. (89) 220
4 vols. Folio. (91) £800
Paris, [1898-1903]. 5 vols. Folio. (88) $1,100

Bauer, Ferdinand. See: Stearn, William T.

Bauer, Ferdinand Lukas, 1760-1826
— Illustrationes florae Novae Hollandiae. L, [1806]-13. Folio. (89) A$120,000
Parts 1 & 2 (of 3) only. (91) £22,000

Bauer, Max Hermann, 1844-1917
— Precious Stones. L, 1904. 4to. (88) $350, $1,200; (90) £120; (91) £150

Baughman, Robert W.
— Kansas in Maps. Topeka, 1961. One of 200. Folio. (89) $110

Bauhinus, Caspar, 1560-1624
— Pinax theatri botanici.... Basel, 1671. 4to. (91) $350

Baum, Dwight James
— The Work of Dwight James Baum. NY, 1927. Ed by Matlack Prices. Folio. Inscr. (91) $140

Baum, Frank Joslyn
— The Laughing Dragon of Oz. Racine: Whitman, [1934]. Illus by Milt Youngren. (90) $140

Baum, L. Frank, 1856-1919
— American Fairy Tales. Chicago: George M. Hill, 1901. Inscr by Baum to his brother. (90) $1,200
— Annabel. Chicago, [1906]. 1st Ed, 1st State. Inscr by Baum (under pseudonym of Suzanne Metcalf) to his brother. (90) $1,600
— Aunt Jane's Nieces on Vacation. By Edith Van Dyne. Chicago: Reilly & Britton, [1912]. 1st Ed, 1st State with ad on verso of half-title listing 7 titles. (90) $275
— The Daring Twins. Chicago, [1911]. 1st Ed, 1st State. Inscr by Baum to his brother. (90) $1,300
— Dorothy and the Wizard in Oz. Chicago, [1908]. 1st Ed, 1st Issue. (89) $130; (90) $140
2d Issue. (88) $80; (89) $110; (90) $140
Chicago: Reilly & Britton, [1914]. (89) $130; (90) $170
Chicago: Reilly & Lee, [c.1926]. (90) $70
— The Emerald City of Oz. Chicago, [1910]. 1st Ed, 1st State. (89) $95; (90) $55, $210, $375
Chicago, [c.1926]. (90) $90
— The Enchanted Island of Yew. Indianapolis, [1903]. 1st Ed, 2d State. (90) $150
3d Ed, 1st State. Chicago: Donohue, [c.1913]. (89) $95
— Father Goose: His Book. Chicago: Hill, [1899]. 1st Ptg. 4to. (91) $90
— Father Goose's Year Book. Chicago, [1907]. 1st Ed. (90) $120
— The Glass City. Syracuse, 1920. Short story in the series "The Wonderful Stories of Oz," pbd in the Syracuse Herald, Magazine Section, Sunday, April 4, 1920. (90) $75
— Glinda of Oz. Chicago, [1920]. 1st Ed. (88) $55; (90) $65; (91) $90
— John Dough and the Cherub. Chicago, [1906]. 1st Ed, later state. (90) $110
Chicago, [c.1914]. (88) $50, $50
— The Land of Oz. Chicago: Reilly & Lee, [c.1941]. Illus by John R. Neill. (90) $50
— The Last Egyptian: A Romance of the Nile. Phila., 1908. 1st Ed, 1st State without ptr's imprint on copyright page. (90) $75
— The Life and Adventures of Santa Claus. Indianapolis, [1902]. 1st Ed. (89) $160
2d State. (88) $150
— The Lost Princess of Oz. Chicago, [1917]. 1st Ed, 1st State. (90) $180
Later State. (89) $55
— The Magic of Oz. Chicago, [1919]. 1st Ed, 1st State. (90) $140
Chicago: Reilly & Lee [c.1925]. (88) $50; (89) $120
— The Magical Monarch of Mo. Indianapolis, [1903]. 1st Ed, 1st State. (91) $220
— The Marvelous Land of Oz. Chicago, 1904. 1st Ed, 1st State. (90) $90, $350
3d State. (90) $110
Martin copy. (90) $7,000
— The Master Key. Indianapolis, [1901]. 1st Ed, 3d State. (90) $80
— Mother Goose in Prose. Chicago: Way & Williams, [1897]. 1st Ed, 1st Issue. 4to. (91) $200
Martin copy. (90) $7,500
1st State. (89) $775
2d Issue but with headbands of fabric of 1st Issue. (89) £700
2d Ed. Chicago: Hill, [1901]. (89) $600; (90) $350
— Ozma and the Little Wizard. Chicago: Reilly & Lee, [c.1932]. 2d Ed, variant issue with Jell-O recipes & ads. 12mo. "Just about an exceptional copy, with itsy-bitsy wear at few edges". (91) $65
— Ozma of Oz. Chicago, [1907]. 1st Ed, 1st State. (89) $140; (90) $70
Chicago, [c.1911]. 2d State. Variant with missing "O" on p 11. (89) $170; (90) $110
Chicago: Reilly & Britton, [c.1913]. 3d State. (89) $95
Chicago: Reilly & Lee, [c.1923]. (90) $60
Chicago: Reilly & Lee, [c.1928]. (90) $60
— The Patchwork Girl of Oz. Chicago, [1913]. 1st Ed, 1st State. (89) $110, $180; (90) $160, $275
— Phoebe Daring. Chicago, [1912]. 1st Ed, 1st State. (90) $130
— Queen Zixi of Ix. NY, 1905. 1st Ed. (90) $60
1st State. (90) $70, $140, $150
— Rinkitink in Oz. Chicago, [1916]. 1st Ed, 1st State. (90) $140
— The Road to Oz. Chicago: Reilly & Britton, [1909]. 1st Ed, 1st Issue. (88) $100; (90)

$175, $180, $200, $350
- Sam Steele's Adventures in Panama. By Capt. Hugh Fitzgerald. Chicago: Reilly & Britton, [1907]. Inscr as Fitzgerald to his brother Henry. (90) $1,700
- The Scarecrow of Oz. Chicago, [1915]. 1st Ed, 1st State. (89) $100; (90) $120, $275
- The Sea Fairies. Chicago, [1911]. 1st Ed, Chicago Issue. (90) $80, $225
- Sky Island. Chicago, [1912]. 1st Ed. (89) $90
- The Songs of Father Goose. Chicago, 1900. 1st Ed. 4to. (90) $140; (91) $120, $160
- The Surprising Adventures of the Magical Monarch of Mo. Indianapolis, [1903]. 1st Ed, 2d State. (90) $100
  2d Ed. Chicago, [c.1913]. ("The Magical Monarch of Mo.") (91) $70
- Tik-Tok of Oz. Chicago, [1914]. 1st Ed, 1st State. (90) $550
  Later State. (89) $65
- The Tin Woodman of Oz. Chicago, [1918]. 1st Ed, 1st State. (90) $190
  2d Ed. Chicago: Reilly & Lee, [c.1919]. (89) $65; (90) $75
  Chicago, [c.1923 or later]. (88) $50
- The Transformation of Old Mombi. Syracuse, 1919. Short story in the series "The Wonderful Stories of Oz," published in the Syracuse Herald, Magazine Section, Sunday, Sept. 28, 1919. (90) $130
- Twinkle and Chubbins. Chicago, [1911]. 1st Ed. (91) $240
- The Woggle-Bug Book. Chicago, 1905. 1st Ed, 1st State. 4to. (90) $50
- The Wonderful Wizard of Oz. Chicago & NY, 1900. 1st Ed, 1st State. 8vo. (88) $700
  Martin copy. (90) $8,000
  2d State. (90) $450
  Martin copy. (90) $2,750
  State Z. (90) $700
  2d Ed. Chicago: Donohue, [1903]. ("The New Wizard of Oz.") 2d Issue. (90) $90
  Indianapolis: Bobbs-Merrill, [1903]. (90) $90
  3d Ed. Chicago: Donohue, [c.1913]. (89) $60
  1st State. (89) $70
  2d State. (90) $100

Bauman, Hans F. S.
- 150 Years of Artists' Lithographs. L, 1953. One of 135. Illus by Graham Sutherland. 4to. (88) £350; (89) £220

Baumann, Gustave
- Frijoles Canyon Pictographs.... Sante Fe, [1939]. One of 500. (89) $280

Baumes, Jean Baptiste Theodore
- Traite de l'amaigrissement des enfans. Paris, 1806. 2d Ed. 8vo. (91) £240

Baur Collection—Geneva
- Chinese Ceramics. Geneva, 1968-77. Compiled by John G. Ayers. Vols I-IV. 4to. (90) $2,600
- Chinese Ceramics. Vol III: Monochrome-Glazed Porcelains of the Ch'ing Dynasty. Geneva, [1972]. Ltd Ed. Compiled by John G. Ayers. 4to. (88) $260
- Chinese Jades and Other Hardstones. Geneva, 1976. Ltd Ed. Compiled by Pierre F. Schneeberger. 4to. (88) £60; (90) $250
- Netsuke. Geneva, 1977. Compiled by M. T. Coullery. Folio. (90) $250

Baur, Johann Wilhelm
- Dem hoch Edlen unnd gestrengen Herrren...[scenes from Ovid's Metamorphoses]. Vienna, 1641. Oblong 4to. (88) $175
- Iconographia.... Augsburg, 1670. 4 parts in 1 vol. Oblong folio. (90) $850; (91) DM3,200

Bautista, Juan
- Confessionario en lengua Mexicana & Castellana.... Mexico: M. Ocharte, 1599. Bound with: Advertencias para los Confessores de los Naturales...Primera parte. Mexico: M. Ocharte, 1600. 8vo. Inscr by Benjamin Blinkhorn to the British & Foreign Bible Society, 1833. (88) £8,000

Bavaria
- Reformacion der bayrischen Landrecht. Munich: Adam Berg, 1588. Bound with: Gerichtsordnung im Fuerstenthumb Obern und Nidern Bayrn. Munich, 1588. And: Bayrische Landtsordnung. Munich, 1598. And: Der fuerstlichen Bayrischen Landordnung weitere Erclerung. Munich, 1598. Folio. (91) £1,400

Baxter, Andrew, 1686?-1750
- Matho: or, the Cosmotheroria Puerilis.... L, 1745. 2d Ed. 2 vols in 1. 8vo. (90) £140

Baxter, Benjamin, Pseud.
- Mr. Baxter Baptiz'd in Bloud, or a Sad History of the Unparallel'd Cruelty of the Anabaptists in New-England. L, 1673. 8vo. (88) £500

Baxter, Evelyn V. —& Rintoul, Leonora Jeffrey
- The Birds of Scotland. Their History, Distribution and Migration. L, 1953. 2 vols. (91) £75

Baxter, George
— The Pictorial Album; or, Cabinet of Paintings, for the Year 1837. L, [1837]. 4to. (90) $160, £130, £180; (91) $90, £140, £320, £320

Baxter, Nathaniel, fl.1606
— Sir Philip Sydneys Ourania, that is, Endimions Song and Tragedie.... L, 1606. 1st Ed. 4to. STC 1598. Grosvenor-Martin copy. (90) $8,500

Baxter, Richard, 1615-91
— The Certainty of the Worlds of Spirits. L, 1691. 1st Ed. 8vo. Wing B1215. (91) £700
— Compassionate Councel to All Young-Men.... L: T. S. & to be sold by B. Simmons & Jonath. Greenwood, 1682. 8vo. (88) £340
— Reliquiae Baxterianae; or, Mr. Richard Baxter's Narrative.... L, 1696. Folio. (88) £65

Baxter, Thomas
— An Illustration of the Egyptian, Grecian and Roman Costume.... L, 1810. 8vo. W. M. Rossetti—Blackmer copy. (90) £80
L, 1814. 8vo. (89) £70

Baxter, William, 1787-1871
— British Phaenogamous Botany.... Oxford, 1834-43. 6 vols. 8vo. (88) £370; (89) £450, £500, £600, £620; (90) £580, £620, £750
Vols I-II only. (89) £180
Vols I-IV (of 6) only. 8vo. (90) £450

Bayard, Hippolyte
— Bayard. Paris, 1943. One of 1,590. 4to. (91) $150

Bayard, Nicholas, 1644?-1707 —& Lodowick, Charles
— A Journal of the Late Actions of the French at Canada. L, 1693. 4to. (88) £3,500

Bayard, Samuel John, d.1879
— A Sketch of the Life of Com. Robert F. Stockton.... NY, 1856. (91) $50

Bayardi, Ottavio Antonio, 1690-1765
— The Antiquities of Herculaneum. L, 1773. 2 vols. 4to & folio. (91) £380
4to. (91) $250
— Prodromo delle antichita d'Ercolano. Naples, 1752. 5 vols. 4to. (89) £85
Kissner copy. (91) £800

Bayer, Gottlieb Siegfried
— Kratkoe Opisanie Vsekh Sluchaev do Azova. St. Petersburg, 1782. 8vo. (88) £190

Bayer, Johann, 1572-1625
— Uranometria. Augsburg: C. Magnus, 1603. 1st Ed. Folio. (88) $4,500; (89) £6,500
Ulm: Johann Goerlin, 1655. Folio. (88) FF15,000
Ulm: Johann Goerlin, 1661. Folio. (88) £550
1st Ed. Ulm: Johann Goerlin, 1665. Folio. (91) £2,000

Bayeux...
— The Bayeux Tapestry. L: Society of Antiquaries, 1819-23. Oblong folio. (90) £320

Bayldon, J. S.
— A Treatise on the Valuation of Property for the Poor's Rate.... L, 1828. 8vo. (88) $150

Bayldon, Oliver
— The Paper Makers Craft. Leicester: Twelve by Eight Press, 1965. Ltd Ed. Folio. (91) $75

Bayle, Pierre, 1647-1706
— Dictionaire historique et critique. Rotterdam, 1697. 4 parts in 2 vols. Folio. (91) £3,600
3d Ed. Rotterdam, 1720. 4 vols. Folio. (89) $300; (91) $150, £80
Amst., 1734. 5 vols. Folio. (90) £65
Amst., 1734-38. 5 vols. Folio. (91) $275
Amst., 1734. 5 vols. Folio. (91) $300, £100
Basel, 1741. 4 vols. Folio. (88) $250
Paris, 1820. 16 vols. 8vo. (90) £90
— The Dictionary. L, 1734-38. 5 vols. Folio. (89) £180; (91) £340
— Nouvelles de la republique des lettres. Amst.: David Mortier, 1715-20. 56 vols. 12mo. (88) FF30,000
— Oeuvres diverses. The Hague, 1727-31. 4 vols. Folio. (89) £90

Bayley, Frank W., 1863-1932
— Five Colonial Artists of New England. Bost., 1929. One of 500. Folio. (88) $110; (89) $130

Bayley, John, d.1869
— The History and Antiquities of the Tower of London. See: Fore-Edge Paintings

Bayley, John Whitcomb, d.1869
— History and Antiquities of the Tower of London. L, 1821-25. 1st Ed. 2 vols. Folio. (91) $300
L, 1825. 2 vols. Folio. (90) £85; (91) $150

Baylis, Edward
— A New and Compleat Body of Practical Botanic Physic.... L, 1791-93. Vol I (all pbd). 4to. (88) £220

Bayliss, Marguerite F.
— Bolinvar. See: Derrydale Press

Baylor, Armistead Keith
— Abdul, an Allegory. NY: Derrydale Press, 1930. One of 500. (89) $225

Bayly, Anselm
— The Sacred Singer, containing an Essay.... L, 1771. 8vo. (88) $110

Bayly, Lewis, d.1631
— The Practice of Pietie. L: Philip Chetwinde, 1668. 24mo. (88) $400

Baynes, Thomas Mann
— The Adventures of a Fox by Moonlight. L: Ackermann, 1836. Oblong folio. (89) £500; (90) £450

Bayros, Franz von
— Ex-Libris. Vienna, 1911. Ltd Ed. 4to. (88) DM800

Baysio, Guido de
— Rosarium decretorum. Venice: Johannes Herbort de Seligenstadt, for Johannes de Colonia & Nicolaus Jenson et socii, 3 Apr 1481. Folio. 416 leaves. Goff B-288. Abrams copy. (90) £15,000

Baz, Gustavo, 1852-1904 —&
Gallo, Edouardo L.
— History of the Mexican Railway. Mexico, 1876. 1st Ed in English. Trans by G. F. Henderson. Folio. (89) £1,300

Bazeley, William. See: Hyett & Bazeley

Bazin, Gilles Augustin, d.1754
— The Natural History of Bees.... L, 1744. 8vo. (88) $150, £160

Beach, Belle
— Riding and Driving for Women. NY, 1912. Inscr to Mrs Vanderbilt. (91) $80

Beach, Joseph Perkins
— The Log of Apollo: Joseph Perkins Beach's Journal.... San Francisco: Book Club of California, 1986. One of 550. (91) $50

Beach, Spencer Ambrose, 1860-1922
— Apples of New York. Albany, 1905. 2 vols. (89) $70; (90) $150; (91) $85

Beach, William Nicholas
— In the Shadow of Mount McKinley. See: Derrydale Press

Beadle, John Hanson, 1840-97
— Life in Utah.... Phila., [1870]. 8vo. (88) $70; (89) $50
— The Undeveloped West; or, Five Years in the Territories.... Phila.: National Publishing Co, [1873]. 8vo. (90) $65

Beagle, Peter S.
— The Last Unicorn. NY: Viking, [1968]. (88) $55; (90) $60, $65

Beale, Edward Fitzgerald, 1822-93
— Wagon Road from Fort Defiance to the Colorado River. Wash., 1858. 8vo. (88) $225
[Wash., 1860]. House Issue. 8vo. (88) $275

Beale, Thomas
— The Natural History of the Sperm Whale.... L, 1839. 2d Ed. 8vo. (89) $250

Beall, Karen F.
— Cries and Itinerant Trades. Hamburg, [1975]. One of 750. Folio. (91) $150, £105

Beals, Carleton
— The Crime of Cuba. Phila. & L, [1933]. Illus by Walker Evans. (89) $55

Beamish, North Ludlow, 1797-1872
— History of the German Legion. L, 1832-37. 2 vols. 4to. (90) $450

Bean, W. J.
— Trees and Shrubs Hardy in the British Isles. L, 1936. 6th Ed of Vols I-II; 2d Ed of Vol III. (91) £55

Beard, Charles R.
— A Catalogue of the Collection of Martinware formed by Mr. Frederick John Nettlefold. L, 1936. Folio. (88) £170; (90) £110; (91) £45, £130

Beardsley, Aubrey, 1872-98
[-] The Brighton Grammar School Annual Entertainment at the Dome. Brighton, 1888. 8vo. (89) £700
— The Early Work. L, 1912. With: The Later Work. L, 1912. Together, 2 vols. 4to, orig cloth. (88) £90
— Fifty Drawings, Selected from the Collection Owned by H. S. Nichols. NY, 1920. One of 500. 4to. (89) $75, $140
— Four Illustrations to the Works of Edgar Allan Poe. [Chicago, 1894-95]. One of 10. 8vo. (89) $2,200
— Grotesques. [L], 1919. One of 25. Illus by Frederick H. Evans. 4to. Sold w.a.f. (91) £160
— Letters from Aubrey Beardsley to Leonard Smithers. L, 1937. (90) $50; (91) $100

BEARDSLEY

— Morte Darthur Portfolio. L, 1927. One of 300. 4to. (88) $110
— A Portfolio of Aubrey Beardsley's Drawings Illustrating "Salome" by Oscar Wilde. [L: John Lane, 1920]. Folio. (89) £150, £250, £260
— Prospectus for the Keynotes Series of Novels and Short Stories. L, 1896. 8vo. (89) £1,300
— Reproductions of Eleven Designs Omitted from the First Edition of Le Morte Darthur. L, 1927. One of 300. 4to. (89) £170, £190
— The Story of Venus and Tannhaeuser. L, 1907. One of 50 on Japan vellum. 4to. (89) $400; (91) $300
— The Uncollected Work. L, 1925. Intro by C. Lewis Hind. 4to. (90) $60, $120; (91) $70
One of 110 on japan vellum. (91) $225
— Under the Hill.... L, 1904. One of 110 on japan vellum. 4to. (91) $175
Beardsley's copy, Aubrey
— KEATS, JOHN. - Poetical Works. L, [c.1890]. 8vo. With 2 inserted ports of Keats by Beardsley & other related material. (88) £2,000

Bearn, Louis Hector de
— Quelques souvenirs d'une campagne en Turquie. [Paris, c.1839]. Folio. (90) £1,400

Beatles, The —&
Rixdorfer, Die
— All you need is Love. Berlin: Hanser, 1968. One of 300. (91) DM850

Beaton, Cecil
— Cecil Beaton's Scrapbook. L, 1937. 4to. (91) $110

Beattie, James, 1735-1803
— Essays on the Nature and Immutability of Truth.... Edin., 1776. 4to. (91) $130
Dublin, 1778. 4to. ESTC 138972. (91) £240
— Poems on Several Occasions. Edin., 1776. 8vo. Inscr with a poem to Susan Logan Park. Adam-Fleming copy. (89) $11,000

Beattie, William, 1793-1875
— The Castles and Abbeys of England. L, [c.1860]. 2 vols. (90) £60
— The Danube. L, [c.1840]. Bound with: Pardoe, Julia. The Beauties of the Bosphorus. L, [c.1845]. Illus by William H. Bartlett. 4to. (91) £450
L, 1842. Illus by W. H. Bartlett. 4to. (89) £140
L, [1844]. 4to. (88) £220, £260, DM1,000; (89) £100, £100, £150, £180, £200, £240, HF750; (90) £220, £240, £240; (91) £550, £210, £320

— Scotland Illustrated.... L, 1838. 2 vols. 4to. (88) £65, £70, £90; (89) $80, £65, £70, £70, £70, £80, £90, £90, £110, £120; (90) £70, £90, £180; (91) $175, £80
L & NY, [1838]. ("Caledonia Illustrated....") 2 vols in 1. 4to. (91) £160
L, 1842. 2 vols. 4to. (89) £85
— La Suisse pittoresque. L, 1836. Illus by W. H. Bartlett. 2 vols. 4to. (89) £300
— Switzerland Illustrated.... L, 1834-36. Illus by William H. Bartlett. 2 vols. 4to. (88) £320
2 vols in 1. 4to. (89) $210
L, 1836. Illus by W. H. Bartlett. 2 vols. 4to. (88) £180, £240, £260, £320, £320, £350, £360, £420; (89) $300, $400, £150, £250, £280, £280, £300, £300, £300, £320, £350, £380, £460; (90) £300, £340, £360; (91) £140, £160, £300, £350, £360, £360, £500
2 vols in the orig 27 parts. 4to. (88) £340
2 vols in 1. 4to. (89) £280; (91) £220
Vol I only. 4to. (88) £95
Vol I only. (88) £110; (90) £120
L, 1838. 2 vols. 4to. (89) £300
L, 1839. 2 vols. 4to. (88) £360; (89) $450, £300
2 vols in 1. 4to. (88) £280
Vol I (of 2) only. 4to. (91) £135
L: Virtue, [1844]. 2 vols. 4to. (89) £360; (90) £340; (91) $450, $500
L, [c.1850]. 2 vols in 1. 4to. (88) $450
— The Waldenses. L, 1838. 4to. (88) £120, £120, £120, £140; (89) $150, £110; (90) £48, £140, £210, £320; (91) £220, £240, £240

Beatty Library, Sir A. Chester
— A Catalogue of the Indian Miniatures. L, 1936. 3 vols. Folio. (88) £650; (90) £580
Inscr by Beatty to Lord Casey. (88) £640
— A Catalogue of the Armenian Manuscripts. Dublin, 1958. 2 vols. (88) £80; (90) £90
— A Catalogue of the Persian Manuscripts and Miniatures. L, 1960-62. Vols II & III only. (88) £40
— A Descriptive Catalogue of the Western Manuscripts. Oxford, 1927-30. Compiled by Eric George Millar. 2 vols in 4 parts. Folio. Martin copy. (90) $2,100
4 vols. Folio. (88) £700
Doheny copy. (88) $2,600
Presentation copy from Beatty to E. H. Dring. (91) £2,200
Vol I & plate vol only. (89) $1,600
— [Sale Catalogue] Catalogue of the Renowned Collection of Western Manuscripts.... L, 1932-33. 2 vols in 1. 4to. (91) $200

Beatty, Charles, d.1772
— The Journal of a Two Months Tour.... L, 1768. 1st Ed. 8vo. (91) $1,100

Beauchasteau, Francois Mathieu Chastelet de.
See: Chastelet de Beauchasteau, Francois Mathieu

Beauclerk, Lord Charles, 1813-61
— Lithographic Views of Military Operations in Canada...during the late Insurrection.... L, 1840. Folio. (91) £1,500

Beauclerk Library, Topham
— [Sale Catalogue] Bibliotheca Beauclerkiana. A Catalogue of the Large and Valuable Library.... L, 1781. 2 parts in 1 vol. 8vo. (88) £160

Beaufort, Emily Anne, Viscountess Strangford
— The Eastern Shores of the Adriatic in 1863.... L, 1864. 8vo. (90) $100
Sligo-Blackmer copy. (90) £325
— Egyptian Sepulchres and Syrian Shrines. L, 1861. 2 vols. 8vo. Blackmer copy. (90) £280

Beaufort, Francis, 1774-1857
— Karamania, or a Brief Description of the South Coast of Asia-Minor. L: R. Hunter, 1817. 8vo. Blackmer copy. (90) £600
L, 1818. 8vo. (91) £260
2d Ed. 8vo. (91) £200

Beaufort, Henry Somerset, Duke of —& Watson, A. E. T.
— The Badminton Library of Sports and Pastimes. L, 1885-96. 26 vols. 4to. (91) £700

Beaufoy, Mark, 1764-1827
— Nautical and Hydraulic Experiments.... L, 1834. Vol I (all pbd). 4to. Inscr to the Marquess of Lansdowne. (89) £100

Beauharnais, Eugenie de, Duchesse de Saint Leu. See: Hortense

Beaujour, Louis A. Felix de, 1763-1836
— Tableau du commerce de la Grece. Paris: Renouard, 1800. 8vo. Blackmer copy. (90) £380
— Voyage militaire dans l'Empire Othoman. Paris: Firmin Didot, 1829. 2 vols. 8vo. Arvanitidi copy. (91) £1,300

Beaulieu, Sebastian de, Sieur de la Pontault
— Plans et profils des principales villes des Duchez de Lorraine et de Bar. Paris, [c.1670]. 8vo. (88) £500

Beaumarchais, Pierre Auguste Caron de, 1732-99
— Eugenie, dram en cinq actes.... Paris, 1767. 8vo. (89) £350
— La Folle Journee, ou Le Mariage de Figaro. Lyons, 1785. 8vo. (89) £60; (90) £350
Paris, 1785. 8vo. (90) £650; (91) £75
Copy on papier fort. (90) £2,200
Louise Contat's copy. (89) $2,500
— Oeuvres. Paris, 1809. 7 vols. 8vo. (89) FF1,000

Beaumont, Cyril William
— The Art of Lydia Lopokova. L, 1920. 4to. (88) £220
— The Art of Stanislas Idzikowski. L, 1926. One of 350. 4to. (89) £80
— The History of Harlequin. L, 1926. One of 325. 4to. (91) $120

Beaumont, Cyril William —& Sitwell, Sacheverell
— The Romantic Ballet.... L, 1938. 4to. (88) £60, £80; (89) £115; (90) £80

Beaumont de Perefixe, Hardouin de. See: Perefixe, Hardouin de Beaumont de

Beaumont, Francis, 1584-1616
— The Dramatic Works of Ben Jonson, and Beaumont and Fletcher. See: Jonson, Ben
— Poems. L, 1640. 1st Ed. 8vo. Huntington-Silver-Newberry Library-Bradley Martin copy. (90) $6,500
— Salmacis and Hermaphroditus. See: Golden Cockerel Press

Beaumont, Francis, 1584-1616 —& Fletcher, John, 1579-1625
— Philaster: or, Love Lies a Bleeding. L, 1652. 5th Ed. 4to. (90) $225
— Works. L, 1647. ("Comedies and Tragedies.") 1st Collected Ed; 1st State of port. Bound with: Beaumont & Fletcher. The Wild-Goose Chase. L, 1652. 1st Ed. Folio, mor gilt by Riviere. Doheny copy. (88) $320
2d state of frontis port. Folio. (89) £680
1st Collected Ed (91) $1,600
1st state of port. Bradley Martin copy. (90) $3,000
2d state of port. (91) £380
L, 1679. ("Fifty Comedies and Tragedies.") Folio. (88) £850; (89) £375, £85; (90) £325, £150
L, 1711. 7 vols. 8vo. (88) $275
L, 1750. 10 vols. 8vo. (88) £300
Edin., 1812. 14 vols. 8vo. (89) £650; (91) $325
L, 1843-46. 11 vols. 8vo. (89) £150; (91) $750

BEAUMONT

Beaumont, John, d.1731
— An Historical, Physiological and Theological Treatise of Spirits, Apparitions, Witchcrafts.... L, 1705. 1st Ed. 8vo. (89) $290; (90) £500; (91) £210

Beaumont, Sir John, 1583-1627
— Bosworth-Field: with a Taste of the Variety of Other Poems.... L, 1629. 1st Ed. 8vo. Hoe-Houghton-Fleming copy. (89) $1,300
STC 1694. (91) £500
STC 1694. Rabinowitz-Bradley Martin copy. (90) $1,200

Beaumont, Joseph, 1616-99
— Psyche: or Loves Mysterie in XX. Canto's.... L, 1648. 1st Ed. Folio. (89) £160
Buxton-Forman—Bradley Martin copy. (90) $650

Beaumont, William, 1785-1853
— Experiments and Observations on the Gastric Juice.... Plattsburgh, 1833. 1st Ed. 8vo. (88) $900; (89) $800, $850; (90) $950, $1,350
Martin copy. (90) $1,200
Bost., 1834. 8vo. (88) $350
Edin., 1838. 8vo. (91) £220
2d Ed. Burlington VT, 1847. ("The Physiology of Digestion....") 8vo. (88) $150; (89) $300
— Further Experiments on the Case of Alexis San Martin. NY, 1826. 8vo. In: The Medical Recorder, Vol IX. (90) $110

Beaumont, William Worby
— Motor Vehicles and Motors. L, 1900-6. 2 vols. 8vo. (91) £130

Beaurain, Jean de, 1696-1771
— Histoire de la campagne de M. le Prince de Conde.... Paris, 1774. Folio. (88) $425, £290
— Histoire militaire de Flandre.... Paris, 1755. 1st Ed. 5 parts in 2 vols. Folio. (89) $1,000
5 parts in 1 vol, the maps bound separately in 2 vols. Folio. (89) £700
5 parts in 2 vols. Folio. (90) £950; (91) £400
6 vols. Folio. (88) £1,200
Parts 3-5 only. Folio. (90) HF1,000
2d Ed. Paris, 1776. 6 vols in 4. Folio. (90) £900

Beauties...
— The Beauties of the Creation: or, a New Moral System of Natural History. L, 1793. 5 vols. 8vo. (91) £220

AMERICAN BOOK PRICES CURRENT

Beauvau, Henri de, d.1684
— Relation journaliere du voyage du Levant. Nancy, 1615. 2d Ed. 4to. Blackmer copy. (90) £3,000

Beauvoir, Roger de
— La Cap et l'epee.... Paris, 1837. 8vo. Martin copy. (90) FF3,800

Beaver, John
— A Letter to the Lords Commissioners for Trade and Plantations.... L, 1720. 4to. (88) £200

Beaver, Philip, 1766-1813
— African Memoranda.... L, 1805. 4to. (88) £150

Beawes, Wyndham, fl.1775
— Lex Mercatoria Rediviva: or the Merchant's Directory. L, [1752]. 1st Ed. Folio. (89) £300

Beccari, Jacopo Bartholommeo
— De quamplurimis phosphoris.... Bologna, 1744. 4to. (90) £280

Beccaria, Cesare Bonesana di, 1738-94
— An Essay on Crimes and Punishments.... Phila.: R. Bell, 1778. 8vo. (91) £130
Edin., 1788. 12mo. (88) £60
— Traite des delits et des peines.... Paris, 1773. 8vo. (91) £110

Beccaria, Giovanni Battista, 1716-81
— A Treatise upon Artificial Electricity.... L, 1776. 1st Ed in English. 4to. (88) £180

Bechai ben Asher
— BIALIK, CHIAM NACHMAN. - Kithvei Ch. N. Bialik Umivchar Targumav. Berlin, 1923. 4 vols. 4to. (89) $450

Bechstein, Johann Matthaeus, 1757-1822
— Gemeinnutzige Naturgeschichte Deutschlands nach allen drey Reichen. Leipzig, 1789-95. 4 vols. 8vo. (91) DM750
Leipzig, 1801-09. 4 vols. 8vo. Martin copy. (90) $2,250
Leipzig, 1795 & 1801-05. Vols I & II, 2d Eds; Vols III & IV, 1st Eds. 4 vols. 8vo. Martin copy. (90) $400

Beck, Jean & Louise
— Le Manuscrit du Roi. Phila., 1938. One of 300. 2 vols. 4to. (88) $110

Beck, Johann Jodocus
— Tractatus de juribus judaeorum. Von Recht der Juden.... Nuremberg, 1741. 4to. (88) $200

Beck, Matthias Fridericus
— Ephemerides Persarum per totium annum. Augsburg, 1695-96. 2 parts in 1 vol. Folio. (91) £550

Beck, Thomas Alcock
— Annales Furnesiensis, History and Antiquities of the Abbey of Furness. L, 1844. 4to. (89) £95

Becker, Carl, d.1859 —& Hefner Alteneck, Jacob Heinrich von, 1811-1908
— Kunstwerke und Geraethschaften des Mittelalters und der Renaissance. Frankfurt, 1852-57-63. 3 vols. Folio. (88) $775

Becker, Felix. See: Thieme & Becker

Becker, George Ferdinand, 1847-1919
— Geology of the Comstock Lode and the Washoe District.... Wash., 1882. 2 vols, including Atlas. (88) $160
Atlas only. (88) $160
Text vol only; lacking Atlas. (89) $110

Becker, Robert H.
— Designs on the Land, Disenos of California Ranchos and Their Makers. See: Grabhorn Printing
— Disenos of California Ranchos... See: Grabhorn Printing

Becker, Wilhelm Bottlieb
— Augusteum ou description des monumens antiques qui se trouvent a Dresde. Leipzig, 1804-11. 3 vols. Folio. Leuchtenberg copy. (89) £420

Beckerath Collection, Adolf von
— Sammlung Adolf von Beckerath. Berlin: Rudolf Lepke, [1913]. (88) $60

Becket, Thomas a, Saint. See: Thomas a Becket

Beckett, Samuel
— All Strange Away. NY: Gotham Book Mart, [1976]. "Apparent proof state". Illus by Edward Gorey. Sgd by Beckett & Gorey. (91) $160
L, 1979. With holograph corrections. (91) £500
— All That Fall. NY, [1957]. Ltd Ed. Sgd on tp. 1958. (90) $325
One of 25 specially bound copies. (90) $800, £750
— Der Ausgestossene. Hamburg: Raamin-Presse, 1976. One of 150. Illus by Roswitha Quadflieg. 4to. (91) DM1,800
— Catastrophe. Northridge CA: Lord John Press, 1983. One of 26. Illus by Joseph Mugnaini. Single sheet, 380mm by 565mm. (88) $150
— Echo's Bones. Paris: Europa Press, 1935.

1st Ed. (88) $200
One of 250. (89) $150; (90) $160; (91) $200, £310
— En attendant Godot. Paris, 1952. (88) $200
Beckett's working rehearsal copy used for the orig production of the play, annotated, marked by him "prompt copy 1953" & later inscr to John & Bettina. John Calder's copy. (91) £30,000
— Endgame.... NY: Grove Press, [1958]. 1st Ed in English, one of 26. (90) $950
— Hinweis auf Pim. Cologne: Hake-Verlag, 1966. One of 100. Illus by Manfred Garstka. (91) DM180
— How It Is (Series A). L, 1964. 1st Ed in English, One of 100, sgd. (90) $325
— Ill Seen, Ill Said. Northridge: Lord John Press, 1982. One of 299. (88) $60, $110; (89) $110; (91) $110, $130
— Imagination Dead Imagine. L, 1965. One of 100. (88) $80
— Krapp's Last Tape. Translated in to Hebrew by Helit Yeshurun. Jerusalem 1983. One of 96 with etching of Beckett port laid in. Illus by Avigdor Arikha. (88) $225; (89) $150
— The Lost Ones. L, 1972. One of 100. (88) $95
— More Pricks than Kicks. L: Calder & Boyars, [1970]. One of 100. (90) £150
— The North. L: Enitharmon Press, 1972. One of 137 with 3 orig etchings. Illus by Avigdor Arikha. Folio. (91) $600
— Poemes. Paris: Editions de Minuit, [1968]. One of 100. Inscr. (88) $200
One of 450. Inscr. (88) $50
— Poems in English. L, 1961. 1st Ed, one of 100. (89) £160; (91) £300
"A mint copy". (90) £280; (91) £200
— Proust. L, 1931. 1st Ed. (88) £120; (89) $120; (91) £120
1st American Ed. NY, 1931. One of 250. (91) $250
L, 1965. Sgd. (89) £65
One of 100. (89) $160; (90) £150
— Waiting for Godot. NY, 1954. (91) $70
— Whoroscope. Paris: The Hours Press, 1930. 1st Ed, One of 100. (88) $950; (90) £1,200
One of 200. (88) £520; (90) £650; (91) $1,800, £500
Bradley Martin copy. (90) $1,000

Beckford, Peter, 1740-1811
— Thoughts on Hunting. Salisbury, 1784. 4to. (89) £190
L, 1796. ("Thoughts upon Hare and Fox Hunting.") 8vo. (88) £110
L, 1802. 4to. Extra-illus with 57 plates. (88) £200

L, [1820]. Illus by Thomas Bewick. 8vo. (88) £75; (90) $130
Extra-illus with 75 plates & with ALs of Richard Tattersall. (90) $325
L, [1911]. One of 350. Illus by G. Denholm Armour. 4to. (89) £110

Beckford, William, d.1799
— A Descriptive Account of the Island of Jamaica. L, 1790. 1st Ed. 2 vols. 8vo. (88) £120; (89) $180, £280; (91) £300

Beckford, William Thomas, 1760-1844
— Azemia, a Novel. L, 1797. 1st Ed. 2 vols. 12mo. Bradley Martin copy. (90) $8,500
— Biographical Memoirs of Extraordinary Painters. L, 1780. 1st Ed. 8vo. Bradley Martin copy. (90) $800
— Italy.... L, 1834. 1st Ed. 2 vols. 8vo. (89) £85; (91) £70, $160
  AL inserted. (88) £360
  Sadleir-Bradley Martin copy. (90) $1,600
— Modern Novel Writing. By Harriet Marlow. L, 1796. 2 vols in 1. 12mo. Bradley Martin copy. (90) $8,000
— Recollections of an Excursion to the Monasteries of Alcobaca and Batalha. L, 1835. 8vo. (88) £130; (90) $90
  "A brilliant copy." Bradley Martin copy. (90) $1,400
  1st American Ed. Phila., 1835. 8vo. (90) $85; (91) $110
— The Story of Al Raoui. L, 1799. Trans by Beckford. 8vo. Bradley Martin copy. (90) $750
— Vathek. L, 1786. ("An Arabian Tale.") 1st Ed. 8vo. (88) £380
  Inserted is a Ds of Beckford's father. Bradley Martin copy. (90) $700
  L.p. copy. J. R. Abbey—Bradley Martin copy. (90) $1,400
  See also: Nonesuch Press
— Vathek. Conte Arabe. Lausanne, 1787. 1st Ed in French. 8vo. Bradley Martin copy. (90) $2,500
  Paris, 1787. 1st Issue (without the Approbation). 8vo. Bradley Martin copy. (90) $550
— Vathek. Eine orientalische Erzaehlung. Beyreuth: The Bear Press, 1985. One of 170. Illus by Gottfried Helnwein. 4to. (91) DM560

Beckford Library, William Thomas
— [Sale Catalogue] The Valuable Library of Books in Fonthill Abbey. L, 1823. 8vo. (88) £180
— [Sale Catalogue] The Hamilton Palace Libraries: Catalogue of the First-[Fourth] Portion of the Beckford Library. L, 1882-83. 4 vols. 8vo. (89) $110

L, 1882-84. 4 vols in 2. 8vo. (91) $120
5 vols in one. 8vo. Martin copy. (90) $600

Beckmann, John, 1739-1811
— A History of Inventions and Discoveries. L, 1817. 3d Ed. 4 vols. 8vo. (89) £55, £60

Becon, Thomas, 1512-67
— The Relikes of Rome. L, 1563. 8vo. Beckford copy. (89) £620

Becque, Henry
— Les Corbeaux. Paris, 1931. One of 130. Illus by Hugues de Beaumont. 4to. (90) $160

Becquerel, Antoine Henri, 1852-1908
— Recherches sur une propriete nouvelle de la matiere.... Paris, 1903. 4to. In: Memoires de l'Academie des Sciences, Vol 46. (88) £260; (89) £160

Beddie, M. K.
— Bibliography of Captain James Cook.... Sydney, 1970. 2d Ed. (91) $200

Beddoes, Thomas Lovell, 1803-49
— Death's Jest-Book; or, the Fool's Tragedy. L, 1850. 8vo. Inscr to Violet Hunt by Andrew Lang. (88) $150
— The Improvisatore, in Three Fyttes, with other Poems. Oxford, 1821. 8vo. Maria Edgeworth's copy. Sadleir-Martin copy. (90) $4,000

Bede, The Venerable, 673-735
— De natura rerum et tempore ratione libri duo. Basel: H. Petrus, Mar 1529. Folio. (90) £460
— Historia ecclesiastica gentis Anglorum. [Strassburg: Heinrich Eggestein, c.1475-78]. Folio. 97 (of 98) leaves; lacking last blank. Goff B-293. Holford-Doheny copy. (88) $32,000
  97 (of 98) leaves; lacking last blank. Goff B-293. The Garden copy. (90) $27,000
  Antwerp, 1550. ("Ecclesiasticae historiae gentis Anglorum.") 12mo. Thomas Smith—Wm. Burton—Fleming copy. (89) $2,600
  L, 1722. Folio. Edward Gibbon's copy, with his ptd book-label. (89) £650
— The History of the Church of Englande. Antwerp: Laet, 1565. 1st Ed in English. Trans by Thomas Stapleton. 4to. STC 1778. (91) £400
  Oxford: Shakespeare Head Press, 1930. One of 475. Folio. (88) $160

Bede, Cuthbert. See: Bradley, Edward

Bedford, Arthur, 1668-1745
— The Evil and Danger of Stage-Plays. L, 1706. 8vo. (91) £75

Bedford, Francis
— Photographic Pictures Made...during the Tour in the East in which...he accompanied His Royal Highness the Prince of Wales. L, [1863]. 1 vol (of 4) only. Folio. (90) £6,500

Bedford, John Russell, 6th Duke, 1766-1839.
See: Corbound & Bedford

Bedier, Joseph
— Le Roman de Tristan et Iseult. Paris: H. Piazza, 1920. 12mo. (91) FF1,500
Paris: H. Piazza, [1933]. Illus by Robert Engels. 4to. (89) SF4,000

Bedos de Celles, Francois, 1706-79
— La Gnomonique pratique.... Paris, 1760. 1st Ed. 8vo. (89) $200

Bee...
— The Bee, or Literary Weekly Intelligencer. Edin., 1791-93. Ed by James Anderson. 18 vols. 8vo. (91) £380

Beebe, Charles William, 1877-1962
— The Arcturus Adventure: An Account of the New York Zoological Society's First Oceanographic Expedition. NY, 1926. One of 50. 4to. (91) £160
Martin copy. (90) $300
— Galapagos: World's End. NY, 1924. 1st Ed, One of 100. 4to. (90) $175
Martin copy. (90) $600
— A Monograph of the Pheasants. L, 1918-22. One of 600. 4 vols. Folio. (89) $1,050; (90) $3,000; (91) $3,000, £1,700
Inscr by Beebe & Anthony Keisle. (91) $2,100
Jeanson copy. (88) FF40,000
Martin copy. (90) $8,000
— Pheasants, their Lives and Homes. Garden City, 1926. 2 vols. (88) $150; (91) $85
NY, 1931. 2 vols. (88) £55; (91) $75, $100

Beebe, Lucius Morris, 1902-66
— Mansions on Rails: The Folklore of the Private Railway Car. Berkeley, Calif., 1959. Ltd Ed. 4to. (90) $55

Beebe, Lucius Morris, 1902-66 —& Clegg, Charles M.
— Legends of the Comstock Lode. Oakland, 1950. Sgd by both on front free endpaper. (91) $55

Beechey, Frederick William, 1796-1856
— An Account of a Visit to California... See: Grabhorn Printing
— Narrative of a Voyage to the Pacific and Beering's Strait.... L, 1831. 1st Ed. 2 vols. 4to. (89) £220; (91) £480, £700, £1,900
2d Ed. 2 vols. 8vo. (88) $160, $650
— A Voyage of Discovery towards the North Pole. L, 1843. 8vo. (90) £260, £300; (91) $375
— The Zoology of Captain Beechey's Voyage.... L, 1839. 1st Ed. 4to. Bradley Martin copy. (89) $9,000

Beechey, Frederick William, 1796-1856 & Henry William
— Proceedings of the Expedition to Explore the Northern Coast of Africa. L, 1828. 1st Ed. 4to. (88) £250; (90) £180; (91) £320, £340

Beeching, H. C.
— A Book of Christmas Verse. L, 1895. Illus by Walter Crane. 8vo. (88) $50
One of 15 on japan vellum. (90) $475
One of 50 L.p. copies. (90) $350

Beeckman, Daniel
— A Voyage to and from the Island of Borneo.... L, 1718. 1st Ed. 8vo. (88) £1,300

Beede, Aaron McGaffey
— Sitting Bull-Custer. Bismarck, [1913]. Inscr to H. P. Goddard. (89) $110

Beer, Johann Georg, 1803-73
— Beitraege zur Morphologie und Biologie der Familie der Orchideen. Vienna, 1863. Folio. (88) £130
— Lehre von den Augenkrankheiten. Vienna, 1813-17. 2 vols. 8vo. (88) £380

Beerbohm, Sir Max, 1872-1956
— Around Theaters. L, 1924. Vols 8 & 9 only. AN by Beerbohm; sgd by Reginald Turner in each vol. (91) £320
— A Book of Caricatures. L, 1907. Folio. (89) $60, £85; (90) £140
— Caricatures of Twenty-Five Gentlemen. L, 1896. 8vo. (90) £220; (91) £130
Inscr to Marcel Boulestin with self-caricature on front free endpaper & with ink drawing affixed to blank following contents leaf. Fleming copy. (89) $3,500
— Cartoons: "The Second Childhood of John Bull." L, [1911]. Folio. (88) £62; (89) £60, £70; (90) £150
— Catalogue of an Exhibition Entitled "Ghosts." L, 1928. One of 55. 4to. (89) $120
— Fifty Caricatures. L, 1913. 4to. (88) £55; (90) £55

BEERBOHM

— The Happy Hypocrite. L & NY, 1897. 1st Ed. 16mo. (90) £160
  With ALs to Stephen Tennant inserted & photo of Beerbohm taken at Villino Chiaro in Apr 1930, so inscr by Siegfried Sassoon. (88) £340
  One of 50. 4to. (89) $130
  L, [1915]. Illus by George Sheringham. 4to. (90) A$160
— Heroes and Heroines of Bitter Sweet. L, 1931. One of 100. Folio. (90) £220
  Plates only. Folio. (90) £260
  One of 900. Folio. (90) £130
— Leaves from the Garland. NY, 1926. One of 72. (89) $250; (90) $200, £120
— More. L & NY, 1899. 1st Ed. 12mo. (90) £120
— The Mote in the Middle Distance. Berkeley CA: Pvtly ptd, [1946]. One of 100. Illus by Lloyd Hoff. (90) £140
— Observations. L, 1925. 1st Ed. 4to. (90) $70, £55
  L, 1926. One of 280. 4to. (88) £65; (91) £170
— A Peep into the Past. [NY]: Privately printed, 1923. One of 300 on japan vellum. (89) $80; (90) $50, $60, £120
— The Poet's Corner. L, 1904. 1st Ed. Folio. (90) £160; (91) $450
— Rossetti and his Circle. L, 1922. (90) $50, $150, £90
  One of 350. (89) £100; (90) £85; (91) £140
— A Survey. L, 1921. 1st Ed, One of 275. 4to. (90) £80
— Things New and Old. L, 1923. 1st Ed, One of 380. 4to. (90) £90, £160; (91) $350
— Works. L, 1896. 8vo. Inscr to Ernest & Ada Leverson & with ACs to Ada Leverson. Fleming copy. (89) $3,800
  L, 1922-28. One of 780. 10 vols. (88) £500; (89) £500; (90) £480, £600, £750; (91) $140
  9 (of 10) vols. Sassoon copy, with watercolor drawing in Vol I by Sassoon, dated 23 June 1940, showing the spines of this set & holograph epigram. (91) £2,100
— Zuleika Dobson. L, 1911. 1st Ed, Issue not stated. (89) $60; (90) £120
  Oxford: Shakespeare Head Press, 1975. One of 750. Illus by Osbert Lancaster. 4to. (88) £80; (90) £130; (91) £60

Beerbohm's annotated copy, Max
— HUNT, VIOLET. - The Wife of Rossetti. Her Life and Death. L, 1932. 8vo. With 2 pencil-sketch ports by Beerbohm at end. (90) £160
— SHAKESPEARE, WILLIAM. - The Sonnets of William Shakespere. L, 1893. 8vo. Inscr by Edward Dowden (the editor) to Beerbohm & with last line of 4 sonnets altered in ink by Beerbohm. (90) £260

AMERICAN BOOK PRICES CURRENT

Beers, F. W.
— Atlas of Long Island, New York. NY, 1873. Folio. (91) $600
— State Atlas of New Jersey. NY, 1872. Folio. (88) $325; (89) $300, $350

Beers, Frederich W. —& Warner, G. E. —& Others
— Atlas of New York and Vicinity. NY, 1867. Folio. (89) $300; (91) $650, $750

Beeton, Isabella Mary
— The Book of Household Management. L, 1861. 1st Ed. 2 vols. 8vo. (88) £60; (89) £160; (90) $550; (91) £240
  L, 1864. Sixty-Fifth Thousand. 8vo. (91) £100
  L, [c.1869]. 8vo. (90) £65
  L, 1889. 8vo. (91) £85

Beever, John
— Practical Fly-Fishing. L, 1893. One of 56 on Dutch handmade paper. 8vo. (90) $180

Beeverell, James
— Les Delices de la Grand Bretagne et de l'Irlande. Leiden, 1707. 8 vols in 9. 8vo. (88) £500, DM1,000; (91) £420
  Leiden: van der Aa, 1727. 8 vols. 8vo. (91) £800

Begbie, Peter James
— The Malayan Peninsula.... [Madras]: Vepery Mission Press, 1834. 8vo. (90) £800

Beger, Laurentius
— Spicilegium antiquitatis. Brandenburg, 1692. Folio. (88) £50
  Kissner copy. (91) £250

Begey, Maria Bersano —& Dondi, Giuseppe
— Le cinquecentine Piemontesi. Turin, 1961-66. 3 vols. 4to. (88) £180

Beggrov, Karl Petrovich, 1799-1875
— Sobranie Vidov S.-Peterburga i Okrestnostei. [N.p., n.d.]. 8vo. (88) £6,000

Begin, Emile Auguste, 1802-88
— Voyage pittoresque en Suisse, en Savoie, et sur les Alpes. Paris, [1851]. Illus by Rouargue Freres. 8vo. (91) £270
— Voyage pittoresque en Espagne et en Portugal. Paris, [1852]. 8vo. (90) £360

Behari Day, Lal
— Folk-Tales of Bengal. L, 1912. Illus by Warwick Goble. (88) $120
  One of 150. (90) £150

Behn, Aphra, 1640-89
— La Montre, or the Lover's Watch. L, 1686. 1st Ed in English. 8vo. (89) $70
— Poems upon Several Occasions. L, 1684. 8vo. (88) £90

Behr, Johann von der
— Diarum oder Tage-Buch, ueber dasjenige so sich Zeit.... Jena & Breslau, 1668. 4to. (90) £120

Behrens, Carl Friedrich
— Histoire de l'expedition de trois vaisseaux envoyes aux Terres Australes.... The Hague, 1739. 2 vols. 8vo. (88) FF14,000

Beiier, Christoph
— Schau-Platz dess Niederlandes oder... Beschreibund der siebenzehen Provincien Desselben. Vienna, 1673. Folio. (88) HF2,400

Beit, Otto
— Catalogue of the Collection of Pictures and Bronzes. See: Bode, Wilhelm von

Beke, Charles Tilstone, 1800-74
— The Late Dr. Charles Beke's Discoveries of Sinai in Arabia and of Midian.... L, 1878. 8vo. Blackmer copy. (90) £130

Beketov, Platon Petrovich, 1761-1836
— Opisanie v litsakh torzhestva...v 1626...pri brakosochetanii gosudaria i velikago kniazia Mikhaila Feodorovicha. Moscow, 1810. 4to. (91) £1,000

Bekhterev, Vladimir Mikhailovich
— Psikhika i Zhizn'. St. Petersburg, [1902]. (90) £350

Belanger, Charles
— Voyage aux Indes-orientales...Zoologie. Paris, 1834. 2 vols in 1 & 7 orig parts. 4to. Martin copy. (90) $1,400

Belany, James Cockburn
— A Treatise upon Falconry. Berwick-upon-Tweed, 1841. 8vo. (88) £125

Belch, ——. See: Langley & Belch

Belcher, Charles Frederic
— The Birds of the District of Geelong, Australia. Geeling, [1914]. 8vo. (89) A$160

Belcher, Edward. See: Simpkinson & Belcher

Belcher, Sir Edward, 1799-1877
— The Last of the Arctic Voyages. L, 1855. 2 vols. 8vo. (88) £280; (90) £400, £480
  Martin copy. (90) $800
  Signet copy. (90) £450
  2 vols in 1. 8vo. Martin copy. (90) $800
— Narrative of a Voyage Round the World.... L, 1843. 1st Ed. 2 vols. 8vo. (88) £360; (89) $300, $550, £360; (90) £800; (91) $350, £260, £480
— Narrative of the Voyage of H.M.S. Samarang.... L, 1848. 1st Ed. 2 vols. 8vo. (89) £80, £800, £1,700; (90) $1,200

Belcher, John, d.1913 —& Macartney, Mervyn Edmund, 1853-1932
— Later Renaissance Architecture in England. L, 1901. 2 vols. Folio. (88) £40; (89) £100; (90) £95, £260; (91) $80

Belcher, Thomas
— The Art of Boxing, or Science of Manual Defence.... L: W. Mason, [c.1815]. 12mo. (88) £110

Belden, Frank A. See: Haven & Belden

Belet, Emilio
— La Vegetation sous Marine: Algues et Goemons. Paris, 1900. Folio. (88) $500

Belgique...
— La Belgique horticole, journal des jardins des serres et des vergers. Liege, [1850]-51-85. Ed by C. & E. Morren. 35 vols (complete set). 8vo. (89) £2,400

Belgium
— Jurisprudentia heroica sive de jure Belgarum circa nobilitatem et insitnia. Brussels: Balthazar Vivien, 1668. 2 parts in 1 vol. Folio. (88) £650
— Jurisprudentia heroica sive de jure Belgarum circa nobilitatem.... Brussels: Balthazar Vivien, 1668. 2 parts in 1 vol. Folio. (91) £105

Belidor, Bernard Forest de, 1693?-1761
— Architectura Hydraulica oder: Die Kunst, das Gewaesser.... Augsburg, 1740-50. Parts 1-12 bound in 2 vols. Folio. (88) DM800
— Architecture hydraulique.... Paris, 1737-53. 4 vols. 4to. (89) £1,600; (91) £900
  Augsburg, 1750-75. ("Architecture hydraulique, Seconde Partie.") 2 vols. 4to. (91) $1,200
  Paris, 1764-78. Vol I in 2 vols. Folio. (89) £100
— Le Bombardier francois. Paris, 1731. 4to. (89) £120
— La Science des ingenieurs.... Paris, 1729. 4to. (89) £420; (91) £300
  The Hague: Pierre Frederic Gosse, 1775. 4to. (88) $175

Belknap, Bill & Frances
— Gunnar Widforss: Painter of the Grand Canyon. Flagstaff, 1969. One of 100. 4to. (88) $180

Belknap, Jeremy, 1744-98
— American Biography.... Bost., 1794-98. 1st Ed. 2 vols. 8vo. (88) $200; (89) $100; (91) $80
Contains 3 signatures of William Plummer. (89) $90
— A Discourse Intended to Commemorate the Discovery of America by Christopher Columbus. Bost., 1792. 1st Ed. 8vo. (91) $140
— The Foresters, an American Tale.... Bost., 1792. 1st Ed. 12mo. Martin copy. (90) $300
Bost., 1796. 8vo. (89) $100
— The History of New-Hampshire. Phila., 1784 & Bost, 1791-92. 3 vols. 8vo. (88) $400

Belknap, Waldron P., Jr.
— American Colonial Painting. Cambr., Mass., 1959. 4to. (89) $60

Bell, Benjamin, 1749-1806
— A System of Surgery. Troy, 1804. 4 vols. 8vo. (89) $275
Benjamin Winslow Dudley's copy. (88) $100
— A Treatise on Gonorrhoea Virulenta, and Lues Venerea. Bost., 1797. 2d American Ed. 2 vols. 8vo. (89) $100

Bell, Sir Charles, 1774-1842
— Engravings of the Arteries.... Phila., 1816. 2d American Ed. 8vo. (88) $100
— Essays on the Anatomy and Philosophy of Expression. L, 1824. 4to. (88) $250
— The Hand.... L, 1833. 1st Ed. 8vo. (89) £70
3d Ed. L, 1834. 8vo. (91) $50
— Illustrations of the Great Operations of Surgery.... L, 1821. 1st Ed. Oblong folio. (89) $2,000; (91) £1,300
— A Series of Engravings, Explaining the Course of the Nerves.... Phila., 1818. 1st American Ed. 4to. (88) $175; (89) $150
— A System of Operative Surgery. L, 1807-9. 1st Ed. 2 vols. 8vo. (90) $650

Bell, Clive, 1881-1964
— Poems. L: Hogarth Press, 1921. 1st Ed. (88) $100; (91) $60

Bell, Currer, Ellis & Acton. See: Bronte, Charlotte, Emily & Anne

Bell, Ellis. See: Bronte, Emily

Bell, Eric Temple. See: Taine, John

Bell, Gertrude, 1868-1926
— The Arab War. See: Golden Cockerel Press

Bell, Horace, 1830-1918
— Reminiscences of a Ranger, or Early Times in Southern California. Los Angeles, 1881. 1st Ed. 8vo. (88) $110, $225; (89) $110; (90) $375; (91) $120, $275
Inscr by Adm. Phineas Banning to Capt. Charles E. Stanley. (88) $170

Bell, James
— A New and Comprehensive Gazetteer of England and Wales. Glasgow, 1836. 4 vols. 8vo. (91) £220
— A System of Geography. L, 1832. 6 vols. 8vo. (88) £85
L, 1844-45. 6 vols. 8vo. (88) £90
L, 1849. 6 vols. 8vo. (89) $130

Bell Collection, James F.
— Jesuit Relations and other Americana in [his] Library. Minneapolis, [1950]. 5 vols, including the 4 Vols of Additions. (91) $100

Bell, James G.
— A Log of the Texas-California Cattle Trail, 1854. [Austin], 1932. Ed by J. Evetts Haley. (89) $130

Bell, John, 1691-1780
— Travels from St. Petersburg in Russia to Diverse Parts of Asia. Glasgow: Foulis, 1763. 1st Ed. 2 vols. 4to. (88) £50, £400; (89) $450, £110; (91) £210, £420
Edin., 1788. 2 vols. 8vo. (89) A$160

Bell, John, 1745-1831
— Bell's British Theatre. L, 1780-81. Vols I-XXI. 21 vols. 8vo. ESTC 014786. (91) £220
L, 1792-97. 34 vols. 8vo. (88) £450

Bell, John, 1763-1820
— Engravings Explaining the Anatomy of the Bones, Muscles and Joints. Edin., 1794. 4to. (91) £320
— The Principles of Surgery as They Relate to Wounds.... L, 1815. 3 vols. 4to. (91) £600

Bell, John, d.1854
— The Wanderings of the Human Intellect.... Newcastle, 1814. 8vo. (91) $50

Bell, John & Charles
— The Anatomy and Physiology of the Human Body. NY, 1834. 2 vols. 8vo. (91) $75
— The Anatomy of the Human Body. NY, 1809 [i.e. 1809-10]. 4 vols in 2. 8vo. (89) $175

Bell, Malcolm
— Edward Burne-Jones, a Record and Review. L, 1892. One of 390. Folio. (88) £170; (90) $80; (91) $250

Bell, Solomon, Pseud. See: Snelling, William Joseph

Bell, Thomas, 1792-1880
— The Anatomy, Physiology, and Diseases of the Teeth. L, 1829. 1st Ed. 8vo. (91) £240 Phila., 1831. 8vo. (91) £100
— A History of British Reptiles. L, 1839. 8vo. (91) $80

Bell, Walter Dalrymple Maitland
— Karamojo Safari. L, 1949. (89) R450
— The Wanderings of an Elephant Hunter. L, 1923. 4to. (89) $110, R1,050; (91) $375 Sgd. (89) £260

Bell, William, 1779?-1859
— Hints to Emigrants; in a Series of Letters from Upper Canada. Edin., 1824. 12mo. (88) £300

Bell, William Abraham
— New Tracks in North America. L, 1869. 1st Ed. 2 vols. 8vo. (88) $110; (91) £240

Bellaire, J. P.
— Precis des operations generales de la division francaise du Levant. Paris, 1805. 8vo. Blackmer copy. (90) £280

Bellamy, Daniel
— Ethic Amusements. L, 1768. 1st Ed. 4to. (88) £100, £160, £360; (89) $150; (91) £260

Bellamy, Edward, 1850-98
— Equality. NY, 1897. 8vo. (91) $200
— Looking Backward.... Bost., 1888. 1st Ed, 1st Issue. 12mo. (89) $120; (91) $100 Martin copy. (90) $375; (91) $85
See also: Limited Editions Club

Bellange, Hippolyte
— Collection des types de tous les corps et des uniformes militaires de la Republique et d'Empir. Paris, 1844. 4to. (90) $350

Bellani, Luigi Vittorio Fossati
— I Libri di viaggio e le guide della raccolta. Rome, 1957. 3 vols. (88) $400

Bellarmino, Roberto Francesco Romolo, Cardinal, 1542-1621
— Disputationes de controversiis Christianae fidei.... Ingolstadt: D. Sartorius, 1596-97-93. 3 vols. Folio. (88) £65
— Dottrina Cristiana. Rome, 1786. 4to. In Italian, Ethiopic & Arabic. (89) £80
— Institutiones Linguae Hebraicae. Venice, 1606. 8vo. (89) $150

Bellasis, George Hutchins
— Views of St. Helena. L, 1815. Oblong folio. (88) £480; (91) £420

Belle Assemblee...
— La Belle Assemblee; or, Bell's Court and Fashionable Magazine. L, 1806-16. First Series, Vols I-VII in 4 vols; 2d Series, Vols I-X, XIII-XIV in 6 vols. 8vo. (88) £500
Vol I, Parts 1 & 2. L, 1806. 8vo. Extra-illus with 14 loose engravings. (88) £110
L, 1814-25. 22 vols in 11; lacking 1823. 8vo. (88) £920
Vols 1-10. L, 1825-29. 10 vols. 8vo. (91) £500
Vol 9. L, 1829. (88) £60

Belleforest, Francois de
— L'Innocence de la tres illustre, tres chaste et debonnaire princesse, madame Marie, Royne d'Escosse. Paris, 1572. 2 parts in 1 vol. 8vo. Kimbolton Castle copy. (91) £380

Belleisle, C. L. A. Fouquet, Comte de Marechal
— Lettres...a M. le Marechal Duc de Contades. [Paris, 1759?]. Bound with: Proceedings of the Committee Appointed to Manage the Contributions...for Cloathing French Prisoners of War. L, 1760. 8vo inlaid to folio & folio. Abbey-Martin copy. (90) $27,000

Bellew, Christopher D.
[-] A Catalogue of Books in the Library of Christopher D. Bellew.... [Galway, 1813]. One of 15. Folio. Martin copy. (90) $4,250

Bellew, Frank
— The Art of Amusinig. NY, 1868. 12mo. (90) $200

Bellew, Henry Walter, 1834-92
— Journal of a Political Mission in Afghanistan in 1857. L, 1862. 8vo. (90) $140

Belli, Lazaro Venanzio
— Dissertazione sopra il Preggi del Canto Gregoriano.... Frascati, 1788. 4to. (88) $600

Belli, Silvio
— Quattro libri geometrici.... Venice: R. Megietti, 1595. 4to. (91) £320

Bellin, Jacques Nicolas, 1703-72
— Description geographique des Isles Antilles possedees par les Anglois. Paris, 1758. 4to. (89) £1,500; (91) $1,400
— Description geographique de la Guyane.... Paris, 1763. 4to. (88) FF8,500
— Description geographique et historique de l'isle de Corse.... Paris: Didot, 1769. 4to. (91) £900
— Description geographique du Golfe de

BELLIN

Venise.... Paris, 1771. 1st Ed. 4to. (88) FF5,800; (91) £650
— Hydrographie francoise recueil des cartes marines. Paris, 1773. 2 vols. Folio. (88) £4,800
Vol II only. Folio. (91) £2,800
— Le Petit Atlas maritime. Paris, 1764. 5 vols. 4to. (88) £5,400; (91) £11,000
Vol IV (of 5) only. 2 parts in 1 vol. 4to. (89) £260

Bellingeri, Carlo Francesco
— Ragionamenti, Sperienze ed Osservazioni Patologiche.... Turin: Gaetano Balbino, 1833. 8vo. (88) $80

Bellingshausen, Capt. T.
— The Voyage of Captain Bellingshausen to the Antarctic Seas, 1819-1821. L: Hakluyt Society, 1945. 2 vols. (88) $275

Bellini, Lorenzo, 1643-1704
— De urinis et pulsibus, de missione sanguinis.... Leiden, 1730. 4to. (88) $250

Belloc, Hilaire, 1870-1953
— Belinda. L, 1928. One of 165. (91) £50
— The Highway and its Vehicles. L, 1926. (90) $50, £70
One of 1,250 numbered copies. 4to. (88) $110; (90) $65
— Verses and Sonnets. L, 1896. 1st Ed. 8vo. Bradley Martin copy. (90) $1,300
Inscr, including sketches of a pig and a rabbit. (90) £460

Bellori, Giovanni Pietro, 1636?-1700
See also: Dorigny & Bellori
— Le Pitture antiche delli grotte di Roma.... Rome, 1706. Folio. (88) $250; (91) £220
— Veteres arcus Augustorum triumphis insignes. Rome, 1690. Folio. (88) £170, £330; (89) £240; (90) $850, £180, £240, £380; (91) £700
Bound with: Bellori & Mantegna, Andrea. C. Iulii Caesaris dictatoris triumphi. Rome, 1692. And: Bellori & Caravaggio, P. Monocromata. Rome, [c.1680]. And: Bellori & Romano, Guilio. Sigismundi Augusti mantuam adventis profectio ac triumphus. Rome, 1680. Kissner copy. (91) £1,000
Bound with: Mantegna, Andrea. C. Iulii Caesaris dictatoris triumphi. Rome, 1692. And: Ghisi, Georgio. 6 double-page plates of the Sistine Chapel spandrels by Michaelangelo. Rome, [c.1690] (91) £1,100
— Veterum illustrium philosopharum, poetarum, rhetorum.... Rome, 1685. Folio. (91) £190
— Le Vite de pittori, scultori et architetti moderni.... Rome, 1672. 4to. (88) $150, £190; (91) £120

AMERICAN BOOK PRICES CURRENT

Rome, 1728. 4to. (90) £160, LIt800,000
Hamilton Palace—Kissner copy. (91) £600

Bellow, Saul
— Dangling Man. NY, 1944. 1st Ed. (91) $110
— Henderson the Rain King. NY, 1959. 1st Ed. (90) $65
— Humboldt's Gift. NY, [1975]. Advance Review Copy. With ANS, sgd with initials. (90) $150

Bellows, George Wesley
— His Lithographs. NY, 1927. 1st Ed. 4to. (90) $100; (91) $50, $110
Charcoal drawing of a beach scene mtd to frontis. (91) $425
NY & L, 1927. Compiled by Emma S. Bellows. Folio. (90) $90
— The Paintings. NY, 1929. Folio. (88) $250; (90) $100; (91) $375

Belloy, Pierre-Laurent Burette de
— Oeuvres. Paris, 1787. 6 vols. 8vo. Beraldi copy. (89) £2,800

Belnos, Mrs. S. C.
— Hindoo and European Manners in Bengal. [N.p., 1832]. Folio. (88) £1,000
— Twenty-Four Plates Illustrative of Hindoo and European Manners in Bengal. L & Paris, [c.1832]. Folio. (89) £380; (90) £700

Beloe, William, 1756-1817
— Anecdotes of Literature and Scarce Books. L, 1807. 6 vols. 8vo. (88) $90
L, 1807-11. Vols I-V (of 6). (90) $120

Belon du Mans, Pierre, 1517-64
— L'Histoire de la nature des oyseaux. Paris: G. Cavellat, 1555. Cavellat issue. Folio. (91) $3,500
Martin copy. (90) $3,750
Paris: Gilles Corrozet, 1555. Corrozet Issue. Folio. (88) FF66,000
— Les Observations de plusieurs singularitez et choses memorables, trouvees en Grece.... Paris, 1553. 3 vols in one. 4to. (90) £620
Paris: Guillaume Cavellat, 1554. 8vo. (91) £1,300
Hagley-Blackmer copy. (90) £4,000
Paris, 1555. 4to. (91) £1,100
Paris, 1588. 4to. (89) £1,350
— Plurimarum singularium & memorabilium rerum in Graecia, Asia, Aegypto.... Antwerp: Plantin, 1589. 8vo. Martin copy. (90) $1,100
— Portraits d'oyseaux, animaux, serpens, herbes, arbres.... Paris, 1557. 4to. (89) £2,000
Martin copy. (90) $5,500

Belperroud, John
— The Vine, with Instructions for its Cultivation.... Geelong, 1859. 8vo. (89) A$650

Beltrami, Giacomo Constantino, 1779-1855
— A Pilgrimage in Europe and America. L, 1828. 1st Ed in English. 2 vols. 8vo. (88) £140

Beltran de Santa Rosa, Pedro
— Arte de el Idioma Maya reducido a succintas Reglas y Semilexicon Yucateco. Mexico, 1746. 4to. (89) $150

Beltran, Francisco
— Biblioteca Bio-Bibliografica. Catalogo de una Importante Coleccion.... Madrid, 1927. One of 100. 4to. (91) $140

Belyi, Andrei —& Others
— Autografy. Moscow, 1921. 4to. (89) £300

Belzoni, Giovanni Battista, 1778-1823
— Narrative of the Operations and Recent Discoveries...Egypt and Nubia. L, 1820-21. 2 vols, including Atlas vol. 4to & folio. (89) £1,800
2d Ed of text, 1st Ed of Atlas. L, 1821-20. 2 vols. 4to & folio. (89) £1,300
— Plates Illustrative of the Researches and Operations in Egypt and Nubia.... L, 1820-22. 2 parts in 1 vol (including Supplement). Folio. (91) £1,900

Bembo, Pietro, 1470-1547
— Gli Asolani. Venice: Aldus, 1505. 4to. (88) £1,400
Issue with dedication to Lucrezia Borgia. 8vo. (91) £3,500
Florence: Giunta, 14 July 1505. 8vo. (88) £100; (90) $1,800
Hall-Stevenson-Abrams copy. (90) £2,800
Venice: Aldus, 1515. 8vo. (90) LIt1,300,000
Venice: Sabbio, 1530. 4to. With Ms material about Bembo bound in at end. (91) £850
— De Aetna. Venice: Aldus, Feb 1495-96. 4to. 30 leaves. Goff B-304. Spencer-Rylands copy. (88) £42,000
Verona: Bodoni, 1969. One of 125. (91) $700
Verona: Officina Bodoni, 1970. One of 125 with text in Latin & German. 8vo. (88) DM520
— Historiae Venetae libri XII. Venice: Aldus, 1551. 1st Ed. Folio. (90) £350; (91) £1,400 Doheny copy. (89) $2,500 Gosford copy. (89) $1,600
— Prose.... Venice: G. Tacuino, 1525. 1st Ed. Folio. (91) LIt1,100,000
— Le Prose. Florence: Lorenzo Torrentino, 1548 [1549]. 12mo. (90) £160

Venice: Andrea Arrivabene, 1557. 12mo. (91) £620
— Rime. Rome: Valerio Dorico et Luigi Fratelli, Oct 1548. 4to. (88) £60

Bemelmans, Ludwig
— The Donkey Inside. NY, 1941. One of 175. (91) $200
— Hotel Splendide. NY, 1941. Inscr. (91) $50
One of 305. (91) $110
— Madeline and the Bad Hat. NY: Viking, [1956]. One of 985. 4to. (91) $160
— Now I Lay Me Down to Sleep. NY, 1943. One of 400. (91) $50
— Small Beer. NY, 1939. One of 175. (91) $225

Bemis, George, 1816-78
— Report of the Case of John W. Webster...Indicted for the Murder of George Parkman. Bost., 1850. 8vo. (88) $100

Bemmel, Abraham van
— Beschryving der Stad Amersfoort. Utrecht, 1760. 2 vols. 8vo. (89) HF2,400

Ben Yehuda, Eliezer
— A Complete Dictionary of Ancient and Modern Hebrew. NY, 1960. 8 vols. 4to. (89) $425; (90) $300

Benavides, Alonso de
— The Memorial of Fray Alonso de Benavides, 1630. Chicago: Pvtly ptd, 1916. One of 300. 8vo. (88) $190

Bendavid, Lazarus
— Beytrage zur Kritik des Geschmacks. Vienna, 1797. 16mo. (89) p$300

Bendire, Charles Emil, 1836-97
— Life Histories of North American Birds. Wash., 1892-95. 2 vols. 4to. (91) $80

Benedetta, Mary
— The Street Markets of London. L, 1936. Illus by L. Moholy-Nagy. (89) HF1,100

Benedetti, Alessandro. See: Alexander Benedictus

Benedetti, Giovanni Battista
— De gnomonum umbrarumque, solarium usu liber. Turin: heirs of Nicolas Bevilaqua, 1574. Folio. (89) £500

Benedict, Carl Peters
— A Tenderfoot Kid on Gyp Water. Austin, 1943. One of 550. Intro by J. Frank Dobie. (89) $190

Benedict, F. G. —& Joslin, E. P.
— Metabolism in Diabetes Mellitus. Wash., 1910. 8vo. (90) $110

Benedict XIV, Pope, 1675-1758
— Bullarium. Venice, 1788. 4 vols. Folio. (88) $70

Benedictiones...
— Benedictiones et gratiarum actiones mensae romani breviarii.... Vienna: Leonhard Nassinger, 1585. 2 parts in 1 vol. 8vo. Ptd on vellum. (91) £3,000

Benedictus
— Nouvelles Variations. Paris, [1928]. Folio. (91) £630

Benegasi y Lujan, Jose Joaquin
— Vida del portentoso negro, san Benito de Palermo. Madrid: Juan de san Martin, 1750. 4to. (88) £200

Benesch, Otto
— The Drawings of Rembrandt. L, 1954-57. 6 vols. 4to. (89) £280, £330
L, 1973. 6 vols. 4to. (88) £220; (89) £240; (91) $550, LIt800,000

Benet, Stephen Vincent, 1898-1943
— Five Men and Pompey. Bost., 1915. 1st Trade Ed, 1st Issue. Inscr to the author's brother, William Rose Benet. Martin copy. (90) $1,000
— John Brown's Body. Garden City, 1928. One of 201 L.p. copies. (88) $60, $120 Sgd. Martin copy. (90) $950
— John Brown's Body: a Poem. See: Limited Editions Club
— Johnny Pye and the Fool-Killer. Weston, Vt., [1938]. One of 750. Illus by Charles Child. (88) $55

Benetti, Antonio
— Viaggi a Constantinopoli di Gio: Battista Donado.... Venice: Andrea Poletti, 1688. Parts 1 & 2 only, in 1 vol. 12mo. Blackmer copy. (90) £350

Benevolent...
— The Benevolent Old Man of the Rock. Bost., [1812]. 16mo. (88) $50

Benezet, Anthony, 1713-84
— Some Historical Account of Guinea.... L, 1772. 8vo. (91) $225

Benezit, Emmanuel, 1854-1920
— Dictionnaire critique.... Paris, 1948-55. 8 vols. (88) $120; (89) £110, £170; (90) £120; (91) $300, £120, £130, £160
Paris, [1954]-59. 8 vols. (89) $250
Paris, 1959-62. 8 vols. (88) £170; (91) £200
Paris, 1960. 8 vols. (88) $200; (89) $250, £160; (91) $150, $325
Paris, 1966. 8 vols. (88) £140, £150, £230; (89) £120, £200; (90) $350, £200; (91) $225, $300, $350, £150, £180, £220
Paris, 1976. 10 vols. (88) $300, £200; (91) $325

Benford, Gregory
— In the Ocean of Night. NY: Dial Press, [1977]. (89) $55

Benguiat Collection, Ephraim. See: Smithsonian Institution

Benham, Daniel
— Sketch of the Life of Jan Ausust Miertsching.... L, 1854. 4to. (88) £480

Benham, Sir William Gurney
— Playing Cards. History of the Pack.... L & Melbourne, 1931. (90) $200; (91) $60

Benivieni, Hieronymo
— Opere. [Venice: Nicolo Zopino e Vicentio comp., 12 Apr 1522]. 8vo. (89) £110

Benjamin, Asher, 1773-1845
— The Practical House Carpenter.... Bost., 1832. 4to. (89) $100

Benjamin ben Jonah, of Tudela
— Itinerarium.... Leiden, 1633. 8vo. (91) £1,400

Benjamin, Israel Joseph
— Acht Jahre in Asien und Afrika. Hannover, 1858. 8vo. (89) $175

Benjamin, Israel Joseph, 1818-64
— Drei Jahre in Amerika.... Hanover, 1862. 3 vols in 1. 8vo. (88) $750

Benjamin, Samuel Green Wheeler, 1837-1914
— A Group of Etchers. NY: Dodd, Mead, [1882]. Folio. (90) $425
— Persia and the Persians. Bost., 1887. 8vo. (90) £80

Benlowes, Edward
— Theophila, or Loves Sacrifice. L, 1652. 1st Ed. Folio. Chew-Kern-Bradley Martin-Hayward-Bradley Martin copy. (90) $11,000

Bennet, Edward
— Shots and Snapshots in British East Africa. L, 1914. (90) $100

Bennett, Agnes Maria, d.1808
— The Beggar Girl. L, 1797. 7 vols. 12mo. (88) £450
— Juvenile Indiscretions. A Novel. Dublin, 1786. 2 vols. 12mo. (91) £260

Bennett, Arnold, 1867-1931
— Elsie and the Child. L: Curwen Press, 1929. One of 100. 4to. (88) £220; (90) £95; (91) £300
  One of 750. (90) A$100
— Journal 1919. L, [1930]. Out-of-series copy. (88) $80
— Lord Raingo. L, [1926]. With ALs. (88) $800
— The Old Wives' Tale.... L, 1908. 1st Ed. Inscr to Grahame & Doris Johnstone. Parsons-Fleming copy. (89) $550
  With card sgd by Bennett. (91) $80
  See also: Limited Editions Club
— Venus Rising from the Sea. L, 1931. One of 350. Illus by E. McKnight Kauffer. 4to. (88) $130; (89) £110; (91) £90, £130, £160

Bennett, Estelline
— Old Deadwood Days. NY, [1928]. Inscr. (88) $55

Bennett, Frank Marion
— The Steam Navy...of the...United States. Pittsburgh: Warren, 1896. (91) $130

Bennett, Frederick Debell
— Narrative of a Whaling Voyage Round the Globe. L, 1840. 2 vols. 8vo. Martin copy. (90) $1,900

Bennett, George, 1804-93
— Gatherings of a Naturalist in Australasia.... L, 1860. 8vo. (88) £65, £120, A$500; (89) A$130, A$380
  Martin copy. (90) $500
— Wanderings in New South Wales.... L, 1834. 2 vols. 8vo. (88) £150; (89) A$130; (91) $200
  Martin copy. (90) $500

Bennett, Ira E.
— History of the Panama Canal.... Wash., 1915. (88) £35
  8vo. (88) $110

Bennett, John Whitchurch
— Fishes. L, 1834. ("A Selection from the most Remarkable...Fishes Found on the Coast of Ceylon....") 2d Ed. 4to. (88) £2,600
  L, 1851. ("A Selection of Rare and Curious Fishes.") 4to. (89) £300
— ("A Selection of Rare and Curious Fishes Found upon the Coast of Ceylon.") (89) £400

Bennett, Melba Berry
— Robinson Jeffers and the Sea. San Francisco, 1936. One of 300. (88) $55; (90) $50; (91) $85

Bennett, Richard, 1844-1900 —& Elton, John
— History of Corn Milling. L & Liverpool, 1898-1904. 4 vols. 8vo. (89) £150

Bennett, Robert
— The Wrath of John Steinbeck or St. John Goes to Church. Los Angeles, 1939. (91) $60

Bennett, Whitman
— A Practical Guide to American Book Collecting. NY, [1941]. One of 100, specially bound in half mor gilt. Inscr to Arthur Swann. (91) $150
— A Practical Guide to American Nineteenth Century Color Plate Books. NY, 1949. (88) $70; (90) $65; (91) $60, $80

Benoist, Felix
— La Normandie illustree. Nantes, 1854-52. 2 vols. Folio. (88) $950, FF5,200, FF6,200
  Nantes, 1864. 3 vols. Folio. (88) FF5,000

Benoist, Philippe & Felix
— Rome dans sa grandeur. Paris, 1870. 3 vols. Folio. (88) FF6,800, FF7,500, FF8,500

Benoit, Elias
— Historie der gereformeerde kerken van Frankryk.... Amst., 1696. Illus by Jan Luyken, with ports by A. Bogaert. 4 parts in 2 vols. Folio. (90) $1,000

Benoit, Pierre Andre, 1886-1962
— L'Atlantide. Paris, 1922. One of 17 on japon imperial with orig pencil drawing & 4 states of the etchings. Illus by Almery Lobel-Riche. 4to. (90) $1,400
  Lyon, 1934. One of 120. 4to. Martin copy. (90) $300

Bensa, Alexander von
— Horses and Coaches in Vienna. Vienna: A. Paterno & A. Berka, 1835. Oblong 4to. Schiff copy. (91) $4,250

Benson, Arthur Christopher, 1862-1925
— The Book of the Queen's Dolls' House. [The Book of the Queen's Dolls' House Library]. L, 1924. One of 1,500. 2 vols. 4to. (88) $80; (89) $80; (90) $250; (91) $90
  Compton Mackenzie's set. (91) $120
  Helena Rubinstein's copy. (90) $150
  Label on front blank records that these vols survived the bombing of the University of London Library, 16 Nov 1940. (89) £140

Walcott-Soliday copy. (91) $325

Benson, Frank Weston
— Etchings and Drypoints.... Bost., 1917. One of 275 with orig sgd etching as frontis. Compiled by Adam E. M. Paff. Folio. (91) $4,600
Bost., 1923. One of 525. Vol III (of 4) only. 4to. (91) $380
Bost., 1929. One of 650. Vol IV (of 4) only. 4to. (88) $400; (91) $300, $350

Bensusan, Samuel Levy. See: Forrest & Bensusan

Bent, Arthur Cleveland
— Life Histories of North American Birds. Wash., 1919-68. 21 vols in 23. (91) $50

Bentham, Edward
— De Tumultibus Americanis. Oxford, 1776. 8vo. (91) $225

Bentham, George, 1800-84 —&
Mueller, Ferdinand, 1825-96
— Flora Australiensis.... L, 1863-78. 7 vols. 8vo. (88) A$1,400; (91) £220

Bentham, James, 1707-76
— The History and Antiquities of the Conventual and Cathedral Church of Ely. Cambr., 1771. 4to. (90) £75
2d Ed. Norwich, 1812. One of 275. 2 vols in 1. 4to. (91) £50

Bentham, Jeremy, 1748-1832
— The Book of Fallacies: From Unfinished Papers.... L, 1824. 8vo. (88) £400; (90) $150, $300
— Codification Proposal...to all Nations Professing Liberal Opinions. L: Robert Heward, 1830. 8vo. (88) £280; (90) £240
— Draught of a New Plan for the Organisation of the Judicial Establishment in France. L, 1790. 8vo. (88) £200
— A Fragment on Government.... L, 1776. 8vo. (89) £900; (91) £1,200
L, 1823. 8vo. (90) £120
— An Introduction to the Principles of Morals and Legislation. L, 1823. 4to. (88) £280; (90) £50
— Justice and Codification Petitions.... L: Robert Heward, 1829. 8vo. Inscr. (90) $900
— Observations on Mr. Secretary Peel's House of Commons Speech...Introducing his Police-Magistrates' Salary Raising Bill.... L, 1825. 8vo. (88) £150
— Official Aptitude Maximized; Expense Minimized: As Shewn in the Several Papers Comprised in this Volume.... L, 1830. 11 parts in 1 vol. 8vo. (88) £750
— Panopticon, or the Inspection-House. L,

1791. Paper fault in 1st leaf of preface. Bound with: Bentham. Panopticon Postscript: Part I/II. L, 1791. 3 vols in 2. 12mo. (88) £680
— The Rational of Reward. L, 1825. 8vo. (88) £420
— Rationale of Judicial Evidence, Specially Applied to English Practice.... L, 1827. Ed by John Stuart Mill. 5 vols. 8vo. George Bentham's copy with his ownership signature. (91) £1,200
— Scotch Reform. L 1807. 8vo. Tp inscr "From the Author". (88) £600
L, 1811. 8vo. Sgd on tp & with holograph notes, some on a bound-in leaf dated 26 May 1818. (91) £580
— Supply without Burthen, or Escheat vice Taxation.... L, 1795. 1 vol bound in its 2 parts. 8vo. (88) £700
— A Table of the Springs of Action. L, 1815. 8vo. Tp inscr "From the Author". (88) £450
— A View of the Hard-Labour Bill. L, 1778. 8vo. (88) £850

Bentivoglio, Guido, Cardinal, 1579-1644
— Della Guerra di Fiandra. Cologne [i.e., Italy?], 1632. Part 1. 4to. (90) $90
— Histoire des guerres de Flandre.... Paris, 1769. 4 vols. 12mo. (89) £3,200
— The History of the Wars of Flanders.... L, 1654. Folio. (88) £220
L, 1678. Folio. (89) £150

Bentley, Edmund Clerihew, 1875-1956
— Trent's Last Case. L, [1913]. (91) $1,400

Bentley, Harry C. —&
Leonard, Ruth S.
— Bibliography of Works on Accounting by American Authors.... Bost., 1934-35. 2 vols. (88) $100; (89) $80

Bentley, Henry
— A Correct Account of all the Cricket Matches from 1786 to 1822 inclusive Played by the Mary-le-bone Club. L, 1823. 8vo. (89) £260, £280

Bentley, Richard, 1662-1742
— Remarks upon a late Discourse of Free-Thinking: in a Letter to N. N. by Phileleutherus Lipsiensis. L: for W. Thurlbourn at Cambr., 1737. 8vo. (90) $200

Bentley, Robert —&
Trimen, Henry
— Medicinal Plants. L, 1880. 4 vols. 8vo. (89) £1,300

Benton, Joseph Augustine, 1818-92
— The California Pilgrim.... Sacramento, 1853. 1st Ed. 8vo. (90) $55
Inscr by the author's wife. (89) $65

Benton, Thomas Hart, 1782-1858
— Discourse...on the Physical Geography of the Country between the States of Missouri and California.... Wash., 1854. 8vo. (88) $70
— Thirty Years' View or a History of the Working of the American Government.... NY & L, 1854-56. 2 vols. With ALs of Benton & cut signature mtd in Vol I. (89) $110

Bentz, Johann
— Thesauri latinitatis purae compendium alterum. Strassburg: heirs of B. H. Jobin, 1596. 8vo. (91) £900

Benyowsky, Mauritius Augustus, Count de
— The Memoirs and Travels.... L, 1790. 2 vols. 4to. (89) £380

Benzoni, Girolamo, b.1519
— De gedenkwaardige West-Indise Voyagien.... Leiden: PIeter van der Aa, 1704. 2 parts in 1 vol. 4to. (91) $500
— Novae novi orbis historiae.... [Geneva]: Vignon, 1578. 8vo. (89) $1,000

Beowulf
— Beowulf. NY, 1932. One of 950. Illus by Rockwell Kent; trans by W. E. Leonard. Folio. (88) $80, $80, $110, $175; (89) $70, $200; (91) $120
Sgd by Rockwell Kent. (91) $130

Beraldi, Henri
See also: Portalis & Beraldi
— Estampes et livres 1872-1892. Paris, 1892. One of 390. 4to. (89) $800
L.p. copy. (90) £440; (91) £580
— Les Graveurs du XIXe Siecle.... Paris, 1885-92. 12 vols. 8vo. (91) $600
Nogent-le-Roi, [1981]. One of 400. 12 vols in 10. (89) $425
— La Reliure du XIXe siecle. Paris, 1894-97. One of 295. 4 vols. 4to. (91) $3,500

Beraldus, Nicolaus
— Sideralis abyssus. Paris: Thomas Kees for H. Fabri, 1514.. Bound with: Martinus Blasius, Joannes. Ars arithmetica.... Paris, 1514. 4to. (88) £800

Beranger, Pierre Jean de, 1780-1857
— Chansons morales ete autres.... Paris, 1816. 18mo. Martin copy. (90) FF1,800
— Oeuvres. Paris, 1847-60. 8 vols. 8vo. (88) $175

Berard, Auguste Simon Louis
— Essai bibliographique sur les editions des Elzevirs.... Paris, 1822. 8vo. (91) $200

Berchoux, Joseph
— La Gastronomie, Poeme.... Paris, 1805. 4th Ed. 12mo. (88) $95

Berdmore, Thomas, 1740-85
— A Treatise on the Disorders and Deformities of the Teeth and Gums.... L, 1770. 8vo. (91) £850

Beregszaszi Nagy, Pal, 1750-1828
— Dissertatio philologica de vocabulorum derivatione ac formatione in lingua Magyarica. Pest: Joannes Thomas Trattner, 1815. 8vo. (88) $140

Berengario da Carpi, Giacomo
— Carpi commentaria cum amplissimis additionibus super anatomia mundini.... Bologna: Hieronymus de Benedictis, 1521. 4to. (89) $28,000

Berenger, Charles Random de. See: Random de Berenger, Charles

Berenger, Richard, d.1782
— The History and Art of Horsemanship. L, 1771. 2 parts in 1 vol. 4to. (91) $350
4to. (90) $350

Berenson, Bernard, 1865-1959
— The Drawings of the Florentine Painters. Chicago, 1938. 3 vols. 4to. (88) $225, £80; (90) $300; (91) $325, £140
Chicago, [1970]. 3 vols. (89) $250; (90) £90; (91) £120
— Italian Pictures of the Renaissance. L, 1957-68. 7 vols. 4to. (88) £300, £950; (89) £800
— Italian Pictures of the Renaissance....Venetian School. NY, [1957]. 2 vols. 4to. (90) $100

Beresford, Capt. George de la Poer
— Twelve Sketches in Double-Tinted Lithography of Scenes in Southern Albania. L, 1855. Folio. (91) £1,700
Blackmer copy. (90) £1,000

Beresford, James, 1764-1810
— The Miseries of Human Life. L, 1806. 8vo. (90) $175
8th Ed. L, 1807. 2 vols. 8vo. (88) $95; (89) £45

Berettini, Pietro. See: Berrettini, Pietro

Berg, Albert, 1825-84
— Die Insel Rhodus. Braunschweig, 1862. 2 parts in 1 vol. 4to. King of Hanover's copy with library stamp of Ernst August II on tp verso. Blackmer copy. (90) £1,000

Berg, Johan August
— Bilder ur Svenska Folklivet. Gothenberg, 1855. Oblong folio. (88) £120; (89) £130; (91) £350

Bergamo, Jacobus Philippus de. See: Jacobus Philippus de Bergamo

Bergamo, Stefano da
— Gli Ornati del coro della Chiesa di S. Pietro. Rome, 1845. Folio. (89) $400

Berganus, Georgius Jodocus
— Benacus. Verona: A. Putelleto, 1546. 1st Ed. 4to. (89) $70

Berge, Friedrich
— Die Fortpflanzung europaischer und aussereuropaischer Vogel. Stuttgart: L. F. Rieger, 1840-41. 2 vols in 1. 16mo. Martin copy. (90) $800

Berge, Friedrich —& Riecke, Viktor Adolf
— Giftpflanzen-Buch. Stuttgart, 1850. 2d Ed. 4to. (91) DM550

Berger, Christoph Heinrich von
— Commentatio de personis, vulgo larvis seu mascheris. Frankfurt & Leipzig: G. M. Knock, [1723]. 4to. (89) £130; (91) £130 Kissner copy. (91) £350

Berger, Thomas
— Little Big Man. NY, 1964. Inscr. (91) $110

Bergeret, Jean Pierre
— Phytonomatotechnie universelle. Paris, 1783-84. 3 vols in 2. Folio. (91) £6,000

Bergeron, L. E. See: Hamelin-Bergeron, P.
— Manuel du tourneur, ou l'art d'apprendre a tourner seul. See: Hamelin-Bergeron, P.

Bergeron, Pierre de, d.1637
— Voyages faits principalement en Asie dans les XII, XIII, XIV, et XV siecles. The Hague: Jean Neaulme, 1735. 11 parts in 2 vols bound in 1 vol. 4to. (88) FF7,000; (91) £430

Berggruen, Oscar
— Cortege historique de la Ville de Vienne, le 27 Avril 1879. Paris: Quantin, [1879]. One of 550. Folio. (90) $90

Bergier, Nicolas
— Histoire des grands chemins de l'Empire Romain. Paris: C. Morel, 1622. 2 vols. 4to. William III's copy. (90) £3,800 Brussels, 1728. 2 vols. 4to. Kissner copy. (91) £1,000
2 vols in 1. 4to. (90) £220

Bergman, Ray
— Fresh-water Bass. NY, [1942]. One of 149. (88) $250; (89) $275
— Trout. Phila., 1938. Inscr by Edgar Burk to Joseph Bates & with 8 orig color drawings of trout flies by Burk on half-title. Laid in is extra suite of color plates inscr to Bates by Angus Cameron. (90) $750 One of 149. (88) $850; (90) $1,300; (91) $700
— With Fly, Plug, and Bait. NY, 1947. One of 249. (88) $225; (90) $200, $225; (91) $70

Bergman, Sir Torbern Olof, 1735-84
— A Dissertation on Elective Attractions.... L, 1785. 8vo. (88) $80

Bergosa y Jordan, Antonio, Bishop of Oaxaca
[A collection of 33 pastoral letters, edicts & proclamations, 1813-15, bound in 1 vol sold at S on 28 June 1991, lot 424] £2,000

Bergstraesser, J. A. B.
— Ueber Signal-,Order und Zielschreiberei in die Ferne.... Frankfurt, 1795. 8vo. (90) $225

Bergstrom, Richard. See: Liljefors & Bergstrom

Berhaut, Marie
— Caillebotte, sa vie et son oeuvre. Paris, 1978. Folio. (90) £1,100

Berington, Joseph
— The History of the Reign of Henry the Second.... Birm., 1790. 4to. (90) $50

Beristain y Souza, Jose Mariano, 1756-1817
— Biblioteca Hispano Americana Septentrional. Mexico City, [1947]. 5 vols in 2. (89) $90

Berkeley, George, 1685-1753
— Alciphron: or, The Minute Philosopher. L, 1732. 1st Ed. 2 vols. 8vo. (90) £190; (91) £115
Whibley-Ivins-Fleming copy. (89) $480
— A Miscellany, Containing Several Tracts on Various Subjects. L, 1752. 8vo. (88) $200; (89) £550
— Philosophical Reflexions.... L, 1744. 8vo. (88) $50
— A Proposal for the Better Supplying of Churches in our Foreign Plantations.... L, 1725. 8vo. (89) $225

- The Querist.... Dublin, 1735-37. 3 parts in 1 vol. 8vo. (91) £3,200
- Siris: A Chain of Philosophical Reflexions and Inquiries.... Dublin, 1744. 1st Ed. 8vo. (90) £230 Inscr "From the Author" apparently in Berkeley's hand. Strachey-Fleming copy. (89) $900
- A Treatise Concerning the Principles of Human Knowledge. Dublin, 1710. 8vo. ESTC 77986. (91) £3,800

Berkhey, J. le Franq van
- Naturlyke Historie van Holland. Amst., 1769-79. Vols I-IV, Part 1, in 7 vols. (89) HF825

Berkowitz, David Sandler
- In Remembrance of Creation. Evolution of Art and Scholarship in the Medieval and Renaissance Bible. Waltham, Mass., [1968]. 4to. (89) $100; (91) $75

Berlese, Laurent, 1784-1863
- Iconographie du genre Camellia. Paris: Cousin, [1839]-41-43. 3 vols. Folio. Doheny copy. (89) $30,000 Vols I & III (of 3). (91) £10,500
- Monographie du genre Camellia. Paris, 1840. 2d Ed. 8vo. Doheny copy. (89) $420

Berlin
- Katalog der Ornamentstichsammlung der Staatlichen Kunstbibliotek Berlin. NY, [1958]. 2 vols. 4to. Reprint of 1939 Ed. (89) $225

Berliner, Abraham Adolf
- Aus meiner Bibliothek. Beitrage zur hebraeischen Bibliographie.... Frankfurt, 1898. 4to. (90) $130

Berliner, Isaac
- La Ciudad de los Palacios: Poemas. Mexico, 1936. Illus by Diego Rivera. 4to. Inscr by Berliner. (89) $600 Inscr to Ben-Zion Goldberg; inscr by Berliner. (91) $450

Berliner, Rudolf
- Ornamentale Vorlage-Blatter des 15. bis 18. Jahrhunderts. Leipzig, 1925-26. 3 vols, including 2 cloth folders of plates. Folio. (91) £110

Berling, Karl
- Festive Publication to Commemorate the 200th Jubilee of the Oldest European China Factory: Meissen. [Dresden], 1910. Folio. (90) $60
- Das Meissner Porzellan und seine Geschichte. Leipzig, 1900. Folio. (88) £220; (89) $325

Berlioz, Hector
- Memoires.... Paris, [1870]. 8vo. Martin copy. (90) FF5,200
- Voyage musical en Allemagne et en Italie. Paris, 1844. 2 vols. 8vo. Martin copy. (90) FF3,800, FF5,500

Berlu, John Jacob
- The Treasury of Drugs unlock'd.... L: J. Harris & T. Howkins, 1690. 12mo. (88) £420

Berluchon, Laurence
- Jardins de Touraine. Tours: Arrault, [1940]. Ltd Ed. Inscr. (91) $70

Berlyn, Annie
- Sunrise-Land; Rambles in Eastern England. L, 1894. 1st Ed, Issue not indicated. 8vo. (88) $140

Bernard, Saint (Bernardus Claravallensis), 1091-1153
- De consideratione. [Augsburg: Anton Sorg, c.1475-77]. 3 parts in 1 vol. Folio. 45 leaves. Goff B-368. (91) $3,800
- Epistola de gubernatione re familiaris. [Rome: Georgius Lauer, c.1470]. 4to. 4 leaves. Goff B-376. (90) $1,000
- Flores. Venice: Giunta, 31 Aug 1503. 8vo. (91) LIt900,000
- Meditationes. [Paris: Louis Martineau & Antoine Caillaut, 1484-85]. 8vo. 16 leaves. GKW 4027. (89) £2,600
- Meditationes de interiori homine. Paris: George Mittelhus, 1493. 4to. 32 leaves. Goff B-406. (88) $600
- Modus bene vivendi. Venice: Bernardinus Benalius, 30 May 1494. 8vo. 106 leaves. Goff B-414. (90) DM4,200
- Opus preclarum suos complectens sermones.... Paris: Jehan Petit, 4 July 1517. 2 parts in 1 vol. Folio. (88) £800
- Opuscula. Brescia: Angelus & Jacobus Britannicus, 18 Mar 1495. 8vo. 344 (of 348) leaves. Goff B-364. Sold w.a.f. (90) £280
 Speier: Petrus Drach, 1501. 8vo. (88) £120
 Venice: Giunta, 1503. 8vo. (90) $225
- Sermones super Cantica canticorum. Rostock: Fratres domus horti viridis ad S. Michaelem, 28 July 1481. Bound with: Homeliarius doctorum. Basel: Nicolaus Kesler, 30 Sept 1493. Folio. 208 leaves, Goff B-427; 247 (of 248) leaves, Goff H-317. The Garden copy. (90) $7,500
 Strassburg: Martin Flach, 1497. Folio. 200 (of 202) leaves; lacking both blanks. Goff B-430. (91) $2,800

BERNARD

Bernard, —
— Nouvelle Maniere de fortifier les places.... Amst., 1689. 12mo. (90) $450

Bernard, Auguste Joseph
— Geofroy Tory: Painter and Engraver.... Bost. & NY, 1909. One of 370. Folio. (88) $200; (90) $250; (91) $225
Doheny copy. (88) $250

Bernard, Claude, 1813-78
— Lecons sur la physiologie et la pathologie du systeme nerveux. Paris, 1858. 1st Ed. 2 vols. 8vo. (88) $750
— Lecons sur les effets des substances toxiques.... Paris, 1857. 1st Ed. 8vo. (88) $200
— Lecons sur les proprietes physiologiques et les alterations pathologiques liquides de l'organisme. Paris, 1859. 2 vols. 8vo. (88) $275
— Lecons sur le diabete et la glycogenese animale. Paris, 1877. 1st Ed. 8vo. (90) $425
— Memoire sur le pancreas.... Paris, 1856. 1st Ed. 4to. (88) $650
In: Academie des Sciences, Paris. Supplement aux Comptes Rendus Hebdomadaires des Seances...Tome Premier. (88) $350
— Nouvelle Recherches experimentales sur les phenomenes glycogeniques du foie. Paris, 1858. 8vo. (88) $175

Bernard, Claude, 1813-78 —& Huette, Charles
— Illustrated Manual of Operative Surgery.... NY, 1855. 8vo. (88) $200
— Precis iconographique de medecine operatoire et d'anatomie chirurgicale. Paris, 1853. 8vo. (88) £220

Bernard de Morlaix
— The Rhythm. See: Hopkins's copy, Gerard Manley

Bernard, Edward
— De mensuris et ponderibus antiquis. Oxford, 1688. 8vo. (88) £90

Bernard, Sir Francis —& Others
— Letters to the Ministry from Governor Bernard, General Gage, and Commodore Hood.... Bost.: Edes & Gill, 1769. 1st Ed. 8vo. (91) $275

Bernard, Jean Frederic
— The Praise of Hell, or a Discovery of the Infernal World.... L: A. Manson, etc., [c.1775]. 12mo. (91) $50

Bernard, John, d.1554
— The Tranquillitie of the Minde. L, 1570. 8vo. (88) $425

Bernard, Pierre —& Others
— Le Jardin des plantes. Paris, 1842-43. 2 vols. 4to. (88) £150; (91) $525
2 vols in 3. 4to. Martin copy. (90) $300
Vol II only. (91) £75

Bernard, Pierre Joseph
— Oeuvres. Paris: Didot, 1797. One of 150. Illus by Pierre Paul Prud'hon. 4to. (89) $550

Bernard, Richard, 1567?-1641
— Ruths Recompence; or, a Commentaire upon the Booke of Ruth. L, 1628. 4to. STC 1962. (91) $175

Bernard, Tristan, 1866-1947
— 60 Annees de Lyricisme intermittent. [Paris, 1945]. Out-of-series copy. Illus by Lucien Boucher. Extra-illus with 5 ink sketches for the illusts. (90) $175

Bernard, William Dallas. See: Hall & Bernard

Bernardin de Saint-Pierre. See: Saint-Pierre, Bernardin de

Bernardinus Senensis
— De contractibus et usuris. [Strassburg: ptr of Henricus Ariminensis, not after 1474]. Folio. 170 leaves. Goff B-345. (88) £2,400

Bernardus Parmensis
— Casus longi super quinque libros decretalium. Bologna: Henricus de Harlem & Johannes Walbeck, 29 Nov 1487. Folio. 203 (of 204) leaves; lacking initial blank. Goff B-462. (91) $4,500

Bernath, Desire de
— Cleopatra. L, 1907. (91) $3,200
L, 1908. 8vo. (90) $450
Boyle-Springs copy. (89) $17,000

Bernatz, Johann Martin
See also: Schubert & Bernatz
— Scenes in Aethiopia. Munich & L, 1851-52. 2 vols in 1. Oblong folio. (91) £1,700
L, 1852. 2 vols in 1. Oblong folio. (89) £620

Bernays, Charles Arrowsmith
— Queensland Politics during Sixty Years. Brisbane, [1919]. (88) A$30, A$35, A$50

Berners, Dame Juliana, b.1388?
— Book of St. Albans. L: for Humfrey Lownes, 1595. ("The Gentlemans Academie. Or, the Book of S. Albans....") 4to. (89) £850
— [Book of St. Albans] The Book Containing

the Treatises of Hawking, Hunting.... L, 1810 [1811]. One of 150. 4to. (88) £110
— Book of St. Albans. L, 1810 [1811]. ("The Book Containing the Treatises of Hawking, Hunting....") One of 150. 4to. (88) £360
L, 1881. 4to. Facsimile of 1486 Ed. (88) $110
L: Elliot, Stock, 1905. ("The Boke of Saint Albans....") 4to. Facsimile of the 1486 Ed. With ALs of Pierre Amedee Pichot about hawking in Turkestan, Bokhara & Khiva. (88) $130
Facsimile of the 1486 Ed. (88) £42; (90) $60
— A Treatyse of Fysshynge wyth an Angle.... L, 1827. 16mo. (91) $75
NY, 1875. 8vo. (90) $90
L, [1880]. 4to. (88) $80; (90) $100; (91) $50, £70
Roosevelt-Fleming copy. (89) $1,000
L, 1883. ("An Older Form of the Treatyse of Fysshynge wyth an Angle.") One of 200. 4to. With ALs from Th. Satchell to Dean Sage. (90) $190
NY, 1903. One of 150 on handmade paper. Doheny copy. (88) $900
NY: Gillis Press, 1903. One of 106. (90) $90; (91) $225
See also: Ashendene Press

Bernhard, Karl, Duke of Saxe-Weimar-Eisenach
— Travels through North America.... Phila., 1828. 2 vols in 1. 8vo. (91) $300

Bernhardt, Sarah
— Dans les nuages: Impressions d'une chaise. Paris, [1878]. 4to. (88) HF500

Bernheim, Hippolyte
— Neue Studien ueber Hypnotismus, Suggestion und Psychotherapie. Leipzig & Vienna, 1892. Trans by Sigmund Freud. 8vo. (91) £140

Bernier, Francois, 1620-88
— Voyages de Francois Bernier contenant le description des etats du Grand Mogol, de l'Hindoustan.... Amst., 1699. 2 vols. 12mo. (89) £150; (90) $250

Bernini, Domenico
— Vita del Cavalier Gio. Lorenzo Bernino. Florence, 1682. 4to. (90) £50

Bernis, Francois Joachim de Pierres de, Cardinal, 1715-94
— Oeuvres. Paris, 1797. One of 250. 8vo. (89) $90

Berno, Abbot of Reichenau
— Libellus de offico Missae. Paris: H. Estienne, 1510s. 4to. (88) $230

Bernoulli, Jacques, 1654-1705
— Ars conjectandi.... Basel, 1713. 1st Ed. 4to. (90) £2,000
— The Doctrine of Permutations and Combinations.... L, 1795. 8vo. (88) $200

Bernoulli, Jean, 1667-1748
See also: Leibnitz & Bernoulli
— Opera. Lausanne & Geneva, 1742. 4 vols. 4to. (91) LIt1,400,000

Bernt, Walther
— The Netherlandish Painters of the Seventeenth Century. NY, 1970. Trans by P. S. Falls. 3 vols. 4to. (91) £190

Beroalde de Verville, Francois, 1556-c.1612
— Le Moyen de parvenir. [Probably Holland, 17th cent]. 2 vols. 16mo. (88) $110

Beroaldus, Philippus, 1453-1505
— De felicitate. Bologna: Franciscus (Plato) de Benedictis, 1 Apr 1495. 4to. 36 leaves. Goff B-482. (90) £1,100
36 leaves. Goff B-482. Broxbourne-Abrams copy. (90) £3,200
— Declamatio philosophi Medici oratoris.... Bologna: Benedictus Hectoris, 13 Dec 1497. 38 leaves. Goff B-473. Bound with 3 other works by Beroaldus: Goff B-487, B-489 & the 24 Dec 1503 Symbola Pythagorae. All were ptd by Hecrotis in Bologna. 4to. Heber-Martin-Manhattan College copy. (91) $5,000
— Opera. [Bologna]: Benedictus Hectoris, 1497-1521. 4to. (90) DM3,600

Berosus
— Berosi sacerdotis Chaldaici Antiquitatum Italiae.... Antwerp: J. Steelsii, 1552. 8vo. (90) £130
— De his quae praecesserunt inundatione terrarum. [Paris: A. E. & G. de Marnef, 1510]. 4to. Kissner copy. (91) £350

Berquen, Robert de
— Les Merveilles des Indes orientales et occidentales.... Paris, 1669. 4to. (91) £1,200

Berquin, Arnaud, 1749?-91
— L'Ami des Enfans. L: M. Elmsley, 1783. 12 vols in 6. 12mo. (91) $150
Paris, 1803. Bound in 4 vols. 12mo. (89) $150
— The Children's Friend. L, 1793. 6 vols. 12mo. (88) £70
— The Family Book, or Children's Journal. Detroit: Theophilus Mettez, 1813. 2 vols.

BERQUIN

8vo. Martin copy. (90) $1,000
— Idylles. Paris, 1775. 16mo. (88) £160
  2 vols. 16mo. (89) $150
— The Looking-Glass for the Mind.... L: E. Newbery, 1787. 1st Ed. 12mo. (89) $50
— Sir John Denham and his Worthy Tenant. New Haven: Sidney's Press, 1817. 32mo. (88) $130

Berquin, Arnaud, 1749?-91 —& Others
— The Friend of Youth.... L, 1788. Ed by Mark Anthony Meilan. 12 vols in 4. 12mo. (88) £180
  12 vols in 6. 12mo. (90) £100

Berquin-Duvallon, ——
— Travels in Louisiana and the Floridas.... NY, 1806. 12mo. (91) $1,200

Berr de Turique, Marcelle
— Raoul Dufy. Paris, 1930. 4to. (88) FF2,200; (91) $500

Berrettini, Pietro, 1596-1669
— Tabulae anatomicae.... Rome, 1741. Folio. (88) DM6,000; (89) £2,200, £2,800

Berrigan, Daniel
— Encounters. NY, 1965. One of 60. Folio. (90) $220

Berry, Harrison
— Slavery and Abolitionism, as Viewed by a Georgia Slave. Atlanta, 1861. 8vo. (91) $1,100

Berry, Wendell
— November Twenty Six Nineteen Hundred Sixty Three. NY, [1964]. Ltd Ed. Illus by Ben Shahn. (88) $60; (90) $55, $60; (91) $80

Berry, William, 1774-1851
— The History of the Island of Guernsey. L, 1815. 4to. (88) $75, $175, £95; (89) £300; (91) £300, £360

Berryman, John
— The Dispossessed. NY, [1948]. (89) $80
— His Thought Made Pockets & the Plane Buckt. Pawlet VT: Claude Fredericks, 1958. One of 526. 4to. (89) $80
— Homage to Mistress Bradstreet. NY, [1956]. Illus by Ben Shahn. 4to. (89) $90
— Love & Fame. NY, 1970. One of 250. (88) $160; (89) $80

Bert, Edmund
— An Approved Treatise of Hawkes and Hawking. L: T. Snodham for Richard Moore, 1619. 4to. Martin copy. (90) $9,000

AMERICAN BOOK PRICES CURRENT

Bertall. See: Arnoux, Charles Albert d'

Bertarelli, Achille. See: Caproni & Bertarelli

Bertaut, Leonard, d.1662
— L'Illustre Orbandale ou l'histoire ancienne et moderne de la ville et cite de Chalon-sur-Saone. Chalon: Pierre Cusset, 1662. 2 vols. 4to. (88) FF6,000

Bertelli, Donato
— Civitatum aliquot insigniorum, et lororum, magis munitorum exacta delineatio. Venice: Donato Bertelli, 1574. Oblong folio. Blackmer copy. (90) £6,000

Bertelli, Pietro
— Theatrum urbium Italicarum. Venice, 1599. Oblong 4to. Kissner copy. (91) £3,800
— Vite degl'imperatori de Turchi.... Venice: Giorgio Greco for Pietro Bertelli, 1599. Folio. Blackmer copy. (90) £1,700

Berthelot, Sabin
See also: Webb & Berthelot
— Antiquites canariennes ou annotations sur l'origine des peuples qui occuperent les Isles Fortunees. Paris, 1879. 4to. (89) $70, $75

Berthier, Alexandre, 1753-1815
— Relation de la Bataille de Marengo.... Paris, 1806. 4to. (90) £1,400

Berthod, Le Sieur
— La Ville de Paris en vers burlesques. Paris, 1655. 4to. (88) £150

Berthold, Arnold A. See: Bunsen & Berthold

Berthold, H.
— Schriftgiessereien und Messinglinien-Fabriken Aktien Gesellschaft. Berlin, [1924]. 4to. (89) $225; (90) $150

Bertholdus
— Horologium devotionis. [Basel: Johann Amerbach, not after 1490]. 8vo. 66 leaves. Goff B-506. (89) $5,000

Berthoud, Ferdinand, 1727-1807
— L'Art de conduire et de regler les pendules. Paris, 1759. 1st Ed. 12mo. (88) £150
— Eclaircissemens sur l'invention, la theorie, la construction...des nouvelles machines proposees en France pour la determination des longitudes en mer. Paris, 1773. 1st Ed. 4to. (89) $110
— Essai sur l'horlogerie.... Paris, 1763. 1st Ed. 2 vols. 4to. (89) £450; (90) $1,900; (91) £850
  2d Ed. Paris, 1786. 2 vols. 4to. (88) $750

Berti, Alessandro Pompeo
— Catalogo della libreria Capponi. See: Capponi Library, Alessandro Gregorio

Bertin, Joseph
— The Noble Game of Chess. L, 1735. 8vo. (89) £380

Bertin, Rene Joseph Hyacinthe
— Oeuvres. Paris, 1824. 8vo. (89) FF7,000

Bertini, A.
— Costumi di Roma e dei contorni. Rome, 1846. 8vo. (89) £280

Bertius, Petrus, 1565-1629
— Tabularum geographicarum contractarum libri septem.... Amst: apud Cornelium Nicolai, 1603. 5 parts in 1 vol. Oblong 8vo. (90) £4,500
Amst., 1606. 5 parts in 1 vol. Oblong 8vo. (90) £3,000
Amst.: Hondius, 1618. 7 parts in 1 vol. Oblong 8vo. (90) £4,800
— Theatri geographiae veteris. Amst.: J. Hondius, 1618-19. 2 vols in 1. Folio. (89) £3,600

Bertoldo...
— Bertoldo, con Bertoldino e Cacasenno in ottava rima.... Bologna, 1736. Illus by J. M. Crespi under the name of Lodovico Mattioli. 4to. (89) $475; (91) LIt3,600,000

Bertrand, Alfred
— Au Pays des Ba-Rotsi Haut-Zambeze.... Paris, 1898. 4to. (88) £150
Inscr. (91) £130

Bertrand, Aloysius, 1807-41
— Dix contes de Gaspard de la Nuit. Paris, 1962. One of 140. Illus by Marcel Gromaire. 4to. (90) £480
— Gaspard de la nuit. Paris, 1842. 8vo. Martin copy. (90) FF30,000
Utrecht, 1956. One of 125. Illus by M. T. Koornstra. 2 vols. 4to. (88) £50

Bertuch, Friedrich Johann Justin, 1747-1822
— Bilderbuch fuer Kinder. Weimar & Gotha, 1790-1830. Parts of Vols II & III in 1 vol. (88) DM900
Weimar & Gotha, 1790. Vol VI only. (88) DM950
Weimar, 1792-1810. Vols I-VII in 4 vols. 4to. (88) DM3,200
Weimar, 1798-1830. 12 vols. 4to. (90) DM15,000
2d Ed of Vol I. Vols 1-12. 4to. (91) £800
3d Ed of Vol I. Weimar, 1798-1821. Vols 1-8 (of 12). 4to. (90) £3,600
Later Ed of Vol I. 25 vols text & 12 plate vols. 4to & 8vo. (91) £3,200

— Bilderbuch fuer Kinder...Thieren, Pflanzen, Blumen.... Weimar, 1803-13. Vol II. (88) DM1,100
Vol V. 4to. (88) DM1,200

Berwick, James Fitz-James, Duke of
— Memoirs of the Duke of Berwick written by himself.... L, 1779. 2 vols. 8vo. ESTC 096937. (91) £80

Besant, Walter, 1836-1901.—& Others
— Survey of London. L, 1902-12. 10 vols. 4to. (90) £140
L, 1903-25. 10 vols. 4to. (88) £140

Beseke, Johann Melchior Gottlieb, 1746-1802
— Beytrag zur Naturgeschichte der Voegel Kurlands. Mitau, [1792]. 1st Ed. 8vo. Inscr to M. Rottiers. Martin copy. (90) $800

Besler, Basilius, 1561-1629
— Hortus Eystettensis sive diligens et accurata omnium plantarum.... Ingolstadt, 1713. 3d Ed. 4to. (88) £150,000
Bound in 3 vols. 4to. (88) £60,000
Nuremberg & Eichstaett, 1713-50. 2 vols bound in 4. Folio. (91) £60,000
2 vols. Folio. (90) DM190,000; (91) DM240,000

Besler, Michael Rupertus
— Rariora Musei Besleriani. See: Lochner, Johannes Henricus

Besley, Henry
— Besley's Views in Cornwall. L, [c.1865]. 8vo. (91) £170

Besly, Jean
— Histoire des comtes de Poictou et ducs de Guyenne. Paris, 1647. Folio. (88) FF4,500

Besnard, Albert
— Elle. Paris, 1921. One of 25. Folio. (88) SF15,000

Besoldus, Christophorus, 1577-1638
— Historia Constantinopolitana.... Strassburg, 1634. 12mo. Blackmer copy. (90) £750

Bessarion, Joannes, d.1472
— In calumniatorem Platonis.... Venice: Aldus, July 1503. Folio. Spencer-Rylands copy. (88) £9,500

Besse, Joseph
— A Collection of the Sufferings of the People called Quakers.... L, 1753. 2 vols. Folio. (90) $110

Bessel, Friedrich Wilhelm, 1784-1846
— Fundamenta astronomiae pro anno 1755.... Koenigsberg, 1818. Folio. (88) £320

Besson, Jacques
— Teatro de los instrumentos y figuras matematicas y mechanicas.... Leon de Francia [Cologne?]: H. Cardon, 1602. Folio. (91) $3,000
— Theatre des instrumens mathematiques & mechaniques.... Lyon: Barthelemy Vincent, 1578. Folio. (88) £2,200; (90) £2,000
— Theatrum instrumentorum et machinarum.... Lyons: Barth. Vincentium, 1578. Folio. (89) £750
Mortimer 58. (90) $4,200
Lyons: Barth. Vincentium, 1582. Folio. (91) £420
— Theatrum oder Schawbuch allerley Werckzeug und Ruestungen. Montbeliard: Jacob Foillet, 1595. Folio. (91) £2,800

Best, C. H. See: Banting & Best

Best, Elsdon, b.1856
— The Maori. Wellington, 1924. 2 vols. (91) £52

Best, Thomas
— A Concise Treatise on the Art of Angling.... L, 1787. 1st Ed. 12mo. (91) $800

Bester, Alfred
— The Demolished Man. Chicago: Shasta, [1953]. 1st Ed. (89) $200

Besterman, Theodore
— The Beginnings of Systematic Bibliography.... L, [1936]. 4to. (91) $140
— Library Catalogue of the Society for Psychical Research. Glasgow, 1927. (91) $100
— Old Art Books.... L, 1975. One of 300. Folio. (88) $110; (89) £65; (91) £60
— A World Bibliography of Bibliographies. L, 1947-49. 2d Ed. 3 vols. 4to. (90) £65
3d Ed. Geneva, [1955-56]. 4 vols. (89) $60; (90) $130
4th Ed. Lausanne, [1966]. 4 vols. (88) $160
5 vols. (88) $200

Bestiaries. See: Destructiorum...

Betagh, William
— A Voyage Round the World. L, 1728. 8vo. (91) $2,000

Bethel, Slingsby, 1617-97
— The Interest of Princes and States. L, 1680. 1st Ed. 8vo. (88) £85
— The World's Mistake in Oliver Cromwell.... L, 1668. 4to. (88) £200; (91) £125

Bethencourt y Molina, Augustin de. See: Lanz & Bethencourt y Molina

Betjeman, Sir John
— Collected Poems. L, 1958. One of 100. (91) £100, £110
— Continual Dew. L, 1937. 1st Ed. (91) £150
— Ghastly Good Taste. L, 1933. 1st Ed. (89) £75
Ls inserted. (91) £75
— Mount Zion, or, In Touch with the Infinite. L: James Press, [1931]. 1st Ed. (88) £90; (91) £200
— An Oxford University Chest. L, 1938. 1st Ed. (89) £85; (91) £120
— Sir John Piers. Mullingar: Westmeath Examiner, [1938]. One of 140. With the autograph Ms setting copy & ANs. Bradley Martin copy. (90) $2,250
— Some Immortal Hours: A Rhapsody of the Celtic Twilight Wrought in Word and Water Color by Deirdre O'Betjeman. L, 1962. One of 12. Folio. Inscr. Bradley Martin copy. (90) $1,700
— Summoned by Bells. L, 1960. With 14 letters from John Betjeman & John Masefield. This copy used by Betjeman for his Argo recording of the work. (91) £130
One of 125. (91) £170

Betten, Henry Lewis
— Upland Game Shooting. Phila., [1940]. One of 124. 8vo. Sgd. (91) $325
Out-of-series copy. Inscr to William K. Harriman. (90) $250

Bettinus, Marius
— Aerarium philosophiae mathematicae.... Bologna, 1648. 3 vols. 4to. (88) £4,000

Bettoni, Eugenio
— Storia naturale degli uccelli che nidificano in Lombardia.... Milan, 1865-[71]. 3 vols, including Atlas. Folio. (88) FF95,000
One of 100. 2 vols. Folio. Bradley Martin copy. (89) $11,000

Betts, Douglas A.
— Chess: An Annotated Bibliography of Works.... Bost., 1974. (88) £190

Beuter, Pedro Antonio
— Cronica generale d'Hispagna, et del Regno di Valenza. Venice: Gabriel Giolito de Ferrari, 1556. 8vo. (88) $225

Beuvius, Adam. See: Wieland, Christoph Martin

Bevan, Edward
— The Honey-Bee; Its Natural History, Physiology and Management. See: Hunt, Leigh

Beveridge, Albert J., 1862-1927
— Abraham Lincoln. Bost., 1928. One of 1,000. With author's signature mtd on front endpaper & with a leaf of orig Ms inlaid. (89) $225
4 vols. (91) $80
— The Life of John Marshall. Bost. & NY, 1916-19. Ltd Ed. 4 vols. (89) $240
Bost. & NY, 1919. 4 vols. Sgd. (89) $200

Beveridge, Erskine
— North Uist.... Edin., 1911. One of 315. 4to. Inscr. (88) £55

Beverley, Robert, c.1673-c.1722
— Histoire de la Virginie... Paris, 1707. 12mo. (88) FF9,500; (89) $110; (91) $90
Amst., 1712. 8vo. (91) £200
— The History of Virginia. L, 1705. ("The History and Present State of Virginia.") 4 parts in 1 vol. 8vo. (88) $5,000; (89) $1,000; (91) $1,100, $1,400, $1,500
L, 1722. 8vo. Phillipps copy. (91) £380

Beverwijk, Johan van, 1594-1647
— Alle de Wercken, zo in de Medicyne als Chirurgie. Amst., 1656. 4to. (89) HFl,600; (90) $425

Bevis, John, 1693-1771
— Atlas Celeste. [c.1750]. Oblong folio. (88) £2,800
— Uranographia Britannica. L, 1750. Oblong folio. (91) £14,000

Bewick, Thomas, 1753-1828
[-] Bewick Gleanings.... Newcastle, 1886. 2 parts in 1 vol. 4to. (89) £130; (91) £280
L.p. copy. (88) £140
— Emblems of Mortality. L, 1789. 12mo. (89) $260
— The Figures of Bewick's Quadrupeds. Newcastle, 1824. 2d Ed. 4to. (91) £240
— Figures of British Land Birds.... Newcastle, 1800. Vol I (all pbd). 8vo. (88) £200; (89) £150, £150
Newcastle, 1825. ("British Land Birds. British Water Birds.") 2 vols. 4to. (88) £260 One of 100 L.p. copies. Inscr by Bewick's daughters. Martin copy. (90) $3,000
— A General History of Quadrupeds. Newcastle, 1790. 8vo. (88) £160; (89) HF750; (90) £240; (91) $300
2d Ed. Newcastle, 1791. 8vo. (89) £170
3d Ed. Newcastle, 1792. 8vo. (91) £55, £80
4th Ed. Newcastle, 1800. 8vo. (88) £50, £65; (90) £170, £50
Ms index inserted at beginning. (89) £50
5th Ed. Newcastle, 1807. 8vo. (88) £50, £50, £160; (89) £85

L.p. copy. (88) £150; (91) £65
8th Ed. Newcastle, 1824. 8vo. (88) £50
— A History of British Birds. Newcastle, 1797-1804. 1st Ed. 2 vols. 8vo. (88) $700; (89) $175
Martin copy. (90) $700
Roscoe 14c. Doheny copy. (89) $850
With: Supplement Part 1. Newcastle, 1821. Together, 3 vols. 8vo. (89) £320
2d Ed of Vol I, 1st Ed (variant F) of Vol II. 2 vols. 8vo. (88) £85
3d Ed of Vol I; 1st Ed variant B of Vol II. Newcastle, 1804-5. 2 vols. 8vo. (89) £70
3d Ed of Vol I, 2d Ed of Vol II. Newcastle, 1805. 2 vols. 8vo. (88) £50, £90, £200
Newcastle, 1809. 2 vols. 8vo. (89) £50
2 vols in 1. 8vo. (90) £75
Newcastle, 1809-22. 2 vols in 1 plus Supplement & Addenda bound in 1 vol. 8vo. Roscoe 20, 25/27c & 28. (88) £80
4th Ed of vol I, 3d Ed of Vol II. Newcastle, 1809. 2 vols in 1. 8vo. (88) £60, £110
5th Ed variant B of Vol I, 1st Ed of Vol II, each vol with accompanying 2d Ed supplement bound in at end. Newcastle 1814-16-4-22. 2 vols. 8vo. Roscoe 21, 17c, 29-30b. (88) £75
Newcastle, 1816. 2 vols. 8vo. (88) £50; (91) £85
Newcastle, 1821. 2 vols. 8vo. (91) £300
7th Ed of Vol I, 5th Ed of Vol II, each with accompanying 1st Ed supplement, Vol II also with the Addenda. Newcastle, 1821-[22]. 2 vols. 8vo. Roscoe 24-25c, 26-27c & 28. (88) £55
Newcastle, 1821. 2 vols. 8vo. Roscoe 24-25a & 26-27a. (88) £180
Newcastle, 1826. 2 vols. 8vo. (89) £110; (91) £70
8th Ed of Vol I, 6th Ed of Vol II. 2 vols. 8vo. Roscoe 31b variant a & 32b. (88) £50
Newcastle, 1832. 2 vols. 8vo. (89) £45, £85; (90) £100; (91) $325
Newcastle, 1847. 2 vols. 8vo. (90) £130, £100; (91) £65
— A Memoir of Thomas Bewick. Newcastle & L, 1862. 8vo. (88) £50; (90) $55
— A Natural History of British Quadrupeds * Foreign Quadrupeds * British Birds * Water Birds * Foreign Birds * Fishes * Reptiles * Serpents & Insects. Alnwick, 1809. Fishes, Reptiles, Serpents & Insects only. 2 vols in one. 12mo. (90) $50
— A New Lottery Book of Birds and Beasts. Newcastle, 1771. 32mo. (90) $1,800
— Select Fables. Newcastle, 1820. 8vo. (88) $175
7th Ed. 4to. (88) £50; (90) £75
Edin.: Pvtly ptd, 1879. One of 100. 4to. (90) £160
— A Supplement to the History of British

BEWICK

Birds Newcastle, 1821. 2 parts in 1 vol. Imperial 8vo. Roscoe 27a. (88) £95
2d Ed. Newcastle, 1821 [1822]. 2 parts in 1 vol. Demy 8vo. Roscoe 29-30c. (88) £65
— Vignettes. Newcastle, 1827. Roscoe 47. 4to. (88) £200
Roscoe 48. 8vo. (88) £520
— The Watercolors and Drawings of.... Cambr. MA: MIT Press, [1981]. 2 vols. Oblong 8vo. (88) $110; (90) $50; (91) $50, $65
One of 13 with 6 engravings ptd from orig woodblocks. (88) £520
L, [1981]. 2 vols. Oblong 8vo. (88) £400
— Works. Newcastle, 1885-87. Memorial Ed. One of 750. 5 vols. 8vo. (88) £220; (89) £190; (91) £170
Out-of-series copy. (89) £170

Beyaert, Henri
— Travaux d'architecture executes en Belgique. Brussels: E. Lyon-Claesen, [c.1892]. 2 vols. Folio. (89) £150

Beyard, Nicholas
— A Journal of the Late Actions of the French at Canada. See: Bayard & Lodowick

Beyer, Adolph
— Otia metallica oder Bergmaennische Reben-Stunden.... Schneeberg, 1748-58. 3 vols. 8vo. (88) DM1,000

Beyer, Edward
— Album of Virginia. [Richmond: Beyer], 1858. Oblong folio. Martin copy. (90) $12,000

Beyle, Marie Henri ("Stendhal") 1783-1842
— L'Abesse de Castro. Paris, 1839. 8vo. Martin copy. (90) FF14,000

— Armance.... Paris, 1827. 1st Ed. 3 vols. 12mo. Martin copy. (90) FF170,000
— Le Couvent de Balano. Paris, 1829. 8vo. Martin copy. (90) FF1,800
— De l'amour. Paris, 1822. 1st Ed. 2 vols in 1. 12mo. (91) FF8,000
Martin copy. (90) FF26,000
— Histoire de la peinture en Italie. Paris, 1817. 1st Ed. 2 vols. 8vo. (89) £65, FF4,000; (91) $200
2 vols in 1. 8vo. Martin copy. (90) FF10,000
— Journal d'Italie.... Paris, [1911]. One of 26 on hollande. 12mo. Martin copy. (90) FF1,600
— Lettres ecrites de Vienne en Autriche, sur le celebre compositeur Joseph Haydn.... Paris, 1814. 1st Ed. 8vo. Martin copy. (90) FF9,500

— Memoires d'un touriste. Paris, 1838. 1st Ed. 2 vols. 8vo. (88) FF16,000
Martin copy. (90) FF15,000
— Promenades dans Rome. Paris, 1829. 1st Ed. 2 vols. 8vo. Martin copy. (90) FF3,600, FF11,000
— Racine et Shakespeare. * Raciine ete Shakespeare No II.... Paris, 1823-[25]. 2 vols. 8vo. Martin copy. (90) FF24,000
— Racine et Shakespeare No. II, ou reponse au manifeste contre le romantisme. Paris, 1825. 1st Ed. 8vo. Martin copy. (90) FF9,000
— Rome, Naples et Florence, en 1817. Paris, 1817. 1st Ed. 8vo. Martin copy. (90) FF4,200
— Le Rouge et le noir.... Paris, 1831. 1st Ed. 2 vols. 8vo. (88) FF180,000
Martin copy. (90) FF160,000
Paris, 1927. One of 1,000. Illus by Daniel-Girard. 2 vols. (89) $140
— Vie de Rossini. Paris, 1824. 1st Ed. 2 vols. 8vo. Martin copy. (90) FF4,000
— Vies de Haydn, de Mozart et de Metastase. Paris, 1817. 8vo. Martin copy. (90) FF7,000

Beze, Theodore de, 1519-1605
— Confessione della fede christiana. See: Mary, Queen of Scots, her copy
— Icones.... [Geneva]: Jean de Laon, 1580. 1st Ed. 4to. (91) $1,000

Bhagvat-Geeta
— The Bhagvat-Geeta, or Dialogues of Kreeshna and Arjoon.... L, 1785. Trans by Charles Wilkins. 4to. (89) £150
The Garden copy. (90) $1,800

Bianchi, Giovanni Paolo Simone
— De conchis minus notis liber. Venice: Joannis Baptistae Pasquali, 1739. 4to. (89) $150
Rome, 1760. 4to. (88) £200

Bianchini, Andrea
— Prove Legale sull'Avvelenamento della Celebre Pittrice Bolognese Elisabetta Sirani. Bologna, 1854. 8vo. (88) £55

Bianchini, Francesco, 1662-1729
— Camera ed Inscrizioni Sepulcrali de' Liberti, servi, et Ufficiali della Casa di Augusto.... Rome, 1727. Folio. (88) £170; (90) £130; (91) £80
Kissner copy. (91) £120
— De tribus generibus instrumentorum musicae veterum organicae dissertatio. Rome, 1742. 4to. (88) $200

1987 - 1991 • BOOKS

— Del Palazzo de Cesari. Verona, 1738. 1st Ed. Folio. (90) £420
Kissner copy. (91) £800
— La Istoria universale, provata con monumenti.... Rome, 1697. 4to. Dedication copy. Kissner copy. (91) £2,200
Kissner copy. (91) £100

Bianchini, Giuseppe Maria
— Dei Gran Duchi di Toscana della Real Casa de' Medici.... Venice, 1741. Folio. (88) £190
L.p. copy. (90) £700

Bianco, Margery Williams, 1881-1944
— Poor Cecco. L, 1925. Illus by Arthur Rackham. 4to. (88) $60, £110
NY, 1925. One of 105. 4to. (89) $2,750

Bianco, Pamela
— Flora. With Illustrative Poems by Walter de la Mare. L: Heinemann, [1919]. 4to. (91) $50
Inscr & with related material inserted. (90) £60

Bianconi, Giovanni Ludovico, 1717-81
— Descrizione dei circhi particolarmente di quello di Caracalla. Rome, 1789. Folio. (88) £180
Kissner copy. (91) £280, £350

Bibaud, Michel, 1782-1857
— Epitres, satires, chansons, epigrammes, et autres pieces de vers. Montreal, 1830. 12mo. (88) $175

Bibelot...
— The Bibelot: A Reprint of Poetry and Prose for Book-Lovers. Portland, Maine, 1895-1915. Ed by Thomas B. Mosher. 21 vols, including Index, 1925. 16mo. (88) $50, $80; (91) $60

Bible in Anglo Saxon
— 1698. - [Old Testament]. Oxford. Bound with: Henshall, Samuel. The First Number of the Etymological Organic Reasoner.... 64, 4, 72, 79 pp. London, 1807. 8vo. D & M 1606. (88) $475; (90) £460

Bible in Arabic
— 1727. - [New Testament]. L: Society for the Promotion of Christian Knowledge. 4to. D & M 1655. Doheny copy. (89) $300

— [Four Gospels]. Lebanon: Monastery of Shuwair, 1776. 1st Ed for Melchite use. Folio. D & M 1661. (89) £900
— [Gospels]. Rome: Typographia Medicea, 1590 [colophon dated 1591]. Folio. (89) $2,800; (90) £2,800; (91) £1,300
— Kitab al-injil al sharif. Shuweir, [1776?].

BIBLE IN DUTCH

Folio. (91) $1,000
[N.p., c.1861]. Folio. (91) $750

Bible in Arabic & Latin
— 1774. - [Four Gospels]. Florence. Folio. (88) £400

— Sacrosancta quatuor Iesu Christi D. N. Evangelia Arabice Scripta.... Rome: ex typographia Medicea, 1619 [1591]. Folio. D & M 1643. (88) £300

Bible in Bohemian
— 1579-1601. - Biblj Ceske. Kralitz: Zacharias Solin. Mixed Ed. 6 vols. 4to. D & M 2186. (88) £3,200

Bible in Cherokee
— 1860. - [New Testament]. NY. 12mo. Doheny copy. (88) $450

— Genesis or the First Book of Moses. Park Hill OK: Mission Press, 1856. 24mo. (89) $200

Bible in Chinese
— c.1823. - Zin yi zhaoshu [New Testament]. Malacca: Anglo-Chinese Press. Trans by Robert Morrison. 8 parts. 8vo. (89) £1,700
— 1854. - Xinyue quanshu. Hong Kong: Yinghua Shuyuan. 8vo. D & M 2514. Robinson copy. (89) £550

Bible in Chippewa
— 1856. - Iu Otoshki-Kikindiuin...The New Testament...translated into the Language of the Ojibwa Indians. NY. 8vo. (91) $120

Bible in Coptic
— 1716. - Novum Testamentum Aegyptium vulgo Copticum.... Oxford.1st Ed in Coptic. 4to. (89) £220

Bible in Danish
— 1550. - Den er den gantske Hellige Scrifft.... Copenhagen: L. Dietz. Folio. (90) £900
— 1589. - Biblia; det er, Den gantske Hellige Scrifft, Paa danske. Copenhagen. 3 parts in 1 vol. Folio. D & M 3156. (88) £600
— 1589-88. - Det er, den Gantske Hellige Scrifft.... Copenhagen: Matz Vingaardt. Issue without the port of Frederick II on verso of tp. 3 vols in 4. Folio. D & M 3156. (88) £2,000

Bible in Dutch
— 1477, 10 Jan. - [Old Testament] Delft: Jacob Jacobszoen van der Meer & Mauricius Yemantszoen. 2 vols. Folio. 642 leaves (of 643); lacking blank in Vol I. Goff B-648. Doheny copy. (88) $95,000
— 1562-61. - Biblia, dat is, de gantsche heylige

BIBLE IN DUTCH

- Schrift.... Emden: Gilles van der Erve. Folio. D & M 3293. (90) HF2,800
- 1599. - [Louvain version]. Antwerp: Jan Moerentorf. Folio. D & M 3300. (90) HF1,500, HF1,500; (91) £220
- 1654. - [States General version]. Amst. 3 parts in 1 vol. Folio. D & M 3313. (90) HF1,500
- 1657-46. - Antwerp: Pieter J. Paets. 2 parts in 1 vol. Folio. (89) $1,200, £150, £300 D & M 3314. (88) HF1,300, HF1,700; (89) HF1,100; (90) £350
- 1660. - [States General Version]. Amst. Folio. (88) £3,600
- 1663. - Leiden: Elzevir. 3 parts in 1 vol. Folio. D & M 3321. (88) HF1,500 Folio. Doheny copy. (88) £650 Bound with a copy of the so-called Saurin Bible. The Hague, 1728. Lacking 1 plate & 1 leaf of text. In 4 vols. Folio. (89) HF3,800
- 1664. - Amst. Folio. (90) £600
- 1686. - Biblia. Dat is de Gantsche H. Schrifture. Dordrecht. Folio. (88) £320, HF1,100; (89) $375
- 1700. - Historie des ouden en nieuwen Testaments. Amst.: P. Mortier. 2 vols. Folio. (88) £450
- 1702. - Amst.: Jacob Lindenberg. Illus by Romeyn de Hooge. Folio. (89) £350; (91) £320
- 1728. - Amst. & Leiden. 3 parts in 1 vol. Folio. (88) £300
- 1729. - Dordrecht. Folio. (88) $700; (90) HF1,600
- 1756-55. - [States General version]. Dordrecht: J. & N. Keur. Folio. (89) £70 D & M 3353. (90) £600
- 1910. - Rembrandt Bibel. Amst. 2 vols. Folio. (89) HF1,600

- Het Hooglied van Salomo. Amst., 1905. Ltd Ed. Illus by B. A. Van der Leck. Folio. (88) HF1,400
- Taferelen der voornaamste geschiedenissen van het Oude en Nieuwe Testament. Amst., 1728. 3 vols. Folio. (88) HF3,400 Sold w.a.f. (89) £250

Bible in English

- 1534. - The newe Testament dylygently corrected and compared with the Greke by Willyam Tindale. Antwerp: Marten Emperowr. 2d completed Ed of Tyndale's NT. 8vo. 412 (of 424) leaves. Herbert 13; STC 2826. West-Gifford copy. (89) £28,000
- 1535, 4 Oct. - [Miles Coverdale's version]. Cologne: Eucharius Cervicornus & Johannes Soter. 1st Ed of 1st complete Bible in English. Single leaf comprising end of Lamentations & beginning of Baruch. Folio. (88) £260
- 1535 or 1536. - Cologne: Eucharius Cervicornus & Johannes Soter. STC 2063, 2063.3 or 2063.5. Folio. Holford-Newton-Doheny copy. (89) $48,000
- 1537. - [Matthew's version] [Antwerp: R. Grafton & E. Whitchurch, L]. 4 parts in 1 vol. Folio. (89) £3,400
- 1537. - L [but Antwerp: Matthew Crom for R. Grafton & E. Whitchurch]. 4 parts in 1 vol. Folio. This copy ptd on saffron-tinted paper. (88) £1,700
- 1539. - L: John Byddell for Thomas Barthlet. Folio. Herbert 45. (88) £9,500
- 1539. - [Great Bible] [Paris: Francis Regnault & L]: R. Grafton & E. Whitchurch. Folio. STC 2068; Herbert 46. Wood-Newton-Doheny copy. (89) $35,000
- 1540, Apr. - L: T. Petyt & R. Redman for T. Berthelet. Folio. Herbert 52. (88) £900
- 1541. - L: R. Grafton or E. Whitchurch. 5 parts in 1 vol. Folio. Herbert 60. (88) £550
- 1541. - [Great Bible] L: Edward Whitchurch. 6th Ed of this version. Folio. Herbert 62. (90) $2,800
- 1541, May. - 5th Ed of this version. L: Edward Whitchurch. Folio. (91) £3,000
- 1546. - The newe testament in Englishe, accordyng to the translacion of the greate Byble. L: Richard Grafton. 8vo. STC2848.5. (89) £10,500
- 1549. - L: T. Raynalde & W. Hyll. Folio. Herbert 75. (88) £900
- 1549. - [Matthew's version] L: John Daye & Wm. Seres. Folio. Herbert 74. (88) £1,200; (89) £1,600
- 1549. - L: Thomas Raynalde & William Hyll. 2 parts in 1 vol. Folio. STC 2078. (91) £550
- 1550. - [Great Bible Version]. L: Edward Whytchurche. 4to. (90) £850
- 1551. - The Byble...faithfuly set forth according to ye Coppy of Thomas Mathewes Translation.... L: John Day. 2 parts in 1 vol. Folio. (91) £3,200
- 1553. - The Newe Testament of Our Lord Jesus Christ. L: Richard Jugge. 8vo. (91) £1,800
- [1553?]. - [Tyndale's version]. L: Richard Jugge. 4to. (90) $2,800 8vo. (90) £3,000
- 1560. - [Geneva version] Geneva: Rouland Hall. 1st Ed of this version. 4to. STC 2093; Herbert 107. Doheny copy. (89) $6,500
- 1566. - [Great Bible]. Rouen: R. Carmarden. Folio. Herbert 119. (89) £1,050
- [1568]. - [Bishops' Bible] L: R. Jugge. 1st Ed of this version. Folio. (88) £600; (89) £50; (90) $2,600

Herbert 125. (89) $2,200; (91) £2,600
STC 2099; Herbert 125. Hogan-Doheny
copy. (89) $6,500
— 1572. - 2d Folio Ed. L: R. Jugge. (90)
£1,800
— 1574. - L: R. Jugge. Folio. (88) £160
Herbert 137. (91) £320
— 1576. - [Geneva version] L: Christopher
Barker. Folio. Herbert 143A. (89) $700
— 1582. - [1st Ed of the Douai New Testament] Rheims: John Fogny. (88) $850,
$850
4to. (90) £580
Doheny copy. (88) $800
Herbert 177. (88) £800
STC 2883; Herbert 177. Doheny copy. (89)
$1,900
STC 2883; Herbert 177. (90) $1,200; (91)
$2,500
— 1583. - [Geneva version] L: Christopher
Barker. Folio. Herbert 178. (89) $750,
£420; (90) £260; (91) £240
STC 2885. (91) £220
— 1583. - The Third Part of the Bible. L: C.
Barker. 8vo. Herbert 181. (88) £300
— 1585. - L: Christopher Barker. 2 parts in 1
vol. Folio. (90) £1,400
Herbert 188. (91) £700
— 1587. - L. 3 parts in 1 vol. 4to. Herbert 194.
(90) £200
— 1589. - [Geneva version] L: Deputies of
Christopher Barker. Incomplete, the
prelims comprising only Title, To the
Christian Reader; imperfect leaf of
Kalendar, 16 leaves of Morning Prayer,
Genesis, with some leaves def & repaired.
Bound with: Metrical Psalms. L, 1590.
Incomplete. Sold w.a.f. (90) £100
Bound with: The Whole Booke of
Psalmes.... L, 1593. Lacking leaves at
end. (90) £190
4to. STC 2150. (91) £220
— 1589. - [New Testament] L: Deputies of
Christopher Barker. Folio. (91) $900
— 1589. - The Text of the New Testament....
L: Deputies of C. Barker. 8vo. (91) £350
— 1590. - L: Deputies of Christopher Barker.
OT & Apocrypha only. 8vo. D & M 157.
(89) $200
— 1592. - L: Christopher Barker. Folio. (89)
£85
— 1595. - [Bishops' Bible] L: Deputies of
Christopher Barker. 4to. D & M 225. (89)
£140
Herbert 225. (89) $450
Folio. D & M 226. (90) £230
— 1597. - [Geneva version] L: Deputies of
Christopher Barker. Folio. (89) £280
— 1599. - L: Deputies of Christopher Barker.
4to. Bound in is undated Sternhold &
Hopkins Metrical Book of Psalmes. (90)
£220
— 1599. - L [but Amst.]. 2 parts in 1 vol.
4to. (90) $800
— 1599. - [Geneva version] L: Deputies of C.
Barker. 4to. (88) £170; (90) $325; (91) £240
STC 2174. (91) £180
— 1600. - [2d Ed in English of Douai New
Testament] Antwerp: Daniel Vervliet. 4to.
(88) $275
— 1600. - [2d Ed in English of Douai Bible]
Douai & Antwerp. New Testament only.
4to. Herbert 258. Doheny copy. (88) $450
— 1601. - The Text of the New Testament of
Jesus Christ Translated...by the Papists of
the Traiterous Seminarie at Rhemes.... L:
Impensis G. B.. Folio. (90) $325
— 1601. - L: Robert Barker. Folio. Herbert
265. (90) £240
— 1602. - [Bishops' Bible] L: Robert Barker.
Folio. (88) £120; (91) £400
Sold w.a.f. (89) £160
— 1603. - [Geneva version] L: Robert Barker.
4to. Herbert 274. (88) $375
Bound in 2 vols. 4to. Herbert 274. (89)
$325
— 1606. - L: R. Barker. Bound with the Book
of Common Prayer (lacking tp & first
leaves) & The Whole Booke of Psalmes
(imperf at end). 4to. (88) £130
— 1607. - L: Robert Barker. 4to. Herbert 289.
(89) £170
1st Issue of this Ed. Bound in is related
material, including the Book of Common
Prayer, Barker, 1607 & The Whole Booke
of Psalmes, 1607. (91) £800
— 1608. - L: R. Barker. 8vo. Bound in is The
Whole Booke of Psalmes, 1610 & Two Right
Profitable and Fruitfull Concordances,
1608. (91) £220
— 1609-10. - [1st Ed in English of Douai Old
Testament] Douai: Laurence Kellam. 2
vols. 4to. (90) $1,600
Doheny copy. (88) $900
— 1609-10-1582. - Douai: Laurence Kellam. 3
vols. 4to. STC 2307 & 2884. (90) £1,800;
(91) £800
— 1610. - L: Robert Barker. Folio. Bound in
are The Whole Booke of Psalmes, by
Sternhold & Hopkins, L, 1615, and The
Booke of Common Prayer, L, 1614. (89)
£220; (91) £300
— 1611. - [Authorized Version] L: Robert
Barker. With "he" reading in Ruth III, 15.
Folio. (88) £5,500; (90) $15,000; (91) £240
Doheny copy. (89) $6,000
Houghton-The Garden copy. (90) $130,000
STC 2216; Herbert 309. Newton-Doheny
copy. (89) $55,000
STC 2216. Downshire copy. (90) £3,000

BIBLE IN ENGLISH

Wren family copy. (90) £11,000
With reading "he" in Ruth III, 15. (91) £160
— 1613-14. - L: Robert Barker. 4to. (89) £520 Herbert 331. (91) £380
— 1613. - [Authorized version] L: Robert Barker. 3 parts in 1 vol. 4to. (88) $1,100
— 1613-11. - L: Robert Barker. With "she" reading in Ruth III, 15. Folio. Herbert 319. (88) £850; (89) $900; (91) £3,800
— 1614. - The Holy Bible.... L: Thomas Barker. 8vo. (90) $200, £140
— 1615. - L: Robert Barker. Bound with: Speed Genealogies, L, 1615. Torn & imperfect. And: The Whole Booke of Psalmes Collected into English Meeter. L, 1615. Imperfect at end. Sold w.a.f. 4to. Herbert 340. (90) £80
— 1616. - [Authorized version] L: Robert Barker. Folio. STC 2244; Herbert 348. (91) £280
With 1616-24 Book of Common Prayer, Psalms & Genealogies bound in. Herbert 349. (89) $500
— 1620-21. - L. 4o. Herbert 379. (88) $500 4to. Herbert 379. (88) $300
— 1630. - L. 4to. H. Rider Haggard's copy. Herbert 429. (90) $200
— 1631. - ["Wicked" Bible] L: Robert Barker. 8vo. Herbert 341. (90) £11,500
Lacking tp; dedication plate detached & glued at edge of upper cover; last leaf of concordance lacking; soiled; marginal stains & tears. (88) $4,200
Tp supplied from anr copy; browned & soiled; hole in 2N8 with loss of a few letters of text. (91) £220
— [1633]. - Cambr.: T. & J. Buck. 4to. With incomplete 1632 prayer book and Book of Psalms [n.d.] bound in. (90) £120
— 1633. - Edin. Bound with: The Whole Booke of Psalmes. London, 1635. 8vo. STC 2311a, 16394, 23039e.13 & 2650. (88) $200
— 1633. - The Text of the New Testament of Jesus Christ. L. Ed by W. Fulke. Folio. (88) $50
— 1634. - L: R. Barker & Assignes of J. Bill. 4to. Herbert 502. (89) $175
— 1637. - Cambr. 4to. (89) £180
— [1638]. - Cambr.: Tho. Buck & Roger Daniel. Bound with: The Whole Booke of Psalmes. Cambr., 1638. Folio. (88) $150
— 1638-39. - L: John Bill. Bound with the Book of Common Prayer [STC 16415] Folio. (88) $800
Bound with the Book of Common Prayer [STC 16415] and The Whole Book of Psalms. (90) $300
— 1639. - L. Folio. Herbert 538. (89) $375; (91) £240, £270
— 1640. - Amst.: Thos. Stafford. Folio. STC

AMERICAN BOOK PRICES CURRENT

2344; D & M 545. (90) £500
— 1640-[39]. - [Authorized version] L: R. Barker & the Assignes of John Bill. Bound with: The Whole Book of Psalms 8vo. (88) $175
— 1643. - The New Testament. L. With The Whole Booke of Psalmes, 1642. 12mo. Doheny copy. (89) $2,000
With: The Whole Booke of Psalmes, 1642. (91) $2,000
— 1646-1645. - L: Assignes of R. Barker. 12mo. Bound in is the Whole Booke of Psalmes, L, 1646. (90) $11,000
— 1649. - L: Companie of Stationers. Bound with: The Whole Book of Psalms. L: Companie of Stationers, 1652. 8vo. (91) £110
— 1650-51. - The Holy Bible.... L. 8vo. (89) $400
— 1652. - L. Bound with: The Whole Book of Psalms. L, 1654. 12mo. Herbert 632. (88) $200
— 1653. - [New Testament] L: John Field. 2 vols. 24mo. Herbert 635. (91) £300
24mo. (88) $110; (90) £230; (91) $625
— 1656. - L: John Field. Bound with: A Brief Concordance and The Whole Book of Psalms. L, 1654 & 1656. 12mo. Herbert 653. (88) $475
— 1657. - Cambr.: John Field. 16mo. (88) £45
— 1660-59. - Cambr. 2 vols. Folio. (88) $800 Herbert 668. (89) £1,300; (90) $1,600
3 vols in 1. Folio. (91) £450
— 1660. - Cambr.: John Field. 3 vols. Folio. D & M 668. (88) £800
— 1660. - L: Henry Hills & John Field. 8vo. Wing B2256A. (91) £1,400
— 1668-66. - Cambr.: John Field. 4to. Bound in are the Whole Book of Psalms and the Book of Common Prayer, both Cambr., 1666. (90) £240
Herbert 697. (89) $140
— 1672-79. - L. Folio. (90) £55
— 1673. - L. 2 vols in 1, including Psalms. 12mo. Extra-illus with c.230 plates. Herbert 714. (89) $750
— 1674. - Cambr.: J. Hayes. Folio. (88) £80
Extra-illust with 6 double-page maps & numerous double-page plates, a few torn. (90) £1,000
— 1675. - [New Testament & Psalms] Cambr. 4to. (91) £160
— 1679. - Oxford: at the Theater. 4to. (88) $350, £150
— 1680. - Oxford. Bound with: The New Testament. L, 1680. And: an unidentified contemp Ed of the metrical Psalms. Folio. (90) $1,000

Herbert 756. Harmsworth-Doheny copy. (89) $380,000
— 1682. - [Amst.?]. 12mo. Herbert 778. (89) $175
Herbert 777. (91) £200
— 1682. - Oxford. Bound with: The Book of Common Prayer & The Whole Book of Psalms of the same date. 4to. Herbert 770. (90) £150
— 1693. - L. 12mo. Herbert 827. (88) $60
— 1696. - New Testament of our Lord and Saviour.... Oxford: University Printers. 12mo. (88) $130
— 1700. - L: Charles Bill. Bound with: The Psalms of David. Edin., 1661. 4to. (90) £120; (91) £250
— 1703. - L: C. Bill & Executrix of T. Newcomb. Bound with: Psalms & Book of Common Prayer. L, 1704. 8vo. (90) $1,600
— 1706. - L. 3 vols in 1. 4to. (89) £75
Bound with: The Book of Common Prayer & The Whole Book of Psalms 4to. (88) $120
— 1715. - Oxford. Folio. (91) £150
Bound in is Book of Common Prayer, also Oxford, 1715. (90) £130
— 1715. - Oxford: John Baskett. Folio. Herbert 935. (89) £65
— 1716. - Edin.: James Watson. 12mo. (88) $100, $140
— 1716-17. - ["Vinegar" Bible]. Oxford: John Baskett. 2 vols. Folio. (88) £1,100
— 1717-16. - Oxford: John Baskett. 2 vols. Folio. Herbert 942. (90) £750, £1,900
— 1719. - Edin. 12mo. (88) £38
— 1723. - Oxford: John Baskett. 2 vols. 4to. (88) £100
4to. Bound in are: The Book of Common Prayer, Oxford, 1719, & The Whole Book of Psalms, L, 1723. Extra-illus with c.250 plates by John Sturt from The Historical Part of the Holy Bible and 6 mtd maps from the 1725 ed of Sacred Geography. (90) $425
— 1726. - Edin.: J. Baskett. 4to. With Thomas Ken's A Manual of Prayers for the Use of the Scholars of Winchester College. L, [c.1705-10]. 12mo, contemp calf. Very worn. Martin copies. (90) $1,600
— 1727. - Edinburgh: J. Mosman & W. Brown. 8vo. D & M 763. (90) £170
— 1735. - L. 3 parts in 1 vol; without Apocrypha. 8vo. Herbert 1028. (88) $140
8vo. Sold as a bdg. Sold w.a.f. (90) £380
— 1750-51. - Oxford. 8vo. (91) £110
— 1753. - L: Thomas Baskett & Assigns of Robert Baskett. Folio. (90) £1,600
— 1762. - Oxford: Baskett. 2 vols. 12mo. Herbert 1145. (91) £800
— 1763. - Cambr.: Baskerville. Folio. Extra-illus with 286 engravings, including 171 of Picart & Hoet from Figures de la Bible & 58 from Mortier's Bible. Bryant-Marlborough-Marjoribanks-Doheny copy. (89) $10,000
1st Issue; list of subscribers ending with Winwood. (91) $1,900
With list of subscribers in 2d State. (89) £320
With list of subscribers in 3d State. Doheny copy. (88) $3,000
— 1769-71. - Birm.: Baskerville. Folio. (88) $100
— 1771-72. - Birm.: John Baskerville. 2 parts in 1 vol. Folio. (89) $400
— 1782-81. - Phila.: R. Aitken. 12mo. Herbert 1283. Doheny copy. (89) $9,500
Herbert 1283. (90) $10,000
— 1788. - Birm.: Pearson & Rollason. 2 vols in 1. 4to. (88) $350; (89) £50
— 1788. - Birm.: Person & Rollason. 4to. Extra-illus with c.190 plates. Herbert 1324. (88) £220
— 1788. - [New Testament] Trenton. 8vo. Hills 17. (89) $750
— 1790. - Phila. 2 vols in 1. 4to. (90) $5,500
Doheny copy. (89) $5,000
— 1791. - Dublin. 2 vols. (91) £380
— 1791. - Trenton: Isaac Collins. 4to. (91) $110
Hills 31. (91) $95
Hills 31; Evans 23184. (91) $250
— 1791. - The Holy Bible. Phila.: W. Young. 2 vols. 12mo. Hills 32. (91) $3,400
— 1792. - The Self-Interpreting Bible. NY: Hodge & Campbell. Folio. (89) $120
— 1792. - NY: T. Allen. Folio. (89) $275
— 1794. - A New Hieroglyphical Bible, for...Children.... Bost.: W. Norman. 1st American Ed. 18mo. (91) $350
— 1795. - L. 4 vols. 4to. (88) £130; (91) £440
— 1795. - L: T. Bensley. Bound with: Fittler. Cartoons of Raphael d'Urbin...a Supplement to the Cabinet Bible. L, 1797. 3 vols. 4to. (91) $425
— 1795. - L: Thomas Bensley. 2 vols. 4to. Herbert 1394. (89) $375
— 1795. - The Holy Bible Abridged... Bost.: S. Hall. 32mo. Martin copy. (90) $550
— 1796. - A Curious Hieroglyphick Bible...for the Amusement of Youth. L: Robert Bassam. 12mo. (88) $160; (89) £45
— 1800-16. - L. 8 vols. Folio. (90) £6,200
— 1800. - L: Thomas Macklin. 6 vols. Folio. (88) £300; (90) £210, £580
6 vols in 7. Folio. Sold w.a.f. (90) £350
— 1800. - L: Thomas Bensley for Thomas Macklin. 1st Macklin Ed. 6 vols. Folio. (91) $3,200
— 1829. - The New Testament L: De la Rue, Cornish & Rock. One of 104. 4to. Ptd in gold on thick enamel paper. (88) £2,800

BIBLE IN ENGLISH

— 1836. - [New Testament]. L: Samuel Bagster. 8vo. Martin copy. (90) $400
— 1837. - Cambr.: Pitt Press. 2 vols. Folio. (89) £4,000
— 1837. - [New Testament] L: S. Bagster. 8vo. George Offor's extra-illus copy. (88) £1,300; (91) £450
— 1838. - L. 4to. (88) £200
— 1846. - The Illuminated Bible. NY. 4to. (88) $150; (89) $200; (91) $135
— 1848. - [New Testament] L. 4to. (88) £350
— 1848. - L: Wm. Pickering. Trans by John Wycliffe. 4to. Herbert 1868. (89) £200; (91) $300, $2,000, £280
— 1850. - Oxford. 4 vols. Folio. D & M 1876. (90) £850
— 1858. - L. Illus by David Roberts. 4to. (91) $700
— 1862-60. - L: Eyre & Spottiswoode. Illus by Francis Frith. 4to. (88) $1,200
— 1862. - The First New Testament Printed in the English Language. Bristol. One of 26, this copy on vellum. Intro by Francis Fry. 8vo. Inscr by Fry to his daughter Caroline & granddaughter Priscilla. (88) £4,800
— 1876. - Hartford. Trans by Julia E. Smith. 8vo. Doheny copy. (88) $280
— 1901. - NY. 24mo. Doheny copy. (88) $800
— 1903. - L: David Nutt. One of 18. 6 vols. (91) $70
— [1908]. - L: Grolier Society. One of 1,000. 14 vols. Herbert 2149. (88) $80
— 1910-11. - L: Ballantyne Press. One of 750. 3 vols. Herbert 2159. (91) $225
— [c.1934]. - Bost: R. H. Hinkley. One of 488. 14 vols. (91) $130, $1,100
— [c.1934]. - The Holy Bible containing the Old and New Testaments and the Apocrypha. Bost.: R. H. Hinkley. One of 500. 14 vols. (91) $750
— 1934-36. - New Testament. L. Illus by Eric Gill. 4 vols. (91) $150, $350
— 1935. - Oxford. One of 200. Designed by Bruce Rogers. 2 vols. Folio. (90) $750; (91) $6,600
Doheny copy. (88) $8,500
2 vols, in 1. Folio. Schimmel copy. (91) $17,000
— 1941. - [New Testament] Paterson NJ: St. Anthony Guild Press. One of 1,000. Doheny copy. (88) $120
— 1949. - Cleveland. One of 975. Designed by Bruce Rogers. Folio. (89) $500; (91) $550 Doheny copy. (88) $400
With William Targ's The Making of the Bruce Rogers World Bible.. (90) $350; (91) $325
— 1950. - The Bible for my Grandchildren.... N.p.: Pvtly ptd. One of 1,000. Ed by Ruth Hornblower Greenough. 2 vols. 4to. (91) $140
— 1953. - Oxford. One of 25 specially bound in mor & on India paper. Folio. (91) $7,500
One of 100 on Nash paper, but this copy in the bdg with the Royal arms. (91) £5,000
— 1958. - NY. 4to. (91) $90
— 1959. - NY: Abradale Press. 4to. (91) $70
— 1965. - Cleveland: World Publishing Co.. Folio. Facsimile reprint of the 1st Ed of the King James version, 1611. (90) $325; (91) $340
— 1970. - The Jerusalem Bible. Garden City. Illus by Salvador Dali. 4to. (88) $65
— 1974. - A Leaf from the First Edition of the First Complete Bible in English, the Coverdale Bible, 1535 San Francisco: Book Club of California. One of 425. Intro by Allen P. Wikgren. 4to. (88) $100; (89) $120, $225; (91) $150
— [n.d.]. - Folio. Presentation copy to Princess Louise Margaret of Prussia from the Maidens of the United Kingdom on the occasion of her marriage to Prince Arthur, Duke of Connaught. With a bound list of the 11,540 subscribers. (89) £5,000

— The Acts of Samson: Judges xiii-xvi. Lexington: Anvil Press, 1975-76. One of 58. Illus by Fritz Kredel. (91) $325
— The Beatitudes. Esher: Penmiel Press, 1984. One of 65. (91) $175
— The Book of Esther. NY: Golden Cross Press, 1935. One of 135. Designed & illuminated by Valenti Angelo. (91) $80, $250
— The Book of Genesis. L: Riccardi Press, 1914. One of 500. Illus by E. Cayley Robinson. 4to. (88) $120; (91) $300
Kentfield: Allen Press, 1970. One of 140. Illus by Blair Hughes-Stanton. Folio. (89) $375; (91) $300
— The Book of Job. L, [1916]. Intro by G. K. Chesterton; illus by C. Mary Tongue. (91) $60
Cummington MA: Cummington Press, 1944. One of 300. 4to. (91) $80, $300
Leigh-on-Sea, 1948. One of 110. Illus by Frank Brangwyn. 4to. (88) £160
— The Book of Jonah. Bronxville: Valenti Angelo, 1969. One of 35. (91) $250
Seal Harbor: High Loft, 1981. One of 20 with an extra suite of the plates. Illus by Elaine Young. ANs of August Heckscher laid in. (91) $175
— The Book of Ruth. Eugene: Univ. of Oregon Fine Arts Press, 1933. One of 90. Folio. (91) $275
L: Read Pale Press, 1934. One of 250. (91) $150

NY: Maverick Press, 1937. One of 40. Scroll, 1,565mm by 50mm. (91) $300
— The Book of Ruth and the Book of Esther. NY: Russell for Will Bradley, 1897. 8vo. (91) $500
— The Book of Ruth and Boaz.... NY: Press of Valenti Angelo, 1949. One of 150. (91) $160, $225
— The Book of the Gospels. L, 1867. 4to. (91) $140
— The Book of Tobit and the History of Susanna. L, 1929. 4to. (88) £60
ANs of Flint laid in. (88) $60
One of 100. (88) £180
One of 100, with an additional suite of plates. (91) $300
One of 875. (89) $55; (91) $60
One of 100. Illus by W. Russell Flint. (90) $70
With an extra suite of plates laid in. (91) $500
— The Book of Tobit. Harrow Weald: Raven Press, 1931. 4to. (89) $225
— The Creation; the First Eight Chapters of Genesis. NY: Pantheon Books, 1948. One of 125. Illus by Frans Masereel; ptd at the Officina Bodoni. Folio. (91) $1,300
— Ecclesiastes. L, 1927. ("Ecclesiasticus; or the Wisdom of Jesus the Son of Sirach.") Illus by Violet Brunton. (91) $110
New York: Spiral Press, 1965. ("Ecclesiastes, or, the Preacher.") One of 285. Illus by Ben Shahn; calligraphy by David Soshensky. (89) $300; (90) $225
Paris: Trianon Press, 1967. One of 200. Illus by Ben Shahn. (91) $800
4to. (88) £480
One of 26 with 2 sgd lithos, ann extra suite of plates & a series of progressive states of 1 of the plates. (88) $1,200
— Ezekiel 47:1-12. N.p.: Mason Hill Press, 1979. One of 35. (91) $130
— The First Tome or Volume of the Paraphrase of Erasmus upon the Newe Testamente. L: E. Whitchurche, 31 Jan 1548. 2 parts in 1 vol. (88) £550
2 vols. Folio. (90) $1,600
Vol I only. Folio. (90) $950
STC 2854.2. (90) $375
— The Four Gospels. L, [1927]. Illus by Vera Willoughby. (91) $150
Lexington KY: Anvil Press, 1954-55. One of 300. Frontis illusts by Victor Hammer. 4 vols. (91) $225
Verona: Officina Bodoni, 1962. One of 320. Folio. (89) £1,600; (90) £1,250; (91) $1,700
Mt. Vernon, [n.d.]. One of 985. Illus by Hans Alexander Mueller. Folio. (91) $60, $120
— The Gospel according to Saint Mark. Market Drayton: Tern Press, 1980. One jf 60.

Illus by Nicholas Parry. Folio. (91) $175
— Grace and Glory. [N.p., mid 19th-cent]. 4to. (91) $80
— The Holy Gospel According to Matthew, Mark, Luke and John. Verona: Officina Bodoni, 1962. One of 320. Folio. (88) $1,400; (89) £1,300; (91) $2,300
— Judith: reprinted from the Apocrypha. L, 1928. One of 100, sgd by W. Russell Flint. 4to. (91) $375
— The Parables from the Gospels. L: Vale Press, 1903. One of 310. Illus by Charles Ricketts. (90) £220; (91) $160, $425
Dedication copy, inscr by Charles Ricketts to T. Sturge Moore. (91) £700
— The Passion of our Lord Jesus Christ according to the four Evangelists. L: Faber, 1934. Eric Gill's copy, with his monogram. (91) $550
— The Proverbs of Salomon, wyth the Rest of the Workes as Ecclesiastes and Sapientia.... L: E. Whitchurche, 1540. 16mo. (89) £8,000
— The Revelation of Saint John the Divine. L, 1931. One of 1,000. Illus by Frances Clayton. (91) $60
Ithaca, [1958]. One of 135. Illus by Elfriede Abbe. Folio. (90) $90
— The Second Chapter from the Gospel According to Saint Matthew. NY: Golden Cross Press, 1936. One of 100. Inscr by Valenti Angelo, the illuminator. (91) $110
[NY, c.1960]. (91) $60
— The Sermon on the Mount. L, 1844. Illus by Owen Jones. 16mo. (88) £65
[L], 1845. 8vo. (90) £60
L: Chatto & Windus, 1911. 4to. (91) $800
NY: Golden Cross Press, 1935. One of 110. Hand-illuminated by Valenti Angelo. 4to. (91) $140
Bronxville: Press of Valenti Angelo, [1963]. One of 50. (91) $120, $180
— The Sixth Chapter of St. Matthew. N.p.: Hammer Creek Press, [n.d.]. One of 85. (91) $150
— The Song of Songs which is Solomon's. L, 1897. ("Song of Solomon.") Illus by H. Granville Fell. 4to. (91) $150, $700, $6,000
L, 1909. ("The Song of Songs.") One of 17 ptd on vellum. Illus by W. Russell Flint. 4to. (88) £380; (91) £85
One of 500. (91) $150, $325
Berlin: Hans Striem Verlag, 1923. One of 100 Illus by Rafaello Busoni. Folio. (91) $100
Jerusalem: Hasefer, 1923. Illus by Zeew Raban. Folio. (91) $375
Phila.: Centaur Press, 1927. ("Song of Solomon.") One of 525, sgd by Wharton Esherick. Illus by Esherick. 4to. (91) $175, $250

BIBLE IN ENGLISH

Chelsea: Swan Press, 1928. ("The Canticles of the Old Testament.") One of 100. (91) $110

Birm.: School of Printing, 1937. ("The Song of Songs as a Drama by Ernest Renan.") One of 55. Trans by Havelock Ellis; illus by Bernard Sleigh. 4to. (91) $200

Frankfurt: Ars Libri, [1962]. ("Canticum Canticorum: The Song of Songs.") One of 200. Illus by Gerhart Kraaz. Folio. (91) $375

L: Circle Press, 1968. ("The Song of Solomon.") One of 150, sgd by Ronald King. Illus by King. Folio. (88) $400

One of 150. Illus by Ronald King. (88) SF16,000; (91) $250

Paris & NY, 1971. ("The Song of Songs of King Solomon.") One of 250. Illus by Salvador Dali. Folio. (88) FF31,000

Austin, 1972. ("The Song of Solomon.") One of 200. Illus by Don Herron. (91) $250

L: Pvtly ptd, 1973. One of 50. Illus by Susan Allix. 4to. (91) DM2,700

Andoversford: Whittington Press, [1976]. One of 6 specially bound. 4to. (88) £700

— ("The Song of Songs.") One of 35. (88) £320; (91) $600

One of 36. 4to. (88) £320

L, 1976. One of 6. Illus by Richard Kennedy. 4to. (88) £700

— The Story of the Exodus. Paris: Leon Amiel, 1966. One of 285. Illus by Marc Chagall. Folio. (88) $22,000, $24,000, $26,000, FF180,000; (89) SF40,500

Bible in Eskimo Labrador

— 1876-78. - [New Testament] Stolpen. 8vo. D & M 3522. (88) $120

Bible in Ethiopic

— 1701. - [Psalms, Biblical Hymns & Song of Songs]. Frankfurt. 4to. D & M 3572. (88) $375

Bible in Fiji

— 1884. - Ai vola tabu, a ya e tu kina na veiyalayalati makawa.... L. 8vo. D & M 3634. (90) $1,200

Bible in Flemish

— 1566. - [Louvain version] Antwerp: C. Plantin. Folio. (88) £160

Bible in French

— 1535. - [1st French Protestant version] Neuchatel [Serrieres, ptd]: Pierre de Wingle, dict Pirot Picard. 4 parts in 1 vol. Folio. Chatsworth copy. D & M 3710. (88) £12,000

— 1541. - La Saincte Bible en francois. Antwerp: Antoine de la Haye. Folio. Martin copy. (90) $28,000

— 1554. - Geneva: Jean Crespin. 8vo. (89) $1,100

— 1567. - La Bible, qui est toute la saincte escriture. [Geneva]: F. Estienne. 8vo. (88) $500

— 1667. - Le Nouveau Testament. Mons: Gaspard Migeot. 1st Ed of the Port Royal version. 2 vols. 8vo. (88) £450

— 1667. - Mons: Gaspard Migeot [but Amst.: D. Elzevir]. 2 vols. 8vo. D & M 3755; Willems 1389. (88) HF1,200

— 1669. - La Sainte Bible. Amst.: Elzevir. 4 parts in 2 vols. Folio. (88) £130
D & M 37611. (90) HF7,500

— 1700. - Antwerp: Pierre Mortier. Issue with nail-marks on final Apocalypse plate. 2 vols. Folio. (90) £650

— 1781-89. - La Sainte Bible. Nimes: Pierre Baume. 24 parts in 25 vols. 8vo. (88) FF5,000

— 1789. - Paris. 4 vols (of 12). 4to. (88) £220
Vols I & II (of 12). 4to. (88) $150

— 1789-1804. - Paris: Peter de Maisonneuve, etc. 12 vols. 8vo. (90) £18,000
Doheny copy. (88) $1,200

— 1866. - Tours. Illus by Gustave Dore. 2 vols. Folio. (91) $130
2 vols extended to 10 vut lacking Vols I & X. Folio. Extra-illus with ptd titles & c.7,900 plates. (88) £5,000

— 1956. - Paris: Teriade. One of 275. Illus by Marc Chagall. 2 vols. Folio. (88) $48,000

— Apocalypse de Saint Jean. Monaco, 1952. One of 270. Illus by Rufino Tamayo. In 36 folders. Folio. (90) $1,200; (91) $550

— Le Cantique des cantiques. [N.p., n.d.]. One of 20 on japon imperial with an extra suite of plates & 2 orig drawings. Illus by Leon Courbouleix. 4to. Schimmel copy. (91) $2,600

Paris, 1886. One of 10 on china with an additional impression of the frontis etching on velin. Illus by Alexandre Bida. Folio. (88) $32,500

Paris, 1925. One of 100. Illus by F. L. Schmied. 8vo. (89) $7,500
Doheny copy. (88) $5,000

Paris: Coulouma Press, 1949. Out-of-series copy stamped "Specimen" on rear cover. 4to. (88) $175

Paris, [1950]. Hors-commerce copy, sgd. Illus by Mariette Lydis. 4to. (90) $250

— La Creation: Les trois premiers livres de la Genese suivis de la genealogie adamique. [lausanne: F. L. Schmied for M. M. Gonin et cie in Paris], 1928. One of 20, this being XV, for Mlle Madeleine Gonin. 4to. (89) $5,500

— Job traduit en francois.... Paris, 1695. 8vo. (90) $325
— Le Livre de Job. Paris: Editions du Seuil, 1946. One of 250. 4to. Schimmel copy. (91) $800
— Ruth et Booz. Paris, 1930. One of 162. Trans by J. C. Mardrus. 4to. (90) £2,200

Bible in French & Hebrew
— Le Livre d'Esther. Paris, [1925]. Copy XII, for M. Viaud-Bruant. Illus by Arthur Szyk. (90) $1,000 One of 775. (91) $650

Bible in Gaelic
— 1685. - [1st Irish Old Testament] L. 4to. D & M 5534. (89) £880 Doheny copy. (88) $800
— 1783-87-1801-1786. - Leabhraiche an t-Seann Tiomnaidh.... [Old Testament]. Dun-Eidin: Uilliam Smellie. Vol I only. 8vo. (88) $50

Bible in Georgian
— 1743. - Moscow. Folio. D & M 4164. (91) £500

Bible in German
— 1466, [before 27 June]. - Strassburg: Johann Mentelin. Folio. 406 leaves. Goff B-624. Martin copy. (90) $300,000
— 1475-76. - Augsburg: Guenther Zainer. 2 vols. Folio. 533 (of 534) leaves; lacking 1st blank. Goff B-627. Penrose copy. (90) £80,000
— 1477, 20 June. - Augsburg: Anton Sorg. Folio. 542 leaves. Goff B-630. Doheny copy. (88) £100,000
— c.1478]. - Cologne: [Heinrich Quentell. Part II (of 2). Folio. 267 (of 274) leaves. Goff B-637. (88) $4,400
— 1483, 17 Feb. - Nuremberg: Anton Koberger. 2 vols in 1. Folio. 583 (of 586) leaves; lacking 3 blanks. Goff B-632. (89) £14,000
Fragment of 112 leaves. (90) DM2,400
— 1487, 25 May. - Augsburg: Johann Schoensperger. Folio. 393 (of 801) leaves; lacking ff. 9, 46-47, 54-55, 62, 290, 399-401. Goff B-634. (88) £2,300
Vol 1 (of 2). Folio. 398 (of 399) leaves. Goff B-634. (88) $4,400
— 1522, Sept. - Das newe Testament deutzch. Wittenberg: Lotter for Doering & Cranach. Luther's "September Testament". Folio. D & M 4188. Furstenberg—The Garden copy. (90) $325,000
— 1524. - [Old Testament - Parts 2 & 3 of Luther's trans] Wittenberg. Bound in 1 vol. Folio. Muther 1619 & 1622; D & M 4189. (90) £5,500
— 1534. - Biblia, das ist die Gantzen Heilige Schrifft Deudsch. Mart. Luth. Wittemburg: Hans Lufft. Parts 1-3 (of 6). Folio. D & M 4199. (91) £2,800
— 1560. - Biblia, das ist die gantze heylige Schrifft.... Frankfurt: Zephelius & Raschen & Feyerabend. Folio. Adams B-1179. (91) £36,000
— 1564. - Lyon: J. de Tournes. Folio. (88) £950
— 1564. - Catholische Bibell.... Cologne: Heirs of Johann Quentel & Gerwinus Calenius. Folio. (91) £450
— 1570. - Biblia das ist: Die gantze Heilige Schrifft Teutsch. Frankfurt: G. Raben & S. Feyrabend & W. Hanen Erben. 2 parts in 1 vol. Folio. Doheny copy. (88) $35,000
— 1576. - [Old Testament from Prophets on & New Testament] Wittemberg: Hans Krafft. Folio. (88) £1,800
— 1599-1600. - Wittenberg: Lorentz Seuberlich. Trans by Martin Luther. 3 parts in 1 vol. Folio. (90) $425
— 1630. - Sacra Biblia, das ist, die gantze H. Schrifft Alten und Newen Testaments.... Cologne: Johann Creps. Folio. D & M 4217 note. (90) £500
— 1630. - Strassburg: Zetzner. Folio. (91) DM3,300
— 1692. - [Luther's version]. Nuremberg. Folio. (88) DM3,600; (89) £420
— 1702. - Nuremberg: J. L. Buggel. 4to. D & M 4225. (91) DM1,600
— 1704. - Frankfurt. Folio. (91) DM7,200
— 1704. - Leipzig. Folio. (91) $80
— 1708. - Biblia, das ist: gantze Heilige Schrift. Nuremberg. Folio. (91) DM1,500
— 1711. - Lueneburg: Stern. Folio. (91) $950
— 1736. - Nuremberg: Endters. Folio. (89) £110
— 1747. - Nuremberg. Folio. (88) £320
— 1763. - Germantown, Pa.: Christoph Saur. 4to. (91) $250
— 1768. - Biblia, das is die gantze heilige Schrifft.... Nuremberg. Folio. (89) £330
— 1777. - Biblia; das ist, die gantze Heil. Schrift.... Wernigerode. 8vo. (90) $175

— Das Buch Judith. Berlin, 1910. One of 310. Illus by Lovis Corinth. Folio. (90) $425
— Das Evangelium nach Matthaeus. Berlin, 1960. One of 300. Illus by Otto Dix. 4to. (88) DM800
— Die heiligen Buecher des alten Bundes. Berlin, 1921-25. One of 12. Trans by Lazarus Goldschmidt. 3 vols. 4to. (91) $950
— Das Hohelied Salomons. Chiemeing am See: Methusalem Presse, 1986. One of 12. Illus by Wilhelm Neufeld. (91) DM500
— Der Prophet Jona nach M. Luther. Leipzig,

BIBLE IN GERMAN

1930. Ltd Ed. Illus by Marcus Behmer. 4to. (88) DM1,300

Bible in Gothic & Anglo Saxon
— 1665. - Quatuor Jesu Christi Evangeliorum.... Dordrecht. 4to. Evelyn copy. D & M 1604. (88) £1,500

Bible in Greek
— [New Testament]. Paris, 1642. "Mazarin" Ed. Folio. D & M 4687. Doheny copy. (89) $2,500
— 1516. - Novum Instrumentum omne [New Testament]. Basel: Johann Froben. Ed by Erasmus, & with his Latin trans. 2 parts in 1 vol. Folio. D & M 4591. Doheny copy. (89) $5,500
— 1518, Feb. - Venice: Aldus. Folio. Grafton-Watson-Davignon - The Garden copy. (90) $32,000
Holford-Newton-Doheny copy. (89) $40,000
— 1526-24. - Strassburg: Wolfgang Koeppel. 3 vols (of 4); lacking Apocrypha. D & M 4602. (91) £250
7 vols. 8vo. D & M 4602. (88) $400
— 1546. - [New Testament] Paris: Robert Estienne. 2 vols. 16mo. (88) $425
Part 2 (of 2). 8vo. (88) $110
— 1550. - Paris: Robert Estienne. 2 parts in 1 vol. Folio. (89) $1,700, $3,800; (90) £2,800 D & M 4622. (90) £4,200; (91) £1,800, £2,800
— 1550. - Novum Iesu Christi D. N. Testamentum. Paris: Robert Estienne. 2 parts in 1 vol. Folio. (91) $3,200
— 1553. - [New Testament] Geneva: Jean Crispin. 8vo. (89) $200
— 1559. - Novum Iesu Christi domini nostri Testamentum. Zurich. Folio. (89) £320
— 1568-69. - Paris: Robert Estienne. 2 vols. 16mo. (90) $150
— 1601. - Frankfurt. Folio. (88) $200
— 1619. - Novum Testamentum Graecum.... Geneva: Petrus de la Rouviere. Folio. D & M 4667. (90) £50
— 1628. - [New Testament] Sedan: J. Janon. 16mo. (89) $350; (91) $170, £190
— 1632. - Cambr.: Thomas & John Buck. Bound with: The Book of Common Prayer. London, 1632 8vo. (88) $200
— 1633. - Amst.: W. Blaeu. One vol in 4. 16mo. (88) £100
— 1642. - Paris. Folio. (90) $275
— 1658. - Kaine diatheke [New Testament]. Amst., Elzevir. 12mo. (90) £70
— 1692. - [New Testament] Venice: Nikolaos Saros. 8vo. (89) £1,400
— 1759. - He Kaine Diatheke. Novum Testamentum. Glasgow: Foulis Press. 4to. Gaskell 363. (91) £100

AMERICAN BOOK PRICES CURRENT

— 1763. - He Kaine Diatheke. Oxford. 8vo. Gaskell Add. 2. (88) $250
— 1763. - [New Testament] Oxford: Clarendon Press. One of 500. 4to. (89) $80, $250; (90) £65; (91) $160, £280
— 1800. - Kaine diatheke [New Testament]. Wigorniae [Worcester], Mass.: Isaiah Thomas, Jr.. 12mo. D & M 4775. (89) $110; (90) $110; (91) $100

Bible in Greek & Latin
— 1519. - [New Testament]. Basel: Froben. Folio. (91) £700, DM12,000
— 1522. - Novum Testamentum omne. Basel: Joh. Frobenius. Ed by Erasmus. Folio. With accompanying vol of Annotations. (91) $1,000
— 1527, Mar. - [New Testament] Basel: Johannes Froben. Folio. D & M 4603. (91) $425

Bible in Hebrew
— 1517. - Venice: Daniel Bomberg. 4to. St. 29; D & M 5084. Kimbolton Castle—Doheny copy. (89) $25,000
— 1536. - Basel: H. Froben & N. Episcopius. Ed by Sebastian Munster. 4to. (90) $1,000
— 1539-44. - Paris: R. Estienne. Last vol only. 4to. Schiff copy. (91) $21,000
— 1539-44. - Paris: R. Stephanus. 24 parts in 2 vols [complete set]. 4to. Adams B-1221. (90) $2,400
— 1543-46. - Paris: Estienne. 2 vols. 16mo. (91) £300
Bound in 6 vols. 16mo. Elkan Nathan Adler copy. St. 115. (89) $5,400
— 1544. - Paris: R. Estienne. 16mo. D & M 5089 note; Adams B-1224. (91) £550
— 1546. - Basel: Michael Isingrin & Henricus Petrus. Folio. (90) $650
— 1565-66. - Antwerp: Plantin. 4to. (91) £500
— 1566-81. - Antwerp: Christopher Plantin. Deuteronomy & Megiloth only. D & M 5099. (88) $110
— 1566. - Antwerp: Plantin. 4to. St. 190, col 34. (88) £750
Hagiographa vol only. 8vo. (90) £70
— 1573-74. - Antwerp: Plantin. 8vo. D & M 5102; St. 227. (88) £700, £1,000
— 1587. - Hamburg: Elian. Folio. D & M 5108. (91) $400
— 1613. - Venice: Giovanni Cajon for Giovanni Bragadin. 4 parts in 2 vols. Folio. Herbert 319. (91) £1,050
— 1617-18. - Geneva: Kafa Ilan. 1 part (of 4) only. 4to. Contains Song of Songs, Ruth, Lamentations, Ecclesiastes, Esther, Job, Isaiah. (90) $120
4to. St. 420. (89) $175
— 1617-18. - Venice. 4 parts in 4 vols. Folio. (88) $850

1987 - 1991 • BOOKS

— 1618-19. - Basel: L. Koenig. Issue with Hebrew general title. Ed by Johann Buxtorf. 2 vols. Variously worn & stained; a few taped repairs; previous owners marks. Bound with: Buxtorf. Tiberias, sive commentarius Masorethicus triplex.... Basel, 1665. Lacking tp. Folio. D & M. 5120. (90) $550

— 1631-35. - Amst.: Menassah ben Israel for Henry Laurentius. 4to. D & M 5124. (89) $175

— 1635. - Amst.: Menasseh ben Israel for Henry Laurentius. 4to. (88) $275

— 1659-61. - Amst: Joseph Athias. 4 vols. 8vo. (89) $1,100; (91) £280

— 1662. - Leiden: J. G. Nissel. 8vo. D & M 5133. (88) $175

— 1677. - Biblia Testamenti Veteris. Frankfurt: B. C. Wustii. 8vo. (88) $275

— 1700-5. - Amst.: David Nunes Torres & Immanuel Athias. 2 vols. 12mo. D & M 5140. (88) $150
Vol I only. D & M 5140. (89) $120

— 1701. - Amst. 8vo. St. 712, col 113-14; D & M 5139. (88) $200; (89) $275; (90) $300; (91) £150

— 1705. - Amst. & Utrecht. 4 vols. 8vo. D & M 5141. (91) $175
8vo. D & M 5141. (88) $175; (90) $550

— 1709. - Cologne: Bartholdi Reuther. Ed by Heinrich Opitz. 4to. D & M 5142. (91) $275

— 1709. - Kiel. Ed by Heinrich Opitz. 4to. (91) £180
D & M 5142. (91) $280

— 1720. - Halle. Ed by Johann Heinrich Michaelis. 2 vols. 4to. D & M 5144. (88) $225; (89) £160
2 vols. 8vo. D & M 5144. (89) $110

— 1730. - Sepher Arba'ah Ve'esrim, Torah Nevi'im Ukethuvim. Venice: Bragadin. 4to. (89) $300

— 1742-44. - Mantua. 4 parts in 3 vols. 4to. D & M 5150. (88) $600

— 1742-44. - Sepher Arbah Ve'esrim. Mantua: Raphael Chaim d'Italia the Physician. 4 parts in 2 vols. 4to. D & M 5150. (89) $550

— 1767. - Tikun Sofrim. Amst.: Leib b. Moses Soesmans. 1 vol only (of 5). 8vo. (91) $500

— 1776-80. - Oxford: Clarendon Press. 2 vols. Folio. (90) £110
D & M 5160. (88) £620

— 1803. - Pisa. 4to. (88) $225

— 1814. - Phila. 2 vols. 8vo. D & M 5168a. (88) $1,200

— The Book of Esther. Jerusalem, 1947. Illus by Ze'ev Raban. Oblong 4to. (89) $200; (90) $300

BIBLE IN HEBREW & LATIN

Jerusalem: for the Miriam Publishing House, 1947. Oblong 4to. Inscr. (89) $325

— Chamisha Chumshei Torah. Antwerp: Christopher Plantin, 1573-74. 16mo. D & M 5102. (91) $950
Antwerp: Christopher Plantin, 1580-82. 4to. D & M 5104. (91) $1,200
Geneva: Kafa Ilan [P. de la Rouviere], 1618. 4to,l. D & M 5118. (91) $850
Amst.: Menasseh ben Israel for H. Laurentius, 1635-36. 4to. D & M 5124. (91) $1,800
Vienna: Anton Schmid, 1815. 4to. Document, 30 May 1818, tipped in, noting this Bible to be used in Court of Law to administer the Jewish Oath, sgd by Eleazar Fleckles & Karl Fischer. (91) $425
Berlin: Soncino Gesellschaft, 1931-33. This copy ptd on vellum except for last 17 leaves & is probably extra to the Ed of 867 (6 on vellum). Folio. (91) $4,800

— Chamishah Chumshei Torah. Antwerp: Christopher Plantin, 1580-82. 4to. (91) $800

— Hosee [-Jonah] cum Thargum id est Chaldaica paraphrasi Ionathan. Paris: Robert Estienne, 1556. 4to. D & M 5097; Adams B-1289. (91) £500

— Neviim Rishonim. Soncino: [Joshua Solomon Soncino], 15 Oct 1485. Folio. 124 (of 166) leaves. Goff Heb-22. (88) £10,000

— Sepher Hamagid. Amst.: Caspar Steen, 1699-1700. 4 parts in 10 vols. 24mo. (91) $1,500

— Sepher Tehillim...Sepher Kinoth. Cambr., 1685. 12mo. (89) $250
Cambr.: John Hayes, 1685. 12mo. (89) $275

— Shir Hashirim. Berlin, 1923. Illus by Ze'ev Raban. Folio. (89) $175; (91) $175
Jerusalem: Ariel Press for the Song of Songs Publishing Co., 1930. Folio. (89) $225

— The Story of Ruth. NY, 1930. Illus by Ze'ev Raban. Folio. (89) $90, $225; (91) $120

Bible in Hebrew & English

— Five Books of Moses. L: Lion Soesmans, 1787. 5 vols. 8vo. (88) $500

Bible in Hebrew & Latin

— 1546. - Basel: Michael Isingrin & Henricus Petrus. Folio. (91) $325

— 1551. - Venice: Marco Antonio Giustiniani. 4to. (90) $350

— 1584. - Antwerp: Plantin. 2 parts in one vol. Folio. Ptd on green paper. (88) £2,800

BIBLE IN HEBREW & LATIN

3 parts in one vol. Folio. (90) $1,100
— 1618. - Geneva: P. de la Rouviere. Folio. (90) £65; (91) £500 St. 420, col 69. (88) $225
— 1668. - [New Testament] Rome. Folio. (90) $120 D & M 5136. (90) $500
— 1699. - Berlin. 8vo. D & M 5138. (89) $325

— Proverbis Salomonis, iam recens iuxta Hebraica veritate translata.... Basel: Froben, 1524. 8vo. Steinschneider I:51. (91) £600

Bible in Icelandic

— 1644. - Biblia Pad er, Oll Heilog Ritning.... Hoolum. 3 parts in 1 vol. Folio. D & M 5491. (88) £6,200
D & M 5491. Doheny copy. (89) $3,300
D & M 5491. (90) £1,200
— 1728. - Biblia ad er oll Heilog Ritning. Hoolum: Marteine Arnoddssyne. 4 parts in 1 vol. Folio. D & M 5494. (91) £300

Bible in Italian

— 1547. - La Biblia laquale in se contiene i sacrosanti libri. Venice: Girolamo Scotto. 4to. Heredia-Tomkinson-Martin copy. (90) $21,000
— 1556. - Lyons: J. de Tournes & G. Gazeau. 16mo. D & M 809. (91) £70
— 1607. - La Bibbia. Coie, i libri del Vecchio, e del Nuovo Testamento [Geneva: Jean de Tournes]. 1st Protestant Bible in Italian. 4to. (90) £190
D & M 5598. Doheny copy. (89) $1,400
— 1833. - Milan: Stella. Atlas vol only. Folio. (88) $160
— 1937. - Milan. Out-of-series copy. 2 vols. Folio. (89) £600
— 1937. - La Bibbia di Borso d'Este. Milan. One of 500. Ed by Giovanni Treccani & Adolfo Venturi. 2 vols. Folio. Inscr by Treccani to Giulio Benedetti. (88) £260

— Epistole et Evangelii che si leggono tutto l'anno alle Messe.... Venice: Galignani, 1602. 4to. (88) $225
Venice: Carlo Conzatti, [1665]. 4to. (90) $50

Bible in Latin

— c.1450-55. - Mainz: Gutenberg. 12 leaves, comprising the whole Book of Daniel. Bluestein - The Garden copy. (90) $360,000
8 consecutive leaves, containing the Epistle to the Romans with the general prologue to Paul's Epistles, the "prologus specialis", the prologue of the Epistle to the Corinthians & Chapters 1 and 2 of that Epistle. Calligraphic presentation page at front, presenting the fragment to John J. Cantwell, 1939, with illuminated border by Graily Hewitt. Doheny copy. (88) $170,000
Five leaves, comprising end of Philemon and Hebrews (complete). Jones-Doheny copy. With: Newton, A. Edward. A Noble Fragment. NY, 1921. (88) $90,000
Single leaf, comprising 4 Kings 2 to 4. (88) £3,800
Single leaf, comprising Isaiah I.1-II.4. (90) $6,000
Single leaf. (90) DM46,000
Single leaf, comprising end of II Paralipomenon, Oratio manasse, St. Jerome's prologue to Esdras & beginning of I Esdras. Binder's waste with recto cleaned & scraped around type columns; verso with minor stain to last 10 lines; 2 small vellum patches on margin. (90) $58,000
Single leaf, comprising Isaiah 38:10 to 41:4. Fleming copy. (89) $13,000
Single leaf, comprising Acts 25:24-27:24. From the Sulzbach-Wells copy. (91) $9,500
Single leaf, Isaiah viii:1 through x:12. Folio. In: Newton, A. Edward. A Noble Fragment. NY, 1921. Goff B-521. (88) $5,250
Single leaf. Folio. In: Newton, A. Edward. A Noble Fragment. NY, 1921. Goff B-521. (89) $8,500
Single leaf, Isaiah XI: 10-13. Folio. In: Newton, A. Edward. A Noble Fragment. NY, 1921. Goff B-521. (89) $9,000
Single leaf, II Kings 4:8 - 5:11. Folio. In: Newton, A. Edward. A Noble Fragment. NY, 1921. Goff B-521. (89) $9,000
Single leaf, Kings III: 21-22. Folio. In: Newton, A. Edward. A Noble Fragment. NY, 1921. Goff B-521. (89) $9,500
Single leaf, Numbers 6:1-7:37. Folio. In: Newton, A. Edward. A Noble Fragment. NY, 1921. Goff B-521. (90) $11,000
Single leaf, comprising Ecclesiastes 3-5. In: Newton, A. Edward. A Noble Fragment. NY, 1921. (90) £6,200
Single leaf, fol 248 (Esdras IV, chapters vi-vii). Folio. In: Newton, A. Edward. A Noble Fragment. NY, 1921. Goff B-521. (91) $12,000
Single leaf, fol 239 (Esdras III, chapter v). Folio. In: Newton, A. Edward. A Noble Fragment. NY, 1921. Goff B-521. (91) $17,000
Single leaf, comprising part of Ecclesiasticus 38-39. Ptd on vellum. Nichols-Saks —The Garden copy. (90) $65,000
Single leaf, comprising Ezechiel 43-45. Trier-Houghton-Greenhill copy. Martin copy. (90) $13,000
Vol I (of 2). Folio. 324 leaves. Goff B-526. Dyson Perrins—Doheny copy. (88) $4,900,000
— not after 1461. - Bamberg: Printer of the

- 36-line Bible. Single leaf only. Folio. Goff B-527. Doheny copy. (88) $30,000
- 1462, 14 Aug. - Mainz: Johann Fust & Peter Schoeffer. 1 leaf, text from Micah, III-VI. Folio. Goff B-529. Doheny copy. (88) $1,400
  1 leaf, text from Zachariah 14:12-21 & Malachi 1:1-4:1. Folio. Goff B-529. (90) $1,500
  2 vols. Folio. Ptd on vellum. 481 leaves. Goff B-529 Doheny copy. (88) $650,000
- not after 1468. - Strassburg: Heinrich Eggestein. Vol I only. Folio. 249 (of 250) leaves; lacking final blank. Goff B-531. (90) $6,500
- c.1473. - Biblia Latina. Strassburg: R-Press type 1. Folio. 425 (of 426) leaves; lacking initial blank. Goff B-534. Doheny copy. (88) $38,000
- 1475. - Basel: Bernhard Richel. Folio. 461 leaves. Goff B-540. Doheny copy. (88) $7,500
- 1475. - Venice: Franciscus Renner, de Heilbronn & Nicolaus de Frankfordia. Folio. 454 (of 455) leaves; lacking 1st blank. Goff B-541. (90) £4,800
- 1475, 16 Nov. - Nuremberg: Anton Koberger. Folio. 474 (of 481) leaves. Goff B-543. (90) $9,000
- 1476. - Naples: Mathias Moravus [& Biagio Romero]. Folio. 454 leaves. Goff B-545. Doheny copy. (88) $9,000
- 1476. - Venice: Nicolaus Jenson. Folio. 470 leaves. Goff B-547. Hogan-Doheny copy. (88) $30,000
- 1476-77. - [New Testament] Paris: Ulrich Gering & Martin Crantz & Michael Friburger. 12 leaves only: Matthew 14-Mark 11. Goff B-550. (91) £1,000
- 1477, 8 Sept. - Basel: Bernhard Richel. Genesis to Psalms only. Folio. (88) £2,200
- 1478. - Venice: Leonardus Wild for Nicolaus de Frankfordia. Folio. 455 (of 456) leaves; lacking initial blank. Goff B-558. (91) $7,000
- 1478, 14 Apr. - Nuremberg: Anton Koberger. Folio. 468 leaves. Goff B-557. Doheny copy. (88) $10,000
- 1478. - Biblia Latina. Venice: Reynaldus de Novimagio & Theodorus de Reynsburch. Folio. 117 (of 456) leaves. Goff B556. (88) $1,200
- 1479. - Basel: Johann Amerbach. Folio. 535 (of 472) leaves. Goff B-561. (91) $3,000
- 1479. - Venice: Nicolaus Jenson. Folio. Ptd on vellum. 451 (of 452) leaves; lacking 1st blank. Goff B-563. Holford-Doheny copy. (88) $95,000
- not after 1480. - Strassburg: Adolf Rusch for Anton Koberger. Fragment of 348 leaves only. Part of Goff B-607. (89) £1,300

Single leaf with text from Hosea. Rubricated. Goff B-607. (91) $325
Vol I only. 253 (of 254) leaves. Goff B-607. (91) £900
- 1480. - Venice: Franciscus Renner, de Heilbronn. 4to & 8vo. 470 leaves. Goff B-566. (88) $3,500
  470 leaves. Goff B-566. Doheny copy. (88) $6,500
  470 leaves. Goff B-566. Abrams copy. (90) £6,000
- 1480, 29 Jan. - Ulm: Johann Zainer. Folio. 430 (of 441) leaves. Goff B-567.. (91) DM2,500
- [c.1481]. - Strassburg:A. Rusch for Koberger. Folio. 12 leaves only, from the books of Judith & Esther. (91) £150
- 1481, 31 July. - Venice: [J. Herbort de Seligenstadt for] Johannes de Colonia, Nicolaus Jenson et Socii. Folio. Part IV (New Testament) only. 386 (of 1,571 leaves). Goff B-611. Doheny copy. (88) $1,600
- 1482-83. - Venice: Franciscus Renner, de Heilbronn. 3 vols. Folio. 1,318 (of 1,322) leaves; lacking 2 blanks. Goff B-612. (90) LIt5,500,000
- 1484, 30 Apr. - Venice: Johannes Herbort de Seligenstadt. 4to. 405 (of 408) leaves; Goff B-580. (88) $1,100
  408 leaves. Goff B-580. (90) DM4,200
- 1486. - [Strassburg: Johann Pruess]. Folio. 538 leaves. Goff B-583. Doheny copy. (88) $6,000
  538 leaves. Goff B-583. (90) DM5,400
- 1487, 3 Dec. - Nuremberg: Anton Koberger. Vol IV only. Folio. 383 (of 384) leaves; lacking initial blank. Goff B-614. (88) £800
- 1489. - Venice: [Bonetus Locatellus for] Octavianus Scotus. Vol IV (of 4) only. Folio. 272 leaves. Goff B-616. (90) £850
- 1491, 27 June. - Basel: Johann Froben. 8vo. 185 leaves only. Goff B-592. (89) £410
  495 (of 496) leaves; lacking blank. Goff B-592. Doheny copy. (88) $3,500
- 1492, Sept 7. - Biblia latina. Venice: Hieronymus de Paganinis. 8vo. 510 (of 552) leaves. Goff B594. (91) LIt1,100,000
- 1495, 27 Oct. - Basel: Froben. 8vo. 460 (of 508) leaves; lacking the Interpretationes, quires A-E, and quire Z. Goff B-598. Doheny copy. (88) $1,500
  506 (of 508) leaves; lacking tp & 2B. Goff B-598.. (91) £900
- 1497. - Strassburg: [J. R. Grueninger]. Folio. 489 (of 492) leaves. Goff B-600. (91) £1,200
- 1497, 6 Sept. - Nuremberg: Anton Koberger. Part 4 (of 4) only. Folio. 351 (of 352) leaves; lacking final blank. Goff B-619. (88) £700
- 1497, 7 Sept. - Venice: Hieronymus de

BIBLE IN LATIN

- Paganinis. 8vo. 511 (of 514) leaves. Goff B-601. (88) $1,200
- 514 leaves. Goff B-601. (88) £420
- 1497, 6 Sept. - Biblia com postillis Nicolai de Lyra.... Nuremberg: Anton Koberger. Part 2 (of 4) only. Folio. 338 leaves. GKW 4294. (88) $2,400
- 1498, 8 May. - Venice: Simon Bevilaqua. 4to. 519 (of 528) leaves; lacking 1st 8 leaves & last leaf. Goff B-603. (89) $1,100
- 528 leaves. Goff B-603. (91) $10,000
- 1504. - Paris: T. Kerver for I. Parvi & I. Scabeller. Folio. (90) $600
- 1510. - [New Testament]. Paris. 8vo. (88) £700
- 1511, 5 June. - Venice: Lucantonio Giunta. 4to. (91) £220
- Doheny copy. (89) $1,800
- 1513, 3 Sept [but 30 Aug]. - Lyons: Jacobus Sacon for Anton Koberger. Folio. (90) £320; (91) £350
- 1515, 12 Jan. - Lyons: Jacob Sacon for Anton Koberger. Folio. (88) £600; (89) £440
- 1518, 10 May. - Biblia cum concordantiis veteris & novi testamenti. Lyons: J. Sacon for A. Koberger. Folio. D & M 6101. (91) £300, £340
- 1519, 15 Oct. - Venice: Lucantonio Giunta. 8vo. (88) £110; (89) $800
- 1521. - Lyons: Jacob Sacon for A. Koberger. 4to. (88) $850
- D&M 6101. (91) $550
- 1526, 6 Nov. - Paris: Widow of T. Kerver. 2 parts in 1 vol. 8vo. (88) £90; (89) $200
- 1528-27. - Lyons: Antonius du Ry. 3 parts in 1 vol. 4to. D & M 6108. Doheny copy. (89) $1,900
- 1528-29. - Lyons: Jacob Mareschal. 7 parts in 6 vols (the Supplementum bound at end of Vol V). Folio. (88) £380
- 1528. - Paris: R. Estienne. Folio. Schreiber 14; D & M 6109. Doheny copy. (89) $3,800
- 1538. - Basel: H. Froben & N. Episcopius. Folio. (89) $750
- 1540. - Antwerp: A. Goinus. Folio. (88) £140
- 1541-42. - Paris: R. Estienne. 8vo. (88) £13,000
- 1542. - Biblia Sacra. Lyons. Folio. (88) $650
- 1545. - Paris: R. Estienne. 8vo. (90) £180; (91) £280
- 1547, Nov. - [1st Ed of the Louvain Bible] Louvain: Bartholomaeus Gravius. Folio. D & M 6129. Doheny copy. (89) $350
- 1555. - [Paris]: R. Estienne. 8vo. (89) £100
- 1558. - Lyons: Guillaume Rouille. 16mo. (89) $175
- 1566. - Frankfurt. Folio. (89) £320

AMERICAN BOOK PRICES CURRENT

- 1566. - Lyons: I. Frellonium. Folio. (90) HF1,300
- 1567. - Antwerp: Plantin. 8vo. (90) $400
- 1567. - Lyons. 8vo. (89) £120
- 1573. - Basel: Petrus Perna. 2 vols in 1. Folio. (88) £200
- 1573. - [New Testament] Paris: J. Kerver. 16mo. (88) £240
- 1576. - Venice: Heirs of N. Bevilaquae & socios. Folio. (91) £200
- Doheny copy. (89) $1,200; (91) $1,600
- 1581. - Lyon: Guillaume Rouille. 8vo. (88) DM700; (90) £55
- 1585. - L: Henricus Middletonus. [New Testament]. 4to. (90) £60
- 1587. - Venice: Hieronymus Polus. 4to. (89) £85
- 1591. - Basel. 8vo. (89) $200
- 1592. - Rome: Typographia Apostolica Vaticana. Folio. Doheny copy. (89) $11,000
- 1592. - [Clementine Ed] Rome: Ex Typographia Apostolica Vaticana. Folio. (88) $700
- Doheny copy. (88) $1,500
- 1600. - Tuebingen: Gruppenbach. Folio. DM 6180. (91) DM1,400
- 1642-40. - Paris: Typographia Regia. 8 vols. Folio. D & M 6217. Lothian-Doheny copy. (89) $900
- 1697. - Venice: N. Pezzana. 4to. (91) $200
- 1748. - Venice. 2 vols. Folio. (90) $150
- 1785. - Bibliorum Sacrorum Vulgatae versionis editio.... Paris: Didot l'Aine. 8 vols. 4to. (89) FF22,000
- 1785. - Novum Jesu-Christi Testamentum. Paris: Barbou. 2 vols. 12mo. One of 3 copies ptd on vellum. Doheny copy. (89) $3,500
- 1961. - Paterson & NY: Pageant Books. One of 1,000. 2 vols. Folio. Facsimile of the Gutenberg Bible of c.1450-55. (88) DM3,200; (89) $1,800; (90) $900, $1,500, £500; (91) $500, $950
- 1977-78. - Munich: Idion Verlag. One of 895. 2 vols plus Kommentarband. Folio. Facsimile of the Gutenberg Bible, reproducing Needham V7. The Garden copy. (90) $6,250
- 1985. - Paris: Les Editions des incunables. 4 vols, including commentary. Folio. Facsimile of the Mazarin Library copy of the Gutenberg Bible. (91) $1,700
- 31 July 1481. - Venice: [J. Herbort de Seligenstadt for] Johannes de Colonia, Nicolaus Jenson et Socii. Folio. 400 (of 1,571) leaves: Goff B-611. (88) $1,100

- Canticum canticorum. Berlin, 1921-22. Facsimile of the 1465 Ed. One of 400.

4to. (91) $200

— Iesu Christi vita, iuxta quatuor Evangelistarum narrationes.... Antwerp: Matthias Crom for Adriaen Kempe van Bouckhout, 24 Dec 1537. Compiled by Willem van Branteghem; illus by Lieven de Witte. 8vo. Ives-Ellsworth-Doheny copy. (89) $2,500; (91) $1,400

— Jesu Syraci liber, qui vulgo Ecclesiasticus dicitur.... Basel: Michael Martinus Stella, [1556]. Bound with: Liber jesu Syrach, ex Germanica translatione D. Martini Lutheri Latine redditus.... Wittenberg: Heirs of Georg Rhau, 1556. 8vo. (91) $550

— [Lefevre's revision of the Vulgate text of Paul's Epistle to the Romans]. Paris: Henri Estienne, 15 Dec 1512. Folio. Schreiber 14. Doheny copy. (89) $1,500

— The Lorsch Gospels. NY, [1967]. Ltd Ed. Folio. (88) £85
One of 1,000. 2 vols. Folio. (88) $225; (89) £120
Facsimile only; lacking explanatory text vol. 4to. (91) $80

— Postille maiores super evangelia & epistolas. Basel: Petrus von Langendorff, Feb 1519. 4to. (88) £480

Bible in Latin & English

— 1538. - Newe Testament both Latine and Englyshe.... Southwarke: James Nicolson. 2d 4to Ed of Coverdale's Diglot New Testament, 2d Issue. 4to. STC 2816.7; Herbert 38. Doheny copy. (89) $5,000

Bible in Latin & French

— 1793. - Le Nouveau Testament. Paris. 5 vols. 8vo. Schuhmann copy. (90) £1,100
Vols I-IV (of 5). Doheny copy. (89) $650

— [Acts of the Apostles only] Paris: Didot jeune, 1798. 8vo. Doheny copy. (88) $320

Bible in Malayan

— 1697. - Amst. 4to. D & M 6490n. (89) £480

Bible in Mohawk

— Nene Karighyoston Tsinihorighhoten ne Saint John. NY, 1818. 18mo. D & M 6798. (89) $200

Bible in Natick

— 1663-61. - The Holy Bible.... Cambr.: Samuel Green & Marmaduke Johnson. 1st Ed of Eliot's Indian Bible. Trans by John Eliot. 4to. "The finest copy known." D & M 6737. Boyle-Phillipps-Fenwick-Doheny copy. (89) $300,000

Bible in Polish

— 1632. - Biblia swieta. Danzig: Andrzeja Hunefelda. 8vo. D & M 7392. (89) £2,500

Bible in Romansch (Lower Engadine)

— 1678-79. - La Sacra Bibla. Scuol: Jacob Dorta a Vulpera. 3 parts in 1 vol. Folio. (91) £2,400

Bible in Rumanian

— 1682. - Svita Shi Dmizeiaska Evangelie. Bucharest: Metropolitan Press. Folio. D & M 7725. (91) £800

Bible in Shorthand

— [1673?]. - L: Samuel Botley. Bound with: The Whole Book of Psalms...Short-writing.... L: Samuel Botley, [1669?] Put into shorthand by Jeremiah Rich. 64mo. (90) £450

— 1687. - Holy Bible in Shorthand by William Addy. L. 8vo. (89) £120; (91) $300

Bible in Sinhalese

— 1776. - [New Testament] Colombo: In 's Kompagnies Drukkery door Johan Fredrik Christoph Dornheim. 4to. D & M 8303. (88) £400

Bible in Spanish

— 1556. - El Testamento Nuevo de Nuestro Senor y Salvador Iesu Christo. Venice: Iuan Philadelpho [Geneva: Jean Crispin]. 8vo. D & M 8468. (90) £580

— 1569, Sept. - [Basel: S. Apairius for Thomas Guarinus]. 1st Ed of complete Bible in Spanish. 3 parts in 1 vol. 4to. D & M 8472. (90) £380
4to. D & M 8472. (89) $1,400
OT only. D & M 8472. (91) £180

— 1602. - Amst.: Lorenco Jacobi. 3 parts in 1 vol. Folio. (88) £500; (89) £320

— 1602. - La Biblia, que es, los sacros libros.... Frankfurt: Wolfgang Richter. 3 parts in 1 vol. 8vo. (88) £900

— 1661. - [Old Testament] Amst.: Joseph Athias. 8vo. D & M 8481. (89) $800

— 1726. - Amst. 4to. D & M 8485. (91) $425

— 1819. - El Nuevo Testamento de Nuestro Senor Jesu Cristo. NY. 12mo. D & M 8495. Doheny copy. (88) $480

— Los Quatro Evangelios de nuestro Senor Jesu Cristo. Buenos Aires: Kraft, 1945. Copy 3 of an unspecified number of copies, with sgd proof of 1 woodcut loosely inserted. Illus by Victor Delhez. Folio. Doheny copy. (88) $450

BIBLE IN SYRIAC

Bible in Syriac
— 1622. - [New Testament] Koethen, near Halle. 4to. (89) £600
— 1664-67. - [New Testamen] Hamburg. 3 parts in 1 vol. 8vo. D & M 8966(d). (89) £400

Bible in Tahitian
[A bound vol containing 6 separately issued translations of parts of the Bible sold at sg on 8 Nov 1990, lot 16] $1,700

Bible in Yiddish
— 1676-78. - Amst.: Uri Feibush Ha'levi. 4 parts in 1 vol plus the Toaliyot by the RaLBa'G on Joshua, Judges & Samuel. Folio. (90) $750
— 1687. - Amst.: Emanuel Atias. Folio. (89) £250

Bible, Polyglot
— 1514-17. - [The Complutensian Bible] Alcala de Henares: Arnald Guillen de Brocar. 6 vols. Folio. D & M 1412. Lyell-Doheny copy. (89) $38,000 D & M 1412. (91) £35,000
— 1568-73. - Biblia Sacra Hebraice, Chaldaice, Graece & Latine [The Antwerp Polyglot]. Antwerp: Christopher Plantin at the expense of King Philip II of Spain. 8 vols. Folio. D & M 1422. Doheny copy. (89) £24,000
— 1569-72. - Antwerp: C. Plantin. 8 vols. Folio. (91) £10,000
— 1569. - [New Testament] [Geneva]: H. Estienne. Folio. Doheny copy. (88) $1,800
— 1570-71. - Biblia Sacra Hebraice, Chaldaice, Graece & Latine [The Second Antwerp, Plantin or Royal Polyglot]. Antwerp: Christopher Plantin at the expense of King Philip II of Spain. 5 vols only (of 8; without the Apparatus). Folio. D & M 1422. Doheny copy. (89) $9,500
— 1584. - Antwerp: Plantin. 3 vols in one. Folio. (90) $500
— 1599. - [New Testament]. Nuremberg. Folio. In 12 languages. (90) $400
— 1629-45. - Paris: A. Vitray. 9 parts in 10 vols. Folio. D & M 1442. Liechtenstein-Doheny copy. (89) $11,000
— 1655-57. - L. Ed by Brian Walton. 6 vols. Folio. Doheny copy. (89) $18,000
— 1657. - Leipzig. Old Testament only. Folio. (89) £60
— 1713. - Hexaplorum Origensis quae supersunt.... Paris. 2 vols. Folio. (90) $275
— 1831. - Biblia Sacra Polyglotta. L: Samuel Bagster. Folio. D & M 1456. Doheny copy. (88) $600
— 1869. - L. 2 vols. Folio. D & M 1456. (90) $275

AMERICAN BOOK PRICES CURRENT

— [Gospels] Stockholm, 1671. 4to. D & M 1448. Doheny copy. (89) $950

Biblia Pauperum
— [Block Book. Scenes from the life of Christ with Old Testament prefigurations & prophecies].Schreiber's Ed VIII. Folio, 276mm by 210mm. 40 leaves. Doheny copy. (88) $2,200,000
— Opera nova contemplativa per ogni fidei Christiano laquale tratta de la figure del testamento vecchio.... Venice: Giovanni Andrea Vavassore, [c.1525]. 8vo. 63 (of 64) leaves; lacking final blank. Block book. Essling 206. (91) £38,000

Bibliografia Medical de Catalunya
— Inventari Primer. Barcelona, 1918. One of 500. 4to. (91) $50

Bibliographica...
— Bibliographica: Papers on Books, their History and Art. L, 1895-97. 12 parts in 3 vols. 8vo. (88) $375; (90) £200; (91) $80, $275, £110, £300
Doheny copy. (88) $300
Facsimile reprint of 1895-97 Ed. Westport, [1970]. 12 parts in 3 vols. (88) $50

Bibliographical Society of the University of Virginia
— Studies in Bibliography. Charlottesville, 1948-76. Vols 1-31, lacking Vol 10. (88) $120
Charlottesville, 1948-86. Vols 1-39; lacking Vol 14. (89) $175
Charlottesville, 1948-88. Vols 1-41, lacking Vols 8 & 10. Martin copy. (90) $250
Vols 1-23. Charlottesville, 1948-70. (90) £80

Bibliophile...
— Le Bibliophile francais. Gazette illustree des amateurs de livres. Paris, 1868-73. Vols I-VII. 8vo. (91) $130

Biblioteca Ambrosiana—Milan
— Hebraica Ambrosiana. Milan, 1972. One of 650. Compiled by A. Luzzatto & L. M. Ottolenghi. 2 parts in 1 vol. 4to. (89) $175

Biblioteca Medicea Laurenziana
— Bibliothecae Ebraicae Graecae Florentinae, sive Bibliothecae Mediceo-Laurentianae Catalogus. Florence, 1757. 8vo. (91) $175

Biblioteca Nationale di Napoli
— Codicum saeculo XV impressorum qui in Regia Bibliotheca Borbonica adservantur catalogus ordine alphabetico digestus.... Naples: Regia Typographia, 1828-41. 4 vols, including Supplement. Folio. (90) $425

Bibliotheca...
— Bibliotheca Americana; or, a Chronological Catalogue of...Books.... L, 1789. 4to. (88) $525, £380
— Bibliotheca Americana, Being a Choice Collection of Books Relating to North and South America and the West-Indies.... Paris, 1831. 8vo. (91) $160
— Bibliotheca Danica; systematisk fortegnelse over den Danske litteratur.... Copenhagen, 1877-1902. 1st Ed. 4 vols. 4to. (91) $225
  Copenhagen, 1961-64. 5 vols. 4to. (91) $90
— Bibliotheca Politica: or an Enquiry into the Ancient Constitution of the English Government. See: Tyrrell, Sir James
— Bibliotheca Sussexiana. L, 1844-45. 6 parts in 1 vol. 8vo. L.p. copy on thick paper. (88) £230
— Bibliotheca scatologica, ou Catalogue raisonne des livres traitant des vertus, faits, et gestes.... Scatopolis [Paris], 5850 [1849]. One of 150. 8vo. (91) $300
— Bibliotheca Spenceriana; or a Descriptive Catalogue of the Books Printed in the Fifteenth Century. See: Dibdin, Thomas Frognall

Bibliotheca Colombina
— BABELON, JEAN. - La Bibliotheque Francaise de Fernand Colomb. Paris, 1913. (91) $140

Bibliotheque...
— Bibliotheque italique ou histoire litteraire de l'Italie. Geneva, 1728-34. 18 vols. 12mo. (91) £120
— Bibliotheque italique ou histoire litterarie de l'Italie. Geneva, 1728-33. Vols I-XVII (of 18). 12mo. (88) FF3,600
— Bibliotheque du Theatre Francois, depuis son Origine. Dresden: Michel Groell, 1768. 3 vols. 8vo. (88) $300; (90) $350
— Bibliotheque cynegetique d'un amateur avec notes bibliographiques. Paris, 1884. One of 300. 4to. (91) £70

Bibliotheque Nationale
— Notices et extraits des manuscrits de la Bibliotheque du Roi [de la Bibliotheque Nationale]. Paris, 1787-1933. 42 vols in 45. 4to. (89) £2,200
— Les Plus Belles Reliures.... Paris, 1929. One of 600. Folio. (89) $225

Bibliotheque Publique de Geneve
— Catalogue.... Geneva, 1834. 2 vols. 8vo. (91) $225

Bibliotheque Publique de Versailles
— PELLECHET, MARIE. - Catalogue des Incunables et des Livres Imprimes de MD. a MDXX. avec Marques Typographiques des Editions du XVe Siecle. Paris, 1889. 8vo. (91) $250

Bicchierai, Allesandro
— Dei Bagni di Montecatini. Florence, 1788. 4to. (89) $325

Bicci, Antonio & Gaetano
— I Contadini della Toscana espressi al naturale. Florence: Miccolo Pagni & Giuseppe Bardi, 1796. Folio. (91) £32,000

Bichat, Marie Francois Xavier, 1771-1802
— Anatomie generale appliquee a la physiologie et a la medecine. Paris, An X [1801]. 4 vols. 8vo. (88) $750
— General Anatomy, applied to Physiology and Medicine. Bost., 1822-23. 4 vols, including Additions. 8vo. (89) $400
— A Treatise on Membranes in General.... Bost., 1813. 8vo. (89) $225
— Anatomie generale, appliquee a la physiologie et a la medecine. Paris: Chez Brosson, 1801-21. 5 vols, including Beclard's Supplement. 8vo. (88) $1,000
— Physiological Researches upon Life and Death. Phila., 1809. 8vo. (89) $150
— Recherches physiologiques sur la vie et la mort. Paris, [1800] An VIII. 8vo. (88) $300
— Traite des membranes en general et de diverses membranes en particulier. Paris, [1800]. 1st Ed. 8vo. (88) $400

Bickerdyke, John. See: Cook, Charles Henry

Bickerstaff, Laura M.
— Pioneer Artists of Taos. Denver, [1955]. (89) $110

Bickham, George, the Younger, d.1758
— A Curious Antique Collection of Bird's-Eye Views.... L, 1796. 4to. (89) £3,800; (91) £3,400

Bickham, George, the Elder, d.1769
— The British Monarchy.... L, 1743. Folio. (88) £140; (91) £450
— The Musical Entertainer. L, [1737]. 2 vols in 1. Folio. (91) £800
— The Universal Penman.... L, 1741. Folio. (88) £350; (89) $300
  L, 1743. Folio. (88) £160; (89) $650, £260; (91) £480, £620

Bickley, Francis Lawrence
— The Adventures of Harlequin. L, 1923. One of 250. Illus by John Austen. (89) $160

Bicknell, Alexander, d.1796
— The History of Edward Prince of Wales. L, 1776. 8vo. (91) $60

Bicknell, Amos Jackson
— Bicknell's Village Builder.... NY, 1872-[71]. Without Supplement. Folio. (89) £100

Bicknell, Clarence
— Flowering Plants and Ferns of the Riviera.... L, 1885. 1st Ed. 8vo. ALs pasted to verso of half-title. (88) £140

Bicknell, John Laurens
— The Hour of Trial; A Tragedy. L, 1824. 8vo. Dedication copy, inscr to Robert Southey. (90) $250

Biddlecombe, Sir George
— Naval Tactics. L, 1850. 4to. (90) £120

Biddulph, William
— The Travels of certaine Englishmen into Africa, Asia, Troy.... L: Th. Haveland for W. Aspley, 1609. 4to. STC 3051. Blackmer copy. (90) £2,000

Bidloo, Govard, 1649-1713
— Anatomia humani corporis.... Amst., 1685. Folio. (90) $2,800; (91) £2,000
  Georges Cuvier's copy, with his stamp on tp. (89) $6,000
— Komste van Zyne Majesteit Willem III...in Holland. The Hague, 1691. Illus by Romeyn de Hooghe. Folio. (88) HF1,400; (90) $2,750
— Ontleding des menschelyken lichaams... iutgebeeld, naar het leven...door G. de Lairesse. Amst., 1690. Folio. (90) $3,500
— Opera omnia anatomico-chirurgica.... Leiden, 1715. 6 parts in 1 vol. 4to. (89) £360
— Relation du voyage de sa majeste Britannique en Hollande.... The Hague, 1692. Folio. (91) £1,000

Bidpai
— The Fables of Pilpay. See: Fore-Edge Paintings

Bidwell, John, 1819-1900
— A Journey to California.... San Francisco: John Henry Nash, 1937. 4to. (88) $110; (89) $70, $80, $85, $90; (90) $60, $95; (91) $75

Bieber, Ralph B.
— Southern Trails to California in 1849. Glendale, 1937. (91) $50

Biel, Gabriel, 1425?-95
— Gabriel in tertium sententiarum. Tuebingen: Johann Otmar for Friedrich Meynberger, [1501]. Folio. (91) £500

Biemmi, Giovanni Maria
— Istoria di Giorgio Castrioto dette Scanderbegh. Brescia: Giammaria Rizzardi, 1756. 8vo. Blackmer copy. (90) £100

Bierbaum, Otto Julius
— Das schoene Maedchen von Pao. Munich, 1910. One of 600. Illus by Franz von Bayros. Folio. (88) DM720, DM760

Bierce, Ambrose, 1842?-1914
— Battle Sketches. Oxford: Shakespeare Head Press, 1930. One of 350. Illus by Thomas Derrick. 4to. (90) $75, $110
— Battlefields and Ghosts. [Palo Alto], 1931. 1st Ed, One of 115. Inscr by James D. Hart. (88) $65
— Battlesketches. L, 19330. One of 350. Inscr by A. J. A. Symons. (88) $75
— Black Beetles in Amber. San Francisco, 1892. 1st Ed. 8vo. (88) $80; (91) $65, $90, $260
  Martin copy. (90) $450
— Can Such Things Be? NY: Cassell, [1893]. (91) $160
— Cobwebs from an Empty Skull. L & NY, 1874. 12mo. (91) $180
— The Cynic's Word Book. NY, 1906. 1st Ed, 1st Issue, without frontis. (90) $175
  BAL state A. (91) $160
— The Dance of Death. San Francisco: Henry Keller, 1877. (91) $50
— The Dance of Death. By William Herman. San Francisco: Henry Keller, 1877. 2d Ed. (88) $60

Bierce, Ambrose, 1842-1914
— The Devil's Dictionary. See: Limited Editions Club

Bierce, Ambrose, 1842?-1914
— Fantastic Fables. NY, 1899. 1st Ed, 1st Ptg. 8vo. (91) $85
  Martin copy. (90) $450
— The Fiend's Delight. L: John Camden Hotten, [1873]. 8vo. (91) $350
— An Invocation. San Francisco: Book Club of California, 1928. One of 300. Folio. Inscr by Oscar Lewis. (91) $60
— The Letters.... San Francisco: Book Club of California, 1922. One of 415. (91) $70
— Nuggets and Dust Panned Out in California by Dod Grile. Collected and Loosely

Arranged by J. Milton Sloluck. L: Chatto & Windus, [1873]. BAL's Printing B. 12mo. (91) $550
Doheny copy. (88) $1,200
— The Shadow on the Dial.... San Francisco, 1909. (89) $160
— Tales of Soldiers and Civilians. San Francisco, 1891. 1st Ed. 12mo. (88) (91) $140, $160, $180
Inscr. Martin copy. (90) $950
Inscr to H. F. Peterson. (88) $800
— Ten Tales. L, 1925. Intro by A. J. A. Symons. (90) $55
— Twenty-one Letters.... Cleveland, 1922. One of 950. (91) $50
Out-of-series copy. (91) $55
— Works. NY & Wash., 1909-12. Out-of-series set with each vol sgd by Bierce. 12 vols. (88) $2,200
Autograph Ed, One of 250. 12 vols. (88) $1,200
— Write it Right: a Little Blacklist of Literary Faults. NY, 1909. (88) $60
San Francisco: Grabhorn-Hoyem, 1971. One of 400. (91) $90

**Bierce, Ambrose, 1842?-1914 —&
Danziger, G. A.**
— The Monk and the Hangman's Daughter. Chicago: F. J. Schulte, 1892. 8vo. Martin copy. (90) $500

Bierens de Haan, David, 1822-95
— Bibliographie Neerlandaise Historique-Scientifique. Nieuwkoop, 1960. One of 300. 4to. (91) $130

Bierstadt, Oscar Albert
— Catalogue. Exhibition of "The Emerald Pool," White Mountains...at Snow & Roos' Art Gallery. San Francisco, 1871. (88) $275
— The Library of Robert Hoe. NY, 1895. One of 350. 8vo. (89) $200; (90) $110, $130; (91) $90

Biese, Nicolas
— De varietate opinionum liber unus. Louvain: Servatius Sassenus, 1567. 8vo. (89) $375

Biet, Antoine
— Voyage de la France Equinoxiale en l'isle de Cayenne. Paris, 1664. 4to. (91) $1,200

Bigelow, Horatio
— Flying Feathers. A Yankee's Hunting Experiences in the South. Richmond, [1937]. (88) $80; (90) $60; (91) $80
— Gunnerman. See: Derrydale Press
— Gunnerman's Gold. Huntington, 1943. One of 1,000. Intro by Nash Buckingham. 4to. (89) $70; (91) $75

Inscr. (88) $70
— Scatter-Gun Sketches. Sport among Upland Game Birds and Waterfowl.... Springfield, Ill., 1922. (91) $195

Bigelow, Jacob, 1787-1879
— American Medical Botany.... Bost., 1817-18-20. 3 vols. 8vo. (89) $2,200
Vol I, Part 2 & Vol II, Parts 1 & 2 only. (91) $475
— Florula Bostoniensis: a Collection of Plants of Boston.... Bost., 1814. 8vo. (89) $140
— A Treatise on the Materia Medica.... Bost., 1822. 1st Ed. 8vo. (90) $100

Bigge, John Thomas
— Report of the Commissioner of Inquiry into the State of the Colony of New South Wales. L, 5 Aug 1822. Bound with: Bigge. Report of the Commissioner of Inquiry, on the Judicial Establishments of New South Wales, and Van Diemen's Land. L, 21 Feb 1823. And: Bigge. Report of the Commissioner of Inquiry, on the State of Agriculture and Trade in...New South Wales. L, 13 Mar 1823. Folio. (89) A$6,000
— Report of the Commissioner of Inquiry, on the Judicial Establishments of New South Wales, and Van Diemen's Land. L, 21 Feb 1823. Folio. (90) A$450

Biggs, William, 1755-1827
— Narrative of William Biggs, While he was a Prisoner with the Kickapoo Indians.... [Edwardsville IL], June 1826. 8vo. (88) $6,000

**Bigmore, Edward Clements —&
Wyman, Charles William Henry**
— A Bibliography of Printing. L, 1880-86. 3 vols. 4to. (89) $200
NY, 1945. 2 vols. Facsimile of the 1880-86 Ed. (88) $70
3 vols in 2. Facsimile of the 1880-86 Ed. (90) $70; (91) $50
L: Holland Press, 1969. One of 350. Facsimile of 1880 Ed. (91) $75
L & Newark DE: Holland Press & Oak Knoll, [1978]. 3 vols in one. Facsimile of the 1880-86 Ed. (91) $50

Bigsby, John Jeremiah, 1792-1881
— The Shoe and Canoe, or Pictures of Travel in the Canadas. L, 1850. 2 vols. 8vo. (89) $60, $375

Bijoux...
— Les Bijoux des neuf-soeurs. Paris, 1790. 2 vols, 24mo. (89) $100

Bilbo, Jack. See: Baruch, Hugo Cyril K.

BILDERLEXICON...

Bilderlexicon...
— Bilderlexicon der Erotik. Vienna & Leipzig, [1928-31]. 4 vols. 4to. (89) $350

Bilguer, Paul Rudolph von, 1815-40
— Handbuch des Schachspiels. Berlin, 1852. 8vo. (89) $50

Biliban, Ivan
— Volga. St. Petersburg, 1904. Folio. (89) $170

Billardon de Sauvigny, Louis Edme
— Histoire Naturelle des Dorades de la Chine.... Paris, 1780. Folio. (91) $9,000

Billings, John D.
— The History of the Tenth Massachusetts Battery of Light Artillery. Bost., 1881. 8vo. Coulter 33. (91) $150

Billings, John Shaw, 1838-1913
— Description of the Johns Hopkins Hospital. Balt., 1890. 4to. (88) $80

Billings, Robert William, 1813-74
— The Baronial and Ecclesiastical Antiquities of Scotland. Edin. & L, [1848-52]. 4 vols. 4to. (89) £90, £240, £400; (91) £160
Edin., 1901. 4 vols. 4to. (89) £130; (90) £130
— Illustrations of the Architectural Antiquities of...Durham.... Durham, 1846. 1st Ed. 4to. (88) £80; (89) £70; (90) £60; (91) £170

Billings, William
— The Singing Master's Assistant.... Bost., 1778. 8vo. (89) $3,200

Billmeir, Jack Albert
— Scientific Instruments (13th-19th Centuries). Oxford, 1955. 2 vols, including 1957 Supplement. 4to. (91) $130

Billroth, Theodor, 1829-94
— Lectures on Surgical Pathology and Therapeutics. L, 1877-78. 2 vols. 8vo. (90) $110

Bilson, Thomas
— The Perpetuall Government of Christs Church. L, 1610. 4to. STC 3066. (90) $100

Bindley Library, James
— [Sale Catalogue] A Catalogue of the very valuable Collection of British Portraits. L, 1819. 3 parts in 1 vol. 4to. (90) £55

Bing, Samuel, 1838-1905
— Artistic Japan.... L, [1888]-91. 36 parts in 6 vols. 4to. (91) $650
6 vols. 4to. (88) £280
— Le Japon artistique. Paris, [1888]. 36 parts. Folio. (88) $325

AMERICAN BOOK PRICES CURRENT

Bing Collection, Samuel
— [Sale catalogue] Collection.... Paris, 1906. 6 parts. Folio. (90) $150
6 parts in 1 vol. Folio. (90) $150

Bingham, Caleb, 1757-1817
— The Child's Companion; Being a Concise Spelling-Book. Bost., 1796. 12mo. (88) $100

Bingham, Helen
— In Tamal Land. San Francisco, [1906]. (89) $225; (90) $180; (91) $110

Bingham, Hiram, 1789-1869
— A Residence of Twenty-One Years in the Sandwich Islands.... Hartford & NY, 1847. 1st Ed. 8vo. (88) $65, $70, $80; (89) $120, $140; (90) $75, $160

Bingham, Joseph
— Works. L, 1726. 2 vols. Folio. Ely Cathedral Library copy. (89) £90

Bingley, William, 1774-1823
— Memoirs of British Quadrupeds. L: Darton & Harvey, 1809. 1st Ed. 2 vols. 8vo. (90) £750

Binion, Samuel Augustus
— Ancient Egypt, or Mizraim. NY, 1887. One of 800. 12 orig parts. Folio. (89) £1,500
2 vols. Folio. (89) $800
Blackmer copy. (90) £1,500

Binney, Amos
— The Territorial Air-Breathing Mollusks of the United States.... Bost., 1851-57. 3 vols. 8vo. Inscr to J. D. A. Cockerell. (88) $750
L.p. copy. (90) $2,400

Binns, Richard William, 1819-1900
— Catalogue of a Collection of Worcester Porcelain...in the Museum at the Royal Porcelain Works. Worcester, 1882. 8vo. (89) $110
— A Century of Potting in the City of Worcester. L, 1877. 2d Ed. 4to. (90) £80

Binny, John. See: Mayhew & Binny

Binos, Marie Dominique de
— Voyage par l'Italie en Egypte au Mont-Liban et en Palestine.... Paris, 1787. 2 vols. 8vo. Blackmer copy. (90) £900

Binyon, Laurence, 1869-1943
— The Art of Botticelli. L, 1913. One of 275. Folio. (88) £50; (91) £100
— Catalogue of the Chinese Frescoes.... See: Eumorfopoulos Collection, George
— Catalogue of the Chinese, Corean and Siamese Paintings.... See: Eumorfopoulos

Collection, George
- Chinese Paintings in English Collections. Paris & Brussels, 1927. 4to. (90) $60
- The Drawings and Engravings of William Blake. L, 1922. Folio. (88) $50; (90) $120; (91) $70
- Dream-Come-True. See: Eragny Press
- The Engraved Designs of William Blake. L & NY, 1926. 4to. (89) $70, $90
- The Followers of William Blake. L & NY, 1925. 4to. (89) £85
  One of 100. (90) $200
- Japanese and Chinese Woodcuts. See: British Museum
- Poems. Oxford: Daniel Press, 1895. 1st Ed, One of 200. 8vo. With 2 A LS s from C. Henry Daniel loosely inserted. (91) £130

Binyon, Laurence, 1869-1943 —& Others
- Persian Miniature Painting. L, 1933. Folio. (88) £280; (89) £420; (90) £260; (91) $225

Binyon, Laurence, 1869-1943 —& Sexton, J. J. O'Brien
- Japanese Colour Prints. L, 1923. 4to. (89) £85

Biographia...
- Biographia Britannica: or, the Lives of the most Eminent Persons.... L, 1747-66. 6 vols in 7. Folio. (89) £110, £120; (91) £100, £320

Biographie...
- Biographie universelle, ancienne et moderne. Paris, 1811-55. Ed by J. F. Michaud. Vols 1-52 only. (88) £340
  Paris, 1811-39. Vols 1-66. 8vo. (89) £600
  Paris, 1811-55. Vols 1-85 (First Series, Vols 1-52; Partie Mythologique, Vols 53-55; Supplement, Vols 56-85, all pbd). (88) $350
  Paris, 1811-62. Vols 1-85; (lacking Vol 26), plus 6-vol supplement. Together, 90 vols. 8vo & 4to. (89) $250
  Vols 1-81, including Supplement. Paris, 1811-47. 8vo. Sold w.a.f. (91) £210
  Vols 1-52. Paris, 1811-28. 8vo. (89) £350

Biologia...
- Biologia Centrali-Americana: Contributions to the Knowledge of the Fauna and Flora of Mexico and Central America. L, 1879-97. Diptera only. 3 vols. 4to. (89) $200
  Zoology: Aves. L, 1879-1904. 4 vols. 4to. Bradley Martin copy. (89) $13,000

Bion & Moschus
- Idylles.... Paris: Didot jeune, 1795. 18mo. L.p. copy on papier velin. (89) £1,000

Bion, Nicolas, 1652?-1733
- The Construction and Principal Uses of Mathematical Instruments. L, 1723. 1st Ed in English. Trans by Edmund Stone. Folio. (88) (91) £480
  L, 1758. Folio. (88) $600; (89) $750; (91) £380
  Trans by Edmund Stone. (88) £310
- Neu-eroeffnete mathematische Werk-Schule. Nuremberg, 1765. 3 parts in 1 vol. 4to. (91) DM950
- Traite de la construction et des principaux usages des instrumens de mathematique. Paris, 1752. 4th Ed. 4to. (89) £90, HF800
- L'Usage des globes celestes et terrestres et des spheres.... Amst., 1700. 4to. (90) £1,050
  Paris, 1728. 8vo. (91) £160

Biondi, Giovanni Francesco, 1572-1644
- Donzella Desterrada, or The Banished Virgin. L, 1635. Folio. (89) £100; (90) £180
  STC 3074. (91) £190
- L'Istoria delle guerre civili d'Inghilterra tra le due case di Lancastro, e Iorc. Venice, 1637-41 & Bologna, 1647. 3 vols. 4to. Kissner copy. (91) £100
  3 vols in 1. 4to. (91) $80

Biondo da Forli, Flavio. See: Blondus, Flavius

Biondo, Flavio. See: Blondus, Flavius

Biondo, Michelangelo, 1497-1565
- Ad Christianissimum Regem Galliae. Rome: Antonio Blado, 1544. ("De canibus et venatione libellus....") 4to. Abrams copy. (90) £1,800

Biorklund, George —& Barnard, Osbert H.
- Rembrandt's Etchings True and False: A Summary Catalogue.... Stockholm, 1955. One of 300. 4to. (90) $375

Biorklung, George —& Barnard, Osbert H.
- Rembrandt's Etchings True and False: A Summary Catalogue.... Stockholm, 1955. One of 300. 4to. (89) $650

Birac, —& Others
- Les Fonctions du Captaine de Cavalerie.... The Hague, 1688. 3 parts in 1 vol. 12mo. (90) £100

Birch, A. G.
- The Moon Terror and Other Stories.... Indianapolis: Popular Fiction Co., [1927]. (90) $50

BIRCH

Birch, George Henry, 1842-1904
— London Churches of the XVIIth and XVIIIth Centuries. L, 1896. Folio. (90) £95

Birch, Samuel, 1813-85 —& Pinches, Theophilus G.
— The Bronze Ornaments of the Palace Gates of Balawat. L, 1880-1902. Parts 1-5. Folio. (90) $500

Birch, Thomas, 1705-66
— The Heads of Illustrious Persons of Great Britain.... L, 1747-52. 2 vols. Folio. (88) £260; (89) £340
2 vols in 1. Folio. (89) £520; (90) $300
Henry Merrik Hoare's copy with his ALs. (90) £420
L, 1813. Folio. (90) £420; (91) £450, £350
— An Inquiry into the Share, which King Charles I had in the Transaction of the Earl of Glamorgan.... L, 1747. 8vo. ESTC 070678. (91) £95
— Memoirs of the Reign of Queen Elizabeth.... L, 1754. 2 vols. 4to. (91) $250, £120

Birch, William, 1755-1834
— Delices de la Grande Bretagne. L, 1791. Oblong 4to. (88) £130; (89) £110

Bird, Horace A.
— History of a Line (Colorado Midland Railway). [NY: Press of the American Bank Note Co., 1889]. (91) $90

Bird, James
— Dunwich; A Tale of the Splendid City. See: Fore-Edge Paintings

Bird, Robert Montgomery, 1806-54
— The Adventures of Robin Day. Phila.: Lea & Blanchard, 1839. 2 vols. 12mo. Waller Barrett—Martin copy. (90) $400
— Calavar. Phila., 1834. 1st Ed. 2 vols. 12mo. Martin copy. (90) $250
— The Infidel; or the Fall of Mexico. Phila., 1835. 1st Ed. 12mo. Martin copy. (90) $475
— Nick of the Woods, or the Jibbenainosay.... Phila., 1837. 1st Ed. 2 vols. 8vo. Martin copy. (90) $500
— Sheppard Lee. Written by Himself. NY, 1836. Copyright notice of Vol I in BAL state A. 2 vols. 12mo. Swann-Martin copy. (90) $550

Biringuccio, Vannuccio
— De la pirotechnia libri X. Venice: Giglio, 1559. ("Pirotechnia.") 8vo. (88) DM1,800
Bologna: Gioseffo Longhi, 1678. 8vo. (89) $375
— La Pyrotechnie, ou art du feu.... Paris: C. Fremy, 1556. 4to. (91) £1,100

AMERICAN BOOK PRICES CURRENT

Paris: C. Fremy, 1572. 4to. (90) £450; (91) £400

Birkbeck, Morris, 1764-1825
— Notes on a Journey in America. Dublin, 1818. 8vo. (88) £90
L: James Ridgway, 1818. 8vo. (90) $70

Birkeland, Olaf Kristian
— Expedition Norvegienne 1899-1900 pour l'Etude des Aurores Boreales. Christiana, 1901. 8vo. With cut signature pasted in on tp. (90) £75

Birken, Sigmund von
— L'Origine del Danubio. Venice, 1684. 12mo. (88) $850
— Spiegel der Ehren des hoechstloeblichsten Kayser- und Koeniglichen Erzhauses Oesterreich. Nuremberg, 1668. Folio. (91) DM1,700

Birnbaum, Uriel, 1894-1956
— Das Buch Jona. Vienna: A. Berger, 1921. One of 300. Folio. (89) $325

Birrell, Augustine, 1850-1933
— Essays. L, 1912. (88) $110

Birtwhistle, John
— The Vision of Wat Tyler. Boughton Monchelsea: Ebenezer Press, 1972. One of 75. Illus by Graham Clarke. Folio. (89) £100, £110, £150
Inscr to Harry Karhac. (91) £450

Bisani, Alessandro
— A Picturesque Tour through Part of Europe, Asia, and Africa. L, 1793. 4to. (88) $110
Blackmer copy. (90) £150; (91) £350

Bischoff, Ignaz Rudolph, von Altenstern
— Grundzuege der Allgemeinen Naturlehre des Menschen.... Vienna, 1838-39. 4 vols in 2. 8vo. (88) $200

Bischoff, James, 1776-1845
— Sketch of the History of Van Diemen's Land. L, 1832. 8vo. (88) A$650; (89) A$480, A$850; (90) A$900

Bischoff, Jan de. See: Episcopius, Johannes

Bisco, John
— The Grand Triall of true Conversion. L: M. S. for G. Eversden, 1655. 8vo. (90) £65

Bishop, Elizabeth
— North & South. Bost., 1946. (91) $350

1987 - 1991 • BOOKS   BLACK

Bishop, George, d.1668
— New-England Judged...Sufferings of the People call'd Quakers in New-England. L, 1702-3. 2 parts in 1 vol. 8vo. (89) $425

Bishop, Isabella Lucy Bird, 1831-1904
— Journeys in Persia and Kurdistan. L, 1891. 2 vols. 8vo. (91) $140, $180, $180
— Unbeaten Tracks in Japan. NY, 1881. 2 vols. 8vo. (91) $120, $160

Bishop, John
See also: Kirby & Bishop
— Beautifull Blossomes, Gathered.... L: Henrie Cockyn, 1577. 1st Ed. 4to. (88) £100, £420

Bishop, John George
— "A Peep in to the Past," Brighton in the Olden Time. Brighton, 1880. 4to. Extra-illus with 22 plates & a folding panorama on 4 sheets joined, by W. Grant. (89) £320

Bishop, Matthew
— The Life and Adventures of Matthew Bishop of Deddington on Oxfordshire. L, 1744. 8vo. (91) £150

Bishop, Nathaniel Holmes, 1837-1902
— Voyage of the Paper Canoe.... Bost., 1878. 8vo. (90) $50

Bishop, Richard Evett
— Bishop's Birds. Phila., 1936. One of 1,050. 4to. (88) $120, $160; (91) $95, $250
— Bishop's Wildfowl. St. Paul, 1948. 4to. (90) $110

Bisselius, Joannes
— Argonauticon americanorum.... Munich, 1647. 1st Ed in Latin. 8vo. (89) $50

Bissell, Alfred Elliott
— In Pursuit of Salar. Wilmington DE, 1966. One of 100. 4to. Inscr. (90) $900

**Bissell, Alfred Elliott —&
Reese, Charles Lee**
— Further Notes on the Pursuit of Salar. Wilmington DE, 1972. One of 100. 4to. (90) $900

Bisset, James
— Abridgment and Collection of the Acts of Assembly of the Province of Maryland.... Phila: William Bradford, 1759. 8vo. (89) $275

Bisset, James, of Birmingham
— A Poetic Survey round Birmingham.... Birm., [1800]. 12mo. (88) £130

Bisset, Sir John Jarvis, 1819-94
— Sport and War or Recollections of Fighting and Hunting in South Africa.... L, 1875. 8vo. (89) R450

Bitaube, Paul Jeremie
— Joseph. Paris: Didot l'Aine, 1786. 8vo. (90) £350, £400, £400

Bitting, Katherine Golden
— Gastronomic Bibliography. San Francisco, 1939. (89) $200; (90) $110, $275, $375
Inscr. (88) $160; (90) $200
L, 1981. Reprint of 1939 Ed. (89) £52; (90) $50
One of 500. Reprint of 1939 Ed. (89) $80
San Francisco, 1981. Reprint of 1939 Ed. (88) $425; (90) $70

Bivero, Pedro de
— Sacrum oratorium piarum imaginum immaculatae Mariea et animae creatae.... Antwerp: Plantin, 1634. 4to. (88) HF1,900

Bizot, Pierre, 1630-96
— Histoire metallique de la Republique de Hollande. Paris, 1687. Folio. (88) $250; (89) $125; (91) $50

Bizozeri, Simpliciano
— Ungria Restaurada, compendiosa noticia, de dos tempos.... Barcelona, 1688. 8vo. (88) £450

Bizzarri, Pietro
— Histoire de la guerre qui c'est passee entre les venitiens et la saincte ligue, contre les turcs pour l'isle de Cypre.... Paris: Nicolas Chesneau, 1573. 8vo. Blackmer copy. (90) £4,000

Blaauw, Frans Ernst
— A Monograph of the Cranes. Leiden & L, 1897. One of 170. Folio. Martin copy. (90) $4,500

Black...
— The Black Art, or Magic Made Easy. NY, 1869. 8vo. Floyd copy. (90) $2,600

Black, Adam & Charles
— General Atlas of the World. Edin., 1822. Folio. (88) £50
Edin. & L, 1844. Folio. (88) £190; (89) £130; (91) $375
Edin., 1851. Folio. (89) £95
Edin., 1865. Folio. (90) $350

Black, Chauncey F.
— Some Account of the Work of Stephen J. Field.... NY, 1881. 8vo. With ALs of Field laid in. (91) $400

BLACK

Black, William
— Some Considerations in relation to Trade....
[N.p.], 1706. 4to. (88) £120

Black, William Henry
— History and Antiquities of the Worshipful Company of Leathersellers. L, 1871. Folio. (91) £170

Blackburn, Henry, 1830-97
— Randolph Caldecott.... L, 1886. 4to. (88) $60
Extra-illus with c.50 items including binding designs, illusts, etc. (90) £550

Blackburn, Mrs Hugh. See: Blackburn, Jane

Blackburn, Jane
— Birds Drawn from Nature. Edin., 1862. Folio. (89) £110
Martin copy. (90) $1,800; (91) £120

Blackburn, Philip C. See: Spiller & Blackburn

Blackburne, E. L.
— Sketches Graphic and Descriptive for a History of the Decorative Painting Applied to English Architecture During the Middle Ages. L, 1847. Folio. (88) $150

Blacker, J. F. See: Gorer & Blacker

Blacker, William
— Art of Angling, and Complete System of Fly-Making. L, Mar 1842. 1st Ed. 16mo. (91) $800
L, [probably the 1843 Ed]. 12mo. With Ms notes. (89) A$1,300
L, 1855. ("Art of Fly Making....") 12mo. (88) $360; (89) $260, A$550; (90) $750, $1,250; (91) $750
— Catechism of Fly Making.... [L], 1843. 8vo. (89) £120; (90) £2,400; (91) £750

Blackmore, John
— Views on the Newcastle and Carlisle Railway. Newcastle, 1837 [engraved title dated 1836]. 4to. (90) $200; (91) £300

Blackmore, Sir Richard, 1654-1729
— A Treatise of Consumptions.... L, 1724. 8vo. (90) £150

Blackmore, Richard Doddridge, 1825-1900
— Erema. L, 1877. 3 vols. 8vo. (90) £80
— Fringilla, or Tales in Verse. Cleveland, 1895. Lacking limitation leaf but one of 600. Illus by Will H. Bradley. 8vo. (89) $30
One of 600 on handmade paper. (88) £230
One of 600. (89) $175
— Lorna Doone. L, 1869. 1st Ed. 3 vols. 8vo. (88) $240; (89) $400

AMERICAN BOOK PRICES CURRENT

Doheny copy. (88) $650

Blackmur, R. P.
— The Double Agent; Essays in Craft and Elucidation. NY, [1935]. (89) $90

Blackstone, Sir William, 1723-80
— An Analysis of the Laws of England. Oxford: Clarendon Press, 1758. 3d Ed. 8vo. (88) $170
— Commentaries on the Laws of England. Oxford, 1765-69. 1st Ed. 4 vols. 4to. (90) $4,250; (91) $6,800, $12,000, £3,600
Doheny copy. (89) $16,000
Martin copy. (90) $12,000
Oxford, 1766-67-70-69. 4 vols. 4to. (89) £850
Vols I-II only. (88) $200
5th Ed. Oxford: Clarendon Press, 1773. 4 vols. 8vo. (88) £100
7th Ed. Oxford, 1775. 4 vols. 8vo. (90) $425, £240; (91) $650, £190
9th Ed. L, 1783. 4 vols. 8vo. (90) £280
Dublin, 1794. 2 vols. 8vo. (91) £120
L, 1803. 4 vols. 4to. (88) $80
L, 1809. 4 vols. 8vo. (88) £120
— An Essay on Collateral Consanguinity.... L, 1750. 8vo. Martin copy. (90) $700
— The Great Charter and Charter of the Forest.... Oxford, 1759. 4to. (89) £600

Blackwall, John, 1790-1881
— A History of the Spiders of Great Britain and Ireland. L, 1861. 2 parts in 1 vol. Folio. (88) £110, £110

Blackwell, Elizabeth, c.1700-58
— A Curious Herbal. L, 1737-39. 2 vols. Folio. (89) $9,000, $9,500; (91) £3,800, £4,200
Vol I (of 2). Folio. Sold w.a.f. (88) £1,700
Vol II only. (89) £2,000
— Herbarium Blackwellianum.... Nuremberg, 1750-65. Vols I-III (of 6). Folio. (88) £4,000
Vols V-VI in 2 vols. (91) $2,400
Nuremberg, 1757-54-73. Centuria III only. (91) $2,200
Nuremberg, 1760-73. 2 (of 6) vols. Folio. Sold w.a.f. (89) £1,500

Blackwell, Thomas, Principal of the Marischal College
— Memoirs of the Court of Augustus. Edin. & L, 1753. 3 vols. 4to. (88) £140; (89) $100

Blackwood, Algernon
— The Empty House and Other Ghost Stories. L, 1906. (90) £85

Blackwood, Lady Alicia
— Scutari, the Bosphorus and the Crimea. Ventnor, Isle of Wight, 1857. 2 vols. Folio. (89) £360; (90) £320, £900 Blackmer copy. (90) £620

Blackwood's...
— Blackwood's Edinburgh Magazine. Edin., 1817-1980. Vols 1-328 (lacking 136-37 & 159). 8vo. (91) £3,700

Blada, V. See: Volck, Adalbert J.

Blades, William, 1824-90
— The Biography and Typography of William Caxton, England's First Printer. L & Strassburg, 1877. 1st Ed. 8vo. (90) $100 L.p. copy. (91) $450
— The Enemies of Books. L, 1888. 2d Ed. 12mo. (90) $50
— The Life and Typography of William Caxton. L, 1861-63. 2 vols. 4to. With related material bound at rear, including 3 A Ls s of Blades. (88) $425

Blades, William F.
— Fishing Flies and Fly Tying. Harrisburg, 1951. 4to. (88) $50 One of 100. (88) $175; (90) $400

Blaes, Gerhard. See: Blasius, Gerardus

Blaeu, Willem, 1571-1638
— The Sea-Beacon. Amst.: Theatrum Orbis Terrarum, 1973. Intro by Ir. C. Koeman. Folio. Facsimile of the 1643 Ed. (90) $80

Blaeu, Willem, 1571-1638 & Jan, 1596-1673
— Atlas major, sive cosmographia Blaviana. Amst., 1662. 1st Ed. 11 vols. Folio. (90) £100,000
Vol I only (91) £8,000
Vol IV only [Netherlands & Low Countries]. ("Geographiae Blavianae....") (91) £7,500
Vol IX only [Africa & Iberian peninsula] (91) £6,500
Vol V only [England & Wales] (91) £9,000, £9,500
Vol VI only [Scotland & Ireland] (90) £1,300; (91) £3,200
Vol VII only [France & Switzerland] (91) £4,800
Vol VIII only [Italy]. ("Geographiae Blavianae....") (91) £9,500
Vol X only [Asia, China & Japan] (91) £5,000
Vol XI only [Americas] (91) £10,000
Vol XI only [America] (90) £9,500
1st Complete Ed; 2d Ed of Vol I. Amst., 1665-62. 11 vols. Folio. (90) £90,000
Vol IX only: [Spain, Portugal, etc]. Amst.:

Blaeu, 1672. (91) $2,750
— Atlas mayor, sino cosmographia Blaviana. Amst., 1658. Vol I only [Scandinavia]. Folio. (91) £4,800
— Le Grand Atlas ou Cosmographie blaviane. Amst., 1667. 2d Ed. Vol II, [America]. Folio. (91) £7,000
2d Ed with French text. 12 vols. Folio. (89) $160,000
Vol VI [Scotland & Ireland]. Folio. (88) £1,400
Amst., 1967-68. One of 500 copies not for sale. 12 vols. Folio. A reprint of the 1st French Ed (1663) of Blaeu's Atlas Major. R. A. Skelton's presentation copy. (88) £1,040
One of 1,000. A reprint of the 1st French Ed (1663) of Blaeu's Atlas Major. (89) $1,200, A$1,550; (90) £1,200
— Nieuw Vermeerderd en Verbeterd Groot Stedeboek van geheel Italie. The Hague: R. C. Alberts, 1724. 1st Ed. Vol I. Folio. (90) $8,000
— Nieuw Vermeerderd en Verbeterd Groot Stedeboek van Piemont en van Savoye. The Hague: R. C. Alberts, 1725. Vol I, Part 2; Vol II, Part 2. Together, 2 vols. Folio. (90) $9,500
— Nouveau theatre d'Italie.... The Hague, 1724. 4 vols. Folio. (89) £14,500
— Nouveau theatre du Piemont et de la Savoye.... The Hague, 1725. 4 vols in 2. Folio. (88) £7,500
Vol I, Part 2 only. Folio. (91) $4,600
— Novum ac magnum theatrum urbium Belgicae.... Amst.: J. Blaeu, [1649]. 2d Ed. 2 vols. Folio. (90) $45,000
— Novum Italiae Theatrum sive accurata descriptio urbium.... The Hague, 1724. 4 vols. Folio. Koeman I, Bl 103-6. (89) £11,500
— Novus Atlas, das ist abbildung und beschreibung von allen Landern des Erdreichs. [Amst., 1635]. Folio. (89) £9,200
— Novus Atlas, das ist, Weltbeschreibung.... Amst., 1641-42. Vol II, Part 1 only [France]. Text in German. (88) £1,000
— Novus Atlas, Das ist Weltbeschreibung.... Amst., 1643-55. 6 vols. Folio. (90) DM130,000
— Novus Atlas. Das ist, Weltbeschreibung. Amst., 1647-56. Vol II only. Orange-Nassau Library. (90) $16,000
Amst., 1654 [but c.1670?]. Vol V [Scotland] only. Robert Louis Stevenson's copy. (90) £4,800
— Theatre des etats de son altesse royale le Duc de Savoye. The Hague, 1700. 2 vols. Folio. (88) FF140,000
— Le Theatre du monde, ou nouvel atlas....

BLAEU

Amst., 1635. Parts 1 & 2 only. Folio. (88) £15,000

Vol II only. Amst., 1640. 2 parts in 1 vol. Folio. (91) $16,000

Amst., 1648. Part 4 only. Folio. (90) £12,000

— Theatrum orbis terrarum, sive Atlas novus.... Amst., 1640-55. 6 vols. Folio. (88) £29,000

Amst., 1645-40-48. Parts I-IV. Folio. (88) £20,000

Vol III only: Italy & Greece. Amst., 1645. Folio. (91) $9,500

Vol IV only: England & Wales. Amst., 1646. Folio. Eglinton copy. (88) £5,000

Vol VI only: China & Japan. Amst., 1649-55. Folio. (91) £3,000

Vol II only. Amst., 1650. (89) £5,500

Vol V only: Scotland & Ireland. Amst., 1654. (89) £1,300, £2,600

Vol VI only: China & Japan. Amst., 1655. (89) £3,600

Folio. (91) £1,400, £3,000

Amst., 1656. Folio. Dutch text. (89) £3,200

— Theatrum Statuum regiae celsitudinis Sabaudiae Ducis. Amst., 1682. 2 vols. Folio. (90) DM38,000

— Tooneel der Heershcappyen...het eerste deel vertoonende Piemont....[—Sabaudia]. The Hague: Adriaan Moetjens, 1697. 2 vols. Folio. Koeman BL 79-80. (88) £6,200

— Tooneel der steden van de Vereenighde Nederlanden.... Amst., 1966. Folio. (88) $150

— Toonneel des aerdrycks oft nieuwe atlas. Amst., 1643-2. Vols I-III. Folio. (88) £16,000

Amst., 1646 [1647]. Vol IV only. Folio. (88) £6,500

Amst., 1650. Vol II only. 2 parts in 1 vol. Folio. (89) £5,200

Vol III only. Folio. (89) £5,000

Blagdon, Francis William, 1778-1819
See also: Williamson & Blagdon

— Authentic Memoirs of the late George Morland. L, 1806 [but 1824 or later]. Folio. (90) £2,500

— A Brief History of Ancient and Modern India. L, 1805. Folio. (88) £5,500; (90) £4,800

Blagrave, John

— The Art of Dyalling.... L, 1609. 4to. (88) £600

AMERICAN BOOK PRICES CURRENT

Blagrave, Joseph, 1610-82

— The Epitome of the Art of Husbandry. L, 1685. Bound with: Blagrave. New Additions to the Art of Husbandry. L, 1685. 8vo. (88) £240; (90) £750

Blaine, Delabere Pritchett

— The Anatomy of the Horse.... L: Sampson Low, [1799]. 9 orig parts (of 12); lacking 4, 5 & 7. Folio. (90) £100

— An Encyclopaedia of Rural Sports.... L, 1840. 8vo. (88) $80

Blainville, —— de

— Travels through Holland, Germany, Switzerland.... L, 1767. 3 vols. 4to. (90) £500

Blair, David

— Cyclopaedia of Australasia. Melbourne, 1881. 4to. (89) $50

— The History of Australasia.... Glasgow, Melbourne, etc., 1878. 4to. (89) A$150, A$440

Blair, Eric Arthur. See: Orwell, George

Blair, Hugh, 1718-1800

— Lectures on Rhetoric and Belles Lettres. Phila.: Robert Aitken, 1784. 4to. (91) $75

L, 1798. 3 vols. 8vo. ESTC 171451. (91) £95

L, 1812. 3 vols. 8vo. (91) $70

— Sermons.... See: Fore-Edge Paintings

Blair, John, d.1782

— The Chronology and History of the World. L, 1754-68. 2 vols. Folio. (88) £800

L, 1768. Folio. (90) £300; (91) £150

L, 1779. Atlas only. Oblong folio. (89) £140

L, 1790. Folio. (91) £80

Blair, Robert, 1699-1746

— The Grave.... L, 1808. 4to. (88) £140; (89) $1,000, £130, HF850; (90) £370; (91) $150 Bradley Martin copy. (90) $1,400 Doheny copy. (89) $1,200

L, 1813 [but c.1870 reprint]. 4to. (89) $200; (91) $325

— The Poetical Works of Robert Blair.... L, 1802. 8vo. Ptd on vellum. Schiff copy. (91) $650

Blake, Andrew

— A Practical Essay on...Delirium Tremens. L, 1840. 8vo. (88) $150

Blake, William, House-Keeper to the Ladies Charity School

— The Ladies Charity School-House Roll of Highgate.... L, [1670]. 8vo. (88) £280

Blake, William, 1757-1827
— America, a Prophecy. Lambeth, 1793 [but mid-1790s]. Folio. Bentley 6, Copy R.. (88) $160,000
— The Book of Ahania. Paris: Trianon Press, 1973. One of 750. 4to. (89) $100; (91) $140
— The Book of Thel. L, 1789. 8vo. Bentley's copy A. Cumberland—Beckford—Hooper —The Garden copy. (90) $145,000
San Francisco: Book Club of California, 1930. One of 300. Illus by Julian Links. (91) $100
— The Book of Urizen. L: Trianon Press, 1958. One of 526. 4to. (91) $190
— Dante. [L, 1838 or c.1892]. ("Illustrations of Dante.") 7 plates on china paper mtd on wove paper c.0.3mm thick. Oblong folio. Biddle-The Garden set. (90) $37,500
L, 1827 [or 1892]. ("Illustrations to Dante's Divine Comedy.") Folio. Doheny copy. (89) $55,000
NY, 1968. ("Illustrations to the Divine Comedy of Dante.") One of 1,000. Folio. (91) $80, $80
— Designs for Gray's Poems. Clairvaux: Trianon Press, 1972. ("Water-Colour Designs for the Poems of Thomas Gray.") One of 18 hors commerce. Ed by Geoffrey Keynes. (91) £800
One of 518. (88) £350; (89) £460; (91) £500
— Europe, a Prophecy. Lambeth, 1794 [c.1830-32?]. 2 plates only (Nos 4 & 5). 4to. From Bentley Copy C. Smith-Biddle-Baskin—The Garden collections. (90) $16,000
L, 1969. Ltd Ed. Folio. (88) £70; (89) $140, £75; (90) £110, £130, £65; (91) $60, $140, $160
— The Gates of Paradise. L, 1968. One of 650. 3 vols. (88) $140
— Illustrations of the Book of Job. L, 1825. Engraved title & 21 plates, all proof impressions. 4to. Still in orig lotting paper; sold as part of the Linnell Collection in 1918 (90) £16,000
L, 1825 [label dated 1826]. Folio. (89) £14,000
Linnel copy. Gilchrist-Mansfield-Seasongood-Bradley Martin copy. (90) $50,000
L, [1874?]. ("Illustrations for the Book of Job.") Folio. (88) $1,000
L: [John Linnell, 1874]. Folio. Doheny copy. (89) $15,000
— Illustrations to the Divine Comedy of Dante. L, 1922. One of 250. Folio. (91) £190
— Illustrations to Young's Night Thoughts. Cambr. MA & L, 1927. One of 500. Folio. (90) $100
— Illustrations of the Book of Job. NY:

Pierpont Morgan Library, 1935. 6 parts. Folio. (90) $400; (91) $600
Doheny copy. (88) $1,100
Proof copy. Parts 2-6 (of 6). (88) £65
— Illustrations to the Bible. L: Trianon Press, 1957. One of 506. Folio. (88) $170
— The Illustrations for Thornton's Virgil. See: Nonesuch Press
— Jerusalem. L: Trianon Press, [1951]. "Apparently a pbr's dummy or specimen copy, with incomplete set of facsimile plates". Folio. (90) $450
One of 516. (88) £380; (89) £850; (90) $650, $800
Doheny copy. (88) $600, $750
L: Trianon Press, 1974. One of 32 for the Trustees of the Blake Trust & the pbrs. (88) $1,400
One of 516. (89) $130; (91) $300
— The Marriage of Heaven and Hell. [L: John Camden Hotten, 1868]. One of 150. 4to. Litho facsimile of 27 leaves, finished by hand. (89) $100
L, Toronto & NY, 1927. (90) $90
— Pencil Drawings. See: Nonesuch Press
— Pencil Drawings. 2d Series. See: Nonesuch Press
— Poems. See: Limited Editions Club
— Poetical Sketches. L, 1783. 1st Ed. 8vo. With 2 holograph corrections. Inscr by John Flaxman to Mr. Long. Bradley Martin copy. (90) $110,000
L: Pickering, 1868. 8vo. Lionel Johnson's copy, sgd by him in 1888. (88) £300
L: Vale Press, 1899. One of 200. Illus by Charles Ricketts. 8vo. (91) $75
— The Song of Los. Paris: Trianon Press, 1975. One of 400. 4to. (89) $100
— Songs of Innocence. [L.]: W. Blake, 1789. 1st Ed. 8vo. Bentley's copy N. Doheny copy. (89) $300,000
Bentley's copy A. McKell copy. (90) $500,000
— Songs of Innocence and Experience. [L.]: W. Blake, 1789-[94?]. 1st Ed. 8vo. Bentley's copy D. Houghton-The Garden copy. (90) $1,200,000
— Songs of Innocence. [L.]: W. Blake, 1789. 1st Ed. 8vo. Bentley's copy H. Fitzgerald-Gaisford-Stirling of Keir copy. (91) £200,000
— Songs of Innocence and Experience. L, 1839. 12mo. (90) £170; (91) £200, £420
— Songs of Innocence. L: Trianon Press, 1954. One of 1,600. Facsimile of the Rosenwald copy of the 1789 Ed. (89) $100; (90) $80; (91) $175
— There is no Natural Religion. L: Trianon Press, 1971. One of 50. 2 vols. 4to & 8vo. (89) £160
— Vala, or the Four Zoas. Oxford: Clarendon

BLAKE

Press, 1963. Ed by G. E. Bentley. Folio. (89) $60; (91) £50
— Works. L, 1893. One of 150 L.p. copies. Ed by Ellis & Yeats. 3 vols. 8vo. (89) £750 One of 500. (88) $325; (91) £700 Doheny copy. (89) $1,200
— The Writings. See: Nonesuch Press
— WILTON, ANDREW. - The Wood Engravings of William Blake for Thornton's Virgil. L: British Museum, 1977. One of 150. 4to. (90) £400

Blake, William Hume, 1809-70
— Brown Waters. Toronto, 1940. One of 1,000. Illus by Clarence A. Gagnon. (88) $90; (89) A$120; (90) $190 4to. (88) $160

Blakeway, John Brickdale, 1765-1826. See: Owen & Blakeway

Blakey, Dorothy
— The Minerva Press 1790-1820. L, 1939. 4to. (89) $60, $80; (90) $100; (91) $50, $150

Blakey, Robert, 1795-1878
— Hints on Angling.... L, 1846. 1st Ed. 8vo. (88) $60
— Historical Sketches of the Angling Literature of All Nations.... L, 1856. 12mo. (89) £90; (90) $85
— The History of Political Literature from the Earliest Times. L, 1855. 2 vols. 8vo. (91) $110

Blakiston, John, 1785-1867
— Twelve Years' Military Adventure in Three Quarters of the Globe.... L, 1829. 2 vols. 8vo. (89) $150

Blakiston, Thomas, 1832-91
— Five Months on the Yang-tsze.... L, 1862. 8vo. (91) $90

Blakston, W. A. —& Others
— The Illustrated Book of Canaries and Cage-Birds.... L, [1877-80]. 4to. (88) £140; (89) £115, £125; (90) £100; (91) £275, £75, £75

Blampied, Edmund. See: Dodgson, Campbell

Blanc, Charles
— L'Oeuvre de Rembrandt. Paris, 1880. One of 80 with an additional vol of proof plates. 3 vols. Folio. (90) £280

Blanc, Louis
— Le Fer forge en France aux XVIe et XVIIe siecles. Paris & Brussels, 1928. Folio. (89) £50

AMERICAN BOOK PRICES CURRENT

Blanch, John
— An Abstract of the Grievances of Trade which Oppress our Poor. L, 1694. 4to. (88) £480

Blanchan, Neltje
— The American Flower Garden. NY, 1909. One of 1,050. 4to. (91) $60

Blanchard, Charles Emile, 1819-1900
— L'Organisation du regne animal. Paris, 1852-64. 38 parts. 4to. Martin set. (90) $1,200

Blanchard, Jean Pierre Baptiste, 1753-1809
— The Principles, History, & Use, of Air-Balloons. NY, 1796. Bound with: Priestley, Joseph. Miscellaneous Observations relating to Education. New London, 1796. And: Barlow, Joel. A Letter addressed to the People of Piedmont.... NY, 1795. And: Priestley, Joseph. A General View of the Arguments for the Unity of God.... NY, 1796 1st Ed. 12mo. (91) $2,600

Blanchard, P. —& Dauzats, A.
— San Juan de Ulua ou relation de l'expedition francoise au Mexique. Paris, 1839. 4to. (88) $325, FF7,500

Blanck, Jacob Nathaniel
— Bibliography of American Literature. New Haven, 1955-92. Vols III-IV only. (90) $70
Vols I-IV only. (91) $180
Vols I-V only. (90) $200
Vols I-VI. (88) $270, $325, £190; (89) $325; (90) $225, £100
Martin copy. (90) $300
Vols I-VII. (88) $300; (89) $475; (91) $400
Inscr. (88) $500
Inscr to Jake Zeitlin as "the other Jake". (89) $450
John Carter's copy. (89) £400
Vols I-VI (90) $325
Vols I-VII. New Haven, 1955-83. (91) £150
— Peter Parley to Penrod.... NY, 1956. 2d ptg. (90) $150

Blanckley, Thomas Riley
— A Naval Expositor. L, 1750. 4to. (88) £1,100

Bland, David
— A History of Book Illustration.... Cleveland, [1958]. (91) $65
L, [1958]. (88) $65; (89) $130; (90) $65, $110, $120; (91) $60, $110
Berkeley, 1969. 4to. (89) £65
Berkeley, [1974]. (89) $60; (90) A$70

Bland, John
— Trade Revived, or a Way Proposed.... L, 1659. 1st Issue. 4to. (88) £1,000

Blandin, Philippe Frederic, 1798-1849
— De l'Autoplastie. Paris, 1836. 8vo. (88) $800

Blane, William
— Cynegetica; or, Essays on Sporting.... L, 1788. 8vo. (88) £65; (89) £50

Blanford, William Thomas, 1832-1905 —& Others
— Scientific Results of the Second Yarkand Mission.... Calcutta or L, [1870s-90s]. 15 orig parts. 4to. Martin copy. (90) $1,300

Blankaart, Steven
— Anatomia reformata.... Leiden, 1695. 8vo. (88) DM1,600
— The Physical Dictionary.... L, 1684. 8vo. (88) £500

Blaquiere, Edward
— Histoire de la revolution actuelle de la Grece. Paris, 1825. 8vo. Blackmer copy. (90) £200
— Narrative of a Second Visit to Greece.... L, 1825. 8vo. Blackmer copy. (90) £380

Blasche, Bernhard Heinrich
— Papyro-Plastics, or the Art of Modelling in Paper.... L, 1825. 2d Ed. Trans by Daniel Boileau. 16mo. (88) £80

Blasche, Bernhard Heinrich —& Boileau, Daniel
— The Art of Working in Pasteboard.... L, 1827. 16mo. (90) £60

Blasius, Gerardus, 1626?-92?
— Anatome animalium. Amst., 1681. 1st Ed. 4to. Martin copy. (90) $700
— Observata anatomica. Leiden & Amst., 1674. 1st Ed. 8vo. (88) DM700

Blason...
— Blason des armes. Paris: Parion de Malaunoy, [after 1500]. 8vo. (91) £500

Blast...
— Blast: Review of the Great English Vortex. L, 1914-15. No 1 only. (88) £380
No 1 only (89) $225

Blatty, William Peter
— The Exorcist. NY: Harper & Row, [1971]. Inscr. (88) $50

Blaue...
— Der Blaue Reiter. See: Kandinsky & Marc

Blaxland, Gregory
— A Journal of a Tour of Discovery across the Blue Mountains in New South Wales. L, 1823. 1st Ed. 12mo. (89) £65,000, A$175,000
Sydney, 1893. One of 55. 8vo. (89) A$3,200

Bledsoe, Anthony J.
— Indian Wars of the Northwest.... San Francisco, 1885. 1st Ed. 8vo. (91) $75, $225

Bleeker, Pieter
— Atlas ichthyologique des Indes Neerlandaises.... Amst.: F. Muller, 1862-[65]. Vols 1-5 only (of 9). Folio. (89) £5,000

Blegny, Etienne de
— Les Elemens, ou premieres instructions de la jeunesse. Paris, 1751. 8vo. (88) £75

Bles, Joseph
— Rare English Glasses of the XVII & XVIII Centuries. L, 1925. 4to. (89) $225; (91) $160

Blessington, Marguerite Gardiner, Countess of
— Conversations of Lord Byron with the Countess of Blessington. L, 1834. 8vo. (89) $250

Blew, William C. A.
— Brighton and its Coaches. L, 1894 [1893]. 1st Ed. 8vo. (88) £90; (91) £90
— A History of Steeple-Chasing. L, 1901. (89) $130

Bleyswijck, Dirck van
— Beschryvinge der Stadt Delft.... Delft, 1667. 4to. (88) £600

Bligh, William, 1754-1817
— The Dangerous Voyage Performed by Captain Bligh.... Dublin, 1824. 12mo. (90) £280
— The Log of H.M.S. Bounty 1787-1789. [Guildford]: Genesis Publications, 1975. One of 50, sgd by Earl Mountbatten of Burma. Folio. (88) £520
One of 50 specially bound in mor. A facsimile Ed. (90) £350
One of 500. A facsimile Ed. (89) A$750; (90) £320
— The Log of H.M.S. Providence 1791-93. L: Genesis Publications, 1976. One of 50, sgd by Earl Mountbatten of Burma. (88) £480
One of 500. (89) A$500
— A Narrative of the Mutiny on Board his Majesty's Ship Bounty.... L, 1790. 4to. (88) $2,600, £1,700
1st Ed. 4to. (89) A$7,600; (91) $2,200

BLIGH

8vo. (89) £500
— A Narrative of the Mutiny on Board H.M. Ship Bounty.... Melbourne, [1952]. Facsimile Ed, one of 1,000. 4to. (88) A$95, A$130
— Relation de l'enlevement du navire le Bounty. Paris, 1790. 8vo. (88) DM510
— Voyage in the Resource. See: Golden Cockerel Press
— The Voyage of the Bounty's Launch. See: Golden Cockerel Press
— A Voyage to the South Sea.... L, 1792. 1st Ed. 4to. (88) £1,500; (89) £1,300, £1,300, £2,100; (90) £1,200, £2,100, A$6,000; (91) £3,200, HK32,000
Ds, 4 Nov 1787, in protective wallet tipped in on endpaper. (89) £4,500
Edge-Partington copy. (88) £2,000
Adelaide, 1969. 4to. Facsimile of 1792 Ed. (90) A$100
— A Voyage to the South Seas. See: Limited Editions Club
— BARNEY, STEPHEN. - Minutes of the Proceedings of the Court-Martial Held at Portsmouth, August 12, 1792, on The Persons Charged with Mutiny on Board His Majesty's Ship the Bounty.... L: J. Deighton, 1794. 4to. (89) £14,000
Bound with: Bligh. A Voyage to the South Sea. L, 1792. (91) $16,000

Blind, Adolphe. See: Clarke & Blind

Blind Tom
[-] Songs, Sketch of the Life...of Blind Tom. NY, [c.1870]. 8vo. (91) $150

Blish, James Benjamin
— Earthman, Come Home. NY: Putnam, [1955]. (88) $60
— The Frozen Year. NY: Ballantine, [1957]. (89) $60
— Jack of Eagles. NY: Greenberg, [1952]. (91) $65

Blismon, Ana-Gramme
— Les mille et Un Amusements de Societe. Paris, [c.1870]. 12mo. (90) $175

Bliss, Carey S.
— A Leaf from the 1583 Rembert Dodoens Herbal Printed by Christopher Plantin. San Francisco: Book Club of Calif., 1977. One of 385. (88) $70, $75; (89) $65, $95; (90) $90, $95, $100; (91) $160, $275
Inscr by Grant Dahlstrom to Jake Zeitlin. (88) $120

AMERICAN BOOK PRICES CURRENT

Bliss, Douglas Percy
— Edward Bawden. Godalming: Pendomer Press, [1979]. One of 200. 4to. (91) £170

Bliss Collection, Robert Woods
— Pre-Columbian Art. NY, 1957. Folio. (89) $170; (90) $150

Bliss, William R.
— Paradise in the Pacific. NY, 1873. 8vo. (89) $110

Blith, Walter, fl.1649
— The English Improver.... L, 1649. 1st Ed. 4to. (88) £280

Blitz, —, Signor
— Fifty Years in the Magic Circle. Hartford, 1871. 8vo. (90) $120

Bloch, E. Maurice
— George Caleb Bingham. Berkeley, 1967. 2 vols. 4to. (89) $175

Bloch, Ernst, 1885-1977
— Spuren. Berlin, 1930. (91) DM360

Bloch, Marcus Elieser, 1723-99
— Allgemeine Naturgeschichte der Fische. Berlin, 1783-87. Vols I-V (of 12). 8vo. (89) £1,100
— Ichthyologie, ou Histoire naturelle des poissons. Berlin, 1795. 2d Ed. 6 vols. Folio. (90) £18,000
— Ichtyologie.... Berlin, 1785-97. 12 parts in 6 vols. Folio. (89) £20,000
Part 2 only (of 12). Folio. (88) £2,400
Parts 1 & 3-4 (of 4) in 3 vols. (90) DM45,000
— Kupfer zu Dr. Bloch's oeconomische Naturgeschichte der Fische deutschlandes. [Berlin, 1782-85]. Oblong folio. (91) £2,600

Bloch, Robert
— The Opener of the Way. Sauk City: Arkham House, 1945. 1st Ed, Ltd Ed. (88) $120
Inscr. (90) $170
— Psycho. NY, 1959. Sgd. (89) $275
— The Scarf. NY, 1947. Sgd. (90) $55
— The Selected Stories of Robert Bloch. Los Angeles, 1987. One of 500. 3 vols. (91) $90

Block, Andrew
— The English Novel, 1740-1850.... L, 1939. (91) $80

Blodget, Lorin
— Climatology of the United States.... Phila., 1857. 8vo. (91) $175

Bloemaert, Abraham, 1564-1651
— Oorspronkelyk en vermaard konstryk tekenboek.... Amst., 1740. 8 parts in 1 vol. Folio. (88) £1,050; (89) $900, £900; (91) £650

Blois
— Commentarius de iis omnibus quae in tertii orginis conventu acta sunt, general trium ordinum concilio Blesis a rege indicto ad decimumquintum Novembris diem 1576. Rignaviae: Jacobum Sterphen, 1577. 8vo. Phillipps copy. (91) $400

Blok, Alexander
— Dvenadtsat'. Skify. Paris, 1920. One of 185 on papier verge d'arches. Illus by N. Goncharova & M. Larionov. 4to. Inscr by Goncharova & Larionov. (88) £550

Blomberg, Carl Johann von
— Description de la Livonie.... Utrecht, 1705. 12mo. (88) $50

Blome, Richard, d.1705
See also: Cox & Blome; Speed & Blome
— L'Amerique angloise. Amst., 1688. 8vo. (88) FF6,500
— The Art of Heraldry.... L, 1685. 8vo. (89) £170
 L, 1730. 8vo. (88) $130, £40
— Britannia: or a Geographical Description.... L, 1673. 1st Ed. Folio. (88) £1,500, £1,500; (89) £3,000; (90) £2,600, £3,000
— A Description of the Island of Jamaica.... L, 1678. 8vo. (89) £650, £950
— An Essay to Heraldry in Two Parts. L, 1684. 8vo. (91) £80
— Hawking or Falconry. See: Cresset Press

Blomefield, Francis, 1705-52 — & Parkin, Charles, 1689-1765
— An Essay towards a Topographical History of the County of Norfolk. Fersfield & Lynn, 1739-75. 1st Ed. 5 vols. Folio. (89) £240
 L, 1805-10. 11 vols. 8vo. (88) £400; (90) £300

Blomfield, Ezekiel, 1778-1818
— A General View of the World. Bungay, 1807. 2 vols. 4to. (88) £35; (90) £100; (91) $160, £60

Blomfield, James
— Rod, Gun, and Palette in the High Rockies. Chicago: W. E. Wroe, 1914. 4to. (90) $350

Blondel, David
— A Treatise of the Sibyls.... L: T.R., 1661. Folio. (89) £70; (90) $325

Blondel, Francois, 1618-86
— Cours d'architecture, enseigne dans l'Academie Royale d'Architecture. Paris, 1698. 5 parts in 1 vol. Folio. (89) £480
 Paris & Amst., 1698. 5 parts in 2 vols. Folio. (89) £1,600
— Resolution des quatre principaux problems d'architecture. Paris: Imprimerie Royale, 1672. Folio. (91) £1,500
— Thermarum aquisgranensium et porcetanarum elucidatio & thaumaturgia.... Aachen, 1688. 8vo. (89) £160

Blondel, Jacques Francois, 1705-74
— Architecture Francoise.... Paris, 1752-56. Vol II only. (91) £340
— Cours d'architecture. Paris, 1675-83. 5 parts in 2 vols. Folio. (90) $2,000
 Paris, 1771-77. 12 vols in 9. 8vo. (88) $450, $700
— De la distribution des maisons de plaisance et de la decoration des edifices en general. Paris, 1737-38. 1st Ed. 2 vols. 4to. (90) £560; (91) £1,300
 Vol I only. (88) £45

Blondus, Flavius, 1388-1463
— De Roma triumphante libri decem. Basel: Froben, 1531. Folio. With ownership inscr of Jacques Malenfant. Kissner copy. (91) £1,100
— Historium ab inclinatione Romanorum imperii decades. Venice: Octavianus Scotus, 16 July 1483. Folio. 370 (of 372) leaves; lacking blank a1 & d6. Goff B-698. Kissner copy. (91) £1,100
 Venice: Thomas de Blavis, 28 June 1484. Folio. 302 leaves. Goff B-699. (91) LIt6,200,000
— Roma instaurata.... Verona: Boninus de Boninis, 1481-82. Issue without the extra prelim leaf & conjugate blank. 2 parts in 1 vol. Folio. 152 leaves. Goff B-702. Kissner copy. (91) £1,500
— Roma Ristaurata, et Italia illustrata. Venice: Tramezzino, 1542. 8vo. (88) £130
— Roma triumphans. Brescia: Angelum Britannicum, 31 July 1503. Folio. Kissner copy. (91) £350

Bloomfield, Robert, 1766-1823
— The Fakenham Ghost. L: Wm. Darton, [c.1813]. Sq 18mo. (89) $100

Blore, Edward
— The Monumental Remains of Noble and Eminent Persons.... L, 1826. 4to. (90) £160

Blore, Thomas, 1764-1818
— The History and Antiquities of the County of Rutland. Stanford, [1811]. Vol I, Part 2 (all pbd). Folio. (90) £65

Blossfeldt, Karl
— Urformen der Kunst. Berlin, [c.1929]. 4to. (88) $80; (91) $90

Blouet, Guillaume Abel
— Expedition scientifique de Moree. Paris, 1831-38. 3 vols. Folio. (89) £1,900
Blackmer copy. (90) £4,800

Blount, Edward
— Notes on the Cape of Good Hope, made during an Excursion in that Colony in the Year 1820.... L, 1821. 8vo. (91) £100

Blount, Sir Henry, 1602-82
— A Voyage into the Levant. L, 1636. 1st Ed. 4to. STC 3136. (90) £1,900
2d Ed. L, 1637. 3d Issue. 12mo. STC 3137. Stirling Maxwell—Blackmer copy. (90) £2,100
8th Ed. L, 1671. 12mo. (90) £550

Blount, Thomas, 1618-79
— Boscobel: or, The History of his Sacred Majesties.... L, 1660. 8vo. (90) £110
Martin copy. (90) $2,500
— Glossographia: Or a Dictionary, Interpreting the Hard Words of Whatsoever Language.... L, 1670. 3d Ed. 8vo. (88) £130
4th Ed. L, 1674. 8vo. (91) £170

Blount, Sir Thomas Pope, 1649-97
— Censura celebriorum authorum.... Geneva, 1694. 2d Ed. 4to. (88) £50
— De re poetica: or Remarks upon Poetry. L: R. Everingham for R. Bently, 1694. 4to. Harvard College—Chevalier copy. (91) $1,000
— A Natural History.... L, 1693. 1st Ed. 8vo. (88) £320; (91) £140, £550

Blow, John, 1648-1708
— Amphion Anglicus. A Work of Many Compositions. L, 1700. 1st Ed. Folio. (90) £500

Blue...
— The "Blue Book": a Bibliographical Attempt to Describe the Guide Books to the Houses of Ill Fame in New Orleans. By Semper Idem. [New Orleans?], 1936. Heartman's Historical Series, No 50. (88) $90, $300; (91) $140

Blum, Andre
— The Origin and Early History of Engraving in France. NY & Frankfurt, 1930. One of 200. Folio. (89) £55

Blum, Andre —& Lauer, Philippe
— La Miniature francaise aux XVe et XVIe siecles. Paris & Brussels, 1930. Folio. (89) £60

Blume, Karl Ludwig, 1796-1862
— Flora Javae. Brussels, 1828-[51]. 3 vols. Folio. (89) $3,750

Blumenbach, Johann Friedrich, 1752-1840
— Handbuch der vergleichenden Anatomie. Geottingen, 1805. 8vo. (88) DM1,600
— Institutiones Physiologicae.... Goettingen, 1787. 8vo. (88) $100
— Ueber die naetuerlichen Verschiedenheiten im Menschengeschichte. Leipzig, 1798. 8vo. (88) DM750

Blumenthal Collection, George & Florence
— Catalogue of the Collection.... Paris, 1926-30. One of 200. Compiled by Stella Rubinstein-Bloch. 6 vols. Folio. (88) C$1,800

Blunden, Edmund Charles
— Poems. Horsham: Price & Co., 1914. One of 100. 12mo. Inscr to P. W. J. Stevenson. Bradley Martin copy. (90) $3,500
— Poems translated from the French.... Horsham: Price & Co., 1914. Inscr to J. Squire. Esher-Bradley Martin copy. (90) $1,200
— Undertones of War. L, 1928. 1st Ed. Inscr to J. Lintott, 28 Mar 1931, & with annotations by Blunden. (89) £800

Blundeville, Thomas, fl.1561
— The Fower Chiefyst Offices belonging to Horsemanshippe.... L: Wyllyam Seres, 1565-66. 1st Ed. 4 parts in 1 vol. 4to. (91) $4,750
— His Exercises.... L, 1622-21. 6th Ed. 4to. (91) $1,100
STC 3150. (91) £200
7th Ed. L, 1636. 8vo. (88) £700; (89) £550; (91) £550

Blunt, Lady Anne, 1837-1917
— Bedouin Tribes of the Euphrates. L, 1879. 1st Ed. 2 vols. 8vo. (88) £70
— The Celebrated Romance of the Stealing of the Mare. See: Gregynog Press

Blunt, Sir Anthony Frederick
— The Paintings of Poussin. L & NY, 1967-68. Vols I-II (of 3). Folio. (91) $160

Blunt, David Enderby
— Elephant. L, 1933. (89) R800; (90) £400

Blunt, Joseph
— A Historical Sketch of the Formation of the Confederacy.... NY, 1825. 8vo. (90) $60

Blunt, Reginald
— The Cheyne Book of Chelsea China and Pottery. L, [1924]. One of 100. 4to. (91) £50

Blunt, Wilfrid Jasper Walter
See also: Sitwell & Blunt
— The Art of Botanical Illustration. L, 1950. (90) $150, A$130; (91) $175
NY, 1951. (89) $90; (90) $100; (91) $120 Inscr to Anita Loos by Aldous Huxley. (90) $160

Blunt, Wilfrid Jasper Walter —& Jones, Paul
— Flora magnifica. L, 1971. One of 506. Folio. (91) £160
Illus by Paul Jones. (91) £180
L, 1976. One of 506, sgd by Jones. Folio. (89) £75
— Flora superba. L, 1971. One of 405. Illus by Paul Jones. Folio. (88) £160; (89) £260, £1,300
L, 1976. One of 406. Folio. (91) £300

Blunt, Wilfrid Scawen, 1840-1922
— The Celebrated Romance of the Stealing of the Mare. See: Gregynog Press
— The Love-Lyrics and Songs of Proteus.... See: Kelmscott Press
— Sonnets and Songs. By Proteus. L, 1875. 8vo. Inscr to Sydney Cockerell. Bradley Martin copy. (90) $2,000

Boaistuau, Pierre, d.1566
— Histoires prodigieuses les plus memorables qui ayenet este observees.... Paris, 1560. 4to. (90) £900
— The Theatre of the World.... L, 1663. 8vo. (91) $250
— Theatrum Mundi. The Theatre or Rule of the World.... L, 1581. 8vo. (89) $425

Bobreau-Deslandes, Andre Francois. See: Deslandes, Andre Francois Boureau

Bobrowski, Johannes
— Maeusefest. Hamburg: Raamin-Presse, 1974. One of 170. Illus by Roswitha Quadflieg. 4to. (91) DM1,800

Bobynet, Pierre
— L'Horographie ingenieuse... Paris, 1647. 3 parts in 1 vol. 8vo. (88) £130

Boccaccio, Giovanni, 1313-73
— Ameto.... Venice: Nicolo Zopino & Vincentio Compagno, 20 Dec 1524. 8vo. (91) LIt420,000
— Amorosa visione.... Milan: Zannotti Castiglione, 1521. 4to. (90) DM3,200
— Amorous Fiammetta. L: Mandrake Press, 1929. One of 550. Folio. (91) $1,400
— De casibus virorum. L: Richard Tottel, 1554. ("A Treatise Excellent and Compendious, Shewing the Falles of Sondry Most Notable Princes....") Folio. (88) £1,700
STC 3117. (91) £1,300
— De claris mulieribus. Ulm: Johann Zainer, 1473. 1st leaf dust-soiled; 9 leaves damp-stained; some browning. 118 leaves. Goff B-716. Bound with: Honorius Augustodunensis. De imagine mundi. [Nuremberg: Anton Koberger, 1472?]. 48 leaves. Goff H-323. And: Cicero, Marcus Tullius. De officiis. Bologna, 1464. Ms on paper. 80 leaves, including 4 blanks. Folio. Abrams copy. (90) £260,000
Bern: Matthias Apiarius, 1539. Folio. (88) $2,000
— Il Decameron. See: Ashendene Press
— Decameron. See: Limited Editions Club
— The Fall of Princes. L: Richard Pynson, 27 Jan 1494. Folio. 206 (of 216) leaves; lacking quire a and H1.4, supplied in photofacsimile. Goff B-710. Waller-Way-Macdonald-Doheny copy. (88) $20,000
— La Fiancee du Roy de Garbe. Paris: H. Floury, 1903. One of 12. Trans by Anthoine Le Macon; illus by Leon Lebegue. 4to. (89) $150
— La Genealogia de gli dei.... Venice, 1574. 4to. (91) £140
Venice, 1581. 4to. (90) £85
— Genealogiae deorum. Venice: Bonetus Locatellus for Octavianus Scotus, 23 Feb 1494. Folio. 162 leaves. Goff B-753. (91) £1,500
— Gencalogie deorum gentilium. Reggio Emilia: Bartholomaeus & Laurentius de Bruschis, Bottonus, 6 Oct 1481. Folio. 355 leaves. Goff B-751. Broxbourne-Abrams copy. (90) £7,500
Paris, 1511. Folio. (90) £90
— I Casi de gl'huomini illustri. Paris, 1765. Bound in 3 vols. (91) £1,400
— Life of Dante. Bost. & NY: Riverside Press for Houghton Mifflin, 1904. One of 265. Folio. (88) $85, $100; (89) $130; (91) $200
See also: Grolier Club
— The Nymphs of Fiesole. Verona: Bodoni,

BOCCACCIO

- 1952. One of 225. 4to. (88) $750, £220, £470; (89) £320, £380; (90) £500; (91) £650
- The Story of Griselda. L: Riccardi Press, 1909. One of 500. (91) $220
- La Theseide innamoramento.... Lucca: Vincenzo Busdraghi for Giulio Guidobono, 1579. Bound with: Boccaccio. Fiammetta. [Florence, 1533]. 8vo. (91) £310
- Tragedies. L: John Wayland, [1554]. ("The Tragedies of Ihon Bochas, of all such Princes as Fell from their Estates through the Mutabilities of Fortune....") Trans by John Lydgate. Folio. (89) £1,150
  L: John Wayland, [c.1554]. ("The Tragedies Gathered by John Bochas, of all such Princes as Fell from their Estates through the Mutability of Fortune....") Folio. Doheny copy. (89) $2,200
  L: John Wayland, [1554]. ("The Tragedies of Ihon Bochas, of all such Princes as Fell from their Estates through the Mutabilities of Fortune....") Folio. STC 3178. (91) $2,200
- Vita di Dante Alighieri. Rome: Francesco Priscianese, 1544. 8vo. (89) £400

Decameron in English

- 1620. - The Decameron.... L.1st Ed in English. 2 vols in 1. Folio. STC 3172. Newdigate-Bradley Martin copy. (90) $7,500
  2 vols in one. Folio. The Garden copy. (90) $14,000
- 1625-20. - L.2d Ed in English of Vol I, 1st Ed of Vol II. 2 vols in 1. Folio. STC 3172-73. (91) £800
- 1625-20. - The Decameron.... L.2d Ed in English of Vol I, 1st Ed of Vol II. 2 vols. Folio. (89) £320, £700
- 1657-55. - Boccace's Tales: or the Quintessence of Wit, Mirth.... L. 2 vols in 1. 12mo. (88) £120
- 1684. - L. Folio. (88) $70, £240
- 1886. - L: Villon Society. Ltd Ed. Trans by John Payne. 3 vols. 8vo. Extra-illus with plates. (89) $375
- 1934-35. - The Decameron. Oxford: Shakespeare Head Press. One of 3 ptd on vellum. 2 vols. 4to. (90) £12,000
  One of 325. (88) £240, £280
- 1949. - Garden City. One of 1,500. Illus by Rockwell Kent. 2 vols. 4to. (91) $60

Decameron in French

- 1697. - Contes et nouvelles. Amst.: G. Gallet. Illus by Romain de Hooghe. 2 vols. 8vo. (88) £440; (89) $200; (90) £260
- 1732. - Cologne. 2 vols. 8vo. (90) £220
- 1779. - Londres [Paris]. 10 vols. 8vo. (88) £160
- [1934]. - Les Contes de Boccace. Paris. Ltd Ed. Illus by Brunelleschi. 2 vols. 4to. (89) $300

Decameron in Italian

- 1573. - Florence: Giunti. 4to. (88) £260
- 1614. - Venice. 4to. (90) $200; (91) £240
- 1725. - L: Thomas Edlin. 4to. Facsimile of the 1527 Giunta Ed. (88) $130
- 1729. - Venice. 4to. Counterfeit of the Giunta Ed of 1527. (91) LIt750,000
- 1729. - Venice: Pasinello. 4to. (88) £110, £110, £130, £150; (90) LIt450,000 Shipperdson-Greg copy. (91) £85
- 1757. - L [but Paris]. 5 vols. 8vo. (88) $110, DM6,000; (89) £650; (90) £2,700, £8,000; (91) £500, £550, LIt1,400,000 Martin copy. (90) $5,500
- [1955]. - Milan. Ltd Ed. Illus by Gino Boccasile. 2 vols. Folio. (91) LIt450,000

Boccalini, Trajano, 1556-1613

- Advices from Parnassus.... L, 1706. Folio. (90) $60

Bocchi, Achille

- Symbolicarum quaestionum, de universo genera.... Bologna: Novae Academiae Bocchianae, 1555. 4to. (91) LIt4,000,000
  2d Ed. Bologna, 1574. 4to. (91) $100, LIt1,700,000

Bocchi, Ottavio, 1697-1749

- Osservazioni...sopra un antico teatro scoperto in Adria. Venice: Simone Occhi, 1739. 4to. Blackmer copy. (90) £320

Boccone, Paolo, 1633-1704

- Icones et descriptiones rariorum plantarum Siciliae, Melitiae... Oxford, 1674. Bound with: Vaillant, Sebastien. Discours sur la structure des fleurs. Leiden, [1718]. 4to. (89) £460
- Museo di fisica e di esperienze variato.... Venice, 1697. 4to. (88) £120
- Recherches et observations naturelles.... Amst., 1674. 8vo. (90) £280

Bochart, Samuel, 1599-1667

- Geographiae sacrae. Caen, 1646. 2 parts in 1 vol. Folio. (89) £200; (91) £600 Frankfurt, 1674. 2 parts in 1 vol. 4to. (90) $275
- Hierozoicon sive bipertitum de animalibus sacrae scripturae. L: T. Roycroft, 1663. Folio. (90) £85
- Opera. Leiden & Utrecht, 1692. In 3 vols. Folio. (91) $200
  Leiden & Utrecht, 1712. 3 vols in 2. Folio. (91) £700

Bochius, Joannes, 1555-1609
— Descriptio publicae gratulationis spectaculorum et ludorum in adventu...Ernesti, Archiducis Austriae...An. MDXCIIII. Antwerp: Plantin, 1595. 1st Ed. Folio. (91) $200
— Historica narratio profectionis et inaugurationis serenissimorum Belgii Principum Alberti et Isabellae, Austriae Archiducum. Antwerp: Plantin, 1602. Folio. (91) $425

Bock, Carl A.
— The Head-Hunters of Borneo. L, 1882. 2d Ed. 8vo. (88) £110

Bock, Elfried, 1875-1933
— Die deutschen Meister. Berlin, 1921. 2 vols. 4to. (89) £250

Bock, Hieronymus, 1489?-1554
— De stirpium. Strassburg: Vendelinus Rihelius, 1552. 4to. (91) LIt5,500,000
— Kraeuterbuch. Strassburg, 1577. Folio. (90) DM32,000
Strassburg, 1630. Folio. (88) HF4,000

Bockstoce, John R. See: Gilkerson & Bockstoce

Bode, Clement Augustus, Baron de. See: De Bode, Clement Augustus

Bode, Johann Elbert
— Uranographia, sive astrorum descriptio. Berlin, 1801. Atlas vol only. Folio. (90) $3,500
— Vorstellung der Gestirne; Representation des astres.... Berlin & Stralsund, 1782. Oblong folio. (88) £460

Bode, Wilhelm von, 1845-1929
— Catalogue of the Collection of Pictures and Bronzes...of Mr. Otto Beit. L: Chiswick Press, 1913. One of 125. Folio. (89) £400

Bode, Wilhelm von, 1845-1929 —& Hofstede de Groot, Cornelis, 1863-1930
— The Complete Work of Rembrandt. Paris, 1897-1906. One of 15. 8 vols. Folio. (91) $1,000
One of 160. (91) £260
One of 575 on japon. (90) £120

Bodenehr, Gabriel, 1664-1758
— Atlas curieux. Augsburg, [c.1704]. Oblong folio. With 2 extra maps inserted. (90) $1,800
— Atlas Curieux oder neuer und compendieuser Atlas. Augsburg: Bodenehr, [c.1720]. Folio. (90) DM7,500
— Force d'Europe oder Die Markwuerdigst- und Fuernehmste.... Augsburg: G. Bodenehr, [1733?]. Folio. (91) £2,000
— Provinciarum Regni Poloniae geographica descriptio. Augsburg: Johann Stridbeck, [c.1730]. 8vo. (89) £350

Bodenschatz, Johann Christoph Georg
— Nufrichtig Deutsch Redender Hebraer.... Frankfurt & Leipzig: Martin Gobhardt, 1756. 4 vols in 1. 4to. (89) $2,600

Bodin, Jean, 1530-96
— De la Demonomanie des sorciers. Paris: Jacques du Puys, 1580. 1st Ed. 4to. (88) £600
— De Magorum Daemonomania. Strasbourg, 1594. 8vo. (91) £400
— De Republica libri sex. Lyons & Paris, 1586. Folio. (91) £380
— The Six Bookes of a Common-weale.... L, 1606. Trans by Richard Knolles. Folio. (91) £380
— Les Six Livres de la Republique. Paris: Chez Jacques du Puy, 1577. Folio. Adams B2234. (88) £450

Bodleian Library
— BURN, JACOB HENRY. - Catalogue of a Collection of Early Newspapers and Essayists, formed by...John Thomas Hope.... Oxford, 1865. 8vo. (91) $90
— MALONE, EDMOND. - Catalogue of Early English Poetry and Other Miscellaneous Works illustrating the British Drama.... Oxford, 1836. Folio. (91) $450

Bodoni, Giovanni Battista, 1740-1813
— Epithalamia exoticis linguis reddita. Parma, 1775. Folio. (89) $2,600
— Manuale tipografico. [L, 1960]. 2 vols. Folio. Facsimile of 1818 Ed. (89) $65; (90) £70
One of—500. 2 vols. Folio. Facsimile of 1818 Ed. (90) £95
Verona: Officina Bodoni, 1968. One of 80 with separate English trans of Mardersteig's intro. 4to. Facsimile of the 1788 Ed. (91) £900
One of 180. Facsimile of the 1788 Ed. (88) £620
— Le Piu insigni pitture Parmensi.... Parma: Bodoni, 1809 [1816]. 4to Ed. (90) $800
— Preface to the Manuale Tipografico of 1818.... L, 1925. Ltd Ed. Inscr by trans, H.V. Marrot. (88) $70
— Serie de' caratteri greci di Giambatista Bodoni. Parma: Bodoni, 1788. 4to. (89) HF2,200

Boeckler, Albert, 1892-1957
— Die Regensburg-Pruefeninger Buchmalerei des XII. und XIII. Jahrhunderts. Munich, 1924. 4to. (88) $200

Boeckler, Georg Andreas
- Architectura curiosa nova.... Nuremberg, [1664]. 4 parts in 1 vol. Folio. (88) £420; (89) £1,900; (90) $3,250
  Nuremberg: Paul Fuersten, 1668. Folio. (89) £780
- Theatrum machinarum novum.... Nuremberg, 1661. Folio. (91) £1,700
  Nuremberg, 1686. Folio. (88) DM620; (91) $2,200

Boehme, Jacob, 1575-1624
- The Epistles.... L, 1649. 1st Ed in English. 2 parts in 1 vol. 4to. (88) £250
- Mysterium Magnum; or an Exposition of the First Book of Moses, called Genesis.... L: M. Simmons for H. Blunden, 1654. 4 parts in 1 vol. Folio. The Garden copy. (90) $1,100
- Works. L, 1764-81. 4 vols. 4to. The Garden copy. (90) $3,250
- XL. Questions Concerning the Soule. L: M. Simmons, 1647. Bound following Boehme's Signatura rerum; or, The Signature of All Things. L, 1651. 4to, modern calf. Extremities rubbed The Garden copy. (90) $1,300

Boehn, Max von, 1850-1921
See also: Fischel & Boehn
- Dolls and Puppets. L, [1932]. (88) £150

Boelen, J.
- Reize naar de Oost-en Westkust van Zuid-Amerika. Amst., 1835-36. 3 vols. 8vo. Inscr by various people connected with the production of the work. (89) $900

Boelker, Homer H.
- Portfolio of Hopi Kachinas. Hollywood, [1969]. One of 1,000. 4to. (88) $190; (89) $100, $150; (90) $100, $160; (91) $80, $110, $110, $120

Boerhaave, Hermann, 1668-1738
- De Viribus Medicamentorum; or, a Treatise of the Virtue and Energy of Medicines. L, 1720. 8vo. (88)
- Elementa chemiae. Leiden, 1732. 2 vols. 4to. (88) $225, $1,300
  2 vols in 1. 4to. (91) $250
  Paris: Cavelier, 1753. 2 vols. 4to. (88) $225
- Elements of Chymistry Faithfully Abridg'd.... L, 1734. 8vo. (90) £140
- Institutiones medicae in usum annuae exercitationis domesticos. [N.p.], 1730. 8vo. (88) $110
- A Method of Studying Physick.... L, 1719. 8vo. (88) £160
- A Treatise on the Powers of Medicines. L, 1740. 8vo. (90) £100

Boersenverein der Deutschen Buchhaendler
- Katalog der Bibliothek. Leipzig, 1902. 2 vols. (91) $80

Boesen, Gudmund —& Boje, Christen Anton
- Old Danish Silver. Copenhagen, 1949. Folio. (89) $75

Boethius, Anicius Manlius Torquatus Severinus, 480?-524?
- Arithmetica. Augsburg: Erhard Ratdolt, 20 May 1488. 1st Ed. 4to. 48 leaves. Goff B-838. (89) £8,500
- Arithmetica, geometria et musica Boetii. Venice: Joannes & Gregorius de Gregoriis de Forlivio, 18 Aug 1492. Folio. (89) $2,500
- Boetius cum triplici commento.... Lyons: Simon Vincent, [c.1510]. 4to. (88) £260
- De consolatione philosophiae. Nuremberg: Anton Koberger, 12 Nov 1476. Folio. 133 (of 140) leaves; lacking leaves 1 & 7 (both blank) & 5 leaves of Tabula. Goff B-771. (88) £4,160
  [Cologne]: Johann Koelhoff, the Elder, 27 Jan 1488. Bound with: Jean Gerson. De consolatione theologiae. 102 plus 24 leaves. Goff B-783. And: Ms of Saint Anselm, Seven Tractates, preceded by Eadmer, Vita Anselmi, c.1465-70 Folio. Doheny copy. (88) $17,000
  Strassburg: Johann Pruess, before 6 Mar 1491. 4to. 188 leaves. Goff B-794. (90) £1,800
  Nuremberg: Anton Koberger, 12 Nov 1496. Folio. 140 leaves. Goff B-771. Von Walderdorff-Kyriss copy. The Garden copy. (90) $60,000
  Cologne: Heinrich Quentell, 31 Dec 1497. ("De consolatione philosophiae, with commentary of Thomas Waleys [here ascribed to Thomas Aquinas].") 218 leaves. Goff-802. Bound with: Pseudo-Boethius, De disciplina scholarium, with anonymous commentary. Cologne: Heinrich Quentell, 5 Mar 1498. 64 (of 66) leaves; lacking D3.4. And: Disticha Catonis. Cologne: Heinrich Quentell, 1496. 48 leaves. 3 works in 1 vol. 4to, Doheny copy. (88) $5,500
  Strassburg: Johannes Grueninger, 1501. ("De philosophico consolati sive de consolatione philosophiae....") Folio. (88) $950
  Rennes: Jehan Mace, 1519. 4to. (90) £460
- De consolatione philosophie. Lyons: Jean Du Pre, 6 & 22 Mar 1493/4. 4to. 185 (of 198) leaves; lacking 2a6 & G1-7. (89) $750
- Della consolatione de la filosofia. Florence: Lorenzo Torrentino, 1551. Trans by Cosimo Bartoli. 8vo. (91) LIt450,000
- Of the Consolation of Philosophy. L, 1695.

Trans by Richard Graham, Lord Viscount Preston. 8vo. (91) $175
— Opera. Venice: Joannes & Gregorius de Gregoriis de Forlivio, 26 Mar 1491. Part 2 only. Folio. 95 (of 96) leaves; lacking initial blank. Goff B-767. (88) $1,100
Basel: Henricpetrina, [1570]. Folio in 8's. (91) £550
— Tetragonismus.... 1503. See: Tetragonismus...

Boetticher, Jacob Gottlieb, 1754-92
— A Geographical, Historical, and Political Description of the Empire of Germany, Holland.... L, 1800. 4to. (89) £190

Bogan, Louise
— Dark Summer: Poems. NY, 1929. (90) $100

Bogan, Zachary. See: Rous & Bogan

Bogatzky, Carl Heinrich von, 1690-1774
— A Gold Treasury for the Children of God.... L, 1762. Oblong 12mo. (91) $70

Boggs, Mae Helene Bacon
— My Playhouse was a Concord Coach.... Oakland, Calif., [1942]. 4to. (88) $275; (89) $90, $200; (90) $150; (91) $130, $160
With photo of Mt. Shasta laid in. (90) $450

Bohatta, Hanns
See also: Weale & Bohatta
— Bibliographie der livres d'heures horae B.M.V., officia...des XV. und XVI. Jahrhunderts. Vienna, 1924. (91) $200
— Katalog der Inkunabeln der Fuerstlich Liechtenstein'schen Fideikommissbibliothek und der Hauslabsammlung. Vienna, 1910. 4to. (91) $300
— Katalog der liturgischen Drucke des XV & XVI Jahrhunderts in der Herzogl. Parma'schen Bibliothek in Schwarzau. Vienna, 1909-10. 2 vols. 4to. (89) $400

Bohn, Dave —&
Petschek, Rodolfo
— Kinsey Photographer: A Half Century of Negatives by Darius and Tabitha May Kinsey. Guildford: Genesis, 1981. One of 25. 2 vols in 1. 4to. (88) £85

Bohn, Henry George
— A Catalogue of Books.... L, 1841. 8vo. (91) $225, £175

Bohny, Nicholas
— Neues Bilderbuch. Anleitung zum Anschauen, Denken, Rechnen und Sprechen. Stuttgart & Esslingen: Schreiber und Schill, [1848]. Oblong folio. (88) $475
— The New Picture Book.... Edin., 1858. Oblong folio. (90) £100, £240

— The New Picture Book being Pictorial Lessons.... Edin., 1866. Oblong folio. (91) £95

Bohr, Niels
— On the Quantum Theory of Line-Spectra. Copenhagen, 1928. 1st Ed. 4to. Facsimile reprint of 1918-22 Ed. (89) £20
— Studier over Metallernes Elektrontheorie. Copenhagen: Thaning & Appel, 1911. 4to. (88) $950, £180; (89) £220

Bohun, Ralph, d.1714
— A Discourse Concerning the Origine and Properties of Wind.... Oxford, 1671. 1st Ed. 8vo. (91) £340

Boileau, Daniel. See: Blasche & Boileau

Boileau, Jacques, 1635-1716
— Historia flagellantium. De recto et perverso flagrorum.... Paris, 1700. 8vo. (88) $80; (89) $60

Boileau-Despreaux, Nicolas, 1636-1711
— Oeuvres. Amst., 1718. 2 vols. Folio. (88) FF4,000; (90) £600
The Hague, 1722. 4 vols. 12mo. (89) $250; (90) £500
Paris, 1740. 2 vols. Folio. (89) $650
Paris, 1747. 5 vols. 8vo. (89) $275
Paris: Crapalet, 1798. 4to. Roederer-Fleming copy. (89) $2,200
The Hague, 1824. 4 vols. 12mo. (91) $120
— Poesies. Paris, 1781. 2 vols in 1. 12mo. Schiff-Fleming copy. (89) $750

Boillot, Joseph
— Modelles, artifices de feu, et divers instrumens de guerre.... Chaumont, 1598. 1st Ed. 4to. (91) £2,600

Boillot, Leon
— Aux mines d'or du Klondike.... Paris, 1899. 8vo. (91) $50

Boisgelin de Kerdu, P. M. Louis de, 1758-1816
— Ancient and Modern Malta. L, 1805. 2d Ed. 2 vols. 4to. (90) £650
— Travels through Denmark and Sweden.... L, 1810. 1st Ed. 2 vols. 4to. (88) £140

Boisonnas, Frederic
— Egypte. Geneva, 1932. Folio. Blackmer copy. (90) £650

Bois-Robert, J. D. de, 1747-1816
— Nil ete Danube, souvenirs d'un touriste. Paris: A. Courcier, [c.1855]. 8vo. Blackmer copy. (90) £190

BOISSARD

Boissard, Jean Jacques, 1528-1602
— Emblematum liber. Frankfurt, 1593. 4to. (91) LIt2,400,000
— Habitus variarum orbis gentium. [Frankfurt, 1581]. Oblong 4to. (89) $1,700
— Icones diversorum hominum fama & rebus gestis illustrium. Metz: A. Faber, 1591. 4to. (91) £1,900
— Icones quinquaginta virorum.... Frankfurt, 1597-99. 4 parts in 1 vol. 4to. (88) $6,000
— Icones variae. Medallions divers. Metz: Jean Aubry, [1584]. 4to. (89) $950
— Topographia Romae. Frankfurt: Matthias Merian, 1627-28-27-1598-1600-2. 6 parts in 2 vols. Folio. (89) £300
— Tractatus posthumus I. I. Boissardi...de divinatione & magicis praestigiis. Oppenheim: Hieronymus Gallerus, [c.1605]. 1st Ed. Folio. (91) £550
— Vitae et icones Sultanorum Turcicorum.... Frankfurt: Theodor de Bry, 1596. 4to. (90) £6,200

Boisseau, Jean
— Typographie francoise, ou representation de plusieurs villes, bourgs.... [N.p., c.1648?]. Oblong 4to. (88) £400

Boissier, Gaston —& Others
— L'Institut de France. Paris, 1909. One of 125. Folio. (88) £130

Boissiere, Jules
— Propos d'un Intoxique. Paris, 1929. Out-of-series copie on japon with 4 suites. Illus by Tsuguharu Foujita. 4to. (88) FF17,000

Boissonas, Fred. See: Baud-Bovy & Boissonas

Boissonnas, Frederic. See: Baud-Bovy & Boissonnas

Boissy, Louis de, 1694-1758
— Oeuvres de theatre.... Paris, 1766. 9 vols. 8vo. (88) FF5,000

Boitard, Pierre, 1787-1859
— Histoire naturelle des oiseaux de proie d'Europe. Paris, 1824. 4to. (88) FF5,000

Bojanus, Ludwig Heinrich
— Anatome Testudinis Europaeae.... Vilnius: J. Zawadzki, 1819-21. 2 parts in 1 vol. Folio. (91) £700

Boje, Christen Anton. See: Boesen & Boje

Boker, George Henry, 1823-90
— The Legend of the Hounds. NY, 1929. One of 200. (88) £35

AMERICAN BOOK PRICES CURRENT

Boldoni, Ottavio
— Theatrum temporaneum aeternitati Caesaris.... Milan, 1636. Folio. (90) $2,750

Boldrewood, Rolf. See: Browne, Thomas Alexander ("Rolf Boldrewood")

Boleluczky, Matthias Benedict
— Rosa Boemica sive Vita Sancti Woytiechi. Prague, 1668. 2 parts in 1 vol. 8vo. (88) £160

Bolingbroke, Henry, 1785-1855
— A Voyage to the Demerary.... L, [1807]. 4to. (90) £180

Bolingbroke, Henry St. John, Viscount, 1678-1751
— A Collection of Political Tracts. L 1775. 8vo. (88) $80
— A Letter to Sir William Windham.... L, 1753. 1st Ed. 8vo. (89) $50
— Letters on the Study and Use of History. L, 1752. 2 vols. 8vo. (89) $225
— Works. L, 1754. 5 vols. 4to. (89) £220; (91) £110, £160

Bollan, William, d.1776
— The Mutual Interest of Great Britain and the American Colonies Considered.... L, 1765. 4to. (91) $600
— The Rights of the English Colonies Established in America Stated and Defended. L, 1774. 4to. (91) $475, $700

Bollanus, Dominicus
— Tractatus...de conceptione...Virginis Marie. Strassburg: J. Gruninger, 1504. 4to. (89) £380

Boller, Henry A.
— Among the Indians. Eight Years in the Far West.... Phila., 1868. 12mo. (91) $325

Boller, Willy
— Masterpieces of the Japanese Color Woodcut. Bost., [1957]. Folio. (88) $65; (90) $90

Bol'shakov, Konstantin
— Serdtse v Perchatke. St. Petersburg, 1913. 8vo. (89) £180
— Solntse na izlete. Moscow, 1916. 4to. (91) £400

Bolton, Arthur T.
— The Architecture of Robert and James Adam. L, 1922. 2 vols. Folio. (88) $300, $400, £90; (89) £180, £200, £200, £220, £300; (90) £320, £1707; (91) $150, $450, £50 Library copy. (91) £100

Bolton, Edmund, 1545?-1633?
— The Elements of Armouries. L: George Eld, 1610. 4to. (91) £280
— Nero Caesar, or, Monarchie Depraved. L, 1624 [engraved title dated 1623]. 1st Ed. Folio. STC 3221. (91) £75

Bolton, Henry Carrington
— A Select Bibliography of Chemistry, 1492-1897. Wash., 1893-1904. Vol I only. (89) $50
With First and Second Supplements and Section VIII -- Academic Dissertations. Together, 4 vols. (91) $475

Bolton, Herbert Eugene
— Anza's California Expeditions. Berkeley, 1930. 5 vols. (88) $325, $350; (89) $200, $275, $375; (91) $400
— Coronado on the Turquoise Trail. Albuquerque, 1949. (88) $130; (89) $120
— Cross, Sword & Gold Pan.... Los Angeles, [1936]. One of 100. Illus by Carl Borg. 4to. (91) $130
— Drake's Plate of Brass. San Francisco, 1937. Sgd by Bolton, Douglas Watson & Allen L. Chickering. (89) $65
— Font's Complete Diary: A Chronicle of the Founding of San Francisco. Berkeley, 1930. Ed by Bolton. (88) $70
Berkeley, 1931. (89) $65
2d Ed. Berkeley, 1933. (88) $60, $75; (89) $60, $60
— Fray Juan Crespi: Missionary Explorer.... Berkeley, 1927. (90) $75; (91) $110
Inscr, 1943. (89) $35
— Guide to Materials for the History of the United States in the Principal Archives of Mexico. Wash., 1913. (91) $225
[-] New Spain and the Anglo-American West. Historical Contributions Presented to.... Los Angeles, [1932]. 1st Ed, One of 500. 2 vols. (89) $160
— Outpost of Empire: The Story of the Founding of San Francisco. NY, 1931. (88) $60; (89) $70
Sgd. (89) $100
— The Rim of Christendom.... NY, 1936. 1st Ed. (89) $90; (90) $110
Sgd & with Ms leaf laid in loose. (88) $85
— Spanish Explorations in the Southwest.... NY, 1916. (89) $150

Bolton, James, d.1799
— Harmonia Ruralis, or, an Essay towards a Natural History of British Song Birds. Stannary & L, 1794-96. 1st Ed, Colored Issue. 2 vols in 1. 4to. Bradley Martin copy. (89) $4,750
2d Ed. L, 1824. 2 vols. 4to. (91) £650
In 1 vol. 4to. (90) £650
Vol I (of 2). 4to. (88) £500
L, 1830. 2 vols in 1. 4to. (91) £750, £1,300
L, 1845. 2 vols in 1. 4to. (88) £1,300, £1,300, £1,400; (89) £1,300, £1,600; (91) £1,200, £1,300
Martin copy. (90) $2,500
2d Ed. 2 vols in 1. 4to. Bradley Martin copy. (89) $4,000
— A History of Fungusses, Growing about Halifax. Halifax & Huddersfield, 1788-91. 4 vols, including Supplement. 4to. (90) £360
4 vols in 1, including Supplement. 4to. (91) £1,200
4 vols in 2, including Supplement. 4to. Dedication copy, inscr to the Earl of Gainsborough noting that this is the only copy ptd on writing paper. de Belder —Fleming copy. (89) $6,000
— Twelve Posies Gathered in the Fields. Halifax, 1792. 8vo. (88) $6,000

Bolton, Robert
— The History of the Several Towns...of the County of Westchester.... NY, 1881. 8vo. (91) $100

Bolton, Theodore
— American Book Illustrators. NY, 1938. One of 1,000. (91) $150, $225

Bolts, Willem, 1740?-1808
— Etat civil, politique et commercant du Bengale. Maastricht, 1775. 2 vols in 1. 8vo. (88) $200; (89) $225

Boltzmann, Ludwig, 1844-1906
— Vorlesungen ueber Gastheorie. Leipzig: Johann Ambrosius Barth, 1896-[98]. 2 vols. 8vo. (89) £80
2 vols in 1. 8vo. (89) £55

Bolus, Harry, 1835-1911
— Icones orchidearum Austro-Africanarum extratropicarum. L, 1896-1913. 3 vols. 8vo. (88) £720, R4,600

Bolyai, Farkas, 1775-1856 —& Bolyai, Janos, 1802-60
— Tentamen juventutem studiosam in elementa matheseos purae.... Maros Vasarhelyini: typis Collegii Reformatorum et Simon Kali, 1832-33. 2 vols. 8vo. (88) £22,000

Bolyai, Janos, 1802-60. See: Bolyai & Bolyai

Bombelles, Henri Francois de
— Traite des evolutions militaires.... Paris, 1754. 8vo. (91) $450

Bomberg, David
— Russian Ballet. L, 1919. 8vo. (90) £2,200

Bon Genre...
— Le Bon Genre; reimpression du recueil de 1827. Paris, [1931]. One of 750. Preface by Leon Moussinac. Folio. (91) $800

Bonafous, Louis Abel de. See: Fontenai, Abbe de

Bonafous, Matthieu, 1793-1852
— Histoire naturelle, agricole, et economique du mais. Paris & Turin, 1836. Folio. (88) £4,800
Inscr. Martin copy. (90) $6,000

Bonanni, Filippo, 1638-1725
— Description des instrumens harmoniques en tout genre. Rome, 1776. 2d Ed. Illus by A. van Westerhout. 4to. (89) £550
— Numismata pontificum romanorum. Rome, 1699. 1st Ed. 2 vols. Folio. Kissner copy. (91) £1,400
— Numismata summorum pontificum templi Vaticani fabricam indicantia.... Rome, 1696. Folio. (88) $650; (89) £220, £280; (90) £110
Rome, 1696-1700. Folio. (91) £280
Rome, 1696. Folio. Kissner copy. (91) £700
Rome, 1715. Folio. (91) £480
Kissner copy. (91) £450
Rome, 1720. Folio. Kissner copy. (91) £400
— Recreatio mentis, et oculi in observatione animalium testaceorum, curiosis naturae inspectoribus. Rome, 1684. 1st Ed in Italian. 4to. (89) FF10,500
— Verzeichnuess der geistlichen Ordens-Personnen in der streitenden Kirches. Nuremberg, 1711. 2 vols. 8vo. (91) LIt400,000

Bonannius, Philippus. See: Bonnani, Filippo

Bonaparte, Charles Lucien, 1803-57
See also: Wilson & Bonaparte
— American Ornithology. Phila., 1825-33. 1st Ed. 4 vols. Folio. (90) $1,100
Vol I only. (88) £100
With rare 1st Issue of Vol I. 4 vols. Folio. Bradley Martin copy. (89) $4,500
— Iconographia della fauna italica. Rome, 1832-41. 3 vols. Folio. (88) £1,500, £2,300
With folded broadsheet, Conspectus Systematis Ornithologiae Caroli-Luciani Bonaparte, Amst., 1850, inserted. Bradley Martin copy. (89) $9,500
3 vols in 1. Folio. (89) £1,300
— Iconographie des pigeons. Paris, 1857-[58]. Folio. (91) £1,300, £2,900

Bradley Martin copy. (89) $5,500
L.p. copy. Jeanson copy. (88) FF26,000

Bonaparte, Charles Lucien, 1803-57 — & Schlegel, Hermann, 1804-84
— Monographie des loxiens. Leiden & Duesseldorf, 1850. 4to. Bradley Martin copy. (89) $1,700

Bonaparte, Joseph, King of Spain, 1768-1844
— Memoires et correspondance politique et militaire.... Paris, 1853. 10 vols. 8vo. (88) $175

Bonarelli della Rovere, Prospero, 1588-1659
— Il Solimano: Tragedia. Florence, 1620. Illus by Jacques Callot. 4to. (90) $4,250

Bonaventura, Saint, 1221-74
— Biblia pauperum. [Venice: Georgius Walch, c.1480]. 4to. 102 leaves. Goff B-850. (88) $750
— Boek van die vier Oefeninghen. Antwerp: Adrien ven Berghen, 1507. Bound with: Dye vijfthiene Bloetstortinghen ons liefs heeren Ihesu Christi. Antwerp: Simon Cock, [c.1540]. 8vo. Six van Vromade —Willems copy. Nijhoff-Kronenberg 2547 & 2520. (91) £8,500
Bound with: Dye vijfthiene Bloetstortinghen ons liefs heeren Ihesu Christi. Antwerp: Simon Cock, [c.1540]. (91) £8,500
— Breviloquium. Augsburg: Anton Sorg, [not after 1476]. Folio. 78 leaves. Goff B-857. Abrams copy. (90) £2,200
— Commentarius in secundum librum Sententiarum Petri Lombardi. Venice: Reynaldus de Novimagio & Theodorus de Reynsburch, 1477. Folio. 328 (of 336) leaves. Goff B-873. (90) DM3,800
— Dieta salutis. Paris: Pierre le Dru, [1500]. 8vo. 152 leaves. GKW 4735. (89) £800
— Legenda maior S. Francisci. Milan: Filippo da Lavagna, 17 Jan 1480. 5 parts in 1 vol. 4to. 90 leaves. Goff B-891. Doheny copy. (88) £14,000
— The Life of Saint Francis of Assisi. San Francisco: John Henry Nash, 1931. One of 385. Trans by E. Gurney Salter. Folio. (89) $90; (91) $160
— The Lyfe of the Gloryous Confessoure of our Lorde Jhesu Criste Seynt Frauncis. L: Richard Pynson, [c.1515]. 4to. Somerfelde —York Minster Library—Doheny copy. (89) $16,000
— Meditationes vitae christi. Strassburg: Johann Reinhard Grueinger, [c.1496]. 4to. 54 leaves. Goff B-897. (91) $950
[Augsburg: Johann Schoensperger, c.1497]. 4to. Leaf count not given. Goff B-895. Doheny copy. (88) $2,000
— Psalterium Beate Virginis. Leipzig: Conrad

Kachelofen, 1516. 16mo. (91) £2,000
— Psalterium divine Virginis Marie. Paris: Etienne Jehannot for Antoine Verard, [before 25 Oct 1499]. 8vo. 44 leaves. Goff B-940. (88) £2,000
— Quaestiones super IV libros sententiarum Petri Lombardi.... [Nuremberg: Anton Koberger, after 2 Mar] 1491. Part 4 (of 5) only. Folio. 272 leaves. Goff P-486. (88) £1,600
  Nuremberg: Anton Koberger, 1500. Part 2 (of 4) only. 192 leaves. Goff P-488. (89) $425
— Tractatus et libri quam plurimi. Strasbourg: Martin Flach, 1489. Folio. 288 leaves. Goff B-927. (91) £3,000
— Vita Christi.... Barcelona: Joan Rosembach, 8 Feb 1522. 4to. Doheny copy. (89) $4,500

Bonaventura, Federico, 1555-1602
— De natura partus octomestris adversus vulgatam opinionem libri decem.... Urbino, 1600. Folio. (88) $400

Bonaveri, Domenico
— Freggi dell'architettura. [Bologna], c.1690. Folio. (89) £320

Bond, Francis, d.1918
— An Introduction to English Church Architecture.... L, 1913. 2 vols. 4to. (91) £60

Bond, Frederick Bligh —& Camm, Bede
— Roodscreens and Roodlofts. L, 1909. 2 vols. 4to. (90) £55

Bond, John Walpole
— A History of Sussex Birds. See: Walpole-Bond, John

Bond, Sir Thomas
— A Digest of Foreign Exchanges... Dublin: Alex. Stewart, 1795. 8vo. (89) £100

Bonde, William
— The Pylgrimage of Perfection.... L: Pynson, 1526. Part 1 only. 4to. (91) £550

Bondi, Clemente, 1742-1821
— La Felicita poema pubblicato in occasione de gloriosi sponsali dell...Alvise Pisani e...Giustiniana Pisani. [Venice, 1753]. 4to. (91) £1,200

Bone, Lady Gertrude
— Children's Children. L, 1908. One of 215 on japan vellum. Illus by Muirhead Bone. 4to. (88) £50

Bone, Sir Muirhead, 1876-1953
— Glasgow. Fifty Drawings.... Glasgow, 1911. One of 200. Folio. (89) £50
— The Western Front. Garden City, 1917. 2 vols, each being a half-cloth folder containing 5 parts. (91) $100

Bone, Muirhead & Gertrude
— Old Spain. L, 1936. One of 265. 2 vols & 1 (of 2) portfolios with 2 drypoints. Folio. (89) £300; (91) £220, £580
  2 vols. Folio. (89) £550
  Folio. Lacking the portfolios. (91) $250

Bonelli, Benedetto
— Animavversioni critiche sopra il notturno congresso delle lammie.... Venice, 1751. 4to. (88) £300; (89) £50

Boner, Charles, 1815-70
— Chamois Hunting in the Mountains of Bavaria. L, 1853. 8vo. (88) $50

Bonet, Theophilus
— A Guide to the Practical Physician.... L, 1684. 1st Ed in English. Folio. (91) £360
— Sepulchretum, sive anatomia practica.... Geneva, 1679. 1st Ed. 2 vols. Folio. (91) £360

Bonfadini, Vita
— La Caccia dell' arcobugio.... Milan: Dionisio Gariboldi for Altobello Pisani, 1648. 12mo. Schiff copy. (91) $1,000
  Ferrara: G. Gironi, [1652]. 12mo. (89) £160

Bonfils, Winifred Black
— The Life and Personality of Phoebe Apperson Hearst. San Francisco: John Henry Nash, 1928. One of 1,000. (89) $55; (90) £60; (91) $85

Boni, Albert
— Photographic Literature. NY, [1962]. 4to. (90) $220

Bonifaccio, Giovanni
— Istoria di Trivigi. Venice, 1744. Folio. (89) £80

Boniface VIII, Pope
— Liber sextus decretalium.... Paris: Jean Prevel, [1523]. 2 parts in 1 vol. 8vo. Terry copy. (89) $950

Boniface VIII, Pope, 1235?-1303
— Liber Sextus Decretalium. Strassburg: Heinrich Eggestein, 1470-72. Folio. 199 (of 201) leaves; lacking f.193 & blank f.105. Goff B-977. (89) £2,800
  Basel: Michael Wenssler, 8 July 1476. Folio. 162 leaves. Goff B-968. (91) $5,000

BONIFACE VIII

Venice: Jenson, 23-24 Nov 1479. ("Sextus Liber Decretalium.") Folio. 120 leaves. Goff B-991. (89) $2,000

121 leaves. Goff B-991. (90) DM5,200

Venice: Nicolaus Jenson, 1487. Folio. 146 leaves. Goff B-984. (91) $23,000

Paris: Thielmann Kerver for Jean Petit & Jean Cabiller, 24 Sept-30 Nov 1511. ("Sexti libri materia cum capitulorum numero....") 4 parts in 1 vol. 4to. (91) £900, £900

Venice, 1600. 3 parts in 1 vol. 4to. (91) £2,800, £2,800

— Sexti libri materia cum capitulorum numero. Paris: Thielman Kerver for Jean Petit & Jean Cabiller, 24 Sept 1511. Bound with: Clement V. Clementinarum materia cum capitulorum & titulorum numero. Paris: Thielman Kerver for Jean Petit & Jean Cabiller, Nov 1511. And: John XXII. Extravagantes XX. Paris: Thielman Kerver for Jean Petit & Jean Cabiller, Nov 1511. And: Extravagantes communes. Paris: Thielman Kerver for Jean Petit & Jean Cabiller, 30 Nov 1511. 4to. (91) $2,750

Bonini, Filippo Maria

— Il Tevere incatenato overo l'arte di frenar l'acque correnti. Rome: Francesco Moneta, 1663. 4to. (88) £350

Bonnaffe, A. A.

— Recuerdos de Lima, Album de tipos, trages y costumbres. [Lima & Paris, c.1856]. Folio. (89) £300

Bonnani, Filippo, 1638-1725

— Museum Kircherianum sive Musaeum a P. Athanasio Kirchero in Collegio Romano Societatis Jesu iam pridem incoeptum. Rome: Georgii Plachi, 1709. Folio. (88) £1,200

Bonnard, Camille

— Costumes des XIIIe, XIVe, et XVe Siecles.... Paris, 1845. ("Costumes historiques des XIIIe, XIVe et XVe siecles.") 2 vols. 4to. (91) £600

— Costumes historiques des XIIe, XIIIe, XIVe, et XVe siecles. Paris, 1860-61. 3 vols. 4to. (88) $225; (89) $425

— Costumi de' secoli XIIIe, XIVe, XVe... Milan, 1832-35. Illus by Paolo Mercuri. 2 vols. 4to. (90) £450

Bonnard, Pierre, 1867-1947

— Correspondances. Paris, 1944. 1st Ed, One of 1,025. (88) $225; (91) $275

— Couleur de Bonnard. Paris, [1947]. Folio. Verve No 17/18. (91) $140

AMERICAN BOOK PRICES CURRENT

Bonnaterre, Pierre Joseph

— Ichthyologie. Paris, 1788. 4to. (88) £150

Bonne, Rigobert —& Desmarest, Nicolas

— Atlas encyclopedique contenant la geographie ancienne et...moderne. Padua, 1789-90. 2 parts in 1 vol. 4to. (91) £1,200

Bonne, Rigobert, 1727-94

— Atlas de toutes les parties connues du globe terrestre. [Geneva: J. L. Pellet, 1780]. 4to. (88) £520, £900; (89) £600; (91) £400, £500

[Geneva: J. L. Pellet, 1780 or 1783]. Folio. (88) $800

— Atlas Maritime ou Cartes reduites de toutes les cotes de France.... Paris, 1778. 8vo. (91) £550

— Atlas moderne ou collection de cartes sur toutes les parties du globe terrestre. Paris: Chez Lattre & Herissant, [1762]. Folio. (88) £680

Paris: Chez Lattre & Delalain, [1762-86]. Folio. (90) £2,400

Paris: Lattre & Delalain, [1762-86]. Folio. (91) $750

Bonnefons, Amable

— Le Petit Livre de vie qui apprend a bien vivre et a bien prier Dieu. Paris: De Hansy & Herissant, 1748. 24mo. Doheny copy. (89) $5,000

Bonnefons, Nicolas de

— Le Jardinier francois.... Amst.: Raphael Smith, 1664. 8vo. (91) £100

Bonnefoy, Yves

— Anti-Platon. Paris: Maeght, 1962. One of 85 on Rives. sgd. Illus by Joan Miro. 4to. (88) FF45,000

Bonnemaison, Fereol

— Galerie de son Altesse Royale Madame la Duchesse de Berry. Ecole Francaise. Peintres modernes. Paris, 1822. Vol I (of 2). Folio. (90) $400

Bonner, T. D.

— The Life and Adventures of James P. Beckwourth, Mountaineer.... NY, 1856. 1st Ed. 12mo. (90) $95; (91) $75

Bonnet, Charles, 1720-93

— Oeuvres d'histoire naturelle et de philosophie. Neuchatel, 1779-83. 8 vols. 4to. (89) HF500

8 vols in 10. 4to. (88) FF14,000

All but the last 3 vols sgd C. Bonnet. (88) £700

Vols I-VII (of 8) bound in 9 vols. 4to. (88) £35
— Recherches sur l'usage des feuilles dans les plantes. Goettingen & Leiden, 1754. 1st Ed. 4to. (89) £320, HF1,000

Bonneval, Claude Alexandre, comte de, 1675-1747
— Anecdotes venitiennes et turques.... Utrecht: Jan Broedelet, 1740. 2 vols. 8vo. Blackmer copy. (90) £1,600
— Memoires du comte de Bonneval.... L: au depens de la Compagnie, 1738. 8vo. Blackmer copy. (90) £1,550
— Memoirs of the Bashaw Count Bonneval.... L, 1750. 8vo. Blackmer copy. (90) £380

Bonney, Edward
— The Banditti of the Prairies. Chicago, 1856. 3d Ed, 30th Thousand. 8vo. (89) $130

Bonney, Thomas George, 1833-1923
— Lake and Mountain Scenery from the Swiss Alps. L, 1874. Folio. (88) £210, £210; (89) £45
— The Peaks and Valleys of the Alps. L, 1868. Illus by Elijah Walton. Folio. (89) £80
— Vignettes: Alpine and Eastern-Alpine Series. L, 1873. Illus by Elijah Walton. 4to. (91) £230

Bonney, Thomas George, 1833-1923 —& Walton, Elijah, 1832-80
— Welsh Scenery.... L, 1875. 4to. (90) $120

Bonnycastle, Sir Richard Henry, 1791-1847
— Spanish America.... L, 1818. 1st Ed. 2 vols. 8vo. (88) $275

Bonpland, Aime J. A., 1773-1858. See: Humboldt & Bonpland

Bonser, Alfred E. —& Others
— The Land of Enchantment. L, 1907. Illus by Arthur Rackham. 4to. (88) $90

Bonstetten, Gustave de, Baron
— Recueil d'antiquites suisses. Berne, Paris & Leipzig, 1855. Folio. (91) £450

Bontekoe, Cornelis
— Korte verhandeling van 's menschen leven.... The Hague, 1684. 2 parts in 1 vol. 8vo. (88) HF600
— Tractat van het Excellenste Kuryd Thee.... The Hague: P. Hagen, 1679. 2d Ed. 3 parts in 1 vol. 8vo. (88) HF750; (89) HF800

Bonvalot, Gabriel
— Through the Heart of Asia. L, 1889. 2 vols. 8vo. (91) $130, $260

Bonwick, James, 1817-1906
— The Bushrangers. Melbourne, 1856. 12mo. Inscr to Dr. Cliffod. (90) A$480
— Curious Facts of Old Colonial Days. L, 1870. 8vo. (88) A$70; (89) A$80, A$100
— Daily Life and Origins of the Tasmanians.... L, 1870. 8vo. Inscr to the Rev. Joseph King. (90) A$120
— Discovery and Settlement of Port Philip. Melbourne, 1856. 12mo. (89) £350, A$1,200
— Early Days of Melbourne.... Melbourne, 1857. 18mo. (89) A$2,500
— John Batman, the Founder of Victoria. Melbourne, 1867. 1st Ed. 12mo. (88) A$110 2d Ed. Melbourne, 1868. 8vo. (88) A$90
— The Last of the Tasmanians.... L, 1870. 8vo. (90) A$450
— The Lost Tasmanian Race.... L, 1884. 8vo. (90) A$300
— The Mormons and the Silver Mines. L, 1872. 8vo. (89) $110 Inscr to his son James. (89) $110
— Notes of a Gold Digger, and Gold Diggers' Guide.... Melbourne, 1852. 12mo. (90) A$1,300
— Port Phillip Settlement. L, 1883. 8vo. (88) A$220, A$300; (89) A$400; (90) A$160
— Resources of Queensland. L, 1880. 1st Ed. 8vo. (90) A$75
— The Tasmanian Lily. L, 1873. 8vo. (90) A$600

Boodt, Anselmus Boetius de, 1550?-1634
— Gemmarum et lapidum historia. Leiden, 1647. In 1 vol. 8vo. (90) £380
— Le Parfaict Joaillier.... Lyons, 1644. 8vo. (88) £260; (90) £480

Book Auction Catalogues
[A collection of c.70 ptd catalogues of late 17th-century English book auctions, bound in 6 vols, containing about one-third of the book auction catalogues known before 1689, sold at S on 13 Dec 1991] £105,000

Book, Booke, or Boke
— The Boke Named the Royall. L: Richard Pynson, 1507. 4to. (89) £10,500
— The Boke of Justices of Peas. L: Robert Redman, 1527. Bound with: Parvus Libellus continens formam multarum rerum prout patet in kalendario. L: Robert Redman, 1527 8vo. STC 14868 & 15581.5. (89) £3,000
— Book Auction Records. L, 1902-74. Vols 1-71 & General Indexes 1-9. (90) £250 Vols 11-28. L, 1914-31. (89) $70 Vols 19-61 in 39 vols. L, 1922-61. (88) £75 Vols 30-74. L, 1933-78. (88) £120 Vols 39-73 & Index vol for 1963-68. L,

BOOK

1944-77. (89) £200
Vols 41-85. L, 1946-89. 8vo & 4to. (90) £340
Vols 69-75 & General Indexes for Vols 46-69. L, 1960-87. Together, 30 vols. (89) $1,100
Vols 60-83. L, 1963-86. (89) £320
Vols 67-69 & Index to Vols 61-65. L, 1971-73. (89) £50
Vols 69-75. L, 1972-78. (88) $140
Vols 72-78, 80 & Index for 66-69. Folkestone, 1975-85. 9 vols. 4to. (90) £80
Vols 72-85. 14 vols. 4to. (89) £420
Vols 75-82. Folkestone, 1977-85. 4to. (88) £260
Vols 75-83. Folkestone, 1977-86. 4to. (90) $475
— The Book Collector. L, 1952-85. Vols 1-232 [complete run], and "mostly" with indexes inserted. With: The Book Handbook. L, 1947-52. Nos 1-9 in 8 orig issues & Vol 2, Nos 1-4. Orig wraps. (91) £280
Vols 1-37, no 2. Lacking only Vol 1, No 2 and Indexes to Vols 1-36. L, 1952-84. With related material. (89) £480
Vols 21-35. L, 1972-86. 60 nos. (90) $300
— A Book Explaining the Ranks and Dignities of British Society.... L, 1809. 12mo. (90) £80; (91) $150
— The Book Handbook: An Illustrated Quarterly for Owners and Collectors of Books. L, 1947-52. Ed by Reginald Horrox. Vols I-II. Together, 13 issues bound in 2 vols. (88) $120
— The Book of English Trades. L, 1821. 8vo. (88) $260; (90) £120
— The Book of Games, or a History of the Juvenile Sports practised at the Kingston Academy. L: Tabart, [plates dated 1804]. 12mo. (88) £480
— The Book of Games, or a History of the Juvenile Sports Practised at a Considerable Academy near London. L: Richard Phillips, 1812. 12mo. (88) £200
— The Book of Kells. See: Codex...
— The Book of Sports, British and Foreign. L, 1843. 2 parts in 1 vol. 4to. (88) £280
— The Book of the Homeless. NY, 1916. 1st American Ed. Ed by Edith Wharton. 4to. (88) $200; (90) $160
— A Book of the Names of all Parishes, Market Towns...and Smallest Places in England and Wales. L, 1657. 4to. (89) £400
— The Book of the Ranks and Dignities of British Society.... L: Tabart & Co., [1805]. 1st Ed. 12mo. (90) £110; (91) £700
— The Book of Trades, or Library of the Useful Arts. L, 1805-6. Mixed Ed. 3 vols. 12mo. (89) £420

AMERICAN BOOK PRICES CURRENT

4th Ed. L, 1811. 3 vols. 12mo. (91) $310

Book Club of California
[See also: Grabhorn Printing & individual author entries]
— Keepsakes. San Francisco, 1946-86. 38 items. (88) $250

Book of Common Prayer
— 1549. - L: Edward Whitchurche. STC 16272. Folio. (88) £1,800
— 1549, 7 Mar. - L: Edward Whitchurche. 1st Ed, 1st Issue. Folio. (89) £4,000 "A magnificent copy." Houghton-The Garden copy. (90) $95,000
— 1550. - L: Richard Grafton. 4to. (89) £10,000
— 1550. - The Book of Comon Prayer Noted. L: Richard Grafton. Bound with: Articles Whereupon it was Agreed by the Archbyshops and Byshops...for the avoyding of the diversities of opinions.... L: Christopher Barker, 1579. And: A Booke of Certaine Canons.... L: John Daye, 1571. 4to. (88) £10,000
— [1570]. - The Booke of Common Prayer and Administration of the Sacramentes.... L: R. Jugge & J. Cawood. 2 parts in 1 vol. 16mo in 8's. Heber-Britwell Harmsworth copy. (88) £2,800
— 1574. - Liber precum publicarum. L: Thos. Vautrollier for Francis Flower. 8vo. (88) £1,100
— 1614. - L: Robert Barker. STC 16342.3. Bound with: The Whole Booke of Psalmes. L: T. Purfoot for the Companie of Stationers, 1618. STC 2560a.4. 4to in 8's. (91) £200
STC 16342.3. Bound with: The Whole Booke of Psalmes. L: T. Purfoot for the Companie of Stationers, 1618. STC 2560a.4. (91) £200
— [1623]. - Liturgia Inglesa. L.1st Ed in Spanish. 4to. (90) £200
— 1629. - L: Bonham Norton & John Bill. Bound with: The Whole Book of Psalmes Collected in to English Meeter.... L, 1630. 24mo. Doheny copy. (89) $2,800
Bound with: The Whole Book of Psalmes Collected in to English Meeter.... L, 1630. (91) $600
— 1637-36. - Edin.: R. Young. Bound with: The Psalmes of King David. L, 1636. 2 parts in 1 vol. Folio. STC 16606 & STC 2736. (89) £260
STC 16606. With the 2 leaves of Certaine Godly Prayers. Folio. STC 16606. (89) $400
— 1638. - Cambr.: Thomas Buck & Roger Daniel. Folio. (90) £2,400
— 1639. - L: R. Barker & J. Bill. 2 parts in 1 vol. 4to. (88) $350

— 1662. - L: By His Majesties Printers. Folio. (89) £500; (91) £500 Martin copy. (90) $2,750 Mostyn-Williams-The Garden copy. (90) $15,000
— 1665. - Cambr.: J. Field. 2 parts in 1 vol. 12mo. In Greek. Isaac Newton's copy. (90) £500
— 1674. - L: Assigns of John Bill & Christopher Barker. 12mo. (88) £335
— 1681. - Oxford. Folio. Martin copy. (90) $19,000
— 1683. - L. 12mo. (89) $350; (90) £100 Folio. (90) £950, £1,700
— 1701. - Oxford. Folio. (90) £420
— 1704. - L. 8vo. (90) £130
— 1707. - L: Charles Bill. 4to. (90) £1,100
— 1709. - L. 12mo. (88) £480
— 1715. - L. Folio. (90) £70
— 1715. - L: John Baskett. Folio. (90) £850
— 1717. - L: John Sturt. 8vo. (88) £140, £340; (90) $350, £280; (91) $600, £350 Doheny copy. (89) $900 Martin copy. (90) $1,800
— 1727. - L: John Baskett. Folio. (90) £550
— 1745. - L. Folio. (90) £65
— 1760. - Cambr.: Baskerville. 1st 8vo Ed. (88) £350, £400; (89) £300; (91) $350, $375 Stephen Tennant's copy. (88) £180
— 1761. - Cambr.: Baskerville. 8vo. (88) $110, $175, £500; (89) $70; (90) £100
— 1762. - Cambr.: Baskerville. 8vo. (88) $110, £120; (89) $100, $450, £180 Gaskell 19. (89) $100; (91) $100 Gaskell 20. (89) $400 Bound with: A New Version of the Psalms of David. Gaskell 20-21. (91) $300
— 1772. - Oxford. 12mo. (91) $70
— 1783. - Oxford. 8vo. (89) £2,600
— 1787. - Ne Yakawea Yondereanayendaghkwa Oghseragwegouh. L. 4to. (89) $1,700
— 1794. - L. 4to. (90) £300
— 1801. - Brooklyn. 8vo. (91) $375
— 1821. - L. 4to. (91) $225
— 1844. - L: William Pickering. Folio. (89) $110; (90) $100
— 1845. - L. Designed by Owen Jones. 8vo. (88) £150; (91) $400
— 1850. - L. Illus by Owen Jones. 8vo. (88) £55; (91) £60
— 1896. - L. One of 300. 4to. Facsimile of 1549 Ed. (90) £50; (91) $1,100
— 1903. - L: Essex House. One of 400. Folio. (91) $550
— 1904. - [NY: Plimpton Press]. Folio. (88) £45
— 1930. - Bost: Merrymount Press. One of 500. Folio. (91) $800

Booker, John, Student in Astrology
— The Dutch Fortune-Teller.... L: Ptd & Sold at the Ptg-Office in Bow Church-Yard [c.1780]. Folio. (91) $15,000

Bookman...
— Bookman: A Monthly Journal for Bookreaders.... L, 1913. Christmas Double Number 1913. Folio. (90) A$70
Christmas Double Number 1915. L, 1915. Folio. (90) A$80
Special Christmas Number. L, 1923. Folio. (90) A$80
Special Christmas Number 1925. L, 1925. Folio. (90) A$130
Special Christmas Number, 1931. L, 1931. Folio. (90) A$110

Bookman's...
— Bookman's Price Index. Detroit, [1964-81]. Vols 1-22. (88) $50
Vols 10-28. Detroit, [1975-84]. 19 vols. (90) $400
Vols 19-28. Detroit, [1980-84]. 4to. (91) £55

Bookworm...
— Bookworm: An Illustrated Treasury of Old Time Literature. NY, 1888-94. Vols I-V & VII. 8vo. (88) $60

Boon, Karel G. See: White & Boon

Boone and Crockett Club. See: North American...

Boosey, Thomas
— Piscatorial Reminiscences and Gleanings, by an Old Angler and Bibliopolist. L, 1835. 2 parts in 1 vol. 8vo. (89) £75

Booth, Edward Thomas
— Rough Notes on the Birds.... L, 1881-87. 3 vols. Folio. (89) £4,200; (90) £3,000, £4,500; (91) £1,000, £4,000, £4,500
Bradley Martin copy. (89) $6,000
Inscr. (89) £4,200

Booth, Edwin Carton
— Australia. L, [1873-76?]. 2 vols. 4to. (88) £420; (89) £280, A$4,000
2 vols in one. 4to. Sold w.a.f. (89) £600
30 orig parts. 4to. (88) £440
8 divisions in 8 vols. 4to. (90) A$1,300
8 orig parts. 4to. (88) A$1,300
Vol II only. (88) £170
L, [1874-76]. 8 vols. 4to. (89) A$900, A$1,000
L, [1886-88]. 2 vols in 8 parts. 4to. (88) £650; (89) £700

BOOTH

Booth, Henry, 1788-1869
— An Account of The Liverpool and Manchester Railway. L. 1830. 8vo. (90) £100

Booth, John
— The Battle of Waterloo, containing the Series of Accounts Published by Authority.... L, 1815. 5th Ed. 8vo. (91) £52

Booth, Stephen
— The Book Called Holinshed's Chronicles.... San Francisco: Book Club of California, 1968. Ltd Ed. 4to. With orig leaf from the 1587 Ed. (88) $70, $75; (89) $65, $100
With orig leaf (the dedication) from the 1587 Ed. (89) $110
With orig leaf from the 1587 Ed. (89) $170; (90) $110; (91) $120

Booth, William, 1829-1912
— In Darkest England and the Way Out. L, [1890]. 1st Ed. 8vo. (89) £110; (91) £160
Inscr to Lady Buxton. Martin copy. (90) $250

Booth, William Beattie, 1804?-74. See: Chandler & Booth

Boothby, Sir Brooke, 1743-1824
— Sorrow, Sacred to the Memory of Penelope. L, 1796. Illus by Henry Fuseli. Folio. (89) $140

Boothby, Guy Newell
— On the Wallaby, or...Across Australia. L, 1894. 8vo. (89) A$100

Bor, Pieter Christiaanszoon, 1559-1635
— Oorspronck, begin ende vervolgh der Nederlantsche oorlogen.... Amst., 1621-[34]. 5 vols in 6. Folio. (88) HF4,800; (90) HF4,000
Amst., 1679-84. 4 vols. Folio. (88) HF3,000

Borao y Clemente, Geronimo, 1821-1878
— La Imprenta en Zaragoza.... Zaragoza, 1860. 8vo. (91) $175

Borba de Moraes, Rubens
— Bibliographia Brasiliana. Amst., 1958. 2 vols. (90) £60; (91) £140
Los Angeles, 1983. 2 vols. 4to. (91) $100

Borcherds, Petrus Borchardus, 1786-1871
— An Auto-Biographical Memoir of Petrus Borchardus Borcherds.... Cape Town, 1861. 8vo. (88) R50

Borchgrevink, Carsten Egeberg, 1864-1934
— First on the Antarctic Continent. L, 1901. 1st Ed. With 3 photos of the expedition & other related material inserted. (91) $160

AMERICAN BOOK PRICES CURRENT

Bordelon, Laurent, 1653-1730
— L'Histoire des imaginations extravagantes de Monsieur Oufle. Paris, 1754. 5 parts in 1 vol. 12mo. (89) $275; (90) £320

Borden, John W. —& Krueger, Janet S.
— Thomas Bewick & the Fables of Aesop. San Francisco: Book Club of California, 1983. One of 518. (88) $55; (90) $65

Borden, William Cline
— The Use of the Roentgen Ray by the Medical Department of the United States Army in the War with Spain. Wash., 1900. 4to. (91) $200

Bordeu, Theophile de
— Recherches sur le Tissu Muqueux.... Paris, 1767. 12mo. (88) £90

Bordini, Giovanni Francesco
— De rebus praeclare gestis a Sixto V Pon. Max. Rome, 1558. 1st Ed. 4to. Kissner copy. (91) £900

Bordona, Jesus Dominguez. See: Dominguez Bordona, Jesus

Bordone, Benedetto
— Isolario.... Venice: Nicolo de Aristotile, detto Zoppino, 1528. ("Libro di Benedetto Bordone nel qual si ragiona de tutte l'isole del mondo.") 1st Ed. Folio. (88) £5,000; (89) £2,200
Venice: Nicolo de Aristotile, detto Zoppino, June 1534. Folio. (91) $6,500, £2,200
Blackmer copy. (90) £5,200
Venice: Aldus for Federico Toresano, 1547. Folio. (91) £4,800
Ownership of Annquetil-Duperron on tp. Later given by Alexander von Humboldt to J. Oltman. Phillipps copy. (90) £2,800

Bore, Eugene
— Correspondance et memoires d'un voyageur en Orient. Paris, 1840. 2 vols. 8vo. Blackmer copy. (90) £500

Borein, Edward
— Ed Borein's West. [Santa Barbara, 1952]. Vaquero Ed, one of 300. 4to. (88) $95
— Etchings of the West. [Santa Barbara, Calif., 1950]. One of 1,001. Ed by Edward S. Spaulding. (91) $55, $60, $60

Borel, Petrus
— Champavert. Contes immoraux.... Paris, 1833. 8vo. Martin copy. (90) FF3,800
— Madame Putiphar. Paris, 1839. 1st Ed. 2 vols. 8vo. With ALs. (88) FF7,000

1987 - 1991 • BOOKS

Copy on papier jonquille. Inscr to Napoleon Thomas. Martin copy. (90) FF120,000
— L'Obelisque de Louqsor.... Paris, 1836. 8vo. Martin copy. (90) FF12,000

Borelli, Giovanni Alfonso, 1608-79
— De motu animalium. Rome, 1680-81. 1st Ed. 2 vols. 4to. Martin copy. (90) $3,250
Leiden, 1710. 2 vols in 1. 4to. (89) £60
— De VI percussionis. Bologna, 1667. 4to. (88) £700; (91) £550

Boreman, Thomas
— A Description of a Great Variety of Animals and Vegetables.... L, 1736. 1st Ed. 12mo. (88) $205; (91) $190
— A Description of above Three Hundred Animals.... Edin.: W. Darling, 1782. 12mo. (88) £80; (90) £170

Borenius, Tancred
— Florentine Frescoes. L, [1930]. 4to. (89) £180

Borg, Carl Oscar
— The Great Southwest Etchings. Santa Ana, 1936. Sgd. (90) $140; (91) $225
Santa Ana: Fine Arts Press, 1936. Ed by E. C. Maxwell. 4to. Sgd on tp by Borg. (88) $100

Borges, Jorge Luis
— Ficciones. See: Limited Editions Club
— Nueve Poemas. Buenos Aires, 1955. One of 50. 4to. Copy 1, with extra frontis, orig sgd gouache, 23 drawings & the cancelled copperplate for frontis mtd inside lower cover. (88) £2,600

Borget, Auguste, b.1809
— La Chine et les chinois. Paris, 1842. Folio. (91) HK60,000
— Sketches of China and the Chinese. L, [1842]. Folio. (90) £5,000

Borgherini, Giovanni Battista
— Esequie di Filippo IV. Cattolico Re di Spagna celebrate in Firenze dal serenissimo Ferdinando II.... Florence, 1665. 4to. (90) $1,600

Borghini, Vincenzo Maria
— Discorsi.... Florence: Giunta, 1584-85. 4to. (89) £100
— Il Riposo. Florence: G. Marescotti, 1584. 8vo. (91) £320

Borgnis, Giuseppe Antonio, b. c.1781
— Traite complet de mecanique applique aux arts.... Paris, 1818-20. ("Composition des machines.") 8 vols. 4to. (89) £520

BORN

Paris, 1818-23. 8 vols plus 2 supplements: Theorie de la mecanique usuelle & Dictionnaire de mecanique appliquee aux arts. Together 10 vols. 4to. (89) HF3,000

Borgo, Pietro
— Aritmetica mercantile. Venice: G. B. Sessa, 10 Dec 1501. ("Libro de abacho....") 4to. Honeyman copy. (88) £550
Venice: Jacobus Pentius de Leucho, 1517. 4to. (88) £280
Venice: F. Bindoni & M. Pasini, 1528. ("Libro de abaco.") 4to. (88) £350
Venice: F. Bindoni & M. Pasini, 1534. ("Libro de abacho.") 8vo. (88) £250

Borgogni, Gherardo, 1526-c.1608
— La Fonte del diporto. Bergamo, 1598. 4to. (91) £450

Borgsdorf, Ernst Friedrich, Baron von
— Neu-Triunphirende Fortification auffallerlen Situationen defensive und offensive. Vienna, 1703. 2 vols. Oblong 4to. (89) £380

Borja, Juan de
— Empresas Morales. Prague: Jorge Nigrin, 1581. 4to. (88) $750

Borlase, William, 1695-1772
— The Natural History of Cornwall. Oxford, 1758. 1st Ed. Folio. (88) £130, £260; (90) £340; (91) £260
— Observations of the Antiquities Historical and Monumental, of the County of Cornwall. Oxford, 1754. 1st Ed. Folio. (91) £180
2d Ed. L, 1769. ("Antiquities Historical and Monumental of the County of Cornwall.") Folio. (88) £220, £320; (89) £130; (90) £320
— Scilly. Oxford, 1756. ("Observations on the Ancient and Present State of the Islands of Scilly....") 4to. (88) £165, £500

Borlase, William Copeland, 1848-99
— The Dolmens of Ireland.... L, 1897. 3 vols. 8vo. (88) £360; (89) £280; (90) £300, £260

Born, Ignaz von, 1742-91
— Catalogue methodique et raisonne de la collection des fossiles de Mlle. Eleonore de Raab. Vienna, 1790. 2 vols. 8vo. (90) $850
— Joannis physiophili opuscula.... Augsburg, 1784. 8vo. (88) $300
— New Process of Amalgamation of Gold and Silver Ores, and Other Metallic Mixtures.... L, 1791. 4to. (88) $400
— Specimen of the Natural History of the Various Orders of Monks.... L, 1783. 8vo. (91) £70
— Ueber das Anquicken der gold- und silberhaeltigen Erze, Rohsteine, Schwarzkupfer und Huettenspeise. Vienna, 1786.

4to. (88) $650, DM1,200

Borneman, Henry Stauffer
— Pennsylvania German Illuminated Manuscripts: a Classification.... Norristown, 1937. Folio. (91) $175

Borra, Luigi
— L'Amoroso Rime. Milan: G. A. Castiglioni, 1542. 4to. (91) £850

Borrer, Dawson
— A Journey from Naples to Jerusalem. L: Madden, 1845. 8vo. Blackmer copy. (90) £200

Borri, Cristoforo, d.1632
— Cochin-China: Containing Many Admirable Rarities.... L: Robert Raworth for Richard Clutterbuck, 1633. Issue with author's name misspelled Barri on tp. 4to. Phillipps-Fleming copy. (89) $4,000

Borrichius, Olaus
— Hermetis, Aegyptiorum ed Chemicorum sapientia ab Hermanni Conringii animadversiones vindicata. Copenhagen: Petrus Haubold, 1674. 4to. (88) £300

Borron, Helie de. See: Helie de Borron

Borrow, George Henry, 1803-81
— The Bible in Spain. L, 1843. 1st Ed. 3 vols. 8vo. (91) $90, £80
— Celebrated Trials.... L, 1825. 1st Ed. 6 vols. 8vo. (91) $110
— Lavengro. L, 1851. 1st Ed. 3 vols. 8vo. (88) $130; (89) £60; (90) £55
  See also: Limited Editions Club
— Romantic Ballads. Norwich, 1826. 1st Ed, 1st Issue. 8vo. (89) £180
— The Romany Rye. L, 1857. 1st Ed. 2 vols. 8vo. (90) $50; (91) £60
— Tales of the Wild and the Wonderful. L, 1825. 1st Ed. 8vo. (90) £500; (91) £500
— Wild Wales.... L, 1862. 1st Ed. 3 vols. 8vo. (90) £55
— Works. L & NY, 1923-24. One of 775. 16 vols. (89) £360

Borthwick, John Douglas
— Three Years in California. Edin. & L, 1857. 8vo. (91) $160, $325, £220
  Oakland, 1948. One of 1,000. (91) $60

Boruwlaski, Count Joseph
— Memoirs.... See: Fore-Edge Paintings

Bory de Saint Vincent, Jean Baptiste G. M., 1778?-1846 — & Schneider, Antoine
— Histoire et description des iles Ionniennes. Paris, 1823. 2 vols, including Atlas. 8vo & folio. (91) £400

Blackmer copy. (90) £1,150

Bory de Saint-Vincent, Jean Baptiste Genevieve Marcellin, Baron de
— Expedition scientifique de Moree. Section des Sciences physiques. Paris & Strasbourg, 1832-36. 6 vols, including Atlas. 4to & folio. (89) £2,000

Bory de Saint-Vincent, Jean Baptiste G. M., 1778?-1846
— Expedition scientifique de Moree. Section des Sciences physiques. Paris & Strasbourg, 1832-36. 6 vols, including Atlas. 4to & folio. Blackmer copy. (90) £4,800
— Expedition scientifique de Moree. Paris & Strasbourg, 1835. Atlas vol only. 4 parts in 1 vol. Folio. (91) £3,200
— Voyage dans les quatres principales iles des mers d'Afrique. Paris, 1804. 3 vols. 4to. Martin copy. (90) $3,250

Bos, Lambert van den
— Keur-stof deses tydts, behelfenden de voornameste geschiedenissen.... Dordrecht, 1672. Illus by Romain de Hooghe. 8vo. (90) $1,400

Bosa, Eugene
— Soggetti pittoreschi e costumi di Venezia. Venice, [1835?]. Folio. (88) £240

Bosbyshell, Oliver Christian
— The 48th in the War.... Phila., 1895. 8vo. Inscr to Mrs. George M. Stull. Coulter 48. (91) $130

Bosca, Petrus
— Oratio...Rome habitae...in celebritate uictorie Malachitane per...Ferdinandum & Helisabeth Hispaniarum principes catholicos.... Rome: Eucharius Silber, 1487. 4to. 6 leaves. GKW 4943. (89) £1,400

Boscana, Geronimo, 1776-1831
— Chinigchinich-Chi-ni ch-nich. A Revised...Version of Alfred Robinson's Translation of...Boscana's Historical Account of...the Indians of...San Juan Capistrano.... Santa Ana, 1933. (89) $170
  Ed by P. T. Hanna. Folio. (89) $110; (90) $170

Boschini, Marco, 1613-78
— L'Arcipelago. Con tute le Isole, Scogli secche, e Bassi fondi.... Venice: Francesco Nicolini, 1658. 4to. (91) £3,000
  Blackmer copy. (90) £2,500
  Coronelli's copy. Fleming copy. (89) $3,000
  Coronelli's copy. (91) $3,200
— La Carta del navegar pitoresco. Venice, 1660. 4to. (89) £250
— Le Minere della pittura.... Venice, 1664. 12mo. (91) £280

— Il Regno tutto di Candia.... Venice, 1651. 4to. (91) $5,500, £5,500
Blackmer copy. (90) £3,800

Bosco, Henri
— Sites et Mirages. Paris, 1950. One of 40 on verge de Montval. Illus by Albert Marquet. 4to. (89) SF2,000

Boscovich, Ruggiero Giuseppe, 1711-87
— De lunae atmosphaera dissertatio. Rome, 1753. 4to. (89) £250
— De observationibus astronomicis.... Rome, 1742. 4to. (91) £320
— Dissertationes quinque ad dioptricam.... Vienna, 1767. 4to. (91) £200
— Philosophiae naturalis theoria. Vienna, 1758. 4to. Honeyman-Garden copy. (90) £4,500
Honeyman-The Garden copy. (90) $12,000

Bosio, Antonio, 1575-1629
— Roma Sotterranea. Rome, 1650. 4to. Kissner copy. (91) £150
— Rome Sotterranea. Rome, 1632. Folio. (91) £800
Kissner copy. (91) £1,400

Bosio, Giacomo
— Histoire des Chevaliers de l'Ordre de S. Jean de Hierusalem.... Paris, 1659-58. In 1 vol. Folio. (90) £2,800
— Histoire des chevaliers de l'order de S. Jean de Hierusalem.... Paris, 1659. In 1 vol. Folio. (90) HF2,400

Bosman, Willem
— A New and Accurate Description of the Coast of Guinea. L, 1721. 2d Ed in English. 8vo. (88) £250; (90) £300

Bosqui, Edward
— Memoirs. See: Grabhorn Printing

Bossche, Gulielmus van den
— Historia medica, in qua libris IV animalium natura.... Brussels, 1639. 1st Ed. 4to. (88) HF1,300

Bosschere, Jean de. See: De Bosschere, Jean

Bosse, Abraham
— La Maniere universelle de Mr Desargues pour poser l'essieu & placer les heures & autres choses aux cadrans au soleil. Paris, 1643. 1st Ed. 8vo. (89) $550; (90) £360
— La Maniere universelle de Mr. Desargues pour practiquer la perspective par petit-pied, comme le geometral. Paris, 1648. 1st Ed. 8vo. (91) $130, £200
— Moyen universel de pratiquer la perspective sur les tableaux.... Paris, 1653. 1st Ed. 8vo. John Evelyn's copy. (91) $700

— Le Peintre converty aux precises et universelles regles de son art. Paris, 1667. 8vo. (90) £50
— Representations geometrales de plusieurs parties de bastiments.... Paris, 1688. Bound with: Traite sur la pratique des ordres de colomnes de l'architecture nommee antique. Folio. Leonard Baskin's copy. (88) £1,000
— Tracte des manieres de graver en taille douce sur l'airin. Paris, 1645. 1st Ed. 8vo. (88) £320
— Traite des manieres de dessiner les ordres de l'architecture antique en toutes leurs parties. Paris, [n.d.]. Bound with: Bosse. Des Ordres de Colonnes. [Paris, n.d.]. And: Representations geometrales de plusieurs parties de bastiments faites par les regles de l'architecture antique. Paris, 1688. Folio, contemp calf. (89) £380

Bossert, Helmuth Theodor
— Ornament.... L, 1924. Folio. (88) $110; (89) £90
— Ornament in Applied Art. NY, 1924. Folio. (88) $110
— Peasant Art in Europe. Berlin, 1926. Folio. (89) £95

Bossewell, John
— Workes of Armorie.... L: Richardi Totelli, 1572. Bound with: Legh, Gerard. The Accedens of Armory. L, 1576. 1st Ed. 4to. (88) £120; (90) £260

Bossi, Benigno
— Mascarade a la grecque. Parma, 1771. Folio. Blackmer copy. (90) £4,600

Bossoli, Carlo, 1815-84
— The Beautiful Scenery and Chief Places of Interest throughout the Crimea. L, 1856. Folio. (91) £850, £1,050
— The War in Italy. L, 1859-60. 4to. (90) £440; (91) £400
L, [1860]. 8vo. (89) £340

Bossu, Jean Bernard, 1720-92
— Travels through that part of North America formerly called Louisiana. L, 1771. 1st Ed in English. 2 vols. 8vo. (88) $1,000, £380; (91) $1,150, £280, £300

Bossuet, Jacques Benigne, 1627-1704
— Discours sur l'histoire universelle.... Paris, 1681. 1st Ed. 4to. (89) £360
Paris, 1784. 4to. (89) £110
— A Discourse on the History of the whole World. L: for Matthew Turner, 1686. 1st Ed in English. 8vo. (90) £50

BOSSUS

Bossus, Matthaeus, 1428-1502
— De instituendo sapientia animo.... Bologna: Francisco (Plato) de Benedictis, 6 Nov 1495. 128 leaves. Goff B-1043. Bound with: Bossus. Sermo in Iesu Christi passionem. Bologna: Franciscus Plato de Benedictis, 11 Nov 1495. 12 leaves. Goff B-1047. Both works ptd on vellum. 4to, Doheny copy. (88) $38,000
— Dialogus de veris et salutaribus animi gaudis.... Florence: Francesco Bonaccorsi, 8 Feb 1491/92. 4to. Ptd on vellum. 90 leaves. Goff B-1041. Medici-Magliabecchi-Doheny copy. (88) $45,000

Bossut, Charles, 1730-1814
— Traite Elementaire de Mechanique et de Dinamique.... Charleville, 1763. 8vo. (90) $425
— Traite elementaire d'hydrodynamique.... Paris, 1771. 2 vols. 8vo. (89) £120
— Traite theorique et experimental d'hydrodynamique. Paris, 1796. 2 vols. 8vo. (89) £85

Boston Athenaeum
— Confederate Imprints. See: Crandall, Marjorie Lyle

Boston Housekeeper. See: Cook's...

Boston Museum of Fine Arts
— The Artist & the Book: 1860-1960. NY, 1982. (91) $70

Boston Public Library
— Catalogue of the Spanish Library...bequeathed...George Ticknor. See: Whitney, James Lyman

Boston Society for Medical Improvement
— Report of a Committee...on the Alleged Dangers which accompany the Inhalation of the Vapor of Sulphuric Ether. Bost., 1861. 8vo. (90) $150

Boswell, Henry
— Historical Descriptions.... L, [1786]. Folio. (89) £700; (90) £220; (91) £560
L: A. Hogg, [c.1790]. Folio. (89) £400; (91) $650
Extra-illus with 427 plates on 329 leaves. (91) £780

Boswell, James, 1740-95
— An Account of Corsica. Dublin, 1768. 12mo. (88) £130; (90) £75
Glasgow: Foulis for Dilly, 1768. 8vo. (88) $175, $280; (89) $150
Inscr to the Earl Marischal of Scotland. Newton-Doheny copy. (89) $8,000
1st Ed. Glasgow: Foulis for Dilly, 1768. 8vo. (90) £240; (91) $160

AMERICAN BOOK PRICES CURRENT

2d Ed. L, 1768. 8vo. (90) £90; (91) $200
— The Journal of a Tour to the Hebrides.... Dublin, 1785. 8vo. (90) £90
1st Ed. L, 1785. 8vo. (88) $180, $220, £120; (89) £105
Doheny copy. (89) $420
2d Ed. 8vo. (88) $120; (89) £280, £480
Bradley Martin copy. (90) $2,000
3d Ed. L, 1786. 8vo. (90) £100
See also: Limited Editions Club
— Letters. Oxford, 1924. One of 100. Ed by Chauncey Brewster Tinker. 2 vols. 8vo. (89) $250
— The Life of Samuel Johnson.... L, 1791. 1st Ed, Issue not given. 2 vols. 4to. (88) $800
With the "give" reading on p. 135 of Vol I. (88) $1,100, $1,600, $2,900; (89) $1,700, $2,000, £1,300; (90) $1,100; (91) $1,600, £1,000
Doheny copy. (88) $2,800
Extra-illus with 26 plates & facsimile letters. (88) $800
Fleming copy. (89) $4,500
2 vols extended to 4. 4to. Extra-illus with 460 ports & views, 23 autographs of persons mentioned in the text, and a 2-line Latin quotation in Johnson's hand. Doheny copy. (88) $4,000
2 vols plus The Principal Corrections and Additions, 1793. 4to. (90) £1,000
With the "gve" reading. 2 vols. 4to. (89) £1,200, £1,600; (90) $2,000, £1,400; (91) $2,600, $5,000, £6,000, £11,000
Bradley Martin copy. (90) $6,500
With address-panel in Johnson's hand of letter to Henry Thrale. The Garden copy. (90) $13,000
2d Ed. L, 1793. 3 vols. 8vo. (88) $230; (89) $175
Owner's stamps embossed on titles, bookplates & booklabels. (90) $175
3d Ed. L, 1799. 3 vols. 8vo. (88) $90
Bost., 1807. 3 vols. 8vo. (88) $75
6th Ed. L, 1811. 4 vols. 8vo. (88) $180
L, 1820. 4 vols. 8vo. (88) £45; (89) $100
L, 1824. 4 vols. 8vo. (88) $160
L, 1826. 4 vols. 8vo. (91) $175
Oxford, 1826. 4 vols. 8vo. With c.125 inserted illusts, some in color. (91) $800
L, 1831. 5 vols. 8vo. (88) $50, £40; (89) £220; (91) $140
5 vols extended to 11. 8vo. Extra-illus with ports & plates & with A Ls s of Mrs. Piozzi, Elizabeth Carter & others. (91) £2,200
L, 1835. 10 vols. 8vo. (89) $375, £70; (91) $75
Vols I-IX (of 10). (91) $115
L, 1839. 10 vols. 8vo. (89) £1,600; (91) £100
L: H. G. Bohn, 1859. 10 vols. 8vo. (89) $140

L: George Bell, 1884. One of 104. Ed by Alexander Napier. 5 vols. 8vo. (88) $425
Reynolds Ed. L, 1885. One of 500. 5 vols. 8vo. (89) £75; (90) $1,200
Extra-illus with over 500 ports, views, etc., inlaid to size. (88) £180
NY, 1891. 6 vols, including Boswell's Journal of a Tour to the Hebrides & Johnson's Diary of a Journey into Northern Wales. 8vo. (91) $375
L, 1896. 6 vols. 8vo. (89) $325
Temple Bar Ed. NY, 1922. Ed by Clement Shorter. 10 vols. 8vo. (88) $90, $175, $180; (89) $700; (90) $160, $600; (91) $90
One of 785. (88) £70
— Private Papers from Malahide Castle in the Collection of Ralph Heyward Isham. L, 1928-37. Ed by Geoffrey Scott. 20 vols, including Index & Journal of a Tour to the Hebrides. 4to & folio. (88) $700, £750; (90) $1,100
With related Ls from Isham & ALs from Frederick Pottle. (89) $1,300
Vols VII-IX only. (91) $110
[Mt. Vernon, 1928]-37. One of 570. 19 vols, including Index. 4to & folio. Doheny copy. (88) $1,900
— William Pitt, the Grocer of London. L, 1790. Single-sheet ptg, 332mm by 138mm. Isham copy. (89) $4,800

Boswell's copy, James
— WOOD, J. G. - Six Views in the Neighbourhood of Llangollen and Bala. L, [plates dated 1793]. Folio. Boswell's subscriber's copy. (88) £920

Botanic...
— The Botanic Garden.... L, 1825-[51]. Vol I. (90) £325
Ed by Benjamin Maund. 18 vols in 16. (90) $8,500
7 vols (of 13). 4to. (91) £1,900
Vol IV. (91) £260
Vols I-V. (91) £1,350
Vols I-VI only. (90) £950
Vols I-XIII (complete set), plus the Auctarium, the Fruitist & the Floral Register. Together, 16 vols. (89) £2,600
Vols I-XIII (complete set) plus The Fruitist, The Floral Register & the Auctarium. Together, 16 vols. (89) £4,200, £5,000
Vol I only (90) $350; (91) $450, £280
Vol II only (88) DM300
Vol IV (88) DM1,200; (89) £270
8vo. (89) £460; (90) £320
Vol IX (89) £320; (91) $450
Vol V only (88) £220, £280; (91) £240
Vol VI only (88) DM1,300; (91) £300
Vol X only (91) $450
Vols I-II (88) £300; (89) £400; (90) £820
Vols I-III (91) $1,100, £720
Vols I-IV. 4 vols. (91) £1,000
Vols I-IV bound in 2 (88) £840
Vols I-VI. 6 vols. (91) £1,700
Vols I-VI in 8 vols (88) $1,700
Vols I-VII only (89) £2,300
Vols I-VIII (88) $4,400; (91) £4,500
Vols I-XIII (91) $6,500
Bound in 7 vols. (88) £4,200
2d Ed. L, 1878. Ed by J. Niven. 6 vols. 8vo. (88) £1,700; (91) £480
Vol III only. (91) £260

Botanical...
— The Botanical Cabinet. See: Loddiges, Conrad & Sons

Botanist...
— The Botanist: Containing Accurately Coloured Figures of Tender and Hardy Ornamental Plants. L, [1837-42]. Ed by Benjamin Maund & J. S. Henslow. 5 vols. (91) £1,700
5 vols. 4to. (90) $3,250; (91) £1,400, £1,400
Vol II only. (89) £340
Vols I & II (of 5) only. 4to. (88) £500; (89) £660
Vols I & III-V (of 5). (89) £1,200
Vols I-II only. (90) £650
Vols I-III only. (88) £440
Vol I only (91) $950
Vol V only. L, [1837-46]. (91) £200
Vols I-IV (91) £1,000

Botero, Giovanni, 1540-1617
— Allgemeine historische Weltbeschreibung. Munich: Nicolaus Heinrich, 1611. Folio. Phillipps copy. (88) £1,400
— Delle relationi universali. Rome: Giorgio Ferrari, 1595. 3 parts in 1 vol. 4to. (88) £100
Rome: Giorgio Ferrari, 1595-97. 4 parts in 3 vols. 4to. (90) £240
— Relations of the Most Famous Kingdoms.... L, 1616. 8vo. (89) £350
— A Treatise Concerning the Causes of the Magnificencie and Greatness of Cities.... L: T. P. for Richard Ockould & Henry Tomes, 1606. 4to. (88) £450

Botley, Samuel
— Maximum in Minimo.... L, 1674. 8vo. (90) £100

Botta, Carlo, 1766-1837
— Histoire de la guerre de l'independence des Etats-Unis d'Amerique. Paris, 1812-13. 4 vols. 8vo. (89) $50

Bottomley, Gordon, 1874-1948
— The Mickle Drede and Other Verses. Kendal: T. Wilson, 1896. 16mo. Inscr to Mrs. James Ashcroft Noble. Bradley Martin copy. (90) $3,750

Bottomley, William Lawrence
— Great Georgian Houses of America. NY, 1933-37. 2 vols. (91) $225

Bottu de Limas, J.
— Six Mois en Orient. Lyons, 1861. 8vo. Blackmer copy. (90) £340

Boturni Benaduci, Lorenzo, c.1702-50
— Idea de una nueva historia general de la America septentrional. Madrid, 1746. 2 parts in 1 vol. 4to. (88) $250

Bouchardat, Apollinaire
— De la Glycosurie ou Diabete Sucre.... Paris, 1883. 8vo. (90) $175

Bouche, Charles Francois
— De la restitution du Comte Venaissin.... Paris: Baudouin, 1789. 8vo. (89) $550

Bouche, Henri. See: Dollfus & Bouche

Bouche, Louis. See: Yarrow & Bouche

Boucher de Crevecoeur de Perthes, Jacques, 1788-1868
— Antiquites Celtiques et Antediluviennes. Paris, 1847-64. 3 vols. 8vo. (88) FF5,800

Boucher de Perthes, Jacques
— Antiquities celtiques et antediluviennes. Paris, 1847-64. 3 vols. 8vo. (88) £80

Boucher, Jonathan
— A View of the Causes and Consequences of the American Revolution.... L, 1797. 8vo. (90) $180

Boucher, Pierre, 1622-1717
— Histoire veritale et naturelle des moeurs & productions du pays de la Nouvelle France, vulgairement dit le Canada. See: Locke's copy, John

Bouchet, Jean, 1476-c.1550
— Les Annales d'Aquitaine. Poitiers, 1644. Folio. (88) FF11,000

Bouchet, Jules Frederic, 1799-1860
— Compositions antiques. Paris, [1851]. Oblong 4to. Blackmer copy. (90) £150

Bouchette, Joseph, 1774-1841
— The British Dominions in North America. L, 1831. 1st Issue. 2 vols. 4to. (89) £200
— A Topographical Description of the Province of Lower Canada.... L, 1815. 8vo. (89) $375
— A Topographical Dictionary of the Province of Lower Canada. L, 1832. 3 vols in 2. 4to. (90) £380

Bouchot, Henri, 1849-1906
— The Book: its Printers, Illustrators, and Binders.... L, 1890. 8vo. (88) $75
— Catherine de Medicis. Paris, 1899. One of 200 on japon. 4to. Extra-illus with c.80 ports & 25 contemp documents & 2 antiphonal leaves. (91) $2,500
One of 1,000. (89) $175
— De la Reliure. Paris, 1891. One of 750. 12mo. (91) $100

Boue, Ami
— Essai Geologique sur L'Ecosse.... Paris, [1820]. 8vo. (88) $275

Bougainville, Hyacinthe Yves Philippe Potentien, Baron de, 1781-1846
— Album pittoresque de la Fregate la Thetis.... Paris, 1828. 6 parts. Folio. (89) A$15,000
— Journal de la navigation autour du globe.... Paris, 1837. 2 text vols & Atlas, 4to & folio. (89) A$16,000
2 vols. Folio. Martin copy. (90) $14,000
2 vols; lacking Atlas. Folio. (91) $550

Bougainville, Louis Antoine de, 1729-1811
— The History of a Voyage to the Malouine.... L, 1773. 2d Ed. 4to. (89) $150
— Voyage autour du monde.... Paris, 1771. 1st Ed. 4to. (91) $3,200
2d Ed. Paris, 1772. 2 vols. 8vo. (91) $900
— A Voyage Round the World.... L, 1772. 4to. (89) $1,500; (91) £850
8vo. (88) £750; (89) A$2,100, A$3,500

Bougard, R.
— The Little Sea Torch. L, 1801. Folio. (88) £780; (90) £400
Blackmer copy. (90) £1,000

Bougeant, Guillaume Hyacinthe, 1690-1743
— Amusement philosophique sur le langage des bestes. Paris, 1739. Bound with: Lettre de Madame De*** a Monsieur De*$...sur le Gout & le Genie. Paris: Prault, 1737 12mo. (91) $80

Bouguer, Pierre, 1698-1758
— De la manoeuvre des vaisseaux.... Paris, 1757. 4to. (89) FF50,500
— Essai d'optique sur la gradation de la lumiere. Paris, 1760. ("Traite d'optique sur la gradation de la lumiere.") 4to. (91) £110
— La Figure de la terre.... Paris, 1744. 4to. (91) $1,200
Paris, 1749. 4to. (88) FF10,000
— Nouveau Traite de navigation, contenant la theorie et la pratique du pilotage. Paris, 1753. 4to. (91) $450

— Traite complet de la navigation. Paris, 1706. 4to. (91) $500
— Traite du navire, de sa construction.... Paris, 1746. 1st Ed. 4to. (89) $700; (91) $1,000

Bouhours, Dominique, 1628-1702
— Histoire de Pierre d'Aubusson grand maistre de Rhodes. Paris: Estienne Michallet, 1691. 8vo. Blackmer copy. (90) £200
— The Life of St. Francis Xavier, of the Society of Jesus.... L, 1688. 8vo. (90) £100

Bouillaud, Jean Baptiste, 1796-1881
— Essai sur la philosophie medicale et sur les generalites de la clinique medicale. Paris, 1836. 8vo. (90) $450

Bouillet, ——, Engineer
— Traite des moyens de rendre les rivieres navigables. Paris, 1693. 1st Ed. 8vo. (88) £160
  Amst.: P. Mortier, 1696. 8vo. (89) £130

Bouillet, Marie Nicolas, 1798-1864
— Dictionnaire Universel d'Histoire et de Geographie.... Paris, 1864. 2 vols. 8vo. (90) $80

Bouillon, Pierre, 1776-1831
— Musee des antiques. Paris, [1811-27]. 3 vols. Folio. (89) £540
  Blackmer copy. (90) £5,800

Boulanger, Nicolas Antoine
— Recherches sur l'origine du despotisme oriental. L: Pvtly ptd, 1762. 8vo. (90) $110

Boulart, Raoul A.
— Ornithologie du salon. Paris, 1878. 8vo. Martin copy. (90) $400

Boulger, George S., 1853-1922 —& Perrin, Ida Southwell
— British Flowering Plants. L, 1914. Ltd Ed. 4 vols. 4to. (88) £100; (89) £80, £80, £80, £100, £105; (90) £70, £100; (91) £60, £90

Boulind, Richard. See: Kraus, Hans P.

Boulton, D'Arcy
— Sketch of His Majesty's Province of Upper Canada. L, 1805. 4to. (89) £450

Boulton, Richard
— A Compleat History of Magick, Sorcery, and Witchcraft. L, 1715-16. 2 vols. 12mo. Senhouse copy. (90) $450

Boulton, William B.
— The Amusements of Old London. L, 1901. 2 vols. 4to. (88) $130; (89) $120

Bouquet, Martin, 1685-1754 —& Others
— Recueil des histoires des Gaules et de la France. Paris, 1738-1904. Vols 1-13 only. Folio. (88) FF8,000

Bourbon, Jacques de
— La Grande & Merveilleuse et Trescruelle Oppugnation de la Noble Cite de Rhodes ...par Sultan Seliman. Paris: Gilles de Gourmont, May 1526. 4to. (89) £1,300

Bourbon, Louis Joseph de, Prince de Conde. See: Conde, Louis Joseph de Bourbon

Bourdet, Bernard
— Soins faciles pour la proprete de la bouche.... Lausanne, 1782. 8vo. (91) £100, £340

Bourdillon, Francis William, 1852-1921
— Ailes d'Alovette. L, 1890-1902. One of 100 & 130. 4to. (90) £100
— Early Editions of the Roman de la Rose. L, 1906. 4to. (89) £40

Boureau-Deslandes, Andre Francois. See: Deslandes, Andre Francois Boureau

Bourgeois, Constant, 1767-1841
— Voyage pittoresque a La Grande Chartreuse. Paris: Delpech, [plates dated 1821]. Folio. (89) £300

Bourgeois, Emile, 1857-1934
— France under Louis XIV.... NY, 1897. 4to. (91) $50

Bourgeois, Louise
— Observations diverses sur la sterilite, perte de fruict, fecondite.... Paris, 1609. 8vo. (90) £1,000

Bourgery, Marc Jean, 1797-1849 —& Others
— Traite complet de l'anatomie de l'homme.... Paris, 1867-71. 9 vols, including Supplement. Folio. (91) £2,400

Bourges, Jacques de
— Relation du voyage de Monseigneur l'Eveque de Beryte, Vicaire Apostolique du Royaume de la Cochinchine. See: Jesuit Relations

Bourgoin, Jules
— Les Arts Arabes. Paris, 1873. Folio. (91) £950
  Blackmer copy. (90) £3,600

BOURGOING

Bourgoing, Jean Francois de, 1748-1811
— Atlas to the Modern State of Spain. L, 1808. 4to. (91) £120
— Travels in Spain.... L, 1789. 3 vols. 8vo. (89) £190; (91) £400

Bourguet, Emilie
— Les Ruines de Delphes. Paris, 1914. 8vo. Blackmer copy. (90) £60

Bourguignon Anville, Jean Baptiste. See: Anville, Jean Baptiste Bourguignon d'

Bourjot Saint-Hilaire, Alexandre
— Histoire naturelle des perroquets, troisieme volume (supplementaire) pour faire suite aux deux volumes de Levaillant.... Paris & Strasbourg: Levrault, [1835]-37-38-[39]. Folio. (88) FF190,000
Bradley Martin copy. (89) $16,000

Bourke, John Gregory, 1843-96
— On the Border with Crook. NY, 1891. 1st Ed. 8vo. (88) $140; (91) $175, $250
With Ds transportation voucher in blank sgd by Bourke as Aide-de-Camp to Gen. Crook, 1873. (88) $170
— The Snake-Dance of the Moquis of Arizona. L, 1884. 8vo. (88) $140, $175
NY, 1884. 8vo. (88) $200; (89) $110, $180, $190

Bourke-White, Margaret
— "Dear Fatherland Rest Quietly" A Report on the Collapse of Hitler's "Thousand Years." NY, 1946. 4to. (89) $225
— Eyes on Russia. NY, 1931. 4to. (90) $225; (91) $110, $175
Sgd on front free endpaper. (88) $140
— Russian War Relief, Inc. Meet Some of the Soviet People. [N.p., c.1940s]. Folio. (89) $300
— Twelve Soviet Photo-Prints [First and Second Series]. [N.p., 1940s]. Folio. (90) $1,300

Bourke-White, Margaret —& Caldwell, Erskine
— Say, Is This the U.S.A. NY, [1941]. 1st Ed. Folio. (89) $75; (90) $175; (91) $90, $150

Bourne, John C.
— The History and Description of the Great Western Railway.... L, 1846. Folio. (89) £2,100; (90) $2,600; (91) £1,600
— A Treatise on the Steam Engine.... L, 1851. 4to. (89) £45

AMERICAN BOOK PRICES CURRENT

Bourne, John C. —& Britton, John, 1771-1857
— Drawings of the London and Birmingham Railway. L, 1839. 4 parts in 1 vol. Folio. (89) £1,800; (90) £2,250
Folio. (90) $2,500; (91) £3,000

Bourne, Vincent
— Poematis. L: Pickering, 1840. 8vo. Sgd on title "W. Cowper 1779". (88) £105

Bourrienne, Louis Antoine Fauvelet de. See: Fauvelet de Bourrienne, Louis Antoine

Bourrit, Marc Theodore, 1739-1819
— Nouvelle Description generale et particuliere des glaciers, vallees de glace et glaciers qui forme la grande chaine des Alpes. Geneva, 1785. 8vo. (89) £220
— Nouvelle Description des glaciers et glaciers de Savoye.... Geneva, 1785. 8vo. Supplementary vol to Bourrit's Description des Alpes Pennines & Rhetiennes. (88) DM600

Boursault, Edme
— Nicht glauben was man sihet. [N.p.]: Widow & Heirs of Paul Fuerst, 1680. 12mo. (90) $200

Boutcher, William
— A Treatise on Forest Trees. Edin., 1775. 4to. Sgd. (88) £130
Dublin, 1784. 8vo. (91) £85

Bouteille, Hippolyte
— Ornithologie du Dauphine ou description des oiseaux.... Grenoble, 1843-[44]. 2 vols. 8vo. (88) FF4,500
Martin copy. (90) $2,500

Boutet de Monvel, Maurice
— Jeanne d'Arc. Paris, [1896]. Oblong 4to. (89) £1,100; (90) $60
One of c30 ptd on japan tissue, this copy for Charles Hemour. (88) $2,500

Boutet de Monvel, Roger
— Beau Brummell and his Times. L: Eveleigh Nash, 1908. 8vo. Doheny copy. (89) $2,500

Boutet, Henri, 1851-1919
— Autour d'Elles. Paris, 1897. One of 100. 4 parts in 1 vol. Folio. (89) $325
— Ces Dames! Paris: Imprimerie Generale Lahure, [1912]. One of 300. (91) $95
— Les Modes feminines du XIXe siecle. Paris, 1901-2. Out-of-series copy. 2 vols in 1. 4to. (91) £360
Paris, 1902. One of 600. 4to. (90) $400
— Pointes seches. Paris, 1898. One of 50 on Japan imperial with orig drypoint, sgd, & with additional suite of the plates on China.

4to. (90) $500

Bouton, Louis, d.1878
— Decades zoologiques de la mission scientifique permanente de l'exploration en Indo-Chine. Hanoi: F. H. Schneider, 1905-[8]. 11 parts in 2 vols. 4to. Martin copy. (90) $7,000

Bovallius, Carl Erik Alexander, 1849-1907
— Nicaraguan Antiquities. Stockholm, 1886. Folio. (89) $60

Bovet Collection, Alfred
— Lettres autographes.... Paris, 1887. One of 500. Catalogued by Etienne Charavay. 4to. (91) $60

Bovet, Richard
— Pandaemonium, or the Devil's Cloyster. L: J. Walthoe, 1684. 8vo. (90) £450

Bovill, E. W.
— Missions to the Niger. Cambr., 1962-66. 4 vols. (88) $65

Bowden, Keith Macrae
— Samuel Thomas Gill. Collary, N.S.W., 1971. 4to. (90) A$140; (91) A$85

Bowdich, Sarah
— The Fresh-Water Fishes of Great Britain. L, 1828-[36]. One of 50. 11 parts in 22. 4to. Martin copy. (90) $31,000

Bowdich, Thomas Edward, 1791-1824
— Excursions dans les isles de Madere et de Porto Santo. [Paris & Strassburg, 1826]. 2 vols, including Atlas. 8vo & 4to. (88) £350
— Excursions in Madeira and Porto Santo. L, 1825. 1st Ed. 4to. (88) £250; (91) £400 Inscr by the author's widow. (89) £580
— Mission from Cape Coast Castle to Ashantee.... L, 1819. 4to. (88) £160, £500; (89) £500, £300, £450; (90) £130; (91) £950, £320, £320, £400 Berkeley Castle copy. (89) £600

Bowditch, Nathaniel, 1773-1838
— The Improved Practical Navigator.... L, 1802. Ed by Thomas Kirby. 8vo. Martin copy. (90) $4,500

Bowe, Nicola G.
— Harry Clarke: His Graphic Art. Mountrath: Dolmen Press, [1983]. One of 250. 4to. Bound in is an extra suite of 8 illusts by Clarke, drawn in 1913 for an Ed of The Rime of the Ancient Mariner, but never pbd. (91) $85

Bowen, Eli, b.1824
— Rambles in the Path of the Steam Horse. Phila., 1855. 8vo. (89) $80

Bowen, Elizabeth
— Seven Winters. See: Cuala Press

Bowen, Emanuel, d.1767
See also: Owen & Bowen
— A Complete Atlas, or Distinct View of the Known World. L, 1752. Folio. (91) $3,500
— A Complete System of Geography. L, 1747. 2 vols. Folio. (88) £1,050, £1,350, £1,800; (89) £1,900, £1,900, £2,400; (91) £2,500

Bowen, Emanuel, d.1767 —& Bowen, Thomas
— Atlas Anglicanus, or a Complete Sett of Maps of the Counties of South Britain. L, [1767]. Oblong folio. (89) £1,100 L, 1777. Folio. (90) £480

Bowen, Emanuel, d.1767 —& Kitchin, Thomas, d.1784
— The Large English Atlas. L: Robert Sayer, [c.1770 or later]. Folio. (88) £600

Bowen, Frank Charles
See also: Parker & Bowen
— The Sea, its History and Romance. L, 1924-26. 16 orig parts. 4to. (88) $60 4 vols. 4to. (89) $50, £75; (91) $150, £54, £100

Bowen, Sir George Ferguson, 1821-99
— The Ionian Islands under British Protection. L, 1851. 8vo. Blackmer copy. (90) £120
— Ithaca in 1850. L, 1851. 8vo. Blackmer copy. (90) £120

Bowen, Thomas. See: Bowen & Bowen

Bower, Archibald
— The History of the Popes. L, 1750-66. 3d Ed of Vols I-II, the rest are 1st Eds. 18 vols. 4to. ESTC 142966 & 144803. (91) £320

Bower, Donald E.
— Fred Rosenstock: A Legend in Books and Art. Flagstaff, [1976]. One of 250. (89) $70

Bowes, James Lord, 1834-99
See also: Audsley & Bowes
— Japanese Enamels. L, 1884. 8vo. (91) £80 L, 1886. One of 200. 8vo. (90) $150
— Japanese Marks and Seals. [L, 1882]. 4to. (91) £60 Liverpool, 1890. 4to. (90) $90, £60
— Japanese Pottery. Liverpool, 1890. 4to. Title & plate versos rubber-stamped. (90) $175

Bowker, J. H. See: Trimen & Bowker

Bowler, Thomas William, d.1869
— The Kafir Wars and British Settlers in South Africa. L, 1865. 4to. (90) £420; (91) £1,000
— Pictorial Album of Cape Town. Cape Town, 1866. Oblong 4to. (88) R5,000

Bowles, Carington, 1724-93
See also: Moll, Herman
— Bowles's New Medium English Atlas. L, 1785. 4to. (89) £1,050
Sir Herbert George Fordham's copy. (90) £1,900
— Bowles's Pocket Atlas of the Counties of South Britain or England and Wales. L, [1785]. 8vo. (88) £750
— Bowles's Post-Chaise Companion. L, [1780?]. 2 vols. 8vo. (88) £360

Bowles, Paul
— Let It Come Down. NY, [1952]. (88) $50

Bowles, Samuel, 1797-1851
— Across the Continent: A Summer's Journey to the Rocky Mountains.... Springfield MA, 1865. 8vo. (89) $65; (90) $55, $90
1st Issue. (91) $90
2d Issue. (90) $60
— Our New West. Hartford, 1869. 1st Ed. 8vo. (91) $70

Bowles, William Lisle
— Fourteen Sonnets, Elegiac and Descriptive. L, 1789. Bound with 23 poetical tracts. 4to. Hayward-Martin copy. (90) $12,000

Bowlker, Charles, d.1779
— The Art of Angling.... Birm.: Baskerville, [1774]. 2d Ed. 12mo. (90) $375
Ludlow, 1833. 12mo. (88) $95; (89) $80
L, 1839. 12mo. (89) $150
Ludlow, 1854. 8vo. (89) A$110

Bowlker, Richard
— The Art of Angling Improved. Worcester, [1746]. 1st Ed. 12mo. (88) £70
Worcester: M. Olivers, [1758?]. 12mo. (89) A$480

Bownas, Samuel, 1676-1763
— An Account of the Life, Travels.... L, 1756. 8vo. (89) $60; (91) $80

Bowring, Sir John, 1792-1872
— The Kingdom and People of Siam. L, 1857. 2 vols. 8vo. (91) £140, £340

Bowyer, Robert, 1758-1834
— The Campaign of Waterloo. L, 1816. Folio. (89) $350, £280; (91) £300
— An Illustrated Record of Important Events in the Annals of Europe.... L, 1815. With map, 4 plain & 19 hand-colored plates.
Bound with: Bowyer, The Campaign of Waterloo. L, 1816. With map & 6 (on 4) colored plates. Folio, 19th-cent half mor gilt (88) £1,150
2 vols in one. Folio. (90) $1,900
Folio. (88) £1,050
With map, 4 plain & 19 colored plates. One leaf torn; some folding plates split. Bound with: Bowyer, The Campaign of Waterloo. L, 1816. With map & 6 (on 4) colored plates. (88) £1,350
Bound with: [Triumphs of Europe]. And: The Campaign of Waterloo. L, 1816. (89) £800
Bound with: Triumphs of Europe. And: The Campaign of Waterloo. L, 1816. (89) £1,100
Bound with: Bowyer. The Campaign of Waterloo. L, 1816. Related material loosely inserted. (88) £1,300
L, 1817. Folio. (88) £450; (91) £380, £680
— An Impartial Historical Narrative.... L, 1823. Folio. (88) £80, £110, £180; (91) £75, £210
— A Selection of Fac-similes of Water-Colour Drawings...of...British Artists. L, 1825. Folio. (88) £1,000
— The Triumphs of Europe.... L, 1814. Folio. (88) DM2,800; (89) £550
Bound with: Bowyer. An Illustrated Record of Important Events in the Annals of Europe. L, 1815. And: Bowyer. The Campaign of Waterloo. L, 1816. (90) £980, £1,100
L, 1915. 2 (of 3) parts in 1 vol. Folio. (91) $1,900

Boxhorn, Marcus Zuerius, d.1653
— Monumenta illustrium virorum et elogia. Amst.: J. Janson, 1638. Folio. (89) £350
— Theatrum sive Hollandiae comitatus et urbium descriptio. Amst.: Hondius, [1632]. Oblong 4to. (88) £750

Boyd, E.
— Popular Arts of Spanish New Mexico. Santa Fe, 1974. 4to. (91) $55

Boyd, James, 1888-1944
— Drums. NY, [1928]. One of 500. 4to. Doheny copy. (89) $900

Boyd, Julian Parks
— Indian Treaties Printed by Benjamin Franklin.... Phila., 1938. One of 500. Folio. (89) $110

Boyd, Martin
— The Montforts. L, 1928. 1st Ed. (89) A$200; (90) A$100
Adelaide, [1963]. (89) A$40

Boydell, John & Josiah
— Graphic Illustrations of the Dramatic Works of Shakespeare.... L, 1792-1803. Folio. (88) $180; (89) $180
L, [plates dated 1798-1802]. Folio. (89) £200; (90) £240, £700; (91) £420
L, 1803. ("A Collection of Prints Illustrating the Dramatic Works of Shakespeare.") 2 vols. Folio. (88) $900, £1,700; (89) $2,000; (91) £240
2 vols in 1. Folio. (91) £1,900
L, 1813. Folio. (91) $2,200
Phila., [c.1850]. 2 vols. Folio. (88) $950
NY, 1852. ("Illustrations of the Dramatic Works of Shakespeare....") 2 vols. Folio. (90) $2,225
Folio. (90) £1,300
Vol I only. Folio. (88) $1,100; (90) £650
— An History of the River Thames. L, 1794-96 [plates watermarked 1827]. 2 vols extended to 3. Folio. Extra-illus with 102 ports. (88) £4,500
L, 1794-96. 2 vols. Folio. (88) $5,500, £1,600, £2,800; (89) £1,800, £2,600, £3,800, £5,200; (91) £2,800
Doheny copy. (88) $4,000
Penrose copy. (91) £2,700
Vol I (of 2) only, Folio. (91) £1,600
— A Set of Prints Engraved after the most Capital Paintings in the Collection of...the Empress of Russia.... L, 1787-88. 2 vols. Folio. (89) $1,700

Boyer, Abel, 1667-1729
— The Draughts of the most Remarkable Fortified Towns of Europe.... L, 1701. 8vo. (89) £240
— Le Grand Theatre de l'honneur et de la noblesse. L, 1729. 4to. (90) £130

Boyer, Jean Baptiste de, Marquis d'Argens.
See: Argens, Jean Baptiste de Boyer

Boyer, Martha Hagensen
— Japanese Export Lacquers. Copenhagen, 1959. Folio. (88) $55, $110; (90) $120

Boyle, Charles, 4th Earl of Orrery, 1676-1731
— Dr. Bentley's Dissertations on the Epistles of Phalaris.... L, 1698. 8vo. (90) $110

Boyle, Eleanor Vere, 1825-1916
— Ros Rosarum ex Horto Poetarum. L, 1885. 8vo. (91) $2,500
— Ros rosarum ex horto poetarum. Dew of the Ever-Living Rose. L, 1896. 8vo. (88) £100

Boyle, Eliza
— Boyle's Court and Country Guide and Town Visiting Directory for January, 1820. L: Eliza Boyle, 1820. 12mo. Doheny copy. (89) $550

Boyle, John, Earl of Cork & Orrery, 1707-62
— Pyrrha. The Fifth Ode of the First Book of Horace Imitated. Dublin, 1742. 8vo. Boyle's own interleaved copy, given by him to his daughter in 1756, so inscr by her. Pforzheimer-Slater-Fleming copy. (89) $3,800
— Remarks on the Life and Writings of Dr. Jonathan Swift. Dublin, 1752. 1st Ed. 8vo. L.p. copy. Inscr to Samuel Madden. (88) $1,800

Boyle, Kay
— Short Stories. Paris: Black Sun Press, 1929. One of 150. (89) $300
— Three Short Novels. Bost., [n.d.]. Inscr "The hard-cover edition of this book, under the title The Crazy Hunter, is dedicated in homage to Katherine Anne Porter. Kay Boyle. January 1972". (88) $50

Boyle, Robert, 1627-91
— A Continuation of New Experiemnts Physico-Mechanical, Touching the Spring and Weight of the Air...The I. Part.... Oxford, 1669. 4to. (88) $475, $1,700
— A Disquisition about the Final Causes of Natural Things. L, 1688. 1st Ed, 1st Issue. 8vo. (88) £620
2d Issue. (88) $850
— An Essay about the Origine & Virtues of Gems.... L, 1672. 8vo. (88) $850
1st Ed. 8vo. (88) $850, $1,600, $2,200; (90) $3,200
— An Essay of the Great Effects of Even Languid and Unheeded Motion.... L, 1685. 1st Ed, Issue not given. 8vo. (89) £800
— Essays of the Strange Subtility...of Effluviums. L: W. G. for M. Pitt, 1673. 8vo. Wing B3951. (88) $250
— Experimentorum novorum physicomechanicorum.... Geneva, 1682. 8vo. (89) £60; (91) £110
— Experiments and Considerations touching Colours.... L, 1664. 8vo. Bookplate of Gilbert Burnet. (89) £1,650
L, 1670. 8vo. (88) $50; (91) £175
— Experiments, Notes, &c. about the Mechanical Origine or Production of Divers Particular Qualities.... L, 1675. 1st Ed, 1st Issue. 8vo. (88) $1,700
L, 1676. 2d Issue. 8vo. (88) $750
— A Free Discourse against Customary Swearing, and a Dissuasive from Cursing. L, 1695. 1st Ed. 8vo. (88) $220
— General Heads for the Natural History of a Country.... L, 1692. 1st Ed. 12mo. (91) £650
— The General History of the Air.... L, 1692. 1st Ed. 4to. (89) $550, £1,100
— An Historical Account of a Degradation of

- Gold, Made by an Anti-Elexir. L, 1739. 2d Ed. 4to. (88) $2,600
- Medicinal Experiments.... L, 1703. "4th Ed". 3 parts in 1 vol. 12mo. (88) $150
- Memoirs for the Natural History of Humane Blood.... L, 1684. 1st Ed, 1st Issue. 8vo. (89) £1,500
- New Experiments Physico-Mechanicall, Touching the Spring of the Air and its Effects.... Oxford, 1660. 1st Ed. 8vo. (88) $1,400
  2d Ed. Oxford, 1662. 3 parts in 1 vol. 4to. (88) $400; (91) $500
- New Experiments and Observations Touching Cold.... L, 1683. 2d Ed. 4to. (88) $75
- Nova Experimenta physico-mechanica de vi aeris elastica. Rotterdam, 1669. 12mo. (88) £190
- Occasional Reflections upon Several Subjects. L, 1665. 8vo. (90) $400; (91) £350 Horblit copy. (91) £700
- Of the High Veneration Man's Intellect Owes to God.... Oxford: M. F. for Richard Davis, 1685. 8vo. (88) $325
- Of the Reconcileableness of Specifick Medicines to the Corpuscular Philosophy.... L, 1685. 1st Ed. 8vo. (91) £300
- The Origine of Formes and Qualities.... Oxford, 1666. 1st Ed. 8vo. (89) £250
- The Sceptical Chymist. L, 1661. 1st Ed. 8vo. (88) £2,300; (89) £15,000
- Short Memoirs for the Natural Experimental History of Mineral Waters. L, 1684/5. 1st Ed. 8vo. (88) $400
- Some Considerations Touching the Usefulnesse of Experimental Naturall Philosophy. Oxford, 1663. 1st Ed, Issue not given. 2 parts in 1 vol. 4to. (88) $1,100, $1,100
  2d Ed. Oxford, 1664. Fulton's "A" Issue. 2 parts in 1 vol. 4to. (88) $175
  2 vols. 4to. (88) $350
- Some Considerations about the Reconcileableness of Reason and Religion. L, 1675. 1st Ed. 2 parts in 1 vol. 8vo. John Evelyn's copy. (89) £1,100
- The Theological Works. L, 1715. 3 vols. 8vo. (88) $50
- Tracts, consisting of Observations about the Saltness of the Sea.... L, 1690. 2d Ed. 8vo. (91) $280
- Tracts...about the Cosmicall Qualities of Things Cosmicall Suspitions, the Temperature of the Subterraneal Regions.... Oxford: W. H. for R. Davis, 1671. 8vo. (89) £1,800; (91) £180
- Works. L, 1744. 5 vols. Folio. (88) $1,200; (89) £400, £1,000; (90) $1,200

L, 1772. 6 vols. 4to. (88) £190; (89) £380

Boyle, Roger, 1st Earl of Orrery, 1621-79
- A Collection of the State Letters.... Dublin, 1743. 2 vols. 8vo. (91) £140
- The History of Henry the Fifth, and the Tragedy of Mustapha. L, 1668. Bound with: Boyle. Two New Tragedies: The Black Prince, and Tryphon. L, 1669. Folio. (88) £170
- A Treatise of the Art of War.... L, 1677. 1st Ed. Folio. (88) £40; (89) £140; (90) $550; (91) £460

Boyle, T. Coraghessan
- Descent of Man: Stories.... Bost., [1979]. Sgd on tp. (91) $120

Boylesve, Rene, 1867-1926
- Les Bains de Bade. Paris, 1921. One of 1,200. Illus by Georges Barbier. (90) $250

Boynton, Charles Brandon, 1806-83
- The History of the Navy during the Rebellion. NY, 1869-70. 2 vols. 8vo. (91) $75

Boynton, Charles Brandon, 1806-83 — & Mason, Timothy B.
- A Journey through Kansas: with Sketches of Nebraska. Cincinnati, 1855. 1st Ed. 12mo. (91) $150
  6th Thousand. (91) $80

Boynton, Edward C., 1824-93
- History of West Point.... NY, 1863. 8vo. (91) $130

Boy's...
- The Boy's Own Conjuring Book. NY, 1860. 16mo. (90) $225, $550

Boys, Thomas Shotter, 1803-74
- Architecture pittoresque dessinee d'apres nature. Paris: Delpech, 1833-36. Folio. (88) £300
- Original Views of London.... L, 1954-55. 2 vols. Folio. Facsimile of the 1842 Ed. Doheny copy. (88) $300
  Guildford, 1972. 2 vols. Folio. (91) £60
- Picturesque Architecture in Paris, Ghent, Antwerp, Rouen. L, 1839. Folio. (90) £5,500
  L, 1928. Folio. (90) $60

Boysleve, Rene, 1867-1926
- Le Parfum des iles Borromees. Paris, 1933. Unique copy with 8 orig watercolor drawings. Illus by Paul Emile Becat. 4to. (90) $2,600

1987 - 1991 • BOOKS

Bracci, Domenico Augusto
— Memorie degli antichi incisori che scolpirono i loro nomi in gemme e cammei.... Florence, 1784-86. 2 vols. Folio. Kissner copy. (91) £1,200
Text in Italian & Latin. Kissner copy. (91) £1,300

Bracciolini, Poggio. See: Poggius Florentinus

Bracebridge, Selina
— Six Views in Lebanon. [L: c.1834]. Oblong folio. Blackmer copy. (90) £1,700

Brachelius, Joannes Adolphus
— Historiarum nostri temporis.... Amst., 1655. 2 vols. 12mo. (91) $375
— Historia sui temporis rerum bello et pace.... Cologne: Joannes Antonius Kinchius, [after 1652]. 4 parts in 1 vol. 8vo. (89) $200

Brackenbury, George
— The Campaign in the Crimea. L, 1855-56. 1st & 2d Series. 8vo. (88) £55
1st Series only. (91) £120

Brackenridge, Henry M., 1786-1871
— Views of Louisiana. Pittsburgh, 1814. 1st Ed. 8vo. (89) $275
Balt., 1817. 12mo. (91) $275
— Voyage to Buenos Ayres.... L, 1820. 2 vols. 8vo. Vol III of Phillips's New Voyages and Travels. (91) £190
— Voyage to South America.... Balt., 1819. 1st Ed. 2 vols. 8vo. (89) $110

Brackenridge, Hugh H., 1748-1816
— The Battle of Bunkers' Hill. A Dramatic Piece...By a Gentleman of Maryland. Phila., 1776. 8vo. (89) $2,400
— Modern Chivalry, or the Adventures of Captain Farrago and Teague O'Regan. Phila. & Pittsburgh, 1792-97. * Modern Chivalry, containing the Adventures of a Captain...Part 2. Carlisle, 1804-5. * Modern Chivalry: Containing the Adventures of Captain John Farrago.... Phila., 1792.1st Eds. Together, 7 vols in 3. 12mo. Waller Barrett-Bradley Martin copy. (90) $6,400

Brackett, Leigh, 1915-78
— The Long Tomorrow. Garden City, 1955. (89) $85
— The Starmen. NY: Gnome Press, [1952]. (89) $50

Bracton, Henricus de, d.1268
— De legibus et consuetudinibus, Angliae libri quinque. L, 1569. 1st Ed. Folio. (89) £1,700
Martin copy. (90) $7,500

BRADBURY

L, 1640. 4to. (88) $110

Bradbury, John, fl.1809
— Travels in the Interior of America. Liverpool, 1817. 1st Ed. 8vo. (91) $1,200
2d Ed. L, 1819. 8vo. (91) $950

Bradbury, Malcolm
— Eating People is Wrong. L, 1959. 1st Ed. (91) £55

Bradbury, Ray
— The Anthem Sprinters and Other Antics. NY, 1963. (88) $130
— Dandelion Wine. Garden City, 1957. (89) $70, $80
Inscr, 23 Sept 1957. (89) $110
Sgd. (88) $150
Sgd. With TLs, 1980, affixed to front pastedown. (90) $140
— Dark Carnival. Sauk City, Wisc., 1947. (91) $140
One of 300. (88) $425; (89) $200; (90) $325; (91) $325
Sgd on label affixed to front pastedown. (91) $250
L: Hamish Hamilton, 1948. (88) $160, £120; (89) $160; (90) $70
— Fahrenheit 451. NY: Ballantine Books, [1953]. (89) $85
Inscr to William Targ & with related material. (88) $300
One of 200 bound in Johns-Manville Quinterra asbestos. (88) $750
See also: Limited Editions Club
— The Golden Apples of the Sun. Garden City, 1953. (88) $55; (89) $55, $95
John Steinbeck's copy. (90) $140
1st English Ed. L, 1953. Inscr by Bradbury with a sketch of an anthropomorphic sun. (89) $110
Sgd & dated. (90) $450
— I Sing the Body Electric! NY, 1969. Inscr to William Targ. (88) $50
— The Illustrated Man. Garden City, 1951. (89) $110
NY, 1951. (88) $130
Inscr with a sketch of an illustrated man. (89) $160
Sgd. (90) $55
L, 1952. Sgd. (88) $90
— The Machineries of Joy: Short Stories.... NY, 1964. Sgd. (88) $50; (90) $85
— Man Dead? The God is Slain! Northridge: Santa Susana Press, 1977. One of 26. Illus by Hans Burkhardt. (88) $350
— The Martian Chronicles. Garden City, 1950. 1st Ed. (88) $375
Inscr. (89) $250; (91) $55
Garden City, 1951. Inscr. (88) $200
— A Medicine for Melancholy. Garden City, 1959. Inscr. (88) $65

BRADBURY

— The October Country. NY: Ballantine Books, [1955]. 1st Ed. (88) $90
L, 1956. (88) $55
— R is for Rocket. Garden City, [1962]. (88) $80
— S is for Space. NY, 1966. In d/j. (88) $80
— A Scent of Sarsaparilla. NY: Ballantine, [1953]. (88) $50
— The Silver Locusts. L, 1951. (88) $80
— Something Wicked This Way Comes. NY, 1962. (88) $180; (89) $100; (90) $100
Inscr. (89) $170
— The Stories of Ray Bradbury. NY, 1980. (88) $50
Sgd with orig drawing of a monster. (91) $75
— This Attic Where the Meadow Greens. Northridge: Lord John Press, 1979. One of 75. Sgd twice. (89) $65
One of 300. Sgd. (91) $50
— Twin Hieroglyphs that Swim the River Dust. Northridge: Lord John Press, 1978. One of 26 lettered copies specially bound in lea. (88) $140
— The Vintage Bradbury. NY, [1965]. (88) $150

Braddon, Lawrence
— Essex's Innocency and Honour Vindicated.... L, 1690. 12mo. (88) £60

Braddon, Mary Elizabeth, 1837-1915
— The Day Will Come. A Novel. L, [1889]. 3 vols. 8vo. (88) £130
Inscr to the author's aunt. Bradley Martin copy. (90) $850
— Phantom Fortune. L, 1883. 1st Ed. 3 vols. 8vo. Slater-Bradley Martin copy. (90) $950

Bradford, Thomas Gamaliel, 1802-87
— A Comprehensive Atlas.... Bost.: American Stationers Co., [1835]. 4to. (88) $500; (91) $1,000
— An Illustrated Atlas.... Bost. & Cincinnati, [1838]. Folio. (88) $1,400; (89) $2,600

Bradford, Thomas Lindsley, 1847-1918
— The Bibliographer's Manual of American History.... Phila., 1907-10. Vols I-IV. (89) $80
— Homoeopathic Bibliography of the United States. Phila., 1892. 8vo. (91) $250

Bradford, William, c.1779-1857
— Equisse du pays, du caractere et du costume en Portugal et en Espagne. L, 1812-13. Folio. (90) £900
— Sketches of the Country, Character, and Costume in Portugal and Spain. L, 1809-10. 2 parts in 1 vol. 4to. (91) £850

AMERICAN BOOK PRICES CURRENT

L, 1812 [text watermarked 1809-10; plates watermarked 1815-16]. With 53 hand-colored plates. Bound with: Chronological and Historical Retrospect of...the War in the Peninsula. L, 1813. 4to. (90) $1,200
L, 1809-10. Folio. (91) £750
L, 1810. 2 parts in 1 vol. Folio. (88) $225; (91) £850, £950
L, 1812. 4to. (90) £900
L, 1812 [plates watermarked 1814-16]. With 53 hand-colored plates. Bound with: Chronological and Historical Retrospect of...the War in the Peninsula. L, 1813. 4to. (88) £400
L, [plates watermarked 1824]. 4to. (90) £850

Bradlaw, Paul
— Observations on the Development of the Alphabet and Printing. Norwich CT, 1940. One of 50. Folio. (91) $450

Bradley, Edward, 1827-89
— Photographic Pleasures, Popularly Portrayed with Pen & Pencil. L, 1855. 1st Ed. 8vo. (91) $250

Bradley, John William, 1830-1916
— A Dictionary of Miniaturists, Illuminators, Calligraphers.... L, 1887-89. 3 vols. 8vo. (91) $300

Bradley, Katherine Harris, d.1914 —& Cooper, Edith Emma
— Julia Domna. L, 1903. One of 240. (91) $70
— The Race of Leaves. L, 1901. One of 280. (91) $70
— Works and Days. L, 1933. Inscr by Max Beerbohm & with 11-line note by him on tp & other notes throughout. (90) £460
— The World at Auction. [L, 1898]. One of 210. Illus by Charles Ricketts. (88) $275

Bradley, Omar N.
— A Soldier's Story. NY, [1951]. One of 750. Tp sgd. (89) $160

Bradley, Richard. See: Furber & Bradley

Bradley, Richard, d.1732
— New Improvements of Planting and Gardening. L, 1739. 5 parts in 1 vol. 8vo. (91) £110
— New Improvements of Planting and Gardening... to which is added... Herefordshire-Orchards. L, 1739. 7th Ed. 3 parts in 1 vol. 8vo. (91) £90

Bradley, Will H.
— The American Chap-Book. Jersey City, N.J., 1904-5. Vols I & II (each with 6 nos), in 1 vol. (91) $475
— Bradley: His Book. Springfield Mass., 1896-97. Vol I only. 4to. (89) $65
— Peter Poodle, Toy Maker to the King. NY, 1906. Martin copy. (90) $800
— The Wonderbox Stories. NY, 1916. 4to. (90) $300

Bradley, William Aspenwall, 1878-1939
— The Etching of Figures. Marlborough-on-Hudson: Dard Hunter, 1915. One of 250. 4to. (90) $425

Bradshaw, George, 1801-53
— Bradshaw's Railway Time Tables and Assistant to Railway Travelling.... L, 1839. 16mo. (89) £80
— Bradshaw's Railway Companion. Manchester, 1842. 16mo. (91) £60
— Map & Sections of the Railways of Great Britain. Manchester, 1839. 8vo. (89) £160

Bradshaw, Henry
— A Catalogue of the Bradshaw Collection of Irish Books in the University Library, Cambridge. Cambr., 1916. 3 vols. 8vo. (88) £220; (89) £150; (90) £300; (91) $175

Bradshaw, Percy Venner
— The Art of the Illustrator. L, [1918]. 18 (of 20) orig parts. Folio. (91) $100
20 orig parts. Folio. (88) £815; (91) £60

Bradshaw, William
See also: Marana & Bradshaw
— Puritanismus Anglicanus. Frankfurt, 1610. 8vo. (88) $80

Bradshaw, William R.
— The Goddess of Atvatabar: Being the History of the Discovery of the Interior World and Conquest of Atvatabar. NY, 1892. (91) $160

Bradstreet, John
[-] An Impartial Account of Lieut. Col. Bradstreet's Expedition to Fort Frontenac. By a Volunteer on the Expedition. L, 1759. 8vo. (91) $2,200

Bradwardine, Thomas, Archbishop of Canterbury, 1290?-1349
— Geometria speculativa. Paris: Guy Marchant, 20 May 1495. Folio. 22 leaves. Goff B-1072. (91) $6,300

Bragdon, Dudley A. See: Denslow & Bragdon

Braght, Tieleman Jans van
— Der blutige Schau-Platz.... Ephrata, 1748-49. 1st Ed. 2 vols in 1. Folio. (90) $2,500

Brahe, Tycho, 1546-1601
— Astronomiae instauratae mechanica. Nuremberg, 1602. 2d Ed. Folio. (88) $5,250; (89) £3,000; (90) £3,800; (91) £2,000, £4,100
— Astronomiae instauratae progymnasmata. Uraniberg & Prague, 1602. 1st Ed. 4to. (91) £2,400
— Epistolarum astronomicarum. Uraniborg & Frankfurt, 1610. 1st Ed, 3d Issue. 4to. (88) DM2,200
— Opera. Frankfurt, 1648. 2 parts in 1 vol. 4to. (88) DM2,200; (91) $2,900

Braid, James, 1795?-1860
— The Physiology of Fascination, and the Critics Criticized. Manchester, 1855. 12mo. (90) $650

Braim, Thomas Henry, 1814-91
— A History of New South Wales.... L, 1846. 2 vols in 1. 8vo. (89) A$350

Brainerd, David
— An Abridgment of Mr. David Brainerd's Journal among the Indians. L, 1748. 12mo. (88) $150

Bramah, Ernest
— English Farming and Why I Turned It Up. L, 1894. 8vo. (88) $110; (91) $70
— The Eyes of Max Carrados. L, 1923. Card sgd by Bramah affixed to title. (88) $85
— The Wallet of Kai Lung. L, 1900. 1st Ed. "A very fine copy". (91) $700

Brambilla, Franz —&
Galvez, J.
— Ruinas de Zaragoza. [Spain, c.1809]. Oblong folio. (89) $200

Bramhall, Frank J.
— The Military Souvenir: A Portrait Gallery.... NY, 1863. Vol I. (90) $140

Bramhall, John, 1594-1663
— Works. Dublin, 1677. Folio. (88) £90

Bramston, James, 1694-1744
— The Man of Taste.... L, 1733. 1st Ed. Folio. (90) £70

Branca, Giovanni
— Le Machine.... Rome, 1629. 1st Ed. 4to. (91) DM6,900
— Manuale d'architettura. Rome, 1772. 8vo. (88) £120; (90) £110
Modena, 1789. 8vo. (91) £180

BRANCACCIO

Brancaccio, Lelio Cesare
— Della nuova disciplina & vera arte militari. Venice: Aldus, 1585. Folio. (91) £250
— I Carichi militari. Antwerp, 1610. 1st Ed. 4to. (90) $1,000

Branch, Douglas
— The Cowboy and his Interpreters. NY, 1926. (89) $110

Brand...
— Brand Book 3 of the Tucson Corral of the Westerners. Tucson, 1976. (89) $50
— Brand Book II. [San Diego: San Diego Corral, 1971]. One of 500. Folio. (89) $65
— Brand Book Number One. [San Diego: San Diego Corral, 1968]. One of 500. Folio. (89) $120; (90) $95
— Brand Book Number Three. [San Diego: San Diego Corral, 1973]. One of 500. Folio. (89) $60
— Brand Book Number Four. [San Diego: San Diego Corral, 1976]. One of 500. Folio. (89) $65
— Brand Book Number Five. [San Diego: San Diego Corral, 1978]. One of 500. Folio. (89) $55
— Brand Book Number Six. [San Diego: San Diego Corral, 1979]. One of 500. Folio. (89) $55
— Brand Book Number Seven. [San Diego: San Diego Corral, 1983]. One of 500. Folio. (89) $55

Brand, Lieut. Charles
— Journal of a Voyage to Peru. L, 1828. 8vo. (88) $75, £70

Brand, John, of Borrowstounness
— A Brief Description of Orkney, Zetland, Pightland-Firth & Caithness. Edin., 1701. 8vo. (88) £90

Brand, John, 1744-1806
— The History and Antiquities of the Town and County of Newcastle upon Tyne. L, 1789. 1st Ed. 2 vols. 4to. (88) £70; (89) £170
— Observations on Popular Antiquities.... L, 1813. 2 vols. 4to. (88) $250; (89) $70

Brand Library, John
— Bibliotheca Brandiana. A Catalogue of the...Library.... L, [1807]. 2 parts in 1 vol. 8vo. (89) £110
Martin copy. (90) $250

Brand, Max
— The Thunderer. See: Derrydale Press

AMERICAN BOOK PRICES CURRENT

Brande, W.
— The Town and Country Brewery Book.... L, 1829. 12mo. (89) £50

Brandi, Giovanni Antonio
— Cronologia de' sommi pontefici. Rome: Guglielmo Facciotto, 1605. Bound with: Sommario, delle vite de gl'imperadori romani. Rome: Luigi Zanetti, 1606. 8vo. (90) £100

Brandon, John Raphael —& Arthur, Joshua
— An Analysis of Gothick Architecture.... L, 1848-47. 2 vols. 4to. (89) $130

Brandt, Bill
— The English at Home. NY & L, 1936. 4to. (89) £50
— Perspective of Nudes. NY, 1961. 4to. (89) $130
— Shadow of Light. NY, 1966. 4to. (88) $80, $80; (89) $140

Brandt, Geeraert, 1626-85
— Het leven en bedryf van den Heere Michiel de Ruiter. Amst., 1687. Folio. (88) $650
— Het leven en bedryf van Michiel de Ruitter. Amst., 1687. Folio. L.p. copy. (88) HF1,200
— Het leven en bedryf van den Heere Michiel de Ruiter. Amst., 1691. Folio. (89) HF600
Amst., 1701. Folio. (89) HF600, HF850
— La Vie de Michel de Ruiter.... Amst., 1698. Folio. (88) FF6,000; (91) £700

Brangwyn, Frank, 1867-1956
— Bookplates. L, 1920. Foreword by Eden Phillpotts. 4to. (89) $90
— Catalogue of the Etched Work.... L: The Fine Art Society, 1912. 4to. (88) £60
— The Historical Paintings in the Great Hall in London of the Worshipful Company of Skinners.... L: Caradoc Press, 1909. One of 300. Folio. (91) $200
— The Way of the Cross. L, [1935]. One of 250. With commentary by G. K. Chesterton. 4to. (89) £160, £250; (91) £120

Brangwyn, Frank, 1867-1956 —& Preston, Hayter
— Windmills. L, [1923]. One of 75. (90) $250; (91) £160

Brankston, Archibald Dooley
— Early Ming Wares of Chingtechen. Peking, 1938. One of 650. 4to. (90) $150

Branner, John Casper
— A Bibliography of Clays and the Ceramic Arts. [Columbus, Ohio], 1906. 2d Ed. (89) $60

Brannon, George
— Vectis Scenery. Southampton, 1825. Oblong folio. (89) £120
Wooton-Common, Isle of Wight, 1827. Oblong 4to. (89) £160
Wooton-Common, Isle of Wight, 1828. Oblong folio. (89) £100
Wooton-Common, Isle of Wight, 1829. Oblong folio. (88) £120; (89) £130, £240
Wooton-Common, Isle of Wight, 1830. Oblong folio. (88) £130
Wooton-Common, Isle of Wight, 1834. Oblong folio. (89) £220
L, 1850. Oblong folio. (91) £160
Wooton-Common, Isle of Wight, 1853. Oblong folio. (89) £130
L, 1864. 4to. (91) £130

Brannon, Philip
— The Park and the Crystal Palace. L: Ackermann, 1851. Folio. (89) £2,600

Bransten, Tommy
— Negroes of America. [San Francisco, 1941]. One of 6 with two sets of wraps. (91) $160

Brant, Sebastian, 1458-1521
— De origine et conversatione bonorum Regum et Laude civitatis Hierosolymae. Basel: Joh. Bergman de Olpe, Mar 1495. 4to. 160 leaves. Goff B-1097. (91) £3,500
— Stultifera navis. Basel: Johann Bergmann de Olpe, 1 Mar 1497. 4to. 148 leaves. Goff B-1086. (90) DM24,000
Basel: Johann Bergmann de Olpe, 1 Aug 1497. 4to. 157 (of 160) leaves; lacking e4-5 & final blank. Goff B1090. (90) £2,600
159 (of 160) leaves; lacking final blank. Goff B-1090. (91) $18,000
Basel: Johannes Bergmann de Olpe, 1 Mar 1498. 4to. 152 (of 164) leaves only. Goff B-1091. (88) £2,000
[Lyons]: Jacobus Sacon, 28 June 1488 [but 1498]. 4to. 155 (of 156) leaves; lacking a 1, supplied in facsimile. Goff B-1093.. (88) $2,500
156 leaves. Goff B-1093. (88) £6,200
Basel: Nicolaus Lamparter, 1507. 4to. (89) £4,200
5 leaves only. 4to. (90) £100
— Stultifera Navis...The Ship of Fooles. L: John Cawood, [1570]. Trans by Alexander Barclay. Folio. (88) £240
Doheny copy. (89) $14,000
STC 3546. (90) £5,000
STC 3546. Bradley Martin copy. (90) $11,000

Edin., 1874. ("Ship of Fools.") 2 vols. 4to. L.p. copy. (89) $75

Brantome, Pierre de Bourdeille, Sieur de, 1535?-1614
— The Lives of Gallant Ladies. See: Golden Cockerel Press
— Oeuvres. The Hague, 1740. 15 vols. 12mo. (88) £240; (90) £320

Braque, Georges, 1882-1963
See also: Vallier, Dora
— Braque lithographe. Monte Carlo, 1963. Text by Francis Ponge; notices & catalogue by Fernand Mourlot. Folio. (88) $425, F2,600; (89) $225, $400, SF1,050; (91) $325, £300
— Cahier de G. Braque 1917-1947. Paris, 1948-[55]. One of 95. 4to. (88) FF4,000; (89) $2,000
One of 750. (88) $60, FF2,500, FF2,500; (89) $110; (91) $160
— Carnets intimes. Paris, 1955. Folio. Verve Nos 31/32. (90) $250
— Catalogue de l'oeuvre de Georges Braque, 1916-1957. Paris: Maeght, 1959-73. 6 vols. 4to. (91) £3,000
Vol I only. (91) $325
Vols I-IV (of 6). (90) £2,000
[-] Hommage a Georges Braque. Paris, 1964. One of 350. Folio. Derriere Le Miroir, Nos 144-46. (88) $75, $425, DM420; (90) $325, $425; (91) $120, £260
— The Intimate Sketchbooks. NY, 1955. Folio. Verve Nos 31/32. (89) $225; (90) $275; (91) $60

Brard, Cyprien Prosper
— Elemens pratiques d'exploitation, contenant tout ce qui est relatif a l'art d'explorer la surface des terrains.... Paris, 1829. 8vo. (88) $250

Brasher, Rex, 1869-1960
— Birds and Trees of North America. Kent, Conn., 1929-32. 1 vol only. Folio. Sgd. (91) $400
12 vols. Oblong folio. Bradley Martin copy. (89) $5,250
3 vols: Game Birds. Oblong folio. (91) $500
6 (of 12) vols plus 2 duplicates. Together, 8 vols. Folio. (88) $1,100
NY, 1961-62. 4 vols. Oblong folio. (88) $80; (89) $225; (90) $200; (91) $180

Brassai, Pseud. of Gyula Halsz
— Paris de nuit. Paris: Arts et Metiers Graphiques, 1933. (90) $280, $440

BRASSEUR DE BOURBOURG

Brasseur de Bourbourg, Charles Etienne, 1814-74
— Bibliotheque Mexico-Guatemalienne.... Paris, 1872. 4to. Inscr. (91) $225

Brassey, Annie, Baroness, 1839-87
— Tahiti: A Series of Photographs. L, 1882. 8vo. (91) £420
Inscr. (88) £160

Brassington, William Salt
— Historic Bindings in the Bodleian Library. L, 1891. 4to. (88) £170; (91) $200
— A History of the Art of Bookbinding. L, 1894. 8vo. (88) $275, $300; (90) $220, £200; (91) £110, £160

Brathwaite, Richard, 1588-1673
— Barnabae Itinerarium, or Barnabee's Journal. L, 1820. One of 125. 2 vols. 12mo. (91) $60
Doheny copy. (89) $220
— Drunken Barnaby's Four Journeys to the North of England...with Bessy Bell. L, 1716. 2d Ed. 8vo. (90) $90
3d Ed. L, 1723. 8vo. (88) £70
L, 1805. Illus by L. W. Harding. 8vo. (91) $50
— The English Gentleman. L, 1630. 1st Ed. 4to. (90) $1,300; (91) $1,000
Huth copy. (88) £900
— The English Gentlewoman Drawne Out to the Full Body.... L, 1631. 1st Ed. 4to. STC 3565.5. Bradley Martin copy. (90) $1,300
— The English Gentleman. L, 1633. Bound with: The English Gentlewoman. L, 1931. 4to. (88) £260
2d Ed. Bound with: The English Gentlewoman. L, 1631. 4to. (88) £1,100
3d Ed. L, 1641. Bound with: The English Gentlewoman. L, 1641. Folio. (88) $350, £120
— The Honest Ghost, or a Voice from the Vault. L, 1658. 1st Ed. 8vo. Sion College —Fleming copy. (89) $580
— Natures Embassie: or, the Wilde-Mans Measures. L, 1621. 1st Ed, 1st Issue. 8vo. STC 3571. (91) £1,000
— Odes.... Lee Priory, Kent, 1815. One of 80. Ed by Sir Egerton Brydges. 8vo. (90) $175
— A Survey of History: or, a Nursery for Gentry. L, 1638. 4to. (88) £60; (89) $225

Bratt, John
— Trails of Yesterday. Lincoln, 1921. (89) $150; (90) $150

AMERICAN BOOK PRICES CURRENT

Braun, Emil
— The Baker's Book. A Practical Hand Book.... NY, 1901. 2 vols. (89) $110

Braun, Georg —& Hogenberg, Franz
— Beschreibung und Contrafactur der vornembsten Stat der Welt. Cologne: G. von Kempen & P. Buchholtz, 1582, 1575-76, 1581-90-[1600]. 5 vols. Folio. (88) £90,000
— Civitates orbis terrarum. Antwerp & Cologne, 1572. Part I. Folio. (88) £4,500; (89) £6,600
Cologne, 1572-1617. 6 parts in 3 vols. Folio. (90) DM130,000
Cologne, 1572-81. Vols I-III (of 5). Folio. (89) £9,900
Cologne, 1572-1606. Vols I-IV. Folio. (90) £3,800
Cologne, [1576-1617]. 6 vols in 2. Folio. (88) £50,000
6 vols in 3. Folio. (89) £47,000
Vol III only. (90) £2,500
Vols III & IV only in 1 vol. (90) £21,000
Parts 3 & 4 only. Cologne, [c.1588]. 2 parts in 1 vol. Folio. (90) $22,000
Amst., 1965. 6 parts in 3 vols. Folio. Facsimile of the 1572-1618 Ed. (88) DM550
Facsimile Ed. Plochingen, 1965. ("Beschreibung und Contrafactur der vornembster Staet der Welt.") Vols 1-2 (of 6). Folio. Facsimile of the 1st German Ed of 1574. (88) $60
NY, 1966. 6 parts in 3 vols. Folio. (88) £120; (90) $300; (91) $170, $650, $750
— Theatre des cites du monde. Cologne, 1579. 4 parts in 2 vols. Folio. (88) FF400,000

Braungart, Richard
— Das Exlibris der Dame. Munich, 1923. One of 200. 4to. (89) $275

Bravo...
— The Bravo. A Venetian Story. See: Cooper, James Fenimore

Bray, Anna Eliza Stothard, 1790-1883
— Life of T. Stothard. L, 1851. 4to. (88) £55
Extended to 2 vols. 4to. Extra-illus with c.97 mtd plates. (89) £180

Bray, William. See: Manning & Bray

Braybourne, Wyndham W. Knatchbull-Hugessen, Baron —& Chubb, Charles
— The Birds of South America. L, [1912]-17. 2 vols, including Atlas. 8vo & 4to. (89) £320; (90) £580

Brayley, Edward Wedlake, 1773-1854
See also: Britton & Brayley; Nash & Brayley
— Ancient Castles of England and Wales. L, 1825. 2 vols. 4to. (91) £300
— London and Middlesex. L, 1810-16. 4 vols in 5. 8vo. (89) £160
— Topographical Sketches of Brighthelmston and its Neighbourhood. L, 1825. 4to. (88) £260
Lacking text. 4to. (90) £160
— A Topographical History of Surrey. Dorking & L, 1841-48. 5 vols. 8vo. (88) £230; (91) £160
Dorking & L, 1850. 4 (of 5) vols. Lacking Vol III. 4to. (90) £100
5 vols. 4to. (91) £100
5 vols. 8vo. (88) £160, £200; (91) £260
L, [1878-81]. ("History of Surrey.") 4 vols. 4to. (89) £200
— Views in Suffolk, Norfolk, and Northamptonshire; illustrative of the Works of Robert Bloomfield.... L, 1818. 8vo. (89) $200

Brayton, Matthew
— The Indian Captive. Cleveland, 1860. 1st Ed. 16mo. (91) $650

Brazil
— Estatutos para os Estudos da Provincia de N. Sra. da Conceicao do Rio de Janeiro.... Lisbon, 1776. Folio. (89) $1,200

Breakenridge, William M.
— Helldorado: Bringing the Law to the Mesquite. Bost., 1928. (89) $70

Breasted, James Henry, 1865-1935
— The Edwin Smith Surgical Papyrus.... Chicago, 1930. 2 vols. 4to. (89) $350

Brebeuf, Jean de, 1593-1649
— The Travels & Sufferings...Among the Hurons of Canada. See: Golden Cockerel Press

Brecht, Bertold
— Gesammelte Werke. L: Malik, [1938]. 2 vols. (91) DM1,100
— Legende von der Enstehund des Buches Taoteking auf dem Weg des Laotse in die Emigration. Frankfurt: Ars Librorum, [1967]. One of 75. Folio. (91) DM480
— Zu den Songs der Dreigroschenoper. Darmstadt, 1969. One of 70. Illus by Eberhard Schlotter. Folio. (91) DM550
— The Threepenny Opera. See: Limited Editions Club

Brechtel, Christoph Fabius
— Nomenclatura pharmaceutica.... Nuremberg, 1603. Folio. (89) £12,000

Bree, Charles Robert, 1811-86
— A History of the Birds of Europe.... L, 1859-63. 4 vols. 8vo. (89) £220, £220; (90) £420
Martin copy. (90) $700
L, 1863-67. 4 vols. 4to. (88) £220; (89) £170, £350
L, 1866-67. 2d Issue. 4 vols. 8vo. (88) DM650; (89) £160; (90) £360; (91) £250
L, 1863 & 1875. 2 vols only. Portions of Vol IV (1st Ed) & Vol V (2d Ed). 8vo. Bree's working copy, interleaved and with extensive notes & references & with drawings, letters, and offprints. Martin copy. (90) $800
2d Ed. L, 1875-76. 4 (of 5) vols; lacking Vol III. With ALs of Francis Orpen Morris tipped in at beginning of Vol I. (88) £220
5 vols. 8vo. (88) $425; (90) £200; (91) £280
Martin copy. (90) $500

Breen, John Richard, 1837-83
— A Short History of the English People. L, 1892-94. 4 vols. 8vo. (91) $90

Breen, Patrick, d.1868
— The Diary of.... San Francisco: Book Club of California, 1946. One of 300. (88) $100; (89) $110, $130, $170
— The Diary of Patrick Breen...the Ordeal of the Donner Party.... San Francisco: Book Club of California, 1946. One of 300. (89) $75; (90) $170; (91) $100
Ls of Lewis Allen laid in. (91) $130

Brees, Samuel Charles
— Pictorial Illustrations of New Zealand. L, 1847. 4to. (88) £750; (91) £300
2d Ed. L, 1848. 4to. (89) £260
L, 1849. 4to. (90) A$600
L, 1948 [Christchurch, 1968]. Ltd Ed. Folio. (88) A$75
— Railway Practice. A Collection of Working Plans.... L, 1837-48. Series 1 plus Appendix, together 2 vols. 4to. (88) £160
L, 1837. Series 1. 4to. (91) $130

Breeskin, Adelyn D.
— The Graphic Work of Mary Cassatt. A Catalogue Raisonne. NY, 1948. One of 550. 4to. (89) $90
— Mary Cassatt.... Wash., 1970. 4to. (90) £3,200; (91) £950, £1,300

Brehm, Alfred Edmund, 1829-84
— Cassell's Book of Birds.... L, [1869-73]. 4 vols. 4to. (89) £100; (90) $225, £110; (91) £70, £70
4 vols in 2. 4to. (89) £55, £75; (90) £90

Brehm, Alfred Edmund, 1829-84 —& Duemichen, Johannes
— Nilbilder...Naturaufnahmen Waehrend zweier Orientreisen 1862 und 1865. Wandsbeck, 1881. 4to. (91) £550

Brehm, Christian Ludwig, 1787-1864
— Beitraege zur Voegelkunde. Neustadt an der Orla, 1820-22. 3 vols. 8vo. Martin copy. (90) $300
— Handbuch der Naturgeschichte aller Voegel Deutschlands. Ilmenau, 1831. 8vo. (90) $900

Breitenbach, Johannes de
— Repetitio elegantissima de statu monachorum et canonicarum regularium. [Leipzig: Gregor Boettiger, [after 22 Nov 1496]. 4to. 32 leaves. Goff B-1107. (91) $3,000

Breitkopf, Johann Gottlob Immanuel
— Versuch, den Ursprung der Spielkarten. Leipzig, 1784. Vol I. 4to. (90) £420

Bremer, Lady J. J. Gordon
— A Mother's Offering to her Children. Sydney, [c.1841]. 12mo. (89) A$11,000

Bremer Press—Toelz, Munich, etc.
— Ballads and Songs of Love. 1930. One of 280. (89) $200
— Bible in German. 1926-28. One of 365. 5 vols. 4to. Doheny copy. (88) $2,000
— Chansons d'Amour. 1921. One of 270. (88) DM3,200
— Lieder der deutschen Mystik. 1922. One of 270. (88) DM1,600, DM2,800
— Der Psalter Deudsch. 1929. One of 150. (88) DM520
— Sonnets. 1931. One of 274. (88) DM1,200
— Walther von der Vogelweide. 1931. One of 250. (88) DM1,200
— AUGUSTINE. - De civitate Dei. 1924. One of 385. Doheny copy. (88) $350 The Garden copy. (90) $900
— BACON, SIR FRANCIS. - The Essays. 1920. One of 270. (91) $250
— EMERSON, RALPH WALDO. - Nature. [Munich: Bremer Press, 1929]. One of 250. (89) $60; (91) $100
— FIELD, W. B. OSGOOD. - John Leech on my Shelves. 1930. One of 155. (88) £650
— HOMER. - Ilias. Odysseia. 1923-24. One of 615. 2 vols. (88) $250; (90) $725 Schimmel copy. (91) $16,000
— HOMER. - Odyssee. 1926. One of 280. (88) DM2,050
— SIMONS, ANNA. - Title und Initialen fuer die Bremer Presse. 1926.. One of 220. (88) $275
— VESALIUS, ANDREAS. - Icones anatomicae. 1934. One of 110. (89) £600
One of 615. (88) £700; (89) $3,400; (91) $2,700
Schimmel copy. (91) $4,200
The Garden copy. (90) $4,000; (91) $3,750

Bremond, Gabriel
— Viaggi fatti nell'Egitto superiore, et inferiore.... Rome: Paolo Moneta, 1679. 4to. Blackmer copy. (90) £420

Brenchley, Julius L., 1816-73
See also: Remy & Brenchley
— Jottings During the Cruise of H.M.S. "Curacoa" among the South Sea Islands. L, 1873. 8vo. (88) £400
Martin copy. (90) $1,100

Brennan, Joseph Payne
— Nine Horrors and a Dream. Sauk City: Arkham House, 1958. One of 1,200. (89) $70
— Scream at Midnight. New Haven: Macabre House, 1963. One of 250. (88) $225

Brentano, Clemens
— Gockel, Hinckel und Gackeleia. Frankfurt, 1838. 8vo. (91) £2,600

Brerewood, Edward, 1565?-1613
— De ponderibus, et pretiis veterum nummorum.... L, 1614. 4to. (88) $200
— Enquiries touching the Diversity of Languages and Religions.... L, 1614. Bound with: De ponderibus et pretiis veterum nummorum.... 4to. (90) $300
L, 1622. 4to. (88) $180
Sir Roger Twysden's copy. (88) £220

Bresadola, Giacomo, 1847-1929
— Iconographia mycologica. Milan & Trento, 1927-80. 32 parts. (89) £500

Brescia
— Statuta communis Brixiae. Brescia: Thomas Ferrancus, 21 May 1473. 5 parts in 1 vol. Folio. 24 leaves. Goff S-709. (91) $8,000

Bresdin, Rodolphe, 1825-85
— Bresdin to Redon; Six Letters, 1870 to 1881. Northampton, Mass.: Gehenna Press, 1969. One of 100 with sgd proof of Baskin's etching laid in. Trans by S. S. Weiner; illus by Leonard Baskin. (90) $190, $250
One of 300. (91) $105

Breslauer, Bernard
— Bibliography: its History and Development. See: Grolier Club

1987 - 1991 • BOOKS

Bressani, Francesco Giuseppe, 1612-72
— Breve relatione d'alcune missioni....
Macerata, 1653. 4to. (88) £2,400

Bretez, Louis
— Plan de Paris. Paris, 1739. Folio. (88) £2,000; (91) $3,500, £1,700

Breton, Andre, 1896-1966
— Arcane 17. NY & Paris, 1944. One of 25 with the etching. Illus by Roberto Matta. 8vo. (89) $3,200
— Constellations. NY, 1959. One of 200 with orig sgd litho. Illus by Joan Miro. Folio. (88) FF38,000
— Introduction au Discours sur le Peu de Realite. Paris, 1927. Copy F of 20 lettered hors-commerce copies on verge d'Arches. 4to. Inscr to Louis Aragon. (89) $850
— Loeslicher Fisch. Berlin: Edition Sirene, 1982. One of 30. (91) DM550 •
— Qu'est-ce que le surrealisme? Brussels, 1934. One of 1,070. Inscr to Rene Cevel. (88) $1,500
— Le Surrealisme et la peinture. NY, 1928. Nos 1-6. 4to. (91) £900
— Young Cherry Trees Secured against Hares. NY: View Editions, 1946. One of 1,000, but with the 2 orig drawings by Arshile Gorky. (91) $110

**Breton, Andre, 1896-1966 —&
Peret, Benjamin**
— Almanach surrealiste du demi-siecle. Paris, 1950. One of 25. Illus by Max Ernst. 8vo. (90) $1,000

Breton de la Martiniere, Jean Baptiste Joseph
— China: Its Costume, Arts, Manufactures....
L, 1812. 1st Ed in English. 4 vols. 12mo. (89) £280
4 vols in 2. 12mo. (91) $600
Mixed Ed. L, 1812-13. 4 vols. 12mo. (89) $160
4 vols in 2. 12mo. (91) £140
6th Ed in English. L, 1813. 4 vols. 12mo. (91) £350
L, 1824. 4 vols. 12mo. (88) £95; (90) $275
4 vols in 2. 12mo. (89) £150; (90) $320
— Le Chine en Miniature. Paris, 1811-12. 6 vols. 18mo. Robinson copy. (89) £420
— L'Egypte et la Syrie. Paris, 1814. 6 vols. 12mo. Blackmer copy. (90) £1,000 Kissner copy. (91) £400
— L'Espagne et le Portugal. Paris, 1815. 6 vols in 3. 12mo. (89) £85
— La Russie, ou moeurs, usages et costumes des habitans.... Paris, 1813. 6 vols. 12mo. (88) £400

BREVIARIUM

Breton, Nicholas, 1545?-1626?
— Englands Selected Characters.... L, 1643. 4to. (91) £600
— The Twelve Moneths and Christmas Day. NY, 1951. (90) $50, $50

Breton, V.
— Essais progressifs sur la composition typographique. Paris, 1893. 4to. (88) £70

Breton, William Henry, d.1887
— Excursions in New South Wales, Western Australia, and Van Diemen's Land.... L, 1833. 8vo. (89) £160, A$280, A$1,800
2d Ed. L, 1834. 8vo. (89) A$500

Brett, Edwin J.
— A Pictorial and Descriptive Record of the Origin of Arms.... L, 1894. 4to. (91) £100

Brett, Oliver, Viscount Esher. See: Escher, Oliver Sylvain Balid Brett

Brett, William Henry, 1818-86
— The Indian Tribes of Guiana. L, 1868. 8vo. (89) $80, $80

Brettingham, Mathew
— The Plans, Elevations and Sections, of Holkham in Norfolk.... L, 1761. Folio. (90) $375
L, 1773. Folio. (89) £100

Brettschneider, E.
— History of European Botanical Discoveries in China. Leipzig, 1935. 2 vols. 4to. (91) $400

Breuil, Henri
See also: Cartailhac & Breuil
— The Rock Paintings of Southern Africa. L, 1955. ("The White Lady of the Brandberg.") Vol I. 4to. (88) R170

Breur, Josef. See: Freud & Breur

Breuvery, J. de. See: Cadalvene & Breuvery

Breval, John Durant, 1680?-1738
— Remarks on Several Parts of Europe.... L, 1726. 2 vols. Folio. Kissner copy. (91) £600
2 vols in 1. Folio. (89) $275
With: Breval. Remarks on Several Parts of Europe...since the Year 1723. L, 1738. Together, 4 vols. Folio. (90) £700

Breviarium
— 1474, 12 Mar. - Breviarium moguntinum. Pars aestivalis. Marienthal: Fratres Vitae Communis. 4to. 340 (of 341) leaves; lacking blank f.204. Goff B-1169. (91) £4,500
— 1478, before 6 May. - Breviarium Romanum. Venice: Nicolaus Jenson.

1003

BREVIARIUM

Folio. Ptd on vellum. 403 (of 404) leaves. Goff B-1112. Doheny copy. (88) $2,600
— 1492, 2 June. - Rouen: Martin Morin. Use of Salisbury. 8vo. STC 15795.5. (91) £5,000
— 1494, 10 Nov. - Breviarium Romanum. Pavia: Franciscus Girardengus. Folio. 335 (of 336) leaves; lacking final blank. Goff B-1114. Doheny copy. (88) $10,000
— 1506, 27 Oct. - Breviarium monasticum secundum ritum congregationis Casinensis. Venice: Bernardinus Staginus. 16mo. (90) £1,400
— 1518, 30 Apr. - Breviarium secundum usum Saltzburgensis. Venice: Lucius Antonius de Giunta imp. Johannes Osvaldi Augustensis. 2 vols. 8vo. (90) £1,200
— 1522. - Breviarium Cartusiense. Paris: Thielman Kerver. 8vo. (90) £650
— 1525, 30 Aug. - Breviarium, use of Sarum, pars Hyemalis. Paris: widow of Thielman Kerver for Franciscus Byrckman. 16mo. STC 15819 (this copy only). (90) £300
— 1544. - Breviarium Romanum. Lyons: Baltazard Arnoullet. 4to. (90) £200
— 1555. - Breviarium, use of Sarum. Paris: Magdalen Boursette. 2 vols. 8vo. STC 1583. (90) £950
— 1555, 7 Mar. - Portoforum seu Breviarium, use of Sarum. L: John Kyngston & Henry Sutton. STC 15839. (90) £700
— 1556. - Portiforium seu breviarium ad insignis Sarisburiensis.... L. 2 parts in 1 vol. 4to. STC 15842. (91) £130, £160
— 1559. - Venice: Heirs of Luc'Antonio Giunta. 8vo. (90) $800
— 1701. - Breviarium Romanum ex decreto Sacrosancti Concilii Tridentini resitutum, et summorum Pontificum auctoritate recognitum. Paris. 4 vols. 8vo. Doheny copy. (88) $450
— 1736. - Breviarium Parisiense. Paris. 4 vols. 4to. Castle Howard copy. (91) £1,400
— 1752. - Breviarium Romanum ex decreto Sacrosancti Concilii Tridentini restitutum.... Antwerp: Ex Architypographia Plantiniana. 4 vols. 4to. Doheny copy. (89) $1,500
— 1768. - Breviarium Romanum. Antwerp: Ex Architypographia Plantiniana. 4 vols. 12mo. (88) $280

Brevoort, Elias
— New Mexico. Her Natural Resources and Attractions.... Sante Fe, 1874. 1st Ed. 8vo. (90) $140

Brewer, James Norris. See: Storer & Brewer

Brewer, Josiah & Emilia A. —& Reynolds, Mary
— First Four Years of the American Independent Smyrna Mission, under the patronage of the New Haven Ladies' Greek Association. Smyrna, 1834. 8vo. Blackmer copy. (90) £1,100

Brewer, Luther
— My Leigh Hunt Library...the First Editions. Cedar Rapids, Iowa, 1932. One of 125. (90) £100; (91) $80

Brewer, Thomas
— A Journeyman Shoemaker's Letter to a Certain Right Honourable. [N.p.], 27 May 1757. Single sheet, folio. (88) £200

Brewer, William H., 1828-1910
— Up and Down California in 1860-1864. New Haven, 1930. (88) $120; (89) $90; (91) $140

Brewerton, G. Douglas
— The War in Kansas. NY, 1856. 12mo. Inscr to Kit Carson (the dedicatee). (89) $325

Brewington, Marion Vernon & Dorothy
— Kendall Whaling Museum Prints. Sharon MA, 1969. 4to. (89) $90
— Marine Paintings and Drawings in the Peabody Museum. See: Peabody Museum

Brewington, Marion Vernon
— The Peabody Museum Collection of Navigating Instruments. See: Peabody Museum

Brewster, Sir David, 1781-1868
— Memoirs of the Life, Writings and Discoveries of Sir Isaac Newton. Edin., 1855. 2 vols. 8vo. (91) £85
— Nouveau Manuel de magie naturelle.... Paris, 1839. 12mo. (90) $225
— The Stereoscope. L, 1856. 8vo. (88) £60

Breydenbach, Bernhard von
— Die heyligen reyssen gen Jherusalem. Augsburg: Anton Sorg, 23 Apr 1488. ("Die fart oder reyss ueber mere....") Folio. 193 (of 194) leaves; lacking final blank. Goff B-1194. (91) DM140,000
— Peregrinatio ad terram sanctam.... Wittemberg: Nicolas Schirlentz, 1536. 8vo. Blackmer copy. (90) £1,000
— Peregrinationes in terram sanctam. Mainz: Erhard Reuwich, 11 Feb 1486. 1st Ed. Folio. 143 (of 148) leaves. Goff B-1189. (91) £4,500
Maps of Venice and Palestine sewn in on stubs. 139 (of 140) leaves plus 8 fold-out sheets. Goff B-1189. Doheny copy. (88) $100,000

— Reise ins Heilige Land. Speyer: Drach, [after 1502]. ("Dis Buch ist innhaltend die heiligen Reysen gein Jherusalem....") Folio. Kloss copy. (91) £22,000

Breyn, Jakob
— Exoticarum aliarumque minus cognitarum plantarum centuria prima. Danzig, [1674]-78. 2 vols, including Atlas in 1. Folio. Caledon copy. (90) $3,600

Briano, Giorgio
— La Siria e l'Asia Minore illustrate. Naples, 1841. 8vo. Blackmer copy. (90) £1,200 Kissner copy. (91) £1,200

Bricaire de la Dixmerie, Nicolas, d.1791
— Les Deux Ages du gout et du genie francais sous Louis XIV & sous Louis XV. The Hague: Lacombe, 1769. 8vo. (91) £280

Brice, Andrew, 1690-1773
— The Grand Gazetteer, or Topographic Dictionary.... Exeter, 1759. Folio. (91) £160

Brice, Germain, 1652-1727
— A New Description of Paris. L, 1598. 2d Ed in English. 2 parts in 1 vol. 12mo. (88) $55

Bricker, Charles
— Landmarks of Mapmaking. Amst., 1968. Folio. (88) $80; (90) $90
NY, [1976]. Folio. (91) $100
Oxford, [1976]. Folio. (91) $100

Bridel, Philippe Cyriaque, 1757-1845
— Voyage pittoresque de Basle a Bienne.... Basel, 1802. Oblong folio. (91) $3,800

Bridgens, Richard
— Sketches Illustrative of the Manners and Costumes of Italy, Switzerland and France. L, 1821. 4to. (90) £400; (91) £400

Bridges, John, 1666-1724
— The History and Antiquities of Northamptonshire. Oxford, 1791 [i.e., 1762-91]. Compiled by Peter Whalley. 2 vols. Folio. (88) £100

Bridges, Robert, 1844-1930
See also: Daniel & Others
— Eros and Psyche. See: Gregynog Press
— The Growth of Love. A Poem in Twenty-Four Sonnets. See: Hopkins's copy, Gerard Manley
— Poems. L, 1873. 1st Ed. 8vo. (88) £75
— Poems Written in the Year MCMXIII. See: Ashendene Press
— Suppressed Chapters and Other Bookishness. L, 1895. 8vo. With ANs & autograph transcript of The Towers of Princeton (From the Train) mtd to front endpapers. (88) $150
— The Testament of Beauty. [Oxford, 1927-29]. One of 25. 5 parts. 4to. Sold with a copy of the 1st Pbd Ed, 1929 & with 4 ANs s to Elkin Matthews & an ANs of Mrs. Bridges. Bradley Martin copy. (90) $3,250
Oxford, 1929. 2d impression. 4to. With caricature of the King by Beerbohm beneath the dedication to him & a spoof letter by Beerbohm from George V to Bridges on rear endpapers. Sassoon copy. (91) £900
One of 250. (88) R60
Inscr. (88) £85

Bridgewater...
— The Bridgewater Treatises on the Power, Wisdom and Goodness of God.... L, 1833-37. 12 vols. 8vo. (88) $550

Bridgewater, Benjamin. See: Dunton, John

Bridgit, Saint, 1303?-73
— Orationes sancte Brigitte, cum oratione sancti Augustini. [Rome: Marcellus Silber, c.1510]. 8 leaves. 8vo. (88) £1,000
— Revelationes. Rome, 1556-57. ("Memoriale effigiatum librorum prophetiarum....") 2 parts in 1 vol. Folio. (91) £200

Brief...
— A Brief Description of the Province of Carolina.... L, 1666. 4to. (88) $25,000
— A Brief Survey of the Growth of Usury in England.... L, 1671. 4to. (88) £650

Brieger, Lothar
— E. M. Lilien: eine kuenstlerische Entwickelung um die Jahrhundertwende. Berlin & Vienna, 1922. One of 100 with orig etching. 4to. (88) £240

Brieger, Peter H. —& Others
— Illuminated Manuscripts of the Divine Comedy. L, 1970. 2 vols. 4to. (88) £60; (90) $110, £65

Briere, Gaston
— Le Chateau de Versailles.... Paris, [1907-9]. 2 vols. Folio. (89) A$220

Brierly, Sir Oswald Walter, 1817-94
— The English & French Fleets in the Baltic, 1854. L: Day, 1854-55. Folio. (90) £4,200

Briet, Philippe, 1601-68
— Parallela geographiae veteris et novae. Paris, 1649. 3 vols. 4to. (89) £520

**Briggs, Clare —&
Newbit, Wilbur D.**
— Oh Skin-Nay! The Days of Real Sport. Chicago: P. F. Volland, [1913]. 4to. Inscr by Briggs with ink sketch, 23 July 1915. (91) $55

BRIGGS

Briggs, Henry, 1561-1630
— Trigonometria Britannica.... Gouda, 1633. Folio. (91) £200

Briggs, Lloyd Vernon, 1863-1941
— Arizona and New Mexico, 1882.... Boston: Privately ptd, 1932. (88) $90
   Boston: Pvtly ptd, 1932. (88) $75
— History of Shipbuilding on North River, Plymouth County, Massachusetts. Bost., 1889. 8vo. (88) $110; (91) $60

Briggs, Richard
— The English Art of Cookery. L, 1791. 2d Ed. 12mo. (90) £290

Brigham, Clarence Saunders
— History and Bibliography of American Newspapers, 1690-1820. Worcester, Mass., 1947. 2 vols. 4to. (88) $140; (89) $120, $140, $150; (91) $120, $175
— Paul Revere's Engravings. Worcester, Mass., 1954. 1st Ed. 4to. (89) $50, $70; (90) $50; (91) $50

Brigham, William Tufts
— Ka Hana Kapa: the Making of Bark-Cloth in Hawaii. Honolulu, 1911. Text vol. 4to. (89) $150

Bright, Richard, 1789-1858
— Address delivered at the Commencement of a Course of Lectures on the Practice of Medicine. L, 1832. 8vo. (90) $120
— Reports of Medical Cases.... L, 1827-31. 2 vols in 3. 4to. (91) £7,000
   Vol I only. 4to. (88) $4,000
— Travels from Vienna through Lower Hungary. Edin., 1818. 1st Ed. 4to. (88) £220

Brigman, Anne
— Songs of Pagan. Caldwell, Idaho, 1949. (88) $140
   Sgd & dated, 1949. (89) $375

Brillat-Savarin, Jean Anthelme, 1755-1826
— Essai historique et critique sur le duel.... Paris, 1819. 1st Ed. 8vo. Inscr to M. le President Moraine. Martin copy. (90) FF2,800
— A Handbook of Gastronomy. L, 1884. One of 500. 8vo. (91) £70
— Physiologie du gout. Paris, 1826. 1st Ed. 2 vols. 8vo. (89) $1,800
   Martin copy. (90) FF7,000
   With ALs. (88) FF15,000
   One of 30 on japon imperial with orig aquarelle by Charles Huard. (88) FF15,000
   Paris, 1839. 8vo. (91) £85
   Paris: Gabriel de Gonet, [1848]. 2 vols. 8vo. (90) $375

AMERICAN BOOK PRICES CURRENT

   Paris, 1879. 2 vols. 8vo. (88) £240
   One of 3 copies with an extra suite of the artist's proofs. Extra-illus with 2 orig drawings. And with ANs by Lalauze about the suites of artists' proofs and ANs by Brillat-Savarin ordering payment to a ptr. (91) £1,400
   Paris, 1926. One of 520. Illus by Pierre Noury. 2 vols. 8vo. (90) $140
   Paris: Piazza, 1930. One of 30 on japan with an orig aquarelle sgd & a suite in black with remarques & a suite in colors. 2 vols. 4to. (89) SF4,800
— The Physiology of Taste.... L, 1925. One of 750. (88) $80, £50; (90) $110
   See also: Limited Editions Club

Brin, David
— The River of Time. Niles IL: Dark Harvest, 1986. One of 400. (89) $65; (90) $80
   One of 520. (91) $150
— Startide Rising. West Bloomfield MI: Phantasia, 1985. One of 375. (89) $110; (90) $95; (91) $100
— The Uplift War. West Bloomfield MI: Phantasia, 1987. One of 475. (89) $85; (90) $80; (91) $100

Brindejont-Offenbach, Jacques
— Les Divertissements d'Eros. Paris, 1927. One of 10 on japon with a watercolor drawing. Illus by Tsuguharu Foujita. 4to. This copy with extra suite in plain & colored states & 7 of the uncolored plates not called for. (89) £3,400

Brindesi, Jean
— Elbicei atika; musee des anciens costumes Turcs de Constantinople. Paris, [1855]. Folio. (90) £1,900
   Blackmer copy. (90) £1,700
— Souvenirs de Constantinople. Paris: Lemercier, [1855-60]. Oblong folio. (90) £3,500
   Blackmer copy. (90) £6,500

Brindley, James
— The History of Inland Navigations. L, 1766. 1st Ed. 2 vols in 1. 8vo. (89) £220

Bringas de Manzaneda, Diego Manuel
— Sermon que en las Solmnes Honras Celebradas en Obsequio do lo VV. PP. Predicadores Apostolicos.... Madrid, 1819. 8vo. (88) $380

Brininstool, Earl Alonzo. See: Hebard & Brininstool

Brinkelow, Henry, d.1546
— The Complaint of Roderyck Mors for the Redresse of Certain Wycked Lawes.... Geneve in Savoye: M. Boys [L?, 1550?]. 8vo. Sgd on flyleaf by Sir Christopher Hatton. (88) £650

Brinkley, Frank, 1841-1912
— The Art of Japan. Bost., [1901]. 2 vols. Folio. (89) £180
  Out-of-series copy. (88) $150
  Satsuma Ed, One of 400. 2 vols. Folio. (90) $400
— Japan. Described and Illustrated by the Japanese. Bost. [1897-98]. 15 vols. Folio. (88) $550
  Orient Ed, One of 500. 10 vols. Folio. (88) $260
  15 vols. Folio. (89) $500; (91) $400
  Orient Ed, One of 500. 10 vols. Folio. (88) $900
  Yedo Ed, One of 1,000. 10 vols. Folio. (89) $650
  Bost.: J. B. Millet, [1904]. 5 vols. Folio. (88) $110
— Oriental Series: Japan and China. Bost. & Tokyo, 1901-2. Artists' Ed, One of 1,000. 12 vols. (91) $250
  Edition not indicated. 12 vols. (89) $60; (91) $150
  Special Artists' Ed, one of 500. 12 vols. (88) $300
  Library Ed. L, 1903-4. 12 vols. (88) $100; (91) £120

Brinley, Francis
— Life of William T. Porter. NY, 1860. 12mo. (89) $80; (90) $60

Brinley Library, George
— [Sale catalogue] Catalogue of the American Library.... Hartford, 1878-93. Parts I-V bound in 3 vols, plus Index & Prices Realized. Together, 5 vols. 8vo. (88) $100
  Parts I-V bound in 2 vols, plus Index & Prices Realized. Together, 4 vols. 8vo. (89) $200

Brinnin, John Malcolm
— Dylan Thomas in America. L, 1956. Proof copy. Sgd & annotated by Edith Sitwell. (89) £450

Brinton, Anna Cox
— A Pre-Raphaelite Aeneid of Virgil in the Collection of Mrs. Edward Lawrence Doheny.... Los Angeles, 1934. Ltd Ed. 4to. With 47 letters & cards thanking Mrs. Doheny for receipt of a copy of the essay by Sydney Cockerell, Graily Hewitt, Ward Ritchie, Bruce Rogers & others. (89) $26,900

Brinton, Daniel Garrison, 1837-99
— Aboriginal American Authors and their Productions.... Phila., 1883. 8vo. (91) $200

Brion de la Tour, Louis
— Atlas general.... Paris, 1766. Bound with: Atlas de France.... Paris, 1767. 4to. (88) £600

Briquet, Charles Moise, 1839-1918
— Les Filigranes.... Leipzig, 1923. 2d Ed. 4 vols. 4to. (88) DM800
  Doheny copy. (88) $550
  NY, 1966. 4 vols. 4to. (88) $200; (89) $275, £180
  Amst., 1967. 4 vols. 4to. (89) $750
  NY, 1984. 4 vols. 4to. (91) £180

Brisbin, Gen. James S., 1837-92
— The Beef Bonanza; or, How to Get Rich on the Plains. Phila., 1881. 8vo. (88) $95; (89) $110; (90) $50

Briscoe, John
— A Discourse on the late funds of the Million-Act, Lottery-Act and Bank of England.... L, 1694. 2d Ed. 4to. (90) £550
  3d Ed. L, 1696. 8vo. (88) £260; (90) £950

Briseux, Charles Etienne
— Traite du beau essentiel dans les parts.... Paris, 1752. 2 vols in 1. Folio. (89) £2,300; (91) DM2,400

Brisseau, Pierre
— Petri Brissoti Doctor Medici Parisiensis praestantissimi Apologetica disceptatio. See: Richelieu's copy, Cardinal Armand Jean du Plessis de

Brisson, ———. See: Saugnier & Brisson

Brisson, Mathurin Jacques, 1723-1806
— Ornithologie.... Paris, 1760. 1st Ed. 6 vols. 4to. (89) £1,800
  Jeanson copy. (88) FF65,000
  Martin copy. (90) $3,000, $5,500
  7 vols in 6, including Supplement. 4to. (88) £900
— Regnum animale in classes IX distributum.... Paris, 1756. 4to. (88) FF7,000

Brissot de Warville, Jacques Pierre, 1754-93
See also: Claviere & Brissot de Warville
— A Critical Examination of the Marquis de Chatellux's Travels in North America. Phila., 1788. 8vo. (91) $225
— New Travels in the United States of America. Dublin, 1792. 8vo. (91) $80
  L, 1792. 2 vols. 8vo. (89) $350
  8vo. (91) $175
  L, 1794. 8vo. (91) $80

1007

Bristed, John, 1778-1855
— The Resources of the United States of America.... NY, 1818. 1st Ed. 8vo. (91) £60

Bristol
— Industrial and Fine Arts Exhibition...September 2nd to November 29th, 1884. Official Catalogue. [Bristol, 1884]. 8vo. Chevalier copy. (91) $130

Britaine, William de
— Humane Prudence, or, the Art by which a Man may Raise Himself...by A. B. L: Robert Harford, 1680. 1st Ed. 12mo. (88) £400

Britania Expirans...
— Britania Expirans or, a brief Memorial of Commerce. L, 1699. 4to. Goldsmiths 35788. (88) £500

Britania Nova...
— Britania Nova: or a Seasonable Discourse Demonstrating how we may Serve our King and Countrey.... L: for Matthew Gilliflower, 1698. 4to. (88) £450

Britanniae Speculum...
— Britanniae Speculum; or, a Short View of the Ancient and Modern State of Great Britain.... L, 1683. 12mo. (89) $150

Britannicus, Probus. See: Johnson, Samuel

British...
— The British American Guide-Book.... NY, Montreal & Glasgow, [1859]. 4 parts in 1 vol. 8vo. (91) $400
— British Apollo, or Curious Amusements for the Ingenious.... L, 1708-11. Vols I-III in 1 vol. Folio. (88) £300
— British Bee Books: A Bibliography, 1500-1976. L, 1979. 8vo. (91) $80
— British Chess Magazine. L, 1895-1966. Vols 15-86. (88) £600
— The British Essayists. L, 1808. 45 vols. 12mo. (89) £170; (91) £170, £750
  L, 1817. 45 vols. 12mo. (89) £60
  L, 1823. Ed by Alexander Chambers. 38 vols. 12mo. (90) £260
— The British Gallery of Contemporary Portraits. L, 1822. 2 vols. Folio. (89) £40
— The British Librarian: Exhibiting a Compendious Review.... L, 1738. Parts 1-6 (all pbd) in 1 vol. 8vo. (91) $200
— The British Poets. L, 1830-45. Aldine Ed. 40 (of 53) vols. 8vo. (89) £260
— British Sports and Sportsmen. L: Sports and Sportsmen Ltd., [1908-33?]. One of 1,000. 15 vols. 4to. (88) £520
  Royal Ed. L: Sports and Sportsmen Ltd., [1908-33?]. Vols I-IX only. (90) £280
— British Union-Catalogue of Periodicals....
  L, 1955-70-64. 4 vols, plus 2 Supplements. 4to. (90) £440

British and Foreign Bible Society
— Specimens of some of the Languages and Dialects, in which the Distribution, Printing, or Translation of the Scriptures...has been promoted by the...Society. L, 1852. 4to. (91) $175

British Association for the Advancement of Science
— Lithographed Signatures of the Members.... Cambr., 1833. 4to. (91) $100
— Report of Meetings. [Continued as]: The Advancement of Science. Vols 1-27. L, 1833-1938 & 1939-70. 8vo. (91) £110

British Chess Magazine
— The British Chess Magazine. L, 1881-1981. Vols 1-101. (88) £1,500
  Vols 21-29. L, 1901-9. (88) £130

British Library. See: British Museum

British Mercury. See: Mallet Dupan, Jacques Francois

British Museum—London
— Babylonian Boundary-Stones and Memorial-Tablets. L, 1912. Ed by L. W. King. 2 vols, including portfolio of plates. Folio. (88) £260
— The Book of the Dead. 1890. Ed by E. A. Wallis Budge. Folio. (88) £130
  2d Ed of Vol I, 1st Ed of Vol II. 1894-95. 2 vols. Folio. (89) £340; (91) £90
  1895. Folio. (91) £60, £300
  1899. By E.A. Wallis Budge. Folio. (88) £180; (89) £110; (90) £70; (91) £75, £85, £100
— Bronze Reliefs from the Gates of Shalmaneser King of Assyria B. C. 860-825. 1915. Ed by L. W. King. 4to. (88) £120
— List of Catalogues of English Book Sales 1676-1900 Now in the British Museum. 1915. 8vo. (88) $100, $130, $140, $160; (89) $100, $200; (91) $275
— Reproductions from Illuminated Manuscripts. 1910. 2d Ed. Series I-III in 3 vols. 4to. (91) $100
— MURRAY, ALEXANDER STUART & SMITH, ARTHUR HAMILTON. - White Athenian Vases in the British Museum. 1896. Folio. (88) £45
— WARNER, SIR GEORGE FREDERIC. - Queen Mary's Psalter. 1912. 4to. (88) £70; (89) $160; (90) £60, £65

Catalogues
— Birds. 1874-98. 27 vols. 12mo. Vols 1-12 & 26 ex-library copies. (89) $1,700
— Bookbindings from the Library of Jean

1987 - 1991 • BOOKS — BRITISH MUSEUM

Grolier.... 1965. (89) $80; (90) $70; (91) $200
— Books in the Library...to the Year 1640. 1884. 3 vols. 8vo. (89) $200
— Books, Manuscripts, Maps and Drawings...(Natural History). 1903-40. 8 vols, including the 3 vol Supplement. 4to. (89) $1,000; (91) $850, $900, £420
— Books Printed in the XVth Century....
    1908-72. Vols I-IX (of 12). Folio. (89) $650
    Vols II-X. Together, 9 vols. Folio. (91) $475
    Vols I-X (of 12). Folio. (91) $750
    Doheny copy. (88) $600
    1963-[62]. 11 vols, including 2 vols of facsimiles. Folio. (88) $875
    Vols 1-10, 12 & 2 vols of facsimiles. Folio. (88) $750
    Vols 1-8 only. (89) $200
    Parts I-X & XII plus facsimiles, Parts I-VII in 2 vols. 1963-[85]. (91) £700
— British and American Book Plates.... 1903-4. Compiled by E. R. J. Gambier Howe. 3 vols. 8vo. (91) $300, £220
— Collection of Playing Cards, Bequeathed... by...Lady Charlotte Schreiber. 1901. (88) $80, $100; (90) $60; (91) $200
— Collection of Birds' Eggs.... 1901-12. Compiled by E. W. Oates & S. G. Reid, with Vol V compiled by W. R. Ogilvie-Grant. 5 vols. (90) $300
— The Collection of English Pottery.... 1903. Compiled by Robert Lockhart Hobson. 4to. (89) $175
— A Description of the Collection of Ancient Marbles.... 1812-61. 11 vols. 4to. Blackmer copy. (90) £1,600
    Vols 3-11. (91) $475
— Drawings by Dutch and Flemish Artists.... 1915-32. Compiled by Arthur M. Hind & A. E. Popham. 5 vols. 8vo. (88) £480; (91) $1,000
— Early German and Flemish Woodcuts.... 1903-11. Compiled by Campbell Dodgson. 2 vols. (88) £200
— Eighteenth Century Short Title Catalogue. 1983. 4to. (88) $300
— Engraved British Portraits.... 1908-25. Compiled by Freeman O'Donoghue & Henry M. Hake. 6 vols, including Supplements & Indexes. (88) £140; (90) £160; (91) $275, $500
— Fifty Manuscripts and Printed Books Bequeathed by Alfred H. Huth. 1912. Folio. (88) £45
— General Catalogue of Printed Books. L, 1936-37. Vols 16-19. Folio. Library copy. (91) $400
    NY: Readex, 1967. 27 vols. 4to. (88) $1,000, £520; (90) $550, $650, $700
    NY: Readex, 1967-69. 27 vols plus 5 Supplements. 4to. (88) $950
    27 vols plus 10 Supplement vols to 1975. 4to. (88) £800
    NY: Readex, 1967. 27 vols plus supplement for 1955-65 in 5 vols. Together, 32 vols. 4to. (89) $1,500
    27 vols plus supplements for 1955-70 in 8 vols. Together, 35 vols. 4to. (90) £920
— The Harleian Collection of Manuscripts. 1808-12. 4 vols. Folio. (88) £100
— Illuminated Manuscripts.... 1903. One of 500. Compiled by Sir George F. Warner. Series I-IV in 1 vol. Folio. (91) $350, £250 Doheny copy. (88) $850
— Irish Manuscripts.... 1926-52. Compiled by Standish Hayes O'Grady & Robin Flower. 3 vols. (91) $120
— Japanese and Chinese Woodcuts.... 1916. Compiled by Laurence Binyon. (90) $250
— Manuscript Maps, Charts and Plans.... 1962. 3 vols. Reprint of 1844-61 Ed. (88) $50
— The Manuscripts in the Cottonian Library.... 1802. Compiled by Joseph Planta. Folio. (88) $70
— Manuscripts in the Spanish Language.... 1875-93. 4 vols. 8vo. (91) £95
— Manuscripts...New Series. 1833-40. Vol I, Parts 1-3. Folio. (89) $200
— Pamphlets, Books, Newspapers, and Manuscripts relating to the Civil War, the Commonwealth, and Restoration, collected by George Thomason.... 1908. 2 vols. 8vo. (90) $300; (91) $175
— Personal and Political Satires.... 1870-1954. Vols 1-11 in 12. (91) $1,100
— Printing and the Mind of Man.... [1963]. (89) $70
— Prints and Drawings. Political and Personal Satires, 1320-1770. 1870-83. 4 vols in 5. 8vo. (91) £320
— Short-Title Catalogue of Books Printed in France.... 1924. (91) $150
— STC Dutch. 1965. ("Short-Title Catalogue of Books Printed in the Netherlands and Belgium....") (91) $100
— STC French. Folkestone, 1969-72. ("A Short-Title Catalogue of French Books, 1601-1700....") 6 parts. 4to. (90) $90
    Folkestone, 1969-73. Compiled by V. F. Goldsmith. 7 parts. 4to. (91) $175
— STC German. 1958. ("Short-Title Catalogue of Books Printed in German-Speaking Countries....") (91) $70
— STC Italian. 1958. ("Short-Title Catalogue of Books Printed in Italy and of Italian Books printed in Other Countries from 1465 to 1600.") (90) $200; (91) $120
— STC Spanish. 1966. ("Short-Title Catalogues of Spanish, Spanish-American, and Portuguese Books printed before 1601.")

(91) $130
— Three Hundred Notable Books Added.... 1899. Folio. (91) $250
— Western Manuscripts in the Old Royal and King's Collections. 1921. 4 vols. 4to. Library markings. (90) £90

Brittannia...
— Brittannia Illustrata or Views of All the Kings Palaces, Several Seats...Publick Buildings and Squares in London and Westminster. L: Henry Overton & J. Hoole, [1727]. Oblong folio. (89) £1,100

Britten, Benjamin, 1913-76
— On Receiving the First Aspen Award. L, 1964. Inscr. (91) £80

Britten, Frederick James, 1843-1913
— Old English Clocks: The Wetherfield Collection. L, 1907. One of 320. Folio. (88) £45

Britton, John, 1771-1857
See also: Bourne & Britton
— The Architectural Antiquities of Great Britain.... L, 1807-26. 5 vols. 4to. (91) £160, £200
L, 1835. 5 vols. 4to. (89) $100, $175, £155
— Bath and Bristol, with the Counties of Somerset and Gloucester.... L, 1829. Illus by T. H. Shepherd. 4to. (91) £340
— Cathedral Antiquities. L, 1836. 5 vols. 4to. (88) £110, £120
— The Fine Arts of the English School.... L: Chiswick Press, 1812. 1st Ed. Folio. (91) $120, £200
— An Historical and Architectural Essay relating to Redcliffe Church, Bristol.... L, 1813. 8vo. (89) £60
— The History and Antiquities of the Cathedral Church of Salisbury. L, 1814. 4to. (89) £60
— The History and Antiquities of the Cathedral Church of York. L, 1819. Folio. (89) $50
— The History and Description with Graphic Illustrations of Cassiobury Park. L, 1837. Ltd Ed. Folio. (89) £320; (91) £650
— Picturesque Antiquities of the English Cities. L, 1830. 4to. (89) £420; (91) £460
One of 12 L.p. copies. (90) £520
L, 1836. 4to. (88) £190; (89) £90, £500; (90) £400
— The Pleasures of Human Life. L, 1807. Illus by Thomas Rowlandson. 8vo. (89) £60
2d Ed. 8vo. (91) $225

Britton, John, 1771-1857 —&
Brayley, Edward Wedlake, 1773-1854
— The Beauties of England and Wales.... L, 1801-18. 18 vols in 26, including Brewer's Introduction. 8vo. (88) £420
18 vols in 25; without Brewer's Introduction. 8vo. (89) £550; (91) £300
18 vols in 25 plus Brewer's Introduction. 8vo. (91) £580
19 vols in 26. 8vo. (88) £400
— Devonshire & Cornwall Illustrated. L, [1829]-32. 2 vols. 4to. (88) £220
2 vols in 1. 4to. (88) £180, £240; (89) £250, £260, £260, £280; (90) £300, £300; (91) £350
L, 1832-37. 2 vols in 1. 4to. (90) £320; (91) $300

Britton, John, 1771-1857 —&
Pugin, Augustus Charles, 1762-1832
— Illustrations of the Public Buildings of London. L, 1825-28 [1823-28]. 2 vols. 8vo. (89) $150, $190
L, 1838. 2 vols. 8vo. (91) £160

Britton, John, 1771-1857 —&
Robson, George Fennell
— Picturesque Views of the English Cities. L, 1828. 4to. (88) £240

Britton, Nathaniel Lord, 1859-1934
— Flora of Bermuda. NY: Scribner's, 1918. 8vo. (91) $80

Britton, Nathaniel Lord, 1859-1934 —&
Brown, Addison
— An Illustrated Flora of the Northern United States.... NY, 1896-98. 1st Ed. 3 vols. 4to. (88) $50

Britton, Nathaniel Lord, 1859-1934 —&
Rose, Joseph Nelson
— The Cactaceae: Descriptions and Illustrations of Plants of the Cactus Family. Wash., 1919-23. 4 vols. 4to. (88) £140, £700
Los Angeles: Cactus & Succulent Society, 1931-37. 4 vols. 4to. (89) $170

Britwell Court Library
— The Britwell Handlist, or Short-Title Catalogue.... L, 1933. 2 vols. 4to. (88) $160, $50; (89) £80; (91) $80
— Catalogue of the Library of Samuel Christie-Miller Esq. Britwell, Bucks., 1873-76. 3 vols in 1. 8vo. (91) $450
— [Sale Catalogue] Catalogue...of the Renowned Library...the Property of S. R. Christie-Miller. L, 1916-27. 19 (of 21) parts in 12 vols. 4to. (91) $325

Britzman, Homer E. See: Adams & Britzman

Brizeux, Auguste
— Marie. Paris, [1832]. 12mo. Bound in is an ALs of Vigny, 25 Mar 1847, asking Ptachat for several copies of this volume. Martin copy. (90) FF3,200

Broad, Amos
[-] The Trial of Amos Broad and his Wife, on Three Several Indictments for Assaulting and Beating Betty, a Slave, and Her Little Female Child Sarah. NY, 1809. 8vo. (91) $1,000

Broadley, Alexander Meyrick
— Napoleon in Caricature 1795-1821. L, 1911. Ltd Ed. 2 vols. Folio. (91) $85, £55 Presentation copy. (89) £60

Broadside
— AMERICAN REVOLUTION. - Advertisement. The Committee of Correspondence in New-York...proceeded to the Nomination of five Persons to go...General Congress at Philadelphia. [NY, 1774]. 4to. (91) $1,200
— The Daily Citizen. [N.p.], 2 [but 4] July 1863. 19 1/4 by 12 1/2 inches. (91) $2,250
— Decrets de la Convention Nationale, du 7 Avril 1793...formation & composition d'un Comite de Salut public. Paris, 1793. 500mm by 370mm. (89) $325
— In Provincial Congress...Recommended to such of the Counties as have not already formed Committees, to do it without delay. [NY: John Holt, 1775]. 4to. Sgd by Philip Livingston. (91) $2,000
— In Provincial Congress...Whereas this Congress has received undoubted Information, that a Number of disaffected Persons in Queen's County, have been supplied with Arms and Ammunition. [NY: John Holt, 1775]. 4to size. (91) $1,100
— ALVARADO, JUAN BAUTISTA. - Juan Bautista Alvarado, Governador Constitucional del Departamento de las Californias; a sus habitantes [warning them against a group of renegades led by Isaac Graham]. [Monterey, c.26 Apr 1840]. 12.25 by 8.50 inches. (89) $4,750
— AMERICAN REVOLUTION. - Advertisement. The Committee of Correspondence in New-York...Nomination of five Persons to go...proposed General Congress at Philadelphia.... [NY, 1774]. 4to. (91) $1,700
— AMERICAN REVOLUTION. - By His Excellency the Hon. Thomas Gage, Esq;...A Proclamation...[promising pardon to everyone except Samuel Adams & John Hancock; orders martial law throughout the Province]. [Bost: Margaret Draper, 1775]. Large folio. (91) $10,000
— AMERICAN REVOLUTION. - A Citizen's Address to the Public. [NY: John Holt, 1769]. Folio. (91) $1,000
— AMERICAN REVOLUTION. - Colony of Massachusett's Bay, 1776. We the Subscribers [declare non-cooperation with the British]. [Watertown: Benjamin Edes, 1776]. Folio size. Evans 14840. Fleming copy. (89) $850
— AMERICAN REVOLUTION. - The Enthusiastic Patriot, or, Cobler of Messina. NY, 1769. Folio size. (91) $1,000
— AMERICAN REVOLUTION. - The Following is a Copy of a Letter which was wrote by a Lady of this City. [NY, 1775]. 4to. (91) $1,100
— AMERICAN REVOLUTION. - General Orders for the Army under the Command of Brigadier General M'Dougall.... [N.p., c.1776]. Folio. (91) $3,000
— AMERICAN REVOLUTION. - Gentlemen, by the last advices from London we learn that an Act has been passed by the British Parliament for blocking up the Harbour of Boston. [Bost., 1774]. 4to. Sgd by William Cooper. (91) $5,500
— AMERICAN REVOLUTION. - In Congress, March 23, 1776 [resolving that Inhabitants of these Colonies be permitted to fit out armed Vessels to cruise on the Enemies of these United Colonies]. Phila.: John Dunlap, 1776. Folio size. Evans 15135. (89) $1,400
— AMERICAN REVOLUTION. - In Convention of the Representatives of the State of New-York.... Fishkill: Samuel Loudon, 1777. Oblong 4to. (91) $1,500
— AMERICAN REVOLUTION. - In Provincial Congress...Sir, in order that timely Assistance may be hand, in case of an Invasion of this Colony. [NY: John Holt, 1775]. 4to size. (91) $1,100
— AMERICAN REVOLUTION. - In Provincial Congress...Resolved, That the Several Committees...purchase or hire all the Arms.... [NY: John Holt, 1775]. 4to size. (91) $1,500
— AMERICAN REVOLUTION. - In Provincial Congress, New-York, May 31, 1776 [asking the colonies to hold general elections]. [NY, 1776]. Folio size. (91) $3,200
— AMERICAN REVOLUTION. - In the House of Representatives, June 7th, 1776 [calling for each town to advise the Person or Persons who should...represent them in the next General Court -- whether, should the honorable Congress...declare them Independant...they the said Inhabitants will solemnly engage...to support them in that Measure]. [Watertown: Benjamin Edes, 1776]. Folio size. Bristol B 4265. Fleming copy. (89) $1,400
— AMERICAN REVOLUTION. - Manifesto and Proclamation to the Members of Congress [offering amnesty]. NY, 3 Oct 1778.

580mm by 470mm. (89) $1,700
— AMERICAN REVOLUTION. - New York. The Following Dialogue being conceived, in some Measure, calculated to advance the Cause of Freedom.... NY, 20 May 1774. Folio. (91) $1,800
— AMERICAN REVOLUTION. - A Plan of the Action at Bunker's Hill.... L, [1775]. Folio. (91) $2,750
— AMERICAN REVOLUTION. - Proceedings of the General Congress of Delegates from the several British Coloniesin North-America, held in Philadelphia, September 1774. NY: John Holt, [1774]. Folio. (91) $1,600
— AMERICAN REVOLUTION. - State of Massachusetts-Bay...Whereas by the Loss of the important Fortress of Ticonderoga. [Bost., 1777]. Folio. (91) $1,100
— AMERICAN REVOLUTION. - To the Freeholders, Freemen, and Inhabitants of the City and County of New-York [reaffirmation of the desire of the Continental Congress that the Colonies cease exporting goods to Great Britain]. [NY: John Holt, 1775]. Folio. (91) $750
— AMERICAN REVOLUTION. - To the Freeholders and Freemen of the City of New-York [assailing Freeman, for trying to shake confidence in the Committee of Observation by his proposition to elect the former delegates]. [NY: John Holt, 1775]. Folio size. (91) $1,400
— AMERICAN REVOLUTION. - To the Freemen, Freeholders, and other Inhabitants of the City and County of New-York. Gentlemen, in Times of Public Danger. [NY: James Rivington, 1774]. Folio size. (91) $1,600
— AMERICAN REVOLUTION. - To the Inhabitants of the City and Colony of New-York. From Mess. Brandford's Paper of the 22d Instant. [NY: John Holt, 1774]. Folio. (91) $1,600
— AMERICAN REVOLUTION. - To the Inhabitants of the City and Colony of New-York...[about the manner of choosing delegates]. [NY: John Holt, 1774]. Folio size. (91) $750
— AMERICAN REVOLUTION. - To the People of New-York [Invective against those seeking peace with Great Britain]. [NY: John Holt, 1774]. 4to size. (91) $475
— AMERICAN REVOLUTION. - To the very respectable and humane Citizens of New-York...At a time when we are all uniting the most strenuous efforts in defence of our just rights and privileges. [NY: John Holt, 1774]. 4to. (91) $2,600
— BESSIRES, JULIEN. - Proclamation. Au nom de Sa Majesté l'Empereur des Francais [on the repair of roads & improvements to communications, agriculture, industry & commerce in Corfu. [Corfu, c.1811]. 470mm by 382mm. Blackmer copy. (90)

£2,100
— BOOTH, JOHN WILKES. - Boston Museum. J. Wilkes Booth as Raphael, the Sculptor. Thursday Evening, May 26, '64. Bost.: F. A. Searle, [1864]. 14.5 by 5.75 inches. (91) $1,600
— BOSTON MASSACRE. - Supplement to the Boston Gazette, &c. of (No. 794). Bost.: Edes & Gill, 25 June 1770. Folio size. (89) $900
— BOSTON TEA PARTY. - Postscript to the Pennsylvania Journal. Number 1618. Phila., 9 Dec 1773. Folio size. (89) $2,400
— BUCHANAN, JAMES. - A Proclamation [on the Utah War]. Wash., 1858. Folio. (89) $200
— BUTLER, BENJAMIN FRANKLIN. - Proclamation. Headquarters Department of the Gulf [announcing that Northern forces control the city of New Orleans & setting forth regulations] [New Orleans, 1862]. 607mm by 190mm. (89) $425
— CALIFORNIA. - Westward the Star of the Empire Takes its Way. [N.p., c.1892-96]. 21.5 by 8.5 inches. (90) $400
— CANADA. - Lands in Upper Canada, to be disposed of by the Canada Company.... L, 1841. 17.75 by 21.75 inches. (88) C$950
— CHARLES V. - Wir Karl der fuenfft... Bischoffen, Prelaten und anderen so zo dem allgemainen Conceili auff den ersten Tage des Monats nachtagligen Zwyspalts unserer hailigen Christlichen Religion gelegen sein woelle.... Augsburg, 23 Mar 1551. 450mm by 330mm. (90) £650
— COOPER, WILLIAM. - By Direction of the Committee of Correspondence for the Town of Boston.... Bost.: Isaiah Thomas, 30 Mar 1773. (89) $1,300
— CORFU. - Eleutheria. Isoths. Politeia Gallikh. Eidhsis [announcing the establishment of the press at Corfu]. Corfu, [1798]. 331mm by 235mm. Blackmer copy. (90) £1,500
— ELIAS, SIMON. - El governador constitucional del departamento de Chihuahua a sus habitantes.... Chihuahua: Cayetano Ramos, 4 Sept 1837. Folio size. (88) $225
— FRANCE. - La Convention Nationale au Peuple francais...18 vendimiaire, An 3. Paris, An III. 420mm by 340mm. (89) $150
— FRANCE. - Decret de la Convention Nationale, du 27 Juin 1793...qui ordonne la convocation des Assemblees primaires.... Paris, 1793. Size not given. (89) $500
— ITURRIGARAY, JOSEPH DE. - Con el importante objecto de fomentar el comercio del nuevo mexico.... Mexico, Dec 1805. Folio size. (88) $130
— JESUITS IN MARYLAND. - An Act for Securing certain Estates and Property, for the support and uses of The Ministers of the Roman Catholic Religion.... Balt.: James Angell, [c.1793]. 350mm by 230mm.

1987 - 1991 • BOOKS   BROCKETT

Doheny copy. (89) $600
— KEARNY, STEPHEN WATTS. - Proclamation. Proclama. To the People of California. The President of the United States....[inaugural address]. Monterey, 1 Mar 1847. 32.1cm by 22cm. (90) $4,000
— LINCOLN, ABRAHAM. - Ford's Theatre...Night 191...Friday evening, April 14th 1865. Benefit! and Last Night of Miss Laura Keene... Tom Taylor's Celebrated Eccentric Comedy...Our American Cousin.... Wash.: Polkinborn & Son, [1865]. 460mm by 127mm. (91) $13,000
— LINCOLN, ABRAHAM. - President Lincoln's Emancipation Proclamation. [San Francisco], 1864. 712mm by 554mm. Sgd. Doheny copy. (88) $65,000
— LINCOLN, ABRAHAM. - [Reward offer of 100,000 dollars for information leading to the arrest of Lincoln's assassin] Wash., 20 Apr 1865. 605mm by 315mm. (91) $17,000
— LINCOLN ASSASSINATION. - $30,000 Reward. Description of John Wilkes Booth! Wash., 16 Apr 1865. 252mm by 200mm. (89) $9,500
— LIVINGSTON, PHILIP. - To the Inhabitants of the City and County [urging attendance at a meeting to appoint delegates to the Continental Congress]. [NY: John Holt, 1775]. 4to size. (91) $1,100
— LOUIS XVI. - Lettres Patents du roi sur le Decret de l'Assemblee Nationale pour l'Admission des Non-Catholiques dans l'Administration.... Poitiers, 1789. (89) $700
— MASSACHUSETTS. - Boston, 26th of June 1775. This Town was Alarmed on the 17th-Instant at the break of Day, by a Firing from the Lively Ship of War.... [Bost.: John Howe, 1775]. Folio. Streeter copy. (90) $5,500
— MASSACHUSETTS. - State of Massachusetts-Bay. A Proclamation for a Day of Public Thanksgiving. Bost., 27 Oct 1778. 420mm by 335mm. (89) $1,100
— MINT. - An Ordinance for the Establishment of the Mint of the United States of America.... [NY, 1786]. Folio size. (91) $1,500, $2,200
— PHILADELPHIA. - Advertisement. At a General Meeting of the Comittee of Mechanicks.... [NY, 1774]. 4to. (91) $1,600
— REGICIDE. - By the King—A Proclamation for Apprehension of Edward Whalley and William Goffe. L, 1660. 430mm by 269mm. (91) $600
— RODNEY, CAESAR. - Delaware State, a Proclamation. Wilmington, [1779]. (89) $475
— SCOTT, WINFIELD. - El General en Gefe de los Egercitos de los Estados-Unidos de America, a la Nacion Megicana. Jalapa, 11 May 1847. 27.1cm by 20.3cm. (90) $250

— SLAVERY. - Injured Humanity, being a Representation of what the unhappy Children of Africa endure.... NY, [c.1831]. Size not given. (89) $475
— WALES. - The Welch-mans Life, Teath and Periall, together with a Long Narrow prod List, of the care her tooke in hers life-time, to make awle hims frend and acquaintance merry at her teath, ascribing the manner of hers funerall, with faire cost bestowed upon them that comes to hims Periall.... [N.p.]: for Richard Burton, 1641. 4to. (88) £60
— WASHINGTON, GEORGE. - By the President of the United States of America. A Proclamation.... NY, 1789. 500mm by 399mm. (91) $35,000
— WASHINGTON, GEORGE. - By the President of the United States of America. A Proclamation [of the first national thanksgiving day under the Constitution]. [NY: Francis Child & John Swaine (?), 1789]. 500mm by 399mm. One of 5 known copies & the only one in private hands. (91) $35,000
— WASHINGTON, GEORGE. - Washington's Farewell Address [to the] People of the United States. [Phila.: G. Fairman & B. H. Rand & C. Toppan, 1821]. Folio. "A first proof no part of which is finished," written at foot, with spaces for vignette & for portrait. (91) $750
— WHIGS. - Let Every True Whig Read This with Attention. [NY, 1791]. Folio size. (91) $650
— WILD MAN OF THE WOODS. - Exhibiting at Niblo's Garden, During the Fair, a Living Orang Outang or Wild Man of the Woods. [N.p., 19th cent]. Folio size. (91) $325

Brocardus, de Monte Sion

— Descriptio terrae sancta exactissima.... Antwerp: J. Steels, 1536. 8vo. (90) £2,400

Brockedon, William, 1787-1854

— Illustrations of the Passes of the Alps.... L, 1828-29. 2 vols. 4to. (88) £320, £400, £500; (89) £230, £300, £360, £420, HF750; (90) £400; (91) £380, £700, £750, £1,500 Inscr, 14 Sept 1834. (91) £650
  L, 1836. 2 vols. 4to. (89) £400
— Italy, Classical, Historical, and Picturesque. L, [c.1847]. Folio. (88) £260, £280, £340, £350; (90) £650
— Road-Book from London to Naples. L, 1835. 8vo. (89) £300

Brockett, John Trotter

— [Sale Catalogue] A Catalogue of the Very Valuable and Extensive Collection of Ancient and Modern Coins and Medals.... L, 1823. 8vo. Sale held on 4 June 1823 & 9 following days. (90) £75

Brockett, Linus Pierpont, 1820-93 —& Vaughan, Mary C.
— Woman's Work in the Civil War.... Phila., 1867. 8vo. (88) $55

Brockett, Paul
— Bibliography of Aeronautics. Wash., 1910. (91) £75

Brockett, William Edward
— Narrative of a Voyage from Sydney to Torres' Straits.... Sydney, 1836. 8vo. (89) A$17,000

Brockhaus, Albert, 1855-1921
— Netsukes. NY, 1924. Trans by M. F. Watt; Ed by E. G. Stillman. (90) $55

Brockway, Thomas
— The European Traveller in America. Hartford, 1785. 8vo. (91) $1,100

Brockwell, Charles, of Catherine Hall, Cambridge
— The Natural and Political History of Portugal. L, 1726. 1st Ed. 8vo. (88) £400

Broder, Patricia J.
— Bronzes of the American West. NY, [1974]. 4to. (91) $130

Brodie, Walter
— Pitcairn's Island and the Islanders in 1850.... L, 1851. 8vo. (88) £90; (89) £65; (90) $120

Brodribb, William Adams
— Recollections of an Australian Squatter.... Sydney, [c.1883]. 8vo. (89) A$250
Melbourne, 1976. One of 350. (89) A$90, A$300

Brodrick, Thomas
— A Compleat History of the Late War in the Netherlands.... L, 1713. 1st Ed. 2 vols. 8vo. (88) £55

Brodrick, William
See also: Salvin & Brodrick
— Falconers' Favourites. L, 1865. Folio. Martin copy. (90) $2,500

Broensted, Peter Oluf
— Reisen und Untersuchungen in Griechenland. Paris: Firmin Didot, 1826-80. 2 vols. Folio. Blackmer copy. (90) £850
— Voyages dans la Grece.... Paris, 1826. Premiere livraison. Folio. Blackmer copy. (90) £160

Brognolus, Candidus
— Alexicacon hoc est opus de maleficis.... Venice: Nicolo Pezzana, 1714. Bound with: Manuale exorcistarum, ac parochorum. Venice, 1714. 4to. (91) £380

Broickwy, Antonius
— In Quatuor Evangelia Enarrationum. Cologne: Petrus Quentell, 1539. Folio. From the Carthusian convent at Wedderen, near Duelmen in Westphalia. (89) £450

Broinowski, Gracius J.
— The Birds of Australia. Melbourne, etc., 1890-91. 6 vols in 3. Folio. (88) £1,650; (91) £3,000
Bradley Martin copy. (89) $7,500

Broiset, Jean
— Retraite spirituelle pour un jour de chaque mois. Paris: Jean Baptiste Coignard, 1743. 12mo. Yemeniz copy. (91) £1,400

Bromley, William, 1664-1732
— Remarks on the Grand Tour of France and Italy. L, 1705. 2d Ed. 8vo. (88) £110

Bromley, William Davenport. See: Davenport, William Davenport Bromley

Bromme, Traugott
— Missouri und Illinois. Taschenbuch fuer Einwanderer.... Balt. & Dresden, 1835. 8vo. Phillipps copy. (88) £480
— Nordamerika's Bewohner, Schonheiten & Naturschaetze. Stuttgart, 1839. 8vo. (88) £260

Bronson, Enos
— An Address to the People of the United States, on the Policy of Maintaining a Permanent Navy. By an American Citizen. Phila., 1802. 8vo. (91) $250

Bronsted, Peter Oluf
— The Bronzes of Siris. L, 1836. Folio. (91) $80
— Voyage dans la Grece. Paris, 1826-30. 1st Ed. 2 vols. 8vo. (91) £600

Bronte, Anne, 1820-49
— The Tenant of Wildfell Hall. L, 1848. 1st Ed. 3 vols. 12mo. (91) $3,250
Normanton-Bradley Martin copy. (90) $32,000
2d Ed. 3 vols. 12mo. (91) £150

Bronte's copy, Anne
— NOEHDEN, GEORGE HENRY. - A Grammar of the German Language. L, 1835. 7th Ed. Annotated throughout by Anne Bronte, partly in miniature script; sgd 14 Sept 1843. (91) £6,500

Bronte, Charlotte, 1816-55
— Jane Eyre. L, 1847. 1st Ed. 3 vols. 8vo. (90) $3,200, £5,800
Bradley Martin copy. (90) $17,000
1st Ed of Vols I & II; 2d Ed of Vol III. L, 1847-48. 3 vols. 8vo. Presentation copy from Bronte's husband, A. B. Nicholls, 1860. Doheny copy. (88) $2,800
— The Professor. L, 1857. 1st Ed. 2 vols. 8vo. (89) £130; (90) £300, £300
Bradley Martin copy. (90) $2,250
Issue not given. (90) £170; (91) $550
2 vols in 1. 8vo. (90) £190
Remainder Issue. Doheny copy. (89) $1,400
— Shirley. L, 1849. 1st Ed. 3 vols. 8vo. (91) £200
Esher-Bradley Martin copy. (90) $2,000
Jones-Newton-Doheny copy. (89) $2,500
— Villette. L, 1853. 1st Ed. 3 vols. 8vo. (90) $110, $5,000, £280, £300, £360
Doheny copy. (89) $3,200
John Addington Symonds's copy. (90) £550

Bronte, Charlotte, Emily & Anne
— Poems by Currer, Ellis, and Acton Bell. L, 1846. 1st Ed, 1st Issue. 8vo. Bradley Martin copy. (90) $9,000
2d Issue. (88) $200, £600; (90) $1,000, £500; (91) £70, £200
1st American Ed. Phila., 1848. 8vo. (90) £400
— Works. L, 1872-73. ("The Life and Works of Charlotte Bronte and her Sisters.") 7 vols. 8vo. (90) £260
L, 1882-84. 7 vols. 8vo. (91) £100
Haworth Ed. L, 1904-6. 7 vols. 8vo. (89) £380
Edin., 1905. 12 vols. (90) £340
9 vols only; lacking Vol I of Jane Eyre. (88) $275
Thornton Ed. 12 vols. 8vo. (90) $700
Edin., 1907. 12 vols. 8vo. (88) £130; (90) $425
L, 1910-20. ("The Life and Works of Charlotte Bronte and her Sisters.") 7 vols. 8vo. (90) £180
Thornton Ed. Edin., 1924. Ed by Temple Scott. 12 vols. (89) £140; (90) £200; (91) £180, £500
Oxford: Shakespeare Head Press, 1931-38. 19 (of 20) vols; lacking Bibliography vol. (88) R2,100; (90) £1,600

Bronte, Emily, 1818-48
— Wuthering Heights. L, 1847. 3 vols (Vol III is Agnes Grey). 8vo. Bradley Martin copy. (90) $37,000
Doheny copy. (89) $30,000

L, 1858. Patrick Bronte's copy, sgd by him on contents page, 22 Nov 1858. (88) £600

Brook, Richard
— The Cyclopaedia of Botany.... L, [c.1865?]. 2 vols. 8vo. (91) £210

Brook, Sir Robert
— La Graunde Abridgement. L: R. Tottell, 1576. 2 parts in 1 vol. 4to. (88) £320
Chambers copy. (89) £320

Brook, Stephen
— A Bibliography of the Gehenna Press, 1942-1975. Northampton MA, 1976. One of 400. Extra sgd impression of the frontis port of Leonard Baskin by Barry Moser laid in. (91) $90

Brooke, Sir Arthur de Capell
— Sketches in Spain and Morocco. L, 1831. 2 vols. 8vo. (88) £160; (89) £130
— Travels through Sweden, Norway and Finmark, to the North Cape. L, 1823. 1st Ed. 4to. (88) £220; (91) $275
— A Winter in Lapland and Sweden. L, 1826. 4to. (89) $110
L, 1827. 4to. (88) £260; (91) £320
— Winter Sketches in Lapland. L, 1826. 1st Ed. 4to. (89) £380

Brooke, Charlotte
— Reliques of Irish Poetry. Dublin, 1789. 4to. (89) £100

Brooke, Frances, 1724-89
— The History of Emily Montague. L, 1769. 4 vols. 12mo. (89) £350
Bradley Martin copy. (90) $1,600

Brooke, Henry, 1703?-83
See also: Moore & Brooke
— The Fool of Quality. L, 1766-69. 1st Ed. 4 vols. 12mo. (89) £190
5 vols. 12mo. (91) £60

Brooke, Henry, 1703?-83 —& Others
— Essays against Popery, Slavery, and Arbitrary Power.... Manchester: R. Whitworth, [1750?]. 8vo. (90) $90

Brooke, Sir James, Rajah of Sarawak, 1803-68
— Narrative of Events in Borneo and Celebes.... L, 1848. 1st Ed. Ed by Capt. Rodney Mundy. 2 vols. 8vo. (91) £200

Brooke, Sir Robert
— Le Liver des Assises & Plees del Corone. L: Richard Tottell, 1580. Folio. (89) £90

BROOKE

Brooke, Rupert, 1887-1915
— 1914 and Other Poems. L, 1915. 1st Ed. 4to. (88) £75, £500; (90) $95, £90, £95; (91) $50
   Fleming copy. (89) $900
   1st American Ed. NY, 1915. One of 87. (91) $500
— "1914." Five Sonnets. L, 1915. 1st Ed. 16mo. (88) $60, $200
— Collected Poems. L, 1919. One of 1,000. Illus by Gwen Raverat. 4to. (88) $175
— Four Poems. L, 1974. One of 100. Folio. (88) $100; (90) £90
   One of 500. (91) £50
— Fragments Now First Collected.... Hartford, 1925. One of 5 ptd on vellum. Fleming copy. (89) $1,400
   One of 99. (88) $225
— Grantchester; the Old Vicarage. Cambr., June 1912. ("Fragments from a Poem to be entitled The Sentimental Exile") 4to. In: Basileon H., No 14, pp 3-4. (89) $350
— Lithuania. Chicago, 1915. (88) $350
— The Old Vicarage Grantchester. L, 1916. 1st Ed. (88) $60; (90) $100
— Poems. L, 1911. 1st Ed. (88) $225; (89) $250, $300; (90) $180
   One of 500. (90) £160
   Inscr & with 5 corrections in ink. With related material identifying the recipients as Bill & Eva Hubbard. Fleming copy. (89) $3,500
   Inscr to Gwen & Jacques Raverat & with ALs tipped in. (91) £2,600
[-] Prize Compositions, Recited in Rugby School, June 24, 1905. Rugby: A. J. Lawrence, 1905. Contains Brooke's The Bastille. Sgd. Bradley Martin copy. (90) $2,750
— "The Bastille." Rugby: A. J. Lawrence, 1905. 1st Ed. Bradley Martin copy. (90) $5,500
— Two Sonnets. With a Memoir of Winston S. Churchill. [The Netherlands, 1945]. One of 100. Vliegend Verzet 1. Bradley Martin copy. (90) $300

Brooke's copy, Rupert
— WELLS, H. G. - First & Last Things. L, 1908. Sgd by Brooke on front free endpaper & dated Nov 1908. (88) $500

Brooke, Sir Thomas
— A Catalogue of the Manuscripts and Printed Books...Preserved at Armitage Bridge House.... L, 1891. Ltd Ed. 2 vols in 4. 8vo. Martin copy. (90) $550

AMERICAN BOOK PRICES CURRENT

Brookes, Iveson L.
— A Defence of the South.... Hamburg SC, 1850. 8vo. (91) $550

Brookes, Richard
— The Art of Angling, Rock and Sea-Fishing. L, 1740. 1st Ed. 12mo. (89) £80; (91) $110, $150
   L, 1766. 12mo. (88) £100
   L, 1781. 12mo. (90) $120
   L, 1785. 12mo. (90) $130
— A New and Accurate System of Natural History. L, 1763. 6 vols. 12mo. (89) £260; (90) £140; (91) £60

Brookes, Samuel
— Anleitung zu dem Studium der Conchylienlehre.... Leipzig, 1823. 4to. (88) DM900

Brookman, Lester G.
— The 19th Century Postage Stamps of the United States. NY, 1947. 2 vols. Sgd. (88) $50

Brooks, Gwendolyn
— A Street in Bronzeville. NY, 1945. (90) $50

Brooks, Hugh Cecil
— Compendiosa bibliographia di edizioni Bodoniane. Florence, 1927. One of 700 on carta a mano vergata. 4to. (89) $375, $400, HF600; (91) £150, LIt800,000

Brooks, Juanita
— The Mountain Meadows Massacre. Stanford, [1950]. (89) $55, $55; (90) $60

Brooks, Noah, 1830-1903
— The Boy Emigrants. NY, 1877. 1st Ed, 1st State. 8vo. Inscr to Emily Hale Perkins. Parsons-Fleming copy. (89) $420

Brooks, Shirley
— London Out of Town, or the Adventures of the Browns at the Sea Side. L, [c.1850]. Oblong 16mo. (91) $70

Brookshaw, George
— Groups of Flowers [Groups of Fruit...Six Birds...]. L, 1819. 2d Ed. 3 parts in 1 vol. 4to. (88) £1,500
   Birds only. 4to. (88) £440
— The Horticultural Repository.... L, [1820]-23. 2 vols. 8vo. (91) £2,200
   2 vols in 1. 8vo. (90) £3,200
— A New Treatise on Flower Painting.... L, 1816. 1st Ed. 4to. (88) $225; (90) £240
— Pomona Britannica. L, [1804]-12. 1st Ed. 4to. (91) £4,800
   L, [1816]-17. 2 vols. 4to. (89) £5,000; (91) £3,500

1016

2 vols in 1. 4to. (91) £4,500
L, 1817. 2 vols in 1. 4to. (90) £5,800
— Six Birds. L, 1817. 1st Ed. 4to. (88) £100, £350; (89) £380
Martin copy. (90) $1,000

Brossa, Joan
— Oda a Joan Miro. Barcelona, 1973. One of 10 hors commerce. Illus by Joan Miro. (90) $425

Brosses, Charles de, 1709-77
— Histoire des navigations aux terres Australes. Paris, 1756. 2 vols. 4to. (88) £1,900; (91) $3,000
— Traite de la formation mecanique des langues.... Paris, 1765. 12mo. (91) £460

Brotherhead, William
— The Book of the Signers.... Phila., 1861. 1st Ed. Folio. (90) £50

Brotherhood...
— Brotherhood Secrets. Troy, 1909-13. Vol I-Vol V, No 4, bound in 2 vols. (90) $600

Brother's...
— The Brother's Gift: or, the Naughty Girl Reformed. Hartford 1811. 32mo. (88) $80

Brothers, Alfred
— Photography: Its History, Processes.... L, 1899. 2d Ed. 8vo. (91) $60

Brouardel, Paul
— Etude critique des diverses medications employees contre le Diabete Sucre. Paris, 1869. 8vo. (90) $60

Brouckner, Isaac
— Nouvel Atlas de Marine.... Berlin, 1749. Folio. (88) £2,900

Brouerius van Niedek, Matthaeus
— Het Zegenpralent Kennemerlant.... Amst.: Leth, [1729]. 2 parts in 1 vol. Folio. (90) HF1,500
— Zederyke zinnebeelden der tonge. Amst., 1764. 8vo. (91) LIt480,000

Brough, Robert Barnabas, 1828-60
— Shadow and Substance. L, 1860. Illus by Charles Bennett. 8vo. (91) $275
— The Turkish Alphabet. L: David Bogue, [1854]. Illus by H. G. Hine. 16mo. (89) £600; (90) £160

Brougham, Henry Peter, Lord, 1778-1868
— Albert Lunel; or, the Chateau of Languedoc. L, 1844. 3 vols. 8vo. (91) $80

Broughton, F. —& Delamotte, William Alfred, 1775-1863
— Views of the Overland Journey to India from Original Sketches. L, [1847?]. Folio. (89) £340, £340

Broughton, Hugh, 1549-1612
— A Concent of Scripture. L: G. Simpson & W. White, [1590]. 4to. (89) $180

Broughton, John Cam Hobhouse, 1st Baron.
See: Hobhouse, John Cam

Broughton, Thomas Duer
— The Costume, Character, Manners, Domestic Habits and Religious Ceremonies of the Mahrattas. L, 1813. 4to. (90) £380; (91) $650

Broughton, Urban Huttleston Rogers
— The Dress of the First Regiment of Life Guards. L, 1925. One of 300. Oblong 4to. (89) £130; (91) £170

Broughton, William Robert, 1762-1821
— Voyage de decouvertes dans la partie septentrionale de l'ocean Pacifique. Paris, 1807. 2 vols. 8vo. (88) $275
— A Voyage of Discovery to the North Pacific Ocean. L, 1804. 1st Ed. 4to. (88) £1,500; (91) $3,400, £2,000, £4,500

Brown, Abbie Farwell, d.1927
— The Lonesomest Doll. Bost., [1928]. Illus by Arthur Rackham. 4to. (88) $275; (91) $375

Brown, Addison. See: Britton & Brown

Brown, Alexander Campbell
— Colony Commerce; or, Reflections on the Commercial System as it Respects the West-India Islands.... L, [c.1785]. 8vo. (91) $275

Brown, Basil J. W.
— Astronomical Atlases, Maps & Charts. L, 1932. 4to. (89) $150, $200; (91) $275

Brown, Charles Brockden
— Wieland: or the Transformation. An American Tale. NY: T. & J. Swords, for H. Caritat, 1798. 12mo. Martin copy. (90) $700

Brown, Christy
— My Left Foot. NY, 1955. (91) $55

Brown, Edward. See: Campbell, John

BROWN

Brown, Eleanor & Bob
— Culinary Americana. NY, [1961]. (90) $80

Brown, Frederic
— Angels and Spaceships. NY, 1954. (89) $95
— The Bloody Moonlight. NY, 1949. (89) $190
— Carnival of Crime. Carbondale & Edwardsville, [1985]. Uncorrected proof. (91) $50
— Martians, Go Home. NY, 1955. (89) $95
— Mitkey Astromouse. NY: Harlan Quist, [1971]. Illus by Helen Edelmann. (91) $50
— Space on my Hands. Chicago: Sasta Publishers, [1951]. Sgd. (88) $110

**Brown, Frederic —&
Reynolds, Mack**
— And the Gods Laughed. West Bloomfield MI: Phantasia, 1987. One of 475. (89) $120

Brown, Fredric
— Space on my Hands. Chicago: Sasta Publishers, [1951]. (89) $85

Brown, Glenn
— History of the United States Capitol. Wash., 1900-2. 2 vols. Folio. (88) $50; (89) $80; (90) $150

Brown, Henry Collins
— Glimpses of Old New-York. NY, 1917. Folio. (88) $55
— The Lordly Hudson. NY, [1937]. Out-of-series copy. Folio. (90) $200

Brown, Horatio F., 1854-1926
— Studies in the History of Venice. See: Clemens's copy, Samuel Langhorne

Brown, J. H.
— Spectropia: Or, Surprising Spectral Illusions Showing Ghosts Everywhere and of any Colour. NY, 1864. 1st American Ed. 4to. (89) $140

Brown, James. See: Lizars & Brown

Brown, James Berry
— Journal of a Journey across the Plains in 1859. San Francisco: Book Club of California, 1970. One of 450. (88) $55; (89) $55

Brown, John, 1735-88
— The Elements of Medicine.... Phila., 1791. 2 vols in 1. 8vo. (89) $50

Brown, John, 1752-1878
— Letters upon the Poetry and Music of the Italian Opera. Edin., 1789. 8vo. (88) $250

Brown Library, John Carter
— Annual Reports. Providence, 1923-68. For 1922-23-1967/68. Together, 42 issues. (88) $60
— Bibliotheca Americana. Providence, 1875-82. One of 100. 2 vols. 4to. (91) $950
Providence, 1919-31. 5 vols. 4to. (88) $275; (89) $450
Mixed Ed. Providence, 1931-61. Vols I-III. 4to. (91) $150
NY, 1975-63 & Providence, 1973. 7 vols. 4to. (88) $325
— European Americana: A Chronological Guide.... NY, 1980. Ed by John Alden & Dennis C. Landis. 2 vols. 4to. (89) $200

Brown, John Ednie
— The Forest Flora of South Australia. L, 1882-[90]. 9 orig parts. Folio. (88) $2,200
Parts 1-8 only. Folio. (89) A$500

Brown, John Henry, 1810-1905
— Reminiscences and Incidents of Early Days of San Francisco. See: Grabhorn Printing

Brown, John J.
— The American Angler's Guide.... NY, 1849. 3d Ed. 8vo. (91) $50

**Brown, Leslie —&
Amadon, Dean**
— Eagles, Hawks and Falcons of the World. [NY, 1968]. 2 vols. 4to. (90) £110

Brown, Louise Norton
— Block Printing & Book Illustration in Japan. L & NY, 1924. Folio. (90) $160, £70

Brown, Paul
— Aintree: Grand Nationals—Past and Present. See: Derrydale Press

Brown, Peter, fl.1776
— New Illustrations of Zoology. L, 1776. 4to. (88) £1,000, £1,600; (90) £950; (91) £1,300
Bradley Martin copy. (89) $5,000
Jeanson copy. (88) FF12,000

Brown, Richard
— Domestic Architecture.... L, 1852. 4to. (91) £50

Brown, Richard, b.1856
— A History of Accounting and Accountants. Edin., 1905. One of 250. (91) $300

Brown, Robert, 1773-1858
— General Remarks, Geographical and Systematical, on the Botany of Terra Australis. L, 1814. 2 vols. 4to. (89) A$250
— The Miscellaneous Botanical Works of.... L, 1866-68. 3 vols, including Atlas. 8vo & folio. (89) £280
Sgd by the Ed, J. J. Bennett, & with Brown's cut signature laid down on tp. (89) £120
— Supplementum primum prodromi florae Novae Hollandiae. L, 1830. 8vo. (89) £120

Brown, Rosel George. See: Laumer & Brown

Brown, Sampson
— Life in the Jungle. Colombo: Herald Press, 1845. (91) $750

Brown, Samuel R., 1775-1817
— The Western Gazetteer, or Emigrant's Directory.... Albany, 1817. 1st Ed, 1st Issue. 8vo. (90) $175
3d Issue. (89) $250

Brown, Thomas
— An Account of the People called Shakers. Troy NY, 1812. 12mo. (88) $80

Brown, Thomas, 1663-1704
— Amusements Serious and Comical.... L, 1700. 8vo. (88) $250
— Natures Cabinet Unlock'd, wherein is Discovered the Natural Causes of Metals, Stones.... L, 1657. 12mo. (88) $700; (90) $500
— Works. L, 1720-21. 5th Ed. 4 vols. 12mo. (90) $325

Brown, Capt. Thomas
— An Atlas of Fossil Conchology of Great Britain and Ireland. L, 1889. 4to. (89) £90
— The Book of Butterflies, Sphinxes and Moths. L, 1832-34. 3 vols. 12mo. (88) £80 Vols I-II (of 3). (89) $275
— Illustrations of the American Ornithology of...Wilson and...Bonaparte.... Edin. & L, [1831]-35. Early issue with Plates XLIV & LXI in states prior to the inclusion of additional figures & with plates with uncorrected misnumbering. Folio. Bradley Martin copy. (89) $55,000
26 orig parts in 23. Folio. "Only known copy in parts." Bradley Martin copy. (89) $60,000
— Illustrations of the Recent Conchology of Great Britain and Ireland. Edin., 1844. 2d Ed. 4to. (88) £600
— Illustrations of the Genera of Birds, Embracing Their Generic Characters.... L, [1845-46]. Parts 1-12 (of 14) bound in 1 vol. Folio. Bradley Martin copy. (89) $1,000

— Illustrations of the Land and Fresh Water Conchology of Great Britain and Ireland. L & Edin., 1845. 4to. (88) £95
— Illustrations of the Fossil Conchology of Great Britain and Ireland. L, 1849. 4to. (88) £200; (89) £180

Brown, William, of Leeds
— America: a Four Years' Residence.... Leeds, 1849. 8vo. (90) $55; (91) $110

Brown, William Henry, 1808-83
— Portrait Gallery of Distinguished American Citizens.... NY, 1931. One of 600. Folio. Facsimile of the Hartford 1845 Ed. (88) $90
Out-of-series copy. Facsimile of the Hartford 1845 Ed. (91) $140

Brown, William Henry, 1836-1910
— The History of the First Locomotives in America. NY, 1871. 8vo. (90) $140

Brown, William Hill
— The Power of Sympathy: or, the Triumph of Nature. Bost.: Isaiah Thomas, 1789. 2 vols in 1. 12mo. Whitman Bennett—Martin copy. (90) $3,500

Brown, William Robinson
— The Horse of the Desert. See: Derrydale Press

Browne, Alexander
— Ars Pictoria, or an Academy Treating of Drawing, Painting.... L, 1675. 2d Ed. 2 parts in 1 vol. Folio. (88) £170

Browne, Daniel Jay, b.1804
— The Sylva Americana.... Bost., 1832. 8vo. (90) $110

Browne, Edgar Athelstane
— Phiz and Dickens as they Appeared.... L, 1913. One of 175. (90) £220

Browne, Edward, 1644-1708
— An Account of Several Travels through a Great Part of Germany. L, 1677. 1st Ed. 4to. (91) $425
— A Brief Account of Some Travels in Hungaria, Austria.... L, 1673. 4to. Blackmer copy. (90) £450
Bound with: An Account of Several Travels through a Great Part of Germany. L, 1677. Kissner copy. (90) £350
L, 1685. Folio. (90) £220
Inscr to William Trumbull. (91) £380
— A Brief Account of some Travels in Divers Parts of Europe. L, 1687. 2d Ed. Folio. (91) £200

BROWNE

Browne, George, A.M.
— Arithmetica infinita; or the Accurate Accomptant's Best Companion.... [L?] 1717/18. Oblong 12mo. (91) £140 Engraved throughout. (91) $650

Browne, Howard
— Return of Tharn. Providence: Grandon, 1956. (89) $65
— Warrior of the Dawn. Chicago: Reilly & Lee, [1943]. (89) $55

Browne, Isaac Hawkins, 1705-60
— Poems upon Various Subjects. L, 1768. 8vo. Presentation copy from the editor. ESTC 116967. (91) £170

Browne, James, 1793-1841
— The History of Scotland: Its Highlands, Regiments and Clans. Edin., 1909. Caledonia Ed, one of 1,000. 8 vols. 8vo. (91) $110
— A History of the Highlands and of the Highland Clans. Edin.: Fullarton, [1851-52]. 4 vols in orig 11 parts. 8vo. (88) £75

Browne, John, Editor
— Browne's Masonic Master-key through the Three Degrees.... L, 1802. 8vo. (91) £280
— Browne's Tracing Boards. Sit Lux, et Lux Fuit.... L, [c.1800]. 3 parts in 1 vol. 4to. With typed trans & ANs of E. H. Dring. (91) £250

Browne, John, 1642-1700
— Adenochoiradelogia: or, an Anatomick-Chirurgical Treatise of Glandules and Strumaes. L, 1684. 3 parts in 1 vol. 8vo. (89) £220
— Myographia Nova, sive musculorum omnium.... L, 1684. Folio. (88) £530; (91) £280

Browne, John Ross, 1817-75
— Adventures in the Apache Country. NY, 1869 [1868]. 1st Ed. 12mo. (88) $80; (89) $110, $110; (91) $110
  NY, 1869. (91) $160
— Crusoe's Island.... NY, 1864. 1st Ed. 12mo. (89) $50; (91) $110
— Etchings of a Whaling Cruise.... NY, 1846. 8vo. (88) $260; (91) $185
— Relacion de los debates de la Convencion de California.... NY, 1851. (88) $75; (89) $85
— Report of the Debates in the Convention of California, on the Formation of the State Constitution.... Wash., 1850. 8vo. (91) $70
— Resources of the Pacific Slope. NY, 1869. (91) $55

AMERICAN BOOK PRICES CURRENT

Browne, Maggie, Pseud. of Margaret Hamer Andrewes
— The Surprising Adventures of Tuppy and Tue. L, 1904. Illus by Arthur Rackham. (88) $450
— Two Old Ladies, Two Foolish Fairies and a Tom Cat. L, 1897. Illus by Arthur Rackham. 8vo. (90) £300

Browne, Moses
— Angling Sports: In Nine Piscatory Eclogues.... L, 1773. 8vo. (89) £130; (90) $130

Browne, Nina E. See: Lane & Browne

Browne, Patrick, 1720?-90
— The Civil and Natural History of Jamaica. L, 1789. 2d Ed. Folio. (89) £400

Browne, T. Egerton
— Trial of Judge Wilkinson, Dr. Wilkinson, and Mr. Murdaugh, on Indictments for the Murder of John Rothwell and Alexander H. Meeks. Louisville, 1839. 8vo. (91) $250

Browne, Sir Thomas, 1605-82
— Certain Miscellany Tracts. L, 1684. 1st Ed, 2d Issue. 8vo. (88) £190; (89) $60
— Christian Morals.... L, 1756. 2d Ed. 8vo. Doheny copy. (89) $150
— Hydriotaphia, Urne-Buriall.... L, 1658. 1st Ed. 8vo. Hayward-Bradley Martin copy. (90) $950
  L, 1932. ("Urne Buriall and the Garden of Cyrus.") One of 215. Ed by John Carter; illus by Paul Nash. (88) £1,200
  Out-of-series copy. (91) £1,200
— Posthumous Works. L, 1712. 1st Ed. 8vo. (89) $250; (91) £70
— Pseudodoxia Epidemica.... L, 1646. 1st Ed. Folio. (88) £130, £190, £260; (89) £70; (90) $300; (91) £110, £80
  2d Issue. (91) $150
  2d Ed. L, 1650. Folio. (88) £90; (89) $175, £150
  Presentation copy, inscr by the recipient, Francis Le Gros. (90) £4,000
  Sold w.a.f. (91) $60
  3d Ed. L, 1658. Folio. (89) £50
  4th Ed. Folio. (88) £70; (89) $130, $150, $200; (90) $60; (91) $100
  L, 1672. 6th Ed. Port cut close & mtd. Bound with: Browne. Religio Medici. L, 1672. 7th Ed. Folio, modern calf (88) £60
  6th Ed. 4to. (88) £70; (89) $175
— Religio Medici. L, 1642. 2d Unauthorized Ed. 8vo. Bradley Martin copy. (90) $1,700
  1st Authorized Ed. [L], 1643. ("A True and Full Copy of that which was most Imperfectly and Surreptitiously Printed before under the Name of: Religio Medi-

ci.") 8vo. (88) $2,200
 1st Ed in Latin. Leiden: Franciscum Hackium, 1644. 12mo. (91) $425
 5th Ed. L, 1659. 8vo. (88) $140, $250
 L, 1669. 3 parts in 1 vol. 8vo. (90) $110
 L: Vale Press, 1902. One of 300. Folio. (90) $110, £50; (91) $100
 See also: Limited Editions Club
— La Religion du medecin. [N.p.], 1668. 1st Ed in French. 12mo. (89) $175
— Works. L, 1686. Folio. (88) £350; (89) $325, $325; (91) £180, £240
 Bemis-The Garden copy. (90) $32,000
 Contemp mor gilt by Queen's Binder A. (90) £2,000
 L, 1836-35. 4 vols. 4to. (88) £90
 L, 1852. 3 vols. 8vo. (91) $50
 L, 1928-31. One of 210. Ed by Geoffrey Keynes. 6 vols. (90) $180

Browne, Thomas Alexander ("Rolf Boldrewood"), 1826-1915
— Old Melbourne Memories. Melbourne, 1889. 8vo. (90) A$130
— Robbery Under Arms, a Story of Life and Adventure.... L, 1888. 1st Ed. 3 vols. 8vo. Bradley Martin copy. (90) $1,700
 Doheny copy. (89) $1,700

Browne, William, 1591-1643?
— Britannia's Pastorals. L, 1616. 2d Ed of 1st part; 1st Ed of 2d part. 2 parts in 1 vol. Folio. (88) £750
 STC 3915, 3915.5. Wilkinson-Bradley Martin copy. (90) $900
 With 160 Ms annotations attributed to John Milton. (90) $2,250
 L: John Haviland, 1625. 2 parts in 1 vol. 8vo. STC 3916. (91) $600
— Circe and Ulysses, the Inner Temple Masque. See: Golden Cockerel Press

Browne, William George
— Nouveau Voyage dans la haute et basse Egypte, en Syrie et dans le Dar-Four.... Paris, 1800. 2 vols. 8vo. Blackmer copy. (90) £700
— Travels in Africa, Egypt and Syria.... L, 1799. 1st Ed. 4to. (90) £200; (91) £420
 Blackmer copy. (90) £2,200

Browne, William Henry James
— Ten Coloured Views Taken During the Arctic Expedition of Captain Sir James C. Ross. L, 1850. Folio. (90) £750

Brownell, Baker. See: Wright & Brownell

Brownell, Charles De Wolf
— The Indian Races of North and South America. NY, 1855. 8vo. (91) $80

Brownell, Henry
— North and South America Illustrated.... Hartford, 1861. 2 vols. 8vo. (88) $60

Browning, Colin Arrott
— England's Exiles; or a View of a System of Instruction and Discipline.... L, 1844. ("The Convict Ship; A Narrative of the Results of Scriptural Instruction and Moral Discipline....") 2d Ed. 8vo. (90) A$140

Browning, Elizabeth Barrett, 1806-61
— The Battle of Marathon. A Poem. L, 1820. 1st Ed, one of 50 & one of 15 known. 8vo. Inscr to her grandmother, Arabella Graham Clarke. Bradley Martin copy. (90) $45,000
— An Essay on Mind, with Other Poems. L, 1826. 1st Ed. 12mo. Currie-Bradley Martin copy. (90) $3,750
 Doheny copy. (88) $650; (89) $750
— Poems. L, 1844. 1st Ed, Mixed Issue. 2 vols. 8vo. (89) £220
 L, 1850. 2 vols. 12mo. Doheny copy. (88) $420
— Poems Before Congress. L, 1860. 1st Ed. 8vo. (89) £65
— The Seraphim and Other Poems. L, 1838. 1st Ed. 12mo. Inscr to Julia Vignoles Martin, Jan 1840. Foot-Fleming copy. (89) $2,200
 2d impression. (89) £100
— Sonnets from the Portuguese. L: Vale Press, 1897. One of 300. 4to. (91) $70, £1,600
 Aiken SC: Palmetto Press, 1900. One of 10. (88) $120
— Sonnets from the Portugese. New Rochelle: Elston Press, 1900. One of 485. (89) $180
— Sonnets from the Portuguese. L: Arthur L. Humphreys, 1913. 8vo. (88) $190; (90) $90
 Montagnola: Officina Bodoni, 1925. One of 225. 4to. (89) £360; (91) $50
 San Francisco, 1927. One of 250. 2 vols, including facsimile. Folio & 8vo. (88) $100; (89) $90
 Tipped in is ALs from Robert Browning to an autograph collector, 27 Dec 1855, containing signatures of both Mr. and Mrs. Browning. Doheny copy. (88) $1,100
 Cambr.: Rampant Lions Press, 1939. One of 5 on vellum. 4to. With pencil note of John Carter saying that the book was a gift to him from the printer (Will Carter). (88) £600
 See also: Limited Editions Club

Browning, Robert, 1812-89
See also: Shelley forgery, Percy Bysshe
— Dramatis Personae. See: Doves Press
— The Flight of the Duchess. L: Essex House Press, 1905. One of 125 on vellum. 12mo. (89) $175
— The Inn Album. L, 1875. 12mo. Inscr to Euphrasia Fanny Haworth. (91) $800
James Russell Lowell's copy. (89) $275
— Last Ride. East Aurora, NY: Roycroft Shop, 1900. Ltd Ed. (89) $80
— Men and Women. L, 1855. 1st Ed. 2 vols. 8vo. (90) $110
Inscr to his wife's brother George. Bradley Martin copy. (90) $4,500
— Paracelsus. L, 1835. 1st Ed. 8vo. (88) $750
— Parleyings with Certain People of Importance in Their Day. See: Clemens's copy, Samuel Langhorne
— Pauline; a Fragment of a Confession. L, 1833. 8vo. Inscr to George Lillie Craik. Bradley Martin copy. (90) $70,000
— Pictor Ignotus, Fra Lippo Lippi, Andrea del Sarto. See: Golden Cockerel Press
— The Pied Piper of Hamelin. L: Robert Dunthorne, 1884. 16mo sheets of rice paper laid down on 4to sheets. With ALs to Edmund Gosse, 16 July 1883, tipped in. (89) £1,600
L, etc.: Routledge, [1888]. Illus by Kate Greenaway. 4to. (88) $140, £95
Inscr by Greenaway to Maud Locker Lampson & with 4 bookplates by Greenaway for members of the Lampson family inserted. (88) £320
Inscr to Helen Brown, 1900 & with pen sketch of a little girl in German dress. Doheny copy. (89) $750
Inscr to Lady Dorothy Nevill, Dec 1888 & with small watercolor drawing of girl holding flowers & a card bearing the inscr on tp. Doheny copy. (89) $4,200
L, 1898. One of 100 on vellum. Illus by Harry Quilter. 4to. (89) £500; (90) $550
One of 400. (89) £125
L: F. Warne, [1910]. Illus by Kate Greenaway. 4to. (91) £50
L, [1934]. One of 410. Illus by Arthur Rackham. (88) $150, $550; (91) $550
One of a few copies specially bound by Sangorski & Sutcliffe containing a sgd ink & watercolor drawing. (90) £4,100
Phila., [1934]. (89) $70
— Pippa Passes. NY, 1900. Frontis & borders by Margaret Armstrong. (91) $60
— The Poetical Works. See: Clemens's copy, Samuel Langhorne
— The Ring and the Book. L, 1868-69. 1st Ed. 4 vols. 8vo. (88) $70

Doheny copy. (89) $1,500
See also: Limited Editions Club
— La Saisiaz: the Two Poets of Croisic. L, 1878. 8vo. Inscr to Mrs. Procter. (88) £620
— Some Poems by Robert Browning. See: Eragny Press
— Sordello. L, 1840. 1st Ed. 12mo. (89) $250
Inscr to Mrs. Basil Montagu & inscr by her to a Mr. Davis. Drinkwater-Doheny copy. (89) $700
Inscr to M. Conan. Fleming copy. (89) $900
Inscr to J. Abel. Doheny copy. (89) $1,700
— Strafford. L, 1837. 1st Ed. 8vo. (88) $200; (90) $250, £420
— Works. L, 1889-90. ("The Poetical Works.") 17 vols. 8vo. (90) $285
Centenary Ed. L, 1912. One of 526. 10 vols. (90) £110

Brownrigg, Marcus Blake
— The Cruise of the Freak. Launceston, [1872]. 8vo. (90) A$450

Brown-Sequard, Charles Edward
— Lectures on the Diagnosis of the Principal Forms of Paralysis of the Lower Extremities. Phila., 1861. 8vo. (88) $325

Bruccoli, Matthew J.
— First Printings of American Authors. Detroit: Gale, [1977-79]. 4 vols. 4to. (88) $250; (89) $275; (90) $190, $250; (91) $110

Bruce, Charles, Viscount
— A Catalogue of the Books...in his Library at Totenham.... Oxford, 1733. 4to. (88) £900

Bruce, Sir James, 1730-94
— Cartes et figures du Voyage en Nubie et en Abyssinie. Paris, 1792. 4to. (88) $175
— Travels to Discover the Source of the Nile. Edin., 1790. 5 vols. 4to. (88) £400, £550; (89) £650
Vols I-IV (of 5). (89) $50
L, 1790. 4 vols; lacking Vol V. (91) £100
5 vols. 4to. (88) £360; (89) £520; (90) £640, £900, £1,100; (91) £800, £1,100
Blackmer copy. (90) £1,500
Martin copy. (90) $1,400
2d Ed. Edin., 1804-5. 8 vols. 8vo & 4to. (88) £110
8 vols. 8vo. (88) £120, £540; (89) £300; (91) £750
3d Ed. Edin., 1813. Atlas vol only. 4to. (88) £70
— Voyages en Nubie et en Abyssinie.... Paris, 1792. ("Cartes et figures du voyage en Nubie et en Abyssinie.") Atlas vol only. 4to. (88) FF3,000

Bruce, Peter Henry, 1692-1757
— Memoirs.... L, 1782. 4to. (88) £100; (91) $260

Bruck, Jacobus a
— Emblemata politica quibus ea, quae ad principatum spectant breviter demonstrantur.... L, 1618. 4to. (90) $1,500

Bruckner, Albert —& Marichal, Robert
— Chartae latinae antiquiores: Facsimile-Edition of the Latin Charters prior to the Ninth Century. Olten & Lausanne, 1954-63. Parts 1-13. Folio. (89) £500

Bruckner, Emanuel Daniel
— Versuch einer Beschreibung historischer und natuerlicher Merkwuerdigkeiten der Landschaft Basel. Basel, 1748-63. 23 parts in 6 vols. 8vo. (89) £3,600

Brue, Adrien Hubert
— Atlas universel de geographie.... Paris, 1822. Folio. (88) FF4,000

Brueckmann, Franz Ernst
— Magnalia Dei in locis subterraneis.... Braunschweig & Wolfenbuettel, 1727-34. Part 3 only. Folio. (88) DM1,000

Bruehl, Anton
— Photographs of Mexico. NY, [1933]. One of 1,000. Folio. (91) $130, $140, $175 Out-of-series copy marked Review in Bruehl's hand. (88) $130

Bruele, Gualtherus
— Praxis medicinae, or the Physitians Practise.... L: R. Cotes for W. Sheares, 1648. 3d Ed. 4to. (91) £260

Bruennich, Morten Thrane
— Ornithologia borealis, sistens collectionem avium.... Copenhagen, 1764. 8vo. Martin copy. (90) $400, $3,250

Brueys, David Augustin de, 1640-1723
— L'Avocat Patelin: a Comedy in Three Acts.... See: Clemens's copy, Samuel Langhorne

Bruff, Joseph Goldsborough
— Gold Rush. NY, 1944. 2 vols. 4to. (90) $75; (91) $160, $225
4to. (88) $170, $225; (89) $110, $140

Bruffey, George A.
— Eighty-One Years in the West. Butte, 1925. (89) $65; (90) $75

Bruguiere, Francis
— San Francisco. San Francisco, 1918. (89) $60

Bruhl, Karl Friedrich Montz Paul, Graf von. See: Hirt & Bruhl

Bruin, Claes. See: Le Brun, Cornelius

Bruin, Cornelius le. See: Le Brun, Cornelius

Brulliot, Franz, 1780-1836
— Dictionnaire des monogrammes, marques figurees, lettres initiales.... Munich, 1832-34. 3 parts & 3 appendices in 1 vol. 4to. (90) $100; (91) $70

Brummell, Beau
— Male and Female Costume...until 1822.... Garden City, 1932. Out-of-series copy. Ed by Eleanor Parker. 4to. (88) $50

Brun, Robert
— Le Livre illustre en France au XVIe siecle. Paris, 1930. 4to. (91) $50

Brune, Johannes de, 1589-1658
— Emblemata of Zinne-werck. Amst., 1661. 3d Ed. 4to. (88) HF1,850, HF3,600
— Emmblemata of Zinnewerck.... Amst: Abraham Latham, [c.1668]. 4to. (90) $900

Brunem, Vojeu de. See: Jouve, Joseph Baptiste

Brunet, Gustave, 1807-96
— Imprimeurs imaginaires et libraires supposes. Paris, 1866. 8vo. (88) $130; (89) $70
— Imprimeurs imaginaires et libraires supposes. * Recherches sur les Imprimeries imaginaires, clandestines, et particuliers. Paris, 1866 & Brussels, 1879. Together, 2 vols. 8vo & 12mo. (91) $50

Brunet, Jacques Charles, 1780-1867
— Manuel du libraire et de l'amateur de livres. Paris, 1814. 2d Ed. 4 vols. 8vo. (88) £75
3d Ed. Paris, 1820-34. 7 vols. 8vo. (89) £140
Brussels, 1821. 4 vols. 8vo. (89) £60
Paris, 1838-45. 5 vols. 8vo. (88) $150; (90) $150; (91) $250, £55, £140
Paris, 1842-44. 5 vols. 8vo. (88) $100; (89) $100, £75, £80
Paris, 1860-65. 6 vols. (89) $250; (90) £360
6 vols in 12 & 2-vol Supplement, 1878-80. Together, 14 vols. 8vo. Doheny copy. (88) $1,000
6 vols plus 1880 Supplement. (88) $400; (90) $500; (91) £200, £220, £260, £420, £440
Martin copy. (90) $400
One of 55 L.p. copies. 6 vols in 12. 8vo. Fleming copy. (89) $1,000

BRUNET

Paris, 1878-80. 8 vols, including 2-vol Supplement. 8vo. (91) $500
Berlin, 1921. 6 vols. Martin copy. (90) $350
6 vols plus the 2-vol Supplement, Paris, 1878. (88) £320
Berlin, 1922. 6 vols plus the Paris, 1878-80 Ed of the Supplement in 2 vols & the c.1925 Ed of Deschamps. Together, 9 vols. 8vo (supplement 4to). (88) $350
Paris, 1964-66. 6 vols plus supplement & Deschamps, Dictionnaire de Geographie. Together, 9 vols in 8. 8vo. Photofacsimile of 1860-80 Ed. (88) £320
Copenhagen, 1966-68. 9 vols. (88) £360; (89) £290; (90) £700, £550, LIt1,800,000
— [Sale Catalogue] Catalogue des livres rares et precieux.... Paris, 1868. 2 vols in 1. 8vo. (91) $325

Brunfels, Otto, 1488?-1534
— Contrafayt Kreueterbuch nach rechter vollkommener art.... Strassburg: J. Schott, 1532. (88) £3,760
— Herbarum vivae eicones.... Strassburg: J. Schott, 1532. 3 parts in 1 vol. Folio. (91) DM2,600
Bound with: Brunfels. Novi Herbarii tomus II. Strassburg: J. Schott, 1532. 1st Ed. Folio. (91) £380
— Precationes Biblicae. Strasbourg: Joannem Schottum, 1528. 8vo. (90) £700

Brunhoff, Jean de, 1899-1937
— Histoire de Babar le petit elephant. * Le Voyage de Babar. Paris, 1931 & 1932. 1st Ed, 1st Issue. Together, 2 vols. Folio. Martin copies. (90) $4,500

Bruni, Leonardo, Aretinus, 1369-1444
— Historia fiorentina. Venice: Jacobus Rubeus, 12 Feb 1476. Bound with: Poggius Florentinus. Historia Fiorentina. Venice: Jacobus Rubeus, 8 Mar 1476. Folio. 217 (of 218) leaves; lacking initial blank. Goff B-1247. 2d work: 115 (of 116) leaves; lacking final blank. Goff P-873. (91) $3,500
Florence: Bartolommeo di Libri, 5 June 1492. ("Le Historie Eiorentine.") Bound with: Poggius Florentinus. Historia Fiorentina. Florence: Bartolommeo di Libri, 1492. Folio. 220 (of 222) leaves (q3 & q6 supplied in 18th-cent Ms) & 116 leaves. Goff B-1248 & P-874. (88) £800
— Libro della Guerra de Ghotti. Florence: Giunta, 1526. 2 parts in 1 vol. 8vo. (91) $750
8vo. (88) £150

AMERICAN BOOK PRICES CURRENT

Brunn, Heinrich, 1822-94 —& Krell, P. F.
— Die Griechischen Vasen, ihr Formen- und Decorationssystem. Leipzig, 1877. Folio. Blackmer copy. (90) £600

Brunner, Johann Conrad A.
— Experimenta nova circa pancreas. Amst., 1683. 8vo. (90) $2,200

Brunner, John
— The Devil's Work. NY, [1970]. (89) $55

Bruno, Giordano, 1548-1600
— De imaginum, signorum & idearum empositione [sic]. Frankfurt: J. Wechel & P. Fisher, 1591. 8vo. (90) £5,800
— De triplici minimo et mensura. Frankfurt: J. Wechel & P. Fisher, 1591. 8vo. (89) £3,800

Brunoff, Maurice de
— Collection des plus beaux numeros comoedia illustre et des programmes. Consacres aux ballets & galas russes.... Paris, [1922?]. Folio. (89) £480; (91) £820

Bruns, Henry P.
— Angling Books of the Americas. Atlanta, 1975. 4to. (89) $110, $160; (91) $50
One of 500. (88) $550
Inscr to Joseph Bates & with sgd Christmas card laid in. (90) $650

Brunschwig, Hieronymus, c.1450-c.1512
— Das Buch zu Distillieren...und das Buch Thesaurus Pauperum.... Strassburg: Johann Grueninger, 1519. Folio. (90) DM7,500
— Dis ist das buch der Cirurgia Hantwirckung.... Milan, 1923. Folio. (88) $175; (89) $60
— Das Distilierbuch, da Buoch der rechten Kunst zu Distilieren.... Strassburg: Johannes Grueninger, 1515. 4th Ed. Folio. (89) $1,300
— The Vertuose Boke of Distyllacyon of the Waters of all Maner of Herbes.... L: Laurens Andrewe, 18 Apr 1527. 1st Ed in English. Folio. (89) £4,000

Brunt, Samuel
— A Voyage to Cacklogallinia: with a Description of the Religion, Policy, Customs and Manners of that Country. L, 1727. 8vo. (89) £450; (90) $475

Brunus, Albertus
— Tractatus de rebus seu dispositionibus dubiis.... Asti: Franciscus Garonus de Liburno, 1536. Bound with: Tractatus de diminutione & deterioratione. Asti, 1536. 4to. (91) LIt1,000,000

Brunus Aretinus, Leonardus. See: Bruni, Leonardo, Aretinus

Brushfield, Thomas N., 1828-1910
— A Bibliography of Sir Walter Raleigh.... Exeter, 1908. One of 250. Author's sgd copy. (91) $140
— The Literature of Devonshire up to the Year 1640. N.p.: Pvtly ptd, 1893. 4to. (91) $120

Brusonius, Lucius Domitius
— Facetiarum exemplorumque libri VII. Rome: Iacobus Mazochius, 15 Sept 1518. 1st Ed. Folio. (90) £100
  Abrams copy. (90) £3,000

Brussel, Isidore Rosenbaum
— Anglo-American First Editions. L, 1935-36. 2 vols. Inscr in both vols. (90) $175
  One of 500. (89) $225
  Out-of-series copy. (89) $55
— A Bibliography of James Branch Cabell. Phila., 1932. One of 100. (89) $50

Brutus, Pseud. —&
Search, Humphrey, Pseud.
— Essays, Historical, Political and Moral. Dublin, [1774?]. 2 vols. 12mo. ESTC 111087. (91) £320

Brutus, Lucius Junius. See: Coleman, William

Bruyerinus Campegius, Joannes Baptista
— De re cibaria libri XXII.... Lyons: Sebastian de Honoratus, 1560. 8vo. (89) $650
  Frankfurt: ex officina Paltheniana, 1600. 8vo. (91) £480

Bruyn, Cornelius de. See: Le Brun, Cornelius

Bruyn, Cornelius le
— A Voyage to the Levant.... See: Le Brun, Cornelius

Bruys, Francois
— The Art of Knowing Women.... L, 1732. 12mo. (88) $275

Bruzen della Martiniere, Antoine Augustin, 1662-1746
— Le Grand Dictionnaire geographique et critique. The Hague, 1726-39. 10 vols. Folio. (88) FF11,000

Bry, Johann Theodor de, 1561-1623
— Florilegium novum, hoc est variorum maximeque rariorum florum.... Frankfurt: Merian, 1641-47. ("Florilegium renovatum et auctum: das ist...Blumenbuch....") Folio. With contemp Ms Index bound in and 1822 Linnaean Ms index loosely inserted. (91) £150,000
— Proscenium vitae humanae sive emblematum secularium. Frankfurt: Wilhelm Fitzer, 1627. 4to. (89) £1,300

Bry, Johann Theodor de, 1561-1623, & Johann Israel de
— Acta Mechmeti I. Saracenorum principis.... Frankfurt, 1597. 4to. Blackmer copy. (90) £6,400
— [Little Voyages]. Frankfurt, 1598-1613. ("Indiae orientalis navigationes.") 6 (of 12) parts in 1 vol. Folio. (90) £480
  Parts 1 & 2 only in 1 vol. Folio. (89) £1,500
  Latin Ed. 6 parts only in 1 vol. Folio. (90) £2,500
  Parts 1-4 only in 1 vol. Folio. (90) £2,300
  Part 10 only. Folio. (91) £2,800

Bry, Theodor de & Johann Theodor de
— [Great Voyages] Collectiones peregrinationum in Indiam Orientalem et Indiam Occidentalem. Frankfurt & Oppenheim, 1590-1625. Part 3 in 2 divisions. (90) £1,400
  Part 5 in 2 divisions only: Americae pars quinta. (90) £1,500
  Frankfurt & Oppenheim, 1590-1625 [1620-25]. Parts 1-12 (of 13). Folio. (91) £36,000
  Parts 1-4 only, in 1 vol. Folio. (88) £9,000
  Parts 1-9 (of 13) only, in 6 vols. Folio. (89) £13,000
  Latin Ed. Parts 4-6 only, in 1 vol: Benzoni's Historia del mondo nuovo. (88) $7,000
  Part 4 only. Folio. (89) £1,700
  Part 6 only. Folio. (88) £750
— [Great Voyages] Wunderbarliche, doch warhafftige erklarung, von der gelegnheit und siften der wilden in Virginia.... Frankfurt, 1594-1620. Parts I-VIII. 3d Ed of Part I, 2d Ed of other parts. Bound in 1 vol. (89) £2,500
— [Great Voyages] Collectiones peregrinationum in Indiam Orientalem et Indiam Occidentalem. Frankfurt: J. Wechel for T. de Bry, 1609. ("Brevis Narratio eorum quae in Florida Americae Provincia Gallis acciderunt....") Part 2 only: Le Moyne's Florida. (89) $3,500

Bryan, Daniel
— The Mountain Muse. Comprising the Adventures of Daniel Boone.... Harrisonburg, [Va.]: Davidson & Bourne, 1813. 12mo. (88) $90

Bryan, Margaret
— A Compendious System of Astronomy.... L, 1797. 8vo. (90) £160

Bryan, Michael, 1757-1821
— Dictionary of Painters and Engravers. L, 1849. 2 vols extended to 7. 8vo. Extra-illus with engravings. Joseph Crawhall's copy, with his signature on title of Vol I. (88) £380
L, 1903-5. 5 vols. 4to. (88) $70, £45; (89) $250; (91) $90, $250
L, 1904-5. ("A Biographical and Critical Dictionary of Painters and Engravers.") 5 vols extended to 24. 4to. Extra-illus with c.4,000 illusts & some orig drawings. (89) £20,000
L, 1909-26. 5 vols. 4to. (89) £60
L, 1913-15. 5 vols. 4to. (91) $190
L, 1920-21. 5 vols. 4to. (89) £50
L, 1930-34. 5 vols. 4to. (89) £90
Port Washington NY: Kennikat Press, 1964. One of 400. 5 vols. (88) $75; (89) $150

Bryant, Edwin, 1805-69
— What I Saw in California.... NY & Phila., 1848. 1st Ed. 8vo. (91) $160
2d Ed. 8vo. (91) $120
Santa Ana, 1936. (89) $90, $160; (91) $50, $130

Bryant, Gilbert Ernest
— The Chelsea Porcelain Toys. L, 1925. One of 650. (89) £65, £110, £120, £180

Bryant, Jacob, 1715-1804
— A New System; or, an Analysis of Ancient Mythology. L, 1774-76. 1st Ed. 3 vols. 4to. (88) £150
3d Ed. L, 1807. 6 vols. 8vo. (91) $250
— Observations and Inquiries Relating to Various Parts of Ancient History.... Cambr., 1767. 1st Ed. 4to. Blackmer copy. (90) £80
— Some Observations upon the Vindication of Homer and of the Ancient Poets and Historians.... Eton: Pote & Williams, 1799. 4to. (88) £55

Bryant, William Cullen
— The Family Library of Poetry and Song. See: Fore-Edge Paintings

Bryant, William Cullen, 1794-1878
— L'Amerique du Nord pittoresque. See: Amerique...
— The Embargo; or Sketches of the Times. Bost., 1809. 2d Ed. 12mo. Martin copy. (90) $700
— Letters from the East. NY, 1869. 1st Ed. 8vo. (91) $50
— Picturesque America, or the Land We Live In. See: Picturesque...
— Picturesque America, or the Land We Live In. 1872-74. See: Picturesque...
— Picturesque America, or the Land We Live In. See: Picturesque...
— Poems. Cambr., Mass., 1821. 1st Ed. 12mo. "An unusually fine copy." Doheny copy. (89) $3,200
One of 750. Martin copy. (90) $1,800
NY, 1832. 8vo. (89) $140
With card sgd by Bryant, 10 Feb 1874. (91) $100
See also: Limited Editions Club
— Thirty Poems. NY, 1864. 1st Ed, 1st State. 12mo. Annotated on pp. 76 & 167. Inscr to Sarah Fairchild Vanduzer. Wakeman-Martin copy. (90) $850
— The White-Footed Deer and Other Poems. NY: I. S. Platt, 1844. 12mo. Terry-Martin copy. (90) $3,750

Bryant, William Cullen, 1794-1878 —& Gay, Sydney H., 1814-88
— A Popular History of the United States. NY, 1876-81. 4 vols. 8vo. (90) $60

Bryce, James, 1838-1922
— The American Commonwealth. L, 1888. 1st Ed. 3 vols. 8vo. (91) $175
ALs to Richard Watson Gilder, 16 Nov 1897, laid in. (89) $225

Bryden, Henry Anderson
— Great and Small Game of Africa. L, 1899. One of 500. 4to. (88) £840; (91) £420
Inscr by Arthur Neumann. (89) £1,000
— Gun and Camera in Southern Africa. L, 1893. 8vo. (88) £50; (89) R400

Brydges, Sir Samuel Egerton, 1762-1837
— Restituta; or the Title and Characters of Old Books in English Literature. L, 1814-16. 1st Ed. 4 vols. 8vo. Anthony Trollope's copy. (89) £230

Brydone, Patrick, 1743-1818
— A Tour through Sicily and Malta. L, 1773. 2 vols. 8vo. (88) £100; (89) £65
2d Ed. L, 1774-73. 2 vols. 8vo. (88) £35
L, 1775. 2 vols. 8vo. (91) £50
L, 1776. 2 vols. 8vo. (88) £55

Bubbled...
— The Bubbled Knights, or Successful Contrivances, Plainly Evincing...the Folly and Unreasonableness of Parents Laying a Restraint upon their Childrens Inclinations, in the Affairs of Love and Marriage. L, [1757]. 2 vols. (89) £750

Buber, Martin, 1878-1965
— Juedische Kuenstler. Berlin, 1903. 4to. (91) $120

Buchan, A.
— Monifieth Gold Links Bazaar Book. [N.p.], 1899. John Kerr's copy, with ALs from Buchan to Kerr, 27 Nov 1899. (88) £2,600

Buchan, John, 1875-1940
— A History of the Great War. Bost. & NY: Houghton Mifflin, 1922. 8 vols. Sgd. (88) $130
— The Pilgrim Fathers. The Newdigate Prize Poem, 1898. Oxford & L, 1898. 8vo. (88) £55; (90) £50
— Scholar Gipsies. L & NY, 1896. 1st Ed. Illus by D. Y. Cameron. 8vo. (88) $100; (90) £160, £200
— Sir Quixote of the Moors. L, 1895. 1st Ed. 8vo. (90) £90, £150; (91) £75
  Card sgd by author inserted. (90) £170

Buchan, William, 1729-1805
— Advice to Mothers, on the Subject of their own Health.... Phila., 1804. 1st American Ed. 8vo. (89) $175
— Domestic Medicine.... Phila., 1772. 2 parts in 1 vol. 8vo. (88) $200
  Phila.: Crukshank, Bell & Muir, 1784. 8vo. (91) $75, $90
  Phila.: Folwell for J. & J. Crukshank, 1797. 8vo. (91) $100

Buchanan, Francis Hamilton, 1762-1829
— An Account of the Fishes Found in the River Ganges.... L & Edin., 1822. 2 vols. 4to & oblong 4to. (89) £425; (91) £420
— Geographical, Statistical, and Historical Description of...Dinajpur.... Calcutta, 1833. 8vo. (88) £360
— A Journey from Madras through the Countries of Mysore, Canara, and Malabar. L, 1807. 1st Ed. 3 vols. 4to. (88) £260, £280; (90) £220

Buchanan, George, 1506-82
— Ane Detectioun of the Duinges of Marie Quene of Scottes.... [L: John Day, 1571]. 1st Ed in English. 12mo. (90) £850
— De iure regni apud Scotus dialogus. Edin.: J. Ross, 1579. 1st Ed. 4to. (89) £140
— The History of Scotland. L, 1690. 2 vols in one. Folio. (90) $95
— Paraphrasis Psalmorum Davidis Poetica.... Strassburg: Josias Rihelius, 1568. 8vo. (91) £420

Buchanan, James, British Consul at New York
— Sketches of the History, Manners and Customs of the North American Indians. L, 1824. 8vo. (88) £100

Buchanan, James, 1791-1868
— A Proclamation [concerning the Utah War and its necessity]. Wash., 1858. Folio. (89) $200

Buchanan, Robert Williams, 1841-1901
— The Piper of Hamelin.... L, 1893. Illus by Hugh Thomson. 8vo. (91) $450, $2,600

Buchanan, Robertson, 1770-1816
— Practical Essays on Mill Work.... L, 1823. 2d Ed. 2 vols. 8vo. (91) £160

Bucher, Francois
— The Pamplona Bibles: a Facsimile compiled from Two Picture Bibles with Martyrologies Commissioned by King Sancho el Fuerte of Navarra. New Haven & L, 1970. 2 vols. 4to. (88) £50; (89) £50; (90) £90; (91) $100, $100

Buchon, Jean Alexandre, 1791-1846
— Atlas geographique, statistique, historique et chronologique des deux Ameriques.... Paris, 1825. Folio. (88) £1,200; (91) $2,250, £1,500

Buc'hoz, Pierre Joseph, 1731-1807
— Centuries de planches enluminees et non enluminees.... Paris & Amst., [1775?]-81. 2 vols. Folio. (89) £4,000
  2 vols in 4. Folio. Jeanson copy. (88) FF50,000
  20 decades in 2 vols. Folio. (91) £3,000
— Collection precieuse et enluminee des fleurs.... Paris, 1776. 2 vols. Folio. (88) £40,000; (89) £17,000
— Les Dons merveilleux et diversement colories de la nature, dans le regne mineral.... Paris, [1779-83]. 2 vols. Folio. (89) £9,500

Buck, Sir George, d.1623
— The History of the Life and Reigne of Richard the Third. L, 1646. 1st Ed. Folio. (88) £150

Buck, Pearl, 1892-1973
— The Chinese Novel: Nobel Lecture Delivered Before the Swedish Academy at Stockholm, December 12, 1938. NY: John Day, [1939]. Sgd on front free endpaper. (91) $60

Buck, Samuel & Nathaniel
— Antiquities; or Venerable Remains of Above Four Hundred Castles, Monasteries.... L, 1774. 3 vols. Folio. (90) £15,000
  Vol II only. (91) £2,200

BUCKBEE

Buckbee, Edna Bryan
— The Saga of Old Tuolumne. NY: Press of the Pioneers, 1935. (88) $55; (91) $150

Bucke, Richard Maurice, 1837-1902
— Cosmic Consciousness: A Study in the Evolution of the Human Mind. Phila., 1901. One of 12 on Holland. 4to. With related holograph material laid in. T. B. Mosher copy. (88) $350

Buckell, George Teasdale Teasdale. See: Teasdale-Buckell, George Teasdale

Buckingham, James Silk, 1786-1855
— America: Historical, Statistic and Descriptive. L, [1841]. 1st Ed. 3 vols. 8vo. (88) $250
— The Slave States of America. L & Paris, [1842]. 2 vols. 8vo. (90) $130
— Travels among the Arab Tribes Inhabiting the Countries East of Syria and Palestine. L, 1825. 4to. (89) £900
  Blackmer copy. (90) £1,700
— Travels in Palestine. L, 1821. 1st Ed. 4to. (91) $550

Buckingham, Nash
— Blood Lines... See: Derrydale Press
— De Shootinest Gent'man and Other Tales. See: Derrydale Press
— Game Bag. Tales of Shooting and Fishing. NY, [1945]. One of 1,250. (90) $85
— Mark Right! See: Derrydale Press
— Ole Miss'. See: Derrydale Press
— Tattered Coat. NY, [1944]. Ltd Ed. (88) $120; (91) $100

Buckland, William, 1784-1856
— Geology and Mineralogy. L, 1858. 2 vols. 8vo. (91) $70
— Reliquiae diluvianae. L, 1823. 1st Ed. 4to. (88) £190
  2d Ed. L, 1824. 4to. (88) £100, £100; (89) £50, £65, £90

Buckland Wright, John
— Cupid's Pastime. L, 1935. One of 31. (90) £900
— Fourteen Wood-Engravings to Illustrate "Le Sphinx." Antwerp, 1960. One of 250. 4to. (90) £580

Buckler, John Chessell, 1793-1894
— Sixty Views of Endowed Grammar Schools. L, 1827. 4to. (91) £120, £125

Buckler, William, 1814-84
— The Larvae of the British Butterflies and Moths. L, 1886-1901. 9 vols. 8vo. (88) £500

AMERICAN BOOK PRICES CURRENT

Buckley, Francis
— A History of Old English Glass. L, 1925. 4to. (89) £48, £70; (90) £55

Bucquoy, Eugene Louis
— Les Gardes d'Honneur du Premier Empire. Nancy, 1908. One of 885. (90) $225
— Les uniformes de l'armee francaise; terre, mer, air. Paris, 1935. Out-of-series copy. Illus by Maurice Toussaint. 4to. (91) £300
— Les Uniformes du Premier Empire. [N.p., c.1920]. One of 250. Vol IV (of 7) only. Folio. With 2 inscr (1935) color plates. (90) $450

Buddingh, Steven Adriaan
— Neerlands Oost-Indie. Reizen over Java, Madura.... Amst., 1867. 2d Ed. 3 vols. 8vo. (89) HF850

Bude, Guillaume, 1468-1540
— Annotationes priores in pandectas. Cologne: J. Soter, Apr 1527. 8vo. (90) $375
— Epistolarum latinarium lib. V. Paris: Jodocus Badius Ascensius, Feb 1531. Folio. Abrams copy. (90) £1,600
— Libri V. de asse, & partib. eius.... Paris: Ascensius, [1514]. ("De Asse et partibus eius....") Folio. Kissner copy. (91) £1,800
  Venice: Aldus, Sept 1522. 4to. (91) LIt1,000,000
  Borowitz copy. (91) $950
  Kissner copy. (91) £950
  [Paris]: Badius, 1527. ("De asse et partibus eius....") Folio. (91) £300, £300
  Paris: Ascensiana, 1532. Folio. (88) £140, £140; (90) £340
— Trattato delle monete e valuta loro.... Florence: Heirs of B. Giunta, 1562. 8vo. (88) $175; (91) $500
  Honeyman copy. (88) £280

Bude, Guillaume, 1468-1540 —& Others
— De philologia studiis liberalis doctrinae.... Leiden, 1696. 4to. (90) $200

Budelius, Renerus
— De monetis, et re numaria, libri duo.... Cologne: J. Gymnicus, 1591. 4to. Bibliotheca Colbertina-A. H. Smith Barry-Honeyman copy. (88) £750

Budge, Sir Ernest Alfred Wallis, 1857-1934
— Amulets and Superstitions. L, 1930. 1st Ed. (90) £85; (91) $80
— By Nile and Tigris. L, 1920. 1st Ed. (88) £90
— The Egyptian Sudan. L, 1907. 2 vols. Blackmer copy. (90) £150
— From Fetish to God in Ancient Egypt. L, 1934. 1st Ed. (89) £150
— The Gods of the Egyptians. L, 1904. 2 vols. 4to. (91) $70

— The Life of Takla Haymanot. L, 1906. One of 250. Trans & Ed by Budge. 2 vols. Folio. (89) £240; (90) $225 Folio. (88) $250
— The Miracles of the Blessed Virgin Mary.... L, 1900. One of 300. Folio. (89) $175; (90) $550
— The Mummy.... Cambr., 1893. 1st Ed. 8vo. (89) $75
— The Book of the Dead. See: British Museum

Budgen, L. M.
— Episodes of Insect Life. L, 1849-51. 3 vols. 8vo. (88) £190; (90) £50; (91) $100

Buechner, Friedrich Karl Christian Ludwig
— Kraft und Stoff. Frankfurt: Meidinger Sohn, 1855. 8vo. (88) £550

Buechner, Georg, 1813-37
— Saemmtliche Werke. Sauerlaender, 1879. 8vo. (91) DM1,050
— Woyzeck. Leipzig: Insel-Verlag, 1920. One of 520. (90) $100

Buechner, Thomas S.
— Norman Rockwell: Artist and Illustrator. NY, [1970]. One of 100 but lacking the suite of collotypes. Folio. (88) $120 One of 1,100. (88) $150; (91) $50, $700, $700

Buek, Friedrich Georg
— Album Hamburgischer Costueme. Hamburg, [1843-47]. (91) £2,200

Buel, Clarence Clough. See: Johnson & Buel

Buel, James William, 1849-1920
— Louisiana and the Fair. St. Louis, [1904-5]. Founders Ed, one of 250. 10 vols. (89) $160

Buenther, Johannes, of Andernach
— De medicina veteri et nova.... Basel: ex officina Henricpetrina, 1571. 1st commentary only (of 2). Folio. Caspar Bauhinus's copy, with his annotations. (89) £400

Buenting, Heinrich, 1545-1606
— Itinerarium Sacrae Scripturae, Das ist, ein Reisebuch.... Magdeburg: Andreas Bessel, 1616. Folio. (89) £2,000; (90) £2,200
— Itinerarium Sacrae Scripturae, oder, Reise-Buch ueber die ganze heilige Schrift. Erfurt: Johann David Jungicol, 1757. 4to. (89) £260

Buergher, Gottfried Augustus, 1747-94
— Leonora. L, 1796. Illus by Bartolozzi after Lady Diana Beauclerk. 4to. (89) HF500 Illus by Bartolozzi after Lady Diana Beauclerc. Folio. (89) £250

Buesching, Anton Friedrich, 1724-93
— A New System of Geography. L, 1762. 6 vols. 4to. (90) £210, £850; (91) £100

Buffet, Bernard
— Jeux de dame. Paris: Andre Sauret, 1970. One of 30. Folio. (88) FF32,000
— Lithographies, 1952-1966. Paris, 1967. Text by Fernand Mourlot. 4to. (88) $80; (89) SF650
— Lithographs, 1952-1966. NY, [1968]. Text by Fernand Mourlot. 4to. (88) $120, $150, $200, $275; (89) $160, $220, $275, $275; (90) $400, $550, $600; (91) $110, $450 One of 125. (91) $1,600 Pbr's proofreader's copy, with pencil notations. (90) $200; (91) $650
— La Passion du Christ. [Paris]: Henri Creuzevault, 1954. One of 140, with a mtd plate sgd by Buffet. Folio. (88) FF16,000 One of 140, with a mtd drawing sgd by Buffet. (89) FF32,500; (91) $1,700

Buffon, Georges Louis Marie Leclerc, Comte de, 1707-88
— Histoire naturelle generale et particuliere. Paris, 1749-1804. 1st Ed. 30 vols, comprising general Vols I-XV, Oiseaux I-IX & the 6-vol Supplement. (91) £1,600
— Histoire naturelle general et particuliere. Paris, 1749-1804. 1st Ed. 38 (of 44) vols; lacking Poissons & Cetacees. (88) $750
— Histoire naturelle generale et particuliere. Paris, 1749-1804. 1st Ed. 39 vols, including Atlas; without fish or cetaceans. 4to. (88) FF28,000
Vols I-XV only. (91) £850
Amst.: H. Schneider, 1766-99. 38 vols. 4to. (91) £3,000
— Histoire naturelle des oiseaux. Paris, 1770-86. 4to Issue. 10 vols. (88) £12,000
— Histoire naturelle generale et particuliere. Paris, 1785-91. 43 (of 54) vols. (90) DM3,200
Paris, 1799-1803. 79 (of 80) vols. 8vo. (88) £700
Paris, 1951. One of 115. Illus by Germaine de Coster. Folio. (89) SF9,000
— Natural History.... L, 1785. 9 vols. 8vo. (91) $130
L, 1791. 9 vols. 8vo. (90) £140
Abridged Ed. L, 1792. 2 vols. 8vo. (89) £75
L, 1793-98. 15 vols. 8vo. (88) $180
L, 1797. 10 vols. 8vo. (88) £80; (91) £70
L, 1797-1816. 14 (of 16) vols. 8vo. (89) £55
L, 1797-1808. 16 vols. 8vo. (88) £190
L, 1812. 20 vols. 8vo. (89) £260, £300; (90) £150
L, 1821. 2 vols. 8vo. (91) £85
— Naturgeschichte der Vogel. Berlin: J. Pauli, 1772-1804. 28 (of 35) vols. 8vo. (91)

BUFFON

£1,100, £1,100
— Oeuvres. Paris, 1839. 8 vols. 8vo. Sold w.a.f. (89) £60
Paris, 1842-45. 6 vols. 8vo. (88) DM650
Paris, [1853-57]. 12 vols. With: Oeuvres de Cuvier et Lacepede...supplement aux oeuvres completes de Buffon. Paris, [1857-58?]. 4 vols. Together, 16 vols. 8vo, modern cloth. Martin copy. (90) $1,300
— Oiseaux. Paris, 1770-86. ("Histoire naturelle des oiseaux.") 10 vols bound in 4. Folio. (91) £20,000
10 vols. Folio. (89) £20,000
Bradley Martin copy. (89) $47,500
With 5 orig drawings inserted. Jeanson copy. (88) FF300,000
10 vols in 15. Folio. (91) £40,000
Bound in 5 vols. Folio. (89) £22,000
Bound in 8 vols. (90) £22,000
Vol I only. (91) £11,000
Vols I-IX. Folio. Martin copy with 262 plates. (90) $3,250
Vols I-VI. (91) £140
Paris, 1770-81. Vols I-VIII (of 9). 4to. Sold w.a.f. (91) £1,500
Paris, 1770-86. Vols VII-X only. (90) £10,000
L, 1793. ("The Natural History of Birds.") 9 vols. 8vo. (88) £140
Paris, [1800-4]. ("Histoire naturelle des oiseaux.") 28 vols. Folio. Martin copy. (90) $1,300
— Storia Naturale.... Livorno, 1829-32. 8vo. (91) £90

Buffum, Edward Gould
— Six Months in the Gold Mines.... Phila., 1850. 12mo. (91) $140, $160

Bugler, Arthur
— H.M.S. Victory. Building, Restoration and Repair. L, 1966. 2 vols, including portfolio of drawings. 4to. (90) £100

Buhle, Christian Adam Adolphe, 1773-1856. See: Naumann & Buhle

**Buhler, Kathryn C. —&
Hood, Graham**
— American Silver in the Yale University Art Gallery. New Haven, 1970. 2 vols. 4to. (88) $130; (91) $550

Buhlman, Josef
— Classic and Renaissance Architecture. NY: William Helbrun, [1916]. Folio. (88) $555

Builder's...
— The Builder's Magazine, or Monthly Companion for Architects, Carpenters.... L, 1774. 4to. (91) $160
— The Builder's Practical Directory or Buildings for all Classes.... L, [1855-57]. 4to.

AMERICAN BOOK PRICES CURRENT

(91) £90

Buist, Robert, 1805-80
— The Family Kitchen Gardener.... NY, 1856. 8vo. (91) $60

Bukowski, Charles
— Bring Me Your Love. Santa Barbara: Black Sparrow Press, 1983. One of 376. (91) $85
— Crucifix in a Deathhand. NY, [1965]. (88) $50
— Factotum. Los Angeles: Black Sparrow Press, 1975. Ltd Ed, sgd. (91) $100, $225, $275
One of 75 with an orig watercolor. (91) $180
— It Catches my Heart in its Hands. New Orleans: Loujon Press, [1963]. 4to. (91) DM550
— There's No Business. Santa Barbara: Black Sparrow Press, 1984. One of 426. (91) $65

Bula N'Zau, Pseud. See: Bailey, Henry

Buleau, Theodore. See: Popp & Buleau

Bulfinch, Thomas, 1796-1867
— The Age of Chivalry. Bost., 1859. 12mo. (89) $65
Martin copy. (90) $500
— The Age of Fable, or Studies of Gods and Heroes. Bost., 1855. 1st Ed, 1st Issue, with names of both ptr & stereotyper on copyright page. Inscr to the Misses Balfour, 25 Dec 1855. Martin copy. (90) $2,000

**Bulkeley, John —&
Cummins, John**
— A Voyage to the South Seas.... L, 1743. 8vo. (89) £360
Issue with authors' names on tp. (90) £900; (91) $800, $850
Phila., 1757. 8vo. (89) $225

Bull, Henrik Johan
— The Cruise of the "Antarctic" to the South Polar Regions.... L & NY, 1896. 8vo. (89) £240

Bull, Henry Graves. See: Hogg & Bull

Bull, John Wrathall
— Early Experiences of Life in South Australia.... Adelaide & L, 1884. 8vo. (88) A$80; (89) £80

Bull, William Perkins
— From Rattlesnake Hunt to Hockey. Toronto: The Perkins Bull Foundation, [1934]. One of 1,000. (88) $50

Bullar, Joseph & Henry
— A Winter in the Azores. L, 1841. 2 vols. 8vo. (88) £50; (89) £70

Bullard Collection, Francis
— A Catalogue of the Collection of Prints from the Liber Studiorum of J. M. W. Turner.... Bost.: Pvtly ptd, 1916. Folio. (90) $175

Bulleid, Arthur —& Gray, Harold St. George
— The Glastonbury Lake Village. Glastonbury, 1911-17. 2 vols. 4to. (90) £75

Bullen, Frank Thomas, 1857-1915
— The Cruise of the "Cachalot". L, 1898. 1st Ed. 8vo. (89) $60; (91) $425
Inscr. (89) $950
Inscr by author & 1 of the illustrators. Martin copy. (90) $475

Bullen, Henry Lewis
— Nicolas Jensen: Printer of Venice. San Francisco: John Henry Nash, 1926. One of 207. Folio. Doheny copy. (88) $300
— The Nuremberg Chronicle: a Monograph. San Francisco, 1930. One of 300. Folio. (88) $75, $200, $400; (91) $300, $450
This copy with an additional laid in leaf from a German Ed. (89) $140

Buller, Sir Walter Lawry, 1838-1906
— Essay on the Ornithology of New Zealand. Dunedin, 1865. 8vo. Martin copy. (90) $400
— A History of the Birds of New Zealand. L, [1872]-73. 4to. Martin copy. (90) $3,500
1st Ed. 4to. (90) £1,000; (91) £950, £1,000
2d Ed. L, [1887]-1888. 2 vols. With: Supplement to the Birds of New Zealand. L, 1905-[06]. 2 vols. Together, 4 vols. 4to, half calf, Martin copy. (90) $3,250
2 vols. 4to. (89) £650, £900, £1,000, £1,100 Martin copy. (90) $1,500
— Manual of the Birds of New Zealand. Wellington, 1882. 8vo. (89) A$140

Bullet, Jean Baptiste, 1699-1775
— Memoires sur la langue celtique. Besancon, 1754-60. 3 vols. Folio. (89) £180

Bullet, Pierre, 1639?-1716
— Architecture pratique, qui comprend la construction...des batimens. Paris, 1774. 8vo. (91) £50
— Verschyde Schoorsteen Mantels. Amst., [n.d.]. Folio. (88) £95

Bulliard, Pierre, 1742-93
— Aviceptologie francaise, ou traite general de tout les ruses...pour prendre les oiseaux.... Paris, 1778. 1st Ed. 12mo. Martin copy. (90) $300
Paris, 1808. 12mo. (89) $300
— Flora Parisiensis, ou descriptions et figures des plantes qui croissent aux environs de Paris.... Paris: Didot le jeune, 1776-83. 6 vols in 4 & Index. Together, 5 vols. 8vo. (91) £5,000
— Herbier de la France.... Paris, 1780-91. 8 vols, including the Dictionnaire elementaire de botanique & the Histoire des champignons. Folio. Sold w.a.f. (89) £4,000

Bulloch, James D., 1823-1901
— The Secret Service of the Confederate States in Europe.... NY, [1959]. 2 vols. 12mo. (90) $130

Bullock, William, fl.1808-28
— Le Mexique en 1823, ou relation d'un voyage.... Paris, 1824. 3 vols including Atlas. 8vo & oblong folio. (89) £250
— Six Months' Residence and Travels in Mexico.... L, 1824. 1st Ed. 8vo. (88) $80, £140; (91) £220
2d Ed. L, 1825. 2 vols. 8vo. (88) $275

Bullock, Wynn
— Wynn Bullock. San Francisco: Scrimshaw Press, 1971. 4to. (88) $100
Sgd on tp, 1973. (89) $180

Bullokar, John
— An English Expositor: teaching the Interpretation of the Hardest Words.... L, 1656. 8vo. (88) £650

Bullot, Maximilien, d.1748. See: Helyot & Bullot

Bull-us, Hector. See: Paulding, James Kirke

Bulwer, John
— Anthropometamorphosis: Man Transform'd. L, 1653. 2d Ed. 4to. (88) £350; (90) £200, £330
— Chirologia, or the Naturall Language of the Hand.... L, 1644. 8vo. Evelyn copy. (91) $3,600
Manchester copy. (90) $1,500
— Philocophus: or, the Deafe and Dumbe Mans Friend. L: for H. Moseley, 1648. 12mo. (88) £520; (90) £950

Bulwer-Lytton, Edward George Earle. See: Lytton, Edward George Earle Bulwer

BUMGARDNER

Bumgardner, Georgia B.
— American Broadsides. Barre, 1971. Folio. (91) $500

Bump, Gardiner —& Others
— The Ruffed Grouse. [Albany], 1947. 4to. (88) $70; (89) $50

Bunbury, Sir Charles James Fox, 1809-86
— Journal of a Residence at the Cape of Good Hope.... L, 1848. 8vo. (91) £60

Bunbury, Henry W., 1750-1811
— An Academy for Grown Horsemen. L, 1787. 1st Ed. Folio. (88) £140; (90) £100
3d Ed. L, 1808. 8vo. (90) £130
Bound with: Annals of Horsemanship. L, 1808. (91) $750
Folio. (91) £65
L, 1809. Illus by Thomas Rowlandson. 8vo. (90) £120; (91) $100
L, 1812. 4to. (88) £60
L, 1825. Illus by Rowlandson. 2 parts in 1 vol. 12mo. (89) $350
— Annals of Horsemanship. Dublin, 1792. 8vo. (88) $250; (91) $400
— Twenty-Two Plates Illustrative of Various Interesting Scenes in the Plays of Shakspeare. L, [1820's]. Folio. (91) $1,400

Bunce, Daniel
— Australasiatic Reminiscences of Twenty-Three Years' Wanderings in Tasmania.... Melbourne, 1857. 8vo. (90) A$850
— Travels with Dr. Leichhardt in Australia. Melbourne, 1859. 12mo. (90) A$550

Bunn, Alfred
— The Stage. L, 1840. 1st Ed. 3 vols. 8vo. (90) $150

Bunnell, Lafayette Houghton, 1824-1903
— Discovery of the Yosemite and the Indian War of 1851.... Chicago, [1880]. 1st Ed. 12mo. (89) $190; (90) $190
Inscr to S. A. Kemp. (89) $225

Bunsen, Robert Wilhelm
— Gasometrische Methoden.... Braunschweig, 1857. 8vo. (88) $500; (90) £150

Bunsen, Robert Wilhelm —& Berthold, Arnold A.
— Das Eisenoxydhydrat, ein Gegengift der arsenigen Saeure. Goettingen, 1834. 8vo. (88) $400

Bunting, Basil
— Loquitur. L, 1965. Ltd Ed. Folio. (88) £420

AMERICAN BOOK PRICES CURRENT

Bunyan, John, 1628-88
— The Acceptable Sacrifice: or the Excellency of a Broken Heart. L, 1691. 12mo. (88) £340
— Bunyan's Pilgrim's Progress...exhibited in a Metamorphosis, or a Transformation of Pictures. Hartford, 1821. 12mo. (88) $80
— A Defence of the Doctrine of Justification by Faith.... L, 1672. 4to. (89) £1,050
— Divine Emblems, or Temporal Things Spiritualized..... L, 1802. 12mo. (88) $180
— The Pilgrim's Progress. L, 1678. 1st Ed. 12mo. 45 (of 124) leaves only, with several missing leaves supplied from modern type facsimile. Bradley Martin copy. (90) $21,000
L: for N. Boddington, 1707. 12mo. (88) £380
Worcester: Isaiah Thomas, 1791. 8vo. (88) $100
Honolulu, 1842. ("Ka hele malihini ana mai keia ao aku a hiki i kela ao.....") 12mo. (88) $425; (91) $750
Doheny copy. (88) $650
L, 1880. One of 500. Illus by the Dalziel Brothers. 4to. (90) $90
NY, 1882. 8vo. (89) $60
NY, 1898. Illus by the Rhead brothers. 4to. (88) £50
L, [1899]. One of 750. Folio. (91) $100
L: Essex House Press, 1899. 16mo. (89) £85
See also: Cresset Press; Limited Editions Club; Nonesuch Press
— Voyage d'un chrestien vers l'eternite. Amst., 1685. 1st Ed in French. 12mo. (91) £4,200
— Works. NY, 1866. 4 vols. 4to. (91) $140

Bunyano, Stephano, Pseud.
— The Prettiest Book for Children. L: Newbery, [c.1795]. 12mo. (89) £600; (91) £250

Buonaiuti, B. Serafino
— Italian Scenery. L, 1806. 1st Ed. Folio. (90) £440
L, 1806 [plates watermarked 1818]. Folio. (89) £400

Buonanni, Filippo, 1638-1725
— Observationes circa viventia.... Rome, 1691. 2 parts in 1 vol. 4to. (90) $650

Buonarotti, Michelangelo, 1475-1564. See: Michelangelo Buonarotti

Buonarroti, Filippo
— Osservazioni sopra alcuni frammenti di vasi antichi.... Florence, 1716. Folio. Kissner copy. (91) £170

1032

Buonaventura, Federigo. See: Bonaventura, Federico

Burbank, Luther, 1849-1926
— Luther Burbank: His Methods and Discoveries and their Practical Application. NY: Luther Burbank Press, 1914-15. 12 vols. (90) $110, $130; (91) $80
14 vols. (88) $200

Burbidge, Frederick William Thomas, 1847-1905
— The Narcissus: its History and Culture. L, 1875. 8vo. (88) $600

Burbury, John
— A Relation of a Journey of Lord Henry Howard...to Constantinople. L, 1671. 12mo. Blackmer copy. (90) £400

Burchardus, Probst von Ursperg, d.1230
— Chronicon abbatis Urspergen a Nino rege Assyriorum magno: usque ad Fridericum II Romanorum imperatorem. Strassburg: Crato Mylius, 1537-38. ("Chronicum abbatis Urspergensis....") 2 parts in 1 vol. Folio. (90) DM2,000

Burchell, William John, 1782-1863
— Travels in the Interior of Southern Africa. L, 1822-24. 2 vols. 4to. (88) $2,250; (91) £320, £1,700
With half-titles present. (91) £2,400

Burchett, Josiah, 1666-1746
— A Complete History of the Most Remarkable Transactions at Sea. L, 1720. 1st Ed. Folio. (90) $375; (91) £320

Burckhardt, John Lewis, 1784-1817
— Arabic Proverbs.... L, 1830. 1st Ed. 4to. (91) £1,000
— Notes on the Bedouins and Wahabys. L, 1831. Ed by William Ouseley. 2 vols. 8vo. (88) £650
— Travels in Arabia. L, 1829. 2 vols. 8vo. (89) £290
4to. (89) $400; (91) £420
— Travels in Nubia. L, 1819. 4to. (88) £100; (89) £280; (90) $500, £350, £700
2d Ed. L, 1822. 4to. (88) £190
Blackmer copy. (90) £700
— Travels in Syria and the Holy Land. L, 1822. 4to. (88) £240; (89) £425, £280; (90) £600
Blackmer copy. (90) £900
— Voyages en Arabie. Paris, 1835. 3 vols. 8vo. Blackmer copy. (90) £700

Burckhardt, Rudolf F.
— Gewirkte Bildteppiche des XV und XVI Jahrhunderts im Historischen Museum zu Basel. Leipzig, 1923. Folio. (90) $350

Burder, Samuel
— Oriental Customs: or, an Illustration of the Sacred Scriptures. See: Fore-Edge Paintings

Burdick, Arthur Jared
— The Prospectors' Manual. Los Angeles, 1905. (88) $160

Burdon, Capt. William
— The Gentleman's Pocket-Farrier. L, 1737. 4th Ed. 12mo. (90) $160

Bure, Guillaume Francois de. See: De Bure, Guillaume Francois

Bureau of Ethnology.
— Twenty-Second Annual Report of the Bureau of American Ethnology to the Secretary of the Smithsonian Institution. See: United States of America

Burges, William
— Law Courts Commission. Report to the Courts of Justice Commission. L, 1867. Folio. Sgd. (89) £800

Burges, William, 1827-81
— Architectural Drawings. L, 1870. Folio. (91) $325

Burgess, Anthony
— A Clockwork Orange. L: Heinemann, [1962. (88) £130, £260
— Coaching Days of England. L, 1966. Oblong folio. (89) $50
— Time for a Tiger. L, 1956. (88) £130
— The Worm and the Ring. L, 1961. 1st Ed. (91) £155

Burgess, Edward
— American and English Yachts. NY, [1887]. Oblong folio. (89) $500

Burgess, Gelett, 1866-1951
— The Lark. San Francisco, 1895-97. Nos 1-24 plus Epilark in 2 vols. (90) $140
— The Master of Mysteries. Indianapolis, [1912]. (89) $110
— The Purple Cow! [San Francisco, 1895]. 1st Pbd Ed. 12mo. (88) $70; (90) $60, $80
Ns laid in. (90) $650

Burgess, J.
— The Rock-Temples of Elephanta or Gharapuri. Bombay, 1871. Photos by D. H. Sykes. 8vo. (90) $170

Burgess, Mike R. See: Reginald, Robert

Burgess, Renate
— Portraits of Doctors & Scientists in the Wellcome Institute.... L, 1973. Folio. (90) $70; (91) $50

Burgkmair, Hans, 1473-1531
See also: Vogtherr & Burgkmair
— Images des saintes de la famille de l'Empereur Maximilien I. Vienna, 1799. Folio. (91) $1,000
— Le Triomphe de l'Empereur Maximilien I. Vienna & L, 1796. Oblong folio. (89) £5,500

Burgo, Joannes de
— Pupilla oculi omnibus presbyteris precipue...summe necessaria. Strassburg, 1516. 4to. (90) £260; (91) £220

Burgoyne, Sir John, 1722-92
— A State of the Expedition from Canada.... L, 1780. 1st Ed. 4to. (88) £680
2d Ed. 4to. (90) $600, £500; (91) £700

Burgundia, Antonius A.
— Mundi Lapis Lydius.... Antwerp, 1639. 4to. (90) $2,000; (91) LIt1,800,000

Buridan, Jean, fl.1338-58
— Questiones super octo libros politicorum Aristotelis. Paris: Nicolaus des Prez for Jean Petit, 24 June 1513. Folio. Abrams copy. (90) £1,850

Burigny, Jean Levesque, 1692-1785
— Histoire des revolutions de l'empire de Constantinople.... Paris, 1750. 3 vols. 8vo. Blackmer copy. (90) £160

Burke & Wills Exploring Expedition
— An Account of the Crossing of...Australia.... Melbourne, 1861. 8vo. (89) A$880, A$1,900; (90) A$1,200
— Supplementary Pamphlet to the Burke and Wills Exploring Expedition. Melbourne, 1861. 8vo. (90) A$4,200

Burke, Edgar
— American Dry Flies and How to Tie Them. NY, 1931. One of 500. (90) $250; (91) $200, $275
12mo. Inscr to Joseph Bates, with Ls & 7 orig watercolor drawings of trout flies by Burke on front pastedown. (90) $900

Burke, Edmund, 1729-97
— An Account of the European Settlements in America. L, 1758. 2 vols. 8vo. (91) £300
3d Ed. L, 1760. 2 vols. 8vo. (91) $180
— A Letter from the Rt. Honourable Edmund Burke to the Duke of Portland on the Conduct of the Minority in Parliament.... L, 1797. 1st Ed, 1st impression. 8vo. (91) $110
— Maxims, Opinions and Characters, Moral, Political and Economical. See: Fore-Edge Paintings
— On Conciliation with the Colonies and Other Papers on the American Revolution. See: Limited Editions Club
— A Philosophical Enquiry into the Origin of our Ideas of the Sublime and Beautiful. L, 1757. 1st Ed. 8vo. (88) £320; (89) $325, £300
9th Ed. L, 1782. 8vo. (90) £170
2d Ed. L, 1790. 8vo. (90) $375
See also: Fore-Edge Paintings
— The Political Tracts and Speeches of Edmund Burke. Dublin, 1777. 8vo. ESTC 039974. (91) £65
— Reflections on the Revolution in France. Dublin, 1790. 8vo. (88) £85
1st Ed. L, 1790. 8vo. (89) $300; (90) £320
Martin copy. (90) $2,600
2d Ed. 8vo. (91) $150
2d impression. (90) $225
3d Ed. 8vo. (90) $90; (91) $60
— Speech of Edmund Burke Esq...Better Security of the Independence of Parliament.... 8vo. (90) £100
— Speech of Edmund Burke, Esq. on American Taxation, April 19, 1774. L, 1775. 1st Ed. 8vo. (90) $900
2d Ed. 8vo. (89) $175
— Speech of Edmund Burke...on Moving his Resolutions for Conciliation with the Colonies, March 22d, 1775. NY, 1775. 1st American Ed. 8vo. (91) $600
— Substance of the Speech...in the Debate on the Army Estimates.... L, 1790. 2d Ed. 8vo. (90) $160
— Two Letters Addressed to a Member of the Present Parliament on...Peace with the Regicide Directory of France. L, 1796. 1st Authorized Ed. 8vo. (88) $120; (90) $180
— Two Letters on the Conduct of our Domestick Parties....., L, 1797. 8vo. (90) $100
1st Ed, 3d impression. 8vo. (90) $180
— A Vindication of Natural Society. L, 1756. 8vo. (88) £380
— Works. Dublin, 1792-93. 3 vols. 8vo. ESTC 052809. (91) £240
L, 1792-1827. 8 vols. 4to. (91) £1,400
Vol III only. (90) $170
L, 1808. 8 vols. 8vo. (90) £130
L, 1823. 8 vols. 8vo. (89) £110
L, 1826-27. 16 vols. 8vo. (90) $130
16 vols in 8. 8vo. (91) £420
Bost., 1894-99. 12 vols. 8vo. (88) $135
Beaconsfield Ed. Bost., 1901. One of 1,000. 12 vols. (91) $70

Burke, H. Farnham
— The Historical Record of the Coronation of their Most Excellent Majesties King Edward VII and Queen Alexandra. Pvtly ptd, 1904. Folio. (88) £60; (90) £80

Burke, John, 1787-1848
— A Genealogical and Heraldic History of the Commoners of Great Britain and Ireland. L, 1836-38. 4 vols. 8vo. (90) $50

Burke, Mary Louise
— Kamehameha, King of the Hawaiian Islands. San Francisco: Colt Press, 1939. One of 90 hand-illuminated copies. Illus by Mallette Dean. Folio. (91) $55

Burley, Walter, 1275-1345?
— Super libros de physica auscultatione Aristotelis. Venice: heirs of O. Scotus, 1524. Folio. (88) £430

Burlington, Charles —& Others
— The Modern Universal British Traveller. L, 1779. Folio. (91) £340

Burlington Fine Arts Club—London

Catalogues of Exhibitions
— Ancient Greek Art. 1904. Folio. (89) $70
— Bookbindings. 1891. 4to. (88) £340; (89) $600; (91) £300
— Carvings in Ivory. 1923. 4to. (88) £70
— Collection of Counterfeits, Imitations and Copies of Works of Art. 1924. 4to. (90) £200
— Illuminated Manuscripts. 1908. 4to. (88) £200; (91) £240
  Doheny copy. (88) $280

Burliuk, David —& Others
— Chetyre Ptitsy. Moscow, 1916. 4to. Inscr by Burliuk. (88) £400

Burmannus, Joannes, 1707-79
— Thesaurus Zeylanicus.... Amst., 1737. 2 parts in 1 vol. 4to. (88) £420

Burmeister, Hermann
— Erlaeuterungen zur Fauna Brasiliens.... Berlin, 1856. Folio. (89) $750
— Genera Insectorum. Iconibus Illustravit et Descripsit. Volumen I. Rhynchota. Berlin, 1838. 8vo. (91) $140

Burn, Jacob Henry
— Catalogue of a Collection of Early Newspapers and Essayists, formed by...John Thomas Hope.... See: Bodleian Library

Burn, Richard. See: Nicolson & Burn, Richard

Burn, Robert, 1829-1904
— Rome and the Campagna: an Historical and Topographical Description.... Cambr. & L, 1871-76. 4to. (91) £55

Burn, Robert Scott
— Working Drawings and Designs in Architecture and Building. L & Edin., [c.1865]. Folio. (89) £110

Burnaby, Andrew, 1734-1812
— Travels through the Middle Settlements in North-America.... L, 1775. 8vo. (89) $150, £380; (90) $200; (91) $350

Burnand, R.
— Reims: La Cathedrale. Paris, [1918]. Pochoir illusts by E. G. Benito. Oblong 4to. (90) $50

Burne-Jones, Sir Edward Coley, 1833-98
— The Beginning of the World. L, 1902. 4to. (91) $175
— The Flower Book. L, 1905. One of 300. 4to. (88) £3,200; (90) $6,500, £5,500, £6,500; (91) £5,100
  Doheny copy. (89) $8,500
— In the Dawn of the World. Bost.: Goodspeed, 1903. One of 185. 4to. (88) $130
— The Work of.... L: Berlin Photographic Company, [c.1900]. One of 200. Folio. (90) $275

Burne-Jones, Lady Georgiana
— Memorials of Edward Burne-Jones. L, 1904. 2 vols. ALs inserted. (91) £80

Burnes, Alexander, 1805-41
— Travels into Bokhara. L, 1834. 1st Ed. 3 vols. 8vo. (89) $180, £190, £220, A$450; (91) £230
  2d Ed. L, 1835. 3 vols. 16mo. (91) $115

Burnes, James, 1801-62
— Narrative of a Visit to the Court of Sinde.... Edin, 1839. 8vo. (91) £300

Burnet, Gilbert, 1643-1715
— History of his Own Time. L, 1724-34. 1st Ed. 2 vols. Folio. (88) £80; (91) £260
  ESTC 144689. (91) £100
  L, 1753. 4 vols. 8vo. (91) £120
  Oxford, 1823. 6 vols. 8vo. (89) $600; (91) $150
  Oxford, 1833. 6 vols. 8vo. (91) $275
— The History of the Reformation of the Church of England. L, 1681-83-1715. 2d Ed. 3 vols. Folio. (90) £90
  Dublin, 1730-33. 3 parts in 3 vols. Folio. ESTC 119677. (91) £190

BURNET

L, 1825. 3 vols in 6. 12mo. (89) $110
Oxford, 1829. 3 vols in 6, plus Index vol. 8vo. (91) $225
— The Memoires of the Lives and Actions of James and William, Dukes of Hamilton and Castleherald.... L, 1677. Folio. (89) $80; (91) £55
— Some Passages of the Life and Death of...John, Earl of Rochester. L, 1680. 1st Ed. 8vo. (91) £65

Burnet, John, 1784-1868
— Practical Treatise on Paintings. L, 1827. 4to. (88) £65; (89) £140

Burnet, John, 1784-1868 —& Others
— Engravings from the Pictures of the National Gallery. L, 1840. Folio. (91) £250

Burnet, Thomas, 1635?-1715
— De statu mortuorum et resurgentium liber. L, 1723. 4to. (89) £165
— The Theory of the Earth. The Two First Books. L, 1684. 2 parts in 1 vol. Folio. (90) $550
  3d Ed. L, 1697. 3 parts in 1 vol. Folio. (91) £70

Burnet, Sir Thomas, 1694-1753
— A Second Tale of a Tub: or, the History of Robert Powel, the Puppet-Show-Man. L, 1715. 1st Ed. 8vo. (88) £280

Burnet, William
— An Essay on Scripture-Prophecy. NY, 1724. 4to. Presentation copy to H. Flynt. (89) $475

Burnett, Frances Hodgson, 1849-1924
— Little Lord Fauntleroy. NY, 1886. 1st Ed. 1st Issue. 4to. (88) $60; (89) $60; (91) $110
  2d Issue. (88) $80
  Issue not given. With ALs by Burnett. Martin copy. (90) $1,500
— Sara Crewe; or What Happened at Miss Minchin's.... L, 1888. 8vo. (88) $90
— The Secret Garden. NY, [1911]. Inscr. (91) $650
  L, [1914]. Illus by Charles Robinson. (88) $90

Burnett, M. A.
— Plantae Utiliores; or, Illustrations of Useful Plants Employed in the Arts and Medicine. L, [1839]-42-47-50. 4 vols in 2. 4to. (89) $2,400

Burnett, Peter Hardeman, 1807-95
— Recollections and Opinions of an Old Pioneer. NY, 1880. 1st Ed. 12mo. (88) $140; (91) $140, $160

Burnett, William. See: Dugdale & Burnett

Burnett, William Riley
— Little Caesar. NY, 1929. 1st Ed. (91) $55

Burney, Charles, 1726-1814
— Abhandlung ueber die Musik der Alten. Leipzig, 1781. 4to. (88) $120
— An Account of Musical Performances in Westminster-Abbey.... L, 1785. 1st Ed. 4to. With 1 additional plate. (89) £300
— A General History of Music. L, 1776-89. 4 vols. 4to. (89) $350, $550; (90) A$1,200
  4 vols. Vol I, 2d Ed; Vols II-IV, 1st Ed. L, 1789-82-89. 4to. (88) £110, £280
— The Present State of Music in France and Italy. L, 1771. 1st Ed. 8vo. (91) $230
  Inscr to H. L. Mencken by Fielding Garrison. (91) $350
— The Present State of Music in Germany, the Netherlands, and United Provinces. L, 1773. 1st Ed. 2 vols. 8vo. (91) $300

Burney, Frances, 1752-1840
— Camilla: Or a Picture of Youth. L, 1796. 1st Ed. 5 vols. 12mo. (88) £170; (89) $80, $140, £160
  Doheny copy. (89) $325
— Cecilia, or Memoirs of an Heiress. L, 1782. 5 vols. 12mo. (88) £90; (89) $175, £120; (91) $50, $160, £1,600
— Diary and Letters. L, 1842-46. 7 vols. 8vo. (88) $220; (91) $180, £170
  L, 1904-5. 6 vols. (88) £35
  Extra-illus with plates. (88) £340
— Evelina, Or, A Young Lady's Entrance into the World. L, 1778. 1st Ed. 3 vols. 12mo. (88) £3,500; (91) £5,200
  L, 1822. 8vo. (91) £280
— Memoirs of Doctor Burney, Arranged from his own Manuscripts.... L, 1832. 3 vols. 8vo. (88) $150

Burney, James, 1750-1821
— A Chronological History of the Discoveries in the South Sea.... L, 1803-17. 5 vols. 4to. (88) £550, £2,200; (89) $5,000, A$16,000
  5 vols in 4. 4to. (89) £5,000
  Vols I-II only. (91) £160
— A Chronological History of North-Eastern Voyages of Discovery.... L, 1819. 1st Ed. 8vo. (91) £250

Burnham, Daniel Hudson, 1846-1912
— Report on a Plan for San Francisco. [San Francisco, 1905]. 4to. (88) $225; (89) $120; (91) $200

Burns, Allan, 1781-1813
— Observations on the Surgical Anatomy of the Head and Neck. Edin., 1811. 1st Ed. 8vo. Inscr. (91) $180

Burns, Edward
— Coinage of Scotland. Edin., 1887. Ltd Ed. 3 vols. 4to. (88) £85, £260 One of 545. (89) $80

Burns, Eugene
— Advanced Fly Fishing.... Harrisburg, [1953]. (88) $60

Burns, John, 1774-1850
— The Anatomy of the Gravid Uterus. Salem & Bost., 1808. 8vo. (89) $80
— Obstetrical Works.... NY, 1809. 3 parts in 1 vol. 8vo. (91) $65

Burns, John Horne
— Lucifer with a Book. NY, [1949]. Inscr. (88) $50
— Memoirs of a Cow Pony.... Bost., [1906]. Inscr. (89) $180

Burns, Robert, 1759-96
— Alloway Kirk or Tam o' Shanter. L, [1795?]. 8vo. (90) $225
— The Fornicators Court. [Edin., c.1823]. Bound with: The Election, a New Song. 8vo. (89) $500
— Letters Addressed to Clarinda.... Glasgow, 1802. 1st Ed. 8vo. (89) £100
— Poems. See: Limited Editions Club
— Poems & Songs. L, 1860. 4to. Chevalier copy. (91) $3,000
— Poems, Chiefly in the Scottish Dialect. Kilmarnock, 1786. 1st Ed. 8vo. (89) $1,900 Glencairn-Bradley Martin copy. (90) $36,000
2d (1st Edin.) Ed. Edin., 1787. 8vo. (91) $140, $3,000, £180
Bradley Martin copy. (90) $2,750
Inscr by W. E. Gladstone. (91) £300
Issue with "skinking" on p.263. (89) $110, $250
Issue with "stinking" on p.263. (88) £130; (89) $200
3d (1st London) Ed. L, 1787. 8vo. (89) $325
NY, 1788. 8vo. (89) $250
Edin., 1793. 2 vols in 1. 12mo. Inscr to Frederick Maxwell. Mills-Benz-Fleming copy. (89) $3,200
Edin., 1794. 8vo. (89) $75
See also: Fore-Edge Paintings; Melville presentation copy, Herman
— Scots Ballads. L, [1939]. One of 320. Folio. (89) £50
— Works. L, 1819. Ed by James Currie. 4 vols. 8vo. George Shepheard's copy, extra-illus with 30 orig watercolor drawings by him. (91) $2,800
L, 1830. 2 vols. 8vo. (91) $80
L, 1834. 8 vols. 8vo. (88) $175; (89) $230
Edin., 1877-79. 6 vols. 8vo. (88) £150
Extra-illus with ports & scenes from poems. (91) $1,300
L, 1879. ("Poetical Works.") One of 500. 2 vols. 8vo. Chevalier copy. (91) $3,000
Edinburgh Ed. Phila., 1895-96. One of 50. 12 vols. 8vo. (90) $450

Burns, Thomas
— Old Scottish Communion Plate. Edin., 1892. Ltd Ed. 4to. (88) £50; (91) £50

Burr, Mrs. A. W.
— Sketches. [N.p., c.1850]. Folio. (90) £2,500

Burr, Aaron, 1756-1836
— The Private Journal.... Rochester, 1903. One of 250. 2 vols. (89) $80
[-] Reports of the Trial of Col. Aaron Burr.... Phila., 1808. In shorthand by David Robertson. 2 vols. 8vo. (91) $60, $250

Burr, David H., 1803-75
— An Atlas of the State of New York.... NY, 1829. Folio. (91) $3,000
— A New Universal Atlas. NY, [c.1835]. Folio. (91) $3,000

Burrell, Mary, d.1898
— Richard Wagner.... L, 1898. One of 100 on paper with watermark facsimile of Wagner's signature. Folio. (91) £170

Burritt, Elijah H., 1794-1838
— Atlas, Designed to Illustrate the Geography of the Heavens. NY, 1835. Folio. (88) $425; (90) £85; (91) £230

Burroughs, Edgar Rice, 1875-1950
— Apache Devil. Tarzana, [1933]. Inscr. (91) $425
— At the Earth's Core. Chicago, 1922. (89) $1,100; (91) $110, $1,700
— Back to the Stone Age. Tarzana, Calif., [1937]. 1st Ed. (89) $120; (90) $550; (91) $200
— The Beasts of Tarzan. Chicago, 1916. (90) $200
— Carson of Venus. Tarzana, [1939]. (89) $60, $225; (90) $70, $180, $200
— The Cave Girl. Chicago, 1925. (91) $90 1st Ed (91) $1,700
— The Chessmen of Mars. Chicago, 1922. Illus by J. Allen St. John. (91) $1,400
— The Deputy Sheriff of Comanche County. Tarzana, [1940]. (89) $140; (90) $140; (91) $275
— Escape on Venus. Tarzana, [1946]. (89) $50; (90) $50, $130; (91) $50, $70

BURROUGHS

- The Eternal Lover. Chicago, 1925. (91) $550
  1st Ed (91) $1,400
- A Fighting Man of Mars. NY: Metropolitan, [1931]. (90) $850; (91) $60
  NY: Canaveral Press, 1962. Galley proof. (90) $150
- The Girl from Hollywood. NY: Macaulay, [1923]. (91) $1,500
  Later Issue, with frontis caption lacking the words "he said". (90) $50
- The Gods of Mars. Chicago, 1918. (91) $100, $2,600
- I Am a Barbarian. Tarzana: Burroughs, [1967]. (90) $55
- John Carter of Mars. NY: Canaveral Press, 1964. Galley proofs. (90) $475
- Jungle Girl. Tarzana, [1932]. (89) $120
- Jungle Tales of Tarzan. Chicago, 1919. Illus by J. Allen St. John. (90) $50; (91) $55, $800
- The Lad and the Lion. Tarzana, [1938]. (89) $135; (90) $85; (91) $300
- Land of Terror. Tarzana, 1944. (89) $110; (90) $250; (91) $90
- The Land That Time Forgot. Chicago, 1924. In d/j. (91) $2,500
- Llana of Gathol. Tarzana, [1948]. (89) $50; (90) $65, $70
- The Mad King. Chicago, 1926. In d/j with small repairs. (91) $1,200
  In worn d/j. (91) $1,200
  1st Ed (91) $1,300
- The Master Mind of Mars. NY, 1927. 4to. In: Amazing Stories Annual, Vol 1. (91) $150
- The Moon Maid. Chicago, 1926. 1st Ed. (91) $2,400
- The Oakdale Affair - The Rider. Tarzana, [1937]. (89) $375
- Official Guide to the Tarzan Clan of America. Tarzana, 1939. (90) $350
- Pellucidar. Chicago, 1923. (89) $950; (91) $50, $80
  NY: Canaveral Press, 1962. Galley proofs. (90) $125
  L: Tom Stacy, [1971]. Sgd by Danton Burroughs, Johnny Weissmuller & Jock Mahoney. (90) $110
- Pirates of Venus. Tarzana, [1934]. (90) $475
  1st Ed. Tarzana, Calif., [1934]. Illus by J. Allen St. John. In torn d/j. (90) $375
- A Princess of Mars. Chicago, 1917. (90) $300; (91) $70
- The Return of Tarzan. Chicago 1915. (89) $80
- Savage Pellucidar. NY: Canaveral Press, 1963. (90) $120
- Swords of Mars. Tarzana: Burroughs, [1936]. (89) $170; (90) $450
- Synthetic Men of Mars. Tarzana, Calif., [1940]. 1st Ed. (89) $130; (90) $350; (91) $130
- Tales of Three Planets. NY: Canaveral Press, 1964. (90) $130
  Galley proofs. (90) $225
- Tanar of Pellucidar. NY, [1930]. 1st Ed. (91) $300, $400
  In d/j. (90) $550
  In repaired d/j. (89) $350
  In worn & chipped d/j. (89) $50
- Tarzan and the Jewels of Opar. Chicago, 1918. (89) $50, $65; (91) $65
  In d/j. (91) $1,200
  NY: Grosset & Dunlap, 1918 [but later]. (91) $50
- Tarzan and the Golden Lion. Chicago, 1923. (88) $250; (90) $225, $1,300; (91) $1,200
- Tarzan and the Ant Men. Chicago, 1924. 1st Ed. (91) $900
- Tarzan and the Lost Empire. NY: Metropolitan, [1929]. 1st Ed. (90) $400; (91) $350, $450
- Tarzan and the City of Gold. Tarzana, [1933]. (89) $100
- Tarzan and the Leopard Men. Tarzana, [1935]. 1st Ed. In d/j. (90) $425
  Illus by J. Allen St. John. (89) $140
  In chipped d/j. (91) $180, $250
  In frayed d/j. (90) $450
- Tarzan and the Forbidden City. Tarzana: Burroughs, [1938]. (89) $90; (90) $190, $425
- Tarzan and the Foreign Legion. Tarzana, [1947]. (88) $55; (89) $50; (90) $55
  Inscr to author's grandson. (89) $65
- Tarzan and "The Foreign Legion." Tarzana: Burroughs, [1947]. (91) $60
- Tarzan and the Madman. NY: Canaveral Press, 1964. Galley proof. (90) $200
- Tarzan and the Castaways. NY: Canaveral Press, 1965. (90) $120
- Tarzan at the Earth's Core. NY: Metropolitan, [1930]. (90) $200
  In d/j. (91) $1,600
- Tarzan, Lord of the Jungle. Chicago: A. C. McClurg, 1928. (90) $1,400
  2d Ptg. (91) $800
- Tarzan of the Apes. [N.p.], 1912. In: The All-Story, Vol XXIV, Oct 1912. Bound at end is New Stories of Tarzan, extracted from Blue Book Magazine, Sept 1916-Aug 1917. (89) $600
  1st Ed. NY, 1912. In: The All-Story. Vol 24, No 2. Martin copy. (90) $8,000
  Chicago, 1914. 1st Ptg. (90) $250; (91) $600
  1st Ed in Book form. Martin copy. (90) $24,000

NY: Grosset & Dunlap, [1927]. (90) $140; (91) $90
— Tarzan the Invincible. Tarzana, [1931]. (89) $80; (90) $140; (91) $50, $225
— Tarzan the Magnificent. Tarzana, [1936]. (89) $150
— Tarzan the Terrible. Chicago, 1921. (91) $110
  In chipped d/j. (91) $1,200
  L: Methuen, 1921. (90) $100
— Tarzan the Untamed. Chicago, 1920. (88) $100; (89) $90; (90) $60, $60
— Tarzan Triumphant. Tarzana: Burroughs, [1932]. 1st Ed. (90) $250, $325; (91) $150
— Tarzan's Quest. Tarzana, [1936]. (89) $160; (91) $250
— Thuvia, Maid of Mars. Chicago, 1920. (89) $70; (91) $65
  In soiled d/j. (91) $1,300
— The War Chief. Chicago, 1927. In d/j. (91) $650
  In soiled & chipped d/j. (89) $850
  In soiled d/j. (91) $1,600
— The Warlord of Mars. Chicago, 1919. 1st Ed, 1st Issue. (89) $50
  Issue not indicated. (90) $55
  In chipped d/j. (91) $1,400

Burroughs, John, 1837-1921
— Notes on Walt Whitman.... NY, 1867. 12mo. Martin copy. (90) $1,600
— Works. Bost., 1904-22. Autograph Ed. One of 750. 23 vols. (88) $80
  Vols 1-15 (of 23). ALs tipped in. (91) $850
  Vols 1-19 (of 23). (89) $475; (90) $700
  Bost., 1904-08. Vols I-XV (of 23). (88) $475

Burroughs, William S.
— Ali's Smile. Brighton, 1971. One of 99. (91) $150
— Blade Runner (a movie). Berkeley: Blue Wind Press, 1979. One of 100. (89) $100
— The Naked Lunch. NY, [1959]. 1st American Ed. (91) $55
  1st Ed. Paris, [1959]. Issue not given. (91) $375

Burrow, J. C. —& Thomas, William
— 'Mongst Mimes and Miners.... L, 1893. 4to. Inscr. (91) £440

Burrows, George Man, 1771-1846
— Commentaries on the Causes, Forms...of Insanity. L, 1828. 8vo. (91) $750
— An Inquiry into Certain Errors Relative to Insanity.... L, 1820. 1st Ed. 8vo. (91) $425

Burrows, Robert
— Extracts from a Diary during Heke's War in the North, in 1845. Auckland, 1886. 8vo. Fragment of ALs inserted. (88) £90

Burrus, Ernest J.
— Kino and the Cartography of Northwestern New Spain. [Tucson], 1965. One of 750. Folio. (88) $170

Bursill, Henry
— Hand Shadows to be Thrown upon the Wall.... L, 1860. 4th Ed. 4to. (91) £85

Burt, William Austin
— Report on the Geography, Topography, and Geology of...the South Shore of Lake Superior. See: Thoreau's copy, Henry David

Burthogge, Richard
— An Essay upon Reason, and the Nature of Spirits. L, 1694. 1st Ed. 8vo. (91) $225

Burton, Alfred. See: Mitford, John

Burton, Lady Isabel, 1831-96
— The Inner Life of Syria, Palestine and the Holy Land. L, 1876. 2 vols. 8vo. Blackmer copy. (90) £200

Burton, John, 1697-1771
— An Essay Towards a Complete New System of Midwifery.... L, 1751. 8vo. (89) £170; (91) £400
  Some plates frayed; some foxing; a few plates torn with peripheral loss. (88) $550

Burton, Sir Richard Francis, 1821-90
— The Book of the Sword. L, 1884. 8vo. (88) £200; (89) £200; (91) $300, £150, £160
  ALs, 29 Nov 1883, inserted at beginning. (91) £340
— The City of the Saints, and Across the Rocky Mountains to California. L, 1861. 1st Ed. 8vo. (88) £140; (89) £80; (90) $200
  2d Ed. L, 1862. 8vo. (88) £65
— Explorations of the Highlands of the Brazil. L, 1869. 1st Ed. 2 vols. 8vo. (90) £350
  Vol II (of 2) only. 8vo. (88) $600
  Proof copy. 2 vols. 8vo. (88) £400
— Falconry in the Valley of the Indus. L, 1852. 1st Ed. 12mo. (88) £650; (89) £340
— First Footsteps in East Africa. L, 1856. 8vo. (88) R2,400; (89) £320; (91) £400
  Martin copy. (90) $1,100
  Memorial Ed. L, 1894. 2 vols. 8vo. (90) £80
— Goa, and the Blue Mountains. L, 1851. 1st Ed, 2d Issue. 12mo. (90) $225; (91) $500, $500
— The Guide-Book. A Pictorial Pilgrimage to Mecca and Medina. L, 1865. 8vo. Martin

BURTON

copy. (90) $7,000
— The Kasidah.... L, 1880. 1st Ed. 4to. Martin copy. (90) $1,200
2d Issue. (88) £180
Portland ME: Thomas Bird Mosher, 1915. One of 20 ptd on japon vellum. Folio. (90) $190
San Francisco, 1919. One of 500. Folio. (90) $65; (91) $55
— The Kasidah of Haji Abdu el Yezdi. See: Limited Editions Club
— The Lake Regions of Central Africa. L, 1860. 1st Ed. 2 vols. 8vo. (88) R1,700; (89) £280; (90) £800; (91) $900, £750
— The Land of Midian Revisited. L, 1879. 1st Ed. 2 vols. 8vo. (88) £300
— The Lands of Cazembe, Lacerda's Journey to Cazembe in 1798. L, 1873. 1st Ed. 8vo. (90) £80, £160; (91) $250
— Letters from the Battlefields of Paraguay. L, 1870. 1st Ed. 8vo. (89) £250
— A Mission to Gelele, King of Dahome. L, 1864. 1st Ed. 2 vols. 8vo. (91) $150
— A New System of Sword Exercise for Infantry. L, 1876. 8vo. Inscr. Martin copy. (90) $6,500
— The Nile Basin. L, 1864. 1st Ed. 8vo. (89) £55; (90) £60
Martin copy. (90) $1,600
— Personal Narrative of a Pilgrimage to El-Medinah and Meccah. L, 1855-56. 1st Ed. 3 vols. 8vo. (88) £650, £750, £750; (89) £650; (90) £1,100, £2,800; (91) £950
Martin copy. (90) $1,900
NY, 1856. 8vo. (89) $75
2d Ed. L, 1857. 2 vols. 8vo. (91) £160
— Scinde; or, the Unhappy Valley. L, 1851. 2d Ed. 2 vols. 8vo. (88) R650
— Ultima-Thule, or a Summer in Iceland. L, 1875. 1st Ed. 2 vols. 8vo. (88) £110, £130; (91) $325
— Vikram and the Vampire. L, 1870. 1st Ed, 2d Issue. 8vo. (90) $130, £150
— Voyage aux Grands Lacs de l'Afrique Orientale. 8vo,.. orig half mor (88) £120
— Wanderings in West Africa. L, 1863. 2 vols. 8vo. (88) R900; (89) $325
— Wanderings in Three Continents.... L, 1901. 1st Ed. (89) £110; (91) $95
— Zanzibar: City, Island and Coast. L, 1872. 1st Ed. 2 vols. 8vo. (88) R1,200; (90) £210, £300

Burton, Sir Richard Francis, 1821-90 —& Cameron, Verney Lovett, 1844-94
— To the Gold Coast for Gold. L, 1883. 1st Ed. 2 vols. 8vo. (91) $250

AMERICAN BOOK PRICES CURRENT

Burton, Sir Richard Francis, 1821-90 —& Drake, Charles F. T.
— Unexplored Syria. L, 1872. 2 vols. 8vo. (90) £280
Blackmer copy. (90) £500

Burton, Robert, 1577-1640
— The Anatomy of Melancholy. Oxford, 1621. 1st Ed. 4to. (88) $3,800
Adam-Leo-Martin-Fleming copy. (89) $3,800
Doheny copy. (89) $5,000
Hazell-Bemis-Greenhill-Bradley Martin copy. (90) $31,000
Houghton-The Garden copy. (90) $40,000
Schiff copy. (91) $6,500
2d Ed. Oxford, 1624. Folio. (89) $80, $500; (91) £55
Ashburnham copy. (90) $900
STC 4160. (91) £350
4th Ed. Oxford, 1632. Folio. (89) $325, £300; (91) £500
5th Ed. Oxford, 1638. Folio. (88) $400, £130, £500; (90) $190
6th Ed. L, 1652. 2d Issue. Folio. (89) £260
7th Ed. L, 1660. Folio. (90) $250
8th Ed. L, 1676. Folio. (89) $175, $250; (91) $135
L, 1800. Extra-illus with 100 ports & views. (88) £260
Bost., 1859. 3 vols. 8vo. (91) $100
L, 1866. Folio. (91) $110
See also: Nonesuch Press

Burton, Sir Richard Francis, 1821-90
— The Kasidah of Haji Abdu el Yezdi. See: Limited Editions Club

Burton, W. K. See: Milne & Burton

Burton, William, 1575-1645
— The Description of Leicester Shire.... L, [1622]. 1st Ed. Folio. (89) £220
With signature of Robert Burton & with notes in his hand. (89) $950

Burton, William, 1609-57
— A Commentary on Antoninus his Itinerary.... L, 1658. Folio. (89) £80; (91) £65
Huth copy. (88) £380

Burton, William, b.1863
— A General History of Porcelain. L, 1921. 2 vols. (88) $85; (89) $50, $55; (90) $70; (91) $110
— A History and Description of English Earthenware and Stoneware. L, 1904. One of 1,450. (91) $60
Out-of-series copy. (89) $90
— Josiah Wedgwood and his Pottery. L, 1922. One of 1,500. (89) $140, $150; (90) $110

Burton Library, William Evans
— [Sale catalogue] Bibliotheca Dramatica. Catalogue of the Theatrical and Miscellaneous Library of.... [NY, 1860]. Compiled by Joseph Sabin. 4to. L.p. copy. (89) $350

Bury, Adrian
— Joseph Crawhall, the Man and the Artist. L. 1958 [1957]. One of 990. 4to. (89) £130

Bury, Lady Charlotte, 1775-1861
— The Three Great Sanctuaries of Tuscany. L. 1833. Oblong folio. (89) £95

Bury, Mrs. Edward
— A Selection of Hexandrian Plants.... L. 1831-34. Folio. (88) £36,000; (89) £30,000

Bury, Priscilla Susan. See: Bury, Mrs. Edward

Bury, Richard de, 1287-1345
— Philobiblon. Oxford: Joseph Barnes, 1599. ("Philobiblon, sive de amore librorum....") 4to. Martin copy. (90) $26,000
— The Philobiblon. L, 1888. One of 50 L.p. copies. Ed & trans by Ernest C. Thomas. 8vo. (88) DM650
Oxford, 1960. 4to. (91) £50
See also: Grabhorn Printing
— Philobiblon. See: Grolier Club

Bury, Thomas Talbot, 1811-77
— Coloured Views of the Liverpool and Manchester Railway. L, 1831. 4to. (88) £1,400; (90) $1,000; (91) £3,500
Part 1 only. 4to. (91) $800

Busbecq, Ogier Ghislain de, 1522-92
— Embaxada y viages de Constantinopla y Amasea.... Pamplona: Carlos de Labayen, 1610. 8vo. Phillipps-Blackmer copy. (90) £300
— The Four Epistles of A. G. Busbequius Concerning his Embassy into Turkey. L, 1694. 8vo. Blackmer copy. (90) £700
— Itinera Constantinopolitanum et Amasianum.... Antwerp: Christopher Plantin, 1581. 8vo. Blackmer copy. (90) £2,000.
— Legationis Turcicae epistolae quatuor. Frankfurt, 1595. 8vo. Blackmer copy. (90) £360
— Opera. Leiden: Elzevir, 1633. 12mo. (90) $70
Blackmer copy. (90) £50

Busby, James
— A Treatise on the Culture of the Vine.... [Sydney], 1825. Thick paper issue. 4to. (89) A$8,800

Busby, Thomas Lord
— Costume of the Lower Orders in Paris. [L, c.1820]. Bound with: Busby. The Fishing Costume and Local Scenery of Hartlepool.... L, 1819. 12mo. (88) $1,300, £160; (89) £550; (91) $425
— Costume of the Lower Orders of the Metropolis. L, [c.1820]. 8vo. (88) £260

Busch, Julius Hermann Moritz —& Loeffler, August
— La Grece pittoresque. Trieste: Julius Ohswaldt, 1871. Folio. Blackmer copy. (90) £200

Busche, Alexander van den
— The Orator. L: A. Islip, 1596. 4to. STC 4182. (91) $1,500

Busenello, Giovanni Francesco, 1598-1659
— A Prospective of the Naval Triumph of the Venetians over the Turk. L, 1658. 8vo. (91) £350

Bush, Martin H.
— The Passion of Sacco and Vanzetti. Syracuse, 1968. One of 200. Illus by Ben Shahn. (88) $110

Bushnell, Stephen Wootton, 1844-1908
— Oriental Ceramic Art Illustrated by Examples from the Collection of W. T. Walters. NY, 1897. One of 500. 10 vols. Folio. (89) $2,250; (91) $1,800

Bustamante, Carlos Maria de
— El Nuevo Bernal Diaz del Castillo.... Mexico, 1847. 2 vols in 1. 8vo. (89) $500; (91) £150

Bustamente Carlos, Calixto
— El Lazarillo de ciegos caminantes desde Buenos Aires.... Gijon [but Lima], 1773. 8vo. (88) £1,900

Busti, Bernardinus de
— Mariale. Milan: Leonardus Pachel, 21 May 1493. 4to. 337 (of 388) leaves. Goff B-1333. (88) $750
388 leaves. Goff B-1333. (89) £1,000

Butcher, Edmund —& Haesler, H.
— Sidmouth Scenery, or Views of the Principal Cottages and Residences of the Nobility and Gentry. Sidmouth, [1816-17]. 8vo. (88) £340, £680; (89) £450

Bute, John Stuart, 3d Earl of
— Botanical Tables Containing the Different Familys of British Plants.... [L, 1785?]. One of 12. Illus by John Miller. 9 vols. 4to. With gilt ownership stamp "E. C. Weymouth," for Elizabeth Cavendish

Bentinck Weymouth, who became the 1st Marchioness of Bath. (89) £32,000

Butler, Alfred Joshua, 1850-1936
— The Ancient Coptic Churches of Egypt. Oxford, 1884. 2 vols. 8vo. Blackmer copy. (90) £260
— Islamic Pottery: a Study Mainly Historical. L, 1926. Folio. (88) $150, £190

Butler, Arthur Gardiner, 1844-1925
— Birds of Great Britain and Ireland. L, [1907-8]. 2 vols. 4to. (88) £140; (89) £170; (90) £140, £150, £300
— Birds of Great Britain and Ireland. Order Passeres. L, [1907-8]. 2 vols. 4to. (91) £80
— Birds of Great Britain and Ireland. L, [1907-8]. 2 vols. 4to. Martin copy. (90) $300
— Foreign Finches in Captivity. L, 1894-[96]. 1st Ed. 4to. (88) £400
"A very fine copy." Bradley Martin copy. (89) $3,500
With 2 Ms corrections to the intro by the author. Arthur Gardiner Butler—Bradley Martin copy. (89) $2,250
2d Ed. L, 1899. 4to. (88) £90, £110, £170, £170; (89) £100, £120; (90) £150, £200; (91) $270
ALs laid in. (90) £180

Butler, Arthur Gardiner, 1844-1925 —& Others
— British Birds, their Nests and Eggs. L, [1896-99]. 6 vols. 4to. (88) £50; (90) £45

Butler, Arthur Stanley George
— The Architecture of Sir Edwin Lutyens. L, 1930. 3 vols. With: Hussey, Christopher E. C. The Life of Sir Edward Lutyens. L, 1950. Together, 4 vols. Folio. (90) £700
— The Architecture of Sir Edward Lutyens. L, 1950. 3 vols. Folio. (89) £640; (90) £250; (91) £220
With: Hussey, Christopher, E. C. The Life of Sir Edward Lutyens. L, 1950. Together, 4 vols. Folio & 4to. (88) £700
With: Hussey, Christopher, E. C. The Life of Sir Edward Lutyens. L, 1950 (88) £700
With: Hussey, Christopher, E. C. The Life of Sir Edward Lutyens. L, 1950 (91) £350
L, [1984]. 3 vols. Folio. (91) £170

Butler, Charles, d.1647
— The Feminin Monarchi, or the Histori of Bees. Oxford, 1634. 1st Ed. 4to. (88) £380; (89) £375; (91) DM1,100

Butler, Ellis Parker, 1869-1937
— Pigs Is Pigs. Copies of the 1905 & 1906 Eds with related material & both inscr, formerly in the Parsons collection, sold in the Fleming sale at CNY in 1989. (89) $1,800

Butler, Henry
— South African Sketches. L, 1841. Folio. (90) £220; (91) $475, £220

Butler, Joseph, 1692-1752
— The Analogy of Religion, Natural and Revealed.... L, 1736. 4to. (90) $175
Butler's copy. (89) $900

Butler, Mann, 1784-1852
— A History of the Commonwealth of Kentucky. Lexington, Ky., 1834. 1st Ed. 12mo. (90) $150

Butler, Richard
— An Essay concerning Blood-Letting. L, 1734. 8vo. (88) $1,100

Butler, Samuel, Settler in Australia
— The Hand-Book for Australian Emigrants.... Glasgow, 1839. 12mo. (89) A$400

Butler, Samuel, 1612-80
— Hudibras. L, 1663-64. 2 vols in 1. 8vo. (88) $90
L, 1694. 2 parts in 1 vol. 8vo. (88) R240; (91) $200
L, 1720. 12mo. Inscr by John Craven, Charles Wesley & Sally Wesley. (88) £380
L, 1726. Illus by Hogarth. 12mo. (89) $110; (90) £70
3 parts in 1 vol. 12mo. (89) $200
Dublin, 1732. Illus by Wm. Hogarth. 12mo. (88) $65
L, 1732. 12mo. (90) $50
Cambr. & L, 1744. 2 vols. 8vo. (89) £50; (90) £60, $140
L, 1793. 3 vols. 4to. (88) £120; (91) $250, £460
4 vols, including Notes on Hudibras. 4to. L.p. copy. Extra-illus with plates. (91) £650
L, 1806. Ed by Zachary Grey; illus by Wm. Hogarth. 2 vols. 8vo. (88) DM600
Ed not specified. L, 1819. 2 vols. 8vo. (88) £40; (89) £55; (90) £50
Extra-illus with c.200 plates. (90) $475
New Ed. 2 vols. 8vo. (91) $175
L, 1822. Illus by J. Clark. 2 vols. 8vo. (88) $1,200, £100; (90) £85; (91) $55
See also: Fore-Edge Paintings
— Hudibras, The First & Second Parts. The Third and Last Part. L, 1674 & 1678. 2 parts in one vol. Folio. (90) $1,100

Butler, Samuel, 1774-1839
— Atlas of Antient Geography. L, 1822. 8vo. (91) £65

Butler, Samuel, 1835-1902
— The Authoress of the Odyssey.... L, 1897. 1st Ed. 8vo. Inscr to Desmond MacCarthy, 1901. (88) $400; (90) $250
— Erewhon. L, 1872. 1st Ed. 8vo. (91) $130

See also: Gregynog Press; Limited Editions Club
— The Way of All Flesh. L, 1903. 1st Ed. (90) $80; (91) £425
— Works. L, 1923-26. Shrewsbury Ed, One of 750. 19 (of 20) vols; lacking Vol IV. (91) £50
20 vols. (88) £220

Butlin, Martin
— The Paintings and Drawings of William Blake. New Haven: Yale Univ., 1981. 2 vols. 4to. (89) £100; (91) £70

Butor, Michel
— Mobile. Paris, 1962. One of 25 on van Gelder. 4to. (90) $4,000
— Les Mots de la Peinture. Geneva, 1969. One of 175. 4to. (88) FF2,000

Butron, Juan de
— Discursos apologeticos en que se defiende la ingenuidad del arte de la pintura. Madrid, 1626. 4to. (89) $475

Butsch, Albert Fidelis
— Die Buecher-Ornamentik der Renaissance. Leipzig: G. Hirth, 1878. Folio. (88) $100

Butterfield, Consul Willshire, 1824-99
— An Historical Account of the Expedition against Sandusky.... Cincinnati, 1873. 8vo. (90) $60
— History of Brule's Discoveries and Explorations.... Cleveland, 1898. 8vo. (91) $80

Butterworth, Benjamin
— The Growth of Industrial Art. Wash., 1892. Folio. (91) £190, £240

Butterworth, Edwin —&
Tait, Arthur Fitzwilliam
— Views on the Manchester and Leeds Railway. L, 1845. Folio. (88) £500

Button, Henry
— Flotsam and Jetsam. Launceston, 1909. (90) A$140

Butts, Mary
— Imaginary Letters. Paris, 1928. One of 250. Illus by Jean Cocteau. 4to. Anthony Butts's copy, with unsgd autograph Ms poem laid in loose. (91) $160

Buttura, Antonio
— A Napoleone il Grande...ode. Paris: Didot, 1807. 12mo. (89) FF12,000

Buxton, Sir Thomas Powell, 1837-1915
— The African Slave Trade. L, 1840. 8vo. (88) $80; (89) $75
ALs inserted. (91) £130
— An Inquiry, whether Crime and Misery are Produced or Prevented, by our Present System of Prison Discipline. L, 1818. 8vo. (89) £240

Buxtorf, Joannes, 1564-1629
— De abbreviaturis hebraicis liber novus.... Basel: L. Regis, 1640. 2d Ed. 8vo. (89) $300
— Epitome grammaticae Hebreae. Basel: Ludovici Regis, 1620. 12mo. (90) $100
— Lexicon Chaldaicum Talmudicum et Rabbinicum. Basel, 1640 [engraved title dated 1639]. Folio. (88) $325, £85
— Schoole der Jooden. Leiden, 1702. 8vo. (89) $500
— Synagoga Judaica. Basel: Koenig, 1661. 8vo. (89) $350
Frankfurt: Kraussen, 1728. 8vo. (89) $2,400
Leipzig, 1738. 8vo. (90) $750

Buxtorf, Johannes, 1564-1629
— Concordantiae bibliorum Hebraicae. Basel, 1632. Folio. (91) $200
— Synagoga Judaica. Das ist Erneuerte jeudische Synagog.... Leipzig, 1738. 8vo. (91) DM1,100

Buy de Mornas, Claude, d.1783
— Atlas methodique et elementaire. Paris, 1761. Vol I (of 4). Folio. (89) £110

Byam, Lydia
— A Collection of Exotics from the Island of Antigua. [L, 1797]. Folio. (90) £1,600
De Belder—Fleming copy. (89) $6,500

Byell, Sir Charles, 1797-1875
— A Second Visit to the United States. L, 1849. 1st Ed. 2 vols. 8vo. (91) $175

Byers, Douglas S. —& Others
— The Pre-history of the Tehuacan Valley. Austin: Univ. of Texas Press, [1967-71]. 5 vols. Folio. (91) $80

Byne, Arthur —&
Stapley, Mildred
— Decorated Wooden Ceilings in Spain. NY, [1920]. Folio. (90) $50
— Majorcan Houses and Gardens. NY, 1928. (91) $140

Bynner, Witter. See: Ford & Bynner

Byrd, Richard Evelyn, 1888-1957
— Alone. NY, 1938. One of 1,000. Illus by Richard E. Harrison. (89) $160
— Discovery: the Story of the Second Byrd Antarctic Expedition. NY, 1935. 1st Ed. (91) $85
Inscr. (91) $80
Out-of-series copy, sgd. (89) $60; (91) $120
— Little America: Aerial Exploration in the Antarctic.... NY, 1930. Sgd. (89) $110
Sgd on flyleaf. (91) $55
Sgd on half-title. (91) $80
One of 1,000. (88) $90; (89) $100; (90) $200; (91) $85, $100
Presentation copy numbered P4. Inscr. (88) $65
— Skyward. NY, 1928. One of 500. 4to. (91) $50

Byrne, J. C.
— Twelve Years' Wanderings in the British Colonies.... L, 1848. 2 vols. 8vo. (88) A$350

Byrne, William. See: Hearne & Byrne

Byrom, John, 1692-1763
— Miscellaneous Poems. Manchester, 1773. 2 vols. 8vo. L.p. copy. (88) $140
— The Universal English Short-Hand. Manchester, 1767. 1st Ed. 8vo. (89) £150

Byron, George Anson, Baron Byron
— Voyage of H.M.S. Blonde to the Sandwich Islands. L, 1826. 1st Ed. 4to. (88) £340; (89) $1,600, £900

Byron, George Gordon Noel, Lord, 1788-1824
— Beppo, a Venetian Story. [Kentfield, Calif.]: Allen Press, 1963. ("A Venetian Story.") One of 150. Oblong folio. (89) $400; (91) $325
— Byron's Letters and Journals. Cambr., 1973-82. Ed by Leslie Marchand. 12 vols. Vol I sgd & inscr by Marchand. (88) $55
[-] The Centenary of Byron's Death in England: Two Addresses Delivered by Demetrius Caclamanos (Minister for Greece). L, 1924. Ltd Ed. (88) $50
— Childe Harold's Pilgrimage. L, 1812-18. 1st Ed, 2d Issue of Canto III, all 5 issues of Canto IV. 4 cantos in 7 vols. 4to. Bradley Martin copy. (90) $1,400
3d Issue of Cantos I & II; 1st Issue of Canto III; Canto IV Issue not specified. 4 cantos in 3 vols. 4to. With Byron's ANs [n.d.] to John Murray, sgd B, bound into 1st vol. (90) $3,500
1st Ed of Cantos I & II. L, 1812. 4to. Spoor-Bradley Martin copy. (90) $400
— Childe Harold's Pilgrimage. Canto the Fourth. L, 1818. 1st Ed, Issue not indicated. 8vo. (88) £30
Mixed Issue. (91) $120
— Childe Harold's Pilgrimage. A Romaunt. L, 1841. 8vo. (91) $350
— Childe Harold's Pilgrimage. See: Fore-Edge Paintings
— The Curse of Minerva. L, 1812. 4to. Terry-Tinker-Martin copy. (90) $14,000
— Don Juan. L, 1819-23. 2d Ed of Cantos I-II, 1st Eds of Cantos III-XVI. 6 vols. 8vo. (88) $100
L: A. M. Philpot, 1924. 8vo. Doheny copy. (88) $750
— Don Juan. Cantos I & II. L, 1819. 1st Ed. 4to. (90) $225, £300
— Don Juan. Cantos I-XVII. L, 1819-24. 1st Ed. 6 vols. 8vo. (90) $1,600
6 vols in 4. 4to & 8vo. Bradley Martin copy. (90) $2,500
— English Bards and Scotch Reviewers. L, [1809]. 1st Ed, 1st Issue. 12mo. Bradley Martin copy. (90) $1,300
2d Issue. (88) £110
Issue not given. (90) $325
With Critique, from the Edinburgh Review, on Byron's Poems which occasioned this book.. (91) $300
— The Giaour, a Fragment of a Turkish Tale. L, 1813. 6th Ed, variant with proper wording to the quote by Moore on tp. 8vo. (88) $80
— Hebrew Melodies. L, 1815. 1st Ed, Issue not stated. 8vo. (88) $150; (91) $600
— Hours of Idleness. Newark, 1807. 1st Ed. 8vo. (88) £600; (89) £420; (90) $1,300, £750; (91) $1,000, £450
L, 1820. 8vo. (89) $225
— The Lament of Tasso. L, 1817. 1st Ed. 8vo. (90) $175
— Letters and Journals of.... L, 1830. 2 vols. (88) $95; (90) £140
2 vols in 4. 4to. Extra-illus with autograph envelope addressed by Byron & an ALs from Lady Anne Byron. (91) $600
3 vols. 4to. Extra-illus with c.200 engraved ports. (89) $400
— Letters Written by Lord Byron during his Residence at Missolonghi...to Mr. Samuel Barff at Zante. Naples: Pvtly ptd, 1884. 4to. Inscr by a member of the Barff family to the Duchess of St. Albans. Newstead Abbey—Blackmer copy. (90) £300
— Manfred, a Dramatic Poem. Brussels: Ptd at the British Press, [c.1817]. Pirated Ed. 8vo. (90) £260
1st Ed. L, 1817. 1st Issue. 8vo. (89) $225; (90) $300
3d Issue. (89) $60
L: Fanfrolico Press, 1929. Out-of-series copy. Illus by Frederick Carter. 4to. (89) £90
— Marino Faliero.... L, 1821. 1st Ed, 1st

Issue. 8vo. (88) $60, £130; (89) $55, £50, £80; (90) $175
Vienna, 1922. Ltd Ed, sgd by the artist & with each plate initialled by him. Illus by Sepp Frank. 4to. (88) $80
— Mazeppa. L, 1819. 1st Ed, 2d Issue. 8vo. (88) $100; (89) $100
— The Parliamentary Speeches of Lord Byron. L, 1824. 8vo. (88) £200
— Poems on Various Occasions.... Newark, 1807. Schiff copy. (91) $20,000
8vo. Sgd on A1; inscr in anr hand "Presented by Lord Byron to William John Bankes". (91) £16,000
— The Poetical Works. L, 1839. 8 vols. 8vo. (90) £110, £650; (91) $225
9 vols. 8vo. (91) $550
Phila., 1839. 8 vols. 8vo. (90) $60
— The Prisoner of Chillon.... L, 1816. 1st Ed, 1st Issue. 8vo. (91) $200
L: Day & Son, [1865]. Illus by W. & G. Audsley. 4to. (89) $130, $280; (90) £45
— Sardanapalus, a Tragedy. The Two Foscari, a Tragedy. Cain, a Mystery. L, 1821. 1st Ed. 8vo. (89) $150; (91) $65
— The Siege of Corinth.... L, 1816. 1st Ed. 8vo. (89) $140, $200; (90) $300; (91) $180
— Waltz: an Apostrophic Hymn. By Horace Hornem, Esq. L, 1813. 4to. (91) $1,900
L, 1821. 8vo. (88) £240
Bound with: Wardrop, James. History of James Mitchell. L, 1813. And: Enigmaticus, Juniophilo, Pseud. Father and Edward. Liverpool, 1810. Bradley Martin copy. (90) $9,000
— Werner, a Tragedy. L, 1823. 1st Ed, 1st Issue. 8vo. (88) $100
Bound with two other works. (91) £170
2d Issue. (88) $130; (89) $100

— Works. L, 1815-20. 8 vols. 8vo. (91) £170
L, 1818-20. 9 vols. 8vo. (91) £70
L, 1832-33. 17 vols. 12mo. (88) $750; (89) $200, £320; (90) $275, $425; (91) $250, DM900
L, 1833. 17 vols. 8vo. (88) £320
Blackmer copy. (90) £400
L, 1834. 17 vols. 12mo. (88) £130
L, 1855-56. 6 vols. 8vo. (91) $190
L, 1898-1904. 13 vols. 8vo. (91) £220
One of 250. (90) $130
Bost.: F. A. Niccolls, 1900. One of 750 for America. 16 vols. (89) $110; (91) $190

Byron, George Gordon Noel, Lord, 1788-1824 —&
Rogers, Samuel, 1763-1855
— Lara, a Tale; Jacqueline, a Tale. L, 1814. 1st Ed. 8vo. (88) $130; (90) $70, $90

Byron, John, 1723-86
— The Narrative of the Honourable John Byron.... L, 1768. 1st Ed. 8vo. (91) $100, $225, £170
L, 1785. 8vo. (90) £70
— Viage del Commandante Byron al Rededor del Mundo.... Madrid, 1769. 2d Ed in Spanish. 4to. (91) £170
— A Voyage Round the World.... L, 1767. 1st Ed. 8vo. (91) $700

Byron, Major
— Letters of Percy Bysshe Shelley. With an Introductory Essay, by Robert Browning. See: Shelley forgery, Percy Bysshe

Byron, Robert, 1905-41 —&
Rice, David Talbot
— The Birth of Western Painting. L, 1930. 4to. (89) £75

A book auction at Sotheby's, circa 1800

WITHDRAWN